Birds of Northern South America

AN IDENTIFICATION GUIDE

Volume 1: Species Accounts

Robin Restall

Clemencia Rodner and Miguel Lentino

with contributions from David Ascanio
Guy Kirwan, Bruno Walther and Olivier Tostain
Discography by Shaun Peters

YALE UNIVERSITY PRESS
NEW HAVEN AND LONDON

For every birder who ever struggled to identify a mystery bird

For those loved ones who supported us so valiantly

Author credits

The plates and captions, and black-and-white line drawings, were all done by Robin Restall, with comments and suggestions, not to mention corrections, by Clemencia Rodner and Miguel Lentino. The distribution maps were compiled and produced by Miguel Lentino. The majority of the text was written by Clemencia Rodner and Robin Restall, but all species and subspecies descriptions were written by Robin Restall. Species accounts for Vireonidae, Corvidae, Alaudidae, Hirundinidae, Troglodytidae, Polioptilidae, Cinclidae, Bombycillidae, Muscicapidae, Mimidae and Thraupidae were prepared by Bruno Walther. The species accounts were reviewed in critical detail by Olivier Tostain and Guy Tudor. All plates were reviewed by David Ascanio, with many captions corrected and additional captions suggested. Shaun Peters produced the discography. The entire text was edited by Guy Kirwan (who also wrote four of the introductory sections), and proofread by Keith Marsh.

Published 2006 in the United Kingdom by Christopher Helm, an imprint of A & C Black Publishers Ltd.
Published 2007 in the United States by Yale University Press.

Commissioning Editor: Nigel Redman
Production and design: Julie Dando, Fluke Art, Cornwall

Printed and bound in China by 1010 Printing International Limited

ISBN: 978-0-300-10862-0
Library of Congress Control Number: 2006933554

A catalogue record for this book is available from the British Library.

The paper in this book meets the guidelines for permanence and durability of the Committee on Production Guidelines for Book Longevity of the Council on Library Resources.

10 9 8 7 6 5 4 3 2 1

CONTENTS

List of families 4

Preface 6

Acknowledgements 7

Introduction 9
- Objectives of this book 9
- Taxonomy 9
- Nomenclature 9
- Geographical area covered 10
- Moult and ageing 10

How to use this book 12
- Concept of the book 12
- The species accounts 12
- References and citations 13
- The plates 13
- The maps 14
- Abbreviated information 14
- Errors and corrections 16
- Bird topography 17

Climate, vegetation and habitats 18
- Glossary of habitats 20

Avifauna of Northern South America 22

Migration 23
- Nearctic migrants 23
- Austral migrants 24
- Intra-tropical migrants 25

Conservation 24

THE SPECIES ACCOUNTS 27

A Discography of Northern South American bird voices
by Shaun Peters 778

Glossary 811

Organisations 812

Bibliography 813

Index 835

LIST OF FAMILIES

TINAMIDAE Tinamous 27
ANHIMIDAE Screamers 34
ANATIDAE Ducks and geese 34
CRACIDAE Chachalacas, guans and curassows 42
ODONTOPHORIDAE New World quails 50
PODICIPEDIDAE Grebes 53
SPHENISCIDAE Penguins 55
DIOMEDEIDAE Albatrosses 56
PROCELLARIIDAE Petrels, prions and shearwaters 57
HYDROBATIDAE Storm-petrels 61
PHAETHONTIDAE Tropicbirds 64
PELECANIDAE Pelicans 65
SULIDAE Boobies 66
PHALACROCORACIDAE Cormorants 67
ANHINGIDAE Anhinga 68
FREGATIDAE Frigatebirds 69
ARDEIDAE Herons, egrets and bitterns 69
THRESKIORNITHIDAE Ibises and spoonbills 77
CICONIIDAE Storks 79
CATHARTIDAE Vultures 80
PHOENICOPTERIDAE Flamingos 82
PANDIONIDAE Osprey 83
ACCIPITRIDAE Kites, harriers, hawks and eagles 83
FALCONIDAE Caracaras and falcons 103
ARAMIDAE Limpkin 109
PSOPHIIDAE Trumpeters 110
RALLIDAE Crakes, rails, gallinules and coots 110
HELIORNITHIDAE Sungrebe 120
EURYPYGIDAE Sunbittern 120
CHARADRIIDAE Plovers 121
HAEMATOPODIDAE Oystercatchers 125
RECURVIROSTRIDAE Stilts and avocets 126
BURHINIDAE Thick-knees 126
SCOLOPACIDAE Snipes, sandpipers and phalaropes 127
THINOCORIDAE Seedsnipes 140
JACANIDAE Jacanas 140
STERCORARIIDAE Skuas and jaegers 141
LARIDAE Gulls and terns 143
RYNCHOPIDAE Skimmers 153
OPISTHOCOMIDAE Hoatzin 154
COLUMBIDAE Pigeons and doves 155
PSITTACIDAE Parrots 170
CUCULIDAE Cuckoos 193
TYTONIDAE Barn owls 199
STRIGIDAE Typical owls 200

STEATORNITHIDAE Oilbird 210
NYCTIBIIDAE Potoos 210
CAPRIMULGIDAE Nighthawks and nightjars 212
APODIDAE Swifts 219
TROCHILIDAE Hummingbirds 224
TROGONIDAE Trogons and quetzals 279
ALCEDINIDAE Kingfishers 285
MOTMOTIDAE Motmots 287
GALBULIDAE Jacamars 289
BUCCONIDAE Puffbirds, nunlets, and nunbirds 293
CAPITONIDAE New World barbets 300
RAMPHASTIDAE Toucans, toucanets and araçaris 304
PICIDAE Piculets and woodpeckers 313
FURNARIIDAE Ovenbirds and woodcreepers 328
THAMNOPHILIDAE Typical antbirds 379
FORMICARIIDAE Ground antbirds 423
CONOPOPHAGIDAE Gnateaters 438
RHINOCRYPTIDAE Tapaculos 439
TYRANNIDAE Tyrant-flycatchers 446
OXYRUNCIDAE Sharpbill 529
COTINGIDAE Cotingas 530
PIPRIDAE Manakins 545
TITYRIDAE Tityras, Schiffornis, becards and allies 554
SAPAYOIDAE Sapayoa 566
VIREONIDAE Peppershrikes, vireos and greenlets 566
CORVIDAE Jays 575
ALAUDIDAE Larks 578
HIRUNDINIDAE Swallows and martins 578
TROGLODYTIDAE Wrens 587
POLIOPTILIDAE Gnatcatchers and gnatwrens 604
CINCLIDAE Dippers 607
BOMBYCILLIDAE Waxwings 607
MUSCICAPIDAE Chats and Old World flycatchers 608
TURDIDAE Thrushes 608
MIMIDAE Catbird, thrashers and mockingbirds 621
STURNIDAE Starlings 623
MOTACILLIDAE Wagtails and pipits 624
THRAUPIDAE Tanagers 625
EMBERIZIDAE New World sparrows, brush finches and allies 683
CARDINALIDAE Cardinals, grosbeaks, saltators and allies 716
PARULIDAE New World warblers 723
ICTERIDAE Oropendolas, orioles, blackbirds and allies 746
FRINGILLIDAE Siskins and euphonias 763
ESTRILDIDAE Waxbills and munias 774
PLOCEIDAE Weavers and allies 776
PASSERIDAE Old World sparrows 777

PREFACE

Over many years of working with others in the field and in a bird museum, we noticed that people fall into a certain behavioural pattern when using field guides; this came to be referred among ourselves as 'the shoehorn syndrome'. We have seen this in action among students as they attempt to identify unfamiliar birds they take from the mist-net at banding stations, we have seen it in the field with birders of every kind and level of experience, and also with visitors to the Phelps Collection when they come to ask about birds they have seen and tried to identify. The 'shoehorn syndrome' is ready to strike whenever a bird comes along that is not instantly recognised, when the observer needs to consult his field guide. Almost invariably, he or she goes straight to the plates and tries to match the bird to one of the illustrations. If the bird is 'not-quite-but-almost' a particular species, it may well get shoehorned into fitting the nearest illustration.

Sometimes, identification by means of illustrations alone may turn out to be correct, but a fair number of times, especially in an unfamiliar country, the foot will have been shoehorned into the wrong shoe. After experiencing numerous instances of these often innocent misidentifications, we became convinced that the reason why the shoehorning of birds into plate illustrations leads to wrong identifications is because, in most guides, fewer than half the *plumages* of birds are illustrated. In some cases, even a number of species are left out of the plates.

Many birders wisely turn to the text to see if there is a species that is not illustrated that fits the description (and we have observed that field-guide users generally *like* plates, but *trust* text). However, it is quite amazing how many people do not check the text, and how often they do not realise that the plates are not as helpful as they should be. The shortcomings of plates in a field guide only become evident if one undertakes a careful analysis of the species concerned, or when some tough confusion species are being examined. Among other problems, 'shoehorning' causes species that are illustrated, invariably the commonest and the ones most likely to be seen, to be recorded more often than they occur in reality, while the ones not illustrated, are recorded rather less often than they have been seen in reality.

The many guides for the countries of northern South America, which we have drawn upon freely in researching for this book, are getting better with every generation, and the most recent ones illustrate almost all the species in their respective countries. However, for many species it is still only the adult male in breeding plumage that is shown, and occasionally a dull female is tucked away behind him, half showing. It is rare indeed to see a complete set of juvenile, immature, female and male plumages, plus different colour morphs, distinct subspecies and non-breeding plumages, all together on a plate, even in the specialised handbooks.

In his wonderfully illuminating book, *The Speciation and Biogeography of Birds* (Newton 2003), Ian Newton says that "…every regional handbook on birds can now give details, not only of the size and colour differences between similar species, but also of the size and colour variation found across the geographical range of a single species, and from one subspecies to another. Such details can often also be given on song and other characteristics. Hence, for birds more than other animals, the geographically definable population has become the customary taxonomic unit of study".

Whilst this may well be true of the Old World and also for North America, it is still not true, unfortunately, for the Neotropics. Vast areas of South American territory are even now waiting for in-depth surveys and detailed population studies. The incredibly useful *Handbook of the Birds of the World* (del Hoyo *et al.*) is sufficiently comprehensive to partially comply with Newton's assertion but, at the time of writing, only two-thirds of the series' volumes have been completed, and it seems unlikely to be finished before 2010. In any case, although each volume seems to be an improvement over the previous one, at least for the Neotropics, it falls a little short of Newton's somewhat Utopian description of the present state of knowledge of avian geographic variation. In the Neotropics, there still remains much to be learned about subspecies and their distributions.

The original inspiration for *Birds of Northern South America* was the recognition that, in the 2,300 or so species that occur in the countries that we selected as our region, there are probably more than 7,000 distinct plumages, very many of which have never been illustrated anywhere, and a considerable number of which are only known, with luck, from one or two specimens. In our everyday work at the Phelps Museum, we were frustrated on an almost daily basis, with inadequate references to identify some taxon or other. RR set out to correct this deficit, by visiting the great collections in North America and making detailed identification drawings. ML joined the project by preparing maps based on known and confirmed specimens, and then CR joined to start making notes on behaviour and status. Christopher Helm and Nigel Redman showed great interest in the proposed book, and the project became a reality.

Work on the book started in 1996, and has taken ten years to complete. The original aim was simply to illustrate as many of the distinct plumages of the species of birds that occur in northern South America as could be found in museums and the literature by the senior author, together with a map for each species and text to assist in identifying and better understanding the variations. Along the way, we also found that illustrating all the species and subspecies would necessarily require an ongoing update of the increasingly fluid taxonomy of Neotropical birds. This led to the interim publication in 2000 of the *Checklist of the Birds of Northern South America* (Rodner *et al.* 2000). This list recognised 2,245 species and included information on all the subspecies found in the region. It formed the basis of the taxonomy for the present volumes, although the number of species has now risen to 2,308. At the time of going to press we believe we are up to date with the latest taxonomic decisions, and certainly we are in step with the SACC list of the AOU. But we are fully aware that further profound changes are on the way, which is likely to increase the number of species in the region, but at least we hope that most of these'new'species will have been illustrated and described in this book, albeit as subspecies at the present time.

It has proved impossible to illustrate and carefully describe absolutely every single distinct plumage, as originally planned, in the same way that it has proved impossible to present a definitive taxonomy. Some 6,388 individual figures have been painted, with work continuing on the illustrations up to the day before the material went off to the printers. We suspect one could add about 1,000 more. However, we trust that we have come as close as possible at the present time in fulfilling the original goal and sincerely hope that this book, in its complete two volumes, with so many subspecies and plumages illustrated for the first time and a much-needed updated taxonomy for the species of this South American region, will make a significant contribution in the direction of that ideal situation described by Professor Newton.

Robin Restall
Caracas, May 2006

ACKNOWLEDGEMENTS

It took ten years to complete this volume. During that time we consulted with countless people – professionals and amateurs, university professors, museum curators, taxidermists, bird artists and illustrators, ornithologists and field researchers, tour guides, birdwatchers, bird trappers and others. We were given advice, problems were solved, leads for follow-up research were given and corrections suggested. All gave encouragement as well as help. We are all ashamed that there are many people who helped at some time, and yet we failed to record their names to include here. To these people most of all, heartfelt thanks for your input.

Firstly, we thank Christopher Helm who had the faith in RR to encourage the project right from the start, regularly offering words of praise and encouragement through the years – and for a mean steak-and-kidney pie! David Ascanio reviewed the plates and plate pulls several times, and made many constructive comments that enabled better captions to be written on the plates; he also reviewed the maps, and his review of the text for Tyrannidae and several other families was invaluable. Shaun Peters did a masterful job in creating a discography of the species in the book. Margarita Martinez drafted text for conebills and several individual oscines, and prepared the list of species that extend into eastern Panamá, northern Peru and northern Brazil; she also helped in countless ways as a research assistant at the Phelps Collection. Guy Kirwan and Olivier Tostain made endless quality comments on the species accounts, sharing unrivalled experience and wisdom with absolute generosity, and patience. Chris Milensky made superb digital photographs of difficult and complicated species, enabling RR to figure out relevant characteristics for many obscure subspecies. Chris Sharpe gave many helpful comments on status during the preparation of the species accounts of non-passerines. Hugh Eva (European Commission Joint Research Centre) kindly prepared the wonderful maps of altitudinal zones and vegetation cover in the introduction. Keith Marsh diligently transposed the various information codes onto the plates as well as pointing out numerous discrepancies between the plates and text.

Warm and heartfelt thanks are also due to the following people for their support and help in so many ways: Alexander Aleixo, Peter Alden, Alan Altman, Jose Alvarez, Phil Angle, Nacho Areta, Dick Banks, Luis Baptista, Gian Basili, John Bates, Steve Beissinger, Francisco Bisbal, Tomas Blohm, Carlos Bosque, Mike Braun, Tom Brown, Rob Brumfield, Daniel Cadena, Diego Calderon F., Peter Capainolo, Steve Cardiff, Yrving Carreño, Clark Casler, Kathy Castelein, Juan Carlos de las Casas, Rob Clay, Mario Cohn-Haft, Charles Collins, Javier Colvée, Dan Cooper, Paul Coopmans, Allen Chartier, Lynn Clark, Nigel Cleere, Tony Crease, Andres M. Cuervo, Maria Rosa Cuesta, James Dean, Robert Dickerman, Donna

Dittman, Thommas Donegan, Carla Dove, Edward Dickinson, Jessica Eberhard, Gunnar Engblom, Patricia Escalante, Diana Esclasans, Ernesto Fernandez, Richard ffrench, Jon Fjeldsaa, John Fitzpatrick, Rosendo Fraga, Juan F. Freile, Anita Gamauf, Adrian Giacomo, Sandra Gines, MaryLou Goodwin, Ivan Goodwin, Gary Graves, Arthur Grosset, Floyd Hayes, Bennett Hennessy, Steve Hilty, Ian Hinze, Josep del Hoyo, Bill Hull, Johan Ingels, Mort and Phyllis Isler, Alvaro Jaramillo, Leo Joseph, Martyn Kenefick, Shannon Kenney, Guy Kirwan, Niels Krabbe, Andrew Kratter, Tim Krynack, Dave Lauten, Dan Lane, Dan Lebbin, Rosemary Low, Jane Lyons, Barry MacKay, Curtis Marantz, Manuel Marin, Larry McQueen, Jeremy Minns, John Moore, Luis Gonzalo Morales, Roy Neilsen, David Nott, Storrs Olson, John O'Neill, Luis O. Nieves, Jorge Pérez, Emma Restall Orr, Joshua Restall Orr, Fernando Ortiz-Crespo, Robert Payne, Ray Paynter, John Penhallurick, Jorge Perez, Luis Perez C., Alison Pirie, Bill Porteous, Dan Porter, Ana Porzecanski, Rick Prum, Nigel Redman, J. Van Remsen, Carlos Rengifo, Luis Miguel Rengifo, Matthew Restall, Carlos Reyes, Jan Hein Ribot, Chris Rimmer, Mark Robbins, Gustavo Rodriguez, Jon Paul Rodriguez, Loretta Rossellini, Tom Ryan, Paul Salaman, Marcos Salcedo, Brian Schmidt, Tom Schulenberg, Chris Sharpe, F. Gary Stiles, Douglas Stotz, Denis Summers-Smith, Paul Sweet, Byron Swift, Stan Temple, Jeremiah Trimble, Francois Vuilleumier, Michael Walters, Sophie Webb, Walter Weber, David Wege, David Weidenfeld, Bret Whitney, Andrew Whittaker, Aisha Williams, Rob Williams, Kevin Winker, Irene Zager and Kevin Zimmer.

In addition to these stalwarts, countless numbers responded to queries made over the years on the NEOORN list server for people working with Neotropical birds. To all those who offered opinions and answers, this book would be less effective in many ways without your contributions, and we are truly grateful.

We also had the privilege of being able to study specimens in the following collections: Museo de Historia Natural La Salle; Museo de la Estacion Biologica, Rancho Grande, Maracay; Louisiana State University Museum of Zoology, Baton Rouge; Harvard University Museum of Comparative Zoology, Cambridge, Mass.; American Museum of Natural History, New York; United States National Museum of Natural History (Smithsonian Institution), Washington, D.C. Our truly profound thanks to the curators and directors of these establishments for their courtesy and help. Without this, it would have been impossible accurately to illustrate nearly half of the birds shown.

Last, but absolutely not least, there are three people without whom the book would not have been finished. The contributions of our Commissioning Editor, Nigel Redman and the designer, Julie Dando, have had a profound and most positive effect on the way the book has ended up. The plates were originally designed with a totally different concept of guide in mind to the way they ended up, but Julie organised and reorganised them, and in the process corrected all sorts of errors, such as changing the angle of a tail, adding protruding wingtips, filling out a throat and slimming down a belly, and so on – in short, she worked absolute wonders. Her good humour and patience was matched only by her professionalism and ability. Nigel not only freely provided the benefit of his bottomless well of experience in editing bird books, but his good-natured persistence, perspective and enviable professionalism kept the senior author from giving up on this project several times, and thus ensured completion of the work - and for feeding me arguably the very best fish and chips in Britain! My wife Mariela lived through my depressions, maniacal highs, angers and sullen doggedness when I was working 15 hours a day for weeks on end. Without her near-saintly support I really would have quit!

This work is essentially the product of the individual enthusiasm of three people. We were not underwritten or supported by anybody, nor any institution. All travel and other expenses for over ten years were paid for by ourselves out of our own pockets – and I regret that this limited our ability to cover all the collections we would have liked to visit. The actual work was done in our homes and on the premises of the Phelps Ornithological Collection, where RR and CR were, and remain, unpaid volunteers. The Phelps Foundation is to be acknowledged and thanked profoundly for allowing us complete freedom of access to the quite magnificent library, and what is probably the finest single-country collection of bird specimens in the world. Despite all the above, the authors of course take full responsibility for any errors that might remain, but it is worth recording that whenever we three disagreed on a point of taxonomy, I made the decision. And I also take sole responsibility for any errors in the illustrations.

RR

INTRODUCTION

Objectives of this book

This book was conceived as, and is primarily intended to be a *visual* guide to the identification of all of the birds one is likely to see within the geographic boundaries of northern South America. It was never intended as a field guide, but as a complement to the various guides that are currently available. It was our ambition to illustrate every distinct plumage of every species in the region, for such has not existed before.

This ambition came to be modified slightly, as there are cases where it was simply impossible to find adequate references, whether they be specimens or original descriptions. Indeed, with some species, there are plumages of females and juveniles that are not even known. But, as it stands, this book contains illustrations of almost every distinct plumage of over 2,300 species and includes many plumages not previously illustrated anywhere, not even in the most eclectic journal. The key word here is 'distinct', for where females and juveniles are sufficiently like the adult male to be indistinguishable in the field they are usually represented by a single illustration. Many flycatchers, for example, fall into this category. We have sought to illustrate every visually distinct subspecies. This permits a comparative look at the full species in the region, and helps identify birds that might be intermediate in a clinal species.

If the user of this book finds that he or she has a good reference for a plumage that is missing, we will be most grateful to receive it and will incorporate it into future editions, along with the inevitable new species that are being described and discovered, even as this book is in production. The cut-off date for new material for this book was the end of May 2006. All data received after that time is being stored for use in a future second edition.

Taxonomy

We have sequenced the families following the American Ornithologists' Union (AOU) Checklist, incorporating the necessary additions of exclusively South American families as revised by the AOU's South American Checklist Committee (SACC). The new order is published on the AOU website (www.aou.org/checklist/index.php3) and was last checked by us in May 2006. The species order within a family generally follows the SACC list but does not always mirror it. The full SACC list is published on the following website: www.aou.org/checklistsouth.php3.

There are occasions when the authors of any guide are faced with the dilemma of the recognition of a species. Whenever this has occurred in our case, we have usually decided to recognise the split, and in this we have gone beyond the SACC list. Since this book has no pretensions to be a taxonomic reference, we feel comfortable in following this policy for the sake of clarification in taxon recognition and prompting more accurate attribution of taxa. One notable example is that of the lumping of Red-backed Hawk with Puna Hawk into a single, indivisible Variable Hawk by Farquhar (1998). There seemed to be an instant wave of agreement with this decision (e.g. Ridgely & Greenfield 2000), but it was not unanimous and we have decided not to follow it. In this case, our decision was subsequently made easier as both the AOU and Dickinson (2003) retained the two as separate species. Subsequently, a new paper presenting a strong case for retaining the two species appeared (Cabot & De Vries 2003), but there is still disagreement about these birds. The plates took ten years to complete and, in some cases, we followed splits proposed by Ridgely & Greenfield (2001), only to find that subsequently these splits were rejected by the SACC on grounds of insufficient published evidence. In some of these cases we have retained the appearance of a split, giving each 'species' its own English name and map, but retained the official scientific name, making the situation clear. In each case of taxonomic uncertainty, the current situation is explicitly mentioned in the species accounts.

We make no pretensions to taxonomic authority. This book should not be quoted as a primary or authoritative source for any taxonomy. Our objective is to aid in the visual recognition of taxa. Our 'recognition' of any taxon is absolutely not an authoritative, formal treatment with scientific credentials. The last thing we would wish is to be accused of having exhibited the 'taxonomy by field guide' syndrome. The species limits presented here are simply what we have accepted, for our purposes of identifying taxa, in as unequivocal way as possible.

Nomenclature

We have followed the most widely used common names throughout. These broadly follow the SACC list, but we have noted alternative English names occasionally. However, we have chosen to follow 'Howard & Moore' (Dickinson 2003) and the new IOC-endorsed list of recommended English names (Gill & Wright 2006) with regard to the hyphenation of English names. Both works explain the rationale for their use of hyphens, but generally they take a minimalist approach, avoiding hyphens unless it is considered essential to use them.

The scientific names follow the SACC list (which in turn follows the names used by the American Ornithologists' Union where possible), unless there is a recent precedent not to do so. Any departures from the SACC list are explained in the Notes sections at the end of the species accounts. These scientific names have gender endings according to the principles set out by David & Gosselin (2000a and 2000b), and in consequence some names will appear to be slightly different from those used in other field guides, or even in our own Checklist (Rodner *et al.* 2000). For example, the Great Green Macaw is now called *Ara ambiguus*, whereas it was formerly known as *Ara ambigua*, and Speckled Crake, formerly *Coturnicops notata*, is now *C. notatus*.

Geographical area covered

The countries covered by the illustrations and the text (but not the maps) are continental Ecuador, continental Colombia, Venezuela and its offshore islands, the islands that were part of the Netherlands Antilles offshore from Venezuela, namely Aruba, Curaçao and Bonaire, and also Trinidad & Tobago, Guyana, Suriname and French Guiana. It should be noted that whilst we recognise Trinidad & Tobago as a single political unit, in distributional terms we accord them separate recognition, thus 'Tr' refers only to Trinidad and 'To' to Tobago, and they are not shorthand for Trinidad *and* Tobago, which is always written 'T&T'.

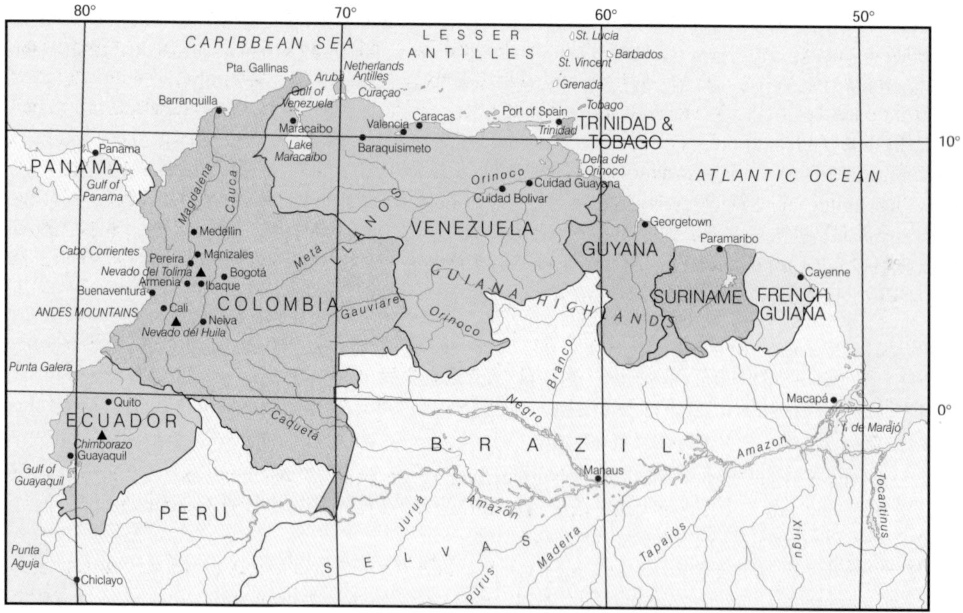

Northern South America, as defined in this book.

The maps are cut off by a straight, latitudinal line eastwards from the southernmost point of Ecuador, at approximately 5° S of the equator. They show the distribution of birds north of this line, as far as we could estimate, thus depicting ranges that extend into or across northern Peru and northern Brazil. We believe that ending a bird's range at the political boundary of a country is not helpful to the user of a book such as this. To observe that a species continues into Peru, Panama or Brazil signals an opportunity for further research, and perhaps a broader understanding of the bird being studied. But please note, we do not identify, nor describe or illustrate, any distinct subspecies that may occur in these extralimital areas. The continuation of the range on the maps into, for instance, northern Brazil means the species occurs there, but we do not identify which subspecies. Nevertheless, this guide may be used (with caution) by birders visiting northern Peru and Brazil north of the Amazon; both these regions still lack a satisfactory field guide.

A few extralimital species have been included for the purpose of reducing possible confusion. An example is the hummingbird, Marvellous Spatuletail *Loddigesia mirabilis* which seems unlikely to occur in southern Ecuador, but for which there has been at least one contentious sighting. Other species occurring just beyond our boundaries will doubtless be recorded in our region in the future, but it has not been possible to include all of these.

Moult and ageing

We have generally avoided mentioning moult in the text, though the effects of age, and wear throughout the year, may be touched upon when they are significant. With some families, the various plumages are so numerous and complex, for example in gulls and hawks, that it is regrettably beyond the scope of this book to be so comprehensive as to illustrate all of these. The reader is invited to refer to specialist books for a more detailed treatment; there are many of these, some of which are very comprehensive and helpful (e.g. *Gulls of Europe, Asia and North America* by Klaus Malling Olsen and Hans Larsson, *Sylvia Warblers* by Hadoram Shirihai, Gabriel Gargallo and Andreas Helbig, *Pipits and Wagtails of Europe, Asia and North America* by Per Alström and Krister Mild, and *Raptors of the World* by James Ferguson-Lees and David Christie). Regrettably, there are virtually no books dealing with Neotropical birds in such detail. However, it is relevant to note that in every species with a distinct contrast between juvenile plumage and the adult (usually male) plumage, there will be a period when the bird is moulting from one to the other, and may look nothing like either. These have been illustrated in only a few cases. In the case of parrots, in most species the sexes and juveniles all look alike, but there is a change of iris colour from juvenile to adult in many species. Juveniles usually have dark brown eyes, whilst adults may develop red, yellow or even white eyes, though many continue to have brown eyes.

Moult may be sudden and dramatic, as in the case of an adult male Mallard Anas *platyrhynchos*, or may be spread over several years, as in the case of wing moult in pelicans and albatrosses. It is important to recognise that, in most cases, the bird needs to be able to fly, and therefore wing-feathers are shed in a steady sequence, with replacement feathers for a few old feathers growing before the old feathers are dropped. Tail- and wing-feathers are usually replaced in matched pairs, a feather or two on each side. At times this might dramatically change the flight profile of a bird; for example, where the central pair of tail-feathers is shorter than those either side, creating a forked-tail impression in a species that normally has a blunt or rounded tail. It is as well to ponder these aspects when faced by a bird that does not quite match the illustrations or descriptions. In most species, post-breeding moult affects the entire plumage. This is true also for birds about to migrate, though many species delay their moult until they reach their wintering grounds. Subsequently, there is a partial moult prior to breeding that only involves body-feathers. There are many different strategies and exceptions to the rules, but below are the various typical plumages and moults, not all of which may be noticeable or significant; note that this sequence does not apply to all species:

> Juvenile plumage followed by post-juvenile moult (usually body-feathers only) → first-winter / immature / intermediate / first adult plumage, followed by pre-breeding moult → first-summer plumage, followed by post-breeding moult → adult (winter / non-breeding) plumage, followed by post-breeding moult → adult summer plumage, etc.

The subject and study of moult of birds in the Neotropics is a very large and complicated one, and merits a dedicated book of its own. The subject has been well covered in North America (e.g. Pyle *et al.* 1987), and thus the moult strategies of Nearctic migrants are comparatively well known.

Migrants usually have a basic (winter) plumage that differs from their alternate (breeding) plumage, but this complicates rather than simplifies identification. Whilst some are only seen in winter plumage, others may be observed in any stage of plumage and moult, from breeding to non-breeding. It has been impossible to illustrate every one of these plumages, but those that may be expected in the region are all depicted.

There are several species that migrate north to spend their non-breeding period in northern South America, and there are considerable numbers of North American species that pass their winter in South America. Some migrants pass overhead, with very few individuals alighting in northern South America, whilst others are generally seen during one passage period and not the other due to their overall routes being elliptical. And, finally, there is the case of altitudinal migrants, where birds breed at higher elevations and move lower when not breeding. All migrants in a non-breeding situation tend to have different feeding habits and vocal behaviour from those on their breeding grounds, and different habitat preferences, which may differ yet again when the birds are in transit.

In some species it is often the case that a few individuals stay in the region the entire following year, returning north only 15–18 months after their arrival. This is particularly true of juveniles that have physiological problems, e.g. illness, parasites or are underweight. These birds do not moult into breeding plumage during their stay, but remain in a basic or winter plumage for the duration, though a few might undertake a partial moult.

HOW TO USE THIS GUIDE

Concept of the book

The concept of the book is to provide as comprehensive a visual guide as possible to the thousands of different plumages of the birds of northern South America, with additional text descriptions and details of subspecies. The text also gives information about the natural history of each species, and the whole should help to resolve all those questions about identification that remain after a bird is identified to species level. As such, it is intended to complement the various country field guides, and be of particular assistance to researchers of plumage variation.

The contents of this book, despite being handled as concisely as we felt possible, have necessitated two volumes. The species accounts appear in the first volume and the plates and maps in the second. The two books are obviously complementary. However, recognising the habits of many field workers and birders to take plates alone into the field, and keep the text back at base for use at the end of the day, we have endeavoured to make the plates more comprehensive than usual with the addition of caption text on the plates themselves and coded information about status and abundance below the maps. In order to keep Volume 2 as portable as possible for field use, most of the introductory material is included in Volume 1, together with the appendices and Discography. However, some parts of the Introduction have been repeated in Volume 2 so that the latter may be used on its own if desired.

The species accounts (Volume 1)

These are short and tight, and are largely complementary to the plates and maps. Species accounts are subdivided into the following sections:

Name A reference to the Plate number in Volume 2 is given after the English and scientific names. Hypothetical species (either unconfirmed for the region or considered to be possible future additions to the list) have their names placed in square brackets.

Identification The accounts begin with the length of the bird, as taken from a live bird or a freshly dead specimen. This is not always recognised by scientists as being a reliable indicator, but in this context it offers a good comparison between species. For some species, such as seabirds, the wingspan (W) is also given. For polytypic species, the description that follows is usually of the nominate form or the most typical race of the region. Distinguishing features of other races are briefly mentioned under Subspecies.

Subspecies (Ssp.) Each taxon's name is followed by abbreviated distributional data. The countries of the region are abbreviated as follows:

Ec	Ecuador	Tr	Trinidad
Co	Colombia	To	Tobago
Ve	Venezuela	T&T	Trinidad & Tobago
Ar	Aruba	Gu	Guyana
Bo	Bonaire	Su	Suriname
Cu	Curaçao	FG	French Guiana
ABC	Aruba, Bonaire & Curaçao		

Distributions are further refined by means of the points of the compass, thus: SC Co = south-central Colombia, NE Ve = north-east Venezuela, NW Gu = north-west Guyana etc. There follows a brief comment that helps discriminate between subspecies. This is particularly useful when not all subspecies are illustrated.

Habits These data have been limited to a few relevant notes. Emphasis has been given to features that assist in the identification of the species.

Status Remarks on status are best read in the context of the map from where a better idea of the distribution of each species will be gained. We have compiled data regarding relative abundance from the main and most current references for each country, which often permits a pattern to emerge, giving an idea of centres of abundance and population densities throughout the range of a species in the region.

Habitat Altitudinal zones or actual altitude figures (sometimes both) are given – see definitions on page 15.

Voice Avian vocalisations are an ever-important contribution to the process of identifying birds, and the technique of responsible playback, to entice a bird close enough to be seen, is increasingly used by birders and ornithologists alike. We have often presented several different versions of a species' vocalisations which in some cases refer to the same calls or songs. These are transcriptions or interpretations, usually by very accomplished ornithologists, and the source of each is given (see 'References and citations') below. The 'Discography' at the end of the book lists all the recordings of relevant bird vocalisations currently available commercially. Furthermore, it also lists bird species whose vocalisations have been recorded (in taxonomic order), cross-referenced to the available compilation and including details of where the recording was made.

Note(s) These are appended (and referenced) when there is an aspect of a species' taxonomy that is relevant to its identification, especially if conflicting data on taxonomy is apparent in other literature. Alternative English or scientific names, or synonyms, are also given here.

References and citations

Throughout the preparation of this book, we have repeatedly referred to the principal guides of the region. These have not been referenced or cited in the species accounts, except in the **Voice** and **Notes** sections. They were invaluable and deserve particular recognition. It is interesting to note that these sources are sometimes contradictory, usually complementary, and invariably informative. It is assumed that ornithologists and birders alike will generally have access to these books, at least the most recent and readily available ones. They give much more local data than will be found herein. The regional guides referred to, together with their abbreviations which have been used to save space, are as follows (complete citations appear in the bibliography):

R&G	*The Birds of Ecuador* by R. S. Ridgely & P. J. Greenfield
H&B	*A Guide to the Birds of Colombia* by S. L. Hilty & W. L. Brown
MdS&P	*A Guide to the Birds of Venezuela* by R. Meyer de Schauensee and W. H. Phelps, Jr.; also the amended Spanish version, *Aves de Venezuela* (P&MdS)
H	*Birds of Venezuela* by S. L. Hilty
Snyder	*The Birds of Guyana* by D. E. Snyder
BFR&S	*A Field Checklist for the Birds of Guyana* by M. Braun, D. Finch, M. Robbins & B. Schmidt
H&M	*The Birds of Surinam* by F. Haverschmidt and G.F. Mees
Tostain *et al.*	*Oiseaux de Guyana* by O. Tostain, J.-L. Dujardin, C. Erard & J.-M. Thiollay.
Voous	*The Birds of the Netherlands Antilles* K. H. Voous
ffrench	*A Guide to the Birds of Trinidad and Tobago* R. ffrench
SFP&M	*Neotropical Birds: Ecology and Conservation* by D. F. Stotz, J. W. Fitzpatrick, T. A. Parker & D. K. Moskovits
F&K	*Birds of the High Andes* by J. Fjeldså & N. Krabbe
Clements	*A Field Guide to the Birds of Peru* by J. F. Clements & N. Shany
Sick	*Birds in Brazil* by H. Sick
S&M	*Taxonomy and Distribution of Birds of the World* by C. G. Sibley & B. L. Monroe, Jr.

Please note that a number of other key references are frequently referred to in the Voice and Notes sections by abbreviations or incomplete citations. These refer to major sources such as family monographs, and they are listed at the ends of the introductory paragraphs as 'Additional references used'. For example, in the tanagers, I&I refers to *Tanagers* by M. L Isler & P. R. Isler. Full citations appear in the bibliography.

The plates (Volume 2)

The purpose of the plates is to show as many different plumages of the birds of the region as possible. Every species recorded in the region has been illustrated, together with almost every distinct subspecies and plumage variation. A few hypothetical species have been included (especially seabirds), on the basis of unconfirmed records for the region or the likelihood of being recorded in the future. Their names are placed within square brackets (as are their text entries in Volume 1).

Species are arranged on the plates more or less taxonomically but, inevitably, concessions have had to be made and some species appear out of sequence. Please note that, *within a family, all of the birds are drawn in proportion to each other.* Thus, the user can view a plate with a familiar species and know at once how much larger or smaller any other related, but unfamiliar, bird in that family is.

Right at the start, we decided to show the birds in a strictly comparative style, somewhat ritualised, but showing jizz characteristics as much as possible. In this way, comparisons of subtle detail in the plumages may be made. The differences in coloration and pattern that are shown between one race and another are not accidents of the printing process, but are deliberate indicators of the differences between one form and another. It would have been beyond my limited abilities as an illustrator to depict every bird in a different and natural pose based on field sketches and photographs. And, whilst the book has taken over ten years to complete, such a requirement would have doubled the preparation time. Another aspect of the birds as drawn is that they are sometimes drawn four-dimensionally in order to show both rump and ventral areas. Most hummingbirds perch with their wing-tips tucked *beneath* their tails, and their bills pointing upwards. In many cases birds have been drawn with their wings in a rarely held position in order to show diagnostic undertail-coverts as well as uppertail-coverts. Many birds hold their wings folded over their lower back and rump, with the tertials concealing the feathers below, including most of the uppertail-coverts, but here they are usually drawn with the wings slightly apart in order to show the lower back, rump and uppertail-coverts. These apparent flaws are a deliberate attempt to draw attention to diagnostic plumage features.

To make the plates more useful, pointers highlight a key feature of the bird in question. Furthermore, additional information is given on the plates themselves by means of caption text. These highlight key habitat preferences or behaviour which, it is hoped, will assist in the identification process and enable Volume 2 to be used on its own in the field.

The threat status of those species listed in *Threatened Birds of the World* is coded next to the English name of each species on the plates (as well as underneath the map). See below for an explanation of these two-letter codes.

The maps (Volume 2)

The areas within which a species occurs are shown in green. The maps also show political boundaries in red and major river systems in blue. The river systems, especially, provide an instant visualisation of whether a species is a bird of high country, for example, or whether it is a bird associated with well-drained lowlands.

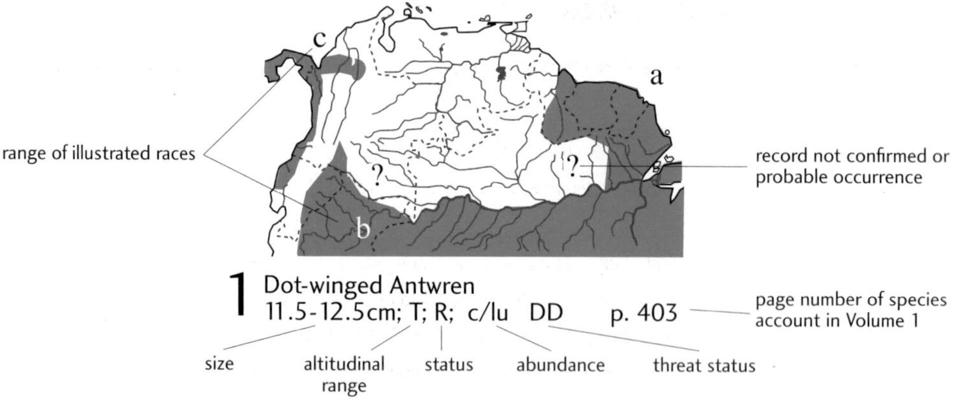

We have avoided as much as possible using blanket ranges within which a particular species might be found, assuming appropriate habitat, altitude, etc. Instead, we have indicated where a bird is confirmed to occur. This is not wholly successful, as there are many species for which it is only possible to prepare a distribution map by relying on the work of others, thereby following their broad strokes, errors or generalisations. Where we have left a simple interrogative '?' on a map, it signifies that a record has not been confirmed, is in doubt, or the occurrence of the species is likely or even probable, but simply not known.

Where more than one race has been illustrated, the approximate ranges of these races are indicated on the map (where possible) with the letters 'a', 'b', 'c' etc. The precise ranges of subspecies in the region is too imperfectly known for this to be done with any great accuracy, and our maps are necessarily rather small.

Abbreviated information

Below each map is a set of data specific to that species. This gives certain basic information in coded form for every species. The purpose of this is to make Volume 2 more useful in the field when used without Volume 1. For fuller details, particularly subspecific differences, please check the species accounts in Volume 1.

The top line has the English name of the species and the page number in Volume 1 where the species account is located. The bottom line presents the following five pieces of information:

Size: approximate or average, or range of, sizes in centimetres (cm). Occasionally, a tail or bill length might also be mentioned, and sometimes the sizes of both males and females, in the case of strongly sexually dimorphic species.

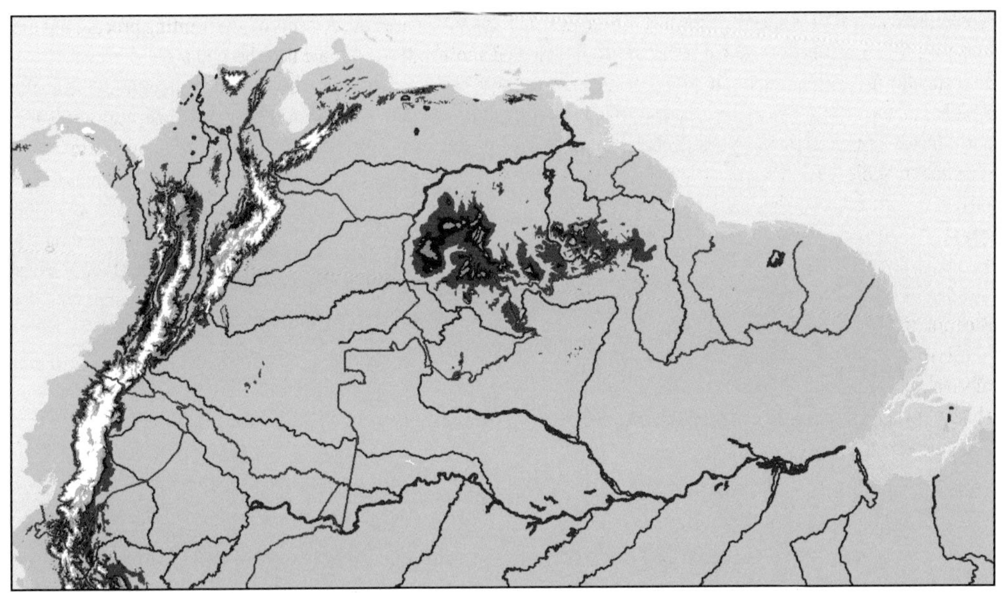

Altitudinal Zones of northern South America as defined in this book. Derived from the US Geological Survey's 30 arc-second database 'GTOPO30' (USGS 1997; Bliss and Olsen 1996).

Altitudinal range: the various altitudinal zones are referred to by name in the species accounts in Volume 1, and by codes in Volume 2:

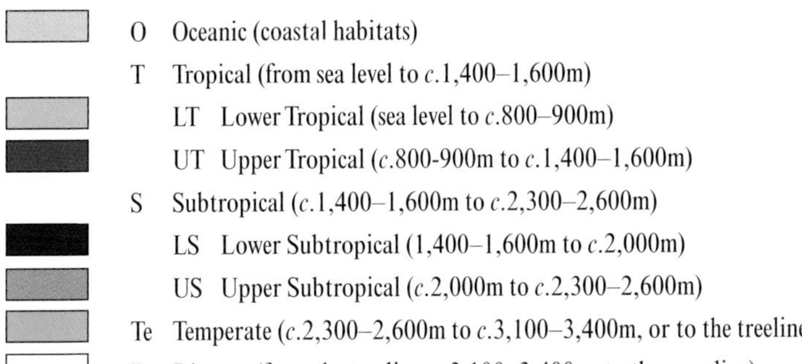

The two lowest zones – Tropical and Subtropical – are each divided into two subzones, in order to be more specific for species that have a narrower altitude range, such as those found exclusively in the lowlands or on lower slopes. When a species ranges throughout the entire Tropical or Subtropical zone, only the general abbreviation is used.

The codes can be used together to indicate a range in altitude, e.g. T-LS indicates Tropical to Lower Subtropical, i.e. sea level to 2,000m.

Status: generally single letters, but combinations are possible (e.g. a species can be both resident and a boreal migrant, thus R/B):

R	Resident	a species that resides within its range throughout the year and breeds
B	Boreal migrant	a species that breeds in the Nearctic region (North America) and migrates to spend the post-breeding season (northern winter) in our region
A	Austral migrant	a species that visits our region from elsewhere in South America
V	Vagrant	a species outside its normal range
I	Introduced	a species introduced into our region, with a self-sustaining population
?	Unconfirmed	status uncertain

Abundance: in order to be as user-friendly as possible, only five codes are used, plus one qualifier (l = local) which may be used with any of the five codes. Thus, lc = locally common etc. Given that abundance will vary considerably in such a huge region, two categories are frequently used, to show the range of abundance within northern South America. The category of the most frequently occurring abundance is generally placed first. Thus, f/s = fairly common to scarce (i.e. the species is more often fairly common than scarce); and u/lc = uncommon to locally common.

c	common	invariably encountered within its normal habitat
f	fairly common or frequent	usually, but not invariably, encountered within its normal habitat
u	uncommon	relatively frequently, but not regularly, encountered within its normal habitat
s	scarce	only irregularly and infrequently encountered within its normal habitat
r	rare	rarely encountered
l	local	only occurs patchily within its range

Threat Status: this gives the status of those species listed in *Threatened Birds of the World* (BirdLife International 2000). The codes are as follows:

CR	Critical	species facing an extremely high risk of extinction in the wild in the near future
EN	Endangered	species facing a very high risk of extinction in the wild in the near future
VU	Vulnerable	species facing a high risk of extinction in the wild in the medium-term future
NT	Near Threatened	species coming very close to qualifying as Threatened (i.e. CR, EN or VU)
LC	Least Concern	species considered to be at less risk of extinction than Near Threatened
DD	Data Deficient	species for which there is inadequate information to make an assessment of its risk of extinction
NE	Not Evaluated	species not assigned a risk category (for example, newly described species with very small ranges or in threatened habitats)

Errors and Corrections

It is hoped that eventually this work will appear in an enlarged and completely revised second edition. When that happens, not only will species new to the region be added, but sexes and juveniles that have been excluded because they were unknown or specimens were unavailable, will be added, as will new descriptions of vocalisations. The reader thus has the opportunity to contribute to this project by informing the authors of any errors on the plates, modifications to the maps, and refinements and corrections to the texts, including vocalisations. Please write to the senior author c/o A&C Black.

Bird Topography

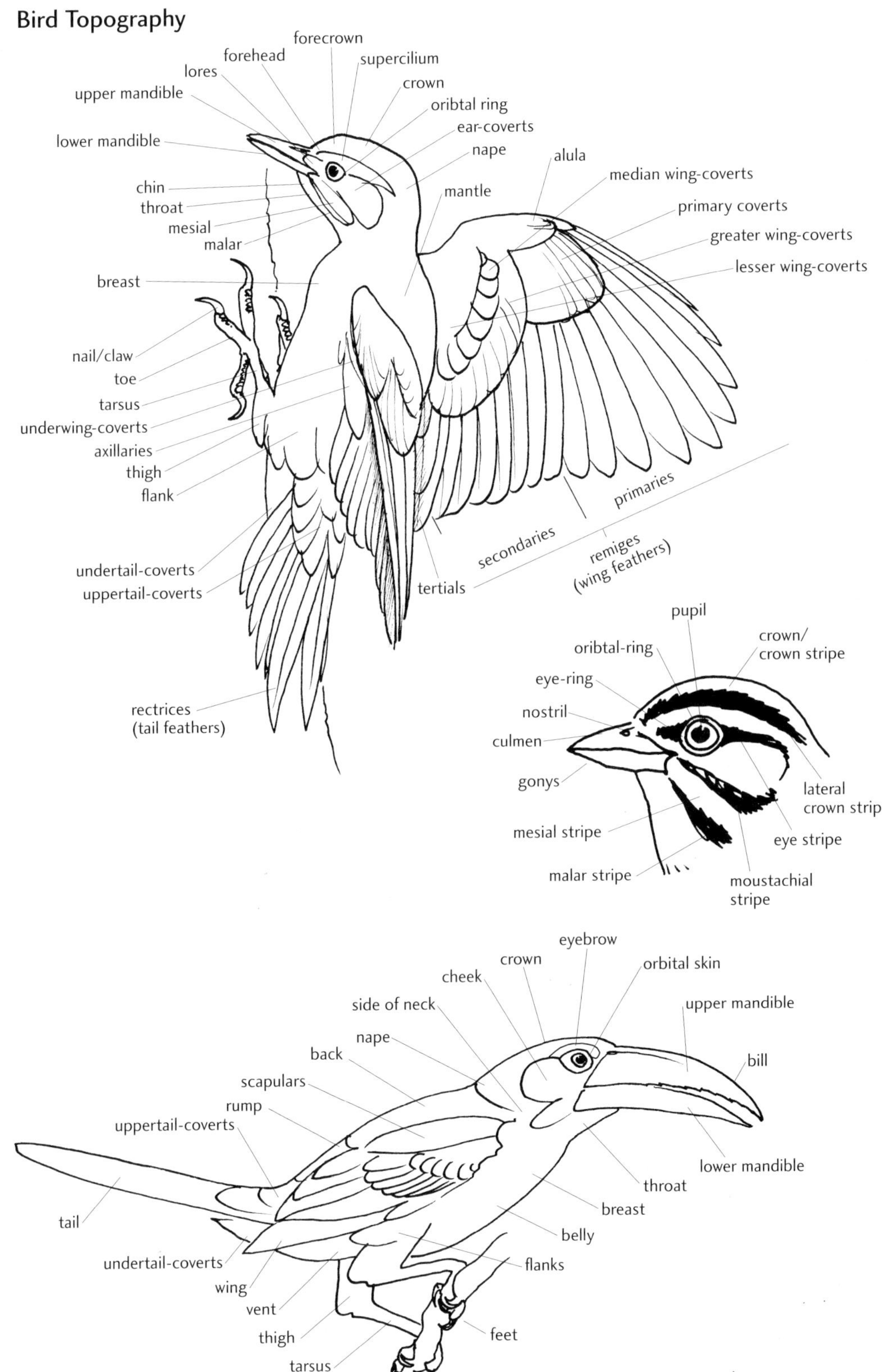

CLIMATE, VEGETATION AND HABITATS

A three-dimensional relief map of northern South America does not provide the most interesting of subjects, for the greater part of region will appear to be rather flat (see map of altitude zones on page 15). The only significant areas of relief are the southern tablelands of the Guianan Shield, the outliers of the Andes along the northern coasts of Venezuela and Colombia (for example, the ornithologically famous Sierra Nevada de Santa Marta, which reach almost 5,800m), and, of course, the Andean chain itself which runs from extreme north-western Venezuela through Colombia (where it divides into three distinct ranges) and throughout Ecuador (where there are just two main ranges), and on to the southernmost tip of the continent. In our region, the Andes reach their peak in Ecuador at the 6,272m Volcán Chimborazo, which is one of the highest summits in the entire continent. Relief is, of course, a major influence on the prevailing climate of this tropical region, and is the principal factor determining temperature, which declines by approximately 6°C per 1,000m. At a single station, for example, in western Colombia, mean temperatures may otherwise only vary by 2°C during the course of a year.

Starting in the west, the climate of Pacific Ecuador and Colombia is chiefly hot, humid and very wet, with annual rainfall at many localities in Ecuador being 3,000–4,000mm per annum. Rainfall to some extent varies with latitude (increasing towards the north), with up to 10,000mm reported in parts of western Colombia, whilst the Quibdó region is the wettest in the Western Hemisphere, regularly receiving up to 13,000mm and a maximum of almost 20,000mm. In Ecuador, most rainfall falls in the first five months of the year and there is also marked variation caused by El Niño events, which can lead to torrential downpours that cause significant infrastructural damage. The original forests in this region, especially in western Ecuador, are very much reduced and development is increasingly affecting the Chocó region of Colombia.

In contrast the north coasts of Colombia and Venezuela are subject to very dry trade winds during December to April, and mean annual rainfall can be as low as 300mm (on the Guajira Peninsula), though at the base of the Andes this might increase to as much as 3,000mm (generally less than 2,500mm in Venezuela, where rainfall totals generally diminish above 2,000m in elevation), and parts of the Santa Marta massif are permanently snow-capped. In the Caribbean lowlands dry deciduous or evergreen woodland, desert scrub and mangrove formations are the most important vegetation types, giving way to montane tropical forests and subsequently cloud forests above about 750m. On the leeward side of the cordillera, one enters another rather drier zone with deciduous or semi-deciduous forests. In areas such as the central-north coast of Venezuela, travellers moving inland will note a swift transition between these habitat types, but elsewhere the coastal plain is often considerably wider. Deforestation has been severe in parts, for example in the Santa Marta massif, and the interior slope of the northern cordillera in Venezuela is one of the most heavily populated regions of the country with the inevitable consequences for the native vegetation.

Rainfall throughout the Andes is much less seasonal, though in the three Colombian cordilleras, two wet and two dry seasons can be identified during the course of the year, with the longest dry period running from June to September (July–August in Ecuador). Annual rainfall varies between 1,500 and 4,000mm per annum, and permanent snow commences at around 5,000m, but even in this region localised drier regions occur (in the rainshadow of mountains) with vegetation dominated by thorn scrub and cacti; as in the north of the region rainfall declines at really high elevations. Major habitats within the Andes include subtropical montane forest, temperate montane forest, elfin and *Polylepis* woodlands, páramo and montane scrub (see the Glossary of Habitats below). Throughout the Andes forest loss has been significant, especially in the valleys (some of which, like Colombia's Magdalena Valley, have served as major trade routes for centuries) and in the foothills.

The vast grasslands of central Venezuela and parts of eastern Colombia, known as the *llanos*, experience a monsoon climate type with a pronounced wet season between May and October and a long dry season from November to April. Rainfall varies between about 1,000mm on the leeward side of the coastal mountains of Venezuela to 1,500mm over most of the region and more exceptionally *c.*3,000mm at the base of Andes in Colombia. Flooding, in season, can be particularly extensive in the south of this region, but for birdwatchers the time to visit is in the late dry season when huge numbers of waterbirds may congregate in the remnant patches of floodwater. Dry forest is a feature of the higher land at the rim of the *llanos*, whilst the presence of pockets of gallery forest leads to a varied passerine avifauna with origins in the adjacent semi-arid zones, but also many others of widespread or Amazonian provenance.

The eastern lowlands of Colombia and Ecuador and thence through southern Venezuela and the Guianas barely, with the exception of a few isolated metas (tablelands) in Amazonian Colombia and the Ptaritepui region of southern Venezuela and Guyana, do not rise much above 500m. Population levels in all of these regions generally remain low, though pressure from development (such as oil exploration) is increasing virtually throughout, and much of these lowlands is still covered in humid forest of various types, principally *terra firme* which is never subject to flooding. Annual rainfall is generally 2,000–3,000mm per annum, though totals in the Gran Sabana of southern Venezuela may locally be considerably less (just over 1,000mm in places), and in southernmost parts of northern South America, in the headwaters of the ríos Negro and Orinoco, may reach 3,500mm, and even 3,900mm around the Macarena highlands in Colombia. The tepui highlands provide the only significant area of relief within this otherwise very uniform landscape, with most of the tablelands reaching a few hundred metres below 3,000m, though most of their famed endemic birds are found much lower, at around 900–1,000m. As mentioned elsewhere, the avifauna of this part of our region has particularly fascinated students of biogeography for almost a century.

There is no clear-cut dry season in many parts of the lowlands, though March and September average slightly drier in Venezuela, and July–August is the driest 'season' in eastern Ecuador. In southernmost Colombia, most rain falls in November to May and, like elsewhere in Amazonia, rain principally falls in short, sharp 'shocks' each afternoon (all-day rain is not unknown, but comparatively infrequent). Amongst the most interesting habitats of the Amazonian part of northern South America are *várzea* (which is seasonally flooded forest along river systems), riparian woodland in floodplains, river islands (of great interest to birdwatchers due to their highly specialised avifaunas), oxbow lakes and their often-related Moriche palm savannas and swamps. Nonetheless, the avifaunas of northern and western Amazonia are generally slightly more depauperate and certainly less endemic-rich than other parts of the Amazon basin. In the east of our region the avifauna is principally defined by a distinctive subset of so-called Guianan species, many of which are habitat specialists of sandy soil regions.

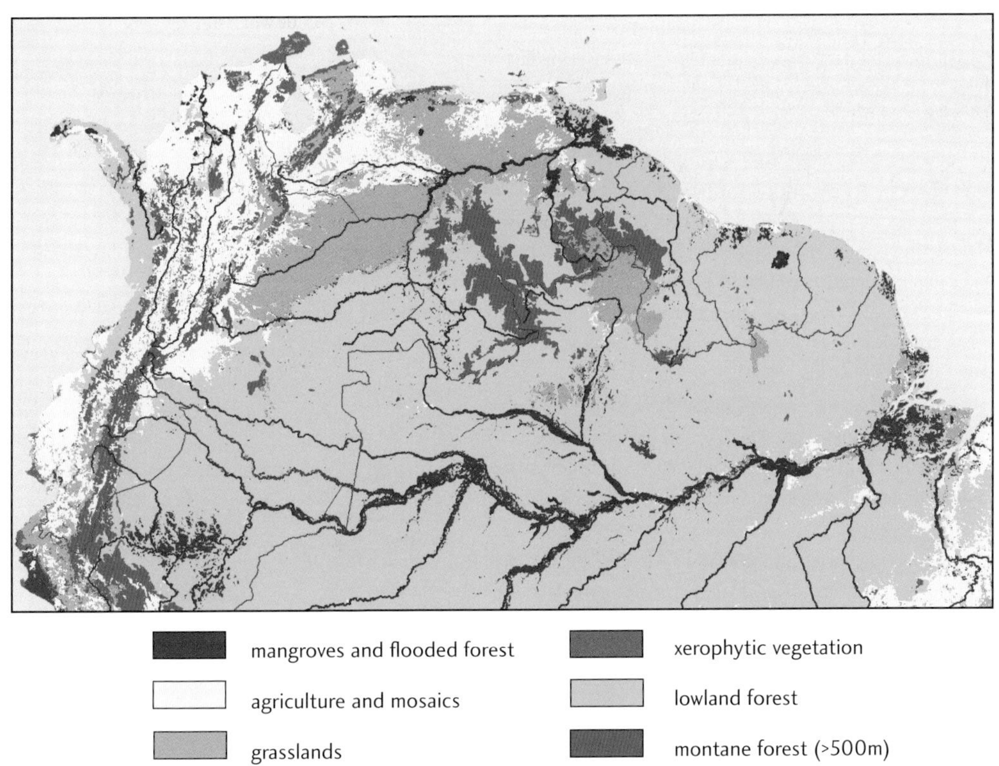

Vegetation map of northern South America. Derived from Eva et al. *(2004) in the GLC 2000 series.*

Glossary of habitats

Arid scrub is fairly open land, albeit sometimes impassable, usually with thorn bushes, cacti and drought-resistant trees.

Borders and edges of forests and woodland form a rather distinct habitat, with species that normally occur in the canopy or upper levels of the forest being found lower at the edges. Some borders have full rounded bushes and low trees that do not occur within forest, others may be densely tangled or simply densely grown. Some species of birds only venture to these marginal areas early in the morning.

Clearings represent similar habitat to borders and edges, but generally offer more security for forest-dwelling species and may be used later in the morning and earlier in the afternoon. Clearings range from natural ones caused by rivers, landslides or treefalls, to others that are man-made along trails and paths.

Cloud forest is, strictly speaking, forest regularly embraced by low clouds. There are both dry and humid cloud forests.

Coastal refers to habitats along the coast, typically beaches and shores, cliffs and rocky coastlines; also coastal waters, including saline swamps and lagoons, etc., though mangrove swamps are usually specified as such.

Cultivation is generally land used for agriculture, including plantations. Birds listed as occurring in cultivation are, by implication, to some extent, tolerant of disturbed habitat and of man's presence.

Deciduous forest is also known as tropical dry forest or just dry forest.

Desert scrub - see Arid scrub.

Dwarf forest and **elfin forest** are terms often used interchangeably, but Fjeldså & Krabbe (1990) separate them neatly.

Espeletia is known locally as frailejon: rosette plants with thick fleshy leaves and yellow flowers on thin stalks that are scattered evenly over vast areas of páramo. They may grow to several metres high.

Gallery forest may be referred to as riparian woodland, but whereas gallery forest occurs alongside waterways, undergrowth and woodland beside rivers is better referred to as riparian.

Llanos are extensive flatlands, often flooded; soil varies from poor to rich and supports open woodland or savanna.

Mangroves are usually found in coastal areas. These dense and usually low forests grow in areas permanently or periodically flooded. There are several species of mangrove, of which those known as red mangrove (genus *Rhizophora*) are commonest and generally most widespread, and typically grow in areas closest to the sea.

Marshes are low-lying areas, permanently wet, sodden or inundated; plant growth consists of stunted low shrubs or scattered bushes, reeds, sedges or even tall grasses, but no trees.

Melastomes (family Melastomataceae) are typical constituent trees of montane evergreen and elfin forests in the Andes, and include widespread genera such as *Miconia* and *Tibouchina*.

Moriche swamp (Morichale) may also be referred to as Moriche marsh, and are forested swamps that are more or less permanently inundated wherein the Moriche Palm *Mauritia flexuosa* dominates. Some bird species are strongly associated with this habitat.

Offshore refers to sea areas, including those within sight of land.

Oxbow lakes develop over long periods and are caused by a meandering river gradually pushing further into a curve until a small crescent-shaped lake is formed, whereupon the river may well form a new course, leaving the lake unfed. The surrounding area may be swampy or marshy and support a distinct plant community, creating a special habitat favoured by some species.

Páramo is open, barren alpine land that occurs from the treeline to the snowline, and may be wet, being often shrouded in cloud or drizzly mist. The characteristic flora of the wetter páramo in Venezuela is *Espeletia* (see above); also endless tufts or clumps of *Stipa* grass. Further south, in drier páramos (e.g. in Ecuador), *Puya* bromeliads and *Chuquiraga* shrubs grow.

Parks and gardens present man-made or man-modified habitats, with ornamental or natural shrubs and trees that offer important habitats for those species that can adapt to some level of disturbance

Pasture is open grassy land where bovines and other mammals periodically graze. Pasture generally has fewer species of birds than ungrazed land.

Pelagic seabirds are those that stay out of sight of land. Truly pelagic species only come ashore to breed, and spend the rest of their lives at sea.

Plantations present various forms, and may have well-spaced tall trees to provide shade for crops or, if the crop benefits from direct sunlight, then there are few trees. Birds that occur in plantations are, by implication, to some extent tolerant of disturbed habitats and of man's presence. Some birds only occur in the canopies of shade trees in such habitat.

Polylepis forest is formed by the woody shrub *Polylepis* which grows at the treeline (roughly 3,000–3,400m) and up to 5,000m. It occurs in ravines and protected gullies, and is favoured by many bird species, some of which are specialists of the habitat.

Riparian wooded habitats evolve gradually along rivers and waterways and in seasonally flooded land, initially with fast-growing plants, typically dominated by *Gynerium* cane and *Cecropia* trees, but gradually become more substantial. Some birds are riverine habitat specialists.

River island scrub or second growth is fast-growing, early succession flora on seasonally flooded or recently exposed islands. Some bird species are specialists of this habitat and are poorly known.

Savanna, also called grassland or campo.

Savanna woodland is open, often scrubby woodland with many gaps and light undergrowth on poor, often sandy soil.

Scrub or scrubby areas: fairly bare land with low rainfall, typically with scattered tough, sparse plants; in dry and desertic areas the dominant plants tend to be thorns, cacti and stunted trees; at higher elevations the character changes a little, but the effect is the same. Never supports a rich avifauna.

Second growth or secondary woodland are usually human-created wooded habitats that are naturally much less species-rich than primary (and thus much less disturbed) woodland and forests.

Shade trees are tall with bare trunks but spreading canopies, planted or left untouched, to provide protection from the sun for cultivated crops such as coffee.

Swamps are usually lowland areas with permanent, often stagnant water. They often have tall grasses, and usually scattered bushes and a few trees, whilst some have strips or patches of woodland where the ground is damp but not inundated and their borders densely grown with shrubbery.

Semi-deciduous forest: also called tropical moist forest.

Tepuis are tall, flat-topped, almost vertically-sided mountains in the states of Bolívar and Amazonas in southern Venezuela. They generally have unique or specific flora and fauna. Many birds described as occurring atop the tepuis really occur on their slopes. Many tepuis have different species or subspecies, and a complete review and comparative analysis of the natural history of the Pantepui region is badly needed.

Terra firme forest is usually referred to simply as *terra firme* and is a type of lowland tropical evergreen forest that typically grows on well-drained upland soils, principally in Amazonia; differs from *várzea* in never being flooded. They are floristically diverse and often statuesque.

Treefall gaps and clearings describe a small area of forest where a large tree has fallen leaving an open area where smaller trees and shrubs have been destroyed by the collapsing branches. The clearing passes through various stages before it is reclaimed by new trees, thus it is a comparatively short-lived microhabitat that particularly attracts border and edge-loving bird species.

Tropical humid forest may be referred to simply as humid forest.

Tropical wet forest, also known as semi-deciduous forest, is rather restricted in extent, being principally found near the base of the Andes and coastal cordillera in Venezuela, as well as in the *llanos* and south of the Orinoco in the same country. It usually occurs on slopes or hilltops.

Várzea forest, usually written simply as *várzea*, refers to forest growing on seasonally flooded land.

Xerophytic areas are dry habitats with low rainfall - see Arid scrub.

AVIFAUNA OF NORTHERN SOUTH AMERICA

Northern South America truly represents a paradise for birdwatchers; it is as if biodiversity has run wild ('megadiversity' as it was described in one recent work). Approximately 2,300 species occur here or, put another way, just a couple of hundred species short of 25% of the global avifauna. Such a staggering total is, of course, unsurprising when one considers that the Colombian avifauna alone consists of over 1,860 species (the highest single total of any country on Earth), that of Ecuador comprises over 1,600 species (an incredible total for such a tiny country), and Venezuela almost 1,400 species, though of course there is considerable overlap between the avifaunas of all three and with the other countries included in this book. What is more, despite the efforts of a legion of past collectors and field workers, all of these totals are still growing. However, unlike the well-known avifaunas of the developed world, the additions are just as likely to be previously overlooked residents (in some cases even species previously unknown to science) as vagrants blown off course. And, virtually no-one has devoted much effort to the marine avifaunas of any of the countries covered in this book; the opportunities for gathering new data on pelagic seabirds, especially off the Pacific coastline, are just waiting for someone to grasp the nettle!

Included here are the islands of Trinidad & Tobago and the Netherlands Antilles, both groups that are ostensibly Caribbean, but in zoogeographic terms unsurprisingly (given their proximity to the mainland) clearly best considered South American. The two former islands, in particular, make an ideal first destination for those who wish to dip a toe into the world's richest avifauna without being completely overwhelmed, for Trinidad & Tobago can truly be said to represent a microcosm of the continent as a whole. They are also amongst the biggest vagrant hotspots in northern South America, and not only regularly produce sightings of boreal visitors more usually to be found further north in the Antilles, but even records of Old World species.

Most of the families endemic to South America occur in our region. In terms of endemic species, the big three countries (Colombia, Ecuador and Venzuela) can muster totals of 60+, 14 and 40+; impressive enough, but certainly less significant than the total of 20 Endemic Bird Areas (EBAs) identified by BirdLife International in the region as a whole, though Ridgely & Greenfield (2001) suggested some modifications to the boundaries of those EBAs in Ecuador. In a different study, Stotz *et al.* (1996) subdivided South America into 34 zoogeographic regions, of which 13 lie wholly or partially within northern South America, despite our region accounting for less than one-third of the total land area of the continent.

What are the reasons for such phenomenal avian diversity? Principally, of course, the answer lies in the tremendous range of habitats that is to be found in northern South America. From coastal wetlands, offshore islands and mangroves to the altiplano of the high Andes, via the full range of forest types to be found in Amazonia. Further diversity is to be found in the forested tepuis (tablelands) of southern Venezuela and adjacent Guyana, the famous 'Lost World' of Arthur Conan Doyle (and the origins of which avifauna have long provoked debate and bewilderment amongst ornithologists), and the Sipaliwini Savanna of southern Suriname, where a number of species more synonymous with the *cerrados* of central Brazil find their northernmost outpost. But, it is the Andes where avian diversity reaches its extraordinary pinnacle, for in these relatively young mountains, which split into three main cordilleras in Colombia, the dynamics of speciation are about as obvious in anywhere in the world, doubtless due in part to the hand of man as habitats are destroyed and fragmented, creating 'island' pockets of native vegetation. The first-time visitor will find the barrage of new species that accompanies each slight change in elevation quite staggering, and even 'old hands' continue to marvel at such richness. Quite simply, anyone with a strong interest in birds should visit this part of the world and experience its wonders at least once.

The first serious investigations of the ornithology of northern South America were made by Alexander Humboldt at the close of the 18th century. Amongst his discoveries was the remarkable Oilbird *Steatornis caripensis* whose nesting grounds at the famous Cueva de los Guácharos, near Caripe, in north-eastern Venezuela, he was shown by local missionaries. Soon, the collectors that followed were sending back to Europe thousands of trade skins from the northern Andes, which were described by Gould, Gray, Lafresnaye and others. Many of these were simply labelled Bogotá and whilst some were almost certainly taken within reasonably close proximity of the city, a great many more were probably or certainly not. In some cases, these skins present still-unsolved problems in identifying the real range of the species in question.

Despite the efforts of those pioneers such as Schomburgk, who reached Roraima in the 1840s, it was not until the first two decades of the 20th century that the work of Frank Chapman and his associates at the American Museum of

Natural History permitted the first syntheses of the avifauna of northern South America, with the publication of classic works on Colombia and Ecuador, both beautifully illustrated by one of the masters of South American bird art, Louis Agassiz Fuertes. Thereafter, others continued the good work, particularly the Phelps family in Venezuela and the truly extraordinary professional collector, Melbourne Carriker, in Colombia, amongst others.

By the mid-20th century, a new era of synthesis was upon us, with Rodolphe Meyer de Schauensee taking the lead by publishing important works on Colombia, then South America as a whole, and finally a field guide to Venezuela - the first to any South American country - in partnership with William Phelps and magnificently illustrated by Guy Tudor. For the first time, field identification of birds in South America was possible, prompting a fresh wave of scientific exploration and the first amateur birdwatchers to visit the continent. Particular mention must be made of the dedicated research into Ecuadorian birds led by Bob Ridgely and the Academy of Natural Sciences at Philadelphia, resulting in a splendid new field guide to this incredibly bird-rich nation, and Steve Hilty's ground-breaking field guides to Colombian and Venezuelan birds. After decades of American-led research in many parts of South America, there is currently a noticeable awakening of interest in birds amongst native South Americans, with particularly vibrant conservation and birding communities springing up in Colombia, Ecuador and Venezuela. Under such favourable circumstances, our knowledge of the avifauna of the entire continent is destined to mushroom.

MIGRATION

The bulk of migrants occurring in northern South America are non-breeding visitors from North America (with a handful also moving south from their breeding grounds in the Caribbean), though overall numbers and species diversity amongst Nearctic migrants are significantly less than further north in Middle America and the West Indies. Other migrants, albeit many fewer, reach the principally southern borders of our region from much further south. So-called austral migration has received greatly increased attention from ornithologists in recent years, but most species that perform such dispersal do not penetrate any further north than the Amazon, thus the phenomenon is relatively inconspicuous in northern South America. Finally, a number of species appear to practice more limited and, to some extent, erratic or altitudinal movements. For both birdwatchers and researchers, perhaps the most interesting subset within the latter group is formed by those species dependent on bamboo seeding events.

Nearctic migrants

More than 420 species of Nearctic breeding birds make seasonal movements to the Neotropics to a greater or lesser degree, of which the greatest diversity occurs in the Central American lowlands, with pine and pine-oak forests representing important winter refuges for many species, especially those that are to some extent restricted to undisturbed forests at this season. Generally speaking, the proportion of Nearctic migrants within Neotropical avian communities decreases with latitude, though south of our region numbers are dramatically reduced, as, for instance, the vast majority of wood warblers (the largest single family of Nearctic migrants) does not regularly reach further south than northern South America. Across much of central and southern South America the number of species is relatively uniform. Quite a number of shorebirds, however, winter principally in Tierra del Fuego, the high Andes of the extreme south or the pampas of Argentina and adjacent countries. Most of these species generally overfly our region and/or are only recorded in certain parts of northern South America at particular seasons, as they perform loop migrations (generally passing further east in autumn and further west on the return route in spring). In addition to latitudinal differences, altitude is also a significant factor in delimiting species distributions amongst such migrants, with rather few species found above 1,500m. Amongst Nearctic migrants, a reasonable number have separate breeding populations within the Neotropics, including northern South America. Many of these are waterbirds, but passerines such as Yellow Warbler *Dendroica petechia* and Red-eyed Vireo *Vireo olivaceus* are other examples. A very small, but somewhat interesting subset of northern migrants moves south to winter in our region (and perhaps beyond) from their sole breeding grounds in the Antilles. Some of these are difficult to identify for one reason or another, e.g. Antillean Nighthawk *Chordeiles gundlachi*, and thus their winter ranges are very poorly known. In the case of Cuban Martin *Progne cryptoleuca*, the wintering grounds are completely unknown but generally speculated to be in South America.

Recent years have witnessed much greater interest in the wintering grounds of Nearctic migrants due to irrefutable declines in many species. Several factors have been identified as the root, but a number of commentators have speculated that loss of tropical forest in the non-breeding quarters is a significant driving force. This has had the happy effect of increasing conservation interest and available resources for preserving such habitats. Nonetheless, as ably argued by Stotz *et al.* (1996), such speculation is not wholly founded on the available facts, which in contrast suggest that rather few Nearctic migrants are habitat specialists and that many passerines are prevalent in secondary and successional habitats. Therefore, their vulnerability to habitat modification on the wintering grounds is somewhat limited, and loss of tropical forest is probably not a key factor in the recent declines of such species, though logging and conversion of lower and mid-elevation forests in the Andes is of real concern for a small suite of Nearctic migrants, including Cerulean Warbler *Dendroica cerulea*. That is not say that those species which are habitat specialists in winter are not at risk. Loss of their winter grassland habitats in southern South America appears to be a significant factor behind the decline in Buff-breasted Sandpiper *Tryngites subruficollis* and may also have limited the ability of Eskimo Curlew *Numenius borealis* to recover from market hunting in North America. Furthermore, as more data become available and the existing information subjected to closer scrutiny, it may be that some species currently believed to be at low risk in their winter quarters are proven to be rather less secure than currently believed. Remsen's (2001) already classic study of the Veery *Catharus fuscescens* in its winter range revealed that, rather than occurring over much of southern Central and South America, as previously believed, the 'true' limits of its distribution at this season were restricted to comparatively small areas of Amazonia, and that most other records were, in fact, probably of migrants. Overestimation of the winter range may be true for many species of Nearctic migrants, and represents a significant 'pitfall' for conservationists attempting to design appropriate conservation strategies. Such over-mapping is probably common even in 'standard' and otherwise highly authoritative works.

Austral migrants

The phenomenon of austral migration has garnered much attention in recent years, though it is rather weakly expressed in northern South America, as most of these visitors from the south tend to stop short of our region in the central and southern Amazon basin. Nonetheless, some species do make it to our region, such as the recently split Sick's Swift *Chaetura meridionalis*, which breeds in northern Argentina to parts of Bolivia and Brazil, and migrates north as far as Colombia and even Panama. Such movements doubtless generally went unnoticed by earlier ornithologists, for many such species are in fact widespread birds, and the austral migrants will easily go unnoticed as they temporarily absorb themselves within the range of their resident counterparts. Nowadays, of course, we recognise the flocks of Tropical Kingbirds *Tyrannus melancholicus* and Fork-tailed Flycatchers *T. savanna* that may line riverbanks in Amazonia in their hundreds for what they really are, southern breeders escaping a cold climate, rather than dismissing them as merely unusual, temporary aggregations.

Unlike Nearctic migrants which comprise a broad spectrum of families and species, austral migration is dominated by representatives of just three groups, namely the Tyrannidae (New World flycatchers), Anatidae (ducks and geese) and Emberizinae (sparrows and finches). The first-named is especially important, as over one-third of those species identified to date as austral migrants are tyrannids. However, these differences are mainly reflective of taxonomic differences in the make-up of the southern South American versus North American avifaunas. Just like Nearctic migrants, those species of austral migrants which perform the longest-distance movements are those which breed at the highest latitudes (in other words furthest south). Nonetheless, there is nothing to compare with the immense distances covered by some arctic tundra-breeding shorebirds which winter in the southern cone. Also in common with the Nearctic breeders, austral migrants generally show little habitat specialisation on their wintering grounds, with the exception of a handful of tyrannids and *Sporophila* seedeaters which seem to be dependent on the steadily decreasing *cerrados* (natural grasslands) of central Brazil.

Intra-tropical migrants

Two forms of intra-regional migration also require a brief summary here. Compared to south-east Brazil and parts of Middle America, e.g. Costa Rica, regular elevational movements (other than local and highly temporary dispersal in response to inclement weather at the highest altitudes) in the tropical Andes are not a pronounced feature. Stotz *et al.* (1996) admitted that some hummingbirds appear to perform regular movements up- and downslope, but pointed to the existence of considerable, year-round field work and collecting at Andean locations that had failed to yield much evidence of such migrations. Nonetheless, it is certainly the case that some species, again often flycatchers, perform seasonal altitudinal movements, albeit usually with an equally strong latitudinal component, and some species, e.g. Dull-coloured

Grassquit *Tiaris obscura*, appear to move west–east from the Andes to the lowlands in winter, leading some more recent authors to question how deep our year-round knowledge of many Andean localities really is.

Finally, a small but highly distinctive set of Neotropical birds depends on bamboo seeds for food, examples in our region being Maroon-chested Ground Dove *Claravis mondetoura* and Slate-coloured Seedeater *Sporophila schistacea*. The very recently discovered Carrizal Seedeater *Amaurospiza carrizalensis* is probably another example of a bamboo-dependent species. Our knowledge of these birds and their ecologies is almost invariably very poor. Their appearances are almost always ephemeral, although they may sometimes occupy certain areas for a number of years before moving on elsewhere. Whether their appearances are more cyclical or truly nomadic is unknown. Even within apparently suitable areas, at times of peak abundance, their usage of, and spatial distribution within, the available habitat is frequently uneven and, to our human eyes, apparently random. Elucidating the mechanisms behind these species' uncanny ability to locate suitable habitat, or even garnering fresh data on their basic life histories, is one of the many special challenges facing Neotropical ornithologists.

CONSERVATION

We perch, somewhat precariously, on the brink of an extinction crisis of potentially epic proportions, a crisis that is, according to some reputable scientists, already irrevocable and driven by sufficiently deep-rooted factors that it threatens our own existence as well as that of the species with which we share this planet. Within such a context, if mankind faces annihilation, why should he devote attention to attempting to preserve birds and other biota? The answer, of course, is rather obvious; the factors at play in the potential extinction of the Earth's biodiversity are, for the main, human-created. The same factors, rising sea temperatures (for example) that wreak havoc upon breeding seabirds, are those at the root of our own precarious position. Threats facing South America's birds include, above all, habitat loss, particularly forest clearance but also conversion of wetlands and grasslands to agriculture and infrastructural development, as well as pollution, the wild bird trade and the threats posed by introduced species.

It has been well known for centuries that natural diversity reaches its pinnacle in the Neotropics. The largest number of species on any of the world's continents occurs in South America. Almost two-thirds of the world's avian families occur there and almost 30% of this total is endemic to the continent. It is, as many before have noted, perhaps as close to paradise as anywhere on Earth. The realisation that all was not well in this other 'Garden of Eden' has been comparatively late in coming. Even now, in the first decade of the 21st century, taxonomists are still kept busy cataloguing new species and finding the best solutions to arrange the existing ones, but nonetheless within the last two decades considerable efforts have turned away from simple cataloguing to conserving. In 1988, Nigel Collar and Paul Andrew, in *Birds to Watch*, listed 350 Neotropical birds as being at risk or potentially at risk of extinction, an increase of 226 species from the second edition of the *Red Data Book*, published just seven years previously. Although overall numbers of species considered globally threatened in the Neotropics had (thankfully) advanced relatively little by 2004, the date of publication for BirdLife International's most recent overview of the state of the world's birds, the number of species regarded as Near Threatened or Lower Risk has been steadily increasing over time. In other words, the warning signs for the next batch of threatened species are already there.

Within the last 20 years, two events might be singled out for their importance in raising awareness of the imperilled conservation status of Neotropical birds. The first was the publication, in 1992, of the magisterial *Threatened Birds of the Americas* (Collar *et al.*), which provided a detailed compendium of our knowledge of 327 species in the Neotropics considered by the authors to be at risk of extinction. The second was the publication four years later of *Neotropical Birds: Ecology and Conservation* (Stotz *et al.* 1996). Though the bulk of the latter book consists of ecological and distributional databases for the birds of the entire region, the introductory chapters to this work provide a series of analyses of the avian communities of Middle and South America and the Caribbean designed to formulate landscape-scale priorities for the conservation of this biological treasure-house. Although the format of these two works and the conservation priority ratings assigned differ, one critical conclusion was reached by both; the time for action was not tomorrow, but now. Both also served to dispel any ongoing misconceptions as to the real battlegrounds for conservationists in South America. It is not the Amazon, but the Atlantic Forests and, in our region, the Northern Andes (amongst others) that demand our attention. These works, and others, have served as clarion calls to field workers to include a greater conservation component in their work and to continue to elucidate the range, biology and threats facing some of South America's most threatened birds.

Other than the Red Data Books for birds, BirdLife has also published a listing of Endemic Bird Areas of the World (Stattersfield *et al.* 1998), of which 20 such regional centres of avian endemism lie either entirely or partly within northern South America. Considerable overlap exists between these priorities for conservation action and those set by Stotz *et al.* Further refining their focus to a finer scale, in 2005, BirdLife in partnership with Conservation International also published (entirely in Spanish) an inventory of Important Bird Areas (IBAs) in the tropical Andes, which covers the countries from Venezuela and Colombia south to Bolivia, a region with 209 globally threatened species. The work listed 455 IBAs, with the largest single total (128) being in Peru. As elsewhere in the world where the BirdLife partnership has been identifying IBAs, the criteria used to establish this network of sites is the same: populations and ranges of globally threatened birds, restricted-range species, and biome-confined and congregatory species. The latter grouping, however, are not particularly well served by the current listing due to a lack of data. An important facet of the IBA work is the establishment of local groups with an interest in preserving and documenting the fauna in their own IBAs.

In other words, the groundwork for the conservation of South America's avifauna has been laid, namely the identification of regions, sites and species that are most at risk. The IBA book suggests that a significant percentage of important sites still lack any form of protection. The challenge currently facing those working in the region is to bring about a change wherein all IBAs, and hence at least the majority of threatened species, enjoy some form of protection. Organisations like ProAves (in Colombia) and Fundación Jocotoco (in Ecuador) have already been grasping the nettle and have purchased a number of areas of land in recent years that protect both important representative avian communities and globally threatened birds.

TINAMIDAE – Tinamous

Tinamous are odd birds, as evidenced by the microscopic structure of their feathers, which is curiously different from that of all other birds. Considered one of the oldest groups of birds on the continent, most tinamous make their home on dense forest floors, where they live solitary, shy and secretive lives, walking silently and deliberately, taking berries and small fruits from bushes or noiselessly turning leaves to find insects and seeds amid the ground litter. A few species have adapted to less secluded habitats, such as brushland and even savannas, where they tend to go around in small parties. But whether in forested or semi-open areas, people seeking them find them vexing and elusive. The calls are easily heard, for tinamous have low, full voices that carry long distances even through thick growth, and they are intriguing – long-drawn, melodious, eerie whistles – surely among the most beautifully haunting sounds of Neotropical forests. In reality, tinamous are often heard but seldom seen, and the rare encounters with them, especially forest species, occur serendipitously in isolated clearings or remote tracks. It is generally by their vocalisations that tinamous are identified and recorded by birders, and differences in calls should be the basis for species comparisons. They are notably poor flyers – the near-absence of tail, short rounded wings and relatively small heart and lung capacity are handicaps that disable them for anything except fast, laborious take-offs and clumsy landings. Thus, it is unsurprising that tinamous constitute an important prey base for many Neotropical carnivores. One wonders how nestlings survive predators, for the simple nests are usually set snugly between buttress roots at the base of a large tree or hidden in thickets or under a bush, where even ground-dwelling animals can easily take them. Hunters consider them prime trophies, and search for them using calling lures, which make females particularly vulnerable. Near human settlements, tinamous are subject to extensive poaching or pressure from subsistence hunting, which has caused severe population reductions in some species. Habitat loss is also a great threat, but where habitat is virgin and remote, they tend to be abundant, thanks to a very efficient breeding strategy, with males polygynous and females polyandrous, and in a reversal of roles that is yet one more odd tinamou trait, the males incubate the eggs and rear the chicks without any help from the female.

Additional references used for this family include Blake (1977) and Cabot (1992).

Tinamus tinamous are large birds of comparatively lower elevations, found on the well-shaded floor of humid and wet forests, shy and likely to walk away at the slightest disturbance. They roost low down, sitting lengthways along a branch.

GREY TINAMOU *Tinamus tao* Pl. 1

Identification 42.5–49cm. Adult is large with a dark brown head and neck finely mottled in pale rows down the neck, chin and throat very pale, mottled dark brown, upperparts mottled very heavily with blackish and rufous, inclining to bars on back, wings and tail; underparts deep grey, rich rufous-orange on undertail-coverts; eyes dark, bill dark grey above, paler below, legs and feet bluish-grey. Immature like adult, juvenile sparsely speckled with white above, heavily barred black, bright cinnamon on nape with pure white stripe on neck-sides.

Ssp. *T. t. kleei* (SC Co: Pacific slope in Cauca, E Ec) similar to *larensis* but greyer, more heavily barred above than *septentrionalis*
T. t. larensis (NC Co: Perijá mts and E slope of E Andes, NW Ve: Perijá mts, Andes from Lara to Táchira, coastal mts Yaracuy to Sucre) as described; browner than *septentrionalis*, undertail-coverts deeper rufous
T. t. septentrionalis (NE Ve, NW Gu) greyer than *larensis*, with whiter throat

Habits Always forages on forest floor, shy and evasive, walking away if approached – and before being seen! Eats mostly fruit, some seeds and insects, and sporadically, small vertebrates. Nests at foot of large trees, amid buttress roots. Usually sings at dusk.
Status Local, very rare in Ecuador, rare in Colombia, and uncommon and local in Venezuela. Not recorded in Guyana in recent times.
Habitat Tropical to Lower Subtropical Zones. Humid *terra firme* forests (occasionally *várzea*); humid pristine or very mature secondary forests on slopes of Andes; cloud forests in Venezuela.
Voice Males utter an abrupt single hoot, often answered by female with a shorter, higher pitched hoot (H&B).

BLACK TINAMOU *Tinamus osgoodi* Pl. 1

Identification 40–46cm. Adult is large, black above, deep grey below, rufous on thighs, vent and undertail-coverts, barred black.

Ssp. *T. o. hershkovitzi* (SC Co)

Habits Unknown.
Status Local and very rare in Colombia.
Habitat Upper Tropical but mostly in Subtropical Zone, 1,500–2,100m. Heavy, humid forest at head of Magdalena Valley, where epiphytes, tree ferns, bromeliads and mosses abound.
Voice Apparently an easily imitated descending whistle (Hardy *et al.* 1995).

GREAT TINAMOU *Tinamus major* Pl. 1

Identification 40–46cm. A large, rather variable, brown bird with pale underparts. Essentially olive-brown above, barred darkly to blackish, bars may be broken or irregular but there is no obvious spotting; crown, head-sides and neck brown to rufous, barred so lightly as to be scale-like, chin and throat pale to white, crest varies in colour and length.

Ssp. *T. m. latifrons* (SW Co, W Ec) like *saturatus*, but pileum sooty black and crest longer
T. m. major (E Ve, Gu, Su, FG) dark head, crest deep chestnut; browner below, heavily vermiculated
T. m. peruvianus (SE Co, E Ec, Ve?) pileum bright rufous, crest very short; heavy dorsal barring, crown rufous
T. m. saturatus (NW Co) distinct occipital crest deep rufous and finely barred; heavily barred above

T. m. zuliensis (NE Co, N Ve) pileum deep rufous, crest very short to lacking; 2 colour phases, yellowish-olive and brown

Habits Persistent hunting has reduced numbers and caused species to become more wary. Sometimes freezes if spotted, but is as likely to flush with noisy wing-flapping. Heard rather more often than seen, and whilst it sings at any time of day or night, is most vocal at dawn and dusk. Nest is a clean spot scratched between buttress roots of a large tree. Will forage in clearings and on dirt trails. Feeds on berries, fallen fruit, small vertebrates and invertebrates.

Status Uncommon to rare in Ecuador. Frequent where forest is intact in Colombia, Venezuela and Guyana, and frequent though more often heard than seen in Suriname and French Guiana.

Habitat Lower Tropical Zone to 1,500m. Tall, dense and undisturbed primary forest, both *terra firme* and *várzea,* and very mature secondary forest. Partial to areas where forest floor is open, but in very wet areas may be found even in dense undergrowth.

Voice One of the most haunting and beautiful Neotropical bird sounds, comprising 7 tremulous whistled notes, the first set sometimes repeated, second note slightly higher pitched but then sliding down, *whoo, who-o-o-o-or*. At times, the last note may be given alone or in series of up to 6 notes that gradually become stronger (R&G). Hilty cautions that *C. soui* copies calls of *T. major*, but *soui* version lacks moving quality and resonance of present species (H&B).

WHITE-THROATED TINAMOU
Tinamus guttatus Pl. 1

Identification 32–36cm. Top of head dark, paler on sides, chin and throat white; above, varies from pale chocolate-brown to dark, with rows of buffy or white spots, and variable dark brown to blackish spotting that may form bars distally; underparts ochraceous to pinkish-brown lightly and narrowly barred on flanks and thighs, possibly also undertail-coverts; eyes brown, legs and feet green. Immature like adult but more heavily spotted above.

Ssp. Monotypic (E Ec, SE Co, S Ve)

Habits Few data available. Feeds on seeds and ants.

Status Uncommon to locally frequent in Ecuador. In Colombia and Venezuela, locally frequent where forest is intact and there is no human pressure or presence.

Habitat Lower Tropical Zone to 400m in Ecuador, 500m in Colombia, 200m in Venezuela. Mainly in *terra firme* wet forest.

Voice A series of very melancholy whistles, the first long and mellow, followed by a shorter, lower one, then a pause followed by several accelerating ones and a repetition of the first two (P&MdS). Song a slow mournful, 2-note whistle, *whuuuUUU, uuuuuuaaaa*, lasting *c*.3.5 s. Also a similar but higher pitched single long whistle, weaker with a faint quaver in the middle, rising slightly at end (Hilty).

Nothocercus tinamous are fairly large, heavily barred and deeply coloured above and below. Very much birds of the interior of wet and humid montane forests.

HIGHLAND TINAMOU
Nothocercus bonapartei Pl. 1

Identification 35–41cm. Somewhat variable and subspecies difficult to separate. Crown and head-sides very dark brown, throat pale rufous or cinnamon, upperparts dark brown finely vermiculated black with additional blackish bars on greater wing-coverts and flight-feathers, wing-coverts having black streaks, pale to whitish spotting may cover all wing-coverts, rump-sides and flanks, or be restricted to wing-coverts; underparts rich deep rufescent ochre, finely barred from sides or flanks to undertail-coverts.

Ssp. *N. b. bonapartei* (NC Co: Perijá mts, Cesar and Norte de Santander, W Ve: Perijá mts, Andes from Lara to Táchira and coastal Cordillera, Carabobo to Miranda) illustrated (note variation)

N. b. discrepans (EC Co: Boyacá and Cundinamarca) darker than *bonapartei* and more rufescent

N. b. intercedens (WC Co: Antioquia to Cauca, Huila and W Caquetá) paler throat than *bonapartei*, generally less rufescent

N. b. plumbeiceps (EC Ec: spottily along E slope) darker than *bonapartei* and less rufescent

Habits Forages alone in marshy or muddy areas and in ravines with thick undergrowth; generally well within cover, but can be surprised walking along a trail, especially during rain. Feeds on fallen fruits or small animals. Shy and difficult to see. Often found where bamboo is seeding. Nest is a small scratched spot in hollow on ground or at base of tree, lined with leaves and blades. Several females may use same nest.

Status Rare to locally uncommon in Ecuador. Uncommon to rare in Colombia, uncommon in Venezuela.

Habitat Subtropical Zone, 500–2,500m, from Amazonian rain forest to cloud forests, mostly in wet, dense, pristine areas, but sometimes in very mature second forest or near clearings.

Voice Vocalisations described as loud, far-reaching, penetrating, deep and whinnying repetitions of *cawoh*. When alarmed, a *quok* scream (H&B).

TAWNY-BREASTED TINAMOU
Nothocercus julius Pl. 1

Identification 35–41cm. Deep rufous crown and nape, long crest, head-sides pale rufous, throat white, neck and upperparts olive-brown, deeply and heavily barred blackish; cinnamon below, rufescent on breast, scalloped and barred from flanks to thighs, black barred undertail-coverts. Immature has brighter orange-rufous pileum.

Ssp. Monotypic (Ec: Andes E slope, E, C & W Co, Ve: S Táchira)

Habits Poorly known. Forages singly or in small groups and keeps well within cover, but might be seen at edges at dawn. Usually heard but not seen.

Status Uncommon to rare in Ecuador, apparently more frequent but only locally so in Colombia. Very locally frequent in Venezuela.

Habitat Subtropical and Temperate Zones 2200–3400m in Ecuador, 1700–3100m in Colombia, 2400–2800m in Venezuela. Wet or very humid forests where tree ferns and epiphytes abound, up to treeline. Sometimes in small clearings. Prefers light, not too tall forest and elfin forest.

Voice Descriptions include a loud, two-note whistle, and a series of high trills, *t'r'r'r'a, t'r'r'r'a*, fluttery and fading towards end (Hilty).

Crypturellus tinamous are smaller than the preceding genera, being generally birds of lowland forests and woodland, and like all tinamous their beautiful songs – typical of lowland forests – are heard far more often than the birds are seen.

BERLEPSCH'S TINAMOU *Crypturellus berlepschi* Pl. 2

Identification 29.5–32cm. Apparently entirely black, but darkest on head and neck; eyes pale reddish-brown or ochre, legs and feet reddish-brown. Eyes reddish or yellowish, bill black above and grey below, legs and feet greyish-brown. Immature barred on wings and sides with cinnamon, scalloped on breast-sides and barred below with same colours but cinnamon more noticeable. Smaller than Black Tinamou, which it almost overlaps, and lacks reddish undertail-coverts.

Ssp. Monotypic (NW Ec: Esmeralda and Pichincha, W Co: W foothills of W Andes and Pacific coast)

Habits Very poorly known. Seems to be fairly solitary on wet forest floor.

Status Scarce in Ecuador. In Colombia, widespread and thought to be quite common in suitable habitat.

Habitat Lower Tropical Zone to 900m, mostly below 500m. Wet primary or mature secondary forests, especially dense second-growth woods of the Pacific coastal lowlands.

Voice Song a short, high-pitched piercing whistle *teeeee* (R&G).

CINEREOUS TINAMOU *Crypturellus cinereus* Pl. 2

Identification 29–32cm. Overall dark ashy brown, becoming fairly reddish on crown and crest, darker on neck and back. Fine white shaft-streaks on neck, bolder on throat, slightly barred dusky on thighs and undertail-coverts. Juvenile barred on wings, rump and tail with cinnamon, darker brown and whitish.

Ssp. Monotypic (E Ec, SE Co, S Ve, Gu, Su, FG)

Habits Shy and elusive, runs to hide at slightest noise. Feeds on berries, fruits and seeds, also ants, crickets and other insects. Does not construct a nest, eggs are simply laid amid thick undergrowth. Reports on their colour vary from salmon to purple to chocolate-brown.

Status Common in Ecuador. Frequent in Colombia, uncommon to locally frequent in Venezuela, frequent in Guyana. Very common in Suriname (especially littoral), common in French Guiana.

Habitat Lower Tropical Zone. Humid forests, especially *várzea*, where generally locally abundant, but also swamp woods, secondary forests and coffee and cocoa plantations. Clearings, borders and even patchy trees provided there is dense undergrowth.

Voice Single tremulous whistles, occasionally in faint series (H&B), or strong, penetrating whistles, resembling a police whistle (P&MdS). A clear, ringing whistle on single pitch, *puuuu*, lasting just under 1 s and repeated every 3–5 s, sometimes for long periods (R&G).

LITTLE TINAMOU *Crypturellus soui* Pl. 3

Identification 21.5–24cm. Highly variable (see plate) and races virtually impossible to separate in field, some are sexually dimorphic with colour phases, others virtually monomorphic. Small; male has crown and head-sides blackish, throat white, neck greyish to brown, upperparts uniform brown, always unbarred and usually unspotted; underparts from bright ochre to bright rufous; eyes vary from grey to pale brown to yellow, bill usually blackish above, and from grey to yellow below, legs and feet greenish-yellow or olive. Female like male but may be much richer rufous both above and below.

Ssp. *C. s. andrei* (NE Ve: E slopes of Andes, coastal mts Lara to Sucre and Monagas, Tr) like *soui* but darker

C. s. caquetae (SE Co: SW Meta and S Putamayo) male similar to *soui*, female darker, browner

C. s. caucae (NC Co: Cauca Valley from S Cordoba and Magdalena Valley to Tolima and Cundinamarca) female darker than *mustelinus* with sooty pileum, male similar to *mustelinus* but paler than *soui*

C. s. harterti (W Co: Pacific coast, W Ec) female more greyish, male darker than *caucae*, greyer above than *caquetae*, weaker barring below

C. s. mustelinus (NE Co: NW Ve Sucre to Cesar to Boyacá and W Arauca, NW Ve: Perijá mts and W slope of Táchira and Mérida Andes) as *soui* but less rufescent above, buffier below; female paler with brownish pileum

C. s. nigriceps (E Ec) the darkest race

C. s. soui (E Co, Ve: Delta, Amazonas and Bolívar, Gu, Su, FG) as described

Habits Forages singly, in pairs or small family groups, searching for fruits, berries, tubers and seeds, as well as ants, termites and other insects. Constantly swallows small pebbles. Shy and elusive, will not flush. Nests at foot of a tree.

Status Locally common in Ecuador. Frequent to common and found in many localities, but subject to severe hunting pressure, in Colombia and Venezuela. Frequent in Guyana, Suriname and French Guiana.

Habitat Tropical Zone, to 2,000m in Colombia, to 1,700m on slopes of tepuis in Venezuela. Dry or humid forests, mostly in dense undergrowth. Edges and clearings, young second growth, plantations, cane fields.

Voice The most frequently-heard tinamou call, said to be an imitation of Great Tinamou but flatter and less resonant. Two main songs described: a two-note song, with first whistle ascending and second descending in tone; and a series of whistles, each higher, louder, more rapid, ending abruptly. Also a slurred call that rises and falls, *pee-ee-ee yer-r-r*, and phrases that resemble Great Tinamou but are never as loud or as resonant, nor low-pitched (R&G). Several song types, and sexual differences, complicate song recognition. At dawn and dusk both sexes give a long song, a slightly quavering series of 5–6 slow whistles, each a half step higher in pitch. Common day calls are various shorter whistles, often doubled, with each note sliding a quarter-tone lower and quavering slightly at end, *weeeeuuuu*, or a single long whistle, sliding up a quarter-tone in middle, trembling and then falling again, *wuuuueeeeuuuu*. Both sexes often counter-call using these different vocalisations (P. Schwartz recording, Hilty).

TEPUI TINAMOU
Crypturellus ptaritepui Pl. 2

Identification 28.5–30cm. Poorly known. Uniformly dark above, with no black or white markings, sides of face grey and throat also pale grey, breast, belly and flanks deep grey, scaled dusky brown, eyes pale creamy to yellowish, bill dark above, yellowish below, legs and feet dark green.

Ssp. Monotypic (Ve: Sororopán, Auyán and Ptari tepui, and possibly other E Bolívar tepuis)

Habits Forages in small groups when not breeding. Swallows small pebbles to aid digestion.
Status Vulnerable. Venezuelan/Pantepui endemic – small range and tiny population. Frequent on tops and high slopes of tepuis, scarcer on lower slopes. Common on Auyán Tepui.
Habitat Upper Tropical and Subtropical Zones, 1,350–1,800m. Dense cloud forests on tops and sides of some tepuis.
Voice Song a long, pure-toned whistle, lasting nearly 4 s, the first half on the same, high pitch, the rest descending and fading (Hilty).

BROWN TINAMOU
Crypturellus obsoletus Pl. 2

Identification 25–30cm. Small, reddish-brown forest tinamou. Adult has blackish crown, grey head, uniform reddish-brown upperparts (somewhat variable, may be quite chestnut), underparts also variable, usually deeper reddish-brown on breast, somewhat greyish on lower breast and belly, more ochraceous from flanks and vent to undertail-coverts, scalloped with long crescents, becoming bars on longest undertail-coverts. Sexes alike, female often more rufescent. Juvenile similar but has small black-and-buffy spots on wings, and soft dusky barring on flanks to undertail-coverts.

Ssp. *C. o. castaneus* (EC Co to E Ec) larger, more uniform chestnut above and below than others
C. o. cerviniventris (N Ve: NW Lara, Falcón, Aragua to Miranda) generally slightly paler than *knoxi*, especially below, barring on flanks brighter and better defined
C. o. knoxi (NW Ve: N Táchira to SE Lara) illustrated; very much like *cerviniventris* but darker below

Habits Main food seeds and insects. Follows army ants; turns up leaf-litter when foraging. Nests at base of a tree.
Status Rare in Ecuador. Uncommon and scarce in Venezuela, but somewhat frequent in a few remote localities. Perhaps extinct in Colombia.
Habitat Tropical Zone on eastern slope of Andes, but reaching Subtropical and even Temperate (cloud forest) Zones on western slope; 1,300–2,200m. Forests, stands of *Alnus*, second growth, edges and clearings, tracks through forest.
Voice Calls mornings and evenings, especially in twilight. Song described as loud, strong and very tremulous *eEEeert* whistled outbursts, repeated at short intervals or in sequences that swell in crescendo (H&B). A long (4 s) high-pitched, pure-toned whistle on same pitch, the second half fading away (D. Ascanio in Hilty).

UNDULATED TINAMOU
Crypturellus undulatus Pl. 2

Identification 28–32cm. Medium-sized; crown sooty, face-sides grey, throat white finely scaled grey, back to tail dark rufous, wing-coverts noticeably paler and more olivaceous, greater coverts basally browner, remiges browner, the entire upperparts finely vermiculated dusky; breast to undertail-coverts creamy to white, flushed tawny on flanks and thighs, finely vermiculated on breast, flanks and thighs broadly barred black, undertail-coverts barred with well-spaced black lines. Eyes pale yellowish-brown, bill black above, grey below, legs and feet yellow. Whitish underparts and strong barring distinctive.

Ssp. *C. u. manapiare* (S Ve) dark, dusky forehead and crown
C. u. simplex (SW Gu, FG) flanks and undertail-coverts paler, duller, less chestnut back
C. u. yapura (SE Co, E Ec) variable, but distinguished by greyish breast

Habits Little known, although less shy and secretive than other *Crypturellus*; seems to prefer riparian habitats and is thus easier to see where there is less undergrowth. Takes small fruits, seeds and insects. Being entirely terrestrial, it moves away from flooded areas during rainy season.
Status Common, though subject to severe hunting pressure near human settlements in Colombia and Ecuador. Locally frequent in Venezuela. Frequent in Guyana. Not recorded yet in Suriname. In French Guiana, sight records only.
Habitat Lower Tropical Zone, to 600m in Ecuador, 500m in Colombia and 200m in Venezuela. Humid forests, less frequently in dry scrub. *Chaco*, gallery and *várzea* forests; young second growth, isolated stands of forest in savannas or river islands, but generally near water.
Voice Sings often during day, described as distinctive, a melodious, melancholy, ascending whistle *whoo, who-who-uh?* or sometimes a twice-ascending *whoo-ho, who-uh?* (H&B).
Note Sometimes called Banded Tinamou.

PALE-BROWED TINAMOU
Crypturellus transfasciatus Pl. 2

Identification 27–29cm. Adult male has dusky brown crown and face-sides with a white eyebrow that broadens behind eye, throat white, neck pale grey frontally, rufescent olive at back to tip of tail, barred from lower back to tail, scapulars and wings, with duskier brown, tipped finely with cream on wing-coverts, tipped broadly on median coverts; breast pale grey to ochraceous, barred black on flanks, thighs and undertail-coverts. Adult female barred from nape to tail, median and greater coverts tipped white; ochraceous buffy below, from foreneck to undertail-coverts, barred broadly with reddish-brown. Difficult to see, but white eyebrow a very good field mark.

Ssp. Monotypic (W & SW Ec: S Manabi to W Loja)

Habits Poorly known. Freezes to avoid detection and thus may be passed by closely. Nests at base of a large tree. Calls mostly during rainy season.
Status Near Threatened. In Ecuador, frequent to uncommon, threatened by deforestation.
Habitat Tropical Zone to 800m, locally to 1,600m in Loja (R&G). Deciduous lowland forests, light woods, scrub.
Voice A distinctive, loud, liquid *ooo-ing* that rings suddenly through the forest, and a loud ringing *ooo-eeé?* (R&G).

[SLATY-BREASTED TINAMOU *Crypturellus boucardi*]

Erroneously listed for Colombia in *Checklist of Birds of Northern South America* (Rodner *et al.* 2000), but species occurs only in Middle America, from south-east Mexico to Costa Rica. It includes races *costaricensis* and *boucardi*, both occurring only in Central America. Colombian records of *C. boucardi* stem from race *columbianus* having been formerly considered as a race of *boucardi*, or because some authors considered it conspecific with *C. erythropus*. Here, *columbianus* is considered a race of *C. erythropus*, but it is very possibly a separate species.

CHOCÓ TINAMOU *Crypturellus kerriae* Pl. 2

Identification 25–27cm. Adult male has blackish front to head and contrasting white throat, becoming slate grey on neck to breast, upperparts deep umber barred slightly blackish on mantle, wings and lower back to tail; underparts rich ferruginous-salmon brown; eyes pale brown, bill dusky, legs and feet bright red. Adult female similar but barring above commences on back and is darker and more noticeable, grey below extends to vent, and breast is faintly barred.

Ssp. Monotypic (W Co: W Chocó in Baudó Mts)

Habits Almost unknown and almost invariably heard but not seen.
Status Rare and fragile due to habitat being seriously imperiled, presumed to have a very small, mostly Colombian range with small populations.
Habitat Lower Tropical Zone (300–800m in Panama). Very humid and dense lowland forests.
Voice Song a low, tremulous, very resonant, 1 s long whistle (H&B), in Panama song is a hollow, mournful *whoh, whoh-ah* (Ridgely & Gwynne).

RED-LEGGED TINAMOU *Crypturellus erythropus* Pl. 2

Identification 27–32cm. Medium-sized and quite variable, especially between races. Essentially, adult male is deep reddish-olive to plain olive or dull chestnut above, variably spotted black and buffy, with barring restricted to rump and tail, or sometimes on flanks and undertail-coverts, throat white, crown dark to blackish, neck brown; breast slate to pale grey, underparts ochraceous to cinnamon; eyes brown, bill blackish above and paler below, legs and feet pink to orange or red. Females invariably more barred above, and usually more reddish and richly coloured.

Ssp. *C. e. columbianus* (NC Co: Caribbean lowlands) pure white chin and pale grey breast in both sexes, female has unmarked deep umber back, lower back to tail rufous with black barring, wings deep brown evenly barred black and cinnamon, underparts cinnamon-ochraceous, barred from flanks to undertail-coverts; male similar but almost entirely unbarred, except faint narrow barring on lower rump, wide -spaced black and cinnamon barring on greater wing-coverts and secondaries, and heavy black barring on undertail-coverts

C. e. cursitans (NW Co, W Ve: Táchira) similar to *columbianus*, but brighter rufescent on neck, with slate grey breast, boldly marked secondaries and buff-tipped axillaries

C. e. erythropus (E Ve, Gu, Su, FG) male has fine black barring on rump to tail, wings olive with scattered black spots and pale buffy tips to wing-coverts, and pale tips to outer edges of secondaries, breast slate grey; female has mantle deep uniform rufous-umber, rest of upperparts evenly and narrowly barred black and rufous; lower neck and breast brown, barred dusky

C. e. idoneus (NE Co, W Ve: Perijá) similar to but paler than *columbianus*

C. e. margaritae (Ve: Margarita I) similar to *erythropus* but smaller and greyer above

C. e. saltuarius (NC Co: Magdalena Valley) similar to Chocó Tinamou but much paler throughout, forecrown sooty black

C. e. spencei (NC Ve) a paler and more spotted version of *erythropus*

Habits Active but solitary forager that is sometimes heard busily moving over leaf-litter. Forages for fallen fruits and berries, seeds, insects and small vertebrates, mostly at dawn and dusk. Curious and not very shy. Apparently breeds in rainy season. Males may amble randomly within their territories when not breeding. Non-territorial females may roam long distances.
Status Although widespread, populations appear small, and are under pressure from hunting and habitat loss in many areas. Very sensitive to deforestation. Relative abundance uncertain in Colombia, uncommon to locally frequent in Venezuela, uncommon in Guyana, rare in S Suriname. Still uncertain in French Guiana, probably rare; requires investigation in the drier parts of the coastal plain.
Habitat Tropical Zone, to 1,700m. Thorny, open woodland, scrub, thickets and second growth; light deciduous forests.
Voice Sings at dusk, a hollow, tremulous whistle – *whooo-hoooa* – repeated every *c.*30 s (H&B, P. Schwartz recording). In Venezuela, song popularly interpreted as *soi-so-la* which serves as the local name.
Notes The taxa included here as ssp. of *C. erythropus* follow the taxonomic arrangement proposed by Blake (1977) and by S&M, also suggested by Carriker (1955) and by P. Schwarz & Eisenmann (*fide* H&B). Both H&B and S&M consider that

races need revision: three are almost certainly separate species *idoneus*, Santa Marta Tinamou; *columbianus*, Colombian Tinamou and *saltuarius*, Magdalena Tinamou (known from a single specimen, is particularly different, and is considered Critically Endangered). In SCJ&W they are listed as separate species. Race *idoneus* sometimes treated as subspecies of Yellow-legged Tinamou *C. noctivagus*, while race *columbianus* is sometimes treated as a ssp. of Slaty-breasted Tinamou *C. boucardi*.

GREY-LEGGED TINAMOU
Crypturellus duidae Pl. 3

Identification 28–31cm. Male has entire head and neck to breast (except white throat) bright rufous, upperparts dark brown, faintly barred dusky, and some white tips to wing-coverts; underparts bright ochraceous, washed rufous on flanks, barred slightly on flanks and thighs; eyes orange to yellow, bill black above, grey to yellowish below, legs and feet grey. Female far more distinctly and obviously barred from back to tail, with paler, broader bars on tertials and remiges.

Ssp. Monotypic (SE Co: S Meta, S Ve: extreme W Bolívar and Amazonas)

Habits Very poorly known.

Status Uncommon to rare in Colombia, uncommon to very locally frequent in Venezuela.

Habitat Lower Tropical Zone, to 500m in Colombia and 200m in Venezuela. Dense, very humid lowland rain forests and forest edges.

Voice Song a slow, monotone whistle that has a brief break near the beginning: *whu-uuuuuuuuuuuuuuuh*, alternately *aah-aaaaaaaah* (Hilty).

VARIEGATED TINAMOU
Crypturellus variegatus Pl. 3

Identification 28–31cm. Adult has black crown, grey head-sides and white throat, neck rufous, darker at back, brighter near breast, entire upperparts heavily barred black on rufous, underparts whitish to ochraceous, barred on flanks, thighs, vent and undertail-coverts; eyes dark brown, bill dark brown above, pale brown below, legs and feet greenish or horn. Juvenile similarly patterned, but barring below paler, tipped white on vent and undertail-coverts, and foreneck and breast spotted with white and black.

Ssp. Monotypic (E Ec: Sucumbios to Morona-Santiago, SE Co: Vichada to W Caquetá and Vaupés, S Ve: Bolívar and Amazonas, Gu, Su, FG)

Habits Very shy. Feeds on insects, seeds and berries. Breeds in rainy season. For nest, uses a small, scratched-clean depression in ground.

Status Uncommon in Ecuador and Colombia, where populations have been severely reduced in many areas by deforestation and hunting. Frequent in southern Venezuela, in Guyana and in the interior of Suriname. Common in forests of the interior in French Guiana.

Habitat Lower Tropical Zone. All types of humid forests, but particularly *terra firme*, thickets and overgrown clearings.

Voice Has a very singular voice. Song a series commencing with a long, tremulous, ascending whistle, then a pause, then 5 shorter, faster whistles, each slightly higher in tone *wuuuuuuuh ...... wuu, wuu, wuu, wuu, wuu* (H&B, P. Schwartz recording).

RUSTY TINAMOU
Crypturellus brevirostris Pl. 3

Identification 25–28cm. Quite distinctive with extensive pale throat, and rest of head, neck and underparts bright rufous; upperparts brown, scalloped black on back, becoming barred on lower back and wings, pale barring on flanks and regular bars on undertail-coverts; eyes dark brown, bill blackish above, paler below, legs and feet greyish-yellow. Juvenile similar but virtually unmarked, but has dark subterminal spots and fringes to lower back and wings, and scattered crescents on flanks.

Ssp. Monotypic (Co?, Gu?, FG)

Habits Very poorly known.

Status Poorly known. Uncertain in Colombia and Guyana. In French Guiana only one recent record (Criquelnini).

Habitat Lower Tropical Zone. Dense humid tropical forests, especially *várzea*.

Voice Described by M. Cohnttaft (1977) as being like *C. bartletti*.

Notes Sight record (1993) in Colombia by J. Newman *fide* SCJ&W. Perhaps conspecific with *C. bartletti*.

BARTLETT'S TINAMOU
Crypturellus bartletti Pl. 3

Identification 25–28cm. Crown and nape uniformly fuscous, throat whitish, foreneck and breast dull brown, upperparts olive-brown heavily barred black, underparts creamy ochre, slightly and faintly barred on flanks, regularly barred dark brown on undertail-coverts; eyes dark brown, bill dark above, pale below, legs and feet pale grey to pale yellowish-horn or greenish. Juvenile duller with blackish crown, sparsely, white- and black-spotted wing-coverts and breast, and indistinct dark flanks markings. Look for contrasting dirty brown upper breast and very pale belly, and obvious barring on back and wings.

Ssp. Monotypic (E Ec)

Habits Poorly known. Forages alone. Extremely shy.

Status Rare, but perhaps under-recorded in E Ecuador (possibly occurs in Colombia).

Habitat Lower Tropical Zone to 400m in Ecuador. Humid lowland *terra firme* forests; in dense vegetation or sometimes in wooded thickets.

Voice Beautiful song is a loud, penetrating series of pure-toned whistles, commencing with long notes separated by long pauses that speed up gradually to shorter, higher notes with shorter pauses (R&G).

Notes First sight records in Ecuador in 1990, first specimen 1991. Possibly conspecific with *C. brevirostris*.

BARRED TINAMOU
Crypturellus casiquiare Pl. 3

Identification 25.5–27cm. Bright rufous head and pure white throat contrast with slate grey neck and breast, which in turn contrasts with white belly, becoming pale ochre on flanks with vestigial barring, and rufescent faintly barred undertail-coverts; upperparts deep black with rufous scalloping and fringes from mantle to tail tip; eyes brown, bill horn with dark tip, legs and feet green. Juvenile/immature duller and browner, less ochraceous, breast flecked rufous, wing-coverts tipped whitish.

Ssp. Monotypic (SE Co: extreme E Guianía and Vaupés, S Ve: extreme SW Amazonas)

Habits Poorly known. Look for grey breast and pale grey belly.
Status Very restricted range, no data on populations. Possibly frequent but quite local in Colombia and Venezuela.
Habitat Lower Tropical Zone to 300m in Colombia and Venezuela. Almost exclusively in white-sand soil forests of the upper rio Negro–Orinoco basin.
Voice The song is described as easily recognised: a long whistle, *wooooa*, then a long series (*c*.30) of shorter whistles that first rise and then fall in pitch and decelerate (H&B, P. Schwartz recording).

TATAUPA TINAMOU
Crypturellus tataupa Pl. 3

Identification 24.5–26.5cm. Quite distinct and unmistakable if seen well. Head, neck, breast and upper belly soft grey, throat white, flanks and thighs creamy buff, undertail-coverts black with whitish-buffy fringes to feathers; upperparts uniform cinnamon-chocolate; eyes brown, bill red, legs and feet pale purplish-red. Juvenile similar but has pale black barring on wings.

Ssp. *C. t. inops* (SE Ec: extreme S Zamora–Chinchipe)

Habits Forages on the ground for seeds, buds and berries, also ants, insects and small snails; less shy than others in family.
Status Uncommon, only recently found in Ecuador.
Habitat Tropical Zone, at 650–950m. Deciduous forests, scrub, edges, clearings and tracks through dense vegetation; occasionally wanders into open grassy areas. Wet, densely vegetated gulleys near forest edge, locally in grassy areas and scrub (Cabot 1992).
Voice Song unlike any other Ecuadorian tinamou, a short, descending series of gravelly notes: *drreeyp? dreey-dri-dri-dri-dri-dru* (R&G).
Note First sight records in Ecuador in 1991, first specimen, taken 1992, erroneously assigned to race *peruviana* in Rodner *et al*. (2000).

Nothoprocta tinamous are distinct both in appearance and habitat. They have decurved bills and somewhat lined or streaked patterns on head, more pronounced on the backs. They are birds of high-altitude, fairly open grassy terrain and are far more likely to flush and fly off when disturbed than other tinamous.

ANDEAN TINAMOU
Nothoprocta pentlandii Pl. 3

Identification 25.5–30cm. Top of head brown with blackish spots or bars, back of neck plain brown, dark line through eyes continues onto neck-sides, eyebrow, face-sides, throat and upper foreneck pale buff, breast grey spotted buff, entire underparts buffy with slight black-spotted chestnut streaking on sides; back streaked whitish, alternating with chestnut that is scaled or spotted black. Rump to tail barred narrowly dark grey and tawny-buff, wing-coverts brown vermiculated and spotted black, greater coverts and all flight-feathers barred rich brown, black and white with fine vermiculations; eyes brown, bill narrow and decurved, dark above and yellowish below, legs and feet yellow. Juvenile has additional pale barring and vermiculations on breast.

Ssp. *N. p. ambigua* (S Ec)

Habits Very secretive, seldom leaves tall grass or scrub cover, but when flushed has distinctive shallow but rapid wingbeats. Feeds on seeds, juicy shoots and fruits; potatoes, alfalfa and barley buds from planted fields; insect larva. Several females lay eggs in 1 nest.
Status Uncommon and local in Ecuador.
Habitat Upper Tropical Zone to Páramo, 1,500–4,000m. Steep, inaccessible slopes and ravines. Semi-arid shrubby, thorny or coarse grass areas, páramos, edge of cloud forests, light woodlands of *Polylepis* or *Carica*, occasionally in planted fields.
Voice Territorial calls include a sharp *cheeleep*, and the song is a long accelerating and descending series of melodic calls, *pyouc-pyuc-pyuc-pyuc...... yucyucyuc*. On western slopes, series shorter (F&K). High-pitched whistled call is an abrupt and shrill *pii-eeng!*, usually given at long intervals and thus difficult to locate (R&G).

CURVE-BILLED TINAMOU
Nothoprocta curvirostris Pl. 3

Identification 26–30cm. Crown black with rufous fringes to feathers, continuing on back of neck, long white supercilium from base of bill to neck-sides, dark line through eyes also continues onto sides of neck, where fragmented by white spots, throat and foreneck whitish-buffy becoming rufous from upper breast back, fading slightly on vent and undertail-coverts, breast lightly barred at sides and spotted irregularly with black and white; upperparts mostly deep chestnut, streaked on back with white lines and rows of heavy, chestnut-edged black spots, wing-coverts brown vermiculated with subterminal black bars and buffy fringes, greater coverts and flight-feathers chestnut barred black, with some narrow white fringes to tertials and innermost secondaries, primaries black barred white; eyes brown, bill dark brown with yellow base, legs and feet dull orange. Juvenile similar but more rufescent above and more spotted on breast-sides and flanks.

Ssp. *N. c. curvirostris* (C Ec: Carchi and Pichincha to E Azuay)

Habits Poorly known. Found around patches of Ericaceae, Compositae and *Hypericum*. Apparently tolerant of human proximity, although human presence very low within its largely inaccessible habitat.
Status Uncommon and local in Ecuador.
Habitat Temperate Zone to Páramo, 3,000–3,900m in Ecuador. Puna and páramo; humid to semi-arid areas of bunch-grass, scrub and evergreen bushes.
Voice Call a series of 3 whistles, *pee-pee-pee*, repeated every 5 s (F&K).

ANHIMIDAE – Screamers

Screamers are large, superficially goose-like birds, related to ducks and flamingos, but anatomically unique. They have sharp spurs on the wing bends and perforated nostrils. Legs and toes are unusually large and long, enabling them to easily walk over floating vegetation, despite weights of several kilos. They make excellent eating and are hunted everywhere. Perch atop bushes and small trees, among tall marsh grasses, but if disturbed fly to top of tall tree, where they call, alerting all wildlife in the area, much to the chagrin of hunters. Calls audible over several kilometres.

Additional references used to prepare this family include Carboneras (1992b).

HORNED SCREAMER
Anhima cornuta Pl. 4

Identification 84–92cm. Black, glossed with green, white scalloping on crown, nape and neck, some white linings to underwing-coverts, belly to undertail-coverts white. A slender 'horn' of firm skin projects from forehead; eyes yellow, bill black, legs and feet grey. Unmistakable. Differs from Northern in white belly and white underwing-coverts, easily visible in flight, and has black cowl with mottled neck.

Ssp. Monotypic, (throughout except ABC)

Habits Usually in pairs in grassy patches near water, sometimes more social. Very wary and flushes at long distance. Occasionally soars, appearing like a vulture, with neck extended and long tail spread.

Status Uncommon to rare in Ecuador, locally common in Colombia and Venezuela, extinct in Guyana and French Guiana. Declining due to habitat loss.

Habitat Tropical Zone to 300m. Remote marshy areas, vegetation-choked lagoons and riverbanks in forested areas, shallow marshes and ponds, but always with bushes and trees.

Voice Very vocal and very loud. An unmistakable and unforgettable, deep throaty *guu-uulp, güü*, usually when perched (R&G). Typically several throaty *u-who* notes, a few *gulp-whoi* calls and a more raucous honking *quik-quoo, quik-quoo, quik-quoo, yoik-yok, yoik-yok*, varied in sequence. Pairs duet, a rhythmic 4-noted *U-WHO-cluk-uak* (Hilty).

NORTHERN SCREAMER
Chauna chavaria Pl. 4

Identification 84–94cm. Black to dark grey on body, head and neck white with a broad black band around neck, red eye-ring prominent, scruffy crest, eyes and bill black, legs and feet greenish-grey. From Horned by red face, white cowl, black neck and scruffy crest.

Ssp. Monotypic (N Co, NW Ve)

Habits Sedentary and sedate, usually singly or in pairs. Not shy but often flushes at some distance. Easily overlooked if resting in tall marsh grasses or in red mangrove.

Status Uncommon and very local in Colombia and Venezuela. Declining due to habitat loss.

Habitat Tropical Zone. Vegetation-choked lagoons in swampy forest, marshes, grassy ponds in open country, banks of slow-flowing rivers with bushes and tall trees nearby or if surrounded by forest.

Voice Often silent for long periods. Recalls Horned Screamer, but less powerful, a rising, high-pitched almost yelping scream. Calling bird usually answered by mate (Hilty).

ANATIDAE – Ducks and Geese

There is a certain gentle artlessness in ducks that makes even the rarest and most 'exotic' species seem familiar and domestic. Among the northern South American species, some are migrants and others residents; some flock in thousands and a few live in distant, solitary pairs. Many are exquisitely dressed in elegant plumage patterns, many have intriguing courtship displays, and yet, with perhaps the single exception of Torrent Duck, none seems to qualify for the appellation wild bird. But they are indeed wild and their conservation is a matter of serious concern. Aside from unrelenting persecution by hunters, they are affected by the destruction of rivers and riparian habitat from damming, pollution (including pesticide run-offs) and silting, and are even the innocent victims of their insatiable appetite for rice. One very interesting aspect of waterfowl life is moult, wherein all flight-feathers are shed simultaneously, rendering the birds literally flightless for some time, until the new ones are in place. Ducks prepare for the energetic demands of growing new feathers by feeding actively (often day and night) to accumulate fat, and by gathering in moulting grounds – wetlands that have been traditionally visited at moulting time, where they may find both an abundance of food and a measure of safety from predators. Rains and water levels are also fundamental. Even the most sedentary species follow seasonal itineraries, journeying, usually between a few not-too-distant wetlands, to take advantage of each when food availability peaks.

Additional references for this family include: Blake (1977), Madge & Burn (1988, referred to here as M&B), Carboneras (1992b), Johnsgard & Carbonell (1996) and Sibley (2000).

Whistling ducks are long-legged and long-necked, short-bodied with a fairly upright stance. Distinctive profile in flight, with legs projecting beyond the tip of the tail, broad wings with black undersides and shallow wingbeats. They walk well and comfortably. Highly gregarious, gathering in close flocks for feeding and roosting. They have shrill canary-like whistles given in flight.

FULVOUS WHISTLING DUCK
Dendrocygna bicolor Pl. 6

Identification 45–53cm. Upright-standing, largely cinnamon with fulvous to brown back barred darkly, paler throat with short thin black streaks, black on back of neck and elongated feathers of flanks are white, edged black; eyes dark, bill blackish, legs and feet grey. Cinnamon from head to belly, with black-and-white streaks on flanks diagnostic.

Ssp. Monotypic (all countries)

Habits Always in flocks that range from small to very large, often mixed with Black-bellied Whistling Duck. Forages mostly at night, dabbling and sometimes diving in open water for seeds, fruits, grass shoots, bulbs and other plant matter in the water.

Status Very local everywhere, always associated with suitable wetlands. Heavily hunted for sport and to prevent crop damage.

Habitat Tropical Zone, occasionally to Subtropical, but generally below 100m. Freshwater wetlands with trees and tall waterside vegetation in *llanos* and other flatlands. Particularly likes rice paddies.

Voice Call repeated continually in flight; a high, reedy *kur-dúr* (Hilty) or a shrill whistle, *ki-weeah* (R&G).

WHITE-FACED WHISTLING DUCK
Dendrocygna viduata Pl. 6

Identification 38–48cm. Adult male has white face and throat, rest of head to halfway down neck black, breast deep ruddy chestnut, back brown streaked black, wings ruddy and grey, flanks finely barred to vermiculated black and white, belly to undertail-coverts black; eyes dark, bill black, legs and feet vinaceous pink. Adult female has white of face dirty and not clean-cut, white throat more extensive, leaving small black band to join black at back of neck, lower foreneck and breast ferruginous, upperparts drab grey lightly spotted and streaked darker, wings like male, entire underparts finely (more so than male) vermiculated black and white; bill dark to blackish, legs and feet dark grey. Juvenile has grey face, breast weaker fulvous. From Black-bellied by head pattern, dark back and black bill.

Ssp. Monotypic (all countries)

Habits Always in small to large groups, often with Black-bellied, forages by day or at night, dabbling or diving for plant matter and some aquatic invertebrates. Flocks stand in tight groups on humid banks, becoming upright when alert. Local movements and breeding season depend on rains, which in turn affect water levels and condition of wetlands.

Status Global population large and widespread in South America and Africa, but very local everywhere, always associated with suitable wetlands. Hunted for sport and to prevent crop damage.

Habitat Tropical and Subtropical Zones, occasionally to Temperate. Freshwater wetlands with or without aquatic vegetation, in *llanos* and other flat, open areas.

Voice A sweet *güi-ri-ri* whistle in flight, with stress on first syllable, e.g. *WEE-te-de* (Hilty).

BLACK-BELLIED WHISTLING DUCK
Dendrocygna autumnalis Pl. 6

Identification 43–53cm. Adult male has grey face, ferruginous crown, grey on back of neck, lower throat white, separated from dull rufescent upper breast by an indistinct greyish bar, lower breast grey, belly and sides black, admixed white on undertail-coverts; entire back bright chestnut, wings grey with a whitish band running lengthways; eyes dark, bill coral red, legs and feet orange-pink. Female has much whiter face and a sandy crown and back of neck, from a soft greyish bar across foreneck to entire breast orange, fading on belly and lightly scalloped with grey, underparts dusky with some buffy on undertail-coverts, back orange-cinnamon, wings pale grey; soft parts like male but slightly paler. Juvenile has duller, greyish-white belly barred darker. From White-faced by chestnut back and coral red bill.

Ssp. *D. a. discolor* (all countries)

Habits Usually in loose flocks, except when breeding. Forages in shallow water, wading and dabbling for vegetable matter, or grazes dry ground near borders of ponds and streams. Flocks move seasonally over large areas to where wetland conditions are adequate.

Status Common, has benefited from forest clearance for pasture and subsequent creation of small drinking ponds.

Habitat Tropical Zone, occasionally to Temperate, but mostly below 200m in Ecuador, to 2,600m in Colombia, to 600m+ in Venezuela. In mangroves, *llanos* and savannas, pastures and agricultural areas, and wetlands with partially wooded borders.

Voice Call is a *güi-ri* whistle, uttered repeatedly by entire flock. Gives variations of *wee*, from *wee-ree* up to 5 notes, e.g. *wee-tee-Wée-te-re* (Hilty). High-pitched whistles, *wi-chi-tee* or *wit-chee, wit-chee-chee* (R&G).

Pair of Masked Ducks swimming (duck on left, drake right); note tail is normally laid on water (as in the duck), but may be raised in display or agonistic situations

MASKED DUCK *Nomonyx dominicus* Pl. 4

Identification 29–36cm. Adult male in breeding plumage has front of head black, nape and throat to breast rich ruddy, becoming more rufescent on back and flanks, which are spotted black, wings have large white speculum, tail short and pointed and may be held vertically at right angles to body. In non-breeding plumage, black face broken up by largely white postocular eyebrow, subocular crescent and irregularly from chin to lower ear-coverts. Eyes reddish-brown, bill pale blue-grey with black tip, legs and feet greyish-green. Female lacks any ruddy or chestnut, having a black crown, white eyebrow, black line through eye, white line from base of lower mandible to ear-coverts, chin and throat whitish; upperparts dull brown, with black crescent-shaped spots; underparts from foreneck ochraceous with black crescent-shaped spots on neck- and breast-sides and flanks. Females and eclipse males from Andean Duck by double white lines on face. From Andean Duck in flight by white wing panels.

Ssp. Monotypic (all countries)

Habits Very wary and secretive. Swims silently into cover or dives at first alarm. Found singly, in pairs or families. Forages by diving for seeds, bulbs and other vegetable matter, and small invertebrates. Tail only occasionally cocked upright.
Status Very local and uncommon, though often considered rarer than it really is due to secretive behaviour.
Habitat Lower Tropical Zone, sea level to 200m. Freshwater swamps and marshes with well-forested borders and abundant water plants. Also in mangrove swamps and rice fields.
Voice Pigeon-like *ouu-goo-goo-ouu* by displaying male (Hilty), also *coo-coo-coo, kirroo-kirroo* and an almost inaudible *oo-oo-oo* (Johnsgard).
Note Previously placed in genus *Oxyura*.

ANDEAN DUCK *Oxyura ferruginea* Pl. 4

Identification 37–43.5cm. Adult male in breeding plumage has entire hood black, almost entire body deep chestnut-brown, becoming sooty on central belly to inner flanks, lower belly to undertail-coverts creamy white, tail dark to blackish, and sometimes held at right angles to body. Eyes dark brown, bill pale blue, legs and feet grey. Adult male in non-breeding plumage is duller and browner with head pattern rather like Masked Duck but with a single white line. Breeding female almost entirely mid brown with fine lateral barring on flanks, central belly to undertail-coverts creamy white. Non-breeding female has head similar to female Masked Duck, but with a single whitish line. Females and eclipse males from Masked Duck by single white line across face. From Masked Duck in flight by lack of white in wings.

Ssp. *O. f. andina* (Co: C & N Andes) variable white patch on cheek, extremes from entirely black to all white are known
O. f. ferruginea (S Co, Ec) as described; no white on head

Habits In small groups that do not join other waterbirds but spend most time on open water, where they forage by diving. Food is mostly aquatic invertebrates and seeds.
Status Uncommon and local; Colombian race *andina* is in decline.

Sample patterns from wide range of variation in head patterns of drake Andean Duck

Habitat Subtropical Zone to Páramo. Partial to montane wetlands with slightly alkaline waters, and also to sites with both deep, open water and large stands of reeds.
Voice Males utter *tic-tic-tic-raah* when displaying (R&G).

GREATER WHITE-FRONTED GOOSE *Anser albifrons* Pl. 6

Identification 65–86cm. A large greyish goose, barred narrowly with white on upperparts, dark heavy bars on belly, white vent and undertail-coverts: white plaque at base of yellowish bill, legs and feet orange. Juvenile lacks facial white plaque and black bars on belly; bill, legs and feet paler. From immature or blue-phase Snow Goose by pink bill and barred plumage.

Ssp. *A. a. elgasi / flavirostris / gambeli*? (Ar) subspecies unknown

Habits Normally in pairs or small flocks, but stragglers likely to be alone. Forages on dry ground, grazing or picking seeds, small fruits, cereals and grain.
Status Northern migrant, abundant in its breeding range, but recorded only rarely in northern South America, where only likely to occur during very cold boreal winters.
Habitat Lower Tropical Zone. Open areas next to wetlands, marshlands and coastal areas.
Voice Noisy. Characteristic flight call is *lyo-lyok*, given repeatedly (M&B).

SNOW GOOSE *Anser caerulescens* Pl. 6

Identification 66–84cm. Typical adult all white with black primaries, reddish-orange bill, legs and feet, and immature is duller white with a grey back and wings, still with black primaries, blackish bill and grey legs and feet. Blue phase is largely deep slate with a white head and clear white fringes to most wing-feathers.

Ssp. *A. c. caerulescens / atlanticus*? (Tr)

Habits In pairs or small groups, forages on dry ground for seeds, grass shoots, berries, grain and cereals.
Status Boreal migrant, abundant in breeding range but rare vagrant to Trinidad.
Habitat Lower Tropical Zone. Open country, always near water and often in rocky terrain or gravel beds, especially on the shore. Agricultural areas.
Voice Very vocal, calling continually in flight, sounds like a small dog barking *la-luk!* (M&B).

ORINOCO GOOSE *Neochen jubata* Pl. 6

Identification 61–66cm. Adult male has head, neck and breast to central belly off-white, streaked slightly buffy on nape and scalloped on breast, mantle grey scalloped white, band across upper mantle, scapulars, breast-sides and flanks orange, wings black with broad white speculum, large crescent of dark brown behind flanks, undertail-coverts white; eyes dark, bill black above, red below, legs and feet bright reddish-orange. Female similarly patterned but has drab wash to crown and back of neck, orange flanks less extensive and dark post-flanks patch borders scalloping on belly sides; bill dusky and pink, legs and feet paler orange. Unmistakable, with proportionately small head and thick neck.

Ssp. Monotypic (Ec Co, Ve, Gu, Su, FG)

Habits In pairs or family groups, or small groups when moulting. Forages by grazing in damp areas, taking variety of vegetable matter and smaller proportions of insects, snails, worms and other invertebrates. Sedentary.
Status Very rare and local in Ecuador. Very local elsewhere. Popular belief that it tastes bad has saved populations of some regions from hunting pressure (e.g. Venezuelan Llanos).
Habitat Lower Tropical Zone to *c*.500m, but recorded to 2,600m. Open areas, gallery forest or wet clearings, most often by large bodies of fresh water (rivers, lakes).
Voice Male's calls include a high whistle and guttural honks in breeding season, whilst female utters a loud cackle (H&B). The male gives a shrill-whistled *zree* and series of hollow reedy whistles, *preep, preep*… like whistling into a barrel. Female a low guttural honking *gur'rump, gur'rump, gur'rump* (Hilty). Both sexes utter a distinctive nasal honking, *unnhh?* (R&G).

MUSCOVY DUCK *Cairina moschata* Pl. 6

Identification 66–84cm. Unmistakable. A large black duck with a white wing patch, male much larger than female, and has pronounced tufted crown and nape, red caruncles on and around face, bill orange with a black band midway along. Female has pink-and-black bill and much smaller tuft on crown. Eyes sepia, legs and feet black. Both sexes have rich purple gloss to neck, and rest of the body may be shot with green and bronze iridescences. Juveniles lack iridescences and are duller with no facial caruncles. Many areas populated by birds that have hybridised, or are several generations on from hybrid breeding with descendents of the white Aylesbury Duck. These birds have variable amounts of white, and the facial caruncles of the male may have grotesque proportions. Even so, they are easily recognisable.

Ssp. Monotypic (all countries except ABC)

Habits Very wary of man, and retires at first suspicion of man's presence. Forages alone, in pairs or in small flocks, picking varied plant matter, as well as small vertebrates and invertebrates. Feeds both by grazing on dry ground or by dabbling in shallow waters.

Pair of Muscovy Ducks in flight, drake at upper left

Status Very extensive range, but only locally common. Populations decreasing due to continual hunting pressure and to its propensity for hybridising with domestic ducks.
Habitat Tropical Zone. Mangroves and coastal lagoons, swamps, slow-flowing rivers with gallery forests, wetlands in or adjacent to forest.
Voice Male hisses, female gives a soft *quack* (Hilty, R&G).

Pair of Comb Ducks in flight, drake at left

COMB DUCK *Sarkidiornis melanotos* Pl. 6

Identification 56–76cm. Rather goose-like, adult male has white head with black crown and small irregular black spots scattered over face and neck, clustering on nape, underparts almost entirely white but for blackish flanks; upperparts uniform black; eyes red, bill swollen at base and has a large flat comb erect from basal two-thirds of culmen, legs and feet greyish-blue. Female much smaller, lacks comb, but does have a prominent basal ridge to culmen and only slight dark brown shading to flanks. Juvenile sandy brown, dusky on back and below, the feathers of the underparts having broad sandy fringes affording a scaled appearance; eyes dark brown, bill, legs and feet grey.

Ssp. *S. m. sylvicola* (all countries)

Habits Wary. Somewhat nocturnal. In pairs or small groups. Forages by grazing on dry ground or by wading and dabbling in shallow water. May occur in flocks of whistling ducks. Journeys seasonally to different wetlands, in accordance with changes in water levels.
Status Rare and very local in Ecuador. Seldom in large numbers, with largest populations in Venezuela. Affected by pesticide use and hunting pressure.
Habitat Tropical Zone. All kinds of wetlands in open and semi-open areas with scattered trees, usually along rivers and open marshland.
Voice Largely silent, but gives wheezy whistles, grunts and hisses in breeding season, particularly in display (M&B).
Note Race *sylvicola* (which may qualify for Near Threatened status) is now often considered specifically distinct from nominate *melanotos* of Africa and Asia (e.g. Kear 2005).

BRAZILIAN TEAL
Amazonetta brasiliensis Pl. 4

Identification 33–38cm. Adult female dark morph has top of head from forehead to nape blackish, with a prominent white spot at base of bill and also just before and over eyes, throat white, dark grey above with wings dark blue and green, and a large white speculum; breast orange-rufous with some irregular black spots on sides, gradually becoming greyer on undertail-coverts; eyes dark, bill black, legs and feet red. Male similar but lacks white spots on face, which is duskier; bill bright red. Pale morph has face largely white and is brighter rufescent below. Red bill and rufescent breast distinctive, whilst double white facial spot on female also distinctive. Bright green-and-blue patch on wing with white trailing edge to secondaries unique.

Ssp. *A. b. brasiliensis* (E Co, Ve: Llanos, Gu) dark and light phases occur equally

Habits Usually in small groups, often with other waterfowl, or in pairs during the breeding season, which is linked to arrival of rains.
Status Common. Adapts to human-induced habitat changes. Under strong hunting pressure in some parts.
Habitat Tropical Zone. Freshwater wetlands partially bordered by woods or within densely forested areas.
Voice Flight-call a fast-repeated *tuwee tuwee* whistle (H&B, P. Schwartz recording), or *pueep-pueep-pueep* with shrill quality. Female has low raspy or grunting *grak* or *unk* (Hilty).

AMERICAN WIGEON

Anas americana Pl. 5 & 7

Identification 45–52cm. Speckled and vermiculated above, with a white forehead and crown in male, and a distinctive black line at base of bill, large white speculum; underparts orange-buffy, mottled somewhat with grey, belly white, and undertail-coverts black (male) or scaled black and white (female).

Ssp. Monotypic (Co, Ve, ABC, T&T)

Habits In pairs or small family groups, but seldom alone, feeds on vegetable matter (aquatic plants as well as green shoots, fresh sedges and grasses), foraging in water (swimming) or on ground, including humid, grassy shores, meadows and ploughed fields that are beginning to sprout.
Status Boreal migrant, reaches northern Colombia, northern Venezuela, and Trinidad & Tobago intermittently (large flocks occasionally occur).
Habitat Tropical Zone. In northern South America, shallow wetlands on or near coast.
Voice Female has low quack *warr warr warr*, male a distinctive 2–3-syllable whistle, *wi-WIW-weew* or *Wiwhew* (Sibley).

EURASIAN WIGEON *Anas penelope* Pl. 5

Identification 45–51cm. More or less entirely soft rufous, subtly patterned with grey and brown, bold white speculum and black flight-feathers. Female slightly less rufous with more dusky marks, slight streaking and vermiculations. Male in breeding plumage easily recognised by rich rufous head, straw-coloured forehead and forecrown, grey mantle and flanks. Eclipse male and female difficult to separate from American Wigeon in field, unless takes flight when grey underwing apparent; also head of Eurasian always warmer in coloration (male especially so), and American has black line at base of bill.

Ssp. Monotypic (Ve)

Habits Very much as previous species.
Status Rare vagrant to Caribbean. Single sight record of male in breeding plumage, in company of Blue-winged Teals in Falcón, Venezuela, March 2002 (Williams & Beadle 2003). Possible that females and eclipse males have been mistaken for American Wigeon?
Habitat Shallow wetlands on or near coast.
Voice Female similar to American, but harsher; male a high-pitched, strong, descending and vibrant *hwEEEEEEr* (Sibley).

GREEN-WINGED TEAL

Anas carolinensis Pl. 5 & 7

Identification 34–43cm. Male and female in non-breeding plumage very much alike, essentially speckled black or dusky on an ochraceous buffy ground; they are readily identified by the white, green and white speculum. Male in breeding plumage quite different, with deep ruddy head and bold, golden-edged green band from eyes to neck-sides, and vermiculated grey upper- and underparts. Female and eclipse males difficult to identify from other generally similar, nondescript female-type teals.

Ssp. Monotypic (migrant from Nearctic: Co, Ve, Ar, To)

Habits Winters usually in pairs or small groups. Dabbles, upends and dips head to pick seeds of water plants, sedges and grasses in shallow water.
Status Boreal migrant: northernmost breeding populations winter to southernmost parts of winter range. Very few scattered records, from Colombia, Venezuela, Aruba, Tobago and possibly Trinidad.
Habitat Tropical to Subtropical Zones. In northern South America, small brackish or saltwater wetlands, on or near coast.
Voice Female shrill and feeble, a high nasal, scratchy *SKEE we we we*. Courting male a ringing whistle, *kreed* or *krick*, which becomes hoarser in non-breeding season (Sibley).
Note Formerly considered conspecific with Eurasian Teal *A. crecca* of Old World.

MÉRIDA SPECKLED TEAL

Anas altipetens Pl. 5 & 7

Identification 40–44cm. Generally brown above and paler brown below, entirely speckled with blackish (feather centres), smaller and denser on head, larger and more spaced on breast, paler and lighter on flanks and undertail-coverts; identifying mark is orange, green and orange speculum; eyes dark, bill, legs and feet bluish-grey. Sexes alike. Generally paler than Andean Teal and browner above, less heavily speckled and barred; green speculum lacks bronze or purple reflections.

Ssp. Monotypic (E Andes of Co, NW Ve)

Habits In pairs or groups, which usually increase in size during moulting period. Feeds on small land and water invertebrates, larvae, seeds and plant matter, foraging both in water and on ground. Nests near water, amidst bushes. Breeding season March–September. Sometimes shares small wetlands with other teals (e.g. Cinnamon, Blue-winged).
Status Fairly common but very local.
Habitat Temperate Zone to Páramo. Montane lakes and rivers; bogs and marshes, usually above 3,000m.
Note Separated from *A. flavirostris* as Andean Teal, together with *A. andium*, by Madge & Burn (1988), but *altipetens* has subsequently been afforded specific recognition (Livezey 1991), though retained in *A. flavirostris* by Carboneras.

ANDEAN TEAL *Anas andium* Pl. 5 & 7

Identification 38–43cm. Generally dull greyish-brown above and greyish below, entirely speckled with blackish spots (feather centres), smaller and denser on head, larger and more spaced on breast, paler and lighter on flanks and mixed with white, drab undertail-coverts; speculum differs from Mérida Teal by being more purplish, with reddish and bronze reflections; eyes dark, bill, legs and feet bluish-grey. Sexes alike.

Ssp. Monotypic (Andes of Ec, C & S Co)

Habits Usually in pairs, sometimes small groups. Feeds on seeds, algae, small aquatic insects and crustaceans, and parts of water plants, by dabbling, dipping head or upending in shallow water, and by filtering mud whilst walking at water's edge. Breeds in marshy areas or in shrubby cover at edge of mountain lakes or in páramos.

Status Uncommon in Ecuador, scarce in Colombia.

Habitat Subtropical Zone to Páramo, usually above 3,000m. Montane lakes, ponds and reservoirs, bogs on high slopes.

Voice Male's call a mellow whistle (H&B). A fast *kree-krik* and a low-pitched quacking (R&G)

Note Separated from *A. flavirostris* as Andean Teal, together with *A. altipetens* by Madge & Burn (1988), but latter subsequently given specific recognition (Livezey 1991). Retained in *A. flavirostris* by Carboneras.

MALLARD *Anas platyrhynchos* Pl. 5 & 7

Identification 50–65cm. Large duck with obvious blue speculum that is diagnostic in all plumages. Female and eclipse male all dark brown with buffy fringes to all feathers, slightly darker line through eyes, and paler eyebrow and upper cheeks; eyes dark, bill dull orange with dark patch, legs and feet dull orange. Breeding male quite distinctive with bottle green head, narrow white neck-band, deep ruddy breast, mid grey above, pale grey below, broad royal blue speculum edged finely with white, 2 central black uppertail-coverts curled upwards, white tail, black undertail-coverts; bill yellow, legs and feet pale orange.

Ssp. *A. p. conboschas / platyrhynchos*? (Ar, Bo, Cu)

Habits Male very retiring and secretive in winter plumage; females may gather in groups on open water but males stay hidden in cover. Takes wide variety of plant parts and also insects and larvae, small crustaceans, worms. Grazes on dry ground and dabbles in shallow water.

The drake Mallard in breeding plumage (right) is easy to identify, but soon after arriving in its wintering grounds it loses all its flight-feathers and moults into 'female-type' plumage (left); the wing- and tail-feathers are replaced before the rest of the body-feathers (centre)

Status Very infrequent winter visitor. Apparently well known, and many reports by hunters on mainland Venezuela, but none confirmed.

Habitat Tropical Zone. Fresh, brackish or saltwater wetlands of all types, with tranquil waters and abundant aquatic or edge shrubbery.

Voice Male generally silent when not breeding. Female utters series of loud rapid quacks on slightly descending scale.

NORTHERN PINTAIL *Anas acuta* Pl. 5

Identification 54–65cm. Adult male quite distinctive with brown front of head, black from rear crown to nape, and bold white line on neck-sides, joining white breast and underparts, vermiculated grey above and below, with long black-and-white scapulars and tertials, and a long narrow tail, the speculum is buff, green and white; eyes dark, bill, legs and feet blue-grey. Female cryptic in ochre and brown, with dark feather centres and pale fringes, a drab 'non-speculum', and a long pointed tail which is not attenuated like the male's.

Ssp. *A. a. acuta* (Boreal migrant: winters to Co, Ve, Ar, Bo, Tr, Gu, Su).

Habits Usually in flocks, from a few to a few dozen birds. Swift flyer. Feeds on vegetable matter (roots, tubers, seeds, leaves) and small invertebrates, by dabbling, tipping up or diving in water, or grazing on dry ground.

Status Boreal migrant, common to abundant in breeding range, but only an occasional winter visitor to Colombia and Venezuela, and more rarely to Guyana and Suriname (southern limit of winter range).

Habitat Tropical to Subtropical Zones. Wetlands in open areas, both fresh and brackish water, and bordered by dense vegetation.

Voice Male utters a mellow *proop-proop*, female a repeated descending series of quacks, weaker than those of Mallard. Female gives a low croak when flushed (M&B).

YELLOW-BILLED PINTAIL *Anas georgica* Pl. 5 & 7

Identification 49–57cm (61–70cm including tail of breeding male). Adult is wholly cryptic dark brown with paler fringes to all feathers, a long pointed tail, yellow bill with a black tip, and grey legs and feet; male has a dark umber-black speculum, bordered buffy. Female marginally paler below, with less bold markings on sides and flanks, and a dull brown speculum; immature has a shorter tail and dull brown speculum. Colour of bill prevents confusion with female Northern Pintail. Often with Andean Teal, which is smaller, shorter tailed and has dark bill (not yellow).

Ssp. *A. g. niceforoi* (SE Co) crown blackish, bill longer, culmen flatter

A. g. spinicauda (S Co, Ec) slightly larger and paler, rufescent brown crown

Habits Usually in pairs or small flocks. Feeds in water, dabbling, upending or diving to pick small invertebrates and vegetable matter, and also sometimes grazes on dry ground.

Status Fairly common to uncommon and very local resident in Colombia and Ecuador, but southern South American populations are austral migrants. Colombian race, *niceforoi* apparently extinct.
Habitat Tropical Zone to Páramo. In northern South America, only in freshwater wetlands of Andean slopes and valleys.
Voice Semi-musical *trrrr*, typical of all pintails (R&G).
Note The taxa treated here were previously considered as different species, but merged without explanation by Meyer de Schauensee (1966).

WHITE-CHEEKED PINTAIL
Anas bahamensis Pl. 5 & 7

Identification 41–50cm. Dark brown crown to wings and tail, the feathers fringed narrowly with ochraceous sepia, sides of face and chin, and front of neck pure white, breast and underparts ochre with dark spots, bolder and more extensive on male than female; male has long attenuated tail, female's tail is not as long nor attenuated; both sexes have bold ochre, green and black speculum; eyes dark, bill bright orange-red with a grey tip, legs and feet grey. From other pintails and females of all other ducks by bright white face, and orange-red base to bill.

Ssp. *A. b. bahamensis* (throughout)

Habits Found alone, in pairs or small (rarely large) groups. Forages in water, upending to pick small aquatic invertebrates, plant matter and seeds. Breeding season varies among localities, in accordance with rains.
Status Fairly common, but distribution is local and spotty
Habitat Lower Tropical Zone, but recorded to 3,900m in Ecuador. Brackish or saltwater wetlands, rarely in fresh water.
Voice Largely silent, but male may give low whistles and female low, descending quacks (M&B).

BLUE-WINGED TEAL *Anas discors* Pl. 5 & 7

Identification 36–40cm. Adult male breeding has grey head with black crown to nape and black-edged white line that runs vertically from above eyes to fill space between eyes and bill, ending in a narrow white line either side of throat; back scaled and scalloped black and grey, lesser wing-coverts bright powder blue, median coverts white and speculum green; underparts from breast to vent warm rufous with black dots, undertail-coverts black. Eclipse male retains essential pattern but is paler on head, above and below, only wings retain same tricoloured pattern. Female streaked black and white, palest on face with pale eyebrow and blackish line through eyes, and wing tricoloured, but white bar has blackish spots on it. Eyes dark, bill dark grey, legs and feet yellow. Breeding male unmistakable. Non-breeding and female from Andean Teal by turquoise, white and green on wing; from Green-winged Teal by turquoise in wing, from female pintails by colour of bill.

Ssp. Monotypic (all countries)

Habits Usually found in large flocks. Forages by dabbling or immersing head to pick seeds and shoots of water grasses, algae and small aquatic invertebrates.
Status Boreal migrant, also local breeding resident. Common to abundant but populations suffer frequent swings.
Habitat Tropical to Subtropical Zones. Mostly saltwater or brackish wetlands, e.g. coastal swamps and lagoons, mangroves, saltmarshes. Occasionally freshwater wetlands.
Voice Male has a thin, whistled *tsee-tsee*, female a high-pitched *quack* (M&B).

CINNAMON TEAL
Anas cyanoptera Pl. 5 & 7

Identification 35–48 cm. Adult male deep reddish-cinnamon from head to vent, dusky on crown; back dark brown with blackish centres to feathers, tertials and lesser wing-coverts sky blue, median coverts white, speculum green, flight-feathers black, tail and tail-coverts black, the coverts fringed dark brown; eyes bright red, bill blue-grey, legs and feet slightly greenish-yellow. Eclipse male resembles the female but has median wing-coverts all white. Female dark, cryptically brown and blackish, a typical pattern amongst many female ducks, lesser wing-coverts sky blue, median coverts basally white, tipped black, speculum green. Breeding male unmistakable. Female and eclipse male warmer, with cinnamon flush, than Blue-winged Teal, and generally lack whitish spot in front of eye. Adults have red eyes.

Ssp. *A. c. borreroi* (Co: E Andes) larger, black spots on flanks and heavily spotted on belly
A. c. tropicus (NW Co) intermediate between others
A. c. septentrionalium (boreal migrant: Co, Ve) as described; unmarked cinnamon below

Habits Usually in small flocks, often mixed with other teal species. Feeds on seeds, algae and parts of aquatic plants, also small aquatic insects, small crustaceans and snails, by dabbling or sometimes dipping head and upending. Flies swift and straight, flocks keeping close together.
Status Boreal migrant *septentrionalium* rare (October–April). Resident races uncommon and local; absent from Ecuador, seriously declining in Colombia, and rare vagrant to Venezuela. Occasional winter visitor on Bonaire.
Habitat Tropical Zone to Páramo. Fresh or brackish wetlands in open country, marshy grasslands, lakes and ponds with abundant water vegetation.
Voice Male has thin, whistled *tsee-tsee*, female a high-pitched *quack* (M&B). Female *quack* like Blue-winged Teal (Sibley).

NORTHERN SHOVELER
Anas clypeata Pl. 5 & 7

Identification 43–52cm. Adult male immediately recognised by large spatulate bill. Entire head dark green, breast white, back blackish with fine pale scaling, scapulars white, wing-coverts blue, speculum white, green and black, flight-feathers black, tail black with white outer feathers; flanks, belly and vent rich cinnamon, finely vermiculated, undertail-coverts black; eyes bright yellow, bill black, legs and feet orange. Female cryptic mix of brown and dark brown, wing-coverts blue, speculum white, black, green and black; eyes brown, bill dusky orange. Breeding male unmistakable, eclipse male retains vestigial characters and still easy to identify. Massive bill is the clincher.

Ssp. Monotypic (Co, Ve, Ar, Bo, T&T)

Habits Usually in pairs or groups of a few to few dozen birds. Sits low in water with bill pointing downwards. Feeds by dabbling or by sieving mud in oozy water edges using highly specialised bill. Main food is tiny aquatic invertebrates and plants. Flight is swift and undeviating.

Status Boreal migrant. Fairly common at southern limits of winter range, on Caribbean coast and offshore islands of northern South America. In Colombia scarce but regular winter visitor.

Habitat Tropical to Subtropical Zones. Fresh and brackish marshes, in shallows.

Voice Female quack is a deep and hoarse *kwarsh*, also a short *gack gack ga ga ga*. Male silent in winter.

TORRENT DUCK *Merganetta armata* Pl. 4

Identification 41–42cm. Adult male has head and neck mainly white, with black from forehead running in broad line over crown and nape to back, and another thinner black line from eye, around ear-coverts to halfway down neck-sides, and joins to rear line behind crown; mantle and uppertail-coverts dark grey, rest of upperparts brown, streaked black; underparts white, with breast to rear flanks streaked black; eyes red, bill bright red with black line at base and on culmen, legs and feet red. Female has similar upperparts, but greyer and less brownish, and lacks line from eyes to neck-sides, and is uniform, unstreaked cinnamon from chin to undertail-coverts. Juvenile recalls female above, white below, broadly barred grey on sides of lower neck to rear flanks, flushed lightly cinnamon on breast-sides; eyes, bill, legs and feet pale brown. No other duck occurs in same habitat.

Ssp. *M. a. colombiana* (Ve, Co, N Ec) as described
M. a. leucogenis (C & S Ec) slightly larger; male distinctly darker above and much more heavily streaked black below, black line from eyes reaches breast; female darker grey above, much ruddier below with some grey and black barring on breast-sides and rear flanks

Habits Usually found in pairs that hold a segment of river as their territory, and sun themselves on rocks or ledges in the middle of streams. In some rivers, densities may reach 1 pair per km of river. Forages by dabbling in pools for larvae and water insects (especially stoneflies), often under rock overhangs, or by diving in torrents. Incredibly nimble in negotiating rapids, even against flow.

Status Widespread. Very local and frequent to uncommon, declining due to damming, silting or pollution, destroying river habitats in many Andean areas.

Habitat Subtropical Zone to Páramo. Tumbling rocky montane streams with pools and stretches of rapids and falls.

Voice A high-pitched *wheek wheek*, in flight and display (H&B). *Weet weet* of male drops at end, clearly audible above the torrent, given perched or in flight. Female has throaty, less carrying *queech* (M&B).

SOUTHERN POCHARD
Netta erythrophthalma Pl. 4 & 7

Identification 46–48cm. Male dark umber-brown with a purple gloss, head-sides washed purplish-chestnut, white wing speculum, breast-sides and flanks washed chestnut; eyes red, long bill grey, legs and feet dark grey. Female browner with white spot at base of bill and broad whitish crescent completely embracing ear-coverts, which are purplish-chestnut like male, some paler brown fringes below, pale undertail-coverts; eyes dark red. Quite distinctive.

Ssp. *N. e. erythrophthalma* (Ec, Co, Ve, Tr, Su)

Habits Alone or in very small (family?) groups, sometimes in company of Jacanas, Common Moorhens and other waterbirds. Forages day or night, by diving, sometimes dabbling or upending, picking seeds and other vegetable matter, and some aquatic invertebrates.

Status Uncommon and very local, with northern South American populations in continuous decline in recent years (apparently still in fair numbers in Venezuela).

Habitat Tropical Zone to Páramo. Freshwater wetlands with open water, submerged plants and border stands of aquatic grasses and shrubs.

Voice Normally silent, male sometimes utters a whirring *perrr-perrr-perrr* in flight; female has a low, hissing *quarrk* (M&B).

RING-NECKED DUCK
Aythya collaris Pl. 4 & 7

Identification 42–43.5cm. Adult male in breeding plumage is entirely black above, including breast and undertail-coverts, and takes its name from brown neck-band that is virtually impossible to see in the field; speculum grey, bordered distally white, and underparts white, finely filigreed (looks grey at distance); eyes white to pale yellow, bill uniquely banded: narrow white base, then grey and white with a black tip, legs and feet grey. Non-breeding male has large white spot at base of bill and brown body-sides. Female almost entirely brown, paler around base of bill and eyes, and on flanks; back, wings and tail dark brown with fine vermiculations, speculum greyish-beige; eyes dark. Immature similar but slightly more buffy. Ring on neck is very poor field mark, but white lines on bill obvious and separate it from Lesser Scaup.

Ssp. Monotypic (Co, Ve, Bo, T&T)

Habits Usually in small groups, forages by diving to sieve the bottom sediment for seeds and other vegetable matters, and aquatic invertebrates. Also by dabbling. Flocks fly in beautiful, very regular, V formation.

Status Northern migrant that rarely reaches northern South America (only a few records).

Habitat Tropical to Subtropical Zones. Fresh or, less frequently, brackish water wetlands in open areas. Partial to larger wetlands with open water as well as extensive reed beds or stands of aquatic plants.

Voice Female has a purring or rough growl *kerp...kerp*. Male silent in winter (Sibley).

LESSER SCAUP *Aythya affinis* Pl. 4 & 7

Identification 41.5–43cm. Adult breeding male has all-black head, neck and breast, back finely vermiculated black and white, flight-feathers black with pale grey speculum; eyes pale yellow, bill dark grey to black at tip, legs and feet grey. Non-breeding male has body-sides brown, irregularly vermiculated white. Female superficially much as female Ring-necked Duck. From Ring-necked Duck by all-dark bill and white in wing in flight, amongst other features.

Ssp. Monotypic (all countries)

Habits Usually in small flocks. Dives to sieve bottom sediment for seeds and other vegetable matter, as well as aquatic invertebrates.
Status Common. Nearctic migrant, winters regularly in northern Venezuela and Trinidad & Tobago, occasionally in Suriname and western Ecuador, sporadically in Colombia, where rare.
Habitat Tropical to Subtropical Zones. Freshwater wetlands in open and semi-open country. In wintering areas, apparently partial to larger wetlands and fairly deep water.
Voice Female has rough, grating *garf...garf...*, male silent in winter (Sibley).

CRACIDAE – Chachalacas, Guans and Curassows

Cracids are among those bird families whose names conjure sylvan images of misty forests dominated by moss, lianas and great, buttress-rooted trees, dimly lit spaces where drops of water glint from every leaf. At one end, we find chachalacas, who thrive in'man-infested'habitats, and at the other, Piping Guans, so very wary of humans they are seldom found outside remote, pristine forests. Cracids include some of the rarest and most difficult to see of all the species in our region. They are quite arboreal and sedentary, although seasonal availability of fruit and water force altitudinal movements in some montane species, whilst lowland ones migrate along the courses of rivers or concentrate in wetter areas. Food is almost exclusively vegetable matter – mostly fruit but also leaves and shoots. Voracious frugivores, they play an important role in seed dispersal within forest ecosystems. Although most are considered diurnal, they are active for long periods in the dark. They stir a couple of hours before daybreak, then from mid-morning roost for most of day. From prior to sundown, they are active for another few hours into the night. Whilst day-roosting, high on the branches of tall trees, they preen and sunbathe. There is very little sexual dimorphism in the family as a whole, although sexes of some of the larger curassows are markedly different. When breeding, they are territorial and males quite vocal. Cracids show some very unique courtship displays: curassows perform sophisticated rituals; chachalacas strut, call antiphonally and tenderly preen and feed each other, but most intriguing are, without doubt, the guans. Their courtship performance is a concert of wing-whirring or drumming, created by modified outer primaries that have 2–3 terminal inches emarginated.

Additional references for this family include Vaurie (1968), Delacour & Amadon (1973), Blake (1977) and del Hoyo (1994).

The chachalacas of the genus *Ortalis* form a homogeneous genus that takes its common name from an onomatopoeic rendering of their calls, given particularly vociferously at and after dawn. They are comparatively small and slender, that is, small heads on slender necks with blue-grey skin around the eyes and bare red skin on the throat, but no wattles or lappets. They have long tails with pale or rufous tips to the outer feathers that can be helpful in identification. They are birds of brush and thickets, foraging both on the ground and in the canopies of flowering and fruiting trees. Urban birds will come to raid dog-feeding bowls and bird feeders alike, though invariably are seen more often when in trees, calling in duet, challenging neighbours and defining territories.

GREY-HEADED CHACHALACA *Ortalis cinereiceps* Pl. 9

Identification 46–58cm. Brown above, with grey head and upper neck, chestnut primaries noticeable when wings folded; dark tail with whitish tips to all but central pair of feathers, pale buffy on sides and flanks. From western race, *ruficrissa*, of Rufous-vented Chachalaca by bright chestnut primaries, conspicuous in flight, but they are allopatric.

Ssp. Monotypic (Co)

Habits Forages at all levels, taking fruit directly from trees, and occasionally insects. Usually in groups of 6–12 or more. Habitually drinks early mornings and evenings.
Status Common or fairly common in Colombia.
Habitat Tropical Zone, locally to 1,700m. Light and humid primary and secondary forests, thickets, stands of *Cecropia*, cleared land gone to waste with fast-growing shrubs and trees.
Voice In twilight, they sing loud, antiphonal choruses of the *cha-cha-laca* phrase common to the genus; calls include soft notes, cackling or clucking.

CHESTNUT-WINGED CHACHALACA *Ortalis garrula* Pl. 9

Identification 53–60cm. Brown above, with rufous head and upper neck, chestnut primaries noticeable when wings folded; dark tail with whitish tips to all but central pair of feathers, pale whitish on sides, thighs and flanks. Distinctive rufous head and bright chestnut primaries. Separated from very similar but larger Rufous-headed Chachalaca by considerable gap in ranges, whilst similar Rufous-vented Chachalaca lacks bright chestnut primaries conspicuous in flight on Chestnut-winged.

Ssp. Monotypic (Co)

Habits Forages in variably sized groups. Diet mostly fruits and berries, seeds, fresh shoots.
Status Common Colombian endemic.
Habitat Tropical Zone. Dry to humid thickets, deciduous forests and mature second growth, woods along rivers, mangroves.
Voice Mainly a loud, reverberating *cha-cha-lac*, given in

chorus with strong rhythm, in twilight. Also squeals and other short calls. A squealing *whooeeell* and *OOEE-chu'uck* in chorus (H&B).

Rufous-vented Chachalaca in flight, showing typical rounded wings and tail, and gliding posture

RUFOUS-VENTED CHACHALACA
Ortalis ruficauda Pl. 9

Identification 55–61cm. Olive-brown above, with greyish head and upper neck; dark tail with greenish and bluish gloss, pale greyish tips to all but central pair of feathers, breast olive-brown, pale olivaceous buffy on sides and thighs. Note, from flanks to vent most birds are rufous, becoming chestnut on undertail-coverts, but varies with locality and some have ochraceous or plain buffy undertail-coverts.

Ssp. *O. r. baliola* (NW Ve) larger than *ruficrissa* and more rufescent, tips of tail pale cinnamon
O. r. ruficrissa (NW Co to NW Ve) as described, distinguished by whitish tips to tail
O. r. ruficauda (N Co, N & NE Ve, To) like *ruficauda* but tail tips deep rufous

Forages in groups of a few to 50+, but in Caracas (where common) it forages in pairs that regularly define their foraging territories most vociferously. Diet: fruits of many plant species, including *Copernicia* palms, *Cecropia*, *Ficus* and others, together with some invertebrates.
Status Common in Colombia, very common in Venezuela.
Habitat Tropical and Subtropical Zones, to *c.*900m in Colombia and 1,600m in Venezuela. Both heavy and open forests, brushland and *llanos* with scattered trees; gallery forests, second growth, and areas near water; parks and gardens.
Voice Both sexes sing loud antiphonal choruses of *gua-cha-raca* phrases, especially at dawn. Pairs and family groups exchange soft whistles and clucks.
Note Race *baliola* synonymised with *ruficrissa*, but description in Blake (1977) says it has white tips to tail – suggesting some confusion. Since our species have pale cinnamon tips, we retain *baliola* pending further research.

Chachalacas have a characteristic way of bursting from a canopy with a momentary whirr of wings, then plane or glide across a gap to another tree; on hillsides, where they can gain extra height, they might cover a considerable distance in this way, following each other at intervals of a few seconds after each bird has landed and safely disappeared into the next canopy

RUFOUS-HEADED CHACHALACA
Ortalis erythroptera Pl. 9

Identification 56–66cm. Brown above, with rufous head and upper neck, chestnut primaries noticeable when wings folded; dark tail with rufous tips to all but central pair of feathers, belly to undertail-coverts creamy. Similar to Chestnut-winged Chachalaca but larger and creamy rather than white below, and has diagnostic rufous tips to tail (white on Chestnut-winged Chachalaca).

Ssp. Monotypic (W Ec, SW Co: Nariño)

Habits Generally quiet and elusive when foraging, and often goes unseen, but can be raucous, especially when groups are communicating. Forages at all levels, usually in small groups. Breeds in rainy season.
Status Uncommon to rare in Ecuador. Threatened by hunting and deforestation.
Habitat Tropical and Subtropical Zones, mostly below 1,000m, but locally to 1,800m. From dry deciduous to humid cloud forests; thickets, savannas, brushland and non-arid coastal areas.
Voice Loud calls may be given throughout day, and often at night. Low phrases include *cha-cha-kaw*, loud includes *kra-kra-ka*. Guan-like honking and yelping calls in alarm (R&G).

SPECKLED CHACHALACA
Ortalis guttata Pl. 9

Identification 45–60cm. Brown above, darker on head, neck and tail, which has outer feathers rufous; breast is spotted white, underparts mid grey-brown, undertail-coverts rufous; legs and feet coral pink. Widespread and only chachalaca in range. Dark head and white speckles on throat are further distinctive features. Similar but larger Colombian Chachalaca has white scallops, not speckles, and is much paler below.

Ssp. *O. g. guttata* (E Ec, S Co)

Habits Forages in small flocks at mid heights and in canopy; often on *Cecropia*. Little known, but quite tolerant of human presence.
Status Fairly frequent in Colombia, common to rare in Ecuador.
Habitat Tropical and Subtropical Zones, usually below 1,100m in Ecuador, but to 2,500m in Colombia. Thickets, grassy slopes, palm groves, low forest, second growth.
Voice Very vocal; rhythmic loud choruses of *cha-cha-laca* phrases in twilight. Various clear soft whistles and clucks. Alarm an ascending squeal (R&G).
Note Included within Variable Chachalaca *O. motmot* by H&B.

COLOMBIAN CHACHALACA
Ortalis columbianus Pl. 9

Identification *c.*50cm. Brown above, greyish on head and darker on tail which has outer feathers rufous; entire throat, neck and breast have white fringes to feathers, affording scaled appearance. Buffy below, with reddish-pink legs and feet.

Scaled appearance to neck and breast feathers separates it from more widespread Speckled, which has white spots on throat.

Ssp. Monotypic (Co)

Habits Forages in pairs or small groups from mid levels to canopy. Prefers *Cecropia* fruits.
Status Colombian endemic, very local. Formerly fairly common but now threatened by hunting. Only small populations remain at a few localities, in pockets of humid forest or scrub.
Habitat Upper Tropical Zone. Borders of humid forests and mature second growth; semi-wooded, humid scrubby areas.
Voice Chorus is typical *chac-a-lac* and variants. Calls *quit* and softer *whit* (M. Álvarez-Rebolledo & S. Córdoba-Córdoba recordings).
Note Included in Variable Chachalaca *O. motmot* by H&B, and in Speckled *O. guttata* by del Hoyo.

LITTLE CHACHALACA
Ortalis motmot Pl. 9

Identification 43–54cm. Tawny brown above, bright rufous on head, rump and uppertail-coverts, and outer 3 pairs of tail-feathers rufous; legs and feet vinous-red. The smallest chachalaca and well separated geographically from other 'rufous-headed'chachalacas.

Ssp. *O. m. motmot* (S Ve, Gu, Su, FG)

Habits Forages in pairs or small groups, sometimes on ground, mainly on berries and small fruits. Dust bathes occasionally, and sunbathes in open patches on ground.
Status Locally frequent in Venezuela, common in Guyana and French Guiana, frequent to common in Suriname.
Habitat Tropical Zone, locally to 1,700m. Where undergrowth is dense in second growth near settlements, patches of forest or clearings amid more extensive woodland, savanna borders, also along rivers and around rocky outcrops (Suriname and French Guiana).
Voice Dawn chorus a loud, coarse and rhythmic *WATCH-a-läk*, over and over, recalling Rufous-vented Chachalaca (though less vocal), but shriller and less raucous (Hilty). Pairs sing antiphonally and may be joined in chorus by all pairs in area.

Guans of the genus *Penelope* are medium to fairly large forest birds. They are generally rich, dark brown, with white fringes (but not tips) to most body feathers, forming unusual rows of inverted Y-like streaks, which vary in extent according to species. They usually have some white grizzling on the face and may have prominent bright crimson face wattles or lappets; the occipital skin is usually extensive, and blue-grey. Primarily arboreal, they perform wing-rattling displays, and glide between trees with a distinct whirr caused by the strongly curved and very stiff narrow outermost primaries.

BAND-TAILED GUAN
Penelope argyrotis Pl. 10

Identification 50–61cm. Entirely dark rufescent brown with short stubby crest; outer tail-feathers dusky and generally contrast with more rufescent central feathers. Tail tip varies from near white (*albicauda*) to rufous (*olivaceiceps*), but this is only visible from below; face heavily grizzled, eye-ring pale bluish-grey, wattle red. Fine white streaking from throat to lower breast, and also on wing-coverts. Legs and feet red to pink. From smaller and darker Andean Guan by frosty head pattern, pale tip (band) to tail, well-developed red dewlap and white-streaked breast.

Ssp. *P. a. albicauda* (Co, Ve: Perijá) whitish tips to outer tail-feathers, white streaks on body extend to flanks
P. a. argyrotis (N Co, NW Ve) tips to tail pale rufescent, shorter crest, fringes on neck and breast are shorter and broader, and appear whiter
P. a. colombiana (N Co) crown feathers narrow, fringed white and somewhat pointed, with less white grizzling above eyes and brownish malar
P. a. mesaeus (N Co, W Ve: Táchira) larger than other races, darker brown head, neck and breast, white streaks reach flanks, narrow rufescent edges to tail
P. a. olivaceiceps (N Ve) rufous tip to tail, looks exactly like *mesaeus* in the field

Habits Forages in small groups (3–5), usually at mid and upper levels, but drops to ground for fallen fruit. Prefers pulpy fruits, especially of laurels and *Cecropia*, and several groups may gather at fruit-laden trees. Breeds late dry season. Wing-rattling display is like'canvas ripping'(P. Schwartz).
Status Locally common in Venezuela, locally frequent to uncommon in Colombia.
Habitat Upper Tropical and Subtropical Zones. Prefers very wet virgin forest, occasionally in mature second growth and coffee plantations.
Voice Only calls during territory establishment: a low *kuak*, mostly at dawn. Alarm *gi-gi-gigigi-gik* or *gu-rr-urr-urrrrr*, loud and rolling (Schäfer *fide* H&B).

BEARDED GUAN *Penelope barbata* Pl. 10

Identification *c.*55cm. Bronzy brown above, darker on head and neck, more dusky below, with distinct grizzling on face, white streaks on neck, breast and sides, tail tip rufous; chin and upper throat fully feathered, tarsus partially feathered; bare wattle and legs coral red. Rufous of tail most noticeable in flight and offers certain identification feature, though it is not always obvious.

Ssp. Monotypic (S Ec)

Habits Forages in pairs or small groups of up to *c.*8, often on ground. Diet: fruits, berries and mostly seeds, which often pass intact in droppings. Whirring-wing display at dawn.
Status Rare in most localities of its small, fragmented distribution, in Andes of southern Ecuador, in Azuay, Loja and Zamora-Chinchipe, mainly on the west slope and very locally on outlying ridges. The most important population is protected in Podocarpus National Park.
Habitat Upper Subtropical and Temperate Zones, usually at 1,900–2,700m. Humid and dry montane cloud forests. Occasionally in small relict forest patches.

Voice Various whistles and honks, often in fast series and higher pitched than other *Penelope* (R&G).
Note Sometimes included in Band-tailed Guan.

BAUDÓ (ORTON'S) GUAN *Penelope ortoni* Pl. 10

Identification 58–63cm. Dark olive-brown above, darkest on head and neck, dark brown below; white streaks on throat to belly. Eyes red, eye-ring slaty, prominent hanging wattle bright red; legs and feet red. Readily confused with much larger, sympatric Crested Guan, but when disturbed Baudó Guan tends to crouch and utter low calls, whilst Crested flees with loud honking (O. Jahn in R&G). Tends to perch quietly in trees. Crested Guan is more clearly streaked on breast, Baudó more scalloped. Andean Guan usually at higher elevations, is darker and more rufescent on belly and vent, and has far less noticeable dewlap.

Ssp. Monotypic (W Ec, SW Co)

Habits Poorly known. Considered rather tame in some areas, but perches quietly in upper near canopy of trees, thus easily overlooked.
Status Recorded at only a few localities and threatened throughout small, fragmented range.
Habitat Upper Tropical Zone, to 1,500m. Humid forests on montane slopes.
Voice Soft, rising whistle lasting *c.*3 s, presumed alarm call (O. Jahn in R&G).

ANDEAN GUAN *Penelope montagnii* Pl. 10

Identification 51–61cm. A small, compact, high-altitude guan with small throat wattles rather than a complete dewlap. Rufous-brown above, more rufous on rump and uppertail-coverts; head grizzling and neck to breast streaking vary with race. White on body feathers are more fringes than solid edges and thus appear greyer; they also almost join, producing more scaled look.

Ssp. *P. m. atrogularis* (SW Co, W Ec) upper throat and chin blackish, streaking on neck and breast finely drawn
P. m. brooki (SE Co, E Ec) white streaking on head most noticeable, duller and darker than others, tip of bill yellow
P. m. montagnii (NW Ve, NE Co) brighter rufescent brown below, the white lines join at the ends of the feathers giving a scaling effect to neck and breast

Habits From Bearded Guan by uniform dark tail. Forages in groups of up to 10, sometimes singly, at mid and upper levels of fruiting trees. Moves altitudinally according to fruiting seasons of trees. Tolerates partially disturbed areas and is observed near settlements. Establishes territory in late dry season, with males making single-rattle wing-whirring displays.
Status Uncommon in Ecuador, locally frequent to uncommon in Colombia.
Habitat Temperate Zone, to 3,650m with a record at 3,900m. Sometimes reaches Subtropical Zone. Dense, epiphyte-rich humid forests.
Voice Calls at dawn, mainly during territory establishment, and honks quite loudly (R. S. Ridgely recording).

MARAIL GUAN *Penelope marail* Pl. 10

Identification 63–68cm. Dark glossy olive-green above, dark rufescent brown below, slight white lining on head, but streaks clearer on neck to mantle and belly and flanks. Rather bushy crest, dewlap deep red, short legs and feet pink. Smaller, darker and shorter legged than similar Spix's Guan.
Ssp. *P. m. jacupeba* (SC & SE Ve: upper Caura) paler, more greyish below
P. m. marail (E Ve, Gu, Su, FG) darker, more rufescent posteriorly
Habits Forages singly or in small groups, mostly in trees but sometimes on ground. Diet is almost exclusively fruit, but has strong preferences including *Euterpe*, *Guatteria*, *Cecropia*, *Eugenia* and *Minquartia*.
Status Frequent to locally common in heavy, undisturbed forest in Suriname and French Guiana (up to 5 prs per sq. km) but declining due to hunting pressure; uncommon in Guyana and Venezuela.
Habitat Tropical Zone, to 600m. Heavy, humid and pristine lowland forests, near water. Occasionally in second growth.
Voice Dawn and dusk, and perhaps at night: a low, muffled rough chachalaca-like *racha, racha, racha*..., usually mixed with other harsh and high notes. Lacks honking of Spix's Guan (Hilty).
Note Confusion in subspecies limits: *jacupeba* is from Brazil, *marail* from Guianas, Venezuelan birds generally considered to be *marail* (e.g. Vaurie 1964, Delacour & Amadon 1973, Hilty).

CRESTED GUAN *Penelope purpurascens* Pl. 10

Identification 72–91cm. Largest guan: like a curassow but less heavily built, and has longer neck and tail. Dark glossy olive-brown above, darkest on head and neck, chestnut rump and bronzy tail; white streaking from throat to mantle and sides of breast. Large red wattle, legs and feet pink. Dark, well-wattled guan that might be mistaken for smaller Baudó Guan. Crested is noticeably rufous posteriorly. Also noisy, unlike almost silent Baudó.

Ssp. *P. p. aequatorialis* (SE Ec, NW Co, NW Ve) uniform dark bronzy tail
P. p. brunnescens (N Co, E Ve) dull chestnut tail, bronzy outer edges

Habits Forages singly, in pairs or small groups (up to 8), usually in upper storey and seldom near ground. Wary and retreats quickly, doubtless due to continued hunting. 'Double-outburst' wing-rattling displays at dawn. Seasonal movements in montane regions.
Status Rare in Ecuador, uncommon and local in Colombia and Venezuela.
Habitat Tropical and Lower Subtropical Zones, to 1,500m in Ecuador, to 1,000m in Colombia with a record to 1,950m, and to 1,100m in Venezuela. Humid forests, borders, most often in hilly areas below 1,000m.
Voice A low guttural *kwee-ooh*, a loud, penetrating *whuuleeur*, also a repetitive *konh-konh-konh-konh*... (R&G). Males call mainly in dry season, when establishing territory; a loud honking, nasal and guttural *quonk, quonk, quonk rrrrrrrrrr* (Hilty).

CAUCA GUAN *Penelope perspicax* Pl. 10

Identification *c.*76cm. Large reddish guan, unmistakable in limited range. Rufescent brown to chestnut, dusky tone to head, neck and breast, which are well lined with white streaks that are more scale-like than usual.

Ssp. Monotypic (SW Co)

Habits Forages at all levels but mainly in mid-storey and understorey branches, in groups of up to 16. Little known.
Status Endangered. Colombian endemic, possibly on verge of extinction.
Habitat Upper Tropical and Subtropical Zones, at 1,300–2,000m. Humid primary forest and mature second growth.
Voice Alarm-call *Quan...Quan*, given in rapid series, short downslurred whistle in contact, whilst the song is a loud, repeated sequence of *chiriwichi, chiriwichi...chiriwichi* notes, sometimes in chorus, and most frequently in February–June (del Hoyo & Motis 2004).

SPIX'S GUAN *Penelope jacquacu* Pl. 10

Identification 70–80cm. Olive-brown with greenish gloss on wings and tail, white streaks on neck and breast, all of which are very variable according to race.

Ssp. *P. j. granti* (E Ve, Gu) larger, generally darker all over, and more blue-green above, rump reddish-brown; some white streaking on foreneck and breast
P. j. jacquacu (E Co, E Ec) distinctly bronze-olive above, rump dull brown, bright rufescent below; well striated with white lines from throat to belly, thighs and flanks, though weaker below, also on mantle and wing-coverts
P. j. orienticola (SE Ve) intermediate, malar stripe variegated greyish-white

Habits Forages singly, in pairs or small family groups, from mid to highest levels, rarely on ground. Diet small fruits, mostly soft, ripe palm fruits. Breeds from late dry season. Nest of leaves high above ground. Displays at dawn with 'double outbursts' of wing-rattling (P. Schwartz recording). Fairly tolerant of human presence, although those near settlements extremely shy.
Status Rare in Ecuador. Frequent in Colombia and Venezuela, except in deforested areas. Frequent in Guyana. Status uncertain in Suriname.
Habitat Tropical Zone. Mostly lowland humid *terra firme* and gallery forests, also *várzea*, but occasionally cloud forests. Borders and clearings.
Voice Calls only in breeding season, at twilight, a loud riotous crowing or howling *kerr-ow, kerr-ow, kerrow, urrrreck, urrrreck, kerrow...* (Hilty).

> Piping Guans of the genus *Pipile* are forest birds with large bodies, long necks with small heads, long loose crests, long tails and comparatively short legs. They are black, glossy brown, green or blue. They have a rattling flight display made even more audible by their stiff, narrow outer primaries.

TRINIDAD PIPING GUAN *Pipile pipile* Pl. 9

Identification *c.*69cm. The only cracid on Trinidad, thus unmistakable. Large with long dark crest that has a few white lines in it, virtually black throughout with a purplish-brown gloss, and perhaps some faint, narrow white streaks on breast; outer wing-coverts each have a heavy white spot, more reduced on inner wing, and producing a series of rows or bars of white spots. Bill black, cere and orbital skin blue, bare throat and wattle dark blue, legs and feet red.

Ssp. Monotypic (Tr)

Habits Forages mostly in evenings until 1–2 hours after midnight, but most active in morning at mid levels. Group size depends on local population, but distinct tendency to forage in large groups, making it vulnerable to hunting. Takes broad variety of fruits, young leaves and insects. Drinks at streams and from water in bracts of forest epiphytes. Breeds February–June, with inter-locality variations. Displays mostly at dawn, with double wing-clap followed by double wing-whirr.
Status Endangered. Rare Trinidad endemic, endangered by loss of forest habitat. Does not tolerate human presence.
Habitat Tropical Zone, 400–900m. Undisturbed primary forest with open ground and closed canopy, and rich in epiphytes and vines; rarely in adjacent mature second growth and coffee plantations.
Voice Calls only in breeding season, a series of clear, high, ascending whistles or piping.
Note Sometimes called Common Piping Guan.

BLUE-THROATED PIPING GUAN *Pipile cumanensis* Pl. 9

Identification 60–69cm. Large with long white crest tinged ochre, virtually black throughout with a blue gloss, and narrow white streaks on breast, bold white streaks on mantle and lesser wing-coverts; outer median and greater wing-coverts each have a heavy white streak, less obvious on inner wing, producing a series of rows of white marks. Bill black, cere and orbital skin white, bare throat and wattle dark blue, legs and feet red.

Ssp. *P. c. cumanensis* (E Ec, C & E Co, S Ve, Gu, Su, FG)

Habits Forages in groups of up to 15, mainly at mid and highest levels, seldom on ground. Prefers palm fruits, flowers of Pui trees and snails. Visits salt licks. Breeds in rainy season; nesting in dense canopy. Moves seasonally along courses of rivers.
Status Uncommon in Ecuador, rare to locally frequent in Venezuela and Colombia, locally frequent in Guyana and Suriname, rare and local in French Guiana.
Habitat Mostly Tropical Zone, but may reach Subtropical Zone seasonally (to 500m in Colombia and 1,000m in Venezuela). Humid *terra firme* and *várzea*; galleries and *cerrado*; coastal lowlands. Partial to riparian forests (up to 100m from watercourses).
Voice Call a long series of feeble, slurred whistles, *fuit, fuit*. Also claps and whirrs wings loudly.
Note Sometimes treated as a race of Trinidad Piping Guan.

Aburria is a monotypic genus, closely related to *Pipile* (and perhaps better subsumed within latter, as suggested by recent genetic evidence), but mainly distinguished by its unusually bright wattle, lack of bare facial skin, crest or dewlap. It does have a noisy rattling-wing display.

WATTLED GUAN *Aburria aburri* Pl. 9

Identification 72–78cm. Large, entirely green-black guan with plain, rounded and feathered head, and a unique, long slender yellow-and-red throat wattle; brown eyes and a bright blue bill.

Ssp. Monotypic (C Ec, C Co, NW Ve)

Habits Very inconspicuous. Usually in pairs or family groups of 3, foraging in mid and upper strata. Breeds from late dry season. Possibly undertakes seasonal altitudinal movements. Wing noises in display similar to Trinidad Piping Guan.

Status Locally rare in Ecuador. Frequent at a few localities but threatened by deforestation in Colombia. In Venezuela only found at a few localities and status uncertain.

Habitat Upper Tropical and Subtropical Zones, at 600–2,500m in Colombia, to 1,800m in Venezuela. Steep terrain. Wet montane forests and mature second growth bordering primary forests. Forest borders.

Voice Song a loud *ba-reeeeer-ah* that rises like a siren and is repeated incessantly (Weske *fide* H&B), transcribed as *bree-ee-ee-ee-ah*, and delivered at intervals throughout the night (R&G). A long, rising buzz, *baaaarrreeeeeeeeeeeer* (the r's trilled), dry, sustained, and snapping over at end, repeated incessantly at dawn and dusk; also irregularly throughout day during breeding season (Hilty).

SICKLE-WINGED GUAN
Chamaepetes goudotii Pl. 10

Identification 50–65cm. Dark brown above and rufous from breast to undertail-coverts; bright blue facial skin with red eyes and pink legs and feet. Rather secretive and seldom seen, thus in a poor sighting could be mistaken for a rufous-bellied *Penelope*, but bright blue facial skin diagnostic, as all *Penelope* have red dewlaps.

Ssp. *C. g. fagani* (SW Co, W Ec) small, dark bronzy green above, scalloped on throat
C. g. goudotii (Co: C, W Andes) paler and brighter rufous below than *sanctamarthae*
C. g. sanctamarthae (Co: Santa Marta) paler, more brownish-olive above
C. g. tschudii (SE Co, E Ec) larger than others, more brownish above, brighter and more ferruginous below than *fagani*

Habits Forages in pairs or groups of 3–5, in mid to upper levels of fruiting trees, at dawn and dusk. Diet small fruits, seeds and leaves. Some altitudinal movements outside breeding season. May displace Andean Guan. Displays with repeated flights between same 2 branches, whilst making single wing-whirr, normally pre-dawn.

Status Uncommon in Ecuador. In Colombia, fairly common at some localities, but threatened in most of range.

Habitat Subtropical and Lower Temperate Zones, at 900–2,600m in Ecuador, and 1,100–2,500m in Colombia, but recorded to 3,000m in Santa Marta. Steep hillsides and inaccessible areas. Tall, wet or humid forest, occasionally mature second growth and coffee plantations, forest borders.

Voice Usually very quiet. Call when foraging a soft *wheet-ta*, but when alarmed, a loud repeated *kée-uck*.

Nothocrax is a monotypic genus that differs from *Crax* by its cryptic plumage and nocturnal behaviour.

NOCTURNAL CURASSOW
Nothocrax urumutum Pl. 10

Identification 50–57cm. Small curassow, rufescent brown on back, wings and tail, finely filigreed with narrow wavy lines, chestnut on head, neck and underparts; long narrow crest from forehead to nape is blackish; eyes chestnut, facial skin whitish above eyes becoming blue below, bill coral pink, legs and feet flesh. Degree of rufescence and crest make this small bird unmistakable, but it is usually known only by its nocturnal vocalisations.

Ssp. Monotypic (E Ec, SE Co, S Ve)

Habits Forages singly, in pairs and small groups of 3–4. Feeds below fruiting trees, at dawn and dusk, but mainly nocturnally. Reportedly roosts in holes in ground during day (R&G) or on low branches above streams.

Status Not considered threatened due to remote habitat, but rare in Ecuador and situation uncertain (possibly frequent) in Venezuela and Colombia. Very rarely seen.

Habitat Tropical Zone, to 400m in Ecuador, 500m in Colombia but only known to 200m in Venezuela. Dense, humid *terra firme*, usually near rivers, also permanently or seasonally flooded forests. Generally favours low-lying, partially flooded areas.

Voice Calls from high perch, mostly a couple of hours after dark and before daybreak. According to Wetmore, a booming, hollow *hoo, hoo-hoo, hoo-hoo-hoo*, followed by a long pause, then a hoot. According to Sick, it is a 2-part, descending *hm-hm-hm, hm-hm-hm-uh*, ending in a long groan (D&A). A deep series of booming notes, far-carrying and ventriloquial, *oo-oo-oó, oo-oo-oóh?* followed after a short pause by a sharp, higher pitched *unh!* (R&G).

Mitu curassows are very similar to *Crax*, and they are sometimes considered congeneric. The main difference is the shape of the bill, which is laterally compressed in *Mitu*, and the crests which are more modest.

LESSER RAZOR-BILLED CURASSOW
Mitu tomentosum Pl. 11

Identification 75–85cm. Mainly black, glossed heavily with blue above, vent to undertail-coverts and tips of tail bright chestnut, bill vermilion-red, very pale at tip, legs and feet vermilion-red. From Razor-billed Curassow by chestnut distal tail-band.

Ssp. Monotypic (E Ec, SE & E Co, S & SE Ve, Gu)

Habits Not shy. Forages mostly on ground but also in trees. Diet fruits and seeds, occasionally small vertebrates or insects. Breeds from early rainy season.

Status Uncommon and local in Guyana. Frequent locally in Colombia and Venezuela. Subject to significant hunting pressure.

Habitat Tropical Zone. Humid forests, especially along rivers and gallery forests, and in areas with dense undergrowth.

Voice Calls most of year, mainly at dawn and dusk and on moonlit nights, a booming *umm – um-m-um*, with a 3 s pause in middle (D&A).

Note Sometimes called Crestless Curassow.

SALVIN'S CURASSOW *Mitu salvini* Pl. 11

Identification 75–89cm. Mainly black with a short recurved crest, blue gloss on mantle, and white vent to undertail-coverts, and tips to tail. Bill vermilion, paler at tip, legs and feet dark grey. Virtually the only curassow in eastern Ecuador. From male Wattled Curassow by broad white tip to tail.

Ssp. Monotypic (E Ec, SE Co)

Habits Forages on ground, singly, in pairs or small family groups, mainly on broad variety of fallen fruit, seeds and leaves, with occasional scavenging. Pairs defend loosely defined territory.

Status Rare in Ecuador. Scarce in Colombia, possibly at low density. Under severe hunting pressure near settlements.

Habitat Lower Tropical Zone. Primary, humid, lowland forests; in *terra firme* away from seasonally flooded areas.

Voice Calls for long periods, crouching on perch. A booming, low-pitched *cronk cronk cronk*, lacking tuba quality of other curassows (D&A). Mostly given at night, described as *oo-oooonh, wooónh-unh…ooóúp-óó-óóóú!* Both sexes give various short, high-pitched squealing calls when nervous or alarmed (R&G).

RAZOR-BILLED CURASSOW
Mitu tuberosum Pl. 11

Identification 83–89cm. Mainly black with bluish gloss above, vent to undertail-coverts deep chestnut, tips of tail white. Crest comparatively long, and bill has expanded culmen that is waxy vermilion-red, legs and feet vermilion. From Lesser Razor-billed by distal white band on tail.

Ssp. Monotypic (SE Co)

Habits Forages singly, in pairs or groups of 3–5. Picks most of its food from ground. Diet includes fruit (main food), seeds, leaves (particularly fern fronds), occasional insects and small vertebrates (frogs, tadpoles). Follows troops of *Saimiri* and *Cebus* monkeys, taking fruit they drop. Visits salt licks.

Status Fairly common but local in Colombia, albeit under intense pressure from hunting.

Habitat Lower Tropical Zone, to 300m. Humid lowland *terra firme* or gallery forests, occasionally *várzea*. Swampy areas and along streams.

Voice Male gives booming *hm-hm…hm, hm-hm…hm*, with last note very strong and pause 2–3 times longer than first notes (Sick *fide* D&A).

HELMETED CURASSOW
Pauxi pauxi Pl. 11

Identification 85–92cm. Combination of coral red bill and grey or pink helmet distinctive. Nearly all black with rich greenish gloss, white vent to undertail-coverts and broad white tips to tail. Eyes chestnut, bill red, legs and feet pink. There is a large bony 'helmet' that is either stone-grey or rather pinkish. Female dimorphic, usually like male, but barred morph has black head, neck and white-tipped tail, from mantle to uppertail-coverts, wings, breast, sides, flanks, and thighs barred chestnut and black, darker above, and white fringes to wing-coverts.

Ssp. *P. p. gilliardi* (Co & Ve: Perijá) smaller and less upright helmet that tilts back

P. p. pauxi (NC & W Ve, E Co) as described

Habits Forages alone, in pairs or small groups, at dawn and dusk. Diet mostly fallen fruit, seeds, leaves and buds, grasses. Moves altitudinally according to food availability. Breeds immediately ahead of rainy season.

Status Endangered. Though occurs in several national parks, threatened due to habitat loss and poaching. Formerly common in northern mountains of Venezuela, but now rare due to intensive hunting.

Habitat Subtropical and Temperate Zones. Very dense, wet, cool montane forests. Humid and steep slopes and gorges with dense undergrowth, dwarf palms and terrestrial aroids (*Philodendron* and other broadleaf plants). Seldom at forest edge.

Voice Males give series of rapid, droning booms, described by H&B as like an old tree groaning. An exceptionally low-pitched humming, typically *uum…uUH a uum…uum…uUH…um-uUH…uum…*, resonating over long distances through forest and difficult to locate (Hilty).

Note Sometimes called Northern Helmeted Curassow.

Crax currasows are distinctive, large, heavily built, black birds with fascinating curly crests, decorated bills and deep booming voices that echo through the night.

GREAT CURASSOW *Crax rubra* Pl. 11

Identification Male 87–92cm, female 78–84cm. Male all black glossed green, and white vent to undertail-coverts; crest long and incredibly curved, each feather forming almost an S-shape; bill grey, the base and swollen, rounded cere or 'knob' waxy yellow. Female has entire head, chin and throat barred black and white, whilst the crest has a broad white band becoming distally black; rich rufous lower neck and breast to uppertail-coverts but grades through cinnamon on belly, sides, flanks and thighs, and vent to undertail-coverts creamy yellow; tail barred chestnut, black and white. Male from male Wattled or Black Curassows by greenish (not blue) gloss, and colour and shape of wattle. Female is unmistakable.

Ssp. *C. r. rubra* (W Co, W Ec)

Habits Forages singly, in pairs or small groups. Diet fallen fruit, but sometimes takes it direct from low branches or shrubs. Also leaves, invertebrates or small vertebrates taken by gleaning foliage and litter. Quite confiding where not hunted.
Status Very rare in Ecuador, possibly extinct at some localities. In Colombia, populations stable only in areas far from settlements, where forest is pristine.
Habitat Tropical and sometimes Lower Subtropical Zone. Heavy humid forests, usually in lowlands. Visits partially cleared areas and plantations.
Voice Male calls include a long, low, booming *oom-m-m* (H&B), so low-pitched you almost feel rather than hear it (R&G). Some whistles (E. Eisenmann).

BLUE-BILLED CURASSOW *Crax alberti* Pl. 12

Identification 82–93cm. Male almost entirely black glossed blue, with white vent to undertail-coverts, the crest is forward-curving; eyes chestnut, bill pale grey with base and round wattle ('knob') at either side bright pale blue, legs and feet flesh-coloured. Female dimorphic. Usually black on head with a partially hidden white band around crest, black breast and entire upperparts, barred with narrow white lines from mantle to tail. Barred morph has black to belly, sides and thighs, and is wholly barred white from foreneck to thighs and mid mantle to tail. From all other curassows by bright blue bill. In either morph, from all other females by white scallop-barring on back.

Ssp. Monotypic (NW Co)

Habits Poorly known. Forages on ground and apparently breeds at end of dry season.
Status Endangered. Very rare Colombian endemic, threatened due to deforestation and severe hunting pressure. Extinct over most of former range.
Habitat Tropical Zone to 600m, but occasionally to 1,200m. Humid lowland forest, foothills and lower montane slopes.
Voice Males give a low boom like others of genus (D&A).

YELLOW-KNOBBED CURASSOW *Crax daubentoni* Pl. 12

Identification 84–93cm. Male from male Great Curassow by blue (not green) gloss, and they are well separated geographically. Forages in family groups or small flocks, from ground to treetops. Breeds in rainy season. Males establish territories and small harems.

Ssp. Monotypic (N Co, N Ve)

Habits Principally forages on ground, sometimes in more open areas, e.g. on tracks, early morning and evening. May gather into small bands of up to 20 in dry season, at other times birds scattered in pairs. Breeds in early wet season (April–June).
Status Often hunted but fairly common in Venezuela, uncommon and local in Colombia. Disappears when land is cropped.
Habitat Tropical Zone. Humid forest surrounded by drier deciduous woodland, or in gallery forests. *Llanos*, foothills and broken country, often near streams and especially in ravines and valleys.
Voice A clear lengthy, arching whistle, rising and falling until no longer audible, *weeeeeeeoooooooo*. Also given as *wheeeeeeee-uuuuuuuuu* lasting *c*.4 s (Hilty).

BLACK CURASSOW *Crax alector* Pl. 12

Identification 85–95cm. All black with forward-curved crest, bluish and purple glosses, and pure white vent to undertail-coverts. Facial skin blue-grey, bill horn and cere and base to mandibles yellow or red (or intermediate), legs and feet pale grey. Female has irregular white barring in crown. From male Yellow-knobbed by smaller cere and grey (not greenish) legs. Cline from east to west in cere colour makes demarcation of races difficult.

Ssp. *C. a. alector* (E Ve, Gu, Su, FG) yellow cere
C. a. erythrognatha (E Co, S Ve) red cere

Habits Feeds on ground and forages alone or in pairs that occasionally stroll along dirt tracks or across clearings. Quite arboreal, takes figs and other fruits (in French Guiana 50% of diet from *Eugenia*), and roosts and sings from branches in subcanopy. Calm and trusting in areas where not persecuted. Breeds in rainy season. Displays by clapping wings and calling.
Status In undisturbed forest, densities relatively low, less than 1 per ha. Locally frequent in Colombia (formerly quite common). In Venezuela, Guyana, Suriname and French Guiana, frequent only where there is no hunting and habitat fairly intact.
Habitat Tropical Zone, locally to 1,700m. Humid *terra firme* and gallery forests. Thickets along rivers and tangled forest borders; sometimes in clearings, roadsides, old plantations. Hillsides with drier ground.
Voice A grave boom, *umm-um* -------- *umm* ---- *um-um*, at dusk and from midnight to dawn. 'A low sepulchral humming' or booming (Hilty).

WATTLED CURASSOW *Crax globulosa* Pl. 12

Identification 82–89cm. Male all black with a forward-curled crest and rich bluish gloss, except white vent to undertail-coverts. Female has vent to undertail-coverts chestnut. Bill black with red cere and base to mandible, the male has an enlarged knob on cere and wattles on sides of mandible. If seen briefly, male could be mistaken for Salvin's but lacks white in tail. Female from either Razor-billed by all-black tail, and crest.

Ssp. Monotypic (E Ec, SE Co)

Habits Poorly known. Mostly arboreal, occasionally feeds on ground. Breeds in rainy season.
Status Vulnerable. Extremely rare. Rapidly declining in Colombia, and possibly still occurs in extreme eastern

Ecuador. Threatened throughout range by hunting, trade and destruction of riparian habitat.

Habitat Tropical Zone, to 300m. Humid forests and *várzea*. Always near water.

Voice A clear, long, arching whistle in series, like Yellow-knobbed Curassow (D&A), a long, leisurely whistle (del Hoyo) thought to be an alarm call (R&G). Calls from branches in subcanopy or at mid levels.

ODONTOPHORIDAE – New World quails

Quails are shy and elusive ground-dwellers, more likely to run than fly, and well designed for secrecy and terrestrial locomotion – robust bodies, short powerful legs and cryptic colouring. They are most frequently seen in family groups (coveys). When alarmed, they hide and crouch in the underbrush. If they do move off, they are more likely to slip away than flush, but when the covey is flushed, it 'explodes', with birds flying in all directions in a steep take-off, and dropping down again after a short distance. Their voices are far-carrying, and are what best reveals their presence. Calls of the bobwhites consist mostly of whistles, whilst wood quails have merry rolling or guttural calls. Quails call mostly at dawn and dusk, with duetting and choruses reported for some species. Many species roost in trees at night. Regarding food, quails are generalists and opportunists. Wood quails search for roots and tubers, foraging in rows and clearing long paths through the leaf-litter. In the dry season, the observer should listen for rustling leaves and flying litter, which will indicate a line of birds clearing a path. Family groups often move in single file. Most species are monogamous and breed during the wet season. Nests are usually a shallow depression lined with leaves and concealed in thick vegetation; some wood quails, however, build a domed nest with a long entrance tunnel. Quails have very high reproductive rate and very low life expectancy, seldom longer than one year.

Additional references for this family include Johnsgard (1998), Carroll (1994) and Madge & McGowan (2002, hereafter M&M).

CRESTED BOBWHITE
Colinus cristatus Pl. 7

Identification 18–23cm. Small, rounded quail distinguished by long, laid-back but outstanding crest, which is usually creamy and contrasts with head. Generally dark brown above with some white fringing to tertials and other feathers, and dark to blackish spots and streaks, paler below usually with large pale spots fringed black. Subspecies vary considerably and individual variation (some races appear to overlap), along with age- and sex-related differences make separation difficult. See plate for examples. Birds in eastern Andes generally much darker. Crested Bobwhite is only savanna quail in region. From all other wood quails by small size (only Tawny-faced is smaller), white speckles on flanks, and crest. Marbled Wood Quail is crested but much larger and has prominent red skin around eyes.

Ssp. *C. c. badius* (Co: W Andes) like *leucotis* but much darker above, the male has throat paler but breast darker

C. c. barnesi (WC Ve) very similar to *sonnini* but darker above, black instead of dark brown and crest is darker (sooty brown with buffy tips)

C. c. bogotensis (NC Co: E Andes) like *leucotis* but darker on throat and less white on rear crown and nape; ear-coverts less white than on *leucotis* but not as dark as on *sonnini*

C. c. continentis (NW Ve) black and cream face, chestnut belly, mid brown back

C. c. cristatus (NE Co: E Andes, Curaçao and Aruba) male has rufous throat with pale malar and ear-coverts but dark on face-sides, and noticeably longer crest

C. c. decoratus (Co: Caribbean coast) similar to *leucotis* but more richly coloured throughout, eyebrow and malar of male heavily variegated with black; throat and breast rich chestnut

C. c. horvathi (NW Ve: Mérida) white crest, male has less rufescent dorsal parts and rather pale underparts with darker shaft-streaks on flanks; female more boldly streaked above

C. c. leucotis (C Co) white forehead and crest, broad rufous eyebrow from just before eye to nape-sides – divided from crest by a black-and-white line; malar and chin white, throat chestnut, lower part of face from eyes to throat rufous with some black dots

C. c. littoralis (NE Co: Santa Marta) like *decoratus* but male paler, with throat less chestnut, being tawny to amber brown; female paler and less spotted below

C. c. mocquerysi (NE Ve) russet breast and belly, few white spots; very close to *sonnini* but crest paler and longer, chin and throat also pale; male has breast bright vinaceous to chestnut, and abdomen less rufous; female whiter below

C. c. parvicristatus (C Co, SC Ve) large; short dark crest, dark ear-coverts and upperparts, heavy black markings

C. c. sonnini (NC & SE Ve, Gu, Su, FG) twin/divided crest dull sepia, face pale buffy or greyish-brown, pale throat spotted dark

Habits Generally very shy and wary of man, but can become very confiding. Sedentary. Coveys of *c.*12+ birds.

Status Frequent to common (populations have benefited from deforestation). In French Guiana very rare and local on coastal plain, and small relict population in the south.

Habitat Tropical Zone, normally below 1,500m, but odd records to 3,200m. Fairly dry to arid lowland grasslands, and locally to Subtropical Zone. Thickets, woodland edges, savannas, roadsides and embankments; pastures, rice and sugarcane plantations. Coveys rest quietly during heat of day tending to sit on ground in shade of bushes or low trees, but may perch among lower branches.

Voice Coveys maintain contact with chirping and cheeping notes; advertising call *pwit pwit pweet* and a wheezy *wheecher* repeated up to 6 times. (M&M). Sings *bob-white*, second note upward-inflected. Call on Curaçao (*cristatus*) *coo-kwee*, often

uttered repeatedly for long periods (Voous). Alarm note *tik! tik! tik! tik! tik!*
Note Race *continentis* is perhaps specifically distinct (M&M).

MARBLED WOOD QUAIL
Odontophorus gujanensis Pl. 8

Identification 23–29cm. Virtually entirely brown with short thick laid-back crest, large orbital red eye-ring, buffy patch immediately behind eye-ring, chestnut chin, whitish throat finely barred black, barred with black over rest of body, with black spots on wings and some white dashes, buffy ends to inner flanks; eyes dark, bill black, legs and feet dark greenish-grey. Bright orange-red bare skin around eyes is distinctive.

Ssp. *O. g. buckleyi* (E Co, E Ec) greyish on sides of head and throat, more heavily barred below
O. g. gujanensis (SE Ve, Gu, Su, FG) as described, most uniformly coloured and barred
O. g. marmoratus (N Co, NW Ve) lacks buffy patch on head, has throat streaked white, more clearly barred, with short white bars fringed black on flanks
O. g. medius (S Ve) uniform grey head, brighter below

Habits Sedentary. Feeds on berries and insects, seeds and fruits. Coveys average 8 individuals. Often betrays presence by vocalisations at dawn and dusk.
Status Locally common, uncommon in Venezuela, frequent in Suriname and French Guiana.
Habitat Tropical and Subtropical Zones. Lowlands. Forest floor of humid forests and mature second growth. Favours ravines and areas with dense tangled undergrowth (R&G).
Voice Duetting pairs call antiphonally: *corocorovado, corocorovado, corocorovado...* Male calls *corocoro* and female *vado* (H&B). A rapidly repeated duet described as *cocoro-kó, cocoro-kó, cocoro-kó...* (R&G). Also a confusingly hollow, repeated *koo-kokoro, koo-kokoro, koo-kokoro* and an advertising call transcribed as *burst-the-bubble, burst-the-bubble, burst-the-bubble* (M&M). Hilty describes two songs from Venezuela: *koo-kee-poo, koo-kee-poo, koo-kee-poo ...* (south of Orinoco) and *buba-wink-kle, buba-wink-kle buba-wink-kle*...from north-west Barinas.

RUFOUS-FRONTED WOOD QUAIL
Odontophorus erythrops Pl. 8

Identification 23–28cm. Brown above from forehead, over crown and back of neck to tail, finely barred and vermiculated dusky and black with some small white accents; sides of head, narrowly down sides of neck, and breast to flanks rich deep cinnamon, chin and broad wedge across throat black; orbital skin grey, eyes dark, bill black, legs and feet greenish-grey. Tacarcuna Wood Quail has extensive white lores and eyebrow. Separated from Rufous-breasted by Central Andes.

Ssp. *O. e. erythrops* (SW Ec) as described; all-black throat
O. e. parambae (W Co, W Ec) white crescent on throat

Habits Wary, but can become confiding. Usually betrays presence by vocalisations. Little known, but presumed to be sedentary. Coveys average 7–8 individuals.
Status Uncommon to fairly common, depending on locality.
Habitat Tropical Zone. Inside humid lowland forests and secondary woodland.
Voice Choruses or duets given repeatedly and enthusiastically in early morning, a fast *chowita, chowita, chowita...* (H&B) or a loud, resonant *koo-klaw, koo-klaw, koo-klaw* uttered in duets or by more birds (M&M, R&G).

BLACK-FRONTED WOOD QUAIL
Odontophorus atrifrons Pl. 8

Identification 24–30cm. Entire head black with bushy, laid-back rufous crest from mid crown to back of head, lower neck and breast greyish, browner on back, brown on wings and rump to tail, all finely vermiculated, wings with long white teardrop spots within each terminal black spot on all feathers; underparts rufous with some irregular vermiculations, mostly on flanks, undertail-coverts barred. Only wood quail in region with all-black face.

Ssp. *O. a. atrifrons* (Co: Santa Marta) as described
O. a. navai (Co & Ve: Perijá) rufous crest smaller, only on nape, underparts entirely greyish, finely vermiculated with black-bordered white streaks on breast and sides to flanks
O. a. variegatus (Co: E Andes) more strongly patterned and browner above; and streaks below reach belly

Habits Shy and furtive, difficult to observe. Little known, but presumably sedentary. Coveys of up to 10 individuals.
Status Uncommon and local.
Habitat Tropical to Lower Temperate Zones, 1,200–3,100m. Floor of montane forests.
Voice Calls repeatedly in early morning, in Santa Marta a whistled *bob-white*. Also, a rhythmical rattling, typical of genus (H&B). Reunited coveys gabble after disturbance (M&M).

CHESTNUT WOOD QUAIL
Odontophorus hyperythrus Pl. 8

Identification 25–28.5cm. Male almost entirely rufous with a long, broad postocular, pale blue to white, which embraces outer edge of ear-coverts, upperparts brown, finely barred black from mantle to tail, wing-feathers have small white teardrop spots and larger black terminal spots. Female has rufous on head only, lacks white spots above, and below is soft buffy grey, more buffy and barred on undertail-coverts. Conspicuous trailing white eyebrow and all-chestnut front are unique.

Ssp. Monotypic (Co)

Habits Little known, but presumably sedentary. Forages on forest floor but may roost in trees. Forages by scratching in leaf-litter and among roots. Very shy and elusive. Coveys may have up to *c.*9 individuals.
Status Rare and local. Regularly heard but difficult to see in Cueva de los Guacharos National Park.
Habitat Subtropical to Temperate Zone. Montane forests.
Voice Merry early-morning choruses of rapid *orrit-killyit, orrit-kilyit, orrit-kilyit* (H&B), presumed to be duet. Also call *peetit peetit* in alarm (M&M).

DARK-BACKED WOOD QUAIL

Odontophorus melanonotus Pl. 8

Identification 24–27cm. Dark crown and head-sides, rear neck and back, all finely vermiculated with black, white spots at tips of greater wing-coverts, tertials and secondaries; chin and malar to lower breast orange-rufous, rest of underparts rufous, heavily washed brown and vermiculated; orbital skin, eyes, bill, legs and feet all dark. Rufous-breasted Wood Quail has black on face and obvious postocular line, whilst Chestnut Wood Quail has entire head rufous.

Ssp. Monotypic (Ec, Co)

Habits Little known, but presumably sedentary.
Status Local Colombian endemic, common in La Planada.
Habitat Upper Tropical to Lower Subtropical Zone, 1,200–1,500m. Very humid montane forests.
Voice Distinctive harsh and throaty, rapidly repeated *keeroro-keeroro-keeroro*…, fast in duet, slower when given by an individual. Also soft, low whistles (M&M, R&G).

RUFOUS-BREASTED WOOD QUAIL

Odontophorus speciosus Pl. 8

Identification 25–26.5cm. Dark brown from forehead to tail, finely vermiculated with black, all wing-feathers have terminal black-and-white spots, lower face and throat black, merging into rufescent ear-coverts and long eyebrow that reaches around ear-coverts is pale blue-grey with small black dots; male rich uniform rufous-chestnut from lower throat to vent and flanks, with sepia undertail-coverts barred lightly; female has lower throat and upper breast rufous, rest of underparts grey, with light buffy barring on undertail-coverts; orbital skin grey, eyes brown, bill black, legs and feet greenish. Black face and pale trailing eyebrow distinctive in range; from sympatric Starred Wood Quail by black on face and eyebrow.

Ssp. *O. s. soederstroemii* (Ec)

Habits Prefers dense tangled undergrowth, and is shy and retiring. Small coveys may run and freeze if disturbed.
Status Rare in Ecuador (M&M), though fairly common locally in Podocarpus National Park.
Habitat Humid tropical and subtropical forests, 800–2,000m.
Behaviour Little known, but presumably sedentary.
Voice Rapidly repeated *keeroroko- keeroroko- keeroroko* similar to Dark-backed, but higher pitched (M&M), and transcribed as *keeoróko-keeoróko-keeoróko* (R&G). Also some soft, low whistling.

TACARCUNA WOOD QUAIL

Odontophorus dialeucos Pl. 8

Identification 22–25 cm. Black crown, white head-sides including loral area around base of bill and chin forms star-like pattern when seen head-on, black cheeks and ear-coverts, continuing across throat to join white lower throat and neck-sides, edged at breast with black, breast and entire underparts brownish-grey, vermiculated blackish and spotted white; nape rufous, upperparts darker brownish-grey, with black-and-white spots and streaks on wings; eyes sepia, bill black, legs and feet greenish-grey. Rather variable with some very dark morphs. Similar to Gorgeted Wood Quail, but well separated geographically. White star of face and throat, with large black cheek patch and narrow black collar distinctive.

Ssp. Monotypic (Co)

Habits Little known, but presumably sedentary.
Status Apparently quite common within very restricted range.
Habitat Upper Tropical Zone, 1,050–1,450m. Restricted to montane forests of Colombia–Panama border.
Voice Unknown, apparently typical *whirr* and chattering notes when flushed (M&M).
Note Subspecies previously named *smithsonianus* proved to be a dark morph (M&M).

GORGETED WOOD QUAIL

Odontophorus strophium Pl. 8

Identification 25.5–27cm. Dark brown crown, back of neck, upperparts and distal underparts all warm rufescent brown, breast reddish-chestnut with bold white streaks; face white with black line through eye, throat largely black with broad white crescent on lower half, and below a broader crescent of black; upperparts dotted and streaked black and white; eyes bright brown, bill black, legs and feet greenish-grey. Female similarly patterned, but grey below, lacks white spots on wings and has small black streaks on white of face and eyebrow. Similar to Tacarcuna Wood Quail but black and white on face more evenly concentric, and they are separated by the Andes.

Ssp. Monotypic (Co)

Habits Sedentary. Forms small coveys of 3 or so birds.
Status Critically Endangered. Very rare and threatened by habitat loss. Endemic to west slope of East Colombian Andes and restricted to two areas: at three sites in Santander (where recently recorded in good numbers) and in Cundinamarca (where last reported in 1923).
Habitat Subtropical Zone, at 1,750–2,050m. Montane forests, especially where *Quercus humboldtii* is predominant; also mature second growth.
Voice Typical loud rollicking song of the genus (M&M), but differs from others in that 3-note refrain falls in pitch, *ti-t-too*, with song phrases lasting *c.*30 s (Donegan *et al.* 2005).

VENEZUELAN WOOD QUAIL

Odontophorus columbianus Pl. 8

Identification 28–30cm. Male has grey crown, rather short, bushy laid-back crest, back of neck to upperparts ruddy brown, darker towards tail, some slight black barring on back, spots and bars on wings, and small white streaks on back and scapulars; chin, malar and throat white with black streaks, clearest in centre, the whole surrounded by a broad black band; underparts ruddy rufous with black-edged white arrowhead streaks on breast and sides, distal underparts brown, as rump and tail; eyes chestnut, bill black with brown base, legs and feet dark greenish-grey. Female lacks any white streaks on back and is washed dark grey below, lacking any streaks. Only quail with white throat in its range.

Ssp. Monotypic (Ve)

Habits Sedentary. Forages and nests on ground, but roosts on branches and palm fronds. Scatters forest floor litter to expose soil and then scratches to find fleshy roots. Also eats seeds, fallen fruits, insects and worms. Breeds in rainy season, building roofed nests at base of palm trees.
Status Near Threatened. Fairly common but very local in 2 national parks of Coastal Cordillera, but future uncertain in national parks of Venezuelan Andes due to illegal logging.
Habitat Tropical to Subtropical Zone, 800–2,400m. Wet montane and cloud forests.
Voice Sings repeatedly at dawn, a loud, rollicking antiphonal duet, *chúrdole-chúr-it, chúrdole-chúr-it, chúrdole-chúr-it…* One bird utters *chúrdole* and the other responds *chúr-it*, the performance having a rhythmic, resonant quality (Hilty).

STARRED WOOD QUAIL
Odontophorus stellatus Pl. 8

Identification 24–26cm. Adult male has grey head with short buffy crest, upperparts sepia with fine brown barring, black streaks on scapulars and tertials, and black-edged white terminal spots on all wing-coverts; underparts cinnamon with rows of small white streaks radiating from centre of lower throat, some fine brown barring on flanks and undertail-coverts; orbital skin pink, eyes dark, bill black, legs and feet grey. Female similar but crown dusky rather than buffy. From Tawny-faced Quail by greyish-olive face and pink eye-ring.

Ssp. Monotypic (Ec)

Habits Shy and difficult to observe, and presence usually only revealed by voice. Very vocal, calling repeatedly at dusk. Keeps within dense forest undergrowth and hides in dense cover when disturbed. Little known but presumed sedentary.
Status Widespread in Amazonia, but rare and little known in Ecuador, perhaps occurs extreme south-east Colombia.
Habitat Tropical Zone, below 400m. Lowland humid forests, including *terra firme* and floodplain forest.
Voice Resonant advertising call repeated for long periods, a low, bubbly, musical *kor-korralo, kor-korralo, kor-korralo*, with a tremor at end of last syllable. Rather similar to Marbled Wood Quail, but slower (M&M). In Peru, sings *koo-kororo, koo-kororo, koo-kororo* (R&G).

TAWNY-FACED QUAIL
Rhynchortyx cinctus Pl. 7

Identification 17–20cm. Small and rounded with small-looking head and proportionately longer legs than wood quail; no crest. Male has bright tawny-orange cheeks and eyebrow, and black line through eyes, chin and throat white, breast grey, belly and flanks to undertail-coverts tawny-orange, paler towards undertail-coverts, which are finely barred black, upperparts grey spotted with black, feathers of wings broadly fringed orange; eyes dark, bill black, legs and feet grey. Female has head, breast and back bright rufous with white line through eyes, white throat, wings spotted black with white lines and fringes broadly rufescent; underparts creamy white with black scallops on lower breast, sides, flanks and undertail-coverts.

Ssp. *R. c. australis* (E Ec, E & NE Co)

Habits Little known but presumed sedentary. Very shy. Takes seeds, worms and insects. Found usually in pairs, but also in coveys of up to 8. When disturbed prefers to run, then freeze.
Status Locally common in Colombia, rare elsewhere.
Habitat Tropical Zone to 1,400m. Lowland humid forests, preferring foothills and adjacent flat ground.
Voice Tinamou-like whistles. Advertising call a sad-sounding, dove-like *cooo* or *toot* lasting a full second. A hollow-sounding, tinamou-like song, *kwoh, kwoh, kwoh-hah* may be preceded by some pure tinamou-like whistles (R&G). If alarmed, utters rapid chirrups like Crested Bobwhite.

PODICIPEDIDAE – Grebes

Exclusively aquatic and partial to clean, freshwater lakes and wetlands with abundant floating and shore vegetation, they are extremely sensitive to pollution. Main food is fish, supplemented by crustaceans and insects, but for reasons not yet clearly understood, they ingest large quantities of feathers, and even feed these to their chicks. The feathers accumulate in the stomach and are eventually egested in pellets. Grebes in general are not particularly social, and many species are solitary, but when breeding even some of these nest colonially. Ungainly on land, they leave water only to visit the wet, cumbersome floating platforms of reeds and grasses that most species construct as nests. Much time is spent grooming the feathers with oil from the uropygial gland at the base of the tail, or sunbathing in a characteristic posture, feathers fluffed, wings slightly raised and back facing the sun. Grebes have several curious habits. They have a unique method of preening the pale belly feathers, exposing them by rolling over in the water. In emergency they use singular diving techniques: sinking (expelling all the air from the body so that the bird disappears instantly, like a stone) or diving by 'folding in the middle', which also requires squeezing out all of the air. Also curious are their courtship displays, which are specific and remarkably elaborate, and often include 'running' on the water (raising the body by paddling at top speed). Chicks are cared for by both parents for a considerable period, and adults are often seen carrying the young on their backs.
Additional references used in the preparation of this family include Llimona & del Hoyo (1992, referred to as Ll&dH here).

LEAST GREBE
Tachybaptus dominicus Pl. 13

Identification 25cm. The smallest grebe. Breeding adult dark, sooty brown above, pale buffy around tail, barred indistinctly on sides and flanks. Eyes golden-yellow. Non-breeding adult has pale whitish throat and white body-sides. Juvenile similar to non-breeding adult but has very distinctive white stripes on head and body-sides streaked, not barred; eyes pale. From Pied-billed by slender bill and small head, from Colombian and Silvery by overall dark coloration.

Ssp. *T. d. brachyrhynchus* (throughout, except W Ec) as described

T. d. eisenmanni (W Ec) slightly smaller

Habits Furtive. Dives to forage and rarely flies, but less reluctant to do so than other species. Prefers to breed in small, temporary pools, dispersing when these dry out.

Status Common to rare, depending on locality, in Ecuador. Locally common in Colombia and Venezuela. In Netherlands Antilles, irregular and absent in dry season. Uncommon in Trinidad & Tobago. Frequent in Guyana, rare in Suriname uncommon and local in French Guiana.

Habitat Tropical to Temperate Zones. Inland lakes and wetlands with much floating vegetation or overgrown shores.

Voice A seldom-uttered, melodious hoot; also loud trills: *dye-dye-ye-ye-e-e...*, or a low *kirrrr-r-r...* (F&K).

Note Races *brachyrhynchus* and *speciosus* often considered synonymous (Ll&dH), based on work of Storer, and due to invalid type locality.

PIED-BILLED GREBE
Podilymbus podiceps Pl. 13

Identification 33cm. A stocky, dusky grebe. Breeding adult is greyish-brown above with black chin and forehead, white tail area, mid greyish-brown on sides and flanks, indistinctly barred; brownish iris with white eye-ring. Bill pale grey with a strong dark band mid-way. Non-breeding adult has white chin and throat, has paler sides and flanks, and bill is pale horn with a faint band. Juvenile like non-breeding adult but differs in having chin and throat irregularly streaked brown, and bill has a vestigial band.

Ssp. *P. p. antarcticus* (throughout region)

Habits Solitary, territorial and quite shy, it escapes by diving and hiding in vegetation. Foraging dives are short. Breeds all year, building platform nests anchored to aquatic vegetation.

Status Locally common to uncommon in Ecuador. Locally common to frequent in Colombia and Venezuela. In Netherlands Antilles irregular and absent in dry season. Uncommon in Trinidad & Tobago. Scarce in Guyana, uncommon in Suriname and French Guiana.

Habitat Tropical to Temperate Zones. Calm or stagnant waters, reservoirs, wetlands and lakes with abundant vegetation and reeds.

Voice Mostly silent, but when breeding suddenly wails, grunts or chatters vibrantly, *eeow-eeow-eeow-keeow*, followed by sequence of *cow* notes. In breeding season, a loud *cuk-cuk-cuk-cuk, cou-cou-cou* (M. L. Goodwin recording).

Notes Tropical populations sedentary, but northern populations migratory. Northern *podiceps* winters to Panama and may occasionally reach northern S. America. Race *antillarum* may occasionally reach Netherlands Antilles, but no records. Both races smaller than *antarcticus*, and paler and greyer.

GREAT GREBE *Podiceps major*

Identification 70–78cm. A distinctive, large slender, long-necked grebe with a long bill and slight crest. Dark blackish-grey upperparts and head, with a grey face, brick red neck and breast, white belly and cinnamon undertail, and black bill. Non-breeder paler on face and neck and often has white on lower neck and breast, with a pale bill. At a distance, more likely to be confused with Neotropic Cormorant than any other grebe due to similar size, but grebe has a distinct profile of very straight neck and head and bill held horizontally. In flight shows white secondaries.

Ssp. *P. m. major* (SW Ec)

Great Grebe non-breeding (behind) and breeding plumages (front)

Habits Dives elegantly and swiftly, springing slightly upwards to do so. Diet principally fish.

Status Vagrant to south-west Ecuador. Sight record, Salinas, March 2005 (B. Haase). Likely to occur only in austral winter.

Habitat Tropical Zone. Large areas of open water without emergent vegetation. In non-breeding season occurs on the sea, inshore and on reservoirs, larger rivers and wetlands.

Voice Silent except when breeding (Jaramillo *et al.* 2003).

Note Sometimes in genus *Podicephorus* (e.g. Fjeldså 2005).

COLOMBIAN GREBE
Podiceps andinus Pl. 13

Identification 33cm. Breeding adult rich dark brown above, with bright yellow-orange tufts sweeping back and up on sides of crest, and deep reddish-orange behind and below eyes to neck-sides, lower throat and breast, becoming rich rufous-orange on body-sides and cream on flanks, heavily washed and irregularly barred orange and brown, more finely dark and white. Non-breeding adult has crest and tufts less developed, and chin, cheeks and throat white. Eyes red and bill dark.

Ssp. Monotypic (C Co)

Habits Reportedly social and sedentary, foraged by gleaning foliage and escaped danger by moving to open water.

Status Extinct. Colombian endemic, formerly abundant at lakes on Bogotá–Ubaté plateau. Last known population, in 1970s, at Lago Tota, near Bogotá, where last reliable report 1978; two thorough searches in early 1980s failed to find any.

Habitat Temperate Zone. Fairly open lakes with reedbeds and expanses of weedy shallows.

Voice Apparently a soft whistle (F&K).

Notes Formerly considered a subspecies of widespread Black-necked Grebe *P. nigricollis*. Sometimes placed in genus *Dytes*.

SILVERY GREBE *Podiceps occipitalis* Pl. 13

Identification 27cm. Breeding adult mid grey above, with silvery grey-buff tufts on ear-coverts, grey crown and black hindneck. Chin to breast and flanks white with grey streaks on sides. Eyes red, bill dark. Non-breeding adult lacks tufts on head and grey is duller. Juvenile like non-breeding adult but back of head and nape slightly paler and duller grey.

Ssp. *P. o. juninensis* (Ec, Co: C Andes)

Habits Not shy, usually in open and often sunbathes with back feathers fluffed up. Diet insects, shrimps and other small aquatic fauna; dives only briefly. Nests in colonies in open, on water weeds. Elaborate displays in breeding season.
Status Very local. Uncommon to rare in Ecuador, uncommon in Colombia.
Habitat Subtropical to Páramo, 2,100m to 4,100m. Open lakes with slightly alkaline waters, shallow reedbeds.
Voice Sudden soft whistles, *dooi'th* or *vit*; also *dzi-dzeee* between each dive during bouts of frenetic diving (F&K).

SPHENISCIDAE – Penguins

Penguins are supreme waterbirds, as even their eyes are adapted for underwater vision. They 'fly' through the water, using their feet and tails as rudders. The wings are reduced to stiff paddles, but are supported by large pectoral muscles that drive the birds through the water at high speed. Densely covered with 3 layers of feathers, evolved to maintain body heat in cold waters. When not breeding they live at sea, often for many months, keeping together in large rafts, for they are highly sociable, and doubtless this strategy offers considerable protection from predators. They overheat easily in tropical waters and Galápagos Penguin, the northernmost species, has larger wings and bare facial skin to enable heat loss. None occur normally in waters off northern South America, and most records are of dead or dying birds on beaches, leaving some doubt as to whether they actually arrived naturally.

Additional references used in the preparation of this family include Martínez (1992).

[HUMBOLDT PENGUIN *Spheniscus humboldti*] Pl.13

Identification 65cm. Adult has reddish face and base of lower mandible, broad white facial line and a single black breast-band. Juvenile dark brown, paler on chin, lower face and throat, and lacks any white lines. From similar Magellanic Penguin by larger deeper bill, more extensive reddish area on face, and single black breast-band. From smaller Galápagos Penguin by reddish facial skin and single black breast-band.

Ssp. Monotypic (Ec, Co)

Habits Usually in small groups, foraging for fish and squid.
Status Accidental in Ecuador and Colombia (Morales 1988). R&G note that only confirmed records in Ecuador are of dead or dying birds on beaches, perhaps dumped overboard by fishermen, and provenance in territorial waters thus uncertain. Breeds north to Lambayeque, Peru, and up to 20 p.a. recorded off Tumbes just south of Ecuador border (Paredes *et al.* 2003), thus natural occurrence in Ecuadorian waters possible.
Habitat Marine, coastal waters.

[MAGELLANIC PENGUIN *Spheniscus magellanicus*] Pl.13

Identification 70cm. Smaller, more slender bill than Humboldt with pink limited to face at base of upper mandible and around eye, broader white band encircling face but not meeting white underparts, and 2 black bands on upper breast.

Ssp. Monotypic (Co)

Habits Often in small, loose groups in waters just offshore in non-breeding season.
Status Accidental in Colombia (Franke & Naranjo 1994), well north of normal range and natural vagrancy considered unlikely. Some disperse when not breeding (April–September). Feeds on pelagic schooling fish. Population declining.
Habitat Mostly pelagic in tropical seas.

[GALÁPAGOS PENGUIN *Spheniscus mendiculus*] Pl.13

Identification 48–53cm. Smallest penguin, with a double black band on upper breast, the lower band often ragged or spotted at its lower edge. Juvenile dark brown with white front, and lacks any bars. From Humboldt which has single black band, by lack of reddish facial skin and small dirty horn-coloured bill.

Ssp. Monotypic (Co)

Habits Forages underwater for small schooling fish.
Status Galápagos endemic. Unconfirmed sighting in Colombia, if valid, could have been human-assisted; natural vagrancy considered highly unlikely. Extremely susceptible to El Niño.
Habitat Marine. Mainly in cool upwelling waters near breeding islands, and only likely to be seen far out to sea.

DIOMEDEIDAE – Albatrosses

Albatrosses are the largest and heaviest seabirds, with wingspans of up to 3.5m and weighing up to 12kg. Their bills are long and involve a complicated structure of bone plates. They have a very keen sense of smell, and share with the other members of the Order Procellariiformes (Procellariidae and Hydrobatidae) tube-shaped nostrils (hence the name 'tubenoses' often attached to members of these families), but the albatrosses' tubes are unique amongst Procellariiformes in that they are separate – a small tube on each side of the bill. Their flight-feathers are dark, which makes them more resistant to wear, and always moulted at sea. To travel thousands of miles, they must keep aloft with virtually zero energy expenditure. Take-off is a clumsy, difficult affair both from water and land, and can only be achieved by flying into the wind – from water, they 'run' a few metres pushing hard with the feet; from land, they use downhill 'runways' that are a feature of every breeding colony. They take up to 10 years to reach maturity and have very slow breeding rates – nesting in colonies on grassy slopes, in scrapes on the ground or mounds of mud and vegetation, they lay only a single egg and many species breed only every other year. They are long-lived with some surviving to 60 years.

As to taxonomy, no one has ever doubted the monophyly of the Diomedeidae. The linear sequence of genera used here follows the SACC, which in turn approximately follows Kennedy & Page (2002). Nowadays, the family is considered to comprise up to 23 species and 4 genera, but *Phoebastria* and *Thalassarche* were formerly subsumed within the genus *Diomedea*. This was changed by Nunn *et al.* (1996) and supported by Penhallurick & Wink (2004). Carboneras (1992c) recognises 2 genera and 14 species, whereas Dickinson (2003) recognises 4 genera and 13 species.

We have attempted to include all of the species that have been recorded or are possible in offshore and coastal waters of northern S. America, but some records do appear unlikely.

Additional references used in the preparation of this family include Harrison (1983, 1987) and Carboneras (1992).

WAVED ALBATROSS
Phoebastria irrorata Pl. 14

Identification 85–93cm, W 230–240cm. Huge. Breast and head creamy white, tinged yellow-buff on crown and nape, rest of body chestnut-brown finely vermiculated black, upperwing and tail browner, central underwing whitish. Juvenile has a whiter head.

Ssp. Monotypic (Pacific: Ec, Co)

Habits Feeds mainly at night, resting on water to take squid, fish and crustaceans, also scavenges in association with cetaceans and undertakes kleptoparasitic attacks on boobies.

Status Uncommon offshore from south-west Ecuador, vagrant to Colombia. A small colony, *c.*10 pairs, breeds on Isla de Plata, Manabí, Ecuador. Main breeding colony on Española, Galápagos. Population (*c.*35,000 birds) is apparently increasing, with nesting areas well protected. At sea ranges to Humboldt Current off Peru.

Habitat Pelagic, though regular off northern Peru.

Voice Shrieks and croaks from feeding groups.

Note Formerly placed in genus *Diomedea* (Nunn *et al.* 1996).

[BLACK-FOOTED ALBATROSS
Phoebastria nigripes] Pl.14

Identification 68–74cm, W 190–210cm. Large, but fairly small by albatross standards. Mostly dusky to dark brown; white band at base of bill and white spot behind eyes, white on long uppertail-coverts and all undertail-coverts. Juvenile darker with less white.

Ssp. Monotypic (N Pacific)

Habits Often follows ships, feeding on kitchen waste and garbage thrown overboard. Feeds by swooping and scooping, diving or sitting on water. Takes crustaceans, especially krill, but squid, fish and carrion.

Status Rare vagrant off coast of northern S America; only a single unconfirmed record for Ecuador.

Habitat Pelagic.

Voice Not known.

Note Formerly *Diomedea nigripes*.

YELLOW-NOSED ALBATROSS
Thalassarche chlororhynchos Pl. 14

Identification 71–82cm, W 180–200cm. Large. Pale grey head with white forehead, and black bill with yellow ridge to culmen becoming orange at tip; upperparts blackish-grey, contrasting with white rump and underparts. Underwing white with black primaries and narrow black leading and trailing edges. Immature has white head and all-black bill.

Ssp. *T. c. chlororhynchos* (Atlantic: FG) as described
Note race *carteri* also has grey on head, mostly on ear-coverts, but this wears rapidly, leaving head effectively all white.

Habits Feeds by seizing fish at surface or in shallow dives just below surface. When attending trawlers, snatches food and flies off to consume it away from the boat.

Status Endangered. Vagrant to French Guiana. The Atlantic nominate population (50,000–100,000 birds) is declining rapidly due to mortality from longline fisheries.

Habitat Pelagic, but frequents warmer, more northern, waters than other Atlantic albatrosses.

Voice Generally silent at sea.

Notes Formerly placed in genus *Diomedea* (Nunn *et al.* 1996). Considered to comprise 2 species (Robertson & Nunn 1998) making Atlantic Yellow-nosed Albatross *T. chlororhynchos* monotypic, which finding was confirmed by the genetic studies of Penhallurick & Wink (2004).

BLACK-BROWED ALBATROSS
Thalassarche melanophrys Pl. 14

Identification 83–93cm, W 210–250cm. Huge. White with contrasting dark grey-black upperwings, back and tail. Underwing white with broad, uneven black leading edge. Distinguished from other albatrosses by all-white head with smudgy dark eyebrow and yellow bill tipped orange. Immature similar but has dusky partial collar, dusky bill and dark underwings. Immature from very similar Grey-headed *T. chrysostoma* (unknown in region) by black tip and ridge to bill.

Ssp. *T. m. melanophrys* (Pacific: Ec)

Habits Feeds by plunging, diving or sitting on water. Takes mostly crustaceans, especially krill, but also squid, fish and carrion. Often feeds in mixed groups with other seabirds or follows cetaceans.

Status Vagrant to waters off southern Ecuador following El Niño events. Global population large (*c.*530,000 pairs) but declining due to mortality from longline and trawl fishing.

Habitat Pelagic, but more often found inshore than other albatrosses. Nests on subantarctic islands in Pacific and Atlantic. Ranges mostly below Tropic of Capricorn, but multiple records from northern latitudes.

Voice Shrieks and croaks from feeding groups; whistles, grunts and cries, and rapid bill-clapping in displays.

Note Formerly placed in *Diomedea* (Nunn *et al.* 1996).

PROCELLARIIDAE – Petrels, Prions and Shearwaters

As much as their cousins the albatrosses, petrels and shearwaters are truly marine birds. Most species are pelagic, but the larger petrels and fulmars, which feed mainly on carrion, prefer continental-shelf waters, wandering only occasionally into high seas. Procellariids occur in all oceans, with the greatest numbers and diversity of species in the Southern Ocean. They are quite compact and of medium to small size, with long narrow wings and dull plumage. Females look exactly like males but are usually slightly smaller and of lighter weight. Like all Procellariiformes, the nostrils are tube-shaped, but instead of two small tubes on the bill-sides, as in albatrosses, the Procellariidae have the two joined as a single tube that runs along the culmen, and which in many species has a single external nasal hole. They have an extraordinarily keen sense of smell. In general, petrels have stouter, longer bills than prions, whilst shearwater bills are the longest and thinnest of the family. In general also, they are magnificent flyers, but flight patterns and favoured manoeuvres vary amongst the various genera, as do preferred strategies of foraging. Flight frequently involves flapping, especially in light winds, but mainly consists of gliding and soaring. In this they differ from albatrosses, which almost never flap, and storm-petrels which flap most frequently of all. Many species are quite gregarious at sea and often occur in flocks of a few to several hundred individuals.

Procellariids are quite difficult to identify, but it helps to subdivide the family into four 'groups' of similar morphological or behavioural characteristics (but no taxonomic value). The first includes the fulmars and all of the larger petrels as well as some smaller species (the genera *Macronectes*, *Fulmarus*, *Thalassoica*, *Daption* and *Pagodroma*). These are the only members of the family that can walk well on land, or need to, for they are mostly scavengers. The next group includes the genera *Pterodroma* and *Bulweria*, which are popularly called gadfly petrels. They fly very fast and low over the water, sometimes rising suddenly and then descending immediately in a flight pattern called 'towering'. The third group comprises *Pachyptila* (prions) and *Halobaena* (Blue Petrel), which are bluish-grey above and mostly white below, and have a dark M-shaped mark on the upperwing. Their flight pattern is extremely restless and erratic, with much twisting from side to side and weaving at great speed. The last group is the shearwaters (*Procellaria*, *Calonectris* and *Puffinus*), spectacular plungers who drop from several metres above the surface to dive in pursuit of prey. Shearwaters also feed by sitting on the water and surface-seizing, and frequently feed at night on the squids and zooplankton that rise to the surface when it is dark. The shearwaters, prions and most gadfly petrels nest in burrows that the birds dig into soft soil or peat, or under boulders, or in abandoned rabbit warrens or deep natural holes on cliffs, lava fields and steep slopes. To visit the burrows, the birds exercise extreme care, coming and going only at night, and avoiding even moonlit nights, for with legs that are poorly adapted to walking, and easily accessible nests, they are virtually defenceless against predators.

Despite their diversity, monophyly of the Procellariidae has never been questioned. The linear sequence of genera used here follows the SACC, which in turn approximately follows Kennedy & Page (2002). Carboneras (1992) recognises 12 genera and 70 species, whereas Dickinson (2003) treats 14 genera and 74 species. One species change is *Puffinus subalaris*: although Murphy noted in 1927 the morphological distinctiveness of this Galápagos taxon, it was traditionally treated as a subspecies of *P. lherminieri* (as in this book). However, genetic data published by Austin *et al.* (2004) strongly indicate that *subalaris* is a separate species, and furthermore that it is only distantly related to *P. lherminieri*, being rather closer to *P. nativitatis*. Thus, the SACC recently approved a proposal to recognise *subalaris* specifically.

We have tried to include all species that have been recorded or are possible in offshore and coastal waters of northern South America, but some records do seem unlikely.

Additional references used in the preparation of this family include Harrison (1983, 1987) and Carboneras (1992).

[SOUTHERN GIANT PETREL *Macronectes giganteus*] Pl.14

Identification 85–100cm, W185–200cm. Fairly large, brownish, with the feathers darker at the tips; pale to whitish head, dark eyes (usually), pale horn-coloured bill with pale grey-greenish tip. Juvenile much browner and more uniformly so, gradually gets lighter and whiter-headed with each moult. Rare white morph is flecked all over with dark brown. Compared to albatrosses thay have shorter, less rounded wings, heavy bills with prominent nasal tube along culmen, and a stocky, hump-backed appearance.

Ssp. Monotypic (Antarctic; moves up both Pacific and Atlantic coasts)

Habits Both a scavenger and predator. At sea, feeds principally by surface-seizing.

Status Possible rare vagrant to Ecuador or French Guiana.

Habitat Marine, usually cold Antarctic waters near ice shores but young birds and immatures follow cold-water currents to subtropical and tropical latitudes off coasts of South America.

SOUTHERN FULMAR *Fulmarus glacialoides* Pl. 15

Identification 46–50cm, W114–120cm. Unmistakable pale petrel. White underparts, head and tail, pale grey mantle and wings, with black flight-feathers and white patch in primaries.

Ssp. Monotypic (Pacific: Ec)

Habits Glides with wings in stiff camber, very distinctive.

Feeds mostly at night on crustaceans, small fish and cephalopods. Often in flocks (sometimes with other seabirds), seizing prey from surface.
Status Accidental to Ecuador. Global population large (*c*.4 million) and apparently stable, although some taken as bycatch by commercial fishing boats.
Habitat Pelagic, usually cold Antarctic waters near icy shores, but young birds follow cold-water currents to subtropical latitudes off western South America.

CAPE PETREL *Daption capense* Pl. 15

Identification 38–40cm, W81–91cm. Unmistakable. Dark brown head and upper back, wings patterned black and white, lower back and rump white dotted black, tail white with black tip; underparts white with underwing edged dark.

Ssp. *D. c. capense*? (Pacific: Ec, Co)

Habits In strong winds, proceeds in bouncing glides very high above waves. Forages day or night, resting on water and pecking to feed. Occasionally dips while on wing and dives. Often accompanies whales. Disperses widely post-breeding.
Status Uncommon off Ecuador and vagrant off southern Colombia. Global population large (*c*.2 million). Some colonies impacted by rats and feral cats; some birds taken as bycatch by commercial fishing boats.
Habitat Pelagic. In austral winter, cold waters of Southern Ocean, in summer, closer to shore near breeding grounds. Often found at tropical latitudes off western South America.
Note Subspecies in our region is assumed to be nominate.

GALÁPAGOS PETREL
Pterodroma phaeopygia Pl. 15

Identification 43cm, W91cm. A large long-winged and long-tailed gadfly petrel; flies with bouncing pattern, typical of genus, up with a few quick strokes, downwards in a glide with wings arched low and backswept. Uniformly dark above except white frontal band on face, all white below with distinctive black line running across wing, primary tips and edges of secondaries black, and has distinctive small black patch on axillaries.

Ssp. Monotypic (Pacific: Ec, Co)

Habits Diet: fish, squid and crustaceans, taken by resting on water or dipping while on wing.
Status Rare but regular off coasts of Ecuador and Colombia, where seemingly more common historically, and population has decreased markedly due to predation by introduced rats, cats, dogs and pigs, and by Galápagos Hawks *Buteo galapagoensis*, trampling of burrows by large mammals and accidental death through ensnarement on barbed wire fences. Although 10,000–30,000 pairs remain, it is considered Critically Endangered.
Habitat Highly pelagic. Breeds in burrows and cavities in humid highlands of the Galápagos.
Notes Previously considered conspecific with Hawaiian Petrel *P. sandwichensis*, which breeds only on Hawaii, under name Dark-rumped Petrel *P. phaeopygia*. The separation was initially suggested based on morphological and vocal differences (Tomkins & Milne 1991), but was only widely adopted following DNA studies (Nunn *et al.* 2000). Three different breeding populations, on different islands in the Galápagos, breed at different times of year and show structural differences, especially in bill size (Carboneras).

BLACK-CAPPED PETREL
Pterodroma hasitata Pl. 15

Identification 40cm, W95cm. Medium-sized, long-winged gadfly petrel (the only species recorded on Atlantic coast of region). Dark cap emphasised by white hindneck (some dark adults have grey hindneck), upperwings grey with dark bar, rump white, tail black, underparts white, with dark primaries, trailing edge and black bar on underwing.

Ssp. Monotypic (Atlantic: Co, Ar, Bo, Cu)

Habits Nocturnal and crepuscular; feeds on fish, squid, and invertebrates associated with *Sargassum* weed reefs and upwellings.
Status Endangered. Vagrant, sight records from Aruba, Bonaire, Curaçao, Colombia and Venezuela. Population has decreased to *c*.2,000 birds, due to habitat destruction, predation by humans (for food) and by introduced mammals (rats, mongoose). Main feeding grounds in Atlantic are between eastern USA and north-east Brazil.
Habitat Highly pelagic. Breeds in cliff burrows within montane forest in highlands of Hispaniola and, perhaps, Cuba.

[KERMADEC PETREL
Pterodroma neglecta] Pl. 15

Identification 38cm, W92cm. Fairly large, long-winged, polymorphic gadfly petrel. Dark morph looks all dusky but is greyish on basal half of primaries and face; yellow legs and feet contrast with dark underparts. Light morph has whitish head with grey nape to mantle and scapulars; white underparts from face to flanks and belly; vent to undertail dark, with contrasting yellow legs and feet; basal half of primaries white.

Ssp. Race not known (Pacific Ocean)

Habits Similar to Mottled Petrel.
Status Possible vagrant to offshore Ecuador.
Habitat Pelagic, occurring in both subtropical and tropical oceans.
Voice *kik-cow-ow-ow-ow*, or a *yuk-kirooo-yuk-yuk*.

[MOTTLED PETREL
Pterodroma inexpectata] Pl. 15

Identification 34cm, W74cm. Medium-sized gadfly petrel. White to grey with dark primaries, and a clearly defined black leading edge to outer wing from ends of primaries to carpal, the line then running diagonally across wings to join patchily across the lower back and rump; tail dark; face paler with an indistinct dark patch on the cheeks; undersides more contrasting white and grey, with broad black band along underwing-coverts; trailing edges of wings black. Bill black, legs and feet yellow. Similar Antarctic Prion is more evenly grey above, has tail grey with black tip, and lacks black bars below.

Ssp. Monotypic (Pacific Ocean)

Habits Flight erratic and weaving; zooms in high arcs, then rapid wingbeats between long glides, low over the waves.
Status Hypothetical and unconfirmed off Ecuador, possibly off Colombia also.
Habitat Pelagic, ranging well to the north in the Pacific, occurring as far as Alaska, but well out in the ocean.
Voice A high-pitched *te-te-te-te-te…* in rapid series.

DOVE (ANTARCTIC) PRION
Pachyptila desolata Pl. 15

Identification 27cm, W61cm. Small and elegant bird, bluish-grey above with a distinct shallow M-shaped black line that runs from wingtip to wingtip; darker on sides of head, with a variable white superciliary line; white below.

Ssp. Monotypic (Circumpolar, S Pacific: Ec?)

Habits Forages by day and may follow ships. Flight erratic and weaving, usually low and often close to the waves; appears to stand or almost sit on the water with wings raised, as it thrusts its head below the surface to feed on near-surface plankton.
Status Rare vagrant to waters off southern Ecuador.
Habitat Essentially a bird of Antarctic and subantarctic seas.

BULWER'S PETREL *Bulweria bulwerii* Pl. 16

Identification 26–28cm, W63–73cm. A distinctive small petrel with a wedge-shaped tail and unique flight action. Flies erratically, with buoyant twists, and wings held slightly forward and down. All dark brown with paler bar on wings and small dark bill.

Ssp. Monotypic (Atlantic: T&T)

Habits Feeds mostly at night, by resting on water to pick fish, squid and surface plankton.
Status Vagrant to Aruba, Bonaire, Curaçao, Trinidad and French Guiana. Recorded off Atlantic coast of northern South America during boreal winter.
Habitat Highly pelagic, except when breeding.

WHITE-CHINNED PETREL
Procellaria aequinoctialis Pl. 15

Identification 51–58cm, W134–147cm. A large, heavy dark petrel. All sooty brown with inconspicuous white chin and heavy pale bill with dark lines. Bulkier and browner than smaller Parkinson's and bill is all pale, lacking dark tip.

Ssp. Monotypic (Pacific: Ec)

Habits Diet mainly squid and crustaceans, picked from surface or by diving. Follows fishing boats. Strong, deliberate wingbeats and sometimes soars high above water.
Status Vagrant to Pacific off Ecuador. Global population very large (*c.*5 million) but decreasing and classified as Vulnerable due to introduced predators at some nesting sites, human exploitation in others, and bycatch mortality in commercial fisheries.
Habitat Marine and pelagic, preferring waters over continental shelf or upwellings. Nests on South Atlantic islands. Follows Humboldt Current to tropical latitudes during austral winter.

PARKINSON'S (BLACK) PETREL
Procellaria parkinsoni Pl. 15

Identification 46cm, W115cm. A medium-sized black petrel. All sooty black, though undersides of primaries may appear silvery, greenish-horn bill with distinct dark tip. Larger and heavier White-chinned lacks dark tip to bill and is browner.

Ssp. Monotypic (Pacific: Ec, Co)

Habits Feeds mostly on squid, fish, crustaceans and invertebrates by picking or diving from surface or by plunging in flight. Mainly feeds in association with small cetaceans, and also around fishing boats.
Status Fairly common in Pacific off Ecuador (March–November). Several recent records off Colombia (February–June). Considered Vulnerable; decline due to predation by introduced rats, cats, dogs and pigs. Population (*c.*10,000) now stable following eradication of cats on main nesting island off New Zealand.
Habitat Highly pelagic, far from land except at nesting colonies.

CORY'S SHEARWATER
Calonectris diomedea Pl. 16

Identification 45–48cm, W100–125cm. Large shearwater with broad, rounded wings. Dusky head, sandy-coloured upperparts with variable white uppertail-coverts, white underparts, and white underwings with dark primaries and trailing edge. Yellow bill. Flight slow and relaxed, with long glides on downward-arched wings. Similar-sized Great is longer and narrower winged with distinct dark cap, black bill, brown belly and variable dark markings on underwings.

Ssp. *C. d. borealis* (Caribbean and Atlantic: Ve, Tr, Gu, Su, FG)

Habits Fishes for squid and fish, mostly at night, and by resting on water or plunging in flight.
Status Rare offshore, with records from Venezuela, Trinidad & Tobago, Guyana, Suriname, French Guiana. Occurs off Atlantic coast of South America during boreal winter. Extensively exploited for food or bait, predated by introduced mammals and has further declined through habitat destruction in most breeding areas, although several colonies are now protected.
Habitat Highly pelagic except around breeding colonies.
Notes Formerly included in *Puffinus* but separation confirmed by DNA studies (Penhallurick & Wink 2004). Only the Trinidad record was certainly identified to subspecies (Collins 1969). Heidrich *et al.* (1996) proposed that race *borealis* is a separate species, and should retain the name Cory's Shearwater, whilst nominate takes the name Scopoli's Shearwater. Hazevoet (1995) proposed species status also for race *edwardsii*, which

would then be known as Cape Verde Shearwater. The latter race has been found in Brazil and could occur in northern South American waters. The nominate winters off South Africa and is seemingly less likely to occur.

WEDGE-TAILED SHEARWATER *Puffinus pacificus* Pl. 16

Identification 38–46cm, W97–105cm. Medium-sized shearwater with wedge-shaped tail. Two colour morphs: one all dark brown, the other with white underparts and dark bars on underwing. Dark morph separated from Sooty by lack of silvery panel on underwing.

Ssp. Monotypic (Pacific: Co)

Habits Fishes by dipping or plunging in flight, sometimes by resting on water. Joins other seabirds and dolphins to prey on schools of fish. Follows fishing boats.

Status Vagrant in Pacific off Colombia. Global population large (2–3 million), but evidence of slight decline.

Habitat Pelagic, seldom near land except at nesting colonies.

PINK-FOOTED SHEARWATER *Puffinus creatopus* Pl. 16

Identification 48cm, W109cm. Large, stocky broad-winged shearwater with slow, relaxed flight consisting of lazy strokes and low glides. Dark brown above with buffy fringes to all feathers, though at distance appears uniform mid brown, and has dusky head, flanks and undertail, white belly and breast, underwings whitish mottled brown, bill pinkish, feet pink. Size, flight action and white belly distinguish it from Sooty.

Ssp. Monotypic (Pacific: Ec, Co)

Habits Fishes by seizing prey while resting on water or by plunge-diving.

Status Considered Vulnerable due to small population (34,000–60,000) and predation by introduced rats, cats, coatis and dogs, harvesting by local people, and erosion of breeding sites through overgrazing. Migrates from breeding islands off Chile north along eastern Pacific coast in austral winter. Uncommon to rare off Ecuador and Colombia.

Habitat Pelagic, mainly in waters over continental shelf.

[BULLER'S SHEARWATER *Puffinus bulleri*] Pl. 16

Identification 45–47cm, W96–99cm. Large striking grey, black and white shearwater with wedge-shaped tail. Upperparts grey with dark cap, tail and wingbar, underparts white, bill grey. Flight graceful and elegant, especially in strong winds: long, high-arching glides and easy strokes.

Ssp. Monotypic (Pacific: Ec)

Habits Feeds mostly at night, taking fish, jellyfish, salps and crustaceans at surface.

Status Considered Vulnerable due to small breeding range. Vagrant to Ecuador (single record of bird washed up on a beach in Guayas). Global population large (2.5 million).

Habitat Marine and pelagic, disperses to northern Pacific during austral winter.

GREAT SHEARWATER *Puffinus gravis* Pl. 16

Identification 43–51cm, W100–118cm. Large shearwater with thin stiff wings. Upperparts dark grey-brown with distinct darker cap emphasised by mostly white neck, thin black bill, narrow white band on uppertail-coverts, underparts white with brown belly, and distinct dark bars on underwings. From Cory's by wing shape, darker coloration, capped appearance and underwing bars. Flies with quick, stiff wingbeats with fairly straight wings.

Ssp. Monotypic (Co? Ve, Atlantic coasts)

Habits Follows trawlers in large noisy flocks to take offal (sounds like a fighting cat – Hilty). Mainly plunge-dives, also dives or picks on surface.

Status Uncommon on passage (doubtless more common than reports suggest). Transequatorial migrant, circling Atlantic, moving north along American coast to Canada and Greenland in Jul–Aug, then east and south along coasts of Britain, Iberia and Africa, to nesting islands in S Atlantic in late September, off northern South America in May–Jun. Recorded off entire coast of Venezuela and must have occurred at least off the eastern end of Colombia's Caribbean coast.

Habitat Cool pelagic waters.

SOOTY SHEARWATER *Puffinus griseus* Pl. 16

Identification 40–51cm, W94–109cm. Mid-sized, slender narrow-winged shearwater. Uniform dark brown with distinctive silvery panels on underwing. Has distinctive flight action with deep slicing beats.

Ssp. Monotypic (Pacific, Caribbean and Atlantic: Ec, Co)

Habits Frequently feeds with congeners, as well as terns and penguins. Flocks, especially of juveniles, follow trawlers. Fishes by diving, plunging and picking from surface.

Status Fairly common, even seasonally abundant, in Pacific off Colombia and Ecuador, and vagrant to Caribbean coast of Colombia. Transequatorial migrant in both Pacific and Atlantic. Large global population (*c.*20 million) but considered Near Threatened based on declines at some colonies and in feeding areas.

Habitat Mostly cold offshore, but also pelagic, waters.

[FLESH-FOOTED SHEARWATER *Puffinus carneipes*] Pl. 16

Identification 43cm, W103cm. Large, typically long-winged shearwater, almost entirely blackish-brown (may appear black) with thick straw-coloured, yellowish-pink or flesh-coloured bill (with black tip), legs and feet. Virtually identical to but slimmer than dark morph of Wedge-tailed Shearwater, which has darker bill, larger head and body. Very similar to dark morph of Pink-footed Shearwater, which is larger and has broader wings. Sooty Shearwater is similar above and has same outline but has pale to silvery wing linings.

Ssp. Monotypic (W Pacific)

Habits Flight slow and languid, with long glides close to the surface and occasional slow, effortless, stiff-winged wingbeats. Dives freely; several may gather at good feeding spot but usually solitary. Seldom follows ships.
Status Rare off the Pacific coast of western USA; unconfirmed vagrant off Ecuador.
Habitat Pelagic.
Voice High-pitched call *ku-ki-ar*.

MANX SHEARWATER
Puffinus puffinus Pl. 16

Identification 30–38cm, W76–89cm. The largest black-and-white shearwater in the region, proportions like larger shearwaters. Entire upperparts blackish, underparts including undertail white, dark auricular area with pale crescent behind. Differs from smaller browner Audubon's in white undertail, darker auriculars and more gliding flight action.

Ssp. Monotypic (Caribbean and Atlantic: Ar, Bo, Cu, T&T)

Habits Feeds alone or in small flocks, by plunging or diving, or by picking from surface while resting on water.
Status Vagrant to Aruba, Bonaire, Curaçao and Trinidad & Tobago. Migrates across equator, found off eastern South America during boreal winter.
Habitat Pelagic waters over continental shelf.

LITTLE SHEARWATER
Puffinus assimilis Pl. 16

Identification 25–30cm, W58–67cm. Smallest shearwater, with auk-like flight action. Black upperparts contrast with white underparts; eye shows clearly, being surrounded by white on face or is at border of black cap. Often flies along troughs between waves, alternating shallow, fluttering strokes and short straight glides. Two subspecies occur in the Atlantic, and either could occur off the Atlantic coast of the region.

Ssp. *P. a. boydi* (Atlantic: FG) dark undertail-coverts
P. a. baroli (Atlantic: FG) white undertail-coverts

Habits Feeds by day. 'Hangs' over water, wings raised above back and feet 'tiptoeing' surface, and then dives or plunges to catch fish and krill. Follows ships.
Status Vagrant off French Guiana, but subspecies unconfirmed. Some nesting sites threatened by introduced cats and rats, and human exploitation of eggs and chicks.
Habitat Marine and pelagic but most frequent near shores and in warm waters at tropical latitudes.

AUDUBON'S SHEARWATER
Puffinus lherminieri Pl. 16

Identification 27–33cm, W64–74cm. Small, short-winged long-tailed black-and-white shearwater. Entire upperparts dark brown, giving capped appearance, underparts white with dusky undertail and tail, bill black, feet pink. From shorter tailed Manx Shearwater by dark undertail, browner upperparts and faster, more flapping flight.

Ssp. *P. l. lherminieri* (Caribbean and Atlantic: Ec?, Ve, Co) as described
P. l. subalaris (Pacific: Ec, Co) underwing-coverts entirely white, lacking broad, dark leading edge of nominate.

Habits Feeds while resting on water, also by pattering, plunging or diving. May join other seabirds. Rarely follows fishing boats.
Status Fairly common in Caribbean off Colombia and Venezuela, where breeds on La Orchila, Los Hermanos and Los Roques groups. Uncommon off Ecuador and Colombia.
Habitat Pelagic, offshore waters.
Notes *P. l. loyemilleri* could also occur in Caribbean and Atlantic waters. SACC now considers *subalaris* as a full species, Galápagos Shearwater.

HYDROBATIDAE – Storm-petrels

Storm-petrels are the smallest of all Procellariiformes. They have long legs and hooked bills with a conspicuous, long, single nostril tube that helps give the birds a distinctive profile and a very keen sense of smell. The colour palette is quite limited – black, dusky, grey, brown, and pure white faces and underparts. The wings are comparatively shorter and broader than the Diomedeidae and Procellariidae, and are, therefore, much better suited for powered flight, but share with those families the characteristic dark flight-feathers, which are more resistant to wear. Like all pelagic birds, moult is a very prolonged, gradual process. Within the family, two subfamilies are often recognised: the Oceanitinae (the genera *Oceanites*, *Garrodia*, *Pelagodroma*, *Fregetta* and *Nesofregetta*), which have shorter, more rounded wings, longer legs and, for the most part, square tails, and the Hydrobatinae (*Hydrobates* and *Oceanodroma*), which have longer, more pointed wings, shorter legs, and forked tails. Most of the breeding sites of Oceanitinae are at southern latitudes, whilst the majority of breeding sites of Hydrobatinae are at northern latitudes. The wing shape of the Hydrobatinae is apparently an adaptation to the relatively calmer conditions of northern seas. In general, storm-petrels fly like swallows – usually direct but sometimes erratic, low over the water, moving restlessly and with great agility, sometimes buoyantly. The Oceanitinae have the curious habit of gliding leisurely over the water with dangling legs, dipping the feet often, whilst the Hydrobatinae fly more energetically, with lots of planing and hovering, sharp banking and, in strong winds, frequent gliding. Storm-petrels rarely rest in the water, but will occasionally plunge from a short height to dive for prey. Most foraging occurs on the wing, by flying low with the long legs dangling, picking food items by barely entering the head into the water. The birds occasionally hover while scanning the water, or sometimes patter the water whilst cruising, which is thought to attract prey to the surface. In fast winds, they can 'walk' on the water, wings outstretched and feet pushing, or even 'stand' on it, the feet serving as anchors and the stiff bird propelled by the wind. Different species and subspecies of storm-petrels occur in areas with marked differences in temperature and salinity, with the greatest numbers found in the cold waters of the Southern Ocean and in the upwellings off South Africa and western South America. They nest in self-excavated burrows in soft soil or peat, abandoned rabbit warrens, burrows of other seabirds or natural holes on cliffs, steep rocky or grassy slopes, caves, and even in ruins and walls. They are always gregarious at their colonies, and at sea often occur in small flocks, but solitary birds are also common. At colonies they are very noisy, making a wide variety of calls and sounds, but are silent at sea. Storm-petrels are remarkably long-lived for their size. Little is known about the populations of most species, but several are of conservation concern, especially where cats, mongoose or rats have been introduced to islands that harbour breeding colonies. Those on large islands or at mainland sites are exposed to a large number of predators, with skuas among the most ferocious. Another danger is sudden, severe storms, which may take a heavy toll on flocks caught in their midst.

We have endeavoured to include all of the species that have been recorded or are possible in offshore and coastal waters of northern South America.

Additional references used in the preparation of this family include Harrison (1983, 1987) and Carboneras (1992).

WHITE-BELLIED STORM-PETREL
Fregatta grallaria Pl. 17

Identification 20cm, W46cm. Blackish-brown above with wing-coverts and back slightly lighter and more greyish; rump white; underwing-coverts and belly to vent white, contrasting well with all blackish head, and vent to tail. The feet do not protrude beyond the squared tail in flight. Very similar Black-bellied Storm-petrel is virtually identical but is distinguished by a thick black line down the centre of the belly and protruding feet. Similar Wilson's Storm-petrel has underwing-coverts grey, belly black, with white vent and undertail-coverts.

Ssp. *F. g. segethi* (S. Pacific: Ec, Co)

Habits Distinctive, wave-hugging flight with bill pointing down, wings stiffly-held, legs dangling and body swinging from side to side; occasionally 'walks on water' and will kick at water, or appear to trail one leg in the water. Accompanies ships, but flies alongside or over bow wave, not over wake.
Status Rare vagrant off Ecuador and Colombia.
Habitat Pelagic.
Voice Usually silent

BLACK-BELLIED STORM-PETREL
Fregatta tropica Pl. 17

Identification 20cm, W46cm. Blackish-brown above with wing-coverts and back slightly lighter and more greyish; rump white; underwing-coverts and belly to vent white, contrasting well with all blackish head, and vent to tail. The feet protrude a little beyond the squared tail in flight. Very similar White-bellied Storm-Petrel is virtually identical but is distinguished by having entire belly to vent white.

Ssp. *F. t. tropica* (Circumpolar: Ec)

Habits Similar to White-bellied Storm-petrel.
Status Rare vagrant off Ecuador.
Habitat Circumpolar, dispersing and wandering north into tropical waters when not breeding, but movements very poorly known.
Voice Usually silent but repeated shrill whistles at breeding grounds.

WILSON'S STORM-PETREL
Oceanites oceanicus Pl. 17

Identification 17–19cm, W38–40cm. Dark brown with prominent white crescent-shaped rump patch and pale carpal bar (upperwing-coverts); feet extend beyond tail in flight and have yellow webs which are occasionally visible in field. From similar White-vented by black belly, dark underwing and more direct, swallow-like flight. From Band-rumped and Leach's by square tail (Leach's has sharp carpal bend and white rump with dark median stripe). Wingbeats faster and glides less than Leach's. Moults April–June (but still renewing some rectrices in August in French Guiana).

Ssp. *O. o. oceanicus* (all coasts) as described
O. o. exasperatus (Ec?) longer-winged and larger-tailed

Habits Follows ships, attends trawlers and feeds in association with cetaceans. When feeding, skips low over surface, with wings raised and patters feet.
Status Vagrant to Ecuador, Venezuela and Trinidad, but breeds in Guianas and common in French Guianan waters March–August. Abundant transequatorial migrant that moves north mainly through eastern Pacific and western Atlantic. Occurs in tropical waters approximately late April–late October. Sometimes in large flocks on migration.
Habitat On migration may be seen over the continental shelf or in more pelagic waters. During breeding season avoids deep oceanic waters, preferring the continental shelf. Widespread, range overlaps with several other storm-petrels, including White-vented, which also occurs in tropical waters off western South America.

WHITE-VENTED STORM-PETREL
Oceanites gracilis Pl. 17

Identification 15–16 cm. Resembles Wilson's but slightly smaller and shorter-winged (has swifter, more erratic flight), pale underwing-coverts, narrower white crescent-shaped rump patch, narrower but paler carpal bar; diagnostic white on belly often hard to see in field. Feet extend beyond tail and have yellow webs.

Ssp. *O. g. gracilis* (Pacific coast: Ec, Co) as described
O. g. galapagoensis (Ec?, Co?) larger with more white on belly

Habits Non-feeding flight is light and zigzagging, usually close to surface. Feeds on wing, dipping periodically but mostly pattering feet just below surface, with wings raised high above back, as if tiptoeing on water. Follows ships, attends trawlers and feeds in association with cetaceans.

Status Rare and irregular off coasts of Ecuador and Colombia.
Habitat Pelagic but more often near land than other species, and is partial to cold waters and upwellings. Disperses through Humboldt Current.
Notes Although only nominate *gracilis* has been recorded with certainty in our region, it is likely that *galapagoensis*, which is resident around Galápagos and presumed to breed there, may also occur in Pacific coastal waters of Ecuador and Colombia. Also called Elliott's Storm-petrel.

WHITE-FACED STORM-PETREL
Pelagodroma marina Pl. 17

Identification 20–21cm, W41–43cm. Distinctive, with conspicuous white forehead and supercilium, white underparts and underwings, grey nuchal collar, grey rump and slightly forked black tail. Could only be confused with larger Hornby's which lacks supercilium and has deeply forked grey tail. In non-feeding flight, weaves and banks constantly in jerky and unpredictable pattern.

Ssp. *P. m. maoriana* (Ec)

Habits Nocturnal feeder. Main diet shrimps and other planktonic crustaceans, as well as small fish and squid. Feeds on wing, by pattering and dipping, but also by resting on water. Seldom approaches ships, but associates with cetaceans.
Status Rare vagrant (no recent records) off Ecuador.
Habitat Mostly pelagic.

LEAST STORM-PETREL
Oceanodroma microsoma Pl. 17

Identification 13–15cm, W32 cm. The smallest storm-petrel, all dark with narrow wings and wedge-shaped tail. Flight fast and direct with deep wingbeats.

Ssp. Monotypic (Pacific coast: Ec, Co)

Habits Feeds on wing, by pattering or resting on water. Main diet planktonic crustaceans (e.g. larvae of Spiny Lobster).
Status Vagrant (December–February).
Habitat Pelagic and prefers warm waters. Found off Colombia and Ecuador during boreal summer.
Note Formerly placed in monotypic genus *Halocyptena*.

WEDGE-RUMPED STORM-PETREL
Oceanodroma tethys Pl. 17

Identification 18–20cm. Extensive white rump and uppertail-coverts diagnostic; otherwise dark brown, and when worn shows distinctive carpal bar (March–July). Distinctive flight action, with wings often held forward and deep slow beats produce fast, steady nighthawk-like twisting and banking flight. Legs do not extend beyond slightly forked tail. Moults August–September.

Ssp. *O. t. kelsalli* (Pacific coast: Ec, Co) as described
O. t. tethys (Ec?, Co?) larger

Habits Feeds on wing, by pattering and dipping or by resting on water, mostly at night. Breeds in crevices or under bushes in lava fields or rock piles, mostly May–June.
Status Regular migrant to offshore Pacific of Ecuador and Colombia (May–October).
Habitat Pelagic. In non-breeding period disperses over Humboldt Current.
Note Although only *kelsalli* has been recorded with certainty in our region, it is likely that nominate *tethys*, which breeds Galápagos, also occurs off Ecuador and Colombia.

BAND-RUMPED STORM-PETREL
Oceanodroma castro Pl. 17

Identification 19–21cm, W44–46cm. Dark brown with paler brown greater coverts forming a prominent, if not dramatic bar, and all-white rump. From Leach's by sharp, clean white rump, and Wilson's by slightly forked tail and shorter legs that do not extend beyond tail. Flies with quick wingbeats and long, slashing glides. Distinctive flight action: banks sideways with half-a-dozen wingbeats, then banks to the other side for half-a-dozen wingbeats, continuing in a sharply defined zigzag.

Ssp. Monotypic (Pacific coast: Ec, Co)

Habits Feeds mainly by day, on the wing, by pattering and dipping, mostly on planktonic crustaceans, and some small fish and squid.
Status Uncertain or vagrant, sight records in January–February off Ecuador. Many breeding sites. Population fairly large but few data.
Habitat Highly pelagic. Partial to warm waters.
Note Also known as Madeiran and Harcourt's Storm-petrel.

LEACH'S STORM-PETREL
Oceanodroma leucorhoa Pl. 17

Identification 19–22cm, W45–48cm. Similar to Wilson's but has forked tail, smudgy rump that does not wrap around onto underside of tail, rump divided by dark central line (hard to see in field), and longer wings with more pronounced carpal angle. From Wilson's by different bouncing and swerving flight action; does not patter surface. Dark-rumped birds in Pacific easily overlooked, as larger Black, but have only slightly forked tail and more fluttery flight. Distinctive flight consists of erratic horizontal turns and sudden vertical jumps.

Ssp. *O. l. chapmani* (Pacific coast) usually has pale rump
O. l. leucorhoa (Atlantic coast) variable rump from pale (north) to dark (south)

Habits On wing, skims, dips and snatches food (mainly small fish, squid and planktonic crustaceans), day or night. Follows cetaceans and, rarely, trawlers, but not other ships. Found in tropical waters during northern winter.
Status Common to uncommon in Atlantic waters off French Guiana (November–May), Suriname, Guyana, Trinidad & Tobago; rare or accidental in Caribbean with records from Venezuela and Curaçao. Predicted but unconfirmed for Pacific waters of Colombia and Ecuador. Widespread and abundant globally; though subject to continuous pressure from natural

(gulls, otters, minks, foxes) and introduced (cats, rats) predators at nesting colonies.
Habitat Pelagic, partial to upwellings and areas at convergence of oceanic currents. Often found in brackish waters of estuaries in French Guiana.

MARKHAM'S (SOOTY) STORM-PETREL
Oceanodroma markhami Pl. 17

Identification 23cm. Large, all dark with paler carpal bar and greater coverts – palest at tips – forming fuzzy but distinct bar which describes a full crescent. Very difficult to separate from Black Storm-petrel, note shorter line of pale fringes to upperwing-coverts. Graceful butterfly-like flight with slow, shallow strokes and long glides.

Ssp. Monotypic (Pacific coast: Ec, Co)

Habits Diet unknown, apparently breeds in coastal deserts of western South America (only known site discovered in 1987) and disperses over Humboldt Current.
Status Uncommon austral migrant or vagrant to offshore Ecuador (only confirmed records for January). Confusion with very similar Black Storm-petrel makes precise status unclear.
Habitat Pelagic, cool waters.

RINGED (HORNBY'S) STORM-PETREL
Oceanodroma hornbyi Pl. 17

Identification 21–23cm, W46cm. Distinctive, large and stocky with swept-back wings; dark cap and chest-band contrast with white underparts, forehead and collar. Brownish-grey upperparts, upperwings have broad paler carpal bar, grey rump and underwings, and longish, notched black tail. Legs do not extend beyond tail. Flight erratic with several deep strokes then a glide.

Ssp. Monotypic (Pacific coast: Ec, Co)

Habits Feeds on wing, pattering, dipping and snatching prey from surface.
Status Vagrant off Ecuador in August–January, with most records from Gulf of Guayaquil; once 130 together (R&G).
Habitat Pelagic. Most records from Humboldt Current.

BLACK STORM-PETREL
Oceanodroma melania Pl. 17

Identification 23cm, W46–51cm. Large and all dark, with pale tips to greater coverts. From very similar Markham's by longer pale carpal bar reaching fore upperwing and flight, which is steady and elegant, with deep vertical strokes and very few glides.

Ssp. Monotypic (Pacific coast: Ec, Co)

Habits Main diet is planktonic crustaceans (larvae of Spiny Lobster), also small fish. Feeds on wing, picking from surface.
Status Fairly common visitor to offshore Ecuador and Colombia, mainly April–November but some present year-round.
Habitat Both pelagic and coastal, generally in warm waters and more regularly seen from shore than most other storm-petrels.
Voice Generally silent at sea.

ASHY STORM-PETREL
Oceanodroma homochroa Pl. 17

Identification 18–21cm. Dark brown, with pale fringes to greater coverts and an indistinct but large pale bar on underwing-coverts, extending from axillaries to edge of wing. Very similar to larger Markham's; differs in indistinct pale underwing bar and is greyer overall. Tail less deeply forked. Flight steady and direct with shallow strokes; seldom glides.

Ssp. Monotypic (Pacific coast: Ec)

Habits Often feeds nocturnally, and is usually gregarious when so doing. Largely takes small cephalopods, fish and crustacea by surface-seizing or dipping whilst hovering. Mainly present at colonies February–April (Brooke 2004).
Status Uncertain and casual vagrant to Ecuador, with sight records in September and January. Total population small but stable in recent years, due to protection of breeding islands off California.
Habitat Marine and highly pelagic, but generally does not disperse far from breeding sites – only rarely reaches Pacific coast of northern South America.

PHAETHONTIDAE – Tropicbirds

Tropicbirds are fairly large, very elegant, long-tailed seabirds. They are usually white, although pinkish birds are often recorded, the colour coming from use of the waterproofing oil gland. Sexes are alike. At distance they look like heavy terns, but the tail always distinguishes them, even the short-tailed young have well-pointed tails. They have a steady graceful flight, with rather fast wingbeats like a pigeon, but alternate periods of flapping with glides. Adults seldom alight on the water, and they cock their tail when they do. Spectacular courtship displays are performed near and over the breeding colonies. Groups display and then pairs separate and perform synchronised acrobatic flights. They breed on rocky islands and coastal cliffs, nesting in crevices, amongst rocks or in scrapes, often under vegetation. Tropicbirds fly *c.*15 m above the surface, from which height they plunge to catch fish and squid; flying-fish may be taken in flight. They are adept at hovering, especially over shallow water, where they also take crustaceans. Their calls resemble the shrill whistle of a ship's bosun and have earned them the vernacular name of Bosunbirds.

RED-BILLED TROPICBIRD
Phaethon aethereus Pl. 18

Identification 90–105cm, tail-streamers 46–56cm, W99–106cm. All white with black on outermost primaries, black line through eye and fine black barring on back, innermost wing-coverts, tertials, rump and uppertail-coverts. Central tail-feathers very long. Bill bright red. Juvenile similar but black eyelines join at nape; bill is yellow and tail much shorter. From smaller White-tailed Tropicbird by faint black scalloping on back, less extensive black on inner wing, and red bill. Juvenile separated from White-tailed by heavier barring on back and wings, black tips to tail-feathers, and more extensive black line through eye joining on nape.

Ssp. *P. a. mesonauta* (Caribbean, E Pacific)

Habits Often in pairs.
Status The rarest tropicbird. Nests on Isla de Plata (Ecuador); on St Giles and Little Tobago (Tobago); on Malpelo I. (Colombia); and on the Los Hermanos and Los Roques (Venezuela). Recorded on Curaçao, but does not nest there. Vagrant to Trinidad. Probably bred historically on Grand Connétable I, off French Guiana (Daszkiewicz & Massary 2006).
Habitat Mostly pelagic in tropical seas, generally only seen near land at breeding colonies.
Voice Calls include loud, repetitive cries or shrieks during courtship flights at colonies, screeching during territorial fights and soft clicking toward chicks in nest.

WHITE-TAILED TROPICBIRD
Phaethon lepturus Pl. 18

Identification 70–82cm, tail-streamers 33–45cm, W90–95cm. All white with black on outermost primaries, heavy black line on wing, from carpal to end of tertials, short black line through eye and orange-yellow bill. Heavier black lines on inner wing, lack of scalloping on mantle, and yellow bill distinguish it from larger Red-billed. Juvenile similar to juvenile Red-billed Tropicbird but has less scalloping on back, white tail tips and shorter black line through eye.

Ssp. *P. l. catesbyi* (Caribbean: Co, To)

Habits Like most tropicbirds, usually encountered in pairs.
Status The commonest tropicbird globally. Numerous nesting sites throughout extensive range but none in northern South America. Recorded in Colombia and Tobago, whilst hypothetical in Venezuela, Aruba, Bonaire, Curaçao and Trinidad.
Habitat Pelagic and coastal waters in tropical and subtropical seas. Mainly in high seas but may feed near coast.
Voice Calls similar to those of Red-billed Tropicbird.

PELECANIDAE – Pelicans

With their extraordinary pouched bills, fat dumpy bodies and short, waddling legs, pelicans seem to be the living caricatures they are so often portrayed as. But these apparently ungainly, malformed birds are amongst the most elegant, skilful and acrobatic flyers. Our two 'brown' pelicans are exclusively seabirds. They prefer shark-infested waters, feeding on fish that have been herded into the shallower waters by the feeding sharks. They dive into the sea, often from a considerable height, crashing into the water breast-first, with a force that stuns the fish in the immediate vicinity, whilst the birds immediately sweep their open bills from side to side to scoop up what they can. The fish are soon swallowed into the gullet, where they are retained until the birds return to the nest to feed the waiting young. They fly high when commuting, in **V** formations or straight lines, synchronising wingbeats and short glides, and are unmistakable at a distance, once their jizz is recognised. Pelicans are colonial breeders, nesting in trees. Young are very vocal, but the adults silent. Mortality is very high in the first year, with few fledglings surviving to adulthood, but those that make it are long-lived.

Additional references used in preparing this family include Gilliard (1958), Harrison (1983), Schreiber & Schreiber (1985), Elliott (1992b) and Johnsgard (1993).

BROWN PELICAN
Pelecanus occidentalis Pl. 20

Identification 105–110cm, W*c*.200cm. Non-breeding adult has all-white head, flushed buffy on face, with some black at base of bill and on throat, entire upperparts grey, underparts sooty with fine white streaking on flanks; eyes pale with broad orange eye-ring, bill dusky horn with paler yellowish base and tip. Breeding has adult rear neck dark brown, the sides just meeting above breast, an ochraceous patch between neck and breast, the white flushed buffy; bill grey with pale orange tip and black spot near culmen tip. Adult feeding young has white lacking any buffy flush, dark eyes, and pale grey bill distally dusky with pale greenish-yellow tip. Juvenile has entire head, neck and upperparts brown, back and wing-feathers fringed slightly paler, underparts creamy white; eyes brown, bill dark grey with horn-coloured cutting edges, black spot near pale tip of culmen.

Ssp. *P. o. carolinensis* (occasional northern visitor)
P. o. murphyi (Pacific coasts) as described
P. o. occidentalis (Caribbean and Atlantic coasts) smaller than *carolinensis*, breeders slightly darker below

Habits Fishes mainly by plunge-diving, occasionally by picking from bottom whilst in shallow water. Main food is fish, especially anchovies and sardines, and also takes scraps discarded by fishermen, and even carrion. Often loses food to piratic seabirds, such as gulls and frigatebirds. Flocks fly stately in loose single-files, often barely above crests of waves. Breeds colonially, normally using same site for generations. Very sensitive to human disturbance at breeding colonies, but quite confident around humans elsewhere in coastal areas, especially ports, where it is frequently seen roosting on posts, boat masts or rigging.
Status Common on Atlantic, Caribbean and Pacific coasts. Rare in the muddy waters of coastal Suriname and French Guiana, mostly juveniles in winter months.
Habitat Prefers coastal waters (never open seas), frequenting ports, bays and estuaries. Breeds on inaccessible cliffs, on small remote, deserted islands and sometimes in mangroves, but very rarely seen inland.

PERUVIAN PELICAN *Pelecanus thagus* Pl. 20

Identification 134–152cm, W*c*.228cm. Much larger that Brown Pelican. When not breeding, generally much whiter on head; during breeding, facial skin much more brightly coloured and has more pronounced straw-coloured crest.

Ssp. Monotypic (Pacific coast: Ec, Co)

Habits Joins other species of seabirds, especially boobies and cormorants in large feeding flocks
Status Common bird of the Humboldt Current.
Habitat Exclusively marine. Prefers coastal waters.
Note Usually treated as a subspecies of Brown Pelican.

SULIDAE – Boobies

Boobies are a family of coastal-oceanic birds comprising just 7 species, but are found throughout the tropical and subtropical waters of the world. They are all very similar, with long, pointed wings, stout but streamlined bodies, and long pointed bills with serrated cutting edges for grasping fish underwater. Being oceanic, they most frequently feed in offshore waters, their diet being almost exclusively fish. Boobies catch fish by diving from some height, hitting the water with sufficient force to stun fish in the immediate vicinity. They fly in formations, sometimes in a long line, alternating flapping with glides. They roost on the water at night, and only come ashore in the breeding season, when they form noisy, busy colonies on steep cliffs and offshore islets. The name booby is said to come from the ease with which sailors slaughtered them for provisions.

Additional references used to prepare this family include Gilliard (1958), Harrison (1983, 1987), Nelson (1985) and Carboneras (1992a).

BLUE-FOOTED BOOBY *Sula nebouxii* Pl. 19

Identification 76–84cm, W152cm. Brown upperwings, head lightly streaked brown and white, back brown with white fringes and large white patch on lower back, tail brown with white central tail-feathers, underparts white, bill grey and has diagnostic blue feet. Juvenile has all-brown head and upper breast, and grey feet. Similar Peruvian Booby is slightly smaller and more slender, more speckled above and lacks large white patch on back.

Ssp. *S. n. nebouxii* (Pacific coast: Ec, Co)

Habits Feeds by plunge-diving for small schooling fish and catches flying-fish on wing. Forages in large flocks, often with other seabirds, sometimes follows dolphins, occasionally in shallow breakwaters along beaches.
Status Global population small. Frequent to common on tropical Pacific coast, with breeding colonies on coastal islands of Ecuador and in Galápagos. Non-breeding resident off Colombia.
Habitat Marine, but inshore waters only. Nesting colonies on barren cliffs and rocky coasts; feeding grounds mostly areas of upwelling or cool waters near coasts.
Voice Silent at sea. At breeding colonies, greeting, territorial and contact calls: hissing, wistful whistles, grunts, growls, etc.

PERUVIAN BOOBY *Sula variegata* Pl. 19

Identification 72–76cm. All-white head contrasts with rest of upperparts, which are brown lightly fringed white, underparts white, bill and legs greyish. Juvenile has streaked brown head and underparts. Similar to larger Blue-footed Booby, but separated by white head and dark blackish feet in adult, and by medium brownish streaking on head and underparts in juvenile.

Ssp. Monotypic (Pacific coast: Ec, Co)

Habits Forages in large flocks, usually with pelicans, cormorants and other seabirds. Rests on water and dives into schools of fish. Low-flying groups plunge on fish, all hitting water simultaneously.
Status Small flocks occur regularly along southern coast of Ecuador north to Santa Elena Peninsula, but large numbers appear during El Niño, fleeing disappearance of food in Humboldt Current off Peru, and may reach north-west Colombia. Population declining due to depletion of anchovy fisheries off Pacific coast of South America.
Habitat Endemic to Humboldt Current. Partial to cool upwellings. Breeds on coastal islands.
Voice Silent at sea. At breeding colonies, greeting, territorial and contact calls: hissing, whistles, grunts, growls, etc.

MASKED BOOBY *Sula dactylatra* Pl. 19

Identification 81–85cm, W152cm. Large, mostly white booby with blackish flight-feathers, greenish-yellow bill and dark face. Juvenile has brown head, back and upperwings contrasting with white mantle, and dark bar on underwing. Does not occur sympatrically with similar Nazca Booby in northern South America.

Ssp. *S. d. dactylatra* (Caribbean and Atlantic coasts)

Habits Forages alone or in small groups, in deeper waters, further from land than other boobies, diving or plunging on fish or squid. Often mobbed by frigatebirds.
Status Global population perhaps large but scattered; Caribbean population small and declining. In Colombia, probably regular offshore on Caribbean coast. Casual, non-breeding visitor to Aruba and Bonaire. In Venezuela a fairly common resident in offshore waters, breeding on several Caribbean islands. Scarce in Trinidad & Tobago, very rare in French Guiana.
Habitat Strictly marine and pelagic, preferring deep waters.
Voice Silent at sea. At breeding colonies, greeting, territorial and contact calls: hissing, trumpeting, whistles, grunts, growls, etc.
Note Nazca Booby was formerly considered a subspecies of Masked Booby.

NAZCA BOOBY *Sula granti* Pl. 19

Identification 90–92 cm, W152cm. Largest booby, mostly white with blackish flight-feathers, orange bill and dark face mask. Juvenile brown on head, upperwing and back with brown underwing bar. Does not occur sympatrically with similar Masked Booby in northern South America.

Ssp. Monotypic (Pacific coast: Ec, Co)

Habits Disperses widely and is mostly pelagic when not breeding.

Status In Ecuador, a common resident with an important nesting colony at Isla de Plata. In Colombia, apparently regular offshore, breeds on Malpelo I.
Habitat Strictly marine, fairly pelagic and prefers deep waters.
Voice Silent at sea. At breeding colonies, greeting, territorial and contact calls: hissing, whistles, grunts, growls, etc.
Note Formerly considered a subspecies of Masked Booby, but separated by Pitman & Jehl (1998), primarily as they do not interbreed, as well as differences in bill colour, size and proportions, and plumage differences at all ages.

RED-FOOTED BOOBY *Sula sula* Pl. 19

Identification 66–77cm, W91–101cm. Highly polymorphic, small booby with red feet. Varies from entirely brown to white with black primaries and secondaries. Most morphs have white tail, which is diagnostic. In Ecuador, most are brown morph, whilst on islands off Venezuela most are white morph. Black-tailed white morph separated from similar Masked and Nazca Boobies by smaller size and all-white head, lacking dark face. Juvenile all brown with yellowish feet.

Ssp. *S. s. sula* (Caribbean and Atlantic coasts) as described
S. s. websteri (Pacific coast) slightly smaller

Habits Forages in flocks, sometimes far from roosts and coasts, most often nocturnally, especially on moonlit nights. Feeds on flying-fish and other small fish, also squid. Frequently robbed by gulls and frigatebirds. Approaches ships and perches on masts and rigs.
Status Global population large and widespread in tropics. In Ecuador breeds on Isla de Plata in small numbers but apparently increasing. Possibly regular in offshore waters of Colombia. Frequent to common resident in Venezuela, where breeds on several Caribbean islands. Rare visitor to Trinidad, but breeding resident on Tobago. Frequent non-breeding visitor to Aruba, Curaçao and Bonaire.
Habitat Marine and pelagic waters when not breeding.
Voice Silent at sea. At breeding colonies, greeting, territorial and contact calls: hissing, whistles, grunts, growls, etc.

BROWN BOOBY *Sula leucogaster* Pl. 19

Identification 64–74cm, W132–150cm. All-brown head and upperparts contrasting with clean white underparts, and has pale yellowish bill and yellow feet. Male has dark slaty face, female a yellowish face. Juvenile uniform dull brown, slightly streaked on underparts; bill, legs and feet dusky. Most likely to be confused with juveniles of larger Masked and Nazca Boobies, which also have all-brown heads, but both have brighter bills and the former a white mantle.

Ssp. *S. l. etesiaca* (Pacific coast) has greyish forehead
S. l. leucogaster (Caribbean and Atlantic coasts) as described

Habits Feeds alone or in pairs, sometimes in small groups, near coasts. Main food is flying-fish, also other small fish and squid, caught by plunge-diving or by picking from surface. May mob other seabirds to steal food.
Status Global population large and widespread in tropics. In Ecuador probably occasional in northern offshore waters. In Colombia the most common booby, where off Caribbean coast breeds on Gorgona and Tonel Is., and off Pacific coast, on Malpelo I. Frequent visitor to Aruba, Curaçao and Bonaire. Frequent to common resident in Venezuela, where breeds on several Caribbean islands. Common on Tobago but uncommon on Trinidad. Recorded in Guyana, where status uncertain. Rare in Suriname, uncommon (juveniles only) but year-round in French Guiana.
Habitat Marine, but always inhabits inshore waters. Several breeding sites in northern South America.
Voice Silent at sea. At breeding colonies, greeting, territorial and contact calls: hissing, whistles, grunts, growls, etc.

PHALACROCORACIDAE – Cormorants

Cormorants are generally slim but robust waterbirds that have evolved to feed on fish by underwater pursuit. They differ from penguins in using their webbed feet, not their wings, for propulsion. They grasp fish with their strong, hooked bills. Soft parts are brightly coloured when breeding. They are highly gregarious, resting, roosting and breeding communally and colonially, on cliffs or in trees; and they often associate with many other species, both on coasts and inland. Cormorants are poorly waterproofed and only enter the water to hunt or to escape danger. They can usually be seen loafing on rocks or trunks of fallen trees over water, often drying their outspread wings.

Additional references used to prepare this family include Orta (1992d) and Sibley (2000).

NEOTROPIC CORMORANT *Phalacrocorax brasilianus* Pl. 20

Identification 58–73cm. The common, widespread cormorant of the region. From much larger Double-crested by white facial skin, dark lores, duller bill, longer tail, rather slender head and neck, and is generally slimmer.

Ssp. *P. b. brasilianus* (throughout)

Habits Usually in flocks commuting to and from roosts in mornings or evenings in irregular, wavy skeins. Diet small fish, frogs and aquatic invertebrates. Flocks gather over fish, and sometimes fish cooperatively, forming fans to herd schools. Dives directly from water surface in pursuit of prey or plunges from air (the only cormorant to do so).
Status Common in west, wanderer to eastern Ecuador, abundant in Colombia, Venezuela and Guyana. In French Guiana, uncommon and local on the coastal plain (mostly Kaw Marshes), very rare elsewhere due to hunting.
Habitat Tropical to Temperate Zones. Waterside areas, from marine (mainly coves, bays and other semi-sheltered coasts) to brackish (estuaries, coastal lagoons) or freshwater wetlands (wide slow-moving rivers, lakes, tarns, reservoirs, marshes). Most abundant in lowlands, but recorded to 5,000m. Swift to colonise reservoirs and temporary wetlands.

Voice Mostly silent, but may emit guttural grunt like a pig (Raffaele *et al.* 1998).
Note Previously named *P. olivacea*, but *brasilianus* is correct name (Browning 1989 and SACC).

DOUBLE-CRESTED CORMORANT
Phalacrocorax auritus Pl. 20

Identification 79–91cm. Adult glossy black with naked, orange-yellow face and gular pouch, small, curled occipital crest, and short tail. Much variation in juvenile plumage, from nearly all-white belly to dark brownish-black. From much smaller Neotropic Cormorant by orange facial skin and pouch, larger bill, and shorter tail.

Ssp. *P. a. floridanus* (Caribbean coast offshore islands)

Habits Principally feeds on schooling fish. Generally coastal.
Status Casual and fairly rare visitor from North America to Aruba, Bonaire, Curaçao, usually in March–August. Hypothetical for mainland.
Habitat Coasts and sheltered coastal wetlands, also inland freshwater wetlands, rivers, lakes and reservoirs in North and Middle America.
Voice Only rarely croaks or grunts, bullfrog-like growling and clean-spoken *yaaa yaa ya* (Sibley), a variety of deep guttural grunts (Raffaele *et al.* 1998), but silent for most part.

GUANAY CORMORANT
Phalacrocorax bougainvillii Pl. 20

Identification 71–76cm. Adult dark brown above, and brown on flanks and thighs. Below, throat white but neck and upper breast brown; rest of underparts white. Broad eye-ring bright red, eyes dark. Unmistakable, the only black-and-white cormorant in the region.

Ssp. Monotypic (Ec, Co)

Habits Highly pelagic, often seen far out to sea, where feeds in deep water. Dives in pursuit of fish, especially anchovies. Frequently in large groups, sometimes with pelicans and boobies. Colonial, with breeding success strictly dependent on anchovy supplies.
Status Rare and irregular on Colombian coast, but regular in small numbers to Ecuador, primarily at Santa Elena Peninsula. Appears in connection with El Niño events. Recorded in Ecuador mostly June–July, on post-breeding dispersal, and in Colombia April–May. Declining recently due to guano extraction and dramatic decline in east Pacific fisheries caused by severe El Niño phenomena and over-fishing.
Habitat Coastal. Feeds in cold waters of Humboldt Current.
Voice Mostly silent, grunts infrequently.
Note It has been suggested that this and several other species should be separated in the genus *Leucocarbo* (Siegel-Causey 1988).

ANHINGIDAE – Anhinga

Anhingas are closely related to cormorants but differ in several respects: they are longer bodied with especially long bills, heads and necks, and long tails that may be fanned. They catch prey underwater by darting the head forward, impaling the target on the sharp, pointed bill. Anhingas fly well and soar readily. They require less take-off distance and can inhabit more sheltered waters than cormorants, but in other respects they behave much as cormorants.

Additional references used to prepare this family included Orta (1992a) and Sibley (2000).

ANHINGA
Anhinga anhinga Pl. 20

Identification 81–91cm. Adult male glossy black with lesser and median wing-coverts pale grey, fringed black, greater wing-coverts near white, tip of tail brown. In breeding condition, white filoplumes on head and neck. Female similar but has pale greyish-buffy head. Juvenile resembles female but has less white in wing. From Neotropical Cormorant by larger size and long snake-like head. Deep wingbeats and occasional glides combined with fanned tail very distinctive.

Ssp. *A. a. anhinga* (east tropical South America)

Habits Often seen in trees or bushes at water's edge, wings outstretched to dry. Usually singly or in pairs, but numbers may congregate at rich fishing spots. On surface, swims with only neck and head above water, looking rather snake-like with a long pointed bill – quite a shock when seen for the first time! Soars with outstretched neck and long tail, giving distinctive profile, though pale neck of female can be hard to see at long distance, giving a headless look.

Anhinga soaring; combination of long neck without any trailing legs and feet is diagnostic

Status Uncommon to rare in Ecuador, locally frequent in Colombia, widespread and common to frequent in Venezuela and Guyana. In French Guiana, although widespread, rare throughout the north with populations drastically diminished by hunting.
Habitat Shallow inland lagoons, reservoirs and marshes, also slow-moving rivers with open water. Occasional in brackish coastal wetlands. Normally to 300m, but sightings to 1,400m.
Voice Usually silent, but sometimes quite vocal when perched, uttering descending series of mechanical clicks, *krr kr krr kr kr krrr krr*, also low, nasal frog-like grunts (Sibley).

FREGATIDAE – Frigatebirds

Frigatebirds are invariably seen in the air, soaring and gliding effortlessly on distinctive bowed wings. They frequent coastal areas of tropical oceans with trade winds. Their requirement of thermals and winds means they favour coasts with high cliffs and mountains. They have the lowest wing loading (weight to wing area ratio) of all birds and prefer to soar, often staying aloft all day, and may even remain at sea all night, soaring high on steady winds. They are unable to walk or swim, and never rest on water; lacking a preen gland their feathers are not waterproofed and they quickly become waterlogged if they inadvertently do so. Usually return at night to a communal roost atop a favoured stand of mangroves or low trees on a remote beach. Frigatebirds forage by swooping onto small fish or carrion at water surface; they follow tuna and are adept at snatching flying fish escaping from underwater pursuit. Their kleptoparasitic foraging methods have given rise to the names, Frigate Bird and Man-O-War Bird, attributed by sailors in tribute to the ferocious manner with which they pursue other seabirds, even pelicans, pecking savagely if they do not quickly disgorge food, and then jinking and spinning to catch the falling food before it hits water. They also take eggs and chicks from seabird nests and feed on carrion and turtle hatchlings on beaches. Adult males have a red gular sac that may be inflated to extraordinary proportions, and which is used in display. They breed colonially, often in mixed colonies with boobies and other seabirds, on oceanic islands, constructing platform nests in bushes and mangroves or sometimes on the ground if no trees are available. Females may be up to 25% larger than males. Young distinguished by their pale head; it takes 2 years to reach adult plumage.

MAGNIFICENT FRIGATEBIRD *Fregata magnificens* Pl. 18

Identification 89–114cm, W217–244cm. Adult male all black with red gular sac and black feet. Subadult male has white crescent on belly and white lines on axillaries; feet dull red. Adult female lacks red gular sac but does have red feet, with white lower throat and breast-sides, and white lines on axillaries; subadult female has white lower throat and breast, longitudinal white crescent either side of belly, white lines on axillaries, and pink feet. Juveniles have buffy heads, which are variable and often quite white, becoming even whiter over next year or so, a white breast and belly, and pink feet. From Great Frigatebird by all dark wings (very occasionally with a brown panel), dark feet and eye-ring. Female has blue orbital skin (not red) and dark throat. Juvenile has whiter head and more white on underparts.

Ssp. Monotypic (Caribbean and Pacific coasts)

Habits Forages alone or in pairs (especially away from shore), or in congregations at abundant food source (schools of fish, seabird rookeries, fishing boats and fishermen's docks, etc.).
Status Fairly common on Caribbean coasts, but populations decreasing. Common on Pacific coasts. Several breeding colonies known throughout the region.
Habitat Marine, mostly in near-shore waters, rarely pelagic. Vagrant inland.
Voice Normally silent in flight, but when attacking other birds sometimes makes fast rattling noise. Nesting colonies very noisy, with birds continually uttering nasal cries, snorts, cackles and bleating.

GREAT FRIGATEBIRD *Fregata minor* Pl. 18

Identification 85–105cm, W205–230cm. Adult male all black with distinct diagonal brown bar across upperwing – not much help when almost invariably seen from below! –, red gular sac and red or brown feet. Subadult male has inverted whitish crescent across lower breast; older juvenile male like juvenile but has blackish markings on mid breast, forming rough bar; adult female has white chin to upper breast and sides of lower breast; subadult female similar with additional white patch on belly. Adult has red eye-ring and subadult red-pink eye-ring. Juvenile has completely buffy head with white throat to belly. Male from Magnificent Frigatebird by red legs, red orbital ring and brown panel on upperwing-coverts (only shown very rarely by Magnificent) and greyish scaling on axillaries. Female has red orbital skin (not blue), pale grey throat and all-black underwing. Juvenile has buffier head and throat.

Ssp. *F. m. ridgwayi* (E Pacific, Ar)

Habits Less piratic than Magnificent Frigatebird.
Status Fairly common in Pacific east to Galápagos, vagrant to western Ecuador and Aruba. Very sensitive to declines in food availability caused by El Niño events.
Habitat Mostly warm tropical waters near island roosts or breeding colonies.
Voice Similar to Magnificent Frigatebird.

ARDEIDAE – Herons, Egrets and Bitterns

Herons and bitterns are waterside fishermen, and as such they move and time their lives with the floods or the tides or, like experienced anglers, seek spots along streams where the catch may be best. Some stand motionless and engrossed, waiting for prey to come within reach of their lightning strike, others run and jab, frantic and erratic, along the muddy edges or in the shallows. Prey is mainly fish, but they take also a fair share of frogs, crabs and other aquatic creatures, as well as insects and small terrestrial vertebrates. The majority of herons and egrets are colonial nesters, often in mixed colonies that may include ibises, cormorants and wood storks. On the trees used for roosting or nesting there is a pecking order, with the larger species helping themselves brazenly to the sturdier spots that will support their greater weight. The bitterns, tiger herons and some of the largest or forest-dwelling herons, however, nest alone. In general, the family is quite poor in its repertoire of vocalisations. Solitary nesters have some vocal displays, but colonial birds tend to be silent except during the breeding season, when the noise in the rookeries is a constant cacophony of croaks, honks, growls and other coarse sounds. A morphological character peculiar to the family are the patches of special down feathers that continually grow and crumble into a dust that the birds use in preening. The long necks curve sharply into two segments, retracted during flight and built to spring like harpoons when fishing, making deadly weapons of the long bills. The long feet and legs give them an idiosyncratic way of walking – long and staid steps, at times casual, at times watchful and stalking. But their beautiful grace is best revealed in flight, when wingbeats that are buoyant and elastic take them across the sky in calm, deliberate and rhythmic movement. Few sights in the world of birds are as memorable as a flock of egrets passing in the distance before the backdrop of a setting sun.

Additional references for this family include Hancock & Kushlan (1984), Martínez-Vilalta & Motis (1992), Porter et al. (1992) Mullarney et al. (1999) and Sibley (2000)

RUFESCENT TIGER HERON

Tigrisoma lineatum Pl. 23

Identification 66–76cm. Entire head and neck rufescent chestnut, barred black from throat-sides and entire lower neck barred, throat and foreneck white, buffy and dark brown, underparts rufous, barred black and white on flanks; eyes yellow, loral skin and base of bill buffy, rest of bill dark brown to blackish, legs and feet pale brown, large scales on fore leg brown, on rear leg greenish. Juvenile almost entirely rufous except white throat and undertail-coverts, barred heavily and irregularly with black throughout.

Ssp. *T. l. lineatum* (all countries)

Habits Feeds alone or sometimes in pairs, standing motionless in shallows or at water's edge. Takes fish, insects, crustaceans, and has been recorded taking small snakes. Most active at dawn and dusk. Roosts and nests on high branches.

Status Scarce over most of range, fairly common in southern Llanos of Venezuela. Uncommon and wary in French Guiana.

Habitat Tropical Zone. Shallow wetlands near wooded areas or gallery forests, as well as marshes, flooded grasslands and slow-moving rivers. Small creeks in primary *terra firme* forest.

Voice Calls described as rapidly repeated *wok-wok-wok*... or *hoo-hoo, hoo-hoo, hoo-hoo*... that fades at end, and a long hoot which shoots higher at end (P. Schwartz, J. V. Remsen, H&B).

FASCIATED TIGER HERON

Tigrisoma fasciatum Pl. 23

Identification 61–71cm. Entire upperparts dark brown scaled buff, ear-coverts washed slightly silvery, throat to breast white with some blackish and brown streaks on latter, rest of underparts cinnamon, thighs grey; eyes yellow, loral skin and base of bill greenish-grey, rest of bill blackish, legs and feet yellowish. Juvenile reddish-rufous with white throat and centre of lower breast to undertail-coverts, heavily spotted and barred black from head to breast and on flanks and thighs, back and wings black with reddish-rufous spots and bars; eyes yellow, facial skin greenish-grey bill, blackish, legs and feet dark greenish-grey. Adult from Rufescent by slate-grey neck; immature very similar to immature Rufescent Tiger Heron, but has shorter, thicker bill and much less barring on flanks.

Ssp. *T. f. salmoni* (Ec, Co, Ve, Gu, Su, FG)

Habits Little known. Solitary; very wary and flushes readily. Usually observed standing on boulders in turbulent water or on gravel bars (R&G). Possibly nocturnal.

Status Range still poorly known, records scarce and scattered. Considered rare and local, and only recently discovered in Suriname and French Guiana. Several recent sight records in rapids of some remote rivers in the interior of French Guiana (Mana river, Camopi river) and Suriname (Raleigh falls).

Habitat Tropical to Temperate Zones. On sandy, gravel or rocky banks along mountain brooks and fast-flowing streams within very humid premontane forests.

Voice An alarm *kwók!* (Straube *et al.* 1993).

BARE-THROATED TIGER HERON

Tigrisoma mexicanum Pl. 23

Identification 71–81cm. Forehead to nape black, face-sides pale grey, back and sides of neck to breast-sides brown, finely and regularly barred black, rest of upperparts darker and duller brown, very finely and evenly barred black; central throat to undertail-coverts rufescent to cinnamon, streaked centrally with black and fringed slightly paler; eyes yellow to pale orange, facial skin, including eye-ring and gular skin, pale green, rest of bill blackish, legs and feet dark green. Juvenile more ochraceous below, with barring on neck reaching pale throat and continuing throughout underparts; darker above with increasingly large, buffy spots on wings forming rough bars.

Ssp. Monotypic (NW Co)

Habits Fishes quietly at dawn or dusk (perhaps nocturnal), usually alone but occasionally in small groups. Not shy.

Status Uncommon near Panama border in Colombia, which marks southernmost limit of its range.

Habitat Tropical Zone. Mangroves and densely wooded salt, brackish or freshwater marshes and swamps. Also, streams and rivers through forested areas.

Voice At twilight and night, calls repeatedly, loud barks or croaks similar to frogs (Wetmore, H&B).

AGAMI HERON *Agamia agami* Pl. 23

Identification 60–76cm. Long thin neck and very long bill. Forehead to crown black, running across ear-coverts and dividing into two lines on deep chestnut neck, one down back of neck, other on sides of central foreneck, which is pale grey, sweeping back over lower neck to join at back, the lower pale grey foreneck – which consists of long slender plumes – divides into a black line that reaches the centre of the breast; upper mantle, body-sides and entire underparts chestnut; back dark green with long grey plumes, wings and tail dark grey, washed dark green; eyes brown, facial skin, including eye-ring and base of bill yellow, distal two-thirds of bill pale greyish-blue, and comparatively short legs and feet yellow. Juvenile from forehead, over rear neck, back and wings, to tail mid brown; and entire underparts from chin (which is whitish) to undertail-coverts pale whitish-buff, streaked dark brown from middle of foreneck to belly and flanks. From smaller Tricoloured Heron by yellow facial skin and chestnut belly.

Ssp. Monotypic (all countries, except ABC)

Habits Feeds quietly and alone by shady watersides. Occasionally in shallow water at edge but never wades. Very shy and wary, and difficult to see.
Status Probably scarce and spottily distributed but so elusive that probably under-recorded. Biggest known nesting colony recently discovered in coastal French Guiana, with more than 2000 pairs (Kaw Marshes) (Tostain & Goguillon). Widespread in French Guiana including forest of the interior.
Habitat Tropical to Lower Subtropical Zones, but mostly in lowlands. Inhabits extensive humid or gallery forests, along shaded streams and by lakes or swamps with dense waterside vegetation, staying well within shadows.
Voice May give sporadic series of low *koo koo koo koo*... notes. Also rattles and short *kwok* calls (H&B). Small groups utter a guttural, clattering, almost frog-like *kur'r'r'r'r*, and a low, rasping *ka-da-dik* to each other.

BOAT-BILLED HERON
Cochlearius cochlearius Pl. 23

Identification 45–51cm. Forehead white, crown black (in form of short laid-back crest), face-sides, neck and breast white, back and wings to tail grey; breast-sides, flanks and thighs black, central belly to undertail-coverts chestnut; large black eyes, bill very broad and flattened, black with a grey tip and horn-coloured lower mandible, legs and feet greyish-yellow. Juvenile has forehead slate grey, upperparts cinnamon to clay colour, buffy below; bill all black. From similar Black-crowned Night Heron by whitish back and massive bill.

Ssp. *C. c. cochlearius* (Co, Ve, Gu, Su, FG) as described
C. c. panamensis (extreme NW Co) entire top of head black, neck and breast grey, rest of plumage much darker than *cochlearius*

Habits Forages alone, from dusk but mainly at night, by standing quietly in muddy or very shallow areas or gravel bars. Feeds by scooping.
Status Common but local.
Habitat Tropical Zone. All types of fresh or brackish wetlands and along rivers, always in areas with forested margins.
Voice Song is *on-onah-aan* and variations of this form principal vocalisation (Kushlan & Hancock 2005). Call a low, guttural *guuk* or *uuk* (Hilty), and in flight a vaguely duck-like *kwa!* (R&G). Roosting birds give a low clucking and bill-clapping (R&G).

ZIGZAG HERON *Zebrilus undulatus* Pl. 24

Identification 28–33cm. Adult very dark above, slightly paler and browner below, forehead to laid-back crest black, upperparts filigreed with pale vermiculations, underparts from cheeks to undertail-coverts also filigreed dark brown, with some spots and scallops overlaid, and irregular narrow black barring. Juvenile lacks crest, has rufous forehead and forecrown grading into black rear crown and nape, otherwise similar to male; from face-sides to undertail-coverts pale rufescent to buffy. Small, dark and inconspicuous; flicks tail. Significantly smaller than rather similar Striated Heron.

Ssp. Monotypic (E Ec, E Co, Ve, Gu, Su, FG)

Habits Very little known. Feeds by day, on fish and insects, perhaps from low overhanging branches or protruding roots, and forages in leaf muck on wet ground.
Status Local and generally very rare, with few records, probably much overlooked due to its way of life.
Habitat Lower Tropical Zone. Undergrowth beside shallow pools, creeks, sluggish streams and swampy areas inside tropical evergreen forests.
Voice Calls consist of a series of nasal, deep *wuannn, wuannn*... varyingly repeated 3 to 7–8 times, then a pause, then more repetitions (G. Rodriguez, pers. comm.). Calls at dusk and into night, a soft but far-carrying *hhoow-oo*, steadily repeated every 4–6 s.

PINNATED BITTERN
Botaurus pinnatus Pl. 23

Identification 64–76cm. Classic cryptic bittern, basically buff throughout with dark brown to blackish barring and streaking (both on wings); eyes orange-yellow, loral skin and bill horn-yellow, legs and feet greenish-yellow. From immature tiger herons by streaked (not barred) wings and back. Females have brown tails.

Ssp. *B. p. pinnatus* (all countries)

Habits Mostly nocturnal and usually alone, but occasionally noted feeding in loose groups. Keeps within dense cover. Probably sedentary. If alarmed, will remain completely still with bill pointing vertically up.
Status Uncommon and local. Rarely seen due to secretive nature and nocturnal habits. Common in rice fields of NW French Guiana.
Habitat Tropical Zone. Shallow freshwater wetlands and flooded grasslands, with thickets of reeds, cat-tails and others. Visits rice fields and sugarcane.
Voice Call a booming *oonng-ka-choonk*, similar to American Bittern *B. lentiginosus* but higher and less resonant (Hilty), *poonk* or *poonkoo* (Stiles & Skutch).
Note Sometimes called South American Bittern.

LEAST BITTERN *Ixobrychus exilis* Pl. 24

Identification 28–36cm. Black crown continues narrowly on nape to back, scapulars and tertials to tail, with white line at edge of mantle; head-sides to undertail-coverts and most wing-coverts buffy, tinged rufous on ear-coverts, neck-sides, greater wing-coverts and outer webs of tertials, primaries black; eyes yellow, bill horn, legs and feet yellowish. Females have brown where males are black (i.e. back, cap). Juvenile much paler, cap is brown and lacks black line on back of neck, and has a brown back. Flushes with slow, laboured wingbeats, revealing black flight-feathers tipped rufous.

Ssp. *I. e. bogotensis* (C Co) much more rufous on sides of neck and breast, white undertail-coverts
I. e. erythromelas (rest of northern South America) as described

Habits Solitary. Feeds on fish, frogs and tadpoles, water insects, crustaceans, usually at dawn or dusk. Generally stays in deep cover. Birds from north of range migrate nocturnally.
Status Very local in Ecuador, fairly common in Colombia and Venezuela. Populations declining in several areas but has colonized some islands of Lesser Antilles in recent years. Juveniles disperse widely. Local populations may move seasonally, depending on rains and condition of wetlands. Locally common in coastal French Guiana.
Habitat Mostly Lower Tropical, but reaches Temperate Zone. Freshwater wetlands with dense vegetation (rushes, sedges, cat-tails, etc.) and overgrown borders. Occasionally in brackish or saltwater marshes and mangroves, and rice fields.
Voice Makes far-carrying, booming calls. An almost guttural, cooing *gruua* or *cuua*, rather like Zigzag Heron but lower (Hilty).

STRIPE-BACKED BITTERN
Ixobrychus involucris Pl. 24

Identification 28–33cm. Generally mid brown with cryptic streaks; dark crown, with pale buffy throat and foreneck and blackish streaks on breast-sides. Back streaked black, brown and pale buffy, wings streaked only slightly on feather centres, but all feathers fringed buffy, shoulder rather tawny; eyes yellowish, eye-ring and lores pale, bill horn, legs and feet pale greenish-yellow.

Ssp. Monotypic (all mainland countries)

Habits Little known. Feeds (probably nocturnally) on small aquatic fauna, keeping within dense cover. Flushes with slow, laboured wingbeats, revealing tawny shoulders and rufous flight-feathers.
Status Vagrant to Ecuador. Almost no data on populations. Generally scarce but locally common at some sites. Seldom seen due to secretive nature.
Habitat Lower Tropical Zone. Freshwater wetlands with dense stands of vegetation and overgrown borders; also rice fields.
Voice Makes far-carrying, booming calls, characteristic of genus. Also 4 low *huu* notes, lower pitched than in Least, and a slow, gargled *g'u'u'u'a'a*, both given night and day (Hilty).
Note Sometimes called Streaked Bittern.

BLACK-CROWNED NIGHT HERON
Nycticorax nycticorax Pl. 23

Identification 61–69cm. Non-breeding adult has forehead and narrow eyebrow white, crown to nape black with a few long white nuchal plumes, face-sides to neck and underparts white, back black, wings and tail grey, slightly buffy on tertials and flight-feathers; eyes red, loral skin greenish, bill black, legs and feet yellow to orange. Breeding adult has much longer nuchal plumes, red loral skin, and red legs and feet. From similar Boat-billed Heron by black back and far less impressive bill.

Ssp. *N. n. hoactli* (northern South America)

Habits Forages from dusk, but mainly at night, in loose flocks, quietly standing or wading in shallows. Days spent roosting in gallery or swamp forests.
Status Locally common and widespread, uncommon in coastal French Guiana.
Habitat Tropical to Temperate Zone, more common at lower elevations. All types of fresh, brackish or saltwater wetlands, always in areas with forested margins or dense waterside vegetation including irrigated agriculture.
Voice Calls a sharp *wuk! wok* or *kwok*, when surprised or in flight (R&G, Hilty).

YELLOW-CROWNED NIGHT HERON
Nyctanassa violacea Pl. 23

Identification 51-71cm. Adult unmistakable due to very bold head pattern, short neck and legs. Crown creamy buffy, with long plumes, rest of head black except white eye-ring and white line running from below eyes to ear-coverts, some black nuchal plumes, but most are white; neck and underparts grey, paler vent to undertail-coverts; upperparts entirely black with broad pale grey fringes to all feathers, including long plumes on back and rump; eyes orange, bill black, legs and feet pale orange with large black scales. Juvenile has brown head, neck and entire upperparts, spotted (on head) or streaked (neck and wing-coverts) white, or feathers fringed white with white terminal spots on greater coverts and flight-feathers; belly and undertail-coverts white, streaked brown; eyes yellow, bill black, legs and feet greenish-yellow. Immature difficult to separate from immature Black-crowned Night Heron, but darker with distinctly smaller white spots on wing-coverts.

Ssp. *N. v. calignis* (W Ec, W Co) much darker grey throughout; distinctive juvenile has very striped head
N. v. cayennensis (Co, Ve, Gu, Su, FG) as described

Habits Forages alone, during day or from dusk to night.
Status In Ecuador, local along coast, rare inland; in Venezuela, fairly common on coast, less common inland. Common in coastal Suriname and French Guiana.
Habitat Tropical Zone. Mostly on coasts, in mangroves, coastal marshes, tidal mudflats and rocky shores, but also beside rivers and all types of freshwater wetlands in open areas, occasionally even urban areas.
Voice Calls a piercing *kwok* in flight. *Quok* given singly or in laughter-like series (Hilty), a nasal *kwak* or *kwek* in flight, higher pitched than Black-crowned (R&G).
Note Sometimes placed in *Nycticorax*.

GREEN HERON *Butorides virescens* Pl. 23

Identification 38–43cm. Crown and head-sides to nape black, the feathers elongated and sometimes raised as a crest, face-sides and entire neck, save a narrow stripe of white, chestnut-brown, upperparts greenish-grey, the feathers lanceolate and paler grey on back and rump, somewhat greener and fringed buff on wings and tail, underparts brown; eyes orange, loral skin grey, bill black, legs and feet yellow to orange. Juvenile like juvenile Striated Heron (which is slightly greyer on neck); from adult by paler bill and lack of rufous on sides of neck.

Ssp. *B. v. virescens* and *B. v. anthonyi* (boreal migrants from N America have occurred in all countries; *virescens* resident on Tobago) as described
B. v. maculata (ABC and offshore islands) only by smaller size

Habits Forages alone, by crouching motionless and then jabbing prey at blinding speed. May wade in deep water.
Status Rare. Races *virescens* and *anthonyi* are boreal migrants, with perhaps small numbers of non-breeding residents. Removed from Guyana list by BFR&S due to lack of evidence; *maculata* is a fairly common breeding resident on offshore islands.
Habitat Tropical to Lower Subtropical Zones. Salt, brackish or freshwater wetlands of all kinds, mostly in lowlands.
Voice Mostly silent, may utter a sharp *kwop* if alarmed.
Notes Formerly included within *B. striata*. Race *maculata* listed in error under *B. striata* in Rodner *et al.* (2000).

STRIATED HERON *Butorides striata* Pl. 23

Identification 35–48cm. Forehead to nape black, the feathers elongated and sometimes raised as a crest, throat white, neck grey, lower throat and central breast streaked black and chestnut, back grey streaked black, wings and tail grey; eyes, loral skin and bill yellow (latter with black tip), legs and feet yellow. Juvenile has less extensive black cap, is brown from nape to tail, and wing-feathers fringed whitish, each with terminal whitish spot; throat white, and face-sides to undertail-coverts whitish, sides of head and foreneck streaked brown; soft parts dull yellow. From Green Heron by grey neck (not maroon-chestnut); juveniles not readily separable in field but Striated has greyer neck-sides. Juvenile Black-crowned Night Heron more heavily streaked below, and more clearly spotted pale above.

Ssp. *B. s. striata* (all countries) as described
B. s. robinsoni (Ve: Margarita I.) indistinguishable in the field

Habits Forages alone, from dusk to night, by perching motionless on branches that touch water or standing just at edge but rarely in water. Very territorial. When nervous raises crest and twitches tail.
Status Common and widespread.
Habitat Tropical to Lower Subtropical Zones. Salt, brackish or freshwater wetlands of all kinds, mostly in lowlands and especially where shore vegetation is dense. Numerous in *várzea* and very fond of muddy waterways.
Voice Mostly silent, but may utter a sharp *keoup!* if alarmed or flushed (Hilty).
Note Was included with *virescens* within cosmopolitan *B. striata*; Green (Green-backed) Heron, separated by Blake (1977) and supported by Monroe & Browning (1992), and retained in *virescens* by Hancock & Elliott (1978) and Martínez-Vilalta & Motis. Some hybridising with Green Heron is known, but case for synonymising not conclusive.

CATTLE EGRET *Bubulcus ibis* Pl. 22

Identification 46–51cm. The smallest all-white heron, adult white with yellow eyes, yellow lores and yellow bill, legs and feet yellowish near thighs, becoming dark green and looking blackish at distance. When breeding, acquires buffy crown, lower back and rump, and lower breast, the feathers are lanceolate and soft parts brighter yellow; for a brief period prior to egg laying, all soft parts are red. Shorter neck and legs than other white egrets, seeming more compact; note all-black legs and feet, although breeding bird changes dramatically (see plate).

Ssp. *B. i. ibis* (all countries)

Habits Diurnal and least aquatic of all egrets, found in loose flocks of varying sizes, foraging for insects and small vertebrates, mostly by walking slowly behind grazing cattle or following plough. Flies daily to roosts. Colonial breeder, rarely in mixed colonies. May nest away from water, sometimes in urban areas.
Status Very common and widespread. Seasonal movements in connection with rains.
Habitat Tropical to Temperate Zones. Particularly associated with agricultural grasslands, e.g. rice paddies, pastures and meadows. Also by streams, freshwater ponds and marshes, and wet, open areas. Often in urban areas but never in forests or salt water.
Voice Mostly silent, but for a few, coarse and simple courtship and nesting calls. A subdued, nasal *brek* or *rick-rak*, occasionally a short soft moan (Sibley). A short *ark* and duck-like *og-ag-ag* (Porter *et al.*).

GREY HERON *Ardea cinerea* Pl. 21

Identification 90–98cm. White head, neck and underparts, black line from supraloral over eye, broadening and extending as 2 long black plumes from nape, front of throat has 2 rows of black streaks that become increasingly lanceolate and hang with lanceolate white plumes from lower breast, broad black line either side of belly, on inside of thighs; back and upperparts grey with extended lanceolate plumes on back, primaries black; eyes yellow, loral skin greenish, bill yellow. First-year is grey where adult is white, otherwise similar but has shorter plumes. From Cocoi Heron by white head with black superciliary and plumes (Cocoi has black crown); from Great Blue by clear, unstreaked, greyish-white underparts, with no trace of buffy or rufous.

Ssp. *A. c. cinerea* (Tr)

Habits Forages alone, serenely, although defends feeding territory.
Status Old World vagrant to Trinidad (specimen in 1959, originally banded in France, and sight record 2001) and Tobago (sight record 1999). (Accidentals also recorded on Barbados, Montserrat, and Pará, Brazil). Makes very extensive (even transoceanic) post-breeding movements.
Habitat Tropical Zone. Coastal wetlands.
Voice Usually calls at dusk when flying to roost, a harsh, loud croaking *kah-ahrk* which may have a singsong, echoing quality (Mullarney *et al.*).

GREAT BLUE HERON *Ardea herodias* Pl. 21–22

Identification 91–137cm. Normal (dark or grey) morph has white head with broad postocular band that ends in a few long black plumes, neck warm vinaceous-buff to tawny, continuing on flanks and thighs, white central foreneck with lanceolate black and white plumes, heavy black line either side of belly, inside thighs, and central belly to undertail-coverts white; upperparts grey with long, paler grey plumes from back, primaries black. Juvenile has buffy head without plumes, paler buffy neck and underparts, more rufescent flanks, wing-coverts fringed buffy, and bill duller yellow. White morph is all white. Soft-part colours almost identical in both morphs; non-breeding adult has eyes yellow, loral skin yellowish-grey to dull green (blue in white morph), bill yellow, legs and feet dull yellow; breeding adult has eyes gradually reddening to bright red in courtship, then yellow once eggs laid, whilst loral skin becomes bright lime green, bill orange, and legs and feet pinkish to red during courtship. White phase has distinctly shorter nuchal plumes than grey morph. Juvenile white morph has buffy-grey legs and feet (juvenile Great Egret blackish).

Ssp. *A. h. occidentalis* (Co, Ve: offshore islands, Ar, Bo, Cu, T&T)

Habits Solitary, quiet and cautious.

Status Boreal migrant, scarce at the southern fringes of its wintering range, which reaches western coastal areas of northern South America.

Habitat Tropical and Subtropical Zones. Mangroves, fresh and saltmarshes, rivers and lakes. Recorded in small wetlands on western Andean slopes.

Voice Call a hoarse *guk uk, guk uk, guk uk uk* (H&B). Flight-call a very deep, hoarse trumpeting *fraahuk* or *braak* (Sibley).

Note White morph sometimes called Great White Heron, and has even been treated as a species.

COCOI HERON *Ardea cocoi* Pl. 21

Identification 97–127cm. Crown black with 2 long black nuchal plumes, rest of head, neck and underparts white with 2 rows of black streaks on foreneck, grey above, paler on back with long plumes, primaries black; eyes yellow, bill dull yellow, legs and feet dull black; when breeding bill becomes brighter yellow and even orange or reddish at base, legs and feet dusky pink. From Great Blue Heron by black crown and lack of any buffy or rufous.

Ssp. Monotypic (all except Ar, Bo, Cu)

Habits Solitary, quiet and cautious; stalks in shallow water or remains still, watching patiently. Takes largish fish, frogs, crabs and insects; occasionally small mammals and even scavenges. Usually territorial, but in receding waters, at onset of dry season, several may feed together.

Status Fairly common.

Habitat Tropical Zone. Freshwater lakes, flooded fields and open marshes, slow rivers. Frequent in coastal areas, in mangroves, coastal marshes, estuaries.

Voice Flight-call a very deep, hoarse trumpeting *fraahuk* or *braak*, like Great Blue but higher in tone.

PURPLE HERON *Ardea purpurea* Pl. 21

Identification 78–90cm. Complex head pattern, basically rufous with black crown and back of neck, black line from below eyes across face-sides and ending in pair of nuchal plumes, black line on neck-sides, throat chin and foreneck black, edged white, with black streaks; base of neck grey, feathers of breast lanceolate, black and white, and hang down, rest of underparts umber; brownish-grey back, becoming paler and browner on lanceolate plumes, wings have deep russet shoulders, rest dark grey; eyes yellow, loral skin greyish-yellow, bill ochraceous horn with black culmen, legs and feet yellow with large black scales. When breeding, lores and bill brighter yellow, tinged orange. Juvenile similar with crown but no black lines on head or neck, but has black streaks bordering white foreneck, upperparts brownish-grey with all feathers fringed buff. From larger Great Blue by rufous head and neck.

Ssp. *A. p. purpurea*? (Tr)

Habits Forages alone, mostly in twilight hours. Stalks prey by waiting motionless, or may stalk slowly forward with neck held at angle of 60°, facing sun, the eyes facing down (Hancock & Kushlan 1978).

Status Western Palearctic species, accidental on Tobago, in 1999 (Kenefick 2004). Accidentals also recorded on Barbados and Fernando de Noronha, Brazil. Makes very extensive (even transoceanic) post-breeding movements.

Habitat Coastal wetlands.

Voice In flight, a gruff monosyllabic *krrek*, like Grey Heron but shorter and slightly disyllabic, deader and less resonant (Mullarney *et al.*).

GREAT EGRET *Ardea alba* Pl. 22

Identification 80–105cm. Adult non-breeding all white with kinked neck that is distinctive; eyes yellow, loral skin dull almost greenish-yellow, bill yellow, legs and feet yellowish near thighs grading into black. In breeding plumage has long extended plumes from back and rump, lores become brighter yellow; in courtship also has plumes from breast, and for brief period before first egg, eyes reddish, loral skin bluish and bill red. Significantly larger than other white herons and egrets; taller and more slender than white-morph Great Blue Heron, and also has blackish legs and feet.

Ssp. *A. a. egretta* (all countries)

Habits Roosts and breeds in mixed colonies but forages alone, standing still and watching quietly. Where food is very abundant may feed in mixed flocks, but otherwise defends a feeding territory.

Status Common and widespread.

Habitat Tropical to Lower Subtropical Zones. Brackish or freshwater wetlands of all kinds, also rice paddies, wet fields and irrigation channels in agricultural areas, and occasionally in grassy pastures.

Voice Grating caws and croaks. Flushes with coarse or raspy *guuk* or *guuk-uuk-uuk*, sometimes given several times (Hilty), a deep, low, gravelly *kroow* or grating, unmusical *karrrr* (Sibley).

Note Sometimes placed in genus *Casmerodius*.

WHISTLING HERON

Syrigma sibilatrix Pl. 21

Identification 50–61cm. Fairly small heron; broad black band over crown and long plumes behind, white chin, buffy neck and breast, blue-grey back and wings, with buffy wing-coverts fringed black, white tail, white belly and undertail-coverts; bright blue orbital skin and pale yellow eyes, orange-yellow bill with black tip, legs and feet blackish. Juvenile quite similar but has paler bill, browner wing-coverts and pale grey breast. The white tail contrasts with the grey and buffy back in flight.

Ssp. *S. a. fostersmithi* (E Co, C Ve)

Habits Forages alone or in pairs, sometimes in small groups. Often perches on fenceposts and may be found in pastures and fields away from water. Widely dispersed individuals commute regularly to roost together in tree rookeries. Northernmost populations (north-east Venezuela) move south in non-breeding season.

Status Patchily distributed but locally common throughout range. Recent sight record in eastern Ecuador (Mena & Jahn 2003).

Habitat Tropical Zone. Generally a dry-land species, found especially in dry pastures, and near streams, ponds, rice paddies and flooded forests, but never wades in open water.

Voice High-frequency calls (whistles) uttered in flight afford species its name. Call a complaining *wueeee wueeee* (Hilty).

CAPPED HERON *Pilherodius pileatus* Pl. 22

Identification 51–61cm. Adult all white with variable pale grey on back and wings, crown black, a few white plumes extending from nape; eyes olive, bill variably blue, legs and feet bluish-grey. When breeding, head, plumes and upper neck are buffy, becoming paler distally. Juvenile has grey cap, no plumes, and buffy tone to back and wings; eyes darker and bill greener. From egrets by bright blue face and black headband, and chunky appearance. Distinctive, bent wings held low flight that appears somewhat laborious.

Ssp. Monotypic (E Ec, Co,Ve, Gu, Su, FG)

Habits Forages alone and is very wary, being quick to flush. Antisocial, but found occasionally near gatherings of other species. Stalks prey at edge of water, motionless or walking slowly.

Status Widespread but generally scarce.

Habitat Tropical Zone. Freshwater wetlands of various types, especially marshes, streams, small ponds, flooded grasslands and smaller rivers; often in or near forest.

Voice Mostly silent, but an occasional croak (Hilty).

Note Sometimes placed in genus *Nycticorax* (e.g. SFP&M), but we follow AOU (1998).

TRICOLOURED HERON

Egretta tricolor Pl. 21

Identification 50–76cm. Distinctive heron; non-breeding adult has short nuchal plumes, long thin neck, and entire upperparts grey, from throat to base of neck rufous with streaks of black and white, underparts white; eyes reddish-brown, facial skin and bill yellow with dark line along culmen and black tip, legs and feet greenish-yellow. Breeding adult has longer, bright reddish-rufous plumes on neck, and much longer, more noticeable buffy plumes on back and rump; bill bright blue with black tip and red legs. Juvenile brown on head, neck and upper back, becoming grey on outer wings, rump and tail, and chin, throat (with some streaks and short plumes) and rest of underparts white. From Little Blue Heron by white belly and yellow legs.

Ssp. *E. t. ruficollis* (boreal migrant to Ec, Co, NW Ve, ABC) larger, with white line on foreneck

E. t. tricolor (NE Ve, Tr, Guianas) as described

Habits Forages alone in feeding territory, occasionally in small groups. Active feeder, frequently fishes by raising and spreading wings, and holding head partially under a wing, walking in shallow water (Hilty).

Status Fairly common to uncommon in northern South America. Migrant race *ruficollis* occurs in northern South America November to late February; local race is sedentary.

Habitat Tropical Zone. Seashores, salt or mudflats; coastal shallows and marshes; mangroves, river deltas and tidal creeks.

Voice Soft nasal moaning, similar to ibises (Sibley).

Notes Previously placed in *Hydranassa* (e.g. SFP&M). Sometimes called Louisiana Heron.

REDDISH EGRET

Egretta rufescens Pl. 21–22

Identification 66–81cm. Adult of normal (grey) morph unmistakable; entire head and neck reddish-rufous with all feathers elongated, rest of body slate grey with long rufescent plumes from back extending beyond tail. In breeding plumage, plumes brighter and longer; pale eyes, bill pink with black tip, legs and feet dark, brighter bluish-grey when breeding. Juvenile has head, neck and underparts drab, grey above, washed drab on back and wing-coverts. White morph from other white egrets by pink-flesh bill with black tip in all plumages.

Ssp. *E. r. rufescens* (N Co, N Ve: offshore islands, Ar, Bo, Cu, T&T)

Habits Forages alone in tenaciously defended territory; constantly active, running and hopping, occasionally holding wings open or raking the bottom for fish.

Status Uncommon, populations have declined in many areas in recent years.

Habitat Tropical Zone. Seashores, coastal shallows or marshes, mangroves and saltflats.

Voice An infrequent soft groan and short grunt, similar to Tricoloured Heron (Sibley).

Note Previously placed in *Hydranassa* or monotypic genus *Dichromanassa* (AOU 1998).

WESTERN REEF HERON

Egretta gularis Pl. 21–22

Identification 55-65cm. Dark-grey morph is uniform slate grey with a white chin; breeding birds have 2 long nuchal plumes, and lengthy lanceolate plumes on breast and back.

Non-breeding adult all white with yellow eyes, yellow loral skin, black bill, black legs and yellow feet. Breeding birds have orange lores and feet. White morph from Snowy Egret by colour of lores and orbital skin (normally bluish-grey but can be yellow, even orange in breeding condition), and slightly drooping bill (*not* easy to see in field). Also, often shows a few dark feathers in wings and tail. From white-morph Little by heavier and dark, greyish-yellow bill. Dark morph has white throat, and separable from rare dark-morph Little by latter, and bill size and colour. Dark morph may show a few white feathers.

Ssp. Monotypic (T&T)

Habits Solitary, defends feeding territory. Typically forages by slow wading in shallows with occasional rushes, also stirs mud with feet.

Status Several records from Trinidad and one from Tobago, perhaps overlooked elsewhere. Mainly an Old World species.

Habitat Tropical Zone. Mainly on reefs and rocky coastal areas, but sometimes at sandy or muddy edges to wetlands of salt or brackish water, less frequently estuaries, mudflats, saltmarshes, etc.

Voice When disturbed may utter a guttural *kawww*.

Notes Treated as a subspecies of Little Egret *E. garzetta* by Martínez-Vilalta & Motis. Sometimes called Western Reef Egret.

Western Reef Heron (lower left) has drooping bill that is not at all obvious, but is a sure discriminator from Little Egret's straight bill (upper right)

LITTLE EGRET *Egretta garzetta* Pl. 22

Identification 55–65cm. Very rare dark grey morph is uniform slate grey with a white chin; breeders have 2 long nuchal plumes, and lengthy lanceolate plumes on breast and back. White morph is all white. Differences in soft-part colours are same in both morphs; eyes always yellow, non-breeders have grey to greenish loral skin and bill dark grey, legs dark grey; breeders have loral skin orange (bright mauve-red during courtship), bill and legs black, the feet become orange then red during courtship. More slender than Snowy. Note dark lores of non-breeder. Breeder from Snowy by 2 nuchal plumes (Snowy has a spray).

Ssp. Monotypic (Ar, Tr, Su, FG)

Habits Solitary, defends feeding territory; when foraging stirs mud with feet.

Status Old World species, well known for its extensive post-breeding dispersal, recorded as an occasional vagrant on some Caribbean islands (where now breeding on Barbados), and Trinidad, Guyana, Suriname and French Guiana. Records for Trinidad and Suriname are of birds banded in Spain. Regular, if sporadic, in coastal French Guiana since 2004.

Habitat Tropical Zone. Open shallow wetlands of salt, fresh or brackish water.

Voice Generally silent away from colony, but may give a short, grunting *raaak* (Porter *et al.*), and on take-off a sharp, hoarse *aaah* (Mullarney *et al.*). Several croaks, growls and sighs (*kre-kre-kre*; *da-wah*; *la-la-la-la-ahhhh*; *kark, gggrow*) in contact, when landing or flying off, and in aggression.

SNOWY EGRET *Egretta thula* Pl. 22

Identification 48–68cm. Adult all white with yellow eyes and lores, black bill, and black legs with yellow feet. In breeding plumage, fine sprayed plumes extend from nape, lower neck and breast, and back and rump. Yellow feet ('dancing slippers') and black legs distinguish it from all except Little Egret. From latter with difficulty, being slightly smaller but more robust; in all plumages, bill black; lores are paler and more yellowish. In breeding plumage, lores feet turn first clear yellow, then briefly pinkish-orange, and it acquires long curving, graceful plumes on neck, head and back (Little has just 2 plumes).

Ssp. *E. t. thula* (all countries)

Habits Forages very actively in flocks; sometimes follows cattle, uses wide variety of methods to catch prey, frequently stirring water with feet to flush aquatic animals.

Status Common and widespread. Wide-ranging seasonal and migratory movements, including post-breeding dispersal.

Habitat Tropical, Subtropical and lower Temperate Zones. All types of shallow wetland with fresh, brackish or salt water, inland and coastal, even in pools on rocky sea shores.

Voice Mostly silent. A hoarse, rasping *raarr* or *hraa*, very similar to Little Blue Heron, and higher and more nasal than Great Egret (Sibley).

LITTLE BLUE HERON *Egretta caerulea* Pl. 21–22

Identification 51–76cm. Non-breeding adult has purple-brown head and neck, rest of body grey; skin of lores dull green, eyes pale yellow, bill base grey with black tip, legs and feet bluish- or greenish-grey. Breeding adult develops long lanceolate plumes on rear crown and nape, lower throat and back (extending beyond the tail), loral skin becomes blue, bill and legs blackish. White (juvenile) phase from white Reddish and other white egrets by colour of bill: base blue-grey with distal two-thirds black, also, intermediate immature is oddly piebald, with grey-smudged back of neck and upperparts. Darker than Reddish Egret, paler than Green Heron, and lacks white underparts of Tricoloured Heron.

Ssp. Monotypic (all countries)

Habits Forages sedately during day, alone or in small groups

and sometimes, in an unusual mutualistic relationship, with manatees or ibises.
Status Common.
Habitat Tropical and Subtropical Zones. Mainly freshwater wetlands of all kinds, but also in brackish and saltwater areas, mangroves and estuaries.
Voice Generally silent, but various hoarse squawks, and a fairly high *raaaaa, raaa…* similar to *raar* of Snowy Egret (Sibley).
Note Previously placed in genus *Florida*.

THRESKIORNITHIDAE – Ibises and Spoonbills

Ibises generally occur in areas with wet soft soil, being mostly seen in open fields that have been recently flooded and left muddy, marshes, swamps, rice fields and other irrigated cultivation. Some are more usually found in coastal areas, mangrove swamps and brackish lagoons, others more inland, sometimes on open savannas and dry areas far from water. They probe and dig for worms, catch small fish, insects, amphibians and other small animals, but most species don't usually wade in water. Several birds are often scattered over a foraging area, frequently involving several different species. Most have a smooth, sustained flight, and fly in long untidy lines and broken skeins.

Additional references used here include Mathieu & del Hoyo (1992), Elliott (1992) and Sibley (2000).

WHITE IBIS *Eudocimus albus* Pl. 24

Identification 56–71cm. All white with tips of outer primaries black; red facial skin, red bill, legs and feet. In breeding condition, distal half of bill is black. When not breeding, the amount of red facial skin is reduced. Juvenile brown above with whitish head and neck, streaked brown, and white underparts. Becomes whiter with age. When foraging on mudflats looks as if it has fallen in the mud. From white egrets by long, decurved red bill and general posture. Flies with neck outstretched (egrets and herons tuck neck back).

Ssp. Monotypic (Ec, Co, Ve, Ar, Cu, Tr)

Habits Notably gregarious, mixing with other ibises and egrets, etc. Flies long distances in skeins from roosts to foraging areas.
Status Locally uncommon to common in coastal Ecuador, local, uncommon and seasonal in parts of Colombia, uncommon to locally fairly common in Venezuela, scarce in Trinidad (no records from Tobago). Casual visitor from mainland to Aruba and Curaçao.
Habitat Lower Tropical Zone. Mainly coastal, mangroves and tidal mudflats. Inland, favours rice fields, rivers, sewage waterways and flooded land.
Voice Nasal grunting *urnk* on ground or in flight (Hilty), and occasional soft honks and grunts (R&G).
Notes Has been considered conspecific with Scarlet Ibis. Hybrids between them are rare. The IOC-recommended English name for this species is American White Ibis.

SCARLET IBIS *Eudocimus ruber* Pl. 24

Identification 54–70cm. Entire plumage vermilion scarlet-red with ends of outer primaries black; red facial skin, entire bill black when breeding, otherwise pinkish-red, and red legs and feet. Juvenile brown above with whitish head and neck, streaked brown, underparts white, but becomes pinker, then redder with age. Adult unmistakable, but immature difficult to separate from immature White Ibis, unless it has some red feathers.

Ssp. Monotypic (Ec?, Co, Ve, Ar, T&T, Gu, Su, FG)

Habits Gregarious, forages and roosts with other large waterbirds, including egrets. Regularly follows grazing cattle and horses. May fly long distances from roost to foraging areas.
Status Hypothetical vagrant to Ecuador, common non-breeding resident east Colombia, locally common Venezuela, casual visitor from mainland to Aruba, abundant in Trinidad but uncommon in Tobago, common to abundant elsewhere, but patchy and declining. Important nesting colonies in coastal Suriname and French Guiana. Heavy human persecution in Venezuela, especially at island breeding colonies where nestlings taken for food.
Habitat Lower Tropical Zone. Mainly coastal, but can occur well inland, e.g. Barinas and Apure in Venezuela. Mangroves, muddy estuaries, sewage ponds, tidal mudflats; inland, rice fields and irrigated cultivation are favoured.
Voice Usually quiet. Nasal *urunk*, similar to White Ibis (Hilty), or *urnk, urnk, urnk* (Sibley).
Note Has been considered conspecific with White Ibis. Hybrids between them are rare.

GLOSSY IBIS *Plegadis falcinellus* Pl. 24

Identification 50–65cm. Entirely dark green with rich bronze, purple and other glossy tones, but looks blackish in poor light; there is a narrow white line framing the blackish facial skin, from base of culmen to dark eye and at base of mandible. Long, decurved bill, legs and feet are also dark. In non-breeding plumage, head and neck become white-streaked. Juvenile similar but duller with a greyish-white wash to head and neck. Green Ibis is chunkier and its shorter legs do not extend beyond tail. Flies in long skeins, alternating series of wingbeats with glides. Legs project beyond tail in flight.

Ssp. Monotypic (Ec, Co, Ve, Ar, Cu, Bo, Tr, To, Gu)

Habits Occasionally wades, sometimes submerging head entirely to probe bottom. May run after prey. Small scattered groups to flocks.
Status Hypothetical visitor to lowland south-west coastal Ecuador, scarce and casual in Colombia, frequent to abundant in Venezuela, frequent non-breeding visitor from mainland to Aruba, Curaçao and Bonaire, scarce in Trinidad & Tobago where sight records only, scarce in Guyana.
Habitat Lower Tropical Zone. Typical ibis habitat but less common in coastal areas, preferring freshwater marshes. Occasionally occurs in dry grasslands, but seldom far from water.
Voice Feeding flocks give soft, nasal, often doubled grunt *wehp-ehp* (Sibley).

WHITE-FACED IBIS *Plegadis chihi* Pl. 24

Identification 46–66cm. Entirely dark green and brown, shot with rich bronzes and other glossy tones. Breeding adult has bill dark horn and facial skin reddish, framed by a broad white line; legs and feet pinkish-red. Non-breeding adult duller with neck strongly streaked white, facial skin and white line duller, bill darker. From very similar Glossy Ibis by red eye, broad white line fringing face, and red legs when breeding. Non-breeder and immature very similar to Glossy but distinguished by streaked head and neck.

Ssp. Monotypic (Ar)

Habits Usually forages in flocks.

Status Vagrant from North America, a casual visitor to Aruba, rare on offshore islands and hypothetical for mainland.

Habitat Tropical to Lower Subtropical Zones. Mainly freshwater marshes, ponds, rice fields, irrigated cultivation and, occasionally, dry fields.

Voice Feeding flocks give soft, nasal, often doubled grunt, *wehp-ehp* (Sibley).

SHARP-TAILED IBIS *Cercibis oxycerca* Pl. 24

Identification 76–86cm. All black, with a greenish gloss and a short, bushy nuchal crest. Long, slightly decurved bill is orange, bright red facial skin forms wattle around eye, mesial line pale, lappet on throat orange, legs and feet orange-red. Large and long-tailed with comparatively and proportionately oddly short legs afford distinctive outline in field. Slow, laboured flight; legs do not extend beyond tail. From Bare-faced by larger size, different shape and tufty nuchal crest.

Ssp. Monotypic (Co, Ve, Gu)

Habits Singly, in pairs or occasionally in small (mixed) flocks.

Status Scarce in Colombia, uncommon to locally frequent, but always in small numbers in Venezuela, and frequent in Guyana.

Habitat Tropical Zone. Damp grassland, savanna at edges of lakes and rivers, open marshes and muddy rice fields.

Voice Loud nasal, bugled *tuur-deee* or truncated *tut-toot*, the second note higher, often repeated constantly in flight. Also calls a nasal *taro-taro* in flight (D. Ascanio recording). Duets, with first bird uttering *tuur* or *tuur-tuur*, the second *deee* (Hilty).

GREEN IBIS
Mesembrinibis cayennensis Pl. 24

Identification 50–58cm. Overall black, head and neck dull black and unglossed, but bushy nape has distinctive turquoise-green gloss, upperparts bronze-olive with greenish gloss; eyes dark brown, bill dull black, legs and feet dark brownish-grey. Appears very dark, but if seen in good light reflects glossy green, especially on neck hackles.

Ssp. Monotypic (all mainland countries)

Habits Wary, most active at dusk and dawn, and normally only in open at these times; probably nocturnal. Short legs do not extend beyond tail in flight. Flies in long, irregular, undulating and erratic lines; wingbeats have stiff upward jerkiness, like Limpkin. Usually singly or pairs, rarely in small loose, scattered groups, and invariably close near forest.

Status Uncommon to locally frequent in Ecuador, uncommon and local in Colombia, frequent to locally common in Venezuela, common in Guyana, fairly common in Suriname, common in French Guiana.

Habitat Tropical Zone. Wet, muddy forested areas, swampy woods and thickets, open stony banks of rivers and streams, mangrove swamps, usually near trees.

Voice Most vocal at dusk: distinctive, loud and rapid, rolling *co'ro co'ro co'ro…* or *kr'u'u'u'u'u'u'u'a*, usually in flight (R&G, Hilty).

BARE-FACED (WHISPERING) IBIS
Phimosus infuscatus Pl. 24

Identification 46–54cm. All-dark ibis with green, bronze purple and red glosses, but actually seems rather dull; pink-red facial skin with horn-coloured bill, pinkish-red legs and feet. Noticeably smaller and shorter tailed than Sharp-tailed Ibis (similar to *Eudocimus* in size). Very short legs do not extend beyond tail in flight. Larger Sharp-tailed Ibis has long tail, giving it a more horizontal stance, and heavier bill; larger Glossy Ibis has longer legs that extend beyond tail in flight.

Ssp. *P. i. berlepschi* (Ec, Co, Ve, Gu)

Habits Social, usually in compact groups. Follows grazing cattle and horses to examine turned-up mud.

Status Movements related to rainfall (breeds soon after rains). Rare visitor to lowland north-east Ecuador, very common Colombia (seasonal in some areas). Very common, especially in *llanos*, in Venezuela. Uncertain status Guyana.

Habitat Lower Tropical Zone. Typical ibis habitat, normally to *c.*500 m, but vagrants to 3,600 m (Hilty).

Voice Rather quiet. Takes alternate common name from soft whispery *cua-cua-cua-cua-cua…*, which swells in volume then diminishes, 12 notes or more, repeated like a soft chant (Hilty).

BUFF-NECKED IBIS
Theristicus caudatus Pl. 24

Identification 71–81cm. Brownish-grey back and wings, the feathers fringed whitish, flight-feathers and tail black; head-sides and throat buffy, with facial skin and mesial lappet black, crown and line down nape joining breast chestnut, merging into black underparts. Eyes red, long decurved bill dark grey, legs and feet orange-red. Seems heavy-bodied and wing pattern lends a goose-like appearance, despite the long, curved bill.

Ssp. *T .c. caudatus* (Co, Ve, Gu, Su, FG)

Habits Forages singly, in pairs or loose and well-scattered small groups. Usually noisy in flight, when black on wings is particularly obvious.

Status Rare west of Andes, frequent but very local east of Andes in Colombia. Common in Venezuela, frequent in Guyana, unknown in Suriname, accidental in French Guiana.

Habitat Tropical Zone. Open country, in savannas, fields and open forests, often far from water, and on dry and recently

burned pastures. Infrequently occurs in more typical ibis habitat, but less often in watery areas than other ibises.
Voice Flight-call a loud nasal *knack-knock*, given repeatedly pre-dawn from roost. Roosting birds may cry in chorus at dawn, before departing for day, *ca-cu-cu-cu-nac-nac-nac-nac*, at first soft but culminating in loud, rhythmic chorus (Hilty), also calls a loud nasal *tau-TAco* at roost, predawn (D. Ascanio recording).

BLACK-FACED IBIS
Theristicus melanopis Pl. 24

Identification 71–76cm. Brownish-grey back and wings, the feathers fringed whitish, flight-feathers and tail black; head-sides and throat buffy extending to breast, which has bar of broken grey crescents across it. Facial skin, mesial lappet and long decurved bill black, eyes red, legs and feet orange-red. Immature has buffy-scalloped wing-coverts. Heavy-bodied and wing pattern lends goose-like appearance, despite long, curved bill. No overlap with Buff-necked Ibis.

Ssp. *T. m. branickii* (Ec)

Habits Forages in pairs or small flocks, rather wary of man. Often wades in comparatively deep water, probing into the bottom mud.
Status Very rare and local in eastern highlands of Ecuador, principally around Antisana and Cotopaxi volcanoes. Has declined through persecution and continues to be hunted for food.
Habitat Páramo. Open country: fields, meadows, pastures, ploughed and cultivated fields in highlands, often near livestock. Also in more typical ibis habitat, but less often in watery areas than other ibises.
Voice Far-carrying, metallic *tur-túrt* usually given in couplets and principally in flight (R&G).
Note The *branickii* subspecies has been considered a distinct species, Andean Ibis (S&M).

Spoonbills are large, heron-like birds that are all white or, in the case of the Neotropical species, a rich reddish-pink. They have a unique style of feeding, swinging the bill, which is long and spatula-shaped, from side to side in the water as they walk slowly forwards. At times the head and even part of the neck may be completely submerged. They may forage singly or in small groups, and are not particularly sociable.

ROSEATE SPOONBILL
Platalea ajaja Pl. 25

Identification 68–86cm. Unmistakable pink bird with unique bill. Essentially white with rosy-pink wings, and pink buff-washed back; lesser wing-coverts and uppertail-coverts crimson, tail buffy. Head bare, greenish with black band at base of neck, long, spatulate bill is horn, mottled greenish; eyes red, legs and feet purplish-red. Immature has yellowish-brown eyes and bill, white-feathered head, and darker legs and feet.

Ssp. Monotypic (all countries)

Habits Forages alone or in small flocks.
Status Local and rare to frequent in Ecuador. In Colombia, fairly scattered and local, but occasionally common on Caribbean coast, rare on Pacific coast and may wander inland. Common on coast and frequent inland in Venezuela. Casual visitor from mainland to Aruba and Bonaire, scarce in Trinidad, rare in Tobago, frequent in Guyana, fairly common in Suriname, rare in coastal French Guiana on mudflats and adjacent young stages of *Avicennia* mangroves.
Habitat Coastal areas: tidal pools, mangroves, areas of salt or brackish water; less often inland, in rice fields, marshes and open watery areas in savannas.
Voice Low ibis-like grunting *huh-huh-huh-huh*..., without changing pitch or volume. Also, a fairly dry, rasping *rrek-ek-ek-ek-ek-ek*..., much lower and faster than ibises (Sibley).
Note Formerly placed in monotypic genus *Ajaia*.

EURASIAN SPOONBILL
Platalea leucorodia Pl. 25

Identification 86cm. Heron-sized, all white with variable yellowish crescent on upper breast and black bill tipped yellow. Dark grey legs and feet. Quite distinct from Roseate Spoonbill.

Ssp. *P. l. leucorodia* (To)

Habits Does not usually mix with other species.
Status Boreal migrant from Old World. Accidental on Tobago, November 1986 (photographed), identified as nominate *leucorodia* by yellow bill tip. Two records from Fernando de Noronha (Brazil). Flies in lines and in V formations at great altitudes on migration, and stray individuals may be blown way off-course.
Habitat Strong preference for sheltered, shallow open water and salt ponds.
Voice Mainly silent in wintering areas.

CICONIIDAE – Storks

Only 3 distinctive members of this family occur in northern South America. They are long-legged, mainly white birds, all of them easily recognised. Omnivorous, they take virtually anything capable of being eaten, from insects to snakes (including small anacondas), from frogs to baby alligators, even some plant material and carrion. Mostly, they feed on fish, even spiny catfish, which are crushed repeatedly in the bill to break the spines. They breed early in the dry season when ponds and rivers are drying, and fish are increasingly trapped in the diminishing waters and thus easiest to catch. Nests are large and conspicuous, but each sufficiently different as to be easily identified. Wood Stork and Jabiru nest in trees, often building platforms atop palms, but whereas Wood Stork nests in colonies, Jabiru breeds in isolation; Maguari Stork nests on the ground. Normally silent, stork vocalisations consists almost solely of bill-clapping, although juvenile Jabiru make a loud whistling when begging, and can be very noisy. Storks fly necks outstretched and are thus easy to separate from herons, which tuck their necks into their shoulders. A soaring stork may look very much like a vulture, but again the outstretched neck is key.

WOOD STORK *Mycteria americana* Pl. 25

Identification 83–110cm. Large white wading bird with black flight-feathers and conspicuously bare head and neck – black in adult, greyish in immature. From Maguari by black head and bill which has downward droop. Similar to King Vulture when soaring, but long neck and legs, and slow wingbeats alternating with glides separate it.

Ssp. Monotypic (all countries)

Habits Gregarious, often in large flocks. Commutes long distances to feeding grounds. Feeds by probing in shallow waters, mostly for fish but pirates from conspecifics and other waders. During non-breeding season, flocks wander widely in search of better food supplies, e.g. Orinoco basin populations may reach Amazonia. (Large flocks regularly recorded over French Guiana – but never land – flying high in the sky in a migratory manner, deep over the forest of the interior or the coastal plain, obviously crossing the country from and to far wetlands.)

Status Populations apparently declining in many areas (quantitative data very scarce), but still quite abundant in Venezuela and to a lesser extent Guyana and Suriname. Rare and sporadic in French Guiana where it does not rest. Rare in Aruba, Bonaire and Curaçao. Threatened by habitat loss and humans taking eggs and chicks.

Habitat Tropical Zone. Wetlands of all kinds, preferably fresh water but sometimes in tidal and brackish waters if food is abundant.

Voice Silent. Grunting and bill-clapping around nesting colonies. Young occasionally give nasal, barking *nyah, nyah, nyah* (Sibley).

MAGUARI STORK *Ciconia maguari* Pl. 25

Identification 97–102cm. Large; all white except black rump to uppertail-coverts and basal half of outer tail-feathers, greater wing-coverts, tertials and all remiges; facial skin red, eyes yellow, bill long, large and has straight culmen and recurved lower mandible, all grey with distal quarter red, legs and feet red. Juvenile similar but has black facial skin, brown eyes and shorter bill.

Ssp. Monotypic (Co, Ve, Tr, Gu, Su, FG)

Habits Forages alone, in pairs or in small groups, especially as waters recede during dry season. Takes small aquatic animals of all kinds (frogs and tadpoles, fish, crabs, etc.). Main threats are agrochemicals and poaching of eggs and chicks for human consumption.

Status Populations believed to be decreasing steadily in Venezuela. Few data from other northern South American countries. Very rare in French Guiana.

Habitat Tropical Zone. Freshwater wetlands of all kinds, including ponds, flooded savannas, rice fields and reedbeds.

Voice Usually silent. Rattles bill. Occasional wheezy, bisyllabic whistling (Kahl 1991).

JABIRU *Jabiru mycteria* Pl. 25

Identification 120–150cm. Largest stork, much larger than others. Long black legs, massive upturned bill, bare head and swollen neck black, red at base. Male is larger, with longer bill. Juvenile all white with feathered head and neck, and black facial skin restricted to around eyes and lores, and black bill. Juvenile Maguari Stork has grey bill with red tip.

Ssp. Monotypic (all mainland countries, T&T)

Habits In dry season tends to prefer shallow open water and may gather in groups. May also fish in unison, the group working together to disturb prey. In wet season prefers deeper water and usually solitary.

Status Fairly common, but now very rare in French Guiana.

Habitat Tropical Zone to 400m. Near water, but often found on dry grassy areas in ranchlands and *llanos*. Wetlands: ponds, marshes, flooded savannas, paddies and banks of rivers in open country or areas of scattered trees.

Voice Usually quiet. Bill-clapping at nest.

CATHARTIDAE – Vultures

Vultures are extremely well designed for the life they live, a sort of 'Bauhaus bird', as illustrated by some of the main characteristics that seem to define this family – all are bare-headed, magnificent fliers, and have either keen sight or keen sense of smell. The various open-area species form guilds, supplementing each other's foraging and feeding abilities. For scavengers, whose main food is carrion, a bare head is just the thing – it can penetrate the innards of carcasses with minimal hindrance. In finding food, their acute sight is of value, but for the guild as a whole the best asset is the extremely keen sense of smell of the Turkey Vultures, which are always first to find a carcass. They guide the others to food, for all tend to spy on the Turkeys, and if they see them suddenly dropping to some spot, they follow. That's when the spectacular flying abilities, where thermals are used to remain aloft for hours with minimum energy cost, become very handy, because the best way to survey the neighbourhood is to be high above it. When all members of the guild are feeding, their different sizes and different bills complement each other well – the larger species (King Vulture, Condors) with more powerful bills, specialize in tearing open the skin and feeding on the harder parts (sinews, muscles), whilst the smaller species take the viscera and finish off the small pieces left on the bones. Greater Yellow-headed Vulture, the only species that is exclusively a forest-dweller and therefore does not often feed in association with the others also has a keen sense of smell. Regarding voice, vultures are generally silent, although they may occasionally grunt or hiss.

In preparing this family we also referred to: Houston (1994, 2001), and Ferguson-Lees & Christie (2001, hereafter F-L&C).

BLACK VULTURE *Coragyps atratus* Pl. 26

Identification 56–68cm. All black. Head and upper neck consists of bare grey and black skin, wrinkled and warty. Legs and feet black. Juvenile has head slightly smoother. From other vultures in flight by shorter tail and whitish patch in primaries. When seen in good light latter appears really white. Wings usually held flat on horizontal plane.

Ssp. *C. a. brasiliensis* (all countries) clear white patch in primaries

C. a. foetens (S Ec) white in primaries much less distinct

Habits General scavenger, visiting carcasses of any size; gathering in large numbers particularly on garbage dumps and refuse piles. Its gape, much larger than Turkey Vulture's, permits it to gulp down muscles and viscera. Hunts small prey (birds, insects, reptiles), but has a predilection for mammal meat. It has no sense of smell, and thus spies on Turkey and other vultures.
Status Very common and widespread. Benefits from human occupation of lands.
Habitat Tropical and Subtropical Zones. Almost always near or within human settlements, common in cities; also throughout lowland open country, especially near rivers. Inevitable at rubbish dumps, sewage outlets and slaughterhouses, etc. In forests, only at edges. Common to 2,700m.
Voice Low hisses, grunts and croaks when feeding and disturbed, or in aggression (F-L&C).
Note Sometimes called American Black Vulture.

TURKEY VULTURE *Cathartes aura* Pl. 26

Identification 64–81cm. All-black plumage, remiges seem dark brown in flight; head bare, reddish (varies according to race) and bill pale. Legs and feet vinaceous-horn. From Black by longer tail and wings held in distinctive shallow V; jinks, rocks and tilts regularly as it glides. Remiges evenly dark brown.

Ssp. *C. a. meridionalis* (boreal migrant to northern South America) largest and brownest with purplish gloss, broad brown fringes above, head red with purplish nape
C. a. septentrionalis (boreal migrant from E USA to Central America and likely N S.Am) larger than *aura*, and pronounced brown edges to feathers of upperparts and primaries
C. a. ruficollis (east of Andes, from N Co, Ve, Gu, Su, FG) the blackest, distinct bluish-white to yellowish corrugations on nape to hindneck
C. a. jota (Co, Ec) smaller, blacker with brown fringes, head bright red
C. a. falklandicus (Ec) like *jota* but larger and browner

Habits Feeds almost exclusively by scavenging (seldom if ever kills), and will even visit carcasses of small birds, although main food is small to medium-sized reptiles and mammals. Finds food through exceedingly sharp sense of smell. At carcasses, tends to be 'overpowered' by other vultures. If pushed out, will return to clean bones when others leave. Avoids carcasses in advanced state of decomposition. Benefits from human occupation of areas, profiting from road kills and pasture burns.
Status Widespread and abundant. The 2 races in North America migrate to northern South America.
Habitat Tropical to Temperate Zones. Less closely associated with human settlements than Black Vulture, but visits garbage dumps.
Voice Usually silent. Low hisses and grunts (F-L&C).

LESSER YELLOW-HEADED VULTURE *Cathartes burrovianus* Pl. 26

Identification 58–66cm. Plumage all black; head bare, reddish on throat, yellow on sides and front, and blue on crown and nape, legs and feet vinaceous-horn. From Turkey and Greater Yellow-headed Vultures by silvery grey tone to remiges, and has white primary shafts when seen from above. Flies with wings in shallow V, like Turkey, also jinks and rocks as it glides, but seldom reaches any height, usually flying fairly low.

Ssp. *C. b. burrovianus* (N & W Co, NW Ve) as described
C. b. urubitinga (SW Co, S Ve, Gu, Su, FG) larger with straw-coloured primary shafts

Habits Feeds almost exclusively by scavenging (seldom if ever kills), and even visits carcasses of small birds, although main food is small to medium-sized reptiles and mammals. Finds food through exceedingly sharp sense of smell. At carcasses, tends to be 'overpowered' by other vultures, but will return to clean bones when they leave. Avoids carcasses in advanced state of decomposition. Benefits from human occupation of areas, profiting from road kills and pasture burns.
Status Fairly large populations; widespread.
Habitat Tropical Zone. Grasslands, *llanos* and savannas. In forest, only at edges.

GREATER YELLOW-HEADED VULTURE *Cathartes melambrotus* Pl. 26

Identification 74–81cm. Plumage all black; head bare, reddish on throat, yellow on sides and front, and blue on crown and nape, legs and feet vinaceous-horn. Tail longer and wings larger than Lesser Yellow-headed. Innermost primaries distinctly darker. Flies on level wings.

Ssp. Monotypic (W & SW Co, S & W Ve, Gu, Su, FG)

Habits Scavenges for forest animals using keen sense of smell and by flying low over canopy. May also soar very high over forests. Joins other vultures at carcasses only rarely and only inside wooded areas.
Status Common in remote, undisturbed forests, but threatened in some areas by deforestation and heavy hunting of potential prey.
Habitat Lower Tropical Zone. Exclusively in pristine, untouched lowland rain forest.

KING VULTURE *Sarcoramphus papa* Pl. 26

Identification 71–81cm. Adult has white back and wings to median coverts, all flushed buffy, white underparts, lower back and tail, rest of wings black, feathered collar on lower neck black, a large blob of flesh-coloured skin protrudes from central breast; head and neck bare, neck reddish-orange on sides and yellowish front, head black overlain with various colours, red on crown, purple at sides, folds and wrinkles yellow, and has a yellowish cere with a bright orange wattle; bill red, legs and feet dark grey with black large scales; eyes white surrounded by red. Juvenile all black with a small black collar and black wattle on cere; eyes dark brown, legs and feet horn-grey. Takes *c.*4 years to reach adulthood via series of intermediate plumages; see plate. Unmistakable close to, but could be confused with Maguari Stork when soaring or at distance. Note stork has extended neck and legs.

Ssp. Monotypic (all countries)

Habits Usually alone, but may be seen in pairs and small family groups. Scavenges with Turkey and both Yellow-headed Vultures, and depends on Turkeys to find carcasses, for it lacks sense of smell. Dominates smaller vultures when feeding, but tears open skin of large animals with its large, powerful bill, thus permitting the smaller vultures to feed. Picks off skin and tougher parts, slowly biting off small pieces.
Status Generally scarce; fairly common locally in Venezuelan Llanos.
Habitat Tropical Zone. Lowland tropics, always in or near undisturbed forest, often in *llanos* and savannas.
Voice Guttural grunts and hisses. Low croaks and bill-snapping when nest threatened (F-L&C).

ANDEAN CONDOR *Vultur gryphus* Pl. 26

Identification 100–130cm, W up to 320cm. Very large. Essentially all black with white collar at base of neck, and white greater wing-coverts and secondaries producing large patch on wings. Head and neck bare, with wrinkles and sagging lobes, pinkish-grey to reddish-grey, bill yellow; adult male has an upright wattle on its crown that is quite distinctive. Juvenile entirely dusky brown with a yellow bill, and takes 4 years or more to reach adulthood, during which time the collar becomes grey, and pink is gradually acquired on the head and neck. Fairly long, rounded tail. Black-and-white pattern and long splayed primaries make bird unmistakable, even at long range. Juvenile is all dark and significantly larger than other vultures. Neck ruff might be detectable. All large eagles have some distinguishing mark, such as a tail-band.

Ssp. Monotypic (Andes)

Habits Ranges widely and flies long distances to forage, but sedentary in general area. Feeds on carrion, on medium to large mammals, including carcasses of farm animals. Large groups (<20) may gather at a carcass. It can easily tear skin and pull off muscles and viscera. Slow breeding rate and may not breed every year.
Status Very rare in Colombia and Venezuela; scarce in Ecuador. Persecuted by local people due to misconceptions.
Habitat Mainly in Temperate Zone and Páramo, but may even descend to coasts (Tropical Zone). Open mountain areas.

PHOENICOPTERIDAE – Flamingos

Flamingos are a small but cosmopolitan family, and immediately recognisable. They all prefer brackish or alkaline waters with few, if any fish. The remarkable, boomerang-shaped bill is held upside-down in the water and swung side to side in a combing-filtering action that traps small crustaceans, algae, diatoms, insect larvae and small fish. They are highly gregarious, gathering in large flocks at feeding grounds and breeding colonially. The black flight-feathers in the wings contrast strongly with the rest of the bird's pale plumage in flight.

Additional references used to prepare this family include del Hoyo (1992) and Sibley (2000).

GREATER FLAMINGO
Phoenicopterus ruber Pl. 25

Identification 120–145cm. Essentially rosy-pink throughout, back paler and contrasting with deeper, reddish wings and black flight-feathers. Bill deep rosy with white base and black tip. Long pink legs and feet. Juvenile greyish-brown with some pink in wings and tail. Unmistakable in range. Very distinctive profile in flight, with swift, steady wingbeats.

Ssp. *P. r. ruber* (Caribbean coast and islands Gu, Su, FG)

Habits Wades in shallow water. Typically wary but may be fairly tame on feeding grounds.

Greater Flamingos are unmistakable in flight

Status Numerous on Caribbean coast and offshore islands, but occurrence erratic and unpredictable. Declining due to habitat loss, disturbance and predation by man. Very rare to very locally regular in small numbers, but no longer breeds, in Colombia. In Venezuela, common and regular in large numbers at several localities on Caribbean coast, and has returned to breed at Ciénaga Los Olivitos, in Zulia. Rare on Trinidad (no records Tobago), situation uncertain in Guyana, fairly common in Suriname, uncommon and erratic in French Guiana where flocks of tens of birds may be seen on the coastal mudflats, or flying to and from the lagoons of Amapá.
Habitat Saline lagoons, estuaries and saltpans.
Voice Rather noisy. Variety of goose-like honks in flight. Also, an incessantly repeated, gabbling *hu-HU-hu* (Hilty). A high, nasal honking, *hooh-hööh-hooh*, like wild geese, but deeper. Courting birds utter *eep-eep* (male), *cak-cak* (female), thus *eep-eep, cak-cak…* (Sibley).
Note Sometimes listed as American Flamingo (e.g. Hilty).

CHILEAN FLAMINGO
Phoenicopterus chilensis Pl. 25

Identification 99–109cm. Pale, rather washed-out pink body with reddish streaks on back, reddish-pink wings and black remiges and tertials. Bill fleshy, with distal half black. Legs whitish with deep pink knee-joints and pink feet. Juvenile essentially whitish with greyish-brown on wings and darker streaks on back. Bill yellowish with distal half black, legs and feet grey. Unmistakable in range. From Greater by smaller size, generally paler coloration and shorter legs, which are grey to pink, and red knees.

Ssp. Monotypic (Ec)

Habits Typically wades in shallow water. Flies strongly on powerful and deep wingbeats, long neck and legs outstretched.
Status Recently recorded in Ecuador, where now present year-round on Santa Elena Peninsula.

Habitat Saltwater lagoons, estuaries and mudflats on coast, preferring water without fish.
Voice Usually quiet in Ecuador; a low howling sometimes heard (R&G).

PANDIONIDAE – Osprey

The Osprey is a large, long-winged and long-legged bird that is quite distinct from the other raptors and is accorded family status because of the extent of the anatomical differences. It is a fish specialist that is usually a boreal migrant visitor to the region, but younger birds often remain year-round. The wings are comparatively narrow for their length, and display a marked angle at the carpal joint when fully open (a sure identification aid). They are adapted for their familiar patrol-hover-dive behaviour, as well as for flying long distances when migrating. Osprey also has a different kind of plumage, dense and oily with considerable water resistance. It has structurally different legs, with the toes all the same length, the outermost reversible, and there are sharp spines on the pads of the soles of the feet. The combination of large and very sharp claws with the spiny under-feet enables the birds to securely grasp large, slippery, wriggling fish. Its nostrils have special valves that close when the bird strikes into the water to snatch large fish swimming near the surface.

Additional references include: Blake (1977), Dunne & Weick (1980), Poole (1994), Sibley (2000) and Ferguson-Lees & Christie (2001).

OSPREY *Pandion haliaetus* Pl. 27

Identification 55–58cm, W145–170cm. Forehead to nape white, broad dark brown wedge on ear-coverts widens on sides, and meets on, back of neck, rest of upperparts dark brown, tail has several dark shadow bars; entire underparts creamy white, underwings essentially white with two broad dark bars, and underside of tail barred brown. Pale to white eyes. Unmistakable once distinctive flight silhouette is known.

Ssp. *P. h. carolinensis* (all countries)

Habits Usually fishes alone, soaring reasonably low over open water or diving, talons outspread, to catch trout-sized fish that constitute their main diet.
Status Boreal migrant, uncommon to rare in Ecuador, frequent in Colombia; winters regularly in Aruba, Curaçao and Bonaire (especially on the leeward side of the islands), common and regular in Venezuela, common in Trinidad & Tobago, and frequent in Guyana, Suriname and French Guiana. In northern South America mainly during Northern Hemisphere winter (October–May), but many reports of immatures staying year-round and even building nests. There is a case in French Guiana (Amana Reserve) where a pair had obviously built a nest (never effectively found), followed a few weeks later by regular come-and-go feeding flights (O. Tostain). Birds from eastern North America that winter in northern South America usually follow Atlantic coast, thence to Cuba and thereafter Hispaniola, and from there cross either to Central America or to the coasts of Colombia and Venezuela, dispersing inland.

Habitat Tropical Zone. Coasts and large rivers, and around large bodies of fresh, brackish or salt water. Most abundant near relatively shallow areas and in coastal wetlands (salt-marshes, mangroves, estuaries, etc.).
Voice Series of upward-inflected whistles, *curlée, curlée, curlée* or a high thin *chur, chee chee chee* in flight or perched (Hilty).

ACCIPITRIDAE – Kites, Harriers, Hawks and Eagles

The Accipitridae is a large and rather diverse family of kites, hawks and eagles, whose names do not connote any kind of similarity of features. They all have hooked bills and bare ceres, sharp talons on their toes and catch prey with their feet. Wings and tail are usually barred and provide the diagnostics for identification of soaring birds. They take live prey, hence the term raptors, which ranges from grasshoppers and moths, through snails and crabs, birds and fish, to monkeys and sloths. In most species females are larger and the sexes play different roles when breeding. Smaller males catch smaller prey nearer to the nest, and are very important when the young are small and the female remains at the nest. The female catches larger prey and travels farther afield in search of it.

Additional references include: Blake (1977), Dunne & Weick (1980), Sibley & Sutton (1988), Pearman (1993), Bierregaard (1994a), Thiollay (1994), White, Olsen & Kiff (1994), Sibley (2000) and Ferguson-Lees & Christie (2001).

Kites are a somewhat diverse collection of species, and the term has no clear taxonomic significance. Rather it groups several genera of elegant and graceful birds that are mostly longer winged than other Accipitridae, often with long, forked tails, and are usually birds of open areas that sometimes hover when hunting.

GREY-HEADED KITE
Leptodon cayanensis Pl. 27, In flight Pl. 29

Identification 46–54cm. Adult has grey head with white throat, underwing-coverts black, rest of underparts white, upperparts all blackish, 3 white bars on tail, the uppermost concealed by uppertail-coverts; eyes blue-grey, cere, facial skin, legs and feet blue-grey. Three colour morphs in immatures: pale phase white on head (small black cap at rear), neck and entire underparts including underwing-coverts, back, wings and tail dark brown with 2 broad paler brown bars on tail and paler fringes to wing-coverts and tertials. Intermediate morph darker above, including entire head except throat, 4 slightly paler bars on tail; and dark morph has entire head, throat and upperparts dark, and streaks on breast, becoming weaker on flanks; bars on tail are fringed above and below with black. Eyes, facial skin, cere, bill, legs and feet yellow in immatures. Pale-phase immature easily confused with Black-and-white Hawk-Eagle but lacks white leading edge to forewing. Adult quite distinct.

Ssp. *L. c. cayanensis* (all countries)

Habits Repeatedly soars above canopy for short periods throughout day. Often perches near treetops. Hunts from exposed perch, mainly at dawn and dusk; also follows troops of monkeys to catch disturbed insects. Flight displays in courtship.

Status Uncommon to rare in Ecuador, uncommon in Colombia (most numerous in Amazonian south-east), uncommon in Trinidad (does not occur in Tobago), uncommon in Guyana, frequent in Suriname, and widespread and locally frequent in French Guiana.

Habitat Tropical and Subtropical Zones. Mainly in lowland rain forests and near water. Gallery forests and partially disturbed, patchy woods.

Voice Apparently calls only during breeding period, when commonest is series of up to 20 loud *wuh wuh wuh*… barks, *kek kek kek*… clucks or guttural *keyo keyo keyo*… notes, which often trigger a response from others in nearby territories. Other calls include a feline *miaow* and, in flight, an *aaaaahh-yal* cry, similar to a gull's. Some calls recall Laughing Falcon (F-L&C).

PEARL KITE

Gampsonyx swainsonii Pl. 27, In flight Pl. 29

Identification 20–28cm. Forehead to crown, lores and face-sides rich buff, back of head and neck and upperparts black, chin to undertail-coverts including underwing-coverts white with a small black patch on breast-sides, rufous patch on lower flanks and thighs; eyes reddish-brown, cere and bill black, legs and feet yellow. Very small hawk, rather falcon-like. Virtually unmistakable but might be mistaken for an American Kestrel given fleeting views, as they are similar in size.

Ssp. *G. s. leonae* (N Co, Ve, Tr, Gu, Su, FG) darker than others, with more conspicuous reddish on flanks and tibia
G. s. magnus (W Co, Ec) like *swainsonii* but slightly larger
G. s. swainsonii (E Ec?) white on flanks, tibia more yellowish-buff

Habits Most often seen singly, sometimes in pairs. Takes lizards and occasionally small birds.

Status Fairly common locally. Uncommon to rare in Ecuador, frequent in Colombia, uncommon and fairly local in Venezuela, uncommon on Trinidad (does not occur on Tobago), and uncommon to rare in Guyana and Suriname. Only one record for French Guiana.

Habitat Tropical Zone. In dry to arid areas, savannas and overgrown pastures, open woodland.

Voice Normally silent. High-pitched scolding *kitt-y, kitt-y, kitt-y* and *kit-kit-kit tsi-ew, ew, ew, ew*, and a low *kee-kee* (F-L&C)

HOOK-BILLED KITE

Chondrohierax uncinatus Pl. 27, In flight Pl. 29

Identification 38–42cm. Adult male is entirely bluish-grey with white vent to undertail-coverts, centres of feathers on back and wing-coverts slightly darker and all feathers of back and wings finely fringed paler, uppertail-coverts barred blackish, tail has 3 broad black bars, the uppermost partially concealed by tail-coverts, flanks finely barred white; eyes vary from yellow to bluish-grey, facial skin, cere, legs and feet yellow, bill black above, white below. Adult female has head and upperparts dark fuscous brown with a narrow pale grey band at base of tail and broad brown bar further down; nuchal collar and entire underparts reddish-rufous, with all but rear collar barred white, and some fine black barring on breast and sides. Dark morph all black except broad white bar at base of tail; eyes brown, facial skin and cere grey, bill black. Immature male dark brown above with narrow white nuchal collar and 4–5 pale bars on tail; underparts entirely white, barred very irregularly brown and black on flanks, undertail-coverts washed slightly buffy, with rufescent bars. Immature female has dark brown cap from forehead to nape, back and wings to tail dark brown, with 3 pale bars on tail and a few white teardrop spots on wing-coverts. Immatures have dark eyes, yellow facial skin, cere, legs and feet, and black bill. Flight profile distinctive: long tail usually held closed and broad wings noticeably narrower at base. Grey morph may be confused with Grey Hawk.

Ssp. *C. u. uncinatus* (all countries except ABC)

Habits It has been suggested that the many different plumages mimic those of other faster or larger raptors, which differ in behaviour or shape. Generally sluggish, secretive and shy, perching inside forest, but will soar high above it. Flies with alternate flaps and glides, then hovers and glides down to seize prey, swooping up again thereafter. Also forages by hopping from branch to branch or hunts from a perch. Feeds mostly on tree snails, complemented with insects and their larvae (especially caterpillars), crabs, frogs, small lizards and salamanders. With snails, it cracks shell to the core and uses hook of bill to extract the body. On the mainland, where different snails are vary in size, birds are dimorphic, with 2 significantly different bill sizes; whilst on islands, where only a single species of snail, all have same-size bill. Breeds later than sympatric kites, almost into rainy season, perhaps to avoid competition over snails.

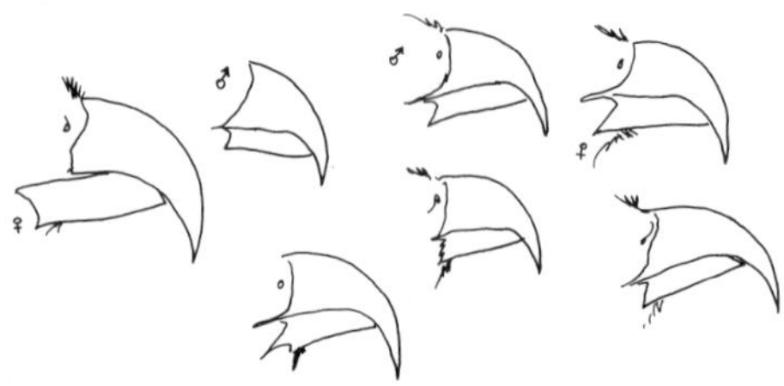

Note the considerable variation in the size and shape of bill of Hook-billed Kite (all drawn in exact proportion from specimens in the Phelps Collection in Caracas)

Status Widespread but scarce and irregular. In Ecuador, rare and local, Colombia thinly spread, Venezuela uncommon, Trinidad infrequent visitor, Tobago rare, Guyana uncommon, Suriname common, and French Guyana uncommon.

Habitat Tropical Zone. Rain forests, mostly below canopy or at edges, in clearings and partially open, disturbed areas.

Voice Apparently silent when not breeding, but quite noisy in protecting nest, at which time (in Panama) calls include a fast musical *wi-i-i-i-i-i-i-i-i-uh* (Hilty).

SWALLOW-TAILED KITE

Elanoides forficatus Pl. 28, In flight Pl. 29

Identification 56–66cm. Striking black-and-white kite with long forked tail; head and underparts snow white, back, wings and tail black (variable white possible on tertials); eyes red, facial skin and cere blue, bill black, legs and feet blue-grey. Juvenile buffy-white rather than pure white, with brown streaks, tail may be shorter. Migrant *forficatus* easily mistaken for resident *yetapa*.

Ssp. *E. f. forficatus* (boreal migrant, Ec) purple gloss above
E. f. yetapa (throughout, except Cu & Bo) green gloss above

Habits Highly aerial, most frequently seen soaring above forest, catching insects alone or in groups that congregate especially where there is a swarm or hatching of winged insects, e.g. termites or *Atta* ants. Gathers in groups of up to 30+ that drift along montane ridges and above lowland forests in sunny weather. Also takes small vertebrates (birds, frogs, lizards) and occasionally fruits. Residents are nomadic over forests through most of South American range, whilst populations at limits of range move to tropical latitudes, making it unclear in our region if birds are resident or migrants.

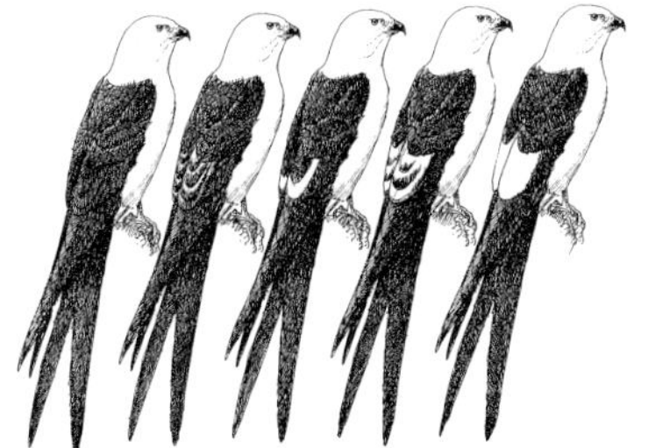

Tertials on Swallow-tailed Kite vary from all black to all white

Status Relatively common throughout. Residents locally common in Ecuador, fairly common in Colombia, common on Trinidad but rare on Tobago, frequent in Guyana, common in Suriname, and frequent in the interior but rather local along coast in French Guiana.

Habitat Tropical to Subtropical Zones. Forested areas, especially with swampy areas.

Voice Normally silent, but utters repeated, shrill high-pitched, twittering whistles. Also, varied series of 2–5 syllables, e.g. *klee-klee…, peet-peet…, kii-ki-ti, bit-dlewit-dlewit* and *gee-wip* (F-L&C).

SNAIL KITE *Rostrhamus sociabilis* Pl. 28

Identification 40–45cm. Adult male deep sooty grey, darker on wings and tail, which has broad white band at base and greyish tip; facial skin, eyes and cere red, bright crimson when breeding, long, very hooked bill is black, legs and feet bright orange. Female dark greyish-brown above with brown fringes that impart barred effect, base of tail white; head, except nape, and underparts buffy white, streaked black, thighs rich buffy, eyes orange to red, facial skin and cere yellow, bill black, legs and feet yellow. Immature like female but much more heavily streaked on head and underparts (to flanks and thighs). Juvenile ruddy brown above, the feathers fringed paler, with rufous front and warm rufous underparts, streaked dark brown to flanks and thighs. Almost unmistakable, with heron-like flight and white tail base, but when quartering or soaring low over marshes is rather harrier-like, with floppier flight.

Ssp. *R. s. sociabilis* (E Ec, N Co, NC Ve, Tr, Gu, Su, FG)

Habits Constantly moves tail. Almost exclusively feeds on medium-sized *Pomacea* snails, using thin, sharply hooked bill to cut the attaching muscles. Juveniles and immatures take smaller snails. Catches prey with feet, sallying from a fixed perch to snatch snails from shallow water or water plants. Also hunts by cruising low over water. Nomadic throughout range according to food availability. Populations at southern limits migrate north to northern South America, but no data on where they go. Nests during rainy season, in colonies of up to several dozen pairs. Communal roosts may comprise up to several hundreds; roosting sites are often loosely associated with heronries, but change as *Pomacea* supplies are depleted.

Status Quite common, but populations subject to local fluctuations according to water and snail situation. Affected by pesticides, drainage of wetlands and, at some sites, introduced *Tilapias*, which affect snail populations. Declining, but locally fairly common in Ecuador and Venezuela, infrequent visitor to Trinidad (not recorded on Tobago), common in Guyana, numerous in Suriname, and rare in French Guiana.

Habitat Tropical Zone. Open, freshwater lowland marshes, rushy lakes and lagoons. Requires abundant stock of Apple Snails (*Pomacea*), thus found only in continuously flooded, mature wetlands and remains in a given area until stocks dwindle, after *c.*2–4 years.

Voice Noisy when breeding but silent when hunting. A rasping bleating *whe-he-he-he-he-he…* (F&K) and clicking *crik-ik-ik-ik,ik, ik, ik* when disturbed. Also a single *kor-ee-ee-a*. In courtship, female utters a 'watch-winding' *weh-heh-heh…* and male a sheep-like bleating (F-L&C, H&B). *Ker-wuck* at roosts, in aerial displays or towards other kites (F-L&C).

SLENDER-BILLED KITE

Helicolestes hamatus Pl. 28

Identification 37–41cm. Adult is slate grey with darker wings and tail; eyes yellow to white, facial skin and cere bright red, bill black, legs and feet red. Immature dull grey with darker wings and brownish tail, fringes to wing feathers rufescent, tail has 2 fairly narrow white bars and buff tip, underparts dark brown-grey, paler distally, barred buffy on thighs and undertail-coverts; eyes brown, facial skin and cere orange, bill dusky, legs and feet yellow. Replaces Snail Kite in forested areas. Could be confused with Slate-coloured Hawk (which has broader head and longer, more rounded tail).

Ssp. Monotypic (Ec, Co, Ve, Gu, Su, FG)

Habits Often soars, not high, in small groups. Hunts from a low perch, mostly taking *Pomacea* snails, which are pulled from the shell by cutting the attachment muscle. Also takes crabs but in much lesser proportion.

Status Poorly known, but restricted habitat and specialised diet make it vulnerable. Very local and scarce in Ecuador and Venezuela, scarce in Guyana, common in coastal region of Suriname, and rare and local in French Guiana.
Habitat Tropical Zone. *Várzea*, edges of swamp forests and flooded gallery and riverine forests; shallow lagoons surrounded by forest; occasionally in plantations.
Voice Call descriptions include a feline *meeeuuu*, similar to a small *Buteo*, and a rising then falling *wheeeeaaaaah*, nasal and buzzy like a kazoo.
Note Traditionally placed in own genus, *Helicolestes*, due to differences from Snail Kite, but recent authors have considered them sufficiently similar to place both in *Rostrhamus* (e.g. Bierregaard 1994, R&G).

DOUBLE-TOOTHED KITE

Harpagus bidentatus Pl. 27, In flight Pl. 29

Identification 31–35cm. Adult has slate grey head with whitish streak either side of central grey of throat, Upperparts grey with 3–4 faint pale bars on tail; breast to flanks, thighs and vent deep rufous, undertail-coverts white; eyes red, cere yellow, bill black, legs and feet yellow. Black morph has entire head, upper breast and upperparts blackish, with 2–3 faint narrow bars on tail, breast to vent deep chestnut, barred finely black and white at rear, and undertail-coverts white. Two immature plumages, both dark brown above with 4–5 faint bars on tail, the first entirely buffy-white below, the other with blackish line on central throat, and black streaks on breast that become shallow V-shaped, broken bars, and narrow black and rufous bars on flanks. More similar to an accipiter than other kites and may be taken for such in flight, especially for female Sharp-shinned or male Bicoloured Hawk, though both have shorter wings and longer legs. Note prominent white undertail-coverts. Wingtips reach halfway down tail and inner web to primaries is bright rufous-chestnut.

Ssp. *H. b. bidentatus* (throughout except western coastal strip) as described

H. b. fasciatus (W Co, W Ec) adult male washed rufous on breast-sides and flanks, barred from breast to flanks with irregular lines of black and white; female has solid rufous breast to flanks, barred finely with white; juvenile male paler grey on head, pale grey from breast to flanks, and barred finely black and grey; eyes red

Double-toothed Kite takes its name from the shape of the cutting edge to the upper mandible

Habits Frequently follows troupes of monkeys, bird flocks and army ants for prey they disturb (lizards, large insects, etc.). Soars in circles, and often in small groups.
Status Uncommon to rare in Ecuador, frequent in Colombia and Venezuela, uncommon in Trinidad (does not occur on Tobago), and uncommon in Guyana, fairly common in Suriname and frequent in French Guiana.
Habitat Tropical Zone, in wet and humid forest, forest edge and open trees such as coffee plantations, wooded savannas and tall secondary woods.
Voice Particularly vocal when breeding, but their high-pitched, thin calls are easily missed. Include *tsip-tsip-tsip-tsip-wheeeeoooip*, a drawn-out *wheeeeoooo*, a whistled *see-wheeeeeep see-weeeet* and a repeated, thin *peeeawe*.... Also a single, high *cheep* (F-L&C).

RUFOUS-THIGHED KITE

Harpagus diodon Pl. 27, In flight Pl. 29

Identification 29–35cm. Dark brown above, with greyish ear-coverts, 3 faint bars on tail, buffy white throat with dark mesial line, greyish breast merging with rufous thighs, white undertail-coverts; eyes orange or red, facial skin, cere, legs and feet yellow, and bill black. Juvenile similar but is entirely buffy white below with rufous thighs, black streaks on breast and central belly, flanks barred. From larger Double-toothed Kite by ferruginous underwing-coverts.

Ssp. Monotypic (E Ec, Ve, Gu, Su, FG)

Habits Very poorly known. Small accipiter-like kite which is relatively tame and sluggish. Usually solitary but occasionally in pairs. Regularly soars over forest, and open areas. Hunts at mid to lower levels
Status Rare but sometimes locally frequent. Only sight records from Ecuador, where very rare and possibly an accidental visitor, uncommon in Venezuela, scarce in Guyana, where possibly an austral migrant, very rare in Suriname, and rare in French Guiana.
Habitat Tropical Zone, in forests of various types, but often in dense primary forest, and is intolerant of disturbed forest and second growth. In French Guiana occurs only in primary forest.
Voice Calls *ëWEEoo-WEEoo-witi* (Sick 1993).

WHITE-TAILED KITE

Elanus leucurus Pl. 28, In flight Pl. 29

Identification 38–43cm. Adult pale grey above, almost white on tail and has black lesser and median wing-coverts, white forehead, eyebrow, face-sides and underparts; eyes red, cere yellow, bill black, legs and feet yellow. Immature similar but head is lightly streaked black, heaviest on nape, upperparts brown with white fringes to all feathers, large black wing patch, and breast to flanks is washed buffy. In flight, resembles a small gull with a long white tail, and at dusk could be taken for a Barn Owl. Sometimes hovers like a kestrel or even flies leisurely on raised wings like a harrier.

Ssp. *E. l. leucurus* (Ec, Co, Ar, Ve, Tr, Gu, Su, FG)

Habits Usually alone though it congregates to roost and

sometimes when hunting. Mainly hunts at dawn and dusk, principally searching for small rodents. Resident populations are nomadic according to prey availability.

Status Both resident and migrant populations occur in northern South America, migrants being both austral and boreal, coming from both ends of range. Populations perhaps increasing over most of range, due to increasing clearance for agriculture. Rare and very local in Ecuador (first sighting 1984, confirmed 1992), frequent in Colombia and Venezuela, sight records in Aruba and Trinidad, frequent in Guyana, and moderately common in Suriname. Rare and very local in NW coastal French Guiana.

Habitat Tropical Zone. Open or lightly wooded areas, savannas with patchy woods, marshes. Areas partially cleared for agriculture.

Voice Calls infrequently, including a *kwep* or *kewp* whistle in greeting, and a 2-note *eeee-grack* whistle followed by a grunt (H&B, Hilty).

Note Formerly *Elanus caeruleus leucurus*, but New World *E. leucurus* now separated from Old World *E. caeruleus* (Clark & Banks 1992).

MISSISSIPPI KITE

Ictinia mississippiensis Pl. 28, In flight Pl. 29

Identification 31–37 cm. Small, falcon-shaped kite. Pale grey head, darker grey back and wings, pale to white greater wing-coverts, black flight-feathers that only just reach beyond tip of tail; underparts entirely bluish-grey; eyes red, facial skin, cere and bill black, legs and feet bright orange. Immature has underparts heavily streaked rufous, but note feathers are pale-fringed, thus streaks appear as large dots; legs and feet yellow. Could be confused with Plumbeous Kite when perched. Mississippi has paler head, secondaries and underparts. Wingtips of Plumbeous protrude well past tip of tail. Very difficult to separate when overhead: look for rufous in wings and barred tail of Plumbeous.

Ssp. Monotypic (E Ec, Co)

Habits Very social, migrating in flocks. Hunts mainly in flight, leisurely gliding to snap up flying insects, but also still-hunts like a flycatcher, returning to the perch to feed. Follows grazing animals to snatch disturbed insects.

Status Boreal migrant, passing through Colombia to winter in Paraguay, northern Argentina and Bolivia. In our region, mainly seen October and March. Winter range and migration routes through northern South America poorly known. Occasional sightings Ecuador (April, December); hypothetical for Venezuela.

Habitat Mostly Lower Tropical Zone, from open grassland to forests, typically agricultural and pasturelands, parks and cultivated areas, open woodland.

Voice Normally silent but birds in flight may chatter to each other.

PLUMBEOUS KITE

Ictinia plumbea Pl. 28, In flight Pl. 29

Identification 33–38cm. Small falcon-like kite that is easily confused with Mississippi Kite, but wingtips project well beyond tip of tail. Head and body plumbeous grey, wings and tail slate to sooty grey with chestnut primaries and white bars on tail; eyes yellow in Ecuador, red elsewhere, cere and bill black, legs and feet bright orange. Immature has whitish head, heavily streaked black, dark grey underparts (feathers fringed pale buffy giving a slightly scaled appearance). Juvenile has entire head and underparts buffy-white, streaked dark grey on head and black on underparts. Young have brown eyes, grey facial skin and cere, darker bills, yellow legs and feet.

Ssp. Monotypic (E Ec, Co, Ve, Tr, Gu, Su, FG)

Habits Often perches on exposed branches and dead trees apparently ignoring human observers, but may also remain concealed in cover.

Status Uncommon to frequent throughout. Ranges from Mexico to Argentina, and birds from both extremes of range visit our region as migrants. In Ecuador uncommon to locally frequent. Frequent to common in Colombia, fairly common in Venezuela, and common in Trinidad.

Habitat Tropical Zone, in fairly open forest; forest edge, secondary woods, gallery forest, forest islands in palm savanna, near rivers and mangroves. Also covers open country.

Voice Usually vocal only when breeding. Mournful, 2–3-syllable whistles descending at end, e.g. *swee-zeeeew* or *fee-eedee*, recalling Piratic Flycatcher. Shrill *shirreeeer* or *sisseeeoo*. Also *hee-hi hee-hi, jip jip* (F-L&C).

Note Sometimes treated as conspecific with Mississippi Kite.

Harriers are medium-sized and slender, with long wings, tails and legs. Flight is buoyant, the wings characteristically held in shallow V, with gull-like glides and sideways rocking rather like Turkey Vultures. They are usually encountered over open country, marshes, swamps, rice fields and cultivated areas where they hunt by quartering the ground, criss-crossing, occasionally hovering briefly before dropping onto their prey.

LONG-WINGED HARRIER

Circus buffoni Pl. 30

Identification 45–60cm. Particularly long wings, and white rump in all but dark morph. Adult male normal morph has head, breast and back to rump black, wings and tail grey with black bars, 4 faint grey bars and grey tip to tail; white eyebrow, fore face, half-ring around facial disc and underparts, with some faint streaking on flanks and thighs; eyes, facial skin and cere yellow, bill black, legs and feet yellow. Female brown above with darker barring, flight-feathers paler with clearer barring, underparts buffy, streaked on breast to flanks; eyes brown. Immature paler brown, more spotted than barred and much more heavily streaked below; more white on face and facial disc more noticeable, soft parts as female. Pale morph is paler and greyer in all plumages. Dark morph is all black with deep ruddy-chestnut thighs and undertail-coverts, immature dark brown above with white facial disc, eyebrow and throat, ochraceous below streaked black and chestnut thighs. The largest harrier with longer wings and more buoyant flight than others. Wingtips nearly reach tail tip. Similar juvenile Cinereous Harrier has barred underwings.

Ssp. Monotypic (Co, Ve, Gu, Su, FG)

Habits Usually rests on ground rather than post or fence.
Status Nomadic and migratory. Widespread but rather local and poorly known in our region. Locally fairly common in Colombia, uncommon and local in Venezuela north of Orinoco. Wanderer and rare breeder in Trinidad & Tobago, and very local in Guyana, Suriname and coastal French Guiana.
Habitat Lower Tropical Zone, in open country, especially marshes, grassland and savannas, small lagoons with emergent vegetation, rice fields and open cultivation.
Voice Usually quiet, but noisy in defence of nest. Utters a fairly rapid series of sandpiper-like notes in alarm (ffrench). Weak squeals in courtship and continuous wader-like chattering.
Note Former name (*Falco*) *brasiliensis*, by Gmelin in 1788, is invalid. Valid name, *Falco buffoni* (=*Circus buffoni*), also by Gmelin 1788, was applied in 1908 by Berlepsch (Banks & Dove 1992).

NORTHERN HARRIER

Circus cyaneus Pl. 30

Identification 45–53 cm. Adult male grey above with faint wing and tail bars, white rump, whitish outermost tail feathers, paler eyebrow, and whitish facial disc; greyish lower throat and upper breast (divided by outline of disc), rest of underparts very pale grey, spotted rufous on flanks; eyes, skin and cere yellow, bill grey, legs and feet yellow. Female has brownish head with whitish eyebrow and throat, buffy outline to facial disc, ochraceous nuchal collar, breast and underparts, streaked brown from head but thinning out on upper thighs and rear flanks. Immature like female, but has more rufescent brown back and almost tawny underparts, with rufous fringes to most feathers, tail bars greyish, and is less heavily streaked below. Juveniles and immatures extremely difficult to separate from other harriers. In adults wingtips fall well short of tail tip.

Ssp. *C. c. hudsonius* (N Co, N Ve)

Habits Perches on ground, poles, fences and reeds, but seldom on trees. Adult males spend very little time on winter grounds, thus most sightings are of ringtails. Usually solitary but prefers to roost communally in winter.
Status Boreal migrant that occasionally visits northern Colombia and Venezuela (the southernmost extent of the winter range), usually in November–December.
Habitat Could occur at any altitude on migration. Open country, avoids woodland. Usually swampy areas with dense, tall reeds and grassy aquatic vegetation. Marshes, wet savannas, rice fields and freshly ploughed land or with young crops.
Voice A fast cackling during aerial displays, whistles and a *kyeh-kyeh-kyeh*... alarm chatter.
Note Recognised as a distinct species, *C. hudsonius* (and *C. cyaneus* then called Hen Harrier) by Ferguson-Lees & Christie (2001), but we follow AOU (1998) in our taxonomy.

CINEREOUS HARRIER

Circus cinereus Pl. 30

Identification 43–50cm. Adult male grey above, darker on wings and tail, which are faintly barred, large white rump patch, white facial disc, underparts evenly and narrowly barred rufous and pale grey; eyes, skin, cere, legs and feet all yellow. Adult female similar, but much deeper grey above and richer rufous to chestnut and white below. Immature dark brown above, paler on neck, whitish eyebrow, fore-face, throat and facial disc, dark brown-streaked breast, reduced on sides, and flanks and thighs streaked pale rufous. Wings shorter and tail longer proportionately than other harriers; rather *Buteo*-like. Look for obvious white rump.

Ssp. Monotypic (Ec, C & S Co)

Habits Usually solitary, but occasionally in pairs, and congregates at roost sites or at abundant food sources. Flies with slow wingbeats, alternating with glides on raised wings. Soars with raised wings but less pronounced than other harriers, circling high. In purposeful flight, sometimes glides with flat or slightly bowed wings between series of 5–10 heavy wingbeats (F&K).
Status Very rare to locally uncommon, being rare in Ecuador and quite uncertain and local in Colombia.
Habitat Temperate Zone to Páramo. Open country, particularly marshes, reedbeds and rushy wetlands, moorland, scrub, pastures and wetlands in humid inter-Andean valleys.
Voice Seldom calls except when breeding. Calls include a fast chatter in aerial displays, in males a *kee-kee-kee*...with females producing a higher pitched *kek-kek-kek*... In courtship, females utter a mournful *pee-u* or *pee-pa*. Also a *kikikikiki*... when alarmed.

Accipiters are relatively small, with a significant difference in size between males and the larger females. They have short, rounded wings for acceleration and long tails, which in combination gives them great manoeuvrability in flight as they pursue prey inside woodland, sometimes through quite dense vegetation. Several species are polymorphic, including dark to virtually melanistic, with different combinations between juveniles and adults.

GREY-BELLIED HAWK

Accipiter poliogaster Pl. 31

Identification 43–51cm. Distinctive. Adult black-faced morph is deep black above with faint bars on tail, face-sides including malar black and pure white below. Grey-faced morph differs in having face-sides grey. Intermediate has rufous flush on breast-sides and vestigial black bars and dots on flanks. Immature has ear-coverts, broad nuchal band and neck-sides bright chestnut, line below eye and malar stripe black, a few black spots on throat, breast and sides well streaked (with some chestnut admixed), and flanks and thighs strongly barred black. All have yellow eyes and cere, black bill, and yellow legs and feet. Pale morph of Bicoloured Hawk has rufous thighs, Slaty-backed Forest Falcon a longer, graduated tail and a black cap. Immature like Ornate Hawk-Eagle, but is half the size and lacks feathered legs and crest.

Ssp. Monotypic (E Ec, NE & E Co, W & S Ve, Gu, Su, FG)

Habits Usually solitary, soaring above forest, and occasionally perches at forest edge or in a clearing. Not shy.

Status A poorly known species. Possibly an austral migrant in some parts of range, where it is found mostly during wetter months. Very rare in Ecuador, widespread but rare in Colombia (few records, mostly March–June), Venezuela, Guyana, Suriname and French Guiana.

Habitat Lower Tropical Zone. Dense, humid lowland forest and mature second growth, especially along rivers.

Voice In flight a rapid cackling *kek-kek-kek-kek-kek-kek* rather like Bicoloured Hawk, slowing or trailing off at end (Hilty).

Note Sometimes called Grey-bellied Goshawk.

COOPER'S HAWK

Accipiter cooperii Pl. 31

Identification 37–47 cm. Adult has dark cap, rest of head washed orange-rufous, throat white, becoming broad scaling on breast to flanks, but barred on undertail-coverts; back to tail grey with faint brownish barring; eyes red, facial skin and cere yellow, bill black, legs and feet yellow. Immature brown above with dark cap, irregular white spots on back, 4–5 counting pale bars on tail; underparts white with brown streaks from throat-sides to flanks and thighs; eyes, skin and cere pale yellow. Similar Plain-breasted Hawk has solid rufous thighs. From Broad-winged Hawk by grey back and many bars on tail.

Ssp. Monotypic (Co)

Habits Quite wary, usually alone, perches within cover of canopy, but occasionally in the open. Sometimes in small groups during migration. Flight like others of genus, alternating glides with a few wing flaps.

Status Boreal migrant with a winter range that normally extends to Costa Rica, but accidental to Colombia, based on a record of a bird ringed in Manitoba that was recovered in Cundinamarca in February.

Habitat Upper Tropical to Temperate Zones. Mostly forested areas, but frequents a variety of habitats in winter: wooded or semi-open areas, often around wetlands and along rivers, borders and clearings of forest, cultivated land with copses and rows of trees, parks and suburban areas.

Voice Usually silent in winter.

SEMICOLLARED HAWK

Accipiter collaris Pl. 31

Identification 30–36 cm. Blackish crown, nape and neck-sides, separated from dark brown back by narrow, slightly irregular or even broken white collar, subtle black bars on wings and tail; head-sides white streaked with tiny black lines, throat and upper breast white, rest of underparts evenly and fairly narrowly barred black and white; eyes, cere, legs and feet yellow. Brown-phase immature is dark brown above with rufous collar, underparts barred rufous-brown, darker on thighs; rufous-phase immature has dark rufous back and head with a bright orange-rufous collar and barring below. Similar Tiny Hawk has very fine barring below and lacks noticeable nuchal collar.

Ssp. Monotypic (Andes: Ve, Co, Ec)

Habits Found usually alone, sometimes in pairs, being wary and shy, and perching mostly within cover. Apparently seldom seen flying in open. Possibly hunts for birds through the forest.

Status Rare in Ecuador, scarce in Colombia and in Venezuela, where precise range and status poorly known.

Habitat Upper Tropical to Subtropical Zones. Humid or wet forests on mid to upper slopes, cloud forests, partially open areas adjacent to forest, light woods.

Voice No description found.

Note Seems to replace Tiny Hawk at higher altitudes.

TINY HAWK *Accipiter superciliosus* Pl. 31

Identification 20–28cm. Adult has blackish cap, grey head-sides and nape, darker grey back and browner wings and tail, throat white, rest of underparts finely and evenly barred black and white; eyes red, cere, facial skin, legs and feet yellow. Two distinct morphs in immatures: brown phase is dark brown above and barred finely brown below; rufous phase is paler and warmer rufescent brown above, with paler, rufous barring below. From Semicollared Hawk by lack of nuchal collar.

Ssp. *A. s. fontanieri* (W Co, W Ec) slightly smaller and darker with bolder bars
A. s. superciliosus (E Co, Ec, Ve, Gu, Su, FG) slightly larger, with fainter and very thin bars

Habits Wary and usually alone, sometimes in pairs, perches in forest or occasionally soars above canopy. Still-hunts for birds which apparently form its main diet. Perches are usually low, but sometimes at mid levels and even in the canopy, and it attacks by swooping onto passing prey.

Status Widespread but scarce: rare in Ecuador (few recent records), uncommon to rare in Colombia, uncommon to locally frequent in Venezuela, scarce in Guyana, rare in Suriname, and frequent in French Guiana.

Habitat Tropical Zone. Humid forests, secondary woods, plantations, deciduous woodland and scrub. At borders and clearings, sometimes in tangles and small forest patches.

Voice Seldom calls. A shrill (?) *kree-ree-ree-ree…* or *keer-keer-keer…* (F-L&C), or a thin *krie-rie-rie-rie* (H&B).

Note Olson (2006) resurrected the genus *Hieraspiza* solely for the Tiny Hawk, based on its distinctively different skeleton from all other *Accipiter*. Its specific name becomes *superciliosa* under this arrangement.

PLAIN-BREASTED HAWK

Accipiter ventralis Pl. 32 In flight Pl. 29

Identification 28–33cm. Very complex number of morphs and plumages (see plate). Normal adult male has dusky head, brown upperparts, barred flight-feathers with 4 pale bars on tail, uppermost concealed by tail-coverts, white below, barred faintly grey and washed rufescent on flanks, thighs rufous; eyes, facial skin, cere, legs and feet yellow. Normal adult female is similar but has fewer bars below and is richer in coloration. Juvenile is streaked black on breast and flanks, thighs rufous, barred black. Dark phase is deep brown above and dark brown below, ruddy on flanks and thighs; black phase is black, and is the only morph to lack rufous thighs. Look for rufous thighs. From Bicoloured Hawk by whitish, somewhat barred or streaked underparts, and Bicoloured Hawk has 3 tail bars.

Ssp. Monotypic (Ec, Co, N & SE Ve, Gu, FG)

Habits Mostly inside forest, perches within cover and is quite wary. Hunts for birds through foliage. May soar occasionally.
Status Uncommon to rare in Ecuador, uncommon to locally frequent in Colombia and Venezuela, situation in Guyana uncertain (possibly rare) but recorded in south-west (M. Robbins & M. Braun, pers. comm.). Rare but probably widespread in the interior of French Guiana.
Habitat Upper Tropical to Temperate Zones. Humid and cloud forests and bushy, mature secondary woods on montane slopes. At borders and clearings.
Voice Calls include fast repetitions of a high-pitch *qui qui qui* cackling (H&B).
Note Formerly considered conspecific with *A.* (*s.*) *striatus* (migrant from North & Middle America and the Caribbean), *A.* (*s.*) *chionogaster* (resident in Mexico and Central America) and *A.* (*s.*) *erythronemius* (resident in south-east South America). Treated as *A. erythronemius ventralis* in AOU (1998) and BFR&S; as *A. s. ventralis* in H&B and F&K. Group separated into separate species in S&M, Bierregaard, R&G, because of differences in morphology, ecology and possibly behaviour (Bierregaard).

BICOLOURED HAWK
Accipiter bicolor Pl. 32 In flight Pl. 29

Identification 35–43cm. Dark grey above, darker on head, wings and tail with 3 somewhat faint bars on tail; grey from throat to flanks, solid rufous thighs, white undertail-coverts; eyes, facial skin, cere, legs and feet yellow. Female notably larger. Whole range of variant plumages in immatures (see plate), main distinction is barring on thighs, 4 tail bars and nuchal collar. From Plain-breasted Hawk by larger size and only 3 pale bars on tail (not 4); immatures most easily separated by nuchal collar. Plumage very variable.

Ssp. *A. b. bicolor* (all countries)

Habits Wary and secretive. Usually alone, sometimes in pairs, soaring above canopy on horizontal wings, or perching quietly within cover, inside forest or sometimes in semi-open spot, spying passing birds. Birds are its main diet and are hunted on wing, chased in weaving flight through foliage. Seldom calls except when breeding.
Status Rare in Ecuador, apparently rare in Colombia (few records, most in drier lowlands), rare to uncommon in Venezuela, uncommon in Guyana, rare in Suriname, and local and uncommon in French Guiana.
Habitat Tropical to Subtropical Zones. Borders of humid and moist forest, and secondary woods, especially beside lakes and rivers, gallery forests and patches of wood in savannas. Plantations and light woodland.
Voice Calls include a fast *cak-cak-cak*... scold near nest (H&B); repeated *waaahh!* squalls between members of a pair; a high-pitched *keh-keh-keh-keh*... or *kow-kow-kow*... bark. Also, groans and soft, clear whistles (F-L&C).

CRANE HAWK
Geranospiza caerulescens Pl. 28

Identification 43–53cm. Lanky and somewhat disproportionate, with long orange-red legs. Adult is entirely blue-grey except black tail with 2 broad white bars; eyes red, facial skin and cere grey, bill dark grey, legs and feet orange-red. Immature similar but has buffy-white tip to tail and faint white barring on throat and lower breast to undertail-coverts. Juvenile grey above, with 3–4 buffy-white bars on tail (including substantial tip); front of head whitish, streaked lightly, heavily at back, with grey, breast to undertail-coverts pale buffy orange, barred faintly grey, eyes orange, facial skin, cere and bill grey, legs and feet orange. Slate-coloured Hawk most similar but has single tail band (juvenile 2) and more patterned underwing. In flight, from any other hawk by white crescent near tip of wings.

Ssp. *G. c. balzarensis* (W Ec, W Co) adult distinctly darker grey overall, bars on tail orange-buffy; immature darker above, more orange-buffy below including tail bars, with whitish eyebrow, bars on underparts broader and darker
G. c. caerulescens (E Ec, N & E Co, Ve, Tr, Gu, Su, FG) as described; smaller and paler

Habits Usually alone, perching semi-concealed at edge of bushes or forest, or in open on posts, fences, bushes, or walks on ground with body horizontal and legs vertical. Hunts around canopy and mid levels, clambering in search of frogs, snakes, nests, etc.
Status Widely but unevenly distributed. Rare to locally uncommon in Ecuador. In Colombia, local and uncommon at most localities, but common in a couple of places. Uncommon in Venezuela, vagrant to Trinidad, frequent in Guyana, moderately common in Suriname and uncommon in French Guiana.
Habitat Very adaptable, in lowlands from dry to humid forests, often near ponds and marshes, streams, open scrub and drier deciduous areas, but usually with water nearby. *Eucalyptus* and coffee plantations.
Voice Call a shrill whistle similar to Roadside Hawk but thinner, e.g. *shreeu, wheeoo, kweeuur*. Calls at dawn and dusk, a long hollow *wo-ow*, repeated at intervals (F-L&C). Infrequent series of soft bleating and downslurred whistles, *ueeoo* or *ueeoo-ueeoo* (Hilty).
Note Race *caerulescens* is sometimes treated as separate species, Grey Crane Hawk. Extensive intergradation between races suggests that they are better treated as a single species.

Fish-eagles are large, long- and broad-winged with fairly short, wedge-shaped tails, and large strong bills. They are primarily fish scavengers, but also catch live fish, mammals and birds. They are birds of coasts, but also lakes and rivers – wherever dead fish might be found. The only fish-eagle to have occurred in our region is Bald Eagle, and only as an offshore vagrant.

BALD EAGLE

Haliaeetus leucocephalus Pl. 40

Identification 80cm. Large eagle, all black with white head and tail, soft parts yellow. Juvenile and intermediate plumages all brown with only latter having a white head, but note underwing pattern and white axillaries. Adult unmistakable. Subadults and older immatures might be confused with Osprey, but wing profile in flight very different and look for all-white underbody of Osprey.

Ssp. *H. l. leucocephalus*? (Curaçao)

Habits Hunts and fishes from a perch, picking fish and waterbirds from open water.

Adult Bald Eagle is unmistakable, but the species is most likely to be seen in intermediate plumage in our region

Status Considered a very rare vagrant, with sightings off the coast of Curaçao in January 1942 and December 1944 (Voous 1957). Has since undergone a considerable decline in USA due to DDT and other causes, but recovery in recent years may lead to future vagrancy.

Habitat Usually near water, in areas with large trees to provide lookout perches.

Voice Weak whistles.

Leucopternis are rather *Buteo*-like hawks but have broader wings and tails, and are all white or pale greyish. They mostly prey on reptiles and amphibians. Four species (Slate-coloured, Plumbeous, Semiplumbeous and Black-faced) are comparatively small and live in forest, and never soar. The other three (White, Grey-backed and Barred) are larger and more conspicuous species that soar regularly (R&G). The black-and-white tail pattern is diagnostic when in doubt.

BARRED HAWK

Leucopternis princeps Pl 32, In flight Pl. 29

Identification 53–59 cm. Entire head and upper breast, back and wings to tail black, tail has 2 narrow grey bars near base and a broad white bar near tip; underparts narrowly barred black and white; eyes dark brown, facial skin, cere, legs and feet yellow. Immature has scapulars and wing-coverts fringed whitish. Plumage pattern – contrast between black head and neck, and pale underparts – unmistakable. Black-chested Buzzard-eagle occurs higher in mountains and is larger, with long, broad wings.

Ssp. Monotypic (W & C Co, N Ec)

Habits Usually found perched calmly on an exposed perch at forest edge, alone, sometimes in pairs or small groups (4–5 birds) soaring high above forest, calling frequently and performing aerial displays. Still-hunts inside forest.

Status Uncommon to rare in Ecuador. In Colombia, rare on Pacific coastal plains, but more common locally in foothills and the south.

Habitat Upper Tropical to Temperate Zones. Humid or wet forests on lower and mid slopes.

Voice Call description includes piercing *wheeeyoor* cries that may sometimes speed-up to into a high-pitched *weep, weep, weep…* laughter (H&B), or loud *wheey-aaar* or *wheeeuu* whistles (R&G).

GREY-BACKED HAWK

Leucopternis occidentalis Pl. 32, In flight Pl. 29

Identification 45–48cm. Head grey with white fringes to feathers, back and wings black, rump to tail white with broad black subterminal bar on tail. Immature similar but dark grey rather than black and has some black streaks on sides. From below as White Hawk.

Ssp. Monotypic (W Ec)

Habits Usually alone or in pairs, or in small groups of 3–4. Still-hunts for small vertebrates and large insects. Perches quietly for long periods in branches of subcanopy or at mid levels.

Status Endangered. Uncommon Ecuadorian endemic, with population subdivided into small, isolated groups inhabiting different forest fragments. Perhaps occurs in south-west Colombia (H&B).

Habitat Tropical Zone, infrequently to Subtropical Zone. Mostly in humid and cloud forests, from lowlands and foothills to upper slopes and especially in humid ravines, and less often in dry deciduous forests or even in mature secondary woodland.

Voice Call include a *keeaar* screech, when perched (F-L&C), but reportedly calls mostly in flight, several fast repetitions of a loud hoarse *shreeeeyr*, reminiscent of White Hawk (R&G).

BLACK-FACED HAWK

Leucopternis melanops Pl. 32, In flight Pl. 29

Identification 31–43 cm. Adult has all-white head and back, streaked black, entire underparts unstreaked white; scapulars and wings black with white spots, rump to tail black, with broad white tail bar midway and narrow white terminal bar; eyes reddish, eye-ring yellow, lores and line through eye black, cere orange-yellow, legs and feet yellow. Immature similar, but more heavily streaked above and lacks white tip to tail. From larger White Hawk by dark head and black tail with white median band, the opposite of White which has a white tail with black median band.

Ssp. Monotypic (NE Ec, S Co, S & SE Ve; Guianas)

Habits Usually alone or in pairs, inside forest, never soaring in the open. Not shy but still-hunts from perch in dense undergrowth or mid level, and in thickest mangrove.

Status Rare in Ecuador, scarce in Colombia (known from only 2–3 localities), uncommon in Venezuela and Guyana, frequent in Suriname, and uncommon in French Guiana; probably partially overlooked.

Habitat Tropical Zone. Humid or wet lowland forest and secondary woodland, *várzea*, mangroves, riparian woods and thickets, forest borders, clearings, occasionally in bushy copses in savanna adjacent to forest.

Voice Occasional call described as a long thin whistle (H&B), or 5 s repetitions of a high-pitched, slurred *keee-u* whistle (R&G).

WHITE HAWK

Leucopternis albicollis Pl. 32, In flight Pl. 29

Identification 46–56cm. Exquisitely beautiful. Entirely white body with a few black streaks on back, scapulars and wings black, all feathers with white tips, tail black with broad white terminal band; eyes orange, facial skin and cere orange, legs and feet yellow. Immature similar but wings dark grey, rather than black, the white fringes slightly broader and black teardrop streaks from rear crown to back. Western races from Black-faced Hawk by white tail with black median band, unlike Black-faced tail, which is black with white median band. Eastern race has all-black tail with white terminal bar. Also has bright orange cere (not grey). Juveniles and immatures have brownish streaking on crown and neck-sides.

Ssp. *L. a. albicollis* (E Ec; E & SE Co; C, E & S Ve; Tr, Gu, Su, FG) as described

L. a. costaricensis (W Co) all-white head and mantle, wing-coverts white except largest, which are black with white tips forming a white bar, white tips to secondaries, tail all white except narrow black subterminal bar

L. a. williaminae (N Co, NW Ve) heavily streaked crown, neck, mantle and scapulars, tail all white with broad black subterminal bar

Habits Usually alone or in pairs, calm and confident, perched on high, exposed spot at forest edge. In early morning and late afternoon, suns and preens for long periods. Single birds or small (family?) groups of 3–4 often soaring in circles above forest. Still-hunts from a perch. Calls often when soaring.

Status Rare in Ecuador. In Colombia, local, most frequent along Orinoco. Locally frequent in Venezuela, uncommon in Trinidad (does not occur in Tobago), frequent in the Guianas.

Habitat Tropical Zone. Pristine, extensive humid forests in hilly lowlands and foothills, forested swamps, pastures with scattered trees adjacent to forest, and sometimes in primary, deciduous or semi-deciduous, forests. In Venezuela, extensive *Mauritia* palm bogs.

Voice Call is a loud whistled scream, variously described as harsh (P&MdS), a husky *shreeeeerrr* (H&B), a scratchy *sheeeeww* or *shhhww*, resembling a Barn Owl (F-L&C), or a rather high, short, tinny *screeea*, like whistle of Piratic Flycatcher (Hilty).

SLATE-COLOURED HAWK

Leucopternis schistaceus

Pl. 32, In flight Pl. 29

Identification 38–43cm. Adult is charcoal grey with broad white band in centre of tail and narrow white tip; eyes red, facial skin and cere red, legs and feet yellow. Immature slate grey above and on head to breast, with white tips to uppertail-coverts, white tail-band and tip; underparts narrowly and evenly barred grey and white; eyes yellow. Dark-morph Hook-billed Kite has deeply hooked bill and very broad white tail-band; juvenile Slender-billed Kite also has deeply hooked bill, and pale fringes to wing-coverts.

Ssp. Monotypic (E Ec, SE Co, S Ve, FG)

Habits Usually alone, sometimes in pairs but seldom soars. Still-hunts at water's edge, to pounce (but not wade) on crabs, frogs, lizards, snakes.

Status Uncommon in Ecuador, common in Colombia and uncommon in Venezuela. Uncommon and local in French Guiana, mostly in NE coastal plain.

Habitat Lower Tropical Zone. Always near slow-flowing or still waters, around forest swamps, ponds and streams, *várzea*, swampy forest, patches of woodland or bushes in seasonally flooded savannas, gallery forest, tall mangroves, riparian woods.

Voice Call a piercing, downslurred *wheeeeeeeeeer* (F-L&C), *kyeeeeeee* (R&G) or *wEEEeeeeeeeeer* (Hilty) whistle. At times a fast (*c*.5 s) sticking *ki ki ki ki ki ki ki* … (P. Coopmans).

PLUMBEOUS HAWK

Leucopternis plumbeus Pl. 32, In flight Pl. 29

Identification 35–38cm. Almost entire body slate grey, thighs barred white; wings and tail black, white tips to uppertail-coverts and broad white tail bar; eyes red, facial skin deep orange, legs and feet pale orange. Immature slightly paler grey, barred grey and white from lower breast back, white tips to uppertail-coverts, narrow white bar near base and broad white bar near tip of tail; eyes yellow. In flight, told by white underwings contrasting with dark body. Completely allopatric with similar-looking Slate-coloured Hawk. From Plumbeous Kite by short wings without rufous that do not reach tail tip.

Ssp. Monotypic (W Ec, W Co)

Habits Usually alone or in pairs that perch in cover at lower and mid levels. Never soars or glides much in open, and is

difficult to see, except that it often perches on high, exposed branches early morning.
Status Poorly known in general, more apt to be found in the foothills than in the lowlands. Rare in Ecuador and Colombia, only a few scattered localities.
Habitat Lower Tropical, occasionally to Subtropical Zone. Humid forests, near streams, ponds and lakes, both inside forest and in clearings and at borders.
Voice Call a long, descending *wheeeeeeeu* whistle (R&G), but rarely vocalises.

SEMIPLUMBEOUS HAWK
Leucopternis semiplumbeus
Pl. 32, In flight Pl. 29

Identification 33–36cm. Mid grey above, darker on wings and blackish on tail which has narrow white bars at base and midway; underparts pale grey; eyes, facial skin, cere, legs and feet yellow. Immature similar but slightly paler grey, with 3 narrow white tail bars and narrow black streaking on breast, flanks and thighs. From Slaty-backed Forest Falcon by orange-red feet and cere (rather than yellow), and tail pattern, and from Short-tailed Hawk by black tail with obvious white median band.

Ssp. Monotypic (NW Ec, W Co)

Habits Usually alone or in pairs, forages within forest, flying fast on shallow wingbeats and making short glides across open areas but rarely soaring. Not shy, but reclusive habits make it very difficult to see.
Status Affected by deforestation. Rare in Ecuador, and frequent to uncommon in Colombia.
Habitat Tropical Zone. Humid or wet forests in lowlands and foothills, mature secondary woodland, cacao plantations, borders and forest patches.
Voice Repeated, high thin whistles, sometimes upslurred (F-L&C); also long *kiak-er-eeeeeeee* whistles, and a monotonous *ooee ooee ooee ooee*…, like an eagle (H&B).

GREY-LINED HAWK
Asturina nitida (*Buteo nitidus*)
Pl. 35, In flight Pl. 34

Identification 38–43cm. Adult has entire head and underparts finely barred dark and pale grey, undertail-coverts unbarred; back and wings medium grey, rump darker, uppertail-coverts and tail black, the latter distinctly barred, with narrow white bar near base, broad white bar lower and narrow white terminal bar; eyes, facial skin, cere, legs and feet yellow. Immature has pale to whitish head and entire underparts, finely streaked blackish on head and throat, the streaks as large extended teardrops on breast-sides and flanks, thighs barred very finely; upperparts dark brown with some irregular buffy highlights, tail has 3 broad buffy bars.

Ssp. *A. n. nitida* (E Co, E Ec, Ve, Gu, Su, FG) as described
A. n. costaricensis (W Ec, N Co) uniform pale blue-grey head and dark blue-grey back, barring on underparts more clearly defined

Habits Usually alone, perched quietly on a bare limb of a solitary tree, or on a roadside pole, or soaring, rarely high. Still-hunts from semi-open perch, but will chase prey through the trees.
Status Uncommon to rare in Ecuador, uncommon to locally frequent in Colombia and Venezuela, uncommon in Trinidad, scarce in Tobago, frequent in Guyana, common in Suriname and in French Guiana.
Habitat Tropical Zone. Partially forested areas, gallery and riparian forests, open woods and deciduous forests, patches of forest in savanna, humid forest edges, tracks or roads through forest, mostly near rivers and streams.
Voice Calls include a loud, sinking *schweeeeeeeer* cry (H&B), a clear *pee-yurrrrr* whistle when displaying, and a descending *keerr-keerr-ker-ker-ker* (F-L&C).
Notes Recently separated from race *plagiata* (Grey Hawk), whilst *A. nitida* is called Grey-lined Hawk. Race *costaricensis* (N Co, W Ec) synonymous under *nitida*: Blake 1977. *Buteo nitidus* retained by some (e.g. Hilty, Thiollay), and supported by genetic data (Riesing *et al.* 2003), with separation into *Asturina* based on unusual moult pattern (AOU 1998).

Buteogallus are large, heavily-built hawks with long yellow legs and short tails. They are lowland birds that soar frequently. The tail bars are diagnostic when in doubt.

RUFOUS CRAB HAWK
Buteogallus aequinoctialis
Pl. 33, In flight Pl. 34

Identification 46cm. Blackish with rufous fringes to upperparts and wing-feathers, secondaries entirely rufous and inner webs to inner primaries also rufous, narrow rufous tail bar positioned centrally, with broad black subterminal bar and narrow terminal white bar; underparts from breast to flanks and thighs barred black and rufous, undertail-coverts have narrow white bars; eyes brown, facial skin and cere yellow, bill horn, legs and feet orange. Immature brown above, streaked, spotted and barred darker; tail has whitish tip and several dark bands; legs and feet yellowish. Unmistakable by virtue of its dark, mainly rufous plumage, with broad rufous wings.

Ssp. Monotypic (W Ve, Tr, Gu, Su, FG)

Habits Usually in pairs, sometimes alone, perched rather low, usually near water. Still-hunts for crabs, which are its sole food, spying for them from a perch and then pouncing in a flash. Also known to hunt on the wing, cruising low over mudflats. Juveniles are especially tame.
Status Frequent in eastern Venezuela, uncommon and local in Trinidad (does not occur in Tobago), frequent in Guyana, common in Suriname and frequent in French Guiana.
Habitat Lower Tropical Zone. Coastal areas, mangroves and marshy river deltas, and adjacent wet grasslands.
Voice Call consists of loud melodious whistles, also a sequence of 6–7 musical laughing notes, the first 3 fast, the

rest slower and lower (F-L&C). Immature gives a harsh, shrill *ke-KEE-KEE-ka-ca*, higher and louder on second and third notes (Hilty).

COMMON BLACK HAWK

Buteogallus anthracinus

Pl. 33, In flight Pl. 34

Identification 46–51cm. All black except broad white tail bar positioned centrally. Immature is browner and has many feathers fringed whitish, which afford a streaked effect, also barred on thighs, and has several irregular bars on tail. From Mangrove Black Hawk mainly by habitat and range, from Great Black Hawk by smaller size, shorter legs and black undertail coverts, but also by distribution.

Ssp. *B. a. anthracinus* (N Co, N Ve, Tr, NW Gu)

Habits Usually alone or in pairs, perching quietly for long periods, semi-hidden or, less often in open. Sometimes a small group (3–4) soars together. Feeds on crabs and small vertebrates, caught by still-hunting from low perch at water's edge or by walking on mudflats or even wading in shallows. May take dead fish and other carrion. Calls often.
Status Frequent in Colombia (especially on Caribbean coast), locally common in Venezuela, common in Trinidad but scarce on Tobago, and situation uncertain in Guyana. Sight records on coastal French Guiana require confirmation.
Habitat Tropical Zone (occasionally to Subtropical). Mostly near streams and wetlands: forested and open swamps, riparian woods, foothill forests, savannas with scattered copses or trees, coastal lagoons, tidal flats, and mangroves on Caribbean coast (mangroves on Pacific coast are in range of Mangrove Black Hawk).
Voice Call, usually in flight, a series of 10–15 sharp whistles, *klee klee klee KLEE KLEE klee klee kle ke ke ki ki*, that increase in loudness and then peter off, becoming softer and slower, and sometimes in shorter version, e.g. *klee KLEE keer ker* (F-L&C). Alternate transcription, an urgent-sounding high, thin, piping *spink-speenk-speenk-spink-spink-spink-spink*, rising then descending slightly (Hilty).
Notes Sometimes treated as conspecific with *B. subtilis* (H&B, R&G). We follow AOU (1998). Call description in H&B (from Slud 1964) corresponds to *B. subtilis*.

MANGROVE BLACK HAWK

Buteogallus subtilis Pl. 33, In flight Pl. 34

Identification 39–47cm. Overall dark brown with paler fringes to feathers affording subtle scaled effect to back, and barring below; wings barred darker as well as having pale-fringed feathers, tail black with narrow white terminal bar and broad white band positioned centrally; eyes brown, skin, cere and most of bill (tip dark), legs and feet yellow. Immature has head and underparts pale buffy, streaked dark brown, thighs barred, tail with buffy tip and several pale grey bars. Difficult to separate from Common Black Hawk, except by habitat and rufous base to secondaries and inner primaries.

Ssp. *B. s. subtilis* (W Co, W Ec)

Habits Usually solitary or in pairs. Perches on low branches or stumps for long periods, calmly surveying surroundings for crabs, which are its main food, or walks on mudflats or even wades in shallows to hunt them. Occasionally feeds on carrion.
Status Uncommon in Ecuador and few records in Colombia.
Habitat Lower Tropical Zone. Coastal mangroves and mangrove swamps on Pacific coast, occasionally in the surroundings and adjacent beach scrub.
Voice Indistinguishable from calls of Common Black Hawk. Also, a loud series of ringing, whistled, 'spinking' notes.
Note Considered a subspecies of *B. anthracinus* in H&B, R&G. We follow AOU (1998). No intergradation between the in areas where they come into contact (F-L&C).

GREAT BLACK HAWK

Buteogallus urubitinga

Pl. 33, In flight plate 34

Identification 64cm. Adult all black except broad white band across basal half of tail, and a narrow white terminal bar; eyes brown, facial skin and cere pale orange, legs and feet yellow. Immature similar but has white fringes to feathers of head, wing-coverts and underparts, becoming distinct bars on flanks and thighs; facial skin and cere dull, almost greenish-yellow. Juvenile dark brown above with rufescent fringes to back and wing-coverts, tertials and flight-feathers barred black, rump narrowly barred black and pale grey, uppertail-coverts white, tail narrowly and evenly barred black and buff; entire head and underparts rufous, with prominent teardrop streaks on crown, neck-sides, lower throat and breast, flanks with double-crossed streaks and thighs finely barred black; eyes dark, facial skin and cere grey, legs and feet yellow. From Common Black Hawk by white uppertail-coverts.

Ssp. *B. u. urubitinga* (all countries) as described
B. u. ridgwayi? (Central American subspecies may wander from Panama to NW Chocó) additional white band on black tail (thus, tail has 2 white bands plus narrow white tips) and white-barred thighs, also white spots and flecks on underwing-coverts and flanks

Habits Usually alone or sometimes in pairs, soaring high. Perches inside canopy or sometimes atop tall trees. Attends savanna fires to prey upon escaping animals. Calls often, both when perched and in flight.
Status Very extensive range, unaffected by human occupation. Uncommon and local to rare in Ecuador, uncommon in Colombia, uncommon to locally frequent in Venezuela, scarce in Trinidad, uncommon on Tobago, frequent in Guyana and common in Suriname and French Guiana.
Habitat Tropical to Lower Subtropical Zones. Humid to semi-dry forests, dry scrub, forest swamps, gallery and riparian forests, mangroves, second growth, open woodland, patchily wooded savanna and pastures. Always near streams or wetlands.

Voice Calls include a high-pitched thin *keeeeeeh*, sometimes extended, with the second half rising *keeeeeeheeeeee*. Also, a loud *wheeeeeeuur* alarm and long series of a rapid *bi... bi... bi... bi...* ticking notes (F-L&C). A high-pitched whistled scream *wheeeeeeeuur* (Hilty).
Note Race *ridgwayi* sometimes considered a separate species, but intermediates occur in Panama.

SAVANNA HAWK *Buteogallus meridionalis*
Pl. 35, In flight Pl. 34

Identification 51–64cm. Adult mainly rufous, some have a greyish wash to head, back and fore underparts, wings with some darker centres to greater coverts, and tertials brown with rufous fringes, tail dark brown with broad white band positioned centrally; underparts finely barred dark brown, bolder on undertail-coverts; soft parts yellow. Immature has dark brown back, median and greater coverts, rufous flight-feathers finely barred darker, 3 white tail bars (narrow, broad and narrow); head and underparts pale buff, streaked brown on head, neck- and body-sides, thighs and undertail-coverts barred buff, rufous and black; soft parts as adult. A large, long-winged hawk; adults mainly rufous, with big, rounded wings that appear too large.

Ssp. Monotypic (all countries except ABC)

Habits Perches very upright on both high and low spots (bare branches, poles, fenceposts, stumps, tops of bushes, dirt mounds), languidly surveying surroundings. Usually alone (quite frequently along roads), occasionally soaring in small groups of 2–3 birds, exceptionally up to a dozen at sites with abundant or easy prey, such as savanna fires, where they walk boldly near the burning grass.
Status Uncommon to locally frequent in Ecuador. In Colombia, common east of Andes but uncommon in north; in Venezuela very common throughout; common in Trinidad but rare in Tobago; common in Guyana, frequent in Suriname and uncommon in coastal French Guiana. Resident in northern South America but larger birds from southern populations move north as far as Colombia and possibly Venezuela.
Habitat Tropical Zone. Open areas with scattered trees or copses, forest edge, savannas and pastures, swamps and marshes, cultivated areas, mangroves, riparian forests.
Voice Seldom calls: a long harsh whistle that ends in a wail, *eeeeee-eh* or *kree-ee-ee-er*, or *skieeeeh* (H&B, P&MdS) and *keeeeeeru* (Hilty). Also a short snarl when alarmed (F-L&C).
Notes Birds from Argentina, *rufulus*, are distinctly larger and darker. Considered monotypic by Bierregaard (where 2 larger, austral races considered invalid), but treated as polytypic in R&G. Formerly placed in *Heterospizias*, a monotypic genus, but here merged in *Buteogallus*, following AOU (1998).

SOLITARY EAGLE
Harpyhaliaetus solitarius
Pl. 35, In flight Pl. 34

Identification 66–71cm. Adult is entirely black except broad white tail band positioned centrally, and narrow white terminal bar; eyes orange, facial skin and cere yellow, legs and feet yellow. Juvenile dark brown instead of black, with pale cinnamon head and breast to flanks, long black streaks on crown, teardrop streaks on nape, breast and flanks (very dense on breast), slight scalloping on back and tail barred finely black; eyes more sepia than orange. Tail is so short that in flight, when fanned, barely extends beyond edge of wing, giving bird a somewhat tailless shape.

Ssp. *H. s. solitarius* (Co, Ve, Ec, FG)

Habits Usually alone, occasionally in pairs, soaring high with wings flat, making wide circles and calling frequently. Behaviour poorly known. Apparently feeds mainly on snakes. Perches on high bare branches and sometimes sweeps downslope in fast glides.
Status Rare in Ecuador, very local in Colombia and Venezuela. Several well circumstanced sight records in French Guiana, at two sites in the north, and around Saül in the interior.
Habitat Upper Tropical to Temperate Zones. Forested valleys and montane slopes with humid, wet and cloud forests.
Voice Calls when soaring or cruising, a series of far-carrying whistled notes: *pee-pee-pee-peeeee, pee-pee-pee-peeeee*...oft repeated (I. Goodwin). Sometimes a slow *weet weet weet* or *yeep yeep yeep* in flight and long, mighty whistles *keeeeeeeeeer looooooooooo* when perched (H&B, F-L&C).
Note Called Black Solitary Eagle in F-L&C, to differentiate it from the Crowned Solitary Eagle of Brazil, which is simply called Crowned Eagle by Sick (1993).

Busarellus hawks are distinguished mainly by having very broad wings and spiny soles to the pads on their feet. They are mainly rufous-coloured.

BLACK-COLLARED HAWK
Busarellus nigricollis Pl. 35, In flight Pl. 34

Identification 46–51cm. Adult has white head, large black patch on central throat and breast, and entire body except primaries, tips of secondaries and tail, black; fine black streaks on nape and back, black lines on centres of median, greater coverts and tertials, and at edge of black throat patch on breast; eyes red, facial skin and cere grey, legs and feet blue-grey. Immature has two distinct morphs, both essentially the same basic coloration as adult, except the tail, which is barred, and breast, which is buffy: dark phase very heavily streaked black and has tail barred evenly black and rufous, with a terminal black band; throat patch extends to neck-sides and rear ear-coverts. The pale phase is only slightly more streaked on head than adult, but heavier elsewhere, and only the basal half of the tail is barred, the rest is all black, and the throat patch larger. Look for whitish head and black throat collar, very broad wings and short tail.

Ssp. *B. n. nigricollis* (all countries)

Habits Usually alone or in pairs, occasionally a small group; soars gracefully or perches indolently, but is not shy, most often near water and in open spots (a high bare branch, roadside pole).

Sometimes cruises over swamps or marshes. Seldom calls.
Status Rare in Ecuador, where only sight records available, but common but fairly local in Colombia, where particularly found on swampy river islands in Amazon. Common in Venezuela, especially in the Llanos. Uncommon and local visitor to Trinidad, frequent in Guyana, common in Suriname, and quite common in coastal French Guiana.
Habitat Lower Tropical Zone. Always around fresh or brackish wetlands with either forested or open shores, and stagnant or slow-moving shallows. Mangroves, marshes, swamps, reservoirs, dykes and borrowing pits along roads, rice paddies, *Mauritia* palm bogs, large marshy river islands.
Voice Calls very varied. A rising and falling *wheeeeeeeah* whistle (J. V. Remsen) or a slow-rising plaintive whistle *wuuueeeeeeeeEEE* and clear downslurred whistle *shreeeuur* (Hilty); a sudden, harsh *BEEyurrr* cry; croaks similar to a heron's; a double cough *he-ehh* and an insect-like buzz that slows into dry ticking (P&MdS, H&B, F-L&C).

BLACK-CHESTED BUZZARD-EAGLE
Geranoaetus melanoleucus

Pl. 33, In flight Pl. 34

Identification 65–80 cm. Very large. Very dark grey above and on breast, with grey lesser and median wing-coverts, greyish face and white terminal tail bar, some small white spots on back and breast; rear underparts white with narrow black bars; eyes red, facial skin, cere, legs and feet yellow. Immature similar but has wing-coverts brownish admixed grey, upper flanks barred narrowly pale grey, and back, flanks, thighs and undertail-coverts finely barred deep tawny and buff; eyes yellow, facial skin and cere greyish-yellow. Juvenile has scapulars barred black and rufous, entire wings brown-grey barred narrowly black; narrow whitish eyebrow, and some fine whitish streaking on face and throat, breast and neck-sides rufous heavily marked with fuscous, upper flanks barred narrowly pale grey and black, rest of underparts barred deep tawny and buff. Adult's wingtips longer than tail. Juvenile separated from juvenile Solitary Eagle by pale chest (vs. streaked) and generally dark underwing.

Ssp. *G. m. australis* (Ec, Co, Ve)

Habits Usually alone or in pairs, flies beautifully, soaring high in graceful circles for long periods, climbing with thermals in front of cliff faces or sometimes cruising over forests, the wings in a slight dihedral with upturned wingtips. May hover occasionally.
Status Uncommon to rare in Ecuador, locally frequent in mountain canyons in Colombia; locally frequent in the Andes and Neblina in Venezuela, where it may occasionally reach lower slopes.
Habitat Tropical Zone to Páramo. Open and semi-open areas, savannas, pastures, xerophytic areas, thorny woods and dry scrub, rocky canyons and ravines, open grassland or shrubby fields on higher slopes and near páramos. In Venezuela, forested slopes.

Black-chested Buzzard-eagle soaring, drawn from photos of the same bird to show how profile and tail can look different on a raptor, depending on the angle (after photos by Rob Williams)

Voice Call a ringing, drawn-out *keeeeuua* or *kiiua*, often repeated several times (F&K, F-L&C). Also, reedy whistles and cackling in alarm. In flight, a high-pitched *ku-keeu* and ringing *ku ku ku ku ku* (R&G). Occasional high, reedy whistles (Hilty).
Notes Called an eagle-buzzard in F-L&C. Perhaps best placed in genus *Buteo* based on genetic data (Riesing *et al.* 2003).

HARRIS'S HAWK *Parabuteo unicinctus*

Pl. 33, In flight Pl. 34

Identification 48–56cm. Entire upper body including wings deep fuscous, with lesser and median wing-coverts deep chestnut, thighs chestnut; vent, under and uppertail-coverts white, tail black with pale tips; eyes brown, facial skin, cere, legs and feet yellow. Immature is browner version of adult, with all feathers rufous-fringed; from chin to belly washed rufous with teardrop streaks, thighs barred.

Ssp. *P. u. harrisi* (W Co, Ec) as described
P. u. unicinctus (NE Co, Ve) faint white barring on lower sides, flanks and thighs; immature has tail conspicuously barred fuscous

Habits Usually in pairs or trios that hunt cooperatively, sometimes in groups of a dozen or more. Still-hunts or walks on ground to catch prey, and may occasionally feed on carrion. Flies very fast and soars often, not very high.
Status Range very extensive, with perhaps migrants from both northern and southern limits of range reaching our region. Rare to locally frequent in Ecuador; common but local in north Colombia, across dry Caribbean region.
Habitat Tropical to Subtropical Zones. Semi-open, drier lowlands and foothills, sometimes in swampy areas, patches of woods in savannas, pastures and grasslands with scattered trees, wooded marshes, dry cactus and thorny scrub.
Voice Infrequent calls described as grating nasal *jiirrr nyaaaah* screams and a soft *eee eee eee eee* in alarm near nest. Also repeated cackling (F-L&C).Call a short, wheezy *hu'u'u'u'u'* like exhaling air (Hilty).
Note Sometimes called Bay-winged Hawk.

Buteo hawks, sometimes called buzzards, form a large genus of medium-sized, stocky raptors with broad wings and broad rounded tails. Several are very polymorphic The group is characteristic of light, open woodland and forest edges, seldom being found inside forest. They are often seen soaring and usually spread their tails wide when doing so. The tail-bands are usually diagnostic. They have short outer primaries with a curved trailing edge, and normally hunt by sitting silently, waiting and watching.

ROADSIDE HAWK *Buteo magnirostris*

Pl. 35, In flight Pl. 34

Identification 33–40cm. Adult dark grey above, from forehead to tail, primaries rufous (barred darker) except black tips, uppertail-coverts have grey fringes, the tail 3 grey bars; throat white streaked finely rufous, breast and rest of underparts dark rufescent grey, barred faintly from lower breast and back with white. Immature mid grey above, from forehead to tail, back and wings fringed rufous, primaries rufous (barred darker) except black tips, uppertail-coverts barred grey and black, tail has 3 grey bars; underparts white streaked finely rufous on throat, barred lightly rufous from breast to flanks, faintly on thighs. Separated from somewhat similar *Buteo* species by fiery yellow eyes and dark bib.

Ssp. *B. m. insidiatrix* (NW Co, N Ve) pale blue-grey head to tail, with rufous on wings and bands on tail, throat to breast and sides pale blue-grey, rest of underparts closely barred grey and white

B. m. magnirostris (E Ec, E Co, S Ve, Guianas) darker, browner grey, with broader, more rufescent barring below

B. m. ecuadoriensis (SW Co, W Ec) upperparts paler, purer grey, tail-bands suffused tawny

Habits Alone, in pairs or occasionally in small (3–4) noisy, circling groups. Perches lazily for long periods in understorey, on roadside poles and wires, fences and bare branches. When excited, wags tail nervously. Attends savanna fires to prey upon escaping animals. Soars only occasionally, flight pattern consists of glides alternated with short wingbeats.

Status Uncommon to locally common in Ecuador. In Colombia and Venezuela, the most common hawk in a wide variety of habitats, frequent in Guyana, common in Suriname and French Guiana. Populations benefit from forest clearance.

Habitat Tropical to Subtropical Zones. Many lightly wooded and semi-open areas and edges of wet, humid, deciduous or dry forests. Gallery forests, scrub, well-treed cities and towns; plantations, wooded savannas, agricultural areas and pastures with scattered groves.

Voice Calls both perched or in flight. Main call is a somewhat angry-sounding, whistled *shweeeeeeeeeee* that drops and fades, but sometimes gives an irritated *ki-ki-ki-ki*… or cackling *cla-cla-cla-cla*… (C. Sharpe, H&B). A nasal, angry-sounding *kzeeeeeer*, buzzy and descending in pitch (Hilty).

Notes Up to 20 races have been described, but most authors regard at least some of these as synonyms. Races *insidiatrix* and *ecuadoriensis* have both been considered synonyms of *magnirostris*, most recently by Bierregaard, but they are clearly differentiated by Blake, and recognised by P&MdS and F-L&C. Riesing *et al.* (2003) proposed resurrection of monotypic genus *Rupornis* for this species.

WHITE-TAILED HAWK

Buteo albicaudatus Pl. 35, In flight Pl. 34

Identification 53–60cm. Confusingly varied, with different morphs varying by subspecies as well as due to individual variation. White-breasted forms may have dark throats. Note that dark-throated morph of race *hypospodius* is very much like race *albicaudatus*, which does not occur in our region. Adult grey morph or normal *colonus* is mid grey from forehead to rump, faintly and regularly barred on wings, scapulars and lesser wing-coverts rufous, fore face whitish, underparts entirely white with faint grey barring on flanks; uppertail-coverts and tail white, finely barred grey with a broad subterminal black band; eyes brown, facial skin, cere, legs and feet dull yellow. A variant (morph?) has entire head grey, with white only on breast and below. Dark morph (rare east of Andes) is similar to the normal in pattern, but is very dark slate grey, including chin and throat. Wingtips obviously longer than tail. From Red-backed by rufous shoulders.

Ssp. *B. a. colonus* (E Co, Ve: E & Margarita I.; Ar, Cu, Bo, Tr, Guianas) as described

B. a. hypospodius (N Co, NW Ve) larger and darker above, immaculate white below; immature has chin and entire throat dark grey

Habits Usually in pairs, soars high over fields and near mountains and cliffs, taking advantage of updrafts. Hunts by cruising leisurely over semi-open areas, hovering stationary on noticing prey, and then diving down. It often attends savanna fires, where it pounces on escaping animals. Perches frequently on or near ground, and on poles and wires.

Status In Ecuador, past reports are considered by R&G to be misidentified Variable Hawks; frequent to locally common in Colombia; present in Aruba, Curaçao and Bonaire, where scarce and local, but most numerous in Curaçao; frequent in Venezuela, scarce in Trinidad (does not occur on Tobago), frequent in Guyana and Suriname, and uncommon in French Guiana.

Habitat Tropical to Subtropical Zones. Open or semi-open drier areas: savannas, dry scrub, cactus deserts, grass and pastureland, very patchy woodland, especially near hills and mountains.

Voice Rarely calls (except when breeding): a series of loud whistles *kee-kee-kee-kee*… (H&B) *kerwee kerwee kerwee*… or *keela keela keela*…, a hoarse, barked *ack kehack kehack*, and a *gliehh klia-klia-klia gheulii* in courtship.

BROAD-WINGED HAWK

Buteo platypterus Pl. 36, In flight Pl. 37

Identification 35–43cm. Either several morphs or much individual variation. Dark morph is rare, black morph very rare. Adult brownish above, from forehead to tail, with some streaking on head, a few paler streaks on back, pale fringes to uppertail-coverts, 2 pale bars on tail, which also has pale tips; slightly rufescent head-sides, streaked brown, breast to flanks pale orange-rufous, but almost white on flanks, with rufous arrowhead streaks, thighs rufous with narrow dark barring, undertail-coverts white; brown eyes, yellow cere, legs and feet. Juvenile dark brown above, heavily streaked, with pale fringes to uppertail-coverts, and *c.*7 narrow black tail bars. Dark (?) morph slightly darker brown above, barred rufous, black and white below, with black spots and streaks on breast and sides. Dark morph also described (F-L&C) as being entirely dark brown with a single broad pale tail bar, and narrow pale terminal wingbar. Black morph (or melanistic individual?) is entirely black. Wingtips reach only halfway down long tail.

Ssp. *B. p. platypterus* (winters all countries) as described
B. p. antillarum (To) smaller and more solidly rufous on breast

Habits On migration, large flocks (several hundred) gather, but by the time they reach Colombia and Venezuela have dispersed, thus in winter range, usually solitary, perching lethargically on poles, wires and subcanopy branches at forest edge. Catches prey by still-hunting from a perch, or by soaring or flying at treetop level to dive upon prey.

Status Boreal migrant, winters mainly in or near Andes, from October to March. Uncommon to rare transient in Ecuador. In Colombia, common both as a transient and winter resident, with stragglers as late as April. Locally common in Venezuela. Uncommon in Trinidad but common in Tobago (where has bred, though unclear if it is a year-round resident, as numbers occasionally swelled by migrants); sight records only in Guyana, where scarce. In Suriname, only known from recent sight records (listed in SFP&M, but not in H&M). Uncommon in French Guiana.

Habitat Partially open areas adjacent to forest but never in forest, plantations, patchy secondary woodland, cultivated areas and fields with scattered groves of trees. Often near water (streams, lakes, ponds, marshy areas).

Voice Calls include a weak, sad whistle, described as *sueeee-oh*, *seeeeeeu* or *siiiiiiu*, and also *kreee eee eee ee, pweeeee* or *kwer-wee-wee-wee* (H&B, F&K, F-L&C). Also, adults and young of both sexes give a piercing *p-teeeeeee* cry, perched or in flight (R&G).

WHITE-RUMPED HAWK

Buteo leucorrhous Pl. 36, In flight Pl. 37

Identification 35–38cm. Mainly black, with narrow white rump (whitish or pale grey fringes to uppertail-coverts) and undertail-coverts; thighs barred evenly rufous, black and white. Dark morph has black thighs, the pale morph a small white forehead patch and white underparts. Two morphs in immature; pale phase has white throat. Pale morph is rare, the dark best separated from dark-morph Broad-winged Hawk by pale creamy wing-linings and undertail-coverts. White rump is a good mark in soaring birds.

Ssp. Monotypic (Ec, Co, N & W Ve)

Habits Usually alone or in pairs, soaring low over forest. At times, gives long repetitions of calls in flight, or from a perch whilst wagging tail.

Status Rare in Ecuador, where mostly found on west slope; scarce, local and spottily distributed throughout Colombia and northern and western Venezuela.

Habitat Subtropical to Temperate Zones, in extensive pristine forests on upper slopes (humid and cloud forests). Clearings, borders and land washes.

Voice Calls include short, whistled *pyee* cries, sometimes repeated endlessly (H&B, F&K); and a high-pitched *squeeeuh* squeal, that may end with a tremolo, *squeeeh-uh-uhuh* (R&G).

Note Riesing *et al.* (2003) recommended this species be transferred to the genus *Percnohierax*.

SHORT-TAILED HAWK

Buteo brachyurus Pl. 36, In flight Pl. 37

Identification 35–41cm. Adult pale morph is dull black above with 5 black bars on dark grey tail, white below, usually with some blackish on sides of foreneck. Wingtips reach tail tip; eyes reddish, skin, cere, legs and feet yellow. Immature finely streaked white on head, upperparts dark brown rather than blackish, with slightly paler fringes to feathers. Dark morph entirely sooty black, perhaps with a small white forehead and fore face, and a few white fringes on nape, tail dark grey with black bars. Immature dark morph streaked below with pale buffy fringes to feathers, and barred on thighs.

Ssp. *B. b. brachyurus* (all countries)

Habits Usually alone, soaring very high. Rarely seen perched exposed, but occasionally perches semi-hidden to still-hunt. Mainly hunts from air, cruising low above canopy or hovering stationary and then diving onto prey.

Status Uncommon in Ecuador, uncommon and thinly spread in Colombia, uncommon in Trinidad, rare on Tobago, uncommon in Guyana, rare in Suriname and frequent in French Guiana.

Habitat Tropical to Subtropical Zones. Always near water (lakes, ponds, rivers) in humid forest, forested marshes, wooded savanna, mangroves, scrubby woods, wet grasslands, pine or oak forests on montane slopes, open areas next to forest.

Voice Seldom calls except when breeding and near nest, these being described as a shrill, piercing *sheee reee eea* and softer *keeeea* or *klee* as well as cackling cries (F&K, F-L&C). When soaring, a short nasal *keeer*, almost like the distant mewing of a kitten (Hilty).

WHITE-THROATED HAWK

Buteo albigula Pl. 36, In flight Pl. 37

Identification 41–48cm. Adult brown above, darker on head, with some subtle buffy fringes to back and wings, tail has 6–7 black bars; underparts white, streaked on sides of face, breast and flanks, thighs barred rufous. Immature very similar but more heavily streaked below (these being more teardrop-shaped), thighs barred black, rufous and white. Apparently, there is a rare dark morph, but we have not seen a specimen. From Short-tailed by longer, many-banded tail and dark trailing edge to secondaries. Juveniles have quite plain underwings.

Ssp. Monotypic (Ec, Co: C & W Andes; N & W Ve)

Habits Seems to soar rather infrequently. Most behavioural aspects similar to Short-tailed Hawk (R&G).
Status Rare in Ecuador, rare and local in Colombia, and scarce in Venezuela.
Habitat Subtropical Zone to Páramo. Humid montane forests, cloud and especially elfin forests, forest patches in páramo, *Eucalyptus* plantations.
Voice Seldom calls except when breeding and near nest, these being described as high, piercing *kee-ah* or *kee-ea* cries (M. Pearman, F&K).
Note High-altitude allospecies of *brachyurus*, and sometimes treated as conspecific, although where they overlap no hybridisation or intergradation has been found.

SWAINSON'S HAWK

Buteo swainsoni Pl. 36, In flight Pl. 37

Identification 46–52cm. Extremely variable with several morphs, the pale being the commonest and easiest to identify, and the dark separated from other dark *Buteo* by dark flight-feathers. Adult pale morph is brown above with buffy-rufous fringes to feathers, pale to whitish tips to uppertail-coverts, *c.*7 narrow dark tail bars and a broader subterminal band, tips of tail whitish; white throat and malar, ruddy breast, rest of underparts white with some brown or rufous barring on flanks and thighs; eyes sepia to brown, facial skin, cere, legs and feet yellow. Immature as adult above but pale fringes more noticeable; head, upper mantle and underparts buffy white, streaked dark brown on head and mantle, finely on face-sides, some heavy spot-streaks on breast-sides and pale brown barring on lower sides; eyes yellowish. Adult red morph has short narrow pale eyebrow, dark brown breast and ruddy flanks and thighs, all narrowly barred dark brown, undertail-coverts white barred ruddy. Dark morph entirely dark brown except lightly streaked pale to whitish throat, and undertail-coverts barred brown and white. Flight outline distinctive: soars high, on stiff, relatively raised, narrow wings with long tips, crisscrossing in wide circles.

Ssp. Monotypic (Ec; Co: E & C Andes; W Ve, To)

Habits Perches on exposed or vegetated branches, and seems lethargic, but is very fast in flight. It is suspected of not feeding during migration.
Status Boreal migrant, winters mainly in Argentina. Rare transient in Ecuador, uncommon on migration and a very rare winter resident in Colombia, and rare transient in Venezuela; rare accidental in Tobago (not recorded in Trinidad). Ecuador and Colombia records are from November and March, stragglers in December and April. Venezuela records are from September and November. Most records are of singles but small groups infrequently encountered in Ecuador and Colombia.
Habitat Upper Tropical to Subtropical Zones. Open and semi-open areas of various types: savannas, grasslands, agricultural fields, montane pastures. Sometimes open areas along rivers.
Voice Usually does not call on migration or in winter.

RED-TAILED HAWK

Buteo jamaicensis Pl. 36, In flight Pl. 37

Identification 47–60cm. Large, broad-winged hawk, all brown above with barred wings, uppertail-coverts and tail cinnamon-brown to rufous above and usually pinkish to almost white below, always with a narrow dark subterminal band and white terminal tip. Underparts range from all white (*borealis*) through white with rufous thighs (*costaricensis*) to entirely rufous (*calurus*); eyes brown, facial skin, cere, legs and feet yellow.

Ssp. *B. j. calurus*? (Co, W Ve)

Habits Frequently soars, sometimes quite high.
Status Boreal migrant, accidental to Colombia and Venezuela, well south-east of its normal winter range in Central America and the Caribbean. In Colombia, sight records from Central Andes (SCJ&W). In Venezuela, sight record from Mérida (Hilty 1999).
Habitat In breeding range, quite varied, from forests to open fields and pastures with scattered trees. In winter, possibly also humid and cloud forests. Always in areas where it can perch high. Recorded to 3,200m.
Voice Calls include a long, fading, sibilant *shee ee eee* whistle, and in alarm, a loud, repeated *chwirk* screech. Juveniles make softer calls.
Notes Possibly 14 valid races; those breeding in boreal regions are migratory. Some western races migrate to Central America, with *calurus* known to reach Panama (Peters, vol. I). Thus, SCJ&W considered that birds observed in Colombia could be *calurus*. The body colour of the bird with a full rufous tail observed by S. Hilty & K. J. Zimmer in Venezuela was not noted.

RED-BACKED HAWK

Buteo polyosoma Pl. 38, In flight Pl. 37

Identification 45–53cm, W *c.*120cm. Extremely polymorphic (see plate). Pale morphs are commonest everywhere. Far more variation among females and juveniles than adult males. Compared with Puna Hawk, it hovers with very floppy wingbeats, inverted on the back strokes but will hang-hover in wind. Flies on shallow stiff wingbeats, and soars with flatter wings (F&K). Appears smaller-winged and longer-tailed in flight than Puna. When perched, wingtips reach halfway down tail (on Puna Hawk to tip of tail).

Ssp. *B. p. polyosoma* (W & C Ec, SW Co)

Habits Hunts mostly mammals.
Status Common in Ecuador and Colombia.

Habitat Open hillsides of coastal lowlands to lower Temperate Zone, 1,600–3,200m, in a variety of open to semi-forested habitats, though mainly in dry, scrubby areas with scattered trees, cliffs, gorges and steep rocky slopes.

Voice Occasional *keeeow-kyow-kyow* (F&K) or shrill *keeyah* when soaring (F-L&C).

Note United with *poecilochrous* under *B. polyosoma* as Variable Hawk by Farquhar (1998), and followed by R&G. We follow AOU (1998), Ferguson-Lees (2001) and Dickinson (2003) in retaining the 2 forms as separate species.

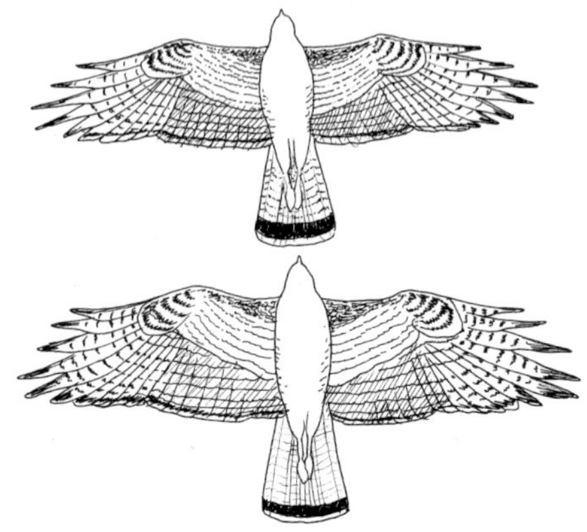

Comparative size and wing formula of lowland Red-backed Hawk P. polyosoma *(above) and the highland Puna Hawk* P. poecilochrous

PUNA HAWK

Buteo poecilochrous Pl. 38, In flight Pl. 37

Identification 50–70cm, W*c*.125–150. Extremely polymorphic (see plate). Pale morphs commonest everywhere. Far more variation among females and juveniles than adult males. Larger-winged than Red-backed and has large rounded wings with short-looking tail in flight. Wingbeats soft and often hang-hovers with a few gentle strokes. When perched, wingtips reach tip of tail (but wings narrower and tail longer on juvenile).

Ssp. Monotypic (W & C Ec, SW & SC Co)

Habits Soars high over ridges and valleys with wings more raised than Red-backed Hawk. Prey is mammals but takes significant quantities of insects and some birds.

Status Generally uncommon in Ecuador, though slightly more frequent to common at a few localities. In Colombia, situation uncertain, with only 1 confirmed record (Cabot *et al.* 2006).

Habitat Subtropical to Temperate Zones, 2,800–5,000m. Cliffs, gorges and steep rocky slopes, forest edges, treeline, stands of *Polylepis*, montane agricultural areas and pastures, almost always between timberline and snowline.

Voice Long, drawn-out *peeeeoo* ranging from a copious cry to a thin whistle. A *hee hee hee* in display (F&K).

Note United under *B. polyosoma* as Variable Hawk by Farquhar (1998), followed by R&G. We follow AOU (1998), Ferguson-Lees (2001) and Dickinson (2003) in retaining the 2 forms as separate species.

ZONE-TAILED HAWK

Buteo albonotatus Pl. 38, In flight Pl. 37

Identification 48–53cm. Slender. Wingtips reach tip of tail. Adult dull black with 3 white tail bars, 2 narrow, near base of tail, the other broader further down, and narrow white tip; eyes pale brown, facial skin and cere dull greyish-yellow, legs and feet yellow. Immature similar but has narrow black-and-white barring over entire tail, and subterminal black bar broader. Glides with wings in a dihedral, like a Turkey Vulture, and easily dismissed as such. Differs in long, narrow tail with visible white band and in underwing pattern.

Ssp. Monotypic (W Ec, N Co, N & SE Ve, Tr, Gu, Su, FG)

Habits Usually alone, forages mostly over open country, soaring leisurely and diving suddenly to pick prey from ground or tree.

Zone-tailed Hawk (left) flies with the same dihedral as Turkey Vulture (right) and may easily be passed off for the latter, but the dark trailing edge to the wing is best field mark, as the barred tail is not always easy to see

Status Both boreal migrants (October–March), and breeding residents occur in northern South America. Rare in Ecuador (sight records only), locally frequent in Colombia and Venezuela, uncommon resident in Trinidad (does not occur on Tobago), uncommon in Guyana, rare in Suriname and locally common in French Guiana.

Habitat Tropical to Temperate Zones. Hilly, broken or montane country of all types: wet to dry or even semi-desertic, densely forested to completely open, but always with water in the surroundings. Montane forests, coniferous, oak and deciduous woods, thorny scrub, marshes, pastures and fields.

Voice Calls include a long, dramatic *keeeeeer* whistle, in typical *Buteo* manner, a high-pitched *kra, kree-kree-kree…* in contact between pairs during display flights, and a lower, more drawn-out *raa aa aa uu* in alarm (F-L& C). An infrequent squealing whistle (Hilty).

Note South American populations are sometimes accorded subspecific status, as *abbreviatus*, but this is not generally accepted.

CRESTED EAGLE

Morphnus guianensis Pl. 39, In flight Pl. 40

Identification 81–86cm. Adult pale morph has head entirely grey with longer crest feathers darker, upperparts fuscous, barred black, tail has 3 broad grey bars, cheeks and throat paler grey, breast as head, underparts white evenly barred rufous, but thighs barred narrower; eyes grey, sepia or dull yellowish, facial skin and cere black, legs and feet dull yellow. Dark morph has head, breast and upperparts charcoal grey with black barring and 3 grey tail bars; underparts barred black and white, more finely on thighs and undertail-coverts. Black morph has underparts dull black with black shadow-barring and fine white fringes to breast and flanks. Intermediates between morphs exist, and between different age-related plumages. Immature mid grey above, spotted and barred black, tail has 6 grey bars, head and breast paler dusky grey, even paler on face, rest of underparts white with some irregular dusky barring on flanks and thighs. Juvenile pale grey above, spotted and barred, tail all grey with 8–9 irregular and narrow black bars, head and underparts white, washed grey over short crest, nape and breast.

Ssp. Monotypic (Ec, Co, Ve, Gu, Su, FG)

Habits Usually alone or in pairs, perched high on an exposed branch, where often remains for long periods, or soars in circles above forest. From Harpy Eagle by smaller, more slender body, proportionately larger head with single-pointed crest (Harpy's split), longer tail and narrower wings.

Status Widespread but generally scarce. Locally rare to very rare in Ecuador, rare and less common than Harpy in Colombia and Venezuela, scarce in Guyana, rare in Suriname, uncommon in French Guiana.

Habitat Tropical Zone. Humid, pristine forests in lowlands and foothills, gallery forests, wet forests in gorges and ravines, tall mature secondary wood and semi-open woodlands.

Voice Calls include shrill 2-part whistles that increase in pitch and resemble those of Great Black Hawk (F-L&C), and loud *wheyr-wheyr-wheyr-wheyr-wheyr-brrr* screams.

HARPY EAGLE

Harpia harpyja Pl. 39, In flight Pl. 40

Identification 86–93cm. Awesome, with a magnificent mien. Adult has grey head, darker on forked crest and nape, black upperparts and breast, and 3 broad tail bars; underparts white, with thighs and upper front part of legs feathered and barred black and white; eyes yellow-grey, facial skin and cere black, unfeathered part of legs and feet yellow. Legs, feet and rear talons thick and huge. Observed at the nest, the female is noticeably larger than the male, the young are downy but with an incipient crest.

Ssp. Monotypic (Ec, Co, Ve, Gu, Su, FG)

Habits Alone or in pairs, cruising and occasionally rising above forests, but does not soar high, circling in accepted sense. Occasionally perches on a high exposed branch. Forages by flying low above canopy or through it, to pick prey from branches, nimbly and with amazing speed. Main prey is monkeys, porcupines, sloths and cracids.

Status Rare and local in Ecuador and Colombia, locally frequent in southern Venezuela, scarce in Guyana, rare in Suriname and uncommon in French Guiana.

Habitat Tropical to Lower Subtropical Zones. Lowlands and foothills: tall, pristine humid or wet forests with vast expanse of continuous canopy, though in some areas, tall secondary woods, savannas adjacent to forest and areas of broken forest with scattered clearings may also be used. Good populations of monkeys, sloths and other prey are a prerequisite.

Voice Calls include a loud *whee ee ee ee ee* or *whee ee oo oo oo* contact cry of the adults, a high-pitched *whee- e-e-e-e, whee-e-e-e-e…* by begging nestlings and dependent juveniles, and also soft croaks, whistles and mewing notes. (F-L&C).

BLACK-AND-WHITE HAWK-EAGLE

Spizastur melanoleucus

Pl. 38, In flight plate 37

Identification 56–60cm. Dark fuscous above with narrow black bars on wings, tail has 3 broad dull, buffy-grey bars and a pale tip, a short, usually laid-back black crest, but rest of head and underparts (including feathered legs) white; eyes yellow, facial skin black, cere orange, legs and feet yellow. Smaller than Ornate Hawk-Eagle with shorter crest and lacks any rufous. Look for pied aspect, large bill and flat head with short bushy crest, and wings extend halfway down tail. Further separated from Ornate Hawk-Eagle by orange (not yellow) cere, black lores and back.

Ssp. Monotypic (Ec, Co, Ve, Gu, Su, FG)

Habits Usually alone, sometimes in pairs, perching rather erect on high exposed branches or inside the canopy, or soaring in leisurely circles. Prey is caught by still-hunting from a perch, tail-chasing and diving from soaring flight.

Status Rare in Ecuador (first report 1980, sight records only), rare and very local in Colombia, uncommon in Venezuela and Guyana, rare in Suriname, and uncommon locally in French Guiana.

Habitat Tropical to Lower Subtropical Zones. Humid and wet lowland and foothill forests adjacent to open country, gallery forests, river and forest borders, patches of forest in wet savannas.

Voice Calls include piping whistles in flight, and shrill *kree-o-wow* screeches (H&B). Less vocal than other hawk-eagles. In flight occasionally gives a shrill, whistled *wheEEeer*, unlike that of Ornate Hawk-Eagle (Hilty).

Note Genus *Spizastur* should be subsumed within *Spizaetus* according to recent genetic data (Helbig *et al.* 2005).

ORNATE HAWK-EAGLE

Spizaetus ornatus Pl. 38, In flight Pl. 37

Identification 58–63cm. Slender but majestic, with rounded wings narrow at base affording butterfly-wing shape. Adult has back dark brown with large black subterminal spots, fringed white, on back and wings, flight-feathers barred, tail has 3 broad grey bars and a narrow pale tip; head bright rufous with a black crest, flat from forehead to crown, but springs erect at right angles, the central 2 feathers being longest, white throat separated by a thin black supra-malar line that forms a series of dashes on throat- to breast-sides, and separating the rufous from white central breast; rest of underparts barred solidly black and white, including entire legs, which are feathered; eyes orange, facial skin grey, cere and feet yellow. Immature has brown back with narrow bars on wings, several broad tail bars, entire head and underparts white, centre of crest feathers rufescent with a central black line, a few emerging rufous feathers on neck- and breast-sides of neck, and a few emerging black (crescent-shaped) bars on flanks and thighs. Look for erectile crest, feathered tarsi and wingtips that extend slightly below tail base. Grey-bellied Hawk has bare tarsi; Black Hawk-Eagle is always darker, the juveniles much less barred below.

Ssp. *S. o. ornatus* (E Co, E Ec, Ve, Tr, Gu, Su, FG) eyebrow and ear-coverts white, rufous only reaches neck-sides, barely to sides of breast, bars on sides broken and include a few spots, rest of bars slightly narrower, and thighs decidedly thinner with white bars broader
S. o. vicarius (W Co, W Ec) as described; brighter, more rufous on head and neck

Habits Usually alone or in pairs, circling and soaring high, especially in mornings, or perching in canopy of tall trees, from where it perch-hunts. Calls frequently.

Status Rare in Ecuador, uncommon in Colombia but slightly more frequent in Venezuela, uncommon in Trinidad, rare on Tobago, uncommon in Guyana, Suriname and French Guiana.

Habitat Tropical Zone. Humid to wet primary forests of lowlands and foothills, gallery and swamp forests, along rivers and roads, and in clearings. Mostly in extensive forest, but often near open country in Venezuelan Llanos.

Voice Calls include a whistled *whit, WHEEEEUU, whep, whep, whep, wheo* that is barely audible at start (H&B); pattern is opposite of Black Hawk-Eagle (Hilty), also cat cries and an excited laughter (F-L&C).

BLACK HAWK-EAGLE

Spizaetus tyrannus Pl. 39, In flight Pl. 40

Identification 63–71cm. Adult all black with 3 broad pale bars in tail, white in short bushy crest; thighs, legs and undertail-coverts finely and evenly barred black and white; eyes orange-yellow, facial skin and cere black, feet yellow. Immature dark greyish-brown above, spotted and heavily barred, with 5–6 bars on tail; crest white with black streaks, face-sides blackish, neck to breast and belly deep sepia with black streaks, flanks dark brown as back, streaked black; thighs, legs and undertail-coverts barred black and white. Look for short bushy crest, rounded wings narrower at base, feathered tarsi and long tail with several bars. Immature much darker below, with distinctive facial markings, than immature Black-and-chestnut Eagle.

Ssp. *S. t. serus* (Ec, Co, Ve, Gu, Su, FG)

Habits Usually alone, soaring high above forest, often circling repeatedly, calling frequently. Perches in subcanopy (seldom near treetops) to perch-hunt for mammals, reptiles and birds (cotingas, tanagers, caciques, araçaris, ducks, chachalacas, tinamous).

Status Rare to locally uncommon in eastern Ecuador (first sighted in west in 1970s), locally frequent in Colombia and Venezuela, infrequent visitor to Trinidad (never on Tobago), uncommon in Guyana, locally regular in Suriname, and common in French Guiana.

Habitat Humid lowland and foothill forests and secondary woodland, around large clearings and along rivers and borders.

Voice Calls frequently in flight, particularly in the morning, including a *wheep-wheep-wheep-waHEEER-er* with last note downslurred. Stressed note near end of series is diagnostic and opposite of Ornate Hawk-Eagle (Hilty). Also bursts of loud, ringing, rhythmic *tee, tee, tee, teeeeee* whistles, and a series of high-pitched, melodious, whistled notes *eee-eee-eh-i, i, i, i, ew-ur* (F-L&C). Responds well to playback.

BLACK-AND-CHESTNUT EAGLE

Oroaetus isidori Pl. 39, In flight Pl. 40

Identification 63–74cm. Adult male has entire head (except short white eyebrow), pointed crest, back and wings to tail-coverts black, tail grey with a broad subterminal black band; breast to undertail-coverts deep reddish-chestnut, thighs blackish, feathered legs deep chestnut; eyes orange-yellow, facial skin grey, cere and feet yellow. Immature has head ruddy brown with black streaks, breast even deeper ruddy with black streaks, throat white, rest of underparts buff with ruddy flushes and a few narrow black streaks, thighs dark brown, legs buffy with faint dusky bars; upperparts dark reddish-brown, tail grey with 2 narrow bars and a broad subterminal band. Juvenile has crown, crest, nape and mantle light brownish-grey with pale fringes to all feathers, scapulars dark brownish-grey with pale fringes, wing-coverts mid brown with pale fringes, tertials and remiges dark brown, with narrow white tips to tertials and secondaries, tail grey with 4 narrow dark bars and a broad subterminal band; underparts from cheeks to undertail-coverts and legs white; eyes yellow. Look for long wings that extend about one-third of way along tail from base, and pale windows in all plumages; crest always raised. Black and Ornate Hawk-Eagles have shorter wings and longer tails; the similar immatures are much more barred below (Black) or paler (Ornate).

Ssp. Monotypic (Ec, Co, Ve)

Habits Perches very upright. Mostly alone or in pairs, circling and soaring high above forest, or, rarely, perching in canopy of tall trees. Hunts in canopy.

Status Rare in Ecuador, local and scarce in Colombia and Venezuela.

Habitat Subtropical Zone. Large tracts of pristine, heavy, humid forest covering entire mountain slopes, valleys and ravines, especially on east-facing slopes with *Cecropia* and *Quercus*, below the treeline.

Voice When caring for eggs or chicks, advertises arrival with a loud *pe-e-e-e-e-eo*, or *chee-chee-chee-chee*… in alarm (H&B). A *keeah-keeah-keeah-keeah*… noted in Ecuador (F-L&C). Also a drawn-out, low-pitched gull-like *quaAAaa* and reedy *kreee, kee-kee* (Hilty).

FALCONIDAE – Caracaras and Falcons

Falcons are immediately thought of as long, pointed-winged, streamlined raptors that streak down from out of the blue to strike an unsuspecting creature with its powerful hindclaw. Of course these are the 'typical' falcons, but the family also includes the bare-faced caracaras that seem more like scavengers than birds of noble mien, the forest falcons, that oddly long-legged group of forest birds that can run through the branches as easily as fly, and the unique Laughing Falcon, seemingly familiar yet not at all well known. They all have a tooth or notch in the upper mandible that is characteristic of the family, as well as less obvious skeletal characteristics that differ from the Accipitridae.

Additional references used for this family include: Blake (1977), Sick (1993), White, Olsen & Kiff (1994), Sibley (2000), and Ferguson-Lees & Christie (2001).

Caracaras are a distinctive and fairly homogenous group, notable for their bare facial skin. Most are omnivorous and they are generally scavengers, always on the lookout for an easy meal. They pirate from other birds, rob nests of eggs and nestlings, scratch the ground and turn over dried cow pats to look for beetles, and lift water lily leaves to peer beneath. They also will take fruit, and Red-throated Caracara can tear apart the fiercest hornets'nest to feed on the grubs. But they can be fierce predators and a pair works most efficiently as a team. Their name is said to be onomatopoeic, deriving from the morning cackling call of the Northern Caracara.

BLACK CARACARA *Daptrius ater* Pl. 41

Identification 43–48cm. Adult is all black but for a broad white band at base of tail; eyes blue, facial skin red, throat bare and yellow, bill brown, cere, legs and feet yellow. Juvenile dull dark brown, spotted and barred black (looks all blackish) with 4 white bars on basal half of tail; eyes dark brown, facial skin, cere, legs and feet yellow. From Red-throated Caracara by yellow skin on throat, but note some white at base of tail.

Ssp. Monotypic (all mainland countries)

Habits Forages in pairs and small noisy bands. Diet includes carrion, fish, insects and fruit.

Status Locally uncommon to common in Ecuador, frequent in Colombia, locally frequent in Venezuela, frequent in Guyana and Suriname, and rare and sporadic along larger rivers of interior French Guiana, very sensitive to hunting along rivers.

Habitat Lower Tropical Zone. Humid lowland forests, partially cleared areas and fallow fields with scattered trees, second-growth woods, mangroves, pastures near forest. Often near rivers and streams.

Voice A long screech *jiiiiiiiii* high-pitched and whistled, similar to Yellow-headed Caracara. A harsh, scratchy scream, *kraaaaaaaa*, descending in pitch and hoarser than same call of Yellow-headed Caracara. Also, in flight, a harsh screaming *sqeeoow, sqeeoow*..., given continually when excited (Hilty).

RED-THROATED CARACARA *Ibycter americanus* Pl. 41

Identification 48–56cm. Adult is all black except pure white belly to undertail-coverts and thighs; eyes red, facial skin red, cere blue, bill yellow, legs and feet red. Juvenile has orange facial skin with rows of small black feathers on throat. From smaller Black Caracara by red legs and very obvious white belly and undertail-coverts.

Ssp. Monotypic (all mainland countries)

Habits Forages inside forest, in pairs or small noisy bands. Diet includes bees and wasps but mostly their larvae, also fruits, berries and seeds. Rather curious and not shy of humans. At times very noisy and loud, with several birds calling together. Perches at all levels, sometimes on treetops at forest borders.

Status Rare in Ecuador, uncommon in Colombia, locally frequent in Venezuela, frequent in Guyana, Suriname and French Guiana, but becomes scarcer in logged forests and hunted areas.

Habitat Tropical Zone. Humid lowland forests, both *várzea* and *terra firme*, and also drier, deciduous forests, second-growth woods, plantations. Often near rivers and streams.

Voice Call is a series of gruff, loud *ca-ca-ca-ca-cao* phrases, repeated, sometimes for long periods and often in raucous chorus. The Spanish onomatopoeia is *co-me ca-cao* ('eat cocoa'). A group may utter different cries, the first, *AH-AH-Aaou*, another a harsh *GRA'OU*, and a third *GRAAHEE'ow*, all at once in cacophony (Hilty).

Note Formerly placed in *Daptrius*, but now known to differ anatomically from *D. ater*, and thus returned to its original genus (Griffiths 1994).

CARUNCULATED CARACARA *Phalcoboenus carunculatus* Pl. 41

Identification 51–56cm. Adult has short, tufty crest on crown to nape; head and upperparts black with white tips to primaries and white fringes to secondaries (not visible in flight), upper breast to flanks white with black fringes to slightly lanceolate feathers producing somewhat arrowhead-like streaking, rest of underparts pure white; eyes dark brown, facial skin and cere bright orange, bill blue at base, yellow at tip, legs and feet rich yellow. Juvenile all brown, facial skin dull orange, bill blue with yellow cutting edges. From Mountain Caracara by more extensive black, streaked white below, but they are rarely sympatric. Juveniles very similar but Carunculated paler, more tawny, and has whitish-buff band at base of primaries.

Ssp. Monotypic (Ec, Co)

Habits Forages alone, in pairs or in small groups that search ground for worms, snails and insects, often around cattle. Strong flier, soaring gracefully on high winds.

Status Uncommon in Ecuador, uncommon to locally frequent in Colombia.

Habitat Temperate Zone to Páramo. Dry or barren open

areas on mountain sides and páramos; montane grasslands.
Voice Infrequent calls are described as harsh barks (F&K).

MOUNTAIN CARACARA
Phalcoboenus megalopterus Pl. 41

Identification 51–56cm. Adult all black except pure white belly, thighs and undertail-coverts, the tail has a white tip; eyes brown, facial skin orange, bill base blue, tip horn, legs and feet yellow. Juvenile entirely brown, paler on vent and undertail-coverts. From Carunculated Caracara by solid black below throat to mid belly.

Ssp. Monotypic (Ec)

Habits Forages alone, in pairs or in small groups that search ground for worms, snails and insects, often around cattle. Strong flier, soaring gracefully on high winds.
Status Rare in extreme southern Ecuador, where first recorded in early 1990s.
Habitat Temperate Zone to Páramo. Dry or barren open areas on mountain sides and páramos, montane grasslands and pastures.
Voice Reportedly similar to Carunculated Caracara (R&G).

NORTHERN CARACARA
Caracara cheriway Pl. 41

Identification 48–53cm. Large and unmistakable. Entire crown, including short crest at rear, black. Rest of head white, with increasingly dense black scallops on mantle and breast; back, rump and wings black with white barring on outer primaries, uppertail-coverts and tail barred black and white; vent and undertail-coverts white; eyes red, facial skin and cere red, bill blue, legs and feet yellow.

Ssp. Monotypic (all countries)

Habits Forages alone, in pairs or in bands that may gather 20+ birds, mostly on the ground. Feeds on carrion, road kills, small mammals and reptiles. Often investigates savanna fires to catch escaping prey.
Status Uncommon to rare in Ecuador, frequent to common in Colombia, very common and widespread in Venezuela; present in all 3 Dutch Antilles, where declining and now scarce (sight records only), Trinidad (but not Tobago), common in Guyana, less so in Suriname, still rare and local in coastal French Guiana where it seems to progress with opening of new pasture areas (recently nested at least once).
Habitat Tropical to Temperate Zones. Partially open areas, borders of deciduous forests, mangroves, savannas with scattered trees, pastures and ploughed fields.
Voice Usually silent. Call a low rattle (P&MdS), a harsh *quick, quick-quick quick querr* (H&B), and a low, toneless, croaking *grrrrk* (Sibley) or very grating *kra'a'a'ak* (Hilty).
Note Previously *Polyborus plancus cheriway*, but we follow AOU (1998) and, thus, revisions by Banks & Dove (1992; name *Caracara* antedates name *Polyborus*) and Dove & Banks (1999; *C. plancus* is best considered 3 species, including *C. cheriway*). Formerly called Crested Caracara. IOC-recommended English name is Northern Crested Caracara.

YELLOW-HEADED CARACARA
Milvago chimachima Pl. 41

Identification 41–46cm. Rather small. Head, mantle and body creamy buff, back and wings brown, tail barred brown and buffy-white; eyes brown, facial skin, cere, legs and feet yellow, bill pale grey. Juvenile almost entirely brown, streaked buffy-white on head, spotted on back and all wing-coverts and tertials have buffy-white terminal spots, tail strongly barred dark brown; throat to flanks have arrowhead streaks, thighs barred basally, vent to undertail-coverts creamy buff; facial skin, cere and bill horn, legs and feet dark grey. Unmistakable. Pale head and white patches on long, rounded wings diagnostic.

Ssp. *M. c. cordatus* (all countries)

Habits Forages alone or in pairs, soaring or perching high to search for prey, or by walking on ground, especially around cattle. Feeds on carrion and road kills, insects (especially ticks), nestlings, small reptiles and mammals, and fruit. Perches on the backs of cattle to pick ticks.
Status Uncommon in Ecuador, very common in Venezuela, sight record from Curaçao, common in Trinidad but scarce in Tobago, common in Guyana, Suriname and French Guiana.
Habitat Tropical to Subtropical Zones. Gallery forests, borders of humid or deciduous forest, shores of larger rivers, open areas with stands of trees, savannas, pastures, urban areas.
Voice Call a high-pitched, whistled, somewhat mournful screech that fades at end: *IIIIIIIIIIIiiiiiiiii*, described as an unpleasant, slowly descending, scratchy scream *SCREEEEEEEEEa* (Hilty).

> Laughing Falcon is a snake specialist that uses exposed perches, usually a bare branch or dead tree, waiting patiently for a snake to come into view. It swoops and grasps its prey behind the head and instantly bites it across the spine. Often seen flying somewhat heavily with a snake dangling and undulating below and behind. The species takes its name from its rather mirthless laughing calls. It has a large head with a black mask that is quite distinctive.

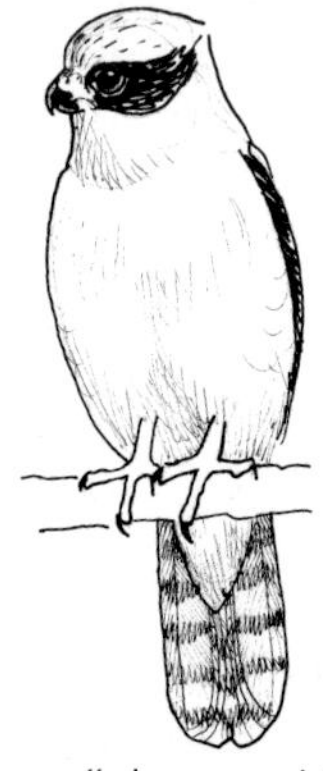

Laughing Falcon normally has an upright pose when perched

LAUGHING FALCON

Herpetotheres cachinnans Pl. 41

Identification 46–56cm. Rounded head with untidy blackish streaks on crown and a bold black mask on head-sides and nape, apart from this, head and body, including rump and tail-coverts, pale creamy buff; back and wings dark brown, tail barred black and white; eyes brown, cere ochre, bill grey, legs and feet yellow. Juvenile has paler body with pale fringes to all feathers. From Yellow-headed Caracara by broad black mask.

Ssp. *H. c. cachinnans* (all mainland countries)

Habits Mostly alone, usually perched high on an exposed branch, and frequently voicing its unmistakable calls that are audible some distance. A graceless flier, it never soars idly like most falcons, but flies with a purposeful, laboured flapping, alternating with short glides. A snake specialist. Not shy of humans.

Status Uncommon to rare in Ecuador, uncommon to frequent in Colombia and Venezuela, uncommon in Guyana, common in Suriname and French Guiana.

Habitat Tropical to Lower Subtropical Zones. Partially open areas, borders of deciduous forests, savanna woodland, second-growth woods, old mangroves, gallery forests and wooded riparian areas. Absent from heavy forest with dense canopy, but occurs in forest with open spaces and clearings.

Voice Calls sound like loud, paced, slightly demented guffaws of laughter: *whaw, whaw, whaw, whaw* or *hahahahahahahaha*. A pair may duet, starting with a low laugh *gogogo*... introducing a series of loud *kwa* notes which continue for *c*.4 minutes, developing into an impressive, equally long series of trisyllabic *a-cua-ahng*. The entire performance may last 9 minutes (Sick 1993).

Forest falcons are distinctly different raptors; slender, with short rounded wings, long legs and tails, they are adapted to hunt on the ground, where they can run fast in pursuit of prey. Perched, they sit very upright but on the ground they run with the body held horizontal and tail straight out behind. The large Collared Forest Falcon hunts chachalacas this way. They can also run along tree branches with great agility, moving through the branches like acrobats, barely using their wings at all. They follow army ants to hunt the animals disturbed by, and the birds attracted to, the swarms. Sexually monomorphic, but most species have different plumage phases (usually grey and rufous), with much variation in juveniles. Forest falcons are cautious and secretive, keeping well concealed and rarely flying across a clearing, preferring to skirt it. They usually occur from mid-levels to the ground. Noisy, pairs maintain contact by their frequent calls, and this is the best means to discover their presence.

BARRED FOREST FALCON

Micrastur ruficollis Pl. 42

Identification 28–35cm. Three morphs in race *zonothorax*. Grey morph is uniform dark grey above, tail black with 3 thin but evenly-spaced white bars (constant in adults of all forms); slightly paler on throat, entire underparts barred black and white, the black bars slightly broader. Brown morph is dark reddish-brown above, slightly rufescent on neck-sides, throat fairly clear, and from breast back barred dark brown and white, the dark bars slightly broader. Rufous morph has dark grey head and rest of upperparts rufous, underparts barred brown and white; eyes ochre, facial skin, cere, legs and feet yellow. Other 2 races occur only in grey form. Juveniles are highly variable and have 4 or more bars on tail. Similar Lined Forest Falcon has yellow eyes and 2 tail bars; Plumbeous Forest Falcon has single, broad white bar on tail.

Ssp. *M. r. concentricus* (S Ve, Guianas) palest, head and mantle paler than back and wings
M. r. interstes (W Co, W Ec) uniform dark grey, upper breast heavily suffused grey
M. r. zonothorax (E Co, Ve) 3 colour morphs; more heavily or densely barred below

Habits Sometimes investigates commotion caused by swarm of ants, and attacks small birds attracted to the swarm, although it normally feeds on lizards. Calling tends to be seasonal, and mostly at dawn and dusk.

Status Uncommon to rare in Ecuador, locally frequent in Colombia and Venezuela, uncommon in Guyana, Suriname and French Guiana.

Habitat Tropical to Subtropical Zones. Humid to wet montane forests, mature second-growth woodland, *várzea*.

Voice Calls described as sharp barks – *ow ow ow*... or *our our our*... – resembling a small dog, and sometimes bursts of *kuop* notes in a descending cackle (H&B).

PLUMBEOUS FOREST FALCON

Micrastur plumbeus Pl. 42

Identification 28–35cm. Slate grey above, slightly paler on head, tail black with a single, broad white band about halfway and narrow white tip, underparts pale grey, darkest on throat, palest on undertail-coverts, barred evenly with darker grey from breast down; eyes, facial skin, cere, legs and feet orange. Juvenile similar above, but slightly warmer or browner grey, underparts white with slight, irregular grey barring on breast-sides and flanks. From Barred Forest Falcon by single white bar on tail.

Ssp. Monotypic (Ec, S Co)

Habits Poorly known. Forages alone, well inside forest, perches within 2m of forest floor which it sits watching intently. Often walks and runs on ground. Food includes snakes, lizards, mice, birds, crabs and large insects.

Status Vulnerable. Rare in Ecuador, where there are conflicting views of the habitat situation: *TBW* considers that very extensive deforestation within small range has left only small fragments; R&G, however, declare that there is still considerable suitable habitat which is likely to remain undisturbed in the future. Rare in Colombia.

Habitat Tropical Zone. Wet or very humid forests.

Voice Calls include series of low, nasal *kew* notes; also, a low-pitched *kiw, ki-kiw, ki-kiw-kiw* phrase, a fast *kiw, ki-ki-ke-kew* and a leisurely *kew... kew... kah-kooh* (R&G).

Note Formerly treated as a subspecies of *Micrastur ruficollis* or *M. gilvicollis*, but taxonomy here follows H&B Bierregaard (1994) and Dickinson (2003).

LINED FOREST FALCON
Micrastur gilvicollis Pl. 42

Identification 25–36cm. Dark grey above with 2 white bars on black tail; face-sides paler grey, even paler on throat, underparts pale grey finely barred dark grey (the darker bars slightly narrower); eyes yellow, facial skin and cere red, legs and feet yellow. Juvenile dark brown above, white below with narrow, widely spaced bars on breast to flanks and thighs; eyes brown. From Barred by white iris and pure white belly and undertail-coverts.

Ssp. Monotypic (all mainland countries)

Habits Much as other forest falcons.

Status Rare in Ecuador, not well known (possibly scarce?) in Colombia, local in Venezuela, uncommon in Guyana and Suriname, common in French Guiana.

Habitat Lower Tropical Zone. Humid *terra firme* forests.

Voice Call 2 mournful, nasal notes: *cow, kah* or *cow, kaw-kaw*, or *cow-kah, kaw-kaw* (H&B, R&G).

Note Formerly treated as a subspecies of *M. ruficollis*, but separated when Schwartz (1972) found *gilvicollis* to be sympatric with *ruficollis* in Amazonas state, Venezuela.

SLATY-BACKED FOREST FALCON
Micrastur mirandollei Pl. 42

Identification 35–46cm. Slate grey from forehead to uppertail-coverts, tail slightly darker with 3 broad grey bands; ear-coverts grey, chin to undertail-coverts white with a few fine, pale, greyish to buff streaks on flanks; eyes sepia, facial skin, cere, legs and feet yellow. Juvenile darker and warmer grey, with darker ear-coverts and bolder narrow dark lines on breast-sides and flanks, eyes brown, other soft parts paler yellow.

Ssp. Monotypic (all mainland countries)

Habits Forages alone, very occasionally in pairs, from mid levels to ground. In areas where sympatric with Collared Forest Falcon, forages at higher levels and may run across canopy branches instead of flying. Normally perches quietly at mid and lower levels, watching for prey, which includes snakes, lizards and birds. Always inside forest.

Status Rare in Ecuador, Colombia and Venezuela, scarce in the Guianas.

Habitat Lower Tropical Zone. Humid lowland forests, near rivers and old second-growth forests.

Voice Calls include a repeated nasal *uiiiit* and long series of strong *jos* notes (P&MdS); also a series of 5–8 nasal, low *aah* notes, sometimes with last 2 notes doubled, *how-au, how-au* (H&B).

COLLARED FOREST FALCON
Micrastur semitorquatus Pl. 42

Identification 46–60cm. The largest forest falcon, with 3 colour morphs. Pale-morph adult is black from forehead to tail, with 3 fairly narrow whitish tail bars, and whitish tips to uppertail-coverts, a bold white collar and white tips to uppertail-coverts; ear-coverts and rest of underparts white; eyes brown, facial skin and cere grey, legs and feet dull greenish-yellow. Tawny morph has 2 variants: first has white replaced entirely by cinnamon, but other has collar white (as in race *naso*). Dark morph is umber below. Immature dark brown above barred darker brown throughout, white barring uppertail-coverts bolder and has 4 tail bars and obvious pale tips to tail. Particularly long-tailed; larger than other forest falcons.

Ssp. *M. s. naso* (N & W Co, Ec) tawny morph is like white-collared tawny morph of *semitorquatus*, but deeper rufous below; all other morphs follow same pattern but are always much darker

M. s. semitorquatus (E Co, Ve, Gu, Su, FG) as described

Habits In late afternoon and at dusk, sometimes calls from forest edge or river border perch.

Status Uncommon to rare in Ecuador, rare or uncommon (though possibly overlooked) in Colombia and Venezuela, uncommon in Guyana, Suriname and French Guiana.

Habitat Tropical Zone. Humid and cloud forests, gallery forests, mangroves.

Voice Call resembles laughter of Laughing Falcon – *cow, cow, cow...* (H&B) or *haw, haw, haw...* – but more unhurried, and always at same slow pace. Another frequent call described as a series of hollow, resonant *oow* notes, repeated every 2–3 s, often for long periods (R&G). Another description states the call to be a long note, repeated severally, each time fainter and lower pitched, rather resembling weak groans of a man in pain. Sometimes a series of clucking notes that increase in frequency to become the call proper. At other times a faint, introductory groan is uttered.

BUCKLEY'S FOREST FALCON
Micrastur buckleyi Pl. 42

Identification 41–46cm. Adult male is black from forehead to tail, except broad white collar, white tips to uppertail-coverts and 3 white tail bars; ear-coverts and rest of underparts white; eyes brown, facial skin, cere, legs and feet yellow. Female similar but has white spots on tertials and inner secondaries. Juvenile similar but collar to breast and rest of underparts orange, with some sparse but even black bars on flanks.

Ssp. Monotypic (SE Ec, Co, Ve)

Habits Poorly known. Forages and flies only inside forests, very secretive and wary.

Status Rare in Ecuador and in Colombia, where H&B note only sight records. Only one specimen from Venezuela. Only a few specimens are available anywhere in range.

Habitat Lower Tropical Zone. Humid lowland forests, especially *várzea* and along rivers.

Voice Calls include a far-carrying *kawa-kaw*, sometimes *kawa-kaw... kow*, repeated slowly with 4–5 s pauses (R&G). Also, a series of 15–16 nasal *anh* notes in crescendo, then fading, and a series of *c.*25 *ko* notes that end with 2 nasal notes (P. Coopmans recording, *fide* R&G).

Falcons of the genus *Falco*, the 'true' falcons, are built for speed. They are streamlined with long tails and long, pointed wings. Most typically, they stoop from a height, plunging at great speed, with wings almost closed, to strike a flying bird from behind or an animal on the ground. Smaller falcons catch insects. Bat Falcons hunt bats, swallows and even swifts in the air. It is common to see a pair hunting, with the one making a capture subsequently passing the prey to its partner, either in the air or on an exposed perch. They are attributed anthropomorphic, romantic values by humans and are considered to have noble qualities.

COMMON (EURASIAN) KESTREL
Falco tinnunculus Pl. 43

Identification 32–39cm. Adult male has grey head with single vertical black line from eye separating grey from pale throat; back, wing-coverts and tertials rich chestnut, rest of wings black, tail grey with black subterminal band and white tip; underparts pale cinnamon, streaked dark brown on breast and flanks. Female chestnut-brown above, streaked on head, barred on wings and tail, primaries and tip of tail blackish; underparts pale cinnamon, more heavily streaked than male. From American Kestrel by significantly larger size, and lack of white on cheeks.

Ssp. Subspecies unknown. Plate essentially depicts European type, *tinnunculus*, but if one of the 4 Atlantic islands races is involved, interesting questions arise. From Canary Islands, *canariensis* is darker and more chestnut than nominate, and more boldly marked, *dacotiae* is much paler than nominate, and female palest of all. From Cape Verdes, *neglectus* is sexually monomorphic with only faint grey on head and tail, and *alexandri* is heavily barred on deep rufous upperparts; both are mooted as species.

Habits Forages by hovering low to pick prey from ground. Sometimes takes insects in air. Feeds on mice and other small mammals, lizards, insects. Disperses after breeding.

Status Vagrant: first-winter photographed in Trinidad (December 2003), and 4 records for French Guiana, possibly ship-assisted from France.

Habitat Tropical to Subtropical Zones? Fields or savannas with scattered trees, outskirts of towns and other fairly open areas, where lamp posts, towers, trees or structures provide perches. Pastures, rice fields and open marshy areas.

Voice Commonest call a shrill *kik-kik-kik*... or *kee-kee-kee*..., in excitement becoming *wik-week wik week* with syllables unevenly stressed (F-L&C). Displaying male gives *keeee, keeee, keeee*.

AMERICAN KESTREL
Falco sparverius Pl. 43

Identification 23–28cm. Small, slender bird. Six races with individual variation plus sex and age differences, but no variant morphs in those races that occur in our region. Typical adult male has grey crown, rufous above, with grey wings and blackish primaries, tail plain rufous with a subterminal bar; face white and neck-sides pale rufous with 3 black markings – a vertical line below the eye, another on the rear ear-coverts and a shorter third on the neck-sides. Breast to flanks rufescent with a few 'teardrops' of black, thighs paler; eye-ring and cere yellow, legs and feet yellow to horn. Female similar but may have rufous on head and is usually barred on back and always on tail, and lacks grey wing-coverts of male. Variable plumage according to age in all races. Larger Common (Eurasian) Kestrel has all-grey head with a single black 'tear' line (no white cheeks).

Ssp. *F. s. aequatorialis* (N Ec) larger; male has rufous centre to grey crown, cinnamon breast, well streaked on sides
F. s. brevipennis (ABC) darker than *isabellinus*, male always has crown dark grey
F. s. caucae (W Co) like smaller *aequatorialis* but has unstreaked back and no rufous crown patch
F. s. isabellinus (Ve, T&T, Gu, Su, FG) fairly pale, considerable variation (see plate)
F. s. ochraceus (E Co to NW Ve) much darker and richer coloured than others
F. s. peruvianus (SW Ec) much paler below than *aequatorialis* with less streaking on flanks (shown as being more heavily spotted in R&G), female more heavily barred than male, with rufous streaks on breast

Habits Forages alone, rarely in pairs, catching large insects in flight. Alert, fast and graceful. Most often seen perched quite upright on posts, fences and wires. Occasionally hovers.

Status Uncommon to rare in Ecuador, frequent in Colombia, common in Venezuela, resident on Aruba, scarce (sight records only) on Trinidad, rare on Tobago, frequent in Guyana but local in Suriname (Sipaliwini savannas and once in the north, Zanderij); accidental in coastal French Guiana.

Habitat Tropical Zone to Páramo. Very varied semi-open habitats, from lowland to xerophytic areas to borders of cloud forests and even páramos, at forest borders, fields with scattered trees, gallery forests.

Voice Calls a high-pitched *killy-killy-killy* or *klee-klee-klee* (H&B) or shrill, clear screaming *kli kli kli kli kli kli kli kli* (Sibley).

MERLIN *Falco columbarius* Pl. 43

Identification 25–33 cm. Grey crown, white nape and neck-sides washed rufous and narrowly streaked black, rest of upperparts grey, flight-feathers and tail darker with 3 broad pale grey bars and a white tip; underparts white, washed rufescent with narrow dark streaks; eyes dark, facial skin and cere yellowish, legs and feet yellow. Female dark brown above, much more heavily streaked below. From all other falcons by lack of black lines or patches on sides of face.

Ssp. *F. c. columbarius* (boreal migrant to Ec, Co, Ve, ABC, T&T, Gu, FG) as described
F. c. richardsoni (boreal migrant to northern South America?) distinctly paler, also has 5–6 pale bars on tail

Habits Forages alone, catching prey in flight with great aerial acrobatics. Main food birds, most often caught on wing, especially flocking species, such as marine birds at colonies, migrant shorebirds on coasts and wintering Dickcissels in Llanos of Venezuela, where Merlins (and Peregrines) are frequently seen circling over the roosts.

Status Rare in Ecuador, uncommon in Colombia, locally frequent to common in Venezuela (winters in north-east Llanos), uncommon in Trinidad & Tobago, rare in Guyana and Suriname, and coastal French Guiana, from where there are only sight records to date.

Habitat Tropical to Temperate Zones. Partially open areas, agricultural lands.

Voice High-pitched whistles. Alarm-call a rapid, accelerating series of strident notes, rising and falling, *twi twitwitwititititititit*, with female's call slower and harsher. Single hard *peek* (Sibley).

BAT FALCON *Falco rufigularis* Pl. 43

Identification 23–30cm. Adult male black above, cinnamon throat runs back as a crescent on neck-sides, around rear ear-coverts, and to upper breast; breast all black with white fringes giving rough barred effect, belly, vent, flanks and thighs deep reddish-rufous, undertail-coverts barred black and white. Female significantly larger, with paler throat and upper breast, black and white more obvious and extensive. Eyes dark, eye-ring, cere, legs and feet yellow. Adult very easy to confuse with larger but much rarer Orange-breasted Falcon, though separable by width of breast bars; however, only sure field discriminator is length of primaries which do *not* reach tip of tail.

Ssp. *F. r. petoensis* (W Co, W Ec) generally slightly paler throughout
F. r. rufigularis (E Co, Ve, Tr, Guianas) as described

Habits Typically seen perched on an exposed branch in crown of tree. Not shy of humans. Tip of tail may appear slightly notched. Forages alone or in pairs, catching prey on wing, and very active at twilight. Main prey is birds, including swifts and hummingbirds.

Status Uncommon to rare in Ecuador, uncommon to locally frequent in Colombia and Venezuela, uncommon on Trinidad (no records Tobago), frequent in Guyana and regular in Suriname, common in French Guiana.

Habitat Lower Tropical Zone. Partially open areas from dry to humid forest borders. Especially along larger rivers in French Guiana.

Voice Calls include a shrill, high-pitched *ke-ke-ke-ke* (H&B) or a loud *kee-kee-kee-kee* (R&G).

Note Subspecific differences clouded by continual cline from palest to richest in colour, with little agreement over divisions. Trend is to recognise just 2 races, and Mexican form *petrophilus* may be regarded as a synonym of *petoensis* (e.g. F-L&C).

ORANGE-BREASTED FALCON
Falco deiroleucus Pl. 43

Identification 33–38cm. Head black with white throat reaching to neck-sides and upper breast, upperparts very dark grey barred black, breast orange-rufous, lower breast, sides and upper belly black with paler tips affording barred effect, rest of underparts orange-rufous. Immature male has undertail-coverts barred black. Female larger. Eyes dark, eye-ring, cere, legs and feet yellow. Fierce and aggressive-looking, noticeably more so than similar but smaller Bat Falcon, though very difficult to separate when perched on distant treetop. Length of primaries a sure discriminator, as they protrude slightly beyond tip of tail, which is unnotched.

Ssp. Monotypic (all mainland countries)

Habits Forages alone, chasing and capturing birds in flight. Often perches in an exposed place, on a tall tree or highest branch of a dead tree. Often nests in palm trees.

Status Rare in Ecuador, very rare in Colombia, scarce and local in Venezuela, scarce in Trinidad (no records Tobago), and scarce in Guyana and Suriname, scarce but widespread in French Guiana, from the remote inselberg to the coastal forests.

Habitat Tropical to Subtropical Zones. Borders of humid forests on montane slopes and in foothills, and along large rivers, and around rocky outcrops.

Voice Call is described as a high *acsiiiiic, asiiiiiic…* (P&MdS, H&M).

APLOMADO FALCON
Falco femoralis Pl. 43

Identification 38–46 cm. Black crown with bold cinnamon postocular stripe reaching base of nape, thick black 'tear line' from eyes and upper cheeks, curling round pale cinnamon-washed lower ear-coverts, neck-sides black; breast to undertail-coverts pale cinnamon, with narrow black lines on breast, sides of lower breast and upper flanks heavily scalloped black with irregular white fringes; upperparts all black, long tail barred evenly with 8+ grey bands, and fine whitish tip. Female distinctly larger; eyes dark brown, facial skin and cere yellow, legs and feet yellow-orange. Immature similar but has dark brown upperparts, more heavily streaked on breast and has brown patch on flanks. Although sexes alike, immature females usually more ochraceous. Larger than Bat and Orange-breasted Falcons, and bars on tail more obvious, whilst postocular line crosses nape.

Ssp. *F. f. femoralis* (N & E Co, Ve, Tr, Guianas) smaller and paler
F. f. pichinchae (SW Co, Ec) darker, more plumbeous above, more deeply ochraceous ruddy below

Habits Forages alone or in pairs, spying prey from an exposed, fairly low perch (fences, wires, bushes), before dashing to strike. When pairs hunt cooperatively, they often resort to a one-two hit method. Feeds on insects, lizards, bats and other small mammals, small birds (caught both aerially and from ground). Often investigates savannas fires to catch escaping prey.

Status Rare in Ecuador, uncommon and local in Colombia, locally frequent in Venezuela, scarce in Trinidad (not recorded Tobago), and uncommon in Guyana and Suriname.

Habitat Tropical Zone to Páramo. Moist to arid, partially open areas, savannas with light woodland or scattered trees, scrub, pastures.

Voice An acrimonious, whistled *eeeee eeeee eeeee*.

PEREGRINE FALCON

Falco peregrinus Pl. 43

Identification 38–51cm. Essentially dark bluish-grey above, darkest on head, with black patch below eyes and white crescent on ear-coverts (the width of the black cheeks and white ear-coverts are diagnostic of subspecies), upperparts darkly barred black; underparts white, washed buffy or pale brown (males barred black, larger females streaked). Could be confused with Merlin in dashing flight, e.g. over Dickcissel roost, but in clear view is unmistakable. It is important to note characters that identify birds to subspecies, because wintering ranges of all 4 races are still uncertain.

Ssp. *F. p. anatum* (breeds in North America, boreal migrant to Ec, Co, Ve, possibly rest of northern South America) slightly paler above than *cassini* and has narrow white auriculars

F. p. cassini (breeds at austral latitudes, and resident breeder in Ec; also, birds from austral populations migrate north along Andes to SW Colombia and possibly W Venezuela, and according to McNutt *et al.* (1980), some are perhaps resident in drier, elevated regions of Co & S Ve) head-sides entirely black separated from neck-sides by a narrow white line

[*F. p. pealei* (breeds Alaska and far north-west North America, rarely migrates to Central America, possibly very rare in our region) broad white ear-coverts streaked laterally with heavy streaking below]

F. p. tundrius (breeds in Nearctic, boreal migrant to Ec, Co, Ve, Tr, and possibly rest of northern South America) paler and smaller than *cassini*, and has broad white ear-coverts

Heads of the four races of Peregrine most likely to be encountered in northern South America, left to right anatum, cassini, pealei *and* tundrius

Habits In winter, forages alone. Soars or perches high to spot prey and then falls upon it with blinding speed. Main food birds, most often caught on wing, especially flocking species, such as marine birds at colonies, migrant shorebirds on coasts and wintering Dickcissels in Llanos of Venezuela, where Peregrines (and Merlins) are frequently seen circling over roosts. Also hunts along forest borders and over savannas, or perches on high exposed spots, such as tops of tall trees, posts and antennas, lighthouses and watch towers. Some individuals may specialise on bats in large cities in the Guianas. In French Guiana some young birds would catch Yellowlegs and Sandpipers when crouching on the mudflats, others have specalised on terns and storm-petrels which they hunt up to 10km offshore. Flies beautifully, light and fast, alternating rapid flapping with short glides.

Status Boreal migrants occur in tropics approximately October–March, austral migrants approximately late April–August. Northern races declined to almost extinction, but following intensive captive-breeding programmes have now recuperated spectacularly. Winter ranges of the 4 races very poorly known. Locally uncommon to rare in Ecuador, uncommon in Colombia, locally frequent in Venezuela, uncommon in Trinidad & Tobago, Guyana and Suriname. Frequent in coastal French Guiana.

Habitat In transit found from Tropical to Temperate Zones, but usually winters in Tropical Zone, mostly at sea level. Coasts, deltas, mangroves, open fields and savannas, oceanic islands.

Voice Calls infrequently. A repeated *hek* (H&B) and alarm described as a slow, scolding, harsh and raucous *rehk rehk rehk*... each note rising a little (Sibley).

ARAMIDAE – Limpkin

Limpkin is the sole member of its family, an unusual bird, commonly described as having characteristics of both a crane and a rail, it is arguably an intermediate between them. Usually found at the edges of marshes and in swampy areas, it is most often solitary, skulking and lifting its feet high (as if limping), and clucking to itself. It occasionally utters a weird and melancholy cry, though this is more often heard at night. Limpkins usually appear hunched, like a rail, but snap their heads upright to survey the surroundings. They probe shallow water and deep mud for *Pomacea* snails and freshwater mussels. Limpkins construct large nest platforms of rushes, reeds and grasses, in trees or bushes just above to a few metres above the water, and the young are able to swim immediately, though they prefer the comfort and seclusion of the nest for a few days.

LIMKPIN *Aramus guarauna* Pl. 24

Identification 55–70cm. Front of head streaked finely dark brown and white, and perhaps flushed slightly buffy, rest of head and neck streaked boldly white on dark umber, entire body has feathers faintly fringed paler; eyes brown, bill horn with darker tip, legs and feet dusky. From immature ibises by noticeably straighter bill (although it is in fact slightly decurved).

Ssp. *A. g. guarauna* (all except ABC)

Habits Principally feeds on apple snails (*Pomacea*) at water's edge, as well as small aquatic invertebrates. Flicks tail frequently on ground.

Status Poorly understood. Generally fairly common despite declines due to loss of habitat. More obvious during rainy season. Uncommon to rare in Ecuador, locally frequent in

Colombia, casual visitor to Aruba (photograph), frequent to locally common in Venezuela, uncommon in Trinidad (does not occur in Tobago), frequent in Guyana, frequent in Suriname, and very local in French Guiana.
Habitat Open freshwater marshes, edges of mangroves, rivers and lakes.
Voice Most unusual, with as wide a variety of anthropomorphic descriptions as it has notes, and reportedly sounds like a human in distress. It cries out at dusk, during the night, and at dawn, often in response to a sudden noise, an unmistakable *ca-rra-ooou*.

PSOPHIIDAE – Trumpeters

A short, velvety feathering covers the graceful neck and exquisitely proportioned head, with large, dark, liquid eyes and a small bill. Peculiar gestures – the way they walk, browsing and leisurely lifting 1 leg to dangle in mid-air for an instant before lifting the other, or running with neck stretched forward as if to take-off. Sometimes kept as beloved pets around dwellings and tiny settlements in deep forests, it is impossible not to find them beautiful and endearing. Trumpeters are ground-dwellers of dense forest interiors, particularly those rich in tree species with a fairly open understorey. Their distinctive full, round body is comparable in size to a large chicken, but the plumage is mostly black with a sheen of electric blue or purple. They take their name from their calls, a booming *oh-oh-oh-oh…oooooo*. The final, drawn-out part is delivered with the bill closed, the sound reverberating in the body, but the threat call is a loud trumpeting. Run fast, but fly poorly. They make a good meal and adults are favourite game for hunters. Largely frugivorous, taking small fruits with soft skins. Arthropods form *c.*10% of the diet and they eat a wide variety of insects. Chicks take almost twice as many insects as fruit. Poisonous millipedes are beaten and repeatedly wiped on the wings prior to being swallowed. They also follow army ants, taking arthropods escaping the advancing swarm.

Additional references used for this family include Colston (1985) and Sherman (1996).

GREY-WINGED TRUMPETER
Psophia crepitans Pl. 48

Identification 45–52cm. Unmistakable. Large round body, blackish with purple and green iridescences on front, rear distinctly pale, with an ochraceous wash grading into pale grey; round head with longish neck, usually held close to hunched body, bill pale grey, legs and feet flesh.

Ssp. *P. c. crepitans* (SE Co, E,S Ve, Gu, Su, FG) as described
P. c. napensis (SE Co to E Ec) sheen much more purple, and grey rump paler

Habits Forages on forest floor or near ground level, in small groups that amble slowly and peaceably, sometimes with Black Curassows. Mainly frugivorous, takes great variety of fruits, but only the pulp – seeds are defecated intact. When alarmed or going to roost, flies to high branch. Breeds in cooperative, polyandrous groups, at end of dry season or well into rainy season. Sedentary and territorial. Groups engage in 'play', including mock fights and rowdy chasing, 'attacks' on twigs and leaves, 'bragging' over food and other behaviours. Shy around settlements.

Trumpeters change from looking rotund and sedate into a speeding ball of apparent fury in an instant. They run towards an item of food or a threat to their chicks equally instantaneously and, when confronting a perceived threat, very effectively. They also do this in play.

Status Threatened by hunting and habitat loss, but frequent in remote areas. Rare in remote areas of Ecuador, uncommon in Colombia, locally frequent in Venezuela, frequent in Guyana, frequent in interior Suriname, locally common in French Guiana.
Habitat Tropical Zone. Pristine, dense, humid lowland *terra firme* forests.
Voice Calls day and night, groups vocalising in unison. Varied, but most typical are sonorous booms that give family its name, described as *umm* notes and uttered in falling sequence: *ummumm-umm-umm, umm, umm, umm…* (H&B, P. Schwartz recording).

PALE-WINGED TRUMPETER
Psophia leucoptera Pl. 48

Identification 45–52cm. Large, round body blackish with rear part distinctly ochre, round head with longish neck, usually held close to hunched body, purplish and green gloss on outer wing-coverts, bill pale grey, legs and feet flesh. Unmistakable as a trumpeter, but risk of confusion with Grey-winged Trumpeter. Look for all-ochre back.

Ssp. *P. l. ochroptera* (SE Co, S Ve)

Habits Behaviour much as previous species.
Status Rare in extreme south-east Colombia, where photographed in Amacayacu National Park (van Leeuwen & Hoogeland 2004), and sighted but unconfirmed at lower río Casiquiare, Amazonas, Venezuela (D. Lauten & K. Castelain, pers. comm.).
Habitat Tropical Zone. Pristine, dense, humid lowland *terra firme* forests.
Voice Calls, similar to Grey-winged, by day and night, groups calling in unison.

RALLIDAE – Crakes, Rails, Gallinules and Coots

All have thick strong legs and feet, and all can swim, but coots alone have lateral membranous lobes on the toes as an additional aid to swimming. All have small wings, and they would seem to need nothing else because, in general, they seem reluctant to fly, preferring to walk, which they do tail cocked with precise, deliberate strides. Most are agile at clambering over reeds, water lilies and rafts of floating plants. When they do fly, the majority do so clumsily, with feet and sometimes head dangling down. However, those species that are migratory fly perfectly well when travelling.

Rallids nest near or on water. Swamp nesters usually have a path or 'gangway' to raised mat of partially interwoven stems, thus always enter the nest from the same side. Some species build high-domed nests, whilst others nest on trees, in deep, well-lined woven cups. Nesting associations involve just a solitary pair to several pairs in relatively close proximity. Pairs often return to regular roosting and nesting sites. Displays include chasing, mock-feeding and leaning forward with open wings. Many species are crepuscular and difficult to see as they keep well hidden within reeds and dank waterside vegetation; they call mostly at dawn and dusk, some nocturnally. It is therefore essential to learn as many vocalizations as possible, as for most species voice is the best clue as to its presence.

Additional references for this section include Ripley (1977), Sick (1993), Taylor (1996), Taylor & van Perlo (1998, referred to here as T&VP).

SPECKLED CRAKE

Coturnicops notatus Pl. 44

Identification 13–14cm. Tiny. Apparently black but there is much rich umber brown in plumage, long blackish rows on upper surface with white crescents at tips of feathers; sides of head and throat heavily streaked white, rows of short, bold white streaks on black breast and umber sides, body-sides to undertail-coverts black with white bars, belly paler; eyes red, bill, legs and feet black. From Black Rail by all-streaked head and white streaks below. White secondaries, visible only in flight.

Ssp. Monotypic (Co: E Andes, NW Ve: Andes, WC Gu)

Habits Forages secretively, always in dense vegetation. Only seen when flushed, usually when almost underfoot. Calls at night.
Status Rare with few records but very large range. Very rare in Colombia, rare and local in Venezuela, and scarce in Guyana.
Habitat Tropical Zone. Swamps and marshes with dense vegetation, flooded pastures and crop fields (rice, alfalfa), wet and coastal grasslands.
Voice Calls very soft and unobtrusive. A *koo weee-cack* phrase that begins high-pitched and ends lower but louder, and occasional *keee* and *kyu* calls (Sick, T&VP).

OCELLATED CRAKE

Micropygia schomburgkii Pl. 44

Identification 14–15cm. Tiny. Unique mottling above, pale buffy below. Buffy olive-brown above with rows of short white dashes fringed black; throat white, underparts pale buffy, white on belly and vent; eyes red, bill black, legs and feet pink. Sexes very similar, male has crown unmarked, but female has black-and-white dashes on crown.

Ssp. *M. s. schomburgkii* (Co, Ve, Gu, Su, FG)

Habits Forages secretively, always in dense vegetation but not necessarily near wetlands. Seen only when flushed, when it jumps up, only to drop down almost immediately. Uses rodent (e.g. *Cavia*) tunnels in tall grass.
Status Local in Colombia, local in Venezuela, uncommon throughout Guianas.
Habitat Tropical Zone. Shallow-flooded, humid or even dry grasslands, *Mauritia* palm bogs. Areas may be quite open or have a few bushes, shrubs or trees, but always with dense, tall grasses.
Voice Sequences of clear, strong *pr-pr-pr* notes, in short spurts. Also harsh whirring *pjrrrr* and *prrrrxxxzzz* phrases (*prrrssss*, like rasping of a grasshopper: Sick), and long sequences mixing these with a *crrraaauuu* phrase. Dawn song is 30 s series of strong *prr-prr-prr*… notes, also uttered at dusk and occasionally by day.

CHESTNUT-HEADED CRAKE

Anurolimnas castaneiceps Pl. 44

Identification 19–22cm. From crown to tail, body-sides and belly to undertail-coverts uniform olive-brown, tail very short, front and sides of head to upper belly and flanks bright chestnut; eyes red, sepia or yellow, bill yellowish-green with blackish tip, legs and feet yellowish-green. From smaller Russet-crowned Crake, by uniform rufous head, yellow-green bill and brown rear-parts.

Ssp. *A. c. castaneiceps* (E Ec) yellowish legs and feet
A. c. coccineipes (S Co, NE Ec) red legs and feet

Habits Forages alone (rarely in pairs), quite erect, within thickets and dense vegetation. Very wary and difficult to see.
Status Uncommon in Ecuador, uncommon in Colombia.
Habitat Lower Tropical Zone. Humid lowland and foothill forests, from *terra firme* to permanently wet ground, edge of *várzea* and streams, tall secondary woodland, stands of *Heliconia*, bananas, and humid, very dense undergrowth.
Voice Soft growls in alarm, and intermittent *tik* and *tuk* notes. Song a raucous synchronized duet – the first sings *ti-too*, the other *ti-turro* – lasting several minutes, given by pair side by side (T&VP).

RUSSET-CROWNED CRAKE

Anurolimnas viridis Pl. 44

Identification 16–18cm. Broad greyish-olive mask, and nape to tail olive-brown; crown, lower face-sides and underparts chestnut; eyes red, bill dark bluish-grey, legs and feet red. From Chestnut-headed Crake by grey (*viridis*) or yellow-brown (*brunnescens*) lores to ear-coverts and dark grey bill (both have pale undertail-coverts). Uniform Crake lacks contrasting grey head-sides and has yellow-green bill.

Ssp. *A. v. brunnescens* (C & E Co) browner olive above from crown, forehead and eyebrow chestnut, mask more yellowish-brown, paler on belly
A. v. viridis (E Ec, S Ve, Guianas) as described

Habits Forages secretively, in thickets or dense vegetation, stepping gingerly over twigs and roots to pick seeds and insects. Runs to flee, never flushes.

Status Very rare in Ecuador, uncommon to locally frequent in Colombia and Venezuela, uncommon in Guyana, frequent in Suriname.
Habitat Tropical Zone. Grasslands, shrubby fallow fields, densely overgrown plantation and crop fields (e.g. manioc) and deforested areas. Not always in wetlands or swampy areas, but sometimes at edge of marshes.
Voice Calls include a loose, slow, well-enunciated, churring rattle that begins with a few 'choked' notes, then flows continually, slowing at end (H&B). Also, a loud high roll (H&M) and a *kewrrr* note in alarm. A long, prolonged, canary-like trill, flowing freely without pause then descending without undulation to end in a few single notes (Sick).
Note Sometimes placed in genus *Laterallus*.

BLACK-BANDED CRAKE
Anurolimnas fasciatus Pl. 44

Identification 18–20cm. Back to tail olive-brown, entire head to breast and sides chestnut, rest of underparts barred evenly black and cinnamon; eyes red, bill black, legs and feet pinkish-red. White-throated Crake is barred black and white.

Ssp. Monotypic (E Ec, SE Co)

Habits Forages secretively, alone or in pairs, in tall grasses, thickets and dense tangles. Calls frequently, especially at dawn and dusk.
Status Rare in Ecuador, locally fairly common in Colombia.
Habitat Lower Tropical Zone. Wet or swampy grassy areas, river edges, clearings overgrown with grasses, borders of oxbow lakes, pools and streams, and on river islands. Mostly in damp or marshy areas, but occasionally far from water.
Voice Call a low churring rattle, given in unison by pair (H&B).
Notes Locality of original description (*Porzana fasciatus* Sclater & Salvin 1867) is Pebas, Peru (quoted erroneously as 'near Caracas, Venezuela' in Taylor & Van Perlo 1998). In Peters (vol. 2), listed as *Laterallus hauxwelli* Sclater & Salvin 1868, but this is a correction of the original name. Some recent authors still place it in genus *Laterallus*.

RUFOUS-SIDED CRAKE
Laterallus melanophaius Pl. 44

Identification 14–18cm. Forehead to tail olive, lores and short eyebrow greyish, face-, neck- and breast-sides form long band of chestnut, chin to flanks white, barred black, undertail-coverts chestnut; eyes red, bill dull yellowish-green, legs and feet yellowish-green. From other barred crakes by white throat and breast.

Ssp. *L. m. melanophaius* (Ve, Gu, Su) as described
L. m. oenops (SE Co, E Ec) rufous front and crown without any grey

Habits Forages in rushes and dense grasses, but sometimes in open or at forest borders. Difficult to flush, but less furtive and shy than other crakes.
Status Uncommon in Ecuador, uncertain in Colombia, local in Venezuela, frequent in Guyana and Suriname.
Habitat Tropical Zone. Densely overgrown edges of freshwater marshes, oxbow lakes, forest swamps, river islands. Also, mudflats, wet meadows, and both flooded or dry grasslands. Freshwater areas with abundant floating algae (macrophytes).
Voice A sudden loose churring or a loud, 6 s long trill *tsewrrrr*; also, high-pitched peeps and a warning *psieh* (Sick, T&VP). Also a *frey-eee, frey-ee, frey-o-o-o* sequence (P&MdS). Calls often answered by other birds nearby.

RUSTY-FLANKED CRAKE
Laterallus levraudi Pl. 44

Identification 14–19cm. Relatively plain. Forehead to tail olive, browner on wings and tail; lores and short eyebrow greyish, cheeks to flanks and undertail-coverts chestnut, chin to vent white; eyes brown, bill, legs and feet dark greenish. Rufous-sided has black-and-white barring on flanks and belly.

Ssp. Monotypic (NC Ve)

Habits Forages stealthily in dense vegetation, where it remains even when responding to playback. Individuals usually forage along a given route, showing up at the same places repeatedly.
Status Endangered. Uncommon and local Venezuelan endemic that perhaps is more numerous than evidenced by the few records, probably increasing, at least expanding in the upper Llanos (D. Ascanio).
Habitat Lower Tropical Zone. Freshwater lakes, marshes, swamps and ponds with bushy borders, rushbeds, and dense aquatic vegetation. Flooded pastures and dry tall-grass fields.
Voice A churring rattle, several seconds long (*TBW*), also, a fast sequence of quiet notes, followed by a loud churring rattle that begins falling but may rise and fall (T&VP).

BLACK RAIL *Laterallus jamaicensis* Pl. 44

Identification 12–15cm. Tiny. Black front of head and breast, chestnut nape, upperparts dark olive with small white spots, distal underparts barred black and white; eyes red, bill black, legs and feet dusky flesh. From Speckled Crake by rufous on crown and nape, white barring below.

Ssp. *L. j. jamaicensis* (Co)

Habits Very few data from winter. In Middle America, occurs in both grassy freshwater marshes and coastal saltmarshes. Very secretive but flies strongly when flushed (Howell & Webb 1995), tucks legs in underparts when flying.
Status Boreal migrant that reaches East Andes of Colombia very occasionally as an accidental.
Habitat Temperate Zone to Páramo. Possibly wet meadows or montane lakes.
Voice Possibly rather silent in non-breeding season, when following may not apply. In response to playback, females utter repeated growls; and a low *croo-croo-croo* in alarm. Also *churt* or *kik* barks, resembling sparrow calls, and a soft, low *twirrr* rattle (T&VP).

WHITE-THROATED CRAKE
Laterallus albigularis Pl. 44

Identification 14–16cm. Almost entire head, mantle and breast chestnut, with white throat and crown washed olivaceous, lower back and wings to tail olive, underparts black, barred with narrow white lines; eyes red, bill greenish with dark tip, legs and feet yellowish-green. From Ruddy Crake by barred underparts, from Grey-breasted by rufous on neck and breast.

Ssp. *L. a. albigularis* (N & W Co, W Ec) as described; white throat

L. a. cerdaleus (N Co: Santa Marta, Córdoba) entire head uniform chestnut, black bars broader

Habits Usually located by call. Remains in dense vegetation, even when responding to playback from very close.

Status Uncommon in Ecuador, locally frequent to uncommon in Colombia.

Habitat Tropical Zone. Humid grass fields, wet pastures, marshes. Wet areas with bushy or tall-grass banks. Clearings and dry stream beds in forests and at borders.

Voice A sudden, bubbly churring *thur'tr'tr'tr'tr'tr'tr'tr'tr'* that falls gradually and is usually answered by neighbouring birds (H&B). Also metallic chips and clear piercing whistles, and a *jeer-jeer-jeer* phrase (T&VP).

GREY-BREASTED CRAKE
Laterallus exilis Pl. 44

Identification 14–15.5cm. Grey head, neck- and breast-sides, with chestnut nape and mantle; back, wings and tail olive with fine white tips to wing-coverts and possibly rump and uppertail-coverts, underparts barred black and white; eyes red, bill yellowish-green with dark tip, legs and feet pale greyish-green. From other crakes with barred flanks by pale grey head to breast, and contrasting bright chestnut nape and upper mantle.

Ssp. Monotypic (Ec, Co, Ve, Tr, Gu, Su, FG)

Habits Forages secretively in dense vegetation, mostly alone or perhaps in pairs. Responds to playback but difficult to flush. Skulks away, but may flush short distance with dangling legs.

Status Uncommon in Ecuador, uncommon in Colombia and Venezuela, uncommon in Trinidad (no records Tobago), scarce in Guyana, locally numerous in Suriname.

Habitat Tropical Zone. Marshes, flooded rice fields and wet grassy habitats with dense, short to fairly tall vegetation.

Voice Includes a sudden, quite musical series of (up to 10) fast whistled *dit*, *tink* or *keek* notes, the first very loud then softer (T&VP). Also a falling musical rattle, and short, low *check* or *chk* churrs (H&B).

CLAPPER RAIL *Rallus longirostris* Pl. 45

Identification 31–41cm. A large rail with long legs and long bill, and considerable variation between subspecies, the only common feature being barred lower breast-sides and flanks. Essentially brown above with long dark streaks from nape to tail, usually greyish on face, a paler throat and pale eyebrow, and foreneck and breast uniform pale brown. From smaller Plain-flanked, by barring on flanks. Virginia Rail is brighter and has definite grey cheeks.

Ssp. *R. l. cypereti* (SW Co, Ec) greyish-olive above with paler and generally more greyish fringes, forehead warm brown, breast pinkish-cinnamon, rear underparts pale buffy barred grey, undertail-coverts barred greyish and white; eyes brown, bill dusky above, horn below, legs and feet flesh

R. l. dillonripleyi (NE Ve) dark brown above with blackish centres to feathers, head-sides grey, rest of head dark, white throat cleanly defined; breast dark pinkish-brown; from breast-sides to rear flanks narrowly barred black and white, undertail-coverts white; legs and feet yellowish

R. l. longirostris (Gu, N Su, FG) paler than all except *phelpsi*, short clear pale eyebrow, grey above with darker streaks, throat white, pale grey on centre of breast and belly, washed slightly cinnamon on sides and barred grey and white, undertail-coverts white; iris reddish, bill flesh-coloured with dusky culmen, legs and feet pale orange-red

R. l. margaritae (Margarita I.) much darker and blacker above, with narrower browner fringes, breast darker, barring on sides dark brown and broader than pale bars, undertail-coverts white with black centres to feathers; lower mandible bright pale orange, legs and feet dull pale orange

R. l. pelodramus (Tr) medium rufescent brown above but very heavily streaked, breast deep cinnamon-grey, barred broadly black and slightly more narrowly white, undertail-coverts white, red legs

R. l. phelpsi (NE Co, NW Ve) palest above, with narrow brown streaks on back, primaries cinnamon-brown, breast more cinnamon, barring cinnamon on pale buff, including undertail-coverts; bill orange-red, legs and feet coral red (lower mandible yellowish), pinkish-red legs and feet

Habits Forages alone, in very shallow water, muddy banks, dense reedbeds, tall grasses on banks. Flies only short distances, with feet dangling. Calls dusk to dawn.

Status Very rare in Ecuador. In Colombia, possibly commoner than sightings suggest; locally frequent in Venezuela, common in Trinidad, frequent in Guyana. Decreasing in Suriname.

Habitat Lower Tropical Zone. Mangroves and coastal marshes. In contrast with North American populations, Clapper Rail in northern South America is very much restricted to coastal mangrove habitats. Voice analysis, playback experiments and habitat preferences seem to indicate that it might be a separate species (D. Ascanio).

Voice Loud, fast series of *kak*, *kek*, *che* or *chack* notes that fall in pitch and speed up at end. In breeding season, males give endless series of *kek* notes, whilst females respond with a few *kek* notes followed by a *burrr*.

Note The dark morphs of *R. longirostris* apparently do not occur in northern South America.

PLAIN-FLANKED RAIL

Rallus wetmorei Pl. 45

Identification 24–27cm. Adult all brown, paler on vent and undertail-coverts, heavily streaked darker brown above; eyes dark, bill dark above, slightly paler below, legs and feet dull greenish-yellow. There is a dark sepia to fuscous 'black' morph. Male has slightly longer bill than female. Juvenile has uniform head; streaking on back only starts halfway down neck. From Clapper Rail by lack of barring on flanks, and smaller size.

Ssp. Monotypic (NC Ve)

Habits Forages in pairs or small family groups, walking through the tangles of mangrove roots and waterplants typical of brackish water.

Status Endangered. Populations extant in states of Carabobo and Falcón, Venezuela, but not seen for many years in Aragua, from where species originally described.

Habitat Lower Tropical Zone at sea level. Mainly Black Mangrove (*Avicennia*), although also occurs in Red Mangrove during dry season. Apparently intolerant of new growth, although it feeds in open areas adjacent to mature mangrove at dawn and dusk (D. Ascanio, pers. comm.).

Voice Very similar to Clapper Rail and sometimes inseparable in field from *R. longirostris phelpsi*. Main difference is an ascending growl at beginning that is lacking in Clapper Rail (D. Ascanio, pers. comm.).

VIRGINIA RAIL *Rallus limicola* Pl. 45

Identification 20–27cm. Dark brown on top of head, nape and upperparts, rufous wing-coverts, streaked back, grey face-sides, slight white eyebrow; chin to breast orange-rufous, rest of underparts barred black and white, white bars half width of black ones; eyes red, bill orange-red with dusky culmen and tip, legs and feet orange. Note long, thin, decurved bill with brownish-red lower mandible, and reddish legs. Rufous-sided has white throat and breast, White-throated has rufous head and breast.

Ssp. *R. l. aequatorialis* (SW Co, Ec)

Habits Quite active, solitary, forages by day in dense cover.

Status Uncommon to rare in Ecuador, scarce and not well known in Colombia.

Habitat Tropical to Temperate Zones. Freshwater (very occasionally brackish or saltwater) wetlands such as ponds and lakes, irrigated fields, páramo bogs, swampy grasslands and wet meadows, always with extensive emergent vegetation, sedges, reeds and tall grasses.

Voice A metallic, fading *keh-keh-keh kehkehkeh* (H&B), also antiphonal duets of grunts in breeding season, and an infrequent advertising *kicker* call. Fast *ki ki ki… krrrrr* or *k-krrrr* sequences are possibly unpaired females, monotonous repetitions of *tik-it* notes perhaps unpaired males (T&VP).

BOGOTÁ RAIL *Rallus semiplumbeus* Pl. 45

Identification 25–30cm. Sepia brown crown and nape, dark brown back with black streaks, rufous wing-coverts, dull brown tertials and secondaries, and primaries have chestnut fringes; white throat, entire face and foreneck to breast and belly bluish-grey, flanks to undertail-coverts barred black and white; eyes dark red, bill red with dusky culmen and tip, legs and feet coral red. From Virginia Rail by larger size, and face to upper belly plumbeous-grey.

Ssp. Monotypic (Co: E Andes)

Habits Forages furtively amid dense vegetation, in open only early morning. Very vocal in breeding season.

Status Endangered. Uncommon to locally frequent Colombian East Andes endemic, threatened by habitat loss.

Habitat Temperate Zone. Ponds, fens, marshes, ditches and wet, rushy meadows on montane slopes and in páramos. Dense, tall reedbeds of *Juncus* and especially *Typha* and *Scirpus*, and also where water's edge has thick vegetation (especially dwarf bamboo) and shallows rich in *Elodea* and other water plants.

Voice A loud, piercing *peep*; if alarmed, a short rapid chattering (Taylor). Also various squeaks, grunts, whistles and piping notes, high-pitched 'battles' and a trilled whistle that rises and falls (T&VP).

RUFOUS-NECKED WOOD RAIL

Aramides axillaris Pl. 46

Identification 28–30cm. Head bright rufous, paler on face-sides, throat white, neck and breast to upper flanks deeper reddish-rufous; mantle grey, rest of upperparts olive with chestnut fringes to primaries; belly and thighs to undertail-coverts dusky black; eyes orange to red with grey orbital ring, bill greenish-yellow, legs and feet coral red. Juvenile almost uniform grey, but has paler buffy wash to face- and throat-sides, olivaceous wash to wings, primaries fringed dark chestnut; eyes dark, bill dusky with orange base, legs and feet orange. From Uniform Crake by larger size and black rear parts. Grey-necked and Brown Wood Rails have grey heads.

Ssp. Monotypic (all countries except ABC, To)

Habits Usually in dense foliage, but visits mudflats when tide out.

Status Uncommon to rare in Ecuador, local and scarce in Colombia and Venezuela, uncommon and local on Trinidad, uncommon in Guyana and Suriname. Sight records only in French Guiana.

Habitat Tropical Zone. Mangroves and coastal wetlands, swamps in forest, forest streams, undergrowth of cloud, humid or drier, deciduous forests, mature secondary woodland.

Voice Recalls Grey-necked Wood Rail (H&B). Descriptions include insistent repetitions of a sharp trio of notes, variously *tuk-tuk-tuk*, *pik-pik-pik* or *pyok-pyok-pyok* (T&VP).

GREY-NECKED WOOD RAIL

Aramides cajanea Pl. 46

Identification 33-42cm. Head, neck and mantle grey, but head-sides paler, throat whitish, mantle darkest; back and wings olive-green with rufous fringes to secondaries and primaries; breast to flanks and belly rufous, thighs grey, vent, tail-coverts and tail black; eyes red, bill yellow distally greenish, legs and feet red. From smaller and allopatric Brown Wood Rail, by grey head and neck, and contrastingly-coloured body, rather than uniformly dark brown; from smaller Rufous-necked by grey head.

Ssp. *A. c. cajanea* (all countries)

Habits Calls loudly and excitedly, often in duets or with birds from wide area joining in riotous chorus.
Status Uncommon in Ecuador, frequent in Colombia, frequent and widespread in Venezuela and on Trinidad, frequent in Guyana, common in Suriname, local in French Guiana.
Habitat Tropical Zone. Humid and deciduous lowland forests, *várzea* and *terra firme*, forest swamps and borders of rivers, streams and oxbow lakes, gallery and second-growth forests, swampy *Mauritia* groves, mangroves and coastal marshes, rice fields, fallow fields, scrubby pastures with wet areas, and wet meadows. Recorded in Henri Pittier NP.
Voice A long, varied series of phrases, e.g. *ko-kirri-ko, chirin-co, chirin-co-co-co, trAY-po-trAY-po-trAY-po-po-po, kook-kooky, cococo-coo-coo, whi-who-wee-wee-wee, kook-kak, kre-co*, etc. Sounds happy and musical. Also a loud cackling distress call and a warning *wett!* (Sick).

BROWN WOOD RAIL *Aramides wolfi* Pl. 46

Identification 33–36cm. Grey head and neck with whitish throat, mantle, breast and belly to flanks dull chestnut, lower back and wings olive-green with rufescent fringes to secondaries and primaries, thighs, vent, tail-coverts and tail black; eyes red, bill yellow distally greenish, legs and feet red. From larger, allopatric Grey-necked Wood Rail by brown mantle.

Ssp. Monotypic (W Ec, W Co)

Habits Poorly known. Forages secretively, keeping in cover, though in coastal areas may venture onto mudflats when tide low.
Status Vulnerable. Very rare in Ecuador. In Colombia, uncertain, possibly uncommon to rare and very local.
Habitat Lower Tropical Zone. Swampy forest and secondary woodland, mangroves and swampy, wooded riparian areas.
Voice Call a rhythmic series of hollow, nasal *cjui-cjui-cjui…* notes (*TBW*). Also, as an oft-repeated *kui-co* or *kui-co-mui* (H&B), sometimes with several birds joining in chorus (T&VP).

RED-WINGED WOOD RAIL
Aramides calopterus Pl. 46

Identification 31–33cm. Crown, hindneck, back and scapulars greenish-olive, head- and neck-sides, and wings rufous; throat white, grading into grey neck, breast, belly and flanks, thighs, vent, tail-coverts and tail black; eyes red, bill yellow distally greenish, legs and feet red. Immature has blackish legs and feet. From all other rails by mahogany red on head-sides and wing-coverts, white throat and dark grey breast.

Ssp. Monotypic (Ec)

Habits Very poorly known.
Status Local and scarce throughout fragmented and very small known range. Very rare in Ecuador. In Colombia, uncertain but possible in Amazonas and Putumayo.
Habitat Lower Tropical Zone. Humid forests, especially flooded forests, but also in *terra firme*. Some confusion as to preferred habitat: J. P. O'Neill (*fide* H&B) considers that it is wet or swampy places *inside* forest, rather than riparian areas, whilst R&G consider that it is mostly found along streams.
Voice Unknown.

UNIFORM CRAKE
Amaurolimnas concolor Pl. 44

Identification 20–23cm. Unique, almost unicoloured. Rufescent-olive above, chestnut below; eyes deep red, bill dull yellow with greener base, legs and feet red.

Ssp. *A. c. castaneus* (Ve, Gu, FG) as described
A. c. guatemalensis (W Co, W Ec) more olivaceous and generally paler

Habits Keeps to dense cover and very reluctant to flush.
Status Very rare and local in Ecuador, uncommon and very local in Colombia and Venezuela, scarce in Guyana, uncertain in French Guiana.
Habitat Tropical Zone. Wet and swampy places with thickets or dense undergrowth in humid or wet forests, flooded forest, streams, oxbow lakes, ravines, swampy stands of palms or *Heliconia* in forest. Mangrove borders. Sometimes in drier areas in secondary woodland or bushy, wooded borders of cultivated plots near pristine forest.
Voice A loud series of slurred *tooee* whistles that first rise and then fall in volume, *tooeee tooeee Tooeee TOOEEE Tooeee tooeee-twee-tui* (H&B); as contact calls between pairs, *tooo* whistles, and when alarmed nasal *kek* or *plik* notes (T&VP).

SORA *Porzana carolina* Pl. 45

Identification 19–25cm. Cryptic plumage. Brown crown, hindneck and upperparts, black patch on rear crown, back and wings streaked black with grey fringes to feathers and small white spots, wing-coverts lack any black; grey eyebrow continues round brown patch on upper ear-coverts, neck-sides pale grey, breast grey, faintly barred paler grey; face black with a black line running down centre of throat to mid breast, small white spot behind eyes; belly whitish and undertail-coverts buffy, flanks and thighs barred black, white and brown; eyes red, bill yellow, legs and feet pale green. Female similar but black line does not reach breast, bill distally greenish. Juvenile lacks black or grey on head and breast, being olivaceous and cinnamon respectively. Look for yellow bill with black around it in face. Juvenile from Ash-throated Crake by lack of any grey and white undertail-coverts.

Ssp. Monotypic (Ec, Co, Ve, ABC, T&T, Gu)

Habits In wintering grounds usually solitary. Comes to edge of reeds or other vegetation early morning. Swims and submerges to feed. Flies with broken, shifting flight.
Status Boreal migrant to north-east South America. Rare in Ecuador, frequent both on passage and in winter in Aruba,

Curaçao and Bonaire (though only sight records from latter 2 islands). As a winter resident, locally frequent to common in Colombia (October–May) and Venezuela (September–May), common in Trinidad but scarce on Tobago, scarce in Guyana and Suriname.
Habitat Lower Tropical Zone, but note there are records at 3,200m in the Andes of Mérida, Venezuela. Winters in fresh or brackish wetlands with extensive reeds and other emergent plants, submerged vegetation, floating plants and shallow open spots. Mangroves and mudflats, rice paddies, drainage ditches, irrigation channels, ponds and lakes.
Voice Main breeding-season call is a series of *c.*12 plaintive, whinnying *whee-hee-hee-hee-hee-hee…* notes, but birds rarely call in winter. Also a rising, complaining *kerwee* or *er-eee* whistle and a metallic *kee* or *kiu* alarm-call (H&B, ffrench, T&VP, Hilty).

ASH-THROATED CRAKE
Porzana albicollis Pl. 45

Identification 21–24cm. Brown above from forehead to tail, streaked darker; chin and upper throat pale grey, and grey from throat to belly, flanks to undertail-coverts barred black and white; eyes red, bill greenish, legs and feet green.

Ssp. *P. a. olivacea* (Co, Ve, Tr, Guianas)

Habits Forages mostly alone, within cover or, quite frequently, at edge of grasses. Shy, may flush suddenly from almost underfoot, but can be curious, peering out in response to noise.
Status Locally scarce to possibly quite frequent in Colombia and Venezuela, rare in Trinidad, frequent in Guyana, locally frequent in Suriname, common in coastal French Guiana.
Habitat Tropical Zone. Tall grasses and reeds around freshwater wetlands: lakes, marshes, *Mauritia* palm bogs, rice paddies, wet pastures, drainage ditches and irrigation channels, wet or boggy grassland.
Voice A sharp *tuk* note (H&B) and loud series of vibrating *d'd'd'd'd'-ou, d'd'd'd'd'-ou, d'd'd'd'd'-ou* phrases, sounding like a machine-gun (P. Schwartz *fide* H&B). Pairs also sing antiphonally, the male a repeated *carrrreau-carrrreau-carrrreau…*, the female a sharp *kere-kere-kere-kere* (T&VP).

YELLOW-BREASTED CRAKE
Porzana flaviventer Pl. 45

Identification 12.5–14cm. Tiny size, buffy-white eyebrow and dark line through eye combined with contrasting buffy scapulars along back are diagnostic. Heavy black-and-white barring on flanks and undertail-coverts.

Ssp. *P. f. bangsi* (N Co) neck-sides much paler; back, rump more heavily variegated
P. f. flaviventer (Ec, Co, Ve, T&T, Gu, Su, FG) as described

Habits Forages alone, sometimes in pairs, clambering on tangles of reeds or mats of floating vegetation or ambling in edge grasses. When flushed, flies short distance with dangling head and feet.
Status Rare and local in Ecuador. Locally common in Colombia, local in Venezuela and Trinidad & Tobago, uncommon in Guyana, abundance uncertain in Suriname.
Habitat Lower Tropical Zone. Freshwater (rarely brackish or saltwater) wetlands with grassy edges and abundant emergent and floating vegetation. Lakes, ponds, marshes, flooded fields and pastures, rice paddies.
Voice A thin *peeep* (P&MdS); a rough, slow, falling *zeee-eee-eee-eee* and loud ringing *clureeoo* (H&B); a churring *k'kuk kurr-kurr* or *je-je-je-jrrr*, a whinny *kreeihr*, a single *krreer* and high-pitched *fi-fi-fuu* in alarm (T&VP).
Note Sometimes placed in genus *Poliolimnas*.

COLOMBIAN CRAKE
Neocrex colombiana Pl. 45

Identification 18–21cm. Grey head with white chin, grey neck and slate grey underparts to flanks and vent, undertail-coverts bright creamy buff; back brown; eyes orange to red, bill yellow with red base, legs and feet red. Distinctive two-toned bill is a great field mark.

Ssp. *N. c. colombiana* (N & W Co, W Ec) as described
N. c. ripleyi (NW Co) paler grey, brown of back extends halfway onto hindneck, undertail-coverts barred cinnamon

Habits Rather skulking though may venture onto open trails and areas with muddy patches. Generally a bird of lush grassland.
Status Very rare in Ecuador and rare in Colombia.
Habitat Tropical to Subtropical Zones. Freshwater wetlands and wet places with grasses, reeds and other dense vegetation. Fields and pastures, rice fields, ponds, marshes, canals and ditches.
Voice Short series of very creaky, 'protesting' squeaks, commencing with a double-noted *uearghk-argk* followed by three creaky squeaks, a short pause, then 4 single *uearghk* notes (O. Jahn recording).
Note Sometimes placed in genus *Porzana*.

PAINT-BILLED CRAKE
Neocrex erythrops Pl. 45

Identification 18–20cm. Brown from crown to tail, grey head-sides, foreneck, breast to belly and flanks, undertail-coverts barred black and white; eyes orange-red, bill has red basal half becoming yellow distally, legs and feet red. Juvenile paler brown above and warmer grey below; eyes brown, bill greyish-yellow, legs and feet pale olive. Similar Grey-breasted is much paler below, has no red on bill and a chestnut mantle. Colombian Crake is allopatric.

Ssp. *N. e. olivascens* (W Ec, Co, Ve, Tr, Guianas) as described
N. e. erythrops (probably in Ec, but unconfirmed) paler with whiter throat

Habits Secretive.
Status Very rare in Ecuador (first record 1992), locally frequent in Colombia and Venezuela, rare and seasonal on Trinidad, uncommon in Guyana, uncommon to rare in Suriname. Sight records only in French Guiana.

Habitat Tropical to Subtropical Zones. Fresh and brackish marshes with dense emergent vegetation, or away from water in dense shrubbery, thickets or tall grasses.
Voice Song a sequence commencing with a long, gradually accelerating and falling series of staccato notes, then 3–4 short churrs, culminating in a 3 s trill (T&VP). Calls loud guttural frog-like *qurrrrk* or *auuuuk* notes, sometimes in series, *qurrrrk auuuuk qurrrrk auuuuk…* (P. Schwartz *fide* H&B). Also, a sharp *twack* in alarm.
Notes Sometimes placed in genus *Porzana* (e.g. Ripley). Specimen from Ecuador apparently is of race *olivascens*, although collected in Manabí, west of the Andes (R&G).

SPOTTED RAIL *Pardirallus maculatus* Pl. 46

Identification 25–32cm. Adult has dark sepia cap, rest of head and neck to upper breast streaked black and white, lower breast to undertail-coverts barred black and white, longest undertail-coverts white; back to tail black with broad olive fringes to all feathers affording a spotted or scaly appearance, the feather shafts white; wing-coverts brown with slight black centres and white shafts, but tertials and greater coverts are black, fringed olive with white lines on outer edges (but not tips); eyes red, long yellow bill with bold red spot at base, legs and feet bright red. Three distinct juvenile morphs: the barred is closest to the adult, and has broader black and white bars on underparts; eyes brown, bill dull yellow with orange base, legs and feet orange. Pale-morph juvenile is medium brown above, beige below with some fine white barring. Dark-morph juvenile is deep dusky brown above with a few scattered white lines, and deep brownish-grey below, with shadow-bars on flanks. Variegated plumage and long greenish bill with red spot at base unmistakable. Juveniles in all morphs from Plain-flanked by shorter, thicker yellowish bill with pink base, and faint barring on flanks.

Ssp. *P. m. maculatus* (Co, Ve, T&T, Su, FG)

Habits Secretive. Sometimes active at night.
Status Rare in Ecuador (first recorded in 1984), locally frequent in Colombia, rare and local in Venezuela and pattern of records suggests a possible migratory behaviour, uncommon in Trinidad, very rare (possibly extinct) on Tobago, frequent in Suriname, local in French Guiana (seemingly unknown in Guyana).
Habitat Lower Tropical Zone. Freshwater marshes with dense emergent vegetation and fringed by woods, tall grasses or thickets. Rice fields, overgrown ditches and canals, wet pastures and grasslands.
Voice A *greech* or *grrrr*, or *krkrreih* or *pump-kreep* grunt, followed by loud repetitions of a groaning screech. Also, a speeding series of deep pumping *wuh-wuh* notes, like a motor being started; also a *gek* note in alarm, and occasional *tick* and *chick* calls.
Note Formerly placed in genus *Rallus*.

PLUMBEOUS RAIL
Pardirallus sanguinolentus Pl. 46

Identification 28–38cm. Fairly large rail; uniform deep brown on forehead, hindneck and upperparts, face from lores to ear-coverts and on flanks and thighs slate grey, vent and undertail-coverts mid brown; eyes orange, long bill greenish-yellow with upper mandible base blue, base of lower red, legs and feet flesh. Juvenile dark brown above, ochraceous below, slightly paler throat; eyes dark brown, bill dusky, legs and feet blue-grey.

Ssp. *P. s. simonsi* (S Ec: Loja)

Habits Secretive. Sometimes active at night.
Status Very rare in Ecuador, where first recorded in 1991.
Habitat Subtropical Zone (in Ecuador). Freshwater marshes with reeds and floating vegetation, especially at mouths of muddy creeks. Ponds, rivers, lakes, swamps, ditches, rice and alfalfa paddies, boggy, rushy pastures, moist to wet cultivated areas.
Voice Sings in duet, the male song a series of penetrating squeals, e.g. *rrueet'e*, *pu-rueet*, *huyr*, *tsewWit* and others, whilst female gives low, deep *hoo* notes.
Note Formerly placed in genus *Ortygonax*.

BLACKISH RAIL *Pardirallus nigricans* Pl. 46

Identification 27–32cm. Long straight bill, greenish with yellowish base. Uniform fuscous from forehead to tail, whitish throat, deep slate grey below, with black undertail-coverts; eyes red, legs and feet coral red. From Plumbeous by reddish legs and dark undertail-coverts.

Ssp. *P. n. caucae* (SW Co) slightly paler, more bluish-grey below, throat whiter, legs, feet brick-red
P. n. nigricans (E Ec) as described

Habits May venture onto muddy banks or mudflats to forage with waders or other waterbirds.
Status Rare to locally uncommon in Ecuador, uncommon in Colombia and in Venezuela, where first records were fairly recent (Caballero *et al.* 1984).
Habitat Tropical to Subtropical Zones. Freshwater marshes and riverine areas with sedges, reeds and floating vegetation, swampy woods, rice paddies, wet meadows and pastures with tall grass.
Voice A fast, metallic *tii'd'dit*, similar to a spinetail, and a plaintive *keeeeeaaa*, like cry of a hawk (H&B). Also, warning whistles, e.g. *tirit*, *kirk* and *PEEEoooo*. Male song a penetrating *whuueeee wheeee wheeee chee chee chee chee chee chee chechch*, often in duet with female, which gives an almost inaudible *bu bu bu bu bu…* (T&VP).
Note Formerly placed in the genus *Ortygonax*.

Gallinules, coots and moorhens are generally rotund, blackish birds with reflections of purple and blue, and have face plaques that range from white to bright red. Unlike rails and crakes they are much more likely to be seen in the open as they forage at the edge of reedbeds or walk on lily leaves and fallen reeds. They fly and swim strongly, bobbing their heads whilst swimming.

SPOT-FLANKED GALLINULE

Gallinula melanops Pl. 47

Identification 22–30cm. Blackish face merges into grey head, neck and breast, upperparts uniform milk chocolate-brown; flanks rufous with round white spots, central belly to undertail-coverts white; eyes red, bill and frontal shield pale green, legs and feet yellowish-green. Juvenile lacks black face and more buffy on throat and breast than grey, back more olive; eyes brown.

Ssp. *G. m. bogotensis* (Co: E Andes)

Habits Forages alone or in pairs. Not secretive. Usually seen swimming in reeds (seldom in open water), or clambering nimbly on reeds and floating plants. Seldom on land. An individual calling on territory will trigger a chain of calls from the surrounding reeds.

Status Locally common in Colombia, where race *bogotensis* has tiny distribution, thousands of miles from the otherwise southern South America range of the species.

Habitat Tropical to Temperate Zones. Freshwater wetlands with abundant emergent and floating vegetation, and dense beds of reeds and rushes. Wet savannas and meadows, marshes, marshy rivers, lakes, ponds, ditches.

Voice Usually silent, but gives clicking and clucking calls, and a *tap-tap-tap*... when foraging. Song is a loud *huh-huh-huh-huh-huh*... burst of hysterical laughs that tails off.

Note Formerly placed in genus *Porphyriops*.

PURPLE GALLINULE

Porphyrula martinica Pl. 47

Identification 27–36cm. Adult has back, wings and tail deep bottle green with turquoise wash to mantle, outer greater coverts and secondaries, and narrowly on flanks; head, neck and underparts rich, almost electric purplish-blue, with black undertail-coverts; eyes dark brown, frontal shield pale blue, basal two-thirds of bill bright red, distal third yellow. Juvenile soft brown above, including head and neck, with pale turquoise wash to wings and rump, breast to flanks and thighs buffy, belly to undertail-coverts white. Adult unmistakable. Immature from adult Azure Gallinule by buffy neck, head-sides and breast, and by bluish frontal shield with brownish bill, and from immature Azure Gallinule by brown back and tail, rather than black or blackish.

Ssp. Monotypic (Ec, Co, Ve, ABC, T&T, Gu, Su, FG)

Habits Forages, usually in pairs but sometimes in flocks of 50+, within or near cover. Sometimes in open, on grassy banks or floating or emergent vegetation, clambering over plants. In rice fields, may much damage, and farmers consider them pests. Occasionally perches on bushes or fence posts near water. Very vocal and excitable, and a calling individual often triggers responses from others.

Status Locally common in Ecuador and Colombia, locally frequent in Venezuela, sight records only for Aruba, Curaçao and Bonaire, where an occasional visitor from both North and South America, common in Trinidad & Tobago, frequent in Guyana, locally numerous in Suriname.

Habitat Tropical Zone. Freshwater wetlands with dense aquatic vegetation, emergents as much as floating and submerged plants. Marshes, lakes and ponds, river deltas, rice fields, overgrown ditches and irrigation canals. Birds in the *llanos* of the river Orinoco have a movement corresponding to the flooding and reducing of the Orinoco and its tributaries (D. Ascanio).

Voice Calls very varied, including reedy cackles, guttural notes (H&B), laughs and grunts. Descriptions include a decelerating *hiddy-hiddy-hiddy, hit-up, hit-up, hit-up*; a sharp *hi-pit kyik* or *ki-lik* that sometimes is given with a booming undertone; and a loud *kur*, often following several *cook* notes, or sometimes *cu-kur-cu*; a Limpkin-like *whiehrrrr* shriek; in alarm, a fast and fading series of *keh* or *ka* notes; and in flight, *kek, kek, kek* notes (T&VP).

Note Sometimes placed in Old World genus *Porphyrio* (e.g. H&B, T&VP). They are very similar, though *Porphyrula* are generally smaller.

AZURE GALLINULE

Porphyrula flavirostris Pl. 47

Identification 23–26cm. Unusually coloured, narrow line of brown from crown to back, wings and tail, with azure or pale bluish-turquoise fringes to feathers, sufficiently broad that almost entire wing appears blue; chin to undertail-coverts white, well washed with azure from sides of face to sides of breast, fading on flanks; eyes reddish-brown, small frontal shield and bill dull, almost greenish-yellow, legs and feet strong yellow. Juvenile browner above and buffy on head, neck and breast. No mistaking adult. Immature Purple Gallinule is rather larger and has green legs, as does Ash-throated Crake.

Ssp. Monotypic (all countries)

Habits Forages in cover or nearby, or on tangles and mats of floating vegetation. Very seldom seen swimming or in open, but occasionally perches on floating mats of emergent plants.

Status Uncommon in Ecuador, uncommon and local and seasonal in Colombia and Venezuela, common in low Llanos November to May but disappearing when rains begin, local in Trinidad (no records Tobago), frequent in Guyana, common in Suriname, locally common in French Guiana.

Habitat Lower Tropical Zone. Freshwater wetlands with dense aquatic vegetation, emergents as much as floating and submerged plants. Marshes, streams and rivers, oxbow lakes and ponds, rice paddies.

Voice Rather silent. Infrequent short trills (H&B), also a *krrrr, krrra, kra* or *ka*, in manner typical of Old World *Porphyrio* (T&VP).

Note Sometimes placed in Old World genus *Porphyrio* (e.g. Ripley, H&B). They are very similar, though *Porphyrula* are generally smaller.

COMMON MOORHEN

Gallinula chloropus Pl. 47

Identification 30–38cm. White upper flanks distinctive in all plumages. Adult has upperparts entirely dark brown; head and underparts black, with broad white fringes to sides and flanks, producing a sketchy line on the middle of the body, and outer undertail-coverts white with black central feathers; eyes dark brown, frontal shield and basal two-thirds of bill bright red, tip yellow, legs above the heel red, rest of legs and feet yellow. Immature fuscous above and brownish-grey below, flecked white on eyebrow, face-sides and throat, and shares adult pattern on undertail-coverts; bill green with yellowish tip. Juvenile olive above, greyish-olive on head, neck and underparts, with white throat and white outer undertail-coverts.

Ssp. *G. c. galeata* (Ve, T&T, Gu, Su, FGu) as described
G. c. pauxilla (N & W Co, W Ec) more greyish-brown, shield much broader

Habits Forages on land and whilst swimming, alone or in flocks of up to 30, by day and on moonlit nights. Less furtive than others (behaviour confident in open), except in Suriname, where rather shy. Walks with high steps and tail horizontal on land, whilst on reeds and floating vegetation clambers gingerly but nimbly with cocked tail. Roosts on trees or bushes at waterside.
Status Common in Ecuador. In Colombia locally frequent resident, with migrants possibly occurring October–April. Local in Venezuela. Irregular in Aruba, Curaçao and Bonaire. Common in Trinidad & Tobago, scarce in Guyana, and rare and local in Suriname.
Habitat Tropical Zone to Páramo. Fresh, very occasionally brackish or saltwater wetlands of many types provided there are wooded shores, a great abundance of emergent and floating water plants, and patches of open water. Marshes, lakes, ponds, rivers and streams, reservoirs and rice fields, sewage farms and seasonal pools.
Voice Varied clicks and chattering calls, often frequently repeated. A sudden loud *krrrrruk!* or *kark!*; a harsh *kik-kik-kik-kik…* in annoyance; a loud *kuk* or *kittick* in alarm; and a *kek-kek-kek-kek…* in flight (Sick, H&B, T&VP).
Note Formerly called Common Gallinule.

AMERICAN COOT *Fulica americana* Pl. 47

Identification 34–43cm. Black head and deep grey (looks black) rest, undertail-coverts white; eyes red, frontal shield and bill white (shield has reddish-brown or dark chestnut callous that covers forehead, and in breeding birds may almost cover shield), and a dark reddish-brown ring around bill near tip, yellow legs have red tibia, feet are yellow with blue-grey lobes. Juvenile olive-brown above, paler ashen below; eyes brown, bill and frontal shield bone-coloured with callous rather faint, legs and feet grey. From Caribbean Coot, by shield, which is large, flat (not bulbous), and by reddish-brown callous atop white shield.

Ssp. *F. a. columbiana* (Ec, Co, N Ve)

Habits Forages in water as well as along shore, where it walks busily with characteristic humpback stance. Feeds on seeds and other vegetable matter, small molluscs and insects, taken by immersing head or upending. When alarmed, rises and opens tail to show white in alarm.
Status Apparently extinct in Ecuador. Locally common in Colombia, where both migrants and year-round residents occur. Casual visitor (sight records only) to Venezuela, Curaçao, Aruba and Bonaire, rare in Tobago (not recorded Trinidad). Presence apparently connected to periods when rains are unusually heavy.
Habitat Tropical to Temperate Zones. Preferably fresh but occasionally brackish wetlands (ponds, lakes, marshes, slow rivers) with reeds along shores and a variety of emergent, submerged and floating water plants.
Voice Calls frequently, varied cackling and clucking notes, often repeated. Males and females separable by voice. Thus, alarm is *puhlk* in males and *poonk* in females; stress is a sorrowful *puhk-cowah* or *pow-ur* in males, and *cooah* in females; intimidation is a *puhk-kuk-kuh* or *cook-uk-ook* in males, and *kaw-pow* or *kra-kow* in females; recognition is *puhk* in males and a low nasal *punk* in females. Courting males call a coughing perk-perk-perk… (T&VP).
Note Formerly considered conspecific with *F. caribaea*. Records for both species difficult to separate in the literature.

CARIBBEAN COOT *Fulica caribaea* Pl. 47

Identification 33–38cm. Black head and upperparts, greyer below, almost mid grey on vent, and white undertail-coverts; eyes orange to red, frontal shield and bill all white with dark chestnut band near bill tip, legs olivaceous yellow, feet darker, greenish-grey. Juvenile uniform grey above, paler below, faintly barred whitish; legs and feet olive-grey. From American Coot, by shield, which is bulbous (not flat), and white or sometimes tinged yellow-orange, never reddish-chestnut.

Ssp. Monotypic (Co, Ve, ABC, T&T)

Habits Forages amid emergents or in areas with beds of bottom-growing plants. Mostly in small groups that confidently swim in open or occasionally walk along shore.
Status Possibly a casual visitor to north-west Colombian coast. Resident in north Venezuela, where frequent but very local. Seasonal resident, and frequent though irregular breeder in Aruba, Curaçao and Bonaire. Scarce in Trinidad & Tobago.
Habitat Lower Tropical Zone. Preferably fresh but occasionally brackish wetlands (lakes, marshes, ponds, slow streams), with reeds and abundant emergent or floating aquatic vegetation.
Voice Various cackling, croaking and clucking notes, similar to American Coot. Also a grating click and rising *krrr-rrrh* in alarm (T&VP).
Note Formerly considered a race of *F. americana*. Records difficult to separate in the literature.

SLATE-COLOURED COOT *Fulica ardesiaca* Pl. 47

Identification 40–44cm. Black head and slate grey body, darker above. Highly variable bill and large, bulbous frontal shield coloration, resulting in 2 morphs being recognised, but other variants occur. Red-fronted morph has shield reddish to chestnut with yellow, white, partially greenish, or any combination-coloured bill, and greenish legs and feet. Pale-fronted morph has bill and shield all white, or shield yellow and bill white, with legs and feet grey to lavender. Juvenile brownish-grey above, quite pale grey on face to white on throat, becoming grey on foreneck and a mix of mid brown and grey lower down, then browner on undertail-coverts (only outer coverts white); eyes brown; bill and small frontal shield grey, legs and feet greenish. From American Coot by paler, slate-coloured body, and different, more bulbous, shield shape.

Ssp. *F. a. atrura* (S Co, Ec)

Habits Forages in areas with much aquatic vegetation, diving to take shoots, leaves, seeds, snails and aquatic insects. Pairs, families or small flocks swim in open water, but seek cover of reeds and other vegetation if approached. Sometimes forages by walking on mats of floating vegetation and, less frequently, along grassy shores.

Status Uncommon to locally common in Ecuador and Colombia.

Habitat In Colombia and Ecuador, Subtropical Zone to Páramo (coastal wetlands in Peru). Freshwater wetlands (ponds, lakes, marshes, slow rivers) with reeds along shores and variety of emergent, submerged and floating water plants. Occasionally in lakes and ponds without reeds. Red-fronted morph tends to dominate at lower altitudes in range, usually well-vegetated wetlands, whilst white-fronted is predominant at higher altitudes, often at montane lakes with no reeds but beds of bottom-growing *Chara* algae.

Voice A low *churrrr* or a frequent, harder *chrrrp, hrrr*, possibly by males, whilst females give low *phyji phyji* chatter (T&VP).

Note Sometimes called Andean Coot.

HELIORNITHIDAE – Sungrebe

Sungrebes are also known as finfoots because of their lobed toes, like grebes and coots, but their tails contain 18 long, rounded rectrices. It is a poorly known family of just 3 species, 1 each in the tropics of the New World, Africa and Asia. Its affinities are far from clear, though DNA evidence suggests it to be closer to Limpkin than any other family. The Sungrebe lives in freshwater streams, slow-flowing rivers and lakes surrounded by dense vegetation. Secretive and shy, they usually occur solitarily or in pairs, swimming low in water or perching motionless for long periods near surface. They are most active early morning and late afternoon, and feed on insects, crustaceans, amphibians, small fish and seeds. To roost, they climb to overhanging branches from where they can drop directly to the water if disturbed. By day, they do not dive to escape danger like other waterbirds but flee onto dry land and run like rails. However, if surprised in comparatively open water they partially submerge and remain motionless. Males possess unique pocket-like folds of skin under the wings where the young are carried.

Additional references used to prepare this family include Gilliard (1958) and Bertram (1996).

SUNGREBE *Heliornis fulica* Pl. 48

Identification 28–30cm. Virtually unmistakable. Resembles a small long-tailed duck or grebe but is instantly recognised by striped black-and-white neck. Male has head black and white, with broad white eyebrow, white lores and below eyes, and white line from white throat diagonally on neck-sides. Above entirely olive with narrow white tips to tail visible in flight, breast pale olive, narrowly on flanks and undertail-coverts; eyes dark, bill dark above and yellow below, legs an extraordinary orange with black bands. Female has orange patch on head-sides, red eyelids and vermilion-red bill, yellowish at base. Note, outside breeding season, both sexes possess male-like plumage, juveniles are duller.

Ssp. Monotypic (Ec, Co, Ve, Tr, Gu, Su, FG)

Habits Shy and secretive, foraging alone, more rarely in pairs, by swimming in still water under or near cover. When disturbed dives or flies off, barely above water. Sometimes swims with just head and neck above water, like an Anhinga.

Status Rare to uncommon in Ecuador, uncommon and local in Colombia and Venezuela, rare in Trinidad (no records Tobago), frequent in Guyana, locally frequent in Suriname, uncommon and local in French Guiana.

Habitat Tropical Zone. Freshwater habitats with slow-moving or still water, and dense marginal or overhanging vegetation.

Voice A series of deep, hollow, honking notes, *ooh, ooh, ooh, ooh, ooh*... (H&B, B. Coffey recording), and *eeyoo, eeyoo, eeyoo-eeyaaa, eeyaa* (M. Álvarez del Toro in Bertram).

EURYPYGIDAE – Sunbittern

The only member of the family, the Sunbittern is a curious and elegant bird of humid forest regions in the New World tropics. It is a long-legged, long-necked, slender bird with unwebbed feet, and a distinctive horizontal stance. Secretive, but often confiding, Sunbitterns favour shady areas at the edges of rivers, streams, lakes and wet areas, though it is also regularly seen in open muddy areas on riverbanks. Its diet includes small fish, insects, snails, small vertebrates and seeds, snatched with jabbing heron-like movements at the water edge. The Sunbittern has remarkably patterned wings which are spread wide in its spectacular courtship and threat displays to reveal a startlingly brilliant pair of 'ocelli' (false eyes). More often, it is observed stalking through the undergrowth beside a stream or river alone or in 'pairs', usually of an adult and nearly grown but still-dependent juvenile. When disturbed, it often flies to perch on a branch. Builds a nest of mud and sticks on the ground or low in a tree; although the young are precocial, they remain in the nest for 2–3 weeks.

Additional references used to prepare this family include Gilliard (1958), Hudson (1985) and Thomas (1996).

SUNBITTERN *Eurypyga helias* Pl. 48

Identification 46–48cm. Unmistakable. Cryptically plumaged, with complex brown and grey mottling and spots, a thin neck and small head, large-looking body and thin, long legs. Reveals exquisite and complex wing pattern in flight and during amazing display, when it raises and bows the wings.

Ssp. *E. h. helias* (E Co, C & S Ve, Gu, Su, FG) larger and greyer above, with narrower dark grey bars; legs and bill perhaps more reddish

E. h. major (W Ec, W Co, NW & N Ve) as described

Habits Stands horizontally, walks elegantly across muddy ground or wet forest litter; does not wade, even in shallow water. Flies buoyantly with rapid beats interspersed by glides.

Sunbittern flying beside a forest stream with characteristic stiff-winged, planing character

Status Rare to uncommon in Ecuador, locally frequent in Colombia, locally frequent to common in Venezuela, frequent in Guyana, and rather scarce in Suriname and French Guiana.
Habitat Tropical Zone. In forested areas beside rivers, streams, lakes, ponds, marshes, and damp areas inside forest. Scarce and local in mangroves. At higher elevations along rushing rivers.
Voice Calls mostly at dawn and dusk, a long high-pitched whistle, *huuuuuuuuuu*. Cackles in contact or alarm, and utters a thin, complaining trill (H&B). Both sexes have varied trills, some rising, others descending, and a loud *kak-kak-kak-kak* in advertisement (Thomas).

CHARADRIIDAE – Plovers

Together, plovers and lapwings form the Charadriidae, a family of small compact waders found on bare or thinly vegetated ground, often near water. They can run swiftly and fly strongly. Their wings are long, for those that live at higher latitudes are all long-distance migrants; some are quite remarkable travellers, covering astonishing distances; they breed in very northern latitudes and winter at the southernmost end of the world. Tails are short and they are clad in strong patterns of black, brown, grey and white – with the occasional yellow or tawny-orange – but are surprisingly cryptic due to the disruptive effect of the contrasting patterns. Many respond to potential danger simply by standing perfectly still, relying on their camouflage. Outside the breeding season they are gregarious, but may still be scattered as they forage on shores or plains, congregating to roost.

Additional references used in preparing this family include Thomson (1964), Hayman, Marchant & Prater (1986, referred to here as HMP), Piersma et al. (1996), Wiersma (1996), Sibley (2000) and Paulson (2005).

PIED LAPWING *Vanellus cayanus* Pl. 49

Identification 21–24cm. Small, black-faced lapwing with broad black band encircling pure white throat and face, continuing over crown, with white rear crown and nape. Scapulars are black, forming a V across back.

Ssp. Monotypic (all mainland countries, Tr)

Habits Quite distinctive. Feeds like a sand plover, running forward in short bursts. Usually in well-dispersed pairs.
Status Generally rare, albeit widespread, but always local resident. Uncommon to locally frequent in Ecuador and Venezuela, uncommon and local in Colombia, vagrant to Trinidad, frequent in Guyana, rather rare in Suriname, and exceptional in French Guiana.
Habitat Swamps and low ground by rivers and sandbars, always surrounded by forest.
Voice Usually quiet, but gives a characteristic *whee-whoot* (R&G) or *kee-oo* (HMP) with the second syllable lower. When flushed utters a *kiee* (HMP) or *wheeyp?* (R&G).
Notes Usually placed with lapwings in *Vanellus* (e.g. HMP, Wiersma, Dickinson 2003), but similar to *Charadrius* plovers in many ways, and often placed in own genus, *Hoploxypterus*, e.g. by H&M and Hilty. We follow AOU (1998). Sometimes called Pied Plover.

SOUTHERN LAPWING
Vanellus chilensis Pl. 50

Identification 31–38cm. Unmistakable, boldly patterned, crested lapwing. Crown, most of neck and upperparts brownish-grey; forehead black and forecrown white, with fine nuchal crest consisting of a couple of black feathers, and bronze scapulars and wing-coverts that are bottle green shot with purple iridescence, median wing-coverts increasingly white towards outer wing and greater coverts all white, which appear as a large white V across spread wings in flight, and white uppertail-coverts; chin and throat black, breast black, rest of underparts white; eyes and eye-ring red, bill red with black tip, legs and feet coral. Juvenile brownish-grey above, barred blackish on crown and nape, fading on hindneck, strongly defined on back and wings, and with white wingbar as adult. Andean Lapwing is paler and lacks crest.

Ssp. *V. c. cayennensis* (all countries)

Habits Noisy, usually in pairs, families or seasonal groups. Pairs usually well dispersed, but occasionally several pairs may nest close together and band together to scold or mob an interloper. Slow-flapping display-flight, but usually has light springy wingbeats. When not breeding flocks maybe large.
Status Widespread and common, except Suriname and French Guina, where very rare.
Habitat Tropical to Temperate Zones. Pastures, damp meadows, open boggy areas, ranchland and unattended grazing land, ploughed areas.
Voice Very noisy and quick to raise alarm, with many different harsh barking cries, *tee-ow* and *pi-up*, often repeated rapidly (HMP), a strident *keh-keh-keh-keh-keh* at the slightest provocation (R&G) or metallic scolding *keek, keek, keek, keek*…or *kee-kee-kee-kee*… (Hilty).

ANDEAN LAPWING

Vanellus resplendens Pl. 50

Identification 33–36cm. Creamy-coloured head with rounded grey mask, lower neck becoming increasingly greyish, ending abruptly in a narrow white collar, and thin black line separates breast from belly and rest of underparts, which are white; back and inner wings dark olivaceous green, with purple lesser wing-coverts; median coverts increasingly white towards outer wing and greater coverts all white, which appears as a large white V across spread wings in flight, with white uppertail-coverts and white outer tail-feathers; eyes and eye-ring red, bill red with black tip, legs and feet coral.

Ssp. Monotypic (Ec, SW Co)

Habits Wary and noisy. On alighting, stands wings raised, showing striking black-and-white pattern.

Status Locally common.

Habitat Temperate Zone to Puna. Breeds at 3,000–4,500m, but occasionally much lower in non-breeding season, when recorded at 300 m in Ecuador. Open short-grassy areas usually near freshwater lakes and rivers (avoids brackish water). Often on partly inundated and hummocky ground.

Voice Noisy, quickly flying up to mob an approaching observer, especially when nesting, a loud *kree! kree! kree!* (R&G). A soft querulous call. Alarm a sharp *wik!* or similar disyllabic cry, often repeated rapidly and noisily as groups mob an intruder (HMP). Mobs with a harsh *criEE-criEE…*, a staccato *cwi-cwi-cwi…*, or more mellow and melodic *didididi – ceLEEC-ceLEEC-ceLEEC…* and sometimes a low, tremulous *kwiwiwiwirrr* (F&K).

Note Listed erroneously for Venezuela by Rodner *et al.* (2000).

Pluvialis or golden plovers are larger than sand plovers, and distinguished by their spangled backs and absence of any white nuchal collar or breast-band. They have large, rounded heads, large eyes and strong black bills, but are not necessarily easy to separate from each other in the field, though on the basis of rarity, any sighting is most likely to be of Black-bellied Plover.

AMERICAN GOLDEN PLOVER

Pluvialis dominica Pl. 49

Identification 24–28cm. In winter plumage, a fairly nondescript plover with fine streaks of golden-buff on black on crown and nape, less well defined on hindneck, bolder and more spotted on back and wings, clear whitish eyebrow, weakly streaked on breast and barred on flanks; long wings protruding well beyond tail characteristic; eyes and bill dark, legs and feet grey. Adult in breeding plumage has crown and hindneck clearly separated from broad white band from forehead down neck-sides, black face, throat and foreneck, becoming narrower on meeting black breast and entirely black underparts. Birds in intermediate plumage have drabber underparts blotched black, and patchy black on face and throat. Generally greyer than other *Pluvialis*, and smaller and darker than Grey Plover. Note wingtips project well beyond tip of tail (Pacific wingtips barely pass tip of tail).

Ssp. Monotypic (all countries)

Habits Usually in small numbers.

Status Uncommon to local passage migrant, stops briefly en route between North America and Argentina. Moves south September–November, mostly overland, but some follow coast, returning north March–April.

Habitat Lower Tropical Zone. Mudflats and shores of brackish and freshwater lagoons, saltmarshes rice fields, air fields, and level ground flooded after rains.

Voice Common flight-call a distinctive *kweedlee* (R&G) or *koweedl* repeated incessantly (Sibley), or *queedleeet* or *que-e-e-a*, falling at end, unlike plaintive call of Black-bellied Plover (Hilty).

Black-bellied Plover (right), is easily separated from other Pluvialis *plovers in flight by its black axillaries, but American and Pacific Golden (left and centre) are virtually identical in non-breeding plumage; toes usually just visible beyond tail-tip in Pacific*

PACIFIC GOLDEN PLOVER

Pluvialis fulva Pl. 49

Identification 23–26cm. In winter/non-breeding plumage very difficult to separate from American Golden Plover: wingtips barely reach beyond tip of tail, more yellowish generally, especially on flanks and face, more spotted on nape, and has different voice.

Ssp. Monotypic (Ec)

Habits As congenerics.

Status Accidental winter vagrant. Normally flies west from North America towards Hawaii.

Habitat Lower Tropical Zone. Most coastal areas, mudflats, etc., open short grassland, with young more likely to be found on mudflats and intertidal flats.

Voice Range of loud calls, a rapid *tu-ee* or *chu-wit* and plaintive *kl-ee* or *ki-wee* (HMP) or *too-EEEE*; *tuee tooEEEE* (Sibley).

BLACK-BELLIED (GREY) PLOVER

Pluvialis squatarola Pl. 49

Identification 30cm. Largest *Pluvialis*, paler than others with more noticeable white spangling above (no yellowish). Note white belly, streaked breast in young, and wingtips falling level with tip of tail. Lack of long hind toe immediately separates this species from other *Pluvialis*. In flight, black axillaries distinctive.

Ssp. Monotypic (all coasts and islands)

Habits Often with sandpipers and Ruddy Turnstones, but usually solitary. Wary and not easy to approach.
Status Widespread, a fairly common transient and winter resident. Arrives from late August and leaves early April. Some remain year-round. Commonest on passage, September–October and April–May.
Habitat Lower Tropical Zone. Coastal areas, accidental inland. Mudflats, beaches, sand strips, muddy shores behind mangroves, tidal pools, extensive lagoons and saltpans.
Voice Distinctive flight call *whee-oo-ee* (R&G), *cleee-er-ree* (Hilty), *tlee-oo-ee* (HMP) or *PLEEooee* (Sibley). Somewhat melancholy and lower pitched than American Golden.

Charadrius sand plovers are characterised by being small and having dark breast-bands, black foreheads and a black line from bill to eye. They forage by sight (rather than probing by feel) and characteristically run forward in short bursts to catch any prey on the sand's surface by surprise, especially sandworms, which are best caught as the receding tide leaves them momentarily exposed. They are generally birds of flat, open ground, typically sand or mud, and favour the intertidal zone.

COMMON RINGED PLOVER

Charadrius hiaticula Pl. 50

Identification 18–20cm. Non-breeding adult has forehead white, white eyebrow along ear-coverts, brown crown, nape and ear-coverts to base of bill, white throat and complete collar, broad brown breast-band broken in the middle, and rest of underparts white; upperparts brown, the greater coverts and leading edge of primaries white, producing a wingbar that is noticeable only in flight; bill all black, legs and feet pale brown. Juvenile much like adult but has fine pale fringes to all feathers. Breeding adult has black band from eye to eye over crown, broad black mask from base of bill to ear-coverts, and a black collar below the white which forms a broad breast-band; bill orange at base with black tip. Very difficult to separate from Semipalmated and side-by-side comparison desirable. Might only be certain by foot comparison: Common has no webbing between outer toes and very little between inner 2; Semipalmated has conspicuous webbing between outer 2 and a little between inner 2. This is a very difficult field mark, but quite apparent in the hand.

Ssp. *C. s. tundrae* (T&T)

Habits Typical of genus.
Status Rare vagrant. Palearctic species that normally winters in southern Europe and Africa. Quite possibly overlooked in the field, mistaken for Semipalmated.
Habitat Tropical Zone. Varied coastal habitats, sometimes on cultivated land and short grassland. Forms large flocks at high-tide roosts.
Voice A highly distinctive, mellow whistle with a rising inflection, *too-li* (HMP) or *toolip*, lower and more wooden than Semipalmated (Sibley). Other calls include a sharper and higher *tooee*. In alarm a low *tooweep* and loud *telee-telee* (HMP) or *towidi, towidi* (Sibley).

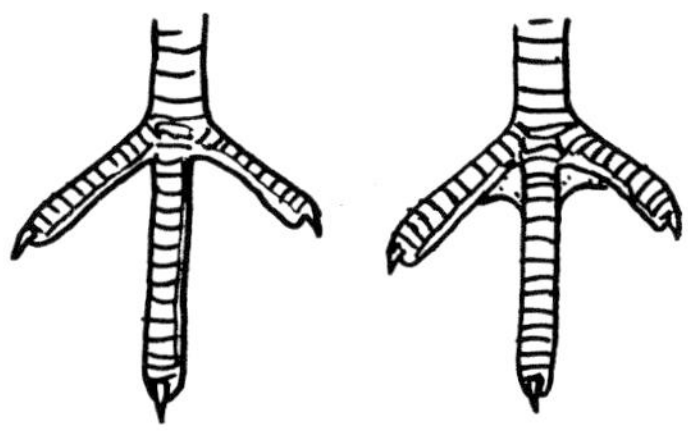

Foot of Common Ringed Plover (left), compared with that of Semipalmated Plover; note distinctive and diagnostic web of latter

SEMIPALMATED PLOVER

Charadrius semipalmatus Pl. 50

Identification 17–19cm. Virtually identical to Common Ringed Plover; differs in having postocular part of eyebrow much shorter, bill smaller and finer, and breast-band narrower in all plumages. Wilson's is larger with all-black bill and pink legs; Collared is smaller, with a finer bill and no nuchal collar; juvenile Snowy is closest but breast-band of latter well broken and restricted to breast-sides (seldom broken in Semipalmated and then only partially). Very difficult to separate from Common Ringed Plover and side-by-side comparison desirable.

Ssp. Monotypic (all coasts and islands)

Habits Scattered along beaches when feeding but flocks to roost. In flight shows white wingbar and white sides to rump.
Status Fairly common. Present year-round, but commonest September–April.
Habitat Lower Tropical Zone. Coastal mud and sand flats, intertidal zone, especially when tide falling, partial to exposed patches of seaweed, sea purslane and *Sesuvium portulacastrum*.
Voice A clear, fairly sharp whistle with a rising inflection, *chee-wee* or *chuwit*, less mellow and fluty than similar call of Common Ringed (HMP), or *ch-veet* (R&G) or *chuWEE* and variations (Sibley).

WILSON'S PLOVER

Charadrius wilsonia Pl. 50

Identification 16.5–20cm. Rather large-headed appearance due mainly to large black bill, proportionately much the heaviest of all *Charadrius*; greyish crown and nape, brownish-grey back; tips of greater coverts and leading edge of inner primaries white, affording wingbar visible only in flight, and rump-sides also white; white forehead and eyebrow, and chin and throat back below ear coverts to nape-sides also white; mask and breast-band vary from gingery to black depending on race and sex, rest of underparts white; eyes dark, bill black, legs and feet dull greenish to dull yellow. The largest of the group, distinguished by its large thick, black bill; from Semipalmated by its pink legs and from Collared by white collar encircling neck.

Ssp. *C. w. wilsonia* (boreal migrant to Caribbean and Atlantic coasts and offshore islands) clear white postocular, mask pale brown; breast-band partial and fragmented in juvenile, pale brown in female and black in male

C. w. cinnamominus (resident; NE Co, Ve, Tr, all offshore islands) bands on head and breast cinnamon/ginger, crown rufous

C. w. beldingi (resident; W Ec, W Co) darker, broadest mask is black on lores and cheeks with less white on face, postocular washed dusky, breast-band black

Habits Its large eyes betray a nocturnal feeding habit, but it catches Fiddler Crabs at any time. Often consorts with Semipalmated Plover. Scattered individuals, seldom small groups, but is gregarious. Feeding action slow and deliberate. Alert, but permits close approach.

Status Race *wilsonia* is a rare passage migrant, pausing en route between North America and Brazil in October, returning in March; *cinnamominus* and *beldingi* are breeding residents, and are uncommon to locally fairly common.

Habitat Lower Tropical Zone. Usually coastal, preferring higher part of beach, sandbars and islands. Occurs on mudflats, edges of coastal lagoons, estuarine flats and freshwater areas near coast.

Voice High, weak, whistled *whit*, less melodic than other small plovers (HMP), an emphatic whistled *phit* or *pheet* (Hilty), *f-whit* or *kwik* (R&G) and, in alarm, *weet!*, *kweet!* and *fü-eet* (Voous), *quit!* or *quit-it!* (HMP).

KILLDEER *Charadrius vociferus* Pl. 50

Identification 23–28cm. Largest of genus and the only species with 2 breast-bands, unique orange rump, strong white wingbar, also voice unmistakable. Eyes dark brown, bill black, legs and feet greenish-grey. Non-breeding adult has rufous fringes to upperparts feathers; juvenile is like duller non-breeding adult.

Ssp. *C. v. vociferus* (Ec, Co, Ve and islands) as described

C. v. peruvianus (S Ec) smaller, with much broader rufous fringes to feathers

C. v. ternominatus (ABC) smaller, greyer, paler

Habits Sometimes in small flocks.

Status Race *vociferus* is rare winter vagrant to all territories; *peruvianus* is spreading north from Peru into Ecuador; *ternominatus* is a vagrant from West Indies, where it is a breeding resident. Sight records only for Trinidad and French Guiana.

Habitat Tropical to Subtropical Zones. Beaches and mudflats but not necessarily near water. Also on open short grasslands, wet pastures, rice fields, agricultural land and wasteland, wet or dry.

Voice Call onomatopoeic, transcribed as, e.g. *kil-deéa* (Hilty), *kill-dee* (HMP), and extended calls, *dee-kill-dee, kill-dee-dee* (Voous) and *deee, deeeyee, tyeeeeeee deew deew, Tewddew* (Sibley).

PIPING PLOVER *Charadrius melodus* Pl. 50

Identification 17–18.5cm. Non-breeding adult and juvenile have pale grey crown, nape and ear-coverts, white forehead, fore face, throat and collar, narrow grey band on breast and pale grey upperparts, underparts white; eyes and bill dark, legs and feet yellow. Breeding adult has black band across white forehead, collar and breast-band black; bill has yellow base and black tip. From similar Snowy Plover by complete breast-band and bright legs, but Snowy always has bill black. In flight shows long, prominent white wingbar and contrasting white uppertail-coverts.

Ssp. Monotypic (all coasts)

Habits Forages night and day, often in small flocks. Feeding action steady and deliberate. May make a scrape in the sand to roost.

Status Vagrant to Caribbean coast, accidental to coasts of Ecuador and western Colombia.

Habitat Lower Tropical Zone. Strictly coastal, preferring sandy beaches, adjacent mudflats and intertidal strips.

Voice A charming, liquid *pee-po* (R&G), a distinctive piping, a plaintive and penetrating *peep* or *peep-lo* (HMP).

SNOWY PLOVER *Charadrius alexandrinus* Pl. 50

Identification 15–17.5cm. Elegant, slim and rather pale coloration, all white below with partial breast-band and grey legs. Adult male breeding has white forehead, a thin white eyebrow that becomes a broad postocular line, white lores and cheeks, but not ear-coverts, forming a fairly broad collar, a black band over crown from behind the eyes, a partial black breast-band, and otherwise white underparts; crown, nape, back and wings pale grey; eyes and bill dark, legs and feet yellowish-grey. Non-breeding adult and juvenile lack black on head and breast.

Ssp. *C. a. nivosus* (Co, Ve, ABC) all black parts narrower and smaller

C. a. occidentalis (S Ec) slightly larger

Habits Feeding action faster than Common Ringed or Semipalmated Plovers, which can draw attention when in a mixed feeding flock.

Status Fairly common to common in Ecuador where resident and sedentary. Breeding resident on Curaçao and Bonaire, but irregular and uncommon on Caribbean coast of Colombia and Venezuela and offshore islands, including Trinidad & Tobago.

Sand plovers all have a characteristic hunched jizz, like this Snowy Plover, which may conceal some plumage characters

Habitat Lower Tropical Zone. In Ecuador margins and vicinity of saltpans. Along Caribbean coast exclusively coastal, preferring flat ground such as beaches and mudflats. On Curaçao visits saline and brackish waters inland, as well as saltpans.
Voice Soft, whistled *puweea* (Hilty), *ku-wheet* (HMP), a dry, gravelly *chrrt* (R&G), *krut* (HMP), and, when excited, a most attractive, soft, melodious trilling *treeee-oo* (Voous).
Note Old World populations known as Kentish Plover. New World races possess several differences, including voice, and it is often suggested that they comprise a distinct species, invariably referred to as Snowy Plover.

COLLARED PLOVER
Charadrius collaris Pl. 50

Identification 14–15cm. Adult male has white forehead with black frontal band and cinnamon crown patch, rear crown to nape and upperparts mid brown with fine cinnamon fringes to all feathers; black lores and cinnamon line from behind eyes to sides of neck, joining black breast-band, small postocular white spot; underparts white; eyes and bill dark, legs and feet flesh. Female has duller and weaker cinnamon on head, immature like adult but lacks any cinnamon. Juvenile lacks both black and cinnamon. The only *Charadrius* to lack a nuchal collar, but has complete breast-band. From similar Semipalmated Plover by lack of white nuchal collar, and cinnamon on head-sides.

Ssp. *C. c. collaris* (throughout)

Habits Often mixes with Semipalmated Plover and Sanderling, although individuals usually well scattered.
Status Widespread but locally common, varying population levels suggest movements but these are not known.
Habitat Lower Tropical Zone. Wide range of habitats, sandy beaches and mudflats, estuarine flats, sand and gravel bars along rivers and sewage farms, airfields, short grassland and open sandy savannas.
Voice Usually quiet, but when disturbed a short *cheep* or *keed-up*, with second syllable lower (Hilty), a frequent, sharp *chip* or *krip* (R&G) and a metallic *chit* or *pit*, sometimes given in series (HMP).

TAWNY-THROATED DOTTEREL
Oreopholus ruficollis Pl. 49

Identification 25–29cm. Largish, fairly nondescript plover, streaked above and white below, and distinguished by orange-tawny throat patch.

Ssp. *O. r. pallidus* (S Ec)

Habits When approached stands erect, turns back to observer and remains still.
Status Effectively hypothetical. Occasional to Ecuador (F&K) but only specimens date from 17th century, from Santa Elena Peninsula (R&G).
Habitat Tropical Zone to Páramo. Semi-arid ridges with open heathland, from coastal plains to Puna grassland. Nowadays more likely to be encountered above 2,000m (to 4,600m) in uninhabited areas (in Peru, Bolivia, Chile and Argentina).
Voice Usually quiet but when flushed gives a *tr-tr-traa-lu*, the last note downward pitched and often repeated when flying overhead (HMP, R&G), or a sad, somewhat reedy, falling *tryyy-y*, often in series (F&K).
Note Formerly placed in genus *Eudromias*.

HAEMATOPODIDAE – Oystercatchers

Oystercatchers are seashore waders and, with one all-black exception, are black and white, giving rise to their old name of Sea Pies. They form a small, remarkably homogenous family that covers most shores of the world, but not oceanic islands (except Galápagos). Their unique bills are long and laterally compressed with a knife-like tip that is used like a chisel, and adapted to feed on marine shellfish and worms. Peak feeding time is the short period when the tide ebbs, and shellfish hold their lips open as they normally do underwater. The oystercatcher drives its bill into the open shell, trying to sever the mussel which instantly paralyses the animal. They are clearly perfectly adapted to deal with bivalves, like mussels, clams and oysters, but also take crabs, cuttlefish and worms. Oystercatchers have an almost unique behaviour in that they will remove their eggs to a safer location when they feel the nest is threatened. They are very noisy in the face of danger, and will feign broken wings, limping off to distract the predator. They also have a false brooding display, wherein they run ahead of a predator and settle as if on eggs or young. This behaviour has fooled many a birdwatcher, who has then spent time searching the spot for the clutch.

Additional references include Gilliard (1958), Hayman, Marchant & Prater (1986) and Knystautas (1996).

AMERICAN OYSTERCATCHER
Haematopus palliatus Pl. 51

Identification 48cm. Unmistakable: large, black and white above, all white below, with long, straight red bill, bright yellow eyes and orange-red eyelids. Juvenile has same pattern but is browner above with pale fringes to all feathers; eyes dark and eye-ring dull orange, bill slightly dusky red, legs and feet brown. In flight, shows a conspicuous white stripe on inner wing, and a white rump. Separated from Black Skimmer (on ground) by all-black head and breast, and long pink legs.

Ssp. *H. p. palliatus* (Ec, Co, Ve, ABC, FG) as described
H. p. prattii (Ve: offshore islands, T&T) bill significantly larger

Habits Usually in pairs, conspicuous but wary, and usually keeps apart from other shorebirds, but may gather in small monospecific groups. Forages in surf, tidal pools and reef shallows, in cracks and crevices amid rocks.
Status Scarce and local in Ecuador; in Colombia, rare and local on Caribbean coast, and few records from Pacific coast. Uncommon in Netherlands Antilles, locally frequent in

Venezuela, rare in Trinidad & Tobago, exceptional in French Guiana. Both residents and boreal migrants form small foraging flocks.

Habitat Lower Tropical Zone (coastal). Sand or rocky beaches, dunes beside sea, reefs and reef walls.

Voice Can be quite noisy, both day and night, giving a loud whistling *wheep!* or *kleep!* with a piping, insistent quality. May be repeated many times or run together as a continuous *kee-ee-ee-ee-ee-ee-ee* (Hilty, R&G), and *klip* or *kwip!* and *piru-piru*, with a song that is a rising trill, falling at end (Sick).

RECURVIROSTRIDAE – Stilts and Avocets

Stilts and avocets are rather delicate and elegant waders, mainly white, with some black and occasional tones of colour. They have long necks and bills, and very long legs that look terribly fragile. Just 7 species occur worldwide, of which the stilts have straight bills, and the avocets are distinguished by their oddly upturned mandibles. Avocets have partially webbed feet with a rudimentary hind toe, absent in stilts. All are sociable birds of shallow lakes, pans and lagoons, often where the water is brackish or salty, and with abundant tiny invertebrates. They usually breed in colonies in shallow wetlands, estuaries and tidal flats. Outside the breeding season they tend to keep in flocks. Occasionally pairs may be found alone, foraging or breeding. Generally silent, unless disturbed, when they emit loud yelping cries.

Additional references include Hayman, Marchant & Prater (1986) and Pierce (1996)

BLACK-NECKED STILT

Himantopus mexicanus Pl. 51

Identification 36–39cm. Crown and head-sides black with a white eye-ring and very broad white eyebrow, hindneck and entire upperparts black; fore face, foreneck and underparts white; eyes red, bill long, thin and slightly decurved, and black, very long legs and feet coral red. Female has back tinged brown. Juvenile like female but has tips of secondaries and inner primaries white. Unmistakable, slim and very long-legged. In flight wings all black with white rump extending to lower back as a wedge. Legs dangle or trail behind.

Ssp. *H. m. mexicanus* (all countries) as described
H. m. melanurus (S Ec) crown white, black hindneck reduced to a thin line becoming an inverted T at base, with a white collar.

Habits Alert and wary, easily aroused to an excited state; flushes and circles calling loudly all the while, especially if young are present. Probes deep in mud, often immersing neck and entire head. May wade into belly-deep water to pick from surface.

Status Irregular everywhere, movements apparently related to water depth and conditions. Frequent in Colombia, common on Aruba, Curaçao and Bonaire, locally common in Venezuela, uncommon in Trinidad, rare visitor to Tobago, and seasonally frequent (occasionally numerous) in Suriname.

Habitat Tropical Zone. Coastal lagoons and rice fields in lowlands, freshwater ponds and marshes.

Voice Sharp, tern-like *yip*, *ruk*, *kik*, and a long, sustained high-pitched *kii-kii-kii-kii-kii-kii*.... and similar (R&G).

Note Formerly included in *H. himantopus* (Black-winged Stilt), but now separated from Old World (*himantopus*) populations. Race *melanurus* regarded as a separate species, White-backed Stilt by some authors (S&M, R&G).

AMERICAN AVOCET

Recurvirostra americana Pl. 51

Identification 43–46cm. Unmistakable with long, slender upturned bill, and very long blue-grey legs. Head and neck flushed orange-cinnamon when breeding. In flight, wings mainly black with white on tertials and at base of wing-coverts.

Ssp. Monotypic (Ec, Ve, ABC, To)

Habits Feeds mainly by sweeping bill from side to side in shallow water. May roost in water, standing on one leg.

Status One record from Ecuador, casual winter visitor to Bonaire, very rare visitor to Venezuela (sight record by T. Ryan) and on Tobago (no records Trinidad).

Habitat Tropical Zone. Coastal lagoons and rice fields in lowlands.

Voice Most frequent call is a loud, oystercatcher-like, disyllabic *kleeyp, kluit* or *kleet*, but is monosyllabic when alarmed (R&G).

BURHINIDAE – Thick-knees

Thick-knees, stone curlews or stone plovers, as they are sometimes called, are large inland shorebirds. Unlike curlews and most plovers, they only have 3 toes, all pointing forwards. Their eyes are yellow and disproportionately large – an adaptation for their nocturnal habits. The 2 species in northern South America are sedentary birds of open country and amongst the least known of the family. It is not uncommon to see thick-knees by day, but most of the time they stand or sit quietly, or even stretch out flat, relying on their cryptic plumage and stillness for protection. They are reluctant fliers, preferring to dash in short spurts, like plovers. When airborne they fly low and fast. Very noisy at night, especially in bright moonlight, and utter mournful, eerie cries. Frequently found at night by the reflection of their eyes.

Additional references used to prepare this family include Gilliard (1958), Pitman (1964), Hayman et al. (1986, hereafter HMP) and Hume (1996).

DOUBLE-STRIPED THICK-KNEE

Burhinus bistriatus Pl. 49

Identification 43–48cm. Large thick-knee plover, long legs, upright posture as a rule, large yellow eyes with broad white supercilium and broad black streak above it. Body and wings generally dusky, all of the feathers fringed broadly buffy or cinnamon-buffy, belly to under tail-coverts white, bill yellow with black distal half, legs and feet yellowish. Back of juvenile has broader pale buffy fringes, legs more greenish-grey. Unmistakable in habitat, far larger than other waders or plovers that might occur nearby. In flight, black wings with white panels on upperwing distinctive, underwing all white.

Ssp. *B. b. pediacus* (N Co, NW Ve) paler, slightly more cinnamon
B. b. vocifer (Cu, Ve: N, E, Margarita I., Tr, Gu) darker; browner and less grey on breast

Habits Quite sedentary.
Status In Colombia, common east of Andes, uncommon and local west of Andes. Common in Venezuela, rare visitor to Trinidad.
Habitat Dry pastures and open areas, with or without scattered trees.
Voice Usually silent by day, but at night a loud *kee-kee-kee*... or shrill *da-ra, da-ra*...like Southern Lapwing, but latter does not call at night (Hilty).

PERUVIAN THICK-KNEE
Burhinus superciliaris Pl. 49

Identification 38–43cm. Regular-size thick-knee plover. Darker back and grey wing-coverts with pale fringes to feathers rarely noticeable at distance. Large pale yellow eyes with white supercilium and black line above it. Juvenile generally darker with broader tawny fringes to all feathers. Bill yellow, distal half dusky, legs and feet greenish-grey. Juvenile browner with buffy fringes to feathers. Unmistakable in range; very large-headed. Distinctive black-and-white panels on wings contrasting with grey wing-coverts, underwing all white.

Ssp. Monotypic (SW Ec)

Habits Typical of genus.
Status Rare and local (apparently declining) in south-west Ecuador (Guayas, El Oro and Loja).
Habitat Open country: semi-desert, arid grassland and dry scrub, fallow agricultural land, etc.
Voice Scolding chattering cries (HMP, R&G).

SCOLOPACIDAE – Snipes, Sandpipers and Phalaropes

Two traits define this family. Long-distance migrations, which make their lives never-ending journeys, autumn and spring spent on the wing with short summer sojourns in subarctic regions, where they only just possess sufficient time to breed, and in the boreal winter just the necessary days to recover body fat for the long return flight. No wonder Peter Matthiessen called them *The Wind Birds*. The second trait is their ever-changing plumage, which makes so many species such a daunting identification challenge, despite the fact that, in general, they are very easy to observe: living on mudflats and sandy beaches, often in large concentrations, and are not particularly wary of humans. But species recognition is a long process, that may take years of frequent observation, because most species undergo several moults during the year, and, on top of that, plumage is slowly but continually changing due to feather wear. The first plumage acquired after the chick down (in autumn of its first year) is called juvenile plumage. When first acquired, this looks very different to some weeks later when feather wear has abraded many feather fringes and the bird is ready for its second moult, which will involve the body- but not the wing-feathers (first basic plumage). A few weeks later comes another body moult, into what is called first alternate plumage. By this time the flight-feathers are extremely worn. As it reaches its second autumn of life, the bird undertakes a complete moult, into definitive basic plumage. The following spring, and all others subsequently, there will be a body moult to definitive alternate plumage, and then every autumn a complete moult to definitive basic plumage. For each of these plumages, there is a gradual change from newly moulted to worn. The extremes are remarkably different, but the stages in between, together with the limited palette of grey, black and brown and the intricacies of their plumage make matters very tough for the observer. On mudflats and beaches, these shorebirds feed on small fish, molluscs, worms and small crustaceans. More inland, some will take insects, spiders and berries. The variety of bill shapes and lengths points to a diversity of food, foraging methods and habitats, and these differences can assist identification. On shores, some species wade knee-deep in shallow water (Dunlin, *Tringa* sandpipers, dowitchers), others swim in deeper water (phalaropes). Some run backwards and forwards with the incoming and receding surf (Sanderling), others prefer soft, muddy soil (*Limosa*), some stay in moist sandy areas (*Numenius*, some *Calidris*, Willet), others rocky beaches (*Arenaria*), some drier, higher areas of beaches or mudflats (some *Numenius*, some *Calidris*, *Actitis*, *Bartramia*). Many species stake out small feeding territories and if another bird approaches make aggressive displays to the intruder. Migrants form flocks that may have from a few to hundreds of birds, usually all of the same species. The first to arrive in tropical wetlands are females, especially those that bred unsuccessfully, followed a few days later by males. Last to arrive are juveniles. To cover the laps of their journeys, the long-distance jumps between each link in the chain of stopovers, they fly extremely fast, on what Matthiessen called 'high-speed wings – blade wings of low camber and high aspect ratio, bearing a minimum of drag'. Without them, their lives would not be possible.

Additional references used for this family include Hayman, Marchant & Prater (1986), Fjeldså & Krabbe (1990), Piersma et al. (1996), Sibley (2000) and Paulson (2005).

Snipe are very difficult to identify to species, even in the hand. They forage in soft, moist soil ideal for earthworms which they hunt by probing their bills into the earth. The bills are long and have a unique, soft and flexible, sensitive tip. Thus, they all occur in similar habitat, including open, freshwater or brackish marshland, swampy meadows, grassy or marshy, mucky or muddy edges of lakes, lagoons, ponds, streams and rivers, especially muddy upper reaches of estuaries. Coastal meadows, sewage farms and rice fields are also snipe habitat; in more open areas, they prefer tussocky vegetation, shrubs and trees of any kind that can provide some protective cover. Their eyes have evolved in an odd-looking position, higher on the head than is normal amongst birds, affording them an extraordinary field of view, and enabling detection of airborne predators whilst their heads are held forward and down, bills probing. When disturbed, they usually crouch motionless and flush reluctantly, but with a rocketing, vertical take-off. The view you are most likely to get then is similar to that shown in the plate! Snipe are secretive, aided by their beautiful, very cryptic plumage, and they are difficult to spot. It is important to check distribution and altitude – and also time of the year – as well as appearance and vocalisations when attempting identification. Snipe have similar display-flights and calls, and their presence may be first noted by territorial activity at twilight. They make a winnowing sound in flight by vibrating the outer tail-feathers, which are held at right angles to the body.

WILSON'S SNIPE *Gallinago delicata* Pl. 52

Identification 25–28cm. Medium-sized with typical coloration. Main diagnostic is 2 pairs of pale lines on either side of back, fine, clear barring on secondaries and rufous tail with 2 bars, the upper being stronger. Very similar to South American Snipe, but generally darker, more boldly striped and darker on the underwing. Short greenish legs, slightly smaller but wing a little longer, and less white on sides of tail.

Ssp. Monotypic (Ec, Co, Ve, T&T, Gu, Su)

Habits Usually freezes or may run for cover when disturbed; flushes explosively at last moment in zigzag flight and may give a nasal call.

Status Boreal migrant, uncommon to rare at limits of its wintering range. Usually arrives October–November and leaves March, but may occur until May, and records from most months.

Habitat Tropical to Temperate Zones. Typical snipe country at 500–3,500m.

Voice When flushed, usually utters a long, harsh *seaaap!* typically rising (HMP), or *khatch* (Snyder 1956), and a distinctive rasping *dzhyt* or *tzhet*. Aerial winnowing is a rich, tremulous *whowho who who who*… sometimes alternating with a vocal *yack*-ing (F&K).

Note This species was formerly treated as a race of Common Snipe *G. gallinago*.

SOUTH AMERICAN SNIPE *Gallinago paraguaiae* Pl. 52

Identification 25–29cm. Small, with strongly barred tertials; main diagnostic is single black bar on rufous tail, and fine white fringes to greater and primary wing-coverts, appearing as a thin white crescent on open wing. Very similar to Common Snipe, but definitely paler on underwing. Wing slightly shorter and has more extensive white on sides of tail. In general, slightly paler, especially below, and more finely streaked pale above. Buff rather than white undertail-coverts.

Ssp. *G. p. paraguaiae* (all except Ar, Bo, Cu)

Habits Very similar to Common Snipe, being very reluctant to flush, taking-off explosively at last moment, in zigzag flight. Best separated by altitude. Generally sedentary.

Status Fairly common throughout. Numbers augmented by austral migrants, May–October.

Habitat Tropical Zone, from sea level to 350m north of Orinoco, to 1,300m south of it. Favours wet savannas and edges of streams, lagoons and marshy coastal areas, generally at lower altitudes than Common.

Voice Alarm-call when flushed and winnowing are similar to Common Snipe.

Note Some authors treat South American Snipe within Common Snipe (e.g. HMP).

NOBLE SNIPE *Gallinago nobilis* Pl. 52

Identification 30–32.5cm. Typical snipe in appearance, but larger with very long bill. Medium-sized; main diagnostics are single black crescent in middle of rufous tail and white line on tips to greater coverts, appearing as narrow white crescent in flight. Restricted to wetlands above and just below treeline. Only Andean Snipe (darker below with all-barred belly) is sympatric. Unbarred white belly gives distinctive 2-tone appearance. Larger, darker, and more heavily mottled than Common Snipe.

Ssp. Monotypic (Ec, C Co, NW Ve)

Habits Usually singly or in pairs, active, restless, but very secretive. Very reluctant to flush, and flight is rather heavy, slow and direct, not twisting like Common Snipe.

Status Fairly common, but undoubtedly under-recorded.

Habitat Temperate Zone to Páramo. Typical snipe habitat at treeline, 2,500–3,500 m, occasionally higher or lower.

Voice Flushes with a nasal, grating *dzhit* and *tzhi-tzhi-tzhi*… (F&K), and a clear melodious call (Piersma *et al.* 1996, P&MS 1978).

GIANT SNIPE *Gallinago undulata* Pl. 52

Identification 35–40cm. Very large snipe with long bill and culmen level with skull, affording flat-headed appearance. Broad, rounded wings, with primaries barred black and sandy-buff, rufous below. Main diagnostic appears to be 4 broad rows of rufous feathers on back and a single black subterminal bar on central tail-feathers.

Ssp. *G. u. undulata* (Co, Ve, Gu, Su, FG)

Habits Very poorly known. Solitary. Quite nocturnal. Seldom flushes, preferring to squat, freeze or slowly stride away.

Status Regular in Suriname, but nowhere common and usually considered uncommon and local, but seldom observed.

Habitat Tropical Zone. Usually in tall vegetation, dry grass, sometimes in dense growth of dry savannas, but also swamps, marshy grasslands, damp pastures and flooded grassland. Recorded 200–2,200m.

Voice When flushed gives a double *kek-kek*, rarely triple, similar to Clapper Rail but softer (Snyder), or a triple *ho-go-go* or similar in nocturnal courtship or territorial aerial display. Also strong, droning *schh*, lasting 4 s (Sick in H&B).

PUNA SNIPE *Gallinago andina* Pl. 52

Identification 22cm. Smallest snipe. Diagnostic are broad buffy lines either side of back, 2 bars on tail (upper broad, subterminal band narrow), and thin white line on tips of greater and primary-coverts, also alula. Note shorter bill, dull yellow legs, almost white underwing, extensive rufous in tail and contrast between blackish back and primaries.

Ssp. Monotypic (S Ec)

Habits When flushed, rises steeply, then flies in small 'jumps', no zigzag, and usually soon drops into cover (F&K).
Status Rare in Ecuador. Some altitudinal migration.
Habitat Temperate Zone to Páramo. High altitudes, along boggy rivers and creeks, and rather open reedy marshes, in Andean puna, 3,000–4,500m.
Voice When flushed a high-pitched *dzeetch*. On ground *dyak dyak dyak* or *dyuc dyuc dyuc*, occasionally *dji didi* (F&K). Display-flight describes wide circles with shallow dives, and winnowing sound uttered when levelling out after a dive, *shushushushushu* (F&K).
Note Treated as a subspecies of South American Snipe in HMP and Piersma.

ANDEAN SNIPE *Gallinago jamesoni* Pl. 52

Identification 29–30cm. Large, high-altitude snipe, with broad rounded wings. Lacks clearly diagnostic characters, but tail has several bars. Lacks clear pale stripes on head and upperparts typical of other snipe. Bill heavier, especially at base; lacks white in wings or tail. Noticeably darker below than Common or Noble Snipes, both of which appear paler below in flight, Andean being barred on belly. Imperial is much darker and heavily barred rufous above.

Ssp. Monotypic (Ec, Co, Ve)

Habits Secretive and solitary, keeping well within cover by day, but active and noisy at dusk and by night.
Status Uncommon, generally very difficult to find. Probably more common than records suggest, usually only seen when displaying.
Habitat Tropical Zone to Páramo. Wide range of habitats; 2,100–4,300m, but typically well within these extremes. Boggy and marshy meadows, especially with *Espeletia*, from open swampy forest to marshy moorland.
Voice Flushes with an explosive *tzhyc!* (F&K). May give long drawn-out series of undulating *jyuk* calls on ground. Calls *whee-tschwu* during wide circling display flight (HMP) or *wic-a* (F&K) at *c.*2 per s, sometimes for up to 1 minute. Winnowing sounds like muffled bellows (HMP).
Note Sometimes considered conspecific with Fuegian Snipe *G. stricklandii* (of southern Chile and Argentina), which is also called Cordilleran Snipe in H&B, F&K and HMP.

IMPERIAL SNIPE *Gallinago imperialis* Pl. 52

Identification 29–30cm. Large, woodcock-like snipe with broad, rounded reddish wings and very short tail, barred upperparts lacking clear pale stripes typical of other snipe, and heavily barred underparts. Lacks white in wings and tail, strongly banded belly. Darker and more noticeably rufous above than Andean Snipe.

Ssp. Monotypic (Ec, Co)

Habits Most likely to be recognised by display-flight and calls given at dusk and dawn.
Status Uncommon, probably local, and generally considered rare, but extraordinarily difficult to find without familiarity of its voice.
Habitat Temperate Zone to Páramo. Varied habitats, but usually around treeline, typically on open marshy páramo, especially grassy areas with *Espeletia*; montane forest country.
Voice Aerial display given high above forest at dusk and dawn, accompanied by a 'shatteringly loud raucous song' that lasts *c.*10 s, repeated after a 6 s pause. Increasingly loud, sharp, single notes followed by a series of double or triple notes, then by single notes decreasing in volume. The song terminates in a shallow dive and winnowing sound (Terborgh & Weske 1972).
Note Called Banded Snipe in H&B, F&K.

The sandpipers form the majority of the Scolopacidae, a large subfamily of some 84 species mainly found in the Northern Hemisphere and most of which are migratory. Thus, our few resident species have their numbers swelled in the boreal autumn starts, as post-breeding birds travel south. Some remain in Central America and the Caribbean, with a few vagrants reaching northern South America, but others are intent on reaching the Southern Cone and pause briefly to feed rapaciously for a few days, then take off again, whilst a few overfly our region completely and are only rare transients. They generally winter on coasts or at nearby wetlands, but some occur well inland in flooded areas or along rivers and lakeshores, as well as at rice fields and sewage farms. All have long wings and short tails, and tend to be rather cryptically coloured. There are many different plumages, ranging from those of the breeding season to non-breeding, with many variations in between. At first, they are bewilderingly alike but with familiarity the individual characteristics become increasingly obvious, like different wing-lengths, bill shapes, head angles, jizz when feeding, and so on.

SHORT-BILLED DOWITCHER
Limnodromus griseus Pl. 54

Identification 25–29cm. Non-breeding adult brownish-grey above, darker on wings, and the upperparts have pale grey fringes to the feathers, cap dark with a long eyebrow from nostril to rear ear-coverts, lower back white, spotted black as it widens on rump, then narrows as long tertials obscure sides, and heavily barred black and white on uppertail-coverts and tail; underparts pale, washed greyish on breast, rest of underparts whitish with faint barring on flanks and undertail-coverts. Breeder much browner and more spotted and barred below. Juvenile brighter than breeding adult. Very much recalls Long-billed Dowitcher, but breast of Long-billed is typically plain, whilst Short-billed is more streaky or flammulated; mantle and scapulars of Long-billed usually longer with darker centres, and tend to be less contrasting in Short-billed, and barring on flanks of Long-billed usually broader and evenly-coloured, but irregular and varied in Short-billed. Note also vocalisations.

Ssp. *L. g. caurinus* (W Ec, W Co) very variable underparts, either spotted, barred or fairly plain
L. g. griseus (Caribbean coast) the greyest race
L. g. hendersoni (Co, both coasts) lacks white on belly, uniform rufous below

Status Transient and winter resident, a few year-round. Local in Ecuador, fairly common in Colombia and Venezuela, common on the islands and in the coastal Guianas.
Habitat Lower Tropical Zone. Usually on intertidal strips, especially tidal mudflats bordering mangroves. Shallow pools in saltmarshes.
Voice Calls year-round, a rapid *tew-tew-tew* or *tu-tu-tu*, variously described as mellow, metallic, sharp, faster than similar call of Lesser Yellowlegs, or with similar cadence but different tone to Ruddy Turnstone (Tostain, ffrench, H&B, R&G, Voous, HMP).

LONG-BILLED DOWITCHER
Limnodromus scolopaceus Pl. 54

Identification 24–30cm. Bill longer than Short-billed Dowitcher, bill of female particularly so, but otherwise very much alike. See previous species and below for separating features.

Ssp. Monotypic (Co, northern coasts and offshore islands)

Status Rare vagrant to northern coast and offshore islands during boreal winter.
Habitat Lower Tropical Zone. When not breeding, differs noticeably from Short-billed in habitat, preferring fresh or brackish pools to intertidal areas, but uses intertidal areas on migration, when may be seen alongside Short-billed (HMP). Intertidal areas, marshes, salt and mudflats.
Voice A thin, sharp *keek-keek-keek* that may run to 5–6 notes, accelerating, especially on taking flight (H&B, Voous, HMP).

BLACK-TAILED GODWIT
Limosa limosa Pl. 53

Identification 36–40cm. Non-breeding adult has grey-brown upperparts with fine buffy fringes to feathers of back and wings, whilst white tips to outermost greater wing-coverts and base of inner primaries only show in flight, as do white underwings; white eyebrow and dark lores, white rump and black tail; long, slightly upturned bill, the basal half pink, legs and feet dark grey. Juvenile generally buffy with browner wings (much darker than juvenile Hudsonian Godwit), all feathers with buffy fringes. Easily identified in flight by combination of long, broad white wingbar (broader than in Hudsonian Godwit), and white underwing, broad white band on lower rump and uppertail, and black tail-band. Similar in size to Willet, but bill noticeably longer and orange basally, the distal third being black. Bill straight with slight upward turn at tip, but straighter than in Hudsonian which is distinctly upturned. Legs longer than Hudsonian Godwit.

Ssp. *L. l. limosa* (Tr)

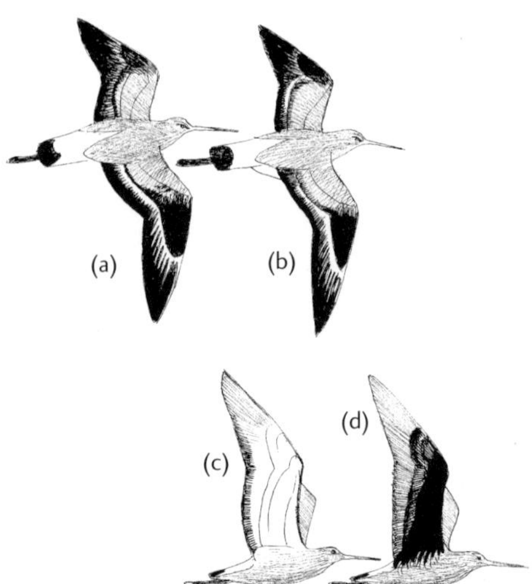

Black-tailed Godwit (a) is not easily separated from Hudsonian Godwit (b) when seen from above or behind, but their underwings are totally different: white in Black-tailed Godwit (c) and black in Hudsonian (d)

Status Palearctic species that winters in south-west Europe and sub-Saharan West Africa. Accidental, photographed on Trinidad, September 2000–January 2001 (Hayes & Kenefick 2002).
Habitat Tropical Zone. On Trinidad in flooded rice fields, coastal mudflats and in Orange Valley. Wet grasslands, shallow wetlands, mudflats; race *limosa* favours freshwater habitats.
Voice Quiet when not breeding. Contact call a short, quiet *tuk* or *kek*, often repeated.

HUDSONIAN GODWIT
Limosa haemastica Pl. 53

Identification 36–42cm. Non-breeding adult has grey or grey-brown upperparts with white tips to outer greater wing-coverts and base of inner primaries visible in flight, as are black underwing-coverts and dark underwing (whitish at base of central secondaries and primaries), white eyebrow, dark lores, white rump and black tail; long, slightly upturned bill with basal third pink, legs and feet dark grey. Juvenile generally buffy, with browner wings and lightly barred scapulars and tertials. In flight shows narrow white wingbar, white rump and black tail. From Willet by bill and blackish legs. Marbled Godwit larger and lacks back-and-white tail.

Monotypic (all countries)

Habits At rest has sedate manner, no bobbing.
Status Rare transient on all coasts except Atlantic – in Suriname, French Guiana – where fair numbers seen. Usually only recorded on southbound passage in October.
Habitat Tropical Zone. Muddy estuaries and tidal pools, coastal lagoons, freshwater lakes and rice cultivations. Will wade in water to 15cm depth.
Voice Usually silent on migration, but may utter a clear, high *toe-wit* or just *whit*.
Note Sometimes treated as a subspecies of Black-tailed Godwit *L. limosa*.

BAR-TAILED GODWIT *Limosa lapponica* Pl. 53

Identification 37–41cm. Prominent white eyebrow, otherwise entire head, neck and breast finely streaked drab brown on white, rest of underparts and underwing white; back and wings blackish with broad pale grey to whitish fringes to feathers (with buffy cast to back and tertials), wedge-shaped rump to uppertail-coverts patch is white, tail has *c.*6 black bars on white ground; bill long, slender and has basal half pink, rest blackish, legs and feet dark. Sexes alike but female larger and longer-billed. Juvenile similar but has a buffier, slightly browner cast. Confusion likely with Whimbrel but upturned bill is certain differential.

Ssp. *L. l. lapponica* (Ve)

Habits Feeds by pecking, stitching and probing. Females have longer bills and tend to feed in deeper water.
Status Vagrant. An Old World species that is a rare accidental to northern South America.
Habitat Tropical Zone. Intertidal areas, preferably sandy parts of estuaries.
Voice Generally not very vocal. Contact and alarm-calls throughout year are a barking *kak-kak*, a deep *kirruc* and variants.

MARBLED GODWIT *Limosa fedoa* Pl. 53

Identification 42–48cm. Large and heavily built; entirely warm ochre with fine dark brown streaks on head (clear eyebrow) and neck, becoming inverted arrowheads on breast; entire upperparts have a distinctly barred appearance; primary-coverts and outer primaries deep brown, underwing-coverts rufescent, rest ochraceous; bill long, slightly upturned, basal half pinkish. Breeding and non-breeding birds similar, bill has more pink and underparts clearer in non-breeders. Juvenile also similar, but has less boldly marked wing-coverts. Bill and legs longer than Bar-tailed Godwit, and very dark primary-coverts create distinctive black patch on outer wings in flight.

Ssp. *L. l. beringiae* (Pacific coast) slightly smaller
L. l. fedoa (Caribbean coast) as described

Habits Feeds in flocks on intertidal mudflats, walking calmly, pecking and probing.
Status Casual vagrant, more likely on Pacific coast, rare on Caribbean. A boreal migrant that rarely wanders south of Central America.
Habitat Lower Tropical Zone. Muddy bays and estuaries, coastal pools and saltmarshes with adjacent grassy borders.
Voice Contact-call a harsh *car-ack*, and a sharp *wik-wik* in alarm (HMP).

ESKIMO CURLEW *Numenius borealis* Pl. 53

Identification 29–34cm. Small curlew with obvious stripe on head, essentially ochre with heavy streaked barring on back and wings, and heavy barring on tail; finely streaked on head and neck, more heavily so on breast and sides, and underwings are cinnamon-buff; comparatively short, curved bill (black with reddish base). Juvenile has underparts unmarked buff. Very much like a smaller *hudsonicus* race of Whimbrel, but more ochraceous, and Whimbrel has barred primaries.

Ssp. Monotypic (Ar, Bo, Cu, T&T)

Status Critically Endangered. Extremely rare, occasional and perhaps extinct. Boreal migrant that passes through easterly South America in September en route to Argentina, returning in March, through western countries. Generally overflies continent, pausing briefly to feed on offshore islands before continuing to far north.
Habitat Lower Tropical Zone. Coastal grasslands.
Voice Poorly known and probably silent in our region. A rippling or fluttering *tr-tr-tr-tr* and a soft whistle *bee-bee* (HMP).

WHIMBREL *Numenius phaeopus* Pl. 53

Identification 40–46cm. Large, conspicuous shorebird that joins flocks of mixed shorebirds, both at roost and when foraging. Broad, dark crown-stripe with narrow pale line down centre, broad pale eyebrow, rest of head to belly and flanks buffy, streaked brownish-grey, belly and thighs to undertail-coverts white, latter lightly and narrowly barred grey; upperparts brownish-grey with broken pale fringes (like dotted lines) to all feathers, primary-coverts solidly dark (forming black patch on outer wing in flight, especially at distance); bill long and decurved, black with a red base to lower mandible. Large, but smaller and darker than Long-billed Curlew with much shorter bill.

Ssp. *N. p. hudsonicus* (all countries)

Habits Flies in single file, occasionally in V formation. Roosts communally, often high in mangroves. Forages alone or in small groups.
Status Fairly common winter visitor and often common transient; some present year-round, but migrants on passage August–October and April–May.
Habitat Lower Tropical Zone. Tidal flats, coastal grasslands (rarely inland), beaches, tidal mudflats and mangrove swamps.
Voice Most frequently heard call, 5–7 liquid piping notes on single pitch, has many transliterations: *whee-whee-whee-whee-whee…*, or *whi-whi-whi-whi-whi…*, *ti-ti-ti-ti-ti-…*, *bi-bi-bi-bi-bi…* and *pee-pee-pee-pee-pee…* well known at northern latitudes, but seldom heard on migration (Voous, R&G, ffrench, H&B, Hilty, HMP and Sibley).

LONG-BILLED CURLEW

Numenius americanus Pl. 53

Identification 50–65cm. Large, cinnamon-coloured curlew with big eyes and droplet-shaped tip to very long bill. Lores and eye-ring white, throat pale, rest of head and upper neck buffy grading into cinnamon neck and underparts, streaked finely with dark brown to breast, upperparts reddish-brown, spotted with cinnamon, whitish edges to wing-coverts, underwing-coverts deep rufous; bill dark with reddish base, legs and feet dark greenish. From Whimbrel by size and lack of head stripes, and bill twice as long.

Ssp. Subspecies unknown. Differences slight and clinal, and both *N. a. parvus* (which is smaller) and *N. a. americanus* (larger) could reach Caribbean coast.

Habits Rather shy, forages in flocks, feeds by striding rapidly, pecking and probing.
Status Rare straggler during boreal winter.
Habitat Tropical Zone. Shallow estuaries, intertidal flats, nearby grasslands and open marshes and farmland (rarely inland).
Voice Normal call is *cur-lee* or *coorLI*, rising in pitch; alarm-call *kee-he-he-he* and *pill-will*, recalling Willet (ffrench, HMP, Sibley).

UPLAND SANDPIPER

Bartramia longicauda Pl. 53

Identification 26–32cm. Short straight bill and long neck diagnostic. Small curlew-like shorebird with a short straight bill, long neck and upright posture. Buffy-ochraceous head to undertail-coverts, paler below, streaked dark brown from forehead to nape, lightly streaked on neck- and breast-sides; back dark brown with ochre to buff fringes and barring, back darker, inner wing paler and outer part, especially primary-coverts and primaries rather dark (contrasting noticeably in flight) and black rump also conspicuous in flight; white underwing and axillaries densely barred black; large dark eyes, yellow bill tipped black, legs and feet yellow.

Ssp. Monotypic (all countries)

Habits Holds wings up for a moment after landing. Forages by walking steadily through grass, often teetering rear body like a Spotted Sandpiper, though not as much.
Status Uncommon passage migrant; overflies region, occasionally transiting en route, September–October and March–May.
Habitat Tropical Zone, but recorded to 4,000m. Open wet grassy areas such as pastures, golf courses, airfields, parks, and sometimes grassy shorelines and sandbanks.
Voice Wide vocabulary, but usual flight-call is *huu-huuit* and alarm *quip-ip-ip-ip* or *kip-ip-ip-ip* (Voous, R&G, ffrench, H&B).

> Tringinae sandpipers have been called tattlers or tattletales, from their custom of acting as lookouts for a feeding flock, the first to sound the alarm at the approach of an intruder. They tend to be solitary or forage in small groups but also join mixed-species flocks. They dip and bob their fronts from time to time.

COMMON GREENSHANK

Tringa nebularia Pl. 54

Identification 30–35cm. Largest *Tringa* with long bill and dull green legs. Non-breeder has head to undertail-coverts white, with grey-streaked crown and hindneck, back brownish-grey with pale blackish spots and fringes to wings, lower back to uppertail-coverts white (in long wedge), tail white with *c.*6 blackish bars; large dark eyes, bill dull greenish with dark tip, legs and feet dull green. Breeder has fine blackish-streaked head and neck, with some spots on flanks; upperparts slightly darker brownish-grey with black scapulars and a few scattered black feathers on back and wings. In all plumages paler than Greater Yellowlegs.

Ssp. Monotypic (Ar, Bo, Cu, T&T, FG)

Habits Usually forages in shallow water in flocks, with steady manner but sometimes makes erratic changes of direction while running and holding bill in water.
Status Accidental vagrant from Europe, most likely to occur September–April.
Habitat Tropical Zone. Winters inland, favouring flooded meadows, marshes, sewage farms and flooded rice fields. Less often in estuaries and sandy or muddy coastal flats.
Voice Usual flight-call a quick, ringing whistle of 2 or more syllables, usually *teu-teu-teu*, and a sharp *tchuk!* or *chip!* in alarm (HMP), similar to yellowlegs.

Rump pattern distinguishes Greenshank (left) from Greater Yellowlegs, in flight.

GREATER YELLOWLEGS

Tringa melanoleuca Pl. 54

Identification 29–35cm. Non-breeding adult has head, neck and underparts white, with grey-brown streaking from crown to hindneck, with less on lower foreneck and breast-sides; back and wings greyish-brown with whitish fringes and black dots, primary-coverts and primaries dark with no white spotting, rump and uppertail-coverts square-shaped and white, tail barred black and white; bill black with greyish base, legs and feet yellow. Breeders more darkly streaked on head and neck, the streaks reaching lower breast and flanks, undertail-coverts narrowly barred black and back blacker with white dots on fringes of feathers. Larger, heavier than Lesser Yellowlegs, stout straight or slightly upturned bill, and more heavily marked below.

Ssp. Monotypic (all countries)

Habits Feeds singly or in small flocks, day and night. Wades in water, often swims, dashing after small fish. When disturbed, runs into deep water with head bobbing, and may flush.
Status Widespread transient and winter visitor that occurs year-round. Uncommon to locally common in Ecuador, elsewhere common, especially so on Atlantic coast of Guianas.
Habitat Tropical Zone to Páramo. Wide variety of habitats, from coastal lagoons and intertidal strip to páramo rain pools. Marshes, rice fields, flooded grassland and along rivers.
Voice Loud ringing *deew-deew-deew*, *tew-tew-tew* or *teu-teu-teu* on a slightly descending scale (Voous, R&G, HMP, Sibley).

Greater Yellowlegs (above) and Lesser Yellowlegs, drawn from median measurements of both in exact proportion; note distance of nostril from base of culmen

LESSER YELLOWLEGS *Tringa flavipes* Pl. 54

Identification 23–25cm. Comparatively short, dark straight bill and orange-yellow legs. Similar to larger Greater Yellowlegs, but has shorter bill, unmarked dark secondaries and more lightly marked body-sides.

Ssp. Monotypic (all countries)

Habits Feeds with delicate, high-stepping gait, dashes like Greater Yellowlegs (Piersma), rarely dashes (HMP), and less likely to run with open bill (Paulson); often feeds with side-to-side movement of bill. Wades in deep water and will walk on water lilies and other floating vegetation.
Status Widespread and fairly common, especially on Atlantic coast of Guianas. Most numerous in boreal winter, but some stay year-round.
Habitat Tropical to Subtropical Zone, rarely higher. Variety of wetlands, coastal and inland, from intertidal strips, where it is commonest on estuaries and mudflats, sewage farms, wet cultivations like rice, flooded pastures, etc. To 2,600m, exceptionally 3,300m.
Voice Characteristic call a double-noted *tew-tew*, sometimes repeated immediately in alarm, alerting entire feeding flock. Like a softer version of Greater Yellowlegs' triple-noted call. Heard year-round (Voous, ffrench, R&G, H&B, Tostain, HMP).

SOLITARY SANDPIPER
Tringa solitaria Pl. 54

Identification 18–21cm. Dark little *Tringa*; non-breeder has brown head with conspicuous white eye-ring, pale lores finely spotted, brown hindneck and breast; back slightly darker with white spots on fringes of feathers, wings dark brown, central tail solid dark brown, outer feathers barred brown and white; bill short and straight, black with grey base, long greenish legs. Two subspecies occur together on wintering grounds. Smaller and darker than Lesser Yellowlegs.

Ssp. *T. s. cinnamomea* (all countries) larger and paler but warmer brown spotting on underparts
T. s. solitaria (all countries) slightly smaller, has blackish lores, pale supraloral spot

Habits Solitary or in twos or threes, rarely flocks (*c*.30 seen French Guiana). Often wades in shallow water, vibrating leading foot to attract fish. In flight, changes direction rapidly. May hold wings aloft when alighting.
Status Fairly common boreal visitor, seen year-round, but rare May–June.
Habitat Tropical Zone. Fresh water of all types, from lakeshores to puddles, usually in fairly open places but along streams and pools in forests where other waders never seen. Ditches, wet meadows, swamps and flooded grassland, wet pastures, farms, even gardens and urban areas.
Voice Most common call a sharp, explosive, *peet!* or *pt-weet*, sometimes doubled or tripled as *tou-tou-twit* or *peet-weet-weet* or in series as in *tee-tee-tee-tee*… (Tostain, Voous, R&G, H&B, HMP, ffrench).

SPOTTED REDSHANK
Tringa erythropus Pl. 54

Identification 29-32cm. Non-breeding adult has grey head with bold white eyebrow, black lores and pale lower sides to white throat, grey hindneck, back and wings with broken white fringes to feathers forming dotted lines; all-white rump (wedge-shaped) very distinctive, uppertail-coverts finely barred grey and white, tail grey centrally, with white outer feathers; underparts and underwings white; long slender bill with red base and slightly drooping tip, bright orange-red legs and feet. Juvenile darker than adult with bold white loral spot but no eyebrow, underparts heavily barred grey and white.

Ssp. Monotypic (To)

Habits Probes and jabs in sand or mud. Sometimes swims in deeper water to feed, occasionally dipping head and neck.
Status Vagrant from Europe. Sight record at Bon Accord Lagoon, Tobago, in February 1983 (Fisher 1998).
Habitat Tropical Zone. Shallow freshwater and brackish wetlands, saltpans and muddy shores on coast.
Voice Flight-call a sharp, rapid whistle, falling then rising, *chu-it* or *ka-wit* (HMP, Sibley) and a short alarm *chip!*

WOOD SANDPIPER *Tringa glareola* Pl. 54

Identification 19–23cm. Rather like Lesser Yellowlegs but is size of Solitary Sandpiper, and separable from both by white superciliary and dull yellowish legs.

Ssp. Monotypic (To)

Habits Fairly solitary.

Status Vagrant to Tobago from Europe photographed at Buccoo, December 1996–February 1997 (McNair *et al.* 2002).
Habitat Freshwater wetlands in winter and flooded fields on migration, rarely in coastal areas.
Voice Call a sharp *chif-chif* (Sibley).

TEREK SANDPIPER *Xenus cinereus* Pl. 54

Identification 19–23cm. Small wader; breeding adult has dark-streaked head (white lores and eye-ring), pale postocular eyebrow, streaked breast, and is generally dark greyish-brown above with irregular white spots on wings and white fringes to all feathers; bill short, straight and dusky. Non-breeder similar but has far less white on back.

Ssp. Monotypic (Tr, FG)

Habits Moves in a frenzied manner, pecking or probing in mud or sweeping bill through water.
Status Vagrant from Europe. Sight record at Waterloo, Trinidad, in June 1999 (Taylor 2001) and a bird photographed, French Guiana, in February 2005 (O. Tostain). There is also a sight record for Barbados, in May 2000 (M. Frost *fide* F. E. Hayes, *in litt.* 2001), and 2 recent records each for Brazil and for Argentina.
Voice Flight-call an emphatic series of high-pitched notes, usually 3+, *pip-pip-pip* (Paulson). Alarm a distinctive *tur-lip!*

SPOTTED SANDPIPER
Actitis macularius Pl. 54

Identification 18–20cm. Small. Breeding bird pale greyish-brown above with white eye-ring and dark lores, pale line through eyes (almost an eyebrow), upperparts have well-spaced black bars; breast to undertail-coverts white with irregular round black spots; bill usually orange, short legs yellowish to orange. Winter plumage usually lacks neatly spotted underparts; juvenile like non-breeder but has bars above tricoloured, cinnamon, black and white. Soft parts dull yellowish but considerable variation, from orange to grey.

Ssp. Monotypic (all countries)

Habits Unique jerky flight, fluttering on stiff wingbeats with regular short glides. Feeds at edge of water, does not wade, and runs with constant teetering action, raising and lowering rear body. Solitary. Sometimes washes food prior to swallowing.
Status Widespread and common throughout region, a transient and winter resident, and commonest August–April, though some seen year-round.
Habitat Tropical to Subtropical Zones. Wide variety of habitats, on coast: sandy beaches, muddy flats, estuaries and mangroves, with a predilection for shrimp farms; and inland, freshwater marshes, riverbanks, streams and ditches. Found to 2,000m, but exceptionally to 3,300m.
Voice Thin piping voice, a plaintive double-whistled *peet-weet*, *peep-peep*, *see-eet* or *weet-weet*, and so on, descending slightly (Tostain, R&G, Voous, H&M, HMP); flight-call a high, clear whistled *twii twii* (Sibley).
Note Generally considered monotypic.

WANDERING TATTLER
Heteroscelus incanus Pl. 54

Identification 26–29cm. Virtually entirely bluish-, almost slate, grey, with white eye-ring, blackish lores, slight white eyebrow, white throat, white belly and undertail-coverts; straight bill black, legs and feet greenish. Breeding bird has entire underparts finely barred grey and white, legs and feet bright yellow. Juvenile differs in having pale grey fringes to all feathers on back and wings.

Ssp. Monotypic (Ec, Co)

Habits Inconspicuous wader, solitary or with turnstones and Surfbirds; dark grey with a white belly, straight black bill and black line through eyes, short yellow legs. Bobs and teeters, moving continually, picking and probing mats of mussels. Low, weaving flight.
Status Scarce and local in boreal winter on Pacific coast, but some stay all year.
Habitat Lower Tropical Zone. Rocky coasts with platforms and piers and offshore islands. Will pause at inland freshwater pools on migration, rarely on estuarine mudflats.
Voice Generally quiet, Characteristic flight-call a plaintive, whistled trill *lidididi* (Sibley) or *ti-lee-lee* (R&G), or a longer call of 6–10 notes on same pitch, accelerating but with decreasing volume, a ringing but hollow-sounding *pew-tu-tu-tu-tu-tu* (HMP).

WILLET *Catoptrophorus semipalmatus* Pl. 56

Identification 33–41cm. Non-breeding adult has grey head with a bold white eye-ring and lores, and grey hindneck and upperparts. Rather like Greater Yellowlegs, but has bluish-grey legs.

Ssp. *C. s. inornatus* (Ec, Bo) less heavily streaked
C. s. semipalmatus (all countries) smaller, darker

Habits Feeds singly and in small, sometimes mixed groups, day and night. Stalks slowly but also runs, scything bill through water; walks with bill angled down. Flight strong with downstroke emphasised.
Status In Ecuador a common migrant (*inornatus*, rarely *semipalmatus*), most numerous November–February; in Colombia and Venezuela, common mainly September–April, and has bred on Los Roques; in Trinidad & Tobago rather uncommon, mostly September–October; in Netherlands Antilles uncommon, mostly August–October; in Suriname numerous with peak in July–August. Occurs on all coasts year-round in small numbers.
Habitat Tropical Zone. Races differ in habitat preferences: *inornatus* is associated with prairie marshes whilst *semipalmatus* is mainly coastal, favouring saltmarshes with short vegetation. However, in transit and winter, this distinction is blurred and both may occur on intertidal strips and saltmarshes.
Voice Like Greater Yellowlegs, only coarser and louder (Voous), usually noisy (ffrench, R&G), loud shrill flight-call *quee-quee-queep* (Hilty) and *whe-whe-whe* (ffrench), *kip-kip-kip* or *kyee-yee-yee* (R&G).

The turnstones are small sandpipers with short legs and dagger-like bills. They are active, sociable and noisy, and have very distinctive wing patterns in flight. The wing-coverts are rather long and protrude over the edge of the wing, particularly in Black Turnstone.

RUDDY TURNSTONE
Arenaria interpres Pl. 56

Identification 21–26cm. Considerable variation in plumage, not least intermediate stages between breeding and non-breeding plumages. Breeding male has very complex plumage that is unmistakable (see plate), even in flight, when reveals broad white lower back and rump, broad line of white feathers at base of wings, and white bases to secondaries and inner primaries. Female similar but duller, with fewer chestnut and more brown tones in wings; the short, dagger-like bill is black and very slightly upturned at tip, legs and feet bright orange. Non-breeder has similar pattern but lacks chestnut in wings and black and white on upper face. Juvenile is even more like a standard sandpiper, but has complete black breast and dull yellowish legs.

Ssp. *A. i. interpres* (unconfirmed in our region) slightly larger, darker streaking, chestnut-red not less intense
A. i. morinella (all countries) as described

Habits Flips stones and shells over with a quick jerky movement to snatch at any life beneath.

Status Widespread and usually common. Boreal transient and winter visitor, with a few present all year. Particularly numerous September–October and March–May.

Habitat Lower Tropical Zone. Coastal, but may occur inland on migration. Rocky, stony shores, mudflats with beds of mussels, etc., prefers stony, shingle and rocky areas, but also on sandy beaches with washed-up seaweed

Voice Flight- and alarm-calls given variously as *katakak* (ffrench) *kutikuk* (R&G), *ut-e-kut* (H&B) and *kuk-kuk-kuk* (Voous).

Turnstones have highly distinctive patterns in flight: Ruddy Turnstone (left), Black Turnstone (centre) and Surfbird (right)

BLACK TURNSTONE
Arenaria melanocephala Pl. 56

Identification 22–25cm. Adult all black above, white below, with white-fringed black feathers forming rows that project onto lower breast; median and greater wing-coverts long and grey-fringed (innermost scapulars, coverts and tertials finely edged white); legs and feet bright orange. Juvenile as adult but dark brown to fuscous, appearing black at distance. From Ruddy Turnstone by apparent lack of white on upperparts, but also has a broad white lower back and rump (concealed by closed wings), broad line of white feathers at base of wings (concealed by scapulars), and white bases to secondaries and inner primaries (concealed by long coverts).

Ssp. Monotypic (Ec)

Habits Forages slowly and steadily over rocks, often with Ruddy Turnstones and Surfbirds. Turns over patches of seaweed, and may follow receding breakers.

Status Rare vagrant to Ecuador.

Habitat Lower Tropical Zone. Rocky coasts, isolated rocky outcrops, occasionally on adjacent beaches or mudflats.

Voice A shrill, high chatter *keeert* and trilling *skirrr*, higher pitched than Ruddy Turnstone (R&G, Sibley, HMP).

Note Listed as a vagrant to Ecuador by SFP&M but not by R&G.

The Calidrid sandpipers or peeps run along beaches and roost in large numbers. They have compact bodies and the long, slender wings of long-distance migrants.

SURFBIRD *Aphriza virgata* Pl. 56

Identification 23–26cm. Robust sandpiper with short thick bill and short-legs, like a turnstone. Non-breeding adult is grey above with a narrow white eye-ring and pale fringes to feathers, dark grey breast, flanks and belly (like Black Turnstone), and rest of underparts white. Juvenile like non-breeding adult, but slightly duller with shorter wing-coverts. White base to secondaries and most primaries obvious in flight (see turnstones), but hidden at rest.

Ssp. Monotypic (Ec, W Co)

Habits Gregarious, and often with other species (turnstones, etc.), but not easy to see among dark rocks.

Status Boreal migrant to Pacific coast, transient and winter resident, with a few staying all year, but most winter in Chile. Rare to locally uncommon, most frequent on southbound passage, in September–October.

Habitat Lower Tropical Zone. Rocky coasts, especially with lots of seaweed, along tidal strip, occasionally on adjacent beaches or mudflats.

Voice Usually silent, but can give a shrill, plaintive whistle, *keee-wee-ah* (HMP).

RED KNOT *Calidris canutus* Pl. 56

Identification 23–25cm. Robust, rather plain bird. Non-breeding adult grey with whitish fringes to upperparts feathers, white eyebrow and grey streaks on foreneck to breast, rest of underparts white; short black bill and olive legs. Juvenile darker and slightly browner. First-year quite distinct, being flushed pale cinnamon on head, with cinnamon foreneck and breast (latter with some whitish scallops), upperparts fuscous with cinnamon to grey fringes to all feathers, centres to scapulars and median coverts black. Adult breeding has whitish and cinnamon spotting on wing-coverts, and face, foreneck and breast bright cinnamon.

Ssp. *C. c. rufa* (all countries)
perhaps also *C. c. roselaari* (in east of region)

Habits Highly gregarious but may occur singly or in large mixed groups, especially with Black-bellied Plovers and turnstones.
Status Uncommon boreal migrant, mainly seen August–October, but remain all winter and a few all year.
Habitat Lower Tropical Zone. Prefers open sandy beaches and sandy outer reaches of estuaries, but occurs on mudflats and occasionally inland at saline lakes on migration.
Voice Two types of call noted, both uttered in flight or when foraging, a sharp single note *kit!* or *kwip!*, *trick!* or *tuit!*, and a softer but still sharp, repeated *kreet-weet* or *twick-twick*, and occasionally a short trill (ffrench, Tostain, Voous, R&G, H&B).

The following sandpipers are generally referred to as stints or peeps. They are the smallest of the sandpipers and can be difficult to identify. Wing-length in relation to tail is important, and can affect the perception of shape; the colour of the legs and feet is also important, but in general, shape and behaviour are more significant than plumage coloration. Flight-calls also helpful, but none of these characteristics is a guarantee of identity by itself.

SANDERLING *Calidris alba* Pl. 55

Identification 20–21cm. Small and the palest of the sandpipers. Non-breeding adult has pale grey rear crown to mantle, brown wings with pale grey fringes, a white trailing edge to secondaries (which shows as a short diagonal bar but appears part of a longer white bar in flight); flight-feathers and tail dusky; bill short and stubby, legs and feet all black. Breeding bird has irregular orange-rufous wash to head and back, and some are rich chestnut. Juvenile is darker than non-breeding adult, with some black feathers on back, scapulars and lesser wing-coverts.

Ssp. *C. a. rubida* (all countries)

Habits Feeds near water's edge, keeping close to waves as they advance and recede, running actively, night and day. Very social, flocks of any size, often mixed with turnstones and plovers.
Status Fairly common, most numerous in September–May, but some occur year-round.
Habitat Lower Tropical Zone. Prefers exposed sandy beaches and sandy outer reaches of estuaries, but also occurs on rocky and muddy shores.
Voice Frequently heard call, in flight and when foraging, a sharp *kit!*, *kwip!*, *trick!* or *tuit!*, and softer *twick* when disturbed. Flight-call may be repeated (ffrench, Tostain, R&G, Voous, HMP).

SEMIPALMATED SANDPIPER
Calidris pusilla Pl. 55

Identification 13–15cm. Non-breeding adult is plain brownish-grey above with fine dark shaft-streaks on back and wings, white superciliary, white below with greyish wash to breast and some faint streaking; bill, legs and feet black, feet semi-webbed (very difficult to see in field). Juvenile darker and more brownish above, with brown fringes to scapulars and tone to crown, buffy to whitish fringes to wing-feathers; underparts white. Very similar to Western Sandpiper and difficult to separate in winter plumage; Semipalmated has shorter bill, broader at base and legs are shorter. Tends to feed by probing mud whilst Western tends to wade into water more.

Ssp. Monotypic (all countries)

Habits Forages socially, and mixed flocks of both species are common. Flocks spread out when foraging, but pack densely at roosts.
Status Abundant, usually the commonest shorebird, especially on northern coasts, more locally common on Pacific coasts. Most numerous August–April.
Habitat Lower Tropical Zone. Mainly on sandy beaches, especially intertidal strips, estuaries, bays and lagoons, but on migration may occur inland at flooded savannas, reservoirs and short-grass marshes.
Voice Flight-call differs from Western, being a shrill and rather indifferent *djjt*, *kyip*, *cherk* or *cher*, *churr* or *pirrrt* – less thin and sharp, slightly lower pitched than Western (ffrench, R&G, H&B, Voous, HMP and Paulson). Other vocalisations include a soft chattering.

Semipalmated Sandpiper (above) and Western Sandpiper

WESTERN SANDPIPER
Calidris mauri Pl. 55

Identification 14–17cm. Non-breeding adult is plain brownish-grey above with fine dark shaft-shafts on back and wings, white superciliary, white below with greyish wash to breast and some faint streaking; bill, legs and feet black, feet semi-webbed (very difficult to see in field). Juvenile darker and more brownish above, with brown fringes to scapulars and tone to crown, buffy to whitish fringes to wing-feathers; underparts white. Very similar to Semipalmated Sandpiper and difficult to separate in winter plumage, but Western has longer bill, more pointed and droop-tipped; legs longer. Feeds by probing mud but tends to wade into water more and may immerse head entirely.

Ssp. Monotypic (all countries)

Habits Forages socially, and mixed flocks of both species common. Flocks spread out when foraging, but pack densely at roosts.

Status Abundant and among the commonest shorebirds, especially on northern coasts, more locally so on Pacific coasts. Most numerous August–April.

Habitat Tropical to Subtropical Zones. Mainly on sandy beaches, especially intertidal strips, estuaries, bays and lagoons, but on migration may occur inland at flooded savannas, reservoirs and short-grass marshes.

Voice Flight-call a sharp *jeep! cheet*, *jyeep!*, *squeep* or *kree-ee-eet*, *jeet*, sharper, slightly longer and higher pitched than Semipalmated (ffrench, Tostain, R&G, H&B, Voous, HMP, Paulson).

LEAST SANDPIPER *Calidris minutilla* Pl. 55

Identification 13–15cm. Very small and tame peep. Pale brown above and on breast, with somewhat irregular blackish centres to upperparts feathers (some appear mottled); whitish eyebrow and throat, white belly; bill black, legs and feet dull greenish-yellow. Juvenile browner with rufous fringes to upperparts, scapulars moult first and appear as a grey diagonal on back. Smallest of all shorebirds, like Semipalmated but smaller with short, thin bill and legs usually yellowish to greenish (not brown) and looks short-tailed. Only small peep with yellowish legs and always looks dark-chested (Semipalmated, Western look white-chested).

Ssp. Monotypic (all countries)

Status Common transient and winter resident with some staying year-round.

Habitat Tropical to Subtropical Zones. On migration occurs in wide variety of wet habitats, both coastal and inland, but more often inland than Semipalmated or Western.

Voice Flight-call is a distinctive, rather drawn-out, high-pitched, rising *peep*, *kree-eep*, *kree-eet* or *treee* (ffrench, R&G, H&B, Voous and HMP).

WHITE-RUMPED SANDPIPER *Calidris fuscicollis* Pl. 55

Identification 17–18cm. Greyish-brown above with dark feather centres (sometimes almost entire feather) and pale fringes, whitish eyebrow and white throat. Breast streaked greyish-brown, rest of underparts white; bill black with pale base to lower mandible, legs and feet dusky brown. Juvenile darker above, blackish on scapulars and outer mantle, with grey fringes, but perhaps a touch of rufous on head and upper (inner) edges to mantle. Resembles Baird's Sandpiper but slightly larger and greyer, white eyebrow slightly longer behind eye and streaks on flanks perhaps more obvious (Baird's is always plain white), whilst wingtips extend beyond tail (like Baird's). Distinctive white uppertail-coverts (not rump, as name suggests) conspicuous in flight but only seen at rest if bird raises wings.

Ssp. Monotypic (all countries)

Status Rare transient that usually overflies region, but small numbers occur in boreal spring and autumn.

Habitat Tropical Zone. Coastal and inland, sandy beaches and mudflats, open fields and marshes, ponds and lagoons.

Voice A light *jeep*, *jeeyt*, *skeet*, *jeeet* or *teep* etc. (ffrench, Voous, H&B, R&G, HMP).

BAIRD'S SANDPIPER *Calidris bairdii* Pl. 55

Identification 14–17cm. Greyish-brown above, the feathers with pale fringes, whitish supraloral spot vaguely separated from short eyebrow, and white throat. Breast streaked greyish-brown, rest of underparts white; bill black, legs and feet dusky brown. Juvenile darker above, with pale brown to pale buff fringes, and head and breast more brownish. Very similar to White-rumped but differs in having breast-band abruptly ending on upper belly, and never has streaks on flanks; also dark centre to rump.

Ssp. Monotypic (all countries)

Status Rare transient that usually overflies region, but small numbers occur in boreal spring and autumn.

Habitat Tropical Zone to Páramo, mainly in Andes at 2,500–4,700m, favouring shallow ponds, lakes and damp grassy areas (R&G), but occasionally on coast, where prefers higher shore and dry fringes of wetlands (HMP).

Voice Flight-calls include a low-pitched *krrrit*, *krrt* or *kurrp*, a low trilling *preeet* and a sharp *tsick!* (R&G, HMP).

PECTORAL SANDPIPER *Calidris melanotos* Pl. 55

Identification 19–23cm. Non-breeding adult has pale brown head, neck and breast, boldly streaked dark brown, rest of underparts white, whitish eyebrow and throat; upperparts dark brown with pale buffy fringes to feathers, and white sides to dark brown lower rump and uppertail-coverts; bill dusky with basal half horn, legs and feet dull brownish-horn. Male is larger than female. From other peeps by buffy-streaked breast sharply demarcated from white belly.

Ssp. Monotypic (all countries)

Habits When disturbed or alarmed, stands still, watching with head up, but flushes reluctantly in a snipe-like zigzag. Highly gregarious, usually with American Golden Plover and other waders. Forages by walking steadily, alternating pecking with rapid probing.

Status Passage migrant (very few birds wintering), usually in August–November, more rarely in spring.

Habitat Tropical Zone to Páramo. Coastal and inland; along Andes at 3,500–4,500 m; saltmarshes, swamps, floodplains, sewage farms and rice fields.

Voice Alarm/flight-call a sharp, rather snipe-like, somewhat low-pitched, throaty note, sometimes repeated, *krrik*, *krurk*, *tr'r'r'k*, *ch'r'r't*, *churk* or *trrit* (ffrench, R&G, H&B, Tostain, Voous, HMP).

DUNLIN *Calidris alpina* Pl. 55

Identification 16–22cm. Dull, with virtually unstreaked grey to grey-brown upperparts, whitish eyebrow, narrow white wingbar (visible in flight), and dark rump and black uppertail-coverts with white sides; white throat, dull brownish-grey head to breast, white underparts (sometimes streaked, depending on race); bill long and droop-tipped, legs and feet black. Juvenile is brighter. Short, with rounded posture; more dumpy than Curlew Sandpiper and bill curved only at end, not entire length.

Ssp. Complete uncertainty as to which subspecies occurs in our region. *C.a. pacifica* has well-defined eyebrow and short streaks on flanks; *C.a. hudsonia* is slightly browner above, typically with streaked flanks and poorly defined eyebrow.

Habits Forages by walking slowly and deliberately, probing into mud or sand.
Status Rare vagrant, with sight records from Ecuador, Colombia and Venezuela.
Habitat Lower Tropical Zone. Estuaries, muddy shores and mudflats, intertidal areas, tidal rivers, flooded fields, marshes, sewage farms
Voice Flight-call a distinctive, slurred, reedy *kreee* or *treeep*. Feeding or roosting flocks make a soft twittering sound (HMP).

CURLEW SANDPIPER
Calidris ferruginea Pl. 55

Identification 18–23cm. Non-breeding adult is pale brownish-grey above with faint shaft-streaks and pale fringes to feathers, head and breast browner, with white eyebrow and throat, uppertail-coverts and rest of underparts white; gently decurved black bill, legs and feet greenish dusky. Juvenile is significantly darker with pale fringes to back feathers contrasting much more; head darker, and eyebrow far more noticeable. Resembles Dunlin, but bill longer and is curved over entire length, with longer legs. Tends to wade in deeper water than Dunlin. When flushed shows white rump and white wingbar, whilst Dunlin has black band on middle of rump to tail.

Ssp. Monotypic (Co, Tr)

Habits Forages night and day; gregarious.
Status Vagrant from Europe, known only from sight records.
Habitat Lower Tropical Zone. Tidal flats and estuaries, coastal lagoons, saltmarshes and saltpans. May occur inland in flooded areas, muddy marshes, etc.
Voice A gentle rippling *chirrup* recalling a very soft Ruddy Turnstone (HMP).

STILT SANDPIPER
Calidris himantopus Pl. 55

Identification 18–23cm. Somewhat like a yellowlegs in plumage, but feeds like a dowitcher. Non-breeding adult rather plain brown above, with narrow dark shaft-streaks and pale fringes, the latter quite prominent in fresh plumage, but soon wear off. Some irregular dark feathers from breeding or juvenile plumage can be retained, and has whitish lores and throat; head-, neck- and upper-breast-sides lightly streaked brown, with irregular dark scallops and bars on flanks; bill longish and slightly decurved at tip, Dunlin-like, and legs and feet greenish-yellow. Juvenile slightly darker brown with white fringes to scapulars and wings. Very similar to Curlew Sandpiper but differs in leg-length and feeding behaviour – usually seen belly deep in water 'stitching', dowitcher-like, but also scythes.

Ssp. Monotypic (all countries)

Habits Often forages with dowitchers and yellowlegs, but usually in deeper water, head down and sometimes submerged completely. Also with stilts but less nervous and more approachable.
Status Boreal transient and winter visitor, varies from very common (Suriname) to rather local (Ecuador), and occurrences not easily predicted. A few stay year-round.
Habitat Lagoons and mudflats on coast, but more frequently at freshwater wetlands slightly inland, and regular in Llanos of Venezuela, saltflats, marshes and sewage farms.
Voice Usually silent but utters a single, plaintive *kiu*, and a soft rattling trill in flight, *kirrr* or *grrrt* (ffrench, R&G, HMP).
Note Formerly placed in monospecific genus *Micropalama*.

BUFF-BREASTED SANDPIPER
Tryngites subruficollis Pl. 55

Identification 18–20cm. Small round head on long neck; runs in very upright manner and is very approachable, often freezing rather than running or flushing. Entirely buff below with paler buffy fringes to all feathers, white underwing-coverts, darker buff crown and hindneck with small dark brown spots (fairly sparse on mid hindneck), upperparts dark brown with broad buffy fringes; short, straight black bill, legs greyish-yellow. Juvenile very similar but more densely spotted on head and neck, and breast-sides; above slightly brighter than adult, with black scapulars and darker back feathers, fringed white or pale buff.

Ssp. Monotypic (all countries)

Habits If flushed flies with erratic, twisting wingbeats. Very often with American Golden Plovers and Pectoral Sandpipers; runs and stops like a plover.
Status Scarce transient, usually only observed on southbound passage in August–September.
Habitat Short-grass country, margins of freshwater wetlands, riverbanks, meadows, páramos and sandbanks, and sometimes found far from water.
Voice Usually silent, but gives a low chirrup, a low, trilled *prrreet*, a low-pitched *tiw* and a sharp *tik* (ffrench, Tostain, R&G, H&B, HMP).

RUFF *Philomachus pugnax* Pl. 53

Identification Male 26–32cm, female 20–25cm. Entire upperparts plain greyish-brown with dark centres and pale fringes to feathers, head to undertail-coverts greyish-white, darker on crown and hindneck, palest on belly and undertail-coverts; eyes dark, bill black (perhaps with a paler base), legs and feet yellow. Juvenile browner and more ochraceous on head and neck, with buffy flanks, and upperparts fringes vary from whitish to rufescent; bill black but legs vary, generally dull greenish-yellow. Like Lesser Yellowlegs but browner, and legs shorter. Tail pattern comprising 2 white ovals, 1 each side of rump, is diagnostic (best seen when flushed), but is not visible at rest.

Ssp. Monotypic (Co, Ve, T&T)

Habits Forages very actively, walking hurriedly or running in bursts, with a characteristic hunched posture.
Status Rare accidental from Europe, with records most likely in August–May.
Habitat Prefers muddy fringes to salt, brackish or freshwater wetlands, and rice fields. Will visit farmland, picking grain, and also freshly mown or short-cropped grassland.
Voice Usually silent but foraging flocks utter low hoarse *kurr*, *kuk-uk* and *kook* notes, and a shrill, rising *hoo-ee* may be heard from migrating groups (HMP).

Two of the phalaropes are more seabirds than shorebirds, as they spend all their time at sea, usually some distance from land. They feed by picking small invertebrates from the surface of the water, and can spin in a circle that causes a whirlpool effect drawing their food towards them. Females are larger than males, and in breeding plumage are more colourful. The third member of the genus is larger and winters principally at high-altitude, saline lakes in the southern Andes.

WILSON'S PHALAROPE

Phalaropus tricolor Pl. 56

Identification 20–25cm. Larger than other phalaropes with more sandpiper-like proportions, but on water unmistakable as a phalarope. Non-breeding adult grey above with broad white fringes to wing-feathers, somewhat dusky primaries, white eyebrow and underparts; bill long, straight and slender, legs and feet yellowish. Juvenile similar but wings brown with pale fringes. Moults to breeding plumage before leaving for North America, in March. Female larger and brighter, with dark grey crown, short white eyebrow, black mask joining black nape and hindneck; chin white, throat and breast rich orange-rufous, rest of underparts white; mantle and wings rufescent brown or chestnut, scapulars grey, flight-feathers and tail brown; legs dark. Male duller or blacker than female, and sometimes appears to be only halfway through moult. Like a small Lesser Yellowlegs but more uniform greyish above, with a whiter head and immaculate white underparts.

Ssp. Monotypic (Ec, Co, Ve, T&T, Su?)

Habits Feeds, by wading or swimming, on brine shrimp and brine flies, pecking, scything and upending. Flocks sometimes spin en masse in water. Occasionally forages on mud, when characteristically walks with tail held slightly aloft.
Status Passage migrant, usually in August/September and again in March. Locally common in Ecuador, where also a winter resident, a rare fall transient in Colombia, and very rare in Venezuela.
Habitat Sometimes in sheltered tidal pools, lagoons and estuaries, but prefers open water of saline lakes in highlands.
Voice Usually silent but may give a soft grunting *aaugh* in flight (HMP).

RED-NECKED PHALAROPE

Phalaropus lobatus Pl. 56

Identification 18–20cm. Smallest phalarope, with a black, needle-like bill. Non-breeder has white head with a dusky crown and postocular line, and small black crescent on lores; back grey with pale fringes to wings and primaries and tail dark. Juvenile similar but dusky crown continues on hindneck to mantle, with pale grey line on inner scapulars, and outer wing-coverts and secondaries dusky.

Ssp. Monotypic (Ec, Co)

Habits Seen in small flocks flying low over sea, or rarely on water. Pecks at prey on water's surface, spins anticlockwise (faster than Red Phalarope) and associates with other birds at sea.
Status Rare Palearctic migrant that is fairly pelagic when not breeding, spending its time on the edge of the Humboldt Current. Irregular and accidental on salt lagoons in Ecuador, and a scarce but regular winter visitor to Pacific coast of Colombia.
Habitat Offshore waters within sight of land, and occurs in small numbers on salt lagoons.
Voice Flight-call is a single *twick* or *clip*, lower pitched than similar call of Red Phalarope.

RED PHALAROPE

Phalaropus fulicarius Pl. 56

Identification 20–22cm. Larger and bulkier than Red-necked Phalarope. Non-breeding adult has white head with small cap on rear crown, dusky postocular line and small black crescent on lores, back pale grey with paler fringes to wings, and primaries and tail dark. Juvenile has larger cap and postocular line, with unmarked neck like adult Red-necked Phalarope, but throat has yellow-orange flush and entire upperparts dusky to black, the feathers fringed cinnamon, with pale grey scapulars forming a contrasting V across the back.

Ssp. Monotypic (Ec, Co)

Habits Usually in small flocks (occasionally large). Feeds by picking from water's surface, but also upends occasionally. Often spins repeatedly.
Status Rare boreal transient and winter visitor. Pelagic, wintering at sea in Humboldt Current. Occurs inshore during bad weather.
Habitat Offshore, rarely in sight of land, in plankton-rich upwellings. May be driven ashore, even inland, by bad storms, when briefly seeks shelter on lakes or reservoirs.
Voice Call is a shrill *wit*, recalling Sanderling (HMP).

THINOCORIDAE – Seedsnipes

Seedsnipes form a small family, restricted to the central and southern Andes. They take their name from being seed-eaters with the rapid, zigzagging flight of snipe, and when flushed, which they do very reluctantly, they utter a sharp, rasping alarm also quite similar to a snipe. Despite this, the Thinocoridae are not especially closely related to the Scolopacidae. They are plump, ground-feeders with long wings, short legs and short tails, and quite unlike snipe they have short conical bills, typical of seed-eating birds. The upperparts are very cryptic, and their defence is to crouch prone, not flushing until the very last moment. Nests are on barren, stony soil, where their eggs are perfectly camouflaged, just like a regular wader's eggs on a pebbly beach. They are birds of inhospitable and unfriendly landscapes, and are very poorly known and understood.

Additional references used to prepare this family include Goodall (1964), Fjeldså & Krabbe (1990) and Fjeldså (1996).

RUFOUS-BELLIED SEEDSNIPE
Attagis gayi Pl. 52

Identification 27–30.5cm. Unmistakable within its habitat. Head and neck buffy with all feathers, except those surrounding eyes, fringed dark brown, affording a close-scaled or vermiculated effect, back to wings and tail dark brown, the feathers fringed buffy; underparts uniform cinnamon; eyes dark, heavy seed-finch-like bill greyish-blue, legs and feet yellowish. One of the larger seedsnipe, rather partridge-like.

Ssp. *A. g. latreillii* (N Ec)

Habits Forages in pairs or small groups on ground, walking to pick seeds and take shoots and small leaves. Shy, when disturbed cowers down and remains motionless. A strong flier. Usually silent.
Status Rare to uncommon, though easily overlooked.
Habitat Páramo, mostly 4,000–4,600m. Rocky fields, high mountain meadows and bogs with *Espeletia* or low bushes and grasses, barren terrain, crags.
Voice Call described as repetitions of a hoarse *gulla-gulla-gulla*... (R&G).
Note The very distinctive and geographically well-separated race *latreillii* may merit species status (R&G).

LEAST SEEDSNIPE
Thinocorus rumicivorus Pl. 52

Identification 16–19cm. A small, lark-like bird that tends to run and crouch, rather than fly if alarmed. Adult male has brown forehead, hindneck, back and tail, the feathers fringed pale buffy to greyish, grey face- and neck-sides, white throat outlined in black, continuing below on central foreneck and joining a narrow black line that separates the grey from white underparts; eyes dark, bill yellow with black tip, legs and feet pink. Female lacks grey neck-sides and black line around white throat tails off above breast.

Ssp. *T. r. cuneicauda* (SW Ec)

Habits Forages on ground, in pairs or small groups. Shy and difficult to see.
Status Very rare, and very poorly known. Something of an enigma in Ecuador, with only a few unconfirmed sightings in the 19th century.
Habitat Lower Tropical Zone in Ecuador. Open expanses of sand or gravel with scanty, scrubby grasses, succulents and bushes.
Voice Call a sudden, low *juk* or *juk-juk*, mostly when flushed. Male gives long series of *kuk* notes, both perched and in flight. Song transcribed as *krii-oko* and *kroo*, also *krro*...*pucui pucui-pucui* from song posts, and *pehooy pehooy pehooy* or an accelerating *tjupo-cooo tjupo-cooo* in flight.
Note The only specimens collected in Ecuador (1898) were described, in 1910, as a new race, *pallidus*, by Salvadori & Festa, but this name was considered a synonym of Peruvian *cuneicauda* by Hellmayr & Conover (1948).

JACANIDAE – Jacanas

An alternative name for jacanas, and indeed the family they belong to, is lily-trotters. It is most apt, for one often sees them stepping over lily leaves in an ornamental lagoon in a park or extensive garden. These plover-sized birds have also been referred to as water-plovers. This walk-on-water ability is a product of the remarkably long toes and toenails, which enable the bird to distribute its weight so extensively that the leaves it steps on barely sink more than a centimetre into the water. Another remarkable aspect of jacanas is that they are polyandrous, with the larger female developing larger and more colourful wattles, displaying to the males and mating with several. The male builds the nest, incubates the eggs and cares for the chicks which are totally precocious and can run across leaves on the water surface soon after hatching. Where a male's territory is small, or in a situation with few other jacanas nearby, the female may well be monogamous and help defend the territory, but that is the limit of her domesticity! Jacanas can be quite noisy, and whilst birds in a park will ignore human observers, in a truly wild situation humans may be greeted with raucous cries, sounding the alarm.

Additional references used to prepare this family include Gilliard (1958), Richford (1985) and Jenni (1996).

WATTLED JACANA *Jacana jacana* Pl. 51

Identification 17–25cm. Black head, (usually) chestnut body and wings with bright yellow flight-feathers very obvious when raises wings, as it often does when foraging; eyes dark brown, caruncled wattle on forehead and bill-sides, and base of bill all red, distal half of bill yellow, long legs and very long toes greyish. Female has larger and brighter wattles, and is larger than male. Juvenile dark brown above with long pale eyebrow, back pale brown, flight-feathers yellow; eyes pale, bill greenish-yellow with orange base, legs pale grey. In flight, with legs stretched back, the feet extend >10 cm beyond tail, giving bird a distinctive flight silhouette.

Ssp. *J. j. hypomelaena* (N Co) blackish above; juvenile dusky from crown to back and wing-coverts, eyes pale yellow, otherwise as juvenile *intermedia*

J. j. melanopygia (W Co, W Ve) dark, dull brown above

J. j. intermedia (E Ec, E Co, N & C Ve) deeper chestnut above; juvenile very different, with dark brown crown and postocular line that reaches dark hindneck, back medium brown, with yellow flight-feathers; eyes and eye-ring pale blue, base of bill orange-red, rest of bill yellow-green, legs and feet pale blue-grey

J. j. jacana (SE Co, S Ve, T&T, Gu, Su, FG) smaller and brighter chestnut above

J. j. scapularis (W Ec) black on scapulars

Habits Forages by walking on floating vegetation or wet ground, or wades in very shallow water, picking small seeds, insects and other invertebrates. Highly sedentary and usually reasonably social. Breeds at end of rainy season. Nest built over shallow water, sometimes in rice fields or wet grasslands. Often seen perched on Capybara to pick ticks from their backs. Flags wings up very frequently, flashing yellow underwing.

Status Common and widespread almost everywhere. Common to uncommon in Ecuador, common in Colombia, abundant in Venezuela, abundant in Trinidad but local in Tobago, common in Guyana, common and locally numerous in Suriname and French Guiana.

Habitat Tropical Zone. Open-country wetlands with shallow water and floating vegetation. Rice paddies, wet fields and pastures, sewage farms.

Voice Often chatters when foraging, and calls when flying across water or away from danger, a squeaky, high, scolding *kee-kee-kee-kee-kee….*

STERCORARIIDAE – Skuas and Jaegers

Skuas and jaegers are the pirates and predators of the seas, the oceanic analogue of hawks and falcons but more pugnacious and daring. They are related to gulls, but there are many differences. Whereas gulls are essentially white, a colour that functions well as a social attraction signal when food is located, skuas and jaegers are cryptically dark, that they may approach gulls and terns without drawing attention. They breed in polar waters, some in the Arctic and others in the Antarctic. Both migrate towards the equator when not breeding, even crossing landmasses on migration, and are irregular visitors to our offshore waters. They are generally silent when not breeding. Females are larger than the males. All are polymorphic, with greyish-white and sooty-brown phases. Generally solitary, although Pomarines occasionally travel in groups. Their bills are hooked and strong, for tearing flesh. The wings have white panels at the base of the primaries, which are large in skuas, small in jaegers. The 7 species in the family reside in 2 natural groupings. The first 4 are the large, heavily built and brown, with short tails. The smaller 3 are the jaegers, more falcon-like birds, slighter of build and long-tailed, which also pick food from the surface of the water. The genus *Catharacta* was brought into *Stercorarius* by Andersson (1999), a proposal that was accepted by the AOU.

Additional references for this family include Harrison (1983), Furness (1985, 1996), Malling Olsen & Larsson (1997), Peterson & McRae (2002) and Murphy (2002).

GREAT SKUA *Stercorarius skua* Pl. 57

Identification 51–66cm. Very large, bulky, brown bird with dark cap; blunt tail; white flash on wingtips formed by white bases to primaries. Juvenile has 2 variants, the usual type dark brown with cinnamon tips to all wing-coverts, and white flash as adult. Dark juvenile is uniformly very dark umber brown, with a smaller white flash at base of primaries. Juvenile dark-morph Pomarine is similar, but has blue-grey bill with black tip, smaller white panel on longer, pointed wings, and a barred rump and underwing.

Ssp. Monotypic (Caribbean offshore waters, Gu, Su?, FG)

Habits Flight direct and purposeful, with shallow, constant wingbeats. They usually approach with a low-level, sneak attack, preying on birds up to the size of a booby. Fast, powerful flyers, they can easily overtake a gull and force it to disgorge, and can kill birds and animals many times heavier, including geese and hare.

Status Most likely in November–February (possible August–March: Hilty). Sight records for Venezuela all from January. Early September–early May in French Guiana, where regular.

Habitat Usually far from land in winter, and seldom seen by seawatchers. Juveniles may be forced inshore by bad weather, but sometimes occurs in unexpectedly large numbers a few kilometres out. Always in continental shelf waters.

CHILEAN SKUA *Stercorarius chilensis* Pl. 57

Identification 53–59cm. Brown above with blackish cap, noticeable white flash in primaries. Juvenile particularly bright cinnamon below, and is distinct amongst skuas in having barred back. Combination of dark cap, cinnamon underparts and underwing-coverts diagnostic at all ages. Similar South Polar Skua (likely to be seen moving south on Pacific coast August–September) tends to be uniform and lacks distinct cap.

Ssp. Monotypic (SW coastal Ec)

Status Accidental to Ecuador. Movements poorly known. Most likely in May–July (May–September: R&G).

Habitat Tends to feed inshore, sometimes even entering harbours, often in channels and straights. May be seen foraging along tidal strip.

SOUTH POLAR SKUA *Stercorarius maccormicki* Pl. 57

Identification 50–55cm. Two distinct morphs, but pale nape distinctive even from a distance. Dark adult is completely fuscous-brown, slightly paler on nape; white flash on wingtip slightly less extensive than on Great Skua. Pale morph has upperparts similar, but head and body creamy or buffy-white. Juvenile recalls pale morph, but is greyer rather than white, and bill has paler base. Lacks contrasting black crown of Chilean. Juvenile dark morph may be taken for Great, but has blue-grey bill. Similar to Great in jizz, but has a smaller head with smaller bill. Pale morph looks almost bicoloured, with pale head and body, dark back, wings and tail.

Ssp. Monotypic (Ec, W Ve, Tr, Su, FG)

Habits Most likely to be seen alone out at sea. Will alight on water, and sometimes follows ships.
Status Passage migrant. Northbound migrants along Atlantic coast in April (they return south along east side of Atlantic), and southbound along Pacific coast August–September (which population moves north through western Pacific). Vagrant to Caribbean waters. (Pacific and Atlantic populations make separate, clockwise transequatorial migrations in post-breeding season.) Dark morph more common than pale morph.
Habitat Pelagic in winter and on migration.
Note Sometimes called MacCormick's Skua.

Three adult jaegers in breeding plumage, left to right, Pomarine, Parasitic and Long-tailed Jaeger

POMARINE JAEGER

Stercorarius pomarinus Pl. 57

Identification 65–78cm, including tail streamers (which lengthen with age). The largest jaeger. Dark morph uncommon. Obvious white flash on long, pointed, dark brown wings, and looks broad-chested and large-headed with powerful, bicoloured bill. Breeding adult has full cap with a buffy collar and neck-sides merging into white throat, dark brown breast-band, whitish underparts and brown undertail-coverts. Non-breeding adult similar, but cap poorly defined and has faint brown barring on flanks, joining on mid breast, and more contrasting on undertail-coverts. Immature has upperparts dark brown but paler than adult, and underwing-coverts tightly barred; lacks dark cap and head and body-barring pale brown. Juvenile similar to immature, with slightly more pale fringes to wing-coverts; broad white and dark brown bars on axillaries. From Great Skua by tail shape.

Ssp. Monotypic (all countries)

Habits Powerful flight interspersed with short glides. Usually solitary, but often in flocks when migrating, and regularly associates with gulls and terns. Often settles on water. Majority of jaeger sightings off Caribbean coast are this species.
Status Regular off Ecuador September–March, but some non-breeders present year-round and probably irregular off all coasts year-round. Most frequently seen off Caribbean coast September–April. Common off French Guiana, especially late October–mid April, but sightings also in May and July.
Habitat Usually pelagic in winter, but somewhat coastal, especially in areas of upwelling.

PARASITIC JAEGER

Stercorarius parasiticus Pl. 57

Identification 46–67cm, including 8–14cm tail-streamers. Non-breeding adult dark brown above with white flash on shafts of outer 5 primaries; dark brown cap, rest of body buffy with dark barring on undertail-coverts, underwing-coverts barred black and brown. First-winter similar but distinguished by also having uppertail-coverts barred, and wing flash covers all primaries, though only shafts are white; darker, dull buff below, with dark bill. Juvenile lacks dark cap, and flash on wing is more intensive, as are white bars on underwing-coverts. Like larger Pomarine in all plumages but less heavy bodied, with more falcon-like, narrower wings and shorter pointed tail-feathers. Rapid and less deep wingbeats than Pomarine and more aggressively harries flying birds, particularly terns. Juvenile particularly difficult to separate from juvenile Long-tailed, but amount of white in wing panels is diagnostic.

Ssp. Monotypic (all countries)

Habits Flight has distinctly jerky upbeats, and is interspersed with glides.
Status Boreal migrant but young birds often stay year-round. The most numerous jaeger off Ecuador. Most sightings reported from Caribbean coast are in January, but occurs year-round. Uncommon off French Guiana, mostly October–April.
Habitat Coastal areas. Gathers at estuaries and bays frequented by numbers of gulls and terns.
Note Also called Arctic Skua or Jaeger.

LONG-TAILED JAEGER

Stercorarius longicaudus Pl. 57

Identification 50–58 cm, including 15–25cm for tail-streamers. Smallest and most slender of the jaegers. Dark phase extremely rare. Non-breeding adult has pale brown wings with back, tail and uppertail-coverts narrowly barred black and white, and 2 central tail-feathers have short to modest extensions (the long tail is a breeding-plumage characteristic); dark brown cap, creamy buff underparts with poorly defined breast-band, and faint barring on flanks. First-winter lacks dark cap, has broad breast-band, is more heavily barred on flanks, has heavily barred undertail-coverts and narrowly barred underwings (dark brown and cream); bill dark. Juvenile has short tail extensions, wing-coverts and back paler brown, and a pale bill. From Parasitic by longer, slimmer wings and noticeably longer tail. White wing panel is smaller, and wing pattern distinct, with dark trailing edge to upper wing (Parasitic has uniform wings). Flight more agile and buoyant, less falcon-like; hovers more frequently.

Ssp. *S. l. pallescens* (Ec) as described
S. l. longicaudus? (Caribbean coastal waters, FG) adults on average are duskier on the belly

Habits Forms strung-out flocks. In bad weather tends to keep low, close to water. Tends to harass smaller birds, but probably less piratic than other jaegers.

Status Seemingly rare off all coasts, but perhaps under-reported; sight record off Venezuela. Definitely very rare off French Guiana (O. Tostain).

Habitat Generally pelagic outside the breeding season.

LARIDAE – Gulls and Terns

Generally thought of as coastal, gulls and terns may also occur inland or, conversely, far out to sea beyond any possibility of being seen from shore. They may be found along all coasts in the region and can be very difficult to identify. Inland species, usually found along large rivers, are much easier to recognise. Some breed in the boreal north, and are seasonal visitors or passage migrants en route to the far south, whilst others are non-breeding visitors from the austral region. A third group consists of residents whose numbers may be swelled by migrants from outside the region. For the purposes of illustration, the gulls divide neatly into two groups, those with black heads for at least part of the year, and those without this feature. Pelagic gulls and terns stay well beyond coastal waters, but may be driven close to shore by bad weather at sea. Coastal gulls are generally highly opportunistic scavenging at sewage processing areas, and pirating food from smaller birds. They are good swimmers and often rest on the water. Most gulls possess a series of plumages, with changes twice per year until adult plumages are reached, contributing to a complexity of plumages that can present enormous difficulties for the non-specialist. Reluctantly, we decided to illustrate only the most typical plumages likely to be encountered in the region. There are several excellent guides to these birds and the serious student is recommended to study them.

Additional references used in preparing this chapter include Harrison (1983, 1987), Malling Olsen & Larsson (1995; here as MOL); Burger & Gochfeld (1996), Gochfeld & Burger (1996), Grant (1997), Mullarney, Svensson, Zetterström & Grant (1999; here as MSZG), and Malling Olsen & Larsson (2004; here as MO&L).

BELCHER'S GULL *Larus belcheri* Pl. 58

Identification 51cm, W120–124cm. Medium-sized, black-backed gull with a heavy bill. Much larger and blacker than any other black-headed gull, with a black tail-band. In flight, has black wings with a white trailing edge to secondaries, black back, and white rump and tail with a black subterminal band. Primaries lack any white spots. Juvenile from juvenile Herring Gull by darker head and contrasting nape.

Ssp. Monotypic (Pacific coast; Ec, Co)

Habits Sometimes accompanies cormorants, which it harries until they regurgitate food. It also steals chicks and eggs, but rarely follows ships.

Status Endemic to Humboldt Current region. Mainly a bird of coasts in Peru, and a casual visitor to coastal Ecuador and, rarely, Colombia.

Habitat Forages along rocky shores, beaches, the intertidal zone and around seabird colonies, scavenging and stealing. Most likely to be seen in harbours and around fishing villages.

Voice Not known.

Note IOU-recommended English name is Band-tailed Gull.

GREY GULL *Larus modestus* Pl. 58

Identification 45–46cm. Distinctive medium- to large-sized gull, mainly dull grey in our region, but breeding adult has a white head. Non-breeding adult is all grey, deeper and bluer grey on wings, slightly paler on forehead and upper ear-coverts. Bill, legs and feet black. All other gulls in our region have white underparts. In flight, mainly blackish flight-feathers with contrasting white trailing edge to secondaries, tail has subterminal black band and white tip.

Ssp. Monotypic (Pacific coast, Ec, Co)

Habits Gathers in large flocks at tide line, running swiftly behind retreating breakers to pick shrimps and sand fleas like a sandpiper. Congregates around trawlers at sea.

Status Regular and locally numerous on south Ecuador coast (May–November), vagrant further north (May–October).

Habitat Forages on sandy coastal beaches but also seen surface-plunging.

Voice Cat-like call.

RING-BILLED GULL *Larus delawarensis* Pl. 58

Identification 45–53cm, W121–127cm. Non-breeding adult has pearl grey back and wings with black primaries, small white 'mirror' near wingtip, white trailing edge, all-white rump and tail, head white with dark crescent on rear ear-coverts and spots on nape; eyes yellowish, bill yellow with black subterminal band, legs and feet yellow. Breeder has all-white head and neck. Second-winter has more extensive black on wingtips, blackish subterminal marks on secondaries, and dark spots on head like non-breeding adult. First-winter has spotted median wing-coverts and tail-coverts. Resembles a small, lightly built Herring Gull but wings longer and wingtips more extensively black with few small white spots. Adult and intermediate separated by banded bill but juvenile has pinkish bill with black tip. Could be confused with larger California Gull, but has more black on wingtips and a larger 'mirror'. Juvenile has fairly clear mantle (streaked on California).

Ssp. Monotypic (Pacific and Caribbean coasts: Ec, Co, Ve, Ar, Bo, Tr)

Habits Usually with other gulls, especially on coasts. To some extent nocturnal.

Status Rare to casual vagrant, more likely to be seen off Caribbean coast, and accidental to Ecuador coast.
Habitat Coastal waters, tidal flats, and reservoirs and estuaries. Highly opportunistic and often forages at garbage dumps.
Voice Call a shrill *ky-ow!* (Hilty), like Herring Gull but more high-pitched and nasal (MSZG).

CALIFORNIA GULL
Larus californicus Pl. 58

Identification 51–58cm, W122–140cm. Large; non-breeding adult is cold grey on back and wings, with black tips to primaries and white spots, and a white trailing edge; head, underparts, rump and tail white, with dusky spots on ear-coverts and hindneck; eyes dark, bill yellow with black subterminal band and red spot on lower mandible. First-winter has brown upperparts with white fringes to feathers, forehead, throat and foreneck white, rest of underparts barred brown and white; bill pale with black tip, legs and feet flesh. Distinctive upright posture noticeable when perched, the wings held low, tips almost touching ground. Likely to be confused with Ring-billed Gull, which has much more black on wingtips and larger 'mirrors'.

Ssp. *L. a. albertaensis*? (Ec) larger with paler mantle
L. a. californicus? (Ec) darker mantle

Status Rare vagrant; only confirmed record from Ecuador (race unknown). Likely to be overlooked or mistaken for Ring-billed Gull.
Habitat Omnivorous and opportunistic; found on coasts, at freshwater wetlands, agricultural fields and even lawns. Eats anything – even fruit.
Voice Call a soft *kow-kow-kow* or *kuk-kuk-kuk* (HMP).

GREAT BLACK-BACKED GULL
Larus marinus Pl. 58

Identification 71–79cm, W152–157cm. The largest gull, black-backed, with heavy flight and slow deep wingbeats. Massive bill, yellow with red spot in adult, yellowish to blackish in subadults and black in juvenile. Immature has black tail-band. First-winter has black bill, dirty nape and hindneck, fuscous back, uppertail-coverts and wings (except primaries) with white fringes and trailing edge. Second-winter similar, but head and rump to tail white, with broad subterminal tail-band. Virtually impossible to misidentify. Its great size and black back stand out.

Ssp. Monotypic (Caribbean coast: Co, Ve, Ar, FG)

Habits Aggressive and domineering. Usually seen singly.
Status Vagrant to Caribbean coast, but number of sightings increasing.
Habitat Coasts and estuaries. Visits large inland waters locally.
Voice A deep *owk!* (HMP), like Lesser Black-backed and Herring *Larus argentatus*, but much deeper and typically hoarse and gruff (MSZG).

KELP GULL *Larus dominicanus* Pl. 58

Identification 58cm, W128–142cm. Breeding adult has black wings with broad white trailing edge, small white 'mirror' near wingtip, white tip to longest tertial, and head, underparts, rump and tail also white. Third-winter similar but has variable streaking on head and breast-sides, and variable dusky subterminal tail bar. Second-winter has broad trailing edge confined to secondaries, greyish rump and uppertail-coverts, all-dark tail, white head with pale streaks. First-year has head and underparts streaked (closest to young Grey Gull but slightly paler on head and uppertail-coverts, with trailing edge white to secondaries bolder on Kelp Gull). Resembles a small Great Black-backed Gull. Very similar to dark-backed *fuscus* race of Lesser Black-backed Gull, but respective ranges well separated. Only large black-backed gull in Ecuador, and only black-backed white-tailed gull breeding in Southern Hemisphere.

Ssp. *L. d. dominicanus* (Ec, Tr, FG)

Habits Aggressive and domineering, usually seen singly or in small groups.
Status Austral migrant to Pacific coast, but also a scarce resident on Santa Elena Peninsula, Ecuador. Two recent records from Trinidad (July–October 2000, February 2001). Vagrant to the Guianas.
Habitat Coastal, often on beaches. May occur on large rivers, large inland lakes, reservoirs and estuaries.
Voice Call a strident *ki-och*, often repeated rapidly (MO&L), also various loud, complaining calls, including a repeated nasal *keeyow* and a *ka-ka-ka-ka-ka* (R&G).
Note Sometimes treated as a subspecies of Lesser Black-backed Gull *L. fuscus*.

AMERICAN HERRING GULL
Larus smithsonianus Pl. 58

Identification 55–56cm, W137–142cm. Large, all-white gull with grey back and wings, wingtips black with white spots, and white trailing edge to entire wing; yellow eyes, yellow bill with red subterminal spot on lower mandible, legs and feet dull yellow. Second-winter similar but has wings darker and slightly browner than back, with black subterminal tail bar. First-winter white except back and wings, and dark markings behind eyes, on rear crown and hindneck, slight barring on tail and a broad dark brown subterminal bar; back grey with some dark centres to scapulars, wings dark brown with broad white fringes to wing-coverts and secondaries, and white centres to outer webs of inner primaries. Juvenile is almost entirely dark brown. All records (with the exception of a second-winter bird at Cayenne, French Guiana), are of first-year birds, which are most likely to be confused with other gulls and photographs are desirable (as with all Holarctic species, MO&L is invaluable; 11 distinct plumages are shown, 7 birds in flight, and 20 photographs). In flight, wings appear proportionately shorter and broader than Lesser Black-backed Gull, very similar to Ring-billed but decidedly larger; larger than Laughing with paler grey mantle and heavier bill.

Ssp. Monotypic (Ec, Co, Ve, ABC, T&T, FG)

Status Casual winter visitor to Aruba and rare on Caribbean coast and the Guianas. Vagrant to Ecuador.
Habitat Mainly coastal, but also visits large inland waters, fields, rubbish tips; highly opportunistic.
Voice Similar to Herring Gull *Larus argentatus* but drier, deeper and quicker: *ci-auww*, often combined with deep cackling, *gag-ag-ag-ag*. Also, a single-noted *klooh* and hollow low *kaaw*.
Note Formerly treated as a race of Herring Gull *L. argentatus*, but mitochondrial work by Crochet *et al.* (2002) and phenotypic analysis (MO&L) suggest species status is more appropriate.

LESSER BLACK-BACKED GULL

Larus fuscus Pl. 58

Identification 51-61cm, W124–127cm. Adult has dark slate back and wings with white leading edge and white trailing edge: non-breeder has dusky streaks from crown to nape; eyes yellow with red eyelids, bill yellow with red subterminal spot on lower mandible, legs and feet yellow. Third-winter like non-breeding adult but has dark tip to bill and dark bar on end of tail. Second-year slightly paler grey and median coverts brown with pale fringes, distal half of greater coverts and tertials the same; bill dull with dark tip, legs and feet flesh. Juvenile dark brown above, paler brown below, all feathers with pale fringes. Similar to Kelp Gull but smaller with a proportionately thinner bill, and adult less black on back. From American Herring Gull and Greater Black-back by proportionately smaller, rounder head and smaller bill which affords gentler facial expression, and longer, narrower wings. Juvenile similar to juvenile Herring Gull. Legs and feet pinkish-brown in first-year but more distinctly yellow thereafter.

Ssp. *L. f. graellsii* (Ec, Ve, Ar, Tr, Su, FG) as described
L. f. intermedius (FG) mantle darker

Habits Usually seen foraging on intertidal strip.
Status Regular visitor to T&T, Guyana and French Guiana, but sight records only, occasional in Venezuela, unconfirmed in Colombia, and vagrant to Ecuador and Suriname. Regular in French Guiana during winter months since mid 1980s, with two or more birds every year, Cayenne harbour being a hot spot.
Habitat Coasts, sandy beaches, estuaries and harbours, may visit inland waters, rice fields and rubbish dumps.
Voice Call similar to Herring Gull *Larus argentatus*, but deeper and more nasal (Hilty, MSZG).

GREY-HOODED GULL

Larus cirrocephalus Pl. 59

Identification 36–38cm, W100–105cm. Adult has pale grey head with a narrow black outline, pale grey back and wings, white 'triangle' from carpal to base of outer 5 primaries, white subterminal spots to outer 2 primaries, underwing entirely darker grey except white at base of central primaries and white subterminal tips visible; rest white; eyes pale to whitish, bill deep carmine, legs and feet coral. Non-breeding adult lacks grey head and has vestigial darkish grey bar on rear crown and around eyes, bill vermilion with a black tip, legs and feet orange. First-summer has wings browner and narrow subterminal tail bar; eyes dark, bill flesh with dark tip, legs and feet dull flesh. Juvenile has darker brown centres to lesser wing-coverts, tips of median and greater coverts, tertials and scapulars; bill mostly dark, legs and feet greyish-flesh. Five plumages illustrated on plate. Distinctive gull with long heavy bill, sloping forehead, tall-looking with an upright posture due to long neck and long legs. Relatively long-winged with a large white wedge on leading edge of outer wing. Most closely recalls Black-headed Gull, but in immature plumages note wing pattern.

Ssp. *L. c. cirrocephalus* (Ec)

Habits Plunge-dives.
Status Locally fairly common breeding resident in south Ecuador, with a recent breeding record in Guayas (Henry 2005).
Habitat Generally coastal but visits freshwater lakes, wetlands and rivers.
Voice Call a long, drawn-out, crow-like *caw-caw* (Hilty), also described as a harsh growling *craw, craw* given incessantly at colonies (R&G).

[BROWN-HOODED GULL

Larus maculipennis] Pl. 59

Identification 35–38cm. Non-breeding adult white with pale greyish-brown markings on ear-coverts and back of head, wings and tail pale grey with white trailing edge, and dark brown leading edge to outer 5 primaries; eyes dark, bill, legs and feet red. Immatures slightly browner grey above with dark brown outermost primaries (subterminal white spots), dark distal third to remaining primaries and secondaries; narrow blackish terminal tail-band. Very similar to Black-headed Gull but has more rounded head, and shorter bill, neck and legs. Also lacks black wingtips and juvenile has black terminal tail bar.

Ssp. Monotypic (Pacific coast)

Status Listed in error for Aruba, Curaçao and Bonaire by Altman & Swift (1993) and by Rodner *et al.* (2000), but is a hypothetical vagrant to Ecuador from the south.
Habitat Coasts and harbours, also rivers, freshwater lakes and marshes, fields, sewage farms and rubbish tips.
Voice Call resembles that of Black-headed Gull.

BLACK-HEADED GULL

Larus ridibundus Pl. 59

Identification 38–43cm, W91–94 cm. Medium-sized gull with grey back, black wingtips and dark brown hood in breeding adult. Non-breeding adult has dark crescent on ear-coverts, grey back and wings with white leading edge that broadens beyond carpal and continues on outermost primaries (blackish tips), most primaries are blackish distally, rest of flight-feathers have white trailing edge; bill red with black tip, legs and feet dark red. First-winter similar but dark secondaries have white edges and tips; all wing-coverts, except inner lesser and greater, brown with pale fringes. From smaller Bonaparte's Gull by red bill (never black). Even immatures have yellowish-red bill, blackish only at tip. From Brown-hooded by black tips to primaries.

Ssp. Monotypic (Caribbean coast and islands and the Guianas)

Black-headed Gull in first-year plumage (left), winter adult (centre), and adult in breeding plumage

Status Vagrant to Netherlands Antilles with sight records from Colombia and Suriname, and a recent photographic record from French Guiana where wintering occurs almost every year – first and second calendar year birds may stay year long.

Habitat Prefers calm shallow waters on coast, harbours, estuaries, rivers, rarely venturing inland. Follows fishing boats and ferries.

Voice Various harsh, rather high-pitched cries, most common *kraah!* Also *krreearr* with many variations and a short, sharp, *kek* or *kekekek* (MSZG). Very vocal all year.

Note IOC-recommended English name is Common Black-headed Gull.

BONAPARTE'S GULL *Larus philadelphia* Pl. 59

Identification 33–36cm, W81–84cm. Small and dainty, resembles a miniature Black-headed Gull, and first-winters very similar to first-winter Black-headed. Differs in all plumages by underwing pattern and black bill. Bonaparte's has a lighter, more buoyant or tern-like flight, recalling Little Gull, especially when surface-feeding with legs trailing. From Sabine's by white (not black) 'triangle' on primaries. Wings more pointed than Laughing Gull.

Ssp. Monotypic (Bo)

Status Casual winter visitor from North America recorded on Bonaire, and hypothetical for Caribbean coast and islands.

Habitat Coasts and estuaries.

Voice Call a nasal *cheer* (Hilty), common feeding call a high, nasal, tern-like *chirp*, quite unlike Black-headed Gull.

ANDEAN GULL *Larus serranus* Pl. 59

Identification 48cm. Breeding adult has grey back and wings, white primary-coverts and bases to primaries, rest of primaries black, with broad black subterminal band on outer 3, white tips to others and trailing edge white; head dark brown with white eye-ring; bill, legs and feet dark red. Non-breeding adult essentially the same but has crescent on ear-coverts rather than all-dark head. Five plumages illustrated on plate. Rather large, stocky, hooded gull in the high Andes, and on the coast. Differs from Laughing and Franklin's by size and wing pattern. In winter plumage from Grey-headed by larger size and ear-spot. In flight, distinctive pattern of white outer wing marked by a black band across black-tipped primaries. Underside of primaries black with white patch.

Ssp. Monotypic (Ec, Co)

Habits Usually in small groups, mainly around water, but sometimes flies high over ridges and slopes in páramo.

Status Uncommon to locally fairly common.

Habitat Breeds in high Andes and occurs at marshes, fields, along rivers and lakes, usually at 4,000–5,300m. When not breeding frequents the Pacific coast.

Voice Call a hoarse *aagh-aagh-kee-aagh* (Hilty), and agitated birds give a tern-like *keeyr*, often repeated (R&G).

LAUGHING GULL *Larus atricilla* Pl. 59

Identification 38–43cm, W99–107cm. Medium-sized gull; grey wings, above and below, with broad white trailing edge and black tips to primaries; breeding adult has blackish head and deep carmine bill, non-breeder a vestigial hood at rear, immatures all have dark secondaries and black tail-bands (see plate). Very social, regularly consorts with Franklin's Gull. From latter by distinctly flatter, longer crown and heavy, drooping bill. In flight appears much larger due to longer, narrower wings which taper to thin points. When perched, wings project well beyond tail. Also has white band separating black wingtip. Dark first-year birds may be mistaken for Parasitic Jaeger. Immature from Franklin's by tail pattern.

Ssp. *L. a. atricilla* (Caribbean coast and offshore islands and the Guianas) as described

L. a. megalopterus (Pacific coast) more black in primaries

Habits Often in large flocks. Aggressive opportunist that pirates food from pelicans. Often seen at tideline where it competes with larger gulls.

Status Passage migrant and winter resident, the most common winter gull, September–May in Caribbean and October–April on Pacific coast. An important and the southernmost nesting population (2,500 pairs) is on Connétable Island, French Guiana. Also occurs year-round with some breeding on Caribbean coast and offshore islands (e.g. Bonaire)

Habitat Usually on coasts, seldom out to sea. Harbours, reefs, estuaries, sewage outlets, rubbish dumps and rice fields. Occasionally inland, e.g. Lake of Valencia, Venezuela.

Voice Call most commonly heard on breeding grounds a strident *hahahaha* (Hilty), *ka-ka-ka-ka-kaa-kaa* or high-pitched 'laughing' *kah-kah-kah-kah*, repeated (ffrench, Voous). Wintering birds may give this call prior to onset of migration (R&G). A yelping *kee-agh* (MSZG).

FRANKLIN'S GULL *Larus pipixcan* Pl. 59

Identification 33–38cm, W86–94cm. Similar to, but smaller than Laughing Gull, with which it frequently associates. Franklin's has shorter wings with rounded tips, but most significant is the white wingtips with subterminal black on 5 outermost. Immature has vestigial head markings like non-breeding adult, black bill and tail-band. All plumages have white trailing edge to wing. Plate shows 4 plumages.

Ssp. Monotypic (Ec, Co, Ve, ABC, FG)

Habits Flight is light and buoyant, rather tern-like, and it will dip to surface of water legs trailing. More pelagic than Laughing and often migrates in flocks well offshore.

Status Boreal migrant, uncommon to rare on all coasts, a transient along Pacific coast and vagrant to Caribbean coasts, with a few birds resident. Usually seen September–March.

Habitat Mainly coastal, but over-wintering birds occasionally venture inland to marshes, lakes, fields and rubbish dumps.

Voice Call a soft *kruuk* (Hilty, MSZG) or a shrill *kuk-kuk-kuk* and nasal *karr, karr* (H&B), a shrill, repeated *guk* when feeding (MSZG).

LITTLE GULL *Larus minutus* Pl. 59

Identification 25–30cm, W63–66cm. World's smallest gull, dainty, round head, short legs, rather tern-like when perched and in flight. Adult quite distinctive, being effectively all white with pale grey back and wings lacking any pattern except white trailing edge, and dark grey underwing; non-breeder has small dark grey crescent on ear-coverts and pale grey rear of head; bill dark, legs and feet coral. First-winter has darker primaries and a brown diagonal from carpal to tip of tertials that forms a V in flight, and a narrow black tip to tail. Juvenile has a dark patch on crown, dark mantle and scapulars finely scalloped white, and black tip to tail, broader in centre and narrower on outer feathers.

Ssp. Monotypic (Co, FG)

Habits Normal flight direct and strong with deep wingbeats, but when feeding becomes hesitant and dips to surface with legs trailing, and will hover with feet pattering surface. Also forages while swimming.

Status Rare vagrant to Colombia, known from a single sight record. Two records for French Guiana (TO).

Habitat Coasts, estuaries and coastal lagoons.

Voice Usually silent outside breeding season but gives a *kek-kek* (MO&L).

Note Sometimes placed in genus *Hydrocoloeus*.

SABINE'S GULL *Xema sabini* Pl. 59

Identification 33–36cm, W86–91cm. Small, with distinctive plumage; breeding adult has slate grey head and bill with bright orange tip, back and 'triangle' from body to carpal and to tip of tertials, grey, another narrow black 'triangle' from carpal to tips of outer 4 primaries, and rest white, underwing has dark subterminal trailing edge to secondaries that reaches almost to outer wing-coverts (pattern unique) with a short black subterminal line on leading four primaries. Non-breeding adult has vestigial hood behind eyes and on nape. Juvenile has back and wing-coverts brown, the feather fringes white, vestigial hood also brown, and a black edge to the gently-forked tail. Distinctive upperwing pattern and forked tail. Swallow-tailed Gull much larger and has different underwing pattern.

Ssp. Races poorly differentiated and species often considered monotypic. All races (*X. s. palaearctica*, *X. s. tschuktschorum* and *X. s. woznesenskii*) could occur in our region (Ec, Co, T&T, FG).

Habits Flight buoyant, graceful with rapid continuous wingbeats, rather tern-like. Often dips to water but does not dive. Usually alone but often associates with terns, e.g. Common, Arctic.

Status Uncommon passage migrant and possible winter resident in Pacific waters. Rare vagrant to Caribbean coast and islands. rare off coast of French Guiana, but possibly overlooked.

Habitat Generally pelagic and rarely seen from coast.

Voice Short grating notes similar to Arctic Tern (MSZG).

SWALLOW-TAILED GULL *Creagrus furcatus* Pl. 59

Identification 55–60cm, W124–139cm. Distinctive gull with broad wings and forked tail; breeding adult has dark grey head with sloping forehead, conspicuous bright red eye-ring and white spot at base of bill, which is black with a pale grey tip; back and 'triangle' from body to carpal and to tip of tertials pale grey, with a narrow white line on outer scapulars, separating back from wings, a black line from carpal to first primary, and distal half of outer primaries and some primary-coverts black, the rest white; underwing-coverts pale grey and underside of remiges darker, rump and tail white, tail more deeply forked than Sabine's Gull. Non-breeding adult similar but has dark grey crescent on ear-coverts, rather than dark hood, first-winter has wing-coverts 'triangle' brown with white fringes, and back is grey; tail has narrow black trailing edge. Juvenile has wing 'triangle' and back dark brown with pale fringes and broad black terminal band on tail. From similar Sabine's Gull by much larger size.

Ssp. Monotypic (Pacific coast: Ec, Co)

Habits Mainly nocturnal, and shy, rarely approaches ships. Undulating flight, broad triangular white patch in centre of wing and deeply-forked tail unmistakable. Singly or small groups, usually seen resting on water.

Status Galápagos endemic, pelagic when not breeding. Scarce visitor to offshore Ecuador and rare off Colombia.

Habitat Pelagic.

Voice Apparently silent when not breeding, otherwise a thin harsh scream and a very un-gull-like rattle (H&B).

Terns are generally slimmer and more graceful in flight than gulls. They are also much more likely to be seen patrolling the sea, parallel to the shore, or flying along a river, plunging for small fish, than gulls. Whilst they also have several plumages these are far less numerous and complicated than those shown by gulls, and thus terns are easier to identify.

BROWN NODDY *Anous stolidus* Pl. 60

Identification 40–45cm. Large and heavily built, whitish forehead grades into dark brown rear, small white mark over eye, full white crescent below, overall dark brown with slightly paler bar on wing-coverts from tips of tertials to outermost lesser coverts, underwing paler with dark fringes to coverts; bill, legs and feet black. Juvenile/immature similar to adult but has forehead and crown spotted and streaked with brown, and feathers of back and wings have paler fringes. From smaller Black Noddy by longer tail that is uniform with body; juveniles have very little white on head, only on lores.

Ssp. *A. s. galapagensis* (Pacific coast) fuscous with pale eyebrow
A. s. ridgwayi (Pacific coast) forehead and crown bluish-grey
A. s. stolidus (Caribbean and Atlantic coasts) larger, forehead and crown ashy white

Habits Very social and mixes with other terns. Flies low over sea and is easy to overlook. Active at night.
Status First documented for Ecuador in September 2004 (F. Félix) and few records for Colombia; offshore Venezuela and islands only in breeding season (February–July), otherwise pelagic. Small and isolted breeding populations in French Guiana (March to September), otherwise at sea with wintering birds from Greater Antilles.
Habitat Many small populations dispersed through tiny islands, seldom seen inshore.
Voice Usually silent. Harsh *kark* or *karr*, a short cluck and low growling notes when foraging, also a sharp *eeyak* (Hilty, MOL).

BLACK NODDY *Anous minutus* Pl. 60

Identification 35–39cm. Adult all black with whitish crown and nape, smaller and shorter tailed than Brown Noddy. Tail is paler than body. Juvenile has sharply defined white cap.

Ssp. *A. m. americanus* (Ve, ABC)

Habits Very social and may occur in large numbers, foraging with fast, fluttering flight over shoaling fish.
Status Rare wanderer to offshore waters, and is casual visitor to Aruba, Bonaire and Curaçao.
Habitat More pelagic than Brown Noddy.
Voice Dry nasal cackles, chatters and squeaky notes, a staccato rattle and a piping whistle, but perhaps largely silent away from colonies.

[WHITE TERN *Gygis alba*] Pl. 60

Identification 28–33cm. Distinctive, all white with rounded head, large black eye set slightly high, and black bill with blue base, legs and feet greenish. Juvenile has irregular brown scalloping on back and lesser wing-coverts, and median and greater coverts have brown terminal spots. Small and delicate, large rounded wings give chunky appearance but is graceful with a light and fluttering flight.

Ssp. *G. a. alba* (Ec? Co?)

Habits Catches flying fish on the wing.
Status Hypothetical for Ecuador and Colombia.
Habitat Pelagic waters off Pacific coast.
Voice Away from colonies, a shrill piping *cheep* or *keek* (Stiles & Skutch 1989).
Notes Sometimes placed in genus *Anous*. Also called Common White Tern and Fairy Tern. More than one species may be involved.

BRIDLED TERN *Onychoprion anaethetus* Pl. 60

Identification 35–38cm, W76–81cm. Adult resembles adult Sooty Tern but distinguished by white forehead that extends over eye as a superciliary, although this is not easy to see at distance! Back grey, wings darker, more brownish and uniform, underparts and underwings white; bill, legs and feet black. Breeding bird has black lores black and white-streaked crown, feathers of back have whitish edges, and tips of outer 2 tail-feathers grey. Juvenile like non-breeder but has wing-coverts fringed white, producing rows of narrow white lines on wings. Black Tern similar but has short grey tail and black on head.

Ssp. *S. a. nelsoni* (Pacific coast) as described
S. a. recognita (Caribbean and Atlantic coasts) in field races indistinguishable

Habits Shy. Singly or in pairs, often rests on driftwood or flotsam. Flies low over sea and plunge-dives without submerging.
Status Generally fairly pelagic, but less so than Sooty Tern. Occasionally numerous offshore (e.g. Chocó, Colombia) but usually irregular. Visits offshore islands of Venezuela.
Habitat Coastal and offshore waters, ranging nearer to coasts when not breeding, and usually within 15 km of shore. Comes inshore to roost on beaches and in trees. Breeds on oceanic islands, and also off north-west Guayas, Ecuador, and Aruba, off Venezuela.
Voice Calls very different from Sooty Tern, a harsh, yapping *wep-wep* or *wap-wap* (Hilty). Locally called *Llorona* (cry-baby) in reference to its low-pitched, often repeated call (Hilty). Around breeding colonies utters a nasal *kyaar* (R&G) and when alarmed, *karr karr* (Voous).
Notes Race *recognita* sometimes considered a synonym of *melanoptera* (e.g. Dickinson 2003). Previously placed in genus *Sterna*.

SOOTY TERN *Onychoprion fuscatus* Pl. 60

Identification 43–45cm, W86–94cm. Adult has white forehead, a black line from base of bill through lores and eye to join black cap, which runs to nape and then, narrowly to sooty upperparts – only white above is on leading edge of inner wing

White forehead does not reach beyond eye in Sooty Tern (left), but extends distinctly beyond it in Bridled Tern (right)

and outer fringe of longest outer tail-feathers; underparts white and underwing white except tips of outermost primaries which are blackish; bill, legs and feet black. First-summer less black, having dusky wash and throat and breast also washed dusky. Juvenile has entire head and breast black, washed out on sides, rest of underparts white, underwings washed dusky and, back and wings have fine white fringes to feathers. Bicoloured tern, long-winged and long-tailed. Much like Bridled at distance, but easily separated close to. White forehead does not extend beyond the eye. Immature is the only all-dark, fork-tailed tern (noddies have wedge-shaped tails).

Ssp. *S. f. crissalis* (Pacific coast) as described
S. f. fuscatus (Caribbean and Atlantic coasts) races indistinguishable in field

Habits Highly social, flocks with other seabirds at shoaling fish, and flies fairly close to water. May also fly high, often in large flocks searching for shoals. Does not plunge-dive, but swoops low to snatch food from surface. Rarely settles on surface, and very rarely swims or rests on water. Does not come to land to roost. Feeds at night.
Status Rare offshore. Breeds on islands off Venezuela in March–July, and French Guiana March–August, then disperses. Movements poorly known but most of Caribbean breeders are assumed to winter off west Africa. Rare off Colombia.
Habitat Pelagic; wanders far and wide at see. Rarely seen near shore except in breeding season.
Voice Call *ker-wacky-wack* (Hilty), a loud *kay-rack* and yelping *wide-a-wake*! (H&B), very noisy night and day (Hilty). A 3–4-syllable, far-reaching *te-wy-da-way*, heard day and night (Voous).
Note Previously placed in genus *Sterna*.

LEAST TERN *Sternula antillarum* Pl. 62

Identification 20–28cm, W50–55cm. Small almost white tern with black cap and 2 outermost primaries black (black leading edge visible on underwing), back and wings pale silvery grey; bill rich yellow with black tip, legs and feet yellow. Non-breeding adult has forehead and lores white, leading edge narrowly dusky, including outer 2 primaries, bill blackish-brown, may be yellow at base. Juvenile/first-winter has back and wings washed greyish-brown with white fringes, acquiring dark leading edge to inner wing and secondaries as moult progresses; bill dark red below, blackish above. Very small (size usually diagnostic), from other small terns by stocky build, buoyant and erratic flight, hurried with rapid, wader-like wingbeats. From larger Yellow-billed Tern by dark tip to somewhat smaller bill.

Ssp. *S. a. antillarum* (Caribbean and Atlantic coasts) darker, more bluish-grey below
S. a. athalassos (Caribbean and Atlantic coasts) all-yellow bill tip

Habits Flies 3–6m above surface and usually hovers before plunge-diving. Mainly marine but occasionally inland along large rivers. Singly or small groups.
Status Uncommon boreal migrant to offshore islands, en route to Brazil. Breeding resident on Aruba and some other islands and occurs locally on northern coasts. Uncommon in French Guiana, mostly on fall migration.
Habitat Often well offshore on passage, but resident birds and occasional migrants may occur at inland bays, salines and coastal areas.
Voice A shrill *kip-kip-kip* and grating *kid-ick-kid-ick* or *krid-ick, krid-ick* (Hilty). A high, penetrating *cherréé-cherréé* and harsh *cheep* (Voous), a distinct *ki-riik* and hoarse *ki-dik* (MOL).
Notes Considered a subspecies of Old World *Sternula albifrons* until separated by Massey (1976). Previously placed in genus *Sterna*.

YELLOW-BILLED TERN
Sternula superciliaris Pl. 62

Identification 23cm. Very small. Adult has white forehead and black cap, silvery grey back and wings, including rump and slightly forked tail; outermost primary-covert and 2 primaries dark; bill bright pale yellow, legs and feet greenish-yellow. Non-breeding adult has crown and lores white. Juvenile has brown marks on forehead, crown and nape, pale brown back and wings with broad white fringes to all feathers. From similar Least by larger bill, always with large amount of yellow. Yellow-billed has shorter and less forked tail.

Ssp. Monotypic (all except ABC)

Habits Flight quick with rapid wingbeats, frequently hovers. Usually solitary or in pairs, occasionally small groups. Often seen on river sandbanks with Black Skimmers.
Status Widespread and fairly common along river systems east of the Andes. Important moulting area in coastal Suriname and French Guiana, where it may gather in very large flocks on mudflats April–September.
Habitat Large inland rivers (Least is mainly coastal or even offshore), but is occasionally (or mostly, in the Guianas) found on coasts and lagoons in non-breeding season. Mouths of tributaries. Rice fields.
Voice Sharp, repeated *kit*, a rapid *kiiti-kitti-kitti* (H&B), nasal *yank* and a reedy, blurred *tee-lee-le* (Hilty), various sharp, penetrating calls, like *keek*, *kik* and *kirrik* (R&G).
Notes Previously placed in genus *Sterna*. Sometimes called Amazon Tern.

PERUVIAN TERN *Sternula lorata* Pl. 62

Identification 23cm. Breeding adult has white forehead and black cap, is entirely pale grey above, including rump and tail, 2–3 outermost primaries have black leading edge; bill yellow with black tip, legs and feet brownish-yellow. Non-breeding adult has crown white-streaked and is whiter below with grey-washed breast; bill blackish with yellow base. Overall greyish tone and black bill separate it from Least Tern, though not sympatric. Least is also paler.

Ssp. Monotypic (Ec, Co?)

Habits Usually solitary or in small groups foraging over shallow water, hovering and plunging. Favours sandy beaches and flats.

Status Scarce austral winter visitor to south-west Ecuador. Very poorly known.

Habitat Humboldt Current zone, coastal, but may venture slightly inland.

Voice Call *chik-chik* and, when excited, a chattering *kerrick-kerrick* and mellow *churi-churi* (Hilty, R&G).

Note Previously placed in genus *Sterna*.

LARGE-BILLED TERN *Phaetusa simplex* Pl. 61

Identification 37cm, W92cm. Mainly freshwater tern with distinctive upperwing pattern. Breeding adult has black cap from forehead to nape, back and 'triangle' on wings (lesser wing-coverts and innermost median and greater coverts) grey; outer median and greater coverts, secondaries and greater primary-coverts white; lesser primary-coverts and primaries black, underwing all white; eyes dark, large, long yellow bill, legs and feet greenish. Non-breeding adult has forehead white, grading into dark grey cap. Juvenile even whiter on head, with a black band from eye to nape; upperparts browner and tail tipped brown.

Ssp. *P. s. simplex* (all countries)

Habits Usually singly or in pairs, but may gather in small flocks to rest or roost. Usually seen flying high over water, follows boats on large rivers and will plunge into wake to feed. Rests and roosts on sandbars with cormorants, skimmers and others, including nighthawks.

Status Common along Orinoco and other large rivers, and Caribbean coast; casual visitor to offshore islands (e.g. just one recent record from Tobago), and very scarce on blackwater rivers. Generally uncommon in Ecuador and western Colombia. Uncommon or rare in Suriname and French Guiana, where found in rice fields and estuaries.

Habitat Rivers, estuaries and coasts, larger lakes.

Voice Quite noisy, especially near colonies, but can be rather silent. Calls include nasal, parrot-like *ink-onk* (Snyder), a loud, reedy *kaay-rak* (Hilty) and loud squealing calls reminiscent of, but shriller than Laughing Gull (R&G).

GULL-BILLED TERN *Gelochelidon nilotica* Pl. 61

Identification 35–43cm, W86–103cm. Breeding adult is all white with silvery grey back and wings, some have blackish tips to primaries and others the outermost primaries darker than rest (slight wedge shape); tail slightly forked, a black cap (no crest) runs from base of bill to nape; eyes dark, bill thick and black, legs and feet black. Non-breeding adult has head white or partially white, perhaps with some black feathers or grey streaks, upperparts often whiter than breeding plumage. Juvenile has sandy tone to upperparts and feathers of back and wings have darker fringes, primaries darker; base of bill deep pink to reddish. Appears white at distance, with broad rounded wings and heavy body, shallow-forked tail. Recalls Sandwich Tern but less graceful with shallower wingbeats. Both have black bills, but Gull-billed is heavier, and Sandwich has yellow tip (not easy to see). Rather gull-like and in flight carries bill straight, not pointed down like other terns.

Ssp. subspecies very similar in the field and not diagnosable
S. n. aranea (all coasts, strictly coastal)
S. n. groenvoldi (FG, from Brazil)
S. n. vanrossemi (Pacific coast)

Habits Flies with smooth, easy strokes, more leisurely than other terns.

Status Passage migrant from North America, fairly common and occurs year-round.

Habitat Generally on coasts but also marshes, lakes, mudflats, shallow brackish coastal waters, saltpans, shrimp farms, beaches, lakes and rivers. Rests on sandbars with other birds. Breeds colonially in freshwater locations, and hawks for food over marshes, fields and water.

Voice Repertoire varied; *kay-tih-did* or *Kay-did*, and a soft nasal *kek-kek* (Hilty), rasping *jeep* and *ra* notes, also *chey-rack*, repeatedly (H&B), a distinctive, sharp and raspy *kay-wek, kay-wek* (R&G), and a deep, double-noted, somewhat guttural and laughing staccato *gek-gek-gek…* or *gir-vit* (MOL).

Note Formerly placed in genus *Sterna*.

CASPIAN TERN *Hydroprogne caspia* Pl. 61

Identification 48–59cm, W127–140cm. Breeding adult has a full black cap (reaching level with eyes) and short crest that gives head an angular appearance, grey back and wings with underside of primaries darker; eyes dark, bill large and heavy, bright red with a black and orange tip. Second-summer very similar but usually has a few white spots in cap, and outer primaries darker. Non-breeding adult has spotted and streaked cap, blackish on lores and below eyes onto ear-coverts, outer primaries washed dusky. First-winter similar but has forehead and forecrown all white. Juvenile has entire cap spotted and streaked, and it extends further on back of head than in adults, back and wings washed slightly buffy, and darker, pale sandy subterminal marks with pale buffy fringes to back and inner wings; rest of wings have white fringes. Largest tern, the size of a Herring Gull with broad wings and a large red bill, and more gull-like than Royal Tern (which has orange bill). Larger and more robust than Royal and tail is less deeply forked. Perched, wings extend well beyond tip of tail (Royal's reach tip).

Ssp. Monotypic (Ec, Co, Ve, ABC, T&T, FG)

Habits Usually associates with other terns, especially Royal and

Gull-billed. Flies up to 15m above water with bill pointing down and hovers before plunging into water. Also pirates from other terns. Roosts with others on sandbars in estuaries and rivers.
Status Regular passage migrant and visitor in small numbers to Caribbean shores and offshore islands. Uncommon to vagrant on Pacific coasts, very rare in French Guiana.
Habitat Coastal lagoons, estuaries, inland lakes and rivers. Seldom out to sea.
Voice Call variously described as a hoarse *kaaa* and shorter *kowk* (Hilty), a deep raucous croaking *kaah, kaah* (H&B), a deep, rough *karr-aa* (Hilty), a distinctive and startlingly loud *krrr-árk* (R&G), and a deep heron-like *aaayayaumm* (Sibley).
Note Formerly placed in genus *Sterna*.

INCA TERN *Larosterna inca* Pl. 60

Identification 40–42cm. Unmistakable. Overall dark bluish-grey with blackish cap, paler on underwing-coverts, broad white trailing edge to wing, conspicuous white moustachial streak; bill, legs and feet bright red and wattle at gape yellow, legs and feet red. Immature similar but has blackish-red bill and short white moustachial streak. Juvenile umber and lacks white moustachial line; back and wing-feathers fringed grey (as is trailing edge); bill blackish, legs and feet blackish-red.

Ssp. Monotypic (Ec, Co?)

Habits Flight graceful and buoyant with shallow, somewhat fluttering wingbeats. Swoops over water with great agility, rather than diving or plunging. Often with cormorants, sea lions and cetaceans, and sometimes occurs in large flocks.
Status Rare and unpredictable visitor to coast of southern Ecuador.
Habitat Humboldt Current endemic. Observed off rocky headlands and occasionally inshore.
Voice Call sounds like a kitten (Hilty).

BLACK TERN *Chlidonias niger* Pl. 60

Identification 22–24cm, W57–66cm. Breeding adult has head, underparts to flanks and vent deep black, undertail-coverts white; black head grades into dark grey mantle; wings and lower back to tail uniform pale grey; eyes dark, bill, legs and feet black. Non-breeding adult and first-summer has head white with a blackish cap and black 'headphones' behind eyes and covering ear-coverts. Juvenile also has cap, but is brown on back and wings, slightly paler on wings, as well as neck- and body-sides to flanks, becoming pale brown on undertail-coverts. Breeding adult unmistakable, in all other plumages cap and ear-coverts markings with uniform wings diagnostic. Often seen in plumage midway between breeding and winter.

Ssp. *C. n. surinamensis* (Pacific and Caribbean coasts)

Habits Flight erratic and nighthawk-like. Frequent jerky undulations, swoops to surface but rarely plunges. Gregarious, often in large flocks.
Status Passage migrant and boreal winter resident. Common to locally abundant off Caribbean and both Colombian coasts, but scarce off Ecuador.
Habitat Fairly pelagic and rarely seen from shore. Occasionally driven into coastal waters by bad weather at sea, when found in harbours and estuaries.
Voice Normally silent, but gives a shrill *kik kik kik* (Hilty), a sharp *keep!* or *kee-ip!* (H&B) and clipped, nasal *kja!* (MOL).

SOUTH AMERICAN TERN
Sterna hirundinacea Pl. 61

Identification 40–44cm, W84–86cm. Similar to Common and Arctic Terns but larger and heavier bill is slightly drooping. Breeding adult has black cap to nape, almost all-grey body, wings and tail (outer edge of outermost primary black), with white face- and throat-sides, and white undertail-coverts; tail forked with long outermost feathers; bill, legs and feet bright red. Non-breeding adult has forehead and crown white, leaving only from behind eye to nape black. First-winter like non-breeding adult, but back, scapulars and wing-coverts scaled brown, bill black. Juvenile has partial cap, back and wings washed pale greyish-brown, darker centres to feathers and whitish fringes, bill, legs and feet dusky.

Ssp. Monotypic (Ec, Co?)

Habits Very social and often in large flocks over open water and kelp beds. Plunge-dives from *c.*6m.
Status Austral migrant, non-breeders casual to Ecuador.
Habitat Coastal, mainly beaches, estuaries, harbours and lagoons.
Voice A metallic *kyick* and screeching *keer* (Hilty) or *kyarrr* (R&G), and *kip*, sometimes repeated (R&G).

ROSEATE TERN *Sterna dougallii* Pl. 62

Identification 35–43cm, W76–79cm. Breeding adult has black cap, pale grey back and wings, outer 3 primaries slightly darker (just visible on underwing), forked tail with outer feathers particularly long, reaching beyond wingtips at rest; bill black with blood red base, becoming even deeper at height of season, legs and feet blood red. Non-breeding adult has forehead and forecrown white; bill all black, legs and feet red. Juvenile has dark brown cap, and pale brownish wash and brown scalloping to back and wings, but soon moults into first-winter plumage, when forehead become whitish, streaked dark brown, markings on wings more irregular, and primaries pale dusky (darker than adults); bill, legs and feet dusky to blackish. Very pale, appearing white from afar. From Common Tern by longer bill, shorter wings and longer tail. From Arctic by uniform pale grey underparts; Arctic has outer 3 primaries dark; Sandwich and Cayenne have darker outer primaries.

Ssp. *S. d. dougallii* (all coasts except Ec)

Habits Almost exclusively pelagic, wintering in east Caribbean and Atlantic, usually in small flocks far out to sea. Coastal records usually of young birds.
Status Rare on Pacific coast of Colombia, breeding resident in Netherlands Antilles and offshore islands, but uncommon, and rarely sighted from coasts. Common in Guyana mostly based on trapped birds banded in the US, but not listed for Suriname and only small numbers occur in French Guiana (overlooked at sea?).

Habitat Generally over deeper water at sea, may be seen resting on buoy or flotsam.
Voice Varied calls, including a soft, wader-like *chew-ick* and high-pitched rasping *aach* (Hilty, Gochfeld & Burger), *chewee* (Voous) or *skivvik* (Sibley) but seldom heard in winter. Alarm-call a high, clear, tinny or scraping *keer* (Hilty, Sibley).

COMMON TERN
Sterna hirundo Pl. 62

Identification 32–38cm, W79–81cm. Adult breeding has black cap, pale grey back and wings, dark outer edge to wing, tips of outer 5 primaries darker on undersides (all plumages, most noticeable in young); 2 outermost tail-feathers *c.*50% longer than others; bill bright red with black tip, legs and feet pale red. Non-breeding adult has forehead and nape white, leaving broad black band behind eyes, leading edge to inner wing brown, outer 4 primaries brownish (long narrow wedge); bill black. First winter leading edge of inner wing darker and secondaries dusky grey. Juvenile darker and warmer grey, with white fringes to all feathers, leading edge of inner wing dusky, forehead streaked brownish; bill black above, dull reddish below with black tip. Very similar to Arctic Tern in all plumages; best discriminator narrow black tips to primaries on Arctic, broader wedge on Common. Juvenile has bicoloured bill (Arctic mostly or all black). Broader winged and shorter tailed than Arctic, and usually seen in flocks, whether foraging, resting or roosting.

Ssp. *S. h hirundo* (all coasts)

Habits Flight buoyant with deep wingbeats, hovers frequently with tail held down, plunge-dives. Seldom in mixed flocks unless resting on beach or rocks. Breeds on offshore islands.
Status Common and widespread, separate breeding resident and wintering populations, with some first-years of latter remaining all year, and passage migrants. Most common October–May.
Habitat Coasts and inland bays, lagoons, saltpans, sandy beaches and scrubby dune areas, islands in estuaries, lakes and rivers, often entering large rivers outside breeding season. Wintering birds offshore French Guiana often associated with trawlers, but may feed in small numbers, and aggregate by thousands in dense floating flocks far from any boat. Seem to come to roost ashore, if ever, at night.
Voice Call a drawn-out *keeargh* (Hilty) or *kee-aarr*, the second note lower pitched (Voous), and varied sharp, hoarse and powerful cries including *kirri-kirri*, rapidly repeated with emphasis on *rrr* sound (MOL).

ARCTIC TERN *Sterna paradisaea* Pl. 62

Identification 33–38cm, W76–85cm. Non-breeding adult has white forehead with black cap essentially forming a broad band over head just behind eyes, pale grey back and wings with dusky leading edge and tips to primaries (visible on underside), grey leading edge to inner wing, and forked tail tapers to wispy point as outermost, longest feathers lie together in level flight; bill blackish, legs and feet blackish-red. First-year has more pronounced dark leading edge to inner wing and trailing edge to outer wing; tail shallowly forked. Very similar to Common Tern but flight more buoyant, with slower, shallower and more graceful strokes; best discriminator is wing pattern, Arctic has only narrow black edge to primaries, which are clearly translucent. Tail entirely white (outer rectrices on Common grey).

Ssp. Monotypic (Pacific coast)

Status Highly pelagic passage migrant; rarely seen off Pacific coast, moving south to wintering grounds (returns north on eastern side of Atlantic). Once in French Guiana.
Habitat Favours cold offshore waters.
Voice Similar to Common Tern, including piping, clear *pi-pi-pi-pi…, pyu pyu pyu pyu*, and a ringing *preee-eh* (MSZG).

ROYAL TERN *Thalasseus maximus* Pl. 61

Identification 50cm, W100–135cm. Large and rather gull-like in flight with slow steady wingbeats. Breeding adult has black cap and shaggy crest, grey wings with inner webs to outer 5 primaries grey, dark to blackish at tips (visible on underwing, in all plumages), tail forked with outer feathers longest; bill plain orange, legs and feet blackish. Bill may appear almost red during few weeks before laying and biggest males with strongest bills recall Caspian Tern. Non-breeders have head mostly white with crest reduced to scraggy ruff on rear crown, black barely reaches eyes. First-winter has head and underwing as non-breeder, but lesser coverts dark grey, greater coverts tipped dark grey and secondaries have subterminal black bar (inner wing has 3 dark lateral lines), lesser primary-coverts to primaries blackish, all wing-feathers have pale fringes, and a white trailing edge. Juvenile has dark grey partial cap, larger than on winter birds, grey to greyish-brown wash to back and wings, with broad white fringes to feathers; bill, legs and feet yellowish. Conspicuous nuchal crest, but most likely to be seen when black is vestigial and forehead and crown are white. Similar, but larger Caspian never has white forehead.

Ssp. *T. m. maximus* (all coasts)

Habits Very social. Usually forages inshore; will feed at sea, but usually within sight of land. Follows ships. Flies high, fishes by diving but does not submerge.
Status Passage migrant en route from south-east USA to Argentina, but some first-years remain all year. Fairly common to common transient on Caribbean coast, occasionally breeding on offshore islands, where occurs year-round on leeward side of islands and there are nesting colonies off French Guiana. Fairly numerous on Pacific coast.
Habitat Coasts, deep bays, lagoons and harbours, but occasionally far up estuaries.
Voice Call *tourreee* and a bleating *ee-ah* (Hilty), a shrill *keer* or *keerlap* (H&B), a raucous, high *kree* or *kgee* (Voous) and distinctive *chirrik* (R&G).
Note Formerly placed in genus *Sterna*.

SANDWICH TERN
Thalasseus sandvicensis Pl. 62

Identification 40–45cm, W86–105cm. Medium-sized tern

that appears all white from afar. Shorter, shallower tail fork than most terns. Crown flat and long, noticeable in flight when head held downwards. Breeding adult has shaggy black crest, pale grey back and wings, with outer 4 primaries dark grey to blackish (blackish tips visible on underwing); bill black with yellow tip, legs and feet black. Non-breeder has crest reduced to scraggy ruff on nape. Juvenile well-marked above and has cap all dark, but this soon becomes partial and first-winter has crest as non-breeder; upperparts slightly brown, most feathers with brown band near edges, and white fringes, but these are soon replaced by much paler ones, only some of which have brownish crescents or V marks; bill shorter and usually all black. From Cayenne Tern by all-black bill, legs and feet, also by delayed moult of black front and cap after laying.

Ssp. *T. s. acuflavidus* (all coasts)

Habits Dives from greater heights than smaller terns and submerges longer than others as well. Often associates with Royal. Roosts on sandy beaches and mudflats.

Status Uncommon passage migrant and boreal winter resident on both coasts, but breeds on Aruba, Bonaire and Curaçao and French Guiana.

Habitat Coastal or offshore waters, often well offshore. Sandy or rocky beaches, mangrove flats, estuaries and harbours. Breeds on open beaches, usually on the highest ground.

Voice A harsh *ki-ki-ki* or rasping *kir-rick*, higher pitched than Gull-billed Tern's similar *kay-weck* (Hilty, H&B). Upwardly inflected, hoarse *kree-it* used frequently (MOL).

Note Formerly placed in genus *Sterna*.

CAYENNE TERN
Thalasseus eurygnatha Pl. 62

Identification 40–43cm, W94–97cm. Only medium-sized tern with all pale yellow bill. Legs and feet also generally yellow. Variants with orange or red bills are mostly birds from southern Brazil and Argentina, they occur in very small numbers among nesting birds in French Guiana. Breeding adult has long shaggy crest, non-breeder has crest reduced to shorter ruff on nape that does not quite reach eyes; back and wings grey, with darker outer primaries, moult of black front begins as soon as the egg is laid in May. Similar Sandwich Tern has all-black bill, legs and feet, and a shorter, less shaggy crest, and where sympatric with latter, Cayenne is smaller (but is larger and has a longer bill in Brazil to Argentina). Similar Elegant Tern is slightly larger with an orange bill.

Ssp. Monotypic (all coasts)

Habits Social but only occasionally mixes with other species. Flight strong, fast and light. Forages by plunging. Rests and roosts on sandy beaches, piers, rocks and tethered boats.

Status Uncommon to fairly common on coasts. Breeding resident locally on offshore islands, and passage migrant from north. Rare on Pacific coast.

Habitat Offshore and coastal waters, sometimes encountered foraging well offshore. Usually along beaches, bays, inlets and coastal lagoons.

Voice Call a shrill, rasping *kee-rack* (Hilty).

Note Formerly placed in genus *Sterna*. Frequently, and probably usually, treated as conspecific with Sandwich Tern, and much confusion exists. At the time of writing (February 2006), this issue is far from resolved and whilst the SACC retains Cayenne Tern within *sandvicensis*, the situation is clearly fluid. Absence of assortive mating on the Virgin Islands is certain (F. E. Hayes *in litt.*). Also in French Guiana where a few Sandwich Terns nest among the Cayenne, retaining their own identity. Observations in French Guiana show different moult chronology between the two species (Tostain). Two independent field studies are being conducted, in Brazil and on Curaçao, and both are employing DNA analysis. Until their taxonomic relationships are proven (hopefully soon), we believe it is better to follow Harrison and others, and treat them as distinct species.

ELEGANT TERN *Thalasseus elegans* Pl. 61

Identification 40–43cm, W76–81cm. Breeding adult has long, drooping, black bushy crest (longest of all terns) and is pale silvery grey above, marginally darker on outer primaries; slightly drooping bill is orange with a yellow tip, legs and feet black. Non-breeder has crest reduced to a ragged ruff on nape, the black extending forward through eyes; bill slightly paler orange and yellow tip more extensive. Slim and elegant, smaller than similar Royal Tern, with proportionately longer, finer and more drooping bill. Prominent black nuchal crest is never streaked white (as in Royal). Crown-feathers longest of all terns, hanging down at nape. Beware breeding adult has subtle pinkish tinge below, like Roseate Tern, but crest totally different.

Ssp. Monotypic (Pacific coast)

Habits Rests in closely packed flocks on sandbars and mudflats. Plunge-dives from 1–3m.

Status Rare to uncommon passage migrant from North America, with a few birds remaining all winter. Sight records should be confirmed as some Cayenne Terns look surprisingly similar.

Habitat Coasts, avoids rough seas. Generally along beaches, at low-lying islands just offshore, estuaries and harbours, saltpans and lagoons. Usually close inshore.

Voice A rasping *karreek-karreek* (Hilty) or *keerik* (Sibley) and recalls Sandwich Tern, but lower pitched (MOL).

Note Formerly placed in genus *Sterna*.

RYNCHOPIDAE – Skimmers

Skimmers take their name from their method of foraging for fish, which entails skimming the water with the lower mandible. Older names include scissor-bill (for the bill action is much like a pair of scissors), razor-bill and shearwater, for they do indeed shear the water. The bill is quite unique in that the upper mandible is compressed laterally into a knife-like flatness and sharpness, and the lower is one-third longer and somewhat flexible. Skimmers fly low, the lower mandible submerged, and after 50–100m double back over the same stretch. The theory is that the first pass causes phosphorescence, which attracts inquisitive fish to be caught on the return. The upper bill rapidly snaps down as the head bends and doubles back into the water, seizing the fish the lower mandible has touched. Black Skimmers forage along calm rivers and lakes, marshes and other pools, and may be found along shores and inlets, but depart elsewhere if the water is rough. Very sociable, they feed, rest and roost in flocks, even breeding in loose, informal colonies. They forage night and day, mostly from dusk to dawn, resting by day. Another unique quality of skimmers is their 'cats eyes', for the pupils open very wide for nocturnal foraging, and appear as vertical slits in the bright light of day.

Additional references used to prepare this family include Erwin (1990) and Zusi (1996).

BLACK SKIMMER *Rynchops niger* Pl. 61

Identification 41–46cm. Large, bicoloured tern-like bird with a long red bill. Breeding adult has all-black upperparts, with a white forehead, from around the base of the bill, fore face and underparts; underwing duller, the coverts being pale grey and flight-feathers light brown, Non-breeding adult has a broad dark brown nape. Bill red, darker at the tip, and legs and feet red. Immature much as non-breeding adult, but dark brown instead of black, bill, legs and feet rather more orange than red. Juvenile is mid brown above with pale fringes to all feathers, underparts buffy-white and underwing-coverts pal brown; bill, legs and feet pink.

Ssp. *R. n. cinerascens* (Ec, Co, Ar, Bo, Ve, Tr, Gu, Su, FG) as described
R. n. niger (boreal migrant to FG, and elsewhere?) small; outer rectrices and underwing-coverts all white, large white trailing edge to secondaries and inner primaries

Habits Social, often seen pairs, but usually in small groups or flocks. Often rests on sandbars with gulls and terns during day.

Status Uncommon in eastern Ecuador and has declined drastically in south-west, somewhat irregular in Colombia, widespread and frequent in Venezuela, common in Trinidad (no records Tobago), common in Guyana, Suriname and French Guiana. In Aruba and Bonaire, a non-breeding visitor from the mainland in April–October. Gradually decreasing everywhere as dams are constructed on rivers, beaches are claimed for human activity and rivers are dredged and sandbars disappear. Does not nest in the Guianas, but large numbers from continental nesting populations use coastal mudflats to moult. In French Guiana, *cinerascens* is by far the most numerous race year-round (but mostly January–September), but recent study has shown that birds with characters of *intercedens* are not rare in March–August, and a few birds typical of *niger* (from North America) are regular in small numbers in French Guiana in December–February (O. Tostain).

Habitat Rivers with placid water, the same for beaches and estuaries, marshes, tidal pools, creeks and lagoons.

Voice In flight a nasal barking *CAaa* (Hilty).

Notes Pacific coast birds tend to be darker below and have broader white tips to primaries. Formerly afforded subspecific status, *R. n. intermedia*, but considered a synonym of *cinerascens* by Blake (1977). Careful analysis of Ecuadorian and other Pacific birds appears warranted. The same is true and under way for those populations visiting the Guianas.

OPISTHOCOMIDAE – Hoatzin

Hoatzins are such extraordinary birds that their taxonomic position has been debated for decades. Long thought to be most closely related to cuckoos, they are now considered closest to the African turacos. They are large, unmistakable birds with rounded, turkey-like bodies, and disproportionately small heads mounted by a great unruly crest. The crop is amazingly large, comprising about one-third of the body, and is used to store shoots and leaves. They live in riverine forests and their nests are invariably placed over water. The young are equally extraordinary. The newly hatched chicks have claws on the second and third digits of the wings, making them effectively legs (or arms). For the first few days, the chicks are able to climb in trees, dive into the water below the nest and swim easily. Hoatzins are usually seen in groups or flocks perched in the tops of tall trees alongside rivers. When they fly, they resemble somewhat grotesque chachalacas with their chestnut colouring and long rounded tails.

Hoatzin chick climbing back to the nest from the water below

HOATZIN *Opisthocomus hoatzin* Pl. 78

Identification 60cm. Turkey-sized and small-headed with an irregular sprayed crest and short, but heavy bill, and red eyes surrounded by a broad orbital of bright blue skin. Head rufescent above with dusky streaks, nape to back, rump and tail dusky with narrow white streaks on hindneck and over mantle, and tail has a broad grey terminal band; wings dark brown with broad whitish tips to lesser and median coverts, narrow white tips to greater coverts; chestnut outer primaries highly attenuated, affording a short, rounded profile to wing; throat to breast pale cinnamon, rest of underparts chestnut.

Ssp. Monotypic (all mainland countries)

Habits Always found in communities. Very clumsy, with limited flight abilities. Nests on branches over water. Sedentary. Exclusively folivorous, taking shoots, buds and

young leaves, and frequently associated with stands of giant Arums, *Cecropia*, leguminous trees or *Avicennia* mangroves. Also feeds on Water Hyacinths.
Status Common but local in Ecuador, Colombia, Venezuela and the Guianas.
Habitat Tropical Zone. Always along slow-flowing streams, in riparian and gallery forests, and also in forests beside brackish water.
Voice Colonies are noisy with constantly uttered contact calls, which consist of series of 3–10 squawks, grunts and croaks. Wheezing raspy *hiss* when defending nest or young.

COLUMBIDAE – Pigeons and Doves

Pigeons and doves are generally stocky, rather plump, birds with short legs, small heads and weak bills. All are instantly recognisable as pigeons or doves, although they vary from large to small, elegant to dumpy, long-tailed to squat. They occur in almost all habitats, from high-latitude temperate regions to tropical desert, high altitude to sea level. Some are highly adaptable, great dispersers and colonisers, whilst others occupy specialised niches that make them vulnerable to habitat change. Songs and calls are variations of the classical cooing call that is their trademark. Their well-developed pectoral muscles give them power for rapid take-off to escape predators, and strength for sustained, fast and direct flight, for they are highly edible and favoured by predators everywhere (including man). They seem defenceless, but have a thick, soft plumage that can be shed at the lightest touch – a kind of shock moult – that can easily leave a fox with nothing but feathers, or a hawk with a talon-load of scattering plumage that enables the victim to escape. Generally, sexes alike and juveniles only differ very slightly, without any of the adult's gloss and often buffy fringes to the feathers. Usually lay 2 eggs, which generally prove to be male and female, hence the expression 'pigeon pair' for human twins that are boy and girl. Pigeons and doves are almost unique among birds in that they produce highly nutritious crop milk for the nestlings, enabling the adults not to switch diet for another source of protein, and assisting the very fast breeding cycle of most species, reducing the time of vulnerability to predators. They swallow their food whole, regurgitating hard seeds and pits of fruit, and take small grits to aid the pre-digestion process. The word pigeon is of Norman-French origin, whilst dove is Anglo-Saxon. Originally both names were applied to the same birds, but general use has come to settle on pigeon for the larger species and dove for the smaller ones.

Additional references used to prepare this family include Goodwin (1983), Baptista et al. (1997) and Gibbs et al. (2001).

FERAL ROCK PIGEON
Columba livia [Not illustrated]

Identification *c.*32cm. Typical *Columba* shape, highly variable with many pied and colour variants. Basic pattern of original wild Rock Pigeon, blue-grey with 2 black wingbars, some white on rump and blackish tip to tail, apparent in many forms and occasionally appears almost identical to wild bird.

Ssp. Domestic and feral (all countries)

Habits Feeds on ground, most commonly where humans leave detritus, grain and crumbs of food. Roosts and breeds under bridges and overhanging roofs.
Status Universal wherever man has settled in numbers. Common to abundant.
Habitat Any altitude with humans: roads, streets, public places, squares and markets, and may occur around farmsteads and agricultural areas close to settlements.
Voice Advertising-call a soft moaning *oorh* or *oh-oo-oor* (Goodwin) or *uu, cu-cuu, cuUUUuua* (Hilty). Display song is a faster and louder, more persistent *coo oo-roo-coo t'coo* (Goodwin).
Note In coastal Chile and Argentina the feral pigeon has taken to the natural cliff habitat of the wild Rock Pigeon and largely reverted to type plumage.

Rock Pigeon does not occur in northern South America; however, the feral domesticated bird occurs in a multitude of varieties in most major cities, many small towns and even villages; the white rump and double wingbars of the wild bird are very often seen in the feral pigeon

New World pigeons of the old genus *Columba* are now placed in the genus *Patagioenas* to separate them from Old World species (Banks *et al.* 2003). They are generally large with vinaceous grey and brownish plumage. Sexes alike, but males have more pronounced rows of iridescent feathers on the neck-sides. Gregarious, arboreal – though some are ground feeders – and strong, direct flight.

WHITE-CROWNED PIGEON
Patagioenas leucocephala Pl. 63

Identification 29–40cm. Large dark pigeon, uniform slate-grey with white forehead and crown, rich purple rear crown and iridescent green on neck-sides and nape; eyes yellow with pale blue-grey eye-ring, cere red, bill horn, legs and feet rose-pink. Juvenile overall drab brown, paler below, with buffy-white forehead, soft parts duller than adult.

Ssp. Monotypic (Co, Ve: Aves I.)

Habits Most often seen flying strongly over forest or mangroves. Shy and retiring.
Status Caribbean species known only from vagrants to Isle of Aves, off Venezuela, and coastal Colombia. Wanders widely among Caribbean islands and probably occurs more frequently than suspected.
Habitat Lower Tropical Zone. Prefers humid evergreen and semi-deciduous hardwood forests and scrubby woodland. Apparently, isolated offshore mangrove islets are preferred for breeding.
Voice A slow, deep 2–3-syllable *coo-curoo-coo* or *coo-croo* (Hilty), the latter probably the nest-call (Goodwin), alternately a deep *whu-cu-cu-cuuuu, cu-cu-cuuuu, cu-cu-cuuuu*… repeated 2–4 times (Gibbs *et al.*), and *cruu, cru, cu-cruuu*, which sounds like *Who took two*, slightly faster and less deliberate than Scaly-naped Pigeon, with second syllable rising (Raffaele *et al.* 1998).

SCALED PIGEON
Patagioenas speciosa Pl. 63

Identification 28–34cm. Adult male has head purplish-brown, neck, mantle and underparts with shades of pinks, gold, buff and light cerise, all scaled heavily with iridescent purple, green and reddish, back and lesser wing-coverts reddish-brown with dark glossy green scaling, rest of wings to tail dark brown with reddish-brown fringes to feathers; eyes brown, broad red eye-ring, cere and bill red, legs and feet coral. Female similar but less colourful with plain brown back and wings to tail. Juvenile plain brown with slight scaling on neck and upper breast, tip of bill horn, otherwise soft parts as adult. Visually unique, the only adult pigeon with scaled white undertail-coverts and bold scaling on neck and breast. Pale-vented Pigeon similar in flight, but usually in groups or flocks.

Ssp. Monotypic (all mainland countries, Tr)

Habits Usually solitary or in pairs in canopy, rarely small groups at fruiting trees. Local in forest, but sometimes gregarious and flocks of 100+ seen in Colombia.
Status Patchily and thinly distributed, and regularly overlooked. In Ecuador, rare to uncommon and local, locally frequent in Colombia, Venezuela and Guyana. Frequent on Trinidad but no records for Tobago, nor Aruba, Bonaire, Curaçao.
Habitat Lower Subtropical Zone. Canopy, edge and semi-open rain and gallery forests, wooded savannas, secondary forests, but favours areas with dense growth and tangles. Appears to tolerate forest fragmentation.
Voice Varied vocabulary or wide geographic variation: *whoo-whoo-whoo-whoo* (Wetmore in Goodwin), *whoooo, wh-wh-whooo, wh-wh-whooo* (R&G), a deep, slurred *caaoo-cuk-ca caaoo, cuk-ca caaa-OOO*, first 2 notes lower then faster, and a much deeper *groo-groo, coo, groo-groo* given by male (Gibbs *et al.*), and a low-pitched, drowsy *coo-OOOOaa cook, cooOOOOaa*…, 4 times, with first note halting, repeated every 15–30 s (Hilty).

SCALY-NAPED PIGEON
Patagioenas squamosa Pl. 63

Identification 32–41cm. Adult male overall bluish slate grey, darker on wings and tail, nape and neck-sides iridescent purple with same-colour scaling extending to mantle, and wash over breast; eyes red with yellow pupils and broad orange eye-ring, cere and bill red, legs and feet coral. Female similar but less purple on nape and weaker mantle scaling, breast grey. Juvenile a duller version of adult, browner grey, more buffy scaling.

Ssp. Monotypic (ABC, Ve: offshore islands)

Habits Rather wary canopy bird. Difficult to observe. Gathers at pools and springs early morning and late afternoon.
Status Caribbean species, known only on offshore islands. Very rare or possibly extinct on Aruba, scarce on Curaçao, common on Bonaire. In Venezuela, on Los Testigos and Los Frailes but probably occurs on all outlying islands, at least irregularly.
Habitat Tropical Zone. Normally a higher altitude counterpart of Bare-eyed (e.g. on Aruba) but recorded to sea level. Well-wooded hillsides, often on and around steep cliffs and fruit plantations, less often in mangroves.
Voice Emphatic *cruu, cruu-cru-cruuu* with first syllable brief, fourth longest and drawn out (Hilty), *who who hoo-oo-hoo* (Wetmore in Goodwin), a deep, resonant *róó-coo-róó or róó-coo-coo-cóórr* (Voous), very strong *rukuku* (Voous in Goodwin), *Ruk-tuh-Coo-oo* and a distinct purring sound (Howe in Goodwin), and *groo…cuk-cuk-coooo-cuk-cuk-coooo, cuk-cuk-coooo*, repeated very slowly at intervals of 20 s or more (Gibbs *et al.*).

BARE-EYED PIGEON
Patagioenas corensis Pl. 63

Identification 30–37cm. Distinctive pigeon with large white wing patch. Head of adult pale grey merging into pinkish mauve that becomes more pink and then buffy on vent, grey on flanks, white undertail-coverts with buffy scallops; nape scalloped black, pale blue and white becoming iridescent golden bronze and black scallops. Lower back, mantle, scapulars and inner wing-coverts pale brown, rump to tail grey, outermost lesser, median and greater coverts white, inner secondaries brown with white fringes, other wing-feathers black; eyes orange with broad pale blue eye-ring and pinkish-brown outer ring, cere whitish, bill pink to yellowish, legs and feet coral. Juvenile has head brown as back, nape with pale bluish scallops; soft parts duller than adult. 'Goggle-eyed' look. In flight by broad white wing patch. When perched recalls a *Leptotila* dove but latter primarily terrestrial whilst Bare-eyed is principally arboreal.

Ssp. Monotypic (Co and Ve coasts, offshore islands, ABC)

Habits Gathers to drink early morning and late afternoon, and makes regular flights to and from foraging areas. Distinctive loud wing-clapping when flushed. Usually in flocks except when breeding.
Status In Colombia, frequent to common on arid north coast.

Local and seasonally uncommon to common in Venezuela, in drier areas of west and central coast, north-central Llanos and Margarita I. Frequent on Aruba, Bonaire and Curaçao, and moves regularly between them and Venezuela mainland.

Habitat Lower Tropical Zone. Xerophytic coastal regions, thorn scrub with *Acacia* and columnar cacti, mangroves, semi-open arid lands.

Voice Territorial and advertising-call a high-pitched not very musical *roo-coo*, with stress on final syllable and often crackling, a more high-pitched *roo-oo-koo* (Voous), slow pigeon-like *coooo, chuck-chuk, cooouu…* (H) and very distinctive *wooo, chuck-chuck* repeated up to 5 times before long *chooouu* (Gibbs *et al.*), the *chuk-chuk* or *wuk-wuk* calls quiet and given in quick succession (H&B).

PALE-VENTED PIGEON

Patagioenas cayennensis Pl. 63

Identification 25–26.5cm. Adult male has mauve forehead, pale green rear crown to nape, upperparts brown with reddish-rufous on back and lesser wing-coverts, greyish on uppertail-coverts; throat white, narrow nuchal collar to upper breast mauve, grading into pink breast and grey flanks, belly grey, undertail-coverts whitish; eyes and eye-ring red, cere and bill dusky, legs and feet red. Female similar, but duller and browner. Juvenile has greyish head, with vinaceous forehead, malar and throat, wings, back and tail darker with white terminal scallops on all feathers, soft parts duller. Medium-sized pigeon with bright red eyes and eye-ring, and grey tail. Plumbeous is browner above with dark brown tail. Ruddy is uniform dark below (race *berlepschi* from Chocó has no white on underwing), and all races have dark tail.

Ssp. *P. c. andersoni* (SE Co, E Ec, Ve) as described

P. c. cayennensis (Gu, Su, FG) crown and nape iridescent green, bronze or mauve depending on light, belly to undertail-coverts grey; lower back, rump and uppertail-coverts dark grey

P. c. occidentalis (W Co, W Ec) very close to *pallidicrissa* and has nearly uniform brownish-grey tail, but lower abdomen and undertail-coverts darker grey; forehead darker vinaceous

P. c. pallidicrissa (N Co) paler overall and whiter below, especially male

P. c. tobagensis (T&T) close to *pallidicrissa* and has nearly uniform brownish-grey tail, and forehead and crown like back, but abdomen and undertail-coverts white, back deeper vinaceous chestnut-rufous

Habits Mainly arboreal and often solitary, but will gather in groups, sometimes large flocks at waterholes, feeding sites and roosts.

Status Widespread. Uncommon to locally common in Ecuador, frequent to common in Colombia. In Venezuela, common and especially abundant in Llanos. Common in Guyana, Trinidad & Tobago, and rather common in Suriname and French Guiana.

Habitat Tropical Zone, in lowlands, but may reach Lower Subtropical Zone. Normally at borders of hill forest, river borders, clearings and partially open gallery forest, generally avoiding closed-canopy and rain forests. Mangroves on Trinidad.

Voice Song slow and drowsy, a low mournful cooing, 3–8 phrases, *oooun…co-woo, tucooo, tucooo* (Hilty), a rather fast *woooh, wok, wuh-woooh, wuk, wuh-woooh*, phrasing similar to Scaled but faster and higher pitched (R&G), and a strong, loud, *cuck-a-coo cuck-a-coo cuck-a-coo…* repeated many times, sometimes preceded by a long *cuooooo*. Also a rough purring *rrRooooo rrRooooo* (Gibbs *et al.*).

Notes Those in eastern Ecuador ascribed to race *cayennensis* by R&G. Listed as Rufous Pigeon in Goodwin (1967) and may also be called Cayenne Pigeon.

BAND-TAILED PIGEON

Patagioenas fasciata Pl. 63

Identification 33–40cm Fairly large, heavily built pigeon with long tail. Adult male dark plumbeous grey, darker on wings, slightly paler on face-sides and below, basal half of tail very marginally darker than uppertail-coverts, with a broad paler bar and terminally darker again; crown and nape have mauve tint, with narrow white line on nape, lower neck and mantle iridescent green, the feathers fringed dark grey; eyes orange-yellow with red eye-ring, cere and bill bright yellow, legs and feet yellow. Female similar but duller and less iridescent above, slightly browner below, tail virtually unbanded. Yellow bill and white nape-band separate it from any feral pigeon that might otherwise be similar. The only *Patagioenas* normally found in highlands, and only highland pigeon that flocks.

Ssp. *P. f. albilinea* (Co, Ve, Ec, Tr) as described

P. f. roraimae (S Ve: Pantepui) more richly coloured, head has iridescent purple gloss, underparts more vinaceous to purple-washed; mid tail has broad blackish band

Habits Canopy species most often seen in flight, it may suddenly burst from cover with loud wing-clapping. Gathers in fruiting trees and on exposed branches.

Status Subtropical Zone to Páramo, occasionally in Upper Tropical Zone. Noticeable seasonal altitudinal movements. Widespread and frequent to common in Ecuador, locally common but decreasing in Colombia and Venezuela, scarce in Trinidad (no records Tobago).

Habitat Tropical to Temperate Zones. Highlands, mostly at 2,000–3,000m, but occurs lower and higher. Usually in humid, heavily wooded hillsides and gulleys but also semi-arid cloud forest, alder woods, second growth and savanna. In Andean region mainly in temperate forests above 2,500m.

Voice Less vocal than other *Patagioenas*. Song a weak series of deep, low-pitched notes, e.g., *cuh-hooo, cuh-hooo, cuh-hooo*, repeated 6–10 times; pitch similar to White-throated Quail-Dove (R&G). Deep mellow cooing, *co-oooh, co-oooh…* repeated several times (Hilty). Flight-calls include a soft rattling *dzrrrr* or *trrrrr* in display (Gibbs *et al.*), throaty *wrrreenh* (R&G), a chirping *dzurrr* and grating *graak* (F&K).

Note The 2 races in our region are included in the *albilinea* group, which is sometimes considered specifically distinct from *fasciata*, White-naped Pigeon (Baptista *et al.*).

MARAÑÓN PIGEON

Patagioenas oenops Pl. 63

Identification 31–34cm. Large, reddish-brown bird, inner wings and tertials reddish-brown, outer wing-coverts grey, secondaries and primaries blackish; short square black tail; eyes outlined black, then red, with blue in pupils, eye-ring lavender, cere and base of bill red, rest of bill pale blue, legs and feet red. Female duller and paler. Somewhat similar Pale-vented Pigeon is paler, particularly on belly, with all-black bill.

Ssp. Monotypic (extreme SE Ec)

Habits Solitary or in small groups, usually in canopy but may take grit on ground.

Status Local and rare in Ecuador. Some seasonal movements.

Habitat Tropical Zone, at *c.*700m. Essentially, riparian forests of Marañón basin, feeding on seeds of *Salix*, *Scinus*, *Ceiba*, *Prosopis* and *Acacia*.

Voice A slow *wa-oooo, wa-wa-oooo* (R&G), a rapidly-delivered *cooo cuck-ca-cooo, cooo cuck-ca-cooo,* and a deep, growling *rrrraaaaooo* (Gibbs *et al.*).

Note Sometimes called Peruvian Pigeon.

SHORT-BILLED PIGEON

Patagioenas nigrirostris Pl. 64

Identification 26–31cm. Male has greyish crown, purple nape to mantle, rest of upperparts deep umber; forehead, face-sides and underparts vinaceous olive – overall impression is of a dark dull bird, more pinkish below; eyes pale, eye-ring red, cere and bill black, legs and feet red. Female similar but head is concolorous with underparts. Juvenile has feathers of upperparts tipped rufescent olive; head and underparts heavily tipped or washed rufescent olive; eyes dark, eye-ring pale brown. From other similar ruddy-grey pigeons by combination of pale eye, black cere and bill, and uniform brownish-grey underparts and underwing.

Ssp. Monotypic (extreme NW Co)

Habits Regularly perches on dead branches at edge of clearing or forest (Gibbs *et al.*); rarely perches conspicuously in open (Ridgely & Gwynne). Mostly arboreal, keeping to mid and upper storeys. In flight appears dull and uniform below. Heard far more often than seen, the call is far-carrying and distinctive.

Status Barely reaches Colombia, where scarce to possibly locally frequent.

Habitat Tropical Zone. Humid lowland forest.

Voice A fluty, melancholy 4-note call, the final note drawn-out, *wuck-ca, ca-cooooo* ('who cooks for you?'), repeated quickly several times (Gibbs *et al.*), and a rapid, purring *rrrroooo*. A characteristic sound of the (Panamanian) forest, typically a mellow, mournful *ho, cu-cu-coóó* or *oh-whit-mo-gó* (Ridgely & Gwynne).

DUSKY PIGEON

Patagioenas goodsoni Pl. 64

Identification 24cm. Small, stocky. Pale grey head, neck and underparts, becoming more vinous (lavender) on flanks and below, with a purplish wash to hindneck; back, wings and tail umber with purplish tone on back to uppertail-coverts; underwing chestnut; eyes pale, eye-ring grey, legs and feet red. Female similar but duller, with less purple and lavender gloss. Juvenile slightly duller than female, eyes dark. From sympatric and rather similar vinaceous race *berlepschi* of Ruddy Pigeon by grey on head. From all other ruddy-coloured pigeons by clearly bicoloured underparts and chestnut underwing, and very distinct call. Plumbeous is larger with longer tail and uniform grey underparts and underwing.

Ssp. Monotypic (W Co, NW Ec)

Habits Display a short upward flight and shallow, rapid gliding descent.

Status In Ecuador, uncommon to locally frequent. In Colombia, rare to only very locally common.

Habitat Tropical Zone to 1,000m, occasionally 1,500m. Humid lowland and foothill forests. In Ecuador in partially logged areas, but always close to primary or little-disturbed forest.

Voice Clearly differs from Ruddy Pigeon's 4-syllable song. Distinctive *cu, wuk-wuk*, last 2 notes fast, repeated regularly and rapidly (Gibbs *et al.*), or fast rhythmic *whoa? pup-pup*, with emphasis on first syllable (R&G).

Note Also called Goodson's Pigeon.

RUDDY PIGEON

Patagioenas subvinacea Pl. 64

Identification 27–32cm. Head to undertail-coverts vary from mauve-grey to greyish-cinnamon depending on race, and glossy or iridescent on sides of neck and breast, back and wings to tail deep umber-brown; eyes red, cere red but bill black, legs and feet dull pale red. Female lacks iridescence of male and has subterminal pale spots on mantle. Juvenile has wing-coverts fringed pale cinnamon, and underparts fringed or scalloped with cinnamon. Similar Dusky Pigeon has lavender-grey body contrasting with chestnut underwings. Plumbeous Pigeon is uniform dark grey below. From all other ruddy-coloured species by combination of red eyes and eye-ring with black cere and bill.

Ssp. *P. s. berlepschi* (W Co, W Ec) bright, paler cinnamon, amethyst gloss to mantle, cinnamon wing-linings

P. s. ogilviegranti (E Ec) more vinaceous (less brownish) with darker, more contrasting bronzy wings than *berlepschi*

P. s. peninsularis (Ve: Paria) smaller, like *zuliae* but more deeply vinaceous on head and underparts; underwing-coverts partially brown

P. s. purpureotincta (SE Co, S Ve, Gu, S Su, FG) darker olive-brown and less purplish above, underwing-coverts dark brown

P. s. ruberrima (N Co: Upper Sinú) synonymised with *bogotensis* by Baptista *et al.* and followed by Dickinson *et al.*

P. s. zuliae (NE Co, NW Ve) Slightly more reddish-purple than *purpureotincta*, particularly on uppertail coverts

Habits Very arboreal and spends most time in subcanopy where very difficult to see unless it calls.
Status Widespread. Uncommon to frequent in Ecuador, frequent in Colombia, Venezuela and Guyana, uncommon in Suriname but common in French Guiana.
Habitat Tropical and Subtropical Zones, seldom above 1,500m, but recorded to 2,200m.
Voice Like Plumbeous, but higher pitched: *wuck, ca, coo-woo* with last syllables well articulated and faster (Gibbs *et al.*), a 4-note mellow, rhythmic *wut, wu-whuú-wu* (R&G), rhythmic, high-pitched *wut wood-woóoo ho* (F&K). Race *berlepschi* gives *wuck, ca, co-oooo* or *wuck ca-ca-coooo*, but where sympatric with Plumbeous a more deliberate *wuck-wuck…wuck-wuck*, the final syllables delivered quickly (Gibbs *et al.*). Also a purring *rrrrooooooo* (R&G).
Note Races very confusing and need review. Race *ogilviegranti* considered synonymous under *purpureotincta*, and *ruberrima* under *bogotensis* by Baptista *et al.* Race *bogotensis* treated as subspecies of Plumbeous Pigeon in MdS&P, H&B, R&G and Hilty, whom we follow here.

PLUMBEOUS PIGEON
Patagioenas plumbea Pl. 64

Identification 33–34cm. Varies considerably according to race; essentially dark brown back, wings to tail, dark vinaceous grey head, underparts and underwings; eyes, eye-ring and cere red, bill black, legs and feet pale red with large darker scales. From other *Patagioenas* in flight by uniform dark greyish underparts and underwing. May be confused with Ruddy Pigeon, but latter has black cere, is smaller and voices are different.

Ssp. *P. p. bogotensis* (C Co) eyes deep red
P. p. chapmani (W Ec, C & W Co) darker, more vinaceous (less grey) on head and underparts than *delicata*; iris pale grey
P. p. delicata (E Ec, E Co, W & S Ve) iris pale yellow
P. p. pallescens (SE Ec) darker and more vinaceous than *delicata*
P. p. wallacei (SE Ve, Gu, Su, FG) much darker on head and neck

Habits Usually in canopy, in pairs or small groups.
Status Frequent in eastern and western Ecuador, frequent to common in Colombia, locally frequent in Venezuela, frequent in Guyana, Suriname and French Guiana.
Habitat Mid Tropical to mid Subtropical Zones. Humid primary forest and well-regenerated secondary habitats.
Voice Varies with subspecies: *chapmani* is similar to *bogotensis* but faster and more clipped, first 2 notes short, last 2 long, *wop-wop-wh-ooh* (R&G); *delicata* gives distinctive *wuck-a-wuck* (Gibbs *et al.*) or *whook a-cóok-huuu* and *whut-whut-whooooa* (Hilty); *wallacei* a *wuck-a-wuck, coooo* (Gibbs *et al.*); and *bogotensis* a 3-noted, rhythmic *whuk-whuk-whuóo* (R&G). All races utter purring *rrrraaaaooo* or *ccrrrooo* before or after main call (Gibbs *et al.*).
Note Races very confusing. MdS&P, H&B, R&G and Hilty treat race *bogotensis* of Ruddy as subspecies of Plumbeous, and Hilty notes that *delicata* may be a synonym of *bogotensis*, and populations in eastern lowland Ecuador (placed here in *delicata*) are ascribed by R&G to *bogotensis*. We follow Baptista *et al.* and Dickinson (2003) in placing *bogotensis* in Ruddy Pigeon. Race *wallacei* considered a synonym of *pallescens* in Dickinson (2003).

EURASIAN COLLARED DOVE
Streptopelia decaocto [Not illustrated]

Identification 31–34cm. Large, elegant dove that is notably pale, uniform buffy-grey, distinguished by black-and-white bar on neck-sides. Undertail white with dark base visible on sides of undertail-coverts. Invariably draws attention when it lands on branch or telegraph wire, as it utters a harsh *krreeeagh* upon alighting.

Eurasian Collared Dove will doubtless be seen in mainland northern South America eventually

Ssp. Monotypic (Tr)

Status Vagrant to Trinidad (one present at Waterloo for 3 months in 2000), presumably from West Indies. A spectacular colonist that has successfully spread west from Asia to Europe and is now colonising the New World, where it is likely to occur increasingly frequently.
Habitat Comfortable in vicinity of man, it forages in towns and gardens in preference to open country. Breeds all year and capable of becoming established very quickly.
Voice Song a trisyllabic *coo* with second syllable stressed and drawn out, third syllable slightly lower-pitched, *doo-doooo-do* (Mullarney *et al.* 1999).

Zenaida doves are medium-sized with pastel buffy colours, spots on wings and graduated tails with white corners. Distinguished from *Leptotila* doves by line across lower ear-coverts and long tails. Birds of open areas and often quite gregarious.

EARED DOVE *Zenaida auriculata* Pl. 64

Identification 22–28cm. Adult male has back, wings and tail medium brown with distinct greyish wash, tail has faint subterminal bar on all but central pair of rectrices, rump and uppertail-coverts grey, tertials and innermost greater wing-coverts have elongated black spot on each feather; forehead pale buffy, crown silvery grey, becoming lilac on sides of face and neck to breast, then pinkish-cinnamon to undertail-coverts, grey flanks; feathers on neck-sides have iridescent patches of bright pale yellow, green and pink; 2 heavy black lines on face-sides, one diagonally across ear-coverts, the other in parallel at base of ear-coverts; eyes brown, bill dusky, legs and feet flesh with large red scales. Adult female similar but has pale buffy face-sides, smaller and exclusively yellow iridescent patches on neck-sides, and more noticeable subterminal bar on tail with orange-buffy tip. Juvenile male a duller version of adult male, lacking neck iridescence, and having pale to whitish tips to wing-coverts; breast brownish with pale centres and dark fringes to feathers. Juvenile female duller version of adult female but has pale shaft-streaks on head, breast, wing- and uppertail-coverts, in addition some breast feathers and all wing-coverts have pale tips, underparts bright cinnamon, subterminal bar and orange tip to tail as female; bill, legs and feet flesh.

Ssp. *Z. a. antioquiae* (Co: NC Andes) similar to *ruficauda* and also like *stenura* but much larger, and darker brown above; abdomen and undertail-coverts like breast (not cinnamon)
Z. a. caucae (W Co) similar to *ruficauda* but has rufous tips to outer rectrices.
Z. a. hypoleuca (W Ec) paler below and more greyish-brown above than others
Z. a. pentheria (Ve: Andes) large with a heavy bill, browner and greyer on back, lower breast to undertail-coverts rufescent
Z. a. rubripes (C Co) dark and uniform brownish, very little vinous wash below
Z. a. ruficauda (Co: E Andes) deep rufous tips to outer rectrices; below, deep almost reddish-pink with bright vinous wash
Z. a. stenura (Ve: all except Falcón, Andes, Tr, Gu) greyer underwing, buffy chin, terminal part of outer rectrices bright vinaceous cinnamon; female paler and greyer
Z. a. vinaceorufa (Ve: Falcón, Ar, Cu, Bo) rufous tips to outer rectrices, otherwise like *rubripes*, and very close to *stenura* but paler brown above, white chin, less deeply vinous below

Habits Usually in flocks, conspicuous, very alert and flushes (with weak wing-claps) at slightest disturbance, yet in some areas is quite tame. Ground feeder, in some areas an agricultural pest.

Status Marked seasonal movements throughout range. Frequent to common in Ecuador, frequent to locally abundant in Colombia, frequent to seasonally abundant in Venezuela, common in Aruba, Curaçao, Bonaire, Guyana and Trinidad & Tobago. Very rare (vagrant?) in French Guiana.

Habitat Dry and semi-arid areas from sea level to 3,500m, occasionally higher. Open grasslands, *Acacia* and cactus scrub, agriculture, aloe cultivations, parks and gardens.

Voice Very deep, growling *ca-ooo…cooo…cooo…cooo… or oh-whoo…whoo…whoo*, the first note disyllabic, the others very deep and'growling'. A deep *whoo* or *ooh-whoo*, the second note accented, often repeated in long series (Gibbs *et al.*, F&K). A low-pitched *ooo-cú-ooo*, rising *coooo* (Hilty) and subdued *whoo-oo* (R&G). Has drum-like timbre, sometimes subdued, and may be heard even during hottest part of day (Voous).

Note Subspecies poorly defined and only subtly different. Race *stenura* treated as synonym of *rubripes* and *pentheria* of *ruficauda* in Baptista *et al.* and Dickinson (2003).

MOURNING DOVE
Zenaida macroura Pl. 64

Identification 27–34cm. Distinctive, mid-sized dove with long graduated, white-edged tail and broad wings. Sandy olive above with black spots on tertials and inner wing-coverts, crown to undertail-coverts buff, more cinnamon on head, nape to mantle silvery grey with small patch of iridescent yellow on neck-sides; eyes brown, eye-ring blue-grey, bill dusky, legs and feet red. Juvenile lacks grey on neck and iridescent patch, head is browner and has some brownish scaling on breast. From *Leptotila* doves by long tail and spots on wings.

Ssp. *Z. m. marginella* (NW Co) as described
Z. m. turturilla (NW Co) pale grey, generally brighter than *marginella*

Habits Terrestrial and generally tame. Flocks to water early morning and late afternoon. Distinctive wing-whirr on take-off. Flight swift and darting, with characteristic whistling sound. Throws tail upwards as flight-intention movement, and also on landing. Feeds on ground, singly (when mate is on nest), in pairs or groups.

Status Boreal migrant that reaches Panama, and is a straggler or rare winter resident in Colombia.

Habitat Tropical Zone. Open grassland and scrub. Thrives in arid or semi-arid areas. Very successful, has taken advantage of urban areas and habitat modification. Sea level to 1,800m.

Voice Low, rather mournful *whoo, ho..hu..hu..hu* or *wrrrhooo, ho..hu..hu,* the first note a growl (Gibbs *et al.*), a mournful *coo-oo, coo-coo-coo*, the second syllable rising sharply (Raffaele *et al.* 1998). Goodwin (1967) describes a very clear, melodious, somewhat sad, romantic *coo-oo OO, OOO*, the first disyllabic note faint, the last 2–3 much louder.

Notes Sometimes called American Mourning Dove. The subspecies to have occurred in Colombia is unclear: *marginella* breeds in western North America and winters in Middle America, *turturilla* breeds Costa Rica to western Panama.

PACIFIC DOVE *Zenaida meloda* Pl. 64

Identification 25–33cm. Heavy-bodied pigeon. Olive-brown above, darker on greater wing-coverts and remiges, leading edge of wing, from carpal to alula thence to greater coverts white, tail has outer pairs of rectrices white and complete broad band about two-thirds on length, head grey with narrow black crescent at base of ear-coverts, throat white, neck-sides to thighs and belly cinnamon, flanks to undertail-coverts grey; eyes brown, eye-ring blue, bill blackish. Paler and greyer than White-winged Dove, and lacks pink on head;

face and neck pale grey rather than buff, and has greyish-pink breast. Geographically well separated. From *Leptotila* doves by line on face and white wingbar.

Ssp. Monotypic (SW Ec)

Habits Perches in trees, regularly in palms, and often in small groups.

Status Uncommon, erratic and fairly local in Ecuador.

Habitat Tropical to Lower Subtropical Zones. Arid and semi-arid agricultural areas, open woodland and urban areas. Mainly on ground in leaf-litter and undergrowth, but also in open fields, parks, gardens and roadsides.

Voice Similar to Pale-vented Pigeon, a distinctive and often-heard, mournful, rhythmic *coo, coo-ooo-poop, coo-ooo-poop, coo-ooo* with little variation in phrasing, repeated at intervals throughout day (R&G).

Notes Sometimes called West Peruvian Dove or treated as a subspecies of White-winged Dove (e.g. by Goodwin, Ridgely & Gwynne), but there are important differences in vocalisations and morphology (Baptista *et al.*).

[WHITE-WINGED DOVE
Zenaida asiatica] Pl. 64

Identification 25–31cm. Heavy-bodied pigeon. Olive-brown above, darker on greater wing-coverts and remiges, leading edge of wing, from carpal to alula thence to greater coverts white, tail has outer pairs of rectrices white and a broad black band on all but central pair; head buffy, with narrow black crescent at base of ear-coverts, throat pale buffy, neck-sides to flanks cinnamon, merging into grey flanks, thighs and belly in a series of scallops, undertail-coverts white; eyes red, eye-ring blue, bill blackish. Distinctive, striking white wingbar. From Pacific by warm buff face and breast (well separated geographically).

Ssp. *Z. a. asiatica* (ABC?) larger and paler.
Z. a. australis (Co?) as described

Habits When nervous jerks tail up and spreads it, as in display. Flight swift and direct, prefers to land in cover than on exposed branch. May gather at feeding area or roost.

Status Vagrant to Aruba, Bonaire and Curaçao; sight records in Colombia (S. Russell *fide* H&B). Race *asiatica* migrates to Greater Antilles, possibly reaches Aruba, Bonaire and Curaçao, whilst race *australis* migrates to west Panama, and possibly reaches Colombia.

Habitat Tropical Zone, locally to 1,500m. Arid to semi-arid scrub, light woodland and second growth.

Voice Call faster and higher pitched than larger Mourning Dove: *caa-coo-cuk…ca-cooo…ca-cooo…ca-cooo…ca-cooo*, final notes drawn and slurred (Gibbs *et al.*), described as a 3-part *who hoo, whoo hoo, hoo-áh, hoo-hoo-áh, who-oo* with first section short and low, second louder and almost merged with third; the third and fourth notes musical and strongly accented, and last part lower and more slurred (Wetmore in Goodwin). Alternate call *wha-uk, cuk…ca-ooo* repeated every 3–5 s, first 3 syllables very close together (Gibbs *et al.*).

Note Often considered conspecific with Pacific Dove but there are important differences in vocalisations and morphology (Baptista *et al.*).

Columbina ground doves are small, plump and short-tailed, generally drab but with bright rufous in wings, noticeable on flushing. Marginally sexually dimorphic and gregarious, they forage in pairs or groups, sometimes small flocks. Reluctant to flush and usually walk from danger. Mostly birds of open places and seemingly trusting of man, as some species forage in towns, cities and gardens.

PLAIN-BREASTED GROUND DOVE
Columbina minuta Pl. 65

Identification 14–16cm. Plain, small and inconspicuous. Adult male is pinkish olive-grey above, greyer on rump to tail, wings have irregular brown spots (each with a purplish iridescence) and inner webs of flight-feathers, including primary-coverts, rich chestnut, all with black tips; crown to nape pale greyish, face to undertail-coverts greyish-pink; eyes yellow to orange, eye-ring blue-grey, bill black, legs and feet coral. Female slightly paler, and distinctly duller on head and breast. Juvenile like female but has fewer spots on wings. Bright rufous wing when flushed. From Common by lack of scaling on neck and breast. Not easily separated from female and juvenile Ruddy, both usually forage in pairs or trios, always with an adult male that secures identification.

Ssp. *C. m. amazilia* (SW Ec) doubtfully distinct from *minuta* but well separated geographically
C. m. elaeodes (WC Co) darker fawn-brown above and pinker below
C. m. minuta (Ve, Tr, Gu, Su, FG, SE Co) as described

Habits Feeds on ground in pairs when breeding, small groups otherwise, often in streets and is tame.

Status Generally increasing with deforestation. Quite scarce but apparently increasing in Ecuador, locally common in Colombia. In Venezuela, frequent, common in lower *Llanos*. Uncommon in Guyana and Trinidad (no records Tobago). Uncommon and very local on sandy soils in French Guiana.

Habitat Tropical Zone to 1,400m. Lowland areas with scrub to light woodland. Favours open fields, agricultural and cultivated areas, parks and urban areas.

Voice Low, steadily repeated series of 2 different calls: a single *wup…wup…wup…* (Gibbs *et al.*) or *wuh wuh wuh* (Astley in Goodwin) repeated up to 40 s without pause, then starts again (Hilty). A 2-syllable *woo-ahk…woo-ahk…* (F&K), *ca-ooo.. ca-ooo…ca-ooo* (Gibbs *et al.*), *woo-ah…woo-ah…woo-ah…* (Wetmore in Goodwin).

COMMON GROUND DOVE
Columbina passerina Pl. 65

Identification 15.5–18cm. Small, plump and scaled. Male has entire head to mantle and breast heavily and regularly scaled, ground colour changes from pink or silvery grey to dark, and fringes of feathers change conversely; upperparts pale greyish-brown with irregular iridescent reddish-umber spots on wings becoming streaks or bands on greater coverts and tertials, inner webs of flight-feathers chestnut, including primary-coverts, all with black tips; underparts greyish-pink, tending to cinnamon on flanks, lower belly to undertail-coverts whitish; eyes red with blue-grey eye-ring, bill orange to pink with black tip, legs and feet orange-pink. Female similar but less bright, spots on wings browner, less strongly iridescent. Juvenile like female but paler and has pale to whitish ends to feathers of upperparts. Bright rufous wing when flushed. From Plain-breasted and female Ruddy Ground-doves by scaling and larger wing spots. May flock with Ruddy, but more wary and easier to flush. Forages with Scaled Dove.

Ssp. *C. p. albivitta* (N Co, Ar, Ve: N & Margarita I., Tr) male has pink forehead, rest of head pink-grey with dark scaling, chin white, deep vinaceous pink from throat to flanks with black centres on throat, sides of neck and breast, vent to undertail-coverts white, bill yellow; female lacks any pink or vinaceous grey – soft pastel brown above, lightly scaled on head and nape, very pale below with black centres to throat, sides of neck and breast; eyes yellow-red, bill yellow with black tip, legs and feet flesh colour

C. p. griseola (S Ve, Gu, Su, FG) male like *albivitta* but slightly more intensely vinous above and below; female duller and darker, greyish-brown to flanks and thighs, undertail-coverts brown with white fringes; juvenile duller than female with no white fringes to brown undertail-coverts

C. p. nana (W Co) crown and nape concolorous with back, suffused vinaceous, no scaling; wing-coverts deeper; vinaceous below; female deeper and duller, no vinaceous on crown

C. p. parvula (C Co) reportedly the smallest race; very dark and very richly coloured

C. p. quitensis (C Ec) pale plumbeous on nape, weakly scaled; like *nana* but larger and darker

C. p. tortugensis (Ve: Tortuga I.) very pale pastel colours, scaling on breast has broad fringes and smaller dark centres, producing more casual spotting than regular scaling

Habits Flies with zig-zag trajectory and quickly lands again. Often with cocked tail when walking. Generally tame and conspicuous, singly when mate brooding, otherwise in pairs and small groups. Permits quite close approach, runs nervously before flushing. In dry country gathers at waterholes.

Status Uncommon to locally frequent in Ecuador, locally common in Colombia, frequent to common in Venezuela and the Guianas, very common in Aruba, Bonaire and Curaçao. Uncommon in Trinidad (no records Tobago).

Habitat Tropical to Subtropical Zones, to 2,900 m. Favours dry, open habitat, e.g. light scrub, brushy and weedy areas, fields, *Acacia* scrub, cactus and thorn scrub, *Rhizophora* mangroves and desolate limestone plateaux. Often seen in roads, parks and gardens.

Voice Calls less often than congeners: *caaOOP!–caaOOP!–caaOOP!* or *whoo-oop! whoo-oop! whoo-oop!* every c.1 s (R&G, H&B, Hilty).

Notes Sometimes called Scaly-breasted Ground Dove (e.g. Goodwin 1967). The many subspecies differ only slightly in extent of red on bill, shade of brown above and white tipping on tail.

SCALED DOVE

Columbina squammata Pl. 65

Identification 18–22cm. Small, distinctive and strikingly long-tailed dove with heavily scalloped, pale plumage. Pale to beige with dark, fine scaling on head and underparts, becoming scallops on lower breast and sides, darker and denser on back and wing-coverts, where outlined in white, outer fringes to outer coverts white, affording a faint wingbar effect; inner webs of primaries deep chestnut, very obvious when bird is flushed; eyes deep red, eye-ring blue-grey, bill grey with blackish tip, legs and feet reddish-flesh. Female virtually identical but slightly paler and less heavily scaled.

Ssp. *C. s. ridgwayi* (N Co, N Ve, Margarita I., Tr, FG)

Habits Most often in pairs on ground, but occasionally forms small flocks. Flushes fairly easily to cover. Rests in open cover. Displays while calling, by bowing, raising and spreading tail, and rocking. Noisy wing-clapping on take-off.

Status Common in Colombia, very common in Venezuela, vagrant to Trinidad. Not listed for Guyana by BFR&S or SFP&M, but Baptista *et al.* indicates that it does occur there.

Habitat Tropical Zone, to 1,200m. Arid and semi-arid savannas and open ground with scattered trees, locally in open woodland. Borders of gallery forest, wasteland, abandoned agriculture and cultivated fields, parks and urban areas with scattered trees. Invades deforested areas.

Voice Different races differ vocally: *ridgwayi* advertising-call is *croo! co-co,* with soft *croo-oo, crr-croo-oo* in aggression (Goodwin). Alliterations of call include (in Venezuela) por-favor and (in Hilty) ál-co'hol and there's no-hope. Also a loud purring *crrrrruu*, repeated continuously.

Note Placed in genus *Scardafella* in MdS&P, H&B and ffrench.

RUDDY GROUND DOVE

Columbina talpacoti Pl. 65

Identification 14–18cm. Rotund little dove that in males appears totally dull chestnut; head grey with pale forehead, upperparts ruddy with black spots on wings, trailing edge to all remiges chestnut and underwing-coverts chestnut with two black bands, axillaries black; greyish-pink throat, underparts strongly vinous, paler on belly and more ruddy on undertail-coverts; eyes red, eye-ring grey, bill grey, legs and feet pink. Female greyish-olive above with black spots on wings, tail darker, back of head grey, forehead to undertail-coverts pinkish-grey, paler on forehead, more vinous on breast and flanks, scalloped slightly pale grey on undertail-coverts. Juvenile generally drab brown with spots on wings less apparent; it has slightly darker scalloping on crown, nape, breast, rump and uppertail-coverts, fringes to wing-coverts are slightly paler. Female from Common and Plain-breasted by black underwing.

Ssp. *C. t. caucae* (W Co) male like *rufipennis* slightly browner above and paler below; female pale umber above with a vinaceous wash on rump and tail-coverts, less rufescent on undertail-coverts
C. t. rufipennis (Co, Ve: N & Margarita I., T&T) as described
C. t. talpacoti (E Ec, E Co, S Ve, Guianas) underwing-coverts black, outer webs of remiges dark brown, causing underwing to look blackish

Habits Terrestrial, tame and confiding, most often seen in streets and gardens. Reluctant to flush, and may freeze before take-off; flies to cover if pressed, but soon returns to foraging. Occasionally singly or pairs but more often in groups. Very aggressive when feeding, with much wing-raising, sharp lunges and pecking.

Status Uncommon to locally frequent and seemingly increasing in Ecuador, common to abundant in Colombia and Venezuela, common in Guyana. Straggler to Aruba, Curaçao and Bonaire. Abundant in Trinidad, common in Tobago, Suriname and French Guiana.

Habitat Tropical Zone, occasionally to 2,600m. Lowlands, savanna, open grassy scrub, edges of forests, marshes, light woodland, cultivation, wasteland, parks and gardens. Generally prefers humid to arid country.

Voice Slow, steadily repeated, rather monotonous series: *oo-oo, oo-oo* (Goodwin), *ca-boo…ca-boo…* (Gibbs *et al.*), *k-whoo, k-whoo….* (R&G) or *ca-HUU, ca-HUU…* (Hilty).

ECUADORIAN GROUND DOVE

Columbina buckleyi Pl. 65

Identification 18cm. Adult male soft pastel grey above, with a delicate lilac tone on back, spots on wing-coverts umber with a carmine iridescence, grey on head, remiges black with dull vinaceous grey outer webs, underwing-coverts black; below greyish-pink becoming mauve-pink on undertail-coverts; eyes dark brown, eye-ring grey, bill blackish, legs and feet grey. Female similar but warmer above and head concolorous with back. Juvenile duller and is more buffy. Similar to Plain-breasted but larger and lacks rufous in wings, and not sympatric. From Croaking Ground Dove by dark irides (latter species has pale eyes and iridescent purplish scapulars), and female Blue Ground Dove has rufous rump and tail.

Ssp. *C. b. buckleyi* (W Ec, W Co)

Habits Singly or in pairs, seldom groups (Gibbs *et al.*); often in large groups, sometimes with Croaking Ground Dove (R&G). Terrestrial in leaf-litter and thickets, and fairly confiding.

Status Frequent and apparently spreading in Ecuador. In Colombia, only recently recorded, on Gorgona I. (Ortiz & von Halle 1990) and in Tumaco (SCJ&W).

Habitat Lower Tropical Zone, to 1,000m. Woodland with patchy thickets and open understorey with thick mosses and lichens, woodland dominated by *Ceiba* and *Acacia*, edges of forest, secondary growth near agriculture.

Voice Monotonous series of relatively high-pitched, almost monosyllabic notes delivered 1 per s, *caooo… caooo… caooo* (Gibbs *et al.*), a slow-paced *whoo-oo… whoo-oo… whoo-oo*, similar to Ruddy Ground Dove (R&G).

Note Not listed in H&B.

PICUI GROUND DOVE

Columbina picui Pl. 65

Identification 18cm. Unmistakable little dove; pale greyish-brown above and greyish-buffy from face to breast, rest of underparts buffy; long, white-edged, rounded tail obvious in flight, as is broad white wingbar, row of lesser coverts alongside scapulars have bold dark iridescent line; eyes pale grey, eye-ring grey, bill blackish, legs and feet flesh. Male is grey on upper head, female has head concolorous with back. Juvenile has pale shaft-streaks on wings and subterminal buffy crescents.

Ssp. *C. p. picui*? (SE Co)

Habits Singly or in pairs, may gather at good feeding spots, in leaf-litter in undergrowth and at edges of woodland. Flight darting and swift.

Status Trans-Amazonian austral migrant, winters occasionally to eastern Peru and rare records (possibly vagrants?) in Colombia.

Habitat Tropical and Subtropical Zones. Light woodland, agricultural and urban areas. In Andes in open *Prosopis* scrub forest.

Voice Series of fairly loud, slightly inflected, even-pitched hollow notes, *ca-OOO…ca-OOO… ca-OOO…* repeated every 1 s or so in series of 3–4 with break of 3–5 s (Gibbs *et al.*).

CROAKING GROUND DOVE

Columbina cruziana Pl. 65

Identification 15cm. Adult male has powdery grey upper head, brownish or warmer grey on back and wings with outer wing-coverts pale grey, line along innermost lesser coverts iridescent reddish-purple, primary-coverts and remiges fuscous with grey fringes to secondaries, underwing entirely dark; throat to undertail-coverts pinkish-grey, greyer on throat, more pinkish-buffy on undertail-coverts; eyes black on outer ring, with white middle ring and red inner, eye-ring orange-yellow, bill base yellow, tip black, legs and feet coral pink. Female very similar but crown concolorous with back. Juvenile like female but has buffy tips to wing-feathers. From female Ecuadorian by bill, pale eye and purplish band on lesser wing-coverts.

Ssp. Monotypic (W Ec, SW Co)

Status Very common to common in Ecuador, sight records in Colombia where possibly spreading.

Habitat Tropical and Subtropical Zones. Arid and semi-arid regions to 2,400m, occasionally 2,900m. Dry deciduous woodland with open understorey, riparian thickets, scrub, open hillsides and agriculture, parks and gardens.

Voice Characteristic, 3-syllable call: a frog-like *kee-wa-wa* (H&B), croaking *qworr* or *tweorr* (F&K), *weeeoop, reeeoop* or *rrroowp* (Gibbs *et al.*), *w-wuwk, w-ouwk, w-ou-w* and a louder, clearer *kow-wow* (Trollope in Goodwin 1977), and a weird, mechanical-sounding *wreeoh* or *creeoh*, repeated slowly but steadily every 2 s (R&G).
Note Also called Gold-billed Ground Dove (e.g. Goodwin 1967).

Claravis ground-doves are forest birds that forage amongst leaf-litter in undergrowth, often with *Leptotila*. They are strongly dimorphic, the males being colourful; both sexes have obvious metallic spots on wings. Larger and longer tailed than *Columbina*.

BLUE GROUND DOVE
Claravis pretiosa Pl. 65

Identification 18.5–21.5cm. Medium-sized dove with profuse blackish metallic spots on wings. Adult male greyish-blue above, primary-coverts and remiges black but underwing-coverts and underwing grey, tail black, forehead, sides of face to undertail-coverts paler blue-grey; eyes red, bill dusky, legs and feet red. Female olive-brown above, dusky on head with pale forehead, wings dusky, blackish on flight-feathers, wing spots deep red, rump to tail deep ruddy rufous; throat to breast pale greyish-cinnamon, rest of underparts pale grey, undertail-coverts ruddy; bill brown. Juvenile like female above but less dark and richly coloured, underparts pale greyish-cinnamon throughout, tending to rufous on undertail-coverts. Female like larger *Leptotila* doves, but latter more bicoloured and lack wing spots. Female from female Ruddy and Ecuadorian by rufous rump and from Maroon-chested by lack of maroon on breast.

Ssp. Monotypic (throughout, except ABC)

Habits Largely terrestrial and shy, usually singly or in pairs, prefers to walk rather than fly from danger.
Status Uncommon to locally frequent in Ecuador. In Colombia, frequent to common and quite local. Frequent in Venezuela (not numerous). Uncommon in Trinidad (no records Tobago). Frequent in Guyana. Very local in French Guiana.
Habitat Tropical Zone to 1,000m. Dry deciduous woodland, sandy forests and scrubby habitats, open scrub, gallery forest and sometimes in more humid forests.
Voice May call from high treetop, but sings from mid-level perch, a slow-paced series of deep notes 1 per s difficult to pinpoint location: *whoop…whoop… whoop…*, or *boop… boop… boop…* (Gibbs *et al.*, R&G, Hilty).

MAROON-CHESTED GROUND DOVE
Claravis mondetoura Pl. 65

Identification 18–24cm. Adult male is dark greyish-blue above with deep red spots on wing-coverts (but not tertials), black primary-coverts and remiges, grey underwing-coverts but rest of underwing dusky; pale grey face with white throat, foreneck to sides of body and upper belly deep purplish-maroon, grey flanks, white belly to undertail-coverts; eyes orange, eye-ring yellow, bill black, legs and feet red. Female dull olive above, rufous-olive on rump and tail, face buffy, breast pale olive, rest of underparts buffy-white, legs and feet red. Unmistakable. From female Blue Ground Dove by paler face and darker breast, much larger and darker wing spots, and white outer tips to tail.

Ssp. *C. m. mondetoura* (N & W Ve, C Co, E Ec)

Habits Usually in pairs, but when bamboo is flowering many gather to feed on ground. Flushes with whistling sound from wingbeats. Keeps to dense cover and usually only located by its song, given from perches well above ground.
Status Nomadic: movements associated with bamboo flowering, making it impossible to estimate status accurately. Very rare, erratic and local in Ecuador, apparently rare and local in Colombia, and rare in Venezuela.
Habitat Subtropical to Temperate Zones, 1,300–2,600m. Follows seeding *Chusquea* and *Guadua* bamboo, in humid montane forests.
Voice Call *coo-ah, coo-ah,* very like Blue Ground Dove, but with rising inflection (Wetmore in Goodwin). Series of long, hollow, slightly inflected notes, c.1 per s *whaoop…whaoop… whaoop…, also da..du..du..du..* and a soft *hoop…hoop… hoop…* (Gibbs *et al.*), a deep but rising *coo-ah* (F&K), resonant hwoop notes, up to 45+ in succession (Hilty) and far-carrying *whoo-oóp… whoo-oóp… whoo-oóp…*, sometimes *whoo-roo-oop, whoo-roo-oop…* (R&G).

BLACK-WINGED GROUND DOVE
Metriopelia melanoptera Pl. 65

Identification 21–23cm. Adult almost entirely pale beige with grey lesser wing-coverts, primary-coverts and remiges black, underwing-coverts and underwing blackish, short tail black, underparts faintly paler with a pale vinaceous lustre; eyes pale blue with red outer circle, eye-ring orange-yellow, bill black, legs and feet greyish-brown. Female effectively the same, slightly duller and less lustrous. Juvenile slightly darker and greyer above with faint buffy fringes to mantle and wing-coverts; eyes blue without red outer circle, yellowish eye-ring less developed. Distinctive pale, stocky dove with black wings and tail, unmistakable.

Ssp. *M. m. melanoptera* (SW Co, Ec)

Habits Usually in small, close groups foraging on ground or huddling among clumps of grass or rocks. Inconspicuous, but when disturbed rockets upwards with rattling *whywhywhywhy* of wings. Flight swift.
Status Uncommon to locally common in highland Ecuador, very locally frequent in Colombia.
Habitat Usually above 3,000m in Páramo, but recorded at 100–4,400m, reaching lower in winter. Arid and semi-arid open grassland and farmland on rocky slopes, usually near treeline, often in or near *Polylepis* woodlands. Often far from trees during day, but returns to roost in *Polylepis* and *Eucalyptus*.

Voice Seldom vocalises. When breeding, an incessant rolling *trrreéé́ooi* (R&G, F&K), and long series every 4–7 s, *rrre-oop... rrre-oop... rrre-oop...* (Gibbs *et al.*).

Leptotila doves are plump, pastel-brown birds with blunt tails, the outer feathers of which are black with white tips that are obvious when the birds flush. All have rufous underwings but these are not especially noticeable. Highly terrestrial, foraging in leaf-litter in forests and woodlands, but perch freely in trees. Shy and retiring, but often forage at edges of forest, and may venture along paths and tracks, where they are usually seen as they scurry along before running or flying into cover.

WHITE-TIPPED DOVE

Leptotila verreauxi Pl. 66

Identification 24–30cm. Uniform-looking terrestrial pigeon; greyish-brown on back to central tail-feathers, rest of rectrices black with broad white tips; head and underparts except underwings pale buffy-grey, whitish on forehead and undertail-coverts, pale purple and green iridescence on neck-sides, underwing entirely chestnut; eyes vary from yellow through orange to red, eye-ring from blue through green to red, bill black, legs pink. Large white corners at ends of tail are main diagnostic – Grey-chested Dove similar but area of sympatry comparatively small and latter is a forest bird. Pallid Dove has more blue-grey on crown and is more rufescent above, more white on belly; Grey-fronted has blue-grey forecrown, distinctly buffy-tinged face and neck-sides; also check distribution. White-tipped Dove is usually seen singly or in pairs, occasionally small groups.

Ssp. *L. v. brasiliensis* (Gu, Su, FG) darker than *verreauxi*, with smaller white tips to tail; foreneck and breast darker (between pale cinnamon-drab and vinaceous fawn)

L. v. decolor (W Co, W & C Ec) like *verreauxi* but much greyer above, forehead whiter, metallic reflections on crown much less pronounced, underparts paler vinaceous, flanks greyer

L. v. hernandezi (SW Co) from *verreauxi* and *brasiliensis* by being generally more olivaceous above, more cinnamon-drab on throat, breast and tail, and drabber on flanks; undertail-coverts dark brown to fuscous; crown and nape mouse grey with metallic green and bronze reflections

L. v. tobagensis (To) similar to *verreauxi* but hindneck and nape bronze-green with very little if any copper reflection; throat white and more extensive; pale vinaceous grey below with ample white abdominal zone

L. v. verreauxi (N Co, N Ve and offshore islands, ABC) as described

L. v. zapluta (Tr) darker on back, wings and tail, being bronze with tinge of green instead of clay brown; front darker vinous

Habits Wary, but ventures into open more than other *Leptotila* and usually seen walking quickly away. Note, when flushed, bird is usually ahead of you, so chestnut underwing not seen, but tail very obvious; bird takes-off with a whirring-wing sound. Flight fast and low. May feed with chickens around homesteads and farms.

Status Uncommon to frequent in Ecuador, common in Colombia, Venezuela, Aruba, Curaçao, Bonaire, Guyana and Trinidad. Abundant in Tobago. Common on coastal plain in French Guiana.

Habitat Drier scrub and light woodland with little understorey, avoids deep forest. Forest edges and open groves, thickets, open areas with scattered trees (*Bombax*, *Carica*, *Ochroma* and thorny leguminaceous species: F&K), aloe fields and dry spots in *Rhizophora* mangroves (Voous).

Voice Mournful, deep and hollow, somewhat booming 2-syllable call (other *Leptotila* have single-note calls), falling and variously described as *ub'OOOOu* (Hilty), *waa-woooo* or *waa-waaoo* (Gibbs *et al.*), *who-whooó* (R&G) and *woob-wooooo* (F&K), like sound of blowing across top of empty bottle.

Notes Race *brasiliensis* sometimes considered specifically distinct, but differences inconsistent (Baptista *et al.*). Birds from humid areas generally richer pinkish and brownish; greyer and paler in drier areas.

GREY-HEADED DOVE

Leptotila plumbeiceps Pl. 66

Identification 23.5–26cm. Forehead to mantle grey, brighter on forehead and crown, wings, back and tail warm olive-brown, tail has 3 outermost tips white; face-sides and underparts to flanks pale greyish-pink, rest of underparts buffy-white, underwing reddish-brown to rufous; eyes yellow, eye-ring red, bill black, legs and feet coral pink. Female duller, lacking pale mauve or purplish iridescence on neck. Juvenile similar above but has buff fringes to back and wing-feathers; neck, breast and flanks richer pink to cinnamon with browner scallops, eye-ring dull, legs and feet pink. From other *Leptotila* by grey mantle.

Ssp. *L. p. plumbeiceps* (W Co)

Habits Shy and wary, flies into cover when flushed. Forages on forest floor, generally keeping in cover but comes out onto trails.

Status Uncommon and local in Colombia, scarce where forests logged.

Habitat Tropical and Subtropical Zones, to 1,800m, rarely 2,600m. Interior of humid forest and forest edges, apparently preferring drier areas.

Voice Distinctive single-note call, a soft mournful *whoooo... whoooo...* A curious, low-pitched *cwuh-h-á* described for race *notius* of west Panama by Wetmore (in Goodwin).

PALLID DOVE *Leptotila pallida* Pl. 66

Identification 25–31cm. Back, wings to central 3 pairs of tail-feathers rufous-olive or chestnut, outer primaries darker, outermost 3 rectrices black with white tips; upper head grey, rest of head, neck and underparts pale greyish-pink, underwing entirely rufous; eyes pale yellow, eye-ring crimson, bill black, legs and feet coral. Female similar but slightly duller and lacks mauve lustre on sides of neck and breast. Juvenile similar but darker on upperparts, with buffy fringes. From White-tipped by whiter mid crown, bluish-grey nape, and mantle and uppertail much more rufous. Belly extensively white.

Ssp. Monotypic (W Ec, W Co)

Habits Usually singly or in pairs, quietly feeding in leaf-litter in undergrowth or at edge of scrub.
Status Uncommon to locally frequent in Ecuador, frequent in Colombia.
Habitat Lower Tropical Zone, to 800m. Lowland evergreen forest and second growth, semi-arid or deciduous woodland and adjacent growth.
Voice Single, short mournful note given every 3–6 s, *hoooo… hoooo*, higher pitched than Grey-fronted, reminiscent of sound produced by blowing across top of bottle. Note ends abruptly, rather than fading (Gibbs *et al.*).

GREY-CHESTED DOVE

Leptotila cassini Pl. 66

Identification 22.5–28cm. Adult male purplish slate grey, dark greyish umber on back, wings and tail, with small white tips to outermost 2 rectrices; crown paler grey and face light bluish-grey; nape, neck, breast to flanks and upper belly rich mauve grey with purplish lustre, vent to undertail-coverts whitish, underwing-coverts rufous, underwing brown; eyes yellow, eye-ring red, bill black, legs and feet red. Female dark greyish umber on nape and neck to breast, becoming browner over rest of underparts. Juvenile like female but has rufous fringes to feathers of upperparts and breast. From much paler White-tipped Dove by lack of broad white band on tail. Dark below.

Ssp. *L. c. cassini* (NW Co)

Habits Shy, terrestrial, usually singly or in pairs, never in flocks.
Status Uncommon and local in Colombia.
Habitat Tropical Zone to 1,300m. Humid or semi-humid lowland forests with preference for second growth. Also shady pastures and gardens. Often in *Heliconia* thickets.
Voice Repeated, sustained mournful cooo (Goodwin) or *whoooo…whoooo…* (Gibbs *et al.*). Very low-pitched and reminiscent of sound made by blowing across top of bottle. End fades away (Gibbs *et al.*).

[CARIBBEAN DOVE

Leptotila jamaicensis] Pl. 66

Identification 30–33cm. Very dark umber back, wings and tail, white tips to all but central pair of rectrices (obvious when flushed), vinaceous grey crown and back of head, red and green iridescent patches on nape to mantle, pale to whitish forehead, warm buffy face-sides and underparts, deepest on breast, chestnut underwing; eyes pale yellow, possibly with red outer circle, eye-ring crimson, bill black, legs and feet deep red. Female similar but slightly duller and lacks iridescence on nape and mantle. Juvenile much duller, with rufous fringes to back and wing-coverts, subterminal crescents on breast feathers; soft parts duller. Larger and notably darker than White-tipped Dove with same amount of white on tip of tail, if not more.

Ssp. Subspecies unknown (mainland Co?)

Habits Feeds on ground, keeping in cover and walking rapidly.
Status Occurs on San Andrés I., but unknown on Colombian mainland.
Habitat Lower Tropical Zone, mostly in lowland scrub and woodland. Most frequent in semi-arid areas.
Voice A *croo; oo, coo-coo-cooo (oo)*, the first note very low and purring, the second very faint (Goodwin), hence description by Bond (1960) of *cu-cu-cuoo*, apparently referring to louder part.
Note Included as San Andrés is Colombian territory, but not part of continental northern South America, and thus outside our region. It is conceivable, but extremely unlikely, that either *neoxena* from San Andrés or *jamaicensis* from Jamaica could occur as vagrants to mainland Colombia.

GREY-FRONTED DOVE

Leptotila rufaxilla Pl. 66

Identification 27–28cm. Male has white forehead to bluish-grey crown, nape greyish-purple with some iridescence; generally olive-brown above with hints of purple and bronze on inner wing-coverts; throat and feathers bordering orbital skin pinkish-white, breast and neck-sides greyish pink; belly and undertail-coverts white; underwing-coverts chestnut; central tail-feathers olive-brown, outer rectrices blackish with white tips. Eyes yellow, but perhaps brown on younger birds, lores and orbital skin red, bill black, legs and feet red. Female browner, more olivaceous on flanks; greenish reflections on flanks, not purple. Juvenile like female but has rufous-orange fringes to upperparts and breast. From similar *Leptotila* by grey crown, buff face and extensively white underparts.

Ssp. *L. r. dubusi* (SE Co, SC Ve, E Ec) like *rufaxilla* but breast more vinaceous, less pink
L. r. hellmayri (NE Ve, Tr) male like *pallidipectus* at rest, but has darker rufous underwing; female like *rufaxilla* but has paler crown and back of head.
L. r. pallidipectus (E Co, W Ve) male has forehead to mid crown white, and is paler and brighter throughout, with paler rufous underwings; female duller and darker below, only slightly darker above and has underwing as dark as *rufaxilla*
L. r. rufaxilla (E Ve, Gu, Su, FG) as described

Habits Inconspicuous terrestrial bird that flushes reluctantly, low and fast. Usually singly or pairs, rarely groups. Forages in leaf-litter of undergrowth.
Status Uncommon to locally frequent in Ecuador, common in Colombia and Venezuela, frequent in Guyana. Common in Trinidad (no records Tobago), Suriname and French Guiana.
Habitat Lower Tropical Zone, to 600m, occasionally 1,400m. Interior humid forest, *terra firme*, *várzea*, bamboo patches,

sandy and gallery forest. Avoids drier areas. Fond of rank growth near water.

Voice Heard more often than seen. A single, deep resonant note that strengthens and fades, repeated every 3–4 s, *whoooo* (Gibbs *et al.*), *whooh* (R&G) or *wooOOOou* (Hilty).

OCHRE-BELLIED DOVE

Leptotila ochraceiventris Pl. 66

Identification 23–25cm. Small, very shy pigeon, more richly coloured than other *Leptotila*. Adult vinous grey on head to mantle, rather cinnamon on head-sides, warm olive-brown on wings, lower back and central 3 pairs of tail-feathers, but outermost 3 pairs black with white tips, pale throat, ochraceous breast, belly and flanks, but vent to undertail-coverts paler; eyes yellow, reddish-purple eye-ring, bill black, legs and feet coral. Female similar but slightly duller and lacks iridescent bloom on nape and mantle. Juvenile olive from forecrown to tail with buffy fringes throughout; underparts pale ochraceous buffy. Pallid Dove more rufous above and whiter below. White-tipped Dove lacks purplish tones to foreparts and has white belly.

Ssp. Monotypic (SW Ec)

Habits On ground, flying to low perch only when disturbed or to call.

Status Vulnerable. Uncommon to rare in Ecuador; habitat fragmentation within its very small range threatens species.

Habitat Upper Tropical to Lower Subtropical Zones.

Voice Slow, distinctive throaty and somewhat explosive *rrroowww* (R&G), a gruff *whaaarr… whaaarr…* (Gibbs *et al.*).

TOLIMA DOVE *Leptotila conoveri* Pl. 66

Identification 22.5–25cm. Pale mauve-grey head (paler on forehead), violaceous grey neck, mantle and breast with purplish lustre; greyish-olive back, wings and tail, of which outer 3 pairs brown with subterminal black band and white tip; throat whitish, belly pale ochraceous, paler on undertail-coverts. Female appears quite similar but lacks lustre on neck. Juvenile unknown. Smaller and more richly coloured than White-tipped.

Ssp. Monotypic (Co: C Andes)

Habits Usually observed singly. Very poorly known, and very shy and hard to find.

Status Endangered. Colombian endemic of uncertain status, but threatened by deforestation.

Habitat Subtropical Zone, 1,600–2,255m. Humid primary forest and adjacent second growth, bushy forest borders and plantations.

Voice Unknown.

Quail-doves are smallish, plump stocky birds with longish legs and short tails, and very largely terrestrial. Inhabit undisturbed, humid primary forest, occasionally adjacent secondary growth, but retreat in face of deforestation. Shy and inconspicuous, keeping well within cover and encountered singly or in pairs, very seldom small groups. Forages in leaf-litter of dense undergrowth in humid montane forests, and prefers to walk rather than fly. When disturbed they tend to freeze, perhaps momentarily, then walk into cover. If flushed they usually fly to low branches with a slight clattering of their wings. They tend to be dark and richly coloured with metallic reflections of purple and bronze. *Leptotila* doves are similar in habitat and habit, but are much paler and have white tips to the outer tail-feathers, which usually obvious when flushed.

SAPPHIRE QUAIL-DOVE

Geotrygon saphirina Pl. 67

Identification 22–26cm. Plump and compact with short tail. Forehead broadly white, crown blue, white from malar to ear-coverts with broad black sub-malar to rear of ear-coverts, white throat, patch of rich orange-bronze on head-sides between bronze-green head-sides and violaceous grey breast; mantle and back deep purple, lower back to uppertail-coverts deep royal blue, tiny stub of tail is black, scapulars, wing-coverts and tertials deep chestnut, single round white spot on upper tertial, remiges dusky; belly and sides whitish to pastel, lower belly and flanks to undertail-coverts ochraceous buffy; eyes pale yellow, eye-ring carmine-red, bill black, legs and feet carmine-red. Female similar but lacks lustre and is slightly duller. Juvenile has grey forehead and ear-coverts, crown rear of head greyish-blue, nape dull pale green, mantle chestnut, round white spot on upper and middle tertials; black malar broadly fringed white, throat buffy-white, breast grey, otherwise as adult. Unmistakable. *Leptotila* have similar habits and habitat but are much paler, and white tips on tail diagnostic.

Ssp. *G. s. saphirina* (E Ec, SE Co)

Habits Shy and inconspicuous, walks into denser cover rather than flying, when disturbed flies to low perch.

Status Rare to uncommon in Ecuador, uncommon in Colombia.

Habitat Lower Tropical Zone, normally to 900m but recorded to 1,100m. Undisturbed humid, primary *terra firme* forest and interior of older secondary woodland. Undergrowth and rank vegetation in damp ravines, near water.

Voice High-pitched series of tremulous disyllabic notes that usually sounds like a single note as first part soft and hard to hear, *ca-whoooo… ca-whoooo…* (Gibbs *et al.*), and repeated for long periods, *c.*3 s apart.

INDIGO-CROWNED QUAIL-DOVE

Geotrygon purpurata Pl. 67

Identification 22–26cm. Plump and compact with very short tail. Forehead white, crown and nape rich indigo, malar to ear-coverts white, sub-malar line black, throat white, nape and neck-sides iridescent orange-bronze, upper mantle indigo, back, scapulars and lesser wing-coverts purple, wings purplish-umber with remiges dusky, rump to uppertail-coverts indigo, tail black; breast vinous grey, belly and sides white, flanks and thighs to undertail-coverts pale buffy. Female duller and lacks iridescence or lustre. Juvenile has grey forehead and facial pattern duller, feathers of upperparts fringed buff with dusky subterminal barring, and breast darker with faint barring. Unmistakable. From Olive-backed by clearly contrasting forehead and crown, and white belly. *Leptotila* share habits and habitat but are larger and paler, and white tips to tail diagnostic.

Ssp. Monotypic (W Co, NW Ec)

Habits Prefers to walk rather than fly, but if disturbed flushes to low perch.
Status Rare to uncommon in Ecuador, somewhat more common in Colombia.
Habitat Upper Tropical Zone, 600–1,100m. Dense understorey of undisturbed primary humid, montane forest.
Voice Not very vocal. Soft, hollow, rather weak *coo* in short series. First note very soft, rises in pitch, last note hard, *whot, whoo-oo-oit*, different from Sapphire Quail-Dove (Gibbs *et al.*, R&G).
Note Formerly considered conspecific with Sapphire Quail-Dove.

OLIVE-BACKED QUAIL-DOVE
Geotrygon veraguensis Pl. 67

Identification 21–24.5cm. Plump and compact with short tail and very dark plumage. White forehead, white face-sides with black malar line and white throat; neck, mantle and breast and sides deep purple with iridescence on neck; back and wings to tail purplish-umber, flanks to undertail-coverts rufous, barred chestnut, vent and thighs grey; eyes pale yellow, eye-ring carmine-red, bill black, legs and feet coral red. Female similar but buffy on forehead and throat, rather than white, dark body-sides extend to flanks. Juvenile like female but scalloped on wings and body with rufous fringes to feathers. From other quail-doves in range by dark breast and underparts.

Ssp. Monotypic (W Co, NW Ec)

Habits Very terrestrial, shy and inconspicuous, but apparently unsuspicious; will freeze at disturbance rather than flush, and walks away rather than taking wing. When flushed flies further into undergrowth, taking flight with distinct wing-rattle (Wetmore in Goodwin).
Status Declining due to deforestation. Rare to locally frequent in Ecuador, uncommon and local in Colombia.
Habitat Lower Tropical Zone, to 900m. Principally in undisturbed primary forest. Prefers dense tangled undergrowth and ravines with dense vegetation, near streams, but will enter advanced secondary growth adjacent to forest.
Voice Not very vocal. Series of deep, resonant mournful coos, repeated about every 5 s, *woOOOouu*, not very different from Ruddy (Gibbs *et al.*). Low, resonant ventriloquial *thum* or *kuunk*, like distant frog (Stiles & Skutch 1989).

RUSSET-CROWNED QUAIL-DOVE
Geotrygon goldmani Pl. 67

Identification 26.5–28cm. Plump and compact, with heavy and longer tail than usual for genus. Crown and nape bright orange-rufous, head-sides rufescent becoming pale grey to whitish on throat with a bold black malar line to neck-sides terminating in a small white triangle; rest of upperparts umber-brown with small patches of golden-bronze iridescence on nape and lustrous purple wash to mantle, but primary-coverts and remiges fuscous; underparts pale grey to belly, pale cinnamon on flanks and thighs to undertail-coverts; eyes red, inner eye-ring reddish but grey on outer part, bill black, legs and feet rose-red. Female duller and lacks iridescence and lustre. Juvenile similar but brown where adult is orange-rufous and is duller grey over entire face, moustachial line shorter, and no white triangle.

Ssp. *G. g. goldmani* (NW Co)

Habits Apparently typical *Geotrygon* in habits, but very poorly known.
Status Apparently scarce in Colombia, with few records.
Habitat Upper Tropical Zone, normally at 750–1,500m, but reported lower and higher. Undisturbed primary forest.
Voice A hollow, cooing sound and long series of low-pitched soft hollow coos, *wa-oooooo*, repeated every 5–7 s (Gibbs *et al.*).

LINED QUAIL-DOVE
Geotrygon linearis Pl. 67

Identification 27–29cm. Forehead warm buffy, becoming umber on crown and nape with a slight purple or bronze-green iridescence; postocular band of pale grey to sides of nape; reddish-brown above with purple iridescence on mantle; narrow black line from base of bill through eye to upper ear-coverts, and broader blackish line from base of bill (sub-malar) below cheeks and ear-coverts to base of nape; breast grey, pale buffy from belly to undertail-coverts with darker greyish-buff wash on flanks. Female similar but has brown-washed breast. Juvenile more rufescent throughout with soft and subtle barring. Larger than other quail-doves, and the only species at higher altitudes in range; when flushed flies higher, up to *c.*15m above ground. Fairly uniform brown but grey flush to nape and breast.

Ssp. *G. l. linearis* (Ve, Co) as described
G. l. trinitatis (E Ve, Tr, To) like *linearis* but decidedly smaller with considerably weaker legs and toes; hindneck chocolate-brown, slightly darker than nape; mantle has bronze-green iridescence; upperwing-coverts and outer webs of remiges less rufescent, being olive to cinnamon-brown; flanks pale brown, and underwing-coverts less rufous
G. l. infusca (C & NE Co, NW Ve) like *linearis* but decidedly paler above with crown cinnamon to light grey, paler purple wash on back; tail less rufescent, rear underparts washed orange-cinnamon

Habits Usually in dense undergrowth, but occasionally at forest edge.
Status Frequent in Colombia and Venezuela, local and scarce

in Trinidad, very rare, possibly extinct on Tobago, where formerly bred.

Habitat Subtropical Zone, 1,500–2,500m. In north-east Venezuela and on Trinidad above 550m, but on Tobago regularly down to *c.*200m. Undisturbed humid, primary and wet forest, including cloud forest. Sings from high perch, but when disturbed, falls silent and glides to forest floor.

Voice Deep hollow *ooUUoo* repeated *c.*20 times per minute. Presumed females have higher pitched version and 2 birds duet. Song resembles Ruddy Quail-Dove and typical *Leptotila*, but lacks booming resonance of latter (Hilty). Long series of deep, hollow *whaoook* or *oooouk* at 15–20 s intervals; recalls Band-tailed Pigeon but steady repetition reveals *Geotrygon* character (Gibbs *et al.*).

Note Generally considered monotypic (e.g. Baptista *et al.*, Gibbs *et al.*, Dickinson).

WHITE-THROATED QUAIL-DOVE

Geotrygon frenata Pl. 67

Identification 30–34cm. Large, large-tailed, plump and compact. Male has forehead flesh-coloured, grading into grey crown to nape, black line through lores to rear ear-coverts, which are flesh colour, black malar line, white throat; neck-sides of stiffened feathers are basally umber and terminally blue-grey, with iridescence, and continue across upper breast as a grey bar; underparts pale buffy, feathers of breast and sides with broad whitish fringes; upperparts reddish-umber; eyes yellow, eye-ring red, bill black, legs and feet coral. Female has shorter black line through eyes, pink of face duller, reduced grey scalloping on neck-sides, and breast entirely buffy with pale whitish fringes; eye-ring orange. Juvenile ruddy brown above, slightly rufescent on head and barred evenly but faintly cinnamon; underparts cinnamon, slightly darker on breast, barred brown from lower throat to flanks; eye-ring orange.

Ssp. *G. f. bourcieri* (W Co, W Ec) as described
G. f. erythropareia (E Ec) more rufescent above and darker, browner below
G. f. subgrisea (Ec: W Loja) paler forecrown than *bourcieri*

Habits Typical *Geotrygon* behaviour. Readily flushes to low branches.

Status Widespread, but probably under-reported. Uncommon to locally frequent in Ecuador, uncommon in Colombia.

Habitat Upper Tropical to Temperate Zones, 900–3,000m, more usually 1,500–2,500m. Seems to prefer undisturbed dense understorey of primary humid montane forest.

Voice Calls from perch, at mid level or higher. More often heard than seen. Low-pitched, hollow call, every few seconds, *Haooooo* or *waooooo* (Gibbs *et al.*), *hooop* (R&G) or *hoo-hooo* (F&K).

Note Races *bourcieri* and *erythropareia* possibly species (S&M), but latter perhaps dark morph of *bourcieri* (Baptista *et al.*, R&G).

VIOLACEOUS QUAIL-DOVE

Geotrygon violacea Pl. 67

Identification 21–24.5cm. Greyish head, paler on forehead, cheeks and throat, pinkish-violet flush to nape, neck-sides and breast, rest of underparts whitish; iridescent bright violet on mantle and upper back, rest of back to tail and wings reddish-brown; eyes orange-brown, eye-ring red, bill carmine-red, legs and feet coral red. Female duller, less violet on back and darker grey on nape. Juvenile orange-rufous on breast, wing-feathers have rufous fringes. Note lack of malar stripe, white belly, bright violet gloss to mantle. Ruddy more reddish-brown above and lacks violaceous iridescence on mantle. Rather like *Leptotila* but lacks white tip to tail.

Ssp. *G. v. albiventer* (Co: Santa Marta, Ve) bluish-grey crown, bluer gloss on breast and back
G. v. violacea (NE Ec, Su) as described

Habits More likely to be seen in trees than other *Geotrygon*. Quiet when flushed, no wing-whirr.

Status Very rare in Ecuador (only a 1992 sight and tape record). In Colombia, local and very uncommon to rare. In Venezuela, uncommon and local. Status uncertain in Suriname.

Habitat Lower Tropical Zone to 1,200m, but recorded to 1,650m. Tolerates some disturbance and will colonise dense second growth and derelict cacao plantations, etc. Heavily shaded undergrowth. In agricultural areas may feed at edge of thicker scrubby growth.

Voice Low *HOOoo*, with last part falling in pitch as if swallowed; higher and mellower than most quail-doves (Hilty). Hollow-sounding *haaoooo* or *woooo* lasting 3–5 s, close to Sapphire Quail-Dove (Gibbs *et al.*).

RUDDY QUAIL-DOVE

Geotrygon montana Pl. 67

Identification 21–24.5cm. Crown violaceous grey, darkening on nape and mantle, and onto breast; back, wings and tail umber with violaceous iridescence; face-sides pale buffy with iridescent carmine-red malar line; underparts whitish; eyes orange-brown, eye-ring red, bill carmine with black tip, legs and feet coral red. Female olive-brown above without violaceous gloss or iridescence, malar line olive-brown; throat pale buffy, breast pale olivaceous becoming buff on belly to undertail-coverts. Juvenile is a duller and slightly more ochraceous version of female, with reddish-brown fringes to upperparts. Sympatric with many other *Geotrygon*; distinguished by reddish-brown plumage and red moustachial line.

Ssp. *G. m. montana* (throughout) those in Tr are intermediate between *montana* and larger, darker *martinica* of Lesser Antilles

Status Widespread, but irregular movements poorly understood (possibly nomadic?). Uncommon to frequent in Ecuador, frequent to common, but quite local in Colombia, uncommon in Venezuela, Guyana and Trinidad (no records Tobago), and French Guiana.

Habitat Tropical Zone, occasionally to Subtropical Zone. Generally to 600m, but 1,900m in Venezuela and 2,600m in Colombia. Regularly forages at woodland edges, and inhabits dense second growth and open woodland, coffee and cacao plantations.

Voice Series of soft, resonant, descending, almost moaning, monosyllabic, cow-like coos; *waooo*, or *wooo* (Gibbs *et al.)*, *oooOOoou* (Hilty), *oooo* (R&G), *hooooooooo* or low *mmmmmm* (F&K).

PSITTACIDAE – Parrots

Parrots are distributed throughout the world's tropics, and some have even extended into colder areas of the Southern Hemisphere. Feral populations in northern countries are also showing they can take the cold, with Ring-necked Parakeets in England for example. Parrots range from very large to very small. Here, the entire family is drawn to the same scale, thus the range can be readily seen between a tiny *Forpus* parrotlet (Plate 74) and the *Ara* macaws (Plate 68). With few exceptions, they are long-winged, fast flyers that often commute long distances from roosting or nest sites to foraging areas. Birds with such behaviour are more often seen early morning and early evening as they fly overhead. Movements are usually driven by fruiting seasons – which can be irregular, and irruptive – leading to speculation about migration, and are generally poorly understood. Parrots are brightly coloured but at the same time astonishingly cryptic. Birds that one moment are noisy and noticeable will suddenly vanish into a canopy, where they forage silently, occasionally maintaining a quiet'conversation'. In fact they may only betray their presence to the would-be observer by dropping half-eaten fruit. Most have ear-splitting shrieks that function as contact calls as they fly high over savanna or forest. Yet in captivity these coarsely raucous birds often learn to utter musical notes, tunes, words and even songs. Most suffer from trapping for the pet trade, some to the point of severe persecution, and several are on the verge of extinction because of this. The custom of cutting tall palms in which there is a nest hole, in order to take the nestlings, is a terribly destructive action that not only removes birds from the wild, but puts a valuable nest site out of repeated future use. With nesting periods lasting as long as 15 weeks, this makes the nests – and the birds – very vulnerable. Juveniles generally have brown irides.

Additional references used for this family include Forshaw & Cooper (1989, hereafter F), Collar (1997), Juniper & Parr (1998, shown here as J&P) and Forshaw (2006).

Macaws are the most dramatic and easily recognisable of the entire family. They are large with long wings and long tails, and fly high overhead, with strong, steady wingbeats. With the exception of Red-and-green Macaw, their tails in flight have a pulsating undulating motion very different from any other long-tailed parrot. Invariably, they fly in pairs or a few pairs together, each pair in echelon, with the female slightly ahead. They shriek in contact as they fly. At times macaws may be seen flying in the heat of the day as they go to rest on the shaded boughs below the canopy of a great tree. They are birds of the Tropical Zone, few occurring above 500m. Macaws lay 2–3 eggs, and the first youngster will fledge 13 weeks after hatching. The parents stop visiting the nest after the first young fledges, and the third chick often dies of starvation if it is too small or behind the others to leave the nest itself. Macaws will gather in large numbers on cliff faces where there is exposed, mineral-rich soil to eat.

BLUE-AND-YELLOW MACAW
Ara ararauna Pl. 68

Identification 75–87cm. Unmistakable, large blue-and-yellow macaw. Forehead green, rest of upperparts rich blue, chin black, underparts rich yellow to flanks, including underwing, blue undertail-coverts, and underside of tail yellow.

Ssp. Monotypic (E Ec, Co, E&S Ve, S Gu, Su, FG)

Habits Usually in pairs or family parties of 3–4 or in small flocks. Often heard before seen overhead as they commute to distant feeding areas. Usually feeds silently in canopy, but may visit ground to pick fallen palm fruits or mangos. Roosts communally, sometimes in large numbers (e.g. in the Orinoco delta).

Status Locally fairly common in eastern Ecuador, locally frequent in Colombia, locally frequent to common in eastern and southern Venezuela, but extinct in Trinidad (no records Tobago), widespread in Guyana, local and now uncommon to rare in Suriname and French Guiana. Thriving number of feral birds in Caracas, Venezuela; not known whether breeding.

Habitat Mangroves, boggy stands of *Mauritia* palm, riparian and swampy areas in lowland forests, *várzea*, edges of gallery forests. In northern Colombia (foothills of Perijá and Santa Marta), dry areas in deciduous forests.

Voice Varied loud shrieking cries, some slightly quivering, *raaaaa, raaaaa... kraaaa, kraaaa...* (R&G), a frequent, penetrating *kewaaaaaaa* (Sick) and a typical flight-call, a rising *raaak* (Munn, in Hilty).

MILITARY MACAW *Ara militaris* Pl. 68

Identification 70–85cm. Forehead red, head green with a bluish tone, mostly on nape, back, inner wing-coverts and innermost secondaries green, outer wing-coverts, remiges, rump and uppertail-coverts blue, basal half of tail red, with a band of green and distal third blue; throat flushed dusky, then green from head to flanks, undertail-coverts blue and undertail yellow. From sympatric all-green macaws by much larger size. Very similar to allopatric Great Green Macaw, but has more prominent bluish tinge on hindneck, smaller all-black bill, dull red base to tail. In flight, Military Macaw has green underwing-coverts and yellowish underside to flight-feathers giving 2-tone effect.

Ssp. *A. m. militaris* (E Ec, Co, NW Ve)

Habits Communal roosts on cliffs and large trees.

Status Vulnerable. Very rare to uncommon everywhere (almost extinct in Ecuador) except northern slope of Santa Marta massif, in Colombia, where fairly common. Major movements, e.g. crossing Andes in Colombia, associated with fruiting seasons.

Habitat All forest-types in foothills of Andes, usually to 600m but to 2,000m in Colombia.

Voice Loud, strident cries audible over some distance, including a harsh *wa-a-ahk*, a drawn-out, raucous *cr-a-a-a-ak* or *kraaak!* (Hilty) and a shrieking *dree-eee-ahy* (J&P), with the most frequent call a loud *rraaah!* (R&G).

GREAT GREEN MACAW

Ara ambiguus Pl. 68

Identification 80–90cm. Forehead red, head, back, inner wing-coverts and innermost secondaries green, outer wing-coverts, remiges, rump and uppertail-coverts blue, basal half of tail orange-red, with a band of green and distal third blue; throat flushed dusky, then green from head to flanks, undertail-coverts blue and undertail yellow. Immature has yellow tip to tail. Very similar to smaller, allopatric Military, but red forehead patch larger, green on head and shoulders have very little bluish tinge, pale tip to proportionately larger bill, and orange base to tail. In flight, Great Green Macaw has all-yellow underwings.

Ssp. *A. a. ambiguus* (NW Co) as described
A. g. guayaquilensis (W Ec) smaller bill

Habits Often flies between forest patches.

Status Vulnerable. Generally common, but retreating due to habitat destruction, and very rare in Ecuador.

Habitat Humid, lower montane forests, usually evergreen, generally in wetter areas than Military Macaw. Recorded in deciduous forest in Ecuador.

Voice Loud, raucous squawks and growls, including *aaaahrk* and *aowrk*. A creaking, groaning *aaa*. Voice is deeper, more resonant and far-carrying than Scarlet (J&P).

SCARLET MACAW *Ara macao* Pl. 68

Identification 80–96cm. Large prominent forehead to mantle scarlet-red, and lines of tiny feathers on white facial skin, also red, underparts to flanks red, lesser wing-coverts red; lower scapulars and median wing-coverts green, rest of wings blue, deeper on primaries; rump, upper- and undertail-coverts cerulean-blue, tail red with fine blue fringes to feathers and dark blue tip. Immature has shorter tail. Large, mostly red, similar in size to widely sympatric Red-and-green, which is slimmer, has all-white facial skin, and broad yellow bar on upperwing-coverts.

Ssp. *A. m. macao* (Ve, Tr, Gu, Su, FG)

Habits Note that tail undulates in flight – a sure discriminator from Red-and-green.

Status Uncommon in Venezuela, sight records only in Trinidad, frequent in Guyana, scarce in Suriname and French Guiana.

Habitat Humid *terra firme* forests, evergreen forest and sometimes in savanna. Tolerant of a fairly wide range of habitats, though prefers undisturbed areas. Often near exposed riverbanks and riverine forest, especially in the Guianas.

Voice Coarse, strident shrieks and squawks, including *rrraaaaa*, a rasping *reck*, *raak* and *rowwwka*, and a harsh growling *scree-e-e-e-t*, a harsh *RAAAAH*, and generally very grating (Sick, Hilty, R&G, J&P).

RED-AND-GREEN MACAW

Ara chloropterus Pl. 68

Identification 75–97cm. From forehead to mantle, scapulars, lesser wing-coverts and underparts to flanks scarlet-red; median and greater wing-coverts yellow with green tips, rest of wing from alula to tertials deep royal blue; rump, upper- and undertail-coverts warm pastel blue, tail red, finely fringed blue, grading to reddish-orange towards end, with a pastel blue tip. Large, mostly red, similar to widely sympatric Scarlet Macaw, which has rows of tiny red feathers on white facial skin, green on upperwing-coverts (although young may show some yellow) and tail tipped blue.

Ssp. Monotypic (all mainland countries)

Habits Note that, unlike Scarlet, tail of Red-and-green does not undulate in flight, but is held rigid. This is a sure in-flight diagnostic.

Status Generally uncommon, even in undisturbed areas: rare and very local in Ecuador, in steep decline in Colombia, heavily persecuted in Venezuela, uncommon in Guyana, but still fairly widespread in interior Suriname and French Guiana.

Habitat *Terra firme* forest, humid lowland evergreen forest, but also sometimes in deciduous forest and gallery woodland in savannas and *llanos*.

Voice Powerful, but less harsh than Scarlet, including a very low, strident raw. A prolonged *ahhra*, a harsh *screeee-ah* and *arAT arAT!* (Sick, J&P, R&G). Like Scarlet but higher pitched and with a falsetto note in middle and slight musical hiccup at end, thus *kaarRRRR UL-a* or *kaaarRRRR O-E-a*, last 2–3 notes high-pitched and slurred (Hilty).

CHESTNUT-FRONTED MACAW

Ara severus Pl. 69

Identification 40–49cm. Medium-sized macaw with long, pointed tail. Skin on face white with rows of tiny black feathers. Forehead deep brown, crown green with bluish tinge most noticeable on nape, back, most of wings, rump and uppertail-coverts, and entire underparts green, except red thighs, deep red underwings with greater coverts brown; corner of wing at carpal, and tip of blue alula bright red, outermost median, most outer greater coverts, secondaries and primaries blue; tail green with clear blue edges and reddish flush either side of shaft of central pair, distal quarter blue; undertail-coverts have bluish centres, undertail dull red; eyes yellow, cere white, bill black. Juvenile has rounder head and lacks blue flush. Similar Red-bellied Macaw has green underwing-coverts and yellowish-olive underwing.

Ssp. *A. s. severus* (Co, Ve, Gu, Su, FG) as described
A. s. castaneifrons (Ec) variably slightly larger

Habits Normally in pairs or groups of several pairs –

occasionally large flocks. More likely to be active during day than other macaws. Flight fast and direct, with wingbeats faster than those of larger macaws – diagnostic when flying high overhead – and regular loud, raucous calls.
Status Widespread in Ecuador, common in Colombia and Venezuela, somewhat irregular in the Guianas, and very rare in French Guiana.
Habitat Generally, forest edges and forest with clearings, second growth, swamp forest with dead trees, *várzea*, wetlands with *Mauritia* palms, gallery forest and savanna with pastures and adjacent trees. Successional growth along rivers and palm-rich borders of slow-moving rivers.
Voice Particularly vocal and typically macaw-like in flight, when gives a *ghehh*, a raspy scream, and scratchy *jaiii* or *kwaaa*. When perched, calls quieter and less harsh, and rather laugh-like including, e.g. *kurrit*, *ka-dak*, *ka-dak*, *keeka*, *keeka*, *keeka* and other cackling notes (J&P, R&G, Sick, Hilty).
Note Differences between subspecies slight and clinal, and species perhaps best regarded as monotypic.

RED-BELLIED MACAW

Ara manilata Pl. 69

Identification 44–50cm. Medium-sized macaw with creamy-yellowish face and cere. Forehead turquoise with yellow shafts on head-sides of head, and grades into green mantle and most of wings; alula, primary-coverts, outermost greater coverts and primaries blue, green underwing-coverts and yellowish-olive underwing, rump to tail green, undertail yellow; throat and breast lavender grey, thighs largely red, flanks to undertail-coverts green; eyes dark, fairly small bill black. Female lacks yellow shafts on head-sides and has less bluish flush. Juvenile has even less blue and a horn-coloured tip to bill. From similar Chestnut-fronted Macaw by green underwing and more streamlined flight profile.

Ssp. Monotypic (Co, Ve, Tr, Gu, Su, FG)

Habits Gregarious, may associate with Orange-winged Amazons and Chestnut-fronted Macaws.
Status Scarce and local in Trinidad (no records Tobago), uncommon in Colombia, Venezuela and Guyana, scarce in Suriname but locally common in coastal French Guiana. Some seasonal movements, but not well understood.
Habitat Sandy savannas and wet areas, swampy and seasonally flooded land, wherever *Mauritia* palms grow, as it is dependent on them for food. Usually below 500 m.
Voice Calls more high-pitched than other macaws and include a repeated *kree-ee-ee* or *kree-ee-ak*, a plaintive, wailing *choiiiaaa* in flight and a loud *sreeet* (Remsen in H&B, R&G, J&P, Hilty).
Note Placed in genus *Orthopsittaca* by some authors, following Sick (1990).

RED-SHOULDERED MACAW

Diopsittaca nobilis Pl. 69

Identification 30cm. The smallest macaw. Adult all green with strong bluish tinge to forehead, red shoulder and carpal on upper wing, extending to underwing-coverts, underside of wing and tail yellowish-olive; cere and skin around eyes and base of bill white, eyes reddish-brown, bill black. Juvenile has less blue on forehead and a horn-coloured bill. Distinct yellow-and-red underwing pattern, tricoloured yellow/red/green in juveniles.

Ssp. *A. n. nobilis* (E Ve, Gu, Su, FG)

Habits Very gregarious, often in large flocks outside breeding season. Locally regarded as a pest, as it feeds on cereal crops and cultivated fruit. Swift flight and weaves through trees, dashing across open spaces at speed.
Status Locally common in Guyana and Suriname, scarce in French Guiana, reported from Trinidad, but assumed to be escapes. Everywhere under great pressure from trappers. Some seasonal movements, but not well understood.
Habitat Variety of rather open woodland, savannas with scattered bushes and palms, sandy soil forests, marshy areas with palms and cultivated areas. A constant feature of preferred habitat is presence of palms, especially *Mauritia*, *Orbignya martiana* and *Maximiliana maripa*.
Voice Noisy and especially vocal in flight. Calls include high-pitched *kreeek-kreeek* and a throatier *ahk-ahk-ahk-ahk-ahk*, often delivered in bursts. Also, a loud honking *yaark yaark… yaark yaark…* At times sounds like an *Aratinga*, and may be mistaken in the field for this genus. A soft nasal, rather high neee given constantly by flocks (Hilty).

> Rose-ringed or Ring-necked Parakeet is an exotic established in Caracas, Venezuela. Originally from the Indian subcontinent, it is a popular species in the international cagebird trade. In the early 1980s a few escaped birds settled in the Parque del Este in the east of the city and after a 20-year period of establishment are now showing signs of spreading west along the valley of Caracas.

ROSE-RINGED PARAKEET

Psittacula krameri Pl. 69

Identification 40cm. Rather macaw-like but slimmer and more streamlined. Look for proportionately large head, long slender wings, long, thin, tapering tail and narrow black 'necklace'. Entirely bright green with nape and neck-sides lightly washed turquoise, narrow yellow nuchal collar bordered in front by a black line that becomes a full bib; primaries blackish, tail washed turquoise; eyes yellow, eye-ring red, cere white, bill bright red on upper mandible, all-black lower, legs and feet grey. Female lacks black chin and yellow-and-black collar. Juvenile has all-green head and is separated from female by yellow eye-ring and flesh-coloured bill.

Ssp. *P. k. manillensis* (Ve, Cu, Bo)

Habits Forages and perches in canopy. Flies fast, straight. Quite noisy – either screeches in frequent squabbles with others, or chatters softly or gives variety of whistles. Roosts communally and nests in tree holes, often in holes on dead palms.
Status Introduced. Population slowly expanding, and now

very locally common in central and north-east of Caracas. In Curaçao, a small flock survived briefly, but has apparently declined, and does not appear established there, although small group is now present on Bonaire. Race(s) there unknown.
Habitat Very adaptable. Prefers semi-open areas with deciduous or humid light woodland, or scattered stands of trees or scrub; urban parks and gardens, orchards.
Voice Calls include a chatter, a flight-call of up to 6 repetitions of a shrill *kee-ak* and a *kreh-kreh-kreh-kreh*... from gathered flocks (J&P).

Aratinga are medium-sized, noisy, largely green parakeets (or conures) with long tails and conspicuous bare ocular skin. They are most often seen in noisy, chattering flocks, sometimes flying quite high. A small flock will fly through trees in an open area, swooping to land in a copse and disappearing completely to forage in silence. Mainly lowland birds of light forest and woodland, and usually seen in pairs or small groups, but they often travel and forage in large flocks when not breeding. Their movements are poorly understood.

BLUE-CROWNED PARAKEET

Aratinga acuticaudata Pl. 70

Identification 33–38cm. Essentially green with a bluish forehead, underwing-coverts green but underwing yellow-olive; undertail dull rusty-orange with red on basal inner webs. On specimens from Venezuela, we found 3 different bill colours: in northern cordillera all yellow, in west (Zulia) flesh-coloured with black tip, and in south (Apure) greyish-horn; eyes orange to yellow, orbital skin very pale grey. Juvenile has no blue on forehead and has more yellow-olive undertail. Only *Aratinga* with blue forehead and crown, although blue not always easy to see in field and is much reduced in immature.

Ssp. *A. a. koenigi* (NE Co, N Ve) has less red to inner webs of undertail
A. a. neoxena (Ve: Margarita I.) paler, more powdery blue on forehead, breast and abdomen bluish-green

Habits Forages on seeds and fruit, in trees and on ground, and may appear at crops in numbers.
Status Fairly common in Colombia and Venezuela, but highly seasonal and variable; race *neoxena* on Margarita seriously threatened by trapping and nest robbing.
Habitat Tropical to Lower Subtropical Zones. Generally in dry to arid country, deciduous forest, gallery forest, *cerrado*, open savanna with *Mauritia* palms, cactus scrub, cultivated areas and pastures. Generally to 600m.
Voice Loud, rapidly repeated *cheeah-cheeah*, unlike Brown-throated Parakeet, which is often in same habitat (J&P, H&B).
Note Arndt (1996) described *koenigi*, based on disjunct distribution (north Venezuela and north-east Colombia) and plumage differences.

SCARLET-FRONTED PARAKEET

Aratinga wagleri Pl. 70

Identification 36cm. All green, paler on underparts, especially undertail-coverts, underwing-coverts also green (no red), underwing and undertail dull, slightly olivaceous green; red forehead and crown extends beyond eyes (but not on lores or orbital skin), and red thighs; eyes yellow, orbital skin white, bill pale horn. Juvenile has red on forehead, not on crown, brown eyes and grey orbital skin. From Blue-crowned by red on head, but also different habitat. From adult Red-masked by less red on head, never on cheeks; may be confused with juvenile Red-masked (see plate), but note ranges.

Ssp. *A. w. frontata* (SW Ec) red on head covers lores and superciliary, also red on carpal and alula, more extensive red on thighs; more evenly green below
A. w. transilis (E Co?, N Ve) almost entirely uniform green, red on crown as *wagleri* but does not extend beyond eyes, irregular red breast-band
A. w. wagleri (W & N Co, NW Ve) as described

Habits Always noisy. Chattering commuting flocks often very noticeable.
Status Locally common, but very variable and movements not well understood. Rare and local in Ecuador, fairly common but declining in Colombia, and locally fairly common in Venezuela.
Habitat Upper Tropical and Subtropical Zones, sometimes reaching Temperate Zone, generally to 2,000m. Humid montane forest, including cloud forest, second growth with *Acacia*, *Prosopis* and *Ochroma*, but prefers virgin forest, though visits orchards, even parks and gardens. Key requirement is accessibility of cliffs for roosting and nesting sites.
Voice Loud and strident, a high-pitched *steak* or *chee-ey*, sometimes repeated. Rather like voice of Red-masked Parakeet (J&P, R&G, Hilty).
Notes Subspecies *frontata* may be a separate species, Cordilleran Parakeet (S&M). Presence of *transilis* in eastern Colombia based on a single specimen, of doubtful identification (Meyer de Schauensee 1949, J&P); *transilis* considered possibly conspecific with Mitred Parakeet *A. mitrata*, from Peru south (Collar). Called Red-fronted Conure in J&P.

RED-MASKED PARAKEET

Aratinga erythrogenys Pl. 70

Identification 33cm. All green with red head, carpal and alula, and thighs, dull yellowish undertail and underwing; eyes orange-yellow, orbital skin white, bill pale horn. Juvenile has green head with red flecks, green thighs; eyes light brown. From partially sympatric race *frontata* of Scarlet-fronted Parakeet by red underwing-coverts.

Ssp. Monotypic (W Ec)

Habits Noisy, especially in flight.
Status Locally fairly common but declining (Near Threatened).
Habitat Lower Tropical Zone, usually below 1,000m, but

recorded to 2,500m. Wide range of habitats from humid evergreen to dry deciduous forests. Often in dry thorn and cactus scrub, farmland and even sparsely vegetated desert. May be seen around urban areas.
Voice Calls include varied nasal and rasping cries, usually bisyllabic with second note longer than first: *sceee-ah* or *squeee-ee-at* and *screee-screéah* or *scrah-scrah-scra-scra* (R&G, Hilty, J&P).

WHITE-EYED PARAKEET
Aratinga leucophthalma Pl. 70

Identification 32–35cm. All green, slightly paler below, with flecks of bright red on head-sides and along carpal and edge of forewing, olivaceous yellow underwing and undertail; eyes orange-yellow, orbital skin white, bill pale horn. From other *Aratinga* by red-and-yellow underwing-coverts.

Ssp. *A. l. callogenys* (SE Co, E Ec) larger and darker, with a heavier bill
A. l. leucophthalma (E Ve, Gu, Su, FG) as described
A. l. nicefori (E Co) paler and more yellowish; red band on forehead

Habits Gregarious and often mixes with other *Aratinga* and Chestnut-fronted Macaws when foraging. Commonly occurs in flocks of up to a few dozen, but even to several hundred. Roosts in large communal gatherings in trees.
Status Uncommon to locally common in Ecuador, common in Colombia, Venezuela and Guyana, and locally common in Suriname and French Guiana.
Habitat Tropical Zone. At edges of all types of lowland forest, *Mauritia* palm groves, seasonally flooded *várzea* forest along rivers, and forest openings.
Voice Wide variety of loud, raspy shrieking calls similar to Red-masked (R&G), also a loud penetrating *neeep neeep,* shrieking *scree-ah screet scree* and a scolding, grating *scraaah scraaah* (J&P), *geeait* or *jeeee-it*, sometimes in long series', much coarser and raspier than corresponding call of Dusky-headed Parakeet (H&B).
Notes Considerable disparity between J&P and Collar on both subspecies and distribution. Race *nicefori* described from a single specimen.

SUN PARAKEET *Aratinga solstitialis* Pl. 70

Identification 30cm. Adult mainly yellow with rich golden-orange tones to front of head and belly; tertials, basal half of greater wing-coverts and tail green, primaries black with solid green patch in centre; underwing-coverts yellow, underwing and undertail grey, tail green with black tip; eyes brown, orbital skin bluish-grey, bill black. Juvenile has green-streaked crown to nape, back and wings green with yellow fringes to feathers, rump and tail-coverts pale green. Unmistakable with bright yellow body, blue-and-green wings and tail.

Ssp. Monotypic (SE Ve?, S Gu, S Su, S FG)

Habits Small noisy flocks melt into foliage when they alight, despite the bright colouring.
Status Very rare in Venezuela, only seen near Santa Elena and sighting contested on grounds of habitat. Local and uncommon in Guyana, only in extreme south of Suriname, but common on Sipaliwini. Accidental in coastal French Guiana.
Habitat Tropical Zone. Savanna and dry forest with *Mauritia* palms and scattered scrub.
Voice A high, shrill grating 2-note *screek-screek*, repeated 3–6 times in rapid succession between pauses. Also, wheezy notes and chuckling sounds. A high-pitched wheezy note, and when perched may emit typical chuckling sounds (H&M, J&P).
Note Has been treated as conspecific with Jandaya Parakeet *A. jandaya*, from north-east Brazil, but best regarded as forming a superspecies (Collar).

DUSKY-HEADED PARAKEET
Aratinga weddellii Pl. 70

Identification 28cm. Head brownish-grey with paler fringes to feathers, rest of body and wings green, slightly brighter and paler below, primaries fuscous with green patch in centre, underwing-coverts bright green, underwing and undertail dark grey; eyes white, orbital skin white, cere flesh-coloured, bill dark grey. Juvenile as adult but has brown eyes. Only *Aratinga* with a (brownish) grey head, and lacks any conspicuous colour in wings.

Ssp. Monotypic (E Ec, SE Co)

Habits Large flocks at abundant food sources, and gathers at mineral soil banks. Often perches where it can be easily seen and less wary than most *Aratinga*. Flies low, just above canopy.
Status Fairly common in Ecuador, common in Colombia.
Habitat Lower Tropical Zone to 750m. Forest edges and open areas, especially *várzea* and floodplain forest, remnants of humid savanna and semi-cleared land. Seen in coffee and sugarcane plantations.
Voice Usually silent at rest, and vocal in flight. Calls include a nasal *je-eek*, 4–5 shrill yapping notes which produce a continuous shrieking when flock in unison (F), similar to White-eyed Parakeet, but less grating, slightly smoother (R&G, H&B, J&P).

PEACH-FRONTED PARAKEET
Aratinga aurea Pl. 71

Identification 28cm. Forehead to point on crown rich orange, surrounded by blue that grades into green on nape and brownish-grey on ear-coverts, back to tail green with rich blue secondaries and primary-coverts, primaries darker blue with green patch in centre; breast mid brown, belly and sides to undertail-coverts pale green, underwing and undertail olivaceous yellow; eyes orange, orbital skin orange, bill black. Juvenile similar but eyes brown and orbital skin grey.

Ssp. Monotypic (S Su)

Habits Generally in small, noisy flocks. Spends much of day in trees and bushes or on ground foraging. Plumage of underparts often soiled and abraded from contact with ground (F). Fairly tame and permits close approach.
Status Common in the Sipaliwini savanna in extreme southern

Suriname, where seems to replace Brown-throated Parakeet; uncertain in SW French Guiana.

Habitat Tropical Zone. Open wooded savanna, *Mauritia* palm groves.

Voice Only voice recorded in our region is a shrill screech, given in flight.

BROWN-THROATED PARAKEET

Aratinga pertinax Pl. 71

Identification 25cm. Essentially green from forehead to tip of tail, variably suffused blue on front of head, and primaries green and blue; underparts have varying amount of grey to brown on face and breast, then pale green to undertail-coverts, underwing-coverts as sides, underwing drab greyish, undertail more yellowish; eyes brown, orbital skin and cere grey, bill varies from horn to black.

Ssp. *A. p. aeruginosa* (N Co, NW Ve) lores to ear-coverts deep umber with short pale shaft-lines, breast well defined pale brown; bill black

A. p. arubensis (Ar) narrow frontal bar by nostrils and medium-sized area surrounding eyes yellow, forehead slightly blue, lower cheeks and ear-coverts to upper breast pale greyish-brown, rest of underparts pale yellowish-green, flushed orange-buffy on belly; bill horn

A. p. chrysophrys (SE Ve) narrow frontal bar orange, crown blue, small area around eyes yellow, lores to ear-coverts and upper breast mid brown, lower breast paler, flushed blue on sides, orange central belly; bill dark grey

A. p. griseipecta (NE Co) lores dark grey, face-sides and ear-coverts mid grey, breast slightly paler, fades into green underparts; bill black

A. p. lehmanni (E Co, W Ve) large orange-yellow area around eyes, lower face-sides streaked brown and yellow, upper breast pale buffy-grey, lower breast green, flanks and belly yellowish-green, undertail-coverts pale green, bill larger, horn-coloured

A. p. margaritensis (Ve: Margarita I.) forehead, area around eyes and upper ear-coverts pale buffy-yellow, lower face-sides grade into breast and become buffy or pale brown, bill brown

A. p. pertinax (Cu) forehead to central crown, around eyes and ear-coverts to lower face and chin orange, breast grey; bill dark greyish-brown

A. p. surinama (NE Ve, Gu, Su) crown powdery blue, narrow frontal line to lores, behind eyes and upper ear-coverts to base of lower mandible rich orange, lower face-sides brown, paler on breast, central belly deep orange, bill dark greyish-brown

A. p. tortugensis (Ve: Tortuga I.) crown bluish, forehead, lores, upper cheeks and ear-coverts orange, lower face-sides and breast pale greyish-buffy, ear-coverts streaked brown, belly yellow with yellowish sides, lower belly orange; bill brownish-horn

A. p. venezuelae (NE & SE Ve) crown dull blue, paler on forehead, medium-sized, irregular area of orange around eyes, face-sides brown, slightly paler on breast; bill blackish; juvenile has whitish forehead with dusky crown, smaller, oval-shaped patch of yellow around eyes; eyes brown and bill dusky

A. p. xanthogenia (Bo) entire head, except narrow bluish-green strip from rear crown to nape, yellow, with orange flush to lores, cheeks, ear-coverts and chin, breast brownish-grey; bill brown; juvenile has orange restricted to forehead, lores, ear-coverts and base of lower mandible; eyes brown, bill brownish-horn

Habits Local name is Cara Sucia (dirty face), very apt as plumage of face and underparts often soiled and stained from contact with fruits. Occasionally in pairs but usually in groups to medium-sized flocks. Noisy in flight, invariably drawing attention as it passes, but usually silent at rest, and difficult to find amongst foliage.

Status Generally common to abundant, often the commonest parrot.

Habitat Tropical Zone. Wide variety of open, wooded habitats including edges of gallery forest, foothill secondary growth, cactus scrub, farmlands and cultivations (where can be a pest), plantations, orchards, parks and gardens. Benefits from forest clearance.

Voice Flight-calls include a constant high-pitched shrieking and harsh grating, *cherr-cheedit* and similar (J&P, H&B, Sick, F, H&M), and a harsh *chzak* or *chrr-chzek* (Hilty).

Note Both F and J&P suggest a thorough revision may reduce number of subspecies, as many are clinal. However, our review of a large series from Venezuelan and offshore populations, suggests races are well drawn, and that the species may be even more fragmented than currently recognised.

GOLDEN-PLUMED PARAKEET

Leptosittaca branickii Pl. 69

Identification 34–35cm. Essentially green, with orange lores and yellow to ear-coverts, the feathers forming a tuft that projects from the neck-sides, broad yellow band on belly with some orange and green fringes, yellow-olive underwing, dull orange-reddish undertail; eyes orange, orbital skin white, bill horn. Juvenile has yellow lores and normal yellow feathering on ear-coverts, belly band narrower and more splotched green; eyes brown, orbital skin grey, bill brown. Generally, the only large, long-tailed parakeet in its habitat; larger but similar Yellow-eared Parrot has far more yellow on head-sides, and a black bill.

Ssp. Monotypic (Ec, S Co)

Habits In pairs when breeding, otherwise small flocks. Vocal in flight but also after alighting in treetops, and often maintains 'conversations' while feeding.

Status Vulnerable. Scarce and local. Movements appear erratic and only recently understood, but undeniably connected to use of *Podocarpus* as source of food. Presence unpredictable.

Habitat Temperate Zone to Páramo, usually 2,400–3,400m. Cloud forest, treeline shrubbery, wherever there is *Podocarpus*. Apparently moves to higher elevations to feed in Ecuador, returning lower to roost, but reverse pattern in Colombia (J&P).
Voice Resembles small macaw or Red-fronted Parakeet (J&P). Calls include vibrant *chree-ah* or *kreeah!* shrieks, similar to Blue-headed Macaw *Ara couloni* (Peru), and a harsh *scraat* when feeding (J&P, R&G, F, H&B).
Note Sometimes placed in *Aratinga* (e.g. R. S. Ridgely in H&B) but usually separated on basis of voice and morphological differences (R&G).

YELLOW-EARED PARROT

Ognorhynchus icterotis Pl. 69

Identification 42cm. Heavy-bodied and macaw-like with a large black bill. Forehead rather macaw-like, clear yellow, lores and face-sides yellow, chin to flanks yellow, rest of body, wings and tail green, but underwing yellow-olive and undertail dull reddish; eyes orange, orbital skin grey, facial skin at base of bill orange-flesh, bill black. Juvenile has yellow of face pale leaf green and yellow of underparts less extensive; eyes duller, brownish-orange. Sympatric and rather similar but smaller Golden-plumed Parakeet has far less yellow on head-sides and a smaller, horn-coloured bill.

Ssp. Monotypic (N Ec, SW Co)

Habits Usually in pairs or small groups. Absolutely dependent on *Ceroxylon* wax palm for roosting and breeding.
Status Critically Endangered. Very rare and local. Movements tied to search for fruiting trees and presence of wax palms (Krabbe & Sornoza 1994, Salaman *et al.* 1999).
Habitat Upper Subtropical to Temperate Zones, usually 2,500–3,000m. Upper humid montane forest dominated by wax palms.
Voice Distinctive flight-call, nasal or goose-like *raanh*, and flocks utter continuous chatter or cacophony (F, H&B, R&G); unusually noisy when foraging and at rest, maintaining 'conversations' of chuckles, squawks and many different cries (P. G. W. Salaman, pers. comm.).

> *Pyrrhura* are small, richly coloured parakeets with small heads, rounded bodies and long tails with rounded tips. They have white eye-rings and reddish tails, and are mainly found in lowland humid forests. Gregarious, they move in small, conspicuously noisy flocks, but are very hard to see at rest or quietly foraging. Sometimes noisy when foraging, but fall silent, often freezing at sign of danger and utter some sharp cries instantly before taking-off. Their flight is swift, usually slightly undulating, and very agile, swerving and wheeling through and around trees. Tend to fly close to the canopy, or the ground when crossing open areas. In general, there is only ever a single species of *Pyrrhura* in a given area, thus their ranges almost fit together like a jigsaw puzzle.

PAINTED PARAKEET

Pyrrhura picta Pl. 71

Identification 22cm. Deep cerulean-blue forehead, grading on crown to reddish-umber on nape and face-sides, with deep maroon-red below eyes, and bold white ear-coverts, upperparts green, primaries largely blue with red wing bend, rump bright red, tail deep red with green wash at sides; breast deep umber, the feathers having broad white fringes affording a perfect scaling effect, flanks and undertail-coverts green, belly deep red; eyes dark, orbital ring white, bill black. Striking pale scales on breast, point of shoulders red, underwing-coverts green (Maroon-tailed has underwing-coverts red).

Ssp. *P. p. lucianii* (SE Ec, S Co) blue forehead very faint, red around eyes forms narrow band of crimson, ear-patch large and dusky green, tiny spot of red at bend of wing, belly patch deep red
P. p. picta (S Ve, Gu, Su, FG) as described

Habits Flocks forage high in canopy of forest interior. Roosts in cavities in rocks and trees.
Status Several disjunct populations. Presence of the *picta* superspecies in Ecuador recently confirmed by specimens (Loaiza *et al.* 2005). Uncommon in northern Colombia, but common in Venezuela, Guyana, Suriname and French Guiana.
Habitat Tropical Zone, generally 100–1,300m but recorded sea level to 2,000m. All forest-types from mature evergreen to second growth, including *terra firme* and seasonally flooded *várzea*, sand ridge and sandy soil forests, also occasionally in partially cleared areas.
Voice Harsh, powerful calls include a descending *ee-ee-m* in flight and single *eeek* in contact. Solitary birds call *peea* to relocate flock. Flight-call *pik-pik* or *pik-pik-pik*. Several notes when perched including *kleek-kleek* and other soft 'conversational' notes (F, H&B, H&M, Sick, J&P, Hilty).
Note Populations in Ecuador were identified as *P.* (*p.*) *peruviana*, rather than *lucianii*, by Loaiza *et al.* (2005), and both these forms were elevated to species level by Joseph (2002), who also redrew the ranges of the parakeets, restricting *lucianii* to central-western Brazil, with *peruviana* in north-west Amazonia.

TODD'S PARAKEET

Pyrrhura caeruleiceps Pl. 71

Identification 22cm. Cerulean-blue forehead and crown, maroon nape, face-sides maroon-red, ear-coverts white with no trace of blue, upperparts green, primaries largely blue with red wing bend and leading edge of distal half of primaries white, rump bright red, tail basally blue, washed green, becoming deep red in centre and then pale red; breast brown, the feathers having broad white fringes affording a perfect scaled effect, and becoming very rounded at rear, flanks and undertail-coverts green, small red belly patch; eyes dark, orbital ring white, bill black.

Ssp. *P. c. caeruleiceps* (N Co: west slope of Magdalena Valley) as described
P. c. pantchenkoi (Perijá: Co & Ve) narrow frontal band

of deep crimson from nostrils across lores and below eyes, but not above eyes (*picta* has crimson above eyes but no frontal band); moustachial dark brown, washed lightly blue and with hint of pale fringes (*picta* and *cuchivera* both have blue moustachial with brown fringes [*picta*] or pale brownish-grey fringes [*cuchivera*], and both have deep crimson belly patches); as *caeruleiceps* below but breast darker brown, leading edge of deep blue primaries turquoise-blue, and small central belly patch is bright red

Status Uncertain.
Habitat Humid montane cloud forest.
Voice Sound-recording from Sierra de Lajas, Perijá (1,200m) in July 2003 is first for Venezuela (D. Ascanio). A harsh whistle, typical of genus but softer than that of Fiery-shouldered and Blood-eared Parakeets. Also, clearly differs from that given by Painted Parakeet, which has a triple-noted vocalisation (D. Ascanio).
Notes Formerly considered part of Painted Parakeet. Vernacular name suggested by Joseph & Stockwell (2002), but renamed Perijá Parakeet by Hilty. Race *pantchenkoi* considered a synonym of *caeruleiceps* by Joseph (2002), but afforded species rank by Rodríguez-Mahecha and Hernández-Camacho (2002).

SINÚ PARAKEET *Pyrrhura subandina* Pl. 71

Identification 22cm. Forehead to nape maroon, narrow red line across forehead, lores and immediately below eyes; ear-coverts buff, lower face-sides somewhat turquoise-blue, upperparts mainly green, primaries blue, rump bright red, tail basally green becoming deep red; breast dark greyish-brown, the feathers having broad buffy-grey fringes affording a perfect scaled effect, flanks and undertail-coverts green, belly deep red; eyes medium brown, orbital ring white, cere grey, bill black.

Ssp. Monotypic (NW Co: Sinú Valley)

Habits Very fond of fruits of *Ficus*, flowers of *Cochlospermum orinocense* and *Erythrina amazonica*, and seeds of various legumes.
Status Rare.
Habitat Only known from the lower Sinú Valley, Córdoba (Colombia).
Voice Unknown.
Note Treated as a subspecies of Painted Parakeet by most previous authors.

VENEZUELAN PARAKEET *Pyrrhura emma* Pl. 71

Identification 22–23cm. Bright blue forecrown, duller on rear crown (washed maroon), nape and neck-sides blue, forehead and face-sides maroon-red with some white streaking on ear-coverts. Back to uppertail-coverts and wings, including secondaries, green, primaries blue with blackish tips, red carpal, tail deep red; chin to upper breast blue, grading green and continuing to undertail-coverts, but entire breast has white scallops on blue and yellow on green, the fringes changing with ground colour, central belly red; eyes deep brown, orbital skin and cere white, bill black above, brownish-horn below. From Maroon-bellied and Red-eared by maroon rump (others green).

Ssp. *P. e. auricularis* (NE Ve, Tr) like *emma* but larger and cleaner white ear-coverts, deeper green and less yellowish above; pale green underwing-coverts, orbital skin and cere grey, bill black
P. e. emma (NW Ve) as described; generally brighter red throughout and brighter or richer coloured; pale green underwing-coverts with red spot on carpal

Habits Fast undulating flight. Restless and apt to move suddenly. Forages at all levels from canopy to ground.
Status Locally fairly common to abundant.
Habitat Tropical Zone, to 1,700m. Forest edge and adjacent clearings with scattered trees, cacao plantations, parkland and even around villages.
Voice Flight-calls include a high-pitched, yelping rather than staccato *chee cheet chee* and *ki ki*, and, when perched, a quieter teet (J&P, F, H&B). Flight-call a loud harsh *KIK-KIK-KIK-KIK* (Hilty).
Notes The Maroon-faced Parakeet *P. leucotis* group comprises 3–4 spp., including the 2 above, but Joseph (2000) proposed to recognise the nominate form (of eastern Brazil) as a distinct species, which was accepted by Hilty, and elevated the range-restricted *griseipectus*, of north-east Brazil, similarly. Joseph further proposed to synonymise *auricularis* under *emma*, but we find these taxa quite distinct.

SANTA MARTA PARAKEET *Pyrrhura viridicata* Pl. 71

Identification 25cm. Basically all green, with red band on forehead continuing onto ear-coverts, another red band on breast, red carpal, most underwing-coverts and distal half of tail, yellow outer underwing-coverts, deep blue primary-coverts and primaries with blackish tips; underwing olive, undertail dull red; eyes brown, cere white, bill pale horn. From Red-fronted by red undertail, and far less red on head.

Ssp. Monotypic (Co: Santa Marta)

Habits Noisy, fast-flying, twisting and wheeling flocks. Shy and flushes with much shrieking if approached closely or disturbed, but may return to same tree.
Status Vulnerable. Fairly common within small range but retreating due to severe loss of habitat.
Habitat Subtropical Zone, apparently mainly 2,100–2,400m, but recorded 1,800–2,800m. Humid montane forest, edges and open areas with shrubs and bracken.
Voice Screeching calls recall Painted Parakeet, with softer chattering notes while clambering in branches (H&B).

FIERY-SHOULDERED PARAKEET *Pyrrhura egregia* Pl. 72

Identification 25cm. Head and body dark green except white scallops on breast, red and orange edge to folded wing that becomes red on inner underwing-coverts, then orange, with band of yellow; underwing and undertail dull olive, primary-coverts and primaries deep blue, tail dark red, deep red central belly patch; eyes dark, orbital ring and cere white, bill bone-coloured. Juvenile paler green with soft brown scalloping below, much-reduced red and orange on wings, underwing-coverts green, centre of belly faintly reddish. From Painted Parakeet by green rump and less obvious scaling on breast. In flight has red-and-yellow underwing.

Ssp. *P. e. egregia* (Roraima: SE Ve, SW Gu) as described
P. e. obscura (S Ve) darker green

Habits A characteristic parakeet of the Pantepui, usually seen in pairs or small noisy flocks of up to 25. Spends much time foraging in canopy.
Status Pantepui endemic. Fairly common to common locally in Venezuela. Frequent in Guyana.
Habitat Upper Tropical to Lower Subtropical Zones, 700–1,800m. Forest and forest edges at bases of tepuis, especially common on their eastern slopes.
Voice Flight-call an unusually harsh, grating *jjaaEEK!* (Hilty).

MAROON-TAILED PARAKEET *Pyrrhura melanura* Pl. 72

Identification 24–25cm. Almost entirely dark green with white scallops on breast, red and orange edge of wing, red primary-coverts with orange tips, green underwing-coverts; outer primaries dull blue, tail deep red; underwing and undertail dull grey; eyes dark brown, orbital ring white, bill grey. Juvenile similar but lacks red, orange or yellow in wings; bill pale horn. From other *Pyrrhura* by lack of red belly patch, though this may show as an infusion in some races.

Ssp. *P. m. berlepschi* (SE Ec) cheeks bright green, broad white scaling on breast and neck-sides (may appear largely white), edge of wing to primary-coverts red
P. m. chapmani (Co: E slope of C Andes) very pale scaling extends to entire neck, upper mantle has bluish tinge
P. m. melanura (S Ve, SE Co, E Ec) as described; very narrow pale scaling on breast
P. m. pacifica (SW Co, NW Ec) narrow, restricted whitish scaling on breast, primary-coverts red, heavy pink suffusion to breast, shorter tail; grey eye-ring and black bill
P. m. souancei (SC Co) fairly broad scaling on breast, primary-coverts red, broad green edges to tail-feathers

Habits Usually in canopy but will come very low in loaded fruit trees.
Status Patchy but generally fairly common and in some areas the commonest parrot. Seasonal movements poorly understood, and temporary presence or absence may account for inconsistency of reports on status. Race *pacifica* never common.
Habitat Tropical to Temperate Zones, generally to 500m (Collar), but to 3,200m (*souancei*), 1,500m (*berlepschi*), 2,800m (*chapmani*) and 1,700m (*pacifica*). Wide variety of habitats from *várzea*, premontane to cloud forests; also secondary growth and partially deforested areas.
Voice Loud, continual raucous shrieking, *screeet screeet screeet* or *keeey keey*, or *kree kree* in flight and when flushed R&G, H&B, J&P).
Note Taxonomic status of all races disputed, with a wide variety of opinions as to which deserve species status and which might be regarded as synonyms. Clearly the species is due a major revision.

EL ORO PARAKEET *Pyrrhura orcesi* Pl. 72

Identification 22cm. Virtually entirely green; broad band of bright red across forehead, a few white scallops on neck-sides, bright red along edge of wing, from carpal to primary-coverts and outermost greater coverts, forms bright red wedge that is particularly obvious in flight, outer primaries blue; broad green basal outer edges of tail, rest of tail dark red; eyes brown, orbital skin white, bill bone-coloured. Female has narrower red band on forehead, not reaching eyes. Juvenile has head all green or a touch of red by nostrils. From allopatric Rose-crowned Parakeet by lack of white in wing. Red-masked Parakeet is larger and has much more red on face.

Ssp. Monotypic (SW Ec)

Habits Usually in small groups, occasionally flocks.
Status Vulnerable. Uncommon to locally fairly common within small range.
Habitat Upper Tropical Zone, at 600–1,200m, but recorded 300–1,550m. Moist, epiphyte-laden cloud forest on west slope of Andes. Receding in face of deforestation.
Voice Rather trilling but harsh, high-pitched and raspy, metallic *tchreeet tchreeet* flight-call, not unlike Maroon-tailed Parakeet (J&P, R&G). Perched birds sound like Budgerigars *Melopsittacus undulatus*.

WHITE-BREASTED PARAKEET *Pyrrhura albipectus* Pl. 72

Identification 24cm. Adult has brown head with buffy fringes to crown that become paler on nape, ear-coverts bright orange-red, outlined yellow, lower face-sides and malar green, the feathers fringed yellow, chin and throat white and wrap back to join at nape, which is scalloped green; back to uppertail-coverts green, wings green with bright red edge from carpal to primary-coverts, primaries mostly blue, tail deep red, basal half with broad green edge; breast yellow, rest of underparts green; eyes dark brown, orbital ring white, bill black. Juvenile has buffy head with pale, yellowy-white fringes, ear-coverts yellow, lower face-sides and malar pale green with white edges, nuchal collar to chin and entire breast white; bill grey, otherwise as adult. Seasonally sympatric with Maroon-tailed Parakeet of race *berlepschi*, from which differs by its solidly pale breast and bright orange ear-coverts.

Ssp. Monotypic (SE Ec)

Habits Flies rapidly just above canopy but flies low when crossing open spaces. Noisy and conspicuous.
Status Vulnerable (*TBW*), Near Threatened (R&G). Locally

common Ecuadorian endemic, but recently reported in adjacent Peru (Navarrete 2003). Some altitudinal movements, not well understood.

Habitat Subtropical to Temperate Zones, mostly 1,400–1,800m, but known 900–2,000m. Prefers montane primary forest, foraging in canopy and edges but also in disturbed forest and partly deforested areas.

Voice Flight-call a constant rapid *screet screet screet*, whilst feeding flocks maintain a constant single *skee* or *week* that makes a chattering chorus (J&P).

Note Sometimes called White-necked Parakeet (Collar).

BROWN-BREASTED PARAKEET

Pyrrhura calliptera Pl. 72

Identification 22–23cm. Entire head and breast mid brown, scalloped or scaled dark brown, but for red ear-coverts and green lower cheeks, rest of body green except bright yellow carpal to primary-coverts, with red fringes to feathers, outer primaries blue and tail red, underwing-coverts green, underwing and undertail grey; eyes brown, orbital ring white, bill yellowish-horn. Juvenile has less extensive brown-scaled breast, edge of wings plain yellow and primary-coverts green. Young adult has edges of wings deeper yellow, including primary-coverts, as only older birds develop red. Noticeable yellow or orange on wing in flight is diagnostic. Tail proportionately shorter than other *Pyrrhura*.

Ssp. Monotypic (Co: E Andes)

Habits Usually in noisy groups.

Status Vulnerable. Colombian endemic suffering from deforestation. Current status assumed as hostilities prevent access to relevant area.

Habitat Upper Subtropical and Temperate Zone cloud forest at 1,700–3,000m, possibly to 3,400m. Elfin woodland and páramo with *Weinmannia tomentosa*, *Quercus humboldtii*, *Clusia* and *Brunellia colombiana*. Also peat-bog páramo, shrubby second growth and cleared areas. More likely at higher levels.

Voice Harsh, far-carrying *screeyr screeyr* (Hilty).

Notes Hypothetical for Venezuela. Sometimes called Flame-winged Parakeet.

RED-EARED PARAKEET

Pyrrhura hoematotis Pl. 72

Identification 25cm. Generally green, with bluish tinge to crown, blood red ear-coverts, faint greyish-brown scalloping on neck and breast, blue outer edge to wing, from carpal to primary-coverts, and primaries, latter with black tips; tail broader than most *Pyrrhura* and rounded at tip, small, deep red belly patch; eyes dark, orbital skin grey, bill bone-white. Juvenile unknown. From partially sympatric race of Venezuelan Parakeet, *emma*, by green rump, red ear-coverts and absence of blue on nape. Red ear-coverts easily seen at rest, brownish-red tail in flight.

Ssp. *P. h. hoematotis* (N Ve) as described

P. h. immarginata (NW Ve) lacks grey-brown pattern on sides of neck and breast

Habits Small groups, occasionally small flocks; daily commute from lowland foraging areas to higher altitudes.

Status Venezuelan endemic. Fairly common, but race *immarginata* has suffered serious loss of habitat; status unknown but expected to be in danger.

Habitat Upper Tropical to Subtropical Zones, 600–2,400m, but mainly 1,000–2,000m. Coastal montane forest edges and open areas with scattered trees. Tends to occupy higher elevations in rainy season and comes lower during dry.

Voice Rapidly repeated *ca ca ca ca ca ca*, the notes sounding like a continual roll (F, J&P).

Note Also called Blood-eared Parakeet.

ROSE-HEADED PARAKEET

Pyrrhura rhodocephala Pl. 72

Identification 24–25cm. Red from forehead to point just beyond crown, ear-coverts red; in older birds, red is more rosy and may be quite extensive, reaching nape and to ear-coverts; rest green except dramatic white edge to wings, from carpal to primary-coverts, that is very obvious in flight, but underwing-coverts green and underwing grey; primaries blue, and broad, rounded tail is deep red; small deep red central belly patch; eyes dark, orbital skin white. Immature has wing edge blue from carpal, with only primary-coverts white, and the red, which may be pinkish, only reaches just beyond the eyes. Juvenile has wing edge blue, pinkish-red forehead and buffy bill. White patch on wing very distinctive. Juvenile could be mistaken for race *immarginata* of Red-eared Parakeet unless its white eye-ring is noticed.

Ssp. Monotypic (Ve)

Habits Gregarious, regularly in flocks, larger at roost sites; travels some distance to and from foraging areas.

Status Near Threatened. Venezuelan endemic. Fairly common but declining due to deforestation.

Habitat Upper Tropical to Temperate Zones, mainly 1,500–2,500m but seen 800–3,400m. Fairly tolerant of disturbance. Humid montane forest edges and elfin forest, second growth, partially cleared areas and páramos.

Voice Apparently quieter than other *Pyrrhura*.

Note Also called Rose-crowned Parakeet.

Bolborhynchus parakeets are small and green, and have wedge-shaped tails. They are birds of the Andean highlands, usually seen flying high overhead, and are very difficult to locate at rest unless seen arriving. Their flight is direct and fast, but flocks can wheel and change direction like small shorebirds. On landing in a tree they disappear and forage silently.

BARRED PARAKEET

Bolborhynchus lineola Pl. 72

Identification 16–17cm. Small, rotund little bird with

sharply pointed tail; entirely green, more emerald on crown, slightly yellowish-green on face-sides, and vent to undertail-coverts, with black scalloping from nape to uppertail-coverts (where become round spots), heavy on lesser and median wing-coverts, but in regular scallops on greater coverts, tertials and secondaries, and fine, overlapping barring on breast-sides and flanks, heavy on undertail-coverts; underwing-coverts green with some black barring; eyes brown with orange orbital skin, bill pale horn. Female slightly less densely marked, and juvenile slightly paler and less boldly marked. *Touit* parrotlets have rounded tails, usually with bright colours; *Forpus* parrotlets have blue in their wings and are never barred, and generally occur at lower elevations. Barring not easy to see in field, but black patch on shoulder diagnostic.

Ssp. *B. l. tigrinus* (Ec, W Co, N & W Ve)

Status Uncommon in Ecuador, local in Colombia, and uncommon and erratic in Venezuela. Strongly associated with seeding bamboo, which means it can appear to be ephemerally common and quite numerous, albeit extremely local. Erratic movements appear migratory-like and distribution perhaps less fragmented than is apparent from available records.

Habitat Upper Tropical to Temperate Zones, to 2,900m in Ecuador, 1,600–2,600m in Colombia, and 900–1,500m in Venezuela. Montane evergreen forest, drier open woodland, clearings and pastures with tall trees, areas where landslides have opened forest to bamboo proliferation, and occasionally in cultivated areas where it takes maize (J&P).

Voice Noisy in flight, with flocks giving a continual sweet chattering overhead. Usually silent at rest but utter rapid *jur-jur-jur…* alarm-calls before flushing (R&G, F, J&P, Hilty).

RUFOUS-FRONTED PARAKEET

Bolborhynchus ferrugineifrons Pl. 72

Identification 18–19cm. Only small parrot within its restricted high-altitude range. Entirely green with bluish-green underwing-coverts, and bright orange-buffy forehead, lores and area at base of mandible, also orange eye-ring and bill is horn.

Ssp. Monotypic (Co)

Habits Usually in pairs, small groups and occasionally small flocks, always noisy, but not shy and is approachable. When flushed soon settles a short distance away. However, it feeds in grasses and is very easy to overlook.

Status Rare Colombian endemic. Endangered, due to habitat destruction.

Habitat Temperate Zone to Páramo, usually 3,200–4,000m, occasionally to 2,800m. Shrubby páramos and their slopes, sparse, open woodland and agricultural areas.

Voice Low-pitched chattering calls, apparently similar to Andean Parakeet *B. orbygnesius* (F).

Forpus parrotlets are tiny, rotund little birds, all bright green with males having blue in the wings. The amount of blue on the underwing-coverts increases, both in size and intensity, with age. Virtually impossible to see when foraging silently in a tree or on ground, but in flight their high-pitched twittering calls draw attention, usually just as they are diving into cover. Flight is swift, somewhat undulating, and usually low, just above canopy or between trees, with agile wheeling and changes of direction. They often feed on grass seeds and will climb tall stems of *Panicum maximus*; they are fond of sunflower and may be a pest to farmers. Generally, they seem to be increasing with deforestation.

GREEN-RUMPED PARROTLET

Forpus passerinus Pl. 74

Identification 12–13cm. Tiny parrot that is almost entirely bright green, rump perhaps more lustrous and slightly emerald, greater wing-coverts pale blue, secondaries blue, primary-coverts and underwing-coverts dark blue; eyes brown, eyelids grey, bill flesh to pale horn. Female all green, paler to yellowish on forehead. Male Dusky-billed Parrotlet has blue rump and grey bill, but female Dusky-billed is all green, though dark bill should still separate them.

Ssp. *F. p. cyanophanes* (N Co) greater wing-coverts and secondaries same shade of blue, forming distinct patch when folded; female has distinctively yellow forehead

F. p. passerinus (Guianas) as described

F. p. viridissimus (N Ve, NE Co, T&T, Cu) slightly darker green and only light blue on upper wing

Habits Gregarious and usually in flocks which suddenly appear, twittering and flying at speed, only to alight into a tree and disappear in silence.

Status Widespread and common.

Habitat Lower Tropical Zone but may reach 1,800m. Wide variety of habitats, but mainly edges of forests, open areas with trees, e.g. ranches, pastures, cultivated and agricultural land, parks and gardens, even tree-lined avenues.

Voice Vocalisations usually described as finch-like. Flight-call *phil-ip, phil-ip, phil-ip…*or *chit-it, chit-it, chit-it….* A *chee…chee…chee…* call and penetrating *tsup-tsup*, accented on second syllable, also described. When feeding or at rest, maintains a constant twittering (F, R&G, J&P, Sick, Hilty).

BLUE-WINGED PARROTLET

Forpus xanthopterygius Pl. 74

Identification 12–13cm. Entirely green with ultramarine-blue rump and outer wing edge from carpal and including greater coverts and primary-coverts, and underwing-coverts same deep rich blue; eyes dark, eyelids grey, bill pinkish-bone. Blue and yellow mutations occur naturally. Dusky-billed Parrotlet has dark bill.

Ssp. *F. x. crassirostris* (SE Co, E Ec) as described

F. x. spengeli (N Co) rump and wing markings pale turquoise-blue

Habits Very gregarious, flocks up to *c.*50.

Status Uncommon and rather local.
Habitat Tropical Zone to 1,200m. Open woodland, light riparian growth, savanna, palm groves, semi-arid scrub, pastures and farmland, parks and gardens. Often seen in *Cecropia* trees feeding on catkins.
Voice A high-pitched chittering in flight.
Notes Erroneously classified under specific name *crassirostris* (Collar 1997, Whitney & Pacheco 1999). Isolated *spengeli* is possibly a race of Mexican Parrotlet *F. cyanopygius*, or more likely a different species (J&P).

SPECTACLED PARROTLET
Forpus conspicillatus Pl. 74

Identification 12–13cm. All green but some variation: face of male more intense and vivid green, female usually paler and more yellowish, and blue around eyes, on wings (above and below) and rump vary with race and individually. Female lacks any blue but tends to be a richer, slightly more emerald-green where male has blue. From allopatric Blue-winged Parrotlet (*F. x. spengeli*) by deeper blue rump and wing patch (*spengeli* is turquoise).

Ssp. *F. p. caucae* (SW Co) paler blue, and larger bill
F. p. conspicillatus (NC Co) bright blue on back and wings
F. p. metae (C Co, SW Ve) brighter green head and more yellow-green below

Habits Twittering flocks often feed on ground.
Status Commonest *Forpus* in Colombia, locally common in Venezuela.
Habitat Tropical to Lower Subtropical Zones. Lightly wooded habitats such as forest edges, clearings with scattered trees, pastures, ranches, *llanos*, second growth, thorn scrub and cultivations.
Voice Continual chattering and twittering.
Note A fourth subspecies, *pallescens*, described as paler than *caucae*, from south-west Colombia, is regarded as a *nomen nudum* (J&P, Collar).

DUSKY-BILLED PARROTLET
Forpus modestus Pl. 74

Identification 12–13cm. Richer and slightly darker green than congenerics, face brighter and rather emerald, rich blue greater coverts, secondaries and primary-coverts, primaries dark with green leading edge, underwing-coverts cobalt-blue, underwing grey; eyes dark, upper mandible dark brown, lower mandible horn. Female lacks blue and has face significantly brighter green. Dark bill separates it from other *Forpus*.

Ssp. *F. m. modestus* (E Co, S & SE Ve, Gu, S FG) paler green, more yellowish below; male has bright emerald-green face, paler violet-blue rump
F. m. sclateri (NE Ec, SE Co, SW Ve) as described

Habits Usually in flocks, sometimes of up to *c.*100 birds.
Status Confusing, but apparently more numerous in west of its range, from local in Ecuador and Colombia to rare in the Guianas.
Habitat Lower Tropical Zone. Forest edge, clearings with scattered trees, pastures and cultivations with trees, second growth and riverine scrub, and seasonally flooded *várzea* forest along rivers.
Voice Flight-call distinctive and enables separation from Blue-winged Parrotlet. Listen for high-pitched, thin whistling, a mouse-like *dziiit*; also when perched (J&P, F, R&G, H&B).
Notes Formerly called *F. sclateri* but see Pacheco & Whitney (in press). *Eidos* is now considered a synonym of *modestus*.

PACIFIC PARROTLET
Forpus coelestis Pl. 74

Identification 12–13cm. Only *Forpus* west of Andes. All green but broad pale blue postocular line merges into greyish nape, rich blue wings, rump and underwing-coverts (like other *Forpus*); eyes dark, bill pale horn. Female lacks blue on rump and wings, and has paler blue postocular line. Juvenile more olive-green on back and wings.

Ssp. Monotypic (W & SW Ec)

Habits Usually in small groups, but these can consolidate into sizeable flocks in dry season. Noisy in flight; when foraging or at rest can be equally noisy, or silent.
Status Fairly common to very common in Ecuador.
Habitat Tropical Zone. Variety of light woodland from deciduous forest to thorn and cactus scrub, mango and other plantations, coastal mangroves, parks and gardens.
Voice High-pitched twittering, *chitit chitit* with metallic tinkling quality (J&P), and chattering *tchit* or *tzit* in rapid series (R&G).

Brotogeris are small, well-built, lowland parakeets, distinguished by a narrow, protruding bill, and differ from *Touit*, which have a similar bill shape, by a short wedge-shaped tail (*Touit* have blunt tails). They are noisy, gregarious birds that travel and forage in flocks, and fly high over the forest. Flight is undulating and somewhat jerky, sometimes short intermittent glides and birds may close the wings momentarily. Several hundred may congregate at roosts. They are generally birds of clearings and forest edges with a preference for flowering trees.

WHITE-WINGED PARAKEET
Brotogeris versicolurus Pl. 73

Identification 22–25cm. Elegant, long-winged and long-tailed parakeet; fairly dull green except for yellow greater and primary-coverts, and white secondaries and inner primaries, outer primaries greenish-blue; lores bare, eyes dark brown, eyelids grey, bill dull horn. Juvenile has white restricted to secondaries. From Golden-winged, *Pyrrhura* and Tui parakeets in French Guiana by extensive white in wings.

Ssp. Monotypic (SE Co, E FG, S Ec - introduced)

Status Common in extreme south-east Colombia (Leticia). In French Guiana known from low valley of Oyapock, but not recently confirmed. Essentially an Amazon river valley bird that ranges along the Pará, Amapá and Guianan coast (Aleixo *et al.* in prep).

Habitat Tropical Zone. Forests and clearings near water, seasonally flooded *várzea*, river islands. Also near habitation.

Voice Flight-calls consist of shrill metallic notes, *chiri… chiri…* and *te-cle-tee* but uncertain which taxa these refer to, possibly *B. chiriri*.

Notes Canary-winged Parakeet is name given to *B. chiriri* (races *chiriri* and *behni*) of Brazil, which has yellow greater coverts and no white in wings, with the largely white-winged *versicolurus* in the north separated as White-winged Parakeet. Has been treated as conspecific with *B. chiriri* but they were mistakenly (Aleixo pers. comm.) understood to have been found sympatrically without interbreeding in Pará, Brazil (Pinto & Camargo 1957) and were separated by Collar; but the split stands. Confusion remains over vernacular names, with the yellow-winged *chiriri* also being called Yellow-chevroned Parakeet, and the white-winged *versicolurus* Canary-winged Parakeet! We follow Sibley and others in our use of White-winged Parakeet.

GREY-CHEEKED PARAKEET

Brotogeris pyrrhoptera Pl. 73

Identification 20cm. Grey forehead and bluish tone to crown, cheeks, from lores to ear-coverts and chin grey, rest of body, wings and mid-length pointed tail green, with olive tone to median coverts and cobalt blue on edge of wing, from alula to primary-coverts; underwing-coverts orange-coral; eyes dark brown with white eyelids, bill yellowish-horn. Juvenile duller with more green and less blue on crown; upper mandible dusky. From Red-winged Parrotlet by pointed not blunt tail, and reddish-orange not yellow underwing.

Ssp. Monotypic (W & SW Ec)

Habits Generally in pairs or small groups and forms mixed groups with Red-masked Parakeet and Bronze-winged Parrot.

Status Near Threatened. Uncommon to locally fairly common.

Habitat Lower Tropical Zone but recorded to 1,400m. Wide variety of forested and semi-open habitats including primary deciduous forest with *Ceiba trichistandra*, secondary woodland, *Acacia*-dominated scrub and semi-cultivated areas. Feeds on seeds and flowers of *Chorisia, Cavanillesia platanifolia*, fruits of *Ceiba* and *Ficus*, and catkins of *Cecropia*.

Voice Flight-call a pleasant *stleet stleet*, otherwise an unmelodious grating *stteeet stteeet* stteee*t*, when perched, repeated rapidly (J&P). Varied shrill chattering calls, more vocal when perched than other parakeets (R&G).

ORANGE-CHINNED PARAKEET

Brotogeris jugularis Pl. 73

Identification 16–18cm. Virtually all-green parakeet with short pointed tail, lesser wing-coverts olive-brown, chin orange; eyes dark, eye-ring white, bill horn. Only small, sharp-tailed parrot with brown wing patch and orange chin. Occasional blue morphs seen.

Ssp. *B. j. exsul* (E Co, W Ve) all green below, olivaceous wash on mantle

B. j. jugularis (N Co, NW Ve) as described; bluish tinge to thighs and undertail

Habits Chatters noisily, especially whilst foraging morning and evening, when large numbers may gather. Normally in the canopy where they feed on flowers.

Status Locally common to abundant in both Colombia and Venezuela.

Habitat Lower Tropical Zone, but to 1,000m in Venezuela and 1,400m in Colombia. Edge of humid forest and plantations to open dry country with scattered trees. Tolerant of disturbance, it occurs in second growth, parks and gardens.

Voice Flight-calls consists of shrill, noisy monotone chattering, suggested as *ack-ack-ack-ack-ack…* (F), and a variety of other calls like *ra-a-a-a-a…* and a more musical *week week kweek-kee roo kee roo*, a harsh, scolding *etchireet!*, a clipped *chi chi chi* and *chee chichit* (F, J&P, H&B).

Note Called Tovi Parakeet in J&P.

COBALT-WINGED PARAKEET

Brotogeris cyanoptera Pl. 73

Identification 18cm. Virtually all green with yellow forehead, reddish-orange chin, cobalt-blue secondaries and primaries; underwing has greater coverts green, lesser coverts blue; eyes dark, eye-ring white, bill pinkish-horn. Male *Forpus* parrotlets also show deep blue in wings, but have blue on rump and entire underwing-coverts blue, and are noticeably smaller.

Ssp. *B. c. cyanoptera* (SE Co, S Ve, E Ec)

Habits Seen in forest canopy more than in clearings and at forest edge like other *Brotogeris*, but often seen overflying clearings! Forages in small, noisy flocks.

Status Common and widespread in Ecuador, locally fairly common in Colombia, and common in Venezuela.

Habitat Lower Tropical Zone. Humid forest, woodland and secondary growth but rarely seen outside woodland.

Voice Noisy as other *Brotogeris*, calls include a clear *splink splink* and complex phrases combining harsh with melodious notes. Said to resemble Tui Parakeet (F, J&P, R&G, H&B).

GOLDEN-WINGED PARAKEET

Brotogeris chrysoptera Pl. 73

Identification 16–18cm. Almost entirely green, with bluish tinge to forehead, orange-yellow primary-coverts, deep blue primaries; underwing coverts green, underside of primaries dull blue; eyes dark brown, eye-ring and cere white, bill bone-coloured. From Cobalt-winged and Tui Parakeets by orange primary-coverts (lacking in juveniles).

Ssp. *B. c. chrysoptera* (NE Ve, Gu, Su, FG)

Habits Normally forages in canopy; in face of danger may freeze silently or kick up a shindig. Has been observed taking algae and snails from fresh water when level very low in dry season.

Status Locally common to abundant throughout range.

Habitat Lower Tropical Zone, to 1,200m north of Orinoco,

to 950m south of it. Most types of forest and woodland, savanna woodlands and sand ridge woods, also urban areas with large trees.
Voice Flight-call a harsh scratchy *tchr tchr tchr*, repeated rapidly up to 6 times, also *chil chil chil* or *chit chit chit* (F, Sick, Snyder, H&M).

TUI PARAKEET

Brotogeris sanctithomae Pl. 73

Identification 17cm. Almost entirely green except yellow patch on forehead, yellow edge to wing and blue greater underwing-coverts; dark brown eyes, white eye-ring, bill brown. From Golden-winged and Cobalt-winged by all-green wings. Dark bill is useful field mark.

Ssp. *B. s. sanctithomae* (NE Ec, SE Co)

Habits Very gregarious, with flocks of up to 500 reported.
Status Rare in Ecuador, where possibly a seasonal visitor, locally abundant in Colombia.
Habitat Lower Tropical Zone, to 100m. Lowland tropical forest, seasonally flooded *várzea* and forests along rivers and other waterways, sugar plantations, disturbed, partially flooded clearings, swampy riverbanks and islands.
Voice Flight-call a high-pitched *screek*, repeated continually; a flock in flight maintains a constant chattering (F, J&P).

Nannopsittaca is a small, slender, almost entirely green parrotlet with an almost square tail and pointed wings, and an irregular ring of yellow feathers around eye. Flight method is diagnostic: direct and fast, with rapid wingbeats which miss a beat at intervals as bird momentarily closes its wings completely, but not long enough to cause undulation in flight pattern. Smaller *Forpus* have blue on rump and tail, and erratic flight. *Touit* are bulkier with square tails, and also have bright colour patches.

TEPUI PARROTLET

Nannopsittaca panychlora Pl. 74

Identification 14cm. Entirely green, save imprecise yellow surrounding eyes, narrow yellow edge to wing at carpal and yellowish-green undertail-coverts, underwing has turquoise tint; eyes brown, eye-ring grey, bill pale to greyish. Juvenile appears like adult.

Ssp. Monotypic (NE, S & SE Ve, S Gu)

Habits Usually seen morning and evening, flying high as it commutes from roosts in tepuis to lowlands of Gran Sabana to feed. Flocks sometimes very large, in continuous waves, or sporadic. These movements are poorly understood.
Status Locally common in Venezuela and Guyana, but erratic movements result in its appearance being unpredictable.
Habitat Upper Tropical to Lower Subtropical Zones.
Voice Lively, twittering sounds. A tinkling, chittering *seize'la* or *tseez'zip* (Hilty).

Touit are small, well-built parakeets, distinguished by a narrow, protruding bill, and differ from *Brotogeris*, which have a similar bill shape, by a short square tail (*Brotogeris* have wedge-shaped tails). They have long tail-coverts that cover most of the brightly coloured tail. All have distinctive bright patches of colour in their wings. Flight noisy, strong and direct with continuous wingbeats and some have in-flight calls that sound like variations on *touit*.

LILAC-TAILED PARROTLET

Touit batavicus Pl. 74

Identification 14cm. Adult has yellowish-green head, shiny on ear-coverts. More yellow around bill and eyes, scaled black on nape, mantle to central uppertail-coverts (and lesser wing-coverts) black with broad green fringes giving scaled effect, median coverts mostly green, greater coverts yellow with purple tips, tertials almost all yellow, remiges black with green leading edge, underwing-coverts blue marked yellow and red; outer tail-coverts slightly greenish-yellow, tail violaceous purple with subterminal black band on all but central rectrices. Breast pastel powder blue, becoming pastel powder green; eyes white to pale yellow, orbital skin white, bill horn with grey tip. Juvenile essentially like adult but duller; more noticeably scaled on mantle, no lustre on ear-coverts, more greyish on breast, and central tail-feathers mauve. Distinctive powdery blue breast and broad yellow bar on dark upper wing.

Ssp. Monotypic (Co: Santa Marta, N & E Ve, Tr, Guianas)

Habits Gregarious and occurs in small flocks, noisy in flight and usually very high in the sky, but generally silent when foraging and at rest in canopy.
Status Local, uncommon and erratic in Venezuela, common in Trinidad, fairly common in Guyana and French Guiana, irregular in Suriname.
Habitat Usually Tropical Zone, but occasionally to Lower Subtropical Zone, to 1,700m in Venezuela. Primary forest and tall second growth, but prefers dense forest and avoids open areas, but on Trinidad comes to roost in large trees in suburbs.
Voice High-pitched *scree-eeet*, rising in pitch over second part, given continuously in flight, also short trills and soft chattering (Snyder), a soft slurred, nasal flight-call, *naaaee*, producing a rather high, whining sound (Hilty).
Note Name spelling changed from *batavica* (David & Gosselin 2002).

SCARLET-SHOULDERED PARROTLET

Touit huetii Pl. 74

Identification 15–16cm. Adult male appears all green but much bright colouring exposed in flight; forehead black, lores extensively rich blue, flushing onto cheeks, crown and head-sides washed pastel cinnamon, outer lesser, median and greater wing-coverts intense sky blue, carpal edge scarlet, alula and primary-coverts black, remiges black with green leading edge, lesser underwing-coverts and axillaries scarlet, greater coverts and underwing bluish-green; rump, uppertail-coverts and central pair of rectrices green, rest of tail scarlet with black terminal band; eyes dark brown, orbital skin white, bill light horn. Female differs in lacking red in tail. Juvenile lacks black forehead and blue lores; juvenile male has weak reddish basal half of tail-feathers; bill paler. From similar parrotlets by striking red underwing-coverts.

Ssp. Monotypic (Co, Ve, Tr, Gu, Su)

Habits Compact flocks have distinctive flight-calls, very difficult to see in canopy and canopy edge, but occasionally visits understorey.

Status Very poorly understood. Reported as rare in Ecuador, rare and local in Colombia and Venezuela, scarce in Trinidad, and uncommon in Guyana and Suriname. Distribution seems oddly fragmented, and movements not at all understood. Appears nomadic, for birds seldom stay in an area for more than a few weeks.

Habitat Lower Tropical Zone, but may reach 1,300m. Lowland humid forest, chiefly in *terra firme* but occasionally in seasonally flooded *várzea*.

Voice Soft disyllabic *touit* (Peru), *witch witch* (Gu), a strident *klooit* (Brazil) and a rasping *juwee* (Bolivia), all of which perhaps different interpretations of same *touit* call, usually given in flight (F, Sick, Snyder, H&B, R&G, J&P, Hilty), and a nasal *reenk* (Hilty).

RED-WINGED PARROTLET
Touit dilectissimus Pl. 74

Identification 15–17cm. Forehead, cheeks and ear-coverts powder blue, bold red crescent from supraloral below eyes, chin and inner throat yellow, nape to uppertail-coverts green, wings green except bright red outer lesser, median and greater coverts (and edge from carpal to alula and onto leading edge of underwing-coverts), primary-coverts black, remiges black above with powdery blue leading edge, tail yellow with black terminal band; underparts paler green, underwing-coverts and axillaries bright yellow, underwing bluish-green, undertail yellow with outer webs of outer feathers green; eyes medium brown, fairly large orbital skin white, bill yellowish-horn. Female has less extensive red on upper wing, being replaced by black. Immature male shows red in wing similar to adult, but very little red and blue on face. Juvenile lacks blue and red on face, wing as female; eyes grey. Only small parrot in its range with red-and-yellow wings.

Ssp. Monotypic (NW Ec, Co, W Ve)

Habits Usually in pairs or small flocks that call softly. Silent when foraging or at rest. Wary in flight, likely to twist and change direction with ease. Known to feed with barbets and tanagers.

Status Near Threatened. Rare to locally uncommon in Ecuador, Colombia and Venezuela. Seasonal altitudinal movements poorly understood.

Habitat Upper Tropical to Lower Subtropical Zones, from 100 to 1,700m, usually at higher elevations in rainy season, and lower in the dry. Seems to prefer wetter parts of Lower Subtropical Zone woodlands.

Voice Flight-call a weak, disyllabic, high-pitched whining, nasal *tuu-eet* or *tuueet* (H&B, Hilty), or a soft, oft-repeated *tuueee* (R&G).

SAPPHIRE-RUMPED PARROTLET
Touit purpuratus Pl. 74

Identification 17–18cm. Almost entirely rich green; crown flushed dark olive-brown to nape and neck-sides, and scapulars same colour, lower back and upper rump rich blue, primary-coverts and remiges black with broad green fringes to primaries, tail maroon-red with narrow black outer fringes to feathers, and narrow black terminal band; underparts green, with axillaries slightly bluish and flanks yellowish-green, undertail dull red; eyes brown, orbital skin grey, bill brownish-horn. Female is paler brown on head and scapulars, tail paler maroon with green subterminal band and narrow black terminal band. Juvenile even paler brown with tail pattern as for each sex but maroon weak. From other *Touit* by green underwing and red undertail.

Ssp. *T. p. purpuratus* (S Ve, Guianas) as described; top of head brown
T. p. viridiceps (SE Co, S Ve, E Ec) crown green, underparts uniform green (undertail dull red)

Habits Rather poorly known; tends to freeze silently when aware of danger and then erupts with alarm-calls. Usually seen in flight close to canopy, between trees or crossing clearings. Forages and rests in canopy.

Status Rare and local in Ecuador, uncommon in Colombia, Venezuela and the Guianas, but inconspicuous, easily overlooked and probably under-reported.

Habitat Lower Tropical Zone, but to 1,200m on Mt. Duida, Venezuela. Montane evergreen forest, humid *terra firme* and seasonally flooded *várzea*, also sand-dune forest and isolated woodlots in cleared areas, and savanna woodland.

Voice Flight-call a distinctive nasal *nyaah*, oft-repeated (R&G), a nasal, horn-like *hoya* or *keree-ke-ke* in flight (J&P), and voice suggests a larger parrot (J. V. Remsen in H&B).

SPOT-WINGED PARROTLET
Touit stictopterus Pl. 74

Identification 17–18cm. All green with brown wings that have white terminal spots on lesser, median and inner greater coverts, outer greater coverts buffy orange, tertials and secondaries have outer webs green, primaries outer edge of basal half green; underwing all green, undertail slightly yellowish-green; eyes orange with outer circle red, orbital skin grey, bill bone-white, greyish at base. Female far more ordinary, lacks white spots and ochraceous patch, and has all feathers edged green. Juvenile similar but duller, and has brown eyes. Completely green below, from other similar parakeets by lack of any clear colour patches.

Ssp. Monotypic (Ec, S Co)

Habits Very gregarious, but extremely cautious and difficult to see when foraging or at rest. Usually flies close to canopy, not high overhead.

Status Vulnerable. Rare and at best locally uncommon. Movements not understood, and apparently fragmented distribution perhaps a function of movements.
Habitat Upper Tropical to Subtropical Zones mainly 100–1,700m, but records from 500 to 2,400m. Few data, but seems to occur in primary montane forest, savanna-like habitat, stunted ridgetop forest or possibly only poor soil forest.
Voice Vocal in flight, otherwise apparently silent (J&P). Flight-call a harsh, repeated *ddreet- ddreet- ddreet- ddreet...* (R&G), and *raah-reh* or *raah-reh* with second syllable higher pitched (F).

Hapalopsittaca are medium-sized, robust-looking parrots with blunt tails and most have bright red on the inner wing, both above and below. Unlike similar, closely related *Pionopsitta* parrots, they are birds of montane forests. Found in pairs or small flocks, usually foraging quietly in canopy. In flight they appear smaller than *Pionus*, with a proportionately longer tail and shallower wingbeats (Hilty). They are poorly known. Three rather similar and confusing species, but well separated by geography.

RUSTY-FACED PARROT
Hapalopsittaca amazonina Pl. 73

Identification 23cm. Forehead and crown crimson, becoming brown then green on nape, lores buffy, front part of lower face, cheeks and area at base of mandible, including chin crimson, becoming brownish then grey on ear-coverts, which have bright buffy shaft-streaks, neck-sides green, mantle green with some brown suffusion, and back to uppertail-coverts green; on wings, inner lesser and median coverts, all greater coverts and secondaries green, most outer lesser coverts bright red, some lesser and outer median coverts, carpal, alula and primary-coverts purple, outer secondaries edged pale blue, primaries deep blue; tail basally red, maroon then finally purple; underwing-coverts and underwing mostly pale green, leading edge scarlet-red, primaries turquoise, undertail basally reddish, distally violet; breast washed yellowish-olive on green, rest of underparts pale green; eyes pale yellowish, cere grey, bill horn with greyish base. Juvenile lacks pale streaks on ear-coverts, has browner breast, and is overall slightly duller.

Ssp. *H. a. amazonina* (Co: E Andes, W Ve) as described
H. a. theresae (E Co, NW Ve) darker green above, with browner and darker head
H. a. velezi (Co: C Andes) golden-olive hindneck contrasts with green mantle, much paler below than others

Habits Observed flying high over forest in flocks of up to 50. Usually forages quietly in canopy, although will descend to lower levels for fruit.
Status Endangered. Very rare in Ecuador, rare and local in Colombia and Venezuela. First discovered in Western Cordillera of northwest Colombia in 2004, on Páramo Frontino.
Habitat Subtropical to Temperate Zones, recorded at 2,000–3,750m, but usually at 2,200–3,000m and mostly at 2,500m. Wet, epiphyte-laden cloud forest, elfin forest, taller stands with broken canopy. Race *velezi* recorded in *Alnus acuminata*.

The red on the wings of Hapalopsittaca *parrots is usually concealed by the scapulars and breast feathers, but shows well in flight*

Voice Flight-call a repeated *chek-chek-chek...* (Ridgely & Gaulin in F) alternately a loud metallic *jiink* or *jeenk* (or *shrEEnk*); when perched a metallic, bisyllabic *EEareek*, like metal scraping metal (Hilty).
Note Formerly included *fuertesi* and *pyrrhops*, which were separated specifically by Graves & Uribe-Restrepo (1989).

INDIGO-WINGED PARROT
Hapalopsittaca fuertesi Pl. 73

Identification 23–24cm. Narrow bright red forehead, forecrown, lores, cheeks and upper ear-coverts buffy-yellow, rear crown blue, merging into green of upperparts, outer wing-coverts and carpal to alula bright red, outer median and greater coverts rich blue, secondaries pale blue with green fringes, primary-coverts and primaries deep indigo-blue; tail basally red, through maroon to purple; lower face-sides green with bright yellow-buffy streaked ear-coverts, rest of underparts bright green; eyes pale yellowish, cere grey, bill pale horn. Juvenile lacks red forehead and streaks on ear-coverts, and blue on head emerges with time. Similar to apparently sympatric Rusty-faced Parrot (*H. a. velezi*) but has contrasting turquoise nape and green mantle (*velezi* has golden nape and green mantle).

Ssp. Monotypic (Co: west slope, C Andes)

Habits Forages in small flocks, in the canopy, feeding on epiphyte berries.
Status Critically Endangered. Colombian endemic thought to be on the verge of extinction, if not already extinct, until a small population was discovered in July 2002 by researchers from the NGO ProAves Colombia.
Habitat Temperate Zone to Páramo, most records 2,900–3,150m. Mature cloud and humid forest, in areas of mossy, epiphyte-laden canopy, with an apparent preference for *Quercus*.
Voice No data.
Notes Sometimes treated as race of Rusty-faced Parrot *H. amazonina*, but *H. a. velezi* might be sympatric. Sometimes called Fuertes' Parrot.

RED-FACED PARROT

Hapalopsittaca pyrrhops Pl. 73

Identification 23cm. Forehead, eyebrow, lores and fore face, including narrow line below eyes, bright red; buffy crown, rear crown and back of head bluish, ear-coverts heavily and extensively streaked yellowish-buffy, rest of body green, wings marked red, blue and indigo as congeners, underwing-coverts bright red, underwing pale greenish-blue; tail green with distal half purple, extensive red patch on central belly; eyes yellow, orbital ring and cere grey, bill bone-coloured. Juvenile has virtually all-buffy face with only a narrow red forehead. No similar species within its limited high-altitude range.

Ssp. Monotypic (S Ec)

Habits Usually in small groups or flocks, and most often seen flying high above canopy. Forages from canopy to understorey.
Status Endangered. Scarce and local, population fragmented due to loss of habitat.
Habitat Temperate Zone to Páramo, range 2,400–3500m but usually at 2,800–3,000m. Temperate forest, edges, woodland and shrubbery near páramos.
Voice Flight-call a rather soft weak *kerree- kerree- kerree…* (Flanagan in R&G). Loud disyllabic *ch-ek ch-ek…* call characteristic, with first part rasping, second part higher pitched. Roosting birds give high-pitched *eek-eek-eek…* followed by more throaty *thrut*. The *eek-eek* notes are uttered by birds when foraging and resting; call of Mountain Cacique *Cacicus leucoramphus* is similar and may be confused (J&P).
Note Formerly treated as race of *H. amazonina*, but separated by Graves & Restrepo (1989).

SHORT-TAILED PARROT

Graydidascalus brachyurus Pl. 73

Identification 24cm. Plump, all-green parrot with bright red triangle at base of upper wing, visible as a small red spot in fold of wing when closed, base of outer 3 rectrices bright red; very short, square tail; red eyes (with distinct, dark'frown'line through eye) and a large dark grey bill. Juvenile lacks red on tail; brown eyes. From similar Amazon parrots by smaller size and all-green wings.

Ssp. *G. b. brachyurus* (E Ec, SE Co, NE FG)

Habits Very gregarious, occurring in groups and flocks. Flight fast and direct, high above canopy. When coming in to land, often appears to tumble in the air, in a very distinctive fluttering pattern, and will flutter from perch to perch in the canopy, all the while chattering, calling and squabbling.
Status Scarce in eastern Ecuador and Colombia, fairly common in coastal French Guiana east of Cayenne. Sometimes locally abundant, but rather ephemeral and unpredictable. Movements poorly understood.
Habitat Lower Tropical Zone, below 400m. Mainly *várzea*, riverine forests and forest bordering lakes, swampy or flooded areas. Avoids *terra firme*. May invade cultivations and plantations.
Voice A very noisy parrot that may be heard some distance away. Flight-calls include a raucous *shreek*, *shreeyk!* or *zhree*, with a grating quality. At rest or feeding, calls include a slightly trilled, horn-like *fuuuuudle* or *fuu-uudle*, also a bisyllabic *zee-craak*, repeated severally, and a sharp, fast *jeek! jeek! jeek!* (J. P. O'Neill in F, J. V. Remsen in H&B, H&B, R&G).
Note Usually treated as monotypic, but birds from east Amazonia have been separated as race *insularis*.

Pionites and *Pionopsitta* parrots are chunky, medium-sized parrots with short, rounded wings and short square tails. There is confusion and uncertainty as to the distinctions between these genera, and some species may be listed in either genus. There are apparently some differences in vocalisations (Hilty). We have followed the AOU here. Their flight is direct, with faster, deeper wingbeats than *Amazona*, but very similar to *Pionus*. The wings often make a whirring sound as the birds pass overhead, and they are gregarious, usually travelling in small groups or flocks, and are very noisy, betraying their presence in this way. Foraging occurs in the forest canopy, but birds come lower at forest edges and in clearings.

BLACK-HEADED PARROT

Pionites melanocephalus Pl. 75

Identification 23cm. Forehead to nape black, lores, narrow line below eyes and small triangle behind them dark green, ear-coverts to throat pale orange, neck-sides and nape deep orange, back deep green with black primaries; breast to vent and flanks creamy, with well-spaced narrow buffy-white shadow-barring, thighs and undertail-coverts deep orange, underwing-coverts green, underwing and undertail dusky; eyes red, orbital skin dark grey, large bill black. Juvenile is more buffy from ear-coverts to undertail-coverts, almost uniform, though darker on face-sides and nape, which is more orange; eyes dark brown. The only white-bellied parrot in its range.

Ssp. *P. m. melanocephalus* (SE Co, NE Ve, Gu, Su, FG) as described

P. m. pallida (S Co, E Ec) face-sides lemon yellow, white from breast to vent, and thighs to undertail-coverts sulphur-yellow

Habits Foraging flocks maintain a lookout system with a few birds always on guard; nonetheless, they are not particularly shy and may be approached closer than most parrots.
Status Fairly common throughout its range.
Habitat Lower Tropical Zone, occasionally to 1,100m. Both *terra firme* and seasonally flooded *várzea* forest, also tall second growth and clearings.
Voice Flight-call a distinctive high-pitched squealing *cleeeooo-cleeeooo* (J. V. Remsen in H&B), or *screeéyr, screeéyr, screeéyr* (R&G, Hilty) and *screee-ah* (J&P). Other calls include a high-pitched *cha-rant*, whistled *toot*, loud *kleek* calls, and a shrill *wey-ak!* alarm that puts flock to flight.
Notes Has been treated as conspecific with White-bellied Parrot *P. leucogaster* of Brazil, on basis of apparent hybrids (Haffer 1977). However, these birds are within range of

individual variation of each species, and they have been kept separate by recent authors (e.g. Sick 1993, R&G, H&M). Sometimes called Black-capped or Black-crowned Parrot.

BROWN-HOODED PARROT

Pionopsitta haematotis Pl. 75

Identification 21–23cm. Head dark brown, grading into buffy-brown neck and breast, with broad bright red postocular line from below eye over ear-coverts, and another around throat, separating dark brown from the buffy-brown; upperparts green, except bluish secondaries with green fringes and dusky primaries; underparts bright green with red axillaries and bluish-green underwing and undertail; eyes yellow, extensive orbital skin from cere to lores and full eye-ring white, cere and bill horn. Juvenile has entire head buffy-brown; eyes brown, orbital skin less extensive and grey. Dark, greyish head with wide-eyed, owlish expression.

Ssp. *P. h. coccinicollaris* (NW Co)

Habits Usually quiet, shy but seemingly tame when feeding, and inconspicuous; stays quiet and still when alarmed. Somewhat vocal when foraging, betraying its presence, but not noisy. Forages at all levels, occasionally with other parrots and toucans. Flight rapid and has distinctive weaving pattern.

Status Scarce to uncommon. Consistently overlooked, perhaps more numerous than recorded. Some possibility of seasonal, altitudinal movements.

Habitat Tropical Zone to 1,200m. Dense primary forest and mature second growth, also forest clearings with trees and grass, and plantations.

Voice Generally rather quiet and more mellow than most parrots. Flight-calls include a *pileek-pileek*, alternating with rough *zapp-zapp* (F), alternately described as *check-check* or *cheek-cheek* with a thin *tseek* (R. S. Ridgely in H&B). Other calls include a musical trill, *tree-lee-eeet* (J&P) or *kree-ee… tee…yer* (F). A possible alarm-call is *screeeah* (J&P).

Note Perhaps best placed in genus *Gypopsitta* (Ribas *et al.* 2005), as currently recognised genus *Pionopsitta* is polyphyletic (Eberhard & Bermingham 2005, Ribas *et al.* 2005).

ROSE-FACED PARROT

Pionopsitta pulchra Pl. 75

Identification 23cm. Very unusual facial pattern and coloration; head mottled buffy-brown and face outlined in dark brown, like facial disc of an owl, within which feathers appear heavily flushed rose-red, there being irregular buffy fringes around eyes and inner edge of ring; rest of body, wings and tail more or less green, upper scapulars yellow-orange with red above, outer wing-coverts and secondaries flushed bluish, primaries dusky; underwing-coverts form small red triangle near body, then mainly yellow-orange, with outermost row turquoise-blue, underwing and undertail green; eyes pale grey, eye-ring grey, bill pale horn. Female similar but lacks dark brown ring around rosy face. Juvenile has crown to nape green and rosy red restricted to a mask. Facial pattern unique, as is underwing pattern.

Ssp. Monotypic (NW Ec, W Co)

Habits Gregarious and usually in flocks in mid storey and canopy where often remains quiet. Noisy in flight.

Status Uncommon to locally fairly common.

Habitat Tropical Zone, generally at 500–1,200m, but recorded to 2,100m. Humid forest, edges, mature second growth, plantations (where sometimes a pest) and clearings with scattered trees.

Voice Flight-call a harsh shrieking *skreek-skreek* or *shreek-shreek*, similar to Blue-headed Parrot (F, R&G, H&B).

Notes Sometimes treated as a subspecies of Brown-hooded Parrot *P. haematotis*. Perhaps best placed in genus *Gypopsitta* (Ribas *et al.* 2005), as currently recognised genus *Pionopsitta* is polyphyletic (Eberhard & Bermingham 2005, Ribas *et al.* 2005).

SAFFRON-HEADED PARROT

Pionopsitta pyrilia Pl. 75

Identification 24cm. Entire hood is yellow, lightly flushed orange or red on ear-coverts and nape, with thin dusky-green line around eyes and lores to base of cere; upperparts green, with bluish tone to outer wing-coverts and secondaries, large patch of yellow on lesser wing-coverts, primaries deep blue, tail has tips dark blue; edge of wings red and underwing-coverts entirely red with narrow orange band at extremes, underwing green with blackish tips to primaries, undertail yellow with green fringes and tips; breast buffy-yellow washed green, distal part of thighs yellow, rest of underparts rather turquoise-green; eyes dark brown, orbital skin white, cere brownish-grey, bill horn. Juvenile has slightly dull yellow head, washed green on crown and chin, but red underwing-coverts stand out. Completely yellow head and shoulders with red underwing diagnostic.

Ssp. Monotypic (N Ec, N & C Co, NW Ve)

Habits Usually in small groups or flocks at or even within treetops, lower when flying along forest edges, calling continuously.

Status Rare in Ecuador, rare to locally uncommon in Colombia and Venezuela.

Habitat Tropical and Lower Subtropical Zones, at lower levels in dry season, to 1,650m in rainy season. Rain forest, cloud forest and tall second growth, in canopy and at forest edge.

Voice Flight-call variously transcribed as *cheweek* (J&P), che-week (H&B), typically doubled *chek-ckek* or *cheeyk-cheeyk* (Ridgely & Gwynne), *skweek*, and also un-parrot-like *keek!* (Hilty).

Note Perhaps best placed in genus *Gypopsitta* (Ribas *et al.* 2005), as currently recognised genus *Pionopsitta* is polyphyletic (Eberhard & Bermingham 2005, Ribas *et al.* 2005).

ORANGE-CHEEKED PARROT

Pionopsitta barrabandi Pl. 75

Identification 25cm. Hood black with yellow-orange cheeks, rest of body, wings and tail mostly green, paler and brighter on undertail-coverts, tail has black tips; patch of yellow-orange on lesser wing-coverts, breast orange, washed dusky and green, distal part of thighs orange; inner webs to outer greater coverts and secondaries blue, primary-coverts and primaries deep blue, outer edge of wing and underwing-coverts bright red with band of orange at extreme, underwing green, undertail yellow with edges and tips green; eyes orange-brown, orbital skin white, bill black. Juvenile lacks black on head but is washed brown and dusky. Orange cheeks on black head are diagnostic and red underwing-coverts noticeable in flight.

Ssp. *P. b. aurantiigena* (E Ec, E Co) cheeks, lesser coverts, bend of wing and thighs deep orange rather than paler yellowish-orange

P. b. barrabandi (SW Co, SW Ve) as described

Habits In small groups or flocks, very wary and secretive, flushes easily. Flocks gather at mineral-rich cliffs and banks along with macaws and others. Normally perches quietly within canopy.

Status Uncommon to fairly common in Ecuador, Colombia and Venezuela.

Habitat Lower Tropical Zone. Mostly in lowland *terra firme* forest, occasionally *várzea*; forest edges, partially disturbed forest, stands of trees in open areas and sandy soil woodland.

Voice Flight-call is a mushy, reedy, bisyllabic *chewt* or *choyet*, and a guttural *kek* or *kuk* (F).

Notes Race *aurantiigena* listed for Ecuador by F, Arndt (1992–96) and J&P but considered not to occur there by R&G. Perhaps best placed in genus *Gypopsitta* (Ribas *et al.* 2005), as currently recognised genus *Pionopsitta* is polyphyletic (Eberhard & Bermingham 2005, Ribas *et al.* 2005).

CAICA PARROT *Pionopsitta caica* Pl. 75

Identification 23cm. Hood black, neck orange-buff with brownish wash and dusky scaling, body, wings and tail almost entirely green, small blue patch on lesser wing-coverts, primary-coverts and primaries deep blue with black tips, tail tipped black; olivaceous breast, rest of underparts green, including underwing and undertail; eyes orange, orbital skin dark grey, cere brown, bill greyish-horn. Juvenile has head green, with some dusky markings from forehead through lores to base of bill, collar orange with light scaling, lacks blue spot on wings; eyes brown, orbital skin grey. Black head with scaly, golden collar diagnostic.

Ssp. Monotypic (SE Ve, Gu, Su, FG)

Habits Gregarious, usually in groups in canopy and at forest margins. Flies very swiftly and agilely through treetops.

Status Widespread and widely dispersed throughout range, being nowhere numerous, generally uncommon to scarce but reportedly common but always in small numbers in French Guiana.

Habitat Tropical Zone. Primarily undisturbed lowland *terra firme*, rarely if ever in *várzea*.

Voice Nasal *screee-ah*, the second syllable higher pitched, followed by a short, sharp *sca*. When foraging or at rest, a scolding nasal *tchneea* and more pleasant, whistled *tooo-eee-eee*, a strident *ewit*, low-pitched, nasal *wee-uck* and *wo-cha* (Sick, J&P). Voice has quality like a child's tin trumpet, in flight an odd nasal *queek!* or *skrek*, and at rest *kunk* or *ank*, every 5 s or so (Hilty).

Note Perhaps best placed in genus *Gypopsitta* (Ribas *et al.* 2005), as currently recognised genus *Pionopsitta* is polyphyletic (Eberhard & Bermingham 2005, Ribas *et al.* 2005).

Pionus are heavy, medium to large parrots distinguished by having red undertail-coverts (though juveniles have virtually no red). They have bare ocular rings, blunt tails and, in most, an odd, unkempt appearance caused by white bases to the feathers being visible. They have fast direct flight patterns with strong, shallow wingbeats, the wings not being raised above the level of the back. Canopy birds of humid forests, they are more likely to be seen singly than other similar-sized parrots, though usually occur in pairs or small groups. Separated from *Amazona* by slightly longer wings and deeper beats. Movements are poorly understood and unpredictable with the possibility of some nomadism.

BLUE-HEADED PARROT

Pionus menstruus Pl. 76

Identification 24–28cm. Entire head rich blue with charcoal-grey patch on ear-coverts and some pink scalloping on chin, grading on mantle, by virtue of some black and pink scallops, into dark green of upperparts, most feathers of which have slightly paler yellow-olive fringes, and on lower breast blending into slightly turquoise-green flanks; undertail-coverts rich red; underwing-coverts green with slight olivaceous tone, underwing and undertail green; eyes brown, orbital skin grey, bill black with sides of upper mandible and base of lower mandible red. Juvenile has turquoise wash to green head, with an olive-green patch on ear-coverts, undertail-coverts green with red centres to a few feathers; eyes dark brown, bill has pink on sides. Blue head diagnostic.

Ssp. *P. m. menstruus* (E Ec, E Co, Ve, Tr, Gu, Su, FG) as described

P. m. rubrigularis (W Co, W Ec) darker green above, deeper blue head, chin patch bright red

Habits Flocks sometimes fly in long straggling lines. Red-billed may look similar in poor light, and is best told by its bright red bill. Dusky has blue on underside of flight-feathers, and quicker, shallower wingbeats.

Status Widespread and common, but patchy and erratic. Movements poorly understood, appears unpredictably and is perhaps nomadic. Deforestation also affects movements.

Habitat Tropical Zone, locally to 1,400m. Mainly lowland forest, mature second growth, seasonally flooded *várzea*, gallery forest, plantations and cultivations; a pest in maize-growing areas.

Voice Several flight-calls including a distinctive, high-pitched *kee-wenk kee-wenk* (E. Eisenmann in F), *keewink*, *kewink* (R&G) or *schweenk* (Hilty), a grating *tchreet*, pleasant whistled *cha-reet*, light wick (J&P) and some harsh screams, a high-pitched *krit-krit* (Snyder, Sick), *chitty-wit-wit* and a more liquid *chil-chil* (F, Sick).

RED-BILLED PARROT

Pionus sordidus Pl. 76

Identification 27–29cm. Plumage quite variable over range (see plate), with all-red bill and all-red undertail-coverts the only constant. Separated from other *Pionus* by all-red bill (race *saturatus* from juvenile Blue-headed Parrot by red undertail-coverts).

Ssp. *P. s. antelius* (NE Ve) bluish-green head, heavily scaled black, throat and upper breast lack scales; nape to uppertail-coverts, wings, and breast to flanks olive-green with paler fringes affording scaled effect; outer wing-coverts, secondaries and primaries green, outermost 2 rectrices dark blue; underwing-coverts turquoise, underwing and undertail green; eyes brown, orbital skin grey, cere brownish-grey, bill coral red; juvenile virtually entirely olive-green with olive fringes to all feathers except outer wing, which are green; eyes dark, bill slightly paler coral

P. s. corallinus (S Co, E Ec) more uniform green with little scaling, clear crescent of rich blue on breast; pale grey to almost white eye-ring

P. s. mindoensis (W Ec) brightest and purest green race, with no scaling, bright blue crescent on breast; dark grey eye-ring

P. s. ponsi (N Co, NW Ve) head green with black scaling, upperparts more evenly coloured and feather fringes less noticeable, upper breast sky blue with dark blue scaling particularly on flanks and abdomen; large, almost white eye-ring

P. s. saturatus (N Co) head green with barely visible grey scaling, turquoise ear-coverts and upper breast, also scaled; upperparts almost uniform green with only slight paler fringes and barely a hint of olive, underparts clearly scaled yellow-olive on green; darker grey eye-ring, bill has upper mandible grey

P. s. sordidus (N Ve) head more blue and very heavily scaled black, darker olive-green, especially on back and wing-coverts which are dusky with greenish fringes

Habits Sometimes congregates with macaws and other parrots at cliff-face mineral fests.

Status Locally uncommon to fairly common; race *antelius* very rare. Local movements occur in Henri Pittier National Park, Venezuela, which may be typical of the species.

Habitat Upper Tropical to Lower Subtropical Zones, with records from 200–2,850m, but 500–1,500m seems most typical. Montane forest and cloud forest, also second growth and partially deforested areas, light woodland, plantations and cleared areas adjacent to forests.

Voice Noisy, especially in flight. Flight-calls include harsh *scree-ah, kee-ank* and *kee-wank*, rather similar to Blue-headed Parrot but thinner and higher (F, R&G, H&B, J&P, Hilty).

Note Validity of *mindoensis* doubted by F, based on misread remark by Bond & Meyer de Schauensee (1943), was erroneously followed by others who dismissed *mindoensis* altogether. The race is perfectly valid.

WHITE-CAPPED PARROT

Pionus seniloides Pl. 76

Identification 29–30cm. Older adult has forehead to crown yellow-white with some red scalloping on crown, rest of head white with heavy and close black scaling, breast grey, undertail-coverts scarlet-red; rest of body dark green; eyes brown, orbital skin white, cere grey, bill yellow. Younger (or more usual?) adult has forehead white, mid crown and back of head green scaled black, nape white scaled black, face-sides, heavily and closely scaled black, breast grey, tapering on sides and onto central belly, vent whitish, undertail-coverts orange-red; bill horn with greyish streaks. Juvenile has forecrown pale green scaled dark green, face-sides whitish to grey, closely scaled dark grey, rest of body green. Difficult to see in a tree, but once seen the white crown ensures identification. Wingbeats somewhat shallower than other *Pionus*.

Ssp. *P. s. seniloides* (NW Ve, CE Co, N Ec)

Status Rare to locally (and seasonally?) common with seasonally shifting populations. Altitudinal movements also appear seasonal. To a large extent nomadic.

Habitat Subtropical to Temperate Zones, 1,400–3300m but most common 2,000–3,000m. Cloud forest, humid forest, elfin forest and open country with scattered trees adjoining páramos. Much time spent foraging in canopy, but visits cultivation and can cause much damage to maize crops.

Voice Quite different from Blue-headed and Red-billed Parrots, more like *Aratinga*, e.g. *kreeyah-kreeyah-kreeyah*, given both perched and flying (R&G). Calls generally rather nasal and unlike other *Pionus* (Hilty), include *reenk* and *careenk* in flight, and nasal *ra-aa* when perched (Hilty).

Note Taxonomy unresolved. Treated as a subspecies of Speckle-faced Parrot *P. tumultuosus* by Collar, J&P and Dickinson (2003), following O'Neill & Parker (1977). However, R&G, F&K, Hilty and Forshaw (2006) maintain it as a full species.

BRONZE-WINGED PARROT

Pionus chalcopterus Pl. 76

Identification 29cm. Head dark green except white throat, entire underparts dark green, back to uppertail-coverts, including wings and tail, darker green with heavy black scaling, wings have distinct bronze wash and lustre, and there is a variable maroon wash above and royal blue below; primary-coverts, primaries and underwing-coverts purple-indigo, with underwing turquoise, central tail purple with green outer feathers, undertail-coverts bright red with dark shaft-streaks, undertail dull turquoise; eyes dark brown, orbital skin pink, bill horn with greyish culmen. Juvenile distinctly greener below, chin pink, lesser and median wing-coverts paler brown. From duller Dusky Parrot by streaky white throat and bronzy back, and from other *Pionus* in lacking any green in plumage.

Ssp. *P. c. chalcopterus* (N & C Co: Andes, NW Ve) distinctly less bluish below, more greenish, paler and more bronze above, larger white bib and more extensive pink scaling on throat
P. c. cyanescens (Ec, SW Co) as described

Habits Shrieks continually in flight.
Status Appears local and fairly common, but is nomadic and appearances irregular, thus true status uncertain.
Habitat Upper Tropical and Subtropical Zones but recorded from sea level to 2,800m, most frequently at 1,400–2,400m. Both wet and dry montane forests, forest edges and clearings, and partially deforested areas.
Voice Similar to Blue-headed (R&G, H&B), but shriller and higher pitched (Hilty), including a repeated flight-call of *kree-ink!* (R&G), *chee-ee chee-ee…* (J&P) and *she'lank* or *she'l'lank* (Hilty).

DUSKY PARROT *Pionus fuscus* Pl. 76

Identification 25–26cm. Brown head with maroon underparts lightly scaled dusky, undertail-coverts and basal half of undertail unmarked bright red, lores red, face-sides and lower ear-coverts dusky, scaled pale greyish-brown, the white bases to feathers showing as irregular lines, upperparts dark brown with maroon and purple wash, scaled slightly paler; primary-coverts, secondaries, primaries and tail rich purple; eyes brown, orbital skin white, bill horn with dark grey culmen and lower mandible. Juvenile greener above, paler and more fringed pinkish below, with red bar on forehead. Uniform dull dark brown relieved by white around head, giving typical *Pionus* unkempt appearance.

Ssp. Monotypic (Ve: Sierra de Perija, to SE Gu, Su, FG)

Habits Usually in canopy but comes lower in fruiting trees.
Status Overall fairly common and widespread but local and unpredictable. Commonest in coastal forests of the Guianas.
Habitat Tropical and Lower Subtropical Zones, usually to 1,000m, but to 1,800m in Perijá and Suriname. Varied habitats from wet montane forest to coastal gallery forest, seasonally flooded *várzea* and cultivations (though avoids more open areas).
Voice Flight-calls include several rough *craáak* or *cra-aak* notes (H&B) and *tellit, tellit, tellit*, a pause, and then repeated (Hilty).

Amazons are among the best-known parrots, not least because of their popularity as cagebirds. They are medium to large in size, generally green, chunky in shape, with short square tails. They have distinctive – if somewhat variable – facial patterns and bright wing speculums that may show in flight. Their rounded wings and stiff, notably shallow, rapid wingbeats appear almost to quiver. They fly high, and are hard to identify in flight unless calls are known. Always fly in pairs (unless the female is at the nest) with the female slightly ahead, maintaining continual contact calls. When foraging in fruiting trees, usually silent and slow as they edge from branch to branch, but are noisy at pre-roost roost gatherings when larger numbers assemble – often inside cities.

FESTIVE AMAZON *Amazona festiva* Pl. 76

Identification 34–35cm. Essentially grass green; adult has thick red line from eye to lores and across forehead, the part from eyes to lores bordered below by a dark line, with some powder blue on head-sides behind eyes, lower back and rump bright red, primary-coverts and primaries deep blue; eyes coloured in series of concentric circles – innermost grey then yellow, then orange then red – the general impression being pale orange, bill horn with grey streaking. Juvenile lacks red rump and has dark eyes. From other *Amazona* by red rump and lack of wing speculum.

Ssp. *A. f. bodini* (E Co, S Ve, NW Gu) more yellowish below, lores grey-black, broad red band across forehead and forecrown, face-sides clearly washed powder blue, yellow edge to wing from carpal to alula; bill blackish
A. f. festiva (SE Co, E Ec) as described

Status Local in Ecuador, common in parts of Colombia, local in Venezuela where it suffers from trapping for international trade, and scarce in Guyana.
Habitat Lower Tropical Zone, to 500m in Colombia but to 1,000m in Venezuela. Variety of lowland forests and woodland but has distinct preference for wet areas, and rarely encountered far from water. Avoids dry-land forest.
Voice Flight-call distinctive, a repeated nasal *wah-wah…* (H&B) and *roww-roww…* (R&G), or an almost laughing *ooínk* or *rank* (Hilty). When perched, calls include *scree-ee-at* (J&P) and a higher pitched version of the flight-call (Hilty).

RED-LORED AMAZON *Amazona autumnalis* Pl. 77

Identification 31–35cm. From upper corner of lores to forecrown and over eyes bright red, intermixed with powdery blue over crown and becomes green on nape; from lores onto cheeks bright yellow, rest more or less green; secondaries bright red with narrow dark blue trailing edge, primaries basally green then dusky, tail basally green, terminally yellowish green with yellow on inner webs, except central pair. Outermost feather has a dark blue outer edge basally, then some red before yellow-green tip; eyes centrally grey, then orange and outer ring is red, generally appearing orange, cere has tiny red bristles, bill dusky to blackish. Juvenile has red restricted to forehead and yellow to lores and just below. Red-feathered cere unique among Amazons, although only visible in the hand. From Yellow-crowned Amazon in flight by longer tail, from Mealy by smaller size.

Ssp. *A. a. lilacina* (W Ec) face more uniform and brighter yellowish-green, red loral patch extends to form a superciliary
A. a. salvini (SW Co, NW Ve) lores black, broad red band to mid crown, top of head to nape bluish with

vinaceous tint, and lightly scalloped, entire face-sides bright green (no yellow), slightly darker green below; paler bill, darker on lower mandible

Habits Keeps still at sign of danger, but noisy when flushed and flies some distance before landing. Keeps to canopy; active early morning and late afternoon.
Status Merits Vulnerable status (R&G). Rare to local, occasionally locally common, but ephemerally so.
Habitat Lower Tropical Zone, to 700m in Ecuador, 800m in Venezuela and 1,000m in Colombia. Wide range of wooded habitats from forest and wooded swamps to gallery forest and scrubby dry forest. Cultivated areas with tall trees and plantations.
Voice Typical loud flight-call *cheek-orak*, *keekorak* or *chikak-oorak* (H&B, R&G, Hilty) and varied calls when perched including *wee-ee-eee-eeet*, a metallic *kalink kalink* and loud scolding *ow-er* (J&P), *yoik-yoik…*, *ack-ack*, *chek-chek* and more (P. Slud in F, J&P).
Notes Races *lilacina* and *salvini* both possibly incipient species (Collar). Also called Yellow-cheeked Amazon.

BLUE-CHEEKED AMAZON
Amazona dufresniana Pl. 77

Identification 34cm. Adult has crown yellow, flushed orange on forehead, grading into green nape, face-sides entirely violaceous blue; rest of bird green except orange secondaries which have delicate violaceous trailing edge; black primaries and yellowish tip to tail; eyes orange tinged red on outer rim, orbital skin pale grey, bill grey with sides of upper mandible pinkish-horn. Juvenile has much less yellow on crown, very little orange and no blue on cheeks. From other Amazons by blue cheeks and yellow wing speculum.

Ssp. Monotypic (SE Ve, N Gu, Su, FG)

Habits Flies higher than most Amazons. In Suriname often with Mealy Amazon (H&M).
Status Near Threatened. Uncommon to scarce everywhere. Some movements, apparently seasonal, but also erratic and poorly understood, possibly between Pantepui in Venezuela and northern Guianas.
Habitat Upper Tropical to Lower Subtropical Zones. From 1,100 to 1,700m in Pantepui, and to 500m in the north of the Guianas. Rainforest and savanna woodlands in Venezuela, gallery and sand-ridge forests in Guianas, also rainforest in the interior of French Guiana.
Voice Distinctly differs from other Amazons: a throaty triplet *queenk-queenk-queen* in flight and when perched is characteristic (Hilty).

YELLOW-SHOULDERED AMAZON
Amazona barbadensis Pl. 77

Identification 33–36cm. Large green bird with entire front of head yellow (forehead so pale as to be whitish), yellow shoulder, and basal half of secondaries bright red, distal half dark blue giving a distinct speculum, primaries dark green becoming distally blackish, thighs yellow; eyes orange, orbital skin grey, bill bone colour. Juvenile less yellow on face and shoulder. Yellow shoulders and red speculum conspicuous in flight.

Ssp. Monotypic (Ve, Bo)

Habits In groups or small flocks. Very noisy at roosts early evening and after dawn.
Status Vulnerable. Heavily trapped for bird trade and under serious threat.
Habitat Lower Tropical Zone. Xerophytic country with cactus and *Acacia*. Also in mangroves and all manner of cultivation. Said to take maize, and mangos.
Voice Loud and raucous with fewer musical calls than other Amazona. A dry rattling screeet and trilling *scree-ee-ee-ak* (J&P), a harsh screeching (F), and throaty, rolling *cu'r'r'r'ak* (Hilty).
Note Race *rothschildi* was applied to birds on offshore islands, which have less yellow on shoulders, but this proved to be just an age-related phase.

YELLOW-CROWNED AMAZON
Amazona ochrocephala Pl. 77

Identification 35–38cm. Adult has forehead to rear crown yellow (not reaching eye level); narrow eyebrow and almost all of rest of bird green, with orange and yellow in bend of wing and secondaries bright red, primaries basally dark green, rest blackish, base of outer tail-feathers dark blue; eyes yellow with red outer ring, orbital skin pale grey, bill dusky with orange sides to upper mandible and black tip. Immature very similar but yellow patch restricted to mid crown and wing speculum orange; orange to brown eyes. Juvenile has smaller yellow coronal patch, grey eye-ring and dark brown eyes. Slightly smaller and sympatric Orange-winged Amazon has blue loral streak and yellow cheeks.

Ssp. *A. o. ochrocephala* (E Co, Ve, Tr, Gu, Su, FG) as described
A. o. panamensis (NW Co) bill pinkish-horn with pale orange sides barely visible, yellow feathers restricted to V-shaped patch on forehead and crown
A. o. nattereri (Ec, S Co) yellow restricted to crown, forehead black; differs from juvenile *ochrocephala* by bluish suffusion to forehead, face and throat, and orange iris

Habits Flushes silently, but wings make flapping sound. Gathers at mineral-rich cliff faces with Mealy, macaws and other parrots.
Status Uncommon and local. In decline everywhere due to loss of habitat and trapping.
Habitat Lower Tropical Zone. Variety of forests and woodland, savanna with scattered trees, *Mauritia* groves, cultivations and agricultural areas, often near habitation. Tends to prefer drier areas.
Voice Flight-call a distinctive, repeated, *kurr-owk…kurr-owk…* (P. Slud in F), *curr-ouw…curr-ouw* or *bow-wow* (Hilty) or *aow-aow*. Wide variety of other calls, notes and whistles, including *screet*, a louder, deeper *graaht, ye-ert* (J&P) and a rapid *ha-ha-ha* (Sick).

ORANGE-WINGED AMAZON
Amazona amazonica Pl. 77

Identification 31–32cm. Adult has broad blue line through eyes, from cere to rear ear-coverts, forehead to crown yellow, face-sides yellow (the shape and extent of yellow and blue rather variable, chin might also be yellow with yellow flecks on throat or back of head, and with age more likely to possess more yellow); rest of bird is green save vermilion-red on 3 outer secondaries and orange trailing edge, black primaries and yellowish tip to tail, but undertail is orange with a green band; eyes orange to red, bill horn. Juvenile has wing patch orange and yellow on face very restricted, with perhaps some blue on lores. From all other Amazons by combination of blue and yellow on head, absence of red or yellow on carpal area, and green band across orange undertail.

Ssp. Monotypic (Ec, Co, Ve, T&T, Gu, Su, FG)

Habits Very noisy at roosts before leaving in morning.
Status Widespread and locally common, considered a pest on Trinidad & Tobago. Hunted for food and sport throughout the Guianas. Heavily trapped for bird trade everywhere.
Habitat Lower Tropical Zone, usually below 500m, but to 1,200m south of Orinoco. Wide variety of forest and woodland, but tends to avoid dense forest where Mealy Amazon is dominant. Frequently forms communal roosts in urban areas, parks and gardens.
Voice Flight-call a distinctive, high-pitched *cm-quick, cm-quick*... or *ca-leek-ca-leek* in Falcón, Venezuela (Hilty), and *kleeak, quick-quick* (H&B), but perhaps most familiar is *kee-wik*...*kee-wik*...*kee-wik* (R&G).
Note Race *tobagensis* described from a single specimen with red speculum on 4 feathers, compared to usual 3. However, most specimens from Tobago have 3, and many birds with 4 feathers occur in Venezuela, showing latter number to be a simple variant, if not an age-related character.

SCALY-NAPED AMAZON
Amazona mercenaria Pl. 77

Identification 32–34cm. A distinctive Amazon with a slightly more protuberant bill than others, and the only highland species. Mainly green with dark bluish fringes to feathers of nape. Almost entirely green; adult male has central pair of rectrices all green, but rest have green base, a mauve band then a broad red band, and terminally pale green on inner webs and yellow on outer; eyes reddish-orange, orbital skin grey, bill grey.

Ssp. *A. m. canipalliata* (Andes: Ec, Co, Ve) male lacks wing speculum, that of female is maroon, very small, and hidden when perched; some have small patches of orange on breast
A. m. mercenaria (SE Ec) has bright red speculum in both sexes

Habits Often flies very high and large flocks may be seen commuting to and from roosts.
Status Local and uncommon throughout, also poorly known. Reported to have seasonal altitudinal movements and be nomadic, but movements simply not well known nor understood.
Habitat Upper Tropical to Temperate Zones, 1,600–3,600m. Montane forests and lightly wooded areas with tall trees, open forest on ridges, wooded ravines in páramos, crosses open areas, flying high.
Voice Flight-call a repetitive *ka-lee*...*ka-lee*...*ka-lee*... often in a long series, similar to Mealy but higher pitched, shriller and faster repeated (H&B). Many other vocalisations including a staccato *chark chark chark*, perched and in flight, and a pleasant *dee-lee-do-de-de-de-dor* (J&P).
Note Presence of race *mercenaria* (which has red speculum) in Ecuador unconfirmed, but sightings seem quite likely (R&G). Most Ecuadorian birds appear either intermediate between *mercenaria* and *canipalliata*, or represent an undescribed subspecies.

MEALY AMAZON *Amazona farinosa* Pl. 77

Identification 38–40cm. Largest and dullest Amazon, distinguished by lack of good field marks! Almost entirely green with subtle whitish fringes to feathers of both upper- and underparts, bluish tone to nape, variable black scalloping on nape or upper mantle, red speculum on outer secondaries and dark blue trailing edge to all secondaries, green undertail-coverts with a whitish wash, distinctly 2-toned tail, with distal half yellowish; eyes orange, orbital skin pale grey, bill varies according to race. Juvenile lacks yellow on head, and has no blue wash on nape or any blackish scaling on nape or upper mantle; bill dusky.

Ssp. *A. f. farinosa* (N & W Co, SC Ve, Guianas) yellow on head, but variable, horn-coloured bill with dusky tip
A. f. inornata (Ec, Co, N & W Ve) richer blue on nape, no yellow on crown, black lores, dusky bill with black tip
A. f. chapmani (E Ec) like *inornata* but larger, occasional touch of yellow on crown

Habits Sits still for long periods and moves slowly along branches.
Status Fairly common throughout.
Habitat Lower Tropical Zone, usually below 500m but recorded to 1,500m. Prefers dense humid forest, often near clearings and edges; frequents plantations and cultivations, where can cause much damage, stands of *Mauritia* palms, gallery forest, sand-ridge forests, semi-open and tall second growth. Joins macaws and other parrots at cliff-face mineral feasts.
Voice Most commonly heard flight call, *CHOaukor CHO-op*, often repeated many times (Hilty). Another characteristic flight-call, a trisyllabic *ta-kah-yee ta-kah-yee ta-kah-yee*... with accent on higher pitched middle syllable (F) and a wide variety of calls, notes and noises, some of which are given perched or in flight. These include *ka-ha, ka-ha* (D. Ascanio, pers. comm.), *kwok-kwok-kwok* on a descending scale immediately upon alighting (F) and *chap-chap-chap-chaow* (R&G).

Note Doubt as to validity of *inornata* expressed by F, and Collar also doubted *chapmani* which he regarded as a synonym of nominate.

RED-FAN PARROT

Deroptyus accipitrinus Pl. 77

Identification 35–36cm. Unmistakable. Adult has forehead and crown white with an extensive crest that is usually laid back, like a cowl around neck, the base grey with white streaks; the feathers of the crest alternate equal bands of carmine-red and blue, lores black, face-sides to throat dusky brown with bold white streaks; upperparts entirely dark green, only the primaries bluish-grey basally, darker towards tips; breast banded carmine/maroon and blue, tapering to a point on lower belly, the blue bands narrower than reddish ones, and sides to undertail-coverts green; underwing-coverts dark, dull green, underwing grey, undertail dusky; eyes yellow, orbital skin buffy-grey, bill dusky. Juvenile has all-brown head with no crest, streaked buffy-white all over, otherwise like adult.

Ssp. *D. a. accipitrinus* (SE Co, E Ec, S Ve, Gu, Su, FG)

Habits Has very distinctive flight, with head lifted, wings angled down and tail fanned, undulating (rather pigeon-like) jizz and frequent glides (unlike any *Accipiter*!). Quite vocal and often heard before seen. Not very gregarious, in pairs or small groups.

Status Rare in Ecuador, uncommon in Venezuela, but more common further east, becoming common in the Guianas. Some seasonal movements, not well known.

Habitat Lower Tropical Zone, below 400m. Rain forests, apparently preferring undisturbed *terra firme*. Also in sand-ridge forests, but mostly riverine forests in Venezuela.

Voice Flight-calls include a distinctive series of *chack* notes, followed by a high-pitched, almost squealing *tak tak heeya heeya*, but only *heeya* notes heard at a distance (McLoughlin & Burton in F), *keeya-keeya-keeya* and a piping *peeu-peeu-peeu-peeu* (R&G). Also, a high-pitched *slit* (F) and varied chattering and whistling notes.

CUCULIDAE – Cuckoos

Cuckoos are a diverse family found throughout most of the world except frozen regions. Most are birds of the tropics or subtropics, but some species everywhere migrate to temperate latitudes to breed. Despite the wide variety of subfamilies, they are characteristically clad in black, brown and white, with some blackish birds displaying bright bronze, green and blue iridescences. They are also zygodactyl, with 2 toes pointing forwards and 2 backwards, permitting clever climbing abilities and fast running on the ground. The aptly-named Squirrel Cuckoo is rufous-chestnut above and has a long tail; it bounds along stout branches, with its tail apparently undulating behind it. The family takes its name from the Eurasian Cuckoo, which has an onomatopoeic call, *cu-coo*, and is very well known for being a brood parasite. Most cuckoos, however, are not brood parasites but monogamous, nest building and rearing their own young. Of the Neotropical cuckoos, 3 beautifully plumaged species, Striped, Pheasant and Pavonine are brood parasites. In considerable contrast, the anis, which are intensely social, build communal nests in which several females may lay up to 2 dozen eggs, and the whole group assists in brooding and rearing the young, including young from the previous brood.

Several North American cuckoos migrate to our region, they are elegant and slim, rather hawk-like in profile with long wings and tails, and typically brown above and white below. Superficially very similar, they merit careful attention to smaller details. Resident anis are all black, sometimes showing deep blue and purple sheens; highly gregarious, they are usually seen in truncated flocks flying follow-my-leader, calling to and highly protective of each other. Should a bird fall into mist-net, the flock will gather around, clumsily mobbing the observer as he struggles to remove the calling and biting bird, and the nasty, vulture-like smell of the bird makes him or her doubly rueful. Most cuckoos are insectivorous, being particularly fond of arthropods, but ground-cuckoos in particular feed on ground-dwelling vertebrates, up to reasonable-sized snakes.

Additional references used for this family include Sick (1993), Payne (1997), Sibley (2000).

American cuckoos are elegant birds with long tails and rounded wings. Their tails usually have pale spots at the tips, and wings may have rufous in the flight-feathers, the combination of which can aid identification. Most *Coccyzus* are boreal or austral migrants. They are slender, somewhat dove-like, elegant birds, apt to sit in the open during the morning and absorb the sun's warmth before becoming active. Mainly feed on large hairy, urticant caterpillars, the hairs of which impact on the birds' stomach linings and must be periodically expelled.

DWARF CUCKOO

Coccyzus pumilus Pl. 79

Identification 20–22cm. Like a mockingbird or thrush, and note strongly defined breast of adult. Adult brownish-grey above with sides of face to breast cinnamon, rest of underparts creamy buff, thighs greyish-brown; tail comparatively shorter than other *Coccyzus*, brownish-grey below with subterminal black bands and terminal white crescents; eyes red, bill black. Juvenile greyish-brown above, sides of face to breast grey, rest of underparts greyish-buff, undertail like adult but white crescents slightly narrower; eyes dark brown.

Ssp. Monotypic (N Co, N & NC Ve)

Habits Usually solitary. Slow and inconspicuous. Sometimes found on ground at foot of bushes.

Status Frequent in Colombia, fairly common in rainy season in Venezuela, but scarce or absent in dry. Movements unknown.

Habitat Tropical Zone. Gallery forest in drier areas, pastures with patches of light forest or shrubs, gardens and parks.

Voice Repeated *trrrr*, *c.*1 per s (Ralph 1975); a mellow early-morning song: *kööa kööa* (P. Schwartz), an occasional churr (Hilty, Payne).

Note Payne (2005) resurrected genus *Coccycua* for this species (spelling of specific name becomes *pumila* under this arrangement).

ASH-COLOURED CUCKOO

Coccyzus cinereus Pl. 79

Identification 24cm. Adult is brownish-grey above, throat and breast greyish-buff, rest of underparts white, washed slightly greyish-buff on flanks and undertail-coverts; undertail dull brownish-grey with subterminal black bars and narrow white terminal tips. Juvenile much browner above, throat and breast greyer; undertail has subterminal black bars but no terminal white tips, eyes brown. Note long tail is not graduated.

Ssp. Monotypic (S Co: Amazonia)

Status Very rare in our region, a trans-Amazonian austral migrant that is occasional/vagrant to extreme south-west Colombia, and possibly elsewhere.

Habitat Tropical Zone. Deciduous and gallery forests, second growth and scrubby areas.

Voice A loud *cowe cowe cow cow* (Wetmore 1926) or *cow-w cow-w cow-w* like Yellow-billed but lacks clucking at end (Payne).

Note Payne (2005) resurrected genus *Coccycua* for this species (spelling of specific name becomes *cinerea* under this arrangement).

BLACK-BILLED CUCKOO

Coccyzus erythropthalmus Pl. 79

Identification 28cm. Greyish-olive above, slightly greyer on head; lower face-sides and chin to undertail-coverts whitish, undertail has outer 2 pairs steeply graduated and all rectrices are grey-olive with dusky subterminal bar and whitish terminal crescents; eyes dark brown with red eye-ring, bill dusky, legs and feet dark grey. Juvenile warmer brown-olive above with pale terminal fringes to inner greater wing-coverts and tertials, rufescent inner webs to remiges; undertail darker than adult with weaker pale tips; eyes dark brown, eye-ring grey, bill dusky above, grey below. From Yellow-billed by tail, which has very little white (Yellow-billed is noticeably contrasting black and white), and uniform wings, whereas Yellow-billed has rufous in flight-feathers.

Ssp. Monotypic (Ec, Co, Ve, Tr)

Habits Furtive, keeps to foliage.

Status Scarce boreal migrant, passing through northern South America in autumn. Uncommon to rare in Ecuador wintering east of the Andes, rare in Colombia and vagrant on Trinidad (no records Tobago).

Habitat Tropical Zone. May use almost any lightly forested or bushy area, but in wintering grounds prefers humid forests.

Voice Generally silent in winter, but characteristic call is 5–6 repetitions of 3-note *cucucu* phrase, a hollow, whistled *po po po po…* and a rolling *kddow kddow kddow…*, higher pitched and less guttural than Yellow-billed (Payne, Hilty).

YELLOW-BILLED CUCKOO

Coccyzus americanus Pl. 79

Identification 30cm. Greyish-olive above with rufous primary-coverts and all remiges (which have with dark tips), dark line through eyes, underparts all white, undertail steeply graduated, dusky to black with white outer webs to outermost feather on each side, 4 outer rectrices have large white terminal spots, but not central pair; eyes dark brown with yellow eye-ring, bill yellow with black line on culmen. Juvenile similar but white spots on tail less distinct and not as clean-cut as on adult; eye-ring and lower mandible grey. Broad white tips to all but central tail-feathers and rufous in wings obvious in flight and distinguish it from Black-billed Cuckoo.

Ssp. Monotypic (throughout)

Habits Secretive and quiet; usually alone, but sometimes in groups on migration.

Status Boreal migrant. More common (locally) September–December and April, scarcer other months; some all year. Very rare in Ecuador, more regular in Colombia, uncommon in Guyana and Trinidad & Tobago.

Habitat Tropical and Subtropical Zones but to 4,000m on passage in Venezuela. Light forests and shrubby areas.

Voice Long, fast series of repeated *ka* and *kowlp* notes, sometimes a single *kddowl*, a deep-swallowed, dove-like *cloom* repeated with long pauses, and slow cooing series, descending and weakening, *too too too too to to to* (Sibley).

PEARLY-BREASTED CUCKOO

Coccyzus euleri Pl. 79

Identification 25cm. Greyish-olive above, lower face to undertail-coverts white, outer web of outermost rectrice on each side white, all rectrices, except central pair, have white V-shaped tips; eyes dark brown, eye-ring grey, bill yellow-orange with black culmen, legs and feet grey. Remiges are concolorous with rest of upper parts, whereas the otherwise very similar Yellow-billed Cuckoo has rufous on flight-feathers.

Ssp. Monotypic (all countries)

Habits Seemingly secretive, perching in dense cover.

Status Rare in Ecuador, very local and scarce in Colombia, Venezuela and the Guianas. Presence erratic and unpredictable, possibly appears in response to caterpillar plagues, perhaps wanderers from extreme north of range, somewhat migratory or combination of all these.

Habitat Tropical Zone to 900m. Sandy soil and gallery forests, scrub.

Voice Recording by P. Schwartz: *tuctuctuctuctuctuc towlp*, tówlp, *tówlp, tówlp*, the last notes similar to *americanus*; song up to 20 slow repetitions of *kuoup* (Hilty).

MANGROVE CUCKOO

Coccyzus minor Pl. 79

Identification 30cm. Two distinct morphs. Pale morph is olive-brown above with black line through eyes, pale buffy underparts; tail steeply graduated and undertail black with large white terminal spots on outer 4 pairs of rectrices; eyes brown with eye-ring variable, yellow to grey, bill black with extensive yellow base to lower mandible. Dark morph is entirely rich cinnamon below, including underwing-coverts. Juvenile has rufescent fringes to wing-coverts and white spots on tail merge into black, not clean-cut like adult.

Ssp. Monotypic (all except Ec)

Habits Quiet, inactive, retiring and solitary.

Status Generally very uncommon. Only a few very old ('Bogotá') specimens from Colombia, sight records in Curaçao and Bonaire, scarce in Venezuela, Trinidad & Tobago, and uncommon in Guyana.

Habitat Tropical Zone. Coasts and islands. *Avicennia* mangrove, forests and xerophytic thickets near streams or sea, few sightings far from water.

Voice Slow series of raspy *ke-ke-ke-ke-ke-ka-ka-ka*... (ffrench) and nasal, unmusical *aan aan aan aan aan urmm urmm*, accelerating slightly, last 2 notes lower and longer (Sibley). Also a low, guttural *gawk gawk gawk gawk*... and single *whit!* (Payne).

Note Race *maynardi*, described from Aruba, is one of 13 based on small samples, but large series show all to be within range of variation found throughout range (Payne).

DARK-BILLED CUCKOO

Coccyzus melacoryphus Pl. 79

Identification 25cm. Olive-brown above with grey crown and black line through eyes, underparts cinnamon (intermediate between pale and dark morphs of Mangrove Cuckoo!), with grey band running narrowly from lower ear-coverts to breast-sides, tail steeply graduated and underside is black with white terminal spots on outer 4 pairs of rectrices. Juvenile is overall duller with brown crown, grey tips to tail and sometimes some rufous in wings, and buff tips to wing-coverts. In coastal region, may be confused with larger Mangrove Cuckoo, especially its dark morph; separated by all-black bill and warmer brown upperparts (not greyish).

Ssp. Monotypic (throughout except ABC and To)

Habits Solitary. Less shy than other *Coccyzus*, may be found on low exposed perches.

Status In northern South America, both resident and austral migrant populations. Uncommon to rare in Ecuador, frequent but local in Colombia, uncommon in Venezuela, scarce in Trinidad, uncommon in Guyana, Suriname and French Guiana.

Habitat Tropical and Subtropical Zones, to 2,800m in Ecuador, 2,400m in Colombia, and in Venezuela to 500m north of Orinoco, 900m south of it. Humid *terra firme*, gallery, secondary and riparian forests, edges of *várzea*, pastures with shrubbery, shade trees in coffee plantations, dry and partially open ranchland.

Voice Seldom sings. Song, a slow *cu-cu-cu-cu-cu-kolp, kolp, kulop*; also, a slow rattle: *dddrrrrrrr* (H&B, Hilty).

GREY-CAPPED CUCKOO

Coccyzus lansbergi Pl. 79

Identification 25cm. Dark grey cap, rest of upperparts dark rufous-brown, throat to upper breast rich rufescent cinnamon, rest of underparts pale cinnamon, tail very steeply graduated and rectrices blunt-ended, undertail black with large white spot at end of each feather; eyes dark brown, eye-ring dull grey, bill black, legs and feet grey. Juvenile similar but has brown crown and less distinct pale tips to rectrices. Intensely coloured. From Dwarf Cuckoo by dark grey cap and richer back and belly; from Little Cuckoo by dark grey cap.

Ssp. Monotypic (S Ec, N Co, N Ve, Bo)

Habits Secretive, tends to stay in cover at low levels.

Status Uncommon to very rare in Ecuador, Colombia and Venezuela, with single record from Bonaire. Apparently migratory from Ecuador to north coast, but movements poorly understood.

Habitat Tropical Zone, to 800m in Ecuador, 600m in Colombia and 1,400m in Venezuela. Dense low vegetation near streams and lagoons, forest borders, very overgrown open areas.

Voice Rapidly repeated call: *cucucucucucucu-cu* (P. Schwartz recording), faster than other *Coccyzus*.

SQUIRREL CUCKOO *Piaya cayana* Pl. 78

Identification 43cm. Unmistakable. Entirely chestnut above, throat and malar to upper breast cinnamon, underparts grey, undertail-coverts dark grey, undertail dull chestnut but each of outer 4 feathers becomes dusky towards tip and has large terminal white crescent, whilst central pair have white tips; eyes red, eye-ring yellow or yellowish-grey, bill yellow, legs and feet dark grey. Juvenile resembles adult, but is (variably) smaller with a (variably) shorter tail; head slightly paler.

Ssp. *P. c. cayana* (S Ve, Gu, Su, FG) slightly paler throat and upper breast, and paler grey underparts; red eye and eye-ring

P. c. circe (W Ve) like *mehleri* but richer rufous

P. c. insulana (Tr, E Ve) like *mehleri* but undertail-coverts black

P. c. mehleri (NE Co, NW Ve) as described

P. c. mesura (E Ec, E Co) like *nigricrissa* but smaller; red eye-ring

P. c. nigricrissa (W Co, W Ec) dark rufous above, chestnut throat and breast, black belly and undertail with bold white crescents at tip of each rectrice; eyes red, eye-ring red, bill yellow, legs and feet dark grey

P. c. thermophila (NW Co) dark rufous above, dark grey belly and undertail; yellow eye-ring

Habits Rather squirrel-like as it bounds along branches, with long, full tail seemingly undulating, pauses unmoving, also like squirrel. Flies short distances, joins mixed flocks and follows army ants.

Status Uncommon to locally common in Ecuador, common in Colombia, Venezuela and Trinidad (no records Tobago), frequent in Guyana, Suriname and French Guiana.

Habitat Tropical and Subtropical Zones to 2,500m, but usually below 1,200m. Dry to humid, light or open woodland, forest edges, second growth, parkland and urban gardens.
Voice Calls rarely, loud, varied and distinct, including *chick, kwah* (H&B), *hic-a-ro* (Payne), *geep-kaweeer* (R&G), all of which are kiskadee-like (Hilty); in alarm, *stit-it*. Song 5–8 loud repetitions of *wheep* (Willis & Eisenmann 1979).

BLACK-BELLIED CUCKOO *Piaya melanogaster* Pl. 78

Identification 38cm. Dark grey cap that runs from malar to nape, white loral spot, rest of upperparts chestnut, throat and breast chestnut, slightly paler on throat, rest of underparts sooty black, undertail black with large white terminal crescent on each rectrice; eyes and bill deep red, legs and feet black. Juvenile has narrower tail-feathers with smaller white tips. From otherwise similar Squirrel Cuckoo by red bill, grey cap and lack of grey on breast.

Ssp. Monotypic (E Ec, SE Co, E Ve, Gu, Su, FG)

Status Rare in Ecuador, uncommon in Colombia, Venezuela and Guyana, and poorly known.
Habitat Tropical Zone. Mostly humid forest canopy, sandy soil forest, edges and overgrown open areas.
Voice Calls, rare and loud, *jjit, jjit-jjir-jjit* and a scratchy, descending *yaaaaa*, followed by a dry rattle (H&B), like Squirrel Cuckoo but harsher and higher pitched (Hilty, Payne).

LITTLE CUCKOO *Piaya minuta* Pl. 78

Identification 25cm. Chestnut above, sides of face and breast cinnamon, rest of underparts grey, tail steeply graduated, the underside dark brown with large terminal white spot on each feather; eyes orange, bill yellow, legs and feet dark grey. Juvenile much darker chestnut above, dark umber-brown below; eyes brown, bill greenish-yellow, legs and feet green. Remarkably like Squirrel Cuckoo but much smaller, and voice very different.

Ssp. *P. m. barinensis* (CW Ve) as described
P. m. gracilis (W Co, W Ec) paler bib and throat, medium grey belly and undertail-coverts
P. m. minuta (E Co, Ve, Tr, Gu, Su, FG) darker, blackish undertail-coverts, eyes red, legs and feet yellow; juvenile dark brown above, sooty grey below with only faint terminal crescents on undertail; eyes dark brown, bill dull yellow, legs and feet black
P. m. panamensis (N Co) like *minuta* but cinnamon-rufous breast smaller and undertail slaty-brown

Status Uncommon to fairly common but local in Colombia, uncommon in Ecuador, very common in north-east Venezuela, fairly common elsewhere in latter country, uncommon in Trinidad, frequent in Guyana, Suriname and French Guiana.
Habitat Tropical Zone, usually below 900m. Near water in low-levels thickets, dense second growth and forest edges, swamps.
Voice Seldom calls, but gives a *tchek* (ffrench), *quienk* (J. P. O'Neill), *wyurr, wreh-reh-reh-reh?* (Ridgely & Gwynne), chattering, descending *anhh-anhh-anhh...*, a whistled *tyoooo* (J. V. Remsen); *geep, were* (H&B) and *tyoooooo* (Payne).
Note Payne (2005) resurrected genus *Coccycua* for this species, along with Dwarf and Ash-coloured Cuckoos.

STRIPED CUCKOO *Tapera naevia* Pl. 79

Identification 28–30cm. Somewhat ragged rufous crest streaked dark, pale to whitish eyebrow, narrow from lores and over eyes but broader behind and reaching around ear-coverts (brown with dark streaks) to join throat-sides, whitish underparts; upperparts ochraceous buff with dusky to blackish streaks and pale tips to tertials and primaries, long graduated tail tapers to twin points, with long uppertail-coverts reaching two-thirds of way from base; eyes hazel, eye-ring yellowish, bill brown above, pale to horn or yellowish below, legs and feet grey. Juvenile has shorter crest with white spots at tips of feathers, above similar to adult but has white spots at tips of wing- and tail-coverts, plus tertials and primaries; eyes brown, underparts warmer buff, especially on face and breast.

Ssp. *T. n. naevia* (all countries)

Habits Well known by its voice, but not easy to locate even when very close. Solitary and furtive, but often sings from exposed perch, raising crest and spreading alula feathers. Runs fast on ground, stopping to display. It is a brood parasite.
Status Uncommon to rare in Ecuador, frequent but quite local in Colombia and Venezuela, common in Trinidad (no records Tobago), common in Guyana, Suriname and French Guiana.
Habitat Tropical Zone. Undergrowth of forests, edges, thickets, and open country with bushes and bogs.
Voice An insistent clear, melancholy, rising whistle, *wüüüü weee* (H&B). Can 'throw' voice very far.

PHEASANT CUCKOO *Dromococcyx phasianellus* Pl. 78

Identification 38cm. Long, laid-back rufous crest, hindneck and upperparts dark brown, the feathers faintly fringed paler, white on tips of median and greater wing-coverts, tail long and slightly graduated with long uppertail-coverts with white terminal spots; cheeks and ear-coverts dark brown with some pale streaking, long pale buffy eyebrow from lores fully embraces ear-coverts and reaches breast- and neck-sides, chin and throat warm buffy, narrow, black-dotted sub-malar line, breast warm buffy, almost cinnamon, finely streaked dark brown, with a few crescents at sides, rest of underparts buffy-white; eyes brown, eye-ring grey, bill dark above, pale below. Might be confused with smaller Pavonine Cuckoo, which is darker and has pale eye.

Ssp. Monotypic (Ec, Co, Ve)

Habits Difficult to see, as keeps in cover and flits across openings or paths discreetly, flight undulating with tail spread. Sings during night and at dawn.

Status Generally uncommon, fairly common locally, but seldom seen due to secretive habits. Rare in Ecuador, uncommon and local in Colombia, Venezuela and the Guianas.
Habitat Tropical Zone, to 400m in Venezuela but to 1,600m elsewhere. Undergrowth of forests, edges, thickets.
Voice A double-whistle, trilled *se-sée-werrrrr*; also *sa, seh, si-see* (Willis & Eisenmann *fide* H&B), *eweerrew*, ending in a tremolo, but tremolo lost if bird excited, and becomes a whistle, *eww eww dewrew*, more like Pavonine Cuckoo (Sick), alternatively transcribed as *pü-püpü-werrrrr*, also an occasional *pa, püh, pe-pee* (Hilty). A series of rattling, clucking notes (Payne).

PAVONINE CUCKOO
Dromococcyx pavoninus Pl. 78

Identification 25cm. Dark brown to blackish above, with sweeping, pointed, rufous crest, pale tips to median and greater wing-coverts, and extremely long uppertail-coverts streaked black centrally with terminal white spots; face- and breast-sides washed cinnamon with dark ear-coverts and cinnamon buffy eyebrow encircling them, and central breast to undertail-coverts white; eyes yellow, bill generally dark, legs and feet grey. Juvenile mid brown above, almost olive with dark rufescent crest, buffy fringes to most feathers and paler streaks at tips of median and greater wing-coverts, brown of ear-coverts continues to breast; eyes dark. Remarkably like Pheasant Cuckoo but significantly smaller and shorter tailed. Pheasant Cuckoo is browner above and has distinctly spotted throat and breast, and dark eyes.

Ssp. *D. p. pavoninus* (E Ec, SE Co, Ve, Gu) pale reddish-chestnut crown and front of head
D. p. perijanus (W Ve) front of head and crown dark chestnut

Habits Skulking and secretive, only reveals presence by voice at night and dawn. Flies with distinctive high-winged, butterfly-like jerkiness, tail somewhat fanned. Perches well concealed within dense vines.
Status In general, uncommon and local. Very rare in Ecuador, sight records in Colombia, uncommon in Venezuela and Guyana.
Habitat Tropical and Subtropical Zones, *perijanus* to 2,000m, *pavoninus* to 900m. Forest edges, dense thickets and thick second growth, lower to mid levels.
Voice A rising *püü, pee, püü-pe-pe* (P. Schwartz). A 4–5-syllable whistle with timbre of Striped Cuckoo, *ew l ew ew, ew-i ew-i i* (Sick). A flat, whistled *püü pee, püü-pe'pe*, first and third notes lowest, the rest half a tone higher (Hilty).
Note Treated as monotypic by Payne, and Dickinson (2003), without comment. Aveledo & Ginés (1950) described *perijanus* on basis of details above. Two years later, Aveledo wrote in the Phelps Collection records (unpublished), that 6 more specimens from Zulia had been collected and confirmed the original diagnosis, but it seems that foxing may have destroyed the evidence. There seems to be no reason to synonymise the race.

Anis and Guira Cuckoo are the antithesis of the idea of cuckoos as brood-parasites, for they not only construct nests and rear their own young, but brooding and rearing are communal efforts, with young from one brood assisting their parents rear the next. Several females lay in same nest, and all those involved rear family together. Anis fly awkwardly, often in single file and land clumsily, as if falling into the bush! In contrast Guira is an elegant flier. Any intruders cause the birds to alarm-call continually. If a bird is trapped or caught in some way, the others fly around trying to assist by their presence and cries. They vocalise continually, keeping in contact as they move about on the ground amongst thick grasses. Their feathers easily become wet as they forage in the grass, and they are often seen on exposed branches, sunning themselves and absorbing the sun's warmth. Usually roost in bamboos, sitting tightly on a horizontal stem, occasionally in clumps.

The three anis, showing variation in bill size and shape within each species, upper birds are juveniles, middle and lower birds drawn from 2 extremes in size, from series in Phelps Ornithological Collection, Caracas, Venezuela; left to right: Greater Ani, Smooth-billed Ani and Groove-billed Ani

GREATER ANI *Crotophaga major* Pl. 80

Identification 46cm. Unmistakable, much larger than other anis, with all-black plumage and violet and bronze sheens, a massive 2-tier bill and bright yellow eyes.

Ssp. Monotypic (throughout except Bo, Cu)

Habits Usually solitary, although pairs or small groups sometimes seen. Very cautious and rather secretive, seeming to judge every move carefully before flying slowly, only to land clumsily.
Status Frequent but local in Ecuador, frequent in Venezuela, local in Trinidad (no records Tobago), common in Guyana. Recently recorded on Aruba (Mlodinow in press).
Habitat Tropical Zone. Near rivers and wetlands, mangroves, humid forests, often seen resting beside a bank of reeds, looking out over swamp or pond.
Voice Weird noises, including hisses, growls and croaks that sound almost reptilian, whirrs and clinks that seem electronic and a fast, repeated *krokroro*, which sounds like a boiling kettle and from which the species derives its Venezuelan name of 'Hervidor'.

SMOOTH-BILLED ANI

Crotophaga ani Pl. 80

Identification 33–40cm. Entirely glossy black with blue and purple glosses, and greyish-fringes to feathers of head and body, which affords bird a distinctly scaled appearance in some lights; eyes brown, bill, legs and feet black. Juvenile smaller and lacks gloss. The smallest ani, with a bulging, well-rounded culmen that surges up in a lateral compression from the forehead, and a fairly smooth bill.

Ssp. Monotypic (throughout except ABC)

Habits Forages near cattle, taking grasshoppers and others disturbed by the grazing animals.

Status Uncommon to locally common in Ecuador, very common in Venezuela, common on Trinidad & Tobago and in Guyana.

Habitat Tropical and Subtropical Zones. Open areas, forest borders, savannas, fields with scattered bushes and trees.

Voice A plaintive, repeated *ooeeeeck*, often given in flight (E. Eisenmann). A monotonous song, *piu, piu, piu*. A querulous *que-lick?* or *queee-ik* (Payne, Sibley)

Groove-billed Ani gliding

GROOVE-BILLED ANI

Crotophaga sulcirostris Pl. 80

Identification 30–34cm. Entirely black with indigo-purple gloss, and greyish fringes to head and body, affording a distinctly scaled appearance in some lights; eyes brown, bill, legs and feet black. Juvenile smaller and lacks gloss, bill smooth. From Smooth-billed Ani by larger size and longer, more symmetrical bill which has usually discernible heavy furrows along it.

Ssp. Monotypic (Ec, Co, Ve, Ar, Bo, Cu)

Habits Invariably seen in noisy and conspicuous groups, up to a dozen or so.

Status Uncommon to locally common in Ecuador, very common in Venezuela. Removed from Guyana list by BFR&S due to lack of documentation.

Habitat Tropical Zone. Open areas, pastures, deciduous and gallery forests.

Voice Series of soft whistles: *swilk, swilk, swilk, swilk*… (E. Eisenmann), a series of *tijo* notes, faster series of *whee-o*, and a long series of rapid whistled *kiw* notes (Payne), sometimes a soft and quite fast *psiiu, psiiu*.

[GUIRA CUCKOO *Guira guira*] Pl. 80

Identification 36cm. Tatty, irregular crest from forecrown to back of head, entire head sandy buff, paler around the eyes, upperparts black with white streaks on back and wing-feathers fringed white, lower back and rump white, uppertail-coverts orange-buff with central tail-feathers darker brown, rest of rectrices black with broad white tips; underparts buffy-white with fine black streaks on throat and breast, usually with yellow eyes and yellow bill, but some birds have orange eyes and bill; legs and feet pink.

Ssp. Monotypic (Cu)

Habits Guira is a communal breeder, like the anis, and groups keep close together. Forages on ground, usually in small flocks. Feeds on small vertebrates, insects, eggs and nestlings.

Status Resident of southern South America that does not naturally occur north of the Amazon River. One record of a lone individual on Curaçao. Extensive enquiries show this to be almost certainly an escapee from captivity.

Habitat Tropical Zone. Dry to xerophytic woodland, scrub and open areas with bushes and trees, parks and gardens.

Voice Calls include sequences of mournful *piiioo, piiioo* whistles. A rough trill and occasional *creeep* notes. Groups sing a scale of descending, warbling notes, producing a cacophony, but in flight may utter groans.

Ground-cuckoos have small heads, long tails and long uppertail-coverts. They communicate using a variety of bill-clicks and bill-pops. Bill-clicks can be extended into a loud continuous rattle. They attend army ants as they pass through their territories, snatching the cockroaches, beetles, other insects and small vertebrates disturbed by the marchers. Ground-cuckoos also follow peccary herds for the same reason. Solitary, individuals will chase intruders from their territory with angry bill-clicking, wing-drooping and tail-spreading displays. The *Neomorphus* species replace each other geographically and are very similar in habits and behaviour, and all are sensitive to habitat disturbance.

RUFOUS-VENTED GROUND CUCKOO

Neomorphus geoffroyi Pl. 80

Identification 46–50cm. Dark maroon-brown from forehead to lower back, becoming redder on rump and tail, substantial, laid-back (but frequently raised) crest is flushed with deep green and cobalt blue, hindneck and back scalloped deep green and tail has deep bronze-green tones to outer fringes of feathers, wings maroon, shot with bronze and green; entire upperparts somewhat metallic and bronzed; chin and malar to breast buff, with paler centres to most feathers and dark lines edging these on some, breast-sides irregularly scalloped black, and rest of underparts cinnamon to rich rufous on undertail-coverts, thighs buff; eyes yellow, orbital skin greyish-blue, bill yellow with bluish flush at base, legs and feet grey-green. Juvenile not found: reportedly duller and darker, blackish with rufous-grey on belly and little gloss on wings and tail, bill dark (Payne).

Ssp. *N. g. aequatorialis* (SE Co, Ec) bronze above, marked scaling on breast with pale fringes

N. g. salvini (Co: NW coast) olive above, very little scalloping on breast

Habits Solitary, shy and secretive, runs like roadrunner. Terrestrial but perches frequently and wings droop to touch perch at rest.
Status Rare in Ecuador, rare and local in Colombia. Disappearing due to forest clearance.
Habitat Tropical Zone to 1,200m. Mostly primary, undisturbed lowland humid forests.
Voice Snaps bill loudly, also sings a plaintive, soft descending *oooooo-oóp*, like a dove, every 3–4 s (H&B, Sick).

BANDED GROUND CUCKOO
Neomorphus radiolosus Pl. 80

Identification 46–50cm. Back and wings chestnut with some black scaling on back and lesser coverts, entire upperparts have bronze and purple iridescences; entire head to mantle and underparts barred black and white, black on thick crest and ear-coverts to back of head, scaled on mantle and breast-sides of breast, with very even bars on flanks and belly to undertail-coverts; rump and uppertail-coverts purplish, tail purple with blackish fringes; eyes red, orbital skin bright blue, legs and feet grey-green. Juvenile has dull black head and upperparts, black underparts with rusty bars and blue and grey bare facial skin. Distinctive combination of chestnut above and black-and-white barring below.

Ssp. Monotypic (Ec, Co)

Habits Very poorly known.
Status Endangered. Very rare in Ecuador, rare and local in Colombia.
Habitat Tropical Zone to 1,500m. Mostly wet foothill forest.
Voice Bill-snaps. Also an *oooooo-wooo*.

RUFOUS-WINGED GROUND CUCKOO
Neomorphus rufipennis Pl. 80

Identification 48–50cm. Two variants, or morphs, the dark morph previously described as race *nigrogularis*. Normal or pale morph in adult plumage has crown, head-sides, hindneck and lower breast deep indigo-blue, throat to upper breast greenish-grey with deep indigo V-shaped markings, least evident on throat, most heavily on upper breast; effect is of graduated, angular scaling. Back to tip of tail, including wings, deep green with a maroon flush to outer fringes of rectrices and on wing-coverts and remiges, latter with purple outer fringes, and entire upperparts have with bronze and purple iridescences; sides and belly greenish-grey, washed greenish-olive on flanks and thighs to undertail-coverts; eyes orange, orbital skin carmine to crimson, bill black with yellowish tip, legs and feet dark grey-green. Dark morph has much less scaling on chin and upper throat, deep indigo to lower breast and mantle, back, wings and rump darker with more purple in iridescence, belly to undertail-coverts dark greenish-olive. Note red skin around eye.

Ssp. Monotypic (Co? Ve, Gu)

Habits Solitary or forages with chicks, generally nervous, and when alarmed escapes by running very fast. Terrestrial, follows army ants and bands of peccaries to take advantage of insects and small vertebrates disturbed by them, a habit that has earned them the name 'Pájaros Baquiros' (peccary birds) in Venezuela.
Status Possibly occurs in Colombia. Uncommon and local in Venezuela and Guyana.
Habitat Tropical Zone to 1,100m. Humid lowland and foothill forests.
Voice Random, intermittent calls consist of hooted *whooo* notes that resemble a pigeon. A *whOOu*, given when walking or perched (Hilty). Snaps bill quite often. Also *ooooooOoóp* (R&G).

RED-BILLED GROUND CUCKOO
Neomorphus pucheranii Pl. 80

Identification 50cm. Top of head has thick, laid-back (but frequently raised) crest that is black with a green-blue gloss, rest of head, neck and underparts white, washed greyish with sparse scallops on throat and foreneck, and broad black breast-band, hindneck washed green, becoming solid green on back, then maroon on rump and tail, with bronze-green iridescence on tail-sides, wings brown, glossed green and bronze on upper wing, rich rufous on greater coverts and tertials, purplish dark brown on remiges; eyes red, eye-ring and orbital skin in front of eye and most of bill bright red, culmen and tip yellow, patch of skin behind eyes bright blue, legs and feet grey. Immature has black throat with patches of green iridescence, brownish-grey breast and underparts, thighs barred black, and rufescent undertail-coverts; hindneck to lower back dark olive with green iridescence, and wings darker than adult.

Ssp. *N. p. pucheranii* (NE Ec?, S Co?)

Status Very rare (sight records only) Ecuador. In Colombia, listed as possible by H&B, but since confirmed there (F. G. Stiles, pers. comm.).
Habitat Tropical Zone. Humid lowland forests.
Voice Calls resemble a curassow's – long, reverberating hums. Snaps bill quite frequently.

TYTONIDAE – Barn Owls

Barn owls form a separate family, Tytonidae, distinct from typical owls. They have large heads with a heart-shaped facial disc, long legs and strong talons. Essentially nocturnal, they usually spend the day out of sight in a box, crevice or dense foliage. At night they fly in ghostly silence, like wraiths appearing from nowhere. They can be vocal with a near-paralysing effect on the unsuspecting human observer, uttering a scream that may be repeated, and pairs hunting together can be quite unnerving as each screams in turn. Barn Owls eat rodents almost exclusively, and have been encouraged by farmers of grain crops in many places. In some areas such encouragement has developed into an organised programme, as in Carabobo, Venezuela, where more than 600 pairs breed in boxes placed on farms.

Additional references for this section include Bruce (1999) and König et al. (1999).

BARN OWL *Tyto alba* Pl. 81

Identification Race *bargei* 29cm, other races 36–38cm. Two morphs: pale morph generally creamy, the other tawny. Pale morph sandy brown above, washed with swathes of grey over crown and mantle, in irregular patches and soft bars on wings and in neat bars on tail; all upperparts very neatly and almost imperceptibly filigreed with vermiculations of black and white, mostly on the grey, individual feathers each have a black-and-white tear or oval streak; facial disc white, edged with small brown, sandy and white feathers, underparts pale buffy with small scattered black-and-white streaks; eyes, bill and feet yellow. Unmistakable, pale and ghostly in flight at night, long-legged and creamy if seen by day.

Ssp. *T. a. bargei* (Cu) (Bo?) significantly smaller than others; eyes very dark brown

T. a. contempta (Ec, S Co) very variable; greyish on back, pale yellowish-brown below with dark spots, facial disc dark with white rim; eyes brown or red

T. a. hellmayri (Ve: E and Margarita I., T&T, Guianas) eyes yellow or brown

T. a. subandeana (Ec, Co) possibly smaller and darker, but lack of barring in dark phase seems to be only consistent difference

Habits Hunts alone at night, occasionally at dusk, often from a low, open perch or sometimes crisscrossing low over open fields. Flies with'leaping'pattern, like a moth, and cruises with strong wingbeats.

Status Often affected when farmers use rat poison. In Ecuador, uncommon to frequent in the west, scarce and local in the east. Local but widespread and possibly frequent in Colombia. Scarce on Curaçao and uncertain, possibly only a very rare visitor to Bonaire. Frequent to common in Venezuela, especially in the Llanos, uncommon on Trinidad & Tobago, uncommon in Guyana, common in coastal Suriname and French Guiana.

Habitat Tropical Zone to Páramo. Partially open areas, especially near settlements, agriculture and pastureland with many trees and patches of light woodland.

Voice Does not hoot. Calls include hisses, snorts, screeches, scraping noises and staccato squeals. In flight, a harsh, vibrating *tsheeerrr*. Snaps bill loudly. (H&B, H&M, R&G).

Note Races poorly defined and best identified by range. Race *subandeana* considered perhaps synonymous with *guatemalae*, race *stictica* synonymised under *contempta* (Bruce).

STRIGIDAE – Typical Owls

The typical owls vary in size from Great Horned Owl to the diminutive pygmy owls. Despite this, they are remarkably similar in being nocturnal, with large eyes set in round discs, large round wings and short tails, and brown or grey, highly cryptic plumage. Most species have colour morphs as well as much individual variation, and, in some instances, it can be very difficult or even virtually impossible to identify a species on plumage alone. It is apparent that species recognition, territory, sexual and mate recognition is much more a matter of voice than plumage. The implications of this for birdwatching and ornithological studies are manifest.

Additional references for this section include Mansell & Low (1980) Howell & Robbins (1995), Robbins & Howell (1995), Marks et al. (1999) and König et al. (1999).

Neotropical screech owls are undergoing continual taxonomic revision. We have veered from the latest AOU Checklist (SACC, May 2006), accepting instead species limits proposed in recent literature (e.g. by Marks *et al.* 1999, König *et al.* 1999, R&G). Our aim has not been to support increasing fragmentation of *Megascops* (formerly *Otus*) taxa, but to ensure that each form with characters that are clearly separable and recognisable is represented here. Descriptions of a species' vocalisations in the literature may be incorrectly attributed due to lumping of taxa by previous authors, and special care must be paid to this subject. Eye colour can be helpful in species identification, but remember that most juveniles have brown eyes, and it is uncertain when those species with yellow eyes as adults acquire that colour. Plumage variation makes visual recognition uncertain, and discriminators for subspecies are strictly comparative. In addition to voice and appearance, a combination of location, altitude and habitat is usually essential for identification. Juveniles are seldom seen, they have the body covered in pale downy feathers, and are barred to a greater or lesser extent (e.g. juvenile Vermiculated Screech Owl on plate 81). Taxonomic note: taxonomy of genus *Megascops* is badly in need of profound study, conmbining extensive field work and comprehensive DNA analysis. Our taxonomy here is not an attempt to pre-judge each study, but is intended to clarify and distinguish the distinct taxa as much as possible so as to facilitate clear taxa data records.

BARE-SHANKED SCREECH OWL *Megascops clarkii* Pl. 82

Identification 20–25cm. Broad head with short ear-tufts, a virtually rimless cinnamon face, crown, back and wings with crossbars, and some spots between them; white underparts barred cinnamon and dark striations (no crossbars); yellow eyes, bill horn, tarsus only feathered halfway, lower tarsus and feet yellow.

Ssp. Monotypic (extreme NW Co)

Habits Usually alone, sometimes in small groups. Hunts at dusk and at night, from canopy to lower levels, in clearings and at forest edges. Day roosts on branch within dense foliage or epiphytes.

Status Central American species that is rare in north-west Colombia.

Habitat Upper Tropical to Temperate Zones. Humid and cloud forests, stunted woods on higher slopes, rows of trees beside roads or fences.

Voice A musical 2-part hooting, *coo, coo-coo-coo* (H&B), a deep *wook wook wook*, repeated every few s (König *et al.*), and a deep *hu-hu, HOO-HOO-hao*, often in duet with female, which has a softer, higher version (Marks *et al.*).

TROPICAL SCREECH OWL

Megascops choliba Pl. 81

Identification 22–25cm. Several morphs, varying with subspecies (7 illustrated). Round head with short ear-tufts, facial disc defined by clear, dark semicircular line on each side; yellow eyes, tarsus fully feathered. The variations in pattern from morph to morph within a given race make description virtually impossible. The main specific characteristics of Tropical Screech Owl are the clear and usually bold double, shallow C – one above the other – bracket either side of face, a usually well-streaked head, significant vermiculations, fine multiple crossbar-streaks below, tarsi fully feathered, eyes always yellow. Ear-tufts usually not evident, but when alarmed, birds adopt 'narrowed' stance, with tufts erect.

Ssp. *M. c. crucigerus* (E Ec, SE Co, Ve, Tr, Guianas) yellowish spots on body feathers
M. c. duidae (S Ve) very dark, with uniform crown and broken white collar on hindneck
M. c. luctisomus (NW Co) larger, like *crucigerus* but (brown phase, at least) paler above, the dark centres both above and below being much narrower, especially on breast
M. c margaritae (N Co, Ve: N and Margarita I.) very distinctly pale grey with bold black lines on head and face

Habits Usually in pairs, hunts only at night, silently fluttering, waving flight pattern, quite different from bounding flight of pygmy owls. Main diet insects. Day roosts in dense cover or tree cavity. Calls mostly before dawn or just after dusk.
Status Uncommon to locally frequent in Ecuador, common in Colombia, Venezuela and Trinidad, frequent in Guyana and coastal Suriname, common in French Guiana.
Habitat Tropical to Temperate Zones. Open, light and secondary woodland in humid to dry areas, from lowlands to mountains, borders of *várzea* and *terra firme*, plantations, gardens and parks.
Voice Varied sequences of short, tremulous whistles, sometimes followed by 2–3 sharp notes, *ou ou ou ou ou ou ook! ook!* Series of bubbling hoots that end in sharp notes, *ho-o-o-o-o-o-o-orr, OOK!* or *bu bu bu bu bu bu kwah! kwah! kwah!*, or a short series of churro notes, repeated at intervals of a few seconds. All are considered territorial songs, and sometimes exchanged in duets by pairs or antiphonally between males (H&B, König *et al.*, Marks *et al.*, R&G).
Notes Subspecies *duidae* morphologically distinct, possibly a separate species, pending analysis of vocalisations (König *et al.*). Race *alticola* (C Co) considered invalid by König *et al.*, who treated it as a morph of *crucigerus*.

VERMICULATED SCREECH OWL

Megascops vermiculatus Pl. 82

Identification 20–23cm. At least 3 distinct morphs with much individual variation; round head with medium ear-tufts, facial disc poorly defined; very noticeable row of white spots on scapulars, less noticeable row of white spots on nape and another, shorter, on outer wing-coverts of closed wing; yellow eyes, tarsus feathered almost to toes.

Ssp. Monotypic (N Co, N Ve)

Habits Hunts at night.
Status Uncertain in Colombia, uncommon to locally frequent in Venezuela.
Habitat Tropical to Subtropical Zones. Mossy, epiphyte-laden humid primary forests, from lowlands to lower slopes.
Voice Male's primary song is a long, fast trill, resembling a toad, rising in volume and pitch, then drops and fades. Female answers with a shorter, higher pitched version. Also *ghoor* or *khoo* calls, and a sad, falling *rreeoorr* purr (Marks *et al.*, König *et al.*).
Notes Formerly considered conspecific with Middle American Screech Owl *M. guatemalae* (e.g. P&MdS), but separated on basis of vocalisations (H&B). Sometimes considered conspecific with Roraima and Río Napo Screech Owls (e.g. Marks *et al.*).

RORAIMA SCREECH OWL

Megascops roraimae Pl. 82

Identification 20–23cm. Generally dark with long ear-tufts that are raised frequently, white scapular spots and short row on outer wing-coverts, heavily marked underparts, thighs barred black and brown, undertail-coverts barred black and white; yellow eyes do not reflect in flashlight.

Ssp. Monotypic (S Ve, Gu, Su)

Habits Nocturnal, may not respond well to playback (Hilty).
Status Pantepui species, locally frequent in Venezuela, uncertain in Guyana (BFR&S), local in Suriname.
Habitat Tropical to Subtropical Zones (*c.*500–2,000m). Humid forest on slopes of tepuis.
Voice Has been described as similar to Vermiculated Screech, but recordings from Venezuela refute this. Male gives ascending, then fading, high-pitched trill, *u'u'u'u'u'u'*… of *c.*50 notes and lasting 5–8 s. Female similar but higher pitched (König *et al.*).
Notes Formerly considered a race of Middle American Screech Owl *M. guatemalae* (e.g. P&MdS), and subsequently within Vermiculated Screech Owl *M. vermiculatus*. Separated by König *et al.* on basis of voice and zoogeography. Considered conspecific with Río Napo Screech Owl in R&G, where listed as Foothill Screech Owl, under which name it is also treated in Hilty.

RÍO NAPO SCREECH OWL

Megascops napensis Pl. 82

Identification 20–22.5cm. Two distinct morphs, rufous and pale brown; well rounded head with short ear-tufts, poorly defined facial disc but well-defined white eyebrows with a few small white spots between them, a long line of clear white spots on scapulars, lower wings broadly barred; eyes pale brown, tarsus fully feathered.

Ssp. Monotypic (EC Ec, SC Co)

Habits Very shy and retiring, mostly hidden when perched. Hunts at night.

Status Rare to uncommon and local in Ecuador, few records in Colombia.
Habitat Tropical to Lower Subtropical Zones. Interior of humid lowland and foothill forests on east slopes of Andes.
Voice A fast, tremulous 5–10 s trill that starts softly and becomes quite loud; reportedly very similar to toad *Bufo marinus* (R&G). Female call similar but higher pitched and shorter. A speeding series that starts with a trill followed by downward-inflected *gurreeoo gyo-gyo-gyo-gyo-gyo* notes (König *et al.*).
Notes Sometimes listed as *M. vermiculatus napensis* (e.g. H&M), but separated by König *et al.* on basis of voice, morphology and zoogeography. Treated as *O. roraimae napensis*, Foothill Screech Owl (but perhaps a separate species) in R&G.

CHOCÓ SCREECH OWL

Megascops centralis Pl. 82

Identification 20–21cm. Round head with short to medium ear-tufts, clear black triple-crossed shaft-streaks on mostly white underparts; yellow eyes, tarsus incompletely feathered.

Ssp. Monotypic (W Ec, W Co)

Habits Shy, nocturnal, roosts in dense foliage by day.
Status Rare to locally uncommon in Ecuador, probably rare in Colombia.
Habitat Tropical Zone. Humid and wet forests and secondary woodland, in foothills and on lower slopes.
Voice Very different from other screech owls, a soft, brief, fast purring trill *kr-r-r-r-r-r-o*, which falls in pitch and ends suddenly (R&G).
Note Taxon *centralis* was described by Hekstra (1982) as a subspecies of Middle (or Guatemalan) American Screech Owl *M. guatemalae*, but Hardy *et al.* (1999) considered it a separate species, based on its very different voice, a treatment followed by R&G, but not by SCJ&W or König *et al.* Taxon not listed by Marks *et al.* (presumably in error). We lack means to evaluate the situation, and have chosen to follow R&G, in order not to dismiss or obscure possibly significant variation.

CINNAMON SCREECH OWL

Megascops petersoni Pl. 82

Identification 21–24cm. Round head, short ear-tufts, faint whitish eyebrow and white chin with dark lines either side, rich colours (in all 3 morphs); dark brown eyes, tarsus barely feathered halfway.

Ssp. Monotypic (S Ec, W Ve)

Habits Hunts only at night.
Status Rare to uncommon and local in Ecuador. In Venezuela presumably rare and local.
Habitat Subtropical to Temperate Zones. Cloud and humid montane forests with dense undergrowth and mossy, epiphyte-laden trees. Possibly replaces Rufescent Screech above Tropical Zone.
Voice A rising and falling series of *bu* or *u* notes, *c.*30–40 in all (female calls higher pitched), and a series of 1–6 explosive notes. Single mournful *wooouuw* and single *whew* perhaps serve for contact (F&K, R&G).
Notes Sometimes considered conspecific with Rufescent *M. ingens* or Colombian Screech Owls *M. colombianus*. Perhaps forms superspecies with extralimital Cloud Forest Screech Owl *M. marshalli*, and both formerly included under invalid name *huberi* (Marks *et al.*, König *et al.*, Weske & Terborgh 1981, Fitzpatrick & O'Neill 1986). Recently discovered in Venezuela (Lentino & Restall in prep.).

NORTHERN TAWNY-BELLIED SCREECH OWL

Megascops watsonii Pl. 81

Identification 19–23cm. Distinctively very dark brown above and deep tawny below, pale spots on scapular cinnamon, quite long ear-tufts; amber eyes.

Ssp. Monotypic (E Ec, SE Co, S Ve, Gu, Su, FG)

Habits Hunts only at night, in forest, mostly in canopy and subcanopy. Shy, roosts in cover and remains half-hidden wherever it perches, even at night. Sometimes calls before dark.
Status Uncommon to locally frequent in Ecuador, uncommon and possibly quite local in Colombia and Venezuela, uncommon in Guyana. In Suriname, rare in north but frequent in south. Uncommon in French Guiana.
Habitat Lower Tropical Zone. Humid lowland primary forest, *várzea* but especially *terra firme*. Mostly forest interiors, seldom at borders.
Voice A long (up to 20 s) series of low, mellow *whoo* or *tuhoot* notes, which begin slowly and softly, swell and then fade (H&B). Similar to Cinnamon Screech, but latter ends abruptly (König *et al.*). Also, a shorter, slower series of sharp hoots that accelerates and rises (R&G).
Notes Treated as *O. atricapilla lophotes* in Haverschmidt & Mees (note correct spelling is not *atricapillus*). Black-capped Screech Owl *O. atricapilla* (in south-east Brazil) now considered a separate species and *lophotes* synonymised under *watsonii*. Specimens from Táchira and Perijá, treated as *watsonii* in Phelps & Phelps (1958), now reidentified as Cinnamon Screech Owl.

RUFESCENT SCREECH OWL

Megascops ingens Pl. 82

Identification 25–28cm. At least 2 morphs; fairly broad head with small ear-tufts, poorly defined facial disc, clear dark-and-pale line on nape; brown eyes, fully feathered tarsus.

Ssp. *M. i. ingens* (SC Co, E Ec) as described
M. i. venezuelanus (NE Co, N & W Ve) paler and smaller

Habits Hunts only at night, roosting by day on thick branch next to trunk, often hidden amid clusters of epiphytes.
Status Generally poorly known, but possibly under-recorded. Uncommon to rare in Ecuador, apparently rare in Colombia.
Habitat Upper Tropical to Subtropical Zones. Humid, wet and cloud forests of mid and high elevations on east slope of Andes, in areas with mossy, epiphyte-laden trees.

Voice A short, mournful *weeeauw*; also, 2 different series of *tu* notes, first fast, with *c.*50 notes and lasting *c.*10 s, the other slower and monotonous, but accelerating at end, *hu-hu-hu-hu-tutututututu* (Marks *et al.*, König *et al.*), or *hu hu, huhu, huhuhuhuhuhu*, female similar but half-pitch higher (Hilty).
Notes Sometimes treated as conspecific with Colombian and Cinnamon Screech Owls (e.g. H&B, R&G). Birds from Coastal Cordillera of northern Venezuela appear morphologically distinct and comparative analysis of vocalisations is required.

COLOMBIAN SCREECH OWL

Megascops colombianus Pl. 82

Identification 26–28cm. Two morphs: rufescent brown and greyish-brown. Uniform plumage with clear narrow dark line defining facial disc, rather poorly defined scapulars; dark brown eyes, tarsus fully feathered.

Ssp. Monotypic (NW Ec, CW & SW Co)

Habits Hunts at night, feeding on large insects and small vertebrates.
Status Uncertain in general: uncommon to rare in Ecuador, probably rare in Colombia.
Habitat Subtropical Zone. Cloud and humid montane forests with dense undergrowth and mossy, epiphyte-laden trees.
Voice Sequence starts with 2 soft notes, followed by series of paced, fluted notes, *bu-bu… bu bu bu bu bu bu bu bu bu*, repeated after a pause of several seconds (König *et al.*).
Note Formerly considered a subspecies of Rufescent Screech Owl but separated by Fitzpatrick & O'Neill (1986) and, although R&G retain older taxonomy, this treatment is followed by König *et al.* and Marks *et al.*

SOUTHERN TAWNY-BELLIED SCREECH OWL *Megascops usta* Pl. 81

Identification 19–24cm. Two morphs; rufous and buffy. Rounded head with mid-length ear-tufts, clear dark lines define facial disc; brown eyes, tarsus fully feathered.

Ssp. Monotypic (SE Co)

Habits Hunts in understorey and mid levels of forest, only at night, although often begins calling early in crepuscular period. Feeds mostly on insects, and some small vertebrates.
Status Uncommon to possibly frequent in some localities of Amazonian Colombia.
Habitat Lower Tropical Zone. Humid lowland primary forest, both *várzea* and *terra firme*.
Voice Series of low *whoo* hoots, at rate of *c.*2 per s, rising, falling and fading, and similar to Northern Tawny-bellied *O. watsonii*. A fast series of *bu* notes that slows to a bouncing pace at end (Marks *et al.*, König *et al.*).
Note Separated from Northern Tawny-bellied by Sibley (1996) and König *et al.*, but retained therein by R&G and Marks *et al.* However, they occur sympatrically in parts of their respective ranges, and DNA studies suggest that *usta* is more closely related to Black-capped Screech Owl *M. atricapilla* (Burton 1992).

TUMBES SCREECH OWL

Megascops pacificus Pl. 82

Identification 17.5 cm. Two morphs, almost equally common, grey-brown and rufous. Fairly small and round-headed with mid-length ear-tufts, facial disc paler and clearly defined, scapular spots white; yellow eyes, bill tip greenish, legs fully feathered.

Ssp. Monotypic (SW Ec)

Habits Hunts only at night. Mainly insectivorous. Day roosts, sometimes in pairs, on high branch, right next to trunk.
Status Uncommon to locally frequent in Ecuador.
Habitat Tropical Zone. Arid scrub and dry deciduous forests of coastal plain and lower foothills.
Voice Fast series of notes – *kwurrrrrrrrrr* – that rise in volume in middle and fade at end. In aggression, a downward-inflected *kew kew kew…* or downslurred *kiu* (Marks *et al.*, König *et al.*). A fast, low-pitched churring trill, which rises in volume before fading to an abrupt end (R&G).
Notes Usually treated as a subspecies of Peruvian Screech Owl (e.g. R&G, Marks *et al.*, König *et al.*), although high probability of them being separate species noted. Differences in size, plumage and voice, plus biogeographic situation whereby the 2 populations are totally allopatric, have led us to revert to older taxonomy, wherein *roboratus* was described as a monotypic species by Bangs & Noble (1918). This taxon was described by Hekstra (1982) as a subspecies of Middle American (Guatemalan) Screech Owl *M. guatemalae*, which clearly it is not. By treating them separately, we seek to highlight the different characteristics of each taxon.

PERUVIAN SCREECH OWL

Megascops roboratus Pl. 82

Identification 20–22cm. Significantly larger (*c.*40% heavier) than Tumbes Screech. Two morphs: grey-brown and a much rarer rufous form. Round head with longish ear-tufts, almost complete black circle defining facial disc, clear scapular spots and short row on outer wing-coverts; eyes yellow, bill yellow, legs and feet fully feathered. Juvenile densely barred.

Ssp. *M. r. roboratus* (extreme S Ec)

Habits Hunts only at night. Mainly insectivorous. Day roosts high up beside trunk, sometimes in pairs.
Status Uncommon in Ecuador.
Habitat Upper Tropical to Lower Subtropical Zones. Dry deciduous forests and semi-open areas with scattered bushes on mid slopes of intermontane valleys.
Voice A rising trill undulating in pitch that accelerates slightly at end and is longer than Tumbes Screech. In aggression, an upward-inflected *kyui, kyui, kyui…* (Marks *et al.*, König *et al.*).
Note See previous species.

WHITE-THROATED SCREECH OWL

Megascops albogularis Pl. 82

Identification 25–28cm. Fairly large, rounded head with very small, non-erectile ear-tufts, facial disc not defined and concolorous with head, line of pale spots on nape, scapular spots cinnamon but well defined, broad triangular chin underscored by a white line, upper breast dark, rest of underparts paler and brighter; eyes orange-amber, tarsus fully feathered.

Ssp. *M. a. aequatorialis* (E Ec) very similar to *albogularis*
M. a. albogularis (N Ec, Co: E Andes, NW Ve) as described
M. a. macabrum (W Ec, Co: W & C Andes) similar to *albogularis* but underparts more finely patterned
M. a. meridensis (W Ve) forehead, eyebrow and belly whitish, crown more spotted
M. a. obscurus (NW Ve) darker than others

Habits Hunts only at night.
Status Uncommon to locally frequent in Ecuador, rare and local but possibly overlooked in Colombia, and possibly frequent locally in Venezuela.
Habitat Upper Subtropical to Temperate Zones. Dense, humid montane, cloud and elfin forests, almost to treeline, especially in areas dense with epiphytes. Bamboo thickets. Sometimes at borders or in glades and clearings, or in semi-open areas with patchy forest.
Voice A long series of high-pitched whistles, *wu wu wu wu wu*… *c.*1 minute long (H&B). A fast, descending series of 10–15 hoots, at rate of 4–9 per s, given by lone birds or duetting pair, the pitch of each bird differing slightly (F&K). A series of barks, sometimes lasting 1 minute or more, *churro churro-churro chu chu chu chu* (König *et al.*). Fast mellow *whop whop whop whodop whodop whodop whodop whoo!* that lasts 10–20 s, with distinctive cadence (R&G), and rhythmic tooting *pu pu púdu-púdu-púdu-*…, 15 couplets at *c.*5 per s (Hilty).
Note The subspecies *aequatorialis* and *obscurus* are considered to be possibly only morphs of *albogularis* (Marks *et al.*). Race *albogularis* not in Ecuador *fide* (R&G).

Great Horned Owl is very large, with prominent ear-tufts and large yellow eyes. They utter maniacal, spine-chilling cries at night in the breeding season.

GREAT HORNED OWL
Bubo virginianus Pl. 84

Identification 48–56cm. Large upright owl with well-developed ear-tufts, broad face with well-defined facial disc surrounded by pale to whitish circle, and broad white band across throat, underparts narrowly and evenly barred; eyes golden-yellow, bill dark. Largest owl in northern South America and unmistakable.

Ssp. *B. v. nacurutu* (N Co, Ve, Gu, Su, FG) as described
B. v. nigrescens (Ec, S Co) noticeably darker
[*B. v. colombianus* (SW Co: Cauca)] perfect intermediate between *nigrescens* and *nacurutu*

Habits Usually alone, hunts at night, or at dawn and dusk, in light woodland and semi-open areas. Roosts in large trees. Often mobbed by small birds, especially when near a nest.
Status Rare to uncommon and apparently local in Ecuador, local but widespread in Colombia and Venezuela, uncommon in Guyana, frequent in coastal Suriname, and French Guiana.
Habitat Tropical Zone to Páramo. Humid or dry, forested or open. Agricultural areas with trees and patchy woodland, often near settlements in rural areas, and sometimes in suburbs. Rocky slopes and hills.
Voice Far-carrying, deep and resonant whoo hoots, 4–5 in males (*whoo-hoo, who, whoo-hoo*, sometimes followed by a soft quivering *chu hu hurr*), 6–8 in females, and pairs call antiphonally. Sometimes, pairs call each other with loud screeches (H&B, M&L).
Note Races *elutus*, *colombianus* and *scotinus* generally considered invalid (Traylor 1958).

BLACK-AND-WHITE OWL
Ciccaba nigrolineata Pl. 84

Identification 35–41cm. Rounded head with no ear-tufts but black-spotted white eyebrows show well, and upperparts black with narrow, fragmented bars on tail, underparts white with narrow, even-width black bars; vivid yellow-orange bill, and brown eyes reflect fiery red in flashlight. Unmistakable in range, no overlap with Black-banded Owl.

Ssp. Monotypic (W Ec, NW Co, NW Ve, FG)

Habits Hunts only at night, but sometimes hawks moths and other insects near outdoor lamps, and by day roosts on branches high in dense foliage.
Status Uncommon in Ecuador, apparently very local in Colombia, uncommon to locally frequent in Venezuela, uncommon to rare in French Guiana.
Habitat Tropical Zone. Humid, semi-deciduous and deciduous forests, and secondary woodland, mangroves, gallery forests, plantations, swampy and riparian areas, forest borders and clearings.
Voice Varying, resonant, hooted phrases, e.g. *hu hu hu hoo-ah*, slurred at end, a series of 10 or more *hu-wah's* or *whoo how's*, with loud deep, single *boo's* during intervals (P. Schwartz). A rising and falling, high-pitched *keeyow*, resembling a hissing cat (H&B, R&G), and fast *buh-buh-buh-buh-buh-buh-bwow,* the last note very strong; female responds with softer *buh-buh-bo*. A loud *whooouw* (R&G). Will respond to playback of Black-banded Owl (Hilty).
Notes Sometimes considered conspecific with Black-banded Owl (e.g. Blake 1958), which occurs east of Andes, as they respond to each other's calls. Both species placed in genus *Strix* by some (e.g. Marks *et al.*, R&G), following DNA studies by Sibley & Ahlquist (1990), which showed generic separation unwarranted. *Ciccaba* separated from *Strix* on basis of differences in external ear (Voous 1964, Norberg 1977), and followed by AOU (1998).

BLACK-BANDED OWL
Ciccaba huhula Pl. 84

Identification 36cm. Rounded head with no ear-tufts, but faint eyebrows may be visible, black above, barred with narrow, somewhat fragmented white lines, underparts barred evenly black and white; deep amber eyes reflect bright red in flashlight, vivid orange-yellow bill. Unmistakable in range, no overlap with Black-and-white Owl.

Ssp. *C. h. huhula* (E Ec, E Co, S Ve, Gu, Su, FG)

Habits Hunts at night, usually in canopy, perching in fairly open spots. Day roost well hidden.

Status Uncommon in Ecuador, except at a few localities. In Colombia, poorly known, locally frequent at some localities and perhaps elsewhere, but goes unnoticed. Locally frequent in Venezuela, uncertain in Guyana, rare in Suriname and French Guiana.

Habitat Lower Tropical Zone. Humid forests, both *terra firme* and *várzea*, occasionally in plantations (cocoa, coffee, bananas) and secondary woodland. Often at borders and around clearings.

Voice Sequence consisting of rising, cat-like *whoeeeruh* scream, followed by a pause, then a loud *booo*, and another sequence that is a deep, resonant *hu hu hu HOOO* (H&B). First call also described as *who ho ho ho whuo* or *who ho ho ho whuo who* (König *et al.*). Responds to playback of Black-and-white Owl (Hilty).

Note See previous species for relationship with Black-and-white Owl.

MOTTLED OWL *Ciccaba virgata* Pl. 84

Identification 30.5–34.5cm. Rounded head without ear-tufts, dark brown to blackish above, facial disc well outlined black and white, very broad blackish areas on breast-sides, with narrow band down centre, heavy streaks below; tail banded black and white; eyes brown.

Ssp. *C. v. macconnelli* (Ve, Guianas) deep rufous-brown above and well barred on wings and tail, rufescent cinnamon below, facial disc clearly outlined in white; lacks black on breast-sides
C. v. virgata (E Ec, Co, Ve, Tr) as described

Habits Hunts only at night, in canopy, subcanopy and mid levels. Calls frequently.

Status Rare in Ecuador, locally frequent in Colombia and Venezuela, uncommon in Trinidad (no records Tobago), uncertain in Guyana, rare in Suriname and French Guiana.

Habitat Tropical to Subtropical Zones. Humid forests, mature secondary woodland, plantations, gallery forest, and thorn forest in drier areas. Both inside forest and at borders.

Voice Series of 2 or more, low, resonant *whooou* or *whoOOOou* notes, slower than Black-and-white or Black-banded Owls, and a rarely used *wheeyow* feline scream (H&B, R&G). Sometimes a few grunts (Marks *et al.*).

Note Placed in genus *Strix* by some authors (see Black-and-white Owl).

RUFOUS-BANDED OWL *Ciccaba albitarsis* Pl. 84

Identification 30–36cm. Rounded head without ear-tufts, short white eyebrow and whitish chin, bold rufous mottling or barring on mantle, nape, wings and tail; breast rufous fading to cinnamon below, variably spotted brown and white. Eyes orange, brown in young (König *et al.*).

Ssp. Monotypic (Ec, Co, Ve)

Habits Hunts only at night, in canopy, roosting during day in dense thickets.

Status Uncommon to locally frequent in Ecuador, rare to locally frequent in Colombia and Venezuela.

Habitat Subtropical to Temperate Zones. Humid montane and cloud forests, in the interior, at borders and in semi-open areas adjacent to forest.

Voice A deep, resonant *hu, hu-hu-hu, HOOOa*, repeated every *c.*10 s (Hilty), resembling Black-banded and Black-and-white Owls. A far-carrying *buh-buh-buh-buh-buh-buuu!* (R&G) and single gruff hoots (König *et al.*).

Notes Placed in genus *Strix* by some authors (e.g. S&M, Marks *et al.*, R&G), but treated as *Ciccaba* in AOU (1998). Spelling of species name as *albitarsus* is incorrect.

CRESTED OWL *Lophostrix cristata* Pl. 81

Identification 36–43cm. Unmistakable: large, impressive white eyebrows meld into long erect, partially white tufts, held very straight (like horns) when nervous or alarmed. Seemingly unmarked but has fine filigreed vermiculations over entire plumage, with short rows of white spots on outer wing-coverts. Patch of white in centre of breast on light (grey) morph of all 3 races, but not on dark morphs.

Ssp. *L. c. cristata* (E Ec, SW Co, S Ve, Guianas) 2 morphs: rufous and grey; brown eyes
L. c. stricklandi (W Co) significantly darker, facial disc better defined with lines below eyes, subtle but dark broad bands on wings and tail, rows of white spots on wings more extensive; deep yellow eyes
L. c. wedeli (NE Co, N Ve) very much darker than *stricklandi*, pileum blackish, blackish-brown above with pale freckling and spotting always darker buff; brown eyes

Habits Usually alone or in pairs. Nocturnal, often calls intermittently throughout night. By day roosts in dense foliage, at low or mid heights, often near streams.

Status Widespread but uncommon in Ecuador, apparently rare and local in Colombia, and Venezuela, uncommon in Guyana, rare in Suriname, common and widespread in French Guiana.

Habitat Tropical Zone. Humid forests, secondary woodland and forest fragments. Mostly in lowlands.

Voice Races *cristata* and *wedeli* give a low, accelerating *k, k, k'k'k'kkrrrrrrr* that may end in a purr, and resembles a frog or 2-note call of Bare-throated Tiger Heron, and is repeated once every 5 s or slower (P. Schwartz, E. Eisenmann recordings, *fide* H&B). Race *stricklandi* utters purring *kworrrrrr*, shorter than that of other races and repeated at irregular intervals (König *et al.*).

Note Race *stricklandi* perhaps a separate species, based on morphology and vocal differences (König *et al.*, Stiles 1999).

SPECTACLED OWL

Pulsatrix perspicillata Pl. 84

Identification 43–48cm. Unmistakable: broad rounded head, head to breast and upperparts deep brown, barred on wings and tail, facial disc white, joining white eyebrows on sides of bill to form large 'spectacles', small dark chin, white throat, belly to undertail buffy-cinnamon; eyes yellow, bill bone-coloured. Juvenile has dark brown face and flight-feathers, but otherwise is covered in creamy down.

Ssp. *P. p. chapmani* (W Co, W Ec) slightly larger and darker than others

P. p. perspicillata (E Co, Ve, Gu, Su, FG) as described

P. p. trinitatis (Tr) has pale buff underparts

Habits Hunts mainly at night, but on dark, overcast days, may occasionally cruise about. Roosts alone, in pairs or with young, on a fairly open thick branch at mid levels to canopy, most often in gallery forest or riparian areas. Nocturnal, calls mostly when there is a full moon.

Status Widespread but not very common in Ecuador, frequent in Colombia, but not often seen, locally frequent in Venezuela, uncommon in Trinidad (no records Tobago), uncommon in Guyana, frequent in Suriname, frequent to locally common in French Guiana.

Habitat Tropical Zone. Humid to drier deciduous forests, secondary woodland, coffee and cocoa plantations, gallery and riparian forests, even urban areas.

Voice An accelerating, descending and fading series of low hoots, *BOO-Boo-boo-boo-boo-boo-boo*, a falling series of muffled *woof* notes, and occasionally a descending whistle (H&B, Hilty). Juvenile has short *woauw* call (R&G).

BAND-BELLIED OWL

Pulsatrix melanota Pl. 84

Identification 35.5–48cm. Somewhat umber-brown, deep chocolate head and breast and upperparts almost entirely narrowly barred black with irregular paler spots; thick white eyebrows, centre of face (either side of bill, and moustachial/chin), together with broad white crescent on throat, dominate head, which has well-defined rufous and chocolate circles around eyes; underparts scalloped rufous, brown and black; eyes brown. Juvenile has eyes set in 2 solid brown discs, rest of face white, flight-feathers brown, narrowly barred with paler or white lines, and rest of body covered in cinnamon down. From Spectacled Owl by brown eyes and prominent even-width bands on underparts; from smaller but rather similar Rufous-banded Owl by very dark head, facial disk and upperparts. No overlap with Spectacled, rather replaces it above c.700m.

Ssp. *P. m. melanota* (E Ec, SE Co)

Habits Hunts at night, often from open perch on large branch. Roosts in fairly open spots.

Status Scarce and local in Ecuador, and poorly known, possibly rare in Colombia. Paucity of records probably due to nocturnal habits in deep forest.

Habitat Upper Tropical Zone. Humid forests and their borders in foothill and lower slopes of eastern Andes.

Voice Series of deep muffled hoots (H&B), reportedly similar to Spectacled Owl but faster and higher pitched (P. Coopmans *fide* R&G).

Pygmy Owls are almost as complex as screech owls, with much confusion caused mainly by variable polymorphism in numerous species. Like screech owls visual identification is usually impossible without at least some knowledge of distribution, elevation, habitat and, most importantly, vocalisations. Bars on tail can be diagnostic, but may be misleading when partially concealed by uppertail-coverts. Most are active night and day. They often call by day, which attracts small birds to mob the caller until it moves away. All have somewhat variable, large eye-like markings on the nape to deter these attackers. The white spots on the head can be an aid to species diagnosis, but are variable between races, morphs and even individuals. Juveniles are seldom seen – they resemble the adults but lack spots or streaks on the head.

SUBTROPICAL PYGMY OWL

Glaucidium parkeri Pl. 83

Identification 14–15cm. Small white spots cover head, scapular spots clear and obvious.

Ssp. Monotypic (SE Ec)

Habits Forages in canopy and subcanopy.

Status Rare and perhaps local on east Andean slope in Ecuador (Cordilleras del Cóndor and de Cutucú). Seems to replace Andean Pygmy Owl below 2,000m. Range possibly larger than currently known, and could extend even as far as south-east Colombia.

Habitat Subtropical Zone. Very humid, mossy, epiphyte-overgrown, primary montane forests – possibly restricted to outlying ridges.

Voice Series of 2–4 toots, *tu-tu-tu – tu,* where last inter-note interval is slightly longer and seems like a hesitation, unique amongst *Glaucidium* (Robbins & Howell 1995).

Note Described by Robbins & Howell (1995) as part of *G. minutissimum* complex, although it ranges higher than all others in the group.

CENTRAL AMERICAN PYGMY OWL

Glaucidium griseiceps Pl. 83

Identification 13–18 cm. Five bars on tail, but only 2–3 normally visible.

Ssp. *G. g. rarum* (extreme NW Co, race in NW Ec uncertain)

Habits Hunts and perches in canopy and subcanopy, where difficult to locate. Has dipping flight pattern.

Status Rare to locally uncommon in Ecuador. Uncommon to locally frequent in Colombia.

Habitat Tropical Zone (to 1,300m). Humid to wet primary forests and their borders in lowlands and foothills of Pacific slope. Occasionally in mature secondary woodland and old cacao plantations.

Voice Song consists of 2–18 unvarying, even-paced notes (Howell & Robbins 1995). A slightly descending, very slow series of toots, usually 3–5, but 12 or more if bird disturbed (R&G). Sometimes the hoots are preceded by trills (Marks *et al.*).

Note Formerly treated as *G. minutissimum griseiceps* (e.g. H&B), but separated by Howell & Robbins (1995), based on vocalisations.

AMAZONIAN PYGMY OWL

Glaucidium hardyi Pl. 83

Identification 14–15cm. Relatively long wings and 5 pale bars on tail, only 3 of which are usually visible.

Ssp. Monotypic (known with certainty from S Ve and FG, but distribution elsewhere in northern South America uncertain)

Habits Only in canopy (Ferruginous Pygmy Owl occupies mid and lower levels). Hunts and calls sporadically dawn to dusk, sometimes active for at least 1 hour beyond sunrise (G. M. Kirwan, pers. comm.); sometimes active during the day.

Status Generally uncommon, but apparent scarcity probably largely reflects lack of appropriate field work. Uncertain in Ecuador (listed in König *et al.*, but not by Marks *et al.* or R&G), apparently absent in Colombia (Howell & Robbins 1995), uncommon to locally frequent in Venezuela, Guyana and Suriname, frequent and widespread in French Guiana.

Habitat Lower Tropical Zone. Humid, primary lowland forest – *várzea* and transitional forests, but especially *terra firme* – in the interior, but sometimes at borders.

Voice Fast series of 10–30 notes, at *c.*12 per s, which run into a loud, tremulous trill. High-pitched trill of 10–20 notes, *c.*2 per s (Hilty). Female higher-pitched, and might be confused with Northern Tawny-bellied Screech Owl *Otus watsonii*.

Note Described by Vielliard (1989).

PERUVIAN PYGMY OWL

Glaucidium peruanum Pl. 83

Identification 16–16.5cm. Lowland population pale cinnamon-rufous with broad pale streaking on crown, whilst highland birds are greyer brown, more spotted on crown, and have white spots on scapulars and wing-coverts larger and more profuse.

Ssp. Monotypic (W & SE Ec)

Habits Active night and day. Sometimes perches on roadside wires. Males very territorial, may dive upon intruders.

Status Widespread, frequent to common in Ecuador, especially in drier areas.

Habitat Tropical Zone to Páramo. Moist to dry woodland, from deciduous forests to arid scrub. Gardens and town parks, agricultural areas with scattered trees, thickets and riparian woodland, elfin forest.

Voice Series of *pew* or *toit* notes that may last several minutes, delivered very fast (too fast to imitate), and more metallic and higher pitched than Ferruginous (H&B, R&G). When excited, high, short *chirrp* notes, singly or in series of 5–10 (König *et al.*), but apparently only given by those at higher elevations.

Notes Formerly considered conspecific with Ferruginous but separated on basis of vocal differences (König 1991) and DNA evidence (Marks *et al.*). Differences in voice and morphology noted between populations on Pacific and Amazonian slopes suggest 2 species might be involved. The type form in Ayacucho and Apurímac (Peru) differs both morphologically and vocally from those on the coast, and there is a significant geographical gap between them. Apparently, a paper describing the coastal form is in preparation (G. Engblom, pers. comm.). Morphological differences exist between lowland and highland birds but their voices are identical (R&G). Sometimes called Pacific Pygmy Owl.

ANDEAN PYGMY OWL

Glaucidium jardinii Pl. 83

Identification 14.5–16cm. Two distinct morphs, rufous (almost entirely rufous below) and dark (spotted white on breast and barred on flanks); small, rounded head with very poorly defined facial mask, spots on head have black 'shadows' and false 'eyes' on nape form 2 narrow lines, white over black; back heavily spotted with paler scallops. From Cloud Forest Pygmy Owl by song, and range.

Ssp. Monotypic (Andes of Ec, Co, Ve)

Habits Hunts by day and night, dashing after prey from perch in canopy, subcanopy or at mid level. Usually alone, perching on semi-open or even an exposed high spot. Flies in dipping pattern, quick wingbeats alternating with short glides.

Status Uncommon and scarce in Ecuador, local and probably under-recorded in Colombia, and uncommon to locally frequent in Venezuela.

Habitat Subtropical Zone (above 2,000m) to Páramo. Humid forests and forest borders to the treeline, elfin and *Polylepis* woods.

Voice A long series of double toots in Colombia (H&B), whilst in Ecuador gives a series of 2–5 *whee-du-du* phrases, followed by toots, *whee-du-du, whee-du-du, tu-tu-tu-tu-tu* (R&G) or 10–30 evenly spaced *poop…poop…poop…* toots *c.*3 per s, higher pitched than Ferruginous (Hilty). In Venezuela song is the same but lacks initial *whee*, thus a series of *du-du* phrases followed by toots.

Notes Only *Glaucidium* on higher slopes, replaced below 2,000m by Cloud Forest Pygmy Owl on Pacific slope of Colombia and Ecuador, and by Subtropical on eastern slope. Has been treated as conspecific with Ferruginous, but calls, plumage and ecology differ.

FERRUGINOUS PYGMY OWL

Glaucidium brasilianum Pl. 83

Identification (16.5–20 cm. Very complex species, with a bewildering variety of morphs and races. See plate, where 12 morphs are shown, for an insight. Extent of individual variation in races makes it impossible to distinguish them in field. All races have a more or less streaked crown, although they may become real spots on back of head. Very likely that there are only 2 races in continental Venezuela: *medianum* north of río Orinoco, *olivaceum* south of it.

Ssp. *G. b. duidae* (S Ve: Mt. Duida, and possibly other tepuis also) very dark, with unspotted mantle; crown has white or ochraceous shaft- streaks, tail blackish with incomplete whitish bars, dense white throat patch

G. b. margaritae (Ve: Margarita I.) all morphs spotted and faintly barred on back, and wings heavily barred, outer scapulars white (pale in rufous morph); rufous morph has short white lines on head, grey morph long white lines and brown morph large, diamond-shaped spots

G. b. medianum (N Co, Ve; north of Orinoco, N Gu, N Su, N FG) smaller with broken whitish tail bars; red morph or birds with rufescent tail bars less common than grey-brown morph; short white streaks edged at sides with black on heads of all morphs; plain unmarked backs, scapulars poorly marked with flattish ovals

G. b. olivaceum (Ve: south of Orinoco) rufous morph has plain unmarked back, 7–8 broad cinnamon bands on tail and tertials; faint streaks on head, poorly-defined'eyes'on nape, heavily streaked below; grey morph has 4–5 narrow white bars on tail, mantle spotted, clear black and white streaks on head, heavily streaked flanks; brown morph heavily spotted on breast-sides, otherwise intermediate between rufous and grey morphs

G. b. phalaenoides (Tr) virtually identical to *margaritae* (see below)

G. b. ucayalae (E Ec, SE Co) red morph has crown indistinctly streaked, tail uniform chestnut or very indistinctly barred darker; brown morph less rufescent, with white throat patch; both morphs have densely streaked underparts

Habits Calls mostly at dusk, but often in day. No other species has same long series of toots at steady pace for so long. Flicks tail with each note. Often answers whistled imitations of song. Perches in semi-open spots. Flies direct, quick wingbeats alternating with short glides.

Status Uncommon to locally frequent in Ecuador, frequent to locally common in Colombia, especially in drier areas. Common and widespread in Venezuela, common in Trinidad (no records Tobago), frequent in Guyana, uncommon in southern Suriname and rare and local in French Guiana.

Habitat Tropical to Subtropical Zones. Deciduous woodland, dry forest and scrub, borders of humid forests (both *várzea* and *terra firme*), gallery forest, gardens and parks.

Voice Long series of toots, *c.*3–4 per s, sometimes lasting more than 1 minute, and series of short purring or trilling *chirrup* notes (H&B). Female higher pitched, often becoming a twitter. Song a long-sustained series *poik, poik, poik,…* (50 or more) just faster than 2 per s (Hilty). Song of *ucayalae* has a distinctly more hollow quality, with more staccato notes.

Notes Subspecies *ucayalae* unrecorded in southern Venezuela, nor are there any records of *phalaenoides* for north-east Venezuela, which is considered synonymous with *margaritae* by some authors, but maintained by Marks *et al.* Based on voice and DNA analysis, *ucayalae* is considered to possibly be a distinct species by Heidrich *et al.* (1995), but König (1991) did not find any molecular differences between *ucayalae* and *brasilianum*. Race *duidae* probably synonymous with *olivaceum*.

CLOUD FOREST PYGMY OWL

Glaucidium nubicola Pl. 83

Identification 16cm. Entire head spotted white, particularly densely at front, and almost entire wings barred with rows of white tips, instead of spotted. From Andean Pygmy Owl mainly by altitude (Andean Pygmy Owl above 2,000m) and voice, but also by shorter tail with several more bars.

Ssp. Monotypic (NW Ec, W Co)

Habits Active in canopy and mid levels.

Status Vulnerable. Uncommon in Ecuador and Colombia.

Habitat Subtropical Zone (1,400–2,000m). Very wet primary montane and cloud forests on steep slopes, in forest and sometimes at borders along trails and on sharp ridge crests.

Voice Distinctive, long series of paired hollow whistles or toots, usually commences with a soft note, *bu, bu-bu, bu-bu, bu-bu, bu-bu…* (Robbins & Stiles 1999, Marks *et al.*, R&G).

Note Described by Robbins & Stiles (1999). Prior to latter publication, it had long been confused with Andean but vocal differences significant.

RIDGWAY'S PYGMY OWL

Glaucidium ridgwayi Pl. 83

Identification 16cm. Very variable, but easily separated from Central American Pygmy Owl by densely barred, longer tail and streaked head.

Ssp. *G. r. ridgwayi* (extreme NW Co)

Habits Active day and night, mainly at dawn and dusk, foraging at mid levels and in low bushes. By day tends to hide in foliage. Flies straight, alternating gliding and rapid flapping.

Status Locally frequent along Pacific and west Caribbean coasts of Colombia.

Habitat Tropical Zone. Dry to moist lowlands with scattered trees or bushes, partially wooded areas with thorn scrub or stands of tall cacti, dry deciduous forest, plantations or secondary woodland.

Voice Long series of hollow toot's at 2.5–3 per s, similar but slower than Ferruginous. A faster series of *whi* notes that sometimes break into bursts of high yelping twitters (König *et al.*). Series variable.

Note Separated from Ferruginous Pygmy Owl by König *et al.*

BURROWING OWL

Athene cunicularia Pl. 81

Identification 18–26cm. Unmistakable. Small terrestrial owl with upright stance and rather longish legs; brown above with whitish spots and streaks; buffy below with some brown across breast and flanks, spotted with white. Eyes yellow. very variable.

Ssp. *A. c. apurensis* (SE Ve) darker than *brachyptera*
A. c. arubensis (Ar, Cu) paler and sandier than *brachyptera* with less barring below
A. c. brachyptera (Ve: N and Margarita I.) smaller, very short wings; pale
A. c. carrikeri (Co: E Andes) small, like *tolimae*, outermost tail feathers white; female overall more tawny
A. c. pichinchae (W Ec: temperate tablelands) dark grey-brown above, finely spotted whitish, dusky barring rather dense
A. c. punensis (SW Ec: lowlands) dark grey-brown above, finely spotted whitish, with less barring below
A. c. tolimae (W Co: upper Magdalena Valley) like *pichinchae* but smaller

Habits Terrestrial and active by day, mostly in early mornings and late afternoons. Usually in pairs or small family groups, standing at entrance of burrow, and often, several burrows form a colony. Flies in undulating pattern. Usually silent. When disturbed, bobs up and down.
Status Widespread throughout South America. Locally frequent in Ecuador, locally common in Colombia and Venezuela. Common on Aruba and a casual visitor to Curaçao, rare and seasonal in Trinidad (no records Tobago), frequent in Guyana. Although listed by Peters, there is no evidence for its occurrence in Suriname (H&M).
Habitat Tropical Zone to Páramo. Savannas, pastures, arid plains and fields with short, sparse vegetation and pockets of bare, sandy soil, both in mountains and lowlands. Sometimes in vacant lots, roadsides, airports, cemeteries and other man-made open spaces.
Voice Calls include a repeated cackling when disturbed. Males sing dusk to dawn, a soft *coo-coo-oo*, females answer with fast series of *eep* calls.
Notes Sometimes placed in genus *Speotyto* (e.g. ffrench 1996a), but skeletal structure and DNA studies support placement in *Athene*. Races *apurensis*, *arubensis* and *punensis* considered invalid by König *et al.*

BUFF-FRONTED OWL *Aegolius harrisii* Pl. 81

Identification 19–20cm. Rounded head, greenish-yellow eyes; forehead and eyebrow, 2 concentric circles around facial disk and entire underparts rich buff. Very dark umber-brown above, with black bars and rows of small white spots.

Ssp. *A. h. harrisii* (Ec, Co, NW Ve, Gu)

Habits Crepuscular and nocturnal. Males sing from canopy, keeping well hidden.
Status Very rare in Ecuador, very rare and poorly known in Colombia and Venezuela.
Habitat Upper Tropical to Temperate Zones. Semi-open areas, clearings with scattered trees, forest borders, both in humid and drier areas. Elfin forest, and *Podocarpus*, *Alnus* and *Polylepis* woodlands.
Voice A fast trill, *tu tu tu tu tu tu tu* that wavers in pitch and lasts 3–4 s (H&B), and a single hooting *oouuu* (Hilty).
Note Population on Cerro de la Neblina (Willard *et al.* 1991) probably a distinct subspecies, but specimens unavailable to us.

STYGIAN OWL *Asio stygius* Pl. 84

Identification 38–46cm. Very dark umber above, with barely visible lines of brown spots on back, scapulars and wings, face outlined by faint buffy and grey feather tips, and ear-tufts very long; underparts buffy with very heavy triple-crossed shafts that look like gross zippers when bird slim in alarm. Pale patch in mid forehead, between prominent ear-tufts. Generally dark, but buff wing-linings visible in flight.

Ssp. *A. s. robustus* (Ec, Co, NW Ve, Gu)

Habits Nocturnal. Day roosts in canopy immediately adjacent to trunk.
Status Uncommon to rare and apparently local in Ecuador, rare and local in Colombia, uncommon and patchily distributed in Venezuela, and scarce in Guyana.
Habitat Tropical to Temperate Zones. Humid forest on montane slopes with adjacent open fields or pastures, patchy woodland in savannas, settlements, parks and cultivated areas next to forest.
Voice A very low, loud *hu* or *hu-hu* and short cat-like *miaow* by female (H&B). Varied screams and squeals (R&G).

STRIPED OWL *Asio clamator* Pl. 84

Identification 30–38cm. Rufous-brown above with darker brown streaks and bars; ear-tufts long and fringed with black that joins very obvious black frame to facial disc; face and underparts buff, heavily streaked on breast but fading quickly on flanks; amber eyes. Much paler coloration than larger Stygian Owl.

Ssp. *A. c. clamator* (Co, Ve, Guianas) as described
A. c. oberi (To) larger, with broader dark bands on primaries

Habits Usually alone or in pairs, hunts at dusk, flying low over open fields or perching on fenceposts, wires and branches to search for prey. By day, sometimes roosts on ground amid tall grasses, and may roost communally in groups of up to 12. Calls infrequently.
Status Rare and local in Ecuador, locally common in Colombia and Venezuela, scarce in Tobago and Guyana, common Suriname, and uncommon in French Guiana.
Habitat Tropical Zone. Light woodland with adjacent open areas, grassland with scattered trees, forested marshes and forest by rivers, plantations, scrub and thickets, agricultural areas with hedges, copses and patchy forest.
Voice A loud *wheeyoo* and series of *ow, ow, ow*… hoots that sound like small dog yapping (P. Schwartz). Squealing notes (R&G) and soft low hoots at pre-dawn roost (D. Rose in Hilty).
Notes Sometimes placed in genera *Rhinoptynx* or *Pseudocops* (e.g. BFR&S, H&M). Race *oberi* considered a synonym of *clamator* by König *et al.*, but retained by Marks *et al.*

SHORT-EARED OWL *Asio flammeus* Pl. 84

Identification 36–38cm. Large with fairly horizontal posture, small head with tiny ear-tufts near centre of head; facial mask well defined by white eyebrow and moustachial that lend a kind of X to centre of face; rufous-brown above, streaked and barred darker brown, buff underparts with a necklace of heavy streaks around throat and scattered fine streaks on breast and sides; yellow eyes encircled by black. Conspicuous black patch at 'wrist' level on upperwing-coverts and dark bars on tips of primaries.

Ssp. *A. f. bogotensis* (Co, Ec) darker, with rusty wash
A. f. pallidicaudus (Ve, Gu) noticeably paler tail, underwing-coverts immaculate ochraceous-buff (streaked fuscous in *bogotensis*)

Habits Flies with 'leaping' pattern, hovers, and when hunting, flies low over open fields quartering like a harrier, wings in a dihedral. Usually alone, sometimes a small group, and most active at dawn and dusk. Always perches low and quite hunched, occasionally on open stumps or fenceposts. Calls infrequently.
Status Rare to locally uncommon in Ecuador, uncommon to local and fairly frequent in Colombia and Venezuela, scarce in Guyana, rare in Suriname, accidental in French Guiana.
Habitat Tropical Zone to Páramo. Open areas: savannas with tall grasses, pastures, páramo.
Voice A cat-like miaowing, a high-pitched *cri-cri-cri…*, series of *yak* or *wak* notes, sometimes drawn-out into *w-a-a-c-k* and a bark-sneeze *like-wow!* (H&B), all used only near nest. In flight, sporadic *toot-toot-toot…, boo-boo-boo…* or *hoo-hoo-hoo…*, especially in display, and females call *ree-yow* or *keee-ow* (H&B, F&K). Also a very harsh *jjjjjeeeaaa* (P. Schwartz).
Note Subspecies *pallidicaudus* considered invalid by König *et al.*

STEATORNITHIDAE – Oilbird

Oilbird is the only bird known to be equipped with a radar system similar to that used by bats, and the only species that can fly in complete dark. Its name is derived from the clear odourless oil obtained from the thick layers of fat in the skin of nestlings; Venezuelan Indians would travel to the caves where the birds breed in order to collect thousands of squabs, which were slaughtered and melted down to extract the oil. The principal food of Oilbirds is palm nuts – and it is the oil from these that is stored by the nestlings. Oilbirds breed on ledges deep inside caves in the ground and hillsides. They emerge as night falls, hundreds to thousands of birds all uttering their echo-locating clicks as they approach the exit from the cave. It is an impressive and never-to-be-forgotten sight. They fly off in loose flocks, screaming and clicking, and may travel up to 100km to find food. They may be observed like great moths, fluttering up and down the trunks of the palms, snatching and swallowing the palm nuts. They return at the very first hint of dawn, to disappear into the abyss of the caves before daylight.

OILBIRD *Steatornis caripensis* Pl. 85

Identification 41–48cm. Large, like a very big nightjar.
Ssp. Monotypic (Ec, Co, Ve, T&T, Gu)
Status Generally considered local and in decline everywhere due to man's activities. Large colonies within protected areas in eastern and southern Venezuela fairly safe and stable.
Habitat Tropical to Subtropical Zones, a colony on Mt. Roraima at 2,600m, and known to 3,000m. Mostly in primary forest but occasionally in coffee or cocoa plantations and other types of mature secondary forest.
Voice In flight, continually emits an electric-sounding *creee, cree, crrree* (F&K), *kerr kerr kerr* or *kur-karr*, (R&G, Hilty); alternately a treble-noted *kuk-kuk-kuk* (C&N). Clicking made within cave, occasionally heard outside, especially when bird is under a large palm.

NYCTIBIIDAE – Potoos

Potoos have melancholic wails of mystical significance for primitive Indians. Their cries are said to sound like those of people being murdered, and were held to be omens of disaster. The birds are nocturnal and rarely seen by day for they have a remarkably cryptic plumage, and a habit of sitting upright and perfectly still on a tree stump or log, leading them to be usually completely overlooked by humans or potential predators. They tend to perch-hunt, capturing large flying insects by sallying and returning, unlike nighthawks which sweep back and forth. They have favoured perches, and may continually use these for several weeks until they are disturbed or local conditions change. These perches may be close to the ground or high in a tree.

The following additional references were used to prepare this family: Gilliard (1958), Cleere & Nurney (1998, hereafter C&N) and Cohn-Haft (1999, hereafter C-H).

GREAT POTOO *Nyctibius grandis* Pl. 86

Identification 45–54cm. The largest potoo, predominately grey and highly varied; with mottles, vermiculations, ragged barring and brown shadings; white barring on tail probably the most consistent mark. Some variation in coloration, from cinnamon-tinged to brown, but as illustrated is typical; it usually appears much larger and paler than other potoos. Common Potoo is smaller and darker. Darker, browner Long-tailed Potoo may appear as large, but tail is longer. Brown eyes reflect yellow-orange and are visible at distance.

Ssp. Monotypic (all mainland countries)

Habits Day roosts on branches up to 40m above ground. Flies with slow, deep wingbeats, and appears awesome when mouth is open as it trolls.
Status Rare to uncommon, but increased knowledge of its voice reveals it to be more common and widespread than thought (R&G).
Habitat Lower Tropical Zone. Lowland forests and partially wooded areas, e.g. evergreen, deciduous and gallery forests, plantations and orchards, patchy woods. Occasionally in Upper Tropical Zone.
Voice Calls mostly at night, a loud far-carrying *waa-ha-oo-oo*, sometimes long sequences of harsh *quacks* and *caws*, and an owl-like *oo-rrooo* (C&N, H&M), a loud, gruff *BUAAaa* that

sounds like a human retching (Hilty), and a short *gwork* in flight (R&G).

LONG-TAILED POTOO

Nyctibius aethereus Pl. 86

Identification 42–56cm. Rufescent brown with black lines, ragged bars, spots and vermiculations; yellow eyes reflect bright orange-red at night. Long tail is a good field mark, but also has some heavy partial barring.

Ssp. *N. a. chocoensis* (W Co) larger; darker and more chestnut, stronger streaking

N. a. longicaudatus (E Ec, SE Co, E Ve, Gu, Su, FG) as described

Habits Roosts in thick cover 4–6m above ground and is very hard to see.

Status Rare, but probably under-recorded.

Habitat Lower Tropical Zone. Interior of humid to semi-dry lowland forests, also evergreen rain forest.

Voice Sings from canopy at night, especially if there is a full moon. Soft rising and falling sequences of *waa-OO-oo*, repeated frequently, first part descending, the second rising (C&N). When disturbed a low, gruff *ruf-ruf-ruf-ruf-ruf*… (Hilty) and a muffled *huh-huh-huh-huh-huh*… (R&G).

COMMON POTOO

Nyctibius griseus Pl. 86

Identification 31–41cm. Considerable variation, including at least 3 morphs; very cryptic indeed, looking utterly non-descript; tail regularly barred and there are pale to whitish bars on primaries that may appear as whitish dots at rest.

Ssp. *N. g. griseus* (Co, rest of Ve, T&T, Gu, Su, FG) as described (330-355mm)

N. g. panamensis (W Ec to SW Táchira, Ve) significantly larger (390-410mm), mostly dark forms

Habits Roosts in canopy or fairly high.

Status Widespread and locally common throughout range.

Habitat Tropical to Lower Subtropical Zones. Mostly low-land forests. In borders and partially wooded areas, second growth, plantations and orchards, with a predisposition for areas near water. Occasionally in mangroves.

Voice A mournful, descending series of hoots, starting loud and fading, e.g. *po-wo-ho-ho-ho* (C&N), *u-wah, wah, who, who, wuh, wüü* (R&G), *BU-OU, Bu-ou, bu-ou, bu-ou* (Hilty), all unbelievably melancholy. Contact-calls are soft whistles, or bark-like in flight.

ANDEAN POTOO

Nyctibius maculosus Pl. 86

Identification 34–40cm. Large and usually brown, under-wing black, and despite individual variation never appears grey. Distinct field mark is 2 white bars, one formed by the scapulars, the other on median wing-coverts; belly to vent pale; otherwise typical vermiculations, barring and irregular spotting; eyes yellow. From dark-morph Common Potoo by white on lesser wing-coverts. Much larger than White-winged Potoo, which has white shoulder.

Ssp. Monotypic (C Ec, W Co, W Ve)

Habits Normally detected by its song on moonlit nights. Males territorial and maintain several singing perches within their territories. Often forages low at edges of forest and in nearby open grassland.

Status Rare throughout range.

Habitat Subtropical to Temperate Zones, 1,800–2,800 m. Humid forest on upper Andean slopes, including montane and cloud forests. Generally at higher elevations than other potoos.

Voice Loud, double-note sequences: *raa-áa* or *aah-aa* repeated every 8–10 s for 2–3 minutes (C&N), with higher pitched ultimate syllable (C-H), *kwaaaanh* (R&G), *waaaaAAAa*, recalling Long-tailed but higher pitched (Hilty) and resembling *WAAuhm* of Great Potoo (F&K).

WHITE-WINGED POTOO

Nyctibius leucopterus Pl. 86

Identification 26–28cm. Small, brown with a pale throat and large (but quite variable) white patch on wing-coverts, usual spotting, streaking and vermiculations, tail neatly and regularly barred, eyes yellow. Noticeable white on wings like Andean Potoo, but is much smaller and hardly likely to occur sympatrically. From dark-brown morph of Common Potoo by white band on wing.

Ssp. Monotypic (C & SW Gu, FG)

Habits Roosts atop stump up to 20m above ground. Usually sings (repetitions of a chipped, high note) from canopy, especially on moonlit nights, but will also call in flight.

Status Recorded in northern South America on the Guianan Shield from a handful of localities, at Iwokrama Reserve in Guyana, and in French Guiana, where only recently found to be fairly common; Palumeu in Suriname and also two sites in French Guiana around the Petif-Saut Lake and at Saül. Probably under-recorded as it sings very occasionally..

Habitat Tropical Zone to 900m. Humid pristine primary forest, especially near watercourses and where *Mora* spp. trees are abundant.

Voice A plaintive whistle *weuuuuuuu*, gradually descending in pitch, mostly at night (C&N), pure-toned *feeeooooo* (C-H), like a falling bomb, *sweeeeeeeuuuuuu*, easily imitated (Hilty).

RUFOUS POTOO

Nyctibius bracteatus Pl. 86

Identification 21.5–24.5cm. Smallest potoo and notably cinnamon-rufous, with obvious, black-edged white spots irregularly on body and tips of tertials, and white gape-line also noticeable; eyes yellow with a black wedge below pupil, lending it an odd keyhole shape.

Ssp. Monotypic (Ec, Co, Ve [has been collected literally at border of Guyana and Venezuela] Gu, Su, FG)

Habits Forages and sings at night.

Status Very rare and local, but probably under-recorded like most other potoos. Now known from a fair number of locations in French Guiana, even close to villages in the interior.

Habitat Tropical Zone. Humid interior of primary forest, including montane and cloud forests. Lower and middle growth of seasonally flooded *várzea* and adjacent *terra firme* and swampy palm forest. Sometimes also in secondary growth. **Voice** Song descending and slightly quavering *boo boo boo boo*...notes (C&N), a bouncy series of *Megascops*-like *WUU, Poo, poo-poo'poo'poo*, comprising *c.*15 notes, slightly accelerating at end and diminishing in volume (C-H, Hilty).

CAPRIMULGIDAE – Nighthawks and Nightjars

Nightjars and nighthawks include a mix of boreal migrants and residents, extremely rare to quite common, widespread and localised, but they all have in common the most complex and subtle cryptic plumages, mottled grey, black and various shades of brown. They are crepuscular, hunting airborne prey at dusk and dawn, and sporadically during the night. By day, they roost silently on the ground, or on a low branch, where their cryptic coloration provides perfect camouflage. Indeed, most are only seen as they fly away as one almost steps on them. Sexes are similar, but males usually have white spots on the wings and tail that separate them and provide important diagnostics for identification. Some males have extraordinarily long decorative plumes.

The following additional references were used to prepare this family: Gilliard (1958), Cleere & Nurney (1998, hereafter C&N) and Cleere (1999).

Nighthawks are beautiful, cryptic, crepuscular birds with long pointed wings and square-ended tails that often fairly short, and fast, erratic flight. They lack the long, stiff rectal bristles around the gape of nightjars. They forage in continual flight, often for lengthy periods. Most commence their hawking in late afternoon, an hour or more before dusk. Each tends to have its characteristic flight pattern and level where it is most often seen. Nighthawks have small weak feet, and roost on the ground or in trees, sometimes quite high, where they are very seldom seen.

SHORT-TAILED NIGHTHAWK
Lurocalis semitorquatus Pl. 85

Identification 21–22cm. Pretty much entirely dark brown with multiple faint spots – black and brown – and bold white and down-curved crescent on throat. Long pointed wings reach beyond short, square tail, and lacks white markings. Erratic flight is bat-like, with bursts of shallow wingbeats and glides. Similar Rufous-bellied larger with an unbarred rufous belly, and is usually found at higher altitude.

Ssp. *L. s. nattereri* (E Ec, Co, W & N Ve) darker below, more densely barred brown

L. s. noctivagus (W Co, NW Ec) darker, more heavily spotted cinnamon and tawny above

L. s. schaeferi (NC Ve: Cordillera de la Costa) blacker below with less pale speckling

L. s. semitorquatus (E Co; WC & S Ve, Tr, To, Guianas) as described

Habits Forages above canopy at dusk, alone or in pairs, and occasionally over water. Roosts in canopy. Poorly known.
Status Widespread but uncommon and local throughout range, but undoubtedly under-recorded. Widely distributed, but always in small numbers, all over the forest of the interior in French Guiana.
Habitat Tropical to Lower Subtropical Zones; *semitorquatus* to 2,250m, *nattereri* to 1,100m and *schaeferi* to 1,150m. Humid forests, borders.
Voice In flight a sharp, *staccato cu-it!* (R&G), *tor-ta, quirrrrt, tor, quirrrt* (F&K), a light *whit-whit-whit-wiss* or chuckling *wup-wup-wup* (ffrench); race *nattereri* has a rising *turreet*, different from *semitorquatus* (H&B).
Notes Race *nattereri* is considered possibly a separate species (Chestnut-banded or Chestnut-bellied Nighthawk) by H&B, S&M, F&K. Races *noctivagus* and *stonei* are probably synonyms (Wetmore 1968, R&G). Sometimes called Semi-collared Nighthawk.

RUFOUS-BELLIED NIGHTHAWK
Lurocalis rufiventris Pl. 85

Identification 23–25cm. All dark with bold white down-curved crescent on throat, underwing-coverts and belly to undertail-coverts deep rufous; tail barred deep rufous and black, with pale tip. Lacks white markings on wings and tail; plain rufous underparts. Very similar Short-tailed has barred underparts and occurs at lower elevations.

Ssp. Monotypic (Ec, C Co, Ve)

Habits Flight bat-like. Forages alone or in pairs around treetops at forest edge or zigzags lower around clearings. Roosts lengthwise on high limb of forest tree.
Status Uncommon in Ecuador, uncommon and local in Andes of central Colombia and Venezuela.
Habitat Subtropical to Temperate Zones, 1,500–2,500m in Ecuador, to 3,000m in Colombia, 1,400–1,800m in Venezuela. Montane forests, forest edge and second growth.
Voice Calls mainly at dawn and dusk. A series of mellow whistled hoots, falling in pitch (F&K), a fast, descending *kwa-kwa-kwa-kwa-ko* in south-east Ecuador (R&G), a high *wuck*, a short *weeop* and slow, descending *qua, QUEE, QUee, qua, qua* (Hilty).
Notes Separated from Short-tailed Nighthawk based on different size, plumage and calls (Parker *et al.* 1991).

LESSER NIGHTHAWK
Chordeiles acutipennis Pl. 85

Identification 19–20cm. Male is dark and rather greyish with rufescent scapulars and pale sub-scapulars; thin, pointed wings that, when folded, reach tip of long, notched tail. In flight, white band on outer primaries, bold white crescent either side of throat, black-tipped tail has shallow fork and a white subterminal band that shows well when flushed; undertail-coverts pale buffy. Female more rufescent below, with a largely pale throat, but no white crescent and no bar on tail.

Ssp. *C. a. acutipennis* (E Ec?, Co, Cu, Bo, Ve, Tr, To, Gu, Su, FG) broader white band on outer 4 primaries
C. a. aequatorialis (resident and austral migrant: SW Co, W Ec) greyer and paler, with paler ochraceous markings
C. a. crissalis (SC Co) paler, less heavily barred below
C. a. micromeris (C Co) like *texensis* but smaller
C. a. texensis (boreal migrant: W Co) paler and larger, most white on wings and tail

Habits Flight extremely buoyant, with short bouts of fast erratic flapping and gliding; forages low with fluttery wingbeats, sometimes in afternoon light.
Status Uncommon to erratically frequent in Ecuador. In Colombia, races *acutipennis* and *crissalis* are resident, *micromeris* a vagrant from Panama (possibly resident?), boreal migrant *texensis* appears December–April in central valleys, and *aequatorialis*, recorded March, perhaps resident in south or is an austral migrant (from Brazil?). In Curaçao and Bonaire, sight records of casual visitors. In Venezuela, *acutipennis* frequent to common resident; *texensis* from North America, whilst *micromeris* from Central America and *aequatorialis* from Brazil probably occur. Common in Trinidad but scarce on Tobago, where probably a seasonal visitor from continental South America. Common in Guyana. Uncommon and local in French Guiana.
Habitat Tropical to Subtropical Zones to 1,200m, occasionally to 2,500m. Grassy, partially wooded areas, scrub, semi-open woodland, parks and gardens, saltmarshes, mudflats and beaches.
Voice A low soft *chuck, chuck* on ground (Hilty) and in flight (ffrench); song a resonant, even-pitched, toad-like trill or slow *churr* that occasionally ends in a deep *tchrrr* or guttural *wahugh* (C&N).

LEAST NIGHTHAWK
Chordeiles pusillus Pl. 85

Identification 15–16cm. Small, very dark with underparts barring only noticeable on vent and undertail-coverts; round white disc on outer primaries, white chin trails back leaving an inverted V. Virtually identical to Antillean Nighthawk, and only be separated with certainty by voice, but if seen roosting, note Antillean Nighthawk's wings only reach tip of tail and do not extend beyond. Band-tailed Nighthawk may look similar but lacks white on wings and has bold white band on upper tail. Lesser Nighthawk much more rufescent; male has white tail-band and female lacks bold white chin.

Ssp. *C. p. esmeraldae* (S Ve, SE Co) as described
C. p. septentrionalis (NE Co, C & E VE, Gu, S Su) finely barred black and white below with white vent and undertail-coverts, white trailing edge to inner wing

Habits Forages alone, in pairs or sometimes in small groups, flying low over open country and sometimes forages alongside Least Nighthawk. Flight is erratic, with fast wingbeats. Roosts in small groups, in low bushes or on ground.
Status Locally frequent in south-east Colombia, frequent to common in Venezuela, common in Guyana. Local in the Sipaliwini savanna in Suriname.
Habitat Lower Tropical Zone to 1,000m. *Llanos*, semi-open savannas, scrub and light woodland, especially in drier areas and *Curatella* scrub. Often abundant in pastures.
Voice Flight-call a short sharp *whit* or *bit*, often repeated in quick succession, *whit-whit-whit-whit*... (C&N). A low *churrr* and nasal *beep* in flight, and a *cur-cur-cur-curry* song (P. Schwartz recording), given as *k-k-k-k-k-kurree* (C&N).

COMMON NIGHTHAWK
Chordeiles minor Pl. 85

Identification 22–25cm. Greyish, black and white; long white curling chin reaches around lower ear-coverts, large white patch on outer 6 primaries fairly close to primary-coverts, vent to undertail-coverts white with vestigial barring; tail barred dark and medium brown and grey, broad subterminal white band, dark tip is notched. Female has white band on wing significantly narrower. From Lesser by larger size, longer, more pointed wings (tips extend beyond tip of tail at rest) with outer primary longest, and white bar on primaries closer to bend in wing. Forages higher than Lesser.

Ssp. *C. m. minor* (ABC, Ve, To?) as described
C. m. aserriensis, *henryi*, *hesperis*, *howelli*, *neotropicalis*, *panamensis* and *sennetti* all possibly winter in northern South America

Habits Bounding flight with deep wingbeats. If flushed in daytime will alight on high perch, such as lamp or overhead cable. Often forages late afternoon.
Status Boreal migrant, arrives late August–September, departs April–May. In Ecuador, uncommon and scarce winterer but occasionally found in numbers on passage. On Curaçao and Bonaire, regular both wintering and transient (sight records in Aruba). On Tobago, uncertain – some sight records, possibly of passage migrants (no records Trinidad).
Habitat Tropical to Subtropical Zones, to 2,600m. Virtually any open or semi-open habitat, from coniferous forest, through sand dunes and beaches to marshes and townships.
Voice Characteristic flight-call a nasal, buzzy *peeent* or *beeehnt* (ffrench, Voous, R&G, H, C&N), and an insect-like, buzzy *beeerp* (F&K, Voous).

SAND-COLOURED NIGHTHAWK
Chordeiles rupestris Pl. 85

Identification 22cm. All but central tail-feathers brown, tipped white, white wing patch with 4 first primaries all black.

Ssp. *C. r. rupestris* (E Ec, SE Co, S Ve) as described
C. r. xyostictus (CE Co) more sandy-coloured and more heavily spotted below

Habits Flies on deep wingbeats (like tern or wader), frequently changing direction but less jerky than Common or Lesser Nighthawks. Often attracted to lamps and town lights. Usually roosts in groups on branches of a fallen tree by water's edge or on river sandbar.
Status Rare to very locally fairly common in Ecuador, locally frequent to common in south-east Colombia, local and uncommon in Venezuela.

Habitat Lower Tropical Zone. Savanna and villages by rivers, grassy river islands, sandbars and sandy beaches along rivers and around lakes.

Voice Territorial song *rrrrr-wo-wo-wo* uttered in flight or when perched, also series of *ow-ow-ow* notes. A soft purring trill, lower growling *gr'r'ow*, spluttering, bubbly *put-put-put-put-put* and quiet, hollow *go-go-go-go-go-go*… (C&N, Hilty).

ANTILLEAN NIGHTHAWK

Chordeiles gundlachii Pl. 85

Identification 20–21cm. Mainly dark grey with black-and-white cryptic pattern above, large white chin patch trails back either side of throat, blackish breast, variably barred underwing-coverts and belly, white undertail, tail barred blackish and white with broad white terminal bar, and dark tip notched into a slight fork. From very similar Common Nighthawk with certainty only by voice, but note if seen roosting – on ground or lengthways along a branch – wingtips do not reach tip of tail (in Common Nighthawk, wings extend beyond tail).

Ssp. *C. g. gundlachii* (Cu, Bo, To, hypothetical for mainland northern South America) 2 morphs, greyish and tawny-ochraceous

C. g. vicinus (hypothetical for northern South America) slightly smaller, no tawny morph

Habits Forages high above beaches and shorelines, fields, pastures and urban areas (streets, gardens), and high over forest. Often dives steeply.

Status Hypothetical winter visitor September–April, almost certainly overlooked among Common Nighthawks. Quite common in breeding range.

Habitat Lower Tropical Zone. Prefers open and semi-open country.

Voice Often-repeated *chitty-chit* or *killikadick*, with short pause between each set, also a more nasal *penk-dick* (C&N).

Note Both races possible but winter quarters unknown.

BAND-TAILED NIGHTHAWK

Nyctiprogne leucopyga Pl. 85

Identification 16–20cm. Dark brown all over, with black and various shades of brown in cryptic markings, small clean white crescent on throat-sides, and broad white band at base of tail. Dark, narrow pointed wings and short tail with broad white band on 3 outer feathers (but appears to cross entire tail in flight). Appears to flutter, with stiff shallow wingbeats and glides, and wings held in dihedral. Short-tailed and Rufous-bellied Nighthawks also have all-dark – but broader – wings, and are much larger.

Ssp. *N. l. exigua* (SW Ve in west Amazonas, E Co) smaller and darker

N. l. latifascia (S Ve in south Amazonas) darker, almost black above

N. l. leucopyga (Guianas) as described

N. l. pallida (C & W Ve, NE Co) smaller and paler

Habits Never abroad in daylight (Hilty), but may be partially diurnal (C&N).

Status Uncommon, local in north-east Ecuador, locally fairly common in Colombia, locally fairly abundant in Venezuela, locally common in the Guianas.

Habitat Lower Tropical Zone to 500 m. Fairly open country, edges of forests, close to water, from streams and ponds to lakes and rivers.

Voice Two songs described: variations on *kwoik kwak* and *ku-woit- kwoit* or *churk…churk…churk*, and a low nasal, frog-like *qurk-ta-ta-ta-ta-ta-ta-ta-ta*… and *wer-CHURK* (C&N, R&G, Hilty).

NACUNDA NIGHTHAWK

Podager nacunda Pl. 85

Identification 23–33cm. Large, sandy-brown above with typical black, camouflaging marks; largely white below, white down-turned, shallow crescent across throat edged below with black, then a broad 'cup' of black, scalloped brown; breast to undertail- white; central tail-feathers brown but rest have large white tips, appearing from below as a broad pale terminal band.

Ssp. *P. n. minor* (resident in N & C Co, Ve, T&T, Gu, Su) as described; smaller and paler

P. n. nacunda (austral migrant from breeding range in Uruguay, winters in Ec, Co, Ve in August–March, FG) larger and darker

Habits Leisurely and graceful flight, sometimes gliding with wings in dihedral. Forages mainly at night, sometimes late afternoon/early evening, often in small groups. Roosts in open by day, on sandbanks, saltflats and in savanna, and on rocky outcrops.

Status Austral migrants, in northern South America mid June–late October, some of which breed in June–October, and residents. In Ecuador, recent sight records (first noted June 1981: R. A. Rowlett *fide* R&G) and occurrence considered uncertain or very rare. Uncommon resident in Trinidad, although some may be seasonal visitors, rare and seasonal in Tobago, but common in Guyana and Suriname. Probably only migrants in French Guiana (O. Tostain).

Habitat Prefers open savannas, as well as marshes, shores and edges of forest, frequently in xerophytic country.

Voice Rarely vocalises when foraging but when flushed utters a low *chuck, cluck* or *cherk-cherk* (ffrench, H&B) and has a slow, low, irregular dove-like *prrrrr-doo* or *dur'du'du'du*… repeated several times in succession (C&N, Hilty).

Nightjars possess amazingly cryptic coloration: at rest on the ground, roosting or brooding, they seem to disappear, as their mottling closely matches the surrounding area. Those that rest on blackish volcanic rock are themselves blackish and can only be seen against the rock by virtue of light and shadow. Crepuscular and nocturnal, they roost by day – usually on or near ground – relying on their camouflage to avoid detection. However, they are easily alerted and watch actively through narrow eye-slits, flushing before an observer comes too close for comfort. Generally insectivorous, but birds and bats have been found in their stomachs. At the other extreme, hundreds of mosquitoes have been found in the stomach of a single bird – indicating that they fly back and forth through clouds of small insects, sieving them with their great gapes, made larger by the long, stiff, rictal bristles – in much the same way that a great whale sieves countless tiny krill in the ocean. They tend to perch-hunt or sally from the ground, but when they fly it is seldom for long, as they soon return to their perch or spot on a road or track. Most nightjars are sedentary but some are migratory, traveling long distances from North America, or Argentina, to spend a few months in northern South America. Males can usually be identified with little difficulty, provided the diagnostic marks are seen, mostly whether there is white in the wing or tail, but females can be very difficult indeed, and habitat, date (to include or eliminate migrants), length of wing and tail can all help.

PAURAQUE *Nyctidromus albicollis* Pl. 86

Identification 22–28cm. Brownish-grey body with clearly defined black and tan scapulars, bright rufous face-sides and white throat patch. When flushed, white on outer 5 primaries near tips of wings, combined with 2 bold white bars on tail, diagnostic. Female less easily identified, the patches on wings are buff, and there are no tail-bands. Two distinct colour morphs, greyish-brown (illustrated) and an uncommon, reddish-brown or tawny morph. Long tail with 2 white feathers between central pair and outer feathers in male is diagnostic; wingtips reach barely halfway along tail.

Ssp. *N. a. albicollis* (E Co? E&S Ve, Tr, Gu, Su, FG) as described
N. a. gilvus (N Co) smaller, paler and greyer

Habits Roosts in leaf-litter. Often sits in roads and tracks at night. Looks like a large moth when flushed, and may fly to a low perch where it sits crosswise.
Status Fairly common to abundant throughout its range.
Habitat Tropical and Subtropical Zones, to at least 2,300m. Wide range of habitats tending to forest edges, cultivated land, scrub with thickets, both xerophytic and swampy, mangroves and *llanos*, plantations, parks and gardens.
Voice Notes and whistles, most of them variants on 'Who ARE you?', e.g. *wheeooo wheeoo-who,* also *wuc wuc whEEeer* and *coo-whEEeer,* or *cuu, cuu, cuu, wheéer* and *wook, wook, wook, wook, wook-a-wéé-ooh* (C&N, F&K, R&G, ffrench, H&M, Hilty).

OCELLATED POORWILL
Nyctiphrynus ocellatus Pl. 87

Identification 20–25cm Overall dark brown, with finely outlined scapulars and rows of paler spots on wing-coverts, and rufous bars on primaries, but all rather subtle; narrow white throat-band, tips of tail white, except central pair. Female similar but slightly browner. A black morph is simply even darker, with same patterns. At rest appears uniform dark brown, lacking any collar on hindneck or white in wings. Chocó Poorwill more heavily spotted blackish above and has noticeable white on inner wing. Similar Blackish Nightjar has blackish, barred pattern above.

Ssp. *N. o. ocellatus* (E Ec, S Co)

Habits Seldom sits on roads or tracks. Sallies from perch 2–5m above ground.
Status Scarce and local.
Habitat Tropical Zone, to 1,350m. Forest interiors, small clearings and open understorey, second-growth forests.
Voice A short *wah, wah, wah* given from ground, and in flight a trilled mellow but somewhat explosive *preeeo, kwr'r'r'ro* or *ddrrreuw* (Ridgely & Gwynne, R&G, C&N).

CHOCÓ POORWILL
Nyctiphrynus rosenbergi Pl. 87

Identification 19–21cm. Very dark with 2–3 bold white spots on inner wing but lacks white on primaries; white crescent on throat, entire tip of tail white. Similar Ocellated lacks white spots on inner wing.

Ssp. Monotypic (W Co, NW Ec)

Habits Foraging birds sometimes fly above canopy like a nighthawk.
Status Presumably often overlooked and locally fairly common.
Habitat Tropical Zone, to 900m. Primary forest, both interior and at edges.
Voice Similar to Ocellated, a resonant, rhythmic, steadily rising *kwor kwor kwor kweeé,* also frog-like *kwok* or *kwi-kwok* and *klaw klaw* (R&G, C&N).
Note Formerly considered a subspecies of Ocellated Poorwill, but separated by Robbins & Ridgely (1992).

CHUCK-WILL'S-WIDOW
Caprimulgus carolinensis Pl. 87

Identification 27–34cm. Large, dark and heavily built; no white in wings, but flight-feathers barred dark rufous and black, and paler scapulars might be noticed in flight; male has inner webs of outer 3 rectrices white. Two colour morphs, brown (illustrated) and greyish-brown. Indistinct tawny-buff collar might be visible at rest. From very similar Rufous Nightjar by greyish crown (Rufous Nightjar has rufous).

Ssp. Monotypic (N Co, N Ve)

Habits May roost at any level.
Status Rare boreal winter visitor.
Habitat Tropical and Subtropical Zones, to 2,600m. Range of habitats from forest interiors and edges to parks and gardens.
Voice Generally silent in winter, but may give in-flight growls or *chuck* notes (F&K, C&N, Hilty).

RUFOUS NIGHTJAR
Caprimulgus rufus Pl. 87

Identification 25–30cm. Large, slight tawny collar, thin white line on throat, no white on wings. Male has all rectrices broadly tipped white, except central pair. From very rare Chuck-will's-widow by rufous on crown (not grey). Pauraque has longer tail, and wing patches.

Ssp. *C. r. minimus* (N Co, W & N Ve, Tr) less rufescent with collar on hindneck tawnier
C. r. rufus (S Ve, Guianas) paler, less rufescent, collar on hindneck often has some white
C. r. subspecies unknown (Ec)

Habits Rarely sits in road or paths at night; sallies from low perch.
Status Uncommon in Ecuador and Colombia, fairly common in Venezuela and Guyana, but rare in Suriname. Race *rutilus* unconfirmed austral migrant, May–August.
Habitat Tropical and Lower Subtropical Zones, to 1,800m. Wide range of habitats; forest and forest edges, scrub and savanna thickets, plantations and cultivation, parks and gardens.
Voice Variously rendered *chuck wee wee weeo* and *chuck wick-wick-WEEoo* (H&M, C&N, R&G, Hilty). Similar to Chuck-will's-widow but faster and higher, and note latter does not sing on wintering grounds.

SILKY-TAILED NIGHTJAR
Caprimulgus sericocaudatus Pl. 87

Identification 24–30cm. Large, dark and long-winged, rufous patch on nape and large white throat patch, scapulars well marked black and white; no white in wings, which are regularly barred rufous and black, tail has large white corners in male and greyish corners in female.

Ssp. *C. s. mengeli* (Ec)

Habits Roosts on ground by day but at night sallies from high perch. Often flies around forest clearings 2–3m above ground.
Status Locally uncommon to fairly common.
Habitat Tropical forest, clearings and edges, bamboo understorey and second growth.
Voice Mournful but melodious and undulating *doh wheeeo weeeo*, repeated for 3 minutes or more with brief pause between each set. Also a treble-noted *gawrr a gawrr* or a longer *gawrr a gawrr a gawrr* (C&N).

BAND-WINGED NIGHTJAR
Caprimulgus longirostris Pl. 87

Identification 20–27cm. In Pantepui, from Blackish and Roraiman by buffy collar; both others slightly smaller and blacker, and have different wing and tail markings. Flushes with jerky, erratic wingbeats and drops suddenly to ground. In Andes is only nightjar at high elevations with white or buff wing-bands.

Ssp. *C. l. roraimae* (Ve: Pantepui) larger and darker with fewer white markings above and very little or no white on tail
C. l. ruficervix (Ec, Co, W & N Ve) as described

Habits Often sits on roads and tracks at night, and hawks insects around street lights and windows. Gives frequent calls before starting to feed at dawn and dusk, usually spending first 20 minutes over river or gallery forest, then dispersing over contiguous savannas.
Status Widespread and fairly common.
Habitat Subtropical and Temperate Zones. In Ecuador at 1,800–3,700m; Colombia 1,600–3,600m; Venezuela 900–3,800m north of Orinoco and 1,300–2,300m to south. Wide range of habitats, from forest edges to stony, semi-desert, shrubby páramo to semi-arid elfin forest, open roads and road cuts.
Voice High-pitched *seeeeeeert sweeeeert seeeeert* (C&N) with variable emphasis, e.g. *seeEEEeert* rising and then downslurred (Hilty), and an occasional nasal *tchree-ee* when flushed (C&N). A very high-pitched *psee-yeet* or *psee-ee-eeyt* given persistently after dusk (R&G).
Note Race *ruficervix* sometimes considered a separate species (C&N), and race *roraimae* probably also specifically distinct (Hilty, D. Ascanio, pers. comm.), whilst birds from Sucre and Monagas, Venezuela, may also merit species status (K. C. Parkes in Hilty).

WHITE-TAILED NIGHTJAR
Caprimulgus cayennensis Pl. 87

Identification 20–22cm. Small and variegated. Male has broad rufous or cinnamon collar on nape and white mark on throat, white band across 4 outer primaries, 2 rows of whitish spots on wing-coverts and white trailing edge to secondaries; 3 outer rectrices have outer fringes white. Female lacks white wing-bands and white on tail, but rufous or cinnamon nape is clear. Female Spot-tailed Nightjar lacks rufous or cinnamon on nape and pale spots on wings less obvious.

Ssp. *C. c. albicauda* (NW Co) heavily tinged buff below
C. c. apertus (W Co, N Ec) indistinguishable from *albicauda* in field
C. c. cayennensis (C & NE Co, Ve, Guianas) very variable, from very dark greyish-brown to pale brown
C. c. insularis (NE Co, NW Ve on Margarita I., ABC) paler and more buffy above
C. c. leopetes (T&T) tawnier above, darker below

Habits Sits on roads and tracks at night, foraging in prolonged, butterfly-like sorties over grassland and pastures. Usually inactive until after dark.
Status Locally fairly common on mainland, scarce on offshore islands.
Habitat Tropical and Subtropical Zones, to 1,600m in Ecuador, 2,100m in Colombia and 1,600m in Venezuela. Generally open scrubby areas, ranchland, pastures, savanna, arid *Acacia* and *Opuntia* scrub.
Voice Whistles all year, a high, thin drawn-out *spit-cheeeeuua*, first note faint then rising and falling (Hilty, R&G, C&N). Flight-calls include high *see-see* and soft *whut* (C&N). Also a tapping or knocking sound by wing-clapping, followed by a *tic-tic* (Voous).

SPOT-TAILED NIGHTJAR
Caprimulgus maculicaudus Pl. 87

Identification 19–21cm. Small and dark with buffy band on outer 3–4 primaries, dark face with strong buff eyebrow and collar, broad white band at tip of tail (except to central rectrices); no white on wing.

Ssp. Monotypic (all mainland countries)

Habits Often sits on roads and tracks. Short sallies from ground and prolonged sorties over grassland.
Status Poorly known. Locally frequent in French Guiana.
Habitat Generally, open pastures, *Thalia* marshland, *Mauritia* groves, burned savannas with scrubby *Curatella* trees, second growth and along woodland and forest edges.
Voice A thin, high-pitched, rising *t-seet* or *t-sweet, pit-suueét* and similar variations (C&N, R&G, Hilty).

LITTLE NIGHTJAR

Caprimulgus parvulus Pl. 87

Identification 19–21cm. Male has full white chin and throat; fringes of scapulars whitish and inner wing-coverts also fringed white, solid white band on outer 4 primaries and large white spots on tips of outer 4 rectrices. Female has buff bar on wings and lacks tail spots. Sometimes rests or roosts near Lesser Nighthawk, which has subterminal tail-band.

Ssp. *C. p. heterurus* (E Co, NW & SE Ve) much broader white band on 5 outer primaries, darker below, larger white spots on tail
C. p. parvulus (extreme SE Co) as described

Habits When flushed usually flies high before returning to ground again, most often behind a bush or tree.
Status Rare in Colombia, uncommon to locally common in Venezuela, but poorly known and probably often overlooked.
Habitat Tropical Zone, to 300m in Colombia and 1,000m in Venezuela. Open woodland, pastures and fields with scrub, scattered bushes and thickets, in foothills and hilly country.
Voice Race *heterurus* gives a few short notes followed by a bubbly roll, *pik-gobble-gobble-gobble-gobble* at short intervals. Race *parvulus* a distinctive warbled series, descending in pitch *dop-dro-dro-dro-dro-dro-dro* (C&N, Hilty).

SCRUB NIGHTJAR

Caprimulgus anthonyi Pl. 87

Identification 18–21cm. Only small nightjar found in semi-open within its range. Male is a small, well-speckled bird with white chin and cinnamon collar, and a broad cinnamon band on primaries. Female has a narrower wing-band.

Ssp. Monotypic (W Ec)

Habits Forages low over bushes. Vocalisations appear to be associated with rain (R&G).
Status Uncommon to locally fairly common.
Habitat Tropical zone, to 750m. Arid scrub, open country with scattered bushes, brushy mesquite, second-growth mesquite, thickets in farmland.
Voice A short, simple *treeow*, repeated steadily every 1–2 s from low perch (R&G), flight-call a soft *tuk-tuk-tuk* and rolling *quaqurr*, rising in pitch at start and again in middle.
Note Sometimes called Anthony's Nightjar.

CAYENNE NIGHTJAR

Caprimulgus maculosus Pl. 87

Identification 22.5cm. Small, brown and variegated; fringes to scapulars well defined and pale fringes to median and greater coverts also obvious. In flight, pointed wings with small white spot on 4 outer primaries, outer 3 tail-feathers broadly tipped white. Female unknown, possibly like male but probably lacks white spots on primaries and tail-corners. Blackish is darker and blacker, with a more spotted appearance and appears round-winged in flight.

Ssp. Monotypic (FG) known only from type specimen and female in plate is hypothetical

Habits Unknown.
Status Apparently extremely rare from the Mana river. Recent searches have failed to locate species near type locality.
Habitat Only specimen was collected near lower reaches of river with numerous boulder-strewn rapids in dense forest and open spaces with sandy or stony riverbanks, large boulders and savanna-like clearings. May be associated with tree-fall gaps in primary forest.
Voice Unknown.

BLACKISH NIGHTJAR

Caprimulgus nigrescens Pl. 87

Identification 19.5–21.5cm. Small, dark brown and spotted with various shades of brown, narrow cinnamon edge to scapulars, white line on throat; male has 3 white spots on outer primaries and 3 small white spots at tips of outer rectrices, but these are not a clear field mark unless bird is studied at rest. Roraiman Nightjar larger with 3 bold white spots on primaries, small white tertial spots and 2–3 subterminal spots on outer rectrices.

Ssp. Monotypic (all mainland countries) birds in west tend to be browner and paler

Habits Roosts on ground or rocks. If approached flattens itself, closing eyes, then may sit upright, open eyes and bob before flying short distance, uttering alarm. Sallies from ground, forages over clearings and streams.
Status Common to locally abundant, but not easy to find.
Habitat Tropical Zone, to 1,100 m. Prefers open stony ground, stony places by rivers, landslides, road cuts, rocky outcrops, large rocks in rivers.
Voice Three or 4 purring, frog-like trills *puurrt…puurrt… puurrt* (Hilty), *pru-r-r-r-t* or *pur-r-r-r-t* (C&N), and in alarm a sharp *ptink* or *prek* (C&N) or *pret!*, like bubble bursting (Hilty).

RORAIMAN NIGHTJAR

Caprimulgus whitelyi Pl. 87

Identification 21–23cm. Quite dark with 3 clear white spots on outer primaries and small white spots on tertials, 2–3 subterminal white spots on tail; wing-coverts have white spots that might give impression of narrow wingbars, but this is not a field mark. Band-winged has larger white patch on throat and buffy collar, Blackish has smaller white spots on wings, lacks white spots on tertials, and spots on tail are at tips. Tail of Roraiman is shorter than both, with wingtips reaching almost to tip of tail at rest.

Ssp. Monotypic (Ve: Pantepui)

Habits Poorly known.
Status Rare and local.
Habitat Forested slopes and upper levels of tepuis, preferring open areas, clearings and tree falls.
Voice A high, thin, ascending *seeeeeEER*, which becomes louder at end, exactly the opposite of Band-winged Nightjar (D. Ascanio recording).

LADDER-TAILED NIGHTJAR

Hydropsalis climacocerca Pl. 86

Identification Male 25–28cm, female 22–23cm. Dark brown with rufous on nape, white edges to scapulars, and white spots on wing-coverts; male has broad white band on outer 5 primaries; tail unique with long central feathers rounded at ends and barred regularly brown and black; next feather shorter, white with a brown tip, next similar but longer, next similar and also longer, but still shorter than central pair, outermost longer than central pair, tapered and have brown and black barred outer webs, inner webs white. Female has 2 cinnamon wing-bands, the outer narrower than the inner, and lacks white spots on back and wings, whilst all-brown and black tail is forked, and central rectrices square-ended. Trident-shaped tail largely white except central pair, distinct from other fancy-tailed nightjars. Easy discriminator in flight is white in wings, though if not seen well might be mistaken for a Pauraque, but note habitat!

Ssp. *H. c. climacocerca* (E Ec, E & SE Co, S Ve) as described
H. c. schomburgki (E Ve, Guianas) darker and browner

Habits Roosts on ground near water, among driftwood, rocks and scrub. At night, best identified by habitat.
Status Uncommon to fairly common across its range.
Habitat Lower Tropical Zone, to 350m. Specialised, on or near sandbars along rivers and river islands, edges of oxbow lagoons and lakes.
Voice Very vocal, flight-call a squeaky *chweeit* (R&G) or snipe-like *cheeit*, also given when flushed (C&N). Also, a high *chip*, repeated monotonously, a slow series of *tsick!* and a repeated *chup!* (R&G, C&N, Hilty).

SCISSOR-TAILED NIGHTJAR

Hydropsalis torquata Pl. 86

Identification Male with tail 50–70cm, female 25–30cm. Generally dark brown with rufous on nape, well spotted and barred rufous, wings all brown and black; long uppertail-coverts barred rufous and blackish, outer pair of rectrices very long and initially broad, gradually tapering to drawn-out point, the outer webs creamy white. Female has long pointed wings, and long rounded tail clearly barred rufous and dark brown. From Ladder-tailed Nightjar by lack of white in wings.

Ssp. *H. t. torquata* (Su)

Habits When flushed flies off silently and alights 20–30m away, in cover. Often sits on roads and tracks at dusk and dawn.
Status Uncommon.
Habitat Sipaliwini savanna, light woodland, *Eucalyptus* and *Acacia* groves, scrubby grassland.
Voice Series of short *tsip* notes, 1 per s, for *c.*3 minutes on end. Flight-call a high-pitched *tsig* (H&M).
Note Pacheco & Whitney (1998) noted that this species is correctly called *torquata*, not the long-used *brasiliana*.

SWALLOW-TAILED NIGHTJAR

Uropsalis segmentata Pl. 86

Identification 22–23cm, male up to 28cm. Generally all brown and black with rufous on nape, but no white marks at all. Adult male has long, rounded tail with 2 outermost feathers twice as long as rest and graduated to point. Female has clearly barred tail and small white spots at tips of greater wing-coverts.

Ssp. *U. s. segmentata* (Ec, Co)

Habits Roosts amid long vines, in gullies or recesses on ground where unmistakable. Both sexes very rufous. Sits on roads at night, short sallies, flying low.
Status Rare, but locally fairly common.
Habitat Mainly Temperate zone, 2,300–3,600m. Forest edges, elfin and cloud forest, often with bamboo, *Espeletia* and páramo. Usually above range of Lyre-tailed Nightjar.
Voice Beautiful song, seldom heard, *wor-r-r-r-e-e-e-e-e-r*, sliding up then down (R&G), or *purrrrr-sweeeee*, lasting 2.5–3 s, first note rising, second descending (C&N).

LYRE-TAILED NIGHTJAR

Uropsalis lyra Pl. 86

Identification 25–28cm, tail of male up to 55cm. Dark brown with subtle brown and black markings, rufous band on nape, outermost 2 tail-feathers extremely long and broad, tapering to thin, buffy-yellow curved tips. Female similar but lacks long outer tail-feathers, instead having a well-forked tail. Very similar to Swallow-tailed but noticeably black and grey on head with rufous collar (both sexes). Moulting male from Band-winged by rufous collar.

Ssp. *U. l. lyra* (Ec, Co, Ve)

Habits Often hovers in flight. Roosts within hanging vines or in crevices of rocky cliffs, in caves or under bridges, where hanging plants offer concealment. Uses same roost sites for long periods.
Status Uncommon and local.
Habitat Subtropical to Temperate Zones, usually 2,500–3,000 m, but to 750m. Humid or damp rocky cliffs, gorges, ravines and bridges, usually close to water.
Voice Flight-call *weep-weep-weep* or *chip-chip-chip*, also given when perched, extended to *weep-weep-weep up up* in courtship (C&N). Unmistakable rollicking song, loud and musical, *wor-pilly-o, wor-pilly-o, wor-pilly-o*… gradually rising in pitch, repeated up to 6 times (R&G), a melodious *wéeou-tee* (or l*iver-pool*) phrase, each slightly higher pitched and stronger, more urgent (H).

APODIDAE – Swifts

Swifts are perfectly adapted to an aerial existence. They never perch and only land when roosting or returning to their nests. Field identification of most species is extremely difficult since they are invariably flying swiftly, and also the similarity of their plumages, particularly if the feathers are worn, whilst the main behavioural differences are very subtle, e.g. slight changes in flight pattern, somewhat dissimilar voices and different nest structures. All are very long-lived. Legs and feet are used exclusively for clinging – they cannot walk and never need to; apart from short intervals spent roosting or incubating eggs, they are constantly flying, some species calling incessantly. Even mating and some roosting is done aloft. Their sole food is insects (flying ants and termites, bees, flies, wasps, beetles), taken in midair with their broad-based bills and given to the nestlings in balls glued with saliva. Their habitats are difficult to define. Definite preferences in roosting and nesting sites – vertical walls, natural or man-made, where small ledges and cracks can be used to anchor a nest in a very shady and frequently wet spot – but in the air, it is possible only to make a general connection to the type of terrain the birds prefer to overfly, presumably air spaces where insects are teeming. Swifts suffer little from natural predators, other than an occasional kill by a falcon, but bad weather can prevent them from feeding.

Cypseloides swifts are quite difficult to identify, but they have longer wings, more swept back than *Chaetura*, without the bulge in the trailing edge and wingtips held slightly down.

Additional references used in preparing this family include Collins (1972), Marín & Stiles (1993, hereafter M&S), Chantler (1999) and Chantler & Driessens (2000, hereafter C&D).

TEPUI SWIFT *Cypseloides phelpsi* Pl. 88

Identification 16.5cm. Overall dark brown with a reddish-rufous collar and full throat – best described as a totally rufous hood with black cap, tail slightly forked, looking notched when closed. Female has rufous slightly paler. Juvenile lacks rufous and is scaled lightly buffy below. From virtually allopatric Chestnut-collared Swift by larger size, more deeply forked tail (juvenile has shallower fork) and more extensive and brighter orange-chestnut.

Ssp. Monotypic (Ve, Gu)

Status Locally frequent Pantepui endemic, recorded once in Coastal Cordillera of Venezuela, and of uncertain status in Guyana, where known from single sites in north and south.

Habitat Upper Tropical to Subtropical Zones. Sightings in montane terrain and high plateaux of the Pantepui, occurs over open grasslands and forests.

Voice Fast, high-pitched chatter.

Note M&S suggest that it might belong in *Streptoprocne*.

BLACK SWIFT *Cypseloides niger* Pl. 88

Identification 18cm, W39cm. All black; slightly paler head, scimitar-shaped wings, tail may appear slightly forked or rounded. Juvenile has pale fringes to all feathers.

Ssp. *C. n. niger* (T&T?, Gu) fringing below may be absent
C. n. borealis (migrant, transient through Co) blackest, with noticeably paler head, white fringing below, larger than *niger*
[*C. n. costaricensis* (migrant, may occasionally reach Co, Ve) smallest; darker than *borealis*]

Habits Fast glides, and much banking and twisting on wings arched below bodyline.

Status Northern migrant that rarely reaches northern South America. Few sight records from Trinidad and slightly more from Tobago, both sight and specimen records from Guyana, where it possibly wanders from West Indies, and one record from an unknown locality in Venezuela (at LSUMZ).

Habitat Tropical to Subtropical Zones. Sighted over steep forested slopes and waterfalls, or over lowlands in very bad weather.

Voice Calls are fast series of raspy chippings and chatter, as well as softer chips and clicks.

Notes Formerly placed in genus *Nephoectes*. IOC-recommended English name is American Black Swift.

WHITE-CHESTED SWIFT *Cypseloides lemosi* Pl. 88

Identification 14–15cm. Dark brown, with distinctive white breast patch that tapers as a narrow line on centre of belly; forked tail. Female has white breast fragmented and underparts scaled paler brown. Juvenile lacks white breast patch, and has entire underparts scaled. Female and juvenile may have slightly shallower tail fork.

Ssp. Monotypic (Ec? Co)

Habits Usually in flocks of 20–25 birds but has been reported within a mixed-species flock of some 150 *Cypseloides* swifts in Ecuador and once a single-species (roosting) flock of 160+.

Status Vulnerable. Uncommon and very local Colombian endemic, recently reported in extreme south-east, with many sight records from Ecuador.

Habitat Upper Tropical to Subtropical Zones. Sightings mostly over bare or grassy slopes with scattered bushes and trees, and even open fields.

Voice Considered similar to Black Swift, a series of steady-paced *chip, chip, chip* calls given by lone birds, which become faster and slightly sweeter and mellower, *chih-chih-chih-chih-chih*, during social interactions (Howell 2002).

SPOT-FRONTED SWIFT *Cypseloides cherriei* Pl. 88

Identification 13–14cm, W31cm. Dark brown with white lores that run in narrow line over eyes to form white spot behind eyes. Tail fairly squared-ended. White spot behind eyes diagnostic.

Ssp. Monotypic (Ec, Co, Ve)

Habits Flight consists of gliding and banking with wings arched below bodyline, and bursts of fast flapping to accelerate.
Status Very rare and local resident in Ecuador, Colombia and Venezuela.
Habitat Upper Tropical to Subtropical Zones. Montane forest areas with wet, shady ravines.
Voice High-pitched, electric chipping or clicking. Described as quiet and slightly nasal, clipped notes, *pihk* or *pi-pihk*, which may be given in, an initially more accelerated, and then steady, rhythmic series of up to 10 notes (Howell 2002).

WHITE-CHINNED SWIFT
Cypseloides cryptus Pl. 88

Identification 14–15cm, W34cm. Small white chin very hard to see in field. Most useful features are overall blackish plumage and short square tail.

Ssp. Monotypic (Ec, Co, Ve, Gu, Su)

Habits When flying in mixed-species flocks, keeps to higher levels.
Status Very rare and local in Ecuador, locally uncommon to frequent in Colombia and Venezuela, locally frequent in Guyana, and only recently discovered in Suriname (Ottema 2004).
Habitat Tropical to Subtropical Zones. Forested mountains with deep, shady ravines or gorges, but sometimes over bare slopes. Frequently near waterfalls.
Voice Sharp, rapid chips and clicks, and fairly musical chirps.

CHESTNUT-COLLARED SWIFT
Streptoprocne rutila Pl. 88

Identification 13cm, W31cm. Dark brown with broad collar of reddish-brown from chin to breast. Tail slightly notched. Female has far less reddish on breast and collar, and might even be collarless. Juvenile is like collarless female. From marginally sympatric Tepui Swift by smaller size, less deeply forked tail and less extensive, darker and duller orange-chestnut collar.

Ssp. *S. r. brunnitorques* (Co, Ec: Andes) as described
S. r. rutila (Ve, Tr?) slightly shorter wings on average

Habits Flight less erratic than *Chaetura*.
Status Northern South American populations are resident, and uncommon to locally frequent in Ecuador, Colombia and Venezuela, and uncommon in Trinidad (no records Tobago, nor in Guyana or Suriname).
Habitat Subtropical to Temperate Zones. Sightings in extensive but broken montane distribution mostly over open or partially wooded areas, or over forests ranging in foothills to highlands. Frequently near waterfalls.
Voice High-pitched, metallic chatter and also buzzes, often resembling insect calls.
Note May appear in genus *Cypseloides*.

WHITE-COLLARED SWIFT
Streptoprocne zonaris Pl. 88

Identification 20cm, W51cm. Very large and dark brown with a complete white collar of more or less even width all round; short forked tail. White collar rather variable, and females tend to have a narrower, slightly broken collar, and juveniles have collar mottled brown. Large size and white collar are unmistakable.

Ssp. *S. z. albicincta* (Ve, T&T, Gu, FG?) smaller; broad breast-band
S. z. altissima (Ec, Co) very large, blackish, with very broad collar, pale throat
S. z. subtropicalis (Ec, N & E Co) smaller, broadest white collar

Status Locally frequent to common throughout range, except in Tobago where rare. Uncommon but widespread in French Guiana, no known nesting site.
Habitat Tropical to Temperate Zones. Sightings mostly over forested slopes and nearby lowlands or, less frequently, open country. Also over old mangroves close to hilly forested ranges in coastal French Guiana.
Voice Flocks very vocal, especially at end of day, when often start singing simultaneously. Chit-chatters and variety of other calls, such as squeaks, clicks, whizzes and whirrs.

Variation in neck pattern of White-collared Swift: male left, female centre, juvenile right

Chaetura is a distinctive genus, fairly easy to identify by virtue of the rounded leading edge to the wings and bulging trailing edge to the primaries and secondaries, but far harder to identify individual species. Careful field notes must be taken, as well as a careful check of known distribution and sympatric species.

GREY-RUMPED SWIFT
Chaetura cinereiventris Pl. 90

Identification 11cm. Dark brown upper head, back and wings with deep indigo gloss, tending to darken on lower back to uppertail-coverts, which are cold bluish-grey; underparts pale grey from chin to grey belly and vent, and dark undertail-coverts and undertail. Distinguished from race *occidentalis* of sympatric Band-rumped Swift *C. s. aetherodroma* by much darker rump (both are uniform below). Other subspecies from Band-rumped by more extensive pale rump and uppertail-coverts.

Ssp. *C. c. guianensis* (E Ve, W Gu) palest, with greatest contrast below

C. c. lawrencei (Ve: N and Margarita I., T&T) like *guianensis*, but marginally darker
C. c. schistacea (E Co, W Ve) darker, with steel blue gloss above
C. c. occidentalis (W Ec, W Co) like *schistacea* but more uniform below
C. c. sclateri (S Ve, S Co) darkest with least contrast below

Habits Forages in small to moderate groups with other swifts, and occasionally with swallows. In mixed flocks tends to feed at lower levels. Sometimes nests and roosts on man-made walls, e.g. concrete bridge supports.
Status Uncommon in Ecuador, frequent to common but local in Colombia, Venezuela, Trinidad, and common in Guyana.
Habitat Tropical to Lower Subtropical Zones. Observed mostly over forests, second growth and semi-open areas on slopes, but occasionally over open lowlands or coastal areas near mountains.
Voice Rapid, high-pitched twittering and bursts of rapid chittering notes (Hilty).

BAND-RUMPED SWIFT
Chaetura spinicaudus Pl. 90

Identification 11cm, W24–26cm. Dark brown with slight blue gloss on head, back and wings; rump buffy-white and does not normally reach uppertail-coverts, which are brown like tail; distinctly pale chin and throat, rest of underparts dark brown. Race *aetherodroma* always appears more contrastingly white-rumped than sympatric Grey-rumped Swift.

Ssp. *C. c. occidentalis* by extensive pale rump and uppertail-coverts. In other races, narrow whitish rump contrasts with rest of upperparts.
C. s. aetherodroma (W Co, W Ec) darker, pale throat, largest rump patch that fades on uppertail-coverts
C. s. latirostris (SE Ve) darker than *spinicauda*, paler below than *aetherodroma*
C. s. spinicaudus (E Ve, Tr, Gu, Su, FG) smallest rump patch

Habits In mixed-species flocks tends to feed at lower levels, often over open stretches of water, particularly early morning and late evening (C&D), seldom seen foraging over extensive tracts of humid forest.
Status Common, often the most abundant *Chaetura* in its range, but uncommon in Ecuador.
Habitat Tropical to Lower Subtropical Zones. Observed over forested and open areas, over montane slopes in Colombia and southern Venezuela, but generally a lowland bird, particularly in northern Venezuela.
Voice Varied squeaks, chattering and distinctive twittering in flight. Rapid, chittering *chsink* (Hilty).
Note Records of race *fumosa* on Panama border (Rodner *et al.* 2000) reassigned to *aetherodroma* (Marín 2000).

CHAPMAN'S SWIFT
Chaetura chapmani Pl. 89

Identification 13–14cm. Dark brown crown to mantle and wings, paler back to tail; below, chin and throat slightly paler, but underparts almost concolorous with underwings, undertail paler. From most similar *Chaetura* by its larger size.

Ssp. *C. c. chapmani* (Co, Ve, Guianas)

Habits Small numbers often associate with other swifts.
Status Poorly known, believed uncommon to very rare throughout range. Populations in 2 separate areas and considered resident in both, although scattered records in Venezuela suggest at least local movements.
Habitat Tropical to Lower Subtropical Zones. Sighted over wooded lowlands, coastal areas and foothills, but mainly over forested higher slopes.
Voice A characteristic, squeezed *che'e'e'e'e'e'd*, which often merge into ticking notes (Hilty).
Note Single sight record, tentatively ascribed to this taxon (admitting possibility of Amazonian Swift) for Ecuador (R&G).

TUMBES SWIFT *Chaetura ocypetes* Pl. 89

Identification 11cm. Dark brown crown to back and wings, pale superciliary, pale grey rump to tail; below, chin and throat pale, breast and belly concolorous with underwings, vent to undertail pale grey. Long wings very arched and pointed, and seem to quiver in flight. Even more distinct profile than Short-tailed Swift, with longer wings and tail, paler grey chin and throat.

Ssp. Monotypic (SW Ec)

Habits Forages relatively low.
Status Uncommon.
Habitat Over lowland woods and lower forested foothills of somewhat dry coastal areas, clearings and forest edges.
Voice Slightly descending series of clear chip notes (R&G).

SHORT-TAILED SWIFT
Chaetura brachyura Pl. 89

Identification 10cm. Very distinctive wing shape and tail appears very short. Dark brown head with slightly pale throat; back, wings, breast, belly and underwings dark brown; tail-coverts and both surfaces of tail pale buffy. Flies differently from other *Chaetura*, like a bat and relatively slow, with a mixture of flapping and short glides.

Ssp. *C. b. brachyura* (Ec, Co, Ve, Tr, Guianas) as described
C. b. praevelox (To) browner with paler throat

Habits Mixes with other swifts, at lower levels of the flock.
Status Locally frequent in all countries.
Habitat Lower Tropical Zone. Most frequent over open lowlands, from arid areas to humid forests, including mangroves. Also plantations and occasionally over urban areas. Often roosts in large numbers in chimneys or large hollow poles.
Voice Sequences of twittering *weeezz* phrases, reminiscent of crickets.

SICK'S SWIFT *Chaetura meridionalis* Pl. 89

Identification 12.5–14cm. Dark olive-brown head, mantle, wings and underwings, small whitish crescent before eyes, pale buffy-grey lower back to uppertail-coverts, dark tail; throat to undertail-coverts pale greyish-buffy, undertail dark. Similar to Ashy-tailed Swift, but paler above and below.

Ssp. Monotypic (Co, Ve, FG)

Status Austral migrant, in small numbers May–August in Colombia and Venezuela. Hypothetical for Guyana and Suriname. Rare in French Guiana.
Habitat Tropical Zone. Forages over montane slopes and foothills, as well as over usual lowland areas. Migrating flocks seen close to the sea in French Guiana (O. Tostain).
Voice A fast excited *tip tip tip* (Sick).
Note Called Ashy-tailed Swift in Hilty.

PALE-RUMPED SWIFT
Chaetura egregia Pl. 89

Identification 11cm, W28.5cm. Dark on head, back and wings; rump to uppertail-coverts bright pale grey, tail contrastingly blackish; throat pale grey, grading into dull brown on breast and underwings, dark brown belly to undertail. From Band-rumped by more extensive whitish rump; from smaller Grey-rumped (*occidentalis* or *sclateri*) by much paler rump, deeper wingbeats and more frequent glides.

Ssp. Monotypic (E Ec)

Habits Flocks with other swifts (especially Grey-rumped), usually at lower levels.
Status Rare to uncommon, but fairly abundant in some localities at higher altitudes on east Andean slopes.
Habitat Tropical to Temperate Zones. Wide variety of mainly humid areas, from open to forested lowlands, and also over forested mountainsides.
Voice Not recorded.

AMAZONIAN SWIFT
Chaetura viridipennis Pl. 89

Identification 14–15cm. Entirely dark brown above, underwings also dark brown, chin to vent slightly paler, undertail-coverts pale grey. Amazonian Swift is larger than Chapman's and has 2 outer primaries the same length, whereas Chapman's Swift has outer primary longer, and also has lower back to uppertail-coverts paler than rest of upperparts.

Ssp. Monotypic (Co)

Status Rare austral migrant to Colombia (from breeding range in central and western Brazil), recorded March–April.
Habitat Forest with clearings or patchy savanna.
Voice Undescribed.
Note Accorded specific status from Chapman's Swift by Marín (1997).

CHIMNEY SWIFT *Chaetura pelagica* Pl. 89

Identification 12–14cm. Back, wings and tail very dark brown, rest of body only slightly paler. Appears almost uniform above and below, but occasionally has pale throat.

Ssp. Monotypic (Ec, Co, Ve, FG)

Habits Always mixes with other swifts, usually at lower levels of the flock.
Status Boreal migrant, regularly recorded on northbound passage in Ecuador, Colombia and Venezuela during boreal early spring. Recently found in north-west French Guiana in late August, over seashore (O. Tostain).

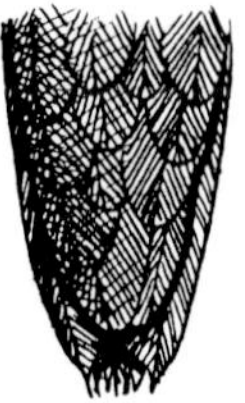

Tail of Chimney Swift, fanned (left) and closed (right)

Habitat Tropical to Subtropical Zones. Through extensive range, occurs over broad diversity of areas, especially urban zones, but on passage observed over montane slopes and lowlands, both forested and open.
Voice Twitters or chips in rising and falling sequences.

ASHY-TAILED SWIFT
Chaetura andrei Pl. 89

Identification 13.5cm. Dark brown above with fine pale crescent in front of eyes, short tail gives distinct flight profile, uppertail-coverts and tail slightly paler; below, a well-defined pale throat but rest dark brown. Paler than Chapman's with less-contrasting rump and paler throat and short pale eyebrow. Flight pattern mixes vibrating wingbeats of typical *Chaetura* and more continued flapping, reminiscent of a bat, like Tumbes Swift. Very similar to Vaux's Swift and virtually inseparable in flight, but habits and habitat are different. Ashy-tailed Swift is fond of forested lowland rivers, while Vaux's Swift prefers mountain slopes.

Ssp. Monotypic (E & SE Ve)

Habits Forages rather low, usually in small flocks, sometimes with other swifts. Migration patterns unknown.
Status Scattered, uncommon and local populations.
Habitat Tropical Zone. Forages over watercourses and contiguous habitats, and a variety of lowland humid forest and open lowland areas.
Voice Rattling, rapid chatter and chippering.
Note Accepted as distinct species until Marín (1997) considered it a synonym of *C. vauxi*. We do not accept this, as it is apparent from comparative examination in COP that they are distinct, and they have different habits and habitat.

VAUX'S SWIFT *Chaetura vauxi* Pl. 89

Identification 12cm. Very dark brown head, back and wings, rump to tail dark brownish-grey; pale throat grades into dusky underparts. Very similar to Ashy-tailed Swift which

Head of Ashy-tailed Swift (left) and Vaux's Swift (race aphanes), showing difference in loral pattern and throat coloration, and Vaux's Swift has a longer bill

has shorter tail and pale eyebrow, but virtually impossible to separate in flight. From Chimney by paler rump and tail, and whiter throat.

Ssp. *C. v. aphanes* (N Ve, possible vagrant to Co?)

Habits Forages in mid-sized to large flocks over montane forests, often with other swifts and sometimes with swallows. Migratory, but pattern not known.
Status Frequent to common in most locations.
Habitat Subtropical Zone, 700m to *c.*1,200m. In Venezuela prefers cloud forest slopes of Coastal Cordillera and the Andes, occasionally lower elevations but most frequently over higher slopes and, occasionally, urban areas.
Voice Varied: fast, high-pitched chipping, squeaking, a chatter, buzzing and whizzing, and soft 2-note sequences.
Note Race *aphanes* considered synonymous with Ashy-tailed Swift by Marín (1997).

WHITE-TIPPED SWIFT
Aeronautes montivagus Pl. 90

Identification 13cm. Piebald pattern. Essentially all blue-black with white chin and throat, a white crescent on flanks, and across vent; tail has small white tips, is forked but usually held closed. Juvenile entirely dusky black with finely speckled throat and small whitish patch on vent. Flight much faster than *Chaetura*. Usually confused with Lesser Swallow-tailed Swift, which has longer tail tips and forages alone or in pairs. *Aeronautes* jizz, once learned, is distinctive.

Ssp. *A. m. montivagus* (Co, N & W Ve, Ec, Gu, Su)

Habits Flocks quite vocal. Always forages in flocks, sometimes with larger congregations of other swifts, where it frequents lower levels of flock.
Status Uncommon to rare in Ecuador, common and even abundant but local in Venezuela, locally frequent in Guyana, with recent sight records and tape-recording from Suriname (Ottema 2004, in press).
Habitat Tropical to Subtropical Zones. Observed over both forest and open terrain, in humid and arid areas, especially along rock walls, ridges, cliffs and sides of tepuis. Not found in lowlands but descends in bad weather.
Voice Calls include buzzing trills in crescendo–decrescendo sequences, wheezy squeaks.

LESSER SWALLOW-TAILED SWIFT
Panyptila cayennensis Pl. 90

Identification 13cm. Generally all black, with white chin and throat that curve up in line either side of head, and small white patch on rear flanks. Long tail usually held closed and appears tapered, but may be fanned in wide shallow fork. From White-tipped Swift by habits and long tail-tip feathers. From Fork-tailed Palm Swift by larger head and more graceful flight.

Ssp. *P. c. cayennensis* (Ec, Co, Ve, Gu, Su, FG)

Habits Flies very high and very fast, like aerial acrobatics. Sometimes joins other swifts, where it tends to forage at top of flock if with *Chaetura*, or at lower levels with *Cypseloides* and or *Streptoprocne*.
Status Uncommon and very local throughout.
Habitat Tropical Zone. In humid regions, over edges and clearings of both primary and secondary forest, as well as large rivers and open agricultural areas, occasionally urban areas.
Voice A soft, high-pitched chatter or chipping.

PYGMY SWIFT *Tachornis furcata* Pl. 90

Identification 10cm. Tiny swift, with narrow wings and spindly tail that may be held closed or open in a prominent fork; brown with pale throat and pale patch on belly. From Fork-tailed Palm Swift by much faster wingbeats smaller size, and distinct upper breast-band. Tail appears shorter and narrower.

Ssp. *T. f. furcata* (NE Co, NW Ve) as described
T. f. nigrodorsalis (W Ve) blacker above, whiter throat

Habits Usually in small flocks flying faster and lower to ground than Fork-tailed Palm Swifts.
Status Uncommon and scarce throughout tiny range, with few known localities.
Habitat Tropical Zone. Observed over forests to open fields with scattered trees, provided there are palms nearby.
Voice Described as a buzzy *bee, beez, beez, beez-be-be-be'be'be*, accelerating and fading at end (around colony) and a churring call (in nest) (Hilty).
Notes Often treated in the genus *Micropanyptila* and sometimes considered monotypic, i.e. *nigrodorsalis* treated as a synonym of *furcata* (Phelps Jr 1973). Sometimes called Pygmy Palm Swift.

Tail of Pygmy Swift fanned (left) and closed (right)

FORK-TAILED PALM SWIFT

Tachornis squamata Pl. 90

Identification 13.2cm. Dark brown with slender, tapered body and narrow wings; pale speckling on underside, and whitish on throat and breast, narrowly on belly and undertail-coverts; tail normally held closed. From Pygmy Swift by slower wingbeats, larger size and more mottled breast (no clear band).

Ssp. *T. s. semota* (Ec, Co, Ve) much darker, with less pale fringing
T. s. squamata (Co, Ve, Tr and Guianas) as described

Habits Associates occasionally with Blue-and-white Swallow, but rarely with other swifts. Forages close to tops of palms and frequently passes close to ground.
Status Common but very local and seldom abundant.
Habitat Always around stands of *Mauritia flexuosa* palms, which grow on sodden or marshy low spots in savannas and beside meandering rivers, as well as (ornamentally) in parks and gardens, where they may harbour groups of palm swifts that can be seen over urban areas.
Voice Vocalises frequently. Calls include a quite unique insect-like buzzing and short trills.

ALPINE SWIFT *Tachymarptis melba* Pl. 88

Identification 20–23cm. Large, dark brown swift with long scimitar-shaped wings, shorter tail than Common Swift, and is less deeply forked, uniform plain brown above; round white throat patch with brown band below it, then pure white breast and belly. Juvenile uniform plain brown above; pale brown below with whitish throat, speckled with darker brown subterminal spots, and entire underparts has pale fringes. Quite unmistakable. Comparatively slow, deep wingbeats and, unlike Common Swift, is more likely to be mistaken for a falcon than a swallow.

Ssp. *T. m. melba* (FG)

Status Vagrant, recorded in June 2002 in north-west French Guiana (Ottema 2004). A summer visitor to Europe and North Africa, and appears to have overshot!
Habitat Normally seen over tall buildings and rock faces.
Voice Drawn-out series of twittering notes, *ti ti titititititititititi-ti-ti-ti tü tü* (Mullarney *et al.* 1999).
Note Frequently placed in genus *Apus*.

TROCHILIDAE – Hummingbirds

When 18th-century naturalists first met with hummingbirds, every gem and sylvan creature they knew was conjured up in the superlatives used to name the magical creatures. No other family has motivated such flights of fancy and imagination. To this day, they ring with those graphic names: Lazuline, Ruby Topaz, amethyst, sylph, coquette, woodstar, sheartail, sungem, fairy, goldenthroat, woodnymph, sapphire, emerald, plumeleteer, Blossomcrown. Happily, modern naturalists see no reason to change the trend. With all we have learned about hummingbirds, their physiology, systematics, metabolism, migrations, we are still in awe of them. As nectar is the main food, several strategies are used to obtain a good supply. Some species stake-out a small 'territory' in a blooming tree or bush, others establish a route, with stages at several bushes and trees, which they faithfully follow daily (trap-lining). Others occasionally even resort to 'parasitism' – taking nectar from holes through the petals, behind the stamina, thus omitting the mutually beneficial ritual of pollination. Such holes are often the work of a *Diglossa* flowerpiercer, but some *Chlorostilbon*, *Phaethornis* and *Anthracothorax* make their own. The other food of fundamental importance to hummingbirds is arthropods. The taxonomy of the Trochilidae has been in turmoil for some years now, with rare birds being classed as hybrids, subspecies being transferred from one species to another, many subspecies being synonymised and others split as separate species. Oddly, there has been little DNA analysis done, or published at least. The taxonomic treatment of the family by K. L. Schuchmann *et al.* in *Handbook of the Birds of the World* (vol. 5) is extensive and far-reaching, and met with very mixed reactions. We have accepted some of the proposed changes and resisted others; in each case, however, we have noted the proposal and given the reference with the name of the author of the species account.

The two sicklebills are remarkable little birds distinguished by their heavily decurved bills. They feed by clinging to the bracts of flowers like *Heliconia*, and glean insects in the lower levels of dark understorey. They seem remarkably alike, but despite several differences they are easiest to separate by their head coloration.

WHITE-TIPPED SICKLEBILL

Eutoxeres aquila Pl. 93

Identification 14.8–15.5cm, bill 3.5cm. All green above with white tips to tail; sides of face, rest of underparts white, streaked black, finely on sides of face, in long regular lines on breast-sides and flanks; bill long and curved, forming almost a semi-circle. Juvenile similar but has clear buff crescents on tips of body feathers from top of head to uppertail-coverts, and on median wing-coverts. From Buff-tailed by white tips to tail (note race *heterurus* well separated geographically from Buff-tailed).

Ssp. *E. a. aquila* (E Co, E Ec) very clear white tips to tail
E. a. heterurus (W Ec, W Co) almost no white tips to tail
E. a. munda (W Co) intermediate between *salvini* and *heterurus*
E. a. salvini (NW Co) broad white fringes to undertail-coverts

Habits Hard to see, in dense forest undergrowth, especially deep, shady thickets. Usually at low levels and singly. When feeding at *Heliconia*, clings to bracts and probes with bill. Gleans insects from low branches. Flies slowly making discernible noise.
Status Common on Pacific slope of Colombian Andes, rare and local in central Colombia; uncommon in Ecuador.
Habitat Tropical and Subtropical Zones. Humid to wet and

mature second-growth forest; most often in *Heliconia* stands.
Voice Squeaks sometimes in flight.
Notes Race *heterura* correctly spelt *heterurus* (David & Gosselin 2002). Race *munda* (*mundus*) considered synonymous under *heterurus* by Hinkelmann (1999).

BUFF-TAILED SICKLEBILL
Eutoxeres condamini Pl. 93

Identification 14.8–15cm, bill 3.5cm. Nearly all green above, but turquoise patch on neck-sides and 3 outer tail-feathers rufous; face-sides and throat buff, very heavily streaked black, with short eyebrow and moustachial, underparts largely white, streaked black, undertail-coverts cinnamon, barred black; bill long and curved, almost in a semi-circle. Juvenile similar, turquoise patch perhaps smaller; all feathers from top of head to uppertail-coverts with buff terminal crescent and black subterminally. From all races of White-tipped by pale superciliary and moustachial, and rufous fringe to 3 outer tail-feathers.

Ssp. *E. c. condamini* (SE Co, E Ec)

Habits Retiring and hard to see. Much like a hermit, with frequent tail-bobbing and other behaviour traits. Shady places, mainly clinging from *Heliconia* and *Centropogon* flowers, but also gleans and hawks insects.
Status Uncommon in Ecuador.
Habitat Tropical to Temperate Zones. Premontane humid forest. Near streams and in humid ravines in primary forest; sometimes thickets around old clearings and overgrown disturbed areas, especially near *Heliconia* stands.
Voice Undescribed.

Glaucis hermits and *Threnetes* barbthroats are typical of the group, without any gloss or iridescence on their plumage. They have long, decurved bills, but lack tail elongations, instead having rounded tails.

BRONZY HERMIT *Glaucis aeneus* Pl. 91

Identification 10.8–11.1cm, bill 2.8–3cm. Small; bronze-green above, including central tail-feathers, outer 4 pairs chestnut with broad dark brown subterminal band, the tips white; head dusky with short white postocular line, underparts uniform pale ochre; bill slightly decurved, lower mandible yellow with dusky tip, feet yellow.

Ssp. Monotypic (Ec, Co)

Habits Normally alone; gleans from under leaves and probes *Heliconia* flowers and moss. Often bold and curious, may approach observers.
Status Uncommon in Ecuador, uncommon to locally frequent in Colombia.
Habitat Lower Tropical Zone. Humid and wet forests; edges and clearings, along streams, lowlands near coast. Most frequently in *Heliconia* stands.
Voice Sharp *zeet* calls in flight (R&G).
Note Correct spelling of name is *aeneus* (David & Gosselin 2002).

RUFOUS-BREASTED HERMIT
Glaucis hirsutus Pl. 91

Identification 13.5–15.3cm, bill 3.3cm. Rich green above, including central tail-feathers, outer 4 pairs deep chestnut with broad blackish subterminal band and white tips, underparts vary significantly by race; bill gently curved, black above, yellow below; feet yellow. From Great-billed Hermit by lack of superciliary and from Tawny-bellied Hermit by lack of white throat; from both by lack of elongated central tail-feathers.

Ssp. *G. h. affinis* (E Ec, C Co and Santa Marta, W Ve) small white chin, cinnamon throat and bold white moustachial, rest of underparts grey
G. h. hirsutus (N & E Ve, Guianas) faint moustachial, rich reddish-cinnamon on breast and sides, rest of underparts paler with some grey in central belly
G. h. insularum (T&T) lacks moustachial, pale ochraceous breast

Habits Usually forages alone, and is often bold, curious and feisty. Feeds at low levels (*Pachystachys*, *Centropogon*, *Hibiscus*), most often in *Heliconia* stands and banana plantations, and also gleans tiny insects and spiders in shrubbery. Males establish territories with 2–3 females.
Status Uncommon to locally common in Colombia, uncommon in Ecuador and Guyana, common in Trinidad & Tobago, Suriname and French Guiana.
Habitat Tropical Zone. Humid and *várzea* forests, thickets, forest edge, second growth; mostly rather wet places along watercourses and creeks; edge of mangroves.
Voice Flight-call a high rising *veep!* or *tseep!* Territorial call *chee-chee-CHee-chee-chee* that rises and falls. When a pair sings in courtship duet, call repeated by female immediately after male (M. L. Goodwin, pers. comm.).
Notes Correct spelling of species name is *hirsutus*; race *affinis* synonymised under nominate by Hinkelmann (1999) who also calls it Hairy Hermit.

SOOTY BARBTHROAT
Threnetes niger Pl. 91

Identification 10–11cm, bill 2.7–2.9cm. Almost entirely dark green, with a diagnostic black mask, fuscous belly and undertail-coverts, and purple undertail; bill black and slightly curved, feet flesh colour.

Ssp. Monotypic (FG)

Habits Forages alone at low and mid levels, visiting several flowers on daily trap-line route. Favoured plants include *Heliconia* and *Monotagma*.
Status Uncommon, often local, but widespread in interior of French Guiana.
Habitat Lower Tropical Zone. Understorey of lowland marshy forests and near streams, associated with plant *Ichnocyphon*, which has large leaves.
Voice Faint *tseep* in flight, in display, male sings short sequences of high notes (R&G).
Note Considered a local dark morph of race *leucurus* of White-tailed Barbthroat by Hinkelmann (1999).

WHITE-TAILED BARBTHROAT
Threnetes leucurus Pl. 91

Identification 13–13.2cm, bill 3cm. Green forehead to central tail-feathers, which have white tips, rest of tail white with dusky tips; black mask, white moustachial, chin and upper throat black, broad band on lower throat orange, breast and sides dusky, belly to vent and flanks buffy-white, undertail-coverts greyish-buffy with white edges; bill black, feet flesh. White outer tail and all-white undertail unique among hermits, and combined with bright rufous bar across throat is diagnostic.

Ssp. *T. l. leucurus* (S Ve, Gu, Su) outer tail-feathers white
T. l. cervinicauda (E Co, E Ec) outer tail-feathers buffy

Habits Feeds at low levels in dense thickets and undergrowth; males display from low perches, singing continuously whilst fanning and wagging tail.
Status Rare to locally common in Ecuador, frequent to locally common in Colombia, uncommon in Guyana, rare in Suriname and French Guiana.
Habitat Tropical Zone. Forests, edges and second growth; *Heliconia* stands.
Voice Song a brief, high *zer-zee-zer-zeri*, repeated frequently; flight-call, a typical, hermit-like *seep!* (H&B).
Note Name *niger* senior to *leucurus* and thus if Sooty Barbthroat regarded as morph of race *leucurus* then latter would be known as *T. niger* (Hinkelmann 1999).

BAND-TAILED BARBTHROAT
Threnetes ruckeri Pl. 91

Identification 13cm, bill 3cm. Black forehead and small mask, rest of upperparts green, including central tail-feathers, rest of tail basally white and distally black, all feathers with fine white tips; black chin and upper throat with drab moustachial, broad band on lower throat orange, breast to vent grey, undertail-coverts buffy with pale grey edges; bill black above, yellow below with dusky tip, feet flesh. Unique undertail pattern separates it from other hermits; separated from White-tailed Barbthroat by Andes.

Ssp. *T. r. darienensis* (N Co) lacks grey belly, is more orange and ochraceous below than *venezuelensis*
T. r. ruckeri (W Co, W Ec) noticeably smaller; clean white moustachial
T. r. venezuelensis (W Ve) as described

Habits Tends to forage at low levels in thickets and undergrowth.
Status Local (uncommon?) in Colombia, uncommon in Ecuador.
Habitat Tropical Zone. Second growth, thickets and borders, favours stands of *Heliconia*.
Voice Males gather in loose leks, where they display by continually flicking tail. Song a rapid sequence of quasi-trills, *srr-srr-srr-srr-srr-srr*.
Note Race *darienensis* invalidated by Hinkelmann (1999) as it is 'from an extensive zone of character introgression' involving 3 subspecies.

Phaethornis hermits are birds of lowland forest, usually encountered in the darkest understorey, but as they fly very quickly between feeding areas along their trap-lines, they may cross open sunny areas. Often found in *Heliconia* stands, but service a variety of flowers. They glean insects from below leaves and also hawk them. Long bills with bright yellow undersides, or bright red, but what separates them from other members of the subfamily is the long tail extensions, and undertail patterns are important in identifing both species and subspecies (see plates). Measurements refer to adult birds in full feather.

GREEN HERMIT *Phaethornis guy* Pl. 91

Identification 17cm, bill 4.3cm. Large green hermit with bright red bill. Female has blackish head with clear cinnamon postocular line and moustachial, throat dusky with pale cinnamon line down centre; nape to basal half of tail green with deep turquoise flush on uppertail-coverts and base of tail, distal half of tail dusky with 2 central feathers having long narrow white extensions; breast to vent grey, undertail-coverts grey with broad white edges; bill bright red with black culmen, feet pink. Male similar but head green with black mask, green reaching to upper breast, undertail-coverts narrowly edged white, bill longer and less curved. From both Long-tailed Hermits by darker underparts.

Ssp. *P. g. apicalis* (E Ec, Co: E Andes, W Ve) richly coloured above and below
P. g. coruscus (NW Co) brightest, with iridescent feathers on breast and flanks
P. g. emiliae (N & C Co) richly coloured above and below
P. g. guy (NE Ve, Tr) largest, brighter green above, paler below

Habits Trap-lines flowers (*Hibiscus*, *Heliconia*, *Tillandsia*, *Centropogon*, *Pachystachys*, *Columnea*, bananas). Gleans leaves and spider webs. Seasonal movements follow flowering, occasionally reaching *Polylepis* forests. Swift flyer, dashing about inside forest.
Status Locally common to uncommon in Ecuador, uncommon and local in Colombia, common in Trinidad.
Habitat Upper Tropical and Subtropical Zones. Wet forest undergrowth and second growth, often in *Heliconia* stands and near water.
Voice Sharp squeaks. Song a loud *tsweep tsweep tswee*, a continuous metallic *heweet-heweet-heweet…* (F&K), a chirping *wartch-wartch-wartch* or *kaneek, kaneek, kaneek* (H&B). Males gather almost year-round at established leks, which may number dozens of birds.

WESTERN LONG-TAILED HERMIT
Phaethornis longirostris Pl. 91

Identification 14–17cm, bill 4cm. Bronze-brown above with purple to maroon wash on wings and bronzy-green on tail, buffy eyebrow and thin moustachial; underparts entirely pale buffy-cinnamon, washed slightly dusky on throat with pale line down centre; undertail purplish-dusky with broad buffy-grey terminal bands, streamers pale grey; bill has orange lower mandible, feet pink. From Green Hermit by paler, ochraceous or grey underparts.

Ssp. *P. l. baroni* (W Ec) greyish underparts, terminal bands on tail pale grey
P. l. cephalus (NW Co) more ochraceous below and on tail tips
P. l. sussurus (Co: Santa Marta, W Ve) as described, larger than others

Habits Solitary forager that follows trap-lines to scattered flowers (*Heliconia*, *Aphelandra*, *Passiflora*). Gleans foliage and spider webs for small spiders and insects.
Status Uncommon to locally common in Ecuador and Colombia.
Habitat Tropical to Subtropical Zones. Understorey of moist, humid and cloud forests, borders and clearings with thickets, mature second growth.
Voice Males gather at leks. A *wheeisk*, repeated quickly and incessantly at leks, and high-pitched *switch* in flight.
Note Split from Eastern Long-tailed Hermit by Hinkelmann & Schuchmann (1997), accepted by AOU (1998). Race *cassini* considered synonymous under *cephalus* by Hinkelmann (1999) as no discernible field discriminator.

EASTERN LONG-TAILED HERMIT
Phaethornis superciliosus Pl. 91

Identification 14cm, bill 4.4cm. Bronze-green above, with broader, browner fringes to rump and paler buffy edges to long tail-coverts, tail and wings umber with purpurescent tone, tail-feathers only thinly tipped white, streamers white, head dark with bold, dull buffy postocular stripe, short dark malar, underparts buffy, washed greyish on throat and breast, and cinnamon on belly and flanks, paler buffy undertail-coverts, bill has orange-red lower mandible, feet pink. From similar western race of Great-billed Hermit, *insolitus*, by clear range separation. Sooty-capped Hermit has obvious pale to white superciliary and moustachial, and rusty uppertail-coverts.

Ssp. *P. s. superciliosus* (Guianas)

Habits Forages at low and mid levels. Follows trap-line to scattered flowers (*Heliconia*, *Passiflora*). Gleans spiders.
Status Frequent in Guyana, common in Suriname and French Guiana.
Habitat Tropical Zone. Undergrowth of moist and humid forests, borders and clearings with thickets, mature second growth, *Heliconia* patches.
Voice Song an ascending trill of 14 notes; an oft-repeated *twich-twtch-twich* (Snyder 1966) or single chirping notes *cheep, cheep*…
Note Split from Western Long-tailed Hermit by Hinkelmann & Schuchmann (1997), accepted by AOU (1998). Race *saturatior* considered synonymous under *superciliosus* by Hinkelmann (1999) as falls within range of variation of *superciliosus*.

WHITE-WHISKERED HERMIT
Phaethornis yaruqui Pl. 92

Identification 17.5cm, bill 4–4.6cm. Pale brown head, scaled darker brown, upperparts green and uppertail-coverts dark brown with cinnamon fringes; tail dark blue, tapers to point, but lacks streamers, though points of central rectrices project 0.5cm, bold orange eyebrow, face-sides black with white moustachial, throat dark grey with short pale greyish line on middle; breast green, belly and flanks dark grey, undertail-coverts dark blue with thin white fringes; bill black with bright red lower mandible, feet pale orange-flesh. Distinctive hermit, more iridescent than others and striking deep blue tail with white tips to rectrices.

Ssp. Monotypic (W Ec, W Co)

Habits Solitary and boldly inspects observers. Follows daily trap-line (Ericaceae, Rubiaceae, bromeliads, *Heliconia*). Swift flyer, dashes about inside forest. Males gather at leks.
Status Common in Ecuador and Colombia. Moves seasonally following flower availability.
Habitat Tropical Zone. Wet forest undergrowth.
Voice Song a raspy *seek*, repeated monotonously at slow pace (J. Fjeldså) while continuously wagging tail.
Note Race *sanctijohannis* apparently described from an immature *yaruqui*, thus invalid (Hinkelmann 1999), accepted by Salaman *et al.* (2001) and Dickinson (2003).

TAWNY-BELLIED HERMIT
Phaethornis syrmatophorus Pl. 92

Identification 17.1–18.1cm, bill 4.1cm. Orange to greenish head with dark brown scaling, back and wings green, rump and uppertail-coverts have loose fluffy cinnamon feathers, tail green with rufous tips to all but central pair which have white streamers; black mask, pale cinnamon malar and black submalar, throat white, underparts cinnamon, darker on flanks; undertail blackish with bold cinnamon tips; bill long and only slightly decurved, black above, red below, feet flesh. White chin and bright rump distinctive.

Ssp. *P. s. columbianus* (EC Co, E Ec) as described, rich cinnamon rump, richer below
P. s. syrmatophorus (W Co, W Ec) pale ochraceous cinnamon rump, nape pale orange with dark scaling, black submalar line short, underparts paler, washed orange on flanks, undertail fringed ochraceous

Habits Forages near ground, inside forest, following routine trap-line. Seasonal movements along slopes.
Status Uncommon in Ecuador, common in Colombia.
Habitat Upper Tropical and Subtropical Zones. Only in highlands. Humid premontane and cloud-forest undergrowth of western Andes, borders and clearings.
Voice Song a high, squeaky *tseep* repeated around 2 per s (H&B, F&K).

GREAT-BILLED HERMIT
Phaethornis malaris Pl. 92

Identification 13cm, bill 3.8–4.2cm. Bronze-green from forehead to base of tail, rest of tail dark purpurescent bronze, small white tips to all but central pair which have white streamers; forehead and mask black with dull buffy postocular, narrow malar buffy, submalar line blackish; throat to undertail-coverts greyish-buffy becoming paler distally, undertail dusky with fine white tips; bill black above, red below, feet vinaceous pink. Similar Tawny-bellied Hermit has white throat. Smaller Rufous-breasted Hermit lacks elongated, white-tipped tail.

Ssp. *P. m. insolitus* (SE Co, extreme S Ve) as described
P. m. malaris (Su, FG) largest and darkest, browner above and more ochraceous below than *insolitus*
P. m. moorei (E Ec, SC Co) larger than *insolitus*, rufescnt flush to lower back and particularly warm fringes to uppertail-coverts, cinnamon edges to tips of tail; underparts deep cinnamon with cinnamon fringes to undertail feathers
P. m. ochraceiventris (S Ec) large, and bright orange below

Habits Feeds mostly on understorey flowers (*Heliconia*, *Pitcarnia*, *Bauhinia*), particularly on lianas. Trap-lines and gleans insects. Leks in higher levels of understorey.
Status Common in Ecuador, very rare in Suriname, frequent in French Guiana. Race *ochraceiventris* apparently collected in south Ecuador, but obviously rare there. Locally frequent in Venezuela.
Habitat Lower Tropical Zone. Primary forests with sandy soils (or lateritic in French Guiana); hills, most often near hilltops. Bamboo stands, second growth, transitional forests. Nest typically on underside of an *Astrocaryum* palm leaf over a stream or small river.
Voice Squeaky *skweep* in flight, repeated by lekking males (R&G).
Note Race *moorei* removed from Eastern Long-tailed Hermit (Hinkelmann 1999).

WHITE-BEARDED HERMIT
Phaethornis hispidus Pl. 92

Identification 16.3cm, bill 3.3cm. Dark greyish head with black mask and white moustachial, grizzled throat, and clear white beard, bronze-geen back and wings, dark grey rump and uppertail-coverts with pale grey to whitish fringes, tail dusky with faint purple tone above and below; breast greyish, blending into pale buffy belly and undertail-coverts with dark centres to latter, very thin pale fringes to undertail, streamers pale grey; bill black above, yellow below, feet vinaceous grey.

Ssp. Monotypic (Ec, Co, S&SW Ve)

Habits Solitary forager at low levels, invariably near ground. Follows routine trap-line. Picks small insects and spiders by gleaning leaves.
Status Uncommon in Ecuador, frequent in Colombia, common in Venezuela.
Habitat Lower Tropical Zone. Always in seasonally inundated areas. Gallery forests and *várzea*, mature second growth. Undergrowth and forest borders.
Voice Lekking males sing endlessly, *tsip-tsip-tsip*… (R&G).

PALE-BELLIED HERMIT
Phaethornis anthophilus Pl. 92

Identification 16–16.8cm, bill 3.8cm. Dark green from forehead to base of tail, long uppertail-coverts with broad white fringes, tail distally dusky, streamers white; black mask with eyebrow and underparts buffy-white, washed greyish on breast, and dark green grizzled streaking on throat, undertail uniform umber-brown; bill black with pale orange lower mandible. Lack of gular stripe diagnostic, but streaking on chin may mislead. Could be confused with Western Long-tailed Hermit, but sympatric race *sussurus* is pale ochraceous below, and more similar *baroni* is out of range.

Ssp. *P. a. anthophilus* (N Co, Ve) as described
P. a. fuliginosus (SE&C Co) see Note below
P. a. fuscicapillus (E Co, Ve) smaller wings and bill

Habits More likely to be seen foraging in open areas than other hermits. Forages alone, trap-lining flowers (*Heliconia*, *Brownea*) and gleaning insects and spiders.
Status Uncommon to locally frequent in Colombia, locally common in Venezuela, where seasonal in some areas. Moves seasonally within range.
Habitat Lower Tropical Zone. Various semi-dry forests: deciduous, gallery, light woodlands and second growth. Forest borders, hedges, thorn scrub, thickets.
Voice No description.
Note Race *fuliginosus* described from single melanistic individual, and is of uncertain validity (Stiles 1995, Hinkelmann 1999).

STRAIGHT-BILLED HERMIT
Phaethornis bourcieri Pl. 92

Identification 15.5–16.3cm, bill 3.3cm. Dull, drab greenish upperparts, uppertail-coverts with black subterminal bars and white termal fringes, face-sides to breast brownish-grey, paler on central belly to undertail-coverts, undertail uniform drab, streamers white; bill black with yellow lower mandible, feet pink.

Ssp. *P. b. bourcieri* (E Ec, SE Co, Ve: Amazonas) whitish throat, pale buffy flanks, more green top of head, golden-buffy edges to uppertail-coverts
P. b. whitelyi (SE Co, Ve: Bolívar, Guianas) buffy throat and flanks; paler edges to uppertail-coverts

Habits Forages alone, mostly in shady undergrowth but sometimes in open, over border shrubbery.
Status Uncommon in Ecuador, common in Colombia and Suriname, frequent in Guyana and French Guiana.
Habitat Tropical Zone. Savannas, forests and hillsides; often close to treefall gaps.
Voice Males at leks perch in loose groups, a few feet above ground, calling sibilantly and moving white tail tips up and down. Song a squeaky *tsee tib-it*, *c.*1 per s, with tail-wagging (H&B), a weak bisyllabic *tsisee…tsisee…* (R&G).
Note Race *whitelyi* considered invalid by Hinkelmann (1999).

STREAK-THROATED HERMIT

Phaethornis rupurumii Pl. 92

Identification 11.9–12.5cm, bill 2.5cm. Small; male bronze-green above, including central tail-feathers which have white streamers rest of tail dark brown; head dark brown to blackish with pale eyebrow and malar; underparts dull pale buffy, palest on undertail-coverts; undertail dark brown with broad cinnamon tips to outer 2 rectrices, broad white edges to next 2. Female has eyebrow and malar more orange than pale buff; bill black above, yellow below, feet orange-pink. From other hermits by black chin.

Ssp. *P. r. rupurumii* (Co, Ve, Gu)

Habits Poorly known. Males gather in leks, sometimes within tangles in undergrowth.
Status Uncertain in Colombia. Frequent in Venezuela, uncommon in Guyana.
Habitat Tropical Zone. Lowlands: undergrowth and thickets in sandy soil forests, also savanna and gallery forests, edges of *várzea*.
Voice In lower Caura region of Venezuela sings a high squeaky *seet, seet, se'se'se'se'se' yrt*, whilst those from lower Amazon sing *etza-squetza, etza-y-yank* (Hilty).
Note Formerly included in Dusky-throated Hermit but separated by Hinkelmann & Schuchmann (1997).

SOOTY-CAPPED HERMIT

Phaethornis augusti Pl. 92

Identification 16.3cm, bill 3.3cm. Dusky head with white eyebrow and long white moustachial, short back malar; drab green on back, rufous rump, uppertail-coverts and basal half of streamers, distal half white, other rectrices basally blackish but distal two-thirds white; throat to flanks grey, paler on belly, palest on undertail-coverts, undertail black with very distinct, large white V-shaped crescents terminally; bill black with orange-red below, feet pink.

Ssp. *P. a. augusti* (E Co, W & N Ve) as described
P. a. curiosus (Co: Santa Marta) pale below
P. a. incanescens (SE Ve, Gu) rufous on uppertail-coverts only

Habits Usually alone; darts about at low levels, occasionally uttering a squeak or flicking tail. Forages by trap-lining, more often in semi-open areas than in thickets.
Status Uncommon in Colombia and Guyana, common in Venezuela. Seasonal vertical movements, recorded in Venezuela to 3,500m.
Habitat Tropical Zone. Forests, from humid to fairly dry; edges and clearings on hillsides.
Voice Song a short, *here-herezee-zee-zeet*, repeatedly uttered every 0.5 s (P. Schwartz recording). A high *tseeo-tseeo, sis-sis-sis*, repeatedly given from favoured song perch whilst marking beat with tail (Hilty, M. L. Goodwin).

REDDISH HERMIT *Phaethornis ruber* Pl. 93

Identification 10.3cm, bill 2.3cm. Tiny hermit; male bronze-green from forehead to back, wings, rump and uppertail-coverts deep reddish-rufous, tail brown becoming black subterminally with rufous tips (no streamers); black mask with white eyebrow and whitish moustachial, throat pale rufous, becoming rich rufous on underparts, with highly variable black crescent on chest. Female similar, less green on head and back, more brownish, and no chest-band. Fairly similar Grey-chinned Hermit has grey throat and long tail.

Ssp. *P. r. episcopus* (E & S Ve, Gu) below more orange than rufous, white tips to tail
P. r. nigricinctus (E Ec, E Co, SW Ve) male intense rufous; female much paler with white tips to tail-feathers
P. r. ruber (Su, FG) as described

Habits Usually alone, at lower levels. Gleans tiny insects and spiders from under leaves. Weaves like a bee when flying. Males gather to sing during breeding season.

Reddish Hermit has an extremely variable breast patch

Status Rare in Ecuador, common in Colombia, frequent in Guianas.
Habitat Tropical Zone. Lowlands: savanna, sandy soil and humid forests; borders, scrub, second growth.
Voice Song thin, descending *zee-zee-zee-zeezeze*, repeated every *c.*3 s (D. W. Snow).

GREY-CHINNED HERMIT

Phaethornis griseogularis Pl. 93

Identification 10.9–11.3cm, bill 2.3cm. Bronze-green forehead to back, rump and uppertail-coverts rufous, tail dusky with green wash and white tips; underparts pale cinnamon. Larger than Reddish Hermit with clear white tips to tail.

Ssp. *P. g. griseogularis* (Co: Andes, S & SE Ve) dark grey chin, rufous fringes to all but central rectrices
P. g. porcullae (SW Ec) larger, white fringes and tips to all rectrices

Habits Usually alone, at lower levels. Gleans tiny insects and spiders from under leaves in undergrowth; visits understorey flowers on trap-line route.
Status Very rare to uncommon in Ecuador, uncommon and local in Colombia.
Habitat Upper Tropical to Subtropical Zones. Wide range of lowland and hillside forests: deciduous, gallery, moist, humid and cloud forests, mature second growth and seasonally dry woodland. Edges and clearings, thickets.
Voice Lekking males sing a high, squeaky *swit-swit-sweeit*… (R&G).
Note Likely to be a separate species (Hinkelmann in R&G, and 1999)

LITTLE HERMIT

Phaethornis longuemareus Pl. 93

Identification 11.4cm, bill 2.4cm. Bronze-brown from forehead to lower back, rump and uppertail-coverts dull rufous but contrast well against dark tail with greenish cast. Tail of male shorter but has longer central feathers; eyebrow above black mask, and malar reaching neck-sides and underparts pale cinnamon, black chin, underparts pale, undertail dusky with white terminal spots; bill black above, yellow below, long and slightly decurved, legs and feet vinaceous. From Reddish Hermit by brown throat and longer, white-tipped tail.

Ssp. *P. l. longuemareus* (Ve, Tr, Guianas)

Habits Usually alone, at lower levels. Gleans tiny insects and spiders from underside of leaves. Trap-lines, favouring *Mandevillia, Heliconia, Palicourea, Pachystachys, Cephaelis.* Wing noise easily discernible.

Status Frequent in Venezuela, uncommon in Guyana, quite common in Suriname and French Guiana, and on Trinidad (no records Tobago).

Habitat Lower Tropical Zone. Wet, humid and secondary forests, edges, mangroves and swamps, gardens and plantations.

Voice Males form leks, using same sites for years. Displays include tail-fanning, jumps, hovering back and forth with jerky turns. Utters soft squeaks. Song a high chitter, *ee-wee-tiddly-weet* in Trinidad (D. W. Snow) and in Guyana an insect-like hiss, *ss-ss-ss-ss-seeoo* (Snyder 1956).

Note Race *imatacae*, described from a single specimen, considered a hybrid Little × Streak-throated Hermit (Hinkelmann 1999).

STRIPE-THROATED HERMIT

Phaethornis striigularis Pl. 93

Identification 11.6cm, bill 2.5cm. Soft sage-green top of head and back, dull rufous eyebrow, nape and rump to uppertail-coverts, dusky tail with white terminal spots, long central rectrices white distally; dusky forehead and mask, pale greyish throat with fine dusky lines, warmer brown on flanks; bill dusky, yellow below with dark tip, feet flesh.

Ssp. *P. s. ignobilis* (NW Ve) as described
P. s. saturatus (NW Co) richer, more orange-coloured, orange moustachial
P. s. striigularis (N Co, NW Ve) palest and greyest underparts, more streaked throat; outer pair of tail-feathers have cinnamon-washed tips
P. s. subrufescens (W Co, W Ec) throat and breast more brownish

Habits Forages at low levels, usually alone, trap-lining small flowers (*Lantana* etc.). Will occasionally 'rob' nectar from flowers.

Status Uncommon to rare in Ecuador, common in Colombia and Venezuela (where seasonal in some areas).

Habitat Tropical, occasionally to Lower Subtropical Zone. Humid to semi-dry forests, mature second growth, plantations, gardens and clearings with shrubs and thickets, borders, humid or moist scrub.

Voice Song a constant, very high-pitched squeaking (easily overlooked) with much local variation in Colombia (H&B). Lekking males utter endless series of high, squeaky *tsit-tsit-tsit*... sometimes adding some tinkling notes (R&G).

Notes Race *nelsoni* considered a synonym of *saturatus* by Hinkelmann (1999) as falls within range of variation of *saturatus*. Latter sometimes treated as a separate species.

BLACK-THROATED HERMIT

Phaethornis atrimentalis Pl. 93

Identification 8–9cm, bill 2cm. Bronzy-brown from forehead to lower back, rump and uppertail-coverts dull rufous but contrast well against dark tail with greenish cast basally, rufous over distal half, with white terminal spots; buffy eyebrow above black mask, and throat buffy with fine dark brown streaking that can look dark, matting together on breast and sometimes forming vestigial breast-band; underparts cinnamon; bill black above and yellow below, long and only slightly decurved, legs and feet vinaceous. Female has less dense streaks on throat and no breast bar. From Reddish Hermit by dark brown throat and pale undertail-coverts.

Ssp. *P. a. atrimentalis* (E Ec, Co: E Andes)

Habits Forages at low levels. Follows trap-line route (*Palicourea, Pitcarnia, Heliconia, Aechmea*). Gleans insects and tiny spiders.

Status Uncommon in Ecuador, frequent locally in Colombia.

Habitat Tropical Zone. Humid lowland forests, borders of *várzea*, second growth and semi-open areas, plantations, often near water.

Voice Lekking males sing repetitively, *psss-psss-psss-psss-psee-u* (R&G).

TOOTH-BILLED HUMMINGBIRD

Androdon aequatorialis Pl. 94

Identification 14.3cm, bill 4.1cm. Top of head metallic copper-red, but varies from deep red to bright orange depending on light, nape green with blue lustre, back metallic green, coppery-bronze rump (varies from copper-orange to purple), broad white band on uppertail-coverts, long coverts dark green; tail basally grey becoming green, subterminally blackish with white tips; underparts entirely grey with blackish streaks from throat to flanks, undertail grey basally then dusky with white tips; bill straight and long, yellow at base below, small hook at tip and several tiny 'teeth' near tip of upper mandible, feet vinaceous. Female duller and browner on head, no blue on nape; streaks below dark grey rather than black.

Ssp. Monotypic (NW Ec, W Co)

Habits Solitary, mid level to subcanopy. Flies swiftly, flicks tail. Hook and serrations on bill adaptation to aid spider hunting, probing into rolled leaves, narrow holes and cavities, main feeding strategy is trap-lining.

Status Rare to locally frequent in Ecuador and Colombia.

Habitat Tropical to Subtropical Zones. Humid and wet primary forests, borders and clearings.

Voice Series of very high notes: *tsit-tsee-tsu* or *tsee-tsu* (R&G, K. Berg recording).

BLUE-FRONTED LANCEBILL

Doryfera johannae Pl. 94

Identification 11–12cm, bill 2.5–3cm. Forehead and crown metallic violet, rest of head and underparts deep indigo-blue to black with green reflections on breast; rear head and nape might reflect purplish or green, back deep indigo becoming green and then bright blue on uppertail-coverts, wing-coverts also metallic with blue or green iridescence; short, broad and slightly rounded tail black; bill needle-like with slight serrations near base, white fluffy feathers at tarsus.

Ssp. *D. j. guianensis* (S Ve, Gu) forecrown less intense violet
D. j. johannae (E Ec, E & C Co) as described

Habits Forages alone, occasionally in pairs (when breeding?), mostly at lower levels, visiting tubular flowers in thickets and bushes or sallying for insects from perch.

Status Uncommon in Guyana, Colombia and Ecuador. Seasonally frequent to common in southern Venezuela. Replaces Green-fronted Lancebill below *c.*1,500 m.

Habitat Upper Tropical to Subtropical Zones. Humid and cloud forests, shrubby borders, clearings, thickets along streams, rocky ravines, crags, areas near caves.

Voice Frequent chittering while flying or perched.

Note Race *rectirostris* considered synonym of *ludoviciae* (Green-fronted Lancebill) by Zimmer (1950).

GREEN-FRONTED LANCEBILL

Doryfera ludovicae Pl. 94

Identification 12–13.8cm, bill 3.5–3.6cm. Forehead bright metallic emerald-green, back of head dull green and nape metallic orange-bronze, rest of upperparts to rump dull green, short uppertail-coverts lustrous turquoise, or bright blue to violet on long coverts, broad and slightly rounded tail black; bill needle-like with slight serrations near base, longer than Blue-fronted Lancebill, white fluffy feathers at tarsus.

Ssp. *D. l. ludovicae* (Ve, Co: Andes)

Habits Forages alone, following trap-line, mostly flowers with long corollas. When perched, bill usually held raised almost vertical.

Status Locally common to fairly common. Uncommon in Ecuador. Replaces previous species above *c.*1,500m, although recorded down to 1,080m in western Venezuela.

Habitat Subtropical to Temperate Zones. Cloud and humid forests on montane slopes. Usually in understorey, wet ravines, occasionally *Polylepis* woodland.

Voice Males sing whilst displaying, with frontlet erect to reveal iridescence.

Note Race *rectirostris* absorbed into nominate as apparently described from immatures of latter (Stiles 1999).

SCALY-BREASTED HUMMINGBIRD

Phaeochroa cuvierii Pl. 94

Identification 13.2cm, bill 1.8cm. Upperparts green (remiges brown); throat to breast medium to pale green, with fine white fringes (rather like females of many hummingbirds), belly cinnamon, white fluffy feathers around tarsi, undertail-coverts brownish-grey with white fringes; bill very slightly curved, black with yellow on base below, feet blackish. Scaly breast not obvious in race *berlepschi*, but undertail-coverts well defined.

Ssp. *P. c. berlepschi* (N Co)

Habits Forages at all levels, solitary, but in rainy season (when breeding) males form loose gatherings to sing. Perches on exposed tip of twig.

Status Local and uncommon.

Habitat Tropical Zone. Partially wooded areas, fields with hedges or bushes, gardens.

Voice Varied and pleasant sequence of trills and chirps, repeated constantly.

Sabrewings take their name from the oddly angled bend in the outermost primaries; they are fairly large and vary in coloration from dull to bright green and contrasting white, and all have a small pale spot behind the eyes.

BUFF-BREASTED SABREWING

Campylopterus duidae Pl. 94

Identification 12cm, bill 2cm. Iridescent green from forehead, grading on lower back and rump into golden-cinnamon of tail, outer rectrices pale cinnamon with dark brown bases; throat to undertail-coverts pale brownish-grey, more clearly grey on belly, undertail pale cinnamon with dark bases; bill comparatively short and black, pale buffy tuft around tarsi, feet brown.

Ssp. *C. d. duidae* (S Ve: Amazonas Yavi, Parú, Duida, Neblina) as described
C. d. guaiquinimae (S Ve: Bolívar, Guaiquinima) flanks flushed rufous

Habits Usually solitary, forages for nectar at lower levels.

Status Endemic to Pantepui. Very common.

Habitat Upper Tropical to Subtropical Zones to 1,700m. Borders of humid and cloud forests, open forest, thickets on slopes and foothills of tepuis, scrub on tops.

Voice No description found.

GREY-BREASTED SABREWING

Campylopterus largipennis Pl. 94

Identification 15.8–16cm, bill 2.8–3cm. Iridescent green from forehead to central tail-feathers, other rectrices basally black, distally white; underparts uniform grey, undertail distinctly black and white; bill slightly curved at tip and black, white tufts over tarsi, feet black.

Ssp. *C. l. aequatorialis* (E Co, E Ec) white only on tips of tail
C. l. largipennis (SE Ve, Guianas) as described; distal half of tail white

Habits Low to mid levels. Perches on tips of exposed twigs. Hawks for insects from perch.

Status Uncommon to locally frequent in Ecuador, Colombia and Venezuela, frequent in Guyana, common in French Guiana.

Habitat Lower Tropical Zone to 400m, but to 800m in French Guiana. Borders of humid forest, both *várzea* and *terra firme*, interior and borders of second growth, plantations and humid scrub. Nests in damp understorey close to small watercourses.
Voice Males may gather in 'circle' of perches to sing. Song comprises 5–10 *soo-eet* notes, continually repeated.

RUFOUS-BREASTED SABREWING

Campylopterus hyperythrus Pl. 94

Identification 12cm, bill 2cm. Bright iridescent green from forehead to tail-coverts, central tail-feathers bronze, outer rectrices cinnamon; entire underparts bright cinnamon, fluffy tufts around tarsi and undertail pale cinnamon; bill fairly short, very slightly decurved at tip, black above, red below, feet deep red.

Ssp. Monotypic (SE Ve, Gu)

Habits Usually solitary, at lower and mid levels.
Status Endemic to Pantepui (Roraima, Uei-tepui, Sororopán, Ptari-tepui, Auyán-tepui, Aprada-tepui and Chimantá). Common in Venezuela, few data from Guyana.
Habitat Upper Tropical to Subtropical Zones, 1,200–2,000m. Cloud forest, open areas with scattered trees and bushes, montane scrub and scrub atop tepuis.
Voice A weak nasal squeak (Hilty).

WHITE-TAILED SABREWING

Campylopterus ensipennis Pl. 94

Identification 14.5–15.8cm, bill 2.5–2.8cm. Male almost entirely lustrous green with purplish cobalt-blue throat; outer rectrices have short black bases and rest white, white tarsal tufts; black bill gently curved, feet black. Female has irregular white malar and smaller blue bib, breast to belly buffy-grey with large, dark-tipped green centres to many feathers, usually in rows; otherwise as male.

Ssp. Monotypic (Ve, To)

Habits Forages alone, at lower to mid levels, occasionally in canopy, impervious to human presence. Visits bromeliads and *Heliconia*.
Status Rare on Tobago since 1963 hurricane, unrecorded Trinidad. Fairly common to uncommon in north-east Venezuela.
Habitat Upper Tropical to Lower Subtropical Zones. Humid forests on montane slopes, cloud forest, second growth and tree cuts.
Voice Calls from perch, repeating rolled note, described by ffrench (1976) as *crrreeet*.

LAZULINE SABREWING

Campylopterus falcatus Pl. 94

Identification 13.9–14.3cm, bill 2.5–2.8cm. Lustrous green forehead to tail-coverts, tail deep rich reddish-chestnut, chin to breast purplish cobalt-blue, becoming green on flanks and belly, tarsal tufts white, undertail-coverts and undertail rich chestnut; bill black and slightly decurved, feet grey. Female has throat to vent grey, with slightly spotty rich blue bib, distal underparts as male.

Ssp. Monotypic (Co, Ve)

Habits Solitary, in subcanopy and at low and mid levels. Marked preference for shady spots in forest, and for *Heliconia*, where it takes both nectar and insects inside bracts. Males perform oscillating display-flights in front of perched females.
Status Locally common in north, increasingly scarcer to south. Very rare in Ecuador.
Habitat Upper Tropical to Temperate Zones, 900–3,000m. Humid forests on montane slopes, cloud forest, coffee plantations, shady gardens (always with canopy cover).
Voice Song a bubbling, varied sequence, *chick, it, chick, it, splek, chat, seet, chik, seet, chik, it, chik, it…* (H&B, P. Schwartz recording).

SANTA MARTA SABREWING

Campylopterus phainopeplus Pl. 94

Identification 15–16cm, bill 2.5cm. Male rich lustrous green from forehead to uppertail-coverts, breast-sides to flanks and belly to undertail-coverts; throat lustrous purplish cobalt-blue, narrowing on centre of lower breast, tarsal tufts pure white; upper- and underside of tail deep indigo-blue; almost straight black bill, feet black. Female similar but is pure white from chin to vent.

Ssp. Monotypic (Co: Santa Marta)

Habits Forages alone, at low to mid levels. Apparently shy of humans, often perches in low bushes. Males perform diving display-flights.
Status Fairly common endemic, Santa Marta, Colombia.
Habitat Upper Tropical to Temperate Zones, 780–4,800m, but usually 1,200–1,800m. Humid forest on slopes, coffee and banana plantations, borders and clearings.
Voice Call a whining double *tweet* in flight, displaying or perching on high twig.

NAPO SABREWING

Campylopterus villaviscensio Pl. 95

Identification 13.5cm, bill 2.1cm. Rich green from forehead to uppertail-coverts and central pair of tail-feathers, throat rich blue with a purplish gloss, breast to belly and flanks green, central belly grey, tarsal tufts white, undertail-coverts blue, fringed white, tail deep blue above and below; black bill straight and needle-like, feet black. Female warm grey from chin to belly, with some green patches on flanks, vent and tarsal tufts white, undertail-coverts blue with grey fringes.

Ssp. Monotypic (E Ec, S Co)

Habits Forages alone, at low to mid levels, visiting flowers for nectar and hawking for insects. Very fond of *Heliconia*.
Status Uncommon to locally common, but suitable habitat within small range threatened by deforestation, and does not seem to adapt to disturbed habitat.
Habitat Upper Tropical to Lower Subtropical Zones, *c.*750–1,800m. Humid forest on montane slopes, usually inside forest, often along watercourses.
Voice No description and no published recordings.

SWALLOW-TAILED HUMMINGBIRD

Eupetomena macroura Pl. 94

Identification 15–17cm, tail 7–9cm; bill 2.1cm. Appears entirely metallic indigo-blue, with purplish gloss and green reflections on back, rump and lesser wing-coverts, and on top of head and ear-coverts; tail deeply forked with tips of outermost rectrices turned slightly outwards; bill black and almost straight, feet black. Female smaller and duller, and juvenile has more brown on wings and brownish on head.

Ssp. *E. m. macroura* (Su: probably only in Sipaliwini area, FG)

Habits Forages alone at low to mid levels, visiting flowers for nectar and hawking for insects. Feeds at variety of plants (bromeliads, Leguminosae, Bombacaceae, Malvaceae, Myrtaceae) and defends feeding territory. Adapts well to man-modified habitats.

Status Very rare in French Guiana but common in Suriname.

Habitat Tropical Zone. Savannas with scattered trees and bushes, borders of forests, plantations, gardens and parks.

Voice No description, but a recording from Brazil listed in Discography.

Note Placed in genus *Campylopterus* by Schuchmann (1999) on basis of song structure and enlarged shaft of primary in male, but resisted by Dickinson (2003) for lack of sufficient evidence.

WHITE-NECKED JACOBIN

Florisuga mellivora Pl. 95

Identification 11.9–13.8cm, bill 1.9–2.3cm. Adult male has head and breast metallic dark blue with greenish reflections on back of head, and green breast-sides, nape has pure white crescent, broadest in centre, tapering on neck-sides; entire upperparts to central tail-feathers lustrous green with golden reflections lower, rest of tail pure white with fine dark blackish tips to central pair; belly, tarsal tufts and flanks to undertail white. Immature male has broad orange stripe from base of bill to lower face-sides; white tail has solid blackish tips to all feathers. Adult female green above with black subterminal band to tail and thin white terminal line, blue reflections on head and gold reflections on back; throat greenish-blue becoming green then bronze on upper belly and sides, all with white fringes giving scaled effect, band across lower belly, vent and sides including tarsal tufts white, rear flanks and undertail-coverts boldly barred black and white. Juvenile much like female but duller and more golden on back, undertail-coverts barred black-brown and white; young male has throat outlined blackish-blue and dark bronze of lower breast continues, barred with white, to undertail-coverts; young female has flanks and belly dull white. Adult and immature males quite unmistakable, female and juveniles best identified by barred undertail-coverts.

Ssp. *F. m. flabellifera* (To) larger
F. m. mellivora (all mainland countries, Tr, Ar) as described

Habits Forages alone, but may gather at blooming tree, where males stage territorial chases. Feeds at coffee-shade *Erythrina* and *Inga*, and vines (*Bauhinia*, *Norantea*), hawks tiny flying insects or picks spiders at mid heights and in canopy, also high above streams or roads. Visits *Heliconia*. Perches exposed on high twigs.

Status Widespread, seasonal in many areas, perhaps due to regional migrations. Uncommon to locally common in Ecuador, Colombia and Venezuela. Uncommon on Aruba, Curaçao and Trinidad & Tobago. Frequent in Guyana, common in Suriname and French Guiana.

Habitat Tropical Zone below 1,000m, but seasonally to *c.*1,500m. Humid to wet forests on montane slopes, plantations, second growth, along streams, at borders and clearings.

Voice In flight a raspy, high-pitched *shit shit shit shit*… Male gives series of brisk *tsip* notes from high perch (R&G).

BROWN VIOLETEAR

Colibri delphinae Pl. 95

Identification 12.4–14.1cm, bill 1.5–1.9cm. Greyish-brown above, darker on rump and uppertail-coverts with terminal orange bands; basal third of tail grey, distally deep brown with grey tip; ear-coverts bright metallic violet, lores and mesial pale buffy, upper throat metallic green and purple-blue lower; breast to vent pastel greyish-brown, tarsal tufts white, undertail-coverts brown with broad orange fringes; bill short, thin and almost straight, feet blackish. Juvenile has head virtually all brown with only vestigial ear-coverts and bib, mesial stripe only slightly paler than rest of head and breast, and entire body subtly scaled (darker fringes and some paler centres).

Ssp. Monotypic (all mainland countries)

Habits Forages alone, mostly in canopy but occasionally at bushes, taking nectar at flowers (especially *Erythrina*) and hawking insects. Males gather to sing in wooded spot, each at a well-defended perch. Also chases at feeding spots and can flare feathers on head-sides as threat signal.

Status Uncommon to rare in Ecuador, rare to seasonally fairly common in Colombia and Venezuela, uncommon Trinidad and Guyana, and locally common in Suriname but very rare in French Guiana.

Habitat Tropical to Subtropical Zones, to 2,800m. Usually in humid or cloud forests on montane slopes, but at lower elevations when trees bloom in lowlands during drier months. Planted fields with scattered stands of woodland.

Voice Calls from high perch repeating sequence of 5–7 occasionally 8 identical chip notes.

GREEN VIOLETEAR

Colibri thalassinus Pl. 95

Identification 11–12cm, bill 1.8–2cm. Male almost entirely bright green with large patch from lores and ear-coverts to neck- and face-sides rich purplish royal blue, some blue and golden reflections on throat and wing-coverts, undertail-coverts broadly edged yellow, tail has bluish reflections and broad black subterminal band; bill black and slightly decurved, feet grey. Female has smaller 'ear' patch, paler reflections on throat and undertail-coverts fringed warm yellow. Female from Sparkling Violetear by all-green underparts.

Ssp. *C. t. cyanotus* (Ec, Co, Ve) as described
C. t. kerdeli (E Ve) metallic coppery-golden reflections on rear crown

Habits Forages alone, but gathers at flowering trees, especially coffee-shade *Inga*, *Erythrina*. Feeds mid level to canopy, and often holds feeding territory. Males sing for hours from high bare twig or gather to sing in 'circle' of perches. Sometimes chase each other or race after same female. Flares out head-side feathers in display or as threat signal. Display-flights undulating.
Status Uncommon and locally frequent in Ecuador, common and widespread but very seasonal in Colombia and Venezuela.
Habitat Subtropical to Temperate Zones, 500–3,000m, at higher levels when breeding. Humid forest, open woodland near páramo, mature second growth, bamboo stands, open terrain with bushes on hillsides, coffee and banana plantations. Thickets in treefalls, clearings and borders.
Voice Song a sequence of sharp notes – *tsup-chip, tsip-chup* – mixed with short rolls and loud whistles (F&K).
Note Races south of Costa Rica may form separate species, Montane Violetear *C. cyanotus*.

SPARKLING VIOLETEAR

Colibri coruscans Pl. 95

Identification 14–15.5cm, bill 2.5cm. Male rich lustrous green from forehead to uppertail-coverts, tail rich royal blue with subterminal black band, face-sides from lores and chin, through eyes and ear-coverts to neck-sides rich purplish-blue; throat green with cobalt centres giving streaked effect, central breast deep lustrous blue, to flanks, white tarsal tufts, undertail-coverts deep turquoise with thin white fringes; bill black and straight, feet black. Female more yellowish-green, or has more yellowish reflections all over, face blackish, ear-tufts much reduced and on lower face- and neck-sides; tail bluish-green with subterminal black band. Similar to but much larger than Green Violetear, which has green chin and breast.

Ssp. *C. c. germanus* (S Ve, Gu?) as described; male has blue tail
C. c. coruscans (Ec, Co, Ve) tail green in both sexes
C. c. rostratus (S Ve) longer tail than *germanus*, otherwise similar

Habits Forages alone, visiting flowering *Clusia* and bushes with erect flowers of any size where corollas open sideways or to sky (*Salvia*, *Lantana*, *Centropogon*, *Guzmania*, *Elleanthus*). Stakes out feeding territories.
Status Common and widespread throughout range.
Habitat Upper Tropical to Temperate Zones, 1,700–4,500m. Deciduous and semi-deciduous forests, humid and cloud forests, second growth, fields with bushes and scattered trees or wooded patches, plantations, gardens and parks.
Voice Males sing for hours from high, exposed twig. In display-flight, lifts sharply from perch, then dives back twittering and fanning tail. Song endless repetition of same sharp *chiip*, mixed with occasional rolls or sometimes a high-pitched whistle.

GREEN-THROATED MANGO

Anthracothorax viridigula Pl. 95

Identification 12.9–15.2cm, bill 2.5cm. Male slightly olivaceous-green from forehead to uppertail-coverts, tail lustrous malachite-green, face-sides to flanks, lower breast to belly and undertail-coverts deep jade green, small white tarsal tufts, chin to throat form extended black 'teardrop' bib; undertail purple with black outer webs to outer rectrices. Female also has deep jade green face- and body-sides, but from chin widens then narrows to almost nothing on lower breast, then broadens on flanks to vent, all white, with single elongated black 'diamond' from mid throat to lower breast, undertail-coverts barred bronzy and white; undertail purple with black outer webs to outer rectrices, black subterminal band and white tips. Female from other female mangos by single black mark on throat.

Ssp. Monotypic (NE Ve, Tr, Guianas)

Habits Forages alone, but groups may form at flowering trees (e.g. *Erythrina glauca*, *Cordia*, *Tabebuia*, *Spathodea*). Males feisty and territorial at feeding spots.
Status Uncommon and local in Venezuela, scarce and local in Trinidad and Guyana, rather common in Suriname, but uncommon in French Guiana. Seasonal movements follow flowering stages of certain trees and birds on 'passage' may turn up in unexpected places.
Habitat Lower Tropical Zone, to 500m. Coastal region, mangroves, marshes, swamps and similar with scattered trees.
Voice Rapid staccato series of pebbly notes (Hilty).

GREEN-BREASTED MANGO

Anthracothorax prevostii Pl. 95

Identification 12.5–13cm, bill 2.5–2.8cm. Adult male has deep green head that continues to central tail-feathers, reflecting bronzy-orange on uppertail-coverts, tail cobalt blue; throat bright metallic green with slight bluish reflection on sides and continuing on flanks, where reflects gold, broad T-shaped black patch in central breast tails off lower, and vent to undertail-coverts black except small white tarsal tufts, undertail deep purple; bill black and slightly decurved, feet black. Female lacks propensity to glow orange on rump and has small white tips to tail; undertail has basal two-thirds purple, distal third deep blue, and white tips. Juvenile very similar but has smaller, green-centred mark in centre of throat; white sides to throat flushed orange, purple only on basal quarter of undertail, and generally duller and less shiny. Female very similar to female Black-throated Mango, but black line on breast is broken and very well separated by white, green and white; chin of Green-breasted is always white, whilst Black-throated is always black.

Ssp. *A. p. viridicordatus* (NE Co, N Ve)

Habits Forages mainly at mid to low levels (*Calliandra*, *Hibiscus*, *Lantana*, *Quassia*, Malvaceae, *Ipomoea*, *Combretum*, *Salvia*), but often in flowering trees (*Ceiba*, *Erythrina*, *Inga*, *Bauhinia*, *Caesalpinia*, *Calycophyllum*), where groups may

gather and males establish feeding territories. Insects picked from air by sallying from perch or by hawking, and from leaves by gleaning. Spiders also taken by gleaning, and their webs visited to glean insects.
Status Very local, but frequent to fairly common where and when found. Seasonal movements follow flowering seasons.
Habitat Tropical Zone. Borders of humid forests and second growth, open woodland, along streams, clearings, scattered trees, coffee plantations, parks and golf courses, gardens.
Voice Male has sequence of whining buzz notes delivered from high bare twig.

Immature female Black-throated Mango (left) has broad tan stripe either side of throat, breast and belly, which at rest tends to obscure black and white front and confuse identification; on the right is an aberrant female with white on the superciliary and all the way to the uppertail-coverts

BLACK-THROATED MANGO

Anthracothorax nigricollis Pl. 95

Identification 12.4–14cm, bill 2.2–2.5cm. Adult male green from forehead to central tail-feathers, outer feathers maroon to purple; chin to vent black, bordered bluish-green, white tarsal tufts, undertail reddish-purple with black outer webs to outer rectrices; bill black and slightly curved, feet dark grey. Female has black of front bordered white and then green, undertail-coverts barred green and white, undertail deep carmine edged black, which increases until end of tail is black, with white tips. Juvenile like female but young male has purple undertail and olive-green undertail-coverts edged white, whilst young female has dull carmine undertail, purer green undertail-coverts and sides of black on throat and breast flushed rufous-orange. Female from female Green-throated Mango by white chin and shorter black line on central breast, with more clean white on sides. Note, young may have aberrant head colouring, with far more extensive orange and white on sides and top of head.

Ssp. *A. n. iridescens* (W Ec, W Co) slightly longer bill, otherwise identical
A. n. nigricollis (T&T, throughout continental northern South America) as described

Habits Forages alone, hovering to hawk insects over open roads and streams, and visits blooming vines, garden bushes (*Ixora*, *Hibiscus*) and trees (*Erythrina*, *Tabebuia*, *Inga*), where may congregate. Shy but adapts easily to sugar-water feeders, and also visits feeders with fruit to take fruit flies. Recorded 'parasitising' *Tabebuia* flowers (ffrench 1976).
Status Uncommon to rare in Ecuador, uncommon to locally common in Colombia and Venezuela. Common on Trinidad, in Guyana, Suriname and French Guiana.
Habitat Tropical Zone to *c.*1,000m, wooded or partially open areas, from quite dry to humid. Borders, clearings and planted fields with scattered trees.
Voice Buzzes frequently in flight and a dry *tshiuck tshiuck* when hovering at flowers.
Note Race *iridescens* sometimes placed in Green-throated Mango but we follow S&M and R&G.

FIERY-TAILED AWLBILL

Avocettula recurvirostris Pl. 95

Identification 9.4cm, bill 1.8cm. Male all green, to central tail-feathers above, rest of tail maroon; metallic brighter green from chin to central breast, and sides to flanks, vent and undertail-coverts dull green, with partially filled black Y in centre of belly, white tarsal tufts; undertail maroon-chestnut; bill black with pronounce upturn at tip, feet black. Female has tail all green, chin to central belly black, bordered broadly white and green at sides, undertail deep maroon with white tips on outer 3 rectrices. Reminiscent of a small mango, but bill shape quite distinctive.

Ssp. Monotypic (Ec, Ve, Guianas)

Habits Forages alone, in open, visiting flowering trees (*Clusia*, *Dioclea*) and bushes, following trap-line.
Status Fragmented range; rare in Ecuador, very rare in Venezuela, scarce in Guyana, uncommon in Suriname and French Guiana, but quite easy to overlook.
Habitat Lower Tropical Zone to 250m, but often to 500m. Borders and canopy of primary forest and adjacent savannas in foothills of tepuis and around granite outcrops, forests along rivers.
Voice No description and no published recordings.
Note Placed in genus *Anthracocorax* by Schuchmann (1999), on basis of plumage and nest structure.

RUBY TOPAZ (HUMMINGBIRD)

Chrysolampis mosquitus Pl. 96

Identification 9.2–10.4cm, bill 1.3–1.5cm. Forehead to nape metallic red (may appear purple or black), similarly, bright pale orange chin to breast can appear glittering gold to dull sepia; entire body and wings umber-brown with blackish mantle and band bordering lower breast, undertail-coverts orange, tail orange with blackish tips; white tarsal tufts, feet black, bill comparatively short and dusky. Immature male has red of head dark greyish-brown with some metallic feathers, orange front is pale greyish-buff with 'teardrop' of dark brown covered in metallic pale orange feathers. Juvenile male pale buffy-brown above with perhaps a few metallic orange feathers, darker on wings, which have greenish tone; throat to undertail-coverts pale greyish-buff with same 'teardrop' pattern, undertail dull violet, darker subterminally with grey terminal band. Adult female soft beige from forehead to uppertail-coverts and central tail-feathers, with metallic pale green that reflects golden, particularly on mantle and wing-coverts; outer rectrices orange with black subterminal band and narrow white tips. Juvenile female is like young male but lacks throat mark. On Trinidad & Tobago differs in that females have 'teardrop' in middle of throat, metallic green with slight gold reflection.

Ssp. Monotypic (Co, Ve, Ar, Bo, Cu, T&T, Guianas)

Habits Forages alone, in canopy and mid level, visiting flowering shrubs and trees (*Samanea*, *Cordia*, *Tabebuia*), searching leaves for tiny spiders and insects. Males aggressive even towards humans and raptors. Displays by spreading tail and raising crown feathers.
Status Uncommon to rare in Colombia, fairly common in Venezuela and Guyana, common in Trinidad & Tobago.
Habitat Tropical Zone to 500m but occurs to *c*.1,700m. Savannas with scattered vegetation, fields, gallery and deciduous forests, xerophytic areas and thorn scrub, mangroves, parks and gardens.
Voice Call a loud *tliii*, oft-repeated from fixed perch (H&B).

Coquettes and thorntails are tiny birds that look like hawk-moths when foraging around a blossoming tree, and are a devil to focus the binoculars on! When moving, they are more like bumblebees, flying comparatively slowly and with a weaving jizz. Larger hummingbirds may have staked territorial claims in these trees, and the coquettes are chased for marauding. All but one have a narrow white band on the rump, some have astonishingly decorative head feathering, others extraordinary tails, one has both! All have short, needle-like bills.

VIOLET-HEADED HUMMINGBIRD
Klais guimeti Pl. 96

Identification 9.1–10.3cm, bill 1–1.3cm. Adult male almost entirely green, brightest and most metallic on rump and uppertail-coverts, subterminal black tail-band; short but erectile, metallic crest that reflects violet, and throat is metallic purplish-blue, reflecting bluish, ear-coverts duller, with a longish white spot behind eyes; underparts grey with some reflective green feathers on breast and scattered on sides, white thighs; bill and feet black. Juvenile male lacks violet and blue, instead green with a slight blue reflection, Adult female green above, reflecting gold on back to tail-coverts, with smaller amount of metallic violet on crown, and grey from chin to undertail-coverts, with scattered metallic green feathers on sides. Juvenile female lacks any violet on head.

Ssp. *K. g. guimeti* (Co, E Ec, N&W Ve)

Habits Forages alone, especially at mid and lower levels (Verbenaceae, Ericaceae, bromeliads), but visits flowering trees of all heights (*Inga*, Rubiaceae, *Warscewiczia*, Guttiferaceae), where sometimes numerous.
Status Uncommon to rare and quite local in Colombia and Ecuador, seasonally fairly frequent in parts of Venezuela.
Habitat Upper Tropical Zone, 800–1,700m in Ecuador, 400–1,450 with a record to 1,800m in Macarena Mts., Colombia, 400–1,300m in Venezuela, sometimes higher or lower. Fields with scattered trees and bushes, mature second growth, borders and clearings of humid forests.
Voice Males sing 2 high notes repeatedly – *pip seet* – from high perch or, in breeding season, at leks. Sharp *tsit tsit* in flight.

TUFTED COQUETTE
Lophornis ornatus Pl. 96

Identification 7.8–8.5cm, bill 1–1.5cm. Adult male has head metallic pale green with a splayed bright orange crest, and spray of orange plumes from face-sides, each with a metallic black terminal disc that reflects emerald-green, forehead and throat reflect emerald-green; orange necklace and rest of body slightly olive-green with orange to gold reflections on rump and uppertail-coverts; narrow white band on rump, orange on outer webs of tail, white thighs; bill red with black tip, feet black. Female has forehead and frontal gorget orange (lacking tufts or crests), rest of upperparts as male, but white rump band washed pale orange; underparts pale green, well washed weak orange; bill basally red, distally black. Juvenile as female but lacks orange frontal gorget, having a pale whitish throat streaked black and orange, and juvenile male has rump band white; bill black with red base.

Ssp. Monotypic (E Ve, Tr, Guianas)

Habits Forages alone, visiting small flowering trees, shrubs (*Asclepia*) and plants in cultivated fields (*Phaseolus*, *Cajanus*). Not shy; an audible wing buzz that differs from other hummingbirds.
Status Uncommon and possibly seasonal.
Habitat Lower Tropical Zone. Humid open areas, savannas with woods and abundant bushes, gallery forests, planted fields, forest borders. In French Guiana in liana-rich canopies of tall humid forest.
Voice Call a soft, dry *chik* (ffrench 1976).

RUFOUS-CRESTED COQUETTE
Lophornis delattrei Pl. 96

Identification 7.9cm, bill 1cm. Adult male has head metallic bright green with abundant bushy crest, the tips of some plumes having tiny black metallic spots that reflect bright green. Number of spots variable and some birds have none; irregular necklace is orange on neck-sides and white in centre of throat, with some black flecks; rest of body green with some orange or golden reflections on back, rump and tail-sides, broad subterminal black band on tail, narrow terminal orange band; white thighs, feet black, bill red with tip black. Female has orange forehead to rear crown (no crest).

Ssp. *L. d. lessoni* (Ec?, C & E Co)

Habits Forages alone, usually on low-flowering shrubs and

bushes in clearings, at borders and edges and overgrown roadsides. Perches on high exposed branches.
Status Rare to very rare and local in Colombia. Unconfirmed in Ecuador.
Habitat Tropical to Subtropical Zones. Borders and clearings of humid forests, hedges and shrubbery adjacent to open fields or roads.
Voice No description found.

SPANGLED COQUETTE

Lophornis stictolophus Pl. 96

Identification 7.2–7.7cm, bill 0.8cm. Adult male has head metallic bright green with an abundant bushy crest, the tips of the plumes having a tiny black, metallic spot that reflects bright green; irregular necklace of orange on neck-sides and white on centre of throat, with some black flecks; rest of body green with some orange or golden reflections on back, rump and tail-sides, broad subterminal black tail-band, narrow terminal orange band; white thighs, feet black, bill red with black tip. Female has forehead and lores to cheeks and throat orange (lacking any tufts or crests).

Ssp. Monotypic (E Ec, E Co, W Ve)

Habits Forages in canopy of tall flowering trees, alone or in small gatherings. Sometimes in mixed feeding groups with Wire-crested Thorntail. Flight seems to drift and weave, and though wings are a blurr of speed, bird seems to be gliding.
Status Uncommon to rare and very local, extensive but very fragmented distribution. Seasonally frequent in Venezuela.
Habitat Upper Tropical Zone. Semi-arid woodland and scrub, second growth, thickets, deciduous forests in foothills.
Voice No description found and no published recordings.

FESTIVE COQUETTE

Lophornis chalybeus Pl. 96

Identification 9.1cm, bill 1.5cm. Head rich deep green with a long crest with red tips, metallic reflections of pale green on forehead and ear-coverts, latter divided from long subauricular tufts by a black line; tufts have white spots at tip of each plume; mantle to lower back reflects golden, with a solid white band and uppertail-coverts deep reddish, tail maroon; underparts green with white thighs; bill and feet black. Female has no crest or subauricular tufts but has a whitish malar; reddish uppertail-coverts less intense and breast reflects golden.

Ssp. *L. c. klagesi* (E Ve) much shorter crest and lacks red tips, less reflective pale green on forehead and ear-coverts, fewer white spots on subauricular tufts
L. c. verreauxii (Ec, E Co, S Ve) long crest, throat and belly blackish-green

Habits Forages alone, mostly in canopy, at flowering trees (*Inga*, *Erythrina*). Perches exposed on high branches.
Status Uncommon in Colombia and Venezuela, very rare in Ecuador.
Habitat Lower Tropical Zone. Humid forest borders, fields with hedges and shrubs.
Voice No description found and no published recordings.

PEACOCK COQUETTE

Lophornis pavoninus Pl. 96

Identification 11cm, bill 1.3cm. Essentially green with white rump band; broad black stripe with orange-red spots over crown, bright metallic pale green at sides, in front a full black oval bib. Subauricular tufts comprise a dozen spatulate plumes with large round black subterminal spots, fringed orange, at base of feathers is patch of bright reddish-orange with several white spots; white thighs. Immature male green with metallic pale green spots on head-sides and a few blackish spots on neck-sides; mask including chin and upper throat black. Female green above, chin to ear-coverts grey, streaked paler, underparts green. Juvenile lacks white rump band, or is restricted to sides; entire underparts grey, with streaked breast- and body-sides. Male Festive Coquette has less dramatic tufts, with small white terminal spots and an all-green forehead and throat.

Ssp. *L. p. duidae* (S Ve) black coronal stripe slightly narrower and lacks orange-red spots, orange-red at base of subauricular tufts small and lacks white spots, and subterminal black spots have no orange fringing
L. p. pavoninus (SE Ve, Gu) as described

Habits Forages alone, but small numbers may gather at flowering trees. Takes nectar from many plants (bromeliads, *Inga*, Rutaceae, *Salvia*, *Lantana*, Compositae, *Rubus*). Perches on high, bare branches.
Status Endemic to Pantepui. Uncommon and seasonal in Venezuela, few data from Guyana.
Habitat Upper Tropical to Subtropical Zones, 500–2,000m. Humid and cloud forests, borders and clearings.
Voice No description found and no published recordings.
Note Race *punctigula* synonymised by Dickerman & Phelps (1982).

WIRE-CRESTED THORNTAIL

Popelairia popelairii Pl. 96

Identification Male 12.7cm, female 8.8cm; bill 1.3cm. Adult male almost all green with a clean white rump band that wraps around to rear flanks, a broader mid blue band immediately below it does not reach beyond flanks; forehead and crown bright metallic green with 2 feathers extending in a lengthy crest, throat and face-sides bright metallic green; central breast black, tapering to vent; uppertail-coverts metallic bright green, but tail deep blue with outer feathers long and tapered, becoming thin shafts at tip, next pair shorter and also pointed, next pair shorter, etc.; bill red with black tip, short white tarsal tufts, feet grey. Female lacks crest and frontal gorget, but has bold white mesial line and is black from chin to centre of lower breast, tail short and blunt, with white tips and central pair shorter than rest, with clear white tips.

Ssp. Monotypic (E Ec, E Co)

Habits Forages alone, mostly in canopy, in tall emergent blooming trees (*Inga*, *Erythrina*). Perches exposed on tip of high branch.
Status Rare and local in Colombia, uncommon in Ecuador.
Habitat Upper Tropical Zone. Humid forest borders.

Voice No description found and no published recordings.
Note Sometimes placed in the genus *Discosura*.

BLACK-BELLIED THORNTAIL

Popelairia langsdorffi Pl. 96

Identification Male 13.5–15cm, female 7.9cm; bill 1.3cm. Adult male almost all green with a clean white rump band that wraps around to behind flanks; throat and face-sides form large gorget of bright metallic green, bordered on breast with bright orange; central breast black, tapering broadly and ending abruptly in white vent, thighs and belly; uppertail-coverts metallic bright green, but tail deep blue with outer feathers long and tapered, becoming thin shafts at tip, the next pair shorter and also pointed, next pair shorter, etc.; bill black tip, feet grey. Female much like male but has bold white mesial line and is metallic black from chin to centre of lower breast, bordered vestigially with orange, and reflecting dark green or dark blue; belly and flanks to undertail-coverts white; tail short and blunt, with white tips and central pair shorter than rest, also with clear white tips.

Ssp. *P. l. melanosternon* (E Ec, S Co, S Ve)

Habits Forages alone, in canopy of flowering trees (e.g. *Inga*), as well as at mid level. Perches exposed on high branches.
Status Uncommon in Colombia and frequent in Venezuela, rare in Ecuador.
Habitat Lower Tropical Zone. Humid forest, at borders and along rivers.
Voice Males display by darting around and above females flashing spread tail, making a loud crack occasionally and whistling rapidly *ti ti, ti, ti*.
Note Sometimes placed in the genus *Discosura*.

GREEN THORNTAIL

Popelairia conversii Pl. 96

Identification Male 11.2cm, female 7.6cm; bill 1cm. Adult male almost all green with clean white rump band that wraps around to rear flanks; vent, thighs and belly white; forehead, throat and face-sides form large gorget of bright metallic green above and metallic blue below; breast and sides green; lower rump metallic green, but uppertail-coverts and tail deep blue with outer feathers long and tapered, becoming thin shafts with a double kink at tip, the next pair shorter and also pointed, next pair shorter, etc.; bill black tip, feet grey. Female lacks bicoloured frontal gorget, but has narrow white mesial line that embraces metallic green chin and upper throat, with a few white feathers, breast green, belly and below white; tail short and slightly forked, with white tips.

Ssp. Monotypic (Ec, Co)

Habits Forages mostly in canopy, visiting flowering trees alone, but often as part of mixed assemblage of hummingbirds and other nectar-feeders at a large tree in full blossom. Apparently partial to flowers with fine filaments (*Inga*, *Mimosa*, *Jambosa*). Hovers under large leafs to pick tiny spiders and insects.
Status Locally common to uncommon in Colombia, uncommon to rare in Ecuador.
Habitat Upper Tropical Zone to 1,000m, perhaps higher. Borders and clearings of humid and wet forests.
Voice No description found and no published recordings.
Note Sometimes placed in the genus *Discosura*.

RACKET-TAILED COQUETTE

Discosura longicaudus Pl. 96

Identification Male 10.7cm, female 8.1cm; bill 1.3cm. Adult male almost all green with a clean white rump band that wraps around to rear flanks; forehead, throat and face-sides form large gorget of metallic green (jade on throat); breast and sides metallic green, reflecting gold, rest of underparts white; lower rump metallic green, but uppertail-coverts and tail deep blue, the outer feathers form thin shafts with an inverted, heart-shaped racket at tip, the next pair pointed, the rest slightly shorter and pointed; bill black, feet vinaceous grey. Female lacks frontal gorget, but has narrow white mesial line that embraces metallic green chin and upper throat, with many white feathers, breast and sides metallic green, reflecting gold on belly, and below white; tail short and blunt, with white tips and central pair slightly shorter than rest.

Ssp. Monotypic (Ve, Guianas)

Habits Forages in the canopy where tall emergent trees are in bloom.
Status Rare in Venezuela, uncommon in the Guianas.
Habitat Lower Tropical Zone, to *c.*200m. Humid primary forest, and scattered scrub or trees in savannas near rivers.
Voice No description found and no published recordings.

> Sapphires and emeralds of the genera *Chlorestes* and *Chlorostilbon* are small, green hummingbirds that all look very much alike, with metallic plumage, mostly with forked tails and straight bills. Females also tend to look very much alike, with white postocular lines and dusky masks. However few are widespread and there is little overlap, so check the distribution maps carefully.

BLUE-CHINNED SAPPHIRE

Chlorestes notata Pl. 97

Identification 10.7–10.9cm, bill 1.8–1.9cm. Almost entirely metallic. Adult male almost entirely metallic green with deep blue chin, paler on sides of face and throat, tail deep blue, white thighs, feet black, bill longer than congenerics, very slightly curved, black above, red below. Female has pale blue chin and white bases to some feathers of throat and breast, and underparts finely fringed white, belly to undertail-coverts white, tail slightly darker and less blue than male. Immature male like female but slightly more olivaceous-green and virtually no blue on chin. Juvenile like female but has greyish chin and throat with fine white fringes, duller than adult. From Copper-rumped and Shining-green Hummingbirds, and by most emeralds by rounded tail (not forked).

Ssp. *C. n. notata* (Ec, SE Co, N & E Ve, T&T, Guianas)

Habits Forages alone, mostly in blooming trees of *Samanea*, *Erythrina*, *Inga*, *Calliandra*, *Bauhinia*, *Stachytarpheta*, and searches for tiny insects and spiders in leaves. Perches on tips of branches in shady spots.

Status Common on Trinidad, rare on Tobago. Mainland distribution fragmented. Uncommon and local in Colombia, rare in Ecuador, widespread but scarce in Venezuela, rather common in Guyana and Suriname.

Habitat Tropical Zone, to *c.*500m. Borders and clearings of humid forests, *várzea* and *terra firme*, mature second growth, gallery and deciduous forests, fields with scattered trees or bushes, coffee and cocoa plantations, gardens.

Voice Sequence of 3–5 repetitions of same *sssooo* note (ffrench). Male has fast series of high *tss* notes (R&G).

Note Traditionally treated in the montypic genus *Chlorestes*, but merged into *Chlorostilbon* by Schuchmann (1999) and followed by Dickinson (2003). We have retained this species in *Chlorestes* (as has SACC).

BLUE-TAILED EMERALD

Chlorostilbon mellisugus Pl. 97

Identification 8.1–9.5cm, bill 1.3–1.8cm. Almost entirely metallic green, forked tail dark blue, white thighs; bill straight and black, feet blackish. Female has white postocular line, dusky lores and ear-coverts forming narrow mask, underparts all grey, palest on vent and undertail-coverts, tail tipped pale grey. Immature like adult female. Juvenile duller olive-green on top of head, postocular line shorter, underparts buff, white vent and tarsal tufts.

Ssp. *C. m. caribaeus* (N, NE & C Ve) very little bluish tinge on throat
C. m. duidae (S Ve) bronzy-orange head and back
C. m. mellisugus (Su, FG) tail only slightly forked
C. m. phoeopygus (E Ec, SC, SE Co) as desribed
C. m. subfurcatus (SE Ve, Gu) more blue-green on throat and uppertail-coverts

Habits Forages alone, at all levels, in shrubs (e.g. *Sesanum*) and flowering trees, where several may gather. Occasional records of nectar 'piracy'. Also insects. Often perches on bush or at low level. Flies swift and direct, not ambling like bumblebee.

Status Common and widespread in Venezuela and Colombia, uncommon to rare in Ecuador, uncommon and local in Trinidad, rather common in the Guianas.

Habitat Tropical to Subtropical Zones. Semi-dry and partially open areas, savannas with bushes or scattered trees, large clearings in *terra firme*, xerophytic scrub and woods, deciduous and gallery forests, agricultural areas with patches of woods or shrubs, gardens and parks.

Voice Song weak *tsip* or *chwep* notes, repeated, with occasional rolls or twitters (F&K, ffrench).

Note Race *napensis* apparently very similar to *phoeopygus* (Stiles 1996a), synonymised by Bündgen (1999) and accepted by Dickinson.

CHIRIBIQUETE EMERALD

Chlorostilbon olivaresi Pl. 97

Identification 8.5–9cm, bill 1.9–2cm. Adult male green above, metallic and reflecting bright green on top and sides of head, chin to throat metallic bright blue, underparts green with white thighs, forked tail deep blue; bill black above, red below, feet grey. Female green above, including central tail-feathers; with white postocular line, blackish mask, underparts ivory white; tail dusky, shorter and less deeply forked than male, with white tips to all but central pair of rectrices.

Ssp. Monotypic (Co)

Habits Forages alone, visiting bushes (*Bonnetia*, *Decagonocarpus*, Melastomataceae) and small trees (*Clusia*, Violaceae) in savannas and forest borders. Picks flies from air by sallying, and small insects from leaves by gleaning. Relatively sedate, pumps tail more slowly than other *Chlorostilbon*.

Status Endemic to Colombia. Common within tiny range.

Habitat Upper Tropical Zone. Savannas with scattered scrub and patches of bare rock atop Sierra de Chiribiquete; occasionally in stunted forests on slopes.

Voice Very quiet, call a short dry *cht* (Stiles 1996).

RED-BILLED EMERALD

Chlorostilbon gibsoni Pl. 97

Identification 8–9cm, bill 1.3cm. Adult male entirely metallic green, with deep indigo, shallow-forked tail, white thighs; bill red with black tip. Female same above, with white tips to tail, short, curved, postocular white line, black mask, underparts pale grey; bill black, feet grey.

Ssp. *C. g. chrysogaster* (N Co, W Ve) larger than other races; malachite green, tail slightly bluer and deeply forked
C. g. gibsoni (C Co) as described
C. g. nitens (NE Co, NW Ve: coast) like *gibsoni* but with slightly golden reflection, less deeply-forked tail

Habits Forages alone, at low to mid levels. Regularly follows trap-line route, over flowers that may be quite dispersed. Often forages at smaller flowers that are insect-pollinated with small nectar yields and usually ignored by other hummingbirds (Hilty).

Status Uncommon and local.

Habitat Tropical to Subtropical Zones. Humid and drier deciduous forests, xerophytic areas and thorny scrub. Coastal areas.

Voice No description found and no published recordings.

Note Included within Blue-tailed Emerald in Bündgen (1999).

WEST ANDEAN EMERALD

Chlorostilbon melanorhynchus Pl. 97

Identification 10.9–11.4cm, bill 1.4cm. Almost entirely metallic green with slightly brighter green face, strong gold to orange reflections on forehead and faint blue on breast; tail forked but outer 2 pairs of rectrices same length. Female all green above, including central tail-feathers, tail more greenish-blue than male, but again outer 2 pairs same length; white postocular line, brownish-grey mask, underparts white with strong buffy tone to centre from throat to belly.

Ssp. *C. m. melanorhynchus* (NC Ec, extreme SW Co) as described
C. m. pumilus (W Co) brighter crown and shorter bill

Habits No behavioural differences between these taxa and those of Blue-tailed Emerald, with which it was previously

considered conspecific, but following are general traits of genus: forages alone, at all levels, in shrubs and flowering trees, where small groups may gather occasionally.
Status Uncommon in west but quite common in northern Ecuador; frequent in parts of Colombia.
Habitat Upper Tropical to Subtropical Zones, *c.*1,000–2,000m. Humid, wet and cloud forests, borders and clearings.
Voice Mostly quiet. Males sing a weak *tsit-trr, tsit-trr, tsit-trr, tsit-trr*… (R&G).

COPPERY EMERALD

Chlorostilbon russatus Pl. 97

Identification 8.4–9.1cm, bill 0.8–1.5cm. Basically metallic green, but reflecting very distinct golden, copper, reddish-copper and reddish-orange (depending on light), most apparent on top and back of head, wing-coverts, uppertail-coverts and forked tail; white thighs, feet black, bill black. Female has tail blunt, almost square, dull purple subterminal band on inner webs of all but central pair, and tiny white tips on outer rectrices; white postocular line, blackish mask, underparts white. Juvenile like female but white only on throat, underparts green.

Ssp. Monotypic (Co, Ve)

Habits Forages from low to mid levels in open areas. Flies swiftly and directly. Visits regularly, in trap-line fashion, a set of flowers that may be quite dispersed.
Status Uncommon and very local. Replaces Red-billed Emerald above 500–600m in Santa Marta range, Colombia.
Habitat Upper Tropical to Temperate Zones. Shrubbery or thickets at forest borders, planted fields with hedges or scattered trees. Humid, shrubby forest.
Voice No description found and no published recordings.

NARROW-TAILED EMERALD

Chlorostilbon stenurus Pl. 97

Identification 9.4–9.8cm, bill 1.8cm. Adult male metallic green, brighter and paler on forehead and from chin to belly, slightly olivaceous and duller on back, but tail bright and richer green, white thighs; feet and bill black. Female similar but tail has 2 central feathers green as male, the rest with a broad, dark blue subterminal band and white tips; buffy-greyish postocular line, dusky-brown mask, creamy buffy underparts. Juvenile similar to female but has top and back of head pale brown. Wingtips reach beyond tip of tail.

Ssp. *C. s. stenurus* (Ve, Co)

Habits Forages alone, at low to mid levels. A trap-liner that usually visits widespread flowers at heights of less than 4m, and specialises in erect corollas that open sideways or to the sky.
Status Data scarce.
Habitat Upper Tropical to Temperate Zones, 1,000–3,000m. On lower slopes, light humid and gallery forests, second growth, open areas with scrub. Cloud and elfin forests at higher elevations. Replaces Short-tailed Emerald above *c.*2,000 m.
Voice No description or published recordings. Mostly silent, possibly sings only in rainy season (D. Ascanio, pers. comm.).
Note Single record for Ecuador believed in error (R&G).

GREEN-TAILED EMERALD

Chlorostilbon alice Pl. 97

Identification 9.4cm, bill 1.8cm. Adult male almost all green except small patch of metallic orange at base of bill, forehead bright paler green, turquoise tone to wing-coverts, white thighs; feet and bill black. A presumed variant, collected in Monagas, is very coppery above with a maroon tail. Apparently a similar bird was collected at a different location (which we have not seen). Adult female has broad dark blue subterminal band on all but central pair of rectrices, and grey tips; grey postocular line, dusky brown mask and underparts brownish-grey. Juvenile male simlar but has green throat-sides to central breast.

Ssp. Monotypic (Ve)

Habits Forages alone, at lower and mid levels. Visits plants (Leguminosae, Ericaceae, Gesneriaceae, Rubiaceae) following trap-line. Hawks insects. Males fiercely defend feeding territory. Perches rather low, in a shady spot. Adapts to human presence.
Status Fairly common but seasonally local Venezuelan endemic.
Habitat Upper Tropical to Lower Subtropical Zones. Borders of humid and cloud forests (not interior), second growth, coffee and banana plantations, parks and gardens.
Voice Thin, soft, high chittering while foraging (Hilty).

SHORT-TAILED EMERALD

Chlorostilbon poortmani Pl. 97

Identification 9–9.4cm, bill 1.8cm. Adult male entirely green, including tail, brighter and purer green at front, slightly reflecting gold on upperparts. Adult female has perhaps slightly more golden reflections, a green forehead, white postocular line, dark brown mask, creamy grey underparts, dark blue tail with white tips except on central pair of rectrices, and slightly more forked than male. Immature male similar but blue on tail forms subterminal band, and has some green on body-sides and centre of throat. Juvenile like female but underparts cinnamon-buffy. Wingtips extend just beyond tail tip. Female has pale grey underparts. From female Coppery and Narrow-tailed Emeralds by blue in tail.

Ssp. *C. p. euchloris* (Co) larger, with more golden sheen
C. p. poortmani (E Co, W Ve) as described

Habits Feeds in flowering trees (*Inga*, *Erythrina*) and trap-lines shrubs with erect, non-pendulous flowers, usually at less than 4m. Flowers on trap-line route usually quite scattered and in open spots.
Status Uncommon in Colombia, uncommon to frequent in Venezuela.
Habitat Upper Tropical to Temperate Zones, to 2,400m. Borders and small clearings of humid and cloud forests, light woods, gallery forests or thickets by streams, mature second growth, fields with scattered trees and bushes, scrub, coffee plantations.
Voice No description found or published recordings. Possibly sings only in wet season.

Lepidopyga hummingbirds are medium-sized birds with metallic green upperparts and brilliant blue foreparts, they have longish, slightly decurved red and black bills.

SAPPHIRE-THROATED HUMMINGBIRD

Lepidopyga coeruleogularis Pl. 97

Identification 10.7cm, bill 1.8cm. Adult male all green except extensive frontal gorget of metallic turquoise; lower back with coppery reflections becoming more intense on central tail-feathers, rest of tail deep blue and deeply forked; bill long and very slightly curved, black above, red below. Female not so intensely coppery above, tail less deeply forked and has white tips; underparts all white.

Ssp. *L. c. confinis* (NW Co) as described
L. c. coelina (NE Co) throat intense electric blue, less bronzy above and paler green

Habits Usually forages alone, mostly at lower and mid levels, in bushes and shrubs of forest edges and semi-open sites, but may gather in canopy of flowering trees (Myrtaceae, Leguminosae).
Status Uncommon and local, more frequent towards coast and near mangroves.
Habitat Lower Tropical Zone. Semi-dry deciduous and partially open woods, edges of mangrove forest, woods near shores.
Voice No description found and no published recordings.

SAPPHIRE-BELLIED HUMMINGBIRD

Lepidopyga lilliae Pl. 97

Identification 11.2cm, bill 1.8cm. Adult male entirely metallic green above, brighter on forehead and face-sides, from throat to flanks purplish-blue, white thighs, undertail-coverts dark blue. Female and immature plumages unknown.

Ssp. Monotypic (Co)

Habits Forages alone, at all levels inside mangrove forest.
Status Critically Endangered. Very rare and local Colombian endemic. Effectively unknown.
Habitat Lower Tropical Zone. Mangrove swamps, rarely in coastal xerophytic scrub.
Voice No description found and no published recordings.

SHINING-GREEN HUMMINGBIRD

Lepidopyga goudoti Pl. 97

Identification 10.9cm, bill 1.8cm. Adult male almost entirely metallic green, tending to bronzy on lower rump, with very dark blue tail, deeply forked, and white thighs, bright emerald reflections on throat; feet black, bill black above, red below. Female similar but has white chin and white belly, less forked tail.

Ssp. *L. g. phaeochroa* (NW Ve) blue forehead and throat (not chin) to upper breast, white belly, less deeply forked tail
L. g. luminosa (N Co: coast) throat yellowish-emerald to gold, back and rump bronzy, uppertail-coverts coppery
L. g. goudoti (C Co) as described
L. g. zuliae (NW Ve) smaller, crown dark and bluish, reddish-coppery on long uppertail-coverts and central rectrices

Habits Forages alone at all levels and at variety of plants (*Heliconia*, *Lantana*, *Hibiscus*), but small groups may gather at *Samanea*, *Inga*, *Erythrina* and *Calliandra*, with frequent chases and bickering. Gleans insects and spiders from canopy and sallies to catch flies, mosquitoes. Moves seasonally, possibly following flowering stages.
Status Fairly common to common but local and seasonal.
Habitat Tropical Zone. Semi-dry deciduous or gallery forests, open woodland and second growth, xerophytic areas and thorny scrub, coffee plantation, gardens.
Voice Song a weak *tsee-dee* (H&B) or *twee-dee*, second note higher, like Green-bellied Hummingbird but shorter (Hilty).

Woodnymphs are a small group of intensely rich blue and bright green birds with deeply forked tails, and smaller, grey-fronted females. They all look very much alike, but are separated geographically.

VIOLET-CROWNED WOODNYMPH

Thalurania colombica Pl. 98

Identification Male 12cm, female 8.4cm; bill 2.3cm. Adult male has forehead deep blue, head-sides and nape green, chin to upper breast brilliant metallic pale green, mantle and neck-sides to breast, belly and flanks electric purplish-blue, lower back to rump green, upper- and undertail-coverts bright pale green, very deeply forked tail dark indigo-blue; thighs white; feet and straight bill black. Immature male has top of head to mantle, to breast and sides reddish-coppery, and green of lower back also coppery, belly and vent pale grey; tail less deeply forked than adult. Adult female smaller, all green above to central tail-feathers, with gold and bronzy reflections on nape and neck-sides; tail quite short and shallowly forked, dull dark blue with grey tips, chin to undertail-coverts brownish-grey.

Ssp. *T. c. colombica* (N Co: C Andes & Santa Marta, NW Ve) as described
T. c. rostrifera (SW Ve; Táchira) back all green, otherwise like adult *colombica*; immature male as adult but wing-coverts green, frontal gorget narrower, and less deep blue underparts with bronzy-brown centres and undertail-coverts fringed white

Habits Forages alone, mostly at lower and mid levels in shady, closed-canopy areas. Only occasionally visits or gathers at flowering trees (*Inga* and others), preferring flowering bushes, small trees, epiphytes and shrubbery (Acanthaceae, *Heliconia*, *Besleria*, Gesneriaceae, *Costus*, *Cornutia*, Ericaceae, *Hamelia*, Bromeliaceae, *Cephalis*, mistletoes). Picks insects and spiders by gleaning leaves, and by hawking in open spaces or sallying from a perch. Males quite fiercely territorial.
Status Common, even abundant, especially in lowlands and

foothills. Threatened by relentless deforestation.
Habitat Tropical to Lower Subtropical Zones. Humid and wet primary forests, both interior and at borders, overgrown clearings, mature second growth, coffee and cacao plantations, always in relatively dense vegetation.
Voice High, dry, fast *kip* or *kyip*, oft-repeated; aggressive note a dry, scratchy *chut-t-t* (Hilty).

FORK-TAILED WOODNYMPH
Thalurania furcata Pl. 98

Identification Male 11–12.7cm, female 9.6–10.9cm; bill 2–2.5cm. Adult male has entire head green, frontal gorget brilliant metallic green, nape and mantle to breast and underparts rich electric blue, undertail-coverts fringed pale blue; back to uppertail-coverts green, wing-coverts blue on shoulder but green lower; very deeply forked tail deep indigo-blue; white thighs, feet and straight bill that is slightly decurved at tip, black. Female smaller, all green above, tail darkening to black distally, with white tips; entire underparts grey.

Ssp. *T. f. fissilis* (SE Ve, W Gu) green above with scapulars and lesser wing-coverts blue, turquoise wash on flanks
T. f. furcata (E Ve, Guianas) as described
T. f. nigrofasciata (SE Co, extreme S Ve) green above with small strip of blue on scapulars, undertail-coverts grey
T. f. orenocensis (S Ve) only a small patch of blue on upper scapulars, otherwise all green above; duller blackish below with little hint of purple in the blue. Female is duller and darker below, no copper on back at all
T. f. refulgens (NE Ve) narrow strip of green on lower back to uppertail-coverts, deep turquoise blue on mid back
T. f. viridipectus (E Ec, E Co) green gorget much deeper, to breast, undertail-coverts fringed white.

Habits Forages alone, mostly at mid and lower levels. Catches flying insects and gleans aphids and spiders. Curious and bold, very aggressive to intruders in feeding territory. Perches exposed on tip of bare twig.
Status Uncommon in Ecuador, common in Venezuela, abundant in Suriname and French Guiana, fairly common in Guyana and Colombia.
Habitat Tropical to Lower Subtropical Zones. Borders and interior of humid and cloud forests, second growth, fields with scattered trees and bushes.
Voice Irregular series of 2–6 insect-like pulsing *sii-sii, sii-sii-sii-sii, sii-sii-sii* notes (Hilty).

GREEN-CROWNED WOODNYMPH
Thalurania fannyi Pl. 98

Identification Male 9.5–10.5cm, female 8.5–9cm; bill 2.1cm. Adult male has entire head green, forehead to crown and frontal gorget brilliant metallic green, narrow collar from nape to breast and underparts rich electric blue, undertail-coverts fringed white; back to uppertail-coverts green, wing-coverts turquoise on shoulder but green lower; deeply forked tail deep indigo-blue; white thighs, bill straight, and feet, black. Female smaller, green above and quite metallic on head, turquoise on wing-coverts, tail very dark blue, and less deeply forked than male; chin, face-sides and breast white, sides and underparts green, undertail-coverts fringed white.

Ssp. *T. f. fannyi* (W Co: Pacific slope) as described
T. f. hypochlora (W Ec) male has blue nuchal collar and breast-sides, rest of underparts green, undertail-coverts fringed white; female grey from chin to white-edged undertail-coverts; juvenile green above with olive forehead and crown, underparts olive-green with irregular white fringes
T. f. subtropicalis (WC Co) nape bronze, less violet on back, tail shorter and fork shallow; female paler grey
T. f. verticeps (SW Co: W Andes, NW Ec) like *fannyi* but back all green

Habits Forages alone, from lower level to subcanopy, in shady, closed-canopy areas. Visits flowering plants (*Inga*, Acanthaceae, *Heliconia*, *Besleria*, Gesneriaceae, *Costus*, *Cornutia*, Ericaceae, *Hamelia*, Bromeliaceae, *Cephalis*, mistletoes). Females glean insects and spiders from leaves. Males quite fiercely territorial at flowering bushes, and to pick insects they hawk or sally from perch.
Status Abundant in Colombia, uncommon in Ecuador, race *hypochlora* threatened by deforestation.
Habitat Tropical to Subtropical Zones. Humid forests, both interior and at borders, and overgrown clearings, mature second growth, coffee and cacao plantations, woody parks and gardens, always with shade.
Voice Mostly silent, sometimes weak *tsip* notes (R&G).

VIOLET-BELLIED HUMMINGBIRD
Damophila julie Pl. 98

Identification 9.4cm, bill 1.3cm. Male has entire head and upperparts to tail-coverts green, forehead and gorget bright metallic emerald-green, rest of underparts rich electric blue, thighs white; tail fairly short and rounded; bill, thin and very slightly curved, and feet black. Female all green above including head-sides, and also breast-sides and flanks, rest of underparts from chin to undertail-coverts grey; tail as male. Very much like almost any woodnymph, but distinctly smaller with a rounded tail.

Ssp. *D. j. feliciana* (W Ec) as described
D. j. julie (N Co) lighter and brighter

Habits Usually forages alone, mostly at lower and mid levels, but also in mixed flocks. Visits flowering bushes (Rubiaceae, Gesneriaceae, Ericaceae), and occasionally flowering trees (*Erythrina*, *Inga*). Hawks flying insects. Males establish feeding territories.
Status Uncommon in Ecuador, fairly common in Colombia, especially in lowlands and foothills.
Habitat Lower Tropical Zone. Humid forests, overgrown clearings and borders, second growth.
Voice Call insect-like, a sequence of hissing notes, *vieiei veii veii veii* (H&B). A thin series of high-pitched, trilled *prrreee* notes (R&G).

Males of the genus *Hylocharis* and closely related sapphires all have bright blue on their heads, and both sexes have red bills with tiny black tips, and shallowly forked tails.

RUFOUS-THROATED SAPPHIRE

Hylocharis sapphirina Pl. 98

Identification 10.9–11cm, bill 2cm. Adult male forehead to rump green, chin bright vermilion, throat rich blue, green to belly and flanks, thighs white; upper- and undertail-coverts and tail rich reddish-chestnut; bill red with tiny black tip, feet black. Female similar but chin orange, fading to cream white on flanks and belly, thighs white, tail-coverts and tail rufous, small white tips to tail on all but central rectrices. Juvenile similar but has green uppertail-coverts and tail, with golden flush to basal half of central retrices, broad subterminal bar across entire tail is slightly darker green, white tips to all but central pair; undertail-coverts cream white.

Ssp. Monotypic (E Ec, E Co, S Ve, Guianas)

Habits Forages at all levels, usually alone but gathers at blooming trees, with frequent chases and bickering over flowers, for it is always pugnacious over feeding territories. Hovers for nectar and hawks open spaces for wasps, beetles and other flying insects. Feeds at Bromeliaceae, Vochysiaceae. Seasonal movements probably connected to flowering seasons and food availability.

Status Very rare in Ecuador, local and uncommon in Colombia and Venezuela, uncommon in Guyana. Locally frequent in Suriname during dry season but scarce rest of year. Uncommon in French Guiana.

Habitat Lower Tropical Zone. Borders and clearings of humid forest and mangrove, tepui foothills, second growth and thickets, fields with bushes and tall trees, coffee plantations.

Voice A thin *zzeee*, repeated intermittently every few seconds. Also *swit, swee-tit, swee-tit, swee-su*, and a gravelly *ch-cht* (R&G).

BLUE-THROATED SAPPHIRE

Hylocharis eliciae Pl. 98

Identification 9–9.5cm, bill 1.8–2cm. Adult male green above, metallic forehead, face-sides and wing-coverts, deep orange uppertail-coverts, brown tail; full gorget is rich bright blue, underparts to belly and flanks green, vent, thighs to undertail-coverts white; bill bright red with black tip, feet black. Female similar but chin and throat white, regularly spotted blue, and white belly more extensive; bill red with black culmen, feet black.

Ssp. *H. e. earina* (extreme NW Co)

Habits Forages alone, in open, usually at lower levels. Visits plants (*Heliconia*, Bromeliaceae, *Stachytarpheta*, *Hamelia*, *Renealmia* and *Thalea*) and trees such as *Inga* and, especially, *Psidium*. Pugnacious over feeding territories, chasing intruders of same or other species. Perches in shady places, on lower branches, where males also sometimes gather to lek.

Status Uncommon to locally common.

Habitat Tropical Zone. Borders and clearings of humid forests, mangroves, swampy woodland, mature second growth, shady gardens.

Voice Song a variable sequence of high-pitched notes.

WHITE-CHINNED SAPPHIRE

Hylocharis cyanus Pl. 98

Identification 10.9–11.3cm, bill 2–2.3cm. Adult male appears to have entire front of head, from rear crown to upper breast rich purplish-blue, but chin is white; rest of head, back, wings and breast to undertail-coverts green; rump reflects orange, red to maroon and purple on longest uppertail-coverts, tail deep indigo, thighs white; eyes chestnut, bill bright red with tiny black tip, feet black. Female similar but lacks blue head, white chin more extensive, underparts buffy-grey and white on tarsi. Young male like female but has emergent blue spots on throat.

Ssp. *H. c. viridiventris* (N & E Co, W & S Ve, Guianas) as described

H. e. rostrata (E Ec) larger

Habits Forages at all levels, alone, but may gather in canopy of flowering *Inga* or *Erythrina* trees. Feeds in flowers by hovering at corollas, not by perching on them (Bromeliaceae, Malvaceae, Myrtaceae, Leguminosae, Loranthaceae, Rubiaceae, Rutaceae, Vochysiaceae). Picks flying insects (beetles, mosquitoes) and spiders among leaves. Males sing from high isolated twigs, and also gather to sing in wide 'circle' (lek?) of scattered perches in canopy.

Status Very rare in Ecuador, fairly common in Colombia, Venezuela and Guyana, and common in Suriname and French Guiana.

Habitat Tropical Zone. Borders and clearings of humid forests, canopy of *terra firme*, second growth and light woods, along streams, coffee, banana and cocoa plantations.

Voice Song fine, high-pitched chirps *tsee-tsee-tsee* (H&M) or incessant *zeit, zeit*… resembling an insect (H&B).

BLUE-HEADED SAPPHIRE

Hylocharis grayi Pl. 98

Identification 10.9cm, bill 2cm. Adult male has entire head except nape, rich purplish-blue, rest of body lustrous green, tail rich blue, thighs white; bill vermilion-red with black tip, feet black. Female has green top and sides of head and back, becoming olive-green, reflecting gold on basal half of tail, then broad subterminal band and white tips. Chin to undertail-coverts white with green spots on throat, breast-sides of breast and flanks.

Ssp. Monotypic (Ec, Co)

Habits Forages at all levels, and gathers at flowering trees. Territorial and aggressive at feeding spots. Picks insects by gleaning leaves and by hawking for flying species.

Status Rare in Ecuador. In Colombia, local and erratic due to seasonal movements.

Habitat Upper Tropical to Subtropical Zones. Dry areas,

planted fields, xerophytic woodland and scrub of rainshadow valleys on Pacific slope of Andes.
Voice Regularly repeated *chu-we-eee* chip notes (H&B).

HUMBOLDT'S SAPPHIRE
Hylocharis humboldtii Pl. 98

Identification 12–12.6cm, bill 2–2.1cm. Male has entire hood deep purple-blue; mantle to lower back and breast to flanks metallic green, rump orange to coppery, uppertail-coverts with some reddish glints, tail coppery-orange; lower belly and vent, thighs white, undertail-coverts orange with white fringes; bill vermilion with black tip, feet black. Female all green from forehead to lower back, rump and tail as male; chin to vent grey, white on thighs, undertail-coverts greyish-buff with white fringes; head has metallic turquoise spots on forehead and crown, and scattered on throat, breast and sides. Immature male like female but has rich blue spots instead of turquoise. Juvenile is like dull, slightly more olivaceous female without turquoise.

Ssp. Monotypic (Ec, Co)

Habits Little known. Forages alone, visiting flowers including *Heliconia* and *Pelliciera rhizophora*, which appears to be a favourite, and others.
Status Very rare in Ecuador, threatened by loss of mangrove. In Colombia very local.
Habitat Tropical Zone. Borders of mangroves, humid forests and mature second growth on or near Pacific coast.
Voice No description found and no published recordings.
Note Formerly considered a subspecies of Blue-headed Sapphire.

GOLDEN-TAILED SAPPHIRE
Chrysuronia oenone Pl. 98

Identification 11.4cm, bill 2cm. Adult male almost entirely metallic green but has face (forecrown to ear-coverts to upper throat) rich metallic blue, central belly to undertail-coverts white, tail deep greenish-blue; bill vermilion with black tip, feet black. Female entirely green above, including tail, all white below.

Ssp. *C. o. longirostris* (E & C Co) bill averages slightly longer
C. o. oenone (E & C Ec, SE Co, N & W Ve, Tr) as described

Habits Solitary, visits flowers at all levels, but mostly in canopy, where may gather at flowering trees. Breeds in rainy season, nests placed on high branches. Migrations involving hundreds, from north to south slope of Venezuelan coastal mountains, recorded in Henri Pittier National Park (M. Lentino).
Status Locally common to rare in Ecuador, locally fairly common in Colombia and Venazuela.
Habitat Tropical to Lower Subtropical Zones. Humid and cloud forests, second growth, lighter woodland and gallery forest, coffee, banana and cocoa plantations, fields with scattered bushes or trees, gardens.
Voice Song described as 2 squeaky notes, repeated steadily (H&B).
Note Race *longirostris* is of doubtful validity.

RUFOUS-CHEEKED HUMMINGBIRD
Goethalsia bella Pl. 99

Identification 10.2cm, bill 1.3cm. Forehead, lores to chin orange, top of head to uppertail-coverts and underparts to belly and flanks metallic green, white thighs and undertail-coverts; patch in middle of greater wing-coverts orange-cinnamon; tail also orange-cinnamon with dark brown central rectrices reflecting green, and dark brown tips to all feathers; bill straight, imperceptibly decurved at tip, feet grey. Female green above from forehead, and lacks orange on wing; underparts orange-cinnamon from chin to breast and sides, but paler and white by vent and thighs.

Ssp. Monotypic (extreme NW Co)

Habits Poorly known. Forages alone at lower to mid levels in forest interior. Visits variety of plants, including woody bushes such as Rubiaceae and Ericaceae.
Status Uncommon, slightly more frequent at higher elevations. Very small range.
Habitat Upper Tropical to Subtropical Zones. Humid forests on montane slopes.
Voice No description found and no published recordings.

VIOLET-CAPPED HUMMINGBIRD
Goldmania violiceps Pl. 98

Identification 10.4cm, bill 1.8cm. Adult male rich metallic green with violaceous electric blue cap; thighs and undertail-coverts white, tail coppery-red; bill deep red with black tip, feet black. Female lacks blue cap and tail only basally coppery-red; entire underparts white, lightly spotted pale green from sides of throat to flanks.

Ssp. Monotypic (NW Co)

Habits Poorly known. Solitary in lower levels and dense, shady haunts. Visits flowers of low shrubs (*Salvia*, *Palicourea*, *Psamisia* and *Pachystachys*).
Status Fairly frequent in small range (from Panama to extreme north-west Colombia).
Habitat Upper Tropical Zone. Humid forests of foothills and lower slopes, both interior and at borders, as well as overgrown clearings.
Voice Males sing a fast, low-pitched series of chip notes.

> Goldenthroats are larger hummingbirds with fairly long bills slightly decurved at the ends, rounded tails; they inhabit fairly open areas.

TEPUI GOLDENTHROAT
Polytmus milleri Pl. 99

Identification 12.5cm, bill 2.5cm. Adult male all green above, somewhat olive-green head to rump, increasingly coppery to reddish on tail-coverts, tail rich bottle green with white tips to all but central pair of rectrices; throat white with green spots, breast to belly green with white fringes, white vent and thighs, undertail-coverts green with broad white fringes, undertail green with bold white tips to feathers; bill gently decurved, and feet black. Female is whiter below and browner above.

Ssp. Monotypic (Ve, Gu)

Habits Solitary forager at variety of low bushes and shrubs (Myrtaceae, bromeliads, Ericaceae and Gesneriaceae). Hawks for insects in open spaces and also gleans tiny spiders from leaves and rocky surfaces.

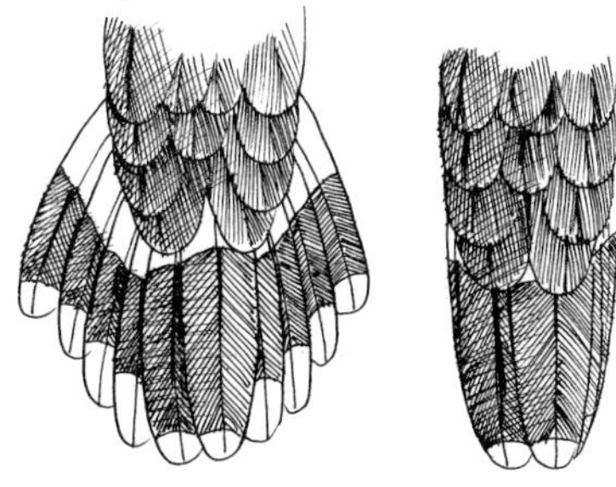

Tail of Tepui Goldenthroat showing distinctive white base when open, which is concealed when tail is folded

Status Locally fairly frequent. Endemic to Pantepui, with sight record in Guyana (Barnett *et al.* 2002).

Habitat Subtropical Zone. Borders of high-elevation savanna with bushes.

Voice Series of loud, intermittent, *tizzie* notes whilst foraging (Hilty).

WHITE-TAILED GOLDENTHROAT

Polytmus guainumbi Pl. 99

Identification 11.5–12.8cm, bill 2.5–2.6cm. Adult male pastel green from forehead to lower back where orange then cinnamon to rufous on uppertail-coverts, tail green with white fringes to outermost pair, varying with sex and age (see plate); white postocular line, ear-coverts brownish, white malar line, green underparts, white vent and thighs, undertail-coverts green with broad white fringes, undertail almost all white (appears all white when closed, but is actually outer 3 pairs) with small amount of green at base of inner webs; bill decurved, bright red with black tip. Female does not have white base to rectrices; more white around green throat and breast, belly and flanks warm buffy, much paler on undertail-coverts, and white vent and thighs. Juvenile male like female but with denser green throat that continues as broad band to mid belly. Juvenile female rich ochraceous-buffy from chin to belly and flanks, rest white.

Ssp. *P. g. andinus* (E Co) more white on inner rectrices
P. g. guainumbi (Ve, Guianas, Tr) as described

Habits Forages alone, mostly low, hovering at small flowers and gleaning insects and spiders in bushes and tall grasses. Feeds at *Heliconia* stands, in Leguminosae, Rubiaceae, Malvaceae, and gardens, visiting *Lagerstroemia* and *Russelia*. May (ffrench) or may not (H&B) feed at flowering trees.

Status Locally fairly common to common, even abundant on mainland, but uncommon and local on Trinidad and in French Guiana.

Juvenile White-tailed Goldenthroat (left) just showing first spots of emerald on throat; immature (right), with full bib; intermediate (centre); adult (not shown) has entire breast green

Habitat Lower Tropical Zone. Open savanna with thickets or bushes, especially in wet grassland or marshes, or near streams, borders of humid and gallery forests, second growth, tepui foothills.

Voice A dry *tsip-tsip* in flight or sequence of 3 squeaky notes from perch atop shrub (ffrench). Fast series of loud, excited *spit* notes (Hilty).

Note Name *andinus* thought preoccupied and renamed *doctus*, but unjustified and returned to *andinus* by Schuchmann (1999), accepted by Dickinson (2003).

GREEN-TAILED GOLDENTHROAT

Polytmus theresiae Pl. 99

Identification 10.6–10.9cm, bill 2cm. Adult male rich green all over, metallic and brilliant from chin to breast, fading on sides, and pure emerald on undertail-coverts, pale gold reflections on back; white thighs; bill reddish-pink with black culmen, feet black. Female has white loral spot and paler chin, belly and flanks have white fringes, vent and thighs white, undertail-coverts green with broad white fringes; undertail green with white tips to outer 3 pairs.

Ssp. *P. t. leucorrhous* (S Co, S Ve, Gu, Su) significantly more gold reflections on mantle to rump, and brighter green throat- and breast-sides; vent white, undertail-coverts green with broad white fringes; female has undertail-coverts entirely white.
P. t. theresiae (E Ve, Guianas) as described

Habits Solitary at low to mid levels, partial to flowers of Melastomataceae (*Rynchanthera*, *Tibouchina*). Follows trap-line route and males sometimes aggressive at certain groups of flowers.

Status Very rare in Ecuador, situation unclear in Colombia, abundant locally in Venezuela. Fairly common in Guyana, common in Suriname and French Guiana,

Habitat Lower tropical Zone. Savanna, fields with scattered bushes and forest edges.

Voice Repeats same *ting* note 10+ times, or sometimes gives 2-note *twit-twit* (H&B).

Note Race *theresiae* collected in Orinoco Delta, Venezuela, by Lentino (2001).

Leucippus are a small group of delicately pastel-coloured hummingbirds, with long, gently-curved bills and white spots behind eyes. Two occur in dry and xerophytic areas, the other an is an Amazon river-island specialist.

BUFFY HUMMINGBIRD

Leucippus fallax Pl. 99

Identification 10.9–11.3cm, bill 2–2.3cm. Pale grey head, bottle green back with pale grey fringes (scaling from lower back to uppertail-coverts), tail darker green with whitish tips to outer rectrices; chin to breast warm cinnamon-buff, belly and flanks to undertail-coverts pure white; bill black above, pink below, feet black.

Ssp. *L. f. cervina* (NE Co: coast, NW Ve) pastel brown head, leaf-green above, becoming grey on uppertail-coverts with pale grey fringes, tail uniform dark green; breast pastel ochre, belly to undertail-coverts pale ochraceous white

L. f. fallax (NC Ve) breast more intensely coloured, more bluish-green above, head darker grey

L. f. richmondi (Ve: NE, Margarita and Tortuga Is.) paler and more pastel grey head, more yellowish-green back with pale yellowish-green reflections on back and wing-coverts, rump and uppertail-coverts uniform grey, tail with white tips to outer rectrices, breast like *cervina* but warmer, belly and below pure white

Habits Solitary, visits flowers of small trees, bushes and cacti (*Agave*, *Opuntia*, *Melocactus*, *Hibiscus*, *Lemairocereus*).
Status Seasonally common when *Agave* flowering. Locally very common in Colombia (Guajira Peninsula).
Habitat Lower Tropical Zone. Xerophytic areas, thorn scrub, borders of mangroves, gardens.
Voice Variety of notes, combinations and variation. Males sing in groups (Hilty).
Note Considered monotypic by Züchner (1999) but series in COP shows clear racial differences.

TUMBES HUMMINGBIRD

Leucippus baeri Pl. 99

Identification 12.3–12.9cm, bill 1.8–1.9cm. Soft pastel green from forehead to tail, slightly darker on tail which has brownish subterminal band and pale tips, all upperparts have subtle grey fringes; from chin to breast and sides pale greyish-cinnamon, greyer on sides, rest of underparts white; bill dusky, feet black.

Ssp. Monotypic (Ec)

Habits Poorly known. Solitary at desert bushes and flowering cacti. Apparently rarely seen at flowering trees (R&G).
Status Uncommon in Ecuador.
Habitat Lower Tropical Zone. Dry woods or xerophytic scrub of coastal deserts and deciduous forests in foothills.
Voice No description found and no published recordings.

OLIVE-SPOTTED HUMMINGBIRD

Leucippus chlorocercus Pl. 99

Identification 10.7cm, bill 1.8cm. Pale olivaceous-green from forehead to tail, rather bronzy-brown on head, paler on rump, all feathers with subtle pale grey fringes, tail has brownish subterminal band and pale tips; chin to undertail-coverts white with bronzy-green spots on throat- and breast-sides; bill blackish, feet black.

Ssp. Monotypic (NE Ec, SE Co)

Habits Forages alone, hovering at small flowers at all heights. Feeds at Malvaceae, Rubiaceae, bromeliads, Leguminosae, Rutaceae, Myrtaceae, Bombacaceae, Loranthaceae. Defends feeding spot from others.
Status Uncommon in Ecuador, locally common in south-east Colombia.
Habitat Lower Tropical Zone. Dense vine-laden thickets and woodland, and more open early second growth on islands of Amazon basin.
Voice Series of 4–7 sharp, high, *yseeyip* notes (R&G).

MANY-SPOTTED HUMMINGBIRD

Taphrospilus hypostictus Pl. 99

Identification 10.5–11.4cm, bill 2.4cm. Male is malachite green from forehead to tail, which has narrow dark subterminal band and pale, almost yellowish tips, underparts entirely green but all feathers clearly fringed white, producing heavily scaled effect, white thighs; bill black above, reddish-pink below, feet grey. Female similar but belly and flanks white. Juvenile like female but has top of head dull orange-green and bill is only pink at base of lower mandible.

Ssp. *T. h. hypostictus* (E Ec, S Co)

Habits Solitary at low to mid heights. Visits flowers of trees, vines, shrubs and terrestrial bromeliads (*Inga*, *Passiflora*, *Pitcarnia*, *Centropogon*, *Palicourea*). Hawks for insects in clearings or over streams.
Status Uncommon in Ecuador and poorly known. Recently discovered on the upper rio Yurayaco in southern Colombia (Cordóba-Cordóba & Echeverry-Galvis 2006).
Habitat Upper Tropical Zone. Interior of humid forests on montane slopes, especially around densely wooded ravines.
Voice No description found and no published recordings.
Note Returned to genus *Leucippus* by Schuchmann (1999).

Amazilia hummingbirds are smallish to medium-sized, invariably green above, fairly metallic, and many have metallic blue on head and or throat, others coppery or orange reflections on the back, and females are similar, usually distinguished by white on front. Generally they inhabit semi-open country at lower elevations, and the few highland species are seldom found inside forest. They tend to forage solo, but will gather in crowns of trees in full blossom, where the more territorial males attempt to maintian a private feeding domain by chasing and bickering with others.

WHITE-CHESTED EMERALD

Amazilia chionopectus Pl. 99

Identification 10.5–11.4cm, bill 2.4cm. Essentially metallic green above with bronze reflections on lower back to tail; birds fall into 2 groups, those that are malachite green with subtle gold reflections, and coppery on nape grading to coppery-red on tail. Tail has a blackish or purplish-brown bar on the outer rectrice about halfway. Underparts pure white; bill straight and black, feet black. Juvenile like adult but more bronze and coppery, especially on head and nape, and lower mandible chestnut-brown.

Ssp. *A. c. chionopectus* (E Ve, Gu, Su, Tr) as described
A. c. orienticola (FG) darker, more bronze underparts
A. c. whitelyi (S Gu) head metallic green, rest of upperparts bronze-green, slightly golden on rump and uppertail-coverts, tail bronze with subterminal blackish bar on outermost rectrices; throat to abdomen pure white with golden- green flanks, undertail-coverts white with pale grey centres.

Habits Solitary. Visits flowers at all levels, from blooming trees (*Erythrina*, *Inga*, *Samanea*, *Calliandra*) to bushes and flowering grasses. Searches for insects in foliage, clicking bill softly as it flies.

Status On mainland, fairly common in west of range (eastern Venezuela and Guyana) to rare in east (Suriname and French Guiana). Common and widespread on Trinidad.

Habitat Lower Tropical Zone. Humid, deciduous and gallery forests, second growth, agricultural fields with hedges and bushes, savannas with scrub or bushes, river borders, coastal woods and scrub.

Voice Variable sequence of raspy notes, including *tche, tchu-tche-tche-tch* (ffrench) and *diidel-ii-didel-ii-didel-ii* (P&MdS). Gathers to sing in small groups.

Notes Treated as *Agytria brevirostris* (Weller 1999, Dickinson 2003), apparently on the basis of Bangs & Penard (1918) who claimed that Lesson's description (1829) of *Argytrina brevirostris* is actually *chionopectus*, making its correct name *brevirostris*. Peters (1945) explicitly rejected Bangs & Penard's conclusion, and retained *brevirostris* under *Amazilia versicolor*, its first use. The illustration in Lesson is impossible to identify with certainty but could be either a juvenile *chionopectus* or female *versicolor*. The description mentions that the bill is black above and white below, with a black tip, and the tail brownish-purple. It is worth repeating that *chionopectus* has an all-black bill, whilst juvenile *chionopectus* has bill black above and chestnut-brown below. *A. v. versicolor* has bill black above and pink or flesh below with a back tip, and tends to fade in old specimens. Race *whitelyi* was described by Boucard in 1883, then again along with *chionopectus* by Boucard (1893–95) but the differences are far from obvious, as birds recalling *whitelyi* are available within a large series of Venezuelan *chionopectus*. We have only been able to examine digital photographs of *whitelyi*. It seems to be geographically separate from *chionopectus*, being restricted to the Anuai Mts., it is greener and has white undertail-coverts with narrow grey centres. We feel that it is an error to discard *whitelyi* until more field data become available and specimens are compared. In any case, the enigma of 2 morphic groups of *chionopectus* must be solved as well.

VERSICOLOURED EMERALD

Amazilia versicolor Pl. 99

Identification 10.4-10.9cm, bill 1.4-1.5cm. Essentially dark green from forehead to tail with turquoise to pale green reflections, their density varying with age and location. Full adult rich blue on head to turquoise on neck- and breast-sides, chin to undertail-coverts pure white (note that green on body-sides extends towards centre of lower breast, before receding to flanks, which is a diagnostic character at all ages). Juvenile has far less blue on head, with irregular turquoise spots.

Ssp. *A. v. hollandi* (S Ve) as described; metallic blue on head and breast-sides of older male
A. v. millerii (E Co, Ve) metallic, bright pale green on head and breast-sides of older male; juvenile more lustrous coppery above, reflecting bronze and reddish gold on rump and uppertail-coverts, ear-coverts slightly metallic green

Habits Solitary forager that visits flowers and gleans insects and small spiders at all levels. Flying insects taken by hawking. Feeds at wide variety of plants, especially those with flat flowers (bromeliads, cacti, Asteraceae, Longoniaceae, Verbenaceae, Bombaceae, *Passiflora*, Labiataceae, *Heliconia*).

Status Uncommon in Colombia, locally frequent in Venezuela (especially *millerii*), insufficiently known in Guyana.

Habitat Lower Tropical Zone. Borders of humid and cloud forests, second growth, gallery and light deciduous forests, savannas with patches of bushes or woodland.

Voice Sequences of whistles and a shrill *che-che-che-che-fii* phrase or *trrri* notes (H&B).

Note Variation in coloration within races is due to age and sex differences, and combined with inadequate or inaccurate illustrations elsewhere has caused much confusion. Races from Brazil are rather different from those in our region.

GLITTERING-THROATED EMERALD

Amazilia fimbriata Pl. 99

Identification 9.8–13cm, bill 1.8–2cm. Dark green from forehead to rump where becomes reddish with golden reflections, and tail dark brown with both greenish fringes and reddish centres, chin to breast, sides and flanks metallic bright green, paler on flanks; white below, starting as a vertical line in middle of lower breast and broadening in an inverted V shape; bill black above, red below, feet black.

Ssp. *A. f. fimbriata* (S Ve) as described
A. f. obscuricauda (Ve: west Llanos) slightly darker; face and breast have blue reflections but centre of breast bows lower in centre, and white of belly more V-shaped or possibly Y-shaped
A. f. apicalis (E Co) like *fimbriata* but bill much longer
A. f. elegantissima (NE Co, N Ve) uppertail-coverts coppery to purple

A. f. fluviatilis (SE Co, E Ec) bright green below extends further and is slightly turquoise, bill longer
A. f. maculicauda (Guianas) inseparable from *fimbriata*

Habits Forages alone, mostly at low and mid levels. Visits flowering bushes or small trees and picks insects from air and foliage, often in gardens. Small groups may gather at feeding spots. Feeds at *Inga, Lantana, Stachytarpheta, Heliconia* and bromeliads. Perches atop bushes or dead twigs in shady spots.
Status Common and widespread throughout range.
Habitat Lower Tropical Zone. Semi-open areas with scattered trees and bushes, wooded patches and gallery forest, xerophytic areas and thorn scrub, mangroves, second growth, planted fields, coffee plantations, suburbs, gardens and parks.
Voice A soft *dz-dz* 'as of pebbles struck together' (Snyder 1966) at dawn, and a loud *piip-piip* in flight (P&MdS).
Note Race *maculicauda* synonymised under *fimbriata* by Weller (1999).

TÁCHIRA EMERALD *Amazilia distans* Pl. 99

Identification 9.5cm, bill 1.6cm. Turquoise forehead then green to rump, becoming dark maroon fringed dark green; chin white with rich blue spots, throat deep purplish royal blue, breast and sides metallic green, rest of underparts white, with pale grey centres to flanks feathers, thighs white; bill very slightly curved, black above, red below, feet grey. Take great care in comparing and noting plumage characteristics. Closest is juvenile and immature male Golden-tailed Sapphire, but present species is white below, whereas young *C. oenone* is grey with spots of green. Look for spots of blue on nape, present in young *C. oenone* but absent on *A. distans*. These discriminators are difficult to see in the field.

Ssp. Monotypic (SW Ve)

Habits Unknown.
Status Venezuelan endemic. Possibly very rare: described from single male collected in 1958. Several reports in recent years (P. Alden, *in litt.*, with M. Gochfeld & M. Kleinbaum, north side of Tamá National Park, in 1964 and 1978; B. Whitney, pers. comm. 1988; D. Cooper, north-east side of Tamá National Park in 1996). It has been suggested (Graves 1998, Weller & Schuchmann 1998) that Táchira Emerald is a hybrid between White-chinned Sapphire and Glittering-throated Emerald. However, neither of these occur in the area, and no collecting or scientific exploration has been done in remote Burgua since the species was collected, nor in the surrounding area, which remains to this day inaccessible by motor vehicle. We maintain *A. distans* in the absence of further fieldwork.
Habitat Tropical Zone. Humid forests.
Voice No description found and no published recordings.

SAPPHIRE-SPANGLED EMERALD
Amazilia lactea Pl. 99

Identification 8–11cm, bill 2cm. Forehead to tail dark green, chin and throat rich purplish-blue with fine pale grey fringes and a few turquoise feathers on neck-sides; body-sides and flanks green, centre of lower breast and belly and undertail-coverts pure white; bill black above, red below, feet grey. In poor light, like all metallic and iridescent hummingbirds, the blue throat can look dull grey. Immature has more obvious pale fringes to blue throat, and green sides do not reach flanks.

Ssp. *A. l. zimmeri* (S Ve: Auyán-tepui & Cerro Perro) as described
A. l. bartletti (E Ec?) bill longer, centre of lower breast and belly green

Habits Forages alone, at all levels, and males defend feeding territory from intruders of same or other species. Takes nectar from wide variety of plant and tree species, including *Heliconia* and bromeliads, Leguminosae, Rubiaceae.
Status Subspecies endemic to Venezuela is frequent to uncommon and very local (3 separate localities). Uncertain in Ecuador, where single sight record in 1995.
Habitat Tropical Zone. Wet to humid forests of tepui slopes, gallery forests.
Voice No description found and no published recordings.

BLUE-CHESTED HUMMINGBIRD
Amazilia amabilis Pl. 100

Identification 8-9cm, bill 1.8cm. Adult male glittering green above with metallic turquoise forehead and crown, tail brown and slightly forked; sides of face and neck, chin and throat metallic bright green; blue breast patch (from lower throat) is comparatively large, some pale greenish on body-sides and grey undertail-coverts fringed white, belly and vent buffy-grey; bill yellowish below, black above. Female green above, slightly bronzy on uppertail-coverts, chin to vent white, spotted on throat- and breast-sides turquoise green, undertail-coverts buffy-grey with white fringes.

Ssp. *A. a. amabilis* (W Ec, W Co)

Habits Solitary forager, seeks nectar and gleans for insects mostly at lower levels, but often gathers at blooming trees, with much bickering over feeding spots. Males gather in loose leks to sing, sometimes pursuing each other aggressively.
Status Uncommon to rare in Ecuador, fairly common in Colombia.
Habitat Lower Tropical Zone. Borders of humid and wet forests, mature second growth, stands of bushes or shrubby edges of fields.
Voice Breeds in drier months, when males form loose congregations to sing, a steady series of squeaky *psee-psee-psee* or *tsit-tsit-tsit* notes (R&G).

PURPLE-CHESTED HUMMINGBIRD
Amazilia rosenbergi Pl. 100

Identification 8-9cm, bill 1.8cm. Male almost entirely shiny green, metallic on sides of head, lower back and wing-coverts, centre of tail green, rest dark indigo; neat breast patch deep purplish-blue, vent and undertail-coverts white; bill black above, pink below, feet dusky. Female similar but tail has white tips, chin to lower breast and sides bright green, the feathers with white fringes, rest of underparts white.

Ssp. Monotypic (Ec, Co)

Habits Solitary, feeds by trap-lining flowers of Ericaceae, Loranthaceae, Gesneriaceae, *Costus* and *Heliconia*.
Status Uncommon in Ecuador and in Colombia.
Habitat Lower Tropical Zone to 200m. Borders and overgrown clearings of wet forests and mature second growth in coastal lowlands.
Voice Male sings sequence of 3 high, brisk notes, *tsip-tsu-tsrit* (R&G). Males not known to gather in singing congregations.

ANDEAN EMERALD

Amazilia franciae Pl. 100

Identification 9.1cm, bill 2.3cm. Green from forehead to rump, uppertail-coverts coppery, tail bronzy; chin to undertail-coverts white, with some green spotting on breast-sides; bill black above, red below, feet dusky. Female similar. From Indigo-capped Hummingbird by brighter green and coppery uppertail-coverts and tail.

Ssp. *A. f. viridiceps* (SW Co, W Ec) as described; green crown and shorter tail
A. f. franciae (Co: Andes) male has forehead to rear crown violet-blue

Habits Follows trap-line route between widely scattered flowers at all levels, especially in mid-storey and canopy. Usually feeds alone, but small, 'argumentative' groups gather at flowering trees, where frequently engages in chases.
Status Uncommon to rare in Ecuador, fairly common at some localities in Colombia.
Habitat Upper Tropical to Subtropical Zones. Borders, overgrown clearings of humid and wet forests, mature second growth, mostly on upper slopes.
Voice Males often sing from tip of high bare branch. Song a loud sequence of squeaky notes, reminiscent of a Bananaquit *Coereba flaveola*.

PLAIN-BELLIED EMERALD

Amazilia leucogaster Pl. 100

Identification 10cm, bill 2.3cm. Adult male shiny green from forehead to tail, with bronzy to coppery reflections on uppertail-coverts and tail; underparts white with only slight green spotting on breast-sides; bill slightly decurved at tip, black above, red below. Female has outer tail-feathers tipped grey.

Ssp. *A. l. leucogaster* (Ve, Guianas)

Habits Forages at all levels, in bushes and small trees (*Heliconia*, bromeliads, Leguminosae, *Verbena*, *Passiflora*, *Hibiscus*, Malvaceae, bananas, Anacardiaceae) and canopy of blooming coffee-shade trees (*Erythrina*).
Status Fairly common in Guyana, common in Suriname and French Guiana.
Habitat Lower Tropical Zone. Mangrove, humid, partially open coastal woodland, coffee and banana plantations, second growth, parks and gardens; borders and thickets.
Voice Fine series of twitters, the central notes declining slightly, the whole immediately repeated several times, *tswit-tswit tsetsetsetsetsetsetsetsetsetsetset tsit tsit ti'ti't* (from recording by J.-H. Ribot).

INDIGO-CAPPED HUMMINGBIRD

Amazilia cyanifrons Pl. 100

Identification 9.1cm, bill 1.8cm. Generally metallic green, distinguished by metallic blue top of head, brightest on forehead and crown; rump and short uppertail-coverts golden-coppery, long uppertail-coverts and tail deep blue, white tibial feathers and greyish-green undertail-coverts broadly fringed white. Female distinctly paler and more turquoise on head; bill slender, basally flesh/pink, distal two-thirds blackish. Juvenile like slightly duller female, with greyish belly. From Andean Emerald by blue tail and darkish undertail-coverts.

Ssp. *A. c. cyanifrons* (N & C Co)

Habits Forages alone and is very territorial and aggressive, but gathers in canopy of flowering *Inga* or *Erythrina*. Feeds in bromeliads and plants (*Eugenia*, *Hamelia*).
Status Very uncommon to locally common in Colombia.
Habitat Upper Tropical to Subtropical Zones. Wet to dry and partially open areas, light woodland and second growth, hedges, overgrown clearings, forest edge, gardens and fields with shrubs or bushes.
Voice No description found and no published recordings.

STEELY-VENTED HUMMINGBIRD

Amazilia saucerrottei Pl. 100

Identification 8.9–9cm, bill 1.8cm. Almost entirely metallic dark green with white vent and thighs, undertail-coverts dark blue fringed white; rump finely and variably washed purple, short uppertail-coverts coppery-golden, long uppertail-coverts violet-blue, tail darker blue; bill black above, red below, feet black. Female similar but has some white scaling on throat.

Ssp. *A. s. braccata* (W Ve) 10 cm; as described
A. s. saucerrottei (W Co) uppertail-coverts blue-black, rest of back green
A. s. warscewiczi (Co: Andes, NW Ve) smaller, more yellowish above and below makes it a brighter green, uppertail-coverts purple-blue

Habits Forages at all levels, but mostly lower, where it fiercely disputes feeding spots. Visits flowering coffee-shade trees (*Inga*, *Erythrina*)
Status Fairly common in Colombia and Venezuela. Can be seasonally abundant at some localities.
Habitat Tropical to Temperate Zones. Humid forests and clearings, second growth and coffee plantations. Also forest borders and cultivated fields in drier areas.
Voice Song a series of agitated *chit* notes, sometimes ending in a trill, and soft peep notes (Hilty).

COPPER-RUMPED HUMMINGBIRD

Amazilia tobaci Pl. 100

Identification 8–9.5cm, bill 1.9–2cm. Metallic green with coppery reflections on lower back to uppertail-coverts, tail cobalt-blue, reflecting purple or violet; white vent and rear flanks, undertail-coverts rufous-orange; bill black above, pink below with black tip. Subspecies rather variable in size and upperparts coloration (see plate).

Ssp. *A. t. monticola* (NW Ve) all green with some reddish-copper in long uppertail-coverts and undertail-coverts green with orange fringes
A. t. feliciae (Ve: northern range) golden-bronze reflections from back of head to rump, slightly more reddish on uppertail-coverts, undertail-coverts orange with white fringes
A. t. caudata (NE Ve) reddish-coppery reflections on all upperparts, less on nape, uppertail-coverts blue with bronzy fringes; undertail-coverts reddish-orange; female smaller with undertail-coverts fringed white
A. t. caurensis (SE Ve) coppery on back and rump, purple uppertail-coverts; undertail-coverts grey
A. t. aliciae (Ve: Margarita I.) much larger, more reddish-coppery above, small white streaks on chin and upper throat, undertail-coverts cinnamon-rufous
A. t. erythronotus (Tr) fairly small; coppery on back and rump but not head, uppertail-coverts purple, undertail-coverts orange
A. t. tobaci (To) large; coppery on rump, maroon on uppertail-coverts

Habits Energetic and feisty, adapts to modified habitats. Forages alone, usually within feeding territory ferociously defended from any bird species that comes near by in kamikaze attacks, but small groups may gather at tree in bloom. Feeds at many flowering trees and bushes (*Erythrina*, *Inga*, *Samanea*, *Calliandra*, *Salvia*, *Lantana*), and seeks small insects in leaves at all levels.
Status Common and widespread.
Habitat Tropical to Lower Subtropical Zones. Humid forests and open areas with trees and bushes, second growth, agricultural areas, parks and gardens.
Voice A wistful, melodious 3-note phrase, popularly described as *erica*, accented on last note, and twitters rapidly in flight, especially in territorial disputes.

COPPER-TAILED HUMMINGBIRD

Amazilia cupreicauda Pl. 100

Identification 10cm, bill 1.5–1.8cm. Head to mantle and underparts to belly and flanks metallic green, with a few white spots on chin; lower back and rump coppery, particularly so on uppertail-coverts and tail; rear flanks, vent and thighs white, undertail-coverts cinnamon; bill black above, red below, feet grey. Female has some white fringes on chin and upper throat. Juvenile dull greenish-olive with metallic green feathers scattered irregularly, maroon rump and uppertail-coverts, tail rather dull maroon, cinnamon undertail-coverts.

Ssp. *A. c. cupreicauda* (SE Ve, W Gu, S Su) as described
A. c. duidae (S Ve) lower back and tail more coppery-red, tail deep blue to violet-blue, intermediate between *cupreicauda* and *laireti*
A. c. laireti (S Ve) richer green, rump to central tail-feathers deep copper-red

Habits Forages alone at blooming shrubs and vines. Often hawks for tiny insects at bromeliads.
Status Frequent to locally common in Venezuela but appears seasonally at many localities. Situation uncertain in Guyana. Rare in Suriname.
Habitat Humid forest and forest borders.
Voice No description found, but a recording is listed in the Discography.
Note Formerly considered a subspecies of Green-bellied Hummingbird *A. viridigaster* (MdS&P).

GREEN-BELLIED HUMMINGBIRD

Amazilia viridigaster Pl. 100

Identification 10.9–11.2cm, bill 1.5–1.8cm. Rich metallic green from forehead to rump and chin to belly, uppertail-coverts purplish-blue with purple/violet fringes, tail rich royal blue, vent white, undertail-coverts orange-rufous; bill black above, red below with lack tip. Female whiter on throat and has paler uppertail-coverts.

Ssp. *A. v. viridigaster* (Ve, Co: E Andes) as described
A. v. iodura (Ve: Táchira) tail-coverts and tail purple with copper fringes

Habits Solitary, visits flowers at all levels. In Andes often at blooming coffee-shade trees, e.g. *Erythrina* and *Inga*. Small groups may gather leading to frequent disputes at feeding spots. Often territorial and belligerent.
Status Uncommon to fairly common in Colombia and Venezuela, uncommon in Guyana.
Habitat Tropical to Subtropical Zones. On slopes of mountains and tepuis. Borders and clearings of humid and cloud forests, partially open woodland, open terrain with shrubbery, coffee plantations, second growth.
Voice A weak *ta-da-titi-da* sequence that is higher pitched for middle *ti* notes (H&B). A high, thin, variable series, *dee-de-deet*, with last note rising sharply (Hilty). Said to be almost a mirror image of song of Copper-rumped Hummingbird.

RUFOUS-TAILED HUMMINGBIRD

Amazilia tzacatl Pl. 100

Identification 11.1–11.4cm, bill 2cm. Body almost entirely green, with grey belly and undertail-coverts; uppertail-coverts and tail maroon with green edges; bill black above, orange below with a black tip, feet grey.

Ssp. *A. t. jucunda* (SW Co, W Ec) longer bill
A. t. tzacatl (E Co, W Ve) as described

Habits Forages mostly at low to mid levels and solitarily, but small groups may gather at flowering trees (*Tabebuia*, *Inga*, *Erythrina*), with frequent disputes over feeding spots. Visits flowering *Costus*, *Thunbergia*, *Hibiscus*, *Heliconia*, *Lantana*, *Hamelia*, *Stachytarpheta* bushes and picks small insects and spiders by gleaning, hawking or dashing quickly from perch. Takes nectar from holes pierced in base of corollas

by flowerpiercers and Bananaquits. Also sips juice from *Clusia* fruits pecked by tanagers and others. Moves to higher elevations during flowering season, even reaching *Polylepis* woods.
Status Common and widespread in Venezuela and Colombia, common to uncommon in Ecuador.
Habitat Tropical to Lower Subtropical Zones. Exceptionally plastic, occurs in dry to humid habitats, more frequently latter but not in forest. Borders, clearings and streams in humid and cloud forests, second growth, cultivated fields with scattered bushes and trees, coffee and banana plantations, dry open woodland, parks and gardens.
Voice Song a sequence of quick *tsip* notes (H&B).

CHESTNUT-BELLIED HUMMINGBIRD
Amazilia castaneiventris Pl. 100

Identification 10.4cm, bill 2cm. Green from forehead to rump with gold to orange reflections from top of head back, uppertail-coverts and central rectrices very bright orange-bronzy, tail green with orange-bronze fringes, forehead, face, chin and throat very metallic with golden-yellow and bright green reflections; breast to undertail-coverts deep orange, with white vent; bill black above, red below, feet black. Female has many white fringes to metallic feathers of chin and throat, and is far less brilliant yellow and green on face.

Ssp. Monotypic (Co)

Habits Poorly known. Solitary forager at variety of plants (*Salvia*, *Trichanthera*) that also takes small insects and spiders.
Status Endangered. Rare Colombian endemic, known from only 2 localities on west slope of East Andes. Threatened by extensive deforestation in small range.
Habitat Upper Tropical to Subtropical Zones, 500–1,500m. Borders of humid forest, bushy ravines and partially open terrain on montane slopes.
Voice No description found and no published recordings.

AMAZILIA HUMMINGBIRD
Amazilia amazilia Pl. 100

Identification 11cm, bill 2 cm. Head to tail green, gradually reflecting more gold or coppery, uppertail-coverts and tail quite densely reflect orange; chin, sides of throat and fore sides of neck bright green with clear white fringes, throat forms a broad wedge of white, breast orange, flanks, belly and vent white, undertail-coverts orange with white fringes; bill red with black culmen, feet grey.

Ssp. Monotypic (SW Ec)

Habits Solitary forager that visits flowers at all levels, especially blooming trees (*Erythrina*, *Psittacanthus*) and takes small insects and spiders by gleaning or hawking in open spaces. Prefers flowers with slightly deep corollas. Males establish feeding territories and chase intruders.
Status Locally common to very rare.
Habitat Tropical Zone. Dry, partially wooded coastal areas, xerophytic scrub and open, arid terrain with bushy patches, parks and gardens.
Voice No description found and no published recordings.

Note R&G are reluctant to accept separation of form *alticola* (see below).

LOJA HUMMINGBIRD
Amazilia alticola Pl. 100

Identification 10cm, bill 2cm. Green forehead to short uppertail-coverts, long uppertail-coverts and tail rufous, coverts fringed green, middle of central rectrices green; throat-sides and lower face bright green scaled white, centre of throat to undertail-coverts white, with touch of orange on breast-sides; bill red with black culmen and tip, feet dark grey. Smaller and much whiter below than Amazilia Hummingbird, tail mainly rufous.

Ssp. Monotypic (SE Ec)

Status Locally common.
Habitat Upper Tropical to Subtropical Zone, 1,500–2,200m. Borders and clearings of humid and cloud forests, and open terrain with bushes on montane slopes.
Voice Reportedly distinct from Amazilia Hummingbird, but no description found and no published recordings.
Notes Separated from Amazilia Hummingbird by Weller (2000) on basis of voice, plumage, distribution and habitat, and accepted by Dickinson (2003). Note that R&G mention another highland form, which they suggest is an undescribed subspecies of *Amazilia*. Being a highland bird, this is perhaps more likely a form of Loja Hummingbird than Amazilia Hummingbird.

SNOWY-BREASTED HUMMINGBIRD
Amazilia edward Pl. 101

Identification 8–10cm, bill 1.8–2cm. Entire head metallic green, to upper breast and mantle, back bronzy-green, increasingly coppery to purplish-rufous on tail; centre of breast broadening to all-white belly, flanks and vent; undertail-coverts rufous. Female is duller above, with white scaling on upper throat and undertail-coverts. Juvenile like female, with grey wash on sides and flanks.

Ssp. *A. e. edward* (extreme NW Co)

Habits Usually solitary, but occasionally in groups at trees in full flower. From mid levels to subcanopy, may defend feeding territory, but several sometimes gather at flowering trees. Apparently particularly fond of *Heliconia*.
Status Occurs rarely near Colombia–Panama border. Very dubious record from foothills in Pichincha, Ecuador (R&G).
Habitat Tropical Zone. Partially open areas, open primary and secondary woodland, coffee plantations, and fallow fields with scattered trees, clearings and thickets. Apparently partial to False Banana.
Voice No description found and no published recordings.

Plumeleteers are fairly large forest hummingbirds, with long, almost straight bills that decurve slightly at the tip. Dull green with some blue, they have broad dusky, slightly forked tails, with noticeably thick, silky white undertail-coverts.

WHITE-VENTED PLUMELETEER

Chalybura buffonii Pl. 101

Identification Male 11.4–11.5cm, female 10.2cm; bill 2.5cm. Adult male almost entirely green, bluish-green on front, tail solid dark blue and undertail-coverts white; bill long, slightly curved at tip, and feet black. Female smaller, warm grey from chin to undertail-coverts, tips of outermost rectrices white, the amount reduced on each feather, until there is only a narrow terminal line on central feathers.

Ssp. *C. b. aeneicauda* (NW Ve, Co: Santa Marta) more golden-green below, central tail bright coppery bronze-green; female has sparse green flecking on breast-sides

C. b. buffonii (C&NE Co, NW Ve) as described

C. b. caeruleogaster (Co: E Andes) largest, male has throat and belly bluish-green, breast blue

C. b. micans (NW Co) larger, central tail deeper blue

Habits Forages alone, in pairs or small groups, in foliage at mid and low levels (*Heliconia*, *Hibiscus*, *Malvaviscus*, *Palicourea*, *Hamelia*, *Aphelandra*), sometimes in canopy (*Inga*, *Erythrina*, *Calliandra*, *Trichanthera*). Adept at piercing long corollas of tubular flowers. At feeding spots, males especially fiercely chase others of same and different species. Picks insects by sallying or darting in open spots or at borders, also by gleaning leaves and spider webs. Perches on tips of bare twigs.
Status Fairly common in Colombia, rare in Ecuador.
Habitat Lower Tropical Zone (may reach Subtropical locally). Borders and clearings of wet, humid, deciduous and dry forests, second growth, open woodland, plantations, humid scrub, marshy areas.
Voice When foraging, *chip* notes (R&G).

BRONZE-TAILED PLUMELETEER

Chalybura urochrysia Pl. 101

Identification Male 11.5cm, female 10.2cm; bill 2.5cm. Adult male virtually all green; glittering green throat and breast, tail bronze-green, belly and flanks grey, vent and undertail-coverts white; bill black above, yellow below with small black tip, feet dull yellow. Female smaller, similar above but all grey below.

Ssp. *C. u. isaurae* (extreme NW Co) bluish-green below with blue throat and breast, tail bright bronze

C. u. urochrysia (W Co, NW Ec) as described

C. u. intermedia (SW Ec) breast greenish-blue, belly grey, tail dark blue

Habits Always forages in forest, in understorey, especially at *Heliconia*, bromeliads, *Cephalis*, Ericaceae, Malvaceae and Gesneriaceae, but also just below canopy or at edges of clearings or tracks (*Inga*, *Hamelia*). Claims feeding rights at groups of flowers and fiercely defends them (especially males). Avid insect eater, hawks or sallies for flies, wasps, bees, mosquitoes, gnats. Females tend more to glean aphids, ants, spiders and other arthropods on leaves.
Status Common in Ecuador, uncommon and local in Colombia.
Habitat Lower Tropical Zone. Borders and interior of humid and wet forests, stands of *Heliconia*, mature second growth, cacao and banana plantations, wooded gardens and parks.
Voice Calls varied, described as twitters, ticking and trilling notes (H&B).

SPECKLED HUMMINGBIRD

Adelomyia melanogenys Pl. 101

Identification 8.4–10cm, bill 1.3cm. Small hummingbird with 6 rather similar subspecies in our region. Essentially brownish-green above, scaled darker, tail dark brown with paler tips; white eyebrow is virtually postocular, dark brown from eyes to ear-coverts, underparts pale buffy with rows of drab or greenish spots and streaks, bill short, straight and dusky, feet flesh colour. Sexes alike, juvenile similar but has pale fringes to feathers of upperparts.

Ssp. *A. m. aeneosticta* (NC Ve) 9.5cm, long bill; greenest above, corners of tail rufous

A. m. cervina (Co: W & C Andes) 10cm, largest, with shortest bill; ruddy brown above, underparts richest buff

A. m. connectens (S Co) intermediate between *cervina* and *maculata*

A. m. debellardiana (W Ve) 9cm, rufescent nape, richest golden on back, corners of tail pale greyish

A. m. maculata (Ec) like *melanogenys* but more buff on inner sides of tail

A. m. melanogenys (W Ve, Co: E Andes) 9cm, green on top of head and back

Habits Solitary, occasionally in pairs, at mid and low levels, often at flowers in thickets along trails and borders (*Fuchsia*, *Impatiens*, *Palicourea*, *Psamisia*, *Lobelia*). Hovers at flowers and also perches on them to feed. Hawks often and vigorously, and sometimes gleans in dense foliage.
Status Common in Ecuador and Venezuela, very common in Colombia.
Habitat Subtropical Zone. Wet and cloud forests, coffee plantations, along streams.
Voice Call a low *dit-dik*, voiced often when foraging.

BLOSSOMCROWN

Anthocephala floriceps Pl. 101

Identification 8.4cm, bill 1.3cm. Forehead bright pale buffy grading into orange-rufous rear crown, then green to central rectrices, rest of tail brown, tips white, tail notched; short, thick postocular line white, upper ear-coverts orange-rufous; front and sides of face to breast and body-sides uniform bright pale buffy, belly to undertail-coverts grey. Female has top of head green and lacks orange-rufous ear-coverts.

Ssp. *A. f. berlepschi* (Co: C Andes) as described

A. f. floriceps (Co: Santa Marta) buff tips to tail, breast-sides darker buffy to undertail-coverts.

Habits Poorly known. Forages alone, mostly at shrubs and small trees at lower levels (Musaceae). Males perch exposed on low twig or gather in small groups (leks?) to sing.
Status Rare, local Colombian endemic.

Habitat Subtropical Zone, race *berlepschi* at 1,200–2,300m, *floriceps* in Santa Marta at 600–2,400m. Humid primary and mature secondary forests, lightly forested areas.
Voice Song consists only of repeated chip notes.

ECUADORIAN PIEDTAIL

Phlogophilus hemileucurus Pl. 101

Identification 7.6cm, bill 1.8cm. Tiny hummingbird with proportionately long bill and short tail; green forehead to rump, uppertail-coverts and central rectrices deep turquoise, rest of tail basally purple, distally white; chin to undertail-coverts white with rows of small green streaks on throat, and a few blurry green streaks on breast-sides; bill like a black needle, feet black.

Ssp. Monotypic (E Ec, S Co)

Habits Solitary forager at low to mid levels. Feeds by clinging to flowers, does not hover. Gleans insects and spiders from dense foliage. Favoured flowers are *Psamisia* and some Rubiaceae, Gesneriaceae.
Status Uncommon in Ecuador, only a few records in Colombia.
Habitat Upper Tropical to Lower Subtropical Zones. Humid forests on lower slopes.
Voice Male repeats sequence of extremely high notes – *tzeee-tzeee-ts-ts* – sometimes adding a *chipper* in display (R&G).

Heliodoxa brilliants are a poorly known group of sparkling rich green, mid-sized to slightly larger hummingbirds with long straight bills and white postocular spots, and well-defined forked tails.

GOULD'S JEWELFRONT

Heliodoxa aurescens Pl. 101

Identification 12–12.2cm, bill 2cm. Forehead to mid crown bright royal blue, then to central pair of rectrices green, rest of tail-feathers chestnut with dark brown outer edges; chin black, face-sides and throat green, breast vibrant reddish-orange, rest of underparts green, white thighs, undertail-coverts fringed orange; bill black, feet grey. Orange breast shield diagnostic.

Ssp. Monotypic (Ec, Co)

Habits Never particularly evident, forages quietly and alone, mostly in understorey but very occasionally at mid levels or in subcanopy.
Status Rare in Ecuador, scarce and local in Colombia, but possibly more common as quite difficult to spot.
Habitat Tropical Zone. Interior of humid *terra firme*, *várzea* and sandy soil woodland, along shady streams and boggy areas, occasionally at borders.
Voice No description found, but a recording from Brazil listed in the Discography.
Note Formerly placed in genus *Polyplancta*.

FAWN-BREASTED BRILLIANT

Heliodoxa rubinoides Pl. 101

Identification 11.2cm, bill 2.3cm. Sparkling green from forehead to tail-coverts, tail brown; chin, throat and sides of face green with some bright paler green spots, and centre of throat has pinkish-violet spots, rest of underparts cinnamon with white thighs; straight bill black, feet grey. Female similar but lacks pinkish-violet on throat and has buffy fringes to some throat feathers.

Ssp. *H. r. aequatorialis* (W Co, W Ec) gold reflections on wing-coverts, lower back and tail-coverts, central rectrices have distinct golden tone, more strongly spotted on throat and breast-sides
H. r. cervinigularis (E Ec) larger; longer bill, throat patch smaller and paler, breast paler, tail slightly more deeply forked
H. r. rubinoides (Co: E Andes) as described

Habits Solitary, mainly at low and mid levels but may visit flowering trees such as *Erythrina* and *Inga*, but never joins gatherings at these. Hawks for insects in open, fairly high.
Status Rare in Ecuador, uncommon and local in Colombia.
Habitat Upper Tropical and Subtropical Zone, from perhaps 1,000 to *c*.2,300m. Interior and shady borders of humid, wet and cloud forests; sometimes in semi-open rural areas, in pastures, fallow fields and gardens.
Voice Male utters series of sharp *tchik!* notes, and a fast and frequent *swi-swi-swi-swu* song (R&G).

VIOLET-FRONTED BRILLIANT

Heliodoxa leadbeateri Pl. 101

Identification Male 13cm, female 10.9–11cm, bill 2.3cm. Forehead and most of crown metallic rich purplish-blue, ear-coverts deep orange, back of head to uppertail-coverts green, gold reflections on back of head and nape, uppertail-coverts gold and coppery to reddish, tail deeply forked and dark brown central 2 pairs of rectrices bronze shot with purple; throat and breast metallic bright green, white thighs, undertail-coverts grey with white fringes; bill black, feet grey. Immature male lacks blue on head and has top of head deep olive-green with orange line from chin to ear-coverts, and lacks golden coppery uppertail-coverts; otherwise similar. Female is bright green above with yellow tips to tail, underparts have white scaling from chin to undertail-coverts.

Ssp. *H. l. leadbeateri* (N Ve) as described
H. l. parvula (N, C & S Co, NW Ve) male intermediate between *leadbeateri* and *sagitta*: frontal patch more violet than purplish-blue, belly paler, central tail greener, rest blackish; female like female *leadbeateri*
H. l. sagitta (E Ec) as *leadbeateri* but lacks coppery tail-coverts and tail is solid deep indigo; female has turquoise fore cap and white belly to undertail-coverts

Habits Forages alone at mid and low levels, mostly in forest or sometimes small clearings or shady borders. Does not gather at flowering trees.
Status Uncommon and local in Ecuador and Colombia.
Habitat Upper Tropical to Subtropical Zones. Undergrowth of borders and clearings of humid and cloud forests, coffee

plantations, second growth, partially open patches of small trees.
Voice Varied series of enthusiastic *chup* notes, doubled or tripled, and sometimes in long strings (Hilty).

BLACK-THROATED BRILLIANT

Heliodoxa schreibersii Pl. 102

Identification 12cm, bill 2.3cm. Dark green above, brighter on uppertail-coverts, tail deeply forked and dark blue; large white triangle behind eyes, velvet black mask from lores and chin to ear-coverts and throat-sides, semi-circular patch of metallic pinkish-violet on throat, with broad band of metallic pale green at base, then rest of underparts velvet black with grey thighs; bill like a black needle, feet grey. Female all green above to central tail-feathers, shorter, less deeply forked tail is dark blue; bold yellowish-white streak from base of bill to ear-coverts, chin green, small semi-circle of pinky-violet on throat and broad patch of yellowish-white, mottled green at base; rest of underparts green with irregular black scalloping, thighs pale grey. Swaggering black moustachial and purple beard with black below diagnostic.

Ssp. *H. s. schreibersii* (E Ec, S & SE Co)

Habits Very poorly known. Solitary in low and mid strata of forest. Visits flowers of Ericaceae, Gesneriaceae.
Status Rare in Colombia and Ecuador.
Habitat Tropical Zone. Humid forests.
Voice Male sings a soft, descending, very high-pitched trill (R&G, J. V. Moore recording).

GREEN-CROWNED BRILLIANT

Heliodoxa jacula Pl. 102

Identification Male 13cm, female 10.9cm, bill 2.3cm. Forehead and front of crown, chin to neck-sides and breast metallic bright green, but round patch of sky blue in centre of throat, underparts green with white thighs; tail bronze-green; black bill and dark grey feet. Female smaller and similar above; metallic pale green from throat and face-sides to belly, with broad white fringes on chin and throat, less so over rest of underparts, undertail-coverts dull green.

Ssp. *H. j. jacula* (N & C Co: E Andes) as described
H. j. jamesoni (W Ec, SW Co) much duller on crown, throat and breast; central tail-feathers glossed green and tail slightly shorter

Habits Solitary, mostly in forest, at low and mid levels. Feeds in *Heliconia* and *Marcgravia*, also *Drymophila*, *Cephalis*, Ericaceae, Gesneriaceae. Hawks for flies, wasps and other flying insects, and gleans tiny insects and spiders from foliage.
Status Uncommon to rare in Ecuador, very local in Colombia.
Habitat Upper Tropical to Subtropical Zones, 300–1,600m. Humid, wet and cloud forests, mature second growth. Both interior and at borders, venturing into adjacent semi-open areas and along streams.
Voice No description found, but a recording from Ecuador listed in the Discography.

EMPRESS BRILLIANT

Heliodoxa imperatrix Pl. 102

Identification Male 14cm, female 12.2cm, bill 2.5cm. Forehead bright metallic green, green from crown to tail, which is very long and steeply graduated, and progressively browner nearer tips; chin and upper throat black bordered bright pale green, lower throat bright pink, rest of underparts green, paler and slightly yellowish on belly and undertail-coverts, with white thighs; bill long and comparatively broad, black, feet grey. Female smaller with long, deeply-forked tail but only half length of male's; chin and throat to face-sides white with reflective green spots, breasts to flanks pale leaf green, centre of lower breast and belly yellow, undertail-coverts bright green. Similar male Pink-throated Brilliant lacks black chin and has bright white undertail-coverts, and female lacks white throat but has rows of small white dots and small pink throat patch, as well as diagnostic white undertail-coverts.

Ssp. Monotypic (NW Ec, WC Co)

Habits Solitary at low and mid levels, in forest and at dense borders, occasionally canopy. With slow wingbeats, hovers at hanging flowers, e.g. epiphytic Ericaceae (*Macleania*, *Cavendishia*, *Psamisia*, *Gaylussacia*), but at small flowers (*Marcgravia* and *Caracasia*) perches on inflorescence, clinging to flower. Drinks water collected in *Heliconia* bracts.
Status Rare in Ecuador, uncommon to locally frequent in Colombia.
Habitat Upper Tropical to Lower Subtropical Zones. Very wet and cloud forests of lower slopes, mature second growth, at borders and clearings.
Voice No description found and no published recordings.

VELVET-BROWED BRILLIANT

Heliodoxa xanthogonys Pl. 102

Identification 10cm, bill 2cm. Forehead, chin and throat to upper breast metallic pale green with pale yellowish reflections, and small pyramidal patch of bright blue in centre of throat; top of head to uppertail-coverts green, with yellowish and bright pale green reflections on back and wing-coverts, becoming bluish to deep turquoise on tail-coverts, tail bronzy on centre of blackish outer feathers; underparts green with white thighs; bill black above, yellow below with black tip. Female smaller with shallow-forked tail, metallic pale green on forehead, then green to uppertail-coverts, tail bronzy-green in centre and dark brown on rest of tail; throat bright green with white scaling, much reduced on lower breast and sides, belly to flanks yellowish-white, undertail-coverts green with white scaling; bill has orange base.

Ssp. Monotypic (Ve, Su)

Habits Geographically well separated from rather similar Green-crowned Brilliant. Very poorly known. Forages on blooming bushes (*Tyleria*) and also feeds on insects.
Status Endemic to Pantepui. Frequent at forest borders, but population status and precise range unclear. Only recently recorded in Suriname (Ottema & Joe in press).

Habitat Upper Tropical to Subtropical Zones, 700–2,000m. Forest and scrub on slopes of tepuis, at borders and clearings.
Voice An occasional nasal *squank* in flight (Hilty).

VIOLET-CHESTED HUMMINGBIRD
Sternoclyta cyanopectus Pl. 102

Identification 11.5cm, bill 3cm. Forehead to uppertail-coverts green, tail olivaceous-green, greater wing-coverts rufous; chin and throat metallic pale green, with paler brilliant reflections; breast metallic purple with pinkish reflections, below green to flanks, centre of belly and undertail-coverts pale ochre, white thighs; bill long and slightly decurved at tip, orange with black culmen and tip. Female similar but has streak of orange from bill base to below eyes, chin to breast and sides bright green scaled white; belly and flanks ochraceous, white thighs, undertail-coverts ochre with white fringes.

Ssp. Monotypic (Ve, Ne Co)

Habits Forages alone, mostly in low and mid strata. Favoured haunts are *Heliconia* patches, shady dense forest, sheltered streams and humid ravines. Feeds on nectar and arthropods.
Status Venezuelan near-endemic. Locally common, tolerates some habitat disturbance. Recently discovered in Tamá National Natural Park in Colombia (Cordóba-Cordóba & Echeverry-Galvis 2006).
Habitat Upper Tropical to Subtropical Zones, to *c.*2,000m. Humid and cloud forests, ravines, mature second growth, coffee and cocoa plantations.
Voice Series of sharp *chit!* notes at *c.*1 s intervals for nearly 30 s, sometimes mixed with *weet* notes and squeaky trills. Staccato chips when foraging (Hilty).

SCISSOR-TAILED HUMMINGBIRD
Hylonympha macrocerca Pl. 102

Identification Male 19cm, tail 9–10cm; female 11.5cm; bill 2.5cm. Full metallic violet cap, chin to neck-sides and upper breast glittering emerald with turquoise and white reflections, rest of body metallic black, reflecting moss green; wings reflect maroon to purple, tail deeply forked with 2 outer feathers very long, each curving outwards and then inwards, and also reflecting maroon to purple; thighs white; bill straight, black above, yellow below, feet black. Female brighter green above with bright green eyebrow; chin to ear-coverts, sides of neck and throat to breast white with rows of metallic green spots, rest of underparts cinnamon (with white thighs); tail long and deeply forked, inner edge straight, outer edge curved, like a pair of scissors; bill longer than male and slightly curved, black above, yellow below.

Ssp. Monotypic (Ve)

Habits Forages at all levels, usually alone but small groups (mostly males?) may gather in canopy of flowering trees. Also nectars at bromeliads (*Guzmania, Pitcarnia, Aechmea, Tillandsia, Vriesea*) and *Heliconia*, and defends feeding territories at flowers.
Status Venezuelan endemic to Paria Peninsula mountains. Frequent, but its small range is seriously threatened by fires and deforestation, slash-and-burn planting of family vegetable plots by local settlers.
Habitat Upper Tropical Zone, 500–1,200m. Humid and cloud forests, mature second growth, in moss-laden areas of tall canopy, borders and small clearings, occasionally in coffee plantations.
Voice Sings short bursts of *tsi-tsi-tsip* notes, repeated at 2–3 s intervals, and sometimes *tsink!* notes at *c.*3 s intervals (Hilty).

PINK-THROATED BRILLIANT
Heliodoxa gularis Pl. 102

Identification 11.4cm, bill 2.8cm. Adult male almost entirely shiny green, with pink patch on throat and pure white undertail-coverts; tail long, well forked and steeply graduated, with a greenish gloss; bill thick and straight. Female slightly smaller but very similar, with smaller pink throat spot and shorter tail; bill very slightly curved. Similar Empress Brilliant male has black chin and green undertail-coverts, the female an extensive white throat and green undertail-coverts.

Ssp. Monotypic (Ec, Co)

Habits Very poorly known, probably similar to congeners. Forages in forest, visiting flowers at low and mid levels, and hawking for tiny insects and spiders. Recorded feeding in various Loranthaceae, especially *Psittacanthus*.
Status Very rare in Ecuador and Colombia.
Habitat Upper Tropical Zone. Humid and wet montane forests on mid-level slopes.
Voice No description found and no published recordings.

FIERY TOPAZ *Topaza pyra* Pl. 102

Identification Male 18cm, female 15cm, bill 2.5cm. Complete black hood to upper breast with brilliant metallic gorget consisting of a gold inner circle and broad leaf green outer circle, but can appear very indistinct in poor light; nape scalloped and scaled blood red, as is breast, and body gradually becomes scarlet to flanks, but on back is vermilion, then orange on rump, and uppertail-coverts are an iridescent patchwork of warm gold and leaf green; central tail-feathers green with orange reflections, rest of tail maroon; next pair of rectrices deep purple, long and curve inwards, slightly spatulate, the outer 3 pairs gradually graduated; undertail has outer edge of outermost rectrices ochre, as is subterminal tip to inner web of same feathers and the penultimate. Thighs pure fluffy white, undertail-coverts leaf green; bill strong, long and slightly curved, feet pink. Female darker green from forehead to rump and flanks, with metallic ruby gorget reflecting pink or violet, scaled orange; rump to uppertail-coverts and undertail-coverts bright apple green, thighs white; bill dusky, feet orange. Young follow same stages as Crimson Topaz (see plate).

Ssp. *T. p. amaruni* (E Ec) tibial feathers either entirely black, or black fringed white
T. p. pyra (SE Co, S Ve: Amazonas) as described

Habits Forages in mid strata or canopy of forest, and in lower strata at borders (*Inga*, *Bombax*, bromeliads, Gesneriaceae, Ericaceae). Hawks for insects high in open at forest border or

above canopy. Fond of rocky areas near black-water streams, and sometimes attaches nest to partially submerged branch, *c.*1 m above water.
Status Rare in Ecuador and Colombia, collected in Venezuela on upper río Asisa, and in virtually inaccessible Quinigua Mts, Ecuador. Perhaps more common than appears, due to preference for canopy.
Habitat Lower Tropical Zone. Humid, sandy soil forests, low, open woodland along blackwater streams, bushes and thickets at edge of savannas, *Mauritia* palm swamps, rocky outcrops and gallery forests.
Voice Loud, fast series of ticking *chip* notes, some single but also doubled and tripled, and even rapid bursts in very irregular sequences characteristic (Hilty, C. Parrish recording).
Note Considered conspecific with Crimson Topaz by Schuchmann (1999).

CRIMSON TOPAZ *Topaza pella* Pl. 102

Identification 18cm, bill 2.5cm. Complete black hood to upper breast with brilliant metallic gorget of apple green, leaf green, yellow and gold reflections; nape scalloped and scaled crimson, as is breast, and body gradually becomes scarlet to flanks and rump, whilst lower rump, uppertail-coverts and central pair of rectrices are mid green with black shafts and coppery-gold reflections, the next pair of rectrices bright reddish-maroon, long and somewhat spatulate, almost like hockey sticks, the outer 3 pairs orange-red and gradually graduated; undertail ochre, central 4 feathers darker. Thighs pure fluffy white, undertail-coverts green with flecks of red; bill strong, long and slightly curved, feet pink. Juvenile male is like a brownish young female with some metallic pink and orange on throat, a few spots of blood red on breast and some orange on flanks. Immature male has longer tail, the 2 plumes being about half length of adult and taper almost to a point at tips, and deep red on breast and nape more established, with a full gorget of golden-yellow with very little green. Female darker green from forehead to rump and flanks, with metallic rosy-pink gorget that reflects yellow and raspberry; rump to uppertail-coverts and undertail-coverts bright apple green, thighs white; bill dusky, feet orange. Juvenile female duller and darker, and lacks pink gorget.

Ssp. *T. p. pella* (Ve, Gu, Su) as described
T. p. smaragdula (FG) significantly longer tail

Habits Forages alone, from mid level to canopy, visiting flowers in tall trees, bushes and branches overhanging water (*Pitcarnia*, *Inga*, *Isertia*, *Eperua*, *Monomoreia*, bromeliads, Gesneriaceae, Ericaceae). Hawks for insects above canopy or in open spots of mid strata. Males defend feeding territories.
Status Widespread but uncommon in Guyana, very locally and seasonally frequent in Venezuela, possibly rare in Suriname, common in French Guiana. May be more common than thought, due to preference for canopy.
Habitat Lower Tropical Zone. Humid forest interiors, in dense, shady areas, especially along black-water streams. Forages and sings in canopy, nests on dead branches in rivers. Males may congregate in late afternoon close to small watercourses.
Voice A loud tweet and descending *s-s-s-s-tk-tk-tk-tk*... (Snyder 1966). Loud continuous chatter and *chip* notes when foraging, and throughout day (Hilty).
Note Race *pamprepta*, originally described from a mislabelled specimen, is a synonym of *smaragdula*. Schuchmann (1999) considered *smaragdula* inseparable from *pella* and synonymised it.

Oreotrochilus hillstars are birds of the Ecuadorian high country, rather sage-green above with turquoise tints, and pale underparts. They favour short-grass rocky slopes which have flowering shrubs such as *Chuquiraga* spp., *Puya* spp. and others.

ECUADORIAN HILLSTAR *Oreotrochilus chimborazo* Pl. 103

Identification 13cm, bill 2cm. Adult male has entire hood purple, nuchal band turquoise, rest of upperparts to tail-coverts olivaceous grey-green, tail dark brown with centre washed strongly dark turquoise, inner webs of next 2 rectrices white, and basal half of inner web of fourth rectrix white, the outermost rectrix all brown, and white bases to outer 3 pairs only visible in flight; breast to flanks and thighs creamy white, undertail-coverts and narrow line down middle of belly greyish-brown, the coverts scaled white; bill slightly decurved, mostly at tip, feet vinaceous-grey. Immature has most of head cobalt-blue with some turquoise reflections, lower throat dark to purple and no nuchal band, otherwise like male. Female same olive greyish-green above from forehead to tail-coverts, central rectrices somewhat greenish-blue, white tips to inner webs of rectrices; throat to face-sides olive-green with white fringes giving scaled effect, breast to flanks pale greyish-brown with white fringes, undertail-coverts greyish-brown with white fringes. Juvenile has darker throat with narrower white fringes, breast to undertail-coverts greyish-brown with faint paler fringes. From smaller Velvet-purple Coronet by white breast and flanks.

Ssp. *O. c. chimborazo* (C Ec: Mt Chimborazo) male has bright turquoise crescent on throat
O. c. jamesonii (N Ec, extreme S Co) as described
O. c. soederstroemi (C Ec: Mt. Quillota) male has few green feathers on throat

Habits Solitary, fiercely defends feeding territory in páramo (*Chuquiraga*, *Puya*, Malvaceae). Spends much time perching in sun, and also long periods spent hawking and gleaning insects. In open páramo, roosts and takes refuge from storms in cracks and caves of rocky outcrops.
Status Uncommon to relatively frequent in Ecuador.
Habitat Páramo, 3,500–5,200m. Semi-arid puna with scattered scrub and bushes, humid wooded ravines, borders of elfin forest at treeline, pastures in páramo.
Voice No description found, but a recording is listed in the Discography.

ANDEAN HILLSTAR

Oreotrochilus estella Pl. 103

Identification 13–15cm, bill 2cm. Male dark green from forehead to tail-coverts, chin to ear-coverts and throat form metallic gorget of deep turquoise-blue in middle to turquoise-green at sides; tail dark brown with central pair of rectrices washed dark turquoise, inner webs of next 2 rectrices white, basal half of inner web of fourth rectrix white, and outermost rectrix brown; breast to flanks and thighs creamy white, with broad blackish line on middle of belly, undertail-coverts greyish-brown, scaled white; bill slightly decurved, mostly at tip, feet blackish. Female green above but is white on gorget, spotted green; breast to vent pale greyish-buff, undertail-coverts dull brownish-grey with bluish-green centres; tail dark brown with white tips to all but central pair, and white bases to outer 3 pairs only visible in flight. Similar to Chimborazo Hillstar but lacks purple on head.

Ssp. *O. e. stolzmanni* (extreme S Ec)

Habits Much as previous species.
Status Mainly Peru, only recently recorded in Ecuador, where seems uncommon.
Habitat Páramo and puna above 3,600m, in open areas and scattered patches of *Puya* and *Polylepis*.
Voice No description found, but a recording from Bolivia listed in Discography.

SWORD-BILLED HUMMINGBIRD

Ensifera ensifera Pl. 103

Identification Male 14cm, bill 10cm; female 13cm, bill 11–12cm. Head wholly lustrous bronze, scaled darker, rest of body and wings dark green with some bronzy reflections and brighter green; large white triangle behind eyes, fluffy white thighs; bill almost as long as bird, dusky and slightly upcurved, feet orange-flesh. Female similar but has white throat to upper breast, with rows of white-edged green feathers. Unmistakable due to incredibly long bill.

Ssp. Monotypic (Ec, Co, Ve)

Habits Forages alone, at mid level and in canopy. Trap-liner that specialises in flowers with long, hanging corollas (*Passiflora*, *Datura*), approached by hovering below petals.
Status Scarce and local in Colombia and Venezuela, uncommon in Ecuador. Presence possibly dependent on abundance of particular food plants.
Habitat Subtropical to Temperate Zones, 1,700–3,500m. Humid montane, wet, cloud and elfin forests, borders, slopes with scattered bushes.
Voice Calls sound like low growls.

GIANT HUMMINGBIRD

Patagona gigas Pl. 103

Identification 23.1cm, bill 4.1cm. Very large. Adult male dark bronzy-green from forehead to lower back, broad white rump, dark continues to forked tail; feathers of head to lower back all have darker fringes, tail-coverts and tail-feathers have subterminal black edging fringed white; chin to belly and flanks deep reddish-cinnamon; thighs and undertail-coverts white; bill straight and dusky, feet grey. Female has throat to upper breast white with fine rows of dark feathers and soft streaks of cinnamon, the dark feathers become large spots on cinnamon lower breast, belly pure cinnamon.

Ssp. *P. g. peruviana* (Ec, extreme S Co)

Habits Largest hummingbird, flies with heavy, flapping wingbeats, reminiscent of a bat, but occasionally glides briefly, when looks more like a swift! Forages mostly alone, mainly on flowers of *Agave* and *Lobelia*. Large percentage of diet consists of insects, and spends long periods hawking.
Status Uncommon in Ecuador, uncommon and seasonal in southern Colombia (sight records).
Habitat Subtropical Zone to Páramo. Open, arid areas, sparse grassland with scattered trees, brush, cacti and thistles, often near water. Hedges of gardens and pastures.
Voice Call an intermittent, forced high *eeep* (H&B). A high *cwueet* when perched or flying (R&G).

GREAT SAPPHIREWING

Pterophanes cyanopterus Pl. 103

Identification 19.3cm, bill 3cm. Very distinctive, large, bluish-green with blue wings. Adult male is entirely lustrous green, washed blue, reflecting turquoise at times, more blue than green undertail-coverts; wings rich blue – even on both surfaces of flight-feathers – reflecting purple at some angles; undertail green; bill straight and blackish, feet pink. Female paler green above with blue only on wing-coverts; chin to vent cinnamon, with flecks of green on breast-sides to flanks, undertail-coverts dull green.

Ssp. *P. c. cyanopterus* (NC Co) as described
P. c. peruvianus (Ec) pale bluish-green above, paler, mostly greenish below
P. c. caeruleus (SC & SW Co) darker blue suffusion on body and wings

Habits Comparatively slow wingbeats, flies strongly and direct, with some glides, when looks swift-like. Feeds by both hovering and perching – when holds its wings sideways.
Status Uncommon to rare in Ecuador, locally frequent in Colombia.
Habitat Temperate Zone to Páramo. Borders of cloud and elfin forests, dry to wet grasslands with shrubbery or scattered trees, or bushes on higher slopes and páramo.
Voice No description found, but 2 recordings from Ecuador listed in Discography.

WHITE-TAILED HILLSTAR

Urochroa bougueri Pl. 103

Identification 14.4cm, bill 3cm. Dark mossy green from forehead to tail-coverts, tail distinctive in having innermost and outermost pairs of rectrices dusky, the rest white; short white postocular line, broad bright reddish-orange moustachial, chin to breast bright royal blue, turquoise at edges; underparts mossy green to grey, grey undertail-coverts fringed white, thighs pale grey; bill straight and needle-like, blackish, feet black. Female similar but moustachial reduced and fragmented on ear-coverts.

Ssp. *U. b. bougueri* (SW Co, NW Ec) as described
U. b. leucura (E Ec, SC Co) greener above, central tail-feathers bronze with black edges, all other rectrices white, small postocular line dull orange, no moustachial

Habits Forages alone or, often, in pairs. Visits flowers at mid and canopy levels. Curious. Takes insects by hawking in open spots within forest. Moves seasonally up and downslope.
Status Uncommon to rare in Ecuador, fairly common in Colombia.
Habitat Upper Tropical to Temperate Zones. Humid, wet and cloud forests of Andean slopes. Inside forest as well as thickets and shrubs at borders. Near streams and in second growth.
Voice Simple *tsit* calls (R&G, J. V. Moore recording).

SHINING SUNBEAM

Aglaeactis cupripennis Pl. 103

Identification 13.2cm, bill 1.8cm. Dark olive-brown from forehead to nape, mantle and back umber, grading deep crimson with a true rainbow of colours to undertail-coverts, tail rufous or dark brown with bronze edges; face-sides, including full superciliary that embraces ear-coverts, and underparts cinnamon-rufous, except white thighs; bill short and fine, dusky above, yellow below with dark tip, feet black.

Ssp. *A. c. cupripennis* (Co, N & C Ec) as described
A. c. parvulus (S Ec) shorter bill, more rufous tail

Habits A chacteristic bird of its habitat, often perching in open and holds its wings aloft for an extended period after landing.
Status Common in Ecuador, locally common but patchily distributed in Colombia.
Habitat Temperate Zone to Páramo, 2,800–3,600m. Borders of elfin and cloud forest and scattered trees or bushes in páramo and subpáramo; hedges, gardens, dense shrubbery or scrub at treeline.
Voice Call, while foraging, *tseep, tsip-tsip*. Also shrill chirping.

MOUNTAIN VELVETBREAST

Lafresnaya lafresnayi Pl. 103

Identification 11–12cm, bill 2.5–3cm. Rich lustrous green from forehead to central tail-feathers, becoming inceasingly bronzy on tail-coverts and tail, rest of tail cream with bronze-green tips; large white triangle behind eyes, lores and ear-coverts black, chin to breast metallic emerald-green, belly, sides and flanks black, thighs contastingly white, undertail-coverts dull bronze-green with paler fringes; bill slightly decurved, feet dark grey. Immature male is slightly more bronzy overall, tail has broad brown tips to white feathers; underparts white, buffy on breast and undertail-coverts, spotted green on chin and throat, and spotted irregularly green and black on sides. Female ore olivaceous-green above, white on basal half of all but central tail-feathers buffy; ear-coverts warm brown, underparts entirely warm buffy with irregular pale green spots on sides of throat to flanks. White at base of tail of juvenile and female good field mark.

Ssp. *L. l. greenewalti* (Ve) paler, more yellowish green; tail white
L. l. lafresnayi (E Co, W Ve) as described
L. l. liriope (Co: Santa Marta) central rectrices coppery, contrast with black
L. l. saul (Ec, Co: W Andes) outer rectrices pure white, tipped greenish-bronze
L. l. tamae (Ve; Tamá) tail horn colour

Habits Forages alone, mostly in subcanopy.
Status Uncommon in Ecuador. Locally common in Colombia, with presence and abundance showing notable seasonal variation.
Habitat Subtropical to Temperate Zones, 1,900–3,400m, but most numerous 2,000–2,800m (Schuchmann). Borders of humid, wet and cloud forests, open fields with scattered trees and bushes, always in or around dense shrubbery.
Voice Call a clear whistle.

Coeligena starfrontlets are a large group of beautiful hummingbirds that range from common and well known to rare and of highly contentious status. They have long bills and occur in montane forests. Fly fast and direct, often high above canopy and may be seen speeding out across valleys and ravines of high country.

COLLARED INCA

Coeligena torquata Pl. 104

Identification 10cm, bill 3.5cm. Crown electric mid blue with some violaceous reflections; lower throat and upper breast solid white, rest of head to upper throat and rear of neck black with metallic deep green feathers spotted around edge of white; rest of body and wings metallic dark green, showing subtle green reflections in good light; thighs white; tail shiny black with basal half of outer 4 rectrices white, and underside entirely white with blackish terminal third; bill long, straight and black, feet fleshy dusky. Female has exactly same pattern but green is paler and crown has no blue.

Ssp. *C. t. fuligidigula* (W Ec) male has brighter blue crown with pale blue reflections, chin and upper throat metallic turquoise, otherwise like *torquata*, but green is paler
C. t. torquata (Ec, Co, Ve: Tamá) as described
C. t. conradii (NW Ve, NE Co) lustrous grass green with white breast and base to tail; female has cinnamon-buffy throat with rufous-brown spots and smaller white breast patch; belly also scaled buffy

Habits Forages alone, in lower to mid levels.
Status Common in Ecuador and Colombia.
Habitat Subtropical to Temperate Zones. Humid, wet and cloud forests, in thickets at borders.
Voice Soft, low, reedy whistle, *tu-tee*, and longer series of low-pitched piping whistles *pip… pip…* and a soft *spit* when foraging (Hilty).

BRONZY INCA *Coeligena coeligena* Pl. 104

Identification 14–15cm, bill 3.3–3.6cm. Six races, all very similar but each distinct. Essentially rich brown (umber to maroon) with green reflections on back, white fringes to throat and perhaps breast, forked tail, long black bill and a white spot behind eyes. Sexes alike, juvenile simply a duller version of adult. Dark and somewhat similar Dusky Starfrontlet is green with no reddish-brown and no white on throat, it has a violet throat spot. From others by overall bronzy-brown plumage, and lack of any bright or contrasting patches.

Ssp. *C. c. obscura* (Ec, S Co) very dark; green and golden reflections on back to rump; throat to breast cleanly scaled pale grey

C. c. ferruginea (Co: W & C Andes) greenish reflections on entire back to tail-coverts, golden reflections on forecrown, underparts cinnamon

C. c. coeligena (N Ve) maroon top of head to mantle and wing-coverts, green reflections on lower back and rump, throat neatly scaled whitish, undertail-coverts fringed orange; juvenile very dark, with pale green reflections on back; white scaling rather blurred and restricted to throat

C. c. zuliana (NW Ve: Perijá) head, mantle and wing-coverts reddish, green reflections on back to tail-coverts; throat and breast have well-defined clear white scaling, undertail-coverts fringed whitish

C. c. columbiana (NE Ve, Ec, Co: C & E Andes) green reflections from mantle to rump and on tail, tail-coverts deep maroon; throat heavily scaled grey that trails down to mid breast

C. c. zuloagae (N Ve: Falcón) very strongly reddish-maroon head, mantle and wings, feathers of mantle fringed gold, bright green reflections on rump; throat feathers fringed white on sides, forming series of curved lines (not scales), undertail-coverts fringed rufous

Habits Forages alone, trap-lining at lower to mid levels of forest edges, but not particularly defensive of feeding areas, though will defend a flowering tree canopy. Favours flowers with long, tubular corollas, including *Fuchsia*, *Cavendishia*, *Heliconia*, etc.

Status Common in Ecuador, seasonal in Colombia and local in Venezuela.

Habitat Upper Tropical to Temperate Zones, 1,500–2,600m. Humid, wet and cloud forests, borders, clearings, fields with scattered trees and bushes, and coffee plantations.

Voice Song a high, short, *tsit sit-it-it*, and call a high, *sweet szeet, zeet, zeet…* (Hilty).

Note Very distinctive race *zuloagae* described from a single specimen.

BROWN INCA *Coeligena wilsoni* Pl. 104

Identification 14.2cm, bill 3.3cm. Bronzy-brown all over, somewhat rufescent on underparts and scapulars, forehead has metallic reflections of paler bronze, whitish patch on neck-sides and undertail-coverts fringed orange, thighs white; the field mark is a reflective pinkish-violet patch on throat, large in male, small in female / immature; bill long, straight and black, feet brown.

Ssp. Monotypic (Ec, Co)

Habits Trap-lines in dense undergrowth and usually seen feeding at epiphytes. Gleans spiders and insects but occasionally hawks.

Status Uncommon in Ecuador. In Colombia, common only at 1,000–1,300 m.

Habitat Upper Tropical to Subtropical Zones. Wet and cloud forests, in thickets at borders.

Voice In flight a descending series of 4–5 high *tseee* or *tsee-deee* notes, also a squeaky *tsik-tsee-uu-tsi-ik* song (P. Coopmans in R&G).

BLACK INCA *Coeligena prunellei* Pl. 104

Identification 13.9cm, bill 3cm. Mostly black or black-looking; head is metallic emerald-green from forehead to crown, with a few reflective spots on upper ear-coverts, a brilliant reflective pale blue throat patch and larger pure white inverted crescent on neck-sides; lesser wing-coverts electric blue and edge of wing from carpal to alula bright carmine-red; nape to rump metallic, reflecting gold and maroon, and on the rump some bright leaf green; uppertail-coverts purple, tail deep indigo-blue and undertail-coverts boldly fringed white; bill black, feet rose. Juvenile duller than adult and lacks blue throat patch.

Ssp. Monotypic (NC Co)

Habits Trap-lines at all levels, to canopy, and favours flowers with hanging corollas like *Fuchsia*, *Aphelandra*, *Macrocarpaea*, etc. Seems not to defend feeding sites but dominates other species anyway.

Status Colombian endemic, locally common.

Habitat Subtropical Zone, 1,000–2,800m. Humid montane slope forests, particularly oak woodland. At borders and along streams.

Voice Call a short *pip*.

PURPLE INCA *Coeligena purpurea* Pl. 104

Identification 14cm, bill 3.3cm. Known only from 2 male specimens. Would no doubt be mistaken for Black Inca, unless seen well, when purple back and wings might be visible, along with pale pink throat and orange-edged undertail-coverts. Basically all black with reddish-purple reflections on top and back of head, becoming rich purple on mantle, back and wing-coverts, rump has metallic bright green fringes, uppertail-coverts purple, tail black with central pair of equal length as feathers either side; pinkish reflections on centre of throat (broader than blue patch on Black Inca), and undertail-coverts fringed broadly reddish-orange.

Ssp. Monotypic (SC Co)

Habits Unknown in life.

Status Unknown, collected in vicinity of Popayán, Colombia.

Habitat Not known.
Voice Undescribed.
Note Considered to be *C. prunellei* × *C. c. columbiana* hybrids by Berlioz (1936) and Züchner (1999), but could as easily be an extinct (?) species.

WHITE-TAILED STARFRONTLET
Coeligena phalerata Pl. 104

Identification 14.2cm, bill 3cm. Male has top of head bright rich blue with turquoise reflections, and triangular patch of rich blue on throat, rest of head, back to upper rump, wings and breast to upper belly and flanks metallic green with turquoise reflections, particularly on back, wings and breast; rest entirely pure white; bill black, feet pink. Female quite different, metallic green from forehead to tail, underparts rich orange-rufous from chin to undertail-coverts, with bright pale orange fringes to undertail-coverts, tail less forked. Juvenile resembles female. Male unique in all-white tail and tail-coverts, though female might be confused with female Golden-bellied Starfrontlet but is darker below and lacks pale patch on wings.

Ssp. Monotypic (Co)

Status Common Santa Marta endemic.
Habitat Subtropical Zone, 1,400–3,700m. Humid and wet forests on montane slopes, thickets, borders and clearings. Apparently, a slight difference in habitat preference by sex, with males preferring clearings in forest interiors whilst females outnumber males at forest edges (Züchner 1999).
Voice Twitters intermittently whilst foraging.

GOLDEN STARFRONTLET
Coeligena eos Pl. 104

Identification 13.5cm, bill 3cm. Male has brilliant metallic leaf green frontlet, top of crown to nape very dark green, throat to ear-coverts and breast metallic with varying reflective colours, centre of throat rich purplish-blue, ear-coverts and breast-sides emerald-green, mantle dark green, greater wing-coverts and secondaries fringed rufous; back to tail coppery with some green reflections but mostly reddish on rump and uppertail-coverts, distal half of tail olive-green; underparts deep rufous with darker scaling; bill black, feet pale orange-flesh. Female paler green, entire underparts orange-rufous with shiny spots of leaf green on face-sides, breast and body-sides, thighs white, feet pink. From Golden-bellied Starfrontlet by deeper rufous suffusion and rufous on tail, Golden Starfrontlet is darker on body but paler on tail.

Ssp. Monotypic (W Ve)

Habits Forages low, trap-lining within a few metres of ground, among trees always at edge of vegetation, around clearings or forest borders.
Status Locally common Venezuelan endemic. Moves seasonally up and downslope.
Habitat Subtropical to Temperate Zones, 1,400–3,200m. Borders of humid, cloud and elfin forests, open fields with scattered bushes and trees, thickets.
Voice No description found and no published recordings.

Note Formerly (i.e. in MdS&P) treated as subspecies of Golden-bellied Starfrontlet.

DUSKY STARFRONTLET
Coeligena orina Pl. 105

Identification 14.2cm, bill 3.3cm. Almost entirely shiny deep green, with a deep purplish-blue throat patch, and white thighs. From Bronzy Inca by violet throat spot, and is generally darker.

Ssp. Monotypic (Co)

Status Presumably very rare Colombian endemic, from Páramo de Frontino, Antioquia. Previously known only from type specimen, described in 1951, and suspected of being a hybrid by some authorities, but rediscovered in 2004.
Habitat At 3,200m, ecotone between Temperate Zone and Páramo. Border of forest at treeline.
Voice No description found and no published recordings.
Note Until recently, usually listed (inexplicably) as race of Golden-bellied Starfrontlet.

GOLDEN-BELLIED STARFRONTLET
Coeligena bonapartei Pl. 104

Identification 13.2–13.9cm, bill 2.5–3cm. Male has full metallic green cap, chin to ear-coverts and breast shiny green, reflecting brightly on sides, with a small blue patch in middle of throat; back of head dark green, brighter on back, becoming gold on rump and bright rufous-orange on uppertail-coverts; tail green with slight coppery sheen at base, belly and undertail-coverts orange; bill black, feet flesh. Female has rufous-orange throat, densely spotted bright green on breast and less on flanks, orange to undertail-coverts, undertail deep rufous. Female from White-tailed Starfrontlet by paler underparts and pale patch on wings, but darker tail.

Ssp. *C. b. bonapartei* (Co: E Andes) as described
C. b. consita (NW Ve; Perijá) female has bright orange spot behind eyes, rufous band on secondaries completely bright buffy orange and brighter green tail; male has pale leaf green cap, deeper blue throat spot, dull rufous secondaries and rufescent discs on lower breast, belly and tail brighter

Habits Forages alone, at lower to mid levels.
Status Uncommon and local in Colombia, local and apparently scarce in Venezuela. Very small distribution split into 2 quite allopatric populations.
Habitat Subtropical to Temperate Zones. Borders of humid, cloud and elfin forests, open fields with scattered bushes and trees, thickets.
Voice No description found and no published recordings.

RAINBOW STARFRONTLET
Coeligena iris Pl. 105

Identification 13–15cm. Male is metallic bright green from forehead to rear crown with line of turquoise on middle and some bright orange discs at rear, back of head to nape very dark green, sides and front of face to breast bright green, back green; lower back and tail cinnamon-orange; wing-coverts green broadly fringed orange, secondaries solid orange; underparts entirely bright orange, except white thighs; bill long like a dusky needle, feet flesh. Female virtually identical, but lacks orange on rear crown. Similar race dichroura of Violet-throated has bold white line on throat.

Ssp. *C. i. aurora* (SE Ec) forehead reflects yellowish-green and crown greenish-turquoise, back more chestnut, some orange on inner primaries

C. i. hesperus (SW Ec) head pattern very complex, central coronal line turquoise, with violet discs on rear of head, crown-sides bright orange like a broad eyebrow, back of neck to nape blackish, neck-sides coppery-orange, chin to lower breast green with small patch of pink surrounded by metallic blue, merging into dull orange belly and orange-brown undertail-coverts; back green, orange reflections on rump, reddish-copper tail-coverts and coppery tail, distally olive-green; wing-coverts shiny green, secondaries solid orange, leading edges of inner 4 primaries orange; female similar but is pale orange on throat and breast, heavily spotted with discs of bright green

C. i. iris (S Ec) as described

Habits Less of a forest bird than congeners and often in more open areas. Trap-lines a wide variey of flowering shrubs and trees, including *Eucalyptus* trees.

Status Common.

Habitat Subtropical Zone to Páramo from *c.*2,000–3,300m. Semi-dry to humid areas, borders of cloud forest, hedges in gardens and highland pastures, scrub and shrubs along streams.

Voice Calls during aerial displays, series of high trills and chips (R&G).

BLUE-THROATED STARFRONTLET

Coeligena helianthea Pl. 105

Identification 14.5cm, bill 3–3.3cm. Adult male essentially all black, but has dark green iridescences all over that catch light; cap is metallic green, throat has patch of purplish-blue on centre, rump and uppertail-coverts reflect both turquoise and electric blue, depending on light even some pale green, lower breast to undertail-coverts shiny violet-pink to rosy-pink, thighs white; bill black, feet vinaceous-flesh. Female is shiny green from forehead to rump where becomes rich blue, brightest on tail-coverts, rump to short uppertail-coverts show range of iridescences, from gold and orange to purple; spot behind eyes orange, chin to vent bright pale orange with green discs on breast-sides, deep reddish-rufous discs on belly to violaceous-pink on undertail-coverts with pale orange fringes.

Ssp. *C. h. helianthea* (Co) as described

C. h. tamai (W Ve) duller and more richly coloured, back more indigo and purplish, belly more purplish-blue to pure purple undertail-coverts

Status Locally frequent in Colombia. Uncommon to frequent in Venezuela.

Habitat Subtropical to Temperate Zones, 1,900–3,300m. Humid, cloud and elfin forests, both interior and at borders and clearings, open fields with scattered shrubs, bushes or trees. Gardens, hedges, often in villages and settlements.

Voice No description found and no published recordings.

VIOLET-THROATED STARFRONTLET

Coeligena violifer Pl. 105

Identification 14.5cm, bill 3.4cm. Head to breast and back shiny green, with forehead metallic green and crown turquoise, ear-coverts metallic green, throat pinkish-violet, obvious white line across upper breast; rest rufescent chestnut, with green reflections on rump, golden and pale green on basal half of tail, becoming increasingly pure chestnut on distal quarter, washed olive-green; underparts rufous with pale orange fringes to undertail-coverts; bill dusky, feet dull flesh. From race *hesperus* of Rainbow Starfrontlet by all-green crown and chestnut tail pattern. From incas by strongly patterned tail.

Ssp. *C. v. dichroura* (S Ec)

Habits Trap-lines flowering plants low down at edges of forests, clearings and treefalls and along forest trails.

Status Uncertain, possibly rare in Ecuador.

Habitat Subtropical to Temperate Zones, 1,500–3,300m, more common at higher elevations. Cloud and elfin forests, borders, treefalls and other openings.

Voice No description found and no published recordings.

Note Listed for Ecuador (Loja) by Züchner, but R&G do not include it.

BUFF-WINGED STARFRONTLET

Coeligena lutetiae Pl. 105

Identification 14.5cm, bill 3.3cm. Essentially all dark green with bright pale buffy secondaries. Male has metallic emerald-green front and a blue bib, upperparts subtly reflect dark green-bronze, brighter on rump and tail-coverts; underparts have green reflections throughout, pale to whitish fringes on undertail-coverts; bill black, feet dark grey. Female greener above and pale buffy from chin to throat, with rows of green discs at sides, rest of underparts green with white to pale buffy scaling. Pale secondaries diagnostic.

Ssp. Monotypic (Ec, Co)

Status Uncommon in Ecuador and Colombia, where patchily distributed.

Habitat Temperate Zone to Páramo, *c.*2,600–3,600m. Humid and wet forests on hillsides and elfin forests near treeline, at borders, clearings, bushy ravines, *Polylepis* woods and thickets.

Voice Occasional flight-call described as a nasal *eernt* or *churt* (R&G).

Boissoneaua coronets are comparatively short-billed birds very similar to, but found at higher levels, than *Coeligena* starfrontlets. They all habitually raise their wings vertically for a few moments upon alighting.

VELVET-PURPLE CORONET

Boissonneaua jardini Pl. 105

Identification 12.7cm, bill 1.8cm. Black hood with purple frontlet to crown and small purple gorget on throat, underparts purple, duskier on undertail-coverts, white thighs and fringes to undertail-coverts; back metallic green with blue and leaf green reflections, tail black with second to fourth rectrices on either side white, tipped black. Female similar, with slightly smaller and duller purple patches on head, underparts fringed violet and pale violaceous grey.

Ssp. Monotypic (Ec, Co)

Habits Forages at mid and lower levels. Solitary, territorial and quite aggressive, but may gather at large flowering trees.
Status Rare in Ecuador. Seldom found and very local in Colombia.
Habitat Upper Tropical to Subtropical Zones, 800–1,700m. Wet and humid forests of lower slopes, woods with moss- and epiphyte-covered trees, borders and clearings.
Voice Courtship song is a series of alternating soft and harsh whistles *si, siii, si, siii, si, siii*... (Ruschi 1973).

CHESTNUT-BREASTED CORONET

Boissonneaua matthewsii Pl. 105

Identification 13.2cm, bill 1.8cm. Metallic green from forehead to central-tail feathers, with paler green reflections and a touch of gold in some lights, tail rufous-orange with outer edge of each rectrix solid green; chin to undertail-coverts rufous-orange, with green discs on throat, almost chestnut on breast; bill straight, needle-like and dusky, feet pink. Female is paler rufous below and has green discs on breast-sides to flanks. Juvenile like female but has more green spotting below and some cinnamon fringes to feathers of back and rump. Similar to several *Coeligena*; look for tail, which has distinctive striped pattern.

Ssp. Monotypic (Ec, Co)

Habits Forages in canopy. Solitary, very territorial and aggressive, but may gather at large flowering trees, where chases frequently occur.
Status Uncommon in Ecuador, rare in Colombia.
Habitat Subtropical to Temperate Zones, 1,200–2,600m. Humid forests, both borders and interior.
Voice No description found, but a recording from Ecuador listed in the Discography.

BUFF-TAILED CORONET

Boissonneaua flavescens Pl. 105

Identification 13.2–13.5cm, bill 1.8–2cm. Adult male shiny green over head and breast to tail, front of face metallic pale green (appears like a frontlet and gorget in some lights), uppertail-coverts fringed pale buffy, tail dark brown washed green, and all but central pair of rectrices fringed pale buffy; belly to undertail-coverts warm buffy with scattered green discs at sides, thighs white, an orange tuft at the shoulder and secondaries paler, more buff than dark brown of primaries; bill short, straight and dusky, feet dusky. Female almost identical but has feathers of chin and throat, and to a lesser extent breast, scaled white.

Ssp. *B. f. flavescens* (Ve, Co) as described
B. f. tinochlora (W Ec) fringes of tail-coverts and tail cinnamon, not pale buffy, and slightly richer cinnamon below

Habits Forages in canopy and mid levels. Solitary, territorial and aggressive, but may gather at flowering trees with others of same and different species. Holds wings up when clinging to flowers to sip nectar. Recorded clinging to vertical trunks like a woodpecker, probably to pick insects.
Status Fairly common in Colombia, uncommon in Ecuador.
Habitat Subtropical Zone to Páramo. Humid montane, wet, cloud and elfin forests, open fields with scattered bushes and trees, forest borders.
Voice Sings fast sequences of *chip* notes and may join others in singing 'circle'.

Heliangelus sunangels are medium-sized, short-billed hummingbirds adapted for feeding at short-corolla flowers. They generally have striking throat patterns and broad tails that are usually only slightly notched. Birds of borders and forest edges of the temperate highlands, they hold their wings up only for a brief moment upon alighting.

ORANGE-THROATED SUNANGEL

Heliangelus mavors Pl. 106

Identification 10.9cm, bill 1.5cm. Male has forehead and full gorget bright metallic orange, spot behind eyes pale orange, upper breast slightly paler buffy than rest, yellowish-buffy to undertail-coverts, flushed orange on sides with a narrow scattering of green discs; crown to tail shiny green with paler reflections (gold on rump and uppertail-coverts); bill orange with black culmen, feet black. Female very similar but lacks frontlet and throat is mixture of metallic orange and green discs.

Ssp. Monotypic (Co, Ve)

Habits Tends to forage fairly low down, both hovering at flowers and clinging to them. Solitary, and aggressive, vigorously defending locations with flowering shrubs. Shows interest in mixed-species flocks; hawks insects.
Status Not well known in Colombia, locally common in Venezuela but seasonal with marked movements up and downslope.
Habitat Upper Subtropical to Temperate Zones, 1,500–3,200m. Usually at edges of cloud and elfin forest, open fields with scattered bushes and trees, overgrown pastures on hillsides.
Voice Foraging call a soft trill that lasts several seconds and is helpful in locating bird (Hilty).

MÉRIDA SUNANGEL

Heliangelus spencei Pl. 106

Identification 10.8cm, bill 1.3cm. Frontlet metallic pale blue, glittering white in some lights, top and back of head dark green, rest of upperparts green; ear-coverts black, gorget purple, scaled pinky-violet, broad white breast-band, underparts yellowish to pale buff, well spotted with green discs, undertail-coverts green, fringed white; bill and feet black. Female has black ear-coverts less extensive, throat maroon with fine white scales on chin and green in centre, with many green discs at sides; less green spotting below and thus seems more yellowish. Similar Amethyst-throated Sunangel has pale green frontlet, raspberry throat and pale buffy breast bar, and is much duller below.

Ssp. Monotypic (Ve)

Habits Forages at lower to mid levels, usually at borders of forest and woodland. Territorial.
Status Uncommon Venezuela endemic.
Habitat Subtropical Zone to Páramo. Cloud and elfin forest, open páramo.
Voice Short, low-pitched, cricket-like *trilltre'e'e'e'e,* very similar to Orange-throated.
Note Recognised specifically in Stotz *et al.* (1966) and P&MdS, but included in Longuemare's Sunangel by Heynen (1999), followed by Hilty, but within Amethyst-throated Sunangel by Dickinson (2003). Until its position becomes definite, we consider the best course is to maintain the taxon as distinct.

AMETHYST-THROATED SUNANGEL

Heliangelus amethysticollis Pl. 106

Identification 11.2cm, bill 1.8cm. Frontlet metallic very pale green, glittering yellowish-white in some lights, top and back of head dark green, rest of upperparts green; ear-coverts black, gorget raspberry, scaled pink, broad yellowish-buffy breast-band, underparts mossy grey, well spotted with green, undertail-coverts fringed paler; bill and feet black. Female has black ear-coverts less extensive, throat buff well spotted with green discs at sides, but thereafter green spotting restricted to breast-sides. Similar but allopatric Longuemare's Sunangel has white breast bar.

Ssp. *H. a. laticlavius* (S Ec)

Habits Forages actively, at low to mid levels, in shrubby clearings, at forest edges and along streams. Usually clings to flowers when feeding, perhaps with outstretched wings. Hawks and sallies for insects.
Status Uncommon to locally fairly common in southern Ecuador.
Habitat Subtropical to Temperate Zones, 1,900–2,700m, but also recorded lower. Cloud and elfin forests, humid overgrown ravines, second growth, open woodland, open fields with scattered bushes and trees, forest borders.
Voice Call a clear whistle and a single, upward-inflected *tsit…tsit…tsit…tsit* lasting *c.*2 s (Hilty).
Note Three northern subspecies separated as Longuemare's Sunangel on distributional grounds (Heynen), a treatment followed by R&G, and Hilty, but not by Dickinson (2003).

LONGUEMARE'S SUNANGEL

Heliangelus clarisse Pl. 106

Identification 11.2cm, bill 1.8cm. Dark green above with dark brown outer rectrices; frontlet metallic emerald-green. Gorget rich rosy-pink with paler pink scaling, broad white bar on breast, lower breast and belly pale yellow-buffy with green discs, vent to undertail-coverts white; bill and feet dusky. Female similar but lacks green frontlet and gorget is maroonish-dusky with green discs.

Ssp. *H. c. clarisse* (Co) as described
H. c. violiceps (Ve: Perijá) male has rich turquoise frontlet and deep purplish gorget; female has duller frontlet and gorget smaller and separated from white breast-band by band of dark green
H. c. verdiscutatus (NE Co, Ve: Tamá) male has emerald frontlet with a deep, bronzy-purple crown that fades on nape and forms dark line through lores, bordering upper edge of rosy-violet gorget; female lacks frontlet but retains loral line; gorget smaller and bordered dark green.

Habits Forages actively, at low to mid levels, and along streams.
Status Frequent in Colombia, uncommon in Venezuela.
Habitat Subtropical to Temperate Zones. Cloud and elfin forests, humid overgrown ravines, second growth, open woodland, open fields with scattered bushes and trees, forest borders.
Voice A clear whistle.
Note Race *verdiscutatus*, invalidated by Heynen (1999) without explanation, is clearly valid.

ROYAL SUNANGEL

Heliangelus regalis Pl. 106

Identification 11–12cm, bill 1.8cm. Small. Male deep indigo-blue with purple gloss, deeply forked tail, white thighs; bill and feet dusky. Female green from forehead to lower rump, becoming deep bluish on tail-coverts, tail deep blue and deeply forked, though less so than male; underparts orange-cinnamon, narrow line over eyes, face-sides with green reflections, throat with paler streaks and rows of small green feathers, cinnamon-washed white breast-band and scattered green discs on body-sides. Female recalls female Orange-throated and Amethyst-throated Sunangels, but forked dark blue tail offers an easy diagnostic.

Ssp. Monotypic (S Ec?)

Habits Main food plant apparently *Brachyotum quinquenerve*, a low shrub with tubular red flowers (Heynen), and males vigorously defend their right to a clump. Often perches to feed rather than hover.
Status Vulnerable. Very small range. Rare or accidental in Ecuador?
Habitat Tropical to Subtropical Zones. Andean ridgetop forests, elfin scrub, dry grasslands with stunted scrub and lichen-covered bushes, succulents and bracken.

Voice No description found and no published recordings.
Note Described in 1979 from Cordillera del Cóndor, Peru (Fitzpatrick *et al.* 1979). Not included in R&G.

GORGETED SUNANGEL

Heliangelus strophianus Pl. 106

Identification 10.9cm, bill 1.5cm. Small bright green frontlet, crown to tail-coverts deep green, Tail deep indigo-blue and well forked; full gorget from chin to line of breast metallic violet, solid white patch on beast, rest on underparts dark green; large white fluffy thighs; bill and feet black. Female has frontlet smaller, chin black with thin white lines, gorget smaller, separated from breast bar by band of dark green, and white breast bar narrower than on male. From Amethyst-throated Sunangel by dark blue, forked tail.

Ssp. Monotypic (NW Ec, SW Co)

Habits Forages in shrubby clearings and at forest edges, but fond of damp, bushy ravines.
Status Uncommon to locally frequent in Ecuador, scarce, only 2–3 old records in Colombia.
Habitat Upper Tropical to Temperate Zones, 1,700–2,300m. Borders and interior of wet or humid forests on montane slopes, especially humid shady ravines, thickets along tracks or at edge of pastures.
Voice No description found, but a recording from Ecuador listed in Discography.

TOURMALINE SUNANGEL

Heliangelus exortis Pl. 106

Identification 10.2cm, bill 1.5cm. Male has metallic emerald-green frontlet, royal blue chin and base of malar, and deep violet throat patch; top of head to forked tail shiny green with malachite tone, breast malachite green, dark green to flanks and belly, large fluffy thighs and undertail-coverts white; bill and feet black. Female lacks frontlet and gorget is white, belly pale buff with green discs, white undertail-coverts. Juvenile like female, with dark, blackish streaks on white gorget which is also fringed black; underparts more buffy. Similar male Gorgeted Sunangel has white band on throat and dark undertail-coverts.

Ssp. Monotypic (E Ec, Co: Andes)

Status Uncommon to frequent in Ecuador, locally frequent to common in Colombia.
Habitat Temperate Zone. Borders and interior of wet and humid, dense mossy forests on montane slopes, overgrown clearings and pastures, thickets and hedges, also often around stands of bamboo.
Voice No description found, but a recording from Colombia listed in Discography.

FLAME-THROATED SUNANGEL

Heliangelus micraster Pl. 106

Identification 10–11cm, bill 1.5cm. Smaller than most congeners. Male has shiny green frontlet, rest of upperparts deep green; chin black, full gorget bright rich orange, breast to upper belly and sides dark green, grading over belly and flanks with diminishing green discs, rest of underparts white; bill and feet black. Female has chin and upper throat white, lower part orange, otherwise like male.

Ssp. *H. m. micraster* (S Ec)

Habits Territorial, defends chosen flowering shrubs vigorously, Forages rather low in forest and at edges but often ventures to flowering shrubs in adjacent open areas.
Status Uncommon in Ecuador.
Habitat Temperate Zone. Borders and interior of humid or wet forests on montane slopes where moss and epiphyte cover is dense. Also fallow pastures or open fields with bushes next to woods.
Voice No description found, recordings from Ecuador and Peru listed in Discography.
Notes Called Little Sunangel by some authors and sometimes considered a subspecies of Tourmaline Sunangel.

PURPLE-THROATED SUNANGEL

Heliangelus viola Pl. 106

Identification 11–12cm, bill 1.4cm. Deep rich green except turquoise frontlet, full pendant gorget rich glittering purple, surrounded by turquoise reflections, especially on breast; thighs white and very fluffy, undertail-coverts fringed buffy, tail long and deeply forked, with outer pair of rectrices black; bill and feet black. Female has black gorget that becomes olive-green at sides, otherwise like male.

Ssp. Monotypic (S Ec)

Habits Very feisty, chases conspecifics and other, usually smaller hummingbirds.
Status Frequent to locally common in Ecuador.
Habitat Upper Subtropical to Temperate Zones, *c.*2,100–3,000m. Humid and cloud forests, *Alnus* woodland, *Eucalyptus* plantations, second growth, fields or pastures with bushes or thickets. Also, relatively dry areas, gardens and orchards.
Voice No description found, but 2 recordings from Ecuador listed in Discography.

BOGOTÁ SUNANGEL

Heliangelus zusii Pl. 106

Identification *c.*12cm, bill 1.8cm. Frontlet metallic yellowish-leaf green, tiny chin black, full gorget metallic emerald-green, rest essentially deep purplish indigo-blue; ear-coverts bright royal blue, tail long and deeply forked, purple; deep blue breast and flanks scaled olive-green, belly and undertail-coverts olivaceous, thighs fluffy and grey; bill and feet black.
Status Data deficient and species status dubious. Redescribed in 1998, from a single 'Bogotá' skin of an apparent male; previously described as *Neolesbia nehrkorni*. Possibly a hybrid, but until genetic studies are undertaken, any statement regarding the validity of this specimen as a bona fide species or a hybrid must be speculation.

Habitat Unknown.
Voice Unknown.
Note The description assumes that the specimen's provenance is Colombia, and discounted a hybrid based on an evaluation of possible Colombian parent species. However, many skins that were shipped to Europe and the US from Bogotá were from Ecuador, thus many possible parents have not been considered. At present, debate is ongoing as to the status of *H. zusii*. Sadly, there are many such 'Bogotá' specimens known, all representatives of lost species or hybrids, and of which effectively nothing is known.

Pufflegs of the genus *Eriocnemis* are small to medium-sized hummingbirds, largely dark green with forked, deep blue tails and straight, needle-like bills. They take their collective name from the large fluffy white feathers on the thighs that cover the tarsi. They are birds of high elevations in the Andes, often at the treeline. Territorial and tend to forage fairly low around shrubby thickets and edges. *Haplophaedia* pufflegs are duller and tend to keep within forest.

BLACK-BREASTED PUFFLEG

Eriocnemis nigrivestis Pl. 107

Identification 8–9cm, bill 1.3cm. Dark green head to back, belly and flanks, with a deep purplish-blue patch in middle of throat, and central breast darker with less greenish reflection; lower back to tail and undertail-coverts deep purplish-blue, large fluffy white thighs cover tarsi and most of feet; bill and feet black. Female almost entirely green with deep purplish-blue undertail-coverts, turquoise uppertail-coverts and dark blue tail; short white line from below lores to below eyes, small blue triangle on throat, golden reflections on nape and neck-sides, soft white scaling on belly and flanks. Juvenile similar but has cinnamon line below eyes, and blue throat spot half the size. Turquoise-throated Puffleg is similar to female, but extremely rare and at lower elevations. Coppery-bellied Puffleg also similar to female but has golden reflections on belly and longer, more deeply forked tail. From woodnymphs by blue undertail-coverts and large white leg puffs.

Ssp. Monotypic (Ec)

Status Critically Endangered. Very rare Ecuadorian endemic, known from 3–4 localities, including slopes of Pichincha and Atacazo volcanos. Severely threatened by habitat loss.
Habitat Temperate Zone to Páramo. Exclusively in very stunted elfin forest on rocky montane ridges, in dense undergrowth rich in epiphytes, mosses, Ericaceae and Bromeliaceae, or at edges overgrown with brambles.
Voice No description found, and no published recordings.

GLOWING PUFFLEG

Eriocnemis vestita Pl. 107

Identification 9cm, bill 1.8cm. Fairly dark green above, turquoise on uppertail-coverts, tail dusky, gorget rich lustrous purplish-blue, dark green breast, belly and flanks turquoise, fluffy white thighs, purple undertail-coverts; bill and feet black. Female has throat to centre of breast golden-yellow with rows of green discs and a band of blue discs across centre, otherwise like male.

Ssp. *E. v. paramillo* (N Co: W & C Andes) throat patch has bright emerald-green crescent either side; belly and flanks black.
E. v. vestita (NW Ve, Co: E Andes) as described
E. v. smaragdinipectus (E Ec, SW Co) broader blue throat patch than others

Status Uncommon in Ecuador, local in Colombia and Venezuela.
Habitat Temperate Zone to Páramo, 2,500–3,500m in Ecuador, 2,250–3,850m in Colombia and 2,600–4,200m in Venezuela. Cloud and elfin forest, scattered bushes and trees in fields, overgrown pastures, bushy slopes and páramos.
Voice No description found, but 2 recordings from Ecuador listed in Discography.

TURQUOISE-THROATED PUFFLEG

Eriocnemis godini Pl. 107

Identification 10-11cm, bill 1.8cm. Adult male has bright pale green frontlet, dark green to rump, uppertail-coverts turquoise, tail deep purplish-blue; throat metallic turquoise with broad band of golden reflections at sides, belly to flanks green with some gold reflections; thighs very fluffy and white, virtually covering feet, undertail-coverts purple; bill and feet black. Female similar but uppertail-coverts and gorget pastel green-turquoise, belly covered with golden reflections.

Ssp. Monotypic (Ec, Co?)

Status Critically Endangered. Very rare Ecuadorian endemic that perhaps formerly occurred in southern Colombia. Known from 4 19th-century specimens and unrecorded for more than 50 years, it could possibly be extinct.
Habitat Upper Subtropical to Temperate Zones, 2,100–2,300m. Possibly in humid to dry forests, both within and at shrubby borders.
Voice No description found (probably unknown) and no published recordings.

SAPPHIRE-VENTED PUFFLEG

Eriocnemis luciani Pl. 107

Identification 13.4cm, bill 2cm. Forehead to forecrown and base of bill, including small chin metallic deep sky blue, quickly green on rest of body and wings; tail long, deeply forked and deep purplish indigo-blue, thighs have long thick fluffy white feathers that conceal tarsi and toes, undertail purple; bill and feet black. Sexes alike, though female has slightly shorter and less deeply forked tail.

Ssp. *E. l. luciani* (W Ec, SW Co)

Habits Solitary, usually in the open rather than in cover, and sometimes seen on ground, feeding at flowers of ground-cover plants. Also hawks for insects. Territorial and very defensive of chosen feeding areas.

Status Uncommon to locally common in Ecuador, uncommon in Colombia.
Habitat Temperate Zone to Páramo, 2,800–4,800m. Open grassy or shrubby areas. Wet montane forest borders, highland fields and pastures, páramo.
Voice No description found, but a recording from Ecuador listed in the Discography.

COPPERY-BELLIED PUFFLEG

Eriocnemis cupreoventris Pl. 107

Identification 11.5cm, bill 1.8cm. Forehead to rump green, uppertail-coverts turquoise sky blue, tail deep indigo; throat to breast and flanks brighter, shiny green, belly shiny golden to coppery, thighs white, undertail-coverts purple; bill and feet black. Female has slight white scaling on throat and less coppery-gold on belly.

Ssp. Monotypic (Co, Ve)

Habits Forages low, searching for flowers with short corollas, clinging to plant while feeding, not hovering. Sallies for insects. Very territorial and aggressive in defence of chosen area.
Status Locally frequent in Colombia and Venezuela.
Habitat Temperate Zone to Páramo, *c.*2,000–3,000m, mostly above 2,500m. Fairly open areas, *Espeletia* and shrubs of páramo, forest borders, hedges and thickets, bushy slopes, occasionally inside montane forest. Occasionally reaches páramo.
Voice No description found and no published recordings.

GOLDEN-BREASTED PUFFLEG

Eriocnemis mosquera Pl. 107

Identification 13.4cm, bill 2cm. Green with golden reflections on throat and breast, long forked tail with bluish reflections, fluffy white thighs, grey undertail-coverts. Female similar but has shorter wings and tail, and undertail-coverts slightly greenish.

Ssp. Monotypic (N Ec, S Co)

Habits Forages at low flowers on bushes in forest, at edges and in clearings, both clinging to flowers and hovering to feed. Territorial and very aggressive.
Status Uncommon to frequent in Ecuador and locally frequent in Colombia.
Habitat Temperate Zone, mainly 2,500–3,500m, with records much lower and slightly higher. Borders and overgrown clearings of humid, wet, cloud or elfin forests, and stunted montane woodland; most often near timberline, between woods and open páramo.
Voice No description found and no published recordings.

COLOURFUL PUFFLEG

Eriocnemis mirabilis Pl. 107

Identification 9.6cm, bill 1.5cm. Male has frontlet glittering turquoise-green and poorly defined gorget a mix of metallic turquoise, leaf green and malachite, rest of head, sides of neck and breast, to tail shiny green, flanks green with shiny red and maroon discs; belly to vent purple, massive silky white thighs with a cinnamon wash on undersides, undertail-coverts a metallic rainbow of pale orange, vermilion-red and leaf green; bill black, feet pink. Female shiny green above and below to breast and body-sides, with heavy white scaling from chin to central belly, clear at sides but like a waterfall of white in middle, thighs massive, silky and white, rest of underparts reddish-bronze with fine white scaling. From other pufflegs by bright purple belly and rainbow-orange undertail-coverts. Quieter female equally distinct.

Ssp. Monotypic (Co)

Status Vulnerable. Uncommon Colombian endemic with a small range.
Habitat Upper Subtropical to Temperate Zones, 2,200–2,500m. Pristine wet and cloud forests, both interior and at borders and clearings.
Voice No description found and no published recordings.

EMERALD-BELLIED PUFFLEG

Eriocnemis alinae Pl. 107

Identification 9.1cm, bill 1.5cm. Tiny hummingbird, with a brilliant emerald frontlet, outlined black, rest green with distinct turquoise wash to uppertail-coverts, tail and underparts, and massive white thighs; large white breast plaque with scattering of shiny, dark green discs; tail has outermost edges slightly convex and indent of fork slightly curved; thin needle-like bill, black, feet pink. Female lacks frontlet.

Ssp. *E. a. alinae* (E Ec, SC Co)

Habits Prefers open spaces within humid and wet forest, groves and glades, treefalls and clearings, all with some canopy cover.
Status Very rare in Ecuador. In Colombia, locally common to scarce.
Habitat Subtropical to Temperate Zones, 2,300–2,800m. Wet and cloud forests, mostly interior but occasionally at borders, oak forests and ridges.
Voice No description found and no published recordings.

BLACK-THIGHED PUFFLEG

Eriocnemis derbyi Pl. 107

Identification 11.7cm, bill 2cm. Green and black with distinctive tail shape. Male green on head, wings and back to uppertail-coverts, which have gold fringes; tail black with outer edge convex, outer 2 rectrices on either side point slightly inwards, rest form a slightly curved indentation to form fork; black underparts start at centre of throat then widen to vent and flanks, sides and centre of belly have scattered green discs, thighs are massive and black! Undertail-coverts green with gold fringes; bill and feet black. Female has much reduced black below, mainly at base of thighs, the outer thighs being pure white; also subtle white scaling over most of underparts. From other pufflegs by black underparts and tail, not to mention tail shape.

Ssp. *E. d. derbyi* (N Ec, Co: C Andes)

Habits Forages for nectar among low-growing flowers, and hawks for insects.
Status Uncommon to rare in Ecuador.
Habitat Temperate Zone to Páramo, 2,500–3,600m. Partially open areas, hedges and woods or bushes in fields and pastures, borders of humid, wet, cloud or elfin forest, overgrown ravines.
Voice No description found, but a recording from Colombia listed in Discography.
Note Formerly included race *longirostris*, based on longer bill, from northern Colombia, but distinction proved clinal and race subsumed in nominate (Heynen).

GREENISH PUFFLEG

Haplophaedia aureliae Pl. 107

Identification 10.5–11.1cm, bill 2cm. Almost entirely dark green with a coppery iridescence, except slightly forked dark blue tail and large white fluffy thighs; bill and feet black. From similar Hoary Puffleg by green underparts and range.

Ssp. *H. a. aureliae* (Co: NC&E Andes) as described
H. a. caucensis (Co: W&C Andes) more coppery on head and rump, larger white patch on belly
H. a. russata (E Ec) brighter coppery above, almost no white below

Habits Moves seasonally up and downslope.
Status Uncommon in Ecuador, frequent in Colombia.
Habitat Subtropical Zone, 1,500–2,500m, sometimes to 3,100m. Humid, wet and cloud forests.
Voice Males may gather in loose groups to sing, an endless repeated *tur seet*, *c.*1 per s (H&B).

HOARY PUFFLEG

Haplophaedia lugens Pl. 107

Identification 10.9cm, bill 1.8cm. Almost entirely dark green, black on face to breast, large white fluffy thighs, greyish undertail-coverts, tail slightly forked and deep indigo-blue; bill and feet black. From similar Greenish Puffleg by dull brown underparts, and range.

Ssp. Monotypic (NW Ec, SW Co)

Status Uncommon in Ecuador, local in Colombia. Range very small and shrinking as habitat disappears, only on Pacific slopes of Andes.
Habitat Upper Tropical to Subtropical Zones, 1,500–2,100 in Ecuador, 1,200–2,500m in Colombia. Humid, wet and cloud forests, mature second growth, borders and small clearings, along wooded montane streams.
Voice Loud *tzik* notes when foraging (P. Coopmans in R&G).

Whitetips are 2 small hummingbirds, one on eastern slopes and the other on western slopes of the Andes, immediately distinguished by the males unique large white spot in the middle of the dark, forked tail. They have sometimes been considered conspecific.

PURPLE-BIBBED WHITETIP

Urosticte benjamini Pl. 107

Identification Male 8.9cm, female 8.1 cm, bill 2cm. Green forehead to tail-coverts, tail brown with distinct green wash, and large rounded white distal half to 2 central feathers; long white triangle behind eyes, chin and throat to ear-coverts form broad gorget of brilliant emerald-green with a shiny bib of raspberry on upper breast and narrow white line encasing them; lower breast to belly and flanks grass green, white thighs, undertail-coverts apple green; bill long and straight, like a dusky needle, feet black. Female all green above, with pale tips to outer 2 rectrices; large white postocular spot, underparts apple green, scaled white, white malar line, thighs and undertail-coverts. Juvenile female like adult but duller and has buffy fringes to head. Juvenile male like adult female but has small white spot on central tail-feathers and complete gorget pale orange. Female and juvenile of allopatric Rufous-vented Whitetip remarkably similar but separated by their buffy undertail-coverts.

Ssp. Monotypic (W Ec, SW & W Co)

Habits Forages within foliage at all levels. Feeds by hovering at small flowers and also gleans insects from leaves and twigs. Gathers at blooming *Inga*.
Status Rare to uncommon in Ecuador, fairly common in Colombia.
Habitat Upper Tropical to Subtropical Zones. Humid and wet forests, borders. Keeps in cover.
Voice No description found, but a recording from Ecuador listed in the Discography.
Note Proposed race *rostrata* (W Co) based on a probably aberrant individual (Schuchmann).

RUFOUS-VENTED WHITETIP

Urosticte ruficrissa Pl. 107

Identification Male 9.4cm, female 8.6cm, bill 2cm. Adult male green from forehead to tail-coverts, tail dark brown with subtle green wash, and large rounded white distal half to 4 central feathers; short white triangle behind eyes, chin and throat, cheeks to breast metallic green with broken white line separating breast and belly; belly and flanks less shiny, white thighs, undertail-coverts buffy; bill long and straight, like a dusky needle, feet black. Female all green above, with white tips to outer 2 rectrices; face-sides (including postocular spot) to flanks, thighs and vent white, spotted green, darker on throat and face, and pale apple on body-sides and flanks. Juvenile female like adult but duller and has buffy fringes to head. Juvenile male like adult female but has small white spot on central tail-feathers, complete gorget pale orange, and rather more green spotting on underparts. Allopatric Purple-bibbed Whitetip female and juvenile remarkably similar, but have white undertail-coverts.

Ssp. Monotypic (E Ec, Co)

Habits Solitary inside foliage at all levels. Hovers at flowers for nectar (*Palicourea*, *Clusia*, *Cavendishia* and other bromeliads),

takes insects by hawking or tiny spiders and insects by gleaning. Moves seasonally up and downslope.
Status Uncommon and local in Colombia, uncommon to rare in Ecuador.
Habitat Subtropical Zone. Humid montane and cloud forest, in semi-open areas.
Voice No description found and no published recordings.

BEARDED HELMETCREST

Oxypogon guerinii Pl. 109

Identification 11.2–11.5cm, bill 0.8cm. Long black crest with white or coloured centre, face-sides black, chin to throat white with long, lanceolate feathers coloured in centre; upperparts bronzy olive-green, tail dark brown with variable amounts of white according to race (see plate), dark face has whitish halo, and underparts brown to dark olive-green; short fine needle-like bill is black, feet grey. Female lacks crest and beard, being all dark on top of head with a white throat. Juvenile like female but lacks white throat. Unique crest and facial pattern easily recognised, despite racial variation.

Ssp. *O. g. stuebelii* (Co: C Andes) blue throat stripe, cinnamon stripe on centre of crest, undertail rufous with outer webs creamy to pale cinnamon; breast scaled cinnamon-buff, increasingly broad until vent, and undertail-coverts almost pure cinnamon-buff
O. g. cyanolaemus (Co: Santa Marta) long purple throat stripe, breast scaled grey, vent to undertail-coverts buffy-white, undertail entirely cream with broad olive tips
O. g. guerinii (Co: E Andes) celadon green throat, undertail dark rufous with pale band on centre of each feather for basal two-thirds, shafts white
O. g. lindenii (Ve) apple green streaks in white beard, underparts very dark olive-green, lightly scaled grey, vent grey, undertail deep maroon with white shafts, narrowly edged white for basal two-thirds of rectrix

Habits Forages in low vegetation, often in fields planted with garlic, onion and other crops. Perches on flowers to feed, especially *Espeletia*, and sometimes even walks on mats of tight, fine grass to pick insects (T. Züchner pers. comm.). Moves widely and swiftly over fields and streams, often flying low. Sallies for and hawks insects.

Bearded Helmetcrest, juvenile male (left), old male (right), showing crests raised

Status Locally common but difficult to find when flowers not blooming on páramo.
Habitat Temperate Zone to Páramo, 3,000–5,200m. Elfin forest, slopes with *Espeletia*, grasses, stands of *Polylepis* and other bushes on páramo and adjacent high valleys in mountains.
Voice Song a short trilled phrase *ti-e-o*, oft-repeated, and a squeaky *seep* (H&B, F&K).

Thornbills and metaltails are small to medium-sized hummingbirds, usually with broad, forked tails, short needle-like bills and often some brilliant spots of colour. They are essentially birds of high country, at the treeline and above, at woodland edges and shrubby thickets, seldom venturing onto open páramo.

VIOLET-THROATED METALTAIL

Metallura baroni Pl. 108

Identification 10–11cm, bill 1.5cm. Adult male is almost entirely shiny deep bottle or bronzy-green, with a deep purplish-violet gorget; undertail-coverts fringed rufous, tail deep blue above, bronze-green below. Female has entire underparts scaled, pale grey on throat, breast and belly; bill black, feet grey.

Ssp. Monotypic (S Ec)

Habits Solitary, with males holding feeding territories. Feeds by hovering in front of flowers. Usually fairly low, and may forage insects from the ground.
Status Vulnerable. Uncommon in Ecuador and very small range threatened by deforestation.
Habitat Temperate Zone to Páramo, *c.*3,100–3,700m. Borders of cloud and elfin forest, *Polylepis* woodland in páramo, fields with rocky outcrops covered by thick mats of mosses, bromeliads and epiphytes.
Voice No description found.

PURPLE-BACKED THORNBILL

Ramphomicron microrhynchum Pl. 108

Identification 8.6cm, bill 0.5cm. Small and slender; male has deep-forked tail and is entirely metallic purple-violet above with blackish lores and dark ear-coverts, brilliant emerald-green gorget and green underparts, fluffy white thighs and greyish undertail-coverts scaled white; small thin bill and feet dusky. Immature male deep purple above with shorter, less deeply forked reddish-maroon tail; throat buffy-white with a few green discs, breast and belly to flanks olive-green, undertail-coverts creamy with narrow dusky centres. Female green above with red uppertail-coverts and maroon tail, most reddish in centre, and white tips to outer 2 rectrices on each side; throat warm ochaceous buff, with white belly and undertail-coverts, spotted green on throat and breast, sides of breast and body have dense green spots, almost joining on upper belly.

Ssp. *R. m. andicola* (W Ve) golden bib fringed green
R. m. microrhynchum (Ec, Co) as described

Habits Tends to forage alone but several may gather at flowering trees; may hover but usually perches on flower to

probe for nectar and to take insects, but also hawks flying insects. Also uses holes in base of corolla made by *Diglossa*.
Status Uncommon in Ecuador, widespread but scarce in Colombia and Venezuela.
Habitat Temperate Zone to Páramo. Cloud and elfin forests, thickets and hedges on slopes and in ravines, páramo with scattered patches of *Polylepis*.
Voice Calls long repetitions of *ti, ti, ti, ti…*

BLACK-BACKED THORNBILL
Ramphomicron dorsale Pl. 108

Identification 9-10cm, bill 0.8cm and very slightly decurved. Male slender with a long, deeply forked tail, velvety black above with subtle purple tone, uppertail-coverts have metallic bronze fringes, tail deep purple; deep gorget of brilliant emerald-green, breast to upper flanks and belly rufescent heavily spotted with shiny green discs, thighs white and undertail-coverts grey; bill and feet dusky. Female rich green above, reddish-rufous on uppertail-coverts, tail deep indigo with white distal half of outer web of outermost rectrix on each side, next 3 rectrices have white tips; entirely white below with a few scattered green discs on throat and breast-sides.

Ssp. Monotypic (Co)

Habits Forages at all levels, usually solitary. Often perches on flowers, takes insects by gleaning ang hawking.
Status Uncommon Colombian endemic in Santa Marta.
Habitat Subtropical Zone to Páramo, 2,000–4,600m. Partially open areas, borders of humid, wet, cloud and elfin forest, hedges, highland fields and pastures with patchy bushes, open páramo.
Voice No description found.

VIRIDIAN METALTAIL
Metallura williami Pl. 108

Identification 10.1cm, bill 1.5cm. Adult male entirely green with metallic green gorget, white thighs, undertail-coverts fringed cinnamon, deep blue tail; thin black bill, grey feet. Female has throat to centre of breast yellow, with rows of green discs, cinnamon scaling below brighter and more extensive.

Ssp. *M. w. atrigularis* (S Ec) male has black bib with extensive metallic green either side; tail entirely green
M. w. williami (Co: C Andes) as described
M. w. recisa (NW Co) all green with metallic green gorget; undertail-coverts scaled cinnamon
M. w. primolina (NE Ec) bib bright green, tail reddish above, green below

Habits Solitary, males defend feeding territories. Forages at all levels, hovers to feed from flowers.
Status Uncommon in Ecuador, uncommon to locally common in Colombia.
Habitat Temperate Zone to Páramo, 2,100–2,700m. Borders of cloud and elfin forest, thickets, stands of bushes or trees and hedges in fields, pastures and open páramo.
Voice No description found.

NEBLINA METALTAIL
Metallura odomae Pl. 108

Identification 10–11cm, bill 0.9cm. Olive above and below, with bronze and gold reflections, full gorget crimson, long uppertail-coverts and tail bright blue, undertail yellowish-green with whitish tips to outer rectrices; white thighs, undertail-coverts fringed cinnamon; bill dusky, feet black. Female very similar but gorget scaled pale grey and underparts scaled buffy to cinnamon.

Ssp. Monotypic (S Ec)

Habits Solitary, with males defending feeding territories. Forages at all levels. Hawks for insects.
Status Uncommon in Ecuador.
Habitat Temperate Zone to Páramo, 2,600–3,400m. Open areas, borders of cloud and elfin forest, wet overgrown ravines, thickets, hedges and scattered stands of woodland in wet and boggy open fields and páramo.
Voice No description found.

RUFOUS-CAPPED THORNBILL
Chalcostigma ruficeps Pl. 108

Identification 8-9cm, bill 1.1cm. Adult male has entire top of head bright chestnut, gorget metallic turquoise and may reflect a partial rainbow (sky blue, turquoise, yellow and leaf green); undertail-coverts rather drab, rest of body green, shining quite brightly on different parts of back at different times, tail olive-green with rufous reflection, undertail bronze; bill black, thighs white, feet grey. Female green above, tail as male, underparts pale cinnamon with some green discs on sides, and white scaling on undertail-coverts.

Ssp. Monotypic (S Ec)

Habits Forages at lower levels, usually clinging to flowers in search of nectar and insects. Takes advantage of holes in bases of corollas made by a *Diglossa*, and apparently makes its own slits (Heindl). Males are territorial.
Status Rare and local, but recorded once in unusual numbers at one locality, which may indicate seasonal movements. In Colombia only a few sightings.
Habitat Temperate Zone, 1,400–3,800m but most numerous *c.*2,500m (Heindl). Borders and clearings of humid and mossy cloud forests, second growth, shrubs along streams.
Voice Calls include high *tzee* notes in flight and muted trills from a perch.
Note Race *aureofastigata* considered too doubtful to maintain (R&G) and synonymised under nominate by Heindl on grounds of clinal progression of throat coloration. Certainly there is variation as no two illustrations in the literature bear much relation.

TYRIAN METALTAIL
Metallura tyrianthina Pl. 108

Identification Male 8.1–9cm, female 7.6cm, bill 1cm. Adult male has green upperparts, with coppery-bronze tail above and below; full gorget metallic emerald-green with turquoise glints, breast to belly and flanks green, thighs white, undertail-coverts dull greenish with buffy scaling; short fine, straight bill and feet black. Female has underparts buffy to pale cinnamon, with shiny green discs, fringed white on throat and breast, becoming irregular and dense on breast- and body-sides, scaled whitish on undertail-coverts, thighs white.

Ssp. *M. t. districta* (Co: Santa Marta, Ve: Perijá) tail violet-blue
M. t. oreopola (Ve) tail golden-red
M. t. chloropogon (N Ve) tail coppery-red
M. t. quitensis (NW Ec) tail bronze-olive
M. t. tyrianthina (E&S Ec, Co, Ve: Tamá) as described; tail bronze

Habits Forages alone, at low to mid levels, aggressively defending feeding spot at shrubs and bushes. Breeding females also defend feeding territory around nest. Perches to feed rather than hovering. Prefers flower with open corollas (Melastomataceae, Ericaceae, Solenaceae), but occasionally punctures holes in base of flowers with long corollas. Not shy, flutters at flowers unworried by observers.
Status Locally common and abundant at certain seasons.
Habitat Temperate Zone to Páramo. Interior, borders and clearings of wet, cloud and elfin forest, stands of woodland in páramo, areas where trees are overgrown with *Tillandsia* and other epiphytes.
Voice Calls from a bare twig, low gurgling chips and short rolled notes.

PERIJÁ METALTAIL
Metallura iracunda Pl. 108

Identification 10.2–10.6cm, bill 1–1.35cm. Larger than Tyrian Metaltail, with much broader, fuller tail only shallowly forked. Dark green head, back and breast to belly and flanks, with contrasting gorget of bright emerald-green with a malachite tone; wings and lower back to uppertail-coverts reddish-bronze with increasingly red reflections to tail-coverts, tail shiny ruby-red above and below; thighs white, undertail-coverts maroon scaled pale buffy; bill has dead straight culmen, appearing slightly upturned, feet black. Female smaller with shorter tail, and less reddish above; pale buffy cinnamon below, with dull greenish wash on breast to undertail-coverts, thighs fluffy white, undertail-coverts scaled white.

Ssp. Monotypic (Co, Ve)

Habits Generally forages at lower levels. Very poorly known.
Status Unknown but probably Near Threatened. Perijá remains inaccessible due to occupation by Colombian terrorists, recent reports warn of extensive habitat loss.
Habitat Temperate Zone, 1,850–3,200m. Open, grassy fields with scattered brush and *Swallenochloa* bamboo; humid and elfin forest borders near tops.
Voice No description found.

BLUE-MANTLED THORNBILL
Chalcostigma stanleyi Pl. 108

Identification 10.8–11.8cm, bill 1.2cm. Rather larger than congeners. Male has dusky head with deep green reflections and brilliant metallic double gorget, outlined black, the larger, upper half emerald-green with leaf green reflections, lower half rosy-violet with pink reflections, rest of underparts dusky with green reflections on breast and undertail-coverts; back to tail deep indigo-blue with purplish gloss and reflections, slightly bronzy on tail-coverts. Female slightly smaller and lacks lower half of gorget. From other thornbills and metaltails by intensity of blue on body.

Ssp. *C. s. stanleyi* (Ec: both slopes)

Habits Forages alone, on shrubs and bushes at mid levels, and in canopy of *Gynoxys*, where gleans insects around and under leaves, and feeds on sweet secretions from stems. Prefers small flowers (*Gentiana*, *Berberis*, *Ribes*, *Guatteria*), perching to feed. Hawks for insects or picks them from ground. Often seen trying to chase Tit-like Dacnis, which shares habitat and competes for same flowers.
Status Uncommon and local in Ecuador.
Habitat Temperate Zone to Páramo. Humid open, steep and rocky slopes with stands of *Polylepis* and *Gynoxys* woods.
Voice Call a weak *dzr* note (F&K).

BRONZE-TAILED THORNBILL
Chalcostigma heteropogon Pl. 108

Identification Male 12.7–13cm, female 8.7–10.2cm, bill 1.3cm. Adult male almost entirely bronze-green except extraordinary extended gorget, which is bright metallic seladon-green with a twin extension of shiny, rosy-pink feathers in an inverted V; rump and uppertail-coverts deep coppery-red; white thighs full and fluffy, undertail feathers fringed buff; tail is full with rounded ends, and deeply-forked. Female slightly smaller and lacks gorget.

Ssp. Monotypic (N Co, Ve: Tamá, Táchira)

Habits Forages alone on low páramo vegetation, mostly flowers of *Espeletia,* but also shrubs of Geraniaceae and Ericaceae, *Hesperomeles*, *Osteomeles*, *Rubus*, *Brachyotum* and *Bartsia*. Clings to flowers to feed, also picks insects by hawking, gleaning amid leaves and even walking or hopping on dense mosses and fine grass on ground. Males often have ruffled appearance. Hovering flight erratic and slow. Very aggressive in defending feeding spot, will not accept company even at flowering trees.
Status Common.
Habitat Temperate Zone. Open rocky fields with grasses, *Espeletia*, scattered bushes and stands of *Polylepis*, gulleys with ferns and bromeliads, borders of elfin forest, cliffs and crags on páramo and adjacent high valleys.
Voice Calls from exposed perch, chipping repeatedly.

RAINBOW-BEARDED THORNBILL
Chalcostigma herrani Pl. 108

Identification 10.8–10.9cm, bill 1.2–1.3cm. Almost entirely dark green; crest long, orange-rufous becoming increasingly golden at tip, gorget is a true rainbow, from celadon-green through turquoise to yellow, orange and vermilion-red at end, varying with light; large broad tail is deep purple, with narrow whitish tips at corners, undertail dusky purple with distal half of feathers white; thighs white; needle-like bill and feet black. Female has solid rufous crest, and lower belly to undertail-coverts pale yellowish-ochre. Immature/juvenile like female but some white streaks and scaling on throat. Male unique, female and juvenile by rufous crown.

Ssp. *C. h. herrani* (S Co, N Ec) as described
C. h. tolimae (Co: W Andes) darker green, throat patch elongated to form narrow beard

Habits Forages alone, mostly low at flowers of páramo shrubs and bushes (*Brachyotum*, *Puya*) and thickets at forest borders. Hangs from or perches on flowers. Very territorial, will chase other birds from favoured clump of flowers, and will not accept other hummingbirds even at large flowering trees. Fans tail often, in what may be a signal, and displays from perch by singing and flapping wings.
Status Uncommon and local.
Habitat Temperate Zone. Elfin forest, open country with bushy patches and stands of *Polylepis* and *Escallonia* woodland, gulleys with thickets of ferns and bromeliads.
Voice Song *cheet-dee-dee-cheet*, a sequence that is oft-repeated (F&K).

WEDGE-BILLED HUMMINGBIRD
Schistes geoffroyi Pl. 109

Identification 8.6cm, bill 1.5cm. Tiny hummingbird with rather complex pattern of colours. Top of head, mantle and wings dark green, back of head rufescent, nape turquoise, lower back to uppertail-coverts rufous, brightest on tail-coverts, tail basally green, becoming blue, the central pair of feathers tipped green, the rest tipped white; long postocular stripe white, lores to ear-coverts blackish, green on face-sides and bright blue on neck-sides; chin and throat metallic emerald or white depending on race, white on sides of neck below blue, breast and sides apple green, belly, flanks, thighs and undertail-coverts white; needle-like bill and feet black. Female and juvenile are not significantly different.

Ssp. *S. g. geoffroyi* (E Ec, E Co, N Ve) chin and throat green
S. g. albogularis (W Ec, Co W&C Andes) chin and throat white, joining white crescent at sides of throat

Habits Always forages alone, never gathers at flowering trees. Feeds at all levels, but mostly at lower levels, in flowers with tubular corollas, following trap-line route.
Status Rare in Ecuador. Frequent to common but very local in Colombia and Venezuela.
Habitat Upper Tropical to Subtropical Zones. Interior of dense humid, wet and cloud forests, where branches are overgrown with mosses and epiphytes.
Voice Reportedly the best singer among hummingbirds, but no description found.

MOUNTAIN AVOCETBILL
Opisthoprora euryptera Pl. 109

Identification 10.2cm, bill 1.3cm. Small brownish-green bird, greener on body, more bronze on head, tail dark green with pale green tips; small buffy-cinnamon malar, underparts white from chin to breast, washed narrowly cinnamon at sides, rest of underparts orange-rufous, spotted and streaked green from chin to flanks; bill needle-like and lightly upturned at tip, and feet black.

Ssp. Monotypic (Ec, Co)

Habits Forages alone at lower levels, in thickets, at small flowers with tubular corollas. Seems lethargic in comparison with other hummingbirds.
Status Rare and local.
Habitat Temperate Zone to Páramo, 2,600–3,600m. Dense, humid and wet montane forests, both interior and at borders or along tracks.
Voice No description found.

Heliothryx are a couple of rather different-looking hummingbirds, remarkably alike, thankfully allopatric, and smooth-feathered, with a silky smooth plumage. They are interesting in having females larger than males, with significantly longer tails.

PURPLE-CROWNED FAIRY
Heliothryx barroti Pl. 109

Identification Male 12.2cm, female 12.9cm, bill 1.5cm. Male has bright purple frontlet, black ear-coverts with purple patch on neck-sides, rest of upperparts bright apple green, with pale yellow-green shafts, becoming turquoise on rump and uppertail-coverts; tail moderately long with central pair of feathers deep blue, darkening at tips, next pair almost as long, the remaining 3 pairs very steeply graduated; a strip of turquoise on malar separates black and purple from white underparts; long needle-like bill and feet black. Female lacks purple frontlet, has patch on neck-sides black and malar white along with rest of underparts; tail half as long again as male's.

Ssp. Monotypic (Ec, Co)

Habits At all levels, always forages alone; groups never gather at flowering trees. Inside forest stays in canopy, but most often found in low shrubbery at edges and in clearings. Favourite flowers include *Inga* and *Erythrina*, *Guzmania*, *Cavendishia*, *Passiflora*. Very vivacious, dashes swiftly between flowers, fanning tail frequently or lifting it stiffly to steer hovering approach to a corolla.
Status Uncommon in Ecuador, frequent in Colombia.
Habitat Tropical Zone, usually to 500m, recorded to 1,000m. Humid and wet forests, mature second growth, borders, clearings.
Voice Only infrequent squeaks.

BLACK-EARED FAIRY
Heliothryx auritus Pl. 109

Identification Male 11.6cm, female 13.2cm, bill 1.5cm. Male has black ear-coverts with purple patch on neck-sides, rest of upperparts bright apple green with pale yellow-green shafts, becoming turquoise on rump and uppertail-coverts; tail moderately long with central pair of feathers deep blue, darkening at tips, next pair almost as long, the remaining 3 pairs very steeply graduated; a strip of turquoise on malar separating black and purple from white underparts; long needle-like bill and feet black. Female has patch on neck-sides black, malar white along with rest of underparts, and grey shaft lines on throat and breast; tail half as long again as male's.

Ssp. *H. a. auritus* (E Ec, N & E Co, Ve, Guianas)

Habits Forages alone, at all levels. Inside forest stays in canopy, but most often found in low shrubbery at edges and in clearings. Gleans insects and spiders from leaves and branches, and catches them midair by hawking. Visits *Heliconia* to pick insects and to drink nectar, as well as water collected in bracts. Known to pierce corollas at base. Favourite flowers include cacti, *Passiflora*, legumes, Rubiaceae, Rutaceae, Zingiberaceae.
Status Uncommon in Ecuador, fairly common in Colombia, uncommon in Venezuela and Guyana, fairly common and widespread in Suriname.
Habitat Tropical Zone to 400m, records to 800m. Humid and cloud forests, patchy woodland in savannas, forests along blackwater rivers.
Voice A single *trix* note, oft-repeated (H&B).
Note Race *major* invalid, represents an immature male, described in error (Schuchmann, R&G).

LONG-BILLED STARTHROAT
Heliomaster longirostris Pl. 109

Identification 14.7cm, bill 3.9cm. Adult male has intense purplish-blue forehead and crown, almost black behind, but deep metallic green over upperparts and breast (green becoming quite bright and reflective on rump, uppertail-coverts and base of tail), tail darker green then turquoise; odd series of white feathers on middle of rump; bold white malar, tiny black chin, gorget bright metallic rosy; breast has malachite gloss, rest of underparts grey with white thighs and centre of belly, white fringes to undertail-coverts; bill, very long and straight, and feet, black. Female lacks rich blue on top of head, and has small, heavily scaled gorget; entirely grey below, with a pale green wash on breast-sides and some yellow scallops on sides and flanks. White line on rump is a good field mark if bird is only seen from behind.

Ssp. *H. l. albicrissa* (W Ec) undertail-coverts white
H. l. longirostris (N Co, Ve, Tr, Guianas) as described
H. l. stuartae (S Co) darker below, smaller bill

Habits Forages in blooming trees (*Erythrina*, *Tabebuia*). Hawks insects high in open spaces. Forages also in bushes (*Heliconia*, bananas) and shrubs, usually alone but sometimes in pairs. Perches exposed on tip of dry twig.
Status Not easily found due to erratic presence. Uncommon in Ecuador, local and scarce in Colombia and Venezuela, frequent in Guyana, uncommon but widespread on Trinidad. Rare in French Guiana.
Habitat Tropical Zone. Clearings and borders of semi-dry to humid forests and second growth, partially wooded areas, plantations, open fields with thickets or hedges.
Voice In Colombia, very quiet, low clipped *tsik* notes (H&B). On Trinidad, sings from perch long repetitions of *weet* notes (ffrench). Clicks bill in flight.

BLUE-TUFTED STARTHROAT
Heliomaster furcifer Pl. 109

Identification 16cm, bill 3cm. Male has top of head bright blue, ear-coverts to nape, mantle and wings apple green, back to tail sea blue with green iridescence; tail has outer feathers convex, and all feathers pointed at angle so deep fork is straight-sided, tail terminally blackish; face-sides from malar consist of long plumes of rich bluish-purple, chin and throat brilliant rosy-red, underparts to belly and sides rich bluish-purple, thighs white and fluffy, undertail-coverts sea blue to turquoise; bill long and slender, and feet, black. Female rich bottle green above with malachite reflections on lower rump to tail, tail forked but lacks odd shape of male's; chin and throat buffy-white, becoming greyer on belly with green sides, white thighs, undertail-coverts greyish-green with white fringes.

Ssp. Monotypic (Ec, Co)

Habits Forages at mid level and in canopy of many flowering bushes and trees (cacti, Leguminosae, bromeliads, verbenas, Loranthaceae, Liliaceae, Lobeliaceae).
Status Scarce in Colombia and Ecuador, perhaps austral migrants that occasionally reach northern South America.
Habitat Tropical Zone. Semi-dry scrub or light woodland. Forest borders and adjacent fields.
Voice Calls a short rolled note, *trrrr*, oft-repeated.

HORNED SUNGEM
Heliactin cornutus Pl. 110

Identification 10.2cm, bill 1.6cm. Male has top of head rich purplish-blue that extends as a long laid-back crest, short bright pale green and long orange-yellow feathers sweep back from rear eyebrow around head to join long blue ones in a beautiful crest; head-sides, ear-coverts to throat and stripe to centre of breast, black, neck-sides to undertail-coverts white (slight leaf green flush on body-sides and flanks); nape to uppertail-coverts metallic green reflecing turquoise and gold; tail consists of extended white feathers, very steeply graduated, with outer webs of outer 3 buff, central pair all buff, next pair all white; bill long and very fine, and feet, black. Female quite distinct; metallic green above with subtle reflections of turquoise and malachite, and less subtle gold and yellow, tail longish and steeply graduated, central pair green, rest white; chin and throat clean yellow-buff, slightly darker and more buffy on face-sides, and finely streaked green, rest of underparts white.

Ssp. Monotypic (S Su)

Habits Solitary forager, mostly on blossoms at low to mid levels. Favourite flowers include Verbenaceae, Malvaceae and Urticaceae, *Lantana*, *Malvaviscus*, *Stachytarpheta*, *Citrus*.

Status Fairly common but local in southern Suriname (Sipaliwini).
Habitat Tropical Zone. Savannas with scattered bushes, gallery or riparian forests, open woods.
Voice No description found and no published recordings.
Note Dickinson (2003) uses *Heliactin bilophus*, presumably from Schuchmann, who states that *bilophus* has seniority of one year over *cornutus*, but *bilophus* is *nomen oblitum* (forgotten name) and thus inapproriate (S&M).

Woodstars are particularly difficult to identify as all are tiny, with the floating, drifting, sometimes pendulum-like flight of bumblebees, their wings audibly whirring. Often seen perched on a thin exposed stem at the edge of a canopy, they are most frequently encountered at large emergent trees in full blossom, neatly nectaring at flowers guarded by some larger, territorial hummingbird. Adult males in breeding plumage are comparatively easy, but in non-breeding plumage can be very difficult and not all post-nuptial plumages are known, let alone with certainty, and few are even mentioned in other guides. Key is the shape of the tail-feathers. Another unexpected plumage aspect is that they have thick and fluffy white thighs, covering the tarsi and practically the feet, sometimes the white extends onto the body-sides and may appear as a white patch either side of the rump. Females and juveniles each have their own characteristics, but require careful study, as there are undescribed plumage phases with them as well. Be sure to check distribution carefully.

PURPLE-COLLARED WOODSTAR
Myrtis fanny Pl. 110

Identification 10cm, bill 2cm. Adult male in breeding plumage metallic leaf green from forehead to uppertail-coverts, with reflections of gold on nape and back, and turquoise on tail-coverts; dark brown tail quite unique in having 4 outer feathers on each side convex with square-cut tips, and central pair so short as to be covered by tail-coverts; lores and large postocular triangle white, with line embracing ear-coverts to neck-sides where it joins white breast. From chin and upper throat over face-sides to ear-coverts brilliant turquoise-blue, and below a broad crescent of violaceous-purple; underparts white with a faint orange-cinnamon flush on rear flanks, with white fluffy thighs, the white extending onto body-sides and sometimes to rump-sides; bill dusky, long and slightly decurved, feet grey. Male in post-nuptial, eclipse or non-breeding plumage similar, but instead of blue and violet gorget is patchy grey with a few dull blue discs; neck-sides to rear flanks pale orange-cinnamon, and flushes undertail-coverts. Female same but tail is slightly rounded, the central pair green, next pair brown, outer 3 basally brown, distally white; face-sides and entire underparts, except white thighs and rear-flanks patch, orange-buffy.

Ssp. Monotypic (Ec)

Habits Forages alone, following trap-line to favourite flowers (cacti, *Malvaceae*, *Cordia*, *Russelia*). Males perform courtship flights in front of females, flying in pendulum motion. Wings make distinct hum as it slowly hovers at flowers.
Status Uncommon.
Habitat Tropical to Temperate Zones, sea level to 3,000m, but most frequent at 1,000–2,000m. Semi-desertic areas of light woodland, agaves or thorn scrub on Pacific slope of Andes. Suburbs and gardens.
Voice Males twitter in display, perched birds sing gurgling or clicking song. Also a *neh-neh-nuh* in flight, quite odd for a hummingbird (P. Coopmans in R&G).

AMETHYST WOODSTAR
Calliphlox amethystina Pl. 110

Identification Male 6.6cm, female 6cm, bill 1.5cm. Adult male rich metallic green above with deeply forked dark brown tail; white spot behind eyes barely joins white line behind ear-coverts that widens on neck-sides into a broad white breast bar; full gorget, covering ear-coverts, is metallic rosy-magenta or reddish-purple, upper belly and sides bright apple green and lower belly and vent to rear flanks white, undertail-coverts greenish, scaled white; bill long, thin and straight, and feet, dusky. Female has shorter, stubby tail, thus appears much smaller; metallic bright green with gold reflections above, including central tail-feathers, rest of tail has basal two-thirds dark brown, distal third orange-ochre; face buffy with dusky ear-coverts and a few discs reflecting red in middle of throat, broad white band on upper breast, orange-buffy breast, centre of belly to vent and rear flanks white; undertail-coverts orange-buffy. Juvenile like female with short tail and central rectrices green, white face with a dusky crescent from ear-coverts to base of throat where disintegrates into spots (juvenile male may show reddish spots on throat, juvenile female never does); breast bar green above orange lower breast; tail has central rectrices green, outer feathers dull olive-green with white tips. Very similar Rufous-shafted Woodstar has very odd tail profile. Purple-throated Woodstar has distinctly purple throat and is usually allopatric.

Ssp. Monotypic (Ec, Co, Ve, Guianas)

Habits Favourite flowers include *Inga*, *Erythrina*, *Calliandra*, *Citrus*, *Convulvus*, *Fuchsia*, *Lantana*, *etc.*
Status Rare in Ecuador. Very locally frequent to uncommon in Colombia and Venezuela, uncommon in Guyana, rare in Suriname. Scarce and irruptive in coastal French Guiana.
Habitat Tropical Zone. From borders of humid forest (but not interior), patches of woods and shrubbery in savannas, parks, gardens, to arid areas and thorn scrub.
Voice Courting male performs in front of female, flying in pendulum motion, making humming noise, seemingly produced by wing vibrations.

PURPLE-THROATED WOODSTAR
Calliphlox mitchellii Pl. 110

Identification 9.5cm, bill 1.5cm. Adult male in breeding plumage is metallic rich green above to tail-coverts, tail maroon, deeply forked with central pair of rectrices very short, but two outermost pairs same length, or outermost slightly shorter, affording distinct profile; thick white postocular line embraces ear-coverts and joins broad band on lower throat and upper breast, complete gorget, including ear-coverts, purple; breast green, belly and flanks cinnamon, thighs and large patch behind flanks white, and undertail-coverts pale green; bill short, straight and dusky, as are feet. Non-breeding male has normal, forked tail and purple gorget replaced by buffy throat and dusky ear-coverts. Female has short stubby tail and looks smaller; tail moderately forked, central pair of rectrices green with dark central band, rest cinnamon with subterminal blackish band; throat richer-coloured than eclipse male, narrow breast band is green, underparts rich cinnamon, with large white rear-flanks white. Juvenile has narrow postocular white line, dusky face-sides with a dusky streak on sides of throat, broad green band on lower breast, throat and neck-sides pale cinnamon-buffy. Belly to undertail cinnamon with a modest white patch on rear flanks.

Ssp. Monotypic (W Ec, W Co)

Habits Forages alone at all levels, generally in canopy with a distinct liking for *Inga* and *Cordia*, and will defend blossoms. Often sits on tips of high exposed branches.
Status Uncommon.
Habitat Lower Tropical to Subtropical Zones, sea level to 2,400m. Humid, wet and cloud forests, at borders and clearings, shrubs or hedges in pastures on lower slopes.
Voice Males perform courtship flights in front of females, flying in pendulum motion whilst whistling softly or snapping bill.
Note Moved from *Philodice* to *Calliphlox* by Schuchmann without explanation, followed by Dickinson (2003) and AOU.

Acestrura woodstars were moved into *Chaetocercus* on grounds that there is no evidence in external morphology to justify treatment in a separate genus (Schuchmann, followed by Dickinson 2003 and accepted by AOU).

GORGETED WOODSTAR

Chaetocercus heliodor Pl. 110

Identification Male 8.7cm, female 7.1cm, bill 1.3cm. Adult male in breeding plumage has upperparts metallic rather bluish-green; oddly shaped dark brown tail, with 2 outer rectrices long and the rest very short; white postocular line; full gorget is bright magenta and extends as ear-tufts, broad white semi-circle on breast, then green to belly and flanks, vent, thighs and rear-flanks patch white, undertail-coverts green; bill long and thin, and feet dusky. Non-breeding male retains tail shape but loses magenta gorget; lores to ear-coverts dusky, buffy throat continues on centre of breast to belly. Female rather more green (less bluish) than male, uppertail-coverts orange, washed green, tail short and stubby with subterminal black band, and outer 2 rectrices slightly longer than rest; ear-coverts dusky, throat pale orange, breast paler, then belly and flanks orange, white from vent to rear flanks, undertail-coverts orange.

Ssp. *C. h. cleavesi* (NE Ec) darker, gorget less purple
C. h. heliodor (Ec, Co, Ve) as described

Habits Forages at all levels, actively buzzing about taking nectar from small flowers, often in dense shrubbery. Usually alone, but may gather at blooming trees such as *Inga* and *Erythrina*. Perches exposed on top of a bush or tree.
Status Uncommon to rare in Colombia, uncommon to locally frequent in Ecuador. Possibly under-reported as easily overlooked.
Habitat Upper Tropical to Temperate Zones. Borders and clearings near edges of humid and cloud forests, thickets and coffee plantations.
Voice When foraging, actively buzzes or hums like a bumblebee.
Note Formerly placed in *Acestrura*.

WHITE-BELLIED WOODSTAR

Chaetocercus mulsant Pl. 110

Identification Male 8.6cm, female 8.1cm, bill 1.6cm. Adult male in breeding plumage is metallic, slightly bluish-green from forehead to central tail-feathers, outermost feather is a short thin shaft, then 2 short and finely pointed rectrices, then feather either side of central pair is longest, tapering to point and curving inwards like pincers. Full gorget, to ear-coverts, brilliant rosy-red, with broad white postocular line around ear-coverts to neck-sides and then across upper breast, entire underparts white, except patch of green either side of breast; bill dusky, long and slightly curved at tip. Eclipse male similar but lacks red gorget and has pale buffy tone to white. Female has short stubby tail, buff with a black subterminal band; is more buffy on face and throat and has broad cinnamon patch on body-sides.

Ssp. Monotypic (Ec, Co)

Habits Forages at *Salvia, Lantana* and other small-blossom bushes, as well as blooming *Agave*, *Inga*, *Erythrina*. Also hawks tiny insects and takes arthropods. Perches in open, atop tree or bush or at tip of exposed branch. Occasionally, several together at flowering tree.
Status Uncommon and local, but possibly under-recorded due to small size.
Habitat Upper Tropical to Temperate Zones, 1,500–4,000m, but most often at 2,000–2,800m. Humid areas. Shrubbery or forest borders next to meadows, pastures or planted fields, coffee plantations, flowering trees.
Voice No description found, but a recording from Ecuador listed in the Discography.
Note Formerly placed in *Acestrura*.

SANTA MARTA WOODSTAR

Chaetocercus astreans Pl. 110

Identification 6.2cm, bill 1.5cm. Tiny; male in breeding plumage is rich green above with mini version of tail of Rufous-shafted Woodstar: central rectrices short, normal shape, green like upperparts, next 2 on either side long, tapering to a point and curving inwards like pincers, next much shorter, thin, pointed and slightly angled outwards, outermost feather reduced to a short bare shaft. Gorget roughly M-shaped, extending on throat and to ear-coverts, brilliant red, bounded from behind eyes to neck-sides and entire underparts, toned cinnamon on undertail-coverts, narrow patch of green on sides forms narrow line that almost joins across breast. Non-breeding male unknown. Female lacks gorget, and has crescent of black on face-sides; slightly forked tail is cinnamon with black subterminal bar and white tips, shorter central rectrices green. Adult male from Rufous-shafted Woodstar by different-shaped red gorget and much shorter tail.

Ssp. Monotypic (Co)

Habits Visits flowering *Inga*, *Erythrina* and other trees. Probably moves seasonally up and downslope, following flowering.
Status Endemic to Santa Marta (Colombia). Variously described as locally common (Schuchmann) or rare to uncommon (H&B).
Habitat Upper Tropical to Temperate Zones. Variously described as occurring at 500–800m (H&B) or 825–2,000m Schuchmann (1999). Humid forests, second growth, coffee plantations, partially timbered areas. Borders, thickets, shrubby clearings.
Voice No description found and no published recordings.
Note Formerly placed in *Acestrura*.

ESMERALDAS WOODSTAR

Chaetocercus berlepschi Pl. 110

Identification 6.5cm, bill 1.1cm. Male uniquely bluish in breeding plumage (non-breeding male unknown). Metallic green above with bluish reflection, stronger on back and rump; brilliant red gorget sweeps back as extensive ear-tufts, large white spot behind eyes, white upper throat and neck-sides, breast grades white to bluish-grey; vent, thighs and rear flanks white; tail short with outer 2 feathers longer (but normally rounded); bill dusky, long and straight, feet dusky. Female all green above to central tail-feathers, rest of tail cinnamon with subterminal black bar; dusky patch on ear-coverts, underparts pale buffy, and white on vent to rear flanks.

Ssp. Monotypic (Ec)

Habits Forages alone, mostly in canopy, visiting flowering trees such as *Inga* and *Munitingia*, or hawking tiny insects. Like congeners, flies in slow, hovering, buzzing manner like a bumblebee.
Status Endangered. Very small range extensively deforested and only small area protected.
Habitat Lower Tropical Zone, to *c*.500m. Edges and thickets of moist or humid lowland forests, mature second growth.
Voice No description found and no published recordings.
Note Formerly placed in *Acestrura*.

SHORT-TAILED WOODSTAR

Myrmia micrura Pl. 110

Identification 6.3cm, bill 1.3cm. Tiny with a very short tail; green above well washed with gold reflections, tail green and rounded without any attenuations; face basically white with a darkish violet patch on upper ear-coverts and metallic, shiny mauve to violet gorget (with pink and purple reflections) that reaches lower ear-coverts, rest of underparts white, flushed buffy and green on sides; bill comparatively long and thin. Non-breeding male unknown. Female has tail centrally green, dark brown laterally, all with broad white tips; below buffy on face-sides to belly and flanks, rest white. Male from other woodstars by very short, rounded green tail; female lacks any dark spots on face.

Ssp. Monotypic (Ec)

Habits Forages alone, mostly at bushes and in lower strata. Favourite flowers are of Malvaceae, cacti and Leguminosae.
Status Common in its tiny range.
Habitat Lower Tropical Zone. Semi-desertic areas of cacti or thorn scrub on Pacific coast. Cultivated plots and gardens.
Voice No description found and no published recordings.

RUFOUS-SHAFTED WOODSTAR

Chaetocercus jourdanii Pl. 110

Identification 7–8.8cm, bill 1–1.8cm. Adult male in breeding plumage is metallic green from forehead to the short central pair of tail-feathers, the next 2 pairs are significantly longer, graduated and curve slightly inwards, dark brown with bright buffy shaft-streaks, the next as short as central pair, narrow and point slightly sideways, and outermost rectrices are tiny vestigial shafts, invisible in the field; short, white postocular line with black line below; chin to ear-coverts and full throat bright rich red (varies by subspecies); broad white pectoral band, belly and sides metallic green, white tibial tufts, rest of underparts green with white bases to feathers giving slightly scaled effect. Non-breeding male loses bright red throat, it being buffy, slightly orange washed dusky, and a broader but less well-defined pectoral band. Juvenile male metallic green from forehead to lower back, rump to uppertail-coverts dusky orange; central pair of tail-feathers shiny green, rest orange-buffy with a broad black band halfway; short white postocular line, ear-coverts and cheeks dusky; underparts from chin to undertail pinkish-buffy, washed dusky on breast-sides and palest on belly, with white tibial feathers. Female metallic green from forehead to central tail-feathers, rest of tail buffy with broad black band across middle; short white postocular line, ear-coverts black; underparts uniform pale cinnamon with white tibial feathers. Note throat colour changes from east to west.

Ssp. *C. j. andinus* (N Co: E Andes, NW Ve: Andes) throat bright red
C. j. rosae (N Ve: Zulia to Northern Cordillera) throat reddish-magenta
C. j. jourdanii (NE Ve, Tr) throat bright purple

Habits Like all tiny woodstars, seems like a buzzing insect at first. Forages at all levels, usually alone, but sometimes several at flowering bush or tree (*Inga*, *Erythrina*).

Status Poorly known, generally scarce but quite common very locally (very rare in Trinidad).
Habitat Upper Tropical to Temperate Zones. Cloud forest, thickets at borders, clearings and treefalls, coffee plantations, mature second growth. Recorded in Caracas seasonally and may be regular visitor.
Voice Calls from high perch, a soft, lisping *tssit, tssit, tssit, tssit* (Hilty, C. Parrish recording).

Tail of male Rufous-shafted Woodstar open, and as normally seen in the field (right)

LITTLE WOODSTAR

Acestrura bombus Pl. 110

Identification Male 8.4cm, female 7.4cm, bill 1.4cm. Adult male metallic green above to central pair of rectrices, outer 4 pairs brown and increasingly long towards centre, with those next to central pair more than twice as long; broad white postocular line completely embraces facial bib, chin to ear-coverts and full throat bright metallic rose-red (almost raspberry), underparts green with white tibial tufts. Bill fairly short, thin, straight and black. Male in eclipse plumage unknown. Female metallic green above, tail cinnamon-buffy with broad black band across middle, the central pair with greenish reflections; chin to ear-coverts and entire underparts orange-cinnamon with white postocular line cleanly separating green, but less from buff; white thighs.

Ssp. Monotypic (Ec)

Habits Forages in canopy and mid levels. Feeds on flowers of bromeliads, *Inga*, *Mutingia*, *Agave* and Ericaceae.
Status Endangered. Appears to be declining due to deforestation, especially in Ecuador.
Habitat Tropical to Subtropical Zones. Deciduous forests of Pacific slope of Andes, at transition between humid and dry areas.
Voice No description found and no published recordings.

> Long-tailed hummingbirds have been collected together on a single plate as this character can often be a source of confusion. Apart from the obvious differences between males and females, it should be remembered that mature, full-grown birds have longer tails. Two species have not been confirmed in our region and will perhaps never, but have been misidentified in the past, and are therefore included. Check the maps if in doubt.

VENEZUELAN SYLPH

Aglaiocercus berlepschi Pl. 111

Identification Male 19.5cm, tail *c.*10cm, female 10.6cm, bill 1.5cm. Adult male has entire top of head brilliant metallic pale green, much darker on lores and from eyes to nape, then metallic green to rump; uppertail-coverts and long tail (outer pair far the longest and usually lie parallel) rich lustrous royal blue; chin and throat royal blue, breast sage to olive-green, belly, sides and flanks green, thighs white, undertail-coverts pale grey-green with darker fringes; bill short, straight and black. Female metallic green above with turquoise-blue reflections on top of head and rump, uppertail-coverts and tail royal blue except outer 2 rectrices which are dark grey with white tips; chin and throat white with variable green discs, breast and sides green, belly to undertail-coverts white.

Ssp. Monotypic (Ve)

Habits Forages at all levels, usually alone, but gathers at flowering trees (*Inga*, *Erythrina*). Follows trap-line. Sometimes defends a particularly rich feeding spot.
Status Uncommon Venezuelan endemic of Caripe–Turimiquire range. No specimens from Paria and reports from that area considered erroneous.
Habitat Subtropical to Temperate Zones. Humid and cloud forests, humid scrub and mature second growth, coffee plantations, especially in areas with moss and epiphyte-covered trees, and along streams.
Voice Possibly *jit* notes, similar to Long-tailed Sylph?
Note Sometimes listed as Berlepsch's Long-tailed Sylph and formerly considered a subspecies of Long-tailed Sylph (Schuchmann & Duffner 1993).

LONG-TAILED SYLPH

Aglaiocercus kingi Pl. 111

Identification Male 19.3cm, tail 11cm, female 11cm, bill 1.3cm. Adult male has entire top of head metallic pale green, rest of body metallic green, darker on face, slight bluish reflections to throat, somewhat olive-green on breast, white thighs; tail long, but only outer feathers very long, and usually held closed, rich royal blue, though shorter rectrices have bright green fringes at tips. Female has rich blue forehead and forecrown, is metallic green above with blue uppertail-coverts and bright royal blue tail, except outer pair which are dark grey with white fringes at tips; chin and throat white with rows of green discs; rest of underparts orange-cinnamon, washed lightly with green on flanks and undertail-coverts, thighs white. Female from female Violet-tailed Sylph by green crown (not blue).

Ssp. *A. k. kingi* (Co: E Andes) as described
A. k. emmae (NW Ec, Co: W & C Andes) tail bright turquoise-blue with bright turquoise-green fringes; female has 3 central pairs of rectrices similarly coloured
A. k. caudata (Ve: Andes, Co: E Andes) no blue throat spot, tail purple-blue
A. k. margarethae (NC Ve) paler green

A. k. mocoa (E Ec, Co: C & E Andes) more glittering green above, throat sapphire-blue to purple

Habits Forages at all levels, alone or in pairs, and gathers with same or other species at flowering trees (*Inga*, *Clusia*, *Erythrina*). Visits flowers on trap-line route or establishes fiercely defended feeding territory at flowering trees or bushes (bromeliads, *Heliconia*, Ericaceae, *Hibiscus*). Recorded piercing holes at base of corollas. Not shy, may be resident in gardens, and in Henri Pittier National Park, northern Venezuela, visits feeders and even perches on visitors' fingers.
Status Uncommon to locally frequent in Ecuador, locally common in Colombia and Venezuela.
Habitat Subtropical to Temperate Zones. Borders and semi-open areas of humid and wet forests or second growth, gardens, fields with woods or bushes.
Voice Foraging call a slow series of buzzy *jit* notes, sometimes a fast *jit-jit-jit*, and 1 s repetitions of a pebbly *bzzt! bzzt!* (Hilty).

VIOLET-TAILED SYLPH
Aglaiocercus coelestis Pl. 111

Identification Male 19–21cm, tail 15cm, female 10cm, bill 1.3cm. Male has brilliant metallic emerald-green top of head, metallic mauve chin and throat; rest of body more or less metallic green, increasingly blue on uppertail-coverts to bright purple tail, inner remiges having pale blue fringes at tips; white thighs; bill short and straight, black. Female has entire top of head metallic blue, dark green lores and through eyes, metallic green above with uppertail-coverts turquoise-green, central tail-feathers blue, outer 2 pairs dark grey with broad white tips; chin and throat white with rows of small green discs, broad white crescent across upper breast, rest of underparts rufous; buffy thighs. Similar Long-tailed Sylph in Ecuador has greeny-blue tail.

Ssp. *A. c. aethereus* (SW Ec) as described
A. c. coelestis (NW Ec, Co: W Andes) male has bright blue throat

Habits Usually forages alone, but also in pairs; however, groups never gather at flowering trees. At all levels, but mostly in shady shrubbery at lower levels, following trap-line route between very scattered clusters of small flowers.
Status Uncommon to locally frequent in Ecuador. Frequent in Colombia.
Habitat Upper Tropical to Subtropical Zones. Interior of dense humid, wet and cloud forests, where branches overgrown with mosses and epiphytes. Infrequently at borders.
Voice Calls from understorey, a single *tez-it* note, oft-repeated (H&B).

BLACK-TAILED TRAINBEARER
Lesbia victoriae Pl. 111

Identification Male 26.5cm, female 14.5cm, bill 1.5cm. Adult male mostly metallic green; deep diamond-shaped bib from chin to upper breast, metallic emerald-green, uppertail-coverts brighter green; thighs white, undertail-coverts buffy; tail long, outermost pair the longest, lustrous deep cobalt-blue, and all rectrices subterminally turquoise-blue with turquoise-green tips.

Ssp. *L. v. aequatorialis* (Ec) longer, bluer tail
L. v. victoriae (Co: E&N Andes) distinctly shorter tail with more greenish tips
L. v. juliae (extreme S Ec) differs from *victoriae* by shorter bill

Status Uncommon to locally common in Ecuador, locally frequent in Colombia.
Habitat Temperate Zone to Páramo. Less humid fields and pastures with hedges or scattered bushes, gardens, densely wooded ravines, *Polylepis* woods, stands of scrub, páramo fields with low shrubbery.
Voice Displaying males dive in front of females and make loud rattle with wings. Song a descending trill, *ti ti tr' t t' tr tic-tic-tic*, and calls include chips and tinkling *zeeet* notes (H&B).
Note Some authors synonymise *aequatorialis* under *victoriae* on grounds that tail-length is variable and *aequatorialis* falls within range of *victoriae*, but no published data comparing fully adult birds reach this conclusion.

GREEN-TAILED TRAINBEARER
Lesbia nuna Pl. 111

Identification Male 17cm, female 12cm, bill 1cm. Adult male metallic green except snow white thighs, vent and undertail-coverts; large bib is bright emerald-green as are uppertail-coverts and central 4 pairs of tail-feathers, outermost and longest are brown with narrow emerald-green tips. Female has white throat with extensive scattering of green discs, densest at sides; green rectrices virtually same length as male, but outer, brown pair much shorter.

Ssp. *L. n. gracilis* (Ec) significantly longer outer tail-feathers with extensive bright green tips
L. n. gouldii (NE & SC Co, Ve: Mérida) as described

Habits Forages at mid levels and canopy, visiting flowers (*Cassia*, *Buddleia*, *Cavendishia*, *Palicourea*, *Rubus*, *Cuphaea*). Spends much time hawking flying insects.
Status No records in Venezuela since 1800s (single specimen from Mérida, BMNH). Fairly common but local in Colombia, uncommon or locally common in Ecuador.
Habitat Subtropical to Temperate Zones. Borders of humid forest, fields with scattered bushes and trees, *Polylepis*, mature but patchy second growth, bushy páramo fields, bamboo-covered landslides.
Voice Flies with audible hum like a bumblebee. Calls sharp, high-pitched buzzes.

RACKET-TAILED PUFFLEG
Ocreatus underwoodii Pl. 111

Identification Male 13.2cm, female 8.7cm, bill 1.3cm. Adult male has blackish lores and subocular area to upper ear-coverts; large metallic emerald-green frontal shield, white thighs and undertail-coverts, rest of body metallic dark green;

Immature male Racket-tailed Puffleg (left) assumes adult plumage but retains some white on chin and female-type tail; middle bird is an adult male in moult, with a partially grown tail; on the right is a fully developed adult male

tail dark with long outer rectrices white on basal half of outer webs, tapering to shafts, with rounded oval rackets. Female similar but has green tail, deeply forked, outermost rectrices dusky with white tips; throat to flanks and belly white with rows of green discs, leg puffs and undertail-coverts white. Races fall into 2 distinct groups; northern races all have white leg tufts, southern races have buffy to rufescent thighs.

Ssp. White tibial puffs

O. u. discifer (NE Co, NW Ve) pale green undertail-coverts; female much whiter below with pale buffy undertail-coverts

O. u. ambiguus (CW Co) black face-sides, chin and upper throat with faint green reflections; tail as long as *underwoodii* but dark rackets smaller, though larger than *melanantherus*

O. u. melanantherus (W Ec: west slope only) bright metallic green, with clearly defined black chin through cheeks to ear-coverts

O. u. polystictus (N Ve) male virtually identical to male *discifer*, but female has well-spotted white underparts

O. u. underwoodii (Ec? Co: East Andes) greener above than *polystictus*, and female less heavily spotted

Rufous tibial puffs

O. u. peruanus (E Ec) distinct from all other races in region by rufous tibial puffs and undertail-coverts in both sexes

Habits Forages alone at low and mid levels, visiting low flowers (*Impatiens*, *Salvia*, *Costus*, *Buddleia*, *Palicourea*, *Cavendishia*) or gathers with same or other species at flowering trees (*Inga*, *Clusia*, *Erythrina*). Perches low, swaying tail gently. Darts in foliage to catch tiny insects. To take nectar, hovers at corolla or clings to petals. Feeding flight wavy and erratic, with occasional spreading and closing of tail rackets.

Status Uncommon in Ecuador. Fairly common to common in Venezuela and Colombia.

Habitat Upper Tropical to Temperate Zones. Borders of wet, humid, cloud and elfin forests, mature second growth, coffee plantations. In dark, humid ravines of forest interior (F&K) or open sunny spots in forest (H&B), often along roads and trails.

Voice Quite noisy, with constant bumblebee-like hum from wings and soft twittering calls.

Note Called Booted Racket-tail by Schuchmann but we follow Dickinson (2003). Race *ambiguus* synonymised under *incommodus* by Schuchmann, but no reasons given. However, *incommodus* used only once, when race *wasa* described by Kleinschmidt(1943), and not used since. On the other hand, since Zimmer described *ambiguus* in 1951, it has been accepted by, among others, Meyer de Schauensee and H&B.

[MARVELLOUS SPATULETAIL *Loddigesia mirabilis*] Pl. 111

Identification Male 10–20cm, tail 1–15cm, female 10cm, tail 5cm, bill 1.2cm. Adult male has metallic bright blue forehead to crest and bib, rest of head black, neck-sides to flanks white, back and wings to tail dark metallic green; tail unique, with central rectrices green, very long and taper to a point, outer pair just shafts, very long and curve round to cross over each other just past tips of stiff central pair, and have large dark blue oval-shaped rackets. Immature male lacks black and blue on head, being green with some white on throat-sides and white on flanks; tail dark with central rectrices extended pale shafts each with a large oval racket. Female like immature male but has belly to undertail-coverts white, tail green and central pair extend as pale shafts (shorter than those of immature male), with brown rackets. Immature male from Racket-tailed Puffleg by white throat-sides and flanks. Female and immature male from Racket-tailed Puffleg by white throat; also note rackets are distinct ovals, whereas Racket-tailed Puffleg has more rounded rackets.

Ssp. Monotypic (does not occur in northern South America, see below)

Habits Forages singly, perching to feed. Males gather in leks to display, but appear to be overall fewer males, and females are more numerous, even at leks. Very agile, flies deftly within thickets, making singular humming noise produced by the odd-shaped wings. Male displays by raising beautiful tail over head so that rackets hang in front of bird.

Status Unknown.

Habitat Subtropical to Temperate Zones. Borders and clearings of humid forest, second growth, open country with thickets of *Rubus* brambles and stands of *Alnus*.

Voice Males, especially immatures, gather in leks to display and call, but voice undescribed.

Note Included here because of an unconfirmed sight record from south-east Ecuador. However, small range in Peru does not appear to extend north of Marañón river, and thus not into Ecuador. We have included all 3 plumages here to resolve future doubts.

[PERUVIAN SHEARTAIL *Thaumastura cora*] Pl. 111

Identification Male 15cm, tail 10cm, female 7cm, bill 1.3cm.

Recalls a woodstar with a long tail. Adult male metallic green from forehead to tail-coverts; white postocular line embraces ear-coverts and throat to centre of breast, and to undertail-coverts, breast- to body-sides green, chin to ear-coverts and throat metallic mauve and purple, edged at ear-coverts rich blue; tail has long outer rectrices that are brown on outer webs and white on inner, tapering almost to shafts, then broaden into pale brown spatulas at tips. Female metallic green above including central tail-feathers, tail longer than woodstars, and all other rectrices basally bright brown, subterminally black with white tips; chin to ear-coverts and underparts white, washed lightly cinnamon-buffy on face. Immature male like female, except that all rectrices but central pair are basally white, and adjacent pair are rather longer, and distally black without white tips; throat to belly pale cinnamon, ear-coverts washed grey, green discs on breast-sides.

Ssp. Monotypic (Ec?)

Habits Forages alone, at all levels, hovering at flowers with a constant wing-hum and flicks tail up and down. Feeds on flowers of cacti, Malvaceae, *Cordia*.

Status. Sightings in Loja, Ecuador, are unconfirmed (recorded in northern Peru to Piura).

Habitat Tropical to Temperate Zones. Mostly coastal; thickets along rivers and in oases, fog-fed brush of Pacific coastal deserts, gardens, farm fields.

Voice Call and song consist of thin chirruping notes that sound insect-like.

TROGONIDAE – Trogons and Quetzals

Trogons and quetzals are a tropical family of medium-sized birds that are mostly brilliant lustrous green, with brightly coloured bellies of red, yellow or orange, despite which they are quite cryptic as they perch motionless at mid levels and in the subcanopy of tall forest. The largely brilliant green quetzals are distinguished by elongated plumes on the wing-coverts and uppertail-coverts of males. Trogons have more varied coloration with fine black-and-white barred wing patches, and boldly barred undertails diagnostic in species identification. Quetzals are largely frugivorous, whilst trogons are more omnivorous, taking large insects on the wing and small animals from leaves and branches. They are all forest birds, and are wholly arboreal, for they are unable to walk on the ground. They make short flights on weak, rounded wings, and freeze upon alighting. Usually found in pairs, these maintain contact by frequent calling and the immobility of the bird changes as the tail moves with each note. They have a knack of sitting back to an observer, watching him with head turned almost completely around. The wings are deeply curved, and the wingtips are often held below the tail-sides, which further enhances the humpback appearance of perched quetzals. Quetzals are mostly vocal during the breeding season, but trogons vocalise year-round. They are all very responsive to playback.

Additional references used to prepare this family include Colston (1985), Sick (1993) and Collar (2001).

Trogon taxonomy may seem confusing, and certainly the birds can be a headache of similarity. We follow R&G and Hilty, who followed Zimmer (1948), and use a more fragmented arrangement of species, thus separating distinctions between various taxa more clearly. But please note these distinctions have not been agreed by the SACC. Note that the barring or vermiculations on the wings usually differ within a species according to age and sex, as do the undertail patterns, and these latter can be enormously helpful in species diagnosis; the outer 3 rectrices are strongly and evenly stepped. Also note eye and eye-ring colour. Trogons often assist the observer by perching in characteristic flat-rumped downturned tail fashion on an exposed limb in the subcanopy. Just be quiet and slow as you get into position.

NORTHERN VIOLACEOUS TROGON
Trogon caligatus Pl. 112

Identification 22–24cm. A small trogon. Adult male has head and breast deep purplish-blue with a barely discernible black face and throat and dramatic yellow eye-ring; back to rump green, tail-coverts turquoise-blue and uppertail sea blue; wing-coverts, tertials and secondaries very finely vermiculated black and white, rest of wings black; belly to undertail-coverts orange, paler distally, narrowly and irregularly edged grey on flanks; undertail white with vestigial black barring on basal half of rectrices, bill slate, feet grey. Immature male has head and breast entirely black, only bluish on nape, and only lesser wing-coverts are finely vermiculated, the rest covered with irregular white lines; inner webs of undertail black. Adult female has entire head, breast and upperparts to tail-coverts charcoal grey, wings and tail black, the wings finely vermiculated black and white, but less finely than adult male; inner webs of rectrices on undertail black; eye-ring incomplete, being bracket-shaped, bill brown, feet olive. Immature female is paler grey with barring on the wings as immature male. Note: wing panels of immature are distinctly more boldly barred white. Amazonian Violaceous is very similar but allopatric, on eastern side of Andes. Amazonian White-tailed is larger; male has no barring on undertail, and a blue-grey eye-ring. Female has much heavier barring on undertail and a complete blue-grey eye-ring.

Ssp. Monotypic (N Co, W Ve)

Habits Perch quietly and sally for fruit and insects, apparently they will attack a wasp nest, staying day after day hawking the insects.

Status Fairly common.

Habitat Tropical Zone, to 1,200m. Borders of humid forest and semi-open areas nearby, but not forest interiors: treefall clearings, clearings with scattered trees, semi-open woodland along streams and at fords, plantations, etc.

Voice A rather fast series of downslurred, steady whistled notes, *cuh-cuh-cuh-cuh*..... (Hilty).

Note Usually treated as conspecific with Amazonian Violaceous Trogon, *T. violaceus*.

AMAZONIAN VIOLACEOUS TROGON

Trogon violaceus Pl. 112

Identification 22–24cm. A small trogon. Adult male has head and breast deep purplish-blue with barely discernible black face and throat, and striking yellow eye-ring; back to rump green, washed blue, tail-coverts turquoise-blue and uppertail dull sea blue; wing-coverts very finely vermiculated black and white, rest of wings black; belly to undertail-coverts rich orange, only slightly paler distally; undertail white with regular black barring and round white spot on tips, bill pale greyish-blue, feet grey. Immature male has head and breast black, only bluish on nape, back pure green, and only lesser wing-coverts are finely and rather obscurely filigreed, the rest are covered with irregular white lines; inner webs of undertail are black with very slight vestigial barring. Adult female has entire head, breast and upperparts to tail-coverts soft dark grey, wings and tail black, wings finely and obscurely vermiculated black and white, and tertials barred white on their fringes; inner webs of rectrices on undertail black, but outer webs have vestigial white bars; eye-ring comprises 2 bright white brackets, bill blue-grey, feet grey. From Amazonian White-tailed by smaller size and significantly less white in undertail of male. Immature male from female White-tailed by green back and turquoise uppertail-coverts. Note wing panels of immatures tend to be more boldly barred white.

Ssp. *T. v. concinnus* (W Ec, W Co) wing panel densely barred grey and white, appearing pale grey

T. v. crissalis (Ec, S Co, S Ve) duller above and head nearly all black, being bright purple-blue only on nape; blue breast separated from denser orange belly by distinct black line, undertail barring has broader black lines

T. v. violaceus (Ve, Tr, Guianas) as described

Habits Sallies for fruit and insects, and often feeds with thrushes and tanagers on fruits in lower trees and bushes.

Status Uncommon in Ecuador, common on Trinidad (no records Tobago), frequent in Guyana, and common in Suriname.

Habitat Tropical Zone, to 1,200m. Generally a forest-edge bird, at borders of sand-ridge forests, patches of forest in savanna, light gallery forest and clearings with scattered trees. Where sympatric with Black-throated Trogon, tends to occur in more open habitats, Black-throated in forests.

Voice Very fast series of 12–15 *chok* notes (H&M). Song 12+ soft *cuh* or *cow* notes steadily repeated without acceleration. Song of Amazonian White-tailed similar but generally faster and accelerates as it progresses.

Note Usually treated as conspecific with Northern Violaceous Trogon, *T. caligatus*.

BLACK-TAILED TROGON

Trogon melanurus Pl. 112

Identification 30-32cm. Adult essentially green above and on breast, with a black face; uppertail-coverts turquoise and tail deep green; wings black with coverts and tertials entirely vermiculated white; green breast separated from rosy-red underparts by a broad white band, thighs dusky; eyes brown, eye-ring red, bill yellow, feet grey. Immature male is grey above and on breast, vermiculations much darker; tail blackish above and below, the pale rosy-red underparts are barely separated from the grey breast by a few white scallops, thighs grey; eye-ring white. Female green above, wings black with coverts finely vermiculated as male, but secondaries fringed white and vermiculated only at edges; dark green tail above, fine grey bars on outer webs of underside; dusky grey face and breast, paler grey below, thighs blackish, vent to undertail-coverts rose-pink; eye-ring red, tip of yellow bill dusky, legs and feet dull flesh. Male from race *temperatus* of Masked Trogon by black line separating breast from belly, whilst female has distinctive grey-and-rose plumage and should not to be confused with any other trogon.

Ssp. *T. m. eumorphus* (SE Co, E Ec) green washed dark blue, lower rump and uppertail-coverts blue, tail rich blue above, blackish underside; entire wing-panel vermiculations very dark

T. m. macroura (N Co, NW Ve) vermiculations on wing panel bright and contrast more with white, breast-band medium width, uppertail-coverts rich blue; female has head to uppertail-coverts and breast paler grey (to mid belly and flanks), vent and undertail-coverts rose-pink; wing panel dark, tail all black

T. m. melanurus (E Co, S Ve, Gu, Su) as described

Habits Usually seen alone, but generally occurs in loose pairs, and sometimes in small groups. Perches quietly, moving head from side to side as it surveys scene, then suddenly sallies upwards to take a hanging fruit or an insect from the foliage or in flight.

Status Uncommon in Ecuador, common in Colombia, frequent in Guyana, frequent and widespread in southern Suriname.

Habitat Tropical Zone to 400m east of Andes in Ecuador, to 500m east of Andes in Colombia and to 100m in Zulia, Venezuela; recorded to 2,200m in Colombia west of Andes, and south of Orinoco in Venezuela to 1,000m. Interior and borders of humid forest and mature, tall second growth

Voice Like bark of small dog, a slow sequence of 20–25 notes, which breaks in middle to continue in lower tone – *waw-waw-waw-waw…wow-wow-wow-wow-…* (H&M).

ECUADORIAN TROGON

Trogon mesurus Pl. 112

Identification 30–32cm. Adult male bright green above, becoming deep turquoise on tail-coverts and deep sea blue on uppertail (blackish below); clear white band separates green breast from bright red underparts, variable in width; wings black with coverts and tertial fringes finely vermiculated; eyes white with bright red eye-ring, bill bright yellow, legs and feet blue-grey. Female uniform grey above and below to breast, wings as male, red belly to undertail-coverts, undertail blackish; bill blackish above, grey below. From very similar Chocó Trogon by white eye and red eye-ring, whilst Chocó lacks narrow white line separating breast and belly.

Ssp. Monotypic (W Ec)

Habits Often at woodland and forest borders and thus more often seen than Chocó, which tends to stay within forest.
Status Fairly common and widespread.
Habitat Tropical and Subtropical Zones, mostly below 800m. Humid and deciduous forests in lowlands, but in western Loja to 2,000m.
Voice Slow, short series of *cow* notes that often starts softly and builds, e.g. *cuh-cuh-cuh-cuh-cow-cow-cow-ców-ców-ców* (R&G).
Note Separated from Black-tailed Trogon (by R&G) on basis of eye colour, vocal differences and disjunct range.

BLUE-CROWNED TROGON

Trogon curucui Pl. 113

Identification 24cm. Small; adult male has head entirely bright purplish-blue with a barely discernible black face, shoulder, back and rump deep green, uppertail-coverts deep sea blue, tail above slate grey, below black with regular narrow white barring and large white terminal spots; broad white band separates blue breast from scarlet belly and undertail-coverts; eyes dark brown, red eye-ring, bill bluish-grey, feet brown. Female uniform grey from head to uppertail-coverts and breast; tail black above, below each rectrice white with long black ellipse on inner fringe to inner web, and black spots on outer fringe of outer web; broad white band separates grey breast from scarlet underparts; eye-ring red, with triangular bracket of white in front of and behind eyes, bill blackish above, grey below, feet brown. Male from all other trogons by combination of largely blue head and red belly, divided by broad white line. Much larger Amazonian White-tailed has rich yellow underparts. Female from female Black-tailed by broad white breast-band and white pattern on undertail.

Ssp. *T. c. peruvianus* (Ec, S Co)

Habits Highly insectivorous, and frequently joins mixed-species feeding flocks at mid and lower levels.
Status Uncommon in Ecuador and Colombia.
Habitat Tropical Zone, to around 1,100m. At all levels in many types of forest and woodland, both humid *terra firme* and *várzea*; appears partial to edges, riverine woodland and scrub.
Voice A fast, even-paced repetition of *cow*, similar to but higher pitched than Amazonian White-tailed (R&G). Much like Amazonian White-tailed but tends to accelerate throughout then stop abruptly (T. A. Parker in H&B).

CHOCÓ TROGON

Trogon comptus Pl. 112

Identification 30–32cm. Adult male has mossy green head and breast, shoulder to lower back, rump and uppertail-coverts bright sea blue, tail dark sea blue; black wings, black face clearly defined, scarlet underparts (note absence of white dividing line); undertail black; eyes white with grey eye-ring, bill bright yellow, feet brown. Female has entire upperparts charcoal grey, including entire tail, face blackish; belly and undertail-coverts scarlet-red; eyes white with grey eye-ring, bill dusky above, yellow below. From Ecuadorian by turquoise rump and uppertail-coverts, and lacks white breast-band. Female very much darker than female Ecuadorian. Superficially similar male Slaty-tailed Trogon has noticeable red eye-ring and bill, and white-vermiculated wing panel, whilst female is much paler grey, and red on eyes and bill is unmistakable.

Ssp. Monotypic (NW Ec, W Co)

Status Uncommon in Ecuador, locally frequent in Colombia.
Habitat Tropical and Lower Subtropical Zones to 1,800m. Interior and borders of humid and wet forests, shady ravines, steep foothills.
Voice Slowly repeated *cow* notes, up to 15 or so, like Ecuadorian Trogon but higher pitched (R&G); similar to Black-tailed, but lower pitched (Collar), similar to Slaty-tailed and Black-tailed but even slower and lower pitched (Haffer 1975).
Note Subject to several changes in English name, from Blue-tailed to White-eyed (S&M), with present Chocó proposed to end confusion (by R&G), as it is not the only white-eyed trogon, neither the most blue-tailed.

AMAZONIAN WHITE-TAILED TROGON

Trogon viridis Pl. 112

Identification 28–30cm. Adult male has head and breast bright purplish-blue, with black bib and lower ear-coverts; shoulder and mantle to upper rump turquoise – bluish on back, bright greenish on shoulder – and lower rump and tail-coverts royal blue as head, tail dull sea blue with terminal black band; underparts rich orange-yellow, and undertail white with basal half of inner webs black, thus base of web appears all black and tip all white, inner rectrices with terminal black band; eyes brown, eye-ring blue, bill pale blue with white culmen. Immature male has mainly black head, moss-green shoulder and back, sea blue tail-coverts and uppertail black and underside as adult; wings have rows of white dots on outer edge of tertials, inner secondaries and basal half of primaries; underparts more yellow, with vague black and white barring on sides; bill darker. Female dark grey above and breast; wings have white vermiculations on coverts, tertials and secondaries; tail black above and below, with regular white bars on underside that are broad on outer edge but narrow on inner edge, outer 3 rectrices have large white terminal spots, underparts orange yellow with grey barring narrowly on sides. Amount of white in male undertail distinctive, otherwise similar to much smaller Amazonian Violaceous, but note latter has yellow eye-ring. Female Amazonian Violaceous has white eye 'brackets'.

Ssp. *T. v. viridis* (E Co, Ve, Tr, Gu, Su, FG)

Status Common throughout range and usually the commonest trogon.
Habitat Tropical Zone, locally to 1,200m. Interior and borders of humid and wet forest and second growth, and in lighter forests of foothills, plantations and sand ridges.
Voice A sequence of 20–25 low notes, slow at first but accelerating at end: *chaw, chaw, chaw, chaw,… cha-cha-cha-cha-…* (H&M). A fast, fairly even series of *cow* or *cowp* notes, up to 20, higher pitched than Black-tailed Trogon (R&G).

WESTERN WHITE-TAILED TROGON

Trogon chionurus Pl. 112

Identification 28–30cm. Essentially rich purplish-blue above with black face, bright green shoulder and few white lines at base of primaries; bright orange belly and undertail-coverts, undertail all white with black terminal band; pale blue eye-ring and bill, brownish-grey feet. Female dark grey above and breast, with white vermiculations on wing panel, undertail white with tiny amount of vestigial barring on basal inner web of outer rectrice, and black terminal band. Similar but much smaller Northern Violaceous has black and some barring in undertail (both sexes) and bright yellow eye-ring (male) or clear white eye 'brackets' (female).

Ssp. Monotypic (W Ec, W Co)

Status Uncommon.

Habitat Tropical and Subtropical Zones, mostly below 500m but occasionally to 800m. Humid forest and borders.

Voice Very fast series of *cow* or *cowp* notes, up to 20 or so, accelerating at end and falling in pitch simultaneously (R&G).

Note We follow R&G in recognising this taxon as specifically distinct from *viridis* based on differences in plumage and vocalisations.

BLACK-THROATED TROGON

Trogon rufus Pl. 113

Identification 25cm. Adult male apple green from crown to rump, uppertail-coverts sea blue, tail pale-olivaceous green with black terminal band, wings black with very fine white vermiculations on coverts and tertials; forehead, face and throat black, breast cobalt-blue, underparts yellow, undertail regularly barred dark grey and yellowish-white, outer 3 rectrices with large white terminal spots; eye-ring pale blue, bill yellow, feet grey. Female rufescent olive on head and tail, wings blackish with very fine buffy vermiculations on coverts and tertials; rest of upperparts and breast olive-brown, underparts yellow; blue eye-ring with white 'brackets' almost forming a complete ring, then black feathering just contrasting with the white, and bill grey on culmen. Immature male like female but has green wash on rear of head. From all other trogons by green head and yellow belly.

Ssp. *T. r. amazonicus* (S Ve) some golden reflections on back, tail more bronzy; vermiculations bolder white, bar-like; black of face reaches to bright bluish-green of lower breast, which is separated from whitish-yellow by a broken black bar

T. r. cupreicauda (W Co, W Ec) like *amazonicus* but has boldly barred undertail like *tenellus*

T. r. rufus (E Ve, Gu, Su, FG) as described

T. r. sulphureus (Ec, extreme S Co, S Ve) reddish-coppery tail with green subterminal and black terminal bands

T. r. tenellus (NW Co) turquoise-blue uppertail-coverts and blue tail, breast green, narrow blackish bar; undertail strongly barred black and white, large white tips to outer rectrices.

Habits Favours vicinity of streams, invariably deep within forest and never at edges.

Status Uncommon in Ecuador, frequent in Colombia, frequent in Guyana, locally frequent but possibly widespread in Suriname.

Habitat Lower Tropical Zone, to 900m, but locally to 1,200m. Damp forests, swampy river-border forests.

Voice Slow, even-paced series of 2–4 *cuh* or *cuk* notes (Hilty), 2–5 clear mellow *cow* whistles decreasing in pitch (Collar), or a very slow, *cuh, cwuh-cwuh*, sometimes with 1–2 extra notes (*sulphureus*), but western-slope birds (*cupreicauda*) may utter 10 or more *cwuh* notes (R&G).

COLLARED TROGON

Trogon collaris Pl. 113

Identification 25cm. Adult male green from crown to tail, which has black tip, shoulder, head and breast also green with black face and sea blue wash, especially to nape and breast, less noticeable on rump and tail, but depends on light; wing-coverts, tertials and secondaries vermiculated with clean, contrasting, fine wavy lines of black and white; broad even-width band of white separates green breast from crimson belly and undertail-coverts, undertail evenly barred, albeit narrowly, black and white, with large white tips, and terminal black band; eyes brown, eye-ring bright red, bill yellow, feet brown. Female has entire head, upperparts and breast rufous-olive, slightly darker on crown and back of head, and tail (which has terminal black band on both surfaces), wings darker sepia-brown with very fine buffy vermiculations; broad white band separates brown breast from salmon-orange underparts, undertail white with irregular grey scribbling on inner webs of outer 3 rectrices. Superficially very similar to Masked Trogon. In areas of sympatry, Masked Trogon has yellow eye-ring and grey and dusky undertail pattern, and all races of Masked Trogon have much darker wing panels. Collared is more bluish-green above and white barring on wing panels and white undertail more obvious. In contrast, Masked Trogon has little or no bluish sheen above, wing panels appear almost uniform, as does undertail – with white tips to outer feathers well contrasting. Vocally different but not dramatically so, thus care required.

Ssp. *T. c. castaneus* (extreme S Co) like *collaris* but wing panel consists of coarser vermiculations (more crudely barred)

T. c. collaris (E Ec, E Co, S Ve, Su) as described

T. c. exoptatus (N Co, N Ve, T&T) upperparts shining coppery-green, undertail evenly barred with thick lines of black and white, and large white tips

T. c. subtropicalis (W & C Co) wing panel more finely vermiculated, very little bluish flush

T. c. virginalis (W Ec, W Co) back richer and slightly brighter green, and tail bars finer than *collaris*

Habits Sociable and associates with mixed flocks.

Status Uncommon in Ecuador, frequent to common in Colombia, uncommon on Trinidad but more abundant on Tobago, frequent in Guyana, locally frequent in Suriname.

Habitat Tropical and Subtropical Zones. Interior and borders of humid and wet forests of foothills and tablelands, second growth and in *várzea* in lowlands.
Voice Short sequences of identical *kyuuw* notes, moderately paced and varying in number between localities (H&M). A soft, melancholy *cu'd cu cu cu cu* (Hilty). Clear, mellow, descending notes, *kyow-kyow-kyow* that may accelerate into a 'laugh', perhaps up to 9 notes. Rather like song of Black-throated (Collar).

MASKED TROGON

Trogon personatus Pl. 113

Identification 25cm. Adult male has head, breast and upperparts, except wing, green (wings black), tail bronze-green above with black terminal band, but below black with fine black and grey lines, and three 3 rectrices are pale grey with whitish tips; rump and uppertail-coverts washed bluish; green breast has broken black line and a broad white band separating it from bright red underparts, eye-ring pinkish-red, bill yellow, feet yellow. Female deep olivaceous-brown on back to tail-coverts but more umber or plain chocolate on head, breast and tail; white breast-band incomplete, being marked with brown at sides, and grades into salmon-orange belly; undertail like male; narrow reddish eye-ring and broad white 'brackets' behind eyes, bill yellow, feet yellow. Very similar to Collared Trogon and care must be taken in areas of sympatry. For differences between them see Collared.

Ssp. *T. p. assimilis* (W Ec, W Co) bill as *personatus* but larger than *temperatus*; wing panel darker than either, and tail has fewer crossbars than *personatus* but more than *temperatus*, finer wing panels
T. p. duidae (S Ve) like *roraimae*, but narrower bars on outer tail-feathers; central rectrices deep coppery-bronze; undertail more narrowly marked white than *roraimae*
T. p. personatus (E Ec, W Ve, Co: C & E Andes) as described; large bill; central tail brassy green with white bars
T. p. ptaritepui (SE Ve) like *roraimae*, but female breast-band more buffy-olivaceous than rich brown
T. p. roraimae (SE Ve, W Gu) undertail has broader white bars and narrower black bars than *personatus*, central tail-feathers deep coppery-bronze,
T. p. sanctaemartae (Co: Santa Marta) male has stronger pale markings on wing than *personatus*, the metallic green reflects peacock blue, thighs black; female like female *personatus*
T. p. temperatus (Co, Ec) like *personatus* but has much smaller bill, more bluish on head, uppertail-coverts and breast, barring on tail faint and restricted to outer rectrices; central tail less brassy, crown more blue; female has white vermiculations (brown on female *personatus*)

Habits Social and associates with mixed flocks. Remains high in tall trees, perching still and silent, but then suddenly zips off 20–40m to snatch a hanging fruit or switch perch.
Status Uncommon in Ecuador, frequent in Colombia, uncertain in Guyana.
Habitat Subtropical and Temperate Zones, 1,200–3,300m. Borders of humid and wet montane forest, and mature second growth.
Voice A soft, steady series of *kwa* notes at higher pitch than Collared Trogon (H&B, Collar). Series of up to 10 soft, cooing notes, *cuu cuu cuu cuu* or longer *wu wh-whu-whu-whu-whu-hu-hu-hu*, louder in middle (Hilty).
Notes There appears to be some confusion as to races in Ecuador; R&G are clear that *assimilis* occurs on west slope and nominate *personatus* at lower elevations on east slope, reaching 2,300m, being replaced at higher elevations by *temperatus*, which occurs at 2,500m and above, but neither Dickinson (2003) nor Collar (2001) list *assimilis* for Ecuador. Race *temperatus* may represent a separate species, having rather different vocalisations as well as morphological differences (R&G).

SLATY-TAILED TROGON

Trogon massena Pl. 113

Identification 30–33cm. Adult male has bright green head, breast and back to rump where it grades into turquoise, which continues on black-tipped tail; wings black with entire wing panel very finely vermiculated, like 'salt and pepper'; face black, underparts pale scarlet, undertail black; eyes reddish-brown, eye-ring and bill red, feet orange-yellow. Female grey above with wings a duller version of male's; face blackish. Grey breast continues on sides, thus initially only central belly is scarlet, but all underparts from flanks are this colour; undertail black with faint rows of grey, vestigial barring; bill red with black culmen. From most other trogons by lack of white in plumage, from Blue-tailed by green tail, red bill, eye and eye-ring.

Ssp. *T. m. australis* (Ec, W Co) as described
T. m. hoffmanni (extreme NW Co) slightly smaller and has distinct golden tone to tail

Habits Hawks insects and may follow troops of monkeys or cacique flocks to catch insects disturbed by them.
Status Very rare in Ecuador, uncommon to common in Colombia.
Habitat Tropical Zone. Interior and borders of wet or humid forests and mature, tall second growth, often around clearings and tree falls.
Voice Song is a steady nasal barking *koh koh koh koh koh…* (Collar) or *cow* or *cue* (H&B).

Quetzals are small-headed, large-bodied birds with a most distinctive hump-rumped posture when perched. They sit still, and despite being brightly coloured with shiny bright green and red, are amazingly cryptic.

CRESTED QUETZAL

Pharomachrus antisianus Pl. 114

Identification 33–35cm. Male bright metallic green from

tufty forehead crest to extended, lanceolate greater wing-coverts, and very long uppertail-coverts, which reach beyond tip of tail; all flight-feathers dark brown, but these are scarcely visible, undertail appears all white, but only 3 outer, stepped rectrices are actually white; breast also bright green, belly to undertail-coverts crimson-red; eyes red, bill and feet yellow. Female has head greyish olive-brown, paler on throat to belly with green reflections on breast; ventral area washed-out pink, becoming richer and redder, and long undertail-coverts almost as red as male, undertail has outer 3 rectrices brown with vestigial whitish barring on outer edges; eyes brown, bill dusky, feet yellowish grey-green. Male from Golden-headed Quetzal by all-white undertail, female less easy to separate but lacks green breast and whitish tips to undertail of female Golden-headed.

Ssp. Monotypic (Ec, Co, Ve)

Habits Forages alone or in pairs, picking fruits or berries by swooping from a perch to surrounding vegetation, and often returning to same perch with fluttery flight.

Status Uncommon to rare in Ecuador, uncommon in Colombia and Venezuela.

Habitat Upper Tropical to Temperate Zones, 1,200–2,700m, occasionally higher. Interior and borders of pristine humid rain and cloud forests and tall, mature second growth.

Voice A slow, melancholy series of whistled *tay, taAAaaao,* easily imitated, and a loud cackling when excited (Hilty); call a loud deliberate *way-way-wáyo*, and alarm-call *ka-ka-ka-ka* (Collar).

WHITE-TIPPED QUETZAL

Pharomachrus fulgidus Pl. 114

Identification 33–34cm. Male has head metallic coppery-green, but can appear completely golden with coppery-red and gold (see plate) or rather dull green; rest of upperparts and breast bright green, all with coppery glints and red or golden sheens, flight-feathers dark brown, but mostly concealed by very long green greater coverts or uppertail-coverts, which extend beyond tip of tail; undertail dark brown, outer 3 rectrices distally white; belly to undertail-coverts scarlet-red; eyes brown, bill and feet yellow. Female similar but browner on head and breast, belly to ventral area creamy, becoming pink and pale red on long undertail-coverts, bill horn, feet greenish-grey. Only quetzal in its range; Collared Trogon separated instantly by white breast-band in all plumages, and usually has strongly barred undertail.

Ssp. *P. f. festatus* (Co: Santa Marta) longer, slightly more golden uppertail-coverts
P. f. fulgidus (NE & NC Ve) as described

Habits Gregarious and vocal in build up to breeding season, with several birds occurring in same vicinity calling.

Status Common in Colombia and Venezuela. Removed from Guyana list by BFR&S due to lack of confirmation.

Habitat Subtropical and Temperate Zones, 900–2,000m. Interior and borders of pristine humid forest and mature, tall second growth, often along shadowy mountain streams and interior of coffee plantations.

Voice A loud *kirra* or *kirra* kip, extended to *kip-kip-kip-a* when excited (H&B). A series of far-carrying, melancholy calls, *WHOOOOOou, ca'who, ca'who, ca'who*, repeated several times without pause, and variations on these notes, e.g. *whOOoou, ca'who, ca'who, ca'who...* sometimes reversed, e.g. *who, caWHOOou* or shortened to a repeated *caWHOou* (Hilty).

GOLDEN-HEADED QUETZAL

Pharomachrus auriceps Pl. 114

Identification 33–36cm. Male is metallic green from head and breast to long uppertail-coverts, which extend beyond tip of tail; small tufty crest on forehead, and head has distinct golden sheen or may look simply bright green (as plate), nape and breast have sea blue or turquoise reflections, and wing-coverts also likely to reflect turquoise-blue; rump reflects more blue; belly to undertail-coverts rich crimson, undertail dark brown; eyes reddish-brown, bill yellow with red at base, feet orange. Female has darker, olive-green head, upperparts similar to male, though wing-coverts less developed and uppertail-coverts not unusually long, thus dark brown flight-feathers more evident; belly pale olive-green, undertail-coverts salmon, undertail has outer 3 rectrices brown with white tips and a few white spots on outer edges. Eyes brown, bill brown with red base, feet dull greyish-yellow. Juvenile male like female, browner on breast and belly, with less developed wing-coverts; eyes darker brown and bill slightly duller yellow with less red than adult male. Male from Crested Quetzal by all-dark undertail, and female by green breast and white tips to undertail. Male Pavonine Quetzal has brown head, the female a yellow bill and solid dark undertail.

Ssp. *P. a. auriceps* (Co, Ec) shorter tail, with less golden sheen
P. a. hargitti (Ve, Co) as described

Habits Usually solitary. Takes fairly large fruits by snatching them as it flies up and hovers momentarily. Flight is fast, with regular, intermittent wing-closing.

Status Uncommon.

Habitat Upper Tropical to Temperate Zones, 1,500–3,100m. Interior and borders of pristine humid forest, mossy cloud forest and occasionally mature, tall second growth.

Voice Melodic, mournful, hawk-like *whe-wheeu, whe-wheuu...* uttered 6–8 times (Collar), or *wheeeu, we-weeeoo, we-weeeoo,* up to four times (Hilty).

PAVONINE QUETZAL

Pharomachrus pavoninus Pl. 114

Identification 33–34cm. The only lowland quetzal and the largest in our region. Bronze-green head has reflections from green to gold and coppery-red, mantle to long uppertail-coverts bright metallic green with larger wing-coverts lanceolate and fringe-like, long uppertail-coverts reach well beyond tip of tail; breast has more yellowish reflections; belly to undertail-coverts pure crimson-red, undertail dark brown; eyes brown, bill rich yellow, feet bright yellow. Female has slightly browner head with less gloss, although it can shine gold or red, and white leading edge to tertials and all remiges;

tail-coverts much longer than on any other female quetzal, but do not reach beyond tip of tail; upper belly olive-green with some brighter reflections, lower belly to undertail-coverts rich salmon-orange, more reddish on belly; bill and feet horn. Juvenile like female but has duller brown head and white, blobby bars on tertials, tail shorter, underparts salmon; eyes dark brown, bill dusky. Possible range overlap at fringe with Golden-headed, which male also has solid dark undertail, but a green head.

Ssp. *P. p. pavoninus* (E Ec, SE Co, S Ve)

Habits Sometimes joins mixed-species feeding flocks.
Status Rare in Ecuador, uncommon and local in Colombia and Venezuela.
Habitat Tropical Zone, to 700m. Humid lowland forests.
Voice A sequence of 5 melodious notes, *ew ewwo-ewwo-ewwo-ewwo*, with warning descending tremolo (Sick), and call a very slow, melancholy descending whistle followed by an emphatic *chok!, thus heeeeear-chok!* (Collar), repeated up to 6 times, *wheeeeear-chok!* (Hilty).

ALCEDINIDAE – Kingfishers

Of the 6 kingfishers in our region, only the Belted is migratory. The others are sedentary residents. Whether a northern breeder or tropical resident, all New World kingfishers nest in burrows that the pairs construct together in riverbanks, landslides, embankments, road cuttings or even compacted dirt at the base of uprooted trees. The entrance is sometimes hidden behind foliage. Except for the pygmy kingfisher's, all burrows overlook water and breeding is associated with the period when river waters recede, exposing the banks. At this time waters are shallower and fish easier to catch. Studies in the Amazon reveal that, in pristine forest habitat, the 4 *Chloroceryle* may occur together without competition, as each takes advantage of a different size of fish and other prey. Thus, on an Orinoco or Amazon tributary, it is not rare to encounter them at seemingly measured intervals, perching on prominent lookouts and patiently scanning the waters like fly-fishermen. All kingfishers call with a repeated *tew* note that is invariably descending, but which varies between species.

We also referred to Fry et al. (1992) and Woodall (2001) in preparing these species accounts.

AMERICAN PYGMY KINGFISHER

Chloroceryle aenea Pl. 115

Identification 13cm. Tiny; dark green above with a short, rufous supraloral line; chin white, throat pale cinnamon, widening and darkening to rich rufous that tapers back on neck-sides, almost but not quite meeting at nape, and on full breast and flanks with a dark green band across centre of breast; central belly and rest of underparts white, and bill black with cinnamon base. Female similar but lacks green breast-band. Juvenile like female but has paler throat and wings covered in rows of white spots. Our smallest kingfisher; Green-and-rufous is almost four times the size.

Ssp. Monotypic (W Ec, Co, Ve, T&T, Gu, Su, FG)

Habits Solitary and unobtrusive but not shy. Perches serenely, spying prey and sallying forth to catch flying insects or dives into water for very small fish and tadpoles. Changes perch frequently.
Status May pass unnoticed as it is very quiet and inconspicuous, but fairly common in suitable habitat. Uncommon in Guyana, uncommon to locally fairly common in Ecuador and Colombia, and fairly common in Venezuela, Suriname and French Guiana.
Habitat Tropical and Subtropical Zones. Always in dense forest, along small streams and pools where the edges are thickly overgrown. Also in gallery forests and old mangroves.
Voice Soft *tik* or *dzit*; also a dry, weak *cht, cht, cht*... In flight gives a clicking *choyt* (H&B).
Note Formerly called simply Pygmy Kingfisher, but now given the qualifier 'American' to differentiate from an African species of same name.

GREEN KINGFISHER

Chloroceryle americana Pl. 115

Identification 20cm. Adult male is rich bottle green above with white terminal spots on all wing-coverts, 2 rows of larger white spots on remiges forming bars, white tips to secondaries, and well-spaced white spots on outer edge of outermost rectrices; white chin and throat with white malar across lower face and neck-sides, joining at nape; breast deep rufous, with patches of dark green on sides forming a partial line below breast, and rest of underparts white. Female like male above, but has warm yellowish-buff neck-sides, throat and belly, rest of underparts white; broad dark green band with some white scaling on upper breast, and an irregular bar of green spots and blotches on upper belly, with a few scattered green spots on flanks and undertail-coverts. Green-and-rufous is larger and entirely rufous below. Similar Amazon Kingfisher is significantly larger and effectively unspotted above and all white below.

Ssp. *C. a. americana* (E Ec, E Co, C & E Ve, Guianas) as described
C. a. bottomeana (N Ve) male as *americana*, female has pale yellow tone to throat and breast, upper-breast bar narrower and more spotted, mesial line thinner and incomplete, less spotting on belly-sides and flanks, and paler throat and lower belly
C. a. cabanisii (W Co, W Ec) white flanks, green spots on undertail-coverts
C. a. septentrionalis (Co) as *cabanisii* but white undertail-coverts

Habits Solitary or in pairs; sedentary and very territorial. In breeding season males frequently engage in fierce territorial disputes. Prey is spied from fixed perch or by hovering. Bobs head and flicks tail at intervals when perched. Diving birds may reach quite deep below surface.
Status The most common and widespread of its genus.
Habitat Tropical Zone. Open, fresh or brackish waterbodies,

mangroves, creeks and streams, ponds, lagoons and flooded forests. Dark or muddy waters, but also rocky mountain streams of sparkling clear water.

Voice Clicks or long series'of softer, more musical notes. In flight, a low raspy *choot*, repeated 2–3 times as if stuttering (H&B).

Note Race *croteta* (Trinidad & Tobago) invalid; apparently described from an aberrant specimen with white throat and lower belly, and was taken on mainland.

AMAZON KINGFISHER

Chloroceryle amazona Pl. 115

Identification 30cm. The largest green kingfisher, with a long, heavy bill. Dark green head with small white crescent below eyes and white supraloral line; white nuchal collar joins white chin and throat, rufous breast, rest of underparts white with a few dark green streaks on flanks. Immature male and juvenile have white terminal spots on all wing-coverts and remiges, breast-sides green and rufous but no breast-band. Female has green breast-sides, but no rufous at all.

Ssp. Monotypic (all countries except Bo and Cu)

Habits Solitary or in pairs, fishes from perch or hovers above water, diving almost vertically. Sedentary but may move seasonally, upstream to subtropical altitudes.

Status Widespread. Uncommon to locally fairly common in Ecuador, fairly common in Guyana, Suriname and French Guiana, common in Colombia and very common in Venezuela.

Habitat Tropical and Lower Subtropical Zones. Wooded shores of broad, placid rivers, lakes and ponds, channels.

Voice Seldom calls. Repeated *tek*; sometimes noises resembling frog calls and also a series of clear, more musical notes that first rise and then fall in pitch and speed.

GREEN-AND-RUFOUS KINGFISHER

Chloroceryle inda Pl. 115

Identification 24cm. Adult male is rich dark green on head broad rufous supraloral streak; nuchal collar cinnamon, joining rufous neck-sides and entire underparts; rest of upperparts green, with wings, rump and tail covered by small white dots. Female similar but has broad green band with white fringes on breast. From American Pygmy by much larger size, whilst rufous underparts, including undertail-coverts, distinguish it from all other kingfishers.

Ssp. Monotypic (Ec, Co, Ve, T&T the Guianas)

Habits Fishes from fixed perch for hours, often bobbing head and flicking tail. Flies away over water when alarmed.

Status Common to uncommon, according to locality.

Habitat Tropical Zone. Edges of rivers and streams in dense forest, swamp forests, *várzea*.

Voice Twitters and chirps reminiscent of a songbird.

Note Race *chocoensis* (western Ecuador and Colombia) was described on basis of buffy spots on wings, but these are inconsistent and appear insufficient reason to warrant subspecific status, thus considered monotypic (Fry *et al.*, Woodall, Dickinson 2003).

Megaceryle kingfishers were formerly placed in the genus *Ceryle*, but this genus is now reserved for Old World kingfishers. The evidence to support this split is slender but is now widely accepted (e.g. Dickinson 2003, SACC).

BELTED KINGFISHER

Megaceryle alcyon Pl. 115

Identification 28–33cm. Adult male has darkish grey head with a rather ragged double crest, first part from crown, second from back of head, black lores and line through eyes, large white supraloral spot; white nuchal collar broadens on neck-sides to chin and throat, broad grey breast-band, rest of underparts white with a few rough scallops on flanks, upperparts mid grey with white spots on wings and tail, primaries black. Immature male has darker head and shorter crests; breast-band has orange scaling, and flanks a few orange streaks amongst the grey ones. Adult female like male but has an additional orange-rufous bar on lower breast and orange narrowly along flanks. Immature female like immature male but has more orange on flanks with a few spots on lower breast. Medium-sized kingfisher, from larger Ringed Kingfisher by white belly in all plumages. Beware band of rufous on flanks in adult female, which may give false impression of rufous belly at distance.

Ssp. Monotypic (Ec, N Co, N Ve, Tr, N Gu, coastal FG)

Habits Singly or in pairs, often watching from a fixed perch, hovering above surface to fish, or flying with long flaps along streams. May commute long distances to fishing spot. Main diet fish, but also takes crustaceans, small reptiles and amphibians, even insects. Usually dives almost vertically. Fish are beaten against perch and then swallowed whole. Bones regurgitated in pellets during night, so a pile often forms under regular roost sites.

Status Scarce boreal visitor (late September–early April). Northern South America marks southern fringe of winter range, thus very rare in Ecuador, rare in Colombia and scarce in Venezuela and Guyana, with a single record in French Guiana, but quite common on most Caribbean islands.

Habitat Tropical and Subtropical Zones. Shores of fresh, brackish and saltwater bodies, mangroves, rivers and steams, and areas of still, clear water with nearby high perches (trees, posts, bridges, aerial wires).

Voice Loud rattle, reminiscent of a child's noise-maker, *kekity-kek-kek-kek-tk-ticky-kek* (Fry *et al.*).

Note Formerly placed in genus *Ceryle*.

RINGED KINGFISHER

Megaceryle torquata Pl. 115

Identification 40cm. Large. Adult male has grey head with large, ragged double crest, and large white supraloral; white nuchal collar joins throat, white malar streaked grey; breast to belly and flanks rufous, vent to undertail-coverts white; mantle to tail grey, and middle of central rectrix blackish with vestigial white barring, tail-coverts barred narrowly white; wings grey with tiny white dots on outer coverts and secondaries, primaries black. Female similar but central rectrices have wavy black centre with white spots in concaves of line, and breast has broad grey band, with a narrower white band separating it from the rufous underparts. Juvenile much darker grey, entirely dotted white, with narrow bars on remiges and tail; similar to female below, but grey breast-band broader and scaled orange, white band also broader, rufous underparts paler. Largest kingfisher. From smaller Belted Kingfisher by all-rufous breast and belly.

Ssp. *M. t. torquata* (Ec, Co, Ve, Tr the Guianas)

Habits Solitary except in breeding season. In some areas (e.g. Orinoco river, Venezuela), small colonies may form. Quite shy; if approached will fly short distance and perch in a more secluded spot. Usually fishes for hours from same high perch, raising crest and cocking tail occasionally while perched. Beats prey against perch before swallowing it whole.

Status Widespread. Fairly common in Ecuador, Guyana and French Guiana, and common in Colombia, Venezuela and Suriname.

Habitat Tropical Zone. Heavily wooded shores of larger fresh, brackish and saltwater bodies and slow-moving rivers. Also rice fields, canals, reservoirs and even ponds in city parks.

Voice A loud *kek* or *klek*, repeated in a rattle if alarmed.

Note Formerly placed in genus *Ceryle*.

MOMOTIDAE – Motmots

The Aztecs from central Mexico gave motmots their name for the calls the birds make. During the 19th century, motmots briefly lost their original name due to the purist zeal of taxonomists, who decided that they should be called Prionites because birds should only have Greek or Latin names. Members of this small family share brightly coloured plumages and almost all have racketed tails. Their beauty and the fact that it is easier to hear than see them, make them prize birds of Neotropical forests. Sexes have similar plumage. The tail-feathers do not possess rackets when they first emerge, but do have a section of barbs near the tip that are quite weak and wear off after a while. They also have 1–3 black feathers in the central breast, of which the variability of these within a species is not understood. Diet consists of a wide variety of invertebrates and small vertebrates, and fruit, usually in smaller quantities. The bills have serrated edges that serve to grasp scorpions and other tricky or largish prey. They hunt in the air with fast sallies from a fixed perch, or on the ground by shuffling in the leaf-litter. Among typical behaviour is a predilection for sitting quietly on a horizontal branch in the subcanopy, watching whilst the tail swings from side to side in a slow, deliberate manner, accelerated if alert. Motmots nest in borrows dug in banks or amid tree roots. These are usually long, narrow tunnels, often a metre or more in length, and the entrance often partially concealed. They can be distinguished from burrows of mammals or other birds because the mouth is broader than it is high. The pair digs the tunnel and take turns incubating, feeding and guarding the young.

Additional references used for this family include Snow (2001).

TODY MOTMOT
Hylomanes momotula Pl. 116

Identification 16.5–18cm. Small and atypical; forehead to nape rufous with a broad turquoise-blue supraloral streak reaching just beyond eyes, broad black line behind eyes to ear-coverts, white from lores to lower ear-coverts, malar, throat and underparts to flanks and vent olive-green with a white sub-malar line and white line on central throat, paler yellowish-olive streaks on breast; vent and undertail-coverts white; back to tail olive-green, the central 4 rectrices longish, rest stepped, with outer pair very short; eyes brown, bill black, legs and feet pink.

Ssp. *H. m. obscurus* (NW Co)

Habits Forages at mid levels and in subcanopy, sometimes even on ground. Fast sallies from a perch to pick spiders, insects, snails and worms from leaves, branches and forest floor, and flying insects, especially dragonflies, cicadas and butterflies (even *Morpho* species), but unlike other motmots, not known to eat fruit.

Status Uncommon in Colombia, with scarce records from just a few localities.

Habitat Tropical Zone to 1,850m. Interior of humid forests and in shady, wet ravines.

Voice A far-carrying *kwa-kwa-kwa-kwa-kwa…* and fast, trembling *coooooooo-o-o-oh*, which resembles the hoot of an *Otus* (H&B).

BROAD-BILLED MOTMOT
Electron platyrhynchum Pl. 116

Identification 33–39cm. Comparatively smaller than other motmots. Completely rufous head and full breast, with black mask and small bib of turquoise-green, 3 black streaks in centre of breast, back and rump including wings (except primaries) and uppertail-coverts pale green, primaries and long tail with rackets turquoise-blue; belly turquoise-green; eyes deep red, bill black, legs and feet grey. Much larger Rufous Motmot lacks turquoise throat and tail is green on basal half at least.

Ssp. *E. p. colombianum* (N Co) throat has larger bib of turquoise-blue and shorter bill, belly to undertail-coverts pale leaf green; tail spatulate and does not develop rackets
E. p. minimus (NC Co) paler than *platyrhynchum*
E. p. platyrhynchum (W Ec, W Co) as described
E. p. pyrrholaemum (E Ec, E Co) throat has large bib of turquoise-green, belly to undertail-coverts leaf green; tail spatulate and does not develop rackets

Habits Forages alone or in pairs, mostly at mid levels. Picks food by sallying into vegetation or air. Follows swarms of ants.

Status Uncommon to fairly common in Ecuador, locally frequent in Colombia. Affected by deforestation.

Habitat Tropical Zone. Humid to wet forests, near borders or around clearings.

Voice Series of loud *oonk* and 3 fast *kruk* notes. Sometimes a bird will only call *oonk* notes, at other times a pair will answer each other with them, and yet other pairs give chorus of *oonk* and another pair a chorus of *kruk* trios (H&B). Calls before and after dawn, a nasal *cwaah* or *cwahnk*, repeated at long intervals (R&G).

RUFOUS MOTMOT

Baryphthengus martii Pl. 116

Identification 42–46cm. Rufous head and full breast to upper belly, with black mask and single black streak in centre of breast, back and rump including wings (except primaries), uppertail-coverts, belly, undertail-coverts and basal half of tail pale green, primaries and distal half of tail turquoise-blue; eyes deep chestnut, bill black, legs and feet grey.

Ssp. *B. m. martii* (E Ec, SE Co) spatulate tail without rackets; 2 morphs, pale and dark
B. m. semirufus (W Ec , NW Co) larger with more blue on belly; tail has rackets

Habits Forages alone or in pairs, from subcanopy to mid levels, with fast sallies from perch; swings tail more than most motmots. Follows army ants, changing perches leisurely above moving swarm. Dawn calls commence long before daybreak, other individuals often answering from different areas of forest.
Status Uncommon in Ecuador, uncommon to locally frequent in Colombia.
Habitat Tropical Zone to 1,400m. Humid to wet pristine forests or mature second growth and areas of lighter forest.
Voice Series of loud, vibrated hoots, *oot hoot-hoot-hoot…* reminiscent of an owl (H&B). From *martii* in west, a loud resonant hooting, *hooó-doo-doo*, sometimes accelerated into a roll, *hoor-r-r-r-ooo,* (R&G). Eastern *semirufus* utters simpler *hó-du* similar to Blue-crowned, but first note shorter (P. Coopmans in R&G).
Note Separated from Rufous-capped Motmot *B. ruficapillus* by differences in voice (Sick 1993).

BLUE-CROWNED MOTMOT

Momotus momota Pl. 116

Identification 39–46 cm; larger in lowlands of eastern Andes, smaller at edges of range. Wide range and considerable variation, with few intergrades (even in voice), make for a complex species that may well prove to be 4 species, perhaps more. In our region, birds fall into 3 fairly well-separated groups. Essentially, recognised by having top of head blue with a black crown. Black mask, body and most of tail green (one or more black breast streaks), distal part of tail turquoise-blue (with rackets); primaries blue; eyes deep chestnut, large heavy bill is black, legs and feet grey with large blackish scales.

Ssp. ***subrufescens*** **group**
M. m. conexus (N & C Co) mostly dull tawny, olive-washed on breast
M. m. osgoodi (NW Ve, NE Co: Norte de Santander) darker below
M. m. spatha (NE Co: Guajira) very pale turquoise forehead, nape and underparts buffy
M. m. subrufescens (Co, Ve: N coast) mostly caramel below, tinged olive
momota **group**
M. m. argenticinctus (W Ec, SW Co) brighter green than *microstephanus* with turquoise in nape
M. m. microstephanus (E Ec, E Co, W Ve) more bronzy and olive below than *argenticinctus*, nape entirely deep glistening violet-blue
M. m. momota (SE Co, C&S Ve, Guianas) rufous nuchal band
M. m. olivaresi (NC Co) like *spatha* but nape concolorous with mantle
undescribed subspecies (C Co: upper Magdalena Valley, listed in SCJ&W)
bahamensis **group**
M. m. bahamensis (T&T) smaller and rufous below

Habits Forages alone or in pairs, from subcanopy to mid levels, mainly in early morning and late afternoon. Follows swarms of ants, hawking the insects that are flushed.

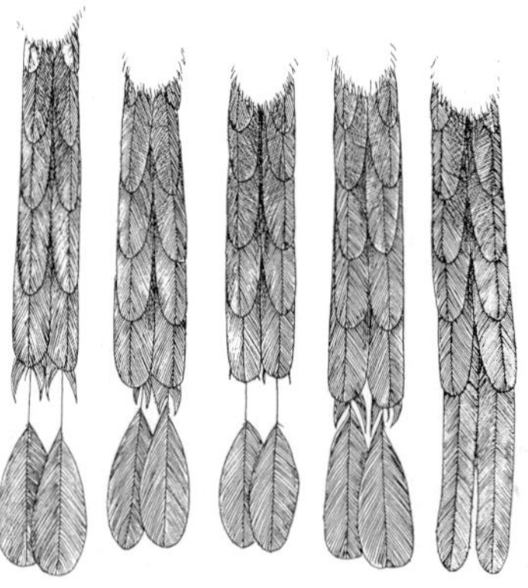

Comparison of how spatulas vary in size and shape, and may not even appear at all; the barbs above the rackets break away gradually once the tail is fully grown, whilst some individuals only develop partial rackets, a few not at all

Status Uncommon to locally common in Ecuador, frequent in Colombia (*subrufescens* quite local), locally frequent in Venezuela, uncommon in Trinidad but common in Tobago, and frequent in Guyana. Uncommon in French Guiana.
Habitat Tropical Zone, to 1,300m. Lower growth and mid level of borders of humid forests, mature second growth and humid semi-open areas with scattered copses or thickets, wooded suburbs, agricultural fields and mining settlements, but generally absent from cleared land or low scrub. Race *argenticinctus* more likely to be seen in open, especially early morning; *subrufescens* in dry forests in coastal areas and moist ravines in desert scrub.
Voice A low *hoo-doot*, similar to an owl's hoot, and also a rolled, vibrating *hrrroo* from lowland birds (H&B), *oüü-doot* at dawn and *h'o'o'o'o'r'r* when disturbed (Hilty), *hooo-do* from *argenticinctus* and *whoooop* from *microstephanus* (R&G).
Note Taxonomy requires revision. Seems likely, based on differences in plumage, size and vocalisations, plus clear

divisions in distribution with no intergradation, that several species are involved (Snow, R&G).

HIGHLAND MOTMOT

Momotus aequatorialis Pl. 116

Identification 46–48cm. Distinctive head pattern: black crown edged white, turquoise-green forehead becoming turquoise-blue on back of head, mask black, with a black line that runs to back of head, separating turquoise-blue from bright green nape; mask complex, being bisected at edge of ear-coverts by a bar of bright shiny pale blue. Malar also bright pale blue with a white line separating it from the mask; rest of body, from chin and mantle to halfway down tail green, distal half of tail and rackets blue; eyes deep red, large heavy bill is black, legs and feet grey with large black scales. Resembles Blue-crowned but they are allopatric, and noticeably larger than nearest race of Blue-crowned, *microstephanus*, which has deep violet nape; also, this is a montane species.

Ssp. *M. a. aequatorialis* (E Ec, Co: Andes)

Habits Forages alone or in pairs, mostly in mid levels and subcanopy.

Status Rare to locally uncommon in Ecuador, locally frequent in Colombia.

Habitat Subtropical Zone, 1,000–2,100m in Ecuador, 1,500–3,100m in Colombia. Humid forests on montane slopes, at borders, clearings and landslides. Known from west Andes in Colombia but only on eastern slope in Ecuador.

Voice A low, owl-like *hoo-doot* (F&K), a fast *hó-doo*, resembling Rufous Motmot (R&G).

Note The SACC has approved the treatment of *M. aequatorialis* as conspecific with *M. momota*.

GALBULIDAE – Jacamars

A small, sun-lit clearing breaks the shadows of a narrow forest trail. On a vine that arches gracefully in mid space perches a Green-tailed Jacamar, shooting glances up, left, right. It waits for a meal of butterflies, feathers glinting in the light. Beautiful jewels of Neotropical forests, jacamars are unmistakable. Common denominators of the family are the metallic glimmer of their plumage, the elongated body and long scissor-nosed bill. All are sedentary forest residents, perch quietly and calmly, to forage by sallying from a favoured perch to catch passing insects in mid-air, dig burrow nests in humid soil of riparian banks, the corky material of a termitarium or, when forests are on flat ground, in the huge clumps of dirt that cling to upended roots of felled trees. The nests are longish galleries that curve into a chamber, to keep young better protected. Both members of the pair excavate, but they are often helped by a third and even a fourth bird, possibly a sibling or older offspring. Jacamars use their bills to break the dirt, and then the feet to remove it from the tunnels. Parents also share in incubating and caring for the brood.

Additional references used for this family include Haffer (1974), Parker & Remsen (1987), Tobias, Züchner & Melo-Júnior (2002, hereafter Tobias).

WHITE-EARED JACAMAR

Galbalcyrhynchus leucotis Pl. 117

Identification 20cm. Unmistakable. Rather kingfisher-like in shape. Head black with bold white face-sides, rest of body deep reddish-chestnut with green-glossed black wings and longish, squared-off tail; eyes red, eye-ring and orbital skin pink, large heavy, dagger-like bill, legs and feet pink.

Ssp. Monotypic (Ec, S Co: E Andes)

Habits Forages singly, in pairs or small groups, from canopy to mid levels.

Status Common in Ecuador, locally common in Colombia.

Habitat Lower Tropical Zone to 500 m. Humid primary forests, both *várzea* and *terra firme*, and mature second growth. At borders, clearings, and particularly along banks of streams and on river islands.

Voice Calls infrequently, a sequence of single *kyew* notes. Small groups perch and call together (H&B). Prolonged rising trill resembling a woodcreeper (Tobias).

Note Sometimes called Chestnut Jacamar.

DUSKY-BACKED JACAMAR

Brachygalba salmoni Pl. 117

Identification 16.5–18cm. Small; entire upperparts rich shiny green, white triangle on chin and throat narrowly reaches neck-sides; underparts cinnamon; eyes chestnut, eye-ring and orbital skin grey, long narrow bill black, legs and feet dark grey.

Ssp. Monotypic (NW Co)

Habits Forages singly or in pairs, catching insects in mid-air, sometimes with long sallies. Perches quite upright.

Status Frequent in Colombia.

Habitat Lower Tropical Zone to 700m. Humid forest and mature second growth, at borders, clearings, treefalls, etc., and beside open streams.

Voice Often calls persistently, a plaintive, upward-inflected *sweet* or *feet*, sometimes in longer series, *pe-pe-pe-peet* (Tobias, H&B).

PALE-HEADED JACAMAR

Brachygalba goeringi Pl. 117

Identification 16–18cm. Crown and head-sides ashy brown, white triangle on chin and throat narrowly reaches neck-sides; breast ashy brown becoming darker at belly, upperparts dark shiny green becoming bluish with wear; underparts white with a rufous band mid belly; eyes deep red, eye-ring grey, bill black, legs and feet dark grey.

Ssp. Monotypic (NE Co, NW & C Ve)

Habits White belly and undertail-coverts with chestnut band distinctive. Forages in pairs or small groups, mainly in canopy, occasionally at mid levels.

Status Near-endemic to Venezuela, scarce and local in Colombia, locally frequent to common in Venezuelan Andes.

Habitat Lower Tropical Zone. Deciduous gallery and savanna forests, light drier woodland.

Voice A varying, rising sequence of high *weet* notes, ending in a trill: *weet, weet, weet, t'weet-t'weet-t'wéet ti'ti'ti't't'...* (H&B, Hilty).

BROWN JACAMAR

Brachygalba lugubris Pl. 117

Identification 14–18cm. Essentially dark brown with blackish wings that are glossed dark green or blue, and pale belly to vent. Juvenile slightly paler, and has vestigial pale eyebrows and throat.

Ssp. *B. l. caquetae* (SE Co, E Ec) rufescent tone to body and fringes to feathers on crown, chin pale to cinnamon, belly cinnamon, blue sheen to wings, all tail-coverts and tail

B. l. fulviventris (CE Co, SC Ve) cinnamon chin, base of malar and belly; green sheen to wings and tail-coverts, but bluish on tail

B. l. lugubris (E & SE Ve, Gu, Su, W FG) tiny white eyebrow, whitish chin and upper throat, pure white central belly and ventral area

B. l. obscuriceps (S Ve) dark with only tiny rufous chin and upper belly

Habits Forages alone, in pairs or small family groups, from subcanopy to mid levels. Often perches on branches above water.

Status Uncommon in Ecuador, locally frequent in Colombia and Venezuela, locally common in Guyana, frequent but patchily distributed in Suriname (more abundant in east), and uncommon but widespread in interior French Guiana.

Habitat Lower Tropical Zone. Gallery forests and savanna woodland, borders and clearings of humid forests, wooded rivers and streams.

Voice Song a falling sequence of notes that ends in a trill, *tick-tick-tick-ti-ti-ti-tit-t-t-t* (H&B), and a high bouncy *plee, plee, plee-plee-plee'ple'ple'pe'pe'e'e'e*, recalling Pale-headed Jacamar. Call a thin, sharply rising *perEET* (Hilty), a high, sharp whistle (H&M) or lower *chewee* (Tobias).

YELLOW-BILLED JACAMAR

Galbula albirostris Pl. 118

Identification 19cm. Male has crown deep maroon, black lores, basal malar and fore cheeks; ear-coverts, nape and rest of upperparts shiny emerald-green with gold and bronze reflections, tail brighter green; chin buff, throat white, rest of underparts cinnamon, quite rufescent on breast to flanks; eyes brown, eye-ring and loral skin yellow, bill yellow with dusky distally on culmen, legs and feet dull yellow. Female very similar but has chin and throat cinnamon, adjoining a deeper and uniform cinnamon breast and underparts.

Ssp. *G. a. albirostris* (SE Co, E Ve, Gu, Su, FG) as described

G. a. chalcocephala (Ve, Co and Ec: Amazonia) crown reddish-purple, chin partially dusky, underparts deeper rufous

Habits Forages alone, in pairs or small family groups, from low to mid levels. Often with mixed flocks. Perches quite upright.

Status Uncommon in Ecuador and Colombia, locally frequent in Venezuela, frequent in Guyana and southern Suriname, and frequent in interior French Guiana.

Habitat Lower Tropical Zone. Well inside humid *várzea* or *terra firma*, in 'dark' tall forest understories, seldom at clearings.

Voice Song a rapid sequence of high notes that ends in a trill: *peea, peea-pee-pee-te-t-t-t-e'e'e'e'e'-e* (H&B) or *peea,-peea-pee-pee-te-t-t-t't't't't'ttttt'r* (Hilty), or series of high whistles that accelerate into a rattle, similar to Bronzy Jacamar (H&M).

BLUISH-FRONTED JACAMAR

Galbula cyanescens Pl. 118

Identification 20–23cm. Forehead and front of crown bluish, rear crown and upperparts shiny green with gold and bronze reflections, fore face dusky and chin spotted whitish and speckled grey and black, underparts uniform rufous including undertail; eyes, bill, legs and feet all dark. Very similar White-chinned has a dusky, slightly purplish forehead and chin is pure white.

Ssp. Monotypic (se Co?)

Status Very scarce in Colombia (sight records only).

Habitat Lower Tropical Zone. Humid lowland forests.

Voice Call a long series of high-pitched kree or kree-ip notes, and full song is *kip kip-kip-kipkikikrkrkrrr-kree-kree-kree-kip-kip-kikikrrrrreeuw*, a series that accelerates into a trill, slows to single notes, then speeds up again in final 'rush' (Tobias).

Notes Sight records from Amacayacu, in Amazonian Colombia (SCJ&W). The species is generally considered to be confined to the basins of the Juruá and Purús rivers, and by the west bank of the Madeira and southern tributaries of the Amazon.

RUFOUS-TAILED JACAMAR

Galbula ruficauda Pl. 118

Identification 23cm. Entirely green above, variable dusky on face according to race; white chin (except *melanogenia*) variable green breast (except *ruficauda*) and cinnamon to rufous below, including undertail; eyes brown, eye-ring and loral skin grey, bill black, legs and feet yellow. Female paler below than male, with buffy throat. Longer, tapered tail separates it from all other jacamars.

Ssp. *G. r. brevirostris* (CE Co: Norte de Santander, NW Ve: S Zulia, Táchira and Mérida) dusky face with some golden reflections, and gold reflections over all green, which is slightly deeper than other races, except tail which is more intense shiny green; very broad breast-band, belly and below deep rufous

G. r. melanogenia (W Co, W Ec) blackish face and chin, medium-width breast-band is highly reflective yellow and gold, yellowish reflections above, tail concolorous with rump and uppertail-coverts; underparts deep chestnut

G. r. pallens (N Co: N Magdalena Valley and Santa Marta, NW Ve: Guajira Peninsula) slightly paler and definitely more bronzy above, including reflections on tail, green breast-band narrow, broader in centre, rest of breast rufous grading into cinnamon of rear underparts and undertail

G. r. ruficauda (C Co: S Magdalena Valley, Arauca, Casanare; NC & E Ve; T&T, Gu, FG) golden-reddish reflections on head-sides and rump; virtually no green breast-band, just a slight green wash on sides, underparts pale cinnamon; female has pale buffy throat, rest of underparts pale cinnamon-buffy

Habits Forages mostly in pairs, from canopy to lower levels. Hunts day and night.

Status Uncommon in Ecuador, common in Colombia and Venezuela, common on Tobago but uncommon in Trinidad. Uncommon and very local in Guyana, and although often listed for Suriname, no reliable records are available. A record for French Guiana is obviously a mistake.

Habitat Lower Tropical Zone. Borders, treefalls and clearings in humid forests, second growth and lightly wooded areas with thickets and bushes, near streams.

Voice A sharp *peeup*; song a speeding sequence *peeo, peeo, peea pee-pee-pee-pe-pe-pe-pe-pe-e-e-e'e'e'e'e* (H&B, Hilty), twittering and chuckling trills and low *bee-bee-bee* (Tobias).

GREEN-TAILED JACAMAR

Galbula galbula Pl. 118

Identification 20cm. Male has upperparts entirely green, malachite tone with golden and pale green reflections on head, touches of malachite and gold reflections on back and wings, and broad green breast-band, tail has distinct bluish band, becoming almost wholly blue at tip, tiny black chin, throat white, breast green, underparts dark chestnut, blackish around lores and eyes, eyes brown, eye-ring and small loral skin dark grey, bill black, legs and feet yellowish. Similar to Rufous-tailed but has shorter tail and dark greenish (not rufous) undertail.

Ssp. Monotypic (SE Co, S & E Ve, Gu, Su, FG)

Habits Forages alone or in pairs, from lower to mid levels.

Status Frequent in Colombia, Venezuela and Guyana. In Suriname, very common in north but scarcer in south. In French Guiana, common on coastal plain.

Habitat Lower Tropical Zone to 700m. Borders and clearings of humid primary forest, gallery forest and mature second growth. Edges of mangroves, coffee plantations and forested sand ridges. Most often in bushes along streams.

Voice Repeated high *peer* or *peet-peet* wistful notes (H&B) or repeated high whistled notes (H&M), a long, accelerating series of high notes, *peea…pee,pee,pee-pee-pee-pe-pe'pe'pep e'p'p'p'e'e'e'e'e e e*, with a complaining quality, ending in a trill. A slow series of steady *peer…peer…peer* reminiscent of Paradise Jacamar (Hilty).

COPPERY-CHESTED JACAMAR

Galbula pastazae Pl. 118

Identification 23cm. Bluish front of head and face, rest of upperparts shiny green with bronze and golden reflections; chin pale whitish, spotted grey and black, throat to breast pale green very much reflecting bronze and gold, rest of underparts rufous, including undertail; eyes dark, eye-ring and loral skin orange-pink, bill, legs and feet dark. No overlap with any other jacamar and reaches much higher altitudes.

Ssp. Monotypic (SC Co, E Ec)

Habits Further distinguished by pinkish-orange eye-ring. Forages alone or in pairs, at mid levels. Returns each day to a few favoured perches.

Status Vulnerable. Uncommon in Ecuador, rare in Colombia. Very small range, threatened by habitat destruction.

Habitat Upper Tropical to Subtropical Zones, from as low as 600m, but usually 1,000–1,700m, with questionable reports higher. Humid montane and cloud forests, mostly in the interior but occasionally at borders.

Voice Calls 3+ repeated loud *quep* notes (Poulsen & Wege 1994). Series of notes on a rising scale, accelerating slightly then dropping down over last 2–3, e.g. *pee-pee-pee-pee-pee-pee-pee-pee-pe-pe-pe-pee-pee-pee-pee-pee* (Tobias).

WHITE-CHINNED JACAMAR

Galbula tombacea Pl. 118

Identification 22cm. Forehead and front of head dusky with slight purplish tone, rear crown and upperparts shiny green with gold and bronze reflections, fore face dusky and chin white, underparts uniform rufous including undertail, eyes, bill, legs and feet all dark. From Bluish-fronted, Purplish and Green-tailed by small white chin, front of head greyish-maroon, and rufous undertail.

Ssp. *G. t. tombacea* (Co, Ec: Amazonia)

Habits Forages alone or in pairs, at low to mid levels.

Status Uncommon in Ecuador, scarce but widespread in Colombia.

Habitat Tropical Zone to 1,200m. Borders of humid and gallery forests, edges of *várzea*, overgrown treefall gaps and clearings.

Voice Repeated *keelip* notes; song a sequence that accelerates gradually: *pee-pee-pee-pe-pe-pe'pe'pe'pe'e'e'e'* (H&B).

PURPLISH JACAMAR

Galbula chalcothorax Pl. 117

Identification 23.5cm. Entire upperparts dark green with iridescent bronze and purple, the head has more cobalt and bluish-purple, the tail more green; chin black, triangular white throat patch reaches narrowly to neck-sides; entire breast, upper belly and sides pure purple, flanks and lower belly black with heavy white fringes, undertail-coverts white; eyes brown, bill, legs and feet black. Very similar to male Bronzy Jacamar but no overlap in range.

Ssp. Monotypic (SE Co, E Ec)

Habits Forages alone or in pairs, often with mixed canopy flocks, from mid levels to canopy.

Status Uncommon to rare in Ecuador, possibly uncommon in Colombia, where only recently discovered (SCJ&W).

Habitat Tropical Zone to 400m in Colombia and 1,000m in Ecuador. Humid forests of lowlands (*terra firme*) and foothills, mostly in the interior, sometimes in clearings and at treefalls.
Voice Song a rising sequence of whistled notes, some doubled, that accelerates into a trill at end: *weeee weeee wi-deee wi-deee wi-deee wi-deee...* (R&G). Call *weeee*, similar to Dusky-capped Flycatcher *Myiarchus tuberculifer* (Tobias).

BRONZY JACAMAR

Galbula leucogastra Pl. 117

Identification 22cm. Head blackish, shot with deep blue and green iridescences, entire upperparts and breast to flanks and upper belly bronze with purple, green and bronze iridescences, tail mostly bronze and green, belly and undertail-coverts white; eyes brown, eye-ring grey, bill, legs and feet black. Female has ochraceous throat and buffy belly and undertail-coverts; wings and body as iridescent as male, but less purple and more a mixture. Male very similar to Purplish Jacamar, but no overlap in range.

Ssp. *G. l. leucogastra* (Co, S Ve, Gu, Su, FG)

Habits Forages in pairs or small (family?) groups, from canopy to lower levels.
Status Locally frequent in Colombia and Venezuela, frequent in Guyana, very rare and local in French Guiana.
Habitat Lower Tropical Zone, below 900m. Sandy soil and humid *terra firme* forest and mature second growth, in clearings, bushy borders and by streams.
Voice A rising series of high whistles that hasten into a trill (H&M). A slow series of 4–5 high *peer* notes that recall Paradise Jacamar but lack initial pauses. Also a slow ticking trill, over and over, t-*t-r-r-r-r-d-d-deet, tadeet, tadeet, tadeet* (Hilty). A rising series of tripled *weeee, weep-pip-pweeeeee, weep-pip-pweeeeee, weep-pip-pweeeeee* notes (Tobias).

PARADISE JACAMAR *Galbula dea* Pl. 117

Identification 30cm. Appears all black with white throat patch. Crown ashy brown, black mask from lores and chin to nape, rest of body, wings and tail glossy black with mainly indigo iridescence on upper surface, and some green on wings; tail very long, tapering to a point; white triangle of throat reaches neck-sides; eyes chestnut, bill long and black, legs and feet grey with large black scales.

Ssp. *G. d. brunneiceps* (Ec, Co, Ve Amazonia) noticeably shorter tail, particularly golden-bronze reflections on wing-coverts, tertials and uppertail-coverts
G. d. dea (Ve, Gu, Su, FG) as described

Habits Forages alone, in pairs or very small groups (3–4, family?), and often joins mixed canopy flocks. May be seen perched on high exposed twigs.
Status Rare in Ecuador, locally common in Colombia, frequent in Guyana, quite common in Suriname, frequent in French Guiana.
Habitat Lower Tropical Zone to 1,000m, but usually below 500m. Sandy soil and humid *terra firme* forest and mature second growth, in clearings, bushy borders and by streams.
Voice A descending sequence, *peep, peep, peep, peep, pee, pee, pe, pe, pe...* (H&B) and series of high, piping tones (H&M). High, thin series that begins slowly then accelerates slightly, *PEEap... PEEap...peeap, peea, pee-pee-pe'pe'pe* (Hilty). Call a single *pip*, and *glewweh*, like a distant woodcreeper or hawk (Tobias).

GREAT JACAMAR

Jacamerops aureus Pl. 118

Identification 30cm. Largest jacamar, wicked-looking, heavy and thick bill. Head green but for small white throat, and intense blue reflections on crown, mixed with small patch of turquoise-blue on nape; rest of upperparts green with heavy gold and coppery iridescences on back and shoulders, central tail bright rich purplish-blue; breast to undertail-coverts deep chestnut; eyes brown with grey eye-ring, bill black, legs and feet blue-grey.

Ssp. *J. a. aureus* (E Co, SE Ve, Guianas) as described
J. a. isidori (E Ec) much paler below
J. a. penardi (W Co, NW Ec) is more green above
J. a. ridgwayi (S Ve) coppery to deep reddish reflections on back, crown more turquoise, underparts deep cinnamon; female more green above, with less colourful reflections, throat and all underparts cinnamon

Habits Forages singly or in pairs, from subcanopy to lower levels. Sallies to pick prey from leaves as well as in air. May join mixed flocks for short periods.
Status Rare to locally frequent in Ecuador, uncommon and local in Colombia, Venezuela and Guyana, scarce in Suriname, rare but widespread in French Guiana.
Habitat Tropical Zone to 700m, locally to 1,100m. Extensive humid forests, usually in the interior but occasionally at well-shaded borders, mature, shaded second growth; often near small streams.
Voice Calls sporadically, wistful long whistles reminiscent of a hawk: *wheeeeeeeer, wheeeeeeeer* from high in canopy (MLG) or *weeeeeeeeewhuuuuu* (Hilty). Call a sequence of 4 low whistles, ending with shorter note (H&M).

BUCCONIDAE – Puffbirds, Nunlets and Nunbirds

Puffbirds and their allies generally present a rather misleading impression. A typical puffbird has a large, broad head with full eyebrows, large, brightly coloured eyes, and a fairly large bill with a hooked tip. It is bulky, fat and sluggish, an appearance created by the soft, coarse and fluffy feathers, but perfectly supportive of the lazy, even stupid image the birds possess. Local names like Bobito and Juan Bobo suggest a dummy without intelligence. They sit perfectly still, with occasional head movements, for hours on end, watching alertly for a passing insect or other suitable creature that it can suddenly snatch quickly from the air, ground or branch. The bird returns to the same perch and beats its prey against the wood until it is dead and the hard parts broken, before swallowing it. This perched, unmoving technique makes the birds easy to overlook, both by human observers and predators, a strategy further enhanced by their generally cryptic plumage. Found both in forests and at edges, but it is the latter where they are most often seen. They build gallery nests with a chamber lined by dry leaves dug in the ground or carved into an arboreal termite nest. The nestlings push the leaves in the nest chamber to the entrance to form a blind that gives the impression the hole is unused and old. Most species vocalise at dawn, or even pre-dawn, but their calls and song by day may reveal their presence. Nunbirds are rather different in many respects and are dealt with below.

Additional references used to prepare this family include Rasmussen & Collar (2002, shown here as R&C).

WHITE-NECKED PUFFBIRD
Notharchus macrorhynchos Pl. 119

Identification 25cm. Large, black-and-white puffbird. Forehead white, top of head to nape black with a thin nuchal line separating nape from all-black upperparts (fringes of all feathers dark brown when fresh); lores black, ear-coverts, lower face, chin and breast white; broad black band across central underparts (scalloped or shallowly scaled whitish when fresh), rest of underparts white with some faint black barring on flanks; orbital skin grey, eyes chestnut, large heavy bill black, legs and feet grey. Similar but smaller Black-breasted Puffbird has all-black forehead and broad black line from lores to breast-sides; Pied Puffbird more similar, but significantly smaller and has white scapulars and noticeable white tips to undertail; also more likely to be seen at forest edge and clearings.

Ssp. *N. m. hyperrynchus* (W Ec, N & NE Co, S Ve) significantly larger; more extensive white forehead runs back as an eyebrow, no scaling; bill proportionately larger and heavier; flanks more heavily barred

N. m. macrorhynchos (SE Ve, Guianas) as described

Habits Forages in canopy and mid levels, wings make low whirring noise. Easily overlooked.
Status Uncommon in Ecuador, frequent in Colombia, widespread and fairly common in Venezuela, uncommon in Guyana, frequent in Suriname, not numerous but widespread in French Guiana.
Habitat Lower Tropical Zone to 1,200m (only to 250m south of Orinoco). Humid forest and tall secondary woodland, inside forest and more obviously at borders and clearings.
Voice Occasional melodious or harsh calls. Song a series of very high, thin twitters (H&B). Descending sequences of melodic whistles, often trisyllabic, sometimes ascending, accelerating or decreasing, e.g. *dibewle-dibewle-dibewle* (Sick), and very weak high trill, usually descending, *ui-ui-ui…wi-dik-dik wi-dik-dik wi-dik-dik* (R&G). Long series of rapid, *pree* whistles (Hilty).
Notes Race *hyperrynchus* may represent a separate species, whilst Santa Marta birds may be an undescribed subspecies (R&C).

BLACK-BREASTED PUFFBIRD
Notharchus pectoralis Pl. 119

Identification 19–21cm. Head and breast almost entirely pure black, except white ear-coverts that taper to a thin nuchal line, and white bib; rest of upperparts black with dark brown fringes to feathers; belly to undertail-coverts white with heavy, regular barring on flanks. Similar to White-necked Puffbird but much smaller with no white on forehead, and more restricted to forest interior.

Ssp. Monotypic (NW Ec, W & WC Co)

Habits Often near running water. Follows army ants.
Status Rare in Ecuador, uncommon in Colombia.
Habitat Tropical Zone to 1,000m. Subcanopy and borders of humid to wet forests and tall secondary woodland. Associated with *Heliconia* and bamboos.
Voice A long, loud series of whistles that begins with 10–30 loud *wheet* or *kwee* notes, then, more slowly, 3–4 lower pitched *whew*, to end with a few *wheet-whew* wolf whistles that fade; also, *chah-chah-chah-chah-chah* as a territorial call (H&B, R&G, R&C).

BROWN-BANDED PUFFBIRD
Notharchus ordii Pl. 119

Identification 20–21cm. Forehead to face-sides white, with a white nuchal line, white neck-sides and breast; blackish upperparts, browner on rump and uppertail-coverts which have black subterminal tips; broad band on lower breast is black above and brown below; rest of underparts white with even-width black bars on flanks; tail black with dirty white tips; eyes dark brown, eye-ring grey, bill heavy and black, legs and feet grey. From larger White-necked by clear brown lower pectoral band and white lores.

Ssp. Monotypic (S Ve, SE Co?)

Habits Forages in canopy, sallying for insects.
Status Very rare in Colombia and uncommon in Venezuela.
Habitat Lower Tropical Zone, 150–300m. Forest edge, humid terra firme, white-sand and transitional forests, and adjacent scrub. Both in forest and at clearings and borders.
Voice A long, loud series of whistles that commences with 10 *wheet* notes, then 3 lower *whew* calls (R&C). Duet *KUEEP! KUEEP, kee-kee-kee-kee-kee, quaaa, kée-kée-quaaa, kée-kée-quaaa…* up to 15 s, with 1 bird calling *KUEEP* and *kee*, the other *quaaa* (Zimmer in Hilty).

PIED PUFFBIRD *Notharchus tectus* Pl. 119

Identification 14–16cm. Head almost all black except fine white spots on forecrown, fading over crown, large white supraloral and narrow eyebrow to rear ear-coverts, and white malar that reaches neck-sides; chin and throat white; upperparts black with large white spots on scapulars forming an irregular line; brownish tail-coverts with whitish tips; breast almost all black save for narrow white line on sides that joins neck-sides; belly to undertail-coverts white with brown and black barring on flanks; undertail has white base to outer rectrices and broad white tips to inner webs of all; eyes brown, bill fairly small, deep-based and black, legs and feet grey. May be confused with larger White-necked but note black forehead with extended white eyebrow and white tips to undertail.

Ssp. *N. t. picatus* (E Ec, SE Co) distinctly larger than *tectus*; entire top of head streaked white; broad black breast-band joins black body-sides, flanks narrowly barred black

N. t. subtectus (W Co, SW Ec) slightly smaller than *tectus*, smaller bill, narrower pectoral band, no spotting on crown

N. t. tectus (S Ve, Guianas) as described; finely spotted forecrown

Habits Forages alone or in pairs, usually in canopy and thus seen from below may look rather like Bronzy Jacamar.

Status Uncommon to rare in Ecuador, uncommon to locally common in Colombia and Venezuela, uncommon in Guyana, frequent in Suriname and French Guiana.

Habitat Tropical Zone to 1,000m. Riverine forest, tall mangrove forest, coffee plantations, edges of dense lowland forest and savanna woodland, also canopy of *terra firme* forest in French Guiana.

Voice Calls frequently. A long *peed-peed-peed, peed-it, peed-it, peed-it, peed-it, peea, pee, pee, pee* that begins high-pitched and falls at end (H&B, Hilty), also described as *pseeee tidit, tidit-tidit*, like a tyrant flycatcher (R&C). Song high and bat-like, a tremulous *peet…rri…bee-bi-bi-bi* (Sick), *pewee pewee pewee* or *wheedeedee-dee-dee, pee-pee-pee-pee-pee-peedi-peedi-peedi-peedi*, speeding-up in middle, slowing at end (R&G).

CHESTNUT-CAPPED PUFFBIRD

Bucco macrodactylus Pl.119

Identification 14–17cm. Entire top of head deep umber-chestnut, lores white, cheeks and ear-coverts black with a white line separating black from large black breast patch; chin and throat yellow-ochre, nuchal band reddish-chestnut; back and wings to tail dark brown with subtle buffy fringes; broad white oval patch on underparts, separating black breast from ochraceous belly, which becomes paler and barred to undertail-coverts; eyes dark brown, bill thick, heavy and black; legs and feet grey. From Spotted Puffbird by lack of eyebrow and 2-toned pectoral band. From larger Collared Puffbird by black bill, white lores and black cheeks.

Ssp. *B. m. caurensis* (SE Ve) smaller bill; much narrower pectoral band, white on neck-sides vestigial, chin, throat and nuchal band cinnamon; more greyish-ochre below; legs and feet vinaceous grey

B. m. macrodactylus (E Ec, E Co, S Ve) as described

Habits Solitary. Favours dense-tangled undergrowth and usually very hard to find.

Status Uncommon in Ecuador and Colombia, locally common in Venezuela.

Habitat Lower Tropical Zone to 600m. Humid forests, both *terra firme* and *várzea*, gallery forests, humid secondary woodland, wet areas and river borders.

Voice Seldom calls. A rising series that ends in a twitter, pup *pup pep pep peep peep pip pip pip piz*; also, a series of sad *weee-a* notes (H&B, Hilty). Calls *weeeeooo*, easily mistaken for Dusky-capped Flycatcher (P. Coopmans in R&G).

SPOTTED PUFFBIRD

Bucco tamatia Pl.119

Identification 18cm. Adult has forehead narrowly cream-coloured, continuing as an eyebrow to rear ear-coverts, lores through and below eyes to ear-coverts dusky, with a white line from base of malar across lower face to become a nuchal band; upper forehead to crown rufous, merging into dark brown back of head and nape, rest of upperparts also dark brown, the feathers more or less fringed buffy, most noticeably on uppertail-coverts; chin and throat rufous widening on neck-sides to embrace black patch on lower-face-sides; underparts white with irregular black scallops except on belly and undertail-coverts; eyes red, bill black, legs and feet vinaceous flesh. Juvenile lacks rufous on forehead and has only loral patch pale creamy, upperparts dark brown, more distinctly fringed buffy than adult, upper breast flushed rufous, underparts less clearly scalloped. From Chestnut-capped Puffbird by creamy eyebrow and heavily spotted belly. White malar with black spot below is distinctive.

Ssp. *B. t. pulmentum* (E Ec, SE Co) paler, sandier throat, slightly paler rufous forehead, heavier and more blurred scaling below

B. t. tamatia (E Co, E Ve, Guianas) as described

Habits Usually solitary in canopy.

Status Very rare in Ecuador, uncommon in Colombia, uncommon to locally frequent in Venezuela, frequent in Guyana, uncommon in Suriname and French Guiana.

Habitat Lower Tropical Zone. Humid lowland forest, sandy soil forest, gallery forest, savanna thickets and palm groves.

Voice Seldom calls. Pre-dawn song a loud, far-carrying, high trill (H&B), a long sequence of high-pitched *chyoi* whistles, followed by a few at lower pitch and ending in *pchooii, pchooii, pchooii, peejowee* whistles (H&B), a soft, long-sustained (up to 30 notes and 15 s) *puweeep, puwéep, puwéep…* weak and plaintive intially but gaining strength, with a whistled *pu'chooee* at end (Hilty), or a long series of monotonous *kueeép* notes, gradually getting louder and lasting up to 15 s (R&G).

Note Placed in genus *Nystactes* by R&C.

SOOTY-CAPPED PUFFBIRD

Bucco noanamae Pl.119

Identification 19cm. Dusky forehead becomes more brown on back of head, broadly whitish on nape; back and wings to tail warm brown, all feathers more or less fringed buffy; malar to neck-sides, chin and throat white, broad pectoral band, rather irregular black scalloping on white underparts; eyes brown, bill black, legs and feet pinky grey. Rather like White-necked and Black-breasted Puffbirds from front, but brown upperparts and grey nape are clear discriminators.

Ssp. Monotypic (NW Co)

Habits Solitary. Very poorly known.
Status Near Threatened. Colombian endemic.
Habitat Lower Tropical Zone to 100m. Humid and wet lowland forests, cocoa plantations, secondary woodland.
Voice Unknown.
Note Placed in genus *Nystactes* by R&C.

COLLARED PUFFBIRD
Bucco capensis Pl.119

Identification 17.5–19cm. Upperparts rufous barred narrowly black, but unbarred around eyes, and more widely spaced bars on tail; broad black nuchal band joins much broader pectoral band; chin and throat buffy-white, underparts buffy-white with ochraceous wash on flanks; eyes bright yellow, bill orange-yellow, legs and feet pale greyish-yellow. Bright bill and rufous head distinctive.

Ssp. *B. c. capensis* (SE Ve, Guianas) as described
B. c. dugandi (E Ec, SE Co, S Ve) noticeably paler though still richly coloured, barring fainter and paler, especially on head, with narrower black pectoral and nuchal bands

Habits Solitary. Still-hunts from shaded perch, sometimes follows mixed flocks. Usually forages at mid levels but often close to ground.
Status Rare in Ecuador, frequent in Guyana, uncommon in Suriname, uncommon but widespread in French Guiana.
Habitat Tropical zone to 500m, but once at 1,700m, undergrowth of primary humid *terra firme* forest.
Voice A far-carrying but difficult to locate, rhythmic *cua-will, cua-will* up to 6 times (Hilty). Usually quiet, but gives a hoarse, rhythmic *cua-will-kú* (R&G).

BARRED PUFFBIRD *Nystalus radiatus* Pl.120

Identification 20–22cm. Resembles a Fasciated Antshrike without solid rufous crown or buff collar. Similar Striolated Puffbird is other side of Andes. Dark brown cap barred blackish, rest of head, from supraloral through extensive eyebrow to broad nuchal band, neck-sides and malar, and entire underparts (except white chin and upper throat) whitish to buffy-cream, mostly barred dark brown (these being well spaced and broken), but on lores, nape, belly and undertail-coverts barring is paler and weaker; dark brown above, barred evenly dark brown except on tail where bars well spaced; eyes pale greyish-yellow, bill greyish-buffy, legs and feet vinaceous grey.

Ssp. *N. r. radiatus* (W Ec, W Co) as described
N. r. fulvidus (C Co: Magdalena Valley) similar in pattern but generally rufous above and pale cinnamon below

Habits Apparently usually solitary, but often in widely spaced pairs sat still for long periods, occasionally flicking tail sideways. Easily overlooked, but is very vocal and may draw attention. Regularly perches on telegraph wires where it is much more likely to be seen.
Status Uncommon in Ecuador, local in Colombia.
Habitat Lower Tropical Zone to 900m, locally to 1,500m above Mindo, Ecuador. Lower storey of lowland humid and wet forest borders, second growth, open streams, overgrown clearings, thickets on open plains and agricultural land.
Voice Long, slow, ventriloquial and very human-like wolf whistle, *phweeeeeet-weeeeeeuuuu*, 4–5 s long, 2 per minute. Similar call of Rufous Mourner is less drawn-out and second note is higher pitched.
Note Race *fulvidus* completely overlooked by Peters' Checklist, and thus disappeared from the literature until mentioned by R&C as a 'probable colour morph'. However, it could even be a separate species, and critical reading of Sclater (1882) and Salvin & Godman (1896) suggests *fulvidus* should be maintained until such time as a fuller review can be attempted.

STRIOLATED PUFFBIRD
Nystalus striolatus Pl.120

Identification 20cm. Forehead to tail dark brown, barred evenly with black, broken only by pale buffy nuchal band; underparts from supraloral and eyebrow to undertail-coverts white, washed buffy on ear-coverts, neck- and breast-sides, and streaked dusky on rear flanks and undertail-coverts; eyes greyish-yellow, eye-ring grey, bill dark greenish-grey, legs and feet grey.

Ssp. *N. s. striolatus* (E Ec)

Habits Similar Barred Puffbird is other side of Andes.
Status Rare in Ecuador.
Habitat Tropical Zone to 1,700m. Canopy, subcanopy, edges, *terra firme* and low-lying swamp forest, transitional forest, second growth, clearings; usually near water.
Voice Soft, sad whistle, *whip, whi wheeu, wheeeeeuu*, with distinct cadence (R&G).

RUSSET-THROATED PUFFBIRD
Hypnelus ruficollis Pl.120

Identification 22cm. A rather variable and confusing species, similar to allopatric Two-banded Puffbird. Races fall into 2 groups, first, those from more humid habitat, then those from xerophytic coastal areas. Juveniles have a slightly paler throat, the pectoral bar a whitish wash and usually slightly broken or irregular; upperparts have buffy fringes. The only puffbird in its habitat.

Ssp. Rufous-throated group
H. r. coloratus (NE Co: Norte de Santander, NW Ve: Carigua, Santa Barbara, Zulia; La Fria, Táchira; El Vigía, Mérida – sea level to 200m) umber-brown above, softly streaked buffy on head and back, becoming barred on rump and uppertail-coverts; all wing-coverts have 'teardrop' buffy spots; lores buffy, cheeks and ear-coverts white; small black triangle behind eyes becomes a thin line around ear-coverts, then a broad crescent below white patch; chin cinnamon becoming deep rufous on throat and upper breast; narrow white pectoral band with a broad black pectoral band below; rest of underparts

cinnamon-buff with a few black spots on lower flanks; eye-ring grey, eyes pale greyish-yellow, bill black, legs and feet grey with larger black scales and claws.

H. r. ruficollis (N Co, NW Ve: Perijá, Mene Grande – 60–120m) noticeably smaller, with a proportionately heavier and deeper bill; upperparts similar; chin paler, throat slightly paler rufous and less extensive, slightly broader white pectoral band; rest of underparts paler with broken spots and bars on flanks

Paler group

H. r. decolor (NE Co: Guajira, NW Ve: Paragua Pen.; Cabimas and Palmarejo, Guajira Peninsula – sea level to 200m) same size as *ruficollis*; paler, more greyish-brown above, streaks and spots whiter and more apparent; face and breast like much larger *coloratus*, but chin white, throat and breast very pale cinnamon, white pectoral band broader and black band narrower; rest of underparts pale whitish-buffy with a few faint bar-spots on lower flanks, bill large and short

H. r. striaticollis (NW Ve: Casigua and Dabajuro, Falcón; Quisiro, Zulia; Quiragua, Cumarebo – sea level) same size as *coloratus*, but colour above like *decolor*; lores pale buffy, continuing as a short eyebrow, and below eyes to ear-coverts; dark crescent from base of mandible to neck-sides brown and blackish; chin and throat white, becoming a broad, greyish-buff band on breast, streaked blackish, grey and white, lower breast broadly creamy-buff, narrow black band between breast and belly; rest of underparts creamy-buff with some large blackish spot-bars on flanks; bill large and long

Status Common to abundant.

Habitat Tropical Zone, mostly at sea level, but a record of *decolor* at 550m. All in similar habitat, low-lying, open deciduous forest and edge, treed savannas, along waterbodies, dense second growth, woodland and scrub with scattered trees, dry thickets.

Voice Noisy. Duets of repeated rhythmic *woduk* notes in crescendo for up to 20 s, then diminishing and ending with just 1 bird calling. Call a high, insect-like *seeeeep* (R&G, Hilty).

Notes Range of recognised races in Venezuela confusing when mapped in detail and it seems very likely undescribed subspecies are involved and even possibly 2 species. Field studies are in hand to map comparative vocalisations and other data. Separated from Two-banded Puffbird in R&C on basis of morphological, plumage and vocal differences, with which we completely agree. Supposed intermediates between them were found to be juvenile and immatures of Two-banded Puffbird (Restall & Lentino in prep.).

TWO-BANDED PUFFBIRD

Hypnelus bicinctus Pl.120

Identification 20–22cm. Adult dark brown above with narrow frontal band of buffy that joins lores and creeps over base of malar to chin and throat, but becomes white on cheeks and ear-coverts, and continues as a narrow white nuchal band; greyish-buffy streaks broad and well spaced, but lower rump and uppertail-coverts narrowly barred; dark brown below ear-coverts and cheeks, and becomes black near base of malar, then leads into broad black pectoral band and equally broad pale cinnamon band, followed by another, narrower and slightly irregular black band on upper belly; rest of underparts pale cinnamon with an incomplete band of black scallops from body-sides and another on lower flanks; eyes pale sulphur-yellow, bill large, long and black, legs and feet dark grey. Juvenile slightly smaller; distinctly paler and browner above, with pale streaks and spots larger; more cinnamon below with upper pectoral band somewhat streaked pale buffy or pale cinnamon, lower band slightly narrower, and the incomplete bands of scallops roughly the same. From Russet-throated by 2 distinct breast-bands.

Ssp. *H. b. bicinctus* (EC Co, S Ve) as described

H. b. stoicus (Ve: Margarita I.) larger, paler greyish-brown above, spots and fringes above whitish; barring below broader but overlaid buffy scallops, legs and feet pale blue-grey

Habits Perches in shade below canopy.

Status Generally common, but not always so, even in suitable habitat.

Habitat Tropical Zone, mostly to *c.*300m or below but a couple of records for each race at 700m. Thinly wooded savanna thickets, abandoned cultivation, open streams with trees.

Voice A rhythmic, repeated *tak-ta-tóoo*. Call a loud croaking, sometimes given in flight (R&C).

Note See previous species.

WHITE-CHESTED PUFFBIRD

Malacoptila fusca Pl.120

Identification 18–19cm. Dark brown above, slightly paler on rectrices, streaked whitish on head and buffy on back, wings and uppertail-coverts; loral and moustachial tufts white; chin to undertail-coverts buffy, densely streaked with long dusky lines from chin to breast, the streaks gradually fading until very faint on flanks and belly; grey-scalloped white crescent across middle of breast; eyes dark brown, bill rich orange with a black tip, legs and feet pale greenish-yellow. From larger Moustached Puffbird by orange-yellow base to bill and white crescent on dark throat and breast. Black-streaked Puffbird occurs at higher elevations, has black bill and lacks white pectoral crescent.

Ssp. *M. f. fusca* (E Ec, SE Co, Gu, Su, FG) as described

M. f. venezuelae (S Ve) darker above with more contrasting whitish streaks, loral and moustachial tufts larger and whiter, streaks on throat and breast narrower and more contrasting, and end almost abruptly, leaving belly and flanks paler and more greyish; cinnamon fringes to primaries and tail-feathers, white pectoral crescent larger and whiter; bill distinctly yellowish-orange

Status Uncommon throughout range. Unobtrusive and probably under-recorded.
Habitat Lower Tropical Zone, mostly below 900m but recorded to 1,200m. Lower level of humid primary evergreen *terra firme* on well-drained soils, second growth, plantations, borders and edges, and clearings with scattered trees.
Voice A high, thin, descending *seeee* or *pseeeeu*, lasting 2 s. Song a prolonged *tsrrrrrrrrrrrr*, repeated at long intervals (R&G, Hilty).

BLACK-STREAKED PUFFBIRD
Malacoptila fulvogularis Pl.120

Identification 19–22cm. Dark brown above with rows of whitish streaks on head, fading to dull buffy on back, with faint pale fringes to lower rump and uppertail-coverts, no streaks or spots on wings; bold white loral and moustachial tufts, outlined black; chin and throat to upper breast cinnamon or rufescent, rest of underparts greyish buffy-white, streaked narrowly black on lower breast to belly and flanks, eyes dark brown, bill black, legs and feet blue-grey. Only *Malacoptila* at its elevation, larger and darker than White-chested Puffbird, and lacks white on breast.

Ssp. *M. f. fulvogularis* (E Ec) as described; whitish streaking on cheeks and belly
M. f. huilae (CS Co) buffy streaks on upperparts, including wings and cheeks, loral and moustachial tufts reduced; chin and throat uniform cinnamon-orange, and belly to undertail-coverts buffy, rows of dark brown streaks on belly and flanks
M. f. substriata (CE Co) loral and moustachial tufts reduced and admixed black and white, chin and throat cinnamon-clay, rows of streaks below distinctively fringed black and cover entire underparts (becoming barring on undertail-coverts)

Habits Sometimes follows ant swarms or mixed flocks.
Status Uncommon to locally fairly common in Ecuador, virtually unknown in Colombia.
Habitat Upper Tropical to Subtropical Zones, 1,100–2,000m in Ecuador, to 1,700m in Colombia. Understorey of humid primary montane forest, open woodland and in east Andean foothills.
Voice Very high-pitched ascending whistle, lasting less than 4 s (R&C). Song rarely heard, a single drawn-out, high-pitched rising *pseeeuueeé*, steadily repeated every 2–4 s (R&G).

WHITE-WHISKERED PUFFBIRD
Malacoptila panamensis Pl.121

Identification 18–21cm. Brown head, back and wings, with cinnamon spots on back and wings, cinnamon eyebrow and streaks on face-sides; loral tufts buffy, moustachial tufts well developed and bright white; chin to breast and rump to tail rufous; underparts whitish washed cinnamon on flanks, with rows of deep cinnamon, fringed black; eyes reddish-brown, bill black above, pale yellow with black tip below, legs and feet bluish-grey. Female greyish-brown on head, darker brown on wings to tail, all well streaked pale buffy; loral tufts well developed and white, duller and paler on breast, underparts more strongly and darker streaked. From White-whiskered Puffbird by grey (not yellow) lower mandible and plain unstreaked rufescent breast. From smaller White-chested Puffbird by rufous throat and breast.

Ssp. *M. p. chocoana* (W Co) darkest, least rufescent In males, spotted white on back and wings, only male with clear white loral tufts; chin and throat patch restricted and weaker, paler cinnamon, streaking below also less extensive
M. p. magdalenae (C Co) spotted on head in both sexes; female more strongly streaked below and male darker above, especially on ear-coverts
M. p. panamensis (NW Co) as described
M. p. poliopis (SW Co, W Ec) throat and breast the brightest orange-rufous, underparts streaked with rows of black, white and rufous, cinnamon eyebrow strongly marked; female darker brownish-grey above with duller rufous breast; more heavily streaked black and white below

Status Uncommon to locally fairly common in Ecuador, common in Colombia.
Habitat Tropical Zone, to 900m in Ecuador. Understorey of humid and wet primary forest near treefalls, edges, older adjacent second growth, and abundant in coffee plantations.
Voice Relatively silent. Weak *peep* or high, thin whistles, difficult to locate. High faint *tsinnnn* in alarm (R&C). A simple, sibilant *pseeeeu*. Song a high-pitched, descending trill like White-chested but shorter, and has emphasised note at end, *tssiirrrrr-tsít* (Coopmans in R&G).

MOUSTACHED PUFFBIRD
Malacoptila mystacalis Pl.120

Identification 20–23cm. Adult brown from forehead to tail, with white supraloral tufts at base of upper mandible and tufts of white feathers at base of lower mandible – forming really splendid moustaches, and white terminal spots on back and wings, becoming white crescentic tips on uppertail-coverts; chin to breast and sides bright rufous; belly and flanks to undertail-coverts buffy-white with a streaky w dusky ash on flanks; eyes dark orange, bill dark above, grey below, legs and feet grey. Juvenile duller, more greyish-brown above with white terminal crescents and whitish streaking on face-sides and ear-coverts; moustache less well developed as tufts blend into sides of drab brown breast; chin to belly streaked slightly rufescent ochre, underparts white with greyish-brown streaks; eyes dark brown. White'pince-nez'and moustachial contrast with brown and rufous, making it unmistakable within its range.

Ssp. *M. m. mystacalis* (Co: Santa Marta, W Ve) as described
M. m. pacifica (SW Co) white lores and supraloral, and breast much richer chestnut-rufous; spots above softer and buffy

Status Uncommon in Colombia, fairly common in Venezuela.
Habitat Upper Tropical to Subtropical Zones, 350–2,100m.

Undergrowth to 6m above ground in dense tangled humid forest, often in gulleys and on slopes, also edges, rarely reaching lower limits of cloud forest.
Voice Usually sings only early morning, an extended thin, high, slow *teez teez teez*… up to 30+ notes in 5–10 s at variable tempo (Hilty).

LANCEOLATED MONKLET
Micromonacha lanceolata Pl.121

Identification 12–15cm. Smallest of family, heavy bill, large eye, black streaks below and black spots on undertail make identification certain. Black frontal band, rest of upperparts uniform rufescent brown; loral tufts white; chin and base of malar to vent white, rows of black streaks from throat to lower belly, sides, flanks and long undertail-coverts orange; undertail pale brown with a black band across middle; eyes dark and large, with a grey eye-ring, bill black, legs and feet grey.

Ssp. *M. l. lanceolata* (SW & WC Co, E Ec)

Habits Seldom follows mixed flocks. Silent, retiring and difficult to detect in mid and upper storeys of humid forest. Likes to perch over streams.
Status Rare in Ecuador and Colombia.
Habitat Upper Tropical to Subtropical Zones, 300–2,100m in Colombia but mostly below 1,100m in Ecuador. Shady, open borders, edges and natural treefall clearings in primary forest and mature second growth, but also small forest patches, coffee plantations.
Voice Rarely heard, 1–5, thin, plaintive, rising whistles, each slightly higher and stronger than preceding note. Thin high-pitched *tsip tsip* in contact (R&G).

RUSTY-BREASTED NUNLET
Nonnula rubecula Pl.121

Identification 14–16cm. Uniform dark brown above with white crescent below eyes and paler lores; chin, malar and neck-sides to upper belly and flanks cinnamon, belly, lower flanks and undertail-coverts white; eyes deep chestnut, bill long and rather drooping, black, legs and feet grey. From Brown Nunlet by whitish eye-ring, and white belly and undertail-coverts.

Ssp. *N. r. cineracea* (S Ec?) grey head and dark greyish-brown above, more greyish on tail, full white eye-ring and lores; chin to flanks clay colour
N. r. duidae (S Ve: Pantepui) dark greyish-brown head, pale buffy-rufous lores; sides of head grade into dark brownish-rufous upperparts
N. r. interfluvialis (Ve: S Amazonas, Co?) paler grey on nape, otherwise like *tapanahoniensis*
N. r. simulatrix (se Co?) like *duidae* but with darker tail
N. r. tapanahoniensis (Su, FG?) as described

Habits Forages alone, sallying to catch insects in open spots within forest, or perches quietly for long periods.
Status Very rare in Ecuador, scarce in Guyana, scarce and patchily distributed in Suriname, very rare in French Guiana (single sighting).
Habitat Lower Tropical Zone. Swampy forest, riparian areas.
Voice A series of *weeip, weeip weeip*… (R&C).
Notes Occurrence in Colombia assigned to races *cineracea* or *duidae* by SCJ&W (1996), and races *interfluvialis* or *simulatrix* by Parkes (1970).

BROWN NUNLET *Nonnula brunnea* Pl.121

Identification 13–16cm. Uniform medium brown above with large loral patch, eye-ring and chin bright pinkish-clay, rest of underparts cinnamon, paler on belly and undertail-coverts; eyes dark brown, bill comparatively long and thin, black with a grey base. From Rusty-breasted Nunlet by pale eye-ring and entirely rufescent underparts.

Ssp. Monotypic (E Ec, SC Co)

Habits Solitary. Often sits well concealed within tangled vines. Occasionally travels with mixed flocks of antwrens and others in understorey.
Status Rare in Ecuador, presumably also in Colombia.
Habitat Lower Tropical Zone, mostly below 400m. Understorey of humid lowland forest.
Voice Series of 20–25 *treeu* notes, repeated steadily, starting quietly, building-up, then fading at end (R&G).

GREY-CHEEKED NUNLET
Nonnula frontalis Pl.121

Identification 14–15cm. No other nunlet in range. Could be mistaken for small tyrannid. From forehead to tail uniform rufescent brown, large area surrounding eyes grey, eye-ring pink, chin to belly and flanks bright pale rufous; eyes dark brown, bill long and slightly decurved, legs and feet pale grey. Grey feathers surrounding eye with pink eye-ring distinctive.

Ssp. *N. f. frontalis* (N Co) as described
N. f. pallescens (NE Co) entire upperparts paler, crown distinctly so; chin to belly and flanks pale buffy orange-cinnamon,
N. f. stulta (W Co) crown very dark, rufous underparts deeper, richer and more extensive

Status Fairly common.
Habitat Tropical zone to 1,000m. Borders and edges of moist to humid gallery forest and second growth, especially in areas with tangled vines.
Voice Usually silent, but gives measured series of up to 20 plaintive notes, *weeip weeip weeip*… (R. S. Rowlett in H&B).

Nunbirds are fairly heavily built with brightly coloured bills that contrast with their black or black-and-grey attire. Birds of lowland forest edges, clearings, trails, road cuts and streams, they frequently use more exposed perches. More active than other puffbirds, they change perches frequently. Rather than short, quick sallies, they seem to sail gracefully, often gliding, catching their prey effortlessly, returning to perch with an upward glide. Also more likely to take prey from the ground, freely taking frogs, lizards, scorpions, etc. Social, occurring in gatherings of up to a dozen, they are very vocal, frequently chorusing excitedly with necks stretched and bills pointing upwards, tails raising and lowering.

WHITE-FACED NUNBIRD

Hapaloptila castanea Pl.121

Identification 23–25cm. White frontal band becomes large triangle of white on lores, black forehead, rest of upper head brownish-grey, back, wings and tail dark brown, rump and uppertail-coverts brownish-grey as head; malar dark chestnut, chin and throat white, underparts chestnut, paling to cinnamon on vent and undertail-coverts. Entirely rufous underparts distinctive, the only montane nunbird.

Ssp. Monotypic (Ec, W Co)

Habits Pairs or small groups.
Status Very rare and local in Ecuador.
Habitat Upper Tropical to Temperate Zones, 1,300–2,400m in Ecuador, usually above 1,500m and ascends to 2,900m in cloud forest.
Voice Infrequent. Series of upward-inflected single or double hoots like *Glaucidium* Pygmy Owl, sometimes becoming a trill. A mournful, downward-slurred *wuooooo* (Sick), flute-like *whoo-doo-doo*, descending *hyoo-hoo-hoo-oo-oo* and loud *yawkl-diddl* or *quee-didada* in duet (R&C). Song a slowly repeated series of rising notes *kwoah…kwoah…kwoah* (M. Lysinger in R&G).
Note Formerly known as White-faced Puffbird

BLACK NUNBIRD *Monasa atra* Pl.122

Identification 25–29cm. Adult black on head and back, charcoal from chin to vent and washed slate on flanks, mainly black wings with pure white lesser wing-coverts, broad white fringes to median wing-coverts, and faint white fringes to distal half of greater coverts; rump and uppertail-coverts slate, tail black, undertail-coverts black with white crescentic tips; eyes crimson, bill scarlet (sealing-wax red), legs and feet grey with large black scales. Juvenile black on head, back, tail and undertail-coverts, rest of body dusky grey, washed brownish on sides and flanks, all wing-coverts grey with broad white fringes and some irregular orange to rusty wash; eyes brown, bill rose-pink. From Yellow-billed Nunbird by red bill. From Black-fronted Nunbird by white on scapulars and wing-coverts. From White-fronted Nunbird by lack of white on face.

Ssp. Monotypic (S & E Ve, Guianas)

Habits Often in small groups which sit in a row and chorus together.
Status Common in Guyana, frequent and widespread in Suriname and French Guiana.
Habitat Lower Tropical Zone to 1,000m. Edges and interior of humid *terra firme* and *várzea*, second growth and along rivers.
Voice A sudden startling cry that begins *weeeeooo weeeoo* and accelerates to a loud, fast *peeteeoo peeteeoo* (H&M). Also a chorus of *wheer-pt'r'e'a'r* cries, transcribed by Hilty as *bring-your-be'e'e'e'r*, lasting *c.*15 s, ending faster and sounding more frantic.
Note Listed as possible in Colombia by R&C.

BLACK-FRONTED NUNBIRD

Monasa nigrifrons Pl.122

Identification 27–28cm. Largest puffbird. Adult all black, orbital skin dark grey, eyes brown, bill crimson-red, legs and feet dark grey with large black scales. Juvenile similar but washed maroon-dusky; eyes dark brown, bill red (noticeably paler than adult).

Ssp. *M. n. nigrifrons* (E Ec, SE Co)

Habits Follows army ants and monkeys to take insects disturbed by their passage. Fast and skilful flyer, but often flies slowly with frequent glides. Solitary, pairs or small groups, at all levels, may be very noisy but can forage silently. Conspicuous in riverine habitats, often in open.
Status Common in Ecuador and Colombia.
Habitat Lower Tropical Zone to 500m. Lowland riverbanks and lake-margin trees and bamboo. Forages low in open understorey riverine woodland, also deciduous woods and *Orbignya mertensiana* palm groves, never far from water.
Voice Full, smooth *kewuh*. A prolonged phrase of complex melodious whistles, accelerating and rising at end; *hewluh… tewrr-tewrr* accompanied by tail movements. Groups sing in chorus (Sick). Song a rapid series of melodious upslurred *clerry* or *curry* whistles, broken by occasional downslurred *turra turra* trill, often in chorus (R&C). Two birds, perched side by side – sometimes facing opposite directions, and swivelling their tails side to side – produce what sounds like a rollicking, gabbling chorus.

WHITE-FRONTED NUNBIRD

Monasa morphoeus Pl.122

Identification 27–28cm. Adult has black head and upper breast, with brightly contrasting white tufty forehead and forecrown, and similarly tufty bib; lower breast to flanks and vent grey, rest black; eyes chestnut, bill bright red, legs and feet grey with large black scales. Juvenile slightly paler all over, like charcoal washed dusky, forehead and bib washed orange to rusty, bill slightly paler and duller red, with dark brown eyes and black streaks along most of culmen. Similar to Black-fronted Nunbird but has yellowish-white mask to forehead and chin, is somewhat greyer and has more orange-red bill.

Ssp. *M. m. fidelis* (NW Co: near Caribbean coast) generally dark grey with black face and ear-coverts, smaller white forehead but full white bib

M. m. pallescens (NW Co: along Pacific coast) white restricted to forehead and forecrown; breast to flanks and vent grey, becoming quite bright on flanks and contrasting with black undertail-coverts, rest of bird black

M. m. peruana (E Ec, SE Co, S Ve) as described

M. m. sclateri (N & C Co) slightly darker below than *peruana*, and undertail-coverts almost concolorous with grey underparts, black chin and lesser wing-coverts pure white

Habits Typical of nunbirds.

Status Uncommon in Ecuador, fairly common in Colombia, common in Venezuela.
Habitat Tropical Zone, mostly below 300m but to 1,350m in Ecuador. Mid levels to canopy of tall *terra firme* and low hill forest, high trees bordering rivers, gallery forest and mature floodplain forest. Unlike Black-fronted not associated with water.
Voice Commonly a blurred, descending whistle with short rippling trill, *peeeur-r-r-r-r-r*, a loud, mournful *how how how* and varied trills, barks and other notes, often sustained for up to 20 minutes at end of day (R&C). Loud rollicking chorus of *dreary, dreary, dreary*… often ending with *dreary-me dreary-me*, repeated for up to 20 s. Alarm-call a series of *wuEEeo-wuEEeo*… very similar to that of Grey Capuchin Monkey *Cebus capella* (Hilty).

YELLOW-BILLED NUNBIRD

Monasa flavirostris Pl.122

Identification 23–26cm. Generally charcoal grey with white lesser wing-coverts; eyes dark brown, bill rich yellow, legs and feet black. Juvenile similar but has less white on wings and washed ochre, bill duller yellow with black streaks along most of culmen. From other nunbirds by yellow bill.

Ssp. Monotypic (E Ec, SE Co)

Habits Often seen on exposed perch high at forest edge. Usually in pairs. Does not follow army ants or mixed flocks.
Status Uncommon in Ecuador, local in Colombia.
Habitat Tropical Zone, usually below 400m but to 750m in Ecuador and 1,400m in Colombia. Borders and edges of forest, subcanopy and understorey, clearings with scattered trees, bamboo stands.
Voice Song consists of full melodious and lengthy phrases in chorus, typically including a frequently repeated *wheekit-wheeyk, wheekit-wheeyk, wheekit-wheeyk* (R&C) and a protracted rollicking gabble (R&G).

SWALLOW-WINGED PUFFBIRD

Chelidoptera tenebrosa Pl.122

Identification 16–17cm. Unique, but could be mistaken for a martin, but rounder head, longer bill and unique silhouette are distinctive. Black head, breast, back, wings and tail; rump and uppertail-coverts white; grey bar between breast and belly; belly, flanks and vent cinnamon; underwing- and undertail-coverts white; eyes brown, bill black, legs and feet grey. Presumed intermediates between 2 races occur across entire Venezuelan Llanos, and all 3 forms occur in Táchira and south-west Barinas.

Ssp. *C. t. pallida* (W Ve: Lake Maracaibo) similar to *tenebrosa* but has white chin and small grey bib, broader grey bar on lower breast then a broad white bar; lower belly, flanks and vent pale ochraceous
Stable intermediate population between other races (Ve; Llanos) pale grey chin, very broad grey band across lower breast, upper belly and sides
C. t. tenebrosa (E Ec, E Co, Ve, Guianas) as described

Habits Usually alone or in pairs, hunts insects in open, by sallying like a martin-cum-flycatcher from a fixed perch on a high bare branch, telephone wire or top of tree. Will catch termites or ants in swarms, hovering or fluttering like a large butterfly. At other times manoeuvres like a bat.
Status Common in Ecuador, common to locally abundant in Colombia, Venezuela and Guyana, frequent to locally common in sandy soil forest and brush in Suriname, quite common in French Guiana.
Habitat Lower Tropical Zone, *pallida* to 500m, *tenebrosa* to 1,000m. Semi-open areas with scattered trees and bushes, light to dense deciduous woodland and humid forest. Much more common on sandy soils.
Voice Rather quiet, occasional plaintive piping *pi pu* or slight *pit-qwit-wit* and harsh squeaky *tzeet* (Hilty). A loud hoarse cry (H&B).
Notes Also called simply Swallow-wing. The enigma of 3 distinct forms occurring sympatrically (at least locally) deserves further investigation and the possibility of more than 1 species being involved cannot be overlooked.

CAPITONIDAE – New World Barbets

Barbets are forest canopy birds. Chubby, with lots of colour and personality, they move through the canopy in pairs or small busy bands, hopping sideways along branches and performing all kinds of contortions, even hanging upside-down, to reach food, somewhat like avian troops of clowns. At times, they perch quietly for long periods on a horizontal branch, leisurely inspecting their surroundings and calling for hours. Mainly frugivorous, they often gather at fruiting trees (*Clusia*, *Guarea*, Lauraceae, *Cordia*, Annonaceae, *Ficus*, *Spondias* and *Psidium*) or pick mistletoe berries, but their diet also includes locusts, beetles and cicadas, as well as small vertebrates. Most species join mixed feeding flocks. Some, the *Eubucco* species in particular, like to search for insects in clumps of dead, curled leaves that often form amid tangles of vines. Barbets are cavity nesters. They carve nest holes in thick dead branches or trunks of soft, decayed wood, or in termite nests, or take over abandoned woodpecker nests and 'fix' them. They may even make holes in soft dirt banks. Occasionally, several nests are relatively close to together. Both adults care for the young, and at least some species are cooperative breeders, with young from the previous year assisting in rearing the brood. Their calls, far-carrying and repeated for long periods, are among the frequent background noises of humid forests on Neotropical montane slopes. Barbet songs have been classified into 3 groups (Lane 1999) – hoots, purrs and purred phrases ('purr-packets'), each species having a single type. Interestingly, when 2 barbets of the same genus co-occur, each has a different song type. This is the case with the White-mantled (a hooter) and Spot-crowned (a purrer), the Five-coloured (a hooter) and Orange-fronted (a purrer), and the Gilded (a hooter) and Scarlet-crowned (a singer of purred phrases). The barbets of Africa and southern Asia are now placed in the Megalaimidae, whilst American barbets form the family Capitonidae (sometimes relegated to the status of subfamily, Capitoninae), closely related to the toucans and containing 3 genera and 14 species (including the newly discovered, stunning Scarlet-banded Barbet *Capito wallacei* from Peru), with 10 occurring in northern South America.

Additional references used to prepare this family include Lane (1999), O'Neill et al. (2000) and Short & Horne (2001, 2002, hereafter S&H).

SCARLET-CROWNED BARBET

Capito aurovirens Pl. 124

Identification 19cm. Male has top of head (forehead to nape) deep crimson-red, head-sides and face sooty olive, black on lores grading to olive on neck-sides, rest of upperparts uniform olive; chin and throat, malar to neck-sides and throat to breast deep bright orange with a reddish wash on sides and breast; rest of underparts olive; eyes red, bill black with silvery base, legs and feet blue-grey. Female has top of head with short white streaks that become less dense on nape, otherwise as male. Uniform olive, with yellow throat and red (male) or white (female) cap distinctive.

Ssp. Monotypic (SE Co, E Ec)

Habits Forages at all levels, alone, in pairs or small groups, searching noiselessly in foliage. Seldom with mixed flocks. Diet mostly fruits. Spends long periods just sitting quietly, looking about.

Status Frequent to common in Ecuador, common in Colombia.

Habitat Lower Tropical zone to 600m. Swamp forests, *várzea* and marshy lowland forests and mature second growth, river islands and margins, sometimes at forest borders or even, occasionally, in drier forest, but almost invariably near water.

Voice Males and females may counter-sing series of fast, frog-like *cruu …, crrrrow…, krowp…, brrawk…* or *trroup…*, 7–15 notes delivered at varying speeds for up to 10 s (S&H, H&B, R&G).

SPOT-CROWNED BARBET

Capito maculicoronatus Pl. 124

Identification 16–18cm. Male has entire upperparts black with feathers of forehead to nape finely edged white; chin, malar and throat white, breast golden-yellow, rest of underparts white with patch of red on sides, irregular black streaks overlaying red and belly-sides, and patch of black on rear flanks; eyes brown, bill black with silvery base, legs and feet blue-grey. Female similar but is black on throat and breast, and more heavily streaked below. From all other black-and-white barbets by heavily streaked flanks.

Ssp. *C. m. rubrilateralis* (W & NW Co)

Habits Forages alone or in pairs, but frequently with mixed flocks or occasionally in small single-species bands. Diet fruits, searching for them methodically in branches of canopy and subcanopy.

Status Locally frequent in Colombia.

Habitat Tropical zone to 900m. Humid to wet forests and mature second growth, at borders and in clearings and landslides.

Voice Quiet for the most part. Two birds will sing simultaneously or duet a series of *kkaaak* segueing into *kkkaakk* (S&H).

ORANGE-FRONTED BARBET

Capito squamatus Pl. 124

Identification 17–18cm. Black above except bright scarlet-red forehead, white crown to nape and white patch on outer webs of tertials; white below, flushed yellow with hint of cinnamon on throat and breast; flanks washed pale grey and have thin black streaks; eyes red, bill black with grey base, legs and feet blue-grey. Female similar but scaled white on back and wings, and is black on front from throat to breast. Black-and-white pattern distinctive.

Ssp. Monotypic (SW Co, W Ec)

Habits Forages alone or in pairs, usually with mixed flocks. Generally a canopy bird, but comes lower at fruiting trees.

Status Locally common to uncommon in Ecuador, where threatened by deforestation; scarce and poorly known in Colombia.

Habitat Tropical Zone, mostly below 800m but locally higher. Canopy and borders of humid and wet forest and second growth, nearby cultivation, orchards, farmland, pastures with fruiting trees, and will cross wide spaces to reach fruiting trees.

Voice A purring species. Song lasts *c.*4 s and consists of very fast series of notes that slur into each other so that they sound like a purr.

WHITE-MANTLED BARBET

Capito hypoleucus Pl. 124

Identification 19cm. Black above except some narrow pale lines on nape and scapulars, top of head red; underparts white with slight yellowish wash and flush of cinnamon on breast; eyes red, bill yellow, legs and feet greenish-grey. Female has a black spot at base of lower mandible. Three races very similar, but consistently distinct. From male Spot-crowned Barbet by lack of streaks on flanks, but has buffy pectoral band.

Ssp. *C. h. carrikeri* (Co: Antioquia) has bold yellow lines on nape and scapulars, and some on mantle; red restricted to forehead, tapering onto forecrown; weak pectoral band, strong yellow wash below

C. h. extinctus (C Co: Caldas) full, bold red coronal stripe, lines on nape and scapulars white, broad pectoral band

C. h. hypoleucus (NC Co) lines on nape white, but those on scapulars yellow; coronal stripe tapers on rear crown, modest pectoral band, slight yellow wash on flanks

Habits Poorly known. Forages in pairs or small family groups, sometimes with mixed flocks. Mostly in canopy, but will come lower and well into open at fruiting trees such as mango and *Cecropia*.

Status Endangered. Uncommon and local Colombian endemic, threatened by habitat loss. Race *carrikeri* known from single specimen; no recent records of *hypoleucus*, but several recent sightings of *extinctus*, which was previously considered extinct (Lane).

Habitat Upper Tropical Zone. Humid forest on montane slopes, forest patches with mosaic of pastures, second growth and plantations mixed with fruiting trees.

Voice Song a series of *hoot* or *poop* notes, 5–6 per s, up to 5 s long, tempo increasing slightly (O'Neill *et al.*). Also *kek-ek* and *tteeaw* (S&H).

FIVE-COLOURED BARBET

Capito quinticolor Pl. 123

Identification 18cm. Forecrown to nape bright crimson, full mask black, rest of upperparts black with clean yellow V-shaped outline to mantle, yellow dash on outer tips of greater wing-coverts and tertials; malar, chin and throat white, breast to vent and flanks rich golden-yellow with a black spot on breast-sides and black streaks on flanks, smudged and dirty-looking at rear; undertail-coverts pale yellow with narrow short black streaks; eyes orange, bill black with grey base, legs and feet grey. Female has top and sides of head and face streaked yellow and black, upperparts as male but wings scaled buffy; throat to breast white, then rich lemon-yellow to undertail-coverts, all streaked with black. Spotted female is unique in range, male difficult to confuse if any of diagnostics seen.

Ssp. Monotypic (W Co, NW Ec)

Habits Forages alone or in pairs, mostly in canopy, very occasionally at low levels. Often with mixed canopy flocks, especially with Masked Tityras *Tityra semifasciata*.

Status Vulnerable. Locally uncommon to frequent, but small range. Formerly considered a Colombian endemic, but now recorded in north-west Ecuador, where rare.

Habitat Lower Tropical Zone, generally below 350m but locally to 600m. Wet forests and mature second growth on Pacific coast.

Voice A hooting species. Call a low-pitched hollow, rolling trill lasting 3–4 s (Pearman 1993). Series of 10–17 deep hollow *oohp* or *oohng* notes that start and end abruptly (O. Jahn in R&G).

BLACK-SPOTTED BARBET

Capito niger Pl. 123

Identification 19cm. Male has top of head black, scaled olive-green, back black, scapulars fringed yellowish on outer webs, lower back to uppertail-coverts black fringed yellow, tail black; wings black with bases of outer webs of greater coverts and tertials also yellow; forehead bright red, narrow yellow eyebrow runs down head-sides to scapulars; malar and throat bright red, chin yellow streaked red; rest of underparts yellow with black patch on breast-sides, and grey streaks on flanks; eyes red, bill black, legs and feet yellowish-grey. Female similar but all black surfaces scaled yellow; yellow breast has long lines of black spots.

Ssp. Monotypic (Ve, Gu, Su, FG)

Habits Forages in canopy and at mid levels, alone, in pairs or small noisy bands. Frequently joins mixed canopy flocks. Sometimes forages clinging to or climbing trunks. Can be very difficult to find, as sits motionless and calls ventriloquially.

Status Fairly common in Venezuela, uncommon in Guyana, frequent and widespread in Suriname and French Guiana.

Habitat Lower Tropical Zone to *c.*250m. Humid *terra firme* and *várzea* forest and mature second growth.

Voice A hoot, different to that of Gilded Barbet (P. Coopmans, pers. comm.), slow, low-pitched and *Geotrygon*-like in quality, faint at first, then stronger and rhythmic, *wu, woot, wú-woot, wú-woot, wú-woot, wú-woot*, lasting up to *c.*8 s, may be repeated several times at 20–40 s intervals, slow, with emphasis on first note of each pair. (Descriptions of Black-spotted Barbet voice in H&B, P&MdS and some recent commercial recordings belong to Gilded Barbet *C. auratus*.)

Note S&H include Gilded Barbet within present species. We follow major revisions to this complex by Haffer, and Lane, accepted by SACC and recently confirmed by DNA evidence (Armenta *et al.* 2005).

GILDED BARBET *Capito auratus* Pl. 123

Identification 19cm. Fairly large and heavy-billed. Three subspecies, but males very much alike, and differences very much relate to underparts in females. Essentially, male has yellowish-olive top of head to nape, rest of upperparts from mantle to tail black with yellow streaking on outer webs of outer mantle, greater wing-coverts have yellowish 'tears' on outer webs, tertials have yellowish patches on basal half of outer webs, rump and uppertail-coverts fringed yellow; malar, chin and throat rich orange, underparts yellow, palest on undertail-coverts, variably streaked or spotted on sides, barred undertail-coverts; eyes red, bill black with grey base, legs and feet greenish-grey. Female basically same, with all wing-coverts fringed orange and has some pale yellow streaks on face-sides and middle of back. See races for different female diagnostics. Very similar to, and easily confused with, Black-spotted Barbet in Venezuela, but latter has red on forehead and throat; no similar species in west.

Ssp. *C. a. aurantiicinctus* (S Ve) male has few black spots on flanks, female an unmarked orange throat and rows of black spots on breast

C. a. nitidior (SE Co, SW Ve) male more reddish on throat than others and no streaks on flanks; female has unmarked, deep reddish-orange throat, heavy black streaks on breast and grey streaks on flanks

C. a. punctatus (E Ec, SE Co) male has black streaks on flanks and most densely barred undertail-coverts; female has clear black streaks on throat and entire underparts

Habits Forages from canopy to mid levels, frequently with canopy flocks. Also joins understorey flocks, mostly

Thamnophilidae and Dendrocolaptidae. Diet principally fruit, with some large insects and small vertebrates. Not shy. Often in copses of mango and in *Cecropia*. Waves tail from side to side when calling.
Status Locally common to uncommon in Ecuador, frequent in Colombia and Venezuela.
Habitat Tropical to Lower Subtropical Zones. Humid forest and mature second growth.
Voice Calls frequently, a 2-note, low and toad-like *juut-uut* (P&MdS), repeated endlessly. From Ecuador a distinctive, measured, repeated *whoo-boop, whoo-boop, whoo-boop...* frequently heard but hard to locate (R&G), and from Venezuela a series of low-pitched hollow, frog-like notes, *oo-dot, oo-dot, oo-dot, o'doot-o'doot-doot-doot* or similar (e.g. *knee-deep...*), the second note of each couplet emphasised (Hilty).
Note S&H include Gilded Barbet within Black-spotted Barbet. We follow major revisions to this complex by Haffer, and Lane, accepted by SACC and recently confirmed by DNA evidence (Armenta *et al.* 2005).

LEMON-THROATED BARBET
Eubucco richardsoni Pl. 123

Identification 15cm. Small; Male has top and sides of head black with crimson spots that almost cover crown, less extensive on sides and ear-coverts, nape turquoise-blue, rest of upperparts olive-green; malar, chin and throat to undertail-coverts golden-yellow, breast washed orange, sides to flanks streaked grey, undertail-coverts banded grey; eyes red, bill golden-yellow, legs and feet greyish-green. Female has top of head and nape concolorous with green back; white eyebrow and orange-yellow line reach round neck-sides of neck to join yellow breast and flanks; malar, chin and throat white, undertail-coverts white, breast-sides to flanks streaked grey; eyes red, bill yellow with blackish culmen. From Scarlet-crowned by contrasting streaks below, grey nape in male and black cheeks of female. From Red-headed by bright yellow throat and breast.

Ssp. *E. r. richardsoni* (SE Co, E Ec)

Habits Forages from mid levels to canopy, alone, in pairs or occasionally small groups, but mostly with mixed canopy flocks including Gilded Barbet, from which distinguished by uniform olive back, wings and tail. Most common near water.
Status Uncommon in Ecuador and Colombia.
Habitat Lower Tropical Zone below 1,100m. Interior of humid forest, dense secondary forest and *várzea*, at borders and near water.
Voice Song a fast series of high *too-doot* notes (H&B), doubled or usually tripled in fast trill-like series (S&H), or 10–12 soft, very rapid *crrruu-crrruu-crrruu* notes (R&G).

RED-HEADED BARBET
Eubucco bourcierii Pl. 123

Identification 16.5cm. Adult male has entire head bright vermilion red, with black lores, tiny black chin, narrow bright pale blue nuchal band separated from red nape by thin black line, rest of upperparts green; red throat grades into orange breast and then yellow underparts that have green streaks on flanks; undertail-coverts whitish-yellow with green lines; eyes red, bill yellow, legs and feet green. Juvenile male has red face with black lores; top and back of head green, concolorous with back, a short thin black line and narrow pale blue line on neck-sides; red throat streaks become green streaks on yellow and, in turn, grey streaks on white over most of underparts. Adult female has black mask, edged pale blue on forecrown and entire ear-coverts pale blue below, small spot at base of malar and chin black, throat pale yellow, top of head to nape yellow-olive, rest of upperparts green as male; breast pale orange, underparts yellow, paler on undertail-coverts, streaked green on flanks, then streaked grey from vent to undertail-coverts. Juvenile female like adult but much greener on head, with only streaks of yellow-olive, throat pale almost grey, throat pastel orange, breast yellow and then grey streaks on white over rest.

Ssp. *E. b. aequatorialis* (W Ec) male has entire head and breast red, with no orange on breast, division between red and yellow of belly is abrupt, and also has fewer grey streaks restricted to flanks; female more yellowish on forecrown and lacks blue division, has deeper orange breast, grey streaking only on flanks
E. b. bourcierii (Co: C & E Andes, N Ve) as described
E. b. occidentalis (Co: W Andes) female lacks blue on crown; male has red breast abruptly meeting rich orange belly, which in turn is clearly divided from pale yellow below, with green streaks on flanks
E. b. orientalis (E Ec) female has blue forecrown; male a red breast merging into pale orange belly

Habits Forages quite actively from undergrowth to canopy, usually in pairs and often with mixed flocks. Frequently passes unnoticed, perching quietly for long periods.
Status Uncommon in Ecuador, frequent in Colombia.
Habitat Upper Tropical to Subtropical Zones, 800–1,900m in Ecuador, to 2,400m in Colombia and 1,500m in Venezuela. Humid to wet and cloud forests, and mature second growth. At borders and clearings.
Voice Mostly silent (H&B). Race *aequatorialis* a soft, low-pitched and resonant *o-o-o-o-o-o-o-o* with quality of Scaled Antpitta *Grallaria guatimalensis* or even a toad; *orientalis* a soft, churring *torrrrrrrrrrrrrrrrr* (P. Coopmans in R&G), a recording by M. Álvarez in Caldas, western Colombia, assumed to be *occidentalis*, is a bold and abrupt *trrrrrrrrrr!* and a soft *grunghk, grunghk, grunghk*; a recording from Quindío, east-central Colombia, by S. Peters (pers. comm.) is *torrrrrrrr-rr-rr*, the final 2 notes separated; *bourcierii* utters a soft note followed by a mellow rolling trill, *d'd'd'd'd'd'd'd'd'd'd* (Hilty). From east slope of Venezuelan Andes (presumably *bourcierii*) comes a soft, rolling *gwrrrrrrrrrr* or *hwrrrrrrrrrr* (P. Boesman, pers. comm.). There is a fourth description (S&H), but no location of origin: a short, fast trill *poooddddddrrrrrr*.

TOUCAN BARBET

Semnornis ramphastinus Pl. 124

Identification 20cm. Largest barbet, unmistakable grey, black and white head, and large bill with black subterminal band. Top of head black (and male has small erectile tuft), at nape widening to become a nuchal collar, finishing at bend of wing; from lores to a point above ear-coverts, then forward to cheeks and base of malar all black, broad white line on head-sides becomes grey on ear-coverts and neck-sides to throat and breast; back and scapulars olive-green, wings grey with olive-green flush to remiges, tail grey, lower back to uppertail-coverts slightly olivaceous-yellow; breast-sides to central belly, then as a wedge to mid flanks scarlet-red, body-sides, rear flanks and vent to undertail-coverts olive-yellow; eyes red, eye-ring grey, large heavy-looking bill pale yellow with blackish subterminal band, legs and feet grey-green.

Ssp. *S. r. caucae* (Co: W Andes) wings all grey; more extensive red below, and vent to undertail-coverts much brighter yellow (as rump)

S. r. ramphastinus (NW Ec) as described

Habits Forages from mid levels to canopy, usually in pairs, sometimes small groups and often with mixed canopy flocks. Lively but will perch quietly for long periods; typically flicks tail, hops sideways and turns about along branches, particularly fond of *Cecropia* fruit.

Status Uncommon in Ecuador, locally uncommon to frequent in Colombia. Threatened by trapping for bird trade.

Habitat Upper Tropical to Subtropical Zones, 1,000–2,400m but mostly 1,400–2,000m. Understorey of wet and cloud forests, dense and bushy secondary forest, and adjacent clearings.

Voice Quite loud. Song a resonant *cuoo*, repeated for several minutes, sometimes by pairs in duets (H&B, F&K); a series of foghorn-like *hawnk* to *aw* notes for up to 3 minutes (S&H). Calls include a reproachful chuckle and low quock notes, *kawk* and *kyak* (H&B, S&H).

RAMPHASTIDAE – Toucans, Toucanets and Araçaris

Toucans and their allies are birds of Neotropical forests. Curiously, whereas rain forests occur on many of the Antilles, the only island where toucans naturally occur is Trinidad. Colonising further islands was probably hampered by their limited flying ability. Often portrayed in popular media as genial, they are among the forest's most ruthless predators of small birds, mice, lizards and frogs, raiding nests and hunting in pairs or packs. This is especially true of araçaris, which fight over prey and tear it apart fiercely. Toucans are omnivorous – they take small vertebrates and invertebrates, but by far the largest part of their diet consists of stone fruits and drupes. Stone-fruit eaters are very different in their ecology from berry-fruit eaters. Their anatomy is highly specialised for eating stone fruits – they have very large throats, in order to swallow large seeds. Sexes often alike, but the bill of the female is usually significantly shorter. Their bills are not only extremely long and deep, but structurally strong, yet very lightweight, and have serrated edges with the 'teeth' leaning forward. This permits an extra-long reach to pick fruit from thin twigs without much increasing their body weight, and gives them a firm grip, so fruit will not be dropped. The zygodactyl feet are also strong, for gripping thin, difficult perches. In a recent study, it was found that many Neotropical palms may have co-evolved with toucans. The toucans afford the palms a good means of dispersing their seeds, because the stony seed is resistant to the avian foregut and passes unscathed through the digestive tract. To attract toucans, palm fruits have an outer layer of pulp that is at once nutritious and thin, so that birds must take several to satisfy their hunger. Individual fruits in a bunch ripen at different times, so that more fruit ripen each day and the fruit change colour as they do so, making the ripe ones easily spotted. Toucans nest in tree cavities, often taking over old woodpecker holes, where both adults care for the chicks. They do not (could not) carve the holes, which are sometimes used also for roosting. Among smaller genera, the birds often roost together in a tree hollow. To sleep, birds turn their heads and lay their beaks on their backs, and flip the tails up and over the bill. The taxonomy of the family is very fluid, with considerable speculation concerning hybrids. We have followed S&M.

Additional references used for this family include: Schwarz (1972b), Haffer (1974), Willis (1983), Stotz et al. (1996), Short & Horne (2001, hereafter S&M).

Aulacorhynchus toucanets are bright green. They generally forage at mid levels to the canopy, in noisy pairs or small bands. They are usually easily noticed by the observer as they clamber and flit among the branches, searching for food. Flight usually short and laboured. They often follow a mixed feeding flock, trailing behind, sometimes seeming aloof or almost indifferent, sometimes secretive. Occasionally move in single file. Diet consists of fruits, arthropods, small vertebrates, eggs and nestlings. They can be fierce predators and will attack cooperatively. When excited they flick their tails and swing their heads from side to side, as well as backwards and forwards.

EMERALD TOUCANET

Aulacorhynchus prasinus Pl. 125

Identification 33–35cm, bill 6.4–7.6cm. Almost entirely emerald green, darker above, paler and brighter below, and undertail-coverts and tip of tail chestnut. Eye-ring and loral skin, including at base of mandible grey, with a narrow edging of sky blue above and behind eyes (which are brown), chin and upper throat pure white. From base outwards, bill has a thin black line at the base, then a broader white line, the upper mandible is black with a black line running the cutting edge to the tip, the culmen is broadly yellow; lower mandible is maroon over the basal third, the rest black; legs and feet green. Female has the bill is noticeably shorter. Juvenile has eye-ring grey with yellow orbital and loral skin, bill all yellow. From all other bright green toucanets by its chestnut undertail-coverts and chestnut tips to tail.

Ssp. *A. p. albivitta* (NE Ec, Co: C & E Andes, Ve) as described; the only race with a white bib
A. p. cognatus (Extreme NW Co) blue-violet bib
A. p. cyanolaemus (SE Ec) reddish-pink skin around eye, full blue bib, yellow tip to black bill
A. p. griseigularis (Co: W Andes) grey bib
A. p. lautus (Co: Santa Marta) grey bib, 2 yellow patches on upper mandible
A. p. phaeolaemus (Co: W Andes) pink skin around eye, blue-grey bib

Status Uncommon in Ecuador, locally common in Colombia.

Habitat Subtropical to Temperate Zones, 1,500–2,600m in Ecuador, 1,600–3,000m in Colombia, 1,700–3,100m in Venezuela. Humid, wet and cloud forests, both interior and borders, and in mature second growth or edges of semi-open fields.

Voice Calls fast repetitions of *took* or *churt* notes (H&B, F&K), or repetitions of a low *crik* note (MdS&P). Variable series of croaking and hoarse, grunting, snore-like, barks and honks, most consisting of a clear element followed by a fast rattling element (S&H).

Note Navarro *et al.* (2001) suggest, within a revisionist study of Mesoamerican forms of this species, that the forms *lautus* and *albivitta*, at least, may warrant specific status.

GROOVE-BILLED TOUCANET

Aulacorhynchus sulcatus Pl. 125

Identification 35–36cm, bill 7.6cm. Almost entirely emerald green, darker above, paler and brighter below; chin and throat white. Eye-ring and loral skin, including at base of mandible blue, eyes red; bill basically entirely blood red, blackish at base of upper mandible and pinkish-orange at base of lower, black on cutting edges of both mandibles but not reaching tip; legs and feet green. Only toucanet in most of its range, but overlaps with Yellow-billed Toucanet in montane north-west Lara and the Cerro Platillón, on Carabobo border with Guárico, where they occasionally interbreed. Hybrids have an intermediate-patterned bill, with characters from each (see plate).

Ssp. *A. s. erythrognathus* (NE Ve) larger, with pale grey to pale bluish throat, heavier bill with extensive bright orange base and black culmen
A. s. sulcatus (NC Ve) as described

Status Locally common Venezuelan endemic.

Habitat Upper Tropical to Subtropical Zones, 400–2,440m but more usually 1,000–2,000m. Humid, wet and cloud forests and mature second growth, woodland borders, suburban gardens.

Voice Described as *croac*, resembling a frog, *cuac* resembling a duck, and even barks like a dog (MdS&P). Most notes are growls (Schwartz 1972), similar in all *Aulacorhynchus* and uttered in series of 8–20 or more notes. Shorter and faster than Chestnut-tipped Toucanet and resembles Crimson-rumped (S&H).

YELLOW-BILLED TOUCANET

Aulacorhynchus calorhynchus Pl. 125

Identification 35–36cm, bill 8.6–9.4cm. Almost entirely emerald green, darker above, paler and brighter below; chin and throat white. Eye-ring and loral skin, including at base of mandible blue, eyes red; bill basically entirely rich yellow, blackish at base of upper mandible and yellow at lower, black on cutting edges of both mandibles but not reaching tip; legs and feet dark grey-green.

Ssp. Monotypic (N Co, NW Ve)

Habits Forages at all levels, noisily or quietly; sometimes trails silently behind a mixed feeding flock.

Status Locally frequent in Colombia, no recent data from Venezuela, though possibly locally frequent. Overlaps with Groove-billed Toucanet in mountains of north-west Lara and the Cerro Platillón, on the Carabobo border with Guárico, where they occasionally interbreed. Hybrids have an intermediate-patterned bill, with characters from each (see plate).

Habitat Upper Tropical to Subtropical Zones, 900–1,900m. Cloud and humid montane forests, both interior and at borders.

Voice Described as 2 per s repetitions of loud, nasal *coank* notes (H&B). Very similar to Groove-billed Toucanet.

Note Considered a subspecies of Groove-billed Toucanet by Schwartz (1972).

CHESTNUT-TIPPED TOUCANET

Aulacorhynchus derbianus Pl. 125

Identification 38–41cm, bill 7.6cm. Almost entirely emerald green, darker above, paler and brighter below, with a small dark brown patch at tip of central rectrices; chin and throat white. Eye-ring and loral skin blue, eyes red; bill has a narrow white line at the base, then basically entirely deep maroon-red, broadly black along cutting edges to tip; legs and feet green. From smaller Emerald Toucanet by red-and-black bill; from larger Crimson-rumped by green rump.

Ssp. *A. d. derbianus* (E Ec, E Co) turquoise nape; bill almost all black, red only at base and tip
A. d. duidae (S Ve) smaller, less blue on head, bill almost all red, with black line on cutting edges
A. d. osgoodi (Gu, Su, FG) lacks chestnut tip to tail; bill black with maroon culmen and at base
A. d. whitelianus (SE Ve, SW Gu) smaller than *duidae*, with smaller chestnut tip to tail, bill exactly intermediate between *osgoodi* and *duidae*

Habits Generally a bird of the canopy where it may be seen alone or in a pair, but occasionally in groups of 6–8 or so.

Status Rare in Ecuador, uncommon in Guyana. Status in Colombia uncertain, very few specimen records. Local on higher mountains in Suriname. Restricted in French Guiana to the extreme SW corner, but possible on some central ranges.
Habitat Upper Tropical to Subtropical Zones, 300–2,400m. Humid to wet montane forests, cloud forests, forests on slopes of tepuis.
Voice Sequence of low barks, *guah, guah, guak, hawk, guak*, at *c*.1 per s, and lacks growl at end (H&B, P. Schwartz recording). Variable song, long series of 1 minute or more, often starts with grunting *gggkk* that quickly becomes *graaa* (S&H).

CRIMSON-RUMPED TOUCANET

Aulacorhynchus haematopygus Pl. 125

Identification 41–48cm, bill 7.6–10cm. Almost entirely green with different tones, bright emerald on flanks and belly to undertail-coverts, darker above, turquoise wash on breast and sides, olivaceous wash to back, basal two-thirds of tail almost malachite in tone, whilst distal third is dark brown; lower rump crimson; chin and throat white. Eye-ring and loral skin deep pink, eyes red; bill has a broad white line surrounding base, then basically maroon-crimson, blackish on basal half of culmen, large black patch in middle of lower mandible; legs and feet green. Largest of the all-green toucanets, from all others by large dark brown tip to tail and bright red rump patch.

Ssp. *A. h. haematopygus* (Co: Andes, Ve: Perijá) 6 terminal tail spots
A. h. sexnotatus (W Ec, SW Co) 4 terminal tail spots

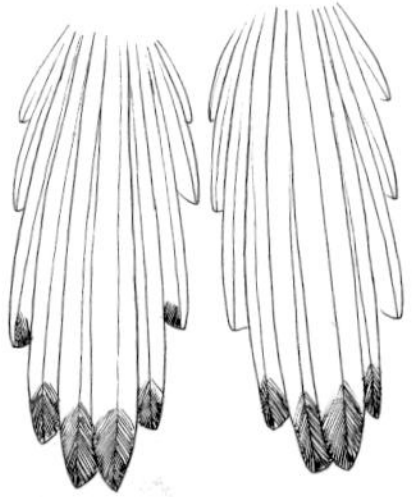

Comparison of terminal spots pattern on Crimson-rumped Toucanet, A. h. sexnotatus *(left),* A. h. haematopygus *(right)*

Status Uncommon to rare in Ecuador, common in Colombia, uncertain in Venezuela.
Habitat Upper Tropical to Subtropical Zones, 300–2,800m, most often 1,000–2,000m. Humid to wet and cloud forests, borders, semi-open wooded fields, to orchards, isolated fruit trees on farms and even gardens.
Voice Endless, 2 per s repetitions of *cua* or *guahk* notes (H&B). Song mainly of barking rattle type (Schwartz 1972), throaty, honking and repetitive. May last up to 2 minutes. Also snark, *bddddiipa* or *pik-ek-ek* (S&H).

Selenidera toucanets are darker, olive-green with significant amounts of black on males, brown on females. They also have golden-yellow ear tufts, and are much more frugivorous than other toucanets.

YELLOW-EARED TOUCANET

Selenidera spectabilis Pl. 126

Identification 38cm, bill 7.6–10.2cm. Only black-fronted toucanet in range. Male has head black with bright yellow ear-coverts-tufts, rest of upperparts rich olive-green, darker and slightly duskier on tail; black of head reaches vent and flanks, but there is a rich golden patch on flanks with orange to reddish tuft, thighs rich reddish-brown, undertail-coverts intense reddish-orange; eyes red, large patch of orbital skin is mixture of turquoise-green, turquoise-blue and yellow, and bill is broadly greenish-yellow on culmen, the rest olive-brown, darkening near tip, with cutting edges red and pale grey; legs and feet dark grey-green. Female essentially same but top of head rich reddish-brown and lacks yellow ear-tufts.

Ssp. Monotypic (Ec, NW Co)

Habits Forages alone or in pairs, always in canopy. During breeding season moves to higher slopes.
Status Very rare in Ecuador, uncommon to locally frequent in Colombia.
Habitat Tropical Zone. Humid and wet forests of foothills and lower slopes.
Voice Slow, rhythmic repetitions of 2 weak notes, *krek-ek* (H&B) or *tik-ekk, tik-ekk...* for up to 12 s or more, sounds rather like hitting 2 stones together twice (S&H).

GOLDEN-COLLARED TOUCANET

Selenidera reinwardtii Pl. 126

Identification 33cm, bill 5.1–6.4cm. Only black-fronted toucanet in range. Male has head black with bright rich yellow ear-coverts flushed reddish near bill, clear yellow nuchal band, rest of upperparts olive-green with a brown tip to tail; black head continues to belly and middle flanks where there is a broad band of yellow, rear flanks olive-green, thighs cinnamon, undertail-coverts red; eyes yellow with an extraordinary horizontal dark line through centre of pupil, eye-ring and orbital skin mixture of turquoise-green, turquoise-blue and yellow, bill bright vermilion-red, distally blackish, legs and feet grey-green. Female similar but has chestnut where male is black and pale olive-green ear-coverts.

Ssp. *S. r. reinwardtii* (E Ec, E Co)

Habits Forages alone, in pairs or with mixed flocks, from mid levels to canopy. Quiet and shy. Sometimes calls from high, bare branch, when makes a display, throwing head forward and down whilst lifting tail over back.
Status Uncommon in east Ecuador and east Colombia.
Habitat Tropical Zone. Humid lowland forests, mostly *terra firme*, but sometimes in *várzea*.
Voice Both sexes sing, often in duet, a series of throaty, frog-like barking *arrowk* notes (H&B), starts high-pitched but quickly drops, and has fast drop of *ak*, *owpor* or *awk* at end (S&H).

TAWNY-TUFTED TOUCANET

Selenidera nattereri Pl. 126

Identification 32–33cm, bill 6.4cm. Only black-fronted toucanet in range. Male has head black with bright rich yellow ear-coverts flushed reddish at edges, clear yellow nuchal band, rest of upperparts olive-green with a small brown tip to tail; black head continues to belly and middle flanks where there is a small patch of yellow, rear flanks and thighs cinnamon, undertail-coverts red; eyes red, with eye-ring and orbital skin a mixture of turquoise-green, turquoise-blue and yellow, and an orange spot near nostrils; bill bright vermilion-red, with a broad vertical dusky band near base, diminishing as dusky bars to about halfway, culmen narrowly greenish-yellow, legs and feet grey-green. Female is similar but has chestnut where male is black.

Ssp. Monotypic (S Co, S Ve, Gu, FG)

Habits Forages from mid levels to canopy, alone or in small bands. Joins mixed canopy flocks.
Status Very local and scarce in Colombia and Venezuela, scarce in Guyana, very rare in French Guiana where only sight records.
Habitat Lower Tropical Zone. Lowland, sandy soil forests.
Voice Soft, low rattles of croaky frog-like notes (H&B), *ggroookk, ggroookk f*or up to 13 s, similar to Golden-collared. Also, croaking rattle of *c.*15 notes, *ggggrik-ggggrik…* (S&H).
Note Sometimes erroneously listed as occurring in Suriname. Considered 'exceptional' in French Guiana (Tostain *et al.*), probably accidental in French Guiana unless a still unknown population.

GUIANAN TOUCANET

Selenidera piperivora Pl. 126

Identification 33cm, bill 7.6cm. Only black-fronted toucanet in range. Male has head black with bright yellow ear-coverts-tufts, rest of upperparts rich olive-green, washed lightly brown on back, greyish on tail with large brown tip; black of head reaches upper belly and sides, lower belly and flanks olivaceous-grey, thighs brown, undertail-coverts red; eyes red, large patch of orbital skin turquoise-green, bill crimson on basal third of upper mandible and basal two-thirds of lower mandible, distally black; legs and feet dark grey-green. Female essentially similar but has broad deep, blood red nuchal band, instead of narrow yellow; underparts from chin to vent and flanks grey, washed latterly olivaceous-green.

Ssp. Monotypic (SE Ve, Gu, Su, FG)

Habits Shy, forages from mid levels to canopy, alone but most often in pairs or small bands. Feeds on small fruits, especially figs, and is partial to *Cecropia* fruits.
Status Local in Venezuela, frequent in Guyana and Suriname, common in French Guiana.
Habitat Lower Tropical Zone. Humid lowland forests, sand-ridge and savanna forests.
Voice Repetitions of a sharp note, reminiscent of a child's rattle (MdS&P), much like mountain-toucans but faster, *bdddt, bdddt, bdddt…* Also other rattle sounds, e.g. *graaak* that may last 1 minute or more (S&H) and whinnying calls (H&B).
Note Formerly called *S. culik*, but see Pacheco & Whitney (2006). *Culik* is now considered to be a synonym.

Araçaris are slender, dark green above with black heads and yellow bellies, all with touches of red or blue, some with yellow eyes, others red. They have long, decurved bills, strongly serrated on the cutting edges. Very confusingly similar but each has its own pattern. Bill coloration is a key to identification. Highly frugivorous.

LETTERED ARAÇARI

Pteroglossus inscriptus Pl. 127

Identification 37cm, bill 6.4–8.9cm. Complete head and upper breast black, back and wings to rump and tail bottle green, uppertail-coverts bright vermilion-red; breast to undertail-coverts rich yellow, with thighs dark brown; eyes red, upper orbital skin bright blue, frontal half of lower skin grey, rear half bright reddish-pink; bill yellow with black culmen, black line inside base, and lower mandible all black except yellow base, with a series of slightly irregular lines curving onto yellow, 1 at each serration. Female similar but has most of head deep brown, leaving only forehead and cap black. From other araçaris in its range by black 'letters' on bill-sides and clear yellow belly.

Ssp. *P. i. humboldti* (E Ec, SE Co)

Habits Forages mostly in small bands which move noisily through canopy in single file, taking short flights and hustling along branches seeking fruits, nests and other prey.
Status Common in eastern Ecuador, locally frequent in Colombia.
Habitat Lower Tropical Zone. Interior, clearings and borders of humid lowland forests, both *terra firme* and *várzea*, and in mature second-growth woodland.
Voice Calls very seldom, described as a low *chak* (H&B) but mostly a fast series of sharp *klik, kkuk* or *kkek* (usually 5–15) notes, punctuated by a double *kkek-ek*. Sometimes in very long series (S&H).
Note Considered to be a subspecies of Green Araçari by Haffer.

GREEN ARAÇARI

Pteroglossus viridis Pl. 127

Identification 30cm, bill 8cm. Complete head and upper breast black, back and wings to rump and tail bottle green, uppertail-coverts bright scarlet-red; breast to undertail-coverts rich yellow, flushed greenish on flanks, with thighs pale brown; eyes red, orbital skin bright blue, with a trailing red upper corner; bill has base yellow, rest of upper mandible red with yellow culmen, and lower mandible all black. Female similar but has head deep reddish-brown. From other araçaris in range by small size and clear yellow belly.

Ssp. Monotypic (SE Ve, Guianas)

Habits Forages in canopy, alone or, most frequently, in small bands, sometimes trailing mixed flocks. Vivacious, very noisy and inquisitive. Raids nests of other birds. Bands may roost together in tree cavities.
Status Locally frequent in Venezuela, frequent in Guyana, widespread but not common in French Guiana.

Habitat Lower Tropical Zone. Lowland forests, sometimes in plantations.
Voice Varied calls and song, including an irregular series of *prip, pridit* or *prrddp* notes up to 6 per s (S&H) and sequence of *tica, tica, tica*... notes, like a child's rattle (MdS&P).

IVORY-BILLED ARAÇARI

Pteroglossus azara Pl. 127

Identification 33–46cm, bill 7.9–10cm. Head entirely black, nuchal band that joins breast-band crimson, back and wings to rump and tail deep bottle-green, uppertail-coverts crimson, lower breast black, belly and upper flanks bright yellow, lower flanks and thighs green, vent to undertail-coverts bright yellow; eyes red, eyelids blue, orbital skin consists of concentric circles of pink and violet, bill pale straw-yellow, legs and feet grey-green. From all other araçaris by all-yellow bill.

Ssp. *P. a. flavirostris* (E Ec, SE Co, S Ve)

Habits Forages in pairs or small bands, in canopy. Bands noisy and spirited, moving through canopy and clearings in single file, taking short flights and hustling along branches seeking fruits, nests and other prey.
Status Uncommon to rare in east Ecuador, frequent in Colombia and Venezuela.
Habitat Lower Tropical Zone. Humid *terra firme*, gallery and sandy soil forests, plantations, patchy woodland in savanna. At borders and in clearings.
Voice Calls differ from congeners, varied series of screams and wails, *kwaa-aa-aa* or *kweee-eee*. Song often starts and occasionally ends with a squawk. Varied contact calls, e.g. *gkek*, alarm *pyeek* and rattles, e.g. *kkkk* (S&H). A fast series of croaking rattles that become shrieks, *cro-ak... co-ak... cro-ak*... (H&B).
Note Species named *flavirostris* in Peters (1948) and followed by most authors, but S&M (1990) determined *azara* has precedence.

CHESTNUT-EARED ARAÇARI

Pteroglossus castanotis Pl. 127

Identification 46 cm, bill 10.2cm. Head black with deep chestnut ear-coverts, the brown merging into the face-sides; back and wings to rump and tail deep bottle green, uppertail-coverts crimson; breast yellow, broad vermilion-red band on upper belly, rest of underparts yellow, thighs brown; eyes yellow, orbital skin rich blue, bill black with yellow base and cutting edges, buffy band starts near nostril and runs to tip of upper mandible, culmen black, legs and feet grey-green. From all other araçaris in range by red band on yellow belly.

Ssp. *P. c. castanotis* (E Ec, E Co)

Habits Forages mostly in small bands, moving noisily through canopy and clearings in single file, taking short flights and hustling along branches seeking fruit, nests and other prey.
Status Uncommon in Ecuador, common in Colombia.
Habitat Lower Tropical Zone. Humid lowland and gallery forests, *várzea*, mature second growth, forest patches in savannas.
Voice Vocalisations for this and 3 following species very similar, including *skeez-up, sneep, pseet, skreek* in irregular series of up to 3 notes per s (H&B, S&H).

BLACK-NECKED ARAÇARI

Pteroglossus aracari Pl. 127

Identification 46cm, bill 11.5cm. Entire hood black to breast, with deep purple gloss, ear-coverts deep chestnut-black, back and wings to rump and tail very dark green; uppertail-coverts crimson; underparts yellow with broad scarlet band on sides and belly, and broad brown band on rear flanks and thighs; eyes red, orbital skin deep violet; base of bill white, upper mandible white with black culmen, lower mandible black; legs and feet grey-green. From much smaller Green by black-and-white bill and red band on belly.

Ssp. *P. a. atricollis* (Guianas) sulphur to orange-yellow breast
P. a. roraimae (S & SE Ve) lemon-yellow breast

Habits Forages mostly in small bands, which move noisily through canopy and clearings in single file, taking short flights and hustling along branches seeking fruit, nests and other prey. Nests in old woodpecker holes, breeds December–January.
Status Locally frequent in Venezuela, frequent in Guyana, frequent and widespread in French Guiana.
Habitat Lower Tropical Zone. Lowland forests, second growth, semi-open woods, at borders and along rivers.
Voice A soft, high *tilin* (MdS&P), *kulik, silik, pssssk* and *pee-it* (S&H). Song a dry chicken-like *tok-toktoktok...toktoktok* (H&M).
Note Race *roraimae* considered invalid by Haffer.

COLLARED ARAÇARI

Pteroglossus torquatus Pl. 127

Identification 41cm, bill 8.9–11.5cm. Only araçari in range. Entire hood black with deep purple gloss, orange-rufous nuchal band, back and wings to rump and tail very dark bluish-green; uppertail-coverts crimson; underparts yellow with indistinct and irregular crimson flush on mid breast with a black patch in centre, and again on body-sides with a somewhat irregular black patch on mid belly; rear flanks and thighs deep cinnamon-brown; eyes yellow with orbital skin mostly crimson but frontal part violet; bill has narrow white band at base, upper mandible yellowish with buffy flush on basal half, base of culmen black, tip blackish; lower mandible black; legs and feet greyish-green.

Ssp. *P. t. nuchalis* (N Co, N Ve) slightly smaller, with cinnamon-rufous parts paler, broader white band at base of bill
P. t. torquatus (NW Co) as described

Habits Forages alone or in small bands, in canopy. Lively, curious and noisy, the bands proceed single file along branches, searching as they go. Roost together in tree cavities.
Status Common in Colombia, frequent in Venezuela.
Habitat Tropical Zone. Humid to drier, lowland forest, tall second growth, deciduous woodland, gallery forests.

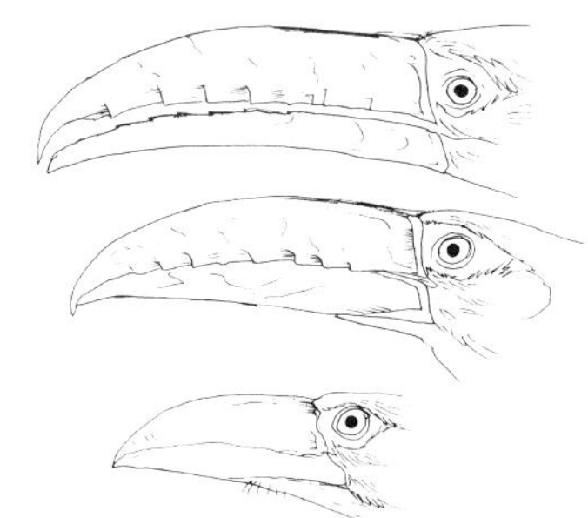

Collared Araçari: adult male above, adult female centre, juvenile below; whilst there is no difference in plumage coloration, females of all araçaris tend to be smaller than males (and juveniles smaller still), and their bills are proportionately smaller, as shown here

Voice Similar to Stripe-billed, a sneeze-like *pitsek!* (H&B). Also *sneep, pseet, sneerp, snee-eep, tzee-zeet, fe-liz* etc. Rattle calls *bddddddt* may be combined with *sneek* calls (S&H).

STRIPE-BILLED ARAÇARI

Pteroglossus sanguineus Pl. 127

Identification 43cm, bill 9–11.5cm. Only araçari in range. Entire hood black with deep indigo tone, back and wings to rump and tail very dark green; uppertail-coverts scarlet; underparts yellow with indistinct and irregular crimson flush on mid breast with large black patch in centre, and again on body-sides with a somewhat irregular black patch on mid belly; thighs yellow; eyes pale yellow with orbital skin mostly crimson, but eye-ring and frontal part violet-blue; bill has narrow white band at base, upper mandible is pale buffy on basal half, culmen broadly pale yellow, tip warm yellow; lower mandible black; legs and feet greyish-green.

Ssp. Monotypic (NW Ec, W Co)

Habits Forages mostly in small bands of 3–15 birds, which move noisily through canopy and clearings in single file, taking short flights and hustling along branches seeking fruit, nests and other prey. Flies with hurried, heavy flapping, and alternating short glides.

Status Common in north-west Ecuador and Colombia.

Habitat Tropical Zone. Humid and wet primary and mature secondary forests.

Voice Much like Collared, Chestnut-eared and Many-banded Araçaris (H&B).

Note Treated as a subspecies of Collared Araçari by Haffer and S&H.

PALE-MANDIBLED ARAÇARI

Pteroglossus erythropygius Pl. 127

Identification 40–43cm, bill 11–13cm. Only araçari in range. Entire hood black with deep indigo tone, back and wings to rump and tail very dark green; uppertail-coverts scarlet; underparts yellow with indistinct and irregular crimson flush on mid breast with large black patch in centre, and again on body-sides with a somewhat irregular black patch on mid belly; thighs yellow; eyes pale yellow with orbital skin mostly crimson, but eye-ring and frontal part violet-blue; bill has narrow white band at base, then mostly ivory, flushed reddish at base, thick black line on cutting edge of upper mandible by 'teeth', and tip of upper mandible orange-yellow, lower mandible black at tip; legs and feet greyish-green.

Ssp. Monotypic (W Ec)

Habits Forages mostly in small bands, which move noisily through canopy and clearings in single file, taking short flights and hustling along branches seeking fruit, nests and other prey. Flies with fast heavy flapping and brief glides. Sometimes calls from exposed perch, especially early morning.

Status Common in western Ecuador.

Habitat Tropical Zone. Humid and wet primary forests, and mature secondary forests.

Voice A sneeze-like *ksiyik!* (R&G).

Note Treated as a subspecies of Collared Araçari by Haffer and S&H.

MANY-BANDED ARAÇARI

Pteroglossus pluricinctus Pl. 127

Identification 43–46cm, bill 11.5–12.7cm. Entire hood black to breast, with deep purple gloss, back and wings to rump and tail very dark green; uppertail-coverts crimson; series of bands of irregular width, from breast: narrow scarlet band, medium yellow band, broader black band, broad yellow flushed red with a few touches of black, broad red with flushes of black, and yellow (sides and vent), and rear flanks, thighs and undertail-coverts brown; eyes yellow, orbital skin bright green; base of bill a narrow yellowish-white line, upper mandible yellowish-white with black culmen and orange tip, lower mandible black; legs and feet grey-green.

Ssp. Monotypic (E Ec, S Co, S Ve)

Habits Forages in pairs or small bands, which move noisily through canopy and clearings in single file, taking short flights and hustling along branches seeking fruit, nests and other prey.

Status Uncommon to locally common in east Ecuador. In Colombia, scarcer in *várzea* than *terra firme*, where locally frequent. Locally frequent to uncommon in Venezuela.

Habitat Lower Tropical Zone. Humid lowland forests.

Voice Most common call much like Collared, Chestnut-eared and Many-banded Araçaris, an emphatic *kissit* (H&B).

Mountain toucans are quite distinctive from other toucans with their brown backs, bright yellow rumps, blue bellies and red undertail-coverts. They have large decurved bills with strongly serrated edges, and perch more erect than toucanets, flicking their tails and moving the heads when calling. Rattle their bills.

PLATE-BILLED MOUNTAIN TOUCAN

Andigena laminirostris Pl. 126

Identification 47–51cm, bill 8.9–10.2cm. Only mountain toucan west of Andes. Top of head black, back dusky brown, rump and tail-coverts bright creamy-yellow, tail grey with brown tip; bright blue from face-sides to flanks and vent, with patch of yellow on mid flanks; thighs dark brown, undertail-coverts bright red; eyes red, orbital skin bright blue above and at sides, yellow below, bill basally bright red with culmen black and distal third black, broad patch of yellowish-cream on sides of upper mandible, legs and feet grey-green.

Ssp. Monotypic (W Ec, SW Co)

Habits Forages alone, in pairs or small bands, mostly in canopy and stands of *Cecropia*. Joins mixed canopy flocks.

Status Uncommon to locally common in Ecuador, uncertain in Colombia, where possibly scarce and local.

Habitat Upper Tropical Zone to Páramo, 300–3,200m, but more usually 1,300–2,500m. Humid, wet and cloud forests, mossy woodland with epiphyte-laden branches, shady ravines.

Voice Sexes call in duets. Male call is loud repetitions of *tryyyyyyk*, the female's a dry *t't't't't'* (F&K). A series of rising, plaintive *quuuuuah, quuuuuah,* and loud *t't't't't'* rattle (H&B). Sounds carry 1km or more. Also *kkrak* and *tek-tek-tek* (S&H).

GREY-BREASTED MOUNTAIN TOUCAN

Andigena hypoglauca Pl. 126

Identification 46cm, bill 8.9–10.2cm. Top of head and face-sides black, back reddish-brown; rump and tail-coverts bright creamy-yellow, tail grey with brown tip; throat to flanks and vent greyish-blue, thighs dark brown, undertail-coverts bright red; eyes brown, orbital skin blue, bill alternating triangular bands, from base: yellow, black, yellow, black and red, the latter from base of culmen to tip of bill, legs and feet grey-green. From Black-billed Mountain Toucan by yellow on bill, black cheeks and dark tail.

Ssp. *A. h. hypoglauca* (Co: C Andes) brown eyes
A .h. lateralis (E Ec) yellow eyes

Habits Forages quietly and alone, in pairs or small bands, mostly in canopy, sometimes in large emergents or occasionally in low berry brambles.

Status Uncommon in Ecuador, uncommon to locally frequent in Colombia.

Habitat Temperate Zone to Páramo, 1,600–3,700m, but mostly 2,500–3,500m. Humid and cloud forests, mossy woodland with epiphyte-laden branches, shady ravines, stands of *Cecropia*.

Voice Loud yelps and whines at dawn and dusk, but is fairly silent by day. Day call a low *kek-kek-kek-kek* (F&K) or loud, nasal, 2 s *kuuuuaat*, repeated at 5 s intervals (H&B). Main song or long-noted vocalisation is a series of *kwaaaaaaa, kweeeeeeeeat* or *kwaaaaaak* notes, which tend to rise then fall at end (S&H).

BLACK-BILLED MOUNTAIN TOUCAN

Andigena nigrirostris Pl. 126

Identification 51cm, bill 9.5–11.4cm. Forehead to mantle deep indigo-blue which might appear black, back and wings olive-brown with tertials and secondaries and most of tail greyish-blue (tail has brown tip); chin, throat and sides of face to upper breast white, merging into pale blue to flanks and vent, thighs brown, undertail-coverts red; eyes red, upper half of orbital skin yellow, lower half blue, bill all black, legs and feet dark grey-green. From Grey-breasted Mountain Toucan by lack of yellow on bill, white cheeks and throat, and blue tail.

Ssp. *A. n. nigrirostris* (Ve, Co: E Andes) as described; bill all black
A. n. occidentalis (Co: W Andes) crescent of red on bill, from base of lower mandible almost to tip of upper mandible
A. n. spilorhynchus (NE Ec, Co: C Andes) crescent of red on basal half of upper mandible

Habits Forages noisily in pairs or small bands, in canopy or tops of bushes.

Status Rare in Ecuador, frequent in Colombia, locally common in Venezuela.

Habitat Subtropical to Temperate Zones, 1,250–3,300m, but mostly 1,700–2,700m. Wet or montane cloud forests, humid scrub and wet, bushy areas with scattered trees. Often near water, along streams and in mossy gulleys.

Voice Song commences with 4–8 *dddt* notes, singly or in couplets, followed by series of low, even-pitched, whistled notes, nasal barks, *kwaaak, cro-ak, co-ak*... or mechanical, nasal, harmonic *tu-aat*, 25–45 per minute. Various rattles indicate contact, alarm and aggression (MdS&P, F&K, H&B, S&H).

Toucans are unmistakable, noisy birds of canopies, and as such need little introduction. However, their taxonomy is by no means clear. The deep-rooted conviction that there is widespread hybridisation is not upheld by a careful mapping of the various taxa and analysis of their distribution. In fact, a look at the plates suggests that there may be more regional populations with genetic integrity than hitherto described. Lumping them into few species only muddies the water of behavioural analysis and can result in completely false conclusions. We believe that the comparative value of field observations is strengthened by clear recognition and unequivocal identification of each taxon. In recognising them here we are not attempting revisionist taxonomy, only clarification of taxon recognition based on actual coloration, and a detailed mapping of individual specimens. All are basically black from top of head to rump, tail and middle underparts, and all have large pale blue legs and zygodactyl feet, thus the descriptions below only describe the variables by which the birds are identified.

KEEL-BILLED TOUCAN

Ramphastos sulfuratus Pl. 128

Identification 48cm, bill 11.3–14.9cm. Distinct chestnut wash to mantle, uppertail-coverts white; face-sides and chin to breast bright lemon-yellow with thin red line separating it from black underparts; undertail-coverts red; eyes pale greenish-yellow, orbital skin blue; bill a kaleidoscope of colours and complex pattern (see plate), essentially pale green with an orange panel on sides and large red tip. From Chocó and Chestnut-billed Toucans by green bill with red tip and orange and blue patches.

Ssp. *R. s. brevicarinatus* (N Co, Ve)

Habits Forages in canopy in pairs or small bands. Calls from tops of trees, often from an exposed perch. Moves bill up and down and from side to side when calling.
Status Common in Colombia, scarce in Venezuela.
Habitat Tropical Zone. Humid to drier forests, gallery forests, light or patchy wooded areas, tall second growth, scrub.
Voice A rapid series of croaks, *krik, krik, krik, krik*... (H&B) or repeated dry, grunted *ue-trek, ue-trek, ue-trek*... (MdS&P).

CHOCÓ TOUCAN

Ramphastos brevis Pl. 128

Identification 44–48cm, 11.4–16.3cm. Uppertail-coverts white; face-sides and chin to breast bright lemon-yellow with thin red line separating it from black underparts; undertail-coverts red; eyes pale yellow-green, orbital skin blue; bill black with a pale greenish-yellow culmen that broadens distally. From Keel-billed and Chestnut-billed Toucans by black bill with broad pale green culmen (also, Chestnut-billed Toucan has green eye-ring).

Ssp. Monotypic (NW Ec, W Co)

Habits Forages alone, in pairs and small bands, in canopy and subcanopy. Sings with head up, swinging in an arc from side to side.
Status Relatively small range. Uncommon in Ecuador, uncommon to locally frequent in Colombia.
Habitat Tropical Zone. Humid to wet forests on foothills and lower slopes, both interior and at borders.
Voice Loud calls from treetops, a series of croaking grunts, varying in pitch and speed of delivery (H&B, S&H).

CITRON-THROATED TOUCAN

Ramphastos citreolaemus Pl. 128

Identification 48–53cm, bill 14–17.8cm. Uppertail-coverts bright pale yellow, face-sides and chin white, becoming lemon-yellow on breast, red band between yellow breast and black underparts. Undertail-coverts bright red, eyes pale blue, orbital skin blue; bill has narrow black line at base, base of each mandible a yellow D-shape with the centre orange, affording a large B-shape, with a wedge of blue and large black panel over most of the bill-sides, and base of culmen pale green, rest of culmen yellow, tip light green. From Keel-billed and Black-mandibled Toucans (race *abbreviatus*) by white of face and yellow uppertail-coverts.

Ssp. Considered monotypic (Co: Antioquia to Tolima, Norte de Santander, Ve: Perijá and W slope of Andes); however...
Birds from Perijá have yellow eyes, an all-blue base to bill and ivory tip, and a much broader red pectoral band
Birds from Venezuelan Andes (Táchira to Lara) have more extensive white, pale green eyes, with a far less-clearly defined pattern at base of bill and pale yellow tip

Habits Forages alone, in pairs or small bands, in canopy and subcanopy.
Status Local in Colombia and Venezuela.
Habitat Tropical Zone. Borders and interior of humid forests.
Voice Loud calls from treetops, a *cree-ops* croaking like a frog (H&B, Hilty).
Note Treated as a subspecies of Channel-billed Toucan by Haffer and S&H.

YELLOW-RIDGED TOUCAN

Ramphastos culminatus Pl. 128

Identification 48cm, bill 10.2–14.7cm. Uppertail-coverts rich yellow, face-sides and chin to breast white, band of red before black underparts, undertail-coverts red; eye colour varies with location, orbital skin blue, base of bill blue, yellowish upper base to upper mandible and culmen to tip. From Citron-throated Toucan by white throat and breast; from Black-mandibled Toucan by white throat and breast, and yellow uppertail-coverts.

Ssp. Considered monotypic (E Ec, Co: Meta and Vichada, Ve: E slope of Andes and Amazonas); however, in Venezuela...
those from Lara have broad red pectoral band, flush of yellow to white breast, red eyes and eye-ring, and orange-yellow base to upper mandible
those from Táchira have yellow-green culmen with blue base to upper mandible, green eyes and green eye-ring
those from Amazonas state have yellow culmen and base of upper mandible yellowish, plus yellow breast and orange uppertail-coverts,

There is likely further variation in Colombia and possibly Ecuador that we have not been able to examine.

Habits Forages in canopy in pairs or small groups. Flies with dipping, heavy flight.
Status Uncommon to locally common in Ecuador, frequent in Colombia and locally frequent in Venezuela.
Habitat Tropical Zone. Borders and clearings of humid or cloud forests, and patches of forest in savannas.
Voice Similar to Citron-throated Toucan: loud, repeated croaks, reminiscent of a frog (H&B).
Note Treated as a subspecies of Channel-billed Toucan by Haffer and S&H.

CHANNEL-BILLED TOUCAN

Ramphastos vitellinus Pl. 129

Identification 48cm, bill 14cm. Uppertail-coverts orange, face-sides and chin white, bright yellow throat to breast, broad red band which merges into black underparts, undertail-coverts red; bill has blue base to lower mandible, yellow base to upper mandible and culmen to yellow tip. From Yellow-ridged

Toucan and much larger Cuvier's Toucan, in fact from all other toucans by orange uppertail-coverts.

Ssp. *R. v. vitellinus* (S & W Ve, Tr, Guianas)
2 morphs occur in Bolívar; first has bill all black with blue base to both mandibles and orange breast; the other has yellowish culmen and reddish-orange breast (both have red uppertail-coverts)

Habits Forages in canopy, mostly in small noisy bands that nimbly hop from branch to branch. Very partial to palm fruits, which they consume in large quantities. Flies in wavy pattern. Nests and roosts in tree cavities. Calls boldly from treetops.
Status Common in Venezuela, Trinidad, Guyana and Suriname, frequent and widespread in French Guiana.
Habitat Tropical Zone. Primary and mature second-growth lowland forests, often near water or in marshy woods.
Voice Repeated loud yelps, *kiok, kiok, kiok*… (MdS&P). Buzzy, frog-like croaking notes, usually of 2+ syllables, e.g. *eeee-okkk* or *eeee arrgh*, etc., notes vary in length. Pair will counter-sing. Other calls include *peeer*, *groaka*, *pwope* and *grunk* (S&H).

BLACK-MANDIBLED TOUCAN

Ramphastos ambiguus Pl. 129

Identification 56–61cm, bill 13.1–19.8cm. Uppertail-coverts white, face-sides and chin to breast rich yellow, then a thin white line and broader red band on breast, undertail-coverts red; eyes brownish-grey, orbital skin rich blue, bill fuscous with rich yellow culmen that widens distally, like a scimitar. From smaller Yellow-ridged and Cuvier's Toucans by all-black base to bill.

Ssp. *R. a. abbreviatus* (W Ve, Co: C Andes) eyes pale greyish-hazel, pale green with touch of yellow in concentric circles around eyes
R. a. ambiguus (E Co, E Ec) as described

Habits Forages in canopy, in pairs or small bands.
Status Rare in Ecuador, locally uncommon to frequent in Colombia, scarce and local in Venezuela.
Habitat Tropical to Subtropical Zones. Humid lowland and lower-slope forests, sometimes to cloud forests, riverine forests, plantations, parks and golf courses.
Voice Loud yelps from treetops. Voice of *abbreviatus* is higher pitched and more 'yippy'.

CHESTNUT-MANDIBLED TOUCAN

Ramphastos swainsonii Pl. 129

Identification 61cm, 13.2–19.3cm. Uppertail-coverts white, face-sides and chin to breast rich yellow, with thin white line then red band, undertail-coverts red; eyes greenish-yellow, orbital skin green; bill deep chocolate-brown with yellow culmen widening distally like a scimitar. Very similar Chocó Toucan has pale green and black bill and blue skin around eye.

Ssp. Monotypic (Ec, W Co)

Habits Forages in canopy, in pairs or small bands. Prefers canopy but will come lower, especially for live prey, and known to pick fallen bananas from the ground. May be very territorially defensive of a fruiting tree.
Status Uncommon in Ecuador, locally common in Colombia.
Habitat Upper Tropical Zone. Humid and wet forests, both interior and at borders, clearings, patches of trees in open land, plantations, orchards, golf courses!
Voice Loud yelps from treetops, reminiscent of a gull, rhythmic repetitions of 2–3 loud notes, *keeyos taday taday* (H&B). Common name in Spanish, *Dios-te-dé* is onomatopoeic. Alternative transcription *kyew, kyu-kik, ki-kik* (S&H).
Note Treated as a subspecies of Black-mandibled Toucan by Haffer and S&H, but we follow H&B, S&M and R&G.

RED-BILLED TOUCAN

Ramphastos tucanus Pl. 130

Identification 53–61cm, bill 16.5cm. Uppertail-coverts yellow, face-sides and chin to breast white, with a tinge of sulphur-yellow low down and broad band of crimson on breast, undertail-coverts red; eyes brown, orbital skin bright blue; bill has black line surrounding base, then a bright blue base to lower mandible and bright yellow base to upper, which continues on culmen to tip, broad black band across bill, then almost entire side panels crimson-red, some rough blackish oscillations on cutting edges and black subterminally. Juvenile a smaller version of adult but deep chestnut on back of head and neck, and bill has large brown side panel. From Channel-billed Toucan by large red panel on bill and yellow uppertail-coverts. Larger Toco may look like '*aurantiirostris*' morph but has black tip to bill and lacks bright blue base to lower mandible, also has different-coloured skin around eye.

Ssp. Considered monotypic (NE & CE Co, Ve, Guianas)
Race described as '*aurantiirostris*' is a rare morph with almost entire sides of bill bright vermilion-red, and sides of throat to breast more yellowish, skin around eyes more violaceous

Habits Forages alone or in pairs. In French Guiana, at end of rainy season, birds from interior migrate to coastal sandy soil and marshy forests, to feed on palm fruits.
Status Uncommon to locally common in Ecuador, frequent in Colombia and Venezuela, common in Guyana, common and widespread in interior of French Guiana.
Habitat Tropical Zone. Humid forests, at borders, along streams and around treefalls. Pine forests.
Voice Often in chorus with several others, a series of alternating higher and lower notes: *kya-khuu, kya-khuu, kya-khuu*… (H&B).
Note Cuvier's Toucan is treated as subspecies of present species in Haffer, and given vernacular name White-throated Toucan.

CUVIER'S TOUCAN

Ramphastos cuvieri Pl. 130

Identification 58–61cm. Uppertail-coverts yellow, face-sides and chin to breast pure white, with clean red band, undertail-coverts red; eyes brown, orbital skin rich blue; bill has black line at base, rich blue base to lower mandible, and rich yellow on upper, running narrowly along culmen to tip of bill, entire middle of bill black. Very similar to smaller Yellow-ridged Toucan and best separated by voice.

Ssp. Monotypic (E Ec, SE Co, S Ve)

Habits Forages most often in pairs or rarely in small bands (up to 20), and always in canopy. Nests in natural cavities in trees.
Status Frequent in Colombia.
Habitat Tropical Zone. Humid forests of lowlands and foothills, plantations, clearings and treefalls, often by rivers.
Voice Loud yelps from treetops are rhythmic repetitions of 2–3 loud whistled yelps, *eeot whew-whew* or *eeot! hue!* (H&B, Hilty).

TOCO TOUCAN *Ramphastos toco* Pl. 130

Identification 60–65cm, 15.8–21.5cm. Uppertail-coverts white, face-sides and chin to breast white, becoming yellowish-tinged near underparts, undertail-coverts red; eyes brown, broad eye-ring blue, orbital skin orange; bill has broad black band at base then orange above, with vermilion-red lower mandible oscillating along lower edge of upper mandible, tip of upper mandible broadly black. Could be mistaken for '*aurantiirostris*' red-billed morph of smaller Red-billed Toucan but has orange-and-blue skin around eye and white uppertail-coverts.

Ssp. *R. t. toco* (Guianas)

Habits Forages alone, sometimes in pairs, rarely bands. Usually in canopy but will visit understorey and even the ground in orchards to take fallen fruit.
Status Uncertain in Guyana, very scarce in Suriname, uncommon to rare in north-east coastal French Guiana from Cayenne region to Brazilian border.
Habitat Tropical Zone. Savanna woodlands, gallery forests, deciduous forests near water, marshy forests and tall mangroves. Often ventures into open areas with scattered trees, the only toucan to do so.
Voice Irregular series of deep grunting notes, from *grrr* to *grunnkkt*, also double grunts as in *ggrekkt-ekk* or *arkkk-rk*. A more melodic *kkrew-yipe (S&H)*.

PICIDAE – Piculets and Woodpeckers

Piculets look almost like wind-up toys. Tiny by woodpecker standards, piculets are found mostly in lowland forests, busily pecking at dead wood on trunks, branches and twigs, to reach the wood-boring insects inside. Their irregular drumming has earned them the whimsical name of 'telegraphists' in Venezuela. They may cling to trunks and upright branches, but are more likely to be seen on a slender limb and particularly on the undersides of branches, often quite slender ones. Their ecology is poorly understood, and it seems likely that there are clear-cut separations of foraging zones within what appear to be identical habitats. Piculets are dimorphic. In males the crown feathers are streaked yellow, orange or red, with white dots or streaks on the nape. Females may follow the same pattern of streaks and dots, but have only white markings. Whether the white is dots, spots or streaks, and the extent that they cover different parts of the top of the head can be an important aid in species identification, for whereas all piculets have some variation of plumage pattern within any given population their head patterns are quite constant. Juveniles lack the black crown, are buffy to pale cinnamon on the head and below, being scaled darkly on the head.

Additional references used to prepare this family include Short (1982), Winkler et al. (1995) and Winkler & Christie (2002, hereafter W&C).

BAR-BREASTED PICULET
Picumnus aurifrons Pl. 131

Identification 7.5cm. Adult male is light olive-green above with yellowish fringes to wing-coverts and remiges, tail fuscous with longitudinal white bars; top of head black with short red streaks on forehead to forecrown, short white streaks from crown to nape; white postocular line to rear ear-coverts; buffy with some dusky barring on face-sides, throat white becoming yellowish to undertail-coverts, sides of throat have V marks, irregular bars on breast, sides and flanks with V marks, more like streaks in central belly. Female has white dots on forehead instead of red, but otherwise is like male. Similar Lafresnaye's has barred back and all-barred underparts.

Ssp. *P. a. aurifrons* (E Ec, S Co)

Habits Believed to prefer foraging in upper tiers.
Status In Colombia, sight records of race *aurifrons* in Leticia (H&B), sight records in Amacayacu (SCJ&W).
Habitat Tropical Zone. Humid forests, *terra firme* and *várzea*, edges and clearings, second-growth woodland.
Voice Calls are hummingbird-like: *tsirrrit-tsit-tsit* (Winkler *et al.*).
Note Formerly named Gold-fronted Piculet, but considered to include *P. borbae* of central Brazil (Short). Thus, Bar-breasted includes *aurifrons* and *borbae*.

ORINOCO PICULET
Picumnus pumilus Pl. 131

Identification 9cm. Male olive above with slightly buffy fringes to tertials, tail dusky with longitudinal white streaks; top of head deep brown, short yellow streaks on forehead and forecrown, back of head has white streaks, becoming buffy on nape; face-sides buffy with dusky barring, entire underparts whitish with irregular yellowish or buffy wash, and neat dusky barring from chin to undertail-coverts. Female like male but has small white dots on forehead instead of yellow streaks. Similar Lafresnaye's has barred back, race *undulatus* of Golden-spangled Piculet has bold white dots on nape and blackish spotting on back.

Ssp. Monotypic (E Co)

Habits Poorly known. Forages at all levels.
Status Rare.

Habitat Tropical Zone. Lowlands. Gallery forests, thickets, edges, open woodland.
Voice No descriptions found.
Note Considered a subspecies of Lafresnaye's Piculet by Short, but they are sympatric in Vaupés, Colombia.

LAFRESNAYE'S PICULET

Picumnus lafresnayi Pl. 131

Identification 9–10cm. Male is green above with golden-yellow fringes to all feathers affording effect of regular barring, tail dusky with longitudinal bars; dusky cheeks, faintly barred, underparts entirely barred dull green on white, washed yellowish; top of head grey with forehead and crown covered with broad little streaks of red, white streaks on nape. Female has small white dots on forehead, but otherwise is like male. From Bar-breasted and Orinoco by barred back. Very similar race *undulatus* of Golden-spangled has spots on back, not barring.

Ssp. *P. l. lafresnayi* (E Ec, SE Co)

Habits Forages from undergrowth to mid levels. Pecks at wood and gleans for insects on bark and surface of leaves. Feeds on termites.
Status Uncommon in Ecuador and Colombia.
Habitat Tropical Zone. Heavily forested and very humid terrain; edges and clearings; mature second growth.
Voice Usually quiet. A 2-note, high-pitched *tseeyt-tsit* phrase (R&G).

ECUADORIAN PICULET

Picumnus sclateri Pl. 131

Identification 8–9 cm. Top of head black with yellow streaks on fore part, white streaks on nape; upperparts brownish-grey with whitish fringes to wing-feathers, tail blackish with white longitudinal lines; underparts white with faint orange tone to ear-coverts, wholly barred grey from chin down. Female as male but has small white dots on forehead. The only other piculet in range is race *harterti* of Olivaceous, which has chestnut ear-coverts.

Ssp. *P. s. parvistriatus* (W Ec) as described; much more finely barred and streaked below
P. s. sclateri (SW Ec) slightly richer coloured, barring distinctly more blackish

Habits Forages at lower levels.
Status Uncommon in Ecuador.
Habitat Tropical Zone. Xerophytic areas, dry deciduous forests with cacti and low thorn scrub. More humid lower montane forests in Loja.
Voice Usually silent. Call a high-pitched *tseee-up* or *tseeet* or *tseeet-tseeet* (P. Coopmans in R&G).

GOLDEN-SPANGLED PICULET

Picumnus exilis Pl. 131

Identification 9–10cm. Greenish-olive above washed rufescent, back and wing-coverts have subterminal black crescents with white 'teardrop' centres, tertials and greater coverts white terminal fringes with black subterminal crescents, tail brown with longitudinal white lines; underparts pale yellowish-buffy, evenly and fairly broadly barred greyish-olive from chin to undertail-coverts; forehead almost solid red, crown black, nape has bold white streaks. Female dotted white on forehead, becoming streaks over whole top of head, back less distinctive, as white spots very much smaller and weaker; underparts more yellowish than male, and more narrowly and densely barred. From Orinoco and Lafresnaye's Piculets by red streaks on crown and spotted back.

Ssp. *P. e. buffoni* (E Guianas) as described; black-edged white spots on wings and back quite distinct
P. e. clarus (SE Ve) orange streaks on forehead and crown, black back of head, white spots on nape; clearer, more yellowish above with yellowish fringing to back and wing-coverts, white spots smaller and restricted to scapulars and coverts; more widely spaced and blacker bars on throat to breast, broken barring on sides becomes scallops on flanks
P. e. undulatus (E Co, S Ve, Gu) bright vermilion-red streaks to rear crown; much browner above, no white spots on back, only on lesser wing coverts

Habits Normally alone or in pairs. Pecks on branches at lower tiers (to 5m). Often hangs from twigs. Eats ants.

Piculets, like this Golden-spangled, are often seen searching the underside of quite narrow branches

Status Sight records only in Colombia, uncommon to locally frequent in Venezuela, frequent in Guyana, frequent and widespread in Suriname, frequent in French Guiana.
Habitat Tropical and Lower Subtropical Zones. In tepuis to 1,900m. Rain and cloud forests, dense growth, along rivers, bamboo stands. Open woodland and savanna.
Voice A *tssilit-tsirrrrr* (Winkler *et al.*).
Note *P. e. salvini* (Venezuela) is considered to be a junior synonym of Scaled Piculet *P. squamulatus obsoletus* (Lentino & Restall in prep.). *P. e. salvini* is known from a single specimen; locality unknown.

BLACK-DOTTED PICULET

Picumnus nigropunctatus Pl. 131

Identification 10cm. Black top of head with vermilion streaks on forehead, black rear to head with white streaks on nape; upperparts olivaceous-green with black 'teardrop' spots on each feather, yellow fringes to tertials and tips of greater coverts; face-sides brown with white spots; entirely yellow below, palest on throat where finely scaled with black dots, becoming round black spots on breast to flanks, more like half-circles or crescents on undertail-coverts. Female similar but top of head covered in small white streaks and spots, below more like half-circles than round spots. From all other piculets in range by (somewhat variable) black dots below.

Ssp. Monotypic (E Ve)

Habits Solitary, in pairs or family parties. Drills obsessively.
Status Endemic to eastern Venezuela. Locally frequent to common, especially in Orinoco Delta.
Habitat Lower Tropical Zone. Lowland forests, mangroves, open woodland.
Voice No description found.
Note Some authors mistakenly attribute this form to *P. e. salvini* (see Scaled Piculet), e.g. Winkler & Christie (2002).

CHESTNUT PICULET

Picumnus cinnamomeus Pl. 131

Identification 9–10.2cm. Top of head black with very pale cinnamon forehead and buffy yellow forecrown that runs into buffy-yellow streaks on rear of head, and bold white streaks on nape; entire body cinnamon, wings and tail darker with cinnamon fringes to wing-coverts and very pale fringes to tertials and tail-feathers. Female has white spots on nape. Rich chestnut coloration quite unique among piculets. Rufous-breasted Piculet has olive-green upperparts and is more southerly.

Ssp. *P. c. cinnamomeus* (N Co, NW Ve) as described; paler than other races, more cinnamon
P. c. larensis (NW Ve: E Zulia) very similar to *perijanus*, but slightly paler above and below, forehead more buffy, streaks on back of head purer yellow
P. c. perijanus (NW Ve: W Zulia, NE Co) dark chestnut with extensive black on top of head to nape, near white, pale cinnamon forehead, heavy buffy-yellow streaks on crown to upper nape, a few white spots at edge of nape; female has crown heavily spotted
P. c. persaturatus (N Co) darkest race; more chestnut than *cinnamomeus*
P. c. venezuelensis (W Ve) dark reddish-brown, with cinnamon forehead, black forecrown, bright yellow streaks on crown, fine white streaks on nape; female has a few small white dots on crown

Habits Alone, in pairs or small family groups. Joins mixed-species flocks. Active and not shy. Forages in thick tangles of vines and dense thickets, at all levels.
Status Common in Colombia. Locally frequent in Venezuela.
Habitat Lower Tropical Zone. Lowlands. Humid and deciduous forest, coffee plantations, xerophytic scrub, open and thorny woodland, mangroves.
Voice Seldom calls or sings. Song a barely audible, fading, insect-like trill *T,I,I,I,I,I,i,i,i,I,I,I,I...* given several times in a few minutes, and calls a series of 3–6 *eeeesk* notes (Hilty).
Note Race *larensis* (Aveledo 1998) overlooked by other authors, possibly synonymous under *perijanus* as the distinction is fairly subtle.

GUIANAN PICULET

Picumnus minutissimus Pl. 132

Identification 9–10cm. Male has top of head black, with red streaks so dense as to obscure most of black on crown, white streaks on nape; back, wings and tail green-grey with paler scaling, becoming whitish on larger coverts and tertials; underparts yellowish to buffy-white washed cinnamon on flanks, tightly scaled on face-sides, barred on throat, rest of underparts scaled, heaviest on flanks; eyes pale brown. Female has a few white dots on forehead, and fine white streaks on nape. Scaled Piculet is similarly scaled but has a completely separate range.

Ssp. Monotypic (Gu, Su, FG)

Habits Forages on small twigs. Very aggressive near nest.
Status In Suriname, frequent everywhere and numerous in coastal region. In French Guiana actual distribution and abundance very confusing, probably much less common than previously thought. For Guyana, listed by SFP&M, but not by BFR&S, who removed it for lack of concrete documentation.
Habitat Lower Tropical Zone. Lowlands. Secondary woodland, mangroves, plantations, along rivers and lakes, occasionally in lower montane forest.
Voice A shrill *kee, kee* or *tjeek, tjeek* (H&M) and thin series of 14 notes *it-it-it-it-it...* (W&C).

WHITE-BARRED PICULET

Picumnus cirratus Pl. 132

Identification 10cm. Male is olive-green above with faint whitish lines/bars on mantle and scapulars, top of head black with rich scarlet streaks on crown, and white streaks on back of head and nape; face-sides also olive-green, with blackish barring; chin to undertail-coverts white, washed pale cinnamon on lower breast and flanks, the whole barred regularly and closely dusky. Female similar but lacks any red on crown, instead has a few small white dots. Pale lines on mantle diagnostic, similar Guianan Piculet has black and white bars. White-bellied Piculet has very little barring on upper breast and perhaps spots on flanks.

Ssp. *P. c. confusus* (Gu, FG)

Habits Tame, found alone, in pairs and sometimes mixed-species flocks. Forages mostly at tips of small branches or twigs, sometimes hanging upside-down, on vines, small trees and bamboo. Flies far when finished at a particular spot.
Status Frequent in Guyana and fairly common in NW French Guiana.
Habitat Tropical and Subtropical Zones. Gallery and transitional forests, open woodland amid savannas; edges.
Voice A high, descending or long, wavering *tsirrrrr*. Also *tsirit, tsick* (W&C). Loud, staccato drumming.

OLIVACEOUS PICULET

Picumnus olivaceus Pl. 132

Identification 8.5–10cm. Male is olive above with yellowish fringes to tertials and faintly on remiges and coverts; top of head black with orange streaks on crown, back of head and nape well streaked with white, ear-coverts washed cinnamon, underparts pale whitish-buffy with fine barring on throat and faintly on breast and flanks. Female similar but streaked only white above. From Ecuadorian and Scaled Piculets by lack of black and white barring, scaling or streaking below, from Chestnut Piculet by pale olivaceous coloration. Races difficult if not impossible to identify in field.

Ssp. *P. o. eisenmanni* (Co and Ve: Perijá) distinctly more yellowish above and below, male has crown tips orange-yellow
P. o. flavotinctus (NW Co: N Chocó) more olivaceous above and below, male has crown tips yellow
P. o. harterti (SW Co, W Ec) smaller; generally darker olive, male has crown tips yellow to golden
P. o. olivaceus (C Co: C & E Andes) as described
P. o. tachirensis (W Ve, E Co) greenish above, male has crown tips orange-yellow

Habits Alone, in pairs or small family groups. Joins mixed-species flocks. Not shy. Forages at low or mid levels, in low tangles and open thickets, preferring thin branches, twigs and vines. Gleans. Drills for grubs and ant nests. Hop-climbs twigs.
Status Uncommon in Ecuador and Colombia.
Habitat Tropical Zone. Forest, open woodland, dense edges and clearings with creepers, gardens and cultivated areas.
Voice Fine, rapid twitters or trills, sometimes soft and clear, sometimes shrill, reminiscent of Black-faced Grassquit. Also sibilant *sst, ssip-ssip* and *peep* (W&C), a single sharp clear note (H&B) and a high, thin trill that falls in pitch (R&G). Does not drum (Skutch).
Note Races *malleolus* and *panamensis*, proposed by Wetmore (1965), inseparable from *olivaceous* and *flavotinctus* (W&C).

RUFOUS-BREASTED PICULET
Picumnus rufiventris Pl. 132

Identification 9–11cm. Male has top of head black with a few small white spots on forecrown, then bright red streaks on crown, short white streaks on nape, upperparts green with cinnamon fringes to all coverts and remiges, including longitudinal lines on tail; face-sides and underparts uniform rufous. Female has black on head spotted white on forecrown, becoming streaks on rear crown to nape. Only sympatric piculet is Plain-breasted, which is totally different colour.

Ssp. *P. r. rufiventris* (E Ec, SE Co)

Habits Alone, in pairs and with mixed-species flocks. Prefers to forage at low and mid levels.
Status Rare or scarce in Ecuador, frequent in Colombia.
Habitat Lower Tropical Zone. Lowlands. Humid *terra firme* and *várzea*, along watercourses, edges and clearings, second growth.
Voice Occasionally a thin, descending *tseeyt-tseeyt-tsit* (R&G).

PLAIN-BREASTED PICULET
Picumnus castelnau Pl. 132

Identification 8–9.2cm. Male has top of head black with red streaks on crown and back of head, nape scaled white, upperparts greenish-grey with faint whitish scaling on back to lesser wing-coverts, yellowish fringes to tertials and greater coverts; face-sides washed brown and dusky with white scaling, underparts yellowish buffy-white, washed brownish on flanks. Female similar with top of head black and less white scaling on nape. Only sympatric piculet is Rufous-breasted, which is totally different colour.

Ssp. Monotypic (Ec, Co)

Habits Alone or in pairs, sometimes with mixed-species flocks. Forages in lower canopy and at mid levels. Inconspicuous.
Status Uncertain in Ecuador, where no recent records and known only from a few very old specimens of doubtful provenance. Rare or scarce (almost no specimens and few sightings), and very local in Colombia.
Habitat Lower Tropical Zone. Swamp and *várzea* forests. Prefers well-developed second growth dominated by *Mimosa* and *Cecropia*.
Voice High-pitched, thin trill *T'E'E'e'e'e'e'e'*, at 20–40 s intervals, falling in pitch after initial triplet, descending, fading at end (H&B).

SCALED PICULET
Picumnus squamulatus Pl. 132

Identification 8–9cm. Male is dark yellowish-olive above with black fringes to back and wing-coverts, each feather having a paler subterminal tip, yellow fringes to tertials and greater coverts; top of head black with bright red streaks on forecrown, black back of crown and white streaks on nape; ear-coverts same as back, with a postocular line that embraces the outer part in a thin crescent; underparts whitish, barred on throat and scaled below, most heavily on flanks. Female similar with a few white spots on forecrown instead of red streaks. From Olivaceous and Chestnut Piculets by rich dark golden-olive back, speckled blackish and obvious black and white pattern below.

Ssp. *P. s. apurensis* (N Ve) whiter, weakest scaling below
P. s. lovejoyi (NW Ve) forecrown streaks yellow, greyish tinge above
P. s. obsoletus (NE Ve) tinged yellowish-green above
P. s. roehli (N Ve, NE Co) variable forecrown streaks, often orange or even yellow
P. s. squamulatus (E Co) as described; strongest scaling below

Habits Alone or in pairs, inconspicuous. Forages in dense scrub, tangled undergrowth and small trees, examining thin branches and twigs. Displays with wing spreads and synchronised movements.
Status Frequent in Colombia and Venezuela.
Habitat Tropical and Lower Subtropical Zones. Gallery and deciduous forests, second growth, xerophytic and other open areas, farms and pastures.
Voice A high-pitched and squeaky *chi-chi-che'e'e'chi*, trill-like towards end (H&B).
Note *P. s. obsoletus* includes *P. exilis salvini* (see Golden-spangled Piculet), Lentino & Restall in prep.

GREYISH PICULET

Picumnus granadensis Pl. 132

Identification 9–10cm. From similar Olivaceous Piculet by white or almost white below, and greyish-brown above. Greyish male has yellow crown streaks, and race *harterti* of Olivaceous Piculet has orange-yellow streaks, but better separated by white throat and pale breast of Greyish Piculet.

Ssp. *P. g. antioquensis* (SW Co) slightly paler and greyer above, slight streaking on breast and flanks
P. g. granadensis (WC Co) entirely white below

Habits Poorly known. Apparently similar in behaviour to Olivaceous Piculet.
Status Uncommon Colombian endemic.
Habitat Upper Tropical and Subtropical Zones. Dry, moderately humid and secondary woodland, scrub and thickets.
Voice Seldom calls. Described as a weak trill at a steady high pitch (H&B).

WHITE-BELLIED PICULET

Picumnus spilogaster Pl. 132

Identification 9cm. Male is brownish-olive above with subtle, faint barring on back and lesser wing-coverts, cinnamon fringes to tertials, secondaries and greater coverts; top of head black with dense red feathers from forehead to crown, white streaks at rear; ear-coverts brownish-olive with white scaling; underparts white, with barring on throat and breast becoming just scattered marks on flanks. Female similar with small white dots in front of black and white streaks on nape.

Ssp. *P. s. orinocensis* (E Ve) spotted darker with cinnamon scaling above, all pale below
P. s. spilogaster (Gu, FG?) as described; barred breast, spotted flanks

Habits Poorly known. Forages alone or in pairs, from undergrowth to subcanopy.
Status Locally frequent in Venezuela, frequent in Guyana. May possibly occur in Colombia but not recorded. For Suriname, included in Haverschmidt (1968), but later removed by H&M. Records for French Guiana very doubtful according to latter, but Tostain *et al.* consider it rare, with only a few, but widespread, recent sightings.
Habitat Lower Tropical Zone. Lowlands. Gallery and deciduous forests, mangroves, open woods and thickets.
Voice No descriptions found.

Despite their often brilliant and attractive colouring, woodpeckers usually draw attention by their drumming on forest trees. The insects and larvae they feed on are more likely to be found in dead wood, which in turn is more likely to have hollows and thus be more resonant. They hammer to chip away bark and wood to find food, but also drum to make noise. Woodpeckers have sharp, chisel-shaped bills, well adapted for thumping strikes against wood, and their tongues are long and barbed to snag and withdraw insect larvae and other creatures. They can also produce a sticky substance from their saliva to coat the tongue and trap insects within crevices. They usually have a pronounced undulating flight and land on a tree at the lower level of their foraging niche. They then work upwards, often spiralling the trunks and boughs unless there is a human observer, when they habitually keep to the other side of the trunk, peeping around occasionally to see if you are still there. Some have harsh cries and laughing rattles, but in general they are quiet, relying on their drumming for communication. A few, such as flickers, forage on the ground where they search for ant nests. Sapsuckers drill holes to cause sap flow, whereupon they both sip the sap and catch insects attracted to it, but our race of Acorn Woodpecker rarely stores acorns in holes it has drilled in tree trunks, as it does to the north.

Additional references used to prepare this section include Gilliard (1958), Short (1982), Winkler et al. (1995) and Winkler & Christie (2002, hereafter W&C).

RED-CROWNED WOODPECKER

Melanerpes rubricapillus Pl. 133

Identification 16–18cm. Adult male barred evenly and regularly from mantle to lower back and tail, black and white; rump and uppertail-coverts white; head and underparts to belly and flanks greyish-buff, with a reddish nuchal band, crown vermilion-red, graduating on back of head; forehead, eyebrow, lores and chin whitish with an orange-buffy supraloral spot; central belly bright red, undertail-coverts barred evenly grey and white; eyes deep red, bill black. Female lacks red on crown, but has a more extensive pale whitish area from forehead.

Ssp. *M. r. paraguanae* (NE Co, N Ve: Paraguaná Peninsula) red patch on crown cut off cleanly at rear crown, no nuchal band, and face more yellowish-buffy; broader white bars above, belly patch golden; female lacks red nuchal band and has face more yellowish-buffy
M. r. rubricapillus (Co, Ve, To, Gu, Su) as described

Habits Forages at all levels, mostly low and mid, acquiring food by hammering in dead wood and probing, gleaning or picking from foliage and bark, and pecking fruits and buds. Diet insects (ants, crickets, centipedes, beetles) and spiders, and a significant portion of fruits (palms, cacti) and nectar (*Balsa*, *Erythrina*). Picks bananas and papaya at feeders. Breeds in wet season, nests and roosts in holes excavated in thin dead trees or palms, large cacti or fence posts, usually so small that the birds enter tail first.
Status Common in Colombia, very common and widespread in Venezuela, uncertain in Guyana, common on Tobago (no records Trinidad), frequent to common in Suriname. Populations tend to increase with forest clearance.
Habitat Tropical to Lower Subtropical Zones. Dry to humid, open and semi-open areas with scattered trees, parks and gardens, patchy woods in savannas. Never in dense forest.
Voice A merry, far-carrying rattle *krrr-r-r-r-r-r* that lasts a few seconds, sometimes a loud *wika-wika-wika-wika*...of excitement (H&B).

YELLOW-TUFTED WOODPECKER

Melanerpes cruentatus Pl. 133

Identification 20cm. Two distinct morphs. Yellow-tufted morph is almost entirely deep indigo-blue or blue-black, male has bright red patch on centre of top of head, and either side a variable (sometimes rich almost orange, usually yellow, maybe even white) eyebrow that reaches neck-sides, projecting slightly as tufts; rump and body-sides to flanks and undertail-coverts barred evenly black and white; central belly red, uppertail-coverts snow white; eyes bright yellow, eye-ring grey, bill black with grey base. Female similar but lacks red on crown. Black morph similar but male lacks yellow on head whist female has barring on sides black and yellowish. Great variability in colour of facial plumage.

Ssp. Monotypic (E Ec, E Co, Ve, Guianas)

Habits Forages in small family groups. Nest holes usually located quite high.

Status Locally common in Ecuador, common in Colombia, frequent in Venezuela and Guyana, common in Suriname and French Guiana.

Habitat Tropical Zone. Drier and deciduous forests, forests on sandy ridges, at borders, in slash-and-burn clearings and timbered plots, where dead or burnt trunks still stand.

Voice Very noisy. Several calls, including a 9-note descending *ih-ih-ih-ih-ih…*, single *chowp* note and loud, raucous *r-r-r-aack-up* (H&B).

Note Formerly considered to comprise 2 subspecies, but *extensus* (Ec, Co, Ve) now regarded as indistinguishable from *cruentatus* (Gu, Su, FG) following Short.

WHITE WOODPECKER

Melanerpes candidus Pl. 133

Identification 24cm. Unmistakable. Male has black back, wings and tail; rest white with a black line running from rear base of eye around ear-coverts to join mantle, nape rich yellow, central belly yellow; eyes white, eye-ring yellow, bill silvery grey, distally black. Female similar but lacks black line on head-sides and yellow nape.

Ssp. Monotypic (Su, FG)

Habits Gleans and pecks insects and raids bee and wasp nests for larvae and honey. Takes berries and fruits. Often flies long distances to remote foraging areas, thus small groups can be spotted flying unwaveringly and directly (instead of usual undulating flight) over open areas. Displays include flights, bobbing and bowing. Quite social. Nest attended by both parents.

Status Frequent in northern Suriname, very local in NW coastal French Guiana.

Habitat Tropical Zone. Mangroves, especially with tall *Avicennia*, dry scrub and forest, open areas with patchy trees, palm groves and orchards.

Voice A 3-note roll – *kirr-kirr-kirr* – in flight, and a slurred *ghirreh* when perched (W&C).

BLACK-CHEEKED WOODPECKER

Melanerpes pucherani Pl. 133

Identification 17–19cm. Male entirely black above with faint and well-spaced white barring on back and wings; forehead yellow, crown to nape scarlet-red; head-sides black with a white postocular line and white ear-coverts, white lores and lower face-sides; underparts all white with weak black broken bars on breast and along sides to undertail-coverts, central belly red; eyes, bill, legs and feet black. Female similar but top of head white.

Ssp. Monotypic (W Ec, W Co)

Habits Forages at mid and upper levels, alone, in pairs, in family groups and, often, mixed flocks. Very agile in probing under bromeliads and epiphytes, clinging or hanging upside-down from vines and twigs. Eats spiders, insects, fruits, berries, shoots and juicy parts of *Cecropia*, and some seeds, especially of bromeliads. Probes in flowers for nectar. Nests in dead trees or palms, and often disputes with tityras over nesting sites. Both sexes drum.

Status Locally common in Ecuador, frequent in Colombia.

Habitat Lower Tropical Zone. Humid or wet evergreen forest, edges, clearings, mature secondary forest and abandoned banana plantations.

Voice Calls somewhat resemble those of Red-crowned, most common a series of 4 short rattles: *cherrr, cherrr, cherrr, cherrr* (W&C).

Note Formerly considered to comprise 2 subspecies, but *perileucos* (C. America) indistinct from *pucherani* (Short).

ACORN WOODPECKER

Melanerpes formicivorus Pl. 133

Identification 23cm. Male almost all black above, except white rump and uppertail-coverts scalloped black, head has unusual pattern of black forehead and chin, pale buffy yellow forecrown and lores running back below eyes to ear-coverts, and forward onto throat, with black around eyes, on top of head and neck-sides to nape; patch of bright crimson on back of head; breast to undertail-coverts black-streaked white, densest on breast, most white on vent and undertail, which is more scalloped. Female similar but lacks red at back of head.

Ssp. *M. f. flavigula* (Co)

Habits Forages busily in canopy or on high dead branches and trunks, in pairs or noisy, chattering groups. Always associated with oaks, but South American race less dependent on acorns and rarely stores these in 'granaries' like northern races. Diet includes fruits, berries and sap drilled from trunks. Also takes insects, gleaning them from leaves, epiphytes and bark, picking ants from ground or sallying from exposed branches or fenceposts to pick them from the air. Social structure, mating and breeding very complex. Groups have communal nests and all help with new brood. Together, groups continually chatter softly among themselves.

Status Race *flavigula* is only race in South America and resident in Colombia, where locally frequent to uncommon.

Habitat Tropical to Temperate Zones. On both slopes of Andes, in pastures, semi-open or partially deforested areas with scattered trees and standing dead trunks, *Quercus* woodland, also mixed *Quercus* and pine.

Voice Repeated raspy or rolling notes, *rack-up* or *r-r-rrrack-up* (H&B), also *karrit* and a repeated *wa-ka* (W&C).

GOLDEN-NAPED WOODPECKER

Melanerpes chrysauchen Pl. 133

Identification 17–19cm. Male all black above with white barring on mantle, white rump and tail-coverts; forehead yellow, crown to back of head scarlet, nape golden-yellow; black postocular line runs down neck-sides to back; ear-coverts to undertail-coverts all white. Female similar but has crown black, leaving red only on back of head.

Ssp. *M. c. pulcher* (Co)

Habits Forages in pairs or small family groups, mostly on dead trunks and thick branches at upper levels. Takes wood-boring insects or, sometimes, winged termites caught by hawking at dusk above canopy. Also, significant amounts of fruits (figs, bananas, *Cecropia* globules, palm fruits). Will visit feeders. Displays include bowing and wing-spreading. Families roost together at nest. Young fed mostly by males.
Status Frequent within small range in Colombia.
Habitat Tropical Zone. Tall humid forests, plantations and slightly cleared areas adjacent to forest, edges and clearings.
Voice Loud *churrr* calls (H&B) and repeated rattling, 'laughing' trills.
Note The race *pulcher* may represent a separate species, Beautiful Woodpecker (S&M).

YELLOW-BELLIED SAPSUCKER

Sphyrapicus varius Pl. 133

Identification 20cm. Upperparts a complex of black and white with solid black scapulars and large white patch on wings; top of head scarlet edged black that joins to form a black line on back of neck, black lores and black postocular line onto ear-coverts that runs down neck-sides, narrow white frontal line between malar and eyes to lower face-sides and on neck-sides, chin and throat scarlet edged black that forms black triangle on central breast; underparts yellow to flanks, then white, all scalloped with deep black V marks. Female lacks red throat, but usually retains red cap, but this is variable, and may be partially spotted or mostly covered with black, and a few individuals may lack any red.

Ssp. Monotypic (NW Co, ABC)

Habits Drills rows, columns or spirals of holes in bark for sap to emerge, and takes both sap and insects attracted to it. Also takes fruits and berries. Favours semi-open areas. Inconspicuous but confiding and usually easy to approach. In winter forages alone. Prefers thick trunks and branches.
Status Boreal migrant that winters in Middle America and West Indies, only occasional in northern South America, at extreme southern limit of winter range. Sighted in extreme north-west Colombia and irregular on Netherlands Antilles November–January. Mostly juveniles in first-winter plumage on latter islands. In Colombia possibly mostly females, as these usually migrate farther south than males.
Habitat Tropical Zone? Partially wooded areas with large trees, gardens, plantations, orchards.
Voice Rarely calls in winter. Alarm a *weetik-weetik*; aggression call *juk-juk-juk* (W&C).
Note Formerly considered conspecific with Red-breasted *S. ruber* and Red-naped Sapsuckers *S. nuchalis* of North America.

GOLDEN-COLLARED WOODPECKER

Veniliornis cassini Pl. 134

Identification 14–16cm. Male has upperparts yellow-olive with large white terminal spots on lesser and median wing-coverts, tail deep olive with whitish barring on outer rectrices; top of head deep olive with red streaks that become very dense then peter out on yellow-ochre nape; face-sides and underparts whitish with dusky barring, which is even and regular from chin to undertail-coverts. Female similar but has deep olive on head instead of red.

Ssp. Monotypic (S&SE Ve, Gu, Su, FG)

Habits Forages singly or in pairs, at all levels, mostly on thin outer limbs, narrow ends of branches in canopy, or on vines. Diet beetles, spiders, berries. Joins mixed flocks.
Status Locally frequent in Venezuela, frequent in Guyana and Suriname. Common in French Guiana.
Habitat Tropical Zone. Sandy soil and sand-ridge forests, stands of woods in savannas.
Voice Seldom calls. Contact-call between pairs a very soft *see-jhrrr-see-jhrrr* (H&M).

SCARLET-BACKED WOODPECKER

Veniliornis callonotus Pl. 134

Identification 13–15cm. Male pomegranate red from forehead to uppertail-coverts, with a few fine dark streaks on top of head, tail blackish with white barring on outer rectrices; sides of face and neck, and chin to undertail-coverts variable buffy-white, eyes deep red, bill yellow. Female similar but has black cap instead of red.

Ssp. *V. c. callonotus* (W Ec, SW Co) as described
V. c. major (S Ec) both sexes have brownish face-sides streaked darker brown and are lightly barred below

Habits Forages alone or in pairs, conspicuously, from low levels to canopy.
Status Uncommon to locally common in Ecuador, rare in Colombia (only a few records).
Habitat Tropical Zone. Partially wooded arid lowlands, scrub with scattered trees and cacti, dry deciduous forests, dense bushes or woods along watercourses.
Voice A *c.*2 s rattle (P. Coopmans) and emphatic 2-note *ki-dik*, once or in short, fast repetitions (R&G).

BLOOD-COLOURED WOODPECKER

Veniliornis sanguineus Pl. 134

Identification 13cm. Adult male pomegranate red from forehead to uppertail-coverts, tail dusky; entire underparts brown with white barring from chin and cheeks to undertail-coverts.

Ssp. Monotypic (Gu, Su, FG?)

Habits Forages alone or in pairs, from canopy to lower levels. Hammers on tree trunks. Diet includes butterflies, beetles, ants and termites.
Status Frequent in Guyana and Suriname; very locally uncommon in coastal W French Guiana, where records very old and require confirmation. Old records for Venezuela considered invalid (H&M).
Habitat Lower Tropical Zone. Mature mangroves, sandy ridge forests, coffee and cacao plantations, lowland forests, savannas with *Curatella* or other scattered trees, gardens and parks.
Voice A shrill *keek!* (H&M).

RED-STAINED WOODPECKER

Veniliornis affinis Pl. 134

Identification 15–18cm. Greenish-olive above with reddish fringes to mantle and wing-coverts, faint barring on remiges and dark barring on all rectrices, head olivaceous with red from forehead to back of head, nape orange; entire underparts barred broadly deep greenish-olive and narrowly white; bill dark grey above, pale grey below. Female has dusky cap instead of red.

Ssp. *V. a. hilaris* (E Ec, SE Co) as described; larger; wings have red tips
V. a. orenocensis (E Co, S Ve) greenish above, less yellowish

Habits Forages from mid levels to canopy, alone or in pairs, regularly with mixed flocks. Diet insects, spiders, fruits and berries. Follows swarms of ants.
Status Uncommon in Ecuador, rare in Colombia (only a few records).
Habitat Tropical Zone. Interior of tall, humid forests, mostly *terra firme*, occasionally in *várzea*.
Voice Seldom calls. A series of nasal, high-pitched *ghi* or *kih* notes (W&C).

CHOCÓ WOODPECKER

Veniliornis chocoensis Pl. 134

Identification 15–16cm. Male olive-green above, narrowly streaked on back with yellowish and red, pale yellowish spots on lesser and median coverts, rump to uppertail-coverts barred yellowish and green, tail dusky with yellowish-green on outer rectrices; forehead to back of head bright red, nape yellow, face-sides pale brown, underparts barred evenly and regularly pale yellow and dusky olive-green; eyes deep red, bill grey above, pale grey below. Female similar but has olive-green cap.

Ssp. Monotypic (W Co, NW Ec)

Habits Poorly known. Forages alone or in pairs, sometimes with mixed flocks.
Status Virtually endemic to Colombia, being rare to uncommon in Ecuador.
Habitat Tropical Zone. Very humid to wet forests of foothills and lower slopes.
Voice No descriptions found.
Note Formerly considered a subspecies of Red-stained (S&M) or Golden-collared Woodpeckers (H&B).

LITTLE WOODPECKER

Veniliornis passerinus Pl. 134

Identification 14–15cm. Very dull but distinctive; almost entirely olive, more yellowish above with rows of white spots on wing-coverts; forecrown to nape scarlet-red, head to breast barred finely yellowish-olive, the bars becoming white and broader on flanks, still white but finer and closer on undertail-coverts; tail dusky with whitish barring on outer rectrices; a pure white line trails from lores to malar and onto neck-sides. Female similar but top of head greyish and streaked slightly whitish. Juvenile like female but is clearly spotted (with dots) on top of head.

Ssp. *V. p. agilis* (E Ec, SE Co) well-marked eyebrow as well as moustache
V. p. fidelis (C & E Co, W Ve) as described; very similar to *modestus*, but bars on tail yellowish and breast tends to be spotted rather than barred
V. p. modestus (NE Ve) as *fidelis*, but slightly more yellowish above, red on head slightly paler, bars on tail whitish, markings on breast tend to be more clearly barred
V. p. passerinus (Gu, FG) small, bill pale, face lacks pale stripes, grey forehead, more warmly coloured below, with more narrow pale bars than other races here

Habits Forages quietly (often unnoticed), at all levels, alone or in pairs, usually with mixed flocks, and in bamboo. Diet includes ants, termites, beetles, grub and insect larvae.
Status Uncommon in Ecuador, frequent in Colombia, Venezuela and Guyana. Not found in Suriname (H&M). Common in eastern coastal French Guiana, much less so in the interior where Golden-collared is more common.
Habitat Tropical Zone. Borders of humid forest, both *terra firme* and *várzea*, old mangroves, gallery and water-edge forests with bamboo, secondary woodland, gardens, forest stands in savannas.
Voice A dry high-pitched rattle, and sometimes long repetitions of same *wika* note (H&B).

YELLOW-VENTED WOODPECKER

Veniliornis dignus Pl. 134

Identification 15–18cm. Male yellowish-olive above with yellow spots on lesser and median wing-coverts, yellow barring on uppertail-coverts and outer rectrices; Top of head to upper mantle (scalloped on mantle) bright red, face-sides dusky with yellowish-white eyebrow and moustachial; underparts yellowish-white with dusky barring, even and close on throat and upper breast, then dark bars wider, but more widely spaced and fading out on flanks; eyes deep red, bill dark grey above, bluish-grey below. Female has red restricted to nape and upper mantle. Rather similar Bar-bellied Woodpecker has continual, even, ochre and white barring.

Ssp. *V. d. abdominalis* (Co and Ve: Tamá) as described
V. d. baezae (E Ec) more evenly barred below, paler barring on throat

V. d. dignus (W Ec, Co: Andes) longer bill than *baezae*; paler abdomen, more lemon, less yellow; less prominent barring on uppertail-coverts, broader and darker barring on breast, the bars being brighter and more sharply defined

Habits Forages calmly, alone or in pairs, from mid levels to canopy. Often joins mixed flocks.
Status Rare to uncommon in Ecuador, frequent in Colombia.
Habitat Upper Tropical to Subtropical Zones. Humid, wet and cloud forests, interior and at borders.
Voice Seldom calls, a *krrrrrrrrr* rattle (P. Coopmans).

SMOKY-BROWN WOODPECKER
Veniliornis fumigatus Pl. 134

Identification 16.5–18cm. Male has upperparts olive-brown, darker on tail-coverts and blackish on tail; forehead to nape bright red with a few dark streaks; face-sides and underparts olive, malar dusky; eyes dark red, bill blackish. Female lacks red on head, instead is a little more dusky brown.

Ssp. *V. f. fumigatus* (Ec, Co, Ve) as described
V. f. obscuratus (SW Ec) darker

Habits Forages quietly, mostly at mid levels, alone or in pairs, usually with mixed flocks.
Status Uncommon to locally frequent in Ecuador, uncommon in Colombia and Venezuela.
Habitat Tropical to Temperate Zones. Interior and borders of humid or wet forests, and dense or light second-growth woodland.
Voice Seldom calls. A high-pitched piping rattle, a single, short *chuck* and gasping *whicker* (H&B), also a loud, fast *chk-skwizazazazah* (R&G).
Note Status and distribution of races uncertain and confusing. Recent publications (including Rodner *et al.*, SCJ&W and W&C) appear in error. Phelps (1972: 28) synonymised *reichenbachi* and *tectricalis*, Chapman synonymised *aureus* (*fide* Zimmer) and Zimmer (1942a) *exsul*, all under *fumigatus*, leaving nominate as only race in Venezuela and Colombia. Race *obscuratus* extends from Peru to southern Ecuador, and birds in central Ecuador apparently are intermediate between it and nominate.

RED-RUMPED WOODPECKER
Veniliornis kirkii Pl. 134

Identification 15–16.5cm. Male yellowish-olive above, with olivaceous-yellow nape, top of head bright red with scattered black streaks, rump and uppertail-coverts bright red, tail dusky with white barring on outer rectrices; face-sides and from chin to undertail-coverts barred dusky and white, chin and throat whitish. Female has dark grey head instead of red.

Ssp. *V. k. cecilii* (W Ec, W Co) as described; smallest race
V. k. continentalis (NE Co, N & W Ve) slightly larger, broader white bars below dark bars, which are blacker
V. k. kirkii (T&T, NE Ve) larger than either above, olive barring below
V. k. monticola (SE Ve: Pantepui, Gu) largest race, heavy dark barring below

Habits Forages from mid levels to canopy, alone, in pairs or small groups, often with mixed flocks. Diet mostly small and mid-sized boring insects and their larvae.
Status Uncommon in Ecuador, Colombia and Venezuela, uncommon in Trinidad & Tobago.
Habitat Tropical to Subtropical Zones. Various lowland and foothill forests, from humid to drier, gallery, deciduous and secondary, plantations and savanna woodland. Edges of mangroves and gardens at edge of towns.
Voice A loud *keeeeer*, like a kiskadee (H&B), a repeated, nasal *quee* or *keee* or *kenh* note, alone or sometimes paired with a *yik* note – *quee-yik, quee-yik* (W&C, H&B, P. Coopmans).

BAR-BELLIED WOODPECKER
Veniliornis nigriceps Pl. 134

Identification 17–19cm. Male yellowish olive-green above, dark brown tail with white barring on outer rectrices, top of head clean bright vermilion-red, extensive white eyebrow from supraloral to rear ear-coverts, which are dusky and have thin white streaks that also reach buffy throat, neck-sides and onto ochre breast and underparts where they become full bars. From Yellow-vented Woodpecker by obvious barring on belly.

Ssp. *V. n. equifasciatus* (Ec, Co) as described
V. n. pectoralis (S Ec?) darker below, with pale bars narrower than the brown

Habits Forages quietly, at all levels (often in undergrowth), alone or in pairs, usually with mixed flocks.
Status Uncommon to rare in Ecuador, uncommon in Colombia.
Habitat Subtropical Zone to Páramo. Humid montane, cloud and elfin forests, especially with dense undergrowth of *Chusquea* bamboo. Stands of woodland in páramo (*Polylepis* and others).
Voice Seldom calls. A long series of *kee* notes (P. Coopmans) or sometimes a single *chik* (R&G).
Note Race *pectoralis* listed for Ecuador by Winkler *et al.*, but not by R&G, Winkler & Christie nor Dickermann.

CRIMSON-MANTLED WOODPECKER
Piculus rivolii Pl. 135

Identification 24–28cm. Much variation in brightness and intensity of red and yellow regardless of age. Adult male almost entirely crimson-reddish above, but feathers have brown bases and bright red fringes, resulting in slightly mottled effect, and black bases to feathers on top of head give different mottled effect; rump tricoloured with olive and yellow-white barring and a crimson wash; uppertail-coverts barred pale sulphur and black; tail blackish. Whitish mask from nostrils slightly above and below eyes to ear-coverts; malar crimson; chin and throat black with white specks; breast has tricoloured scaling, each feather has black base, a white V crescent, broad black outer edge and red fringes, whilst over rest of underparts the red fringing is replaced by yellow, becoming pale ochraceous-yellow on undertail-coverts. Adult female has forehead to crown black and malar also all black; chin and throat black with less white spotting than male, and less red on breast. Juvenile browner above, the feathers having darker, dusky bases, with brightest red on nape, forehead to back of head black, malar is black, chin and upper throat profusely barred black and white, becoming scaling on lower throat to lower breast, then pale yellowish-buffy. Immature acquires patchy red on top of head and brighter red fringes to back, and males have patchy red on forecrown and malar as well.

Ssp. *P. r. brevirostris* (Ec, SW Co) shorter bill; male flecked black from forehead to rear crown, whilst female is black on top of head, flecked black on red nape; mask pale yellow

P. r. meridae (W Ve) shorter bill; male has black chin and deeper yellow below, rump and uppertail-coverts almost entirely black (slight olive barring on rump); female has chin and throat well spotted white and buffy underparts like female *rivolii*

P. r. quindiuna (NC Co) like *rivolii*, female has a little red on crown

P. r. rivolii (W Ve, EC Co) as described

P. r. zuliensis (Co, Ve: Perijá) male has rump and uppertail-coverts black, chin and throat well spotted white; female is blacker on breast and brighter red above

Habits Forages from low levels to canopy, alone or in pairs, often with mixed flocks. Searches for insects and grubs on mossy, epiphyte-covered branches, exploring, gleaning and probing cracks, crevices and leaves. Also takes ants from ground. Rarely hammers.

Status Uncommon to rare in Ecuador, frequent in Colombia, locally frequent in Venezuela.

Habitat Subtropical Zone to Páramo borders. Humid, wet, cloud and elfin forests, sometimes in scrub above treeline or even in *Espeletia* bushes at edge of open páramo.

Voice Mostly silent. Occasionally a rising *kre-ep* or series of rapid *kick* notes (H&B). A rolling *churrrr-r-r* (F&K).

GOLDEN-OLIVE WOODPECKER

Piculus rubiginosus Pl. 135

Identification 18–23cm. Quite variable age, sex and individual variation within any race. Adult male has entire upperparts yellowish-olive, barred narrowly whitish on uppertail-coverts, tail distally black. Female lacks red malar, and has black and white streaks on chin and throat. Top of head from forehead to back of head mid grey, darker at sides; postocular line and nape crimson-red; mask from nostrils through eyes to ear-coverts buffy-white, flecked faintly grey; malar crimson, blackish at base; chin and throat finely streaked black and white; underparts grade from black with well-spaced narrow yellowish lines on breast through even bars to yellow undertail-coverts with well-spaced black bars.

Ssp. *P. r. alleni* (Co: Santa Marta) large; golden-bronze above with reddish tone; rump unbarred, weak vestigial barring on uppertail-coverts; black throat with some white spots, breast bars narrow

P. r. buenavistae (E Ec, Co: E Andes, east slope) very large; back reddish-bronze, whitish cheeks, rump and uppertail-coverts well barred

P. r. coloratus (extreme SE Ec) more golden greenish-olive above, belly and flanks bright yellow, barred only on flanks

P. r. deltanus (E Ve) small; more greenish above, throat has large white streaks

P. r. guianae (S Ve: Gran Sabana to Amazonas) darker grey crown and darker yellowish-olive back; mask buffy, grey on ear-coverts, red malar shorter than other races, male well barred with blackish

P. r. gularis (Co: C Andes) fairly large; throat black with sparse spotting; paler below

P. r. meridensis (Co: Perijá, Ve: Perijá to Táchira) larger than *rubiginosus*; male has more red on nape (less grey); more golden-olive above, barring below more grey and yellow than blackish and whitish; rump and uppertail-coverts barred as underparts, throat well streaked, upper breast has heavy white barring

P. r. paraquensis (SC Ve) larger; very bronzed above; very little red on head which is largely dark grey, red only on nape; very little red on female, and may lack red altogether

P. r. rubiginosus (NC, NE Ve) as described

P. r. rubripileus (W Ec, SW Co) like *gularis* but smaller and has blacker breast bars

P. r. tobagensis (To) slightly larger than *trinitatis* with a heavier bill; breast bars broad and more greenish than blackish

P. r. trinitatis (Tr) smaller than *tobagensis*, with smaller bill; bronze-olive above, band below blackish to brownish-black, mask yellowish white; smaller than *rubiginosus* but very similar in general appearance

P. r. viridissimus (SE Ve: Auyán-tepui) rather large; dull greenish-olive above, dusky wash to mantle, with very weak pale and narrow barring on uppertail-coverts; forehead blackish becoming grey on crown, mask very dull, pale buffy-grey on lores, barred blackish and grey on ear-coverts; chin and throat black, more spotted white than streaked; breast black with narrow whitish bars, barring becoming greyer and more evenly spaced on flanks and belly to undertail-coverts

P. r. nigriceps (Gu, Su, FG) top of head black (no grey), red of nape reduced to an obscure broken line on male (missing on female); back and wings bright yellowish-green.

Habits Forages alone or in pairs, in canopy and at mid levels, often with mixed canopy flocks. In arid areas forages on cacti. Hammers into bark in search of grubs and wood-boring insects. Picks ants and termites from nests, and tears into bromeliads and cacao pods to reach insects inside. Very occasionally, takes fruits or berries.

Status Locally common in Ecuador, frequent in Colombia and Venezuela, common in Trinidad & Tobago, frequent in Guyana, common in Suriname; uncommon and local in French Guiana.

Habitat Tropical to Subtropical Zones, 200–3,100m over region, but fair variation within it. Humid montane and cloud

forests, wet mossy forests with epiphytes, humid mature second growth, clearings and treefalls with tall scattered trees, dry deciduous forests (pine, oak and others), mangroves, riparian woods, coffee plantations, lines of trees along fences.
Voice Contact a hoarse, loud shriek, and also a loud rattle call (H&M). A very loud and strong *geep* or *keer*, and an odd *utzia-deek* (H&B). A ringing, strident *tree- tree- tree- tree- tree- tree*, from exposed perch (R&G).

YELLOW-THROATED WOODPECKER
Piculus flavigula Pl. 135

Identification 18–20cm. Male green above with dark primaries and tail, barred yellowish on uppertail-coverts, green fringes to rectrices; entire top of head vermilion-red, smallish red malar, rest of head yellow; breast to undertail-coverts scaled, scalloped and barred black and white. Female has only nape red, rest of top of head yellow, streaked green.

Ssp. *P. f. flavigula* (E Co, Ve, Gu, Su, FG) as described
P. f. magnus (E Ec, SE Co, S Ve) male lacks red malar, female has red from rear crown to nape

Habits Forages alone or in pairs, often with mixed flocks, from mid levels to treetops. Diet includes termites and ants.
Status Rare in Ecuador, frequent in Colombia, locally frequent in Venezuela, frequent in Guyana and Suriname, uncommon in French Guiana.
Habitat Lower Tropical Zone. Humid *terra firme* and *várzea* forests, sandy ridge forests, riverine habitats, stands of woods in savannas.
Voice A 2-note *queea queea* and decelerating *kee kee kee kee*… (H&B).
Note Reported specimens of an apparently undescribed subspecies from south-west Colombia (Winkler *et al.*) are actually Lita Woodpecker.

LITA WOODPECKER
Piculus litae Pl. 135

Identification 17–18cm. Male dull and dark olive-green above, reddish-brown on primaries; entire top of head crimson-red, lores and mask through ear-coverts dark olive-green, large moustachial, supramalar yellow, malar crimson; underparts from chin to undertail-coverts first white becoming yellow, barred dark olive-green, the bars formed by shallow Vs, darkest and heaviest on lower breast and flanks. Female only has red on nape, lacking red on front and top of head, and also red moustachial. Juvenile lacks all red, but has emergent yellow moustachial. Duller and washed green below.

Ssp. Monotypic (NW Ec, W Co)

Habits Forages from mid levels to subcanopy, alone or in pairs, and regularly with mixed flocks.
Status Uncommon in Ecuador and Colombia.
Habitat Tropical Zone. Humid and wet forests on lower slopes, in foothills and lowlands.
Voice A hissing *peessh* or *shreeyr* (W&C).
Note Formerly considered a subspecies of White-throated Woodpecker (S&M).

GOLDEN-GREEN WOODPECKER
Piculus chrysochloros Pl. 135

Identification 18–24cm. Male golden, washed green above; entire top of head bright scarlet-red, lores to ear-coverts yellowish-green, lower face-sides golden-yellow with red malar, and rest of underparts golden-yellow with some dark olive barring from breast to flanks; eyes pale yellowish-grey. Juvenile similar but has red-orange to vermilion crown, and malar has more green than red. Female lacks red on head, instead is golden-yellow, washed over head-sides, nape and malar with green. Juvenile female similar but has green wash over top of head, with ear-coverts and malar darker.

Ssp. *P. c aurosus* (N Co) like *xanthochlorus*, breast blacker barring, brighter golden-yellow
P. c. capistratus (Ec, C Co, S Ve, Gu, Su) above much greener, throat barred. Largest race
P. c. guianensis (FG) like *capistratus* but throat unbarred
P. c. xanthochlorus (NE Co, NW Ve) as described

Habits Forages alone or in pairs, often with mixed canopy flocks, and usually in canopy. Gleans amid branches and foliage and also digs grubs from under bark. Diet includes spiders and insects, especially ants and termites, often taken from nests.
Status Rare in Ecuador, frequent in Colombia, uncommon in Guyana and French Guiana, rare in Suriname.
Habitat Lower Tropical Zone. *Várzea*, humid to drier *terra firme*, deciduous woods, xerophytic woodland or scrub. Often near water. Restricted to the canopy of the tall *terra firme* forest in French Guiana.
Voice Seldom calls, one to several piercing *shreeyr* notes (R&G).

WHITE-THROATED WOODPECKER
Piculus leucolaemus Pl. 135

Identification 19–20cm. Male olivaceous-green above with top of head vermilion-red bordered by olive-green to nape; lores to ear-coverts and neck-sides golden-yellow with green crescent on ear-coverts; large red malar, chin and throat white; breast blackish becoming white with black V-shaped scallops on undertail-coverts. Female only has red on rear of head – crown, forehead and malar olive-green.

Ssp. Monotypic (E Ec, NW Co)

Habits Usually forages alone, sometimes with mixed flocks, from mid levels to subcanopy.
Status Rare in Ecuador, uncommon in Colombia.
Habitat Tropical Zone. Humid and wet forests on lower slopes, and *várzea* and *terra firme* in lowlands, forest borders and river edges, second-growth woodland.
Voice Seldom calls, a grating, sibilant *piiissh* or *shreeeyr* (W&C).

SPOT-BREASTED WOODPECKER
Chrysoptilus punctigula Pl. 134

Identification 18–21cm. Highly variable in all races, both above and below; bars above and spots below vary in size and shape. Male dark bronze-green above, barred black, from mantle to tip of tail; forehead and crown black, rear crown to nape vermilion-red, eyebrow and head-sides white, malar bright red, chin and throat black with white speckles, underparts yellow, flushed red on breast with slightly irregular rows of round black spots to undertail-coverts. Female similar, but lacks red moustachial.

Ssp. *C. p. guttatus* (Ec) male duller and darker green above; forehead and crown black, back of head to nape red; female has black on head reaching farther back; black streaked red moustachial, breast warm olive with heavy spotting

C. p. punctigula (Guianas) as described, smallest race

C. p. punctipectus (Ve) bright greyish-olive above with widely spaced bars; rump and uppertail-coverts yellowish-buff; red malar infused black on entire length; underparts lack red flush; scattered round black spots, but none on belly and undertail-coverts more sparsely spotted

C. p. speciosus (Ec, SE Co) like *guttatus*

C. p. striatigularis (WC Co) paler olive-green above, reddish tinge to rump and breast; throat white with a few black streaks, below heavily spotted

C. p. ujhelyii (N Co) breast bright reddish-orange, crown almost entirely red with black restricted to forehead and forecrown (variable), back almost unbarred

C. p. zuliae (NW Ve) yellowish-olive above, barred black; rump and uppertail-coverts buffy-yellow with black heart-shaped spots; forehead to crown black with red bases, back of head and nape red; chin and throat black with nearly triangular-shaped white spots, malar red with black base, breast well spotted with heart-shaped spots

Habits Forages alone or in pairs, from subcanopy to lower levels, sometimes on ground for brief periods, where it may pick ants, even by breaking open anthills.

Status Uncommon to rare in Ecuador, locally frequent in Colombia and Venezuela, frequent in Guyana and Suriname and French Guiana.

Habitat Lower Tropical Zone. Often near water. Open areas with scattered trees, scrub, light primary and secondary woodland, coffee and other plantations, mangroves, riverine woods.

Voice A repeated *week-a, week-a*… to greet conspecific, series of high-pitched notes that begin and end with lower notes, *wha-whe-whe-whe-whe-whe-whe-whe-wha*, and *ta-wick* (H&B); a repeated high-pitched, nasal *wha* or *kah*, or *keeh* notes (W&C). A loud yelling cry (H&M).

Note Placed in *Colaptes* by some authors on basis of similarity, but differences are greater and we agree with R&G and Hilty in retaining *Chrysoptilus*.

CAMPO FLICKER

Colaptes campestris Pl. 136

Identification 28–31cm. Male mid-brown above with long pointed tail, feathers of back and wings have broad white fringes affording completely scaled appearance, rump and uppertail-coverts barred black and white, tail with white barring on outer fringes of outer rectrices. Top of head black, head-sides to nape, neck-sides and breast golden-buffy; malar red with a few black and white spots, chin, throat and bib black, with a few white marks on throat; belly to undertail-coverts white barred blackish; eyes bright red, long bill black, legs and feet greenish-grey. Female similar but has black malar, flecked with white.

Ssp. *C. c. campestris* (Su)

Habits Forages alone or in pairs, occasionally in small groups, on trunks or canopy of trees, but mostly on ground, searching termite and anthills, around rocks, fallen logs or base of trees or cacti. May be seen flying long distances between solitary trees.

Status Mainly southern South America, and occurs in our region only in Sipaliwini savannas of Suriname, where fairly common.

Habitat Tropical to Subtropical Zones. Open savannas with scattered trees or copses.

Voice Calls mostly in flight, a loud *kyoo-kyookyoo-kyek, kyek, keyk, kyek* (H&M).

ANDEAN FLICKER

Colaptes rupicola Pl. 136

Identification 32cm. Adult black above, barred whitish on back and white on wings; top of head black, head-sides, chin, throat and breast cinnamon, black malar with patch of bright red at end, breast has shallow black scallops; sides and belly to undertail-coverts, rump and uppertail-coverts, golden ochraceous yellow with a few, small and vestigial blackish bars on flanks and long uppertail-coverts; edges of long back tail spotted yellow; eyes bright yellow, bill black, thighs, legs and feet yellow.

Ssp. *C. r. cinereicapillus* (extreme SE Ec)

Habits Forages on or near ground, in groups of 4–5 to more than a dozen. Feeds on large insects (beetles, moths, crickets and their grubs or larvae), dug from soil or plucked from base of bushes or grass tussocks. Fond of grassy, rock-strewn slopes, where perches on high spot and then drops to walk or hop around stones, even in dense grass. Nests in holes that it digs out in cliffs, road cuts or riverbanks.

Status Rare or occasional in Ecuador, where first recorded in 1991.

Habitat Temperate Zone to Páramo. Open, rocky montane areas with bushes and grasses, ravines, puna, copses of *Polylepis*, edge of treeline forests.

Voice A loud *tew-tew-tew* whistle, similar to Greater Yellowlegs; *peek* or *keek* notes in contact; long, descending, musical trills in advertisement from a rock lookout; and a loud *kwa-kwa-kwa wee-a wee-a* in display (W&C). One or several loud, piercing *kweeir!* whistles and a *kli-kli-kli* series (R&G).

WAVED WOODPECKER

Celeus undatus Pl. 136

Identification 23–24cm. Entirely rich reddish-brown, paler on head, darker above, darkest on breast, barred evenly black on back and wings, slightly more sparsely on uppertail-coverts and tail, a few black spots on lower throat, dense black scaling on breast, becoming barring on belly and sides; large vermilion-red malar; eyes red, bill yellow with pale blue base and cutting edges, legs and feet grey. Female lacks red moustachial and is finely spotted on sides of face and throat.

Ssp. *C. u. amarcurensis* (NE Ve) as described, darker and crest plain
C. u. undatus (E Ve, Guianas) head paler, finely barred throughout

Habits Forages in pairs, in canopy and upper mid levels. Searches for insects (ants, termites, beetles, grubs) on foliage and under bark, and takes seeds and berries. Often heard hammering.
Status Uncommon to fairly common in Venezuela. Frequent in Guyana and Suriname and French Guiana.
Habitat Lower Tropical Zone. Lowland forests and stands of forest in savannas, often in riparian areas.
Voice Not noisy. Call a repeated double note, the first liquid and musical, the other a descending growl (H&M), also a loud *wit-koa* and a very soft, ascending *kowahair* (W&C). Voice virtually identical with that of Scaly-breasted Woodpecker, with each species responding to playback of the other (D. Ascanio pers. com.).

SCALY-BREASTED WOODPECKER

Celeus grammicus Pl. 136

Identification 23–26cm. Male entirely reddish-brown, cinnamon on undertail-coverts, nape to lower back and wings, throat and flanks barred black, breast, belly and sides double-scaled; rump and uppertail-coverts pale yellowish sage-green and unmarked, as are cinnamon undertail-coverts; eyes red, very large, fish-tail moustachial is crimson-red; bill yellow with pale blue base and cutting edges; legs and feet greenish-grey. Female similar, but lacks moustachial, and scales on breast bold but single.

Ssp. *C. g. grammicus* (SE Co, S Ve) more heavily barred
C. g. verreauxii (E Ec, E Co) less heavily barred

Habits Forages on trunks and thick branches from mid levels to canopy. Alone, in pairs or often small family groups, and regularly with mixed flocks. Drills for wood-boring insects and gleans from bark. Diet also includes fruit.
Status Uncommon in Ecuador and Colombia, uncommon to locally frequent in Venezuela.
Habitat Lower Tropical Zone. Humid lowland forests, *várzea* and *terra firme*, mature secondary woodland, stands of trees in savannas.
Voice Several clearly enunciated whistles, a fast, nasal *curry-kuuu* and *doit-gua*. Also, 2–4 metallic *pring!* notes (H&B, W&C). Voice virtually identical with that of Waved Woodpecker, with each species responding to playback of the other (D. Ascanio pers. com.).

CREAM-COLOURED WOODPECKER

Celeus flavus Pl. 136

Identification 24–28cm. Male almost entirely rich golden cream with brown smaller wing-coverts and cinnamon greater coverts and remiges, tertials fringed broadly cream; tail black; broad malar bright red with small white streaks; eyes red, bill yellow with touch of pale blue near base of lower mandible. Female similar but lacks red moustachial.

Ssp. *C. f. flavus* (E Co, S Ve, Guianas) as described; most rufous in wing
C. f. semicinnamomeus (E Ve) wing-coverts yellowish-white instead of chestnut or brown, and remiges are cinnamon instead of chestnut or brown
C. f. peruvianus (Ec, SE Co) brown on wings instead of rufous

Habits Forages in pairs, occasionally a lone bird or small family group, at mid levels and in subcanopy. Picks termites by breaking into arboreal nests, and also feeds on ants, seeds, small fruit and grubs.
Status Uncommon in Ecuador and Colombia, locally frequent to common in Venezuela, frequent in Guyana, scarcer in Suriname. Locally common in coastal French Guiana.
Habitat Lower Tropical Zone. Wet, swampy forest, mangroves, humid plantations (coffee), wet riparian areas.
Voice A loud, high laugh (H&M) or a laughing *wutchuk… kee-hoohoo-hoo-hoo, pueer, pueer, purr, paw* (W&C).
Note Short recognised just 4 races, mentioning problems with intergrades, difficulty of assigning races and considered racial limits to be arbitrary. He does not even mention *semicinnamomeus*, which was synonymised by Peters (1948), but maintained by Phelps & Phelps (1958), who believed Peters made the change in error. R&G suggested combining all Amazonian populations under one name, whilst Dickinson (2003) followed Short. An unresolved aspect and not discussed, is the extent of variation within a given population, and reasons for the variation. Clearly, much further study is needed to avoid further assumptions.

CINNAMON WOODPECKER

Celeus loricatus Pl. 136

Identification 19–23cm. Male reddish-rufous above to rump, barred black from mantle to rump and wings, uppertail-coverts creamy with black bars, tail black with well-spaced, narrow white bars; head and breast to flanks cinnamon with black spots on forehead and forecrown, washed russet on crown and chin whilst throat is scarlet red; barred black from breast to flanks, rest of underparts creamy white with pale scallops; eyes red, bill dark horn. Female lacks red throat.

Ssp. *C. l. innotatus* (N Co) head lacks spotting and barring, red throat patch slightly smaller, underparts pale creamy with faint grey spots and scallops on breast and sides; wings and back cinnamon, tail barred broadly white, narrowly black
C. l. loricatus (W Ec, W Co) as described; well barred
C. l. mentalis (NW Co) spotted black on forehead and

crown, fairly uniform cinnamon head and upperparts, lightly and sparsely barred above, mostly on uppertail-coverts, underparts pale creamy white, regularly barred black, tail barred evenly black and white

Habits Forages in canopy, alone or in pairs, seldom with mixed flocks. Feeds on termites and ants by gleaning and drilling into bark and termite nests, and also on fruits and berries.
Status Uncommon in both Ecuador and Colombia.
Habitat Lower Tropical Zone. Interior of humid and wet forests and mature second growth. Occasionally at borders and even in partially open areas next to forest.
Voice Calls 4–5 sudden, descending *PHET! phet! phet! phet! phet!* notes (H&B). Also, a fast, descending *peee-peew-peu-peu* that sometimes begins with *chuweeoo* or *chikikikirik*, a squeaky *tititit-too* and *chwee-titit* (W&C). Hammering slow and short.

RINGED WOODPECKER
Celeus torquatus Pl. 136

Identification 26–28cm. Male has entire head buffy-cinnamon with broad supramalar red and very broad black collar from nape and upper mantle to lower throat and upper breast; rest of upperparts rich reddish-brown, with black subterminal crescents on wing-coverts, bars on remiges and rectrices, tail tipped black; underparts uniform cinnamon, eyes red, bill drab horn. Female as male but lacks red on head-sides.

Ssp. *C. t. occidentalis* (E Ec, Co, S Ve) black only on breast, heavily barred above and below
C. t. torquatus (E Ve, Guianas) as described

Habits Forages from mid levels to canopy, on thick trunks and branches. Diet insects (ants, termites), and also takes berries, small fruits, catkins.
Status Rare in Ecuador, rare (few records) and possibly quite local in Colombia, uncommon to rare in Venezuela, uncommon in Guyana, rare in Suriname.
Habitat Lower Tropical Zone. Tall, humid *terra firme*, mature second growth and gallery forest, and drier sandy soil and savanna forests.
Voice Loud whistled notes – *kuu kuu kuu kuu kuu kuu* – resembling Least Pygmy Owl *Glaucidium minutissimum* (W&C) or very loud, ringing *kuu! kuu! kuu! kuu! kuut!* (H&B).

RUFOUS-HEADED WOODPECKER
Celeus spectabilis Pl. 136

Identification 26–28cm. Male has head chocolate-brown with broad crimson postocular band to back of head, the sides joining on incipient crest, and a broad crimson malar; breast and tail black; rest of body and wings (except cinnamon tertials and remiges) creamy yellow with brightly contrasting black bars, except patch on neck-sides, rump and uppertail-coverts, and body-sides (covered mostly by folded wings) yellow. Female similar but lacks red on head.

Ssp. *C. s. spectabilis* (E Ec)

Habits Poorly known. Forages at lower levels, including fallen trees, to subcanopy, alone or in pairs. Apparently drills bamboo in search of boring insects.
Status Rare in Ecuador.
Habitat Lower Tropical Zone. Humid forests, mostly riparian (river edge, river islands), where *Heliconia*, *Cecropia* or *Gynerium* canes abound, and also in bamboo (thickets of *Chusquea* or stands of *Guadua*).
Voice Sequence of a loud, squeaky *skweeeak!* or *squeeeah!* followed by a bubbling *kluh-kluh-kluh-kluh-kluh*… (W&C, R&G).

CHESTNUT WOODPECKER
Celeus elegans Pl. 136

Identification 26–32cm. Extremely variable geographically, from all cinnamon with cream head to entirely deep brown. Common elements are: very broad and extensive crimson malar and black tail; eyes dark brown with pale blue orbital skin, bill yellow with pale blue-grey tip. Like most woodpeckers, female is the same, but lacks red on head.

Ssp. *C. e. citreopygius* (Ec, Co) deep chocolate-chestnut head and upperparts, rump and uppertail-coverts dull orange, underparts deep umber-brown
C. e. deltanus (NE Ve) intermediate between *hellmayri* and *jumanus*
C. e. elegans (Su, FG) crest pale buffy, rest of bird cinnamon, paler on rump and uppertail-coverts
C. e. hellmayri (E Ve, Gu, Su?) like *jumanus* but has cream-coloured crest
C. e. jumanus (SW Ve, SE Co) reddish-chestnut crest, rump yellow; uppertail-coverts orange; rest deep chocolate-chestnut
C. e. leotaudi (Tr) like *elegans* but smaller and brighter, and crest more orange

Habits Forages alone or in pairs, on trunks and thick branches, from mid levels and subcanopy to top of trees. Often in mixed canopy flocks. Feeds on insects, especially ants and termites, taken from bark or by hacking into arboreal nests. Also takes *Cecropia* catkins, berries and fruits. Hammers loudly in double taps.
Status Uncommon in Ecuador, frequent in Colombia, locally frequent in Venezuela, frequent in Guyana and Suriname, uncommon on Trinidad (no records Tobago), uncommon in French Guiana.
Habitat Lower Tropical Zone. Mangroves, sand-ridge, gallery and humid *terra firme* forests; *várzea*, stands of forest in savannas, mature second growth, coffee and cocoa plantations.
Voice Descending series of musical notes: *wewa ew-ew-ew-ew-ew*. Also, some short, screechy calls: *whee-jar* and *keeeaaaa* (H&M).
Note Race *hellmayri* listed as occurring in Suriname by Peters (1948), but not by H&M.

LINEATED WOODPECKER
Dryocopus lineatus Pl. 137

Identification 30–36cm. Top of head scarlet, running a short way on back of neck, face-sides black, lores and ear-coverts to back of neck black, as is mantle and lower back, wings and rump to tail; white supramalar to head-sides and down neck-sides; scapulars broadly white, converging but not joining: \ /; black chin and throat to breast; rest of underparts white with black V marks forming rough bars; eyes yellow, eye-ring red, bill black with grey base to lower mandible. Female similar but lacks red malar. From other large black-and-white woodpeckers by distinct white lines on scapulars that do not join in V; Crimson-crested has white scapulars in V, as does Guayaquil Woodpecker, which also has boldly barred rump.

Ssp. *D. l. fuscipennis* (W Ec) smaller and distinctly browner, underparts orange to buffy
D. l. lineatus (W Co, Ve, Tr, Guianas) as described

Habits Forages mostly in pairs, mid levels to canopy, on thick trunks and limbs. Sometimes in mixed flocks of understorey birds (antwrens, woodcreepers). Roosts in tree holes.
Status Uncommon in Ecuador, common and widespread in Colombia and Venezuela, frequent in Guyana, common in Trinidad (no records Tobago), common in Suriname.
Habitat Tropical Zone. Mangroves, tall, humid forests, scattered woods in savannas, sand-ridge and deciduous forests.
Voice Calls frequently, a loud, unmistakable *keck! krrrrrrrrrrrr!*, which betrays presence instantly. Hammers intermittently, but often for several minutes, tapping very loudly 6–7 times and then rapping.
Note Race *nuperus* one of 6 considered insufficiently differentiated from nominate to warrant recognition (W&C, Dickinson 2003).

POWERFUL WOODPECKER
Campephilus pollens Pl. 137

Identification 32–37cm. Male has top of head in pyramid-shaped tuft of crimson; bold white line from base of bill (malar) and lores and to neck-sides, then on neck-sides to corners of breast; chin to throat and breast black, rest of upperparts black with white scapulars that join in V shape; rump white. Underparts heavily barred with V-shaped rows of rough barring, black on cinnamon; eyes pink, bill black. Female similar but lacks red on head, black instead. White rump diagnostic. Female from other large woodpeckers by black-and-white head. Male from female Lineated by converging white stripes on back, and from males of all other large woodpecker by thickly barred red-and-black underparts. Crimson-bellied has all-black back and wings.

Ssp. *C. p. pollens* (Ec, Co, W Ve)

Habits Forages alone or in pairs, from understorey to subcanopy, on thick trunks and branches.
Status Rare in Ecuador, locally frequent to scarce in Colombia and in Venezuela.
Habitat Subtropical to Temperate Zones. Humid to wet forests, mostly interior but sometimes at borders.
Voice A loud *udd'daa-da-da*, quite different from congeners (H&B). A frequent, nasal *kyaaah* or *peeyaw*, a fast *kikikikikawh* in flight and descending *kikikiki-keh-keh-kah-kah* when excited (W&C). Hammers a doubled *tap-tap* with both equally loud.

Note All northern South American *Campephilus* woodpeckers were formerly placed in genus *Phloeoceastes*.

RED-NECKED WOODPECKER
Campephilus rubricollis Pl. 137

Identification 30–32cm. Male has small bicoloured, black-and-white ellipse below ear-coverts, rest of head and neck bright scarlet-red, upperparts black with rufous at base of primaries; underparts reddish-cinnamon; eyes white to pale sulphur-yellow, bill ivory to yellow-bone. Female has extended broad white malar, edged above and below with black. From all other large, red-crested woodpeckers by reddish-cinnamon underparts and no white markings on back. Crimson-crested has bold white lines and V on back.

Ssp. *C. r. rubricollis* (C Co, S Ve, Guianas) as described; rufous in wings
C. r. trachelopyrus (S Ec) large red basal patch on primaries and outer secondaries

Habits Forages mostly in pairs, sometimes in small family groups, from mid levels to subcanopy. Feeds on larvae, grubs and wood-boring insects.
Status Rare in Ecuador, locally frequent in Colombia, frequent in Venezuela and Guyana, common in Suriname and French Guiana.
Habitat Tropical Zone. Humid forests from lowlands to lower slopes, cloud and sandy soil forests, *várzea*, savanna woodlands, gallery forests, mature second-growth woodland.
Voice A loud, nasal, drawn-out *khiaaaah* (H&M); also a sudden loud *querra-querra* (W&C). Hammers with a hard and soft tap, the 2 repeated at a slow pace, sometimes for long periods.

CRIMSON-BELLIED WOODPECKER
Campephilus haematogaster Pl. 137

Identification 33–34cm. Male has black eyebrow, yellowish-buffy patch over nostrils, lores and broad line on face-sides that joins yellowish-buffy postocular line behind ear-coverts, the 2 separated by a broad black postocular line; chin and throat black, trailing down foreneck in a series of scallops, and rest of head and neck scarlet-red; underparts red with black barring on flanks; eyes reddish-brown, bill dark grey. Female very similar, but has yellowish-buffy ear-coverts continuing as a line on neck-sides, with solid black foreneck. Only large woodpecker with 2 clear, pale-coloured stripes on face: a broad malar and thinner superciliary. All-red rump also distinctive. Lineated and Guayaquil Woodpeckers both have V-shaped white lines on back, and black or barred rumps.

Ssp. *C. h. haematogaster* (E Ec, E Co) as described
C. h. splendens (W Ec, W Co) red tips on throat and foreneck; narrowly barred blackish on upper rump and entire underparts

Habits Forages alone, sometimes in pairs, quietly climbing and exploring large trunks at lower levels. Where vegetation is dense, keeps to underbrush.
Status Rare in Ecuador, uncommon in Colombia.

Habitat Tropical to Subtropical Zones. Interior of humid and wet forests, from lowlands to montane slopes.
Voice Race *haematogaster* utters a low rattle (H&B) or loud *stk! st-kr-r-r-r-r-r-r-r*. Race *splendens* drums with a strong double tapping (W&C).
Note Form *C. h. splendens* sometimes considered a separate species, Splendid Woodpecker.

GUAYAQUIL WOODPECKER

Campephilus guayaquilensis Pl. 137

Identification 32–34cm. Male has small bicoloured, black-and-white ellipse below ear-coverts, rest of head bright scarlet-red, chin and throat black with some red flecks; neck black with broad white line either side; back black with white scapulars that join in V, wings dark brown; rump and uppertail-coverts black with broad buffy fringes affording scalloped or barred effect, tail brown, with black fringes; underparts barred black and buffy. Female similar but lacks black-and-white ellipse on face-sides and has small white frontal bar that joins white malar that, in turn, joins white lines on neck-sides. Lineated Woodpecker has white on scapulars not joining in a V and rump all black.

Ssp. Monotypic (W Ec, SW Co)

Habits Forages in pairs, at upper levels and in canopy, on thicker limbs and dead branches. Feeds on grubs, larvae and wood-boring insects.
Status Very small range on Pacific coast, from Colombia to northern Peru, rare to uncommon throughout.
Habitat Tropical Zone. Mangroves, humid to dry, deciduous forests, mature second-growth woodland.
Voice Hammers a doubled tap-tap with both taps equally loud.

CRIMSON-CRESTED WOODPECKER

Campephilus melanoleucos Pl. 137

Identification 33–38cm. Male has small bicoloured, black-and-white ellipse below ear-coverts, rest of head bright scarlet-red, lores and spot at base of malar white, chin and throat black; neck black with broad white line either side, back black with white scapulars that join in V, wings, rump, uppertail-coverts and tail black; underparts boldly barred black and white. From Red-necked Woodpecker by white in neck and barred breast and belly, from Lineated Woodpecker by white V on back.

Ssp. *C. m. malherbii* (N & W Co, W Ve) black and white barring below
C. m. melanoleucos (E Ec, E Co, Ve, Tr, Gu, Su, FG) black and buffy-tan barring below, but distinguished from Powerful Woodpecker by black rump

Habits Forages mostly in pairs, at upper levels and canopy, on thicker trunks and limbs. Takes insects (butterflies, beetles, termites, grubs, larvae) and berries.
Status Common in Ecuador, frequent in Colombia, uncommon on Trinidad (no records Tobago), frequent in Guyana, Suriname and French Guiana.
Habitat Tropical to Subtropical Zones. Humid, swampy and riparian lowland forests, wetter areas of sandy ridge forests, mangroves, coffee plantations, savanna woodland.
Voice Mostly quiet. Series of fluted notes resembling a tree-frog, *kweer, kweer, kai-ai-ai-ai* in contact (W&C), a reedy, vibrating *chis-sic* and reedy, lisping *tttt-he-he-he* (H&B). Hammers a short roll of 5 taps (compared with long roll of Lineated and 2 single taps of Red-necked), with the first tap stronger.

FURNARIIDAE – Ovenbirds and Woodcreepers

Traditional furnariids are indeed a motley crew – tails, bills, crests and caps, leg-length, facial marks, general jizz, and attitude change from one genus to the next. Their colours, however, remain rather similar, brown, white and grey. Often referred to rather sweepingly as ovenbirds, only a few species really build 'ovens', i.e. round nests of clay or mud. According to the latest revision of the family, that by Remsen (2003), of 236 furnariids 210 species are endemic to South America. In woodcreepers, plumage also takes the form of subtle variations on rufous, brown, buff and black. Bills, on the other hand, range from short and straight to unbelievably long and curved, from very thin to very broad and strong. The tail-feathers have very strong shafts and often terminate in spines that make them perfect props when the birds hop-climb tree trunks. Woodcreepers occur from central Mexico to northern Argentina, with the greatest number of species in northern South America and Brazil. Under traditional taxonomy (Peters' *Check-list*, for example), furnariids were placed as the second family in the order Passeriformes, following woodcreepers (Dendrocolaptidae). Such placement 'felt' suitable for woodcreepers, which may appear superficially intermediate between woodpeckers and more passerine-like ovenbirds. Nowadays, Dendrocolaptidae and Furnariidae are known to be offshoots from the same origin. For a while, accepted treatment was to invert the order of the two families, but more recently, following genetic studies by Chesser (2004b) and others, the SACC has elected to include them all under the Furnariidae, where genera that formerly comprised Dendrocolaptidae are placed at the end, following those of the original Furnariidae. Under the present arrangement, however, genetic studies indicate that the genera *Sclerurus* and *Geositta* are basal to all others, in other words, they are source of all other genera, and, if Dendrocolaptidae and Furnariidae were to be treated separately, then *Sclerurus* and *Geositta* would have to be separated as well, and form the family Scleruridae. In sharp contrast to some families that are close relatives within the Passeriformes (i.e. Thamnophilidae), there is little sexual dimorphism, that is, birds of both sexes are, for most part, identical. One aspect of behaviour that shows remarkable variety in furnariids is nest architecture: mud 'ovens' in horneros, balls of sticks with sock-like tubular entrances in *Synallaxis* spinetails, concealed, massive clumps of grass in *Cranioleuca* spinetails, large well-woven baskets in canasteros, cosy domed cups of *Espeletia* leaves and soft mosses in thistletails, burrows dug into earth banks in leaftossers, foliage-gleaners and treehunters, holes on trees in *Xenops*, fantastically huge contraptions of twigs that defy gravity in thornbirds. This variety made for a most interesting study of relationships within the family based just on nest architecture (Zyskowski & Prum 1999). Woodcreepers, on the other hand, all nest in tree-trunk holes, hollows, nooks and crannies, some building flimsy cup nests in small sheltered spots.

Additional references for this family include: Vaurie (1971, 1980), Marantz (1997), Zyskowski & Prum (1999), Remsen (2003, hereafter Remsen) and Marantz, Aleixo, Bevier & Patten (2003, hereafter as Marantz).

Geositta miners are birds of open terrain that fly straight and strong, and display with song-flights (a character unique within Furnariidae). All have notched tails and wings with distinctive markings. They nest in self-excavated tunnels or burrows that they take over from other small vertebrates, within which they place a simple platform of grasses and leaves or soft bark strips.

SLENDER-BILLED MINER

Geositta tenuirostris Pl. 138

Identification 16cm. Rather rotund with short tail and long bill. Adult uniform brown above with paler fringes to median and greater coverts and rufous secondaries that form a longitudinal stripe on closed wing, but solid block of rufous in flight, basal two-thirds of tail-feathers, except central pair, also rufous; underparts white, washed faintly pale buffy and well covered on breast and sides with faint brown streaks. Bill long, thin, slightly decurved, dark horn with a pale horn base, legs and feet grey. Juvenile has dark centres to feathers from forehead to uppertail-coverts, most noticeable on back.

Ssp. *G. t. kalimayae* (C Ec: Cotopaxi, Chimborazo)

Habits Forages alone or in pairs, walking or running to dig out or pick insects and worms from ground. Flight strong and straight. As well as in flight, males often also perch atop a rock or boulder to sing. Not shy.

Status Rare and local in Ecuador, where first found in 1990.

Habitat Temperate Zone to Páramo, *c.*3,300–4,000m. High Andes in open, arid areas, scrub, grasslands and cultivated fields or highland pastures, usually near streams or ponds.

Voice Song is accelerating repetitions of *jit* or *keek* notes, lasting 30 s or so. Various sharp notes, including *keeeeek, week-week, chwea* and a nasal *kyeenh* (Remsen).

Note Race *kalimayae* recently described by Krabbe (1992).

Cinclodes always live at high altitudes in partially open areas and near water, with the exception of Surf Cinclodes which occurs on rocky Peruvian beaches, running on the sand or in the trail of waves. They are somewhat reminiscent of thrushes – sturdy birds that stand upright and proud – but with shorter legs. In flight, they show characteristic rufous wingbars and rufous tail-corners. The genus is particularly southern – most of the 13 species occur south of the equator. A characteristic is the slow wing-flapping displays made while singing from a perch, which serve well to show the highly contrasting wingbars. Nests are pads of grass and soft bark or leaf strips, placed at the end of burrows excavated in dirt banks or mud walls, sometimes even in old buildings.

BAR-WINGED CINCLODES

Cinclodes fuscus Pl. 138

Identification 15–18.5cm. Adult heavily built, olive-brown above, darker on flight-feathers; some rufous on median wing-coverts and fringes of greater coverts, base of remiges rufous, showing as band across wing in flight, white supercilium and black cheeks striated white; chin and throat to centre of belly white with rows of dusky marks, rest of underparts olive-brown as back, feathers from breast to flanks having olive-brown fringes, giving faint scaled effect.

Ssp. *C. f. albidiventris* (Ec) back has reddish tone, outer web of outer rectrices and tips of all but central pair pale grey, deep cinnamon wingbars, fore supercilium buffy, chin and throat pure white without spots, browner breast with obvious pale centres to feathers

C. f. heterurus (W Ve: páramos from Mérida to Lara) differs from *oreobates* in that 3 outer rectrices are almost all bright cinnamon, middle rectrices more rufescent

C. f. oreobates (Co: Santa Marta & E & C Andes, Ve: Páramo de Tamá) less rufescent above, webs of outer pair and tips of all rectrices except middle pair white, eyebrow buffy, throat spotted, underparts entirely white with slight olive wash on flanks and thighs

C. f. paramo (extreme N Ec?, SW Co: Nariño) see below

Habits Forages on ground, alone or in loose pairs, walking or running in short spurts to pick insects and seeds from ground in both dry and muddy spots, or glean them from low foliage. Digs only rarely, unlike Stout-billed Cinclodes, which digs and probes constantly. Flicks tail and wings frequently and when singing. Often perches on a rock or boulder to survey area.

Status Frequent to common in Ecuador, locally frequent in Colombia, frequent to common in Venezuela, where range recently extended; found on Páramo de Tamá, Táchira (Calchi 1995). More numerous higher in altitudinal range.

Habitat Temperate Zone to Páramo, *c.*3,200–5,000m. Páramo grasslands and bushy, rocky, barren or scrubby fields. Usually near streams or ponds or in wet, boggy meadows, especially at lower elevations. May be found around villages and settlements.

Voice Song a short, rising, fast and high trill, *tetet't't't't't't't* (H&B) or *t-r-r-r-r-r-r-r-r-r-t* (Remsen); call a sharp *pfip!* (H&B), or a sharp *tsip* whistle and high tinkling notes (Remsen).

Notes Race *paramo* considered invalid by Remsen, based on extensive overlap in measurements of wing and tail, which were characters used to differentiate it from *oreobates*.

STOUT-BILLED CINCLODES

Cinclodes excelsior Pl. 138

Identification 20–22cm. Sturdy with long black bill. Adult olive-brown above with base of remiges rufous forming a bright, poorly defined wingbar in flight, long white eyebrow bordered black above and below, cheeks black well striated white; chin and throat white, rest of underparts buffy, washed olive-brown with dark fringes to breast and flanks giving a weak scaled effect. Eyes brown, bill black and slightly decurved, legs and feet brown.

Ssp. *C. e. columbianus* (Co: C Andes) darker above, paler below, rufous wingbar better defined
C. e. excelsior (Ec) as described, finely barred throat

Habits Forages on ground, in pairs or small family groups. Walks about probing and poking in ground, in wet or dry spots, looking for insects, seeds and small frogs. Displays from a perch by flapping wings and singing.

Status Uncommon to frequent in Ecuador, locally frequent (but scarcer than Bar-winged) in Colombia.

Habitat Temperate Zone to Páramo, 3,000–4,500m. Rocky, bushy or grassy fields on páramo, wet, boggy meadows, and barren areas, woodland borders at treeline, elfin forest and copses of *Polylepis*.

Voice Song a high *tr-r-r-r-r-r-r-reet* trill, and in flight, a *trrip-reep-reep* trill. Calls include a nasal *kiu*, *druut* and *ken-eek*, and in flight low twittering notes (Remsen).

Notes Formerly placed in *Upucerthia* and by Vaurie (1980) in *Geositta*, but F&K found this incorrect based on behaviour. Formerly, also treated as race of Royal Cinclodes *C. aricomae*, of south Peruvian Andes. Correct spelling of subspecies is *columbianus*, not *columbiana* nor *colombianus* (David & Gosselin 2002)

Being its oldest genus, *Furnarius* gives its name to the family, even if comparatively speaking it is a small genus (six species). Horneros are stocky and strut about, with fairly long, slender bills, short tails and long legs, reminiscent of thrushes. They inhabit open and semi-open areas, and forage on ground but are not entirely terrestrial. Main colours are rufous and white. Pairs sing loud, boisterous duets. They build remarkable 'oven' nests, spherical, smooth and made of mud, with a side opening, placed atop a post or horizontal branch and lined with pads of grass and soft vegetable matter. A nest may weigh as much as 5kg, whilst the birds' weight may be no more than 50g.

LESSER HORNERO *Furnarius minor* Pl. 138

Identification 15cm. Bright orange-rufous above, crown grey, white eyebrow, dusky ear-coverts with fine white streaks becoming rufous then white on malar, chin and throat white, breast, sides, flanks and thighs cinnamon, central belly to undertail-coverts white. Eyes dark brown, short black bill slightly decurved, legs and feet dusky. Much paler and smaller than Pale-billed Hornero which has buffy eyestripe, long thin yellow bill and pale horn-coloured legs and feet.

Ssp. Monotypic (E Ec, SE Co)

Habits Forages quietly on or close to ground in vegetation near water edge.

Status Rare to uncommon in Ecuador, where first recorded 1975. Scarce to possibly frequent in parts of Colombia, where mostly known from sight records.

Habitat Lower Tropical Zone, to 300m. *Várzea* and riparian forests, river islands of Amazonian basin.

Voice Song a fast and falling sequence of high *kee* notes, call a scratchy *krik* (R&G).

PALE-BILLED HORNERO

Furnarius torridus Pl. 138

Identification 18.5cm. Deep rufous above with slate grey crown, long white eyebrow, greyish at lores, head-sides grey becoming rufous on malar, chin and throat white, breast and sides deep rufous, belly, flanks and thighs cinnamon, undertail-coverts cream. Eyes brown, bill horn, grey on culmen, legs and feet flesh.

Ssp. Monotypic (NE Ec, SE Co: Amazon tributaries)

Habits Forages on or near ground, usually alone, often near water. Likes leaf-litter and flips leaves over as it goes.

Status In Ecuador, very rare and possibly just only wanders to extreme north-east. In Colombia, uncommon or scarce (recent sight records from Amacayacu National Park).

Habitat Lower Tropical Zone. *Várzea* and riparian forests, river islands of Amazonian basin.

Voice Song like Pale-legged Hornero (race unknown); call a loud *chek* (Remsen).

Notes Formerly treated as dark morph of *F. leucopus* (Vaurie 1973, 1980) or a race of *F. leucopus* (H&B, following Cory & Hellmayr (1925). Present treatment follows Zimmer (1936a), R&G and SACC. Called Bay Hornero in R&G. Recent data on this species from Peru in Rosenberg (1990).

PALE-LEGGED HORNERO

Furnarius leucopus Pl. 138

Identification 16.5–19cm. Essentially rufous above with grey crown, pale eyebrow, rufous head-sides, white chin and throat, rufous breast and sides, pale belly and vent. Eyes brown, bill long and yellowish, legs and feet horn. Juvenile has dark flecks on breast. Some confusion over taxonomy (see below). We acknowledge 3 groups that might be recognised as species.

Ssp. Pacific Hornero, *cinnamomeus* group
F. (l.) cinnamomeus (SW Ec) bright orange-rufous above, crown buffy-grey, broad pale buffy eyebrow, malar area, chin and throat white, breast to undertail-coverts creamy white, washed very lightly cinnamon; eyes very pale orange, surrounded by

vague grey ring, long rather decurved bill black above, horn below, legs and feet pale brown

Pale-legged Hornero, *leucopus* group

F. (*l.*) *leucopus* (SW Gu, possibly SE Ve?) bright orange-rufous above, white eyebrow, only breast rufescent, belly to flanks and thighs pale cinnamon, undertail-coverts white with dusky streaks, pink legs and feet

F. (*l.*) *tricolor* (E Ec: Río Morona) has greyer crown, more ochraceous back, paler than wings and tail, dark eyes, pink legs and feet

Caribbean Hornero, *longirostris* group

F. (*l.*) *longirostris* (N & NE Co: Caribbean region, NW Ve: N Zulia, W Falcón & Lara) greyish-olive crown, buffy eyebrow, bright rufous below with white throat, centre of belly and vent, undertail-coverts pale cinnamon, flesh-coloured legs and feet. Birds from state of Lara, N Venezuela have grey crowns, white eyebrows, and are distinctly paler, almost entirely white below (see below)

F. (*l.*) *endoecus* (NC Co: Middle & Upper Magdalena basin & Antioquia; NW Ve: S Zulia) has darker, more brown/less ochre upperparts, dark undertail-coverts

Habits Forages alone or sometimes in pairs, searching for insects mostly on ground, inspecting grass and leaf-litter, sometimes flipping leaves, and often checking anthills. Walks as if showing off, with big steps, or hops on lowest twigs of shrubbery. Sometimes on dirt tracks.

Status Race *cinnamomeus* common to very common in lowland west Ecuador. Race *endoecus* frequent and race *longirostris* common in Colombia. In Venezuela and Guyana, a frequent species.

Habitat Tropical to Temperate Zones, *c.*1,500–2,500m. Partially wooded areas and semi-open terrain with bushes, deciduous forest in dry to moist areas with muddy borders of streams or wetlands, pastures and agricultural areas.

Voice Races *longirostris* and *endoecus* sing a sudden, rising then falling sequence of notes: *teer-teer-teer-teer*… (H&B). Race *leucopus* has an explosive, descending staccato series; call a loud *chet* or *kyeek* (Remsen). Race *cinnamomeus* sings frequently, call a frequent, loud and clear *kyeek* and scratchy *krik*. Frequently heard song an arresting and almost raucous fast series of loud, piercing and descending *kee* notes, sometimes uttered by pair together, heads tilted back (R&G).

Notes Range of *F. leucopus* quite disjunct and there are significant differences between races in size, habitat, behaviour and voice, but no formal revision has been published. Race *cinnamomeus* perhaps a separate species and might include races *longirostris* and *endoecus*, though these may constitute a separate species of their own (Remsen). *Cinnamomeus* treated specifically, as Pacific Hornero, in R&G, whilst race *longirostris* (and *endoecus*) similarly, as Caribbean Hornero, in Hilty, both following on R&T. Clements & Shany (2001) also point out that more than one species may be involved, specifically naming Pacific Hornero, and Remsen mentions that *tricolor* has been treated specifically. Race *tricolor* recently recorded in Ecuador, in Río Morona region (Krabbe 2004). Birds labelled *longirostris* from Lara, Venezuela, are visually distinct, and currently under investigation for vocalisation comparisons, etc. (Restall & Ascanio in prep).

Leptasthenura tit-spinetails occur in bushy areas on high mountains. All are small and nimble, and very pretty. They have tiny stubby bills and their tails are highly graduated, the 2 central feathers very long and almost streamer-like. Nests vary slightly within this genus of 10 species – small open cups or domed balls of grasses, placed in narrow rock crevices, treeholes, abandoned domed nests or in well-protected nooks between a branch and the trunk.

ANDEAN TIT-SPINETAIL

Leptasthenura andicola Pl. 142

Identification 16.5cm. Rounded body and head, tiny bill and long bifurcated tail. Dusky above with rufous streaks on head, white streaks on nape and back to uppertail-coverts, wings have rufous fringes, tail uniformly dark. White eyebrow, head-sides dark finely streaked pale, underparts dusky, streaked white from chin to breast, belly to undertail-coverts unstreaked. Juvenile and immature resemble adult but have top of head only rufous and dusky streaked, whilst adult has some buffy and whitish admixed, also young have warmer, tawny wash on flanks, with feathers having dusky fringes, but not easy to see; young juveniles have tail square-ended.

Ssp. *L. a. andicola* (Ec, Co: C Andes) as described

L. a. certhia (W Ve) like *extima* but wing-band is smaller, wing-coverts have almost no fringes, crown-stripes paler, belly greyer, and throat, chest and streaks on back whiter

L. a. exterior (Co: E Andes) upperparts much browner, rufous streaks on head brighter, underparts buffy to cinnamon with dark streaks rather than white, undertail-coverts white

L. a. extima (Co: Santa Marta) smaller than nominate, with broader and more rufescent fringes to wing-feathers, white streaks on mantle broad and bold, narrower and buffier eyebrow, throat densely spotted, breast virtually unstreaked, some pale streaks on flanks, undertail-coverts pale buffy-grey

Habits Forages in pairs or small groups usually inside foliage. Gleans small insects from low bushes and grasses, or picks from ground, moving nimbly and restlessly. Pokes into epiphytes, seed heads and flowers. Flies furtively through tall grasses and low bushes, or flushes rapidly to hide low. Sometimes joins mixed flocks of thistletails, *Catamenia* seedeaters and other small birds, or forages in company of White-throated Tyrannulet, which is amongst most ubiquitous species in such habitat.

Status Uncommon to frequent in Ecuador, where there is an isolated population on Cordillera of Las Lagunillas (Zamora-Chinchipe). Frequent in Colombia and Venezuela.

Habitat Temperate Zone to Páramo, *c*.3,200–4,400m. Elfin forest and stunted woodland near treeline, copses of *Polylepis*, patches of scrub on steep slopes, open fields in páramo in arid, moist or humid areas, fields of *Espeletia* and other low bushes.
Voice A feeble tinkling *tez-dit* or *tez-dit-dit*; a high squeal that resembles a mammal (H&B). Song a very high, descending series of notes beginning and ending in a trill. Call a hesitating series of short high trills, a monotone trill, a weak, high *tee-zit*, and in contact, a *zit* or *tik*, or *tzi-dik* (Remsen).
Note Isolated population in Ecuador may be a separate subspecies (N. Krabbe in R&G).

Schizoeaca thistletails occur in shrubbery near treeline. They are small and plump, with thin stubby bills and heads that resemble a wren. Their most striking feature are their tails, which are very graduated and loose, and often described as 'attenuated' or 'decomposed'; in reality they look like someone stuck them onto the bird in a hurry. To date, nests of only 2 of 8 species in the genus have been described – in both cases, a ball of grasses, mosses and other soft vegetable matter, with a side entrance, covered on outside with mosses and placed on low vegetation. In all probability, the others have similar nests.

PERIJÁ THISTLETAIL

Schizoeaca perijana Pl. 142

Identification 20.5–22cm. Fairly uniform dark brown above with a buffy eyebrow and narrow white eye-ring; tiny patch of orange on chin, otherwise is slightly paler and more greyish below. Eyes dark, bill thin and pointed, pale grey at base, legs and feet grey; long tail well over half total length and is a ragged-looking bundle of shafts.

Ssp. Monotypic (Ve & Co: Perijá)

Habits Forages alone or in pairs, moving briskly to glean insects in shrubbery.
Status Vulnerable. Tiny range on highest ridges of Cordillera de Perijá, on Venezuela/Colombia border. Possibly locally frequent to common. Specimens from both sides of border, but no-one has surveyed area since early 1970s, as it is controlled by Colombian terrorists. Recent expeditions to lower elevations by Phelps Ornithological Collection have ascertained that higher-elevation forests are apparently still quite intact, at least on Venezuelan side.
Habitat Temperate Zone to Páramo, 2,900–3,400m. Elfin forest, thickets, bushy fields and open grassy areas around treeline.
Voice No recordings or published descriptions found.
Note In revision by Vaurie (1980), all taxa in *Schizoeaca* were treated as races of single species, *S. fuliginosa*, contrary to traditional treatment. However, F&K, R&T continued to maintain them as separate species following Remsen's revision. We follow Remsen (1981, 2003) in maintaining traditional species.

OCHRE-BROWED THISTLETAIL

Schizoeaca coryi Pl. 142

Identification 18cm. Uniform brown above with rufous-orange face and chin and slightly paler eyebrow, whitish throat, rest of underparts greyish-buffy. Juvenile similar but has white chin and finely barred underparts. Tail is long and looks split and somewhat dishevelled; bill dark above, pale horn below.

Ssp. Monotypic (Ve: Andes)

Habits Forages alone or in pairs, gleaning insects as it moves briskly through foliage at lower levels. Seldom seen in open and is very secretive. Often forages on ground under bushes. Sometimes joins mixed flocks of small páramo birds, e.g. Plain-coloured Seedeater, Plumbeous Sierra Finch and Andean Tit-Spinetail.
Status Venezuelan endemic. Irregularly distributed in páramos from northern Táchira to northern Trujillo, it is locally common in many places, especially at higher elevations.
Habitat Temperate Zone to Páramo, 2,500–4,100m. Thickets and hedges around treeline, elfin and *Polylepis* woods, *Espeletia* fields and bushy páramo.
Voice Fairly quiet. While foraging, a high, nasal *meeeow* and mouse-like *peeeap*. In alarm, a high *PEE'd'deet*. Song a trill that speeds up then slows, *pipipi'pi'pi'pi'pi'pi-pi-pi-pi pi pi pi pt pt* (Hilty).
Note See previous species.

WHITE-CHINNED THISTLETAIL

Schizoeaca fuliginosa Pl. 142

Identification 18–19cm. Uniform ruddy brown above with a pale greyish eyebrow and narrow white eye-ring; white chin and grey underparts, becoming browner on flanks and undertail-coverts; tail long, pointed and somewhat dishevelled, eyes whitish.

Ssp. *S. f. fuliginosa* (N & C Ec, Co: C & E Andes, W Ve: S Táchira) reddish-brown back, grey underparts, white eyes, grey eyebrow
S. f. fumigata (S Co) darker back, browner underparts, dark eyes, white eyebrow, smaller chin spot

Habits Forages in pairs, flitting restlessly through dense foliage at lower levels. Fairly shy, cocks tail in alarm. Flight mostly relatively short spurts between bushes.
Status Uncommon to locally frequent in Ecuador. In Colombia locally frequent, but more common at upper end of altitudinal range. Locally frequent to common in Venezuela.
Habitat Temperate Zone to Páramo, 2,800–4,000m. Thickets, patches of bracken and hedges at treeline, elfin and *Polylepis* woods, treeline fringes of *Espeletia* fields and bushy páramo.
Voice A high, penetrating *tik*, sometimes in a long series; song a high, rising trill (H&B) or a speeding, rattled trill, *tik, tik, te te'te'tr't't'r'r'rrrrr* (Hilty). Also, a rising series of triple notes *tididit tididit, tididit!* and sharp *pyeek* or *chink* calls (P. Coopmans).
Notes We maintain traditional species limits, as in Remsen

(1981, 2003), rather than revision by Vaurie (1980), in which all taxa of *Schizoeaca* were treated as races of *S. fuliginosa*. *S. griseomurina*, whose range intersects the 2 northern races of *S. fuliginosa* (*fuliginosa* and *fumigata*) and 2 southern subspecies (*peruviana* of north Peru and *plengei* of central Peru), very probably evolved in parallel and is closely related to *S. fuliginosa* (Remsen).

MOUSE-COLOURED THISTLETAIL

Schizoeaca griseomurina Pl. 142

Identification 18.5–19cm. Uniform olive-brown above with noticeable white eye-ring, white chin, rest of underparts mouse grey, somewhat paler grey on central belly to undertail-coverts.

Ssp. Monotypic (S Ec)

Habits Forages in undergrowth, alone or in pairs, rarely with mixed flocks, flitting through dense foliage, sometimes coming briefly into open. Has habit of cocking tail and flapping wings.
Status Uncommon to locally frequent in Ecuador.
Habitat Temperate Zone to Páramo, 2,200–4,000m. Thickets and hedges at treeline, elfin and *Polylepis* woodland, grassy or shrubby páramo.
Voice Song a sequence of inflected notes followed by a trill, *sweei, sweei, swi, ti-ti-titi-trrrrr* (P. Coopmans). Calls include a descending *pseeeuw* and a sharp *peent* (R&G, Remsen)
Note See previous species.

Synallaxis spinetails are widespread and numerous – 33 species, with a few pending description, and undoubtedly others awaiting discovery. Most skulk in thickets near ground, are difficult to see and very similar: comparatively small, with long, graduated, double-pointed tails, lots of rufous in plumage, and in many, crown and shoulder patches of matching colours. Note that, in comparison, *Cranioleuca* are treetop specialists, at mid levels to canopy. Though many have very small ranges, 2–3 sympatric species is a common phenomenon. Their simple 2–3-note songs can be heard all day, making voice the best character for identification. Nests are large globes of grass and straw with a side entrance and reinforced ('thatched') roof. Some have long entrance tubes that may hang or curve outside or wind inside nest structure.

AZARA'S SPINETAIL

Synallaxis azarae Pl. 141

Identification 17–18cm. Entire body mouse grey, paler on belly and throat, rufous crown, wings and tail, dusky ear-coverts, blackish patch on centre of lower throat. Juvenile has paler throat with black and white barring on lower throat, buffy superciliary bordered above and below with dusky, underparts ochraceous except white belly

Ssp. *S. a. elegantior* (Co: E Andes, W Ve) much darker greyish on back, head-sides and breast, darker rufous and more brownish tail; 10 rectrices
S. a. media (N Ec, Co: W & C Andes) as described, 8 rectrices
S. a. ochracea (SW Ec) longer tailed, sometimes shows faint eyebrow and much paler below, 8 rectrices

Habits Look for rufous tail, wings and back of head, down to nape, that give upperparts a 2-tone contrast with olive-brown back. Forages in underbrush, alone or in pairs, flitting secretively inside thickets and vine tangles. Seldom found in mixed flocks.
Status Frequent to common and widespread in Ecuador, Colombia and Venezuela.
Habitat Subtropical to Temperate Zones, at 1,000–3,000m. Fallow fields and overgrown pastures, open areas with bracken, thickets along roadsides and at fringes of montane and cloud forests.
Voice Sings incessantly at dawn and in early morning, then frequently throughout day, a nasal 2-note call *be-quick* or *mac-white*, second note higher and more emphatic (Hilty). Also, a *trrrt* trill and infrequent, fast *kakakakakaka*.... (R&G). Song of *ochracea* similar but higher pitched.
Notes *S. azarae* presently treated as including 8 populations between western Venezuela to north-west Argentina. Formerly, *superciliosa* group (*superciliosa*, of north-west Argentina, and *samaipatae*, of south Bolivia) was considered a separate species (Buff-browed Spinetail), whilst *elegantior* group (all races in our region plus *fruticicola* from north Peru) was also treated specifically by Vaurie & Schwartz (1972), followed by F&K. Remsen *et al*. (1988) returned *superciliosa* group to *S. azarae*, based on vocal similarity and plumage variation found in all populations. For *elegantior* group, R&T considered that basis for separation used by Vaurie & Schwartz (vocal differences) was apparently inaccurate.

PALE-BREASTED SPINETAIL

Synallaxis albescens Pl. 141

Identification 16.5cm. Above mid greyish olive-brown with noticeable rufous patch on crown and somewhat brighter rufous lesser and median coverts. Below, whitish with black bases to throat-feathers, which show as spotty patch of variable size. Breast suffused warm, perhaps pinkish-grey, with some olive-brown wash on flanks. Look for long, greyish-brown tail (most other spinetails have rufous tails). Juvenile lacks rufous patches above and is much warmer brown below. Immature shows traces of rufous on crown and is more or less greyish-brown below with warm brown only on breast. Tepui Spinetail has wings and tail all brown, and Azara's Spinetail is similarly patterned but has body distinctly grey and a rufous tail.

Ssp. *S. a. inaequalis* (FG) pale greyish olive-brown above with bright orange-rufous crown patch and wing-coverts, breast and flanks greyish
S. a. insignis (EC Co, Ve: S Apure) has blackish centres to feathers of forehead that contrast with rufous crown patch, back fairly pale greyish-brown, and orange-rufous wing-coverts but not tertials
S. a. josephinae (S & SE Ve, Gu, Su) dark, warm grey

forehead and head-sides, contrasting with small dark rufous crown patch, above darkest and richest coloured, and crown patch and wing-coverts same dark rufous

S. a. latitabunda (NW Co) darker than nominate, with a browner tail, and similar to *josephinae* above, but browner on breast and flanks

S. a. littoralis (N Co: coast) is like *occipitalis* but browner above and paler below

S. a. nesiotis (Ve: Margarita & Cubagua Is.) dark forehead contrasting with orange-rufous crown patch, pale greyish-brown back, and pale orange-rufous lesser and median wing-coverts

S. a. occipitalis (N Co: Norte de Santander & Santander, NW Ve: Sierra de Perijá, Andes of Mérida & Táchira) very similar to *trinitatis* but paler, wing-coverts more orange-rufous, fuller and richer breast patch with undertail-coverts same colour (much paler on *trinitatis*)

S. a. perpallida (NE Co: Guajira Peninsula, NW Ve: coasts of Zulia & Falcón, Lara) pale yellowish-buffy forehead, extensive, bright, pale orange-rufous crown patch, and pale yellowish-buffy back; pale orange-rufous on wing includes greater coverts

S. a. trinitatis (Ve: Llanos, extreme N Amazonas, N Bolívar, Sucre & Monagas, Tr) shows almost no contrast between buffy forehead and rich rufous crown patch, warm buffy back, bright rufous on wings to greater coverts and, often, fringes of tertials

Habits Forages in undergrowth, usually in pairs, keeping in cover whilst looking for insects and spiders in foliage. Favours dense stands of *Borreria verticilata*. Seldom flies more than a few metres. Builds very large ball nests lined with snake skins. A favoured host of Striped Cuckoo.

Status Common in Colombia, common and widespread in Venezuela. In Trinidad, decreasing: considered frequent and widespread by ffrench (1976), but uncommon by ffrench (1996); does not occur on Tobago. Frequent in Guyana, common in Suriname, locally frequent to common in French Guiana.

Habitat Tropical Zone, to 2,100m. Humid forest borders, coffee plantations, undergrowth of sandy soil forest and scrub, savannas, fallow fields, open areas with dense grasses or bushes, shrubby road borders, marshes with reeds, mangrove.

Voice Calls rhythmically, in duets, repeated obsessively, a 2-note *wer-choo,* with second note higher and sharper. Said to sound like *wake up!*

Notes According to Vaurie (1980), geographic variation is so gradual as to invalidate all races. However, we found that characteristics of each to be consistent, if allowing for juveniles and immatures, and we follow Dickinson (2003). Race *hypoleuca* synonymised under *latitabunda* by Wetmore (1972) and Remsen; race *trinitatis* synonymised under *nesiotis* in Remsen, but not in Dickinson (2003). We maintain *trinitatis* based on specimens in Caracas, which show racial differences described above. On other hand, birds of Santa Marta, Colombia, cannot be assigned to extended *nesiotis*, as proposed in SCJ&W and Remsen, for then, extended range (including traditional range of *trinitatis*) would be divided into two by ranges of *occipitalis* and *perpallida*. Thus, we leave Santa Marta population unassigned to *occipitalis*, *perpallida* or *littoralis* until a comparative analysis is available for the species' entire range. *S. albescens* formerly included *S. albigularis*, but this taxon was split by Chapman (1931) and Zimmer (1936b). Thus, texts that show *S. albescens* in Ecuador reflect its former status as conspecific with *albigularis*.

SLATY SPINETAIL

Synallaxis brachyura Pl. 139

Identification 16.5cm. Body entirely grey with rufous wings and rufous crown to nape, tail dusky brown. Eyes brown, bill dark, legs and feet grey. Juvenile a straightforward paler and duller version of adult. Looks very slaty, much darker than other spinetails.

Ssp. *S. b. brachyura* (N Co: Antioquia, Magdalena Valley) deep rufous-chestnut crown, paler grey eyebrow, some silvery grey streaks on throat

S. b. caucae (C Co) generally paler grey and paler on head and wings

S. b. griseonucha (SW Ec) similar to *nigrofumosa*, with more silvery throat and whitish belly

S. b. nigrofumosa (NW & CW Ec, W Co) uniform deep slate grey and darker rufous than other races

Habits Forages in pairs or sometimes in small family groups, from undergrowth to mid levels, keeping mostly inside foliage.

Status Frequent to common in Ecuador and Colombia, where race *brachyura* mostly below 300m, whilst *caucae* and *nigrofumosa* are more common above 1,000m.

Habitat Tropical to Subtropical Zones, to *c.*2,000m. Light woodland, coffee plantations, shrubby borders and clearings, sometimes in gardens.

Voice Does not call obsessively like some others in genus. Song a low, churring sequence – *chut-chut-churrr* – that resembles a wren, and a grating, descending *turrrrrr* (H&B).

Notes Race *griseonucha* Chapman, 1923, synonymised under *chapmani* by Hellmayr (1925), but like R&T we consider it to be a valid race. Name *chapmani* was applied by Wetmore (1972) to populations in west Colombia and north-west Ecuador, but by Wiedenfeld *et al.* (1985) to those in south-west Ecuador. We follow Slud (1964) and Remsen in placing west Colombian and north-west Ecuadorian birds in *nigrofumosa*, as characters described for *chapmani* are within variation of *nigrofumosa*.

DARK-BREASTED SPINETAIL

Synallaxis albigularis Pl. 141

Identification 15–16cm. Adult has dark grey back, including dark grey wings with rufous fringes to coverts, all-rufous crown from dusky forehead to nape, grey head-sides, white throat, small black bib between throat and breast, grey becomes white on belly, but sides and flanks grey merges into buffy thighs and undertail-coverts. Look for comparatively short, olive-brown tail.

Ssp. *S. a. albigularis* (SE Ec: from S Napo, SE Co: extreme S Amazonas) as described
S. a. rodolphei (NE Ec: N Napo, C Co: Meta to Putumayo) generally darker

Habits Forages secretively, usually in pairs that search for insects at lower levels and sometimes on ground under bushes. Displays by raising feathers on throat so that it looks solid black.
Status Frequent to common in both Ecuador and Colombia.
Habitat Lower Tropical Zone to *c.*1,800m. Thickets and bushes at forest borders, overgrown clearings, bushy borders along roads, shrubbery and reeds near water, river islands, especially where there are patches of *Gynerium* cane and bushes of *Tessaria*.
Voice Calls frequently, usually from in foliage, but sometimes from a fairly visible spot. Call a short dropping sequence, *dit-dududu?* (H&B).
Notes Formerly treated as a race of *S. albescens*, but treated specifically by Chapman (1931) and Zimmer (1936b). Race *rodolphei* Bond, 1956, was not included in Peters.

DUSKY SPINETAIL *Synallaxis moesta* Pl. 141

Identification 15.5–16.5cm. Entire body and head slate grey, mantle darker, except deep rufous wings and crown, chin and throat darker with white spots, dark brown tail. Eyes brown, short sharp-pointed, black bill, dark legs and feet. No overlap with Slaty Spinetail; relatively thick-billed, shorter-tailed and much darker than other spinetails.

Ssp. *S. m. brunneicaudalis* (E Ec, S Co: SE Nariño) as described
S. m. moesta (Co: E slope of E Andes in S Casanare & NW Meta) paler and duller than *brunneicaudalis*, little or no contrast between nape, mantle and wings, is generally greyish-olive.
S. m. obscura (SE Co: E slope of Andes in Caquetá & Putumayo) darkest race, and deeper, browner on back, tail and underparts, face throat and breast uniform

Habits Forages in pairs or more rarely alone, keeping always to dense undergrowth, skulking secretively. Gleans insects from leaves and small twigs.
Status Uncommon to frequent and quite local in Ecuador, apparently scarce in Colombia.
Habitat Tropical Zone, 300–1,350m. Humid montane forest, secondary woodland, forest borders. Quite partial to stands of bamboo.
Voice Call a low, nasal churr, *rha-a-a-a-a-a-a-a-a* (R&G).
Note Race *brunneicaudalis* treated specifically in Cory & Hellmayr (1925).

MCCONNELL'S SPINETAIL
Synallaxis macconnelli Pl. 140

Identification 15–17cm. All brown with rufous wings and tail, ear-coverts to throat grey with some white spotting or barring. Juvenile paler, more prominently barred white on lower face rather than spotted.

Ssp. *S. m. macconnelli* (S Ve: tepuis of NE Amazonas and NW Bolívar, Cerro Neblina?) dark olive-brown, cheeks pale grey, bib blackish, both with white spots.
S. m. obscurior (SE Ve: tepuis of SE Bolívar, Guianas) darker olive-brown, lower face and bib blackish with reduced white spotting
S. m. yavii (S Ve: Cerro Yavi, NE Amazonas) pale olivaceous-brown underparts

Habits Usually forages in pairs, deep in dark undergrowth and very difficult to see. However, recorded singing at dawn from very low, somewhat exposed perches. Does not join mixed flocks, but very active and calls frequently when a flock passes through.
Status Uncommon but possibly frequent in Venezuela, where quite common on Escalera Road, eastern Bolívar. Scarce and local in Guyana, widespread and locally common in Suriname, uncommon to locally frequent in French Guiana.
Habitat Tropical Zone, 100–1,900m. Humid and wet forests on slopes of tepuis, wooded riparian areas with dense underbrush or dense bushes at borders of slow-moving rivers. Sometimes near small villages. In Venezuela, mostly above 1,000m, whilst in Guianas mostly in lowlands.
Voice Calls frequently throughout day, a repeated loud rattle or trill: *tir.r.r.r-ti-r.r… ti-r.r…* (H&M). Also, described as a low, weak, gravely churr, *trtrtrtrtr-dek!* (Hilty).
Notes Correct spelling of English name is McConnell's, not MacConnell's, but misspelling in scientific name comes from original description and therefore valid. Race *yavii* based on a single specimen, and Remsen suggests might be invalid. Race *griseipectus* synonymised under *macconnelli* by Remsen, but Hilty maintained *griseipectus* for east Bolívar birds, and did not assign birds from Cerro Neblina to any race. Race *macconnelli* formerly considered either under *S. cabanisi* or *S. moesta*; taxonomy confusing: first described as race of *cabanisi*, where it appears in Peters, then *cabanisi* was united with *moesta*, and thus became *S. moesta obscurior*. Then Vaurie (1980) pointed out that populations included in *S. moesta* have different numbers of tail-feathers (some 8, some 10) and separated eastern populations (8 rectrices) into separate species *S. macconnelli*, including *moesta* (which has 8 rectrices). Vaurie dismissed all existing races, but *macconnelli* type differs from *obscurior*. Race *macconnelli* has brown underparts and is a montane form, found at 1,000–1,900m, whilst *obscurior* has grey underparts and is a lowland bird found only below 700m. However, Vaurie stated that *S. cabanisi griseipectus* on Ptari-tepui (1,700–1,900m), near Roraima, is virtually identical to *obscurior*. This could mean that birds from Suriname should be called *S. macconnelli griseipectus* (which name has precedence). On other hand, Phelps Jr. (1972) had withdrawn that name, synonymising it under *macconnelli*. Thus, *obscurior* remains correct name for taxon in Suriname. To avoid a change in nomenclature that may prove to have been mistaken, Dickinson (2003) retains name *obscurior* for Suriname.

SILVERY-THROATED SPINETAIL

Synallaxis subpudica Pl. 139

Identification 17–19cm. Pale brown upperparts, including head-sides, pale cinnamon-rufous crown to nape, and wings; narrow buffy superciliary separating cinnamon crown from brown cheeks, malar whitish, chin and throat dark brownish-grey, rest of underparts buffy. Eyes brown, bill, legs and feet, grey.

Ssp. Monotypic (Co: E Andes)

Habits Forages mostly in pairs, gleaning insects at lower levels and in undergrowth.
Status Common Colombian endemic, especially numerous in Sabana de Bogotá above 2,100m.
Habitat Upper Tropical to Subtropical Zones, 1,200–3,200m. Montane forest and secondary woodland, in clearings and border thickets.
Voice A loud, falling, chipping chatter – *chi-chi-chi-ti-ti-ti-i-i* – often answered instantly by another (H&B). Calls include a sharp *kik* and a low trill in alarm (Remsen).

BLACKISH-HEADED SPINETAIL

Synallaxis tithys Pl. 140

Identification 14.5cm. Entire body and head slate grey, darkest on head, black on throat, bright rufous wings, brownish-grey tail; brown eye contrasts against dark grey of face. Look for black face and bright cinnamon-rufous wing-coverts in marked contrast with olivaceous-grey back.

Ssp. Monotypic (SW Ec)

Habits Forages in dense undergrowth and vine tangles, alone or more frequently in pairs that glean insects from lower foliage or pick them from ground. Furtive, rarely comes out in open or moves to mid levels. Has been recorded apparently foraging with mixed flocks.
Status Endangered. In Ecuador, generally rare to uncommon, but locally frequent at a few localities (Machalilla National Park). Range very small, severely fragmented and declining.
Habitat Tropical Zone, to *c*.1,000m, in drier evergreen, deciduous and secondary woodland with thickets and dense undergrowth.
Voice Very distinctive. Song a short, rising trill, *t-t-t-t-t-trit*, and then pauses few seconds, the sequence repeated over and over. Alarm-call *wee-di wee-di wee-di*… (P. Coopmans).

WHITE-BELLIED SPINETAIL

Synallaxis propinqua Pl. 139

Identification 16–17cm. Even grey above, from forehead to tail-coverts, bright rufous wings and tail, whitish malar and black bib, breast grey, fading into buffy over rest of underparts. Look for fairly long bill, a large patch of black on lower throat, white belly and grey breast.

Ssp. Monotypic (E Ec, Co: extreme S Amazonas, FG)

Habits Forages alone or in pairs, in lowest foliage or on ground, always keeping well inside vegetation. Quite fond of dense patches of *Gynerium* cane.
Status Very locally uncommon to frequent in Ecuador, probably uncommon and very local in French Guiana. In Colombia, recent sight records (Pearman 1993, SFP&M).
Habitat Lower Tropical Zone, to *c*.300m, always on river islands in Amazonia, in stands of cane, reedbeds and early growth (especially *Tessaria*).
Voice Calls very frequently. For Ecuador, described as an unusual low *ch-r-r-r-r-r-r-r-r* churr; a slower, scratchy *krreenh-kreeenh-kre-kre-kre-kre-kre* sequence, that is fast when bird nervous, and a doubled *kr-krreenh*.

PLAIN-CROWNED SPINETAIL

Synallaxis gujanensis Pl. 139

Identification 15–16.5cm. Warm brown above, from forehead to tail, with rufous wings and tail (contrast between back and wings not large), but looks concolorous in some lights. Underparts entirely buffy, nearly white on throat, washed brown from sides to undertail-coverts. Juvenile much darker below and finely barred dusky throughout.

Ssp. *S. g. columbiana* (Co: E Andes) much whiter underparts than nominate.
S. g. gujanensis (Ve, Guianas) as described
S. g. huallagae (E Ec) darker and greyer

Habits Forages in loose pairs, very low or on ground, in thick undergrowth. Very secretive, seldom, if ever, in open, but pairs constantly call. Moves with short, bouncy hops, cocking tail. Builds a large nest lined with shed snake skins and is often parasitised by Striped Cuckoo.
Status Frequent in Ecuador, frequent to locally very common in Colombia. In Venezuela, locally frequent in Bolívar, but scarcer and only at wide-scattered localities in Amazonas. Frequent in Guyana, common in Suriname, frequent in French Guiana, where widespread in littoral and local in interior around settlements.
Habitat Tropical to Lower Subtropical Zones, to 550m in Venezuela, *c*.400m in Ecuador and 1,200m in Colombia. Always at riverbanks, in riparian woodland or scrub, stands of *Gynerium* cane, early successional bushes and stands of *Cecropia*, wet areas, swamps, *várzea*, river islands.
Voice Song an abrupt *KEW!.. huaa*, with long pause between notes and usually elicits reply from mate (H&B, Hilty). In Suriname, sings in duets, rhythmical repetitions of *ke he* (H&M).
Note Race in Ecuador uncertain, provisionally assigned to *huallagae* by R&G (only a few specimens, collected in Río Aguarico in 1992).

MARAÑÓN SPINETAIL

Synallaxis maranonica Pl. 139

Identification 15.5cm. Entirely mousy brown, rather more greyish on breast, except rufous wings, with fine white streaking on throat.

Ssp. Monotypic (Ec)

Habits Usually forages in pairs, on ground or in undergrowth and lower levels of forest, always skulking in cover.

Status Vulnerable. Uncommon, but very locally frequent in Ecuador, where first recorded 1991. Range very small and declining, and has apparently been extirpated locally.
Habitat Upper Tropical Zone, 500–1,200m. Moist forest and deciduous woodland, occasionally wanders to higher, more humid forests.
Voice Song a very slow *kiweeu keeu*, then pauses several seconds, before sequence is repeated (R&G).
Note Formerly treated as a race of *S. gujanensis*, but now considered a species based on plumage and vocal differences (Vaurie 1980, S&M).

RUDDY SPINETAIL *Synallaxis rutilans* Pl. 139

Identification 14–15cm. Deep umber crown to uppertail-coverts, dark brown tail and undertail-coverts; black lores and throat, rest of face, from frontal band to ear-coverts, and below to flanks rich dark rufous-chestnut. Juvenile very dark brown, reddish-chestnut only on face, with buffy spots on throat and streaks on belly.

Ssp. *S. r. caquetensis* (E Ec, SE Co) deep mahogany-red of crown extends to back, flanks and belly olive-fuscous with hint of mahogany
S. r. dissors (Co & Ve: Orinoco basin, Gu, FG) mantle warmer than *rutilans*, less olivaceous; less rufous laterally and interscapular region lacks strong chestnut, being often entirely brown; scapulars mainly brown with much less chestnut; hindneck lacks rufous collar
S. r. rutilans (Su) like *dissors*, but more reddish-brown above, less dark, more extensive rufous below

Habits Forages in pairs for insects, near or on ground, searching leaf-litter and tangles of vines. Sometimes joins mixed understorey flocks.
Status Rare to uncommon and very local in Ecuador, where first recorded in 1936 but inadvertently omitted from the country's avifauna for many years after. Uncommon and local in Colombia, uncommon to locally frequent in Venezuela, uncommon in Guyana, rather common on sand ridges in coastal region of Suriname. In French Guiana, rare and possibly very local, first recorded only recently (1984).
Habitat Tropical Zone, race *caquetensis* to 250m in Ecuador, to 500m in Colombia; race *dissors* to 1,200m in Venezuela. Humid lowland *terra firme* and secondary woodland, slopes of tepuis. Often in dense bushes in treefall gaps, but not at forest borders. Absent from sandy soil forests.
Voice A nasal *kit-naaa* or *bik-waaa* (Venezuela, P. Schwartz recording), or a *kee-kawow* or *kee-kow* (Ecuador), repeated frequently (R&G, H&B).
Note Occurrence of race *rutilans* in Suriname considered doubtful, as it mainly occurs south of Amazon.

CHESTNUT-THROATED SPINETAIL
Synallaxis cherriei Pl. 140

Identification 14cm. Look for rufous throat and breast contrasting with dark grey belly. Ruddy Spinetail very similar, though deeper in coloration, with a black bib.

Ssp. *S. c. napoensis* (E Ec, SE Co: extreme S Amazonas) dark belly and patch of rufous on forehead small and bright

Habits Forages in pairs, at lower levels and on ground; checks clumps of dead leaves and tangles of lianas.
Status Near Threatened. Scarce throughout: very rare and local in Ecuador, where most records made in second growth, and possibly rare in Colombia, where first sighted recently, at Puerto Nariño, on Amazon, near Leticia and Amacayacu National Park (SCJ&W).
Habitat Tropical Zone, 200–1,000m, in humid forest and especially secondary woodland, forest borders, stands of *Guadua* bamboo.
Voice Song a 2-note frog-like trill, *trrrr tuuit, trrrr tuuit, trrrr tuuit*…, repeated frequently (R&G).
Note Race *napoensis* described from a specimen of uncertain locality, taken in Napo basin in 1930. Recent specimens from 2 localities in eastern Ecuador are different (as illustrated) and we agree with R&G that race *saturatus*, which was synonymised under *napoensis*, probably merits restoring.

RUFOUS SPINETAIL
Synallaxis unirufa Pl. 141

Identification 18cm. Entirely rufous, with black lores, black bill and reddish eyes.

Ssp. *S. u. meridana* (Co: Páramo de Tamá, on Ve border with SE Norte de Santander: Ve: Andes from Trujillo to Táchira) rich reddish-rufous, vestigial black spot on throat, bill all black; juvenile warm brown above, warm ochraceous below, washed brown on flanks, thighs and undertail-coverts; 10 rectrices
S. u. munoztebari (Ve & Co: Perijá) relatively pale cinnamon-rufous forehead and underparts, pale eyebrow, longer tail of only 8 rectrices, bill black with pale base to lower mandible
S. u. unirufa (Ec, Co: all 3 Andean ranges) paler rufous body, shorter tail of 10 rectrices, all-black bill

Habits Races *unirufa* and *meridana* both forage in pairs or small family groups that follow mixed canopy flocks whilst remaining at low and mid levels, and both glean small insects from leaves and twigs, keeping well inside foliage, but perhaps less secretive when following mixed flocks. Race *munoztebari* forages in undergrowth, sometimes to mid levels, in pairs or small family groups, and apparently does not join mixed flocks.
Status Race *unirufa* uncommon to locally frequent in Ecuador and Colombia; race *meridana* locally frequent in Colombia and Venezuela. Race *munoztebari* endemic to Perijá, rare to uncommon in Colombia and uncommon to possibly locally frequent in Venezuela.
Habitat Subtropical to Temperate Zones, races *meridana* and *unirufa* at *c.*1,200–3,500m; race *munoztebari* 1,900–2,900m. Humid and wet montane and cloud forests, in mossy, epiphyte-overgrown areas, borders, and especially in *Chusquea* and areas with bracken.

Voice Races *unirufa* and *meridana* give a loud nasal *queeeik* or *quee-queeeik*, or sometimes *quee-quee-queeik* and in alarm a low churr (H&B, Hilty). Voice of *munoztebari* unknown.
Notes Formerly included *Synallaxis castanea* (Black-throated Spinetail), separated by Vaurie & Schwartz (1972) on basis of vocal and plumage differences. Race *munoztebari* was missed by Peters, and we failed to list it in Rodner *et al.* (2000). It was described as, and has to date been considered a race *S. unirufa*, but we suspect it is specifically distinct, as it differs in plumage from all other races of *S. unirufa*, especially in having only 8 tail-feathers vs. 10 in all others.

BLACK-THROATED SPINETAIL
Synallaxis castanea Pl. 141

Identification 18–18.5cm. An entirely rich rufous bird, except fine black eye-ring, black lores, rufous chin and black throat. Comparatively long tail has only 8 rectrices, 2 outermost being quite short.

Ssp. Monotypic (N Ve: mountains from Carabobo to Miranda)

Habits Forages at lower to mid levels, in pairs or small family groups that do not follow mixed flocks, but briefly become more active when they pass by. Usually remains in shrubbery, gleaning insects from leaves and small twigs, but comes into open occasionally, if only for a few seconds. Apparently does not forage on ground.
Status Venezuelan endemic, frequent to locally common in its tiny range in the central Coastal Cordillera.
Habitat Subtropical to Temperate Zones, 1,300–2,200m. Humid to wet forests, cloud forests, thickets on mountain trails, patches of *Chusquea* and bracken fern.
Voice Calls mostly in early morning, a loud series of 4–6 *kik* notes, sometimes in rhythmic variations (Hilty), also interpreted as *ke-che-che-che-che-che* (Remsen).
Note Formerly treated as a race of *S. unirufa*, but separated by Vaurie & Schwartz (1972), based on their quite different voices, and plumage differences.

RUSTY-HEADED SPINETAIL
Synallaxis fuscorufa Pl. 139

Identification 16–18cm. Soft mid brown from back to tail, rest orange-rufous; faint brown lores and eye-ring, orange-brown eyes, grey bill, paler below.

Ssp. Monotypic (Co: Santa Marta)

Habits Forages at low and mid levels, in pairs or small family groups, and often with mixed flocks. Systematically checks dense bushes, thickets and vines for insects. Less secretive than congeners, coming into open fairly regularly.
Status Colombian endemic, common in its tiny range, especially above 2,000m.
Habitat Upper Tropical to Temperate Zones, 800–3,000m. Humid montane forest and secondary woodland and scrub, forest borders, treefalls and clearings, patches of *Chusquea* and bracken.
Voice Calls incessantly, a short, nasal *dit-dit-du* (H&B).

STRIPE-BREASTED SPINETAIL
Synallaxis cinnamomea Pl. 140

Identification 14cm. Olive-brown above, rufous wings; white throat streaked black (varies from all white with few fine black streaks to all black with few white streaks, according to race), rest of underparts brown streaked black. Juvenile varies by race, but essential difference is that feathers below have black fringes rather than streaks. Boldly streaked underparts are a sure discriminator. Several races with considerable variation (see plate).

Ssp. *S. c. aveledoi* (NE Co: E slope of E Andes in Norte de Santander; W Ve:) vestigial white eyebrow, paler below, whitish on belly, thin black streaks from chin to rear; birds from Perijá differ in being significantly ruddier all over
S. c. bolivari (NC Ve) whitish eyebrow, white throat with virtually no streaks, underparts centrally quite orange, palest on centre of belly
S. c. carri (Tr) small white chin, black throat extends to breast, with thin white streaks, belly has some buffy streaks, rest of underparts unstreaked
S. c. cinnamomea (Co: E Andes in Cundinamarca, Boyacá and Santander, Ve: Perijá) rufous above and below, white throat streaked black, underparts streaked buffy
S. c. pariae (E Ve) buffy supraloral spot, uniform dark brown below, white throat with thin black streaks, thin black streaks to flanks, undertail-coverts have thin white streaks
S. c. striatipectus (E Ve) underparts uniform with deep brown back, white throat thinly streaked, underparts streaked to flanks, undertail-coverts have thin whitish streaks
S. c. terrestris (To) pure white throat, breast streaked black and white, belly flammulated brown and white, sides to belly and rest of underparts even brown

Habits Forages in undergrowth, usually in pairs that glean insects and spiders from foliage, although it is less secretive than congeners and comes into open fairly regularly. During rainy season, sings constantly, but in dry season only sings intermittently.
Status Frequent in Colombia and Venezuela. Uncommon on Trinidad, where population has declined, formerly frequent and widespread, but now uncommon; on Tobago, quite common and widespread.
Habitat Upper Tropical to Subtropical Zones, 900–2,100m. Humid to drier, deciduous forests, secondary woodland and dry deciduous scrub on montane slopes.
Voice A plaintive 2-note call, with second note rising, *me too?*. Also, a querulous *chew*, short, repeated *mik, mik, mik*… and in alarm a quick *chee-chee-chee* (ffrench). Also, a fairly high, nasal, liquid *churt-wert*, interpreted as *keep-going?* (H&B).

NECKLACED SPINETAIL
Synallaxis stictothorax Pl. 140

Identification 12.5cm. Very small and handsome. Buffy-brown above with orange-rufous wings and long, white eyebrow, black and white stripes on forehead, snow white throat, and band of profuse dusky streaking across white breast; sides and belly to undertail-coverts pale orange-cinnamon.

Ssp. *S. s. stictothorax* (SW Ec: coastal Guayas and Manabí) rufous tail with central feathers dusky, giving 2-tone effect, and dusky brown back

S. s. maculata (S Ec: extreme S Loja and perhaps coastal El Oro) mainly rufous tail with only tips dusky, and back more rufescent

Habits Forages in underbrush and at low levels, in pairs that nimbly glean insects from leaves and mossy thin branches. Less skulking than others in genus.

Status Frequent in Ecuador.

Habitat Lower Tropical Zone, to *c.*200m. Arid areas, dry deciduous woodland and arid scrub.

Voice Song a variable sequence of stuttering *ch* or *che* notes that begins loud then fades, *ch-ch-ch-che-che-cheh-cheh-che-ch-ch ch, ch, ch…* (R&G). Also, a *tr-r t-rik t-rik t-rik* (P. Coopmans).

Notes R&G suggest this species is not a *Synallaxis*, as its behaviour, nest and eggs are more like *Cranioleuca*, whilst vocalisations and plumage are more like *Siptornopsis* of northern Peru. Race *maculata* only recently recorded in Ecuador.

WHITE-WHISKERED SPINETAIL
Synallaxis candei Pl. 139

Identification 16–17cm. Adult pale rufous above with top of head grey, from lores to nape, postocular line orange-rufous, upper cheeks and ear-coverts black, just bordering end of white malar, black apron across lower throat, breast, sides and flanks orange, central belly to undertail-coverts pure white. Juvenile has small white supraloral spot, is barred on head rather than streaked, slight black scalloping where white of throat joins black apron, and slight grey scalloping on central breast and belly. Outer 2 pairs of tail-feathers pale rufous, inner 3 pairs dusky rufous. All races have unmistakable head pattern and 2-tone tail.

Ssp. *S. c. atrigularis* (N Co: Magdalena Valley from S Bolívar to S Magdalena) black head, cheeks divided from black throat by diffuse malar of white flecks, and brown back

S. c. candei (N Co: Caribbean coast from Sucre to Santa Marta) bold rufous eyebrow, black cheeks divided from black throat by bold white malar, and bright rufous back

S. c. venezuelensis (NE Co: Guajira to central Cesar, NW Ve: N Zulia, E & C Falcón & N Lara) narrow rufous eyebrow and 2-tone effect in tail most striking, white throat markedly contrasts with black cheeks and narrow black border below throat, and has bright rufous back

Habits Forages in pairs, picking insects from ground or gleaning them at lowest levels of foliage, in thickets or tangled vines. Flicks tail up and down frequently, carrying it cocked most of time when foraging. Sometimes comes out from under bushes, hopping nervously and erratically.

Status In Colombia, race *venezuelensis* common and even numerous locally, races *candei* and *atrigularis* scarcer, though locally frequent. In Venezuela, frequent to common, perhaps locally numerous.

Habitat Tropical Zone, to *c.*1,000m. Arid wooded areas with cacti, thorn scrub, borders of mangrove, bushy fringes of saltflats, scrubby borders of dry stream beds.

Voice Most frequent is an oft-repeated, nasal *a-DIT-DIT-du*, where first and last notes are feebler (H&B). Otherwise a nasal *paa pip!*, a scolding *paa-pip pu pip-a pip pip'pip'pip'pip* in alarm, and *naaaa* and *keeea* also in alarm (Hilty).

Note Formerly treated in genus *Poecilurus*, but *Poecilurus* was merged into *Synallaxis* by Vaurie (1980), and followed by S&M and Hilty, but not in R&T or BFR&S. However, Remsen points out that it is very doubtful that 3 species placed in *Poecilurus* (*scutatus* of Brazil, *kollari* and *candei*) form a monophyletic group, thus rendering genus invalid.

HOARY-THROATED SPINETAIL
Synallaxis kollari Pl. 140

Identification 15–16cm. Grey-brown from frontal band to nape and mantle, lores and malar, weak whitish-buffy eye-ring; throat black with noticeable white specks, head- and neck-sides, scapulars, wings and breast bright rufous grading into orange sides and belly to undertail-coverts. Distinctive bright rufous bird with black bib, unlike any other *Synallaxis* in its range.

Ssp. Monotypic (SW Gu, Ve?)

Habits Forages low in dense, vine-rich understorey of seasonally flooded gallery forest only 500m wide.

Status Endangered. Considered a Brazilian endemic by Sick (1993) and restricted to gallery forest at headwaters of rio Branco, northern Brazil, and extreme western Guyana, being amongst the least known of its genus. Nonetheless, it is locally fairly common and has recently been collected in Guyana (BFR&S), with sight records dating from 1993 (Forrester 1995), and was considered possible in extreme south-east Bolívar, Venezuela, by Hilty. Its very small range is possibly much affected by fires, and there are records from only 5 localities, with a total population of perhaps no more than 1,000 individuals.

Habitat Lower Tropical Zone, to *c.*100m, in seasonally flooded riparian forests, areas of dense undergrowth with thickets and abundant vines.

Voice Song a 2-note phrase, repeated at 1 s intervals (Remsen).

Note See previous species.

WHITE-BROWED SPINETAIL
Hellmayrea gularis Pl. 145

Identification 11–13.5cm. Rufescent brown above; black-bordered white eyebrow from frontal band to rear ear-coverts, short blackish streaks on ear-coverts merging into blackish edge, white chin and throat fringed black; underparts a paler shade of rufous than upperparts; bicoloured bill, black above and yellowish below. Juvenile has dark tips to feathers of breast and belly.

Ssp. *H. g. brunneidorsalis* (Ve & Co: Perijá) quite distinct, brown above, with white eyebrow (no black borders) reaching upper ear-coverts, rear ear-coverts strongly marked with black, lores black, large white supraloral spots converge on forehead, mouse greyish below

H. g. cinereiventris (Co: Norte de Santander; Ve: N Táchira, Trujillo & Mérida) darker, richer brown above, white supraloral spots converge on forehead, lores black, eyebrow heavily lined black, and smaller white bib heavily lined black as well, fine white streaks on ear-coverts; brownish-grey underparts

H. g. gularis (Ec; Co: W & C Andes, E Andes in Boyacá & Cundinamarca; Ve: S Táchira) as described; birds from Tamá (nominally *gularis*) brighter rufous above than *cinereiventris* with rather similar facial pattern, but forecrown black and few white streaks on cheeks; pale greyish on breast and belly

Habits Forages in undergrowth to mid levels, usually alone. Occasionally joins mixed flocks. Movements like a wren, hopping through dense foliage to glean insects or searching mosses and tangles, especially in tall bamboo and *Chusquea*. Inspects curled-up dead leaves. Quite nimble, hangs upside down from twigs, hitches up trunks.

Status Uncommon to frequent in Ecuador. In Colombia, most frequent at ecotone between high-montane forest and open páramo. In Venezuela, frequent to locally common near treeline.

Habitat Temperate Zone to Páramo, *c*.2,300–3,800m. Humid to wet highland forest, cloud, elfin and stunted forests near treeline, stands of bamboo, thickets and vine tangles.

Voice Song at dawn, rarely during day. In Táchira, Venezuela, a speeding sequence of high notes, *zit, zit, zit, zit-zit-zit-zit'zit'i'i'i'iii-zit-zit*, with last 2 highest. In Trujillo, Venezuela, a sequence of buzzy notes, *tz tz-tztztztz'tz'tz'ti'ti'tic'tic tic, tic*, rising then falling. Calls include a low, odd, descending *trrrrrrrrr* trill and *chip* when foraging (P. Schwartz, H&B).

Notes Formerly placed in *Synallaxis* by some authors (e.g. Meyer de Schauensee 1970), but Braun & Parker (1985) found that differences in voice, morphology (short tail, lack of rufous wing patch), and foraging behaviour justified use of monotypic genus, as in Peters and in Phelps & Phelps Jr. (1950). Race *gularis* treated specifically by Borrero & Hernández (1958), but limits of *cinereiventris* and *gularis* in Boyacá and Norte de Santander require clarification. In Venezuela, it is clear that those in Tamá (southern Táchira) are *gularis*, but birds on Colombian side assigned to *cinereiventris* (H&B), which led Remsen to consider *cinereiventris* as possibly invalid. In contrast, race *brunneidorsalis* very distinct. A complete revision is needed. Nest apparently unknown. *Hellmayrea* is 1 of 27 monotypic genera in Furnariidae.

Cranioleuca spinetails are very similar in form and behaviour to *Synallaxis*, but are generally smaller with shorter, more graduated, stiffer tails ending in 'spines', which they often use as a prop when hitching up trunks. They are treetop specialists – quite unlike *Synallaxis*, which are understorey skulkers. Their coloration is quite plain, except for rufous wings and tails. Found from lowlands to mountains, and all except Parker's and Speckled forage in mid and upper strata of forest. Songs are descending chipping trills, heard much less frequently than *Synallaxis*. Nests are rounded or oval masses of mosses, grass, thin sticks and vegetable fibres, usually with an entrance passage that opens near bottom, and covered on outside with moss. They usually hang from tip of a branch. Nine species occur in our region, none is endemic, but 2 (Tepui and Streak-capped) are quite range-restricted. Vaurie (1980) merged *Cranioleuca* under *Certhiaxis*, but this has not accepted subsequently.

RED-FACED SPINETAIL

Cranioleuca erythrops Pl. 145

Identification 14–15cm. Adult has brown back, paler nape and neck, top and head-sides, wings and rump to tail bright rufous, throat white, underparts brown and only slightly paler than back; eyes orange to reddish-brown or brown, but unknown if variation is age- or sex-related. Immature similar but nape and neck concolorous with back, and buffy eyebrow distinctive. Juvenile has entire head concolorous with back, except buffy eyebrow and throat. Look for rufous forehead and head-sides, framed with paler brown.

Ssp. *C. e. erythrops* (W Ec: Esmeraldas to NW Azuay and W Guayas) as described; 2 central rectrices dull reddish-brown

C. e. griseigularis (Co: W Andes & W slope of C Andes, Antioquia to Quindio) 2 central rectrices brighter and more cinnamon, and breast noticeably greyer

Habits Forages from mid levels to canopy, alone or in pairs, and usually with mixed flocks. Nimble and restless, searches for insects in tangled vegetation and on epiphyte-laden branches.

Status Uncommon to locally common in Ecuador, frequent in Colombia.

Habitat Upper Tropical to Subtropical Zones, 700–1,800m in Ecuador, 700–2,100m in Colombia. Humid foothill and montane forests, deciduous foothill forest and mature secondary woodland, in vine tangles, dead-leaf clumps and border thickets.

Voice Song a fast sequence of high chattery or scratchy notes, *seet-seet-seet-se'e'e'e'e'e'e* (H&B). Also, a series of *ukukuki, ukukuki, ukukuki, ukukuki, ukukuki, ukukuki*, and fast, rising series of squeaky *sfi* notes that sometimes end in a twittering chatter (Remsen).

Note Some uncertainty as to whether race *erythrops* ranges from Esmeraldas south to El Oro, or only reaches east Guayas and north-west Azuay (F&K, R&G).

LINE-CHEEKED SPINETAIL

Cranioleuca antisiensis Pl. 145

Identification 14–15cm. Brown above with brown ear-coverts, bright rufous crown to nape, wings and tail, whitish eyebrow and broad, brown postocular stripe, white throat merges into mouse grey breast and buffy underparts.

Ssp. *C. a. antisiensis* (S Ec: N Azuay to Loja & El Oro)

Habits Forages alone or in pairs, and regularly with mixed flocks. Hitches up trunks and hops sideways on branches. Nimble and quick-moving; gleans insects, picking them from leaves, small cracks in bark, and epiphytes or bromeliads.
Status Frequent to common in Ecuador.
Habitat Subtropical to Temperate Zones, 1,000–2,900m. Humid and semi-humid montane forest, secondary woodland, montane scrub, fallow fields and pastures with hedges or scattered bushes and trees.
Voice Song a loud, falling and fading series of sharp notes that lasts 1–1.5 sec. Also, a longer, more irregular sequence that sometimes ends in a series of long, loud notes. Contact a *tsi-chick* note (R&G, Remsen).
Note Separated from *C. baroni* (Baron's Spinetail of Peru) based on plumage, size and vocal differences.

ASH-BROWED SPINETAIL

Cranioleuca curtata Pl. 145

Identification 14–15cm. Warm, mid brown above, somewhat rufescent on wings, more so on rump to tail, crown bright rufous, broad superciliary faint grey, head-sides to undertail-coverts ochraceus-buffy. Eyes pale greyish-white. Juvenile darker and grey eyebrow more contrasting; eyes dark. Best separated from Line-cheeked by darker, richer brown on back and darker, brownish-grey throat, because, despite vernacular name, Line-cheeked does not have more streaking on cheeks.

Ssp. *C. c. cisandina* (E Ec, S Co: E slope of E Andes) as described, greyish-white eyes
C. c. curtata (Co: W slope of E Andes in W Caquetá and SE Nariño) darker and greyer below; brown or chestnut eyes

Habits Forages from low levels to canopy, often with mixed flocks including other furnariids. Agile and restless, hops on branches inspecting tufts of moss and epiphytes, or pokes tangled clumps of vines and dead leaves.
Status Uncommon to frequent in Ecuador, uncommon in Colombia, but possibly more frequent than records suggest in some areas.
Habitat Upper Tropical to Temperate Zones, *c.*500–1,700m in Ecuador, 1,000–2500m in Colombia. Humid montane forest and secondary woodland, in tangled vines or brambles and border thickets.
Voice Fast series of high strident notes followed by a fading trill with a bouncing rhythm that usually lasts *c.*2 s, but sometimes is slower and longer, *c.*5 s (R&G, Remsen).
Notes F&K considered that *curtata* might be better treated as a subspecies group under *C. erythrops*. Vaurie (1971) validated Fork-tailed Spinetail *C. furcata* (a species described by Taczanowski), but Graves (1986a) showed that plumage described by Vaurie belonged to immature *C. curtata*. Specimens collected since confirm Graves' diagnosis, but bear in mind that some older lists for Ecuador include Fork-tailed Spinetail. Race *cisandina* formerly treated specifically, but Peters placed it under *C. curtata*, which arrangements has persisted until the present.

TEPUI SPINETAIL

Cranioleuca demissa Pl. 145

Identification 14cm. Olive-brown above with slight rufescence on wings and rump, bright rufous top of head and tail, narrow white eyebrow, dark greyish cheeks with some white streaks, underparts grey, brown from flanks to undertail-coverts.

Ssp. *C. d. demissa* (S Ve: Bolívar, on all eastern tepuis, Amazonas on Duida, Paraque, Neblina and Parú; W Gu on Mts. Kowa and Ayanganna; extreme N Brazil on Roraima) grey underparts and white eyebrow
C. d. cardonai (S Ve: Bolívar on Guaiquinima and Cerro Tabaro, Amazonas on NE cerros) darker, narrow white streaks on throat; olivaceous-brown underparts

Habits Forages from mid levels to canopy, alone or in pairs, and regularly with mixed flocks that include antwrens, tanagers, woodcreepers, other furnariids and even woodpeckers. Main diet small insects gleaned from foliage and twigs, or picked from cracks in bark and mosses or bromeliads. Also pokes into curled dead leaves and tangles of vines and debris. Quite active and nimble, hitches up trunks like a woodcreeper.
Status Frequent in Venezuela, but status uncertain in Guyana.
Habitat Upper Tropical to Temperate Zones, 1,100–2,450m. Humid and wet forests on slopes of tepuis, less frequently in gallery forest and mature secondary woodland in surrounding plains.
Voice Song a speeding, descending series of high, bouncy notes, *TEE TEE' Te'ti ti'ti'ti'ti'i'i'*, and call is a much-repeated short harsh rattle (Hilty).
Notes Formerly treated within *Certhiaxis* and also included *C. hellmayri*, but latter split by Vaurie (1971). Race *cardonai* recently described (Phelps Jr. 1980). In Guyana, only specimen record is from Mt. Ayanganna (1960) with sight record for Mt. Kowa (Barnett *et al.* 2002), but quite probably occurs on Guianan side of Roraima.

STREAK-CAPPED SPINETAIL

Cranioleuca hellmayri Pl. 145

Identification 15cm. Brown above with rufous wings, tail and top of head, black streaks on crown, cheeks and ear-coverts, with whitish streaks that run onto neck-sides, buffy eyebrow and throat, becoming brown below, almost concolorous with back. Eyes pale brownish to pale grey, bill horn, darker on culmen.

Ssp. Monotypic (Co: Sierra de Santa Marta; NW Ve: Sierra de Perijá)

Habits Forages from mid levels to subcanopy. Moves restlessly through foliage to glean insects, probing into cracks and inspecting bromeliads, in pairs, families or small groups, most often with mixed flocks.
Status Common in Colombia, especially at 1,700–1,800m. In Venezuela, possibly uncommon, but status unclear: a specimen was collected in 1991 in Río Lajas, but area is very dangerous and of difficult access, and no further surveys since.
Habitat Tropical to Temperate Zones, 1,520–3,000m in Colombia, at 700m in Venezuela, where range unknown. Humid montane forest, mature secondary woodland, borders and clearings.
Voice Call a squeaky trill, *ti ti't't'tttt*, repeated frequently (H&B, F&K).
Note Formerly considered a race of *C. demissa*, but separated by Vaurie (1971).

CRESTED SPINETAIL
Cranioleuca subcristata Pl. 145

Identification 14–15cm. Almost entirely brown except rufous wings and tail, feathers on crown to nape rather long and streaked black, head-sides and throat washed whitish and finely streaked black, fading on upper breast. Crest is not raised, and bird never looks crested in field. Eyes chestnut to cream, but unknown whether variation is age-related. Juvenile similar but has warm, almost orange, tone on centre of breast and belly.

Ssp. *C. s. subcristata* (NE Co: E slope of E Andes from Norte de Santander to Boyacá; NW Ve: northern mountains and E slope of Andes in Barinas and Lara, foothills around Lake Maracaibo) as described
C. s. fuscivertex (W Ve: E slope of Andes in Táchira & Apure) blacker, more noticeable crown streaking

Habits Forages from low levels to subcanopy, alone or in pairs, and often with mixed flocks. Gleans insects from foliage and bark, probing mosses and epiphytes, inspecting tangles, twisting, hanging and stretching nimbly to reach prey.
Status Uncommon to locally frequent in Colombia. In Venezuela, common in Coastal Cordillera, frequent and local on Andes.
Habitat Tropical to Subtropical Zones, 300–1,500m in Colombia, 50–1,950m, but mostly above 400m in Venezuela. Moist to humid montane and foothill forests, mature secondary woodland, plantations.
Voice Sings frequently, a sequence of 3–4 high, bouncy notes followed by a short trill, *pzeep, pzeep, pzeep, pee'pe'pe'e'e'e* (P. Schwartz recording, H&B). Call a sharp *tsink* and slow rattle.

RUSTY-BACKED SPINETAIL
Cranioleuca vulpina Pl. 145

Identification 14.5–16cm. Dark brown above with rich rufous wings, tail and top of head, except pastel brown forehead, buff eyebrow and dark narrow postocular line, whitish streaks on face-sides; entirely brownish-buff underparts. Eye colour perhaps variable: yellowish-grey in H&B (Colombian birds?), dark reddish-brown in Venezuelan specimens we examined.

Ssp. *C. v. alopecias* (E & SE Co: NE Meta, E Vichada & S Amazonas, C & S Ve: Portuguesa to Delta Amacuro, along Orinoco, Amazonas,, W Gu) white throat clearer, and virtually no scaling on underparts, though slightly more in juveniles, bill black above and pale grey below, legs greenish, whilst feet and claws yellow
C. v. apurensis (SW Ve) slightly warmer below, with more pronounced scaling, quite strong in juvenile; bill all dark grey, legs and feet yellow

Habits Forages in close-knit pairs or small family groups, usually from mid levels to tops of waterside vegetation. Gleans insects from both live and dead leaves, picks and probes bark. Does not follow mixed flocks but may briefly join those that pass by. Quite active but often quiet and pass unseen.
Status Frequent in Colombia and Venezuela, of uncertain status in Guyana.
Habitat Lower Tropical Zone, to 400m. Waterside vegetation, tall grasses and reeds, bushes and young trees, vine thickets, on river islands and along rivers, gallery forest, ponds, oxbow lakes.
Voice Song may last several seconds and pairs often sing together, a loose, gradually falling series of rattle notes, *kuee-kuee-kuee-kuee-quaa-quaa-qua-quaquaquaquaqua* (H&B, Hilty), a speeding, fading series of emphatic notes, *ch-ch-ch-chchchchchewewewewewew*, or a series of scolding *choy* notes (Remsen).
Note Formerly included *vulpecula*, which was treated specifically by Zimmer (1997).

PARKER'S SPINETAIL
Cranioleuca vulpecula Pl. 144

Identification 13–14cm. Entirely rufous upperparts, narrow whitish eyebrow, finely streaked greyish cheeks, white throat, and underparts greyish-buffy. Eyes brown to chestnut. From Rusty-backed Spinetail by significantly paler breast.

Ssp. Monotypic (E Ec: along Napo, Aguarico and Pastaza rivers).

Habits A cane specialist usually found amongst thin vertical stems and has exceptionally long claws to assist grasping such perches. Forages in thickets and dense undergrowth, up to subcanopy, in close-knit pairs. Agile and restless, tends to remain in tangles and it can be quite hard to see, though often heard. Gleans insects from crannies at base of leaves, in bark and twigs, and in clumps of debris amidst crisscrossing branches.
Status Frequent in Ecuador.
Habitat Lower Tropical Zone, to 400m. Riparian woodland and early successional scrub on river islands, especially on young to medium-age river islands, and especially in patches of *Tessaria* and/or *Gynerium* cane, also in *Cecropia*.
Voice Frequently vocalises. Song a speeding, falling series of nasal notes, *tew-tew-tew-tew-trrrrrr*, ending in a chortled

trill, and gives sharp *chut* notes, sometimes doubled or tripled (R&G).

Notes Formerly considered a race of *C. vulpina*, but separated by Zimmer (1997), based mainly on voice but also plumage differences. Also differences in habitat: Parker's Spinetail occurs only on river islands of Amazon basin, whilst Rusty-backed is widespread in riparian scrub outside Amazonia, but they are widely sympatric.

SPECKLED SPINETAIL

Cranioleuca gutturata Pl. 144

Identification 13–14.5cm. Olive-brown above with deep rufous wings and tail, dark chestnut crown contrasts with dark olive-brown upperparts, short buffy eyebrow and buffy-white chin; head-sides and entire underparts buffy-white with rows of dusky arrowheads merging into faintly greyish-barred flanks, belly and undertail-coverts. Eye colour whitish or yellow to brown. Juvenile as adult, but less rufous on wings and almost clear pale buffy below – no streaks on breast.

Ssp. *C. g. gutturata* (E Ec, E Co) brighter and more contrasting, longer whiter eyebrow, more extensive and whiter throat with more clearly defined black stripes and spots, underparts brighter, buffier and more clearly barred dusky; pale eyes

C. g. hyposticta (S Ve, Su, FG) as described; dark eyes

Habits Somewhat wren-like and the only lowland spinetail with speckled underparts. Forages in tangled understorey, from mid levels to subcanopy, alone or in pairs and regularly with mixed flocks of include antwrens, flycatchers, woodcreepers and other furnariids. Agile, gleans insects from leaves and twigs, inspects and pokes curled dead leaves and clumps of dead creepers.

Status Rare to uncommon and apparently quite local in Ecuador, uncommon in Colombia and Venezuela. Rare in Suriname, where known from a specimen collected in 1965 and more recent sight records; widespread but uncommon to rare in French Guiana.

Habitat Lower Tropical Zone, to 600m in Ecuador but mainly below 400m; to *c*.750m in Colombia and Venezuela. Only in lowland forest with abundant lianas and vines, and usually near water; *várzea*, marshy areas, riparian woodland, boggy *terra firme*.

Voice Not very vocal. Song 2–7 repetitions of a very high thin *seeeeeee* note that may be unnoticed, and sometimes end in low, sputtering trills. Also a quavering, falling trill with an initial note, *tch-t-t-t-t-t-t-t-t-t-t...* (Hilty, Remsen).

Notes Treated within *Certhiaxis* by H&M and Tostain *et al.* Peters, Vaurie (1980), R&G and Remsen (2003) consider the species to be monotypic.

Certhiaxis spinetails frequent lowland wetlands (marshes, ponds, ditches, mangrove borders) and sing rattling or churring notes. They are very similar in form to *Cranioleuca*, but have thinner, longer bills and rather thick legs. Nests are bulky globes of grasses and thorny sticks, lined with soft materials, with long entrance tubes and reinforced ('thatched') roofs, constructed on low branches above or adjacent to water. The two species are sympatric in some areas.

YELLOW-CHINNED SPINETAIL

Certhiaxis cinnamomeus Pl. 144

Identification 13–15cm. Essentially bicoloured: pale cinnamon-rufous above and white below, with a greyish forecrown and lores, pale eyebrow and hard-to-see yellow chin. Juvenile like adult but greyish on top of head and duller on mantle and wings. Red-and-white Spinetail has lower face and breast pure white. Rusty-backed Spinetail is darker below, and is found in trees and bushes, not in reeds and grasses.

Ssp. *C. c. cinnamomeus* (NE Ve: N Sucre & N Anzoátegui, Tr, Guianas) greyish-brown forecrown, dusky rear ear-coverts and hard-to-see greyish eyebrow, white chin

C. c. fuscifrons (N Co) near black forecrown and complete white eyebrow, faint yellow chin

C. c. marabinus (NW Ve: Lake Maracaibo basin) dusky greyish forecrown, very short white eyebrow and brightest reddish-brown upperparts; chin quite yellow, flushed on throat, flanks and undertail-coverts washed pale cinnamon

C. c. orenocensis (EC Ve: Orinoco from N Amazonas) has forecrown as rest of pale brown upperparts, face and sides washed brown, flanks to undertail-coverts washed buffy, pale yellowish chin

C. c. valencianus (C Ve: Falcón & Lara to Aragua & Guárico) dusky forehead reaches forecrown, greyish cheeks and pale greyish wash on sides, pale yellowish chin

Habits Forages alone or in very loose pairs. Sometimes skulks, but often hops about in open on top of grasses and low bushes, or on muddy ground by water's edge. May fly off suddenly. Often parasitised by Striped Cuckoo.

Status Common in Colombia, Venezuela, Trinidad (does not occur Tobago) and Guyana. In Suriname, locally common and quite numerous. Common in littoral of French Guiana.

Habitat Lower Tropical Zone to *c*.500m. Grasses, reeds and shrubs at borders of marshes, mangroves, ponds and ditches. Always near water.

Voice Rattling call (H&M). Song a rising *churr*; call a thin buzzy trill, a series of ticking notes, and a sharp *chip* (H&B, Hilty). Song resembles that of *Laterallus* rails, which share same habitat.

Note Correct spelling is *cinnamomeus*, not *cinnamomea*, as *Certhiaxis* is masculine, and names of subspecies follow suit (David & Gosselin 2002). Called Yellow-throated Spinetail in most older texts, present common name proposed by H&B.

RED-AND-WHITE SPINETAIL

Certhiaxis mustelinus Pl. 145

Identification 14–15cm. Two-colour bird: bright rufous above and white below (with pale buffish tinge to belly), and sharp black lores. Greyish cheeks and white eyebrow of Yellow-chinned separate them, with grey forehead and yellow chin clinching features in good views.

Ssp. Monotypic (SE Co: Amazonas)

Habits Forages in open, on reeds or grasses, or on muddy ground of banks at water's edge.

Status Locally frequent to common in Colombia.

Habitat Lower Tropical Zone to *c.*100m. Grasses and tangled vegetation at borders of freshwater marshes, ponds and ditches, and river islands of Amazonia. Always in grasses next to water.

Voice Song a churring rattle; call a 3-note *chuck, chuck, check* (H&B).

Note Correct spelling is *mustelinus*, not *mustelina* (David & Gosselin 2002).

Asthenes canasteros are birds of páramo and puna in the high Andes. Of 22 species in genus, most occur from Peru to Chile and Argentina. Canasteros are relatively small with dull plumage and a patch of orange on throat, and sing trilled songs. They are terrestrial and usually quite shy and difficult to see, but for their habit of singing from exposed perches. The name canastero (basket weaver) comes from habit of weaving large domed nests of sticks and grasses, accessed by side entrances or fairly long tubes. Vaurie (1980) merged *Asthenes* under *Thripophaga*, and Remsen considers the genus to be possibly polyphyletic.

STREAK-BACKED CANASTERO

Asthenes wyatti Pl. 140

Identification 15–18cm. Olive-brown above, streaked black, i.e. feathers dusky to blackish with broad olive-brown fringes, wing-coverts fringed deep reddish-rufous, basal half of remiges also deep reddish-rufous which shows as an extensive bar in flight, outer webs of tail-feathers except central pair bright reddish-rufous, also noticeable in flight, buffy eyebrow. Underparts buffy with variable rufous to orange patch in centre of throat.

Ssp. *A. w. aequatorialis* (C Ec: Pichincha to Chimborazo) greyish below, tail blacker than nominate

A. w. azuay (S Ec: Azuay to Zamora-Chinchipe & Loja) distinctly larger than other races; buffy below with more extensive rufous in wings and tail than *aequatorialis*, crown and back darker than nominate

A. w. mucuchiesi (Ve: páramos of Merida and Trujillo) crown and back more greyish, less brownish than nominate, undertail cinnamon-brown

A. w. sanctaemartae (N Co: Santa Marta) broader but less contrasting streaks above, darker orange chin and a longer bill than nominate

A. w. wyatti (C Co: E Andes in Santander) as described

A. w. perijanus (NE Co & W Ve: Sierra de Perijá) crown and back darker than *azuay*, undertail dark chestnut-brown

Habits Forages on ground and in low bushes, alone or in very loose pairs. Inspects grass and gleans insects from leaves and twigs, picks them from ground, or snaps them as they fly by. Secretive and skulking, runs hurriedly between bushes or rocks, but will perch on a low exposed spot to sing. Cocks tail frequently.

Status Uncommon and local in Ecuador, locally common in Colombia and Venezuela.

Habitat Páramos, at 2,900–4,400m in Ecuador, 2,400–5,000m in Colombia, 3,600–4,100m in Venezuela. Fields of *Espeletia* and other low bushes in open páramo.

Voice Unclear from literature whether songs vary racially. For Venezuela, Hilty describes a short, rising and speeding trill, *wu'u'ur'ur'd'd'd'd*. For Colombia, H&B describe 2 types of song, both lasting *c.*1 s and both apparently used indistinctly: one a single insect-like trill, other of 3 short insect-like trills. For Ecuador, R&G describe a rising, very fast trill lasting several seconds and a doubled or tripled short trill. According to N. Krabbe, 2 races in Ecuador have similar song.

Notes *A. wyatti* has a confusing taxonomic history. Past authors grouped races included here, and those presently included under *A. sclateri* (southern Peru to north-central Argentina) and *A. anthoides* (southern Chile & south-west Argentina) in several different ways. More recently, these taxa were grouped into 4 species by F&K (*A. wyatti*, *A. punensis*, *A. sclateri* and *A. anthoides*) or into 3 species by Navas & Bo (1982: *A. wyatti*, *A. sclateri* and *A. anthoides*, with *punensis* included under *A. sclateri*). The latter treatment is followed here and by Remsen, although Remsen points to possibility that *A. wyatti* and *A. sclateri* may not be separate species.

MANY-STRIPED CANASTERO

Asthenes flammulata Pl. 140

Identification 15–16.5cm. Generally very dark brown, broadly streaked buffy-white above and below, with rufous wings and tail. Flight-feathers rufous at base, with distal half blackish, whilst tail has 4 central feathers dusky and all outer ones dull rufous, and looks slightly dishevelled. Appearance more contrastingly streaked than Streak-backed Canastero.

Ssp. *A. f. flammulata* (Ec: páramos from Carchi to Loja; S Co: Nariño) buffy-orange throat and white eyebrow

A. f. multostriata (Co: E Andes from Norte de Santander to Cundinamarca) deep rufous throat and eyebrow ochraceous-white

A. f. quindiana (Co: C Andes from Caldas to Cauca) white chin with pale rufous throat and eyebrow pale rufous

Habits Forages on ground and in low vegetation, running hurriedly between bushes or rocks. Perches on low, exposed spots to sing. Tail held cocked most of time. When flushed, flies very low for a short stretch and then dives into cover.

Status Frequent in Ecuador, where more abundant than Streak-backed Canastero (they are sympatric at only a few localities); uncommon to frequent but only very locally

in Colombia, (occurs with Streak-backed Canastero in Santander).
Habitat Páramo, at 3,000–4,200m in Ecuador, 2,800–4,200m in Colombia. Humid to drier open, grassy páramos with scattered bushes or rocks, sometimes in open fields slightly below treeline.
Voice Call a soft meowing *peeow*. Song a series of whining notes and a rattle (H&B) or a speeding series of trills that end in a chipper: *trree-trree-trree-trreetrreetrreetritritritrotitititi* (R&G).

Thripophaga are called softtails because their tails are relatively short and rounded, and their remiges lack spine tips of many other furnariids. Remsen points out that though 4 species in genus share similar tail structure and head pattern, and an affinity for dense vine tangles, some authors (R&T, Mazar Barnett & Kirwan 2004) have expressed doubts as to it being monophyletic: the 4 seem to fall into 2 groups: *T. macroura* and *T. cherriei*, which apparently are closer to *Asthenes*, and *T. fusciceps* and *T. berlepschi* (Andes of Peru), which Vaurie (1980) considered to belong in *Phacellodomus*. Name change to soft-tail currently being considered by SACC.

ORINOCO SOFTTAIL
Thripophaga cherriei Pl. 145

Identification 16–17cm. Olive-brown above with dark rufous wings and tail (comparatively short with rounded tips to feathers); white eyebrow, patch of deep orange on chin, underparts tawny, streaked buffy-white from head-sides to flanks and belly; eyes dark red.

Ssp. Monotypic (S Ve)

Habits Foraging behaviour and other details of ecology and biology, including nest shape, virtually unknown.
Status Vulnerable. Locally frequent Venezuelan endemic, recorded only along río Capuana, a small affluent of the Orinoco, approximately halfway between mouths of the Ventuari (Venezuela) and Vichada (Colombia) rivers. Its very small range is possibly affected by itinerant agriculture and lies within Sipapo Forest Reserve, an area that may eventually be subject to timber extraction.
Habitat Lower Tropical Zone to *c.*100m. *Várzea* and riparian forests with dense understorey.
Voice Unknown.
Note Together with *T. macroura* of coastal SE Brazil, *T. cherriei* has been considered by some to be more closely related to *Asthenes*, based on the bright orange chin patch.

PLAIN SOFTTAIL
Thripophaga fusciceps Pl. 145

Identification 15cm. A very plain olive-brown or rufescent brown bird with hazel eyes and rufous wing and tail.

Ssp. *T. f. dimorpha* (E Ec: ríos Napo and Pastaza)

Habits Forages in pairs or small groups, from subcanopy to mid levels. Whether it joins mixed flocks is unclear (R&G, Remsen). Gleans insects from dead leaves and twigs, and is perhaps a dead-leaf specialist. Favours tangled vines, where it forages well out of sight. Nest of *T. f. dimorpha* a ball of small twigs, soft fibres and leaves, *c.*20cm in diameter, with 2 entrance tubes converging from above on interior chamber. This is apparently unique within the Furnariidae.
Status Apparently rare and very local in Amazonian lowlands of eastern Ecuador.
Habitat Lower Tropical Zone to 400 m. Flooded evergreen forest, *várzea*, riparian forests. Often around treefalls, at borders or in areas with dense tangled vines. May wander into drier, deciduous forest.
Voice Song of *T. f. dimorpha* a loud, sharp, descending *churrrr*. Both members of pair often sing simultaneously (R&G). Song of nominate race quite different (see Remsen).
Note Remsen suggests that 3 races may be separate species, based on size differences (other races are 18cm long) and disjunct ranges. We agree that together with marked difference in size, unique nest architecture may indicate that *dimorpha* is a separate species.

RUFOUS-FRONTED THORNBIRD
Phacellodomus rufifrons Pl. 143

Identification 15–17cm. Highly nondescript: olive-brown above, pale buffy brown below, forehead slightly rufescent, slightly buffy supercilium, chin whitish. Juvenile darker and warmer brown below.

Ssp. *P. r. castilloi* (Ve: western Llanos) as described
P. r. inornatus (NE Co: Llanos in E Boyacá to Arauca & Vichada; N & NC Ve: SE Falcón to Miranda) lacks any rufous on forehead, pale cinnamon below
P. r. peruvianus (extreme S Ec) bright rufous forehead that grades into crown, pale creamy below with bright pale fulvous flanks

Habits Forages mostly on ground in cover, in pairs or groups of up to a dozen that include nest helpers. Gleans insects and spiders from leaf-litter or dried leaves on low branches, but does not toss or flick leaves. Frequently at mid levels or canopy when not foraging. Builds a remarkable nest: a huge cylindrical 'tower' of sticks and thorn twigs, hung from end of a branch in a very exposed location, such as a roadside, and branches often break from weight of nest, which can reach a length of more than 2m and a girth of more than 0.5m. From entrance holes, tunnels lead to several interior chambers, lined with feathers, reptile skin, hairs and leaves. Nests are re-used and often upper chambers are occupied by other species (Stripe-backed Wren, Saffron Finch, Cattle Tyrant, etc.), which either share 'condominium' or expel owners, as is case with Troupials. Some young from preceding brood act as nest helpers for more than one year, joining in nest building or nest expansion, and sometimes even feed new brood. Thornbirds are frequently parasitised by Striped Cuckoos.
Status Frequent in Ecuador, where first recorded 1986

(first specimens 1989), frequent to common in Colombia and Venezuela.

Habitat Tropical to Lower Subtropical Zones, 650–1,500m in Ecuador, to 950m in Venezuela. Savanna, *llanos*, ranches and pastures, dry to moist scrub and deciduous forest, secondary woodland, gallery forest. In general, open areas with abundant dense bushes and thickets and a smattering of large trees.

Voice Sings frequently, with mate often joining excitedly, a loud bright series of *chit* notes that speed up at first and then slow to a sudden end. Calls include lengthy, loud twittering, and a sharp *chek* or *chip* in alarm (H&B, Remsen).

Notes Taxonomy long discussed, mainly due to extremely disjunct ranges of 4 groups of subspecies presently included in *P. rufifrons* (*castilloi* and *inornatus* in *llanos* of Venezuela and Colombia; *peruvianus* in southern Ecuador and northern Peru, *sincipitalis* in eastern Bolivia, south-west Brazil, northern Paraguay and north-west Argentina; and *specularis* and *rufifrons* in eastern Brazil). S&M suggested separating them as 3 species, and R&T also noted same possibility. In R&G and Hilty, Rufous-fronted Thornbird *P. rufifrons* (including *peruvianus* and other southern races) is treated as specifically distinct, whilst northern races in *llanos* of Colombia and Venezuela are treated as *P. inornatus* (Plain Thornbird) based on very disjunct range and differences in plumage and voice. We maintain traditional taxonomy until a formal analysis is published. Extended species called Plain-fronted Thornbird in P&MdS and Common Thornbird in R&T, who also suggested that *peruvianus*, if placed in a separate species, could be called Marañón Thornbird, a suggestion followed by R&G.

SPECTACLED PRICKLETAIL

Siptornis striaticollis Pl. 143

Identification 11–12cm. Tawny-brown above with rufous wings and tail, postocular white eyebrow, black lores, white crescent below eyes, dusky-edged white streaks from throat to breast, short tail ends in two points. Resembles a xenops, not only in plumage but in acrobatic habits, though easily separated by lack of a conspicuous white malar.

Ssp. *S. s. nortoni* (E Ec) shorter postocular stripe, streaks on throat and breast to upper flanks, much more conspicuous, lores buffy-grey to grey instead of dark grey or black

S. s. striaticollis (C Co: Magdalena Valley & E Andes: W slope from Cundinamarca to Huila, E slope from Cauca to Caquetá) white streaks barely reach breast

Habits Forages mostly at mid levels, occasionally to subcanopy or canopy, alone, in pairs or sometimes in small groups, and often with mixed flocks. Agile, moves like a warbler or piculet, but always fairly quietly, and may pass unseen. Climbs on smaller branches, gleaning insects from bark and leaves or in larger branches inspecting epiphytes and mosses or tangled bunches of dead leaves. Sometimes checks underside of large leaves (i.e. *Cecropia*, *Balsa*) by hanging upside-down. When hitching up, braces itself with tail.

Status In Ecuador, uncommon to fairly frequent in some parts of Podocarpus National Park, but rare and local in rest of range. Rare and local in Colombia.

Habitat Subtropical Zone, at 1,300–2,300m in Ecuador, 1,650–2,400m in Colombia. Humid montane and cloud forests.

Voice A high trill.

Notes *Siptornis* is one of 27 monotypic genera in Furnariidae. Race *nortoni* was described by Graves & Robbins (1987) from a specimen collected by D. Norton on Volcán Sumaco, Napo, in 1964. Until recently, species known only from 'Bogotá' skins, a few specimens from Magdalena Valley (Colombia) and single different specimen from Mopoto, on east slope of Ecuador (Chapman 1917) that belongs to new race.

ORANGE-FRONTED PLUSHCROWN

Metopothrix aurantiaca Pl. 143

Identification 10.5–11.5cm. More like a finch or warbler in appearance. Yellowish-green above, slightly browner on wings and tail, full orange patch on forehead, with a pale, whitish-yellow postocular line, underparts warm yellow, washed with green of back on breast to vent. Juvenile essentially same but has yellow forehead.

Ssp. Monotypic (NE Ec: Napo, Sucumbíos, SE Co)

Habits Forages from mid levels to canopy, in pairs or small family groups. H&B and Remsen consider that it occurs with mixed flocks fairly frequently, but R&G that it generally forages independently of them. Behaves like a warbler, flitting nimbly and restlessly in outer, thinner twigs to glean insects from leaves or pick small fruits or flowers.

Status Uncommon to locally frequent in Ecuador. In Colombia, very locally frequent, especially in interior of mature secondary woodland in Putumayo.

Habitat Lower Tropical Zone to *c.*600m. Mature secondary woodland, humid *terra firme* and *várzea*, borders and clearings, gardens.

Voice Variable high, distinct, sibilant notes, *tswit-tsweet* or *tsweet-tsweet-tsweet-tsweet*... (R&G).

Notes *Metopothrix* is one of 27 monotypic genera in Furnariidae. Correct spelling is *aurantiaca*, not *aurantiacus*, (David & Gosselin 2002). Coloration quite unique amongst Furnariidae, and in shape it bears certain resemblance to warbler, thus some authors questioned its placement (e.g. Vaurie, who suggested that *Metopothrix* might be part of Pipridae), until Feduccia's (1970) study of cranial and palate morphology confirmed its placement in Furnariidae.

Xenerpestes greytails are tiny canopy birds that behave and look slightly like warblers. The 2 species inhabit wet forests and have fairly small ranges. There are few data available for either; both are difficult to find and are considered amongst rarest and least known of furnariids. Both have dark grey, graduated tails. The few nests that have been found were of sticks, cylindrical or rounded, or shaped like a light bulb, and hung from a branch *c.*10 m high. Placement of *Xenerpestes* in Furnariidae has been questioned: Berlepsch placed it therein due to similarities with *Metopothrix*, and Vaurie (1971) found similarities in bill shape with *Xenops*, whilst considering that similarities with *Metopothrix* did not give sufficient reason to state that the 2 genera are close. He suggested that *Xenerpestes* could be an antbird, but nonetheless maintained it in Furnariidae.

DOUBLE-BANDED GREYTAIL

Xenerpestes minlosi Pl. 143

Identification 10.5–11cm. Grey above, darker on top of head, wings and tail, 2 white wingbars, white eyebrow, underparts entirely creamy white. Eyes pale brown, yellowish bill with a dusky tip, legs and feet greyish-horn. Juvenile lacks wingbars and is duller, washed grey below.

Ssp. *X. m. minlosi* (NW Co: Caribbean lowlands in W Córdoba to NW Santander) as described

X. m. umbraticus (NW Ec: Pichincha, W Co: Chocó Pacific lowlands) wings, tail and upperparts darker than nominate

Habits Forages from upper mid levels to canopy, in pairs or small family groups, and frequently with mixed flocks of antwrens, antbirds and other furnariids. Somewhat warbler-like, flitting nimbly and restlessly in outer, thinner twigs to glean insects from leaves or pick small fruits or flowers, but also creeps up trunks like a xenops, and inspects tangles of dry leaves and vines.

Status Rare and local in Ecuador, where first recorded in 1995. Uncommon to very locally frequent in Colombia, where occurs at a few, widely scattered localities.

Habitat Lower Tropical Zone, 400–500m in Ecuador, to 900m in Colombia. Wet forests, secondary woodland with scattered large trees.

Voice Song a fast dry, reeling trill (R&G); a sharp inflected note (Remsen).

Notes According to R&G, allocation of Ecuadorian birds to race *umbraticus* is unconfirmed.

EQUATORIAL GREYTAIL

Xenerpestes singularis Pl. 143

Identification 11–11.5cm. Small, warbler-like bird. Soft grey above, darker on wings and tail, postocular white eyebrow, orange forehead, underparts white, streaked grey from chin and cheeks to flanks and vent, undertail-coverts grey.

Ssp. Monotypic (E Ec: Napo to Zamora-Chinchipe)

Habits Forages in canopy of very tall trees, where pairs or small groups usually occur within mixed flocks and are easily overlooked. Inspects tangles of vines and dead leaves and is most often seen at ends of small stems on outer branches.

Status Rare to locally uncommon in Ecuador, where range increasingly deforested.

Habitat Upper Tropical to Lower Subtropical Zones, 1,000–1,600m. Wet and mossy foothill and montane forests. Tall trees heavily laden with epiphytes, mosses and bromeliads.

Voice Frequent call is a single *tsit* note. Song a dry *tzzzzzzzzzzz* trill, monotone and insect-like, lasting *c*.5 s (R&G).

RORAIMAN BARBTAIL

Roraimia adusta Pl. 142

Identification 14.5cm. Four very similar races that would be virtually impossible to separate in field. Adult deep rufescent brown above with dusky top of head, deep red frontal band that runs back in an ever-widening eyebrow to neck-sides, but in poor light looks almost black, mantle to tail increasingly reddish, wings dusky with reddish fringes; face-sides from lores black; throat and malar white, breast buffy with sepia streaks that become denser until flanks and belly are entirely sepia. Juvenile similar but far less reddish. Look for a striking head pattern: deep umber-brown top of head with deep reddish eyebrow that extends and widens towards nape, and a blackish mask bordered below by a bright white throat.

Ssp. *R. a. adusta* (S Ve: tepuis of SE Bolívar, W Gu) frontal band and postocular less bright than others, buffy underparts fairly pale

R. a. duidae (S Ve: tepuis Duida, Huachamacarii and Parú, C Amazonas), brighter above, eyebrow and nape brighter reddish, and brightest race above; below like *obscurodorsalis*

R. a. mayri (S Ve: Cerro Jaua, SW Bolívar) frontal band strongly reddish (more so than others), all upperparts redder, throat white, buffy underparts almost as weak as *adusta*

R. a. obscurodorsalis (SE Ve: Cerro Sipapo, NW Amazonas) generally darker, reddish above not very distinct, very buffy washed orange below, streaks virtually flammulations, throat off-white to pale buffy

Habits Forages alone or in pairs, mostly with mixed understorey flocks. Quietly moves up low and mid segments of small trunks and on low branches, zigzagging or circling up with short hops, checking mosses and epiphytes. Very fond of berries of Melastomataceae, which often grow at forest borders. Quite silent and very easily overlooked.

Status Endemic to Pantepui. In Venezuela, uncommon in lower parts of altitudinal range, but quite common higher. In Guyana, situation uncertain, due to paucity of records. A recent survey of Potaro Plateau (Barnett *et al*. 2002), relatively close to Roraima, produced no records.

Habitat Subtropical Zone, 1,000–2,500m. Wet montane and cloudy sand soil forests with abundant mosses and epiphytes, stunted forest on higher slopes of tepuis.

Voice Sings rarely, a slow series of metallic, scraping notes, *tlink, sink, sink, tslink… sink*, with second and third notes lower (Hilty).

Note Formerly placed in genus *Premnoplex*, but in monotypic genus *Roraimia* by Phelps Jr. (1977). Vaurie (1980) merged *Roraimia* in *Margarornis*, but present treatment confirmed by Rudge & Raikow (1992). *Roraimia* is one of 27 monotypic genera in Furnariidae.

RUSTY-WINGED BARBTAIL

Premnornis guttuligera Pl. 142

Identification 13.5–14.5cm. Dark brown above, more rusty on rump to tail, with pale buffy streaks on back, whitish eyebrow, white throat, whitish streaks on head-sides and breast, becoming broad and buffy on sides, belly and flanks; eyes brown, horn-coloured bill with dark culmen, legs and feet brown. Look for streaked back and broad buff scallop-streaking below. Very like *Premnoplex* barbtails, but (despite English name) lacks barbed tips to tail-feathers.

Ssp. *P. g. guttuligera* (Andes: Ec & Co) more rufous on crown and back

P. g. venezuelana (W Ve: Perijá & SW Táchira) darker, more olivaceous on crown and back, blacker fringes to crown-feathers make it appear more scalloped

Habits Forages mostly alone, often with mixed understorey flocks, from low levels to subcanopy. Inspects clumps of dead leaves and tangled vines. Does not hitch up trunks, like Spotted Barbtail, but flits actively and nimbly like foliage-gleaner. Quite silent and inconspicuous.

Status Uncommon in Ecuador, uncommon to locally frequent in Colombia, uncommon in Venezuela.

Habitat Subtropical Zone, 1,600–2,900m. Humid montane forest with abundant mosses and epiphytes.

Voice Sings very rarely, a bouncy, accelerating *tsi-tsi-tsi-si-si-sisisisisisi* or *tsip'tsip'ti'ti'ti'ti'ti'ti'i'i'i'i'i*; calls include a sharp *tseep* or buzzy *zeet-zeet,* occasionally when foraging, and less frequently, an emphatic *tsip-tsip-tsip-tsip-tsip* (R&G, Hilty).

Note *Premnornis* is one of 27 monotypic genera in Furnariidae. Vaurie (1980) merged *Premnornis* with *Margarornis*, but not accepted by AOU (1998), R&T, R&G, Hilty or Remsen.

SPOTTED BARBTAIL

Premnoplex brunnescens Pl. 142

Identification 13–14cm. Deep rufescent brown above with some tawny streaking, underparts dark tawny-brown, throat tawny-orange, with streaks that become teardrop spots on dark brown. Look for rows of rich buff, drop-shaped spots over underparts, dark tail with spines on tips of feathers.

Ssp. *P. b. brunnescens* (Andes: Ec, Co & Ve: Perijá in Zulia, Andes of Táchira, Mérida & NW Barinas) tail fuscous, heavily streaked, pale tawny-ochraceous throat, and dark brown back with feathers edged blackish

P. b. coloratus (Co: Santa Marta) browner tail, rich tawny-ochraceous throat that extends well onto chest, and back has a rufous tinge

P. b. rostratus (NC Ve: N mountains from Lara to Miranda) black tail, noticeable rich tawny-ochraceous throat, deeper rufous back

Habits Forages at lower levels, alone or in pairs, in shady areas with dense undergrowth. Moves quietly along first few metres of trunks and low-lying branches, zig-zagging up with short hops. Very easily overlooked. Occasionally joins mixed understorey flocks.

Status Frequent in Ecuador and Colombia. In Venezuela, uncommon but probably more frequent than records indicate.

Habitat Upper Tropical to Subtropical Zones, 700–3,000m. Wet montane and cloud forests where mosses and epiphytes abound and lower levels are fairly dense.

Voice Call a sibilant *pseEK!* or sharp *teep!* as bird flies to next tree (Hilty, R&G). Rarely sings. Hilty describes song in Venezuela and Colombia as a high, racing *eep eep eep ti'ti'ti'tititi* and song of *brunnescens* in Ecuador as a flat, slowing trill, *ti ti'ti'ti'ti'ti'ti'ti'ti'ti'ti'i'i.* In R&G, song for *brunnescens* described as a short descending trill, *pseerrr*, sometimes following several high, emphatic notes.

Note Race in Trujillo, Venezuela, uncertain. Vaurie (1980) merged *Premnoplex* within *Margarornis*, but not accepted by AOU (1998), R&T, R&G, Hilty or Remsen.

WHITE-THROATED BARBTAIL

Premnoplex tatei Pl. 142

Identification 14–15cm. Dark rusty olive-brown above and below, with pale to whitish streaks on head and back, whitish streaks below to flanks. Two rather different races.

Ssp. *P. t. pariae* (NE Ve: Cordillera de Paria) very white throat which extends through streaks and then teardrop spots to upper belly and upper flanks

P. t. tatei (NE Ve: Cordillera de Caripe/Turimiquire) completely dark brown below with rows of small whitish spots on chin and throat, becoming larger and reaching lower flanks

Habits Forages alone, in pairs or small family groups, always at lower levels, in dense undergrowth. May forage on ground. Flits through foliage nimbly and restlessly.

Status Vulnerable. Uncommon to very locally frequent Venezuelan endemic, with 2 disjunct populations. Classified as threatened due to its very small range, which is increasingly affected by deforestation, fires and itinerant agriculture.

Habitat Upper Tropical to Subtropical Zones; race *tatei* at 1,100–2,400m, *pariae* at 800–1,200m. Wet and cloud forests where mosses, epiphytes and understorey palms abound and lower levels are fairly dense.

Voice Song of race *tatei* a rapid series soft, reedy whistles, *we-whur, we-whur, wee-heet…*, with some variations, including *be-be-bur, be-be-bur…* and *pi, pr-pr-pr-prip!* (Hilty). Race *pariae* calls *we-whúr* and *szzzz, szzzz, szzzzz, szzzzzzz!* and song is *be'be'bur* (D. Ascanio).

Notes Formerly considered a race of *P. brunnescens* but Meyer de Schauensee (1970) treated it specifically. Remsen considered published evidence for such treatment as weak, but their voices are quite different. S&M felt *pariae* might represent a separate species (Paria Barbtail).

Margarornis treerunners are beautiful inhabitants of Andean forests. They behave much like woodcreepers, using their tails as a brace when hitching up trunks or hopping on horizontal branches. Their nests are small balls of moss with a side entrance.

FULVOUS-DOTTED TREERUNNER

Margarornis stellatus Pl. 143

Identification 15cm. Bright chestnut with white throat and radiating black-bordered white streaks on face- and body-sides and breast, rest of underparts have darker fringes giving a slightly scaled effect. Look for bright chestnut upperparts, white throat, pointed spots edged black, and scattering of spots, white with black borders, obvious against rufous-chestnut background of upper chest.

Ssp. Monotypic (NW Ec: Carchi to Chimborazo, Co: W Andes)

Habits Forages from mid levels to subcanopy, alone, in pairs or small groups, and usually with mixed flocks. Scales tree trunks like a woodcreeper (frequently using tail for support), inspecting mosses and epiphytes, resolutely peering and probing them in search of insects.

Status Very rare and local in Ecuador, where threatened by human encroachment and loss of forest. Frequent in Colombia.

Habitat Upper Tropical to Lower Subtropical Zones, 1,200–1,900m in Ecuador; 1,200–2,200m in Colombia. Very humid, wet and cloud forests, in areas of permanent humidity with abundant mosses and epiphytes.

Voice No description found and apparently no recordings exist, possibly because silent most of time.

Note R&T proposed name Star-chested Treerunner, given that 'dots' are not fulvous but white (bird is fulvous) and they form a star-shaped pattern.

PEARLED TREERUNNER

Margarornis squamiger Pl. 143

Identification 15–16cm. Bright chestnut back to tail, head olive with black-bordered white eyebrow, white throat and rows of black-fringed white spots over entire olive underparts. Juvenile a duller and slightly less well-patterned version of adult. Look for long white eyebrow and striking white throat, bright rufous back, and numerous tear-shaped spots that stand out boldly against olive-brown background of underparts – a very handsome bird indeed.

Ssp. *M. s. perlatus* (Andes: Ec, Co & Ve)

Habits Forages from mid levels to canopy, alone, in pairs or small family groups, and almost always with mixed canopy flocks. Moves like a small woodcreeper, scaling trunks with short hops, but also creeps nimbly along underside of mossy branches or flits restlessly through foliage like a foliage-gleaner. Easy to see but very quiet.

Status Widespread and frequent in Ecuador, frequent in Colombia. In Venezuela, common in Táchira, frequent elsewhere. Also, more common everywhere at higher altitudes.

Habitat Subtropical Zone to Páramo, 1,500–3,800m, but mainly 1,800–3,500m. Humid, wet and cloud forests, secondary woodland, elfin forests and *Polylepis* copses at treeline. Areas with abundant mosses and epiphytes.

Voice Foraging call a high, thin *tik* or *tsit*. Song a trill formed by long series of same *tik* note at a very high pitch (Hilty, R&G). Also a *trrrr-trrrr* trill (Remsen).

Pseudocolaptes are beautiful and comparatively large furnariids. In part, their handsome looks derive from the conspicuous pale tufts that flare backwards on neck-sides and provide their common name. They represent an unusual case of sexual dimorphism: females' bills are longer than males'. They are birds of montane forest canopies, and are considered epiphyte specialists because they are quite adept at foraging in bromeliads growing on larger horizontal branches. Their nests are balls of vegetable matter with a tube entrance, placed in a tree hole or crevice, often in abandoned woodpecker holes.

BUFFY TUFTEDCHEEK

Pseudocolaptes lawrencii Pl. 143

Identification 19.5–20.5cm. Deep rich rufous above (blackish centres to wing-feathers) and below, except head and breast; top of head and mask from lores to a point on rear ear-coverts, nape and neck-sides dusky; eyebrow and extended, tufty ear-coverts creamy white, chin and throat buffy, heavily streaked white, entire breast blackish-fringed white producing pattern of streaks or scales; subtle buffy streaking on nape and underparts; eyes dark brown, bill horn with dusky culmen, legs and feet brown. Look for beautiful plumage pattern and rich colours. Best separated from Streaked Tuftedcheek by dark breast and heavy scalloping, but they occur at different altitudes, with very little overlap.

Ssp. *P. l. johnsoni* (W Ec, W Co: W Andes)

Habits Forages in canopy and subcanopy, alone or in pairs, usually with mixed flocks. Probes and climbs inside epiphytes and mosses on large horizontal branches, feeding on insects, spiders and small amphibians inside bromeliads. Pokes noisily in debris around clumps of epiphytes. Often uses tail to prop itself.

Status Uncommon and seemingly very local in Ecuador, where mostly in south-west (Azuay and El Oro); uncommon in Colombia.

Habitat Upper Tropical to Subtropical Zones, 700–1,700m in Ecuador, 800–2,000m in Colombia. Very humid to wet montane and cloud forests, both interior and at borders.

Voice Sequence of high, loud notes and trills (R&G) or an ascending then descending and fading series of gurgling trills: *peek peek prrrrrrrrreeeeeeeee* (Remsen).

Notes Formerly called Lawrence's Tuftedcheek, or considered a subspecies of *P. boissonneautii*, but treated separately by Peters (1951) and subsequent authors. Zimmer (1936c) placed *johnsoni* as a race of *P. lawrencii*, but Robbins & Ridgely (1990) suggested species was warranted, and treated thus (under name Pacific Tuftedcheek) in R&T and R&G, on basis of plumage differences and disjunct distributions.

STREAKED TUFTEDCHEEK

Pseudocolaptes boissonneautii Pl. 143

Identification 20–22cm. Varies racially, but essentially dark ruddy brown above, paler rufous below, top and sides of head fuscous, ear-coverts pure white, extended and tufted, cheeks to throat white. Bill size varies by race, eye colour possibly as well. Look for conspicuous snowy white ear-covert tufts that may be flared outwards.

Ssp. *P. b. boissonneautii* (W Ec: W slope from Esmeraldas to N El Oro, Co: W & C Andes, E Andes S from Cundinamarca) very deep reddish-umber above, deep reddish-rufous rump to tail, postocular eyebrow reddish-rufous, throat washed buffy with pale dusky scaling, breast and underparts reddish-rufous, scaled black on upper breast, bill short and black, eyes dark brown

P. b. meridae (W Ve: Andes & Perijá, E Co: Perijá & E Andes in Boyacá & Santander) eyebrow narrow, starts in front of eye, white washed buffy; ear-coverts long and tufted, chin, throat and malar creamy buff, slightly scaled dusky on lower throat, breast pale cinnamon, black fringes only on sides of neck and breast; bill thin and pointed, black with horn-coloured base, eyes dark brown

P. b. oberholseri (Ec: all E slope, W slope in S El Oro & W Loja) darker crown, buff eyebrow, buffy streaks on back, heavier blackish fringes on neck and breast feathers, chin, throat to tufted ear-coverts white, bill long and pointed, black with pale grey base, eyes mid-brown

P. b. striaticeps (N Ve: Coastal Cordillera) head not as dark and streaked buffy, full eyebrow orange-buffy, chin and throat buffy, malar and long-tufted ear-coverts pure white; underparts paler cinnamon with pale centres from breast to flanks, richer undertail-coverts; eyes brown, bill long and horn-coloured with dusky culmen

Habits Forages in canopy and subcanopy, alone or in pairs, usually with mixed flocks. Climbs inside epiphytes and mosses on large horizontal branches, taking insects, spiders and small amphibians inside bromeliads. Pokes noisily in debris around clumps of epiphytes, hammers on wood energetically, or clambers nimbly over leaves and mosses. Often uses tail to prop itself.

Status Uncommon to frequent in Ecuador, frequent and widespread in Colombia, uncommon in Venezuela.

Habitat Subtropical Zone to Páramo, 1,800–3,400m in Ecuador, 1,800–3,200m in Colombia, 1450–3,000m in Venezuela, but mostly above 2,500m to treeline. Humid to wet montane, cloud and elfin forests, always where bromeliads abound.

Voice Sings mostly at dawn, rarely during day, a sequence of 1–2 sharp notes followed by a trill, *chut, chut, ch'iiiii'e'e'e'e'e-e-e-e-e*, starts very fast, slows and ends suddenly (H&B, Hilty, P. Schwartz recording). Foraging calls include a single, flat *chut* and loud *chink!* and *cheeyk!* (H&B, R&G).

Note Race *orientalis* of eastern Ecuador synonymised under *oberholseri* in Remsen. Zimmer (1936c) considered that specimens of this race from south-west Ecuador were somewhat different or atypical.

POINT-TAILED PALMCREEPER

Berlepschia rikeri Pl. 143

Identification 21.5–22cm. Quite unique: head and underparts black with heavy white streaks, whilst mantle, wings and tail contrast sharply in plain chestnut-rufous; bill straight, long and thin with a narrow ridge; wing- and tail-feathers quite pointed, eyes reddish-orange.

Ssp. Monotypic (NE Ec: Napo and Sucumbíos, SE Co, S Ve, Guianas)

Habits Forages in canopy of palms, in very loose pairs or small family groups of 3–4 that seek insects and spiders deep in fronds. Moves over and under leaves with great agility. Very handsome, but very shy and quiet, and difficult to find unless singing, as it occasionally does from very tip of a palm.

Status Rare to locally uncommon in Ecuador, where first recorded 1988. Rare in Colombia where first sight records also recent (Pearman 1993). Uncommon to very locally frequent in Venezuela and Guyana. Uncommon in north but increasingly frequent in southern Suriname, where first recorded 1974. Uncommon to locally common in coastal French Guiana.

Habitat Lower Tropical Zone, to 650m in Ecuador, to 200m in Venezuela. Found only in boggy or marshy stands of Moriche Palm *Mauritia flexuosa* in savannas, occasionally in stands of *Bactris* palms and in palm marshes in forests.

Voice Sings or calls mostly at dawn and dusk. Song a loud *chwee-chwee-chwee-chwee-chwee-chwee* whistle (H&M) or a fast, far-carrying series of ringing notes, *dedede-kee!-kee!-kee!-kee!-kee!-kee!-kee!-kee!* that may last 3–5 s (R&G), or a loud *kree!-kree!-kree!...* series of up to 30 ringing notes, lasting 5–7 s (Hilty); mate joins in almost immediately.

Notes *Berlepschia* is one of 27 monotypic genera in Furnariidae.

CHESTNUT-WINGED HOOKBILL

Ancistrops strigilatus Pl. 143

Identification 18–19cm. Dark olive-brown above with dark rufous wings and tail, narrow pale to whitish streaks on top and sides of head, broader and whiter on back. Underparts greyish-buffy, streaked brownish on centre, and whitish on sides and flanks. Eyes brown, bill large and heavy (small hooked tip very hard to see), dusky above, bluish-grey below. Resembles a *Philydor* but is more heavy built.

Ssp. Monotypic (E Ec: Napo & Sucumbíos; SE Co: S Meta & W Vaupés to Amazonas)

Habits Forages from mid levels to canopy, alone or in pairs, quite often with mixed canopy flocks of nunbirds, woodcreepers, other furnariids, etc. Slow and deliberate, inspects epiphytes and vine tangles, moving along thicker branches and near trunk. Not shy.

Status Rare to locally frequent in Ecuador, uncommon in Colombia.
Habitat Lower Tropical Zone, to 600m locally in Ecuador but generally below 450m. Humid *terra firme*, occasionally in *várzea*.
Voice Song a long quavering trill that can last over 30 s. Calls include a nasal *tyew-tyew* followed by bouts of chatter, a short ascending trill and harsh *bzzzzt* buzz (H&B, R&G, Remsen).
Notes We follow Remsen in considering *A. strigilatus* monotypic, as characteristics of only other race (in Brazil) apparently occur throughout range. Vaurie (1980) merged *Ancistrops* within *Philydor*. *Ancistrops* is one of 27 monotypic genera in Furnariidae.

Hyloctistes has been considered a monospecific genus subdivided into 2 groups of subspecies with disjunct ranges; west of Andes from Nicaragua to west Ecuador (races *nicaraguae, virgatus, assimilis* and *cordobae*), and east of Andes in southern Venezuela and upper Amazonia (races *lemae* and *subulatus*). Remsen considered them almost certainly separate species, and there is a study in preparation. R&T had suggested that trans-Andean populations and Amazonian populations merit species rank based on vocal differences; and R&G, SCJ&W and Hilty treat them as separate species. Vaurie (1980) included *Hyloctistes* within *Philydor*. Woodhaunters are forest understorey birds. For a nest, they make small pads of leaf rachises at end of a burrow dug in a bank.

EASTERN WOODHAUNTER

Hyloctistes subulatus Pl. 146

Identification 16.5–19cm. Dark olive-brown above, slightly rufescent on wings and more rufescent on rump to tail, streaked buffy from head to back; olive-brown below with buffy chin and throat, some pale streaking on sides, more rufescent on undertail-coverts.

Ssp. *H. s. lemae* (SE Ve) streaking on crown, throat and underparts more marked than in nominate, chin yellowish.
H. s. subulatus (E Ec, SE Co, S Ve) chin buffy

Habits Forages alone or in very loose pairs, from undergrowth to mid levels, searching clumps of dead leaves that have accumulated in tangles of vines or criss-crossing branches, and inspecting debris in epiphyte clusters on thick branches and trunks. Often found in canopy, in company of mixed flocks with other furnariids, as well as flycatchers, antwrens and antshrikes. Returns to favourite perches to sing every morning, and pairs are territorial.
Status Uncommon to frequent in Ecuador; uncommon but perhaps locally frequent in Colombia and Venezuela.
Habitat Tropical Zone, recorded to 1,500m but more numerous below 500m in Venezuela, and mostly below 1,100m in Ecuador. Humid and wet *terra firme* and mature secondary woodland in lowlands and foothills.
Voice In lowlands of east Bolívar, Venezuela, dawn song, repeated after pauses, is 2–3 rough whistles followed by a rattle, *chaw, cheee, t'r'r'r'r'r'r'r'r*, whilst in foothills gives a continually repeated, slow, plaintive *kalEEp-cleer* (Hilty). In Ecuador, 2–4 loud, ringing *teeu* notes, often followed by a *tr-r-r-r-r-r-r* rattle, and call is a sudden, clear *squirp!* (R&G).
Note Often treated within an expanded *H. subulatus* (Striped Woodhaunter). As here, split into 2 species by some recent authors (R&G, Hilty, SCJ&W), but no formal revision published.

WESTERN WOODHAUNTER

Hyloctistes virgatus Pl. 146

Identification 16.5–17cm. Dark olive-brown above, contrastingly rufescent on wings and rump to tail, streaked buffy from head to nape, clear buffy eyebrow; olive-brown below with buffy chin and throat that extends in soft streaks to breast-sides. Apart from voice, main differences from Eastern Woodhaunter are lack of streaking on mantle, throat more ochraceous and fewer flammulations below; upperparts quite dark.

Ssp. *H. v. assimilis* (W Ec, W Co) generally dark, with almost no streaking
H. v. cordobae (NW Co: Córdoba & N Antioquia) paler, more yellowish throat and face than *assimilis*

Habits As previous species.
Status Uncommon to frequent in Ecuador, uncommon but perhaps locally frequent in Colombia.
Habitat Tropical Zone (to 1,100m). Humid *terra firme* and mature secondary woodland.
Voice Sings long, paced repetitions of same sharp nasal *keeu* or *kyip* note: *keeu-keeu-keeu-keeu…* or *kyip-kyip-kyip-kyip…* and call a sudden, clear *squirp!* (R&T, R&G).
Notes Those races listed here, and *virgatus* (of western Panama) and *nicaraguae* (eastern Nicaragua), formerly placed under *H. subulatus* (Striped Woodhaunter).

Syndactyla foliage-gleaners inhabit the understorey of montane forests. The genus has been merged by some into *Philydor* and considered by others to possibly belong with *Thripadectes* (see Remsen). They move along horizontal branches turning about-face with each little hop, and are dead-leaf specialists. All have very streaked underparts and contrasting throats that are whitish or paler than rest, and a bill that is slightly to quite wedge-shaped. Nests are shallow cups of twigs, placed in various holes, e.g. abandoned woodpecker holes, drainage pipes, holes in walls, etc.

GUTTULATED FOLIAGE-GLEANER

Syndactyla guttulata Pl. 146

Identification 19cm. Entirely olive-brown with deep rufous rump to tail and rufescent undertail-coverts; distinct buffy streaks on back, eyebrow of buffy dots and streaks, buffy streaks on malar, and other, smaller buffy streaks on head- and neck-sides; chin and throat creamy buff, extending more faintly onto breast, sides and flanks. Dark eyes, stout grey bill, dark grey legs and feet. Juvenile has bright rufous eyebrow; face-sides and throat have rows of black-fringed white spots; bill dark above, horn below.

Ssp. *S. g. guttulata* (NC Ve: Falcón and Yaracuy to Miranda) adult has very orange postocular stripe, rounded scales on breast and deep orange undertail-coverts

S. g. pallida (NE Ve: Anzoátegui and N Monagas) far less rufous-orange, postocular buffy; juvenile has postocular much warmer and orange-tinted, but still paler than adult *guttulata*

Habits Forages at low to mid levels, alone or in very loose pairs, often with understorey mixed flocks of antwrens, warblers and bush-tanagers. Often secretive, keeping behind foliage, but quite active and very nimble, often hangs upside-down to inspect bark or dead leaves. Sometimes attends army ants.

Status Endemic to northern Venezuela, where uncommon to locally frequent.

Habitat Upper Tropical to Subtropical Zones, 900–2,100m. Wet montane and cloud forests.

Voice Sings only a few times per day, a speeding sequence of rough notes, *cjak…cjak..czak'czak'zak'zak'zak'za'za'za'za…* Foraging call a coarse *chak* (Hilty).

BUFF-BROWED FOLIAGE-GLEANER

Syndactyla rufosuperciliata Pl. 146

Identification 18cm. Brownish-olive from forehead to back, very fine buffy streaks on back, dark rufous-umber wings and rump to tail, faint buffy eyebrow, buffy head-sides, white streaks on ear-coverts, chin and throat white with fine dusky vermiculations, underparts brownish-olive with white streaks on sides of neck and breast fading on belly and flanks.

Ssp. *S. r. cabanisi* (SE Ec: Cordillera del Cóndor, Zamora-Chinchipe)

Habits Forages in undergrowth, alone or in pairs, mostly with mixed flocks that often include Lineated Foliage-gleaner.

Status Uncommon in Ecuador, where first found 1990 (Krabbe & Sornoza 1994).

Habitat Tropical to Subtropical Zones, 1,700–1,900m. Humid montane forest, in patches of *Chusquea* bamboo.

Voice Males sing frequently, a fast sequence of rough notes, *kuh-kuh-kuh-kihkihkihkikikikiku*, similar to Lineated Foliage-gleaner, but apparently less nasal (R&G).

LINEATED FOLIAGE-GLEANER

Syndactyla subalaris Pl. 146

Identification 18–19cm. Quite variable, but essentially olive-brown with slightly rufescent wings, dark rufescent rump to tail and undertail-coverts. Pale to whitish streaks from top of head and throat, radiating over back and breast. Juvenile much warmer, flushed orange on breast.

Ssp. *S. s. mentalis* (E Ec) much darker crown and nape, with buff streaks more abundant and marked; more abundant streaks on underparts

S. s. olivacea (Ve: Táchira) most olivaceous underparts

S. s. striolata (Co: E Andes, W Ve) top and sides of head much darker, effectively fuscous, entire head streaked white (black on throat), most heavily streaked with broader buff streaks on back

S. s. subalaris (W Ec, Co: W & C Andes) virtually unstreaked crown, white streaks to upper mantle only, white chin and throat, soft narrow white streaks on breast-sides

S. s. tacarcunae (NW Co on border with Panama) pale yellowish throat and greyish underparts

Habits Forages from undergrowth to mid levels, alone or in pairs, mostly with mixed flocks. Keeps inside foliage, but is quite noisy. Moves along horizontal branches inspecting mosses and leaf debris, or probes clumps of dead leaves. Like others in genus, constructs nest of vegetable matter at end of a burrow excavated in a dirt bank.

Status Uncommon to frequent in Ecuador, uncommon and local in Venezuela.

Habitat Upper Tropical to Subtropical Zones, 100–2,100m in Ecuador, 1,300–2,400m in Colombia and 800–2,000m in Venezuela. Humid montane forest with abundant vines.

Voice Sings frequently, a fast sequence of rough notes that start with a stuttering. In Ecuador, *anh, anh, anh-anh-anh-anhanhanhanh*. In Venezuela, *bzert, bzert, jzut, jzut-jj-jj-jj*. A sudden *skanh!* and *kr-kr*, sometimes run into a series. Also, a scratchy *jzert*. (R&G, Hilty).

RUFOUS-NECKED FOLIAGE-GLEANER

Syndactyla ruficollis Pl. 146

Identification 18cm. Look for bold, broad orange-rufous eyebrow that circles neck-sides, and contrasting buffy cinnamon throat. Rufous-brown above with fine whitish streaks, broad bright orange eyebrow wraps around ear-coverts and joins orange throat (chin paler), and this colour extends as streak over olive underparts, becoming paler and buffy on belly and flanks. Eyes dark, bill dark above, grey below, legs and feet dark horn.

Ssp. Monotypic (SW Ec: Loja)

Habits Usually forages in undergrowth to subcanopy, alone or in pairs, or in dry season sometimes in small family groups and usually with mixed flocks. Hops along larger horizontal branches overgrown with epiphytes, inspecting them for insects. Also recorded foraging on ground, searching leaf-litter or fern patches and stands of bamboo.

Status Vulnerable. Uncommon to frequent and local in south-west Ecuador. Its very small range is very fragmented and declining rapidly.

Habitat Tropical to Temperate Zones, 400–2,900m but mostly 1,300–2,300m. Moist deciduous, semi-deciduous and humid evergreen forest, secondary woodland, stands of bamboo, often along streams.

Voice Call and song nasal and sharp. Call an *ank* note (R&G) and song lasts *c*.2 s and drops at end, *chick, chick, che-che, tirrrrrr* (Remsen).

Notes Formerly placed in *Automolus*, but removed on basis of voice, plumage and distribution characteristics (see Remsen). Race *celicae* (south-west Ecuador) now considered invalid as plumage characters that supposedly define it occur in all populations (Remsen, R&G). Sighting in El Oro unconfirmed (R&G).

Anabacerthia foliage-gleaners are relatively small and slender, arboreal, and their lack of secretive or furtive habits makes them comparatively easy to see. They have a distinctive head pattern, a bill with a straight culmen, and fairly thick eyebrow and eye-ring. They nest in abandoned woodpecker holes or holes in stumps of dead trees or palms, which they line with a thick mat of moss and lichen.

SCALY-THROATED FOLIAGE-GLEANER

Anabacerthia variegaticeps Pl. 146

Identification 16.5–18cm. Entirely rufescent olive-brown above, with small black streaks on top of head, distinct, bold, black-edged, bright orange eye-ring and postocular streak; chin and throat white with white streaks radiating onto olive head-sides and breast, rest of underparts olive-brown with faint narrow streaks throughout.

Ssp. *A. v. temporalis* (W Ec, Co: W Andes)

Habits Active and conspicuous, forages for insects and spiders from subcanopy to lower levels, alone or in pairs, frequently with mixed-species flocks. Hops on branches, inspecting them above and below. Checks bromeliads and other clumps of epiphytes. Often hops sideways.

Status Frequent in Ecuador, uncommon and very local in Colombia.

Habitat Upper Tropical to Subtropical Zones. Humid to wet montane and cloud forests and mature second growth, both at borders and interiors

Voice Song a rising then descending series of scratchy squeaks; call a sharp, sudden *kweeeeah*, and a rusty rattle. Also, a fast series of 15–20 penetrating *skee* or *tjik* notes, or a single sharp, dry *skeeyh* or *skek* (R&G).

Notes Formerly considered conspecific with *A. striaticollis*, but separated by Wetmore (1972) on basis of plumage differences. Formerly called Spectacled Foliage-gleaner, but there are many spectacled foliage-gleaners in South America, so present name seems more appropriate (R&T 1994, AOU 1998), although our race lacks scaly throat. Race *temporalis* formerly treated as a separate species and later a race of *A. striaticollis*, but is probably a separate species. Genus *Anabacerthia* merged into *Philydor* by Vaurie (1980) and Hilty suspects that *Anabacerthia* may belong in *Philydor*.

MONTANE FOLIAGE-GLEANER

Anabacerthia striaticollis Pl. 146

Identification 16–16.5cm. Olive-brown above, rufous rump to tail, head greyish-olive with dusky fringes to feathers, white eye-ring and postocular line, dusky ear-coverts with narrow white streaks, white chin and whitish throat, underparts cinnamon. Bill slightly more xenops-like than usual with culmen flat and mandible upturned over distal third, black above, greyish below. Look for conspicuous eye-ring and postocular line.

Ssp. *A. s. anxia* (Co: Santa Marta) eye-ring, postocular line, throat and breast all yellowish

A. s. montana (E Ec) more rufescent brown above, eye-ring and postocular line bold, white streaks from throat to upper breast and sides

A. s. perijana (W Ve) back yellowish-brown, throat more yellowish and underparts yellowish-olive

A. s. striaticollis (Andes: Co, Ve) as described

A. s. venezuelana (NC Ve) greyish-olive above, back concolorous with head, underparts pale greyish-buffy on sides and breast, with white streaks reaching flanks

Habits Forages for insects and spiders from subcanopy to lower levels, alone or in pairs and frequently with mixed-species flocks. Hops on branches, inspecting them above and below. Checks bromeliads and other clumps of epiphytes. Often hops sideways.

Status Frequent in Ecuador. In Colombia and Venezuela, the commonest montane foliage-gleaner.

Habitat Upper Tropical to Subtropical Zones. Humid forest and mature secondary woodland in foothills and on lower and middle Andean slopes. Sometimes at borders and in clearings.

Voice Does not call or sing often. In Ecuador, song similar to Scaly-throated, but softer and more irregularly paced (R&G). In Colombia, a single sharp, raspy *chek* note, or a fast staccato series (H&B). In Venezuela, coarse *chit!* or *skip!* notes, doubled when foraging, and song a staccato repetition of same rough *chuk* note (Hilty).

Notes Formerly considered conspecific with *A. variegaticeps*, but separated by Wetmore (1972) on basis of plumage differences. Genus *Anabacerthia* merged within *Philydor* by Vaurie (1980) and Hilty considers that *Anabacerthia* might be best placed in *Philydor*.

Philydor foliage-gleaners are slender inhabitants of humid lowland forests. Most are arboreal, but a few species forage in undergrowth. They are active and energetic, but not very vocal. Quite distinctive with bold pale eyebrow underlined by striking dark eyestripe. Nest a simple flat plate of rootlets, placed, depending on species, within a hole dug by adults in rotten wood of a snag, or a tunnel excavated in a soft dirt bank or slope cut.

RUFOUS-TAILED FOLIAGE-GLEANER

Philydor ruficaudatum Pl. 144

Identification 17–18cm. Olive-brown above, tail rufous; eye-ring, postocular line, streaks on cheeks, chin and throat to below creamy white, with olive streaks on ear-coverts and sides, increasing until undertail-coverts are more olive than creamy.

Ssp. *P. r. flavipectus* (S Ve) clean sulphur-yellow chin and throat, flammulated breast, diffuse on belly, underwing-coverts ochre, flanks yellowish-olive; juvenile has rufous eyebrow, duller throat with orange tinge on malar, breast flammulations very diffuse

P. r. ruficaudatum (E Ec, SE Co, S Ve, Guianas) similar above but greyer below, throat pale straw yellow, sides and flanks greyish-olive, underwing-coverts buffy

Habits Always found with mixed canopy and subcanopy flocks of insectivorous birds, including other furnariids and woodcreepers. Restless, forages from mid levels to canopy, where searches for insects in outer, higher branches and twigs. Probes hanging curled-up dry leaves and bundles of dead leaves trapped by vines.

Status Rare in Ecuador, where many records probably reflect confusion with Rufous-rumped Foliage-gleaner *P. erythrocercum subflavum*. Uncommon to possibly frequent very locally in Colombia, frequent in Venezuela, uncommon in Guyana and in Suriname, scarce or uncommon in French Guiana.

Habitat Tropical Zone. Humid lowland forest, *terra firme* and, less frequently, *várzea*; foothills and lower slopes; slopes of tepuis.

Voice Song a single note, repeated continuously (H&M). No descriptions from Ecuador, Colombia or Venezuela found. In south-east Peru, staccato notes that become lower and faster at end, *te- te- te- te- te- te- te- te-t-t-t-r* (R&G). In southern Brazil, a loud clatter *ke-ke-ke-kee-kee-kee-kee-… ke-ke-ke-ke-ke* that accelerates at beginning and slows down at end, and also a variable *wt-pt-pt, wit-wit-wit, d'd'd'd'd'd'd'd* (Hilty).

Notes Considered by some to be closer to *Anabacerthia* than to other *Philydor*. As *Philydor* is neuter, correct spelling is *ruficaudatum*, not *ruficaudatus* (David & Gosselin 2002).

CINNAMON-RUMPED FOLIAGE-GLEANER

Philydor pyrrhodes Pl. 144

Identification 16.5–17cm. Slaty wings contrast with rufescent brown upperparts, bright cinnamon rump and tail, and bright orange-cinnamon underparts.

Ssp. Monotypic (E Ec: Napo; SE Co, S Ve, Guianas)

Habits Forages alone, in pairs or small groups, only occasionally with mixed flocks, at lower levels, searching *Heliconia*, palms and other large-leaf plants, or inspecting bundles of dead leaves trapped by criss-crossing branches or tangles of vines. Very shy and secretive.

Status Rare to locally uncommon in Ecuador, uncommon in Colombia, uncommon and very local in Venezuela, uncommon in Guyana, widespread but scarce in Suriname and French Guiana.

Habitat Lower Tropical Zone. Pristine humid forest, *terra firme* and *várzea*, usually near water, and often with dense tangled vines or abundant palms in understorey, where dead, dry fronds are searched for insects and larvae.

Voice In Peru, a loud, short trill (H&B). Song a long buzzy trill of varying length that rises in pitch to a crescendo with an abrupt drop and end, and both sexes give a harsh *chek* (Hilty). In Suriname a 2-note alarm *tratra… tratra…* and song is a toneless loud rattle *tr.r.r.r.r.e.e.e – r.r.r.r.e.e.e* (H&M).

SLATY-WINGED FOLIAGE-GLEANER

Philydor fuscipenne Pl. 146

Identification 16.5–17cm. Slate brown or dusky wings contrast with rufescent body and tail, slate brown head with dusky-bordered, very long and noticeable, broad cinnamon-buff eyestripe. Pale eye-ring; ear-coverts edged dusky, buffy-ochraceous underparts palest on throat. Juvenile generally similar but warmer and more rufescent.

Ssp. *P. f. erythronotum* (NW Ec, Co: Andes)

Habits Forages alone or in pairs, often with mixed flocks in undergrowth, occasionally to lower midstorey. Restless, searches branches and twigs from mid levels to undergrowth, inspecting clumps of epiphytes and curled dead leaves.

Status Rare to uncommon and local in Ecuador, very common in Colombia, especially in foothills.

Habitat Tropical Zone, 500–1,000m, occasionally to 1,200m. Humid forests and mature secondary woodland.

Voice A sharp *chef!* between foraging birds (R&G), song a monotone accelerating trill (Remsen).

Notes As *Philydor* is neuter, correct spelling is *fuscipenne* not *fuscipennis* (David & Gosselin 2002). Formerly considered conspecific with *P. erythrocercum*, but they differ in foraging habits and habitat preference: *fuscipenne* in understorey, whilst *erythrocercum* lives in canopy (H&B), and *fuscipenne* is probably closer to *P. pyrrhodes* (R&T); this is a return to classification by Cory & Hellmayr (1925). Race *erythronotum* has been treated specifically and sometimes as a race of *P. erythrocercum*, but present placement follows Zimmer (1935a) and Vaurie (1980). Populations in Colombia possibly represent a separate subspecies (R&G).

RUFOUS-RUMPED FOLIAGE-GLEANER

Philydor erythrocercum Pl. 144

Identification 16.5–17cm. Olive-brown above with rufescent rump to tail, dusky-edged eyebrow and eye-ring, whitish throat and buffy underparts. Juvenile distinctly more rufescent, with eyebrow, neck-sides and throat more orange.

Ssp. *P. e. erythrocercum* (S Gu, S Su, FG) generally more rufescent than *subflavum* and more rufous on rump to tail, eyebrow more orange

P. e. subfulvum (E Ec, SE Co) generally paler, with eyebrow and throat pale buffy, underparts washed more greyish-olive

Habits Forages from mid levels to canopy, but mostly in subcanopy, alone or in pairs that are usually part of mixed flocks of antbirds, other furnariids, flycatchers, etc. Very acrobatic, looks for insects in curled dead leaves and bunches of dead leaves ensnared in tangled vines; a dead-leaf specialist (Remsen). Breeds in dry season.
Status Uncommon to locally frequent in Ecuador, frequent and widespread in Amazonian Colombia, frequent in Guyana, common in Suriname, common to frequent in French Guiana.
Habitat Lower Tropical Zone to 1,300m. Humid lowland forest, especially *terra firme* and humid forests of foothills and lower slopes.
Voice Song a slightly rising then falling sequence of high notes, *chu, chee, chee, chee, chu;* calls include a *cheeyu*, *chak* and *wheeeeyk* (Remsen).
Notes As *Philydor* is neuter, correct spelling is *erythrocercum*, not *erythrocercus* (David & Gosselin 2002). Race *subfulvum* formerly treated as a separate species in past, but is better considered under *P. erythrocercum* (Zimmer 1935a).

CHESTNUT-WINGED FOLIAGE-GLEANER
Philydor erythropterum Pl. 146

Identification 18–18.5cm. Rufous-chestnut wings and tail contrast with dark greyish-olive upperparts, bright orange-ochre eyebrow and throat with streaked greyish-olive ear-coverts; underparts cream with pale olive wash on breast and flanks, more so on undertail-coverts.

Ssp. *P. e. erythropterum* (E Ec, SE Co, S Ve)

Habits Forages alone or in pairs, always with mixed canopy flocks. Restless and vivacious, tends to search for insects in outer, higher branches and twigs. Probes hanging curled-up dry leaves and bunches of dead leaves trapped by vines.
Status Uncommon in Ecuador and Colombia. In Venezuela possibly uncommon, but situation not well known due to remoteness of area where it occurs.
Habitat Lower Tropical Zone to 1,200m, but most records below 500m. Tall humid lowland forest, both *várzea* and *terra firme*.
Voice Seldom calls or sings. Male's song a descending trill that lasts 2–3 s (R&G).
Note *Philydor* is neuter, thus correct spelling is *erythropterum* not *erythropterus* (David & Gosselin 2002).

BUFF-FRONTED FOLIAGE-GLEANER
Philydor rufum Pl. 146

Identification 19cm. Dark greyish-olive top of head and solid olive back to uppertail-coverts, wings and tail rufous, frontal band, eyebrow and head-sides to breast and sides rufous, olivaceous from belly and flanks to undertail-coverts.

Ssp. *P. r. colombianum* (N Ve) lores and eyebrow pale, streaks on crown reach base of culmen, rufous throat becomes paler as it merges into greyish-rufous belly
P. r. cuchiverum (S Ve) pale around eyes and postocular, but lores olive, uniform rufous from chin to belly
P. r. panerythrum (E Ec, N Co) like *colombianus* but longer wings, darker, tawnier back, more ochraceous than ochraceous-buff below
P. r. riveti (NW Ec, Co: W Andes) smaller, darker crown, darker, more sepia back, breast and belly washed brown in clean contrast with clear ochraceous throat

Habits Forages from mid levels to canopy, alone or in pairs, usually with mixed canopy flocks. Restless, flits around canopy, hops along horizontal branches and inspects both green leaves and dead ones. Probes bundles of dead leaves ensnared in tangles of vines. Nest a burrow dug in a vertical bank.
Status Uncommon to frequent in Ecuador, uncommon and local in Colombia. In Venezuela both races frequent in their respective ranges.
Habitat Tropical to Subtropical Zones. Tall humid to wet forests and mature secondary woodland.
Voice Sings infrequently. In Ecuador, a fast, falling series of metallic notes, *whi-ki-ki-ki-ke-ke-ke-kuh-kuh* (R&G). In Colombia, 2 types of *churrr*, the first a snort, the other harsh and sounds like a frog's croak. In Venezuela, a loose, coarse, rising then falling rattle (Hilty).
Note As *Philydor* is neuter, correct spelling is *rufum*, not *rufus* (David & Gosselin 2002).

DUSKY-CHEEKED FOLIAGE-GLEANER
Anabazenops dorsalis Pl. 147

Identification 18–18.5cm. Dark greyish-olive head and back contrast clearly with rich rufous rump to tail, clean white eyebrow, chin and throat white, rest of underparts creamy, washed greyish-olive on sides and flanks. Bill rather thick and chisel-shaped, horn-coloured. Juvenile warmer throughout, pale cinnamon below and eyebrow distinctly cinnamon.

Ssp. Monotypic (E Ec: base of Andes from Napo to Zamora-Chinchipe; S Co: W Caquetá & Putumayo)

Habits Forages in undergrowth, alone or in pairs, sometimes with mixed understorey flocks. A dead-leaf specialist that seeks insect food mostly in *Guadua* bamboo, inspecting dead leaf debris around rings of spines and stem bases. Climbs and moves along vines and thin stems using tail for support.
Status Rare to locally uncommon in Ecuador, uncommon to locally frequent in Colombia.
Habitat Tropical Zone to 1,000m, but in some areas to 1,300m in Ecuador, 200–500m in Colombia. Humid foothill forest, *várzea*, mature secondary woodland, seasonally flooded riparian forests and river islands, always in stands of *Guadua* bamboo or *Gynerium* cane.
Voice Song a paced *tcho, tcho, tcho, tcho, tcho, tcho…* that varies in number of notes (R&G).
Notes Formerly placed in *Automolus* (e.g. in H&B), but in *Anabazenops* by Kratter & Parker (1997) based on voice, plumage of juveniles and adults, measurements, habitat, and especially, nest architecture, as builds its nest above ground, in cavities of bamboo trunks, whilst all *Automolus* have nest burrows. Called Crested Foliage-gleaner in H&B, but see R&T, and Bamboo Foliage-gleaner in R&G. Genus *Anabazenops* merged into *Philydor* by Vaurie (1980).

Thripadectes treehunters are quiet, somewhat lethargic birds of Andean slope forests, where they occur mostly in understorey *Chusquea* and other bamboos. They are difficult to separate as all are comparatively large and robust, with stout black bills, and their furtive habits make them difficult to see. The nest, a flat plate exclusively constructed of rachises of compound leaves, is placed in a burrow excavated in a dirt bank. Called leaf-gleaners by some authors in the past.

UNIFORM TREEHUNTER

Thripadectes ignobilis Pl. 147

Identification 19cm. Entirely dark brown, slightly paler and more reddish on wings, rump and tail, but only discernible in good light, faint buffy eyebrow, lines on ear-coverts and broad streaks on breast, sides and flanks; eyes dark brown, dark grey bill comparatively short and slightly decurved, legs and feet dark brown. The only member of genus that is virtually unstreaked above.

Ssp. Monotypic (NW Ec, SW Co)

Habits Forages alone, hopping along branches and in vine tangles, poking debris and dry leaves in dense undergrowth, especially in patches of *Chusquea*. Occasionally joins mixed understorey flocks.

Status Uncommon to locally frequent, and usually more numerous at lower altitudes in Ecuador and Colombia.

Habitat Upper Tropical to Temperate Zones, 700–1,700m in Ecuador, 200–2,500m in Colombia. Humid and wet montane and foothill forests.

Voice Song is 6–8 sharp *kik* notes, higher and faster than Streak-capped Treehunter (R&G).

STREAK-CAPPED TREEHUNTER

Thripadectes virgaticeps Pl. 147

Identification 21.5–22cm. Essentially brown above, more rufescent on wings and tail, dusky to blackish on head with whitish streaks, ochraceous through cinnamon to rufous below with some scaling on breast. Eyes dark brown, bill black, large and wedge-shaped, legs and feet olive. Look for a few fine white shaft-streaks on blackish crown and nape, and obscure brown or dusky streaks on cinnamon or ochraceous-buff throat and chest.

Ssp. *T. v. klagesi* (N Ve) rather greyish on crown, back and rump paler rufous, eyebrow quite pronounced, very clear **V**-shaped fringes to streaks on throat, underparts change from olive of breast to rufous of belly

T. v. magdalenae (C Co) as described

T. v. sclateri (Co: W Andes) short slender bill, olive above with rufous on rump weak, pale ochraceous below

T. v. sumaco (E Ec: Napo) olive above, with crown poorly demarcated from back, generally less rufous

T. v. tachirensis (W Ve) like *klagesi* but streaks on throat diffuse, and merges very gradually through olive breast to rufescent belly

T. v. virgaticeps (NW Ec: Carchi to Pichincha) longer and heavier bill than others

Habits Usually forages in pairs or small family groups, in dense undergrowth. Quite active but secretive, hops about inside cover, probing mossy clumps, tangles and debris. Rarely in company of mixed understorey flocks.

Status Uncommon in Ecuador but fairly common in Colombia, uncommon and local in Venezuela.

Habitat Upper Tropical to Temperate Zones, 1,300–2,100m in Ecuador, 1,200–2,500m in Colombia, most numerous at 1,700–2,000m. Humid and wet montane and cloud forests, where mosses and epiphytes abound.

Voice Alarm or scold a raspy, nasal *jwick* and contact call a hard, low, fast *ju-dut* or *chidik*. Song a short, flat series of distinct notes, *chup-cheyp-cheyp-cheyp-cheyp-cheyp* (H&B, R&G).

Notes Sighting in El Oro, Ecuador, unconfirmed.

BLACK-BILLED TREEHUNTER

Thripadectes melanorhynchus Pl. 147

Identification 20–20.5cm. Rufescent dark brown above, streaked heavily buff on top and sides of head, back and scapulars, streaks over eye form ragged eyebrow, chin and throat cinnamon with distinct scaling due to dusky fringes to feathers, rest of underparts deep tawny-cinnamon. Bill black, but other large treehunters also have black bills.

Ssp. *T. m. melanorhynchus* (E Ec) darker and sootier above, streaks narrower

T. m. striaticeps (Co: E & C Andes) as described

Habits Forages alone in undergrowth, seldom if ever with mixed flocks. Very secretive and difficult to see.

Status Uncommon to locally frequent in Ecuador. In Colombia, rare to uncommon and very local, known from 3 localities: in Meta (1,200m), east Cauca and Putumayo.

Habitat Upper Tropical to Lower Subtropical Zones, 1,000–1,700m. Humid montane forest and secondary woodland.

Voice Vocalises infrequently. Song a loud series of sharp *kyip* notes, sometimes paired (R&G).

STRIPED TREEHUNTER

Thripadectes holostictus Pl. 147

Identification 20–20.5cm. Wings and rump to tail dark rufous with faint pale streaks to centres of wing-feathers; back, entire head and breast dusky, streaked pale buffy on top and head-sides, and back, underparts orange-cinnamon, with broad dusky fringes to feathers giving scaled effect. Similar and larger Flammulated Treehunter entirely streaked below, not scaled.

Ssp. *T. h. holostictus* (E Ec, Co: Andes, Ve: S Táchira) as described

T. h. striatidorsus (W Ec, SW Co) more rufescent and less blackish

Habits Forages in undergrowth. Secretive and quite difficult to see.

Status Uncommon to locally frequent in Ecuador; rare or

scarce in Colombia and Venezuela.

Habitat Subtropical to Temperate Zones, 1,500–3,000m but mostly 2,000–2,300m in Ecuador, 100–2,700m in Colombia, 1,800–2,000m in Venezuela. Humid to wet montane and cloud forests, with abundant mosses, epiphytes and dense understorey, especially *Chusquea* and other bamboos.

Voice A fast sequence, *kl'li'li'li'li'li'lip*, reminiscent of a flycatcher, and song a low staccato rattle that peters off (Hilty).

FLAMMULATED TREEHUNTER

Thripadectes flammulatus Pl. 147

Identification 24cm. Wings and rump to tail rufous, back, top and sides of head dusky to blackish, streaked buffy to white (on ear-coverts); underparts bright orange-cinnamon, heavily streaked black to dusky. Legs and feet olive with pale claws.

Ssp. *T. f. bricenoi* (Ve: páramos of Mérida) buff throat with vestigial streaking

T. f. flammulatus (Ec, Co: Andes & Santa Marta, Ve: páramos of Táchira) very heavily streaked black on throat and underparts

Habits Forages in dense, tangled undergrowth, mostly alone and does not join mixed flocks. Restless and energetic, but quite difficult to see, as it moves quite secretively in tangles. Inspects debris and dead leaves.

Status Uncommon and local in Ecuador, Colombia and Venezuela.

Habitat Upper Tropical Zone to Páramo, 2,000–3,500m in Ecuador, *c*.1,000–3,000m in Colombia, 2,700–3,000m in Venezuela) Humid to wet montane forest, patches of bamboo, especially *Chusquea*, mossy areas with very dense understorey.

Voice Seldom vocalises. Song is an even-paced slow rattle that speeds up or sometimes slows towards end, *t-a-a-a'a'a'a'a'a'a-a-a-a*... (Hilty).

Notes F&K suggested that *T. flammulatus* should be considered conspecific with Rufous-backed Treehunter *T. scrutator* of Peru and Bolivia.

> *Automolus* foliage-gleaners are large and drab and remain in undergrowth, whilst *Philydor* are smaller, more slender and arboreal. *Automolus* are considered dead-leaf specialists, as they mostly forage by probing curls of dead leaves. Some species are very skulking and more often heard than seen. Difficult to identify, key field marks are colour of eyes and throat, and presence of an eye-ring or eyebrow. Calls are loud and consist of 1–2 notes, much repeated. Nests are shallow plates woven exclusively with rachises of compound leaves, constructed in a long tunnel excavated in a bank or road cut.

BUFF-THROATED FOLIAGE-GLEANER

Automolus ochrolaemus Pl. 147

Identification 18.5–19cm. Olive-brown above, rufescent rump to tail, pale eye-ring and postocular line, pale throat, ochraceous underparts tending to rufous on undertail-coverts. Juvenile duller with distinct orange tinge to eyebrow and face.

Ssp. *A. o. pallidigularis* (NW Ec: Esmeraldas to SW Manabí, W Co: Antioquia to Nariño & mid Magdalena Valley) white throat and plainer, dull brown, unflammulated underparts

A. o. turdinus (E Ec, SE Co: Amazonian lowlands; S Ve: Bolívar & Amazonas, Guianas) buffy throat and pale flammulations on breast

Habits Forages in understorey and at low to mid levels, alone or, more often, in loose pairs or groups, and responds very well to playback. Regularly with mixed flocks. Not shy; hops energetically through tangles and on low branches, searching for insects, spiders and tiny invertebrates in debris and curled dead leaves.

Status Uncommon to locally frequent in Ecuador, where western *pallidigularis* occurs mostly in secondary woodland and is scarce in wet forests, whilst eastern *turdinus* is found mainly in swampy and riparian forests. In Colombia widespread and frequent; uncommon to locally frequent in Venezuela; frequent in Guyana; common in Suriname; uncommon but widespread in French Guiana.

Habitat Tropical Zone, 800–1,300m in Ecuador, to 1,200m in Colombia and 1,000m in Venezuela. Humid lowland forest, *várzea* and *terra firme,* swampy forest, secondary woodland. In treefalls, overgrown clearings, along streams and at fringes. Always in thick tangled undergrowth.

Voice Sings mostly at dawn and dusk. Song a frequently repeated, very emphatic, loud *tarrr*... *tarrr*... *tarrr*... (H&M) or a brief falling series of distinct notes *kee-kee-ke-krrr* or *ki, ki, ki, ki, ke, ke, krrr* or *KEE Kee krr kr ka.* Alarm-call a loud falling rattle or buzzy *durrrrrrr* (H&B, R&G, Hilty).

OLIVE-BACKED FOLIAGE-GLEANER

Automolus infuscatus Pl. 147

Identification 19cm. Greyish olive-brown above with dark rufous wings and rump to tail, fringes of olive are sharply divided from pure white of malar and throat, rest of underparts depend on racial character.

Ssp. *A. i. badius* (E Co, S Ve: Amazonas, W & C Bolívar to Paurai-tepui) back somewhat richer, redder brown, fine white streaking on ear-coverts with a few white spots on lower cheeks, underparts soft grey

A. i. cervicalis (SE Ve: NE Bolívar; S Gu, S Su, FG) top and head-sides slightly rufescent and all feathers have blackish fringes, underparts pale creamy buff, washed olive on breast-sides and flanks

A. i. infuscatus (E Ec, SE Co) breast-sides washed grey, belly and flanks pale ochre, undertail-coverts cinnamon

Habits Forages at low to mid levels, alone, in pairs or in groups and regularly with mixed flocks usually of other furnariids, antwrens and *Thamnomanes* antbirds. Hops on low branches or lurks in thinner undergrowth looking for insects, spiders and tiny vertebrates, and poking of debris and dead leaves. Tends to be difficult to see and best found by call. Non-breeders undertake seasonal and post-breeding wandering movements.

Status Frequent in Ecuador, common and widespread in Colombia, uncommon to locally frequent in Venezuela, frequent in Guyana. In Suriname, frequent, but less common than Buff-throated Foliage-gleaner. In French Guiana, one of most common foliage-gleaners of interior.

Habitat Lower Tropical Zone, to 700m in Ecuador, 400m in Colombia and 1,100m in Venezuela. Humid lowland *terra firme*, occasionally in borders of *várzea*.

Voice Calls frequently while foraging. A very loud, short call followed by a hoarse drawn-out cry, and a much-repeated, loud, 2-note *tchau-ho…tchau-ho…* (H&M). Also, a sharp *chikah* (R&G); single, loud, nasal *chikwuk* in alarm or same note repeated over and over while foraging (H&B). Song a fast loud staccato rattle of varying length, *ch-r-r-r-r-r-r-r-r-r-r…* or *tu'tu'tu'tu'tu'tu'tu'…* or *du'du'du'du'du'du'du'du'du'…* (H&B, R&G, Hilty).

WHITE-THROATED FOLIAGE-GLEANER

Automolus roraimae Pl. 148

Identification 18cm. Olive-brown back and wings, rufescent rump to tail. Top and sides of head dusky with dark-edged whitish eyebrow, whitish throat and brown underparts. Juvenile more tawny-orange on eyebrow and underparts, the feathers fringed dusky, giving a well-scaled effect. Immature has colouring of juvenile but lacks scaling. Look for long buffy-white eyestripe and creamy white throat that contrasts with rest of body.

Ssp. *A. r. duidae* (S Ve: C Amazonas, Cerros Yaví, Parú, Gimé, Duida, Huachamacari and Neblina) deep rufous-brown above, dark umber on top of head and sides, fringes of tertials and secondaries more deep rufous, rump to tail deep rufous, long narrow white eyebrow, chin, throat and malar white, breast cinnamon, sides brown, rufous from vent to undertail-coverts; immature similar above but richer rufous on breast, and weakly scalloped/barred/mottled rufous to flanks and belly, dull eyebrow, pale buffy throat, and breast and belly washed rufescent

A. r. paraquensis (S Ve: N Amazonas, Cerros Paraque, Sipapo) indistinguishable from *duidae* in field, slightly less reddish on back and below

A. r. roraimae (S Ve: E Bolívar, eastern tepuis; CW Gu: Mt Roraima) white eyebrow and throat, underparts concolorous with back

A. r. urutani (S Ve: SW Bolívar & SE Amazonas, Cerros Jaua, Sarisariñama and Urutani) indistinguishable from *duidae* in field, though generally paler and slightly brighter throughout; immature has pale eye-ring, eyebrow very long and rufous with a few white feathers, and around and over eyes; juvenile similar but has feathers of throat to belly fringed blackish, rufous eyebrow

Habits Forages from low levels to subcanopy, alone, in pairs or small family groups, and regularly joins mixed flocks. Seeks insects in dead leaves or gleans them from foliage, mostly in dense undergrowth but sometimes in vine tangles or on mossy branches, occasionally climbing trunks briefly.

Status Pantepui endemic. In Venezuela, frequent to common above 1,800m on tepui slopes, local and scarce at lower altitudes. In Guyana scarce at 800m and uncommon above 1,200m. First Guianan specimens collected 2001.

Habitat Subtropical to Temperate Zones, 1,300–2,500m in Venezuela, 800–2,500m in Guyana. Only in humid, mossy forests with dense undergrowth, on sandy soils on slopes of tepuis; not found in red-soil forests.

Voice Foraging calls include rough *tzik* and *chezk* notes, which are also incorporated in song. Song a long, rising and speeding sequence of very harsh notes, *tzik… chek… tzik… jjza-jjza-jjza-jza-jza- ja'ja'ja'ja'ja*. Voice considered similar to *Syndactyla* and *Anabazenops* (Hilty).

Notes Treated as *A. albigularis* in Peters. Specimens from Cerro Neblina, originally described as Neblina Foliage-gleaner *Philydor hylobius*, found to be juvenile *A. roraimae* by Dickerman *et al.* (1986). Recent sight records from Potaro Plateau (Barnett *et al.* 2002) and specimen records from Guianan side of Mt. Roraima (Braun *et al.* 2003), tentatively assigned here to race *roraimae*. Called Tepui Foliage-gleaner in Hilty, which seems apt, but not accepted by SACC.

BROWN-RUMPED FOLIAGE-GLEANER

Automolus melanopezus Pl. 147

Identification 18–20cm. Upperparts rich intense rufous, slightly darker on wings and tail, lores and ear-coverts perhaps even darker, throat and malar deep orange, merging into rufous underparts. Juvenile slightly darker and browner with dark fringes to all feathers; eyes brown. Look for bright eyes and bright ochraceous-orange throat sharply contrasting with dark brown face and ear-coverts.

Ssp. Monotypic (E Ec: Napo & Sucumbíos to Morona-Santiago, SE Co: Putumayo).

Habits Forages in dense, tangled undergrowth, frequently along rivers and streams, often with flocks of antbirds and other furnariids. A dead-leaf specialist that searches for insects, spiders and small frogs in curled-up dead leaves and is partial to foraging in clumps of leaves in bamboo stands.

Status Rare to uncommon and local in Ecuador, scarce and not well known in Colombia.

Habitat Lower Tropical Zone, to *c.*500m. Humid lowland *terra firme*, swampy forests and mature secondary woodland, usually along streams or near water, often in stands of bamboo.

Voice Song a fast rhythmic sequence comprising 2 emphatic notes and a rattle, *whit-whit-wu-trrrrrrrrr* or *whit-whit-whidididididit* (H&B, R&G).

RUDDY FOLIAGE-GLEANER

Automolus rubiginosus Pl. 147

Identification 18.5–19cm. Very dark and unmarked with contrasting cinnamon-rufous throat. Juvenile similar but has generally paler and more extensive throat. Races very much alike.

Ssp. *A. r. brunnescens* (E Ec: Napo to Morona-Santiago) dark chestnut tail and paler, more rufescent brown belly

A. r. caquetae (SE Co: E base of Andes from Arauca to Putumayo; NE Ec: Sucumbíos) browner, much less rufous underparts, contrasting more with rich rufous throat.

A. r. cinnamomeigula (Co: E base of Andes in Meta) dark olive ear-coverts, very cinnamon-rufous below

A. r. nigricauda (W Ec: Esmeraldas to Azuay; W Co: W slope of W Andes from Baudó Mts in Chocó to Nariño) dark with a blackish tail and dark greyish-brown upperparts

A. r. obscurus (Guianas) significantly smaller, with smaller bill and feet, slightly more olivaceous above and paler below

A. r. rufipectus (Co: Santa Marta) rather reddish-brown with tail distinctly dark rufous

A. r. sasaimae (C Co: W slope of E Andes in Cundinamarca)

A. r. saturatus (NW Co: N Chocó & W Antioquia) quite dark brown

A. r. venezuelanus (S Ve: W Apure to SE Bolívar & S Amazonas) dark olive ear-coverts, very deep reddish throat

Habits Forages alone or in pairs that seek insects mostly close to ground, skulking restlessly and keeping always inside cover. Seldom joins mixed flocks.

Status In Ecuador, rare to uncommon and local in eastern lowlands but uncommon to locally frequent in western foothills. Locally frequent in Colombia, uncommon and local in Venezuela, Guyana, Suriname and French Guiana.

Habitat Tropical to Temperate Zones, to 1,300m in west Ecuador and 1,000m in the east, to 1,800m in Colombia. Humid and wet lowland *terra firme*, secondary woodland, in shrubby fringes and areas with many lianas.

Voice Sings frequently, endlessly repeating a 2-note phrase, first soft and short and second long and louder *ke-keeeuh… ke-keeeuh…* and both sexes give a *tr… tra… trrra…* alarm-call (H&M). A nasal, rising whining *keeaaah* repeated after a short pause (H&B). Song also described as a querulous, nasal, rising *kweeeeahhhhh* (R&G).

Notes AOU (1998), Remsen and Hilty consider that races presently included in *A. rubiginosus* very probably represent more than one species. Race *obscurus* from Guianas significantly smaller and is vocally different. Race *caquetae* first found in Ecuador 1993. West of Andes races *nigricauda* and *saturatus* were formerly considered a separate species under *A. nigricauda*, a treatment that is very probably more correct.

CHESTNUT-CROWNED FOLIAGE-GLEANER *Automolus rufipileatus* Pl. 148

Identification 19–20cm. Olive-brown back and wings, rump to tail rufous, top of head chestnut, head-sides pale olive-brown, chin, throat and malar creamy buff, rest of underparts pale olive-brown, rufescent on undertail-coverts; eyes orange-yellow. Juvenile has distinctly duller crown, and most feathers of head and underparts fringed dusky giving slightly irregular scales. Look for pale underparts that contrast with darker, mainly uniform brown upperparts, and bright orange-yellow eyes; bill slenderer than that of other *Automolus*.

Ssp. *A. r. consobrinus* (E Ec: E lowlands; E Co: E slope of E Andes from Arauca to Putumayo and E lowlands from Meta to Amazonas, Ve: E slope of Andes from Táchira to S Lara, C & S Amazonas and S Bolívar, Guianas)

Habits Forages in dense undergrowth and vine tangles, especially along rivers and streams, in loose pairs or small family groups. Disagreement as to whether forages with mixed flocks: H&B consider that it regularly joins mixed flocks of antbirds and other furnariids, whilst R&G state that it does so only rarely. Quite active and nimble, but also very wary and secretive, so hard to see despite it singing frequently.

Status Uncommon to locally frequent in Ecuador, Colombia and Venezuela; frequent in Guyana; widespread but only locally common in Suriname; rare and very local in French Guiana.

Habitat Lower Tropical Zone, to 700m in Ecuador, 500m in Colombia and *c*.900m in Venezuela. *Várzea*, stands of *Gynerium* cane in seasonally flooded riparian forests, river islands, stands of *Guadua* bamboo, damp to wet mature secondary woodland. Not found in *terra firme*.

Voice Sings mostly at dawn, repeating song frequently at regular intervals with brief pauses. A loud nasal rattle, *tr,rr,r,r,r,r,roh* (H&M), *d-r-r-r-r-r-r-r-r-r-…* (R&G) or *d'd'd'd'd'd 'd'd'd'…* (Hilty).

HENNA-HOODED FOLIAGE-GLEANER *Hylocryptus erythrocephalus* Pl. 148

Identification 21–22cm. Very distinctive furnariid, with olive back, rufous wings and rump to tail, entirely rufous head (paler on throat), pale olive-grey breast to flanks, thighs and vent, and pale rufous undertail-coverts. Eyes orange to hazel, bill long and pointed and pale horn with dusky culmen, legs and feet greyish-olive with pale claws.

Ssp. *H. e. erythrocephalus* (SW Ec: Loja and El Oro)

Habits Forages terrestrially or very near ground, alone or in pairs, often with mixed flocks. Very noisy when searching for prey in dry leaves. Sometimes climbs up lowest metre of a trunk, in short hops like a woodcreeper. Nest is of dry grasses and leaves at end of 1m horizontal burrow in a dirt bank.

Status Uncommon and very local in Ecuador.

Habitat Upper Tropical to Lower Subtropical Zones, 400–1,800m. Dry to moist tropical forest and deciduous woodland in lowlands and foothills, riparian and gallery woods, partially cleared or disturbed woodland. Partial to areas with a thick layer of dried leaves on ground.

Voice Song described as a continuous *dee-dee-dee-dee… dee-dee-dee-dee…* (Berg 1994) or a persistent, far-carrying staccato churr, *kree-kruh-kruh-kruh-kruh-kruh-kruh-kurrrr*; also *tok-tok-tok-tok-tok-tok-tok-tok-tok-tok* that sounds like cranking machinery (R&G, Remsen).

Note Vaurie (1980) merged *Hylocryptus* within *Automolus*.

Sclerurus are dark, with short but broad black tails and long, fairly straight and slender bills. Usually found alone, well inside forest. Their songs, which comprise clear whistles, are quite different from all other furnariids. Nest is small pad of rachises of compound leaves, placed at end of a burrow dug in a bank , a road cut or a treefall mount. All leaftossers are amongst first species to disappear with deforestation, being very susceptible even to selective logging.

TAWNY-THROATED LEAFTOSSER

Sclerurus mexicanus Pl. 148

Identification 15–16.5cm. Rich dark brown upper back becomes rufescent brown on rump, black tail; head concolorous with back, rich tawny-rufous or cinnamon-rufous chest and throat becomes deep brown on belly; eyes dark brown, long, slender bill slightly decurved at tip, short grey legs. Juvenile similar but duller and has dusky fringes to feathers of throat and breast. Similar Short-billed Leaftosser has shorter straighter bill and throat is paler and less rufescent, but where they overlap are extremely difficult to identify except by voice.

Ssp. *S. m. andinus* (N Co: Chocó & Antioquia to Perijá, W & S Ve: Perijá, N & C Amazonas, C & E Bolívar, W Gu: tepui region) as described

S. m. macconnelli (E & S Gu, S Su, FG) rump and uppertail-coverts bright rufous, orange-rufous of throat extends to breast and only gradually darkens to vent

S. m. obscurior (W Ec, Co: W Andes) rump and uppertail-coverts almost concolorous with back, orange only on throat, rest of underparts as back, but with narrow orange fringes to breast, sides and upper belly

S. m. peruvianus (E Ec, CS Co: W Meta, Caquetá & Putumayo) very similar to *obscurior*, but not quite as dark

Habits Forages alone or sometimes in very loose pairs, very low or on ground. Searches for insects in leaf-litter and on fallen logs in damp forest, moving with little hops (not really walking). Never joins mixed flocks. Furtive and quiet but not shy, may go unnoticed, but often located by noise it makes when flicking and tossing dry leaves. If flushed, flies to a low branch, where freezes for a few seconds before disappearing. Flicks wings often and sometimes perches on tree trunks like a woodcreeper.

Status Rare to uncommon and local in Ecuador, uncommon and local in Venezuela and Colombia, uncommon in Guyana, Suriname and French Guiana.

Habitat Tropical to Lower Subtropical Zones, to 1,600m in Ecuador, 2,000m in Colombia, 1,400–2,000m in north Venezuela and 300–1,100m in south. Humid lowland *terra firme* to forests in foothills and on lower slopes, in damp, shady areas.

Voice Sings mostly at daybreak and early morning, loud, shrill notes (H&M) or a descending series of sharp *squee* notes (H&B), or a falling sequence of 4–5 high, increasingly short wheezy notes or slurred whistles, *peeeeee-peeeee-peeee-peee* or *pseeer-pseeer-pseer-psee-pse*, often followed by a lively chatter (R&G, Hilty). Alarm a loud *squeek!* or sharp *chick* (H&B, Hilty).

Notes Former English name for all *Sclerurus* was leafscraper, but recent authors have taken to more accurate leaftosser proposed by A. Skutch. In Venezuela, a recent sight record in northwest Barinas was apparently of this species (Boesman 1998).

SHORT-BILLED LEAFTOSSER

Sclerurus rufigularis Pl. 148

Identification 15–16cm. Completely dark olive-brown with pale orange throat that merges into face-sides and breast, eyes brown, bill shorter than other leaftossers, and straight, legs and feet grey. Similar Tawny-throated Leaftosser has a longer, curved bill and throat is richer and more rufescent, but extremely difficult to identify in area of overlap; best separated by voice.

Ssp. *S. r. brunnescens* (E Ec, SE Co) slightly darker

S. r. fulvigularis (S & SE Ve, Guianas) as described

Habits Forages only very low or on ground. Very similar to Tawny-throated Leaftosser.

Status In Ecuador, rare and local, and possibly very scarce but widespread in *terra firme* of eastern lowlands. Found there only recently, although there are specimens dating from 1920s, which went unrecognised due to confusion with race *peruvianus* of Tawny-throated Leaftosser. Scarce in Colombia. In Venezuela, widespread and frequent to locally common around tepuis. Uncommon in Guyana, widespread and uncommon to locally frequent in Suriname, common in French Guiana.

Habitat Lower Tropical Zone, to 300m in Ecuador, 500m in Colombia but locally to 1,800m, and to 900m in Venezuela. Humid lowland *terra firme*, sandy soil and swampy forests.

Voice Song a high, shrill chatter, *tseet-tseet… tseet-tseet…* (H&M) or a descending sequence of 3–5 high, slow and deliberate whistles *TZEET, SEEer, Seeer, seea* (Hilty). Alarm a sharp *squeek*.

GREY-THROATED LEAFTOSSER

Sclerurus albigularis Pl. 148

Identification 16.5–18cm. Olive-brown above, including top and sides of head and wings, tail blackish, rump and uppertail-coverts dark rufous, faint greyish eyebrow, short pale grey streaks on rather dark ear-coverts, chin and throat grey, breast dull orange-rufous, rest of underparts olive-brown like back; eyes dark, bill long and straight, with upturned distal third of lower mandible, blackish with grey base, legs and feet dark brown. Juvenile similar but has somewhat speckled or scaly-looking throat and dark fringes to feathers of malar area, bill horn.

Ssp. *S. a. albigularis* (E Co: ; N Ve: S Táchira & Lara to Sucre; Tr) as described

S. a. kunanensis (Ve: Perija) very much like *albigularis* but definitely more richly coloured throughout

S. a. propinquus (Co: Santa Marta) darker above and below than *albigularis*, throat more greyish

S. a. zamorae (E Ec: W Napo to Zamora-Chinchipe) brighter rufous breast, duller chestnut rump and uppertail-coverts, clearer and better defined eyebrows; much darker belly

Habits Forages alone, very low or on ground, searching leaf-litter and tossing leaves right and left as it does so.
Status Very rare (scarce) and local in Ecuador, scarce in Colombia, frequent locally in Venezuela, uncommon in Trinidad, scarce or occasional on Tobago.
Habitat Tropical to Subtropical Zones, at 1,000–1,700m in Ecuador, 1,500–2,100m in Colombia and 450–2,200m in Venezuela. Humid foothill and montane forests, in ravines and beside streams.
Voice Song a rising sequence of 4–6 notes, *kwu-kwu-kwe-kwe-kwi-kwi?*, rather complaining and sometimes followed by a trill and chatter (P. Coopmans). Also, *tuee tuee tuee tweeep* or *tuee tuee tuee tweeep tweeep*, with each note inflected. Alarm a very fast *chuee-chuee-chuee chue'e'e'e'e'e'e'e* (P. Schwartz, H&B).

BLACK-TAILED LEAFTOSSER

Sclerurus caudacutus Pl. 148

Identification 18cm. Almost entirely dark brown, suffused rufous on rump and uppertail-coverts, face and breast suffused orange-rufous, chin white and throat buffy. Eyes dark brown, fairly long, thin and straight blackish bill with pale base to lower mandible, short dark legs.

Ssp. *S. c. brunneus* (E Ec, SE Co, SW Ve) white throat lightly scaled dusky
S. c. caudacutus (Guianas) whitish throat lightly scaled rufous-brown
S. c. insignis (S Ve) similar to *caudacutus* but slightly darker above, and orange suffusion with dark scaling on throat and face-sides more extensive

Habits Forages alone or in very loose pairs, on forest floor or very close to it, often hopping on or around fallen logs or mossy rocks, turning over dead leaves or probing soft soil. Shy and very easy to overlook.
Status Uncommon to locally frequent in Ecuador, where, despite scarce records, considered most numerous *Sclerurus* in eastern lowlands. Uncommon to very locally frequent in Colombia, uncommon to locally frequent in Venezuela, uncommon in Guyana, uncommon to locally frequent in Suriname, common in French Guiana.
Habitat Tropical Zone, to *c.*900m in Ecuador, *c.*500m in Colombia and 1,100m in Venezuela. Humid, primary *terra firme*, moist shady forests and forests on foothills of tepuis.
Voice When disturbed, a loud, shrill chatter (H&M). Song a loud, speeding then slowing series of emphatic notes: *queet, queet, queet-queet, queet'queet'ke'ke'ke'keke'queet'queet-que-queet* (H&B).

SCALY-THROATED LEAFTOSSER

Sclerurus guatemalensis Pl. 148

Identification 16–17cm. Very dark ruddy brown with rufous suffusion to face and breast, with dark fringes to feathers; chin and throat well-defined white with clean black fringes to feathers; bill horn, darker at tip and with slight droop at tip.

Ssp. *S. g. salvini* (W Ec: Esmeraldas & Manabí, W Co: Chocó & Nariño) as described
S. g. ennosiphyllus (NW Co: Antioquia & Bolívar) more grey above, generally paler above and below

Habits Forages alone or in very loose pairs, on forest floor or very close to it.
Status Rare to uncommon and local in Ecuador, uncommon and local in Colombia, where range of *salvini* in Pacific lowlands and foothills is interrupted in wettest areas.
Habitat Tropical Zone, to 800–900m. Humid primary forests in lowlands and foothills, but apparently not in wet forests.
Voice Song an endlessly repeated falling series of emphatic whistles, *whit whit peet peet peet peet pert pert*; alarm-call a fast *wheeeek!* (H&B).
Notes Race *guatemalensis* incorrectly listed for northern Colombia in SCJ&W. Race *ennosiphyllus*, described by Wetmore in 1951, not included in Peters or in SCJ&W.

SHARP-TAILED STREAMCREEPER

Lochmias nematura Pl. 148

Identification 13–15cm. Dark umber above, with black tail with narrow, stiff, spiny tips, and dark brown underparts covered in profuse white spots resembling scales. Eyes dark brown, thin, slightly decurved bill, and dark legs and feet. Races differ by presence of eyebrow (which varies in size, and is not age-related) and extent and density of white markings below. Juvenile resembles adult.

Ssp. *L. n. castanonotus* (SE Ve; CW Gu) full thick postocular stripe of many small white dots
L. n. chimantae (S VE) very small vestigial eyebrow, lots of white spotting on chin and throat but malar dark, dark brown wash on sides
L. n. sororius (Co: Andes, NC Ve) larger, no eyebrow, far fewer white spots below and has longer bill than others

Habits Forages alone or in loose pairs, searching and probing ground, on rocks and fallen logs, in mossy or muddy spots and even wading in very shallow water of brooks and rivulets. Often found in *Heliconia*, vine tangles and thickets by streams. Scatters dead leaves to find insects. Fairly quiet, slow and shy. Flies erratically. Nest unique: a ball of plant matter with an entrance hole, built at end of a burrow dug in a bank.
Status Rare to locally uncommon in Ecuador, uncommon and local in Colombia. In Venezuela, rare and local in north, but more widespread and frequent south of Orinoco. Rare in Guyana, where only recently reported for first time (Barnett *et al.* 2002).
Habitat Tropical to Temperate Zones. In Ecuador, 700–1,300m, Colombia at 1,300–2,100m and in Venezuela at 850–1,300m in north and 1,000–2,500m in south. Humid forest and secondary woodland, in areas of dense undergrowth and abundant mosses and epiphytes by rocky streams. In Guyana found on and around giant boulders in riverine habitats (D. Ascanio).

Voice Sing infrequently, mostly at dawn, a flat sequence of high trills (H&B) or an accelerating rattle, *pit, pit-pit-pit'pt'pt' pt'pt'pt'pt'pt*, chattering and on a flat, low pitch (Hilty). A loud *sea-sick*, and *chet-chet-chet* in alarm (Remsen).

Notes Birds from Guyana assigned here to *castanonotus*, which is closest race, but no specimens from there. Relationships and placement of *Lochmias* within Furnariidae controversial – placed next to *Sclerurus* based on morphology, but recent molecular studies have found it closer to *Furnarius*. Correct spelling of races *castanonotus* and *sororius*, not *castanonota* and *sororia*, but *nematura* and *chimantae* do not vary because they are nouns (Dickinson 2003). *Lochmias* is one of 27 monotypic genera in Furnariidae.

Xenops are small, arboreal inhabitants of humid lowland and foothill forests, which forage exclusively in upper branches. With one exception, their bills are quite curious and unique: flattened at sides with an obviously upturned lower mandible. All have a broad diagonal cinnamon wingbar best seen in flight, and 3 species in our region have a conspicuous silver white malar. They build their nests in small cavities in rotten wood or holes made by piculets.

RUFOUS-TAILED XENOPS

Xenops milleri Pl. 144

Identification 10–11cm. Tiny nondescript xenops with all-rufous tail and bill that is thin and straight (lower mandible not upturned), upper back olive-brown with buffy streaks, thin pale eyebrow and underparts pale olive-brown with whitish streaks; olive or brown legs. Main difference from other *Xenops* is lack of malar stripe. From race *acutirostris* of Slender-billed Xenops, which also has white streaks on mantle, by virtual lack of white eyebrow.

Ssp. Monotypic (E Ec, E Co, S Ve, Guianas)

Habits Forages high in canopy, clambering nimbly sideways on thin bare branches like a piculet, and frequently turning about face with a jerky jump. Picks at bark and probes small cracks to get small insects. Joins mixed flocks of canopy birds.

Status Rare and apparently local in Ecuador, where first recorded in 1972. In Colombia, possibly fairly frequent but records scarce. Locally frequent in Venezuela, scarce in Guyana, uncommon in Suriname, widespread but rare in French Guiana.

Habitat Lower Tropical Zone, locally to 1,000m in Ecuador, lowlands to *c*.500m elsewhere. Humid primary *terra firme* and tall sandy soil forests, often with abundant lianas and usually near water.

Voice Song a bouncy sequence that rises in volume in middle then fades, *chit-chit, chit, chuEET, chuEET, chuEET, chueet, chueet, chueet, chu ee* (K. J. Zimmer recording, Hilty).

Notes Formerly placed in monotypic genus *Microxenops*, based on differences in bill shape and tail (simpler pattern). Treated as *Xenops* since Peters' Checklist, but revision is needed.

SLENDER-BILLED XENOPS

Xenops tenuirostris Pl. 144

Identification 10.5–11.5cm. Thin, pointed and very slightly upturned bill, white malar stripe, upperparts cinnamon-brown with buffy streaks, a black line runs length of tail, either side of central rectrices; dark slate or black legs.

Ssp. *X. t. acutirostris* (E Ec, SE Co, S Ve: C & S Amazonas, W & SE Bolívar) crown brown with dark shaft-streaks, eyebrow buffy-white, mantle cinnamon-rufous streaked buffy or white, rump and uppertail-coverts cinnamon-rufous, central tail-feathers black; throat white, breast and belly greyish-olive streaked white, undertail-coverts greyish-buff, outer tail black with basal cinnamon band

X. t. hellmayri (Su, FG) streaks on back weak and greyish, eyebrow, neck and throat bright buff and has darker crown with sharper streaks, decidedly buffy below

X. t. tenuirostris (S Ve: NW Amazonas) rufous-brown above, white shaft-streaks from forehead to mantle and bright rufous suffusion either side of white, rump to tail rufous-red, outer web of third rectrix on each side black, wings dark brown with rufous bar on distal half of primaries, basal half of secondaries and tertials rufous; chin whitish, malar white, all underparts greyish-olive with soft white streaks

Habits Forages in close-knit pairs, high in canopy. Active and nimble, hops sideways along thin bare branches, constantly turning about face with little jumps, or briefly climbs trunks and vertical branches, or inspects vine tangles. Most often seen on outer stems and twigs.

Status Generally scarce; rare to locally uncommon in Ecuador, uncommon in Colombia, frequent in Venezuela. Scarce in Guyana, where first specimen record 2001 on Mt. Roraima (Braun *et al.* 2003), uncommon in Suriname (scarcer than Plain Xenops) and rare in French Guiana.

Habitat Tropical Zone, locally to 1,000m in Ecuador, at 1,100m in Guyana, lowlands to *c*.500m elsewhere. Humid lowland and swampy forests; in Suriname, in boggy or swampy grassland; in Guyana, transitional forest between lowlands and cloud forest.

Voice Song a flat sequence of 10–12 *chit* notes, *ch-ch-chit-chit-chee-chee-chit-chit-chit-chit* (K. J. Zimmer recording, Hilty).

Notes Remsen considered that race *tenuirostris* does not occur in Venezuela, and assigned all Venezuelan birds to *acutirostris*, but acknowledged differences from typical specimens. It seems strange that birds from north-west Amazonas, Venezuela, would be *tenuirostris*, as type of this race is from Rio Madeira, south of Amazon. Race *acutirostris* appears to have a peri-Amazon distribution, as known for other species, making it indeed odd that *tenuirostris* should be found at both ends of crescent-shaped range of *acutirostris*. If this were true, *tenuirostris* would have 2 populations isolated from each other. Specimens in COP show some differences between those from north-west Amazonas and those from Bolívar and southern and central

Amazonas. Although we believe they might prove to represent an undescribed race, we continue to list those from north-west Amazonas as *tenuirostris*, until a more thorough revision sheds light on this confused situation. Remsen was also uncertain as to whether to place birds from Guyana in *hellmayri*, as these could very well be *acutirostris*.

PLAIN XENOPS *Xenops minutus* Pl. 144

Identification 12–12.5cm. Unstreaked olive-brown top of head and back, with rufous wings and tail, black line either side of central tail-feathers, white eyebrow and malar stripe, whitish chin, otherwise generally uniform olive below; dark grey legs. Differs from other xenops mainly in lack of streaking, so look for plain back and almost unmarked underparts, but birds with some streaking on breast should be observed carefully as they could be another species.

Ssp. *X. m. littoralis* (W Ec, W Co) darker than other races, with relatively extensive white throat
X. m. neglectus (NE Co, NW Ve) yellowish throat and olivaceous underparts
X. m. obsoletus (E Ec) whitish throat more extensive, and feathers have fine brownish fringes; wing-band dark ochraceous.
X. m. olivaceus (W Ve) mostly olivaceous below, instead of grey-brown
X. m. remoratus (E Co, W Ve) generally duller, with crown that *looks* unstreaked, but an obviously streaked breast
X. m. ruficaudus (E Co, S & E Ve, Guianas) darker crown with very narrow buff streaks and broader brown fringes to throat feathers; obvious streaking on chest

Habits Forages at low to mid levels, rarely to subcanopy, clambering acrobatically on thin twigs like a piculet. Pecks at ends of broken twigs in search of tiny spiders. Joins mixed flocks.

Status In Ecuador, uncommon to frequent in west, uncommon in east. Frequent in Colombia, frequent to common in Venezuela, frequent in Guyana and Suriname. Widespread and common in French Guiana.

Habitat Tropical Zone, locally to 1,300m in Ecuador, to 1,800m in Colombia, lowlands to *c*.900m elsewhere. Humid lowland and savanna forests, mature secondary woodland, dry to moist deciduous woodland, plantations. Areas with vine undergrowth.

Voice Song a fast, chittering trill, *fit fit fit-ft'ft'ft'f'f'f'f'f'f'f'i 'i'i* or *chit, chit, chi-ch'ch'e'e'e'e'i'i'i* or *dit dit dit-dit'dt'd'd'd'd' d'd'da'a'a*, at first fast then slows and drops . Also, soft *chit* calls, and a lively *fst, fist-fist-fist* (Hilty).

STREAKED XENOPS *Xenops rutilans* Pl. 144

Identification 11.5–12.5cm. Dark head streaked dusky and buffy, rufous back lightly streaked, rufous wings and tail with black in tail varying by race, underparts well streaked white and brown.

Ssp. *X. r. guayae* (W Ec) small, buffy underparts narrowly streaked white, black only on inner web of fourth rectrix
X. r. heterurus (NE Ec, Co, Ve, Tr) white-centred rufous streaks on deep brown head which become vestigial on upper mantle, white chin and throat, malar and postocular stripe, soft greyish-cinnamon breast to faint orange-cinnamon vent and undertail-coverts, all streaked narrowly whitish, black on third and fourth rectrices
X. r. perijanus (W Ve) like *heterurus* above, below more extensively white throat, extending as streaks to olive breast, rest of underparts rufescent olive with narrow pale streaks
X. r. phelpsi (NE Co: Santa Marta) all-rufous tail and much less black on third rectrix
X. r. peruvianus (SE Ec) like *heterurus* but less black on tail – has black on third and fourth rectrices but inner webs only, bright ochraceous below, throat less whitish and has tinge of yellow, undertail-coverts rufous.
X. r. purusianus (FG?) crown dark, rest of upperparts and tail like *heterurus*, but much paler below and more broadly streaked white

Habits Forages in close-knit pairs or family groups, from mid levels to subcanopy, occasionally in undergrowth. Often in mixed flocks of insectivorous birds (woodcreepers, flycatchers and other furnariids). Clambers nimbly on twigs and vines, hopping sideways on thin bare branches, poking into cracks and clumps of mosses, or sometimes chipping off bits of bark. Often seen upside-down as it forages.

Status Uncommon to locally frequent in Ecuador, frequent in Colombia and Venezuela, uncommon in Trinidad (no records Tobago), rare in French Guiana.

Habitat Tropical to Subtropical Zones, to 2,000m in west Ecuador, 800–2,000m in east Ecuador; 1,500–2,800m in Colombia; 700–2,200m in Venezuela and seldom below 1,000m in west. Humid to wet montane forest and secondary and deciduous woodland and forest borders.

Voice Song a chattery sequence of 5–6 metallic *zeet* notes, fast then slows down and drops (H&B, Hilty).

Note Those in French Guiana hesitantly assigned here to northernmost race in Brazil, but this race, *purusianus*, and indeed all other Brazilian races, occur south of the Amazon, thus designation is likely incorrect.

WOODCREEPERS (formerly Dendrocolaptidae)

Plain, uniformly coloured *Dendrocincla* woodcreepers lack bars, spots or streaks, and are considered the most primitive of woodcreeper genera. Mid to large in size, their bills are straight and their tail-feathers less rigid, with smaller spiny tips than other woodcreepers. As they forage mostly by sallying, there is no need for stiffer tails. Most species live in lowlands and are inveterate army ant followers.

TYRANNINE WOODCREEPER

Dendrocincla tyrannina Pl.149

Identification 23–26.5cm. Only large unstreaked, uniformly warm brown woodcreeper in its altitudinal range, with a large, heavy bill.

Ssp. *D. t. hellmayri* (Co & Ve: Táchira) smallest race, more olivaceous, feathers on crown more clearly fringed dusky than *tyrannina*

D. t. macrorhyncha (extreme NE Ec) significantly larger and marginally paler, with significantly larger, longer bill

D. t. tyrannina (Ec: N to S on both slopes, Co) more rufous than *hellmayri*

Habits Follows mixed flocks. Forages fairly quietly at lower levels, usually alone, hitching up trunks or hopping on lower branches.

Status Rare to locally frequent in Ecuador, rare and local in Colombia and Venezuela.

Habitat Subtropical and Temperate Zones (rarely to Tropical Zone), at 1,400–3,100m, most abundant at 1,800–2,700m in Ecuador; 1,900–3,000m, but from 1,500m on Pacific slope in Colombia; and 1,800–2,800m in Venezuela. Humid to wet montane and cloud forests.

Voice A long rattle that starts with a few slow hollow notes, then speeds up to end slow and hollow, and a shuddering *tr'E'E'E'E'A* alarm (Hilty).

Note Race *macrorhyncha,* described from 2 specimens, of uncertain status – has been considered a species. R&G consider it invalid, F&K to involve aberrant individuals or a separate taxon and Marantz thinks it likely to be aberrant nominate *tyrannina*. We recognise it in absence of conclusive evidence otherwise.

PLAIN-BROWN WOODCREEPER

Dendrocincla fuliginosa Pl. 149

Identification 20–22cm. Uniform brown with slight crest (crown-feathers frequently raised), but has subtle markings on face, greyish cheeks, diffuse pale malar, and dark, straight bill, and varies according to subspecies. Differences between races subtle, and most unidentifiable in field, only nominate *fuliginosa* is really distinctive.

Ssp. *D. f. barinensis* (WC Ve: W Llanos) olivaceous-brown, lacks whitish chin, bill horn, legs and feet olive

D. f. deltana (NE Ve: Orinoco delta) slightly more gingery above, slightly flecked dark on chin and upper throat, bill black above, grey below, legs and feet vinaceous-grey

D. f. fuliginosa (SE Ve, Guianas) chin and throat buffy, noticeably flecked dusky and white (rough barring) and has pale shaft-streaks, pale spots around eyes and a postocular row of tawny-orange spots; bill, legs and feet black

D. f. lafresnayei (N & E Co, NW Ve) greyish chin reaching to breast, bill, legs and feet grey; juvenile slightly brighter, bill black above, flesh below, legs and feet grey

D. f. meruloides (N Ve: coast & E Llanos, T&T) like *deltana*, but slightly more gingery brown above, bill brown above, grey below, legs and feet blue-grey

D. f. neglecta (E Ec) larger than *phaeochroa*, slightly darker and more olivaceous above, paler and less rufescent below; whiter throat and brown more rufescent than *ridgwayi*

D. f. phaeochroa (E Ec, E Co, S Ve) slightly darker above than others, pale greenish-buffy chin and throat, bill black above, grey below, legs and feet blue-grey

D. f. ridgwayi (W Ec, W Co) chin and throat pale grey-brown, narrow buffy postocular line; juvenile generally slightly brighter and more cinnamon

Habits Follows army ants noisily, sometimes in groups that bicker amongst themselves. Often follows mixed flocks or forages alone or in pairs, searching for insects on vertical trunks at low and mid levels, and sometimes inspecting fallen logs. Flaps wings and hops about when excited. Nests during dry season.

Status Widespread and frequent to locally common in Ecuador, frequent in Colombia and Venezuela, common in Trinidad, uncommon in Tobago, frequent in Guyana, common in Suriname, uncommon but widespread in French Guiana.

Habitat Tropical Zone, to 1,400m but mainly below 1,000m in west Ecuador, to 1,100m in east Ecuador; to 1,200m, locally 1,500m in Colombia; to 1,800m but mainly below 1,300m in Venezuela. Humid to wet forests, mature secondary woodland, sand and savanna forests. Not found in mangroves.

Voice Like congeners, a long bubbling rattle that rises and falls. Also, a loud sudden *squeeeeik*, and song consists of up to 30 whinnying, descending notes: *ke-te-te-te-tu-tu-tu-tu-tue-tue-tue-tue-chu-chu-chu-chu-chew-chew* (H&B, Hilty). Metallic *cheeng* notes (H&M).

Notes R&G consider race *neglecta* (Todd 1948) possibly synonymous with *phaeochroa*.

WHITE-CHINNED WOODCREEPER

Dendrocincla merula Pl. 149

Identification 18–21cm. Generally smoky with rufous wings and tail, unstreaked plumage, and sharp white upper throat. Bill highly variable, usually blackish above, below blackish to yellowish-green. Juvenile has duller throat and is generally darker below, with all-dark bill. From Plain Brown Woodcreeper by white throat.

Ssp. *D. m. bartletti* (NE Ec: Napo & Sucumbíos, E Co: S Meta, Vaupés & Amazonas, S Ve) eyes bluish-grey in Colombia, brown in Venezuela, but birds with grey eyes recorded in Roraima and Orinoco areas

D. m. merula (Guianas) reddish-brown eyes

Habits Forages alone or in pairs and nearly always following army ants, picking insects mostly on ground. Nests during dry season.

Status Rare in Ecuador, where first recorded 1976; uncommon in Colombia, scarce and local in Venezuela, uncommon in Guyana, very rare in Suriname (where known from only 1 specimen dated 1866), uncommon in French Guiana.
Habitat Lower Tropical Zone, to 300m in Ecuador, 500m in Colombia and 300m in Venezuela. Humid *terra firme* and sandy soil forests.
Voice Song a descending, slowing *kue, kue, kue, ku, ku, ku, ku, ku, ku*.... In alarm, irregular rattles: *shu-shu, shu-shu-shu-shu*... (Hilty).

RUDDY WOODCREEPER

Dendrocincla homochroa Pl. 149

Identification 20–20.5cm. Bright ruddy cap, with rest of body dark rufescent brown, brighter rufous on wings and tail. Juvenile like adult but belly and undertail-coverts more rufescent.

Ssp. *D. h. meridionalis* (E Co: Perijá Mts., W Ve: Perijá Mts. & Andes) crown darker chestnut, back darker and more olive-brown than *ruficeps*
D. h. ruficeps (NW Co: N Chocó) paler, larger with heavier bill than *meridionalis*

Habits Follows army ants quietly, sometimes in small groups, or forages alone, clinging to trunks at low levels. Rarely sings or rattles.
Status Possibly scarce, with few records in Colombia. In Venezuela, frequent, but foothills and lower slopes of Andes and in Perijá are being deforested relentlessly.
Habitat Tropical Zone, to 800m in Colombia; to 1,250m but mostly below 450m in Venezuela. Humid forests, clearings, partially logged areas.
Voice A short *chu-chu-chuchuchuchu-chut* rattle, similar to congeners (H&B). Song a dozen or so, slow-paced *wheet* notes, and a *churrrr*, nasal, falling *deeeeah* and squeaky *kink* notes (Hilty).

Deconychura woodcreepers are birds of the Amazon watershed, where they have extensive ranges but always seem to occur at low density. They have very long tails and are amongst the few woodcreepers that show differences between males and females (the former being considerably larger).

LONG-TAILED WOODCREEPER

Deconychura longicauda Pl. 149

Identification 19.5–22cm. Fairly slim-looking, olive-brown head, back and body, with longish rufous wings and tail, including uppertail-coverts. Pale buffy lores and supercilium, thin buffy spot or stripe behind eye, streaky spots of pale buffy on head-sides, throat and breast. Bill fairly short, dark above and bluish-grey below. Juvenile has brownish scaling on throat and breast spots are larger, but diffuse. Larger than Spot-throated, crown almost unstreaked and breast markings more spotted, longer and more slender bill. Spot-throated far less rufous.

Ssp. *D. l. connectens* (E Ec: W Napo to Zamora-Chinchipe, SE Co: SE Guainía, E Vaupés, E Amazonas, S Ve) paler, spots on breast smaller and sharper than *longicauda*
D. l. darienensis (NW Co) more heavily and extensively streaked below, streaks reaching flanks
D. l. longicauda (Guianas) smaller and slightly paler than *connectens*
D. l. minor (N Co: Santander) similar to *typica*
D. l. pallida (E Ec: lowlands?) paler, breast has thinner streaks than *longicauda*
D. l. typica (NW Co?) smaller and more heavily spotted on breast

Habits Forages quietly alone or in pairs, sometimes following understorey mixed flocks but not army ants.
Status Rare and local in Ecuador, uncommon and local in Colombia and Venezuela, uncommon in Guyana, rare in Suriname (few records), uncommon in French Guiana.
Habitat Tropical Zone, to 1,700m in Ecuador, 1,300m in Colombia and 400m in Venezuela. Humid lowland primary forests, *terra firme* and *várzea*, and forests in hilly areas.
Voice That of *connectens* in Ecuador is a simple, colourless and fast trill, descending at first then rising at end, lasting *c.*2 s. In Venezuela, also *connectens*, song described as dramatic, a dozen or so slow, falling whistles: *PEEE.. peee.. peuu puu tuu tuu tuu tu*. Also, fast, low *trrrr-trrrr*... trills in alarm (Hilty). These vocalisations are typical of *connectens* and *pallida*.
Notes Race *pallida* unconfirmed in Ecuador (no specimens) but considered likely in lowlands (R&G). Race *minor* (with *typica* of Central America) formerly treated specifically. Marantz consider that present races may include more than one species, as there are vocal differences between different groups of subspecies, and that *typica* and *minor* are possibly closer to *D. stictolaema* than to Amazonian races (*longicauda* and others). Race *typica* listed for Colombia in Peters, SCJ&W but not in Marantz.

SPOT-THROATED WOODCREEPER

Deconychura stictolaema Pl. 149

Identification 19–20.5cm. Olive head, back and entire underparts, wings and tail rufous, chestnut-rufous rump; plain, unstreaked crown and breast; lots of broad buff streak-spots on throat. Look for short, thin and straight bill. Smaller than Long-tailed Woodcreeper, with better-marked spots on breast and has rufous rump.

Ssp. *D. s. clarior* (Gu, E FG) as described
D. s. secunda (E Ec: W Napo, SE Co: W Putumayo to Guianía & Amazonas, S Ve: C & S Amazonas) more rufescent above, olive below

Habits Forages quietly at low levels, alone or, more usually, with mixed flocks.
Status Rare and local in Ecuador. First recorded in Colombia 1969, where rare but possibly frequent. Uncommon to possibly very locally frequent in Venezuela, where found in only 4 localities of southern Amazonas. Uncommon in Guyana, uncommon to rare in French Guiana. Not listed for Suriname

in H&M, but recent sight record near Tafelberg listed on J.H. Ribot's website.

Habitat Lower Tropical Zone, 200–350m in Ecuador; to 400m in Colombia and 200m in Venezuela. Humid lowland forests.

Voice Song a rising and falling series of vibrating notes: *wuee-ee-ee-EE-EE-EE-ee-ee-ee-ee-e-e-e…* (Hilty). Rarely heard singing.

Notes Race *secunda* formerly treated specifically by some authors. Race in Guyana uncertain, population apparently isolated from those in Venezuela and French Guiana (and perhaps Suriname), assigned here to *clarior* following Marantz.

OLIVACEOUS WOODCREEPER

Sittasomus griseicapillus Pl. 149

Identification 15–16.5cm. Rather variable, but essentially greyish-olive head, back and wing-coverts, underparts to upper belly and flanks greyish-olive, tertials, rump, tail and tail-coverts bright rufous (those from Anzoátegui, Venezuela, have yellowish wash to head and underparts). Lores and eye-ring pale. Bill slender and straight, black above, dark to grey below with pale cutting edges. In flight, pale band at base of flight-feathers very obvious and a good field mark if bird flies overhead. Juvenile brighter above, with rufous fringes to wing-coverts, paler below. Lack of streaks or spots makes for easy identification.

Ssp. *S. g. aequatorialis* (W Ec: Pacific coast W Esmeraldas to El Oro & W Loja) browner above and more buffy-olive below than nominate, with paler remiges; more buffy-olive below than *amazonus*, with cinnamon-rufous tail and wings

S. g. amazonus (E Ec; SE Co: S Meta, Vichada & Guainía; S Ve: W & S Amazonas) similar to nominate but bill larger and generally darker and greyer, less olive; larger, generally darker, more greyish below than *aequatorialis* with rufous tail and wings

S. g. axillaris (S Ve: N & C Amazonas & Bolívar; Guianas) upperparts and tail more rufescent than *amazonus*

S. g. enochrus (N Co) similar to *griseus*

S. g. griseus (To, N Ve: Andes SW Lara to Mérida & SW Barinas, coastal ranges of C & E Falcón to Sucre & N Monagas) smaller, with shorter bill, head and underparts more olive, back russet-brown, wingbar whitish and diffuse

S. g. levis (NW Co) similar to *griseus*, but wingbar buffy

S. g. perijanus (NE Co: NW Magdalena & W Guajira, NW Ve; Perijá Mts.) like *griseus* but wingbar buffy, head more olive-green, back russet-brown

S. g. tachirensis (NC & NE Co: S Bolívar & Santander; W Ve: SW Táchira)

Habits Forages quietly, alone or in pairs, sometimes with mixed flocks, obsessively searching thick trunks from low to mid levels, climbing with mechanical little hops.

Olivaceous Woodcreeper has inner webs of secondaries and inner primaries white, buffy or pale rufous, evident as a bar in flight, which aids recognition

Status Frequent to locally common in west Ecuador, rare to uncommon in east, uncommon to frequent in Colombia, common and widespread in Venezuela, uncommon in Tobago (no records Trinidad), uncommon and local in Guyana, widespread but quite scarce in French Guiana. In Suriname, only sight records, reported in SFP&M and by J.-M. Thiollay (along upper Itany River, in south-east of country).

Habitat Tropical Zone, to 1,100m, locally to 2,000m in west Ecuador, to ±1,700m in east; to 1,000m in Colombia; and to 2,300m north of Orinoco and 1,600m south of it in Venezuela. Humid to moist forest and mature secondary woodland, at borders and interior, and more open areas.

Voice Song a fast, raising then falling trill, *wu-wu-wu-we-we-we-ee-ee-ee-e-e-e-ee-ee-ee-we-we-we-wu-wu-wu*. Also a long rattling chatter, and in south, a rising speeding *jowe, jowe, jowee, jowee, joweet, joweet* (H&B, Hilty). Voice in Amazonas state (Venezuela) distinctly differs from birds of Northern Cordillera (D. Ascanio).

Notes Race *enochrus* recently described by Wetmore (1970) but considered synonymous with Central American *sylvioides* by Marantz. Race *levis* which is listed in Dickinson (2003) but not in SCJ&W is considered synonymous with *sylvioides* by Marantz. R&G consider that races in Ecuador are probably separate species (their calls are strikingly different) and Marantz considers that *aequatorialis*, which is geographically isolated, most probably represents a species. Present arrangement may well include several species (R&T, R&G, Hardy *et al.* 1998), possibly up to 5 (Marantz).

WEDGE-BILLED WOODCREEPER

Glyphorynchus spirurus Pl. 149

Identification 14cm. Smallest woodcreeper. Olive to rufescent above, with dull rufous-brown tertials and tail, pale streaks on head and throat, with clear partial eye-ring and distinct supercilium, throat pale, becoming rows of pale dots across lower face-sides and breast, somewhat variable according to race, and may be whitish or orange-rufous. Bright cinnamon bar on wing also varies according to race, on all remiges except outer 5, which are distinctly longer. This should prove a useful field mark. Bill short, wedge-shaped but with straight culmen, and upcurved lower mandible, pale blue-grey. Juvenile indistinguishable from adult. Very small and rather like a xenops, though tail very different. Look for small head with buffy eyebrow and small, wedge-shaped bill. Xenops have bright pale line behind eyes and/or bold white mesial, they also lack typical woodcreeper tail of stiff spines (several xenops have black lines on tail as well), and have proportionately larger, wedge-shaped bill with obvious pale base to mandible.

Ssp. *G. s. amacurensis* (NE Ve: Sucre & Delta) pale orange throat becoming rows of inverted-triangle-shaped spots on breast

G. s. castelnaudii (E Ec, SE Co: Amazonas) extremely variable, throat cinnamon, generally darker, more olivaceous below, and shorter, stouter bill

G. s. coronobscurus (Ve: Neblina Mts., S Amazonas) marginally darker head, pale rufous throat, thin buffy streaks on breast

G. s. integratus (NE Co: mid Sinú river E to middle Magdalena Valley S to W Boyacá, E of Andes from Norte de Santander to NW Arauca, W Ve: Perijá Mts. & Andes) chin and throat buffy-white, flecked slightly pale orange and olive, spots on breast broad, diamond-shaped

G. s. pallidulus (NW Co: Cerro Pirre & E slope of Cerro Tacarcuna) pale cinnamon throat, long triangular spots on breast, generally pale

G. s. rufigularis (NW Ec, E Co: Meta & Vichada S to Putumayo & Vaupés, S Ve: N & C Amazonas & S Bolívar) chin and throat pale rufous (dull orange), narrow buffy inverted triangular spots on breast

G. s. spirurus (E Ve: NE & E Bolívar, Guianas) chin and throat pale orange, scaled dark olive, pale buffy spots on breast large and diamond-shaped, fine streaks on belly

G. s. sublestus (W Ec, Co: Andes) throat more cinnamon than ochre, pale streaks below narrow and sparse

G. s. subrufescens (NW Co: Pacific coast & lower Atrato Valley E to upper Sinú river) similar to *sublestus*, but smaller, more rufescent (less brownish) and less extensive streaking on breast

Wing surfaces of Wedge-billed Woodcreeper (upperside on right), showing wingbar and unusual shape, and note the small white bar on underwing-coverts

Habits Forages at low and mid levels, alone or in pairs, often (almost always) with mixed flocks. Searches obsessively around thick trunks, chipping off flecks of bark.

Status Uncommon to sometimes common in Ecuador, frequent to common in Colombia, common to very common in Venezuela, frequent in Guyana, common in Suriname, frequent in French Guiana.

Habitat Tropical Zone, to 1,700m, locally to 2,000m in Ecuador; to 2,100m but most numerous below 1,200m in Colombia; to 1,800m in Venezuela. Humid to wet forests, both *várzea* and *terra firme*, and mature secondary woodland. Wooded sand ridges and savanna forests in Suriname. Not found in mangroves.

Voice Calls *chief!* and *chief-beef!* that sound like sneezes. Song a rising series, *too-e, too-e, tu-tu-tu-tue'tue'twu'twee'twee* (Hilty), or a fast series of *tiff* notes, followed by a few sneezes (H&B). Call a short chatter: *chet… chet-chet* (H&M).

Notes Race *rufigularis* possibly a synonym of *castelnaudii* (R&G, Marantz). On basis of voice, it is probable that present arrangement may include more than one species (Marantz). Correct spelling is *Glyphorynchus*, not *Glyphorhynchus* (SACC).

LONG-BILLED WOODCREEPER

Nasica longirostris Pl. 153

Identification 36cm. Snake-like, with long bill, long neck, long body and tail. Upperparts rich rufous, upper part of head dark to sooty with long whitish supercilium and streaked nape, chin to upper breast white, becoming pale streaks on dusky breast, and continuing on cinnamon belly and flanks. Vent and undertail-coverts rufous. Long and almost straight, strong, cream-coloured bill is about one-fifth of total length. All other long and slender-billed woodcreepers have curved bills.

Long-billed Woodcreeper has a long neck and bill that it uses to dart at spiders and other large insects as it forages amongst growth on tree trunks (after B. Walther)

Ssp. Monotypic (E Ec: along Napo, Aguarico & Pastaza rivers, E Co: S from W Caquetá & E Vichada, S Ve: Amazonas, FG)

Habits Forages for spiders, large insects and small vertebrates in canopy and subcanopy, alone or in pairs, usually climbing on trunks or thick branches, searching nooks, crannies and epiphyte clumps. Follows mixed flocks.

Status Uncommon to locally frequent in Ecuador, frequent in Colombia, locally frequent in Venezuela. In French Guiana, especially frequent in marshy, seasonally flooded forest.

Habitat Lower Tropical Zone, to 400m in Ecuador, 500m in Colombia and 200m in Venezuela. Almost always near water, in *várzea*, swampy forest or along rivers and streams in *terra firme*.

Voice Song a long series of loud, sorrowful whistles *whoooOOOooo… whoooOOOooo… whoooOOOooo...* easy to imitate (Hilty). Usually responds to an imitation of song or playback.

CINNAMON-THROATED WOODCREEPER

Dendrexetastes rufigula Pl. 150

Identification 24 –25cm. Large woodcreeper with a heavy, pale bill. Cinnamon-olive above and below with bright rufous wings and tail. Pale bluish-grey eye-ring, eyes reddish. Pale streaking on nape and underparts varies by race. Look for very thick, straight, pale yellowish-green bill. From all other streaked woodcreepers by bill and lack of streaks on head.

Ssp. *D. r. devillei* (E Ec, SE Co: W Caquetá S to Amazonas) only faintly streaked on upper mantle, more clearly so on breast, streaks fading on sides and upper belly
D. r. rufigula (Ve: NE Bolívar & S Delta Amacuro, Guianas) strongly streaked on mantle, breast, particularly on sides, also rest of underparts to undertail-coverts

Habits Forages alone or in pairs at mid levels and in outer branches of canopy, and a regular member of mixed flocks. Probes fruits and leaf clumps. Calls at dawn, amongst first to do so, and at dusk, almost night.
Status Uncommon to locally frequent in Ecuador and Colombia, uncommon in Venezuela (first recorded Bolívar in 1998), uncommon and local in Guyana, uncommon to locally frequent in Suriname, widespread and frequent in French Guiana.
Habitat Lower Tropical Zone, to 500m, locally to 1,200m in Ecuador; to 500m in Colombia and 300m in Venezuela. Humid lowland forests, both *terra firme* and *várzea*, river islands. Coastal sandy soil and savanna forests in Suriname, often in areas with palms. Also in old mangrove in French Guiana.
Voice Loud penetrating whistles (R&G); a falling trill in Amazonas (H&B); in Venezuela and Suriname, haunting, anguished *tew* notes that rise in volume and then fade (Hilty).
Note Race *devillei* formerly considered a separate species, but now treated as conspecific, based on vocal similarity (Marantz).

RED-BILLED WOODCREEPER

Hylexetastes perrotii Pl. 151

Identification 29cm. Large, heavily built woodcreeper with large and heavy, distinct red bill. Entirely olive, including wing-coverts, except rufous tertials and remiges, rump and tail, with somewhat diffuse whitish stripe from lores to edge of ear-coverts, also whitish chin and throat. Centre of belly to undertail-coverts barred finely paler buffy, but variable. Grey eye-ring, eyes reddish, bill dull carmine to crimson. Bill and strong facial marks separate it from all other woodcreepers.

Ssp. *H. p. perrotii* (E Ve: NE Bolívar & S Delta Amacuro, Guianas)

Habits Forages alone or in pairs, climbing thick trunks from low levels to subcanopy, joining mixed flocks and also attending army ants. Prefers low, dark, dense areas. Diet includes bees, wasps, beetles, ants. Nests in niches or large holes on dead trees, during dry season.
Status Rare or very scarce in Venezuela (few records), uncommon in Guyana, uncommon to rare in Suriname, rare in French Guiana.
Habitat Lower Tropical Zone, to ±200m in Venezuela. Humid lowland and savanna forests.
Voice Song a rising series of loud whistles (Hilty), e.g. *kyuu-hee…. kyuu-hee…* (H&M).
Note Listed as possible for east Colombia in H&B. Voices of this species and Brazilian *H. stresemanni* are quite similar, and they are possibly conspecific (Marantz).

STRONG-BILLED WOODCREEPER

Xiphocolaptes promeropirhynchus Pl. 150

Identification 28–33cm. Large, heavily built woodcreeper with long, strong bill. Olive-brown except rufous tertials and inner webs of remiges, rump and tail, streaked on head, back and underparts; prominent pale buffy lores become whitish streaks below eyes and on ear-coverts, and streaks run over eyes in a rough supercilium, chin and throat buffy-white, becoming streaks on breast. Extent to which streaks are bold or weak, edged dark to blackish, or not at all, and extent of streaking on back and underparts vary subspecifically. Similarly, belly and undertail-coverts might be finely barred dark brown; eyes amber to red to dark brown. Blackish bill is slightly decurved, laterally compressed and has very pale horn-coloured cutting edges and, in some cases, pale base to mandible. Much individual variation in all races. Juvenile darker and has ochraceous tips to wing-coverts. A very large, bulky and long bird, with a long, strong bill and noticeable pale loral spot and throat, streaked from head to body.

Ssp. *X. p. crassirostris* (SW Ec: El Oro & Loja) smaller, throat unstreaked and whiter than nominate; like *procerus* with fuscous crown and white throat, postocular stripe pale buffy, streaks below broader, belly and vent heavily spotted, bill slender
X. p. fortis (N Co?, N Ve?) known from single specimen, very similar to *rostratus*, more rufous than *sanctaemartae*, raw umber below, bill pale brown
X. p. ignotus (Ec: Subtropical Zone and above) rufous above, rump and tail dark chestnut, raw umber below, belly and vent heavily spotted, large pale horn bill
X. p. macarenae (CE Co: Macarena Mts. to Caquetá) fine streaks on crown extend only to nape
X. p. neblinae (S Ve: Neblina, Amazonas) dark above, throat heavily streaked
X. p. orenocensis (Ec: E lowlands, Co: E Vichada & SE Nariño, S Ve: Amazonas), crown blackish heavily streaked buff, supramalar almost erased by buff streaks, plumage more rufescent than nominate; eyes red, bill larger and longer, pale greenish- or greyish-horn

X. p. procerus (N & C Ve: montane W Zulia, N Mérida, NW Lara E to Sucre & N Monagas) slightly redder above, thicker streaks on head have reddish flush, but only thin lines on mantle, markings below soft and diffuse spots on belly, bill heavy, greyish-brown

X. p. promeropirhynchus (Co: Perijá Mts. & E Andes of Norte de Santander to S Huila, W Ve: Perijá Mts, & Andes of Táchira to Trujillo) fine dusky barring on belly, and blackish or grey bill, streaks on crown extend to upper mantle; bill thin, black above, grey below

X. p. rostratus (N Co: lowlands in Córdoba & Bolívar, Sinú Valley E to San Lucas Mts., Magdalena Valley) like *sanctaemartae* but bill much larger and stouter, throat plain buff, not edged brown

X. p. sanctaemartae (NE Co: Santa Marta) larger than *procerus*, unbarred belly, slight brown streaking on buffy throat, breast has very fine pale streaks that extend less than on nominate, streaks on crown extend only to nape, bill longer, pale horn

X. p. tenebrosus (SE Ve: Amazonas & Bolívar: Chimantá & Roraima tepuis, Guianas) differs from all others by dark breast and back, striped chin and straight culmen

X. p. virgatus (C Co: C Andes S to W slope in Cauca) like nominate

Habits Forages in pairs, occasionally alone, sometimes with mixed flocks, at all levels. Sometimes follows army ants or searches for prey while hitching up trunks or by inspecting clumps of epiphytes on branches. In some areas seems to specialise in searching bromeliads.

Status Uncommon and local in Ecuador, rare to locally common in Colombia, rare to uncommon in Venezuela, uncommon in Guyana, widespread but very rare in French Guiana. Two records for Suriname records mentioned by J.H. Ribot on his website: a bird captured by E.R. Blake, in 1939, in western border territory claimed from Guyana, and a sighting by J.-M. Thiollay in the south-east, near the Litani River, in territory disputed with French Guiana.

Habitat Tropical to Temperate Zones; montane races, mostly 1,100–3,000m, eastern races to 600m in Ecuador; 100–3,000m, most numerous above 1,500m, in Colombia; 400–2,800m north of Orinoco and to 1,800m south of it in Venezuela. Venezuelan races in Amazonas separated altitudinally: *neblinae* occurs in Subtropical Zone, *orenocensis* in Lower Tropical Zone, and *tenebrosus* in Upper Tropical Zone. Humid lowland and cloud forests, mature second growth, deciduous and semi-arid woodland, and sandy soil forests.

Voice Calls early morning and late evening, an unmistakable descending series of double whistles that often begins with a single high note, *WEE-uut, WE-uut, We-uuh, we-uuh, we-uuh* (H&B, Hilty).

Note Races *neblinae* and *fortis* known from single specimens, latter without type locality and possibly a variant of *rostratus*. Race *ignotus* synonymised with *promeropirhynchus* by Chapman (1926), followed by R&G, who place all montane populations in Ecuador (except in south-west) in nominate. All races presently included in *X. promeropirhynchus* can be divided into 3 groups, and were treated separately in past; for example, former treatment of Amazonian race *orenocensis* (with *neblinae*, *tenebrosus*, *macarenae*) as a species considered possibly correct by R&T and R&G. Races in Middle America also formerly treated specifically, and Marantz considers a thorough study necessary, given differences in plumage but strong vocal similarities.

Dendrocolaptes are relatively large woodcreepers with stout straight bills, barred plumage and rounded tails. The bill is broad-based with a slight hook tip. Some are barred on belly, or have streaked or barred patterns, and most have pale throats. Ruffed crowns indicate males and sleek crowns females.

NORTHERN BARRED WOODCREEPER

Dendrocolaptes sanctithomae Pl. 150

Identification 25–28cm. Large, with black fringes to feathers of head and underparts affording barred appearance. Back, lesser and median coverts brown, barred blackish, head and underparts buffy (washed orange on top of head and flanks) barred brown; rest of wings, rump and tail rufous. Eyes vary from amber to brown, bill blackish, somewhat flesh-coloured at base of mandible. Female larger than male. Juvenile has all-black bill, underparts with more diffuse barring. Look for even dusky barring on pale brown head, back and underparts.

Ssp. *D. s. punctipectus* (Co: Perijá & E Andes in Norte de Santander, Ve: S Zulia, NW Táchira, NW Mérida) larger, darker on breast with strong triangular marks with pale centres giving streaked effect

D. s. sanctithomae (NW Ec: Esmeraldas to Pichincha, N & W Co: Pacific coast & Gulf of Urabá to Sierra of San Lucas) as described

Habits Forages alone, in pairs or occasionally in small groups, from low to mid levels and even subcanopy, inspecting cracks on trunks and clusters of bromeliads and other epiphytes. Sometimes with mixed flocks, but most commonly at swarms of army ants, where it clings to trunks above ants and sallies to catch insects of all sizes and even small lizards or frogs. Occasionally in middle of frantic activity will stop still, perched a long while, as if to catch its breath.

Status Uncommon to locally frequent in Ecuador and Colombia, uncommon or scarce (few records) in Venezuela.

Habitat Tropical and Subtropical Zones, to 800m in Ecuador, 900m in Colombia and 450m in Venezuela. Humid lowland forests, mature secondary woodland, foothill forests.

Voice In Ecuador race *sanctithomae* sings most at dawn and dusk, an excited-sounding and somewhat rising series of forceful clear whistles that gradually become much louder, *oowít, oowít, oowít, OOWÍT, OOWÍT!* Also snarling calls at ant swarms (R&G). Song of *punctipectus* quite different, a series of long whistles on single pitch that ends in harsh chatter. Various calls described as *oiynk* or *awwynk*, a snarling *wikaih* and *caa*, grunting *eh*, murmured *auh-auh-auh-auh-auh*, quiet *wh-whe*, nasal *kyarr* sometimes in series; and when agitated, a series of gobbling notes that rise and fall in pitch (Marantz).

Notes Formerly *D. certhia sanctithomae*, but separated by Willis (1992) and Marantz (1997); latter considered races *nigrirostris* and *colombianus* (Ecuador) synonyms of *sanctithomae* and *hyleorus* a synonym of *punctipectus*. Race *punctipectus* might be a full species based on vocalisations (Marantz).

AMAZONIAN BARRED WOODCREEPER

Dendrocolaptes certhia Pl. 150

Identification 27–28cm. Barred dark brown and orange or buffy, except flight-feathers, rump and tail-coverts; bill dark brown with reddish base, eyes reddish to dark brown. No overlap with Northern Barred Woodcreeper, which has rufous to orange top of head and nape, where Amazonian Barred Woodcreeper tends to dark brown.

Ssp. *D. c. certhia* (E Co: E Vichada, SE Ve: Amazonas & Bolívar, Guianas) barring on dark brown back less clear

D. c. radiolatus (E Ec, SE Co: SW Meta & Vaupés to Amazonas) barring on mantle and shoulders much clearer and contrasting

Habits Forages at all levels, alone or in pairs, infrequently in small groups but often with mixed flocks. In subcanopy, inspects cracks in bark as well as clusters of epiphytes. Also follows army ants, staying alert on trunks a few metres above swarm and sallying to catch insects that fly up. Diet includes many types of insects.

Status Uncommon to locally frequent in Ecuador, uncommon to frequent in Colombia and Venezuela. Frequent in Guyana, frequent to common in Suriname, widespread but uncommon in French Guiana.

Habitat Tropical Zone, to 600m (locally 900m) in Ecuador; to 900m (locally 1,200m) in Colombia and to 1,400m in Venezuela. Humid *terra firme* and mature second growth. Riparian forests, sometimes in *várzea*. Sandy soil and savanna forests in Suriname. Not in mangroves.

Voice Sings mostly in crepuscular hours. a descending sequence of high notes that sound like demented laughter *whee-whee-EE-Ee-Ee-ee-ee-ee-ee-eu eu eu*, fading at end (Hilty). Calls at ant swarms include various snarls and snorts.

Notes Revision by Marantz (1997).

BLACK-BANDED WOODCREEPER

Dendrocolaptes picumnus Pl. 150

Identification 25–28cm. Stout, fairly straight, dusky bill, dusky brown crown and underparts from lower breast covered with fine, even barring. Buff-throated Woodcreeper lacks barring below.

Ssp. *D. p. multistrigatus* (Co: all 3 Andean ranges from N to Cauca & Huila, Perijá Mts., W Ve: Perijá Mts. & Andes of Trujillo to Táchira) small; streaks on head reach upper mantle, back to rump lightly barred blackish; streaks on throat have rows of dusky spots at fringes which appear as heavy barring: eyes brown, bill black above, brown below; legs and feet greenish

D. p. picumnus (S Ve: Amazonas & Bolívar, Guianas) large; brown back with pale shafts, deep rufous wings, rump and tail; head dark brown with very pale shafts broadening into small teardrop spots, denser over and behind eyes, small on face-sides but becoming rows of large buffy spots on throat, malar and neck-sides, changing abruptly to cinnamon-olive breast with broad dusky streaks; changing abruptly again to narrow dusky barring on rufescent buffy posteriorly; eyes dark, bill black above, grey below, legs and feet grey; very extensive and conspicuous barring below; all-black bill

D. p. seilerni (N Co: Santa Marta, N Ve: Falcón to Sucre & N Monagas) less barred below than nominate, buffy streaks on breast narrow and shorter but continue on sides to belly; barring closer (but not equal) and slightly finer on centre of belly and flanks; bill horn above, pale greyish-horn below

D. p. validus (E Ec, SE Co: W Meta & W Caquetá to Amazonas) streaks on head to upper mantle, back and lesser coverts lightly barred, streaks on throat extend to breast and merge with regular black and buffy barring; bill black above, greyish below

Habits Forages alone, in very loose pairs or in small groups, at all levels. In canopy and subcanopy, joins mixed flocks of insectivores, picking insects from bark or sallying to catch others in flight. Forages also quite low, following army ants by flying from trunk to trunk, staying not too high above swarm to catch all types of insect prey.

Status Rare to very locally frequent in Ecuador. Rare in Colombia, uncommon in Venezuela and in Guyana, frequent in Suriname, rare in French Guiana.

Habitat Tropical to Lower Subtropical Zones, to 1,500–1,900m in Ecuador; 1,300 to ± 2,800m west of Andes, lowlands to ± 2,800m east of Andes in Colombia; 400–2,700m north of Orinoco and 500m south of it in Venezuela. Humid *terra firme* and *várzea* forests and mature second growth. Sandy soil and savanna forests in Suriname. Clearings.

Voice Song a sequence of *c.*20 *whin* notes that lasts 4–5 s and starts fast and then slows at end. Also, a shorter sequence (*c.*2 s) of *chu-we-we-we-we-we-we-we* (H&B).

Notes Much discussion concerning treatment and relationships of this and Brazilian *D. hoffmannsi*, and *D. platyrostris*. Marantz (1997) proposed that *D. picumnus* was not close to *D. hoffmannsi*, but subsequently changed his opinion on basis of voice and distribution (Marantz).

The genus *Xiphorhynchus* is the most numerous of the woodcreepers. Its members, very diverse in size and habitat, use varied foraging strategies – some specialise in foraging at bromeliads and other epiphytes, some prefer moss-covered trunks, and yet others rummage and probe clusters of dead leaves. Many are regular attendees at moving swarms of army ants (*Eciton* and *Labidus* spp.) where they are amongst the most competitive, often behaving aggressively to other attending birds.

STRAIGHT-BILLED WOODCREEPER

Xiphorhynchus picus Pl. 151

Identification 20–20.5cm. Mid-sized woodcreeper, highly variable but essentially has rufous back, wings and tail, olive top of head, neck and lower body, face, throat and breast heavily scaled pale buffy-white; face may appear white. Bill very straight, colour varies racially. Juvenile generally darker, throat buffier, and markings more diffuse, with dark to black bill. The only woodcreeper in coastal areas of northern Colombia and Venezuela. Elsewhere, look for whitish cheeks, ear-coverts, foreneck and throat, and straight bill; in most parts of range the only woodcreeper with superciliary, face-sides and throat all pale. Races separate into 2 morphological groups, but significant regional differences in vocalisations could lead to recognition of several species.

Ssp. **The *picus* group** is generally more rufescent, and more heavily and extensively streaked.

X. p. altirostris (Tr) like *picus* but wings and bill longer, latter also heavier and more decurved; more extensive spots below

X. p. deltanus (NE Ve: Delta Amacuro) similar to *duidae* but darker, streaks on head pale buffy, vestigial fringes to throat feathers, bill blackish above, bone white below (see Notes below)

X. p. duidae (SE Co: E Vichada, S Ve: upper Orinoco & upper rio Negro) back more chestnut, spots on head narrow and whitish, clear white postocular line; body paler olive, almost greenish, with white spots to belly and flanks, bill black above, pale horn below

X. p. peruvianus (SW Co: Caquetá region) brighter and more rufescent above, throat deeper buff

X. p. picus (E Co: Orinoco region, S Ve: S Anzoátegui, S Monagas, E Bolívar, Guianas) whitish spots on forecrown become teardrop-shaped on rear crown and cluster on nape, sandy below, bill grey above, pale below

X. p. saturatior (E Co: Norte de Santander to Meta, W Ve: lowlands of C & S Zulia, NW Táchira & W Mérida) postocular stripe off-white, narrow spots on crown pale tawny, rich ruddy body, bill ivory

The *picirostris* group is paler above with much bolder white or near-white face and throat.

X. p. choicus (coastal NC Ve: E Falcón to Miranda) back almost uniform rufous, only hint of brown on upper mantle, spots on head vinaceous-tawny, bill bone-coloured

X. p. dugandi (NW Co: lowlands of Cesar to Bolívar & Magdalena Valley to N Huila) dark markings on head extensively black, but paler than on *extimus*

X. p. extimus (NW Co: N Chocó to S Córdoba in lower Atrato & upper Sinú Valleys) overall browner rather than rufous

X. p. longirostris (Ve: Margarita I.) richer, deeper rufous on back, including rich rufous-brown upper mantle, bill all white

X. p. paraguanae (NW Ve: Falcón & N Lara) brighter rufous above with only slight brown on upper mantle, spots on crown vinaceous-cinnamon, body paler, almost orange, bill white; juvenile more richly coloured and buffy, bill dark

X. p. phalara (C Ve: Llanos from W Apure to NW Bolívar & N Anzoátegui and coast from Anzoátegui to NE Sucre) spots on head tawny, extremely buffy face and throat, bill dull ivory-horn

X. p. picirostris (N Co: coastal lowlands of Atlántico to Guajira, NW Ve: Guajira to C Zulia) spots on head orange-cinnamon, throat rather buffy, feathers edged black, bill ivory; juvenile warm buffy, bill black

Habits Forages alone, in pairs and often with mixed flocks, hitching up medium and thinner trunks at low to mid levels. Diet includes all kinds of insects (including flying termites), small lizards. Nests in holes or crevices on trees, and also in arboreal termite nests.

Status Frequent to common in Ecuador and Colombia. In Venezuela, very common in arid regions, less numerous in more humid regions. Frequent in Guyana. In Suriname, commonest in coastal forests and mangrove. Common in coastal plain of French Guiana, especially mangroves.

Habitat Lower Tropical Zone, to 500m in Ecuador, 600m in Colombia and to 1,400m north of Orinoco, and to 200m south of it in Venezuela. Humid lowland forest, *várzea*, river and forest borders, clearings, swampy forests, mangrove, but also drier savanna forests and in plantations.

Voice In Amazonia and south Venezuela, a fast series of 30–40 intermediate notes (21khz) in 2–3 s, starting with a few stuttered notes, followed by series of descending slow notes that speed up in middle and then slow again at end: *chip, chip, chip, dip-dip-dii-dii-di-di-di-di-di-di dew, dew, dew*, or also *stit-ste-e-e-e-e-e-e-ee-eerp-eerp-eerp*. In north Venezuela, voice varies by race, *phalara* is similar to above but at slightly lower frequency (1.8khz) and is longer (4.1 s). Race *deltanus* occurs in red mangrove and song is fastest and most explosive with a frequency of 2.0–2.5khz and lasts 4 s. Starts with an initial chip followed by a series that speeds up slightly in middle and ends in a series of slowly repeated, up-and-down notes: *chip. chip-chip-chip-dip-dip-dip-di-di-di-di-di-di-di, dip, dip, wik-up, wik-up, wik-up* (Marantz, D. Ascanio, pers. comm.).

Notes Race in Ecuador uncertain (R&G). Race *borreroi* considered invalid by Marantz. *X. picus* formerly included *kienerii* (see below) of Amazon and its tributaries, but *kienerii* now recognised as separate species. In past, *X. picus* and *X. kienerii* (=*necopinus*) were placed in genus *Dendroplex*, but merged into *Xiphorhynchus* (Peters 1951). Northern races (*altirostris*, *choicus*, *dugandi*, *longirostris*, *phalara*) formerly treated as a separate species under *picirostris*, but Peters included them all in *picus*. On basis of vocalisations, *deltanus* is a candidate for separation (D. Ascanio, pers. comm.).

ZIMMER'S WOODCREEPER

Xiphorhynchus kienerii Pl. 151

Identification 21–25cm. Dark rufous upper body, wings and tail, brightest rufous on secondaries; head very dark, dusky olive heavily marked with rows of blackish-edged pale spots, palest and most concentrated on chin and throat. Underparts rufous-olive with paler, dark-edged streaks. Eyes pale brown to brownish-grey, orbital ring mustard yellow, bill greyish-horn to whitish, blue-grey base of upper mandible. Juvenile similar but has less well-defined markings below, and bill blackish.

Ssp. Monotypic (E Ec: río Napo?, extreme SE Co)

Habits Forages alone or with mixed flocks of insectivores, from mid levels to subcanopy and canopy, hitching up trunks, gleaning insects from cracks in bark, rotten wood and termite tunnels. Sings on and off during day.

Status Uncertain but very probable on río Napo in Ecuador, locally frequent in Colombia.

Habitat Lower Tropical Zone to 200m. *Várzes*, swampy seasonally flooded forests of Amazon, river islands.

Voice Song a fast, steady series of high notes, *tr'r'r'r'r'r'r'r'r*, on even pitch (Marantz).

Notes Known as *Dendroplex necopinus* since description in 1934, but found to be identical to specimens identified as *Dendrornis kienerii*, described in 1856 and subsequently mistakenly assigned to *X. picus*. Recognised as a separate species from *X. picus* by Marantz, based on vocal, morphological, ecological and molecular evidence. Aleixo & Whitney (2002) showed that *kienerii* has priority over *necopinus*.

STRIPED WOODCREEPER

Xiphorhynchus obsoletus Pl. 152

Identification 19–20.5cm. Dark olive with rufous tertials, rump and tail; streaked from forehead to lower back and throat to flanks with dark-edged, pale buffy-white spots; chin whitish. Vent and undertail-coverts plain. Bill dark above, bluish-grey below with whitish cutting edges. Juvenile like adult but streaks more diffuse and less clearly defined. Far more streaked on back than Ocellated and much duller on throat than either Spix's or Elegant Woodcreepers.

Ssp. *X. o. caicarae* (C Ve: along Orinoco from Caicara to Altagracia) paler above, brighter rufous, extended teardrop streaks on back less heavily defined, markings of throat and chest more like scales than drops

X. o. notatus (E Co: upper rio Negro basin in Guainía, W & S Ve: SW Táchira, Barinas, W Apure to N Amazonas, N Bolívar from upper Caura to Cuyuní rivers) more rufescent than *obsoletus*, with throat and streaks more buffy and ochraceous (Marantz) but a large series of both in COP show no differences

X. o. obsoletus (E Ve: Delta Amacuro, Guianas) as described, specimens from Venezuela more richly coloured than *notatus*, but not noticeable in field; bill paler and more uniform than other races

X. o. palliatus (E Ec: basins of Napo, Aguarico and Pastaza rivers, SE Co: Meta & Caquetá) more richly rufescent, with back almost all rufous, bill heavier

Habits Forages alone or in pairs in dense understorey, at low and mid levels. Nests in holes on stumps or in arboreal termite nests.

Status Uncommon to frequent in Ecuador and Colombia, uncommon to locally common in Venezuela, locally frequent in Trinidad (no records Tobago), frequent in Guyana, locally frequent to uncommon in Suriname, uncommon in French Guiana.

Habitat Lower Tropical Zone, to 300m in Ecuador, 400m in Colombia and 500m in Venezuela. Humid lowland forest, *várzea*, wet areas along streams, swampy forests. Not in mangroves.

Voice Sings early morning and erratically through day, a loud energetic rattle or trill, *tr'e'e'a'a'a'e'e'e'e'eP!*, which starts suddenly, descends and then jumps up at end (Hilty).

OCELLATED WOODCREEPER

Xiphorhynchus ocellatus Pl. 152

Identification 20–22.5cm. Dark rufous wings, rump and tail, unstreaked mid-brown mantle and back, dark rufous-olive head profusely marked with small buff drops on crown, becoming fine lines on nape that fade on upper mantle, buffy eye-ring runs into postocular line, chin almost completely buffy, with fringes gradually becoming darker on throat, lower throat and chest buff with dusky scalloping that affords a scaled look, but rest of underparts unmarked. Bill dark above pale below. Juvenile has less extensive streaking below and a darker breast, bill all dark.

Ssp. *X. o. lineatocapilla* (SC Ve?) bill markedly heavier and crown more blackish, back less rufous

X. o. weddellii (E Ec?, E & SE Co: E Guainía, E Vaupés, S Amazonas, S Ve: SW Amazonas) as described

Habits Forages alone or in very loose pairs, at lower levels, searching up trunks and probing masses of dead leaves and in mosses. Joins understorey mixed flocks. Not easy to see.

Status Uncommon to locally frequent in Ecuador and Colombia, scarce but perhaps locally frequent in Venezuela.

Habitat Tropical Zone, to 1,100m, most numerous below 800m in Ecuador; to 500m in Colombia and 200m in Venezuela. Interior of humid *terra firme*, along rivers, occasionally in *várzea*.

Voice Sings only occasionally, a scolding sequence commencing with several harsh nasal notes, then 1–2 sharp notes and a falling whine, *qeek-qeek-qeek-qeek-qeek-qeek, CHIK! CHIK! neeeeea*... (Hilty). Also, a fast trill that descends slightly at very start and then rises to end, *t'r'r'r'r'r'a'a'a'a'eik!* (H&B).

Notes Population in south Venezuela treated in some references (P&MdS, Hilty) as race *ocellatus* because *weddellii* was considered a synonym, but genetic and vocal data show that they are separate. Race *napensis*, formerly included in this species, now placed under Tschudi's Woodcreeper *X. chunchotambo*. Race *lineatocapilla* known from single specimen from somewhere in central Orinoco. Correct spelling is *lineatocapilla*, not *lineatocapillus* (David & Gosselin 2002).

TSCHUDI'S WOODCREEPER

Xiphorhynchus chunchotambo Pl. 151

Identification 21–24.5cm. Dark brown crown with very

small buff drop-shaped spots, olive-brown back with narrow but well-defined buff streaks, throat rich buff with extensive dusky scaling.

Ssp. *X. c. napensis* (E Ec: E slope & lowlands, S Co: W Caquetá, SE Nariño to W Amazonas)

Habits Forages alone or in loose pairs, at low and mid levels, searching trunks and probing masses of dead leaves and mosses. Regularly joins understorey mixed flocks, but follows army ants only occasionally.

Status Uncommon to locally frequent in Ecuador and Colombia.

Habitat Tropical Zone to 1,800m. Humid forests on lower slopes and adjacent lowland *terra firme* and seasonally flooded forests, occasionally in wooded swamps.

Voice Sings at dawn and dusk and only sporadically by day; a fast descending sequence of nasal notes, *whe-whe-whe-whe-whe-chechecheow*, and call is series of squeaky notes, *wik-di-di-di-di-di-dit* (Marantz)

Note Race *napensis* formerly treated as a race of Ocellated Woodcreeper (H&B), but considered best placed here on basis of external morphology (Marantz).

[SPIX'S WOODCREEPER
Xiphorhynchus spixii] (not illustrated)

Monotypic (Brazil: S of lower Amazon river). Listed in Rodner *et al.* (2000), as formerly considered part of a polytypic species (with races *ornatus* and *buenavistae* amongst its subspecies). Haffer (1997) separated *spixii* from all subspecies west and north of Amazon, placing these under *X. elegans*. Now considered monotypic, range of *X. spixii* is south-central Brazil and therefore does not occur in our region.

ELEGANT WOODCREEPER
Xiphorhynchus elegans Pl. 152

Identification 18–23cm. Mid brown above and below, with rufous rump, lower wings and tail, upper head dark brown. All brown areas covered with rows of tear-shaped spots, usually dark-edged, and varying in size from smallest on forehead to largest on back, sides and flanks; small and paler over eye and behind (vestigial superciliary). Look for a long, thin, almost straight pale bill, barely hinted eyebrow and buffy-white throat. Female slightly smaller and juvenile darker, with pale shaft-streaks on scapulars and wing-coverts.

Ssp. *X. e. buenavistae* (SE Co: E slope of E Andes in W Meta & Caquetá) greyer than *ornatus*, with spots smaller and less ochraceous

X. e. ornatus (E Ec: Napo & Sucumbíos, SE Co: E Vaupés & S Amazonas) has rump, wings and tail deeper rufous than *buenavistae*, with all spots larger, and generally is richer and warmer

Habits Forages in undergrowth to mid levels and even subcanopy, alone or sometimes in pairs, almost always with mixed understorey flocks, where it is a core species, especially with *Thamnomanes* antshrikes. Very feisty, defends flock territory. Gleans or pecks insects from bark, dead leaves and mosses. Only sporadically follows army ants, usually in pairs.

Status Rare to apparently very local and uncommon in Ecuador, uncommon to locally frequent in Colombia.

Habitat Lower Tropical Zone, to 400m in Ecuador; to 1,400 m (race *buenavistae* locally to 2,400m) in Colombia. Humid forest, mainly *terra firme*, but sometimes in *várzea* and riparian forests, wooded river islands, sandy soil forests, stands of *Guadua* bamboo.

Voice: Song at dawn and dusk, only sporadically, a long, falling series of *c.*30 ringing whistles, *whit, whit, wit, wit, wit… wit, wit, wee, wee, wee, wit, wit, wit, wit, wew*. Also, a tapering series of 10–20 sharp whistles *chip, chip, cher-cher-che-che-che-che-che-che-che-che, weeur* that ends in a whine. Also, long series of *eek* notes that goes up and down and varies in tone (Marantz).

Notes Race *buenavistae* placed in *spixii* by H&B. Revision by Haffer (1997) defined taxonomy employed here. However, in R&T both *buenavistae* and *ornatus* were included in *X. spixii*, with *buenavistae* considered probably synonymous with *ornatus*, and in R&G *ornatus* was also placed under *spixii*. Marantz states that recent genetic and morphological studies support recognition of *X. elegans* (with *buenavistae, ornatus, insignis* and *juruanus*) as a separate species.

CHESTNUT-RUMPED WOODCREEPER
Xiphorhynchus pardalotus Pl. 152

Identification 21–23.5cm. Warm mid brown above and below, with rufous rump, lower wings and tail, upper head dark brown. All brown areas covered with rows of teardrop-shaped spots, usually dark-edged and varying from smallest on forehead to largest on back, sides and flanks. Buffy eye-ring and postocular line. Look for buff eyebrow and eye-ring, blackish-brown crown and nape covered in small buffy drop-shaped spots that lengthen and become scantier on upper back. Very similar Ocellated Woodcreeper virtually unstreaked on back, Buff-throated is larger and more heavily built, with grey ocular skin and race *polystictus* has white throat. Chestnut-rumped has much richer buffy throat than either Ocellated or Elegant Woodcreepers.

Ssp. *X. p. caurensis* (S Ve: tepuis of Amazonas & Bolívar, W Gu) as described; more rufescent above, with streaks softer, more narrowly edged than nominate

X. p. pardalotus (Guianas) less rufescent, more heavily streaked

Habits Always forages with mixed flocks of forest understorey and is a persistent follower of army ants. Nests during dry season.

Status Uncommon to frequent in Venezuela, frequent in Guyana, common in Suriname, very common in forests of interior in French Guiana.

Habitat Tropical and Subtropical Zones, mostly to ± 500m, to 1,800m on tepui slopes in Venezuela. Humid to wet *terra firme*, forests on slopes of tepuis, mature secondary and savanna woodlands, sometimes near rivers. Not found in mangroves.

Voice Call a weak *tjeep… tjeep-tjeep…* always heard in mixed flocks (H&M). Song a sequence of *c.*15 notes that speeds into a rattle and then fades, *chip! chip, chip, chi-i-i-i-i-i-ip* or *zut, zut, zut-zut-zut-t't't't'e' e e e*. Loud *peet* notes, tweeting *ik* notes, chips and a long *che-e-e-e-e-eep-eep-pool-pool-eep-e-e-e…*, typical of many woodcreepers (Marantz).

BUFF-THROATED WOODCREEPER

Xiphorhynchus guttatus Pl. 151

Identification 26–29cm. Fairly large, heavily built woodcreeper with dark rufous wings, rump and tail, dark brown head with clear white or buffy throat, cinnamon-olive below, with pale buffy spots on head and face-sides, rest of back, breast and sides have long rows of buffy streaks. Heavy, decurved bill is pale blue-grey with brown at base of culmen. Eyes dark reddish, eye-ring grey. Female smaller and juvenile more clearly and heavily streaked on back and upper breast, bill shorter and blackish.

Ssp. *X. g. guttatoides* (E Ec: Sucumbíos to Zamora-Chinchipe, SE Co: Meta & Guianía S to Amazonas, S Ve: S & W Amazonas) bill pale (both mandibles)
X. g. polystictus (E Co: E Vichada, S Ve: N Amazonas, Bolívar, SW Anzoátegui & Delta Amacuro, Guianas?) dark upper mandible, pale lower mandible
X. g. connectens (FG?) more deeply streaked buff above and below

Habits Easy to see. Forages from subcanopy to mid levels, alone or in loose pairs, and often with mixed flocks. Climbs on trunks and thicker branches, inspects dead leaves, and probes bases of palm leaves and epiphytes.

Status Frequent to common in Ecuador. In Colombia, the commonest woodcreeper in most humid forests. In Venezuela, the commonest woodcreeper south of Orinoco. Frequent in Guyana and Suriname, where it overlaps with *X. picus* but is much less common in forests of interior. Locally common in French Guiana, where replaces *X. pardalotus* in old mangroves and swampy forests of littoral or in seasonally flooded riparian forests in interior.

Habitat Tropical Zone, to 700m, locally to 1,000m in Ecuador; to 1,100m in Colombia; to 500m in Venezuela. Mostly in mature forest, also *Avicennia* mangrove, sandy soil and humid lowland forests (both *várzea* and *terra firme*), savanna forests and old plantations.

Voice One of the most striking, loudest voices in forest, an explosive loud series of 20–25 whinnying notes that fade at end (H&M). In east Bolívar, Venezuela, at dawn, a rhythmic, dropping *chev-re, chev-re, chev-re, chev-re*, during day, a speeding then slowing series of whistles, *dui-dui-kui'kui'kui 'kui'kui'kui'ku'u'u'ut, ut*, and an unhurried, melancholy *tep. tep, tep teep-twee-tweep-tweep-tweep-teep-teep-tee-tee-toe-toe-toe* (Hilty). In Ecuador, a loud, speeding series of even, ringing whistles, mostly at dawn and dusk but also sporadically during day, a short fast series of laughing notes, *wheeyer, wheep-wheep-wheep-wheep-whip*, and a loud, descending *kyoow* (R&G).

Note Race in French Guiana uncertain: assigned to *polystictus* in H&M, but considered possibly *connectens* in Marantz. In Peters, this and *X. susurrans* were treated together, but revision by Willis (1983) showed that differences in size and song merit maintaining 2 species (AOU 1998, Dickinson 2003). Race *polystictus* formerly considered a separate species. Recent studies by Aleixo (2002) and Marantz have revealed further problems in *X. guttatus* and *X. susurrans* as treated here, involving vocal differences and similarities, as well as relationships between races, so further studies are required.

COCOA WOODCREEPER

Xiphorhynchus susurrans Pl. 151

Identification Two distinct subspecies groups:
***Susurrans* group** 22.5–25.5cm. Adult dark brown above with wings, rump and tail more similar in colour than most woodcreepers. Rows of pale spots do not form streaks as feathers have complete dark fringes, eye-ring and postocular spot clear and distinct, chin and upper throat whitish. Bill large and heavy, decurved and generally dark. Female slightly smaller.

Ssp. *X. s. jardinei* (NE Ve: highlands of NE Anzoátegui, Sucre, N Monagas) long, all-black bill; juvenile has throat and underparts deeper buff, and is more rufescent above
X. s. margaritae (Ve: Margarita I.) smaller than *susurrans* and *jardinei*, with no scaling on throat but larger spots on underparts; juvenile has fewer and larger spots on throat and breast
X. s. susurrans (NE Ve: lowlands of SE Sucre, T&T) long, all-black bill

***Nanus* group** 18.5–24.5cm, smaller, more olive above and more richly buff below. Juvenile darker than adult, with throat faintly scaled dusky, crown less spotted and streaks below broader.

Ssp. *X. s. nanus* (N & E Co: Gulf of Urabá to W Guajira, to lower Cauca Valley, upper Magdalena Valley in S Tolima, Catatumbo lowlands & NW Arauca, N & W Ve: Zulia, Táchira to Lara & Falcón, Yaracuy to Miranda, Apure to Portuguesa & N Guárico)
X. s. rosenbergi (W Co: Cauca Valley in Valle)

Habits Forages from low levels to canopy, alone and sometimes in pairs, often joining understorey flocks of other woodcreepers and many antbirds, and regularly attends army ant swarms. When not following latter, found mostly at mid levels to canopy. Gleans insects from bark, inspects mosses and epiphytes, probes dead leaves and rotting stumps, sallies for escaping insects at ant swarms. Quite feisty, disputes prey and position at ant swarms with antbirds, ovenbirds and other woodcreepers. Very vocal, sings from a concealed spot in canopy. Often sings during day when breeding, and sometimes incessantly at dawn and evening.

Status Widespread and common in Colombia and Venezuela, common in Trinidad & Tobago.

Habitat Tropical to Lower Subtropical Zones, to 1,100m, locally to 1,350m in Colombia; to 1,800m, locally to 2,400m in Venezuela. Moist to humid forests, mature secondary woodland, coffee and cocoa plantations.

Voice In northern mountains of Venezuela, song a varied sequence of speeding then slowing notes, *tu-wee, tuwee, tuwee, Wee Wee, Wee, wert, wert, wert, wert, wer, wer*, mostly at dawn, and a series of clear whistles, *peer-peer-peer-peer-peer-peer-peert*, at dawn and during day. Race *jardinieri* has faster song (Hilty). Another song is also of clear whistles, *ki, ki, kuee, kuee, whe, whew, whew, whew, whew* and another is *she-you, she-you, cherp chew* or *che-e-e-r, che-e-e-r, che-e-e-r* (Marantz).
Notes Following Peters, all races were included under *X. guttatus* in H&B and MdS&P, but see *X. guttatus*. Race *demonstratus* of north-east Colombia and north-west Venezuela, considered synomynous under *nanus* (Phelps & Phelps Jr. 1963).

BLACK-STRIPED WOODCREEPER

Xiphorhynchus lachrymosus Pl. 153

Identification 22–25cm. Entirely fuscous, spotted and streaked buffy, except lower wings (greater coverts, tertials and remiges), rump and tail. Rows of spots and streaks from top of head to lower back, scapulars and wing-coverts; cream-coloured chin and throat, becoming spots then streaks over entire underparts. Bill large, heavy and slightly decurved, pale blue-grey but dark on culmen and base above nostrils.

Ssp. *X. l. alarum* (N Co: lowlands in Antioquia & Santander) has spots of both back and underparts smaller, and fringes to outer webs of greater coverts are brown instead of black
X. l. lachrymosus (NW Ec: Esmeraldas to NW Pichincha, W Co: Pacific coast from Chocó) as described

Habits Forages alone or in pairs, occasionally with mixed flocks, at mid levels to canopy, spiraling up trunks and inspecting branches. Prey includes insects, spiders and tiny frogs and lizards. Attends swarms of army ants regularly, where it perches a couple of metres above swarm watching intently, and sometimes is aggressive to other birds at swarm (woodcreepers, antbirds, puffbirds, etc.).
Status Frequent in Ecuador, uncommon and local in Colombia.
Habitat Tropical Zone, to 450m in Ecuador; to 1,500m in Colombia. Wet and humid forests, borders, mature secondary woodland, plantations, mangroves.
Voice A descending series of 3–4 very loud whistles, *whee, hew, hew*, and song is a speeding and then falling series of 10–30 very soft *we* or *di* notes, fast enough to sound like a trill. Other calls include a loud, energetic *doweeet* or *choo-reep* (H&B, Marantz).

SPOTTED WOODCREEPER

Xiphorhynchus erythropygius Pl. 152

Identification 20–23cm. Brown head and body, with small pale buffy spots on head and back, larger on head-sides and underparts. Relatively long bill and conspicuous buff eye-ring, buff throat, and crown seems uniformly dusky. Underparts covered in large triangular buff spots.

Ssp. *X. e. aequatorialis* (W Ec: Esmeraldas to Guayas, El Oro & W Loja, W Co: W slope of W Andes from S Chocó and upper Atrato Valley to Nariño) as described
X. e. insolitus (NW Co: N Chocó & C Antioquia S to N Caldas) brighter rufous above and deeper olive, more densely spotted below

Habits Forages alone or in pairs (sometimes adult and fledged juvenile), from mid levels to subcanopy. Usually with mixed canopy flocks, especially those that include Golden-crowned Warbler, Common Bush Tanager and Lineated Foliage-gleaner. Climbs moss-covered trunks and hops along mossy larger branches, to pick insects by inspecting moss and epiphytes, and probing dead leaves, bark and crevices. Forages alone at marching swarms of army ants, perching on trunks above swarm to keep an alert eye on escaping insects as well as on other attendees.
Status Frequent to locally common in Ecuador. Locally frequent in Colombia, apparently replaces Olive-backed at lower elevations.
Habitat Tropical and Subtropical Zones, mainly to 1,400m, locally to 1,700m in north-west, to ± 2,000m in south-west Ecuador; to 1,500m, mostly 200–1,400m in Colombia. Humid to wet forests, mature secondary woodland on montane slopes.
Voice Sings intermittently, mostly crepuscularly, a series of 3–4 long, descending whistles, each lower than previous and sometimes followed by 1–2 sad notes, *wheeeoo, wheeeoo, wheeeoo, wheeeo* (Marantz), or *d'ddrrear, d'ddrrear, d'ddrrear, whew, whew* (H&B).
Notes Formerly included in *X. triangularis*.

OLIVE-BACKED WOODCREEPER

Xiphorhynchus triangularis Pl. 152

Identification 23cm. Olive-brown with inner webs of flight-feathers, rump and tail rufous, rows of dark-edged pale spots, fine and small on head, fading on nape, obvious pale eye-ring and postocular spot, cheeks and chin, spots reaching across underparts to undertail-coverts, though only strongly marked on face, throat and breast. Buffy throat has striking olive scallops.

Ssp. *X. t. hylodromus* (N Ve: Andes in Trujillo & S Lara, Coastal Cordillera in Yaracuy to Miranda) darker, less reddish secondaries, paler throat and paler, more heavily spotted underparts
X. t. triangularis (E Ec: E slope of Andes, Co: all Andes, W Ve: Andes in Mérida & Táchira, Perijá Mts.)

Habits Forages alone or in pairs and frequently with mixed flocks (especially if with Lineated Foliage-gleaner), from lower levels to subcanopy, but mostly in upper half of trees. Looks for insects around moss-covered trunks and larger branches.
Status Frequent in east Andes of Ecuador. In Colombia, especially frequent in West Andes. Uncommon to locally frequent in Venezuela.
Habitat Subtropical Zone, 1,000–2,100m, locally to 750m in Ecuador; 1,500–2,700m, locally to 800m in west Cauca and to 400m in east Nariño, in Colombia; and 1,000–2,500m

in Venezuela. Wet to humid montane and cloud forests, and secondary woodland slopes, including borders.

Voice Vocalises infrequently; a penetrating, loud slurred *wEEeeeu*, song a sharp sequence that speeds up initially then slows and dies: *we we we-we-we-we-we-WE-WE-we-we wa* (Hilty).

Notes Formerly, *X. triangularis* also included X. *erythropygius* and its races, but they were separated in Peters' Checklist and by Wetmore (1972), which arrangement was recently confirmed by genetic evidence (Marantz).

Lepidocolaptes woodcreepers tend to forage with mixed flocks, mostly in canopy, especially in areas where they are sympatric with any *Xiphorhynchus*, which forage more in the subcanopy and at mid levels. All are small to mid-sized woodcreeper with thin, small and only slightly decurved bills (but more so than *Xiphorynchus*), and tips of their flight-feathers are contrastingly dark, especially in more humid habitats. *Lepidocolaptes* forage mostly from bark of vertical trunks, perching skillfully with legs splayed outwards using the tail as a prop.

STREAK-HEADED WOODCREEPER

Lepidocolaptes souleyetii Pl. 152

Identification 20cm (*littoralis* 18cm). Pale olive back, wing-coverts and body, lower wings, rump and tail somewhat more pale rufous; head and upper breast fuscous with blackish-edged whitish streaks varying from fine and indistinct on top of head, strengthening slightly on nape, but none on back, bolder supercilium, near-white chin and bold streaks over face-sides, neck, throat and breast, becoming pale buffy streaks to undertail-coverts. Bill greyish-horn, darker above, paler below, somewhat variable. Juvenile has bill duskier and is less strongly or clearly marked below. Slightly smaller Lineated Woodcreeper is paler above, has paler bill and generally looks less boldly spotted above. Spot-crowned Woodcreeper distinctly spotted on head but otherwise very similar.

Ssp. *L. s. esmeraldae* (W Ec: Esmeraldas to N & C El Oro, SW Co) shorter bill than nominate, deeper buff throat

L. s. lineaticeps (N Co, W Ve: foothills of Andes in Táchira, Mérida & Barinas) like *uaireni*, throat finely streaked

L. s. littoralis (N Co, Ve: rest of N, N & NE Bolívar; Tr, Gu) smaller and paler than nominate

L. s. souleyetii (SW Ec: S El Oro & Loja) as described

L. s. uaireni (SE Ve: S Gran Sabana in Bolívar) darker above and below, white on head obscure

Habits Forages alone or in pairs from mid levels to canopy, climbing trunks and on branches, inspecting holes and crannies, mosses and epiphytes. Often with mixed flocks of insectivores.

Status Frequent in Ecuador and Colombia, common and widespread in Venezuela, uncommon in Trinidad (no records Tobago); uncommon, sight records only in Guyana.

Habitat Tropical Zone, to 800m, locally to 1,800 in west Loja and to 1,300 at Mindo in Ecuador; to 1,500m in Colombia; and to 1,600m north of Orinoco and 1,100m south of it in Venezuela. Semi-humid to dry areas: deciduous and partially deforested areas, xerophytic scrub.

Voice Song a high, musical trill: *chi-chi-chi-chi*... (H&B) or a rapid, falling *p'e'e'e'e'e'e'eeeeaaa* (Hilty). A short rattle in alarm.

NARROW-BILLED WOODCREEPER

Lepidocolaptes angustirostris Pl. 152

Identification 20cm. Very distinctive, rufous above, fuscous top of head with fine whitish streaks, bold white supercilium from supraloral to nape-sides, blackish line from lores to rear ear-coverts, and creamy white underparts, including undertail-coverts.

Ssp. *L. a. griseiceps* (S Su: Sipaliwini savanna)

Habits Forages alone or in pairs, sometimes in small groups, and regularly with mixed flocks, but very rarely at ant swarms. Spirals up trunks and hops on branches, picking insects from holes and cracks, inspecting mosses and epiphytes, and probing curled dead leaves.

Status In our region, only in Sipaliwini savanna, Suriname, where it is uncommon.

Habitat Tropical Zone, to ±500m in Suriname. Open savanna, stands of *Mauritia* palm.

Voice Song a musical, descending sequence of 4–8 notes, sometimes whistled or rolled and slurred, *peer, peer, peer, peeer, peeeer, pweeeer* and variations such as, *peee, pee-pee-pee-pee-peepeepeepeepeepupupu* (Marantz).

MONTANE WOODCREEPER

Lepidocolaptes lacrymiger Pl. 152

Identification 19cm. Pale olive nape, back and wing-coverts, rest of upperparts cinnamon-olive, nape has faint buffy spots; entire head, except nape, fuscous to blackish with white spots and streaks, bold white eye-ring and postocular stripe, bold white spots become black-edged streaks running from face and chin, forming rows that reach undertail-coverts. Long, fairly slender, decurved bill pale blue-grey, darkish on culmen above nostril. Female slightly smaller and juvenile less strongly marked below, streaks being weakly edged with black, with shorter, darker bill.

Ssp. Two groups, based on morphology:

***Lacrymiger* group** have throat feathers fringed black and streaks more rounded distally, tipped and fringed black, giving a scaly effect.

L. l. lacrymiger (E Co: Perijá & N of E Andes, W Ve: Perijá & Andes) more olive above, spots on head diamond-shaped with arrowhead black fringes, feathers from chin downwards fringed dusky, giving scaled effect

L. l. lafresnayi (N Ve: Coastal Cordillera from Carabobo to Miranda) pale buffy chin, warmer rufous-olive above, streaks on head have only slightly darker tips

L. l. sanctaemartae (N Co: Santa Marta) weakly marked throat, greyish below with broader streaks

L. l. sneiderni (C Co: W & C Andes & W slope of E Andes) darker, more olive-grey, less spotted below

***Warscewiczi* group** is darker and more rufescent, both above and below, back more streaked, throat buffy, spots below more streaked and fringed, but not tipped, black.

L. l. warscewiczi (extreme S Ec: S Zamora-Chinchipe) deeper buff below

L. l. aequatorialis (Ec: E slope in Sucumbíos to N & C Zamora-Chinchipe, W slope in Carchi to W Loja, SW Co: Pacific slope in Nariño) more rufescent than *warscewiczi*, throat more buffy and streaks broader

L. l. frigidus (SW Co: E slope in Nariño) more olivaceous above, darker bill

Habits Forages alone or in pairs from mid levels to canopy, climbing trunks and on branches, inspecting mosses and clumps of epiphytes. Often with mixed canopy flocks.

Status Uncommon to frequent in Ecuador, common in Colombia and in Venezuela.

Habitat Subtropical and Temperate Zones, 1,100–3,000m, mostly above 1,500m in Ecuador; 1,800–3,000m, locally to 1,200m in Colombia; 900–2,900m, mostly above 1,500m in Venezuela. Humid to wet montane, cloud and elfin forests.

Voice Quiet, sings infrequently, a speeding, rhythmic sequence of slurred whistles: *tseu-tseu, tsip-tsip- tsee-tsee-tsee-tsee-tsee* (R&G). In Venezuela, a thin, high, speeding chatter: *swit-swit-swit-swiz-swiz'is'is'it'it't't't*, with song in northern mountains smoother than in Andes (Hilty).

Note Placed under *L. affinis* (Spot-crowned Woodcreeper, of Middle America) by Meyer de Schauensee (1966; followed by S&M), but now returned to specific status (AOU 1998, Dickinson 2003). Although no formal study has been published, they are quite different in plumage and calls.

LINEATED WOODCREEPER

Lepidocolaptes albolineatus Pl. 152

Identification 18cm. Olive back and wing-coverts, rest of wings, rump and tail pale rufous-olive; head and underparts slightly greyish-olive with black-edged warm buffy spots and lines or streaks on top of head, with rounded blackish tips, rich buffy streaks on throat and breast. Juvenile darker above, more streaked and streaks extend to back.

Ssp. *L. a. albolineatus* (E Ve: NE Bolívar & possibly SE Sucre; Guianas) crown has fine, buffy-white spots, bill all dark

L. a. duidae (S Ve: Amazonas & W & S Bolívar) generally darker, crown unspotted, pale buffy throat with narrower streaks below, bill larger and dark above, pale grey below

L. a. fuscicapillus (E Ec: Sucumbíos to Morona-Santiago) cinnamon-brown above, underparts more fulvous with rich buff streaks and rich buff throat

Habits Forages in pairs, climbing trunks and main branches from mid levels to canopy. Does not join mixed flocks in French Guiana, but joins canopy flocks in Venezuela. Diet includes many types of insects and spiders. Nests during dry season, in holes of dead trees.

Status Rare to uncommon and local in Ecuador. Sight records in Colombia (SFP&M) are supposedly of race *duidae* (SCJ&W) and listed for Vaupés in Marantz. In Venezuela, quite frequent in Amazonas, but less common in Bolívar. Frequent in Guyana, common in Suriname and French Guiana.

Habitat Tropical Zone, to 1,000m but mostly below 600m in Ecuador; to 1,300m in Venezuela. Humid and savanna forests and *terra firme*.

Voice In Venezuela, west Amazonas birds (*duidae*) sing a fast, descending sequence of thin, high, nasal notes: *pe-pee-pee-pee-peer-peer-peer-pear*; in Bolívar (*albolineatus*), song faster, chattering and though higher pitched for first few notes, drops much lower pitch over most of notes (Hilty). In Ecuador (*fuscicapillus*), a pretty, descending and accelerating sequence of soft notes: *ti,ti,ti-ti-tee-tee-teh-teh-tutututututu* (R&G).

Note Southern races, such as *duidae* and *fuscicapillus*, possibly represent a separate species.

With their astonishingly long, downward arching bills to probe deep, difficult spots, forest-dwelling *Campylorhamphus* scythebills are very adept at foraging in thickets and stands of bamboo, especially *Guadua*, as well as in bromeliads and other epiphytes. R&G warn that neither colour nor shape of bill can be used to identify species in field. Curvature of their bills seldom as dramatic as portrayed in most field guides. Juveniles have shorter bills and could be confused with *Lepidocolaptes* woodcreepers.

GREATER SCYTHEBILL

Campylorhamphus pucherani Pl. 153

Identification 29cm. Entirely ruddy brown with broad white eye-ring and postocular stripe, and broad white line running irregularly from gape to lower ear-coverts; also pale whitish, buffy or cinnamon streaks on sides of neck, throat, breast and body-sides to flanks. Bill long, pale but dark on culmen above nostrils, and curved. Remarkably large for a scythebill and separated from others by pale bill and conspicuous moustachial and eyebrow.

Ssp. Monotypic (Ec: spottily in W Napo, Morona-Santiago & Loja, and Pichincha on E slope; W Co: W Andes on W slope in Valle & Cauca, upper Magdalena Valley in W Huila)

Habits Forages alone, rarely in pairs or with large mixed flocks, at low and mid levels. Climbs tree ferns and thick, mossy trunks and branches, taking insects and spiders.

Status Generally quite scarce. Very rare and local in Ecuador, rare and local in Colombia.

Habitat Subtropical and Temperate Zones, at 2,000–2,800m in Ecuador; 900–2,500m in Colombia. Humid to wet montane and cloud forests.

Voice Quite different from congeners. A sequence of alternating twitters and nasal *ik* notes, sometimes a loud, rising *oo-eeek* (Marantz). A weak, rising series of nasal notes: *ee-ee-ee-ee-ee-enh* (R&G).

RED-BILLED SCYTHEBILL

Campylorhamphus trochilirostris Pl. 153

Identification 23–23.5cm. Generally olive-brown, more ruddy on wings, rump and tail, dark brown-edged white streaks on head, breast and sides (head looks blackish with pale streaks). Bill long and slender, curved and pinkish-red. Female smaller and juvenile duller, with shorter bill that is dark and only shows pinkish-red at tip.

Ssp. *C. t. brevipennis* (W Co: Pacific coast in Chocó) darker and smaller than *venezuelensis* but has proportionately longer bill

C. t. napensis (E Ec: Amazonian lowlands) bill shorter and more strongly decurved than *thoracicus*

C. t. thoracicus (W Ec: Esmeraldas to W Lojam SW Co: SW Nariño) streaks have distinct black borders

C. t. venezuelensis (N Co: Caribbean lowlands, Magdalena Valley to N Huila, lowlands in Norte de Santander to W Meta, Ve: N & SE Zulia, Andes & Apure to Sucre, NW & C Bolívar) larger and brighter than *brevipennis* or *napensis*, but note that in a large series variation in coloration and strength of white streaks both above and below is noticeable

Habits Shy. Forages with mixed flocks of insectivores in understorey, to level of lowest branches in canopy. Checks mossy branches, and clumps of orchids, bromeliads and other epiphytes, and also tangles of vines and lianas, and crevices on trees in drier areas, or may even pick prey from ground.

Status Rare to locally frequent in Ecuador. Uncommon and very patchily distributed in Colombia. Frequent in Venezuela, especially in gallery forests and isolated patches of tall forest in Llanos. (Report of an uncommon but regular scythebill in French Guiana wrongly assigned to this species, in fact is Curve-billed *C. procurvoides*).

Habitat Tropical Zone to 800m, locally in south to 1,500m in west Ecuador; to 400m, locally to 900m in east Ecuador; to 1,300m in Colombia; and to 2,000m north of Orinoco and 950 m south of it in Venezuela. Humid to moist, undisturbed lowland forest (up to cloud forests), swampy forests, deciduous and mature secondary woodland, drier, deciduous woodland, gallery forests.

Voice In Venezuela, song at dawn a fast rising trill: *dedede'e'e'e'e, dedede'e'e'e'e*, or a fast-dropping trill that ends in several slow notes (P. Schwartz, H&B); also (in Portuguesa) a 5–10 minute-long fast, dropping *we'he'he'he'he'he'he'e'e'e'e 'e* (Hilty); also a loud, rapidly rising and rattled *stri'i'i'i'I'I'I'K* (Hilty; Aragua). In Colombia, sings during day a descending *twe-whee, whew, wheew, whuuew* (H&B). A continuous *pee-ep* in alarm. In Ecuador, song a *tuwee-tuwee-toowa-tew-tew* that sometimes commences with a trill (R&G).

BROWN-BILLED SCYTHEBILL

Campylorhamphus pusillus Pl. 153

Identification 22–23cm. Small. Generally pale warm brown, more bright ruddy on lower wings, rump and tail, streaked buffy on head, and finely so on back and wing-coverts, face, chin and throat streaked whitish-buffy, warmer streaks on breast and sides, extending finely to undertail-coverts. Bill slightly heavier than congeners, and is dark horn to blackish-brown. Juvenile darker and more olivaceous, streaking less distinct, bill shorter. From Red-billed Scythebill by deep buff (instead of whitish) upper throat, and from Greater Scythebill by lack of white on face (malar and postocular streaks).

Ssp. *C. p. guapiensis* (SW Co: coastal lowlands in Cauca) more generally rufescent than nominate, no streaks on back or wing-coverts

C. p. pusillus (Ec: spottily on both slopes, to lowlands in N Esmeraldas, Co: W Andes from Antioquia to W Nariño, C Andes in Valdivia to Valle on W slope & Huila on E slope, E Andes in Cundinamarca on W slope & Norte de Santander & N Boyacá on E slope) as described

C. p. tachirensis (E Co: Perijá Mts., W Ve: Perijá Mts. & Andes in Táchira) more olive below than others; juvenile darker below, though streaks are same; bill short and black

Habits Difficult to detect, as forages in dense foliage, at low and mid levels. Follows understorey flocks alone or, more frequently, in pairs, inspecting every nook and cranny on trunks, base of large leaves and clumps of epiphytes.

Status Rare to uncommon in Ecuador, uncommon and local in Colombia and Venezuela.

Habitat Tropical and Subtropical Zones, 600–2,100m, locally to 100m in Ecuador; 300–2,100m in Colombia; 1,800–2,175m in Venezuela. Mossy areas with many epiphytes in humid to wet forest and mature second growth. Mossy forests of foothills and lower slope in Colombia, to cloud forests in Venezuela.

Voice Sings infrequently, a tremulous, lamenting sequence that increases in volume in middle and varies with each following outburst: *twe-twe-weo. WEO-weo weo-we-we-we-we-we* (H&B). A sweet, variable series of *tuwee* and *teeur* notes and trills, rising and falling, and rather tremulous (R&G).

Note Birds from east and west slopes of Ecuador apparently do not differ significantly (R&G).

CURVE-BILLED SCYTHEBILL

Campylorhamphus procurvoides Pl. 153

Identification 23cm. Warm brown all over, more rufescent on wings, rump and tail, rows of short, whitish streaks over head, neck, throat and breast, lengthening slightly and fading on belly and flanks. Bill dark red to reddish-brown, perhaps with paler base to mandible. From Brown-billed by lack of streaks on back and, usually, redder bill.

Ssp. *C. p. procurvoides* (Su, FG) as described,larger than *sanus* and more olivaceous

C. p. sanus (NE Ec: lowlands in Sucumbíos, E Co: E Norte de Santander, W Meta & W Caquetá to Guainía, Vaupés & Amazonas, S Ve: SW Amazonas & NE Bolívar, W Gu) distinctly smaller, warmer, with shorter and more decurved bill, streaks below are finer and more separated; 2 presumed immatures have shorter bills, but not as short as juvenile, with streaks ending on nape, not on upper mantle as in adult, also, more distinctly spotted (rather than streaked) below

Habits Forages at low and mid levels, to subcanopy, often with mixed flocks.

Status Very rare and local in Ecuador, where first recorded 1992–93. Uncommon to locally frequent in Colombia, where apparently replaces Red-billed in east (they meet along east base of Andes). Uncommon, but possibly locally frequent in Venezuela; uncommon in Guyana; widespread but uncommon in Suriname; frequent but easily overlooked in French Guiana. (Report of an uncommon but regular scythebill in French Guiana evidently is this species, but previously wrongly assigned to Red-billed Scythebill *C. trochilirostris*).

Habitat Lower Tropical Zone, to 400m in Ecuador, 500m in Colombia and *c.*500m in Venezuela. Humid, lowland *terra firme* and savanna forests.

Voice Calls at dawn, a bubbly sequence of 7–9 high notes: *keeea, kee-ke-ke-ke-ke-ke* (H&B).

THAMNOPHILIDAE – Typical Antbirds

Theirs is a half-lit world of vines, dim forest floor, dappled thickets and clearing edge. In this shadowy world, evolution has fostered a group of birds of astonishing variety, surpassed in numbers only by flycatchers, and divided nowadays into 2 families: Thamnophilidae and Formicariidae. Amongst Formicariidae, most species are entirely terrestrial, whilst Thamnophilidae use a wider range of levels, some even the subcanopy. They forage mostly for insects and drink rain water collected in hollows of leaves. Only a handful take ants, but their common name springs from intriguing strategy some species have developed, of following marching swarms of army ants, to take their pick of arthropods (and occasional small vertebrates) that flee in all directions as the horde approaches. Amidst these swarm followers, there exists a precise hierarchy – some species dominate and take the best spots along the advancing front, others stay behind. Some species exclusively feed around ant swarms and are often referred to as 'professional' antbirds. Thamnophilid antbirds blend beautifully with their surroundings – males almost always in elegant black and white, like flecks of light dancing in the shadows; females in the warm ochre, brown and rust of decaying leaves. Antbirds construct open basket nests, usually low in shrubbery or even on the ground, and as they are most often found in close-knit pairs, some species are believed to pair for life. Much of their biology remains to be researched and understood, whilst their complex taxonomy, especially geographic variation, continues to pose challenges and vex systematists. One characteristic that is providing new insight into their lineages is voice; birds that live permanently in low-visibility terrain must locate each other by sound. Thus, songs and calls are quite distinctive. As gaps in vocal information are filled, differences and similarities between species are slowly emerging.

Additional reference for this family: Zimmer & Isler (2003, hereafter Z&I).

FASCIATED ANTSHRIKE

Cymbilaimus lineatus Pl. 154

Identification 17–18cm. Heavy hooked bill, red eyes and minimal crest in both sexes. Adult male all black with white bars, most strongly barred on underparts and least strongly on crown (nominate *lineatus*), female has dark brown/buff barring, with distinctive rufous crest. Juvenile male has broader white bars. Undulated Antshrike is larger with fainter barring, and male has a black throat whilst female is more rufous; female Black-throated Antshrike lacks barred upperparts, whilst all similar *Thamnophilus* antshrikes have coarser barring and yellow eyes.

Ssp. *C. l. brangeri* (W Ve: E Andes, Táchira, Mérida to Barinas) male has white lines on forehead, rest of crown black

C. l. fasciatus (NW Ec, W & N Co) larger than *intermedius* with more powerful bill, male has variable strong white barring on forehead, crown black; both sexes have broader black bands below, female cinnamon tail bars

C. l. intermedius (E Ec, E Co, S Ve) male has few and very narrow white bars on forehead whilst crown is black, and pale bars on tail broader; female distinctly more gingery or orange-flushed on vent and undertail-coverts than *brangeri*

C. l. lineatus (E Ve, Guianas) male has fine white lines on forehead, and usually on crown-sides, occasionally right across crown, black lines below heavier and closer than on other races, i.e. white lines thinner; female has blacker lines on breast

Habits Moves deliberately and rather sluggishly, by short hops through dense vegetation, sometimes pausing for long periods to scan foliage, quickly gleans invertebrates and small vertebrates using quick stabs and short sallies. Usually in pairs and regularly with mixed-species flocks, and sometimes attends army ants.

Status Uncommon to frequent in Ecuador, Colombia and Venezuela, frequent in Guyana, locally frequent in Suriname, common in French Guiana.

Habitat Tropical Zone, to 1,000m, rarely to 1,600m, mostly in canopy but sometimes lower, in dense midstorey and lower levels when breeding. Frequents vine tangles of evergreen forest, forest edge and gaps, second growth and riverine habitats.

Voice A slow sequence of 4–6 resonant whistles, *cüwe-cüwe-cüwe-cüwe-cüwe*, and fast rattles in alarm (H&B). A rattle-like staccato chatter, plaintive downslurred whistle (Z&I), complaining *teeeou* (R&G) and nasal alarm, *wanyurk* (H&B). Song a steadily repeated series of 3–10 loud plaintive ventriloquial downslurred *ouee* whistles, notes longer than spaces, with middle notes sometimes slightly longer and higher pitched (H&B, Z&I).

Note Race *brangeri* described by Aveledo & Pérez (1991), but considered indistinguishable from other races (Z&I) and not recognised by Hilty. It is clearly distinct based on material at COP. Z&I consider *fasciatus* and *intermedius* indistinguishable. Hellmayr (1924) found *fasciatus* to be an ill-defined race yet listed several discriminating characters. We prefer to maintain all 3 races until further evidence becomes available.

Frederickena antshrikes are large, heavily built birds with hooked bills. They are generally dark, and heavily barred above and below. Skulkers, they occur in pairs in dense undergrowth.

BLACK-THROATED ANTSHRIKE
Frederickena viridis Pl. 154

Identification 19–22cm. Heavy hooked bill, red eyes and distinct crest in both sexes. Adult male is dark grey with black head, throat, breast, and tail (faintly barred white) and dusky wings. Female rufous above, including wings, with black tail barred white, and forehead, head-sides and underparts white with narrow black bars. Juvenile male like female but rufous upperparts gradually replaced by dark grey. Female Fasciated Antshrike has barred upperparts, and all other similar antshrikes are smaller, e.g. female Lined Antshrike (no overlap) is smaller and has yellow eyes and rufous tail.

Ssp. Monotypic (SE Ve, Guianas)

Habits Moves slowly, alone or in pairs, sometimes with mixed-species flocks and following army ants, by short hops through dense vegetation, occasionally pausing for long periods to scan foliage, then quickly gleans invertebrates and probably small vertebrates, using quick stabs and short sallies.
Status Uncommon to rare, uncommon in Guyana, widespread but scarce or even rare in French Guiana, and a low-density resident in suitable habitat.
Habitat Lower Tropical Zone, to 700m, in dense understorey (sometimes on ground) of evergreen forest, with preference for sandy soil and *terra firme* forest, especially dense vine-tangled gaps created by treefalls or streams within undisturbed forest, also patches of savanna with dense bushes in forest clearings.
Voice Nasal downslurred *churr*, song a steadily repeated series of 6–15 (usually 9–11) loud plaintive downslurred *peeeur* whistles, so closely spaced that they almost run together, with volume often increasing slightly, female slightly higher pitched (Z&I, Hilty).
Note Forms a superspecies with Undulated Antshrike (Z&I).

UNDULATED ANTSHRIKE
Frederickena unduligera Pl. 154

Identification 23cm. Heavy hooked bill and prominent crest in both sexes, eye colour varies from reddish-brown to pale yellow. Adult male black with irregular buffy to white barring and black throat, adult female rufous with wavy black barring and dusky tail with greyish barring. Juvenile male like female but darker and more heavily barred. Other similar antshrikes are smaller, e.g. Fasciated Antshrike is smaller with stronger barring, and male has barred throat, whilst female is paler below.

Ssp. *F. u. fulva* (E Ec, S Co) as described
F. u. unduligera (extreme SE Co) both sexes a little lighter and brighter than *fulva*

Habits Moves slowly, alone or in pairs, rarely with mixed-species flocks or following army ants, by short hops through dense vegetation, sometimes pausing for long periods to scan foliage, then quickly gleans invertebrates and probably small vertebrates, using quick stabs and short sallies.
Status Rare to uncommon and local, low-density resident in suitable undisturbed habitat, being generally absent from disturbed habitat.
Habitat Tropical Zone, to 700m, rarely to 1,100m, in dense understorey (sometimes on ground) of evergreen forest, with preference for *terra firme*, especially dense vine-tangled gaps created by treefalls or streams within undisturbed forest, rarely in dense second growth or away from deep cover.
Voice A nasal squeal followed by a sharp note, short scratchy calls repeated in short series, a nasal downslurred *churr* (Z&I) and long high-pitched and descending *keeeeeeeeyur* (R&G). Song a steadily repeated series of 7–20 (usually 11–16) plaintive *uué* whistles, commencing downslurred and becoming upslurred (R&T, Z&I).
Note Forms a superspecies with Black-throated Antshrike (Z&I).

The *Taraba* antshrike is a large and bold, bicoloured bird with several distinct subspecies that have different voices, and almost certainly more than one species is involved. It responds well to playback.

GREAT ANTSHRIKE *Taraba major* Pl. 154

Identification 19–20cm. Heavy hooked bill, red eyes and prominent crest in both sexes. Adult male black above with 2–3 white wingbars and white below. Female rufous above with brownish ear-coverts and cinnamon-tinged white below, whitest on throat. Juvenile has cinnamon bars above and below, becoming more indistinct with age.

Ssp. ***Transandeanus* group:**
T. m. granadensis (NE Co, N Ve) male has black head-sides not extending below gape and vent tipped extensively white
T. m. obscurus (W Co) male has 3 wingbars and undertail-coverts black with white tips; female uniform above, only slightly darker on ear-coverts, and has vent to undertail-coverts pale rufous
T. m. transandeanus (SW Co, W Ec) more white tips of vent
***Major* group:**
T. m. duidae (Ve) like *semifasciatus* but larger, female darker with underparts indistinctly streaked and barred blackish
T. m. melanurus (SE Co, E Ec) male has 2 wingbars, black tail and is all white below
T. m. semifasciatus (E Co, S & NE Ve, Tr, Guianas) has least white in tail, no or thin white wing fringes, deeper grey on vent

Habits Moves sluggishly, usually in pairs, by short hops through dense vegetation, pausing to scan foliage, carefully inspecting leaves, often where there are many vines, then quickly gleans invertebrates and small vertebrates using quick stabs and short sallies. There are a few, rare records of feeding in association with mixed flocks. Follows ant swarms sporadically and only in some localities, but is amongst the few antbirds that regularly consumes ants of all kinds (aside of *Sciton* and *Labidus* in armies). Moves tail sharply whilst singing.
Status Uncommon to fairly common and widespread in suitable habitat, more abundant in west than east Ecuador, frequent in Guyana, and very local in littoral but frequent in interior in French Guiana.
Habitat Tropical Zone, locally to 2,200m (southern Venezuela) but mostly below 1,500m, in dense understorey of gallery forest, savanna woodland, second growth (e.g. plantations) and gaps, clearings and edge in primary forest (mostly *varzéa* and riparian woodland in eastern Ecuador). Ranges from dry (but not arid) regions, to humid or swampy forests; bamboo stands and humid thickets; dense grassland; edges of tracks through forest, borders, clearings.
Voice Calls vary geographically and include a decelerating rolling series of whistles, shorter rattles often repeated rapidly, evenly paced series of harsh and more musical notes, a downslurred growl, clear high-pitched whine (Z&I), throaty alarm, *cah* notes (Hilty), harsh scolding *churr* (ffrench) and gravelly *chrr-krr-krr-krr-krr* (R&G). Song a long accelerating series of up to 40 loud hooting nasal *cuk* or *pook* whistles, usually ending in a nasal snarl, *nyaah* (H&B, Z&I, R&T, ffrench), or a series of *qwoks*, increasing in speed and resembling trogon calls but ending in a nasal snarl (Hilty).
Notes Z&I consider that races west of Andes, e.g. *transandeanus* and *oscurus*, and those in Central America (collectively the *transandeanus* group), may merit recognition as a separate species from nominate and all other races east of Andes (the *major* group), based on significant vocal differences between them. M. Martínez (unpublished thesis, filed in COP) showed that *granadensis* and *semifasciatus* are almost certainly distinct species, based on morphological and vocal differences, and distinct zone of overlap without interbreeding in Miranda State, Venezuela.

Sakesphorus is a small genus of antshrikes that are mostly crested, with strongly barred wings. They wag their tails frequently.

BLACK-CRESTED ANTSHRIKE
Sakesphorus canadensis Pl. 155

Identification 15.7–16cm. Extremely variable. Male has complete black hood with long, bushy crest, heavy black bill and chestnut eyes, white line separates head from back, which is brown, becoming paler on rump and uppertail-coverts, wings and tail black with white fringes; black throat reaches centre of breast, with sides and underparts whitish; legs and feet grey. Female has large bushy rufous crest, not quite as generous as male's, is generally pale rufous or buffy to cinnamon above, with black and white wings and tail, below more or less buffy. Juveniles are weaker, duller versions of adults with much shorter crests.

Ssp. *S. c. canadensis* (Su, FG) male has chestnut back streaked black, ochraceous rump and uppertail-coverts, pale grey below, yellowish flanks and undertail-coverts; female has face speckled black and white, with black streaks reaching neck and throat, above rufous, buffy below, washed rufous on sides and flanks

S. c. fumosus (S Ve) male sooty brown above with neck and body sooty grey, undertail-coverts black with white tips; female darker brown above than other races, darker face, with black streaks on breast quite heavy

S. c. intermedius (C & S Ve) male very much like *canadensis*; female much brighter ochraceous, particularly paler on face and forehead, crest reduced and more cinnamon

S. c. loretoyacuensis (S Co) male has maroon-grey back and grey wash on sides and flanks, otherwise white below with few black streaks on breast; female dark on back, like *pulchellus* but not as dark as *loretoyacuensis*, and almost as heavily streaked on breast as *loretoyacuensis*

S. c. paraguanae (NW Ve: coastal xerophytic areas) varies; males from Paraguaná have small white streaks over entire head, back and rump pale ochraceous-cinnamon, in Lara have throat completely white-flecked, and in Falcón have throat white with black flecks, white flecks on forehead become bold streaks on forecrown; female has deep rufous crest, back warmer and more cinnamon than underparts, pale face, some dark streaking on breast; juvenile/subadult male slightly paler than male, with shorter crest admixed rufous and black, black of head appears as vestigial streaking

S. c. phainoleucus (NE Co, NW Ve) male has almost all-white throat with black patch on centre of breast

S. c. pulchellus (N Co, NW Ve: dry forest) variable; males have white streaks on face and throat-sides, but centre of throat black, crest has white streaks on forehead and forecrown, back uniform brown with black streaks; female generally pale cinnamon with streaking restricted to face, but from río Sucuy, Zulia, are richly coloured above, rich ochre below with fine black streaks on breast, from Adícora, Paraguaná peninsula creamier throat, paler below, much less streaking on breast, and slightly paler above than females from Guajira peninsula, which have pale upperparts, especially crest, very pale throat, medium-coloured breast and streaks; females in Falcón west of peninsula have black-streaked crown, dark back and bold blackish breast streaks.

S. c. trinitatis (NE Ve, Tr, Gu) male like *canadensis*; female rich brown above with reddish crest, facial streaks heavy and reach lower on breast

Habits Forages quietly in pairs, mostly from ground to mid levels, hopping amidst branches or occasionally joining mixed flocks. Both sexes wag tail.
Status Fairly common to common. Frequent in Guyana, common in littoral of French Guiana.
Habitat Tropical Zone to *c.*800m, in patchy woodland and savanna with scattered bushes, scrub and farmland near lightly forested areas; gallery woodland and mangrove; cactus forest. Locally, in gardens and parks.
Voice A rising, speeding series of some 10 *tok* or *wok* notes (Hilty) and a variable, more slowly delivered series that sometimes accelerates slightly (Z&I). Series of *woh, woh, woh-who-wehwehwehwehweh?* may be echoed by female (R&T).

COLLARED ANTSHRIKE
Sakesphorus bernardi Pl. 155

Identification 17cm. Crested hood all black, with some having white specks on face, white collar separates black from bright rufous back (few white feathers in centre) and continues to all-white underparts, wings dusky with white spots on lesser coverts and white fringes to all other feathers, rump and uppertail-coverts rufous, long uppertail-coverts have white tips, tail black with white tips. Female has shorter, rufous crest, face speckled black and white, upperparts as male, collar and underparts ochraceous-creamy.

Ssp. *S. b. bernardi* (W Ec: Manabí & Guayas) as described
S. b. piurae (SW Ec: El Oro & Loja) slightly larger, and male more rufescent on back and more rufous on wings

Habits Not shy and easy to see, though it avoids settled areas. Forages from undergrowth to canopy; wags tail almost continually.
Status Frequent to common in Ecuador.
Habitat Tropical Zone, to 1,500m, locally to 1,850m in Ecuador. Arid scrub and thickets, dry deciduous forest and open woodland in lowlands and on lower slopes.
Voice Both sexes utter *ank* (R&G). Loudsong a rapidly delivered, 2 s burst of staccato notes, beginning and ending with longer emphatic notes (Z&I).
Notes Genetic data published by Irestedt *et al.* (2004) suggest that *Sakesphorus* (represented by *S. bernardi*) may be embedded within *Thamnophilus*.

BLACK-BACKED ANTSHRIKE
Sakesphorus melanonotus Pl. 155

Identification 15.5–16cm. Male all black except white breast-sides and flanks, and white spots on lesser coverts, white fringes to median and greater coverts, forming 2 wingbars, fringes of tertials and remiges, and tips of uppertail-coverts. Outer webs of outer tail-feathers white and tips of all rectrices white; eyes dark brown, bill black, legs and feet grey. Female brown above with dark centres to feathers on top of head giving scaled effect, ochraceous on uppertail-coverts and rufescent on tail; wings dusky with white like male; underparts ochraceous below, palest on belly. Both sexes have partially concealed irregular white feathers in centre of back. Juvenile like female with all-dark top of head, immature male usually has emergent black. Male Black-crested Antshrike has much more prominent crest and white collar; female closer, but has prominent rufous crest and black tail.

Ssp. Monotypic (W & N Ve, NE Co)

Habits Forages in pairs, quietly and intently, at low to mid levels in denser tangles or may hop on ground occasionally. Shakes tail all the time.
Status Uncommon.
Habitat Tropical Zone to 1,300m but mostly below 500m. Thick, dry scrub and thorny woodland, streamside thickets in semi-arid lands.
Voice Call a short *rrrrrrrrr* rattle (P. Schwartz, Hilty). Possible loud song a descending *aawr* repeated regularly. Also a short, rapid, rolling series of notes descending in pitch, apart from first, lower note. Also *ee-ohr* and various abrupt *pip* notes (Z&I).

BAND-TAILED ANTSHRIKE
Sakesphorus melanothorax Pl.155

Identification 17cm. Male all black with small white terminal spots on wing-coverts and outer fringes of scapulars, broad white band at tip of tail. Female entirely rufous with full black mask that extends to centre of breast. Male easily confused with very similar eastern race of Blackish-grey Antshrike, but latter has no white in tail; female also similar but has blackish top of head only, and is darker above, not all rufous.

Ssp. Monotypic (Su, FG)

Habits Forages quietly and discreetly in pairs.
Status Poorly known in Suriname, locally frequent in French Guiana.
Habitat Tropical Zone, to 650m, in humid forest, treefalls and dense undergrowth with an abundance of lianas or vines. In the Guianas, in dry tangled growth between large boulders.
Voice A slow series of *kaw* notes. (T. Davis, R&T). Loudsong a short series of deep, downward-inflected, somewhat muffled notes that speed up and end with 2 more abrupt notes. Call a muffled nasal growl, sometimes doubled (Z&I).

Thamnophilus antshrikes are a large group of often-distinctive birds, with males of several species barred black and white with crested heads and pale eyes, and females being bright rufous above, often barred black and white below. In others, males are shades of grey to blackish, some with small spots on wings, and females much darker rufous. All have robust bills with a small hook at tip. They are generally very vocal, and their presence often first detected by their calls.

BARRED ANTSHRIKE
Thamnophilus doliatus Pl. 156

Introduction 15–16.5cm. Five distinct plumage phases in males and 4 in females. Old adult male entirely barred transversally with black and white, and has black crest with white patch on rear crown (obvious when crown raised); chin and throat streaked rather than barred. Black bars much broader above, but on underparts equal-width with white bars. Young adult has white bars slightly broader above and below. Subadult male exactly like young adult, but is barred black and pale cinnamon, and throat more heavily streaked than in adults. Immature male barred rufous and black above, with lightly streaked throat, and below cinnamon-buffy with narrow black bars on breast to flanks. Juvenile male dark above (though paler than juvenile female) with vestigial dark bars from forehead to rump; chin and breast orange, belly to undertail-coverts creamy, with shadow bars. Old adult female rufous above, darkest on crest, head-sides and face streaked rufescent buffy and black, underparts cinnamon, palest on throat, with subtle black streaks and rufous wash on breast and sides. Younger adult female similar but paler on crown and paler below. Subadult or immature female has streaks on head-sides extending to form a collar, and streaks on throat extend to upper breast as small dots. Juvenile female dark umber above, orange-cinnamon below, streaks on throat become vestigial broken bars (like spots) from breast to flanks. Eyes vary from pale yellow to dark brown (tendency for older birds to have paler eyes). Bill black above, grey below, legs and feet slightly greenish-grey. Much racial variation (6 of 12 races occur in our region) in which main differences are broadness of bars.

Ssp. *T. d. albicans* (C Co) male has all-black crown, centre of belly white; female unbarred below

T. d. doliatus (SE Ve, Guianas) very similar to *fraterculus*

T. d. fraterculus (E Co, Ve, Tr) virtually identical to *doliatus* but smaller, with a shorter tail

T. d. nigrescens (NE Co, NW Ve) male has broad black bars above and below, crest all black

T. d. nigricristatus (N Co) male has crown all black, centre of belly unbarred or faintly barred

T. d. tobagensis (To) larger, with a stronger bill; male whiter on forehead and has narrower black barring below; female paler, more cinnamon-rufous above with a buffy forehead, throat clear and pale ochraceous below

Habits Always in pairs that forage within fairly well-defined territory, hopping slowly in shrubbery, occasionally in open, parsimoniously seeking large insect prey and calling infrequently. Occasionally follows ant swarms.

Status Common. Sight records in Ecuador, frequent in Guyana, Suriname and French Guiana.

Habitat Tropical to Lower Subtropical Zones, usually below 1,250m but records to 2,000m. Humid to dry densely tangled forest borders, thickets and clearings (seldom in forest); gardens and parks in urban areas.

Voice Vocalisations vary subspecifically (Z&I), but basic song a merry, rolling series of nasal notes, always: *ha-ha-ha-ha-hahahahahahahaha-haaah* (Rodner) or *hu, huh u hu, hu'hu'hu'u'u-wank* (like bouncing ball) and occasionally a nasal, strained and upscale *cuee, uee, uee* and a low growl *graaaaa* typical of genus (Hilty).

Notes Formerly included *T. zarumae*, but latter separated by R&T and Parker *et al*. (1995).

CHAPMAN'S ANTSHRIKE

Thamnophilus zarumae Pl. 156

Identification 15.5cm. Male heavily barred black and white above, with some buffy on uppertail-coverts, crest almost entirely black, spotted white on forehead, face-sides streaked white; throat to breast and sides have broken black bars on white, rest of underparts pale buffy. Eyes pale brown, bill black above and grey below, legs and feet slightly greenish-grey. Female rufous-brown above, streaked black and cinnamon on face- and neck-sides, tending to black and white on ear-coverts, whitish throat to warm buffy below with some dark streaking on sides.

Ssp. Monotypic (SW Ec)

Habits Like Barred Antshrike, always in pairs within a territory and forages in same slow, deliberate manner.

Status Fairly common.

Habitat Upper Tropical to Lower Subtropical Zones, at 800–2,000m, locally in east Loja to 2,550m, in arid to moist forest borders, semi-open second growth and scrub.

Voice A 2-part phrase consisting of several low-pitched *chup* notes, then several much higher and nasal ones (R&T). Loudsong is 3-parted: an accelerating series of 12–13 sharp nasal notes, 3 longer, louder notes at higher pitch, and a short, lower pitched trill. An abrupt *chup* and highly variable squeals (Z&I).

Notes Formerly considered a race of *T. doliatus*, but treated as a separate species by R&T and Parker *et al*. (1995) based on voice and plumage differences; followed by Z&I.

BAR-CRESTED ANTSHRIKE

Thamnophilus multistriatus Pl. 156

Identification 15–16.5 cm. Adult male barred black and white except chin and throat which are streaked. Above, black bars broader than white ones, broadest on wings and tail, but on underparts white broader. Adult female rich rufous above, barred black and white on face-sides, streaked on chin and throat, barred black and white below with some rufous wash on flanks and undertail-coverts. Eyes pale grey, bill dark grey above, paler below, legs and feet olive-grey.

Ssp. *T. m. brachyurus* (C Co) similar to *multistriatus* but tail much shorter, black barring below less heavy in either sex, thus looks whiter; female has streaks on face-sides forming complete collar of black spots, partially concealed on nape

T. m. multistriatus (Co: E slope of W Andes, C Andes, W slope of E Andes)

T. m. oecotonophilus (Co, Ve) larger, with longer tail; white on forehead more spotted than barred, male has broader white bars from central belly to undertail-coverts

T. m. selvae (Co & Ve: Perijá; Co: W slope of W Andes) like *multistriatus* but back darker, throat more heavily streaked and below barred darker, crown much less heavily spotted than *brachyurus* and black bars on back broader

Habits Forages calmly, peering around for prey. Understorey to canopy, but mostly in subcanopy.
Status Fairly common.
Habitat Upper Tropical Zone, in humid to dry dense forest borders, thickets, clearings, overgrown fields with scattered trees, hedges, parks and gardens in urban areas.
Voice Song similar to Barred Antshrike but shorter and slower (Hilty). Loudsong a rapidly accelerating series of 16–20 nasal notes, pitch falling obviously at end, terminating in unaccented, slightly slurred note (Z&I).

LINED ANTSHRIKE

Thamnophilus tenuepunctatus Pl. 156

Identification 15–16.5cm. Male barred black and white except all-black crown (full loose crest), white bars narrower than black ones, though streaked black and white on sides of face, chin and throat. Immature or subadult male resembles adult but has orange wash to white bars. Eyes pale, yellowy or grey, bill black, legs and feet grey. Female bright rufous above and streaked black and white on sides of face, chin and throat, and barred over all underparts. Female very similar to female Bar-crested Antshrike, but seldom has any rufous wash on flanks and undertail-coverts, if anything is washed whitish. No overlap with Barred Antshrike in Ecuador.

Ssp. *T. t. berlepschi* (SE Ec) black and white bars on back of equal width and not interrupted as in *tenuifasciatus*, white spots on lores and forehead, but blacker on crown-sides

T. t. tenuepunctatus (Co) as described; black bands on tail are 2–3 times as broad as white bars

T. t. tenuifasciatus (Ec, Co) broader white bars than *tenuepunctatus*, denser white spotting/streaking on lores and forehead, black and white bars on tail equal-width; female deeper brown above

Habits Territorial and always in pairs; foraging similar to Barred Antshrike but more retiring, making it more difficult to see.
Status Uncommon to locally fairly common.
Habitat Upper Tropical Zone, 400–1,400m in Ecuador and to 1,200m in Colombia. Humid forests borders of lower Andean slopes, clearings with early successional bushes, plantations and gardens; in dense vine undergrowth and thickets.
Voice Frequently heard song given by both sexes, with female echoing male's louder effort, a fast, accelerating series of nasal notes with a strongly emphasised and lower pitched final note, *heh-heh-ha-ha-hahahahahahaha-hánh*. Also several other growling or guttural calls, including a short nasal *nah!*

BLACK ANTSHRIKE

Thamnophilus nigriceps Pl. 156

Identification 15–16cm. Adult male all black, with dark grey flanks and white underwing-coverts; eyes dark, bill black and legs and feet grey. Adult female rufous-brown above, dark, dusky on head and breast and sides, heavily streaked whitish or pale buffy. The width and strength of streaks ranges from narrow and whitish to broader and more buffy-edged black, in a cline from north to south. Flanks and belly to undertail-coverts ochre. Immature male like female but has pale fringes to wing-coverts and black barring on flanks and vent. Young female has broader streaks below.

Ssp. Monotypic (N Co, S to Tolima)

Habits Pairs forage deliberately, for large insects in fairly open view, hopping in dense vine borders of woods, at mid levels. Frequently pauses to search for likely prey. Jerks tail when alarmed.
Status Common to fairly common.
Habitat Tropical Zone to 600m. Humid forests and open woodland, in borders, thickets and successional vine shrubbery in clearings.
Voice A long, nasal and slightly accelerating sequence of *kuck* notes with tail pumping downwards, *kuock, kuock, kuock, kuock-ku-ku-ku-ku-ku*. A hollow, nasal *peero* that may be uttered several times, a rapid querulous *kuo-lu-lu-lu-lu* and a nasal growl (H&B).

COCHA ANTSHRIKE

Thamnophilus praecox Pl. 156

Identification 16cm. Male all black, except white underwing-coverts; eyes dark, bill black, legs and feet dark grey. Adult female entirely bright rufous above, paler cinnamon below, with a complete black hood that may or might not have white shafts to some or many feathers of chin, throat and face-sides.

Ssp. Monotypic (NE Ec)

Habits Pairs usually forage together but may separate for short periods or move with other species of antbirds, but not mixed flocks. They glean parsimoniously in dense foliage. Males spread and vibrate tail when singing.
Status Uncommon to fairly common and very local.
Habitat Lower Tropical Zone, to 300m. Restricted to black-water watersheds, in *várzea* and dense vegetation along creeks; always at lower levels and close to water.
Voice Song a long series (e.g. 18) of hollow, rather liquid notes of even pitch, intensity and pace, *ko-ko-ko-ko-ko-ko-ko-ko-ko-ko…*, uttered by male, with bird motionless except vibrating tail, sometimes repeated by female, albeit song shorter and slightly higher pitched. Both sexes give a mellow *pwow-pwow* and a more trilled *krrrr* (R&G, Z&I).

BLACKISH-GREY ANTSHRIKE

Thamnophilus nigrocinereus Pl. 157

Identification 16.5cm. Adult male charcoal grey above with white fringes to wing-coverts, a few white feathers in centre of back, and white fringes to uppertail-coverts, below, slate grey, slightly paler on chin, slight white edging to flanks, grading to white on lower belly and vent; eyes dark, bill black, legs and feet grey. Adult female olivaceous above, top and sides of head slate grey, brighter and paler cinnamon from chin to undertail-coverts.

Juvenile dark olive-brown above, greyish on head, with white feathers in centre of back, and pale buffy fringes to wing-coverts; from chin to belly mid grey with rows of short white streaks, becoming pale brown on flanks and vent to undertail-coverts.

Ssp. *T. n. cinereoniger* (NE Co, SE Ve: Orinoco basin) as described
T. n. kulczynskii (E FG) male almost uniformly dark charcoal, with white fringes to wing-coverts and white feathers in centre of back; female darker above and richer below, with slate-coloured head

Habits Forages in pairs at mid levels, often joining mixed understorey flocks or making sporadic forays to ground. Languid and constant tail-wagging interspersed with vibrations when bird sings.
Status Common but quite local.
Habitat Lower Tropical Zone. Habitat varies subspecifically. In Colombia and Venezuela, *cinereoniger* is most common in seasonally flooded, stunted (low-canopy), dense savanna woodland on white-sand soil, and in gallery forest along seasonally flooded creeks, sometimes in dense scrub in non-flooded regions. In French Guiana *kulczynskii* occurs in young and middle-stage coastal mangrove, with highest densities in mixed stands of both white and red mangrove, and in densely vegetated river edges away from coast (Hilty, Z&I).
Voice Race *cinereoniger* utters slow, bouncy sequence of *chook* notes; also growls and plaintive *caw* calls (Hilty) and a strongly accelerated but slowly delivered series of low- and even-pitched, mellow, punchy notes (Z&I).
Notes Formerly included *T. cryptoleucus*. Vocal differences indicate that *T. nigrocinereus* may include more than one species (Z&I).

CASTELNAU'S ANTSHRIKE
Thamnophilus cryptoleucus Pl. 157

Identification 16-17cm. Adult male all black, with white fringes to outer edges of scapulars and wing-coverts, and white flecks in centre of back; dark grey sides and flanks; white underwing-coverts; eyes deep red, bill black, legs and feet dark grey. Female all black with just a few white feathers in centre of back. Juvenile resembles female but is brownish-black.

Ssp. Monotypic (SE Co)

Habits Forages in pairs that are very timid and evasive, and rarely join mixed flocks. Wags tail languidly, but constantly, and flicks downwards when singing.
Status Uncommon to fairly common but very local.
Habitat Lower Tropical Zone, in *várzea* and swampy forests along rivers, but is essentially a river island specialist, fond of *Cecropia*-dominated woodland.
Voice A short, rapidly accelerating series of resonant nasal notes, usually but not always with a growl at end, *keok, keok, keok-keok'kuk'ku'ku'ku'ku, raa*. Also a low, nasal *káou, káou, káou, káou*, given slowly and deliberately, and an alarm-call, *káou, raaaaa* (H&B),
Notes Formerly considered a subspecies of *T. nigrocinereus*, but treated as a separate species in R&T, Z&I and SACC.

WHITE-SHOULDERED ANTSHRIKE
Thamnophilus aethiops Pl. 157

Identification 16cm. Adult male *aethiops* all black except terminal white spots on lesser wing-coverts; eyes dark red, bill black, legs and feet dark grey. Adult female deep reddish-brown, darker brown on wings and tail. Juvenile slightly paler than female above with buffy terminal spots on wing-coverts and tertials, below, whitish on chin and deep ochraceous-buffy, more rufescent on breast, and more pale ochre on central belly and vent.

Ssp. *T. a. aethiops* (Ec) as described
T. a. polionotus (E Co, S Ve) body deeper yet, darker on cap, wings and tail, with terminal whitish dots on wing-coverts; female brighter than *aethiops*, particularly on undertail-coverts; juvenile presumably slightly paler as well
T. a. wetmorei (Co) male closest to *polionotus* but darker grey above and especially so below, where is blackish-grey; from *aethiops* by deep dull grey body (not uniform black) and heavy white terminal spots on upperwing-coverts; female differs markedly from female *polionotus* by having mantle much paler, so rufus cap contrasts more clearly; tail brown

Habits Pairs forage by gleaning at lower levels, but do not join mixed flocks; tend to be sedentary within a territory.
Status Uncommon.
Habitat Tropical to Lower Subtropical Zones, in lowland *terra firme*, but up to lower fringes of montane forests in parts of range; partial to small treefall clearings and dense successional regrowth inside forest borders.
Voice Rolling calls. Songs differ between various subspecies; e.g. in Ecuador, a slow-paced sequence of *anh* notes; in Venezuela, a fast and high-pitched series of *kah* notes.

UNIFORM ANTSHRIKE
Thamnophilus unicolor Pl. 157

Identification 15.5–16cm. Adult male uniform blackish-grey, occasionally with small white tips to outer tail-feathers; eyes pale grey, bill black, legs and feet blackish. Adult female almost entirely rufous-brown, paler below, with top of head bright rufous, head-sides and forehead grey, chin and upper throat ochraceous. Juvenile like female but has buffy tips to greater wing-coverts.

Ssp. *T. u. grandior* (E Ec, Co) longer tail, more likely to have white tips to outer rectrices
T. u. unicolor (W Ec) shorter tail, seldom has white tips to outer rectrices

Habits Forages quietly in pairs, gleaning from low to subcanopy levels; very seldom with understorey mixed flocks.
Status Uncommon.
Habitat Upper Tropical to Subtropical Zones, mostly 1,000–2,000m in Ecuador, 900–2,300m on Pacific slope in Colombia, 1,400–2,300m, occasionally to 2,700m elsewhere. Interior of humid and wet montane forests and cloud forests.

Voice Short series of 3–5 soft nasal *ahn* notes, each with a rising inflection, reminiscent of sound of bouncing ball, a rattled *kar'r'r'r* (R&T, R&G, H&B) and a *mew* (H&B).

BLACK-CAPPED (PLAIN-WINGED) ANTSHRIKE

Thamnophilus schistaceus Pl. 157

Identification 14–14.5cm. Male all grey, darker above and on wings and tail, with a blackish cap; eyes deep red, bill black, legs and feet grey. Adult female slightly yellowish-olive above with rufous crown, ochre below. Juvenile like female above but paler below, variably buffy to yellowish. Very similar Mouse-coloured Antshrike has grey eyes and pale dots on wing-coverts.

Ssp. *T. s. capitalis* (Ec, Co) as described
T. s. dubius (Ec) less black on crown than *capitalis*
T. s. heterogynus (E Co) male has crown only slightly darker than nape and back; female rich rufous above and rich ochre below

Habits Pairs forage by gleaning intently from foliage, hopping calmly inside tangles as well as more in open, at low to mid levels.
Status Fairly common to common throughout.
Habitat Tropical Zone, mostly below 1,000m in Ecuador and to 500m in Colombia. Humid primary and mature secondary *terra firme*, usually in interior but near borders with dense shrubs or adjacent *várzea*.
Voice Males sing intermittently throughout day when forests generally quiet, a rapid sequence of nasal notes, *anh-anh-anh-anh-anh-anh-anh-anhanh* finishing with a signature lower pitched double note at end. Female answers, starting halfway through male's song or maybe with small delay, a similar but higher pitched sequence. Another call is a series of bark-like notes reminiscent of a forest falcon (Sick 1993, R&T, R&G, Hilty).

MOUSE-COLOURED ANTSHRIKE

Thamnophilus murinus Pl. 157

Identification 13.5–14cm. Adult male dark grey above with white feathers on centre of back and white tips to long uppertail-coverts, wings dark brown with white terminal spots to wing-coverts, tail blackish, underparts mid grey; eyes grey, bill blackish above, mid grey below, legs and feet grey. Adult female olive-brown above with terminal buffy spots to wing-coverts and tertials, rufescent on head, pale ochraceous below, flushed darker on sides and flanks. From Black-capped Antshrike by grey eyes and white dots on wings (Black-capped has red eyes).

Ssp. *T. m. cayennensis* (FG) male has chestnut wings with buffy spots
T. m. canipennis (E Ec, SE Co) male has dusky wings with white spots
T. m. murinus (EC Co, S Ve, Gu, Su) as described

Habits Forages in pairs, examining twigs and leaves in canopy. Quite independent, does not usually join mixed understorey flocks or visit ant swarms.
Status Fairly common to common. Frequent in Guyana, common in French Guiana.
Habitat Tropical Zone to 450m in Ecuador and Colombia, but to 1,300m in Venezuela. Humid forest, both *terra firme* and white-sand; patchy forests in savannas and along black-water streams.
Voice Slightly accelerating series of up to 15 similar, short notes, descending only slightly in pitch (Z&I). Song and forest falcon-like barking call similar to Black-capped Antshrike, but song slower paced (Hilty, R&T).

EASTERN (GUIANAN) SLATY ANTSHRIKE

Thamnophilus punctatus Pl. 158

Identification 14.5–15cm. Adult male essentially grey with black cap, wings and tail. Above is darker grey, with a few black and white feathers in centre of back, wings have large white terminal tips, forming bars, and tertials and outer fringes of remiges also edged white, long uppertail-coverts and tail black with white tips; below grey, becoming paler on belly, flanks and undertail-coverts; eyes dull red, bill black with grey base to mandible, legs and feet bluish-grey. Female warm, yellowish-olive above with both black and white feathers in centre of back, crown rufous, wings dark brown with black-edged white tips to wing-coverts and tertials, and white fringes to remiges, long uppertail-coverts and tail rufous, with black-edged white terminal spots, face-sides, chin and central belly are pale, rest of underparts ochraceous-buffy, washed yellowish-olive on sides and flanks.

Ssp. *T. p. interpositus* (E Co, W Ve) male charcoal grey on back, almost concolorous with black cap, rest of body dark grey, slightly paler on undertail-coverts; female darker throughout, black feathers on back obscured by white; blue-grey eyes.
T. p. leucogaster (extreme S Ec) male mid grey above with clear white feathers in centre of back, and few or no black ones, underparts paler grey than *punctatus*, white vent to undertail-coverts; eyes pale grey; female much paler below than *punctatus*
T. p. punctatus (S & E Ve, Guianas) as described

Habits Pairs skulk in scrubby foliage and may easily pass unnoticed. Wags tail constantly, especially when excited. Does not follow ant swarms.
Status Common. Frequent in Guyana, common in coastal French Guiana.
Habitat Tropical Zone, to 650m in Ecuador, 500m in Colombia and 1,500m in Venezuela. All types of forest: humid evergreen or deciduous, second growth, *terra firme* or white-sand, but always at borders, never interior. Old second growth stands and forest patches along savanna belt in northern French Guiana.
Voice Each race reportedly has slight variation of same paced sequence of 6–10 *ahn* notes, some rising, others dropping or rolled at end or ending in a muffled tremolo (Sick 1993,

R&T); however, differences may be greater than similarities: e.g. *leucogaster* song in Ecuador an accelerating series of *anh-anh- anh- anh-ah-ah-ahahah* (R&G); song of *interpositus* in western Andes 10–30 rapidly accelerating whistled *hu* or *du* notes ending in a nasal *dwenk* (H&B); *punctatus* in Venezuela gives a nasal and leisurely series of *c.*10 notes (first few longer) that gradually accelerate and rise in pitch, *oank, oank, ank, ank, ank, ank-ank-ankank* (Hilty).

Note Common name problematic, with Eastern and Northern Slaty Antshrike both in use. Race *leucogaster* called Peruvian or Marañón Slaty Antshrike and given specific status in R&G. Slaty Antshrike refers to complete superspecies, which embraces 6 species (or more).

WESTERN SLATY ANTSHRIKE

Thamnophilus atrinucha Pl. 158

Identification 14.5–15cm. Adult male essentially grey, darker above, with black cap and blackish marks on head-sides with a little grizzling on face-sides, wings black with white spots on lesser coverts, and broad white fringes to median and greater coverts producing two clear wingbars, fringes of scapulars white producing line either side of mantle, with a fair number of black feathers scattered on back and a few white ones interspersed, long uppertail-feathers black with white tips, tail black with bold white tips, below uniform mid grey, possibly with a few white feathers on belly. Female clay brown above, rufescent on crown and uppertail-coverts, darker on centre of back, wings and tail (former has whitish feathers fringed dark brown), wing-coverts have white fringes with subterminal dark brown marks, as do long uppertail-coverts and tips of remiges. Immature male a darker, less rufescent version of female with black feathers emerging on head, nape and mantle.

Ssp. *T. a. atrinucha* (W Ec, W Co, SW Ve) as described
T. a. gorgonae (W coast Co: Gorgona I.) forecrown of male extensively grey, female tawny-cinnamon below
T. a. subcinereus (N Co, NW Ve) generally paler in both sexes

Habits Pairs forage by gleaning calmly up vines and on branches and trunks. Easier to see than other antshrikes as not timid. Joins mixed understorey flocks and occasionally visits ant swarms.

Status Fairly common.

Habitat Tropical Zone. Humid primary and mature secondary forest, especially in not too dense forest borders.

Voice A sequence, in crescendo, of 10–30 *huh* or *han* whistles, ending in an emphatic *wenk*. Calls include *cah* and grumbled rolls (Sick 1993, R&T, Hilty). Loudsong a rapidly delivered series of emphatic notes, too fast to count, nearly level in frequency and constant in pace, ending with a longer note at slightly higher pitch. Softsong a long series that begins slowly and then accelerates. A loud bark may be followed by a roll of abrupt notes. A *caw* that may be given in groups of up to 4 notes (Z&I).

Note Isler *et al.* (1997) synonymised *subcinereus* under *atrinucha*.

STREAK-BACKED ANTSHRIKE

Thamnophilus insignis Pl. 158

Identification 16.5–17cm. Adult male black above with white dots on forehead, small streaks on nape, irregular white feathers in centre of back, outer fringes to scapulars forming a line, full spots on tips of all wing-coverts, outer fringes of tertials and distal outer edges of secondaries; grey below; eyes dark, bill black with grey base to mandible, legs and feet grey. Adult female has chestnut rear crown. Juvenile like female but paler, rufescent or cinnamon rear crown with dark scaling. A tepui endemic that is only grey to black antshrike with white streaks on nape, and in fact only antshrike in its range.

Ssp. *T. i. insignis* (extreme SW Ve) male has variable number of small white flecks on forecrown, ranging from none, 1–2 to 15; nape has many larger broad white flecks, also variable
T. i. nigrofrontalis (S Ve: Pantepui) male has entire top of head pure black with a few small flecks on nape and sides; grey of belly to undertail-coverts washed softly olive, undertail-coverts fringed broadly whitish

Habits Pairs or small family groups forage low, often in small bands with other tepui endemics, gleaning unconcernedly in typically dense understorey of tepui forests. Singing birds mark each note of song with downward movement of tail.

Status Uncommon, but fairly common in some localities.

Habitat Upper Tropical to Subtropical Zones, 900–2000m, in stunted forests of tepui slopes.

Voice Generally less vocal than other antshrikes. Sometimes sings at dawn. Song of male a slowly accelerating, very nasal *cunk, cuk cuk-cucucucucucu'cu'cu'cucurank*. High-pitched *rank* at end characteristic. Female sings a similar but higher pitched song (Hilty).

AMAZONIAN ANTSHRIKE

Thamnophilus amazonicus Pl. 158

Identification 14–15 cm. Adult male grey, with a black cap, heavy black markings on back and a few white feathers in centre, black wings with large white terminal spots to coverts, outer fringes of scapulars, tertials and remiges; long uppertail-coverts black with white terminal spots, tail black with white tips and median spots on outermost feathers; underparts uniform grey, barely paler than upperparts; eyes, bill, legs and feet all dark. Adult female has back tawny-olive with black streaks and a few white feathers, wings black with bold white spots on tips of coverts, white outer fringes to scapulars and tertials, tail black with white tips and median spots on outermost feathers; entire head and underparts bright orange-rufous. Immature male like adult but has strong orange-rufous flush to head, paler on sides of face and breast, belly and flanks barred white on grey. Female is unlikely to be confused, but male needs to be separated from Pearly Antshrike (very distinct white spots on lower wings and tail), Spot-winged Antshrike (black on entire upper head to nape) and Guianan Slaty Antshrike (black cap).

Ssp. *T. a. amazonicus* (SE Co, extreme E Ec) as described
T. a. cinereiceps (EC Co, SW Ve) male lacks black cap and black marks on back, is paler on rump and lower underparts; eyes deep red; female has lower breast to flanks warm yellow-ochre, undertail-coverts white
T. a. divaricatus (extreme E Ve, Guianas) like *cinereiceps* but uniform grey with black streaks on rear crown, nape and back; female washed olive-grey on flanks and barred on vent to undertail-coverts

Habits Pairs inspect foliage for insects, mostly at upper mid levels, and join mixed understorey flocks at forest borders. Shakes and spreads tail when singing.

Status Uncommon to locally common. Frequent in Guyana, uncommon in French Guiana.

Habitat Tropical Zone, to 200m in Ecuador, 500m in Colombia and 400m in Venezuela, with a record at 1,300m on Cerro Yapacana. Habitat varies subspecifically. Race *amazonicus* almost exclusively occupies vine borders and light gaps in seasonally flooded *várzea*; *cinereiceps* occurs in sandy soil habitats, both stunted savanna woodland on white-sand and shrubby borders of taller *terra firme*; *divaricatus* inhabits liana-rich *terra firme*, locally in open forest near tepui summits and at river edges (Z&I).

Voice Male sings a fast, accelerating sequence of *kuh* notes that sound like trogon calls, growing louder in middle then slowing at end (Hilty, R&T), final notes may change in quality, and or strengthen or fade (Z&I); female may join in or follow with a higher pitched version. Also a querulous, nasal *keeunh?* (R&G).

SPOT-WINGED ANTSHRIKE
Pygiptila stellaris Pl. 158

Identification 14cm. Adult male all grey, black from forehead to nape, wing-coverts dark to blackish with white spots on tips, including primary-coverts, affording unique wing pattern (no white at all on tertials or remiges); eyes dark, bill blackish with grey base to mandible, legs and feet grey. Female grey from crown to tail, outer wing-coverts and remiges (not tertials, which are grey) pale rufous, entire underparts pale orange-cinnamon. Juvenile like female, with white interscapular patch. Immature male intermediate between juvenile and adult male, brownish-grey on head with rest of upperparts dark brownish-grey, like female but shows black on head first and then some on mantle; white interscapular patch ranges from entirely hidden to quite obvious. Pattern of spots on wing separates male from any other black-capped grey antshrikes.

Ssp. *P. s. maculipennis* (E Ec, SE Co) paler grey than *occipitalis*, female suffused brown on upperparts
P. s. occipitalis (S Co, S Ve, Su, FG) darker in both sexes than *maculipennis*

Habits Pairs or small groups forage with mixed flocks in upper middle tiers and subcanopy, especially at ends of branches, hopping and looking for prey intently.

Status Fairly common. Uncommon in Guyana, rare in French Guiana.

Habitat Lower Tropical Zone, mostly below 400m in Ecuador, to 500m in Colombia and to 700m in Venezuela. *Várzea*, swampy and humid *terra firme* forests and borders, occasionally ranging into mature second growth.

Voice Distinctive but brief song a sharp and piercing *t-t-t-t-t-t-teéuw*, repeated after intervals of a few seconds. A sharp *chet!* may be followed by *keeeuw* (R&G). An excited pair will repeatedly utter *tu-di-dit?* with other bird responding with a fast, raspy *kr-kr-kr-kr-kr-kr-krrreeet-kr-kr* (P. Coopmans in R&G). Sings repeatedly for some minutes a phrase consisting of a short trill followed by loud whistle (Hilty).

Note Race *maculipennis* merged with *stellaris* by Z&I on grounds of being clinal.

PEARLY ANTSHRIKE
Megastictus margaritatus Pl. 158

Identification 12-13cm. Adult male pale grey with black wings and tail, large white terminal spots to wing-coverts, tertials and long uppertail-coverts, and tail tipped white; eyes pale yellowish-grey, bill dark with pale base to mandible, legs and feet pale grey. Female pale olive above, ochraceous below; wings and tail dark brown with buffy terminal spots to coverts. Only 1 juvenile (unsexed) found, it had less reddish on head and was greyer on crown, paler cinnamon below.

Ssp. Monotypic (SE Co, S Ve)

Habits Forages in pairs or small groups, intently searching fairly open branches of mid levels, picking prey by gleaning or sallying to nearby leaves. Usually quiet, may pass unobserved. Occasionally joins mixed understorey flocks. Flips tail up and down intermittently.

Status Rare and local in Ecuador, fairly common but local in Colombia, and uncommon in Venezuela.

Habitat Lower Tropical Zone, to 500m in Colombia and 400m in Venezuela, in *terra firme* and mature second growth, and especially white-sand forests.

Voice A soft, sad and slow *wheet* (Hilty). Loudsong 2–3 slowly delivered whistles, slurred up and down and followed by 6–7 flat, raspy notes delivered much faster, altogether lasting up to 3 s. Also whistled, upslurred *wheet* notes as contact between pair (Z&I).

Bushbirds are very poorly known, with virtually nothing recorded as to their natural history and the rationale for their distinctive bills. They appear to be dead-wood specialists, hacking at rotting wood and digging channels under bark of dead wood.

BLACK BUSHBIRD
Neoctantes niger Pl. 159

Identification 16cm. Adult male all black with small white interscapular patch; bill has culmen effectively horizontal, with base of mandible curving upwards, affording upturned look; eyes dark, bill black with bluish-grey base, legs and feet dark grey. Female like male but has large chestnut patch on breast. Male's bill distinctive, female unique.

Ssp. Monotypic (E Ec, extreme SC & E Co)

Habits Forages in pairs that hop furtively within thick tangles,

from lowest to mid tiers. Pecks holes on rotting logs, presumably in search of insects. Also looks about intently in foliage.
Status Rare to locally uncommon. Pairs apparently well spaced and seldom together.
Habitat Lower Tropical Zone, to 600m in Ecuador and 400m in Colombia, in *várzea*, swampy and humid *terra firme* forests, and early successional growth; especially borders, treefall clearings and streamsides with fallen logs.
Voice Sings ventriloquially, repeating a fluty *querk* note with a steady rhythm for minutes on end (Hilty). Distinctive song an often slightly rising series of semi-musical *werk* notes, uttered 1 per s, for a minute or more (R&G).

Recurve-billed Bushbird specialises in extracting invertebrates from the bark of dead branches: it first hammers an incision into the bark (upper), then inserts the bill and pushes forward with a rocking motion, moving its head a little from side to side (middle), gouges along, splitting the bark open, exposing the dead wood and whatever grubs or beetles may be there (lower)

RECURVE-BILLED BUSHBIRD
Clytoctantes alixii Pl. 159

Identification 16.5cm. Adult male all black, with small white interscapular patch; heavy black bill with flat, horizontal culmen and upcurved mandible; eyes dark, legs and feet dark grey. Immature/subadult male has small white-tipped wing-coverts, and black slightly duller. Juvenile male dark brown above with larger pale tips to wing-coverts, paler, more tawny from face-sides and chin to breast, duller below. Adult female rich rufous, darker on wings, with buffy interscapular patch and buffy tips to coverts, tail darker still. Juvenile female duller and less rufous, with larger buffy spots on wings. Separated from all other black antbirds by unique bill.

Ssp. Monotypic (N Co, NW Ve)

Habits Very furtive. The odd-shaped bill serves a specialist function (see line drawing above). Has been seen attempting to split bark along branches, and desisting, presumably because resistance too great, thus wood less likely to be rotten and insect-infested (D. Ascanio, pers. comm.) Has been observed at an ant swarm.
Status Rare.
Habitat Tropical Zone, *c*.250–1,250m, in humid primary and mature secondary forest, borders and treefall clearings, always at lowest levels, especially in *Cecropia*-dominated, decaying secondary woodland, abandoned plantations or any land that has been cleared but subsequent vegetation has matured and started to decay to point of being replaced by next growth.
Voice Female recorded in Colombia uttered a chirring *ke'e'e'ew* (Hilty, Z&I).

SPECKLED ANTSHRIKE
Xenornis setifrons Pl. 158

Identification 15cm. Adult male deep reddish-umber above, streaked from forehead to rump buffy-orange, wings darker with buffy-orange tips to coverts and tertials; lower rump, tail, face-sides and underparts slate grey, faintly streaked paler grey; eyes pale grey-brown, bill slightly wedge-shaped, black above, grey below, short black bristles at base, but invisible in field, legs and feet dark grey. Female similar, including grey uppertail-coverts and tail, but is a slightly paler brown, streaked buffy below, becoming darker and less streaked from flanks to undertail-coverts, chin whitish. General coloration like a foliage-gleaner but lacks rufous tail.

Ssp. Monotypic (NW Co)

Habits Very furtive and easily overlooked. Forages in pairs that stay close, and with mixed flocks. Perches still then sallies abruptly to grab prey from nearby leaves. Very odd bird, Wetmore theorized that it may be a relict of a very old group.
Status Rare.
Habitat Tropical Zone, usually at 350–800m, in understorey of undisturbed humid forests on foothills and slopes.
Voice Series of 5–10 high, rhythmic, rising notes (B. Whitney & G. Rosenberg).
Note We follow Ridgely & Gwynne and Z&I in retaining English name Speckled Antshrike as being far more appropriate than alternate Spiny-faced Antshrike.

RUSSET ANTSHRIKE
Thamnistes anabatinus Pl. 158

Identification 14.5–15cm. Male rufous-brown above, rufescent on head, bright rufous patch on mantle, wings and tail rufous; soft buffy supercilium and face-sides, pale to creamy buff below, washed rufescent on breast. Bill long and heavy, eyes dark, legs and feet grey. Female slightly paler than male with less dramatic rufous patch on back.

Ssp. *T. a. aequatorialis* (E Ec, SE Co) rufescent top of head, greyish wash to dark olive upperparts and pale grey tone to sides and belly to undertail-coverts.
T. a. gularis (NE Co?, NW Ve) darker more olivaceous, less yellowish throat
T. a. intermedius (W Ec, W Co) upperparts, wings and tail dark brown, not rufous, back has russet tinge, tail hazel rather than cinnamon or rufescent

Habits Forages alone or in pairs with mixed flocks, at upper mid levels and in canopy. Quite active but not very vocal, finds prey by gleaning and looking intently in dense foliage and clumps of dead leaves, especially at ends of branches.

Status Uncommon to fairly common locally.

Habitat Upper Tropical to Lower Subtropical Zones, in humid and wet forests of lower Andean slopes and foothills.

Voice Loudsong west of Andes (*intermedius*), a short countable series (e.g. 6 notes, 2 s) of abrupt, downslurred notes that decline in pitch preceded by an abrupt, lower pitched, softer note. Calls west of Andes include variable, short, thin *weep* notes with pitch sharply rising and falling, strung together doubly and triply and in combination with downslurred squeal. East of Andes (*aequatorialis*, *gularis*) loudsong a short (e.g. 1.8 s) trill that mostly rises in pitch and slows (Z&I).

Note Z&I positive that two species may be involved based on vocalisations, morphology and distribution, but defer decision until further information becomes available, with western *intermedius* part of one species and eastern birds, including *aequatorialis* and *gularis* other.

Dysithamnus antvireos are generally small birds with short, thick bills and a rather upright posture. They forage rather deliberately, gleaning from foliage, but do not sally, and are found in foothill and montane forest.

PLAIN ANTVIREO

Dysithamnus mentalis Pl. 159

Identification 11.5cm. Many subspecies, with clear but subtle distinctions. Essentially, male grey above, darker on top of head, with ear-coverts even darker, mantle, scapulars, wing-coverts and alula darker to dusky with white fringes forming 2 thin wingbars (not all races), underparts paler, usually buffy to whitish depending on race; eyes brown, bill black to greyish-brown or blackish above and grey below, legs and feet largely grey, but vary from vinaceous to bluish or greenish-grey. Female varies above, from soft olivaceous-grey with a brown tinge and browner wings with no wingbars, to olive-rufous with darker rufescent top of head and clear pale eye-ring; underparts from buffy to yellowish-white according to race. Juvenile generally like female but more uniform above (less distinct on top and sides of head) and paler or whiter below. Immature male browner above than adult, particularly on wings, and more likely to have buffy or olivaceous wash on flanks.

Ssp. *D. m. aequatorialis* (W Ec: Pacific slope) male has yellowish belly; both sexes considerably paler below than *napensis* (of E slope), with darker ear-coverts and yellow-washed belly

D. m. andrei (NE Ve: S Sucre, N Bolívar, Tr) male drab mouse grey above, dusky top and sides of head contrast well with grey mantle, wings brownish and wingbars obvious; white below, washed grey on sides to flanks, hint of yellowish-buff on belly to undertail-coverts; female pale warm olive above, slightly richer and rusty on top of head, warmer on wings, especially scapulars, coverts and alula, with buffy fringes (wingbars)

D. m. cumbreanus (N Ve: coastal range from Falcón, Lara to N Sucre) male like *ptaritepui* above but slightly warmer and paler below (almost greenish-grey), dusky top and sides of head, especially scapulars, coverts and alula, which are terminally blackish with white fringes; dingy white below with pale sulphur-yellow tinge to undertail-coverts; female mouse grey above, with broad eye-ring, rufescent on wings and tail, with only faint, vestigial wingbars; dingy white chin to breast, sulphur-yellow to buffy belly and flanks to undertail-coverts, narrowly washed olivaceous-grey on sides and flanks

D. m. extremus (Co: W & C Andes, Mid Cauca Valley) male uniform slate grey above, including fringes of rectrices and remiges, with slight olive wash on wings; white below, greyish on flanks (no olive wash); female has chest and sides white without any yellow, buffy undertail-coverts

D. m. napensis (E Ec, extreme S Co) darker than *aequatorialis* (of W slope), being uniform pale grey below but darker than *extremus*; flanks and rump always washed olivaceous; female lacks yellow on belly and is just like female *extremus*

D. m. oberi (To) closer to *cumbreanus* of Venezuela than *andrei* of Trinidad; larger bill than *andrei*; male has back dull greyish olive-green and lacks any cinereous wash on body-sides; female browner above and more yellow below than *andrei*; compared to *cumbreanus*, male more pure white below, only faintly tinged olive on sides; female browner on back, more russet on wings and tail, and more yellow below

D. m. ptaritepui (SE Ve: Ptari-tepui, Sororopán-tepui) male like *spodionotus* above, but paler below with white flecks on throat and belly; immature male slightly browner above, especially on wings; flecked white on throat and belly, flanks to undertail-coverts olive; female olive above, dull rufescent top of head and mid-brown suffusion on wings and tail, whitish throat and belly, olive head-sides to flanks, buffy undertail-coverts; juvenile like female but duller and generally slightly paler

D. m. semicinereus (WC Co, W Ve) male almost pure grey above, including tail, ear-coverts as top of head, throat and underparts grey, breast darker, centre of belly white, flanks pale grey with yellow tinge; female has crown more tawny and is less grey above, wings and tail fringed clay, throat pale olive-brown, white belly becomes yellow on vent

D. m. spodionotus (S & SE Ve: Amazonas, S Bolívar) illustrated; male is slate grey above, near black on top and sides of head, scapulars, coverts and alula dusky with black line inside white edges; mid grey below with white flecking on chin and throat, undertail-coverts fringed pale grey; immature male similar above, but whiter on chin and throat, becoming mostly white on central belly, flanks washed olivaceous; female soft rufescent olive above, slightly more rufescent on wings, crown more rufescent, underparts rufescent buffy, slightly denser on breast; immature/juvenile female like adult but slightly duller and paler below, with more white on throat to belly

D. m. suffusus (extreme NW Co) male more deeply coloured below, with yellow extending well onto chest, flanks brownish rather than greenish-olive; female darker, more brownish-olive breast and body-sides, underparts strongly washed dull citrine

D. m. viridis (N Co, W Ve: Perijá to Mérida, Táchira) male dark greenish-olive above, top and sides of head only slightly darker, narrow white wingbars, whitish throat to yellowish belly washed broadly mid grey to flanks, buffy-yellow vent to undertail-coverts; female drab olive-brown above, browner wings and tail, faint buffy wingbars, rusty top of head, more rufescent on forehead, dingy white throat to yellowish belly broadly washed olive to pale buffy-olive on flanks

Habits Usually in pairs or small (family?) groups that forage unhurriedly and unobtrusively, hopping along branches to glean from both surfaces of leaves, hovering briefly to glean from undersides, or perching quietly at lower levels. Continually flicks both wings as it forages. A regular participant in mixed understorey flocks, particularly with antwrens, foliage-gleaners, greenlets and warblers. Occasionally forages on ground.
Status Fairly common to common. Uncommon in Guyana.
Habitat Tropical to Lower Subtropical Zones, to 1500m on west slope in Ecuador but 700–1,700m on east slopes; 600–2,200m in Colombia (from 300m near Panama border); and to 2,200m in Venezuela. Lower growth of humid to moist forests, montane, secondary, deciduous and gallery.
Voice Male sings a short accelerating roll that is soft, bouncy, and downscale, *buu, bu bu-bu-bu'bu'u'u'u'*. A continually repeated, weak nasal *naa* (Hilty) and a soft, querulous upward sliding *bu-u-u-u-u-ef?* (K. J. Zimmer in Hilty).

SPOT-CROWNED ANTVIREO

Dysithamnus puncticeps Pl. 159

Identification 11.5cm. Male grey above, darker on head with rows of white specks, white terminal spots to coverts and faint brown fringes to tertials and remiges, and tail also has faint brown fringes. Chin and breast pale to whitish, flecked blackish, becoming grey on sides and flanks then faint brown on vent and tail-coverts. Eyes pale grey, bill grey, darker distally, legs and feet grey. Female brown above, more tawny on head, uppertail-coverts and fringes to tertial and remiges, pale cinnamon-buffy tips to wing-coverts, black flecks on head, chin to breast streaked dark brown, underparts cinnamon. Plain Antvireo has dark eyes lacks streaks on head.

Ssp. Monotypic (NW Ec, W Co).

Habits Always in pairs that quietly glean in undergrowth and often join mixed understorey flocks.
Status Uncommon, but fairly common in some localities.
Habitat Tropical Zone to 1,000m. Humid and wet forests of foothills.
Voice Song longer and faster with more even cadence and less abrupt delivery than Plain Antvireo (R&G), a soft, tremulous roll, accelerating, descending slightly and fading (H&M). A rapid trill (e.g. 28 notes in 2.7 s), first rising slightly, falling slightly terminally, pace constant then accelerating slightly at end. A short, descending *chirr* (Z&I) or descending trill (P. Coopmans).
Note Three subspecies formerly recognised, *flemmingi*, *intensus* and *puncticeps*, but broad areas of intergradation have diffused distinctions to point where better considered taxonomically monotypic (Z&I) – see plate.

WHITE-STREAKED ANTVIREO

Dysithamnus leucostictus Pl. 159

Identification 12.5–13cm. Adult male dark grey, darkest on wings, tail and head, with white terminal spots on wing-coverts, soft, paler grey streaks on face-sides, e.g. postocular and ear-coverts, chin and throat, slightly broader and longer on lower breast. Juvenile male dark brown above, tinged dark grey on head and breast, with buffy spots on wing-coverts and paler streaks from face to lower breast. Adult female dark brown above (though not as dark as juvenile male), rufescent on top of head, grey face and underparts to flanks, streaked white, buffy vent to undertail-coverts. Bicoloured Antvireo darker, especially female, with much more obscure streaks below and paler rufous on head.

Ssp. *D. l. leucostictus* (EC Co, E Ec) as described

D. l. tocuyensis (N Ve) male lacks pale grey streaks and thus appears darker; female noticeably paler and brighter above and below

Habits Most frequently found in mixed understorey flocks, and always in pairs that forage in deliberate, noiseless fashion typical of genus.
Status Uncommon, but fairly common in a few localities.
Habitat Upper Tropical to Lower Subtropical Zones. Humid montane forests.
Voice A descending sequence of 7–8 soft whistles.

BICOLOURED ANTVIREO

Dysithamnus occidentalis Pl. 159

Identification 13.5cm. Adult male blackish-grey, only slightly paler below, partially obscured white interscapular patch, whitish spots on wing-coverts; eyes, bill, legs and feet dark. Younger adult male brownish-black with fine white shaft-streaks on face and breast. Juvenile male like female but darker and more heavily streaked and spotted. Female dark brown above, rufous on top of head, white on back and wings as male, face to flanks dark grey, with fine white shaft-streaks, flanks and vent to undertail-coverts dark rufous-brown. Male White-streaked Antvireo is paler below and has clear grey streaks below, female clearly streaked.

Ssp. *D. o. occidentalis* (extreme N Ec, S Co) as described

D. o. punctitectus (E Ec) both sexes paler, lesser wing-coverts all white

Habits Forages alone or in pairs, by gleaning quietly around stems and foliage of lower levels. Perhaps only joins mixed understorey flocks more rarely than congeners (Ágreda *et al.* 2005).
Status Vulnerable. Rare to probably very uncommon and local.
Habitat Upper Tropical to Subtropical Zones, 1,500–2,050m in Ecuador, with single record on west slope at 2,200m, and at 900–1,200m in Colombia. Humid montane forests, especially in dense tangles around treefall or landslide clearings.
Voice Male calls *jeer-deer-drr* and also *peer* (B. M. Whitney), distinctive, fast throaty *jeer-deer-dur*, also a clear *peeu* call (R&G) and a fast ascending *pu-pu-pooyeh?* (M. Lysinger).
Note Sometimes called Western Antvireo *Thamnomanes occidentalis*, e.g. H&B.

Thamnomanes are rather plain grey birds with bicoloured females. They are a regular component of mixed-species flocks, where they can be found perching rather upright, often at the edges of flocks where they act as lookouts. But their prime role in flocks is that of leader – when either of these species is heard is time to wait for a flock.

DUSKY-THROATED ANTSHRIKE
Thamnomanes ardesiacus Pl. 159

Identification 13–14cm. Adult male uniform grey with chin and throat ranging from a few blackish tips to full black, depending on race plus individual variation and age! Both adults have white interscapular patch, but juveniles do not. Underwing-coverts dark grey with whitish fringes, affording a barred effect. Eyes, bill, legs and feet dark. Female olive-brown above, whitish on chin, to warm olive-brown breast and ochraceous-buffy below.

Ssp. *T. a. ardesiacus* (E Ec, SC & SE Co) adult male has black restricted to chin

T. a. obidensis (S & E Ve, Guianas) adult male has full black chin and throat, though we found adults in same area ranging from blackish with rough white barring to a small sooty bib or a large all-black bib; immature male has whitish flecks and short streaks on face-sides, and paler grey fringes to wing-coverts, also slightly brownish to buffy on undertail-coverts; we found adult females ranging from those with buffy-white throat to barred irregularly with blackish and brown, to blackish and white

Habits Forages in pairs or small family groups, at lower levels, regularly with mixed understorey flocks and occasionally at ant swarms. Perches almost vertically, leaning slightly forward, unlike Cinereous Antshrike, which perches quite upright. From perch, sallies to nearby foliage for prey.
Status Fairly common. Frequent in Guyana, common in Suriname and French Guiana.
Habitat Tropical Zone, mostly low but recorded to 1,100m. Humid *terra firme* forests.
Voice Song in Ecuador (*ardesiacus*) a series of raspy but musical notes that accelerate obviously, and rise in pitch before (often but not always) ending in a drawn-out growl, *grr, grr, grr-grr-gee-gee-geegeegeegeegigigi, greeeyr*. A sharp, raspy *greeeyr* and sneezing *tchif*! (R&G). Song in Venezuela (*obidensis*) a sharply ascending series of coarse, raspy whistles, *jaaw, jaaw, jaw, jay, juu, ju, j-j-j*, accelerating before ending abruptly; an incisive *skéap!* (louder and sharper than corresponding call of Cinereous Antshrike), also a buzzy *juueeer* (like snarl of *Gymnopithys*); and flat *week-week, week*, rather like Cinereous Antshrike but lacking loud rattle quality (Hilty).

CINEREOUS ANTSHRIKE
Thamnomanes caesius Pl. 159

Identification 14.5cm. Adult male dark bluish grey with small whitish chin that barely shows, and white underwing-coverts; eyes and bill dark, legs and feet grey. Immature male dark grey, but paler than adult, with brown fringes to wing-coverts and tertials, belly to undertail-coverts bright rufous. Female olive-brown above with whitish chin, olive-brown breast and bright rufous belly to undertail-coverts. Both sexes have large, but well-covered white interscapular patch. Male rather darker than male Dusky-throated Antshrike. Female quite distinct with abrupt change of colour from grey to rufous on breast.

Ssp. *T. c. glaucus* (E Ec, E Co, S Ve, Guianas)

Habits Perches quite erect on horizontal stems, compared to Dusky-throated Antshrike, which perches at slight angle. Signals frequently by lifting wings to display white underneath. Mostly at mid levels in forests, in pairs or small family groups, foraging very noisily and nervously, twitching body and flicking wings and tail. Oft-given loudsong appears to serve as a clarion for other species to form mixed understorey flocks, where it serves as central species. Occasionally follows ant swarms. Picks insects from air by sallying and returning to perch like a flycatcher.
Status Fairly common to common and widespread. Frequent in Guyana, Suriname and French Guiana.
Habitat Tropical Zone, mostly to 600m in Ecuador, 500m in Colombia and 500m in Venezuela, with occasional records to 850m and a specimen collected at 1,500m on Cerro Neblina. Humid primary and secondary *terra firme* and *várzea* forests.
Voice A soliloquy of low, whistled notes, *wert-wert* phrases, often interrupted by loud staccato rattles, *d'd'd'd'd*. Contact-call an oft-repeated, whistled *tuee, tuee*.... The less-often heard song is several slow, wheezy whistles accelerating into a rapid, bubbly trill fading at end, *squeet...squeet, wheet, wheet, whee, wheesp wheesp whes whes we we e-e-e-e-u-u-u-r*, lasting *c.*6 s (Hilty).

Myrmotherula antwrens are tiny, short-tailed birds with long, thin bills, and are bewilderingly alike. They are essentially birds of lowland forests east of the Andes, forage at all heights, from ground to canopy, and are very frequent within understorey mixed-species flocks. Juveniles are like females, and immature males are intermediate between the adults in plumage.

PYGMY ANTWREN

Myrmotherula brachyura Pl. 160

Identification 8.5cm. Black streaked white above, wings black with 2 white bars and finely fringed tertials and remiges; face-sides white divided by black malar, throat white, underparts creamy buffy-white. Female similar but is suffused buffy on head and breast, breast streaked slightly dusky. From Yellow-throated Antwren by throat colour. From Moustached Antwren by smaller white cheeks and narrower malar.

Ssp. Monotypic (E Ec, C & E Co, S Ve, Guianas)

Habits Pairs forage restlessly in small territories, joining mixed flocks as they pass through, especially at edges and borders. Usually in dense tangles of vines and shrubs around treefall clearings or edges of small rivers, up to subcanopy, more likely at forest edge than interior of forest.
Status Common and widespread in Ecuador, local on Pacific slope but common east of Andes in Colombia and Venezuela, frequent in Guyana; locally common in French Guiana.
Habitat Tropical Zone, to 600m in Ecuador, 900m in Venezuela, though usually below 500m. Lowland evergreen forest, including *terra firme* and *várzea*, second-growth woodland.
Voice Male song a fast, accelerating and slightly husky *chree-chree-chree-chee-chee-ee-ee-ee-ee-rrr*, rising at first then descending. Female may join in or might follow with a shorter version (H&B, R&G). Described as a 'bouncing ball' song by Hilty, a series of notes on same pitch, *peeup, peeup-peeup-pee-pee-ee-e-e"e'e'e'e'eeee*. Contact a doubled, *cheer-cheer* or *peer-peer*.
Notes Closely related to Moustached Antwren, but differs in voice and plumage (Z&I).

MOUSTACHED ANTWREN

Myrmotherula ignota Pl. 160

Identification 7.5-8cm. Black streaked white above, wings black with 3 white bars and finely fringed tertials and remiges, face-sides white divided by black malar, throat white, underparts creamy buffy-white. Female similar but suffused buffy on back of head (streaks on forehead and forecrown white) and breast, and latter streaked slightly dusky. From Pygmy Antwren by clearer white cheek-patch and heavier moustachial, Yellow-throated Antwren is more like Pygmy Antwren, and throat is distinctly buffy-yellow.

Ssp. *M. i. ignota* (W Co: Pacific slope) as described
M. i. obscura (SE Co, E Ec) fewer white lines on back, thus mantle noticeably blacker

Habits Forages restlessly in dense tangles and overlapping layers of leaves in mid to upper levels in forest, but comes lower at edges and in clearings, such as treefalls. Pairs and small (family?) groups stay close. Less inclined to join mixed-species flocks than Pygmy Antwren.
Status Uncommon and local in Ecuador, fairly uncommon in Colombia.
Habitat Lower Tropical Zone, to 900m on Pacific coast and 500m east of Andes. Generally in lowland *terra firme* and *várzea*, usually found at forest borders with tall trees, also along streams in forests.
Voice Song of both races in Ecuador similar to, but differs from, Pygmy Antwren in being more moderately paced with less acceleration, notes clearer, more musical, and lacks Pygmy Antwren's rolled ending (R&G), and *obscura* in Colombia same (H&B).
Notes Races *ignota* and *obscura* formerly considered races of Pygmy Antwren. Race *obscura* has been treated specifically (H&B, Isler & Isler 2003). Races *ignota* and *obscura* treated as separate species in SCJ&W (Griscom's Antwren *M. ignota* and Short-billed Antwren *M. obscura*), followed by R&G on grounds of different vocalisations although R&G do not describe any differences. However, Z&I state categorically that no differences in vocalisations exist.

YELLOW-THROATED ANTWREN

Myrmotherula ambigua Pl. 160

Identification 8cm. Black streaked white above, wings black with 2 white bars and finely fringed tertials and remiges; face-sides white, finely streaked black, divided from throat by narrow black malar, throat and underparts pale yellow. Female similar but suffused buffy on head, back and breast-sides. From similar Pygmy, Short-billed and Moustached Antwrens by yellow throat.

Ssp. Monotypic (extreme E Co, SW Venezuela)

Habits Pairs stay close together and are often, if not usually, in mixed-species flocks in canopy.
Status Uncommon to fairly common. Most often found in white-sand soil forests.
Habitat Tropical Zone, to 200m, in both areas of high-canopy trees on poor soil and low-canopy forest on white-sand soil.
Voice Song a slow steady series of 10–15 (less than 2 notes per s), thin, high-pitched whistles, at constant pitch, *weeeu, weeeu, weeeu*… (or *peeeu, peeeu, peeeu*…) (C. Parrish in Hilty).

GUIANAN STREAKED ANTWREN

Myrmotherula surinamensis Pl. 160

Identification 9.5cm. Streaked black and white above, wings black with white terminal spots to median and greater coverts, thin white fringes to tertials and remiges, white below, streaked black, weakest on flanks; bill long, dark above, pale below. Female like male on back, wings and tail, but entire head (chin white) and breast orange-cinnamon, with black streaks on crown and nape, with orange grading into mantle, underparts white, washed orange, and pale orange-cinnamon streaks on flanks. Very similar, though allopatric, male Amazonian Streaked Antwren indistinguishable in field, though streaks below tend narrower; female different, being suffused orange on back and streaked black over entire head to breast and sides, fading on flanks. Male Cherrie's Antwren is more heavily streaked black, and looks slightly blacker as a result, and female Cherrie's is a much paler orange, more warm ochre.

Ssp. Monotypic (S Ve, Guianas)

Habits Forages most actively, seldom at rest for more than 1–2 s and constantly flicks wings. Gleans from both sides of leaves, sallying up to glean from undersides. Occasionally joins mixed flocks, but only as they pass through its territory.
Status Uncommon to fairly common throughout its range, and frequent in Guyana and French Guiana.
Habitat Lower Tropical Zone, to 400m. Gallery forests, low bushes and vine-tangled walls along rivers in French Guiana.
Voice A bubbly series of 6–8 notes that quickly rise and fall; like Amazonian Streaked Antwren, but faster, with more notes, *tu-tu-HEE-HEE--hay-hay-ha*. Entire phrase repeated 4–8 times in rapid succession without pause, and given in duplicate if female joins in. Other vocalisations, given by both sexes, include a vibrating trill of *c.*50 notes in 2.5 s, a short, breezy *weet-weet-weet-weet* and a faster, rattling *tu-tu-tu-tu-tu*. Contact a soft, nasal *nay-who* (Hilty).
Notes Formerly considered conspecific with Amazonian Streaked Antwren, but separated on basis of vocal and morphological differences; they are sympatric at least in south-west Amazonas state, Venezuela. Common name sometimes written Streaked-Antwren to denote superspecies group.

AMAZONIAN STREAKED ANTWREN
Myrmotherula multostriata Pl. 160

Identification 9.5cm. Streaked black and white above, wings black with white terminal spots to median and greater coverts, thin white fringes to tertials and remiges, white below, streaked black, weakest on flanks; bill long, dark above, pale below. Female like male on lower back, wings and tail, but entire head (chin white), mantle and breast orange-cinnamon with black streaks, underparts white, washed orange. Male indistinguishable from Guianan Streaked Antwren in field, but female Guianan lacks streaks on face-sides and underparts. Male Stripe-chested Antwren is similar (but in hand, note has 10 rectrices, Amazonian 12).

Ssp. Monotypic (E Ec, E Co, extreme S Ve)

Habits Understorey and midstorey, foraging in pairs, on move whole time, constantly changing direction.
Status Uncommon and local.
Habitat Tropical Zone, to 300m. Usually at edges and borders of seasonally flooded lowland evergreen forest and *várzea*, and adjacent shrubby second growth.
Voice A vibrating loudsong of *c.*40 notes in 2.5 s, apparently only uttered by male. A territorial song given by both sexes in Peru, *way hey HEE, hay-aa*, rises then falls in large slow steps with mid note highest – like Guianan Streaked Antwren but simpler and has slightly different pattern (Hilty). A lilting and musical song, *pur-pur-peé-peé-peé-pur*, with unusual cadence. Both sexes also give a contact *chee-pu*, like that of White-flanked Antwren (R&G).
Note See Guianan Streaked Antwren.

PACIFIC ANTWREN
Myrmotherula pacifica Pl. 160

Identification 9.5cm. Male streaked black and white above, wings black with white terminal spots to median and greater coverts, thin white fringes to tertials and remiges, white below, streaked black, weakest on flanks; bill long, dark above, pale below. Female like male on lower back, wings and tail, but entire head (chin white) to breast and sides orange-cinnamon, with black streaks on rear crown and nape, underparts white, washed orange. Male indistinguishable from male Cherrie's Antwren, but they do not overlap. The female with an almost entirely clear orange head is quite distinct.

Ssp. Monotypic (W Ec, W & N Co)

Habits Forest edges and riparian thickets, but is not tied to environs of water and does not occur in forest interior. Pairs forage together and do not join mixed-species flocks. Favours vine tangles and dense, multi-layered foliage at lower and mid levels of forest edges.
Status Fairly common throughout.
Habitat Tropical Zone, mostly below 800m in Ecuador and Colombia. Under- and midstorey of lowland and foothill evergreen forests, and second growth.
Voice Song a fast, sprightly chipper that rises slightly, e.g. *chee-chee-chi-chich-ch-ch-ch-chch-ch*. Both sexes utter *chee-pu* and *chee-cher* calls (R&G), and there is a strident, even-pitched *chrreee-chrreee-chrreee-chrreee* (P. Coopmans). In Panama, song a fast, accelerating chipper, rising lightly, *chee-chee-chee-chee-chee-chee* (Ridgely & Gwynne).
Note Until recently, considered conspecific with Guianan and Amazonian Streaked Antwrens, but separated on basis of voice and plumage, and now seems most closely related to Cherrie's Antwren (Z&I).

CHERRIE'S ANTWREN
Myrmotherula cherriei Pl. 160

Identification 9.5cm. Male streaked black and white above, wings black with white terminal spots to median and greater coverts, thin white fringes to tertials and remiges, white below, streaked black, weakest on flanks; bill long, dark above, pale below. Female like male on lower back, wings and tail, but entire head and underparts pale cinnamon-buffy, streaked as male. Male inseparable from Amazonian Streaked Antwren in field, but female pale buffy underparts. Smaller Yellow-throated Antwren female has clear, unstreaked underparts. Male heavier streaked above and below than Guianan Streaked Antwren and (in hand) a longer bill and longer tail. Female Guianan is far more intense orange on head and breast.

Ssp. Monotypic (SE Co, SW Ve)

Habits Forages in pairs that stay low in understorey, but frequently join mixed-species flocks.
Status Fairly common.
Habitat Lower Tropical Zone, to 550m. Two main habitats: seasonally flooded, low-canopy and fairly dense scrub forest on white-sand-soil, and thickets and palm-filled borders of low-canopy, seasonally flooded gallery forest along small creeks in savanna (Hilty).
Voice Apparently an infrequent songster, a fast ascending rattle, *trddddddddddddd*, unmusical with a hard, flat quality.

Call a flat, dull *tsuu* (Hilty). Loudsong similar to Guianan and Amazonian Streaked Antwrens, but pitch rises more noticeably throughout and pace is constant (Z&I).

STRIPE-CHESTED ANTWREN

Myrmotherula longicauda Pl. 160

Identification 9.5cm. Male streaked black and white above, wings black with white terminal spots to median and greater coverts, thin white fringes to tertials and remiges, white below, streaked black, weakest on flanks; bill long, dark above, pale below. Female like male on lower back, wings and tail, but entire head (chin white), back, breast and sides pale orange-cinnamon, whitish on throat, with black streaks on head, face- and neck-sides, and entire underparts, densest on breast. Male like Amazonian Streaked Antwren (but in hand, note 10 rectrices, Amazonian has 12); female differs in having back and wings black and white, all flushed buffy on Stripe-chested Antwren.

Ssp. *M. l. soderstromi* (N Ec, S Co: E slopes) belly white
M. l. pseudoaustralis (S Ec: E slope) as described

Habits Usually in pairs, but often alone, foraging at mid and upper levels (higher than Amazonian); seldom joins mixed flocks (R&G, H&B), but stated to often occur in mixed-species flocks by Z&I.
Status Fairly common in Ecuador, common in Colombia.
Habitat Tropical Zone, at 400–1,000m in Ecuador and Colombia. Lowland evergreen forest and second-growth borders, particularly with tangled vines. Also regenerating clearings and swampy riparian habitats. In Peru, in permanently flooded low forest with areas of stagnant black water.
Voice Distinctive song, a fast-repeated musical phrase, *chidu-chidu-chidu-chidu…* of up to 12+ notes. A double note and short, descending trill, *chiwi-chrrrrrrrt* (P. Coopmans in R&G).

PLAIN-THROATED ANTWREN

Myrmotherula hauxwelli Pl. 160

Identification 9.5cm. Adult male all grey, darker above, especially on wings and tail, whitish chin, with white terminal spots on median and greater coverts, and tertials and long tail-coverts, and tail also tipped white. Adult female soft grey above, washed cinnamon, spots as male but pale cinnamon; from face-sides to undertail-coverts cinnamon, washed slightly olive on sides and flanks. Male is only small, all-grey antbird without black markings (Grey Antwren has black bars above white wing dots, and Leaden Antwren probably does not occur in our region). Female less distinct, look for clear white spots on tertials, but like male is rarely found very far above ground.

Ssp. *M. h. suffusa* (E Ec, SE Co)

Habits Usually in pairs that stay close together on or near ground, regularly perches horizontally on slender upright stems, like a *Hylophylax* antbird. Seldom found with mixed flocks.
Status Uncommon but widespread in Ecuador,
Habitat Tropical Zone, to 400m in Ecuador and Colombia, in *terra firme* and *várzea* and frequently in wet habitats, like swamps or near meandering streams (R&G).
Voice Male song a series of 6–10 high-pitched, penetrating *chwee* notes that start slowly and increase in volume, lasting *c.*2–3 s; rising slightly in pitch (H&B). Initial notes sound more musical and higher pitched, remaining notes shorter and more hollow-sounding, first speeding up and then even-paced (Z&I). Contact and alarm a repeated, sharp *chik!* and a stuttered *ch-ch-ch-ch-ch-ch-ch* (R&G).
Note R&G found specimens from Ecuador that matched *hauxwelli* and proposed synonymising *suffusa*.

RUFOUS-BELLIED ANTWREN

Myrmotherula guttata Pl. 160

Identification 9cm. Adult male soft grey on head, with whitish chin, back and breast, rump and uppertail ochraceous, wings and tail dark fuscous with large ochre spots on wing-coverts (2 wingbars), tertials and uppertail-coverts, and tail broadly tipped ochre; belly and flanks to undertail-coverts cinnamon. Female similar but fawn – like cinnamon-washed grey. Juvenile apparently inseparable from female. One male-plumaged female lacked white interscapular patch. This species' pattern is unique and the large pale spots on tertials and uppertail-coverts should prove conclusive.

Ssp. Monotypic (S & SE Venezuela, Guianas)

Habits Usually in pairs that forage very close to ground in forest, seldom with mixed flocks. Shy and not easily seen. Regularly perches horizontally on slender upright stems, like a *Hylophylax* antbird.
Status Uncommon to locally fairly common in Venezuela. Frequent in Guyana, fairly common in Suriname and French Guiana.
Habitat Tropical Zone, to 800m, in humid lowland *terra firme*, sometimes in damp or swampy areas within forest.
Voice Song a highly penetrating, slow series of whistles (*c.*2 per s) on constant pitch, or slightly rising, *wheeee, wheeee, wheeee, wheeee*, with 10–20 notes, sometimes slightly faster and more urgent at end (Hilty). Common call given variously as *pyir,r,r,r,r,r* (H&M), a rattling *j'r'r'r'r'r* (Hilty) or an ascending rattle-like call repeated irregularly or rapidly in series, and a short, slightly descending rattle (Z&I).

BROWN-BELLIED ANTWREN

Myrmotherula gutturalis Pl. 161

Identification 11cm. Male tawny above, wing-coverts dark brown with bold white terminal spots, face-sides striated brown and white, suffused grey, chin and throat black with white inverted triangular spots, sides of neck, breast and body grey, rest of underparts paler brown than above. Tail longer than usual for genus. Eyes yellowish-grey, bill blackish with pale base, legs and feet grey. Female lacks black and white bib and grey breast and is paler brown throughout; pale brown eyes. Very similar to Stipple-throated Antwren, though slightly paler and brighter with complementary distribution; also has pale brown eyes, and wing-coverts blackish rather than brown.

Ssp. Monotypic (E Ve, Guianas)

Habits Usually at low and mid levels in pairs or small groups and often in *Thamnomanes*-led mixed flocks (Hilty). A dead-leaf specialist that is often seen clinging to bunches of hanging dead leaves, in vine tangles, and also dead or dying ends of live leaves.
Status Uncommon to fairly common in Venezuela, frequent in the Guianas.
Habitat Tropical Zone, to 1,000m, but usually lower. Lowland and foothill *terra firme* interiors.
Voice A fine *t't'r'r'r'r* (H&M), song a thin, chattery trill of *c.*2 s, quite high-pitched with a slight squeak at start, first rising, then descending, *pe-e-e-e-e-ee-ee-ee-e-e-e-e-u* (Hilty).

CHECKER-THROATED ANTWREN
Myrmotherula fulviventris Pl. 162

Identification 11cm. Olive-brown above, wing-coverts dark dusky with bold buffy tips that form 3 wingbars, full bib checkered black and white, rest of underparts pale brown; eyes pale buffy-yellow. Female lacks checkered throat but otherwise similar. Male is only checker-throated antwren in its range, west of Andes. Female might be confused with other females, but Slaty Antwren has uniform wing-coverts; White-flanked has whitish throat and white flank plumes.

Ssp. *M. f. fulviventris* (W Ec, NW & W Co) as described
M. f. salmoni (C Co, Magdalena Valley) more olive-brown

Habits Very much as previous species.
Status Rare in south, but more common in north Ecuador and common in Colombia. More common in lowlands than foothills.
Habitat Tropical Zone, to 900m in Ecuador, locally to 2,000m in Colombia, in understorey of humid foothill and lowland forests.
Voice Song a descending series of high-pitched notes, *seee, seee, seeu, seeu* (R&G); a loud, high-pitched *tseek-seek-seek-seek* (Hilty), variable series of abrupt, almost staccato notes (e.g. 11 notes in 2.5 s), variable in pace, pitch and intensity, but often accelerates and intensifies initially, and decelerates and dies off slightly at end (Z&I).
Note Four races described, two in our region, but not recognised by Z&I due to conflicting information concerning discriminating features and ranges. Race *salmoni* apparently intergrades with *fulviventris*.

BROWN-BACKED ANTWREN
Myrmotherula fjeldsaai Pl. 162

Identification 10–11cm. Male yellowish olive-brown above, darker on wings (with rufous tone), coverts tipped buffy-white, more buffy on greater coverts; cheeks and around eyes slightly grizzled white, grey and brown, sides of neck, breast and body grey, rest of underparts pale ochraceous; eyes pale amber. Female lacks checkered bib and grey on breast and sides, being indistinctly streaked whitish and brown, overall paler brown than male with wing-coverts buffy.

Ssp. Monotypic (SE Ec)

Habits As Rufous-bellied Antwren.
Status Fairly common.
Habitat Lower Tropical Zone, to 1,000m, but just 150–300m in Yasuní National Park, in lowland and foothill *terra firme* forest interior.
Voice A trill of abrupt, high-pitched and thin, sibilant notes, first ascending and then gradually dropping, *zee-ee-ee-ee-ee-ee* (R&G, Z&I).
Note Called Yasuní Antwren in R&G.

[WHITE-EYED ANTWREN
Myrmotherula leucophthalma] Pl. 162

Identification 9.5–11cm. Male olive-brown above, darker on wings (with rufous tone), coverts tipped warm buffy; cheeks and around eyes slightly grizzled white, grey and brown, sides of neck, breast and body grey, rest of underparts pale ochraceous; eyes slightly greyish-white. Female like male above, below lacks checkered bib and grey on breast and sides, instead being uniform cinnamon-buffy. Very much like Brown-backed but different eye colour a sure discriminator.

Ssp. *M. l. dissita* (extralimital; comes closest to Peru/ Ecuador border)

Status Not known to occur in Ecuador, but a specimen of Brown-backed Antwren had been misidentified as White-eyed, and Ecuador was included in range by Meyer de Schauensee (1970). On that basis was painted for this book, but once mistake was clarified – with discovery and description of Brown-backed Antwren (Krabbe *et al.* 1999) – we decided to retain it to ensure comparative value and help resolve possible confusion.
Habitat Tropical Zone, to *c.*1,000m but usually below 700m, in understorey of lowland evergreen forest and transitional second growth. Very much a dead-leaf specialist.
Voice A moderately long series (15 notes in 4 s) of downslurred notes, first usually drawn out, subsequent notes shorter as series speeds up and drops slightly in pitch, somewhat variable (Z&I).

STIPPLE-THROATED ANTWREN
Myrmotherula haematonota Pl. 161

Identification 11cm. Adult male has dark brown head with slight dark scaling, deep reddish-chestnut back, fuscous to blackish wing-coverts with large white terminal spots forming 2–3 wingbars, primary-coverts and alula also tipped buffy, brown tail, around eyes and ear-coverts slightly grizzled grey, white and brown, sides of neck, breast and body grey, merging into soft buffy underparts, chin and throat black with white arrowhead streaks; eyes amber, bill, legs and feet dark grey. Female lacks grey and bib, being yellow-ochre on sides of head and throat, lightly streaked buffy on otherwise uniform warm cinnamon underparts. Juvenile same above, but has cinnamon spots and bars on wings (vs. white) and is well washed ruddy below; bill black above, orange-brown below. Male Ornate Antwren has clearer grey head and solid black bib (watch for variant Stipple-throated Antwren), but contrasting pale undertail-coverts a sure discriminator.

Ssp. *M. h. pyrrhonota* (extreme NE Ec, SE Co, S Ve)

Habits Usually in pairs that stay close, foraging close to ground in dense undergrowth and tangled vines in forest. A dead-leaf specialist (see Rufous-bellied Antwren).

Status Fairly common but local in Ecuador, common in Colombia, uncommon in Venezuela.

Habitat Tropical Zone, to 250m in Ecuador, 500m in Colombia and 1,300m in Venezuela.

Voice Trill of abrupt, high-pitched and thin, sibilant notes, first ascending then gradually dropping, *zee-ee-ee-ee-ee-ee* . Regional variation in pace and length (R&G, Z&I).

FOOTHILL ANTWREN

Myrmotherula spodionota Pl. 161

Identification 11cm. Entire head and back olivaceous-grey, rufescent dark olive on wings and tail, wing-coverts blackish with white terminal spots to coverts, chin and throat black with white arrowheads, breast and sides paler and cleaner grey than back, flanks and belly to undertail-coverts cinnamon; eyes grey to greyish-hazel, bill dark grey, paler at base of mandible, legs and feet grey. Female rufescent olive above with wing-coverts as male; underparts paler, cinnamon, streaked slightly olivaceous on throat and breast. Very similar to Stipple-throated and Brown-backed Antwrens, but occurs at a higher elevations.

Ssp. *M. s. spodionota* (Ec: E slope, S Co)

Habits Usually in pairs that stay close, foraging close to ground in dense undergrowth and tangled vines in forest; often flocks with Slaty Antwren. A dead-leaf specialist (see Rufous-bellied Antwren).

Status Uncommon to fairly common throughout.

Habitat Tropical to Subtropical Zone, at 500–1,500m, in dense understorey of foothill *terra firme*.

Voice Loudsong a trill of abrupt, sibilant notes, first ascending then gradually dropping in pitch. Very similar to Brown-backed and Stipple-backed Antwrens.

ORNATE ANTWREN

Myrmotherula ornata Pl. 161

Identification 11cm. Male grey on head, upper back and wings, tail dusky; wing-coverts black with white terminal spots (also alula and primary-coverts), lower back and rump solid rufous; chin and throat black, underparts pale grey, becoming pale buffy on flanks and undertail-coverts; eyes and bill dark, legs and feet grey. Female olive where male is grey above, and buffy where male pale grey below, black bib streaked with white arrowhead spots. The contrasting rufous back patch is quite distinct in both sexes. From Foothill Antwren by dark eyes (Foothill pale). Also male Foothill Antwren has speckled bib, female no bib.

Ssp. *M. o. ornata* (C Co) as described
M. o. saturata (E Ec, SC Co) male darker grey below; both sexes deeper brown above, especially chestnut on rump

Habits Usually in close pairs, foraging low in understorey, and joins mixed flocks. A dead-leaf specialist (see Rufous-bellied Antwren).

Status Fairly common.

Habitat Tropical Zone, to 1,200m in Ecuador and Colombia, in *terra firme*, favouring vine tangles in lowlands and stands of bamboo in foothills (R&G).

Voice A short emphatic trill (T. A. Parker in H&B). Song a thin, high-pitched chipper that fades away, *tsee-tsee-tsi-tsi-tsitsitsi* (R&G) and lasts *c*.1.5 s, starting with an emphatic note, descending slightly in pitch and often in intensity. Call, a sharp, high-pitched *seet* (Z&I).

RUFOUS-TAILED ANTWREN

Myrmotherula erythrura Pl. 161

Identification 11.5cm. Brown above, olivaceous on head, brighter, more rufescent on lower back, rump and tail; wing-coverts deep brown with white terminal spots, grey on face, sides and breast, whitish chin with small black-and-white bib, underparts buffy; eyes brown, bill blackish, legs and feet grey. Female similar but grey restricted to face, small white chin, throat to undertail-coverts pale cinnamon-ochre. More rufescent and slightly longer tail than similar antwrens, and lacks significant bib.

Ssp. *M. e. erythrura* (E Co, E Ec)

Habits Forages in pairs or small groups, and joins mixed species flocks in understorey. A dead-leaf specialist.

Status Uncommon to locally fairly common in Ecuador, uncommon to common in Colombia.

Habitat Lower Tropical Zone, to 700m in Ecuador and 500m in Colombia, in understorey of *terra firme* and *várzea*.

Voice Male song a high-pitched *swee, swee-sei-swi-seeseesees* with a squeaky, almost hummingbird-like quality (R&G) or an even-paced series of high-pitched *wheet* notes (e.g. 9 notes in 3.5 s), variable but mostly upslurred. Length varies continually, usually 5–12 notes (Z&I). Alarm-call a short bubbling rattle like Stipple-throated Antwren (H&B).

WHITE-FLANKED ANTWREN

Myrmotherula axillaris Pl. 161

Identification 10.5cm. Male slate grey above with white outer fringes to scapulars, wing-coverts nearly black with large white terminal spots, tertials black with fine white outer fringes; below black from chin to central belly and thighs, flanks to undertail-coverts long and silky white, undertail-coverts grey, subterminally black with white fringes; tail has white tips on underside only; eyes and bill dark, legs and feet grey. Immature male mostly slate grey with black only on throat and an irregular black line to belly, white on flanks much reduced; wings and tail dark brown, wing-coverts with buffy terminal spots. Female uniform rufescent olive above, with rufescent wings and tail, pale cinnamon terminal spots on coverts; whitish throat, almost uniform pale cinnamon below, washed narrowly olivaceous on sides, and rufous undertail-coverts. Juvenile exactly like female. The white underwings, with long axillary plumes are often hidden or partially obscured at rest, but flashed when bird vocalises. No other antbird has this feature.

Ssp. *M. a. albigula* (W Co, W Ec) male much blacker (albeit variable), white fringes to scapulars broader and undertail-coverts black, with white edges; female greyer above, wing-coverts tipped buff
M. a. axillaris (SE Ve, Tr, Guianas) as described
M. a. melaena (E Ec, E Co, W Ve) male much blacker above, charcoal rather than slate (albeit variable), and black more extensive on vent, wings and tail darker and undertail-coverts grey, with a little black on centres, less white on flanks; immature male indistinguishable from immature male *axillaris*; female distinctly olive above (not rufescent olive like *axillaris*), darker on sides and paler below

Habits Understorey but also forages as high as lower canopy. Active, in pairs and small groups, and sometimes the most numerous species in mixed-species flocks. Flicks its wings frequently.
Status Fairly common to common in Ecuador, common in Colombia and Venezuela, frequent in Guyana and French Guiana, and common in Suriname
Habitat Tropical Zone, to 900m in Ecuador and Colombia, and 1,000m in Venezuela. Tall primary *terra firme* forest where it is always within mixed-species understorey flocks; but also old second growths where it is usually in solitary pairs.
Voice A short, jerky trill (H&M). In Ecuador and west Colombia a descending *cheep-doo* or *cheep, cheep-doo*, east of Andes *nyaa-whop*. Dawn song of 6–10 descending whistles at 2 per s, *pyee, pee, piy, pey, puh, pu* (H&B, R&G). Song of *axillaris* a rapid series of abrupt, low-pitched notes, dropping sharply in pitch and gaining in intensity at start, then more or less level; pace varies geographically, *merula* and *albigula* give a slower, even-paced series, dropping in pitch, gaining then dropping in intensity (Z&I).

SLATY ANTWREN

Myrmotherula schisticolor Pl. 162

Identification 10cm. Male entirely slate grey with black wings that have white tips to coverts, black tail, and an extensive black bib from chin to centre of breast. Immature male like female but has black bib and whitish spots on wings; juvenile male like female but has vestigial black bib. Female olive-brown with distinct greyish tone above, and barely discernible buffy tips to wing-coverts and fringes of tertials and remiges, paler buffy below. Similar Long-winged Antwren paler grey and black bib contrasts more strongly, white fringes to scapulars show as white line along wing and has pale fringes to undertail-coverts. Females can be very similar but Long-winged occurs at lower elevations.

Ssp. *M. s. interior* (E Ec, E Co) male darker, charcoal grey, black more extensive; female more bluish-grey above with clear buffy tips to wing-coverts, brighter below, paler on throat but more ruddy on breast and sides, belly and flanks
M. s. sanctaemartae (NE Co, N Ve) male slightly paler grey, black less extensive; female generally warmer and more rufescent below
M. s. schisticolor (W Ec, W Co) as described

Habits Usually in close pairs in understorey, foraging acrobatically, often in and among dead-leaf tangles. Frequently joins understorey mixed flocks.
Status Uncommon in Ecuador, fairly common in Colombia and fairly common to common in Venezuela.
Habitat Upper Tropical to Subtropical Zones, 400–1,450m on west slope and 900–1,700m on east slope in Ecuador; 900–2,100m in Colombia, but to 400m on east slope in Caquetá; 350–2,000m in Venezuela, occasionally lower. In undergrowth, inside humid and wet foothill and montane forests, and adjacent second growth.
Voice Song an upward-inflected *wheeyp*, often doubled or tripled (P. Coopmans in R&G), a short *tee-up* (H&B), a rather high, forced series of 2–3 slow whistles on same pitch, *swEEErt, swEEErt, swEEErt* (Hilty), an upslurred whistle, *wheet*, repeated singly at intervals up to 2 s or in groups of 2–4 at shorter intervals (Z&I).

RÍO SUNO ANTWREN

Myrmotherula sunensis Pl. 162

Identification 9cm. Male all grey, with black wings and tail that have broad grey fringes to tertials, remiges and rectrices, wing-coverts black with bold white spots, extensive black bib that covers chin and malar to breast (but not sides); eyes and bill dark, legs and feet grey. Female olivaceous-grey above, with buffy spots on wing-coverts, buffy drab below. Rather like Long-winged Antwren but smaller, with shorter tail, overall paler grey with very large black bib. Female small and comparatively nondescript compared to female Long-winged, which is larger and longer tailed, more distinctly grey above and less drab below.

Ssp. *M. s. sunensis* (NE Ec)

Habits Forages in pairs, small groups and often, possibly usually, with mixed-species understorey flocks. Most often near ground.
Status Rare to locally uncommon.
Habitat Lower Tropical Zone, to 500m.
Voice Song a clear melodic *wi-weedy-weedy-weedy* (P. Coopmans), also described as a series of 2–5 similar, even-paced, long thin whistles (e.g. 4 notes in 1.5 s) at moderate pitch, first note often slightly higher, intervals between notes shorter than notes themselves (Z&I).

PLAIN-WINGED ANTWREN

Myrmotherula behni Pl. 161

Identification 9.5cm. Male uniform grey with an extensive black bib that extends to central belly, slight white grizzling on face-sides and around eyes. Female almost uniform olivaceous-brown above, slight whitish grizzling on face and chin, rest of underparts pale brown. The lack of any spots of bars on wing is distinctive.

Ssp. *M. b. behni* (E Co: Sierra Macarena) as described

M. b. camanii (S Ve: Cerro Camani, N Amazonas) slightly paler in both sexes; female from female *inornata* and *yavii* by pale olivaceous upperparts instead of rufous-brown; underparts more olivaceous, less brownish; male from *yavii* by paler grey underparts and crown uniform with back, without blackish tips to feathers
M. b. inornata (SE Ve: Roraima, Gu: Roraima) larger than *behni*; larger black throat, tail longer
M. b. yavii (Ve: Amazonas) male darker, more bluish-grey, throat deeper black; female more olive above and darker, more olivaceous flanks to undertail-coverts

Habits Always seems to occur in undergrowth on slopes of humid foothills.
Status Rare and local in Ecuador, uncertain status in Colombia and Guyana – Guyana records require confirmation. Several sight records for Suriname and French Guiana. Locally fairly common in Venezuela.
Habitat Upper Tropical to Lower Subtropical Zones, at 800–1,600m in Ecuador, 1,300–1,800m in Colombia and 950–1,800m in Venezuela.
Voice A sharp *sweeik*, more nasal *kyunh* (N. Krabbe in R&G) and sharp *wheet* (Z&I). Loudsong in Ecuador a series of simple, slightly downslurred notes on approximately same pitch; notes longer then intervals between them (Z&I).

LONG-WINGED ANTWREN
Myrmotherula longipennis Pl. 162

Identification 10cm. Male is slate grey with black bib that reaches centre of breast, wing-coverts black with white tips, and tail blackish, narrowly tipped white; eyes dark brown, bill long and black, legs and feet plumbeous grey. Female olive-brown above with slight greyish tone, rufous-buffy fringes to wing-coverts and tips of tail, small buffy eye-ring, buffy on throat and breast, greyish sides and flanks, whitish belly to undertail-coverts. Progression of plumages in male, from juvenile, which is like female with very weak spots on wings and grey of sides continuing to belly and undertail-coverts, to a more distinct grey from lower breast over rest of underparts, darker on head and clearer spots on wings, to all grey with dark brown wings and partial black bib. Slaty Antwren is darker with more extensive black breast. In Ecuador, female Slaty has paler face/throat and lacks grey on sides. Male Grey Antwren is paler and lacks black bib, female Grey most likely to be confused in Ecuador, but elsewhere is greyer above and paler below.

Ssp. *M. l. longipennis* (SE Co, S & E Ve, Guianas) as described
M. l. zimmeri (E Ec) female has head darker greyish-olive, back bluish-grey, wings and tail darker with more contrasting cinnamon spots on wings, cinnamon below

Habits Generally forages in pairs, and most often seen in more open, tall forest. Very active and habitually forages in leaves at ends of branches, unlike Grey and White-flanked Antwrens. Usually with other antwrens and in mixed-species understorey flocks (always so in French Guiana). Flicks and shivers wings like White-flanked Antwren.
Status Rare to locally fairly common in Ecuador, fairy common in Colombia, uncommon to fairly common in Venezuela, frequent in the Guianas.
Habitat Lower Tropical Zone, to 1,300m in Venezuela but mostly below 900m, in understorey and midstorey of humid *terra firme* and *várzea*.
Voice Male song a rather harsh *chuwey-chuwey-chuwey-chuwee-chuwee-chuwee* that gradually increases in strength and intensity before ending abruptly (T. A. Parker, R&G, H&B), or *weary-weary-weary-weary-weary*, slightly buzzy or raspy, on same pitch or slightly rising (Hilty). Call a nasal, reedy and somewhat hoarse *néw-newt* or *náa-new* (2–4 notes) (Hilty). Both song and call similar to White-flanked Antwren.

GREY ANTWREN
Myrmotherula menetriesii Pl. 162

Identification 10cm. Male uniform grey except wing-coverts which have subterminal black band and white tip, producing fairly unusual wingbars. Female grey above, tinged olive, wings slightly darker and only faint pale tips to coverts, underparts rich cinnamon. Plain-throated Antwren has bold white spots on tertials and longer uppertail-coverts, whilst Leaden Antwren lacks black subterminal bars on wings and occurs in different habitat.

Ssp. *M. m. cinereiventris* (E Ve, Gu, FG) male slightly darker, may have occasional black dot on breast; female brownish-olive above, distinctly paler ochraceous below with slight grey wash on flanks
M. m. pallida (E Co, S Ve: NW & W Amazonas, E Ec) as described

Habits Forages very actively, hardly ever pausing. Usually in pairs and small groups at mid to upper levels and often joins subcanopy and understorey flocks. Frequently flicks tail sideways and also flicks wings. Has a habit of leaning forward to stretch for potential prey.
Status Fairly common in Ecuador and Venezuela, common in Colombia, frequent in Guyana, common in Suriname and French Guiana.
Habitat Tropical Zone, to 600m in Ecuador, 1,300–1,800m in Colombia and 1,000m in Venezuela. Mid levels and subcanopy of lowland *terra firme* forest.
Voice Thin song a wavering series of 10–12 *ree* or *shree* notes that rise in pitch and accelerate slightly. Contact a sprightly *chir, whi-whi-whi-whi, chik* (R&G).

[LEADEN ANTWREN
Myrmotherula assimilis] Pl. 162

Identification 9cm. Small and short-tailed. Male all grey, with slightly darker wings and tail, and white terminal spots on coverts, white interscapular patch and a whitish chin. Female greyish-olive above with pale buffy terminal spots to coverts, lower face-sides, chin and throat whitish, rest of underparts cinnamon-ochre. Distinctive in that male is virtually uniform pale grey, not significantly darker on wings or wing-coverts, female's whitish throat and cinnamon underparts that serve as useful identification pointers. In their habitat, semi-open *várzea* scrub on river islands and riverbanks, unmistakable.

Ssp. *M. a. assimilis* (extreme SE Co)

Habits Often seen on outer branches and tends to forage vertically, up and down hanging vines, frequently flicking wings and tail.

Status Several sight records in Colombia, but no confirmation.

Habitat Lower Tropical Zone. All sightings on or near I. Corea, on Colombian border with River Amazon.

Voice Very fast, descending trill, e.g. 55 notes in 3.5 s (Hilty, Z&I).

BANDED ANTBIRD

Dichrozona cincta Pl. 167

Identification 10–10.7cm. Reddish-brown above, wing-coverts black with 2 bold pale buffy wingbars, and lesser coverts sometimes show a third, white bar, rump to uppertail-coverts black with white bar that shows well in flight; face-sides greyish-white, chin to undertail-coverts white, washed variably buffy or greyish, with few large black spots on breast and sides. Female slightly buffier than male, juvenile buffier still, with spots on flanks as well. Contrasting chestnut upperparts with 2 bold wingbars, and white underparts with large black spots identify this little ground bird at once. Wings comparatively long and strong for a Thamnophilid.

Ssp. *D. c. cincta* (E Co, S Ve) as described
D. c. stellata (E Ec) darker grey on forehead and lores, washed grey on flanks, spots on breast larger and more profuse

Habits Pairs maintain fairly large territories. They walk on forest floor, wagging tail continually and simultaneously fluffing back and wings, flashing a ribbon of paler colour formed by wing and rump bands in curious display. Eats ants occasionally.

Status Rare to locally uncommon in Ecuador, uncommon in Colombia and fairly common in Venezuela.

Habitat Lower Tropical Zone. Humid *terra firme*, always on ground or in lowest vegetation.

Voice Long buzzy trills and long crescendos of soft *zee* notes (Sick 1993, T. A. Parker, Hilty). No details of song in region, only from south-east Peru: a distinctive series of 12+ high, thin and drawn-out notes, *psszueeé, psszueeé,...* delivered slowly, ascending fractionally and with an insect-like quality (R&G), e.g. 16 notes in 15 s, drawn out and becoming more intense, shortening slightly and rising in pitch gradually, with intervals much shorter than notes. A short whistle that rises, falls then rises upscale, *wheee-up* (Z&I).

Note Validity of race *stellata* queried by Z&I on grounds of insufficient comparative documentation.

Herpsilochmus antwrens are canopy-dwellers that are rarely seen lower down; mostly black and white above, with a bold white eyebrow and comparatively longish tails, they are vaguely like gnatcatchers. Usually only one species occurs in any given area, making it essential to study distribution and learn songs to identify them with certainty

SPOT-TAILED ANTWREN

Herpsilochmus sticturus Pl. 163

Identification 10.5cm. Adult male grey above, with top of head, interscapular patch, wings and tail black, and black line through eyes; bold white supercilium, a few white streaks in black patch on back, white fringes to scapulars and tertials, terminal white spots on wing-coverts (2 dotted wingbars), 3 white streaks on inner webs of central tail-feathers, and white outer fringes to outer tail-feathers and white tips to rectrices. Underparts pale grey, whitest on belly and undertail-coverts. Female similar but has top of head flecked rufous and breast gently suffused yellowish-buffy. Juvenile like duller female, white spots on wings far less bold and even more yellowish-buffy below. Male Spot-tailed has 3 white streaks on inner webs of central rectrices, whereas male Dugand's Antwren has a single long streak; otherwise they are similar. Male virtually identical to Spot-backed Antwren, and best separated by voice, but female has white spots on black crown and is warm buffy on supraloral and sides of neck and breast. Todd's Antwren presents another problem, as they often forage together in same mixed-species flocks; Todd's has row of 4 white spots on upperside of central tail-feathers, and female Todd's has white streaks on black crown.

Ssp. Monotypic (SE Ve, Guianas)

Habits Usually found in mixed flocks in canopy, but also frequently in solitary wandering pairs.

Status Uncommon to fairly common in Venezuela, frequent in Guyana and fairly common in Suriname, very common in French Guiana.

Habitat Lower Tropical Zone to *c.*300m. Humid lowland evergreen forest, particularly gallery forest along or near water.

Voice Short bouncy series that starts slowly but accelerates slightly, *chwnk chwnk chwnk chi chi-chi'chi'ch'ch'ch'ch'ch 'ch'ch'ch* (Hilty). Series of short notes (e.g. 28 in 2.8 s) that accelerates and becomes more abrupt, initially rising, then pitch and intensity drop at end (Z&I).

Note See Dugand's Antwren.

DUGAND'S ANTWREN

Herpsilochmus dugandi Pl. 163

Identification 10.5cm. Adult male grey above, with top of head, interscapular patch, wings and tail black, and black line through eyes; bold white supercilium, a few white streaks in black patch on back, white fringes to scapulars and tertials, terminal white spots on wing-coverts (2 dotted wingbars), a single white streak on inner webs of central tail-feathers, and white outer fringes to outer tail-feathers and white tips to all rectrices. Underparts pale grey, whitest on belly and undertail-coverts. Female similar but has top of head bright rufous, faintly flecked brown, and head-sides to body-sides gently suffused buffy. Juvenile like duller female, white spots on wings far less bold and more yellowish-buffy below. Male Spot-tailed Antwren has 3 white streaks on inner webs of central rectrices, whereas male Dugand's has single long streak; otherwise they are similar. Ancient Antwren distinctive in having yellow underparts.

Ssp. Monotypic (S Co, NE Ec)

Habits Usually in pairs within mixed-species flocks in canopy. Very difficult to see and usually located by vocalisations; male shivers and vibrates tail while singing.

Status Uncommon to locally fairly common.

Habitat Lower Tropical Zone to 450m, but recorded to 600m. Humid lowland evergreen forest.

Voice Accelerating series of fast, chippered semi-musical notes that drop slightly in pitch, e.g. *ch, ch, ch-ch-chchchchchchchch*, often followed by shorter version from female. Both sexes give distinctive *chut-chut* or *tu-tuk* in contact (R&G).

Note Formerly treated as subspecies of *H. sticturus*, but voice and female plumages differ, and there are differences in plumage and habitat preference (Whitney & Alvarez 1998, Z&I).

TODD'S ANTWREN

Herpsilochmus stictocephalus Pl. 163

Identification 11cm. Adult male grey above, with top of head, interscapular patch, wings and tail black, and black line through eyes; small white spots on forehead, bold white supercilium, a few white streaks in black patch on back, white fringes to scapulars and tertials, terminal white spots on wing-coverts (2 dotted wingbars), 4 white spots on inner webs of central tail-feathers, white outer fringes to outer tail-feathers and white tips to all rectrices. Head-sides, cheeks and ear-coverts streaked faintly black, underparts pale grey, whitest on belly and undertail-coverts. Female similar but has top of head softly flecked white, and neck- to body-sides gently suffused buffy. Male Spot-tailed Antwren is darker above, but very similar and counting spots on tail is neither easy or reliable, unless in the hand, due to unknown length of long uppertail-coverts; however, lacks white spots on forehead. Females different, with Spot-tailed having chestnut on crown. Note also vocal differences.

Ssp. Monotypic (E Ve, Gu, Su, FG)

Habits Usually in pairs high in canopy, often in outer foliage and usually in mixed-species flocks that may also include Spot-tailed Antwren.

Status Fairly common in Venezuela and the Guinanas.

Habitat Lower Tropical Zone to *c*.300m in humid lowland evergreen forest.

Voice Fairly rapid, descending whinny of *c*.12 notes, *we'he'he-e-e-e-e-e-e-e-e-a*, soft and laugh-like, and much higher pitched than Spot-tailed Antwren (Hilty), or a moderately long series (e.g. 13 notes in 2 s), initial notes delivered slowly, with a change of pitch as song progesses (Z&I).

SPOT-BACKED ANTWREN

Herpsilochmus dorsimaculatus Pl. 163

Identification 11cm. Adult male grey above, with top of head, interscapular patch, wings and tail black, and black line through eyes; bold white supercilium, a few white streaks in black patch on back, white fringes to scapulars and tertials, terminal white spots on wing-coverts (2 dotted wingbars), 3 white streaks on inner webs of central tail-feathers, white outer edges to outer tail-feathers and white tips to all rectrices. Underparts pale grey, whitest on belly and undertail-coverts. Female similar but has top of head flecked white, supraloral, head- and neck-sides and breast suffused cinnamon-buffy. Juvenile like duller female, white spots on wings far less bold and more cinnamon-buffy below. Very similar Spot-tailed Antwren darker grey above, but otherwise same and best told by voice; female Spot-tailed much whiter below, only flushed slightly yellowish-buffy, and has crown chestnut-streaked and eyebrow all white.

Ssp. Monotypic (S Ve)

Habits Usually forages in pairs in midstorey upwards and less inclined to stay exclusively in canopy, but most often found in and below vine-tangled canopy of seasonally flooded black-water forest.

Status Uncommon.

Habitat Lower Tropical Zone, usually below 400m but up to 600m. Lowland evergreen forest and *várzea*.

Voice Song a short, 2 s 'rubbery lipped' fast trill rising slightly then falling, with last notes more distinct, *eeeeieieieieiei eeeeeeeeeee'e'e'r*, soft and ventriloquial (Hilty). Somewhat short, e.g. 1.5 s, trilling rattle, intensity and pitch rise then fall, final notes with overtones imparting harsh quality (Z&I).

RORAIMAN ANTWREN

Herpsilochmus roraimae Pl. 163

Identification 12.5cm. Adult male grey above, with top of head, interscapular patch, wings and tail black, also black line through eyes; bold white supercilium, a few white streaks in black patch on back, white fringes to scapulars and tertials, terminal white spots on wing-coverts (2 solid wingbars), 6 white streaks on outer webs of central tail-feathers, white outer edges to outer 2 tail-feathers, which are steeply graduated, and white tips to all tail-feathers. Underparts pale grey, whitest on belly and undertail-coverts. Female similar but has entire top of head to nape flecked white, below, washed buffy on breast. Juvenile has white spots on head larger and arrowhead-shaped, greyish-brown above and cinnamon-buffy below. Largest *Herpsilochmus* in Venezuela, and also occurs at higher elevations with no overlap.

Ssp. *H. r. kathleenae* (S Ve) male fresher, colder grey above and has grey undertail-coverts; female has sides of breast pale grey
H. r. roraimae (SE Ve, S Gu) as described

Habits Usually solitary or in pairs, occasionally small groups that follow mixed-species flocks. Forages generally on upper surfaces of topmost leaves in canopy, and may be seen fluttering out after an insect that has been flushed.

Status Fairly common in Amazonas and common in Bolívar, Venezuela; frequent in Guyana.

Habitat Upper Tropical to Lower Subtropical Zones, at 900–2,000m, in humid to wet evergreen forest and borders, on tepui

slopes, and in Melastome forests near top of tepuis.
Voice Song a hard, fast, staccato series of *c*.20 notes in 2.5 s, slightly louder in middle and decelerating at end, *ch che'che'ch e'che'che'che'che'che'che'che' ch ch ch*, recalling song of Spot-tailed Antwren but latter accelerates in finale (Hilty).

YELLOW-BREASTED ANTWREN

Herpsilochmus axillaris Pl. 163

Identification 11cm. Adult male grey above, paler on uppertail-coverts, grey central tail, rest black with white tips and outer web of outermost feathers white, wings black with white tips to coverts (2 clear bars and a third variable), top of head black with white spots on centre, eyebrow comprising a series of small white dots, cheeks and ear-coverts streaked white and black; throat whitish, edged with grey or blackish flecks on malar, underparts pale yellowish and grey (see below). Female similar pattern but different colour, top of head rufous, back to uppertail-coverts and all remiges brown, wing-coverts and underparts as male.

Ssp. *H. a. aequatorialis* (E Ec) throat white, breast grey merging to yellow below, washed olive on sides
H. a. senex (SW Co: W slope of Andes) throat and upper breast greyish-white, sharply divided from yellow underparts

Habits Forages in pairs in midstorey and subcanopy, particularly in vine tangles, occasionally in canopy or lower at forest borders. Usually in mixed-species flocks.
Status Rare to uncommon in Ecuador and uncommon in Colombia.
Habitat Upper Tropical to Lower Subtropical Zones, 800–1,700m.
Voice Song of male a chippered trill that descends in pitch steadily and evenly, *tree-ee-ee-ee-ee-ee-ew*, and is often followed by female with shorter version (R&G). A rattle-like trill of dry notes (e.g. 30 notes in 2.2 s), flat then decreasing in pitch and intensity while accelerating slightly (Z&I).

RUFOUS-WINGED ANTWREN

Herpsilochmus rufimarginatus Pl. 163

Identification 11.5cm. Two distinct and well-separated morphs. **Pale morph:** adult male pale grey from mantle to tail, with a few black streaks in centre of back, white tips to tail and outer webs of outermost tail-feathers also white, wing-coverts and tertials black, former with terminal white spots, latter fringed white, outer fringes of secondaries and primaries bright cinnamon-rufous; top of head black, with long bold white eyebrow, black eyestripe, cheeks and ear-coverts white with some flecking and streaking, underparts white, tinged yellowish. Female similar but has rufous cap instead of black, back clear olivaceous-grey and is flushed rusty on breast. **Dark morph:** adult male dark grey above from mantle to tail, with black streaking that almost covers back, tail dark grey, blackish on central feathers (white spots and tips same), outer fringes of secondaries and primaries bright rich rufous; top of head black, long bold white eyebrow, black eyestripe, cheeks and ear-coverts white with some flecking and streaking, underparts white, flushed grey on throat and breast, rest of underparts more rich yellowish. Female differs in being deeper rufous-brown on head and having back more honey-brownish, with an extensive rusty wash below. Juvenile appears indistinguishable from adult. The 2 morphs appear to be distributed in parallel, each becoming darker from north to south. The rufous patches on wing are large and very distinctive and cannot be confused with another antwren.

Ssp. *H. r. exiguus* (N Co) small (10cm); male clear grey above, female olive-grey above, both have secondaries and primaries fringed amber
H. r. frater (NW & E Ec: E slope of Andes, Co, Ve, Gu, Su) as described

Habits Forages in pairs in canopy, but often at edges of forest and ventures to trees separated from but close to border. Frequently joins mixed-species flocks.
Status Uncommon and local in Ecuador, main population (*frater*) on east slope at 600–1,300m, but a smaller population, possibly of Colombian race *exiguus*, in north-west. Very uncommon in Colombia, fairly common in Venezuela but rather unevenly distributed and tends to be local. Restricted to the Tafelberg in Suriname.
Habitat Tropical Zone, below 200m on north-west slope in Ecuador, 1,000–1,200m in Colombia. To 860m in Venezuela, but most records below 500m. Lowland and foothill forests, both interior and at borders.
Voice Song of *frater* in Ecuador a fast, descending and accelerating series of nasal, almost gravelly notes, *chu, chu, chu-chu-chu-ch-ch-chchch-rrr-chúp*, with accented final note. Female often follows with shorter version (R&G). In Venezuela, *ku, ku ku-ku-ku'ku'we'e'e'e'e'djt*, bouncy with a rough note at end (P. Schwartz recording, Hilty). Race *exiguus* gives a short complex series of *c*.6 notes that accelerate and drop in pitch before being overtaken by rapid series of higher pitched notes that decelerate (Z&I).

ANCIENT ANTWREN

Herpsilochmus gentryi Pl. 163

Identification 11.5cm. Adult male grey above with concealed white interscapular patch and some black streaks on back, wings and tail black with white outer fringes to scapulars, tertials and secondaries, white terminal spots to coverts, tail has white outer fringes to central and outermost pairs, top of head black, long white eyebrow, thick black eyestripe, cheeks, ear-coverts and entire underparts yellow, ear-coverts flecked grey, washed lightly olive on sides and flanks. Female similar but has white spots on crown and slight ochraceous tone to breast and sides.

Ssp. Monotypic (SW Ec)

Habits Frequently flicks wings. Often joins mixed-species flocks.
Status Rare to uncommon and local.
Habitat Tropical Zone, to 200m, in tall *terra firme* forest, presumably on white-sand soil.
Voice Male song a series of chippered notes that slow

markedly and fall slightly in pitch, e.g. *chedidididi-di-di-deh-deh-deh*, often followed by female with shorter version (R&G); alternatively, a moderately long series (e.g. 15 notes in 2.1 s) that increases then decreases in pitch and intensity, and decelerates throughout (Z&I).

DOT-WINGED ANTWREN

Microrhopias quixensis Pl. 164

Identification 11.5–12.5cm. Small bird with a long tail. Adult male virtually all black, charcoal grey on wings, with large white terminal spots on very graduated tail (distal two-thirds of underside appear white), long white but mostly concealed interscapular patch, outer fringes of scapulars white, large round tips to wing-coverts. Female is blackish-grey, rather than pure black, and has breast on down reddish-chestnut. Juvenile duller, dark brownish-grey with underparts chestnut-brown, and white on wings reduced to paler fringes and spots on greater coverts.

Ssp. *M. q. consobrinus* (N & W Co, W Ec) male as *quixensis*; female lacks black throat and is dark brownish-grey above, entire underparts rufous with slight olive-grey wash on flanks

M. q. microstictus (Guianas) male has larger tips to tail-feathers (entire undertail appears white) and female also has entire undertail white, is slightly more reddish-rufous than *consobrinus*, but also has more extensive grey flanks

M. q. quixensis (E Ec, SE Co) as described

Habits Pairs or small groups may be found with mixed understorey flocks or foraging independently, at lower to mid levels. Usually at forest edge and in second growth, and favours vine tangles and dense creeper growth. Captures prey by gleaning. Regularly raises its tail slowly while spreading rectrices, showing large flash of white. Displays by erecting interscapular patch.

Status Fairly common to common in Ecuador, fairly common west of Andes in Colombia, less so to east. Uncommon in Guyana but fairly common in Suriname, locally common in southern and central French Guiana, very local in the north.

Habitat Tropical Zone to 800m in Ecuador but mostly below 500m, to 900m on west side of Andes in Colombia. Humid to wet primary and mature secondary *terra firme* and *várzea*; in south of range partial to large stands of bamboo. In Guianas found in upper levels of dry, tangled growth between large boulders of Guianan shield.

Voice A musical sequence of 5–10 whistles, ending with lower tone note, e.g. *wee, tsee-tsi-tsi-tsi-tu-tu*, sometimes with rougher *zhait* or *zheeeit* notes mixed (R&G). Calls include *peep* (in falsetto), *chew* and almost inaudible buzzes (Hilty). Most striking call a loud and harsh rattle (H&M).

Note Race *boucardi* (Middle America) erroneously listed in Rodner *et al.* (2000).

WHITE-FRINGED ANTWREN

Formicivora grisea Pl. 164

Identification 12–13cm. Much variation between races, more so for females than males. Adult male brownish-grey above, wing-coverts black with white tips, long uppertail-coverts black with white terminal spots, steeply graduated tail black with white outer fringes to outer feathers and all feathers have white tips; broad white line separates grey upperparts from all-black underparts, starts as frontal band, runs over eye and around ear-coverts, along sides and flanks, and may cover vent and undertail-coverts, depending on race. Female essentially pale brown above with wings and tail like male, and underparts ranging from uniform very pale yellow to white, heavily streaked black. Juvenile generally pale, washed-out version of female, with immature males showing emergent black on face and breast. Occasionally seen with Rusty-backed Antwren in Sipaliwini, but latter prefers lower scrub. Otherwise, white fringe makes it unmistakable. Two groups which are almost certainly species, with distinct vocalisations as well as morphological differences. In absence of formal SACC recognition, we acknowledge them here thus.

Ssp. **Northern White-fringed Antwren** *intermedia* group, female has streaked underparts:

F. g. intermedia (Co: Santa Marta, N Ve, Tr) clear white fringe to scapulars, thin white fringes to tertials, sides and flanks broadly white, vent and undertail-coverts black, female has white head-sides to undertail-coverts with some black streaks on breast and belly

F. g. fumosa (E Co, W Ve) male very dark brownish-grey above, white fringe small and reduced, underparts extensively black, and vent and undertail-coverts black, female extensively streaked black below

F. g. orenocensis (S Ve: Bolívar) tawny-brown above, undertail-coverts white softly barred blackish; female has black streaks on face, throat, breast and belly, rather than solid black, undertail-coverts white, softly barred blackish like male

F. g. tobagensis (To) like *intermedia* but male has white undertail-coverts; female more heavily streaked on breast

Southern White-fringed Antwren *grisea* group, female has unstreaked underparts:

F. g. grisea (Guianas) male has small white spots on wing-coverts and vestigial white fringe to scapulars, also vent and undertail-coverts black, female bright buffy-yellow below, white undertail-coverts

F. g. hondae (C Co) bold white fringe to scapulars, large white spots on coverts, white broad on sides and flanks, undertail-coverts black; female has large white spots on wings, pale yellowish below, white undertail-coverts

F. g. rufiventris (E Co, S Ve: Amazonas) male like *grisea*, but has dark brown undertail-coverts; female has underparts rufous, undertail-coverts faintly barred rufous and white

Habits Always in pairs at borders and low levels, sometimes with small mixed flocks. Not shy, but difficult to see as it stays in thickets, methodically examining twigs and leaves for insects. Although avoids coming into open, often perches very low in

light cut-over forest. Recorded avidly sallying with several other species at explosions of winged termites above canopy. Signature gestures include 'swivelling' spread rectrices sideways and drooping wings to expose white underwing.
Status Common and widespread throughout its range; restricted to the coastal plain in French Guiana.
Habitat Tropical Zone to 1,100m in Colombia. Dry scrub, patches of thicket or shrubby woods in savannas, gallery forests. In moister areas, low shrubby woodland or early second growth.
Voice Southern White-fringed Antwren group: in Guianas, loud long repetitions of a sharp *chup* note, ending with a *chedep-chedep-chedep* sequence; in Suriname a low, husky *chuup, chuup, chuup…*, up to 50 notes in 13 s, often repeated 2–3 times with little more than a 1 s pause between; also *c.*10–20 low, coarse *qlip-qlip-qlip* at rate of 3 per s, and a liquid *queek, chuup* (R&T, Hilty); distinctive call, *kyúk-kyúk-kyúk* (H&M). Northern White-fringed Antwren group: in Venezuela, 3+ repetitions of a mellow *tu*, ending with a soft descending trill; also a mushy bi-syllable *chúret*; song a weak pianissimo phrase, slightly descending, *juup, tu-du-du-du-du-du* (inhale, exhale) and 2–5 soft syncopated notes, *ju-ju… ju-ju-ju-ju-…..ju-ju-ju* in little Morse Code patterns, oft-repeated or followed by a short trill (Hilty); in Trinidad, a sequence of sharp *tu-ik* notes, alternating fast and slow repetitions, a single whistled *tu*, followed by a soft trill (ffrench).
Note R&T pointed out that species falls into 2 groups, those races in which females have uniform clear underparts and those where females have black streaks on white; difference is underlined by 2 distinct vocalisation types which split on same lines. Hilty came to same conclusion and recognised 2 species, Southern White-fringed Antwren, and Northern White-fringed Antwren, which we acknowledge here.

RUSTY-BACKED ANTWREN
Formicivora rufa Pl. 164

Identification 12.5cm. Adult male completely rufous above with black face, throat and central belly, fringed white like White-fringed Antwren, flanks and vent to undertail-coverts white, washed rufous; wings and tail black, with terminal white spots on coverts, rufous fringes to tertials and remiges, tips of graduated tail-feathers white. Female similar but has face and breast streaked black on white, instead of solid black. Juvenile resembles female, with weaker streaking and paler below.

Ssp. *F. r. chapmani* (Su)

Habits Occasionally seen with White-fringed Antwren, but latter generally prefers taller scrub (H&M). Pairs or small groups forage well inside foliage at low to mid levels. Joins mixed flocks only occasionally.
Status Common in low scrub in Sipaliwini Savanna.
Habitat Lower Tropical Zone. Stands of shrubbery or thicket in savannas, gallery forests, open woodland with thicket patches; often near water.
Voice Some 10–15 hurried, rhythmic repetitions of *chedede* phrase; also an even faster *ch-ch…*

Drymophila antbirds represent a small genus of easily recognised birds almost exclusively found in areas where *Guadua* and *Chusquea* bamboos dominate undergrowth. They have small bodies and long tails, black-streaked white foreparts and rufous rear parts. Tails are black, steeply graduated and heavily spotted white terminally.

STRIATED ANTBIRD
Drymophila devillei Pl. 163

Identification 14cm. Adult male has back and head white, streaked heavily black, throat, breast and sides white, streaked heavily on sides but lightly on breast, rest of body rufous with black streaks on rump and uppertail-coverts. Wings black with white terminal spots on coverts and bright rufous fringes to tertials and remiges; steeply graduated tail black with 4 white spots on outer edges of central pair, and large terminal white spot on each rectrix, appearing from above as a series of white scallops on sides of tail. Female similar but has top of head and neck rufous, and rufous flush on sides. Juvenile is olive-grey instead of white above and flushed grey on breast, rufous of posterior parts much weaker. Very similar Long-tailed Antbird has clear, unmarked rump.

Ssp. *D. d. devillei* (NE Ec, SC Co)

Habits Forages in pairs and small groups at lower and mid levels, particularly amongst nodes of bamboos and vine tangles.
Status Rare and local.
Habitat Tropical Zone, 300–700m, in *Guadua* bamboo-dominated undergrowth of lowland humid forest.
Voice Song a moderately long series (e.g. 17 notes in 3 s), with 2 weak introductory notes followed by 3 emphatic long raspy notes, then a rapidly accelerating series of clear notes rising and falling in pitch (Z&I).

LONG-TAILED ANTBIRD
Drymophila caudata Pl. 163

Identification 15cm. Adult male has back, head and breast white, heavily streaked black, rest of body rufous. Wings black with white terminal spots on coverts and bright rufous fringes to tertials and remiges; steeply graduated tail black with large white terminal spot on each rectrice, appearing from above as series of white scallops on sides of tail. Long uppertail-coverts black with white terminal spots. Female similar but has top of head and neck rufous, and rufous flush on sides and breast. Juvenile olive-grey instead of white above and flushed grey on breast, rufous of posterior parts much weaker. Very similar Striated Antbird has heavily streaked rump.

Ssp. *D. c. aristeguietana* (W Ve) much heavier streaking, particularly on top and back of head
D. c. caudata (Co & Ec: Andes) as described, fully streaked on breast
D. c. hellmayri (N Co) streaking very heavy on top of head and mantle, but very light on throat and breast, and tail is dusky with rufous wash
D. c. klagesi (N Ve) both sexes have white throat to

breast with very light streaking, and clean division with rufous belly and flanks

Habits Frequently calls and sings as it forages in dense undergrowth. Usually in pairs, very seldom joins mixed-species flocks.
Status Uncommon to locally fairly common.
Habitat Upper Tropical to Subtropical Zone, 1,500–2,600m and to 1,100m along road to Loreto north of Archidona, with a very low record at 750m in Azuay (R&G). Montane evergreen and secondary forests with plentiful bamboo, also in vine tangles and overgrown plantations.
Voice Song a distinctive, raspy *cheeyt-cheeyt, wheezy-wheeyz-wheeyz*; and male may be joined by female with several *cheet* calls R&G). Two very clear, rhythmic notes followed by 3 very wheezy phrases, accented note higher pitched, *chuet, chuet, pa-fjéee-jt, pa-fjéee-jt* (H&B). number of notes, their shape, length and quality varies both regionally and individually (Z&I).

Terenura antwrens are somewhat warbler-like in behaviour, and distinctive in their rufous, tan, grey and yellow plumage, thankfully well-separated geographically with little or no overlap, as they all look and sound alike! Generally in the canopy where they are seldom seen, but they sing continually.

RUFOUS-RUMPED ANTWREN
Terenura callinota Pl. 164

Identification 11cm. Pale sandy olive-brown back, wings, tail and uppertail-coverts, with bright orange-rufous rump and concealed orange interscapular patch, outer fringes of scapulars white and dusky wing-coverts with whitish-yellow terminal spots forming 2 bars; top of head to nape blackish, eyebrow white, head-sides grey with a blackish eyestripe, soft white streaking on cheeks and ear-coverts to white chin and throat, pale greyish breast, rest of underparts pale yellow, to whitish on undertail-coverts. Female similar but has top of head and nape concolorous with back, lacks interscapular patch and white outer fringes to scapulars. No overlap with Chestnut-shouldered Antwren.

Ssp. *T. c. callinota* (Andes: Co & Ec) as described
T. c. guianensis (Gu) rump darker, rufous-chestnut; lacks interscapular patch
T. c. venezuelana (Ve: Perijá) male as *callinota*, female has back olive-grey and underparts paler

Habits Usually in pairs and often in mixed-species flocks, in outermost branches, where acrobatic and warbler-like in its restless searching above and below leaves (when its bright orange rump can be seen to advantage).
Status Uncommon in Ecuador and Colombia, virtually unknown in Venezuela, scarce and local in Guyana.
Habitat Upper Tropical to Subtropical Zones, 900–1,800m in Ecuador, 1,450–1,900m in Venezuela. Canopy and subcanopy of humid and wet cloud forests, often lower at edges.
Voice Frequent song a rapidly uttered, high-pitched, *tsii-tsii-tsi-tsi-tititititititititi*, that accelerates into a fast chipper or trill (R&G). A very high, thin, chipping *ti-ti-ti'ti'i'i'i'ti'tzzs, tzzs, tzss, tzss* with number of buzzing notes at end varying (B. M. Whitney in H&B), a 2-part trill, starting slowly then accelerating into a staccato *sue-see-wee-st'e'e'e'e'e'e'e'e'e*, recalling Tennessee Warbler (Hilty). In Colombia 26 notes in 2.6 s of initially distinct, countable notes that rise in pitch and shorten to become a high-pitched trill (Z&I).

CHESTNUT-SHOULDERED ANTWREN
Terenura humeralis Pl. 164

Identification 11cm. Pale sandy olive-brown back, wings, tail and uppertail-coverts, with bright rufous-chestnut rump, wing bend and partially concealed rufous-chestnut scapular patch, dusky wing-coverts with whitish terminal spots forming 2 bars; top of head to nape blackish, eyebrow white, head-sides grey with blackish eyestripe, soft black and white streaking on cheeks and ear-coverts to pale greyish chin, throat and breast, rest of underparts white, pale yellow on flanks. Female similar but has top of head and nape concolorous with back, eyebrow pale grey, lacks concealed patch on scapulars. No overlap with Rufous-rumped Antwren.

Ssp. *T. h. humeralis* (E Ec)

Habits Pairs or small groups keep close and are almost invariably encountered in mixed feeding flocks. Forages from understorey to canopy, often in outermost branches, where acrobatic and warbler-like in its restless searching above and below leaves (when rufous-chestnut rump shows to advantage).
Status Rare to locally fairly common.
Habitat Lower Tropical Zone, to *c*.600m. Canopy and subcanopy of lowland evergreen forest.
Voice Like Rufous-rumped Antwren, perhaps slightly slower.

ASH-WINGED ANTWREN
Terenura spodioptila Pl. 164

Identification 10.5cm. Upper mantle and nape grey, back chestnut, rump rufous-chestnut, wings, uppertail-coverts and tail brown, with large white terminal spots on wing-coverts forming 2 wingbars, top of head black merging into nape, long eyebrow white, head-sides greyish with black eyestripe, neck-sides to flanks grey, whitish throat and centre of breast to undertail-coverts. Female similar but crown brown, merging into chestnut mantle, face- and body-sides washed slightly brown with yellowish tinge to breast. Juvenile softer brown above and almost all yellowish below.

Ssp. *T. s. signata* (SE Co) much smaller white terminal spots on wing-coverts
T. s. spodioptila (S Ve, Gu) as described

Habits Pairs or small groups keep close and are almost invariably encountered in mixed flocks. Forages from understorey to canopy, often in outermost branches, where acrobatic and warbler-like in its restless searching above and below leaves (when chestnut back and rump show to advantage). Also flicks wings frequently and opens wings and fans tail.
Status Rare to locally uncommon in Ecuador and Colombia, fairly common in Venezuela and Guyana. Uncommon in French Guiana, but probably much overlooked.

Habitat Lower Tropical Zone, to *c.*600m but to 1,100m in Venezuela. Canopy and subcanopy of lowland evergreen forest.
Voice A high-pitched bouncy series of emphatic notes that accelerate into a fast trill, *tsip, tsee tsee tse te'ti'ti'ti'ti'ti'tititi*, recalling Tennessee Warbler (Hilty) or a long introductory note quickly accelerating into a very rapid trill that descends in pitch, ending with 2–3 distinct, countable and abrupt notes (Z&I).
Note Race *elaopteryx* (French Guiana) considered inseparable from *spodioptila* and synonymised by Z&I.

Cercomacra antbirds are a homogenous lot, with all males dark grey to blackish, and females olive above and cinnamon below. Intermediate males are like females but with grey patches. They have steeply graduated tails with a large white spot at tip of underside of each rectrix. Generally skulking and retiring birds of tangles and dense foliage and thus difficult to spot, but they respond well to playback.

GREY ANTBIRD
Cercomacra cinerascens Pl. 165

Identification 16cm. Adult male charcoal grey, with a partially concealed interscapular patch, white body patch at wing bend (usually concealed by scapulars), slightly greyer underparts and bold white terminal spots on undertail. Female olive-brown above with hardly any interscapular patch, cinnamon eyebrow, darker wings and tail with paler, somewhat yellowish tips to wing-coverts, cinnamon below, paler on undertail-coverts. Immature male like female but has larger interscapular patch. Juvenile like female but lacks white dots on wing-coverts, instead has buffy fringes. Dusky Antbird has smaller tail spots.

Ssp. *C. c. cinerascens* (E Ec, Co: E Andes) as described
C. c. immaculata (SE Ve, Guianas) male has row of small white dots on tips of greater coverts

Habits Usually in pairs well inside cover of tangles and vine- and liana-strewn foliage, foraging quietly. White spots on undertail best signal. Do not appear to join mixed-species flocks but are vocal when they pass by, and may travel with them for a short while.
Status Fairly common to locally common throughout its range.
Habitat Tropical Zone, to 900m but usually below 600–700m. Dense tangles in subcanopy and midstorey of lowland evergreen forest.
Voice Male song unmistakable: 2 hoarse notes: *kuk-kcheeh, kuk-kcheeh, kuk-kcheeh*; call a loud, machine-gun-like *kga-ga-ga-ga-ga* (H&M) or somewhat hiccup-like *ch-krr, ch-krr, ch-krr…* up to 7–8 times. A sharp, nasal *keeyr*, sometimes repeated steadily and fast, growling, *kr-kr-kr-kr-kr-kr….* (R&G).

DUSKY ANTBIRD
Cercomacra tyrannina Pl. 165

Identification 13.5–14.5cm. Adult male slate grey, with large white interscapular patch, white body patch at wing bend (usually concealed by scapulars), slightly paler on throat and below, small white terminal dots on wing-coverts and small white spots on undertail; eyes dark brown to brownish-grey. Female greyish olive-brown above, with lores and tips to wing-coverts buffy-orange, below bright orange-rufous; bill all black. Juvenile and immature similar to adult female, but juvenile female has white-flecked throat, almost forming irregular bars; juvenile male has both black and white flecks on throat, distinctly more bar-like than juvenile female, and is distinctly greyer olive above than adult female. Immature male as juvenile, but has variable grey underparts, and we assume it becomes completely grey below.

Ssp. *C. t. saturatior* (E Ve, Guianas) male generally darker to blacker, clear white fringes to all feathers, some variable white barring on centre of belly
C. t. tyrannina (W Ec, SE Co & W Andes, SC Ve) as described
C. t. vicina (Andes: Ec, Co & Ve) male washed brownish-olive on sides and flanks, wings and tail, female paler below, more ochraceous on throat and undertail-coverts

Habits Forages in pairs and sometimes in mixed-species flocks, keeping close to ground in dense undergrowth, thickets and shrubby borders, and at edges of humid forest and second-growth woodland.
Status Fairly common to common across its range.
Habitat Tropical to Lower Subtropical Zones, to 800m in Ecuador, occasionally to 1,400m, to 1,800m in Colombia with records to 2,100m, and to 1,200m in Venezuela, occasionally to 1,800m. Undergrowth and dense understorey of humid lowland and foothill forest edges, seldom within forest, and often in thickets along streams.
Voice Song 5–6 slow notes that become a trill, *pee-pee-pee-pee-pee-peepeeh'r'r'r'rrrrrrrr* (H&M). Male song *pü, pü, pee-peepipipi?* with female chiming in with a softer, higher pitched version (R&G). Another song, a loose, nasal, rattling series of *klu* notes, slightly accelerating as female joins in or follows with unsynchronised series of 3–4 *jut-ut' jut-ut' jut-ut' jut-ut'* notes (H&B, Hilty).
Note Species revision by Bierregaard *et al.* (1997).

PARKER'S ANTBIRD
Cercomacra parkeri Pl. 165

Identification 14cm. Adult male slate grey above, slightly paler below, with white interscapular patch, white body patch at wing bend (usually concealed by scapulars), whitish terminal spots to coverts. Adult female greyish-olive above, more greyish on head, merging into olive on scapulars, with cinnamon fringes to wing-coverts, ochraceous chin merging through throat to underparts, washed olive-grey from flanks and vent to undertail-coverts.

Ssp. Monotypic (Co: C & W Andes)

Habits Usually in pairs, most often in young, shrubby patches at borders, also in densely vegetated light gaps in forest and bamboo (*Chusquea*) thickets (Z&I).

Status Uncommon.
Habitat Tropical and Subtropical Zones, *c.*1,100–2,000m, in borders of wet montane cloud and rain forest, and tall second-growth woodland, with an affinity for bamboo thickets.
Voice Song a muted note followed by series of more intense, higher pitched notes, initially flat-pitched then descending and accelerating as final notes shorten (10 notes in 2.3 s). Song of female similar but higher pitched and shorter (e.g. 6 notes in 1.6 s) and notes downslurred, usually given in duet after start of male loudsong (Z&I).
Notes Recently described species (Graves 1997).

WILLIS'S ANTBIRD
Cercomacra laeta Pl. 165

Identification 13.5–14.5cm. Adult male pure dark grey, with white interscapular patch, white body patch at wing bend (usually concealed by scapulars) and no pale tips to rectrices. Adult female greyish-olive above, more greyish on head, merging into olive on scapulars, with cinnamon fringes to grey wing-coverts, ochraceous chin merging through throat to cinnamon head-sides and underparts, washed olive-grey from flanks and vent to undertail-coverts.

Ssp. *C. l. waimiri* (extreme S Gu)

Habits Forages at lower levels, in thickets and dense shrubbery, alone, in pairs or family groups, and seldom with mixed flocks, searching for insects systematically, by hopping a little then stopping. Gives little wing-flicks continually while foraging. Attends passing armies of ants, but follows only briefly.
Status Locally fairly common.
Habitat Lower Tropical Zone, to 300m. Undergrowth of edges and borders of tall lowland evergreen forest and second growth, often near water. In west of range, where partially sympatric with Dusky Antbird, seems to prefer shrubby borders of white-sand forest, especially poorly drained and swampy land (Z&I).
Voice Male sings sequence of single note, then 4–6 double notes, high then low. Female joins in with a rising series of 4 long notes (Z&I). Song a bright, clear almost bubbly *pee'dánk, pee'dánk, pee'dánk, pee'dánk* (A. Whittaker in Hilty).
Note Formerly considered a subspecies of *C. tyrannina* (Bierregaard *et al.* 1997).

BLACKISH ANTBIRD
Cercomacra nigrescens Pl. 165

Identification 14–15cm. Adult male dark slate grey, slightly paler below, darker on wings and tail, with white interscapular patch, white body patch at wing bend (usually concealed by scapulars), wing-coverts have black subterminal bar and white terminal spot, tail all blackish. Female somewhat rufescent olive-brown above, slightly darker on wings and tail, with paler tips to wing-coverts, rufescent cinnamon below. Easily confused with Black Antbird, male of which is uniform black above and below, and female is more olive, less rufescent, especially on face- and neck-sides. In area of overlap in eastern lowlands, R&G state Black Antbird absent from riparian woodlands, whereas Blackish is more a bird of riparian habitats and swampy areas.

Ssp. *C. n. aequatorialis* (E Ec & S Co on E slope) male slate grey with black and white bars on wings much more noticeable
C. n. nigrescens (Gu, N Su, FG) as described
C. n. fuscicauda (E Ec & SE Co in lowlands) slightly paler than *nigrescens*

Habits Forages at lower levels, in thickets and dense shrubbery, alone, in pairs or family groups, sometimes with mixed flocks, looking for insects systematically, by hopping a little then stopping. Attends passing army ants. Visits bamboo and *Heliconia* stands to search for prey.
Status Uncommon to frequent in Ecuador, uncommon to locally frequent in Colombia, uncommon and local in Guyana, scarce in Suriname. Uncommon and local in French Guiana.
Habitat Lower Tropical Zone (*nigrescens* and *fuscicauda*) or Upper Tropical to Subtropical Zones (*aequatorialis*). Humid lowland forest, both *várzea* and *terra firme* (*nigrescens* and *fuscicauda*), and montane forest (*aequatorialis*). Mature second growth, dense edges and bushy clearings, stands of bamboo, overgrown plantations, wet areas. In Suriname, in mangrove and swamps between forested sand ridges of coastal region.
Voice Vocalisations differ subspecifically. Male *nigrescens* gives a loud chatter alternating with a high, melancholy whistle (H&M) and sings a single, low *wup* note followed by a short rattle of variable length, female joins in with a rising series of distinct *wup* notes. Race *fuscicauda* is most distinct, rattle condensed into a single note dropping in pitch and intensity, *What cheer!* (Z&I), or a loud drawn-out *wor-cheeéyr*, often given independently, but female sometimes follows with a rising series similar to female *aequatorialis* (R&G). Montane *aequatorialis* commonly sings a fast, mainly falling, *wor, chih-chih-cheh-cheh-cheh-cheh* and female usually follows with clearly enunciated series of 4–5 rising notes, *pur, pu-puh-peh-pih-pi?*
Note Presently includes 6 races that quite possibly represent more than 1 species (Z&I). It seems clear that montane *aequatorialis* is a prime candidate for species recognition.

BLACK ANTBIRD *Cercomacra serva* Pl. 165

Identification 14cm. Adult male uniform black with partially concealed white interscapular patch, white body patch at wing bend (usually concealed by scapulars) and white tips to wing-coverts. Adult female olive-brown above, washed slightly grey on head, with a vestigial interscapular patch and slight greyish wash to rump and tail, orange-rufous below. For separation from Blackish Antbird see that species.

Ssp. *C. s. serva* (E Ec)

Habits Close pairs or small groups forage in dense undergrowth near ground and seldom join mixed-species flocks.
Status Uncommon to fairly common.
Habitat Tropical Zone, to *c.*1,300m. Borders of lowland and foothill forests, secondary growth, tangles in treefall gaps and stands of understorey bamboo.

Voice Call an accelerating *drrr-drr-dr-dr-d'd'd'd* (P. Coopmans in R&G). Male song a distinctly rising series of loud, rather harsh notes that accelerate at end, *wor, chur, cheh-cheh-chi-chi-chi?* Female sometimes joins in or follows on with a similar but lower pitched version, often followed by 2–4 soft, abrupt notes (Z&I).

JET ANTBIRD

Cercomacra nigricans Pl. 165

Identification 15cm. Adult male all black, with white interscapular patch, white body patch at wing bend (usually concealed by scapulars), outer fringes of scapulars white, wing-coverts all tipped white, tail steeply graduated, with large white terminal spots on underside; eyes dark brown, bill black, legs and feet grey. Female deep slate grey to blackish, with black wings and tail, in addition to white markings of male, also has white tips to long uppertail-coverts, narrow whitish eye-ring, and some thin white streaks on throat and breast. Several clear stages of plumage development in female (see plate), from juvenile through 2 intermediate plumages to adult; it seems male goes direct from juvenile to all-black adult. First intermediate retains dark brown flight-feathers of juvenile, but wing-coverts are black with buffy tips, above dusky grey, with paler grey eye-ring and grizzling on face; underparts mid grey with black scallops from chin to belly, and white scallops on belly. Next stage similar above, with darker flight-feathers, body now almost as dark as adult, but with much black and white streaking from throat to flanks, then white bars on central belly. Juvenile is greyish-olive above (no white spots on coverts) with white interscapular patch, paler greyish head-sides, white from chin to belly, grading into yellowish flanks, vent and undertail-coverts.

Ssp. Monotypic (Co, W Ec, SW Ve)

Habits Pairs stay close as they forage in deepest undergrowth and scrub. Very seldom join mixed-species flocks and virtually impossible to find unless frequently uttered song is recognised.
Status Uncommon to locally common in Ecuador, locally common in Colombia and Venezuela.
Habitat Lower Tropical Zone, to *c.*600m in Ecuador and Venezuela, and 1,500m in Colombia. Deep tangled undergrowth, vines and thickets at forest edges, alongside pastures, overgrown plantations, swampy areas and riparian habitats.
Voice Male song in Ecuador (and Panama) a loud, measured series of 4–5 harsh, paired notes, second part lower pitched, *tch-ker* (R&G, Ridgely & Gwynne). Also an emphatic series, *chak chak chak*… (P. Coopmans in R&G). In Colombia song a persistently repeated, guttural, *chek-wah, chek-wah, chek-wah, chek-wah*, occasionally with more notes (H&B). In Venezuela, male sings solos or duets with female, a harsh, halting *chék-off, chék-off, chék-off, chék-off* (last note swallowed) and female starts at end, her first note overlapping male's last, a rhythmic, gravelly *karump, karump, karump, karump*, thus song heard is *chék-kor-rump, chék-kor-rump*… Female also sings solo in gaps between male's (Hilty). Each pair of notes in male's consists of a sharp, abrupt note followed by a longer burry note (5 notes in 2.8 s); when female interjects complex double note, male shifts to single buzzy note, lower pitched than female's, and 2 notes are alternated (Z&I).
Note Despite very fragmented distribution, considered monotypic, with race *atrata*, described for north-west Colombia, considered inseparable from nominate.

RIO BRANCO ANTBIRD

Cercomacra carbonaria Pl. 165

Identification 14cm. Adult male all black, with white interscapular patch, white body patch at wing bend (usually concealed by scapulars), outer fringes of scapulars white, wing-coverts tipped white, tail steeply graduated, with large white terminal spots on underside; eyes dark brown, bill black, legs and feet grey. Female is very different from other *Cercomacra*, being olive-brown above with white interscapular patch, white body patch at wing bend (usually concealed), outer fringes of scapulars white, wing-coverts black with white tips; chin and throat white with black streaks, forming black line on malar, breast to undertail-coverts ochraceous, palest and yellowish on centre of breast and belly, olivaceous on undertail-coverts. Only overlap is with Grey Antbird; male distinctly grey, albeit dark, and has virtually no white on wings, female and juvenile entirely ochraceous below.

Ssp. Monotypic (Gu)

Habits Close pairs and small groups forage in dense undergrowth and tangles in brush and forest edge along banks and islands of rivers. Tail is wagged up and down, and wings flicked frequently. Apparently occupies a band no broader than 100m from riverbank.
Status Vulnerable. Uncommon and local along Ireng river, which forms part of border between Brazil and Guyana, and which then runs south into rio Branco, Brazil.
Habitat Lower Tropical Zone. Undergrowth and understorey of riparian habitat.
Voice Male sings a series of (up to 10) paired notes, a short buzzy note and longer, clear note. Female duets by interjecting a loud buzzy note, whereupon male switches to single buzzy note, lower pitched than female's, and they are alternated antiphonally for 3–5 s (Z&I).

Pyriglena fire-eyes are aptly named, as they all have bright red eyes. They have an odd, small-headed and rather paddle-shaped tail appearance, lending a subtle but distinct profile.

WHITE-BACKED FIRE-EYE

Pyriglena leuconota Pl. 165

Identification 18cm. Adult male entirely black with semi-concealed white interscapular patch, tail steeply graduated; eyes bright red, bill, legs and feet black. Female differs dramatically by race.

Ssp. *P. l. castanoptera* (Co, E Ec) female entirely black except uniform chestnut back, to short uppertail-coverts, and wings; white interscapular patch

P. l. pacifica (E Ec) female entirely olive-brown, rufescent on wings, tail dusky to blackish, small white interscapular patch

Habits Forages in pairs or small groups, and frequently visits ant swarms, though hard to see due to skulking nature. Moves about mostly in dense foliage, languidly raising and lowering tail.
Status Locally fairly common.
Habitat Tropical and Subtropical Zones, *pacifica* from coast to *c.*1,350m, *castanoptera* at 1,000–2,000m on east slope in Ecuador, but found at 400–2,700m in Colombia. Humid to deciduous primary and mature secondary forest, sometimes at borders and in bamboo stands. Often found in understorey of gallery forest (*pacifica*).
Voice Song frequently uttered and far-carrying, *peer-peer-peer-peer-peer-peer-peer-peer-peer-peer*… fading and descending at end, female sometimes follows with her own softer and shorter version (R&G). A loud *chik* or *chi-djik*, and when excited a *chi-dji-djik* (P. Coopmans in R&G).

Myrmoborus antbirds are stocky, rotund birds with short tails and inhabit undergrowth; they are distinguished by having black faces and red eyes.

WHITE-BROWED ANTBIRD
Myrmoborus leucophrys Pl. 166

Identification 13.7 cm. Adult male dark bluish-grey with slightly darker wings (no white spots) and tail, whitish forehead and long eyebrow, face and throat black. Adult female rufescent olive above, top of head to back rusty-brown with a bright, long eyebrow, wings have buffy terminal spot to coverts forming 3 wingbars, olive runs onto neck-sides and washes down sides, flanks and undertail-coverts, throat to vent white. Juvenile indistinguishable from adult.

Ssp. *M. l. angustirostris* (S & SE Ve, Guianas) white of forehead extends to exactly middle of eyes, belly grey to undertail-coverts; female has forehead and fore eyebrow, bright cinnamon-rufous, becoming cream-coloured postocularly, with a few black spots on breast-sides
M. l. erythrophrys (W Ve, Co: E Andes) whitish forehead extends to crown and ends just beyond eyes, underparts entirely dull charcoal; female has dark fringes to breast feathers, giving slight scaled effect, eyebrow only slightly paler rufous postocularly
M. l. leucophrys (E Ec) like *angustirostris* but male darker

Habits Very territorial. Forages in pairs that often join mixed flocks and occasionally visit army ants in early second growth. Likes to hop on vertical twigs and sally to catch prey. Also hops on ground in dense undergrowth. Raises and lowers tail frequently and deliberately.
Status Uncommon to locally fairly common in Ecuador, fairly common in Colombia, common in Venezuela, fairly common in Guyana and rather common in Suriname. Uncommon and local in central and southern French Guiana.
Habitat Tropical Zone, generally below *c.*500m but occasionally recorded higher, reaching 1,400m. Borders of *várzea* and *terra firme*, deforested areas with early second growth and bamboo, in wet areas and along creeks, in tangled foliage in mid storey.
Voice Rattles and *huah* calls. Song an explosive, loud whinnying, uttered by both sexes (H&M). Also, a very fast, loud but falling series of *c.*30 *pee'* or *ee'* notes that slowly fades, e.g. *pi'pi'pi'pi'pi'pi'pi'pi'pi'pi'pi'p'p'p'p'p'p'rr* (R&G, Hilty).
Note Revision by O'Neill & Parker (1997).

ASH-BREASTED ANTBIRD
Myrmoborus lugubris Pl. 166

Identification 13.2cm. Adult male bluish-grey above, full black mask from forehead to ear-coverts and throat, breast and underparts white; bill black, eyes red, legs and feet vinaceous-grey. Female rufescent brown above, with greyish wash to head and mantle, faint pale tips to wing-coverts, black mask only covers forehead to cheeks and ear-coverts, throat to undertail-coverts white; bill blackish above, greyish-horn below.

Ssp. *M. l. berlepschi* (extreme NE Ec)

Habits Forages alone or in pairs at lowest levels, perching on vertical stems or hopping on ground, catching prey by sallying to air or picking from foliage or floor. Not shy, seen calling, raising and lowering tail slowly.
Status Occurs in our region only on one island at confluence of ríos Aguarico and Napo, where it is apparently fairly common.
Habitat Tropical Zone at 150m, in *várzea* forest along rivers, soggy riverbanks and swampy areas, especially on river islands, with a liking for *Heliconia* stands.
Voice Rattles and *jeet* calls, or a loud, fast and falling series of *tew*, *peeyr* and *peeyr-pur* notes (R&G, J. V. Remsen, Hilty).

BLACK-FACED ANTBIRD
Myrmoborus myotherinus Pl. 166

Identification 13cm. Adult male blue-grey above, wings darker, wing-coverts black with clear white tips forming 3 wingbars, full black mask, including throat, is fringed white from supraloral to rear ear-coverts; eyes bright red, bill black, legs and feet vinaceous-grey. Variant male from SW of range has darker grey underparts and was formerly named as race *napensis*. Female has white chin and black mask, cinnamon from forehead to sides of neck in a face-framing crescent, rich olive above with three cinnamon wingbars; underparts rich bright cinnamon.

Ssp. *M. m. elegans* (E Ec, Co: E Andes, S Ve)

Habits Forages at low level, mostly in pairs but sometimes in families, sallying from vertical perches or searching leaves or forest floor.
Status Common.
Habitat Tropical Zone. Interior of primary *terra firme* and mature second-growth forests. Thickets and overgrown treefall gaps with many saplings.
Voice Sharp *peea*; also a loud, slow and falling series of *cheep* or *jeep* notes, usually 10+ (Hilty)
Note Race *napensis*, previously listed in Rodner *et al.* (2000), falls within a range of variation of *elegans*, and was synonymised by Haffer & Fitzpatrick (1985).

WARBLING ANTBIRD

Hypocnemis cantator Pl. 167

Identification 12cm. Greyish-brown above with dark streaks, wings and tail dark with subterminal blackish triangles and white terminal spots on coverts, brown fringes to tertials and flight-feathers, rump clear rufous-brown, head black above with line of short white streaks on central crown, and white streaks forming eyebrow, head-sides grizzled black and white, with black and white forming streaks on neck- to breast-sides; chin to belly white, with some streaking, flanks to undertail-coverts rich rufous. Eyes brown, bill dark above, pale below, legs and feet pale grey. Female similar but black generally replaced by dark brown on head, back and wings.

Ssp. *H. c. cantator* (SE Ve, Guianas) as described
H. c. flavescens (Ve, E Co) brighter than *cantator*, with heavier white streaking on head continuing on back, and less streaking on breast, pale yellow flush to throat and breast, flanks and undertail-coverts light orange
H. c. saturata (SE Co, E Ec) similar to *cantator* above, but distinctly yellow on throat to breast, with a few deliberate black streaks on sides, and brighter rufous below

Habits Forages in pairs or groups, often with mixed flocks or occasionally at ant swarms. Catches prey by examining foliage and sallying from perches in low to mid tiers.
Status Common. Frequent in Guyana and French Guiana.
Habitat Tropical Zone, in *várzea*, borders of primary *terra firme* and mature second-growth, and forest stands in savannas; bamboos or thick, vine vegetation along creeks and wet areas. Typical of old tree-fall gaps in French Guiana.
Voice Male song a series of clear notes that become raspy rather abruptly (all races), but otherwise variable among populations, in pace, change of pace, pattern of peak frequencies and shapes of notes; female song usually starts just before or just after male's finishes, typically 6–9 notes that descend in frequency, but differs between populations in pace, etc. Each population has its own call notes (Z&I). In Ecuador (*saturata*), song a raspy, almost snarling, *peer, peer-peer-peer-peer-pur-pur-pyur*, descending, and sometimes female chips in halfway through with shorter, higher pitched version. A distinctive *wur-cheeé*, or *wur-cheeé-cheeé* call (R&G). Song in Colombia (*flavescens*?) a slow descending, buzzy, *tew-zew-zew-tzy-tzzu*, rough at end, of up to 8 notes, also a slow, wheezy *whew, tew tew*, unhurried and gasping, resembling Black-chinned Antbird (J. V. Remsen in H&B). In Venezuela (*flavescens*) song *tew, tzew-tzew-tur pur paw*, husky and rough, almost snarling at end, up to 12 notes, and female responds with a similar, shorter and higher pitched version, and contact-call *wur-tew* or *wur-tew-tew*. Song of *cantator* similar but higher pitched, cleaner (much less buzzy) and faster (Hilty).
Note Race *notaea* (south-east Venezuela), synonymised under *cantator* on grounds of indistinguishable plumage and voice (Z&I), though Hilty states that songs are different.

YELLOW-BROWED ANTBIRD

Hypocnemis hypoxantha Pl. 167

Identification 11.7cm. Olive-green above from mantle to tail, wing-coverts black with terminal white spots, pale yellowish fringes to flight-feathers and small white terminal spots on tail. Top of head black with row of white streaks on central crown, long yellow eyebrow, black eyestripe and fine yellow eye-ring, cheeks and ear-coverts yellow with black and yellow streaks on neck-sides reaching breast-sides, narrow black malar; underparts yellow with some pale black streaking, greenish-olive wash on flanks. Eyes dark, bill black, legs and feet dark grey. Female similar but streaking on crown yellow, wing-coverts brown with large subterminal black spots and terminal buffy-white spots.

Ssp. *H. h. hypoxantha* (SE Co, E Ec)

Habits Forages in pairs or groups and sometimes with mixed flocks. Fairly active, hops about examining leaves and stems for prey.
Status Uncommon.
Habitat Tropical Zone, in humid *terra firme*, in dense parts of subcanopy and mid levels, at tangled borders and treefall gaps.
Voice A fast *dree-pu* or *dree-pu-pu*, and a scratchy *kreeéuk* (P. Coopmans in R&G). Sings rapid *queequequeeet*, repeated after brief pause (H&B), or a descending series becoming raspy, somewhat like some races of *H. cantator* but, most audibly, notes change gradually, rather than abruptly, from clear to raspy; female similar but typically shorter and descending more sharply (Z&I).

BLACK-CHINNED ANTBIRD

Hypocnemoides melanopogon Pl. 166

Identification 11.5cm. A well-rounded bird with a short tail, long black bill and pale blue-grey eyes. Male generally dark, dull grey with a black throat, wing-coverts black with white tips that form wingbars, and a white-tipped black tail. Female almost same grey above, but below is pale grey, washed white on centre from chin to undertail-coverts, spotted and dappled white on grey from malar to flanks. Juvenile entirely umber-grey, darker on wings and tail, dappled white on chin and throat, white on undertail-coverts. Intermediate male said to resemble female (Z&I). Slate-coloured and Spot-winged Antbirds have dark eyes and longer tails, females are deep rufous. Male Spot-winged of race *leucostigma* may have pale eyes, but is contrastingly sooty above and mid grey below without black on throat. Amazonas Antbird is larger and has a longer, slightly notched tail without white tips, and female is very different.

Ssp. *H. m. melanopogon* (CE Ve, Guianas) as described; intermediate male exactly like adult female *occidentalis*
H. m. occidentalis (S Ve, SE Co, NE Ec) male much paler grey below; female white below, spotted grey (rather than grey, spotted white)

Habits Forages in pairs or sometimes in groups, hopping in low vegetation, seldom on ground. Perches on fallen logs and occasionally on vertical twigs. Groups are noisy. Lowers and raises tail slowly, with rectrices spread, exposing white spots otherwise not visible.

Status Uncommon to locally fairly common across range.
Habitat Tropical Zone, to 200m in Ecuador, 500m in Colombia and 400m in Venezuela. Likely wanders higher throughout, as recorded to 950m in Venezuela. Always near quiet or slow-flowing waters, in swamps, *várzea* or very wet *terra firme* and gallery forests (not in well-drained areas) and mangrove.
Voice A long phrase, loud and accelerating as it becomes raspier, *cheé-chee-chi-chi-chichichichichichechechechez*, descending at end (R&G), or *psheep psheep eep ep-ep-e-e-e'e'e'e'e weep-weep-jeep-jeep* slowing and descending slightly at end (H&B, Hilty). A rising and falling series (e.g. 13 notes in 2 s) accelerating as notes become shorter, except emphatic final notes that slow but typically do not become raspy (Z&I).

BLACK-AND-WHITE ANTBIRD
Myrmochanes hemileucus Pl. 167

Identification 11.5cm. Very distinctive, chubby little bi-coloured bird with short tail. Entirely black above with white, partially concealed, interscapular patch, white outer fringes to scapulars, white tips to median and greater coverts, small white tips to long upperwing-coverts and to tail, underparts pure white. Female virtually identical but has white supraloral spot and lemon flush to lower underparts.

Ssp. Monotypic (E Ec)

Habits Forages in pairs, fairly actively, flitting around in thickets from near ground to mid storey. Sings often and is not shy. Rises crown feathers when excited.
Status In Ecuador, uncommon to locally fairly common in younger successional growth on islands in río Napo (R&G). In Colombia known only from islands in Amazon opposite Leticia (H&B).
Habitat Tropical Zone. Thick, early second growth and bushy *Cecropia* stands on river islands.
Voice Short, speeding and tremulous series of *bip* notes that recall bouncing ball and answered by mate (H&B). Frequently given song a fast *tu-tu-u-u-u-u-u*, first notes lower pitched; mate often replies with an inflected *toot!*, sometimes doubled or tripled. Call a slurred rattle (R&G) or low-pitched *chuck* and scolding series of squeals (e.g. 9 notes in 0.9 s), decelerating slightly and decreasing in intensity.

BARE-CROWNED ANTBIRD
Gymnocichla nudiceps Pl. 167

Identification 16cm. Male all black, with partially concealed white interscapular patch and white fringes to wing-coverts forming bars; bare skin of crown and ocular area to base of bill blue; eyes brown, bill black, legs and feet pale grey. Female entirely olivaceous-rufous above and rufous below, with a smaller, mostly concealed interscapular patch, and paler fringes to wing-coverts forming faint, barely discernible bars; ocular area and lores blue, eyes brown, bill grey.

Ssp. *G. n. nudiceps* (NW Co) as described
G. n. sanctamartae (N Co) male has white spots on wings, female paler rufous affording greater contrast with olivaceous wings and tail

Habits Forages, usually in pairs, often at army ant swarms, where several pairs may occur together, hopping about. Secretive, but bolder at ant swarms. Occasionally zaps tail downwards or rattles it as it sings.
Status Uncommon to fairly common locally.
Habitat Tropical Zone, in humid and mature second-growth forest; low-level tangles at borders and overgrown clearings and dense vines in subcanopy, by streams through thick undergrowth.
Voice Male sings series of 7–9 ringing, quivering, accelerating *cheeep* notes. Rattles and *skeep* calls (H&B, R&T).

SILVERED ANTBIRD
Sclateria naevia Pl. 167

Identification 15cm. Adult male slate grey above with small white tips to wing-coverts, throat white, breast white with broad grey fringes to elongated feathers giving very streaked appearance, darker on flanks and undertail-coverts; eyes grey or sometimes brown, long bill black, legs and feet pale horn. Female olive-brown above with pale cinnamon spots on wings, below white, with breast feathers fringed brown, lending same streaked appearance of male. Immature male female-like but has grey on sides of head, body and flanks, whilst juvenile is a duller version of female, but larger pale spots on wings. Grey eyes at all ages. In Yapacana National Park, on south bank of río Ventuari, Amazonas state, male of race *argentata* could easily be confused with male Yapacana Antbird which is smaller with a shorter bill and lacks distinct scalloping on sides.

Ssp. *S. n. argentata* (E Ec, SE Co, S Ve: W & S Amazonas) like *naevia* above, but all white below with only vestigial grey and streaking on sides and flanks, legs and feet flesh; female uniform slightly rufescent olive above, with small cinnamon dots on wings, bright olive on sides of neck, body and flanks, paler on undertail-coverts; immature male like female but has grey on body-sides and undertail-coverts; juvenile male duller, more flushed with olive and some white streaking on breast-sides and belly, undertail-coverts greyish-olive
S. n. diaphora (SC Ve: NW Bolívar) duller slate above with duller, barely discernible spots on wings, almost entirely grey below with whitish streaks on throat and breast, far more restricted than on *naevia*, legs and feet yellowish-grey; female warm olive-brown above with faint pale spots on wings, white throat, rest of underparts rufescent brown, with faint vestigial streaks on breast
S. n. naevia (E Ve, Tr, Guianas) as described

Habits Forages alone or in pairs, rarely hopping on muddy leaf-litter, more often very low through foliage right at water's edge, a habitat often shared with Black-chinned Antbird. Swings tail slowly either upwards or sideways.
Status Fairly common to common locally. Frequent in Guyana. Common in French Guiana.
Habitat Tropical Zone, in *várzea*, swampy forest or dense,

swampy riversides, always in undergrowth near water. Locally in mangrove.

Voice Song a series of 2 rising whistles that become long cheerful trills *weeea-tri-tr-tr'tr'tr'tr'tr'tr'tr'tr'a'a'* which grow louder and then softer till fading. Also, various chips and gurgling calls (Hilty).

Note Race *diaphora* reported to represent cline between *argentata* and *naevia* and requires further investigation (Z&I), but specimens in Phelps Collection do meet characteristics one would expect of an intermediate (see plate and description).

BLACK-HEADED ANTBIRD

Percnostola rufifrons Pl. 166

Identification 14–15cm. Two species proposed and partially accepted. Grounds for resisting split unclear and appear to contradict evidence. We present them as incipient species.

Amazonas Antbird Pl. 166

P. (*r.*) *minor* (SE Co, S Ve) Adult male slate grey, long black cap from forehead to nape has grey fringes to longer, rounded feathers of crown giving scaled effect, wing-coverts black with white fringes forming 2 clear albeit narrow wingbars and possibly a third on lesser coverts. Tail slightly shorter than *rufifrons*. Chin to throat has full black bib; eyes pale grey. Female greyish olive-brown above, dark brown wings and tail with bright rufous tips to coverts forming 2 pale bars, head dark rufescent, brown or slightly greyish ear-coverts, rufous below, becoming paler on belly and flanks, washed olivaceous on vent and undertail-coverts. Immature male like female above but has median coverts dusky with narrow buffy fringes; below patchy, somewhat mottled greyish-tawny.

Black-headed Antbird Pl. 166

P. (*r.*) *rufifrons* (E & S Guianas) Adult male slate grey, long black cap from forehead to nape, wing-coverts black with white fringes forming 2 clear albeit narrow wingbars and possibly a third on lesser coverts. Tail slightly fuller and longer than *minor*. Chin to throat has black bib; eyes clear red. Female olive-brown above, dark brown wings and tail, with bright rufous tips to coverts forming 2+ bars, head bright rufous including eyebrow, but has long black cap exactly like male; bright rufous below, washed lightly olivaceous on flanks, vent and undertail-coverts.

Habits Forage singly or in pairs, from ground to lower mid levels, and regularly at ant swarms. Pick insects from ground, foliage and branches. Not shy, observed tossing leaves, dashing towards prey and jumping onto perch. Regularly pumps tail down then raises it slowly.

Status Frequent in Colombia, Venezuela and widespread in Guyana. In Suriname, frequent in savanna forests and very common in interior. Common in French Guiana.

Habitat Tropical Zone. Humid *terra firme* and mature second-growth forests, especially white-sand forests. Also savanna forest and mangrove in coastal regions of Suriname and French Guiana, dense undergrowth and borders, overgrown clearings and treefalls.

Voice Race *rufifrons* in Suriname sings rapid succession of 5–6 identical high notes, among most frequent songs in forest (H&M). Race *minor* in Colombia gives loud, whistled *pa, peer-peer-peer-peer-peer-pear-pear*, slightly dropping in pitch at end (H&B). Sings a short, countable series (e.g. 8 notes in 2.3 s) of strident downslurred whistles at even pitch that become slightly longer as song decelerates (neither race nor location given) (Z&I).

Notes Capparella *et al.* (1997) described race *jensoni* (Brazil) and, in revising species complex, proposed that *minor* with *jensoni* be treated as a separate species, Amazonas Antbird (song of *jensoni* is distinctly faster than *rufifrons*). This was followed by Dickinson (2003) and Rodner *et al.* (2000), but not by Isler *et al.* (2001) or Hilty, who considered *minor* to be too similar in plumage and voice to *rufifrons* to merit separation, but did not offer any Venezuelan or Guianan vocalisations, and ignored significant differences in female plumages. Z&I suggested to await evidence from field studies in possible contact zone, if there is one, as well as molecular research in order to determine extent to which they are isolated and possibly genetically distinct.

Genus *Schistocichla* (Zimmer 1931, Phelps & Phelps 1950) was subsumed within *Percnostola* (Meyer de Schauensee 1966), but resuscitated by R&T, followed by R&G, Hilty and Dickinson (2003). They differ from *Percnostola* antbirds by having rounder heads and no long crest feathers; tips of wing-coverts have spots, not fringes. They are inconspicuous birds that frequent undergrowth of *terra firme* forests.

SLATE-COLOURED ANTBIRD

Schistocichla schistacea Pl. 166

Identification 14.5cm. Adult male uniform slate grey, with wings slightly darker and white tips to coverts; eyes dark brown, bill blackish, legs and feet dark grey. Adult female dark olive above, dark rufous-chestnut on head-sides, including eyebrow, and underparts, bill slightly horn-coloured below. Spot-winged is paler below and darker above in both sexes.

Ssp. Monotypic (extreme SE Co, Leticia area)

Habits Forages alone or in pairs and sometimes in small groups, on or near ground. Seldom joins mixed-species flocks. Hops on ground and onto low perch, then down again, stopping regularly to look up and around, at which point it flicks its tail up then lowers it slowly.

Status Rare to locally common.

Habitat Lower Tropical Zone, to 400m, in undergrowth of humid *terra firme*, near water and in swampy areas.

Voice Musical series of loud, unhurried notes: *teuw, teuw, teuw, teuw, teep, teep...* (R&T), a short, countable series (e.g. 6 notes in 2.5 s) in which notes become more intense and rise slightly in pitch, but shorten throughout, whilst intervals remain constant. Calls include unclear *tchick* notes in pairs, or in a short (e.g. 1.2 s) twittering series; also a long (0.5 s) downslurred whistle (Z&I).

SPOT-WINGED ANTBIRD

Schistocichla leucostigma Pl. 166

Identification 15cm. Male dark slate grey above, paler slate below, with darker wings that have white spots on tips of coverts; bill blackish above, pale on base of lower mandible. Female dark rufescent brown above, darker on wings and tail with pale rufous tips to coverts, brighter rufous on neck-sides and underparts. Juvenile appears to resemble female, but male becomes grey below (paler than adult male), with whitish throat and pale grey barring on belly, flanks and undertail-coverts, and upperparts as adult female. Three subspecies all very similar above, only differing in size and shape of terminal spots on wing-coverts, and shade below. Male Roraiman Antbird is much darker below.

Ssp. *S. l. infuscata* (Ve: S Amazonas, E Co) male has triangular-shaped terminal spots on coverts, and is pale grey below; female bright rufous below, with medium-sized cinnamon triangles on coverts

S. l. leucostigma (S Ve, Guianas) as described, palest grey below and has round white spots on coverts, grey eyes, dark bill paler at base, legs and feet pink

S. l. subplumbea (SW Ve, E Co, E Ec) darker and more evenly coloured, less contrast between upper- and underparts, white dots on wings much smaller and duller, eyes dark brown, legs and feet pale bluish-grey; female has smaller wing spots and is more uniformly deep rufous below, darker on vent to undertail-coverts

Habits Seldom found at ant swarms. Hops about, flicking tail upwards and sometimes perching horizontally on vertical twigs.

Status Locally common to uncommon.

Habitat Tropical Zone, to 700m, though usually much lower. Humid *terra firme*, particularly in white-sand forests; low foliage in damp spots, wet treefall gaps and slow-flowing streams in level terrain.

Voice Bubbling rattles, soft rising trills and *chip-pip* calls (Hilty). Alarm-call a loud chatter (H&M). Song a rapid trill (*leucostigma*, 40 notes in 4.5 s,) accelerating at start but slows then holds steady. Long calls not preceded by a high note.

RORAIMAN ANTBIRD

Schistocichla saturata Pl. 166

Identification 15cm. Male uniform dark slate grey, eyes dark brown, bill entirely blackish, legs and feet dark bluish-grey. Female dark chocolate-brown above, deep but bright ferruginous below. Both sexes of Spot-winged Antbird are paler below, and female is chocolate above and bright ferruginous below.

Ssp. *S. s. saturata* (Roraima: SE Ve, CW Gu) adult male blackish slate above and below, with black wings and clean white tips to coverts, female has throat and breast chestnut

S. s. obscura (SE Ve: 120–240km N of Roraima) male slightly blacker, female slightly darker

Status Locally fairly common.

Habitat Upper Tropical to Subtropical Zones, usually above 1,000m, though occurs to 700m on Roraima and as low as 250m on Sierra de Lema. Within low foliage in damp places, e.g. beside fast-flowing montane streams.

Voice Song a fast trill, both races producing 19 notes in 2.8 s, accelerating throughout and dropping sharply in pitch at end. The long calls of both races are typically preceded by an abrupt, higher pitched note (absent in *leucostigma*).

Note Race *saturata*, which was formerly treated as a race of *S. leucostigma*, was considered a separate species by Braun *et al.* (2005), based on morphological, vocal and genetic data. However, race *obscura* was not subjected to same DNA analysis, but comparative data on plumage, behaviour, habitat and distribution imply very strongly that it is much closer to *saturata* then *leucostigma*.

CAURA ANTBIRD

Schistocichla caurensis Pl. 166

Identification 17.5cm. Adult male slate grey with sooty tone above, wing-coverts blackish with white subterminal spots, eyes red, bill black, legs and feet grey. Female deep rufescent olive above, greyish on head, with rufous tips to coverts, deep rufous below, browner on flanks and undertail-coverts; eyes dark brown. Juvenile and immature lack pure coloration, but are virtually indistinguishable from adults. In hand they are browner, with browner underwing-coverts and pale grey fringes to belly. Differences in races subtle, and only visible in old adults. Rather similar to Spot-winged and Roraiman Antbirds but significantly larger, and different habitat.

Ssp. *S. c. australis* (Ve: NW & SE Amazonas) male a colder charcoal colour above

S. c. caurensis (Ve: N Bolívar) male slightly greyer

Status Few data, but apparently somewhat common locally.

Habitat Tropical Zone, 100–1,350m but more often at 350–700m. Dense, humid forests with tall trees on slopes of tepuis and other hills, with fairly open understorey of bamboo and abundant large boulders covered with mosses, bromeliads and ferns (Z&I).

Voice Loudsong a short series (e.g. 11 notes in 4 s) of short, buzzy notes, initially flat, then dropping in pitch as intervals between notes shorten; female similar but notes fewer and often begins as male finishes (Z&I).

Myrmeciza antbirds comprise a rather confusing, polyphyletic group that may well shake down into several distinct genera. They vary in size and patterns, with several black taxa and many with bright rufous and chestnut. Several have red eyes. Wings vary from plain to a variety of spots and dots.

STUB-TAILED ANTBIRD

Myrmeciza berlepschi Pl. 168

Identification 13.2cm. Adult male sooty black, with white interscapular patch, tiny pale tips to wing-coverts, stubby tail; dark red eyes, large black bill and grey legs and feet. Adult female very similar but dots on wings larger and whiter, with short white streaks on chin to belly that start as narrow arrowheads but widen gradually to become fringes. Male Esmeraldas Antbird is obviously grey and black, with clear white wing spots, and found at higher elevations; all other similar black antbirds are east of Andes.

Ssp. Monotypic (SW Co, NW Ec)

Habits Neither shy nor skulking. Characteristically pumps tail up and down.
Status Locally common.
Habitat Tropical Zone to *c.*500m but usually lower. Wet forests in lowlands and lower foothills.
Voice Song a rising series of *c.*8 downslurred *peer* notes that first drop then rise in pitch, also rendered *chi-chu-chu-chu-chew-chéw-chéw-chéw* (R&G); also a high, sharp rattle, *tr'rt'rt'it* (H&B).
Notes Formerly placed in genus *Sipia* (Robbins & Ridgely 1993).

ESMERALDAS ANTBIRD
Myrmeciza nigricauda Pl. 169

Identification 13-13.5cm. Adult male slate grey with white interscapular patch, black wing-coverts with white tips; bright red eyes, fine black bill and grey legs and feet. Female dark reddish-brown from back to tail, and flanks and belly to undertail-coverts, entire head and breast slate grey with rows of small white marks on blackish throat. Male Stub-tailed Antbird is uniform sooty and lacks visible spots on wings; also at lower elevations.

Ssp. Monotypic (SW Co, NW Ec)

Habits Forages alone, in pairs or family groups, hopping on vertical stems of low foliage (seldom on ground) and searching for food deliberately. Occasionally attends ant swarms. Habitually pumps tail downwards.
Status Uncommon and local.
Habitat Tropical Zone, at 500–1,100m. Dense and very humid or wet primary and mature second-growth forest on steep slopes, especially in overgrown ravines and clearings caused by treefalls or landslides.
Voice Rattles and *chip* calls. Sings occasionally 6+ very high-pitched but not very far-carrying notes, *psee-pseé-psi-psi-psi-pseé*, usually with second and always with last note higher pitched and emphasised. Female sometimes gives shorter version; both sexes give a sharp, but nasal and falling *skweeyr* or *sk-kweeyr* (R&G).
Notes Formerly placed in genus *Sipia* (Robbins & Ridgely 1991).

WHITE-BELLIED ANTBIRD
Myrmeciza longipes Pl. 168

Identification 14.5–15cm. Adult male bright rufous-chestnut above, with a vestigial grey eyebrow that widens around ear-coverts and narrows on breast-sides to become buffy on flanks and undertail-coverts, lores, cheeks, ear-coverts and breast black, belly white; eyes reddish-brown, bill long, straight and black, legs and feet flesh. Female similar above, but has weak subterminal blackish spots on wing-coverts; lacks black face being somewhat grizzled sooty, grey and cinnamon on head-sides, grey eyebrow continues around ear-coverts but not lower, throat whitish, breast cinnamon, flushed cinnamon on sides and flanks to undertail-coverts, belly white. Juvenile like female but has weaker to vestigial black spots on wings, and males start to show black on throat. Ferruginous-backed Antbird has orange-cinnamon underparts. Bright chestnut above and white belly should separate this species from all others.

Ssp. *M. l. boucardi* (C Co: Upper Magdalena Valley) top of head to nape and breast on male grey, also in female but flushed rufous, and easy to separate from *panamensis*, which has rufous on head
M. l. griseipectus (SE Co: E of Andes, S & E Ve, Gu) top of head darker and slightly greyish, blackish subterminal spots on wing-coverts, face black as *longipes*, but grades into dark grey breast that washes onto sides and belly
M. l. longipes (extreme NE Co, N Ve, Tr) as described
M. l. panamensis (N Co) male has black of breast like *longipes*, with extension of grey on flanks and belly like *griseipectus*, and female has more sooty on face-sides, but above is brighter, paler rufous and has no spots on wings

Habits Forages alone or in pairs, hopping on ground or through low foliage. Follows ant swarms occasionally. Shy. Has been observed eating ants. Lowers tail.
Status Fairly common to locally common.
Habitat Tropical to Lower Subtropical Zones, to 1,750m in Colombia (*boucardi*) and 1,300m in Venezuela. Dry to slightly humid deciduous and semi-deciduous forests and second growth; in dense undergrowth and tangled borders.
Voice Song a loud ringing crescendo of 15–25 rapid *jeer* notes, falling, trailing off and ending with a few *cherr* notes on same pitch (H&B). Alarm a single downslurred *jeeeeeer* (Hilty). Song of *longipes* a long (e.g. 4 s) ringing trill that decelerates, and decreases in pitch and intensity (Z&I); apparently song varies slightly by race.

CHESTNUT-BACKED ANTBIRD
Myrmeciza exsul Pl. 168

Identification 13cm. Adult male deep chestnut above, wings darker (with white tips to coverts in some races), slate grey head and breast, dark chestnut belly to undertail-coverts; eye surrounded by pale blue skin, irides brown, bill black, legs and feet grey. Adult female like male above, head slate grey, underparts chestnut. Juvenile like female but has head all brown, concolorous with back. Female Esmeraldas Antbird has red eyes, and Chestnut-backed Antbird has distinct blue skin around brown eyes.

Ssp. *M. e. cassini* (N Co) brighter rufous than others, particularly on back, white spots on wing-coverts bold and clear

M. e. maculifer (W Co, W Ec) darker chestnut above, small white spots on wings, darker grey on head and breast; female has small, pale buffy spots on wings

M. e. niglarus (extreme NW Co) intermediate chestnut, but generally like *maculifer*, and wings uniform brown without spots

Habits Forages alone or in pairs, at low levels and occasionally at ant swarms. Hops on vertical perches, looking attentively for insects in foliage. Seems very shy, but occurs in open understorey as well as dense undergrowth. Likes tangled and vine-strewn areas on sides of ravines near streams and treefall gaps. Lowers tail slowly, but faster when alarmed.
Status Fairly common to locally common.
Habitat Tropical Zone to *c.*900m but occasionally to 1,200m. Humid and wet primary and sometimes mature secondary forests.
Voice Song easily recognised and easily imitated, 2–3 slightly downslurred whistles, *peh, peeea* or *peh, peh, peeéa* (paraphrased as 'come…here' or 'come…right…here'), intervals between notes typically longer than notes, final note longest and lower pitched (Z&I). A soft nasal churring, *kreeuyr*, and sharp, fast, *whit-it* (R&G). Loud and strong whistles: *cheap, cheap, cheer.* Also, rattles, nasal cries and *quit-it* calls (H&B).

FERRUGINOUS-BACKED ANTBIRD
Myrmeciza ferruginea Pl. 168

Identification 15cm. Adult male bright ferruginous chestnut above, wings and tail darker, wing-coverts black with pale buff tips that form clear dotted bars, full deep black mask from supraloral in a narrow line, broadening behind eyes onto face, throat and central breast, with a white line bordering it from just behind eyes, across neck-sides, and dividing breast from belly, underparts rich bright rufous; skin around eyes blue, eyes dark brown, bill blackish above, grey below, legs and feet grey.

Ssp. *M. f. ferruginea* (Ve, Guianas)

Habits Forages in pairs, hopping or walking on ground and lowering tail deliberately. Runs about like small rail, hopping onto fallen logs and low branches, seldom more than 1m above ground. Does not join mixed flocks.
Status Common throughout.
Habitat Tropical Zone. Humid *terra firme* and stunted, sandy-soil forests; brushy savannas, edges.
Voice Male sings a rather fast-paced and loud, *weehee-weehee-weehee-weehee-weehee*, with variations but always same pattern (R&T), or a high double note, repeated 5 times, slightly descending at end, *sééye-sééye-sééye-sééye-sééye*, or a high tinkling series of rhythmic couplets, typically, *ti-WHEEty, WHEEty, WHEEty, WHEEty, whee*, falling slightly in pitch, often faster when excited; occasionally a rapid *te-de'de'de'de'de-de*, like an accelerated main song with rhythm lost. Recalls Spot-backed Antbird. Alarm-call a loud chattering (H&M) or a dry, thin rattle, like several other *Myrmeciza* but higher pitched (Hilty).

DULL-MANTLED ANTBIRD
Myrmeciza laemosticta Pl. 168

Identification 14cm. Adult male dark brown above, with some black patches on back and largely concealed interscapular patch, median wing-coverts distal half black with clear white tips, entire head and underparts to belly dark grey, black on throat and breast, flanks and vent to undertail-coverts rufescent brown; eyes red, bill long and black, legs and feet grey. Female similar but white spots on wings less bold, grey of head and breast perhaps not quite as dark, chin and throat checkered white. May be confused with Chestnut-backed Antbird, which has blue skin around brown eyes, also, race *niglarus* in north-west Colombia has no white spots in wings, race *cassini*, further east is much brighter rufous, in neither do females have checkered throat.

Ssp. *M. l. palliata* (Co, W Ve?) as described

M. l. venezuelae (NW Ve) black on male restricted to chin, median wing-coverts terminal third dusky with white terminal spots. Female throat has inverted Y spots not the squarish ones on female *palliata*.

Habits Forages in pairs, flitting through lowest tiers but seldom on ground, often perching on vertical twigs and occasionally visiting ant swarms. Lowers tail slowly.
Status Uncommon and local.
Habitat Tropical Zone to 1,100m. Dense and very humid or wet forests on steep slopes, especially in densely overgrown ravines and along streams.
Voice Song different to rest of genus but similar to closely related Esmeraldas Antbird, *c.*6 measured, high, thin notes, *eek, eek, zeet, zeet, eek, eek*, first 2 very high, next 2 slightly lower and last 2 extremely high (H&B). Song a series of short notes (e.g. 8 notes in 1.8 s), begins with 3 upslurred or flat notes and abruptly switches to 5 even-paced downslurred notes; female's song has first 3 notes longer and raspier than male, followed by 2 or 4 abrupt terminal notes (Z&I).
Notes Races *bolivari* and *venezuelae* synonymised under *palliata* (Robbins & Ridgely 1991), but Hilty pointed out that Venezuelan birds are paler and differ in other minor ways. We find very little difference between *bolivari* and *venezuelae* but a significant difference between the latter and *palliata*.

YAPACANA ANTBIRD
Myrmeciza disjuncta Pl. 169

Identification 13.5cm. Adult male blackish-grey above, with vestigial white eyebrow and irregular gradations on head-sides, large white but largely concealed interscapular patch, wings slightly darker with small white tips to coverts; underparts white, washed pastel grey on sides to flanks. Female similar above, but buff wing spots less bold, underparts warm ochraceous, slightly paler on throat and warmer on breast. Juvenile indistinguishable. Male could be confused with male Silvered Antbird, which is larger, has a distinctly longer bill and clear grey scalloping on sides.

Ssp. Monotypic (Ve: Cerro Yapacana)

Habits Forages in pairs at lower levels.

Status Very restricted range, but locally common.
Habitat Tropical Zone, to 100m. Restricted to humid white-sand forests of upper Orinoco–Casiquiare–Negro basins. Undergrowth and scrub, dense, seasonally flooded, scrubby savanna woodland with bamboo, dense mats of sawgrass and other impenetrable and spiny vegetation at Yapacana National Park, on south bank of río Ventuari (Hilty).
Voice Song of male rather loud, a buzzy *kzzzzzzzzzZZZZZZ, ki-ki-kzzzzip*, which may be repeated severally. Female song similar but usually a shorter single buzz, i.e. *kzzzzZZZZ* (K. J. Zimmer in Hilty). Song, 2 prolonged (0.8–1.5 s) harsh, frequency-modulated elements separated by a short pause with 1–2 abrupt *pip* notes, first harsh element longer and rising in pitch and intensity, second more even; occasionally 3 harsh elements (Z&I).

GREY-BELLIED ANTBIRD
Myrmeciza pelzelni Pl. 169

Identification 13cm. Very distinctive antbird, despite being apparently drab. Adult male reddish-brown above, darker on wings and tail, with wing-coverts darkest, scapulars spotted pale buffy, wing-coverts and tertials have large white spots, head-sides grey, merging into black chin and breast, with white spots on face- to breast-sides, flanks to undertail-coverts brown, belly grey; eyes dark brown, bill black, legs and feet grey. Female similar above, throat white, bar of dark grey from face-sides across upper breast, spotted white, underparts white, washed brownish on sides and flanks to undertail-coverts, belly greyish.

Ssp. Monotypic (Co & Ve: Amazonas)

Habits Very territorial and pairs noisily defend their area. They walk steadily across leaf-litter and moss-covered stems and branches of fairly open evergreen forest floor, and also densely wooded sandy soil forest floor thick with terrestrial bromeliads.
Status Uncommon to locally fairly common.
Habitat Tropical Zone, to 200m, in humid, predominantly white-sand forests of upper río Negro basin.
Voice Song *c.*12–15 high, shrill, slightly buzzy and penetrating whistles, *shree, shree, shree, shree… shrEE, shREE, SHREE*, series growing louder and more insistent, and increasing slightly in pitch at end; each song lasts 4–4.5 s, with a 5-s pause. In agonistic response or alarm, both sexes give a low, rubber-lipped rattle that is almost spat out (K. J. Zimmer recording in Hilty).

NORTHERN CHESTNUT-TAILED ANTBIRD *Myrmeciza castanea* Pl. 169

Identification 13cm. Adult male ruddy brown above with partially concealed white interscapular patch, wing-coverts blackish, buffy-white tips to lesser and median coverts, greater coverts have rufous-buffy tips. Head and breast grey, darker on crown with blackish centres to, becoming brownish on nape, grey sides merge into paler grey flanks, white belly and rufous undertail-coverts. Eyes dark brown, bill black, legs and feet grey. Female similar if slightly paler above but rufescent from chin to breast, washed olive to rufous on flanks and undertail-coverts, belly white.

Ssp. *M. c. centunculorum* (extreme S Co, E Ec) more even grey on head, extensive white belly and paler undertail-coverts; female generally paler
M. c. castanea (SE Ec) as described

Habits Forages singly or in pairs, hopping on or near ground, always within dense undergrowth. Very rarely with mixed flocks or at ant swarms. Lowers tail slowly.
Status Uncommon to fairly common locally.
Habitat Tropical Zone, *centunculorum* to 350m in Ecuador and 400m in Colombia, *castanea* to *c.*1,500 in SE Ecuador. Humid primary and mature second-growth forest in foothills, also in overgrown semi-dry savannas.
Voice Ascending and only slightly accelerating series of clear, rather high-pitched notes, e.g. *teeeee-teee-tee-te-tit* (P. Coopmans in R&G). Loudsong a series (e.g. 7 notes in 1.4s) of long sharp whistles that dramatically shorten while rising in pitch, abrupt final note drops in pitch (Z&I).

PLUMBEOUS ANTBIRD
Myrmeciza hyperythra Pl. 169

Identification 18cm. Adult male deep slate grey, darker on wing-coverts with small white tips; blue skin surrounding eye, trailing back to point; eyes brown, bill black, legs and feet grey. Female like male above, bright rufous below, with olivaceous vent to undertail-coverts. Combination of blue skin around eyes and white spots on wings ensures identification.

Ssp. Monotypic (NE Ec, SE Co)

Habits Forages in pairs, searching deliberately around stems and leaves from low tiers to subcanopy. Rarely at ant swarms. Equally likely to perch upright on horizontal or vertical stems. Moves tail downwards. Not timid.
Status Fairly common to locally numerous.
Habitat Tropical Zone, to 300m in Ecuador and 500m in Colombia, in *várzea*, densely overgrown clearings or advancing second growth; shares drier parts of habitat and edges of *várzea* with White-shouldered Antwren.
Voice Loud song a fast rattling *wo-wu-wh-wr'wr'wr'wr'wr'wr'wr' wr'wr*, an accelerating *whir dudududududu dudududu…* slowing and fading at end, a *wut* in alarm, and repeatedly repeated *puok-bubu* (H&B). A slightly rising series of very fast notes that accelerate into a rattle, *wo-wu-wu-wu-wu-wu-wu-wrrrrrrrrrr* (R&G).

WHITE-SHOULDERED ANTBIRD
Myrmeciza melanoceps Pl. 168

Identification 18cm. Adult male all black, with solid white patch under uppermost scapulars that is partially hidden; skin around eyes dull blue, appearing grey, eyes red, bill long and black, legs and feet dark grey. Female distinctive with entire body rufous, richer above and slightly darker and browner on wings and tail, brighter more orange-cinnamon below; entire head black. Cocha Antshrike very similar in both sexes, but has white underwing-coverts, is smaller and lacks blue skin around eyes; it is usually found in thickets along small black-water streams.

Ssp. Monotypic (SE Co, E Ec)

Habits Forages singly, in pairs or in small groups, hopping within dense low to high mid-level foliage, peering for insects on twigs and leaves, and moving tail downwards. May attend army ants swarms occasionally, or join mixed flocks. Sings often.
Status Fairly common.
Habitat Lower Tropical Zone, in semi-dry to humid *terra firme* and *várzea*; often along streams. May be found with Plumbeous Antbird.
Voice Loud penetrating series of whistles (e.g. 7 notes in 2.1 s), readily recognised: begins with 2 soft notes: *sit-up pe-ter, pe-ter, pe-ter, pe-ter, pe-ter* (C. Rodner), *sit-up peter, peter, peter, peter, peter* (H&B), *pur, peeur-peeur-peeur-peeur* (R&T, R&G), or 2 soft notes, first longer than second, followed by mostly flat notes that become more intense and lengthen slightly (Z&I). In alarm an abrupt *cheedo-cheeo-cheeo-cheeo-cheeyo* (R&T, R&G).

SOOTY ANTBIRD *Myrmeciza fortis* Pl. 169

Identification 18.3cm. Male entirely sooty, somewhat dusky but blacker on head, with a concealed white line on lesser coverts; skin around eyes blue, reaching to point behind eyes, eyes red. Female dark reddish-olive, richer on head, greyish on sides of head and breast. Male White-shouldered Antbird is black, and has small white patch at shoulder, but both characters not easy to see. Plumbeous has white dots on wings. Immaculate Antbird is other side of Andes.

Ssp. *M. f. fortis* (E Ec, SE Co)

Habits Habitual ant swarm follower that forages in pairs or small groups. Perches in dense cover at low to lower mid levels and drops to ground to quickly snap up an insect and then dash back to cover. Lowers tail slowly.
Status Uncommon, but fairly common locally.
Habitat Tropical Zone, to *c.*600m, in humid primary and mature second-growth *terra firme*, but more on drier, higher slopes and ridges away from streams. Shares more humid parts of habitat with White-shouldered Antbird.
Voice A loud penetrating *teeuw-teeuw-teeuw-teeuw-teeuw-teeuw-teeuw-teeuw-teeuw*, slightly ascending and lasting *c.*2–4 s (R&G). Like White-shouldered but faster and beginning notes slightly rising, *pi-peer, peer-peer-peer-peer-peer* (T. A. Parker in H&B). Series of similar, resonant, slightly downslurred whistles (e.g. 11 notes in 2.8 s) on same pitch, first note less intense, and notes shortening slightly (Z&I).

IMMACULATE ANTBIRD
Myrmeciza immaculata Pl. 169

Identification 18cm. Male all black, with concealed white line at wing bend, skin around eye blue, eyes red. Female deep ruddy brown, richer on head and neck, dusky on face and tail. No confusion species on Pacific slope, to east virtually no overlap with other large black, red-eyed antbirds, and is at higher elevations. Three races differ only in female plumage.

Ssp. *M. i. macrorhyncha* (W Co, W Ec) brighter brown
M. i. brunnea (Co & Ve: Perijá) duller brown above, underparts more olivaceous
M. i. immaculata (C & E Co, W Ve) as described

Habits Forages in pairs or small family groups, hopping in dense low foliage, searching deliberately around stems and leaves, frequently perching sideways on vertical twigs and moving tail downwards. Regularly found at ant swarms.
Status Fairly common to uncommon.
Habitat Tropical Zone, to 1,500m in west, 400–2,000m on eastern slope, in very humid primary and mature second-growth foothill forests, especially in dense undergrowth in ravines or borders.
Voice In Ecuador (*macrorhyncha*), gives a rapid, loud-ringing and slightly descending series of clear whistles, *peer-peer-peer-peer-peer-peer-peer-peer*, slowing slightly at end (R&G), apparently delivered at faster rate than other races (Z&I). A rapid but decelerating series of *peep* whistles and loud *chirk* calls (H&B, Hilty).
Notes Name *macrorhyncha* is a new name for *berlepschi*, the latter being no longer valid (Robbins & Ridgely 1993).

GREY-HEADED ANTBIRD
Myrmeciza griseiceps Pl. 169

Identification 13.5–14cm. Adult male olive-brown with all-grey head and blackish breast, wings and tail dark brown with blackish wing-coverts tipped white, and white tips to tail, head darker grey with narrow pale eye-ring, paler at sides, fading to whitish on belly, olive on flanks and undertail-coverts; eyes dark brown, bill black, legs and feet grey. Female paler throughout with buffy spots on wings, no black on breast (flammulated grey and white). No confusion species in its small range.

Ssp. Monotypic (extreme SW Ec)

Habits Forages inconspicuously, alone or in pairs, at mid levels and seldom on ground. Habitually moves its tail slowly downwards whilst spread, revealing white spots. Regularly in mixed flocks (with Line-cheeked Spinetail, Grey-breasted Wood-wren, Rufous-naped Brush-finch and others).
Status Rare to locally uncommon. Apparently not a bamboo obligate, but in Ecuador, where seems to have suffered from habitat destruction, doing well in bamboo-dominated second growth in abandoned pastures and deforested areas (R&G, Z&I).
Habitat Tropical and Subtropical Zones, at 600–2,500m, in humid primary and second-growth forests with stands of *Chusquea* bamboo and dense undergrowth.
Voice Regularly gives a nasal, querulous, *squee-squirt?*, repeated every few seconds, sometimes only *squeey*? (R&T). Song a short clearly descending trill, *trrrrrrrrr* (R&G). Presumed loudsong a moderate length (e.g. 0.8 s) rattle dropping in pitch and intensity, typically starts with a single lower note; female similar but often with a brief break (Z&I).

BLACK-THROATED ANTBIRD
Myrmeciza atrothorax Pl. 169

Identification 14cm. Adult male dark brown on back with partially concealed white interscapular patch, brown top of head, wings also brown, wing-coverts darker, each with a subterminal black spot and triangular white tip, rump to tail sooty; lores, cheeks, ear-coverts, sides to flanks and belly dark grey, chin, throat, breast and undertail-coverts black; eyes dark brown, bill black and legs and feet flesh to pale grey. Female similar above, albeit slightly warmer, with white throat, rufous to sides and belly, olivaceous on flanks and dull black undertail-coverts. Juvenile resembles slightly paler female, but young male has mix of black and grey feathers on throat, and grey flanks. Immature male like a dull adult with pale spots on wing-coverts and patchy black on throat and upper breast.

Ssp. *M. a. atrothorax* (SE Co, S Ve, Guianas) as described
M. a. metae (E Co) male has black feathers on sides and flanks fringed grey, female like *atrothorax*
M. a. tenebrosa (NE Ec) male much darker above, with wing-coverts black, and white spots on wings tiny, black below; female slightly darker and lacks pale spots on wings

Habits Forages in pairs or small family groups, low in undergrowth with tangles or dense foliage. Rarely attends ant swarms or joins mixed flocks. Hops about noisily on horizontal branches and lowers tail slowly.
Status Common to fairly common locally.
Habitat Tropical Zone, to 400m in Ecuador. Humid *terra firme*, *várzea*, forested savanna, early or advancing second growth and riparian woodland; always near water. In Suriname occurs in both old plantations and savanna forests of interior, and *Mauritia* swamps of Sipaliwini savanna.
Voice In Ecuador (*tenebrosa*) a fast, incisive and ascending series of sharp, high-pitched notes, *chee-ch-chee, chi-chi-chi-chí-chí* (like cheeping chicks), sometimes answered by female's more even-pitched song. A *cheeyt* call (R&G). In Venezuela and Colombia (presumably *atrothorax*), rather loud, high-pitched, forced *pe'pee-pee-pee-pee-pee-peep*, unmusical and slightly ascending at end (H&B, Hilty). A sharp noisy *PSEEyap!* when disturbed, also a *chip* and flat rattle, *chip-chip't't't't* (Hilty). In Suriname (also *atrothorax*), series of 5–6 high notes, of which last 3 ascend and are uttered slightly slower than first.

WHITE-PLUMED ANTBIRD
Pithys albifrons Pl. 170

Identification 12–13cm. Adult mid grey on back and wings, rest of body and tail rich rufous-chestnut, head black with white facial crest that fans out from forehead in a long bifurcation, and from sides of bill and chin. Eyes brown, bill black and legs and feet salmon-pink. Immature has entire head grey, concolorous with and joining back at nape, with no crest.

Ssp. *P. a. albifrons* (S Ve, Guianas) narrow white postocular line and black of head merges into grey of mantle
P. a. peruvianus (Co, Ve, Ec) as described

Habits Always at ant swarms (an obligate ant-follower), where often the most numerous species, catching insects fleeing from oncoming ants. Frantic and distrustful, its restlessness makes it difficult to see as it flits between vertical twigs, and it readily retreats to cover, where it churrs in alarm. Usually within 1m of ground, sallying to ground or low foliage, sometimes hopping after prey or snapping its bill characteristically.
Status Fairly common.
Habitat Tropical Zone, mostly below 500–600m, but to 1,100m in Ecuador and 1,350m in Venezuela. Lower levels of humid *terra firme* and mature second-growth forests.
Voice Very vocal when foraging. Loud alarm-call a sharp *STIK!-STIK!,* of 1–3 notes. Utters a thin, descending and listless-sounding *tseeee* or *seeeeea* (R&T, R&G, Hilty).
Note Race *brevibarba* described on basis of shorter plumes considered to fall within range of *peruvianus* by R&G and was synonymised by Z&I.

[WHITE-MASKED ANTBIRD
Pithys castaneus] Pl. 170

Identification 14cm. Entirely rich rufous-chestnut, except white lores, eyebrow, eye-ring and connecting line to chin and upper throat, contrasting with black forehead to rear crown and behind ear-coverts to throat-sides. White-plumed Antbird has grey back and wings.

Ssp. Monotypic (NE Peru)

Habits Always at ant swarms, usually in vanguard of attendant antbirds.
Status Hypothetical for Ecuador. Recorded north of río Marañón, but not into Ecuador (one sighting unconfirmed), though seems possible there, thus included here.
Habitat Tropical Zone. Lower levels of humid *terra firme* and mature second-growth forests on white sand soil.
Voice Song a long (e.g. 1.6 s) whistle, rising slightly in pitch and ending in a brief upslur. A short *chirr* and abrupt *chip-chip* notes (Z&I).

RUFOUS-THROATED ANTBIRD
Gymnopithys rufigula Pl. 170

Identification 15cm. Adult male olive-brown above with a white interscapular patch, paler and more ochraceous below, throat and head-sides tinged rich orange-rufous; large area of bare skin around eyes is very pale blue, eyes brown, bill blackish above, paler below, legs and feet flesh. Female similar but has interscapular patch pale cinnamon; juvenile darker below, almost concolorous with back and paler on throat, lacking orange-rufous.

Ssp. *G. r. pallidus* (S Ve) as *pallidigula*, but also paler olive-brown above
G. r. pallidigula (S Ve) paler below, being rather ochraceous on centre of breast and belly, female much paler, almost whitish from throat and on centre of breast to vent
G. r. rufigula (E Ve, Guianas) as described

Habits Obligate ant-follower, only at ant swarms unless in non-feeding transit or while breeding, when remains in territory and may be seen foraging away from ant swarms. Generally a few pairs, and often with a larger number of White-plumed Antbirds, attend a swarm. Suspicious and cautious of human presence. Partial to vertical stem perches, sallying to and from

them to ground or low bushes. *Gymnopithys* signature gestures include bill-snapping and lifting tail very slowly then zapping it back as if pulled by a spring.
Status Fairly common.
Habitat Tropical Zone, to *c.*900m, at lower levels of humid primary and mature second-growth *terra firme*.
Voice Series of soft *chirr* notes in mild alarm, and sharp staccato *stit-tit!* and *stit-it-it!* in high-intensity alarm. Loudsong a high, whinny-like series that quickly rises and falls, *we-whe-whee-HE-He-he'hu'we'we*, recalling Bicoloured Antbird (Hilty).

BICOLOURED ANTBIRD

Gymnopithys leucaspis Pl. 170

Identification 14.5cm. Races comprise 2 morphological groups, those with a broad grey streak from eyes to neck-sides, and those without. Essentially, this is basis for recognising 2 species, though this lacks sufficient substantiation for acceptance by AOU. We treat them thus:

Ssp. Bicoloured Antbird *bicolor* group (east of Andes): broad and widening grey postocular streak, skin around eyes striking pale blue, legs and feet plumbeous to bluish-grey.

G. l. aequatorialis (SW Co, W Ec) back and wings to tail dark chestnut-brown with contrasting rufous top of head, broad grey postocular streak, black cheeks and ear-coverts that develop as a broad black vertically line on sides, becoming deep brown on flanks and undertail-coverts, chin to belly white

G. l. bicolor (NW Co) chestnut above with top of head concolorous with back, line from neck-sides to flanks umber-brown

G. l. daguae (W Co) much darker brown above, top of head concolorous with back

G. l. ruficeps (C Co) top of head to nape bright rufous, back deep chestnut, narrow grey line around ear-coverts

White-cheeked Antbird *leucaspis* group (west of Andes): legs and feet rarely pink, skin around eyes dull blue-grey, females have a concealed cinnamon interscapular patch.

G. l. castaneus (E Ec) darker than *leucaspis*, top of head concolorous with back

G. l. leucaspis (E Co) chestnut above, brighter on top of head, cheeks and fore ear-coverts white

Habits In pairs, sometimes several pairs aggressive to each other, and always with other inveterate ant swarm followers – often bickering with Ocellated and Spotted Antbirds, though both subspecies groups have different suite of companion species. Sallies to and from vertical perches to ground or other branches, eager but wary. Snaps bill and lifts and zaps tail.
Status Uncommon to locally fairly common.
Habitat Tropical Zone, below 1,000m. Humid *terra firme* primary and mature second-growth forests.
Voice West of Andes (*leucaspis* group), a series (10 notes in 2.1 s) starting with long, slightly upslurred whistles that shorten rapidly and gain intensity, followed by shorter notes that drop in pitch and intensity before becoming harsh (Z&I). East of Andes (*bicolor* group), a series (20 notes in 3.7 s) commencing with upslurred even-pitched whistles that shorten into rather abrupt notes dropping in frequency and intensity, then lengthen and increase again, finally decreasing in intensity and becoming harsh (Z&I).
Notes Race *bicolor* (with *aequatorialis*, *daguae* and *ruficeps*) treated as a species separate from *leucaspis* (with *lateralis* and *castanea* White-cheeked Antbird) in H&B and SCJ&W. AOU (1998) and Z&I follow Hackett (1993); preliminary study suggests they are at least moderately differentiated genetically, but further molecular studies and analysis of vocalisations are required before taxonomic changes can be recommended (Z&I).

LUNULATED ANTBIRD

Gymnopithys lunulatus Pl. 170

Identification 14.5cm. Adult male bluish-grey with black lores and short line through eyes, vestigial white eyebrow, white chin and throat; eyes dark brown, bill black, legs and feet vinaceous-grey. Female ochraceous-olive with vestigial white eyebrow, white chin and throat, also, dark brown subterminal bars on lower back, wing-coverts and tertials, and fainter subterminal bars on sides and flanks, each feather with a pale rufescent buffy terminal bar; tail has pale spots on outer fringes of central rectrices and inner webs of all others. Juvenile resembles female, but lunules not as sharply defined, and lacks white in face and throat. The white throat is an excellent field mark.

Ssp. Monotypic (SE Ec)

Habits Always at ant swarms (almost certainly an obligate ant-follower). Usually a few individuals or pairs, not shy. Snaps bill and lifts and zaps tail.
Status Locally uncommon to rare.
Habitat Tropical Zone, mostly below 300m in Ecuador. Exclusively in *várzea*.
Voice Song a fast series of even-pitched notes, slowing into several consecutively lower pitched notes (R&G).

WING-BANDED ANTBIRD

Myrmornis torquata Pl. 167

Identification 15.5–16.5cm. Rotund, long-billed and short-legged ground-dweller that is easy to recognise, but not describe! Adult male soft brownish-grey above, feathers of back with broad chestnut fringes that afford strong scaled effect, several irregular black feathers, mostly in centre of mantle and lower back, wings black with buffy-rufous tertials and distal outer fringes of secondaries, coverts fringed broadly pale pinkish-buff, duller on lesser, brighter, forming 2 wingbars on median and greater coverts, outer fringes of central primaries buffy, forming longitudinal bar that joins bright tips of secondaries, rump and tail rufous (latter held cocked like an antthrush); chin, cheeks and throat black with postocular crescent that reaches onto sides, formed of black and white scallops that spread slightly on lower breast and belly, but extremely variable and less developed in younger birds, though still vary in adults; breast to vent soft grey, undertail-coverts rufous. Skin around eyes trails back to a point, blue-grey, eyes chestnut, bill black, legs and feet yellowish to pinkish-grey. Female similar but has deep rufous-orange throat and scalloping on breast is usually less strongly contrasting. Juvenile has top of head soft brownish-grey with dark grey fringes giving scaled effect, less black on back and chestnut fringes narrower (often vestigial), and may be some white flecking at edges of slightly smaller bib. Juvenile male has dull blackish bib, whilst that of female is paler and slightly duller rufous. Intermediate bird like adult but has pale striations to centres of feathers on head.

Ssp. *M. t. stictoptera* (N & NW Co) scalloping does not extend to sides and breast
M. t. torquata (SE Co, E Ec, S Ve, Gu, FG) as described

Habits Upturned tail may recall an antthrush, but hops whilst antthrushes walk. Forages quietly on ground or barely above it, in close pairs, tossing leaves energetically and searching leaf-litter. Unworried by human presence, but in alarm may fly up to perch a couple of metres above ground. Does not follow ant swarms.

Status Uncommon to rare. Apparently quite local. Widespread and not uncommon in Suriname. Widespread but always at low density in French Guiana.

Habitat Tropical Zone, to 400m in Ecuador, 900m in Colombia and 1,200m in Venezuela. Floor of tall humid forests.

Voice A faint, wooden insect-like trill, *wrrr* (Snyder 1966). More musical than most antbirds, a series of some 7 loud, whistles in an ascending crescendo, uttered from ground or low branch, with an uncanny resemblance to song of Bright-rumped Attila (H&M). Song mainly at dawn, a fairly loud series of 10–14 whistled and strongly inflected *préea* notes, each rising then falling sharply, evenly spaced, the series gradually rising and lasting up to 4 s. In alarm, a rough *churr*. Mostly vocal in rainy season (Hilty).

HAIRY-CRESTED ANTBIRD

Rhegmatorhina melanosticta Pl. 170

Identification 15cm. Adult male entirely olive-brown, with greyish tinge on underparts, top of head to nape greyish-buffy, the feathers having a hair-like texture, generally laid back but may be raised as a crest, black mask, including chin and throat, surrounds bright pale bluish-white ocular skin; eyes brown, bill black, legs and feet vinous-grey. Female distinguished by barred back and wings, formed by blackish subterminal bars and pale tips. Immature similarly barred but lacks pale crest of adult, being dark brown on crown, merging into back. Nothing quite like it in range.

Ssp. *R. m. melanosticta* (E Ec)

Habits An obligate ant-follower, alone or in pairs, foraging by sallying from vertical twigs and stems, snapping up fleeing insects on ground and in air. Raises crest aggressively at other antbirds, and flicks tail occasionally.

Status Uncommon to locally fairly common.

Habitat Tropical Zone, to 1,000m but more common below 700m. Humid *terra firme*, far from flooded areas and riverbanks. Always near ground.

Voice Nasal *wheeerrrs* and snarls. Song a rhythmic, descending series of whistles with a long, increasingly loud first note.

CHESTNUT-CRESTED ANTBIRD

Rhegmatorhina cristata Pl. 170

Identification 15cm. All brown, with a broad black mask and large bluish-white eye-ring of bare skin, wings and tail slightly darker, and female has dark scalloping on back. Feathers on top of head long, projecting slightly at rear, giving slightly right-angled look to back of head, but is seldom raised and is not prominent.

Ssp. Monotypic (E Co: Vaupés)

Habits Obligate ant-follower, always found attending swarming ants (or in transit, non-feeding). Regularly flicks tail upwards.

Status Uncommon.

Habitat Tropical Zone to 250m. Undergrowth of humid, sandy soil, stunted forests.

Voice Contact chips; soft, 3-whistle songs used mostly at ant swarms; also churrs. Song has structure typical of genus and closely related *Gymnopithys* and *Phlegopsis*, a series of whistles with strong second note and following notes dropping until they fade: *Eeee, HEEER, you, you, you, you* (H&B).

> *Hylophylax* are small, rotund little birds that forage actively near ground, using vertical stems as perches. They are usually in pairs and may follow ant swarms in humid lowland forests.

SPOTTED ANTBIRD

Hylophylax naevioides Pl. 171

Identification 11.5cm. Adult male chestnut-rufous above, with black wings and tail, white tips to lesser coverts, orange-rufous tips to median and greater coverts, and fringes of tertials and all but basal secondaries and distal primaries, fringes of basal primaries being paler; broad orange-rufous terminal spots and fringes to rectrices; head slate grey with chin and throat black, underparts white with rows of large black spots, flanks and undertail-coverts grey. Eyes dark grey, legs vinaceous. Female paler rufescent brown above, wings and tail black with spots, bars and fringes like male, from chin white, streaked rufescent brown on breast, and washed lightly on flanks and undertail-coverts.

Ssp. *H. n. naevioides* (W & N Co, W Ec)

Habits Frequently follows swarms, but also forages independent of them. Quite active, alone or in pairs, at lower levels, sallying for prey on ground or in underbrush. Often fans and flicks tail upwards. Distinct propensity to perch on vertical stems.

Status Uncommon and local.
Habitat Tropical Zone, to 300m, occasionally higher. Lowlands and lower slopes, in wet or humid primary and mature second-growth forests.
Voice Contact *peep*, buzzes and chirps. Song a descending and fading series of high-pitched wheezy notes: *peetee, weety, weety, weety, weety, weety...* or *peezee, wheezee, wheezee, wheezee, wheeya* (R&G, H&B, Willis & Eisenmann 1979). Song a long series (e.g. 19 notes, 4.5 s) typically commencing with longer note and intensity usually increases at start and decreases at end; typical female song is shorter (Z&I).

SPOT-BACKED ANTBIRD
Hylophylax naevius Pl. 171

Identification 11.5cm. Adult male olive-brown above, tail distally blackish with white tips; centre of back black with concealed white interscapular patch, pale streaks on mantle and scapulars, wing-coverts and basal secondaries black, white tips to coverts and tertials, fringes of flight-feathers cinnamon; head-sides grey, chin, throat and malar black, breast white, merging into pale buffy flanks and undertail-coverts, a few short rows of large black spots on sides and breast. Eyes grey or dark grey, bill black, legs and feet flesh. Female has black on back streaked far more heavily, black mesial, white chin and throat, breast and underparts creamy buffy with rather more extensive black streaks. Juvenile more richly washed brownish below. No overlap with Spotted Antbird, but may be very difficult to separate from Dot-backed Antbird, and only certain discriminator is song.

Ssp. *H. n. naevius* (S Ve, Guianas) as described
H. n. theresae (SE Co, E Ec) more extensive black and more extensively streaked pale on back (except juvenile which has no black), and more extensively streaked black below, larger white tips to tail

Habits Lower levels, usually near floor, alone or more frequently in pairs, sometimes family groups. Sallies to ground or low vegetation, taking insects from both top and undersides of leaves. Flicks tail. Follows army ants but not assiduously, and often perches on thin vertical stems. Sings from perches 2+m above ground. Once in Suriname, several males singing together.
Status Common to fairly common, but often goes undetected.
Habitat Tropical Zone, to 1,000m in Ecuador but usually below 700m, and usually below 500m in Colombia, to 1,100m in Venezuela. Humid primary and mature secondary *terra firme*; occasionally in *várzea*. Usually close to small water courses.
Voice Song of *naevius* in Suriname a very high, thin double note, repeated 6–9 times rapidly and becoming slightly weaker and lower at end, *sééyee séëyee séëyee séëyee séëyee*.... (H&M). In Venezuela *naevius* song transcribed as *pfée-be, pfé-be, PFEE-BE, pfée-be*..... (Hilty). Loudsong of *naevius* a long series of doubled notes (9 pairs in 3.8 s), each of 2 clear whistles of similar length and shape, peak of first initially at higher frequency, but lower at end, intensity and pitch typically gain initially, fall at end, and pace nearly constant (Z&I). In Ecuador, *theresae* gives a fast high-pitched and somewhat wheezy, *wur, weépur-weépur-weépur-weépur*... Song of *theresae* in Colombia a soft but high-pitched, fast and rhythmic: *pée-bee, pée-bee, PEE-BEE, pée-bee, pée-bee, pée-bee, pee-bee* (H&B). Race *theresae* also sings 9 doubled notes in 3.8 s with second much shorter than first, longer notes shorten and change shape throughout, short note peaks at higher pitch than long note at beginning and end, but not in middle (Z&I).
Notes Race *consobrinus* considered indistinguishable from nominate (Hilty, Z&I), but in a series of 58 specimens in Phelps Collection, female *consobrinus* definitely had more rufous-washed underparts than *naevius*, though Phelps himself synonymised them. Spelling of *naevius* and *consobrinus* is correct, changed from *naevia* and *consobrina* (David & Gosselin 2002).

DOT-BACKED ANTBIRD
Hylophylax punctulatus Pl. 171

Identification 11cm. Adult male dark olive-brown above with central back to uppertail-coverts black with white spots, wings and tail black with white tips to wing-coverts, tertials and tail, fringes of remiges brown; lores, narrow eye-ring and ear-coverts white, throat black, underparts white with black streak-spots on breast and sides, flanks and undertail lightly washed buffy. Female has throat white, malar black. Juvenile resembles female but much more buffy below and has streaks extending to and fading on belly and flanks. May be very difficult to separate from Spot-backed Antbird, except by song.

Ssp. *H. p. punctulatus* (Co, E & S Ve) as described
H. p. subochraceus (E Ec) spots on upperparts and wings cinnamon-buff, not white, and underparts washed cinnamon from flanks and belly to undertail-coverts

Habits Forages mostly in pairs, in undergrowth and at mid levels. Does not join mixed flocks. Not shy, said to respond easily to playback by approaching then perching quietly.
Status Rare to uncommon locally.
Habitat Tropical Zone, below 300m, in *várzea*, swampy, stunted forests and riparian areas.
Voice Male *subochraceus* gives a distinctive, leisurely series: *whee-beéyr, whee-beéyr, whee-beéyr, whee-beéyr*..... (R&G), and in Venezuela, *punctulatus* a *whee-pEEo, whee-pEEo, whee-pEEo*... over and over, speeding up when excited (Hilty). Song a series of doubled notes each *c*.0.5 s long and both somewhat similar sharp whistles, first an upslur and second a downslur, sounding like *free beer*, delivered at *c*.1 every 2 s, sometimes for several minutes; often given singly (Z&I).
Note Z&I synonymised *subochraceus* under *punctulatus* as they appear to intergrade south of Amazon.

SCALE-BACKED ANTBIRD
Hylophylax poecilinotus Pl. 171

Identification 13cm. Old male is lead grey, mantle, lower back, wing- and tail-coverts have black subterminal bars with white tips that afford a barred effect across upperparts, tertials have white fringes and tips, rest of remiges black, tail has white spot in centre of each of central pair, narrow white outer edge to basal half of outermost remiges ending in a white spot halfway along, and white tips to all rectrices. Some whitish mottling on central belly and faint barring on undertail-coverts; eyes dark brown, bill black, and legs and feet pale grey. Immature or younger male has rufescent wash to rear crown and nape, rufescent edges to white fringes of wings and back, and rufous thighs. Female similar, but base colour of upperparts substantially browner, top and sides of head deep rufous, chin tinged pale rufous, throat white, breast to undertail-coverts grey, tinged pale rufescent on flanks, thighs rufous. Juvenile similar to female, but duller and browner on head, and chin and throat ochraceous, underparts less clean grey, mottled lightly with an ochraceous wash. Males vary only slightly between races, but females may vary substantially.

Ssp. *H. p. duidae* (E Co, S Ve) male significantly darker, belly and vent rufescent, more clearly barred on undertail-coverts; female like *poecilinotus* but has entire underparts rufous

H. p. lepidonotus (SE Co, E Ec) male as nominate; female has entire underparts paler rufous than *duidae*, and is yellowish-ochre on belly

H. p. poecilinotus (S Ve, Guianas) as described

Habits Forages most frequently in pairs, for arthropods amid low foliage or by sallying briefly to ground. Perches mostly on vertical stems. Follows army ants, though generally only 1 pair present at a swarm, usually near its fringes, deferring to other, more dominant ant-followers.

Status Uncommon to fairly common locally.

Habitat Tropical and Lower Subtropical Zones. Undergrowth of *terra firme*; occasionally in mature second growth.

Voice Songs of 3 subspecies in region similar. A series (e.g. 10 notes in 7.1 s) of long upslurred notes with little space between them, each rising in pitch and gathering intensity, though final note or notes decrease; much individual variation in length of song and extent to which final notes rise (Z&I). Given as *tew, tueeé? tueeé? tueeé? tueeé?* … (R&T) and in Ecuador, *teeuw, tuweeé tuweeé tuweeé…* (R&G). Song at Mitú, Colombia, up to 10 slow quavering *preeeeee* whistles, each a half-tone higher than preceding note (H&B), and in Venezuela, 5–10 slow, slightly quavering whistles, *pureeeeee, pureeeeee…* each note a quarter to a half-tone higher than preceding note (Hilty). In Suriname, a mewing hoarse trill, *tyeerreeh… tyeerreeh… tyeerreeh…* and a high shrill *tseet – tseet* (H&M).

Note Correct spellings are *poecilinotus* and *lepidonotus* (David & Gosselin 2002).

> *Phlegopsis* and *Phaenostictus* bare-eyed antbirds are obligate ant-followers and are dominant at antswarms, Ocellated Antbird over all. Wary and shy of observers but with patience can become used to their presence.

BLACK-SPOTTED BARE-EYE

Phlegopsis nigromaculata Pl. 171

Identification 17–18.5cm. Adult rufescent brown above, more rufescent on wings and tail, with black terminal teardrop spots on all feathers except remiges and rectrices, entire head and underparts to belly and flanks black, grading into same brown as back; broad ring of red skin around eye, eyes brown, bill black, legs and feet dark grey. Juvenile similar but has less bare skin around eyes and this is dull greyish-brown.

Ssp. *P. n. nigromaculata* (E Ec)

Habits Obligate ant-follower, dashing between low perches and to floor, to flick litter about in search of prey. Frequently in close pairs or small families. A good number may gather at a swarm, bickering over foraging territories and waving their open tails. Very nervous of observers.

Status Uncommon to fairly common, though always attending ant swarms.

Habitat Tropical Zone, to 400m, in lower levels of both primary and mature secondary *várzea*, occasionally in primary or secondary *terra firme*.

Voice Male has distinctive slow song, a simple raspy *zhweé, zhwu*, or *zhweé, zhwu, zhwu*. Both sexes utter a drawn-out *zhheeeuw*, especially at swarms (R&G). Moderately long, flat, rich whistles, each slightly lower pitched and becoming harsher; final note less intense, and number of notes variable (Z&I).

ARGUS BARE-EYE

Phlegopsis barringeri Pl. 171

Identification 18cm. Adult male has back reddish-brown with small, blackish-rimmed buff spots, remiges, tail and undertail-coverts largely chestnut, with blackish patch on central primaries, and tail distally blackish with chestnut tips, head and breast to flanks and vent glossy black. Skin around eyes red.

Ssp. Monotypic (SW Co: Nariño)

Status Unknown. Possibly an aberrant individual, a hybrid, extremely rare or extinct.

Habitat Presumably as congeners.

Voice Unknown.

Notes Known from only single specimen, taken in south-east Nariño, on Colombia/Ecuador border, in 1951. Following Willis (1979), Graves (1992) considered it to represent a hybrid *P. nigromaculata* × *P. erythroptera*.

REDDISH-WINGED BARE-EYE

Phlegopsis erythroptera Pl. 171

Identification 18.5cm. Adult male black, with white scallops on back continuing to short uppertail-coverts where they become rufous, white fringes to lesser coverts, chestnut on median and greater coverts, tertials have chestnut tips and broad band of chestnut on central secondaries and primaries; large area of bare skin around eyes red, eyes brown, legs and feet brownish-grey. Immature male has broader but duller chestnut on wings, so that greater coverts and most of remiges this colour. Female largely rufous-chestnut, darker above, and darker on wings and tail with whitish tips to median and greater coverts and tertials, and narrower, whitish bar across central remiges. Black-spotted Bare-eye is clearly spotted and lacks bands in wings, and wing-bands separate it from all other black antbirds.

Ssp. *P. e. erythroptera* (SE Co, E Ec, S Ve)

Habits Rarely seen away from army ants, with seldom more than 2–3 at any swarm, where they dominate all other antbirds except Ocellated Antbird. They forage by hopping between low perches and floor, where they toss forest litter while moving their open tails in a gesture characteristic of genus.
Status Uncommon.
Habitat Tropical Zone, to 750m in Ecuador, 500m in Colombia and 350m in Venezuela. Mainly in *terra firme* (rarely in *várzea* or near streams), but occasionally in mature second growth.
Voice Song a short, descending series of 4–6 harsh piercing notes, *whee-wheerp, wheerp… wheeur…wheeur….* descending, slowing and becoming buzzy; Black-spotted's is similar but shorter and slower. Both sexes give a snarling, downslurred *skíyarrr* (R&G). In alarm a loud sharp, metallic *pchiirr* with buzzy quality (Hilty).

OCELLATED ANTBIRD

Phaenostictus mcleannani Pl. 170

Identification 19.5–20cm. Adult mainly black, with a bright orange-rufous collar that wraps around neck-sides onto upper breast where it becomes fringes to black feathers; almost entire body above and below, including wings, scalloped with buffy-rufous fringes, tail black; top of head buffy and large amount of bare skin around eyes blue, eyes brown, bill black, legs and feet flesh. Juvenile is more richly coloured, with crest dusky and pale fringes to feathers.

Ssp. *P. m. chocoanus* (W Co) as described
P. m. pacificus (SW Co, NW Ec) generally more richly coloured, crest deep rufous, darker than nape; juvenile has blackish crest with pale fringes

Habits Obligate swarm follower that forages alone, in pairs or small family groups. Dominates all other antbirds following ants. Dashes between perches and ground, flicking tail upwards occasionally and looking about warily.
Status Uncommon and local, almost exclusively in association with army ants.
Habitat Tropical Zone, to 750m in Ecuador and 900m in Colombia, but generally lower in both countries. Lowlands and lower slopes, in humid to wet forests. Always in undergrowth.
Voice A nasal *dfzurrr* or *dzeerr* often given at ant swarms (R&G). Alarm a sharp *wheerrr chirr* (Eisenmann 1952) and loud *chip-ip-ip*. Faint song an ascending then descending *whee, hu, hee, choo*; loudsong a long series of high whistles that ascend then descend, and often end with rough *charr, pee, pee, pee, pee, pee, pee-pe-te'e'e'e'e'e'pe-peer peer charr* (Willis 1973, H&B), or a series (15 notes in 15.1 s) of short, rich whistles that gradually become even shorter, except final notes which lengthen, pitch and intensity increase but drop at end, number of notes variable, final note sometimes repeated and becoming harsher (Z&I).

FORMICARIIDAE – Ground Antbirds

The Formicariidae and Thamnophilidae were long considered a single family, until DNA-DNA hybridisation studies by Sibley & Ahlquist confirmed what had been suspected by some: that within the Formicariidae there were at least 2 very distinct families. This separation has been supported by the AOU (1998) and, subsequently, by Zimmer & Isler (2003). The name used for the single family belongs to the 'terrestrial' group, in which *Formicarius*, the nominate genus, is placed. However, the most recent genetic study, by Chesser (2004), suggests that the Formicariidae might best be divided into 2 families: the first, which is apparently closer to tapaculos, would be led by the genus *Formicarius*, and the other would include the genera *Grallaria*, *Grallaricula* and *Myrmothera*. A subsequent study (Rice 2005) found that most antpitta genera occupied two subclades forming a monophyletic grouping, but that *Pittasoma* appears to be a sister genus of *Conopophaga* (Conopophagidae)! Thus, as with so many Neotropical families and groups of genera, the matter remains unresolved.
The antthrushes and antpittas that form the ground antbirds all feed on the ground, picking invertebrates amid the litter of leaves. They hop and bound, walk and run, and often move quickly, affording only a fleeting glance, but sometimes move deliberately, turning leaves and moving mosses in search of worms and insects. The majority forage within dense cover, often on slopes or in ravines, and are much easier to discover by their vocalisations than by seeing them. The smallest, in the genus *Grallaricula*, are less terrestrial, foraging amongst the dense undergrowth near the ground, perching sideways on vertical stems of vines and mossy roots, occasionally on the forest floor. The genus *Hylopezus* and some (perhaps all?) species of *Grallaricula* habitually stand with their legs and head quite still, whilst moving the body from side to side. Some species sing from a low perch, others from either a perch or on the ground.

Most seem more likely to be seen foraging in comparatively open places in early morning. They do not join mixed feeding flocks. In the main, there are no plumage differences between the sexes. Chicks are fluffy and barred, but very soon acquire juvenile and then immature plumage, usually distinguished by spots or barring on head, back and wings. They are quite territorial and as most species breed during the wet season, the return of the rains also marks the start of the song periods of antthrushes and antpittas in the forests, which are some of the most intriguing and beautiful vocalisations of these shady realms. All antpittas are easier to see when it is raining, for then, they must feel safer, less likely to encounter predators, and may be found walking or hopping along a trail where they would never be seen otherwise.

Being essentially birds of forest floor, almost every one is, virtually by definition, threatened by the non-stop forest clearance throughout the region, and the inevitable range fragmentation and habitat loss. Knowledge of status and range is often based on outdated information, and species that have not been seen for many years are insufficiently known for anything other than guesswork.

Additional reference for this family: Krabbe & Schulenberg (2003, hereafter K&S).

Formicarius antthrushes walk graciously on the forest floor and in leaf-litter, with tail cocked, appearing confident and jaunty, but in reality are shy and retiring. They are birds of humid forests, both lowland and montane, and respond well to playback.

RUFOUS-CAPPED ANTTHRUSH

Formicarius colma Pl. 172

Identification 18cm. Adult male has chestnut crown and nape, olive-green upperparts and black below, becoming olive-green on flanks and undertail-coverts; bill black, eyes brown, legs and feet grey-brown. Females show some white on chin and throat, but this is very variable (see plate), and whitish scaling on flanks and undertail-coverts. Juvenile/immature much browner, with paler legs and feet, whilst young males have variable amount of chestnut suffusion on the throat, females virtually none, and both have black scaling on front of head.

Ssp. *F. c. colma* (E Co, S Ve, Guianas) indistinguishable from *nigrifrons* in the field, but on average has black restricted to forehead; legs and feet dark vinaceous

F. c. nigrifrons (E Ec, S Ve) black usually to forecrown; legs and feet vinaceous

Habits Characteristic head-bobbing walk on forest floor; often follows army ants.

Status Uncommon and rather local in Ecuador, uncommon in Venezuela, frequent in Guyana and common in French Guiana.

Habitat Lower Tropical Zone, to 1,100m but most often below 500m. At higher elevations than Black-faced Antthrush, to 1,700m in Venezuela.

Voice An eerie, wavering glissando that falters and drops slightly in pitch at first, then slowly and steadily rises to finale, *wu-u-u-u-er-er-u-u-u-u-u-u-u-u-u-u-u-u-u-u-u* varies locally (Hilty).

BLACK-FACED ANTTHRUSH

Formicarius analis Pl. 172

Identification 17–20cm. Black face with chestnut patch behind ear-coverts that may be quite noticeable (*crissalis*) to virtually absent (*zamorae*), dark brown above with ruddy rump and uppertail-coverts, grey below varies according to race, chestnut undertail-coverts. Legs and feet also vary racially, from pale to deep purplish-vinaceous. Juvenile/immature paler than adult with some pale scalloping on belly and variable white on throat according to race. Adults have pale bluish bare skin around eye, somewhat vestigial and duller in young.

Ssp. *F. a. connectens* (E Co) dark above like *zamorae*, but paler grey on breast

F. a. crissalis (S Ve, Guianas) palest race, bright pale chestnut patch behind ear-coverts and large white loral spot

F. a. griseoventris (extreme NE Co, W Ve) long bill, bright chestnut patch behind ear-coverts, lacks white loral spot

F. a. panamensis (NW Co) paler below, with small chestnut patch

F. a. saturatus (C Co, N & W Ve, Tr) richly coloured, dark chestnut patch, very small loral spot

F. a. virescens (Co: Santa Marta) more olivaceous above and pale below

F. a. zamorae (E Ec) very dark with intense colours, very small white loral spot

Habits Retiring, but responds well to playback. Will follow ant swarms.

Status Uncommon to locally common in Ecuador, common in Venezuela and Trinidad (no records Tobago), frequent in Guyana and common in French Guiana.

Habitat Tropical Zone, usually to 500m. Floor of humid forests and tall secondary woodland of lowlands and foothills.

Voice Characteristic of lowland and foothill forests year-round; typically, song starts with a strong whistle, then a pause followed by a series of notes at 2 per s. Song given by both sexes, with that of the female slightly higher pitched, and is repeated every 15 s. Dawn songs longer than those uttered during day. Song length may vary regionally and sometimes even more locally (Hilty, K&S).

Notes Voice and plumages vary considerably across range, but neither well documented nor correlated. Two or more species probably involved (K&S). Races *saturatus*, *virescens* and *panamensis* perhaps form part of a separate species (Howell 1994).

BLACK-HEADED ANTTHRUSH

Formicarius nigricapillus Pl. 172

Identification 18cm. Not black-headed, but actually dark slate. Back, wings and rump dark chestnut-brown with uppertail-coverts dark rufous and tail dark brown. Grey of head extends to belly and flanks, undertail-coverts rufous. Bill black, eyes brown with surrounding skin pale blue, legs and feet grey. Some olive on lower belly, more noticeable on female. Juvenile plumage not found.

Ssp. *F. n. destructus* (W Ec, W Co)

Habits Not easy to see due to nature of behaviour and habitat, usually found by its vocalisation.

Status Uncommon to frequent in Ecuador.

Habitat Tropical to Lower Subtropical Zones, rarely above 900m. Favours wet, dense undergrowth, particularly in ravines.

Voice Loud resonant series of rapidly uttered, short notes, lasting up to 5 s, rising in pitch and becoming a little faster, then slowing and falling slightly.

RUFOUS-BREASTED ANTTHRUSH

Formicarius rufipectus Pl. 172

Identification 18.5–19cm. Three well-marked subspecies, each with a slightly different song. Black bill, pale bluish-white skin around eyes and greyish feet. Juvenile duller below and show variable white on throat (see plate for juvenile Black-faced and Rufous-capped Antthrushes). From other antthrushes in region by rufous breast.

Ssp. *F. r. carrikeri* (W Ec, Co: W & C Andes) bright rufous, especially noticeable on neck-sides and uppertail-coverts
F. r. lasallei (NW Ve) dark umber-rufous on breast and uppertail-coverts
F. r. thoracicus (E Ec) rich rufous restricted to breast and undertail-coverts

Habits Difficult to find and usually located by its song.
Status Uncommon to frequent in Ecuador, frequent in Venezuela.
Habitat Upper Tropical to Subtropical Zones, 850–2,500m, locally to over 3,000m. Favours dense undergrowth of ravines and steep slopes in humid montane forest and tall second growth.
Voice Song a short 2-note *toot-toot* (K&S) or *üü, üü* (Hilty), given by both sexes. Second note usually slightly higher pitched in *carrikeri*, sometimes slightly higher in *lasallei*, but both even in *thoracicus*.

Chamaeza antthrushes inhabit the floors of humid forest interiors; they are rounded, short-billed birds, rather like short-tailed thrushes, but whilst the body angle may recall that of a thrush, the legs tend to be more vertical – they are designed for walking, not hopping. The genus is quite vocal, but the birds are surprisingly inconspicuous.

SHORT-TAILED ANTTHRUSH

Chamaeza campanisona Pl. 173

Identification 19-20.5cm. Very thrush-like, albeit with a short tail. Fawn above with a postocular line that varies from white to buffy, vestigial to prominent, depending on race. Underparts white, with black streaks on outer fringes of feathers sometimes forming full scallops; undertail-coverts usually cinnamon or pale rufous. Usually, subterminal tail band with whitish tips, but much racial and individual variation. Bill black above, lower mandible yellowish with dark tip. From larger Striated Antthrush by fawn not ruddy back, and neck patch, which is very weakly defined in Striated. From Schwartz's Antthrush by generally clean postocular line and throat (both streaked black in Schwartz's); also whiter, much less marked central breast and belly, which is always well scalloped on Schwartz's Antthrush.

Ssp. *C. c. columbiana* (Co: E Andes) like *venezuelana* but more heavily streaked below
C. c. fulvescens (SE Ve, W Gu) rich deep fulvous above, deeper than any other race, with rufous bar on breast, and undertail-coverts very richly coloured
C. c. huachamacarii (S Ve) pale fawn above with small, almost vestigial white postocular line and poorly defined patch on neck-sides; rufous on breast and flanks
C. c. obscura (E Ve) very similar to *yavii*
C. c. punctigula (E Ec) well-defined postocular line and neck patch; only tinge of rufous on breast
C. c. venezuelana (N Ve) palest race, mostly white below with few black streaks; postocular line and neck patch bright and very well defined
C. c. yavii (Ve: N Amazonas) well-defined postocular line reaches around auriculars to join clearly defined neck-patch; rufous on breast, but not body-sides

Habits Keeps within undergrowth on forest floor and sings frequently.
Status Uncommon and fairly local in Ecuador, frequent in Venezuela, scarce in Guyana.
Habitat Tropical to Lower Subtropical Zones, premontane forest mostly 500–1,200m, rarely to 1,500m, where perhaps overlaps slightly with Schwartz's Antthrush.
Voice Distinctive, ventriloquial and trogon-like series of rising *woo* notes, slowing abruptly and falling *woop* notes (H&B). Race *obscura* on Sierra de Lema is similar but first half decidedly faster (Hilty). Race *punctigula* described as beautiful series of *cow* notes that start slowly but quickly accelerate and become louder, then abruptly shift into descending series of 4–6 lower pitched *wo* or *wop* notes that gradually become weaker and fade (R&G).
Notes Formerly known as *C. brevicauda* (Peters 1951). Possibly includes up to 4 species (K&S). Race *huachamacarii* (Phelps & Phelps Jr. 1951) known from a single specimen.

STRIATED ANTTHRUSH

Chamaeza nobilis Pl. 173

Identification 22–23cm. Entire upperparts deep rufescent brown with white postocular line and buffy loral spot. Vestigial whitish patch on neck-sides rarely noticeable. Throat white, rest of underparts white with outer fringes to feathers black, usually forming streaks but sometimes appearing as complete scallops; slight rufous flush to breast-sides and flanks. Larger than Short-tailed Antthrush, with more boldly contrasting black and white markings below; Schwartz's Antthrush has fine black streaking on throat and postocular line, and markings below are complete scallops.

Ssp. *C. n. rubida* (E Ec, SE Co)

Habits Inhabits floor of *terra firme* forest where undergrowth is sparse, but amazingly difficult to see, even when using playback. Heard far more often than seen.
Status Rare to locally frequent in Ecuador.
Habitat Lower Tropical Zone, to 1,000m, but most frequent below *c.*700m.
Voice Song recalls Short-tailed Antthrush but notes faster, and is longer and lower pitched: a series of hollow-sounding notes increasing in volume and accelerating slightly, followed

by series of whooping notes fading in volume, *whoo-whoo whoo, whoo-whoo-whoo-whoop-whoop-whoop-whoop*.
Note Called Noble Antthrush in R&T.

SCHWARTZ'S ANTTHRUSH

Chamaeza turdina Pl. 173

Identification 19cm. Brown above, white superciliary line with fine blackish flecks, throat and ear-coverts whitish, also flecked blackish. Pale to whitish lores connected to superciliary line. Below, buffy with brown scallops (*chionogaster* brown morph) or white with black scallops and bars. Bill black with basal half of mandible horn-coloured, eyes brown, legs and feet olivaceous. Two morphs: buffy has base colour of underparts rich buffy, black-and-white morph has black vermiculations on white base. From Short-tailed Antthrush by more heavily marked underparts and complete scallops, with no unmarked centre to belly; from Striated Antthrush by clear scalloping pattern below, rather than streaking.

Ssp. *C. t. chionogaster* (N Ve) white morph has breast, belly and flanks black and white with no buffy at all, scallops mostly doubled on flanks, giving distinctive pattern; no pale loral spot; brown morph has buffy underparts with brown scallops, double scalloping less extensive, undertail-coverts buffy, and feathers of flanks, vent and undertail-coverts olive-green with black terminal bars

C. t. turdina (Co: C & E Andes) white underparts washed lightly olive-green, heaviest on flanks; scalloping light and single, flanks and undertail-coverts with fine, fairly dense terminal bars

Habits Walks and runs on forest floor.
Status Frequent in Venezuela.
Habitat Subtropical to Temperate Zones, in humid to wet montane forest. Found at higher elevations than Short-tailed Antthrush, 1,500–2,100m, rarely 1,100–1,500m where they might overlap slightly.
Voice Two song-types. The first is a noticeably long series of *cu* notes that gradually increase in intensity, pitch and speed, and lasts up to 50 s; it might slow slightly and even fall off at the end. The other is a descending series of loud *cuu* or *cuuk* notes that slow into a chuckling gurgle that might stop abruptly, or segue into the first type (Hilty, K&S).
Notes *C. turdina* formerly considered conspecific with *C. ruficauda*, but Willis (1992) separated northern races under *C. turdina* from the southern races, which are now placed in *C. ruficauda*. Called Scalloped Antthrush in S&M and in R&T.

BARRED ANTTHRUSH

Chamaeza mollissima Pl. 173

Identification 20cm. Chocolate-brown above with 3 sets of distinctive barring on head – above eye, below eye and the mesial stripe. Chin and throat also barred in same distinctive black-and-white, and this continues over entire underparts. Barring close and dense, unlike any other antthrush in our region. Small, pointed bill is black, eyes brown and legs and feet pale pinkish-brown.

Ssp. *C. m. mollissima* (E Ec, C Co)

Habits Like rest of genus, more often heard than seen, as it forages in dense undergrowth.
Status Very rare to rare and apparently local in Ecuador.
Habitat Upper Subtropical to Temperate Zones, undisturbed cloud and wet montane forest, 1,800–3,100m.
Voice Song a fast, extended series of same *cuh* note for perhaps 20 s, increasing in volume and pitch. Similar to Schwartz's Antthrush but at a higher pitch and faster, ending abruptly (H&B, K&S, Hilty).

Pittasoma antpittas are rounded birds with very short tails, rich brown with some spots and some barring below. Their bills are proportionately large and heavy. They inhabit floors of wet lowland forests.

BLACK-CROWNED ANTPITTA

Pittasoma michleri Pl. 174

Identification 18–19cm. Rotund with tiny downturned tail. Male has top of head black, rest of upperparts olive with black streaks on back and white subterminal spots with black terminal tips to wing-coverts; bold white lores, orange face-sides, black chin, white rest of underparts washed olive-green, barred black; bill black above, orange-horn below, eyes brown, legs and feet grey. Female similar but has chin rusty rather than black. Juvenile differs in having loral spot grey, orange cheeks dirty, rufous wash on breast and barring consists more of irregular scalloping. Wing-coverts have white terminal tips without black fringes, and bill horn-coloured. Boldly barred underparts distinguish it from all other antpittas.

Ssp. *P. m. michleri* (NW Co)

Habits Hops and bounds across forest floor, but will remains still for periods on a low perch, and is generally difficult to see. Follows ant swarms.
Status Rare and local.
Habitat Tropical Zone, to 1,000m. Floor and undergrowth of humid and wet forests of lowlands and foothills.
Voice Long series of harsh notes slowing at end, *wakwakwakwakwak wakwakwakwakwak-wak-wak-wak* Song is a series of level *tu* notes, also slowing towards end (Ridgely & Gwynne).

RUFOUS-CROWNED ANTPITTA

Pittasoma rufopileatum Pl. 173

Identification 16–17.5cm. Rotund with tiny downturned tail, large head and bill. Forehead to nape rufous, black bar from lores through eyes to nape-sides, rest of upperparts fawn with black streaks on back and wing-feathers usually have terminal white spots. Female has small white streaks in black eyestripe. Underparts light rufous to pale, depending on race, and heavily, lightly or unbarred also according to race.

Ssp. *P. r. harterti* (SW Co) pale rufous below, juvenile and male lightly barred on breast-sides and flanks, and female only slightly barred

P. r. rosenbergi (W Co) pale buffy below, with pale rufous of the face cleanly cut at throat
P. r. rufopileatum (NW Ec) paler below, washed olive on flanks and heavily barred on breast and centre of belly; female has vestigial bars

Habits Walks or bounds rapidly across forest floor and then may pause and remain still for a while. Individuals may follow ant swarms.
Status Rare to uncommon and possibly local in Ecuador, generally uncommon in Colombia.
Habitat Tropical Zone, to *c.*1,100m. Wet lowland and foothill forests.
Voice Single whistle, descending at end, given at short intervals for several minutes.

Grallaria antpittas are rounded, very short-tailed birds with long legs that walk, run and bound across floor of humid montane forests. Usually in pairs and heard far more often than seen, but may respond well to playback.

UNDULATED ANTPITTA
Grallaria squamigera Pl. 174

Identification 20–24cm. Large, rotund bird with white throat and black moustachial, and heavily barred black on ochraceous-orange head-sides and underparts. Bill heavy and black with horn-coloured base, eyes brown, legs and feet vinaceous-pink. Juvenile has entire head barred and spotted, and underparts less cleanly barred than adult. Feathers of back and wing-coverts have terminal orange fringes with subterminal blackish bars. Bill horn-coloured. Immature has top of head grey, but retains orange and black, barred nuchal band, and orange and blackish terminal markings on back and wings. From slightly larger Great Antpitta by clear markings on head-sides and neat white throat, all-dark bill and pale legs and feet. Larger Giant Antpitta lacks white throat in all races, is richer rufous below with finer barring, and has pale grey legs and feet. Serious confusion with Great Antpitta has led to probable overstating of sightings of latter. Note that Undulated Antpitta is usually found at higher levels than Great Antpitta (1,700–2,300m).

Ssp. *G. s. canicauda* (SE Ec) all grey above
G. s. squamigera (Andes: Ec, Co, Ve) grey head, rest of upperparts olive

Habits Rather shy and retiring though will briefly walk from cover into relatively open spaces when foraging.
Status Uncommon to locally frequent in Ecuador, local in Colombia, locally frequent in Venezuela.
Habitat Upper Subtropical Zone to Páramo. Humid, wet montane forest, mossy woodland, clumps of *Chusquea* bamboo and *Neurolepis* cane, also very disturbed, semi-humid shrubbery (K&S), mostly at 2,400–3,000m.
Voice Rather *Megascops*-like series, *huhuhuhuhuhuhuhuhu' hu'hu* on level tone but rising at end (P. Schwartz recording, Venezuela). Or, in Ecuador, a fast, hollow, quavering trill, *hohohohohohohohohohohoho* with the last few notes more enunciated (R&G), very similar to, but slightly slower, than Giant Antpitta. Song lasts 4–5 s and notes are uttered at rate of 14–16 per s (K&S). Rarely heard call, *rrhooh-rrhooh-rrhooh* (K&S).

GIANT ANTPITTA
Grallaria gigantea Pl. 174

Identification 25cm. Large, rotund bird with long legs, grey cap and nape, brown above and rich rufous face, cheeks and underparts, barred black. Bill heavy and 2-toned, black maxilla, dark horn mandible, legs and feet pale grey. Juvenile is paler brown from forehead to tail, with no grey on head. Irregular spotting on back and wings formed by black subterminal spots and orange fringes. Bill horn-coloured, legs and feet vinaceous. Immature acquires grey head but retains spotting on back and wings.

Ssp. *G. g. gigantea* (E Ec) olive-brown above, medium rufous on face and underparts, barred black throughout except vent and undertail-coverts
G. g. hylodroma (NW Ec, SW Co) dark brown above, very rich reddish-rufous on face and underparts, barred on breast and flanks
G. g. lehmanni (Co: C Andes) paler throughout, with markedly paler throat and lighter, more widely spaced barring

Habits Little-known bird of wet or muddy highland forest floors with a preference for level ground, though occasionally found on slopes. Hops and bounds onto and over fallen branches. Sings from a low perch.
Status Endangered. Rare and local in Ecuador, and race *lehmanni* possibly extinct in Colombia (K&S).
Habitat Subtropical to Temperate Zones, 1,400–2,300m on west slope in Ecuador, and 2,000m on east slope; 2,300–3,000m in Colombia, and 1,700–2,300m in Venezuela. Humid and wet primary montane forest.
Voice Song of *hylodroma* 4–6 s series of rolling, owl-like notes evenly paced (16–18 per s), gradually increasing in volume and sometimes ending with a sudden rise in pitch. Song of *gigantea* longer (8 s) and faster (19–20 notes per s: K&S). Song virtually indistinguishable from Undulated Antpitta, which is slightly shorter (4–5 s) and slower (14–15 notes per s).
Notes *G. gigantea* possibly conspecific with *G. excelsa* (Hilty, K&S); alternatively, race *lehmanni* might be placed under *G. excelsa*, whilst race *hylodroma* could be treated as a separate species (K&S). Notes on species were provided by Krabbe *et al.* (1994).

GREAT ANTPITTA
Grallaria excelsa Pl. 174

Identification 24–25.5cm. Large, rotund bird with long legs. Forehead olive-orange becoming grey on crown to nape, rest of upperparts olive; white throat, rest of underparts rufous with black barring. Bill blackish above, flesh-coloured below, eyes brown, and legs and feet dark olive-grey (*excelsa*) or pale olive-brown (*phelpsi*). Juvenile undescribed but probably very similar to juvenile Undulated Antpitta with similar progression of plumage. Race *excelsa* very similar to race *squamigera* of Undulated Antpitta and difficult to separate in field. Undulated Antpitta has blacker bill with only base of lower mandible pale, the mesial blacker and better defined, the ear-coverts more clearly striped black on orange, and legs and feet violaceous-flesh.

Ssp. *G. e. excelsa* (W Ve) white lores, mesial and throat, extending to upper breast (key field mark)
G. e. phelpsi (N Ve) white on head restricted to chin and centre of throat

Habits Surprisingly frustrating to track by its voice, as it will fly into canopy, then a short distance over the forest, back to the canopy and then drop to the ground to call again.
Status Scarce Venezuelan endemic, but difficult to find and possibly more numerous than records suggest. However, K&S note that many reports of Great Antpitta involve misidentified Undulated Antpitta.
Habitat Subtropical Zone. Dense cloud forest on highest ridges, from 1,700m (usually above 2,000m) to 2,300m, in dense understorey and at lower levels than Undulated Antpitta (which is mostly at 2,400–3,000m).
Voice Song a low-frequency vibrating hollow (K&S) or rubber-lipped (Hilty) trill lasting 4–5 s, with notes delivered at 14–20 per s. Very similar to Undulated Antpitta, but ends abruptly, not slowing at end.
Notes *G. excelsa* is possibly conspecific with *G. gigantea* (Hilty, K&S).

VARIEGATED ANTPITTA
Grallaria varia Pl. 175

Identification 20.5cm. Forehead olivaceous, forecrown to nape grey, rest of upperparts olive-brown, scaled black on back. Lores and mesial cream, with streaks of cream on ear-coverts. Throat to breast cinnamon or russet, palest on belly, with irregular spot-streaks on breast. Eyes brown, legs and feet pinkish-grey. Easily confused with Scaled Antpitta (race *roraimae*), in eastern Venezuela and western Guyana, but has paler underparts and clear streaking on breast-sides. In western Venezuela might be confused with smaller Táchira Antpitta, which is darker and has a clearly defined moustachial and necklace without streaks on body-sides. From Plain-backed Antpitta by scaling on back and streaks on breast.

Ssp. *G. v. cinereiceps* (S Ve) more cinnamon below with heavier scaling on back, bill dark grey
G. v. varia (Guianas) darker throat and breast with stronger cream-coloured streaks; bill horn

Habits A retiring, somewhat crepuscular bird, most active pre-dawn and at dusk, usually found foraging on forest floor.
Status Uncommon to locally frequent in Venezuela, uncommon in Guyana. In French Guiana, widespread in the interior but uncommon.
Habitat Tropical Zone, to 640m on Sierra Parima, Venezuela. Humid or wet lowland forests and mature secondary woodland.
Voice Song a series of low-pitched hoots with a penetrating, vibrant quality and audible over some distance, *whü whü whü whüü-WHU-WHU WHü whü*, lasting *c*.2.5 s, accelerating slightly, swelling, fading and ending abruptly (Hilty).

MOUSTACHED ANTPITTA
Grallaria alleni Pl. 176

Identification 16–17cm. Whitish lores, top of head to nape grey, rest of upperparts olive-brown including head-sides, mesial white. Two races differ notably in coloration of underparts. Both have irregular white spots, fringed black, on centre of breast. Bill grey above, pinkish below; eyes brown, legs and feet grey. From Variegated and Táchira Antpittas by considerable gap in ranges, and from Scaled Antpitta by paler, virtually unmarked grey head, and also is found at higher elevations.

Ssp. *G. a. alleni* (Co: C Andes, W slope) throat and breast pale olive-cinnamon, fading to white with some olive wash on body-sides and thighs, undertail-coverts cinnamon
G. a. andaquiensis (N Ec, Co: E Andes) throat and breast rufous, becoming cinnamon over entire underparts

Habits Difficult to encounter as it prefers ravines and steep slopes.
Status Endangered. Rare to local in Ecuador, very rare to local in Colombia.
Habitat Upper Subtropical Zone, 1,850–2,500m. Dense undergrowth of humid and wet cloud forest.
Voice Song a gradually ascending series of hollow notes that also become louder and higher pitched (R&G), 2–3 s long, delivered at 17–25 notes at 8–9 per s (K&S). Similar to song of Scaled Antpitta but shorter.
Note *G. alleni* and *G. guatimalensis* possibly conspecific (S&M).

SCALED ANTPITTA
Grallaria guatimalensis Pl. 175

Identification 18cm. Considerable variation and diagnostic characters may be missing from some individuals and some taxa require confirmation. Essentially olive-brown above with grey nape, and rufous below; may have pale or white lores, mesial white or pale, and upper breast may have necklace and or white or pale streaks. Bill varies from all black to distinctly bicoloured (mandible entirely or partially horn, yellow, grey or ochraceous); eyes brown, legs and feet from vinaceous through pale olive to pure, pale grey. Juvenile all brown with pale, pinkish belly, short pale streaks over most of body, with terminal spots on wing-coverts; tail barred. Could be confused with several other species, but take careful note of comparative ranges and elevations. Race *regulus* from very rare Moustached Antpitta of race *andaquiensis* in northern Ecuador and southern Colombia by buff malar and buffy markings on dark brown breast, and race *alleni* quite distinct with creamy-white belly. From Plain-backed Antpitta by black scaling in all races.

Ssp. *G. g. aripoensis* (Tr) smaller than mainland birds, very rich rufous below with clearly defined moustachial and necklace

G. g. carmelitae (NE Co: Santa Marta, NW Ve: Perijá) very brownish with dull underparts; lores dark, moustachial and necklace dull greyish-buffy

G. g. chocoensis (NW Co) similar to *carmelitae*, very dark with heavy black scaling on back, lores dark, weakly defined moustachial and necklace

G. g. regulus (Ec, N & SW Co, W Ve) malar stripe, necklace and streaks on breast-sides buffy, dark brown breast grades into dark-streaked belly

G. g. roraimae (S Ve: tepuis, W Gu) top of head more grey, brighter rufous below, moustachial and necklace white and usually well defined (see plate)

There is a single specimen in the Phelps Collection, from Isla Margarita that could prove to be yet another variant of *roraimae*, or a distinct form.

Habits Prefers slopes and ravines where tangled and dense undergrowth makes it difficult to find.

Status Rare to locally frequent in Ecuador, local in Colombia, widespread but quite local in Venezuela, rare in Trinidad (no records Tobago). Generally widespread but habitat now fragmented, and current distribution and status known only approximately.

Habitat Tropical to Temperate Zones. Humid and wet foothill forests, rain and cloud forests. From 250 to *c.*1,000m, but may occur to 2,000m and rarely to 2,800m.

Voice Song in Ecuador a low-pitched, hollow and resonant trill that gradually increases in pitch and volume, slowing in middle then accelerating again (R&G). In Venezuela a quavering rubber-lipped vibrato of low, hollow notes that gradually slides up scale and ends abruptly, lasting *c.*4 s (Hilty). In Colombia (*regulus*) a rolling series of 30–50 notes at 14–17 per s, volume and pitch increasing over first two-thirds then levels and falls slightly at end (K&S).

TÁCHIRA ANTPITTA

Grallaria chthonia Pl. 176

Identification 17–18cm. Distinctive and well-marked antpitta, greenish-olive above with some bluish-grey on nape, and black fringes afford a wholly scaled appearance from lores to uppertail-coverts. Bib and throat fuscous, with clean warm buffy-yellow malar and necklace, the spots of latter fringed fuscous. Underparts pale buffy-cinnamon, suffused greenish-olive from breast to flanks, with slight barring throughout, and cream-coloured shafts to feathers of breast-sides. Bill all black, eyes brown, legs and feet distinctly vinaceous. From Scaled Antpitta (race *regulus*) by cleaner and more clearly defined moustachial and necklace, together with comparatively evenly coloured underparts, lacking buffy and dark brown streaks. From Variegated Antpitta by lack of buffy streaks below and much neater moustachial and necklace, and note that Variegated Antpitta is more likely to be encountered at lower elevations, e.g. below 1,000m.

Ssp. Monotypic (W Ve: río Chiquito, Táchira)

Status Endangered. Apparently extremely rare Venezuelan endemic, though range has not been visited by ornithologists since 1956, as it is extremely dangerous due to permanent menace of Colombian guerrillas, narcotics traffickers and timber thieves. Efforts to find the bird on the Colombian side of Tamá, in 1990 and 1996, were unsuccessful, perhaps because the bird is truly endemic to the very small río Chiquito area, which lies wholly in Venezuela, and is part of the watershed of Lake Maracaibo.

Habitat Subtropical Zone, at 1,800–2,100m. Río Chiquito, the only location where it has been found, is just 5km long. The precise location was not well described by the collectors, and is not known today.

Voice Unknown.

Notes Specific status of *G. chthonia* has been questioned, e.g. that it might be a subspecies of *G. guatimalensis* (Hilty), but also considered to be more closely related to *G. alleni* than to *G. guatimalensis* by K&S.

PLAIN-BACKED ANTPITTA

Grallaria haplonota Pl. 175

Identification 17cm. Generally uniform brown above and paler, more rufous or cinnamon below. Mesial paler and may continue round head-sides below ear-coverts, throat also paler but usually grades into upper breast. Bill bicoloured, with blackish maxilla and pale below (latter varying according to race or morph), eyes brown, and legs and feet grey, vinaceous grey or vinaceous. Juvenile mostly dark brown, rufous on belly and undertail-coverts; streaked above, the short streaks inclining to spots on tips of feathers above; feathers of back fringed darker brown, lending a softly scaled appearance. Breast also spotted with slightly darker brown fringes to feathers.

Ssp. *G. h. chaplinae* (E Ec, SE Co) like *haplonota* but more back more greenish-olive, crown lightly scaled with black

G. h. haplonota (NC Ve) brown morph olive-brown above with buffy mesial and throat, grading into rufous below; bill has mandible yellowish, legs and feet vinaceous grey; green morph is greenish-olive above with fine whitish feathers around eyes and on lores, mesial and throat white and there is a vestigial necklace formed by blackish fringes to green-olive upper breast; mandible flesh-coloured, legs and feet cool grey

G. h. parambae (NW Ec, W Co) rufous-brown above, slightly reddish on crown and paler lores, mesial, throat and underparts uniform cinnamon; mandible grey basally, flesh-coloured distally, legs and feet pale grey

G. h. pariae (NE Ve) rich ruddy brown above with fine yellowish feathers around eyes, mesial and throat bright rufous, paler on throat, underparts rufous, richer on breast-sides and flanks; mandible horn-coloured, legs and feet rich vinaceous

Habits Very difficult to find as keeps well within cover in densely vegetated areas.

Status Rare to locally frequent in Ecuador and Colombia, locally common in Venezuela
Habitat Upper Tropical to Subtropical Zones. Dense undergrowth in cloud forest, favouring steep slopes and treefalls, 700–1,800m.
Voice Sings from low perch, a series of low, hollow, mournful notes that gradually become louder and rise in pitch before falling at end (R&G). A slow, measured series of 5–9 low notes, rising slightly in middle, *wü, wüü, wüü, whüü, whüü, whüü, wüü, wüü, wü* (Hilty). Song 4–5 s long, 10–18 notes at rate of 3 per s, pitch and volume increasing initially and falling somewhat at end (K&S).
Note Race *parambae* considered possibly a separate species by Stiles & Álvarez-López (1995).

OCHRE-STRIPED ANTPITTA

Grallaria dignissima Pl. 176

Identification 19cm. Brown above, white lores, ochraceous-rufous face and upper breast, rest of underparts white, streaked black on breast-sides and flanks, the stripes being formed by the black outer fringes to the lanceolate white feathers. Bill grey, darker above, eyes dark, legs and feet grey. From Chestnut-crowned, Spotted and Thrush-like Antpittas by rufous on throat (all others have broad white throats).

Ssp. Monotypic (E Ec, SE Co)

Habits Walks, runs, hops and bounds rapidly, sings from a low perch.
Status Rare to uncommon in Ecuador and Colombia.
Habitat Lower Tropical Zone, to 450m. Humid *terra firme* forest, with a propensity for areas with running streams in uneven terrain.
Voice A mournful and far-reaching 2-part song, *whü, wheeeow*, the second part turning downward. Repeated at intervals of 5–10 s.
Notes Formerly placed in genus *Thamnocharis*, but later merged into *Grallaria* by Lowery & O'Neill (1969).

CHESTNUT-CROWNED ANTPITTA

Grallaria ruficapilla Pl. 178

Identification 19.5–20.5cm. Top and sides of head rufous, back and upperparts tawny, entire underparts white with streaks varying according to subspecies; streaked feathers on the breast-sides and flanks are somewhat lanceolate, thighs brown. Bill largely blackish with grey base to lower mandible, eyes brown, legs and feet vary from pale bluish-grey to dark grey. Immature has black barring on head that gradually becomes rufous, wing-coverts and many back feathers have tips fringed orange with subterminal black spots. Flank feathers somewhat rounded at tips, not lanceolate as in adult. Chick has wings and tail of immature, but body feathers mostly fluffy, and barred rufous and black. Throat white, belly and undertail-coverts sandy, but thighs barred. Bill rosy, eyes dark, legs and feet dark grey.

Ssp. *G. r. albiloris* (S Ec) white lores, moustachial and mostly white ear-coverts
G. r. avilae (N Ve) head rufous with no blackish streaks, feathers from breast-sides to flanks have pale olive outer edges, then black with a white stripe on centre; legs and feet olive-grey
G. r. connectens (SW Ec) like *ruficapilla* but slightly paler with white lores and white-streaked ear-coverts
G. r. nigrolineata (Ve: Andes) darkish lines on face-sides and black streaks on breast, feathers on flanks white with black streaks on outer half; legs and feet pale blue-grey
G. r. perijana (NW Ve, NE Co) creamy-white below, with a few brown streaks on throat-sides and on breast, feathers on breast-sides olive with white central streaks, becoming all white on flanks with an olive line on outer edge; legs and feet dark blue-grey
G. r. ruficapilla (Ec, Co: Andes) pale lores, streaks on body-sides tricoloured like *avilae*, with black streaks on centre of breast and belly; legs and feet pale blue-grey

Habits Probably tolerates human disturbance more than any other member of family.
Status Frequent and widespread in Ecuador, widespread and common in Colombia and Venezuela.
Habitat Upper Tropical to Temperate Zones. Foothill forest, paths, borders and clearings, disturbed land, even gardens and scrub, and secondary woodland alongside human developments.
Voice Song very short, barely 1.5 s, a series of 3 different notes but very distinctive and well-known throughout range. In Ecuador and Colombia rendered *com-pra pan* but in Venezuela as *Com-pa-dre*. Responds very well to playback and will even walk up to tape recorder to examine where other bird is hiding (M. L. Goodwin, pers. comm.).

WATKINS'S ANTPITTA

Grallaria watkinsi Pl. 176

Identification 18cm. Rufous on top and sides of head streaked both whitish and dark; rest of upperparts olive, also streaked on back. Throat white and rest of underparts whitish with broad dark olivaceous streaks on breast and body-sides. Bill horn-coloured, darker on maxilla, eyes brown, legs and feet salmon-pink. From Chestnut-crowned, which it replaces at lower levels, by paler, streaked crown and salmon-pink legs.

Ssp. Monotypic (SW Ec)

Status Frequent in Ecuador.
Habitat Tropical and Lower Subtropical Zones to 1,800m. Tends to prefer dry woodland, semi-deciduous and montane forest, and may occur in regenerating scrub and second growth, usually in cover but often comes into open while foraging.
Voice Responds well to playback, but reportedly sings only in breeding season, July–August, at dawn and dusk (K&S). Song distinctive, a series of 4–7 well-enunciated and emphatic notes, the last rising sharply, *keeu, kew-kew-kew k-wheeeeī?* (R&G). Call outside breeding season like last part of song, only faster (K&S).

Notes Formerly considered a subspecies of *G. ruficapilla*, but their songs are very different, they differ in plumage and bare-parts details, and intermediates are unknown from the area where they overlap (K&S).

SANTA MARTA ANTPITTA

Grallaria bangsi Pl. 176

Identification 18cm. Undistinguished and easily overlooked; brown above with some subtle pale feathering before and behind eyes and a touch of rufous on ear-coverts. Below, white with some bright rufous-orange on chin and brownish streaks throughout except centre of belly. Bill dark horn above, pale horn mandible, eyes dark brown, legs and feet grey. No other similar antpitta in its range.

Ssp. Monotypic (NE Co: Santa Marta)

Habits Apparently less retiring than congeners and more likely to be seen in clearings, treefalls or at edges of forest, particularly in early morning.

Status Fairly common within its restricted range, but obviously at risk from deforestation and habitat loss.

Habitat Subtropical Zone, 1,200–2,400 m, usually above 1,600 m. Cloud forest, mature secondary woodland and undergrowth tangles at forest edges.

Voice A frequently heard call, *c.*1 s in duration given every 10 s. Two notes, a loud flat *bob white*, not strongly upslurred (H&B), or, 2 similar whistles, the first slightly rising, the second distinctly so (K&S).

CUNDINAMARCA ANTPITTA

Grallaria kaestneri Pl. 176

Identification 15–16cm. Particularly dull and undistinguished antpitta. Dull brown above and streaked dull brown over greyish underparts, paler on throat and belly, both of which are unstreaked. Bill grey, eyes brown, legs and feet vinaceous pale grey. Unlikely to be confused with any other antpitta in its range.

Ssp. Monotypic (Co: E Andes)

Status Fairly common within its highly restricted range.

Habitat Upper Subtropical Zone, 1,800–2,300m. Cloud forest and mature secondary woodland with a preference for dense dark understorey. Apparently tolerates considerable forest disturbance.

Voice Song consists of 2–3 short whistles, the first slightly shorter, the series rising in pitch and lasting 1 s.

GREY-NAPED ANTPITTA

Grallaria griseonucha Pl. 177

Identification 16–17cm. Appears entirely deep reddish-brown, but crown olive and nape grey. Lores grey and underparts more rufescent. Bill dark, pale horn at base of mandible, eyes brown, legs grey. Closest confusion species is Rufous Antpitta, from which separated by grey nape, deeper rufous underparts and grey legs, but ranges not known to overlap.

Ssp. *G. g. griseonucha* (Ve: Mérida) very little grey on lores and mandible has base only slightly paler; pale shafts to long feathers of ear-coverts, breast and flanks; legs and feet brownish-grey

G. g. tachirae (Ve: Táchira) grey lores paler than grey of nape, mandible pale horn, slightly more olive-brown above, pale throat, buffy scalloping on belly and vent, legs and feet grey

Status Venezuelan endemic, locally frequent to common in its Andean range.

Habitat Temperate Zone, at 2,300–2,800m. Floor of dense and tangled undergrowth of cloud forest, often in or near stands of *Chusquea* bamboo.

Voice Sings year-round: primary song is a rapid series of hollow, low but rising notes, loudest at end, *wü, wü-wü-wü wu'wU'WU* delivered quickly and ending abruptly (Hilty). Also given as a series of 10–16 similar hollow notes increasing in volume to near end, then fading on final note, the pitch even or falling slightly during first half then rising. Lasts less than 2 s, uttered roughly every 10 s (K&S). Call a single whistled *whüüt?* uttered singly at long intervals or in irregular series (Hilty). Alternatively 2–3 notes, the first usually weakest, given every few seconds for several minutes, often with a pause before last note (K&S).

BICOLOURED ANTPITTA

Grallaria rufocinerea Pl. 176

Identification 15–16cm. Head and upperparts deep rufous, breast and underparts slate grey. Bill blackish, eyes brown, legs and feet grey. Chestnut-naped Antpitta is larger, bright rufous head contrasts with darker back, has paler bill and grey eyes with a spot of postocular white skin.

Ssp. *G. r. romeroana* (S Co: Magdalena Valley and W Putumayo, NW Ec: NW Sucumbíos) rufous chin and throat

G. r. rufocinerea (Co: SC Andes, S Antioquia to W Huila) black chin and throat

Habits Behaviour little known, presumably much like other *Grallaria*.

Status Vulnerable. Rare in Ecuador, where first recorded 1999, fairly common within very limited range in Colombia, where threatened by forest clearance, although appears reasonably tolerant of disturbance.

Habitat Temperate Zone, 1,950–3,100m, usually above 2,150m. Understorey of temperate forest in Ecuador, cloud forest in Colombia, also in secondary woodland and undergrowth at edges of forest.

Voice Song a high, clear whistled *treeeee* or slurred *treeeeeaaaa* given at short intervals (H&B), slurred upwards or downwards. A descending series of 6–7 whistles, 5–6 s long, given in duet, perhaps between male and female (K&S).

JOCOTOCO ANTPITTA

Grallaria ridgelyi Pl. 178

Identification 20–22cm. Very distinctive, unmistakable antpitta. Top and sides of head glossy black with large white patch of bristle-like feathers from lores to fore ear-coverts and covering base of mandible. Nape greyish-olive, back and wing-coverts greenish-olive, wings and tail rufous. Chin white, grading into grey underparts. Heavy bill black, eyes dark red, legs and feet grey.

Ssp. Monotypic (S Ec)

Habits Poorly known and difficult to see. Seems to forage in pairs and is very shy, but responds well to playback.

Status Endangered. Ecuadorian endemic, threatened due to vulnerability of tiny (known) range (180km^2); uncommon and extremely local (Heinz *et al.* 2005).

Habitat Upper Subtropical Zone, 2,300–2,680m. Moss-rich montane forest with ample bamboo, preferring steep, overgrown areas near streams.

Voice Series of low-pitched *hoo* notes, uttered by male every *c.*1 s, which may continue for 15 s to over 1 minute. Most frequent at dawn or dusk (R&G). Reminiscent of a dog bark or Rufous-banded Owl. Both sexes call a similarly pitched but softer *ho-co*, with the second note usually lower, occasionally higher; alarm similar but second note churred (K&S).

Note A recently described species (Krabbe *et al.* 1999).

CHESTNUT-NAPED ANTPITTA

Grallaria nuchalis Pl. 177

Identification 20cm. Top of head and nape rufous, darker (or grey) on ear-coverts, back, wing-coverts and tail brown, with tertials and remiges rufous, fringed brown; bill grey to dark grey, eyes grey with spot of white postocular skin, legs and feet grey. Race *obsoleta* most like Bicoloured Antpitta, which is more easterly in its distribution; range of *nuchalis* lies slightly south of Bicoloured, but more likely to co-occur, though separable by much brighter rufous head, with clearly contrasting nape and mantle.

Ssp. *G. n. nuchalis* (E Ec) palest race
G. n. obsoleta (NW Ec) darkest race, top of head darker and more olivaceous than nape as a broad rufous band, blackish on face and ear-coverts
G. n. ruficeps (Co: E & C Andes) uniformly rich rufous top of head and nape

Habits Responds well to playback, but difficult to see within dense stands of bamboo. Like many antpittas, most likely to be seen in open early in morning.

Status Uncommon to locally frequent in Ecuador, uncommon in Colombia.

Habitat Temperate Zone, 2,000–3,000m. Cloud forest, particularly with dense stands of *Chusquea* bamboo.

Voice Song of *obsoleta* a distinctive and far-carrying series of somewhat metallic notes, at first hesitating, gradually accelerating, ending in short series of rapidly rising tinkling notes, *tew; tew, tew, tew-tew-tew-the-te-ti-ti-tititit?* Song of *nuchalis* has different pattern, starting with a fast phrase, *tew-te-te-tew, tew-tew-tew-tew-tew-titititititi?* Song of *ruficeps* in Colombia is quite different, it consisting of 2 phrases up to 15 s apart. The first is short, the second twice as long. Each starts with a single, easily missed hiccup note, followed by a series of even notes, then 2–3 rising, slightly faster and slightly sharper notes, e.g., *whu'ert, whert whert whert, whet-wheet ...... whu'ert, whert* (9–10 times), *whit-wheet-wheet* (C. D. Cadena recording). Birds from Medellín sound slightly different, with hiccup more pronounced and series rising gently throughout song, which is repeated every 10 s. First song had 8 *wheert* notes and ended with same hiccup that preceded it, with subsequent songs extended by an additional note each time, but end hiccup dropped (D. Calderon Franco recording).

Notes Northern race, *ruficeps*, formerly considered a separate species, but placed within *G. nuchalis* by Peters (1951). On basis of voice, it appears much more different than currently recognised, and might be returned to species rank. Also, race *obsoleta* is perhaps best treated specifically, also based on differences in voice, (K&S).

YELLOW-BREASTED ANTPITTA

Grallaria flavotincta Pl. 176

Identification 17cm. Cleanly contrasting, bicoloured bird, dark rufous-brown above and yellow below, the yellow fading to off-white on flanks and undertail-coverts, with slight brown wash on flanks. Bill blackish, eyes dark brown, legs and feet mid grey. From White-bellied Antpitta by yellow underparts; White-bellied is all white below with noticeably browner wash to breast-sides and flanks (*castanea*).

Ssp. Monotypic (NW Ec, Co: W & C Andes)

Status Rare to locally uncommon in Ecuador (where first recorded 1984) and Colombia. A restricted-range species vulnerable to habitat loss through deforestation.

Habitat Upper Tropical to Lower Subtropical Zones, 1,500 (1,300 in K&S) to 2,350m. Favours humid dense undergrowth of montane forests, often in bamboo, but may be found at forest edges, particularly early in morning.

Voice Short fast song given every 15–20 s, a whistled *pu-püüü-puuh*, with first note soft and easily missed (R&G). Responds to playback, when might utter a shrill shriek, *eeeeeeeee-yk*! (R&G, K&S).

Notes Formerly considered a subspecies of *G. hypoleuca* (H&B, S&M), when carried name Bay-backed Antpitta, but also separated by some earlier authors. Due to differences in voice, treated as a separate species in R&T, R&G, and K&S.

WHITE-BELLIED ANTPITTA

Grallaria hypoleuca Pl. 176

Identification 17cm. Cleanly contrasting, bicoloured bird, dark rufous-brown above and white (perhaps with a soft grey tone) below. Bill blackish, eyes dark brown, legs and feet pale grey. From Yellow-breasted by complete lack of yellow. Race *castanea* has considerably more brown on body-sides.

Ssp. *G. h. castanea* (E Ec, SW Co) noticeably smaller, brighter chestnut above and more chestnut wash on breast-sides and flanks
G. h. hypoleuca (Co: E Andes) very little chestnut wash on flanks

Habits Seems tolerant of habitat degradation and occurs in fragmented areas, landslides and treefalls, as well as at forest edges.
Status Uncommon to frequent, fairly common at some localities in Ecuador and Colombia.
Habitat Upper Tropical to Lower Subtropical Zones, 1,400–2,200m. Humid montane forests.
Voice Short fast song, *too, téw-téw* repeated every *c.*10 s, sometimes sounding like a *Glaucidium* pygmy owl (R&G, K&S).
Note Formerly considered conspecific with *G. flavocincta*, when known as Bay-backed Antpitta.

RUFOUS ANTPITTA

Grallaria rufula Pl. 177

Identification 14–14.5cm. Very variable: rufous throughout, or with white belly, or rather olive above and buffy below. Bill blackish above, flesh-coloured mandible with dark tip, eyes brown, legs and feet greyish. Unmistakable in Ecuador and parts of Venezuela where plumage all rufous. Similarly, on Santa Marta easily recognised. Race *saltuensis* (north-east Colombia and north-west Venezuela) may be confused with a poorly marked Scaled Antpitta or Tawny Antpitta, though latter has noticeable pale eye-ring.

Ssp. *G. r. rufula* (Andes: Ec, Co & Ve) rufous throughout, paler below; legs and feet vinaceous
G. r. saltuensis (NE Co & NW Ve: Perijá) olive above, pale ochraceous to creamy-white below; legs and feet pale brown
G. r. spatiator (Co: Santa Marta) mainly rufous, paler below with white belly; legs and feet pale grey

Status Uncommon to frequent in Ecuador, and locally fairly common in Colombia, very locally frequent in Venezuela.
Habitat Temperate Zone to Páramo, 2,300–3,600m. Montane cloud forest, favouring areas near streams and other damp spots, particularly likely to be found in or around stands of *Chusquea* bamboo.
Voice Race *rufula* has a series of *tu* notes given so rapidly as to almost run together as a single trill up to 4 s (R&G) or 7 s long (K&S), and a clear ringing *pih*, *piopee* or *peé pipipee* (R&G). Sings infrequently (K&S). Race *spatiator* has a shorter song, some 30 notes in 3 s and falling gradually in pitch. Song of *saltuensis* unknown (Hilty).
Notes Possibly includes more than one species, as indicated by significant regional variation in song (K&S) and plumage. Race *saltuensis* has different size and plumage, and is perhaps a separate species (Hilty); it may be more closely related to *G. quitensis* and possibly best treated as a subspecies of latter (K&S). *Saltuensis* was treated as a separate species, Perijá Antpitta, in SCJ&W.

TAWNY ANTPITTA

Grallaria quitensis Pl. 177

Identification Race *alticola* 16cm, *quitensis* 18cm. Uniform warm brown above, underparts rufescent with paler (*alticola*) or darker (*quitensis*) flammulations. Bill blackish, eyes brown, legs and feet pale olive-grey.

Ssp. *G. q. alticola* (Co: E Andes) smaller and brighter with more white below
G. q. quitensis (Ec, Co: C Andes) larger, with heavier bill; somewhat darker and more richly coloured below

Habits Comparatively easy to see in semi-open areas, being fairly tolerant of habitat disturbance and agriculture. Runs and hops, and will perch on poles and stems in open to call. Quite vocal.
Status Frequent to common in Ecuador, locally common in Colombia.
Habitat Temperate Zone, 3,000–4,500 m in Ecuador, 3,000–3,700 in Colombia, rarely lower, to 2,700 in both countries. Elfin forest and páramo with scattered bushes, shrubs and *Espeletia*, pastures with shrubs and bushes, and areas near water.
Voice Song of *quitensis* in Ecuador is a loud, far-reaching *took, tu-tu* (R&G), given perched in open, almost in manner of a meadowlark. In Colombia, *alticola* has a lively *pit-wheer perwheedit*, with stress on first syllable, which may be omitted (K&S).
Note On basis of different vocalisations, *alticola* might be better treated as a separate species (K&S).

BROWN-BANDED ANTPITTA

Grallaria milleri Pl. 178

Identification 17cm. Essentially bicoloured, brown above and white below, with rufous-brown wash forming band on breast, and along flanks and thighs. Bill black, eyes dark brown, legs and feet bluish-grey. Juvenile barred and flecked blackish all over (K&S). Despite apparent similarity to some other antpittas, there is no other similar within its range. From Tawny Antpitta by clear white underparts with breast-band, whereas Tawny is clearly flammulated rufous.

Ssp. Monotypic (Co: C Andes)

Status Endangered. Entire known range either deforested or under threat, but species not well known. Appears fairly tolerant of disturbance and possibly exists in areas not yet surveyed.
Habitat Temperate Zone, 1,800–3,140m. Dense undergrowth of humid montane forests, and second-growth woodland with dense undergrowth.
Voice Song a series of 3 whistles given within *c.*1 s, pause between first and second note, last note slightly higher pitched. Also a slightly rising *wooee*, given frequently (K&S).

Hylopezus antpittas are small, rotund birds with stubby, downturned tails, a large pale eye-ring and pink legs; bright ochre underwing-coverts. They may fly up several metres into cover when disturbed, and will sing from an exposed branch well above ground. Apart from foraging quite close to the ground, they are apparently very fond of hopping through branches at about (human) eye level. May flick their wings when nervous, and also move their body from side to side without moving the head. They are inhabitants of lowland rain forests.

STREAK-CHESTED ANTPITTA

Hylopezus perspicillatus Pl. 177

Identification 14cm. Rotund little antpitta. Top of head and nape grey, large ring of whitish feathers around eyes, lores and ear-coverts cream with black mesial line, upperparts dark brown with buffy streaks on mantle and buffy spots on tips of median and greater wing-coverts. Underparts whitish to cream with some rufous suffusion on breast, and blackish streaks on breast and body-sides. Bill grey with pale base to mandible, eyes dark brown, legs and feet pinkish-grey.

Ssp. *H. p. pallidior* (C Co) pale grey top of head, pure white throat and underparts, narrow streaks on mantle
H. p. periophthalmicus (W Ec, W Co) rufous suffusion over breast, mesial and streaks on breast and flanks bold black; rufous terminal spots on wing-coverts
H. p. perspicillatus (NW Co) pale rufous wash to breast, tear-shaped streaks on mantle, and buffy crescent-shaped terminal spots on wing-coverts

Habits Hops, walks and runs, and not easy to see unless singing, when it may remain on an exposed perch, often several metres above ground.
Status Rare to locally frequent in Ecuador, uncommon in Colombia.
Habitat Tropical Zone, to 800m in Ecuador and to 1,200m in Colombia, more common at lower elevations. Prefers light undergrowth of humid forests.
Voice Race *pallidior* utters a series of whistled notes, repeated persistently, *pay-pee-pee-pee-pay-pay-paaw*, rising slightly, then last 3 notes falling melancholically. Race *perspicillatus* sings *deh, dee, dee, dee, dee, deé-eh, déh-oh, dóh-a*, last 3 couplets falling away (H&B). Race *periophthalmicus* gives melancholy song, rising at first then fading away, *poh, po-po-po-po-po-po-peu-peu-peu* (R&G).
Notes Genus *Hylopezus* separated from *Grallaria* by Lowery & O'Neill (1969). Called Spectacled Antpitta in AOU (1983), but Streak-chested Antpitta in most field guides and in SACC list.

SPOTTED ANTPITTA

Hylopezus macularius Pl. 177

Identification 14cm. Grey top of head and nape, back brown with slight pale fringes to wing-coverts, large pale eye-ring, black streaks on head-sides (mesial and ear-coverts), all white below with some rufous on body-sides and black streaks on breast and body-sides. Bill black above, horn-coloured on mandible, eyes brown, legs and feet horn.

Ssp. *H. m. diversus* (SE Co, S Ve: Amazonas) fine buffy streaks on mantle, heavy black mesial and facial streaks, brownish eye-ring, olivaceous flanks, black streaks and spots over breast and belly
H. m. macularius (SE Ve, Gu, FG) paler olive-brown back, uniform, paler streaks on head-sides, streaks below restricted to breast, rufous wash on flanks

Habits Hops, walks and runs, alternating stops, may fly some metres up when disturbed, but returns to ground and may run into cover. Generally shy, but occasionally bold and may rarely be seen singing from an exposed perch.
Status Uncommon and very local in Venezuela, uncommon in Guyana, frequent in French Guiana.
Habitat Lower Tropical Zone to 500m. Dense undergrowth of lowland forests, areas around treefalls and gallery forest.
Voice Race *macularius* sings mostly at dawn and dusk, a low, rhythmically whistled *wü-whoo, wü-whee-whee*, first and third notes lower pitched (Hilty), given as *whoa-whoa-wok-whoa-wok-wok*. Song, presumed to be *diversus*, *hoor-hoor-hoor-hoor-ho-ho* (K&S).
Notes Genus *Hylopezus* separated from *Grallaria* by Lowery & O'Neill (1969). *H. macularius* possibly includes more than one species (Hilty, K&S).

THICKET ANTPITTA

Hylopezus dives Pl. 177

Identification 14cm. Top of head and nape olive-grey, rest of upperparts dark brown. Lores and ear-coverts buffy with vague blackish spots and streaks, Underparts white with rufous wash on breast and body-sides, black streaks on mesial, breast and flanks. Bill blackish, pale horn on mandible, eyes brown, legs and feet pale brownish-grey. Rather similar to Spotted Antpitta, but considerable gap in ranges, also similar to smaller Streak-chested Antpitta but lacks spots and streaks above, and large pale eye-ring.

Ssp. *H. d. barbacoae* (W Co)

Habits Forages low in tangled thickets and on logs, walking, running and bounding. Sings often, throughout day, often using a fallen log as perch.
Status Common on disturbed coastal plain and actually seems to favour light habitat disturbance.
Habitat Tropical Zone to 900m. Tangled thickets and shrubs at edges of younger, second-growth woodland and forest borders. Normally shuns forest interior except at large treefalls and small abandoned clearings.
Voice Song a series of mellow notes, rising at first, then levelling, *oh-oh-ou-oü-oü-üü-üü-üü!* ending abruptly (H&B).
Notes Genus *Hylopezus* separated from *Grallaria* by Lowery & O'Neill (1969). *H. dives* was formerly considered a subspecies of *H. fulviventris*, but separated on basis of vocal differences. In R&T, confusingly called Fulvous-bellied Antpitta, the name that was used when species included *fulviventris*. Name Thicket Antpitta proposed by AOU (1998) to emphasise the split and to avoid use of Fulvous-bellied for *H. dives*, as may suggest that it corresponds instead to *H. fulviventris*, White-lored Antpitta.

WHITE-LORED ANTPITTA

Hylopezus fulviventris Pl. 179

Identification 14.5cm. Head grey with pale lores and triangular white postocular spot, rest of upperparts rich brown. Throat and malar white with thin black mesial, underparts white with soft fulvous flush to breast and body-sides with faint, blackish streaks on breast and belly-sides. Bill black, pale base to mandible, eyes brown, legs and feet salmon-pink. From Thrush-like Antpitta by white around eyes and fulvous on underparts.

Ssp. *H. f. caquetae* (Co) head pale grey, lores cream
H. f. fulviventris (E Ec) head dark grey, lores white

Status Uncommon in Ecuador and local in Colombia.
Habitat Lower Tropical Zone, to 750m in Ecuador, 600m in Colombia. On or just above ground in very dense, tangled undergrowth at borders of lowland forest and in overgrown, tangled clearings; heard far more often than seen.
Voice Sings frequently, a short, slow series of 3–4 abrupt hollow notes, *kwoh-kwoh-kwoh*, with first note soft and inaudible at distance (R&G), or series of 4–6 downslurred *cuock* notes (K&S).
Note Voice is similar to that of *H. berlepschi* (Amazonian Antpitta), and they might be conspecific (K&S).

Myrmothera antpittas are fairly small, *Grallaria*-like but with smaller bills, and like *Hylopezus* in habits. They sing from an exposed perch 1m or more above ground, and may fly up when disturbed, but usually are well hidden in dense undergrowth.

THRUSH-LIKE ANTPITTA
Myrmothera campanisona Pl. 178

Identification 15cm. Brown above, white below, with streaks according to subspecies. Bill 2-toned, dark horn maxilla and pale horn mandible with darkish tip, eyes brown, with pale ocular ring and small triangular, whitish spot behind eyes.

Ssp. *M. c. campanisona* (SE Ve, Guianas) paler version of *dissors*
M. c. dissors (SE Co, S Ve) pale olive-brown above, with paler olive-brown streaks on breast and body-sides; legs and feet olive-brown
M. c. modesta (Co: E Andes) chestnut above with grey streaks below; legs and feet pale pinkish-brown
M. c. signata (E Ec) rufous-brown above with similar-coloured streaks below; legs and feet flesh

Habits Very shy and skulking in dense second growth and at treefalls.
Status Frequent and widespread in Ecuador. Locally frequent in Venezuela, frequent in Guyana and French Guiana.
Habitat Lower Tropical Zone, mostly below 700m in Ecuador, below 600m in Colombia and below 800m in Venezuela. Found in dense thickets at borders of humid *terra firme* forest, rarely savanna forest; areas where regeneration is at early stage and very thick on ground, often along streams.
Voice Song in Ecuador (*signata*) 4–6 hollow whistles delivered quickly, *whoh-whoh-whoh-whoh-whoh*, for protracted periods (R&G). In Colombia, a trogon-like series of *c.*10 accelerating and rising *woo* notes followed by an abruptly slowing and falling series of *woop* notes (H&B). In Venezuela, a short series of 5–6 hollow, resonant whistles *wüh wüh WUH Wüh wü*, increasing in volume and then fading at end. May sing from same thicket for days on end (Hilty).

TEPUI ANTPITTA
Myrmothera simplex Pl. 178

Identification 16–16.5cm. Head, except white throat, and upperparts dark brown, underparts white with brown to grey on breast and body-sides according to race; bill black, eyes brown, legs and feet grey. Juveniles vary considerably, again according to race. From other antpittas by broad breast-band.

Ssp. *M. s. duidae* (S Ve: Yaví, Duida and Neblina massifs) very much like *guaiquinimae* but has more white on belly, although this is flecked
M. s. guaiquinimae (S Ve: Cerro Guaiquinima and Paurai-tepui) dark umber above, pale throat finely streaked cinnamon, broad cinnamon band on breast and body-sides to undertail-coverts; juvenile almost wholly deep rufous-brown with whitish chin, base of mandible yellow-horn
M. s. pacaraimae (SE Ve: Cerro Pacaraima) very much like *simplex* but less densely coloured on breast and flanks
M. s. simplex (SE Ve: Gran Sabana, Roraima, CW Gu: Roraima) dark brown above with white throat finely marked with dark grey streaks, broad olive-grey band on breast and body-sides to undertail-coverts; juvenile like adult but has white belly heavily flammulated rufous and undertail-coverts rufous

Habits Found singly in dense undergrowth on tepui summits and in stunted forest of upper slopes. Hops and runs, sometimes curious and boldly comes into open, but is equally adept at staying concealed.
Status Frequent in Venezuela, uncommon and local in Guyana.
Habitat Upper Tropical to Temperate Zones, 600–2,400m, but mostly above 1,200m. Dense mossy undergrowth of thick rain and cloud forest, with a liking for treefalls.
Voice Song consists of 6–7 deliberately-paced hollow notes, rising slightly at first and increasing in volume, last notes on same pitch, *whu-whu-whu-WU-hu-hu* (Hilty).
Notes Formerly called Brown-breasted Antpitta. Recent sight records in Guyana (Barnett *et al.* 2002) were tentatively assigned to race *simplex*.

Grallaricula are the smallest of the antpittas, tiny, rotund birds with scarcely any tail, brown and rufous above, and ranging from rich rufous to white below, with small, fine bills. They inhabit the lower undergrowth, performing wing-assisted hopping or short flights through bushes and shrubs within 1m or so of the ground, but only occasionally visiting the ground. Most often seen at (human) eye level or slightly lower. May flick their wings when nervous, and also move their body from side to side without moving the head.

OCHRE-BREASTED ANTPITTA

Grallaricula flavirostris Pl. 179

Identification 10cm. Rotund little bird with greyish top of head and nape, greenish-olive above, rufous on head-sides and breast with blackish fringes to feathers of breast and flanks, resulting in streaks that may be dense and bold, or faint; white belly and undertail-coverts, dark bill, brown eyes with ring of paler feathers, and vinaceous-pink legs and feet. Much variation within any population, though some seem more prone to vary than others (see plate). Confusion could arise between races or individuals with weak or poorly defined streaks on breast and Slate-crowned Antpitta, which never has black streaks on breast. In Ecuador, Slate-crowned is usually found at higher elevations, but in Colombia they species do overlap on Pacific coast, where Ochre-breasted has the strongest streaking on breast and flanks.

Ssp. *G. f. flavirostris* (E Ec, Co: E Andes) breast variably streaked, bill bicoloured in some, totally dark in others

G. f. mindoensis (NW Ec) face-sides to breast and body-sides rich rufous, throat may be paler, breast boldly streaked; pale variant or morph has white throat and ochre on upper breast and sides, also streaked black; 2 variations in bill colour, independent of morph, pale brown and dark brown

G. f. ochraceiventris (Co: W Andes) white throat and belly with rich ochre breast, black streaks across entire breast and on white sides; bill black

G. f. zarumae (SW Ec) plain ochraceous underparts with subtle (and variable) flammulations slightly darker; dark variant, or morph has underparts significantly paler, but both morphs have all-yellow bill

Habits Active and tolerant to indifferent of observers, but small and difficult to see in foliage. Forages amongst mossy branches low down and will drop to floor. Also sallies for insects. Be alert for sudden little movements.

Status Uncommon to locally frequent in Ecuador and Colombia.

Habitat Upper Tropical to Subtropical Zones, 800–2,000 m in Ecuador, 500–2,100m in Colombia. Fairly open undergrowth (Hilty), and dense lower growth (R&G) of wet, mossy forest in foothills and on mountains.

Voice Song a simple *weeeuu*, repeated at 8–10 s intervals (R&G). A short, ascending series of 5–8 mellow whistles, *wuwu-wu-wu-uu-uu-uu-ueet*, faster at end (Hilty). Rarely heard song 7 s long, an evenly paced series of 30 notes, over first half rising in volume and pitch, then steady. Call a single, emphatic whistle (K&S).

RUSTY-BREASTED ANTPITTA

Grallaricula ferrugineipectus Pl. 179

Identification 10–11cm. Small, rotund bird, pale olive-brown above, lores orange, head-sides and chin to breast and flanks rufous, with white belly and undertail-coverts. Bill horn-coloured, darker above, eyes dark brown, legs and feet flesh-coloured. Similar Slate-crowned Antpitta has grey on top of head and nape.

Ssp. *G. f. ferrugineipectus* (Co: Santa Marta, W & N Ve) white crescent on upper breast

G. f. rara (E Co, NW Ve) top of head ruddy brown, white spot or patch in centre of upper breast

Habits Usually in pairs, forages amongst mossy branches near ground and sallies for insects like a flycatcher.

Status Uncommon and local in Colombia, frequent to common in Venezuela.

Habitat Upper Tropical to Temperate Zones, 1,750–3,050m. Undergrowth of humid montane forest, often associated with large stands of bamboo. May be seen in drier areas than other *Grallaricula*.

Voice Dawn song *twa-twa-twa-twa-twa-twa-cwi-cwi-cwi-cwi-cwi-cwi-cwi*, the second half louder and higher pitched (H&B).

Notes More than one species may be involved (R&T). Race *rara* formerly treated as a separate species, but placed within *G. ferrugineipectus* by Peters (1951), though H&B suggested to treat it specifically again. Southern race *leymebambae* has different voice may also be better treated specifically (K&S).

SLATE-CROWNED ANTPITTA

Grallaricula nana Pl. 179

Identification 10.5–11cm. Small rotund bird, with top of head and nape slate grey, rest of upperparts green-olive, lores, head-sides and entire underparts rufous, but some races have white belly and or vent. Bill horn-coloured, dark on maxilla, eyes brown, legs and feet salmon.

Ssp. *G. n. cumanensis* (NE Ve) significantly different in that chin, lores and undertail-coverts are orange, sides of head and body deep reddish-rufous, with a breast-band, throat, upper breast and belly pure white; legs and feet grey

G. n. kukenamensis (SE Ve) almost entirely rufous below, orange lores, eye-ring, centre of belly and undertail-coverts

G. n. nana (E Ec, Co: E Andes, W Ve) like *kukenamensis* but has white belly and undertail-coverts

G. n. olivascens (NC Ve: Turimiquire) olive-green above, underparts orange with white patch in centre of upper breast and white belly, irregular dark olive fringes to some feathers of throat and breast

G. n. pariae (NE Ve: Paria) like *kukenamensis* but has solid pure white patch on throat, and white of belly slightly larger and clearly defined

Habits Usually inside dense undergrowth within 1–2m of ground, perch-gleaning, occasionally sallies to forest floor. May hop on forest floor and stop suddenly. Seems to wander rather than stay in one locality.

Status Uncommon in Ecuador. Frequent to common in Venezuela.

Habitat Subtropical to Temperate Zones, 2,000–2,900m in Ecuador, 1,900–2,100m in Colombia, perhaps to 1,300m on

Pacific slope, and 700–2,800m in Venezuela. Undergrowth of humid forests, particularly stands of *Chusquea* bamboo.

Voice Varies only slightly racially. A P. Schwartz recording from Venezuela is rendered by H&B, *we'ti'ti'ti'ti'ti'tee'too*. Generally comprises *c*.30 notes, rising gradually over first half and then steady, the whole lasting only 2–3 s (K&S).

Notes Races of Coastal Cordillera of Venezuela, *olivascens* and *cumanensis*, possibly represent a separate species, but no significant vocal differences exist, compared to other races. Race *occidentalis* synonymised under *nana* as similar birds occur in north Peru (K&S).

SCALLOP-BREASTED ANTPITTA
Grallaricula loricata Pl. 179

Identification 10.8cm. Small, rotund bird with orange head, pale creamy mesial and throat, washed olive-green from forehead to nape and on ear-coverts, lores rich yellow-buff, and rest of upperparts olive-green. Breast to undertail-coverts white, lightly scalloped black on breast and body-sides. Bill brown on maxilla, cream mandible, eyes brown, legs and feet vinaceous-grey. Juvenile brighter and paler, having orange head unmarked olive-green, breast scalloping soft brown, and legs and feet pale pink-grey.

Ssp. Monotypic (NC Ve)

Habits Solitary and sedentary. Mainly active at dawn and dusk, in cloud forest understorey with diversity of dense and semi-open vegetation. Forages actively amongst low branches, especially those covered with moss, searching for small insects.

Status Common but local Venezuelan endemic, with many recent records by C. Verea (*in litt.*), though was formerly considered very scarce.

Habitat Subtropical Zone, from 800 to 2,100m, but mainly above 1,400m. Where range overlaps with Slate-crowned Antpitta, Scallop-breasted occupies higher elevations. Lower growth and understorey of humid montane forest, occasionally second growth.

Voice Song mostly consists of melancholic *shiiiuu* notes, repeated successively 3–5 times, or separated by 3 s intervals. Males produce a second vocalisation *shiiiiiiiiiuuuuuu*, a single, longer, descending melancholy note, probably used in territory defence (Verea 2004).

PERUVIAN ANTPITTA
Grallaricula peruviana Pl. 179

Identification 10cm. Small, rotund bird in which male has top of head and nape rich orange, lores black, ear-coverts and rest of upperparts olive-green; white below with a black malar that joins black scalloping over entire breast. Bill bicoloured, blackish above and flesh below, eyes brown with orange eye-ring, legs and feet olive. Female lacks any orange on head and eye-ring is creamy orange. Recalls Scallop-breasted Antpitta, but well separated geographically.

Ssp. Monotypic (SW Ec)

Habits Virtually unknown but presumably like congeners.

Status Rare and local in Ecuador, where first recorded 1984 (F&K).

Habitat Subtropical Zone, 1,750–2,100m. Moderately open undergrowth of humid montane forest.

Voice Not known.

Notes Considered possibly a race of Scallop-breasted Antpitta (Meyer de Schauensee 1966), but more likely forms a superspecies with Ochre-fronted Antpitta *G. ochraceifrons* of Peru (K&S).

CRESCENT-FACED ANTPITTA
Grallaricula lineifrons Pl. 179

Identification 11.5cm. Diagnostic facial pattern, top, nape and sides of head deep slate grey, with triangular orange spot on neck-sides and a broad white crescent that curves from just over lores above eye and across lower ear-coverts, and fringed black on mesial and around eye, with a triangular white postocular spot. Upperparts olive-green; chin to undertail-coverts white tinged orange and streaked black from throat to belly; bill black, eyes brown, legs and feet grey.

Ssp. Monotypic (NE Ec, N Co: C & E Andes)

Habits Hops through undergrowth, perch-gleaning, often clings sideways to stems and vines. Sallies to, and occasionally descends to forest floor.

Status Rare to frequent in Ecuador, and locally uncommon to fairly common in Colombia. Small, restricted range.

Habitat Páramo, from 2,900 to 3,400m. Undergrowth of humid montane forest. Where range overlaps with Slate-crowned Antpitta, Crescent-faced occupies higher levels.

Voice Sings 3–4 times per minute, 14–20 notes increasing steadily in pitch and volume, leveling at end (K&S), or, an ascending trill of piping notes, the last few rather shrill, e.g. *pu-pu-pe-pe-pee-pee-pi-pi-pi?* (M. B. Robbins recording, R&G).

HOODED ANTPITTA
Grallaricula cucullata Pl. 179

Identification 10.5cm. Head entirely bright orange-rufous, back olive-green, wings olive-brown and underparts greyish-white with orange-rufous thighs. Bill salmon, eyes brown. Unique plumage with all-rufous head and pale bill, and confusion unlikely.

Ssp. *G. c. cucullata* (Co: Andes) narrow crescent of white on throat, breast pale grey with short, faint flammulations below white crescent, belly white; legs and feet pale grey

G. c. venezuelana (SW Ve) (NE Co) white crescent on throat is broad, breast pale olive with pale olivaceous wash on flanks; legs and feet pale olive

Habits Poorly known. Usually seen foraging in undergrowth, hopping from perch to perch and occasionally on ground.

Status Vulnerable. Very local and uncommon to rare in Venezuela, uncommon to fairly common in Colombia, but threatened by continuing forest clearance.

Habitat Subtropical to Temperate Zones, 1,800–2,135m in Colombia, to 2,550m in Venezuela, with a possible extreme range of 1,500–2,700m. Understorey of rain and cloud forest.
Voice Undescribed, although apparently known in Colombia (Downing & Hickman 2004), where recorded as giving a di- or trisyllabic high-pitched, liquid call, repeated 2–3 times.

CONOPOPHAGIDAE – Gnateaters

Gnateaters are boldly marked inhabitants of the dense tangles that form at landslides or treefalls in South American forests. They are plump, long-legged and visually attractive, but are seldom seen, for they are quiet and elusive, keeping low and well inside the thick foliage. They are recognisable by their silvery white postocular stripe, longer and ending in a tuft in males. Fledglings show a short, rough postocular line, but are otherwise dark brown and barred, but acquire adult-like plumage very soon afterwards. Gnateaters usually perch silently on a horizontal branch, waiting for a passing insect. They do not follow mixed flocks, but seem to join the excitement when a band passes through their territory. However, at least one species has been recorded attending a swarm of army ants. Nests are cup-shaped, quite bulky and somewhat straggly. Gnateaters are now settled into their own family, Conopophagidae, but have endured an adventurous taxonomic history, having been shuffled in and out of the Formicariidae over time. Separation from the Formicariidae is based on DNA studies, first by Sibley & Ahlquist (1985, 1990), subsequently by Rice (2000).

Additional references for this family: Whitney (2003).

CHESTNUT-BELTED GNATEATER
Conopophaga aurita Pl. 180

Identification 11.5–13cm. Male has a mostly black head, white postocular line, dark brown back with barely discernible rufous tips to wing-feathers, and black fringes to those of back. Breast rich rufous, belly to undertail-coverts white, with olive-washed body-sides. Female lacks black on face and has vague white lores and a pale chin. Both sexes have long, pale blue legs.

Ssp. *C. a. aurita* (Guianas) fine black scallops on back and belly mainly clear white; female has white chin and throat

C. a. inexpectata (SE Co) very similar to *aurita* but less white, more brownish below; female has creamy-rufous chin and throat

C. a. occidentalis (E Ec) darker above with heavy black scallops, rufous more extensive on breast

Habits Forages in dense undergrowth and sometimes follows army ants. Very shy and easily missed. In threat displays, vibrating wings produce a whine.
Status Uncommon in Ecuador and Colombia.
Habitat Lower Tropical Zone, to 300m in Ecuador, 500m in Colombia and 1,300m in western Guyana. Humid lowland *terra firme* forests. Often around overgrown treefalls.
Voice Call a sneeze-like *cheff!* and a loud rattling trill, rising slightly in pitch and then levelling (R&T, R&G).

ASH-THROATED GNATEATER
Conopophaga peruviana Pl. 180

Identification 11.5–12cm. Male has notably grey head and underparts, with contrasting white postocular line, back also grey but has bold, somewhat irregular black scalloping; bill black, eyes dark, legs and feet variable grey, from pinkish to dark. Female has rufous face and breast, dark brown upperparts with rufous terminal spots on tertials and wing-coverts, and some variation, with some birds having less distinct spots on wings and throat concolorous with breast (possibly older birds).

Ssp. Monotypic (E Ec)

Habits Very furtive and easily overlooked. Forages alone or in pairs at lower levels and often found around overgrown treefalls, occasionally in lighter clearings.
Status Uncommon in Ecuador.
Habitat Tropical Zone. Lowland, humid *terra firme* forests, in areas with dense, tangled undergrowth.
Voice Calls a sharp, loud *chink!* or *zhweeik!* and a softer *cheff* (R&T, R&G).

CHESTNUT-CROWNED GNATEATER
Conopophaga castaneiceps Pl. 180

Identification 13–13.5cm. Distinguished from other gnateaters by chestnut forehead and pale lower mandible; long, tufted, bold silver-white postocular stripe; long, pale blue legs.

Ssp. *C. c. castaneiceps* (NE Ec, Co: C & E Andes) slightly greyer mantle than *chocoensis* and *chapmani* in both sexes; female darker, black feathers with subtle blackish fringe, more olivaceous-brown above, undertail-coverts plain

C. c. chapmani (SE Ec) much darker grey, more olive-brown on flanks; undertail-coverts barred; female richer, more olive brown below with white patch in centre of belly

C. c. chocoensis (W Co) above blacker on cheeks and nape, scalloping on mantle heavy; uniform grey below with gingery wash on undertail-coverts; female similar to *chapmani* but lacks any scalloping on mantle

Habits Very furtive and easily overlooked. Forages alone or in pairs in dense undergrowth, sallying from a low perch, which is changed frequently. Wings make whirring sound in flight.
Status Uncommon in Ecuador, uncommon to locally frequent in Colombia.
Habitat Upper Tropical to Subtropical Zones. Humid and wet montane forests and secondary woodland. Often at borders or around old clearings.
Voice Calls occasionally, a rattle of raspy chip notes, *chit, chit-it, chit-it-it-it-it*. Also, *check* notes in alarm (H&B)

RHINOCRYPTIDAE – Tapaculos

Tapaculos are secretive little forest-dwellers, who move about like mice on the forest floor, searching for insects through thickets and tangles in the lowest levels of the understorey, and also in more open spots such as rocky outcrops, fallen logs and dirt tracks, though never straying far from cover. They are closely related to the ground-dwelling antbirds, Formicariidae, and to the gnateaters, Conopophagidae, which relationships have been confirmed by recent genetic studies (Chesser 2004b). On the other hand, the same research has thrown into doubt inclusion of the genus *Melanopareia* within the Rhinocryptidae. However, for now, it is retained herein until further revisions are published.

All tapaculos cock their tails regularly, or keep it cocked most of the time. Their flight abilities are relatively poor, for they seldom fly but short distances, and never move far above ground. In contrast, their legs are quite strong, as would be expected of birds that mostly walk or hop. Main food is insects found in the leaf-litter or on logs or rocky outcrops, supplemented occasionally by berries and buds. The nest is a ball of grasses with an entrance hole at the side.

Rhinocryptidae is exclusively a mainland family, but is also absent from all three Guianas. The genus *Scytalopus* underwent a taxonomic revolution in 1997, when Krabbe & Schulenberg published the first findings of a major study; many taxa were reassessed and quite some recognised specifically. Additional results and further were included in Krabbe & Schulenberg (2003). Even more recently, a paper describing Stiles's Tapaculo (Cuervo *et al.* 2005) brings news of still more new species. We are confident that many more taxa in this extremely complicated and obscure family await full recognition.

Additional references for this family: Krabbe & Schulenberg (1997, 2003, hereafter K&S 1997, K&S 2003).

RUSTY-BELTED TAPACULO
Liosceles thoracicus Pl. 181

Identification 19–19.5cm. Adult male dark reddish-brown above, median and greater wing-coverts have black subterminal spots enclosing a smaller white spot, tail grey-brown, head grey with white superciliary that wraps around ear-coverts as small, irregular white spots and streaks; throat and malar white, breast white, separated from throat by broad orange patch, flanks to undertail-coverts deep rufous, barred strongly black, the bands starting on lower breast and sides; eyes dark brown, bill dark to blackish above, pale horn below, legs and feet horn. Female similar but has eyebrow narrower and much-reduced orange breast patch. Juvenile has white eyebrow broken irregularly, and lacks white spots around ear-coverts, throat and breast pale grey, scalloped dusky. Beautifully marked: look for white eyebrow, heavy brown barring on flanks and belly and wing-coverts spotting.

Ssp. *L. t. dugandi* (SE Co: W Putumayo) breast-band rufous, broad and reaches throat and neck-sides

L. t. erithacus (E Ec, SE Co: SE Nariño) breast-band orange-brown, narrower, rest of underparts washed pale yellow

Habits Forages alone or in pairs, on ground, hopping or walking inside thickets or on fallen logs and more open spots, looking for insects that crawl on litter.

Status Uncommon to locally common in Ecuador, locally frequent in Colombia.

Habitat Tropical Zone, to 600m, occasionally higher. Humid *terra firme* forest. Favours small clearings, treefalls and areas with fallen logs.

Voice Sings from ground or on fallen log, fluffing throat feathers and pushing head forward with each note. Calls include loud series of sharp *cree* notes and single, lower *tchrc*. Song a hollow *woouk*... whistle, followed by a 3–4 s pause, then a descending series of 4–6 low whistles, *wu, wu, wu, wu, wu* (H&B). Also, 1+ whistles, every 3–5 s, followed by fading whistles (K&S).

ASH-COLOURED TAPACULO
Myornis senilis Pl. 181

Identification 14cm. Adult medium grey, paler below, with duskier wings and longer, fuller tail than most tapaculos, and variable cinnamon to rusty wash on flanks and undertail-coverts; bill short and blackish above, browner below, legs and feet brown. Immature dark brown above, with slight cinnamon tone to lower rump and uppertail-coverts, pale cinnamon terminal spots on wing-coverts; chin buffy, then grey like adult to lower breast, and rest of underparts cinnamon. Juvenile rufous-brown above, ochraceous brown below, with faint darker barring on wings and tail. From other tapaculos by absence of any barring in adults.

Ssp. Monotypic (Ec, Co: C & E Andes, Ve?)

Habits Hops and creeps through dense tangles of bamboo or cane, foraging amongst dead leaves, from close to ground to *c.*4m up, but rarely on ground (K&S).

Status Uncommon to frequent in Ecuador, almost certainly occurs in Venezuela in same mountains of Tamá where occurs in Colombia.

Habitat Upper Subtropical to Temperate Zones, 2,300–3,500m in Ecuador and 2,400–3,100m in Colombia. Invariably in stands of *Chusquea* bamboo and *Neurolepis* cane in humid montane forest.

Voice Sings a low, nasal, *c.*10 s series that begins spaced, speeds up in middle and ends in a squealing trill: *chup...... chup...... chup... chup-chup... che-chup-chup.. che-che-a-chup, chik-a-da-dup, chik-a-da-dup, che-e-e-te-te-te-tetetetetetEEEEEEEeeer, terr* (Hilty).

Notes Placed in *Scytalopus* by H&B, but F&K point out that, aside from the longer tail, there exist differences in juvenile plumage and bill shape, plus a larger vocabulary than *Scytalopus*. Furthermore, K&S indicate that *Myiornis* is closer to *Merulaxis* than to *Scytalopus*. *Merulaxis* does not occur in our region.

BLACKISH TAPACULO

Scytalopus latrans Pl. 181

Identification 12–12.5cm. Male uniform dark grey or blackish-grey; eyes dark brown, bill blackish, legs and feet dark brown. Female uniform dark grey, with slight olive wash at rear. Immature browner on wings and tail, with reddish-brown outer fringes to tertials and coverts, and paler terminal spots; subtly barred brown and black on flanks and undertail-coverts. Juvenile dark brown above, almost medium brown below, barred medium brown above, from mantle to long uppertail-coverts, and barred dark brown below; wings dark brown with medium brown edges to tertials and coverts, all with diffuse terminal spots.

Ssp. *S. l. latrans* (E Ec, Co: Andes, W Ve) as described
S. l. subcinereus (SW Ec) male uniformly blackish; female much paler than female *latrans*, with extensively brown flanks; juvenile quite different from juvenile of nominate, being finely and closely barred black on dark brown above, including wing-coverts, and below

Habits Very difficult to see and presence usually revealed by its voice, though is attracted by playback. Forages alone or in loose pairs, on ground or dense, low vegetation, moving incessantly in search of insects.

Status Frequent to common in Ecuador, locally frequent in Venezuela.

Habitat Subtropical Zone to Páramo. Borders and clearings of humid or moist montane forests, in dense shrubbery, thickets, tangles of blackberry or bracken, and in hedges or bushes in open fields adjacent to forest, and montane scrub in drier, rockier areas.

Voice Pairs often duet, with female song higher pitched. In Táchira, Venezuela, song of *latrans* differs at 2 localities: in Bramón (1,800m), a series of *unk* notes, very low, hollow and nasal; and above Betania (2,200m), a slow (1 per s), series of nasal double notes, *cueep-cueep, cueep-cueep*… (Hilty). In Ecuador, a fast series of *pir* notes, lasting almost 30 s, and calls a rising *huir-huir,* but on east slope of Andes, sings a fast series of sharp *pur* notes, steadily on same level (R&G).

Notes Formerly, both races were included under *S. unicolor*, Unicoloured Tapaculo, but were separated on basis of vocalisations by Coopmans *et al.* (2001) and K&S (2003). They were treated under *S. unicolor* in Hilty, following K&S (1997). K&S (1997) and R&G suggested that *subcinereus* might deserve species-level treatment. The existence of 2 different songs in race *latrans* in Venezuela, as noted by Hilty, and of 2 different songs in *subcinereus* in Ecuador, further suggests that more than one species is involved! Note Unicoloured Tapaculo is now considered endemic to Peru.

SANTA MARTA TAPACULO

Scytalopus sanctaemartae Pl. 181

Identification 11cm. Adult grey above, with brown wings and tail, and, usually, a plain white patch on forecrown, but which may be barred black and white; underparts paler grey with some whitish mottling on sides and belly that appears as barring on some individuals, flanks to upper- and undertail-coverts closely barred rufous and dark grey; eyes brown, bill black, legs and feet flesh-brown. Female similar but has distinctly smaller forecrown patch and less whitish on sides and belly. Juvenile heavily and closely barred dark brown and rufous above; rufous on head-sides and underparts, with fringes and tips dark brown, giving a subtly barred effect to face and throat, becoming scaled on breast to flanks, but more like bars on flanks and tail-coverts, legs and feet dark horn.

Ssp. Monotypic (Co: Santa Marta)

Habits Forages on or near forest floor, and generally lower than other tapaculos.

Status Locally frequent but highly range-restricted Colombian endemic.

Habitat Subtropical Zone, 600–1,700m. Dark tangled undergrowth of mossy humid forests, in shady ravines and along montane streams.

Voice Sings a long rising and falling trill; call a sharp squeak, repeated over and over (K&S).

Note Formerly treated as a subspecies of Rufous-vented Tapaculo *S. femoralis*, but separated on basis of vocalisations by K&S (1997), and had earlier been considered a species by Cory & Hellmayr (1924).

LONG-TAILED TAPACULO

Scytalopus micropterus Pl. 183

Identification 13.5cm. Adult male dark grey with dark brown wings and tail, deep rufous-brown lower rump and uppertail-coverts, with or without blackish barring; flanks, lower belly and vent to undertail-coverts deep rufous-reddish brown with black barring; eyes dark brown, bill dusky, legs and feet horn to dusky. Female duller. Immature variably washed brownish above and has variable grey sides to breast, sides and belly. Juvenile not found.

Ssp. Monotypic (C & E Co, E Ec)

Habits Forages alone or very occasionally in pairs, on forest floor and at lower levels. Shy and secretive.

Status Frequent in Ecuador, uncommon to locally frequent in Colombia.

Habitat Upper Tropical to Temperate Zones. Borders and clearings of humid montane forest, in dense shrubbery, thickets, tangles of blackberry or bracken, and often near streams

Voice Sings a long, accelerating series of notes, *chu-dok, chu-dok, chudok, chudok, chudok-chudok, chudok-chudok*, which may last for nearly 10 s (R&G).

Notes Formerly treated as a subspecies of Rufous-vented Tapaculo *S. femoralis*, but separated on basis of vocalisations by K&S (1997). Called Equatorial Rufous-vented Tapaculo in R&G.

WHITE-CROWNED TAPACULO

Scytalopus atratus Pl. 44

Identification 12–12.5cm. Adult male blackish-grey above with deep reddish-brown rump and variable white patch on crown, chin sometimes white or grey, underparts dark greyish-black with white tips to lower belly, and flanks to undertail-coverts deep reddish-brown, scalloped black on flanks, becoming black barring distally. Female paler, washed brown above, with smaller and duller crown patch; may have large grey patch on throat and grey mottling, scalloping or broad bars on belly, and upper- and undertail-coverts brighter reddish-brown than male, barred dusky to blackish. Immature lacks white or grey throat patch, has deep reddish-brown fringes to tertials and secondaries, wing-coverts deep reddish-brown with black subterminal bars. Juvenile bright rufous-brown, darker above, especially on wings and tail, barred on top of head and uppertail-coverts; barred finely and closely on throat and cheeks, rest of underparts barred uniform dusky and rufous.

Ssp. *S. a. atratus* (E Ec, Co: E Andes) as described
S. a. confusus (Co: C & W Andes) male slaty above, brownish on lower back, flanks and undertail-coverts more strongly barred reddish-brown and black
S. a. nigricans (Ve: Perijá & Andes of Táchira & Mérida) darker than nominate, bill smaller; female has rufous tips and dusky subterminal bars to tertials and wing-coverts, grey throat more extensive

Habits Forages alone or very occasionally in pairs, at lower levels.
Status Uncommon to frequent in Ecuador, frequent in Colombia, locally frequent in Venezuela.
Habitat Upper Tropical to Subtropical Zones. Humid, wet and cloud forests, dense forest edges, treefalls, overgrown clearings, mountain roads.
Voice In Táchira, Venezuela, slow series (2–3 per s) of low, nasal notes: *keyouk, keyouk…* (Hilty).
Notes Formerly all 3 races were included under *S. femoralis*, Rufous-vented Tapaculo, but were separated on basis of vocalisations by K&S (1997). Treated as subspecies under *S. bolivianus* in R&T, but *atratus* was treated specifically by Cory & Hellmayr (1924). Race *nigricans* was described by Phelps & Phelps (1963). Called Northern White-crowned Tapaculo in R&G and Hilty.

PALE-THROATED TAPACULO

Scytalopus panamensis Pl. 183

Identification 11.5cm. Adult dark grey above, except rump to uppertail-coverts which are deep rufous with fine, close black barring; softer and paler grey from throat to belly, indistinctly but heavily scaled paler grey, flanks and belly to undertail-coverts rufous, barred closely black; eyes dark brown, bill black, legs and feet dusky brown. Female similar, slightly browner above. Juvenile undescribed. Look for white eyebrow; the only tapaculo with such a mark in our region.

Ssp. Monotypic (extreme NW Co: Cerro Tacarcuna, on Panama border)

Habits Forages alone or very occasionally in pairs, at lower levels.
Status Vulnerable. Locally common. Endemic to 2 mountains on Panama–Colombia border (Cerro Tacarcuna and Cerro Mali).
Habitat Upper Tropical Zone, 1,100–1,500m. Humid montane forests, at borders and overgrown clearings.
Voice Sings series of piping notes: *tseety-seety seety seety…* (H&B).
Notes Formerly, e.g. in Peters' Checklist, *S. panamensis* included several forms now considered species on the basis of vocal differences (K&S 1997), for instance Nariño Tapaculo. Called Tacarcuna Tapaculo in R&T.

CHOCÓ TAPACULO

Scytalopus chocoensis Pl. 183

Identification 11.5cm. Adult male dark grey above, somewhat brownish on wings and tail, rump and uppertail-coverts deep reddish-rufous brown, barred finely and closely black; throat paler grey than rest of head, but head-sides to breast and belly as back, with subtle and faint paler grey scalloping; flanks and belly to undertail-coverts deep reddish-rufous barred black; eyes dark brown, bill black, legs and feet dusky. Female similar but has brownish wash to upperparts and pale grey throat tends to continue on centre of breast to belly. Juvenile dull dark brown above, with rump and uppertail-coverts and from throat to undertail-coverts deep reddish-rufous, finely and closely barred black.

Ssp. Monotypic (NW Ec, W Co)

Habits Forages on the ground and at lower levels.
Status Frequent in Ecuador and Colombia.
Habitat Tropical Zone, 350–950m in Ecuador, 250–1,250m in Colombia. Dense undergrowth of wet primary foothill forest, occasionally at forest borders.
Voice Song a series of high, clear notes that commence with a stutter: *p-d-d-d-pi-pi-pi-pi-pi-pi-pi-pi…* Also a scolding *chiu-chiu-chiu-chiu…* (R&G).
Note A recently described species (K&S 1997).

ECUADORIAN TAPACULO

Scytalopus robbinsi Pl. 181

Identification 11–11.5cm. Adult male slate grey above, washed brown from nape to uppertail-coverts, head sides and underparts to belly pale mid grey, perhaps with some irregular paler grey scalloping on central belly; flanks and vent to undertail-coverts rufous barred black; eyes brown, bill black, legs and feet grey. Female similar but paler on throat and centre of belly.

Ssp. Monotypic (SW Ec)

Habits Forages on ground and at lower levels.
Status Uncommon and local Ecuadorian endemic.
Habitat Upper Tropical Zone, 700–1,250m. Humid forests on foothills and lower slopes.
Voice Similar to Chocó Tapaculo, but notes much faster, almost sounding doubled (R&G).
Notes A recently described species (K&S 1997). Called El Oro Tapaculo in R&G.

STILES'S TAPACULO

Scytalopus stilesi Pl. 183

Identification 10–11cm. Male has forehead to back, wings and tail, and from chin to breast charcoal-grey, slightly paler on chin and throat, rump and uppertail-coverts dull brown; belly and sides to undertail-coverts bright brown with dark charcoal-grey barring; eyes dark brown, bill blackish, legs and feet greyish-brown. Female similar but browner on wings and tail, and immature female distinctly paler with pale tips to wing-coverts, brighter unbarred rump and uppertail-coverts, and more obviously barred, brighter rear underparts. Juvenile male all brown, darker above and paler below, barred throughout dark grey and grey. Blackish Tapaculo is darker and lacks any barring at rear, White-crowned has distinctive white patch on top of head, and Spillmann's is slightly brighter and has whitish scalloping on belly; all are larger, particularly Spillmann's, which is perhaps closest in coloration.

Ssp. Monotypic (C Co: Caldas to Antioquia)

Habits Typical of genus.

Status Near Threatened (Cuervo *et al.* 2005), albeit fairly common in remnants of unspoilt habitat in range, but threatened by ongoing habitat destruction.

Habitat Subtropical and Temperate Zones, at *c.*1,400 to over 2,100m. Tracts of primary and mature cloud forest in range are subject to severe pressure and fragmentation.

Voice Song a long series of short *churr* notes, each lasting 3–5 s, occasionally up to 15 s, repeated monotonously up to 35 times; female advertisement is given in duet with male. Compared to *S. robbinsi*, faster and lower pitched. A 2–3-note call, *cu-wi?, cu-cui-wi?* or *cu-wi-wi?* has last note rising.

Notes Recently described (Cuervo *et al.* 2005). Considered to be most closely related to Ecuadorian Tapaculo.

UPPER MAGDALENA TAPACULO

Scytalopus rodriguezi Pl. 182

Identification 10–11cm. Male has forehead to back, wings and tail, and from chin to lower breast dark grey (more blackish on upperparts), rump and uppertail-coverts variably barred dark brown, and tertials either washed dark brown or with dark brown tips; belly and sides to undertail-coverts barred cinnamon and blackish, and belly feathers may show variable pale grey tips; eyes dark brown, bill black, legs and feet dusky brown. Female undescribed but presumably similar, and juvenile also undescribed. Only likely to be confused with Spillmann's Tapaculo, which replaces it at higher elevations in same region, but latter is slightly paler overall.

Ssp. Monotypic (C Co: Huila, at head of Magdalena Valley)

Habits Typical of genus; usually within 50cm of ground, where seems to feed exclusively on small insects.

Status Endangered (Krabbe *et al.* 2005), albeit fairly common in remnants of unspoilt habitat in tiny range, but threatened by ongoing habitat destruction.

Habitat Temperate Zone, at 2,000–2,300m. Dense understorey of humid forest.

Voice Song considered amongst the simplest of the genus: a single note repeated at pace of 4–5 per s, usually given in bouts of 2–5 (or more) phrases, but occasionally singly. Phrases may be initiated by a slightly lower pitched note Both volume and pitch rise over first 4–6 s, but then remain steady, ending abruptly and occasionally fading at end. Calls comprise single rising *cui* notes (lasting 0.1 s) and a less accentuated *brzk*.

Notes Recently described (Krabbe *et al.* 2005). Considered most closely related to Ecuadorian and Stiles's Tapaculos.

NARIÑO TAPACULO

Scytalopus vicinior Pl. 183

Identification 12–12.5cm. Slate grey forehead to lower back and wings, rump and uppertail-coverts rufous with narrow, dark brownish-grey barring, below grey to belly, sometimes with slight white barring on sides, vent and flanks to undertail-coverts rufous with black barring. Female very similar but paler grey throat and some whitish on central belly. Juvenile dark brown barred black above, except on wings and tail which are dark brown, underparts rufous with black barring from chin to undertail-coverts, very fine on throat, scalloped on flanks and broad on undertail-coverts.

Ssp. Monotypic (NW Ec, W Co)

Habits Forages secretively, on ground and in lower undergrowth, both in forest and occasionally at borders or along paths.

Status Frequent in Ecuador, scarce to locally frequent in Colombia.

Habitat Subtropical Zone to Páramo, 1,250–2,000m. Humid, mossy montane forests, occasionally at their borders.

Voice Series of clear, ringing notes commencing with a brief stutter: *pididi-ü- ü- ü- ü- ü- ü- ü- ü- ü- ü*... Contact call consists of a single, brief note.

Note Formerly treated as a subspecies of *S. panamensis*, but separated on basis of vocalisations (K&S 1997).

BROWN-RUMPED TAPACULO

Scytalopus latebricola Pl. 183

Identification 13cm. Adult brownish-grey from forehead to lower back, wings and tail, rump and uppertail-coverts sandy brown with soft dusky barring, pale grey from chin to belly with some faint white scallops on sides and belly, flanks and vent to undertail-coverts rufous, barred dusky, the rufous bars broader; eyes brown, bill horn with dark culmen and tip, legs and feet horn to flesh. Juvenile rufous with dark brown bars and scallops – the feathers are rufous with dark brown centres and narrow fringes, the tertials and greater wing-coverts have a subterminal spot and bar. Effect is of varied spots, scallops and bars (see plate); legs and bill flesh.

Ssp. Monotypic (Co: Santa Marta)

Habits Forages on ground and in lower levels of dense thickets and tangled undergrowth.

Status Locally frequent Colombian endemic.

Habitat Subtropical Zone to Páramo, 1,900 to *c.*3,700m.

Humid and wet forests and mature secondary woodland, at thick borders and tangles of briars and bracken.

Voice Song a sequence of single notes followed by a rapid trill; has a scolding call and a nasal, high *szeow* (K&S 2003).

Note Formerly included *S. meridanus*, *S. caracae* and *S. spillmanni* as subspecies, but these taxa separated on basis of vocalisations by K&S (1997).

MÉRIDA TAPACULO

Scytalopus meridanus Pl. 182

Identification 12.5cm. Adult male brownish-grey above, from forehead to tail, somewhat paler grey from chin to belly, with silvery whitish mottling or diffuse scalloping, vent and flanks to undertail-coverts rufous with sparse black scallops (loose barring). Bill dark, legs and feet darkish horn. Female similar but slightly paler, more silvery on belly, brighter and paler rufous below with even sparser scallops on flanks. Immature lacks silvery white on belly and is sparsely barred on rear flanks and undertail-coverts; bill paler at base. We found 3 distinct juveniles, first scalloped and barred brown and blackish above, with buffy terminal spots on wing-coverts and tertials, latter also with subterminal black bars, very pale buffy to pale rufescent on sides, finely barred on throat and breast, becoming spotted and scalloped on flanks and regularly barred on undertail-coverts. Another is more richly coloured, darker and more rufescent, and third very dark indeed, somewhat greyish, and finely barred on throat. From Matorral by larger size, longer bill and darker rufous and slightly barred underparts; from White-crowned by lack of white spot on crown; and Brown-rumped by plain rump and irregular, sparse barring on flanks.

Ssp. Monotypic (Ve: Andes in Perijá, Táchira, Mérida, Trujillo, Lara)

Habits Forages alone or sometimes in loose pairs, searching lowest vegetation or ground. Very territorial.

Status Considered a Venezuelan endemic by K&S, but Hilty suggests that it possibly occurs in East and Central Andes of Colombia. Frequent to locally common in Venezuela.

Habitat Subtropical Zone to Páramo, 1,600–3,600m or higher. Humid or wet montane forests, mature secondary woodland, in dense borders and undergrowth, thickets and brambles.

Voice Song varies: in Guaramacal National Park (Trujillo), fast trills that may last 1–15 s, in Yacambú National Park (Lara), a loud, squeaky *knee-deep,* followed by an accelerating *tidip, tidip, tidip, tidip*... In Táchira, song is slower, of 6–8 notes (Hilty).

Notes Formerly treated as a subspecies of *S. latebricola*, but separated on basis of vocalisations by K&S (1997). Hilty's voice descriptions suggest the possibility that more than one species is involved.

CARACAS TAPACULO

Scytalopus caracae Pl. 182

Identification 12.5cm. Adult male dark brownish-grey above, slightly paler on lores, underparts slightly paler grey, somewhat buffy on belly, almost creamy in centre, flanks to undertail-coverts dull rufescent brown with diffuse, sparse barring; eyes dark brown, bill blackish, legs and feet dark grey. Adult female has brown of flanks and undertail more extensive, starting on lower belly, and clearly distinct from grey body-sides and upper belly, and is also clearly but sparsely barred black. Immature like adult but has dark subterminal bars on tertials and coverts, plus terminal pale rufous tips, white barring over both grey belly and rufous lower belly to vent, and rest of underparts pale rufous with indistinct brown barring. Two distinct juveniles were found, the first dark tawny brown above with pale rufescent fringes affording a scaled or barred appearance; very bright pale rufous below with fine grey barring on sides of face and throat, somewhat irregular and slightly sparse dark brown barring over rest. The other is deep ruddy brown above, regularly barred darker brown, and rich reddish-brown below, barred and scaled dark brown. All young have brown bills, somewhat variable leg and feet colour, but generally dark greyish-horn.

Ssp. Monotypic (Ve: Coastal Range)

Habits Forages alone or much less frequently in loose pairs, searching restlessly with short runs, hops and fast, brief flights through lowest vegetation or on ground. Curious and very vocal, but elusive. Very territorial.

Status Venezuelan endemic, common to locally very common.

Habitat Subtropical Zone, 1,200–2,400m. Humid or wet montane forest, cloud forest, mature second growth, dense borders and undergrowth, thickets and brambles.

Voice Song quite different from other *Scytalopus*: a loud, scolding *ka KICK-ka-ca,* endlessly repeated (Hilty).

Note Formerly treated as a subspecies of *S. latebricola*, but separated on basis of vocalisations by K&S (1997).

SPILLMANN'S TAPACULO

Scytalopus spillmanni Pl. 183

Identification 12.5 cm. Adult male dark grey from forehead to lower back, wings and tail, with all feathers fringed slightly darker and too dark for any scaling or barring to be obvious, rump and uppertail-coverts dull rufous-brown; sides of face and chin to belly and body-sides paler grey, strongly scalloped white on centre of lower breast and belly, whilst flanks, belly to undertail-coverts rufous, heavily scaled black. Eyes brown, bill blackish, legs and feet greyish-horn. Adult female usually washed brownish above and brighter rufous on flanks. Juvenile dark rufescent brown above, barred throughout darker brown, pale rufous tips to wing-coverts and tertials; paler rufous-brown below, fairly clear on sides of face and throat, but boldly scaled black from breast to undertail-coverts, centres of flank feathers brighter and slightly paler. Darker and more boldly marked in all plumages than Chusquea Tapaculo. From Nariño Tapaculo by white scales on belly, and Nariño has barred rump and uppertail-coverts.

Ssp. Monotypic (Ec, Co: Andes)

Habits Forages alone, and very secretive.
Status Frequent to locally common in Ecuador and Colombia.
Habitat Upper Subtropical to Temperate Zones, *c.*1,900–3,700m in Ecuador, to 3,200m in Colombia. Humid montane forest, in border thickets and especially patches of *Chusquea* bamboo.
Voice Song a series that begins with a few short notes, then continuous in a long, very fast, high trill. Calls include a short rising trill and scolding *keekeekeekee* call (R&G).
Note Formerly treated as a subspecies of *S. latebricola*, but separated on basis of vocalisations by K&S (1997).

CHUSQUEA TAPACULO

Scytalopus parkeri Pl. 183

Identification 12.5cm. Adult medium grey from forehead and ear-coverts to lower back, wings and tail, with all feathers narrowly fringed darker grey, giving a faint scaled effect, rump and uppertail-coverts dull rufous, with fine dusky barring on coverts; paler shade of same grey from chin to belly, with a little silvery grey and whitish tips and mottling, vent buffy, flanks to undertail-coverts bright rufous with sparse bars or scales. Eyes dark brown, bill black, legs and feet greyish-brown. Juvenile sandy rufous with darker wings and tail, barred dark brown, finest on chin and throat, appearing as scales on back and broadly barred on wings. Distinctly paler and slightly brighter than Spillmann's Tapaculo in all plumages.

Ssp. Monotypic (SE Ec)

Habits Forages alone, almost invariably in or close to *Chusquea* bamboo, where it searches tangles of dead leaves that collect near bases and in forks of stems, from ground level to *c.*2m.
Status Uncommon to locally frequent in Ecuador, uncommon to locally common in Colombia.
Habitat Subtropical and Temperate Zones, 2,250–3,150m in Ecuador. Humid montane forests, in border thickets and especially in tangled patches of *Chusquea* bamboo.
Voice At dawn sings a descending trill and then gives low-pitched trills during day (R&G).
Note A recently described species (K&S 1997).

MATTORAL TAPACULO

Scytalopus griseicollis Pl. 182

Identification 10–11.5cm. Two very different races but have same bicoloured pattern of grey head, back, wings and breast, and rufous rump to flanks and tail-coverts. Juvenile cinnamon brown, more or less evenly barred throughout. Quite unique with plumage divided into silver grey front half and a bright rufous rear, without any barring or scaling (similarly unmarked, but much paler Lara Tapaculo occurs only in Lara, Venezuela).

Ssp. *S. g. griseicollis* (C Co: E Andes), back dusky grey, rump orange-brown, tail brown, wings fuscous grey
S. g. infasciatus (Co: C & E Andes), larger, darker than nominate; back washed brown, rump and tail-coverts bright tawny, wings dusky brown

Habits Inhabits low scrub, close to ground, very tolerant of disturbed habitat.
Status Local and frequent to common Colombian endemic.
Habitat Temperate Zone; *griseicollis* occurs in humid and moist scrub near treeline, including heavily disturbed and fragmented habitats, 2,600–3,900m; *infasciatus* occurs in humid forest at treeline, 2,000–3,300m, distinctly favouring patches of *Chusquea* bamboo (K&S 2003).
Voice Sings a single note followed by a rising trill 10+ s long (K&S 2003).
Notes Race *griseicollis* formerly treated as a subspecies of *S. magellanicus*, but separated on basis of vocalisations (K&S 1997). Treated as separate species by Cory & Hellmayr (1924). Race *infasciatus* problematic: variously treated as synonym of *griseicollis* or of *S. meridanus*, then, by K&S (1997), specifically, who subsequently (2003) considered it a subspecies of *S. griseicollis*. With this split, and those of Lara and Páramo Tapaculos, Magellanic Tapaculo becomes endemic to southern Chile and southern Argentina. IOC-recommended English name is Rufous-rumped Tapaculo.

LARA TAPACULO

Scytalopus fuscicauda Pl. 182

Identification 10.5–11cm. Head to rump grey, washed rusty on uppertail-coverts, paler grey below, almost whitish in centre; sides, flanks and vent to undertail-coverts bright pale rufous; eyes brown, bill dusky, legs and feet horn.

Ssp. Monotypic (Ve: Andes)

Habits Forages on or near ground, more in open than congeners.
Status Uncommon to very locally frequent Venezuelan endemic.
Habitat Temperate Zone, 2,500–3,200m. Stunted woodland, elfin forest and open fields with thickets and bushes near treeline, humid shady ravines.
Voice A short, ascending trill lasting *c.*1.5 s, repeated various times (D. Ascanio).
Notes Formerly treated as a subspecies of *S. magellanicus,* but separated on basis of vocalisations and placed within *S. griseicollis* by K&S (1997). Present treatment follows K&S (2003), although they suggest that *S. fuscicauda* may be conspecific with or even a synonym of *S. meridanus*. Hilty treats it as a subspecies of *S. griseicollis* and calls it Rufous-rumped Tapaculo (as formerly treated by Cory & Hellmayr 1924).

PÁRAMO TAPACULO

Scytalopus canus Pl. 182

Identification 10.5-11cm. Dark grey with slightly paler throat and breast, some subtle mottling or scaling on rear underparts, but not distinctive. Female similar to male, juvenile undescribed.

Ssp. *S. c. canus* (Co: W Andes) as described

S. c. opacus (Co: C Andes, E & S Ec) male like *canus* but has variable amount of deep rufous on flanks and undertail-coverts, with variable amounts of black barring, belly variably mottled grey or pale grey; female dark rufous-brown above with faint darker fringes, whilst wing-coverts and tertials have subterminal blackish bands and buffy tips, tail barred; face to lower breast mid grey, flanks to undertail-coverts rufous with variable dusky barring, paler on belly; variant from extreme southern Ecuador has white primary-coverts

Habits Forages in undergrowth and at lower levels.
Status Uncommon and local in Ecuador, frequent in Colombia.
Habitat Temperate Zone to Páramo, 3,000–4,000m. Undergrowth at edges of humid montane forests near treeline, *Polylepis* forest, Páramo scrub, *Blechnum* fern and patches of *Chusquea* bamboo.
Voice Sings a fast dry *trrrrrrrrr* trill. Sometimes male sings trill while female gives descending series of high notes. Calls include a scolding *kee-kee-kee-kee* or short churrr notes (R&G).
Notes Both races were formerly treated as subspecies of either *S. magellanicus* or *S. unicolor*, but were separated on basis of vocalisations by K&S (1997). Subsequently, K&S (2003) considered that *opacus* might prove to be a separate species, but called for further studies.

OCELLATED TAPACULO

Acropternis orthonyx Pl. 183

Identification 22–23cm. Large, uniquely patterned tapaculo. Top of head to back, wings, tail, neck-sides and breast, belly and thighs dark rufescent brown, each feather, including wing-coverts, with a 'teardrop' of black and white; face, chin and throat deep burnt orange, rump to lower flanks and tail-coverts the same. Juvenile apparently blackish on top of head and lacks spots on belly.

Ssp. *A. o. infuscatus* (Ec) white spots on rear crown washed deep orange, undertail-coverts rufescent brown with pale rufescent spots

A. o. orthonyx (Co: E Andes, Ve: Andes) spots on top of head to nape washed burnt orange, undertail-coverts burnt orange

Habits The elongated and very straight (dagger-like) hindclaw is used to find insects, as bird scratches ground, pushing backwards with both feet at once in a clumsy jump, sometimes creating quite a pile of dirt, pausing to check what has surfaced and then moving to another spot. Forages alone or in very loose pairs and occasionally seen in groups of 3, probably a small family. Scurries or hops on ground and lowest branches, almost always in thickets of bamboo.
Status Everywhere spottily distributed, being uncommon to frequent in Ecuador, uncommon to very locally frequent in Colombia, and very locally frequent in Venezuela.
Habitat Subtropical to Temperate Zones. Humid and wet forests, stands of tall bamboo and thickets of *Chusquea*, patches of forest at treeline with lots of bamboo.
Voice Loud, piercing *queeow* notes, reminiscent of a jay, uttered singly or repeated at a fast pace for *c.*1 minute (P. Schwartz recording, Venezuela). Also in Venezuela, sharp *kueeee!* or *KEEa,* or *phEEEeo!* whistles (Hilty). In Peru, a rising and falling *weeeoou* whistle, followed sometimes by a few *tu* notes (T. S. Schulenberg).
Note Correct spelling is *infuscatus*, not *infuscata* (David & Gosselin 2002).

Melanopareia crescentchests are quite different from the typical tapaculos described here, boldly and brightly patterned, with long tails. However, they are as shy and skulking in their behaviour, but are responsive to playback. They occur in dry scrub country in south-west Ecuador.

MARAÑÓN CRESCENTCHEST

Melanopareia maranonica Pl. 181

Identification 16cm. Adult male greyish-olive above, including lesser and median wing-coverts, with black wings and tail, broad white outer fringes to greater wing-coverts and off-white fringes to tertials, remiges and rectrices; top of head and mask to neck-sides black, supercilium and throat to neck-sides creamy-buff, suffused rufous on neck-sides; broad black crescent on breast, rest of underparts chestnut grading to tawny below; eyes dark brown, long pointed bill is pale bluish grey with blackish tip, legs and feet flesh. Female differs only in having narrower black crescent on breast. Juvenile undescribed.

Ssp. Monotypic (extreme SE Ec)

Habits Forages alone, on ground and at lowest levels in dense dry scrub.
Status Only recently documented in Ecuador (Navarrete *et al.* 2003), where a small population, first reported in 1992, appears to be present in the extreme south (R&G).
Habitat Lower Tropical Zone, to *c.*700m. Secondary arid scrub.
Voice Song a series of *chuck* notes at slow pace and a faster paced series, both are loud and resonant; calls include a scolding *churr*, a *cree* and a high-pitched *tseet* (K&S).
Note Considered conspecific with *Melanopareia elegans* in S&M.

ELEGANT CRESCENTCHEST

Melanopareia elegans Pl. 181

Identification 14.5cm. Adult male greyish-olive above, including lesser and wing-coverts, with black wings and tail, broad chestnut fringes to median and greater wing-coverts, tertials and secondaries, off-white fringes to primaries, greyish-olive fringes to rectrices; top of head and mask to neck-sides black, supercilium and throat to neck-sides creamy-buff, suffused rufous on neck-sides; breast black, grading chestnut on belly; eyes dark brown, short pointed bill is blackish, legs and feet flesh. Female differs only in having narrower black breast-band, with uniform tawny underparts. Juvenile undescribed.

Ssp. *M. e. elegans* (SW Ec)

Habits Forages alone, on ground and lowest levels. Shy, scurries and hops about under cover, and only rarely shows for a few seconds on the open.
Status Uncommon to locally frequent in Ecuador.
Habitat Tropical to Temperate Zones. Arid to moist scrub and light woodland with dense undergrowth, less frequently in fairly humid areas with thickets and dense scrub, and in second growth in sparsely vegetated regions.
Voice Song a far-carrying, paced series – *cho-cho-cho-cho-cho-cho-cho-cho-cho* – that sounds like a laughing frog (R&G).
Notes Considered conspecific with *Melanopareia maranonica* in S&M. Race *paucalensis* from north-west Peru mentioned in R&G, but unclear if it possibly occurs in Ecuador, or if birds from southern Loja are similar to this race.

TYRANNIDAE – Tyrant-flycatchers

Tyrannids seem to embody the very meaning of biodiversity. Virtually an explosion of evolutionary variety, the Neotropical tyrant-flycatchers evolved by exploring the region's plethora of food niches and learning to exploit virtually all of them and, in doing so, becoming the most numerous of all bird families in the tropics, *c.*540 species, 250 of which occur in our region. Such numbers represent a great organisational challenge. Thus, it is unsurprising that their taxonomy has been complicated and convoluted. Here, we follow the AOU's Checklist. Remember that wingbars, pale fringes and tips to the tertials and tail-sides are often invaluable diagnostics, but are most noticeable in fresh plumage; in all species the tips and outer fringes to the tertials tend to wear as the breeding season advances, and in some the wingbars and pale fringes to the uppertail-coverts and tail-feathers may also wear to the point where they all but disappear.

In most species sexes are alike and juveniles very similar to adults. In the hand the latter have a softer and coarser texture to some body-feathers, especially the chin and undertail-coverts, as well as much sparser underwing-coverts feathering. Subspecific differences may be subtle, where the main distinction is size, but in some species races may be quite distinct.

Additional references for this family include Lanyon (1988) and the family and species accounts edited by Fitzpatrick (2004) in HBW vol. 9; 16 authors contributed to the species accounts in the latter volume, but we have attributed all to Fitzpatrick, as editor. The family essay and species accounts in HBW present a major revision to the family, in which Fitzpatrick and his collaborators found, through access to often-larger numbers of specimens than available to past workers, considerable intraspecific variation that did not conform to previously recognised geographic variation. As a result, many subspecies – often entire groups – have been subsumed within a single race. The resulting simplifications may confuse users of other guides, and we have not accepted all of Fitzpatrick's changes. In all cases where a change from existing lists was made we have referenced the fact.

Mionectes flycatchers are fairly slender in form with narrow-based bills. They share an emarginated outer primary in males, presumably an adaptation for producing the soft whirring wing-rattles given in display. This odd-shaped feather also occurs in females but does not appear until older and its function, if any, is unknown. They perch upright and some habitually nod their heads nervously and flick/fan one wing upwards – a behaviour more typical of *Leptopogon* flycatchers. They usually occur alone, though in the post-breeding season may form family parties, and may also be found in mixed-species feeding flocks. A lek system of courtship is employed, vocalising from near the ground, and birds are generally silent except when at the lek. Usually they occur in the lower growth of light woodland, but can be present in the canopy at forest edge.

STREAK-NECKED FLYCATCHER
Mionectes striaticollis Pl. 184

Identification 12.5–13cm. Bright greenish-olive above, darker on head, with small white spot behind eye and heavily streaked underparts, but yellow belly unstreaked. Typically perches upright. From very similar race *hederaceus* of Olive-striped Flycatcher by yellow breast and underparts. *M. o. hederaceus* more mid greyish below with grey streaks extending further on belly, larger white spot behind eye is more noticeable and also has all-black bill (R&G). Race *venezuelensis* of Olive-striped very similar, but distinct by range. Usually occurs at higher elevations than Olive-striped Flycatcher.

Ssp. *M. s. columbianus* (E Ec, E, C & W Co) greyish-olive on crown and generally slightly darker
M. s. viridiceps (W Ec, SW Co) rather greener, with striping on breast broader and yellower

Habits Forages mostly for berries and small fruits, alone, in family groups or with mixed flocks, rarely in pairs, from low to mid levels and subcanopy. Shy and inconspicuous.
Status Uncommon in Ecuador, locally uncommon to common in Colombia.
Habitat Subtropical Zone to Páramo, 600–3,400m but commonest at 1,300–2,500m. Humid, wet and cloud forests, mature second growth, inside forest in areas with abundant epiphytes and mosses, but also in dead shrubbery at borders and clearings.
Voice Generally silent. Dry sequences of high and low paired notes (H&B), a sharp *tzie* and a repeated *tselee* (F&K); opens bill wide, exposing orange gape, and sways head from side to side (R&G).
Note Race *selvae* synonymised under *colombianus* by Fitzpatrick (2004); though tends to show more intense olive on crown and represents a diffuse intergradation between *colombianus* and *viridiceps*.

OLIVE-STRIPED FLYCATCHER

Mionectes olivaceus Pl. 184

Identification 13cm. Uniform greenish-olive above with prominent white postocular spot, and heavily streaked underparts. Dull yellow belly mostly streaked grey. Juvenile perceptibly duller and browner on head and duller, less greenish on back, with faint whitish streaks, throat and breast olive-grey with off-white streaks and rest of underparts less bright yellow (more sulphur than primrose); bill all dark. Generally perches upright, but leans forward at times. From similar Streak-necked Flycatcher, with which occasionally sympatric (but altitudinally separated, with Olive-striped usually at lower elevations), by streaked belly, more greenish head and all-dark bill.

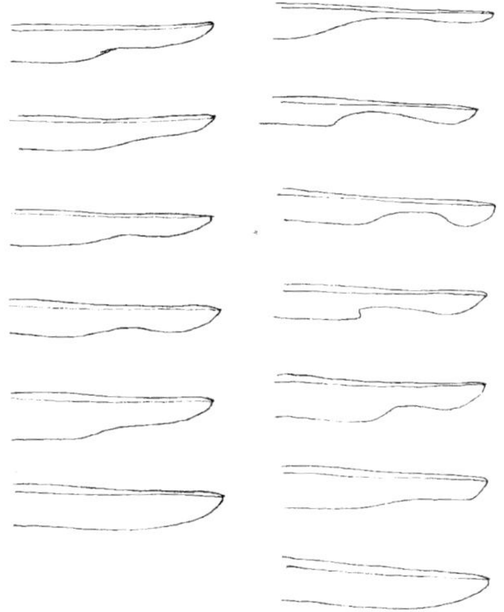

Olive-striped Flycatcher may be sexed by wing-chord and the ninth primary. There is no attenuation in first-years, but partial attenuation in second-years which is roughly similar in both sexes. In third-years, that of male is very narrow, whilst females are less so. Wing-chord in females is 60–65mm, whilst in males it is 65–70mm. Females on left, males on right. In both columns, bottom feather is of a juvenile bird

Ssp. *M. o. galbinus* (Co: Santa Marta) paler back with golden tone, throat streaks very fine, rich yellow

M. o. hederaceus (W Co, NW Ec) darker above, streaks below more grey and white

M. o. meridae (NE Co, NW Ve) brighter green above with weak wingbars, underparts yellower, birds from Mérida have yellow on throat more like points than streaks

M. o. pallidus (Co: E Andes) like *meridae* but paler with weaker yellow below

M. o. venezuelensis (Ve: N Mts., Tr) like *meridae* but more olivaceous above and seldom has wingbars, which are rich yellow; less yellow on chin and breast

Habits Forages mostly for berries and small fruit, alone or with mixed flocks, very rarely in pairs, from mid levels to canopy. When breeding forages at lower levels. Gleans small insects or fruits from foliage, sometimes by hovering briefly below leaves. Nest an untidy globe of straw with a side entrance, suspended from aerial roots. Shy and inconspicuous, seldom vocalises.

Status Uncommon to rare in Ecuador, very common locally in Colombia and Venezuela, and scarce in Trinidad.

Habitat Tropical to Lower Subtropical Zones, 600–1,600m, rarely to 3,000m. Humid, wet and cloud forests, mature second growth, in shady, humid ravines and areas with abundant epiphytes and mosses, borders with Melastomaceae, and clearings.

Voice An intermittent, high-pitched, dry *zeeeeee* repeated every few seconds (H&B), and a descending *seeeeu* (R&G).

Note Races *pallidus*, *meridae* and *venezuelensis* all synonymised under *venezuelensis* by Fitzpatrick (2004).

OCHRE-BELLIED FLYCATCHER

Mionectes oleagineus Pl. 184

Identification 13cm. Distinctive, olive above with 2 rather diffuse, ochraceous wingbars, greyish on throat and cinnamon-ochraceous below. Eyes brown, bill black with pale base, legs and feet slate. Many subspecies very difficult to identify, even in hand. Similar to Streak-necked and Olive-striped Flycatchers above but unmarked cinnamon-ochre below. Similar to McConnell's Flycatcher but with wingbars.

Ssp. *M. o. abdominalis* (NC Ve) mid green above with uppertail-coverts as back, and slight ochraceous tinge

M. o chloronotus (E Co, W & S Ve) mid green above with uppertail-coverts slightly infused brownish-ochre, deep ochraceous below

M. o dorsalis (SE Ve: Roraima & Chimantá) below like *chloronota* and *intensa*, above dull brownish-green like *abdominalis* but fringes and tips of greater coverts and tertials more cinnamon

M. o hauxwelli (E Ec) more richly coloured and ochraceous below than *pacificus*

M. o intensus (Se Ve, W Gu) not visually separable from *chloronotus*

M. o pacificus (SW Co, W Ec) brighter and more yellowish green than *parcus*, rump tinged buffy, abdomen even paler, more yellowish and less buffy

M. o pallidiventris (NE Ve, T&T) bright green above with hint of ochre to uppertail-coverts, bright creamy ochre below

M. o parcus (N Co, NW Ve) bright green above with uppertail-coverts ochraceous, pale ochraceous below

M. o. wallacei (Guianas) as described; streaks on breast fade, leaving flanks and underparts clear and uniform

Habits Upright stance on perch and habitually nods head and flicks/fans a wing up. Forages alone or with mixed flocks, from low to mid levels, and frequently sings. Gleans small insects or fruits from foliage, sometimes by hovering briefly below leaves. Nest shaped somewhat like an avocado, covered with mosses with a side entrance. Calls and displays alone from a perch, at display grounds (leks) in light undergrowth.

Status Uncommon to rare in Ecuador, common in Colombia and Venezuela, frequent in Guyana, common in Suriname, French Guiana and Trinidad (uncommon in Tobago).
Habitat Tropical Zone, to 1,800m. Essentially a forest-edge bird, seldom within forest, but occasionally a few hundred metres away from it. Sandy soil forest, partially cleared areas, second growth, agriculture and plantations with shade trees, large clearings. Always near running water.
Voice An intermittent sequence of varied chirps and twitters, interspersed with bouts of 'sneezing' (*choo* or *pitchoo*) and punctuated by wing flashing and crest ruffling (H&B).
Note A wide-ranging species usually divided into 2 subspecies groups, *assimilis* in Middle America and *oleaginous* in northern South America and Amazonia. Fitzpatrick (2004) found geographical variation in nominate group minimal but individual, age and sexual variation to be considerable, and synonymised *intensus*, *wallacei*, *chloronotus* and *hauxwelli* under *oleagineus*.

MCCONNELL'S FLYCATCHER

Mionectes macconnelli Pl. 184

Identification 12cm. Uniform olive-green above with no wingbars, rich cinnamon-buff below (colours vary sub-specifically, *macconnelli* duller and darker, others much brighter). Not easily separated from Ochre-bellied Flycatcher, but latter has 2 rather diffuse wingbars.

Ssp. *M. m. macconnelli* (E Ve, Gu, FG) dark olive-green above, sienna below
M. m. roraimae (S Ve, W Gu) very similar to *mercedesfosterae*, bright olive-green above, slightly richer, more intense cinnamon below
M. m. mercedesfosterae (SE Ve: Cerros Duida and Jimé, Paurai-tepui and Sierra de Lema) slightly brighter than *roraimae*, both above and below, green above, almost yellow-ochre on breast

Habits Forages alone or in pairs, in undergrowth up to subcanopy. Usually quiet and inconspicuous. Takes insects, spiders, small fruits and berries. Female constructs small sack of dry fibres and grasses with side entrance, always above a stream. Unusual is that, despite not being sexually dimorphic, males sing in fixed leks, usually *c.*1m above ground in understorey, sometimes near a large tree. Race *macconnelli* gathers in groups of *c.*10, whereas *roraimae* and *mercedesfosterae* lek in groups of 4–5 males, and their voice is very different.
Status Uncommon in Venezuela, where race *macconnelli* rare. Frequent in Guyana, Suriname and French Guiana.
Habitat Tropical to Lower Subtropical Zones: *macconnelli* in lowlands to 400m, with a specimen from 950m; *roraimae* at 800–2,000m but moves lower to breed, sometimes to 700m, with a specimen from 500m. Humid and cloud forests, both inside and at borders, on slopes and atop tepuis, second growth and plantations. Race *roraimae* apparently restricted to sandy soil forest (D. Ascanio, pers. comm.).
Voice Race *macconnelli* utters several series' of notes, all rather parakeet-like, e.g. *tzztzztzztzz* or *tziptziptziptzip*, each series on slightly different pitch and only a few seconds apart. Race *roraimae* quite different, a galloping continual series of mostly complex accelerating *tik* notes, appearing jumbled and as if bird cannot utter them fast enough, *tdrik'tdrik'tdrik'tdr ik'tdrik*, each set rising slightly then falling back, sometimes a series followed by a musical *twzzeeee*, which in turn may be repeated at a different pitch (D. Ascanio).
Note Fitzpatrick (2004) found that characteristics defining *mercedesfosterae* (southern Venezuela) were within range of variation of *roraimae* and thus synonymised it. Hilty & Ascanio (in prep.) consider *roraimae* and *mercedesfosterae* to represent a separate species, and a new Pantepui endemic.

Leptopogon flycatchers generally perch upright and, like *Mionectes*, flick or fan a wing over the back while perched. All have irregular pale feathers on the face, affording a grizzled appearance, and have a dark vertical crescent behind the ear-coverts. They also appear to have a large head in comparison to the body.

RUFOUS-BREASTED FLYCATCHER

Leptopogon rufipectus Pl. 184

Identification 13–13.2cm. Combination of upright posture and rufous breast with warm yellow underparts distinctive. Two wingbars and pale fringes to tertials and flight-feathers may be indistinct in worn plumage.

Ssp. *L. r. rufipectus* (NE Ec, S Co: C & E Andes) crown slate grey, back olive-green
L. r. venezuelanus (W Ve: Táchira) paler grey head and olive-brown back

Habits Forages alone or in pairs, often with mixed flocks, at low levels to subcanopy. Highly frugivorous, especially in non-breeding season. Gleans food whilst briefly hovering before underside of leaves. Nest a long, hanging, woven structure with a small chamber and side entrance.
Status Uncommon in Ecuador, locally frequent to common in Colombia, frequent but very local in Venezuela.
Habitat Subtropical to Temperate Zones, 1,500–2,700m. Humid, cloud and elfin forests, mossy areas and areas of low vegetation on higher slopes.
Voice Calls frequently, an abrupt *kweek* (F&K).
Note Race *venezuelanus* synonymised under nominate by Fitzpatrick (2004).

SEPIA-CAPPED FLYCATCHER

Leptopogon amaurocephalus Pl. 184

Identification 13–14cm. Brown crown, rest of upperparts olive with 2 wingbars and whitish fringes to tertials and remiges; face grizzled, with whitish line behind eye embracing dark rear ear-coverts crescent. Yellow below, washed olive on breast. Very similar to Slaty-capped but longer tail and wingbars formed by whitish tips to median and greater coverts. Broad pale whitish fringes to tertials obvious. More often found at forest edges than Slaty-capped Flycatcher, and gives only single wing-flicks.

Ssp. *L. a. diversus* (NC & NE Co, NW Ve) rufous head and tail, paler greenish-olive on back, paler yellow belly
L. a. pileatus (NW Co) cinnamon-brown uppertail-coverts and tail
L. a. obscuritergum (S Ve, Guianas) darker back, notably olive chin to lower breast with some grizzling on chin and throat, paler more sulphur-yellow belly
L. a. orinocensis (C & WC Ve) brighter green above than *obscuritergum*; virtually lacks any olivaceous wash on breast
L. a. peruvianus (SE Co, E Ec) crown dark olive, dark grey back

Habits Forages in pairs, from undergrowth to mid levels. Very territorial, and pairs duet frequently in territorial defence. Joins mixed-species flocks, but only within their territory. Quietly picks insects and small spiders from leaves, using short sallies from fixed perch. Nest a ball of grasses and fibres, sometimes suspended below a log, sometimes under overhang of a bank.
Status Uncommon in Ecuador, generally uncommon but locally frequent in Colombia, uncommon in Venezuela and Guyana, frequent in Suriname, apparently widespread but uncommon in French Guiana.
Habitat Tropical Zone, to 450m in Ecuador, 600m in Colombia and Venezuela north of Orinoco but to 1,600m south of it. Moist, light forest, *várzea* and humid, denser montane and cloud forests, second growth, shady plantations and humid scrub.
Voice Vocalisations variously described as rather quiet, with a low *pree-ee-ee-ee* (H&B), to frequent, with a strong trill (H&M) to a fast chatter *dret-deedeedeedeedeuw* (R&T). Sick mentions a *psewrrr*, fuller *rrr-EEo, psorriulT*, weak *wet*, and an ascending sequence of limpid soft whistles ending in a *coarse ew ew ew ew ewe w…PSEEoo*, presumably of race *obscuritergum*.
Note We follow Fitzpatrick (2004) in merging race *faustus* of north-west Colombia within Middle American *pileatus*, but we retain *obscuritergum*, which we find distinct from *orinocensis*.

SLATY-CAPPED FLYCATCHER
Leptopogon superciliaris Pl. 184

Identification 13.5–14cm. Slate grey crown, rest of upperparts olive with 2 wingbars and whitish fringes to tertials and remiges; wingbars formed by teardrop-shaped terminal spots to median and greater coverts. Face grizzled, with whitish line behind eye embracing dark rear ear-coverts crescent. Yellow below, washed olive on breast. Very similar to Sepia-capped Flycatcher but tail shorter, often gives single wing-flick immediately after flicking other wing. Less often found at forest fringes.

Ssp. *L. s. superciliaris* (E Ec, SE Co, W Ec, Co: W Andes) slightly darker than *venezuelensis*, with much variation in colour of wingbars; light grizzling on chin and throat
L. s. venezuelensis (C & CE Co, N Ve) grizzling on face-sides whiter than *pariae* and has additional whitish spots on nape-sides; no grizzling on chin and throat; all those from Sucre are paler below, but similar individuals occur throughout northern region
L. s. pariae (NE Ve, Tr) darker grey nape; noticeably more olive from chin to breast, with some black and white grizzling on chin and throat

Habits Forages alone or in small groups, at low to mid levels but mostly in subcanopy; frequently in mixed flocks. More vivacious and vocal than congeners, but also perches upright and raises wing behind back continually when perched. Nest often hung under a bank, log or aerial roots, an irregularly shaped structure of grasses and straws, with a side entrance that may occasionally be covered by an eave.
Status Locally common to uncommon in Ecuador, frequent in Colombia.
Habitat Upper Tropical to Subtropical Zones, to 1,500m on west slope, 600–1,500m on east slope in Ecuador, 120–2,100m on Pacific slope but 600–2,100m on east slope in Colombia, and 400–2,000m in Venezuela. Humid, wet and cloud forests, humid borders and clearings, shady plantations.
Voice An assertive *skeet'de'e'e'e'er!* (H&B)
Note Due to degree of variation within any population, Fitzpatrick (2004) synonymised all of the above subspecies into a single, yellow-bellied, *superciliaris*. We agree with synonymising *transandinus* under *superciliaris* but retain *venezuelensis*, including *poliocephalus* within latter.

Pseudotriccus pygmy tyrants are small, montane flycatchers, inconspicuous and easily overlooked. Usually noticed foraging low inside forest but occasionally at forest edges. Two common habits are bursts of bill-snapping, often in alarm, and wing-whirring in flight. The sound of the snapping bill is quite noticeable when an insect is taken in a sally.

BRONZE-OLIVE PYGMY TYRANT
Pseudotriccus pelzelni Pl. 184

Identification 11.2cm. Rather inconspicuous and easily overlooked, olive, bronze or brown above (depending on race), washed heavily with same colour on breast and flanks, with a yellow throat, belly and undertail-coverts. The eyes are reddish.

Ssp. *P. p. annectens* (NW Ec, SW Co) bronzy brown above and bright yellow on belly; intergrades with *berlepschi*, birds being intermediate in characters
P. p. berlepschi (NW Co) darker brown above with blackish crown
P. p. pelzelni (E Ec, E Co) smaller than *annectens* and distinctly more olivaceous

Habits Mostly forages in undergrowth and at mid levels, alone and does not join mixed flocks. Very vivacious, flits about snapping insects or picking berries.
Status Uncommon in Ecuador, locally frequent in Colombia.
Habitat Upper Tropical to Subtropical Zones, at 300–2,500m but mostly 600–2,000m (R&G). Undergrowth of humid, wet and cloud forests; dense, humid borders.

Voice Song an abrupt sequence of 4–6 *piff* notes, uttered at 1 per s (H&B). A shrill high-pitched *preeeeeeee*, sometimes with a separate note at end, and a drier descending trill (R&G).

RUFOUS-HEADED PYGMY TYRANT

Pseudotriccus ruficeps Pl. 184

Identification 10.9–11cm. Bright orange-rufous head and rich chestnut wings and tail contrast with olive back and breast, yellow belly and undertail-coverts. Juvenile distinct, being olive on head and chestnut of wings and tail duller, yellow below is duller. Orange-rufous gradually becomes apparent, starting on forehead.

Ssp. Monotypic (NE & W Ec, W & S Co)

Habits Forages for insects alone or in pairs, sallying and flitting quietly and furtively in undergrowth, sometimes dropping to ground under dense foliage. Bill-snapping is commonest habit.

Status Uncommon to fairly common in Ecuador, uncommon to locally frequent in Colombia.

Habitat Subtropical to Temperate Zones, 2,000–3,300m in Ecuador, mostly 1,400–2,800m in Colombia, but to 400 m in south-east Nariño and 3,600m in Nevado Santo Isabel. Wet and cloud forests, tangles of vines, dense, humid borders and overgrown clearings.

Voice Song a bright, high *teeeeeaaaaaeeeee-ip* trill that dips and rises to end with a snap (H&B), or falling and rising *trrrrrrr* trills, 2–3 s long, interspersed with longer, high notes (F&K). A loud, explosive buzzy trill of several seconds, *tzzzzzzzzzzzzeuw*, sometimes ending in a snap; often snaps bill repeatedly (Fitzpatrick).

> *Poecilotriccus* tody-tyrants are easily overlooked and usually heard before seen. They seem to prefer edges of primary forest and second growth, but not to tolerate extensive deforestation. They are less active than other tody-tyrants and perch inside foliage, relaxed and singing. Members of *Poecilotriccus* are named tody-flycatcher in R&G.

RUFOUS-CROWNED TODY-TYRANT

Poecilotriccus ruficeps Pl. 185

Identification 9–9.7cm. Head either (a) has rich rufous crown bordered black, grey nape, pale pinkish-rufous ear-coverts, with black malar, throat and upper breast buffy-white; or (b) all rufous with paler throat. Back greenish-olive, wings blackish with yellow tips to median and greater coverts forming 2 bars, fringes of tertials also yellow. In all 4 races there is a greenish, poorly defined band on breast which has some black; rest of underparts yellow. Sexes alike; juvenile generally paler on throat.

Ssp. *P. r. melanomystax* (NC Co: C Andes) bold black line separating crown from grey nape also encircles ear-coverts, whitish cheeks may be washed slightly pinkish-rufous

P. r. ruficeps (NE Ec, Co: E Andes, Ve: Táchira, Trujillo) head rufous, ear-coverts paler, chin paler still, separated from white throat by broad rufous band; olive band on breast has black marks, and narrow greyish nape

P. r. rufigenis (W Ec, SW Co) head entirely pale rufous, malar bar vestigial, narrow greyish nape

P. r. peruvianus (S Ec) like *melanomystax* but ear-coverts washed more noticeably pinkish-rufous, with bolder black lines on head, breast-band blackish

Habits Forages for insects alone or in pairs, sallying and flitting quietly and furtively in undergrowth, sometimes dropping to ground under dense foliage. Bill-snapping is commonest habit.

Status Uncommon in Ecuador, uncommon to locally common in Colombia, uncommon in Venezuela.

Habitat Subtropical to Temperate Zones, mostly 1,500–2,500m in Ecuador, from 1,000 but more usually 1,600–2,700m in Colombia, 1,800–2,900m in Venezuela. Tangled edges of humid and cloud forests, hedges, thickets and bushes in highland pastures, apparently partial to stands of bamboo, vines and mature second growth.

Voice Feeble, stuttering sequences of *patreer* or *patreer-pit* (H&B), with frequent *tick-trrrr* calls when foraging (F&K). Additionally, a low-pitched flat *chak*, *ttrew*, *pip-prrrrr*, and song rendered *pa-treer-pit-pit-pit*, with *melanomystax* uttering a gravelly *stick-di-dik* (Fitzpatrick).

Notes Differences of plumage comprise 2 groups: those with a black line or bridle over head (a) above, and those plain-headed, with little or no black on head (b) above. The bridled group comprises *melanomystax* and *peruvianus*, which might prove to be specifically distinct (Fitzpatrick). However, there appears to be sometimes considerable individual variation within populations across entire range, e.g. a specimen resembling Johnson's Tody-Tyrant *P. luluae* was captured in Tamá National Park by the authors, and specimens of race *ruficeps* resembling *rufigenis* were collected in Táchira, Venezuela; rather than 2 species, it could prove to be a monotypic polymorph.

BLACK-AND-WHITE TODY-TYRANT

Poecilotriccus capitalis Pl. 185

Identification 9.4cm. Male very distinctive; glossy black above with white outer fringes to tertials, producing bold white line on wing, white below with grey or blackish wash to breast-sides and yellowish undertail-coverts. Female has rufous-chestnut top of head, grey cheeks and olive upperparts, with same white line on tertials; below, as male. Juvenile recalls female but has olive instead of rufous-chestnut top of head. Adults have dark red eyes, juvenile brown.

Ssp. *P. c. capitalis* (E Ec, S Co)

Habits Poorly known. Forages within dense undergrowth, usually alone and does not join mixed flocks. Sallies to glean insects from underside of foliage. Quiet but not shy.

Status Rare in Ecuador; uncertain, possibly rare in Colombia.

Habitat Tropical Zone, to 1,350m, in dense thickets at borders of humid forest, particularly bamboo stands and mature second growth along streams.
Voice A sharp, fast *tik t-r-r-r-r-r-ew*, becoming a more explosive *tk tk tk wey-wey-wey-whuh* when agitated (Fitzpatrick).

Taeniotriccus is a monotypic genus that generally perches upright with tail drooped, and is a bird of riverine to humid forest. It is easily overlooked.

BLACK-CHESTED TYRANT
Taeniotriccus andrei Pl. 185

Identification 11.7cm. Distinctive, crested flycatcher. Male has top of head in form of an irregular black crest, rest of head rich, pinkish-rufous, paler on throat. Upperparts and breast black, except bright yellow bases to primaries and remiges forming a wingbar that extends on outer fringes of tertials. Rest of underparts white, flushed grey on body-sides, and yellowish undertail-coverts. Female similar, though less bold, with back olive-grey, rufous of head more pinkish, and duller below. Two reports of females in Delta Amacuro with a clear grey nuchal band (D. Ascanio & A. Whittaker, pers. comm.).

Ssp. *P. a. andrei* (SE Ve, Gu? Su)

Habits Forages in small open areas of understorey, often perching still for a while, tail slightly drooped, sallying at a passing insect and alighting on another bare branch.
Status Usually considered rare, but uncommon or even locally common in Venezuela; in Suriname known from single specimen taken very near border with Guyana in north-east.

Male Black-chested Tyrant at rest, showing crest raised and laid back; note how yellow outer fringes to tertials form very distinctive field mark (after Zimmer & Whittaker 2004)

Habitat Lower Tropical Zone to 350m. Swampy tidal forest in southern Delta Amacuro. Understorey of humid forest, particularly *várzea*, and areas well endowed with bamboo in *terra firme*. Also stands of bamboo, mature second growth with *Cecropia*, overgrown clearings, often near streams and rivers.
Voice A reedy *chewp* or *chert*, repeated every few seconds for up to 5 minutes or more. Less often, a *k'dink, k'dink*, which may be interspersed with *chewp* series, only given by male (Zimmer & Whittaker 2004).

Note Taxonomic position debated, with sound arguments for retaining monospecific genus, as well as for bringing it into *Poecilotriccus*.

Hemitriccus tody-tyrants are small flycatchers that are ever-active, fast-moving and always alert. They have fairly long bills that are flat and wide, and may offer a good field mark when seen from below. Most species have pale eyes.

SNETHLAGE'S TODY-TYRANT
Hemitriccus minor Pl. 186

Identification 10cm. Small with very wide bill and short, narrow tail. Olive-green above, wings brownish with yellowish-white tips forming 2 wingbars that join broader whitish-yellow outer fringes to tertials, to form obvious line on wing; fringes of remiges yellowish-green, brighter on secondaries. Brownish tail has green fringes to feathers. Below, pale, yellowish-white, heavily flammulated olive or greyish-olive from chin to vent. Eyes white, bill black and legs dark grey. Sexes alike, but juvenile smaller, with brown eyes and base of bill pale orange to horn, far less greenish and yellowish in plumage, both above and below, and thus appears more drab. Adult very much like White-eyed Tody-Tyrant, but much smaller and lacks white eye-ring. In shape and jizz, recalls a tody-flycatcher.

Ssp. *H. m. pallens* (S Ve, FG)

Habits Forages alone or in pairs, in dense or vine-laden thickets, mostly at mid levels, occasionally to subcanopy. Not known to join mixed flocks. Easily overlooked.
Status Precise range unknown, but undoubtedly uncommon in Venezuela (4 specimens from 2 localities in Amazonas). Few records from French Guiana suggest it is frequent at a few localities, but possibly widespread throughout forest block.
Habitat Tropical Zone, to 220m. Dense borders of humid forests, tangled second growth.
Voice Vocalisations in French Guiana and Venezuela unknown. In Brazil, a set of usually 3 even-spaced, gravelly trills, sometimes prefaced by *pik* (K. J. Zimmer in Hilty).
Notes Differences exist between Venezuelan birds and *pallens* in Brazil, and the former may warrant separate taxonomic recognition, though further data (including vocalisations) are required. Thus, Brazilian data may not be relevant here. A report of the species in Suriname was based on a misidentified specimen.

BOAT-BILLED TODY-TYRANT
Hemitriccus josephinae Pl. 186

Identification 11cm. Not boat-billed, but note lack of wingbars. Uniform dull greenish-olive above and pale yellow below, with reddish-brown eyes. The only tody-tyrant or similar in its range with dark eyes and no wingbars. Bill not as wide as name suggests, and is certainly not a field mark.

Ssp. Monotypic (Guianas)

Habits Forages alone or in pairs, in understorey and mid levels. Perches quietly in secluded spots, sometimes for a relatively long time, and is very easily overlooked. Most likely to be detected by voice.

Status Scarce and local in Guyana east of Essequibo (does not range further west), rare in Suriname. Uncommon to locally frequent but widespread in French Guiana.

Habitat Lower Tropical Zone, to 200m. Borders and clearings of humid forest with second growth, especially where there are thick tangled vines and lianas on a rocky substrate.

Voice A descending *pic, pic, pic* (R&T). In Suriname song a descending 4 (not 3) notes, *pic, pic, pic, pic!* (D. Ascanio recording).

WHITE-EYED TODY-TYRANT

Hemitriccus zosterops Pl. 186

Identification 11–11.2cm. Bright olive above, with wings dusky olive; pale yellowish fringes to wing-feathers give 2 indistinct wingbars. Throat whitish with fine streaks, rest of underparts yellowish to pale brown, flammulated olive on breast and flanks. Eyes pale (yellowish), legs and feet are also variably pale.

Ssp. *H. z. zosterops* (E Ec, S Co, S Ve, Su, FG)

Habits Very territorial. Forages from mid levels to subcanopy, often near streams. Takes beetles, flies, wasps and caterpillars, by sallying to undersides of leaves. Does not join mixed flocks, being very territorial. Perches for long periods. Low hum from wings in flight.

Status Uncommon in Ecuador, scarce in Colombia, locally frequent in Guyana and Suriname; locally common and widespread in French Guiana. Overall local in our region.

Habitat Lower Tropical Zone, below 1,000m in Ecuador. Interior of humid *terra firme*, in shady, dense areas. Typically in mid understorey, on well-drained soils with tall primary forest in French Guiana (O. Tostain).

Voice Race *zosterops* gives an oft-repeated, fast *tic, tic, tic, tididididit*, sometimes just several repetitions of *tic* note (Hilty), e.g. *pik, pik-pik* etc. (R&G). A fast staccato trill with separate introductory note, *tik-trrrrrrrrrrrrrree*, rising at end (Fitzpatrick).

JOHANNES'S TODY-TYRANT

Hemitriccus iohannis Pl. 186

Identification 11cm. Uniform bright olive above with somewhat weak to indistinct wingbars; may have white supraloral spot but lacks white eye-ring, and eyebrow also variable; throat whitish with fine dark streaks, rest of underparts yellow with olive wash to breast. Eyes vary from white to clear or dull yellow. From Stripe-necked Tody-Tyrant by wingbars more clearly marked, and less clearly streaked throat.

Ssp. Monotypic (E Ec, S Co)

Habits Forages, alone or in pairs, at mid levels to canopy, sallying for insects unobtrusively, under cover of foliage. Often in tangles alongside rivers. Presence best detected by call.

Status Very rare in Ecuador and Colombia (main range in Amazonian Peru and extreme central-west Brazil).

Habitat Lower Tropical Zone, to 200m in Ecuador. Forests and shrubbery beside rivers, humid second growth, tangles of vines and lianas.

Voice A melodious trill that begins with a sharp note and tends to fade at end, *tik-trrrrrrrrrrrrreee* (R&T), or rises at end (Fitzpatrick).

STRIPE-NECKED TODY-TYRANT

Hemitriccus striaticollis Pl. 186

Identification 10.9–11cm. Bright olive above, somewhat darker and greyish on crown, virtually no wingbars but fringes of tertials whitish; yellowish below, streaked brownish on throat and breast. From Johannes's Tody-Tyrant by virtual lack of wingbars, presence of clear white supraloral spot and white eye-ring, and more obviously streaked throat.

Ssp. *H. s. striaticollis* (E Co: Meta)

Habits Forages alone or in pairs, in undergrowth and at mid levels. Often perches in open, with posture not completely erect, but fairly upright.

Status Uncertain in Colombia, where records few and population believed to be small and isolated.

Habitat Lower Tropical Zone, to 700m. Gallery forest, overgrown borders and thickets at edges of *várzea* and wet or marshy woodland.

Voice A repeated *whi-didit* that sometimes begins with a fast *pit, pit, pit, pit* sequence (R&T).

PEARLY-VENTED TODY-TYRANT

Hemitriccus margaritaceiventer Pl. 186

Identification 10–10.6cm. Comparatively drab little fly-catcher, with pale eyes and long bill; drab to olive-brown above with wingbars and pale fringes to tertials, whitish below, washed and streaked brownish on breast and flanks. Races distinctly differ. Width of bill is most distinctive field mark and is obvious from below, but note colour of back may vary with light conditions.

Ssp. *H. m. auyantepui* (SE Ve) greyish-olive above, pale greyish breast and underparts; eyes hazel

H. m. breweri (S Ve: Sarisariñama) dark above with wing markings somewhat obscure, whitish throat contrasts with dark breast and flanks, eyes white

H. m. chiribiquetensis (SE Co) lines on throat darker and heavier, back greyer than *impiger* or *septentrionalis*, wingbars paler and more contrasting

H. m. duidae (S Ve) dark above but wing markings contrasting, underparts warm cream to pale orange, bill reddish; orange eyes with bloodshot effect

H. m. impiger (NE Co, Ve: N & Margarita I.) buffy-brown above with yellow eyes, streaked buffy-brown on breast

H. m. pyrrhops (S Co: Caquetá) deep cinnamon

preocular spot; like *impiger* but lines stronger and much greyer above

H. m. septentrionalis (S Co) grey-olive above, black bill

Habits Forages in pairs but occasionally alone, in undergrowth and bushes, up to mid levels. Distinctive mode, moving through tangles purposefully, pausing momentarily to scan below leaves, making small sallies to pick insects from underside of leaves or from air, or gleaning from twigs and bark.

Status Frequent in Colombia and Venezuela.

Habitat Tropical to Subtropical Zones, to 1,000m north of Orinoco but to 2,000m south of it. Varied humid to dry habitats, including humid and cloud forests, forests on slopes and tops of tepuis, second growth and light woodland, savannas with scattered trees, arid areas with thorn scrub.

Voice Often heard, and several calls described: 3–4 *tuk* notes followed by a rising, varied series of *queek* notes; a sharp *tick* note and descending *t'r'r'r'r'r'* trill; short trills and buzzes (H&B); a brief *pik* or *tuk* and *sput-spik!* Race *impiger* gives a short, rising *tuk-tuk-tu-tu're're'et*, other races a thin, fast downscale *tic-tic-ter'r'r'r'r'r'r'r'r'r'r* (Hilty). The long musical trill may rise but more often descends. Also a frog-like buzz when foraging (Fitzpatrick). Voice of races *auyantepui* and *duidae* appear different from general pattern of others, and these 2 may represent a separate species (D. Ascanio recording).

BLACK-THROATED TODY-TYRANT

Hemitriccus granadensis Pl. 186

Identification 10–10.7cm. Very distinctive face pattern, with white (buffy or deep cinnamon) mask and black neck- and throat-sides. Generally yellowish-/greenish-olive above, wings and tail brownish, with coverts and remiges fringed yellow but no wingbars, white below with brownish or grey wash on breast and body-sides and flanks usually tinged yellow. Races quite distinct.

Ssp. *H. g. andinus* (N Co: E Andes, Ve: Táchira) smaller; dark buffy lores

H. g. federalis (NC Ve) paler below, slightly brighter above, grey breast much paler

H. g. granadensis (NE Ec, Co) white eye-ring

H. g. intensus (W Ve) white lores, darker breast with pure grey below (no buffy or brownish infusion)

H. g. lehmanni (Co: Santa Marta) larger, breast somewhat brownish

H. g. pyrrhops (SE Ec: Loja) eye-ring and loral patch deep cinnamon

Habits Forages in undergrowth and bushes, to mid levels, occasionally joining mixed flocks. Perches quietly for long periods. Takes insects and berries, sallying to underside of leaves or gleaning in a systematic and parsimonious manner. Wings make humming noise in flight, which is swift and direct.

Status Uncommon to rare in Ecuador, uncommon in Colombia.

Habitat Tropical to Subtropical Zones, 1,800–3,300m. Humid and cloud forests, mature second growth, areas of mossy, epiphyte-laden trees, and at borders.

Voice Calls variously described, in Ecuador as *whididik* and a sharp *wheep-wheep-wheep-wheep*; in Colombia as repetitions of 2 stuttering *dut't't't'* notes, sometimes a nasal *tip-buuuuu* or a sharp *pik, peet peet* (H&B). Dawn song given as *kee kee kee krrrrrrt*, ending in a hard, sharp trill, and a sharp trilled *krrrt* while patrolling territory; also, in alarm, a repeated *keep keep* (Fitzpatrick).

BUFF-THROATED TODY-TYRANT

Hemitriccus rufigularis Pl. 186

Identification 12cm. Plain olive above with no wingbars, warm buffy throat and breast, white belly with dull olive flanks; eyes yellow.

Ssp. Monotypic (E Andes, Ec)

Habits Forages from understorey to subcanopy on insects, hopping on branches, which it inspects and gleans, sallying from a fixed perch to pick from undersides of leaves. Probably maintains permanent, monogamous, territorial pairs. Like congeners, male sings mostly during hotter part of day, less so at dawn or in late afternoon (M. Cohn-Haft pers. obs.).

Status Scarce to rare in Ecuador.

Habitat Upper Tropical Zone, 1,300–1,500m. Dark, humid, relatively open forest interiors on lower slopes. Sometimes along wooded ridges.

Voice Song a series of clear, monosyllabic and inflected *kyek* notes, i.e. *kyek, kyek, kyek, kyek* …; usually with 4–10 notes in a series, followed by a pause of up to a few minutes, then another series (P. Coopmans, pers. comm.), e.g. *kik-keek-keek keek-kéék* or *kw-díp kw-díp kw-díp kw-deep* (Fitzpatrick).

CINNAMON-BREASTED TODY-TYRANT

Hemitriccus cinnamomeipectus Pl. 186

Identification 10cm. Small, dark olive above without wingbars, but white fringes to tertials form distinct mark on inner wing, face and breast cinnamon, rest of underparts yellow; eyes reddish. Smaller than similar Buffy-throated Tody-Tyrant, more richly coloured and lacks pale eye of latter.

Ssp. Monotypic (SE Ec)

Habits Poorly known. Forages alone or with mixed understorey flocks (in association with some antbirds). Makes brief sallies from perch to pick insects from underside of leaves then moves on, or flits about shrubbery.

Status Very rare in Ecuador (2 separate populations with very small ranges in northern Peru, the northernmost one barely reaching southern Ecuador).

Habitat Subtropical Zone, 1,700–1,900m. Humid montane and cloud forests, in areas with mossy, epiphyte-laden trees, and often in *Chusquea* bamboo.

Voice A fast, falling rattle *prrrrrrrrrrr* (Fitzpatrick).

Tody-flycatchers comprise 2 closely related genera, *Poecilotriccus* and *Todirostrum*. *Todirostrum* are distinctive, noticeably small, rounded birds that draw attention by their constantly active, lively behaviour. *Poecilotriccus* generally remain hidden in foliage, are relaxed and less active. They tend to perch still and sing. Both genera are brightly coloured with contrasting patterns, and have broad, flat bills used to snatch insects from the underside of leaves; bills are longer in *Todirostrum*, and this is a good field mark. They generally have a horizontal jizz with their tails often held above the horizontal. Eye colour varies from white or pale to brown within species, but the reason for such variation is unknown, though in some cases juveniles have brown eyes.

RUDDY TODY-FLYCATCHER

Poecilotriccus russatus Pl. 185

Identification 9.5–10cm. Dark olive above with 2 bold, cinnamon wingbars, forehead and face, chin to lower breast cinnamon, olive flanks and white belly to undertail-coverts; eyes dark. Sexes appear alike in field, but female is dark greyish on crown. Combination of cinnamon front and wingbars very distinctive.

Ssp. Monotypic (SE Ve, W Gu)

Habits Forages alone, in pairs or in small (family?) groups during immediate post-breeding period, mostly in undergrowth and at borders, but up to subcanopy.
Status Pantepui endemic, frequent only very locally in Venezuela. In Guyana found on slopes of Mt. Roraima and the environs of Sierra de Lema.
Habitat Subtropical Zone, 1,200–2,500m, in mossy, wet understorey of dense forests, adjacent thickets and thickets along streams in humid, cloud and stunted forests on slopes of tepuis.
Voice Quiet but not shy, utters an explosive *tik-tik-tr-r-r-r-r-r*, sometimes a fast, additional *tik-a-doo* (R&T), a weak, dull *tsuk, sick, tr'r'r'r'r'r'r'r*, followed sometimes by other calls in various combinations. When disturbed, *chip-t'b'r'r'r, squeeeeo, t'b'r'r'r* with a squeak in middle (Hilty).
Note Formerly placed in genus *Todirostrum* (Lanyon 1988).

RUSTY-FRONTED TODY-FLYCATCHER

Poecilotriccus latirostris Pl. 185

Identification 9.4–9.5cm. Rather dull-looking, olive above, darker on wings with 2 bright buffy wingbars, grey crown and neck, forehead and face-sides warm ochraceous, greyish-white below, flammulated olive on breast and flanks; eyes hazel. Easily confused with other tody-flycatchers in similar habitats, but best separated by warm ochre or rusty-buff of face and buffy wingbars.

Ssp. *P. l. caniceps* (E Ec, SE Co) dark grey crown and rich rusty face
P. l. mituensis (S Co) brownish-grey crown and neck, face less richly coloured

Habits Difficult to see as it forages inside tangled undergrowth, sallying to pick insects from undersides of leaves or by hopping between twigs, gleaning. Perches for long periods, spying surroundings intently.
Status Uncommon in Ecuador, uncommon to locally frequent in Colombia.
Habitat Tropical Zone, mostly below 700m in Ecuador, to 500m in Colombia. Borders of partially open areas, mature, dense second growth and *terra firme* or *várzea* forests; in thickets, along streams, tangled edges.
Voice Resembles a frog: several low, brief *trrrrr* trills, often commencing with a sharp *chup* (H&B). Sometimes just utters *tik* (Fitzpatrick).
Note Formerly placed in genus *Todirostrum* (Lanyon 1988).

SMOKY-FRONTED TODY-FLYCATCHER

Poecilotriccus fumifrons Pl. 185

Identification 9cm. Nondescript little bird with no distinguishing features, olive above, wings darker with clear yellowish wingbars, greyish head with pale lores and hint of pale superciliary. Yellowish below with dull olive wash and slightly flammulated breast and flanks; eyes pale reddish-brown.

Ssp. *P. f. penardi* (Su, FG)

Habits Forages mostly in pairs, in low shrubbery and bushes where very difficult to see even at very close range. Takes small insects by sallying from fixed perch or by gleaning.
Status Rare in Suriname, uncommon to common in French Guiana.
Habitat Tropical Zone, to 400m, in dense forest borders, overgrown clearings with tangled vines and climbing weeds, thickets and bushes in savannas and open areas near forest.
Voice A dry rattle *kerrr… kerrr…*, repeated rapidly in alarm (H&M), or as typical trill preceded by 1+ *tic* notes, e.g. *tic, tic, trrrrr* (R&T).
Note Formerly placed in genus *Todirostrum* (Lanyon 1988).

SLATE-HEADED TODY-FLYCATCHER

Poecilotriccus sylvia Pl. 185

Identification 9–10cm. Fairly distinct, despite lack of obvious field marks; olive above with greyish head and neck, whitish eye-ring, broken in front by grey lores, but noticeable white supraloral that joins upper part of eye-ring sometimes referred to as spectacles. Very clear yellow wingbars and fringes to tertials. Below whitish, with soft grey streaks on breast and flanks. Eyes white, through grey, pale yellow or brown, but juveniles seem always to have brown irides. Juvenile has buffy wingbars and buffy fringes to tertials and remiges, and is brighter, sulphur-yellow below. Smaller Pale-eyed Pygmy Tyrant is noticeably streaked on breast and always has a distinctive bright eye, with a smaller bill. Even smaller Short-tailed Pygmy Tyrant has a much shorter tail, and occurs in higher forest strata.

Ssp. *P. s. griseolus* (SE Co, Ve) grey head and nape with whitish supraloral spot and vestigial eye-ring; eyes usually dark

P. s. superciliaris (Co) white eye-ring and supraloral contrast well against darker grey head; overall rather whitish below, with less greenish suffusion on breast and less yellow

P. s. sylvia (Gu, FG) grey restricted to top of head (not on nape); eye-ring and supraloral buffy

Habits Forages in pairs that maintain contact by continually calling, and is most likely to be detected by its vocalisations. Not shy, but forages in lower levels of shrubbery, thus difficult to see. Picks insects by gleaning them from foliage. Typically forages in dense foliage, searching undersides of leaves for prey.

Status Frequent in Colombia, Venezuela and Guyana, rare (overlooked?) in French Guiana.

Habitat Tropical Zone, to 1,100m in Colombia and 1,000m in Venezuela. Dense borders and tangled, overgrown clearings in drier to moist forests, gallery forest and secondary woodland.

Voice A soft rolled *tuk grrrt* (H&B) or *tk, tr-r-r-r-t* (R&T), which could be mistaken as a frog or an insect. Also an excited *tic-a-turr!* (Fitzpatrick).

Note Formerly placed in genus *Todirostrum* (Lanyon 1988c).

SPOTTED TODY-FLYCATCHER

Todirostrum maculatum Pl. 185

Identification 9.7–10cm. Greenish-olive above with dark wings and yellow fringes to wing-coverts and remiges which tend to form bars, head grey with white supraloral and whitish streaks over top of head and across head- and neck-sides; throat white, becoming yellow below, streaked blackish from chin to breast and flanks. Eyes generally yellowish, sometimes whiter or grey, or warmer to orange or hazel. From Painted Tody-Flycatcher by streaked underparts and no overlap; Spotted is an understorey edge species, whilst Painted is a canopy species.

Ssp. *T. m. amacurense* (NE Ve, Tr) dark greenish-olive above, dark streaks on breast

T. m. maculatum (Su, FG) like *signatum* with much blacker crown

T. m. signatum (SE Co) lighter and brighter than other races

Habits Forages in pairs or family groups, always near water in edge habitats, including fringes of mangroves. Occurs from low to mid levels, darting to pick spiders and insects on foliage or in flight, catching then with loud snaps of bill. More curious than timid, quite easy to see, though never as frequent as Common Tody-Flycatcher. Dishevelled globular nest often located at end of hanging branch near a wasp's nest.

Status Uncommon in Ecuador, but common in Colombia, Venezuela, Guyana, Suriname and northern French Guiana. Local in Trinidad.

Habitat Lower Tropical Zone, to 250m in Ecuador and 100m in Venezuela. Humid wooded areas, always near water: mangroves, borders of *várzea* forest, bushy river fringes or river islands.

Voice A surprisingly loud *churrp* (P&MdS) or *peep* (H&B), a loud clear *tee* or *peek*, repeated up to 12 times at 2 s intervals, often immediately answered by mate (Fitzpatrick), sung in varying repetitions and in syncopated duets.

COMMON TODY-FLYCATCHER

Todirostrum cinereum Pl. 185

Identification 9.7cm. Readily recognised in being dark above and yellow below, the long broad black bill is noticeable and eyes are usually bright pale yellow. Juvenile has similar pattern but is not so dark above, and eyes are dark. Maracaibo Tody-Flycatcher could look similar from below, but has shorter tail, a much brighter, greener back, and dark eyes; they are largely allopatric. From Black-headed Tody-Flycatcher by pale eyes and longer tail, but juveniles very difficult to separate in field. Black-headed Tody-Flycatcher more likely to be found calling from canopy.

Ssp. *T. c. cinereum* (N & E Co, C & E Ve, Guianas) slate grey nape and upper back, all yellow below

T. c. peruanum (E Ec) darker grey above with much more black on head than other races, including malar; all yellow below; sometimes has dark eyes

T. c. sclateri (W Ec, SW Co) nape grey with back all olive, white throat

Habits Forages alone or in pairs, at all levels, very actively darting about in foliage at all heights, but most often at mid levels. Feeds on flies, wasps, beetles and small spiders, mostly by gleaning underside of leaves. Habitually wags tail sideways, and in display cocks it while hopping sideways on branch.

Status Locally common to rare in Ecuador, common in Colombia and Venezuela, frequent in Guyana, Suriname and French Guiana.

Habitat Tropical Zone, occasionally to Lower Subtropical Zone, mostly below 1,500m, at 400–1,900m in Ecuador, to 1,900m in Colombia, to 1,650m north of Orinoco in Venezuela and to 1,300m south of it. Semi-open, relatively humid areas with scattered bushes as well as forest interiors, borders and clearings; farmland, gardens, parks and villages with large trees; old plantations.

Voice A sharp, continual *tic, tic, tic* (H&M) or a brightly trilled *te'e'e'eet!* (H&B).

MARACAIBO TODY-FLYCATCHER

Todirostrum viridanum Pl. 185

Identification 8.6–9cm. Fairly nondescript, with none of distinguishing marks of other tody-flycatchers, but note short tail. Pale olive above with blackish wings that have buffy fringes to wing-coverts and remiges, but wingbars not particularly obvious; head grey with blackish forecrown, a few irregular yellowish marks on forehead, and whitish lores and postocular spots. Pale yellow below. The only tody-flycatcher in its range, but small overlap with Common possible. Latter has whitish eyes contrasting with black head, and a darker back.

Ssp. Monotypic (NE Ve)

Habits Forages alone or in pairs, usually at lower levels. Habitually snaps bill loudly on snatching an insect and also wags tail. Curious rather than shy.
Status Venezuelan endemic, locally frequent.
Habitat Lower Tropical Zone, to 200m, perhaps reaching 400m. Arid and semi-arid regions, coastal xerophytic woodland and thorny scrub.
Voice Advertising call a series of 6 sharp notes, *seek-seek-seek-seek-seek-seek* (Hilty)

BLACK-HEADED TODY-FLYCATCHER

Todirostrum nigriceps Pl. 185

Identification 8.9cm. Small, bright yellowish-olive above, blackish wings with yellow fringes to wing-coverts and remiges with a strong wingbar, short tail; head black with contrasting white throat and rest of underparts yellow. Bill black and eyes dark brown. Juvenile distinctly duller with yellowish throat and paler underparts. From Common Tody-Flycatcher by dark eye and shorter tail, but juveniles very difficult to separate in field. Look for darker head and shorter tail in Black-headed which is more a bird of upper levels to canopy, whereas Common is more usually found at mid to lower levels.

Ssp. Monotypic

Habits Forages alone or in pairs, at all levels often along thick limbs or just inside foliage. Fairly shy, often passing unnoticed. Nest a typical unkempt ball of plant materials, suspended from a branch, sometimes quite high.
Status Uncommon in Ecuador. In Colombia, frequent in north but rare on Pacific side. Frequent in Venezuela.
Habitat Tropical Zone, to 900m in Ecuador, rarely to 1,100m in Colombia and 1,000m in Venezuela. Moist, humid or wet forests and mature second growth, at borders and large clearings; open woodland, second growth, plantations.
Voice A loud series of sharp, positive, *peep* notes, given singly or doubled (H&B, Hilty). Song a slow series of usually 5–8 (–12) high-pitched, sharp, *tsip* or *jyip* notes, first somewhat lower, final ones accelerating and increasing slightly in volume (Fitzpatrick).

PAINTED TODY-FLYCATCHER

Todirostrum pictum Pl. 185

Identification 8.5cm. Yellow-olive above, black wings with yellow fringes to wing-coverts and remiges, showing as 2 wingbars, head black with white supraloral spot and mesial stripe. Below, bright yellow, with strong black streaks on breast and sides. Bill looks rather large. From Yellow-browed Tody-Flycatcher by lack of yellow superciliary, but they would only overlap in south-east Amazonas, Colombia. From Black-headed by pale eyes and black streaks on breast, but both not easy to see in canopy and confusion possible.

Ssp. Monotypic.

Habits Forages at all levels. Individuals and pairs sally for flies and wasps, other insects, small spiders. Nest a tousled pouch with a side entrance, suspended from a limb, often quite high and sited near a wasp nest.
Status Frequent in Venezuela and Guyana, extremely local in Suriname, common in French Guiana.
Habitat Lower Tropical Zone, to 400m. Humid, partially forested areas, second growth, thickets, plantations. Exclusively in canopy of tall *terra firme* in French Guiana.
Voice A low, penetrating whistle *teeng-teeng-teeng* (H&M), also *che-vik* (H&B) and series of feeble *chiip* notes (P&MdS).

YELLOW-BROWED TODY-FLYCATCHER

Todirostrum chrysocrotaphum Pl. 185

Identification 8.5–9cm. Bright yellowish-olive back, black wings with yellow fringes to coverts and remiges forming strong wingbars, head black with strong yellow postocular superciliary and mesial, and white supraloral spot. Underparts yellow with black streaks on throat and breast-sides. Eyes yellow. From Painted Tody-Flycatcher by postocular superciliary and mesial, but they would only overlap in south-east Amazonas, Colombia. From Black-headed by yellow stripes on head, yellow eyes and black streaks on breast, but not easy to see in canopy and confusion possible.

Ssp. *T. c. guttatum* (E Ec, E Co, extreme S Ve).

Habits Forages alone or in pairs, very occasionally with mixed flocks, from low levels to canopy but almost invariably in treetops, usually where foliage is particularly lush. Hops with tail cocked, peering about and picking insects.
Status Uncommon in Ecuador, Colombia and Venezuela.
Habitat Tropical Zone, to 600m in Ecuador and 500m in Colombia. Borders of humid *terra firme* and *várzea*, mature second growth, semi-open spots adjacent to forest.
Voice A sequence of 10+ *pip* notes (H&B).

GOLDEN-WINGED TODY-FLYCATCHER

Poecilotriccus calopterus Pl. 185

Identification 9.7cm. Bright olive-green above with black head, wings and tail; median wing-coverts bright golden-yellow forming strong bar, lesser wing-coverts maroon, this pattern being an unmistakable field mark.

Ssp. *P. c. calopterus* (E Ec, SE Co)

Habits Forages in pairs, often near ground, always in dense foliage, including bushy second growth in abandoned pastures and clearings (Fitzpatrick).
Status Uncommon to rare and local in Ecuador, scarce in Colombia.
Habitat Tropical Zone, to 1,300m in Ecuador, 350–450m in Colombia. Undergrowth, thickets and smaller trees at borders of humid forest, mature second growth and regenerating clearings.
Voice Several rapid repetitions of a fast, dropping *tsk-t-t-t-t-t-t* (H&B) or equally rapid repetitions of a raspy *drededeuw* (R&T).
Note Race *calopterus* may be specifically distinct from *pulchellus* of Peru (as in Fitzpatrick).

Antpipits were long considered part of the Conopophagidae. They are terrestrial, walking on the forest floor and sallying upwards to snap insects from the underside of leaves. Bill-snapping is characteristic of genus and is often given in alarm or in contact between a pair.

RINGED ANTPIPIT

Corythopis torquatus Pl. 186

Identification 14cm. Pipit-like in shape and posture, olive-brown above, white below with bold black patch in centre of breast and black streaks trailing to breast-sides; flanks washed greyish. Eye colour somewhat variable, from off-white to pale brown or grey, bill has black upper mandible and flesh-coloured lower mandible. Juvenile has breast patch browner and more diffuse, as are vestigial streaks.

Ssp. *C. t. sarayacuensis* (E Ec, SE Co) crown concolorous with brownish-olive back
C. t. anthoides (S & SE Ve, Guianas) slightly smaller; crown slate grey

Habits Forages alone or in pairs on forest floor from where follows movements of mixed flocks and sometimes joins other species at ant swarms. Feeds on beetles and crickets. Walks quietly on ground with short sprints in horizontal position, bobs head and wags tail continually, snapping its bill loudly. Not shy, perches in open low above ground.
Status Uncommon in Ecuador and Guyana; infrequent in Colombia and Venezuela; frequent in Suriname and French Guiana, where widespread.
Habitat Tropical Zone, mostly below 600m in Ecuador, to 500m in Colombia and 1,400m in Venezuela. Humid forest, dry stream beds and wet borders of streams or rivers, *terra firme* and seasonally flooded areas.
Voice Song is clearly somewhat variable, a 2-note whistled *chweeee-chee*… (H&M), or *peeeur-prayer* (H&B) or *peeew-prayeur* (Fitzpatrick), and *peeur, peeur-peépit* (R&G) with second note lower pitched.

Phyllomyias flycatchers are a very homogeneous-looking genus, greenish-olive above with dark wings and (with a single exception) clear wingbars, and mostly yellow below. They sometimes perch horizontally but mostly maintain an upright position at rest, the tail held level with body. Taxonomically, they are complex and have been the subject of various revisions that in some cases have resulted in confusing nomenclature. There is a paucity of juveniles in museum collections, but they are probably all rather like that illustrated for Sooty-capped Tyrannulet – browner and duller with pale fringes to most parts and clear wingbars.

ROUGH-LEGGED TYRANNULET

Phyllomyias burmeisteri Pl. 187

Identification 11.4–11.5cm. Back and tail olive, wings dusky with 2 yellow wingbars and fringes of tertials and remiges yellow to whitish, pileum grey and face-sides somewhat grizzled; throat white, rest of underparts yellow. Eyes vary from whitish to pale reddish-brown.

Ssp. *P. b. bunites* (SE Ve) grey of crown dark and extends to nape; bill very small.
P. b. leucogonys (Ec, E Co) duller and paler back, with paler wingbars, also paler below, bill larger
P. b. viridiceps (CN Ve) crown olive, only forehead grey
P. b. wetmorei (NW Ve) overall noticeably darker than other races

Habits Forages alone or in pairs, from mid levels to canopy but usually in canopy, only coming lower to visit rich food source. Often joins mixed flocks. Hops vivaciously, sometimes flagging up a wing or pausing to spy about, then darting off.
Status Rare in Ecuador, scarce in Colombia, uncommon and local in Venezuela.
Habitat Upper Tropical to Subtropical Zones, 600–1,500m in Ecuador, 600–1,200m in Colombia and 475–1,800m in Venezuela. Borders and clearings of humid forests on montane slopes.
Voice Rapid repetitions of a buzzy *t'e'eeeeszip* and an insistent *psss psss psss* (H&B) or *psee-psee-psee-psee* (Fitzpatrick); also a high-pitched, endless, *tzee-yeep* (R&T) and single *péééza* (Fitzpatrick).
Notes Earlier taxonomy placed this species in its own genus *Acrochordopus*. Treated as *Phyllomyias zeledoni*, White-fronted Tyrannulet, in S&M, R&T, R&G and Hilty, due to differences in voice. Races *burmeisteri* and *zeledoni* also treated as separate species by some earlier authors, but grouped into single species by Meyer de Schauensee (1966, 1970) and Traylor (1977, 1979), which treatment also followed by Dickinson (2003) and Fitzpatrick due to insufficient data to justify split.

URICH'S TYRANNULET

Phyllomyias urichi Pl. 187

Identification 13cm. Bright yellowish-olive above, with dark wings and longish tail, pale yellow fringes to wing-coverts produce 2 bold yellow wingbars, top of head grey, with distinct supraloral stripe, head-sides and chin pale yellow to whitish, rest of underparts pale yellow with faint olivaceous flammulations on breast-sides. Eyes brown, bill small and bicoloured, base of lower mandible pale, flesh-coloured with a black tip. In poor light, head appears grey, but in sunlight appears concolorous with back. Easily confused with Southern Beardless Tyrannulet which has distinct bushy crest, white lores and broken white eye-ring, and is generally duller, Forest Elaenia (race *venezuelae*) has small, white-centred crest and noticeable olivaceous streaking on breast, Yellow-olive Flycatcher (race *aequatorialis*) has a larger all-black bill, and a noticeable, large white loral spot, and Golden-faced Tyrannulet has a clear yellow supraloral that runs into a short superciliary. All these lack bold white wingbars.

Ssp. Monotypic (NE Ve).

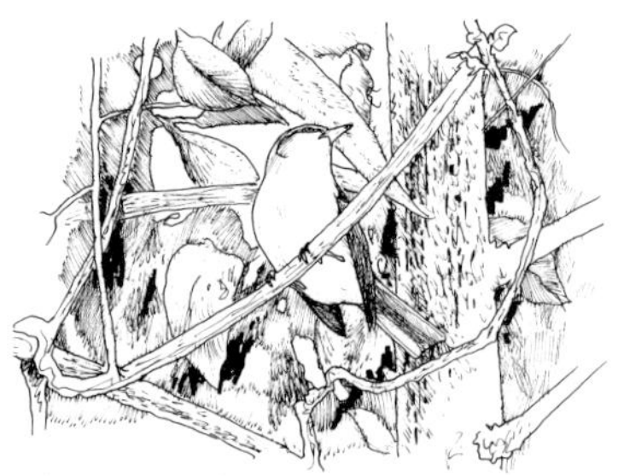

Urich's Tyrannulet forages restlessly in understorey, with tail cocked and wings drooped (based on a photograph by D. Ascanio)

Habits An extremely active bird, restless and continually on the move, tail cocked and wings drooped. Turns leaves and explores bunches of dead leaves. Forages alone and with mixed-species flocks. Does not visit canopy but forages in understorey of light woodland contiguous with coffee plantations (D. Ascanio, pers. comm.).

Status Uncommon Venezuelan endemic.

Habitat Tropical Zone, 900–1,100m. Understorey of humid and cloud forests, both interior and at borders.

Voice Unknown.

Notes Formerly included under *P. virescens*, but separated by Cardoso da Silva (1996), followed by Dickinson (2003) and Fitzpatrick. *P. virescens*, with *urichi*, *reiseri* (principally of Brazil) and *sclateri* (Peru and Bolivia), formerly placed in genus *Xanthomyias*, but latter merged under *Phyllomyias* by Traylor (1977, 1979).

SOOTY-HEADED TYRANNULET

Phyllomyias griseiceps Pl. 187

Identification 10–10.6cm. Rather nondescript, greyish-olive above, darker on crown, with paler, whitish fringes to wing-coverts and tertials varying with age, wear and subspecies, but never bold and never forming clear wingbars (usually none at all); slightly grizzled on face, white supraloral reaches back as a semi-superciliary; whitish throat grading to yellowish below, washed dull olive on breast and flanks. Eyes dark brown, bill small and dark. Juvenile browner and has pale fringes to feathers of upperparts, strongest on wings (giving tatty scaled effect) but most noticeable on crown. Best identified by combination of short eyebrow and lack of wingbars. Posture upright, especially when at rest.

Ssp. *P. g. caucae* (CW Co) paler than *griseiceps*

P. g. cristatus (N Co, N Ve) compared to *pallidiceps*, irregular and variable wingbars, but tips of median wing-coverts weaker and inconsistent, tips of greater coverts brighter

P. g. griseiceps (Ec) darker above than *caucae*, especially on crown

P. g. pallidiceps (SE Ve, Gu) compared to *cristatus*, browner back with darker wings and 2 irregular, variable wingbars

Habits Forages alone or in pairs in canopy, only lower at forest edge; does not join mixed flocks. Picks insects by gleaning and by sallying to undersides of leaves. Also takes small fruit and visits fruiting trees for both fruit and insects these attract. Often missed as tends to flit about inside vegetation, but sings from exposed perch in canopy.

Status Uncommon to rare in Ecuador, locally common in Colombia, locally frequent in Venezuela, uncommon and local in Guyana, uncommon and very local in French Guiana where only recently discovered (sight records only).

Habitat Tropical Zone, mostly below 1,100m in Ecuador, 1,300–2,200m in Colombia, to 1300m north of Orinoco, but only to 460m south of it. Borders and clearings of humid forests, drier deciduous and white-sand forests, plantations, partially open areas with stands of trees or bushes. Large clearings and disturbed canopy in submontane forest (600–750m) in French Guiana.

Voice Sings frequently, *whit, wheet-wheet-wheeu* and also a *tee'p'p'pip* trill, endlessly repeated (H&B). Main song said to be a bright, rollicking *whip, whip-dip-irip* (R&T).

Note Fitzpatrick found racial differences insignificant and synonymised all described variation.

PLUMBEOUS-CROWNED TYRANNULET

Phyllomyias plumbeiceps Pl. 187

Identification 11.5–11.7cm. Olive above with darker wings and yellowish wingbars; crown grey with white superciliary wrapping around ear-coverts, with dark crescent and grizzled cheeks; throat white, rest of underparts yellow, washed olive on breast and flanks. From Ecuadorian Tyrannulet by eyebrow and dark crescent on cheek; from Ashy-headed Tyrannulet by less well-defined ear-coverts and white throat (Ashy-headed has yellow throat).

Ssp. Monotypic (C Co, C Ec).

Habits Forages in mossy canopies and upper levels, often with mixed flocks. Picks insects with brief sallies from perch. Quiet for long periods, peering around and occasionally flagging up one wing.

Status Rare in Ecuador, uncommon and local in Colombia and Venezuela.

Habitat Subtropical Zone, 1,200–2,200m. Humid and wet forests on montane slopes.

Voice A series of some 8 sharp notes reminiscent of furnariid calls, given intermittently through day (R&T).

Note Formerly placed in *Oreotriccus* (with *griseocapilla* of south-east Brazil), but merged within *Phyllomyias* by Traylor (1977, 1979).

BLACK-CAPPED TYRANNULET

Phyllomyias nigrocapillus Pl. 187

Identification 11–11.7cm. Bright olive above with darker wings and 2 boldly contrasting yellowish-white wingbars, crown dark to blackish, white supraloral spot with narrow superciliary that tends to wrap faintly around dark crescent on ear-coverts (less clearly defined than Plumbeous-crowned or Ashy-headed Tyrannulets). Perches fairly horizontally, frequently with tail slightly cocked. From Ecuadorian Tyrannulet by whitish line around ear-coverts and shorter tail.

Ssp. *P. n. aureus* (W Ve) similar to *flavimentum* but generally more golden wash, crown slightly dusky greyish
P. n. flavimentum (Co: Santa Marta) buffy fringes to secondaries, deep yellow supraloral streak, no white on chin, deeper yellow below
P. n. nigrocapillus (Ec, Co: Andes, W Ve) whitish supraloral streak

Habits Forages alone or in pairs, from mid levels to canopy, often within dense foliage, thus hardly noticeable. Quite vivacious, dashes and hops sprightly about, often with mixed-species flocks.
Status Uncommon in Ecuador, uncommon to fairly common in Colombia.
Habitat Temperate Zone, 2,300–3,300m but sometimes lower in Colombia. Dense cloud forest, lighter montane woodland and mature second growth.
Voice A high *peeeep* unlike a typical flycatcher call (H&B, F&K). Also an emphatic series of high-pitched notes *tzi-tzi-tzrr*, repeated persistently (Fitzpatrick).
Note Formerly placed in genus, *Tyranniscus* together with species *cinereiceps* and *uropygialis*, but transferred to *Phyllomyias* by Traylor (1977, 1979).

ASHY-HEADED TYRANNULET
Phyllomyias cinereiceps Pl. 187

Identification 10.2–11cm. Olive-green above with dark wings that show 2 weak but clear wingbars, crown bluish-grey with white supraloral spot running back behind ear-coverts, which have clearly defined black crescent; cheeks grizzled greenish-yellow, throat white, rest of underparts yellow, flammulated greenish on breast and sides; eyes dark red. From similar species by distinctly blue-grey crown, very clear black crescent on rear ear-coverts, distinct flammulations on breast and reddish eye (not easy to detect in field).

Ssp. Monotypic (C Ec, C Co)

Habits Forages alone or in pairs, at lower and mid levels, often with mixed-species flocks. Takes flying insects by chasing in foliage or gleans from leaves with brief hover. When perched, straight but slightly hunched and watches surroundings intently. Occasionally flicks 1 wing over back.
Status Uncommon in Ecuador. In Colombia situation poorly known but possibly quite local, records spotty.
Habitat Upper Tropical to Temperate Zones, mostly 1350–2,500m in Ecuador and 1,900–2,300m in Colombia. Humid forest.
Voice Call has 2 segments: a loud, high *pseee* followed by a fast, descending trill, *sweeeee, see-ee-ee-ee-eew* (F&K, Fitzpatrick).
Note Formerly placed in genus *Tyranniscus*, together with species *nigrocapillus* and *uropygialis*, but transferred to *Phyllomyias* by Traylor (1977, 1979).

TAWNY-RUMPED TYRANNULET
Phyllomyias uropygialis Pl. 187

Identification 11.2–11.5cm. Brown-olive above with darker wings and 2 bright, buffy wingbars, rump and uppertail-coverts cinnamon (diagnostic but difficult to see), tail dark brown; dark brown crown with white lores and superciliary; sides of face and throat greyish-white, breast and flanks olive, yellow central belly becoming whitish below. From similar species by generally browner appearance, buffy wingbars and with certainty by cinnamon rump and uppertail-coverts.

Ssp. Monotypic (C Ec, C Co, W Ve)

Habits Forages in pairs or small groups, from low levels to subcanopy, but most often in treetops. Joins both mid-level and canopy mixed flocks. Takes flying insects or gleans them from leaves with brief hover. Raises crown frequently. Usually first species to start pre-dawn/dawn chorus
Status Uncommon to rare in Ecuador, scarce in Venezuela. In Colombia situation not well known, records spotty.
Habitat Subtropical Zone to Páramo, 2,100–3,100m in Ecuador, 1,500–2,600m in Colombia, to 3,100m in Venezuela. Bushy borders, thickets and clearings of humid forest on upper slopes.
Voice A *pzit* in contact and a 2-note song (F&K), or an infrequent *tseep-tseep*, occasionally in fast repetitions (R&T). Also *tseep, zéé-u* singly or in series, especially in early morning (Fitzpatrick).
Note Formerly placed in genus *Tyranniscus*, together with species *nigrocapillus* and *cinereiceps*, but transferred to *Phyllomyias* by Traylor (1977, 1979).

Zimmerius tyrannulets formerly constituted part of the genus *Tyranniscus*, of which the other members are now placed in *Phyllomyias*. They are distinct in that all have well-marked golden-yellow fringes to the wing-coverts and remiges, but these never form clear wingbars as in *Phyllomyias*. Also they tend to perch horizontally with the tail slightly cocked. Sexes are alike, but males have slightly longer tails.

PALTRY TYRANNULET
Zimmerius vilissimus Pl. 187

Identification 10cm. Greenish-olive above with dark wings and tail, pale yellowish fringes to wing-coverts and remiges, crown dark brownish-grey, bold white supraloral and superciliary, head-sides greyish-olive, throat whitish, becoming pale grey flammulated darker grey on breast and sides, pale yellow below; eyes dull yellow. Female smaller. Juvenile has duller crown and brown eyes. From Golden-faced Tyrannulet by prominent white superciliary (short, yellowish line in latter), and from all other tyrannulets in range by lack of wingbars.

Ssp. *Z. v. parvus* (NW Co: Chocó)

Habits Forages in canopy, usually inside foliage, thus often passing unnoticed. Joins mixed flocks. Partiality to

Loranthaceae berries has led some authors, who considered race *parvus* to be possibly a separate species, to suggest name Mistletoe Tyrannulet.
Status In Colombia situation uncertain.
Habitat Tropical Zones, to 100m. Borders and clearings of humid forest and mature second growth.
Voice A loud *peeayik* or *pee-areet* repeated for long periods, and *pyeu* (R&T, Fitzpatrick).
Note Race *parvus* perhaps a distinct species from *vilissimus* (H&B, Fitzpatrick).

VENEZUELAN TYRANNULET

Zimmerius improbus Pl. 187

Identification 11.5–12cm. Olive above with dusky wings which have sharply defined yellow fringes to terminal half of secondaries, forming a block of yellow (but not wingbars). Outer fringes of wing-coverts yellow, but not tips – juvenile differs in having lores dark, with grey legs and feet (black in adults). Whitish edge to basal half of primaries may form another block. Head mostly dark brown with white supraloral spot and superciliary, and white half-ring below eye, cheeks and malar grizzled (not in *petersi*); throat pale greenish-white, breast, sides and flanks flammulated olive-grey, rest of underparts yellow; eyes dark brown.

Ssp. *Z. i. improbus* (N Co, NW Ve) ear-coverts concolorous with crown and merge into neck-sides, white half-ring below eye merges with grizzled cheeks and malar; inseparable from *tamae* in field; juvenile like adult but has very dark eyes and pale, large whitish tips to greater coverts, forming clear wingbar

Head of petersi *on left, compared with* tamae / improbus *on right; note clearly defined auriculars of* petersi

Z. i. petersi (Co: Santa Marta, Ve: Perijá & Tamá) distinct from others, pale olive above with dark grey crown and clearly defined auriculars that contrast abruptly with irregular white malar and off-white throat, breast soft pale grey, rest of underparts pale sulphur-yellow; juvenile has white supraloral duller and crown more soft olivaceous grey; wings and tail mid brown, with pale fringes to greater coverts; eyes very dark brown

Z. i. tamae (N Ve) like *improbus*, perhaps slightly paler yellow below, but crown browner and more clearly defined; juvenile duller mid brown above with yellow outer fringes to greater coverts reaching tips of feathers; differs from juvenile *petersi* in being noticeably darker and having only forehead dark, crown concolorous with back, more olive-washed on breast

Habits Forages alone or in pairs, picking small fruits or gleaning and sallying insects in outer branches, from mid levels to canopy. Joins flocks. Globular nest with side entrance, most often attached to or inside clumps of hanging moss.
Status Frequent in Colombia, common in Venezuela.
Habitat Tropical to Temperate Zones, 1,200–2,300m in Colombia. Humid primary and secondary forests, at borders and in clearings and partially open areas, sometimes where Spanish moss is abundant.
Voice Calls include *pier-he-he-he-he*, a dawn-call of *beef-beer*, *chee-yip* and other loud long chips (H&B).
Note Venezuelan Tyrannulet was previously considered conspecific with Paltry Tyrannulet, and appears under this name in H&B.

RED-BILLED TYRANNULET

Zimmerius cinereicapilla Pl. 187

Identification 12cm. Inappropriately named for bill not red but black above and basal half of lower mandible flesh-coloured and not easy to see. Eyes straw yellow (a good field mark). Otherwise a typical *Zimmerius*, olive above with darker brown wings sharply fringed yellow, top of head greyish with short whitish superciliary; throat pale grey becoming olive-grey on breast and bright yellow below. From Golden-faced Tyrannulet by pale eyes; latter also has yellow on face and is whiter below.

Ssp. Monotypic (Ec)

Habits Forages alone, usually in canopy, with mixed flocks. Gleans insects from foliage by hovering briefly.
Status Very rare in Ecuador, where a small-range population occurs, widely disjunct from larger range in Peru.
Habitat Tropical Zone, 800–1,350m. Humid forests of mid-montane slopes and foothills, both at borders and in interior.
Voice A rapid, quite musical *chirchededede-whet-whet* (R&T) or a descending series beginning and ending with more emphatic notes, including *wheet-wheet* at end; also a single, soft *cheet* (Fitzpatrick).

SLENDER-FOOTED TYRANNULET

Zimmerius gracilipes Pl. 187

Identification 10.2cm. Olive-brown above with brown wings; wing-feathers fringed yellow but no bars formed, tail brown, edged olive; eyes pale, legs and feet black. Juvenile slightly paler and duller than adult, with brown eyes and grey legs and feet. Lack of wingbars separates it from all otherwise similar tyrannulets.

Ssp. *Z. g. acer* (Guianas) whitish face, clear white to pale sulphur-yellow throat, becoming more sulphur-yellow to undertail, breast and sides washed warm, olivaceous-grey; eyes white or pale grey

Z. g. gracilipes (SE Co, S & SE Ve) grizzled cheeks and throat, yellow below, washed olive-green on breast, sides and flanks; eyes pale blue

Habits Forages quietly, alone or in pairs, gleaning or

sallying for insects in outer branches and picking berries from mid levels to canopy. Often passes unnoticed. Feeds on Loranthaceae. Perches with tail slightly raised. Joins mixed canopy flocks.

Status Uncommon in Ecuador. Frequent in Colombia, Guyana and Suriname, common in French Guiana.

Habitat Tropical Zone, to 2,000m in Venezuela but mostly below 1,000m. Primary forest, both *várzea* and humid *terra firme*, mostly at borders and clearings and in forest stands in savannas, gardens and parks in villages and suburban areas.

Voice Day song of *gracilipes chu, ch-chu'RE?* (Hilty) and of *acer* a 5-note series of weak, high-pitched whistles *fee, fee, fee, fee, fee* (H&M), with dawn song a short, hard whistle, *tuu, de'de* (Hilty).

Notes Race *acer* formerly considered a separate species, but placed as race of *Z. gracilipes* by Zimmer (1941b). S&M treat it as a separate species. Fitzpatrick notes that differences among named populations extremely subtle, apparently clinal and recognisable only as averages; on other hand, apparent vocal differences across range imply that more than one taxon is involved. Apparently, both races listed above have been collected at same locality in Brazil.

GOLDEN-FACED TYRANNULET

Zimmerius chrysops Pl. 187

Identification 10.9–11.5cm. A rather ordinary little tyrannulet with a yellow foreface that separates it from all other tyrannulets.

Ssp. *Z. c. albigularis* (SW Co, NW Ec) yellow on head paler, with less yellow below, throat almost white, breast pure grey
Z. c. chrysops (E Ec, Co: Andes, NW Ve) as described
Z. c. cumanensis (NE Ve) reportedly washed pale greenish-yellow below, but looks exactly like *chrysops*
Z. c. flavidifrons (SW Ec) like *albigularis* but darker throughout
Z. c. minimus (Co: Santa Marta) smaller; slightly paler green above and more yellow on abdomen

Habits Forages alone or in pairs, conspicuous in outer branches from mid levels to canopy. Often with mixed canopy flocks. Perches in open, leaning forward. Flicks tail upwards slightly and sometimes makes fluttering noise with wings in flight (courtship display?).

Status Common in Ecuador and Colombia, locally frequent in Venezuela.

Habitat Upper Tropical to Temperate Zones, to 1,600m in west Ecuador, to 2,200m in east, 100–2,700m in Colombia, usually at 300–2400m, and 450–1,500m but may occur to 2,400m in Venezuela. Humid to wet primary forest and adjacent clearings of lower slopes and foothills, coffee plantations, both older and light second growth and gardens.

Voice Plaintive *hueer?* characteristic of species and canopy habitat. Also *chu-de-de'e'e'e*, a typical *teer-tif* dawn-call (H&B) and slow, drowsy *cheeee* (4–5 times) (R&G).

Tyrannulets of the genus *Ornithion* are inconspicuous, short-tailed and heavy-looking little birds with clear supercilia, and characteristic, piercing voices. They are birds of treetops.

WHITE-LORED TYRANNULET

Ornithion inerme Pl. 188

Identification 8.5–9cm. Olive above with dusky brown wings and tail, wings have 2 rows of large white spots that form distinctive wingbars, top of head slate grey with white line from lores over eyes and another below eyes like spectacles; throat whitish, becoming yellowish below. Female slightly smaller. Juvenile duller and, whilst has pale fringes to wing-coverts, with no bright white spots, a weak superciliary and no spectacles. Thick, black bill. Distinguished by its small size and character of wingbars.

Ssp. Monotypic (E Ec, E Co, S Ve, Gu, Su, FG)

Habits Vivacious and restless, forages alone or in pairs in canopy and higher mid levels, gleaning insects and hopping about in foliage. Joins canopy feeding flocks.

Status Uncommon to locally frequent in Ecuador, possibly scarce (few records) in Colombia, locally frequent in Venezuela, frequent in Guyana, scarce (few records) in Suriname, common (but easily overlooked) in French Guiana.

Habitat Tropical Zone, mostly below 600m in Ecuador, to 1,200m in Venezuela. Borders of humid, gallery, savanna, *várzea* and even sandy soil forests and other wooded areas. Canopy of tall forest in French Guiana.

Voice Sings from highest branches, a series of high *whee* notes (H&B) or endless repetitions of *pee-dee-dee-deet* (R&G). Also, a loud, penetrating and persistently repeated, high metallic and ringing *sree-de-de-de*, and when excited a faster, longer *di-di-di-di-d'd'd'd'd'ddd*, ending in a metallic accelerating trill that is somewhat attenuated (Hilty).

BROWN-CAPPED TYRANNULET

Ornithion brunneicapillus Pl. 188

Identification 7.6–8.4cm. Olive above with brown crown, white lores and superciliary; yellow below with slight olive wash on breast. From other tyrannulets by lack of any wingbars or distinguishing marks above, bold eyebrow and virtually clear yellow underparts. Juvenile brown above, olive on crown and lacks clear superciliary.

Ssp. *O. b. brunneicapillus* (W & C CO, NW Ec) as described
O. b. dilutum (NE Co, NW Ve) slightly paler

Habits Vocalisations draw attention to this little bird. Forages alone or in pairs, from undergrowth to canopy. Joins mixed flocks. Seems quite restless when gleaning twigs and leaves. Nest an open cup, quite flat and dishevelled.

Status Uncommon in Ecuador and Colombia.

Habitat Tropical Zone, to 1,200m in Venezuela. Humid forest, mature second growth, open woodland, plantations; at borders and clearings.

Voice Distinctive song is a descending series of quick whistled notes: *peee, pih-pey-peh-pūh* (H&B) and the call is a single *peeep* (Fitzpatrick).

Notes Formerly, *O. brunneicapillus* and *O. semiflavum* of Middle America were placed in separate genus *Microtriccus*, but this was merged under *Ornithion* by Zimmer (1941b). Also, 2 races in O. *brunneicapillus* formerly placed in *O. semiflavum*, but separated by Slud (1964) based on differences in voice. Wetmore (1972) considered that morphological differences merited maintaining *Microtriccus*. Correct spelling is *brunneicapillus* not *brunneicapillum* (David & Gosselin 2002). Fitzpatrick considered *dilutus* not reliably distinguishable from *brunneicapillus* and synonymised them.

SOUTHERN BEARDLESS TYRANNULET

Camptostoma obsoletum Pl. 188

Identification 9.7cm. Above greyish-brown to olive-brown, browner and slightly darker on crown which is short-crested, wings darker with 2 clear wingbars; short weak whitish superciliary and eye-ring; whitish throat and yellowish below. Combination of short, bushy crest, 2 strong wingbars and horizontal posture with cocked tail distinguish it from other tyrannulets. From Mouse-colored Tyrannulet by white wingbars and by its nest (a small ball shape with a side entrance; Mouse-coloured's nest is cup-shaped).

Ssp. *C. o. bogotensis* (E Co) like *caucae*

C. o. caucae (C Co: W Andes) darker than *pusillum*, more greyish above with a sooty cap, throat and breast greyish, belly sulphur-yellow

C. o. napaeum (C Co, S & SE Ve, Guianas) darker above with clearly defined sooty-brown cap, wingbars whitish primrose-yellow; more greyish, powdery olive on breast

C. o. olivaceum (E Ec, SE Co) paler green above than *napaeum*, crown virtually concolorous with back (only slightly darker), below, only chin white, rest yellow

C. o. pusillum (N Co, & NW Ve) olive cap and deep olive-buff wingbars

C. o. sclateri (W Ec) tail, rump and fringes of flight-feathers fringed buffy

C. o. venezuelae (NC, NE& C Ve, Tr) from *pusillum* by off-white wingbars

Habits Forages alone or in pairs, quite unafraid and vivacious. Flits about with tail cocked, making short dashing sallies infrequently. Feeds on ants, wasps, cicadas and spiders, and also many berries, especially of Loranthaceae. Nest often located near a wasp's nest.

Status Locally common to uncommon in Ecuador. Frequent in Colombia, Venezuela and Guyana, quite common in Suriname, Trinidad and French Guiana.

Habitat Tropical Zone, to 2,300m in Ecuador but mainly below 300m in east, and to 1,600m in Marañon catchment, to 2,000m in Colombia but mainly below 1,200m, and to 1,000m in Venezuela. Wide variety of dry or humid, semi-open areas with scattered trees or bushes; gardens and parks, plantations, edge of mangroves. Locally in canopy of tall forest in French Guiana.

Voice Long, drawn-out whistles and wistful song also comprises high whistles *peeh... peeh... pee-hee-heeheeheehee... peeh...* (H&M), and a plaintive *peeeeee-tee* (Hilty).

Notes Species has been conveniently separated into 4 groups, each of which has some distinct characteristic. Three of these occur in our region, and include following races: in northern South America *venezuelensis, pusillum, caucae* and *napeum*; western South America *sclateri*; and western Amazonia *olivaceum*. One or more of these may prove to be distinct species. Fitzpatrick found *bogotensis* to be a poorly defined intermediate between *caucae* and *pusillum* and synonymised it under *caucae*. He also synonymised *venezuelae* under *pusillum*, but a series of 12 *pusillum* examined by us appears sufficiently distinct to maintain both.

MOUSE-COLOURED TYRANNULET

Phaeomyias murina Pl. 188

Identification 13cm. Rather undistinguished flycatcher, mouse-brown above, long greyish-white superciliary from bill to well beyond eye, 2 well-defined but dark wingbars, and fringes to tertials; sides of head, throat and breast greyish-white, rest of underparts yellow. Distinctive flat-headed appearance and wingbars distinctly buffy or cinnamon. Nest is cup-shaped. Southern Beardless Tyrannulet's nest is ball-shaped with side entrance. Look for very long greyish-white eyebrow, relatively long, often slightly drooped tail, 2 wide buffy wingbars and flattish head.

Ssp. *P. m. incomta* (N & W Co, Ve, Tr) duller than *wagae*, between drab and hair brown, wingbars broader and rich cinnamon; foreneck, breast and sides dingy greyish with only mid abdomen very pale yellow

P. m. tumbezana (SW Ec) olive-brown above with rufescent tone to back and pale cinnamon wingbars, white below with pale buffy tinge, rather than yellow, grey wash to breast and flanks

P. m. wagae (Guianas, Ec?) bill slightly larger; darker above, more olivaceous than *incomta*, less rufescent, yellow below more extensive, reaching foreneck, leaving only upper throat white

Habits Forages alone or in pairs, quietly, gleaning and flitting about in canopy. Main diet berries, especially of Loranthaceae, taking seeds by wiping fruit against a twig. Also picks small beetles and other insects. Small cup nest is mostly of mosses with dense feather lining, in fork of bush or small tree.

Status In Ecuador race *tumbezana* uncommon to locally frequent; birds with yellowish bellies sighted in north-east considered possibly of race *wagae* (R&G), uncommon and local. Common in Colombia, common and widespread in Venezuela, locally frequent in Trinidad, frequent in Guyana and Suriname, very common in French Guiana.

Habitat Tropical to Lower Subtropical Zones, to 600m in Ecuador, 1,000m in Colombia (once at 1,700m), and in Venezuela to 1,900m north of Orinoco and 950m south of it. Open woodland, light deciduous forest, scrub and second growth in savannas and on lower slopes, edge of mangroves, plantations, parks and gardens.

Voice In Ecuador race *tumbezana* has sharp squeaky, *sque'ky, squeky-kit!* and also gives weird, mechanical-sounding *kit-wrzzzzzzzzzz*, whilst probable dawn song is a high-pitched *kzeeeeet* interspersed with squeaky notes. In contrast, race *wagae* (?) has dry *jejejejejéjew* or *jejejejejéw* (R&G). In Colombia *incompta* vocalisations include song attributed to *wagae* (?) in north-east Ecuador, also a weak *czert*, a *td td'd'd'd'd'd'd* rattle and run of rising *pip* notes followed by a tumbled chatter (Ridgely, Hilty and Fitzpatrick in H&B). In Venezuela a nasal *teetep* and a rattle, often in duet, and in morning a long, enthusiastic rambling *tu-tu-tu-tu-tu… tu-tu-Tu-Te-Teep!* for several minutes. In Guyana, race *wagae* described (N.Howe in Snyder 1966) as calling *ik-ik* and *tit-tit-tit-TIT-tittit*, and in Suriname a trembling chatter (H&M).

Note Race *tumbezana* (and *inflava* and *maranonica* of north-west Peru) treated as a separate species, Tumbes Tyrannulet, in R&G, but retained in *P. murina* by Fitzpatrick.

YELLOW TYRANNULET

Capsiempis flaveola Pl. 189

Identification 11.4–11.5cm. Yellowish-olive above with dusky wings and 2 bold yellow wingbars, superciliary varies according to race but can be good field mark, yellow below. Juvenile duller and more mid brownish above, wing-coverts buffy-brown. In Guianas race *amazona* could be confused with Olive-green Tyrannulet, but note all-yellow superciliary (lacking in Olive-green Tyrannulet).

Ssp. *C. f. amazona* (Guianas) smaller size with slightly duller and darker upperparts

C. f. cerula (NE Ec, E Co, E & S Ve) all-yellow superciliary; juvenile has back and crown soft brownish-olive and wing-coverts whitish with no trace of cinnamon; lacks wingbars by time of first full moult

C. f. leucophrys (CN Co, NW Ve) lores, supraloral and chin white

C. f. magnirostris (SW Ec) larger bill; greener above and yellow superciliary distinctly pale

Habits Forages in pairs or small (family?) parties, gleaning and sallying from undergrowth to canopy. Seldom joins mixed flocks. Feeds on insects, as well as significant percentage of berries. Cup nest is sometimes adorned with moss. Calls frequently as if 'chatting' with others.

Status Uncommon to rare in Ecuador. Frequent in Colombia. Scarce and local in Guyana, uncommon in Suriname, rare and local in French Guiana.

Habitat Tropical Zone, to 1,500m in Ecuador, 500m in Colombia and to 600m north of Orinoco in Venezuela, but only to 300m south of it. Borders of drier forest and second growth, patches of bamboo, sandy soil woodland and thickets, gallery forests.

Voice Pairs maintain contact with each other through duets. Short trills and varying series of pleasant rolling notes (R&G), e.g. *pee-tee* or *peeteetee*, usually accelerating (H&B, R&T). In Venezuela, song transcribed as 'pretty cake', repeated rapidly 10+ times when excited (Hilty).

Note Race *amazona*, described from few specimens, merged into *cerula* by Fitzpatrick.

Scrub flycatchers of genus *Sublegatus* were previously considered conspecific, under *S. arenum*, but were separated into 3 species on the basis of vocalisations and plumage differences. Further splits may be forthcoming. They look much like *Myiarchus*, but all have stubby black bills. All have an upright posture at rest.

NORTHERN SCRUB FLYCATCHER

Sublegatus arenarum Pl. 189

Identification 15cm. Greyish-brown above, including crown (no white) with 3 pale greyish wingbars in fresh plumage. In worn plumage that on lesser coverts virtually lost. Greyish-white loral spot and superciliary with narrow eye-ring; chin white, throat and breast grey and rest of underparts yellow. Juvenile similar but browner above. Pale whitish fringes to all feathers of upperparts, giving scaled appearance, uppertail-coverts ruddy-coloured.

Ssp. *S. a. atrirostris* (N Co) crown much darker than *glaber* and forms distinct cap, pale fringes to wing-coverts less conspicuous; throat and breast deeper grey and abdomen paler yellow

S. a. glaber (Ve: N coast & Margarita I., Tr, Su, FG) as described

S. a. orinocensis (E Co, C Ve) crown less dark and merges into nape, like *glaber* below but yellow richer and breast slightly browner grey

S. a. pallens (Ve: Los Roques, ABC) very pale pure grey from chin to breast and sulphur-yellow below

S. a. tortuguensis (Ve: Tortuga Is.) slightly paler, more yellowish-brown above and yellow below richer

Habits Forages alone or in pairs, always in undergrowth or at mid levels. Feeds on insects, spiders, and occasionally berries and small fruits, by gleaning or with short sallies from a perch, always keeping in foliage. Forages sometimes on ground, sedately picking ants. Perches vertically, tail pointing down. Constructs delicate, exquisite cup nest of lichens, spider webs and animal hairs.

Status Frequent in Colombia, Guyana and Suriname, small numbers in French Guiana. Frequent and widespread in Curaçao and Bonaire, but scarcer on Aruba. Locally frequent in Trinidad.

Habitat Tropical Zone, to 500m in Colombia and 600m in Venezuela. Coastal areas and lowland dry, semi-open areas with cacti, *Acacia*, *Piptadenia*, *Prosopis*. In mangroves, dry scrub, deciduous and thorny woodland.

Voice A thin but sweet and cheerful *pee-wee*, and varied rattles, e.g. *pee-weereereeree* or *peepereepeewee-peewee* (Vous). Also, a sad *cheee* (H&B).

SOUTHERN SCRUB FLYCATCHER

Sublegatus modestus (not illustrated)

Identification 14cm. Greyish-brown above with short, bushy crest, wings darker with 2 wingbars and pale fringes to tertials, ear-coverts slightly browner, clear supraloral spot and poorly defined greyish superciliary and eye-ring; below whitish, with a grey-suffused breast, and yellowish below. Race *modestus* very similar to, but smaller than Amazonian Scrub Flycatcher, bill shorter and division between greyish breast and yellow belly more abrupt in Southern. However, identification uncertain without in-hand examination. Extremely unlikely this taxon has occurred in our region. The migratory race *brevirostris* is distinguished from other scrub flycatchers by its bold white wingbars, and longer wings and tail.

Ssp. *S. m. brevirostris* (SE Co: Mitú) has bold white wingbars.

Habits Difficult to see, quiet, and forages inside foliage.

The migratory race of Southern Scrub Flycatcher is just like Amazonian Scrub Flycatcher, but has bold white wingbars

Status Breeds in northern Argentina and Uruguay to southern Brazil and eastern Peru, but presence unconfirmed in northern South America (Fitzpatrick), though mentioned from as far north as Mitú, Amazonian Colombia.

Habitat Tropical Zone. Dry, arid scrub and light open woodland, and densely wooded savannas.

Voice A high-pitched *see-pee…peeepeeepeee…seee* (de Peña & Rumboll 1998), a repeated *pseee-ú* and *cheer* (Fitzpatrick). Unknown to what extent it vocalises on migration and in winter, and is possibly silent, apart from occasional calls.

Note Erroneously listed as a regular, if local visitor, to Colombia, Venezuela and Guianas (H&B), but we suspect this reference inadvertently refers to Amazonian Scrub Flycatcher.

AMAZONIAN SCRUB FLYCATCHER

Sublegatus obscurior Pl. 189

Identification 15cm. Particularly nondescript: dark greyish-brown above with faint, pale superciliary and narrow eye-ring, wings and tail dusky, and 2 indistinct wingbars; chin to breast grey, rest of underparts dull yellow. Very little overlap with Northern Scrub Flycatcher, but is distinctly duller and almost grubbier looking.

Ssp. Monotypic (E Ec, E Co, S Ve, S Gu, S Su, S FG).

Habits Forages quietly, mostly in pairs, gleaning or sallying for insects and picking berries and small fruit.

Status Rare in Ecuador, uncommon and local in Colombia and Venezuela, uncommon in Guyana, and scarce and local in Suriname.

Habitat Tropical Zone, to 900m in Ecuador, 500m in Colombia and 460m in Venezuela. Scrub, woodland in savannas, gallery forest, open, overgrown lots in humid forest and also at borders.

Voice Song a sweet *chwedee… chwedee… chuweee…* (R&T).

SUIRIRI FLYCATCHER

Suiriri suiriri Pl. 189

Identification 15.5–16cm. Distinctive and not easily confused due to its pale yellow rump and uppertail-coverts. Back olive, contrasting with grey head, dusky tail and wings, with clearly defined pale grey wingbars and fringes to tertials, dark line from lores through eyes and white supraloral spot forms superciliary that reaches behind eyes; face slightly grizzled grey and white, from chin to breast and sides white, with rest of underparts bright yellow.

Ssp. *S. s. affinis* (S Su: Sipaliwini)

Habits Forages in pairs or small groups, making short sallies from a low exposed perch and by gleaning. Takes insects. Perches upright, mostly on low branches and sometimes drops to ground. May occasionally hover above grass, with fanned tail. Pairs sing joyfully in duet.

Status Uncommon in Suriname.

Habitat Tropical Zone. Open scrub on rocky hills, savanna with scattered trees or scrub, edge of gallery forests.

Voice Song a rapid sequence of nasal *dya* notes and gives a sudden *dyrrr* scold (R&T).

YELLOW-CROWNED TYRANNULET

Tyrannulus elatus Pl. 188

Identification 10.2cm. Small and plump, a discreet little flycatcher heard more often than seen. Darkish olive above with dusky wings and 2 bold pale yellowish-white to white wingbars, and olive tail; head all grey, much darker on crown with partially concealed orange-yellow central stripe and bright orange fringes to feathers of rear crown, whitish eye-ring and some pale grey grizzling on face, underparts washed olive on breast and sides, becoming yellowish on central belly. Juveniles differ by race. Similar but larger Greenish Elaenia lacks wingbars; yellow phase and female Grey Elaenia similar but lack eye-ring.

Ssp. *T. e. elatus* (S Ve, Guianas) as described, slightly browner upperparts, less extensive and paler yellow below; juvenile resembles adult above but white fringes to wing-coverts narrower; feathers of crest shorter, and crown-sides same olive as back, yellow more concealed; throat and breast slightly darker

T. e. panamensis (NW Ec, Co, N Ve) paler grey-green

back with pale yellowish wingbars, paler throat and brighter, pure yellow underparts and undertail-coverts; juvenile slightly browner on back and wingbars (a series of spots) white; feathers of crown shorter and browner than adult and yellow more concealed

Habits Difficult to see, forages alone at mid levels and in low canopy, making short flights amidst leaves. Feeds mostly on berries (*Capsicum*, *Phthirusa* and Lauracae), with some small insects. Does not join mixed flocks. Occasionally perches in open atop bushes or trees. Normal posture fairly horizontal with slightly cocked tail, but may droop tail at rest.

Status Uncommon in Ecuador. Common in Colombia, frequent in Guyana, common in Suriname, frequent in French Guiana.

Habitat Tropical Zone, mostly below 600m in Ecuador, to 1,000m in Colombia and to 1,200m in Venezuela. Semi-dry to humid areas. Edge of gallery forests, savanna woodland, gardens and parks, borders and clearings of denser forest, and *várzea*. Also canopy of tall *terra firme* in French Guiana

Voice Calls often and throughout day, a short *wee wheer*, resembling a wolf whistle (H&B).

Note Fitzpatrick does not recognise any races, finding all those described indistinguishable in large series, but we found constant differences between a large series of specimens of the 2 races from Venezuela.

Myiopagis elaenias are similar to *Elaenia*, but are usually slightly smaller, tend to be more green and yellowish, and have white or yellow coronal patches that are usually concealed within dark caps. They vary in posture and tend to forage within cover.

FOREST ELAENIA
Myiopagis gaimardii Pl. 188

Identification 12.5–13cm. Olive above, dark grey crown with white coronal stripe, forming a loose but short crest, wings brown with 2 yellowish-white wingbars and sharply defined yellow fringes to tertials and secondaries, tail only slightly browner than back; white throat, olive flammulations on breast, underparts yellow. Juvenile *guianensis* olive-brown above with crown only slightly darker and coronal stripe absent, or just appearing as small spot or streak, wingbars buffy-white but fringes to secondaries and tertials sharply defined in yellow. Juvenile *bogotensis* similar but has fringes to secondaries and tertials white. Best separated from similar elaenias by voice; from Yellow-crowned Elaenia by streaked breast (rather than suffused grey), from Greenish Elaenia by wingbars, some plumages of Grey Elaenia similar but latter always has 3 wingbars.

Ssp. *M. g. bogotensis* (NE Co, N Ve) larger than *guianensis*, brighter green above, white in crown often suffused yellow, pastel olive throat to breast, underparts sulphur-yellow

M. g. gaimardii (austral migrant to S Ec, CE Co) grey crown with semi-concealed white stripe, breast broadly flammulated olive, underparts bright yellow

M. g. guianensis (E Co, SE Ve, Guianas) like *gaimardi* but darker and duller above, coronal stripe yellowish-white; primrose-yellow below with breast flammulations richer

M. g. macilvainii (N Co) like *bogotensis* but crown-stripe bright yellow

M. g. trinitatis (Tr) like *guianensis* but distinctly larger, more extensive white throat and breast greyer

Habits Forages in canopy and often joins mixed flocks. Gleans and flits about in foliage. Takes berries and small fruits, beetles and small insects. Perches fairly horizontally. Constructs cup nest high in canopy.

Status Uncommon in Ecuador, frequent in Colombia and Guyana, common in Trinidad and French Guiana.

Habitat Tropical Zone, usually below 1,000m but occasional to 1,500m in Venezuela. Rarely in forest, despite name, frequents mangrove, borders of humid, gallery and deciduous forests, and forest stands in savannas, plantations, gardens, beside streams. Typically in canopy of tall *terra firme* in French Guiana.

Voice Calls frequently and emphatically, a very distinctive sharp *pitchweet* or *pill-dweet* (H&B), also *pill'drEET!*, the second part slightly buzzy and rising, typically given at long intervals (Hilty), and *pitcheeet*, typically isolated calls or at intervals of *c*.30 s (Fitzpatrick).

GREY ELAENIA *Myiopagis caniceps* Pl. 188

Identification 12–13cm. A unique, polymorphic elaenia, with 3 distinct colour variants in adult male. In all plumages, birds in fresh plumage have blackish wings with 3 white wingbars; fringes to lesser coverts may be somewhat worn and also might be somewhat obscured by scapulars. Adult male grey morph *cinerea* very distinct and unmistakable, pure grey above with very dark brown wings, well-defined wingbars and white fringes to tertials. Crown fuscous with very small, mainly concealed white patch in centre. Face slightly grizzled; below, soft grey from chin to breast, becoming white over rest of underparts. Green morph male and adult female very similar, but male has duller, greyer back and wingbars slightly whiter; coronal streak more obvious, white bar on lesser coverts weaker than others as white restricted to tips of feathers; pale yellow below. Yellow-morph male is like female but green back duller, wings medium (not dark) brown and wingbars less well defined; far less yellow below, more greyish on breast and tending to buffy below. Female olive above with fuscous to blackish wings and yellowish wingbars, paler on sides of greyish head and has less grey or olive on breast.

Ssp. *M. c. cinerea* (E Ec, E Co, NW&S Ve, Gu, FG) female has yellow crown streak

M. c. parambae (NW Ec, W Co) similar to *cinerea*, but much smaller; adult grey-morph male has more grey on breast, green-morph male has ash-grey crown with white (not yellow) coronal streak, whiter throat and paler yellow underparts; female has white crown patch

Habits Forages alone or in pairs, always in canopy, often in outermost twigs. Takes insects and berries, gleaning them amid foliage. Typically leans forward on perch (but is sometimes straight) and cocks tail sporadically.

Status Locally uncommon to rare in Ecuador, uncommon in Colombia (few records), scarce and local in Guyana, rare in French Guiana.

Habitat Tropical Zone, mostly below 600m in Ecuador and Colombia but in Venezuela to 1,200m north of Orinoco and to 300m south of it. Humid to dry and cloud forests, deciduous woodland, borders and clearings.

Voice A fast shrill chippering that descends and fades at end, introduced by several sharper notes, e.g. *swee swee swee wee-ee-ee-ee-ee-ee-ee-ee-ee*. In east Ecuador *parambae* also gives a *tsi-si-tseeuw, tsi-tseeuw* not uttered by *cinerea* (R&G). In Venezuela, song of *cinerea* is *e-e-p-p-p-pepepepe....pepepepupupupu* (*c*.40 notes in 3 s), slightly descending. When excited a snappy *ee-ee-ee-pit-chew, pee-chew* (K. J. Zimmer in Hilty).

Notes Fitzpatrick mentions that species is considered by some to not belong in *Myiopagis* (e.g. Hilty) due to sexual dimorphism.

FOOTHILL ELAENIA

Myiopagis olallai Pl. 188

Identification 12–13cm. Olive above with dusky wings and 3 yellowish-white wingbars, yellow fringes to tertials and secondaries; head grey with white semi-concealed coronal patch, lores, eye-ring and cheeks mottled whitish, throat white, rest of underparts yellow with some olivaceous flammulations on breast. Could be confused with female Grey Elaenia but range and habitat differ.

Ssp. Monotypic (N&S Ec).

Habits Forages and sings in canopy and at mid levels, in pairs, usually with mixed-species flocks. Frequently sallies to pick from both above and below leaves. Generally perches horizontally.

Status Local and threatened at lower elevations due to ongoing deforestation, but less threatened and little known in higher wetter forests, where deforestation has, thus far, had less impact.

Habitat Tropical Zone, 800–1,500m. Very humid to wet primary forest on lower slopes of eastern Andes.

Voice Song comprises series of introductory notes, followed by varied sequence ending in a harsh, ascending trill, distinctly rising in pitch and lasting 2 s. Calls and sings frequently while foraging, especially in morning (Coopmans & Krabbe 2000, Fitzpatrick).

PACIFIC ELAENIA

Myiopagis subplacens Pl. 189

Identification 13.5–14cm. Olive above with dusky wings and tail, 2 faint wingbars, but whitish fringes to tertials and secondaries form noticeable pale block on wings, crown and head-sides dark brown with large, bright yellow coronal patch, irregular, grizzled whitish superciliary that wraps around dark ear-coverts, with some grizzling on fore cheeks; chin to breast grey, grading pale yellow below. Greenish Elaenia similar but lacks pale wing-patch and is greyish on head, not brown, and usually found at much lower elevations.

Ssp. Monotypic (W Ec)

Habits Forages at lower to mid levels and at borders, mostly alone. Rarely with mixed flocks. Perches distinctly upright.

Status Uncommon to rare in Ecuador.

Habitat Tropical to Subtropical Zones, to 1,750m. Drier deciduous forest and second growth.

Voice Song a sharp *cheet! woorrr-it... cheet! woorrr-it*, oft-repeated (R&T), and dawn song is *chrrr, chrrr, chi-wik... chrrr, chrrr, chi-wik...* (P. Coopmans).

YELLOW-CROWNED ELAENIA

Myiopagis flavivertex Pl. 189

Identification 13cm. Olive above with dusky wings and 2 yellow wingbars, grey of throat, breast and flanks quite extensive, and division with yellow on belly abrupt. Juvenile quite distinct, being greener above, with mid-brown wings and buffy to cinnamon wingbars and fringes to tertials and secondaries. Yellow crown vestigial, and there is a pale supraloral spot. From Greenish Elaenia by wingbars.

Ssp. Monotypic (NE Ec, NE & S Ve, Guianas)

Habits Forages at mid and lower levels, alone or in pairs, seldom joining mixed flocks. Takes caterpillars, termites, beetles, wasps, bees. Perches vertically.

Status Rare in Ecuador, unrecorded in Colombia but possible in extreme east, frequent but local in Venezuela and Suriname, frequent in Guyana and uncommon in northern French Guiana.

Habitat Tropical Zone, below 300m in Ecuador and to 200m in Venezuela. Swampy forests in coastal and sandy soil areas, and *várzea*.

Voice Call variously described as an intermittent startled *WEECHECHe'e'e* (Hilty), a sharp, loud *jew, jee-jee-jew* (R&T) or a weak trilled *pyeew, pi.hi.hihihi* (H&M).

GREENISH ELAENIA

Myiopagis viridicata Pl. 188

Identification 13–15cm. A large elaenia, widespread, with much geographic variation but always lacks wingbars. Olive above with dusky wings (pale fringes to tertials and secondaries), head generally greyish, darkest on crown with semi-concealed yellow stripe, face grizzled but pale superciliary apparent; throat pale grey, breast greyish or olivaceous and rest of underparts yellow. Female similar but slightly smaller and has paler coronal patch. Despite clear differences between subspecies, there is much individual variation within any population. Juveniles vary by race. From similar Pacific

Elaenia by lack of wingbars, on Pacific they are weak and poorly defined; Pacific also has pale fringes to secondaries appearing more as a block lacking on Greenish. Pacific Elaenia also favours drier habitats and usually perches vertically.

Ssp. *M. v. accola* (NW Co) as described, has larger bill and is greener above than others

M. v. implacens (W Ec, SW Co) like *pallens* but much smaller with same-size bill, dull black rear crown, richer olive-green above, wing fringes bright yellow.

M. v. pallens (NE Co) very similar to *accola* but bill larger and slightly paler all over

M. v. restricta (Ve) olive above, browner wings with yellowish fringes, crown brown with bright yellow fringes to feathers, faint pale lores, clear eye-ring; bright, pale sulphur-yellow below with olive flammulated throat to breast; juvenile a softer, uniform powder brown above, with slightly yellowish-white fringes to wing-coverts and remiges but no wingbars, crown almost concolorous with back and has no yellow patch; eye-ring clear but no pale loral patch or superciliary; soft pastel brownish-grey chin to breast, and faintly yellowish-white below

M. v. zuliae (Ve: Perijá) paler above than *restricta*, no wingbars but indistinctly paler wing-coverts producing vestigial wingbar, lores white with clear superciliary and eye-ring; soft, pastel brownish-grey flammulations on breast; juvenile warmer, paler brown above with distinct, broad buffy wingbars and browner crown, but not as contrasting as adult, and no coronal patch

Habits Forages alone or in pairs, in shady areas at all levels from undergrowth to canopy. Takes insects and berries, gleaning from a perch the surrounding foliage. Joins mixed canopy flocks. Perching usually somewhat across branch.
Status Uncommon in Ecuador, locally frequent in Colombia and Venezuela, uncommon in Guyana.
Habitat Tropical to Subtropical Zones, mostly below 500m but to 1,000m in Ecuador and 1,300m in Colombia. In Venezuela reaches 1,000m north of Orinoco, but only 300m south of it. Moist to deciduous forests, partially open areas with patchy woodland or scrub, at borders and along streams, gallery forests, clearings.
Voice Weak, a buzzy, slurred *screechit*, and dawn call *peer-pee, peer-pee, peer-peer-pee*… (H&B). A slow downslurred *peeuur*, oftern embroidered with additional low-pitched *peeuur* notes, *tseepurr* and similar notes (W. Belton). A high-pitched strident song, slurred and burry *cheerip* or *cheeyree*, and *zrreeeeer* (R&G).
Note Zimmer (1941c) failed to find differences between *pallens* and *accola*, and Fitzpatrick found differences between *pallens*, *zuliae*, *restricta* and *accola* minimal, and suggested merging all under *accola*. Comparing fresh specimens, we found differences between *zuliae* and *restricta* significant. Under the circumstances we suggest retaining all races until fresh specimens of various plumages can be compared.

GREY-AND-WHITE TYRANNULET

Pseudelaenia leucospodia Pl. 188

Identification 12.5cm. Greyish-brown above with dusky wings and tail, pale fringes to wing-feathers but no wingbars, crown dark with irregular, usually exposed white patch; surrounding feathers longer and form a bushy crest divided into 2, a white supraloral spot and small white eye-ring that joins white lores. Below, white with slight tinge of greyish or olive on sides and flanks. Juvenile has smaller white crown patch. From all similar tyrannulets and elaenias by bold white on head and lack of wingbars, and breast notably lacks dark flush.

Ssp. *P. l. cinereifrons* (SW Ec)

Habits Forages alone or more usually in pairs, gleaning insects from foliage. Perches in forward-leaning position, and shakes slightly or cocks tail from time to time.
Status Rare in Ecuador.
Habitat Tropical Zone, to 100m. Arid scrub and sparse, dry woodland, especially in pebbly clearings such as desert washes and along dry creeks and riverbeds.
Voice A sharp *chevit* and *chevit-chet* (R&T).

Elaenia elaenias are a rather homogenous group of species that all more or less resemble each other. They are olive-brown above, greyish on the breast with pale yellow bellies. Heads are fairly small, but they have bushy crests, usually with white centres. When the crest is relaxed, especially at rest, white may be obscured. They have 2–3 wingbars, more prominent in fresh plumage, and may have thin or faint whitish eye-rings and loral areas, with short rounded bills. Active in relatively sparse cover, despite appearing quite drab they are usually quite noticeable. When not foraging they will perch still, usually upright, and are easily overlooked.

CARIBBEAN ELAENIA

Elaenia martinica Pl. 189

Identification 15cm. Rather drab-looking elaenia, brownish-grey above with a short, bushy crest. Greyish below, darker on breast and sides. Three wingbars, whitish fringes to tertials and secondaries, and a small white coronal patch that is fairly well concealed. Throat to lower belly soft grey, becoming pale yellow. Plumage may be very worn and bleached, with tail appearing as shafts. Race in our region is smallest of species, and very easily confused with Lesser Elaenia which is slightly smaller still, paler and greener above, and has a yellow belly.

Ssp. *E. m. riisii* (ABC)

Habits Rather retiring, usually within scrub; often in dense bushes of *Croton flavens*, copses of *Guaiacum officinale* and *Hippomane mancinella* and locally in rhizophore mangroves. In open country may be found in lone acacias and thorn scrub (Voous 1983). Forages quietly for insects, fruits and berries, and smaller percentage of insects. Perches horizontally, sometimes for long periods, surveying surroundings quietly.

Nest a small, not very neat cup, placed in a branch fork or rock wall cranny. Raises crest frequently, often when singing.

Status Locally frequent in Curaçao and Bonaire, but very rare in Aruba.

Habitat Tropical Zone. Semi-humid hill forests and drier areas of sparse woodland or scrub, mangroves, planted fields with scattered trees.

Voice A strong, cheerful whistled *wee-wee-weew*, and *pee-wee-reereeree* or *peeweetprr* (Voous), latter being the dawn song (Fitzpatrick).

YELLOW-BELLIED ELAENIA
Elaenia flavogaster Pl. 189

Identification 16.5cm. Fairly variable, olive-brown to greyish-brown above and yellow to pale or faint yellow below. Crest dark brown, full, long and bushy with white on inner fringes of longest feathers which show well, but core white patch well covered. Wingbars white, occasionally yellowish and either 2–3. Third bar, on lesser coverts, may be white and noticeable but duller than others (individual variation), or worn to whitish fringes, even non-existent. Throat grey, rarely pure white, breast soft grey grading yellow, rarely very pale olive-grey. Juvenile is distinctly paler overall, greenish-olive above, with wings and tail mid brown (much paler than near fuscous of adult). No crest and no hidden white coronal patch, and crown is concolorous with back.

Ssp. *E. f. flavogaster* (Co, Ve, Margarita I., T&T, Guianas) as described

E. f. semipagana (W Ec) quite distinct; decidedly greyish face, blackish crest without any white (or very small traces), much paler and greener back, purer white throat and paler yellow below; shorter bill

Field sketches showing Yellow-bellied Elaenia, in repose (left) and active (right); head appears smaller when crest fully depressed; bird with crest fully erect (lower right) had breeze from behind that pushed feathers further forward

Habits Very vivacious, forages in canopy and at mid levels, alone, in pairs or sometimes in small groups. Takes berries and insects by gleaning, sallying or flycatching (for flying termites, wasps etc.). Bathes in shallow water and then sunbathes to dry.

Status Locally common to rare in Ecuador, very common and widespread in Colombia and Venezuela, common in Tobago and abundant in Trinidad, frequent in Guyana and Suriname, common in French Guiana.

Habitat Tropical to Subtropical Zones, to 1,300m in Ecuador, locally higher in south, to 1,700m in Colombia and occasionally to 2,100m, and to 1,750m in Venezuela. Open, shrubby areas with scattered trees, borders of dry to humid forest, parks and large gardens, plantations.

Voice A loud hoarse *breeeer*, rapid sequences of *dreer-tree* (H&B), a screaming *gheeuw* (H&M). Pairs often call and answer excitedly.

LARGE ELAENIA *Elaenia spectabilis* Pl. 189

Identification 18cm. Dull brownish-olive above with modest crest that shows little white, 3 prominent whitish bars on dusky wings, throat pale grey, becoming grey on breast, pale yellow below. From similar but smaller Yellow-bellied Elaenia by smaller crest that often shows no white at all, and has only 2 wingbars.

Ssp. *E. s. spectabilis* (E Ec, extreme SE Co).

Habits Forages alone, in bushes and thickets around clearings and at borders, at low and mid levels. Feeds by gleaning from perch and also searching foliage.

Status Austral migrant, wintering in middle to north-west South America from approximately mid May to mid September. Rare in Ecuador, where regular June to late August, but always in small numbers in Colombia.

Habitat Tropical Zone, to 600m. Borders and clearings of lowland forest, gardens and urban parks, and beside watercourses.

Voice Rather quiet in winter, occasionally a sad, faint *weeoo* (H&B) or soft *cleeuw* (R&G).

WHITE-CRESTED ELAENIA
Elaenia albiceps Pl. 190

Identification 14.5–15cm. Quite difficult to identify. Dusky olive above with darker wings and 2–3 (depending on wear) whitish wingbars, small crest that is rarely displayed though white coronal line is often visible, vague, narrow eye-ring; throat white, becoming grey on breast and then white below. Sierran Elaenia very similar but definitely yellowish below. Southern race *E. a. chilensis*, is a poorly known austral migrant that is mostly overlooked in winter range and may occasionally reach south-west of our region; darker above, with 2 narrow but prominent yellowish-white wingbars and a pure white coronal line. Very difficult to separate from another austral migrant, Small-billed Elaenia, which has 3 wingbars, and is greyish on throat as well as breast. May also be confused with Plain-crested Elaenia, but shorter crest and white coronal line definitive.

Ssp. *E. a. griseigularis* (SW Co, W & NE Ec) larger, abdomen and belly dingy with no trace of yellow

E. a. chilensis (SW Co? E Ec?) smaller, flanks, belly, abdomen and undertail-coverts whitish, tinged yellow

Habits Hover-gleans for berries at fruiting trees, and several may forage together. May accompany mixed flocks. Often perches quietly for long periods.

Status Uncommon to locally frequent in Ecuador, locally frequent in southern Colombia.
Habitat Subtropical Zone to Páramo, 1,900–3,400m in Ecuador and generally at 2,100m to treeline in Colombia. Partially open areas and forest borders, low shrubbery, planted fields near woodland or with scattered trees.
Voice Often like Sierran Elaenia. An abrupt *peyr*, *wheeo* and burry *brreeo* (R&G). For most part, austral vistors do not vocalise.

SMALL-BILLED ELAENIA
Elaenia parvirostris Pl. 190

Identification 14.5–14.7cm. Olive-brown above, darker wings with 3 wingbars, small crest with mostly concealed coronal line, large white eye-ring, grey throat to lower breast and flanks, and lacks yellow on underparts. Easily confused with *chilensis* race of White-crested Elaenia, but large white eye-ring a clincher. May be confused with Plain-crested Elaenia, but shorter crest and white coronal line definitive.

Ssp. Monotypic (all countries E of Andes).

Habits Forages alone and quietly in low vegetation and shrubs. Perches inconspicuously.
Status Austral migrant, wintering north to our region from approximately mid May to mid September. Uncommon in Ecuador, uncommon to fairly common in Colombia and Venezuela, rare in Trinidad, uncommon in Guyana, scarce (rare) in Suriname and probably rare in French Guiana.

On left bird in fresh plumage, that on right has worn plumage; note reduced wingbars and even white eye-ring is diminished

Habitat Tropical Zone, migrates through Andean foothills to 400m in Ecuador, 1,800m in Colombia and 1,250m in Venezuela. Open areas, forest borders and shrubby clearings, low scrub, gardens. In coastal areas and foothills and beside streams. May occur in numbers on Amazonian river islands.
Voice Rarely vocalises in winter, but sporadically calls *cheee-oh* (H&B) or *cheeu* (R&T).

SLATY ELAENIA *Elaenia strepera* Pl. 190

Identification 16cm. The only *Elaenia* in which both female and juvenile differ from male. Male is effectively slaty grey throughout, darker on wings with 3 faint wingbars (that on lesser coverts barely noticeable at rest), white coronal line (also rarely noticed) and white belly that does not show at rest. Small crest and small-headed character especially noticeable in this species, lending it a large-eyed appearance. Female olive-dusky above, fuscous wings with more noticeable, cinnamon wingbars; below, creamy yellowish with greyish-olive suffusion on throat and breast. Juvenile male much like male but has pale cinnamon wingbars (distinctly lighter than female) and pale light yellowish tone to belly. Species unique among elaenias, but might be confused with a *Contopus* pewee, though all these have large heads and proportionately larger and longer bills. Black of large race *ardesiacus* of Greater Pewee contrasts with fuscous back, other races almost same size as Slaty Elaenia but dark cap still noticeable, as are proportionately larger head and bill, and all races lack white belly. Western Wood Pewee, Eastern Wood Pewee and Tropical Pewee are all browner grey and have a pale throat.

Ssp. Monotypic (austral migrant to Ve)

Male Slaty Elaenia appears uniformly dark grey, small-headed and large-eyed; it perches for long periods on an exposed branch within an open bush or low tree, still and silent

Habits Usually forages alone in mid levels, treetops and canopy. Takes insects and berries by sallying from open treetop perches and hover-gleaning. May perch quietly on bare branch within but near edge of open tree or bush.
Status Austral migrant, winters to Venezuela where local March to early October. Records of birds on passage few and only from Colombia, but must pass through eastern lowlands of Ecuador as well.
Habitat Subtropical to Temperate Zones, to 900m in Venezuela. Partially open areas near forests, in overgrown clearings, fields with shrubs or bushes, pastures.
Voice Wintering birds are mostly silent, but may vocalise in response to playback of song.

MOTTLE-BACKED ELAENIA
Elaenia gigas Pl. 190

Identification 19cm. Large, dusky olive above with darker centres to feathers of back, affording a somewhat mottled effect, with darker wings and 2 white wingbars, white outer fringes to tips of secondaries; crest well divided and frequently raised, showing white in centre which gives bird a somewhat horned aspect. Below, white on throat, flammulated olive on sides of throat and breast, and flanks, yellow over rest. Similar to Yellow-bellied Elaenia, but definitely larger and mottled back and flammulations below separate it, whilst forked crest is diagnostic.

Ssp. Monotypic (E Ec, S Co)

Habits Forages alone or in pairs, from mid levels to canopy.

Often perches atop isolated bush in middle of a field or clearing.
Status Uncommon to rare in Ecuador, and rare (very few records) in Colombia.
Habitat Tropical Zone, 250–1,250m in Ecuador, but recorded to 1,800m. Humid foothill forest borders and overgrown clearings, patches of shrubs in fields and pastures; overgrown shores of river islands.
Voice A loud *wurdít* (H&B), *direet*, a shrill *pert-chéér* (Fitzpatrick) and *wor-eet!* (R&G).

BROWNISH ELAENIA
Elaenia pelzelni Pl. 190

Identification 18–19cm. Large, dull brown above with 3 dull wingbars, that on lesser coverts particularly so, no crest and white coronal line usually obscured (absent in female); whitish below, washed brown on breast, sides and flanks. Could be confused with Large Elaenia but latter has brighter, whiter wingbars, noticeable crest and underparts pale grey and yellow.

Ssp. Monotypic (SE Co)

Habits Forages at all levels, often in fringe shrubbery. Shy. Possibly moves seasonally in areas bordering rivers, in connection with flood patterns; often seen in *Cecropia* on river islands.
Status Included here based on sight record of 4 birds near Letitia, Colombia (S. L. Hilty in H&B). Effectively hypothetical for northern South America.
Habitat Tropical Zone to 200m. Essentially an Amazon river island specialist, found in scrub and early second growth with dense underbrush at river borders and in shrubs or stands of succesional trees on river islands.
Voice Varied burry and clear notes, e.g. low *chick-ert* or *chick-ert-ert*, the first note slightly higher, a clearer *chick-urp* or *per-cheet*, the second note higher, a repeated liquid *whit* and a high metallic *chick-eep* (Fitzpatrick).

PLAIN-CRESTED ELAENIA
Elaenia cristata Pl. 190

Identification 14.5cm. Smallish elaenia with comparatively large bill. Long crest with no white, usually held partially raised and noticeable on rear of head. Dull olive-brown above with darker wings, 2–3 white wingbars and whitish distal fringes to remiges. Equal numbers of birds have 2 or 3 wingbars, but white fringes to lesser coverts always narrow and they wear easily or may be concealed by scapulars. Greyish-white throat, olive-grey breast and pale yellow below. Juveniles all have 3 somewhat buffy wingbars, and are slightly paler, less brown on back and slightly browner on breast, and overall less olive. May be confused with both Small-billed and White-crested Elaenias, but long, backswept crest lacking any white definitive.

Ssp. *E. c. cristata* (SE Co, C & E Ve, Guianas) pale greyish back

E. c. alticola (SE Ve: Tepuis) browner and darker above, abdomen pale yellow

Habits Forages conspicuously in low vegetation for berries. Apparently nomadic, following food resources. Beautifully woven nest of fine mosses and lichens, lined with plant wool.
Status Rare in Colombia (only a couple of records: Rojas *et al.* 1997), locally frequent in Venezuela, Guyana, Suriname and French Guiana.
Habitat Tropical Zone, to 400m north of Orinoco and to 1,350m in tepuis. Sandy soil scrub in savannas with scattered bushes and thickets, often near streams. Very characteristic of this habitat.
Voice Shrieking and diagnostic, described as *jer-jehjeh* (R&T).

RUFOUS-CROWNED ELAENIA
Elaenia ruficeps Pl. 190

Identification 14.5cm. Dark brownish-olive above (darker than most elaenias), with dusky wings and 2 white wingbars, bushy crest lacks white centre but has bright rufous patch on rear, which varies in size and may be completely obscured at rest; white eye-ring. Pale yellow below, heavily flammulated greyish-olive on breast. Combination of rufous nape patch, white eye-ring and streaked breast quite distinctive. Juvenile has little or no rufous on head and rufous wingbars, with barely noticeable rufous tips to tail (whitish in adult).

Ssp. Monotypic (SE Co, SE Ve, Guianas)

Habits Forages conspicuously in bushes and thickets, in pairs or sometimes in small groups. Takes berries and small fruits, also bees, beetles and small insects. Joins mixed flocks.
Status Distribution apparently very fragmented; uncommon to locally common in Colombia and Venezuela, uncommon in Guyana, locally common in Suriname, scarce and very local due to habitat loss in French Guiana.
Habitat Tropical Zone, to 500m in Colombia but to 1,400m in Venezuela. Mostly in sandy soil areas with dense scrub: savannas with scattered bushes and thickets, stands of spiny palms, borders of light woodland.
Voice A low, growling *d-rr-rr-rr* (R&T) and weak *pyerrr… pyerrr…pyerrr-tsee* (H&M).

LESSER ELAENIA
Elaenia chiriquensis Pl. 190

Identification 14cm. Smaller, typical elaenia with no distinguishing characters. Greyish-brown above, wings slightly darker, with *c.*75% having 2 white wingbars, the rest 3, rarely wingbars wear off almost completely. Crest very modest and usually laid back, thus rear crown appears squared-off. Juvenile slightly paler brown above, with faint transverse barring and 3 wingbars, below less yellow, with slightly creamy tint. Juvenile female has thighs barred brownish. From Yellow-bellied Elaenia by smaller size and smaller, undivided crest; from Small-billed by yellowish belly and narrower eye-ring; similar Sierran Elaenia has yellowish wingbars and is more yellow below.

Ssp. *E. c. albivertex* (Co, Ve, Guianas) more greyish-olive above, pale yellow below
E. c. brachyptera (SW Co, NW Ec) more brownish-olive above, throat and breast tinged greyish-olive, yellow below

Habits Forages on tops and at mid levels of tall bushes and thickets, taking berries and small fruits, but is not very noisy or conspicuous.
Status Rare in Ecuador, uncommon to fairly common in Colombia and Venezuela, frequent in Guyana, locally frequent in Trinidad, scarce and local in Suriname, rare and very local in French Guiana. Central American and austral populations move seasonally, but migrations poorly understood, and may reach Colombia occasionally, albeit at different times of year.
Habitat Tropical Zone to Páramo, 700–2,800m in Ecuador, to 2,200m in Colombia. Sandy soil savannas with light woodland, open grassland with scattered bushes and thickets.
Voice A purring plaintive *chibu* or *jwebu*, soft sequences of *weeb* or long, burry *freeeeee* notes (H&B). Commonest call in Venezuela a clear, whistled *weEEa* (K. J. Zimmer in Hilty). A burry *beer-ta* or *chí-bur* (Fitzpatrick).

MOUNTAIN ELAENIA
Elaenia frantzii Pl. 190

Identification 14cm. Yellowish olive-brown above, with dusky wings and 2 whitish wingbars; white fringes to tertials, distal half of secondaries and all primaries quite noticeable and may appear as patch of white. Effectively no crest or coronal line and head appears small and rounded; underparts yellowish, heavily olivaceous on sides of face to breast. From White-crested, Sierran and Lesser Elaenias by rounded head and lack of both crest and white on head.

Ssp. *E. f. browni* (NE Co, NW Ve) smaller, paler above (more greenish-olive), somewhat browner on breast
E. f. pudica (Co, N Ve) virtually impossible to separate in field

Habits Forages fairly quietly, alone, in pairs and sometimes in groups at fruiting bushes and trees. Quite frugivorous, feeds mostly by perch-gleaning and hover-gleaning for berries and fruits, but taking some insects and sometimes sallies to catch them. Perches with somewhat forward-leaning posture. Appears to move seasonally at regional levels, possibly following fruit availability.
Status Locally common to frequent in Colombia and Venezuela.
Habitat Subtropical Zone to Páramo, 1,500–2,500m in Colombia (with records to 3,000m, and 900–3,600m on Santa Marta and 1,700–2,250m in Perijá). Partially open areas on higher slopes, clearings, cultivation and pastures, scattered bushes or copses.
Voice A sad, drawn-out *peeeeerr* and short, sharper *peeee-oo* whistle (H&B). Dawn song a breezy, constantly repeated *WEeu-tic* (Hilty).

HIGHLAND ELAENIA
Elaenia obscura Pl. 190

Identification 18cm. Large, dark elaenia with small, plain rounded head, no crest or coronal line, and short stubby bill. Dark olive above with darker wings, 2 yellowish wingbars and yellow eye-ring; yellow below, well washed dull olive on throat and breast. Large Elaenia has noticeable crest, as does smaller Sierran Elaenia.

Ssp. *E. o. obscura* (extreme S Ec).

Habits Forages alone or in pairs, mostly in vegetation or undergrowth. Takes insects, berries and small fruits. Shy and furtive, tends to remain in cover but calls frequently.
Status Rare in Ecuador.
Habitat Upper Tropical to Temperate Zones, 2,150–3,000m. Humid montane forests, at borders and clearings, as well as in the interior.
Voice A rolled *burrrrr* (R&T) or *burreep* (R&G).

GREAT ELAENIA *Elaenia dayi* Pl. 190

Identification 20cm. Noticeably large elaenia, unmistakable despite its dark dull appearance. Dark brownish-grey above with slightly darker crown (no white), 2 buffy-white wingbars in fresh plumage tend to wear and all but disappear as season advances. Juvenile like adult above, but lacks eye-ring, is browner on breast-sides, greyish on flanks, vent and undertail-coverts (pale in adult); thighs barred dark brown and buffy. Three races form perfect cline, with *auyantepui* darkest and *dayi* palest. Juvenile could be mistaken for Black-billed Thrush!

Ssp. *E. d. auyantepui* (S Ve: Auyán-tepui) fuscous above including crown, greyer on breast
E. d. dayi (SE Ve: eastern tepuis) slightly paler above and below, crown brown, and brownest above, more yellowish below, a faded greyish-sulphur
E. d. tyleri (S Ve: Amazonas tepuis) crown fuscous, in other respects intermediate

Habits Poorly known. Confiding, forages alone or in pairs, at mid levels to canopy, sometimes in forest border thickets. Takes berries and insects.
Status Endemic to Pantepui of Venezuela. Rare on Gran Sabana, locally frequent to common on tepuis.
Habitat Upper Tropical to Temperate Zones, at 1,800–2,600m with occasional records to 300m; above 1,650m on Auyán-tepui, above 2,000m on Huachamacari, Cuquenán and Roraima. Humid forests on tepui slopes and scrub and stunted woodland on their tops, and in impenetrable stands of *Bonnetia*.
Voice Mostly quiet, song a loud *SQUEE'ch'ch'ch'cheet'cheet*, first note high, middle notes rattling (D. Ascanio recording).
Notes Race *tyleri* of Cerro Duida described as separate species by Chapman (1929).

SIERRAN ELAENIA
Elaenia pallatangae Pl. 190

Identification 14.5–14.7cm. Small, olive above with dusky wings and 2 white wingbars, tertials edged broadly white and distal half of secondaries also fringed white, slight crest with central coronal line usually visible towards rear, pale yellowish eye-ring and lores, pale yellow below, slightly flammulated olive on breast and sides. Juvenile distinctly more reddish-brown, with very slight well-concealed coronal stripe; greyish-brown breast, belly very pale with no greenish suffusion on sides and flanks.

Ssp. *E. p. davidwillardi* (S Ve, Cerro Neblina) darker greyish-olive above than *olivina* and brighter yellow below
E. p. olivina (S Ve: tepuis, Gu) longer bill, browner above and more olivaceous below
E. p. pallatangae (Ec, S Co) as described

Habits Forages quietly alone or in pairs, but occasionally joins mixed-species flocks when it seems to prefer forest edge and upper canopy, not the interior. Also joins flocks of Olive-backed Tanagers at fruiting trees. Takes insects and perch-gleans berries and small fruits; often perches in light cover for long periods.

Status Uncommon in Ecuador, scarce but widespread in Colombia, locally frequent to uncommon in Venezuela, frequent in Guyana.

Habitat Subtropical Zone to Páramo. Andean race occurs at 1,500–2,100m in Ecuador and 1,600–2,500m in Colombia; at borders and clearings of montane forests, fields and pastures with scattered bushes and stands of trees. Pantepui races occur at 950–2,400m, and *olivina* is found to 1,300m on the Sierra de Lema; at borders of humid forest on tepui slopes and in low vegetation on their tops, preferring areas of stunted and scrubby forest around rocky openings and borders of melastome-dominated regrowth (Hilty).

Voice Call of *pallatangue* a sharp, lucid *wheeu* whistle (R&T), also an abrupt, burry *breeyup* or *wree-yr* (Fitzpatrick). Pantepui *olivina* calls a simple *pfeEEu*, like Mountain Elaenia (Hilty), or a short, explosive *peeut!* or *tseeerp!* Song reportedly typical of large elaenias but less musical, a loud outburst, *chierp chierp chrrrrrrrrt-chup-chup pt tchweeeeerrp* (D. Ascanio rcording).

Note Two well-separated populations, the first, on the Venezuelan tepuis, may prove to be more diverse than hitherto recognised, and the other in the Andes, from central Colombia south. Race *olivina* of Mt. Roraima formerly considered a separate species, but removed to *E. pallatangae* by Zimmer (1941c), though a recent field study suggests Venezuelan birds are indeed better regarded specifically (Ascanio in prep.).

Mecocerculus tyrannulets are birds of montane forests in the Andes. They invariably have well-marked wingbars and a pale loral stripe that forms a superciliary, broken and dark in juveniles. With the notable exception of White-throated Tyrannulet, this genus perches rather horizontally. White-throated Tyrannulet possibly comprises more than one species (F&K, Fitzpatrick), and the genus *Mecocerculus* possibly includes species best separated into other genera (Lanyon 1988).

WHITE-THROATED TYRANNULET

Mecocerculus leucophrys Pl. 189

Identification 14–15cm. Somewhat variable, essentially brown above, with dusky wings, 2 wingbars and pale fringes to tertials and remiges, whitish loral mark over eye and, in some cases, shortly behind, white crescent below eye; throat whitish, rather full and puffy, extending below and onto fore cheeks, heavily streaked brown on darker races, breast and sides brownish-grey and underparts yellow. Much variation within any given population due to combination of age and condition of plumage. Loss of wingbars with wear is typical of dark races, *parui* (see plate), *roraimae* and *chapmani*. Ochre outer fringes to secondaries also abrade, thus birds in worn plumage quite different from fresh birds, but this does not seem to occur to same extent in paler races. Juvenile has wingbars darker than adult, but differs in small details racially. Fluffy white throat (rather like Bearded Flycatcher) and comparatively long tail are good diagnostics. Differs from other *Mecocerculus* by upright posture and white throat.

Ssp. *M. l. chapmani* (S Ve: Amazonas, Duida and Marahuaca) darkest of 3 dark races, with breast darker and more olive (less grey), belly richer yellow
M. l. gularis (NW Ve: Andes & Perijá) back brownish-olive, wingbars white, pileum slightly darker, softly grading into mantle, cheeks mostly white; white of throat grades into pale olive-grey breast, belly pale sulphur-yellow; juvenile has head concolorous with back, wingbars ochraceous-buff
M. l. montensis (Co: Santa Marta) similar to *nigriceps* but longer tail and bill, back olive, pileum much darker, wingbars and fringes of tertials dull tawny-ochraceous, breast dark greyish-olive, belly primrose
M. l. nigriceps (NE Ve: Eastern Cordillera) smallest race, back brownish-olive, wingbars whitest, pileum slightly darker and softly grades into mantle; cheeks mostly white, breast rather paler than *gularis* and *palliditergum*, yellow underparts pale sulphur; juvenile has cap slightly darker, grading into mantle, wingbars clay
M. l. notatus (Co: W & C Andes) similar to *setophagoides* but more richly coloured above, darker and more sooty olive, wingbars and fringes of tertials and secondaries ochraceous-buff
M. l. palliditergum (CN Ve: Coastal Cordillera) from *nigriceps* by paler back, more yellowish, less olivaceous; crown paler, more nearly uniform with back; from *gularis* by shorter tail and wings, and slightly richer yellow belly; pileum seems slightly chocolate-coloured; juvenile has pileum concolorous with mantle, wingbars clay
M. l. parui (S Ve: N Amazonas, Cerro Paru) back fuscous-olive, slightly darker and more brownish-, less greyish-olive above than *roraimae*, wingbars white, suffused clay; pileum darker and well defined; juvenile has pileum slightly paler than adult but still contrasts well with mantle, wingbars tawny

M. l. roraimae (SE Ve) back deep sepia, cap darker and clearly separated from mantle, wingbars white, cheeks well striated dark brown; juvenile has pileum clearly divided from mantle, wingbars, fringes of tertials and secondaries tawny

M. l. rufomarginatus (SW Co, Ec) back deep umber-brown with wingbars ochraceous-rufous, breast richly coloured brownish

M. l. setophagoides (Co: E Andes) largest but apart from size virtually identical to *nigriceps*, slightly darker above, a little less olivaceous

Habits Forages alone, in pairs or more frequently in small groups often with mixed canopy flocks; never at lower levels. Restless, noisy and conspicuous. Takes insects in short sallies from perch and by gleaning from twigs and leaves. Perches very upright, tail held straight down. Very vocal and draws attention by its vocalisations.

Status Uncommon in Ecuador, common and widespread in Colombia, common to frequent in western Venezuela, locally frequent to uncommon in tepuis.

Habitat Subtropical Zone to Páramo, mostly 2,800–3400m in Ecuador, locally to 3,600m, 1,900–3,800m in Andes of Colombia though usually at 2,600–3,400m. Borders of humid montane forest, elfin woodland and stands of *Polylepis* above treeline, fields and pastures with hedges, scattered bushes or copses.

Voice A frequent *pip-pip-pip or pit-pit-pit* in contact and a rarely heard, soft complex warble (H&B), also dawn call described as *whichiry, whichiry, whichiry-chew* (R&T) and an excited *ch'd'dik, ch'd'dik, ch'd'dik,chew*, with first note sometimes accented (R&G).

Note We have retained all 10 subspecies described for our region. Fitzpatrick suggested merging *montensis* and *pallidLitergum* into *nigriceps*, and *gularis* with *setophagoides*. We have studied over 500 specimens of 5 races and found no significant difference between *gularis*, *palliditergum* and *nigriceps* which implies going significantly further than Fitzpatrick. However, unpublished notes by W. H. Phelps make it clear that racial differences are only reliably distinguished in fresh specimens. The racial characters given above thus include points taken from type descriptions and notes by Phelps. There is such variation within any given population that, as noted by Dickerman (1984), comparisons are only valid if made between birds of same age, sex and condition.

WHITE-TAILED TYRANNULET

Mecocerculus poecilocercus Pl. 191

Identification 10.4–11cm. Smallish flycatcher that is rather warbler-like. Back olive-green with contrasting bright greenish-yellow rump and uppertail-coverts, wings dusky with 2 white wingbars and white fringes to tertials and primaries and yellow distal fringes to secondaries, tail grey with 2 outer rectrices white on inner webs (appear all white from below); throat and underparts white, flammulated somewhat grey on breast, and often tinged yellow on rear flanks and undertail-coverts. White on tail not obvious when seen from side or above, but frequently droops wings and fans tail, exposing pale rump and uppertail-coverts, as well as white in tail. More likely to be mistaken for a warbler (e.g. Blackburnian) than a tyrannulet. White-banded Tyrannulet usually at higher elevations, has far more boldly marked wingbars and lacks pale rump.

White-tailed Tyrannulet showing pale rump

Ssp. Monotypic

Habits Forages alone or in pairs, most frequently within mixed canopy flocks, from mid levels and subcanopy to canopy. Takes insects by sallying to nearby leaves and by gleaning from perch. Tends to be in periphery of canopy. Perches quite horizontally, leaning forward.

Status Locally common to uncommon in Ecuador, uncommon in Colombia.

Habitat Subtropical to Temperate Zones, 1,500–2,500m in Ecuador and mostly 2,000–2,400m in Colombia but occasionally to 2,700m. Humid montane forests, both in interior and at borders.

Voice A *wheezy wee, weez-weez-weez*, often used when foraging (H&B), and a frequent, fading series of 4 notes, *pee, pee-pee-pee* (R&T).

RUFOUS-WINGED TYRANNULET

Mecocerculus calopterus Pl. 191

Identification 11cm. Small warbler-like tyrannulet. Back greenish-olive with dusky wings, 2 white wingbars that may be washed slightly rufous, bright rufous fringes to tertials and secondaries present solid rufous patch in closed wing, primaries fringed whitish, 2 outer tail-feathers white, long white superciliary, grey crown and black eyestripe joining black ear-coverts; throat and breast greyish-white grading into yellow undertail-coverts.

Ssp. Monotypic (W Ec, Andean slopes)

Habits Forages alone or in pairs, from mid levels to canopy, mostly with mixed canopy flocks. Sometimes in hedges and bushes away from forest edge. Quite lively, flits about in foliage, gleaning insects.

Status Uncommon to rare and local in Ecuador.

Habitat: Upper Tropical to Subtropical Zones, 700–2,000m. Borders and clearings of humid to drier deciduous forest and partially open areas, fields and pastures with scattered bushes or trees, plantations.

Voice A gruff *pur-chee*, *chi-chichu* and descending series of rapidly uttered notes, *kuw-ki-ke-ke-ku-ku* (R&G).

SULPHUR-BELLIED TYRANNULET

Mecocerculus minor Pl. 191

Identification 11–12cm. Dark olive above with dusky wings, 2 broad buffy wingbars and fringes to tertials and rectrices (except base of secondaries) also buffy. Dark grey crown, grizzled face; chin white, rest of underparts yellow, suffused olive on breast. Juvenile has paler cap, at nape merging into mantle. Only member of genus with yellow underparts. Resembles Variegated Bristle Tyrant but differs in posture, as latter perches upright.

Ssp. Monotypic (E Ec Andean slopes)

Habits Forages at low to mid levels, alone, in pairs or sometimes groups of 3 (perhaps families). Most often loosely associated with mixed canopy flocks, following them but remaining at mid levels. Forward-leaning, quite horizontal posture, typical of genus.
Status Uncommon to rare in Ecuador, locally frequent in Colombia, quite scarce in Venezuela.
Habitat Subtropical to Temperate Zones, 1,600–2,800m. Humid montane and cloud forests, and mature second growth, always at borders or brushy clearings.
Voice A sharp, rapid *chew-chew-chew-chew-chew* (R&T).

WHITE-BANDED TYRANNULET

Mecocerculus stictopterus Pl. 191

Identification 11.7–13cm. Dark brown back with dusky wings and 2 white wingbars, fringes of tertials also white, distal fringes of secondaries yellowish, but fringes to primaries whitish, tail olive; pileum grey, long white superciliary; throat whitish, greyish-olive breast and sides, belly white, undertail-coverts yellowish. Juvenile has wingbars buffy-white washed slightly cinnamon, and pileum brown, only slightly darker than back. From distinctly smaller White-tailed by longer tail, bolder white eyebrow and uniform rump and tail (no white in tail of Ecuadorian or Colombian birds), and white in tail of White-banded is buffier.

Ssp. *M. s. albocaudatus* (Ve: Andes) outermost 2 tail-feathers whitish-buffy
M. s. stictopterus (Ec, Co) as described

Habits Forages alone, in pairs or most frequently with mixed flocks, from mid levels to canopy. Noisy, calls often and flits about searching for insects on thinner twigs in outer branches. Perches horizontally with a forward-leaning posture and feeds by gleaning from foliage.
Status Uncommon in Ecuador, frequent in Colombia.
Habitat Temperate Zone to Páramo, 1,800–3,600m in Colombia but mostly 2,500–3,300m. Humid and mossy montane cloud and elfin forests, secondary woodland and adjacent partially open areas. Groves of alders. Borders, clearings, fields with copses, hedges or scattered bushes.
Voice Descriptions vary: R&T note a slurred, repeated *squeeyh?*, sometimes *squeeee-e-e-eyh? squeh-deh-deh-deh-deh* – a descending series beginning with a high note; H&B a high *zeet tu* and longer series *zeeeeet, zeeeeet, zeeeeet…* (*albocaudatus*), or a loud descending *skeee! dr'e'e'e'e'e'e* when foraging (*stictopterus*).

TORRENT TYRANNULET

Serpophaga cinerea Pl. 191

Identification 11.2cm. Unmistakable: only along Andean watercourses. Above grey with fuscous wings that have white bars and white fringes to tertials, pileum blackish with white in centre, largely covered, and grey of mantle continues below. Wingbars of juvenile slightly less well formed and softer white, slightly washed brown; pileum greyish-brown with no trace of white.

Ssp. *S. c. cinerea* (Ec, Co, NW Ve)

Habits Forages alone or in pairs, moving restlessly amidst mossy rocks and boulders beside streams, sallying for airborne insects or those on vegetation. Pairs maintain territory along a stream and perched on rocks or overhanging vines or branches, flicking their tail up and down frequently.
Status Uncommon to rare in Ecuador. Locally frequent to common in Colombia and Venezuela.
Habitat Upper Tropical to Temperate Zones, 700–3,100m in Ecuador, 100–3,200m in Colombia and 1,500–3,000m in Venezuela. Mountain brooks and rocky, fast-flowing streams on slopes of Andes, from treeline to foothills.
Voice A piercing *chip* audible over rushing of water, often in fast repetition and pairs often call in duet.

RIVER TYRANNULET

Serpophaga hypoleuca Pl. 191

Identification 10.7cm. Only along lowland watercourses. Dark grey above, fringes of wing-coverts and tertials brownish, crest usually laid back with some white visible on rear crown, partially white lores, chin and fore-face white, breast grey, rest of underparts white. Flicks tail up and down frequently, and alights with body horizontal.

Ssp. *S. h. hypoleuca* (E Ec, SE Co) as described
S. h. venezuelana (C & E Ve, CE Co) smaller, soft powder brown above, tinged cinnamon on rump

Habits Presence erratic; as moves between sites responding to food availability. Forages mostly in pairs, searching shrubs, saplings and weeds. Feeds by gleaning insects from foliage or by sallying to pick them in air.
Status Scarce and local in Ecuador, rare in Colombia (sight records only of *hypoleuca*, whilst *venezuelana* first recorded in Arauca, in 1993: Rojas *et al.* 1997), and uncommon to locally frequent in Venezuela.
Habitat Tropical Zone, to 400m. Borders and islands of Orinoco and some of its larger northern affluents (Apure and Meta), and also of Amazon and some of its larger affluents (Napo, Ucayali, Tocantins), in early successional vegetation on river islands and adjacent savannas.
Voice Thin weak *see-blik!* or *pit-chik* and *tsit* while foraging. Song a chattery duet in defence of territory, *p'dit-p'dit-p'dit* or a rapid bubbly *pik-up pik-up pik-up…*, also a sputtering,

rattling *chip-skép! prfffffffft'ft'ft'-chip! chip!* with second note highest (R&G).

SLENDER-BILLED INEZIA

Inezia tenuirostris Pl. 191

Identification 9.4cm. Tiny, nondescript little flycatcher. Greyish-olive above with dusky tail, 2 narrow whitish wingbars, thin whitish eye-ring and narrow supercilium, face and throat whitish, rest of underparts yellow; bill short and thin.

Ssp. Monotypic (NE Co, NW Ve)

Habits Forages alone or in pairs, from undergrowth to subcanopy, gleaning from foliage of bushes and trees. Apparently avoids thickets. Cocks tail when foraging. Quite confiding.

Status Locally frequent in Colombia and Venezuela.

Habitat Tropical Zone, to 300m in Colombia and 800m in Venezuela. Arid or dry areas: essentially a bird of thorny desert scrub, but may be found in dry low woods and scrubby pastures nearby.

Voice Song a long, dry trill that fades at end, and an arcing series of whistles *teer-TEER-teer-teer-teer* (Fitzpatrick), or a flat insipid *trilltleeeeeeee'e'e'e'e'e'e'e* lasting *c.*2 s (Hilty).

Notes Formerly placed in genus *Phaeomyias*, but changed to *Inezia* by Zimmer (1941b). Zimmer & Whittaker 2000 recommended use of Inezia as English name, which we follow here.

PALE-TIPPED INEZIA

Inezia caudata Pl. 191

Identification 12cm. Olive-brown above, dusky wings with 2 narrow wingbars and whitish outermost fringes to tail; in worn plumage, wingbars all but disappear. White eye-ring, lores, face and chin whitish, yellowish with buffy tinge on throat and breast, rest of underparts yellow. White outer fringes to tail are good field mark.

Ssp. *I. c. caudata* (C Ve, Guianas, CE Co?) darker back, darker wings with white-fringed tertials; below, paler, more sulphur-yellow; eyes brown

I. c. intermedia (NE Co, NW & NC Ve) slightly paler back, paler brown wings with less white on tertial fringes; whiter throat; eye colour varies from dark to white; breeding birds, especially males, generally have white, yellowish or grey eyes, young have brown eyes

Habits Forages alone or in pairs, from subcanopy to undergrowth but mostly below 2m and often on ground. Cocks tail when foraging. Takes ants, termites, spiders by perch-gleaning. Joins mixed-species flocks of woodpeckers, spinetails, flycatchers and greenlets. Constructs cup nest high in tree fork or on vine.

Status Frequent in Venezuela and Guyana, common in Suriname, locally frequent in French Guiana.

Habitat Tropical Zone to 400m. *Avicennia* mangrove, borders, humid to wet areas, coffee plantations. Light deciduous woodland or scrub.

Voice Very vocal: a descending *teep tee'r'r* and clear *peep, pe-de-de-de…* with often a fast 12+ *de* notes (H&B) or *TEEP! Tedede* (Hilty). Also a short series commencing with 2 louder, slightly separate notes *cheep chee-deleet* (Zimmer & Whittaker 2000).

Notes Formerly considered a subspecies of *I. subflava* and composite species was called Pale-tipped Tyrannulet, but separated by Zimmer & Whittaker (2000) based on vocal differences. Zimmer & Whittaker also recommended use of Inezia as English name, which we follow here.

AMAZONIAN INEZIA

Inezia subflava Pl. 191

Identification 12cm. Brown above with dusky wings and 2 thin wingbars, longish dusky olive tail has pale ochraceous outer fringes and tips; face and chin whitish with rest of underparts yellow and vague olive flammulations on breast and sides. Eyes usually brown but some older birds, especially males have pale grey or whitish irides.

Ssp. *I. s. obscura* (S Ve, extreme E Co).

Habits Forages alone or in pairs, from subcanopy to undergrowth. Cocks tail when foraging. Takes ants, termites and spiders by perch-gleaning. Apparently does not join mixed flocks.

Status Locally common in Colombia and Venezuela.

Habitat Tropical Zone, to 400m in Colombia and 200m in Venezuela. Humid and gallery forests, and *várzea*. Always near water or along streams, often in bushes at water's edge and in thickets on river islands.

Voice Shrill repetitions of *cher-dup* (H&B), loudsong is dry rattle on single pitch with closely spaced notes at rate of 26 notes in 2 s (Zimmer & Whittaker 2000), and duet between pair comprises explosive series of *pit-chew* notes, thought to be from male, with slightly lower pitched series of *kut-chup* or *kutterup* at slightly faster intervals, presumed to be from female. Duet may be prefaced by a short rapid series of *kip* notes by male (Fitzpatrick).

Note Formerly included northern taxa *caudata* and *intermedia*, and composite species called Pale-tipped Tyrannulet (Zimmer & Whittaker 2000).

LESSER WAGTAIL-TYRANT

Stigmatura napensis Pl. 191

Identification 13.2cm. Fairly typical olive and yellow tyrant but for its long rounded tail. Greyish-olive above with dusky wings and 2 broad wingbars, tail long and dark, with all but central pair of feathers having broad yellow-white bases and large yellow-white spots at tips. Below yellow with an olive wash on breast and sides.

Ssp. *S. n. napensis* (Ec, SE Co: Leticia, Ve: upper Orinoco)

Habits Forages alone or in pairs, from undergrowth to mid levels, flitting excitedly in foliage to pick insects by perch-gleaning or with quick sallies. Continually cocks tail energetically when foraging.

Status Uncommon in Ecuador. In Colombia, status unknown but many sight records along Brazilian border.

Habitat Tropical Zone, to 300m. Low successional vegetation (brush, grasses, creepers, saplings) on sandy river islands and banks of rivers of Amazon basin.
Voice Loud whistles, *weeeert?* and *weeeEE!*, and a tapering rattle *sque'e'e'e'e'e* (H&B).

AGILE TIT-TYRANT

Anairetes agilis Pl. 192

Identification 13cm. Long-tailed flycatcher. Above warm brown heavily streaked black, dusky wings with faint wingbars and narrow white fringes to tertials, crest long and usually laid back, with long white supercilium; yellow below heavily streaked blackish on face, throat, breast and sides. Juvenile slightly paler brown above with dull buffy wingbars and buffy fringes to tertials, streaking below more extensive but less black. Tufted Tit-Tyrant is smaller and has crest prominently recurved upwards.

Ssp. Monotypic (N Ec, E & C Co, Ve: Mérida, Táchira)

Habits Forages in pairs or small groups of 3–5 (families?), mostly with mixed-species flocks at treeline forests. Not shy, picks insects from foliage by rapid gleaning, mostly near tips of branches.
Status Uncommon in Ecuador and locally common in Colombia.
Habitat Temperate Zone to Páramo, mostly at 2,500–3,600m in Ecuador, Clearings, areas of brush and partially open areas at borders of elfin and other temperate forests near treeline, frequently in stands of *Chusquea* bamboo.
Voice Reminiscent of Cinnamon Flycatcher, an even trill *pti'i'i'i'i'i'i*. A single soft *speew-it!* and a short chattery trill, sometimes descending slightly and ending in a hiccup, *t-t-t-t-t-t-t-t-t-e-e-e-spew-it* (Fitzpatrick).
Note Formerly placed in genus *Uromyias*. Lanyon (1988a), R&T and R&G maintained *Uromyias* on basis of morphology and voice, but Roy *et al.* (1999) found genetic data to show that *Uromyias* is embedded within *Anairetes*.

BLACK-CRESTED TIT-TYRANT

Anairetes nigrocristatus Pl. 192

Identification 13cm. Dramatically plumaged and quite distinct, crested flycatcher, white with dense black streaks. Body, back to rump and breast to undertail-coverts white, streaked black. Face, chin and crest all black, with rear crown and nape white. Wings black, with 2 white bars and white fringes to remiges, tail black with white outer fringes. Bill coral red with a blackish tip. Female similar but has shorter crest. Crest of juvenile brownish and shorter still; back is olivaceous streaked blackish, buffy lores and partial eye-ring, underparts dirty white streaked obscurely dark brown; bill brown.

Ssp. Monotypic (extreme S Ec: S of Utuana, S Loja)

Habits Forages alone or in pairs, sometimes with *A. parulus*. Takes insects by gleaning in shrubbery or with short sallies. Occasionally shakes wings with shuddering motion.
Status Very rare and local in Ecuador.
Habitat Temperate Zone to Páramo, 2,400–2,500m. Humid, fairly open areas: cultivated slopes with hedges and copses of small trees, highland pastures, fallow fields with scattered bushes, groves of *Polylepis*, but in Ecuador appears to occur only in regenerating scrub.
Voice A series of fast, explosive notes: *wheek-tititittttttiti* (R&T) and a shorter *wheek-tic tit ititi* (Fitzpatrick).
Notes Formerly treated as a race of Pied-crested Tit-Tyrant *A. reguloides*, but separated on basis of larger size (F&K). Population in southern Ecuador might be subspecifically distinct, being much darker than specimens from central and northern Peru (R&G).

TUFTED TIT-TYRANT

Anairetes parulus Pl. 192

Identification 10.9cm. Cute, with white eyes and recurved crest. Greyish-olive above streaked lightly darker, with dusky wings and tail and 2 narrow but clear white wingbars. Top of head black with bold white loral line and superciliary, crest also black perhaps with some white (usually invisible) on crown; head-sides and underparts white at throat and cheeks, becoming yellow below, all boldly streaked black. Juvenile duller and slightly browner, with a shorter crest lacking any white on crown. Difficult to confuse, Agile Tit-Tyrant is larger, with a longer tail and laid back crest; Black-crested is much larger, and always separable by black face and eyes.

Ssp. *A. p. aequatorialis* (S Co, Ec)

Habits Forages alone or in pairs in undergrowth or mid-level foliage, usually keeping to cover but calling frequently. Seldom joins mixed flocks. Picks insects with short sallies or by perch-gleaning. Constructs small, neatly lined cup nest in a bush or bamboo, often at water's edge.
Status Uncommon to rare in Ecuador and uncommon to frequent in Colombia.
Habitat Subtropical Zone to Páramo, 2,500–3,500m in Ecuador and 2,100–3,600m in Colombia. Varied habitats, including partially open slopes, fields with hedges or scattered bushes and trees, elfin and other woodlands at treeline, *Polylepis* woodland and stands of *Chusquea* bamboo.
Voice Contact-call a thin *pluit-pluit* (Fitzpatrick). Other calls include a fast toneless trill and feeble rising *pee-de-dit* whistle. Song comprises loud variations of *chew wit titititi wit* (H&B), sometimes in duet, e.g. *chuit-chuit-chuit-chuit-chuit-chidi-didi* (R&G).

BEARDED TACHURI

Polystictus pectoralis Pl. 192

Identification 9.7cm. Essentially buffy-brown above, tending to rufous on rump and uppertail-coverts, wings darker brown (with or without wingbars) and below warm ochraceous-yellow with cinnamon wash. Male has white lores and heavy black streaking on chin, face and top of head, lacking in female, which has ochraceous lores. Perches vertically, hanging sideways to stems, with tail held straight down for balance. Flies low, undulating over grasses, to perch at some distance atop a stem. Two subspecies rather different.

Ssp. *P. p. bogotensis* (C Co: Andean savannas of Bogotá and upper Dagua Valley) much larger, with longer crest feathers, less well-defined face markings (male), more rufous above, with deep tawny wingbars

P. p. brevipennis (E Co: eastern llanos, S Ve, Gu, Su) dark head of male almost forms hood, wingbars pale tawny to whitish

Habits Forages with small flocks of grass finches including *Sporophila* seedeaters, taking insects disturbed by others, hopping between stems of tall grass. These flocks sometimes include *Ammodramus* and *Emberizoides*, and, in Brazil, *Coryphaspiza melanotis*.

Status Race *brevipennis* frequent but very local in Colombia, rare, very local and declining in Venezuela, uncommon in Guyana and Suriname, and rare in French Guiana. Race *bogotensis* very rare and perhaps extirpated, with no recent reports.

Habitat Tropical Zone, *brevipennis* to 1,500m, *bogotensis* 2,600–2,700m. Dry savanna with low bushes and tussock grasses, and fringes of open marshes or boggy areas.

Voice A feeble *feee* whistle (H&B).

Notes Race *bogotensis* perhaps merits species status, but also possibly extinct (Fitzpatrick), and *brevipennis* is also possibly specifically distinct (F&K).

CRESTED DORADITO

Pseudocolopteryx sclateri Pl. 192

Identification 10cm. Adult male olive-green above with dark striations, wings brown with pale buffy fringes and 2 ragged wingbars, tail brown with yellowish fringes; crown feathers fairly long, usually laid back on nape, either buffy-yellow with brown line on centre, buffy-yellow on inner part and fuscous on outer, or completely fuscous with a partially concealed yellow patch; white superciliary. Entire underparts intense, rich yellow, with a few green or dusky striations on sides. Adult female very similar, but has more striations on sides, sometimes even on breast. Juvenile slightly duller above, with cinnamon wingbars and fringes to remiges and rectrices, richer and deeper than adult; feathers of crown shorter and coronal patch slightly orange, superciliary buffy-yellow; below not quite such an intense yellow.

Ssp. Monotypic (Ve, Tr, Gu)

Habits Forages alone or in pairs, discreetly perch-gleaning insects in shrubbery or grasses at water's edge. Constructs deep cup nest of grasses, weeds and soft fibres.

Status Fragmented distribution. Sporadic and very local in Venezuela, rare to scarce in Trinidad and uncertain in Guyana. Northern South American populations (in Venezuela at least) seem to appear suddenly, breed and then disappear. Some authors (e.g. Olrog, ffrench, Hilty) have wondered if these can be considered migrants, but we consider them nomads or more possibly irruptive due to severe flooding.

Habitat Tropical Zone, to 1,500m. Freshwater marshes, reedbeds and wet savannas (tall grasses near water). Prefers permanent marshes but will use seasonal wetlands.

Voice A squeaky *tsik-tsik-tsee-lee* and soft, thin *sik* (R&T).

SUBTROPICAL DORADITO

Pseudocolopteryx acutipennis Pl. 192

Identification 11.7cm. Bright olive-green above with dusky tail and wings, and fringes of greater coverts and tertials rather dull cinnamon, sometimes appearing like wingbars, whilst underparts entirely yellow. Male has central primaries oddly attenuated. Juvenile has more prominent wingbars and base of lower mandible pale.

Ssp. Monotypic (N Ec, C Co)

Habits Forages discreetly in grasses and reeds, and in adjacent shrubbery. Feeds on insects by perch-gleaning atop grass stems. Very shy and quiet.

Central primaries in male Subtropical Doradito are oddly attenuated and pointed

Status Erratic in our region being rare in Ecuador and scarce in Colombia (few records). Some authors (e.g. Olrog, ffrench, Hilty) consider it possibly an austral migrant, but when species appears in our region, it breeds, suggesting that these are irruptive movements, possibly associated with floods or other habitat changes.

Habitat Upper Tropical to Subtropical Zones, 2,400–3,500m in Ecuador and 1,500–1,900m in Colombia. Wet or boggy grasslands, shrubby, wet savannas, open marshes.

Voice Series of buzzy, irregular introductory notes followed by a short nasal snort, *tzit-tzit-tzit t-konk* (B. M. Whitney in F&K), with call while foraging *tzit* (R&G).

TAWNY-CROWNED PYGMY TYRANT

Euscarthmus meloryphus Pl. 191

Identification 10.2cm. Two rather distinct subspecies, well separated geographically.

Ssp. *E. m. paulus* (NE Co, N, C& SE Ve) brown above, wings and tail slightly darker with 2 faint cinnamon wingbars, a bright rufous patch on crown, the feathers of which are slightly elongated and often form small crest, face buffy-brown with an indistinct eye-ring, throat whitish, breast somewhat fulvous and belly pale yellow

E. m. fulviceps (W & SE Ec) olive above, darker on wings and tail, with 2 prominent buffy wingbars, small, semi-concealed rufous coronal patch, forehead fulvous and face bright buffy; throat white, breast slightly greyish and underparts pale yellow, washed greyish on flanks

Habits Forages in low vegetation, alone or in pairs. Takes insects, perch-gleaning briefly from stems or skittering about on ground searching in leaves and litter. Shy and quiet. Constructs dainty, thin cup nest of dry grasses in a low bush.
Status Locally common to uncommon in Ecuador, locally common in Colombia and Venezuela.
Habitat Tropical to Subtropical Zones, to 1,500m in Ecuador but to 2000m in south, and to 1,000m in Colombia and Venezuela. Dry open areas with low vegetation: grassy or weedy savannas with patchy bushes, thickets or scrubby trees.
Voice Call of *fulviceps* in Ecuador *plee-tirik* or *plee-ti-re-tik*, with song a repeated fast *re-tr-tr-tr-tr-tr-trreétrrt*. For *paulus* in Colombia and Venezuela, a varied chatter: *plitick* and *plick* and similar pebbly noises (H&B), and an abrupt, dry stuttering *ple'bik!*, lengthened to *ple-plit'erick* in locust-like song, repeated frequently, even during heat of day (Hilty).

RUFOUS-SIDED PYGMY TYRANT

Euscarthmus rufomarginatus Pl. 191

Identification 11cm. Fairly uniform dull brown from forehead to lower back, with uppertail-coverts more rufous, wings and tail dull blackish-brown with rufous-buff tips to wing-coverts and tertials, producing 2 wingbars, no crest, but longer coronal feathers can be raised and partially conceal vestigial orange-rufous coronal patch; supraloral streak buffy-white, chin and throat white, sides, flanks and undertail-coverts ochraceous-tawny, centre of breast and belly pale yellow.

Ssp. *E. r. savannophilus* (Su: Sipaliwini savanna)

Habits Forages alone or in pairs close to ground, in low-level vegetation and occasionally on ground.
Status Locally fairly common in Sipaliwini savanna to which the race is endemic.
Habitat Tropical Zone. Open areas, in savannas and grassland.
Voice Musical, high-pitched song (H&M, Mees 1994). Vocalisations in Fitzpatrick refer to nominate: unmusical *tik* notes followed by a buzz, *tic-tic-tic, tiker-trrrrrk*, also longer series of buzzes ending with emphatic *trrrrriker*. Unknown whether races differ vocally, and if so to what extent.
Note Race *savannophilus* represents an extraordinarily isolated small population, described by Mees (1968), but Fitzpatrick considered it inseparable from nominate.

Bristle tyrants were formerly placed in *Pogonotriccus* but were moved to *Phylloscartes* by Traylor (1977), though their separation is perhaps valid but no such proposal has been received by the SACC. They are separated from *Phylloscartes* by their upright posture, tail held vertically down, and habit of flicking 1 wing, and a moment later the other. This flick may be considerable, up over the back, not just a sideways movement. They forage deliberately with the tail held downwards, unlike the flitting, tail-cocking and darting style of tyrannulets, in the canopy and midstorey, but not in sunlit areas, and they hawk for insects rather than glean. All except Spectacled Bristle Tyrant have bold black patches on the ear-coverts. They are also usually found in mixed-species flocks.

MARBLE-FACED BRISTLE TYRANT

Phylloscartes ophthalmicus Pl. 193

Identification 11.5cm. Above yellowish-olive with brown wings and tail, wings have pale yellow fringes to coverts and tertials, appearing as 2 bold but slightly diffuse wingbars, and solid pale yellowish patch on remiges, tail-feathers have greenish-yellow outer fringes, crown slate grey with white lores and superciliary extending around ear-coverts, which are distally black. Face-sides grizzled with a bold white spot on cheeks that enhances black crescent on ear-coverts; below yellow, with heavy olive wash on breast. Bill black with base of lower mandible slightly paler. Juvenile similar but duller. From Venezuelan Bristle Tyrant by dull wing-coverts (not black) and complete (i.e. continuous) wingbars.

Ssp. *P. o. ophthalmicus* (NW & E Ec, Co: W & C Andes) as described

P. o. purus (N Ve: northern Cordillera and inland range of Aragua) generally more yellowish, cheek spot bright yellow, as are wingbars and underparts

Habits Forages alone or in pairs, always with mixed flocks of insectivores and frugivores in subcanopy and canopy. Makes short sallies to hover-glean insects from leaves, then pauses to scan around with tail held down. Perches vertically. Foraging pairs occasionally occur with 2–3 immatures, presumably family parties. Typical gestures include flagging up one wing, often followed by flicking the other and sometimes both wings.
Status Uncommon in Ecuador, locally frequent to uncommon in Colombia and Venezuela.
Habitat Upper Tropical to Subtropical Zones. Humid to wet montane and cloud forests, in interior of forest and at clearings and borders.
Voice A high-pitched unmusical *skeek e' ti'ti'ti'ti'ti'ti* (H&B). Contact when foraging *ju-E!* Song a bubbly trill descending slightly then ascending and starting and / or ending with same call-note, *ju-E, pit'pe'e'e'e'a'a'a'e'e'e'e'e'pit'pit…ju-E* (Hilty).
Note Placed in genus *Pogonotriccus* by Fitzpatrick and R&G.

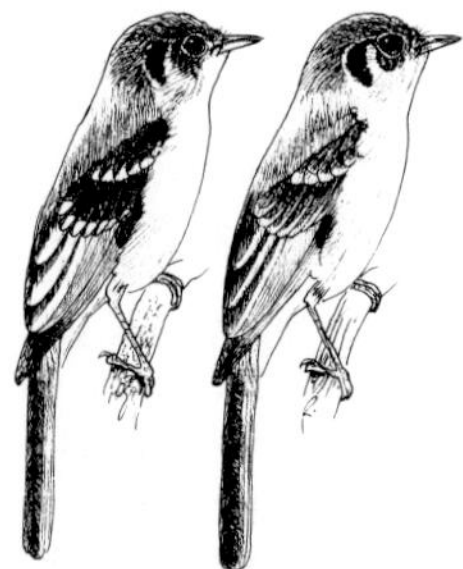

Comparison of wingbars of Venezuelan Bristle Tyrant (left) and Marble-faced Bristle Tyrant

VENEZUELAN BRISTLE TYRANT

Phylloscartes venezuelanus Pl. 193

Identification 10.5cm. Olive above with dusky wings that have 2 clear yellow wingbars formed by pale yellow spots on terminal outer half of wing-coverts (note these are often incorrectly drawn in the literature, and difference between this wingbar and those of other bristle tyrants is diagnostic). Tail-feathers have greenish-yellow outer fringes; grey crown, yellowish-white lores and broken eye-ring, and pale, vestigial superciliary extends around ear-coverts, which are distally black. Face-sides grizzled and yellow spot on cheeks enhances black crescent of ear-coverts; below yellow, with heavy olive wash on breast. Bill black with base of lower mandible flesh-coloured. Very easily confused with Marble-faced Bristle Tyrant, which has dusky wing-coverts and soft, slightly diffuse, continuous wingbars.

Ssp. Monotypic (N Ve: Northern Cordillera and inland range of Miranda and Aragua)

Habits Forages alone, mostly at mid levels to subcanopy, often in flocks with woodcreepers, antbirds and other insect-eaters, where it frequently occurs with Marble-faced Bristle Tyrant. Sometimes in small family groups. Flags one wing up, in gesture typical of genus. Vertical perching posture.
Status Uncommon and local Venezuelan endemic.
Habitat Upper Tropical Zone, 950–1,400m. Humid and cloud forests on upper slopes of coastal cordillera.
Voice Calls cheerfully and often, rendered *tree-ee-ee-ew, tee-tee-tee*, but reportedly similar to *P. ophthalmicus* (R&T). Soft, double-noted *chee'dip*. Song a fast trill, descending then ascending, *ch'e'e'e'e'd'd'd'd'd'e'e'eWEEP!* and rather like Marble-faced Bristle Tyrant (Hilty).
Note Placed in genus *Pogonotriccus* by Fitzpatrick and R&G.

SPECTACLED BRISTLE TYRANT

Phylloscartes orbitalis Pl. 193

Identification 10.7cm. Slightly smaller than other bristle tyrants. Olive-green above with olive tail and dusky wings that have 2 yellowish-white wingbars and fringes to tertials; crown grey with clear white eye-ring that distinguishes it from congeners, face-sides grizzled yellow, slightly darker on cheeks but lacks solid black patch of other bristle tyrants; below all yellow.

Ssp. Monotypic (Ec, extreme S Co: SW Putumayo)

Habits Forages alone or in pairs, invariably with mixed-species understorey flocks, which consist mainly of insectivores (antbirds, flycatchers, woodcreepers etc.). Makes short sallies to hover-glean insects from leaves, then pauses to scan with tail held down. Frequently flags up one wing.
Status Rare in Ecuador, status unknown in Colombia as there are few records (its range only just enters the country).
Habitat Tropical Zone, 700–1,400m in Ecuador, in Colombia mainly at 900m. Humid forest on foothills and mid slopes on Amazonian side of Andes.
Voice A fast chirpy trill that descends slightly to start and ends in 2–3 sharp notes (R&G).
Note Placed in genus *Pogonotriccus* by Fitzpatrick and R&G.

VARIEGATED BRISTLE TYRANT

Phylloscartes poecilotis Pl. 193

Identification 11.4cm. Olive above with darker tail and dusky wings that have 2 broad buffy wingbars, crown and nape grey, head-sides grizzled, with irregular whitish line from lores to embrace dusky ear-coverts, underparts pale yellow. Similar to Chapman's Bristle Tyrant but has whitish on face, and well separated geographically. From Marble-faced and other bristle tyrants by buffy wingbars.

Ssp. *P. p. pifanoi* (Perijá: Co & Ve) crown and nape slate grey, contrasting more with back
P. p. poecilotis (Andes: Ve, Co & Ec) as described, crown and nape neutral grey

Habits Forages alone, in pairs and occasionally in small families, invariably with mixed flocks. Some dispute over foraging height: mid levels to canopy (H&B, Fitzpatrick) or low to mid levels (R&G). Where sympatric, often occurs in same flocks with Marble-faced Bristle Tyrant.
Status Uncommon in Ecuador, frequent in Colombia and Venezuela.
Habitat Upper Tropical to Subtropical Zones, 1,500–2,000m in Ecuador, 1,500–2,300m in Colombia and Venezuela. Humid, wet and cloud forests on upper slopes.
Voice Two thin notes, *whee-see* on same pitch (H&B), and a *tsit!*, reminiscent of a tanager (R&G).
Notes Placed in genus *Pogonotriccus* by Fitzpatrick and R&G. Fitzpatrick considers race *pifanoi* to simply represent individual variation and synonymised it.

ANTIOQUIA BRISTLE TYRANT

Phylloscartes lanyoni Pl. 193

Identification 11cm. Poorly known. Olive above, with dusky wings that have 2 broad yellow wingbars, fringed and tipped pale yellow, grey crown, yellowish lores and broken eye-ring, face-sides grizzled yellow with blackish crescent on ear-coverts.

Ssp. Monotypic (Co: Central Andes)

Habits Forages at mid levels to canopy, with behaviour similar to congeners. Probably breeds during March–June rains.
Status Endangered. Colombian endemic described in 1988 from single male and female specimens taken by Carriker in 1948. Total range just 600 km^2.
Habitat Tropical Zone, 450–900m. Borders of humid low-land semi-deciduous forest and second growth, clearings.
Voice Unknown.

CHAPMAN'S BRISTLE TYRANT

Phylloscartes chapmani Pl. 193

Identification 11.5cm. Poorly known. Dull olive above with dusky wings that have 2 buffy wingbars, whitish fringes to tertials and yellowish fringes to remiges, crown and nape slightly darker olive, with pale loral line that fades behind eyes, white eye-ring. Face-sides grizzled with black crescent on rear cheeks, throat and breast olive-yellow, rest of underparts yellow. From congeners by buffy wingbars and eye-ring.

Ssp. *P. c. chapmani* (SE Ve) dull, paler wingbars, below washed-out yellow; juvenile has wings more mid brown with paler, almost white wingbars; throat grizzled, throat and breast duller grey-olive

P. c. duidae (S Ve) slightly more rich green above, richer cinnamon wingbars and brighter, cleaner yellow below

Habits Forages singly, sometimes with mixed-species flocks, in canopy and subcanopy. Flags up wing and cocks tail. Very quiet and inconspicuous.

Status Venezuelan and Pantepui endemic, Locally frequent.

Habitat Upper Tropical to Subtropical Zones, 1,000–2,000m. Primary humid and cloud forests on slopes and tops of tepuis.

Voice Call a short *wheee*. Song like first phrase of Marble-faced Bristle Tyrant, a short fast *psit!* followed by a trill (D. Ascanio).

Phylloscartes tyrannulets are slender, long-tailed birds with a horizontal stance and characteristically hold the tail horizontal if not cocked, and sometimes flick it upwards. They frequently flick one wing upwards, often followed by the other. Alert and lively when foraging, their manner recalls that of gnatcatchers. *Phylloscartes* tyrannulets forage in the canopy and midstorey but often, especially when not in feeding flocks, are found at the canopy edge even in fully sunlit areas. They do not hawk like *Pogonotriccus* bristle tyrants, instead search for insects in foliage and, because this requires them to be more nimble, it has been speculated that this is the reason for their longer tails.

BLACK-FRONTED TYRANNULET
Phylloscartes nigrifrons Pl. 193

Identification 12–13cm. Dark olive above with blackish wings that have 2 bold yellowish-white wingbars and fringes to tertials, whilst fringes to remiges yellowish, crown dark grey with white nasal plumes, and narrow superciliary line that embraces ear-coverts, which are distally black forming a crescent, face-sides grizzled; underparts white, mottled grey on throat, washed grey on breast and yellowish-grey on sides and flanks. Juvenile duller above, slightly browner on crown; lower belly and undertail-coverts lack any yellow wash, but are buffy.

Ssp. Monotypic (S & SE Ve & Guyana: Cerro Roraima)

Habits Forages alone, sometimes in pairs and mostly with mixed flocks. Takes spiders and insects by gleaning them from leaves. Horizontal on perch. Flags up wing and cocks tail. Very quiet and inconspicuous.

Status Locally frequent Pantepui endemic in Venezuela and Roraima region of adjacent Guyana.

Habitat Upper Tropical to Subtropical Zones, 900–1,800m. Humid forests on slopes of tepuis.

Voice Song a long, very thin trill lasting 2–3 s, descending over second half (D. Ascanio). When foraging, a thin sharp *tsuk-cheez-tr'r'r'r'r'r'r'r'r'r'r'r'r* with *cheez* note highest, and tail vibrated during trill at end (Hilty).

ECUADOREAN TYRANNULET
Phylloscartes gualaquizae Pl. 193

Identification 11.5cm. Greenish-olive above, wings and tail dusky with 2 yellow wingbars, crown grey with weak whitish superciliary and eye-ring, face and head-sides whitish with indistinct black crescent on ear-coverts; throat whitish, breast pale yellow mottled olive and rest of underparts pure yellow. Bill long and black. Difficult to separate from White-fronted or Plumbeous-crowned Tyrannulets. White-fronted has shorter bill with clear flesh-coloured lower mandible, narrow white band on forehead and no black crescent on ear-coverts. Plumbeous-crowned is slightly larger with both a shorter bill and tail, and also lacks any black on ear-coverts.

Ssp. Monotypic (E Ec)

Habits Forages alone, mostly with mixed canopy flocks, usually in outer twigs and branches of treetops. Typical gestures include tail-cocking and flicking a wing in sail-like gesture.

Status Rare in Ecuador.

Habitat Tropical to Lower Subtropical Zones, 700–1,400m. Humid forest of foothills and lower slopes, at borders and clearings as well as interior.

Voice A thin *feeeeee* whistle and *sp-i-i-i-i-i* rattle similar to Cinnamon Flycatcher (R&T); a thin wheezy trill that descends, ascends then descends again (Fitzpatrick).

RUFOUS-LORED TYRANNULET
Phylloscartes flaviventris Pl. 193

Identification 11.5cm. Olive above, dusky wings and tail with 2 yellow wingbars and yellow fringes to tertials and remiges, crown slightly darker olive, rufous lores and eye-ring continue as white line that embraces black rear ear-coverts, which are slightly grizzled yellow; entire underparts yellow. Usually with Marble-faced and Venezuelan Bristle Tyrants which are quite similar, but both perch upright whilst Rufous-lored is horizontal and sallies for insects.

Ssp. Monotypic (Ve: northern coastal range)

Habits Forages in canopy, alone or in pairs, mostly with mixed canopy flocks. Typical gestures include forward-leaning posture, and holds tail horizontal and wings slightly away from body, like a gnatcatcher, while foraging (Fitzpatrick & Stotz 1997).

Status Locally frequent to uncommon Venezuelan endemic (Peruvian and Bolivian populations now recognised as *P. parkeri*: Fitzpatrick & Stotz 1997). Previously reported

fragmented range (P&MdS), with separate Andean and coastal range populations, incorrect, as very old Mérida specimens now considered erroneous.
Habitat Tropical Zone, 300–1,000m. Humid forest on lower slopes and in foothills.
Voice Short series of loud, merry whistles. A fussy call while foraging, a high, thin jangling *teep-teep-teep* (1–4 notes) uttered rapidly, also a jangled *te'te'skeek!* (Hilty).
Note Sometimes erroneously listed under Yellow-bellied Bristle Tyrant (e.g. by Rodner *et al.*, Meyer de Schauensee & Phelps Jnr.).

OLIVE-GREEN TYRANNULET

Phylloscartes virescens Pl. 193

Identification 12cm. Poorly known. Olive from crown to tail, with dusky wings that have 2 white wingbars. Bill long and pointed, black above, grey below. Readily confused with Yellow Tyrannulet, but latter has yellow superciliary from lores back.

Ssp. Monotypic (NE Gu, N & C Su, FG)

Habits Forages very actively in canopy, often with mixed flocks. Typical gestures include flagging wing up and cocking tail slightly. Constructs enclosed nest with side entrance.
Status Scarce in Guyana, Suriname and French Guiana.
Habitat Tropical Zone, to 500m, in humid forest, mostly along rivers but also at borders.
Voice Song by both of foraging pair, series of high, reedy notes, preceded by a higher, exclamatory note, *queet! peet-peet-peet*. The *queet!* note is sometimes uttered alone or followed by a disorganised chatter.

RUFOUS-BROWED TYRANNULET

Phylloscartes superciliaris Pl. 193

Identification 11.5cm. Above bright greenish-olive, wings and tail dusky olive, yellowish fringes to coverts and remiges, producing narrow wingbars in fresh plumage, crown dark grey with supraloral and supercilium contrastingly rufous. Pure white spot at base of bill and black line from lores through eye to encircle white ear-coverts, running back up to gape between cheek and mesial. Underparts white, suffused grey on sides and flanks, undertail-coverts pale yellow. Juvenile slightly paler on head with buffy-white fringes to greater coverts. Largely unmistakable, only similar species is Rufous-lored Tyrannulet which has white postocular superciliary and both wingbars significantly bolder than Rufous-browed.

Ssp. *P. s. griseocapillus* (S Ec, NC Co, Ve: Perijá)

Habits Forages in canopy, often with mixed-species flocks. Takes small insects by gleaning and flitting about in foliage, and also fruits and berries; often vocal while foraging. Typical gestures include raising a wing sail-like, and keeping tail horizontal or slightly cocked when moving about.
Status Very rare in Ecuador, very local and uncommon in Colombia, and local in Venezuela.
Habitat Upper Tropical to Lower Subtropical Zones, 1,300–1,700m in Ecuador and Colombia, and 1,650–2,000m in Venezuela. Humid forest of foothills and lower slopes, both at borders and in interior.
Voice A loud, energetic *wiss wreewreewreewreewree* or *wree tititititi* (H&B) or *spee-ee-ee-ee-ee, spee-didi-dee* (R&G).

Pygmy tyrants are small, often tiny, with varied vocalisations that sound mechanical or insect-like. They sometimes have extravagant crests. *Myiornis* are rounded, tiny birds with very short tails and frog-like songs.

BLACK-CAPPED PYGMY TYRANT

Myiornis atricapillus Pl. 192

Identification 6.9cm. Tiny, upperparts bright olive, short tail blackish, wings dusky with bright olive fringes (yellowish on remiges), and male has black cap that grades into mantle, head-sides greyish, lores black with bold white supraloral and eye-ring; white below, washed grey on breast and sides, yellowish-olive on flanks. Bill long and black, legs and feet flesh. Female has black restricted to forehead, with cap washed slightly sooty. Within range it is unique. Male might be confused with a tody-flycatcher, but these all have clear yellow wingbars, and Common Tody-Flycatcher has whitish eyes and juvenile is much greyer above and yellow below.

Ssp. Monotypic (NE Ec, E Co: Pacific slopes)

Habits Forages alone, from low to mid levels. Moves abruptly and is difficult to see (could be confused with a large insect!). Perches quietly scanning foliage above, then makes lightning sally to underside of a leaf. Takes small beetles and spiders. Constructs large, untidy ball-shaped nest with side entrance, of fibres and mosses, suspended from a twig.
Status Uncommon in Ecuador, locally frequent in Colombia.
Habitat Lower Tropical Zone, to 800m in Ecuador and 900m in Colombia. Humid and wet forests, at borders, in clearings or in adjacent semi-open areas.
Voice Essentially same variety of mechanical trills that sound like a frog starting up or a cricket on trial run as its congener. Repetitions of a feeble *eeeeek*, a soft trilled purr and a repeated *tseeyp* (H&B, R&G, Fitzpatrick).
Note Treated as conspecific with *M. ecaudatus* in H&B.

SHORT-TAILED PYGMY TYRANT

Myiornis ecaudatus Pl. 192

Identification 6.6cm. Tiny with very short tail. Bright olive above, tail and wings dusky with yellow fringes to wing-coverts and remiges, but no clear wingbars; head grey, lores black with a bold white supraloral and eye-ring; below white, flushed yellow-olive on sides and flanks. Bill long and black, legs and feet flesh.

Ssp. *M. e. miserabilis* (E Co: east side of Andes, N & C Ve, Tr, Gu, Su)

Habits Forages alone, at low to mid levels. Diet and feeding behaviour as congener. Diminutive and easily overlooked. Males chase competitors.

Status Rare in Ecuador; uncommon in Colombia and Trinidad, locally frequent in Venezuela; frequent in Guyana, Suriname, French Guiana.
Habitat Tropical Zone, to 400m in Ecuador, 500m in Colombia and Venezuela north of Orinoco, but to 900m south of river. Humid forests, at borders and near water.
Voice Like previous species, utters mechanical trills that sound more like a frog starting up or a cricket on trial run. Call in Suriname a high-pitched, fine trill *trrree... trrree...* (H&M), and in Colombia a series of squeaky chirps (H&B). In Venezuela, Hilty describes a high-pitched series of up to 15 *c'r'e'eek* notes, at first hesitant, then accelerating and descending slightly.

Lophotriccus pygmy tyrants are small, inconspicuous birds with full-bodied crests, and often loud voices, of lower growth and fringes of forests and woodland.

Male Scale-crested Pygmy Tyrant displaying crest

SCALE-CRESTED PYGMY TYRANT
Lophotriccus pileatus Pl. 192

Identification 9.5–10cm. Small; male has distinctive, surprisingly large crest. Olive above with dusky wings and tail, fringed yellow forming 2 pale wingbars. Crest of long, rounded feathers is black with narrow, bright orange-rufous fringes that are usually laid back but may be erected. Below, throat whitish, rest of underparts pale yellow, variously flushed and streaked on breast and flanks according to race. Bill grey and eyes yellow. Female has slightly shorter, but orange-rufous fringes distinctly broader, thus appears redder than in male. Juvenile has 2 plumages, perhaps better labelled juvenile and immature. Young juvenile has crown olive, concolorous with back. A few crest feathers may appear on rear crown or nape, and sex determinable by width of cinnamon fringes. Paler below than adult and more streaked on flanks. Immature has crest feathers developed, but short, with narrower fringes, those of male very thin, affording a dusky-looking crown; those of female with fuller fringes. Only a very few, longest feathers on rear crown have fringes as broad as adults.

Ssp. *L. p. pileatus* (E Ec) throat and upper breast white, streaked olive, fringes of crest feathers rufous
L. p. sanctaeluciae (NE Co, NW Ve) throat and breast pale yellow, indistinct yellow wingbars, flight-feathers fringed olive
L. p. squamaecrista (Andes: Co & Ec) wing-coverts have less conspicuous greenish fringes, throat and breast white with broader and darker streaks, flanks and undertail-coverts yellow

Habits Forages alone, in understorey and at mid levels, making short sallies to glean insects from leaves. Males call intermittently throughout day and can occur in very loose aggregations like an incipient lek. Nest a ball, suspended from end of a twig, with a side entrance and eave above, and a long, crudely woven tail.
Status Locally common to uncommon in Ecuador, frequent to common in Colombia, and locally frequent in Venezuela.
Habitat Upper Tropical to Lower Subtropical Zones. Race *pileatus* on east slope of Andes in Ecuador, at 700–1,700m, *squamaecrista* on Pacific side from lowlands to 1,700m, and 300–1,500m in Colombia but occasionally to 2,300m, and 400 (rarely lower) to 2,500m in Venezuela. Wet and humid forests and mature second growth on lower Andean slopes.
Voice Main call charmingly described by Hilty as 'like slowly winding a watch' – an amazingly loud, slightly rising series of metallic *trik* notes. Also sometimes makes a purring call. An extremely loud trill, like a police whistle, given throughout day, and a series of sharp *preek* notes, sometimes widely spaced (Fitzpatrick).

DOUBLE-BANDED PYGMY TYRANT
Lophotriccus vitiosus Pl. 192

Identification 9.5–10cm. Very small. Olive above, wings dusky with 2 pale wingbars, crown bushy and long, extending beyond nape when laid flat, black with grey fringes; below varies racially. Bill long and grey, legs flesh, eyes straw yellow. Female similar but has less well-developed crest. Could be confused with Scale-crested on eastern slopes but latter has rufous fringes to crest-feathers, is more greenish above and generally occurs at higher elevations.

Ssp. *L. v. affinis* (E Ec, SE Co) crown-feathers fringed dark grey, yellow below, greyish-olive flammulations on sides of throat and breast
L. v. guianensis (Guianas) crown-feathers fringed pale grey, white below, tinged yellow on breast-sides and flanks, more heavily flammulated olive-grey on throat, breast and sides

Habits Forages mostly alone, at low and mid levels. Joins mixed flocks occasionally in Suriname but infrequently in Colombia. Takes beetles, flies, wasps, small caterpillars, moths and spiders from underside of leaves in a quick sally. Small ball-shaped nest of mosses is attached to a leafy branch; entrance at bottom and has an eave.
Status Uncommon in Ecuador. Frequent in Guyana, Suriname and French Guiana.
Habitat Lower Tropical Zone, to 600m in Ecuador. Savanna and humid forests. Strictly associated with old treefall gaps in *terra firme* in French Guiana.
Voice A toneless trill *tir'r'r'r'er... tir'r'r'r'er* (H&M) and series of buzzy *turrrrrrrrr* trills (H&B). Not as loud as Scale-crested Pygmy Tyrant.

HELMETED PYGMY TYRANT

Lophotriccus galeatus Pl. 192

Identification 9.5–10cm. Very small. Olive above, with dusky wings that have indistinct olive fringes to coverts and tertials producing faint wingbars, crest long (feathers narrow and extending beyond rear crown) and black edged olive. Head-sides grey, lores pale, throat and underparts pale yellow vaguely streaked or flammulated grey. Bill grey above, flesh-coloured below, legs and feet flesh, and eyes pale yellow to pale orange. Pale-eyed Pygmy Tyrant is paler on back and completely lacks crest. White-eyed Tody-Tyrant has bold yellow wingbars and olive crown.

Ssp. Monotypic (E Ve, Guianas)

Habits Forages alone, usually at mid levels. Builds pouch nest at end of thin twig, with small tunnel entrance low on side.
Status Locally common in Colombia and Venezuela, frequent in Guyana, common in Suriname, frequent in French Guiana.
Habitat Tropical Zone to 1,100m. Coastal woodland, coffee plantations, savanna and swamp forests, sandy soil woodland., second growth and forest borders
Voice Calls include a series of soft single notes (H&M) or sequence of *pick* notes in slight crescendo, sometimes followed by a warble (H&B).

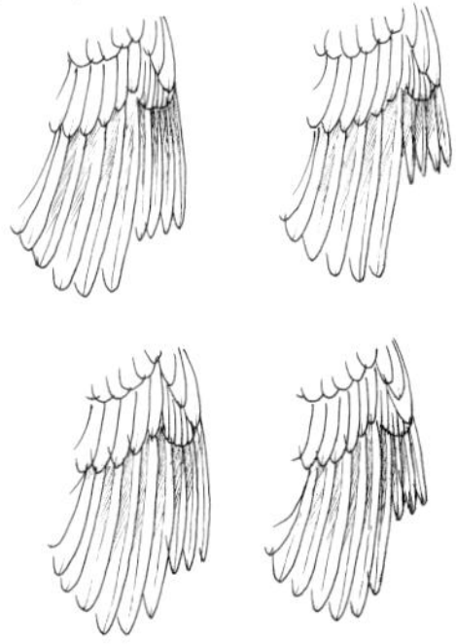

Pale-eyed Pygmy Tyrant has the 4 outer primaries shorter and attenuated, whilst the similar Helmeted Pygmy Tyrant has the 3 outermost primaries so. This occurs in adults of both sexes of both species equally. In juveniles the attenuated feathers are longer. From left to right, Pale-eyed Pygmy Tyrant juvenile and adult, and Helmeted Pygmy Tyrant juvenile and adult

PALE-EYED PYGMY TYRANT

Atalotriccus pilaris Pl. 192

Identification 8.9–9.5cm. Tiny, nondescript bird. Olive above, including crown and neck-sides, head-sides pale buffy, wings and tail dusky with pale yellowish fringes to wing-coverts, tertials and remiges, producing somewhat indistinct wingbars, white below, tinged warm grey on throat and breast. Similar Pearly-vented Tody-Tyrant has longer bill and brown upperparts.

Ssp. *A. p. griseiceps* (E Co, C & E Ve, W Gu) crown smoky grey, contrasting with back
A. p. pilaris (N & C Co) crown concolorous olive with back
A. p. venezuelensis (N & C Ve) crown grey, back brighter green

Habits Forages in pairs, usually at mid levels, sallying to undersides of leaves to pick insects or by gleaning foliage. Lively and at times restless, perches quite vertical and alert.
Status Frequent in Guyana.
Habitat Tropical Zone. Arid areas, in thorny or deciduous woodland, xerophytic scrub.
Voice Long variable trills: *trrrrrrrrr* or *ti, tit, trrrrrrrtreeeet* or *trrreeeet* (H&B).
Note Placed in *Lophotriccus* by Hilty.

Bentbills form a tiny genus notable for the peculiar downturn to their rather deep-based and slightly long bills. They are tiny, olive-green above with yellow underparts, and frequent dense thickets at forest edges in humid lowlands; not easy to see. Their voices have been likened to sounds emitted by toads.

NORTHERN BENTBILL

Oncostoma cinereigulare Pl. 193

Identification 9.5cm. Tiny, olive above with dusky wings that have yellow fringes to coverts, tertials and remiges; the 2–3 variable wingbars may not be apparent at all. Head usually greyish (though may be more olive), streaked grey and white on throat, merging into yellow underparts washed olive on sides and flanks. Bill unusually large for such a tiny bird and bent downwards halfway towards tip; eyes pale. Only likely to be confused with Southern Bentbill, which has no grey on throat or breast and is more yellowish on head-sides.

Ssp. Monotypic (NW Co: NW Antioquia)

Habits Forages in dense undergrowth and thickets. Perches quietly and sallies suddenly to pick insects from underside of leaves.
Status Middle American species, very rare in north-west Colombia (one record?).
Habitat Tropical Zone. Thickets at humid forest borders and in second growth.
Voice Calls often, a guttural trill, *grrrr* or *chiurrrrrrrr*, sometimes prefaced by *t-trrrrrr*.

SOUTHERN BENTBILL

Oncostoma olivaceum Pl. 193

Identification 9.1cm. Tiny, olive above with dusky wings that have yellow fringes to coverts, tertials and remiges; the 2–3 indistinct greenish-yellow wingbars may not be apparent at all. Head olive but may be tinged grey, throat pale yellow, vaguely streaked or flammulated olive, merging into yellow underparts, whitish on centre of belly and undertail-coverts. Bill seems large and is bent downwards halfway towards tip; eyes pale. Only likely confusion is with very rare Northern Bentbill, which is greyish on throat and breast.

Ssp. Monotypic (NW Co)

Habits Forages alone, mostly skulking at low levels in

undergrowth and border thickets. Perches quietly, sallying suddenly to pick insects from underside of leaves. Builds a small ball-shaped nest, the entrance hole at the top and has an eave.

Status Locally frequent in Colombia.

Habitat Tropical Zone to 1,000m. Borders and overgrown clearings of moist to humid forests and second growth.

Voice Males form loose, lek-like aggregations, calling almost continually, a feeble, nasal, frog-like *gurrrrrrrrr* trill (H&B), sometimes prefaced by *pt-trrrrrrr*.

BROWNISH TWISTWING

Cnipodectes subbrunneus Pl. 194

Identification 18cm. Large flycatcher with slightly longish tail, and outer primaries have uniquely stiffened and twisted shafts in adult male. Above dull brown, more rufescent on rump to tail, wings darker brown with bright buffy-rufous fringes to coverts, producing 2 wingbars, tertials and secondaries; head slightly darker than back with paler loral spot, throat pale brown becoming warmer, richer brown on breast then greyish or yellowish below. Bill broad and flat, black above, pale below; eyes pale orange. Similar Thrush-like Manakin has large dark eyes and plain wings.

Ssp. *C. s. minor* (SE Co) slightly paler and more olivaceous above

C. s. panamensis (NW Co) indistinguishable from *subbrunneus* in field

C. s. subbrunneus (W Co, W Ec) as described

Habits Forages alone, at mid levels. Takes insects using short sallies. Nest a bulky cylinder of fibres with a side entrance hole, suspended from a vine or branch.

Status Uncommon to rare in Ecuador, uncommon in Colombia.

Habitat Lower Tropical Zone, to 600m in Ecuador, and to 1,200m west of Andes but to only 400m on east slope in Colombia. Humid forest and mature second growth, in areas where understorey is well shaded but open. Often near streams.

Voice Males form lek-like aggregations (albeit quite dispersed) and call a loud *kuuuit!* all day. Song a sharp, loud *kuuheeer* or *keeéuw*, doubled or occasionally trebled whistle (H&B, R&G, Fitzpatrick), often preceded by bill-snapping and accompanied by wing-lifting.

Ramphotrigon flatbills constitute a genus of unassuming flycatchers found in humid forests, distinguished by their wide, flat bills, ochraceous wingbars and distinctive calls.

LARGE-HEADED FLATBILL

Ramphotrigon megacephalum Pl. 194

Identification 13.2–13.5cm. Medium-sized flycatcher which, despite name, does not have a remarkably large head. Dull olive from forehead to tail, with dusky wings that have 2 ochraceous wingbars, and ochraceous fringes to tertials and secondaries. In fresh plumage some have vestigial ochraceous fringes to lesser coverts, producing 3 wingbars, but this is unlikely to be noticeable. Also, colour of wingbars varies from buffy to cinnamon, irrespective of age or sex. Dark lores and white supraloral spot runs into prominent eye-ring, with vestigial superciliary. Throat pale, slightly yellowish-grey, breast light yellow softly flammulated ochraceous and olive, rest of underparts yellow. Very similar to larger Dusky-tailed Flatbill but separated by habitat, and Large-headed Flatbill has significantly more white before and around eye.

Ssp. *R. m. pectorale* (SE Co, S Ve) paler above but darker, more ochraceous on breast, with a more striped throat and richer yellow belly

R. m. venezuelense (WC Ve) darker above with more cinnamon wingbars

Habits Forages alone or with mixed flocks. In Ecuador only found in bamboo thickets, and in Venezuela and Colombia mostly so. Tends to avoid dense foliage, but will perch quietly for long periods, and thus easily overlooked. Takes insects by gleaning or sallying upwards to leaves and branches.

Status Rare in Ecuador, very local in Colombia, frequent in Venezuela.

Habitat Tropical to Lower Subtropical Zones, 300–1,300m in Ecuador, to 500m in Colombia and 600m in Venezuela. Interior and borders of humid forest, mostly where bamboo is abundant.

Voice Slow and sad, a double-noted *whoo… whoo*, also interpreted as *baaam… booo*.

Note Rather appropriately called Bamboo Flatbill by Hilty.

DUSKY-TAILED FLATBILL

Ramphotrigon fuscicauda Pl. 194

Identification 15.5–16.5cm. Brownish-olive above, slightly darker on head; wings dusky with cinnamon fringes to feathers, producing 2–3 wingbars (that on lesser coverts may be vestigial). Vestigial supraloral spot and eye-ring. Below yellow, streaked and flammulated olive on throat, breast and sides. Very similar to smaller Large-headed Flatbill which is a bamboo specialist, and thus distinguishable by habitat, whilst Dusky-tailed has much less white before and around eye.

Ssp. Monotypic (NE Ec, S Co)

Habits Forages alone or very occasionally with mixed flocks, at low and mid levels, usually in vine tangles.

Status Very rare in Ecuador and Colombia (only one record?).

Habitat Tropical Zone, 250–700m in Ecuador, to 300m in Colombia. Swamp forest and *várzea*, and dense shady ravines. Reportedly frequents bamboo thickets (e.g. Fitzpatrick) but presumably elsewhere in range as appears not to be found in bamboo in Ecuador or Colombia.

Voice A long, increasingly slurred note with sharp upturned finale, *peeeeewwwEEP* or *peeyooo-wheé*; song a mellow, mournful *peeeeu,tr'r'r*, *treey-treey-treey-treey*, increasing in volume at end. Also a lazy *peeeeow-whoóðw* repeated several times (Fitzpatrick).

RUFOUS-TAILED FLATBILL

Ramphotrigon ruficauda Pl. 194

Identification 15–16cm. Large flycatcher with somewhat large head. Olive forehead to lower back, rufous rump and tail, wings dusky with bright rufous fringes to feathers producing 2 clear wingbars, supraloral and eye-ring indistinct, yellowish-white, below yellow from throat to vent, heavily flammulated olive on throat, breast and sides, undertail-coverts ochraceous. Juvenile very similar but has throat spotted pale yellow, not streaked, is slightly paler and browner above (most noticeably on lower rump which is orange-buffy), but uppertail-coverts rufous like tail, as in adult.

Ssp. Monotypic (NE Ec, SE Co, S & E Ve, Guianas)

Habits Forages alone or in pairs, only rarely with mixed flocks, in undergrowth and at mid levels. Takes insects and berries by sallying upwards to leaves and branches from perch. Flutters languidly or perches idly for long intervals. Nests in dry season, using cavities in broken trunks or large fallen branches near ground.

Status Rare in Ecuador, frequent in Colombia and Venezuela, uncommon in Guyana, frequent in Suriname, infrequent but widespread in southern French Guiana.

Habitat Lower Tropical Zone, below 300m in Ecuador, to 600m in Colombia and 500m in Venezuela. Humid lowland *várzea* and *terra firme* as well as savanna forests.

Voice Song 2 whistled notes, first sad, second low and flute-like (H&B), or a long melancholy whistle (H&M).

Rhynchocylus flatbills are all full-headed, large, dull, greenish flycatchers with very broad bills, blackish above and flesh to whitish below.

EYE-RINGED FLATBILL

Rhynchocyclus brevirostris Pl. 194

Identification 15cm. Olive-green above with dusky wings and tail with yellowish-olive fringes, head, throat and upper breast dull olive-green, bold white eye-ring, belly yellow flammulated olive-green, undertail-coverts olive-green. Male has comb-like barbs on outer primaries (lacking in female and juvenile). Juvenile less streaked below and more yellow. Similar to Olivaceous Flatbill, but much greener above and below, and duller on wings.

Ssp. *R. b. hellmayri* (NW Co: NW Chocó)

Habits Forages lethargically, usually alone or with mixed understorey flocks. Perches idly, very straight, inspecting foliage. Picks insects by sallying to underside of leaf.

Status Scarce in Colombia where restricted to Cerro Tacarcuna on Panama border.

Habitat Tropical to Temperate Zones, to 1,100m, but 700–1,500m on Cerro Tacarcuna. Montane forest, usually in mossy shaded ravines, sometimes at borders.

Voice A buzzy, rising *bzzeeeep* (H&B), high-pitched, squeaky and rising *zweeip* or *sweeip*, cicada-like *zzrrip*, shrill lisping *ssiir* or *ssssi*, and longer *weep weep wip-wip-wip* (Fitzpatrick).

PACIFIC FLATBILL

Rhynchocyclus pacificus Pl. 194

Identification 15cm. Dark olive-green from head to tail, wings dusky with buffy-ochraceous fringes to all feathers, yellow below, heavily streaked or flammulated olive-green except centre of belly. Bill wide and flat. Very much like Eye-ringed Flatbill, but lacks eye-ring.

Ssp. Monotypic (NW Ec, W Co: Chocó)

Habits Forages alone, in undergrowth and at low levels. Often with mixed understorey flocks of antbirds and furnariids. Perches morosely, darting suddenly to take an insect from underside of a leaf.

Status Rare in Ecuador, uncommon in Colombia.

Habitat Tropical Zone, to 800m in Ecuador and 1,100m in Colombia. Lower growth of humid forests and mature second growth.

Voice Calls occasionally, a sudden loud *whust* (H&B) or hissing *scheeeuw* (Fitzpatrick). Song a fast descending series of clear or blurry notes *tchwee-tee-tee-te-tu-tu-tu* (recordings by O. Jahn and N. Krabbe in R&G).

OLIVACEOUS FLATBILL

Rhynchocyclus olivaceus Pl. 194

Identification 15–17cm. Dark olive from head to tail, variably greenish according to race, with dusky wings that have pale fringes to wing-coverts, tertials and secondaries. Again, fringes produce vague wingbars that may be very clear, or less so, according to race. Underparts yellow, streaked and flammulated greenish-olive. Juvenile duller above, with wingbars slightly paler, more ochraceous uppertail-coverts and paler yellow below.

Ssp. *R. o. aequinoctialis* (SE Co, E Ec) like *guianensis*, but wing markings yellow

R. o. bardus (NW Co) like *flavus*, bright green above, wing markings dull yellow, throat and breast more yellowish, streaks less distinct and more greenish

R. o. flavus (NE & E Co, W Ve: W Zulia) bright, more yellow from throat to vent, breast grey washed slightly olive and flammulated pale yellow, belly and abdomen pure yellow, undertail-coverts very pale; mandible flesh; juvenile duller and darker above, wingbars dull yellow-ochre, duller below, and mandible pale greyish-flesh

R. o. guianensis (S & SE Ve, Guianas) smaller, olive-green above, yellow-ochre fringes to wing-coverts, quite darkly streaked greyish-olive below and heavily flammulated to flanks, central belly lightly streaked, undertail-coverts pale olive; lower mandible flesh; juvenile darker above, more greyish-olive below and brighter yellow; lower mandible orange

R. o. jelambianus (W Ve: E & S Zulia) more olive above, fringes of greater wing-coverts yellow, yellow below flammulated olive from throat to breast, washed olive on sides, flanks to undertail-coverts, with central belly clear; juvenile slightly warmer, almost brownish above; distinct apricot wash to throat and breast

R. o. mirus (NW Co) secondaries and tertials deep buff rather than pale yellow, uppertail-coverts olive-brown, contrasting with back, tail darker brown

R. o. tamborensis (Co: Santander) similar to *flavus* but brighter yellow below, including green flammulations on breast which are less distinct and more blurred

Habits A contemplative, aloof bird, forages alone at low and mid levels and also joins mixed flocks. Perches very straight and very quiet, but sallies quickly to pick insects from foliage, changing perches often. Nest a large, crude, pear-shaped balloon with a woven entrance tube that protrudes near bottom.

Status Uncommon in Ecuador, Colombia and Guyana; rare in north but locally frequent in southern Suriname; uncommon but widespread in French Guiana.

Habitat Tropical Zone, to 700m in Ecuador, to 600m in Colombia and in Venezuela to 1,000m north of Orinoco, but 500m south of it. Humid, swampy and *várzea* forests, savanna woodland, borders of mature second growth, plantations, often by marshy areas.

Voice A loud *skreeeek*, similar to Grey-crowned Flycatcher (J. V. Remsen in H&B), or *tshret* (in R&G). Song in Ecuador an ascending *tuu tee tee ti ti?* (P. Coopmans in R&G). In northern Venezuela (race?) 5–7 nasal, upslurred notes *tree-tree-tree-tree-e-e-e*, ascending and faster at end, heard mainly at dawn (Fitzpatrick).

FULVOUS-BREASTED FLATBILL

Rhynchocyclus fulvipectus Pl. 194

Identification 15cm. Dark olive above, wings dusky with ochraceous fringes but no clear wingbars, vestigial eye-ring, underparts pale yellow, dull tawny wash on breast. Juvenile unknown.

Ssp. Monotypic (NW & E Ec, W & NC Co, W Ve)

Habits Forages alone or with mixed flocks. Perches pensively and quietly then dashes off through foliage. Constructs bulky balloon-shaped nest with a tube entrance.

Status Uncommon in Ecuador and Colombia.

Habitat Upper Tropical to Subtropical Zones, 900–1,800m in Ecuador, 200–1,200m on Pacific slope in Colombia, 1,900–2,300 on west slope of eastern Andes in Colombia, and to 1,800m in western Venezuela (Táchira). Lower growth of humid and wet montane forests, coffee plantations, mature second growth. Borders as well as riparian and semi-open, bushy areas.

Voice Call in Ecuador an infrequent wheezy and upslurred *zhreeyp* (R&G).

Tolmomyias flycatchers have broad flat bills, but less broad than flatbills, neither are their rictal bristles so well developed. Similar in coloration but have plain underparts, never streaked. Species identification is difficult and a bewildering number of races does little to assist matters. Where 2 species overlap, it is better to rely on voice for identification. Confusion where Yellow-olive Flycatcher, Yellow-margined and Grey-crowned Flycatchers occur sympatrically can be chronic. In addition to voice, check distribution, altitudes and habitat preferences. All are called flatbills by Hilty and R&G, reverting to their name in Cory & Hellmayr (1927) but this change of English name to flatbill has not yet been adopted by AOU.

YELLOW-OLIVE FLYCATCHER

Tolmomyias sulphurescens Pl. 195

Identification 14cm. Olive-green above with very dark, fuscous wings that have yellow fringes forming 2 wingbars, and yellow fringes to tertials. Distinctive is that yellow fringes to remiges are broad and even-width, giving wing very evenly marked appearance. Head darker with distinct pre-loral spot, white supraloral over nostrils. Below, evenly yellow from chin to undertail-coverts. Bill dark above and warm flesh below, but ranges from orange to bone-coloured; eyes vary but usually pale greyish-brown. Juvenile like adult above, but far less yellow below, being pale mousey washed sulphur-yellow on belly and undertail-coverts. Major confusion, where they are sympatric, with Yellow-margined and Grey-crowned Flycatchers, but Yellow-olive has evenly marked remiges and white supraloral; Yellow-margined has yellow fringes to remiges finer, primaries less yellow with whitish base, and lacks white supraloral; bill dark above and cold marble below. Grey-crowned is smaller, more yellowish-green above, with all-black bill and prefers drier habitat. In field, all three look alike below, though *assimilis* is slightly greyer.

Ssp. *T. s. aequatorialis* (W Ec) dark grey crown, supraloral spot very noticeable, dull yellow-green breast

T. s. asemus (W Co) grey crown and greyish throat and breast, duller yellow belly

T. s. berlepschi (Tr) greyish-olive crown and greyish throat, dull olive breast and dull yellow belly

T. s. cherriei (S & NE Ve: Bolívar to Delta Amacuro, Guianas) good supraloral and eye-ring, black lines on cheeks, throat grizzled white, grey and yellow, primrose below, well washed olive on breast and sides

T. s. confusus (NE Ec: east slope, Co: E Andes, W Ve) grey crown, supraloral spot vestigial, grey crown, distinct patch on ear-coverts; indistinguishable from *peruvianus*

T. s. duidae (S Ve: Amazonas) very dull supraloral and eye-ring, cheeks darker, throat, breast and sides washed greyish-olive, rest primrose-yellow

T. s. exortivus (NE Co, N Ve) back bright yellowish-green, supraloral small, grizzled fore-cheeks, bright rich yellow below washed slightly olivaceous

T. s. flavoolivaceus (NW Co) smaller, greener on crown and throat, and brighter yellow belly

T. s. peruvianus (SE Ec: east slope) grey crown,

supraloral vestigial, grey crown, distinct patch on ear-coverts; indistinguishable from *confusus*

Habits Forages in upper canopy, usually with mixed flocks (H&M), or in subcanopy and at mid levels, taking insects from air and foliage. Also feeds on small fruits and berries. Often draws attention by its shrill, hoarse calls. Usually perches quite upright, more so than congeners. Constructs hanging, bulky bag-like nest, of fine fibres and shaped like teapot with a longish tube entrance.

Status Locally uncommon to frequent in Ecuador and Colombia; fairly common in Venezuela; common in Suriname and on Trinidad; situation uncertain in Guyana; very locally common in coastal plain of French Guiana.

Habitat Tropical to Lower Subtropical Zones, to *c*.800m but mostly to 500m on west slope and 900–1,700m east of Andes in Ecuador, to 1,200m in Colombia with occasional records to 1,800m, and in Venezuela to 1,900m north of Orinoco and to 1,500m south of it. Diverse forest types, wooded slopes, plantations and semi-open areas, from fairly dry to very humid.

Voice Calls frequently, typically issuing from a mixed flock and often announcing its arrival. Race *aequatorialis* in Ecuador a thin well-enunciated series of quick notes, *psee-pset-psey-pset*. Birds east of Andes, *confusus* and *peruvianus*, have notes slightly longer, *swit-swit-swit-swit* (P. Coopmans). In Colombia (no location) calls said to resemble Yellow-margined Flycatcher but more staccato and less penetrating, usually 1–2 occasionally to 6, high-pitched, emphatic and slightly lispy *pipt* or *tsipt* notes; in longer sequences always a pause between first 2 notes, and final note, or 2 emphasised more than others, *tsip… tsip tsip TSIP* (Hilty, and J. Fitzpatrick in H&B).

Notes Called Yellow-olive Flatbill in Hilty and R&G. Very widespread and some races clearly distinct whilst others appear part of a cline; species merits in-depth revision as it seems quite likely that 2+ species are involved. Fitzpatrick recognises 16 subspecies, but only 9 occur in our region.

YELLOW-MARGINED FLYCATCHER

Tolmomyias assimilis Pl. 195

Identification 13cm. Olive above with fuscous wings that have fringes to coverts and remiges yellow, fringes of primaries duller and basally white, contrasting with black primary-coverts. No wingbars, leading fringes of coverts yellow but tips plain. Head dark olivaceous-grey, with a fuzzy eye-ring. Throat pale grey, greyish-olive breast and sides, rest of underparts yellow. Major risk of confusion is with Yellow-olive and Grey-crowned Flycatchers. In plumage, Yellow-olive has evenly marked remiges and a white supraloral spot, Yellow-margined yellow fringes to remiges finer and primaries less yellow with whitish base to primaries, and lacks white supraloral; bill dark above and cold marble below. Grey-crowned is smaller, lacks supraloral, is more yellowish-green above, has all-black bill and prefers drier habitat. In field, all three look alike below, though *assimilis* is slightly greyer.

Ssp. *T. a. examinatus* (SE Ve, Gu, FG) olive crown and very dull olive breast; juvenile dark drab olive above with cinnamon wingbars; pale greyish-olive below lightly flammulated creamy yellow, with creamy yellow central belly

T. a. flavotectus (NW Ec, W Co) pale grey throat and grey breast, yellow fringes to greater wing-coverts

T. a. neglectus (E Co, SW Ve) olive crown and dull olive breast; juvenile duller above and yellow fringes to wing-feathers very narrow with no wingbars; darker on head with a vestigial eye-ring, slightly buffy on throat, olive-green flammulations on flanks broader than adult

T. a. obscuriceps (NE Ec, SE Co) greyish-olive crown

Habits Usually forages in pairs, almost always with mixed flocks of antbirds at mid levels of forests. Fairly active, tends to perch fairly horizontally, cocks tail occasionally. Nest a hanging bag, mostly *Marasmius* fibres and constructed at mid levels, in open spots of understorey in undisturbed forest.

Status Uncommon in Ecuador. Frequent in Colombia, Guyana and French Guiana.

Habitat Tropical Zone, to 750m in Ecuador, 800m in Colombia and 1,200m in Venezuela. Interior of *terra firme*, humid forests, occasionally at borders.

Voice Race *flavotectus* in Ecuador gives harsh emphatic series of short notes, *zhweyk, zhwek-zhwek-zhwek-zhwek* with characteristic slight pause after slightly lower piched first note (R&G). In Colombia, common call (presumably *flavotectus*) is *zhweek, zhweek, zhweek* or *tsish, tsish, tsish*, followed by pause of several seconds before being repeated (H&B). Fitzpatrick gives song as leisurely series of 3–5 nasal buzzy whistles, ascending in pitch and shrill, *weeeuw weeeu weee* or *znuuznuu znuuu, znuuu-pik*, latter also given by Hilty for Venezuela.

Notes Given English name of Zimmer's Flatbill in Hilty and R&G. Race *flavotectus* recognised as separate species by R&G, Yellow-margined Flatbill, based on its radically different voice. In Rodner *et al.*, we listed *T. a. obscuriceps* for Suriname, but Haverschmidt & Mees (1994) found all existing records to relate to *T. sulphurescens cherriei*.

GREY-CROWNED FLYCATCHER

Tolmomyias poliocephalus Pl. 195

Identification 11-12 cm. Smaller than similar flycatchers with an all-black bill. Olivaceous-green above, fuscous wings with narrow yellow fringes to coverts and remiges. Primaries fringed paler yellowish, becoming white basally and contrasting with blackish primary-coverts. Head grey without supraloral and narrow eye-ring. Throat greenish, breast and flanks olive, rest yellow. Eyes pale greyish-brown. Major confusion with Yellow-margined and Yellow-olive Flycatchers, but Yellow-olive has evenly marked remiges and white supraloral, Yellow-margined has finer yellow fringes to remiges and primaries less yellow with whitish bases, lacks white pince-nez, and bill is dark above and cold marble below. Grey-crowned smaller, more yellowish-green above, with all-black bill and prefers drier habitat. In field, all three look alike below, though *assimilis* is slightly greyer.

Ssp. *T. p. klagesi* (CE Ve) greyish-olive above, eye-ring yellowish-white and dull greyish-white throat grades into breast flammulated grey and yellow, with yellow belly to undertail-coverts; breast-sides olivaceous-grey, to flanks and sides; bill black above, bone white below; juvenile duller above, creamy yellow below, with dull thighs and undertail-coverts (yellow in adult)

T. p. poliocephalus (E Ec, SE Co, SW Ve) as described, like Yellow-olive Flycatcher but smaller, with smaller bill

T. p. sclateri (Guianas) back duller green, crown uniform grey, pale greyish-white throat, underparts pale yellow; generally duller above and paler below; juvenile slightly greyer below, but virtually identical to adult

Habits Forages at mid levels and in subcanopy but most often in canopy, frequently with mixed flocks. Breeds in dry season. Takes flies, beetles, gnats and other insects. Bag-shaped nest has entrance hole near bottom and is usually suspended from vine or horizontal branch in a clearing or at forest edge, almost always near a wasp nest.

Status Uncommon to fairly common in Ecuador. Frequent in Guyana, common in Suriname, frequent in French Guiana.

Habitat Lower Tropical Zone, to 600m in Ecuador, 500m in Colombia and 1,000m in Venezuela. Forests, from marshy or humid to drier, deciduous and savanna woodland, preferring *várzea* and second-growth *terra firme*, coffee plantations, gardens and parks.

Voice Distinctive series of high whistles. Song of *poliocephalus* in Ecuador a repeated, inflected, somewhat wheezy *fiwee?* Sometimes given at intervals of 1–2 s, at other times in a short series, then a pause (R&G). In Colombia (Amazonas) a somewhat wheezy, rising, high-pitched whistle, *fweee!* (H&B), or a series of soft, inflected whistles *pchoi-pchoi-pchoi* (J. V. Remsen in H&B). In Venezuela *klagesi* gives a leisurely, slightly husky series, *teeawe…teeawe..teeawe.teawe*, which tends to accelerate. Dawn song often repeated over and over for several minutes (Hilty). In Guianas, *sclateri* utters a very different, flatter, piping series of 5–6 whistles, *pfee… pfee… pfee… pfee…* with last 3 notes often higher pitched (Hilty).

Note Given name Grey-crowned Flatbill in Hilty and R&G.

YELLOW-BREASTED FLYCATCHER

Tolmomyias flaviventris Pl. 195

Identification 12–12.5 cm. Bright yellowish-olive from forehead to lower back, wings and tail dusky to fuscous, fringes of wing-coverts and remiges yellow with 2 wingbars; supraloral and slight eye-ring ochraceous, face dull ochraceous-olive, yellow below with warm olive wash on breast. Bill dark above, below pale (marble or bone, occasionally flesh). Juvenile both duller and slightly darker above, with wings like adult; throat and breast paler brownish-yellow, rest of underparts sulphur-yellow flammulated white. From all congeners by crown concolorous with back and all-yellow underparts. Fairly similar Yellow Tyrannulet has clear yellow superciliary.

Ssp. *T. f. aurulentus* (N Co, NW Ve) compared to *collingwoodi*, evenly pale greenish-yellow back and crown with occasional yellow streaks and fringes, supraloral clear and bold, warmer on breast, often flushed slightly peach

T. f. collingwoodi (E Co, C, N & E Ve, T&T, Guianas) many have soft, irregular grey scalloping on mantle, supraloral weak, cleaner and slightly more greenish below

T. f. dissors (SW Ve) darker, more olive-green above, supraloral weak, base of bill orange

T. f. viridiceps (E Ec, SE Co) pure green above, yellow loral streak vestigial, throat and breast washed greenish

Habits Forages alone or in pairs, mostly in canopy, but may be found at mid levels, rarely lower, gleaning in foliage. Found in mixed flocks occasionally, but also in lightly wooded areas where mixed flocks do not occur (Fitzpatrick). Perches fairly upright. Takes flies, bees, gnats, beetles and other flying insects. Female constructs ball nest with entrance spout that arches to open near bottom, similar to a retort; usually hung from end of very high branch and often near a wasp nest.

Status Fairly common to common in Ecuador, frequent to locally common in Colombia. Common in Trinidad and Tobago, frequent in Guyana, common in northern Suriname. Locally frequent in north-west French Guiana.

Habitat Lower Tropical Zone, mostly below 800m in Ecuador, to 500m in Colombia and 900m in Venezuela, only in coastal regions of Suriname and French Guiana. Mangroves, coffee plantations, parks and gardens, clearings with scattered trees. Shrubby borders and prefers *Cecropia*-rich second growth, streams and river islands.

Voice Song of *viridiceps* in Ecuador a series of 2–5 sharp shrill notes that gradually become louder (R&G), and a faster series of 3–4 rising *cheeyp* notes (Fitzpatrick). In Colombia, song an emphatic chirruping (H&M) or loud intermittent *surreep… surreep… surreep…* (J. Fitzpatrick in H&B). Hilty found all Venezuelan races to give same vocalisation: song 3–5 rather loud, penetrating whistles, *sweEP! ….sweEP! …sweEP!...* with a pause of 1+ s between notes; call a single *sweEP*! Race *collingwoodi* apparently gives sequences of 2 notes on Trinidad, *peeeet* or *peeeit*, but sequences of 3 notes on Tobago (ffrench).

Notes Fitzpatrick subsumed *collingwoodi* within *aurulentus* without explanation, but our series of 235 specimens of these 2 suggests separation is justified. Given name Ochre-lored Flycatcher by Hilty. West Amazonian race *viridiceps* given species status by R&G, under name Olive-faced Flatbill, following Bates *et al.* (1992) on account of plumage and vocal differences.

ORANGE-EYED FLYCATCHER

Tolmomyias traylori Pl. 195

Identification 13.5cm. Dark olive-green above with somewhat darker wings and tail, yellowish fringes to feathers afford 2 wingbars, grey crown with dark lores and pale buffy supraloral, throat whitish-buff and breast ochraceous-buff, rest of underparts yellow to creamy-buff on undertail-coverts. Bill dark, eyes pale orange.

Ssp. Monotypic (E Ec, SE Co)

Habits Forages at mid levels, alone, in pairs and sometimes with mixed flocks. Sallies to pick insects and spiders from leaves. Both adults feed young at nest.
Status Rare in Ecuador, possibly frequent in Colombia, where specimens from at least 2 localities.
Habitat Tropical Zone, to 300m. Subcanopy of *várzea* and riverine forest. Range, as presently known, suggests possibility that this and *T. sulphurescens insignis* replace each other in river-edge habitats.
Voice Song a series of (3–8) short notes, each rising sharply in intensity and slightly in pitch (Schulenberg & Parker 1997). Call a distinctive 2-parted and buzzy *wheeeeezzz-birrt* or *psi-trrrrrrrr*, given at rather long intervals sometimes with a few other buzzy notes appended. Song also described as a series of 5–7 well-enunciated *zhreee* notes, fairly similar to race *viridiceps* of Yellow-breasted Flycatcher, but notes somewhat longer and wheezier (R&G).
Note Recently described (Schulenberg & Parker 1997).

Spadebills are chubby little birds with grossly disproportionately broad bills, long stiff rictal bristles and short tails. Generally brown above and pale yellow below, they have partially concealed contrasting coronal patches. They forage in understorey, where they dart up to scoop an insect from the underside of a leaf, but generally do not join mixed-species flocks. Despite beng rather active, they are fairly inconspicuous.

CINNAMON-CRESTED SPADEBILL

Platyrinchus saturatus Pl. 195

Identification 9.4cm. Dull little bird, brownish from forehead to tail, with cinnamon coronal patch that may be partially concealed, buffy-white supraloral and eye-ring, white throat, rest of underparts sulphur-yellow, washed olive on breast-sides and flanks. Female is similar but has coronal patch less developed and perhaps slightly duller; juvenile lacks coronal patch altogether.

Ssp. *P. s. saturatus* (E Co, S Ve, Guianas)

Habits Not well known. Forages alone, mostly low but occasionally up to mid levels. Sometimes follows mixed flocks but remains in understorey.
Status Rare in Ecuador and Colombia, locally uncommon to frequent in Venezuela, uncommon in Guyana, frequent and widespread in southern Suriname and scarce in French Guiana.
Habitat Tropical Zone, to 300m in Colombia and 900m in Venezuela. Humid, sandy soil forest, marshy woodland, tangles of vines and thickets, treefall gaps.
Voice Repetitions of a single sharp note: *chit... chit... chit... chit...* (H&M), and a distinct nasal *chip-it* or *squik-it* (Fitzpatrick). Song in our region unknown.

WHITE-THROATED SPADEBILL

Platyrinchus mystaceus Pl. 195

Identification 9.4cm. Tiny, olive-brown above with partially concealed golden-yellow coronal patch. Lores, stripe from behind eye around ear-coverts and running below eye all dark olive, supraloral, eye-ring, mesial and stripe on inner ear-coverts and cheeks buffy, depending on race. Throat white, well defined or less so, depending on race, breast warm buffy, to nearly cinnamon on sides and flanks, or yellow. Bill dark above, either dark or pale below, again depending on race. Female similar but coronal patch absent, though sometimes has single, elongated cream feather; juvenile sometimes more rufescent above than adult and throat and breast paler and tinged greyish, though mostly indistinguishable from adult female. Similar Golden-crowned Spadebill has black-edged coronal patch and dingy yellow throat. Races form 2 groups, the *albogularis* group in Middle America and Andes which has lower mandible dark; and nominate from the lowlands and tepuis which has lower mandible pale to white.

Ssp. Group (a):

P. m. albogularis (W Ec, Co: W Andes) back dull brownish-olive, much darker than *neglectus* and wing-feather fringes rufous, white throat cleanly divided from breast which is rich yellowish, belly whitish, dark lower mandible with white tip

P. m. neglectus (Co, Ve: Táchira) paler and more olivaceous above than *albogularis*, with coronal patch less obscured and fringes of wing-coverts much less rufous, bright pale yellow below with less buffy on breast than *albogularis*

P. m. perijanus (W Ve) dull white throat, almost pale grey, breast dirty or dingy, slightly flammulated olive and ochraceous, pale sulphur-yellow flanks, olivaceous upperparts otherwise like *albogularis*

P. m. zamorae (E Ec) similar to *albogularis* but back slightly rufescent, and wing-feathers fringed rufous; paler below, more creamy, tinged buffy only at sides, mandible has distinctly grey tip

Group (b):

P. m. duidae (S Ve, Gu, FG?) greenish-olive back like *insularis* but slightly darker, white throat contrasts cleanly with warm buffy breast

P. m. imatacae (E Ve) mid greenish olive-brown above, crown slightly tinged grey, almost uniform pale below, throat tinged creamy yellow, no buffy on breast, just a gentle wash, sides, flanks and belly pale yellowish with faint wash of ochre and olive

P. m. insularis (N Ve, T&T) greenish-olive above, throat slightly yellowish, breast has buffy-ochre wash over yellow, rest of underparts yellow; 8 of 50 birds examined had all-dark bills, unrelated to age or sex

P. m. ptaritepui (SE Ve) sepia above with rufous fringes to wing-feathers, white throat contrasts well with warm ochraceous breast which merges into warm yellow belly

P. m. ventralis (Ve: Neblina) sepia back slightly darker than of *ptaritepui*, with rufous fringes to wing-feathers, bright yellow coronal patch, pure white throat contrasts with rich ochre wash below, almost pure cinnamon, extending to undertail-coverts

Habits Forages alone, very quietly, at low levels and may perch for long periods. Picks insects from undersides of leaves by sallying quickly usually from a well-covered perch in understorey. Sometimes joins understorey mixed-species flocks. Constructs sturdy little cup nest of fine fibres, in fork at low height.

Status Uncommon in Ecuador, uncommon to frequent in Colombia and Venezuela. Uncertain in Guyana, uncommon in Trinidad & Tobago, and French Guiana (only sight records).

Habitat Tropical to Subtropical Zones, mostly 600–2,000m on west slope and 1,000–2,000m on east side; in Colombia mostly 900–2,000m, occasionally lower on west slope, and in Venezuela reaches 1,800m. Humid and wet forests and mature second growth.

Voice Rarely calls or sings, a sharp *squeep!* or *skip!* is most often heard in Venezuela, and song is an arcing feeble trill *pe'e'e'e'e'e'e'e'e'e'e'e't*, recalling an insect buzz (H&B). Song lower pitched and more nasal than Golden-crowned Spadebill (J. Fitzpatrick in Hilty). Song on east slope of Ecuador an ascending, rattled trill (R&G).

GOLDEN-CROWNED SPADEBILL

Platyrinchus coronatus Pl. 195

Identification 8.5–9cm. Olive above with rich chrome-yellow coronal patch that becomes cinnamon at fringes, the whole edged broadly with black; lores, stripe behind eye and around ear-coverts, and running down from eye all black; supraloral, eye-ring, mesial and stripe on inner ear-coverts pale yellowish-white. Throat pale, slightly dingy whitish-yellow and underparts straw yellow with slight greenish-grey flush to sides and flanks. Bill blackish above, pale yellow below. Female has coronal patch entirely orange-cinnamon. Juvenile more greyish above, with rufous fringes to wing-feathers and lacks coronal patch altogether. From similar White-throated Spadebill by black edge to coronal patch.

Ssp. *P. c. coronatus* (E Ec, SE Co, SW Ve) as described
P. c. gumia (SE Ve, Guianas) smaller with brighter yellow belly
P. c. superciliaris (W Co, NW Ec, Ve: N Amazonas) brighter yellow below

Habits Forages alone, in pairs or small family groups, in shaded understorey, at low and mid levels. Picks insects and spiders from leaves by sallying from perch. Does not follow mixed flocks. Constructs tiny cup nest of moss and fine fibres, in fork at low height.

Status Uncommon in Ecuador. In Colombia and Venezuela, locally uncommon to frequent, especially in *várzea*. Uncommon in Guyana, scarce but widespread in southern Suriname and quite frequent in French Guiana.

Habitat Lower Tropical Zone, mostly to 700m in Ecuador but recorded to 1,650m, to 900m west of Andes in Colombia and 400m on east side. In Venezuela reaches 1,500m. Humid *terra firme* and *várzea* forests.

Voice Song an extended but rather weak and colourless, high-pitched but rising and falling trill, easily passed over as an insect (R&G). Fitzpatrick gives opposite structure; *se'e'e' e'e'e'r'r'r'r'e'e'e* or *bzee-eee-eép*, descending in pitch slightly in middle and rising at end. At dawn, sings *se'e'e'e'e'e'a'a'a'e 'e'e'pip! pip!* (H&B). For Suriname, call a high-pitched trill: *t,r,r,r,r,reee-hee* (H&M).

YELLOW-THROATED SPADEBILL

Platyrinchus flavigularis Pl. 195

Identification 10.2cm. Olive above with darker tail and wings which have faint rufous fringes to feathers, rufous-olive crown with large irregular white coronal patch in male, black fringes distally, white appearing cut off; yellowish loral spot, throat bright pale yellow, with olive-green breast and yellow underparts. Male has throat slightly richer yellow with hint of orange, on female and juvenile yellow is pure. Bill dark above, yellow below. Female has very little white in crown, with hint of yellow, juvenile almost no white at all and crown is mixed with olive of back and merges seamlessly from nape to mantle.

Ssp. *P. f. flavigularis* (NE Ec, Co: E Andes) as described
P. f. vividus (W Ve) generally paler with less olive on breast

Habits Forages alone, inconspicuously and mostly in undergrowth. Flits quietly and abruptly between branches. Often sits motionless on an exposed perch.

Status Rare in Ecuador and Colombia, but possibly more common locally in north-west Venezuela.

Habitat Lower Subtropical to Temperate Zones, 750–1,700m in Ecuador, 1,800–2,300m in Colombia and 1,250–2,100m in Venezuela. Undergrowth of humid and wet forests of upper montane slopes.

Voice A sharp *peeeyr*, typically repeated every 4–5 s (R&G).

WHITE-CRESTED SPADEBILL

Platyrinchus platyrhynchos Pl. 195

Identification 11.4cm. Amazonian species, larger and proportionately chubbier than other spadebills in our region, with the broadest bill. Deep rufous-brown above with wings slightly darker and deep tawny fringes; head grey with large white coronal patch, partially concealed, pale supraloral spot and small eye-ring; chin and throat pure white, contrasting with all-cinnamon breast and underparts. Bill dark above, pale below. Female has less white in crown and brighter uppertail-coverts. Juvenile has rufous fringes to greater coverts, forming ragged wingbar, and narrow paler rufous fringes to all other wing-feathers.

Ssp. *P. p. platyrhynchos* (E Co, S Ve, Guianas?) all-cinnamon breast
P. p. senex (E Ec) pale cinnamon below, washed greyish-brown on breast

Habits Forages alone or in pairs, mostly at mid levels. Not known to join mixed flocks. Tends to perch in dense foliage, making short sorties upwards to snatch insects from undersides of leaves. Confiding. Constructs very small cup nest, anchored to fork in an understorey sapling.
Status Rare in Ecuador and Colombia, uncommon to locally fairly common in Venezuela, uncommon in Guyana, scarce in Suriname, quite rare in French Guiana.
Habitat Tropical Zone, to 300m. Open understorey of humid, sandy soil forests.
Voice Sharp 4 s repetitions of a *spip!*, note reminiscent of *Sclerurus*, and sometimes a short arcing buzz like a small engine (H&B) or burry trill that gradually rises in pitch, becoming louder, before falling at end. Singing birds have display-flight in which they angle steeply down before recovering another perch with manakin-like wing-whirr. Most frequent call an explosive *skeep!* or *skeeuw!* given every 2 s (R&G). For Suriname, described calls include dry *kyuk… kyuk…* in contact and more musical *tyweep… tyweep…* (H&M).

Royal flycatchers are large, comparatively short-legged birds that seldom raise their crests except when displaying in territorial defence or threat, as well as in courtship and post-copulation. However, they seem to raise the crest readily when handled. The laid-back crest extends beyond the nape, lending a fairly unique hammerhead or woodpecker-like appearance. At rest may perch rather horizontally. They have long, noticeable rictal bristles. Birds of undergrowth in lowland forests, all nest in long, rambling structures of woven straw and plant fibres wrapped around a drooping limb. Near the bottom is a small chamber with a side entrance, replete with a long 'tail' that may serve as an anchor in wind. *Onychorhynchus* formerly contained the various forms within a single species *O. coronatus*, but the various subspecies (including *swainsoni* in Brazil) have more recently been recognised as 4 species (AOU 1998, Collar *et al.* 1992, 1994, R&G).

When the crest is raised, the head is twisted sideways and up and down

AMAZONIAN ROYAL FLYCATCHER

Onychorhynchus coronatus Pl. 194

Identification 15–16.5cm. Deep umber-brown above with soft whitish spots, basally bordered black, at tips of wing-coverts and tertials, lower rump buffy, becoming bright cinnamon on short uppertail-coverts and rufous on tail, darkest at tip. Long, crimson crest with large black spot broadly bordered violet-blue at tip of each feather. Head-sides grizzled ochraceous-buff and brown, with underparts same ochraceous-buff, finely barred brown from throat to breast and sides. Legs yellow. Female differs in having crest cinnamon-orange, but is otherwise similar. Juvenile has entire upperparts barred slightly darker brown, extending over rump to tip of tail; terminal black and white spots on wing-coverts much larger, forming 2 bars; slightly shorter crest is bright orange, and each feather carries a black-and-blue spot. Below, slightly darker than adult, with barring darker and more heavy; legs and feet brown.

Ssp. *O. c. coronatus* (S & E Ve, Guianas) as described
O. c castelnaui (S Ve, SE Co, E Ec) distinctly different crest pattern, scarlet, grading to fiery orange at tip, black spots with much broader royal blue borders

Habits Easily missed as it forages quietly, occasionally in pairs, in understorey. Perches upright, tail held down. Occasionally follows mixed-species canopy flocks, but remains in understorey.
Status Rare to uncommon and local in Ecuador, uncommon in Colombia, locally frequent to common in Venezuela, uncommon in Guyana, Suriname and French Guiana.
Habitat Lower Tropical Zone, to 300m, occasionally to 400m in Ecuador and 1,200m in Colombia. In Venezuela restricted to upper Delta Amacuro, where main habitat is seasonally flooded riverine forest.
Voice Rarely vocalises. Calls include a sometimes excitedly repeated *preee-o* or *keee-you* whistle (R&G), and low-pitched *sur-lip*, reminiscent of a jacamar, sometimes repeated over and over (H&B). Also a 2-syllable *curr-lep*, slurred upwards (Hilty).

PACIFIC ROYAL FLYCATCHER

Onychorhynchus occidentalis Pl. 194

Identification 16.5cm. Cinnamon-brown above, with darker brown wings and soft whitish spots, basally bordered black, at tips of wing-coverts, and tertials, rump to tail pale cinnamon. Crest, invariably laid back and protruding beyond nape, scarlet with subterminal black spots, edged royal blue at tip of each long feather. Underparts paler cinnamon, richest on breast, palest on belly. Legs and feet yellow. Female differs by having red of crest yellow. Juvenile has entire upperparts barred slightly darker brown, extending over rump to tip of tail; terminal black and white spots on wing-coverts larger than in adult, forming 2 bars whilst slightly shorter crest is yellow, with each feather carrying a black-and-blue spot. Below, slightly darker than adult, with barring marginally heavier; legs and feet brown.

Ssp. Monotypic (W Ec)

Habits Alone or in pairs, foraging in undergrowth and at lower levels.

Status Endangered. Rare and local in Ecuador, where threatened by habitat loss.
Habitat Tropical Zone, below 600m in dry western lowlands. Drier or semi-humid deciduous and semi-deciduous forests, secondary woodland. Apparently shows no association with water (R&G).
Voice Calls similar to Amazonian Royal Flycatcher (R&T, R&G).

NORTHERN ROYAL FLYCATCHER

Onychorhynchus mexicanus Pl. 194

Identification 16–16.5cm. Dark brown above, with wings only slightly darker and soft buffy spots, basally bordered black, at tips of coverts, and tertials, rump to tail contrast strongly with back, being bright creamy buffy-yellow. Crest, which is invariably laid back protruding beyond nape, is crimson with subterminal black spots, edged blue-violet at end of each long feather. Underparts buffy-yellow, softly barred and mottled olive on breast, palest on belly. Legs and feet yellow. Female differs by having red of crest yellow-orange. Juvenile has entire upperparts barred slightly darker brown, extending over rump to tip of tail; terminal black and white spots on wing-coverts larger than in adult, forming 2 bars. Slightly shorter crest is pale orange, with each feather carrying a black-and-blue spot. Below yellowish-buffy, with barring slightly heavier than in adult; legs and feet brown.

Ssp. *O. m. fraterculus* (NE & N Co, NW Ve)

Habits Forages alone and in pairs during breeding season. Moves quietly in understorey, only occasionally higher. In Costa Rica, Slud (1964) found it accompanied mixed flocks, but Hilty states that while it might occasionally be seen within a flock it is as likely to be below. Forages on wing, making dashing sallies that resemble a redstart, taking insects with a snap, and with hanging head and tail flutters indirectly to land on another perch some distance from where it took off (Slud).
Status Uncommon in Colombia, uncommon to locally frequent in Venezuela.
Habitat Lower growth of forest borders and second-growth woodland, near streams in lowlands and occasionally in foothills, to 1,100m (Ridgely & Gwynne 1989). In Belize forages at mid levels to subcanopy (Jones 2003).
Voice Very quiet, occasionally gives series of *cur-lip* notes at *c.*1 per s (Hilty). Call, *eonk!* and song (in Belize) *duh whew whew whew whew…* (Jones 2003). A squeaky to hollow, plaintive *whee-uk'* or *see-uk'*, suggesting a muffled jacamar. Song (in Middle America) a descending series of plaintive whistles, usually 5–8, following a shorter introductory note, *whi' peeu peeu peeu peeu…* or *wh' wheeu wheeu…*(Howell & Webb 1995).

ORNATE FLYCATCHER

Myiotriccus ornatus Pl. 196

Identification 11.5cm. Head grey, slate to blackish on top with partially concealed rich yellow coronal patch, palest on throat, and contrastingly white preocular spot, back greenish-olive, rump and short uppertail-coverts golden-yellow, long uppertail-coverts and basal half of tail bright rufous, becoming fuscous distally; wings dusky with buffy fringes to feathers; breast olive, becoming golden-yellow over rest of underparts.

Ssp. *M. o. ornatus* (N Co: C & E Andes) easily recognised by 2-tone tail
M. o. phoenicurus (S Co: E Andes, E Ec) tertials and secondaries edged rufous, tail all bright cinnamon
M. o. stellatus (W Ec, W Co) long uppertail-coverts and tail dark brown

Status Common in Ecuador, locally frequent in Colombia.
Habitat Tropical to Subtropical Zones, 350–2,000m on west slope in Ecuador, from 500m on east, but usually 800–2,000m; 400–2,300m on Pacific slope in Colombia, 600–2,300m elsewhere. Very humid, wet or cloud forests and mature second growth on Pacific slope of Andes; at borders, in clearings such as old treefalls, and along streams, particularly in dark ravines.
Voice Frequently uttered is a high, sharp *peet!*, and sometimes a fast run of blurry *skeep* notes (H&B), also *peek!* and *wheep!* (Fitzpatrick), oft-repeated.

FLAVESCENT FLYCATCHER

Myiophobus flavicans Pl. 197

Identification 12–13cm. Olive above, wings dark brown with fairly broad rufous fringes and tips producing 2 wingbars and near block of rufous on remiges; partially concealed yellow or orange coronal patch varies with race, and broken eye-ring; underparts yellow, flushed and flammulated olive on breast and sides, warm buffy wash on flanks. Bill dark above, pale below. Female similar but lacks coronal patch. Juvenile also lacks coronal patch, is duller above and slightly paler below, and lacks warm buffy wash of adults on flanks. Similar Orange-crested Flycatcher has complete eye-ring, less noticeable preocular spot and an orange crest. Posture and shape rather like boreal migrant Alder and Acadian Flycatchers.

Ssp. *M. f. caripensis* (E Ve: Turimiquire Range) more yellow below, with olive less extensive
M. f. flavicans (Co, Ec) coronal patch yellow to orange
M. f. perijanus (NE Co, Ve: Perijá & Tamá) like *flavicans* but all-dark bill and orange coronal patch
M. f. venezuelanus (N Ve) crown patch yellow and underparts less flammulated; bill black above and lower mandible brown

Habits Forages alone or in pairs, at low to mid levels. Preferred foraging haunts variously mostly forest borders (H&B) or mostly forest interior (R&G). Shy and mostly quiet, occasionally calls at dawn but rarely during day.
Status Uncommon to rare in Ecuador, locally frequent in Colombia and Venezuela.
Habitat Tropical to Subtropical Zones, 1,300–2,500m in Ecuador, 1,200–2,700m in Colombia, and 1,300–2,300m, occasionally to 900m in Venezuela. Humid, wet and cloud

forests, on mossy slopes where branches and trunks are thick with epyphites, or in dense stands of bamboo.
Voice Call a sharp *tsink!* (Hilty). Song a fast rhythmic series of 5–8 *kawick* notes (P. Coopmans).

ORANGE-CRESTED FLYCATCHER
Myiophobus phoenicomitra Pl. 197

Identification 11.5–13cm. Dark olive above, wings and tail dusky, 2 rather dull rufous wingbars and fringes to tertials, complete yellow eye-ring, partially concealed orange coronal patch is almost red to golden-yellow, underparts all yellow with olive flush and flammulations. Bill black above, pale yellowish below. Somewhat sympatric with Flavescent Flycatcher, but at lower altitudes; separated by complete eye-ring and weak preocular spot, 2-tone bill (all black in Flavescent) and darker, more greenish back.

Ssp. *M. p. litae* (W Ec, W Co: W Andes) smaller, brighter rufous wingbars and brighter yellow below
M. p. phoenicomitra (E Ec, E Co) as described

Habits Forages in border thickets as well as in underbrush and open mid levels.
Status Uncommon to rare in Ecuador, frequent to uncommon (few records) and very local in Colombia.
Habitat Upper Tropical Zone, 600–1,550m in Ecuador, to 1,100m in Colombia. Humid and wet forests of lower slopes (occasionally to lower cloud forests). At borders.
Voice Call an ascending series of 3 buzzy chips, *bzip, bzip, bzip!* (H&B), or a weak, thin, high-pitched *tsut-tseép-tsu* (R&G).

[UNADORNED FLYCATCHER
Myiophobus inornatus] (not illustrated)

Listed erroneously in Rodner *et al.* for southern Ecuador, but only occurs from south-east Peru to northern Bolivia.

RORAIMAN FLYCATCHER
Myiophobus roraimae Pl. 197

Identification 13.2–13.5cm. Rich umber-olive above, duskier on wings and tail, but with rich rufescent-brown fringes to remiges and rectrices, 2 wingbars; coronal patch bright rufescent-brown bordered dusky, narrow yellowish-white eye-ring and slightly pale lores; throat and underparts yellowish-white, washed greyish-olive on breast, sides and flanks. Bill long, as are rictal bristles. Female lacks coronal patch but has dusky crown. Juvenile lacks coronal patch but has crown rufous-brown, concolorous with back; duller below, with more extensive and warmer olive-grey breast and sides, and yellow belly paler. Euler's Flycatcher lacks coronal patch and is less richly coloured.

Ssp. *M. r. roraimae* (SE Co, S Ve, W Gu) as described
M. r. rufipennis (E Ec) paler and warmer above
M. r. sadiecoatsae (S Ve) paler brown above with more reddish wingbars, paler on throat and lighter on breast

Habits Forages at mid levels and in subcanopy, often at edges.
Status Rare and very local in Ecuador; uncommon and very local in Colombia; uncommon in Venezuela; scarce and situation uncertain in Guianas.
Habitat Upper Tropical to Subtropical Zones, 1,100–1,700m in Andes, 1,300–1,800m in tepuis. Cloud, humid montane and tepui slope forests, scrub forest in sandy lowlands.
Voice Call of Venezuelan races unknown, voice described in Fitzpatrick as an explosive and buzzy series of spluttered *tschew* notes, rising and descending, with a softer sharp *pit* or *tschit*, sometimes doubled or tripled, and occasionally a sputtered series of chattering between individuals, *jjttt-jjjttt-jjttt-tschit* (possibly *rufipennis*).

HANDSOME FLYCATCHER
Myiophobus pulcher Pl. 197

Identification 9.5-11cm. Olive back with darker brown wings and tail, 2 distinct wingbars and fringes to tertials, head grey with partially concealed orange coronal patch (reduced, duller or absent in female and lacking in juvenile), pale lores that join full eye-ring; below yellow with warm ochraceous flush to throat and breast. Grey cap diagnostic compared to other *Myiophobus*; short tail and lack of rufous on head-sides separates it from Rufous-breasted Flycatcher. Orange-banded has longer tail, yellow coronal patch and noticeably whitish eyes.

Ssp. *M. p. bellus* (NE Ec, Co: C & E Andes) larger race, darker grey-green above, with rich ochraceous wingbars and full warm flush to breast that contrasts with paler yellow below
M. p. pulcher (NW Ec, SW Co: W Andes) smaller, pale ochraceous wingbars and richer, more uniform yellow below, with less well-marked breast

Habits Forages in canopy and subcanopy, sometimes at mid levels in edge shrubbery. Mostly with mixed canopy flocks, occasionally seen perched semi-concealed. Gleans busily or makes short sallies for insects.
Status Rare to locally frequent in Ecuador, common to frequent but spottily distributed in Colombia.
Habitat Subtropical Zone, 1,500–2,400m in Ecuador, 1,800–2,600m on Pacific slope in Colombia (to 800m in west Cauca) and 1,400–2,600m in east. Middle and upper levels of humid and wet montane forests, in mossy areas, sometimes at forest borders and in second growth.
Voice Song a bright *tsi-tsi-tsi* (R&G).

ORANGE-BANDED FLYCATCHER
Myiophobus lintoni Pl. 197

Identification 12.5–13cm. Dark brownish-olive above, wings and tail dusky, 2 strong cinnamon wingbars, partially concealed ochre-yellow coronal patch (dull brown or absent in female, lacking in juvenile), throat whitish, rest of underparts yellow, washed olive on breast. Bill black above and orange below; eyes appear whitish, but are actually greyish-yellow or pale yellow (also in juvenile). Yellow iris diagnostic compared to other *Myiophobus*.

Ssp. Monotypic (SE Ec; eastern slope)

Habits Forages busily in canopy, sometimes at mid levels, calling frequently.
Status Rare to locally frequent in Ecuador.
Habitat Upper Subtropical to Temperate Zones, 2,250–3,200m. Cloud, elfin, humid or wet montane forests, mature second growth, sometimes at fringes and landslide clearings.
Voice Incessant *chip* or *peeyk* notes, whilst dawn song consists of endlessly repeated *tsin* notes (F&K, R&G).

BRAN-COLOURED FLYCATCHER
Myiophobus fasciatus Pl. 197

Identification 11.4cm. Quite variable in coloration, but generally dark brown above with dusky wings and tail. Two well-defined wingbars are pale buffy to light rufous, regardless of age or sex. Semi-concealed bright yellow coronal patch, and whitish below with pale greyish-brown flush to breast, well streaked darker brown, and yellowish tinge to belly. Female has coronal patch smaller or absent, but given significant variation in size and colour of patch, this is not a reliable diagnostic; breast comparatively less heavily streaked. Juvenile distinct, paler and richer reddish-brown above, paler and brighter on rump where young female is particularly pale cinnamon; wingbars, fringes to remiges and uppertail-coverts rufous. Besides voice, streaked breast is a good field mark.

Ssp. *M. f. crypterythrus* (W Ec, SW Co) brownish-grey above with 2 rich rufous wingbars, and pale almost white fringes to tertials, breast fairly densely streaked brown
M. f. fasciatus (E Ec, Co, N & SE Ve, Tr, Guianas) more umber-brown above with 2 buffy-white wingbars and whitish tips to tertials

Habits Forages alone or in pairs, taking ants, termites, beetles, flies, bees and wasps with sallies or by gleaning. Also takes berries and may be found at fruiting bushes.
Status Uncommon to rare in Ecuador, locally frequent to uncommon in Colombia and Venezuela, uncommon in Trinidad (but unrecorded on Tobago), scarce in Guyana, rather common in Suriname and uncommon and local in French Guiana.
Habitat Tropical to Subtropical Zones, at 300–1,100m on east slope, to 1,500m in west. Borders of deciduous and humid forest, open areas with scattered bushes and trees, fallow fields, hedges and thickets.
Voice Varied calls and songs described: in contact, a soft *whisp*; melodious, leisurely trills or a fast *whee seety seety*; dawn song *wisk wee-wee-wee* (Wetmore, H&B) or *weé, wu-du…weé, wu-du*, or *jili-ju…* day song a rattled trill, *whee-yee-yee-yee-yee-yee* (Fitzpatrick).

OLIVE-CHESTED FLYCATCHER
Myiophobus cryptoxanthus Pl. 197

Identification 12.2cm. Dark olive above, wings and tail dusky with 2 well-defined pale wingbars, greyish olive-brown crown with well-concealed pale yellow coronal line, throat whitish, rest of underparts yellow, streaked grey-brown on breast and sides. Could be mistaken for Bran-coloured Flycatcher, but more yellowish below and, where sympatric, Bran-coloured is markedly more rufescent.

Ssp. Monotypic (E Ec)

Habits Forages alone or in pairs, at mid to low levels. Perches upright. Sallies to catch insects, both in air and from foliage. Not noisy or obvious, and easily missed.
Status Local and uncommon to rare in eastern Ecuador.
Habitat Tropical to Lower Subtropical Zones, 400–1,400m. Borders and clearings of humid light woodland, second growth and fields with scattered bushes.
Voice Call a cheery *weee d'd'd'd'd'*; dawn song a long series of *chwee… chwee… chwee…* (P. Coopmans *fide* R&G).

RUDDY-TAILED FLYCATCHER
Terenotriccus erythrurus Pl. 196

Identification 10.9cm. Small cinnamon flycatcher, though back and head actually greyish, wings slightly darker brown with 2 cinnamon wingbars, rump bright cinnamon and tail rufous; slight pale eye-ring, cheeks buffy and throat pale, slightly greyish, underparts cinnamon, slightly paler on undertail-coverts. Bill short, black above, yellowish below; eyes large and dark; legs and feet horn-coloured. Juvenile generally brighter, tail darker distally with dark tip, and breast washed olive. From Cinnamon Flycatcher by wingbars and horn-coloured legs and feet; Cinnamon has grey legs and feet. Also, Cinnamon Flycatcher perches on exposed branches of forest edge, whilst Ruddy-tailed Flycatcher is more a bird of forest interior.

Ssp. *T. e. erythrurus* (SE Ve, Guianas) cinnamon below
T. e. fulvigularis (NW Ec, N & W Co, W & NC Ve) bright orange-buff below
T. e. signatus (E Ec, E Co) throat whitish-buff
T. e. venezuelensis (extreme E Co, S Ve) paler grey-olive on crown and back

Habits Usually forages alone, sometimes with mixed flocks, in undergrowth, gleaning insects from foliage or sometimes picking them from air. May perch quietly for long periods, often flagging both wings at once with quick flick. Constructs dark bag-shaped nest with a side entrance, suspended from a vine or tip of a branch.
Status Uncommon in Ecuador, frequent in Colombia and Guyana, fairly common in Venezuela, locally frequent in Suriname and French Guiana.
Habitat Tropical Zone, to *c.*1,000m throughout our region. Usually at edge of savanna and humid lowland forest or mature second growth.
Voice Call an prolonged whistle, followed by a short trill (H&M), also a high double-note whistle, *tsee, peet*, or a long, descending single *peeeeea* (H&B). Call repeated at dawn, a high, thin rather faint *teeu-téép!* Song insect-like, though

slightly more musical, a relatively soft, clear penetrating series of 6–7 high thin whistles, first 2–3 louder, then accelerating and ascending in pitch, *keek, keek, eek-eek-eek-eek-eek*; occasionally rising then falling, *wi wi wi keek…keek, keek keek keek keek*. Also an urgent *pee peew peew peew peew peew* during interactions (Fitzpatrick).

Note Removed from *Terenotriccus* to *Myiobius* by Lanyon (1988) and *Terenotriccus* found to be monophyletic with *Myiobius* by Mobley & Prum (1995), but thereafter *erythrurus* was considered sufficiently different from other *Myiobius* to merit recognition at generic level by AOU (1998).

Myiobius is a distinctive genus of mid-sized flycatchers with blackish tails and contrasting bright yellow rumps, all very much alike. They have broad bills with long rictal bristles, are usually quiet or silent, but acrobatically hawk flying insects and frequently fan their tails. The latter is so constant that they might well be termed fan-tailed flycatchers. Forest birds that build hanging, pear-shaped bag nests, with an entrance hole at bottom, usually attached to the end of a branch and suspended over water. Habitat is often a key to field identification.

Sulphur-rumped Flycatcher; Myiobius *flycatchers frequently fan their tails like Australian* Rhipidura *fantails*

TAWNY-BREASTED FLYCATCHER

Myiobius villosus Pl. 196

Identification 14-15cm. Mid-sized flycatcher with contrasting yellow rump. Back and wings olive-brown, slight rufous fringes to feathers but no wingbars, rump bright sulphur-yellow, tail dusky to black, head olive-brown with an irregular and partially concealed yellow coronal patch, pale lores, whitish eye-ring extends slightly behind eye; neck-sides to breast and sides, thighs and undertail-coverts all ochraceous-tawny, centreal belly yellow. Female has coronal patch cinnamon or absent. Juvenile lacks coronal patch and is browner, less greenish-olive above and duller ochraceous below. From congeners by underparts, Black-tailed Flycatcher has buffy throat, Sulphur-rumped Flycatcher shows much more yellow on its belly.

Ssp. *M. v. clarus* (E Ec, SE Co) greener above
M. v. schaeferi (E Co: E Andes, W Ve) breast more intensely coloured giving impression of a band
M. v. villosus (W Ec, W Co, W Ve) as described

Habits Forages alone or in pairs, usually with mixed flocks, from mid levels to canopy. Lively and quick, flits from perch to perch, gleaning or sallying, and constantly fanning tail and flicking wings.

Status Uncommon to rare in Ecuador, uncommon in Colombia, local in Venezuela.

Habitat Upper Tropical to Subtropical Zones. Humid, wet and cloud forests, wooded montane slopes, along streams.

Voice Call a sudden, loud *espit!* similar to Whiskered Flycatcher (H&B).

SULPHUR-RUMPED FLYCATCHER

Myiobius sulphureipygius Pl. 196

Identification 12.5–13cm. Mid-sized flycatcher with contrasting yellow rump. Back and wings olive-brown, slight rufous fringes to feathers but no wingbars, rump bright sulphur-yellow, uppertail-coverts black and tail dusky to black, head olive-brown with an irregular and partially concealed yellow coronal patch, pale lores, cheeks greyish-buffy, whitish eye-ring extends slightly behind eye, breast, sides, thighs and undertail-coverts ochraceous-tawny, belly and undertail-coverts broadly yellow. Female has coronal patch cinnamon or absent. Juvenile lacks coronal patch and is browner, less greenish-olive above and duller ochraceous below. From congeners by underparts, Black-tailed Flycatcher has buffy throat, Tawny-breasted far less yellow on belly.

Ssp. *M. s. aureatus* (W Co, W Ec) as described
M. s. semiflavus (Co: Antioquia) rump more intense yellow (lemon-coloured), throat very pale yellow, breast and sides brighter soft greenish

Habits Forages in understorey, alone or in pairs and often with mixed flocks. Very active and quick, jumps from perch to perch or sallies to pick insects from foliage or air. Fans tail and flicks wings often, or drops wings to reveal yellow rump.

Status Uncommon and local in Ecuador, locally frequent in Colombia.

Habitat Tropical to Lower Subtropical Zones. Humid forest and mature secondary woodland, mostly in lowlands.

Voice Call a low, sharp *psit!* (H&B) or *psik!* (R&G). Song a clear series of 4–6 *tschew* notes or *tseeu tseeu tseeu tseer tseer*, quiet, rising then falling, remininscent of Dot-winged Antwren. Dawn song a rapid, repeated *chu-wee-da-wiit* or *chu wee-da-wit* (Fitzpatrick).

Notes Sometimes considered a race of *M. barbatus* but recognised specifically by AOU (1998). Race *aureatus* apparently considered by some to be separate species, race *semiflavus* not mentioned by Fitzpatrick.

WHISKERED FLYCATCHER

Myiobius barbatus Pl. 196

Identification 12.5–13cm. Mid-sized flycatcher with contrasting yellow rump. Back and wings olive-green, with fine rufous fringes to feathers but no wingbars, rump bright sulphur-yellow, uppertail-coverts black and tail dusky to black, head greenish-olive with an irregular and partially concealed yellow coronal patch, pale lores, cheeks pale greyish-olive, whitish eye-ring extends slightly behind eye, throat dirty white, rest of underparts pale yellow, washed olivaceous-grey on breast and sides. Female lacks coronal patch. Juvenile slightly browner above, uppertail-coverts same dusky as tail (not black) and lacks coronal patch; breast distinctly buffy-brown. From congeners by underparts, Black-tailed Flycatcher has buffy throat, Tawny-breasted shows far less yellow on belly, having an ochraceous wash covering flanks.

Ssp. *M. b. barbatus* (E Ec, SE Co, S Ve, Guianas)

Habits Forages at low to mid levels in undergrowth, usually with mixed-species flocks, gleaning or catching insects. Fans tail frequently. Nest a dishevelled, drop-shaped mass, attached to vertical vines, twigs or aerial roots, of grass, twigs, dead leaves, moss, and appears like a mass of vegetation rubbish.
Status Uncommon in Ecuador, frequent at many localities in Colombia, uncommon to fairly common in Venezuela, frequent in Guyana, rare to locally common in Suriname and common in French Guiana.
Habitat Tropical Zone, mostly below 600m in Ecuador but recorded to 1,300m, mostly below 1,000m in Colombia and Venezuela, with occasional records to 1,300m. Dry deciduous to humid *terra firme* forests.
Voice Call a clear *geet... geet... geet...* (H&M) or sharp *tsip* or *psik!* (Fitzpatrick).
Note Considered a separate species from *M. sulphureipygius* (AOU 1998).

BLACK-TAILED FLYCATCHER
Myiobius atricaudus Pl. 196

Identification 12.5–13cm. Mid-sized flycatcher with contrasting yellow rump. Back and wings olive-green, faint rufous fringes to feathers but no wingbars, rump bright sulphur-yellow, uppertail-coverts and tail black, head greenish-olive with irregular and partially concealed yellow coronal patch, pale lores, whitish eye-ring extends slightly behind eye, throat buffy-white merging into dull buffy-olive breast, rest of underparts pale yellow, but vary with subspecies. Female has coronal patch smaller or absent. Juvenile lacks coronal patch. From congeners by underparts, Whiskered Flycatcher has white throat contrasting with greyish-olive breast, Sulphur-rumped has rich ochraceous wash to breast and flanks, and Tawny-breasted has ochraceous wash covering breast, flanks and undertail-coverts.

Ssp. *M. a. adjacens* (E Ec, S Co) palest race with near-white rump
M. a. atricaudus (W Co) as described
M. a. modestus (SE Ve) breast-band tinged ochraceous
M. a. portovelae (W Ec) warm ochraceous breast, not on flanks, which with belly are bright yellow

Habits Forages mostly alone, often with mixed flocks, in understorey and occasionally in border thickets and bushes. Busy, agile and quick, gleans or sallies to pick insects. Fans tail occasionally. Constructs bag nest, always suspended over water.
Status Uncommon to rare in Ecuador, uncommon to locally frequent in Colombia, infrequent in Venezuela.
Habitat Tropical Zone, to 600m in Ecuador, 1,400m in Colombia and 200m in Venezuela. Borders of humid forest, lighter woodland, bushy fields and second growth, often near streams. More a bird of drier forest than Whiskered Flycatcher.
Voice Call a soft *whit* (R&G) or *tsit* (Hilty).

CINNAMON TYRANT
Neopipo cinnamomea Pl. 196

Identification 8.5–9cm. Tiny flycatcher resembling a manakin in shape (large, rounded head, large eyes) and posture. Above cinnamon-rufous with darker wings that have rufous fringes to feathers, creating 2 blurry wingbars, head grey with partly concealed bright yellow coronal patch that is difficult to see as bird is usually in mid canopy; entire underparts cinnamon; legs and feet grey, bill black above and orange below, and no rictal bristles. Female has coronal patch smaller and may be slightly duller overall. Easily mistaken for similar-sized Ruddy-tailed Flycatcher, which has much broader bill and long rictal bristles, but clinching difference is short yellow legs. Voice also useful in identification.

Ssp. *N. c. cinnamomea* (E Ec, extreme E Co, S Ve) as described
N. c. helenae (Guianas) face-sides and ear-coverts ash-grey, throat greyish-white (instead of cinnamon)

Habits Forages alone in undergrowth and at lower levels, sometimes with mixed flocks where observed with Ruddy-tailed Flycatcher. Perches still at lower and mid levels, upright and slightly hunched-looking.
Status Rare in Ecuador, scarce and poorly known in Colombia, uncommon in Venezuela, uncommon in Guyana, rare in Suriname (only 2 specimen records) and French Guiana. Easily overlooked and may well be under-reported.
Habitat Lower Tropical Zone, to 400m in Ecuador, 300m in Colombia and 200m in Venezuela. Humid *terra firme*, but possibly mainly in sandy soil forests; in eastern Venezuela in tropical humid forest.
Voice Descriptions vary: R&T mention a short, low-pitched *weeeeo* whistle, whilst (R&G) describe paced repetitions of a high-pitched *pseeeeu* whistle. A rising then falling and fading series of *psee* notes perhaps represents the song (R&G).
Notes Formerly placed in the Pipridae (manakins), under name Cinnamon Manakin (e.g. H&B) or Cinnamon Tyrant-Manakin, based mostly on lack of rictal bristles. DNA studies, by Mobley & Prum (1995), have found that it is more closely related to tyrant-flycatchers. Given English name Cinnamon Neopipo by Hilty, but referred to as Cinnamon Tyrant in R&G.

CINNAMON FLYCATCHER
Pyrrhomyias cinnamomeus Pl. 196

Identification 13cm. Quite unmistakable in range and habitat. Cinnamon-rufous above with orange-cinnamon band on lower rump, black wings with 2 broad rufous wingbars, rufous fringes to tertials and secondaries form large rufous patch; uppertail-coverts dusky with broad rufous fringes, tail dusky, also with some rufous edges; head darker brown (depending on race) with partially concealed yellow coronal patch. Below entirely cinnamon. Female slightly smaller with a smaller bill. Juvenile male has yellow in crown, female does not, and rump band rufous; feathers of lower back and uppertail-coverts lightly edged paler.

Ssp. *P. c. assimilis* (Co: Santa Marta) back orange-rufous and crown reddish-brown, olive band on upper rump, lower rump band orange-buff, tail rufous with dark subterminal band

P .c. pariae (NE Ve: Paria) deepest chestnut underparts, rump band rufous

P. c. pyrrhopterus (Ec, Co, W Ve) slightly smaller, distinctly olive above, and crown tinged olive, rump band cinnamon-creamy, uppertail-coverts black edged rufous

P. c. spadix (NE Ve) bright rufous fringes to secondaries join greater coverts wingbar to form solid patch of rufous on wing; differs from *vieillotoides* in having throat, belly and undertail-coverts paler, effectively leaving broad breast-band.

P. c. vieillotioides (NW Ve) bright rufous fringes to secondaries join greater coverts wingbar to form a solid patch of rufous on wing

Habits Forages at mid levels and in shrubbery, perching quite straight on horizontal twigs and sallying to catch passing insects or picking them from leaves. Usually in pairs that may join passing mixed flocks but apparently do not follow them. Sings continuously from perch and is usually heard before seen.

Status Common in Ecuador. In Colombia, one of the commonest flycatchers in mountains. Quiet common and widespread in Venezuela.

Habitat Upper Tropical to Temperate Zones, 1,200–3,000m in Ecuador, 1,500–2,700m in Colombia, and 700–2,900m in Venezuela. Humid or wet montane forests, cloud and elfin forests, coffee plantations and secondary woodland. At borders and clearings and along trails and roads through forest.

Voice A flat, low, sudden *pti-i-i-i-i-i* rattle and *pit, pit-pit-pit-pit* stuttering scold (H&B); a 1 s long *trrrrrrrt* rattling trill and *tjip tjip tjip*… flight-call (F&K).

CLIFF FLYCATCHER

Hirundinea ferruginea Pl. 196

Identification 18–19cm. Quite unmistakable large, slender flycatcher, but often very easily missed as it perches on rock faces, unless it suddenly makes a swallow-like sortie or vocalises. It is also swallow-like when perched. Dark brown above, from crown to tail; wings have cinnamon-rufous base to secondaries and primaries, forming roughly triangular shape on remiges. Underparts uniform cinnamon-rufous.

Ssp. *H. f. ferruginea* (E Co: Guainia & Vaupés, S & SE Ve, SW Gu, S Su, FG) crown to face-sides mottled brown, not really noticeable in field, white chin grades irregularly into cinnamon throat

H. f. sclateri (E Ec, Co: E Andes and Perijá, Ve: Perijá) white mottling on face forms superciliary and white chin contrasts abruptly with cinnamon-rufous underparts

Habits Singles, pairs or small groups, always near or on rocky escarpments sallying to pick passing insects or gliding and banking gracefully. Calls and chatters throughout day.

Status Highly fragmented range which, combined with its movements, makes its appearances fairly unpredictable. In Guianas, apparently moves between large bare rocky outcrops in otherwise continuous tracts of humid lowland forest. Resident in northern South America, but southern South American populations migratory with northern limits of winter range unknown. Comparatively recently recorded in Ecuador, where becoming established at rocky road cuts on east slope. Locally frequent in Colombia and Venezuela, uncommon and local in Guyana, frequent in southern Suriname and French Guiana.

Habitat Upper Tropical to Lower Subtropical Zones, 900–1,700m in Ecuador, to at least 1,500m in Colombia, 750–2,500m in Andes of Venezuela, but south of Orinoco from 100m to 1,900m. Invariably favours vertical rocky areas, e.g. cliffs, canyons, rock walls, tall road cuts, quarries, steep slopes of tepuis. Sometimes in cities, where associated with tall buildings.

Voice A twittering whistle (P&MdS); varied twittering *killy, killy, killy*… or *ka-lee, ka-lee, ka-lee*… chatter (H&B); repetitions of a 1 s excited *tee-trrr-rrr* (F&K); *wheeeyp* or *whee, dee, dee, ee, ee, ee* or *wheeuw-d'd'd'd'dr* (R&G). Dawn song a rapid, high, tinny *kit-ti-LEE*, repeated continually. Day calls similar but uttered singly, also an insistent *killy, killy, killy*… or *kaleé, kaleé, kaleé*… and other variations, all nasal, metallic and ringing. Some calls resemble a Bat Falcon, others a kestrel (Hilty).

FUSCOUS FLYCATCHER

Cnemotriccus fuscatus Pl. 198

Identification 14cm. Retiring inconspicuous flycatcher. Plain mid brown above with very slightly paler supraloral running into whitish superciliary and narrow eye-ring; wings slightly darker and browner with 2 variable wingbars (generally dull cinnamon), pale, dull yellowish throat and greyish-olive breast slightly flammulated pale sulphur-yellow, rest of underparts pale sulphur-yellow. Bill all black. Juvenile impossible to separate in field; slightly more powdery brown above and slightly paler below, yellow being more whitish. Wingbars are paler and buffier, but they are generally rather variable making this is an unreliable diagnostic. Race *cabanisi* easy to confuse with Euler's Flycatcher, having not only same plumage pattern and coloration, but same upright posture; however, comparatively larger with a slightly longer tail, and Euler's is also comparatively rare and is probably more likely to be mistaken for Fuscous Flycatcher than vice versa. Voice is key.

Ssp. *C. f. cabanisi* olive phase (N & E Co, NW to NE & E Ve: NE Bolívar, T&T) as described

C. f. cabanisi grey phase (C Ve: Orinoco belt) darker brown above, whitish throat, grey breast, extremely pale sulphur-yellow below (appears white)

C. f. duidae (S Ve: SW Amazonas) like *cabanisi* but warmer and slightly darker olive breast, lower mandible orange; juvenile has buffy wingbars, is flammulated yellow on breast and paler on belly; lower mandible flesh

C. f. fumosus (NE Ve: Delta Amacuro, Guianas) slightly larger, wingbars dull brown, bill all black, breast dark greenish-olive, lower breast and belly intense sulphur-yellow; juvenile has rufous back a shade paler, slightly paler below, wingbars slightly richer

C. f. fuscatior (SW Ve: Guasdualito, SE Co, E Ec: border with Peru) like *duidae*, but slightly denser brown above, and richer olive breast and richer sulphur-yellow below, wingbars brown, throat pale

Habits Perches quite upright and forages quietly in shady undergrowth, picking insects from foliage.

Status Uncommon in Ecuador, locally frequent in Venezuela, local in Trinidad, common in Tobago, uncommon in Guyana, frequent in coastal Suriname and French Guiana.

Habitat Tropical Zone, to 400m in Ecuador, 900m in Colombia and Venezuela north of Orinoco, but south of river to only 250m. In Ecuador, lower growth of riparian woodland and on river islands, but in Colombia, drier deciduous forest borders, shrubby second growth, humid forest and overgrown clearings. In Venezuela, varied habitats, including dry to humid forests, gallery forest, thickets along *várzea* forest creeks and dense vegetation on river islands. In Suriname restricted to dark undergrowth of swamp forests in coastal region.

Voice Most frequent call of *fuscatior* in Ecuador a low-pitched gravelly *wor, jeer- jeer- jeer- jeer- jeer- jeer-jew*, with number of *jeer* notes varying, lasting up to 2 s. Also a *wheeéeu* at more leisurely intervals (J. V. Moore recording, in R&G). In Colombia, dawn song an excited series of clear high notes, *p-pit-pit-PEED-it*, and full song *chip-weeti-weeti-weetiyee, chip-weety-weety-weety-cheetip* (J. Fitzpatrick in H&B). In Venezuela, a strident whistle, unexpectedly loud (P&MdS). Advertising-call a soft but explosive *feeew!* repeated irregularly, and song is a more repetitive *thew! thew! thew! thew! thew!* repeated up to 9 times. Agonistic call a louder and more explosive *whew! t't'-t't tue-he!* (D. Ascanio).

Notes Most authors comment that more than one species may be involved due to differences in vocalisations. In Venezuela, race *cabanisi* appears to have 2 colour morphs and this is currently being investigated by Restall & Lentino.

Lathrotriccus and *Empidonax* flycatchers are a confusing group that include some species virtually impossible to identify with certainty. The essential difference is that *Empidonax* are boreal migrants, and thus are normally found in our region only seasonally whilst *Lathrotriccus* are year-round resident, though southern populations of *euleri* move north to northern South America. Previously, all were included in *Empidonax*, but *euleri* is now known not to be an *Empidonax*, with *Lathrotriccus* being erected to embrace the South American residents (Zink & Johnson 1984, Lanyon & Lanyon 1986, Lanyon 1986).

EULER'S FLYCATCHER

Lathrotriccus euleri Pl. 198

Identification 13.5cm. Olive-brown above, wings dusky with 2 pale buffy wingbars and buffy fringes to tertials and secondaries, pale lores and superciliary and whitish eye-ring; throat pale greyish-white grading into light olive-brown on breast, belly white or pale yellow; eyes dark brown, bill dark above and flesh below, legs and feet dark. From *Empidonax*, with much difficulty, by very buffy wingbars and darker back. Willow and Alder Flycatchers never as brown and have white wingbars. Fuscous Flycatcher is larger (check location and habitat for race) and Euler's has distinctly darker breast. **Voice**, habitat (more in forest) and time of year (not a boreal migrant) also useful.

Ssp. *L. e. bolivianus* (E Ec, S Ve, migrant to SE Co) less olivaceous above, pale yellow belly

L. e. lawrencei (E Co, WN & C Ve, Tr, Su, FG) more olivaceous above, more yellowish belly

L. e. argentinus (not recorded) greyer breast and white belly

L. e. euleri (not recorded) brownish-olive breast, white belly with variable yellow flush

Habits Usually in undergrowth; forages alone, sallying for passing insects and flitting from perch to perch. Perches upright, flicks tail and calls often.

Status Rare in Ecuador, scarce and poorly known in Colombia, Uncommon to locally fairly common in Venezuela, uncommon in Trinidad (no records Tobago), uncommon and local in Guyana, rare in Suriname and very rare in French Guiana. Possible that southern races (*argentinus* and *euleri*) reach our region on migration, but neither yet recorded.

Habitat Tropical Zone. Humid and cloud forests, slopes of tepuis, cocoa and coffee plantations, light and secondary woodland, swampy forest.

Voice A shrill *PYEEW, pyeew, pyee hee hee* (H&M) or *chee, chi-wi-wi-wi-wi* (ffrench), or *peeeur, peer-per-per-peeur* (R&T), *peer, peeer-wheer* or *quee, di-di-di-di* (H&B) and *FEEEU! pe'pe'pe'p'p*, first note loudest, last notes buzzy and run together downscale (Hilty). Song in breeding season transcribed as *BEER dearlE*. Other weak and wavering calls, *seeeeeeoo – tee-tee, seeeeeeoo-teeteetee* and often a simple *cheeur* are best means of locating this inconspicuous species (W. Belton). In swamp forests of Venezuela and Suriname voice of this and that of Yellow-crowned Elaenia almost identical. Look for wingbars in Euler's and note song of latter is longer.

Notes Formerly placed in *Empidonax* (H&B, P&MdS). Race *flaviventris* is perhaps a separate species (Lawrence's Flycatcher: Banks 1997).

GREY-BREASTED FLYCATCHER

Lathrotriccus griseipectus Pl. 198

Identification 13–13.5cm. Greyish-olive above including tail, wings fuscous with 2 broad white wingbars and white fringes to tertials, head grey with white lores and broken white eye-ring, chin whitish, throat and breast soft grey, belly and underparts yellowish-white. Juvenile warmer, with buffy wingbars and more yellowish belly. From Tropical Pewee (race *punensis*) by white eye-ring and very prominent wingbars.

Ssp. Monotypic (SW Ec)

Habits Usually in woody vines and tangles. Forages in understorey and at mid levels. Calls most often during rainy season.

Status Generally uncommon to rare in Ecuador, but slightly more frequent at 2 sites, populations apparently declining due to loss of habitat.

Habitat Tropical Zone to 1,700m. Moist to fairly dry deciduous and semi-deciduous forests.

Voice Resembles Euler's, fast varying sequences of burry notes, e.g. *peeeur, peer-per-per-pur* (R&T) and *zhweeur zhweer-zhwer-zhwer* (R&G).

Note Formerly placed in *Empidonax*, but as similar to *L. euleri* in voice, form and behaviour moved to *Lathrotriccus*. Also, see Parker *et al.* (1995).

BLACK-BILLED FLYCATCHER

Aphanotriccus audax Pl. 198

Identification 13–13.5cm. Greenish-olive above, with greyish tinge to head, tail brown, wings dusky with 2 pale buffy wingbars and fringes to tertials, whitish lores and slight superciliary and eye-ring; whitish throat, underparts pale yellow washed olive on breast. Bill and legs black. Like an *Empidonax* but has all-black bill and somewhat horizontal posture, features that are sufficient to separate it visually.

Ssp. Monotypic (NW Co)

Habits Usually in pairs foraging in undergrowth, sallying to pick insects from foliage and flitting between perches.

Status Locally frequent in río Sinú basin.

Habitat Lower Tropical Zone, at 100–600m. Humid forest, usually near streams, in swampy and riparian areas.

Voice Song a loud wheezy *bee BEE, be-be-be-bez*, sometimes a fainter *bee beez bez baw* (H&B).

TUFTED FLYCATCHER

Mitrephanes phaeocercus Pl. 199

Identification 12.5–13cm. Olive-green above, wings and tail dusky, crest slightly darker than nape, pale loral spot and eye-ring, 2 pale buffy wingbars, cheeks olive, chin pale, throat and breast buffy to cinnamon, rest of underparts yellow. Juvenile has crown dark brown with buffy fringes to feathers and entire upperparts, like a juvenile *Contopus*. Pointy crest characteristic, but also look for ochre throat and breast. The only smallish crested flycatcher in its range.

Ssp. *M. p. berlepschi* (W Co, NW Ec) light olive-green above, buffy, olive-yellow lores; paler, more yellowish (less tawny) throat and chest, bright canary-yellow below

M. p. eminulus (Co: Chocó) darker green above, with dingy yellow lores and eye-ring, dull olive-fulvous throat and breast, with greenish sides

Habits Forages at lower and mid levels, usually in pairs that perch in open, sallying to catch passing insects and often returning to same perch. Brisk and alert, perches quite upright and shakes tail when alighting. Calls frequently.

Status Rare in Ecuador, frequent in Colombia.

Habitat Tropical Zone, 100–1,200m. Borders of humid and wet forests, shrubby clearings on lower slopes.

Voice A fast, enthusiastic sequence of 4–7 *pee* or *pik* notes (H&B); fast high notes, e.g. *tsu-tsu-tseet*, with soft notes sometimes inserted between sequences (P. Coopmans).

Note Called Common Tufted-Flycatcher (R&T) or Northern Tufted-Flycatcher (R&G).

[OLIVE TUFTED FLYCATCHER

Mitrephanes olivaceus] Pl. 199

Identification 13cm. Olive above, wings and tail dusky with 2 subtle, buffy wingbars and fringes to tertials, distinct pointy crest similar to Tufted Flycatcher; pale lores and eye-ring, and face-sides dull orange. Chin pale, throat, breast and flanks olivaceous, rest of underparts yellow.

Ssp. Monotypic (extreme SE Ec?)

Habits As previous species.

Status Generally uncommon and uncertain in Ecuador, where only a few unconfirmed sight records (H&B, R&T, R&G).

Habitat Upper Tropical to Subtropical Zones. Humid montane forest on east slope of Andes.

Voice Two variations of song from Peru are *chp-chi-chup'chup'chup'chup* or *tcht-chiii-cht'cht'cht'cht'cht*, a rolling series of 5–7 notes which may be uttered without prefacing notes (T. Schulenberg recording).

Note Called Olive Tufted-Flycatcher in R&T and R&G.

Contopus pewees are nondescript grey to blackish birds that nonetheless are fairly noticeable as they perch at forest edges, roadsides and clearings, sallying into open in pursuit of flying insects. Three species are boreal migrants, the rest are residents. They perch upright and have a distinct profile with their short but well-defined crests. Juveniles are scalloped above and have wingbars, but those species with wingbars in adults often have them obscure and poorly defined. Voice may be a critical factor in identifying some species.

OLIVE-SIDED FLYCATCHER

Contopus cooperi Pl. 198

Identification 18-20cm. Large-headed, long-winged and short-tailed pewee, with distinctive contrasting pattern on underparts. Brownish or greyish-olive above with pale fringes to wing-coverts and tertials, and 2 indistinct, greyish wingbars; underparts white on centre from chin to undertail-coverts, sides and flanks brownish or greyish-olive, with white tuft on flanks. Large flat bill is black above and yellow to orange below. Juvenile similar but slightly browner and has fringes to wing-feathers washed buffy.

Ssp. Monotypic (Ec, Co, Ve, Tr, Guianas)

Habits Forages in canopy, making long sallies from a favourite exposed perch on a dead branch to pick passing insects.
Status Uncommon to rare in Ecuador and Venezuela, uncommon in Trinidad (no records Tobago), a scarce vagrant to Guyana and Suriname, and recorded in small numbers in French Guiana (where sometimes found in same tree year after year). A boreal migrant that arrives in our region from October, with most records in Colombia. Departure commences in April and the last leave by May.
Habitat Tropical and Subtropical Zones in Ecuador, mostly 400–1,500m. In Colombia to 3,300m and in Venezuela 200–2,200m. Forest fringes, forest openings and treefalls in humid montane forest.
Voice Usually quiet, but might give a fast, whistled *pip-pip-pip* or *bik-bik-bik* (Hilty, Fitzpatrick). In boreal spring sometimes gives full song, *whit, whee-pew* (Fitzpatrick) or *hic, three-beers* (Hilty)
Note Formerly placed in *Nuttallornis* and specific name *borealis* used (e.g. H&B), but *cooperi* has precedence (Banks & Browning 1995).

SMOKE-COLOURED PEWEE

Contopus fumigatus Pl. 199

Identification 16–17cm. Large smoke-grey flycatcher with crest usually held erect, giving pointy appearance to head. Crown slightly darker than back. Bill black above, yellow to orange below. Juvenile quite distinct, being dusky above with buffy fringes to feathers and broad pale band on nape, below pale buffy, scalloped lightly with brown. Possible confusion with Olive-sided Flycatcher due to size and crest, but latter has distinct white 'parting' down underparts. Identical to Blackish Pewee, but latter smaller with less well-developed crest, and is generally finer and more delicate-looking.

Ssp. *C. f. ardosiacus* (E Ec, Co, NW Ve) paler vent than *duidae*, outer web of outer tail-feathers pale grey
C. f. cineraceus (N Ve) crown almost concolorous with back, paler grey overall with distinct brownish flush
C. f. duidae (S Ve, S Gu) almost completely uniform below, outer web of outer tail-feathers as rest of tail
C. f. zarumae (W Ec, SW Co) as described

Habits Usually forages alone, from an exposed perch, making lengthy sallies and returning to same perch, which may be used many times.
Status Common in Ecuador, fairly common in Colombia, common in Venezuela, uncertain in Guyana, very scarce and uncertain in Suriname.
Habitat Tropical to Subtropical Zones, 800–2,600m in Ecuador, 300–3,000m in Colombia and 500–2,800m in north-west Venezuela, but 900–1,900m south of Orinoco. Generally at humid montane forest fringes, clearings with scattered trees and treefalls, sides of roads and open trails.
Voice Frequent loud *pip-pip-pip*, sometimes *pip-pip-pip-pip*. Might be confused with Blackish Pewee, which is often repeated irregularly but is *not* tripled, as Smoke-coloured Pewee's call typically is, and is more high-pitched. Dawn song in Ecuador, a rapid series of fast, variable phrases, *wudidit*, *weeu* and *weeeuw-wu-didit* (R&G). Also a clear whistled *peeew*. Song in Andes (race?) a hoarse *zur zur zur zúr zur zur zur* (Fitzpatrick). Song of race *cineraceus* in Venezuela *whueer, whu-u'whuet!* (Hilty)
Note Previously named Greater Pewee and considered conspecific with *C. pertinax* of Middle and North America.

WESTERN WOOD PEWEE

Contopus sordidulus Pl. 199

Identification 14–16cm. Greyish-brown above, faintly pale lores and eye-ring, wings dusky with 2 pale wingbars and fringes to tertials; throat pale grey to whitish, breast, sides and flanks grey, belly white with yellow tinge, undertail-coverts have dark centres. Bill black with base of lower mandible usually flesh. Juvenile similar but maybe slightly browner, less olive both above and below, and belly and vent whitish rather than yellow. Vestigial wingbars slightly bolder and a little buffy. Very difficult to separate from Eastern Wood Pewee, but generally Western in fresh plumage is darker and browner, with no olive and less greyish; also darker and browner below with duller throat, vestigial wingbars and darker underwing-coverts. In worn plumage differences less apparent. If vocalisation heard, problem is solved.

Ssp. *C. s. saturatus* (winters to SE Ve) darker and more olive above, with darker crown
C. s. sordidulus (winters to Co, Ec) as described
C. s. veliei (winters to S Ve) more greyish, no yellow on belly
C. s. peninsulae (winters to NW S Am) paler, with narrow grey breast-band, shorter wings and tail, longer bill

Status Boreal migrant that arrives from August; leaves Ecuador in March and Venezuela and Colombia by late April. Status can only be guessed due to problems with identification and transient nature. Common at some localities in west Ecuador, fairly common in Colombia and uncommon in Venezuela.
Habitat To 1,000m in south-east Venezuela.
Voice Calls often, a melancholy and burry *preeeer* or *freeeer* (R&G) or a harsh or hoarse nasal *peeyee* or *peeeer* (H&B),

sometimes followed by a rapid, rolled, *chu-i-lit* (Fitzpatrick). Song seldom heard, a burry *preé-ur*, which may be repeated or with *pur-didi* interspersed (R&G).

EASTERN WOOD PEWEE

Contopus virens Pl. 199

Identification 13.5–15cm. Greyish-brown above, crown almost concolorous with back, wings dusky with 2 pale wingbars and fringes to tertials; throat paler grey to whitish, breast, sides and flanks grey, belly white with yellow tinge and undertail-coverts clear yellow. Bill black with most of lower mandible yellow or grey, perhaps even flesh, with dark tip. Juvenile similar but wingbars stronger and pale buffy; bill dark above and yellow below. See Western Wood Pewee for separation from latter.

Ssp. Monotypic (Ec, Co, Ve)

Status Boreal migrant that arrives in August; departs Ecuador in March and Venezuela and Colombia by late April. **Status** can only be guessed due to problems with identification and bird's transient nature. Uncommon to rare in Ecuador, Colombia and Venezuela, scarce in French Guiana.
Habitat Tropical and Lower Subtropical Zones, to 1,200m in Ecuador, 1,700m in Colombia and in Venezuela to 1,300m north of Orinoco and to 700m south of it. May reach higher altitudes on migration.
Voice Calls frequently and throughout day, a sweet plaintive *pee-wee?* which may be repeated, or interspersed with a burrier downslurred *pee-ur*. Full song, mostly given in April, *pee-a-wee* (R&G), second note lower and alternating with *peeeur* (Fitzpatrick).

TROPICAL PEWEE

Contopus cinereus Pl. 199

Identification 14cm. Rather variable in colour and size, with subspecies; 2 fairly dark whilst *surinamensis* is significantly paler. Generally grey above with darker crest held erect most of time, wings dusky with 2–3 wingbars (fringes to lesser coverts pale and form slight bar especially in fresh plumage) and whitish fringes to tertials and distal half of secondaries. White chin and throat, greyish breast and sides, rest of underparts white. Juvenile softer in coloration and fringes to wing-feathers buffy. In Ecuador *punensis* only occurs in dry western lowlands and might occasionally be seen near Western Wood Pewee, but separated by whitish lores and smaller size, and especially voice. Also has habit of shivering tail on alighting which is an important field mark. In Colombia main confusion are wood pewees, both of which are larger whilst Tropical has pale loral spot. Similar *Empidonax* flycatchers have bolder wingbars and tend to perch in cover whilst pewees usually use exposed perches.

Ssp. *C. c. bogotensis* (N & E Co, NW & NC Ve, Tr) large and dark
C. c. punensis (W Ec) larger and darker with a larger bill, dark above, yellowish below
C. c. surinamensis (SE Ve, Guianas) smaller, mid grey and paler below; bill dark above, orange below

Status Uncommon in Ecuador, common in Trinidad (no records Tobago), widespread in Venezuela, scarce in Guyana, locally frequent in Suriname and French Guiana.
Habitat Tropical and Subtropical Zones, to 1,500m in Ecuador, commonly to 1,000m in Colombia, but wanders to 2,600m, in Venezuela to 1,900m and in Suriname to 100m. In Ecuador at borders and clearings of deciduous and semi-humid forests and woodland; forest fringes and clearings in humid areas and fringes of gallery woodland in drier parts in Colombia; similar in Venezuela but mostly in foothills and hilly areas; though generally distributed in hilly country, also found in tropical dry forest of upper *llanos* and in farmland contiguous to forested areas. In Suriname appears to occur only in coastal lowland forests, particularly in mangroves.
Voice Call of *punensis* a clear *pee-pit* or *peee, pidit* (R&G). In Colombia, *bogotensis* has a short, slightly trilled *tirrip* or *treee* (H&B). In Venezuela (race unknown) *tre'e'e'e* or *tir'r'r'ip* or similar, and like Streak-headed Woodcreeper. At dawn may sing a series of rising *weet* notes (Hilty). In Suriname, song of *surinamensis* an unpretentious, not very musical *kyeer,r,r... kyeer,r,r... kyeer,r,r...* (H&M).
Note Race *punensis* afforded species status as Tumbes Pewee by R&G due to striking vocal differences.

BLACKISH PEWEE

Contopus nigrescens Pl. 199

Identification 13cm. Comparatively small and entirely sooty grey. Wings and tail slightly darker, top of head also darker, crest tidy and usually laid back giving head pointy look. Bill black above, yellowish below, eyes, legs and feet dark. Juvenile has pale, whitish fringes to wing-coverts. Much smaller than virtually identical Smoke-coloured Pewee which has bushier crest and looks more top-heavy. Calls also differ, whilst Blackish Pewee occurs at higher levels and in canopy.

Ssp. *C. n. canescens* (S Gu: extreme SE) slightly but obviously paler above
C. n. nigrescens (E Ec) as described

Habits Often in pairs or family parties, and a pair may use same tree, even same perch for days on end, making long sorties for insects. Perches upright and usually shivers tail on alighting.
Status Rare in Ecuador, locally frequent in Guyana, in Acari Mts. on Brazilian border.
Habitat Tropical Zone, 400–900m in Ecuador, 800–1,000m in Guyana. Generally in canopy at forest edge, in treefalls and clearings along streams and rivers.
Voice Song a snappy but somewhat burry *chi-bew*, repeated at 3–4 s intervals. Both sexes often give a sharp *pip!* or *peep!* sometimes in an irregular series, but typically not tripled, unlike Smoke-coloured, whose call is lower pitched R&G).

WHITE-THROATED PEWEE

Contopus albogularis Pl. 199

Identification 13cm. Very distinctive being all grey with a white throat. Entirely slate grey with darker wings, tail and crown; chin and throat contrasting pure white. Bill black above with dull orange mandible. Juvenile has buffy wingbars and fine buffy fringes to tertials and secondaries. The only all-dark grey bird with bright white throat in range.

Ssp. Monotypic (Su, FG)

Habits Apparently holds territory for a few years then disappears suddenly. Typically uses exposed perches, but easily overlooked, making long sorties for prey and returning to same perch.

Status Locally common in Suriname, uncommon and patchy in French Guiana.

Habitat Tropical Zone, 100–700m. Treefalls, forest edges and clearings contiguous to extensive forest. Seems to favour mesa-like terrain, avoiding lowland humid forest.

Voice In Suriname a monotonous, toneless *chép… chép… chép…* uttered throughout day, and song is *peeyoo, peeyoo* followed by a trill (H&M).

Empidonax flycatchers are fairly nondescript boreal migrants with 2 bold white wingbars and are often very difficult to separate. Vocalisations are an enormous help, but they are fairly quiet whilst in our region, rarely singing.

ACADIAN FLYCATCHER

Empidonax virescens Pl. 198

Identification 14cm. Greenish-olive above, dusky wings with 2 bold whitish wingbars and broad white fringes to tertials and distal half of secondaries that form solid panel on closed wing, whitish or yellowish-white lores and eye-ring, throat white grading into pale olive wash on breast, slightly flammulated on sides and flanks, belly and undertail-coverts white. Bill black above, orange-yellow below. The only *Empidonax* with grey legs and feet and also has longest wings and largest bill. Moults on breeding grounds pre-migration, arriving in fairly fresh plumage with clearly yellowish underparts. Seems to undertake body moult prior to departing as specimens from January–February are very white below, then in March are bright yellow and green above. Juvenile usually still shows buffy on wingbars and some buffy fringes to body-feathers. Greener above and yellower below than slightly smaller Willow and Alder Flycatchers.

Ssp. Monotypic (W Ec, NW Co, NW Ve)

Status Boreal migrant that arrives in August–September and leaves in March–April. Uncommon to rare in northern South America.

Habitat Tropical to Lower Subtropical Zones, to 1,200m in Ecuador, 2,700m in Colombia and at least 1,200m in Venezuela. Generally in lower growth of lowland humid and semi-humid forests, woodland and plantations, thickets and treefall gaps.

Voice Frequent call a rather sharp, inflected *wheeyk* uttered every few seconds for long periods. Rarely heard song is an explosive *ka-zeép!* (R&G). Call also described as a rising *fweep!* (H&B), and song as *spit-chee!* (R. T. Peterson in H&B).

ALDER FLYCATCHER

Empidonax alnorum Pl. 198

Identification 13cm. Drab olive or brownish-olive above, slightly darker on head, wings dusky with 2 white or yellowish-white wingbars and fringes to tertials and distal half of secondaries, an indistinct loral spot and variable whitish eye-ring; chin and throat whitish with brownish-olive wash on breast, rest of underparts whitish. Usually arrives in fresh plumage, more olive above and whiter on wingbars and belly. Body moult to breeding plumage in our region, becoming greener above and white on wings and belly is brighter with slight yellow cast. Juvenile usually still shows yellowish-buffy wingbars. Easily confused with Willow Flycatcher, but in fresh plumage is greener above, with more contrasting wingbars, slightly longer tail, more pointed wings and shorter bill though these difficult to judge even in the hand.

Ssp. Monotypic (Ec, Co)

Status Boreal migrant. Rare in eastern Ecuador. In Colombia probably frequent in Andean foothills and adjacent lowlands, but much confusion with Alder Flycatcher. Uncertain in Venezuela, with no records but possibly transits (AOU 1998).

Habitat Tropical Zone, transients possible at higher elevations. Semi-open areas with thickets, overgrown clearings, fallow fields and pastures with bushes and scrub.

Voice Frequent call in winter is a short, dry *whit!*, *pip!* or *pit!* Song, infrequent in winter, a blurry, semi-whistled *fee-zwee-o*, *we-be-o* (H&B) or *fee-béé-o* (Fitzpatrick).

Note Formerly considered a race of *E. traillii*, but they differ in voice, ecology and winter range (AOU 1998).

WILLOW FLYCATCHER

Empidonax traillii Pl. 198

Identification 13cm. Drab olive or brownish-olive above, slightly darker on head, wings dusky with 2 white or yellowish-white wingbars and fringes to tertials and distal half of secondaries, an indistinct loral spot and variable whitish eye-ring; chin and throat whitish with brownish-olive wash on breast, rest of underparts whitish. Arrives in fresh plumage when more olive above and whiter on wingbars and belly. Body moult to breeding plumage in our region, becoming greener above, and white on wings and belly brighter with light yellow cast. Juvenile usually still shows yellowish-buffy wingbars. Easily confused with Alder Flycatcher, but in fresh plumage less greenish above with less contrasting wingbars, slightly shorter tail and longer bill though these differences are difficult to observe even in the hand.

Ssp. *E. t. traillii* (Ec?, Co?) darker than *brewsteri*
E. t. brewsteri (Co?) slightly paler than *traillii*

Status Boreal migrant: rare in eastern Ecuador, where only identified by song (no specimens), and probably frequent in

north-west Colombia, but records uncertain due to confusion with Alder Flycatcher.
Habitat Tropical Zone, transients possible at higher elevations. Semi-open areas with thickets, overgrown clearings, fallow fields and pastures with bushes and scrub.
Voice Frequent call in winter a soft *pit* or *pip* (R&G), a mellow, upturned *whuit* or *whit* (Fitzpatrick). Song, infrequent in winter, a two-note *fitz-bew* (H&B).
Notes Races that reach South America uncertain: R&G, SCJ&W and Dickinson (2003) list *traillii*; SCJ&W also list *brewsteri* and Dickinson (2003) also lists *extimus*. Race *campestris* mentioned in R&G but not listed in Dickinson.

There is just one species of black phoebe in our region, a distinct and characteristic black tyrannid of montane watercourses.

BLACK PHOEBE *Sayornis nigricans* Pl. 200

Identification 15–18cm. Unmistakable, though we believe a bird in unusual moult was misidentified as an American Dipper. Sooty black save 2 white wingbars and white fringes to tertials and remiges, 2 outermost tail-feathers and pure white belly. Considerable range in density of black on body and amount of white in wings and tail which appear unrelated to wear, but may be function of age. Bill, legs and feet black. Immature slate grey, with bar on lesser coverts slightly ochraceous, whilst white on greater coverts and tertials less than adult; belly off-white to grey, with perhaps vestigial buffy fringes to some body-feathers, most often on rump and uppertail-coverts. Juvenile duller yet, wingbars ochre to buffy, and has pale buffy fringes to grey body.

Ssp. *S. n. angustirostris* (Ec, Co, W & N Ve).

Habits Both sexes flick tail constantly. Males display spreading wings forward and upwards in wide arc while fanning tail. Usually in pairs, perches in open on boulders, gravel and sandbanks, bridges, walls and buildings on or alongside rivers and streams in foothills and montane areas, rarely by still or slow-moving water. Sallies to snatch passing insects, always fairly low and often over water.
Status Fairly common and widespread in Ecuador, Colombia and Venezuela.
Habitat Tropical and Subtropical Zones, 500m or lower to *c.*2,800m throughout range. Riverine montane habitat, in open areas but may occur on streams through tall forest provided there are open areas nearby.
Voice A bright, rising *peeert*, accompanied by an upward tail-flick (H&B), song a rather shrill *zhrreeee, pseekiyu* (R&G) and song-flight, during which bird flutters vertically up then down, *t't't'-esk-u t't't'-esk-u psip t't't'-esk-u*… (Hilty). A 2-peaked *tweedle-deedle-eek* uttered while chasing mate or an intruder (Fitzpatrick).

Vermilion Flycatcher is a stunningly coloured and wide-spread species that occurs from Mexico to Argentina. It is singularly sexually dimorphic.

VERMILION FLYCATCHER
Pyrocephalus rubinus Pl. 198

Identification 13cm. Male sooty black above, including wings and tail with fine fringes to wing-feathers. Lores and line through eye to upper ear-coverts and nape also black. Top of head and forehead, chin to undertail-coverts scarlet. Crest not long, but fairly bushy and affects head profile depending on whether laid back or erect. Bill, legs and feet black. Thirteen subspecies recognised, but in our region only 3 occur, and male similar in each. Variation comes with females. Two colour variants in females of some races, with pink flush of rear underparts replaced by yellow. Female greyish-brown above, warmer than juvenile with lighter fringes to wing-coverts and tertials only. Chin to belly whitish with light streaks on lower throat and breast, fading to pink on lower underparts. Juvenile greyish-brown above, feathers having slightly paler fringes, giving overall scalloped effect. Below, white, with lines of streaks on breast, sides and to flanks, each feather having a white edge, producing lines of scallops. Vermilion Flycatcher is unique in its habitat.

Ssp. *P. r. piurae* (W Ec: widespread, C & W Co) female extensively pink below
P. r. rubinus (austral migrant: winters to E Ec, SE Co) female very pale pink or often simply white like juvenile; frequently birds are yellow below
P. r. saturatus (NE Co, N & SE Ve, Gu) female rosy pink below

Habits Males perch in open, on stem of shrub or bush, or upper strand of wire fence. Seldom perches very high and usually sufficiently near ground to sally down to snatch insects over grass and herbage. Frequently in pairs. Often pumps tail downwards.
Status Race *piurae* common in western Ecuador, *rubinus* scarce in east, *saturatus* common in Colombia and Venezuela, and frequent in Guyana.
Habitat Tropical and Subtropical Zones, to 3,000m or more. Wide variety of habitats but more often found in dry or arid open areas regardless of altitude.
Voice Both sexes call a high, sharp *peep!* or *peent!* Song-flight *pid'd'd'reeeit*, performed at any time of day; male flutters vertically upwards, hovers a while, then flutteringly descends. In Venezuela sings mostly at dawn and dusk, rarely in daytime. Also *ching-tink-a-le-tink* and *pt-pt-pre-ee-seee*, and other variations (Fitzpatrick), including *titi'tre'e'e'E* (Hilty).

Chat-tyrants of the genus *Ochthoeca* (including *Sylvicultrix*) are montane flycatchers, rotund, attractively coloured with a distinctive, bold superciliary. They have short bills and long rictal bristles, a vertical posture and all flick their tails frequently. Do not join mixed-species flocks, but usually occur low and often near streams and montane watercourses.

CROWNED CHAT-TYRANT

Ochthoeca frontalis Pl. 200

Identification 12.5cm. Unmistakable in range. Dark brown above, somewhat dusky wings and tail, greyish tinge to head and neck, blackish on crown, bold yellow frontal band on forehead running into white superciliary on sides of crown and nape, grey below, paler on throat, richer on breast, undertail-coverts dull cinnamon. Female has paler crown and more extensive, somewhat paler cinnamon rear underparts. Juvenile paler and brighter throughout, with cinnamon frontal band and superciliary, and more yellowish undertail-coverts.

Ssp. *O. f. albidiadema* (Co: E Andes) frontal band and superciliary white
O. f. frontalis (N Ec, Co: C Andes) frontal band yellow and superciliary white

Habits Usually forages alone, perching low in undergrowth. Usually silent. Rarely joins mixed flocks.

Status Uncommon to rare in Ecuador, uncommon in Colombia.

Habitat Temperate Zone to Páramo, 2,800 or lower, to 4,000m in Ecuador, 2,300–3,600m in Colombia. In Ecuador, *Polylepis* woodland and dead bamboo on mossy ground (Fitzpatrick), in Colombia, most often in elfin forest below treeline where flits among mossy trunks and limbs rather than in foliage (H&B).

Voice Song a drawn-out, high-pitched, descending trill, *sesrrrrrrrrrrrrrrrrrrrrrrrrrrrrrr* (P. Coopmans in R&G) or *ti-tirrrrrrrrrr…* (H&B).

JELSKI'S CHAT-TYRANT

Ochthoeca jelskii Pl. 200

Identification 12cm. Olive-brown above with wings and tail dusky, 2 rufous wingbars, head dusky to blackish with bold yellow frontal band and white superciliary reaching beyond ear-coverts; grey chin to breast and sides, then white, with rufous flush to flanks. Female buffier below. Juvenile has rufous wash above and more ruddy flush below than adult female, and superciliary changes from light ochraceous to rufous above ear-coverts. From Crowned Chat-Tyrant by wingbars and white belly, but they are apparently allopatric as Jelski's does not occur on east slope.

Ssp. Monotypic (S Ec: Loja)

Habits A bird of dark undergrowth where it is easily overlooked. Usually forages alone but occasionally follows mixed flocks.

Status Rare in Ecuador.

Habitat Upper Subtropical to Temperate Zones, from 1,300m or 2,200m to 2,800m. Borders of montane forest and secondary woodland and adjacent shrubby areas.

Voice Song *c.*1 s long, a high-pitched, sharp *tseeeee!* When agitated or excited a *tseee-krrrr* or *tsetsirrekerr* (P. Coopmans in R&G).

YELLOW-BELLIED CHAT-TYRANT

Ochthoeca diadema Pl. 200

Identification 12cm. Olive above, slightly darker on wings, tail and top of head, with frontal area and superciliary bright yellow; entire underparts yellow, washed on breast, sides and flanks yellowish-olive according to race. Juvenile has rufous wash above, with rufous wingbars; more olivaceous on throat, sides and flanks, and yellow below bright; there may be a light ochraceous wash to vent. The only chat-tyrant with yellow underparts and looking so yellowish. Frontal bar and superciliary diagnostic.

Ssp. *O. d. diadema* (SW Ve: Páramo de Tamá, N Táchira) as described; cap darker than *meridana*
O. d. gratiosa (N Ec, Co: Andes) much darker, more rufous-brown, and darker and more olive below, yellow tint only on abdomen
O. d. jesupi (Co: Santa Marta) crown uniform with back, below not as bright yellow
O. d. meridana (Ve: Andes of Trujillo) slightly warmer brown, less olive above, deeper yellow below than *diadema*, darker and more dusky, less olivaceous crown than *tovarensis*; from *diadema* by brighter, deeper yellow underparts
O. d. rubellula (Páramo de Perijá: Co & Ve) crown paler than *diadema*, back lighter, more reddish-brown, underparts paler yellow
O. d. tovarensis (NC Ve: Northern Cordillera) from *diadema* by more olivaceous crown and nape, less suffused sooty brown; deeper brownish-olive back and tertials

Habits Forages quietly in dark undergrowth, perches fairly upright and flicks tail upwards. Usually solitary but may follow mixed flocks without actually joining them.

Status Uncommon in Ecuador and Venezuela.

Habitat Upper Subtropical Zone to Páramo, 2,200–3,100m in Ecuador, 1,700–3,100m in Colombia. In Venezuela, *rubellula* in Perijá, *diadema* and *meridana* in Andes, 2,100–3050m, and in Northern Cordillera (*tovarensis*) at 1,950–2,200m.

Voice In Ecuador, *gratiosa* gives very dry trill, slightly inflected at start, *tsueéurrrrrr*. Dawn song a shorter *psi-uw*, repeated every few seconds (R&G). In Colombia a long, buzzy trill that sags in middle (H&B). In Venezuela, *diadema* dawn song is a fast, thin trill that ascends slightly, *chiiiiiiiiiiiiiiit* or *prrrreeeeeeeeeeee* like fingers running a comb, uttered only a few times at first light. Further east, *meridana* has a thin trill that sags in middle then ascends at end, *chiiiiiiiiaaaaaaaaiiiiiiii*, and a much longer *ppprrrrrreeeeeeeeeeeeeeaa* that slowly rises then drops at end (Hilty). Voice of *tovarensis* is very similar to *meridana*, but longer at end (D. Ascanio recording).

Note Fitzpatrick considered *meridana* inseparable from *diadema* and synonymised them. They are quite alike and extremely difficult to identify in field, but we found the original descriptions to be valid.

SLATY-BACKED CHAT-TYRANT

Ochthoeca cinnamomeiventris Pl. 200

Identification 12cm. Slate grey above, wings and tail slightly browner, head to breast blackish, breast and belly deep chestnut, flanks and undertail-coverts charcoal grey. Frontal band is formed by 2 large supraloral spots that do *not* join at base of culmen. Superciliary reaches over eye, but does not extend as far as other chat-tyrants. Rather unique in its habitat; note unusual eyebrow. Might be confused briefly with Black Phoebe, but latter has no white on head, but does have white in wings. Normally, Black Phoebe has much longer tail than Slaty-backed Chat-Tyrant and posture differs clearly. Also, although both occur along watercourses, the chat-tyrant is a forest species whereas Black Phoebe occurs on boulders and in exposed areas.

Ssp. *O. c. cinnamomeiventris* (Andes: N Ec, Co, Ve: W Táchira) deep bay breast; juvenile similar, with slightly less intense bay colour on belly and vent

O. c. nigrita (Ve: Andes in E Táchira, Mérida) no chestnut at all; older birds have a faint white superciliary that reaches 1cm past eye; juvenile browner below, grey has light rufous wash, and supraloral narrower

Status Uncommon in Ecuador. Fairly common in Colombia. Locally common in Venezuela.

Habitat Subtropical Zone to Páramo, 1,700–2,800m in Ecuador, 1,600–3,000m in Colombia and 1,800–2,800m in Venezuela. Bushy forest borders and shrubs along streams, and dense tangles in ravines with falling water.

Voice In Ecuador, a drawn-out, high-pitched, sharp and surprisingly loud *dzweeéyeeuw*, often repeated endlessly. Dawn song is same note followed by 3–4 *tseét* notes (R&G). In Colombia and Venezuela, a loud, often-heard high, burry whistle, *sweeeeeea*, rising slightly then falling, easily heard above rushing mountain streams (Hilty).

Note Venezuelan birds treated specifically, as Blackish Chat-Tyrant *Ochthoeca nigrita*, in Hilty (2003).

RUFOUS-BREASTED CHAT-TYRANT

Ochthoeca rufipectoralis Pl. 200

Identification 13cm. Varies by race. Basically dark brown above with dusky wings and tail, broad rufous wingbar, and pale fringes and tips to tertials that disappear with wear; dusky head, dark crown contrasting with back; frontal band and long superciliary white (except *poliogastra*), throat grey, breast orange-rufous, rest of underparts grey (or white). Rufous breast quite distinctive, but might be confused with larger Brown-backed Chat-Tyrant, though latter has entire underparts rufous and extended superciliary also fairly rufous.

Ssp. *O. r. obfuscata* (Ec, Co: C & W Andes) occasionally 2 wingbars, ochraceous fringes to tertials, whitish below

O. r. poliogastra (Co: Santa Marta) head concolorous with back, pale fringes to tertials, frontal bar and superciliary tinged ochraceous, narrower breast band, mid grey below

O. r. rubicundulus (Perijá: Co & Ve) paler brown above, whitish chin, paler grey below; juvenile has crown almost concolorous with back, just slightly greyer and darker, wings and tail not as dark brown; supraloral slightly buffy and diffuse on frontal band, breast much paler, being a smaller area washed olivaceous

O. r. rufopectus (N Co: E Andes) very dark above without wingbars, darkest grey below

Habits Usually at mid to upper levels, more so than other chat-tyrants. Forages by sallying from exposed, fairly high perch. Flicks tail up, especially if alert or alarmed. Occasionally follows mixed flocks.

Status Uncommon in Ecuador.

Habitat Temperate Zone to Páramo, 2,500–3,300m in Ecuador. Stunted forest and scattered thickets near treeline, *Polylepis* above treeline and *Espeletia* in open páramo.

Voice Dawn song in Ecuador, *tirip, weé-eeuw, tirip, weé-eeuw…* (N. Krabbe in R&G). In Colombia, song an abrupt *ch-brrr, ch-brrr, ch-brrr*, with some clucking notes (J. Silliman in H&B), a faint *cleeoo* and *pt'pt'pt'pt'pt'pt'pt'pt'p y'cleeoo, cleeoo* (Smith & Vuilleumier in H&B). Other songs, mentioned by Fitzpatrick, include *tjrt-tjrrrrt-tjt-trrrt* and *chic-chic-chica*.

BROWN-BACKED CHAT-TYRANT

Ochthoeca fumicolor Pl. 200

Identification 15cm. Large and very ruddy-looking. Rufescent-brown above, dusky wings and tail, with outer webs of outer tail-feathers white, and broad rufous bar across greater coverts; in most races a second bar on median coverts, frontal band and long superciliary buffy to rufous, lower face and upper throat greyish, lower throat and below cinnamon to rufous. Female tends to be paler below, and juvenile warmer with no grey on chin. Unlikely to be confused, a large chat-tyrant that is completely rufous below. In all races long superciliary is clincher.

Ssp. *O. f. brunneifrons* (Ec, S Co: C & W Andes) 2 broad rufous wingbars, full superciliary buffy, richest rufous underparts

O. f. ferruginea (N Co: C & W Andes) shorter superciliary buffy, more white on outer tail-feathers

O. f. fumicolor (N Co: E Andes, Ve: Táchira) palest race, cooler brown on head; no frontal band, white superciliary barely reaches base of culmen, clear grey chin, pale ochraceous flanks and undertail-coverts

O. f. superciliosa (Ve: Andes) darkest race, with single broad wingbar, dark on head-sides with broad rufous frontal band and superciliary that broadens at rear, rich olive of throat merges into deep chestnut-rufous breast and belly, white undertail-coverts; juvenile paler on throat and belly, wingbar narrower and slightly paler, frontal bar and superciliary noticeably paler, more ochraceous

Habits Usually easy to see, often in pairs on an exposed perch.
Status Uncommon to locally common in Ecuador. Common in Colombia and Venezuela.
Habitat Temperate Zone to Páramo, 2,800–4,200m in Ecuador, 2,500–3,600m in Colombia and 2,200–4,200m in Venezuela. Essentially semi-open montane habitats, thickets and shrubby areas, stunted trees and *Polylepis* woodland, *Espeletia* in open páramo.
Voice Generally quiet but occasionally utters a soft *pseeu* (R&T) or soft *prip!* when foraging (Hilty). Also a loud abrupt clear whistle, *kleeeip*, perched or in flight (H&B). Dawn song in Ecuador a fast, chattered *keé-ke-de keé-ke-de keé-kedu-keékeé-ke-du-keé* (P. Coopmans in R&G), and in Venezuela at dawn, pairs sing a fast rhythmic duet, *plee, plít'ter'tew, plít'ter'tew, plít'ter'tew…* with variations including *cháp'pa, cháp'pa…* or *cháp'pit'dip…* (Hilty).

WHITE-BROWED CHAT-TYRANT

Ochthoeca leucophrys Pl. 200

Identification 14.5cm. Brownish-grey above, with dusky tail and wings, very faint rufous fringes to wing-feathers but no wingbars, outer web of outer tail-feathers white, frontal band and superciliary white, chin to lower breast and sides grey, rest below, white. Juvenile has rufous wingbars. Could be confused with smaller Jelski's Chat-Tyrant, particularly juvenile, but Jelski's has yellow frontal band and rufous wash on flanks. Adult White-browed is grey and white below and lacks wingbars.

Ssp. *O. l. dissors* (extreme S Ec)

Habits Usually alone or in pairs, sallies from prominent perch atop bush and may return to same perch, or to ground. Fairly conspicuous and often flicks wings and tail.
Status Rare in extreme southern Ecuador, in highlands of Azuay and northern Loja..
Habitat Upper Temperate Zone to Páramo, 2,200–2,800m. Scrub, hedges, open woodland and *Polylepis*; fond of ravines and gullies, and usually found near water.
Voice Call a sharp *queeuuw*! (R&G). Sometimes calls in flight, *keeu keu keu keu keu*, and *tee teeti* in alarm (Fitzpatrick).

DRAB WATER TYRANT

Ochthornis littoralis Pl. 202

Identification 13cm. Generally drab and nondescript, pale rump, top of head and nape, wings and tail darker, crown contrasting slightly with nape, pale superciliary and darker loral stripe; below slightly paler and more sandy. Variation with some paler above and others have paler throats, whilst many have vestigial paler fringes to wing-coverts, and coloration of crown not consistent. Such variations might be age-related. Also moult appears quite rapid, with several birds moulting an entire row of wing-coverts simultaneously. Blake (1950) found 3 specimens from southern Guyana to be browner and darker than series from Brazil and Peru, and their remiges and wing-coverts also lacked buffy- or pale-coloured fringes of Peruvian birds. Juvenile has crown concolorous with back, and wing-coverts and remiges have paler fringes, producing irregular but fairly broad wingbars. Rather like Spot-billed Ground Tyrant, but completely different altitude! Also similar to Little Water Tyrant, but separated by whitish lores and pale rump, and latter has pale spot at base of lower mandible.

Ssp. Monotypic (E Ec, S Co, S & SW Ve, S Gu, FG)

Habits Often encountered in pairs along riverbanks, usually perching 1m from surface of water.
Status Common in Ecuador, Colombia and Venezuela, locally uncommon to common in Guyana. Confirmation from French Guiana needed.
Habitat Tropical Zone, to 400m in Ecuador, 500m in Colombia and 600m in Venezuela. Always near water, particularly fond of exposed roots projecting from eroded river banks, and driftwood, fallen trees, etc., occasionally on sandbanks.
Voice Usually quiet but an occasional *free* or *fweet*. Displaying birds, sometimes pairs, posture with wings outstretched while giving a fast excited *weet-weedidee, weet-weedidee, weet-weedidee…* (R&G), or *wee-chiddle-chee…* (H&B).

Bush tyrants are large flycatchers of forests and borders in the high Andes. Two genera are represented in our region, *Myiotheretes* which has rufous in the wings or tail, and *Cnemarchus* with extensive rufous on body and tail.

RED-RUMPED BUSH TYRANT

Cnemarchus erythropygius Pl. 201

Identification 23cm. Large, distinctive bush tyrant, dark brownish-slate on back, fuscous tail with bright orange-rufous outer fringes to basal half of all but central rectrices, and fuscous wings with distinctive white outer fringes to basal half of tertials. Entire head and breast grey, powdery grey on forehead (white in juvenile), with some white flammulations on chin and throat, darker on breast; rump, sides and underparts orange-rufous. Underwing-coverts cinnamon, may show in flight. Streak-throated Bush Tyrant lacks grey head and bright rump, also cinnamon on inner webs of all remiges show well in flight. Santa Marta Bush Tyrant much smaller and like Streak-throated. Neither has white on tertials.

Ssp. *C. e. erythropygius* (Ec, S Co) as described
C. e. orinomus (N Co: Santa Marta) lower back and rump paler brown, back of head and nape greyer, underwing-coverts paler

Habits Mostly in open páramos with scattered bushes of *Berberis* and *Verbena*, *Polylepis* groves and puna grassland. Perches exposed, on branches to fences and atop shrubs,

sallying into air or to ground. Often in pairs but appears to be alone as 2 birds may be some distance apart.
Status Uncommon to rare in Ecuador and Colombia.
Habitat Upper Temperate Zone to Páramo, 2,800–4,100m in Ecuador, 3,100–3,600m in Colombia and to 3,900m on Santa Marta massif though Wetmore (1946) described *orinomus* as being found on Santa Marta between 1,060 and 1,200m.
Voice Usual calls include a high-pitched *kyeee* and higher *shyeik* (N. Krabbe in R&G), and a high-pitched plaintive whistle, *wheeeu*, in Peru (P. Coopmans).
Note Fitzpatrick synonymised *orinomus* under *erythropygius*.

STREAK-THROATED BUSH TYRANT
Myiotheretes striaticollis Pl. 201

Identification 23cm. Brown above, with wings and tail darker, fringed rufescent on wing-coverts and greyish on tertials and secondaries. Head-sides narrowly streaked white, chin and throat white with black streaks; rest of underparts orange-rufous. In flight, cinnamon on wings and tail shows well, inner webs of all remiges and rectrices rufous above and cinnamon below, with dusky tips forming terminal band to both wings and tail. From below, effect is all bright cinnamon. In coloration and pattern could be a thrush, but upright posture distinct. Generally unmistakable, though Red-rumped Bush Tyrant can look similar in flight, cinnamon rump should serve as a discriminator. Santa Marta and Smoky Bush Tyrants have similar wing patterns but lack any white in wing and also lack bright rump.

Ssp. *M. s. striaticollis* (Ec, Co, W Ve)

Habits Forages alone or in pairs, often perches quite high.
Status Uncommon in Ecuador and Colombia, but still most widespread and frequently seen bush tyrant. Common in Venezuela.
Habitat Subtropical Zone to Páramo, mostly 2,400–3,200m in Ecuador and Colombia. Semi-open terrain, including cultivation, open pastures and areas with scattered trees.
Voice A loud, rising *sweeeeeeee*. Song *tsi-seeee-rit* or *tsi-si-see-rit*, rather like Tropical Kingbird. In Venezuela, local name Chifla Perro derives from call, which sounds like whistle one hears when someone is calling a dog.

SANTA MARTA BUSH TYRANT
Myiotheretes pernix Pl. 201

Identification 19cm. Like Streak-throated Bush Tyrant but much smaller and only outer web of outer tail-feathers fringed rufous. Wing-feathers fringed rufous, producing 1–2 bars depending on feather wear. Streaks below extend to cinnamon breast.

Ssp. Monotypic (Co: Santa Marta)

Habits Usually forages alone, sallying from perch at edge, sometimes fairly high up.
Status Colombian endemic. Uncommon.
Habitat Temperate Zone, 2,100–2,900m. Shrubby forest and second-growth borders, shrubby clearings, always in borders, not in open.
Voice Short but descending loud whistle, *weeuuu, heeuuu, heeuu*, repeated continually for up to 1 minute or more (Fitzpatrick).

SMOKY BUSH TYRANT
Myiotheretes fumigatus Pl. 201

Identification 18–20cm. Large, dark and rather thrush-like, uniform sooty brown with whitish superciliary and whitish flammulations on throat. Wings dark brown with basal half of inner webs of all remiges cinnamon. Juvenile similar but rufescent fringes to wing-feathers produce rather fuzzy wingbars. In flight might recall much larger Streak-throated Bush Tyrant, but note lack of rufous in tail.

Ssp. *M. f. cajamarcae* (S Ec) darker overall, short supercilium
M. f. fumigatus (N Ec, Co) as described
M. f. lugubris (W Ve: Andes) crown darker and more contrasting with back, shorter superciliary, streaking restricted to chin and uppermost throat, and has cinnamon vent and undertail-coverts
M. f. olivaceus (Perijá: Co & Ve) supercilium grey and fairly prominent, vent and undertail-coverts brown

Habits Rather shy and usually perches discretely at edge of foliage to sally after insects. In contrast, Streak-throated Bush Tyrant perches more exposed way. Forages alone, in pairs or small groups and often follows mixed flocks.
Status Uncommon in Ecuador.
Habitat Humid montane and elfin forests, usually at fringes and well below treeline.
Voice Amongst earliest pre-dawn performers, a long-sustained but halting series of clear whistles, *cheea, cheea, cheea, chuEE*, or more often an alternated series, *chura, chura, chEEea, chura, chura, chura, chEEea…* with scarcely a break between songs. During day an occasional soft, downslurred whistle, *peeeee* (like Dusky-capped Flycatcher). Infrequently a soft, 3-noted whistle that slurs down then rises (Hilty).

Grey Monjita is the only representative of a genus of large, grey, black and white flycatchers of open country that forage by dropping to ground.

GREY MONJITA *Xolmis cinereus* Pl. 201

Identification 23cm. Ash-grey above with blackish wings and tail; grey of long uppertail-coverts contrasts against black tail with broad grey tip, wings have pale grey fringes to coverts, tertials and secondaries, and bright white base to primaries. Throat white with broad moustachial streak of black and white lines. Breast flushed warm grey, rest of underparts white. Juvenile has brownish wash to grey of plumage. Quite distinctive at rest, quite unmistakable in flight, especially as legs hang down, toes clenched, reminiscent of a White-tailed Kite, and is sometimes mobbed by smaller birds which appear to think it is indeed a raptor.

Ssp. *X. c. cinereus* (Su: extreme south)

Habits Usually forages by dropping to ground where takes *Coleoptera* beetles.

Status Common on Sipaliwini savanna where a breeding resident.

Grey Monjita in flight; note distinctive wing pattern and dangling legs

Habitat Tropical Zone, below 1,000m. Essentially a bird of grassland and *cerrado*, though Mees (H&M) encountered it in forest in Kabalebo.

Voice High, with timbre of domestic chick, *PEEa*. Song is *PEEeh-PEEeh-ili-dew-dlee-ew*, a limpid whistle given at dawn and during day (Sick).

> *Agriornis* shrike-tyrants are large, heavy-bodied flycatchers of the high Andes which take their name from the hooked bills used to take comparatively large vertebrate prey. They make long, gliding flights with their contrastingly patterned tails half-spread, sometimes dropping to ground for prey. They perch conspicuously on boulders and walls, are territorial and usually seen alone or in well-spaced pairs.

BLACK-BILLED SHRIKE-TYRANT

Agriornis montanus Pl. 201

Identification 23cm. Large brown bird noticeable for its striking blackish and white tail. Overall dark greyish-brown with 4 central tail-feathers fuscous above, (only 2 central ones from below), rest of tail white. Wings greyish with remiges dusky, white fringes to tertials and secondaries. Whitish supraloral patch becomes an eyebrow, lores dark and continuing through eye as dark line, rest of face and chin white, streaked black and fuscous. Below, slightly paler greyish-brown, gently flammulated darker brown, undertail-coverts and undertail white. Eyes bright pale yellow, bill all black. Juvenile rather less greyish and more brownish, darker on breast; bill mostly yellow, eyes brown. Very much like White-tailed Shrike-Tyrant, but much smaller, lacks clear superciliary and has yellow eyes.

Ssp. *A. m. solitarius* (Ec, S Co)

Habits Usually seen perched on a boulder or prominence overlooking adjacent ground, and may take-off with long glides between vantage points, dropping onto prey as opportune. Prefers rocks rather than bushes. Often hovers briefly, when white tail particularly obvious, before dropping to ground.

Status Uncommon to rare in Ecuador.

Habitat Temperate Zone to Páramo, 2,500–4,000m in Ecuador and 2,800–3,600m in Colombia. Open grassy areas, pastures or agriculture with scattered trees and bushes, edge of *Polylepis* forest, *puna* grassland, rocky slopes, cliffs, even village gardens.

Voice Occasionally gives a loud ringing, rising and falling *wheee, wheeeu* or just *wheeeu* (R&G). Also a loud whistled *pyuk* (Fitzpatrick).

WHITE-TAILED SHRIKE-TYRANT

Agriornis andicola Pl. 201

Identification 26–28cm. Amongst the largest flycatchers, like a large thrush except dark and white tail. Dark grey-brown above with narrow pale fringes to greater coverts and tertials. Central tail-feathers dark, rest white, lores pale, with full whitish superciliary, whitish streaking on ear-coverts, chin and entire throat flammulated blackish and white. Upper breast to flanks warm grey, subtly flammulated darker, grading into white belly and undertail-coverts. Bill dark above with mandible horn-coloured. Juvenile undescribed. Much like Black-billed Shrike-Tyrant, but much larger, with clear white superciliary, brown eyes and a proportionately heavier bill.

Ssp. *A. a. andicola* (Ec).

Habits Prefers open slopes of high valleys, with scattered rocks, boulders and dry stone walls on which it perches, cliffs with rocky outcrops.

Status Rare in Ecuador with few sightings.

Habitat Páramo, 2,400–3,100m. Open dry scrubby country with rocky outcrops.

Voice Usually silent, but occasionally a loud melodic *teeu, tcheeu-tcheeu-tcheeuw* (R&G).

> Ground tyrants are rather graceful flycatchers of the high Andes, remarkably similar in appearance to Old World wheatears and pipits, with long legs and upright posture. They inhabit dry open country and pursue prey on the ground with short, bouncy flights, or short runs on the ground, pausing frequently and fanning their tails to flash white outer feathers.

SPOT-BILLED GROUND TYRANT

Muscisaxicola maculirostris Pl. 202

Identification 14–15cm. Sandy brown above with dusky wings, feather fringes buffy producing 2 faint wingbars; clear pale supraloral spot reaches above eye, lores dusky. Lower rump and tail black with outer web of outer tail-feathers whitish. Throat buffy-white and rest of underparts uniform pale cinnamon-buff, underwing-coverts pale buff. Bill black with base of lower mandible orange-yellow, but rather inconspicuous. Juvenile similar with rufous fringes to wings.

Similar Little Ground Tyrant lacks whitish supraloral and eyebrow, and is white below; also occurs at lower elevations with no known overlap.

Ssp. *M. m. niceforoi* (N Co: E Andes) slightly more rufous above, tawny-buff underwing-coverts
M. m. rufescens (Ec) as described

Habits Runs on ground with crouched, horizontal jizz, standing erect when pauses to look around. Usually alone or in pairs, but occasionally in loose groups.
Status Uncommon in Ecuador, uncommon and local in Colombia.
Habitat Páramo, 2,400–3,500m in Ecuador, 2,600–3,200m in Colombia, possibly higher in both countries. Open terrain and dry, sparsely vegetated slopes with rocks and dry stone walls. Seldom seen near water.
Voice A short, usually repeated *tek* (Hilty). In display-flight flutters upwards uttering series of *t-tk* notes, stalls with wings held high and utters *cleeeoo*, then swoops to ground (F&K, Smith & Vuilleumier 1971, Fitzpatrick).

DARK-FACED GROUND TYRANT
Muscisaxicola maclovianus Pl. 202

Identification 15cm. Dark brownish-grey above with lower rump and tail black, outer web of outer tail-feather and outer edge of next feather white. Wings slightly darker with fringes as back, face and forehead blackish becoming dark umber on crown. Chin flushed umber, throat to flanks grey, white lower belly and undertail-coverts. Juvenile has buffy fringes to wing-coverts and whitish fringes to primaries, is paler on head and lacks umber flush on chin.

Ssp. *M. m. mentalis* (austral migrant: vagrant to Ec).

Status Rare vagrant to Ecuador.
Habitat Tropical Zone in April–October. Breeds in high Andes and descends to lowlands in winter where occurs in pastures, open scrub, deserts and beaches. Also moves further north, usually only as far as La Libertad, Peru (08°S). Two birds recorded in Ecuador were on coast at El Oro (03°30'S), but were oddly seen in January, when they would normally be breeding in highlands of Chile!
Voice Alarm-call a rapid series of *cheep!* notes, also a hard *tu!* which also may be repeated rapidly (F&K).

LITTLE GROUND TYRANT
Muscisaxicola fluviatilis Pl. 202

Identification 13cm. Greyish-brown above, tail black with outer web of outer feathers white; wings dusky with narrow greyish-buffy fringes to coverts and tertials, 2 wingbars, lores and eye-ring buffy (but not as obvious as line over eye in Spot-billed), throat buffy-white, breast pale greyish-buff, rest of underparts white. Similar to Spot-billed Ground Tyrant but occurs much lower and is riverine bird. Similar to Drab Water Tyrant, but readily separated by contrasting white belly and lack of loral distinction. Easy to overlook as its coloration is very cryptic, and usually only spotted when it moves.

Ssp. Monotypic (E Ec)

Habits Occurs singly and in pairs.
Status Rare and local in Ecuador.
Habitat Tropical Zone, to 1,150m. Usually on sandbars and along riverbanks.
Voice Usually quiet, utters a high-pitched, rising *peeeép* (Fitzpatrick).

WHITE-BROWED GROUND TYRANT
Muscisaxicola albilora Pl. 202

Identification 16cm. Greyish-brown above, browner on crown, with rear crown and nape tawny; tail black with outer webs of outer tail-feathers whitish, wings dusky with pale fringes, grey below, whiter on undertail-coverts. Juvenile has crown brown and narrow rufous fringes to wing-feathers. From Plain-capped Ground Tyrant by grey underparts and lack of distinct white supraloral spot.

Ssp. Monotypic (Ec)

Habits Generally forages on ground, running and stopping, rather like a pipit. Flares tail infrequently.
Status Austral migrant, uncommon to rare in southern Ecuador, at northern limit of winter range, and a vagrant to Gorgona I., off south-west Colombia (Ortiz-Von Halle 1990).
Habitat Páramo, 2,400–3,700m. Normally found on barren rocky slopes, in winter (April–September) often prefers wetter areas than those used by most ground tyrants, e.g. marshes and around lakes.
Voice Call a soft *chwip!* (Jaramillo 2003) and *tut!* (F&K).

PLAIN-CAPPED GROUND TYRANT
Muscisaxicola alpinus Pl. 202

Identification 18–19cm. Dark greyish-brown above, lower rump and tail black, crown very dark; supraloral and short eyebrow white, lores dark; white below, washed pale greyish-brown on breast and sides. Juvenile has upperparts faintly streaked darker, wing-coverts and remiges narrowly fringed cinnamon, belly and vent washed buffy, breast to vent flammulated white on pale buffy-grey.

Ssp. *M. a. alpina* (N Ec) as described
M .a. columbianus (N Co: C Andes) darker on back, almost concolorous with crown, greyer below
M. a. quesadae (C Co: C Andes) as *alpina* but smaller

Status Common in Ecuador.
Habitat Páramo, 3,800–4,600m. Puna and páramo grasslands with low vegetation, *Espeletia*, and sometimes on drier rocky soil with sparser vegetation, from treeline to snowline.
Voice Usually silent, an occasional soft *tik* or *zit* (F&K, R&G).
Note Called Páramo Ground Tyrant by R&G.

An enigmatic bird of uncertain affiliation, Short-tailed Field Tyrant is a long- and pale-legged, short-tailed, plump little bird that was formerly considered to be a cotinga, then an antbird, then a *Muscisaxicola* ground tyrant, but its distinctions were distilled by Lanyon (1986) and whilst now undoubtedly secure in its own genus, its position in Tyrannidae is far less certain.

SHORT-TAILED FIELD TYRANT

Muscigralla brevicauda Pl. 202

Identification 11cm. Pale brownish-grey above, rump pinkish-buff, uppertail-coverts rufous-chestnut, tail dusky with narrow buffy tips, wings dusky with white fringes to tertials and 2 white wingbars. Semi-concealed yellow coronal spot, supraloral spot and short eyebrow white. Underparts all white, flushed buffy on breast and yellowish on sides and flanks. Legs and feet flesh-coloured. Quite distinct in habitat.

Ssp. Monotypic (SW Ec: lowlands)

Habits Always on ground, running and stopping, seizes insects on ground or as they fly up. Upright posture and appears very short-tailed.

Status Uncommon in Ecuador.

Habitat Tropical Zone, to 1,500m but commonest near sea level. Dry to barren country, agricultural land that is bare, scattered weeds and scrub with a few trees.

Voice Song a weak sibilant *tizztízzz*, sometimes preceded by a few *tik* notes, usually given while standing on a rock but may be uttered in display-flight (R&G).

Knipolegus tyrants are represented in our region by 3 species with all-black males and brown females, and a single monomorphic species. Two have red eyes, all are notably quiet and discreet, and are primarily birds of lowland forests.

AMAZONIAN BLACK TYRANT

Knipolegus poecilocercus Pl. 203

Identification 13cm. Adult male entirely glossy blue-black, with brown eyes and blue bill. Female olive above with dusky tail, uppertail-coverts and fringes of tail rufous, wings dusky with 2 buffy wingbars and fringes to tertials and secondaries, pale lores and area around eyes, buffy-white below with dark streaking on breast and sides, yellowish on belly. Bill and eyes brown. Juvenile has head tawny concolorous with back, fringes of wing-feathers, uppertail-coverts and tail tawny; below, both more intensely and diffusely streaked, with an overall pale tawny wash. Similar Black Manakin has more rounded head and different habitat. Female more problematic, resembles several other flycatcher, e.g. Bran-coloured, Vermilion and Riverside; all lack rufous uppertail-coverts and occur in different habitats.

Ssp. Monotypic (Ec, Co, Ve, Gu)

Habits Quiet and retiring, but active, flitting from shaded perch onto stem protruding from water, or lily leaf, and is manakin-like in movements. Distinctive display consists of single male jumping few centimetres to return to same perch. Most active during heat of day. Nest record in Venezuela (November 2005) was an open basket (unlike that described for Colombia: H&B) in a side of root in flooded forest, *c.*1m above water; only one chick (D. Ascanio).

Status Rare and local in Ecuador, uncommon and local in Guyana. Widespread but local in llanos of Colombia and Venezuela.

Habitat Tropical Zone, to 350m. In Ecuador, only in blackwater drainages. Undergrowth and shady thickets around shallow water and in seasonally flooded *várzea*. In Venezuela in seasonally flooded forest.

Voice Usually silent and display vocalisations barely audible more than a few metres. Male utters high-pitched *tsik* and female louder *pit-pit* (Fitzpatrick). In Venezuela, a very soft double *ptee-reek* while displaying in air (D. Ascanio).

RUFOUS-TAILED TYRANT

Knipolegus poecilurus Pl. 202

Identification 15cm. Brownish-grey above, tail and wings slightly darker, amount of rufous in tail varies by race; 2 broad buffy wingbars, pale buffy below, washed or streaked on breast, sides and flanks. Undertail-coverts cinnamon. Eyes red, bill, legs and feet brownish-black.

Ssp. *K. p. paraquensis* (S Ve: Paraque) no rufous in tail
K. p. peruanus (SE Ec) very similar to *poecilurus*, but dusky apical markings on tail far less extensive
K. p. poecilurus (Co) greyer on back, deep ochraceous below; intermediate between *salvini* and *venezuelanus*
K. p salvini (S Ve) 2 different types of plumage or morphs; first has cinnamon ground to underparts with grey wash on breast; other pale creamy buffy below
K. p venezuelanus (W & N Ve) tail mostly rufous, like *poecilurus*, but much paler below, buffy instead of deep ochraceous

Status Rare in Ecuador, uncommon and local in Venezuela and Guyana.

Habitat Tropical to Temperate Zones, mostly 1,600–2,000m in Colombia, 1,000–2,000m north of Orinoco in Venezuela and 900–2,400m south of river. Forest borders and shrubby clearings, semi-open scrub by rivers and lakes, and especially on seasonally flooded islands with early successional growth like *Tessaria* and *Cecropia* saplings. In southern Venezuela occurs mostly on slopes of tepuis.

Voice Call, a short metallic trill, *tzteeer* or *triit* (Fitzpatrick).

ANDEAN TYRANT

Knipolegus signatus Pl. 203

Identification 15cm. Adult male uniform sooty black with white patch on underwing, eyes dark red, bill black. Female warm olive-brown above, cinnamon-rufous on uppertail-coverts and very narrow fringes to tail, wings dusky with 2 ochraceous wingbars and fringes to tertials and secondaries forming patch, underparts olive, streaked and flammulated olive-brown and pale, especially on belly and flanks. Eyes red. Juvenile similar to female but has brown eyes, is warmer brown above and wingbars whitish with patch on secondaries yellowish; streaking below paler, slightly yellowish and more extensive.

Ssp. *K. s. signatus* (S Ec: Cordillera del Cóndor)

Habits Tends to forage alone, perches upright and frequently vibrates tail from side to side. Keeps to darker areas in forest, along paths, clearings and in alder thickets and slopes along montane streams.
Status Uncommon in southern Ecuador, at extreme northern limit of range.
Habitat Subtropical Zone to Páramo, in humid montane forest.
Voice Unknown.
Note Race *signatus* formerly considered a distinct species, Jelski's Bush Tyrant *Myiotheretes signatus*, but included with *K. cabanisi* (Plumbeous Tyrant) by Traylor (1982), followed by most subsequent authors.

RIVERSIDE TYRANT

Knipolegus orenocensis Pl. 203

Identification 15cm. Male uniform sooty to blackish, brownest on wings, darkest on head, with slight crest; eyes dark, deep-based pale blue-grey bill, legs and feet blackish. Immature male a shade lighter, more fuscous or brownish. Female dark olivaceous-brown. Juvenile like female with some pale buffy streaking on throat, buffy underwing, belly and ventral area.

Ssp. *K. o. orenocensis* (Co: Meta, C Ve) as described
K. o. sclateri (E Ec) male uniform dull black, female dull olive-grey above with rufescent rump; paler below with light olive-grey streaks, fine on throat, darker on breast, paler and broader on belly and flanks; juvenile brownish-grey with pale rufous wash on rump and rufescent fringes to wing-coverts (weak wingbars) and soft pale streaking or flammulations below

Habits Display in Venezuela comprises sheer vertical flight while vocalising, usually from scrub and returns to same perch (D. Ascanio).
Status Rare in Ecuador and Colombia, uncommon and local in Venezuela in *llanos* of middle and lower Orinoco.
Habitat Tropical Zone, below 300m. Scrub and early successional growth like *Tessaria* and *Cecropia* saplings, grasses and bushes on seasonally flooded islands, and along riverbanks and by lakes. Shows greater preference for open areas than Amazonian Black Tyrant.
Voice A contact *tuk*, soft musical *peééo*, soft stuttering *pi-weet* or *pi-piweet* (Fitzpatrick) and several high-pitched raspy *tzreeet* notes followed by some jumbled notes (P. Coopmans in R&G). In Venezuela, a very soft *tsik-tsik* followed by an explosive *tschue-up!* while displaying in air (D. Ascanio).

Water tyrants are small, pied birds, always found near water. They are constantly active and are fairly social, pairs and family groups are frequently seen, and it is rare to see a lone bird, except in height of dry season when they are usually solitary.

PIED WATER TYRANT

Fluvicola pica Pl. 202

Identification 13cm. Perky, black and white birds found on ponds of all sizes. Nape, mantle and lower back black, scapulars, rump and uppertail-coverts white, tail black with white tips, wings black with broad white fringes to tertials; crown, forehead and entire underparts white; eyes, bill, legs and feet black. Juvenile has forehead dirty white becoming dark buffy on crown and nape, mantle and wing-coverts brown, remiges darker with whitish tips to tertials, tail dusky with narrow white tips. Might be confused with female White-headed Marsh Tyrant, which is much more aerial, whereas Pied Water Tyrant is more terrestrial with more contrasting plumage.

Ssp. *F. p. pica* (Co, Ve, Tr, Guianas)

Habits Flits in and out of bushes and grasses around water, wandering onto protruding sticks of semi-submerged trees, onto water lilies, etc. hunting insects. One of few birds seen in open on water at midday. Display similar to Riverside Tyrant, but flights much shorter.
Status Accidental in Ecuador, locally common in Colombia, common in Venezuela and Trinidad, frequent in Guyana and common in Suriname and French Guiana.
Habitat Tropical Zone, normally to 450m occasionally to 1,000m. Marshy areas, ponds and wetlands with aquatic vegetation, including rice cultivations. Typically also in brackish-water marshes, lagoons and seashore flats in French Guiana.
Voice A nasal, buzzy *zhweeoo* or *dreap*, mostly at dawn or dusk, a soft *pik*, like imitating sound of bubble bursting; song a repeated, buzzy *choo-wer* (Fitzpatrick).

MASKED WATER TYRANT

Fluvicola nengeta Pl. 202

Identification 14.5cm. Unmistakable. All white with black wings (tertials tipped white), tail (also has white tips) and black streak through eyes; back washed pastel brownish-grey. Bill, legs and feet black.

Ssp. *F. n. atripennis* (SW Ec)

Habits Forages alone or in pairs on ground or on water, walking on floating aquatic plants such as water hyacinth and lilies, and using dead branches of partially submerged trees, etc., to catch insects.
Status Uncommon to locally common in Ecuador.
Habitat Tropical Zone, to 800m. Marshy areas, ponds and wetlands with aquatic vegetation, including rice cultivations.
Voice Call a sharp *kirt!* Song a repeated soft, *dewdelewdel-dewdel* (Fitzpatrick).

WHITE-HEADED MARSH TYRANT

Arundinicola leucocephala Pl. 202

Identification 13cm. Male has head all white, with slightly bushy short crest that gives head rounded look, rest of bird fuscous to black. Bill black with basal half of mandible yellow. Female brownish-grey above, with dusky tail and wings, latter with brownish-grey fringes producing 2 faint wingbars; white face and throat, underparts white with brownish-grey wash to breast, sides and flanks. Juvenile is like female.

Ssp. Monotypic (N & E Co, N & C Ve, Tr, Guianas)

Habits Perches low, near ground or water, on exposed stems, and sallies to hawk flying insects. Any possible confusion with Pied Water Tyrant dispelled as latter is a terrestrial forager.

Status Rare in Ecuador, common in Trinidad, frequent in Guyana.

Habitat Tropical Zone, to *c.*500m. Marshes, shrubby, damp grasslands, and open riverine habitats including islands.

Voice Usually silent but occasionally utters a high, sharp *sedik!* or low *dewde-lewde*, repeated at short intervals in display-flight (Fitzpatrick).

YELLOW-BROWED TYRANT

Satrapa icterophrys Pl. 203

Identification 16cm. Dark olive-green above, wings and tail dusky with outermost tail-feathers partly white, wings have clear whitish fringes to wing-coverts (2 wingbars), tertials and secondaries, head tinged greyish, long conspicuous superciliary, lores and cheeks blackish-olive; throat to undertail-coverts yellow, flushed olive on breast-sides of breast, with paler undertail-coverts. Female similar, but has paler eyestripe and paler yellow below, slightly flammulated on breast and sides. Juvenile has spots on breast. Most likely to be mistaken for *Myiozetetes* flycatcher, but is separated by yellow eyestripe.

Ssp. Monotypic (Co, Ve)

Habits Forages alone. Diet insects (especially caterpillars), Probably, for most part, migrates across central Amazonian watershed.

Status Uncommon and local breeding resident in southern Venezuela. Also, an austral migrant that occasionally winters to Colombia (first recorded 1991 in Arauca: Rojas *et al.* 1997), probably in Venezuela and perhaps to the Guianas.

Habitat Tropical to Subtropical Zones, to *c.*500m. Open and semi-open areas: borders of marshes and gallery forests, by streams and lagoons, in bushes or stands of tall trees in savannas.

Voice Usually silent, but occasionally utters a mild but sharp *wheee!* Song a rising laughter-like *whuee…whee whee whee* (Fitzpatrick).

Colonia is a very small, mostly black flycatcher with a short stubby bill and variably long black tail-streamers depending on age and sex. A bird of forest edge, widespread in tropical lowlands.

LONG-TAILED TYRANT

Colonia colonus Pl. 203

Identification Male 9cm, female 8cm, tail 1–12cm, rarely longer, longest in old males, shorter in females and from 0 to several cm in juveniles. Unmistakable. Male basically all black with white forehead, crown and rump. Female similar with duller crown and whitish mottling on belly. Juvenile duller, sootier grey with pale grey belly, central tail-feathers barely project.

Ssp. *C. c. fuscicapillus* (N Ec, CE Co: E Andes) small white rump, darker crown on female

C. c. leuconota (NW Ec, W Co) like *fuscicapillus* with mottled white on back

C. c. niveiceps (SE Ec) pale grey crown

C. c. poecilonota (E Co, S Ve, Guianas) grey crown, streaked black, black back streaked grey, large white rump

Habits Usually in pairs, using an exposed favourite perch, from where sallies to hawk passing flying insects. Sedentary, a pair will occupy a clearing for long periods, possibly indefinitely if conditions remain favourable.

Status Fairly common in Ecuador, common but fairly local in Colombia, Venezuela and Guyana. Uncommon in French Guiana.

Habitat Tropical Zone, mostly below 1,200m. Borders of humid forest and secondary woodland, early successional forest, clearings and plantations.

Voice A distinctive, soft, and smooth, rising, *sweet*. May call several times and flicks tail upwards at same time. (R&G). Also a soft *tweet-a-tweet-a-tweet-a…* (H&B).

Machetornis flycatchers are ground tyrants that may be seen on pastures everywhere, running around beneath cattle and horses, but are also found on almost any open dry land. Seasonal movements, probably in response to changing weather, with result in birds temporarily occupying atypical areas at times, such as parks and gardens.

CATTLE TYRANT

Machetornis rixosa Pl. 202

Identification 19.5cm. Sandy above, with wings and tail slightly darker and fringes faintly cinnamon, scarlet crest usually largely concealed by longer and darker, olive feathers; underparts yellow. Female has coronal patch smaller, slightly paler and well concealed, crown concolorous with back, thus birds can be sexed by tone of top of head. Below, slightly paler yellow with faint buffy wash to breast. Juvenile notably paler sandy above and equally paler yellow below, lacks any red on head and has pale rufous-tawny fringes to secondaries and uppertail-coverts. Intermediate adult female plumage in which bird has tawny of secondaries and uppertail-coverts of juvenile, but sandy above and yellow below of adult. Could be confused with a kingbird, but has terrestrial habits.

Whilst kingbirds will drop to ground, they soon return to an exposed perch on high. When not foraging on ground, Cattle Tyrants will perch high, but their posture and profile, smaller headed with no grey on head, separates them. Scarlet crown usually completely obscured, but is raised when excited and is then surprisingly apparent.

Ssp. *M. r. flavigularis* (E Ec, N Co, Ve)

Habits Will often attack own image in a window or side mirror of a car. Confiding and seldom afraid of man, forages in pairs and loose groups. Propensity for ground under and around grazing herbivores, often perching on their backs.
Status Straggler or vagrant to eastern Ecuador, common and widespread across northern Colombia and Venezuela.
Habitat Tropical Zone, to 1,000m. Dry pastures, savanna, agricultural and farmland, occasionally in towns and even city parks and gardens (often on fairways of golf courses).
Voice Call and dawn song like Tropical Kingbird, but higher pitched, softer and perhaps more squeaky. Dawn song *t'te'te'ree*, repeated endlessly. Commonest call, a thin squeaky note with a rising inflection. At dusk utters series of rising and falling *tic* notes and short trills (Hilty).
Note Race *obscurodorsalis*, originally described by Phelps & Phelps (1948), synonymised with *flavigularis* by Phelps Jr. & Aveledo (1966).

Cattle Tyrant has a fasination for reflective surfaces especially car mirrors and will display to its own reflection repeatedly

Attilas are big flycatchers with large heads that are rather difficult to see, despite being quite vocal.

RUFOUS-TAILED ATTILA
Attila phoenicurus Pl. 204

Identification 18cm. Rufous above with brighter orange-rufous rump and tail, wings darker (except tertials) and primaries blackish, head grey with pale ochraceous chin and upper throat, lower throat and breast rufous, forming slightly diffuse band, rest of underparts ochraceous. Bill all dark with pale spot at base of lower mandible, eyes dark reddish-brown, legs and feet grey. From Citron-bellied Attila by contrasting grey head with rufous back, darker rump and rufous breast.

Ssp. Monotypic (S Ve)

Habits Forages in canopy and at mid levels.
Status Uncommon austral migrant, rare or scarce in southern Venezuela, where possibly winters May–October. Threatened by continuing deforestation in its breeding range in south-east Brazil and north-east Argentina.
Habitat Tropical to Subtropical Zones, to 1,500m. Lighter areas in humid forests and mature second growth.
Voice Mostly silent while in winter range.
Note Several morphological differences (in tarsus, wing, bill) compared to others in genus led past authors to place *phoenicurus* in separate, monotypic genus *Pseudattila*. Present treatment follows Traylor (1977, 1979).

CINNAMON ATTILA
Attila cinnamomeus Pl. 204

Identification 20cm. Rufous above, including wings and tail, rump brighter orange-rufous but contrast not striking, primaries dusky; cinnamon-rufous below, perhaps slightly yellowish on belly; eyes chestnut-red. Sexes quite alike. Could be confused with Greater Schiffornis, which has more compact body and is smaller. Smaller Cinnamon Becard has bright, pale supraloral spot and superciliary.

Ssp. Monotypic (E Ec, SE Co, E Ve, Guianas)

Habits Forages sedately at mid levels and subcanopy, most often in pairs. Will perch quietly for few minutes, tail characteristically hanging down. Takes berries, frogs, wasps, crickets, flies, cicadas and weevils. Breeds early in rainy season, building cup nest of dry sticks, semi-concealed behind bromeliad or in crack in trunk.
Status Uncommon and local in Ecuador and Colombia. Locally common in Venezuela. Frequent in Guyana, quite common in Suriname and French Guiana.
Habitat Tropical Zone. *Várzea*, marshy forests with *Euterpe* palms and *Symphonia* trees, mature mangrove.
Voice Both birds of pair sing, long repetitions of a slow, clearly whistled phrase *twe-tueeeeeer, twe-tueeeeeer…* (H&B, H&M). Gives ringing, hawk-like whistle, *pü-puéééeeear*, rising then descending and fading. Song often repeated persistently (Fitzpatrick).

OCHRACEOUS ATTILA
Attila torridus Pl. 204

Identification 22cm. Unique and unmistakable. Cinnamon-ochraceous head and back, scapulars, lesser wing-coverts and tail cinnamon, rump and short uppertail-coverts paler ochraceus-cinnamon, wings dusky with ochraceous fringes to coverts, tertials and secondaries, primaries fuscous; entire underparts ochraceous-yellow.

Ssp. Monotypic (W Ec, SW Co)

Habits Forages in pairs, in canopy and at mid levels. Perches upright, often exposed, very quiet, idly lifting tail now and then. Sallies to pick insects from air or foliage. Also takes fruits and berries.

Status Uncommon in Ecuador and possibly rare in Colombia (only 1 record?). Threatened by deforestation in its small, Pacific coast range.
Habitat Tropical Zone to 1,500m. Borders and clearings of humid lowland forests, cocoa plantations.
Voice Far-carrying loud repetitions of *whoeeeer* notes (R&T), downslurred and similar to Black Hawk-Eagle, and sometimes extended to *whoeeeer, wheéu whit-whit*; also a sharp *wheek* or *keek* call. Song a rising series of whistles, *wuuu-wuuu-weee-weee-weeé-weeé-wuyeép* with cadence similar to Cinnamon Attila (Fitzpatrick).

CITRON-BELLIED ATTILA

Attila citriniventris Pl. 204

Identification 20.5cm. Rufous-olive back and wing-coverts, tertials, rump and tail cinnamon, uppertail-coverts yellow-ochre; head grey, grading into ruddy back, lores whitish, chin grey with white flammulations, ochraceous throat and breast, rest of underparts yellow-ochre. Sexes appear alike, but female has more yellow on belly, where male is mostly rufous. Bill dark above, pale horn to flesh below, dark reddish-brown eyes, legs and feet grey. From Rufous-tailed Attila by duller back and ochraceous breast without band-like quality. Pale lower mandible also diagnostic. Possibly confusion with smaller Greater Schiffornis, which has stubby bill and lacks pale, contrasting lower rump.

Ssp. Monotypic (E Ec, E Co, S Ve)

Habits Forages in canopy, alone or in pairs. Inconspicuous, perches quietly for long periods or sings, repeating song over and over.
Status Rare in Ecuador and Colombia, locally frequent in Venezuela.
Habitat Tropical Zone, to 300m in Ecuador. Humid forests, both interior and at borders and clearings.
Voice Song a series of *cuee* notes, ending in a lower-pitched *cuu* note (P. Schwartz recording *fide* H&B). A loud, rapid and slightly rising *whee-whee-whee-wheewu*, last note lower. Also a flat *whee- whee- whee- whee- whee…* on same pitch (Hilty).

DULL-CAPPED ATTILA

Attila bolivianus Pl. 204

Identification 22cm. Rufous-brown above, including wings, but primaries dusky, rump to tail cinnamon-rufous, top of head dark brown, rufous-cinnamon below, intense and rich on throat to cinnamon on undertail-coverts. Eyes straw to white, bill horn above, flesh below, legs and feet blue-grey. From Cinnamon Attila by white eyes.

Ssp. *A. b. nattereri* (extreme NE Ec, extreme SE Co)

Habits Forages alone at low and mid levels. Very sedate and shy, so even if singing is quite difficult to see, as tends to perch hidden. Nest of mosses similar to plumage colour.
Status Sighted in Ecuador, where possibly a vagrant. Locally frequent in Colombia.
Habitat Tropical Zone, to 250m in Ecuador, 500m in Colombia. Wet areas: swamp forests, *várzea*, boggy islands of larger rivers.
Voice Song similar to *A. spadiceus*, a series of rising notes *wheet, wheet, wheet, wheet, wheet, weeu* (H&B), or *whee-whee-whee wee-per, wee-per, wee-per, wheu* (T. A. Parker).
Note Called White-eyed Attila in R&G.

BRIGHT-RUMPED ATTILA

Attila spadiceus Pl. 204

Identification 19cm. Polymorphic, with 3 main morphs but intermediates confuse situation. Of 35 specimens from Venezuela alone, we found 13 different plumage types representing 5 distinct groups (see plate). Almost all have bright yellow rump (species' characteristic) and 2 wingbars. Note eye colour extremely variable, from pale yellow, through orange and red to dark brown, regardless of morph. Bill dark above, mandible also varies, from whitish to dark. Legs and feet generally blue-grey, but vary from pale to dark. From other species by yellow rump and wingbars, both characteristics which are somewhat obscure in some individuals.
Olive morph (common) olive above, with pale yellow rump, bright orange-rufous tail, yellowish lores and area around eyes, below entirely pale yellow with dark-streaked breast and sides, fading out on upper belly and flanks.
Grey morph has grey back, neck and head with white-streaked chin to breast, white belly and flanks, dark reddish-brown tail and undertail-coverts sulphur-yellow.
Rufous morph is deep rufous above, and on throat and breast, with rufous fringes to wing-feathers, deep orange-ochre of rump infuses upper tail, head dull dark rufous-grey, chin has white streaks, breast uniform. Belly, flanks and undertail-coverts buffy. All our specimens had orange eyes.
Rufous-and-white morph very deep rufous above with ochre rump and bright rufous tail, buffy fringes to wing-feathers; all white below, streaked rufous-brown from chin to breast, becoming soft greyish, fading on flanks; undertail-coverts white. All specimens had bright orange eyes.
Grey-and-yellow morph is slate grey above with deep pure yellow rump, tail dark rufous-brown, pale grey fringes to wing-feathers; grey chin to breast, streaked yellow, rest white streaked olive-grey, undertail-coverts pale yellow.

In view of extreme variation within our region, and the fact that races are differentiated on minor characters we find racial descriptions only confusing.

Ssp. *A. s. caniceps* (N Co)
A. s. parambae (NW Ec, W Co)
A. s. parvirostris (NE Co, NW Ve)
A. s. sclateri (NW Co)
A. s. spadiceus (S Co, C & E Ve, Tr, Guianas)

Habits Forages sedately, at all levels but mostly mid, usually solitary but occasionally with mixed flocks. Sallies for passing insects or gleans foliage, and will sing from concealed perch for many minutes. Very noisy and vocalises frequently; more often heard than seen.

Status Uncommon to rare in Ecuador. Frequent in Colombia, Venezuela, Guyana and French Guiana, frequent and widespread in Suriname, uncommon in Trinidad (no records Tobago).

Habitat Tropical to Subtropical Zones, usually below 1,500m but recorded to 2,100m. Wet and humid forests and mature second growth.

Voice In Colombia, main songs described as a short phrase that sounds like *beat-it* and a longer whistled *weed-we-two*, oft-repeated (H&B). In Ecuador, song a far-carrying, forceful ascending series, higher pitched in west, *whup, whip, wheédip, wheédip, wheédip, wheédip, wheédip……wheeeyr*, with distinctive slur at end. Frequent call a fast, laughing *weer-weer-weer-weer-weer-weer……weerpo*. Also some staccato notes in flight (R&G). In Venezuela, main song *whé-tit, whé-tit, whé-tit, whé-tit, whé-tit… wheeuu*, last note lower and downslurred, sometimes alternated with *weed we-to, weed we-to, weed we-to, weed we-to, weed we-to, weed we're-took*, swelling and rising then sliding at end, with numerous variations. Finally, a loud, angry rattle when alarmed or disturbed, *di-di-di-di-dit!* (Hilty).

Note Differences in dawn song enable subspecies to be placed in 2 groups, Middle and South American, which suggests that more than one species is involved (Leger & Mountjoy 2003). But, there are also apparent vocal differences within our region anyway, and indeed as much variation in song as there is plumage variants.

RUFOUS MOURNER

Rhytipterna holerythra Pl. 204

Identification 20cm. Rich rufous, darker on crown and slightly paler below, wings and tail dusky with rufous fringes. Bill dark, pale at base of mandible, eyes dark, feet and legs black. Very similar Rufous Piha larger, with round head and fuller body. Also tends to perch more angled when at rest, whereas Rufous Piha perches more upright. Similar Speckled Mourner has faint black spots on fringes of lesser and median coverts, and juvenile has black fringes to median and greater coverts forming clear black bars.

Ssp. *R. h. rosenbergi* (NW Ec, W Co) darker than *holerythra*
R. h. holerythra (N Co) as described

Habits Furtive and difficult to find. Forages alone or in pairs, from canopy to low levels, leisurely sallying or moving through foliage to pick insects, berries and fruits. Perches on top branches to sing or view surroundings. Possibly nests in holes in dirt banks.

Status Rare in Ecuador, uncommon and local in Colombia.

Habitat Tropical Zone, to 700m in Ecuador and 1,000m in Colombia. Wet and humid forests and mature second growth. Rarely at forest edges.

Voice One call very similar to a wolf whistle (H&B) a rising then falling, drawling *wheeeip-wheeeur* (R&G) that sounds mournful (Fitzpatrick). A brighter and somewhat more cheerful song, *wheee-per, wheeéur* (R&G).

GREYISH MOURNER

Rhytipterna simplex Pl. 203

Identification 20cm. Uniform grey body, dusky wings and tail with grey fringes to all feathers, paler and more yellowish-grey belly is variable, with some paler than others, regardless of sex or age. Eyes red, bill legs and feet black. Juvenile generally paler, particularly on flanks, belly and undertail-coverts which are pale sulphurous grey. Wings and tail dusky with cinnamon to rufous fringes. Eyes chestnut to dark, bill black with paler base to mandible, legs and feet dark grey. Screaming Piha very similar and may be very difficult to separate in field, but is slightly larger, more slate grey and has browner eyes. Best way to separate them is by voice.

Ssp. *R. s. frederici* (E Co, S Ve, Guianas)

Habits Forages alone, in pairs or family groups, usually very quietly, and may pass unnoticed. Sallies from perch to pick passing insects, but also hover-gleans for berries and small fruits in subcanopy and at mid levels. Joins mixed feeding flocks.

Status Locally common to uncommon in Ecuador, uncommon in Colombia, frequent in Guyana, Suriname and French Guiana.

Habitat Tropical Zone, mostly below 700m in Ecuador and 500m in Colombia, but to 1,300m in Venezuela. Humid to semi-dry forests and savanna woodland.

Voice Both sexes sing, a yodel (H&B) or sequence of toneless notes ending in a loud whistle (H&M). A loud, fast, rather sneeze-like *r-t-t-t-t-t-t-tchéw*, somewhat explosive and sometimes repeated severally, or *tchew!* uttered a few times (R&G). Also a rising series of notes that slows at end, *tu-tu-te-te-tee tee teeuw teeuw* (P. Coopmans).

PALE-BELLIED MOURNER

Rhytipterna immunda Pl. 203

Identification 19cm. Greyish-olive above with darker wings and tail, buffy fringes to coverts, more rufescent fringes on rectrices and remiges, face, throat and upper breast paler grey, pale yellow below, ochraceous on undertail-coverts. Bill dark with pale base to lower mandible, eyes red, legs and feet grey. Might be confused with a *Myiarchus* flycatcher, but has completely rounded head with no crest, concealed or otherwise, a far less upright posture, perches at right angles, and is far less active.

Ssp. Monotypic (E Co, Ve, Su, FG)

Habits Forages alone or in pairs in canopy or upper level of bushes, where perches for long periods, usually inside foliage. Feeds on berries and fruits.

Status Scarce and local in south-east Colombia (very few records), Guyana, French Guiana and uncommon to locally fairly common in Venezuela (sight records on Cerro Neblina), rather frequent in Suriname.

Habitat Tropical Zone to 300m. *Cerrados*; semi-open, sandy soil woods and scrub.

Voice Song a loud ringing 3-note phrase, *kerr-WEE-chew… kerr-WEE-chew…*, with middle note stronger and richer.

SIRYSTES *Sirystes sibilator* Pl. 205

Identification 18–19cm. Two distinct races. Essentially grey above with white rump and grey uppertail-coverts, wings and tail black, with pale fringes to wing-feathers, head and nape black, feathers bushy and *Myiarchus*-like, head-sides grey, underparts white, washed grey on throat and breast. Bill, legs and feet black. Juvenile similar but has buffy wash. Likely to be mistaken for a becard or a *Myiarchus*, but grey back and white rump diagnostic, and only Swainson's Flycatcher has whitish underparts.

Sirystes is very much like Myiarchus *in shape and profile – it frequently raises its crest and lowers its head forward, but the white rump is diagnostic*

Ssp. *S. s. albocinereus* (E Ec, E Co, SW Ve) brownish-grey back and wing-coverts, feathers fringed paler, including back, uppertail-coverts dark brownish-grey; flammulated soft grey from chin to lower breast and sides; eyes dark chestnut

S. s. albogriseus (NW Ec, NW Co: Chocó) more grey above, only long uppertail-coverts darkish grey, tail black with white tips, wings black with white fringes, chin and throat white, breast washed clean grey; eyes red

Habits Forages in pairs, in canopy, sallying to air or foliage to pick insects, fruits and berries, and moves through treetops with mixed flocks. Posture similar to a canary and frequent gestures include raising crest and nodding head.

Status Uncommon in Ecuador, uncommon and local in Colombia and Venezuela, scarce in Guyana, uncommon in Suriname and French Guiana.

Habitat Tropical Zone, to 1,000m. Canopy of humid primary and secondary forests, particularly in *várzea* and riparian forest.

Voice In Ecuador, *albocinereus* (Eastern Sirystes) utters loud calls including *wheeer-péw* and *wheer-péw-pu*, sometimes in an excited series, *wheeer-pe-pe-pew-pew-péw* or *wheeer-péw-péw-péw* (R&G). In contrast, *albogriseus* (Western Sirystes) gives a husky *chup-chip-chip* or *prup-prip-prip-prip*, and excited birds a much faster *che-che-che-che-che-che-chut* (P. Coopmans). In Venezuela, Hilty notes calls of Eastern Sirystes as *wheer whit-it*, *wheer whit* or *wheer, pe-pe-pe*, and excited acceleration as *wheeer, pi-pi-pi-pi-pi-pi*.

Notes Formerly placed in the Cotingidae but better placed in Tyrannidae adjacent to *Myiarchus* (Lanyon & Fitzpatrick 1983). Race *albogriseus* treated as separate species, Western Sirystes, in R&G, with remaining races called Eastern Sirystes in R&G and Hilty, based on different plumage and voice.

Myiarchus flycatchers comprise a remarkably homogeneous genus that is notoriously difficult to identify to species. Fairly upright though not vertical in posture, they have large-looking heads due to the full, bushy crests, and are dark greyish-brown above, greyish on throat and breast and yellow below. Differences are subtle and quite confusing when subspecific variation is considered. Indeed, many subspecies appear to be simple intergrades between more distinct populations. Undertail pattern and coloration can be key; beware of relying on rufous in plumage as all juveniles have rufous fringes to wing-feathers. Check distribution, as this can be critical, and voice is an invaluable aid. They all build nests in cavities or holes, and use an inordinate amount of trash in construction, from discarded snake skins to plastic.

[RUFOUS FLYCATCHER *Myiarchus semirufus*] Pl. 205

Identification 18cm. Grey-brown above, wings and tail all rufous with central tail-feathers and tertials having fuscous centres; chin to undertail-coverts ochraceous-cinnamon. Eyes, bill, legs and feet dark. Characteristically *Myiarchus* in posture and demeanour, but quite distinct in its rufous colouring.

Ssp. Monotypic (extreme S Ec: hypothetical)

Habits Forages in pairs, in upper levels.

Status Endemic to coastal Peru, listed for Ecuador by Altman & Swift (1993), clearly in error (SFP&M, R&T, R&G), but was listed in Rodner *et al.* and hence here.

Habitat Tropical Zone. Dry, semi-open areas: thorn scrub, deciduous woodland, cultivated fields along rivers.

Voice Calls intermittently, a whistled soft *huit* (R&T). Male's dawn song alternates *huit* notes with rasping whistles (Lanyon 1978).

DUSKY-CAPPED FLYCATCHER *Myiarchus tuberculifer* Pl. 205

Identification 16–17cm. Fairly small. Generally greenish-olive above with dusky wings and tail, pale fringes to feathers form indistinct wingbars, undertail mid brown, head darker, being slate grey on bushy crown (looks black in field), pale grey to whitish chin, clean pale grey on throat and breast, bright pale yellow below. Eyes, bill, legs and feet dark to blackish. Juvenile has rufous fringes to wing-feathers. From other

Myiarchus by small size, dark crown (distinctive) and absence of rufous in tail.

Ssp. *M. t. atriceps* (S Ec) larger with black crown and greyish-washed nape, paler yellow below
M. t. brunneiceps (W Co) greenish back
M. t. nigriceps (W Ec, SW Co) blackish crown with greyish-washed nape, richer yellow below
M. t. pallidus (N Co, N&WC Ve) paler above, crown smoky olive
M. t. tuberculifer (E Ec, E Co, S Ve, Guianas) as described

Habits Usually in pairs. Forages from mid levels to canopy, mostly alone but often with mixed flocks. Feeds by sallying, usually in open, sunlit spots above foliage. Often perches in open tangles. Habitual gestures include raising crest and nodding. Main diet insects and their larvae. Breeding season of nominate race August–Oct., *atriceps* in Ecuador February–April, other races March–June.
Status Widespread in Ecuador, fairly common in Colombia, Venezuela, Guyana, Suriname and French Guiana.
Habitat Tropical Zone to Páramo, to 1,500m in Ecuador but to 2,500m in south, to 1,800m in Colombia with record to 2,400m in Nariño, in Venezuela to 2,000m north of Orinoco and 1,300m south of it. *Várzea* and dry to humid lowland and montane forests, coffee and banana plantations and second growth, along watercourses and at borders and clearings, but not in dense forest.
Voice A wistful, tapering whistle, *keeuh… keeuh…* (H&M) or *peeeerrr…* (H&B). At dawn, males alternate whistles and *huit* notes (H&M). Most distinctive and key for identification is a double *wheet-peeert*, uttered repeatedly when excited (D. Ascanio).

SWAINSON'S FLYCATCHER

Myiarchus swainsoni Pl. 205

Identification 19.5–21cm. Generally considered dullest of genus, quite variable racially. Look for bill colour to differentiate austral migrants (maxilla light brown, mandible deep pink or orange) from residents (maxilla black, mandible brownish). Dark olive-grey above with sooty cap, white fringes to wing-coverts, tertials and distal part of secondaries, undertail dark brown, grey throat and breast with yellow to belly, white undertail-coverts. Juvenile and immature have rufous fringes to wing-feathers. From congeners by very dark undertail and pale sulphur belly.

Ssp. *M. s. albimarginatus* (N Su) intergrade between *pelzelni* and *phaeonotus*
M. s. ferocior (austral migrant to SE Co, W Ve?) pale olive-green above, brownish-olive ear-coverts darker than rest of head, more extensive and paler yellow below
M. s. pelzelni (Guianas) olive-green above, paler yellow below
M. s. phaeonotus (E & S Ve, S & W Gu) dark smoky olive, olivaceous breast and dingy tinge to entire underparts, bill black
M. s. swainsoni (austral migrant to E Co, N Ve, Su, Tr) as described
M. s. amazonus (Su, FG) intergrade between *pelzelni* and *phaeonotus*
M. s. fumosus (SE Ve, synonymous with *phaeonotus*)

Habits Forages alone, in pairs or small groups, from mid levels to canopy, often with mixed flocks. Sallies or flits to pick insects, fruits and berries. Like congeners, does not perch erect, but rather forward-leaning. Not shy. Nests in cavities (woodpecker and natural tree holes), recesses in broken limbs or stumps, or under eaves. Lines nests with variety of soft materials: hair, fur, feathers and pieces of shed snake skins.
Status Uncommon in Ecuador (austral migrant), in Colombia both migrants and residents, locally common in Venezuela, especially south of Orinoco. Resident populations frequent in Guyana and Suriname, but austral migrants (*swainsoni*) scarce.
Habitat Tropical to Subtropical Zones. Austral migrants mainly keep to lowlands, typically below 400m, but residents reach 2,600m in Colombia and 1,800m in Venezuela. In different parts of our region, migrant and resident races use different habitats. Migrants select borders, clearings and riverbanks in humid and *várzea* forests in Colombia; mangroves and coastal woodland in Suriname; fields with scattered trees, scrub, woods in savannas, mangroves, gallery and deciduous woodland and second growth in Venezuela. Residents occur in humid forests of tepui slopes in Venezuela, but drier, partially open areas, e.g. sandy soil savannas with *Curatella*, in Guyana and Suriname.
Voice Main calls a melancholy *phweeeee* whistle (H&B) or doubled *wiherr… wiherr…* for *pelzelni* (H&M); also outbursts of whistles (Lanyon *fide* H&B). Breeding season of residents is February–May. Males have 2 dawn songs: whistles of varied length alternating with occasional *huit* notes, and same plus complex combinations of modulated whistles and a central *huit*.
Notes Both *pelzelni* and *phaeonotus* were formerly accorded species status whilst a recent genetic study (Joseph *et al.* 2004) found that all races, except nominate, are closest to *M. tuberculifer*. Races *albimarginatus* and *amazonus*, described from Suriname and French Guiana, apparently relate to fresh-plumaged intergrades between *pelzelni* and *phaeonotus* (Fitzpatrick).

VENEZUELAN FLYCATCHER

Myiarchus venezuelensis Pl. 205

Identification 18–18.5cm. Dark olive-green above, central crown darker, giving slightly streaked effect, wings dusky, 2 pale wingbars, fringes of tertials and secondaries yellow, fringes of primaries usually rufous, undertail pale olive, and outer webs to outer tail-feathers whitish below with white quills and narrow rufous fringes, throat and breast grey flammulated white, underparts pallid yellow. Juvenile has narrow rufous fringes to secondaries, long uppertail-coverts also rufous. Panama Flycatcher paler on back, with darker brown undertail, less rufous on primaries and richer yellow below including undertail-coverts. Race *brunnescens* of Short-crested Flycatcher has darker brown undertail and warm buffy undertail-coverts, with a brownish, olive-buffy wash on breast.

Ssp. Monotypic (NE Co, N Ve)

Habits Forages alone or in pairs, at mid levels and in canopy. Sallies for insects in air or picks them from foliage with a short hover. Breeding season possibly March–June.
Status Locally frequent in Colombia, uncommon and local in Venezuela but under-reported due to identification problems, and locally frequent on Tobago.
Habitat Tropical Zone, to 500m in Colombia. Generally in partially open areas, deciduous woodland, savannas with scattered stands of trees or bushes, rocky, forested ridges. On Caribbean coast edges of humid to moist forests. South of Orinoco moist forest usually near water.
Voice Rasping whistles, hiccups and *wheer-r-r* notes in aggression, with melancholy whistles in contact, and male's dawn song comprises sad isolated whistles (Lanyon 1978). No rolls, trills or *huit* notes (Hilty).

PANAMA FLYCATCHER
Myiarchus panamensis Pl. 205

Identification 18–19cm. Greyish-olive above, wings and tail slightly darker with paler, yellowish-white fringes to wing-coverts and tertials, outer webs of undertail whitish and quills white, same feathers above buffy on outer webs and quills dark brown. Centres to crown-feathers dark, creating streaked effect, throat and breast pale grey and rest of underparts pale yellow. Eyes, bill, legs and feet dark. Juvenile has rufous fringes to wing-coverts. Venezuelan Flycatcher has heavier, somewhat dingy grey throat, and outer webs of outer tail-feathers narrowly rufous with rufous quills. Short-crested Flycatcher of race *brunnescens* has brownish olive-buffy wash to breast, throat paler and slightly yellowish, outer webs to outer tail-feathers rusty with brown quills on upperside.

Ssp. *M. p. panamensis* (W, C & N Co, NW Ve)

Habits Forages alone or in pairs, from mid levels to canopy, occasionally on ground. Takes insects and fruits by sallying. Also runs on ground like a thrush to snatch insects.
Status Frequent in Colombia and Venezuela.
Habitat Tropical Zone. Semi-arid, partially open areas: scrub, light woodland, mangroves, borders and clearings in dry forest.
Voice Dawn song consists of isolated, short, vibrato whistles, and same used as infrequent contact-calls between foraging birds (Lanyon 1978). Day call a short modulated whistle at infrequent intervals, sometimes in pairs or rapid series' which may become modified *huit* notes or short rolls or trills (Hilty). Repeated hiccups, rasping whistles and rolls in response to intruding conspecifics (Fitzpatrick).

SHORT-CRESTED FLYCATCHER
Myiarchus ferox Pl. 205

Identification 18-19cm. Dark brown above with dusky wings and tail, pale fringes to wing-coverts and tertials, greyish on throat and breast may reach sides and flanks, yellow below. Juvenile has rufous fringes to wing-coverts. Venezuelan Flycatcher has more reddish-rufous fringes to outer webs of outer tail-feathers from above, and whitish with white quills below. Panama Flycatcher has back paler olive and undertail-coverts are same yellow as underparts.

Ssp. *M. f. brunnescens* (Llanos: Ve & Co) much browner with mid brown undertail, breast brownish-olive with marked wash to flanks, slightly richer yellow below, buffy undertail-coverts; juvenile has secondaries rufous, not tawny, undertail-coverts buffy, outer webs of outer tail-feathers pale below with pale brown quills, and rusty above (not as reddish as *venezuelensis*) and brown quills
M. f. ferox (E Ec, E Co, S Ve, Guianas) darker olive above with particularly well-defined upper wingbar, sootier head, throat and upper breast cooler grey with pale olivaceous wash on sides and flanks

Habits Forages alone or in pairs, from mid levels to canopy, in sunlit area. Picks insect, fruits and berries by sallying and quickly hovering in foliage. Other typical gestures include nodding head and raising tail slowly. Calm and sluggish.
Status Uncommon in Ecuador; frequent in Colombia, Venezuela, Guyana; common and widespread in Suriname, and common in French Guiana.
Habitat Tropical Zone, mostly below 500m but occasionally to 1,000m. Partially open areas, borders and overgrown clearings of humid and mangrove forests, stands of bushes in sandy soil savannas, gallery forests, coffee and cocoa plantations.
Voice Most frequent is a soft purring *prrrrt*, sometimes a descending trill (H&B), *turrrt* (Hilty), also a toneless rattle *jhirrrr* (H&M). At dawn, males sing isolated whistles with an explosive vibrato modulation, *trrrrrrrrrrrr-rrr-rrr*, also given during day (D. Ascanio).

PALE-EDGED FLYCATCHER
Myiarchus cephalotes Pl. 206

Identification 18–20cm. Dark brown above, white fringes to wing-feathers form 2 wingbars, with white-edged tertials and tail-feathers, head virtually concolorous with back, head-sides slightly lighter, throat and breast pale grey, rest of underparts yellow. Eyes, bill, legs and feet dark. Juvenile has rufous fringes to secondaries. From others of genus in range by whitish outer fringes to tail-feathers.

Ssp. *M. c. caribbaeus* (N Ve) smaller and outer fringes of tail paler
M. c. cephalotes (E Ec, C & S Co) as described

Habits Forages alone or in pairs, from canopy to lower levels, often perching on exposed branches at mid levels; occasionally

with mixed-species flocks. Sallies to hover-glean from foliage and sometimes in air.
Status Uncommon in Ecuador, uncommon to locally common in Colombia and Venezuela.
Habitat Tropical Zone to Páramo, 1,400–2,100m in Venezuela. Borders and clearings of dense to light primary montane forest.
Voice At dawn, males give sharp, piercing whistles, whilst during day calls include rasps and descending whistles (Lanyon 1978) or a vigorous if slightly sad *wheep, pip-peer-peer-peer* (H&B).
Notes Races *caucae* and *gularis* are synonymous with *cephalotes*.

SOOTY-CROWNED FLYCATCHER
Myiarchus phaeocephalus Pl. 205

Identification 18–19cm. Greyish-olive above, with dusky wings and 2 greyish wingbars, pale greyish fringes to tertials and outer tail-feathers. Head blackish on hindcrown with grey forehead, throat and breast pale grey, underparts pale yellow.

Ssp. *M. p. phaeocephalus* (W Ec)

Habits Forages alone or in pairs, at mid and upper levels, sallying conspicuously to foliage, occasionally to ground. Takes insects and berries. Nests in deep (>30 cm) cavities in broken branches or trunks of trees at ±2 m above ground, with lining of fur, bits of plastic and snake skin, feathers and cloth. Season February–April.
Status Uncommon to rare in Ecuador.
Habitat Tropical to Subtropical Zones. Borders and clearings of mangrove and arid or semi-arid deciduous forests, dry scrub.
Voice Males sing series of melancholy whistles at dawn. During day, calls include repetitions of 2-syllable hiccups and high-pitched or rasping whistles, whilst contact-calls are rapid, descending sequences of whistles (Lanyon 1978). Most frequent is a querulous *freeee?* or *whreeee?* Song is combination of this note and low burry *tr-tret* notes (hiccups). Also a descending *wheeé-dee-dee-de-du-du* (P. Coopmans).

APICAL FLYCATCHER
Myiarchus apicalis Pl. 206

Identification 18–19 cm. Dark olive above with dusky wings and tail (white tips and pale greyish-olive underside), wings have whitish fringes to tertials and coverts (2 wingbars), crown brownish-olive with dark centres giving streaked appearance. Throat and breast pale grey, sides to flanks washed olive, rest of underparts pale yellow. Juvenile has rufous fringes to wing-feathers. From congeners in range by whitish outer fringes to tail and pale underside.

Ssp. Monotypic (C Co)

Habits Forages alone or in pairs. Sallies to foliage, to air and occasionally to ground, to catch insects or pick fruits or berries. Breeding season January–April.
Status Locally frequent Colombian endemic in upper basins of Cauca, Patía, Magdalena and Dagua rivers.
Habitat Tropical to Temperate Zones, 400–1,700m but has occurred to 2,500m. Arid and semi-arid open areas, savannas, fields and pastures with scattered trees or light woodland, along rivers.
Voice Dawn song unknown, possibly whistled notes, but day calls include hiccups, whistles and varied *huit* calls, especially if alarmed. Appears capable of changing between these calls seamlessly. Does not use rasp notes (Lanyon 1978). Typically gives a long series of rolls without interjecting any other vocalisations (Fitzpatrick).

GREAT CRESTED FLYCATCHER
Myiarchus crinitus Pl. 206

Identification 20cm. The largest *Myiarchus* and a boreal migrant. Olive-green above with rufous-tinged uppertail-coverts and tail largely rufous, wings dusky with whitish wingbars, rufous fringes to primaries, fringes of secondaries greyish-white and fringes of tertials yellowish-grey. Crown and nape darker brown with darker centres affording a well-streaked appearance, head-sides slightly paler than back, chin whitish, throat and upper breast grey, lower breast and underparts bright yellow. Iris, legs and feet dark. Bill dark above with pale horn mandible. Female slightly smaller, juvenile a little duller. From congeners by combination of size, amount of rufous in wings and tail, and bright, contrasting underparts.

Ssp. Monotypic (N Ec, N Co, NW Ve)

Habits Forages alone, from lower to top levels but mostly in canopy, at fruiting trees and bushes, and picks insects in flight, from cracks in bark and ground. Character variously described as peaceful and sluggish, perching quietly on top branches (P&MdS), or as active and aggressive, hawking for prey (F&K).
Status Irregular boreal migrant (October–May) with sight records in Ecuador, and uncommon in Colombia and western Venezuela.
Habitat Tropical Zone. Borders and overgrown clearings of humid primary forest, mature second growth, plantations. Also drier forests.
Voice An ascending, loud whistle, *wheeeep* (H&B) or *wheee-eep* occasionally in series (Fitzpatrick), frequently heard in our region.

BROWN-CRESTED FLYCATCHER
Myiarchus tyrannulus Pl. 205

Identification 20cm. Large. Greyish-brown above, head, wings and tail only slightly darker. Rufous lower rump to basal sides of tail. Two white wingbars, upper stronger, rufous fringes to primaries and whitish fringes to tertials and secondaries. Throat and breast pale grey, underparts pale sulphur-yellow. Bill particularly large and heavy, dark often with pale base to mandible. Juvenile slightly warmer on head, fringes of wing-coverts tawny, tertials creamy buff. From congeners by combination of size, heavy bill, amount of rufous in wings and rufous uppertail-coverts.

Ssp. *M. t. tyrannulus* (N & E Co, N Ve, T&T, Guianas)

Habits Forages alone or in pairs, by sallying from perch to air or ground. Takes insects and spiders. Often perches in open. Constructs twig nest in cavity on trees or posts, at >1m from ground, lined with feathers, hairs and discarded snake skins.

Status Common in Colombia, frequent in Guyana, Suriname and French Guiana. Usually the commonest *Myiarchus* encountered in open country.

Habitat Tropical to Subtropical Zones. Mangrove, arid and semi-arid areas with light deciduous or thorny woodland or scrub, deciduous gallery forest, savanna woods.

Voice Very vocal. A long, low sequence of *whip* notes (H&B), also *week-week-week-wee-hee-hee-hee-heeuw* (H&M). Male's dawn song alternates isolated *huit* notes with complex series of *whay-burg* notes (Lanyon 1978). The *huit* note is that most frequently used in calls and songs and is characteristic (Fitzpatrick). No long whistled notes. Dawn song also described as a whistled roll, *WHEE'p'peer* (Hilty).

Kingbirds (genus *Tyrannus*) are amongst the better known groups of Neotropical flycatchers due to their habit of sitting proudly on an exposed perch, from whence they sally forth after passing insects. The commonest and most widespread by far is Tropical Kingbird. With the exception of long-tailed species, all look more or less the same, so that other species may be dismissed too readily as the common congener.

SNOWY-THROATED KINGBIRD

Tyrannus niveigularis Pl. 206

Identification 19cm. Clean, almost bluish-grey above, becoming slightly olivaceous on lower rump and uppertail-coverts, black wings and tail, whitish fringes to wing-coverts and tertials form 2 white wingbars; semi-concealed yellow coronal crest may be raised, giving top of head a bushy appearance, black lores through eye in broad band ending on ear-coverts; chin and throat pure white, breast grey and underparts pure light yellow. From larger Tropical Kingbird, by square tail (not forked), white throat and grey breast very noticeable.

Ssp. Monotypic (W Ec, SE Co)

Habits Usually alone, perching atop vegetation but not on most prominent branches, as congeners often do. Sallies for insects or picks small fruits and berries.

Status Fairly common breeder Ecuador but disperses post-breeding, some to Colombia, where apparently uncommon and poorly known (H&B).

Habitat Tropical Zone, below 500m in Ecuador but to 1,200m in Colombia. In breeding season, semi-desert scrub and dry open areas with scattered trees or light woodland, stands of *Acacia*, forest borders or uninhabited clearings. Post-breeding in more humid areas, where more likely to be seen with Tropical Kingbird, e.g. clearings and borders of forested areas.

Voice Shorter and drier than similar calls of Tropical Kingbird, a sharp, *kip!* that may be extended into *kip-krr-ee-ee-ee* (R&G). Dawn song a fast jumbled *ki-ki-ki-krr-reé-it!* (P. Coopmans). In Colombia gives a soft twitter (Marchant *fide* H&B).

WHITE-THROATED KINGBIRD

Tyrannus albogularis Pl. 206

Identification 21cm. Yellowish-olive above, with dusky wings and tail, feathers having fine whitish fringes but no wingbars, pale grey head with semi-concealed short orange crest that may be raised, giving top of head bushy appearance; broad black band from lores through eyes forms clear mask, chin, upper throat and head-sides white, underparts lemon-yellow. Tropical Kingbird has darker grey head and olive breast, but when perched high in sun might appear paler. Look for contrasting pale head and distinctly contrasting broad white throat of White-throated, and lack of olive on breast.

Ssp. Monotypic (NE Ec, SE Co, SE Ve, Guianas)

Habits Perches in open on high branches and telegraph wires. Forages by sallying from perch.

Status Northern South American populations are: a) resident in south-east Venezuela and southern Guianas; or b) austral migrants from central Brazil to extreme southern Colombia and easternmost Ecuador (sight records only), and north-east and south Venezuela. Scarce to rare, but frequent at a few localities, and migrants present May–August. Sight records in French Guiana need confirmation and may involve austral migrants only.

Habitat Tropical Zone, below 100m. Always near water. Open or lightly wooded areas and palm groves, especially Moriche palm *Mauritia flexuosa* stands, sometimes in swamp forests.

Voice Similar to Tropical Kingbird, but does not call often. Typically a shrill, trilled, *tic tic tic i'i'i'i'i'i'i'i'i'i'* (Fitzpatrick).

TROPICAL KINGBIRD

Tyrannus melancholicus Pl. 206

Identification 22cm. Greyish-olive above, darker on rump and uppertail-coverts, wings and tail fuscous with faint pale fringes to feathers but no wingbars; head mid grey with partially concealed orange crest that gives head bushy aspect when raised, broad black band from lores through eye, rarely with sufficient contrast with top of head and pale grey cheeks to appear bold; chin whitish, upper throat and fore-face grey, olive breast and lemon-yellow below. Juvenile is like adult female but lacks any coronal line; chin and throat are pure white, breast is a narrow dusky bar and underparts paler yellow; all wing-coverts, uppertail-coverts and edges of rectrices cinnamon. From congeners by combination of larger size, larger and heavier bill, less white throat, and olive breast,

Ssp. *T. m. melancholicus* (Ec, Co, Ve, Guianas) as described
T. m. satrapa (N Co, Ve, T&T) crown pale grey, throat white, chest-band pale yellowish

Habits Forages usually alone, sallying from a prominent perch or chasing and swooping on insects; will also pick spiders, and catches small fish by hovering like a tern over a pond or stream. May be seen on its perch throughout day. In breeding season, often mobs raptors that approach its nest, which is a neat open cup of dry sticks, often quite exposed. Sing from before daybreak, from high exposed perch.

Status Abundant throughout range. Birds from south of range (Argentina, south Brazil) winter to Amazonia, including French Guiana and might rarely reach extreme southern Venezuela and south-east Colombia.

Habitat Tropical to Subtropical Zones, to 1,800m in Ecuador and 2,700m in Colombia. Man-made or natural open areas with scattered trees or patches of light woodland (including in cities). In forest, at clearings, borders and riversides.

Voice In Ecuador (*melancholicus*), varied high-pitched, twittering calls, e.g. *pee, ee-ee-ee-ee*, a dawn song of *pip* or *pee* notes, followed by a rising twitter, *piririree?* which may be repeated a few times. One of first birds to sing, often before first light (R&G). In Colombia and Venezuela (race?) a high, trilled, *tre'e'e'e'e'eip* with a more elaborate dawn song as in Ecuador (H&B, Hilty).

SCISSOR-TAILED FLYCATCHER

Tyrannus forficatus Pl. 207

Identification 35cm (including tail ±18cm). Grey above, often tinged pinkish on lower back, brown rump, elongated tail black with white (flushed pink or yellow) outermost tail-feathers with black tips, wings black with whitish fringes to feathers, perhaps with vestigial wingbars, head to breast grey, palest on throat, underparts flushed salmon or pink. Some variation due to age and development of tail, and some have shorter tail and are yellow instead of pink or salmon. Female slightly duller and pink weaker, tail also slightly shorter. Immature has even shorter tail and is less colourful. Fork-tailed Flycatcher easily separated by black cap and white underparts.

Ssp. Monotypic (NE Ec, E Co, Pacific seaboard)

Habits Forages mostly by flycatching insects. Perches in open, even on fence wires and posts.

Status Boreal migrant that normally only just reaches Panama, mostly on Pacific side. Sight records from eastern Ecuador and perhaps the north-west coast of Colombia.

Habitat Tropical Zone, coastal lowlands. In winter, open, moist areas (pastures, agricultural land, semi-humid scrub), but no data from Ecuador.

Voice Does not sing while in the region.

FORK-TAILED FLYCATCHER

Tyrannus savana Pl. 207

Identification 28cm. (including male's tail ±10cm). Pale grey above with black wings and tail, pale whitish fringes to feathers but no wingbars. Top and sides of head and nape black, with semi-concealed yellow coronal patch; all white below. Female and juvenile have shorter tails, but as adult males moult tail, only sure males are those with long tails! Unmistakable due to its long slender tail, but even juvenile with its essentially 2-tone plumage is easy to recognise.

Ssp. *T. s. monachus* (Central American migrant to, and resident in N & C Co, Ve, Su, FG) cleaner, more pure grey above than *savana*
T. s. sanctaemartae (resident in NE Co, NW Ve) like *monachus*, but has differently emarginated outer primaries
T. s. savana (austral migrant: winters to E Co, Ve, T&T, Guianas) slightly dingy grey above

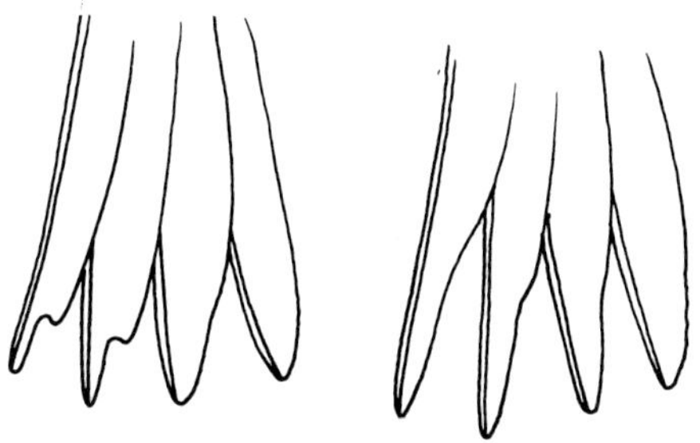

There is significant difference in emargination of outer primaries of Fork-tailed Flycatcher, race monachus *(left) and* sanctaemartae, *though in the field birds appear alike (after Zimmer 1937c)*

Habits Found alone or in loose flocks that may seem to pass in waves. Perches mostly in open. At night, thousands may gather to roosts on trees, palms, in reedbeds or their fringes. Feeds at fruiting trees and Royal Palms (*Roystonea*), often gathers at swarming termites and also picks beetles, wasps, butterflies, berries. Chases hawks and others that may be perceived as a threat. Flight measured and elegant, with long tail lending a certain special grace to all movements.

Status Populations in our region are: a) residents (*T. monachus* breeds in Llanos, March–May, Sipaliwini, Suriname, January, and once recorded breeding in coastal French Guiana, February–March); b) migrants from Middle America that winter east and west of Andes from October to April; and c) austral migrants that winter east of Andes, from Colombia to Trinidad and the Guianas from late March to October. Migrant races are frequent, with austral breeders usually most numerous. Both boreal and austral migrants may occur together in March and October. Rare in Ecuador. Quite common in Colombia, Venezuela, Guyana, Suriname and French Guiana.

Habitat Tropical to Subtropical Zones, usually below 1,000m but migrants recorded to 3,000m in Andes. Moist to

dry savannas, pasture and agricultural land. In forests occurs on or above treetops, in clearings and along open roads and river.
Voice Calls consist of soft *tic* notes and twittering.

EASTERN KINGBIRD

Tyrannus tyrannus Pl. 206

Identification 22cm. Entire upperparts blackish with white tips to tail and partially concealed bright vermilion coronal patch, chin to undertail-coverts white, washed grey on lower throat and breast. Immature browner with no coronal patch, and dirty brownish smudges on neck-sides, lower throat to breast, and flanks. Much darker above than Grey Kingbird, and from all other congeners by white not yellow below.

Ssp. Monotypic (Ec, Co, Ve, T&T, Guianas)

Habits In our region mostly in compact migrating bands that most often perch high on outer branches of canopy or on wires. Sometimes flies erratically.
Status Migrant from North America, passing through our region to winter further south, as far east as French Guiana. Moves south September–October and north in March–May, but is never numerous, and stragglers may occur between two periods; sometimes with flocks of Fork-tailed Flycatcher.
Habitat Tropical to Subtropical Zones, mostly below 800m but occasionally much higher, to 3,700m in Ecuador, 2,600m in Colombia and 1,700m in Venezuela. Partially open areas: parks, gardens, plantations, fields with trees, light woodland, forest edge.
Voice Does not call on migration.

GREY KINGBIRD

Tyrannus dominicensis Pl. 206

Identification 23cm. Grey above, darker wings and tail, with pale grey fringes forming vestigial wingbars, head grey with partially concealed orange to yellow coronal patch, black lores and band through eye to ear-coverts forms somewhat masked appearance. White chin to undertail-coverts, washed grey (mostly) on breast-sides; bill dark, and quite large and heavy. Juvenile browner above with buffy to rufous fringes to wing-coverts and tail-sides and washed rufous on uppertail-coverts. From Eastern Kingbird by grey not black upperparts, and from all other congeners by white underparts instead of yellow. Also, Eastern Kingbird has 2 distinctive white terminal spots on tail.

Ssp. *T. d. vorax* (Tr) larger, slightly darker and heavier bill
T. d. dominicensis (boreal migrant, breeds on SE coast of USA and in Greater Antilles, winters in northern S America) as described

Habits Residents usually occur alone or in pairs, migrants in small loose bands; perches on conspicuous perches at mid to high levels to sally for insects and forages in bushes and canopy for fruits and berries. Can be quite aggressive towards smaller birds, and observed mobbing finches to rob them of food.
Status Vagrant to Ecuador, locally fairly common in northern Colombia, local breeding resident in Venezuela, becoming locally frequent to very common in mid September–March or mid April. Fairly common in coastal French Guiana late September–early April.
Habitat Tropical Zone (occasionally to Subtropical Zone or higher), with records to 3,000m in Colombia and 1,700m in Venezuela. Generally in moist to dry open areas with scattered trees and bushes or stands of light woodland, urban areas, pastures.
Voice Three-note call is a rolling, cheerful *pe-cheer-ry* (R. T. Peterson *fide* H&B). Noisy, shrill, chattering *pitch-chir'r'r'e* (Hilty).

VARIEGATED FLYCATCHER

Empidonomus varius Pl. 207

Identification 18cm. Dark brown above with paler fringes creating a slightly streaked appearance, lower rump and uppertail-coverts rich rufous with black centres, outer fringes of tail-feathers also rufous; wings blackish with white fringes forming 3 wingbars in fresh plumage, upper far less noticeable in worn plumage; head dark, blackish on top with partially concealed yellow coronal patch, white spot on lores forms long superciliary around ear-coverts and across lower nape (where joins), lower cheeks to chin and throat dingy white, divided by dusky malar stripe; throat tinged yellow becoming dingy buffy-yellow, heavily streaked dusky on breast and sides, rest of underparts yellow. Juvenile lacks yellow coronal patch but has rufous fringes to feathers of crown; in all other respects resembles adult. Resident *rufinus* very like smaller Piratic Flycatcher, but separated by rufous tail, and migrant *varius* also told by this character. Eyebrow far less noticeable than on Piratic whilst Streaked Flycatcher is significantly larger and much more clearly streaked. Juvenile might be confused with juvenile Crowned Slaty Flycatcher.

Ssp. *E. v. rufinus* (resident of WC, S & E Ve, Guianas, possibly extreme SE Co) compared with *varius* has softer, more diffuse flammulations, ending at breast and sides
E. v. varius (austral migrant: winters in E Ec, E Co, N Ve, Tr, Guianas in March–August) darker brown above, mainly because fringes darker than in *rufinus*, below, streaks darker, bolder and more pointed, reaching flanks

Habits Residents alone or in pairs, migrants often in small groups. Nest a shallow cup of dry, fine twigs and rootlets, placed on a *Curatella* or other low bush.
Status Uncommon in Ecuador, locally frequent to uncommon in Colombia, widespread and frequent in Venezuela, Guyana and Suriname, scarce in French Guiana. Migrants occur late February–August, most frequent May–July.
Habitat Tropical Zone, mostly below 1,200m though recorded to 1,900m in Venezuelan Andes. Race *rufinus* in open areas and savannas with scattered trees and bushes or patchy woodland.

Race *varius* in borders and brushy clearings of humid forest, mangrove and plantations.
Voice Song weak, and may be confused with insects. A high-pitched *zreeee* whistle, 3-note *chee-chee-chuum* (Snyder 1964) and thin *pseee* (R&T) at irregular intervals. Migrants vocalise only occasionally.

CROWNED SLATY FLYCATCHER

Griseotyrannus aurantioatrocristatus Pl. 206

Identification 18cm. Dull brown above with dusky wings and tail, fringes to wing-feathers slightly paler (faint wingbars), top of head blackish with large yellow, partially concealed, coronal patch, but longer feathers, with black central streaks, extend to nape; grey supraloral almost forms frontal band and extends in a clear superciliary, lores black with dark streak running through eye, and cheeks grey. Below soft grey, becoming paler and increasingly yellowish on belly and undertail-coverts, but rather dingy. Juvenile browner on head and lacks yellow crest, with rusty fringes on wings, uppertail-coverts and basal sides of tail.

Ssp. *G. a. aurantioatrocristatus* (austral migrant: occasionally winters to Ve, Gu) as described
G. a. pallidiventris (austral migrant: winters to E Ec, SE Co) slightly paler above and below, with cleaner and paler whitish-yellow belly and undertail-coverts

Habits Forages alone, quite sedately and almost lethargically. Perches exposed high at forest edge. Sallies to pick flying insects.
Status Fairly common March–September in Ecuador, but less common in Colombia and scarce in Venezuela and Guyana.
Habitat Tropical to Subtropical Zones, below 1,100m in Ecuador, to 400m in Colombia and to *c.*1,000m in Venezuela (once to 2,500m). Humid and partially open areas: borders of humid and *várzea* forests, fields with scattered trees or bushes.
Voice Does not sing while in the region.

SULPHURY FLYCATCHER

Tyrannopsis sulphurea Pl. 209

Identification 20cm. Dark olive above, dusky grey on head with concealed yellow-orange coronal patch, blackish lores and stripe through eye to fuscous cheeks, white throat, streaks on sides extend to breast, rest of underparts yellow. Like a dark Tropical or White-throated Kingbird but smaller-headed and smaller-billed, and neither has dark streaking on sides of throat and breast.

Ssp. Monotypic (E Ec, SE Co, S & SE Ve, Tr, Guianas)

Habits Forages alone, in pairs or small family groups, sallying from tops of Moriche Palms *Mauritia flexuosa* for spiders, bees, termites and ants, or picks nuts. Cup nest of dry sticks, high in palm. Very vocal.
Status Very local Moriche Palm specialist, very seldom found away from these trees, but may occur even within boundaries of urban areas. Rare in Ecuador, local in Colombia, uncommon and local in Venezuela, frequent in Guyana and French Guiana.
Habitat Tropical Zone, to 400m. Open areas, both natural and man-made, but always associated with Moriche Palms.
Voice Calls often and loud, like pulses of electric energy, *zhrEEEEEEEE!, zhr-zhrEEEEEEEE!* with pairs rapidly counter-calling in fast repartee. Song a similar-sounding, high-pitched, penetrating series of blurred trills, *zhr'dek…zhr'r'r'e'k…zhr'dek'dek…* (Hilty) or *jweez, jweez-z jweez, jee-peet, jee-peet-teet, jeepeet, ks, ks, ks, ks-ksi-gay* (Fitzpatrick).

BOAT-BILLED FLYCATCHER

Megarhynchus pitangua Pl. 208

Identification 23cm. Large, large-headed and even larger-billed. Olive above with buffy fringes to wing- and tail-feathers, top of head black with mostly concealed orange coronal patch, bold white supercilia from supraloral to nape where they join. Lores black reaching back in broad band across head-sides to rear ear-coverts, trailing off below superciliary. Chin and throat pure white, rest of underparts pure primrose-yellow. Bill massive and very broad, eyes brown, legs and feet dark grey. Juvenile similar though browner above, with rusty fringes to wing- and tail-feathers, head dark brown without coronal patch, and yellow underparts paler. Easily mistaken for Great Kiskadee when in canopy, but massive bill is significantly broader and longer when seen from above or below. Side-on, back less rufescent and fringes to wing-coverts, remiges and rectrices also less rufescent. Voices are also different.

Ssp. *M. p. chrysogaster* (W Ec) fringes to wing-coverts, tertials and secondaries more rufous, coronal patch tawny-orange
M. p. mexicanus (NW Co) more greenish-olive above, coronal patch tawnier
M. p. pitangua (E Ec, C & E Co, Ve, Guianas) as described

Habits Forages alone or in pairs, mostly quite high and perches in canopy, usually in cover and often heard before seen. Takes large insects, spiders and small vertebrates, berries and fruit. Build shallow cup nest of dry twigs, high on a limb.

Boat-billed Flycatcher (left) is often confused with Great Kiskadee in the field, but a view of their heads from above shows how different they are

Status Widespread in Ecuador, frequent in Colombia, Venezuela, Guyana, Suriname and French Guiana.
Habitat Tropical to Subtropical Zones, to 1,300m in Ecuador, 1,400m in Colombia and 1,900m in Venezuela though mostly below 1,000m. Partially open areas, forest borders and clearings with trees, plantations, second growth.
Voice Quite vocal. In eastern Ecuador, most frequent call (*pitangua*) a strident, nasal *kryeeeh-nyeh-nyeh-nyeh* sometimes pumping head as it calls, in west (*chrysogaster*) a fast *kreh-kreh-kreh-kreh- kreh-kreeeenh*, and series of *kirrr-wick* calls (R&G). In Colombia (*mexicanus*?) frequently utters distinctive nasal mocking, *nya-nya-nya-nya-nya…* (H&B). In Venezuela (*pitangua*), a wavering *kwée'le* and dawn song, *whé-dic*, repeated continually (Hilty). Voice may recall somebody continually complaining!

Conopias flycatchers are tree-top dwellers, usually found in twos or threes. They perch still on tops of emergent trees and are easier to see from forest edges or from a canopy observation point.

WHITE-RINGED FLYCATCHER
Conopias albovittatus Pl. 209

Identification 16.5cm. Olive above, slightly darker on wings and tail with white fringes to tertials and secondaries, top and sides of head black with semi-concealed yellow coronal patch, white frontal bar runs back and broadens behind ear-coverts and across nape, forming complete diadem. Throat white, underparts all yellow. Juvenile browner above, with rusty barring on head instead of yellow patch, wing-coverts and rump have rusty fringes, and fringes to tertials and secondaries more yellowish. From Lemon-browed Flycatcher by white brow, which might not be noticeable in poor light, but white fringes to tertials and secondaries of White-ringed diagnostic.

Ssp. *C. a. albovittatus* (NW Ec, W Co)

Habits Forages alone, in pairs or small family groups, always high in canopy. Active and vivacious. Nests in holes in tree trunks, lined with grass.
Status Uncommon in Ecuador and Colombia.
Habitat Tropical Zone, mostly below 1,000m. Borders of wet and humid forests, mature second growth, clearings with tall scattered trees.
Voice Call consists of a rattling trill, a short note and another rattling trill *qua-tre'e'e'e'e* (Skutch *fide* H&B) or as a fast *tre-r-r-r-r, tre-r-r-r-r* (R&T, R&G).

YELLOW-THROATED FLYCATCHER
Conopias parvus Pl. 209

Identification 16.5cm. Olive above, slightly darker on wings and tail with pale or yellowish fringes to tertials and secondaries, top and sides of head black with semi-concealed yellow coronal patch, white frontal bar broadens behind ear-coverts and across nape, forming complete diadem. Throat and underparts yellow. Juvenile browner above with fringes on head, instead of yellow patch, back, wing-coverts, rump and uppertail-coverts have rufous fringes, and much paler yellow, almost white below. Three-striped Flycatcher has white brow ending on rear ear-coverts whilst Lemon-browed has full diadem, broad on nape, and bright yellow.

Ssp. Monotypic (E Ec, E Co, S & SE Ve, Guianas)

Habits Usually forages in pairs in canopy, frequently in recently burnt areas. Sallies for insects and picks berries and fruits. Weaves cup nest of fine grasses inside abandoned woodpecker hole, usually on dead tree, and will also fix abandoned cacique nests.
Status Rare in Ecuador, uncommon in Colombia, uncommon to locally common in Venezuela, frequent in Guyana, Suriname and French Guiana.
Habitat Tropical Zone, to 1,300m. Borders of wet and humid forests.
Voice Calls loudly and frequently, a rhythmic *queelele* (H&B), *quee-le-le* (Hilty) or *tre-tree-tree* (R&T) and *weedle-de-wee* (Fitzpatrick).

THREE-STRIPED FLYCATCHER
Conopias trivirgatus Pl. 209

Identification 16cm. Olive above, paler on upper mantle and nape, rest of upperparts have paler fringes affording slightly mottled effect and palest on tertials. Head blackish with white supraloral over eye and around ear-coverts, almost joining on nape, but not as broad and noticeable as in other *Conopias*. Entire underparts yellow. Eyes dark red. Juvenile has upperparts paler and fringes slightly rustier, remiges and rectrices decidedly paler brown. Underparts paler yellow. Social and Rusty-margined Flycatchers similar but both have white throats and far more clearly marked fringes to wing-feathers, and uniform backs.

Ssp. *C. t. berlepschi* (NE Ec, S Ve: upper río Caura)

Habits Forages in pairs or small family groups, and with mixed canopy flocks. Perches in open on high branches and calls frequently.
Status Only sight records in extreme north-east Ecuador, where rare and local, first recorded in 1992 (P. Coopmans). Very rare in Venezuela, (one specimen and a few recent sight records).
Habitat Tropical Zone, mostly below 300m. Humid lowland forests, *várzea*. At borders and along rivers.
Voice A vigorous, raspy *jeeuw* in fast repetitions or as single notes (R&T).

LEMON-BROWED FLYCATCHER
Conopias cinchoneti Pl. 209

Identification 16cm. Greenish-olive above, wings and tail dusky with 2 narrow rusty wingbars and rusty fringes to tertials, secondaries, uppertail-coverts and basal half of tail-feathers. Top and sides of head darker olive-green with broad frontal band extending over eye and around ear-coverts to nape-sides (narrower than most congeners). Underparts entirely olive, more sulphur on throat. Juvenile undescribed. From similar congeners by vivid yellow superciliary.

Ssp. *C. c. cinchoneti* (E Ec) broader superciliary and bar on nape, no wingbars
C. c. icterophrys (Co: Andes, Ve: Andes in Mérida and Barinas; Perijá) narrower superciliary and paler throat

Habits Forages in canopy, alone, in pairs or small family groups, sometimes with mixed flocks. Quite noisy. Perches on canopy top, jumping between perches. Sallies to take insects or picks fruit by briefly hovering.
Status Uncommon in Ecuador, very local in Colombia and Venezuela.
Habitat Tropical to Subtropical Zones, 1,000–2,000m in Ecuador, 900–2,100m in Colombia with records to 400m, and 450–2,150m in Venezuela. Humid, wet and cloud forests on montane slopes, at borders and clearings.
Voice Distinctive far-carrying call of *cinchoneti* a series of shrill notes, e.g. *pi-dee* or *prid-d'reeee*, often rapidly repeated with head pumping (R&G); of *icterophrys* a quavering *ptreeer-ptreeer-ptreeer* (H&B) and *pa'treeeer* or *pa'treeeer'pa treeeer'patreeeer* with peculiar nasal and complaining quality; distinctive once learnt (Hilty).

GOLDEN-CROWNED FLYCATCHER
Myiodynastes chrysocephalus Pl. 209

Identification 19–20cm. Olive above, wings, tail and uppertail-coverts darker with rufous fringes forming 2 wingbars and well-defined tertials and secondaries, fringes of uppertail-coverts and basal half of tail-feathers. Top and sides of head fuscous with only partially concealed long yellow patch, white superciliary from supraloral to behind ear-coverts. Underparts yellow, with buffy wash to throat and olive flammulations on breast and sides. Juvenile browner above, fringes to feathers brighter and slightly buffier, head brown with no coronal patch, yellowish superciliary reaches around ear-coverts to join broad yellow malar. Paler yellow below, faint flammulations on breast. From Great Kiskadee by incomplete white superciliary and broad white malar. Also occurs at higher elevations and probably replaces Streaked and Boat-billed Flycatchers in highlands.

Ssp. *M. c. cinerascens* (Co: Santa Marta, W Ve) as described
M. c. minor (Ec, Co) very similar, darker above

Habits Forages alone or in pairs, mostly in canopy and occasionally joins mixed flocks. Feeds on insects and fruits. Perches upright but with head slightly sunk, exposed at mid heights or in canopy, nodding, or will sing from treetop.
Status Uncommon in Ecuador, common in Colombia and Venezuela.
Habitat Tropical to Temperate Zones, mostly 1,000–2,100m in Ecuador, 900–2,400m in Colombia and 600–2,300m in Venezuela. Humid, wet and cloud forests, in clearings with trees and borders.
Voice Very vocal, with a loud raucous and squealing *skweé-ah!* or *squeeé-yu!*, repeated insistently (R&G), like squeezing a rubber bath toy (Hilty), and a loud energetic *kiss-u* (H&B). Dawn song a repeated *squeeé-yu-d'r'r'r* (P. Coopmans). Also a melancholy *pee-ah* or *peeeir*, similar to Social Flycatcher (Fitzpatrick).

BAIRD'S FLYCATCHER
Myiodynastes bairdii Pl. 209

Identification 23cm. Brown above with darker wings and tail; wings have buffy fringes forming two wingbars, well-defined on tertials and secondaries, becoming rufous on secondaries, and fringes to rump, uppertail-coverts and tail-feathers all rufous. Head sandy brown with yellow coronal patch and yellowish supercilia, blackish band from lores to rear ear-coverts, chin whitish, rest of underparts yellow with pale sandy wash to throat and upper breast. Bill blackish, large and heavy. Golden-crowned Flycatcher has markedly more streaked head and is generally at higher elevations.

Ssp. Monotypic (SW Ec)

Habits Forages alone or in pairs, mostly in canopy, sallying for airborne insects or in foliage. Perches on bare branches or wires, but to sing tends to perch partially hidden.
Status Uncommon in Ecuador.
Habitat Tropical Zone, to 1,000m. Dry, partially open areas, deciduous forest, arid scrub, along streams, parks and gardens.
Voice Rarely sings except at dawn and dusk, bowing with each phrase. Described as *tuie-wee, tuieweet* (F&K) or *wrryeeit… wrryeeit… wrryeeit…* every 2–4 s (R&G).

STREAKED FLYCATCHER
Myiodynastes maculatus Pl. 207

Identification 22cm. Widespread with considerable racial variation. Essentially dark above with pale fringes giving streaked appearance, wings darker with pale fringes, rump, uppertail-coverts and basal fringes to feathers of dark tail, all rufous with dark centres; partially concealed yellow coronal patch, narrow white superciliary, underparts white perhaps with yellowish suffusion, streaked dusky. Bill large, blackish with flesh-coloured base to mandible. Juvenile browner on head and lacks yellow patch, rufous-tawny fringes on wings, is paler, creamier white below with more diffuse streaks. In northern Ecuador and southern Colombia, very similar Sulphur-bellied Flycatcher has stronger yellow belly and streaks of malar joining across breast in band. Elsewhere, no other flycatcher as large and prominently streaked, and large bill is noteworthy.

Ssp. *M. m. chapmani* (W Ec, W Co) nearest to *difficilis* but differs from it and all other races by unusually broad and clear superciliary, most of which unstreaked, and streaks on breast slightly heavier than *difficilis*
M. m. difficilis (NW Co, W Ve) very close to *tobagensis*

but streaks lighter and only extend to upper flanks, marginally more rufous in wings, belly whitish-yellow

M. m. insolens (boreal migrant to NW Co?) pale olive above with yellow supercilium and little streaking

M. m. maculatus (Su, FG) as described

M. m. nobilis (NE Co) fairly pale and buffy, more yellow below

M. m. solitarius (austral migrant to Co, Ve, Guianas) most crisply contrasting black and white, streaked from chin to undertail-coverts; juvenile slightly more yellowish below

M. m. tobagensis (C & E Ve, T&T, Gu) very broadly edged pale brown above and on head, giving much paler appearance, broad and heavy dusky streaks on breast, extending to flanks, belly clear warm yellow

Habits Forages alone or in pairs, in canopy and at mid levels, on berries, fruits and large insects by sallying from branches. Residents breed in rainy season. Nests in abandoned woodpecker holes, lined with grass, or builds cup nest on palm or tree, occasionally under eaves of house.

Status Uncommon in Ecuador, frequent in Colombia and Venezuela, fairly common on Trinidad, less so on Tobago, uncommon in Guyana, fairly frequent in Suriname and French Guiana.

Habitat Tropical to Subtropical Zones, mostly below 1,500m but higher, to 3,000m in Venezuela. Resident races in mangroves, especially Red *Rhizophora mangle* and White Mangroves *Avicennia nitida*, and in borders and clearings of *várzea*, humid *terra firme*, forest along rivers, river islands, coffee plantations. Migrant races in drier, lighter woods in savannas, from late April–early September.

Voice Residents usually silent (H&M) or as often noisy (H&B), with calls including a loud, sometimes repeated *dit*. Calls in Ecuador *kip! chup!* and *eechup!* all sometimes repeated intermittently (R&G), in Colombia a loud *dit!* (H&B), in Venezuela *sqUEE-zik!* (Hilty) and, on Trinidad, *chip chip chip* at rate of 1 per s (ffrench). A musical *wheet-siddle-whit* at dawn and dusk (J. V. Remsen in H&B). Dawn song in Ecuador *wheeé-cheederee-wheé* (R&G) and in Venezuela *WEET, wiggle-your-feet!* without pause (Hilty), on Trinidad, *scree-per-cher-wee* (ffrench).

Note Race *solitarius* perhaps a separate species, Solitary Flycatcher, but possibility discounted by Fitzpatrick.

SULPHUR-BELLIED FLYCATCHER

Myiodynastes luteiventris Pl. 207

Identification 20cm. Dusky above with pale yellowish fringes giving streaked appearance, including lesser coverts; lower rump, uppertail-coverts and fringes of tail-feathers rufous, wings fuscous to black with white outer fringes to coverts, tertials and secondaries, forming wingbar on median coverts; broad blackish bar from lores to ear-coverts, with white superciliary and malar; chin and throat white, rest of underparts yellow, with blackish teardrop streaks on throat-sides, across breast and sides and flanks. From Streaked Flycatcher by yellow infusion to upperparts, and streaks that form a sort of necklace across breast.

Ssp. Monotypic (Ec, Co)

Habits Forages mostly alone, occasionally in pairs, at all levels, mostly on fruits and berries.

Status Boreal migrant, (winters in west and south-west Amazonia), uncommon to rare transient through Colombia in October and March–April, both transient and winter resident in Ecuador, October–April.

Habitat Tropical to Subtropical Zones, to 2,600m on passage, but residents in Ecuador below 400m. Borders of humid forests, semi-open second growth.

Voice Rather silent in winter but sometimes gives *squeez! ya* call or plain *squeez!* (R&G).

Myiozetetes flycatchers are medium-sized olive-and-yellow birds with black-and-white striped heads, much as many other flycatchers, and are often quite common in open areas at edges of lowland forests and clearings. Two are regularly confused and often found around habitation, particularly farms and buildings. They construct enclosed nests high among branches of trees.

RUSTY-MARGINED FLYCATCHER

Myiozetetes cayanensis Pl. 208

Identification 16.5–17cm. Essentially greenish-olive above with dark brown wings and tail, rusty fringes to wing-feathers, uppertail-coverts and tail-sides; block of cinnamon-rufous in secondaries. Head black with partially concealed yellow-orange coronal patch, broad white frontal band continuing as a superciliary, white throat and yellow underparts. Juvenile lacks coronal patch and has broader rusty margins, and is slightly paler below. Social Flycatcher is very similar and, in Ecuador, differences not readily apparent; elsewhere, rufous in wings of *rufipennis* sufficient to prevent confusion.

Ssp. *M. c. cayanensis* (S Ve, Guianas) medium-width rufous fringes to tertials, remiges, uppertail-coverts and tail, pale greenish wash on breast, crown patch mostly yellow, orange hidden below yellow

M. c. hellmayri (W Ec, W & C Co, W Ve) slightly paler back, narrow buffy-tawny fringes to wing-coverts, narrow rufous fringes to remiges, more intense yellow below, crown patch centrally orange, yellow at sides

M. c. rufipennis (E Ec, E Co, N & C Ve) broad rufous fringes to wing-feathers, uppertail-coverts and tail, shafts of breast feathers form fine dark lines, crown patch entirely orange; juvenile has wing almost all rufous

Habits Forages in canopy and at mid levels, sallying in

open and over streams to catch insects. Berries and fruit also important in diet. Bathes in rain or by plunging in flight like kingfishers. May be multi-brooded. Quieter and less bold than *M. similis*. Pairs often sing in duet, while displaying.
Status Common virtually throughout our region.
Habitat Tropical to Subtropical Zones, mostly below 1,000m in Ecuador, to 1,500m in Colombia (rarely to 2,100m), and to 1,900m north of Orinoco in Venezuela, below 1,000m south of river. Always near water. Partially open areas, forest borders, clearings, riverbanks or stream sides, along roads, in orchards, parks and gardens.
Voice Most frequent call, which identifies species, a high-pitched and plaintive, sad-sounding *freeeea* (R&G) *wheeeee* (R&T), *cheeeeeeuw* (H&M) or *peeeeeeea* (H&B). Other, faster and more excited calls may be uttered in duet, but sound much like Social Flycatcher, *cheepcheeree-chew* and a fast, repeated *keewit* (R&G). Also a loud and emphatic *puuuuureeeéé-éét-éét* or *too-eeéet*. Dawn song a repeated *fweee*, sometimes in short couplets or with an additional note (Fitzpatrick).

SOCIAL FLYCATCHER
Myiozetetes similis Pl. 208

Identification 16.5–17cm. Essentially greenish-olive above with dark brown wings and tail, rusty fringes to wing-feathers, uppertail-coverts and tail-sides; block of cinnamon-rufous on secondaries. Head sooty grey with partially concealed red coronal patch, broad white frontal band continuing as a superciliary, white throat and yellow underparts. Juvenile more greyish-brown above with wing-coverts more buffy than rufous, lacks coronal patch and has broader rusty fringes to wings and tail. Very similar Rusty-margined Flycatcher also varies racially. In west Ecuador, Rusty-margined *hellmayri* is buffy-olive above with tawny fringes to secondaries and primaries, and is least rufous-winged of its species, but most intense yellow below. In comparison, Social Flycatcher race *grandis* is slightly deeper yellow below, and has paler wing-coverts more conspicuous than other races. Elsewhere, differences between them greater, with Rusty-margined being more obviously rusty-winged. Also, note that Social lacks calls similar to mournful and plaintive *peeeeeea* of Rusty-margined. In Venezuela, race *similis* easily confused with Rusty-margined; north of Orinoco separation easier as Rusty-margined looks like a bleached Social Flycatcher. Note cheeks of Social are dusky, but black in Rusty-margined.

Ssp. *M. s. columbianus* (N Co, N & C Ve) paler and greener above, finer fringes to tertials and secondaries, faint sulphur wash on throat; juvenile has buff fringes to tertials, tawny fringes to rest of wing- and tail-feathers, on breast, feather shafts form fine lines

M. s. grandis (W Ec) pale tips to greater coverts more noticeable, secondaries more yellow, and more intense yellow below

M. s. similis (E Ec, E Co, S & SW Ve) darker and browner above, fringes of tertials and secondaries broader and slightly yellowish, superciliary slightly yellowish, pale yellow wash to throat; juvenile has narrow buffy fringes to wings and tail, crown darker with vestigial orange-red in centre

Habits Forages alone, in pairs or, most often, in vocal, exuberant (family?) groups. Feeds at all levels, by sallying for insects or gathering at fruit- or berry-laden trees. Picks berries by hovering in front of them.
Status Common in Ecuador, Colombia and Venezuela.
Habitat Tropical Zone, below 1,400m in Ecuador, below 900m in Colombia though to 1,200 on east slope of Andes, and to 1,500m in Venezuela north of Orinoco but only below 500m south of it. Open areas with patchy woodland or scattered trees and bushes, forest borders and clearings. Well adapted to urban areas.
Voice Calls varied, oft-repeated, and rather unmusical. Race *grandis* gives chattering *kree-kree-kree*, whilst *similis* has a chattered *ti-ti-ti-ti-chew*, *techedew* and plain *tchew*. Race *colombianus* calls *cre-u*, a series of *chur* notes and a lightly trilled *triiu*.

GREY-CAPPED FLYCATCHER
Myiozetetes granadensis Pl. 209

Identification 16.5–17cm. Olive above, darker on wings and tail with very narrow pale yellowish fringes to wing-coverts and tertials; head greyish, only marginally darker than back, with red, partly concealed, coronal patch, short white superciliary and black mask, outer web of outer tail-feathers tawny, underparts yellow. Female has red coronal patch reduced or perhaps absent. Eyes pale brownish-grey. Juvenile browner above with yellowish fringes to tertials and rusty fringes to wing-coverts, lacks coronal patch and head has olive wash, and is paler yellow below. Eyes dark. From Social Flycatcher by rather than sooty grey head and much shorter superciliary that barely reaches ear-coverts.

Ssp. *M. g. obscurior* (E Ec, E Co, CS Ve) slightly larger and darker than *occidentalis*

M. g. occidentalis (W Ec, W Co) slightly smaller and paler

Habits Forages alone, sometimes in pairs or small noisy groups, mostly at mid levels. Sallies to catch passing insects or picks them from foliage, as well as berries and fruit.
Status Common in Ecuador, frequent in Colombia, local in Venezuela.
Habitat Tropical Zone, usually below 1,000m. Humid, partially open regions with light woodland, second growth or scattered trees or bushes, agricultural areas with scattered trees. Often near water.
Voice More piercing than Social Flycatcher, sometimes recalling Great Kiskadee, with varied sequences of *kip!*, *kip-it!* and *kip-keeuw, kip-keer, k-beer, kip-kee-chew, kip-kip-kip-it* (R&G). Race *obscurior* utters a loud, coarse dawn

song, *kip, kip, ki, kip, kip, kip, ke-ke-kree-yí* (P. Coopmans), whilst *occidentalis* has dawn song *kip kip kip keeuwkreh* (O. Jahn).

DUSKY-CHESTED FLYCATCHER

Myiozetetes luteiventris Pl. 207

Identification 14–15cm. Dark olive above, wings and tail dusky with barely discernible rufous fringes to wing-feathers, head slightly greyish and streaked darker, with a partially concealed longish yellow patch, chin and upper throat white, lower throat merges into yellow underparts, with darkish streaks across breast, sides and upper flanks. Female has coronal patch reduced and concealed. Juvenile distinctly browner above, notably on nape and upper mantle, broader fringes to wing-feathers, like adult below but slightly paler yellow and streaks fainter. From congeners by no white lines on head, and streaks on breast. Piratic Flycatcher paler and has bold white lines on head.

Ssp. *M. l. luteiventris* (E Ec, SE Co, S Ve) as described
M. l. septentrionalis (Su, FG) fringes of wing-feathers less rufous, more greenish-tawny

Habits Forages from upper mid levels to canopy; usually in pairs, picking small fruits and berries or sallying to leaves, hover-gleaning and gleaning for insects. Apparently does not associate with mixed flocks. Lifts tail or, less often, head and tail.

Status Rare in Ecuador, uncommon and local in Colombia where possibly seasonal in some areas, uncommon in Venezuela, scarce in Guyana, locally frequent in Suriname, and uncommon in French Guiana.

Habitat Tropical Zone, to 600m in Ecuador, 250m in Colombia and 350m in Venezuela. Humid forest, both *terra firme* and *várzea*; canopy and borders (especially along roads), treefalls or overgrown clearings with some trees.

Voice Excited-sounding calls resemble Grey-capped Flycatcher, e.g. a fast, nasal *nyeeuw-nyeeuw-keep-kít*, sometimes given in jumbled duet (R&G). Other vocalisations are cat-like, soft miaows (*nyeeuw*) and a nasal *chauw…chauw…* (H&B, H&M), a whining *meeow* and softer *neea*, and when excited a rapid *neea-ne-wít!* (Hilty).

Note Formerly placed in genus *Tyrannopsis*.

PIRATIC FLYCATCHER

Legatus leucophaius Pl. 207

Identification 15cm. Variable, dingy bird with no colourful characters. Dull brown above with slightly darker wings and tail, irregular pale fringes to feathers, especially in fresh plumage, give unkempt appearance, whitish on greater coverts, yellowish on tertials and secondaries, with fine rufous fringes to uppertail-coverts and tail. Top and sides of head darker brown than back, but barely contrast; white line encircles crown, becoming greyish and diffuse on nape, and is not a strong field mark; concealed yellow coronal patch. White malar stripe separated from dull whitish throat by narrow black line. Underparts variable, from yellowish to almost dull white, streaked dusky from lower throat and breast to sides and flanks. Juvenile very similar but paler, looking more washed out especially on head and mask, wings have buffy fringes, and pale, barely noticeable tawny fringes to uppertail-coverts and tail, throat is more dingy and streaks more diffuse. Easy to identify by voice. White eyebrow more obvious than in similar Variegated Flycatcher.

Ssp. *L. l. leucophaius* (NW & E Ec, Co, Ve, Guianas)

Habits Forages alone or in pairs, in canopy and subcanopy, or perches on high exposed spot, singing endlessly. Takes berries and fruits, and large insects, but adult diet mostly frugivorous. Takes over abandoned cacique nests or usurps ball nests of *Myiozetetes*, *Pitangus*, *Pachyramphus*, even hanging pouches of *Tolmomyias*, by mobbing owners and then removing eggs.

Status Populations from Middle and southern South America migrate to our region during their respective winters, but movements and wintering ranges not well known. Usually found near colonies of caciques (*C. cela*, *C. haemorrhous*) and oropendolas. Uncommon in Ecuador, locally frequent in Colombia and Venezuela, frequent in Guyana, common in Suriname and French Guiana.

Habitat Tropical Zone to 1,000m. Open areas with scattered trees or bushes, borders of humid forest and second growth.

Voice Loud whistles, *tjeee…ee* (H&M), *tee-u* (H&B), *wee-yee* (R&T) and an upslurred *weeEEE?* sometimes followed after a pause by a whistled *wiririre?* all heard throughout day in first half of year. A rarely heard, frog-like song, *reek-reek-reek…* (Hilty).

LESSER KISKADEE

Philohydor lictor Pl. 208

Identification 17–18cm. Comparatively slender compared to rounder allied species. Warm dark brown above, wings and tail dusky with rufous fringes, top and sides of head black with partially concealed coronal yellow patch. White throat, all yellow below. Bill black, noticeably long and thin. Juvenile slightly darker brown above with rusty fringes to wing-coverts, slightly more rusty than adult, paler below, washed-out sulphur. Very similar to Social and Rusty-margined Flycatchers though larger and less rotund, and both others have short bills and orange (Rusty-margined) or red (Social) coronal patches.

Ssp. *P. l. lictor* (E Ec, E & SE Co, Ve, Guianas) as described
P. l. panamensis (N Co) similar but smaller

Habits Forages alone or in pairs, sallying from low perches at water's edge. Sometimes drops to ground. Takes insects and spiders. Displays with trembling wings and builds cup nest of twigs low over water.

Status Common in Ecuador, south-east Colombia, Venezuela and Guyana. Locally common in Suriname and French Guiana.

Habitat Tropical Zone, below *c.*500m with unconfirmed sight records higher. Always near water, beside lakes, ponds, streams and in mangrove, in waterside vegetation or on emergent dead trunks or branches.

Voice Calls nasal, *dzay-dzwee-zwee-zwee* (R&T), *queeee-be* (H&B), *dzreeéy, dzweee* or *dzreeéy-dzwee-dzwee-dzwee* (R&G). Song softer and faster, a more repetitive version of Great Kiskadee. Hilty unforgettably transcribes the common call *SQUEEZE me, ba'by!*, sometimes repeated several times in succession, or a shorter *SQUEEZE me!* Also an excited chattered greeting, *ca-déde*, varied to *ca-déde-er*.

Note Formerly placed in *Pitangus*, but despite DNA implying that it might be closer to *Phelpsia*, currently placed in monotypic genus, *Philohydor* (Lanyon 1984), partly because of significant differences in nest construction.

GREAT KISKADEE

Pitangus sulphuratus Pl. 208

Identification 22cm. Brown above varies racially. Fringes of wing and tail-feathers rufous, top and sides of head black with partially concealed coronal yellow patch, white supraloral becomes a superciliary, which join at nape; throat and chin white, rest of underparts pure yellow with small olive patch on breast-sides. Similar Boat-billed Flycatcher has larger head and massive bill, and voice is unmistakable clincher.

Ssp. *P. s. caucensis* (W & S Co) distinctly browner, less rufous above

P. s. rufipennis (N Co, N & C Ve) dark olive back with bright rufous fringes to wings and tail, yellow coronal patch may reach nape, pure lemon-yellow below

P. s. sulphuratus (E Ec, SE Co, Guianas) warm olive back with broad rufous fringes to wings and tail

P. s. trinitatis (E Co: Meta, E Ve, Tr) less warm brown above than *rufipennis*, rufous fringes narrower, slightly paler below, more sulphur-yellow

Habits Forages in canopy, alone or in pairs, flycatching from exposed perches. Omnivorous: takes all kinds of insects, spiders, fish (plunging across surface rather like a kingfisher, but not submerging) and small vertebrates (regularly raids nests of small birds), fruits and berries. Bathes in heavy rain or by dipping in flight. Quite bold, has no fear of chasing hawks or vultures away from nest. Both adults build large, straggly ball nest with side entrance, high on a limb or telephone pole.

Status Widespread, fairly common to abundant throughout.

Habitat Tropical to Subtropical Zones, to *c.*1,000m in Ecuador, 1,500m in Colombia, and in Venezuela to 1,750m north of Orinoco and usually below 500m south of it. Urban and agricultural areas, light forest borders and partially wooded areas. Totally adapted to urban habitats.

Voice Loud call is unmistakable and often heard, it paraphrases its onomatopoeic name, *kiskadeeee!*, and curiously, has an interpretation in all of the region's languages: 'qu'est-ce qu'il dit', 'cristofué', 'bemtevé', 'grietjebie'. Pairs often call in duet and even in flight. Male bows flashing coronal crest while singing in courtship, and aggression. May give a *ka-dee!* or simple *deee!* Dawn song a raucous *kyah k-yah zzk-zzik ky-ar* or *beeeww-biew-prrrr-beeeww* (Fitzpatrick).

Phelpsia is very much like *Myiozetetes*, but has a noticeably smaller bill and larger head with a fuller throat (the so-called beard).

WHITE-BEARDED FLYCATCHER

Phelpsia inornata Pl. 208

Identification 16.5cm. Brown above, wings and tail darker, outer webs of outer tail-feathers pale creamy sienna, tertials and secondaries finely fringed yellow, head black with white frontal band continuing as a superciliary around ear-coverts, widening as it joins on nape and thus encircling blackish crown. Lores, ear-coverts and head-sides blackish, chin and full throat pure white, rest of underparts pure yellow. Juvenile has warm buffy back, wings and tail, fringes to wing-feathers buffy, yellowish on secondaries, crown dark brown with paler subterminal spots; white encircling superciliary and throat washed faintly buffy and yellow underparts less intense. From similar *Myiozetetes* and allies by disproportionately larger head with full white throat, and smaller bill.

Ssp. Monotypic (NE Co, C Ve: N of Orinoco)

Habits Forages in pairs or small family parties, gleaning foliage quite inconspicuously, but calls loudly, often fluffing wings and back. Often perches on an exposed branch, typically sallying down to ground and returning to same spot. Pairs often sing antiphonally.

Status Locally frequent in both Colombia (Arauca) and Venezuela. First specimen records for Colombia in 1991 (Rojas *et al.* 1997).

Habitat Lower Tropical Zone, to 450m. Gallery forests, isolated woods (typical in low *llanos*), and light woodland or scattered trees in savannas, even near dwellings.

Voice Contact consists of repetitions of *churup* or *cheerurit* phrases, and is also given in alarm. Pairs will duet enthusiastically, with a staccato to and-fro *CHEE'ter, CHEE'ter, CHEE'ter...* repeated up to 12+ times (Hilty).

OXYRUNCIDAE—Sharpbill

The SACC posted this comment (January 2005) after the proposal to resurrect Oxyruncidae was approved: 'The relationships of *Oxyruncus* remain unresolved. It was previously included in the Cotingidae in this classification, as in Snow (2004), based on Sibley *et al.* (1984), Sibley & Ahlquist (1985, 1990), and Prum *et al.* (2000). *Oxyruncus* had been formerly placed in a monotypic family Oxyruncidae (e.g. Hellmayr 1929, Phelps & Phelps 1950a, Wetmore 1960, Meyer de Schauensee 1970, Ames 1971, AOU 1983, 1998) or in the Tyrannidae (Mayr & Amadon 1951). Lanyon (1985) found no relationship between *Oxyruncus* and traditional members of the Cotingidae, but rather a relationship between *Oxyruncus* and the Tyrannidae or *Tityra* and *Pachyramphus*. Prum (1990a) found some morphological evidence for a relationship to *Pachyramphus* but concluded that *Oxyruncus* was not a member of the 'Schiffornis assemblage' that includes *Pachyramphus* (Prum & Lanyon 1989). Recent genetic data (Johansson *et al.* 2002, Chesser 2004b) found no strong support for any of these relationships. Thus the traditional ranking of *Oxyruncus* as a monotypic family is the best portrayal of our understanding of its relationships at this time.'

Additional reference for this family: Snow (2004).

SHARPBILL *Oxyruncus cristatus* Pl. 210

Identification 15–17cm. Adult olive-green above, darker on wings and tail, top of head greyish with subtle white flecks from forehead over supercilium, becoming whitish on head-sides with grey fringes; semi-concealed orange-red crest from crown to nape; underparts white with somewhat blurred and ill-defined dark grey scalloping; eyes vary from orange to yellow, bill has fairly straight culmen and is sharp-pointed, black above and grey below with black tip, short legs and feet blue-grey. Does not appear crested and concealed crest reportedly red in males, orange in females race *tocantinsi*? (R&G), but a large series of two races from Venezuela shows more individual variation than sexual differences. Juvenile resembles adult, but more prominent white markings on forehead and head-sides, lacks any red on crown, though rear crown is sepia with black scales; large yellowish to white oval spots on terminal outer fringes of median and greater wing-coverts and tertials, white terminal spots on longer tail-coverts, and white tips to tail; fewer dark grey markings below. Races poorly defined, being separated mainly on basis of crest colour, and fall into 2 groups, yellow-bellied and white-bellied – only latter races occur in northern South America.

Ssp. *O. c. hypoglaucus* (Ve: Roraima, Gu: Marumé) lores and cheeks white, median upperwing-coverts well margined with yellow; flame-scarlet crest

O. c. phelpsi (E Co?, Ve: Bolívar & N Amazonas, Gu: Acari Mts.) heavily marked white underparts; scarlet-red crest

O. c. tacarcunae (NW Co: Serranía de San Lucas) orange-red crest

O. c. tocantinsi (extreme SE Ec?) like *hypoglaucus* with white underparts, black marks less pronounced and more rounded

Habits Acrobatic foraging behaviour resembles a vireo, at upper levels, often with mixed flocks, taking insects, berries and fruit, using its sharp bill to probe fruit or clumps of dried leaves. Often in pairs. May perch quietly for long periods. Males may gather in loose leks to sing in breeding season. In non-breeding season, usually moves to lower altitudes.

Status Sight record by T. Parker & A. Luna in southern Ecuador (1993, Zamora-Chinchipe). Uncommon to rare in Colombia, where only recently recorded; uncommon to fairly common in Venezuela where local on slopes of tepuis; and uncommon in Guyana, the mountains of interior Suriname and French Guiana.

Habitat Upper Tropical to Subtropical Zones, at *c.*900m in Ecuador and 500–1,800m in Venezuela. Humid forests and their edges in foothills, on montane slopes and tepuis.

Voice An extended, high-pitched, descending *zeeeeeeeeeuuuu u'u'u'u'u'u'* trill (H&M, H&B, Hilty).

Notes *Oxyruncus* is sufficiently odd to require a monotypic genus, and was frequently placed in its own monotypic family Oxyruncidae. Recent treatments placed it in the Tyrannidae (Lanyon 1985) or the Cotingidae (Sibley, Lanyon & Ahlquist 1984), which we followed in agreement with the SACC, until the latter changed to its present position, sustaining treatment in a separate family as explained above. It was included in the Cotingidae by Dickinson (2003) and Snow (2004). Ericson *et al.* (2006) recommended that *Oxyruncus* be treated as the basal member of the Tityridae, but we have retained it in its own family here as it remains a problematic tyrannoid.

O. cristatus has a number of subspecies and a range that extends from Costa Rica to Bolivia, Paraguay and southern Brazil. Race *phelpsi* was considered a synonym of *hypoglaucus* by Mees (1974), a treatment rejected by Traylor (1979) but followed by Dickinson (2003). Race *tacarcunae* recorded in Colombia by P. G. W. Salaman (SCJ&W), but not listed in Dickinson (2003). Race in Ecuador unknown – perhaps *tocantinsi*?

COTINGIDAE – Cotingas

Cotingas are exclusively Neotropical and, for the most part, are birds of humid forest canopy and subcanopy, who feed mainly, if not exclusively on fruit. Some cotingas are very sedentary, remaining their whole lives in a given area. Others move seasonally up and down or along slopes, following the fruiting seasons of various trees, and still others, such as bellbirds, may disperse surprisingly long distances. In size, some cotingas are amongst the largest of all Neotropical Passeriformes, and many are adorned with strange crests, fancy feathers and odd wattles. Amidst their voices are some of the loudest, farthest-carrying and most unusual sounds of the New World tropics. Nests are cup-shaped and, generally, delicate and comparatively small, but some species construct fairly large, sturdy nests. They are usually placed in the fork of some tall horizontal branches or well hidden in dense bushes or vines. Exceptions are the cocks-of-the-rock, whose nests are of mud and vegetable matter, plastered to humid rock walls over waterfalls or amidst boulders.

As a family, Cotingidae has undergone many changes in recent years. Formerly, it included the genera *Tityra* through *Pachyramphus*, but recent genetic data (Irestedt *et al.* 2002, Chesser 2004b) confirm these genera to form a monophyletic group apart from cotingas and more closely related to Pipridae than to Cotingidae (Chesser 2004b). Thus, these genera have been removed from Cotingidae and considered separately as Incertae Sedis (uncertain placement, but presently between

Sharpbill and manakins), pending a decision for its possible treatment in a new family. Other changes include the removal of the genus *Oxyruncus* to its own, monotypic family Oxyruncidae, and the inclusion of the genus *Rupicola*, thereby eliminating the family Rupicolidae. Prum (1990) found the genus *Phytotoma* (which occurs entirely in Peru, Bolivia and the Southern Cone) to be monophyletic with Cotingidae, thus eliminating the family Phytotomidae. Within our region, and considering the cotingas in their present composition, Tobago and the Netherlands Antilles harbour no representatives of the family, but 2 occur in Trinidad.

Additional references for this family: Prum & Lanyon (1989), Prum (1990), Prum et al. (2000, 2001) and Snow (2004).

Red-crested Cotinga, crest laid back as normal, crest raised when excited, crest raised in display – sides of neck and upper breast also erected.

RED-CRESTED COTINGA

Ampelion rubrocristatus Pl. 212

Identification 21–23cm. Mostly dark grey with blackish tail and white subterminal bar on underside, blackish head and wings, white fringes to feathers of rump, belly and tail-coverts give streaked effect. Long loose crest may be laid flat on nape, protruding slightly, or oddly erect when fanned at sides. Eyes brown, bill white with black tip, legs and feet brown. Juvenile similar but has vestigial brown crest. Quite unique in its altitude range. Look for large white spots on tail-feathers (may seem like a band).

Ssp. Monotypic (Ec: both slopes of Andes; Co: Andes & Santa Marta; Ve: Perijá Mts. & Andes from NE Trujillo to Táchira).

Habits Serene, perching alone atop of trees or bushes, spying environs. Forages alone, in pairs or small groups, picking fruits and berries while perching on a branch or twig, or takes insects from air during a quick sally. In flight, its wings make a dull *whirr* sound. If excited, e.g. during courtship or aggressive encounters, raised and spread-open crest is like a fancy head ornament. Simultaneously, displays with series of fast bows and tail flips.

Status Uncommon to frequent in Ecuador, frequent in Colombia and uncommon to locally frequent in Venezuela.

Habitat Subtropical to Temperate Zones, 2,500–3,500m, locally to 3,900m in Ecuador; 2,200m to treeline, more common above 2,700m in Colombia; 2,500–3,250m in Venezuela. Humid montane forests, semi-open woodland, suburban areas with patchy woodland, bushy hedges in high pastures, borders of elfin forest and *Polylepis* woods.

Voice Usually silent, may occasionally give an odd *trrrrrrr* trill, both perched and in flight (H&B, Hilty).

Notes Correct spelling is *rubrocristatus*, not *rubrocristata*, as *Ampelion* is masculine (David & Gosselin 2002). Formerly placed in genus *Heliochera*.

CHESTNUT-CRESTED COTINGA

Ampelion rufaxilla Pl. 212

Identification 20–23cm. Look for chestnut shoulders, short bluish bill, olive-grey upperparts with dusky streaks. Long crest has chestnut tip and usually lies flat, but may be raised fan-like; throat, head-sides and back of neck bright cinnamon, underparts pale yellow with blackish streaks.

Ssp. *A. r. antioquiae* (Ec: N Sucumbíos; Co: C Andes Quindío to Huila & W Andes in Valle & Cauca), slightly larger, broader streaks on underparts, chestnut on neck and shoulder darker

A. r. rufaxilla (extreme S Ec: S Zamora-Chinchipe) as described

Habits Forages alone or in pairs, but not with mixed flocks. Often perches exposed high above canopy, from where it sallies to catch passing insects.

Status Rare and very local in Ecuador, where first observed 1984 and confirmed 1992, and rare and local in Colombia.

Habitat Subtropical Zone, 1,800–2,700m in Ecuador; 1,900–2,700m, most common above 2,300 m in Colombia. Pristine humid forests on higher montane slopes.

Voice Calls include a guttural *ch-ch-ch-rrrrrrreh* and short *reh* notes (Snow). Also, a *trrrrrrr* trill, similar to Red-crested (H&B).

Notes Correct spelling is *rufaxilla*, as this term is invariable (David & Gosselin 2002). Formerly treated in genus *Heliochera*.

CHESTNUT-BELLIED COTINGA

Doliornis remseni Pl. 212

Identification 20–21.5cm. Dark brownish slate grey above and over entire breast, top of head black in male, grey (black feathers extensively fringed grey) in female; rich rufous-chestnut belly to undertail-coverts (unmarked). Both sexes have erectile crests, though neither raises them very often.

Ssp. Monotypic (E Ec: E Carchi, Zamora-Chinchipe & E Loja; Co: S of C Andes in Quindío)

Habits Forages in canopy, sometimes in loose association with mixed canopy flocks of tanagers and others. Perches quietly on very tops of trees, particularly those with dense canopies and fairly flat tops. Feeds on small fruits and berries, especially *Escallonia*, *Miconia* and other Melastomataceae.

Status Rare to very locally frequent in Ecuador and Colombia.

Habitat Temperate Zone to Páramo, most numerous above 3,100m; 2,900–3,500m in Ecuador; 2,900–3,650 in Colombia. Humid high-montane forests, elfin forests, treeline scrub.

Voice No description found.

Notes Species recently described by Robbins et al. (1994) and placed in *Doliornis* based on size, shape and general coloration similarities with *D. sclateri*. Genus *Doliornis* was formerly merged in *Ampelion*. Lanyon & Lanyon (1989) suggested that they were best separated, especially given differences in bill structure. Proven to be a valid genus by analysis of syrinx characters (Prum 1990) and by clarification of juvenile plumage in *D. sclateri* (Robbins *et al.* 1994).

Fruiteaters of the genus *Pipreola*, together with their sister genera *Laniisoma* and *Ampelioides*, are rather rotund birds with short tails, bright olive-green above with patterns of yellow and green below (*P. whitelyi* being an exception); some have black heads and several have red bills. They are distinctive and easily categorised. Most vocalise at quite high frequencies. Differences between species are less easily appreciated. They are birds of montane forests, generally shy, seemingly lethargic, probably with little need to be active as their fruits and berries do not require pursuit.

GREEN-AND-BLACK FRUITEATER

Pipreola riefferii Pl. 211

Identification 19–20 cm. Male has shiny greenish-black head, throat and upper breast with narrow yellow border at front and sides, and breast and belly yellow with greenish markings at sides; eyes brown, bill, legs and feet orange-red. Female has shiny green head, throat and upper breast, lower breast and belly streaked yellow and green. Juvenile darker, washed grey on head and breast, streaked grey below to flanks and belly, bill tipped black, legs and feet flesh. Often seen in same fruiting trees as Barred Fruiteater, which is larger and has very clearly barred underparts, with large yellow spots on tertials and coral legs and feet – but they sound similar!

Ssp. *P. r. confusa* (E Ec: Sucumbíos to Zamora-Chinchipe) smaller, male has greenish upper breast, sides, flanks and belly washed green and streaked darker

P. r. melanolaema (N & NW Ve: Andes from N Táchira to S Lara & Coastal Cordillera from Aragua to Miranda),white fringes to tertials and pale tips to median and greater coverts, more yellow on central underparts, and male's hood is glossy black

P. r. occidentalis (SW Co: W & C Andes, W Ec: Esmeraldas & Carchi to Bolívar & N El Oro) male has narrow yellow nuchal collar, white tips to tertials, underparts almost entirely yellow and reddish legs

P. r. riefferii (C Co: E Andes & Perijá Mts; W Ve: Perijá Mts & S Táchira) like *confusa* but brighter green above and less heavily marked below

Habits Quiet and elusive. Forages in pairs or loose groups of up to 6, from low to mid levels in densest parts of forest, moving lethargically, occasionally joining mixed flocks. Perches to pick fruits and berries, sometimes lazily or clumsily, and spends long periods perching 'contentedly' while leisurely scanning surroundings.

Status Uncommon to frequent in Ecuador, common in Colombia and frequent to common in Venezuela.

Habitat Subtropical to Temperate Zones, at 1,700–2,500m, locally to 3,300m in Ecuador; 1,500–2,700m in Colombia, but to 900m on Pacific slope; 1,800–3,050m in Andes and 1,700–2,150m in Coastal Cordillera, Venezuela. Humid, wet and cloud forests, misty, mossy woodland, clearings, forest edge, isolated copses near forest edge.

Voice A high, fading *ti-ti-ti-ti-ti-ti...* lasting *c.*5 s (Snow) and a fading *tic-tic-ti-ti-ti-tiseeeeeeeeeeeeeeeeaa* and *ti-tsi-tsi-tsi-tsi-tsi-tsi-...* song, by both sexes, easily confused with insect calls (F&K, Hilty).

Notes O'Neill & Parker (1981), Sibley & Monroe (1990) and Snow all suggested that above races, together with *chachapoyas* of N Peru, may prove to represent a separate species from isolated race *tallmanorum* of C Peru (Huánuco). Formerly placed in genus *Euchlornis* but in *Pipreola* by Zimmer 1930. Formerly included *P. intermedia* of Peru (east slope).

BARRED FRUITEATER

Pipreola arcuata Pl. 210

Identification 22–23cm. Adult male bright olive-green above with all-black hood and fine black and yellow barring below. Greater wing-coverts have large subterminal orange-yellow spots and are fringed black, tertials black with large orange-yellow spot on outer web of each and small yellow tip. Uppertail-coverts have subterminal black spots, tail black with central feathers green, subterminal black bar and white tips. Eyes pale yellowish, bill crimson, legs and feet scarlet. Female lacks black head, being green to forehead, and barred to chin. Immature male like female but has some blackish on face and cheeks, and may show some extra black in barring on throat. Juvenile much like duller female with irregular black and ochraceous-yellow spots on lesser wing-coverts and back, some green suffusion on breast overlaying barring; pale brown eyes, bill very dark red. Often seen in same fruiting trees as Green-and-black Fruiteater, which is smaller and lacks large spots on wings and black and white on tail, and has pale flesh-coloured legs and feet, the latter being the most important field mark when seen only briefly; they sound similar!

Ssp. *P. a. arcuata* (N Ec: W slope, Co: W Andes in Cauca, C Andes, E slope of E Andes & Perijá Mts.; NW Ve: Andes & Perijá Mts.)

Habits Quiet and elusive, forages from mid levels to subcanopy, alone, in pairs or in small parties of 3+ that may sometimes include Green-and-black Fruiteaters. Seldom joins mixed flocks of other birds. Spends long periods perching 'contentedly' while leisurely scanning surroundings. Not shy.

Status Uncommon to locally frequent in Ecuador, uncommon in Colombia and in Venezuela. Generally much less common than Green and-black Fruiteater.

Habitat Subtropical to Temperate Zones, 2,500–3,300m,

locally to 2,250m in Ecuador; 1,500–3,100m, more numerous above 2,200m in Colombia; and 1,800–3,100m, more numerous above 2,300m in Venezuela. Humid and wet montane forests, dense forest edge.

Voice A very high-pitched, descending with slight rise at end, almost hissing, *s-seeeeeeeeeeeeaaaaaee*, lasting *c*.2–3 s (R&G, Hilty, Snow). Often gives a drawn-out, high-pitched *wheeeeeen* and occasionally a high-pitched shriek (F&K).

GOLDEN-BREASTED FRUITEATER

Pipreola aureopectus Pl. 211

Identification 16.5–17.5cm. Adult male entirely bright olive-green above, tertials darker distally with white tips, face blackish at base of bill and around eyes, like a small, diffuse mask; throat to undertail-coverts rich golden-yellow, green on breast-sides becoming streaked on flanks. Eyes orange-yellow, bill orange-red and legs greenish-grey. Female like male above with vestigial tips to tertials; yellow underparts have dense green streaks or flammulations. Juvenile duller lacking tips to tertials and even more heavily streaked on face and breast; eyes brown.

Ssp. *P. a. aureopectus* (Co: Perijá Mts. & N end of all 3 Andean ranges, Ve: Perijá Mts. & Andes male only narrowly streaked on body-sides but completely streaked on flanks and belly, becoming faint flammulations on undertail-coverts

P. a. decora (Co: Santa Marta) smaller than nominate; bright yellow line across neck-sides

P. a. festiva (N Ve: Coastal Cordillera) as described

Habits May forage alone but usually in pairs, from mid levels to subcanopy. Joins mixed flocks for short periods. Moves calmly, leisurely picking berries and small fruit while perched on branch.

Status Locally common in Colombia, fairly common in Venezuela.

Habitat Subtropical Zone, in Colombia at 600–2,300m but usually above 1,700m; and in Venezuela at 1,700–3,100m in Perijá Mts., 100–2,300m in Andes and 800–2,050m in Coastal Cordillera. Humid montane forests and secondary woodland. In Venezuela, where occurs sympatrically with Green-and-black Fruiteater, tends to occupy mid altitudes, with Green-and-black more in wet cloud forests.

Voice A high *seeeeeéééé* or a sibilant rising, then falling and then rising again and fading at end, *pseéééeeeeeeeeaaaeeeéé tic tic* (Hilty, Snow). Contact is a short *pseeeéé* (D. Ascanio recording).

Note Formerly included *jucunda* (Orange-breasted Fruiteater), *lubomirskii* (Black-chested Fruiteater) and Peruvian *pulchra* (Masked Fruiteater), but these are all considered separately on basis of parapatric distributions and in some cases, apparent sympatry without intergradation (Snow).

ORANGE-BREASTED FRUITEATER

Pipreola jucunda Pl. 211

Identification 18 cm. Male has complete glossy black hood, in sharp contrast with entirely bright olive-green upperparts. Lower throat and centre of breast bright yellowish-orange, extending as a narrow line across neck-sides to behind ear coverts, bordered below by a diffuse narrow black band. Central breast and belly yellow, washed green on sides, with a narrow, sometimes broken green band on centre of breast. Yellowish-white eyes, red-orange bill, greenish-grey legs. Female entirely green above, with underparts streaked green and yellow from chin to undertail-coverts.

Ssp. Monotypic (NW Ec: Esmeraldas to Pichincha; SW Co: Pacific slope from S Chocó to Nariño)

Habits Forages from low to mid levels, alone or in loose pairs, very occasionally with mixed flocks. Picks fruits and berries only from perch. Slow and quiet.

Status Rare to locally frequent in Ecuador, frequent to common in Colombia.

Habitat Subtropical Zone, 600–1,700m in Ecuador, 900–1,400m but mostly 1,100–1,300m in Colombia. Usually more numerous at upper elevations of range. Humid, wet and cloud forests, mossy, foggy, epiphyte-overgrown areas, forest borders.

Voice A very high *se-e-e-e-e-e-e-e-e* hiss that lasts 2–3 s and is easily missed (H&B, Snow); song an infrequently heard, sharp and piercing *psii* (R&G).

Note Formerly considered a race of *P. aureopectus* (Snow 1982, S&M).

BLACK-CHESTED FRUITEATER

Pipreola lubomirskii Pl. 211

Identification 17–18 cm. Male has glossy black hood reaching upper breast, in sharp contrast to entirely green upperparts; underparts yellow, with some green and black scalloping on sides and washed green on flanks; eyes yellowish-white, bill orange-red, legs and feet greenish-grey. Female all green above and below to breast, rest of underparts streaked heavily green and yellow; bill dusky orange.

Ssp. Monotypic (E Ec: E slope; S Co: head of Magdalena Valley in Huila & SE Nariño, possibly in W Caquetá & W Putumayo)

Habits Forages from low to mid levels, both alone and in pairs, very occasionally in small groups. Of slow and quiet habits.

Status In Ecuador, uncommon and scarce in most of range, but slightly more numerous on both slopes of Cordillera de Guacamayos. Rare and local in Colombia.

Habitat Subtropical Zone, at 1,500–2,100m in Ecuador and 1,600–2,300m in Colombia, in humid montane and cloud forests.

Voice A high, rising, *pseeet* (Snow). Male has very thin, high-pitched song, drawn-out and ascending, becoming stronger towards end (R&G).

Note Formerly considered a race of *P. aureopectus* (Snow 1982, S&M).

FIERY-THROATED FRUITEATER

Pipreola chlorolepidota Pl. 211

Identification 12–13cm. Male all green above with dusky lores, broad white tips to tertials and small white tips to remiges and rectrices, orange throat merging with scarlet breast, and rest of underparts green, except yellowish centre of belly; greyish-white eyes, orange-red bill with black tip and orange legs. Female has small white terminal spots on tertials and tail, a yellow chin and rest of underparts evenly and narrowly barred green and yellow, with green wash overlaying sides, bill dusky orange. The smallest of the genus.

Ssp. Monotypic (E Ec, Co: W Caquetá).

Habits Forages from lower to mid levels, alone or in pairs. Often joins mixed flocks. Gathers at fruiting trees.
Status Near Threatened. Rare and local (possibly under-recorded) in Ecuador, unconfirmed in Colombia.
Habitat Upper Tropical Zone, 600–1,250m, locally to 300m in Ecuador. Humid foothill forests.
Voice A high *tsi,* very brief and sharp (Snow, P. Coopmans).

SCARLET-BREASTED FRUITEATER

Pipreola frontalis Pl. 211

Identification 15–16.5cm. Adult male has entirely green upperparts with tertials tipped white, dark green head, chin and upper throat bright yellow, lower throat and neck-sides below cheeks and upper breast bright fiery orange, and rest of underparts yellow with lower body-sides, flanks and thighs green; pale yellow eyes, orange bill and legs. Female all green above, white tips to tertials, and look for some yellow on supraloral and sides of forehead, and entire underparts barred dark green and yellow.

Ssp. *P. f. squamipectus* (SE Ec: E slope)

Habits Forages alone, in pairs or small groups, from mid levels to subcanopy, picking fruits and berries from perch or with short hover-sallies. Perches still and quiet for long periods. Joins mixed flocks of canopy birds.
Status Near Threatened. Uncommon to locally frequent in Ecuador.
Habitat Subtropical Zone, 1,000–1,700m in Ecuador. Humid to wet montane forests.
Voice An infrequently heard, thin and very high short *psiii* (R&G, Snow)
Notes R&G believe species not in danger, as substantial portion of range is remote and very little threatened by human activities, and a significant part is within Podocarpus National Park. They further suggest that *squamipectus* may be a separate species (Bluish-fronted Fruiteater) but do not offer any rationale.

HANDSOME FRUITEATER

Pipreola formosa Pl. 211

Identification 16–17.5cm. With its black hood, fiery orange-red chest and yellow underparts, male is unmistakable. Female has bright green head, small crescent-shaped yellow patch on upper breast and yellow underparts barred and spotted green. In both sexes, look for bright green upperparts, orange-red bill, olive legs and large white tips to tertials, which are best field marks from female Golden-breasted Fruiteater, though usually prefers wetter habitats. Subspecies comprise two groups, separated as follows.

Ssp. ***Formosa*** **group,** larger (17.5cm) large round white spots on tertials, red patch on chest formed of strips

P. f. formosa (CN Ve: N cordilleras from Falcón to Miranda) female has all-green throat with crescent-shaped patch below orange-yellow; adults have yellow-orange eyes, juveniles dark yellow

Pariae **group**, smaller (16.5cm) tertials largely black with white crescentic tips, red patch on breast a single suffuse unit

P. f. pariae (NE Ve: Paria Peninsula, E Sucre) female has yellow throat with fine green barring and crescent-shaped patch scarlet instead of yellow, whilst red on chest of male is brighter and more extensive; male has orange eyes, immature male with throat patch, orange; female yellow; all-green juvenile brown to orange

P. f. rubidior (NE Ve: Cerros Turimiquire & Negro, NE Anzoátegui, N Monagas & W Sucre) female has yellow throat with fine dark green barring and crescent-shaped patch reddish instead of yellow; adult and immature with throat patch have orange-yellow eyes, all-green juvenile brown eyes

Habits Quiet, very calm, sluggish and thus easy to miss, forages at mid levels, alone, in pairs or sometimes in small family groups, moving through foliage or sallying briefly to pick fruits and berries. Occasionally appears within mixed flocks of canopy birds, such as tanagers and warblers, in fruiting trees, but it is the flock that effectively joins the fruiteaters! The flock moves on, fruiteaters remain.
Status Venezuelan endemic, frequent in central Coastal Cordilleras, common on Paria Mts. Easier to see in rainy season, when scrub in understorey laden with berries, and birds visit lower levels.
Habitat Subtropical Zone, at 800–2,200m. Humid to wet montane and cloud forests.
Voice Race *formosa* gives a high *pik* and a *ti-ti-ti-ti-ti-ti…* Song of *rubidior* and *pariae* a high, fading *peeééé-eeeeee-e-e-e-e* (Snow, D. Ascanio), or *peeEEEeeeeee'e'e'e'e*, louder at start but smooth, slowing at end, and varies little in pitch (Hilty, D. Ascanio). Vocalisations differ in pitch, with those of *formosa* being at high frequency, those by *rubidior/pariae* medium frequency (D. Ascanio, pers. comm.).
Note Proposal recognising *pariae/rubidior* group as distinct species (Paria Fruiteater) (D. Ascanio, C Reugifo & J. G. Leon in prep.).

RED-BANDED FRUITEATER

Pipreola whitelyi Pl. 210

Identification 16–17.5cm. Male has greenish-grey upperparts, orange fringes to wing-coverts, tertials and inner secondaries, grey head with tawny-buff eyebrow and neck-side streaks, rusty cheeks and grey underparts with striking coral red breast and sides, orange eyes, coral red bill, legs and feet. Female more greenish above, underparts yellowish-white with black streaks, overlaid with yellowish-white wash that reduces contrast of streaks; eyes yellowish, bill yellow-orange, legs and feet horn. Immature/juvenile like a pallid female with dark streaks on top and rear of head, irregular dark streaks with pale centres on wing-coverts and back. In plumage, this unusual *Pipreola* is among the most distinctive of the eastern tepui endemics (Braun *et al.* 2003).

Ssp. *P. w. kathleenae* (SE Ve: Sierra de Lema, Mt. Aprada, Ptari, Sororopán, Uaipán, Chimantá, Cuquenán & Roraima) male slightly paler and less green above, and paler grey below, eyebrow and neck streaking yellowish, with buffy-orange tips to wing-coverts and series of broad streaks and spots of yellow and bright orange on breast; female darker above with slight green flush, and more contrastingly black and white on underparts, only vent and undertail-coverts have yellowish wash; bill yellowish-coral.

P. w. whitelyi (SE Ve: Roraima, W Gu: Roraima, Mt Twek-quay, Mt. Kowa) as described

Habits Forages quietly, sluggishly and inconspicuously, alone or in pairs, from mid level to subcanopy. Sometimes with mixed flocks of canopy birds, such as tanagers and warblers, but there are many more sightings in fruiting trees than in mixed flocks.

Status Pantepui endemic (*kathleenae*) with tiny distribution, uncommon to locally frequent at higher elevations (though never numerous) in Venezuela, where seemingly most abundant on Ptari-tepui and Auyán-tepui. On Mt. Roraima (*whitelyi*) in Guyana, situation uncertain, hopefully more frequent than scarce records indicate, as few ornithologists visit the region. Uncommon and seldom seen on Sierra de Lema, on Venezuela/Guyana border.

Habitat Subtropical Zone, *kathleenae* at 1,300–2,100m and *whitelyi* at 1,800–2,250m. Humid to wet montane and cloud forests where branches overgrown with mosses and epiphytes. Dense secondary woodland, especially where Melastomataceae abound.

Voice A long, very high *tseeaaaaeeeeeeeeee* or *pss-ee-ee-ee-ee-ee-ee* trill, at first descending, then rising steadily, and in excitement 4–6 thin *ti* notes (Hilty, Snow). Very similar to Golden-breasted Fruiteater. Duet slower, with both individuals producing a short call that is steady at first, then rises at end, *peeeu-ééu* (D. Ascanio recording).

SCALED FRUITEATER

Ampelioides tschudii Pl. 210

Identification 19–20.5cm. Adult male black above with olive yellow fringes almost throughout, affording strongly scaled effect to back, wing-coverts and to long uppertail-coverts, greater wing-coverts entirely olive joining broad olive outer fringes to tertials and secondaries, producing longitudinal bar on wing, primaries black, as is tail which has terminal yellow tips to central pair of rectrices; top of head black, from forehead, around eyes and back to nape; ochraceous nuchal collar divides black from scaled back. Large whitish loral spot, lower face-sides to throat white, with small black streaks on malar forming rough stripe, and scattered streaks on throat; rest of underparts buffy with black vermiculations giving scaled effect. Eyes creamy yellow, bill has upper mandible black, lower mandible olive, legs and feet dark grey. Female same, smaller and lacks black of head, being olive-buffy streaked black.

Ssp. Monotypic (Ec: both slopes of Andes, Co: Pacific slope of W Andes, Perijá Mts., both slopes of E Andes, Macarena Mts.; NW Ve: Perijá Mts., SE Táchira & SE Lara)

Habits Forages alone, in pairs or sometimes in small groups, seeking berries and small fruits (occasionally insects) amid epiphytes and mosses. May be found within mixed canopy flocks in fruiting trees, but likely to remain when flock moves on. Possible seasonal movements up and downslope. Extremely territorial during breeding season when sings frequently from within canopy.

Status Rare to uncommon in Ecuador, uncommon and local in Colombia and uncommon to rare in Venezuela.

Habitat Upper Tropical to Subtropical Zones, at 900–1,900m, locally in west and in smaller numbers to 650m in Ecuador; 650–2,700m in Colombia; and 1,250–2,000m in Venezuela. Humid, wet and cloud forests.

Voice A series of long, high whistles – *wheeeEEEEEaaa* – that rise then fade away, reminiscent of a raptor (H&B, Hilty, Snow).

GUIANAN COCK-OF-THE-ROCK

Rupicola rupicola Pl. 216

Identification 28–32cm. Male unmistakable: bright orange plumage and remarkable rounded crest along centre of head, of stiff bright orange feathers from culmen to nape; eyes orange. Female smaller, with similar profile but much smaller crest, only over forecrown; deep coffee colour, slightly paler on vent and undertail-coverts; eyes yellowish-white. Juvenile not as dark, paler cheeks and distinctly paler (cinnamon) from central breast to undertail-coverts, with dark thighs; brown eyes.

Ssp. Monotypic (E Co; S Ve: Amazonas & Bolívar; Guianas)

Habits Both sexes forage from mid levels to canopy, alone or in very loose groups. Males form leks where groups of 20–30+ birds display to watching females, and they spend much time at these locations. Large leks in Venezuela and Guianas, but quite rare in Colombia. Diet includes berries, fruits, insects and small vertebrates. Follows troops of *Cebus* monkeys. Flight fast and direct. Nests are cups of mud and vegetable matter, plastered to humid rock walls, in crevices and niches, constructed and tended by female.

Status Very locally fairly common in Colombia, locally frequent to common in Venezuela, frequent in Guyana, widespread and common in Suriname, and rather common in French Guiana.

Habitat Tropical to Subtropical Zones, to 300m in Colombia and 2,000m in Venezuela. Humid forest on tepui slopes, sandy soil forests and near waterfalls and rocky outcrops, especially karstic. Rocky walls and mountainside boulders are essential for nesting.

Voice Leks are totally silent, with display being totally visual. Song is uttered away from lek, and is a sequence of very loud raucous cries at irregular intervals: *khauw*... *khauw*... (H&M). Commonest call a loud *kreeayouu*, much less frequently a *keeow* or *waaow* (Hilty), reportedly sounding like'keep going!'.

Notes Some authors formerly treated *Rupicola* in family Rupicolidae, but now again included in Cotingidae (Snow 1979). Correct spelling is *rupicola*, as this term is invariable (David & Gosselin 2002).

ANDEAN COCK-OF-THE-ROCK

Rupicola peruvianus Pl. 216

Identification 30–32cm. Adult male unmistakable, being almost entirely red or orange, with black wings and tail, rounded longitudinal flat crest being the clincher. Adult female is rich brown, with dusky wings and tail, and a smaller, lower profile crest.

Ssp. *R. p. aequatorialis* (E Ec: W Sucumbíos to Zamora-Chinchipe, Co: C & E Andes, Ve: Andes of Mérida & Táchira) males reddish-orange with brighter, paler orange crest and yellow eyes; female chocolate-brown with dark brown wings and yellow eyes

R. p. sanguinolentus (NW Ec: E Esmeraldas & Carchi to Cotopaxi, Co: W Andes) male brilliant blood red with scarlet-orange crest, eyes usually red, sometimes orange; female has deep orange-brown body, cinnamon-brown head, and generally redder than female *aequatorialis*; yellow to orange eyes

Habits Forages alone in forest, always near streams, but groups may gather at fruiting trees. May be observed crossing clearings or flying across gorges or ravines. Males gather to display for females at traditional leks, apparently used for many years. The oldest known lek in Venezuela, at San Isidro, has been in continual use since 1960s. Leks based on same satellite system as in Capuchinbird, with central lek of a dozen or more males, and several satellites each up to a couple of hundred metres away, at which only 2–3 males gather. The satellite leks are usually active only in breeding season. Leks are inside forest near ravines or gorges where females nest, at sites with many low branches and lianas 2–5m above ground.

Status Uncommon to locally frequent in Ecuador; locally frequent in Colombia; frequent in Venezuela, but only very locally.

Habitat Upper Tropical to Subtropical Zones, at 600–2,500m, most numerous 900–2100m in Ecuador; 1400–2400m but to 500m on Pacific slope and on east slope of East Andes in Colombia; and 1,000–1,500m in Venezuela. Humid forest of shady ravines and rocky, forested, mossy mountainsides with gorges and waterfalls.

Voice Usually very quiet away from display grounds. At leks, male calls sound like pig squeals and grunts, and also loud stuttering squawks. In flight, birds give infrequent loud, plaintive *wankk* calls (Hilty, Snow).

Note Correct spelling of names is *peruvianus* not *peruviana* (and *sanguinolentus* not *sanguinolenta*), as *Rupicola* is masculine (David & Gosselin 2002).

> *Phoenicircus* red cotingas are experts at choosing the darkest parts of forest to forage. They make a distinct whispering noise with their wings as they fly. Males gather in leks rather ephemerally, moving locations and using more than one site.

BLACK-NECKED RED COTINGA

Phoenicircus nigricollis Pl. 212

Identification Male 22cm, female 24cm. Adult male entirely crimson-red, except black throat and lower head-sides, nape to mantle, wing-coverts and tip of tail, greater wing-coverts brown-edged black. tertials black fringed brown, secondaries brown, primaries black finely fringed brown. Feathers on top of head slightly elongated, pointing forward on forehead and erectile on top. Female slightly larger, with same pattern but red less bright, more rosy and black replaced by brown. Eyes brown, bill orange, legs and feet orange-horn.

Ssp. Monotypic (E Ec: E Sucumbíos to E Pastaza; SE Co: W Caquetá, W Putumayo, Vaupés, Guainía & Amazonas; S Ve: extreme SW Amazonas)

Habits Forages noisily from low levels to subcanopy, often gathering at fruiting trees. Males gather in very loose leks to display and sing, with most singing from dawn through first couple of hours of daylight. At leks each male holds small circular territory with 3–5 favourite perches, often hanging loops of lianas, and display consists of fast twisting flights between perches and head-bobbing. Modified primaries permit them to accompany display-flights with whistling trills made by wings.

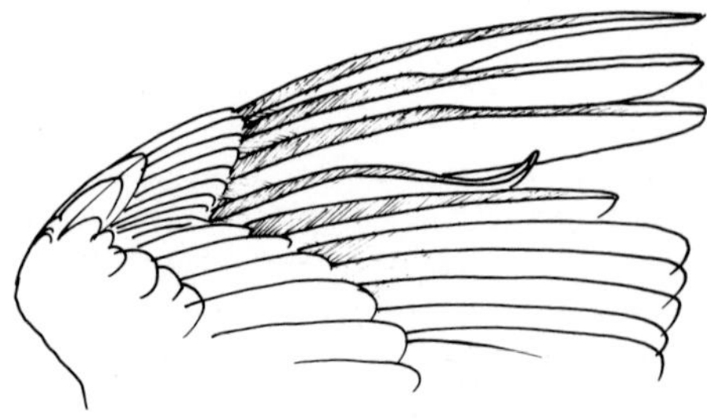

Males of both red cotingas have the outer primaries modified as illustrated; this adaptation produces a special and unique noise during display-flights

Status Rare to uncommon and very local in Ecuador, rare in Colombia, and rare and local in Venezuela. In some areas, red feathers especially sought-after by indigenous people to make headdresses and other artefacts, and hunting has virtually wiped out species locally.
Habitat Lower Tropical Zone, to 400m in Ecuador and Colombia; to 200m in Venezuela. Humid lowland *terra firme* forest, forest borders in well-drained areas.
Voice In Colombia a loud *qua-a-a*, like a crow (H&B), and in Venezuela a loud sudden *SKREEA!*, harsh and metallic, and accompanied by head-bobbing (Hilty). Males advertise with a loud *wheaa* and there is a soft *wur* and *yip* alarm-call. In display-flight, males give a short *whea* and make whistling trill with wings (Snow).
Note Snow (1973) suggested the species might be a manakin (Pipridae) based on plumage characteristics, its communal displays and morphological characteristics (the toes are partially united).

GUIANAN RED COTINGA
Phoenicircus carnifex Pl. 212

Identification Male 22cm, female 24cm. Male has a flat, shining red crest, with rest of head, neck and throat glossy blackish-maroon, wings and tips of tail dark rufous, breast, belly, rump and tail bright scarlet. Female has same plumage but much more subdued, in brownish-olive and pinkish-brown, with raspberry red crown. Female slightly larger and male has modified outer primaries (see drawing) like Black-necked Red Cotinga.

Ssp. Monotypic (E Ve: NE Bolívar in ríos Cuyuní & Grande basins; Guianas).

Habits Forages from mid level to subcanopy, alone or in small groups that gather at fruiting trees to pick fruits from a perch or uses short hover-sallies or swooping snatches. Does not join mixed flocks. Feeds only on berries and small fruit. Males form very loose leks to sing, and call very loudly and noisily at dawn and during first 2 hours or so of daylight. Frequent swooping flights between several fixed perches (*c.*12) at *c.*10m above ground, with rattling sound produced by wings, are probably territorial displays. In courtship male bounces up and down, in stretch–sit–stretch… motion as it sings (D. Ascanio).
Status Very local in Venezuela, locally frequent to common in Guyana, uncommon to locally frequent in interior of Suriname, common in interior of French Guiana.
Habitat Lower Tropical Zone, to 250m in Venezuela. Humid *terra firme* forest.
Voice Song a loud high note, followed by a high whistle that changes tone in middle: *wuuk-peeyeweet… wuuk-peeyeweet* (H&M). Also, at dawn a loud *pee-chew-eet* in advertisement, and when alarmed, *wheep* notes, singly or in long series (Hilty). In French Guiana calls somewhat reminiscent of *Piculus rubiginosus* (O. Tostain).

Blue cotingas are often found alongside araçaris, foraging for ripe fruit in *Euterpes* palms, where they sally for fruits. They are plump and rather dove-like with small, rounded heads and larger rotund bodies; shortish tails and long wings. Vocally, they are fairly quiet, but colours of males are very 'loud' and can appear almost electrical in some lights. Females are more cryptic and can be tricky to identify.

BLUE COTINGA *Cotinga nattererii* Pl. 213

Identification 18–20 cm. Quite plump, male is shiny turquoise-blue with black eye-ring, black tail and 2 very dark purple patches, on throat and on chest to mid belly. Wings black with blue fringes, except to median and lesser wing-coverts which are all blue. Eighth to tenth primaries modified by constricted inner webs. Female is brown with buffy scaling above, buffy with brown spots and scaling below. Throat plain buffy and underwing-coverts, which are conspicuous in flight, are cinnamon.

Ssp. Monotypic (NW Ec: Esmeraldas to Pichincha; W & NC Co: Pacific coast & N lowlands to mid Magdalena Valley; W Ve: base of Andes in NW Táchira & W Mérida)

Habits Forages in canopy, alone or in groups at fruiting trees. Feeds exclusively on fruit and berries of many trees, including mistletoes, figs, *Ficus*, and *Euterpe* palms. Spends long periods perching quietly, sometimes quite erect on a bare, exposed branch at very top of canopy. Builds tiny cup nest in canopy. In flight, male's wings give an audible whistle through modified flight-feathers.
Status Rare to locally uncommon in Ecuador, uncommon but possibly under-recorded in Colombia, rare to possibly uncommon with very few records in Venezuela, where prime habitats mostly replaced with pasture for cattle.
Habitat Tropical Zone, to *c.*300m in Ecuador, 1,000m in Colombia and 1,000m in Venezuela. Humid and wet forests of lowlands and foothills, secondary woodland.
Voice Males do not call, females give loud shrieks at nest (Hilty, Snow).
Note Formerly called Natterer's Cotinga.

PLUM-THROATED COTINGA
Cotinga maynana Pl. 213

Identification 19–20cm. Male is shiny turquoise-blue with a plum-purple throat, and tail blue above and black on underside. Primaries black and wing-coverts and rest of remiges black with blue fringes. Female is greyish brown with buffy scaling above, mottled pale greyish-brown below, and dappled bright cinnamon on belly, undertail and underwing-coverts, which are conspicuous in flight.

Ssp. Monotypic (E Ec, S Co: E Andes)

Habits Forages in canopy, alone or in groups at fruiting trees. Feeds exclusively on fruits and berries of many trees, including mistletoes, figs, *Ficus*, and *Euterpe* palms, picked from perch or in short sallies. Spends long periods perching quietly, sometimes quite erect on bare, exposed branch at very top of canopy. Builds tiny cup nest in canopy. Where they occur sympatrically, often found with Spangled Cotinga at same fruiting tree. In flight, male's wings give audible twitter or whistle. Males display by dropping from perch at an angle and then flying with loud wing whistle 40–50m over open spaces (including water), breaking in midair with loud wing whirr and then returning to perch.

Status Uncommon to locally frequent in Ecuador, where has declined dramatically at some localities in recent years. Uncommon to frequent in Colombia.

Habitat Tropical Zone, to *c.*800m in Ecuador and 500m in Colombia. Humid lowland forests, both *terra firme* and *várzea*.

Voice Apparently silent, no recordings exist (H&B, Snow).

PURPLE-BREASTED COTINGA

Cotinga cotinga Pl. 213

Identification 18–19cm. Male has deep violet-blue upperparts and lower belly, black wings and tail, and dark reddish-purple patch from throat to mid belly; unmistakable. Female dark brown with feathers fringed buffy above, pale brown with feathers fringed clean white below, and dull cinnamon underwing-coverts; looks entirely and strongly scaled. From female Plum-throated by crisp scaling below instead of diffuse dappling, and by lack of cinnamon on lower belly.

Ssp. Monotypic (SE Co: Guainía & Vaupés; S Ve: S Amazonas & NE & CN Bolívar; Guianas)

Habits Perches exposed, e.g. dead treetops (especially in early morning or late in day), or inside canopy, remaining quiet and still for long periods. Forages in canopy. Diet mainly berries and small fruits, including mistletoes and *Euterpe* palms, taken while perched or in short sallies. In flight, male's wings give an audible whirr. Flies fast, undulating, and has quite unique jizz.

Status Rare to possibly uncommon in Colombia, rare to uncommon in Venezuela and uncommon in Guyana. In Suriname, uncommon to rare in both savanna forests and the interior. In French Guiana, uncommon but widespread in forests of interior.

Habitat Tropical Zone, to 250m in Colombia and 600m in Venezuela. Humid sandy soil forests in basins of black-water rivers.

Voice Usually silent, seldom-used call is a plaintive *preeeeeeer* (Hilty, Snow).

SPANGLED COTINGA

Cotinga cayana Pl. 213

Identification 20–20.5cm. Male brilliant turquoise-blue with scattered spots of black, throat and upper breast shining reddish-purple; black tail, black wings with coverts and remiges fringed turquoise-blue. Female dark brown with feathers fringed pale brown above, looks quite scaled, greyish unmarked throat and dull cinnamon-brown underwing-coverts.

Ssp. Monotypic (E Ec; E Co; S Ve: SE Táchira, Amazonas & Bolívar; Guianas)

Habits Forages from high perch, hawking passing insects, and attends swarms of flying termites. Perches exposed, such as dead treetops, and also in canopy foliage, remaining quiet and lethargic for long periods. Food includes berries and insects. Where sympatric, often found with Plum-throated or Purple-throated Cotingas at same fruiting trees. Males gather daily in very loose leks, sitting very straight atop tall emergent trees, mostly in early morning and late afternoon, their glorious plumage radiant in the sunlight. They display by dropping from perch at shallow angle and flying with loud wing whistle 40–50m over open spaces, breaking in midair with loud wing whirr, then returning to perch. Flies fast with shallow undulations.

Status Uncommon to locally frequent in Ecuador, uncommon in Amazonia and scarce in savannas of Colombia, frequent in Venezuela, uncommon in Guyana, and in Suriname frequent in both savanna forests and forests of interior, whilst in French Guiana, frequent but difficult to observe in the interior.

Habitat Tropical Zone, to 400m, locally 600m in Ecuador; to 500m in Colombia; and to 500m in Venezuela. Humid *várzea* and *terra firme*, gallery, savanna and sandy soil forests.

Voice Male calls a soft *hooo, hooo* (Snow).

WHITE BELLBIRD *Procnias albus* Pl. 213

Identification Male 28–29cm, female 27cm. Male all white with a long, black, chord-like wattle from base of lower mandible that wraps over and around bill, always from left to right; black bill and eyes. Length of wattle varies according to whether bird is foraging or in display mode. When singing, it is at its longest, but is half length at other times. Female has no wattle, is uniform olive-green above, crown uniform with back, yellow heavily streaked olive-green below, and has plain yellow undertail-coverts.

Ssp. *P. a. albus* (SE Ve, Tr, Guianas)

Habits Forages alone, in canopy and subcanopy, feeding on fruits, especially of Lauraceae and Burseraceae. Males polygamous: they gather in very loose leks comprising a few individuals, and call all day from permanent, completely exposed perches. Females may gather at fruiting trees. Seasonally conspicuous when males calling but otherwise difficult to find.

Status Uncommon to quite locally frequent in Venezuela and scarce and seasonal (vagrant) on Trinidad (no records Tobago). In Guyana, considered uncommon in BFR&S, with recent sight and tape records from Potaro Plateau (Barnett *et al.* 2002). In Suriname, widespread and common in hill forests of interior. In French Guiana, locally frequent in montane interior and seasonal on coastal plain (Île de Cayenne, Montagne de Kaw, Forêt sur Bale Blancs de Mana).

Habitat Tropical Zone, 450–1,500m in Venezuela and 0–850m in French Guiana. Tall humid forest of lowlands and lower slopes; in breeding season on higher slopes, but at other times moves to lowlands. In French Guiana in marshy and white-sand forests in non-breeding season.

Voice Only males sing, from treetops and turning on branch to call in another direction after each call. Their songs resonate through forests, a sound like the metallic, ringing clang of a gong: a 2-note *donng-geh*, first note long, second brief (H&M), or a loud *kong-kay* like 2 strikes of a bell, and a more melodic reverberating *duaaaaaaaaa... deeeeeee* with second note like echo of first. Sometimes, *kong-kay* song may be very loud and wattle swings momentarily to left side. Vocal from September or as late as December, depending on location, to late March or early April, or where birds start later until June. Rest of year silent, except in French Guiana, where sings infrequently on non-breeding grounds.
Notes Correct spelling is *albus* not *alba*, as *Procnias* is masculine (David & Gosselin 2002). White Bellbird seems to gradually replace Bearded Bellbird at lower elevations.

BEARDED BELLBIRD
Procnias averano Pl. 213

Identification Male 27–29cm, female 26–27cm. Adult male mainly silvery or greyish-white with very contrasting brown head and black wings, and a wiry, straggly beard formed by several black wattles of varying lengths. Takes 4 years for male to reach adult plumage. In display, breast expands and beard is fuller. Juvenile much like female, duller below and above. Female has no beard, is fairly uniform olive-green above, darker to dusky on crown, with greenish-yellow throat, breast heavily streaked dark olive and plain yellow vent; legs and feet dark. First-year male has darker head and notably darker back, the feathers fringed paler, but barely discernible; legs and feet grey. Second-year male has no yellow on white underparts and dusky streaking is reduced to sides, breast and upper belly. Back and wings still dusky but now have broad pale grey fringes. Head has clearly defined dusky hood but some brown feathers apparent, usually on sides and nape. Third-year male has brown head and wattles, but back to uppertail-coverts are dusky, with grey fringes, wings and tail are blackish.

Ssp. *P. a. carnobarba* (NE Co: Perijá Mts. & possibly NW Santander, Ve: all ranges, Tr, Gu) as described, white plumage washed silvery grey, instead of snowy white of nominate form

Habits Forages in canopy and mid levels, usually alone, feeding on fairly large fruits, mostly Lauraceae and Burseraceae. Seeds are regurgitated almost intact, which makes bellbirds important in dispersal and re-seeding. Females may gather at fruiting trees. Males have permanent territories and are polygamous, and call through day from exposed spots on top of canopy or display and call inside forest, but as calls are ventriloquial, bird may prove impossible to find.
Status Uncertain, probably uncommon in Colombia. In Venezuela uncommon and local, though possibly under-recorded due to it being commoner at higher elevations. Uncommon in Trinidad (no records Tobago). Situation in Guyana uncertain, although perhaps locally frequent – recently observed atop Mt. Kowa and heard many times on its slopes (Barnett *et al.* 2002).
Habitat Upper Tropical to Subtropical Zones, at 150–600m in Colombia, 350–1,600m in northern Venezuela and at 700–1,900m in southern Venezuela. Moist to humid forests on montane and tepui slopes.
Voice A loud, very far-carrying, dull *bock... bock... bock...* every few seconds; a series of *tonk, tonk, tonk, ...* metallic notes like hammering on an anvil (Hilty) and given *c.*2 per s; sometimes, a loud, somewhat melodious *kerong-kerong...* or *tic-tock, tic-tock, tic-tock...* combined with a high, ringing *eeee* that echoes *tic* notes. Females apparently are silent. Males sing year-round, but with less frequency and intensity when not breeding. Sings most of year in Trinidad, except October when moulting and these birds have modified song. In Venezuela, from January (or at least March) to mid July in north, and in Bolívar from November to early September.
Note Bearded Bellbird seems to gradually replace White Bellbird at higher elevations.

DUSKY PIHA
Lipaugus fuscocinereus Pl. 214

Identification 33cm. Large, entirely grey bird with long grey-washed brownish tail and darker grey wings. Males have fifth to seventh primaries modified, barbs of middle elongated, stiffened and not interlocking.

Ssp. Monotypic (E Ec: E slope; Co: W Andes)

Habits Forages in canopy and subcanopy, alone or sometimes with mixed flocks, picking fruits and berries with a sally and short flutter. A calm, lethargic bird that perches for long periods but has been recorded flying back and forth between 2 trees calling persistently.
Status Rare to uncommon and possibly local in Ecuador, uncommon and local in Colombia.
Habitat Subtropical to Temperate Zones, at 1,700–2,600m in Ecuador and 2,000–3,000m in Colombia. Humid forests on montane slopes, borders and clearings, and alder wood groves.
Voice A loud downslurred *pee-a-weeee* or *pee-a-weeee-a-weeee*, also interpreted as *whee-a-wheeee* or *whee-a-wheeee-a-wheeeea*, similar to Screaming Piha, and usually triggers replies by others (H&B, Snow).
Note Genus *Lipaugus* was placed in Tyrannidae (Wetmore 1972) on basis of plumage and form similar to *Laniocera* and *Rhytipterna*, but now considered to best placed in Cotingidae (Warter 1965, Prum *et al.* 2000).

CHESTNUT-CAPPED PIHA
Lipaugus weberi Pl. 214

Identification 24–25cm. Adult entirely slate grey except pale cinnamon undertail-coverts and conspicuous deep chestnut crown in male; eyes dark brown, legs grey, bill blackish. Male has sixth and seventh primaries modified; barbs on outer web stiffened and do not interlock, rather like very fine teeth in comb. Juvenile very similar but chestnut on crown duller and reduced.

Ssp. Monotypic (N Co: C Andes in Antioquia)

Habits Forages alone in canopy and subcanopy, picking fruits (Lauraceae, Melastomataceae, Rubiaceae) and invertebrates with short sallies or by reaching from perch. Sometimes joins mixed canopy flocks.

Status Endangered. Colombian endemic, uncommon to very locally frequent. Recently discovered, it has been found at *c.*25 localities, but at several of these is affected by forest fragmentation, and total range is very small (*c.*100 km²).

Habitat Subtropical Zone, at 1,400–1,900m. Wet montane and cloud forests, including slightly disturbed areas, but not in secondary woodland.

Voice A loud *sreeck* that rises and falls sharply, and a nasal *gluck-gluck* in contact (Snow).

Note A recently described species (Cuervo *et al.* 2001).

SCREAMING PIHA
Lipaugus vociferans Pl. 214

Identification 24–28cm. Adult entirely grey, throat and belly slightly paler, reminiscent of a thrush in size and shape, with a relatively long tail, grey eyes and dusky bill and legs. Throat has concealed yellow-orange patch that is revealed when bird sings. Juvenile slightly softer grey with cinnamon greater wing-coverts and lower back flushed cinnamon, gradually becoming pure cinnamon on uppertail-coverts; undertail-coverts lightly washed cinnamon. Difficult to separate from Greyish Mourner, which is smaller, more slender, does not have paler underparts and usually accompanies mixed flocks. Voice is very distinctive.

Ssp. Monotypic (E Ec, SE Co, S & E Ve, Guianas)

Habits Forages in canopy and subcanopy, picking fruits and berries by hovering. Rarely joins mixed flocks. Forms broad singing leks where 20+ gather in branches of subcanopy, individuals always keeping 30–50m from each other. Singing alternates between long periods of silence with a sudden burst of song that make forests ring for a few minutes. Calls seem ventriloquial, thus singing individuals away from leks are very difficult to locate even when close. Male sings with mouth wide open showing bright orange gape.

Status Uncommon to locally common in Ecuador, common and widespread in Colombia and Venezuela, common in Suriname. Very common in French Guiana.

Habitat Tropical Zone, to 500m, locally and less numerous to 900m in Ecuador; to 600m in Colombia; and to 1,400m, but mostly below 900m in Venezuela. Humid, wet or swampy lowland forests, *várzea* and *terra firme*, occasionally in foothills and on lower slopes of tepuis.

Voice One of first vocalisations that visitors to region learn. Song is a sequence of low, gurgling notes followed by 3 loud, resonant whistles, *peee-pee-yow*, the defining call of lowland forests of the entire Orinoco and Amazon basins. It is unmistakable.

RUFOUS PIHA *Lipaugus unirufus* Pl. 214

Identification 23–24cm. An entirely cinnamon-brown bird, throat paler and crown and wings brighter, reminiscent of a thrush in size and shape, with a relatively long tail, brown eyes, blackish bill and dark greenish-grey legs. Sexes are alike. Difficult to separate from Rufous Mourner which is smaller, more slender and has flat top to head, instead of a rounded head (see plate 204).

Ssp. *L. u. castaneotinctus* (NW Ec: Esmeraldas, SW Co: Pacific slope in Cauca & Nariño) darker and generally more chestnut.

L. u. unirufus (NW Co: from Pacific coast in Chocó across Antioquia & Bolívar to Santander, Guajira?) brighter and more orange-cinnamon

Habits Forages in canopy and subcanopy, sallying to pick fruits (*Euterpe* and other palms, Lauraceae, *Ficus*), and small invertebrates. Occasionally joins mixed flocks. Placid and lethargic, perches still for long periods, watching surroundings from mid level and subcanopy.

Status Uncommon to locally common in Ecuador and uncommon to frequent in Colombia.

Habitat Tropical Zone, to 700m in Ecuador and 1,000m in Colombia. Humid and wet lowland forests, occasionally in foothill woodland.

Voice Calls at lek include a ringing *peer*, soft *cheer-weet* or *whee-er-wit,* also interpreted as *quir-a* or *pee-hear-wit* (H&B, Snow). Other calls include a loud *trrt-trrt-trrt-trrt* rattle, musical trills and series of *cla* notes.

Notes Range in Ecuador formerly extended to southern Pichincha. In Colombia, race of isolated population in Serranía de Macuira, east Guajira, unknown, tentatively assigned here to nominate.

ROSE-COLLARED PIHA
Lipaugus streptophorus Pl. 214

Identification 22–23cm. Entirely grey, slate grey above and pale pearly grey below, except striking, broad magenta collar in male, magenta undertail-coverts in male and cinnamon-rufous undertail-coverts in females and juveniles. Eyes dark brown, legs grey, bill blackish. Female and juvenile lack rose collar and thus closely recall Screaming Piha (juveniles have been seen being fed by adults; D. Ascanio).

Ssp. Monotypic (SE Ve: E Bolívar in tepuis Roraima, Aprada, Acopán, Uei and Ptari, and Sierra de Lema; S Gu: Potaro, Roraima).

Habits Forages in canopy and subcanopy, mostly in fruiting trees, feeding mainly on fruits (especially Melastomataceae), but also insects, picking food by short sallies and mashing fruits before swallowing. Usually in pairs or in small family groups at fruiting trees. Perches for long periods inside canopy and is usually very quiet, thus easily missed, but will often perch in open more briefly. Males make a *pow, pow* during displays that are possibly produced by the wings. Tends to live in pairs, though leks are very loose, with 2–3 calling males (D. Ascanio).

Status Endemic to tepui region: uncommon and local in Sierra de Lema, frequent to common in Aprada, Acopán and Ptari tepuis in Venezuela, and in Guyana, frequent to common on Mt. Kowa and Potaro Plateau.
Habitat Subtropical Zone, at 1,000–1,800m but mostly above 1,300m in Venezuela. Humid and wet tepui slope forests and mature dense secondary woodland, especially where Melastomataceae abound.
Voice A clear, rising and falling *sueeet-suéééeeeoo* whistle and a sharp *skreeyr* trill (Snow).

GREY-TAILED PIHA

Snowornis subalaris Pl. 214

Identification 23–24cm. Thrush-like bird with bright olive-green upperparts, greyish-green wings, grey rump and tail, whitish chin, dull olive-grey throat and chest with pale grey shaft-streaks, grey belly and yellow underwing-coverts; eyes dark brown with pale eye-ring, bill dark horn and legs and grey. Male has semi-concealed black patch on crown, but this is not visible in field. From Olivaceous Piha by grey tail and belly, yellower underwing-coverts.

Ssp. Monotypic (NE Ec: Sucumbíos to Morona-Santiago & Zamora-Chinchipe, S Co: E slope of E Andes in W Caquetá & W Putumayo?)

Habits Forages at lower to mid levels, alone or sometimes in pairs, feeding mainly on fruits (especially Melastomataceae), but also insects, picking food items with short sallies. Joins mixed flocks only occasionally. Sits for long periods in understorey and is usually very quiet, thus easy to miss, but often perches for short periods in open.
Status Rare to uncommon and possibly local in Ecuador and Colombia. Occupies elevations below those of Olivaceus Piha.
Habitat Tropical Zone, at 500–1,400m in Ecuador and 800–1,000m in Colombia. Humid montane and foothill forests.
Voice Sings a clear, ringing, 2-note whistle: *churrrrrr-ee* or sometimes *chreeee* (Snow).
Note Formerly placed in *Lipaugus* or *Lathria*, but represents a distinct clade, meritorious of a new generic name (Prum 2001).

OLIVACEOUS PIHA

Snowornis cryptolophus Pl. 214

Identification 23–25cm. Thrush-like (though tail is short) with olive-green upperparts, yellow-olive underparts, bright yellow belly, sulphur-yellow on bend of wing and dull yellowish underwing-coverts, large dark brown eyes with pale eye-ring, grey legs and dark horn bill. Semi-concealed black patch on crown is not visible in field. From Grey-tailed Piha by greenish tail and olive-green belly, and duller, paler yellow underwing-coverts.

Ssp. *S. c. cryptolophus* (E Ec, S Co: E Andes) as described
S. c. mindoensis (NW Ec: Esmeraldas to Pichincha, SW Co: Pacific slope in Valle, Cauca & Nariño), slightly smaller, base of crown feathers white, not brown

Habits Forages at lower to mid levels, alone or sometimes in pairs, feeding mainly on fruits (especially Melastomataceae), but also some insects, picking food with short sallies. Joins mixed flocks only occasionally. Perches for long periods in understorey and is usually very quiet, thus easy to miss, but often perches for short periods in open.
Status Uncommon and possibly local in Ecuador, uncommon to frequent but local in Colombia.
Habitat Upper Tropical to Subtropical Zones, at 1,000–1,800m in Ecuador and 900–2,300m in Colombia. Humid and wet forests on montane slopes, and mossy, epiphyte-overgrown areas.
Voice Apparently no recordings exist.
Note Formerly placed in *Lipaugus* or *Lathria*, but represents a distinct clade, meritorious of a new generic name (Prum 2001).

PURPLE-THROATED COTINGA

Porphyrolaema porphyrolaema Pl. 212

Identification 16.5–18.5cm. Male unmistakable: black above with feathers fringed white imparting scaly effect from mantle to uppertail-coverts; deep rosy-purple throat, and rest of underparts white with some black barring on flanks. Eyes dark brown, a short broad black bill with a highly arched culmen, blackish legs and feet. Unlike any other female cotinga, female has rufous throat and rest of underparts barred buff and dusky or black. Above, brown fringed buffy-white and crown has uneven buffy and dusky barring.

Ssp. Monotypic (E Ec: E Sucumbíos to E Morona-Santiago, S Co: C & E Caquetá, E Putumayo & Amazonas).

Habits Forages from mid levels to subcanopy, alone, in pairs or sometimes in small groups at fruiting trees. Feeds on fruits of *Cecropia*, *Ficus* and other forest trees by reaching from perch.
Status Rare to uncommon and local in Ecuador; uncertain in Colombia, but perhaps locally frequent.
Habitat Tropical Zone, to *c*.400m in Ecuador and 500m in Colombia. Humid forests, *várzea* and *terra firme*, although apparently more numerous in former. Borders and clearings.
Voice Calls from perch on treetop, repeating very loud, plaintive *preeeeeeer* or *wheeeeeeeur*, over and over, every couple of seconds (R&G, Snow).

POMPADOUR COTINGA

Xipholena punicea Pl. 212

Identification 19–20.5cm. Spectacular male is entirely glistening (seems lacquered) deep crimson-purple with white wings. Primaries tipped black and greater wing-coverts crimson-purple and elongated and stiffened, with pointed tips and heavy white shafts. In flight, white wings appear almost transparent. Male takes 4 years to acquire this plumage, prior to this similar, but flammulated below with crimson-purple on rose-red, wings black with broad white fringes to greater coverts and secondaries, tertials black, fringed rosy, long uppertail-coverts grey and tail black. Intermediate plumage is much like female, which is dark ash-grey above with paler fringes, wings and tail dusky with broad white outer fringes to innermost greater wing-coverts, tertials and secondaries; narrow white eye-ring, paler grey below, with white undertail-coverts. In all plumages, eyes pale yellowish to white, flat bill is dark horn, slightly hooked at tip, and brownish-black legs and feet have pale buffy soles. Juvenile like female, but softer brown, greater wing-coverts and tertials fringed whitish, but not secondaries; eyes brownish and bill horn.

Ssp. Monotypic (E Ec: E Pastaza, E Co: extreme NE Guainía to SE Guainía & Vaupés, possibly Vichada, S Ve: Amazonas & Bolívar, S Gu, Su, FG).

Habits Forages alone, very quietly, searching for fruits and berries in canopy and upper levels, or sometimes in groups at fruiting trees. Favourite fruits include those of *Euterpe* palms, Moraceae and Lauraceae. Also sallies from treetops to catch flying ants and termites. Hilty considers it to generally not join mixed flocks, but Snow states that females and juveniles often occur in mixed canopy flocks, and that only adult males rarely join them. May move large distances following fruiting seasons of various trees. Flight is undulating, intermittently flashing out wings; a very important field mark, as light makes white in wing highly visible. Usually rather silent, perching calmly for long periods on exposed treetops.

Status Uncertain, apparently very rare in Ecuador (1 specimen record), frequent in Colombia, uncommon to frequent in Venezuela, and uncommon in Guyana. In Suriname, common in both savanna forests and forests of interior, in French Guiana, frequent and widespread in the interior.

Habitat Tropical to Lower Subtropical Zones, to 200m in Ecuador, 200m in Colombia and 1,300m in Venezuela. Particularly common in watershed of upper Caroni river, near El Paují. Sandy soil forests in white-sand areas with savanna and gallery forests, *terra firme*, swampy forest and *igapó*. Seems more common in sandy soil forest, and less common in humid lowland forest.

Voice Mostly silent: a gurgling note (H&M), reminiscent of a *Tityra* (O. Tostain), and males very infrequently give a loud, rattling croak, like a frog (Snow).

BLACK-TIPPED COTINGA

Carpodectes hopkei Pl. 213

Identification Male 24–25cm, female 23.5–24cm. Male entirely snow white except narrow black tips to outer primaries and central tail-feathers. Female greyish-brown above, with brownish-black wings and tail, wing-coverts and inner remiges fringed white, throat and breast pale grey, and belly whitish. Broad, rounded wings are a good field mark in flight.

Ssp. Monotypic (NW Ec: Esmeraldas to Pichincha, W Co: Pacific slope, from Chocó to Nariño)

Habits Forages in canopy and subcanopy, alone, in pairs or in small groups of *c.*3–10 at fruiting trees (*Cecropia*, *Ficus*, *Persea*). Perches calmly in canopy during day, or in early morning (and mainly in males) in high, open spots where sometimes remains for long periods. Sometimes males fly with long bounds and slow wing-flapping, possibly in display, as otherwise recorded flying faster and more direct.

Status Rare to locally frequent in Ecuador, locally frequent in Colombia.

Habitat Tropical Zone, to 500m, seasonally in some areas to 700m in Ecuador; mostly below 300m in Colombia, but recorded to 1,450m. Humid and wet forests of lowlands and foothills, mangroves, secondary woodland with scattered tall trees.

Voice Not known to vocalise.

Notes Called White Cotinga in Wetmore (1972). Sometimes considered a subspecies of Snowy Cotinga *C. nitidus* of Central America.

BARE-NECKED FRUITCROW

Gymnoderus foetidus Pl. 215

Identification Male 34–38cm, female 30–34cm. A large, mainly black bird with a small head, large eyes (greyish to dark crimson), blue-grey bill tipped black, and long tail. Male has large patch of blue, crinkled bare skin covering entire throat and neck-sides, and silvery grey wings, whilst female's patch of bare skin is much smaller, confined to neck-sides, and wings are very dark grey, only slightly paler than back. Both sexes have short, soft, plush-like feathers on crown and face. Juvenile like female, though slightly smaller and distinguished by grey fringes to wings, uppertail-coverts and most of underparts. Easily identified, even at distance, by its unusual shape – large body, thin neck and small head like a vulture's.

Ssp. Monotypic (E Ec: E Sucumbíos to Pastaza, E Co: W Meta to SE Vichada, S to Amazonas, S Ve: along upper Orinoco & tributaries from extreme W Bolívar to Amazonas, S Gu, Su, FG).

Habits Forages alone or in small groups, searching for fruits (Melastomataceae and Lauraceae) in canopy, where often seen hopping along thick branches, moving very much like a toucan. Often flies in open above forest, with distinctive rowing wingbeats, and silver flash of male's flight-feathers can be identified at long range. In dry season, wanders to areas where otherwise absent. Males display by aggressively ousting each other from a perch, chasing through canopy with slow, deliberate flight.

Status Frequent in Ecuador, common in Colombia, uncommon in Venezuela, uncommon in Guyana. In Suriname, frequent in forests on sand ridges, along rivers, but very scarce in the interior. In French Guiana, uncommon to locally frequent in marshy forests of coast rich in *Euterpe* palms and along rivers of interior.

Habitat Tropical Zone, to 300m and locally to 400m in Ecuador; to 500m in Colombia and *c.*200m in Venezuela. Wet and swampy forests, *várzea* and *terra firme*, borders of lakes, rivers and streams, *Cecropia* patches, river islands. Always near water, especially large rivers.

Voice Calls a deep booming *ooooooo*, like a foghorn (Snow).

CRIMSON FRUITCROW

Haematoderus militaris Pl. 215

Identification 33–36cm. Quite large, with big head and powerful, dark red bill, chestnut eyes and black legs. Male is mostly shiny crimson with dusky wings and tail, female has rosy-red head, neck and underparts, with dark brown back, wings and tail. In male, feathers of crown, upper back and breast are quite different, being very narrow and long.

Ssp. Monotypic (Ve: extreme S Amazonas in Serranía de la Neblina; S Gu, S Su, FG)

Habits Forages in canopy and subcanopy, alone or sometimes in small groups. Unlike rest of family, diet consists mainly of insects and spiders, and only recently found to occasionally take *Cecropia* fruits and possibly those of other trees. Males display by rising 30m above canopy with very shallow slow wingbeats, then spiral down with wings raised and tail spread. Seems to take ownership of favourite perch and use it for several years.
Status In Venezuela, status uncertain, scarce, probably rare. Scarce in Guyana. In Suriname, rare to uncommon, though widespread in both savanna forests and those of interior. In French Guiana, scarce but probably largely overlooked in interior.
Habitat Tropical Zone, to *c*.200m. Humid forests.
Voice Fairly quiet. Males call a short, low *bock* (Snow); also a short, single or sometimes double low hoot, like an owl's, that is repeated intermittently (Hilty).
Note Recorded on Cerro Neblina, Venezuela (Lentino 1994).

PURPLE-THROATED FRUITCROW

Querula purpurata Pl. 215

Identification 28–30cm. Stocky black bird with short legs and tail. Males have a striking, shiny, reddish-purple or magenta 'cravat' on throat, of highly modified feathers that can be raised into a wide gorget in display. Eyes red, bill grey, legs and feet vinous grey. Female lacks red gorget and eyes are dull red. Juvenile as female but has dark brown eyes. Bounding flight on broad, rounded wings is good field mark.

Ssp. Monotypic (NW & E Ec: N Esmeraldas to S Pichincha, E Sucumbíos to NE Morona-Santiago, Co: Pacific coast, Cauca & Magdalena Valleys to Caldas, S Meta & Vaupés to Amazonas, Ve: lowlands of Bolívar & S Amazonas, Guianas)

Habits Forages in noisy, agitated family groups of 3–8 that move through upper levels, dashing from branch to branch, calling each other. Seeks insects by perching quietly to scan around, plucks berries and other small fruits from branches in swooping sallies. Quite curious, will sometimes perch above observers, as if inspecting them. Vibrates tail frequently when perched. Snow (1971) observed breeding in Guyana and found that a single, fairly flat and loose cup nest is attended by all group members, who feed the single chick an exclusive diet of insects; the fledging period is comparatively long.
Status Uncommon to locally common in Ecuador, common in Colombia, frequent to common in Venezuela, frequent in Guyana. In Suriname, common in forests of sand ridges and those of interior. In French Guiana, common in mangroves and forests of coastal region and interior.
Habitat Tropical Zone, to 500m and locally to 700m in Ecuador; to 1,200m in Colombia; to 500m in Venezuela. Humid lowland and foothill forests and secondary woodland, borders, partially timbered areas, sandy soil forests.
Voice A loud, yodelling, low double note, *ka-hoowa... ka-hoowa...* (H&M), paced repetitions of a mellow, 2-note *oo-wa*, and in alarm, a loud *wak-wak-wak-wak-wak* (Snow), like a barking dog, low mellow *oo-waa* or *ooouuua* whistles and a longer, rising *wheeooowhoo* or *weeooowhuu* (H&B, Hilty). Barks especially in response to playback or whistling by intruders (D. Ascanio, pers. comm.).

RED-RUFFED FRUITCROW

Pyroderus scutatus Pl. 215

Identification Male 43–46cm, female 38cm. Unmistakable: a large black bird with bright red and orange barred breast, and pale eyes. Eyes pale grey, blue-grey or pale buffy, stout, silvery grey bill in male or dusky in female, sturdy legs and feet dark vinaceous. The orange and red 'neck-piece' that covers throat, chest and neck-sides with curly, stiff feathers has air sacs that can be inflated and projected forward like an apron. Female has throat and breast slightly less colourful. Juvenile mostly brown on breast with brown eyes.

Ssp. *P. s. granadensis* (Co: E slope of C Andes, E Andes & Perijá Mts, W & N Ve: Perijá Mts, Andes & Coastal Cordillera) slight chestnut mottling on lower breast
P. s. occidentalis (Co: W Andes & W slope of C Andes) breast, belly and flanks solid chestnut
P. s. orenocensis (E Ve: NE Bolívar; N Gu) bright chestnut on breast and belly, mottled orange-buffy

Habits Forages alone or occasionally in pairs, from mid levels to canopy, often spending some time at fruiting trees. At dawn, males gather at leks, where each holds a small display territory. Display includes bowing then straightening up, and sometimes vibrates wings, accompanied by calls, repeated after long intervals or when others arrive at lek. Flies in an undulating, heavy pattern, and usually through forest, not above trees.
Status Very rare and local in Ecuador, locally uncommon to frequent in Colombia, very local and rare to uncommon in Venezuela, scarce in Guyana.
Habitat Upper Tropical to Lower Subtropical Zones, at 1,600–2,700m in Colombia, occasionally to *c*.1,000m; 1,200–1,900m north of Orinoco in Venezuela, at 50–500m south of it. Humid, wet and cloud forests, mature second growth, deciduous and dry forests, borders, small fields with scattered trees adjacent to forest, clearings. South of Orinoco it is a bird of moist forest, but on Andean slopes in cloud forest (D. Ascanio).
Voice Mostly silent. Male's call at lek a sequence of 3 resonant, booming double notes – *umm-umm-umm* – that sound like someone blowing across top of a bottle (H&B, Hilty), or like a bull, which accounts for Spanish name *Pájaro Torero*. Males advertise with a duo of deep, hollow booms (Snow).

CAPUCHINBIRD

Perissocephalus tricolor Pl. 214

Identification 34–36cm. Unmistakable: large and uniformly cinnamon-brown (almost same colour as a howler monkey) with bare head and face slate grey, a large, sturdy black bill and short rounded tail. May recall a small Black Vulture with its bare head and uniform mantle.

Ssp. Monotypic (S & SE Ve: S Amazonas & E Bolívar, S Gu, S Su, FG)

Habits Forages alone in canopy and subcanopy, picking fruits by sallying upwards and slowing for an instant. Main diet is fruits of Lauraceae, Burseraceae and palms, but also takes insects and spiders. Seeds are regurgitated shortly afterwards, bird perching in a shady spot to digest its meal. Males gather to sing at dawn and dusk in leks that apparently may have existed in same spot for centuries. Usually, several females come to attend lek, behaving quite aggressively to each other. Satellite lekking system, like Guianan Cock-of-the-rock, comprising nuclear lek with many birds in attendance and small satellite leks within a radius of up to 1km, each attended by 2–3 birds. Leks seem to be associated with *Cecropia* trees (D. Ascanio, pers. comm.). Dawn gatherings last *c*.1 hour, then birds disperse to forage, but continue giving contact calls through the day. Displaying males bow as they begin to sing, then straighten up as tall as possible while expanding neck in a ruff, cocking tail and flaring 2 bright rufous puffs at base of tail, as they reach finale.

Status In Colombia, occurrence uncertain, sight records listed in SFP&M and listed for extreme E Vaupés in Snow, but no reference found. Locally frequent or even common in Venezuela, frequent in Guyana. In Suriname, frequent in forests of interior, occasional in sand ridge forests during dry months. In French Guiana, frequent in all areas where *terra firme* forest remains intact.

Habitat Tropical to Lower Subtropical Zones, to 1,400m in Venezuela. Humid lowland forests and forested slopes of tepuis.

Voice Sing rounds of calls, answering each other, producing an eerie sound like the distant rumour of a motor or a chainsaw. The call – *oh-wa-a-oo-oow* – resembles lowing of a cow mixed with hoarse grating growls. In Suriname, these have earned it local name'bush-cow'. Between songs, especially at midday, male utters a short, frog-like croak, *rounhh* (D. Ascanio, pers. comm.).

LONG-WATTLED UMBRELLABIRD

Cephalopterus penduliger Pl. 216

Identification Males 41–51cm, females 36–46cm. Large, entirely purplish-black birds with large full crests. Male has crest that leans forward almost entire length of bill, and a long feathered wattle from lower throat that can extend to 30cm in display. Female's crest is smaller and does not hang forward, and wattle very small. The wattle is narrow from but deep front to back. Males have a relatively large crest with black shafts to feathers, females a small crest also with black shafts. Both sexes have brown eyes.

Ssp. Monotypic (W Ec: Esmeraldas to El Oro, Co: W Andes: Pacific slope in Valle, Cauca & Nariño)

Habits Forages in canopy and subcanopy, usually alone, often perching briefly on exposed spots. Diet includes large insects, small frogs and lizards, fruits of palms, laurels and other trees. Quite wary. Flight undulating, like a woodpecker, with wattle held close to body, and seen most often as it flies across rivers. In display, males make large jumps between branches, perch and lean forward to call while distending wattle, and crest is held erect. Males gather to sing at long-established leks. Suspected to migrate up and downslope, but leks at lower altitudes seem to be occupied year-round, so movements uncertain.

Status Rare to locally uncommon in Ecuador, rare and local in Colombia.

Habitat Upper Tropical to Subtropical Zones, 150–1,100m and locally to 1,500m in Ecuador; 700–1,800m in Colombia. Humid, wet and cloud forests. Sometimes on solitary trees in clearings.

Voice Mostly silent. Males advertise with a loud, far-carrying *booooh* grunt, females give an *aaugh* alarm-call (Snow).

AMAZONIAN UMBRELLABIRD

Cephalopterus ornatus Pl. 216

Identification Male 50–51cm, female 42–46cm. Male very large and purplish-black with very large crest and comparatively short, full-bodied wattle. Crest is quite tall with forward-curving tips to feathers and conspicuous white shafts rising from forehead; usually raised, but it can be brought down over bill. In flight, some authors claim crest is laid back, but others state that it is held erect. Male's wattle is fairly wide, some 15cm long and densely feathered, and usually held close to body, thus not very noticeable at distance. Female also entirely back, with much smaller and conical, almost pointed crest, whilst wattle is very small or entirely lacking.

Ssp. Monotypic (E Ec: Amazonian lowlands, Co: Amazonian lowlands, S Ve: NW & S Amazonas, S Gu)

Habits Forages in canopy and subcanopy, alone, in pairs or, more usually, in groups of 8+ that move with large hops between branches or cross open spaces in undulating flight, like a woodpecker. Watchful and quite wary, perches impassively behind foliage, but sometimes perches briefly in open. Males display by bowing and then raising head to call. Nest is a flat cup of twigs where single egg is brooded.

Status Rare to locally frequent in Ecuador, uncommon in Colombia, uncommon to locally frequent in Venezuela, situation in Guyana uncertain.

Habitat Tropical Zone: Amazonian population to 400m, base of Andes population 900–1,300m in Ecuador; to 1,200 m in Colombia; to 200m in Venezuela. In Amazon and Orinoco basins, riparian forests along large rivers and around lakes or marshes, *várzea* and river islands. At base of Andes, foothill forests and lowland *terra firme* forests.

Voice Males advertise with a far-carrying *booooo* boom,

females give series of 2-note calls, *goh-ahh* or *go-uh* (Snow).
Notes According to R&G, there seems to be no contact between Amazonian/Orinocan population and that at base of Andes.

PIPRIDAE – Manakins

Manakins being found only in Neotropical forests, have odd, very interesting displays and social behaviour and, in most species, the males are beautifully colourful, even gaudy. In general, females and immatures are cryptic olivaceous-green, and some are very difficult to distinguish if not accompanied by a male. Manakins live inside forest, foraging for small fruits, berries and insects, mostly in the lower and midstoreys. Melastomaceae berries are a tremendous attraction for these birds. They construct small cup nests hung on low branches or amidst shrubbery. Courtship is a complicated affair – males gather at a 'community' display site, called a lek, to dance and call with raspy unmusical voices. Females attend these to choose a partner. The males' dancing displays are often spectacular, intriguing and varied.

In recent years, a few genera formerly included in this family have been found, mostly through DNA studies, to be more properly placed elsewhere (*Schiffornis*), or even in their own monotypic family (*Sapayoa*). Present taxonomy of the family follows the SACC.

Among many papers on parts of the family, we took into account the comprehensive revisions of Prum & Johnson (1987), Prum (1992, 1994), and Snow 2004 (hereafter Snow).

Neopelma tyrant-manakins are rather undistinguished, tyrannid-like birds, olive above and yellowish or pale grey to white below. They tend to be solitary, even singing males, though there may be more than one bird singing within earshot of another. Rather flycatcher-like in their foraging behaviour, they search for insects in foliage and sally for fruit.

SAFFRON-CRESTED TYRANT-MANAKIN
Neopelma chrysocephalum Pl. 220

Identification 13.5cm. Rather flycatcher-like; dull olive-green above, with broad golden-yellow streak on crown (not easily seen), also dull olive-green on face, grading to yellowish below; eyes pale orange to off-white. An orange-crowned variant from extreme north-west of range in Venezuela might represent a distinct population. Juvenile like adult but slightly paler and smaller or vestigial coronal stripe. Larger than immature male Golden-headed Manakin, which usually shows patchy black in plumage. Lack of wingbars separates it from similar flycatchers, e.g. Forest Elaenia.

Ssp. Monotypic (S Ve, Guianas)

Habits Forages alone, searching for small insects in thin-stemmed underbrush, and hover-gleans for small fruits. Frequently utters monosyllabic note that aids its location.
Status Uncommon in Colombia, uncommon to possibly locally frequent in Venezuela, frequent in Guyana and Suriname. Uncommon in French Guiana.
Habitat Tropical Zone, in savanna forests and white-sand forests.
Voice Single-note call, regularly repeated (H&M). Song a loud, nasal *jewee-jewEE-JEWEE-JEwee-jewee* or *buuu jewy, jewy, jew, squick, squick, squick...* repeated for long periods. Song ventriloquial.
Notes Systematic position of the genus *Neopelma* is unclear and it was formerly placed in the Tyrannidae. It is perhaps closest to *Tyranneutes* (indeed, they were formerly merged under *Neopelma*: Hellmayr 1929), and Whitney *et al.* (1995) suggested that 'true' *Neopelma* might be restricted to *aurifrons* of eastern Brazil, with the remainder of species currently treated therein requiring a new genus. IOC-recommended English name is Saffron-crested Neopelma.

PALE-BELLIED TYRANT-MANAKIN
Neopelma pallescens Pl. 220

Identification 14cm. Rather flycatcher-like; dull, slightly greyish olive-green above, with broad plain yellow streak on crown (not easily seen), also dull, paler greyish-olive on face, grading on centre of breast to whitish below; eyes pale brown to off-white, bill blackish above, pinkish-grey below, legs and feet bluish-grey. Juvenile like adult, but has vestigial coronal stripe. Slightly larger than Saffron-crested, which is distinctly yellow below.

Ssp. Monotypic (S Gu)

Status Uncommon in Guyana where only recently recorded, in northern Rupunumi (Robbins *et al.* 2004).
Habitat Tropical Zone, in savanna forests.
Voice Males call a low, nasal *wraah, wra-wra* in advertisement (Snow).
Notes Genus *Neopelma* was formerly placed in the Tyrannidae. IOC-recommended English name is Pale-bellied Neopelma.

Tyranneutes tyrant-manakins are very small birds, rather like miniature *Neopelma*, to which they are closely related. They have longish, pointed wings and tiny bills. Being small and drab, with the habit of perching still for long periods, they are not at all easy to locate.

DWARF TYRANT-MANAKIN
Tyranneutes stolzmanni Pl. 220

Identification 8–9cm. Tiny olive-green bird with pale yellowish throat and yellow belly to undertail-coverts; noticeably pale grey (occasionally yellowish or pale orange) eyes, bill dusky, legs dark grey. From all other female and juvenile tyrant-manakins, and larger manakins, by whitish eyes. Much like a miniature Saffron-crested Tyrant-Manakin with dark eyes, but safely separated by voice.

Ssp. Monotypic (E Ec, E Co, S Ve)

Habits Very shy or skulking and difficult to see, but frequently heard; calls continually from favourite perch on thin, bare horizontal branch, but also perches quietly for long periods. Forages alone at all levels.

Status Frequent in Ecuador and Colombia, frequent to common in Venezuela, where especially abundant in sandy soil forests of Amazonas.

Habitat Tropical Zone, mostly below 500m in Ecuador, 400m in Colombia and 300m in Venezuela. Humid *terra firme* forests or rarely *várzea*, sandy soil forests.

Voice Male calls persistently, sounding very similar to Blue-crowned Manakin but stronger: an incessant, loud, twangy *tjur-HEET* (H&B), *jew-pit!* (Snow) or *Ur-jit!* (R&G). Advertising-call a hoarse *tjur-heet!* or *du-veet!* (Hilty).

Notes Genus *Tyranneutes* was formerly placed in the Tyrannidae. IOC-recommended English name is Dwarf Tyranneutes.

TINY TYRANT-MANAKIN

Tyranneutes virescens Pl. 220

Identification 8–8.5cm. Very small, dull olive above with partially concealed yellow coronal streak; throat to flanks and thighs greyish, slightly flammulated, with yellow centre to belly. Dark eyes, dark legs and feet. Female similar but has yellow crown much reduced. Less yellow below than slightly larger, pale-eyed Dwarf Tyrant-Manakin; note that yellow coronal patch of Tiny Tyrant-Manakin is not easy to see.

Ssp. Monotypic (E Ve, Guianas)

Habits Usually solitary. May be found throughout day, calling persistently from a horizontal stem. Generally forages at lower levels but occasionally found in canopy.

Status Uncommon and local in Venezuela, frequent in Guyana and Suriname, and common in the interior of French Guiana.

Habitat Tropical Zone, to 500m. Humid to drier, deciduous primary forest, savanna forest, humid *terra firme* and sandy soil forests. Restricted to lowland wet forests in French Guiana.

Voice A melodious, persistently repeated *teedleeoo* (H&M). Advertising-call is a much-repeated, melancholy *weedle-de-dee*, rendered 'Nicky the Greek' (Hilty).

Notes Genus *Tyranneutes* was formerly placed in the Tyrannidae. IOC-recommended English name is Tiny Tyranneutes.

GOLDEN-WINGED MANAKIN

Masius chrysopterus Pl. 218

Identification 10.5–11 cm. Male mostly black with bright yellow crown that develops into a short crest that curls over bill. Nape uniform, rich pink-rose to umber-red, spotted pink or ochre, depending on race. Feathers on head-sides tuft-like and may be directed upwards. Most races have small yellow bib, but size and shape vary (including individually). Juvenile male resembles female, but most show some yellow on throat, and immature has vestigial forehead, crown and nape coloration, varying with race and age. Called 'golden-winged', the extensive yellow in wings and tail rarely show except in flight. Several forms, possibly undescribed subspecies, require formal description. Females similar, regardless of race, uniform olive-green, but may show some pale greenish-yellow on throat and belly. Legs of all forms pinkish-orange and irides are invariably dark.

Ssp. *M. c. bellus* (Co: W & C Andes), hindcrown and nape brown to reddish-brown
M. c. chrysopterus (NC & E Co, Ve: Andes) hindcrown and nape broadly tipped orange
M. c. coronulatus (W Ec, SW Co: W slope) centre of nape flame orange, hindcrown brown to reddish-brown
M. c. pax (E Ec, S Co: E slope) centre of nape feathers scale-like, browner and very shiny
M. c. peruvianus (SE Ec) hindcrown and nape orange-red

Habits Forages alone, in small groups and frequently with mixed flocks, searching for small insects, fruits and berries, from lower levels to subcanopy. Inconspicuous, mostly at mid levels, but may be found at borders when Melastomataceae have berries. Leks form around fallen log on forest floor. Males fly to it at low angle, alight and then sits bolt upright, perch still with tail raised and bill down, then bow low, moving head right and left while raising crest 'horns'.

Status Uncommon to frequent in Ecuador, uncommon to locally frequent in Colombia and uncommon in Venezuela.

Habitat Upper Tropical and Subtropical Zones, 400–2,000m in Ecuador, 600–2,300m in Colombia, and 1,000–2,100m in Venezuela. Humid and wet forests from foothills to high slopes, mossy areas, borders and clearings.

Voice Mostly silent when not displaying, call a weak *teeeee* trill or low *nurrrt* grunt. During display, a 3-note *pk-k-ker* during jump or thin *seee* in flight (Hilty).

Notes Revisions by Prum & Johnson (1987) and Prum (1992). Race *peruvianus* only recently found in Ecuador (R&G).

> Male *Corapipo* manakins are glossy blue-black with throats of pure white silky feathers. The females are typically olive-green.

WHITE-THROATED MANAKIN

Corapipo gutturalis Pl. 217

Identification 9.5cm. Male all black with brightly contrasting white front from chin and malar to centre of breast. Eyes dark brown, bill dusky to blackish above, paler to flesh below, legs and feet dark purplish. Juvenile and female olive-green above, paler to pale greyish on throat and central belly; immature male resembles female, though olive above slightly darker and colder, it mainly differs by having entire underparts whitish. Lack of any yellowish below separates species from other similar manakins and is well separated geographically from other *Corapipo* manakins.

Ssp. Monotypic (S Ve, Guianas)

Habits Forages in upper levels, generally sallying for insects and fruits. Regularly joins mixed flocks.

Status Uncommon to locally frequent in Venezuela, frequent in Guyana and Suriname, common in the interior of French Guiana.

Habitat Tropical Zone, 200–1,100m in Venezuela and 400–700m in Suriname, 20–800m in French Guiana. Humid forests on slopes of the tepuis and nearby mountains.

Voice Contact a high, bubbly, slightly trilled *tseeu, tseeu, tseee* or *tseeu, tsee-tsee* (Hilty). Not unlike *Taenotriscus erythrurus* in French Guiana (Tostain); mechanical sounds over courtship on mossy logs.
Notes Race *carminae* from Cerro Marahuaca, Amazonas, Venezuela (Barnes 1955) synonymised under nominate by Phelps & Phelps Jr. (1963). Revisions by Prum (1986, 1992).

WHITE-RUFFED MANAKIN
Corapipo altera Pl. 219

Identification 9.5cm. All black with blue sheen, especially on upperparts, contrasting with white crescent across lower cheeks, chin and upper throat; line where white meets breast is concave, leading inwards towards bill. Female mainly dark olive with slight greyish throat and distinct yellowish tone to centre of lower breast and belly. Juvenile like female. Immature male shows some white on chin and throat-sides, and acquires full white throat with black mask as second-year. Very distinctive and unmistakable, though almost identical to White-bibbed Manakin, which has entire throat white, they are separated geographically. Outermost primary is very short and narrow.

Ssp. *C. a. altera* (NW Co)

Habits Like other manakins, often seen in fruiting trees.
Status Uncommon and local in Colombia.
Habitat Tropical Zone, 200–1,500m, favouring dense undergrowth.
Voice A sharp *prrreep* given by both sexes (Ridgely & Gwynne).
Notes Western races *altera* and *heteroleuca* (SW Central America) formerly considered subspecies of *C. leucorrhoa*, but separated on basis of differences in wing characters (Wetmore 1972, followed by S&M, AOU 1998 and Dickinson 2003), but retained as single species by Snow. Mistakenly called White-bibbed Manakin in R&T.

WHITE-BIBBED MANAKIN
Corapipo leucorrhoa Pl. 219

Identification 9.5cm. Male all black with blue gloss, especially above, contrasting with bold white band across front of lower face, from rear edge of ear-coverts to chin and throat; line where white meets breast is level to convex, curving down towards breast. Female olive-green with greyish throat and face-sides, and yellowish below. Immature male is like female with white on throat only just emerging. Male unmistakable in range.

Ssp. Monotypic (NC & W Co, NW Ve: Perijá)

Habits Sallies for insects and fruit, and sometimes joins mixed-species flocks.
Status Uncommon and local in Colombia, uncommon to very locally frequent in Venezuela.
Habitat Tropical Zone, to 1,200m. Humid to wet foothill forests and mature second growth.
Voice A very high trill that resembles an insect: *s-e-e-e-e-e-e-e*, also *seet't't'u-u-u* in display-flight (Hilty).
Notes Revision by Prum (1992). Mistakenly called White-ruffed Manakin in R&T.

Machaeropterus manakins are very small, mostly dark olive-green, with some bright colours in males, usually including red on top of head. They are distinguished generically by the modified inner remiges that contribute unique sounds during displays, when held erect and vibrated.

CLUB-WINGED MANAKIN
Machaeropterus deliciosus Pl. 220

Identification 10–10.5cm. Tiny; male quite distinctive in mostly chestnut body with scarlet crown, black flanks and wings, with white fringes to oddly-shaped tertials and secondaries, which are narrow at base, club-shaped, and twisted as if malformed. They produce the strange *tip-tip-beeuuwww* sounds in display. Female dull olive-green, paler below, and not easily separate from female-type congeners and tyrant-manakins, but is virtually uniform, with no streaks or flammulations, and a subtle cinnamon tinge to face and yellowish on belly.

Ssp. Monotypic (NW Ec, SW Co)

Habits Found at lower levels of montane forest, usually at forest edges.
Status Uncommon to frequent in Ecuador, very local in Colombia.
Habitat Tropical and Lower Subtropical Zones, to 1,600 m. Very humid to wet and cloud forests. In mossy, epiphyte-laden areas, at borders, sometimes in mature second growth.
Voice High-pitched *seet seet* followed by several loud and strident *keah!* notes (Snow).
Note Formerly placed in monotypic genus *Allocotopterus* (Snow 1975b).

STRIPED MANAKIN
Machaeropterus regulus Pl. 220

Identification 8.5–9cm. Male olive-green above with bright red cap from forehead to nape, whitish throat, red breast, the feathers becoming lanceolate, striped chestnut with white shaft-streaks; eyes reddish-brown, bill blackish above, pale below, legs and feet vinaceous-flesh. Female entirely olive-green above, dingy white below washed olive on sides and flanks, brownish on breast. Immature male like female, but show some partial adult characteristics, e.g. a few red feathers on head. Iris, leg and feet colours vary subspecifically.

Ssp. *M. r. antioquiae* (C & W Co) male like *striolatus* but slightly more yellowish above with darker red on head and broader white streaks on breast
M. r. aureopectus (SE & SC Ve, Gu) male has red eyes and bright red crown and nape, upper breast yellowish, chestnut streaks below have black centres; female whitish below flushed yellow on breast, eyes red; immature male has some olive flush on breast, eyes brown
M. r. obscurostriatus (W Ve: Mérida) male has some reddish streaking on upper breast and rufous streaks over rest of underparts; female has dull olive throat

and upper breast; legs and feet greyish olive-green, irides orange-yellow

M. r. striolatus (E Ec, E Co: E Andes) as described

M. r. zulianus (NW Ve) male has red breast and white centres to dark chestnut streaks; female whitish below, softly streaked weak chestnut, eyes orange; immature male similar but streaks darker, eyes yellow

Habits Usually within forest but occasionally at borders and edges, sallying for insects and fruits.

Status Uncommon to frequent and apparently local in Ecuador, very local and scarce in Colombia, frequent but very local in Venezuela, uncertain in Guyana.

Habitat Tropical and Lower Subtropical Zones. Usually found at borders of humid forest and in mature second growth.

Voice Apparently varies geographically, but more details required. In Venezuela (race unknown), a soft, sharply enunciated *pit-sink*, in eastern Colombia (presumably *striolatus*) a fast series of short notes followed by a short buzz, *whit whit whit whit skeeezz*. Also, presumably *striolatus*, from western Brazil, a soft, insect-like *whoo-cheet* (Snow).

Notes Race *aureopectus* recently recorded in Guyana (Agro & Ridgely 1998). Race *regulus* of south-east Brazil treated as a separate species in Snow (Eastern Striped Manakin), thus placing all taxa included here under *M. striolatus* (Western Striped Manakin).

FIERY-CAPPED MANAKIN

Machaeropterus pyrocephalus Pl. 220

Identification 9.5cm. Tiny; male lacks bright red cap of other races outside our region. Top of head pale orange, somewhat reddish on nape, with superciliary pure yellow and reaching base of neck, upperparts brownish, with olive-green wings and olive-green ear-coverts; neck- and body-sides pinkish-brown with warm, slightly rufous streaks on breast-sides and flanks; eyes red, bill dusky, legs and feet flesh. Female olive-green above, browner on wings, with whitish throat, greyish chest and pale saffron belly to undertail-coverts. Immature male like female but has top of head (not nape) yellow. Immature and female could be confused with those of Striped Manakin, but latter distinctly more orange-buffy below, compared to greyish and white of Fiery-capped.

Ssp. *M. p. pallidiceps* (SC Ve)

Habits Fairly solitary away from leks and even at leks, males well spaced and out of sight of each other. Usually found in fruiting trees, particularly Melastomaceae.

Status Uncommon and very local, but possibly under-recorded and more frequent than seems in Venezuela.

Habitat Tropical Zone, at 100–200m. Normally in various kinds of foothill forest, mature secondary woodland and transitional forest (favoured?).

Voice Advertisement a high, delicate and soft, frog-like *tiink*, often at rate of once or twice per minute (Hilty). High-pitched *pling* that sounds like a tree-frog uttered at long intervals. Rattling mechanical sound in flight, like that of a large beetle (Snow).

BLUE-CROWNED MANAKIN

Lepidothrix coronata Pl. 218

Identification 9–10cm. Small, all-black male distinguished by bright blue top of head and nape; eyes reddish-brown, legs and feet dark. Female olivaceous-green above, with greyish-green chin to breast, and yellow belly and undertail-coverts; eyes red. Immature male resembles female but slightly paler and greyer on chin and throat, and soon start to show random black feathers. Four races are very similar, and females impossible to separate in field. Male from other bright-crowned, black manakins by lack of any bright colour or white on rump. Female from most other female manakins by reddish eyes and yellow underparts; female White-crowned is yellowish from chin on down. Females of both White-fronted and Orange-bellied Manakins have pale throats.

Ssp. *L. c. caquetae* (SE Co) cool blue on top of head, uppertail-coverts lack blue gloss

L. c. carbonata (C & SE Co, S Ve) male has paler blue on top of head and tinge of greenish-blue on belly and undertail-coverts

L. c. coronata (E Ec) warmer blue, also more bluish on uppertail-coverts

L. c. minuscula (W & NC Co, NW Ec) smallest race, deepest blue on top of head

Habits Often joins mixed-species foraging parties, feeds by sallying to snatch fruits and berries, or insects. Males display and call from some oft-used slender branches.

Status Frequent to common in Ecuador, uncommon to locally common in Colombia, locally common in Venezuela.

Habitat Tropical Zone, most often below 1,000m but records to 1,400m. Humid lowland forests, forests on lower slopes of tepuis.

Voice Males advertise with a hoarse, slow *tho-wiik… tho-wiik… tho-wiik…* A soft *treereereeree* trill used by both sexes.

Note Formerly placed in the genus *Pipra* (Prum 1992, 1994).

WHITE-FRONTED MANAKIN

Lepidothrix serena Pl. 218

Identification 9cm. Small. Male mainly velvety black with bright patches of colour: forehead and crown silvery white, rump and uppertail-coverts intense powder blue, chest and belly rich yellow, divided by a black bar, undertail-coverts olive-green. Female olive-green above with pure green rump and uppertail-coverts, crown tinged bluish and face tinged greyish; below all yellow with diffuse bar of green across breast, thighs green, undertail-coverts washed faintly green. Immature male similar but usually shows some irregular patches of black. From apparently very similar Orange-bellied Manakin by range, but female Orange-bellied has more extensive olive wash on breast and smaller yellowish throat.

Ssp. Monotypic (Guianas)

Habits Forages by sallying for insects and fruits, particularly berries of Melastomaceae (H&M).

Status Widespread and frequent in Guyana, very common in forests of interior Suriname and French Guiana.
Habitat Lower Tropical Zone, to 700m. Humid lowland forest, mostly at edges.
Voice A series of soft, throaty *whreee* notes (Snow), loud voice of displaying male best compared with note of a referee's whistle, *pyeer…pyeer…pyeer…*, irregularly interrupted with a very frog-like, slow *whôk?… whôk?…* (H&M).
Note Formerly placed in the genus *Pipra* (Prum 1992, 1994).

ORANGE-BELLIED MANAKIN

Lepidothrix suavissima Pl. 218

Identification 9–9.5cm. Male velvety black above, with silvery white forehead and crown, slightly tinged blue, bright pale blue rump and uppertail-coverts, orange belly and olive-green undertail-coverts. Female olive above with pure green rump and uppertail-coverts; rich, orange-yellow below, with olive suffusion on breast and olive thighs. Immature male resembles female but usually shows irregular patches of black; juvenile like female. Similar White-fronted Manakin has larger yellow patch below, divided by black bar. Ranges do not overlap. Small area of overlap with Blue-crowned Manakin and females might be confused, but slightly smaller Blue-crowned is uniform and slightly greener above, and lacks brighter green rump and uppertail-coverts.

Ssp. Monotypic (E & SE Ve, Gu)

Habits Forages alone, very restlessly, picking berries and small fruits from bushes and small trees in the understory or at borders. Joins mixed flocks as they pass through territory, but apparently does not follow them. Flashes wings frequently when calling or singing.
Status Endemic to Pantepui. Locally frequent in Venezuela, frequent in Guyana.
Habitat Upper Tropical and Lower Subtropical Zones, 250m to *c*.1,800m. Humid and wet forests on slopes of tepuis and surrounding mountains.
Voice Main advertising call is very soft and frog-like, a short nasal *aank*. Males also sing varied sequences of warbling notes, e.g. *whee-pee-pee-pi-pi-pe-pee* or *wu WE WE wa we we wit* (Hilty)
Notes Formerly placed in the genus *Pipra* and considered a subspecies of White-fronted Manakin (Prum 1994, Snow). Sometimes called Tepui Manakin.

BLUE-RUMPED MANAKIN

Lepidothrix isidorei Pl. 217

Identification 7.5–7.6cm. Very small, mostly black with blue gloss, extensive white top of head from forehead to nape, and powder-blue rump and uppertail-coverts; eyes bright red, bill black (greyish at base), legs and feet dark grey. Female olive-green, with yellowish forecrown and emerald green rump that contrasts with brownish tail; centre of lower breast to undertail-coverts yellow, washed olive on sides and flanks, thighs olive. Juvenile like female but slightly duller on rump and underparts. Male from White-crowned Manakin by contrasting blue rump. Female White-crowned Manakin lacks yellow forehead and bright green rump.

Ssp. *L. i. isidorei* (E Ec, Co: E Andes)

Habits Forages alone at small fruiting trees, often at forest edge.
Status Uncommon to locally frequent in Ecuador, rare in Colombia.
Habitat Upper Tropical and Lower Subtropical Zones. Humid foothill forests.
Voice Males give continual, rising *koooit* or *wreee* in display (L. Navarrete recording, in R&G and Snow).
Note Formerly placed in the genus *Pipra*.

Manacus is a small genus of black, yellow and olive-green manakins whose taxonomy is somewhat confused. Currently, 1–2 species are recognised (both of which occur in our region), but it is possible that Golden-collared Manakin should in fact be considered as 2 species.

GOLDEN-COLLARED MANAKIN

Manacus vitellinus Pl. 219

Identification 10.5cm. Male has top of head and nape (but not neck), mantle, wings and tail black. Entire neck, head-sides and throat to upper breast bright yellow, and throat feathers are elongated (directed forward beyond tip of bill in display), with rest of body olive-green; eyes dark brown, bill blackish, legs and feet orange, but nails brown. Female entirely olive-green, with brown eyes, black bill and orange legs. White-bearded Manakin is white instead of yellow, except race *flaveolus* of Upper Magdalena Valley, which is very pale yellow below, extending lower (to belly) than on race *milleri* of Sinú and Cauca valleys. Otherwise quite distinct. Seems probable that 2 species will be recognised as follows (see Notes, below):

Ssp. **Golden-collared Manakin *vitellinus* group**
M. vitellinus (NW Co) as described
Orange-collared Manakin *aurantiacus* group
M. (*v.*) *milleri* (N Co) no significant difference from *vitellinus* in field according to Snow, but the yellow is a clearer, brighter lemon than *vitellinus*, and belly, undertail-coverts and uppertail-coverts are paler olive-green, washed yellow
M. (*v.*) *viridiventris* (NW Ec, W Co) throat more lemon-yellow according to Snow, but yellow is much more orange and belly is solid olive-green

Habits Behaviour at lek is like that of White-bearded, but lacks fanning display. They forage in the understorey, sallying for fruits and insects.
Status Very common in Colombia.
Habitat Tropical Zone, to 1,200m. Found in thickets at borders of humid forests, wet secondary and dense regenerating lowland woodlands.
Voice A slightly trilled *peeerr* and clear *chee-pooh* at lek (H&B, Snow).

Notes Treated as a separate species from *M. manacus* by AOU (1998) and Snow, but retained under *M. manacus* by R&G, the SACC (as of February 2005) and by Dickinson (2003) whilst recognising paraphyletic nature of species. Brumfield & Braun (2001) and Brumfield *et al.* (2001) found that races east of Andes are not sister to those west of Andes, on this basis we have shown them separately on the plate.

WHITE-BEARDED MANAKIN

Manacus manacus Pl. 219

Identification 10.5–11cm. Distinctive black cap, back and tail contrasts with white body in male, and separates it from all other black-and-white manakins. Blue gloss on mantle varies racially. Female greenish-olive and much less yellow below, but not safely separable from female congenerics. Juvenile resembles female but immature male has some black on cap and patchy black on back. Irides dark brown, legs bright orange with black nails in all plumages.

Ssp. *M. m. abditivus* (CN Co) very small, white nape and underparts
M. m. bangsi (NW Ec, SW Co) small, white nape, white upper breast fairly cleanly separated from grey rear underparts
M. m. flaveolus (CE Co) very small, distinctly yellowish-white underparts
M. m. interior (E Ec, E Co, NW & SC Ve) white nape, grey below, from *umbrosus* by smaller cap
M. m. leucochlamys (NW & W Ec) softly barred blackish on grey mantle
M. m. manacus (S Ve, Guianas) white nape fairly narrow and cap broader, grey from upper breast down
M. m. maximus (SW Ec) like *leucochlamys* but white throat-feathers longer
M. m. trinitatis (Tr) large, all-white nape and underparts, female larger and somewhat paler than others
M. m. umbrosus (Ve: C Amazonas) very like *bangsi* but white grades into grey on breast

Habits Displaying males construct a performance ring or court by clearing even smallest debris from small circle of forest floor around a thin vertical sapling. The display involves jumps to and from the sapling, with whirrs and snapping noises like twigs breaking, produced by the wings. The firecracker-like sounds draw attention to the lek.
Status Frequent in Ecuador, locally common in Colombia, locally frequent in Venezuela, common and abundant in Trinidad (not on Tobago), frequent in Guyana, Suriname and French Guiana.
Habitat Tropical Zone, to 1,900m, but usually below 1,000m and mostly below 800m. Lowland secondary and gallery forests. Typically in the forest borders along roads, rivers, human settlements, pastures and savannas.
Voice Plaintive *peeerr* at lek, becoming a louder, high-pitched *chwee*. Also a distinct *chee-poo* at start of display (Snow).
Notes Our taxonomy follows AOU (1998) and Snow, where *M. manacus* includes all black-and-white races in north and central Colombia and east of Andes, with yellow-and-black taxa grouped under *vitellinus* and *aurantiacus* groups of Golden-collared Manakin (which see).

The 2 *Chiroxiphia* manakins are distinct and recognised by their bright red caps and powder blue backs. Whilst having complex and different displays, in general their behaviour is typical of the Pipridae. The males cooperate, jumping over each other sideways (Lance-tailed) or backwards (Blue-backed), in what are possibly the most sophisticated, evolved displays amongst Neotropical birds.

LANCE-TAILED MANAKIN

Chiroxiphia lanceolata Pl. 218

Identification 13–13.5cm. Male grey with black wings, scarlet crown and powder-blue back. Crown-feathers slightly elongated, forming modest crest, and 2 central tail-feathers are also elongated. Legs and feet orange. Immature male lacks blue back and has olive-green wings, but does have red crest and grey body. Female olive-green with pale buffy underparts, pale greyish on chin and washed olive on breast. Juvenile male resembles female but develops red crest. Female and juvenile have yellowish legs and feet. Blue-backed Manakin appears very similar but differs in some respects and there is no overlap in range. Female and juvenile Blue-backed Manakins have pink-salmon legs and feet.

Ssp. Monotypic (N & NE Co, N Ve)

Habits Rather shy as it forages in dense lower growth using sorties and sallies, taking small fruits and insects in flight, but not shy at leks. Reacts very actively to call of a pygmy owl.
Status Locally common in Colombia, common in Venezuela, especially on north slope of central Coastal Cordillera.
Habitat Tropical Zone, to 850m in Colombia and *c.*1,200m in Venezuela. Dry to humid deciduous forests, secondary woodland, old coffee and cocoa plantations or mature second growth around plantations.
Voice Advertising-calls sound like a mechanical toy, a short sequence of whistled notes: *to-leeo, to-leeo-leeo*… repeated incessantly. Sometimes, a single, mellow *kow* note, and in displaying an incessant, nasal frog-like *na-a-a-a-a-a-a-a* (Hilty). Males duet *too-wit-dooo* (Snow).

BLUE-BACKED MANAKIN

Chiroxiphia pareola Pl. 218

Identification 12.5–13cm. Male all black with scarlet crown that forms short crest, back cerulean blue and legs and feet pink-salmon. Female olive-green, greener than female Lance-tailed, with pink-salmon legs and feet. Juvenile male like female but has red cap and some blackish on face; immature male similar but develops blue mantle. No overlap with Lance-tailed Manakin.

Ssp. *C. p. atlantica* (To) larger than nominate, with slightly more extensive red cap and blue cape, blue is more turquoise
C. p. napensis (E Ec, SE Co) brighter red, duller blue
C. p. pareola (E Ve, Guianas) as described

Habits Calls often, especially in breeding season (just before and during early part of rains, around March–July), but not at all easy to see. Very shy and easily disturbed.
Status Uncommon to locally frequent in Ecuador, rare or scarce in Colombia, very locally frequent in Venezuela, uncommon on Tobago (does not occur Trinidad), common in Guyana and in French Guiana, frequent in littoral, but very rare and local in the interior.
Habitat Tropical Zone, to *c.*500m, in lowland and foothill *terra firme* forest with abundant undergrowth, from dry deciduous woodland to bushy second growth.
Voice A soft *chirrup* in contact or when foraging. Advertising-call from displaying males a whistled *queenk!* or *wheet-weet!* Other calls include a *clock-clock-clock* and nasal *naaaaaaaa* (Hilty). Advertising-call given by Snow as a rolling *wrrr*, often followed by an abrupt single or double *chup!*
Note Differences in voice across range suggest that perhaps more than one species is involved (Hilty).

JET MANAKIN *Xenopipo unicolor* Pl. 221

Identification 12cm. Male is all black with blue gloss on upperparts and white underwing-coverts; eyes brown, bill bluish-grey and legs and feet usually dark. Female greenish-olive above, slightly paler greyish-olive below, with dark eyes, bill, legs and feet. Juvenile resembles female and immature male has irregular black feathers. Well separated geographically from Black Manakin. Female could be confused with Green Manakin but never shows yellow belly of that species.

Ssp. Monotypic (S Ec)

Habits Very poorly known.
Status Uncommon and local in Ecuador, where first recorded in 1979.
Habitat Upper Tropical to Lower Subtropical Zones, 1,450–1,700m, in humid montane forest.
Voice Call a descending, slurred whistle: *peeeeer* (R&G, Snow).
Note Formerly placed in genus *Chloropipo* (see Prum 1992).

OLIVE MANAKIN
Xenopipo uniformis Pl. 221

Identification 13.5cm. Dull, olive bird with all ages and sexes alike; underwing-coverts pale greenish drab. Eye, bill, legs and feet all dark. Look for faint yellowish eye-ring and closed wings reaching tip of tail. Readily confused with female Scarlet-horned Manakin, which has orange-horn legs. Female Black Manakin has pale eyes and yellowish central belly.

Ssp. *X. u. duidae* (S Ve) slightly smaller and brighter
X. u. uniformis (SE Ve, W Gu) as described

Habits Forages mostly alone, at mid and low levels.
Status Endemic to Pantepui. Frequent in Venezuela (especially where Melastomataceae are abundant), but in Guyana its status is not well known.
Habitat Upper Tropical and Subtropical Zones, 800–2,100m, in humid to wet forests on slopes of tepuis, both interior and borders.
Voice Advertising-call a clear, rising whistle *preeeeeeeéé* (Snow), usually given at long intervals, and occasionally preceded by a few low, stuttering *stu-tu-tu-tu-tu* notes (Hilty). Frequently utters a *zurrt!* call (D. Ascanio).
Note Formerly placed in the genus *Chloropipo* (see Prum 1992).

GREEN MANAKIN
Xenopipo holochlora Pl. 221

Identification 12cm. Olive-green above with yellow belly and undertail-coverts. Eyes and bill dark, legs and feet vinaceous-grey. No differences in age or sex. Three subspecies differ mainly in extent and pattern of yellow below. From female Jet Manakin by yellow belly.

Ssp. *X. h. holochlora* (E Ec, SE Co) green above, with pale greyish-yellow chin to upper breast that grade into saffron-yellow belly
X. h. litae (NW Ec, W Co) olive-green above and on entire head, breast and flanks, rich yellow from centre of breast to belly and undertail-coverts
X. h. suffusa (NW Co) olive-green above, with head and breast darker, greyish olive-green; fairly abrupt change to strong yellow of belly and undertail-coverts

Habits Forages alone, in undergrowth and lower levels.
Status Uncommon to frequent and quite local in Ecuador, uncommon but possibly frequent in Colombia.
Habitat Tropical Zone. Humid to wet lowland forests, *holochlora* mainly in hilly *terra firme* forests in east Ecuador.
Voice Soft sputtering calls (O. Jahn in R&G) and an aggressive *arrn* (R. Prum).
Notes Formerly placed in genus *Chloropipo* (see Prum 1992). Two species may be involved, either side of the Andes, with race *litae* perhaps inseparable from *suffusa* (R. Prum in R&T, Snow).

YELLOW-HEADED MANAKIN
Xenopipo flavicapilla Pl. 220

Identification 12.5cm. Uniform olive above, from mantle to tail, and wings, with white underwing-coverts, all-yellow head and body, flushed olive on face of male, whilst female is flushed faintly olive on back of head and nape, more so on face, breast and sides; eyes orange to red, bill dark above and bluish-grey below, legs and feet pinkish-grey. Juvenile has duller eyes and heavier olive wash over almost all yellow parts, being clear yellow only on belly and undertail-coverts.

Ssp. Monotypic (Ec, S Co; Andes)

Habits Very poorly known, usually solitary although may forage with mixed flocks.
Status Very rare in Ecuador, uncommon and possibly local in Colombia.
Habitat Subtropical Zone, at 1,500–2,100m. Undergrowth of humid forest and tall second-growth woodland. Not a river island specialist, but can usually be found on islands with mature forest.
Voice Unknown.
Note Formerly placed in the genus *Chloropipo* (Prum 1992).

BLACK MANAKIN

Xenopipo atronitens Pl. 221

Identification 12.5cm. Male dull black, more brownish on wings and back, with bluish fringes to feathers giving scaled appearance in some lights, underwing-coverts black; eyes dark brown, bill blue-grey with black tip, legs and feet black. Female olive-green with yellowish belly and undertail-coverts; eyes pale, bill black, legs and feet grey. No overlap with Jet Manakin, which has white underwing-coverts. Pale eye separates female from other similar olive-green manakins.

Ssp. Monotypic (SE Co, SC & SE Ve, Guianas)

Habits May accompany mixed flocks, sallying for small fruits and insects.

Status Local but frequent in Colombia, Venezuela, Guyana and Suriname; very rare in French Guiana, where known only from a few sight records.

Habitat Tropical Zone, usually to 700m but to 1,200m. Deciduous savanna forests, savanna scrub and woodland, borders and outlying stands of bushes. Almost exclusively in sandy soil forests in Venezuela. In Suriname commonly found at lower levels and in thickets of open savanna forests.

Voice Mostly quiet, but can be quite vocal at times, giving variety of rattles and loud sequences of sharp notes: *skee! kep-kep-kep- kep* (Hilty). Also a dry, rattling *trrrrrrrup* (Snow).

YELLOW-CROWNED MANAKIN

Heterocercus flavivertex Pl. 221

Identification 14–14.5cm. Male is richly coloured: olive-green above, with partially concealed yellowish-orange crown, dusky mask from lores to ear-coverts, large, clean white bib that includes malar of silky, elongate feathers that extend over ear-coverts forming a slight tuft, narrow band of darkish olive between white and ruddy below; eyes reddish, bill black, legs and feet grey. Female lacks yellow crown, bib is smaller (does not extend over ear-coverts) and duller to greyish-buffy, bar across breast is more diffuse and underparts are cinnamon. Juvenile is like a dull female with bib grey and underparts faintly washed olive; eyes brown. Similarly patterned Orange-crested Manakin is well separated geographically.

Ssp. Monotypic (E Co, S Ve)

Habits Forages alone in small trees and dense, scrubby vegetation, picking berries and small fruits.

Status In Colombia scarce but very locally frequent in Meta basin. Locally frequent in Venezuela.

Habitat Tropical Zone, to 300m. Sandy soil, seasonally inundated forests along black-water streams and rivers and oxbow lakes, sandy soil *várzea*, wet riparian woods and scrub.

Voice Male gives a weak *t-t-t-t-t-t-t-t* trill when perched and an explosive, rising and falling sequence that sounds like a sneeze in the middle, *speeeeeeeeEEEEEits-spit-cheeeeeeeeeu* (Hilty)

Note Called Yellow-crested in R&T, R&G and Hilty.

ORANGE-CROWNED MANAKIN

Heterocercus aurantiivertex Pl. 221

Identification 14cm. Male is warm olive-brown above with partially concealed bright orange crown that may extend into a small, loose crest, narrow pale eye-ring, grey mask from lores to ear-coverts, and large white bib including malar of long silky feathers that border lower ear-coverts in a sparse tuft; pale cinnamon below variably washed olive; eyes dark, bill dark bluish-grey paler at tip, legs and feet grey. Female similar to male but lacks orange crown and bib is less well developed, below lightly washed olive. Juvenile and immature resemble female. Similarly patterned Yellow-crowned Manakin is well separated geographically.

Ssp. Monotypic (E Ec)

Habits Quiet and discreet, usually found on favourite perch near or overlooking water. Sallies for fruits and insects, apparently preferring small *Ficus* fruits.

Status Rare to locally uncommon in Ecuador.

Habitat Tropical Zone, below 300m. Shows distinct preference for seasonally flooded, black-water drainages, usually being found along rivers and streams.

Voice Long, penetrating trill, descending then rising (J. V. Moore recording); also a high-pitched sibilant *wsiii* (R&G). Advertising-call a thin meandering trill of 1–3 s. Display-flight over forest has rapid descent with a hissing sound that becomes louder and ends with a loud *pop!*, probably caused by both wings and tail (Snow).

Note Called Orange-crested Manakin in R&T and R&G.

WHITE-CROWNED MANAKIN

Dixiphia pipra Pl. 217

Identification 9–10cm. Adult male all black with white cap; blue gloss varies racially and becomes richer with age. Red eyes, black bill, legs and feet in all plumages and sexes. Immature male soon has some white on crown and subsequently develops irregular black feathering. Juvenile male resembles female but is more pure grey below. Adult and juvenile females alike, olive-green above with greyish tone to head and grey underparts washed olive-green, slightly paler on belly and vent. An adult female with black wings was taken in Suriname and another with black on breast. Also, adult males have been collected with white feathers on flanks and vent, and it seems possible other variants might occur (H&M). From slightly smaller Blue-rumped Manakin by pale blue rump of latter.

Ssp. *D. p. bolivari* (NW Co) blackish bases to white feathers of nape lend slightly striated appearance, rich blue gloss

D. p. coracina (E Ec, Co: E Andes, NW Ve) grey bases to all white feathers; female quite distinct, with clean grey top of head and nape, whitish-yellow head-sides and bright yellowish below

D. p. minima (S Co: W Andes) like *unica* but with shorter nape-feathers

D. p. pipra (E Co, S & E Ve, Guianas) dullish, steel blue gloss, pure white cap

D. p. unica (NC & S Co) small, longer, all-white feathers on nape, grey legs and feet

Habits Birds seen at fruiting trees in undergrowth are usually female-plumaged, sallying for berries and insects. Males territorial, with well-dispersed lek system, the birds perching quietly, regularly calling and occasionally spurred to action.
Status Rare to locally frequent in Ecuador. In Colombia, common in the Orinoco and rio Negro basins, frequent to uncommon in Amazonia, and local on Pacific slope. In Venezuela, uncommon and very local in Andes and Perijá, but quite frequent and widespread south of the Orinoco, frequent in Guyana and common in the forested interior of Suriname and French Guiana.
Habitat Tropical and Subtropical Zones, to 1,600m, but occurs in lowlands as well as foothills. Humid forests, '*matas*' (isolated, nearly circular patches of tall forest in savannas), tall secondary woodland, and palm groves or areas of *várzea* in sandy soil forests.
Voice Males advertise their presence from a mid-level perch. Calls vary geographically, with *pipra* giving a thin, insect-like *chrrrrr* (Snow) and *coracina* a loud *drrrrrr-éuw* (R&G). Birds on Pacific slope in Colombia (*bolivari*?) give a thin, cicada-like *shre-e-e-e-e-e* slightly trilled, at intervals of 15–20 s (H&B). A long trill, *jeeeeeeeee*, every *c*.30 s (Hilty), presumably either *coracina* or *pipra*. Calls of other subspecies apparently not transcribed.
Notes Apparently, this species' origin differs from that of all other *Pipra*, and it was placed in the monotypic genus *Dixiphia* by Prum (1992, 1994), followed by, e.g. Hilty, R&G and Snow. Possibly more than one species is involved (AOU 1998), as western races from Central America and western South America differ vocally (Snow), and race *coracina* has a different display.

CRIMSON-HOODED MANAKIN
Pipra aureola Pl. 217

Identification 11.5cm. Male unmistakable in range, with black wings and lower body, crimson head, upper mantle and breast, and variable suffusion of yellow on face, mantle and lower breast, thighs yellow; bill vinaceous-red, eyes white and legs and feet vinaceous-red. Female dull, pale olive-green above, yellow on throat and upper breast with dull ochre wash; eyes pale brown, bill, legs and feet grey. Fully adult females with red feathers on breast have been collected in Suriname (H&M). Young male like female but readily separated by white eye, vinaceous-red bill, legs and feet, and begins to acquire spots of red, noticeable first on breast. White eyes and red bill also distinguish young males from other species, although a solitary female would be an identification challenge.

Ssp. *P. a. aureola* (E & SE Ve, Guianas)

Habits Very fond of *Ficus* fruits.
Status Locally frequent in Venezuela, very local in Guyana, common in Suriname, locally abundant in coastal French Guiana.
Habitat Tropical Zone, mostly lowlands to 300m but occurs to 1,200m near Roraima, in Venezuela. Swampy forests, lowland riparian forests, deciduous and semi-deciduous woodland near bogs or wetlands, and always near water, especially in areas with many vines and lianas in the understorey or stands of palms.
Voice Males advertise by calling a nasal, dropping *neeeeeeeeer* that is instantly answered by others and, in display, a soft *eeer-teet* (Hilty).

WIRE-TAILED MANAKIN
Pipra filicauda Pl. 217

Identification 11.5–11.8cm. Male, with its black back and wings to tail, flaming scarlet crown, nape and upper mantle and bright yellow forehead to undertail-coverts, impossible to confuse; eyes white or whitish, bill blackish and legs and feet sooty reddish. Immature male resembles female, but usually shows yellow on forehead and scarlet on crown first, then small amounts of scarlet on nape; eyes as adult. Female olive-green from forehead to tail, yellow from chin to vent, washed olive-green on sides and flanks, and olive-green undertail-coverts, eyes as adult male. Juvenile like female but with barely developed tail and brownish eyes. From female and immature male of larger Crimson-hooded Manakin and smaller Golden-headed Manakin by long tail; from all other olive-green manakins by white eyes and pale yellowish belly.

Ssp. *P. f. filicauda* (E Ec, SE Co, S Ve) 3 outermost rectrices steeply graduated, less intense yellow below, palest on vent and flanks, olive-green thighs, eyes white, legs deep vinaceous

P. f. subpallida (Co: E Andes, W & NC Ve) 3 outermost rectrices gently graduated, intense yellow below, eyes pale brown, black thighs, legs and feet

Status Frequent to locally common in Ecuador, scarce and local in Colombia, locally frequent to very locally common and numerous in Venezuela.
Habitat Tropical Zone, mainly below 500m in Ecuador and Colombia (but recorded to 750m), in Venezuela to 300m south of the Orinoco and to 1,000m north of it. Foothill deciduous forests, lowland dry to moist forests, swampy forests, mature secondary woodland, old coffee and cocoa plantations. Mostly along streams, and in *várzea* in the south.
Voice Claps or snaps wings, making a funny *plok* or *klop* sound. Advertising-call in Ecuador a distinctive, nasal, descending *eeeeuw* (R&G), *eeeeeeeeeaa* in Colombia (H&B), *eeeeeeu* in Venezuela (Hilty) and simply *eeew* (Snow).
Note Formerly placed in the unique genus *Teleonema* (Haffer 1970, Prum 1992).

RED-CAPPED MANAKIN
Pipra mentalis Pl. 217

Identification 10cm. Male unique within its range; bright red head except black chin and throat, yellow thighs and rest of body entirely black with blue gloss; eyes white, legs and feet grey. Female olive-green, paler below and yellowish on belly; eyes brown, legs and feet pale brown. Immature male resembles female but soon acquires pale eyes and a few small, scattered red and black feathers. Juvenile resembles female. No overlap with Scarlet-horned Manakin. Male similar to race *flammiceps* of parapatric white-eyed Golden-headed Manakin, which has variable head coloration, sometimes entirely orange-red. Female Golden-headed separated by salmon-orange legs, horn-coloured bill and pale brown eyes. Hybrids between the 2 species are known.

Ssp. *P. m. minor* (NW Ec, W Co: west slopes in both countries)

Habits Forages mostly in at lower to mid levels, but males gather in loose groups, several to many metres apart, 5–15m up and call insistently.

Status Frequent to locally common in Ecuador, frequent to locally common in Colombia.

Habitat Tropical Zone. Mature secondary and humid forests.

Voice Usual call a tight, sharp *psit!* (H&B) or *psip!* sometimes preceded by a high *p'tsweeee* or *sick-seeeeeee* (Ridgely & Gwynne). Full display-call is *psit psit psit p'tsweeee psip* (Snow) or *pit-peeeeeEEEEaaa-psick* (H&B).

GOLDEN-HEADED MANAKIN

Pipra erythrocephala Pl. 217

Identification 9.5cm. Small, all black with blue gloss, except bright orange-yellow head and red thighs; white eyes, pink bill, legs and feet. Female olive-green, paler below, with pale greyish or pale brown eyes, and pale pinkish-brown bill, legs and feet. Juvenile female resembles adult female, juvenile male similar but has white eyes. Immature male shows irregular black feathering first, then acquires full yellow cap (these are genuine interim plumages, not conditioned by moult). While young males in the Phelps Collection are labelled as having white eyes, H&M state that males retain pale brown eyes until moulting to adult plumage. Combination of pale eyes, bill and legs and feet generally separates them from other female and young male manakins. Larger Saffron-crested Tyrant-Manakin separated from yellow-capped immature male by yellow underparts; male Sapayoa is much larger and has dark eyes; immature Golden-winged Manakin also has dark eyes (vocalisations of the 2 are similar).

Ssp. *P. e. berlepschi* (E Ec, SE Co) uniform yellow head with narrow, sharply defined red border

P. e. erythrocephala (N Co, Ve, Tr, Guianas) orange head with variable reddish suffusion

P. e. flammiceps (E Co) yellow to orange head, often orange on sides and nape, or nape only, usually with fringe of red between nape and mantle

Habits Forages mostly at lower levels, snatching insects from leaves in flight. Diet also includes wide variety of small fruits and berries, especially Melastomataceae.

Status Frequent in Ecuador. In Colombia, uncommon and local, but frequent in basins of Orinoco and rio Negro. In Venezuela, uncommon and local north of the Orinoco, but common and locally abundant south of it, especially in upper basins of Orinoco and rio Negro. Abundant on Trinidad (does not occur on Tobago), frequent in Guyana. In French Guiana, common in both interior and coastal woodlands.

Habitat Tropical Zone, to 500m in Ecuador and Colombia, with records to 900m. Humid *terra firme* in lowlands and foothills, secondary woodland, riparian and sandy soil forests.

Voice Varied buzzy trills and whistles (ffrench), and very noisy when displaying. Calls commence with a *pu* note then a trill, then 1+ final whistles: *pu-prrrrrr-pt* (Hilty). A variety of sharp calls include a protracted *tzik-tzik-tzeeeeeeeeuw-tzik!* given in flight between 2 display branches, the final sharp *tzik!* as the bird lands.

Notes Race *flavissima* (Trinidad) considered invalid by ffrench (1976), being synonymised with *erythrocephala*. Race *flammiceps* considered indistinguishable from *berlepschi* by Snow without accounting for orange-red infusion. There is considerable variation of head colour within *erythrocephala*.

SCARLET-HORNED MANAKIN

Pipra cornuta Pl. 218

Identification 12.5cm. Large black manakin with slight blue gloss to upperparts, entire head scarlet with feathers on sides elongated as trailing tufts or 'horns', thighs scarlet; bill grey above with yellow mandible, eyes, legs and feet yellow. Unique within its range. Female olive-green above, paler below; bill grey, paler on lower mandible, eyes brown, legs and feet orange or ochraceous-yellow. Juvenile similar to adult female but has pale bill. Female looks like any typical female manakin, but separated by larger size in combination with brown eyes and pale orange legs and feet. From Olive Manakin by pale legs and feet. Invariably heard first, thus important to learn call.

Ssp. Monotypic (S Ve, S Gu)

Status Endemic to Pantepui. Frequent to common in Venezuela. In Guyana, recorded but status uncertain.

Habitat Upper Tropical to Subtropical Zones, 500–1,800m. Humid to wet forests on lower slopes of tepuis and mountains.

Voice Males advertise their presence by vibrating their wings very fast, producing a noise like electricity short-circuiting between 2 wires. In display, they bill-snap loudly. Calls are squeaky – a *squee-ke-slick!* and *ee-slick!* (Hilty).

Note Formerly placed in the genus *Ceratopipra* (Prum 1990, 1992).

TITYRIDAE – Tityras, Schiffornis, Becards and Allies

In 1990, Sibley & Ahlquist found that the genera *Tityra*, *Schiffornis* and *Pachyramphus* formed a distinct group, which they considered to be most closely related to the Tyrannidae, thus most subsequent authors placed what became known as the Schiffornis assemblage within the tyrant-flycatchers. In the late 1990s, work by Prum *et al.* (2000) wrought a change, and genera *Tityra* through *Phibalura* were placed tentatively in Cotingidae. Even more recent genetic studies (Irestedt *et al.* 2002, Chesser 2004b) have confirmed that genera *Tityra* through at least *Pachyramphus* indeed form a monophyletic group, and furthermore, Chesser (2004b) found this group to be more closely related to manakins (Pipridae) than to cotingas. In consequence, the SACC recently (February 2005) removed these genera from the Cotingidae and placed them as Incertae Sedis (of undecided position) following Pipridae. Thus, this group, comprising here *Tityra*, *Schiffornis*, *Laniocera*, *Iodopleura*, *Laniisoma*, *Xenopsaris* and *Pachyramphus*, is inserted after manakins. More recently, Ericson *et al.* (2006) have established that the group should be placed in a new family, Tityridae. A review of the various genera reveals the following.

Tityra is a group of 3 very distinctive species that differ from *Pachyramphus*, in which they were formerly included, in some morphological characters of skull and syrinx.

Schiffornis was formerly included in the Pipridae, but morphological (Prum & Lanyon 1989) and genetic data (Chesser 2004b) indicate that it forms a group with the genera *Tityra* through *Pachyramphus*. Until 1998, all *Schiffornis* were called manakins, but most subsequent authors have followed AOU (1998) in changing their English name to schiffornis.

Laniocera was formerly placed in the Cotingidae and then transferred to Tyrannidae based on anatomical analysis (Ames 1971) and on rationale for its removal from Cotingidae provided by Snow (1973). However, most recent morphological (Prum & Lanyon 1989), nesting biology (Londoño & Cadena 2003) and genetic data (Chesser 2004b) indicate that *Laniocera*'s closest relatives are *Schiffornis* and *Laniisoma*.

Iodopleura had traditionally been placed in Cotingidae, but like *Laniocera*, all recent data place it unmistakably in the Schiffornis group.

Laniisoma was also placed traditionally in the Cotingidae, but recent data (Prum & Lanyon 1989) places it in the Schiffornis group and indicates that it probably is sister to *Laniocera*.

Since its description, *Xenopsaris* had always been a genus of particularly uncertain and controversial affinities. Some authors considered it closely related to *Pachyramphus*, whereas others considered the plumage resemblance between them to be superficial or convergent. Traylor (1977) considered that *Xenopsaris* was either closely related to Serpophagine tyrannids or *incertae sedis* within Tyrannidae. But Prum & Lanyon's morphological analysis (1989) afforded strong support to a sister relationship with *Pachyramphus*, and Fitzpatrick (2004) provided rationale for maintaining the separate genus pending further data.

With *Pachyramphus*, like all other genera in this group, there is a history of controversy over its relationships, with authors such as Traylor (1977) including it in Tyrannidae whilst others placed it in Cotingidae. Morphological (Prum & Lanyon 1989) and genetic data (Chesser 2004b) indicate that *Pachyramphus* is better placed in this group of genera close to *Tityra*.

Additional references for this group: Prum & Lanyon (1989), Chesser (2004b), Remsen/SACC and Snow (2004)

BLACK-TAILED TITYRA

Tityra cayana Pl. 224

Identification 20–22cm. Look for broad red bare patches around eyes. Bill red on basal half, black on distal half of upper mandible and grey on distal half of lower mandible, eyes dark brown, and legs are black or greyish-black. Male has black head, pure white underparts, soft pearl grey upperparts and black tail and wings. Female similar but has brownish crown and variable amount of black streaking on much greyer upperparts and on chest. Juvenile male like female but has blackish-brown head and pale buffy tinge to underparts. Male separated from male Masked by all-black head and tail, and from Black-crowned by red on face and bill.

Ssp. *T. c. cayana* (E Ec, E Co: E Andes, Ve, Tr, Guianas)

Habits Forages in canopy, usually in pairs, occasionally a loose band containing a few individuals. Recorded in mixed canopy flocks and with Yellow-tufted Woodpeckers and Long-tailed Tyrants, but H&B note their aggressive nature and that they are seldom found with other birds. Mainly frugivorous, specialises in juicy berries and fruits with a lot of pulp (Lauraceae, Meliaceae), and complements diet with large insects caught in flight as well as swarming ants and termites. Flies swiftly across broad open spaces, perches frequently on tall bare snags and branches. Nests in dead-tree holes, which female lines with leaves. Tostain *et al.* state that male remains nearby during entire nest building process, but does not assist, whilst H&M claim that both adults participate in construction. H&M recorded a pair furiously chasing a large woodpecker that began to hammer in nesting tree.

Status Frequent in Ecuador, Colombia, Venezuela and Suriname, but uncommon in Guyana. Common in Trinidad (no records Tobago). Frequent in French Guiana, where widespread in interior and by far the commonest of genus in this country. In Suriname, found mostly in sandy soil forests away from coast.

Habitat Tropical Zone, to 500m in Ecuador and Colombia; to 1,100m in Venezuela. Humid lowland forests (*terra firme* and *várzea*), moist and humid foothill forests, sandy soil forests, river borders and forest edges, clearings, semi-cleared areas around settlements, tall, mature mangroves, plantations, areas that have been recently burned but large trees are still standing.

Voice A dry toneless rattle (H&M); soft, nasal pairs of croaking notes (H&B); an odd, brief nasal grunt – *urt* – often doubled and second note higher (R&G); paired or tripled buzzy *neebit* notes, and a nasal *weenk, weenk*… grunt (Hilty). Some authors claim it calls frequently, both perched and in flight, but others (Hilty) that it is not very vocal.

MASKED TITYRA

Tityra semifasciata Pl. 224

Identification 20–21cm. Look for broad rosy-red bare patches around eyes; bill mostly rosy-red with black tip. Male has front of head (and face) black, back of head white, tail-feathers black with white tips and base, upperparts very soft pearly grey, black wings and pure white underparts. Female similar but has brown head, darker grey back and pale grey underparts. Best separated from female Black-tailed by lack of streaking.

Ssp. *T. s. columbiana* (N Co: W Andes, NW & N Ve: Perijá Mts., Andes, Coastal Cordillera) very similar to *semifasciata*, less white at base of tail; female browner above

T. s. fortis (E Ec, SE Co: base of E Andes in W Meta) longer and heavier bill

T. s. nigriceps (NW Ec, SW Co: Nariño) male slightly whiter than nominate, with more extensive black on face and broader white tip to tail

T. s. semifasciata (FG) as described

Habits Conspicuous. Forages in canopy, usually in pairs or sometimes in small groups. Often found at fruiting trees. Although sometimes found with mixed flocks, it is rather aggressive and bullish towards other birds. Mainly frugivorous, specialises in juicy berries and fruits with a lot of pulp (Lauraceae, Myristicaceae, Meliaceae) which are picked while perched or in brief sallies, and complements diet with large insects caught in flight, as well as swarming ants and termites. Often seen flying swiftly across broad open spaces or perched on snag or bare branch at treetop height. Nests in dead-tree holes or abandoned woodpecker holes which are sometimes violently seized from other birds.

Status Frequent in Ecuador, common in Colombia, frequent to locally common in Venezuela. Race *semifasciata* from eastern Brazil is rare in interior of French Guiana.

Habitat Tropical Zone, to 1,500m but mostly below 1,100m in Ecuador; to 1,700m but mostly below 1,200m in Colombia; to 1,800m in Venezuela. Humid and moist forests of foothills and adjacent lowlands at base of Andes, but not in lowlands away from Andes. Secondary woodland, forest edges, clearings with scattered trees.

Voice Calls include an odd, brief nasal grunt – *urt* – often doubled and second note higher; a nasal 2-syllable *gurank-gureek* grunt (Hilty); and odd nasal *kuert* croak, sometimes doubled (H&B).

BLACK-CROWNED TITYRA

Tityra inquisitor Pl. 224

Identification 18–19cm. Lacks bare patches on face. Eyes dark brown, legs black, bill all black or black above and blue-grey below. In male look for complete lack of red on face or bill, and solid black crown to eye level. Males have white back with pearly tone, black primaries and black distal half of tail. In female, look for rusty cheeks, buff forehead and brownish back with dusky streaks.

Ssp. *T. i. albitorques* (W Ec, N & W Co) male has mainly white tail, with black only as broad subterminal band

T. i. buckleyi (E Ec, SE Co:) male has white cheeks and ear-coverts and an almost all-black tail

T. i. erythogenys (E Co: Norte de Santander & Llanos, Ve, Gu, N Su, FG) male smaller than nominate, with black on head extending to cheeks and ear-coverts and a mostly black tail

Habits Forages in pairs or small family groups that do not join mixed flocks but are often aggressive to other species. Main diet fruit, with a special fondness for largish and more nutrient-rich species, supplemented with insects, especially crickets and termites, particularly when nesting. Rather calm when perched, spending long periods on bare twigs in canopy, but flight is fast and direct. Nests in holes on large dead trees or atop stumps. In Colombia, recorded nesting in same tree as Masked Tityra.

Status Uncommon in Ecuador. In Colombia, uncommon to frequent in West Andes, frequent to common in East Andes. Locally frequent in Venezuela, uncommon and local in Guyana. In Suriname, widespread in north but much scarcer than Black-tailed Tityra, and absent from south. Rare in the *massif forestier*, seems more connected with old mangroves in French Guiana.

Habitat Tropical Zone, to 700m in Ecuador, 800m in Colombia and 1,100 in Venezuela. Pristine humid and moist forests, secondary woodland, clearings, forest edges and river borders.

Voice Very quiet. Both perched or flight, occasionally issues a strange, buzzy *uurnt* grunt, sometimes doubled (Hilty). Calls include *zick* and *squick* notes (H&B).

Notes Although similar to other tityras in vocalisations and general plumage, *T. inquisitor* shows differences in skull and tarsal structure, bill shape and lack of bare skin on face, which led Ridgway (1907) to place it in monotypic genus *Erator*. Thereafter, Hellmayr (1929) merged *Erator* within *Tityra*, which was followed by most subsequent classifications, even when Wetmore (1972) proposed resurrection of *Erator* based on these differences, and gave it the name Black-crowned Becard.

VÁRZEA SCHIFFORNIS

Schiffornis major Pl. 223

Identification 15cm. A plain, mostly bright cinnamon-rufous bird with rounded head and very large dark eyes, surrounded by a patch of grey on cheeks and ear-coverts; chin and belly paler than rest of underparts.

Ssp. *S. m. duidae* (E Co?, S Ve: S of Caño Capuana) has grey head and brown back.

S. m. major (E Ec: basins of ríos Napo & Aguarico, SE Co: extreme SE Amazonas) as described

Habits Similar to Thrush-like Schiffornis. Forages alone, occasionally in pairs, keeping well hidden in undergrowth. Very difficult to see – recorded mostly by voice and sings mostly at dawn and dusk.

Status Uncommon and local in Ecuador, where first recorded in 1970s. Uncommon in Colombia, where found in 1975. Uncommon to frequent but always quite local in Venezuela.

Habitat Tropical Zone, to 300m in Ecuador, 100m in Colombia and 200m in Venezuela. Exclusively in *várzea* and along streams (absent in black-water areas).

Voice Sings a slow, whistled *tee, towee-tee, towee?* or *teeoo, teewee? ... teeoo... teeoo, teeweet* or *twoweeo, tweeEET, teeu-dewEE, tweeEET... teeu... dewEET... teeu... dewEET* that is quite distinctive and similar in quality to Thrush-like Schiffornis (R&G, Hilty). Alarm or excitement call is a *chrrrrrrrt* rattle.

Notes The genus *Schiffornis* was formerly included in the Pipridae, but the morphological analysis by Prum & Lanyon (1989) revealed that it belongs with the *Tityra–Pachyramphus* group. *Schiffornis major* was occasionally placed in monotypic genus *Massornis*, but Zimmer (1936d) unequivocally established the correct placement to be within *Schiffornis*, and subsequently its vernacular name was changed from Greater Manakin to Várzea Mourner (as proposed by Prum & Lanyon 1989 and followed by R&T and Snow). Present name follows proposal in AOU (1998) of changing English group name to schiffornis which has been followed by most subsequent authors.

THRUSH-LIKE SCHIFFORNIS

Schiffornis turdina Pl. 223

Identification 15.5–16.5cm. Very plain-looking and featureless, with a vaguely 'daft' appearance; look for rounded head with very large dark grey eyes set off by diffuse pale eye-ring, black bill and dark grey legs. Upperparts brownish-olive, browner on wings, and throat and breast also brownish-olive, but belly paler and greyer; sexes identical.

Ssp. *S. t. acrolophites* (NW Co: highlands of Panama–Colombia border) dark olive-brown and almost uniform above and below.

S. t. aenea (E Ec: E slope of Andes) has browner crown than *amazona*

S. t. amazona (E Ec: NE lowlands, SE Co: Vichada, Guainía, Vaupés, S Ve: Amazonas) has rufescent brown crown and is generally paler, less brown and more olive above, more greyish below, than *aenea* or *rosenbergi*

S. t. olivacea (SE Ve: Bolívar & Delta Amacuro, Gu) very dull and uniform olive-brown

S. t. panamensis (NW Co: lowlands of N Chocó & W Córdoba) bright brown crown, wings and tail; cinnamon throat, greyish below

S. t. rosenbergi (W Ec: N Manabí & Esmeraldas to Loja, W Co: Pacific slope) dark brownish-olive below, with no grey

S. t. stenorhyncha (N & NE Co: Guajira, Caribbean lowlands, W & NC Ve: W Zulia, Andes, Yaracuy) more rufous-brown above than *olivacea*, especially wings, and underparts have throat and chest yellowish-brown and belly and vent greyish-olive

S. t. wallacii (Su, FG) like *amazona*

Habits Usually alone, forages secretively in undergrowth, where seldom seen, so most records are vocal, due to males' whistled calls. Seldom joins mixed flocks. Main diet insects (including butterfly larvae, crickets, beetles), taken from twigs or leaves with short sallies, but also berries and other small fruit. Often perches sideways on a vertical twig, like antbirds. Flies with whirring wings and when flushed jumps to nearby perch giving a cackling cry. Nest a bulky cup, well hidden in dense foliage on a stump or in corner of a leaf and palm trunk.

Status Uncommon to locally frequent in Ecuador, frequent and widespread in Colombia, frequent in Venezuela and Guyana, common in Suriname. In French Guiana, widespread in the interior, but always at low densities.

Habitat Tropical Zone, to 1,300m in west Ecuador, race *aeneus* 900–1,700m in eastern Ecuador, race *amazona* 200–300m in eastern Ecuador; to 1,400m in Colombia and, in Venezuela, to 1,800m north of Orinoco and to 800m south of it. Lower levels of humid evergreen to drier deciduous forests, savanna forest, mature secondary woodland.

Voice Varies geographically but always recognisable. Calls include melodious 4-note whistle *teee-ooo-eee-toooo*, sometimes 3 notes *toooo-ee-toooo* in Suriname (H&M). Also, a very slow, rising *teeeeu... weee-ti?* in western Ecuador (*rosenbergi*), a faster, sadder, more rhythmic *teeeu, wheeu-whee-tu-tu* on east slope of Ecuadorian Andes (*aeneus*), and *teeeeu, weee, tu-weee* in eastern lowlands of Ecuador (*amazona*) (R&G). In Colombia, *rosenbergi* calls *eee, creEEK*, *amazona* a more deliberate mellower *pee-ree-ret*, race *acrolophites* a *twick-sweet-twee*, delivered very slowly. In Venezuela, race *amazona* sings *weeeeee... PREE, a-weET!* (H&B).

Notes Formerly called Thrush-like Manakin. Genus *Schiffornis* was formerly included in the Pipridae, but morphological analysis (Prum & Lanyon 1989) has shown that it belongs in the *Tityra–Pachyramphus* group. As *Schiffornis* is feminine, the correct spelling of the species name is *turdina*, not *turdinus* (David & Gosselin 2002). *S. turdina* almost certainly comprises more than one species (Stiles & Skutch 1989, R&G, Snow 2004). The many subspecies constitute a very complicated group, with differences in voice, plumage and altitudinal range, and there are dark and pale forms. Snow recommends an extensive study.

SPECKLED MOURNER

Laniocera rufescens Pl. 204

Identification 19–20cm. Rufous-brown above, wings browner with broad rufous fringes to feathers, lesser and median wing-coverts have subterminal buffy spots with blackish basal spots creating 2 wingbars, primaries darker brown, tail all rufous, greyish tone to head; chin to undertail-coverts warm cinnamon, paler and slightly ochraceous on chin. Yellow tufts on body-sides may show well, or be (partially) hidden by folded wings; throat to flanks it is softly and faintly barred greyish-brown. Juvenile greyer and slightly darker on head, with black fringes to median and greater wing-coverts creating 2 wingbars, but different from those of adult, and body-sides have random round, black spots.

Ssp. *L. r. griseigula* (coastal NW Co) smaller, darker and duller than nominate

L. r. rufescens (NW Co: Chocó in Córdoba, N Antioquia & Santander) as described

L. r. tertia (NW Ec: Esmeraldas & NW Pichincha, SW Co) more richly chestnut above

Habits Perches morosely and forages quietly in undergrowth and at mid levels. Picks insects from foliage or air with short sallies.

Status Generally scarce and rare to locally uncommon in Ecuador, where threatened by habitat destruction; uncommon and local (scarce?) in Colombia.

Habitat Tropical Zone, to 500m in Ecuador and 1,000m in Colombia. Humid to wet forests and mature secondary woodland in foothills and adjacent lowlands. Swampy areas, mossy, shady areas such as ravines and along forest streams.

Voice Males gather to sing (leks?), the same sites being used for generations. Calls endlessly throughout day, repeating a ringing phrase described as *tlee-yeei* (R&T) or as a clear, slow, lamenting *wheeeep deeeur*, first rising and then falling – rather like a languid wolf whistle (H&B). Also a plaintive, drawn-out and slightly mewing, *peeeeeeeu* stopping abruptly (Fitzpatrick 2004).

Note Previously placed in *Rhytipterna*.

CINEREOUS MOURNER

Laniocera hypopyrra Pl. 203

Identification 20–21cm. Obvious confusion exists concerning plumage of this widespread but little-known bird, resulting in erroneous descriptions of plumage variation. Three distinct plumages progress logically and naturally, from juvenile through an intermediate to final adult. Moult sequence and period in each plumage unknown. Adult grey above, slightly darker on wings and tail, median and greater wing-coverts and tertials have pale cinnamon terminal spots creating 2 apparent wingbars, tail slightly barred, throat and upper breast slightly paler grey, rest of underparts pale grey, barred faintly with grey of breast. Tuft of bright orange-cinnamon on body-sides that either shows well or is covered by folded wing. Sexes alike. Immature or young adult has same bright cinnamon wing spots fringed with black, with a few, random spots of same colour fringed black on lower body. Body-side tufts yellow. Juvenile quite distinct, subterminal cinnamon spots fringed black on wing-coverts and tertials are more rufescent, and form cinnamon tips to secondaries as well; uppertail-coverts are lightly marked with cinnamon and have small, faint black spots, tail tipped cinnamon-rufous and body-side tufts yellow. On lower belly, in a seemingly random pattern, is a series of cinnamon-rufous spots, fringed black, roughly forming a V from yellow body-side tufts and effectively joining on vent; undertail-coverts cinnamon-rufous with black spots. Separable from other grey mourners by spotted wingbars and body-side tufts.

Ssp. Monotypic (E Ec, SE Co, S & E Ve, Guianas)

Habits Forages in understory and at mid levels, catching insects (caterpillars, butterflies, flies, wasps) by sallying to foliage and sometimes to air, or picking fruits and berries. Sometimes joins mixed understory flocks that include antbirds and woodcreepers. Most often seen on a favourite singing perch, where a few males gather in a loose, barely connected lek.

Status Rare to locally uncommon in Ecuador, frequent in Colombia, uncommon and local in Venezuela, and uncommon in Guyana and Suriname. Rare in French Guiana.

Habitat Tropical Zone, to 500m. Fairly dry to humid and light to dense forests, *terra firme*, sandy soil forests and savanna woodland. Often found on humid wooded slopes of ravines.

Voice Males gather in shady spots, forming loose leks to sing endlessly all day, a thin and melodious sequence of high slurred whistles, repeated 10–15 times in a singsong: *seea-weh* (H&B) or *chee-hooeet* (H&M); or a *seee-a-way* phrase delivered with a drowsy hypnotic quality, first part often a long, drawn-out *cheeeeee, a-wee*, then bird settles into a singsong rhythm (Hilty); also a series of 3–4 plaintive *teeéuw* whistles (R&G) or a repeated *weet-jeh* shriek (P. Coopmans).

Note Previously placed in *Rhytipterna*.

[BUFF-THROATED PURPLETUFT

Iodopleura pipra] Pl. 212

Identification 9.5cm. Very small plump bird with dark grey upperparts, darkest on crown, and white band across rump. Wings are dusky, long and swallow-shaped; tail dusky and very short. Underparts include warm buffy throat, upper breast and undertail-coverts, with white lower breast and belly barred grey; breast-sides also grey, but males have beautiful violet tufts on upper flanks, which differentiate them from females.

Status Although sometimes listed for French Guiana, Tostain *et al.* notes it does not occur in the Guianas and that specimens supposedly from French Guiana in reality are more probably from eastern Brazil. For Guyana, listed by Snyder (1966) and as uncertain by SFP&M, but BFR&S considered it amongst the 13 species removed from the country's checklist for lack of concrete documentation.

Habitat Tropical Zone, to 1,000m. Humid forests, cacao plantations.

Voice Fast repetitions of a weak, high *se-se-see* (Snow 2004).

Note Two races: *leucopygia* (coastal forests in NE Brazil) and *pipra* (littoral of SE Brazil).

WHITE-BROWED PURPLETUFT

Iodopleura isabellae Pl. 212

Identification 11–12 cm. A plump little bird with entire upperparts, wings and very short tail brownish-black, wings quite long and shaped like a swallow's, face handsomely marked with snow white eyebrow, moustachial and lores, and also a snow white band on rump; underparts white centrally, dusky brown on breast-sides, white barred dusky on flanks. Males have beautiful violet tufts on upper flanks, unlike females, but practically invisible in field. Eyes dark brown and legs dark grey; bill very short, with broad base and hooked tip, a black upper mandible and lead grey lower mandible.

Ssp. *I. i. isabellae* (E Ec, S Ve: Amazonas)

Habits Forages in pairs or small groups, mostly in canopy but sometimes at mid levels. Gathers at fruiting trees (mistletoes and others with berries or small fruits) and sallies for insects from perch, which is usually a bare twig at very top of canopy. May perch quietly for long periods. Thought to move through large tracts of forest, as rarely noted in the same place more than once. Nest resembles a hummingbird's – tiny and constructed of mosses and spider webs.

Status Uncommon in Ecuador and Colombia (possibly under-recorded), and uncommon to possibly locally frequent in Venezuela.
Habitat Tropical Zone to ±700m, but mostly to 500m in Ecuador and Colombia; to 200m but perhaps higher in Venezuela. Humid forest, *várzea* and *terra firme*, clearings and forest edge, white-sand forest.
Voice Not very vocal. Song a very weak high *jeee-jee-jee* or sometimes *eeee* (H&B), a soft high *tre'e'e'd* trill, a shrill, rising, much-repeated *eeeEE*, soft repetitions of a *sr'r'r--sr'r'r...* trill, and thin *ti-ti'ti-ti-ti-ti-ti...* rattle (Hilty).

DUSKY PURPLETUFT

Iodopleura fusca Pl. 212

Identification 11.5–12cm. Plump little bird with entire upperparts, wings and very short tail black, except white band across rump. Wings quite long and shaped like a swallow's. Underparts dark brown at sides, white centrally. Males have beautiful glossy violet tufts on upper flanks, unlike females, but practically invisible in field. Eyes dark brown and legs dark grey; bill very short, with broad base and hooked tip, a black upper mandible and lead grey lower mandible.

Ssp. Monotypic (SE Ve: E & SE Bolívar, SE Delta Amacuro, Guianas)

Habits Forages in pairs or small groups, in canopy and at forest edge, searching for fruiting trees. Main diet berries, but also frequently sallies for insects. Perches for long periods on exposed twigs atop tall trees.
Status Rare to possibly uncommon in Venezuela (very few records), uncommon in Guyana. In Suriname, situation is uncertain – possibly rare or uncommon. In French Guiana, uncommon (perhaps under-recorded) but widespread in the interior.
Habitat Tropical Zone, to 500m in Venezuela. Humid forests, forest and river borders.
Voice Rather quiet. Calls very similar to soft, high, thin trills and whistles of White-browed Purpletuft.
Note Genus *Iodopleura* still placed within the Cotingidae by Hilty, and Snow.

ELEGANT MOURNER

Laniisoma elegans Pl. 210

Identification 17–18cm. Bright olive-green upperparts and golden-yellow underparts with some dusky scaling. Eyes dark brown and legs brownish to greyish-olive. Two-toned bill: black upper mandible and pale horn lower mandible. Male has black crown reaching to eye level, female no crown patch. In male of races *buckleyi* and *venezuelense*, only throat- and breast-sides and flanks are scaled, whilst in female scaling covers almost entire underparts. Descriptions of immature vary: according to H&B, upperparts are ochraceous-buff with a few black spots, and wing-coverts are dusky with ochraceous tips, but Snow states that it resembles female, except wing-coverts are broadly tipped cinnamon.

Ssp. *L. e. buckleyi* (E Ec) smaller than nominate
L. e. venezuelense (C Co: E Andes in N Boyacá, SW Ve: E base of Andes in Táchira & Barinas) very bright green upperparts

Habits Forages alone, occasionally in pairs or small groups, from low to mid levels. Diet mostly fruit, with preference for berries of Melastomataceae. Very quiet and apathetic and thus easily overlooked. Knowledge of its song is essential for finding this species.
Status Very rare to rare and apparently local in Ecuador, rare and local in Colombia. In Venezuela, rare but possibly locally uncommon or even frequent, uncertainty caused by lack of recent records, as range unsafe due to presence of Colombian guerrillas.
Habitat Tropical Zone, 400–1,350m in Ecuador, to 700m in Colombia and 200–530m in Venezuela. Humid forest of both lowlands (*terra firme*) and foothills, forest edge. Seems to occur mostly in hilly regions, especially at base of Andes.
Notes R&G and Hilty treated Andean races *buckleyi* and *venezuelense* (with *cadwaladeri* of Bolivia) as a separate species (Andean Laniisoma) from *L. elegans* of south-eastern Brazil, returning to species limits of Hellmayr (1929), but this was not followed by Snow nor by SACC. Although range is extremely disjunct, there is virtually no difference in voices and plumage differences are considered insufficiently marked to warrant treatment as species. Name Elegant Mourner proposed by R&T to replace Shrike-like Cotinga, and followed by Snow, but not yet by SACC. We use it here in recognition that species is no longer considered a cotinga and because, as noted by R&T, it is not at all shrike-like.

WHITE-NAPED XENOPSARIS

Xenopsaris albinucha Pl. 224

Identification 12.5–13 cm. Slender little bird with a proportionately large white head, glossy blue-black crown, white eye-ring, narrow white forehead, pale grey nape, brownish-grey upperparts and snow white underparts, dusky grey-brown wing-feathers narrowly fringed white, and a long, dark brown-washed tail. Immature has a brownish crown, upperparts washed brown and often scalloped, and a creamy-yellowish belly. Best separated from Cinereous Becard by pure white rather than grey underparts, smaller size and slender proportions.

Ssp. *X. a. minor* (C Ve: NW Falcón, Llanos from Apure, Barinas & Portuguesa to W Delta Amacuro, N Bolívar, NE Co?) much smaller than nominate, but otherwise identical; male has wing 60–62mm, tail 53–57mm
X. a. albinucha (S Gu) male has wing 64–66mm, tail 58–61mm

Habits Forages alone or in very loose pairs, from canopy to ground. Picks insects from foliage or from air in fast sallies, or chasing after them in twisting flight, even dropping briefly to ground to make a strike. Sits quietly, very straight and upright in outer branches and is quite easily overlooked.

Status Uncommon and local in Venezuela, scarce in Guyana. Not yet recorded in Colombia, but could occur in Arauca or Vichada.
Habitat Tropical Zone, to 550m in Venezuela. Copses and isolated stands of trees in savannas and pastures, gallery woodland, scattered trees and light woodland in open or semi-open areas near water, patches of tall sedge grasses beside streams, ponds or marshes.
Voice Sings mostly in rainy season, a high, variable, tentative series of sweet trills, *teep, tre'e'e'e'a... eea... wu'u'u'e'e'e-e-e-e-e-p*, that rises and then falls, culminating in a long, rising and quavering trill.
Notes Called Reed Manakin in Prum & Lanyon (1989). Xenopsaris is maintained in a genus separate from *Pachyramphus* because of its lack of sexual dimorphism, several morphological differences, including much smaller size and odd-shaped ninth primary, and differences in nest shape; *Xenopsaris* constructs an open cup, whilst *Pachyramphus* builds a closed ball.

Pachyramphus becards are beautiful, relatively small canopy birds of tranquil disposition. Some live mainly in lowlands, others at higher elevations. All have comparatively large heads, which give them a very distinctive jizz. Their nests are large untidy balls of dry grasses with a side entrance hole, usually placed high in the canopy, sometimes in a very conspicuous spot, and in several species in close proximity to nests of bees or wasps. In P&MdS, H&B and H&M they appear with cotingas, whilst in AOU (1998), R&G, BFR&S and Hilty they are included with tyrannids.

GREEN-BACKED BECARD
Pachyramphus viridis Pl. 222

Identification 14.5–15cm. Distinctive, large-headed chunky bird with dark eyes and narrow yellowish eye-ring, dark grey legs and broad bill with a small hook, bluish-horn in colour. Male has glistening black crown, which extends over nape to back, and pale grey throat. Ear-coverts and neck-sides bright olive. Rest of upperparts olive, and primaries and secondaries dusky with olive fringes; mere hint of pectoral band and rest of underparts greyish. Female similar but crown, nape and face-sides dull yellowish-olive (as back) and lesser wing-coverts bright rufous-chestnut.

Ssp. *P. v. griseigularis* (SE Ve: tepuis of E Bolívar, W Gu: Mt. Roraima)

Habits Forages in canopy, alone or in very loose pairs, often with mixed flocks of tanagers, warblers, flycatchers and others. Searches for insects with calm deliberation or hops about watchfully and without hurry.
Status Very disjunct range: in our region, uncommon and local in Venezuela and Guyana.
Habitat Tropical to Lower Subtropical Zones, to 1,000m in Venezuela. Mostly in partially open areas of tall, moist to humid forest, light woodland, forest edge with bushes, forests on slopes of tepuis.
Voice Male sings soft, musical series of whistles that rise in a very musical crescendo – *trididideededeedee* – and also long, rising repetitions of a thin, nasal *q-wink* note (Hilty). Another call is an occasional *jew* note (Fitzpatrick *et al.* 2004).
Note R&T and R&G considered Andean race *xanthogenys* specifically distinct from *P. viridis*, followed by Fitzpatrick (2004).

YELLOW-CHEEKED BECARD
Pachyramphus xanthogenys Pl. 222

Identification 14.5–15cm. Distinctive, chunky, large-headed bird with dark eyes, dark greyish legs and broad bluish-horn bill that is slightly hook-tipped. Sexes similar. Male has glossy black crown and narrow whitish forehead or loral area. Entire upperparts olive-green, wings blackish with broad olive fringes to wing-coverts and inner remiges, tail dark olive, face bright yellow, breast olive-yellow, belly and undertail-coverts white. Female has olive crown, darkest at front, narrow grey forehead or loral area, greyish-olive upperparts, rufous-chestnut lesser coverts, pale greyish face and throat, greenish chest, and white belly and undertail-coverts washed pale grey.

Ssp. *P. x. xanthogenys* (E Ec: E base of Andes , S Co?)

Habits Forages in pairs, from mid levels to canopy and usually where foliage is densest, but always at borders. Seldom joins mixed flocks and rarely found in forest interior.
Status Small range apparently comprising a few disjunct segments. In Ecuador, uncommon to locally frequent, especially in Zumba, where very frequent. In Colombia, not yet recorded but could occur in extreme south, in hilly country of west Putumayo and east Nariño (H&B).
Habitat Tropical to Subtropical Zones, 650–1,700m in Ecuador. Humid forests of montane slopes and foothills, clearings with scattered tall trees, light woodland, forest edge.
Voice Male sings unmistakable series of soft whistles – *du-de-de-de-dididididi* – quite musical, given at long intervals and sometimes commencing with 1+ ascending *te-wik* notes (Fitzpatrick 2004).
Note Formerly conspecific with *P. viridis*, but treated as a separate species by R&T and R&G, based on plumage differences and their very disjunct ranges.

BARRED BECARD
Pachyramphus versicolor Pl. 222

Identification 12.5–13 cm. Small and chunky with large head, dark eyes, narrow pale yellow eye-ring, thick bill with black upper mandible and bluish-grey lower mandible, grey legs and lovely plumage. Male is glossy black from crown to back, becoming slate grey on rump, tail and wings, but inner remiges and greater coverts strikingly black with white tips and fringes; yellow lores, face, throat and neck-sides butter yellow and rest of underparts pale greyish-white, all barred dusky. Female is olive from crown to tail, with blackish wings but coverts almost completely rufous-chestnut and secondaries fringed rufous; underparts pale yellow, very finely barred like male. Immature male much greener, with dull olive admixed sooty black, becoming dark greenish-grey on crown and nape, and has underparts as female but paler and duller.

Ssp. *P. v. meridionalis* (SE Ec: Zamora-Chinchipe) male is distinctly more softly and faintly barred below
P. v. versicolor (N & C Ec:, Co, W Ve: Perijá Mts. & Andes) as described

Habits Forages in canopy, in pairs that move calmly and are usually with mixed flocks. Perches quite upright and attentive, and makes short sallies to pick insects from leaves or from air, also to pick fruits and berries. Dashes between branches or moves along them with small hops.
Status In Ecuador, Colombia and Venezuela uncommon to locally frequent, and populations always modest.
Habitat Subtropical Zone to Páramo, 1,500–2,600m, occasionally to 1,200m or 3,500m in Ecuador; 1,600–2,600m, rarely to ±500m in Colombia; and 2,000–2,900m in Venezuela. Humid montane forests, mature secondary forest, light woodland, forest edge.
Voice Male sings mostly at dawn, a rising *we-pi-pi-ti'ti'tre'tre'ree*, sad but sweet and musical, and there is a 2-note *tu-duu* whistled call (Hilty).
Note R&G doubt validity of race *meridionalis* but give no reason.

CINNAMON BECARD
Pachyramphus cinnamomeus Pl. 222

Identification 14–14.8cm. A mainly cinnamon-rufous or chestnut-rufous bird with dark eyes, blackish bill with paler grey lower mandible and dark grey legs. Sexes identical except that males have a shorter, narrower ninth primary; upperparts to tail rufous, darkest on crown, lores blackish with a buffy-white or grey supraloral line, and wings rufous or cinnamon-rufous, darkest on primary-coverts, with primaries dusky or blackish with rufous fringes; underparts tawny or pale cinnamon to cinnamon-buff with a whitish throat and belly. Immature similar but generally paler above and brighter rufous below. Juvenile male lacks modified ninth primary.

Ssp. *P. c. badius* (W Ve: E slope of Andes in E & SE Táchira) darker brown on wings, paler below
P. c. cinnamomeus (W Ec: Esmeraldas to El Oro & NW Azuay, Co: Guajira to W Meta, S Antioquia & Pacific coast) as described
P. c. magdalenae (N Co: Magdalena to Cordoba to N Antioquia, W Ve: S & W Zulia, W slope of Andes in SE Zulia, W Mérida & NW Táchira) darker brown on top and rear of head and wings, underparts tinged cinnamon on sides of breast

Habits Forages in canopy and at mid levels, but mainly subcanopy. Alone, in pairs and sometimes in loose groups that may visit fruiting trees. Main diet insects, small fruit and berries, all picked by sallying to foliage. Spends long periods perched quietly, watching and singing occasionally. A typical gesture is frequent nodding of head.
Status Frequent to common in Ecuador, common in Colombia, frequent to locally common in Venezuela.
Habitat Subtropical to Temperate Zones, to 800m, scarcer to 1,500m, in Ecuador; to 1,300m in Colombia; and to 1,200m in Venezuela. Humid forests of foothills and lowlands, forest edge, clearings with tall scattered trees, secondary woodland.
Voice Sings often, a fading, fast *tee-dear-dear-dear-dear*, very sweet and musical (H&B). Resembles song of Chestnut-crowned Becard.
Note In Ecuador, apparently one specimen from Loja but identification not certain.

CHESTNUT-CROWNED BECARD
Pachyramphus castaneus Pl. 222

Identification 14–14.5cm. Mainly cinnamon-rufous with conspicuous grey postocular band that extends round back of head from eye to eye, blackish bill, dark eyes and dusky legs. Sexes identical: upperparts to tail rufous, darkest chestnut on crown, lores dusky with buff supraloral line, and wings dusky cinnamon, remiges with pale cinnamon-rufous fringes and wing-coverts dusky rufous; underparts cinnamon-rufous, slightly paler on throat and belly.

Ssp. *P. c. intermedius* (N Ve: NE Lara to Sucre) as described
P. c. parui (S Ve: Amazonas on Cerro Parú) generally richer colour and darker, with dusky chestnut crown
P. c. saturatus (E Ec, SE Co: Macarena Mts. & río Guaviare to Amazonas, SE Ve: extreme SE Bolívar) paler, dull cinnamon on back to tail, dark wings contrasting, otherwise similar to *intermedius*

Habits Forages in canopy and at mid levels, alone or in pairs that seldom join mixed flocks. May visit fruiting trees. Main diet insects (some fairly large), small fruit and berries, all picked by sallying to foliage or by gleaning from leaves while perched. Spends long periods perched quietly, sometimes in fairly open spots, watching morosely and singing occasionally. A typical gesture is frequent nodding of head.
Status Rare to locally frequent in Ecuador, uncommon (perhaps under-recorded) in Colombia, frequent to common in Venezuela, where 3 well-separated races occur.
Habitat Tropical to Lower Subtropical Zones, to 1,000m, locally to 1,500m in Ecuador; to 500m in Colombia; and to 1,700 in Venezuela. Humid forests of foothills and lowlands, *terra firme* and *várzea*, secondary woodland clearings with tall trees, forest edge.
Voice A sad, descending *deeeeu, deeu-dee-de-de,* (Hilty) or *teeeer, tee-tee* (H&B) musical, slow, soft and dainty. Resembles song of Cinnamon Becard but is shorter.

WHITE-WINGED BECARD
Pachyramphus polychopterus Pl. 222

Identification 15cm. Large-headed and chunky, with brown eyes, and plumbeous bill and legs. Male has shining blue-black crown, head-sides dark grey, rest of upperparts black except grey rump, black wings with conspicuous white scapular bars, wing-coverts fringed and tipped white, forming 2 wingbars, inner remiges fringed white, underparts dark grey, tail black, graduated, with large white tips which appear, from below, as pairs of white spots. Female has greyish-olive crown, dusky lores, whitish supraloral stripe that becomes an incomplete whitish eye-ring, dusky wings with broad cinnamon-buff fringes to scapulars, wing-coverts and inner remiges, underparts pale greyish-yellow, black tail with large cinnamon-buff tips that appear as spots from below. Juvenile like female, but juvenile male has dark grey centres to feathers of crown and nape.

Ssp. *P. p. cinereiventris* (N Co: S & C Chocó to Cordoba, Sucre, Bolívar & Magdalena to Cesar) smaller than *tristis*, with uniform grey rump, uppertail-coverts and entire underparts

P. p. dorsalis (NW Ec, C & SW Co: Pacific slope, C Andes & W slope of E Andes) large; very pale; male has pale grey nuchal collar and is clear pale grey on rump and underparts; female more olivaceous above and rich yellow belly to undertail-coverts

P. p. nigriventris (CE Co: W Meta to Vaupés, S Ve: Amazonas in Mt. Duida region) male all black above and below, with white fringes to wing-coverts and tail tips; female has greyish-olive upperparts

P. p. similis (NW Co: N Chocó) all black above and pale grey below, and fairly small

P. p. tenebrosus (E Ec: lowlands of Sucumbíos to SE Morona-Santiago, SE Co: W Caquetá to SE Nariño & Amazonas) male black, very glossy, with bold white wingbars and tail spots; female very olivaceous above

P. p. tristis (NE Co, Ve: throughout, except Mt. Duida region, T&T, Gu, N Su, FG) slaty grey underparts with sprinkling of white on belly

Habits Forages at mid levels and in canopy, alone or in pairs. In wooded areas, usually with mixed canopy flocks, but also alone in partially open areas. Picks insects and fruit by scanning surroundings from perch and then sallying briefly to pick from foliage. Main diet insects, including butterfly larvae, bees, wasps, crickets, locust, beetles, termites, but also fruits and berries. Spends long periods perching quietly, as if taking a rest. Nest a large untidy ball of dry grasses with a side entrance typical of genus, usually located close to a wasp nest and placed in an outer fork of a very high main limb. Nest building undertaken only by female. In French Guiana, nests found on thorn bushes bordering rivers through mangroves. Possibly breeds twice a year.

Status In Ecuador, frequent in east and uncommon in northwest, where absent from lowlands. Common in Colombia, common and widespread in Venezuela, frequent in Guyana and Suriname, and locally frequent on coastal plain in French Guiana. Uncommon in Trinidad & Tobago.

Habitat Tropical Zone, to 900m in east and 600–1,500m in western Ecuador; to 2,000m, occasionally 2,700m in Colombia, and to 1,900m in Venezuela. Wet, humid and moist forests, secondary woodland, coffee plantations, forest edge, gallery and riverine forests, clearings with scattered tall trees, light swampy woodland, tall mangrove, gardens and suburban areas, degraded forests in cultivated areas. Does not occur in savanna or in dense forest.

Voice Song given by both sexes is a sweet series of warbled notes: *teeur, tur-tur-tur-turtur?*; also a soft, falling *tew te tu tu tu tu* (Hilty).

Notes Race *niger*, listed by H&B for western Meta to Vaupés, was considered invalid by Fitzpatrick (2004), synonymised under *nigriventris*.

BLACK-AND-WHITE BECARD

Pachyramphus albogriseus Pl. 223

Identification 13–14 cm. Conspicuous, short white supraloral stripe and partial eye-ring, blue-grey bill with black tip, and blue-grey legs. Male has 3 distinct plumage phases. Adult has entire top of head from lores and forehead to nape black with cobalt-blue gloss, narrow white line from base of nostrils over supraloral to form short eyebrow; upperparts clean mouse grey, wings and tail fuscous to blackish, tips of median coverts white, tips of outer greater coverts white (abrade) fringes and tips of inner greater coverts white and fringes of tertials white, combining to give impression of broad white bar running length of wing; distal half of outer rectrices white, the white patch becoming smaller on each successive pair inwards, until central pair have very small white tips; entire underparts white, washed faintly pale grey, thighs grey; eyes dark brown, bill all dark grey or black above and grey below, and legs and feet grey. Intermediate male is brownish-olive green above, wings and tail fuscous to blackish with whitish outer webs to outer rectrices; spots, tips and bars on wings and tail orange-rufous; cap rich brown, framed in black from nostrils over eyes then in a broad band across nape; small whitish supraloral and short eyebrow, lores black; underparts sulphur-yellow, whitish on chin, gradually becoming more yellow over throat; bill blackish above and pale flesh below, legs and feet grey-green. Juvenile male like intermediate but distinctly paler and brighter brown on head, underparts more pure sulphur; duller green above. Adult female like juvenile male but is notably darker brown on head, like intermediate male; bill black above, grey below. Juvenile female like adult but decidedly greyer and more drab on back, duller and darker brown on head, paler rufous bars on wings and spots on tail; throat and breast washed greyish-buffy. Male best separated from male White-winged Becard by bold white supraloral stripe, grey back (black in White-winged) and lack of white scapulars (very prominent in White winged. From male Cinereous Becard, by bold white marks on wings.

Ssp. *P. a. albogriseus* (Co: E slope of E Andes, W & N Ve: Andes & Coastal Cordillera) as described

P. a. coronatus (N Co: Santa Marta & Perijá Mts., NW Ve: Perijá Mts.) male virtually identical to male *albogriseus*, but has distinct 2-tone bill, black above, blue-grey below and legs and feet dark grey; female paler yellow below, supraloral spot and eyebrow cinnamon-buffy, brown of top of head almost totally lacks border (just darkish brown) and back is more olive, less yellowish-green

P. a. guayaquilensis (W Ec: Esmeraldas to Loja in lowlands & foothills) smaller, all colours seem lightly washed with dusky

P. a. salvini (E Ec) smaller with shorter bill; male has whiter belly and much smaller spots on wing-coverts, female has duller, more greyish-olive back

Habits Forages from mid levels to subcanopy, alone or in pairs and usually with mixed flocks. May visit fruiting trees. Main diet insects, small fruit and berries, picked by sallying to foliage. Spends long periods perched quietly, watching morosely and singing occasionally. A typical gesture is frequent nodding of head.

Status Uncommon in east, uncommon and quite local in western Ecuador, possibly frequent in Colombia, frequent but local in Venezuela.

Habitat Tropical to Subtropical Zones, at 900 to ±2,500m in east, to 2,000m in western Ecuador; 900–2,700m in Colombia; 1,200–2,200m, occasionally to ±1,000m in Venezuela. Humid to wet forests and secondary woodland on montane slopes and foothills, drier, deciduous woodland on lower slopes. Usually not at forest edge, but rather well inside forest.

Voice Sings only sporadically, a short, variable series of soft warbled notes – *t'you, t'you-duEET?* or *chu-chu, chu-EE?*, or *chu-u-RE?* – all quite melodious and sweet, and rising suddenly at end (Hilty).

BLACK-CAPPED BECARD

Pachyramphus marginatus Pl. 223

Identification 13–14cm. Male is black, grey and white, female is rufous-chestnut, olive and pale yellow; eyes dark brown, bill and legs plumbeous. In male, note glossy bluish-black crown the shine creating an odd scaly effect, black tail tipped white, narrow white eye-ring, black wings with white scapulars, 2 white wingbars and fairly broad white fringes to wing-coverts and remiges; grey back contrasts sharply with black of head, rest of body mostly grey. Female has chestnut crown, dusky lores, conspicuous but incomplete white eye-ring, greyish-olive upperparts, black wings with ochraceous-buff fringes to wing-coverts and inner remiges, black tail with large cinnamon-buff tips, and yellowish grey-olive underparts. Immature male like female, but has poorly developed cap and crown dull green like mantle. Very young birds have dark grey bars on upperparts. Male best separated from male White-winged Becard by much paler underparts and smaller size.

Ssp. *P. m. nanus* (E Ec, E Co, Ve: Amazonas & Bolívar, S Gu, Su, FG)

Habits Forages from mid levels to canopy, alone or in pairs and usually with mixed flocks. May visit fruiting trees. Main diet insects and spiders, fruit and berries, picked by sallying to foliage. Spends long periods perched quietly, watching morosely and singing occasionally. A typical gesture is frequent nodding of head.

Status Uncommon to locally frequent in Ecuador, possibly frequent in Colombia, frequent in Venezuela, Guyana and Suriname, and widespread but uncommon in the interior of French Guiana.

Habitat Tropical Zone, to 700m in Ecuador, 500m in Colombia and 1,000m in Venezuela. Interior of humid lowland forest (mainly *terra firme*) and mature secondary woodland, forests of coastal sand ridges (but not in mangrove), savanna forests.

Voice Very beautiful and varied warbling song (H&M), both musical and melancholy – *teeu, whee-do-weet,* or *twee-twee-tee-eet, dear-dear,* or *tewtewtewtee, dew-dew* – often quickly repeated, sometimes varying scale as if practicing. Also, several variations of rapid trills, *teeu, tee-tee-tee-te-ti, or tre-tre'tre-e-e-e-e-it*, with last note lower. Dawn song a fragile, soft *tew, tew-tweet!* rising sharply at end (Hilty, Fitzpatrick 2004).

GLOSSY-BACKED BECARD

Pachyramphus surinamus Pl. 223

Identification 13–14cm. Upright bird with a comparatively large head, dark brown eyes, lead-coloured bill and black legs. Male has all-black upperparts with a bluish sheen and completely snow white underparts. Female's crown-feathers black with broad chestnut fringes (appears chestnut spotted black), and has small whitish forehead, pale grey nape and back, white rump and blackish tail with whitish or buffish tips to outermost rectrices, extensive broad rufous fringes to black wing-coverts, tertials and some flight-feathers, and white underparts from throat down. Juvenile light olive back, streaked dusky black wings and tail, all feathers broadly edged with dull rufous; greyish rufous head and nape, grey cheeks, neck-sides; yellowish below, light streaks on throat and breast.

Ssp. Monotypic (SE Ve?, Guianas)

Habits Forages in very loose pairs, from subcanopy to highest parts of canopy and in tops of emergents, picking spiders, as well as caterpillars, crickets, beetles and other insects, and some fruit. Usually with mixed flocks, flitting purposely amid branches, and inspecting surrounding foliage to pick prey or fruit with a brief hover. Nest is a ball of dry grasses with a side entrance, typical of *Pachyramphus*, but with interesting difference that *surinamus* build them atop bottle-shaped nests of bees or wasps, most often of sting-less bees of genus *Trigona*.

Status Scarce and local in Guyana, uncommon in Suriname, rare in the interior of French Guiana. In Venezuela, only a sight and tape record from lower río Caura, Bolívar.

Habitat Tropical Zone, to 300m. Humid and savanna forests, clearings, forest edge, old forests in coastal areas with well-drained soils.

Voice Dawn song a sweet musical series of soft notes – *wuweet, weet-weet-weet-weet* – of 5–9 notes, repeated after short pauses. When foraging, gives a *kweee, kew-kew-kew…* in contact, and when excited thin *wee, tee-tee-te- ti-ti-ti-ti'ti'ti'* (A. Whittaker *fide* Hilty).

CINEREOUS BECARD

Pachyramphus rufus Pl. 224

Identification 13–14cm. Male has pearl grey upperparts with glossy black crown, pale grey underparts that become paler, almost whitish, on belly, whitish throat, wing-feathers blackish with white fringes, narrow on primaries and broad on secondaries and greater coverts, and slaty grey tail with narrow white tips. Female has rufous-cinnamon upperparts with chestnut crown and whitish lores, pale cinnamon face, cinnamon-buffy underparts that become paler, almost whitish, on belly, primaries and secondaries blackish with rufescent margins, greater coverts cinnamon-rufous and cinnamon tail. Both sexes have dark brown eyes, lead-coloured bill and legs. Juvenile and immature male like female but usually have cap somewhat grey. Male best separated from White-naped Xenopsaris by grey rather than pure white underparts, shorter tail and chubbier shape, and from male Black-and-white Becard by all-grey tail (not black with large white tips). See plate for progression of plumage.

Ssp. *P. r. rufus* (N Co: Guajira to Sucre, Huila & Valle & E Andes in Norte de Santander, Ve: entire N & N Bolívar, Gu, N Su: coastal plain to N savanna region, FG) as described

P. r. juruanus? (SE Ec?, SE Co?) black crown extends to nape on male; female more extensively rufous below

Habits Forages alone or more often in pairs, high in canopy (in Colombia from low scrub to subcanopy), where sallies for insects, picking them from foliage, often from undersides of leaves. Also takes berries and other small fruit. Slow and deliberate, perches for short while inspecting surroundings before sallying for food or to change perch. Only very occasionally with mixed flocks. Nests have been found atop a palm by edge of a mangrove in French Guiana, and wedged in fork of high branch in northern Venezuela.

Status Uncertain in south-east Ecuador (very old records). Uncommon and local in northern Colombia (sight records from Leticia by J. V. Remsen possibly of race *juruanus*). Uncommon to locally frequent in Venezuela, frequent in Guyana, common in Suriname. In French Guiana, common on coastal plain, but more local in interior. Never very numerous.

Habitat Tropical Zone, to 1,500m in Colombia and 1,300m in Venezuela. Dry to moist light woodland, second growth, borders of woodland and mangrove, degraded areas, woodland around inselbergs and along rivers, open country, pastures and agricultural areas with scattered trees and copses, coffee plantations.

Voice Several different songs given by both sexes, most somewhat melancholy. A sweet series of whistles in Colombia, *tuwee-tuwee-tuwee-tuwee-tuwe-wee*, and a rising speeding series in Venezuela, *twee, twe, twee-twee-tweetwee-ti'ti'ti'ti'ti*, reminiscent of a woodcreeper, also a *twee-twee-twee-tweedo* (P. Schwartz *fide* H&B), a short delicate, sharply rising trill – *tuwe'e'e'e'e'e'e'e* – or a longer trill – *we de-de-de-DE'DE'De'di'di'dididi* – and in Delta Amacuro, a husky *we-p-pe-pe-pe-pe-pe-pe* – that runs up scale. Calls include a metallic *eeeeE* and *breez-det* buzz (Hilty).

SLATY BECARD

Pachyramphus spodiurus Pl. 223

Identification 14cm. Small, large-headed bird with dark eyes, blackish bill with base of lower mandible pale grey and blackish legs. Male has black crown, very dark grey nape and back, blackish wings with remiges narrowly fringed white, all-black primary-coverts, and tail is dusky black above, grey below; underparts grey, slightly paler than back. Female similarly patterned but in cinnamon-rufous and cream: crown dark rufous, rest of upperparts bright cinnamon-rufous, with black remiges fringed bright rufous and tail cinnamon above, buffy below; small whitish supraloral spot, whitish throat and buffy-cinnamon face, rest of underparts cinnamon-buff becoming whitish on belly. Male best separated from male One-coloured Becard by pale lores and white fringes on wings.

Ssp. Monotypic (W Ec: W Esmeraldas & W Pichincha to W Loja)

Habits Forages in pairs, from low levels to canopy. In many areas, bushes and trees are fairly small, so often found foraging at low levels. Little is known of its diet. Inconspicuous, perches quietly in canopy and subcanopy.

Status Endangered. Very small range, mostly in Ecuador, where rare to locally uncommon, though possibly, due to its very unobtrusive habits, more numerous than records suggest.

Habitat Tropical Zone, to 600m and locally to 1,100m in Ecuador. Semi-humid and deciduous forests, cultivated areas, plantations and clearings with scattered tall trees or copses, dry washes in arid scrub areas.

Voice Male sings a series of musical whistles, *tu, tu, tee-tee-titititititri*, that begins slowly but speeds up and increases in pitch and volume. Also a short slurred trill that also starts low and rises in pitch (R&G).

Note Until early 20th century was considered a subspecies of *P. rufus*, under name Crested Becard, but Zimmer (1936f) returned it to species level, as it had been treated in Hellmayr (1929), and this has been followed since.

ONE-COLOURED BECARD

Pachyramphus homochrous Pl. 222

Identification 16–17cm. Despite name, a 2-tone bird with dark eyes, stout blackish bill with slight hook at tip and dusky legs. Male slate black above, with crown, wings and tail darker, underparts dark grey. Female cinnamon-rufous above, primaries dusky with cinnamon fringes, secondaries and wing-coverts rufous with narrow, pale cinnamon fringes, and cinnamon-buff underparts fade to whitish-buff on throat and centre of belly. Juvenile like female but paler, gradually becoming black on crown and back, then wings and tail.

Ssp. *P. h. canescens* (NE Co: N Magdalena & NE Bolívar, NW Ve: Lake Maracaibo area) paler throat and belly

P. h. homochrous (W Ec: Esmeraldas to El Oro & W Loja, W Co: Pacific slope of W Andes to S Chocó)
P. h. quimarinus (NW Co: S Magdalena, C & SW Bolívar & E Antioquia) like *homochrous*

Habits Forages from mid levels to subcanopy, in pairs that occasionally join mixed flocks. Diet insects and fruit. A typical gesture is pumping head while raising crown-feathers, which make it appear to have a large crest.
Status Locally frequent in Ecuador, common in Colombia, scarce in Venezuela.
Habitat Tropical Zone, to 1,000m and locally to 1,500m in Ecuador, to 900m in Colombia and to *c*.500m in Venezuela. Humid to dry forests of lowlands and foothills, deciduous and secondary woodland, light woods, semi-humid to dry scrub with scattered tall trees or small copses. Prefers forest edge and areas where forest is lighter.
Voice A loud, sharp, variable chatter, *ske-e-et'et'itTT, tseer, tsrip*, in Colombia, a *stet-ee-ee-teet-tsit-tsit-tsitts-tsit* and frequently a squeaky, high *tweiuu* (H&B, Fitzpatrick 2004).
Notes Together with *P. minor* and *P. validus*, formerly placed in genus *Platypsaris* but Snow (1973, 1979) merged *Platypsaris* under *Pachyramphus*. However, P&MdS, H&B, R&G, and Hilty retain *Platypsaris* due to several differences (larger and less vocal, heavier bills and shape and placement of nest – hanging from, instead of supported by, large branch).

PINK-THROATED BECARD
Pachyramphus minor Pl. 223

Identification 16–17cm. A large-headed, slightly crested bird with dark brown eyes, blackish-grey legs, and bill has black upper mandible and blue-grey lower mandible. Male almost entirely black, but greyish-black on face and underparts, with small white patch at bend of wing and conspicuous rosy crescent between throat and chest. Juvenile male has dull brownish back, and lacks white interscapular line; underparts cinnamon with patchy grey and emergent rosy feathering on throat. Female has medium grey or slate grey crown, nape and back, sharp contrasting with rufous cheeks and neck-sides, greyish-rufous rump, dark rufous wings and tail, underparts pale cinnamon-rufous becoming buffy on throat and centre of belly. Female best separated from female Chestnut-crowned Becard by grey crown, nape and back.

Ssp. Monotypic (E Ec, SE Co, S Ve, Guianas)

Habits Forages alone, in pairs and sometimes in small family groups, from mid levels to canopy. Usually with mixed feeding flocks. Nods head frequently, like many in genus. Main diet insects taken by sallying in air or to foliage from a perch, but also takes fruit, both with sallies and by gleaning. Slow and deliberate, changes perches a few times in a tree, then moves to another. Nest an untidy ball of dry grasses typical of genus, most often placed on a large, high branch of a tall tree.
Status Rare to locally uncommon in Ecuador, uncommon to frequent in Colombia, uncommon in Venezuela, frequent in Guyana and Suriname, and common in the interior of French Guiana.
Habitat Lower Tropical Zone, to *c*.600m in Ecuador, 500m in Colombia and 800m in Venezuela. Lowland, mainly *terra firme* forests (occasionally in *várzea*), savanna forests, forests of coastal sand ridges, forest edge.
Voice Rarely calls or sings. A clear, rising whistle, *tuuuueeeE* or *tyoooeee*, also *tic* or *pick* notes (H&B, Hilty).
Notes Together with *P. validus* and *P. homochrous*, formerly placed in genus *Platypsaris* but Snow (1973, 1979) merged *Platypsaris* under *Pachyramphus*. However, P&MdS, H&B, R&G, and Hilty retain *Platypsaris* due to several differences (they are larger and less vocal, have heavier bills, and shape and placement of nest are different).

CRESTED BECARD
Pachyramphus validus Pl. 223

Identification 18–19cm. Male almost entirely black, with glossy black crown, slaty black tail, dark grey cheeks and smoky grey underparts, palest on throat. Female has dark grey crown, rufous nape, back and tail, dull buff supraloral spot, cinnamon face, dusky wings with primaries narrowly fringed rufous and inner remiges entirely rufous, yellowish-cinnamon throat and pale yellowish-cinnamon or buffy-cinnamon underparts.

Ssp. *P. v. audax*? (SE Ec: S Zamora-Chinchipe)

Habits Forages in canopy and borders.
Status Possibly rare in south-east Ecuador, where first found in 1998.
Habitat Temperate Zone, 2,550–2,600m. Humid montane forests and mature secondary woodland.
Voice Very quiet, occasionally gives squeaky or twittering note, or sings series of clear, descending whistles: *sui-sui-sui-sui*… (R&G).
Notes Called Plain Becard in Fitzpatrick (2004). Together with *P. minor* and *P. homochrous*, formerly placed in genus *Platypsaris* but Snow (1973, 1979) merged *Platypsaris* under *Pachyramphus*. However, P&MdS, H&B, R&G, and Hilty retain *Platypsaris* (see previous species). If treated in *Platypsaris*, *validus* is called *Platypsaris rufus*, but when genera are merged, it is necessary to use *validus* because *rufus* is preoccupied. Birds in Ecuador, assigned here to race *audax* following R&G, may represent a new race, as closest population is more than 1,000 km away in southern Peru.

GENUS INCERTAE SEDIS

The genus *Piprites* also has a history of controversy. It was traditionally placed in Pipridae, thereafter Ames (1971) suggested it belonged in Tyrannidae and was closely related to *Myiobius*, but Prum (2001) was unable to find support for either relationship. It may belong to Tityridae but is placed as *incertae sedis* for the time being.

WING-BARRED PIPRITES

Piprites chloris Pl. 221

Identification 13–14cm. Large 'manakin' that looks like a vireo with a manakin head, or recalls certain flycatchers. Bright olive-green above, varying from bright yellow to soft grey below, depending on race. Large white terminal spots on tertials and prominent wingbar also vary according to subspecies. Note bright pale yellow eye-ring. Iris dark brown, legs grey.

Ssp. *P. c. antioquiae* (Co: C Andes) bright green back to uppertail-coverts, wingbar of medium width, lores yellow; bright yellow below

P. c. chlorion (E Co, N, E & S Ve, Guianas) dark green back to uppertail-coverts, wingbar narrow, all-grey head with greenish forehead, lores barely yellow; yellow bib and undertail-coverts

P. c. perijana (W Ve: Perijá & Táchira) slightly duller green than *antioquiae* with pale olive wash on breast and sides; wingbar very broad

P. c. tschudii (E Ec, extreme E Co, extreme S Ve) dull dark green back to uppertail-coverts, greyish-green crown and grey nape; underparts pale saffron-yellow washed pale greyish-olive on sides and flanks

Birds from Ríos Casiquiare and Guainía, Ve, are intermediate between *tschudii* and *chlorion* and were presumed to be hybrids by Phelps (description in prep)

Habits Very calm and slow demeanour. Usually found foraging alone or less often in pairs, though not in undergrowth (as is common in manakins), but more at mid levels and in subcanopy. Also differs from manakins in diet and manner of feeding; mostly takes insects by perch-gleaning, with only small proportion of fruits and berries, and rarely sallies. Often with mixed flocks of insectivores.

Status Uncommon and apparently local in Ecuador and Colombia, uncommon to locally frequent in Venezuela, frequent in Guyana, uncommon to rare in Suriname, and widespread and common in French Guiana.

Habitat Tropical Zone, mostly below 1,000m in Ecuador, with records to 1,500m; to 1,500m in Colombia, and at 350–2,000m north of Orinoco and to 1,700m south of it in Venezuela. Humid to drier, deciduous forests, sandy soil forests, savanna forest. A typical member of understorey mixed flocks of *terra firme* forest.

Voice Infrequent song is quite distinctive, a loud, nasal and varying sequence of *kuep kuep kuep kuep kue-di-le kuep?* notes (H&B), or *quee, quee quee queedle-le-quee, quee?* (Hilty). Tends to sing more during early rainy season. In Ecuador, a loud rhythmic *whip, pip-pip, pididip, whip, whip?* (R&G).

Notes Race *antioquiae* does not occur in Ecuador, and species is entirely absent from west Ecuador (R&G), though mapped there by some previous references. *P. chloris* was formerly known as Wing-barred Manakin and placed in the Pipridae. Ames (1971) proposed to place it within the Tyrannidae and that it was closely related to *Myiobius*, but Prum (2001) was unable to find support for either relationship, and thus the SACC consider it incertae sedis within the *Schiffornis* group.

SAPAYOIDAE – Sapayoa

The traditional treatment of this oddest of species, *Sapayoa aenigma*, was to place it in the Pipridae, although some authors, e.g. Wetmore (1972), expressed their doubts. Subsequently, Lanyon (1985) found that *Sapayoa* did not lie within the Pipridae, or in any other closely related New World families, which led him to suggest that it might be more closely related to Old World suboscines – broadbills, pittas and asities. Support for this came from Sibley & Ahlquist (1990). Irestedt *et al.* (2006) confirmed this view, but recommended treatment in a family of its own.

BROAD-BILLED SAPAYOA

Sapayoa aenigma Pl. 221

Identification 14–15cm. Male is rich, deep ochraceous-olive above with a semi-concealed yellow-orange coronal stripe; paler ochraceous olive below, almost orange on centre of underparts; eyes chestnut, broad, flat, dark-coloured bill with spiky rictal bristles, legs and feet grey. Plumage has an oily appearance. Female and juvenile are like male, but lack coronal stripe; immature male has emergent yellow on crown. Very similar in coloration and shape to most female manakins, but larger and longer tailed.

Ssp. Monotypic (NW Ec, W & NW Co)

Habits Forages unobtrusively, alone or less often in pairs, at low to mid levels. Perches quietly, spying surroundings and then sallies for passing insects and also to pick insects, berries and small fruit from foliage. Often found with mixed understorey flocks, especially those with *Myrmotherula* antwrens. Nest quite unique, and is amongst the traits that set it apart from the Pipridae, being pear-shaped, constructed of fibres and strips of bark, with a longish 'tail' hanging down, also of fibres. The nest is hung from a low branch, over water.

Status Rare to locally uncommon in Ecuador, where few records, and uncommon to locally somewhat frequent in Colombia.

Habitat Tropical Zone, to 500m in Ecuador and 1,100m in Colombia. Humid forests, along streams and in shady ravines.

Voice Calls include a soft trill and louder chirping: *chip, ch-ch-ch* (R&G).

Note Formerly placed in the Pipridae, and called Broad-billed Manakin by some authors or Broad-billed Sapayoa by S&M, R&T and R&G, but found to be much closer to Old World suboscines than to New World representatives (Fjeldså *et al.* 2003, Chesser 2004b, Irestedt *et al.* 2006).

VIREONIDAE – Peppershrikes, Vireos and Greenlets

One of the least distinguished and more problematic families for field identification, the vireos occupy 3 groups. Peppershrikes are the possible exception, with their bold eyebrows and heavy hooked bills, they are also exclusively perch-gleaners, working along branches and through foliage, particularly towards the outer, thinner stems, searching for arthropods and rolled-up dead leaves which offer good protection for a pupating insect; their bills are particularly strong, as any field worker who has taking a bird from a mist-net will testify.

Vireos are generally warbler-sized, olive-green or yellow-green above with grey, white or yellow below. Slightly larger than greenlets, the other group of vireos, they are distinguished by having eyebrows and eye-rings. Sexes are usually similar. Their voices are rarely musical, and usually repetitive, with some species having a large vocabulary of different calls. They are either canopy foragers or work the lower levels. Nests are bag-like, cup-shaped affairs, suspended from the rim of a horizontal fork and, in the case of the Neotropical species, usually lay 2 eggs, and the young leave the nest in as few as 11–12 days after hatching.

Greenlets are more nondescript, being greenish above and pale below, slightly smaller than vireos with more slender bills. They are confusingly similar in appearance, so attention must be paid to distribution, habitat and small details. They are very warbler-like and regularly sally for flying insects.

Peppershrikes are large vireos with very strong bills hooked at the tip. They forage steadily and rather deliberately in the canopy and at mid levels, searching for rolled dead leaves used by insects as protection to pupate. They take free-living insects as well, especially those with heavy shells and wing-cases, and are partial to toxic, spiny caterpillars. Peppershrikes are remarkably cryptic and usually hard to spot, but also vocalise ceaselessly, drawing the observer's attention.

RUFOUS-BROWED PEPPERSHRIKE

Cyclarhis gujanensis Pl. 225

Identification 14.5–16cm. Chunky and bull-headed; heavy bill with strong hook. Adult has grey head with distinctive rufous forehead and supercilium, olive upperparts, dull greyish-white chin and upper throat, greenish-yellow lower throat and breast, becoming whitish over rest of underparts, but plumage varies between subspecies (look for combination of body shape, heavy bill and rufous brow). Eyes orange-red, bill dusky to dark horn, perhaps paler on base of mandible, legs and feet flesh. Juvenile has paler brow, buffy-tipped crown-feathers and wing-coverts. Similarly shaped but duller and darker Black-billed Peppershrike has smaller rufous brow, black (not pale brownish) bill, greenish or greyish-yellow (not orange) eyes, bluish-grey (not pink) legs, mostly grey (not yellow) underparts, and is usually found at higher altitudes and in closed forests. Green-backed Becard lacks rufous brow.

Ssp. *C. g. cantica* (N & E Co, Santa Marta) close to *flavipectus* but richer and brighter yellow on throat and breast; less greenish below (more buffy)

C. g. contrerasi (extreme S Ec, east slope) very close to *virenticeps* but feathers on top and back of head broadly fringed chestnut; ear-coverts more greenish; mainly olive throat and breast, grey belly

C. g. flavipectus (Ve: Paria, Tr) dark forehead and eyebrow; whitish chin and dull yellow throat to breast and body-sides; rest of underparts buffy-white washed greyish on lower breast and flanks

C. g. gujanensis (E Co, S Ve, Guianas) as described; medium rufous forehead and eyebrow

C. g. parvus (E Andes in Co, N & C Ve) paler forehead and eyebrow; white throat, bright yellow breast and body-sides, rest of underparts creamy white

C. g. virenticeps (SW, W & SE Ec) yellowish-olive above extending to crown (which lacks grey), chestnut forehead and supercilium, ear-coverts olive-yellow or yellowish-green; bright yellow breast very extensive

Habits Forages alone or in pairs rather sluggishly, usually high in dense vegetation where hard to see, but easier to observe when lower at forest edges and in arid vegetation. Only occasionally joins mixed-species flocks. Specialist in cracking tightly rolled dead leaves to reach pupating larvae within.

Status Fairly common to common and widespread.

Habitat Tropical to Temperate Zones, to 3,100m but usually below 2,000m, in various arid to humid and semi-open to wooded habitats, including degraded and urban areas, usually restricted to edge of continuous forest, e.g. *várzea* in Amazonia, but even there sometimes in canopy.

Voice A descending series of 3–7 slurred notes (first usually loudest), e.g. *dreeu-dreeu-dreeu*. Song variable, consisting of several hurried phrases of 5–7 descending whistles, e.g. *do-you-wash-every-week*, each phrase sometimes repeated for several minutes before switching, and often sings throughout day even when foraging (R&T, R&G, Hilty).

BLACK-BILLED PEPPERSHRIKE

Cyclarhis nigrirostris Pl. 225

Identification 14.5–15cm. Chunky and bull-headed; heavy bill with strong hook. Adult deep olive-green above with a long deep crimson eyebrow, head-sides and underparts mostly mid grey with mustard yellow wash on sides, forming broken breast-band, vent to undertail-coverts whitish; eyes pale yellow, bill black, legs and feet grey. See Rufous-browed Peppershrike (especially rather similar races *contrerasi* and *virenticeps*).

Ssp. *C. n. atrirostris* (W Ec, SW Co: Pacific slope in Nariño) mid grey underparts

C. n. nigrirostris (NC Ec, C & W Co) slightly paler and brighter above, almost white below, with mustard yellow wash on head-, neck- and body-sides and flanks

Habits Hard to see as it forages alone or in pairs, from midstorey to canopy, rather deliberately. Often joins mixed-species flocks, when more likely to be found. Calls continually.

Status Uncommon to locally fairly common.

Habitat Tropical to Temperate Zones, at 650–2,700m, in humid to wet forests (including cloud forest), edges and mature second growth.

Voice Similar to Rufous-browed Peppershrike, although song somewhat richer and more melodious, typically a series of fast, loud whistles, e.g. *teetoo-tooa-chéwit* or *come-right-here-RIGHT-now*, and sometimes also very like song of Slate-coloured Grosbeak. Often sings throughout day, even when foraging (H&B, R&G).

YELLOW-BROWED SHRIKE-VIREO

Vireolanius eximius Pl. 225

Identification 13.5–14cm. Chunky, large-headed and short-tailed; heavy bill with strong hook. Adult male bright grass-green above with blue crown and nape and yellow supercilium, throat and breast, becoming more yellowish-green on rest of underparts. Adult female slightly duller with crown admixed green. Duller Slaty-capped Shrike-Vireo does not overlap. Similarly coloured chlorophonias or female honeycreepers are much smaller and have different body shape.

Ssp. *V. e. eximius* (NE Co, NW Ve) as described
V. e. mutabilis (NW Co) central belly to undertail-coverts yellow

Habits Hard to see as it forages sluggishly in dense foliage, usually high in canopy. Often joins mixed-species flocks.
Status Uncommon to locally fairly common in north-west Colombia and in restricted range in extreme north-west Venezuela (Sierra de Perijá and south-east Táchira).
Habitat Tropical to Lower Subtropical Zones, at 100–1,700m but mostly in foothills, in humid forest, edges and mature second growth.
Voice Song in eastern Panama (*mutabilis*) is a loud, far-carrying series of 3–4 *peer* whistles, sometimes endlessly repeated throughout day, faster paced than Slaty-capped Shrike-Vireo (R&T).
Notes Formerly placed in genus *Smaragdolanius* and sometimes considered a subspecies of Green Shrike-Vireo *V. pulchellus* of Central America (R&T). S. Olson does not consider *mutabilis* a valid subspecies (H&B).

SLATY-CAPPED SHRIKE-VIREO

Vireolanius leucotis Pl. 225

Identification 14–15cm. Chunky, large-headed and short-tailed; heavy bill is black above and blue-grey below with strong hook. Adult has olive-green upperparts and distinctive head pattern; slate grey with long yellow eyebrow from supraloral to nape-sides, short, bold crescent below eyes and base of malar yellow, joining yellow throat and yellow underparts, tinged olive on sides, flanks and belly. Distal half of malar slate grey, as are lower cheeks and ear-coverts. Eyes bright lime-green, legs and feet flesh. Brighter Yellow-browed Shrike-Vireo does not overlap.

Ssp. *V. l. leucotis* (E Ec, SC Co, S Ve, Guianas) legs usually bluish-grey, white continues from patch below eyes, forming a cheek-stripe (shorter in female and does not reach neck-sides); female also has short green breast streaks, becoming clines on belly and flanks; juvenile has supraloral ochraceous and is heavily streaked with green lines from breast to undertail-coverts
V. l. mikettae (W Ec, W Co) as described; no white cheek-stripe, pink legs

Habits Hard to see as it forages deliberately in canopy for invertebrates. Usually observed singly, but also occurs in pairs or small flocks, and frequently joins mixed-species flocks when it is most likely to be seen.
Status Uncommon to locally fairly common.
Habitat Tropical to Subtropical Zones, at 200–2,100m but mostly below 1,100m in Ecuador; 300–1,800m in Colombia with sparse records to 2,100m; and 200–1,300m in Venezuela. Humid to wet forests (including mossy forests), edges and mature second growth.
Voice Calls include a soft *whit*. Song a loud, far-carrying series of *tyeer* whistles (descending in *leucotis*, longer and even-pitched in *mikettae*), sometimes endlessly repeated throughout day, even when foraging, at rate of *c*.1 per s, similar to Brown-headed and Tawny-crowned Greenlets (R&T, R&G, Hilty). A single whistle, repeated at short intervals, *wheeuw… wheeuw…* (H&M).
Note Formerly placed in genus *Smaragdolanius*.

YELLOW-THROATED VIREO

Vireo flavifrons Pl. 226

Identification 14–14.5cm. Large-headed, short-tailed and heavy-billed. Adult has bright olive-green head and mantle, grey scapulars, lower back and rump, and uppertail-coverts; tail and wings blackish with 2 white wingbars (lacking in all other vireos), distinctive yellow eye-ring ('spectacles') that commence in a supraloral patch that joins across nostrils, with a short postocular extension; chin and throat to breast and body-sides rich golden-yellow, sharply demarcated from rest of white underparts, thus appearing more clean-cut than any other vireo in northern South America (similar tyrannids distinguished by body shape, posture, behaviour and voice). However, breast sometimes appear patchy white. Birds in fresh plumage have leading edge to greater wing-coverts white and broader white fringes to tertials. In worn plumage pattern much reduced and only median coverts wingbar maybe noticeable.

Ssp. Monotypic (boreal migrant to Co, N & W Ve, Cu, T&T)

Habits Slowly and deliberately forages (mostly alone) from midstorey to canopy for invertebrates; often joins mixed-species flocks.
Status Winters in Central America and north-west South America, rare to uncommon on Trinidad (April–May) and Tobago (December), in Venezuela (November–March) and Colombia (November–March; June), where most frequent in Santa Marta; once on Curaçao (March 1957).
Habitat Tropical to Subtropical Zones, to 1,800m but once to 2,700m, in forest edge, mature second growth, plantations, riparian and other lighter woodlands, but anywhere on migration.
Voice A rapid, harsh, often-repeated *shep*. Song consists of phrases with 2–3 short slurred whistles, e.g. *rrreeyoo, rreeooee, three-eight…*, at rate of *c*.1 phrase every 3 s, regularly gives subsong in winter (R&T, Sibley).

PHILADELPHIA VIREO

Vireo philadelphicus Pl. 226

Identification 12cm. Adult dull medium olive-brown above with distinct white supercilium, grey crown and dark lores and eyestripe; pale yellow throat and breast, rest of underparts paler yellow. Eyes dark brown, bill dusky, legs and feet brown. Similar Brown-capped Vireo is usually overall brighter with obviously browner cap and back, and crisper facial pattern, which is even sharper in larger Red-eyed Vireo which also has red (not dark) eyes and yellow restricted to body-sides, flanks and vent. Larger Yellow-green Vireo has longer bill, reddish-brown (not dark) eyes and fainter white supercilium.

Ssp. Monotypic (boreal vagrant to Chocó & Bogotá in Co)

Status Winters in North and Central America, vagrant to Colombia (October–April).

Habitat Tropical to Subtropical Zones, to 2,600m, in various wooded habitats, but anywhere on migration; most likely in foothills and highlands.

Voice A soft, nasal, slightly descending *weeej-weeezh-weeezh-weeezh*. Song similar to Red-eyed Vireo, but higher, weaker and choppier with longer pauses (Sibley).

RED-EYED VIREO *Vireo olivaceus* Pl. 226

Identification 14–15cm. Different populations: some are boreal migrants, others austral migrants and still others resident. Adult olive above, grey on head, slightly olivaceous-grey on cheeks and ear-coverts, solid white supercilium from supraloral to just behind eye, edged narrowly darker grey, white crescent below eyes; underparts white with warm olivaceous wash to sides, becoming buffy to yellowish on flanks and very pale yellow from belly rearwards. Eyes bright reddish, bill dark to blackish above, grey below, legs and feet grey. Juvenile has dark brown eyes, faint supercilium and pale brown crown-sides, mantle, scapulars and secondary wing-coverts. See Philadelphia Vireo above. Very similar Yellow-green Vireo has less crisp facial pattern (lacking distinct dark border to supercilium), slightly more olive-tinged crown and upperparts, and more extensive and brighter yellow underparts (but can be quite drab in some adults, and equally some races of Red-eyed Vireo, e.g. *griseobarbatus*, can be quite bright yellow below). Very similar Black-whiskered Vireo has duller and browner upperparts with less contrasting grey crown and less crisp facial pattern with faint dark whiskers (sometimes hard to see, and moulting or wet Red-eyed Vireos may appear to have whiskers too). Smaller Brown-capped Vireo has obviously browner cap and back, less obvious face pattern and all-yellow rear underparts.

Ssp. *V. o. diversus* and *chivi* (throughout northern South America; southern birds are austral migrants) olive-brown above with poorly defined grey supercilium lined above with black, greyish-olive wash from face- to breast-sides, off-white breast and rest of underparts pale yellowish-buffy, eyes brown (not red)

V. o. caucae (W Co) chin to belly white, narrowly washed olive-brown on sides and flanks, undertail-coverts pale buffy-yellow

V. o. griseobarbatus (W Ec) well-defined supercilium with black line above and dark grey eyestripe, underparts white with yellow tone, becoming quite yellow on undertail-coverts, washed narrowly with olive on sides and flanks

V. o. olivaceus (boreal migrant to our region, including Cu and Bo) as described

V. o. pectoralis (extreme S Ec) greenish-olive above, with yellowish-white supercilium, bordered black above and below, throat pale greyish-olive extending to face-sides, with faint white crescent below eyes, sides and flanks washed greenish-olive, undertail-coverts yellow

V. o. solimoensis (extreme S & E Ec) plain white below with slight buffy tinge to flanks and undertail-coverts

V. o. tobagensis (To) olive-brown above, with bold white supercilium bordered above with dark grey, and dark grey eyestripe; white below, undertail-coverts pale yellow

V. o. vividior (NE Co, Ve, Tr, Guianas) narrow white supercilium, bordered above with black, underparts white, vent and undertail-coverts yellow

Habits Usually solitary but sometimes in pairs. Forages slowly and deliberately for invertebrates and fruits in variety of habitats. Usually in canopy. Often joins mixed-species flocks.

Status Fairly common to common and widespread, with 6 records from Bonaire (September–October) and Curaçao (October–November, February).

Habitat Tropical Zone, to 3,600m but usually below 1,650m. Various dry to humid semi-open to closed woodland and forests, e.g. humid forest canopy and edge, lighter woodland, second growth, shrubby clearings, plantations, thickets, parks and gardens, and may be seen anywhere on migration.

Voice A rather nasal, descending *jeeeyr*. Residents sing a simple *cheewit* or *cheep-cheup* repeated more or less continuously whilst migrants from North America and southern South America are probably silent on wintering grounds (R&T, ffrench, R&G).

Note Subspecies *chivi* also called Chivi Vireo and is perhaps a separate species (Johnson & Zink 1985, Johnson *et al.* 1988).

YELLOW-GREEN VIREO

Vireo flavoviridis Pl. 226

Identification 14–15cm. Adult bright olive-green above, grey on head, slightly olivaceous on cheeks and ear-coverts, vague grey supercilium from supraloral to well behind eye, only slightly paler than grey crown, narrowly outlined above darker grey; underparts white with warm yellowish wash on sides, becoming richer yellow from vent to undertail-coverts. Eyes bright reddish, bill dark to blackish above, grey below, legs and feet grey. Juvenile has crown cinnamon-buff with whitish supercilium; very pale yellow below. Adult very similar to Red-eyed Vireo, from which not always safely separated, which also applies to very similar Black-whiskered Vireo, though latter overall duller (less yellow) with browner upperparts and has faint dark whiskers (can be hard to see). See also Philadelphia Vireo. Most likely to be confused with race *chivi* of Red-eyed Vireo, which is duller on breast and buffy on belly, and apparently occurs only in south of region between March and August.

Ssp. *V. f. flavoviridis* (migrant from Central America) as described

V. f. forreri (migrant from Tres Marias Is., Mexico) larger, greenish-olive above with only faint supercilium, slightly paler grey than crown; all white below, washed from rear ear-coverts to sides and flanks with greenish-olive

V. f. insulanus (migrant from Pearl Is., Panama) greenish-olive above with only faint supercilium, slightly paler grey than crown; all white below, washed from rear ear-coverts to sides and flanks with yellow

Habits Behaviour much like Red-eyed Vireo and they often forage together (adding to potential for confusion), although Yellow-green Vireo is less likely to occur in canopy.
Status Breeds in Central America and winters in north-west South America, where uncommon to fairly common in Colombia (July–December, March–April) and eastern Ecuador (September–April), with 1 record from southern Táchira, north-west Venezuela, but certainly overlooked.
Habitat Tropical to Temperate Zones, usually below 1,500m (but possibly higher on migration) and in Ecuador usually below 400m in eastern lowlands. Humid forests, edges, second growth, clearings, lighter woodlands, but anywhere on migration.
Voice Migrant populations sing short snatches of song on South American wintering grounds. Song shorter, faster, less musical and jerkier than Red-eyed Vireo, e.g. *ch-ree, chree, swee, chr-ee*… (R&G, Hilty).
Note Formerly considered a subspecies of Red-eyed Vireo (e.g. H&B; see Johnson & Zink 1985 and Johnson *et al.* 1988 for taxonomic comments).

CHOCÓ VIREO *Vireo masteri* Pl. 226

Identification 10cm. Adult greenish-olive above with broad yellow supercilium contrasting with greyish-olive crown and dark eyestripe, dark brown wings with olive fringes and 2 broad creamy wingbars; whitish throat, creamy white below with yellow breast, flanks and undertail-coverts; eyes brown, bill has black maxilla, pale mandible, and bright bluish-grey legs. Similar Brown-capped Vireo has browner upperparts and lacks wingbars. See also Rufous-rumped Antwren which has rufous rump and longer tail.

Ssp. Monotypic (C Co)

Habits Forages singly, in pairs or small flocks, exclusively in canopy, for invertebrates, and sometimes joins mixed-species flocks.
Status Endangered. Endemic to Pacific slope of West Andes of Colombia, where known from only 3 sites: Alto de Pisones, Risaralda, and two in Junín area, Nariño, where fairly common in suitable habitat. Habitat fragmented and much reduced by road building, logging and agriculture.
Habitat Upper Tropical to Lower Subtropical Zones, at 1,100–1,600m, in undisturbed cloud forest, usually on steep slopes, with a rather broken canopy and natural treefall gaps, preferably with an abundance of palms, epiphytes, ferns and moss.
Voice Calls include a brief *chip* in contact. Song a series of 6–20 variable, high-pitched notes lasting 1–3 s (BirdLife 2004).
Note A recently described species (Salaman & Stiles 1996).

BLACK-WHISKERED VIREO
Vireo altiloquus Pl. 226

Identification 14–16cm. Adult olive above, greyish-brown on head, slightly olivaceous-grey eyebrow, cheeks and ear-coverts, with dark eyestripe; variable but fairly narrow dusky line at outer edge of malar ('whisker'); underparts white with olivaceous-grey wash on sides, and pale yellow from vent posteriorly. Eyes bright reddish, bill dark to blackish above, grey below, legs and feet grey. Juvenile duller and buffier with brown malar streak. Adult very similar to Red-eyed and Yellow-green Vireos, from which not always be safely separated, unless (sometimes faint) diagnostic black 'whiskers' observed. Behaviour much like that of Red-eyed Vireo (adding to potential for confusion). Migrants do not sing.

Ssp. *V. a. altiloquus* (boreal migrant to Co, Ve, Guianas) as described

V. a. barbadensis (migrant on Tr) distinctive, whitish supercilium with black upper border, whitish face with bold blackish eyestripe and malar, underparts white

V. a. barbatulus (boreal migrant in transit through Co, Ve, Tr) dull, drab supercilium and face-sides, shorter eyestripe and malar, well washed with drab at sides and flanks, undertail-coverts pale sulphur-yellow

V. a. bonairensis (ABC, N Ve: Margarita & Los Roques Is., Tr) paler olive above than other races, with primaries contrastingly dark; pale brown supercilium has narrow black upper border, similar pale brown face-sides, narrow eyestripe and malar, sides and flanks narrowly washed pale grey, undertail-coverts pale yellow

Confirmed on Tobago, but subspecies uncertain (M. Kenefick, pers. comm.)

Habits Like Red-eyed Vireo also found in wide variety of habitats. Fairly tolerant of disturbed areas.
Status Breeds in Florida, West Indies, and various islands off northern Venezuela (subspecies *barbadensis* and *bonairensis*), and winters across most of northern South America (August–April, once in June in Colombia), where rare to uncommon (possible but not yet recorded in Ecuador).
Habitat Tropical to Temperate Zones, to 3,000m but usually below 2,000m. In moist to humid forest edges, second growth, clearings and lighter woodlands on mainland and

in mangroves, coastal vegetation, scrubby woodland and overgrown plantations on islands where it breeds.

Voice A nasal *waink*. Residents have a somewhat faster, hoarser and more clipped song than Red-eyed Vireo, e.g. an endlessly repeated, cheerful *veer-o* or *whip, Tom-Kelly*, whilst migrants are probably silent in winter (Voous 1983, H&B, R&T).

BROWN-CAPPED VIREO

Vireo leucophrys Pl. 225

Identification 12–13cm. Adult olive-brown above with top of head slightly darker brown, barely contrasting with mantle, and tapering white supercilium contrasting with prominent black eyes, ear-coverts brownish, washed slightly paler on lower throat and breast, chin whitish becoming buffy-yellowish on rear underparts. Bill dark horn with pink base to lower mandible. Sexes alike, but juvenile clearly distinct, paler brown above with very short supercilium and darker cap, and below white with only a flush of sulphur-yellow on rear underparts. All other *Vireo* species lack brown cap, although not equally contrasting in all races. Smaller greenlets with brown caps lack white supercilium, have less heavy bills, exhibit different behaviour and are usually at lower altitudes.

Ssp. *V. l. disjunctus* (C & W Andes in N Co, C & S Co) like a darker *josephae* but throat patch smaller and less white

V. l. josephae (W Ec, SW Co: Nariño) exactly like *leucophrys* but pileum fuscous in Colombian, and black on Ecuadorian birds

V. l. leucophrys (E Ec, E Andes in E Co) as described

V. l. mirandae (Santa Marta in Co, Perijá, Andes and coastal range in Ve) very close to *leucophrys* but averages paler yellow below and is slightly paler (less brownish) above

Habits Forages deliberately, alone or in pairs, at all levels, but usually high. Often joins mixed-species flocks.

Status Fairly common to common.

Habitat Tropical to Subtropical Zones, at 500–3,150m (usually below 2,600m), in humid to wet forests (including cloud forest), edges, mature second growth, clearings and plantations.

Voice A rising, buzzy *zreeee* call, sometimes repeated 2–4 times. Song a short, fast, musical warble, emphatically rising in pitch at end, e.g. *here you sée me hear me sing so swéet* (R&T, Hilty).

Notes Formerly considered conspecific with Warbling Vireo *V. gilvus*. Race *dissors* synonymised with *disjunctus* by Olson (1981b).

Greenlets are rather small, warbler-like birds much alike in appearance, generally olive above and pale below; they have pointed bills and forage with great agility. They fall into two groups, those of forest canopies and those of edges, borders and scrub, and it has been suggested these might prove to represent separate genera. Currently however, all are placed in *Hylophilus*.

LEMON-CHESTED GREENLET

Hylophilus thoracicus Pl. 227

Identification 12–13cm. Adult bright olive-green above with grey hindcrown and nape, and grey below with broad yellow pectoral band and yellow undertail-coverts; eyes whitish to pale yellow-orange, bill dark above, pinkish below, legs and feet vinaceous-flesh. Juvenile differs in having head duller greyish, washed olive; throat and pectoral band duller, as if lightly washed drab over the grey and yellow, undertail-coverts dull pale buffy. Grey-chested Greenlet is much greyer below (with only slight yellow at breast-sides). Ashy-headed Greenlet has dark reddish-brown eyes, all-grey head, more diffuse and extensive yellow underparts, and different voice and habitat preferences. Tepui Greenlet has all-grey head and wings and usually occurs at higher altitudes. Much commoner Dusky-capped Greenlet has dark eyes, brownish upperparts and mostly yellow underparts.

Ssp. *H. t. aemulus* (E Ec, SE Co) head concolorous with back, underparts white with yellow pectoral band and washed grey on flanks, legs and feet slightly paler.

H. t. griseiventris (E Ve, Guianas) as described

Habits Forages singly or in pairs from midstorey to canopy for invertebrates and fruits, almost always with mixed-species flocks.

Status Uncommon to locally fairly common, somewhat uncertain in south-east Colombia, but probably overlooked as it is in eastern Ecuador, where only a handful of records in lowlands. Common in the interior of Suriname and French Guiana.

Habitat Lower Tropical Zone, to 900m, in moist to humid forests (mostly *terra firme* in Venezuela, but also *várzea*), edges and mature second growth.

Voice High buzzy *chip* notes when foraging. Song a bright, penetrating series of *c.*6–10 even-pitched rhythmic notes (*c.*3 per s), e.g. *peeer-peeer-peeer…*, *chewee-chewee-chewee…*, or *peedit-peedit-peedit-peedit-peedit…*, sometimes louder, lacking trilled finale typical of Ashy-headed Greenlet (H&B, R&T, R&G, Hilty).

GREY-CHESTED GREENLET

Hylophilus semicinereus Pl. 227

Identification 12cm. Adult olive-green above, greyish on nape but no clear contrast with back, underparts almost entirely pale grey, lightly washed brown on sides and across breast, and yellow on undertail-coverts; eyes pale greyish to white, bill clearly contrasting dusky above, pink below, legs and feet pinkish-grey. Juvenile similar but washed brownish on head and nape, more brown-washed below, and tinged yellow on sides and vent to undertail-coverts; bill dusky, legs and feet grey. Except lemon pectoral band, very much like Lemon-chested Greenlet. Ashy-headed Greenlet has dark (not whitish-grey) eyes, all-grey head and yellower underparts. Brown-headed Greenlet has dark (not whitish-grey) eyes, all-brown head and even more uniform grey underparts.

Ssp. *H. s. viridiceps* (SE Ve, FG)

Habits Behaviour much like Lemon-chested Greenlet: usually in mixed-species canopy flocks and tends to keep to outer branches where it is agile on slender stems and tips.
Status Probably fairly common to common, but uncommon and local in southern Venezuela, though probably overlooked. A few scattered sight records for French Guiana.
Habitat Lower Tropical Zone, to 350m, in humid forests (mostly scrubby *várzea*), edges, and mature second growth, especially in areas of sandy soil with lower-canopy forests.
Voice Song similar to Lemon-chested and Scrub Greenlets, but more a repetition of a single, slightly downslurred note at rate of *c.*1 note per s, e.g. *seeur-seeur-seeur-*..., repeated 20 times or more (R&T), or *peeer, peeer, peeer*... (Hilty).

ASHY-HEADED GREENLET
Hylophilus pectoralis Pl. 227

Identification 12cm. Adult dark olive-green above with ash-grey head and nape, entirely grey below with dull greenish-yellow wash from breast to sides and flanks; eyes bright to pale orange or pale vermilion, bill dark grey above, medium grey below, legs and feet greyish-flesh. Juvenile slightly duller. Similar to Lemon-chested and Grey-chested Greenlets. Tepui Greenlet has greyish-white (not dark reddish-brown) eyes, contrasting grey (not olive) wings and tail, and usually occurs at higher altitudes.

Ssp. Monotypic (E Ve, Guianas)

Habits Forages alone or in pairs at all levels, but mostly from midstorey to canopy, and mostly for berries. Calls persistently, thus drawing attention to its presence. Sometimes joins mixed-species flocks.
Status Known only from one specimen, from Delta Amacuro, in eastern Venezuela, though probably overlooked. Fairly common in the Guianas where it is commonest greenlet of coastal region.
Habitat Lower Tropical Zone, to 400m. Mostly in coastal mangroves and edges of moderately humid forests, light woodland and scattered shrubs and trees on sandy soil coastal plains, but also in scattered vegetation more inland, e.g. in coffee plantations and gardens.
Voice Song a persistent series of melodious rhythmic notes (*c.*4 notes per s), similar to Lemon-chested or Scrub Greenlets, but usually has diagnostic trilled, descending finale, e.g. *churée-churée-churée-*..., *chewchewchewrrréét* (H&M), *a-wirra-wirra-wirra-wirrawooor*, or rolling *weedlee-weedly-weedly-weedly-weedly* (Snyder), an agitated *weedá-weedá-weedá-weedá-chewchewchéëuw* and brisk *chureé-chureé-chureé*... with up to 8–10 notes in 2–2.5 s (Hilty).

TEPUI GREENLET
Hylophilus sclateri Pl. 227

Identification 12cm. Similar to Lemon-chested and Ashy-headed Greenlets, but perhaps more 2-toned appearance, upperparts grey, from forehead to tail, with strong olive-green wash on back to rump, and underparts very white, with a warm yellow band across breast and narrow greenish-yellow wash on sides.

Ssp. Monotypic (S Ve, S & W Gu, C Su)

Habits Forages singly, in pairs or small flocks almost invariably in canopy (lower at edges), and quite frequently joins mixed-species flocks. Restless and very agile, acrobatically working slender stems at tips of outer branches.
Status Uncommon to locally common in tepuis. Only recently discovered in Acari Mts., Guyana (M. B. Robbins *et al.*), and on the Tafelberg, Suriname (Ottema & Joe in press).
Habitat Tropical to Subtropical Zones, at 600–2,000m, in humid to wet forests, edges, low woodland and thickets.
Voice A nasal, downslurred scold. Song a distinctive, short, clear, oft-repeated *suuWEEEeeuu* whistle, rising then quickly falling, similar to a *Sporophila* seedeater (R&T, Hilty).

BUFF-CHEEKED GREENLET
Hylophilus muscicapinus Pl. 227

Identification 11.5–12cm. Dull-coloured adult is olive above with grey crown and nape, distinctive buffy cheeks extending to neck-sides and breast (often hard to see), otherwise whitish below. Bill dark above, pinkish-grey below, usually with brown eyes. Despite distinctive buff coloration, can be hard to separate from other dull-coloured greenlets in range, e.g. Brown-headed Greenlet, which has brownish head, yellowish wing fringes and mostly grey underparts (only tinged buffy on throat and breast), thus best field mark is characteristic song.

Ssp. *H. m. muscicapinus* (S Ve, Guianas)

Habits Forages in pairs or small flocks mostly from midstorey to canopy (lower at edges) for invertebrates, almost always in mixed-species flocks.
Status Fairly common to common, but easily overlooked unless song is known.
Habitat Tropical Zone, to 1,100m, in humid forest (*terra firme* and *várzea*) and edges.
Voice Song a distinctive, snappy, incessant *whitchy-ta-whEEu*, *split-your-Ear* or *weechy-weechy* (H&M, Hilty).

BROWN-HEADED GREENLET
Hylophilus brunneiceps Pl. 227

Identification 11.5cm. Greenish-olive above with rufescent brown head (slightly richer brown in adult male), buffy-brown face-sides and whitish throat; somewhat yellowish on rump and tail-edges and fringes to tertials and secondaries; pastel brownish-grey on breast; pale grey flanks, belly and vent, undertail-coverts yellow. Eyes reddish to bright chestnut or dark brown, bill dark above, pinkish below, legs and feet flesh. Sexes and juveniles appear alike, but male is slightly warmer and more intense grey on breast, female washed brown on breast, and juvenile washed buffy on throat and breast. Dull-coloured adult can be hard to separate from other dull-coloured greenlets in range, e.g. Grey-chested, Buff-cheeked or Dusky-capped Greenlets, which latter is browner (not olive) above and more yellowish below (see Tawny-crowned Greenlet), thus best field mark is characteristic song.

Ssp. *H. b. brunneiceps* (E Co, S Ve)

Habits Forages in pairs or small flocks mostly from midstorey to canopy (lower at edges) for invertebrates, sometimes joining mixed-species flocks.
Status Seemingly uncommon, but probably often overlooked.
Habitat Lower Tropical Zone, to 400m. In forests along edges of streams and tall *várzea* forest, savanna woodland and scrubby low-canopy forest on sandy soil and along black-water rivers.
Voice Song a loud, slow, downslurred and even-pitched *seeeeaarn* or *peeeern*, incessantly repeated at rate of *c.*1 note per s, after playback changing to series of twitters followed by 4–5 soft notes and louder, descending *swe'swe'swe'swe'swe' swe'peer-peer-peer-PEEERN PEEERN PEEERN*, also a more excited, faster and ringing *ree-ree-ree*... at rate of *c.*3 notes per s, similar to song of Scrub Greenlet (Hilty).

DUSKY-CAPPED GREENLET
Hylophilus hypoxanthus Pl. 227

Identification 11.5–12cm. Adult dusky brown above, chin and throat including malar pale to whitish, rest of underparts pale yellow, washed brown on sides and breast; dark eyes, bill dark above, pinkish below, legs and feet grey. Only Amazonian greenlet with mostly yellow underparts (compare Lemon-chested and Brown-headed Greenlets).

Ssp. *H. h. fuscicapillus* (E Ec) paler brown above (not dusky)
H. h. hypoxanthus (SE Co, S Ve) as described

Habits Forages noisily alone or in pairs, mostly from midstorey to canopy (lower at edges), almost always within mixed-species flocks.
Status Fairly common to common, but easily overlooked unless song is known.
Habitat Lower Tropical Zone, to 600m, in humid forest (mostly *terra firme* but also *várzea*) and edges.
Voice Song a fast, bright, distinctive *purcheechoweér* or *itsochuwéet*, with last note sometimes dropped and uttered constantly while foraging (H&B, R&T, Hilty).

RUFOUS-NAPED GREENLET
Hylophilus semibrunneus Pl. 227

Identification 12–12.5cm. Mid brown above, with variable wingbars formed by pale buffy fringes to greater coverts; birds in fresh plumage have obvious bars, those in worn plumage virtually none, but majority have something between extremes. Head deep rufous becoming paler on face-sides but cleanly divided on mantle, short but clear white supercilium, underparts entirely greyish-white washed pale lemon on breast, faint cinnamon wash at sides and narrowly washed pale drab on flanks, undertail-coverts yellowish; eyes varying shades of brown, bill dark above, pinkish below, legs and feet grey. Juvenile appears duller below, with a paler crown; some are intermediate with darker feathers emerging on crown. Distinctive rufous crown and nape excludes confusion except with juvenile Golden-fronted Greenlet, which lacks solid rufous top of head. See Tawny-crowned Greenlet and female Plain Antvireo which both forage in undergrowth.

Ssp. Monotypic (E Ec, Co, Zulia & Perijá in NW Ve)

Habits Forages alone, in pairs or small flocks, mostly from midstorey to canopy (lower at edges) for invertebrates. Often joins mixed-species flocks.
Status Rare to uncommon and local, but probably often overlooked.
Habitat Tropical to Subtropical Zones, at 450–2,100m, in humid to wet forests, edges and mature second growth.
Voice Song a weak, fast, musical, ascending and oft-repeated *wa-chee-ra-dit'it* or *cheedodoweédidideét*, similar to Dusky-capped Greenlet but slightly longer and faster (H&B, R&G, Hilty).

GOLDEN-FRONTED GREENLET
Hylophilus aurantiifrons Pl. 227

Identification 11.4–12cm. Uniform yellow-olive above with yellowish forehead, pallid brown top of head that grades into back, almost uniform pale below, depending on race; eyes dark brown, bill dark above, pinkish below, legs and feet grey. Distinctive reddish-brown crown and nape and buffy face with conspicuous dark eyes excludes confusion except with Rufous-naped and duller Scrub Greenlets, which latter has pale brownish-olive (not yellowish-brown) crown and nape, less yellow on underparts and different voice.

Ssp. *H. a. aurantiifrons* (N coast in Co) pale sulphur-yellow below, paler on throat and undertail-coverts
H. a. helvinus (W Ve) crown darker reddish-brown, almost white throat, rest of underparts pale yellow, flushed rufous on breast and sides, becoming an almost greenish-olive wash on flanks, undertail-coverts pale yellow
H. a. saturatus (E Co, NC & NE Ve, Tr) white throat and around base of bill, ochraceous yellow, slightly flushed rufescent on sides and breast, becoming rich warm yellow on belly and flanks to undertail-coverts; juvenile pale sulphur-yellow below, warmer and slightly ochraceous on undertail-coverts

Habits Noisily forages alone, in pairs or small flocks, at all levels, for invertebrates, often joining mixed-species flocks.
Status Uncommon to locally common (e.g. Trinidad).
Habitat Tropical to Subtropical Zones, to 1,900m, in various dry to wet habitats (but usually in moister habitats than Scrub Greenlet), e.g. *terra firme*, *várzea* and gallery forests, edges, second growth, scrubby clearings, scrub, plantations and gardens.
Voice Calls include a rapid, frequently uttered *cheetsacheéyou*, a simpler, less frequent *cheevee* or *choo-chwee*, and a more nasal scold. Song a short, quick, semi-musical and oft-repeated *de-wichy-de-whéter* (R&T, ffrench, Hilty).

SCRUB GREENLET
Hylophilus flavipes Pl. 227

Identification 11.5cm. Olive-brown above with faint buffy supercilium, throat whitish, underparts buffy, slightly darker on breast, creamy on belly and flanks, slightly yellowish on undertail-coverts; eyes white or dark, pinkish bill, legs and feet grey. Juvenile much like adult, but has pale supercilium and brown eyes. Eye colour of adults varies, with brown eyes commonest in some areas and white in others, but seem somewhat inconsistent with racial distribution; colours given below and on plate seem usual for race concerned, but are not absolute. Possible that all brown-eyed birds are juvenile or intermediates, i.e. immature, but several had enlarged gonads. Separation of races not easy with some variation within populations, e.g. race *flavipes* does not cross East Andes of Colombia, but many specimens from range of *acuticauda* look like *flavipes*. This essentially dull greenlet is most easily confused with warmer coloured Golden-fronted Greenlet (see above), but also check other dull-coloured greenlets.

Ssp. *H. f. acuticauda* (Ve: Llanos, C & E, Margarita I.) more yellowish below; eyes white to yellow and pale brown, but all from Margarita I. had brown eyes

H. f. flavipes (N Co) yellowish tone to back and underparts, white eyes

H. f. galbanus (W & NW Ve) browner above, most specimens had pale grey or pale yellow eyes, but birds from Lara state had brown eyes

H. f. insularis (To) like *acuticauda*, brown eyes

H. f. melleus (Guajira in Co) slightly darker on top of head and back, and buffier below, eyes white

Habits Rather deliberately forages alone, in pairs or small flocks at all levels for invertebrates, sometimes joins mixed-species flocks.

Status Fairly common to common (e.g. Tobago).

Habitat Tropical Zone, to 1,200m, mostly in drier scrubby habitats (especially degraded areas with emerging second-growth trees), but also in dry to moist deciduous to semi-deciduous forests (including gallery forests), woodlands and edges.

Voice A nasal, oft-repeated *nyaa* scold, and various churrs and high squeaks. Song a rapid, penetrating series of 4–35 (usually *c.*10) *turee* or *peer* notes (R&T, Hilty), transcribed as *weary* or *weet* notes for Tobago (ffrench).

Note Central American subspecies *viridiflavus* is sometimes considered a separate species called Yellow-green Greenlet (R&T, AOU 1998).

OLIVACEOUS GREENLET

Hylophilus olivaceus Pl. 226

Identification 12cm. Adult dull olive above with yellowish forehead and yellowish-olive below (brightest on belly); white or pale yellow eyes, pinkish bill, legs pale flesh. Juvenile pale greyish-brown above with olive wings and tail (brighter green fringes than adult), and white below. Similar Scrub Greenlet does not overlap (see also Tawny-crowned Greenlet).

Ssp. Monotypic (CE Ec)

Habits Unobtrusively forages alone, in pairs or small flocks, mostly from midstorey to canopy (lower at edges), and sometimes joins mixed-species flocks.

Status Uncommon to locally fairly common.

Habitat Tropical Zone, at 600 to *c.*1,500m, at edges of humid forest and woodland, in second growth and overgrown clearings.

Voice Calls probably similar to Scrub Greenlet. Song a distinctive, fast and loud series of up to 10–12 musical *suwee, twee* or *peer* notes, also similar to Scrub Greenlet (R&T, R&G).

Note Formerly considered a subspecies of Scrub Greenlet (S&M).

TAWNY-CROWNED GREENLET

Hylophilus ochraceiceps Pl. 227

Identification 11.5cm. Adult olive above with distinctive tawny forecrown and cinnamon-brown wings and tail, and pale greyish-olive below with diffuse dull yellowish-olive breast-band. Eyes either yellowish-white or dark, according to subspecies, bill dark above, pinkish-grey below. Despite being only understorey greenlet and having distinctive pale eyes and tawny forecrown (both lacking in race *luteifrons*), could be confused with female Plain Antvireo, or female antwrens or greenlets, e.g. Brown-headed Greenlet, which has dark (rarely pale) eyes, less contrasting brown head, more buffy (not yellowish-olive) underparts, and forages mostly high; thus best field mark is Tawny-crowned Greenlet's characteristic voice.

Ssp. *H. o. bulunensis* (W Ec, W Co) tawny-yellow forecrown, more uniformly olive below with yellow undertail-coverts; pale eyes

H. o. ferrugineifrons (E Ec, SE Co, S Ve, W Gu) grey underparts washed narrowly olive on sides and flanks, undertail-coverts yellow; usually pale but sometimes has brown eyes

H. o. luteifrons (E Ve, Guianas) brown eyes, yellowish-rufous forecrown, throat greyish or yellowish-white, buffier below, especially on breast; eyes dark brown

Habits Active and quick as it forages alone, in pairs or small flocks mostly in dark undergrowth of understorey (never in canopy and rarely at borders and edges). Almost always joins mixed-species flocks where could be mistaken for a female *Myrmotherula*.

Status Uncommon to fairly common (seemingly rarer in Ecuador), but easily overlooked unless song is known.

Habitat Tropical Zone, to 1,600m, in humid to wet forests (e.g. *terra firme*) and adjacent mature second growth, rare or absent in scrubby sandy belt forests.

Voice A frequently uttered, harsh, nasal *nyahh* scold. Song a loud, clear, penetrating, plaintive and ventriloquial *teeeeuw* or *teee-yeeé*, with second note slightly rising or falling, repeated frequently at rate of *c.*2.5 s (R&T, Hilty).

Note Subspecies *luteifrons* belongs to *rubrifrons* group which may constitute a separate species (R&T).

LESSER GREENLET

Hylophilus decurtatus Pl. 227

Identification 9.5–10cm. Small, plump greenlet with short tail. Yellowish-olive above with narrow whitish eye-ring, and greyish-white below with greenish-yellow tinge to sides and flanks. Eyes dark brown, bill dark above, pinkish-grey below, legs and feet grey. Best separated from other greenlets by distinctive small, plump, large-headed and short-tailed body (similarly coloured Tennessee Warbler also has different body shape and white supercilium).

Ssp. *H. d. darienensis* (W Co) top of head, nape and sides of neck brownish-grey, contrasts with brown of mantle
H. d. minor (W Ec, Nariño in SW Co) top of head and nape concolorous with back

Habits Active and quick as it forages, mostly in small flocks, from midstorey to canopy (lower at edges), and often joins mixed-species flocks.
Status Uncommon to locally common.
Habitat Tropical Zone, to 1,400m but usually below 1,100m, in drier deciduous to humid evergreen forests, edges and mature second growth.
Voice Calls include various nasal *nyah* scolds and a constantly repeated, rapid, musical *wichee-cheeu* (*minor*), and *deedereét* or *itsacheét* (*darienensis*) (R&T, R&G, H&B).
Note The Central American races are sometimes considered a separate species called Grey-headed Greenlet (AOU 1998).

CORVIDAE – Jays

The sole representatives of the worldwide crow family to occur in northern South America are jays. With the exception of Green Jay, which combines green and yellow with striking touches of black and blue, all are mainly blue, accented to a greater or lesser degree with black and white. Juveniles are just like adults, but are slightly smaller and duller. At a glance, some species may appear similar, but in general they are well separated geographically and there is little sympatry, thus combined use of the distribution maps and plates should reduce identification problems to a minimum. All of the New World jays have large vocabularies that can only be described as buzzes, clicks, whistles, warbles, ripples and so on, and birds use creative combinations. Jays tend to travel in small foraging groups, possibly adults and juveniles, although second-years sometimes assist the rearing of a clutch, so they may be extended family groups. These foraging groups maintain loose flock cohesion by continually uttering penetrating cries, and each species has its typical contact calls. In this way, they draw attention to themselves and observers can draw them closer by mimicking calls or using playback. However, they are generally suspicious and utter frequent alarm-calls to draw attention of the observer before melting away.

Additional references used to prepare this family include Goodwin (1986) and Madge & Burn (1993, hereafter referred to as M&B).

The *Cyanolyca* collared jays represent a homogenous genus with no dramatic differences between species, being rich blue with paler heads and black masks that form a necklace across the throat. They generally replace each other ecologically, although there is some overlap between Turquoise and Black-collared. Their voices are quite distinct.

BLACK-COLLARED JAY
Cyanolyca armillata Pl. 228

Identification 30–34cm. A rather long-tailed jay. Adult is rich, deep blue with slightly paler, more rose-purple crown and throat; black mask from frontal band and mesial over ear-coverts, narrows and sweeps down to embrace throat. Eyes brown, short bill, legs and feet black. Juvenile duller and lacks rose-purple tone on head. Similar and much more common Turquoise Jay is more cerulean blue rather than royal blue, and has much paler crown and throat, narrower necklace, shorter tail and different voice. Beautiful Jay does not overlap.

Ssp. *C. a. armillata* (Co, SW Ve) as described; slightly brighter than others and purer blue
C. a. meridana (W Ve) darker and more purplish-blue
C. a. quindiuna (N Ec, Co) larger with heavier bill, darker mauve head and throat contrasting with green-tinged body, wings and tail

Habits Forages in pairs but mostly in small flocks, from midstorey to canopy, working branches covered with epiphytes, and sometimes joins mixed-species flocks.
Status Rare and local in most of its range, especially in Ecuador, commonest in west Venezuela and also fairly common in Nariño, Colombia.
Habitat Subtropical Zone to Páramo, at 1,600–3,250m. In humid to wet, mossy cloud forests and edges, mature second growth, also stunted and dwarf forests near treeline, and occasionally in gulleys with bamboo and fern thickets, but less tolerant of degraded forest than Turquoise Jay. More likely to be found inside forest than Turquoise Jay, which likes open forest.
Voice Calls include a rising, querulous, almost twanging *schree!*, a sharp upward staccato *reek!*, loud, piercing *eek!-eek!-EEK!* or *chzak-eek!*, a metallic *tnk! tnk!*, soft downward *craagh!*, sharp stuttered *jet-jtjtjtjt*, low guttural *wowr* and several high, thin notes. The unusually large repertoire of calls may be uttered in various rapid combinations (Goodwin, R&T, M&B, Hilty).

TURQUOISE JAY
Cyanolyca turcosa Pl. 228

Identification 30–34cm. Body entirely cobalt-blue, with broad black mask below line from rear ear-coverts to curving round as a necklace. Top of head and nape and throat paler, slightly mauve-blue. Juvenile duller, somewhat greyish and lacks black collar. Shorter-tailed than Black-collared Jay, and colder, slightly more greenish-blue. Smaller, rarer and more violet-blue Beautiful Jay has much paler whitish crown and nape, and shorter tail, lacks black collar and usually occurs at lower elevations.

Ssp. Monotypic (Ec, S Co)

Habits Forages for invertebrates and fruits, in small flocks at all levels, but mostly from midstorey to canopy. Often joins mixed-species flocks. More likely to be encountered in open forest than Black-collared Jay which is more closely bound to forest interiors.

Status Fairly common in Ecuador, apparently rarer in Colombia.
Habitat Subtropical Zone to Páramo, at 1,500–3,500m, in humid forest, woodland, edges, clearings and second-growth, e.g. *Alnus* stands, also elfin forest close to treeline, and fairly tolerant of disturbed, semi-open second-growth forests.
Voice A loud, hissing *jeeyr*, clear, descending *hye*, loud, piercing descending *tsrrrp*, an explosive *kworrr* and snarling *wharr*, all which may be repeated severally, and various other short, less raucous notes and clicks (Goodwin, R&T, F&K, M&B, R&G).

BEAUTIFUL JAY

Cyanolyca pulchra Pl. 228

Identification 27cm. Deep royal blue, top of head, nape, chin and throat powdery blue bordered black, bisected by black mask that joins black neck-sides. Adult female and juvenile usually tinged brownish above, and juvenile distinctly duller. Much darker blue, with much paler head than either of other collared jays, and pale chin and throat is sufficient to separate it from any other jay in region.

Ssp. Monotypic (NW Ec, W Co)

Habits Inconspicuous but readily located by voice as it forages alone, in pairs or sometimes in small flocks, mostly at lower levels.
Status Near Threatened. Rare to locally uncommon in Ecuador, where appears to have declined for largely unknown reasons since 1970s, and may deserve higher conservation status. Almost exclusively dependent on primary forest and extremely sensitive to human disturbance which is accelerating conversion of its habitat, with over 40% of Chocó forests already cleared or degraded.
Habitat Tropical to Subtropical Zones, at 900–2,300m but mostly 1,300-2,000m, in extremely wet forest (including mossy cloud forest) and edges on Pacific slope, favouring dense understorey, particularly along watercourses and in marshy areas.
Voice Common calls include a double *click* followed by a rising whistle, an oft-repeated *chee*, loud, inflected, oft-repeated *chewp* or *tjik*, quickly repeated, mellow *chew-chew-chew*… which can become louder and more explosive, a short, dry, oft-repeated *graasp*, and various guttural smacking and clicking notes, sounding clearer and more staccato than Turquoise Jay (H&B, M&B, R&G).

Cyanocorax jays are large, heavily built birds with bristly tufts on their foreheads, some white on their underparts and white on the tail – the exception being Green Jay, where white is replaced by yellow. Social and garrulous, they maintain contact by continually calling. Their breeding behaviour is poorly known, but it is thought they are at least partly social, with members of previous broods assisting in raising young of current brood.

Cyanocorax *jays all have small bristle tufts on their foreheads, left to right, Cayenne Jay, Green Jay of race* guatemalensis, *and Azure-naped Jay*

VIOLACEOUS JAY

Cyanocorax violaceus Pl. 228

Identification 33–37cm. Virtually only jay of Upper Amazon and Orinoco. Adult dull violaceous-grey with blue tinge on wings and tail, grey nape and black head separated by a white fringe, throat and breast also black but grading into violaceous-grey body. Eyes mid brown, bill black, legs and feet dark grey. Juvenile duller and greyer; head sooty grey, rather than black, and black of throat does not extend to mid breast as in adult. Azure-naped Jay (overlaps only in south-east Colombia and southern Venezuela) has pale yellowish-white eyes, more extensive pale blue nape, white vent and undertail-coverts and tip to tail.

Ssp. *C. v. pallidus* (NC Ve) generally paler overall
C. v. violaceus (E Ec, E Co, W & S Ve, S Gu) as described

Habits Noisy and conspicuous as it forages for invertebrates, small vertebrates and fruits, mostly in flocks of up to 12 and usually from midstorey to canopy. Sometimes joins mixed-species flocks.
Status Fairly common to locally common.
Habitat Tropical Zone, to 1,350m, usually in semi-open habitats near water and avoids dense *terra firme*, e.g. *várzea* edges, gallery and savanna forests, mangroves, edges of lakes and rivers, second growth, clearings with standing trees, frequenting *Scheelea macrolepis* palms and *Cecropia* stands, and even degraded dry woodland and xerophytic scrub in northern Anzoátegui; more tolerant of dry habitat than other jays.
Voice Chortling gurgles, descending ripples, guttural clicks, a loud, harsh and oft-repeated *jeeer*, a scream-like, loud, raspy, descending *peeough*, and, less frequently, a sharp, oft-repeated *clop* (Goodwin, H&B, R&T, M&B).

AZURE-NAPED JAY

Cyanocorax heilprini Pl. 228

Identification 33.5–36cm. Dark brown above with rear crown and nape bright lavender blue, front and sides of head black with feathers of forecrown and forehead curled up and forwards in short brushy crest, mesial bright blue, chin to centre of breast dark violaceous-grey, sides, lower breast and belly violaceous, vent to undertail-coverts white. Eyes pale to yellowish-white, bill, legs and feet black.

Ssp. Monotypic (SE Co, S Ve)

Habits Found in noisy groups that travel slowly, foraging at

all levels. Wary of observers and utters alarm cries, moving around with various members of group, taking it in turns to observe at intruder before moving on, or all simply melt into surrounding woodland.
Status Rare and local.
Habitat Lower Tropical Zone, to 250m, in stunted forests, edges and second growth on sandy belts in upper río Negro basin, and in lighter savanna woodland.
Voice A loud, harsh *jeer* very similar to Violaceous Jay, but thinner, higher and more descending, also a nasal, honking *duk-duk*, smooth, abrupt *keop*, liquid *puk*, rapid *je-je-je*, staccato clicking and various other calls (M&B, Hilty).

CAYENNE JAY
Cyanocorax cayanus Pl. 228

Identification 33cm. Mid brown on back, wings and tail dark brown, distal third of tail white; rear crown and nape white, continuing on neck-sides to underparts, front of head to central crown, ear-coverts, throat and centre of breast black, highlighted by short, broad white line above rear of eyes, a small broad crescent behind and slightly below eyes, and broad mesial stripe is also white. Juvenile paler brown above, with mantle grading into white of nape, and white tip at to tail narrower; face dusky rather than black and does not extend as far onto breast as on adult. White around eyes missing and mesial is less well developed. Eyes pale brown and bill blackish with pale grey base to mandible. Unique within its range.

Ssp. Monotypic (SE Ve, Guianas)

Habits Noisy but wary and difficult to observe, forages in family groups in treetops, seems to glide between trees with minimal wingbeats. Generally wary, but where undisturbed tolerates observers.
Status Fairly common. Sparsely distributed in French Guiana.
Habitat Tropical Zone, to 1,100 m. Woodland and scrub, secondary and savanna forests, edges; especially in white-sand areas of upper río Negro and Orinoco basins
Voice A melodious *tjeeeooo* (H&M) or *keyow* (M&B) and varied typical jay-like notes.

BLACK-CHESTED JAY
Cyanocorax affinis Pl. 228

Identification 35.5cm. Mid brown back and nape, wings and tail dark brown, distal third of tail white; front of head to central crown, ear-coverts, throat and breast black, highlighted by short, broad violet line above rear of eyes, short broad line behind and slightly below eyes and broad mesial stripe also violet. Sides and belly to undertail-coverts white. Eyes yellow, bill, legs and feet black. Juvenile paler brown above, with dusky brown head extending only to throat, white tip to tail slightly narrower and no violet spots on face; eyes pale brown and bill blackish with pale grey base to mandible. First-year intermediate. Unique within its range, white belly and tip of tail distinctive.

Ssp. *C. a. affinis* (N Co, NW Ve)

Habits Small family groups forage within dense foliage, usually at mid levels.
Status Relatively common but tends to be local.
Habitat Tropical Zone, to 2,600m but mostly in foothills. From dense secondary forest to edges, clearings and plantations.
Voice Sequences of 3 *Kyoop!*, *peeo!* or *cheo!* notes, also *chow, chow, chow!* sequences and clicks, squeaks and rattles (Goodwin, Hardy, H&B).

WHITE-TAILED JAY
Cyanocorax mystacalis Pl. 228

Identification 35.5cm. White from nape to mantle continues as line on neck-sides to breast, rest of underparts to undertail-coverts, outer tail-feathers and distal quarter of tail also white. Lower back to central tail-feathers and wings rich violaceous-blue; forehead, ear-coverts, chin, throat and centre of breast black, highlighted by white crescent above and slightly behind eyes, white triangle from base of mandible to behind eyes and a point at end of mesial. Eyes yellow. Juvenile has slightly less extensive black on head, lacks white rear eyebrow and white triangle is replaced by violet mesial; eyes pale brown. Unique in its range, white border to tail offers distinctive field mark, looks almost all-white in flight, with dark central line.

Ssp. Monotypic (SW Ec)

Habits Small family groups, forages at all levels but mostly near ground, readily comes into open and easily observed. Often resident close to habitation.
Status Uncommon and local.
Habitat Tropical Zone, to 1,200m. Dry secondary forest and edges, clearings, park-like mesquite forest and cactus steppe.
Voice Calls include typical but variable, scolding chatter *cha-cha-cha-cha-cha*… and a double-noted, high-pitched *clewp-clewp* (M&B).

GREEN JAY *Cyanocorax yncas* Pl. 228

Identification 30cm. Green above, with 3 outermost tail-feathers yellow, nape white or blue (depending on race), prominent violet-blue tufty frontal crest, face, neck-sides and centre of breast black, highlighted by violet-blue crescent above eyes and odd-shaped violet-blue mesial (midway between triangle and letter Y on its side). Underparts yellow. Bill black, but eyes, legs and feet colorations depend on race.

Ssp. *C. y. cyanodorsalis* (C & E Co, NW Ve) large, frontal crest and hindneck deep blue, back washed blue; eyes yellow, legs and feet brownish
C. y. galeatus (W Co) like *yncas* but crest larger; eyes yellow
C. y. guatemalensis (N Ve) crest smaller than *cyanodorsalis*, no blue wash on back, eyes orange-yellow, legs and feet grey
C. y. yncas (E Ec, SW Co) hindneck white, eyes brown, legs and feet coral orange

Habits Literally calls attention as foraging flock maintains contact. Conspicuous, noisy, social and very tolerant of

disturbance. Often very curious and will closely approach an observer, responding to an imitation of its contact call. Forages at mid and lower levels, occasionally to ground.
Status Common but local.
Habitat Tropical to Temperate Zones, at 800–3,000m, in humid montane and secondary forests, clearings and forest edges.
Voice Large varied vocabulary of metallic clicks and plinks, buzzes and mewing notes, varying in pitch, often given in triplicate. A double or treble *cleeop*, nasal *nyaa-nyaa-nyaa* (M&B). In Venezuela, commonest call, *querr, querr, querr!* adapted as local name 'Querre-querre'.
Note Green Jay ranges from Texas (USA) to Nicaragua, then from Colombia and Venezuela south to Bolivia. Northern populations are often referred to as the *luxuosus* group (Green Jay), and South American population as the *yncas* group (Inca Jay), and they are occasionally considered as specifically distinct.

ALAUDIDAE – Larks

The only member that occurs in our region is a very local race of Horned (or Shore) Lark, a species of astonishing distribution, from Colombia to Alaska and Arctic coasts of Canada, as well as Europe south to North Africa and east to China, with a total of 42 races regularly recognised. Whilst the facial pattern and unique 'horns' are distinctive, its behaviour is that of a fairly typical lark, foraging in a typical low crouch, with legs hidden, and several may be feed together quietly and unseen. Juveniles are very cryptically plumaged, but begin moult into adult-like plumage within weeks of fledging. The Horned Lark's song is fairly weak and often given at considerable height above ground, the bird rising vertically and hovering while singing. On completion it drops like a stone to the ground.

HORNED LARK
Eremophila alpestris Pl. 240

Identification 15cm. Adult has distinctive facial pattern (much duller in female) of white forehead and eyebrow topped with black horn-shaped feathers, and yellowish throat bordered at sides and on breast with black; upperparts pale brown with dusky streaks ('sparrow-like'), the white outer web of the outer tail-feathers conspicuous in flight, and underparts whitish. Juvenile much greyer with many small white spots or scales above. All similar pipits and finches lack white in tail (except Stripe-tailed Yellow Finch) and facial pattern (all).

Ssp. *E. a. peregrina* (Co: Cundinamarca & Boyacá)

Habits Forages alone, in pairs or small flocks for invertebrates and seeds, mostly on relatively open ground, e.g. barren fields and short-grass pastures.
Status Uncommon and local in East Andes of Cundinamarca and Boyacá, Colombia, e.g. around Bogotá airport, and declining rapidly (probably <1,000 individuals) as result of agricultural practices, pesticide use and the introduction of kikuyu grass.
Habitat Temperate Zone, 2,500–3,100m, on almost barren high-altitude plateaux, but not páramos.
Voice Undescribed, but presumably similar to North and Central American populations which have high, soft *see-tu* and *see-titi* calls, and a high, weak, chirping, tinkling song (Sibley 2000).

HIRUNDINIDAE – Swallows and Martins

Swallows and martins are graceful and elegant, long-winged, fork-tailed birds that spend much of their time foraging for aerial insects. Although the term swallow is more often applied to blue-and-white birds, and martin for brown-and-white birds, there are many exceptions, and the names refer to exactly the same group of birds. Totally unrelated to swifts, to which they bear only a superficial resemblance, they can perch and land on the ground normally, like other passerines. Many species breed in temperate countries and migrate towards and often beyond the equator on migration each year. In northern South America both boreal and austral migrants occur, as well as residents, which in turn may be altitudinal migrants. They often have short, sweet songs and build nests in holes or crevices, or construct a nest of wattle, mud and saliva, attached to a cliff face or wall of a house. They are largely unafraid of man and several species live in the middle of cities.

Additional references for this family: Turner & Rose (1989, hereafter T&R).

The nominate race of Sand Martin is the only representative of this Old World genus that occurs in North America, where it breeds, and South America where it winters.

BANK SWALLOW / SAND MARTIN
Riparia riparia Pl. 231

Identification 12cm. Adult greyish-brown above (becoming browner with wear) and white below except diagnostic and well-defined greyish-brown breast-band, with slightly notched tail. Sexes alike. Juvenile has pale cinnamon to creamy feather fringes above and buffy tinge below (but these are variable and disappear with wear), and white extends upwards behind ear-coverts. Juvenile Tree, Northern and Southern Rough-winged Swallows lack breast-band, Black-collared Swallow has more deeply forked tail and black vent, and Brown-chested Martin is much larger, has different flight pattern and white visible either side of tail base.

Ssp. *R. r. riparia* (boreal migrant; in transit through our region)

Habits Fast and erratic flight pattern with shallow rapid fluttery wingbeats is diagnostic, foraging usually relatively low over ground or water.
Status Locally fairly common to common throughout our region, seen singly, in pairs, small or even fairly large flocks on migration, but more dispersed in winter.

Habitat Lower Tropical Zone, to 3,700m on migration but usually below 1,000m, in open and semi-open habitats, e.g. wetlands, grassland, farmland, usually avoiding forested and built-up areas, but may be seen anywhere on migration. Often roosts in reedbeds.
Voice Calls include single or repeated *tschr* in flight, a confrontational *schrrp* and high-intensity repetitive alarm-call given at colony. Song is an unmusical twittering broken into phrases (T&R).
Notes The species, which is widespread across Eurasia, wintering across Africa and Asia, is known in the Old World as Sand Martin, but in the New World as Bank Swallow. It is possible that our race, *riparia*, is a distinct species (S&M).

Tachycineta swallows are small, dark above glossed blue or green, white or whitish rumps, with the exception of juvenile Tree Swallow, and white below. All have fairly short, forked tails. Gochfeld *et al.* (1980) pointed out the difficulty in identifying *Tachycineta* on the wing and referred to sightings of birds in Suriname and Colombia where certain species identifications were not possible, but where the genus was certain.

TREE SWALLOW
Tachycineta bicolor Pl. 229

Identification 13–15cm. Adult black above with green-blue gloss on head, back, wing- and tail-coverts, tail slightly forked, pure white below with a small white crescent on sides of rump, and some females are duller and less glossed than males. Juvenile drabber grey-brown above lacking any gloss, but has distinctive partial whitish collar and diffuse pale grey-brown breast band (usually more diffuse and incomplete than Bank Swallow). Only swallow without white rump (cf. white rump-sides in Violet-green Swallow) combined with pure white underparts (cf. Blue-and-white Swallow's black vent). Juvenile differs from juvenile rough-winged swallows by having white throat and generally white underparts, from juvenile Violet-green Swallow by sharper separation between brown upperparts and whitish underparts, and from juvenile Bank Swallow by its less distinct breast-band.

Ssp. Monotypic (boreal migrant; occasional in EC, Co, occasional sight records in Ve, Ec, Tr, and Gu)

Status Rare winter visitor, usually in flocks, sometimes with other swallow species.
Habitat Tropical Zone, most records from sea level, along coasts, but recorded at 2,800m in Colombia. Open, semi-open and wooded habitats (including mangroves), often near water, but anywhere on migration, even at high elevations. Roosts in marshes and trees.
Voice Calls include high chirps and twitters, e.g. dry rough *chee* or *chrip*, *buli-duli-dulit* or a liquid *churdle-churdle*, antagonistic call *zjiht* or *tick-tick-tick*, alarm-call a harsh chatter *peeh* or *pee-deeh*. Song a series of clear, sweet whistles *twit-weet twit-weet liliweet twit-weet*… also a clear *tsuwi tsuw* (Sibley). In large flocks, thin scratchy *tzeev* notes.

MANGROVE SWALLOW
Tachycineta albilinea Pl. 229

Identification 11–12cm. Adult has green-blue gloss on head, back, wing- and tail-coverts, white supraloral and rump, dark grey-brown tail and wings with white-fringed tertials, pure white below including underwing-coverts. Sexes similar. Juvenile drabber grey-brown above lacking any gloss, white underparts washed grey-brown with brownish tinge on breast-sides. Lacks Violet-green Swallow's white face and divided white rump and White-winged Swallow's white wing patch, whilst Blue-and-white Swallow has black rump and vent, and bluer gloss.

Ssp. Monotypic (Caribbean coastal Co, and possibly S and E along coast)

Habits Nests in tree cavities, often in partially submerged trees, also nest boxes. Usually forages low in rapid direct flight, alone or in pairs during breeding season, but also in small flocks during non-breeding season.
Status Rare on Colombian coast (and perhaps further south and east), seen in singles and pairs up to small (rarely large) flocks.
Habitat Lower Tropical Zone, coastal lagoons and beaches, mangroves, rivers, lakes, ponds, marshes, damp fields, meadows and savannas, almost always near water and even over salt water near shores.
Voice Calls include a sharp alarm note (T&R), *chrit* and *chiri-chrit* and a buzzy *dzreet*, song is a series of soft trills, chirps and burry chips.
Note Sight records in Colombia and Suriname (Gochfeld *et al.* 1980).

TUMBES SWALLOW
Tachycineta stolzmanni Pl. 229

Identification 11.5–13cm. Adult like Mangrove Swallow, but has smaller bill, less to no white on supraloral, greyish underwing-coverts, and greyer underparts with some dusky shaft-streaking. Sexes similar. Juvenile drabber grey-brown above lacking any gloss. Lacks Violet-green Swallow's white face and divided white rump; Blue-and-white Swallow has black rump and vent, and bluer gloss.

Ssp. Monotypic (SW Ec)

Habits Often seen perched on snags or wires. Seen in singles, pairs or flocks.
Status Uncommon and very local in south-west Ecuador.
Habitat Lower Tropical Zone, to 150m, in open and semi-open habitats, e.g. over arid scrub, farmland and coastal lagoons, but unlike Mangrove Swallow shows little association with water.
Voice Buzzy *dzeet* around nests (M. B. Robbins in R&G).
Note Formerly considered a subspecies of Mangrove Swallow but separation confirmed by AOU (1998).

WHITE-WINGED SWALLOW
Tachycineta albiventer Pl. 229

Identification 13.5–14cm. Adult has green-blue glossed

upperparts, except white rump and blackish wings with distinctive large white wing patch formed by white fringes to inner flight-feathers, tertials and upperwing-coverts; pure white below. Sexes alike. Juvenile drabber brown above lacking any gloss, has little or no white in wings and greyer underparts. No other similar swallow has diagnostic white wing patch, but compare similar Mangrove Swallow.

Ssp. Monotypic (E Ec, N & E Co, Ve, T&T, Guianas)

Habits Nests in, e.g. tree holes, rock crevices, cliffs and eaves of houses. Often perches on snags, branches and rocks over water, from where makes leisurely and graceful zigzag flights low above water. Only occasionally flies high. Forages over more open areas than White-banded Swallow.

Status Fairly common to common and widespread in appropriate habitat within its range, seen in singles, pairs or small flocks.

Habitat Lower Tropical Zone, to 500m, along rivers and around larger lakes and reservoirs, and open and semi-open habitats, e.g. pastures, clearings, mangroves, beaches, flooded *llanos*, and even pastures, airstrips, sewage ponds and dry savannas away from water, but usually near water.

Voice Most frequent call is a rather pretty *wreeeeet* (R&G). Soft buzzy *twe'e'e'd* in flight or perched, nesting birds utter soft gurgles, gives long series of metallic *jee-reek* notes during pre-dawn flight over water, short harsh alarm-call, song is a trilled *zweeed* (T&R).

[CHILEAN SWALLOW
Tachycineta meyeni] Pl. 229

Identification 12–13.5cm. Adult has dark blue glossed upperparts, except black wings and tail and white rump (some individuals also have inconspicuous white supraloral), pure white below. Sexes similar. Juvenile duller brown with slight gloss, often with narrow white line above lores.

Ssp. Monotypic (austral migrant; Cu)

Habits Flies fast and low over ground, usually singly, but sometimes in small flocks.

Status Accidental austral visitor that usually winters as far north as Peru. Inexplicable record of 2 on Curaçao (Voous 1983), likely a misidentification.

Habitat Lower Tropical Zone, to 1,000m, in open and semi-open habitats near water, e.g. marshes, lakes, lagoons, rivers, coasts, open woodland, clearings, scrub, forest edge and human habitation, but may be seen anywhere on migration.

Voice Call unknown; song high-pitched gurgle followed by lower guttural sounds (T&R).

Note Species name formerly *leucopyga* but name pre-occupied.

VIOLET-GREEN SWALLOW
Tachycineta thalassina Pl. 229

Identification 11.5–14cm. Adult has violet-green gloss on upperparts, except black wings and tail, and white face and sides of rump, pure white below. Female and juvenile drabber grey-brown above with little or no gloss, juvenile more greyish below. From Mangrove Swallow by more white on face and continued green on centre of rump. Tree Swallows lacks white face and side of rump.

Ssp. Subspecies unknown (boreal migrant; sight record in Co)

Status Vagrant, a January sight record from Santa Marta Mts., Colombia. Usually winters as far south as Costa Rica.

Habitat Recorded at 2,200m in Colombia, usually in various open and semi-open habitats to 4,000m, e.g. over coniferous, deciduous or mixed woodlands, and often near habitation, but may be seen anywhere on migration (when often near water).

Voice Calls include sharp hard *chilp* and *chip-lip* notes and a contact *chee-chee* (T&R).

Progne martins are large, robust birds with forked tails, all dark above with dark heads and breasts, most have a white belly and undertail-coverts, but some adult males are entirely dark blue. The genus includes many migratory species.

BROWN-CHESTED MARTIN
Progne tapera Pl. 230

Identification 16–19cm. Adult dull grey-brown above with duskier wings and tail, white below with distinctive broad grey-brown breast-band that extends as narrow band of pear-shaped spots (*fusca*) or greyish throat merges into indistinct breast-band without band of spots (*tapera*). Long silky undertail-coverts usually protrude sideways, thus visible from above either side of tail base. Sexes alike. Juvenile has grey-brown throat-sides and slightly squarer tail. All other *Progne*, even juveniles, have dark violet-blue gloss above and lack distinct breast-band, and Bank Swallow is smaller with different flight pattern.

Ssp. *P. t. tapera* (SW & E Ec, N & E Co, Ve, Guianas) greyish throat merges into indistinct breast-band and lacks pear-shaped spots below

P. t. fusca (austral migrant; E Ec, N & E Co, Ve, Guianas) slightly larger, darker sides and flanks, white throat clearly distinct from breast-band, which extends as narrow band of pear-shaped spots below

Habits Often takes over hornero nests, but also nests in cavities in trees, sandbanks, termite nests, buildings and bridges. Especially when nesting, performs characteristic slow, fluttery, circular flights with down-held wings. Foraging flights swift and swooping and almost invariably near ground, but often seen resting for long periods on fences, wires or branches at forest or water edge.

Status Fairly common to common and widespread, seen in singles, pairs or, in non-breeding season, in sometimes very large flocks (when occasionally mixed with other swallows).

Habitat Tropical to Lower Subtropical Zones, to 1,600m (even 4,000m on migration), in open and semi-open habitats with scattered trees, often near water, e.g. along riverbanks and sandbars, or in clearings and over farmland, grassland, savanna and habitation.

Voice Calls include a flat weak *chu-chu* or *chu-chu-chip* contact call and series of rough buzzy *j'jrt*, *djuit-djut* or *dchri-dchrie-dchrruid* (T&R), also a harsh, guttural song with gurgling sounds (Turner 2004).
Note Sometimes placed in monotypic genus *Phaeoprogne* due to lack of blue in its plumage and various morphological characters, but placement in *Progne* confirmed by DNA studies (Turner 2004).

PURPLE MARTIN

Progne subis Pl. 230

Identification 18–20cm. Male all dark with purple-blue gloss, black tail and wings. Female (eastern USA) overall sooty brown with less gloss, grey collar and forecrown, grey throat and upper breast, becoming paler grey below with dingy grey-brown markings, whilst female (western USA) is even paler overall, with whitish collar and forecrown, pale cheeks, throat and underparts. Juvenile also sooty brown with distinctive grey collar, throat and upper breast, becoming whiter below with fine dark streaks. Male indistinguishable from male Cuban or Southern Martins in field (though Southern Martin has slightly longer, more deeply forked tail). Female Caribbean, Cuban, Grey-breasted, Sinaloa and Southern Martins all lack pale collar and forecrown, and female Cuban, Caribbean and Sinaloa Martins possess more distinct contrast between dark breast and white belly, and lack scaly breast of female Purple Martin, whilst female Southern Martin is darkest below (female Grey-breasted and Purple Martins are paler, with female Caribbean, Cuban and Sinaloa Martins being palest below). First-summer male Purple Martin is similar to Caribbean or Sinaloa Martin overall, but has more uneven, blotchily distributed blue-black spots on underparts.

Ssp. *P. s. subis* (boreal migrant; transits through our region) as described
P. s. hesperia (boreal migrant; perhaps transits through our region) slightly smaller than *subis*, female more extensively white below and on forehead than *subis*, with distinct pale collar
P. s. arboricola (boreal migrant; perhaps transits through our region) slightly larger than *subis*, female more extensively white below and on forehead than *subis*

Habits Flight pattern alternates between long periods gliding in circles with short bursts of flapping flight, often quite high (30–60m).
Status Migrates relatively rapidly through northern South America to wintering areas further south, mostly August–October, but continuing until November, returning north mostly January. Varies from uncommon to locally abundant, seen in singles or small to large flocks, frequently accompanying other migrant swallows, either in steady migratory flight or at large roosts, e.g. in city parks or on buildings.
Habitat Tropical Zone to Páramo, to 3,600m, but mostly in lowlands, in open, semi-open or forest-edge habitats, e.g. ponds, wetlands, grassland, farmland, usually near water, but seen anywhere on migration.

Voice Calls include melodious low whistles, e.g. a rich descending *cherr*, given once or in series, an alarm sounding like a buzzy *geerrt*, also a *zweet* and *zwrack*, and rich gurgling song, including a high *twick-twick* (Turner 2004, Raffaele *et al.* 1998).
Note Sometimes considered conspecific with Cuban Martin.

CARIBBEAN MARTIN

Progne dominicensis Pl. 230

Identification 17–19cm. Male all dark with purple-blue gloss, except distinctive, sharply demarcated white lower breast, belly and vent. Female similar, but rather dark grey-brown on forehead, neck, head-sides and underparts. First-year male like adult female. Juvenile like adult female but even less glossed. Male has more extensive blue-black on flanks than male Sinaloa Martin, creating smaller white belly patch (difficult to determine in field). Female Grey-breasted and Purple Martins have less breast/belly contrast, female Cuban Martin has white extending to upper belly (instead of lower belly in female Caribbean), but appears very similar in field, as does female Sinaloa Martin which is slightly smaller and has darker throat, whilst first-year male Purple Martin has faint greyish collar and blotchy dark glossy feathers on breast and flanks, which may somewhat resemble overall pattern of female Caribbean Martin.

Ssp. Monotypic (ABC, T&T, FG, also boreal migrant; perhaps in transit through or wintering in our region)

Habits Alternates long periods of gliding in circles with short bursts of flapping flight, often quite high, but may forage low amongst cattle.
Status Nests on Tobago and most of West Indies, where fairly common to common in breeding season (February–September) but absent in non-breeding season. Collected on Aruba, Curaçao and Bonaire, sight records in Colombia, Venezuela, Guyana and French Guiana indicate migrates (rarely?) to northern South America in non-breeding season.
Habitat Tropical Zone, only seen at, or marginally above, sea level, in open, semi-open but also forested habitats in Tobago, e.g. mangrove, second growth, farmland, towns and cliffs, especially near water and on coasts, but also near water further inland.
Voice Probably similar to Grey-breasted and Purple Martin. *Zwoot* is used as contact call, *kweet* in antagonistic encounters, *wheet* in alarm, *croot* in courtship, *peak* as high-pitched alarm-call and *wrack* for mobbing predators. Song is gurgling and warbling (Turner 2004, T&R).
Notes Also called Snowy-bellied Martin. Sometimes considered conspecific with Sinaloa Martin or Cuban Martin.

[SINALOA MARTIN

Progne sinaloae] Pl. 230

Identification 17–18.5cm. Male has less extensive blue-black on flanks and purer white vent than male Caribbean Martin, thus creating larger white belly patch (but difficult to determine in field). Female Caribbean Martin slightly larger and has more extensive pale throat, but appears very similar in field, as does female Cuban Martin. Flight pattern as Caribbean Martin.

Ssp. Monotypic (boreal migrant; perhaps in transit through or wintering in our region)

Status Endemic breeder in west Mexico; unrecorded but hypothetical in northern South America.
Habitat Presumably Tropical Zone, in similar habitats as Caribbean Martin. Breeds in semi-open habitats and pine–oak forests in Mexico, to 2,000m.
Voice Probably similar to Caribbean Martin.
Note Sometimes considered conspecific with Caribbean Martin.

CUBAN MARTIN

Progne cryptoleuca Pl. 230

Identification 18–19.5cm. Male like male Purple Martin, only separable in the hand by concealed, extensively white abdomen (also indistinguishable from male Southern Martin in field). Female resembles female Grey-breasted Martin but throat, breast and body-sides duskier brown, and belly whiter, creating more distinct breast/belly contrast. Female Southern Martin darker below, female Purple Martin has pale collar and forecrown, and less distinct contrast between dark breast and white belly, female Caribbean Martin has white reaching lower belly (upper belly in female Cuban Martin), but appears very similar in field, as does female Sinaloa Martin. Flight pattern as Caribbean Martin.

Ssp. Monotypic (Cu; boreal migrant, perhaps in transit through or wintering in our region)

Status Common endemic breeder in Cuba and some offshore islands. Specimen records from Curaçao, otherwise unrecorded but possible on mainland (its wintering areas are unknown).
Habitat Presumably Tropical Zone, in similar habitats as Caribbean Martin.
Voice Probably similar to Caribbean or Purple Martins. Song is a rich gurgling, including a high *twick-twick* (Turner 2004).
Note Sometimes considered conspecific with Caribbean or Purple Martins.

GREY-BREASTED MARTIN

Progne chalybea Pl. 230

Identification 16–19cm. Male all dark above with steely blue gloss, black tail and wings, distinctive grey-brown throat and breast merging into white underparts, sometimes with a few narrow dark shaft-streaks. Female duller and less glossed above. Juvenile sooty brown above with less contrast below. Male distinguished from male Caribbean and Sinaloa Martins by less contrast between grey (instead of dark bluish) throat and breast and white belly. Both sexes lack brown upperparts and pale throat of Brown-chested Martin, and female lacks pale collar and forecrown of female Purple Martin, all-dark underparts of female Southern Martin, and whiter underparts more sharply demarcated from darker breast of female Caribbean, Cuban and Sinaloa Martins. Juvenile Grey-breasted Martin lacks breast-band of juvenile Brown-chested Martin.

Ssp. *P. c. chalybea* (Ec, Co, Ve, Tr, Guianas) smaller, shorter-tailed (*c*.5.5cm), dingy to buffy-white underparts with few or no shaft-streaks
P. c. macrorhamphus (austral migrant; winters Ve, Cu, Su) larger, longer-tailed (*c*.8.5cm), paler underparts

Habits Conspicuous, often perching on wires and buildings and nests under eaves of buildings, but also in other natural cavities, e.g. tree holes. Often flies quite high in loose flocks, gliding leisurely for long periods, interspersed with short bursts of flapping flight. Seen in large flocks during non-breeding migration and roosting.
Status Most common and widespread *Progne*, locally abundant in semi-open habitats. Southern *macrorhamphus* abundant May-Sept in French Guiana, with some roosts containing up to 40,000 birds.
Habitat Tropical to Lower Subtropical Zones, to 2,000m but even higher on migration (2,400m), in open and semi-open habitats, fond of farmland, habitation and, especially, water, e.g. rivers and swamps, also mangrove, grassland, savanna and woodland, but less often over closed forests, though it quickly uses clearings.
Voice Calls include a rich *chu* or *chu-chu* (R&T 1994), a staccato *cree* in courtship (Turner 2004), and a loud *churr* or *chreet* in flight (R&G). Males utter a rattle call, *zwat* in antagonistic encounters, *krack* when mobbing predators and *cluck* when territorial intruders appear (T&R). Song is series of rich gurgling sounds (R&T).
Note Subspecies *domestica* synonymous with *macrorhamphus* (Brooke 1974).

SOUTHERN MARTIN

Progne elegans Pl. 230

Identification 17–20.5cm. Male all dark with steely blue gloss, black tail and wings. Female is less glossed above and sometimes has grey-brown forecrown, dusky brown below, sometimes appearing scaly due to pale feather fringes, and belly sometimes slightly paler. Like female, juvenile also dark above and dusky brown below, with juvenile male sometimes having a few glossy blue feathers. Male indistinguishable from male Cuban and Purple Martins in field (though Purple Martin has slightly shorter, less deeply forked tail), but female is only Progne with essentially uniform dark underparts. Female Purple Martin has slightly paler underparts (especially belly), pale collar and forecrown. Behaviour and flight pattern similar to Grey-breasted Martin with which often associates on migration and in winter.

Ssp. Monotypic (austral migrant; winters SE Co, Su, FG and perhaps adjacent areas)

Habits Forages both high and low.
Status Vagrants overshooting winter range in west Amazonia occasionally reach northern South America (April–October).
Habitat Tropical to Lower subtropical Zones, mainly in lowlands, but much higher on migration (2,600m), in open and semi-open habitats, e.g. wetlands, grassland, farmland,

woodland, scrub and habitation, often roosting and feeding along rivers in wintering areas, sometimes in large numbers, but may be seen anywhere on migration.

Voice Probably similar to Grey-breasted and Purple Martins. Short harsh contact call, high-pitched alarm-call, and short gurgling or warbling song (T&R, Turner 2004).

Note Formerly treated as conspecific with Galápagos Martin *P. modesta*.

Notiochelidon are small swallows, similar to *Tachycineta*, but generally with longer, more deeply forked tails, and all have dark rumps. They all have dark vent and undertail-coverts, and some species are entirely dark.

BROWN-BELLIED SWALLOW

Notiochelidon murina Pl. 229

Identification 13.5–14cm. Adult all dark above with blue-green gloss, dusky tail and wings, tail long and deeply forked, and dull sooty brown below except bluish-black vent. May look all dark in field. Juvenile sooty brown above, greyish-white below with dark brown throat and shorter tail. Only somewhat similar species is White-thighed Swallow, which is smaller, has distinctive white thighs, pale rump and occurs at lower altitudes than present species. Juvenile Blue-and-white Swallow is smaller and paler below.

Ssp. *N. m. murina* (W Co, Ec) greener above, paler below
N. m. meridensis (W Ve) bluer above, smoky grey-brown below

Habits Nests in crevices on cliffs, road cuts or eaves of buildings (but less associated with habitation than Blue-and-white Swallow). Flies rapidly and fluidly at various heights (but usually closer to ground than Blue-and-white Swallow), typically in large circles before moving on.

Status Fairly common to common, usually nesting, roosting and foraging alone, in pairs or small flocks (*c*.5–30); numbers may change due to daily and seasonal movements in response to weather.

Habitat Temperate Zone to Páramo, 1,800–4,300m (occasionally higher) but usually 2,500m to treeline, in open and semi-open highlands, e.g. grassland, farmland, shrub, elfin forest, *Polylepis* woodland, and often around habitation and near water.

Voice Usually quiet, flight-call a rather scratchy *tjrrp* (R&G), contact call a chirp-like *tjrip-tjrip-tjrip-tjrip*, a harsh alarm and a weak buzzy song (T&R).

Note Sometimes placed in genus *Orochelidon* or *Atticora*.

BLUE-AND-WHITE SWALLOW

Notiochelidon cyanoleuca Pl. 229

Identification 12–13.5cm. Adult all dark above with steel blue gloss, dusky tail and wings, tail slightly forked, pure white below except a few dusky spots on breast and bluish-black vent. Juvenile brown above, white below except pale pinkish-buff throat merging into grey-brown breast-band or spots, and dull brown vent (diagnostic in comparison to those species with pale vents, e.g. Tree and Southern Rough-winged Swallows). Tree Swallow has white vent, and Pale-footed Swallow is smaller and has pinkish buff-throat and upper breast, and sooty sides and flanks. Juvenile Blue-and-white Swallow more easily confused with other swallows, especially juvenile Pale-footed Swallow (use voice and habitat).

Ssp. *N. c. cyanoleuca* (Ec, Co, Ve, Tr, Gu, FG?) smaller; smoky blue-black underwing-coverts, bluish-black flanks and vent
N. c. patagonica (austral migrant; winters Ec, E Co, N Ve, Su, FG) slightly larger (13.5cm), whitish-mottled pale grey-brown underwing-coverts, black on vent more restricted to sides

Habits Nests in all kinds of natural and artificial crevices, e.g. on cliffs, road cuts, eaves of buildings, and holes dug in sand banks. Usually in loose flocks, flies leisurely at various heights (but usually higher above ground than Brown-bellied Swallow), typically circling and zigzagging before moving on. Readily sits with other species when at rest.

Status Common and widespread, usually nesting, roosting and foraging in small to large flocks (common in non-breeding season), and migrants may form flocks of up to *c*.1,000 birds. Numbers may change due to daily and seasonal movements in response to weather. Austral migrants usually in lowlands or foothills (late March–October).

Habitat Tropical Zone to Páramo (although not on actual páramos), to 3,500m. Most abundant in foothills at 400–2,500m, over open and semi-open habitats, closely associated with habitation and cultivation, cliffs and road cuts, and benefits from deforestation, often foraging around cattle.

Voice Calls include thin, rapid and oft-repeated *chit-chit* (Hilty 1986), thin buzzy *tzee* in flight (Hilty 2003), and, most commonly, a scratchy *rising tree-ee-ee-ee* or *dzzzrheee*, sometimes starting with a sputter (R&G). Song a buzzy monotonous trill *tizi'zi'zi'zi'tzz-tzz-tzz-tzzi-zzi-zzi-zii-zii-zzzz* or *tizzzzzzzzzzzziiiiiiiii*, often repeated over and over (Hilty). Most vocal at the end of the day.

Note Sometimes placed in *Atticora* or *Orochelidon*.

PALE-FOOTED SWALLOW

Notiochelidon flavipes Pl. 229

Identification 11.5–12.5cm. Adult all dark above with steel blue gloss, dusky tail and wings, tail slightly forked, pure white below except pinkish-buff throat, sooty sides and flanks (diagnostic in field, as buff throat often goes unseen), and bluish-black vent (pale feet are not diagnostic). In addition to these differences from Blue-and-white Swallow, Pale-footed Swallow is smaller, less common, more associated with forests and has different voice and faster, straighter and more erratic flight pattern, often with incessant backtracking (Hilty).

Ssp. Monotypic (Ec, Co, W Ve)

Status Uncommon to locally fairly common in appropriate habitat (and probably still often overlooked), usually foraging in small flocks (*c*.5–15, occasionally 50+). Numbers may change due to daily and seasonal movements in response to weather.

Habitat Upper Subtropical Zone to Páramo, 1,500–3,600m, usually 2,200–3,000m, but even at 200m in bad weather, and usually low over Temperate Zone forest and forest-edge habitats on east Andean slopes, e.g. upper cloud forest or elfin forest (on average higher than Blue-and-white Swallow and lower than Brown-bellied Swallow, but can be seen with either species, and more associated with closed forest than either of others).
Voice Flight-calls include crisp, crackling *tszeet* and soft trilled *tr'e'e'e'e'e'd* (unlike thin, buzzy notes of Blue-and-white Swallow: Hilty).

Atticora swallows are small, slender birds with long, extended forked tails that may appear pointed when closed. They are dark above, one is distinguished by a white breast-band across a dark blue throat and breast, the other in reverse, having a dark blue band across white underparts. Even juveniles carry these discriminators.

WHITE-BANDED SWALLOW

Atticora fasciata Pl. 231

Identification 14.5–15cm. Adult all dark with steel blue gloss, except distinctive white breast-band and white thighs (hard to see in field), with dusky tail and wings, and long, deeply forked tail. Juvenile browner overall, especially below, where breast-band is less distinct, but retains adult's overall pattern.

Ssp. Monotypic (E Ec, SE Co, SE Ve, Guianas)

Habits Nests in small colonies, in holes dug into riverbanks. Often seen perched singly, in pairs or small flocks, on snags, branches and rocks over water, from where they perform rapid, darting, zig-zag flights low above water, only occasionally flying high. Prefers more closed areas nearer forest edge than White-winged Swallow.
Status Uncommon to locally common.
Habitat Tropical Zone, to 1,400m but usually below 900m, along forest-fringed rivers and larger streams, with preference for clear 'black' over muddy 'white' rivers, and sometimes over clearings adjacent to or even away from water, and rarely found at lakes.
Voice Calls include a fast *trrrdt*, often drawn-out or repeated several times (R&G), a fine buzzy *z-z-z-z-ee-eep* (H&B), harsh buzzy *bzrrrt* often given in flight (Hilty) and sharp *tschra* in alarm (T&R).

BLACK-COLLARED SWALLOW

Atticora melanoleuca Pl. 231

Identification 14–15cm. Adult all dark above with steel blue gloss, dusky tail and wings, tail long and deeply forked, pure white below except distinctive blue-black breast-band and vent. Juvenile retains adult pattern, but blue areas are brown, with brown breast-band smudged and slight brown tone to throat. Bank Swallows have less deeply forked tail and white crissum, and juvenile Barn Swallows have pale reddish forecrown and throat.

Ssp. Monotypic (SE Co, SE Ve, Guianas)

Habits Like White-banded Swallow, but also quite often circles high over rivers, rocky outcrops and adjacent forest. Nests in rock crevices or holes in riverbanks, in pairs or small flocks, and often perches in small flocks beside rivers, e.g. on rocks or sandbanks.
Status Uncommon to locally fairly common (sometimes large flocks up to 80 after rains), with some seasonal and irregular movements due to changes in weather and water table.
Habitat Lower Tropical Zone, to 300m, along rivers and larger streams with torrents created by waterfalls or rapids.
Voice Calls include a buzzy *jtt*.

Neochelidon swallows are medium-sized, entirely dark and unmistakable by having white-tufted thighs. They have a distinct jizz, flying and jinking much like a typical bat.

WHITE-THIGHED SWALLOW

Neochelidon tibialis Pl. 229

Identification 10.5–13cm. Adult brownish-black above with slight green-blue gloss on head and mantle, the rump distinctly paler grey-brown, similarly pale below with distinctively darker brownish-black vent and tail (moderately forked). Diagnostic white thighs sometimes visible when perched. Juvenile has faint pale feather fringes below. Southern Rough-winged Swallow is larger and has paler underparts with buff throat and yellowish belly.

Ssp. *N. t. minima* (W & C Co, W Ec) smaller (10.2cm), shorter tailed, upperparts darker brown with less gloss, rump and underparts darker brown showing less contrast with upperparts

N. t. griseiventris (E Ec, S Co, SE Ve, Su, FG) larger (13cm), longer tailed, upperparts paler brown with more gloss, rump and underparts paler greyish-brown thus showing more contrast with upperparts

Habits Diagnostic fast erratic bat-like flight when foraging low in pairs or small flocks, usually near water but sometimes low above canopy. Nests in natural but not in artificial cavities, e.g. tree holes, sandbanks.
Status Uncommon to locally fairly common, with some seasonal movements possible. More numerous west of Andes, and uncommon to rare and rather local in Venezuela.
Habitat Tropical Zone, to 1,600m but mostly below 1,000m, over humid tropical forests, along forested rivers, roads and forest edges, and in small forest gaps, clearings, second growth, gardens, and even in relatively open habitat around habitation.
Voice Calls include a thin, high-pitched *tsee-tit*, a *chit-it*, *chee-dee-dit?* (R&G), a soft trilled *pe'e'e'e'd* (Hilty) and constantly uttered soft *zeet-zeet* whilst foraging (T&R).
Note Race *minima* formerly was frequently spelled (incorrectly) *minimus* (David & Gosselin 2002).

Alopochelidon and *Stelgidopteryx* are medium-sized swallows, sandy brown above, white below, rather like large Bank Swallows, but lacking any band across chest. The rough-winged swallows are not easy to separate, but Tawny-headed Swallow, with its restricted distribution is usually easily eliminated. All have distinct calls.

TAWNY-HEADED SWALLOW

Alopochelidon fucata Pl. 231

Identification 12cm. Adult has brownish-black crown with tawny-rufous forehead, eyebrow and hindcrown, merging into cinnamon-buff ear-coverts, head-sides, throat and breast, which frame darker brownish lores; remaining upperparts grey-brown, with slightly paler rump just contrasting with dark brown, almost square tail, dark-brown wings, and rest of underparts dull white with pale grey-brown sides. Sexes alike. Juvenile has less rufous, buffier head and yellowish rather than rufous feather fringes, affording a paler and scalier appearance. Southern Rough-winged Swallow is larger and lacks rufous on head.

Ssp. Monotypic (N & SE Ve, E Co)

Habits Nests mainly in sandbanks beside rivers, ditches and other watercourses (rarely uses artificial sites), usually nesting and foraging in pairs or small flocks, flying low with frequent swoops.

Status Very local in Colombia and Venezuela, larger flocks (>100) in non-breeding season indicate some seasonal movements, and Colombian records exclusively relate to migrants.

Habitat Tropical to Lower Subtropical Zone, to 1,600m, over open and semi-open habitats, e.g. along streams, over grassland, marshes and ponds, and forest clearings.

Voice Calls include a soft trilled *treeeeb* in flight (Hilty).

Note Formerly placed in genus *Stelgidopteryx*.

NORTHERN ROUGH-WINGED SWALLOW

Stelgidopteryx serripennis Pl. 231

Identification 12.5–14.5cm. Adult grey-brown above, with darker lores, wings and square tail, and pale greyish-white below with throat buff in fresh plumage, becoming white on belly and vent. Sexes alike. Juvenile has 2 bright cinnamon wingbars and buffy throat. Flight pattern more rapid and direct, less twisting and turning than Bank Swallow, which is further distinguished by smaller size and brown breast-band.

Ssp. *S. s. ridgwayi / stuarti* (boreal migrants; winter normally in Yucatán Peninsula but seen regularly in West Indies, vagrants to ABC) *ridgwayi* is larger and darker above than *psammochrous*; *stuarti* very dark and has rufous-tinged throat

S. s. psammochrous (boreal migrant; winters Middle America to Panama, and apparently often seen in West Indies, could reach our Caribbean coast of our region) paler above and below, particularly on crown and rump

S. s. serripennis (boreal migrant from W USA, winters Central America to Panama, assumed record for Bonaire, possible Co and Ve) as described

S. s. fulvipennis (vagrant or migrant? from northern Central America, recorded Valle, Co) much duller than other races

Habits Perches and forages in small flocks, flying low above ground or water. Roosts in mangroves, marshes and sugarcane fields.

Status Vagrants may reach northern South America, as they winter regularly in Panama and the West Indies, and have been recorded in Aruba, Curaçao and Bonaire.

Habitat Tropical to Temperate Zone, to 2,500m, over open and semi-open habitats near water, e.g. grassland, wetlands, rocky gorges, exposed sand or gravel banks, road cuts, but may be seen anywhere on migration.

Voice Calls include a low, coarse *prriit*, song a steady repetition of rough, rising *frrip* notes (Sibley), chirps during chases and a harsh alarm-call (T&R).

Notes Wetmore *et al.* (1984) point out that the Panamanian race, *uropygialis*, is subject to much individual variation, tending towards more northern and duller Middle American race *fulvipennis*, with paler individuals found throughout range of *uropygialis*, leading to description of race *decolor*, which was rejected by Wetmore *et al.* It seems possible that the record of *S. serripennis fulvipennis* (Downing 2005) relates to the race *decolor* or duller variants of *uropygialis*. Ridgely & Gwynne speculate that *fulvipennis*, which they list as breeding in Panama and which appears to transit near the southern edges of its wintering range, could occur in Colombia; they do not mention *decolor*/*uropygialis*.

SOUTHERN ROUGH-WINGED SWALLOW

Stelgidopteryx ruficollis Pl. 231

Identification 13–13.5cm. Adult like Northern Rough-winged Swallow, but smaller with paler rump, distinctly cinnamon throat and yellowish belly. Sexes alike. Juvenile has duller throat and pale feather fringes to upperparts, giving it a paler, scalier appearance. Tawny-headed Swallow is smaller and has rufous head with dark crown, Bank Swallow smaller with a brown breast-band, White-thighed Swallow smaller and more uniformly dark below, and juvenile Blue-and-white Swallow has darker vent and more deeply forked tail.

Ssp. *S. r. ruficollis* (E Ec, SE Co, SE Ve, Guianas) darkest form, with underparts even darker than *uropygialis*, rump almost concolorous with upperparts

S. r. uropygialis (W & C Co, W Ec) contrasting whitish rump, cinnamon-rufous throat, yellowish belly

S. r. aequalis (N Co, Ve, Tr) tawny-buff throat, paler upperparts, rump and throat than *ruficollis*

Habits Nests in natural cavities, e.g. sandbanks, and perches and forages alone, in pairs or small flocks, flying low above ground or water somewhat erratically, but more in lines than in circles.

Status Generally common and widespread, with numbers usually largest near water. Restricted to areas with natural nest sites. More abundant west of Andes. Austral migrants from central South America have been recorded in Colombia and Suriname. Uncommon and local in French Guiana.
Habitat Tropical to Subtropical Zone, to 3,600m but usually below 1,000m, over open and semi-open habitats, e.g. savanna, forest clearings and areas of habitation.
Voice Calls include a rough buzzy upslurred *djreet* (R&T) or *sureee* (Hilty), twittering notes, and harsh buzzy calls during chases at nest sites (T&R).

BARN SWALLOW *Hirundo rustica* Pl. 231

Identification 14–18cm, depending on length of outer tail-feathers. Adult black above with steel blue gloss except rufous forehead, rufous throat separated from remaining cinnamon to pale buff underparts by narrow blue breast-band, deeply forked tail with diagnostic long outer tail-feathers in breeding adults. Sexes similar, but female whiter below and has shorter tail-feathers. Juvenile duller, with even shorter tail and often ill-defined (or almost lacks) breast-band, but retains rufous on head (albeit slightly paler than adult), distinguishing it from juvenile Black-collared Swallow, whilst juvenile Cave Swallow has very pale creamy-white throat and juvenile Cliff Swallow has grey-brown cheeks with grey-brown or greyish throat.

Ssp. *H. r. erythrogaster* (boreal migrant; winters in northern South America) as described

Habits Swift flight pattern with much banking and turning, foraging usually relatively low over ground or water.
Status Locally fairly to very common throughout northern South America (August–May), seen singly, in pairs, small or even very large flocks. Most common boreal migrant swallow, with large roosting concentrations observed, e.g. around sugarcane fields.
Habitat Tropical to Temperate Zone, to 3,700m on migration but usually below 1,000m, in open and semi-open habitats, e.g. wetlands, grassland, farmland and around habitation, and often near water, but may be seen anywhere on migration.
Voice Calls include a chirping contact, a screeching *witt tititititi* threat, several alarm-calls, e.g. *chir-chir*, *tsi-wit*, and muffled *dewihlik* (T&R). Song is a melodious twittering mixed with a grating rattle (T&R), but usually silent on wintering grounds except a soft rising *tweet* (Hilty).

The two *Petrochelidon* swallows are large martin-like birds with combination coloration above and below. They occur at considerable heights on migration, but wintering birds are usually found in lowlands.

CLIFF SWALLOW
Petrochelidon pyrrhonota Pl. 231

Identification 13–15cm. Adult has buffy-white forehead, crown and mantle black with blue gloss, separated by pale greyish collar, pale cinnamon rump, blackish wings and tail, rufous cheeks separated by black central throat stripe, rest of underparts pale greyish with faint cinnamon tinge to upper breast; broad wings and square tail (used for more soaring flight than other swallows). Sexes alike. Juvenile much duller without blue gloss, grey-brown cheeks, grey-brown or greyish throat, and lacks distinctive pale forehead and dark throat stripe. Juveniles collected in Venezuela showed pale buffy rump and uppertail-coverts clearly, in contrast to rufous rump of juvenile Cave Swallow. Cave Swallow has much paler cheeks and throat (except Mexican race *pallida* and Greater Antillean race *fulva* which may have similarly coloured cheeks and throat) and lacks dark throat stripe. Barn Swallow has forked tail and lacks pale rump.

Ssp. *P. p. pyrrhonota* and *melanogaster* (boreal migrants; transits northern South America) *melanogaster* smaller than *pyrrhonota*, *melanogaster* has deep cinnamon forehead and rump

P. p. tachina and *hypopolia* (boreal migrants; winter range unknown) *tachina* is smaller and *hypopolia* larger than *pyrrhonota*, *tachina* has cinnamon forehead, *hypopolia* larger, whiter frontal band, white breast, greyer flanks and pectoral region, paler rump and more rufescent underparts than *pyrrhonota*

Status Locally common in western part of northern South America (August–October, March–April), generally a passage migrant through northern South America, traveling south August to October, returning northwards February to April, with a few birds over-wintering in Ecuador seen in singles, pairs, small or often quite large flocks, especially during migration, e.g. at mountain passes. Rare in Suriname and French Guiana, among flocks of Barn Swallows in fall migration.
Habitat Tropical to Temperate Zone, to 4,000m on migration but usually much lower, in open and semi-open habitats, e.g. wetlands, grassland, farmland, forest clearings and habitation, especially near water, but may be seen anywhere on migration.
Voice Calls include a *chur* in contact, a plaintive *purr* alarm-call and *squeak* indicating food (T&R). Song is a rapid, squeaky twittering (Turner 2004, T&R).
Notes The various races show much intergradation, forming more of a cline from north to south than in typically distinct races. Sometimes placed in genus *Hirundo*, but DNA studies support retention of *Petrochelidon*.

CHESTNUT-COLLARED SWALLOW
Petrochelidon rufocollaris Pl. 231

Identification 12cm. Adult has narrow rufous forehead and hindcrown and broad rufous rump, remaining upperparts black with blue gloss and grey streaks on back, broad black wings and shallow-forked tail tail, white underparts (including cheeks and throat) except for rufous breast band and sides joining rufous hindcrown. Sexes alike. Juvenile is much duller, with dull rufous forehead, and very pale creamy-white throat, sometimes with dusky spots. Cliff Swallow has dark rufous cheeks and throat, greyish collar and usually a pale forehead. Cave Swallow has rufous cheeks and throat.

SSp. *P. r. aequatorialis* (SW Ec) as described

Habits Nests colonially in cliffs or eaves of buildings. Usually forages low over ground or water in small to large flocks.
Status Uncommon to locally common in southwest Ecuador (*aequatorialis*), dispersing after breeding season and then sometimes gathering in very large flocks.
Habitat Tropical to Subtropical Zone, up to 2,100m, in agricultural, human-inhabitated and other open and semi-open habitats.
Voice Calls include a gravelly *chrrt* often given in flight (R&G).
Note Sometimes placed in the genus *Hirundo*.

CAVE SWALLOW
Petrochelidon fulva Pl. 231

Identification 13-14cm. Adult has broad rufous forehead, narrow rufous hindcrown and rufous rump, remaining upperparts black with blue gloss and grey streaks on back, broad black wings and shallow-forked tail; cheeks and throat buffy-rufous, rest of underparts white except for vestigial pale rufous and grey breast band and sides joining rufous hindcrown. Sexes alike. Juvenile is much duller, with dull whitish forehead, and very pale creamy-white throat, sometimes with dusky spots. Cliff Swallow has dark rufous cheeks and throat, greyish collar and usually a pale forehead. Chestnut-collared Swallow has white cheeks and throat.

SSp. *P. f. pallida* (boreal vagrant to ABC) as described
P. f. cavicola (hypothetical vagrant from Caribbean to ABC and possibly T&T) smaller and much darker than *pallida* with deeper blue crown, rufous cheeks and throat, and dark rufous rump

Habits Forages in open areas, often near cliffs and in ravines.
Status Rare vagrant to southern Caribbean. North and Central American races of Cave Swallow may occur anywhere in northern South America during migration, but only substantiated record so far is one specimen of *pallida* taken on Curaçao in 1952.
Habitat Tropical Zone, up to 1,500m, in open areas, often near water.
Voice Calls *che*, *weet*, or *cheweet*. Song initially some squeaks, then a warble and some two-tone notes (Turner 2004).
Note Sometimes placed in the genus *Hirundo*.

TROGLODYTIDAE – Wrens

Wrens range in size from quite small to the size of a thrush. Males and females are the same, with virtually no differences between the sexes, whilst juveniles are usually only minimally different, except a few *Thryothorus* and *Campylorhynchus* species that differ significantly. Many studies of wrens have focused on vocalisations and dialects in recent years, for some species possess amazing vocabularies, consisting of dozens or even hundreds of phrases and songs. All respond well to playback. Some of the Neotropical forest species, such as those in the genera *Cyphorhinus*, *Microcerculus* and *Thryothorus* have hauntingly beautiful songs. Pairs sing antiphonal duets, filling the forest with their glorious music. Those species in the genus *Cistothorus* have incredibly large repertoires, and studies have found that migratory populations acquire songs from local ones, or, in other words, they travel and learn languages! They have been studied in particular depth by Don Kroodsma and his research team (1985). Wrens inhabit bushes, hedgerows, thorn scrub, gardens and house roofs (especially the eaves), forest undergrowth, rocky, shrubby terrain, even stonewalls and rock faces. Foraging is busy with much systematic checking of appropriate nooks and crannies or amidst the foliage, all done apace. Nests are quite varied; some simple and others quite complex in respect of their construction and materials, but most are domed or covered. Many species also build roost nests, which they take advantage of year-round. As for their classification, the Troglodytidae were traditionally placed near nuthatches (Sittidae), creepers (Certhiidae), mockingbirds (Mimidae) and dippers (Cinclidae), (Sibley & Ahlquist 1990, Sheldon & Gill 1996, Barker *et al.* 2004, Voelker & Spellman 2004), recent genetic studies however, suggest close relationships to gnatcatchers and gnatwrens (Polioptilidae), followed by creepers and nuthatches. The introduction of the Donacobius into the family (following Wetmore *et al.* 1984 and Kiltie & Fitzpatrick 1984), was rejected by Barker (2004), whose genetic data supported monophyly of the Troglodytidae, once that very controversial genus was removed. Barker's data also pointed to a sister relationship between Troglodytidae and Polioptilidae, which proposal has recently approved by the SACC, and suggested that two genera, *Microcerculus* and *Odontorchilus*, are the origin of all the others that occur in South America.

Additional references for this family include Brewer & MacKay (2001), hereafter B&M, and Kroodsma amd Brewer (2005) here as K&B..

Campylorhynchus wrens are the largest of the family, more like mimids in shape, but thoroughly wren-like in behaviour, keeping discretely within cover, but with loud vocalisations that immediately draw attention to their presence. They are social and breeding pairs are often assisted by youngsters from an earlier brood.

BICOLOURED WREN
Campylorhynchus griseus Pl. 232

Identification 20–22cm. Large size combined with dark upperparts, long white-tipped tail, faint shadow-barring on tail-coverts and tail, black eyestripe and long bold eyebrow, and white underparts make adult unmistakable. Eyes orange to brown, long and slightly decurved bill is blackish-grey above, variable below according to race, legs and feet grey to black depending on race. Juvenile much paler with buffy tips to feathers of head and pale greyish-buffy underparts.

Ssp. *C. g. albicilius* (N Co, NW Ve) mantle and wings fuscous to black, with deep rufous fringes to feathers, lower back, rump and tail also deep rufous; creamy white below, whiter on sides and flanks, dull buffy vent and undertail-coverts, thighs banded black and sepia;

faint shadow-barring on tail-coverts and tail; bill all blackish, legs and feet dark grey

C. g. bicolor (C Co) similar to *albicilius* but has colder and slightly darker brown fringes to feathers above, pure white eyebrow and underparts to flanks, vent to undertail-coverts buffy, thighs banded black and buffy; bill grey, legs and feet dark grey

C. g. griseus (S & SE Ve, Gu) raw umber above with some dusky barring on tertials and secondaries, uppertail-coverts and tail, much fainter and barely noticeable barring on wing-coverts, whitish-buffy underparts, including undertail-coverts and thighs; eyes pale reddish-brown, bill blackish above, pale bluish-grey below, legs and feet grey

C. g. minor (CE Co, N Ve) smaller than nominate, lower back tawny with faint dusky barring on wings and tail-coverts; underparts pure white, only slightly greyish-buffy undertail-coverts, thighs whitish with dusky barring; barred wings, tail-coverts and tail; eyes dark, bill dark grey with flesh-coloured base to mandible, legs and feet blackish

C. g. pallidus (Ve: NE Amazonas) dark drab grey above with rather pale, somewhat vestigial, dusky grey barring from nape to tail; underparts uniform white, eyes orange-brown, bill blackish above with flesh-coloured mandible, legs and feet bluish-grey

C. g. zimmeri (Co: Huila and Tolima) markedly less rufescent and darker than *albicilius*, reduced cinnamon in wings; cinnamon outer fringes to tail; short deep bill with olive-buff base

Habits Noisy and conspicuous as it forages for invertebrates and fruit in vegetation, especially palms, on ground with tail characteristically held high. Often breeds cooperatively.
Status Fairly common to common.
Habitat Tropical to Subtropical Zones, to 2,100m, in arid to semi-humid habitats with scattered vegetation, e.g. cactus-dominated scrub, semi-open dry woodland or seasonally flooded savanna woodland, but also disturbed habitats, e.g. coffee plantations, farmland and gardens with large trees.
Voice Calls include various harsh, grating or scolding notes, e.g. *rud*, *awk-chook* or *ook-a-chuk*. Song a series of loud gurgling or grating notes, 2–5 in each phrase, e.g. *oh-chook-acha-chak*. Birds sing alone, in duet or as a chorus of 3+ birds (H&B, B&M, Hilty).Marked geographical variation in song type (K&B).

THRUSH-LIKE WREN
Campylorhynchus turdinus Pl. 232

Identification 20–20.5cm. Large. Adult dark drab from forehead to lower back, plus lesser wing-coverts, each feather with a dusky to blackish centre; rather chestnut on wings and tail, with bold blackish barring on wings, rump to tail; narrow, pale grey eyebrow, black lores, ear-coverts as back; from chin to sides and belly dull white with rows of spots almost forming continual streaks, lower belly and flanks to undertail-coverts pale buffy to cinnamon, with darker spots forming bars. Eyes pale brown to ochraceous, bill yellow with dusky culmen, legs and feet greenish-grey. Juvenile duller, with reduced spots below. Not very thrush-like but perhaps most likely to be mistaken for a juvenile thrush, e.g. Pale-breasted.

Ssp. *C. t. aenigmaticus* (SW Co) russet above, unbarred, paler and slightly greyish on head, forehead, eyebrow and ear-coverts drab; chin to belly dull white, narrowly washed pale russet on sides, broadly on flanks and from vent to undertail-coverts, dusky spots on sides gradually become bars on flanks and fully barred over rest of russet underparts

C. t. hypostictus (E Ec, E Co) as described

Habits Not wary as it forages, usually in pairs or small flocks, in dense vegetation of vines and epiphytes in higher parts of trees, where quite hard to see. Very vocal, suddenly and explosively bursting into duets. Sings from prominent perches, e.g. treetops and wires. Rarely joins mixed-species flocks.
Status Fairly common to common.
Habitat Tropical Zone, to 1,300m, in *várzea* and *terra firme* forest, edges, second growth and clearings.
Voice Calls include a loud rough, scolding *jiff*. Song a distinctive series of very loud cheerful chortling notes, e.g. *chew-yoo-choop, chew-yu-yu-yu-chup…*, often repeated and often the sexes duet. (B&M). A very loud, rhythmic, staccato duet, *chooka-cookcook, chooka-cookcook…* resembling an oropendola (H&B). Phrases complex and variable, *chookedadoh, choh, choh or choh-do-do-dit*, often repeated several times (R&T), and markedly more musical than other *Campylorhynchus* in Ecuador (R&G). Both sexes sing.
Notes Race *aenigmaticus* described as a race of Thrush-like Wren by Meyer de Schauensee (1948) who, in view of variation among individuals, expressed view it was possibly an intermediate between White-headed and Thrush-like Wrens. Subsequently considered a White-headed Wren × Band-backed Wren hybrid (Haffer 1967, 1975). R&T agreed with Haffer, and further suggested that Thrush-like and White-headed Wrens are conspecific. Clearly, there is an opportunity for further investigation, in the absence of which we follow Dickinson (2003) in maintaining the original taxonomy.

WHITE-HEADED WREN
Campylorhynchus albobrunneus Pl. 232

Identification 18.5–19cm. Adult unmistakable. Deep olive-brown back and wings to tail, head white, underparts white with slight buffy wash and vestigial barring on undertail-coverts. Eyes orange-brown, bill dark with lower mandible horn-coloured, legs and feet slightly olivaceous-grey. Juvenile drab to grey-brown on rear crown, darkening on nape to join back, front of face white, to sides and breast, belly buffy, washed warm drab and barred like adult over vent to undertail-coverts. Some show faint barring on nape and mantle.

Ssp. *C. a. harterti* (W Co)

Habits Forages in pairs or more often in small flocks, in dense vegetation of vines and epiphytes, from midstorey to canopy, rarely to ground, tail held high and swung sideways. Rarely joins mixed-species flocks.

Status Uncommon and local.
Habitat Tropical Zone, to 1,500m but mostly below 1,000m, in humid forest and edges with lots of epiphytes, also adjacent second-growth and clearings.
Voice Calls a very harsh scratchy *kahk* (B&M) and oft-repeated *cawk* (H&B). Song a guttural scraping, e.g. *too-da-dick, tadick*, often repeated, by individual or pair; sexes often duet (H&B).
Note See comments on taxon *aenigmaticus* of Thrush-like Wren, listed as subspecies of White-headed Wren in B&M.

BAND-BACKED WREN

Campylorhynchus zonatus Pl. 232

Identification 18.5–20.5cm. Adult boldly patterned above with black and white bands on back and wings to tail, top of head to nape and neck-sides pale cinnamon-brown with dark spots or streaks, broad white eyebrow, dark line through eye and pale eye-ring, ear-coverts washed pale cinnamon and streaked blackish; chin to breast and sides white with black crescentic spots from neck- to body-sides, belly and rest of underparts pale cinnamon, the black crescents becoming bars, thighs pale cinnamon, perhaps with black spots; eyes brown, bill slightly shorter than other *Campylorhynchus*, blackish above and pale horn below, legs and feet grey. Juvenile cinnamon above streaked and spotted dusky, forming bars on wings and tail, but rump and uppertail-coverts comparatively unspotted; top of head heavily fringed black, less prominent eyebrow than adult, dark line through eye and pale eye-ring, underparts unmarked white to flanks, undertail-coverts washed buffy; eyes brown, bill horn, legs and feet horn. Fasciated Wren has no cinnamon in its plumage, neither does Thrush-like Wren, which has uniform dark back, and both are parapatric. Noisy Stripe-backed Wren has longitudinal stripes on back and pale eyes.

Ssp. *C. z. brevirostris* (NW Ec, N Co) as described
C. z. curvirostris (Santa Marta in Co) slightly smaller, white bars above slightly narrower and only on back and upper wings, barring becoming cinnamon and black, narrower eyebrow; below, spots start on throat, are heavier and more 'teardrop' shaped than crescentic, distal underparts more heavily barred dusky and cinnamon to rufous

Habits Conspicuous, usually in flocks of up to 12, foraging from ground to canopy, very often in dense vines, epiphytes and especially palm fronds. Searches for invertebrates, turning leaf-litter, prising bark and probing epiphytes. Sometimes joins mixed-species flocks. Usually roosts in communal nests high up in trees, and breeds cooperatively.
Status Uncommon to locally fairly common.
Habitat Tropical to Lower Subtropical Zones, to 1,600m, in dry but mostly humid forest and edges, also adjacent second growth and clearings with tall trees, in northern Ecuador also around habitation.
Voice Calls include a churring note, uttered incessantly in flocks, also several *chak* calls. Song a jumbled series of harsh scratchy rapid notes in phrases lasting 2–3 s, e.g. *zwit-took-to-zueer*, often repeated, and sexes often duet (H&B, B&M, R&G).

STRIPE-BACKED WREN

Campylorhynchus nuchalis Pl. 232

Identification 17.5–18cm. Adult is striped (i.e. longitudinal lines) black and white on back, barred black and white on wings with whitish spots on outer edges of otherwise black rectrices. Top of head brown with black spots/streaks, broad eyebrow; warm, creamy white below with sparse black spots; eyes pale yellow, long and slightly decurved bill dark above, paler below, legs and feet dark grey. Juvenile dark brown, streaked crown appearing virtually black, patterned above like adult but dusky and pale buffy instead of black and white; pale buffy underparts with narrow, vestigial barring; pale eyes as adult, bill horn with dark culmen, legs and feet olive-grey. Fasciated and Stripe-backed Wrens geographically well separated. Band-backed Wren has lateral bands on back and cinnamon and black bands on distal underparts.

Ssp. *C. n. brevipennis* (N Ve) distal half of tertials all black; sparsely and erratically spotted below, but distinct bars on lower body-sides, flanks and undertail-coverts
C. n. nuchalis (W, C & S Co) pale fringes to tips of tertials; almost pinkish-buff below with erratic blackish spots all over, tending to bars on flanks, thighs barred brown or creamy white and black
C. n. pardus (N & C Co) pale drab brown head with whitish eyebrow, only sparsely spotted on crown, short row of blackish spots on malar and a few random spots on underparts and thighs

Habits Noisy and conspicuous as it forages in small to large flocks at all levels for invertebrates, even on trunks, breeds cooperatively with up to 14 individuals in such groupings.
Status Fairly common to very common.
Habitat Lower Tropical Zone, to 800m, usually in dry to semi-humid habitats (drier than Band-backed Wren above), but sometimes in very wet habitats with scattered bushes, trees and open woodland, and forest, including gallery forests, agricultural areas, parks and gardens, and around ponds and small lakes.
Voice Calls include loud, harsh, guttural and chucking notes, e.g. a sharp *klip* uttered when foraging. Song a series of hollow scratchy notes, e.g. *zhewit-here* or *arrowak-gero-kick*. Birds sing in duet or as a chorus (H&B, B&M, Hilty).

FASCIATED WREN

Campylorhynchus fasciatus Pl. 232

Identification 19cm. From head to lower back evenly striped deep grey and pale grey, extending also across wings and rump, to tail, where bars are heavy and broad; face- and neck-sides striped, top of head washed mid grey with rows of dark grey spots; underparts have rows of spots from throat to breast where they increasingly become bars, dark grey bars being broader than pale grey ones. Eyes yellow to pale orange, longish, slightly decurved bill dark grey with pale base, legs and feet greenish-yellow. Juvenile very similar, with a darker cap but slightly duller barring above and paler markings below, tending to larger and more continual rows of spots; eyes dark brown, bill dark horn with a dusky tip. Adult should be unmistakable in its range, as somewhat similar Band-backed Wren is distinctly rufous-buffy on top of head and distal underparts, and is spotted and barred with black.

Ssp. *C. f. pallescens* (SW Ec)

Habits Noisy and conspicuous as it forages in pairs or flocks in bushy vegetation and on ground with raised tails, often around habitation, for invertebrates, fruits and seeds.

Status Fairly common to very common.

Habitat Tropical to Subtropical Zones, to 2,500m but usually below 1,500m, in arid and semi-arid habitats with bushy vegetation, e.g. thorn scrub, second growth and gallery forests, shrubby, thorny or *Bombax*-dominated deciduous woodland, crops and pastures with hedgerows and scattered vegetation, orchards and gardens.

Voice Calls include a sharp *churr* and other harsh notes. Song a series of short harsh *churr* notes, repeated many times, often interspersed with gurgling notes, and often the sexes duet (B&M, K&B).

GREY-MANTLED WREN

Odontorchilus branickii Pl. 233

Identification 12–13cm. Very distinctive little wren, gnatcatcher-like with its long tail. Soft French grey above, washed pale cinnamon on forehead to crown, finely striped darker grey on nape, and grey and white on head-sides, wings slightly darker grey, tail evenly barred faint, slightly diffuse darker grey, including on white outermost rectrices, central feathers unbarred; underparts white, washed pale buffy on breast with soft grey streaks on flanks, undertail-coverts barred black and white. Eyes pale brown to orange-brown, bill, legs and feet grey, Juvenile has throat and breast finely streaked dark grey and lower breast to belly washed noticeably more warmly than adult, more buffy on breast and duller brown forehead; eyes darker brown. Distinctive long barred tail is constantly twitched and cocked, lending superficial resemblance to *Polioptila* gnatcatchers (see also *Xenerpestes* greytails).

Ssp. *O. b. branickii* (E Ec, S Co) tail barred dark grey, including central feathers, and underparts decidedly paler (undertail-coverts black and white)

O. b. minor (NW Ec) as described

Habits Forages alone or in pairs in subcanopy and canopy for invertebrates, mostly along larger branches, searching lichens, mosses and epiphytes, but not in terminal foliage. Often joins mixed-species canopy flocks.

Status Rare to uncommon and local (perhaps under-recorded), fairly common in north-west Ecuador).

Habitat Tropical to Subtropical Zones, 100–2,400m, in humid to wet forests and edges.

Voice Generally fairly quiet, but calls include a high, often-repeated *si* when foraging. Song a weak high rapid, even-pitched metallic trill (B&M), also *swe-swe-swe-swe-swe*… (R&G).

RUFOUS WREN

Cinnycerthia unirufa Pl. 233

Identification 16.5–18cm. Adult bright rufous-brown with subtle black barring on wings and fainter barring on tail; eyes brown, bill dark grey, legs and feet dark grey. Juvenile almost identical but overall slightly paler, lacks black lores, sometimes has whitish flush to forehead, base of malar and throat; eyes brown, bill yellow with dark culmen, legs and feet brownish-grey. Adult similar to Sharpe's Wren but usually much paler and more rufous with far less noticeable barring, but habits similar, though Sharpe's usually travels only in pairs or small groups. Rufous Wren travels in bands that may number 20+. In Ecuador, Sharpe's (*olivaceus*) is paler than Rufous (*unibrunnea*) and they do not overlap, with Rufous Wren at higher elevations. In Colombia, north of Caldas, where they are near, they are closer in coloration, but Sharpe's is clearly heavily barred whilst barring on Rufous Wren is hardly noticeable, and presumably the elevational difference holds good.

Ssp. *C. u. chakei* (Perijá in Co, Ve) richer, more reddish-rufous than *unirufa*, softer and more subtle barring, pale eyes (usually pale ochre, but varies to pale grey), legs and feet very dark grey

C. u. unibrunnea (Ec, Co) deep umber-rufous with dusky barring on wings and tail, eyes brown, legs plumbeous

C. u. unirufa (C & N Co, Ve) as described

Habits Not wary and often curious as it forages in large flocks in dense undergrowth near or on ground for invertebrates, joins mixed-species flocks.

Status Uncommon to locally common in suitable habitat.

Habitat Subtropical Zone to Páramo, 1,800–3,800m but usually above 2,200m, in dense humid to wet cloud and mossy forests and edges, most numerous in *Chusquea* bamboo stands, and even in shrubbery slightly above timberline.

Voice Calls include a soft *churr*, short *whit-whit*, sharp *tsip* or *tsap*, and loud harsh *geeea* and *jeer* mobbing calls. Song is typically a startling duet, consisting of rapidly repeated notes, e.g. *chew-tu, chew-tu, whoo-hee…, ee-o, t-e-e-e-e-e-e-e-e-e-e, wuh-todaly-todaly-todaly-woo* or *wuu-tweedie, wuu-tweedie, wuu-weedie-weedie-weedie*, overlaid with a loud metallic trill and accompanied by other group members' *whit* and *whort* calls (H&B, R&T, B&M, Hilty), the whole lasting about 10 s, other members of group sometimes joining in (K&B).

SHARPE'S WREN

Cinnycerthia olivascens Pl. 233

Identification 16cm. Adult deep rufescent brown with solid, fine and even-width black barring, slightly paler and more rufous on face and breast, and some have whitish foreheads, base of malar and chin/throat; eyes brown, bill deep dusky, legs and feet pale grey. Juvenile similar but has a small greyish postocular patch. Adult similar to Rufous Wren but much blacker and more noticeable barring, and usually travels only in pairs or small groups. In Ecuador, Sharpe's (*olivaceus*) is paler than Rufous (*unibrunnea*) and they do not overlap, with Rufous Wren at higher elevations. In Colombia, north of

Caldas where they come close, they are closer in coloration, but Sharpe's is clearly heavily barred whilst barring on Rufous Wren is barely noticeable.

Ssp. *C. o. bogotensis* (E Andes in Co) much darker than *olivascens*, slightly paler around face, but never has whitish on forehead and or chin/throat of latter
C. o. olivascens (Ec, W & C Andes in Co) as described

Habits Much as previous species, but habitually forms smaller flocks.
Status Uncommon to locally fairly common in suitable habitat.
Habitat Upper Tropical Zone to Páramo, 900–3,100m but usually 1,500–2,500m, in wet cloud and mossy forests and edges, also second growth, often in *Chusquea* bamboo.
Voice Calls include a sharp *zit* or *zee*, wheezy excited *tziee*, alarmed *treek*, chattering *trrr-trrr-tjk-trrr*..., and low, soft *wurt* when foraging. Song a series of rich melodious variable phrases and trills, e.g. *bububububububu, qua-keep, qua-keep, qua-keep, wa-teer-cup, tutututututu*... (H&B, F&K, R&G).
Notes Formerly called Sepia-brown Wren *C. peruana*. Forms superspecies with Peruvian Wren *C. peruana* and Fulvous Wren *C. fulva* of Peru and Bolivia (Brumfield & Remsen 1996).

SEDGE WREN

Cistothorus platensis Pl. 234

Identification 9–11.5cm Tiny, striped wren with frequently cocked tail. Somewhat rufescent brown above, evenly barred blackish on wings and tail, lower rump and uppertail-coverts, white lines on back, cutting across black markings that may be bar-like or streaks, top of head uniform brown, denser than on back and less rufescent, gentle eyebrow, pale buffy creamy white below, washed darker buffy on flanks, becoming dense cinnamon-buffy on undertail-coverts; eyes dark brown, bill horn with dark tip, legs and feet flesh. Juvenile has barring narrower, and thus more bars on wings and tail, but unbarred rump, head paler brown with small pale streaks; bill yellow with dark tip. Similar Apolinar's Marsh Wren occurs in different habitat and is larger with uniform olive-brown (not faintly streaked brown) crown, grey (not faint buffy) supercilium, stronger tail barring and dull buffy (not cinnamon-buffy) flanks. Similar Páramo Wren has strongly (not faintly) streaked crown, pronounced white (not faint buffy) supercilium, barred rump, and stronger flank, wing and tail barring. See also slightly larger House Wren which has no stripes on back and streaked *Asthenes* canasteros.

Ssp. *C. p. aequatorialis* (Ec, SW Co) similar to *alticola* but longer wings and legs, bright buffy lores, broad buffy supercilium, heavier bars on rectrices
C. p. alticola (Co: Santa Marta, N & SE Ve, E Gu) as described; very short supercilium
C. p. tamae (CE Co, Táchira in Ve) narrow dark streaks on crown, more rufous above and more cinnamon below, with pale throat and belly
C. p. tolimae (C Co) pale streaks on forehead, whitish throat to central belly

Habits Forages alone or in pairs, mostly in wet grass, bulrushes, sedges and bushy tangles close to ground, for invertebrates and some seeds. Usually breeds in loose colonies.
Status Very local but fairly common to common in suitable habitat.
Habitat Tropical Zone to Páramo, to 4,500m and usually above 2,800m in Ecuador, 2,400m in Colombia and 900m in Venezuela, in humid to wet grassy and sedge areas with scattered bushes, also in clearings and agricultural areas in Ecuador with tall rushes and grasses, partially flooded *Alnus* forest, mossy bogs in elfin forest and *Chusquea* bamboo bogs in páramos.
Voice Calls include a nasal oft-repeated *meur* or *tchew* and an alarmed *rrreh-rrreh*. Songs vary individually, and pairs frequently duet, a complex series of clucking notes, churrs, rattles and buzzes, typically beginning with an insect-like buzz and ending in a trill, e.g. *cheh, cheh, cheh, ti-ti-ti, prrr-titititi*... (*tamae*) or *tu-tu-tu-tu, tee-tee-tee, ter-ter-ter, tsee-ee-ee-ee*.... Often sings from exposed perch (H&B, F&K, R&G, Hilty). Songs often contain imitations; successive songs usually different. Females do not sing (K&B).
Note Also called Grass Wren or (Short-billed) Marsh Wren.

APOLINAR'S MARSH WREN

Cistothorus apolinari Pl. 234

Identification 12–13 cm. Bright rufous-brown above, back streaked blackish and white, wings barred evenly black, tail bars broad and well spaced on central rectrices, but narrower on outer feathers. Juvenile has bluish-grey head, no supercilium, buff lower nape and less streaked back. See similar Sedge Wren.

Ssp. *C. a. apolinari* (Boyacá and Cundinamarca, E Andes in C Co)
C. a. hernandezi (Sumapaz massif, C Co) significantly longer bill, wing and tarsus, but shorter tail; whiter below with no buff, and generally paler below

Habits Retiring as it forages in pairs or small flocks by gleaning invertebrates from vegetation, principally reeds, near water level; often breeds in loose colonies. Race *hernandezi* occurs in small groups that defend small territories
Status Endangered. Endemic to Colombia with very small range and population just a few thousand individuals; declining rapidly due to degradation and loss of its severely fragmented habitat. Current strongholds are Laguna de Tota (Boyacá), Laguna de Fúquene (Cundinamarca), and several remnant wetlands around Bogotá, e.g. Parque La Florida near the international airport.
Habitat Subtropical Zone to Páramo, 1,800–4,000m but usually above 2,500 m, in tall, dense, emergent vegetation fringing marshes, lagoons and lakes (mostly reedbeds with *Typha* cattails and *Scirpus* bulrushes). Recently discovered race *hernandezi* inhabits swampy páramo at 3,800–3,900m, and is dependent on *Chusquea tessellata* for nest sites.
Voice Calls include a scolding low *churr* and harsh grating *chahh-chahh*. Song a short series of bubbling low-pitched *toe-a-twée* interspersed with short *churr* notes, or a rapidly

repeated sequence of 6–7 harsh *churr* notes, usually starting with a low note and then alternating up and down. Often sings from exposed perches (H&B, B&M). Race *hernandezi* vocalisations described in detail (Stiles & Caycedo 2002), female song different, given more frequently, and groups sing in duet and chorus. Apparently, there are 11 distinct forms of song – more than race *apolinari* which has 6–7.
Notes Cadena (2003) questioned whether *hernandezi* might be better regarded specifically. Also called Apolinar's Wren.

PÁRAMO WREN

Cistothorus meridae Pl. 234

Identification 10cm. Tiny striped wren with frequently cocked tail. Adult rich brown from forehead to tip of tail, with bold white lines diminishing and terminating on rump, face-sides, including bold supercilium, neck-sides as back but with bold white dots instead of lines; lower cheeks and ear-coverts greyish-buffy, continuing to body-sides, flanks and undertail-coverts, throat, centre of breast and belly whitish, closely and evenly, but very faintly, barred black on flanks. Eyes, bill, legs and feet brown. Juvenile slightly paler brown, heavily streaked black on head and nape, only a few narrow white lines on mantle, rump unmarked, eyebrow short and rufescent buffy; bill dusky above, flesh below, legs and feet flesh. Immature like juvenile but has all-dark bill. Similar Sedge Wren (race *tamae*) is much richer rufescent, especially underparts, eyebrow similar colour and streaks on back pale buffy, not white. Mountain Wren is unmarked on the back and has much longer tail.

Ssp. Monotypic (Ve: Mérida, Táchira & Trujillo)

Habits Not especially wary as it actively forages near ground for invertebrates. Usually flies low and apparently weakly, and not far. Usually in pairs and easily overlooked, unless singing. Very territorial, and responds well to playback.
Status Endemic to Venezuela. Fairly common in suitable habitat but somewhat local, e.g. at Laguna Mucubají or Pico de Aguila near Mérida city.
Habitat Páramo, 3,000–4,100m, in damp and boggy habitats with mix of dense grasses, mosses, bromeliads and bushes, and also in mossy low open forest and wheat fields.
Voice Calls consist mostly of churrs and buzzing scolds, and a high *jeet*. 20-25 different songs, varying both individually and geographically (K&B). Songs vary individually, often a series of high, clear, trilling notes interspersed with harsh buzzy scolds, e.g. *ts-ts-tseee-ts-tseeeu* or *tseee-teeeeu-tee-ee-ee-ee-ee*, may be in duet with female simply uttering simple dry rattles. Often sings from exposed perches (R&T, B&M, Hilty).
Note Also called Mérida Wren.

Wrens of the genus *Thryothorus* are distinguished mainly by the presence and structure of their vocal duets. A recent paper by Mann *et al.* (2006) presents a compelling hypothesis based on a comprehensive DNA analysis of all but four species of the genus, that reduces *Thryothorus* to a monotypic genus. All but the type species are placed in three genera, *Thryophilus*, and two newly-resurrected, *Phengopedius* and *Cantorchilus*. We properly retain the current use of *Thryothorus* here, but indicate where possible, the likely future change of name.

SOOTY-HEADED WREN

Thryothorus spadix Pl. 238

Identification 14.5–15cm. Adult rich reddish-brown above, completely unmarked except tail which is strongly barred black, head dark grey with a barely discernable black mask, pure white supraloral spot, white eyebrow that breaks up in white streaks to nape-sides, narrow white crescent below eye, a few white lines over ear-coverts, and a short, possibly broken white line at base of malar; breast and sides bright chestnut, becoming sepia-brown on flanks and thighs, belly to undertail-coverts grey with irregular black spots on belly that become regular black bars on undertail-coverts; eyes dark brown, bill, legs and feet grey. Juvenile equally distinct in being adult-like but lacks black mask and white marks, instead having hood dark grey, breast, sides and flanks sepia-brown, belly to undertail-coverts grey as head. Adult unmistakable with diagnostic black head and throat, chestnut breast and unbarred wings.

Ssp. *T. s. spadix* (W Andes in NW & C Co)

Habits Forages in pairs close to ground in dense undergrowth for invertebrates, probing dead leaves. Also follows army ants.
Status Uncommon to locally common. Possibly occurs but not reported from extreme north-west Ecuador.
Habitat Tropical to Lower Subtropical Zones, 400–1,800m but usually above 800m, in humid and cloud forests with much mossy growth, also edges, overgrown clearings and mature second growth.
Voice Calls include a sad *tee-dooo* or *chur-doo, chur-daw*, the second and fourth notes lower. Song a loud series of *c.*12 clear gurgling whistles, with one motif often repeated; apparently the sexes duet (H&B, B&M). Series of *c.*6 gurgling whistles with one phrase frequently repeated (K&B).
Note Formerly considered a subspecies of Black-throated Wren (Wetmore *et al.* 1984).

BLACK-BELLIED WREN

Thryothorus fasciatoventris Pl. 238

Identification 15cm. Adult is chestnut from forehead to tip of tail, barred closely and finely dusky on wings, and more broadly and evenly black on tail; black mask with slightly irregular white supercilium, eye-ring and lines over ear-coverts; chin and malar to breast pure white, lower breast to undertail-coverts flushed chestnut on fore sides, washed chestnut from lower flanks to undertail-coverts, the whole evenly barred black, the black bars broader than underlying colour. Juvenile essentially a dull version of adult, mask grey (not black), white facial marks pale grey with only a touch of white on eyebrow, throat warm greyish-white, underparts sepia with fine shadow-barring from breast to undertail-coverts. Soft parts as adult but base of bill horn.

Ssp. *T. f. albigularis* (W Co: Chocó) similar to nominate but slightly richer and redder above, much denser coloration below, appearing almost black with paler barring on flanks

T. f. fasciatoventris (N Co) as described

Habits A skulker, usually solitary, very retiring and wary as it forages at all levels, from ground to canopy, but usually lower. Sometimes in pairs.

Status Uncommon to locally common.

Habitat Tropical Zone, to 1,000m, in dense low humid to wet vegetation, especially thickets along streams and other waterbodies and young second growth at forest edges and in overgrown pastures. May be quite common in overgrown clearings, thickets and hedges along pastures.

Voice Calls include a *jeer-whoop*, *bubu-whoop* and raspy chatter in alarm. Song a beautiful and varied series of low liquid gurgling and slurred phrases, e.g. *cheer-ful, whip-por-warble*, a set phrase repeated many times before moving to next; pairs often duet (H&B, B&M).

Note May be revised to genus *Pheugopedius* (Mann *et al.* 2006).

PLAIN-TAILED WREN

Thryothorus euophrys Pl. 237

Identification 16–16.5cm. As its name suggests, tail unbarred, but in fact entire bird is unbarred. Adult bright rufous above. Top of head brown, blackish from forehead to crown, bold white superciliary edged finely black above, broadly below by black line from lores to sides of nape, ear-coverts pale grey with black lines and some white, mesial white, lower malar black, chin to throat creamy white, rest of underparts sandy brown (slightly paler than upperparts) with short rows of large black spots from where throat joins breast; eyes brown, bill grey above, horn-flesh below, legs and feet dark grey. Juvenile has head to undertail-coverts almost uniform sandy brown (as adult) with grey mask and pale chin and upper throat – essentially looks all rufous with a grey mask. Stripes on head may recall Whiskered Wren, but latter is slightly smaller, usually found at lower altitudes and has barred tail.

Ssp. *T. e. euophrys* (W Ec, Co) as described

T. e. longipes (E Ec, Co) very similar to *euophrys* but breast markings much reduced and grey rather than black

T. e. atriceps (SE Ec) like nominate but crown decidedly greyish, and breast unmarked and washed grey

Habits Usually in pairs and very retiring as it forages for invertebrates near ground in dense undergrowth. Does not join mixed-species flocks, but responds very well to playback.

Status Uncommon to locally common in suitable habitat.

Habitat Subtropical Zone to Páramo, 1,800–3,500m but mostly at 2,000–3,300m. Montane woodland and dense edges, especially disturbed areas such as recent landslides or clearings overgrown with *Chusquea* bamboo.

Voice Calls include a wheezy *zwee*, loud *choo-chip, choo-chip, choo-chip-chip*, an alarmed *tje tjekrrtejrr te tekrrr…*, and sharp *tju-tju* with second note lower. Song consists of varied phrases of loud gurgling whistles, e.g. *cheery-cheery-cheo, tu hehuhui-hu hehu*, or *tuie huit huihui, hu hui huhe hui*, each phrase repeated many times; often the sexes duet (F&K, H&B, B&M).

Note May be revised to genus *Pheugopedius* (Mann *et al.* 2006).

WHISKERED WREN

Thryothorus mystacalis Pl. 235

Identification 15.5–16cm. Essentially deep rufescent brown above, most races having black-barred tail, head dark with long whitish supercilium, white mesial and black malar, throat creamy, underparts from grey and sepia to cinnamon. Eyes hazel, bill black above, yellowish below, legs and feet dark flesh. Juvenile duller, with head pattern less distinct. In Ecuador, might be confused with similar Plain-tailed Wren, but relevant races are different; Plain-tailed has plain tail, whereas all ages of race *mystacalis* of Whiskered Wren are distinctly barred on tail and lack bright rufous colour. Coraya Wren is slightly smaller and lacks distinctive white malar streak, as do other similar overlapping congeners in Venezuela.

Ssp. *T. m. amaurogaster* (NE & E Co) back and wings raw umber (darker than other races), top of head fuscous, head-sides unmarked black, underparts creamy buff on throat, rest deep cinnamon to tawny; eyes dark brown, bill dark with horn base

T. m. consobrinus (NW Ve) adult deep, slightly reddish-chestnut above, top of head grey, off-white supercilium bordered black above and below, ear-coverts black, strong white crescent below eyes and many small white lines over ear-coverts, mesial creamy to buffy, malar black, throat buffy, rest of underparts buffy drab, greyish on sides, tending to dull cinnamon on flanks and undertail-coverts; eyes orange to reddish-brown, bill black above, grey below; juvenile is Mikado brown above, top of head concolorous, but grey on neck-sides and slightly onto nape, eyebrow narrow and slightly broken, pale mesial thin, black malar with some grey, chin to belly pale greyish-buff, rest cinnamon

T. m. macrurus (C & E Andes in CE Co) like *mystacalis* but much larger, disproportionately longer, very differently coloured and virtually unbarred tail

T. m. mystacalis (Ec) adult deep, slightly reddish-chestnut above with greyish nape and grey upper mantle which continues over neck-sides to breast, albeit slightly paler, dotted white crescent below eye and white lines on ear-coverts, underparts distally drab clay; bill black above, grey below

T. m. ruficaudatus (NC Ve) tail barring distally very faint, basally virtually absent (no overlap with Plain-tailed Wren), head dark grey with narrow and slightly broken superciliary, bold white lines on face-sides and ear-coverts, pale mesial buffy and short, malar black and equally short, chin pale cinnamon grading through cinnamon-rufous to deep rufescent cinnamon-tawny on undertail-coverts; juvenile virtually concolorous above, slightly duller than adult, and greyish on nape and face-sides to breast, becoming dull cinnamon over rest of underparts

T. m. saltuensis (W Andes W Co) like nominate but clearer grey crown, greyer breast and sides more mouse grey (less buffy); black malar broader with white supramalar narrower; less distinct tail barring

T. m. tachirensis (Táchira in Ve) was synonymised with *consobrinus* by Phelps & Phelps (1963)

T. m. yananchae (Nariño in S Co) closest to *mystacalis* but has slaty grey crown (vs. brownish-grey) extending over mantle; from *macrourus* by greyer crown and upper mantle, rest of underparts paler chestnut

Habits Very retiring and wary as it forages, usually in pairs, from under- to midstorey of dense undergrowth. Does not join mixed-species flocks. Inevitably heard before seen.

Status Uncommon to locally fairly common.

Habitat Tropical to Temperate Zones, sea level to 2,800m but mostly at 800–2,400m, at forest edge and second growth, overgrown treefalls and clearings, often in *Heliconia* thickets, only rarely interior of forest.

Voice Calls include a low throaty *bong-bong*, liquid bubbly *whick-whick-whick* and frog-like *kwi*, sometimes repeated 3–4 times. Song a series of loud gurgling whistles, e.g. *to-wit-toweebo*, *chuwee-boo-bop-chuweebo*, *whee-ha-whee-ha* or *too-whee*; often sexes duet (H&B, B&M, R&G, Hilty).

Notes Formerly considered conspecific with Moustached Wren *T. genibarbis*, but the Andean subspecies are now considered specifically as *T. mystacalis* whilst Amazonian subspecies retained in Moustached Wren complex (R&T, R&G, Hilty). May be revised to genus *Pheugopedius* (Mann *et al.* 2006).

CORAYA WREN

Thryothorus coraya Pl. 237

Identification 14.5cm. Adult rather dark above with unbarred wings and distinctive black-faced head, including broad black malar (but lacks white stripe above of Whiskered Wren). Juvenile has dull blackish-grey head with indistinct pattern, grey throat and breast, and greyish-brown (not orange-brown) eyes. Similar *Henicorhina* wood wrens are much smaller and shorter tailed, and all have barred wings.

Ssp. *T. c. barrowcloughianus* (Ve: Cerros Roraima & Cuquenán) dark rufous-brown above, somewhat clearer and brighter on lower rump and tail-coverts, tail barred black and, more narrowly, brighter rufous, top of head grades from dusky forehead to nape which is concolorous with back; mask black with narrow postocular eyebrow and a very few tiny white lines on supraloral and ear-coverts, with vestigial crescent of white dots below eyes, chin and throat pure white with a few tiny black streaks on chin and throat-sides, underparts almost uniform bright rufous, slightly paler on breast, only distal-most undertail-coverts barred black

T. c. caurensis (E Co, S Ve) 3 variants, somewhat more common is brown or normal – deep rufous-brown above, uppertail-coverts faintly barred, tail broadly and unevenly barred, those halfway down tail slightly broader, blackish streaks from forehead fading by mid crown, short white eyebrow above eye scarcely reaches rear ear-coverts, narrowly bordered black above with black mask below, a few white feathers on supraloral, crescent of white dots below eyes and short white lines over ear-coverts; chin and throat white, breast-sides umber becoming deep rufous on flanks, and rather closely barred rufous and black on undertail-coverts; eyes brown, bill black, legs and feet grey; juvenile much as adult above except bars on tail narrower towards sides and eyebrow is just a few white dots, a very few dull, whitish feathers on supraloral, and short lines on ear-coverts; chin and throat buffy, rest of underparts umber-brown; base of bill horn, legs and feet vinous grey; grey variant has more extensive and clearer white lines on head-sides, longer eyebrow, dots below eyes bolder, tail is slightly heavier and more evenly barred with faint barring on uppertail-coverts, breast and sides to belly grey, undertail-coverts regularly barred dusky and warm grey; third variant, birds from Neblina, have tail almost entirely dusky, with paler brown spots at basal sides; only underparts are like normal, but darker; legs and feet blackish

T. c. coraya (E Gu, Su, FG) medium rufous-brown above, with very broad black bands on tail, dusky greyish forehead, crown to nape rather sepia, white eyebrow longer and clearer than any other race, few tiny white feathers on supraloral, rows of white across cheeks and ear-coverts, chin and throat pure white, with fore neck-sides to central upper breast and centre of belly pale grey, breast-sides chestnut, rest of underparts dusky rufous, with broad dusky bars on undertail-coverts

T. c. griseipectus (E Ec, S Co) slightly brighter rufous above, tail evenly and regularly barred black; clear white supraloral spot, long thin eyebrow clean white, row of white dots below eyes, white streaks on cheeks and ear-coverts form almost solid white lines, chin and throat white, neck-sides to upper breast, grading down centre of belly mid grey, chestnut breast-sides become dark rufous-brown on flanks to undertail-coverts, only distal undertail-coverts barred dusky

T. c. obscurus (SE Ve: Auyán-tepui) dark rufous-brown above, top of head slightly darker, tail broadly barred black, full mask black, including forehead, a vestigial postocular eyebrow, and few thin white lines on ear-coverts, black of ear-coverts extends to neck-sides and separates breast from white throat, with several black streaks on lower throat, rest of underparts reddish-rufous, distal undertail-coverts narrowly barred black

T. c. ridgwayi (Gran Sabana in SE Ve, W Gu) somewhat

variable, but uniformly deep rufous-brown with virtually black tail with narrow, well-spaced rufescent bars; black mask bordered by narrow, short eyebrow and fan of short white lines over supraloral; white streaks over ear-coverts broader and less clean-cut than other races, crescent of white dots below eyes well defined; chin and throat pure white with scattered black streaks at border with bright rufous breast; distal underparts brown as described, barred regularly black; variants include those with longer white eyebrow and white-spotted black ear-coverts reaching upper breast which has a faint grey band

Habits Not especially retiring and wary as it forages for invertebrates and some seeds, in dense undergrowth from near ground to midstorey. Usually in pairs or small flocks and joins mixed-species flocks.

Status Fairly common to common.

Habitat Tropical to Temperate Zones, to 2,400m but mostly below 1,000m, in *terra firme* and *várzea* forest, edges and mature second growth, especially near water, e.g. gallery forests in savannas, often in lianas.

Voice Calls include *who-oor-wheeeer,* followed by a rapid *wop-wop-wop-wop* or *chuchuchuchuchu*, an alarmed *cut-cut-coo*, and distinctive *chidip chidip choopu* or *tu-dk tu-choow*, often repeated. Song a prolonged series of varied bubbling trills and whistles, some phrases repeated many times before moving on to next, interspersed with occasional high harsh notes, e.g. *seeeEEEyou, ear-ear-ear-ear*; pairs usually duet (H&B, R&T, B&M, R&G, Hilty).

Notes May be revised to genus *Pheugopedius* (Mann *et al.* 2006). Race *barrowcloughianus* described by Aveledo & Pérez (1994). Lowland and highland birds may be 2 species based on plumage and vocal differences (Hilty). Species is undeniably variable within any given population, and we found *caurensis* to be particularly variable and perhaps involves more than one race. Unfortunately, there do not appear to be sound-recordings of all of the different taxa and certainly none tied to voucher specimens; in any case, wrens are notoriously creative and expansive in the development of vocabularies, thus it seems that only a species-wide analysis of DNA will explain the multiple and complex fragmentation of plumages.

RUFOUS-BREASTED WREN

Thryothorus rutilus Pl. 237

Identification 14cm. Adult rich olive-brown above, distally spotted on tail, roughly in bars, face black with rows of white spots, breast intense rich rufous becoming paler on flanks, a few small black spots from edge of throat to upper breast, but probably not visible in the field; belly white with scattered black spots, thighs olive, undertail-coverts pale olive with narrow black bars; eyes deep reddish-brown, bill long and slim, finely pointed and black, legs and feet grey. Juvenile is a pallid version of adult, with vestigial barring on tail and white throat. Similar Stripe-throated Wren has barred wings and does not overlap. Speckle-breasted Wren, race *colombianus*, could overlap with race *interior* of Rufous-breasted Wren, but it has from chin to sides and belly regularly and narrowly barred black and white, and a bold white eyebrow which should separate it satisfactorily.

Ssp. *T. r. hypospodius* (E Andes in Co) similar to *rutilus* but blacker tail barring, the bars on central tail being particularly broad, throat and malar clearly barred with black bars being narrower than white ones, lending a whiter aspect to throat

T. r. intensus (NW Ve) black line above eyebrow and bordering ear-coverts, regular, even and slightly narrower bars on tail, sides and flanks more olive than rufous, undertail-coverts plain

T. r. interior (E Andes in N Co) pale, cinnamon-brown upperparts, tail has even, closely spaced, narrow black bars; ear-coverts streaked white, malar clearly spotted white, throat barred, breast pale rufous, body-sides and flanks olive, centre of belly pale to white, undertail-coverts plain buffy

T. r. laetus (NE Co, NW Ve) very distinct, pale sandy cinnamon above (the palest race), tail with broad grey bars, upper breast bright orange to pale orange on sides, merging into pale olive on flanks and undertail-coverts which are evenly barred with same grey as tail; a few large white spots on black malar, whilst chin and throat have broad white bars, black spots scattered from throat down centre of breast and spread over white belly; bill blackish above, grey below, legs and feet pale vinaceous-grey

T. r. rutilus (C, N & NE Ve, Tr) as described

T. r. tobagensis (To) similar to *rutilus* but has stronger bill, longer wings and duller breast

Habits Actively forages for invertebrates and seeds, in dense vegetation from understorey to subcanopy. Usually in pairs or groups, and sometimes follows army ants.

Status Fairly common to common in suitable habitat (less common on Tobago than Trinidad).

Habitat Tropical to Lower Subtropical Zones, to 1,900m, in scrubby thickets, vine tangles, and edges of seasonally dry, semi-deciduous to moist forests and lighter woodland, as well as second growth.

Voice Calls include a short rising trill, sharp *curr* or *chweep* and distinctive rising *chip-reeez*. Song consists of clear whistles interspersed with trills, e.g. *eer-tosee-towhep*; sexes often duet (H&B, ffrench, B&M). Call a rising *tip-breeeeze*, like running fingers up a comb. Vigorous antiphonal songs recall those of Buff-breasted Wren but are higher pitched, flatter (less musical) and notable for many slurred notes, typically a rollicking phrase delivered in lively, musical tempo, repeated 2–3 times, e.g., *too-see-HEEear to-see, too-see-HEEear to-see*, then song changes (Hilty).

Notes May be revised to genus *Pheugopedius*, (Mann *et al.* 2006). Sometimes considered conspecific with Speckle-breasted Wren (Wetmore *et al.* 1984, AOU 1998).

SPECKLE-BREASTED WREN

Thryothorus sclateri Pl. 237

Identification 13–14cm. Adult brown above, faintly barred on wings, boldly barred blackish and drab grey on tail, eyebrow bold and white, face-sides black with white streaks, colour of back varies racially; underparts also vary significantly by race, but undertail-coverts boldly barred black and white. Eyes reddish-brown, bill deep grey, legs and feet pale grey. Juvenile slightly duller above, buffy instead of brown or rufous on belly and flanks, spotting or barring less extensive, eyes brown. Rather similar, larger Rufous-breasted Wren (race *hypospodius*) might be confused with race *colombianus* of Speckle-breasted, but has tail barred brown and blackish, and bright rufous breast. Stripe-throated Wren has much broader barring on wings, throat streaked black and white and does not extend onto breast, and undertail-coverts concolorous with underparts.

Ssp. *T. s. columbianus* (Co: C Andes in Valle & E Andes in Bogotá) similar to *sclateri*, slightly duller and uniform above, and more evenly and finely barred below, flanks more olivaceous-brown

T. s. paucimaculatus (SW Ec) slightly smaller, uniform pale reddish-brown above, white chin and upper throat, spotted somewhat irregularly on lower throat and upper breast, then to vent pale rufous.

T. s. sclateri (río Marañón drainage, SE Ec) reddish-brown on head, olive-brown back without any reddish tones, boldly and densely barred black and white below, extending onto reddish-brown flanks

Habits Not particularly retiring or wary, forages from near ground to midstorey, favouring dense undergrowth and vine thickets. Usually in pairs and sometimes joins mixed-species flocks.

Status Fairly common to locally common in Ecuador. Apparently benefits from expansion of human cultivation, spreading north in Ecuador.

Habitat Upper Tropical to Lower Subtropical Zones, 1,100–2,000m, in deciduous and semi-humid forests, woodland and edges.

Voice Calls include one similar to sound made by running one's fingers along a comb. Song a series of fast, repeated phrases which are less musical than many congeners (R&T), probably sings antiphonally (K&B).

Notes May be revised to genus *Pheugopedius* (Mann *et al.* 2006). Sometimes considered conspecific with Rufous-breasted Wren (Wetmore *et al.* 1984, AOU 1998), and formerly considered a subspecies of Spot-breasted Wren *T. maculipectus* (R&T, B&M). Parker & Carr (1992) considered race *sclateri* a separate species, and given name Marañón Wren by R&G. If accepted, this would leave *T. paucimaculatus* as Speckle-breasted Wren.

BAY WREN *Thryothorus nigricapillus* Pl. 235

Identification 14.5–14.7cm. Adult bright rufous-brown above, barred strongly black on wings and tail, head black with large white supraloral spot, white eye-ring and short postocular line, large white spot on ear-coverts, broad white mesial separated from white throat by narrow black line; underparts white from throat to central belly, becoming bright rufous-brown on flanks and vent to undertail-coverts. Black barring on sides and flanks to undertail-coverts. Eyes reddish-brown, bill black, legs and feet grey. Juvenile similar but black of head duller and grades into mantle, brown of flanks duller; eyes dark brown.

Ssp. *T. n. connectens* (SW Co) throat white, rest of underparts from breast are broadly barred black

T. n. nigricapillus (W Ec) as described; barred broadly on sides of breast and body

T. n. schottii (NW Co) like *nigricapillus*, but throat and entire underparts narrowly barred black

Habits Forages actively for invertebrates in dense undergrowth. Usually in pairs that are very vocal. Often confiding and curious.

Status Common.

Habitat Tropical to Lower Subtropical Zones, to 1,800m but usually below 1,400m, in rank undergrowth, treefalls and other overgrown clearings near edges of forests, woodland and second growth. Especially likes damp low-lying tangles and *Heliconia* thickets near watercourses, only rarely interior of forest; sometimes in well-vegetated gardens.

Voice Calls include a distinctive loud *heetowip*. Song consists of various fast loud ringing phrases, e.g. *see-me, how-wet-I-am*, a set phrase repeated many times before moving on to next; sexes often duet (R&T).

Note May be revised to genus *Cantorchilus* (Mann *et al.* 2006).

STRIPE-THROATED WREN
Thryothorus leucopogon Pl. 237

Identification 12–13cm. Olive-brown above with pale orange-buffy bars from mantle to tip of tail; broad superciliary, bordered narrowly above and below with black, lores and chin to ear-coverts and throat white, with long, irregular black lines, breast and body-sides to undertail-coverts cinnamon, washed olive on flanks; eyes hazel to golden, bill dark grey with paler base, legs and feet grey. Juvenile similar but has less clearly defined black and white on face, eyes brown. Smaller than somewhat similar Rufous-breasted Wren, separable by barred wings. Speckle-breasted Wren has shorter tail, barred black and grey, with black and white barred undertail-coverts, and brown eyes.

Ssp. *T. l. grisescens* (NW Co) evenly olive from forehead to uppertail-coverts, with barring only on wings and tail, olive wash far more extensive below, with only central breast and belly bright orange-buffy, undertail-coverts shadow-barred

T. l. leucopogon (W Ec, W Co) as described

Habits Forages in dense undergrowth and vine tangles from near ground to midstorey, and often joins mixed-species flocks.

Status Uncommon and local, more common north in Ecuador.

Habitat Tropical Zone, to 900m, in edges of humid to wet forests and second growth.

Voice Calls include well-spaced *teeee* whistles and distinctive, fast *chu, ch-chu* or *chu, ch-chu, ch-chu* phrases; song apparently a run-together version of same phrases (R&T, R&G). Song a tuneless repetition (K&B).

Notes May be revised to genus *Cantorchilus* (Mann *et al.* 2006). Formerly considered conspecific with Stripe-breasted Wren *T. thoracicus* (Wetmore *et al.* 1984, AOU 1998).

RUFOUS-AND-WHITE WREN

Thryothorus rufalbus Pl. 235

Identification 14.5–16.5cm. Adult bright medium rufous-brown above, barred finely and evenly on wings, rather more boldly on tail, with long white supercilium bordered above and below with black, white cheeks lightly streaked black, and tear-shaped streaks on neck-sides; white underparts washed sandy on flanks, barred black and white on undertail-coverts. Juvenile slightly darker above, almost dusky on top of head, has more obscure facial markings and some brown-washed grey mottling on breast. Slightly smaller Buff-breasted Wren has duller upperparts and buffy underparts (though quite pale in race *venezuelanus*). Niceforo's Wren is duller olive-grey on head and upper back, and has more greyish-brown sides and flanks. Similar *Henicorhina* wood wrens are much smaller and shorter tailed.

Ssp. *T. r. cumanensis* (N coast in Co, N Ve) paler brown above, eyebrow plain white, only bordered faintly black below, very few black and white markings on neck-sides, mesial more clearly defined with black
T. r. minlosi (Ne Co, CN & W Ve) as described

Habits Very retiring and wary as it forages for invertebrates, alone or in pairs (briefly in small flocks after fledging) in dense undergrowth and vine tangles, from ground to lower midstorey, Does not join mixed-species flocks.
Status Fairly common to common.
Habitat Tropical to Lower Subtropical Zones, to 1,500m, in dry deciduous to moist semi-deciduous forests, woodland, edges and second growth, rarely in forest interior, also in gallery forests and plantations.
Voice Calls include a harsh scold and castanet-like chattering. Very distinctive song is a series of variable but very melodic, hooting owl-like whistles, e.g. 4–5 low slow whistles preceded and followed by a higher note, *weee-boo-boo-boo-boo-whit*; sexes often duet (B&M, Hilty, K&B).
Note May be revised to genus *Thryophilus* (Mann *et al.* 2006).

NICEFORO'S WREN

Thryothorus nicefori Pl. 235

Identification 14.5–15cm. Adult dull olive-grey on head and mantle, becoming slightly more rufescent on back, finely barred on wings, more broadly barred on tail; long superciliary bordered black above and below, rows of black lines on head-sides, underparts white becoming greyish on sides and flanks, barred broadly black and white on undertail-coverts. Juvenile undescribed.

Ssp. Monotypic (W slope of E Andes in Santander, Co)

Habits Very poorly known, but presumably similar to Rufous-and-white Wren.
Status Critically Endangered. Endemic to Colombia. Known only from type locality (near San Gil, on río Fonce south of Bucaramanga) where found in 1945–48, 1989 and 2000. Known range extremely small (*c.*3km^2), population tiny (<50?) and inferred to be declining because region's environment is highly modified and habitat degradation is apparently ongoing, with *Acacia* scrub threatened by seasonal burning for farming and goat and cattle grazing.
Habitat Upper Tropical Zone, in dense xeric *Acacia* scrub in semi-arid valley of large, intermontane río Sagamosa drainage, at 1,095m, but not in adjacent coffee plantations.
Voice Very similar to Rufous-and-white Wren. Song consists of several low-pitched, slow, mellow, bouncing whistles, preceded by higher notes (BirdLife 2004).
Note Sometimes considered a subspecies of Rufous-and-white Wren, a suggestion supported by playback experiments showing that Niceforo's Wren responds to recordings of Rufous-and-white Wren's song (Collar *et al.* 1992, BirdLife 2004).
Note May be revised to genus *Thryophilus* (Mann *et al.* 2006).

BUFF-BREASTED WREN

Thryothorus leucotis Pl. 236

Identification 14–14.5cm. Much variation between and within races; essentially, adult brown above with barred wings and tail, the bars more widely spaced on tail than wings, variable white supercilium, even more variable face-sides, which may be almost entirely whitish or black with white streaks; white throat and buffy underparts. Eyes brown, bill from black to orange-horn with dark tip, legs and feet vary from pale grey to dark brown. Juvenile tends to have slightly more diffuse facial markings and is variably streaked grey on breast. Larger and longer-tailed than similar *Henicorhina* wood wrens.

Ssp. *T. l. albipectus* (NE Ve, Guianas) a highly variable race, intermediate between most colourful *bogotensis* and palest *hypoleucus*, but some individuals match these extremes; white supercilium from base of nostrils to rear of brown ear-coverts heavily streaked white, bill dark grey above, pale grey below, legs and feet dark grey
T. l. bogotensis (E Co, C Ve) reddish-brown above, long thin eyebrow from lores to nape-sides, bordered narrowly black above and below, face-sides black streaked white and a few white dots on neck-sides; bill dark grey, legs and feet medium grey; juvenile slightly darker above, broken eyebrow from above eye to rear ear-coverts, lores black, ear-coverts streaked with short white dashes, throat and breast streaked with rows of short grey dashes, bill orange-horn with a greyish tip, legs and feet dull horn
T. l. collinus (Guajira in Co) restricted to isolated Macuira Mts., at northern tip of Guajira peninsula; specimens not examined by us
T. l. galbraithii (extreme NW Co) much more rufescent below than *leucotis* and overall darker
T. l. hypoleucus (NC Ve) very much like *albipectus* but significantly paler below, whitish; only flanks and uppertail-coverts washed buffy-brown, olivaceous above (less rufescent); tail paler, less tawny; juvenile

has lores brown and eyebrow thin and short

T. l. leucotis (NC Co) differs from *venezuelanus* in pale brown dorsal surface with slight clay-coloured tone to rump and tail-coverts; much paler wing and tail bars; distal underparts paler

T. l. peruanus (NE Ec) nearest to *albipectus* but smaller and tail much shorter; duller above, underparts decidedly darker (deep pinkish-buff to pale tawny-olive), becoming olive-brown on flanks and tail-coverts.

T. l. venezuelanus (NE Co, NW Ve) somewhat variable and possibly 2 different races; northern birds (NW Zulia) mid brown above (like *albipectus*), fairly lightly barred on wings; long narrow white eyebrow separated from white streaks on ear-coverts by black lores and black line along top of ear-coverts, breast very pale sandy, merging into pale rufescent underparts; upper mandible black, lower orange-yellow, legs and feet dark grey; southern birds (Barinas) darker brown above (like *bogotensis*) with bolder black line through eyes, breast cinnamon and rest of underparts more rufescent; bill all grey, paler below, legs and feet medium grey; juvenile has darker top and sides of head with rows of small white dashes over cheeks and ear-coverts, long grey streaks from lower throat to sides and breast, white belly, brown flanks; bill dark grey, legs and feet dark grey

T. l. zuliensis (N Santander in Co, Maracaibo basin in Ve) the darkest race, more rufous above and wing and tail bars darker; with long white supercilium, narrowly outlined above and below with black, face-sides and malar black, with rows of short white dashes, throat has rows of grey streaks, breast and sides to undertail-coverts uniform brown

Habits Somewhat retiring as it forages in dense undergrowth and thickets, but active and curious. Sometimes on or near ground but more usually in vine tangles in subcanopy. Usually in pairs or small flocks. Rarely joins mixed-species flocks.

Status Uncommon to locally common.

Habitat Lower Tropical Zone, to 950m, in dry deciduous to humid forests, woodland, second growth, edges and clearings, often near water (more so than Coraya Wren), e.g. along lakes or streams or in *várzea*, gallery and mangrove forests and other flooded areas.

Voice Calls include a *chunk*, and distinctive rapid *totok*, *chit-cho* or *chit-cho-cho* (*albipectus* has slow musical oft-repeated *ee-yurk*). Hilty notes call as a loud, incisive *pssEET-CHOO!* Song a complex series of abrupt sharp notes with numerous short clear whistles, with up to 12 notes per phrase, e.g. *chee-chongchong*, *choreewee*, *Amelia-choke* or *tseEE-now, don't give'me'CHURT now*, repeated many times over, and usually given by pairs. Pairs frequently sing antiphonal duets (R&T, H&M, B&M, R&G, Hilty). Juvenile male sings antiphonally with mother, juvenile female sings antiphonally with father (K&B).

Note May be revised to genus *Cantorchilus* (Mann *et al.* 2006).

SUPERCILIATED WREN

Thryothorus superciliaris Pl. 235

Identification 14.5cm. Sandy brown above, faintly barred on wings, more broadly on tail; long bold white supercilium from bill to neck-sides, blackish line through eyes, head-sides and underparts white, washed pale pinkish-sandy on flanks and distal underparts. Juvenile has duller and paler crown, and less rufous upperparts. Adult similar to Buff-breasted Wren (no overlap) but more rufous above, and much whiter on cheeks and underparts, with stronger supercilium and only trace of buffy on flanks and lower belly. Overlapping Speckle-breasted Wren is quite dissimilar.

Ssp. *T. s. baroni* (SW Ec: El Oro) brighter and slightly more rufous above than nominate, with darker flanks and vent

T. s. superciliaris (SW: Manabí & Guayas) as described

Habits Similar to Buff-breasted Wren, but easier to see in its more open habitat.

Status Uncommon to fairly common.

Habitat Tropical Zone, to 1,850m but usually below 1,500m, in dry scrub, thickets, hedgerows and undergrowth of deciduous to humid woodlands, occurring far from water.

Voice Calls include several churrs. Song similar to Buff-breasted Wren but phrases usually not as fast or musical (B&M, R&G). A series of short repeated phrases of 2–3 notes, sometimes extended (K&B).

Note May be revised to genus *Cantorchilus* (Mann *et al.* 2006).

SOUTHERN HOUSE WREN

Troglodytes musculus Pl. 234

Identification 11–12.5cm. Adult greyish sepia-brown above, barred finely and faintly on mantle, darker on lower back and well defined on rump to tail, and wings; faint buffy eyebrow, with dark line through eyes; throat white, rest of underparts pale, washed buffy on sides. Juvenile has darker scalloping on flanks and undertail-coverts. Santa Marta Wren has bolder supercilium, buffy-white eye-ring, and barred flanks and vent. Mountain Wren has shorter tail, bolder supercilium and is more rufous above, and more forest-based. See Sedge Wren also.

Ssp. *T. m. albicans* (W Ec & La Plata & Puna Is., S & SE Co, Ve) rich tawny-olive above, washed on sides and flanks, vent and undertail-coverts (latter spotted black and white); juvenile pale tawny-olive above, regularly and evenly scalloped below

T. m. atopus (N Co) more deeply ochraceous below than *striatulus*

T. m. columbae (E Andes in Co) similar to *striatulus* but darker greyish-brown above with fine dusky bars, and darker below

T. m. effutitus (Ve: Andes from Táchira to Lara) definitely more greyish-brown above than *albicans*, washed cinnamon-buff below, undertail-coverts barred brown; juvenile pale cinnamon below and faintly scalloped

T. m. striatulus (W & C Andes in Co) as described; large, greyish-brown above, whitish to pale buffy below

T. m. tobagensis (To) longer wings, heavier bill, whiter below

Habits Often cocks tail. Conspicuous and confident as it forages alone or in pairs for invertebrates on ground or in low vegetation. Does not cock tail when it sings.
Status Uncommon to common and very widespread, although declined in Venezuela due to use of DDT in 1980s.
Habitat Tropical Zone to Páramo, to 4,000m, in all open and semi-open arid to humid habitats, near or away from habitation; avoids closed forest and clearly benefits from forest clearance. In French Guiana found only away from man in old *Avicennia* mangroves.
Voice Calls include a nasal *jeeyah* and rasping repeated *wheep* or *eeeeh* in alarm. Song a cheerful gurgling warble and chatter given year-round, sometimes sexes duet, males often singing from high exposed perches (F&K, B&M, R&G), female song distinct, a low, rapid twittering, maybe followed by a high clear trill (K&B).
Note Formerly part of (Northern) House Wren *T. aedon* (e.g. R&T).

SANTA MARTA WREN
Troglodytes monticola Pl. 234

Identification 11.5cm. Adult is evenly brown above with fine regular barring throughout, faintest on head, darkest and clearest on wings and tail, underparts pinkish-cinnamon, warmest and most intense on breast, a faint eyebrow of same colour borders ear-coverts; fine black barring on lower sides covers flanks becoming almost black and white on undertail-coverts. Juvenile instead of barring has dark feather tips above and on ear-coverts, superciliary tinged greyish; underparts paler with no intensification on breast, brown barring begins on rear flanks and covers undertail-coverts. The similar, slightly smaller, longer-tailed Mountain Wren has a longer bill and a conspicuous long, broad pale eyebrow. The common Southern House Wren is larger, with a longer and fuller tail and is singularly paler below.

Ssp. Monotypic (Santa Marta in Co)

Habits Retiring and wary, and easily overlooked.
Status Endemic to upper levels of Santa Marta, Colombia.
Habitat Páramo, 3,200–4,600m, in low dense shrubbery at timberline of high-altitude forests and in sheltered areas higher in páramo.
Voice Call a constantly given *di-di* (K&B).
Note Formerly considered a subspecies of Mountain Wren (S&M).

MOUNTAIN WREN
Troglodytes solstitialis Pl. 234

Identification 9–11cm. Adult is mid brown above with fine, regular dusky barring on wings and tail, long broad, creamy superciliary from lores that reaches nape-sides where becomes spots, dark brown postocular patch on upper ear-coverts; chin white, merging into warm creamy or pale sandy lower face-sides and throat to flanks, undertail-coverts barred dusky and white; eyes dark brown, bill dark grey with pale base, legs and feet grey. Juvenile similar but barring above less crisp, white of chin extends across central underparts to vent, with sides to undertail-coverts washed brownish, entire underparts speckled and flecked with broken, vestigial bars, and undertail-coverts barred dusky. Santa Marta Wren has a shorter tail, is also barred on back, but upperparts are more richly toned. Southern House Wren is larger, with a longer, fuller tail and lacks broad pale eyebrow.

Ssp. *T. s. solitarius* (Andes in Co & Ve) very similar to nominate but darker above, lores, cheeks and ear-coverts washed brown (slightly paler than back), underparts much paler, whiter on belly, narrowly washed olive on flanks; juvenile also similar to nominate but slightly darker.
T. s. solstitialis (Ec, SW Co) as described

Habits Sometimes cocks tail. Not particularly retiring and wary as it forages alone, in pairs or small flocks, in dense, tangled vines at borders and edges, and openings such as treefalls, etc. from understorey to subcanopy. Often seen searching moss-covered and epiphyte-laden limbs and trunks. Regularly seen attending understorey mixed-species flocks.
Status Uncommon to fairly common in Ecuador, uncommon to common (at higher elevations) in Colombia, fairly common in Venezuela, and commonest in slightly disturbed forests.
Habitat Tropical Zone to Páramo, 700–3,600m, in humid to wet cloud and elfin forests, stunted woodland, edges and clearings, sometimes in bamboo.
Voice Calls include a distinctive, constantly given trill, *tchr-r-r*, *dzz* or *didi*, and an alarmed *zri-di-di* or *zri-dr-dre-drrr*. Song a rather quiet unmusical series of high fast notes, *treee-treeee-tititiki* or *wiss'lee'ree*, like breaking of fine glass, and descending and fading at end (R&T, F&K, B&M, R&G, Hilty).

TEPUI WREN *Troglodytes rufulus* Pl. 234

Identification 12–13cm. Appears uniform brown above, but actually softly barred on wings and tail; underparts vary from near-concolorous brown to white. Much variation between populations on different tepuis (see below), including juveniles which are much darker and always have dusky scaling below. Southern House Wren is paler with longer fuller tail and longer pointed bill.

Ssp. *T. r. duidae* (S Ve: C Amazonas & S Bolívar) very similar to *fulvigularis* above but superciliary slightly broader and paler; throat to belly whitish, rest of underparts rufescent brown, faintly barred on undertail-coverts; eyes dark brown, bill black above, yellow below; juvenile like adult but darker and less reddish above, and white underparts regularly and densely scaled black
T. r. fulvigularis (SE Ve: SE Bolívar) deep, slightly rufescent brown all over, slightly darker on wings and tail which are barred blackish, outer fringes of ear-coverts dusky, with paler rufescent superciliary, faint barring on flanks, darker on undertail-coverts; eyes dark brown, bill black, legs and feet grey

T. r. marahuacae (SE Ve: C Amazonas) like *duidae* but has back and tail dark greyish-brown, less reddish and more olivaceous on sides and underparts

T. r. rufulus (SE Ve: E Bolívar on Guyana border) larger than *solstitialis* and more intensely coloured, more rufescent brown below

T. r. wetmorei (S Ve: S Amazonas) dark brown above, finely barred black on wings and tail, reddish tone to top of head, superciliary and chin to sides and belly deep, slightly violaceous-grey, flanks and thighs dark rufescent brown, undertail-coverts finely barred black on deep rufous; eyes reddish-brown, bill black with yellow base, legs and feet dark horn; juvenile similar but slightly darker above, and grey underparts scaled black with white shafts; legs and feet dark grey

T. r. yavii (S Ve: N Amazonas) deep brown above, darker on wings and tail which are also finely barred black, lores and superciliary, running around ear-coverts and face-sides, rufous, dark postocular line borders outermost ear-coverts; chin, malar and throat, upper body-sides, breast and belly pale grey, rufescent brown on lower sides, darker on flanks, thighs and vent, undertail-coverts barred pale rufous and dusky; bill dark grey above, dull horn below, legs and feet fleshy horn; juvenile much deeper reddish-brown above, thus barring almost obscured, deep reddish-rufous below, paler, greyish on chin and centre of breast and belly, all scalloped blackish; eyes dark brown, bill dusky above, dull horn below, legs and feet dark grey

Habits Conspicuous and confident as it forages alone or in pairs on ground or in low vegetation.

Status Locally common. Only recently recorded on Mt. Kowa, NE Guyana (Barnett *et al.* 2002).

Habitat Upper Tropical to Temperate Zones, 1,000–2,800m, in humid to wet forests, edges, and bushes in open rocky areas.

Voice Calls unknown. Song on Cerro Roraima a series of high thin notes given in a slow choppy manner, *slick... seeleet... seet... slick... t'slik... slick... seeleet...*, sounding like musical scrapes from a violin, and may continue for several minutes (D. Ascanio). Song (race and location not given) a series of high, thin whistled twitters, sometimes continuing for several seconds, sometimes disjunct separate phrases (K&B).

WHITE-BREASTED WOOD WREN

Henicorhina leucosticta Pl. 233

Identification 10–11.5cm. Adult deep umber-brown above, barred black on wings and tail, top of head black, including supraloral; bold white superciliary; face-sides black with white streaks on cheeks and inner ear-coverts; chin, throat and malar to sides and belly pure white, flanks to undertail-coverts rufous. Eyes brown, bill dark grey, legs and feet pale grey. Similar Coraya, Rufous-and-white and Buff-breasted Wrens are all much larger and longer tailed.

Ssp. *H. l. albilateralis* (C Co) bright rufous above with rather faint broad barring on tail and slightly stronger barring on wings, top of head olive, broad and conspicuous superciliary, lores to neck-sides, with white-streaked ear-coverts; chin, throat and malar to sides and belly pure white

H. l. darienensis (NW Co) black pileum

H. l. eucharis (Valle in W Co) large, dull upperparts, less prominent barring on wings and tail, no malar streak

H. l. hauxwelli (E Ec, E Co) as described

H. l. inornata (NW Ec, W Co) rufous above from top of head to tip of tail, bold black bars on wings and tail, forehead black with some streaking to forecrown, and black line forming upper border to white superciliary and supraloral, face-sides including malar black, well streaked with white; chin to upper belly dull, slightly off-white, grading into grey lower belly, deep brown rest of underparts

H. l. leucosticta (S Ve, Gu, Su) deep reddish-brown above with black barring on wings and tail, top of head black; bold white line over supraloral and superciliary to neck-sides where there are a few white spots; sides of face and neck black with much white spotting and streaking; malar and chin to centre of breast white, sides and broad band across belly grey, distal underparts deep rufous, bill black, legs and feet dark grey; juvenile almost entirely deep umber-brown, blackish on top of head, deep grey on sides; narrow white postocular eyebrow, a few small white spots on face-sides, throat grey, upper breast dull, dark violaceous-grey; bill has orange base, legs and feet very dark

Habits Often cocks tail. Not particularly retiring or wary as it forages for invertebrates, on ground or in understorey. Alone, in pairs or small flocks; sometimes follows army ants.

Status Fairly common to common. Uncommon to rare and local in French Guiana.

Habitat Tropical Zone, to 1,800m but usually below 1,000m, in humid to wet forests, edges and mature second growth, especially in dense vegetation of ravines and treefalls, also savanna forests in Suriname.

Voice Calls include a *chut*, scolding *churrr* and rattling trills. Song a series of loud relatively short phrases, e.g. *weee-wyi-tee-tuuw*, *cheery-cheery-cheee*, *we-per-chee-purty-choo*, *GEEeear-hurry-hurry* or *sKEEET, purty-purty-purty*, usually repeated several times (up to 4–6), more melodic but with shorter phrases than Grey-breasted Wood Wren (R&T, R&G, Hilty).

GREY-BREASTED WOOD WREN

Henicorhina leucophrys Pl. 233

Identification 10–11.5cm. Rufescent brown above, more chestnut on lower back and rump, faintly barred on wing-coverts, slightly bolder on tertials and secondaries, and brighter on outer fringes of primaries; tail short and barred regularly greyish-brown; top of head dark grey streaked and fringed brown, white eyebrow bordered black above and below; face-sides streaked black and white; white throat to belly, washed faintly greyish, sides and flanks to undertail-coverts rusty brown; eyes chestnut, bill black, legs and feet drab to fuscous. Juvenile similar but has less contrasting face-sides, the streaks being more diffuse, and throat greyish. Generally at higher altitudes than White-breasted Wood Wren. Similar Coraya, Rufous-and-white and Buff-breasted Wrens are much larger and longer tailed.

Ssp. *H. l. anachoreta* (tops of Santa Marta, Co) differs substantially from *bangsi* by streaked throat, grey forehead and breast, less rufous flanks

H. l. bangsi (slopes of Santa Marta, Co) similar to *hilaris* but has paler throat and breast

H. l. brunneiceps (N Ec, W Andes of SW Co) similar to *leucophrys* but heavier bill, brighter upperparts, distinctly streaked throat, darker breast, and flanks and pileum deeper brown

H. l. hilaris (SW Ec) like *leucophrys* but much paler foreneck and breast, nearly greyish-white; fulvous of flanks more extensive leaving only narrow buffy or pale rufous line down abdomen

H. l. leucophrys (Ec, E, C & W Andes of Co) as described

H. l. manastarae (W Ve: S Zulia) closest to *venezuelensis* but paler greyish below (less reddish), and from *bangsi* by having crown darker (more olive less yellow), back darker and less rufous

H. l. meridana (Andes in Ve) similar to *leucophrys*, but throat profusely and often regularly streaked black, breast deeper, almost slate grey; flanks and undertail-coverts much richer and more rufescent

H. l. sanluisensis (NE Ve: San Luis range, Falcón) from other Venezuelan races by darker back and uropygium, more brownish, less reddish

H. l. tamae (E Andes in NE Co, W Táchira in Ve: Páramo de Tama) nearest to *meridana* but flanks, lower abdomen and undertail-coverts paler, more yellowish-brown, back averages paler brown

H. l. venezuelensis (Coastal Cordillera, N Ve) like *leucophrys* in having unstreaked throat, but breast and belly fairly whitish, deepening into grey on sides of breast only; central abdomen faintly marked greyish; flanks much more brown, less rufescent and less extensive; similar to *bangsi* but much darker breast-sides and flanks less rufescent

Habits Often cocks tail. Confiding, sometimes quite curious and bold as it forages for invertebrates on ground or in understorey. Usually in pairs or small flocks, often joins mixed-species flocks. Responds well to playback.

Status Common.

Habitat Upper Tropical to Temperate Zones, 400–3,600m but usually above 1,000m, in dense, damp, mossy undergrowth of humid to wet cloud forests, edges, treefalls, overgrown clearings and mature second growth, often along streams.

Voice Calls include an oft-repeated dry gravelly *churrr* and, in alarm, rapid hard ticking or a softer *trriut-trriut-trriut*. Song a series of rhythmic, loud and long phrases (more staccato than White-breasted Wood Wren), e.g. *put-on-your-nightie*, *you're witty stee* or *cheerooeechee-cheewee-cheerooweechee*, often repeated several times, sometimes in duet. Sings throughout day and year-round (R&T, F&K, Hilty). Much individual and geographic variation (K&B).

BAR-WINGED WOOD WREN

Henicorhina leucoptera Pl. 233

Identification 11cm. Back dark brown grading to rufous on rump and uppertail-coverts, wings and tail extremely dark with black bars, the wings having broad white tips to median and greater coverts, forming 2 obvious bars, outer fringes of outer 2 primaries white; top of head grey becoming darker to near blackish on nape, long white superciliary from nostrils to nape-sides, face-sides black with white streaks forming lines that reach rear ear-coverts, white throat, grey breast and sides, becoming rufous on flanks and undertail-coverts which have dusky bars; eyes dark brown, bill grey with pale base, legs and feet grey. Juvenile much darker, with bars on wings and tail quite obscure, head almost entirely dark vinous-grey, grading on breast to darker rufescent brown than adult; lacks wingbars (paler brown tips) but has small white mark near alula that is absent in juvenile *leucophrys*; narrow, faint white supercilium from eye to nape, few thin white streaks on face-sides and throat; underparts dark umber-brown, more cinnamon on belly and undertail-coverts, with dark tips to feathers.

Ssp. Monotypic (SE Ec)

Habits Similar to other *Henicorhina* wood wrens.

Status Near Threatened. Fairly common in its very small, apparently disjunct range in extreme south-east Ecuador (north end of Cordillera del Cóndor) and northern Peru. Although its habitats are reasonably intact, they may be threatened by grazing and burning in the future.

Habitat Lower Subtropical Zone, 1,700–1,950m. Dense, mossy cloud forests and their edges, especially favouring dense understorey of stunted elfin forest on exposed ridges, but also in tall moist hill forests and fern-covered slopes in savanna woodland.

Voice Calls include a rapid, high-pitched chattering alarm. Song higher, faster, more melodic, less staccato and with more frequent trills than Grey-breasted Wood Wren; another song type consists of longer phrases, beginning and ending with a trill; the sexes often duet (F&K, B&M, R&G).

Note More information can be found in Fitzpatrick *et al.* (1977) and Krabbe & Sornoza (1994).

MUNCHIQUE WOOD WREN

Henicorhina negreti Pl. 233

Identification 11.5cm. Adult dark brown above, brighter on rump and uppertail-coverts, narrow black barring on wings and tail, tail tipped white; top of head dark brown with black tips, long, broad white superciliary to nape-sides, broad black line from lores to neck-sides, ear-coverts covered with short white streaks, broad white throat with rows of short black streaks. Throat medium grey merging into brown body-sides to flanks, becoming paler, almost rufous on undertail-coverts, belly pale grey barred black; eyes hazel, bill black with pale blue-grey base. Juvenile much darker with dull greyish superciliary and only faint streaking on ear-coverts and small whitish spots on throat. Closest to Grey-breasted Wood Wren, which lacks white tip to tail and has belly and vent unmarked, also race *leucophrys*, has a white throat.

Ssp. Monotypic (Co: W Andes)

Status Critically Endangered (Salaman *et al.* 2003).

Habitat Temperate Zone, 2,250–2,640m. Naturally disturbed forest, with mosaic of landslides and treefalls; extremely wet, stunted montane cloud forest, rich in epiphytes and continuously foggy.

Voice Quite vocal, like congeners, calling and singing throughout day. Responds to playback with harsh churring alarm-calls. Song a jumbled series of melodic notes, remarkably so compared to Grey-breasted Wood Wren. Song consists of lengthy repetitions of repeated phrases of 6–12 pure notes, each phrase lasting *c.*2 s, following on without a pause, and a typical song may contain 10+ phrases, some curtailed (Salaman *et al.* 2003).

Note A recently described species (Salaman *et al.* 2003).

Microcerculus wrens have a distinctive profile, almost a caricature wren, with long bill and short cocked tail. They have the most beautiful voices, combined with the frustrating habit of being easy to hear but most difficult to see.

SOUTHERN NIGHTINGALE-WREN

Microcerculus marginatus Pl. 236

Identification 11cm. Upperparts entirely dark brown, scaled black in some races; pure white below, scaled black and white in some races. Eyes dark brown, bill dark grey, yellow-horn lower mandible or paler at base, legs and feet dark grey. Juvenile has obscure barring on crown and back, and brown and white scalloping on throat and upper breast (resembling Speckle-breasted Wren which has white supercilium, black and white scalloping and longer tail). Unmistakable due to combination of body shape with long bill, long legs, short stubby tail and diagnostic song. Very small area of overlap with Flutist Wren, which is all brown.

Ssp. *M. m. corrasus* (Santa Marta, Co) very dark brown above, fine black barring on wings and tail, subterminal black spots and terminal white spots on wing-coverts, faint rufescent eyebrow; throat to lower breast pure white, belly to undertail-coverts rufous with clear black scallops almost forming bars

M. m. marginatus (E Ec, SE Co, SW Ve) mid brown above, terminal white spots on wing-coverts, subtle black barring on outer fringes of tail-feathers and tertials; slightly greyish ear-coverts, throat to vent white, flanks to undertail-coverts pale brown irregularly scalloped black; juvenile has more clearly grey ear-coverts, throat to belly white, sides and flanks rufescent, barred grey on upper breast, becoming darker scallops on flanks and belly, darker still as bars on undertail-coverts

M. m. occidentalis (NW Ec, W Co) dark brown above, deeply and obscurely barred black from top of head to tail; chin white, throat to sides and belly white with fine vermiculations, rest of underparts rufous-brown with black scallops that become bars distally

M. m. squamulatus (NE Co, NW & N Ve) almost uniform dark brown with black barring, but throat to belly white, vermiculated black on throat and scaled black on breast, flanks and belly; juvenile same above, slightly paler brown with distinct pale tips to greater wing-coverts; whitish washed finely warm brown from chin to belly, darker distally, all finely barred darker brown

M. m. taeniatus (W Ec, W Co) dark brown above, barred black from top of head to uppertail-coverts; white throat, neck-sides and centre of breast and belly heavily vermiculated with black, rest of underparts deep rufescent brown scalloped or barred black

Habits Often cocks tail and constantly teeters rear end. Very retiring and wary as it forages alone or in loose pairs, in dense undergrowth on or near ground, looking for small invertebrates. Does not join mixed-species flocks.

Status Fairly common to common.

Habitat Tropical Zone, to 1,800m, in humid to wet forests and mature second growth, particularly wooded ravines and other dense tangles along streams.

Voice Calls unknown. Song a series of up to 10+ pure-toned whistles, first 2–4 rapidly delivered, rising then descending, then abruptly slowing and becoming very long-drawn, each note barely a quarter-tone lower than the preceding and given at progressively longer intervals, with intervals of up to 10 s at end, e.g. *we-ee-EEE-EEt eee, eee… eee… eee… eee……* and so on for up to *c.*1 minute (Hilty), 2.5 minutes (K&B).

Note Called Scaly-breasted Wren in Rodner *et al.* (2000).

FLUTIST WREN

Microcerculus ustulatus Pl. 236

Identification 11.5cm. Adult is dark reddish-brown above, paler and slightly rufescent below, and sometimes scaled (depending on race). Eyes dark brown, bill long and thin, blackish above, orange-yellow below, legs and feet dark grey. Juvenile slightly darker with generally obscure dark barring above and below. Effectively solid brown without any white, which distinguishes this bird from all others. Subtle but quite distinct racial differences.

Ssp. *M. u. duidae* (S Ve: W Bolívar & Amazonas) almost entirely ruddy brown, scaled on top and sides of head, barred finely on lower back and tail-coverts, scaled on sides, lower breast and centre of belly with pale brown, darker spots in centres of feathers

M. u. lunatipectus (S Ve: C Bolívar) fine dark scaling on top of head, scaled below with feathers from lower throat to belly having blackish subterminal crescents (lunar scaling), rest of underparts barred

M. u. obscurus (Gran Sabana tepuis in Ve) almost uniformly dark umber-chocolate, no barring or scaling

M. u. ustulatus (SE Ve, W Gu) small amount of scaling on top of head, some irregular lunar scaling on sides and belly

Habits Generally found alone, feeding on invertebrates on

forest floor, and only rarely in vegetation just above ground.
Status Fairly common.
Habitat Upper Tropical to Subtropical Zones, 850–2,100m but usually below 1,500m, in dense humid to wet forests, especially mossy forests on slopes of mountains and tepuis.
Voice Like a piccolo; song a series of lovely, flute-like whistles, typically slow and melancholic lasting 10–20 s, e.g. *wee, püü, wee püü, tee, tee, tee, tee, tee*, with first and third notes highest and *tee* notes slowly ascending, but songs highly variable individually, though usually a few patterned notes are followed by a long series that trail off downscale (R&T, Hilty).

WING-BANDED WREN

Microcerculus bambla Pl. 236

Identification 11.5cm. Adult dark, slightly greyish-brown above with regular and even black bars on rump to uppertail-coverts, large clean white terminal spot on greater wing-coverts, small terminal white spot on median coverts, throat broadly mauve-grey, finely barred darker, merging into deep rufous-brown of rest of underparts, evenly barred with narrow black lines. Eyes dark brown, bill long and black above, orange-yellow below, legs and feet dark grey. Adult unmistakable due to combination of body shape and bold white wingbar (the smaller wingbar is less obvious).

Ssp. *M. b. albigularis* (E Ec) similar pattern to *bambla*, but evenly and finely barred from forehead to uppertail-coverts, very pale grey chin and throat, grey breast and sides, rest of underparts as described; juvenile slightly brighter above and finely barred brown over entire underparts

M. b. bambla (SE Ve, Gu, FG) as described

M. b. caurensis (S & SC Ve) barred on top of head and uppertail-coverts; fairly uniform grey from chin to lower breast, paler on belly, rest of underparts barred black on rufous-brown

Habits Similar to Scaly-breasted Wren, but more often found exploring rotten logs, searching for invertebrates and small vertebrates, such as young frogs, and less often in leaf-litter. Sometimes joins mixed-species flocks.
Status Uncommon to fairly common in Ecuador, uncommon and local in Venezuela and Suriname, apparently more common in Guyana and French Guiana.
Habitat Tropical Zone, 150–1,500m, in humid primary forests and mature second growth, preferring wet understorey rich in rotting logs and avoids drier forests.
Voice Calls include a sharp metallic *chek* and loud rattle in alarm. Song a series of 3–7 well-spaced high long whistles separated by short pauses, usually followed by a long, accelerating (sometimes decelerating) slowly descending and quavering glissando, *eee… … ee… ee.. ee. ee-e-e-e-e-e-e-e-e-e-e-e-e-e-e-e-e-e-e-e-e-e*, trailing off at end, described as 'the shrieks emitted by a whistling kettle' (H&M, B&M, R&G, Hilty).

Cyphorhinus wrens are rather solid-looking birds found on or near the ground, distinguished by their slightly odd-shaped pointed bills, some usually pale blue skin around eyes and bright chestnut-red breasts; they often cock their tails and might be mistaken for tapaculos rather than wrens. Usually in family groups. Beautiful and accomplished songbirds that sound quite unreal when first heard, transfixing the listener, but are very difficult to see as they move silently in the dark interior of the undergrowth. They sing as well singly or in duet, and respond well to playback, but don't expect the curious bird to stay long.

CHESTNUT-BREASTED WREN

Cyphorhinus thoracicus Pl. 238

Identification 13.5–15cm. Deep brown above, around eyes, neck-sides, lower flanks and vent to undertail-coverts, feathers above obscurely and narrowly fringed black, affording a scaled (not barred) appearance; throat, ear-coverts, breast, sides and belly bright chestnut-red; eyes dark brown with narrow blue-grey eye-ring, blackish bill has an undulating culmen caused by swollen-looking base, and seemingly upturned distal half of lower mandible, legs and feet dusky. Juvenile has paler lower belly. Closely related Song and Musician Wrens have noticeably barred wings and tails. See Tawny-throated Leaftosser.

Ssp. *C. t. dichrous* (Ec, C & W Andes in Co)

Habits Retiring and wary as it skulks in pairs or small flocks on or near ground in piles of accumulated leaf-litter and tangled undergrowth. Does not join mixed-species flocks, but sometimes active on ground below such passing groups.
Status Uncommon and local in Ecuador, fairly common in Colombia.
Habitat Tropical to Temperate Zones, 700–2,600m, in humid to wet forests and mossy cloud forests, sometimes near streams.
Voice Calls include a raspy harsh oft-repeated *churr*. Song a haunting flute-like series of 2–4 minor-key notes, 1 per s, ascending then descending, perhaps alternating in half-tone steps, e.g. *here-see, here-see…*, first note a half-tone higher, lacking harsh *churr* notes typical of congeners, often repeated for several minutes; after playback song may jump an octave higher (H&B, F&K, R&G).
Note Also called Chestnut Wren.

SONG WREN

Cyphorhinus phaeocephalus Pl. 238

Identification 13cm. Dark brown above, barred evenly on wings and tail paler brown, flanks and belly to undertail-coverts the same brown; chin and face-sides to breast and body-sides bright chestnut-red, merging into brown belly; skin around eyes from lores to a point above rear ear-coverts bright pale blue, bill with slightly concave-looking culmen (due to slight bump above nostrils), pale greyish-blue, legs and feet brownish-grey. Juvenile undescribed, but apparently similar to adult.

Ssp. *C. p. chocoanus* (Chocó, W Co) very deep chocolate-brown, chestnut front also heavily washed with same dark brown

C. p. lawrencii (NW Co) bright chestnut of breast contrasts with white central belly and vent; distinct propensity to have part of chin or throat pure white (see plate)

C. p. phaeocephalus (W Ec, W Co) as described

C. p. propinquus (N Co) paler brown, like *lawrencii*, but throat contrasts abruptly with paler brown belly

Habits Usually on or near ground, often found probing decaying bark and wood of rotten logs and leaf-litter gathered at sides. In pairs or small groups. Sometimes follows ant swarms, and may also join mixed-species understorey flocks.

Status Locally fairly common.

Habitat Tropical Zone, to 1,000m, in humid to wet forests and mature second growth.

Voice Harsh frog-like calls and continuously repeated *churr* notes when disturbed. Song a series of guttural *churr* notes, harsh *chowk chowk-a-chowk* noises, tremolos and loud, melodic whistles that may vary enormously in pitch, e.g. *ong cutta cutta, whong cutta cutta glut, WHOO HEE*.... Pairs duet frequently. Song somewhat simpler than Musician Wren (H&B, B&M, R&G).

Note Formerly considered conspecific with Musician Wren (S&M).

MUSICIAN WREN
Cyphorhinus arada Pl. 238

Identification 12.5–13cm. Adult is deep chestnut above, barred regularly and evenly on wings and tail, nape and mantle distinctively streaked with long 'teardrops' of white, fringed black, black streaks on top of head and face-sides, postocular white eyebrow washed chestnut, lores to breast only slightly brighter brown than upperparts, centre of lower breast and upper belly pale buffy, breast-sides, flanks and lower belly to undertail-coverts brown with black streaks on sides, and barring on undertail-coverts; skin around eye blue, extending to point behind eyes, but far less extensive than Song Wren, bill dark grey, pale blue base of lower mandible, legs and feet blue-grey. Juvenile has only vestigial eye-ring, lacks eyebrow, has fainter streaks on mantle washed chestnut, and faint barring on lower belly.

Ssp. *C. a. arada* (SE Ve, Guianas) as described

C. a. salvini (E Ec, SE Co) quite distinct as lacks bold streaks on mantle, bright chestnut eyebrow starts at lores and supraloral, same bright bars on wings and from chin to breast and sides; rest of underparts deep chestnut-brown but not as dark as upperparts

C. a. transfluvialis (SE Co) similar to *rufogularis* but smaller; generally paler and less rufescent

C. a. urbanoi (SE Ve) darker and more uniform brown above (black bars on wings and tail less contrasting), but eyebrow and streaks on back brighter; face and breast paler chestnut, contrasting with very pale to whitish belly, flanks, thighs and vent to undertail-coverts same brown as upperparts; legs and feet brown; juvenile more uniform brown above with buffy streaks on back, barring barely discernible, dull reddish-brown on breast merges into brown of distal underparts; bill dark brown above, yellow basal half of lower mandible, legs and feet brownish-grey

Habits Similar to congeners. Responds well to playback, but may as quickly disappear having seen source! Forages on or near ground, especially in well-overgrown treefalls with rotting logs and collections of leaf-litter. Sometimes follows army ants or joins mixed-species flocks.

Status Fairly common, but rare to uncommon and somewhat local in Ecuador.

Habitat Tropical Zone, to 1,000m (or 1,300m in west Napo and Podocarpus National Park, Ecuador, and to 1,400m on Sierra de Lema, Venezuela), in *terra firme* and *várzea*.

Voice Calls include a harsh *churk* and continuously repeated *churr* notes when disturbed. Song a series of pure, clear, haunting whistles, especially *E-O*, varying over entire scale, the same phrase repeated with minor variations many times before moving to next, usually interspersed with guttural *churr* notes, e.g. *grr, E-O-pu-ho-who-E...grr-grr, pu-E-O-who-ho...grr, E-pur-E-O-Le-ho...chik-grr...E-O, who-E-ho, Le-ho*...; sexes often duet (R&T, B&M, Hilty).

Note Formerly considered conspecific with Song Wren (S&M).

POLIOPTILIDAE – Gnatcatchers and Gnatwrens

This small Neotropical family was formerly treated as a subfamily of Old World warblers, Sylviidae. They are essentially active little birds of lowland forests, always on the move, prying crevices and bundles of partially dried leaves, and also sallying to catch insects on the wing. Typically grey with black and white highlights, their bills are long to very long and tails are also long, and held cocked.

COLLARED GNATWREN
Microbates collaris Pl. 239

Identification 10.5–11cm. Adult unmistakable by long thin bill, distinctive black markings, and short stubby, usually cocked tail which is constantly wagged. Dark sepia-brown above with long thin white supercilium starting at lores, bordered above with black, and below by black mask, white lower face-sides, black malar; throat white, broad black band on breast, rest of underparts pale grey, washed brown from thighs and rear flanks to undertail-coverts. Eyes brown, bill variable, usually dark horn, legs and feet grey. Immature slightly brighter brown above and black facial and breast markings reduced; juvenile brighter brown still, has all-white face-sides with no black markings below.

Ssp. *M. c. paraguensis* (SE Ve) head darker brown, lores black, black markings slightly more extensive, with a vestigial breast bar both above and below band

M. c. collaris (SW Ve, SE Co) as described

M. c. columbianus (NE Ec) head much darker brown, white eyebrow bordered above with black, other black lines on head and breast heavier; breast-sides and flanks broadly

grey, causing breast-band to be narrower
M. c. torquatus (S Su, FG) entire upperparts dark brown, black breast-band broader

Habits Difficult to see as it forages alone, in pairs or small flocks in lower vines and tangled undergrowth, sometimes follows ant swarms and often joins mixed-species flocks.
Status Rare and local in north-east Ecuador, locally common in Colombia and uncommon to locally common in Venezuela. Uncommon and widespread in French Guiana.
Habitat Lower tropical Zone, to 900m, in humid *terra firme* forest, rarely at edges.
Voice Calls include harsh scolding *jipp*, an alarmed loud chatter, and a continuous high chirping when foraging. Song is a high, thin drawn-out *eeeeeeea* whistle, repeated every 3–5 s for long periods (H&M, R&G, Hilty).

TAWNY-FACED GNATWREN

Microbates cinereiventris Pl. 239

Identification 10.2–10.5cm. Adult unmistakable due to long thin bill, distinctive tawny face (may be hard to see in dim forest light; cf. Scaly-breasted Wren and Collared Gnatwren), and short stubby, usually cocked tail is constantly wagged. Brown above, face-sides, including eyebrow and neck-sides bright tawny orange, malar black, throat white, becoming grey on breast, sides and flanks, streaked on body-sides both black and white, centre of belly white, undertail-coverts orange as face.

Ssp. *M. c. cinereiventris* (W Ec, W Co) has a short black postocular stripe
M. c. hormotus (E Ec) dark brown on top of head, back and wings, darker grey on sides and flanks, more boldly streaked black and white
M. c. magdalenae (N Co) slightly paler brown above, less streaking on sides, undertail-coverts paler
M. c. peruvianus (E Ec, S Co) uniform grey breast and abdomen, lacks postocular mark; somewhat rufescent above, weakly defined black malar and breast streaks

Habits Similar to Collared Gnatwren.
Status Uncommon to locally fairly common in Ecuador (especially in west), fairly common to common in Colombia.
Habitat Tropical Zone, to 1,000m, in humid to wet forests and mature second-growth, rarely at edges.
Voice Calls include a rapid chatter, *tsek-tsek-tsek*, sometimes accelerated into *chrichrichrichrichri*, and a complaining *nyeeeh* given whilst foraging. Song is a high, thin, drawn-out *teeeeeea*, repeated many times every few seconds, sometimes preceded by a few rough nasal *jik* scolds (H&B, R&T, R&G).
Note Also called Half-collared Gnatwren.

LONG-BILLED GNATWREN

Ramphocaenus melanurus Pl. 239

Identification 12–13.2cm. Adult has longer bill and tail (usually cocked and constantly wagged) than congeners. Quite varied racially, but in general brown above with a darker tail, and white below, washed brown or grey. Eyes dark brown, bill horn, darker distally, legs and feet grey.

Ssp. *R. m. albiventris* (SE Ve, Guianas) dark brown above with clear white eyebrow, white below, washed irregularly grey on sides, flanks and undertail-coverts
R. m. duidae (NE Ec, SW Co, S Ve) rufescent brown above, faint buffy eyebrow; white below washed pale orange-tawny on sides of face and breast, flanks and undertail-coverts
R. m. griseodorsalis (WC Co) back slaty smoke grey, head less rufous-grey, slightly tinged cinnamon which is stronger and more ochraceous on forehead; head-sides strongly ochraceous-buff, olivaceous-buff underparts deeper
R. m. rufiventris (N Co, E Ec) dark brownish-grey above, with entire head rufous-brown except pure white throat; rest of underparts rufescent, with central belly white
R. m. pallidus (NE Co, N Ve) paler underparts than *trinitatis*, only inner sides and flanks much less washed with lighter buff; back more smoky grey, less brownish
R. m. sanctaemartae (N Co, NW Ve) medium brown above, lower cheeks and ear-coverts orange-tawny, paler on breast and even paler over rest of underparts
R. m. trinitatis (E Co, Tr, NE, C & W Ve) brown back, slightly darker wings, head more tawny, underparts almost all white, with slight orange wash on sides and flanks

Habits Similar to other gnatwrens but forages somewhat higher, from understorey to canopy, and less often with mixed-species flocks. Canopy dweller, but nests close to the ground in tree-fall gaps.
Status Fairly common to common.
Habitat Tropical to Subtropical Zones, to 1,700m, in moist to humid *terra firme* and *várzea*, second growth, overgrown clearings, edges and gaps, also in lighter dry deciduous woodlands and shrubby areas (less forest-based than other gnatwrens), provided large arboreal vine tangles are present.
Voice Calls include a slowly rising trill *tic-tic-tre-e-e-e-e-e* and a rapid even-pitched *tre-ee-ee-ee-ee-ee*. In Colombia, song a loud *wheit-wheit-wheit-wheit-wheit-wheit*, often preceded by *skee-er* or *chert*, *chert-sweet*; in Venezuela, a slow dry rattle *td r'dr'dr'dr'dr'dr'dr'dr'dr'dr*, smoother and faster south of Orinoco (H&B, Hilty).

TROPICAL GNATCATCHER

Polioptila plumbea Pl. 239

Identification 11–12.7cm. Adult male French grey above with tertials and remiges black, greater wing-coverts blackish with white tips; white outer fringes to tertials, tail black, with outer 3 feathers all white (black base varies racially, see plate); top of head black with deep blue gloss from forehead to nape, face-sides and underparts white, washed faintly grey on breast, sides and flanks. Eyes dark brown, bill black, legs and feet dark grey to blackish. Adult female has grey cap, concolorous with upperparts. Juvenile male as female, but top of head darker. Black cap and white underparts separate it from Guianan Gnatcatcher, which has prominent white eye-ring and mostly grey underparts.

Ssp. *P. p. anteocularis* (NW Co) outer fringes of tertials narrowly white, underparts almost entirely white
P. p. bilineata (W Ec, N Co) like *anteocularis* but has white postocular eyebrow; female also has postocular eyebrow
P. p. daguae (W Co) very dark grey above, almost concolorous with head
P. p. innotata (E Co, S Ve, Gu) pale bluish-grey above, broad white fringes to tertials
P. p. plumbea (Su, FG) as described, outer half of tertials white – unique
P. p. plumbeiceps (N Co, N Ve) dark bluish-grey above, greater wing-coverts blackish, prominent black base to outer 3 remiges

Habits Often cocks and wags tail. Not wary as it forages in pairs on outer foliage in subcanopy and canopy for invertebrates, often joins mixed-species flocks.
Status Fairly common to common in Ecuador (less so in east), common in Colombia, Venezuela, Suriname and French Guiana. More common in drier habitats, except in French Guiana where it favours swampy forests and humid *terra firme* forest.
Habitat Tropical Zone, to 1,900m but usually below 1,500m, in semi-dry deciduous to humid forests, second growth, edges, clearings and savannas with scattered vegetation, lighter woodlands (e.g. *Acacia*), mangrove, scrubby areas, arid scrub, plantations and gardens, and in Amazonia lower *várzea* growth along rivers and on river islands.
Voice Calls include a buzzy *gezzzzzz* and mewing *meaa*. Song is a clear high rhythmic *peet, peet, peet peeti peeti, ti'ti'pee, pee pee*, usually slightly falling and rising in pitch, but also *chup-chup-chup…* or *wees-wees-wees…* with *c.*6–10 notes on same pitch (H&B, H&M, Hilty).

GUIANAN GNATCATCHER
Polioptila guianensis Pl. 239

Identification 11cm. Adult male dark grey above with outer 3 rectrices white-grey, white eye-ring and lores; face-sides and neck to breast including sides bluish-grey, chin and upper throat, and belly to undertail-coverts white; eyes dark brown, bill, legs and feet dark grey. Adult female is less dark on back or top of head, and white throat is more extensive, but less clearly defined. Tropical Gnatcatcher has black or grey cap contrasting with all-white underparts.

Ssp. *P. g. facilis* (S Ve) warmer grey, with very little soft white streaking on throat, white lores and eye-ring much reduced, only 2 outer rectrices white, with black bases
P. g. guianensis (Guianas) as described

Habits Often cocks and wags tail. Habits similar to Tropical Gnatcatcher.
Status Rare to uncommon and local.
Habitat Lower Tropical Zone, to 500m, in humid *terra firme* forest and edges.
Voice Calls unknown. Song of *facilis* is a high thin *sii-sii-sii…* of *c.*8–15 notes in 1–2 s, often repeated over and over (A. Whittaker recording in Hilty). Race *facilis* starts with highest note, followed by lower second note, and rest given at steady, slower pace, whereas song of *guianensis* is more evenly paced and pitched throughout (Whitney & Alvarez Alonso 2005).
Note Whitney & Alvarez Alonso (2005) regarded all 3 taxa within the Guianan Gnatcatcher at specific level, on the basis of vocalisations and morphology, which equal to species-level differences recognised elsewhere within the genus. The names Guianan Gnatcatcher (*guianensis*) and Rio Negro Gnatcatcher (*facilis*) are suggested for those taxa in our region.

SLATE-THROATED GNATCATCHER
Polioptila schistaceigula Pl. 239

Identification 10.2–11cm. Adult mostly deep plumbeous-grey with white borders to undersides of outermost 2 rectrices; fine white eye-ring, central belly is pale grey, vent to undertail-coverts all white. Individual variation in plumage including small white lores and eyebrow, and or white spots on chin and throat. Eyes dark brown, bill black, legs and feet dark grey. Female less deeply coloured on head, with a small white eyebrow and thicker black line through eyes. Overlapping Tropical Gnatcatcher all white below and has white fringes to tertials. No overlap with similar but paler Guianan Gnatcatcher.

Ssp. Monotypic (W Co, W Ec)

Habits Often cocks and wags tail. Habits similar to Tropical Gnatcatcher, but forages more warily and sometimes lower in understorey to midstorey.
Status Rare to uncommon and local. Considered Near Threatened in Ecuador.
Habitat Tropical Zone, to 1,000m, in humid and wet forests, mature second-growth and edges.
Voice Calls include a nasal mewing and short faint, slightly ascending trill *trrrrrrrt*. Song a weak but long and higher pitched trill, more descending in pitch than congeners (H&B, R&G). On the basis of vocal differences, probably involves different species (O. Tostain).

GENUS INCERTAE SEDIS – Donacobius

Taxonomy still uncertain, formerly considered a member of the Mimidae, and called Black-capped Mockingbird, then the Troglodytidae, and currently associated with the latter, pending sufficient DNA-based data to establish its true affinities. Apparently an aberrant 'sylvioid', related to Old World babblers (Timaliidae) and warblers (Sylviidae) (K&B).

BLACK-CAPPED DONACOBIUS
Donacobius atricapilla Pl. 238

Identification 21.5–22cm. Adult has distinctive black cap, deep brown upperparts and long white-tipped tail; underparts pale ochre, affording unmistakable bicoloured pattern; yellow-orange eyes, bill blackish, legs and feet vinaceous grey. Juvenile paler above with vestigial white eyebrow, crown and head-sides dusky rather than pure deep brown, eyes yellow, base of bill creamy-yellow, legs and feet grey.

Ssp. *D. a. atricapilla* (Ve, Guianas) ruddy uppertail-coverts

D. a. brachyptera (N Co) slightly smaller than others, with paler brown rump and underparts

D. a. nigrodorsalis (E Ec, SE Co) dark brown above, including uppertail-coverts, fine, well-spaced black bars on body-sides and flanks

Habits Vociferous, greeting intruders with raucous calls often from atop vegetation growing in water, and forages actively and vocally on ground at edges of ponds and lagoons, and at low to medium heights in vegetation above water. Disappears into bushes overhanging water, emerging a few moments later, vocal and active as before. Usually seen in pairs or trios (latter usually involving a juvenile).

Status Fairly common to common in suitable habitat.

Habitat Tropical Zone, to 1,400m but mostly below 1,000m, mainly in brushy marshy areas at edges of rivers, lagoons, oxbow lakes and other standing water, even artificial ones, and apparently spreading to higher elevations with creation of damp pastures due to deforestation.

Voice Calls include a loud *quoit-quoit-quoit-quoit*, a low *chirru*, a harsh *jeeyaa*, sometimes repeated, and a grating scolding alarm-call. Song is an antiphonal duet, with each sex singing differently and waving their tails from side to side; male utters a series of ringing upslurred whistles, *who-it who-it who-it*, with female answering with lower sizzling and grating noises (R&T, Brewer & Mackay 2001).

CINCLIDAE – Dippers

Of all Passeriformes associated with water, none are more water bound than dippers, which never cease to surprise the observer with their uncanny ability to walk and feed in turbulent water. They are well built for the task – a chunky, brawny-looking body, short tail that does not encumber its owner, muscular stubby wings that serve well for paddling, very strong legs and feet for maintaining their position in powerful currents, a thick layer of down under a profuse coat of contour feathers for insulation, very high oxygen capacity in the blood for holding their breath, nostrils that can be shut tight, and last, but not least, the most amazing of all, eyes that can adapt to perfect vision both in and out of the water by changing the curvature of the lens! Dippers only live along clean mountain rivers and brooks with bottoms of rocks, pebbles and sand, where they find an abundance of water insects and other small prey, and wet, algae-covered boulders and rocky outcrops beside and in the middle of the stream, where they perch as well as forage between dips. They also nest near streams, building a globe of grass and moss in some unreachable rocky nook. Their most typical characteristic and that which gives them their name is dipping – moving the entire body up and down. But they are also regularly seen preening, and it seems logical that feathers which are regularly wetted require extra care. For this very important purpose, dippers have an oil gland that is comparatively larger than that of other birds of equal size, and must be the source of the odd, stale smell noticeable when the bird is held in the hand. Bouts of wing flexing and tail bobbing are other frequent gestures, thought to be part of a series of visual signals they use to communicate with partners or offspring in an environment of almost deafening noise. In this murmur-filled habitat their voices are necessarily loud, high-pitched and brassy, used both to attract partners and to repel intruders from territories. Recent genetic studies have yet to determine the closest relatives of the Cinclidae: the study by Barker (2004) suggests the thrushes (Turdidae) and Old World flycatchers (Muscicapidae) whilst that of Voelker & Spellman (2004) suggests the starlings (Sturnidae) and mockingbirds (Mimidae). However, a close relationship to wrens, which was traditionally considered to be the case, has now been discarded. Worldwide, the family consists of 5 species, 2 are found in the Old World and 3 in the Americas, from Canada to northern Argentina.

WHITE-CAPPED DIPPER

Cinclus leucocephalus Pl. 240

Identification 15cm. Adult has forehead to mantle white, with a band of black dividing the nape and mantle; broad mask and rest of upperparts black, with small white dots around eyes forming an eye-ring that joins white crown; chin to flanks and belly white, rear flanks, thighs and vent to undertail-coverts black, scalloped grey. Eyes deep red, bill black, legs and feet grey. Juvenile has some dark streaking on white of head, back entirely fuscous with black fringes to all feathers; chin and throat white, breast and rest of underparts dark brownish-grey with subtle darker streaking. Unmistakable coloration and habits.

Ssp. *C. l. leuconotus* (Andes in Ec, Co & Ve) as described

C. l. rivularis (Co: Santa Marta) from forehead to lower back streaked grey, rump and uppertail-coverts barred grey and fuscous; chin to flanks and belly white, thighs and distal underparts whitish with grey barring

Habits Presence often betrayed by white faeces on boulders and rocks, from which it commences foraging expeditions in water and at water's edge (but does not dive), also forages in vegetation nearby. Singles or pairs defend territory along section of running water.

Status Fairly common where water is clear, but susceptible to pollution.

Habitat Tropical Zone to Páramo, 100–3,900m, along rushing mountain streams and rivers with boulders, both small and large, and in open and forested areas.

Voice Calls include a sharp *tjik*, *zeet* or *zeet-zeet* (H&B, F&K, Brewer & MacKay 2001). Song is a lengthy, loud musical trill (R&T).

BOMBYCILLIDAE – Waxwings

In temperate America where they breed, Cedar Waxwings are birds of partially open areas, but in tropical America they inhabit humid forests. In the north, they are mostly found in tight flocks, often visiting orchards or fruiting trees; in northern South America, most records are of singles, tiny groups at most, for this species only very rarely straggles as far south as our region. In the tropics, they continue to visit fruiting trees and probably attend termite eruptions, for their diet also includes insects. Exquisitely elegant, waxwings derive their name from the modified secondaries, which have bare tips, extending beyond the filaments, that are flattened, glossy bright red and artificial-looking, but only present in adults. In flight they form a sort of bar across the wing, but are not visible in flight. They are handsome birds and, as such, often chosen as subjects for schmaltzy Christmas cards. In the early decades of the 20th century waxwings suffered due to the widespread use of DDT. The substantive population recovery of recent years brings the possibility of an increase in records in northern South America.

CEDAR WAXWING

Bombycilla cedrorum Pl. 240

Identification 18cm. Adult deep cinnamon-brown above with greyish wings, rump and tail which is short and square and has black subterminal band and yellow (or sometimes orange) terminal band, tertials and secondaries have bright red tips; head, neck-sides and breast cinnamon, chin blackish, distinctive long, backswept crest also cinnamon, distinctive white-bordered black mask sweeps back to join below crest; distal underparts yellowish-white. First-year lacks red tips to secondaries, whilst juvenile is much duller grey with a shorter crest, brown-streaked white face and black lores rather than a mask, breast and flanks streaked brown.

Ssp. Monotypic (boreal vagrant to Co, N Ve)

Habits In North and Central America, forages at fruiting trees and shrubs in large flocks in winter, but usually only in small flocks or singles in Panama.

Status Winters in North and Central America and Caribbean, rare even in Panama (January–March), and only accidental in northern South America. Vagrants noted at Nuquí, Chocó, in February, and near Buenaventura, Valle, in January (both Colombia: H&B), and Cerro Pejochaina (1,650m), Sierra de Perijá, Venezuela (Hilty).

Habitat Tropical to Subtropical Zones, but may be seen anywhere on migration.

Voice Calls an irregular series of high thin *eeeeee*, slightly quavering, repeated over and over (Hilty).

MUSCICAPIDAE – Chats and Old World Flycatchers

The only representative of this Old World family to have occurred in our region is Northern Wheatear. It is a typical member of the large and diverse but homogeneous genus *Oenanthe* which occurs across northern temperate latitudes and ranges to the tropics. They are generally of a similar size, grey above, with a distinctive white rump and white basal halves to the outer rectrices forming a bright white T that is obvious in flight. They prefer open areas and occur from beaches to deserts, open farmland and pastures with stones walls to submontane rocky outcrops. Typically, they stand upright, tail tightly closed, the dark wings obscuring the white rump, often for some time, giving the observer chance to take careful notes.

NORTHERN WHEATEAR

Oenanthe oenanthe Pl. 241

Identification 16cm. Breeding adult male has distinctive black mask, whilst non-breeding adult male, adult female and juvenile require more careful identification, but distinctive black-and-white tail pattern, constant bobbing, and preference for open stony habitats should identify the species (although it might turn up anywhere on migration).

Ssp. Subspecies unknown (boreal vagrant to Bo, Cu)

Habits Runs suddenly and quite fast, stands with distinctive upright posture. Perches atop dry stone walls, boulders and lone stems.

Status Two vagrant records: on Curaçao, November 1962, and Bonaire, December 1975 (Voous 1983).

Habitat Tropical Zone, usually in open habitats with scattered bushes, especially along coasts and watersides.

Voice Calls include a whistled *hiit* and a tongue-clicking *chack*. Song is an explosive fast chirpy verse with occasional *hiit* notes (Mullarney *et al.* 1999).

TURDIDAE – Thrushes

With air still frozen, a birdwatcher threads silently along an Andean trail, at a turn in the track, from somewhere ahead, a bird breaks into dreamy, limpid song, its voice a flute-like, liquid and beautiful. It is an Andean Solitaire. Shy, like most thrushes, the singer may prove difficult to see, but the birder will forever remember the song. Rare is the birdwatcher in Neotropical regions that has not had some variation of this experience; in our collective mind, thrushes are music. Some voices are metallic, some like flutes or pan pipes. At times, haunting melodies come from thin air, as if moss or trees were singing; at times, they are hesitant, remote and eerie, like ghostly noises from distant ruins. And, even if voices of a few species are quite mediocre, glorious melodies are the family's signature. There are members of Turdidae in all corners of planet, especially in Holarctic regions – they comprise one of most widespread and well-known bird families in the world. In our region, some rank, together with larger icterids and cotingas, amongst the largest of our Passeriformes. Few species show bright colours, they are most often clad in attractive shades of brown, grey, buffy or black, frequently highlighted by bright yellow bills and yellow or pink eye-rings, legs and feet. Typically, juveniles are spotted on the wings and body, and, if the juvenile plumage is not known, it is a reasonable supposition that the back, breast and wing-coverts, at least, will carry large spots of buffy or orange. Some Neotropical thrushes live exclusively in forests, whilst others occur in open and semi-open areas, from bare scrub to humid pastures and even urban parks and gardens, and have adapted well to all elevations, from the Andes to lowlands and coasts. In their diet, berries and fruits figure very prominently, especially outside of the breeding season, but they also take insects, snails, earthworms and grubs, chasing them with bold hops on the ground or by foraging at all levels. Certain mannerisms, such as the way they hop and tail- and wing-flicking, are so typical of thrushes that they permit instant identification of the family.

By and large, thrushes construct open-basket nests with plant materials and mud, where they lay their lovely blue or greenish-blue, spotted eggs.

Additional references used to compile this family include Clement & Hathaway (2000, hereafter C&H), and Collar (2005).

Solitaires are modest-sized thrushes, quiet and retiring and usually difficult to encounter but for their beautiful songs. They have broad, short bills, and are mainly arboreal, but place their nests close to ground.

VARIED SOLITAIRE

Myadestes coloratus Pl. 241

Identification 16–18cm. Entire head and underparts clean slate grey, with contrasting black mask from forehead and chin to ear-coverts, mantle to uppertail-coverts bright rufous; remiges black with silvery grey band across inner webs that flashes like a bar in flight, tail black with outer feathers greyish; bill, legs and feet yellow-orange. Juvenile dark brown above with buff spots covering entire body, more greyish below with paler buff spots; terminal spots on wing-coverts produce 2 wingbars. Like Andean Solitaire, but with black face, grey tail (no white tips) and orange bill and legs.

Ssp. Monotypic (Cerro Tacarcuna in NW Chocó, NW Co)

Habits Like Andean Solitaire, usually remains hidden in dense undergrowth but occasionally comes out in open at lower levels.
Status Uncommon to fairly common at a few localities in north-west Colombia near Panama border.
Habitat Upper Tropical to Subtropical Zones, 800–2,200m, in moist to humid and cloud forests and edges.
Voice Calls include single harsh notes. Song consists of beautiful, drawn-out, unhurried flute-like phrases with long pauses, similar to Andean Solitaire (Ridgely & Gwynne), e.g. *see-see, see-at you… seeeeleeeuu… see, see-at-you* (C&H). Sings mostly in twilight or foggy conditions year-round.

Solitaires have a whitish band across the basal inner primaries and the secondaries that is concealed at rest, but as the bird flits silently away becomes clearer

ANDEAN SOLITAIRE

Myadestes ralloides Pl. 241

Identification 16.5–18cm. Adult dull rufous-brown above and slate grey below, silvery grey bases to inner webs of remiges visible in flight; tail has outer feathers grey, also noticeable in flight. Short but broad bill, dusky above and yellow-orange below (to some extent depending on subspecies). Juvenile all brown, darkest on wings and palest on undertail-coverts, covered with buff spots with terminal spots on wing-coverts producing 2 wingbars. Slimmer and perches more upright than *Turdus* thrushes.

Ssp. *M. r. candelae* (C Co) above dark tawny, breast dark grey
M. r. plumbeiceps (W & C Andes in Co, W Ec) above rich rufous, crown to nape slate grey (tinged brown in Ec)
M. r. venezuelensis (E Andes in Co, N Ve, E Ec) above paler brown, flanks strongly tinged olive

Habits Very retiring and wary as it forages alone or in pairs for invertebrates by gleaning or sallying at all levels, then perches motionless for long periods, eluding observers by flying away quietly, easier to see when, as it does regularly, following army ants and visiting fruit trees, rarely with mixed-species flocks.
Status Fairly common to common.
Habitat Upper Tropical to Temperate Zones, at 800–4,500m but usually 1,200–2,900m, in humid to wet montane, cloud and elfin forests, edges and mature second growth, especially near streams.
Voice A throaty *rroau* (F&K). Song loud but also ventriloquial, thus does not help in locating bird as it sits very still. Beautiful, musical and fluted sequences of varied phrases, with pauses of a few seconds, e.g. *lee-day… leedle-lee… lulee… ur-lur… turdelee… see-see… eee-oh-lay… teul-teul…*, song shriller and less flute-like on east slope of Andes (R&T, C&H, R&G). Sings in twilight year-round. Also has flight song, uttered as bird flies over forest, essentially a highly speeded-up version of perched song that sounds more like a jumble of notes reminiscent of an *Atlapetes* brush finch (Collar).

Cichlopsis solitaires are more thrush-like in appearance, with a longer bill than *Myadestes* solitaires, and no wing markings, and also tend to perch somewhat more angled, like a *Turdus*.

RUFOUS-BROWN SOLITAIRE

Cichlopsis leucogenys Pl. 241

Identification 20.5–21cm. Adult mostly rufous-brown, with ochraceous throat and vent and greyish belly. Bill black above, yellow-orange below. Juvenile has fine buff terminal spots on head, tawny-buff fringes to back and wing-coverts, the latter combining with terminal spots to produce 2 faint wingbars. Distinguished from *Turdus* thrushes by short bicoloured bill combined with grey belly and unstreaked ochraceous throat and vent.

Ssp. *C. l. chubbi* (W Ec, Co) brighter reddish-rufous throat, richer on breast, grey belly well defined, undertail-coverts bright orange-buff
C. l. gularis (SE Ve, Gu) grey belly merges with breast and flanks, undertail-coverts pale orange-buff

Habits Hard to see as it forages, often alone, sometimes in pairs, inside forest. Usually sings from perch in mid canopy, and may flutter its wings while singing.
Status Mostly rare to uncommon, fairly common only at a few localities. Sight record in Suriname (R&T, SFP&M). Considered Vulnerable in Ecuador.

Habitat Tropical Zone, at 500–1,300m, occasionally to 100m in Ecuador, in humid to wet, mossy montane forests on slopes of mountains and tepuis.
Voice A thin sharp *tsr-reeee* whistle, louder *sueeet* alarm (C&H), and a high, thin *iiiiiiii* (Collar). Song consists of long, fast, continually varying, rambling, unmelodious phrases which include musical notes, chattering, whistles and twitters (R&T). Highly seasonal and usually uttered early morning, rendered *tliiowit-tsiii-trrrrr-tr-tr-tiio* (Collar).
Note Placed by most authors in monotypic genus *Cichlopsis*, but Ripley (1964) and Meyer de Schauensee (1966, 1970) merged *Cichlopsis* with *Myadestes*, though R&T returned to placement in *Cichlopsis* and this followed by most recent authors. Genetic data (Klicka *et al.* 2000) indicate that *Cichlopsis* is not closely related to *Myadestes* but rather sister to *Entomodestes*, leading to recommendation that *Cichlopsis* and *Entomodestes* be merged. SACC moved *Cichlopsis* into linear sequence with *Entomodestes*.

Black solitaires are larger than *Myadestes* solitaires and have slightly longer tails with prominent white on the outer feathers, noticeable when the birds are in flight. They are black with white panels on face-sides. Juveniles are unspotted, being effectively paler and duller then adults.

BLACK SOLITAIRE

Entomodestes coracinus Pl. 241

Identification 23cm. Adult unmistakable, all black with white face-sides, from base of bill to ear-coverts, underwing-coverts and axillaries, and distal halves of outermost 2 tail-feathers; eyes red. Juvenile duller and browner than adult, and lacks white tuft on breast-sides, usually apparent in adult.

Ssp. Monotypic (W Ec, W Co)

Habits Forages alone or in pairs from low levels to subcanopy, although several may gather at fruiting trees, where it joins mixed-species flocks and is easier to see, as it is normally extremely wary.
Status Mostly uncommon, but fairly common in some localities. Considered Near Threatened in Ecuador, as it appears sensitive to habitat disturbance.
Habitat Tropical to Lower Subtropical Zones, at 400–1,900m but usually 600–1,600m, in mossy, wet and cloud forests, edges, clearings and mature second growth.
Voice A weak, slightly buzzing high-pitched *tzeeeeeeeee* or *wreeeeeeeenh*, lasting 1–2 s and hard to locate because of its ventriloquial quality and bird's tendency to call from dense cover (H&B, C&H, R&G). Song poorly known, a weak, yet far-carrying, high, buzzy, nasal *wreeeeeeeenh*, lasting just over 1 s and very similar to White-eared Solitaire *E. leucotis* of N. Peru to Bolivia (Collar).

ORANGE-BILLED NIGHTINGALE-THRUSH

Catharus aurantiirostris Pl. 242

Identification 15.5–17cm. Considerable racial variation. Warm olive above, slightly brighter on rump, but remiges and rectrices a little darker, front of face greyish, chin and upper throat white, grizzled or flammulated grey, merging with much greyer breast, sides and flanks, latter washed olive. Centre of belly and undertail-coverts white. Bill coral to orange, legs and feet flesh to pale orange-brown. Juvenile overall darker brown than adult, with buffy centres to feathers, affording spotted appearance, throat paler, undertail-coverts buffy-white, with darkish horn-coloured bill, legs and feet. All nightingale-thrushes have orange bill, eye-ring and legs, but this species' brown back is diagnostic. Other brown-backed *Turdus* and *Catharus* thrushes lack orange bill, eye-ring and legs.

Ssp. *C. a. aurantiirostris* (E Co, N & SW Ve) note clear contrast between grey breast and white belly
C. a. barbaritoi (Perijá in Ve) like *aurantiirostris*, but more rufous on wings and tail
C. a. birchalli (NE Ve, Tr) head and nape dark grey, tinged rufous, rump rich brown, throat pale grey, breast to flanks olivaceous-grey, undertail-coverts pale olivaceous-grey
C. a. inornatus (E Andes in Co) like *phaeoplurus* but lacks any rufous tinge above and paler below
C. a. insignis (C Co) similar to *birchalli*, but somewhat greyish on nape and flight-feathers
C. a. phaeoplurus (W Co) richer rufous above, pale grey face and almost uniform pale grey below

Habits Retiring as it forages alone or in pairs in dense undergrowth and sometimes on ground for invertebrates, rarely venturing into small cleared spot or path, flicks leaves to expose insects. Occasionally ventures to mid levels for berries and seeds, and often follows ant swarms. Perches still or sings continually for long intervals from inside low, thick tangles and thickets.
Status Fairly common to common but local.
Habitat Tropical to Temperate Zones, 600–2,200m in Colombia, 1,500–2,900m in Venezuela, above 750m in Trinidad. Dense undergrowth of humid and cloud forests, edges, clearings and second growth, but also in lighter semi-deciduous woodland, bamboo thickets, coffee plantations, drier thorn scrub, and tangles and thickets in overgrown pastures, field margins, and large gardens in towns and villages.
Voice Calls include *chirp* and *chirr-chrit*, a *chuck* followed by a nasal wheeze, scratchy or squeaky *mew* or *miaow*, dry or nasal *waa-a-a-a*, often prolonged into a chatter, and an alarmed *chirr-rr* (C&H). One of the poorest singers in genus, song comprises high-pitched chirps, squeaks, trills and warbles, grouped into short jumbled phrases and interspersed with long pauses, delivered year-round and throughout day, though mostly at twilight; song has many geographic variations (F&K, H&B, C&H).
Note Race *phaeoplurus* of west Colombia formerly considered part of a separate species that included *griseiceps* subspecies-group of Central America, but all these were gathered into a single, extended species by Zimmer (1944c).

SPOTTED NIGHTINGALE-THRUSH
Catharus dryas Pl. 242

Identification 16.5–19cm. Olive above, with no markings on wings, tail slightly darker, top and sides of head black, chin, throat and underparts warm yellow with dusky arrowhead spots. Intensity of coloration and strength of spotting vary, possibly becoming richer with age. Paler birds, presumed first-years, also have far less greyish-olive on sides and flanks, being generally whiter below. Bill, legs, feet and narrow eye-ring orange. Juvenile dark brown above with buff streaks, most prominent on back and wings, where spots on coverts tend to form bars; below, dusky olive on breast, fading to olive on sides and flanks, with buff streak-shaped spots. Somewhat similar Slaty-backed Nightingale-Thrush has head and upperparts uniform dark grey, unspotted grey underparts and white (not dark) eyes, and generally occurs at higher elevations.

Ssp. *C. d. maculatus* (Ec, E Co, W Ve)

Habits Retiring as it forages alone, in pairs or small flocks in dense undergrowth and on ground, searching leaf-litter for invertebrates, follows ant swarms.

Status Uncommon to fairly common in Ecuador and Colombia (more common on west Andean slopes), uncommon and very local in Venezuela.

Habitat Tropical to Subtropical Zones, 650–1,800m in Ecuador, tending lower on west slope; 700–2,100m in Colombia and 900–2,200m in Venezuela. In humid or wet, mossy cloud forests and edges, especially near streams and dense ravines.

Voice A dry, nasal *rrehr*, *rreh'hu* or *reh'chew*; also loud bill-clacking. Ventriloquial song best indicator of presence, a beautiful, liquid sequence of whistles, e.g. *cholo-chu, ee-o, tuEE-o, lur-we and clo-EE-o*, some quite similar to Wood Thrush, interspersed with short pauses (P. Schwartz recording, T. A. Parker in H&B, C&H).

Notes Race *dryas* listed by Peters and Dickinson as occurring in Ecuador, but only occurs in Central America. Race *ecuadoreanus* described by Carriker (1935) for Andes in west Ecuador considered unworthy of recognition by Robbins & Ridgely (1990), as poorly differentiated and falls within range of *maculatus*.

SLATY-BACKED NIGHTINGALE-THRUSH
Catharus fuscater Pl. 242

Identification 17.5–19.5cm. Male dark slate grey above, including head, with narrow orange eye-ring; underparts vary significantly by subspecies. Bill, legs and feet orange. Juvenile has dark eye, dark brown upperparts with soft buff streaks on head and back, buffish-brown underparts, paler on chin and undertail-coverts, streaked more noticeably with lighter buffy. Somewhat similar Spotted Nightingale-Thrush has dark eyes and is well spotted below. Male Pale-eyed Thrush larger, all black and arboreal.

Ssp. *C. f. fuscater* (Ec, E Andes in Co, Andes in Ve) chin and throat white, breast and patch behind flanks grey, belly, flanks and undertail-coverts pale yellowish, thighs dark slate.

C. f. opertaneus (W Andes in Co) dark brown above, vinaceous-buffy below, richest on breast, paler, more greyish on flanks.

C. f. sanctaemartae (N Co) darkest race, with blackish head and dark grey underparts from chin to undertail-coverts

Habits Flicks wings constantly. Retiring as it forages alone, in pairs or small flocks in dense undergrowth and on ground, searching leaf-litter for invertebrates, flicking leaves; follows ant swarms, may venture into clearings and other open areas at dawn.

Status Uncommon to fairly common in Ecuador and Colombia (more common on west slope), locally common in Venezuela.

Habitat Tropical to Temperate Zones, at 600–3,250m, in humid or wet cloud forests and edges, especially near streams and dense ravines.

Voice A cat-like *meeow*, buzzier *wheeety* or *whewty-weer*, a high *poeeeee* whistle, and low grating *khroum-khroum* growls when alarmed. Ventriloquial song a beautiful, unhurried and haunting sequence of fluted whistles and raspy phrases, less hurried and more flute-like than Spotted Nightingale-Thrush (C&H). A haunting, ethereal flute-like *eer-lee, ur-eee-lee* like a distant rusty gate (Collar).

North American thrushes that migrate south to winter in South America may be winter residents in our region or transients en route further south. They are not easy to separate if seen briefly, and Grey-cheeked versus Swainson's Thrush can be a particularly vexing identification challenge.

VEERY *Catharus fuscescens* Pl. 242

Identification 17–19.5cm. Rufescent above, with grey lores and partial pale eye-ring; white below, washed buffy on throat and breast, lightly spotted with arrowhead marks on breast. Juvenile has buff spotting on head and back but not on wings, below, spots formed by olive fringes to feathers. More rufous above, greyer (not olive) on flanks with weaker throat stripe and breast spots than Grey-cheeked or Swainson's Thrushes.

Ssp. *C. f. fuscescens* (boreal migrant to Co, Ve, Bo, Cu, Tr, Gu) as described

C. f. fuliginosa (possible boreal migrant to South America) too poorly defined to separate from *fuscescens* in field, but some birds reddish above with clearly triangular breast spots

C. f. salicicola (boreal migrant to Co, Ve) more olive above, grey of upper lores and eye-ring absent, breast spots darker and rounder

Habits Retiring as it forages alone in dense undergrowth or on ground for invertebrates and fruits, sometimes follows ant swarms. Sometimes forms migratory flocks with other thrushes. Sings well on wintering grounds, especially at dawn and dusk. Does not sing en route south, but possibly whilst on passage north.

Status Winters in south-central and south-east Brazil (Remsen 2001), and transient through northern South America. Very uncommon between September and April, most records in September and October. rare in Trinidad (October, April), Bonaire (October–November) and Curaçao (Oct, April–May).

Habitat Tropical to Subtropical Zones, to 2,300m but mostly below 1,500m, in closed forest and more open woodland, edges and second growth, but anywhere on migration.

Voice A nasal rough *jerrr*, a slow downslurred *pheuw* or *hee-oo*, nasal *waaa-a-a-a*, rapid harsh *ho-ch-ch-ch-ch* chuckle, an alarmed low *wuck*, often repeated, and fluted *veer* or *veeyer* in flight. Generally silent in northern South America but may utter smooth, rolling and fluting *vrdi vrreed vreed vreer vree* song, descending in 2 stages (R&T, C&H, Sibley), especially prior to departure in March–April.

GREY-CHEEKED THRUSH

Catharus minimus Pl. 242

Identification 16–19.5cm. Dull olive above, cheeks greyish, no eye-ring; white below, sides of throat and breast washed slightly greyish-olive, heavily spotted dusky, rest of underparts white. Adult uniform above but first-year has buffy tips to greater wing-coverts. Juvenile spotted on head and back, with pale terminal spots on greater wing-coverts, below heavily spotted brown and dusky. Cold greyish cheeks and lack of eye-ring separate it from Veery, also more heavily spotted below. Immature separated by pale spots on greater wing-coverts. From Swainson's Thrush with difficulty: unmarked grey cheeks and lack of eye-ring give impression of cold grey face (often hard to see), whilst Swainson's Thrush sports distinct spectacles formed by buffy lores and eye-ring (much more so than Veery, which has narrow pale greyish-buff lores and partial eye-ring). Grey-cheeked also has slightly greyer upperparts and more heavily spotted breast than Swainson's. Juvenile has extensive buff spotting above and grey spotting below.

Ssp. *C. m. minimus* (boreal migrant to E Ec, Co, Ve, Tr, Gu, Bo, Cu) as described

C. m. aliciae (boreal migrant to E Ec, Co, Ve, Tr, Gu, Bo, Cu) slightly larger, washed brownish-olive on flanks

Habits Retiring as it forages alone or in pairs in dense undergrowth or on ground, often in damp areas, for invertebrates, fruits and seeds. Sometimes forms migratory flocks with other thrushes.

Status Present September–May. Uncommon as transient and rare as resident in east Ecuador (October–April), apparently uncommon in Colombia (October–May), fairly common in Venezuela (October–May), rare in Trinidad (November–January, March), Bonaire (October–November) and Curaçao (April–May), with sight records from Suriname.

Habitat Tropical to Temperate Zones, to 3,000m but mostly below 1,500m, in woodlands, from humid closed to semi-open semi-deciduous forests, edges and second growth, overgrown clearings and plantations, often in riverine thickets and other wet areas, but anywhere on migration.

Voice A downslurred *vee-er* and *weeah* (higher and more nasal than Veery), thin *wheesp* calls on migration, a short *chuck*, light *pheeeu*, and high, nasal *jee-er* in flight. Song high, thin and nasal with stuttering pauses, e.g. *ch-ch zreeew zi-zi-zreeee zi-zreeew* (F&K, C&H, Sibley). Generally silent in winter, but may begin to sing in late season.

Note Bicknell's Thrush *C. bicknelli* (formerly considered a subspecies of Grey-cheeked Thrush: see Ouellet 1993) has not yet been recorded in northern South America; it winters exclusively in West Indies, but could occur.

SWAINSON'S THRUSH

Catharus ustulatus Pl. 242

Identification 16–19.5cm. Uniform olive above, though first-year has pale buffy tips to greater wing-coverts, with clear, complete eye-ring. Chin and throat pale buff becoming creamy buff on breast with distinct line of wedge-shaped spots on malar, becoming heavy wedge-shaped spots on breast, rounder as they fade on lower breast, fading out on upper belly, sides and flanks washed heavily olive. Cf. Veery and Grey-cheeked Thrush, but note buffy spectacles not apparent in some (especially juveniles) during southbound migration (in hand, Swainson's usually has shorter wing than Grey-cheeked: 88–105 vs. 97–109 mm). Juvenile has extensive buff spotting above and olive spotting below; very similar to juvenile Grey-cheeked Thrush and only separated safely by pale eye-ring.

Ssp. *C. u. swainsoni* (boreal migrant to Ec, Co, Ve, Gu)

Habits Retiring as it forages usually alone, sometimes in pairs, from understorey to canopy (rarely near or on ground) for invertebrates and especially fruits (often in fruiting trees, especially during spring migration), sometimes joins mixed-species flocks or follows ant swarms. Sometimes forms migratory flocks with other thrushes.

Status By far commonest of North American migrant thrushes, both a transient and winter visitor to northern South America (mid October to late April), and fairly common to very common at some localities (outnumbers Grey-cheeked Thrush in Ecuador, Colombia and Venezuela), but only rare transient in Bonaire (October–November, April) and Curaçao (October, April).

Habitat Tropical to Temperate Zones, to 3,800m but mostly below 2,000m. Winters mostly in submontane and montane regions, in closed forests and more open woodland, edges and second growth, clearings, riverine thickets, plantations and gardens, but anywhere on migration.

Voice A low, liquid *quip*, a chatter introduced by *qui-brrrrr*, a burry, descending *heep* or *queev* in flight, and soft *twink*, *twip* or *wit*, all ventriloquial and given with nervous wing-flicks. Song smooth, rolling and rising (C&H, Sibley). Sings well on wintering grounds, night and day, but very little during migration.

Note Comprises 2 groups, a russet-backed group including nominate *ustulatus*, and olive-backed birds known as *swainsoni* group, with several differences besides upperparts coloration, including breeding habitat, some vocalisations and wintering areas. Only *swainsoni* has been recorded in northern South America.

WOOD THRUSH
Hylocichla mustelina Pl. 242

Identification 19.5–21.5cm. From other migrant thrushes by size, bright chestnut nape, white eye-ring and large black spots below to flanks. Juvenile has narrow buffy streaks above.

Ssp. Monotypic (boreal migrant to Co, Cu)

Habits Behaviour presumed similar to that in Central America, frequently flicking wings, retiring as it forages alone or in small flocks in dense undergrowth for invertebrates and fruits, joins mixed-species flocks and follows ant swarms.
Status Winters in Central America, rare in east Panama and an accidental overshoot to region, only confirmed records are from Colombia (December) and Curaçao (October).
Habitat Tropical to Subtropical Zones, in forested foothills in Colombia, presumably in undergrowth and thickets of moist lowland forests, second growth and plantations, as in Central American wintering grounds.
Voice A distinctive *whip-whip-whip* and buzzy, nasal *jeeen* in flight. Gives weaker version of breeding song, a rich varied fluting that begins with soft *po po po* notes, rising and ending with a rich buzzy whistle, especially in late winter (Ridgely & Gwynne, Sibley).
Notes Whether monotypic genus *Hylocichla* should be recognised or merged in *Catharus*, as by Sibley & Monroe, is controversial; see Winker & Rappole (1988) and AOU (1998), but recent genetic data (Klicka *et al.* 2005) support retention of *Hylocichla*. *Catharus fuscescens*, *C. minimus* and *C. ustulatus* were also formerly included in *Hylocichla* (e.g. Hellmayr 1934, Pinto 1944, Phelps & Phelps 1950a, AOU 1957), but most classifications have followed Ripley (1964) and Meyer de Schauensee (1966), based on Dilger (1956), in placing them in *Catharus*. Other genetic data (Outlaw *et al.* 2003) strongly support their inclusion in *Catharus* rather than *Hylocichla*.

Typical thrushes, *Turdus*, represent by far the largest and most widespread genus in the family. They occur across Asia, Europe, Africa and the Americas and are arguably the most successful genus of any family of birds. They are predominantly brown and black, and many species have yellow bills, legs and feet and occasionally a yellow eye-ring. All are quite vocal, singing strongly and persistently, but with variable ability. They occur in many habitats, from open to darker recesses of forests. Klicka *et al.* 2005, found *Platycihla* to be embedded within *Turdus*, and we follow Collar in using *Turdus* for Yellow-legged and Pale-eyed thrushes.

YELLOW-LEGGED THRUSH
Turdus flavipes Pl. 243

Identification 19–22cm. Males, females and juveniles differ racially. Intermediates cause havoc and there is much variation. Dark brown eyes and yellow eye-ring and legs (dull yellow in female); bill usually yellow in male, dusky in female (often with some yellow on culmen or base). Very similar Pale-vented Thrush does not overlap; Cocoa Thrush much more rufous above (not olive) with more whitish throat; Clay-coloured Thrush lacks eye-ring and has reddish-brown eyes, olive bill, and paler, more uniformly buffy-brownish coloration. Male Glossy-black Thrush all black (no overlap with all-black *xanthoscela*) and female slightly larger, darker and more uniform below. Female Pale-eyed Thrush has pale eye without eye-ring; female Black-hooded Thrush slightly larger and paler uniform tawny-buff below.

Ssp. *T. f. melanopleura* (NE Ve, Margarita I., Tr) male has all-black head, mantle scalloped black and grey, lower back to uppertail-coverts grey, wings and tail black; breast black, belly scalloped dusky and black, undertail-coverts grey, scalloped lightly pale grey (dark morph on Margarita has grey deep slate); female olive-brown above, chin to upper breast scalloped buffy and olive, rest of underparts warm brownish-buff; juvenile rich rufous-brown above, darker on wings and tail, heavily spotted buffy on head, back and wings, below gingery-buff, spotted and scalloped dark brown

T. f. polionota (S Ve, W Gu) male like *venezuelensis*; female darker and greyer above, darker brown on wings and tail, buffy spots on median wing-coverts, below greyish, streaked black on throat, becoming spots on upper breast, warm brownish-buff on sides and flanks, barred grey and whitish on undertail-coverts, centre of belly whitish; juvenile very dark, fuscous on nape and upper back, wings and tail, spotted on back and wings with tawny, heavily spotted and barred tawny and fuscous below

T. f. venezuelensis (N Co, W & N Ve) male has black head, breast, wings, tail and thighs, rest of body grey, upper back scalloped black, undertail-coverts scalloped white; female olive above, buffy below, slightly streaked on chin and upper throat dusky, centre of belly white, with white scallops on undertail-coverts; juvenile dusky above, palest on uppertail-coverts, fuscous on wings and tail, and spotted buffy on head, back and wings; below greyish-buffy, spotted and barred dusky, darkest on breast and thighs

T. f. xanthoscela (To) male all black with blue gloss, female and juvenile duller below but similar to *melanopleura*

Habits Wary as it forages alone or in pairs, from lower mid-storey (rarely lower) to canopy for invertebrates and fruits, often at fruiting trees.
Status Fairly common, although some races have very restricted distributions in which suitable habitat is rapidly being destroyed. Also captured for bird trade. Believed to migrate seasonally within South America, possibly responding to fruit availability.
Habitat Tropical to Subtropical Zones, at 350–2,500m (to 300m and 100m on Tobago and Margarita, respectively), in

humid rain and cloud forests, edges, second growth and clearings, lighter deciduous woodland, plantations and gardens.
Voice Calls include *tsrip*, *cuck* and in alarm *sreeet*. Song loud, musical and varied, with many high notes, mimicking phrases of other songbirds and most common phrases a liquid *swet-to weeea*, *sweet to-weeea-speet* and *tsreep, tsreh-tsreh-tsreh, tsrip-tsrip-tsrip*, often repeated, males sing for lengthy periods from treetops with only brief breaks. Much variation with individuals having their own unique blend that includes phrases mimicked from other species and changing order of notes (P. Schwartz recording, ffrench, H&B, C&H, Hilty).
Notes Formerly considered conspecific with Pale-eyed Thrush, but Phelps & Phelps (1946) found them to be sympatric in Venezuela. Formerly placed in genus *Platycichla*, but merged in *Turdus* by Klicka *et al*. 2005.

PALE-EYED THRUSH
Turdus leucops Pl. 241

Identification 18–22cm. Adult male all black with yellow bill and legs; pale eyes (whitish-blue in male, pale grey to grey-brown in female and juvenile). Female olive-brown, paler below, becoming greyer on belly, and easily confused with other female thrushes (e.g. Yellow-legged Thrush). Juvenile has buffy spots above and blackish spots below. Female Pale-vented and Black-billed Thrushes have extensively white bellies. Glossy-black Thrush has dark eye with yellow eye-ring, and female is also slightly larger, darker and more uniform below. Female Black-hooded Thrush slightly larger and paler uniform tawny-buff below, with yellow bill and narrow eye-ring. Cocoa Thrush much more rufous above and has more whitish throat. Clay-coloured Thrush has reddish-brown eyes, olive bill, and paler and more uniformly buffy-brownish coloration.

Ssp. Monotypic (Ec, Co, Ve, Gu)

Habits Very retiring as it forages alone or in pairs from understorey to canopy, sometimes in subcanopy, for invertebrates and fruits, often at fruiting trees with other frugivores, but does not join mixed-species flocks.
Status Rare to uncommon and local, but often overlooked and possibly more common, and may migrate seasonally, possibly responding to fruit availability.
Habitat Upper Tropical to Lower Subtropical Zones, at 900–2,000m, in cloud and humid to wet (especially mossy) forests, edges and mature second growth, also well-wooded ravines.
Voice Song an unusually variable series of fairly musical or squeaky phrases, with many high notes, some imitations and brief to long pauses, e.g. *wheero-weet, chup-e, ez-t, e-ta, ti't, eez, cheur-ez-wee.t*…, males sing from treetops (H&B, C&H, Hilty).
Notes Formerly considered conspecific with Yellow-legged Thrush, but Phelps & Phelps (1946) found them to be sympatric in Venezuela. Formerly placed in genus *Platycichla*, but merged in *Turdus* by Klicka *et al*. 2005.

CHIGUANCO THRUSH
Turdus chiguanco Pl. 244

Identification 26–28cm. Adult entirely uniform dark greyish-brown, very slightly paler below. Immature like adult, with pale spots on wing-coverts and pale barring on belly, duller barring from vent to undertail-coverts. Yellow bill and legs (no eye-ring). Eyes described as red to chestnut to hazel, but we have found range even broader, to include grey and greyish-hazel. Juvenile has buffy streaks on head and buffy underparts with brown spots. Similar Great Thrush favours more humid conditions, is larger and longer tailed, usually with more orange bill and legs and, in adults, yellow eye-ring.

Ssp. *T. c. conradi* (Ec) larger and paler than nominate.

Habits Typical very erect stance, with protruding breast, raised tail and slightly drooping wings, frequently flicks wings and tail. Not wary when close to humans as it forages alone, in pairs or small flocks, often on fields and lawns, for invertebrates, but also in fruiting trees.

Chiguanco Thrush in typical upright, full-breasted posture

Status Uncommon to common, more common in south, possibly spreading north. Short-distance movements, possibly responding to fruit availability.
Habitat Upper Tropical Zone to Páramo, at 1,500–3,200 m, in semi-arid to arid, relatively open terrain with scattered vegetation but usually near water, e.g. ravines, hedgerows, orchards, town parks and gardens, but also fairly open deciduous forests, light montane woodlands and, at higher elevations, *Polylepis* stands.
Voice Calls include *weeeh*, an oft-repeated *cluck*, a thin, high wheezing alarm *wheen*, and a loud sharp *tsi-tsi-tsi* when flying away from disturbance. Song a simple sequence of musical whistles, e.g. *wee-see-seeu*, interspersed with short trills and repeated many times (F&K, C&H, R&G). Sings mostly in twilight, often from exposed perches (even wires), but only during breeding season; weak and relatively unmusical, a series of short and simple melodic phrases that end in a jumble or twitter, each phrase repeated 2–3 times, eg. *siblisirrilé, seblesierilli*…. (Collar).
Note Race *conradi* considered invalid by R&T, R&G, but maintained by Dickinson (2003) and Collar.

GREAT THRUSH *Turdus fuscater* Pl. 244

Identification 28–33cm. Very large; varies according to race. Dark brown above, wings and tail slightly darker, a little paler below, underwing-coverts uniform with body-sides. Legs long and sturdy. Bill, eye-ring and legs yellow-orange to orange. Eyes reddish-chestnut. Juvenile varies also, usually has fine buffy streaks above and heavy brownish mottling below; eyes dark. Largest South American thrush.

Ssp. *T. f. cacozelus* (Santa Marta, N Co) palest subspecies, olive-brown above, buffy-olive below becoming whitish on belly, buffy to orange underwing-coverts

T. f. clarus (Perijá, Co & Ve) slightly warmer olive above, with warmer pale olive underparts; juvenile warmer brownish-olive above, with pale throat and buffy underparts, washed warmer, almost tawny on breast with mid brown subterminal spots and dusky edges; bill and eye-ring greyish

T. f. gigas (E Andes in Co, Andes in W Ve) largest subspecies, uniform dark olive-brown above and slightly paler, greyish-olive, below, with narrow dark mesial line and subtle dark centres to feathers of throat and breast, paler on belly; immature has very subtle spotting above, but breast has whitish subterminal spots with dusky terminal fringes, fading out on sides and flanks

T. f. quindio (N Ec, C & W Andes in Co) darkest subspecies, sooty olive above, and only slightly paler on rear underparts; immature marginally paler below, with blackish fringes from chin to flanks, giving scalloped appearance

T. f. gigantodes (S Ec) only slightly paler than *quindio*, sooty brown below, occasionally with buffy streaks on chin and throat, underwing-coverts concolorous with body-sides

Habits Flicks tail up on landing and when foraging on ground, e.g. on lawns and roadsides. Walks and runs forward, standing very upright and tilting head to look at ground, as if listening, in classic garden thrush manner. Makes frequent short flights from rock to bush or other promontory, and flash of yellow of its legs against dark body gives impression of a small hawk. Bold and seldom wary, and quite vocal, as it forages alone or in small flocks (communal roosts of up to 40 individuals), or in pairs in breeding season when very territorial, from ground to canopy by sallying for invertebrates or picking fruits from bushes and trees.

The yellow legs are very noticeable as one glimpses a Great Thrush darting from rock to rock on a hillside, leaving the impression of a hawk

Status Common to very common, expanding its range due to forest clearance. Short-distance movements, possibly responding to fruit availability.

Habitat Subtropical Zone to Páramo, at 1,400–4,200m but usually above 2000m, in open country, e.g. *páramo* grasslands, especially around isolated montane scrub or woodland or *Polylepis* stands, to semi-open areas, and common on farmland and pastures with scattered vegetation, hedgerows, ravines and gardens (even in large cities), and edges of and clearings in woodland, e.g. humid cloud forest and second growth, but absent from large undisturbed forests.

Voice Various loud calls, e.g. an incessant *kweep*, a robin-like *see-ert*, thin wavering *eeeee*, throaty *chee-yop* or sharp *keeyert* in flight, and *kee*, *chuck* and *kuet* (often repeated in alarm and/or flight), and clear whistles. Song varies between subspecies and is infrequently heard, a fairly limited series of rapid but weak musical whistles, e.g. *ooweetyu* or *so clear-e*, often repeated and interspersed with clear high whistles, dry trills and nasal *nwee* notes (F&K, R&T, H&B, C&H, R&G, Hilty). Sings in twilight (usually pre-dawn) from midstorey to canopy, but only during early breeding season. Song in Venezuela loud thick whistles *so-clear-e, so-clear-e, so-clear-e*, often mixed with a nasal *nwee-nwee*, high notes and dry trills, and after a few phrases drifting slowly and fluidly to new ones (Collar).

GLOSSY-BLACK THRUSH

Turdus serranus Pl. 244

Identification 23–25.5cm. Adult male (except *cumanensis*) glossy black with dark eyes, bright yellow-orange eye-ring, bill, legs and feet. Females vary by subspecies. Juvenile has fine buffy streaks above and buffy mottling below. No overlap with Yellow-legged Thrush and Pale-eyed Thrush has pale eyes but no eye-ring. Dark races of Great Thrush are much larger, longer tailed and far less secretive forest birds than Glossy-black Thrush (though they may occur together); also male Glossy-black is deeper black than Great Thrush, female Glossy-black Thrush browner than Great Thrush.

Ssp. *T. s. atrosericeus* (NE Co, N Ve) as described, adult female dark, somewhat greyish olive-brown above, slightly paler below, with pale yellow bill and legs, and narrow, dull orange-yellow eye-ring

T. s. cumanensis (NE Ve) male dark chocolate-brown with blackish tail and wings, narrow rufous wing fringes; female darker above and below than *atrosericeus* with darker wings and tail, bill, legs and feet yellowish-horn, eye-ring dull yellowish-grey

T. s. fuscobrunneus (Ec, Co) all glossy black, smaller bill and shorter wings and tail than nominate, female similar to *cumanensis* but slightly richer in tone, bill greyish-horn, legs and feet yellow

Habits Wary as it forages for invertebrates and fruits, from midstorey to canopy, rarely near or on ground. Solitary or in pairs, rarely joins mixed flocks. Occasionally makes short forays to trees in open fields, swiftly crossing the open space.

Status Fairly common to locally common. Some short-distance movements, possibly in response to fruit availability.

Habitat Tropical Zone to Páramo, at 320–3,750m but usually 1,500–2,800m, in humid to wet primary and mature secondary forests, cloud forests and edges, adjacent clearings and gardens, sometimes in dry deciduous forest (south-east Ecuador).

Voice A typical repeated *chip* or *tchi* in flight, and sharp rasping *rrrrrt-rrrrrt* alarm. Song comprises persistent repetitions of very fast, high, shrill and rising phrases, e.g. *tee-do-dede-do-deet* or *ee-te-jeete-o*-et, sometimes including slurred notes or short trills, with short intervals (P. Schwarz recording, F&K, H&B, C&H). In breeding season, males sing almost continuously in twilight from high, concealed perches (often amid epiphytes in canopy).

ANDEAN SLATY THRUSH

Turdus nigriceps Pl. 245

Identification 19–23cm. Male slate grey above, slightly darker on wings, black on tail, top and sides of head; throat white with rows of streaks reaching pale slate grey breast to belly, flanks and thighs, vent white, undertail-coverts white streaked black; pale yellow eye-ring, bright yellow bill, legs and feet. Adult female solid olive-brown from top and sides of head to tail, throat white, streaked rufous-brown to ruddy breast, sides and flanks ruddy, washed greyish-olive, belly and vent white, undertail-coverts white streaked brown. Bill, eye-ring, legs and feet yellowish or buffy-horn. Juvenile olive above with fine buffy-orange streaks, pale buffy throat grading through pale yellowish-buffy to undertail-coverts, with buffy-brown scaling from chin to undertail-coverts, white only on central belly, thighs and vent. Adult male is only grey thrush in Ecuador, but quite distinctive in any case. White-necked Thrush has broad yellow-orange eye-ring and white crescent on lower throat. Black-billed Thrush has black (not yellow) bill and no eye-ring. Ecuadorian Thrush has olive-yellow bill and weaker throat streaking.

Ssp. *T. n. nigriceps* (resident and austral migrant in S Ec)

Habits Very wary and retiring as it forages alone or in pairs from midstorey to canopy.

Status Uncommon and local in southern Loja, south Ecuador when breeding (January–May), and 2 non-breeding records of presumed migrants in Zamora-Chinchipe, south-east Ecuador (June–July). Breeding population considered Near Threatened because of extensive deforestation in region.

Habitat Upper Tropical to Lower Subtropical Zones, at 1,400–1,800m, in humid forests, edges and second growth on Andean slopes, especially along streams in shady ravines and in stands of alder.

Voice A dry *tsok* and frequent harsh *kraa* in contact. Song consists of repetitions of a monotonous high *tiji-tijihe*, interrupted by long pauses, but also described as rather drawn-out, musical, high whistles combined with variable series'of metallic notes, often including *tooee, too-oo*… before repeating whistled phrases (C&H). Sings from dense cover of midstorey to canopy, and ventriloquial song makes bird even harder to find.

Note R&T consider that *T. nigriceps* could be monotypic, as race *subalaris* (southern Brazil, north-east Argentina, Paraguay) apparently has quite different voice and may prove to be a separate species.

PLUMBEOUS-BACKED THRUSH

Turdus reevei Pl. 243

Identification 23–24cm. Adult blue-grey above, slightly darker on wings, paler fringes to uppertail-coverts, darker tail, chin and throat white, finely streaked blackish, breast greyish, becoming pale buffy to peach below, white on vent and undertail-coverts. Bill, legs and feet yellow, eyes pale blue. Female has brownish tinge to head and face. Juvenile dark brown above, with fine buffy streaks from head to uppertail-coverts including wing-coverts, white on chin and undertail-coverts, pale buffy over rest with irregular dark spotting and scaling. Pale blue eye of adult diagnostic, separating it from any possible confusion with White-necked or Dagua Thrushes.

Ssp. Monotypic (SW Ec)

Habits Apparently unwary as it forages from midstorey to canopy at fruiting trees. May be solitary, in pairs or small flocks, sometimes on ground, in flocks of up to 30 but does not join mixed-species flocks.

Status Uncommon to locally common. Some seasonal movements, possibly in response to wet season and food availability, appearing in first half of year in drier regions.

Habitat Tropical to Subtropical Zones, to 2,500m but usually below 1,600m, in fairly dry and deciduous to humid primary and mature secondary forest and woodland, edges and clearings, gulches and ravines, adjacent scrub, roadsides and fallow fields near forest.

Voice A piercing, descending *pseeeu* (sometimes even-pitched or ascending). Song (given from canopy) a series of rapid musical whistles in a jumbled manner, often interspersed with descending whistles, sometimes several singing together (C&H, R&G).

BLACK-HOODED THRUSH

Turdus olivater Pl. 245

Identification 23–24cm. Dark olive brown above, entire head and upper breast black, sides of breast to belly ochraceous, becoming dark buffy-olive on undertail-coverts. Bill, narrow eye-ring, legs and feet yellow. Female has chin and throat flammulated ochre, grading into ochraceous breast. Immature has brown hood and orange tips to wing-coverts, fine buffy streaks on scapulars, and black spots on throat that do not reach breast. Juvenile olive above, with buffy streaks and spots on wing-coverts, ochraceous below with warm brown flush and scaling on breast and flanks, some blackish scaling on breast. Male unmistakable, but female may be confused with females of Yellow-legged or Pale-eyed Thrushes. Male of race *caucae* from male Black-billed Thrush, race *murinus*, by black hood and paler, more yellowish-grey underparts, and Black-billed has black bill. Female Glossy-black Thrush darker and more uniform below. Clay-coloured Thrush paler, is found at lower altitudes and has olive bill.

Ssp. *T. o. caucae* (Co: Andes) like *olivater* above but quite distinct below, dingy whitish throat with black streaks, rest of underparts yellowish-buffy, female similar but has brown (not black) hood

T. o. duidae (SE Ve) black on throat appears as streaks, bright rufous below, longer bill, tail and wings than *roraimae*, female like *olivater* but dark olive on head and richer, more cinnamon below
T. o. kemptoni (Ve: Neblina) black on throat appears as streaks, bright rufous below, darker abdomen than *duidae* or *paraquensis*
T. o. olivater (N Co, N Ve) as described
T. o. paraquensis (S Ve) black on throat appears as streaks, bright rufous below, darker above and paler below than *duidae*
T. o. roraimae (SE Ve, Gu) less black on head, merging with darker olive-brown upperparts, broad streaks extend across lower throat, breast to belly pale orange; female has pale throat with black streaks
T. o. sanctaemartae (Co) black of upper breast grades into lower breast in spots, below, paler and yellowish-grey

Habits Apparently unwary as it forages, usually alone, from ground to canopy for invertebrates and fruits. Several may gather in a fruiting tree; follows army ants.
Status Fairly common to locally common, sight records in Suriname (SFP&M, C&H). Numbers appear to shift seasonally.
Habitat Upper Tropical to Temperate Zones, at 600–2,600m. Humid primary and mature secondary and cloud forests, edges, clearings, but also more open woodland, plantations and even open country with scattered vegetation.
Voice Song comprises mellow sequences of slow musical 2–3 syllabled phrases, e.g. *too-doo*, *too-dee*, *chur-dee*, or *turwere*, with ringing *clee* or high thin *ee-ee* interspersed; also softer, more melodious song. Sings mostly in twilight from midstorey to canopy (P. Schwartz recording, H&B, C&H, Hilty).
Note R&T suggested that *T. o. caucae* might deserve recognition as a separate species, but there are no recent records of that race and it could be extinct.

MARAÑÓN THRUSH
Turdus maranonicus Pl. 243

Identification 21.5–23cm. Adult olive-brown above, faintly scaled darker brown, pure white below with distinctive brown crescents. Juvenile slightly paler brown above with fine buffy streaks from head to uppertail-coverts, below whiter on belly and thighs than adult. Juvenile from juvenile Plumbeous-backed Thrush by pure white underparts, not washed buffy-yellow.

Ssp. Monotypic (SE Ec)

Habits Apparently unwary as it forages alone, in pairs or small flocks of up to 6, in vegetation or on ground.
Status Fairly common to common and conspicuous at a few localities in its small range.
Habitat Tropical to Lower Subtropical Zones, at 650–1,600m, in drier areas, e.g. arid scrub, dry deciduous and thorny woodland, secondary woodland, edges and clearings, mango groves, irrigated agriculture and gardens, even foraging on ploughed fields and grassy areas.
Voice A frequent nasal contact *bip*, series of *chup* notes, and typical thrush-like alarm. Song comprises melodious, flute-like, leisurely phrases (C&H), slower than Black-billed Thrush with more slurred notes (P. Coopmans in R&G). Sings from canopy, often well hidden.

CHESTNUT-BELLIED THRUSH
Turdus fulviventris Pl. 243

Identification 23–25cm. Adult male dark olive-brown above, head black, breast dark grey, running up neck-sides to divide black head from dark brown back in a narrow collar, belly and flanks rich ruddy rufous, thighs and undertail-coverts warm grey. Bill yellow, eye-ring orange, legs and feet horn. Female similar but head fuscous and grades into back and chest, with some buffy flecks on chin and throat. Juvenile dark olive above, paler on mantle with head dusky, paler on cheeks; throat buffy, breast greyish and belly to flanks rusty-cinnamon, barred dusky, though much less on flanks and more on thighs, undertail-coverts warm grey. Adult unmistakable, reminiscent of American Robin.

Ssp. Monotypic (Ec, E Andes in Co, Andes in Ve)

Habits Forages alone or in pairs from ground to canopy, tossing leaves inside forest, foraging on small patches of bare or grassy ground, e.g. in clearings, or sometimes feeding in fruiting trees. Rarely joins mixed-species flocks. Generally shy and retiring.
Status Uncommon to locally fairly common. Numbers appear to shift seasonally.
Habitat Upper Tropical to Temperate Zones, at 1,300–2,700m, once to 1,000m in Ecuador. Humid to wet and mossy cloud forests, edges, second growth and adjacent clearings, particularly on steep hillsides, and even in shrubby areas.
Voice A dull *peen*. Song, not particularly beautiful, consists of very varied, hesitantly delivered short trills, buzzes, high notes and more thrush-like phrases, e.g. *che'e'e'e-chert chee-rt-ee'e'r'r, chu-wurt, titi,t't't, eet* (P. Schwartz recording, H&B, F&K), but not often heard (R&G). Usually sings from within canopy.

PALE-BREASTED THRUSH
Turdus leucomelas Pl. 245

Identification 23–27cm. Warm medium brown above, becoming soft grey on head, rump and uppertail-coverts, white throat with fine blackish streaks, breast, sides, flanks and thighs warm grey, belly and undertail-coverts pure white. Female warmer, with streaks on throat and breast-sides. Juvenile same brown above, but streaked and spotted warm buffy, with spotty barring below from chin to flanks, streaked on undertail-coverts. Cocoa Thrush much warmer rufous-brown.

Ssp. *T. l. albiventer* (Co, Ve, Gu, Su, FG) has rusty-brown on forehead, gingery wash to mantle and tertials
T. l. cautor (Guajira in Co) as described

Habits Not wary as it forages alone, in pairs or small flocks from ground to canopy for invertebrates and fruits, often

hopping around or under bushes and occasionally on open grass, but never far from cover. Often in fruiting bushes and trees.
Status Fairly common to locally common.
Habitat Tropical to Lower subtropical Zones, to 2,000m, in various semi-open and disturbed habitats and common around habitation, in dry to humid forest edges and clearings, deciduous woodland, second growth, plantations, dense thickets, gallery forest and forest islands in open grassland, often near water and even in cultivated areas, roadsides, pastures, parks and gardens with or near patches of forest.
Voice A distinctive single or repeated harsh guttural *wert*, growling *quwaak* and alarm *cha-cha*, *zit* or *zeezit*. Song quite melodious with many *hereit-hereit-tuweee* and *tuwee-tuwee* phrases, often repeated (R&T, C&H, Hilty). Sings usually at twilight from within dense midstorey to canopy (mainly December–July).

BLACK-BILLED THRUSH
Turdus ignobilis Pl. 245

Identification 21.5–24cm. Varies racially; basically olive-brown above with white throat, variably streaked, and greyish to brown breast and flanks, with white belly and undertail-coverts. Juvenile has slight streaking above, whitish below with arrowhead streaks from throat to flanks, densest on breast. Despite distinctive dark bill, this dingy thrush may be confused with several others (see Pale-eyed and Andean Slaty-thrushes), but lack of obvious field marks distinctive. Following 4 species all more forest-tied: Lawrence's has warmer brown coloration, yellow bill and eye-ring; Pale-vented has warmer brown coloration and more finely streaked throat; Hauxwell's has warmer brown coloration; White-necked Thrush similar to subspecies *debilis* but has more contrast between dark upper- and grey underparts, paler bill, narrow yellow eye-ring, and more heavily streaked throat with broader white crescent below.

Ssp. *T. i. arthuri* (S Ve, NE Gu, NW Su, FG) slightly greyish face and upperparts, olive-tinged wings and tail, buffy-olive breast to flanks

T. i. debilis (E Ec, E Co, W Ve: E side of East Andes) smaller bill, white crescent below throat and pure white belly and vent

T. i. goodfellowi (W Co: Cauca to Quindío) chin and throat whitish, prominently streaked diffuse brown, breast much deeper brown-buff than *ignobilis*, white belly and vent

T. i. ignobilis (E Co: W Central Andes) sides of chin and throat white, diffusely streaked pale brown, breast-sides dull grey-brown, becoming a wash on flanks, belly and vent whitish, undertail-coverts buffy-white

T. i. murinus (E Ve, W Gu, south of río Cuyuní to Roraima) darkest race, streaks on throat fuscous to blackish and extend slightly onto breast, breast to flanks brownish-buff, including thighs

Habits Constantly flicks tail downwards. Not wary as it forages from ground to canopy for invertebrates and fruits, often at fruiting trees, solitary or in pairs, rarely joins mixed-species flocks. Often hops on lawns or open grassy ground around habitation.
Status Common and widespread in Colombia but only uncommon to locally fairly common in Ecuador and Venezuela.
Habitat Tropical to Temperate Zones, 700–2,800m. Mostly in semi-open habitats, often near water, e.g. edges of humid forest (on tops of some tepuis) and mature second growth, riverine thickets, light woodland, plantations, gallery forest and scattered vegetation in savannas, but also quite conspicuous near habitation, in pastures, parks and gardens with patches of trees nearby.
Voice A soft *blok*, loud upslurred *weea*, evenly-pitched *kweet*, *scree* alarm and loud *quee-kipper-kipper-kipper* in flight. Song a soft, not particularly notable, but typical thrush-like continuous sequence of rapid notes and phrases, e.g. *wert*, *tu-lee*, *su-wee* and *your-your-we*, often repeated; once, in southern Venezuela song included a nasal, rising *queek*. Sings from treetops mostly in twilight, especially at dawn (H&B, C&H, R&G, Hilty).

LAWRENCE'S THRUSH
Turdus lawrencii Pl. 246

Identification 21.5–23cm. Adult olive-brown with bright yellow-orange bill and eye-ring (darker bill and narrower eye-ring in female), streaked white throat, and whitish belly and vent. Juvenile has pale orange-buffy streaks above and brown spots below. Pale-vented Thrush has pale grey head without eye-ring (no overlap), Cocoa Thrush warmer rufous-brown and has dark bill and no eye-ring, Hauxwell's Thrush paler brown and has dark bill and no eye-ring.

Ssp. Monotypic (E Ec, SE Co, S Ve)

Habits Very difficult to see as it forages in humid leaf-litter or from midstorey to canopy, often in fruiting trees. Takes invertebrates and fruits. Sometimes joins mixed-species flocks.
Status Uncommon (certainly under-recorded unless song known) to locally fairly common.
Habitat Tropical Zone, to 600m in Ecuador and Colombia and 1,200m in Venezuela, along streams in seasonally flooded ecotone between *várzea* and *terra firme* forest.
Voice A soft *kup* or *kup-kip*, sharp piercing *peer*, also plaintive *perwheee*, abrupt *weecheee* or loud *pedep-peep-peep*. An extraordinary mimic, with songs and calls of up to 50 other bird species (and even frogs and insects) having been mixed with its own sequences. A male in full swing may improvise with only short pauses, for hours, like a practicing musician. Sing from frequently used perches on treetops or inside canopy (C&H, Hilty).

Taxonomic note on Pale-vented, Cocoa and Hauxwell's Thrushes. Species limits in *Turdus obsoletus*, *T. fumigatus* and *T. hauxwelli* have been controversial and confusing. Hellmayr (1934), Phelps & Phelps (1950)

and Snow (1985) treated all 3 as conspecific under *T. fumigatus*. Ripley (1964) treated *obsoletus* under *T. fumigatus* but *T. hauxwelli* as a separate species, because it was by then known to be sympatric with *T. fumigatus* in western Brazil. Meyer de Schauensee (1966) considered *fumigatus* and *hauxwelli* as separate species, but *obsoletus* under *T. hauxwelli* rather than *T. fumigatus*. Then, in 1989, R&T treated *T. fumigatus*, *T. obsoletus* and *T. hauxwelli* as separate species based on plumage, habitat, and elevational differences, and this treatment has been largely followed since. However, both Meyer de Schauensee (1966) and R&T noted that assignment of races *parambanus*, *colombianus* and *orinocensis* is problematic. Here, we place *parambanus* and *columbianus* under *T. obsoletus* and *orinocensis* under *T. fumigatus*, following Dickinson and Collar.

PALE-VENTED THRUSH
Turdus obsoletus Pl. 246

Identification 21.5–23cm. Adult rufous-brown above, slightly paler below with dark bill, no eye-ring, streaked whitish throat and contrasting pure white lower belly and vent; bright orange underwing-coverts in flight. Juvenile rufous-brown with pale buffy streaks above, whitish chin and throat, streaked finely with dusky, tawny on breast with broad, brown arrowhead mottling, belly and undertail-coverts pure white. Dark bill and dark throat, overall dull except strongly contrasting white vent and undertail-coverts distinctive. Ecuadorian Thrush separated by yellow eye-ring and whitish throat, Hauxwell's Thrush closest, but only occurs west of Andes.

Ssp. *T. o. colombianus* (E slope of W Andes in Co) paler above and on fringes of wing-coverts and flight-feathers than nominate
T. o. obsoletus (NW Co) as described
T. o. parambanus (NE Ec, W Co) darker above, central tail-feathers uniform with rest of tail

Habits Wary as it forages for invertebrates and fruits alone or in pairs from understorey to canopy, sometimes joining mixed-species flocks. Only rarely forages in leaf-litter.

Status Rare to uncommon and local in Colombia and Ecuador.

Habitat Tropical to Lower Subtropical Zones, at 200–1,900m. Wet to humid forests, mostly in interior and rarely visits edges and mature second growth, sometimes in gallery forests.

Voice A thin dry *bzeeek*, throaty *wuk*, rising *weep*, often repeated several times, also a *zhweek*. Song consists of fast, musical thrush-like sequences, frequently with *tewee* or *weeooweet* phrases and squeaky notes (H&B, R&G, C&H), delivered from a usually hidden perch in subcanopy or mid level; considerably faster than Dagua Thrush (R&G).

Note Three subspecies were formerly considered to belong to *T. hauxwelli*, namely *colombianus*, *obsoletus* and *parambanus* (see Snow 1985 and above).

COCOA THRUSH *Turdus fumigatus* Pl. 246

Identification 21.5–24cm. Warm, uniform rufous-brown above and cinnamon-brown below, throat paler, streaked brown on breast, vent and undertail-coverts whitish, feathers edged cinnamon. Underwing-coverts rich cinnamon and basal half of inner webs of remiges also cinnamon. Bill and eyes dark brown, legs and feet yellowish. Juvenile similar but has orange-buffy streaks above and slightly brown-mottled breast. Subspecies are poorly separated, with much individual variation within any given population; distinctions below are those which characterise race, but are not certain identifiers. Nearest confusion species is Hauxwell's Thrush, which is darker above and olive-tinged below.

Ssp. *T. f. aquilonalis* (NE Co, N Ve, Tr) paler brown above and paler orange-brown below than nominate
T. f. fumigatus (Gu, Su, FG) colder, more greyish tone throughout
T. f. orinocensis (SE Co, S Ve) warmer, more chestnut coloration

Habits Shivers tail upon landing. Very wary as it forages for invertebrates and fruits, keeping in dense cover of forest (but less wary when foraging in cultivated or urban areas, e.g. roadside ditches on Trinidad). May be alone or in pairs from ground to midstorey. Also in fruiting canopy trees.

Status Uncommon to locally fairly common.

Habitat Tropical to Lower Subtropical Zones, to 1,800m, in dense tropical forest, especially humid *terra firme* and *várzea* near water, particularly streams or swamps, but more easily seen at forest edges and clearings, in gallery and savanna forests, deciduous second growth, plantations and cultivated areas such as parks and gardens.

Voice A harsh *bak*, scolding *squeak*, harsh rapid *chat-shat-shat* or *kik-ik-ik-ik* and *chuck* in flight. Song consists of fast, loud and varied sequences of musical phrases, e.g. *teew-too*, *john-pierre-oh* or *mi-yes*, often repeated, ending in a *sree*. Sings in twilight, especially at dusk and during breeding season, from midstorey to canopy, when several males may gather to sing (C&H, Hilty).

HAUXWELL'S THRUSH
Turdus hauxwelli Pl. 246

Identification 23 cm. Dark olive-brown above, with a yellow eye-ring, paler, almost greyish-olive below, underwing-coverts bright cinnamon, centre of belly to undertail-coverts white. Bill black, eyes dark, legs and feet horn. Juvenile has fine orange-buffy streaks above and brown-mottled breast. Very similar to Pale-vented Thrush, but no overlap. Also, possible confusion with Cocoa Thrush but no overlap in region, though they could do; Cocoa is much warmer, more orange-cinnamon below compared to greyish-olive underparts of Hauxwell's Thrush.

Ssp. Monotypic (E Ec, SE Co)

Habits Wary as it forages alone or in pairs from understorey to subcanopy, usually keeping in thickets, only rarely coming out at edges and in clearings. Sometimes in canopy of fruiting trees.

Status Rare to locally uncommon in east Ecuador and southeast Colombia.
Habitat Lower Tropical Zone, to *c.*400m. Dense humid *terra firme* and *várzea*, second growth, edges and clearings, usually near water, also forested river islands and gallery forests.
Voice An ascending *dree* and querulous upslurred *kweeeow*. Song a distinctively slow, rambling series of rising and falling whistled phrases, e.g. *see-you*, *wit-tuu*, *woo-it* or *see-it-ooo*, interspersed with softer churrs, trills and imitations (C&H, R&G). Apparently an accomplished mimic, and 1 individual responded to playback with a subsong that comprised imitations of at least 10 bird species found in that habitat (Collar).

CLAY-COLOURED THRUSH

Turdus grayi Pl. 246

Identification 23–26.5cm. Dull olive-brown above with pale leading edge to remiges, throat whitish finely streaked dusky, yellow below, washed olive on breast, with pale undertail-coverts. Bill olive-yellow distally, more greenish-horn at base, paler on mandible; colour depends on season, brighter when breeding. Eyes dark, legs and feet olive-grey. Juvenile lacks pale leading edge to remiges, has buffy spots and streaks from head to lower back and spots on wing-coverts, pale ochraceous below with fine arrowhead marks on throat, bolder and heavier on breast, fading on flanks.

Ssp. *T. g. casius* (NW Co) as described
T. g. incomptus (N Co) similar but slightly duller on breast and belly

Habits Flicks wings and raises tail on landing. Apparently unwary as it forages alone or in pairs (sometimes small flocks to roost) from understorey to canopy, in fruiting trees, and sometimes on ground.
Status Uncommon to locally fairly common.
Habitat Lower Tropical Zone, to 300m, in dry to wet semi-open woodland, plantations, edges and clearings, cultivation with scattered trees, e.g. orchards and gardens, but also interior of primary and secondary forests outside breeding season.
Voice A cat-like rising *sreer*, *quirre* or *jerereeee*, drawn-out nasal *wee-ee-gwa*, nuthatch-like *ung-ung-ung*, chuckling *tock-tock*, sometimes varied with *kluh-kluh* or *pup-pup*, and high thin *siii* in flight. Song a very musical, mellow series of clear, rhythmic notes including trills, warbles, whistles and some high-pitched piercing notes. Sings often and all day, but mostly in twilight and during breeding season (H&B, C&H).
Note English name Clay-coloured Thrush used by Meyer de Schauensee (1970), R&T, S&M and Clements (2000), but AOU (1998), Wetmore *et al.* (1984) and SACC use more traditional Clay-coloured Robin.

BARE-EYED THRUSH

Turdus nudigenis Pl. 246

Identification 23–24cm. Olive above, slightly greyish on uppertail-coverts, below also olive, but paler, streaked white on throat, thighs brown. White on centre of belly and undertail-coverts. Conspicuous, bright yellow-orange, over-sized bare eye-ring that may be quite swollen and irregular. Juvenile has fine pale buffy streaks above, whitish on throat, tawny on breast and yellow on flanks, belly and undertail-coverts white, throat and breast with arrowhead brown streaks. Bill yellow to yellow-horn in adult, more greenish-horn in juvenile, eyes dark brown, legs and feet yellowish-horn. Large and exaggerated eye-ring of adult quite unmistakable, juvenile's eye-ring smaller, but still sufficient to be unmistakable. Lawrence's Thrush is darker richer colour below and has narrower eye-ring. Clay-coloured and Ecuadorian Thrushes do not overlap.

Ssp. *T. n. nudigenis* (E Co, Ve, Margarita I., T&T, Guianas)

Habits Fairly retiring as it forages usually alone but sometimes in pairs, mostly in canopy, frequently numerous at flowering or fruiting trees. Sometimes forages on ground for invertebrates and may be seen warily prospecting a garden lawn.
Status Uncommon to locally common, but abundant on Trinidad & Tobago. Apparently benefits from expansion of cultivation and is a common thrush of city gardens.
Habitat Tropical to Lower Subtropical Zones, to 1,800m but mostly below 1,000m, in semi-open habitats, e.g. edges and clearings of rain forest, deciduous and gallery forests, mature second growth, semi-open woodland, bamboo stands, savannas with forest patches, dry scrub and cultivation, especially fruit, cocoa and coffee plantations, open fields, town parks and gardens.
Voice A cat-like rising *keer-leee*, *shuh-ey* or *pee-ou-wa*, a more musical *chareera*, harsh *tak-tak-tak* and monosyllabic frog-like note. Song a series of musical fluted phrases similar to Cocoa Thrush, but slower and lower, including *ture-too-too*, *cheerily-cheer-up-cheerio* and ringing trills, with few repetitions but frequent pauses (C&H). *Cheery-peep, cheerio!* is a frequently uttered phase while warming up for a serenade (Restall). Will sing throughout day during breeding season.
Note Also called Yellow-eyed or Spectacled Thrush (Collar).

ECUADORIAN THRUSH

Turdus maculirostris Pl. 246

Identification 21.5–23cm. Uniform dull olive-brown above, paler olive below, streaked white on throat, slightly flammulated on lower breast and flanks, which are washed buffy, belly, thighs and undertail-coverts whitish, undertail-coverts with olivaceous centres. Bill yellow to greenish-yellow or horn, eye-ring yellow to yellow-orange, legs and feet grey. Juvenile has fine pale orange-buffy streaks above, yellow below, with heavy arrowhead markings on breast, fainter on sides and flanks. Similar to Bare-eyed Thrush but has narrow yellow eye-ring. Female Pale-eyed and Glossy-black Thrushes darker and more uniform brown and occur at higher elevations. Dagua Thrush darker above with white crescent below throat and narrower eye-ring. Clay-coloured and Bare-eyed Thrushes do not overlap.

Ssp. Monotypic (W Ec)

Habits Wary as it forages alone or in pairs from midstorey to canopy (rarely on ground), sometimes in small flocks at fruiting trees.
Status Uncommon to locally fairly common, most common

Turdus in western Ecuador. Has apparently spread due to deforestation.
Habitat Tropical to Lower Subtropical Zones, to 2,200m, in deciduous, semi-deciduous and humid forests, edges, second growth and clearings, particularly damp areas, sometimes in open areas with grass, scattered trees and hedges.
Voice A *chuck* and distinctive thin whining querulous cat-like *queeoww*. Song comprises sequences of musical phrases (C&H, R&G).
Note Formerly considered a subspecies of Bare-eyed Thrush.

DAGUA THRUSH *Turdus daguae* Pl. 246

Identification 21.5–23cm. Adult deep olive-brown above, with narrow yellow eye-ring, distinctive white crescent below heavily streaked white throat, breast, sides and flanks dull orange-brown, white belly and vent. Juvenile dark brown with fine orange-buffy streaks above, buffy throat with malar streaked heavily dark brown, breast, sides and flanks orange-brown with dark brown arrowhead mottling, pale buffy belly, vent and undertail-coverts. Much darker above than Ecuadorian Thrush and more contrastingly patterned below. Similar White-necked Thrush does not overlap.

Ssp. Monotypic (W Ec, W Co)

Habits Apparently unwary as it forages alone or in pairs from understorey (rarely on ground) to canopy, where often in fruiting trees.
Status Uncommon to locally fairly common but decidedly local in Ecuador, fairly common in Colombia.
Habitat Lower Tropical Zone, to 900m, in humid to wet forests, mature second growth, edges and clearings, also cultivated areas, e.g. plantations.
Voice A *krrup*, and excited, repeated *queeyrp*. Song a long continuous, somewhat monotonous musical carolling, similar to but slightly faster than that of closely related White-necked Thrush. Sings from high perches (R&G).
Note Formerly considered a separate species from *T. assimilis* but, more recently, R&T and S&M treated them as conspecific. Both treatments lack sufficient evidence in support. R&G considered *daguae* a separate species, based on voice, which resembles that of *T. albicollis* more than *T. assimilis*. It is retained within White-throated Thrush by Dickinson and Collar; SACC awaiting proposal.

WHITE-NECKED THRUSH
Turdus albicollis Pl. 243

Identification 20.5–24cm. Deep brown above, including top and sides of head, narrow yellow eye-ring, throat white, heavily streaked black, ending in sharp black line across throat, immediately below is a pure white area patch quickly grades into grey breast, sides and flanks, thighs dark, rest of underparts white. Bill dark above, yellow below, eyes dark, legs and feet dark horn. Juvenile streaked and spotted above pale buffy, slightly larger streaks on scapulars; entire throat white, with a few small arrowhead marks on chin, upper breast tawny, heavily spotted and barred dark brown, lower breast, sides and flanks olivaceous-grey, spotted on sides with faded brown, thighs grey, rest of underparts white. Adult and juvenile very similar to Dagua Thrush (no overlap). Cf. Andean Slaty Thrush and Black-billed Thrush.

Ssp. *T. a. phaeopygoides* (NE Co, N Ve, Tr, To) like *phaeopygus* but longer wings, reddish eye-ring, more olive above
T. a. phaeopygus (E Co, S Ve, Gu, Su, FG) eye-ring ochraceous-yellow, bill black, legs and feet grey
T. a. spodiolaemus (E Ec) more rufous-olive above and heavier throat streaking than nominate, lower mandible yellow

Habits Very wary as it forages for invertebrates, alone or in pairs in dense cover from ground to midstorey, sometimes ventures into canopy, e.g. at fruiting trees where can occur in small flocks, and sometimes follows ant swarms, but even then usually difficult to see, though in some places (e.g. Trinidad or Henri Pittier National Park, northern Venezuela) forages in open along trails and roadsides, and in pastures and gardens.
Status Fairly common in Ecuador and Colombia, uncommon to locally fairly common in Venezuela, common throughout Suriname, but scarce in savanna forests. Common in the interior of French Guiana.
Habitat Tropical to Lower Subtropical Zones, to 1,900m, in primary and mature secondary humid *terra firme* and *várzea* forests, edges and clearings.
Voice A low *chack* or *wuk*, an oft-repeated *jup*, *jig-wig* or *jig-wig-wig*, thin high *tsri* and sharp *youp* or *yoow-up* alarm. Song quite monotonous with a low–high phrase *oo-ee* tirelessly repeated, though always slightly altered. Sings throughout day from under- to midstorey, but often difficult to locate in dense cover (C&H, R&G, Hilty).
Note Sometimes called White-throated Thrush (e.g. Collar).

MIMIDAE – Catbird, Thrashers and Mockingbirds

This exclusively New World family consists mostly of medium-sized birds (rather thrush-like) with long rounded tails, shortish rounded wings and longish, slightly decurved bills. They are generally unremarkable in coloration, usually grey or brown, with some having distinctive white patches on the tips of the tail, most noticeable in flight. Sexes are alike and juveniles differ very little. They are often remarkably good singers, and the mockingbirds of South America have long been favourite cagebirds for this reason. They usually forage on the ground, favouring leaf-litter, often in undergrowth, taking insects and small fruits, e.g. of *Prunus* species. Some, however, fearlessly forage in the open.

Additional references used in the preparation of this family were: Brewer & Mackay (2001, hereafter B&M) and Cody (2005, hereafter Cody).

GREY CATBIRD
Dumetella carolinensis Pl. 247

Identification 20–22cm. Adult is all grey with fairly long tail (often cocked), black crown and chestnut undertail-coverts. Once known, the *mew* call is unmistakable.

Ssp. Monotypic (boreal vagrant to N Co)

Habits Not shy but tends to skulk in bushes and shrubbery, moving quietly, foraging in lower levels of semi-humid and semi-deciduous forest, but higher in fruiting trees.
Status Winters in North and Central America and the Caribbean, uncommon in eastern Panama, but small numbers may regularly reach north-west Colombia, with records from Ciénaga, Magdalena (March), Katíos National Park, north-west Chocó (January), north of the same park (also January), and near Acandí, Chocó (January: H&B).
Habitat Tropical to Subtropical Zones, in dense thickets, but could be seen anywhere during migration.
Voice Calls include a hoarse, cat-like *mwee* or *meeurr*, loud crackling *kedekekek* when startled, harsh and rapid *chek-chek-chek*, soft low-pitched *whirt* or low deep *whurf*. Song mixes melodious, nasal and squeaky notes interspersed with *mwee* notes and other cat-like sounds, which may also be uttered individually. Pairs duet. Mimics other species to some extent, including regular mechanical noises, like a squeaking gate (Sibley, Cody).

TROPICAL MOCKINGBIRD

Mimus gilvus Pl. 247

Identification 23–25.5cm. Adult mid grey above with blackish wings and tail, white tips to greater and median wing-coverts, tertials and inner secondaries, giving slight double wingbar effect, tips of all tail-feathers except central pair also white, white eyebrow with dark line through eyes; underparts entirely white, washed grey on face- to breast-sides. Eyes vary from yellow to orange, bill, legs and feet blackish. Juvenile slightly browner grey and slightly buffy below with faint streaking from breast to flanks; eyes olive to hazel. Adult unmistakably bicoloured and long-tailed.

Ssp. *M. g. gilvus* (Su, FG) as described
M. g. melanopterus (NE & E Co, Ve, Gu) larger and paler than *gilvus*, distinctly buffy and browner in tone, white on outer rectrices more extensive, dark line through eye more mask-like; eyes dark
M. g. rostratus (ABC, Margarita, Orchila, Tortuga, Blanquilla, Hermanos & Testigos Is., N of Ve) like *melanopterus* but mask bolder and bill heavier
M. g. tobagensis (T&T) darker above than *gilvus* with black shafts, broader wing-covert markings, lateral rectrices have more extensive white tips, and eyebrow more contrasting, no mask, darker wash to breast; eyes yellow
M. g. tolimensis (NW Ec, W & C Co) like *melanopterus* but larger with longer wings and tail buffy to ochraceous, wash on breast, brown streaks on flanks

Habits May 'flash' wings by raising and spreading them, but flashes white undertail when alighting, and regularly when foraging. Occurs in pairs or family groups that defend nest sites. Forages both in vegetation and on ground for invertebrates, small vertebrates, fruits, berries and even eggs. Frequently pauses and stands rather upright with tail momentarily cocked upwards, and then lowers it gently.
Status Fairly common to common in semi-open habitats, expanding its range to higher altitudes and south (recently recorded in Ecuador), as it benefits from forest clearance.
Habitat Tropical to Temperate Zones, to 2,600m, but usually much lower, in semi-open habitats such as savannas, ranchlands, arid scrub, plantations, parks and gardens.
Voice Calls include a harsh *chek* and *jeeop* alarm-call. Song is a rambling series of musical phrases, often repeated several times, together with clucking or wheezing notes (R&T, Hilty, B&M).

CHALK-BROWED MOCKINGBIRD

Mimus saturninus Pl. 247

Identification 23.5–26cm. Brownish-grey above with buffy fringes to feathers of mantle to uppertail-coverts, wings and tail darker with well-defined white terminal spots on median coverts, white tips to greater coverts and tertials, broad buffy-white eyebrow, thick black line through eyes, underparts white washed buffy-grey on breast. Juvenile slightly browner above, eyebrow narrower, distinctly washed buffy-grey on underparts, with darker streaks on breast; eyes hazel, bill horn on lower mandible. Adult unmistakable, as similar Tropical Mockingbird is grey (not brownish) above with a far less prominent supercilium behind eye.

Ssp. *M. s. saturninus* (S Su, S FG)

Habits Often holds tail raised over back, but other habits similar to Tropical Mockingbird.
Status Fairly common to common at the Sipaliwini Savanna, in southern Suriname.
Habitat Tropical to Temperate Zones, to 2,500m but usually much lower, in swampy habitats in Sipaliwini.
Voice Calls include *chripp-chripp*, *scha-scha-scha*, *krrra*, a frequent *chert* and *check-check* alarm-call. Song exceptionally variable, with numerous phrases jumbled together, some imitations, and many phrases are often repeated several times (R&T, B&M). Jumps into air while singing.

LONG-TAILED MOCKINGBIRD

Mimus longicaudatus Pl. 247

Identification 26–29.5cm. Dark brown above with white tips to tail, distinct blackish and white facial pattern, underparts all white with dark brown wash to breast; eyes yellowish-hazel, bill, legs and feet blackish. Juvenile has facial pattern less distinct and black-streaked breast; eyes hazel. Only mockingbird in its range and has very distinctive facial pattern.

Ssp. *M. l. albogriseus* (SW Ec) as described
M. l. platensis (Isla de la Plata, Ec) larger, especially bill; eyes yellowish

Habits Hops on ground with raised tail and glides for long distances over ground, but other otherwise similar to Tropical Mockingbird.
Status Fairly common to common in Ecuador, most common near coast and in arid areas.

Habitat Tropical to Subtropical Zones, to 1,900m but mostly below 1,500m, in desertic and coastal scrub, undergrowth of light woodlands, farmland, hedgerows, riparian thickets, gardens and towns, strongly favouring arid habitats, occurring even in almost barren areas provided some vegetation is present.
Voice Song is a long series of chuckling, chortling and gurgling notes with no obvious pattern, given even during hottest periods when other birds are silent (R&T, R&G).

BROWN THRASHER

Toxostoma rufum Pl. 247

Identification 25–29cm. Adult bright rufous above, and has long rufous tail and wings with 2 black and white wingbars, head-sides brown with line of black spots on malar; underparts bright buffy-white with heavy 'teardrop' streaks that are rufous on breast and gradually become dark brown on belly and flanks; eyes yellow, bill black above, dark horn below, legs and feet brown. Juvenile similar but has brown eyes.

Ssp. *T. r. rufum* (boreal vagrant to Cu)

Habits Usually skulks in undergrowth of scrub and on ground.
Status Winters in North America: only 3–4 records from Cuba (Kirkconnell *et al.* in prep.) and few elsewhere in West Indies. In our region a single record from Curaçao, October 1957 (Voous 1983), but the species clearly does not usually move this far south.
Habitat Tropical Zone, probably in similar habitats as in North America., e.g. hedgerows, brush and woodland edges. In Mexico in arid to humid brushy scrub, and woodland understorey (Howell & Webb 1995).
Voice Calls include a sharp *spuck* or *chakk*, a low toneless growling *chhr*, sharp *tssuk*, and rich low whistle *peeooori* or *breeeew*. Song is a long series of varied melodious phrases, each usually given 2–3 times with pause between each (Sibley, B&M).

PEARLY-EYED THRASHER

Margarops fuscatus Pl. 247

Identification 27–30cm. Adult greyish-brown above streaked darker brown throughout, long dark brown tail with narrow white tips above, broader below, white underparts with coarse brown V-shaped streaks; white or pale yellow eyes, large yellowish or flesh-coloured bill.

Ssp. *M. f. bonairensis* (Bo, Los Hermanos archipelago, Ve)

Habits Raucous and conspicuous, forages in trees for fruit, invertebrates and small vertebrates, including eggs and nestlings of other bird species, sometimes on ground.
Status Local but widespread on Bonaire, but more restricted to around springs and wells during dry spells. Sight record from Rio Canario, Curaçao. Last record on Isla Horquilla (=La Orchila), Los Hermanos archipelago, Venezuela, in 1908, where presumed extinct (although there have been no birdwatcher reports from the islands for decades).
Habitat Tropical Zone, in thickets, scrub, woodland, forest, mangrove, coastal palm groves and even in urban habitats.
Voice A guttural *craw-craw*, harsh *chook-chook* and many other raucous calls. Song is a series of 1–3-syllable phrases (e.g. *pio-tareeu-tsee*) with long pauses separating them (Raffaele *et al.* 1998). Often sings well into day and during clear nights (B&M).

STURNIDAE–Starlings

The European Starling belongs to the Old World family of Sturnidae, and is completely unrelated to the New World starlings and blackbirds (Icteridae). It is another tremendously successful coloniser, ranging in the New World across the whole of North America and into Mexico. It is an aggressive and noisy bird that is very adaptable to all kinds of conditions. It readily, aggressively and usually successfully, takes nesting holes whether already taken by other species or not, and thus is competitive for scarce resources. In Jamaica it is documented as having replaced woodpeckers at their nest holes (Raffaele *et al.* 1998). Lever (1987) is in no doubt about its impact, '…the good they do by probing the ground for insects, grubs, wireworms and Japanese beetles during the breeding season is far outweighed by their depredations on fruits, berries, corn, maize, grain, seed, rice…. In addition they can transmit diseases such as avian tuberculosis, toxoplasmosis, psittacosis, cryptococcal meningitis, avian malaria and Newcastle Disease'. It is clearly the least desirable of the exotics listed here.

EUROPEAN STARLING

Sturnus vulgaris Pl. 306

Identification 20cm. Breeding adult is black with a long, pointed bill and long legs, feathers of nape and upper breast lanceolate, and entire plumage glossy, the colours changing with the light, but can appear dazzling purple on head and neck, bronze on back, green on scapulars and blue on flanks. Bill yellow, with base of mandible pale blue in male. In non-breeding season, in fresh plumage, almost every feather has an arrowhead-shaped pale tip and wing-feathers fringed cinnamon to buffy; bill dark horn to blackish. Juvenile soft sandy drab or grey-brown, the centres of wing- and tail-feathers darker, with darker flammulations on breast, sides and flanks; bill dark. As moults to winter plumage, young acquires very distinctive patchwork of the different plumages, whilst new feathers cause juvenile plumage to appear paler. In flight has a very distinctive triangular shape to wings.

Ssp. Unidentified subspecies (casual visitor to ABC)

Habits Forages by walking sedately on ground, probing into the substrate and opening it, the forward-directed eyes looking straight down. Will run at any other bird successfully feeding and will either join in or flush the other away. Uses exposed perches (rooftops are typical), singing and ruffling the lanceolate feathers out in all directions.
Status Casual visitor to Aruba, Curaçao and Bonaire, presumably from other parts of the Caribbean or from North America. Both sedentary and migratory across Europe

and North America, the northernmost birds displace more southerly populations, which move further south.

Habitat Tropical Zone, at sea level in our region.

Voice Calls include a buzzing *churrr* on take-off and *kyett!* in alarm e.g. a passing hawk. Song (usually a sign of nesting intention or activity) a medley of sweet whistles and raucous squeaks, it is an accomplished mimic and an old male can have a very entertaining repertoire, challenging the listener to identify all of the original musicians (and squeaking gates!) (Mullarney *et al.* 1999).

European Starling in flight has a distinctive arrowhead silhouette

MOTACILLIDAE – Wagtails and Pipits

The Motacillidae fall into 2 distinct groups, the long-tailed, unstreaked wagtails, and the brownish, streaked pipits. Wagtails are easily recognised: they are slender, elegant birds with long tails and fairly long dark-coloured legs that forage on the ground, walking and running, and constantly bobbing their tails. The tail-bobbing becomes faster when the bird is anxious. Wagtails are usually associated with water, but the only member of the genus to have occurred in our region can forage far from water. During the day, they perch on telegraph wires, walls and rocks but rarely, if ever, in trees; however, at night they roost communally in trees or tall reedbeds. Pipits are cryptically coloured in shades of brown, invariably well streaked, with regular-length tails, pale legs and feet, and a long hindclaw. Birds of open country, primarily scrubby areas with short grasses, they too forage on the ground, occasionally pausing to stand upright and still. They fly up to perch on exposed wires and cables, and on walls, etc., but unlike wagtails also readily perch on trees and bushes. They have aerial song-flights, culminating in parachuting glides to the ground. Pipits invariably roost and nest on the ground.

WHITE WAGTAIL *Motacilla alba* Pl. 240

Identification 16.5–19cm. Long slender body and distinctive coloration combined with constant tail wagging while foraging on open ground make species unmistakable. Adult male has distinctive head pattern of white forehead and eyebrow bordered by black crown, eyestripe and hindcrown, white head-sides and black throat, remaining upperparts grey, with long black tail and distinctive white sides, and whitish underparts. Female somewhat duller with grey hindcrown, juvenile much duller with less distinctive facial pattern.

Ssp. Subspecies unknown (Palearctic vagrant to Tr)

Habits Runs quickly, stopping suddenly, head and tail bobbing rapidly. Seems fairly tame and confiding.

Status Single vagrant record on Trinidad, December 1987–January 1988 (ffrench 1991).

Habitat Tropical Zone, but could be seen anywhere. Usually in damp or wet habitats like swamps, bogs, sewage farms, banks of waterways, but also visits gardens with lawns.

Voice Easily recognised *tsli-vitt* or *zi-ze-litt* calls, whilst song is a few twittering notes separated by brief pauses (Mullarney *et al.* 1999).

PÁRAMO PIPIT *Anthus bogotensis* Pl. 240

Identification 15cm. Adult ochraceous above with broad black streaks, dusky tail with buff outer tail-feathers (appearing whitish in flight), wing-coverts dusky with buff tips forming 2 narrow wingbars, below rather uniform dark buffy (paler on throat and greyer in worn plumage), with a few blackish spots or short streaks on breast. Sexes alike. Juvenile lacks buffy tinge, with white streaks above and outer tail-feathers buffy-white on outer web. Larger than Yellowish Pipit, which occurs only in lowlands and is usually more streaked and more yellowish (not buffy) on underparts.

Ssp. *A. b. bogotensis* (Ec, Co: E & C Andes) narrow buff wingbars

A. b. meridae (Andes in Ve) broad buff wingbars, heavier streaks on breast, no streaks on sides

Habits Forages alone, in pairs or small flocks, for invertebrates and seeds, mostly on ground but also in grass and low shrubs. Sings from elevated perch.

Status Locally fairly common to common, with some elevational movements, and perhaps less common in Ecuador.

Habitat Temperate Zone to Páramo, at 2,100–4,500m, in dry as well as wet treeless bogs, fields, pastures and grasslands (both *páramo* and *puna*), often where short and bunch grasses are mixed.

Voice Calls include a thin *tjirp*, *pit-sit* or *chit-chit* when flushed, sometimes a chattering *triee-chi-chi* in territorial disputes (F&K); song from perch is a simple *tseedle-tseedle-tslee* (R&T, Hilty), but in flight is exuberant and musical, with a wheezing note followed by a high chattering *nyeeezzzzz, dziit-it, dziit-it, chit-it-it-it-it-it* or *sweet-sweet-sweez-twee'e'e'e'e'e'e'e'e'sr'r'r-tsee-tseez-tseez* (Hilty, F&K).

YELLOWISH PIPIT *Anthus lutescens* Pl. 240

Identification 13–13.5cm. Adult dark brown above with buff and black streaks (becoming speckles on neck-sides), and a relatively short dusky tail with white outer tail-feathers (conspicuous in flight), wing-coverts blackish-brown with buff tips forming 2 narrow wingbars, below buffy- to yellowish-white (whiter in worn plumage) with brown streaks on chest (cf. Páramo Pipit). Sexes alike. Juvenile virtually identical to adult. Smaller than Páramo Pipit which occurs only in highlands and is usually buffier on underparts.

Ssp. *A. l. lutescens* (CE Co, C, E & SE Ve, Guianas)

Habits Forages alone or in pairs for invertebrates and seeds,

mostly on ground.
Status Locally fairly common to common and widespread. Appears loosely colonial both during breeding and non-breeding seasons. Rare and local on the northern coastal savannas of French Guiana.
Habitat Tropical Zone, to 1,300m, in grasslands with rather short grass and adjacent barren areas, e.g. near rivers, lakes, lagoons, but also on pastures, farmlands and seasonally flooded grasslands (*llanos*).
Voice Calls include a *wisst*, a *chit-chit* when flushed and *tsitsirrit* given from ground or perch (probably a short territorial song). Song in flight commences with series of *tsit* notes as bird flies up to 10–20m, then slowly descends uttering a long slurred *dzeeeeeeeeeeeeeu*, often followed by a *dzip* (Ridgely & Gwynne, R&T, H&B, Hilty).

THRAUPIDAE – Tanagers and Allies

Thraupidae is amongst the best-known families in the Neotropics, due to the brilliant and often kaleidoscopic colours of many species. Their taxonomic history is complex, and until recently tanagers were regarded as a subfamily within Emberizidae. The current taxonomic status is fairly clear, thanks largely to the work of Burns (1977, 1998, 2002 and unpublished data referred to by the SACC), which has wrought some profound changes to traditional systematics. Euphonias and chlorophonias have been transferred to Fringillidae, the bush tanagers, North American *Piranga* and the dull red *Habia* are currently suspended as Incertae Sedis, undoubtedly en route to Cardinalidae, itself also once a subfamily of Emberizidae. Essentially Neotropical, tanagers are far more diverse than might be assumed; they range from sea level to just below the snowline, from xerophytic deserts to lush, moss-laden rain forest, from ground level to the upper canopy. In some species the sexes and ages alike, in others males and females are quite different, and in coloration they range from cryptic green to dramatic combinations of colours. They can be silent and solitary, or travel in noisy bands of mixed species. As if to underscore all this variation, they can be shy and retiring, preferring only undisturbed areas, or bold and fearless of man, foraging in parks and gardens. The implication of all this diversity is that whilst there may be similarities in appearance and behaviour within a genus, essentially every species warrants careful recording of its characteristics. The family is widespread and generally common. Had they been accomplished songsters, there is no doubt that trapping for the cagebird trade would have brought many populations to a threatened state. As it is, despite being favourites in aviculture, they are generally only sought by experienced and dedicated aviculturists, as their diet of fruits, nectar and insects tends to discourage most cagebird keepers.

Additional references for this family include Isler and Isler 1987, hereafter referred to as I&I.

BLACK-FACED TANAGER
Schistochlamys melanopis Pl. 248

Identification 17–19cm. Adult dark grey above, darkest on wings, tertials have grey fringes, forecrown to ear-coverts and full bib black, below paler grey, palest on belly and undertail-coverts, bill bluish-grey with black tip. Immature similar but grey is dull, slightly olivaceous-grey, black on face restricted to lores, base of mesial and smaller bib than adult, below mid grey, tinged yellowish at bib with paler belly and undertail-coverts. Juvenile dark olive above, darker on wings and tail, with paler fringes to coverts, tertials and outer fringes of rectrices; no black on face, but ample diffuse crescents above and below eyes, like broken eye-ring; paler yellowish-olive below, palest on belly and undertail-coverts. Whilst adult is quite unmistakable and immature virtually so, unaccompanied juveniles can be quite confusing (cf. similar saltators, finches, *Conothraupis*, *Tachyphonus* or *Piranga* tanagers), but look for uniform coloration combined with yellowish broken eye-ring, pale belly and rounded tail.

Ssp. *S. m. aterrima* (SE Ec, E Co, Ve, W Gu) face entirely black
S. m. melanopis (E Guianas) mask not all black, deep brown crown, ear-coverts and throat

Habits Often perches atop bushes or small trees. Forages for invertebrates, fruits and seeds, in pairs or sometimes small flocks in canopy of small trees and low shrubs. In open country, e.g. Gran Sabana, Venezuela, may be encountered in tall grass and weedy shrubs, working vertical stems like an over-sized seedeater.
Status Uncommon to locally fairly common. Benefits from forest clearance and has recently spread into south-east Ecuador.
Habitat Tropical to Subtropical Zones, to 2,000m, but usually below 1,700m, in semi-open dry to humid habitats, e.g. gallery forests and scattered shrubbery in savannas, open woodland, low second growth and edges, *Mauritia* palm stands and, in more humid areas, forest and woodland edges and shrubby clearings.
Voice A sharp *swit* and sometimes a rather weak *tee-tseet-tseet-tseet*. Song a rich, melodic, grosbeak-like and rhythmic series of 3–4 flute-like whistled phrases, e.g. *tu-whit-WHEER, tu-whit-WHEER, tu-whit* or *swéet right here for mé*, repeated every *c.*10 s (R&T, I&I, Hilty).
Note Genetic data (Burns 1997, Burns & Naoki 2004) indicate that *Schistochlamys*, *Cissopis* and *Neothraupis* are close relatives.

WHITE-RUMPED TANAGER
Cypsnagra hirundinacea Pl. 248

Identification 16–16.5cm. Adult generally black above with lower back, rump, median wing-coverts and patch at base of primaries white; short buffy supraloral spot does not become an eyebrow, chin, throat and upper breast pale buff, rest of underparts buffy-white. Juvenile dark brown above with white of adult replaced by dull, buffy-white, below entirely buffy.

Ssp. *C. h. pallidigula* (S Su, FG)

Habits Forages in pairs or small flocks (family groups?), low in vegetation or sometimes on ground, mainly for invertebrates and sometimes for fruits and seeds.
Status Fairly common in Sipaliwini savanna, southern

Suriname (H&M), but only single record (January 1984) from Petit Saut, in French Guiana (Tostain *et al.*, SFP&M).
Habitat Tropical Zone, to 1,100m, in savanna swamps as well as in drier parts with scattered, stunted trees.
Voice A flat *chak*. Pairs duet loudly from low treetops, most often in early morning, male commencing with an unmusical churring that becomes a vigorous staccato rattle, joined by female with a musical vigorous series, e.g. *wee-o ta-CHEE-o chee-o...*, repeated again and again (I&I). R&T state that female begins and male answers.

BLACK-AND-WHITE TANAGER

Conothraupis speculigera Pl. 248

Identification 16–16.5cm. Adult male glossy blue-black except grey rump and flanks, and white belly, vent and speculum. Dark red eyes, bill black above, blue below with black tip. Adult female greyish green-olive above with yellow lores and eye-ring, pale yellowish below with short, fine dusky olive streaks on breast and flanks. Juvenile duller and seemingly darker above, less yellow below and more heavily streaked darker olive from throat to flanks. Larger Streaked Saltator has conspicuous white eyebrow whilst female *Piranga* tanagers lack streaked breast.

Ssp. Monotypic (W Ec)

Habits Forages for invertebrates and seeds, alone, in pairs or small to large flocks, in low bushes and herbs below taller trees, and also higher in trees.
Status Near Threatened. Usually rare to uncommon in disjunct range on western slope of Andes, mostly in western Loja, with scattered records, probably of migrants, from further north as far as south-west Pichincha. Probably nomadic as it may be locally fairly common during wet season, but is absent from same areas during dry season.
Habitat Tropical to Subtropical Zones, to 1,950m but usually at 500–1,700m, in deciduous woodland, edges, clearings and mature second growth, gallery forests, riparian thickets and semi-open arid scrub.
Voice Song a loud distinctive series of ringing double notes *chee-ong* repeated 3–6 times, delivered by males perched atop bushes and trees, and often given for protracted periods, even at midday (I&I, R&G).

RED-BILLED PIED TANAGER

Lamprospiza melanoleuca Pl. 248

Identification 17cm. Adult male black above including head, underparts pure white, with thick black diagonal line, like an inverted V, from edge of black throat, to breast-sides; eyes brown, bill scarlet-red. Adult female grey above, with black wings, tail and head, below as male, also with red bill. Juvenile female like adult female but has pale fringes to wing-coverts and washed grey on sides and flanks. Juvenile male like juvenile female but has black scalloping on grey back, from mantle to uppertail-coverts.

Ssp. Monotypic (Guianas)

Habits Forages for invertebrates, fruits and seeds in small flocks, usually in canopy but sometimes lower in fruiting trees, joins mixed-species flocks, sometimes with Yellow-green Grosbeak in treetops (H&M).
Status Fairly common. Widespread in the interior of French Guiana.
Habitat Tropical Zone, to 600m. Mostly in *terra firme* forests and edges, but also in savanna forests and woodland.
Voice Flocks noisy, e.g. a high buzzy *tzee-tzee* or *tzee-tzee-tzee*, or a clearer louder moderately pitched *cheer* or *chee-cheer*, often followed by a high *chi-de-de-dit* that may become a lengthy trill, also a moderately pitched *per-CHEE-chee-chee* in flight (I&I).
Note Placement of this species in Thraupidae has been questioned (Yuri & Mindell 2002).

MAGPIE TANAGER

Cissopis leverianus Pl. 248

Identification 25.5–29cm. Quite unmistakable. Adult white from mantle to uppertail-coverts, wings and tail black (graduated tail with white tips, wings with white lesser and median coverts, white terminal spots to greater coverts and tertials fringed white); head black with feathers of nape and breast lanceolate, extending over white mantle and below, to belly, rest of underparts white. Bill black, eyes bright yellow, legs and feet vinaceous-grey. Juvenile slightly smaller, head sooty black, mantle and wing-coverts washed grey, otherwise as adult.

Ssp. *C. l. leverianus* (E Ec, E Co, W & SE Ve, Guianas)

Habits Often wags long tail. May perch for long periods on isolated high perch. Noisy as it forages for invertebrates, fruits and seeds alone, in pairs or small flocks of up to 10 at all levels. Sometimes joins mixed-species flocks and is very conspicuous as they travel slowly at forest edge, Magpie Tanager visiting open areas more than most flock members.
Status Fairly common to common, but rare in Suriname and French Guiana. Has apparently spread due to forest clearance.
Habitat Tropical Zone, to 2,000m but usually much lower. Riparian thickets in semi-open floodplains and *várzea* edges along rivers, and open woodland, edges, mature second growth and overgrown clearings, plantations, parks and gardens.
Voice A hard, loud metallic and oft-repeated *chek*, thin squealing *sweeeee* and squealing *eeCHUK*. Song variable but always combines low raspy rattles, jerky whistles and chatters with moderately pitched squeaky notes, e.g. *t-t-t-t-t-t-t-TEEK TEEK TEEK, titl-titl-tleechuk ee-CHUK*...or *t-t-t-t, chu-chu tweéte, chu-chu-tweéti*, usually delivered for long periods (R&T, I&I, Hilty).
Note Correct spelling of species name is *leverianus* (David & Gosselin 2002b).

GRASS-GREEN TANAGER

Chlorornis riefferii Pl. 248

Identification 20–20.5cm. Adults have unmistakable grass-green plumage, with rich mid blue glaze on wing-coverts, chestnut mask, vent and undertail-coverts, and red eyes, bill, legs and feet. Juvenile duller with brown bill.

Ssp. *C. r. riefferii* (Andes in Co & Ec)

Habits Moderately active and conspicuous as it forages alone, in pairs or small flocks at all levels for invertebrates, fruits and seeds, often joins mixed-species flocks.

Status Usually fairly common to common but somewhat local.

Habitat Subtropical Zone to Temperate Zone, at 1,700–3,500m but mostly 2,000–2,900m. Usually in humid to wet mossy and cloud forests and edges, often with dense undergrowth and bamboo, less common in mature second growth.

Voice A distinctive squeaking, finch-like *enk*, sometimes repeated 2–3 times or in stuttering series, also a stuttering *du-du-du* and longer whinny *dut-du-u-u-u-u-u* fading in volume, and a slow *t-e-e-e-e-e-k* in flight (H&B, I&I). Dawn song begins with 1–2 *enk* notes, followed by 1–5 harsh double squeaks like a rusty gate (I&I), but also described as a snarling *de-dede-detúitúi-detúitúi-…*, last part repeated 3–5 times (F&K).

WHITE-CAPPED TANAGER

Sericossypha albocristata Pl. 248

Identification 23–24cm. Adult male all black with distinctive white cap that embraces forehead and lores, and clearly defined, crimson-red apron from chin to upper breast. Female has far less extensive bib of dark crimson that fades out on throat, white cap has grey base to feathers, giving slightly less pure white look. Immature resembles female, but has duller, slightly buffy-toned cap, and males have red more extensive. Juvenile has buffy-grey tint to top of head, and only vestigial red on chin and upper throat.

Ssp. Monotypic (Ec, Co, SW Ve)

Habits Often perches in open for long periods. Usually noisy and conspicuous as it forages in jay-like manner for invertebrates, fruits and seeds, in small flocks (usually 4–8, but sometimes up to 20) mostly in canopy. Sometimes joins mixed-species flocks. May respond to playback.

Status Rare to uncommon and local. Appears to have large home range or is perhaps even nomadic.

Habitat Subtropical Zone to Temperate Zone, at 1,400–3,200m but mostly 1,900–2,700m, in humid cloud and mossy forests, edges and second growth.

Voice Piercing notes such as *cheeeyáp*, *cheeeyp*, *kip*, *keep*, *peeeaap*, *peeer* and *peeeur* strung together erratically, often for several minutes at *c.*40 notes per minute, with several flock members often calling simultaneously (R&T, I&I).

Note Taxonomic placement problematic, as has long been thought to perhaps be a cotinga, despite having nine primaries (suboscines have ten). Morony (1985) established that it was certainly oscine, but raised fresh doubts over its position. Burns (1997) support its placement within Thraupidae and furthermore suggest it is a sister taxon to *Nemosia*.

GREY-HOODED BUSH TANAGER

Cnemoscopus rubrirostris Pl. 249

Identification 15–17cm. Adult olive above with complete grey hood, yellow below with olive-tinged flanks; eyes brown, bill and legs distinctively pink. Juvenile similar but duller. Ashy-throated Bush Tanager, race *conspicillatus*, has pale throat and white belly, and most other *Chlorospingus* have pale eyes, any vaguely similar *Hemispingus* has pale superciliary.

Ssp. *C. r. rubrirostris* (Andes in Ec, Co, W Ve)

Habits Forages for invertebrates, fruits and seeds, in pairs or small flocks (rarely alone) from understorey to canopy, but usually high. Constantly wags tail. Has distinctive jizz, creeping from centre of tree along limbs towards outer foliage. Often joins mixed-species flocks.

Status Fairly common to locally common, less common in Ecuador.

Habitat Subtropical Zone to Páramo, 1,900–3,300m but mostly at 2,200–3,000m, in mossy humid to wet cloud forests, edges and clearings, especially in alder (*Alnus* spp.) stands.

Voice A high *swit*, *tsit-tsit…*, *zit*, *pist*, and sharp high *tseeet* or *swit*. Song a rapid series of moderately to high-pitched squeaky notes lasting 3–4 s, sometimes twittering, then changes to several smacking *chip* notes before starting over again, e.g. broken jumble *tchee-tchee wee zt-z-tchee…*(F&K, I&I). Dawn song a simple, high-pitched and endlessly repeated *tswee-tsur*, sometimes *sweee swee tsur* (R&G).

Note Sometimes placed in either *Chlorospingus* or *Hemispingus*.

> *Hemispingus* are rather dull-coloured, mostly olivaceous-greenish birds with touches of grey and black, occurring in understorey of montane forests and often found in mixed-species foraging flocks.

BLACK-CAPPED HEMISPINGUS

Hemispingus atropileus Pl. 250

Identification 15–18cm. Adult has brownish-olive upperparts, long narrow buffy-white supercilium on blackish-brown head, buffy orange-yellow throat and breast with rest of underparts yellowish-olive. Juvenile has paler maxilla and more fuscous head. Smaller Superciliaried Hemispingus has less black on head, shorter supercilium and brighter yellow underparts. Black-eared Hemispingus has grey upperparts and narrow white supercilium (often lacking). Slaty-backed Hemispingus is darker above and bright ferruginous below. See also Citrine and Black-crested Warblers and Tanager Finch.

Ssp. *H. a. atropileus* (Andes in Ec, Co, W Ve)

Habits Restlessly forages for invertebrates, berries and seeds, in pairs or small to large flocks of to 12, in dense undergrowth from under- to lower midstorey. Often joins mixed-species flocks.

Status Fairly common to common.

Habitat Temperate Zone to Páramo, at 1,800–3,600 m but mostly at 2,250–3,200m, in humid to very humid cloud forests and dense, shrubby edges, preferring *Chusquea* bamboo and other dense second growth, sometimes in semi-open treeline elfin forest.

Voice A high hissing *tsit* and lively high-pitched chattering and squeaking notes and trills when foraging. Song consists of phrases of rapid high notes, e.g. *d-d-d-d-d-dit* or *z-z-z-z-zeet*, sometimes running into a rapid ascending or descending trill (F&K, I&I, Hilty).

Note Race *auricularis* may occur in southern Ecuador (R&G).

SUPERCILIARIED HEMISPINGUS

Hemispingus superciliaris Pl. 250

Identification 13–14cm. Adult has olive-green upperparts, blackish wings and tail with olive-green fringes, head concolorous with back, clean white supercilium and greyish-black forecrown and cheeks, yellow underparts with olive-tinged flanks. Subadult has less contrasting head and more olive breast and sides. Oleaginous Hemispingus is dingier with less distinct supercilium, more ochraceous underparts and usually occurs at lower elevations. See also Grey-hooded Bush Tanager, Black-capped Hemispingus (race *nigrifrons*) and Citrine Warbler (very similar race *chrysophrys* which has black triangular patch at base of flight-feathers and dusky grey, not pale legs).

Ssp. *H. s. chrysophrys* (Andes in Ve) yellow supercilium, olive crown

H. s. maculifrons (SW Ec) white supercilium, pale greyish-olive forecrown and cheeks

H. s. nigrifrons (N and C Ec, Co) white supercilium, greyish-black forecrown and cheeks

H. s. superciliaris (Ec, C Co) as described

Habits Restlessly forages for insects, berries and seeds, alone, in pairs or small to large flocks of up to 20. Mostly in canopy, lower at edges and in shrubbery. Often joins mixed-species flocks.

Status Uncommon to common.

Habitat Temperate Zone to Páramo, at 1,900–3,700m but mostly 2,100–3,200m, in humid to wet forests, edges, hedgerows and second growth (*maculifrons* also in tall *Polylepis* woodland and other montane shrubbery).

Voice High *tsit* or *tsick*. Song (mostly just after dawn) of *maculifrons* and *leucogaster* an accelerating series of rapid, moderate- to high-pitched dry harsh *tsit* notes that becomes louder but slows at end, lasting *c*.3–4 s, and often sung simultaneously by pair or several birds (I&I, Hilty).

Note Genetic data (García-Moreno *et al.* 2001) indicate that *H. superciliaris* clusters with group of *Hemispingus* that includes *H. verticalis*–*H. xanthophthalmus* and *H. trifasciatus*; plumage similarities also suggest that *H. reyi* belongs in this group.

GREY-CAPPED HEMISPINGUS

Hemispingus reyi Pl. 250

Identification 14cm. Adult has grey crown contrasting with olive upperparts, pale yellow ear-coverts, and underparts yellow with olive-tinged sides and flanks. See Citrine Warbler and sympatric *Hemispingus*, all of which have a supercilium.

Ssp. Monotypic (Andes in W Ve)

Habits Forages mostly in small flocks, but sometimes in pairs or large flocks of up to 20, mainly at lower levels, and often joins mixed-species flocks.

Status Near Threatened. Endemic to Venezuela, where locally fairly common from west Táchira and Mérida to Trujillo on Cordillera de Mérida. Although some large tracts of forest remain within its limited range, deforestation has been locally severe due to road building, logging, cattle ranching, other agricultural colonisation and mining.

Habitat Subtropical Zone to Temperate Zone, at 1,900–3,200m, in wet and mossy cloud, elfin and dwarf forest and shrubby forest edges, especially with dense *Chusquea* bamboo, e.g. along roadsides, where often easy to see, also in clearings, open woodland and páramo with bushes.

Voice High thin *seep*, longer *seeeep*, thin chittering notes and buzzy *bzit* notes when foraging. Song may be a sharp scratchy, moderate- to high-pitched *tee chew chew*, followed by several *chew* notes or *sit-sit, seet* (F&K, I&I, Hilty).

OLEAGINOUS HEMISPINGUS

Hemispingus frontalis Pl. 250

Identification 13–15cm. Fairly nondescript adult has dull olive upperparts with pale cinnamon fringes to brownish wing- and tail-feathers, indistinct yellow-ochre supercilium most pronounced in front of eye, and dingy yellow-ochre underparts, brightest on throat and olive-tinged on sides. Best distinguished by its drab, dingy appearance lacking conspicuous field marks except long, narrow eyebrow (see e.g. Yellow-green Bush Tanager, Superciliaried Hemispingus and smaller Citrine Warbler).

Ssp. *H. f. flavidorsalis* (Perijá, Ve) uniform olive-green above, wings and tail brown with olive-green fringes, superciliary buffy-yellow, yellowish-buffy throat, rest pale olive-green; legs and feet grey

H. f. frontalis (E Ec, Co) supercilium weak and pale yellow-olive, underparts pale orange-yellow becoming buffier on lower breast and belly with olive-brown sides

H. f. hanieli (N Ve) olive above with a noticeable rufous tone to tail, warm ochre supercilium and orange-buffy throat, belly to undertail-coverts pale olive with breast a rich mixture of throat and belly; legs and feet pale brown

H. f. ignobilis (Andes in Ve) olive-green above, dull greenish-yellow superciliary, pale buffy throat well demarcated from pale olive breast and underparts; legs and feet slightly vinaceous grey-brown

H. f. iteratus (NE Ve) olive-green above, pale buffy-orange superciliary and throat, warmer on breast where blends into warm orange-flushed belly and flanks

Habits Often twitches and flicks tail. Forages, often with jerky movements, alone, in pairs or small flocks mostly in understorey to lower midstorey, and often joins mixed-species flocks.

Status Fairly common but often overlooked as it prefers dense forest undergrowth, rarer and more local in Ecuador.
Habitat Subtropical to Temperate Zones, at 1,300–2,900m but usually 1,900–2,400m, in cloud and humid to wet forests, edges and clearings, also mature second growth, most often in dense undergrowth, thickets, vine tangles and other shrubbery.
Voice A harsh moderately- to high-pitched *chip* and soft *chit* when foraging. Song (mostly just after dawn) a series of moderately- to high-pitched squeaky rattles, e.g. *chip chip chi-chi-chi-ch-ch-ch-ch-ch…*, rapidly accelerating and usually ending in a drawn-out, squealing *wa-CHEW wa-CHEW…*, usually uttered 3–4 times, and often sung simultaneously by pair or several birds (F&K, I&I, Hilty).
Note R&T suspected that Venezuelan races (as *H. ignobilis*) might deserve species status from *Hemispingus frontalis*; Hilty however, noted that their vocalisations and behaviour were similar.

Black-eared Hemispingus can be confused with Slaty-backed Hemispingus: white on head of Black-eared can vary considerably, but never reaches beyond eyes; here a well-marked example (right) is compared to a typical Slaty-backed Hemispingus

BLACK-EARED HEMISPINGUS

Hemispingus melanotis Pl. 250

Identification 14cm. Adult greyish-olive above with black mask, frontal band and chin, usually has very short and narrow white supercilium (sometimes lacking, occasionally pronounced), and is cinnamon-rufous below, paler on belly. Longish, pointed black bill. Juvenile duller above with more extensive olive wash to nape, white superciliary absent, but has pale, buffy supraloral spot. Most likely to be confused with Slaty-backed Hemispingus, if seen poorly, e.g. inside canopy with sun behind, but Slaty-backed always has very long, narrow white superciliary and rich cinnamon to rufous underparts. Similarly, young Black-headed Hemispingus might be confused; the central coronal stripe being taken for a superciliary, but grey underparts with whitish belly separates it.

Ssp. *H. m. melanotis* (E Ec, Co, SW Ve)

Habits Forages for insects and seeds, alone, in pairs or small flocks, mostly in understorey to midstorey. Often joins mixed-species flocks.
Status Rare and local in most of range and often overlooked as it prefers dense forest undergrowth.
Habitat Subtropical to Temperate Zones, at 1,800–2,800m, in cloud and humid to very wet forests and edges, mature second growth and plantations, most often in dense undergrowth, particularly dense understorey of *Chusquea* bamboo, *Dryopteris* tree ferns, vine tangles and other shrubbery.
Voice A *tje*. Song a rhythmic *didadidadidadida* lasting 2–3 s (F&K).
Note Genetic data (García-Moreno *et al.* 2001) indicate that distinctive race *piurae*, currently treated as a subspecies of *H. melanotis* (e.g. Meyer de Schauensee 1970), is more distant from latter than *H. frontalis*. R&G treated *piurae* and *ochraceus* as a separate species from *H. melanotis* based on plumage and vocal differences.

WESTERN HEMISPINGUS

Hemispingus ochraceus Pl. 250

Identification 14cm. Olive above with top of head grey, dusky mask runs from supraloral above and gape of bill below beyond ear-coverts, bordered above with a pale, greyish line that is not quite a superciliary. Below, uniform yellow ochre.

Ssp. *H. m. ochraceus* (W Ec, SW Co: west slopes of Andes)

Habits Forages in undergrowth and tangles within forest. Shows no predilection for bamboo.
Status Rare and local. Few records and poorly known.
Habitat Subtropical Zone, 1,600–2,200m. Undergrowth of montane and secondary forest.
Voice Reportedly similar to song of Black-eared Hemispingus (R&G).
Note Previously treated as a subspecies of *H. melanotis*.

PIURA HEMISPINGUS

Hemispingus piurae Pl. 250

Identification 14cm. Olive-grey above, wings and tail darker with grey fringes on back, hood black with clear white superciliary from supraloral to neck-sides; underparts orange-rufous. Looks much like a pale Slaty-backed Hemispingus, but well separated geographically.

Ssp. *H. m. piurae* (SE Ec) black crown with long, broad white supercilium, black chin, rufous underparts

Habits Usually forages in pairs, seldom joins mixed flocks.
Status Uncommon and very local in southernmost Loja, Ecuador,
Habitat Temperate Zone, at 2,000–2,500m in dense undergrowth of *Chusquea* bamboo.
Voice No details; reportedly like Black-eared but delivered at a slower rate (P. Coopmans).
Note Previously treated as a subspecies of *H. melanotis*.

SLATY-BACKED HEMISPINGUS

Hemispingus goeringi Pl. 250

Identification 13–15cm. Adult male has dark grey upperparts with black cheeks and crown, separated by long, conspicuous white supercilium, and orange-rufous underparts with olive-brown flanks. Female same above but paler below, being ochraceous, pale to whitish on central belly and vent. Dark eyes, bicoloured bill, dark above and grey below, horn-coloured long tarsi and large feet, short bill. Black-eared Hemispingus lacks black crown and conspicuous supercilium, with duller underparts. See also Black-capped Hemispingus.

Ssp. Monotypic (Andes in W Ve)

Habits Forages for insects and berries, alone, in pairs or small flocks, on or near ground in dense undergrowth. Often joins mixed-species flocks. At dawn, may feed on ground near forest edge.

Status Vulnerable. Endemic to Venezuela, with very small range in south-west half of Cordillera de Mérida, in Táchira and Mérida, western Venezuela, where locally common along Pico Humboldt trail, Sierra Nevada National Park, and recent records also from Páramo Batallón on Mérida/Táchira border and Páramo Zumbador, and older records from just 2 other areas. As is easily overlooked, it might, however, still occur in these areas and other contiguous tracts of suitable habitat, though it has doubtlessly declined due to extensive deforestation wrought by road building, agricultural conversion and mining.

Habitat Temperate Zone, at 2,300–3,200m, in humid to wet cloud and elfin forests, especially dense shrubby borders and stunted vegetation, near bamboo stands, most commonly near treeline and in scattered trees at edge of humid páramo.

Voice Song a continuous stream of moderate-pitched, harsh notes, *ch-d-d-d-d-d-d…*, interspersed with *plink* notes, and a more pleasant high-pitched stream of musical, almost tinkling *chi-ti-tee chi-ti-tee …*, both probably given in duet, sometimes lasting 3 minutes (I&I, Hilty).

BLACK-HEADED HEMISPINGUS

Hemispingus verticalis Pl. 250

Identification 14–15cm. Adult has dark grey upperparts with blackish wings and tail, black hood with clay-coloured crown-stripe and pale grey underparts becoming whitish on belly, pale eyes, thin bill. Female like male but has coronal line more buffy. Juvenile has grey throat with greyish spots and dark eyes. Compare similar *Atlapetes* brush finches.

Ssp. Monotypic (Andes in E Ec, S & C Co, Ve)

Habits Forages for insects, berries and fruits, alone, in pairs or small and sometimes large flocks, from midstorey to canopy (often *walking* on top of outer vegetation). Often joins mixed-species flocks.

Status Uncommon and local, but common in Podocarpus National Park, southern Ecuador.

Habitat Temperate Zone to Páramo, at 2,350–3,600m, in dense humid to wet cloud and elfin forests and shrubby edges, also stunted shrubbery and tree groves in humid páramo near treeline, especially in alder (*Alnus*) and bamboo stands, but mostly at or just below treeline.

Voice Song a moderately to high-pitched, squeaky, rapid twitter with no fixed theme, overlain with a continuous stream of thin high *seet* notes, lasting 5–15 s, and often given simultaneously by pair or several birds and repeated for several minutes; twitter may cease for intervals of to 12 s during which *seet* notes continue at slower pace (F&K, I&I).

Note Genetic data (García-Moreno *et al.* 2001) support traditional view based on plumage, morphology, and biogeography (Parker et al. 1985, F&K, S&M) that *H. verticalis* and *H. xanthophthalmus* are sister taxa and form a superspecies; they were formerly (e.g. Hellmayr 1936, Phelps & Phelps 1950a) placed in a separate genus, *Pseudospingus*, but Zimmer (1947b) merged this into *Hemispingus*.

Thlypopsis are small, rather warbler-like tanagers, mostly grey with contrasting touches of fulvous, rufescent and orange.

FULVOUS-HEADED TANAGER

Thlypopsis fulviceps Pl. 251

Identification 12–13cm. Adult has rufous-chestnut hood sharply separated from dark grey upperparts and paler grey underparts, becoming whitish on belly and undertail-coverts. Short bill is dark with pale base to mandible, legs and feet grey. Female has paler throat. Juvenile has paler hood tinged olive on crown and is pale buffy below.

Ssp. *T. f. fulviceps* (NE Co, N & W Ve) as described
T. f. intensa (NE & C Co) deeper chestnut hood and cinnamon undertail-coverts
T. f. meridensis (Mérida, Ve) similar to *fulviceps* but paler grey below, pale grey undertail-coverts
T. f. obscuriceps (Perijá, Ve) similar to *fulviceps*, darker grey above, whitish undertail-coverts

Habits Forages for insects, berries and fruits, alone, in pairs or small to large flocks of up to 10, at all levels. Often joins mixed-species flocks.

Status Uncommon to locally fairly common, commonest in moist to semi-humid forests, with numbers decreasing sharply in more humid zones.

Habitat Tropical to Subtropical Zones, at 750–2,380m, in dense thickets, vine tangles and *Chusquea* bamboo stands at shrubby forest edges, and adjacent semi-open areas, also inside humid forests, open woodlands and suburban areas.

Voice Thin high *tsit* and *chik* notes. Song a rarely heard, accelerating series of high notes, e.g. *chi chi cht-cht-tit-t-t-t-t-t-t*, trailing off at end (Hilty).

BUFF-BELLIED TANAGER

Thlypopsis inornata Pl. 251

Identification 12.5–13cm. Adult has greenish-grey upperparts, darker on wings and tail, rufous crown and nape contrasting with buffy frontal band, head-sides and underparts. Female has more olive crown and nape less contrasting with upperparts, and paler underparts. Juvenile has more olive upperparts and yellower underparts. Rufous-chested Tanager (no overlap in southern Ecuador) has deeper orange-rufous underparts concolorous (not contrasting) with cap, and usually occurs at higher elevations.

Ssp. Monotypic (S Ec)

Habits Forages, usually in pairs and sometimes in small

flocks, mostly near ground (even in tall grass), and sometimes joins mixed-species flocks.

Status Uncommon to locally fairly common in río Marañón drainage around Zumba in extreme southern Zamora-Chinchipe.

Habitat Tropical to Subtropical Zones, at 650–1,200m, in dense shrubby second-growth woodland, clearings and thickets, e.g. along forest edges, rivers and ravines.

Voice A soft *seet-a* repeated several times, and *sip* or *seep* when foraging (I&I).

RUFOUS-CHESTED TANAGER

Thlypopsis ornata Pl. 251

Identification 12–13cm. Short bill. Adult has olive-grey upperparts, orange-rufous hood and breast, sides and thighs grey, belly white, undertail-coverts cinnamon. Juvenile has hood paler, more orange with pale olive tinge, and is yellower below with olive-tinged flanks. Larger Rufous-crested Tanager has grey head with only crown-stripe rufous and is forest-based. See Buff-bellied Tanager.

Ssp. *T. o. media* (S Ec) similar, but larger
T. o. ornata (W Ec, SW Co) as described

Habits Continually on the move, forages for insects at all levels, alone, in pairs or small flocks. Often joins mixed-species flocks.

Status Rare to uncommon and local in Ecuador but increasingly common in south. Fairly common but very local in Cauca, south-west Colombia, where has undoubtedly decreased due to habitat loss.

Habitat Subtropical Zone to Páramo, at 1,200–3,400m but mostly 1,800–3,000m, in dense shrubby second-growth woodland, clearings and bamboo thickets, e.g. at forest edges, steep slopes and ravines, also *Polylepis*; often in semi-open habitats away from continuous forest, locally even in relatively arid scrub.

Voice A *seep*, also an occasional, somewhat metallic and jumbled *see-sje-se-seek-sje-se-seek-se-sjuk*. Song a warbling *tzee-wee-dee-zi* (F&K, I&I, R&G).

ORANGE-HEADED TANAGER

Thlypopsis sordida Pl. 251

Identification 14cm. Adult has greyish-olive upperparts contrasting with orange-rufous head, becoming pale yellow on lores, ocular area and throat; very pale greyish-cinnamon underparts. Dark eyes, short grey bill, legs and feet. Juvenile paler, more greyish-olive above, including top of head, yellowish lores, ocular area, throat and upper breast, contrasting with paler olive-tinged underparts and almost white undertail-coverts.

Ssp. *T. s. chrysopis* (E Ec, S Co) pure grey above, with less olive wash, much less buffy below breast and sides pale greyish-brown
T. s. orinocensis (C Ve) as described

Habits Continually active, forages for insects, seeds, fruits and berries, alone, in pairs or small flocks, at all levels. Sometimes joins mixed-species flocks.

Status Uncommon and somewhat local along Orinoco in Venezuela, uncommon to locally common in southern Colombia and east Ecuador, apparently benefiting from habitat conversion.

Habitat Tropical Zone, to 500m in Ecuador and Colombia, 200m in Venezuela. Early second growth, shrubs and trees along rivers and on river islands in Venezuela, also other shrubby areas, parks and gardens in Colombia and Ecuador, where spreading into cleared areas and second growth away from riparian areas. In Peruvian Amazon, race *chrysopis* has predilection for water hyacinth beds. In comparison, *orinocensis* in Venezuela seems to prefer open scrub and grassland (D. Ascanio, pers, comm.).

Voice High thin, often doubled or tripled *seet* or *sit* notes, and an occasional slower-paced *see-ta*. Song a high-pitched stuttering series, usually preceded by several longer notes, e.g. *seet seet t-t-t-t-t-t-t-t-t-t-d-dit* (I&I, R&G, Hilty).

Note S&M (1990) considered *T. sordida* and *T. inornata* a superspecies; Meyer de Schauensee (1966) suggested they might be best treated as conspecific, but they may be sympatric at some localities (Zimmer 1947a).

GUIRA TANAGER

Hemithraupis guira Pl. 251

Identification 13–14cm. Adult male yellow-olive from crown to lower back, rump orange-rufous, uppertail-coverts bright orange, wings and tail dusky, fringed yellow-olive; dusky mask from lores through eyes to ear-coverts and down to throat, bordered above by bright orange superciliary, and slightly brighter or more yellowy orange on ear-coverts. Breast deep orange-rufous, sides and flanks grey, belly to undertail-coverts cream, washed olive on belly. Immature or subadult male has far less orange-rufous on rump and breast, mask is browner and paler, and uppertail-coverts weakly washed yellow. Adult female has yellow-olive upperparts, including rump, with yellowish uppertail-coverts, lacks mask but has faint yellowish eye-ring and eyestripe, yellow underparts with grey flanks and thighs, washed grey belly. Eyes dark, bill horn-coloured above and yellow-orange below, legs and feet grey. Juvenile yellow-olive above, slightly duller than adult, with no orange nor yellow above, face greyish and underparts weak yellow, washed pale grey on flanks, thighs and belly. Female Yellow-backed Tanager lacks eye-stripe but has whitish eye-ring, darker greenish upperparts with more distinctly yellow-fringed wings, more uniform bright yellow underparts with olive flanks, and is rarely found outside continuous forest. Female Yellow Warbler lacks eyestripe, eye-ring and grey flanks and is brighter yellow overall.

Ssp. *H. g. guirina* (W Ec, W & C Co) face-sides, chin and throat dark brown, orange of breast adjoins, with no yellow between, has more ochraceous eyebrow than *huambina*; female darker above with yellowish tail-coverts and much paler below, brighter than female *huambina*

H. g. huambina (E Ec, SE Co) male has yellower superciliary than *guirina*
H. g. nigrigula (NC Co, N Ve, Guianas) lower mask tends to bisect yellow fringe that separates it from orange breast, female yellowish-olive above, canary yellow below
H. g. roraimae (SE Ve, Gu) yellow fringe across breast complete, female darker greenish-olive above, yellowish uppertail-coverts very weak

Habits Forages restlessly, in pairs or small and sometimes large flocks of up to 25 in outer canopy, for insects, fruits and seeds, and often joins mixed-species flocks.
Status Fairly common in Ecuador and Guianas, uncommon to fairly common but local in Colombia and Venezuela.
Habitat Tropical Zone, to 1,450m. Tall humid *terra firme* forest and edges, but in drier, moist or moderately humid forests and second growth in Venezuela, also plantations with tall trees, gallery forest, open woodland, isolated tree stands, second growth, orchards and tall scrub.
Voice An *auck* and *chit* notes. Dawn song a moderate- to high-pitched cadence reminiscent of a drummer's roll, e.g. *TIT-de-de-DIT TIT TIT, tit-de-de-dit dit*, lasting *c*.2.5 s and repeated after 3 s pauses. Day song a rapid moderate- to high-pitched series of nasal *chee* or *chut* notes accelerating into a trill of *chit* notes, slowing at end, lasting *c*.2 s and repeated after 5 s pauses. Song in northern Venezuela a series of 6–7 rather weak, but sharp notes, e.g. *sa-sit-sit-sit-sit-sit* (I&I, Hilty).

YELLOW-BACKED TANAGER
Hemithraupis flavicollis Pl. 251

Identification 12.7–13cm. Adult male black from forehead to back, lower back, rump and short uppertail-coverts pure yellow, wings and tail black with noticeable white spot at base of primaries; chin, face-sides and throat yellow, breast and sides grey, whitish from central breast to vent, undertail-coverts yellow; eyes brown, thin bill is blackish above, yellowish below, legs and feet greenish-grey. Immature male olive-green above, slightly darker than female, and often shows some black, below yellow, with sides and flanks mottled grey and olive. Adult female has brownish-olive upperparts with narrow white eye-ring, yellow-fringed wing-feathers and yellow-tinged rump, yellow underparts lightly flammulated olive-green, and washed on sides. Juvenile like female but slightly paler and more washed yellow than adult, paler below, with a washed-out appearance. See female Guira Tanager.

Ssp. *H. f. albigularis* (C Co) male has central throat white, barred and spotted black on breast-sides and small yellow supraloral spot; female has whitish belly
H. f. aurigularis (SE Co, S Ve) male like *flavicollis* but irregular black mottling on body-sides; immature has same pattern, female lightly mottled olive on flanks
H. f. flavicollis (Su, FG) as described; only race without black mottling on body-sides
H. f. hellmayri (SE Ve, W Gu) yellow throat extends to breast, central breast lacks black scallops (only on sides); female slightly browner above, with head more brown and distinct from back; juvenile as female but back concolorous with head
H. f. ornata (NW Co) yellow replaced by rich yellow-orange
H. f. peruana (E Ec, SC Co) outer row of lesser wing-coverts yellow, like a wingbar or shoulder patch, yellow supraloral streak and half-crescent below eyes

Habits Forages in pairs or small flocks in outer canopy for insects, fruits and berries, and often joins mixed-species flocks.
Status Uncommon to fairly common in Ecuador, fairly common in rest of range.
Habitat Tropical Zone, to 1,000m, mainly in humid *terra firme* and *várzea* and edges, sometimes in adjacent clearings, second growth, plantations, lighter woodlands and parks.
Voice A high *tseep*, *tseet*, *tsick*, *tut* or *tyoo* notes, often combined, given when foraging (H&B, I&I, Hilty).

BLACK-AND-YELLOW TANAGER
Chrysothlypis chrysomelas Pl. 251

Identification 12cm. Male bright yellow with black lores and narrow eye-ring, upper back, wings and tail. Female yellow-olive above and all yellow below. Male quite unmistakable, but female is much like female Yellow-backed Tanager, though is brighter yellow-olive above and cleaner yellow below.

Ssp. *C. c. ocularis* (NW Colombia)

Habits Very mobile, usually in small groups which often join mixed-species flocks. Perch-gleans, hover-gleans and probes hanging bunches of dead leaves.
Status In Panama fairly common, but is only a rare wanderer across border into Colombia.
Habitat Tropical Zone, 400–1,200m, mostly below 1,050m, in canopy and at borders of humid forest and mature second growth in foothills, occasionally clearings or isolated trees just outside forest edge.
Voice Sharp, high-pitched *tzeee*, sometimes doubled, a weak *tsiss* or *tsiss-it*, and rapid *tzee dit-dit-dit* or *tzee-di-zit zit zit* (I&I).

SCARLET-AND-WHITE TANAGER
Chrysothlypis salmoni Pl. 251

Identification 12-13cm. Adult male unmistakable, almost entirely bright red body with brown wings and tail, pure white sides and flanks, vent and undertail-coverts rosy. Dark eyes, dark, rather long thin bill, grey legs and feet. Adult female greyish-olive above with slightly paler, yellowish-green fringes to flight-feathers and greyish-white underparts with buffy-tinged throat and breast. Juvenile like female. Subadult male resembles female for at least one year, but becomes progressively mottled scarlet, white and brownish-olive.

Ssp. Monotypic (NW Ec, W Co)

Habits Often perches upright. Forages in pairs or small flocks, mostly from midstorey to canopy, for insects, fruits, berries and seeds, and often joins mixed-species flocks.
Status Uncommon to locally fairly common.

Habitat Tropical Zone, to 1,100m but mostly at 200–800m, in tall humid to wet semi-open forests, edges and second growth (sometimes in continuous forest), also dense scrub on ridges and in steep canyons.
Voice A weak sibilant *chip* or *sciip* in flight or foraging (H&B, I&I), but also a distinctive, brief, fast, descending series of fairly high notes, e.g. *tsi-tsi-tse-tsu-tu* (R&G).
Note Sometimes placed in genus *Erythrothlypis* (R&G).

HOODED TANAGER
Nemosia pileata Pl. 251

Identification 12–13.5cm. Adult male has greyish-blue upperparts with short white supraloral and distinctive black hood extending to breast-sides in an irregular line; white underparts with blue-grey wash on sides and flanks. Duller adult female has greyish-blue head concolorous with upperparts, and buffy-tinged throat and breast. Yellow eyes, legs and feet, short-tailed. Immature male like female. Smaller Bicoloured Conebill lacks black hood and white supraloral, and has reddish-brown eyes, dusky pinkish legs and duller underparts. Even smaller, male White-eared Conebill lacks white supraloral and has dark eyes and legs, conspicuous white ear patch, inconspicuous white rump band and duller underparts. Female White-eared Conebill lacks white supraloral and has dark eyes and legs, different head pattern, whitish rump and duller underparts.

Ssp. *N. p. hypoleuca* (N Co, N Ve) male entirely white below, female very pale buffy
N. p. pileata (FG) as described, breast, abdomen and sides of body pale lavender blue
N. p. surinamensis (Gu, Su) similar to but larger than *pileata*, and darker above

Habits Forages deliberately, in pairs or small flocks, on rather substantial open branches in relatively open trees and also in outer foliage, gleaning invertebrates but rarely picking fruits and berries (e.g. *Miconia*). Sometimes joins mixed-species flocks.
Status Uncommon in Colombia and Venezuela, where seasonal movements may occur in *llanos*, and common in coastal Suriname and Guyana, but uncommon further inland.
Habitat Tropical Zone, to 600m, mostly in semi-open moist semi-deciduous and humid evergreen woodland and edges (e.g. *Avicennia* mangrove and *várzea*), also gallery forest, wooded sand ridges, tall scrub, shrubby clearings, pastures with scattered trees, second growth, plantations, parks, gardens and trees (e.g. *Cecropia*, *Mimosa*) along riverbanks and on swampy river islands, often near water.
Voice Rapid, loud, sharp, high *tic*, *chip* and *tsip* notes, sometimes given in rapid succession, especially in flight, or as trills and rattles when agitated; also softer, moderate-pitched *sip*, trembling, nasal *ts-sn-sn-sn-sn* and various sharp moderate- to high-pitched notes, e.g. *ss-chit*. Dawn song a high, insistent, explosive, moderate-pitched *tsip-tsip ti-CHEW ti-CHEW*, or similar variation, *c.*7 songs per minute, when excited also other chips, twitters and trills, e.g. *tic, tic-tttttttttttttttt*, by which it often draws attention (H&B, I&I, Hilty).

ROSY THRUSH-TANAGER
Rhodinocichla rosea Pl. 252

Identification 19–20cm. Adult unmistakable, very dark brown above and on flanks, rosy-carmine over rest of underparts and lores, long superciliary becomes white beyond eye, and note rather long thin bill. Subadult or immature male has faint superciliary and is extensive dark brown below, with well-framed gorget of rufous-ochre, belly white, undertail-coverts ochre. Female has rosy colours replaced by rufous-ochre. Juvenile like female but duller.

Ssp. *R. r. beebei* (NE Co, NW Ve: Perijá and Zulia) postocular stripe either completely absent or very faint; female ochraceous-orange below
R. r. harterti (C Co) male dark, deep mouse grey with grey fringes to remiges and wing-coverts less noticeable; female darker above, without olivaceous tinge, deep rufous below
R. r. rosea (NW Ve: Coastal Cordillera, Falcón to Miranda) as described, with clear white postocular line

Habits Very wary as it forages alone, in pairs or small flocks on or near ground, flicking leaf-litter with bill to pick invertebrates, fruits and seeds, rarely joins mixed-species flocks. Also sings from within cover and in so doing betrays its presence. Responds extremely well to playback and comes right up close, but may still remain hidden!
Status Uncommon and local, but locally common, e.g. Cundinamarca, Colombia, and Urbanización San José or at Hotel Tamanaco, Caracas, Venezuela.
Habitat Tropical to Subtropical Zones, 100–1,700m. Thickets, shrubbery and dense tangled undergrowth of deciduous woodland, edges, second growth, clearings, plantations and scrub in both dry and humid regions. Occurs in gardens and parks in towns and cities.
Voice A short, dry *tur-ta'tup*, ringing, jay-like *eeoo* when foraging and low- to moderate-pitched *too-wee* or *ter-wee* whistle, second note higher, sometimes followed by a downward-inflected *ta-woo* or brief, mellow chatter. Song a rich, loud, ringing low- to moderate-pitched *pa-CHEW* or *cho-oh, chowee* or *wheeo, chee-oh, chweeo* or similar variation (e.g. *cholo, cheela, cholo, cheela…* or *tor-CHIL-o, waCHEer, tor-CHIL-o…*), repeated every 3–4 s, reminiscent of *Thryothorus* wrens, with both members of pair often singing separately and antiphonally (only tanager known to do so). Both sexes also utter a monotonously repeated, loud and harsh *chew*, at *c.*1 note per s (R&T, I&I, Hilty).
Notes Also called Rose-breasted Thrush Tanager. More than one species is speculated to be involved (Peterson *et al.* 2004).

DUSKY-FACED TANAGER
Mitrospingus cassinii Pl. 252

Identification 18cm. Adult has blackish-grey upperparts extending to head-sides and throat, forming a mask outlined olive-yellow, with underparts also olive-yellow, tinged buffy on belly. Greyish-white eyes. Juvenile duller with vestigial olive-yellow on crown and crown, and buffy-tinged underparts.

Olive-backed Tanager (no overlap) has olive upperparts and brighter underparts, and forages more deliberately. Ochre-breasted Tanager has less conspicuous bluish-grey eyes and ochraceous underparts. Slightly smaller Grey-headed Tanager has all-grey head with inconspicuous dark eyes.

Ssp. *M. c. cassinii* (W Ec, W Co)

Habits Difficult to see as it forages for invertebrates, seeds and fruits rapidly and noisily in small flocks of up to 12 in undergrowth. Constantly twitches wings and tail, rarely joins mixed-species flocks (often with Tawny-crested Tanager).
Status Fairly common in Ecuador, common in Colombia.
Habitat Tropical Zone, to 1,100m but usually below 800m. Thickets, shrubbery and dense undergrowth at edges of humid forest, woodland and especially streams, rivers and swampy places, sometimes in adjacent low dense second growth.
Voice An incessant, gravelly, harsh, moderate-pitched *cht-cht-cht…* or *chet-ut*, and sometimes high *wss* or *sszeet?* notes, rapid *swiss* notes, and jumbled sharp notes, e.g. *spssnks* or *sptzks* (R&T, I&I).

OLIVE-BACKED TANAGER

Mitrospingus oleagineus Pl. 252

Identification 18.5–19.5cm. Adult basically greenish-olive, darker on wings and tail, with a grey mask and olive-yellow belly; grey eyes. Juvenile distinctly duller, lacks grey mask and has brownish-grey eyes. See Dusky-faced Tanager (no overlap). Smaller female White-shouldered Tanager has dark eyes, grey crown and whitish throat.

Ssp. *M. o. obscuripectus* (E Ve) slightly darker and more olive above
M. o. oleagineus (E Ve, W Gu) as described

Habits Sluggishly and quietly forages in small to large flocks of up to 20 and often joins mixed-species flocks. Searches from under- to midstorey for invertebrates, fruits and seeds.
Status Locally common, e.g. on the Sierra de Lema, eastern Venezuela.
Habitat Tropical to Subtropical Zones, at 900–1,800m, in humid to wet forests and edges on slopes of tepuis and mountains, also in dense, stunted, Melastome-dominated second growth on white-sand soils.
Voice A thin, ticking, oft-repeated *tic* in contact, a soft *chip*, high, thin *seeep*, thin, drawn-out rising *seeeeeek*, an often rapidly repeated, loud, harsh *zwer* or *zwee* sometimes accelerated into a rattle, and a buzzy, oft-repeated *pzzzzz* when foraging. Song a short high squealing *zweee-eet?* or *zwee-er-eet?* often repeated every 1–3 s, with 2–3 group members sometimes singing simultaneously (I&I, Hilty).

OLIVE TANAGER

Chlorothraupis frenata Pl. 252

Identification 17cm. Adult male entirely olive, slightly paler below with yellowish throat. Female similar but has paler underparts and yellow lores. Heavy black bill. Yellow-green Bush Tanager is remarkably similar but has smaller bill, and does not overlap. Red-crowned Ant Tanager is much browner with orange crown-stripe. Lemon-spectacled Tanager (no overlap) has yellow spectacles. Broad-billed Sapayoa is more uniform dull yellow below and forages alone and quietly.

Ssp. Monotypic (S Ec, N Ec, SW Co)

Habits Rapidly and noisily forages for invertebrates, seeds, fruits and berries, mostly in small flocks in vine-tangled understorey to midstorey. Often joins and at times even appears to lead mixed-species understorey flocks.
Status Poorly known in Colombia, in foothills along east slope of Andes in west Caquetá to east Nariño, and locally common just across border in Bermejo oil field area north of Lumbaquí, Sucumbíos, northern Ecuador, with one record from Loja–Zamora road, just above Zamora, southern Ecuador.
Habitat Tropical Zone, at 400–1,100m, in lower and middle growth of humid foothill forests and edges.
Voice Song in Ecuador (mainly at dawn) a series of lovely, ringing, loud notes, each repeated severally before continuing to next, with an initial phrase reminiscent of Buff-rumped Warbler (H&B, I&I, R&G).
Note Formerly considered conspecific with Carmiol's Tanager. Separation based on their disjunct ranges and different behaviour and vocalisations (S&M, R&G).

CARMIOL'S TANAGER

Chlorothraupis carmioli Pl. 252

Identification 16–17cm. Adult male entirely olive, slightly paler below, yellowish throat with vague olive throat streaks. Female similar but lacks throat streaks, with paler underparts and yellow lores. Heavy black bill. Yellow-green Bush Tanager remarkably similar but has smaller bill, and does not overlap. Red-crowned Ant Tanager is much browner with orange crown-stripe. Lemon-spectacled Tanager (no overlap) has yellow spectacles. Broad-billed Sapayoa is more uniform dull yellow below and forages alone and quietly.

Ssp. *C. c. lutescens* (NW Co)

Habits Forages rapidly and noisily looking for invertebrates, seeds, fruits and berries. Mostly in small flocks in vine-tangled understorey to midstorey. Often joins mixed-species flocks.
Status Poorly known in Colombia, occurring on slopes of Cerro Tacarcuna in north-west Chocó.
Habitat Tropical Zone, in undergrowth of humid forests and edges in foothills.
Voice Incessantly repeated harsh chatters and squeaks, e.g. *skwick*, *squeak* or *squirr*, also metallic trebled *wrss* and hurried *eep-eep-eep-eep*. (H&B, Ridgely & Gwynne, Slud 1964).
Note See previous species.

LEMON-SPECTACLED TANAGER

Chlorothraupis olivacea Pl. 252

Identification 17cm. Adult entirely dark olive above with distinctive yellow spectacles, lightly streaked throat, slightly paler below, becoming yellowish on belly and vent. Heavy black bill, reddish-brown eyes. Female slightly paler and more yellowish on vent and undertail-coverts. From Olive Tanager by its yellow spectacles. Juvenile lacks spectacles, and may be confused with similar Ochre-breasted Tanager, which is more ochraceous below and usually occurs at higher elevations.

Ssp. Monotypic (NW Ec, W Co)

Habits Forages noisily alone, in pairs or small flocks of up to 6, looking for invertebrates, fruits and seeds, in understorey to midstorey. Often joins mixed-species flocks.

Status Fairly common to locally common, southern limit of its range being the río Verde, south of Chontaduro, Esmeraldas, in north-west Ecuador.

Habitat Tropical to Subtropical Zones, to 1,500m in Colombia but usually below 450m, in dense undergrowth of humid to wet forests, edges and mature second growth, especially along streams.

Voice A *jee-ut*, *eep* and other notes, e.g. a nasal *nyaah-nyaah-nyaah-nyaah-nyaah!*, but most commonly heard is an incessantly repeated, harsh, moderate-pitched chatter, e.g. *cheat*, *treu* or *turee*, uttered at *c*.4–8 notes in 1–2 s, repeatedly uttered after a short pause at a slightly different pitch. Musical song similar to Olive Tanager (H&B, I&I, R&G).

Note Also called Yellow-browed Tanager.

OCHRE-BREASTED TANAGER

Chlorothraupis stolzmanni Pl. 252

Identification 17–18.5cm. Notably drab adult dark olive above and dull ochraceous below with pale chin, olive-tinged throat- and body-sides and flanks. Heavy dusky bill, often with a pinkish gape, pale bluish-grey eyes. From other *Chlorothraupis* by pale eyes, pale bib and ochraceous breast. Smaller female Tawny-crested Tanager entirely brownish-olive with dark eyes.

Ssp. *C. s. dugandi* (N Ec, SW Co) has greyer crown and slightly paler underparts
C. s. stolzmanni (W Ec) as described

Habits Forages rapidly and noisily looking for invertebrates, fruits, berries, even frogs and lizards, mostly in under- to midstorey but sometimes to subcanopy. In small to large flocks of up to 15, and sometimes joins mixed-species flocks.

Status Uncommon to locally common.

Habitat Tropical to Subtropical Zones, at 200–2,100m but usually 400–1,500m, in dense undergrowth of humid to very wet forests, less often at edges.

Voice Almost incessantly repeated, rough, very rapid, moderate- to high-pitched *jeep* chatters given when foraging, also mobs loudly with *jee'ut* and other notes. Dawn song a fast series of loud, harsh, high notes, often sung for half an hour or more from canopy perch, with each individual singing a different repertoire, e.g. *geegeegee wit'er wit'er tututu, weep, TWEER-TWEER-TWEER, eep'eep k' eep eep eep TWEER-TWEER-TWEER jeep-jeep TWEER* …, with unmusical *eep* almost too high for human ears; also continuously repeated, single loud lower *wheeu* notes (often doubled) interspersed with jumbles, and often incorporates imitations of other species (H&B, I&I, R&G).

GREY-HEADED TANAGER

Eucometis penicillata Pl. 252

Identification 16–18.5cm. Adult has grey head with short, bushy crest and white feather bases (visible when crest raised) with remaining upperparts olive, and yellow underparts with whitish throat. Remarkably similar female White-shouldered Tanager is smaller and slightly duller, lacks crest and usually forages higher.

Ssp. *E. p. affinis* (N Ve) crest shorter and white more concealed, very pale grey throat, with streaks or flammulations of grey
E. p. cristata (N & NW Co, W Ve) crest moderate, somewhat greyish, pale grey, olive-tinged throat
E. p. penicillata (E Ec, SE Co, Ve, Guianas) as described, has largest crest and full white chin and throat

Habits Often twitches tail, flicks wings, and raises crest. Retiring as it forages alone, in pairs or small flocks in dense understorey. Mostly seeks invertebrates, but sometimes fruits, berries and seeds. Often attends army ant swarms (north and west of Andes). Sometimes joins mixed-species flocks (east of Andes).

Status Rare to uncommon and local in Ecuador and Colombia, fairly common but somewhat local in Venezuela, and uncommon in Guianas.

Habitat Tropical Zone, to 1,700m, in wide range of habitats with dense tangled undergrowth and shrubs, e.g. humid forests and edges, especially *várzea* and swampy forests (e.g. *Mauritia* palm swamps and mangroves), but also in light woodland, plantations, gallery forest, scrub in cultivation and even riparian woodland in fairly dry regions.

Voice Almost incessantly repeated, sharp, smacking, unmusical, moderate- to high-pitched *stet*, *chup* and *chip* chatters, a more musical, high *pseet*, also an alarmed *schip!* Song a jumbled series of high, buzzy, sputtering notes, e.g. *pzzzt-buzzt-buzzt-fzzzt* (H&B, I&I, R&G, Hilty).

FULVOUS SHRIKE-TANAGER

Lanio fulvus Pl. 253

Identification 15–18cm. Adult is generally apricot yellow above, brightest on nape, with rich orange breast, but hood, wings and tail black. Eyes reddish-brown, heavy, shrike-like bill. Adult female has greyish-brown head, rufescent back, wings and tail, and paler rufous rump, upper- and undertail-coverts, greyish-buffy throat, ochraceous breast and ochraceous-rufous belly and vent; eyes dark brown. Juvenile male rather like female but has blackish smudges on head and is paler, slightly more yellowish on belly, flanks and uppertail-coverts. Adult male unmistakable but female less certain. Female Flame-crested Tanager has more uniform ochraceous underparts. Female Fulvous-crested Tanager has spectacles, olive upperparts and paler underparts. Both lack shrike-like bill and behave differently.

Ssp. *L. f. fulvus* (S Ve, Guianas) as described
L. f. peruvianus (E Ec, S Co, W Ve: Táchira) generally more fulvescent with only nape bright yellow

Habits Usually sits rather upright on larger branches in midstorey and subcanopy. Noisily forages alone or in pairs usually just below canopy. Catches invertebrates flushed by mixed-species canopy flocks, with flycatcher-like sallies.
Status Fairly common to common, less common in Colombia and Ecuador.
Habitat Tropical Zone, to 1,750m but usually below 1,000m, in tall humid *terra firme* and *várzea* and sometimes at edges.
Voice Frequently uttered loud, sharp, slightly descending, moderate-pitched *tchew*, *tcha* or *tyoo* notes, doubled or tripled in alarm and sometimes varied to a strongly descending *tchee-yee*, also sharp, high *skeep!* notes and short rattles. Dawn song a high *tzee-a*, doubled or tripled, repeated after a pause of 5–17 s (H&B, I&I, R&G, Hilty).

RUFOUS-CRESTED TANAGER

Creurgops verticalis Pl. 253

Identification 15–16.5cm. Adult male uniform brownish-grey above and cinnamon-rufous below, with black-bordered cinnamon-rufous crest only visible when excited; pale brown eyes and heavy bill. Female lacks cinnamon crest and is slightly paler below, with brown eyes. Juvenile like female but slightly paler and tinged buffy on upperparts. Black-eared Hemispingus very similar, but has black chin and mesial, warmer breast and greyer sides and flanks. Fawn-breasted Tanager more bluish above with black mask and usually in edge habitats. Much smaller male Rusty Flowerpiercer has proportionately slimmer body, different-shaped bill and different behaviour.

Ssp. Monotypic (E Ec, W Co, SW Ve)

Habits Forages rather deliberately, alone or in pairs, in subcanopy or canopy for invertebrates (sometimes sallying) and sometimes fruits, almost always in mixed-species flocks.
Status In Ecuador, uncommon to locally fairly common. In Colombia, much commoner in Upper Magdalena Valley in Huila (e.g. at Finca Merenberg) than in Central and West Andes. In Venezuela, known only from a few records at Hacienda La Providencia, upper Río Chiquito Valley, southern Táchira, but probably also occurs in adjacent Colombia.
Habitat Tropical to Temperate Zones, at 1,600–2,700m, in humid mossy and cloud forests and edges.
Voice Unknown, apparently very silent (I&I, R&G).

SCARLET-BROWED TANAGER

Heterospingus xanthopygius Pl. 253

Identification 17–18cm. Adult male all black or blackish, with a lemon rump and line on lesser wing-coverts, extraordinary supercilium, white just in front of eyes then bright red above eyes and sweeps back with feathers slightly elongated and tuft-like; axillaries and body-sides white, showing variably as a tuft on sides. Eyes chestnut, substantial, hooked bill, legs and feet black. Female also very distinctive; all-black with yellow rump. Male Lemon-rumped Tanager differs from female Scarlet-browed by silvery, blue-grey bill with white at base of mandible. Some male Flame-rumped Tanagers are equally similar, albeit warmer, almost orange on rump, but also have silvery grey bill, legs and feet. Male Flame-crested Tanager could well be mistaken, if scarlet crest is thought to be a supercilium.

Ssp. *H. x. berliozi* (NW Ec, W Co) deep slate instead of black; female lacks pale line on sides of body
H. x. xanthopygius (N Co) as described

Habits Often perches motionless on tree crowns and exposed branches for long periods, but may move rapidly whilst foraging. Looks for invertebrates, fruits, berries and seeds, alone, in pairs or small flocks, mostly in canopy (lower at edge). Often joins mixed-species flocks.
Status Uncommon to locally fairly common, and may have decreased due to widespread deforestation, especially in southern Ecuador.
Habitat Tropical Zone, to 1,100m but mostly below 800m, in dense humid to wet forests and edges, and sometimes in mature second growth and clearings with scattered trees.
Voice A sharp far-carrying *dzeet* or *dzip*, or loud, forceful *chip*, often given when foraging. Song in Chocó, Colombia, a squeaky twittering, e.g. *cheero-bitty, cheero-bitty, cherro-pit-sup* (H&B, R&T, I&I).
Note Also called Sulphur-rumped Tanager.

FLAME-CRESTED TANAGER

Tachyphonus cristatus Pl. 254

Identification 15–16.5cm. Adult male all black with bright orange crest, pale orange rump and dull orange throat. Female all rufous, richer but paler ochraceous below, with whitish throat. Throat colours of both sexes may be difficult to see in field. Fulvous-crested Tanager has thinner, 2-tone bill and usually forages at lower levels. Male Fulvous-crested has shorter but bushier crest, black throat, more conspicuous white pectoral tufts and rufous flank patches. Female Fulvous-crested much more olive above with grey head and conspicuous broken yellow eye-ring, dingy buffy below, more yellowish-ochraceous on belly. Also compare female Flame-crested with much larger female Fulvous Shrike-tanager.

Ssp. *T. c. cristatellus* (SE Co) crest entirely scarlet, bib dull
T. c. cristatus (FG) as described, crest paler at very front
T. c. fallax (E Ec, S Co) crest bright yellow, bib dull yellow
T. c. intercedens (E Ve, Gu, Su) varies, on Gran Sabana, Venezuela, crest pale orange with deep orange centre, bib clear yellow-orange, in Imataca and upper río Cuyuni, rich warm yellow with dull yellow bib, in Guyana, crest pale yellow and bib greyish-yellow; rump is pale yellow-orange; female much paler below and lacks any rufous above, bill horn, slightly paler on mandible
T. c. orinocensis (E Co, S Ve) male has 2-tone crest, front and sides rich yellow, centre and rear bright red, bib pale orange, yellow on upper rump and more orange on lower rump; female quite rufous above and below, bill 2-tone, dark above, pale horn below

Habits Sometimes perches rather upright. Forages for invertebrates, fruits, berries and seeds, usually in pairs but

sometimes in small flocks from midstorey to canopy (lower at edge). Often joins mixed-species flocks.
Status Uncommon to locally fairly common in Ecuador, fairly common to common in Colombia, Venezuela and Guianas, but easily overlooked because of canopy-dwelling habits.
Habitat Tropical Zone, to 1,400m but usually below 600m, in humid forest, edges and mature second growth, especially *terra firme*; in Suriname, also in sand ridge and savanna forests.
Voice Thin *seeep* notes when foraging, also *cher* and insignificant *chat, tseh, tseh, tseh, tsititi* (I&I, Hilty).

FULVOUS-CRESTED TANAGER
Tachyphonus surinamus Pl. 254

Identification 15–17cm. Male all black, with orange rump, white line on lesser wing-coverts, short bushy crest, pale orange, flushed reddish at front, buffy-white pectoral tuft and deep rufous patch on flanks. Bill black above, grey mandible, legs and feet grey. Female olive-green above, grey on head with buffy, broken eye-ring, pale buffy below, richer on breast and undertail-coverts, greyish on flanks. Juvenile browner, lacks grey on head, and is much warmer below, almost rufescent. In Guyana, race *intercedens* of Flame-crested Tanager has yellow crest, but lacks rufous on flanks and yellowish pectoral patch, with a dull yellowish bib, though differences are not noticeable. Female Fulvous Shrike Tanager has distinctly longer, more shrike-like bill. White-shouldered Tanager has no eye-ring, better-defined grey head and white throat contrasting with yellow underparts.

Ssp. *T. s. brevipes* (E Ec, E Co, S Ve: El Carmen, S. Amazonas) as described; female paler below, creamy buff to pale cinnamon on undertail-coverts
T. s. surinamus (E & S Ve, Guianas) crest longer with a few black tips to central feathers, pectoral tufts white in both sexes; female pale cinnamon below with cinnamon undertail-coverts, and eye-ring more prominent

Habits Often flicks wings. Forages for invertebrates, fruits, berries and seeds. Usually in pairs and small flocks, and mostly in midstorey (sometimes lower at edge or in canopy, but usually lower than Flame-crested Tanager). Often joins mixed-species flocks.
Status Uncommon to locally fairly common, more common eastwards, in western Amazonia mostly in sandy soil forests.
Habitat Tropical Zone, to 1,400m, in humid forests, edges and adjacent scrub and second growth, especially *terra firme* and sandy soil forests, wooded edges on rocky outcrops, also in open low-lying forests, e.g. *várzea*; in Suriname, also savanna forests but rarely in sand ridge forests.
Voice Low- to moderate-pitched, gravelly, abrupt notes, e.g. *chur, chur-dit*, also a rattled *chu-di-di-di-dit*, high, weak *steep*, sometimes combined with lower pitched *steep!-didit*, high, oft-repeated *tseek* or *tcheeu-cheeuw*, and buzzy rattles when foraging. Song in Venezuela a sibilant, almost hissing and extremely high *sieeeee-siiiiiiii*, with second note higher, sometimes with another *sii* added (H&M, I&I, Hilty).

WHITE-SHOULDERED TANAGER
Tachyphonus luctuosus Pl. 254

Identification 13–14cm. Adult male all black with large white shoulder formed by entire lesser wing-coverts, and has white underwing-coverts; eyes, bill, legs and feet dark. Adult female entirely greyish-olive above, whitish on chin and throat, with rest of underparts yellow; bill dark above and pale grey below. Juvenile even duller, with olive wash on sides and flanks, and all-black bill. All-black adult male with white underwing-coverts and conspicuous white shoulder patches might well be confused with much larger male White-lined Tanager, which is not forest-based and has much less white in wing. (Also compare somewhat similar male White-winged Becard). Female similar to Ashy-throated Bush Tanager, Olive-backed Tanager and especially Grey-headed Tanager.

Ssp. *T. l. flaviventris* (NE Ve, Tr) like *luctuosus* but has slightly longer bill, and longer wing
T. l. luctuosus (E Ec, SE Co, Ve, Guianas) as described
T. l. panamensis (W Ec, N & W Co, W Ve) female brighter, more yellowish-green above, and brighter yellow below, with whiter chin and throat

Habits Forages for insects and some fruits (regularly seen at fruiting trees). Usually in pairs, sometimes small flocks mostly from midstorey to subcanopy. In forests, joins mixed-species flocks.
Status Uncommon to fairly common in Ecuador, but more common in Venezuela and French Guiana, and very common in western Suriname; uncommon in Trinidad.
Habitat Tropical Zone, usually below 1,300m but sometimes to 2,200m in Colombia. Tall, deciduous or humid to wet forests, especially in dense foliage and vine tangles in treefalls, at edges and in mature second growth, shaded plantations and clearings with scattered trees.
Voice Rather insignificant, but high, sharp and almost hissing *tseer* (in Trinidad, an unmusical *tchirrup* or squeaky, oft-repeated *tswee*), also an accelerating 6-syllable *ch-ch-ch-chchch*. Song a thin, high *seet* repeated 2–4 times (ffrench, I&I, Hilty).

TAWNY-CRESTED TANAGER
Tachyphonus delatrii Pl. 254

Identification 14–14.5cm. All-black adult male has conspicuous tawny crest. Female dark olive-brown, becoming blackish posteriorly (and thus darker than any other female tanager in range, but see Ochre-breasted Tanager, much larger Dusky-faced Tanager and even dark grosbeaks or foliage-gleaners), and almost always accompanied by males. Subadult like female but darker, immature male may show tawny crown before becoming all black.

Ssp. Monotypic (W Ec, W Co)

Habits Forages very rapidly for insects and fruits, mostly in large flocks of 8–20+ (smaller flocks at higher elevations) in under- to lower midstorey. Sometimes in mixed-species flocks.
Status Fairly common to common, somewhat rarer and more local in Ecuador.

Habitat Tropical Zone, usually below 800m but sometimes to 1,500m, in humid to very wet forests, shrubby edges and mature second growth.
Voice A loud, squeaky or smacking *chit* or *tswik*, singly or repeated severally, and constantly uttered when foraging (H&B, R&T, I&I).

WHITE-LINED TANAGER
Tachyphonus rufus Pl. 254

Identification 17–19cm. Adult male usually appears all black, but in display lesser coverts appear like white line on wing, and in flight, white wing bend and underwing-coverts may show (note male White-shouldered Tanager also has white underwing-coverts). Bill black above, lower mandible bluish-grey at base. Adult female uniform rufous milk chocolate, and slightly paler below. Juvenile distinctly paler, especially on throat and central breast. Immature male has irregular black patches in plumage. Smaller male Red-shouldered Tanager often looks rather similar, but female Red-shouldered has duller brownish-grey upperparts, darkest on head, and contrasting greyish-white underparts, more whitish on throat (thus, White-lined best identified by unique combination of black male and rufous female and habitat). Also compare female White-lined Tanager to female becards and Rufous Mourner, which have different bills.

Ssp. Monotypic (NW Ec, Co, Ve, T&T, Guianas)

Habits Often flicks wings before flying, exposing white underwings. Forages restlessly. Takes invertebrates, fruits, berries, seeds and sometimes nectar, restlessly, usually in pairs. Keeps fairly low (but sometimes higher in fruiting trees) within shrubby vegetation. Rarely joins mixed-species flocks.
Status Rare to locally fairly common in Ecuador, common in rest of range (including Trinidad & Tobago), apparently spreading due to deforestation.
Habitat Tropical Zone, to 2,700m but usually below 1,500m, in forest edges and borders of mangroves, shrubby clearings, second growth, gallery forest, lighter woodland and cultivation with thickets, rarely in *llanos*, also in light forest on Trinidad & Tobago; often near water and mainly in humid areas. Common in urban areas, parks and gardens where it is invariably seen in pairs.
Voice A short *check*, weak, thin *seep*, and *wist-wist* in flight. Song in Venezuela a bouncy, chattery *chuEE, chuit, chuit-chuit-chuit*…, with first syllable strongest; in eastern Mérida, a softer, more leisurely and continuous *cheewank, wink,* …, whilst in Ecuador and Colombia a continuously repeated *cheeru*… or *cheép-chooi,* … (ffrench, H&B, I&I, R&G, Hilty).

RED-SHOULDERED TANAGER
Tachyphonus phoenicius Pl. 254

Identification 15–16cm. Thin bill. Adult male usually appears all black, with narrow white line on bend of wing tipped red (at rest, red hard to see, but in flight, diagnostic red in bend of wing and white underwing-coverts may show). Female dark greyish-brown above with broad blackish mask that is not obvious in field, chin, throat and mesial white, breast and sides to flanks pale olivaceous-grey, belly to vent pale yellow, undertail-coverts pale buffy-yellow. Juvenile lacks any yellow below, being entirely white with dusky streaks.

Ssp. Monotypic (C Co, S Ve, Guianas)

Habits Often flicks wings. Forages for invertebrates, fruits, seeds and sometimes nectar, restless, usually alone or in pairs (occasionally in small flocks) and usually fairly low. Occasionally joins mixed-species flocks.
Status Uncommon to locally common in Colombia, Venezuela and Suriname, more uncommon and local in French Guiana.
Habitat Tropical to Subtropical Zones, to 2,000m in Venezuela but usually below 400m, in scrubby forest edges, gallery forest, lighter woodland, second growth and scattered vegetation in bushy, semi-open savannas on white-sand soils, also rocky outcrops and granite plates.
Voice Weak, low- to moderate-pitched *chup* or *cheup* calls, high *tsit* calls and soft chips when foraging (I&I, Hilty).

[YELLOW-CRESTED TANAGER
Tachyphonus rufiventer] Pl. 254

Identification 15cm. Adult male mostly black above, from black frontal band to tail, with contrasting bright yellow crest, lower rump and short uppertail-coverts, with narrow white scapular line; bright yellow chin and throat, separated from orange or yellowish-cinnamon breast and sides to undertail-coverts by variable black bar. Female olive-green above, bright yellow on chin and throat to flanks, with cinnamon undertail-coverts. Juvenile similar but underparts grade from whitish throat, through yellow breast and sides to dingy orange flanks and undertail-coverts. Whilst upperparts are typical of *Tachyphonus*, underparts of male, with clear black band on chest should ensure correct identification.

Ssp. Monotypic (reported S Co, in southernmost Amazonas, but perhaps only seen on south bank of Amazon, opposite Leticia, in Brazil)

Habits Highly sedentary and apparently spends most time in mixed-species flocks in canopy. Thus seems unlikely to cross river into Colombia.
Status Probably hypothetical.
Habitat Tropical Zone (to 1,400m in Peru) in *terra firme* and low-lying forest including tall second growth and *várzea*.
Voice A raspy, moderate-pitched *jjit*, and high-pitched, less raspy *zzeep* and combined *zzeep? jjit jjit jjeep* (T. A. Parker in I&I).
Note Originally included on basis of sight record, but no subsequent confirmation and now listed as hypothetical; illustration retained to assist identification.

VERMILION TANAGER
Calochaetes coccineus Pl. 257

Identification 17–18cm. Adult male entirely deep carmine-red, with all-black wings and tail, and small black mask from lores to just behind eyes and chin. Bill black with pale bluish-grey base to mandible. Adult female is slightly duller. Very much like *Ramphocelus* in jizz and behaviour. Adult male has red mantle and mid belly whilst rather similar Masked Crimson Tanager (which does not overlap in habitat) has black mantle and belly. Male Scarlet Tanager very similar but lacks mask, has a paler bill and is more scarlet than carmine.

Ssp. Monotypic (E Ec, S Co)

Habits Forages for invertebrates, fruits, berries and seeds, often searching moss and epiphytes on horizontal branches. Usually alone, in pairs or small flocks, mostly in canopy. Almost always joins mixed-species flocks.
Status Uncommon to locally fairly common in Ecuador, rare in Colombia (perhaps overlooked?); regularly found in Romerillos area, Podocarpus National Park and near San Rafael Falls, both in Ecuador.
Habitat Tropical to Subtropical Zones, at 1,100–1,800m in Ecuador but 320–600m in Colombia (but doubtless also higher), in humid, mossy cloud forests and edges.
Voice A sharp high *chip* and *zit*, sometimes accelerated as a trill, e.g. *chip chip zit-t-t-t-t* (I&I, R&G).

Ramphocelus are distinguished by stunning lustrous red and black (or in one case, yellow and black) plumage in males, together with a swollen, silvery white base to mandible. They are birds of borders and light woodland, usually in cover but also open spaces, as they forage for insects and fruit. The feathers of head are erect and plush, like velvet. Bills are pointed upwards to reveal the white bases and rumps are raised in display.

MASKED CRIMSON TANAGER
Ramphocelus nigrogularis Pl. 257

Identification 17–19cm. Mostly lustrous, rich crimson body with black wings and tail, black mask and central belly, vent and thighs also black; bill black above with lower mandible pale, bright silvery white and slightly swollen at base. Female slightly duller, belly dark brown and lower mandible normal size and darker. Subadult male resembles female. Juvenile dull reddish-brown, with dark wings and tail, paler and more cinnamon below, bill all black. Silver-beaked Tanager is much more maroon; Vermilion Tanager has red back and belly.

Ssp. Monotypic (E Ec, SE Co)

Habits Noisily forages for invertebrates, fruits, berries and seeds. Usually in pairs or small flocks of up to 14+ at all levels and often found high in *Erythrina* flowers along riverbanks. Sometimes joins mixed-species flocks, and occasionally roosts in large flocks.
Status Fairly common.
Habitat Tropical Zone, to 600m, mostly at shrubby edges of *várzea* and in streamside and oxbow shrubbery, also adjacent second growth, clearings and cultivated areas, usually near water, apparently avoiding larger *terra firme* forests.
Voice A distinctive, sharp, metallic, moderate- to high-pitched *tchi*, *tsit* or *tchink*, often given in flight, also in hostility or alarm, and *whi-it* or *wheeeeet*, probably in contact. Dawn song a series of weak, but sweet and musical, low- to moderate-pitched *whee-chu* (second note lower) or *chuck-wheet* whistles repeated at *c.*1 per s for long periods, sometimes interrupted with single notes and brief pauses. Day song of rich, slow, low- to moderate-pitched phrases like *wheeet, chu-chu wheeet wheeet, chu-chu wier wheeet*, and *chu-chu wheeet, chu-chu whirt*, interrupted by occasional pauses (H&B, I&I, R&G).

CRIMSON-BACKED TANAGER
Ramphocelus dimidiatus Pl. 257

Identification 16–18cm. Adult male lustrous deep crimson-red, deeper on rounded, plush head, with black wings, tail and central belly. Female darker, deep rich brownish-red with a duller bill. Immature even duller and browner, approaching cinnamon-red on underparts, bill blackish and not swollen. Adult male unmistakable as no overlap with Silver-beaked Tanager (east of Andes). Adult female more reddish-brown anteriorly and more scarlet-red posteriorly than male, but contrasting red rump and belly should distinguish it from somewhat similar Red-crowned and Red-throated Ant Tanagers. Subadult male resembles female. Theoretically could be confused with Scarlet Tanager, but red completely different, Scarlet being brighter red, with less rounded head and lacks black belly.

Ssp. *R. d. dimidiatus* (NW Co, W Ve) as described
R. d. molochinus (NW Co) throat and chest darker, more clearly defined from rest of underparts; crown and nape much darker shade of crimson.

Habits Noisily forages in pairs or small flocks (sometimes alone or in larger flocks) from under- to midstorey at edges, for invertebrates, fruits and seeds. Sometimes joins mixed-species flocks, and occasionally roosts in large flocks in bushes and trees.
Status Fairly common to common. Benefits from deforestation.
Habitat Tropical to Subtropical Zones, to 2,200m but usually below 1,200m, in shrubby edges of moist to humid forest and woodland, also adjacent clearings, thickets, cultivation, plantations and gardens, less common in dry second growth and rarely inside dense forest.
Voice High, loud and sometimes doubled *wheeeeet* or *sseeeeeeeet* contact, a distinctive, nasal, moderate-pitched *chank*, *wah*, *whanh* or *anh*, whilst foraging or in hostile situations, also a highly variable, hoarse *whaah*, *wheeaah* or *zhawhee*, uttered in series of 2–4 (–10) notes, uttered in aggressive situation or to greet mate. Song a long, slow series of rather clipped and slightly buzzy (or clear and melodious), moderate-pitched, single or double notes, e.g. *reet, skréa, seek, reé-a, séea, bz-weet, wit-weet, fzeet, reéza, bzeep, skeéa*..., rising and falling, for up to several minutes; when agitated, somewhat shrill and squeaky *tew-wheet sweeee* (I&I, Hilty).

SILVER-BEAKED TANAGER
Ramphocelus carbo Pl. 257

Identification 16–18cm. Adult male sooty black above with lustrous crimson wash (appears all black in poor light), deep crimson on chin to breast, with brownish-black rest of underparts. Adult female red rusty-brown on lower rump and tail-coverts, warm brown below with pale streaks on chin and throat, greyish-brown suffusion on breast. Bill black with swollen silvery white base to lower mandible (duller and less swollen in female). Crimson-backed Tanager very similar, but is distinctly brighter red and does not overlap. Masked Crimson Tanager also much brighter red and has distinct black mask.

Ssp. *R. c. capitalis* (NE Ve) male pure black above, deep red only on head, bright deep crimson chin and breast, rest of underparts black with faint red wash; female has deep rich red lower rump and tail-coverts; red-washed brown below, with pink-red streaks on chin and throat

R. c. carbo (E Ec, SE Co, S Ve, Guianas) as described

R. c. magnirostris (NE Ve, Tr) male like *carbo* but with larger, heavier bill and white base larger; female also like *carbo* but more uniform reddish below

R. c. unicolor (E Co) comparatively uniform, abdomen and back only slightly darker than breast

R. c. venezuelensis (E Co, W Ve) deep red on head, rest of upperparts black with faint crimson wash, deep crimson chin to breast, grading to crimson-washed charcoal on rest of underparts; female has deep reddish-brown chin to throat, redder on breast, rest as *capitalis*

Habits Often flicks wings and tail as it forages noisily, usually in small flocks of up to 10+ (with adult males in minority). At all levels but usually in undergrowth at forest edges, searching for invertebrates, fruits, berries, seeds and nectar. Sometimes joins mixed-species flocks.

Status Common to locally very common, although rare to locally absent in *llanos*. Spreading due to deforestation.

Habitat Tropical Zone, to 1,900m but usually below 1,200m, in bushy edges (especially beside *várzea*, lakes or rivers), light, semi-open woodland, shrubby clearings, second growth, gardens and thickets in savanna, cultivation and abandoned plantations, mostly in humid areas and near water, and rarely inside dense forest.

Voice An often-heard, loud, metallic, sharp, moderate-pitched *chank* or *chink*, a more musical high-pitched *zweep* or *tseeet*, and quickly repeated *wek-wek-wek*. Dawn song an energetic but repetitive series of short, semi-musical, harsh and squeaky moderate-pitched phrases, e.g. *tu tu tweep, chip-tup tweep, tu tu tweep, chip, sput, wheer…* or *tchu-wee tchu wee chyeét…*, repeated over and over at *c.*1 phrase per s, sometimes broken by pause or harsh *chak*. Day song a monotonously repeated moderate-pitched *CHICK chit-ti-wee*, sometimes shortened to *CHICK*, delivered at *c.*20–25 phrases per minute (H&B, ffrench, I&I, R&G, Hilty).

FLAME-RUMPED TANAGER

Ramphocelus flammigerus Pl. 256

Identification 18–18.5cm. Definitive adult male all black with scarlet lower back, rump and short uppertail-coverts. However, many variants in rump colour, some age-related, others probably diet, others simply genetic variation – from warm yellow (including ochraceous, cinnamon-tinged and orange) to deep crimson. Bill dark above, pale bluish-silver below with black tip, legs and feet pale grey. Juvenile male dark olive-grey above, blackish on wings and tail, with warm yellow rump; below yellow, with warm to orange flush on breast to near whitish undertail-coverts. Immature and subadult gradually acquire adult rump colour, chin and throat become black, and black feathering gradually appears over rest of underparts. Adult female dark greyish-olive above with orange-red lower back, rump and short uppertail-coverts, below, primarily yellow, usually with orange-red band on breast, but variants lack red and might have orange or ochraceous flush, others a pure white chin and throat and lemon-yellow below. Juvenile female much paler above than juvenile male, with a less distinct rump, more ochraceous-yellow, pale saffron-yellow below with usually some orange or ochre on breast, and paler vent and undertail-coverts. Major confusion where Lemon-rumped and Flame-rumped Tanagers overlap, with any bird that is not pure crimson or pure yellow being regarded as a hybrid. However, it seems that any warmth in yellow, whether orange or ochraceous indicates Flame-rumped Tanager. Female *Piranga* tanagers lack bright rump. Scarlet-browed Tanager has dark bill, legs and feet and shorter tail, and white tufts at sides might also be evident.

Ssp. Monotypic (W & C Co)

Habits Often flicks wings and tail. Noisily forages at all levels for invertebrates, fruits, berries and seeds. Usually in small flocks of up to 12+, with adult males in minority; sometimes, young or even adults seen alone. Rarely joins mixed-species flocks but joins feeding aggregations at fruiting trees.

Status Fairly common to very common, especially in Pacific lowlands.

Habitat Tropical to Subtropical Zones, to 2,100m, at forest and wooded edges, shrubby clearings, second growth, plantations, overgrown pastures, thickets and gardens.

Voice Not reliably known due to confusion with Lemon-rumped Tanager, but reportedly similar to latter. Dawn song a series of evenly-paced, identical notes *kioo* or *klioo*, similar to Lemon-rumped, but given less frequently. Solitary birds call a soft *tzzheet*, softer and more melodious than similar but hoarser call of Lemon-rumped. Also a range of bisyllabic notes (Moynihan 1966).

Note Has been assumed to hybridise freely with *R. icteronotus*, but there is little or no solid evidence to support this, and tremendous variability of *flammigerus* on western slope (totally absent in *icteronotus* in plains) has been taken as evidence for hybridisation. Certainly, variation in rump colour of *flammigerus* has been viewed as a problem in species identification (Nørgaard-Olesen 1974). They were synonymised in AOU 1983 Checklist, but continue to be treated as separate species elsewhere (e.g. R&G, H&B).

Note on relationship between Flame-rumped and Lemon-rumped Tanagers. These sibling species clearly separated from their ancestral root comparatively recently in evolutionary terms. Flame-rumped Tanager is established at roughly 1,000–2,000m on the eastern slope of the West Andes and in the Cauca Valley, whilst Lemon-rumped Tanager occurs in the coastal plain from Panama to Ecuador. At some point, during the last century there was significant forest destruction on the slopes between the two ranges (R&T) and it seems that Flame-rumped Tanager began to expand downslope. Clearly, replacement habitat was second growth and different from that occupied in the hills and on the Cauca side, but whatever factors had contributed to the evolution of a red rump weakened or ceased, and Flame-rumped Tanagers appeared with orange rumps and variations from the original red to pale orange. Several possible reasons exist for this change in appearance, none of which has been researched. One of these is change of diet. Many examples exist where birds have changed colour significantly in accordance with a marked shift in diet. Changes can be wrought by addition of one element or deprivation of another. Birds can gain colour or lose it; addition of carotene or xanthacanthin to the diet of a yellow bird, such as a canary, will lead to it developing reddish feathers at next moult, whilst a Troupial will change from vivid orange to plain yellow if deprived of these elements in its diet. Another explanation is Gloger's Rule, which predicts that birds in humid, forested regions will be darker than their counterparts in arid, non-forested regions. The hypothesis here is that lemon-rumped birds are those from sunlit, arid coastlands, with red-rumped birds in highlands. An adequate example of this occurs in Flame-crested Tanager where the amount of red, or lack of it, correlates exactly with environment. Finally, there is the possibility of hybridisation with Lemon-rumped Tanagers, which presumably likewise invaded newly available habitat, this time moving upslope.

Whatever circumstance produced red originally was not present on the newly opened western slopes, or it was diluted by some factor. Whether red-rumped birds interbred with lemon-rumped birds is unknown as there are no records of nests attended by different parents. No experiments have been conducted under controlled conditions to see whether one colour is dominant. Or, as apparently assumed, they mix following Mendel, with, for example, one-quarter being red-rumped, one-quarter lemon-rumped, and half orange-rumped.

Careful comparison shows that the 2 species differ subtly in both behaviour and vocalisations. They are perhaps subspecies of a single species or different species. The orange variants may well be hybrids, the result of 2 sibling species meeting before separating mechanisms were fully established, or intergrades between races. We have regarded the variants as Flame-rumped Tanagers, as when examining an extensive series of specimens it is hard not to come to that conclusion. But whatever proves to be true, it seems to be of no utility to classify them as either hybrids or intergrades solely based on assumptions, and it is much better to consider them different until proven otherwise.

One of the differences between Lemon-rumped and Flame-rumped Tanagers is the way they ruffle their feathers; Lemon-rumped (left, after Moynihan 1966) does not ruffle the head- and body-feathers simultaneously, but Crimson-rumped Tanager (right, after Brosset in Nørgaard-Olesen 1974) does so

LEMON-RUMPED TANAGER

Ramphocelus icteronotus Pl. 256

Identification 18–18.5cm. Definitive adult male all black with yellow lower back, rump and short uppertail-coverts; bill pale bluish-grey, legs and feet pale grey. Immature and subadult male like juvenile but with black feathering appearing. Adult female greyish-olive above, (marginally darker and perhaps more olivaceous than female *flammigerus*) with pale lemon yellow lower back, rump and short uppertail-coverts, below, pale lemon-yellow. Juvenile paler below, rather sulphur-yellow, washed white on chin and throat, faintly flammulated olive on breast. Juvenile male has dusky undertail-coverts with yellowish tips. No similarity in yellow with juvenile *flammigerus*, neither does latter have faint striations or flammulations on breast. Clearly, there is major confusion where Lemon-rumped and Flame-rumped Tanagers overlap. Any warmth in yellow feathering, whether orange or ochraceous, indicates a variant Flame-rumped Tanager. Female *Piranga* tanagers lack bright rump.

Ssp. Monotypic (W & C Co)

Habits At rest, constantly jerks tail and often flicks wings. Noisily forages in small flocks of up to 12+, with adult males in minority. At all levels. Rarely joins mixed-species flocks but attends feeding aggregations at fruiting trees.

Status Fairly common to very common, especially in Pacific lowlands.

Habitat Tropical to Subtropical Zones, to 2,100m. Second growth and wooded edges, shrubby areas, thickets and clearings, plantations, parks and gardens.

Voice A scolding *chewp!* and note from female exactly like female House Sparrow (Wetmore *et al.* 1984). An oft-heard low- to moderate-pitched, nasal *anh* or *cha*, and high, hard *tzzheet*, also hoarse *zraa*, various bisyllabic notes (e.g. *tseeee-yah*) and rapid, low rattles. Dawn song consists of same phrase repeated in regular cadence, *kioo* or *klioo*, uttered far more frequently than by Flame-rumped Tanager. A range of bisyllabic notes, including *tseeee-yah*, *tseee-up*, *eee-ya*, *kheezoo*, etc. (Moynihan 1966).

Thraupis are medium-sized tanagers of light woodland and fairly open areas, usually seen as they swoop between trees, often landing on an exposed perch to scan around. They are great fruit eaters and are numerous and frequent visitors to mangos and other fruiting trees in urban and suburban parks and gardens. Usually seen in pairs or small family groups, they are highly animated, social birds always bickering and frequently betray their presence in a treetop by their squeaky voices.

BLUE-GREY TANAGER

Thraupis episcopus Pl. 258

Identification 16-18cm. Adult blue-grey, with head brighter or paler than back, and underparts typically paler and bluer, with wing-coverts varying by subspecies; bill dark or blackish, legs and feet dark grey. Juvenile duller and especially greyer on head and wing-coverts, brightens with first body moult at a few months, but fails to attain distinct wing coloration until first complete moult. Glaucous Tanager appears duskier, distinctly more blue-grey on back, and head concolorous (though juvenile Blue-grey has head almost concolorous with back), conspicuous dark blue patch at base of outer flight-feathers, sharply contrasting white belly, and greenish-turquoise fringes to flight-feathers.

Ssp. *T. e. berlepschi* (To) brighter and darker blue on rump and lesser wing-coverts
T. e. caerulea (SE Ec) lesser and median wing-coverts white, greater wing-coverts tipped white
T. e. cana (Co: from Panama to Perijá, N Ve: Perijá along entire Northern Cordillera) lesser wing-coverts rich lustrous blue
T. e. coelestis (NE & EC Ec, SE Co) whitish lesser wing-coverts
T. e. episcopus (Guianas) white shoulders (lesser wing-coverts)
T. e. leucoptera (C Co) lesser wing-coverts pale bluish-white
T. e. mediana (SE Co, SE Ve) lesser wing-coverts whitish, median coverts fringed white
T. e. nesophilus (E Co, E Ve: S of Orinoco, Tr) lesser and median wing-coverts concolorous with back
T. e. quaesita (W Ec, SW Co) richer, deep blue on wing-coverts

Habits Forages noisily, usually in pairs but sometimes in small flocks, at all levels but mostly high in trees or shrubs. Takes invertebrates, fruits, berries, leaves, flowers and nectar, sometimes joins mixed-species flocks, but more often joins feeding aggregations at fruiting trees.
Status Common and widespread, especially in lowlands, except in continuous forest, has greatly benefited from deforestation.
Habitat Tropical to Subtropical Zones, to 2,700m but usually below 1,500m. Various habitats, e.g. gallery forest, mixed, light woodland, river and oxbow lake edges, young and mature second growth, plantations, parks, gardens and other cultivated and settled areas, even in cities, in both dry and humid regions.
Voice An often-heard rising, squeaky *seeeee* or *che-eup*, and a dry, strained *tsuup*, sometimes followed by a few twitter notes. Song a complex series of fast, high, squeaky twittering or drawn-out notes, typically mixed with *tsuup* or *tsuee* notes, and typically alternating between 1–2 high- and 1–2 moderate-pitched notes, e.g. *seee seee chaa chaa sweez cha sweez cha-cha*, delivered at 2–5 notes per s and usually speeding at end, with some songs ending in a trill; this pattern may be repeated or changed with every series; females deliver briefer and weaker songs, and sometimes 2 birds sing together, producing a jumble of notes (F&K, I&I, Hilty).
Note Also called Blue Tanager.

GLAUCOUS TANAGER

Thraupis glaucocolpa Pl. 258

Identification 16–17cm. Adult grey above with a bluish tinge, especially noticeable on rump and uppertail-coverts, pale greenish-blue fringes to wing-coverts and outer tail-feathers, with particularly bright broad fringes to remiges; grey below, whitish on chin, washed powdery blue on breast and flanks. Pure white from vent to undertail-coverts. Female has slightly greener-fringed flight-feathers. Juvenile paler and duller with green tone to fringes. Any confusion with Blue-grey Tanager diminished by white undertail-coverts.

Ssp. Monotypic (N Co: NE Bolívar to E, N Ve: E to Sucre and Margarita I.)

Habits Forages for invertebrates and fruits, sometimes alone or in small flocks, but usually in pairs. Found at all levels but mostly high in trees or shrubs.
Status Uncommon to locally fairly common, commonest in arid regions, appears to move seasonally with rainfall, e.g. much more common in east Falcón, Venezuela, in May–July.
Habitat Tropical Zone, to 800m but usually below 500m, in gallery forest, deciduous woodland, mature second growth, dry scrubby and thorn vegetation, plantations, gardens and trees and scrub in agriculture, mostly in dry and arid Caribbean lowlands, but also in tree groves in *llanos*.
Voice A high, thin *sweEEeeeee*, descending at end, given at intervals of *c.*10 s, or a high, sibilant and ascending *seeeep*. Song a pulsating series of very high notes swelling in volume, e.g. *e-e-e-ee-ee-eee-eee-see-SEE-SEE-SEE*, most often heard in early rainy season (I&I, Hilty).
Note Formerly considered a subspecies of Sayaca Tanager *T. sayaca*.

PALM TANAGER

Thraupis palmarum Pl. 258

Identification 16.5–19cm. Essentially grey with maroon to dusky wings and tail, with pale green tone to head and wing-coverts, which contrast strongly with dark flight-feathers. Plumage silky and glossy. Juvenile distinctly duller and lacks pale green tone to head, and is very much reduced on wing-coverts. In poor light, adult somewhat similar to Blue-grey Tanager (sometimes together), but always distinguished by distinctive 2-toned wing pattern, clearly visible in flight and at rest. Behaviour similar to Blue-grey Tanager, but more often in canopy of large forests and less often in urban areas.

Ssp. *T. p. atripennis* (N Co, NW Ve) forehead and crown conspicuous pale yellow-olive contrasting with hindneck, wings quite blackish; body gloss bluish

T. p. melanoptera (E Co, Ve, T&T, Guianas) bright yellow-citrine head, dull sepia wings and tail, sepia back, dull citrine below with purplish gloss all over

T. p. violilavata (W Ec, SW Co) little or no green on forehead and crown, with less contrasting black wings, lesser wing-coverts glossed bluish; generally glossier with more strongly bluish gloss above and below

Habits Often seen in palms in gardens and parks, searching undersides of leaves for insects. Also particularly fond of fruits of *Cecropia*. Sometimes roosts in small to large flocks.

Status Common and widespread, especially in scrubby woodland and gallery forest in Gran Sabana, Venezuela.

Habitat Tropical Zone, to 2,600m but usually below 1,300m, in forests, edges, second growth, savannas, pastures, clearings, gardens and other cultivated or populated areas with scattered large trees, especially fond of palm trees, in both fairly dry and humid regions.

Voice A lisping rising moderate- to high-pitched *seeeee?*, downward-inflected *see-you*, upward-inflected low- to moderate-pitched *wheerst?*, piercing metallic *weert* or *whit*, and rapid *pip-pip*. Song often delivered from atop palm tree, a fast stream of sputtering, squeaky, sibilant, twittering or clear, moderate- to high-pitched notes, lasting 3–6 s, e.g. *SU-suri SU-suri, sit-IT sit-IT sit-IT, seet seet wheerst?, sreee sreee*, slightly less musical than Blue-grey Tanager, lacking dry, strained *tsuup* notes characteristic of latter (I&I, Hilty).

BLUE-CAPPED TANAGER

Thraupis cyanocephala Pl.258

Identification 16–19cm. Rich yellow olive-green above, royal blue head varies by subspecies, grey below (also varies racially), and usually has yellow undertail-coverts and thighs, and underwing-coverts and underwings yellow. Eyes chestnut-brown, bill black, legs and feet grey. Juvenile slightly duller above, with less extensive blue than adult and more extensive grey below. Plumage varies geographically, but blue cap and greenish back, and yellow underwing coverts in flight should distinguish all races.

Ssp. *T. c. annectens* (C Co) slightly darker below with more bluish tinge

T. c. auricrissa (NC Co, W Ve) slightly darker below with distinct bluish tinge, centre of belly and thighs to undertail-coverts strongly yellow

T. c. buesingi (NE Ve, Tr) top of head blue, head-sides blackish, darker grey below with prominent pale-grey moustachial underlined blackish, vent to undertail-coverts greenish with yellow edges

T. c. cyanocephala (W Ec) blue top and sides of head, grey chin to flanks, thighs, vent and undertail-coverts yellow

T. c. hypophaea (NW Ve) underparts strongly suffused blue

T. c. margaritae (N Co) smaller, with dull blue on throat and foreneck, sharply demarcated from remaining grey underparts

T. c. olivicyanea (N Ve) entire hood and underparts to breast-sides and upper flanks blue, belly grey, thighs yellow, vent to undertail-coverts greenish

T. c. subcinerea (NE Ve) like *cyanocephala*, but has prominent pale-grey moustachial line

Habits Forages for invertebrates, but mostly takes fruits, berries and seeds. Usually in pairs or small flocks, often noisy, but sometimes alone or in flocks of up to 15. At all levels, but mostly high. Sometimes joins mixed-species flocks or, more often, feeding aggregations at fruiting trees.

Status Uncommon to fairly common in Ecuador, fairly common in Colombia, common to locally very common in Venezuela, but uncommon and local in Trinidad.

Habitat Subtropical to Temperate Zones, at 800–3,000m but usually 1,800–2,300m, above 550m on Trinidad. In disturbed habitats, e.g. shrubby forest and roadsides, patchy second growth, open woodland, coffee plantations, clearings and pastures with some trees, hedges and tree-lined fences.

Voice A sharp, high *tsit*. Song a twittering, unmusical jumble of sharp and squeaky high notes, consisting of 2–3 short, piercing, high whistles followed by a jumble of moderate- to high-pitched notes, somewhat reminiscent of Blue-grey Tanager or Lacrimose Mountain Tanager, e.g. *tsuee-tsuee-tee-ee-ee-seet* (H&B, I&I, R&G, Hilty).

Note Also called Blue-headed Tanager.

BLUE-AND-YELLOW TANAGER

Thraupis bonariensis Pl. 258

Identification 16.5–17cm. Adult male has blue head with black around bill, olive back, orange-yellow rump, black wings and tail with blue fringes, and orange-yellow underparts, paler on belly and olive on sides. Adult female greyish-olive to greyish-brown above with paler rump and blue-tinged crown and shoulders, blue-grey wings and tail, and dingy yellowish-buffy below with greyish-brown throat. Subadult male like female, but whole head tinged blue, with more yellowish rump and underparts. Juvenile like female but rump duller and less extensive, and lacks blue tinge on head. Adult female, subadult male or juvenile, if alone (rare), may be confused with female or immature Scrub Tanager, female Hepatic Tanager or female Fawn-breasted Tanager, but look for bluish head and drab plumage.

Ssp. *T. b. darwinii* (W Ec)

Habits Usually forages in pairs or in small flocks (sometimes alone) and usually within cover at all levels. Searches for invertebrates, fruits, berries, seeds, flowers, leaves, buds, pods and flowers. Sometimes joins mixed-species flocks or feeding aggregations at fruiting trees.

Status Uncommon to locally fairly common, in more arid portions of central and inter-Andean valleys, from Carchi and Imbabura to southern Azuay and northernmost Loja, apparently spreading due to deforestation, and may eventually be recorded in southern Colombia.

Habitat Tropical to Temperate Zones, at 1,800–3,000m, in roadside edges, lighter woodland, second growth, scrub, orchards, hedgerows, gardens and agricultural regions.

Voice Incessantly repeated high *sweet* and *tick* notes, sometimes joined in a jumbled series. Song, delivered from treetops, a series of 4–6 sweet, doubled, moderate- to high-pitched notes, e.g. *purseé, purseé, purseé, purseé*…, with no squeaky quality but may begin or end with short trill or single note, repeated after 10–20 s (F&K, I&I, R&G).

BLUE-BACKED TANAGER

Cyanicterus cyanicterus Pl. 258

Identification 17cm. Entire upperparts including hood to breast and sides rich cerulean-blue, deeper on head and breast, slightly greenish on back, underparts rich yellow with blackish thighs; eyes bright orange-red, bill long and somewhat decurved, black, legs and feet flesh. Female slightly paler, more turquoise above, top of head and nape paler cerulean-blue, forehead and supercilium, face-sides and underparts yellow, tinged ochraceous on face and breast; eyes orange-red, bill dark but not black. Juvenile significantly duller and young male has some blue streaking on head-sides and mesial; eyes pale brown, bill brown. Unmistakable in its lowland range (compare to Andean mountain Tanagers).

Ssp. Monotypic (E Ve, Guianas)

Habits Forages noisily and deliberately, usually in pairs but also in small flocks. Usually from subcanopy to canopy, often joins mixed-species flocks.

Status Rare to uncommon and local, but perhaps often overlooked.

Habitat Tropical Zone, to 650m, in tall humid forests and edges, and sometimes isolated trees in adjacent clearings, more rarely in savanna forests.

Voice Calls or song include loud, high, mostly 2–3-note (sometimes 5) phrases perched or in flight, e.g. *keeee, kuuu* or *keeee, ksuuu-ksuuu*, also a high and thin but penetrating *tseet-tseet* (or *tseee-tsew-tsew*) with second note lower, and sometimes preceded by a *pit* note which is also delivered in a series when excited (R&T, H&M, I&I, Hilty).

Note Taxonomic placement possibly uncertain (I&I, Hilty).

Bangsia and *Wetmorethraupis* are mid-sized, rather stocky tanagers with comparatively short tails and bright contrasting patterns, of understorey and mid levels of wet, mossy forests, where they are quiet and rather inactive.

BLACK-AND-GOLD TANAGER

Bangsia melanochlamys Pl. 257

Identification 15–16cm. Adult all black above with blue lesser and median wing-coverts and uppertail-coverts; orange-yellow breast, then yellow to undertail-coverts. Eyes dark, bill black with paler base to mandible, legs and feet grey. Juvenile undescribed. Golden-chested Tanager has dark blue tinge, is only orange-yellow on upper breast, vent and underwing-coverts, and usually occurs at lower elevations.

Ssp. Monotypic (W Co)

Habits Forages alone or in pairs at all levels, for invertebrates, fruits and seeds. Sometimes joins mixed-species flocks.

Status Vulnerable. Threatened due to its small range, which is declining owing to continued habitat destruction and fragmentation. Endemic to Colombia, where only occurs in 2 disjunct areas: on north and west slopes of Central Andes in Antioquia, where rediscovered in 1999 west of río Nechí after 51 years and is common in Reserva la Serrana; and on Pacific slope of West Andes in Chocó, Risaralda and Valle del Cauca, around Cerro Tatamá and Mistrató, including Alto de Pisones, where also common.

Habitat Tropical to Subtropical Zones, at 1,000–2,450m but usually 1,400–1,750m, in humid to wet cloud forest with heavy undergrowth, adjacent second growth and other disturbed habitats, e.g. forest borders and fragments, and even cultivation.

Voice A sharp, staccato *tst* or *pit*, uttered in flocks; lone birds sometimes utter a longer *pseee* or *pseeyee*. Song consists of 3–5 phrases, *pit-psEEyee* or *tst-tzEEee*, delivered rapidly and followed by a pause (I&I, BirdLife 2004).

Note Formerly placed in genus *Buthraupis*.

GOLDEN-CHESTED TANAGER

Bangsia rothschildi Pl. 257

Identification 15–16cm. All blue-black with blue gloss, large warm yellow crescent on breast, and yellow vent to undertail-coverts. Eyes dark chestnut, bill black, legs and feet grey. Juvenile undescribed. See Black-and-gold Tanager. Moss-backed Tanager has greener upperparts and underparts, bluer head and smaller yellow breast patch, and usually occurs at higher elevations.

Ssp. Monotypic (NW Ec, SW Co)

Habits Sluggish forager and may perch quietly for long periods. Often moves barbet-like, hopping along open branches with 180° turns. Alone or in pairs, mostly from midstorey to subcanopy. Searches for invertebrates, fruits, berries, seeds, and flowers, and often follows mixed-species flocks.

Status Rare to uncommon and local in Ecuador where considered Near Threatened (R&G), but fairly common in Colombia.

Habitat Tropical Zone, at 100–600m in Ecuador and 250–1,100m in Colombia, in humid to very wet forests and edges,

Voice A shrill, high *kjeee*. Song a buzzy, insect-like *tiz-ez-ez-ez-ez-ez-ez*, repeated up to 10 times per minute (I&I, R&G).

Note Formerly placed in genus *Buthraupis*.

MOSS-BACKED TANAGER

Bangsia edwardsi Pl. 257

Identification 15–16cm. Generally moss-green with dark blue head, blackish wings and tail with blue fringes to feathers, and small but prominent yellow crescent in centre of breast. Eyes dark brown, pale dusky upper mandible, yellowish-flesh lower mandible, legs and feet grey.

Ssp. Monotypic (NW Ec, SW Co)

Habits Moss-green coloration may recall a fruiteater as it forages sluggishly for invertebrates, fruits, berries, in barbet-like manner, hopping with 180° turns. Usually found from understorey to subcanopy. Alone or in pairs, it often joins mixed-species flocks.

Status Locally uncommon to common in Ecuador, becoming rarer in south, locally fairly common to common in Colombia.

Habitat Tropical to Subtropical Zones, at 400–2,100m but usually below 1,100m in Ecuador and above 900m in Colombia. In wet and mossy cloud forests, edges, sometimes second growth and trees in adjacent clearings.

Voice A short, spitting, high *psheee*. Song, usually delivered from prominent perch and mostly heard just after dawn, a series of simple, unmusical, bubbly and rattling trills, ascending and descending, e.g. *tr'e'e'E'E'e'e'r r'e'e'E'E'e'e'r…* lasting up to 1 minute (H&B, I&I, R&G).

Note Formerly placed in genus *Buthraupis*.

GOLD-RINGED TANAGER

Bangsia aureocincta Pl. 257

Identification 16cm. Mostly dark green adult with yellow central breast should be unmistakable by black head (olive in female) with conspicuous and diagnostic yellow ring formed by postocular supercilium curving behind ear-coverts and joining malar to base of bill (though Slaty-capped Shrike-vireo looks somewhat similar). Bill blackish above and yellowish below.

Ssp. Monotypic (W Co)

Habits Forages mainly for fruit but also invertebrates. Sometimes joins mixed-species flocks.

Status Endangered. Threatened due to small range, with ongoing habitat destruction, degradation and fragmentation. Endemic to Colombia, where known from only 4 localities on Pacific slope of West Andes: from headwaters of río San Juan, in vicinity of Cerro Tatamá (Risaralda/Chocó/Valle del Cauca border) where unrecorded since 1946; Alto de los Galápagos (Valle del Cauca/Chocó border), the Caramanta massif at Alto de Pisones (Risaralda), where it is common to abundant, and, recently, Las Orquideas National Park (Antioquia).

Habitat Subtropical Zone, at 1,600–2,200m. Humid to wet, mossy and dense cloud forests on steep ridges with numerous natural treefalls breaking canopy.

Voice Calls include *chip* and *chit* contact notes, and a short, twittered, low-pitched trill often given in alarm or excitement. Song consists of sharp, penetrating, high-pitched whistles or thin, watery trills, *tseeuurr*, delivered in groups of 3–6 (I&I, BirdLife 2004).

Note Formerly placed in genus *Buthraupis*.

Buthraupis are commanding tanagers of high Andes. Large of body, with fairly long tails and strong compact bills, like many mountain tanagers they have yellow underparts and blue or green upperparts.

HOODED MOUNTAIN TANAGER

Buthraupis montana Pl. 259

Identification 21–23cm. Bright deep blue above, dark wings and tail with blue fringes; hood black; breast to undertail-coverts bright yellow, with some black scalloping on sides. Red eyes, bill, thighs, legs and feet black. Juvenile paler yellow below. Adult easily distinguished from smaller Black-chested Mountain Tanager which has dark eyes, different behaviour and lacks black thighs. Juvenile has duller black and yellow pattern.

Ssp. *B. m. cucullata* (W Ec, W Co) head all black, greyish violet-blue nape, back bright blue, blackish wings and tail fringed green and blue – blue outermost; entire underparts from breast to undertail-coverts pure yellow, thighs noticeably black

B. m. gigas (NC Co, NW & SW Ve) duller and less purple than *cucullata*; lustrous but dull Tyrian blue above (like a pastel purple)

B. m. venezuelae (Sierra de Perijá, NE Co & NW Ve) blue of back is lustrous but duller than *gigas*, with more green showing through

Habits Forages sluggishly or rapidly but always noisily, in pairs or small to large flocks of up to 10–25. Occurs at all levels, but usually in subcanopy to canopy of tall vegetation seeking invertebrates, fruits, berries and seeds. Sometimes joins mixed-species flocks. Often seen flying long distances across open spaces.

Status Fairly common.

Habitat Subtropical to Temperate Zones, at 1,800–3,300m (once to 1,100m in Colombia), in tall, epiphyte-laden, humid to wet cloud forests, edges and mature second growth on steep slopes and canyons, also nearby clearings and shrubby hillsides.

Voice A characteristic loud *tee tee tee…* flight-call, a hoarse, nasal *zhhi* alarm-call, loud, sharp, moderate-pitched and usually rapidly repeated *weeck*, *toot*, *weeck-toot* and *toot-weeck* notes when foraging, a high, thin *tseep* contact, also high, thin, single or trilled *ti* notes, and weaker *zit-zit* notes similar to other tanagers. In flight-display high above forest, a rapid, exuberant *chip'ut-chip'ut…* or series of high *seet* or *ti* notes. Dawn song may be a *weeck* or *toot-weeck* monotonously repeated at *c*.1 per s. Dawn choruses of flocks can be heard over long distances, and later in day, sometimes eliciting outbursts from other groups (H&B, F&K, I&I, Hilty).

BLACK-CHESTED MOUNTAIN TANAGER *Buthraupis eximia* Pl. 259

Identification 18–22cm. Back moss-green, rump lustrous violet-blue, long uppertail-coverts deep dark green, wings and tail black with lesser and median wing-coverts lustrous violet-blue, distal half of greater coverts moss-green; top of head to nape lustrous violet-blue, forehead to lores, sides of face to breast dull black, rest of underparts golden-yellow, basal half of thighs black; eyes dark brown, bill, legs and feet black. Hooded Mountain Tanager is not only significantly larger, but is very blue above without any moss-green. Lacrimose Mountain Tanager has yellow crescent below eyes and another on neck-sides. Blue-winged Mountain Tanager has distinctive yellow crown and nape.

Ssp. *B. e. chloronota* (NW Ec, SE Co) larger, dull blue head, dark moss-green rump, black of mask, throat and upper breast less extensive; underwing-coverts lack yellow fringes; lacks stiff bristles on chin apparent in other races

B. e. cyanocalyptra (SC Ec) dull blue nape bordered by broader band of deeper blue, dark moss-green rump; black of throat and breast extends deeper, mid throat has concealed pure white patch; underwing-coverts have yellow fringes

B. e. eximia (NC Co, SW Ve) as described

B. e. zimmeri (WC Co) rump cress-green, top of head bright lustrous blue, face intense black with conspicuous sheen

Habits Moves jerkily with some tail-flicking along mossy limbs, searching epiphytes or foliage. Less social and much quieter than Hooded Mountain Tanager when it forages alone, in pairs or small flocks of up to 6 at all levels, but usually fairly high for invertebrates, fruits, berries and seeds, and rarely joins mixed-species flocks.

Status Rare to locally uncommon and seemingly local, just reaching extreme south-west Venezuela.

Habitat Temperate Zone to Páramo, at 2,000–3,800m but mostly 2,800–3,400m, in humid to wet, mossy cloud forests and edges, and elfin woodland and shrubbery at or near treeline.

Voice Soft *zit*, *seep* and *chip* notes when foraging. Dawn song a simple series of alternating *tchew syéeuw* notes, with second note higher. Song a loud, repetitive *tititi-turry-tititi-tee-ter-turry*… delivered for to 30 s (F&K, I&I, R&G, Hilty).

MASKED MOUNTAIN TANAGER

Buthraupis wetmorei Pl. 259

Identification 20–21.5cm. Yellowish-olive upperparts with prominent yellow rump make adult much more yellowish above than other mountain tanagers. Female slightly duller than male.

Ssp. Monotypic (SC Ec, SW Co)

Habits Rather slowly and quietly forages alone, in pairs or small flocks, usually in cover close to ground, but sometimes atop scrubby epiphyte-laden trees. Looks for invertebrates, fruits and berries, and often joins mixed-species flocks. Often spotted flying between patches of cover.

Status Vulnerable. Threatened due to its small disjunct range, which is declining owing to continued habitat destruction, degradation and fragmentation. Rare and local in Colombia, with records from Puracé National Park and environs, Cauca, and recently from Nariño; restricted to East Andes in Ecuador (Carchi, Napo, Morona-Santiago, Azuay, Loja and Zamora-Chinchipe) where generally rare to uncommon and local, but fairly common at Cajanuma, Podocarpus National Park.

Habitat Temperate Zone to Páramo, at 2,900–3,650m, in very humid upper reaches of cloud forest, low stunted woodland and mossy elfin forest, scattered bushes, bamboo, giant grasses and dense shrubbery near treeline at páramo–forest ecotone.

Voice Song a fairly long series of high and rather weak but variable *tsee* notes (R&G).

ORANGE-THROATED TANAGER

Wetmorethraupis sterrhopteron Pl. 259

Identification 17–18cm. Essentially black above, from forehead to tail, with deep cerulean-blue wing-coverts and broadly fringed tertials and secondaries; tiny black chin, throat to breast bright rich orange, pale yellow-buffy underparts with black thighs. Orange throat (much duller in subadult) should be diagnostic within its limited range.

Ssp. Monotypic (SE Ec)

Habits Forages in pairs or small flocks of up to 6 in canopy for invertebrates and fruits (e.g. *Cecropia*), sometimes joins mixed-species flocks, and often hops along larger limbs probing moss and epiphytes.

Status Vulnerable, but considered endangered in Ecuador (R&G), threatened due to its small range, in which suitable habitat is declining because of road construction and human settlement. Known only from upper río Nangaritza Valley and nearby Miazi, on west slope of southern Cordillera del Cóndor, in south-east Zamora-Chinchipe, Ecuador (where rare to uncommon and very local), and adjacent Peru.

Habitat Tropical Zone, 450–1,000m, primarily in mature, humid *terra firme* and edges where slopes are neither steep nor wet, but also in disturbed mature forest.

Voice A penetrating *seet*. Dawn song a deliberate, steadily repeated *in-chee-tooch* or *we-tsi-tsoo*, delivered from high perch (I&I, R&G, BirdLife 2004).

SANTA MARTA MOUNTAIN TANAGER

Anisognathus melanogenys Pl. 259

Identification 18–18.5cm. Adult blue above with diagnostic black cheeks surrounding yellow crescent right below eye, orange-yellow below with black crescents on flanks joining black thighs. Compare Santa Marta Brush Finch which has entire head black with silver cheeks.

Ssp. Monotypic (Santa Marta in Co)

Habits Forages rapidly, may be in pairs or small flocks of up to 6 at all levels, but usually below subcanopy; often joins mixed-species flocks and aggregations at fruiting trees.

Status Endemic to Colombia, where fairly common to common, moving to lower altitudes in wet season.

Habitat Subtropical to Temperate Zones, at 1,200–3,200m, in mossy forest edges and second growth, but only occasionally in forest or adjacent shrubby overgrown clearings and pastures.

Voice A weak chirping note (F&K, I&I).
Notes Also called Black-cheeked Mountain Tanager. Formerly considered a race of Lacrimose Mountain Tanager.

LACRIMOSE MOUNTAIN TANAGER *Anisognathus lacrymosus* Pl. 259

Identification 17–19cm. Adult varies geographically (from dark blue-grey to olive above and from yellow to tawny-orange below), but all have distinctive darkish cheeks surrounding a yellow crescent right below eye and larger triangular spot on neck-sides. Juvenile is duller, slightly paler above; duller yellow below, slightly flammulated and washed olive.

Ssp. *A. l. caerulescens* (S Ec) similar to *palpebrosus*, usually with yellow crescent right below eye
A. l. intensus (SW Co) forecrown and head-sides darker than *palpebrosus*, paler below than *palpebrosus*
A. l. melanops (Andes in Ve) back slaty, forecrown and head-sides darker than in *palpebrosus*, paler below than *palpebrosus*
A. l. olivaceiceps (W Co) like *palpebrosus*, but forecrown, supercilium and head-sides tinged olive, hindneck and back paler and browner, underparts paler
A. l. pallididorsalis (Co & Ve, Sierra de Perijá) above dull blue-grey, rump and shoulders blue, forehead and head-sides dusky green, dark yellow below, often lacking yellow spot right below eye, otherwise paler than *tamae*, especially on back
A. l. palpebrosus (E Ec, SW Co) bluish-slate above, rump and shoulders purplish-blue, flight- and tail-feathers fringed blue, head-sides greenish slate, yellow spot behind ear-coverts, underparts bright warm yellow
A. l. tamae (NC Co, W Ve) forecrown and head-sides dark yellow-olive (darker than *palpebrosus*), back dusky bluish-grey, underparts darker than *melanops* but paler than *palpebrosus*

Habits Forages rather deliberately for invertebrates, fruits and berries. Forages alone, in pairs or small flocks and often joins mixed-species flocks. From understorey to subcanopy.
Status Fairly common to common in Ecuador, common in Colombia and Venezuela.
Habitat Subtropical Zone to Páramo, at 1,800–3,800m but usually above 2,600m, in humid cloud and mossy forests, edges and second growth, and, at higher elevations, in stunted and elfin forests and edges, and sometimes on scrubby hillsides nearby.
Voice A tanager-like *zit*, also longer *tziit*, and high, thin *see* or *seeek* notes when foraging, and sometimes short bursts of staccato chipping (2–8 notes) repeated frequently. Song, usually just after dawn and from a high perch atop shrub or a tree, a jumbled and complex series of 2–6 (or more) high, sputtering and excited phrases, usually *ee-chut-chut-ee* but also *chuck-zit-it*, *swiik-id-dee-it-it* or *suick-id-dit*; pauses variable and last up to 1 minute, and may be interrupted by soft high *see* or *swee* notes (F&K, I&I, Hilty).

SCARLET-BELLIED MOUNTAIN TANAGER *Anisognathus igniventris* Pl. 259

Identification 16–19cm. Adult unmistakable, large with a long tail, jay-like jizz and entire head, breast and upperparts black with crescent of bright red on ear-coverts, bright lustrous blue rump and uppertail-coverts; lower breast, belly to vent and flanks scarlet-red; thighs and undertail-coverts black. Juvenile has underparts rich orange-rufous.

Ssp. *A. i. erythrotus* (Ec, S Co) above black, rump and shoulders blue, spot behind ear-coverts scarlet, throat, breast, vent and undertail-coverts black, rest of underparts scarlet; juvenile and immature have duller black upperparts and scarlet breast admixed tawny-orange, with feathers tipped more or less conspicuously dark
A. i. lunulatus (NC Co, W Ve) as described

Habits Forages in jay-like manner but rather quietly, often alone or in pairs. Sometimes in small flocks of up to 15+ and sometimes joins mixed-species flocks. Forages at all levels for invertebrates, fruits, berries, seeds, flowers, leaves and buds, Often remains in cover, and often only seen in flight between patches of dense vegetation.
Status Fairly common to common in Ecuador and Colombia, uncommon to locally fairly common in Venezuela, may migrate seasonally or nomadically.
Habitat Temperate Zone to Páramo, at 2,200–3,900m but usually 2,500–3,500m, in wet cloud and mossy forests, edges and second growth, also elfin, dwarf and *Polylepis*-dominated forests, and humid *páramo* shrubbery near or slightly above treeline; also hedgerows, thickets, trees and bushes in clearings and pastures.
Voice A tanager-like *tit* and characteristic *trrt tit*, sometimes prolonged to *trrr-tit-trrr-trrr-tit tit trrr trrr trrr*. Song, from concealed or semi-open perch except at dawn, a tinkling, bell-like jumble of rapid, complex, rising and falling notes mixed with lower nasal notes, almost sounding like cranking an old engine (F&K, I&I, Hilty).

BLUE-WINGED MOUNTAIN TANAGER *Anisognathus somptuosus* Pl. 259

Identification 16–18cm. Adult has back black, rump and uppertail-coverts green, wings black with bright blue shoulders, and fringes to remiges and rectrices blue, head black with broad yellow streak from crown to nape, underparts yellow; eyes brown, bill black with silvery base, legs and feet dark grey. Juvenile has yellow parts slightly duller, with feathers of smaller nape patch fringed narrowly dark. Adult unmistakable in most of its range, but on Pacific slope compare slimmer Black-chinned Mountain Tanager which has much less blue on wing and much brighter yellow-olive back contrasting sharply with black head, which has yellow only on rear crown.

Ssp. *A. s. alamoris* (SW Ec) smaller; like *antioquiae*, back black but mantle mixed green and rump greener, flight-feather fringes paler sky blue
A. s. antioquiae (N Co) interscapular area tinged

greenish, rump green, fringes of wings and tail medium sky blue
A. s. baezae (E Ec, S Co) like *victorini* but darker, more olivaceous back, mossy green, nuchal region suffused black, pale turquoise-blue fringes to wings and tail
A. s. cyanopterus (W Ec, SW Co) black back, rump very dark olive-green to black, flight-feather fringes cobalt-blue, like shoulder patch, extensive yellow nape
A. s. somptuosus (SE Ec) black back and head-sides with central crown and nape yellow, flight-feather fringes paler cerulean-blue, uropygial brownish-olive (not mossy green), purplish-blue shoulders
A. s. venezuelanus (N Ve) smaller; back sooty black, lower rump to uppertail-coverts sooty black washed basally green and yellow; juvenile has smaller yellow patch on back of head, feathers fringed black; back browner
A. s. victorini (C Co, SW Ve) larger; moss-green back from mantle to uppertail-coverts, basally washed darker green and deep turquoise
A. s. viridiorsalis (N Ve) back to uppertail-coverts sooty black, feathers washed basally green

Habits Conspicuous as it forages at all levels but usually from midstorey upwards. Typically runs and hops along branch until it reaches terminal foliage, searching for invertebrates, fruits, berries and seeds. In pairs or flocks of 3–10, rarely up to 25, and often joins mixed-species flocks.
Status Fairly common to common in Ecuador, common in Colombia, fairly common in Venezuela, and tolerant of some habitat disturbance but locally uncommon wherever habitat loss has been severe (e.g. west Loja, Ecuador).
Habitat Tropical to Subtropical Zones, at 900–2,600m, in humid to wet forests, edges, mature second growth and adjacent clearings.
Voice Faint, slightly buzzy ticking, chipping and trilled notes, a soft *seeet*, long, harsh *veeeeee*, and soft, high *tic* or *tic-it* notes when foraging, sometimes becoming short bursts or trills. Song high, rapid and almost twittering *ti-ti-ti-ti ti'ti'ti' TI'TI'TI'ti'ti'ti'ti'ti'ti ti ti*, a little louder and faster in middle part (H&B, F&K, I&I, Hilty).
Notes Formerly called *A. flavinucha* or *A. flavinuchus*, but older name *somptuosus* Lesson, 1831, has priority (S&M). Sometimes placed in genus *Compsocoma* (F&K).

BLACK-CHINNED MOUNTAIN TANAGER *Anisognathus notabilis* Pl. 259

Identification 18–18.5cm. Adult should be unmistakable, but may be confused with Blue-winged Mountain Tanager, which has a dark back.

Ssp. Monotypic (NW Ec, SW Co)

Habits Forages alone, in pairs or small flocks of up to 6, at all levels but usually from midstorey up, for invertebrates and fruits, and often joins mixed-species flocks. Perches rather upright for some time, then runs and hops rapidly along branch until reaches terminal foliage.
Status Uncommon to locally fairly common in Ecuador, uncommon and very local in Colombia.
Habitat Tropical to Subtropical Zones, at 800–2,200m (once at 300m), in humid to wet (sometimes mossy) forests and edges.
Voice Calls include high thin *tic* notes. Song a series of high notes repeated frequently, e.g. *tsit-tsit-tseeéu-tsit-tsit-tseeu-tsit* (H&B, I&I, R&G).

Iridosornis are comparatively small tanagers, with rich iridescent plumage, bright yellow throats and orange undertail-coverts and are surprisingly cryptic. Usually found in undergrowth of montane forests. Keeps body horizontal when active.

PURPLISH-MANTLED TANAGER *Iridosornis porphyrocephalus* Pl. 260

Identification 14–16cm. Deep blue above, purplish gloss on back, more greenish-blue on rump and tail but looks virtually black in poor light, continues to breast, sides and flanks, central belly and vent buffy white, undertail-coverts dull orange. Female has belly greyish-buffy. Adult is only similar to Yellow-throated Tanager, which has breast, sides, flanks and belly dull ochraceous-buffy. There is no overlap.

Ssp. Monotypic (W Ec, W Co)

Habits Forages quietly and rather sluggishly, mostly in pairs but also alone or in small flocks, and often joins mixed-species flocks. Usually in shrubby lower growth searching for invertebrates, fruits and berries,
Status Near Threatened. Uncommon to locally fairly common in Colombia where confined to West Andes (principally on Pacific slope north to southern Chocó) and north end of Central Andes (in Antioquia), but very rare in north-west Ecuador (where only certainly known from Carchi and Imbabura, with an uncertain record from Loja) and considered Vulnerable (R&G). Threatened by rapid and ongoing deforestation, largely the result of intensive logging, human settlement, cattle grazing and mining, with severe destruction in its core elevational range.
Habitat Subtropical Zone, 750–2,700m but usually at 1,500–2,200m, in humid (especially mossy) cloud forests, edges and second growth, but sometimes in less humid areas.
Voice A buzzy, downscale and mostly high-pitched *seeeer*, repeated every 3 s for long periods is perhaps song (delivered upright with head thrown back), and a high, slightly raspy *tsit*, sometimes runs into a trill (H&B, I&I). Song in Colombia a very high *ts-ts-tseéuit tseeuwee* (R&G).

YELLOW-THROATED TANAGER *Iridosornis analis* Pl. 260

Identification 15–16cm. Adult a variable dull blue above, richer and warmer on head to narrow blackish mask, rather more greyish-turquoise on rump, wings and tail dusky with broad turquoise fringes; lower cheeks, chin and throat bright yellow (narrow dusky edge at base of bill), underparts buffy to cinnamon undertail-coverts. Eyes dark red, bill grey, whitish at base, legs and feet flesh to grey. Adult similar to Purplish-mantled Tanager, but no overlap.

Ssp. Monotypic (E Ec)

Habits Forages quietly and rather sluggishly. Usually in pairs or small flocks in lower growth (sometimes to canopy) looking for invertebrates, fruits and seeds. Often joins mixed-species flocks and feeding aggregations in fruiting trees.

Status Rare to fairly common and seemingly local in Ecuador, but apparently more common in south. Uncertain in Colombia, where known only by an unconfirmed sight record from western Putumayo, in 1978.

Habitat Tropical to Subtropical Zones, at 1,400–2,300m, in humid to wet, especially mossy cloud forests, edges and second growth with dense undergrowth, and stunted forests at higher altitudes.

Voice A downward-inflected *tseeeer*, from high to moderate pitch, repeated after 2–13 s, is perhaps a song, but is also heard infrequently when foraging (I&I, R&G).

GOLDEN-CROWNED TANAGER *Iridosornis rufivertex* Pl. 260

Identification 16.5–18cm. Adult is almost entirely rich blue with a black hood, bright orange crown patch, and chestnut undertail-coverts; eyes deep red, bill black with whitish base to lower mandible, legs and feet grey. Juvenile blackish with wings and tail as adult, but coronal patch duller and smaller. Adult unmistakable in good light (compare Plushcap which is rufous below), but may appear blackish in poor light.

Ssp. *I. r. caeruleoventris* (N Co) crest cadmium-orange, no chestnut on underwing-coverts, vent and undertail-coverts dark blue and concolorous with belly

I. r. ignicapillus (SW Co) crown patch cadmium-orange, underwing- and undertail-coverts chestnut

I. r. rufivertex (E Ec, C Co, W Ve) chestnut vent

I. r. subsimilis (W Ec) broad frontal band and coronal patch paler and duller

Habits Forages for invertebrates, fruits, berries and seeds rather quietly but rapidly. Usually alone, in pairs or small flocks in lower growth, and often joins mixed-species flocks.

Status Uncommon to locally fairly common in Ecuador, fairly common in Colombia (where easily found in Puracé National Park), but only a few records in Venezuela at extreme northern end of its range.

Habitat Temperate Zone to Páramo, at 2,250–3,800m, in dense undergrowth and edges of low, dense, mossy elfin and cloud forests, especially stunted treeline vegetation, and nearby tangled thickets, trees and shrubbery in *páramo*, less often in taller forest at lower elevations.

Voice High thin *seeeep* notes, high *tsip* or *tsick* notes when foraging, and a finer *tee tee* (F&K, I&I, Hilty).

Note Race *subsimilis* considered doubtfully distinct by F&K and R&G.

BUFF-BREASTED MOUNTAIN TANAGER *Dubusia taeniata* Pl. 260

Identification 18–20cm. Adult dull blue above, blackish wings and tail with broad blue fringes black hood with conspicuous long broad eyebrow of frosty pale blue freckles and streaks, inconspicuous buff breast-band visible when close, belly and flanks yellow, thighs black, undertail-coverts buff. Eyes dark brown, bill black, legs and feet dark grey. Juvenile has dull olive back and ochraceous breast and vent.

Ssp. *D. t. carrikeri* (N Co) smaller, with deeper buff breast that extends spottily from chin, through throat to lower breast

D. t. taeniata (Ec, Co, W Ve) full black throat

Habits Forages rather deliberately and sluggishly, for invertebrates, fruits, berries and seeds. At all levels, but usually fairly low in dense vegetation, though visits fruiting trees. Usually alone or in pairs, sometimes joins mixed-species flocks.

Status Uncommon to locally fairly common in Ecuador, uncommon and local in Colombia and Venezuela.

Habitat Subtropical Zone to Páramo, at 2,000–3,600m but usually above 2,500m, in humid to wet and usually mossy forests, edges, and elfin and stunted woodlands to treeline (where most numerous), sometimes in denser second growth, adjacent clearings and isolated scrubby patches; in some areas favouring *Chusquea* bamboo.

Voice Calls include loud chatters. Song a very loud, clear, sweet, moderate-pitched *peeoueee-paaaay* whistle, lasting 2–3 s, with first note slurred downward then upward, second note slightly lower and sliding down, sometimes repeated frequently at intervals of 3–7 s for several minutes in morning (H&B, F&K, I&I, R&G, Hilty).

Note Sometimes placed in genus *Delothraupis*.

FAWN-BREASTED TANAGER *Pipraeidea melanonota* Pl. 260

Identification 13–15cm. Adult male has dusky bluish upperparts, much brighter on head and rump, black mask and fawn-buffy underparts. Short, swallow-like bill with small hook, red eyes, relatively long wings and short tail. Female duller above. Juvenile like female, but throat-feathers have faint dark tips, and is more brownish-grey above. See Black-eared Hemispingus and Rufous-crested Tanager. Much smaller male Rusty Flowerpiercer has dark eyes, no mask, proportionately slimmer body, different-shaped bill and different behaviour.

Ssp. *P. m. venezuelensis* (Ec, E Co, Ve)

Habits Often perches for long periods on exposed branches, then sallies in pursuit of prey. Quietly forages for invertebrates, fruits, berries and seeds, alone or in pairs, and at all levels. Rarely joins mixed-species flocks, but often joins feeding aggregations in fruiting trees.

Status Uncommon to locally fairly common, and may be spreading due to deforestation.

Habitat Tropical to Subtropical Zones, at 400–3,100m, in

forest edges and bushy second growth, pastures, clearings, gardens and other cultivated areas with large scattered trees.
Voice Song usually given from high perch, a squeaky, unmusical series of strong, monotonous, high *see* or *sweee* notes, varying from a few slow notes to 12 or more very fast ones (like a pulsating trill), but always lasting only 2–3 s and often repeated after 2–3 s; also a more jumbled, euphonia-like song (H&B, I&I, R&G, Hilty).

Conirostrum conebills are rather delicate little birds with fine pointed bills, more warbler-like than tanager. They are predominately blue above and pale below, with a few exceptions. Whilst the males are easy to identify, females may be a problem. The *Oreomanes* Giant Conebill is significantly larger and is like a Nuthatch *Sitta* sp., creeping along trunks and branches.

CHESTNUT-VENTED CONEBILL

Conirostrum speciosum Pl. 268

Identification 10.2cm. Adult male dull greyish-blue, slightly paler below with chestnut vent and (usually) a small but distinctive small white spot at base of primaries. Adult female bright olive above with contrasting greyish-blue crown and nape, brownish wings and tail with yellowish-green fringes, and greyish-white below with variable buffy tinge, including lores and head-sides. Juvenile like female, but has crown and nape concolorous bright olive with back. Whilst male is rather unmistakable, nondescript female best separated by attendant male (compare female and juvenile White-eared and Bicoloured Conebills, Tennessee Warbler, Scrub Greenlet, female Blue Dacnis).

Ssp. *C. s. amazonum* (E Ec, E Co, SW Ve, Gu, FG) slightly darker above, much darker below
C. s. guaricola (C Ve) as described

Habits Active and quick as it forages for invertebrates in canopy. Usually in pairs or small flocks, rarely alone. Sometimes joins mixed-species flocks.
Status Uncommon and local, but perhaps often overlooked.
Habitat Tropical Zone, to 1,200m, in deciduous woodland and scrub, gallery forest and other scattered groves of large trees in *llanos*, favouring drier, strongly seasonal areas in Venezuela, also *várzea* edges, swampy river islands and second growth in Amazonian Colombia and Ecuador, also swampy forests on sand ridges near coast in Suriname and French Guiana.
Voice Calls include high *tic* and *ti* notes. Song a high, thin, leisurely *tidé, tidé, tidé, tidé, ti'dee'rít* (Hilty).
Note R&T point out that this species, along with other lowland conebills, is rather different from montane conebills and merits separate genus, *Ateleodacnis*.

WHITE-EARED CONEBILL

Conirostrum leucogenys Pl. 268

Identification 9.5–10.2cm. Tiny with a proportionately short tail. Adult male dark slate grey with shiny black crown and nape, wings and tail black with grey fringes to greater wing-coverts and white fringes to tertials, conspicuous white ear-patch and inconspicuous white rump band; throat to breast mouse grey, paler grey sides and flanks, yellowish-white on belly and vent; undertail-coverts chestnut, but longest pair of feathers pale grey; eyes and bill black with grey base; legs and feet grey. Adult female mouse grey above with faint green wash, yellowish-white rump, whitish ear-patch and yellowish below, washed slightly greyish on sides of face and breast, perhaps with hint of orange on breast. Juvenile like female but slightly warmer, more brownish-grey above and lacks pale ear-patch. Whilst male is rather unmistakable, nondescript female best separated by attendant male (compare female and juvenile Chestnut-vented and Bicoloured Conebills, and Tennessee Warbler).

Ssp. *C. l. cyanochroum* (W Ve) male slightly darker above and more deep grey on breast; female and juvenile appear olive-washed from malar on down, suffused across breast, and lacking any pure yellow
C. l. leucogenys (N Co, NW Ve) as described
C. l. panamense (NW Co) similar to *leucogenys* but adult male much darker above and below; adult female slightly darker above with little or no green tones

Habits Active and quick as it forages alone, in pairs or small flocks from midstorey to canopy for invertebrates (lower at edges or in smaller flowering trees), and sometimes joins mixed-species flocks. In Panama, race *panamense* found in flocks at tops of giant trees.
Status Uncommon to locally fairly common, but easily overlooked unless song is known.
Habitat Tropical Zone, to 800m, rarely to 1,300m, in dry to moist open woodlands, edges, cacao plantations, gallery forest, second growth with scattered tall trees, and tall legumes in pastures.
Voice Usually persistently repeated song, a high, thin, tinkling, unmusical series of notes, e.g. *tsing-le, tséet-e-tséet*, lasting *c.*1.5 s, often slowing and fading at end (Hilty).

BICOLOURED CONEBILL

Conirostrum bicolor Pl. 268

Identification 10.2–11.5cm. Adult soft blue-grey above with brownish tertials and rectrices, all with fine grey fringes; underparts soft pinkish, buffy-grey, with underwing-coverts paler, slightly darker on sides, flanks and thighs; eyes reddish-brown, bill black above and grey below, legs and feet grey. Juvenile yellowish-olive above, browner wings and tail; narrow buffy fringes to greater wing-coverts, narrow fringes to tertials; entire underparts yellow, paler on undertail-coverts. Breeds in intermediate plumage: female same as juvenile above, slightly paler below; male duller and darker, more greenish-olive above; below very much paler, washed-out yellow with wash of warm pinkish buffy-grey on sides and flanks. Easily confused, especially females and juveniles (compare Yellow Warblers, which have dark eyes, dusky legs and yellow undertail; also female and juvenile Chestnut-vented and White-eared Conebills, Tennessee Warbler and female Hooded Tanager).

Ssp. *C. b. bicolor* (N Co, N Ve, Guianas, Tr) as described
C. b. minus (E Ec, S Co) buffier below

Habits Active and quick as it forages for invertebrates and seeds, from midstorey to canopy, lower at edges or in second growth. Usually in pairs or small flocks, rarely joins mixed-species flocks.
Status Fairly common to common along entire north coast of South America including Trinidad, but very rare and local in eastern Ecuador and southern Colombia.
Habitat Lower Tropical Zone, near sea level in coastal mangrove and rarely in adjacent riverine vegetation, but to 300m in Ecuador and Colombia. Early to late second growth on swampy river islands (rarely along riverbanks) in Amazonia.
Voice A soft, high, sibilant *tsik*, *pit-sik* and *few-it-sip* when foraging. Song a rapid, high, even-pitched, squeaky and somewhat buzzy series, e.g. *pfits, t'wit'wit'wit'chit* (H&B, Hilty).

CINEREOUS CONEBILL
Conirostrum cinereum Pl. 268

Identification 10.5–12.5cm. Adult dull greyish-brown above (darker on crown) with buffy forehead and supercilium, and blackish wings with conspicuous L-shaped white patches, and is dull buffish-ochraceous below. Immature has buffy tone to wing-patches. Juvenile has faintly dark-tipped feathers on back and breast, and yellowish-tinged supercilium and underparts. Male Rusty Flowerpiercer lacks conspicuous supercilium and wing-patches.

Ssp. *C. c. fraseri* (Ec, SW Co)

Habits Active and quick as it forages alone, in pairs or small flocks at all levels, but often quite low for invertebrates and fruits, and sometimes joins mixed-species flocks.
Status Uncommon to fairly common in Ecuador and uncommon in Colombia.
Habitat Temperate Zone to Páramo, 2,300–4,000m but mostly at 2,500–3,600m, favouring more arid, semi-open habitats but also in more humid habitats, e.g. bushy woodlands and edges, dense stunted shrubbery, including *Polylepis*, hedgerows, fields and gardens with scattered vegetation, riparian thickets and sometimes in shrubby páramo. Avoids densely forested areas, and may benefit from forest clearance.
Voice A fine twitter and fine *tsip-tsip*, *zee* or *zee-zeet*. Song a fast jumbled series of twittering notes and phrases, sometimes given when foraging (H&B, F&K, R&G).

RUFOUS-BROWED CONEBILL
Conirostrum rufum Pl. 268

Identification 12–12.5cm. Adult dark bluish-grey above with blackish tail and wings (faint whitish wingbar and white-fringed tertials), distinctive rufous forehead and supercilium contrasting with dusky lores, and rufous below. Juvenile duller with paler underparts.

Ssp. Monotypic (Co, W Ve)

Habits Forages for invertebrates, in pairs or small flocks. Sometimes joins mixed-species flocks.
Status Uncommon to fairly common in Colombia, in Venezuela only reported from atop Cerro El Retiro, southern Táchira.
Habitat Temperate Zone to Páramo, at 2,650–3,400m, in shrubby non-forest habitats and stunted woodland, cloud forest edge and adjacent second growth to treeline, occasionally in semi-arid cultivation with scattered vegetation.
Voice Song a complex, fast series of high, squeaky notes, similar to Blue-backed Conebill (Hilty).

BLUE-BACKED CONEBILL
Conirostrum sitticolor Pl. 268

Identification 12–13cm. Male black above, with broad blue fringes to all except hood, sides of breast, belly and rest of underparts rufous-chestnut. Eyes dark, bill black, legs and feet grey. Female similar but has blue on nape and neck-sides. Immature duller, with greyish-blue back and throat. Adult distinctly tricoloured and unmistakable if seen well (see Rufous-browed Conebill, Black-throated, Chestnut-bellied, Coal-black and Rusty Flowerpiercers).

Ssp. *C. s. intermedium* (W Ve) blue postocular stripe
C. s. pallidus (Perijá in Ve) paler and more cinnamon below
C. s. sitticolor (Ec, Co) as described

Habits Active and quick as it forages alone, in pairs or small flocks at all levels, for invertebrates and seeds, almost always joins mixed-species flocks.
Status Uncommon to common, commonest just below tree-line.
Habitat Temperate Zone to Páramo, at 2,300–3,800m, in humid to wet forests, woodland, second growth and especially stunted and elfin forests (including *Polylepis*) and shrubbery to treeline.
Voice A fine, oft-repeated *zit*. Song mostly heard early morning, a complex jumbled series of high, thin rapid chips and twitters lasting to 6 s, e.g. *chipapita-chipapita, jeet, chipapita*…, often persistently repeated (F&K, Hilty).

CAPPED CONEBILL
Conirostrum albifrons Pl. 268

Identification 13–13.5cm. Basically 2 groups, those in which male has white crown and those where crown is blue. Immature like female. Nominate adult male has back black with slight deep blue gloss, lower back to rump deep rich violet-blue, wings and tail deep brown; top of head white; entire underparts sooty black; eyes brown, bill black above, sepia below, legs and feet black. Immature male is a mix of grey and sooty black, lower back and rump pale grey/violet-blue; white crown narrower (with black eyebrow); eyes brown, bill black, legs and feet dusky. Female totally different, olive-green above with yellow admixed on rump, head grey, darker above with sky blue wash to forehead and crown, grey on nape; chin to breast paler grey, rest of underparts pale greyish-yellow, richest on undertail-coverts. Adult male with blue crown may look all black in bad light, and could be confused with all-black flowerpiercers. Compare female with Grey-hooded Bush Tanager, Tennessee Warbler and female Blue Dacnis.

Ssp. **White-crowned group**
C. a. albifrons (NE Co, SW Ve) as described
C. a. centralandium (N Ec, C Co) male has crown either pure white or white with a few blue feathers; upperparts generally slightly bluer and rump brighter blue; female as *albifrons*
Blue-crowned group
C. a. atrocyaneum (Ec, SW Co) male has crown purplish-blue; female as *albifrons*
C. a. cyanonotum (N Ve) male has crown deep violet-blue, some with a few white feathers admixed, others with a few pale blue feathers; female like *albifrons* above, but paler, warmer grey on throat and breast, slightly buffy on rest of underparts

Habits Creeps along branches, often at their tips, constantly wags tail. Forages for invertebrates in canopy, alone, in pairs or small flocks. Often joins mixed-species flocks.
Status Uncommon to locally common in Andes, but rare to uncommon in north Venezuela.
Habitat Subtropical to Temperate Zones, at 1,800–3,000m, in humid and mossy forests, edges and mature second growth.
Voice A *chit* while foraging. Dawn song in Venezuela a high, leisurely *wee-see-wee-see-wee-see-weez* with first note stronger, also *swee-ty, swee-ty, swee-ty, tit'til'tit* with last part trilled (Hilty), in Ecuador a high, penetrating *tsu-tseeu, tsu-tseeu, tsu-tseeu*, usually preceded by a jumbled *tsududuit* (R&G).

GIANT CONEBILL
Oreomanes fraseri Pl. 268

Identification 16.5cm. Adult grey above with chestnut supercilium and distinctive white ear-patch, and chestnut below. Immature has duskier crown, white supercilium, lower cheek and throat, dusky mottling or streaking on throat and breast, and slightly paler underparts. Juvenile even browner above, with whiter throat.

Ssp. *O. f. fraseri* (Ec, SW Co)

Habits Forages on *Polylepis* trunks and branches, searching for invertebrates under bark (listen for birds scaling off bark). Often alone, in pairs or sometimes small flocks, and occasionally joins mixed-species flocks.
Status Near Threatened. Perhaps already extinct in Nariño, south-west Colombia, but rare to locally uncommon in Ecuador, where uncommon even in apparently optimal habitat. Its decline is attributed to destruction and fragmentation of *Polylepis* woodlands due to uncontrolled use of fire, firewood collection, intense grazing, unsound agricultural techniques and forestation with exotic trees (especially *Eucalyptus*).
Habitat Temperate Zone to Páramo, at 3,000–4,500m, in *Polylepis* at or usually above timberline.
Voice A soft, high *seep*, *whee* or *zit* when foraging. Song a musical twitter, e.g. *cheet, cheeveét, cheeveét* (H&B, F&K, R&G).

Flowerpiercers have slender, upturned bills, hooked at the tip, that have evolved for the purpose of piercing flowers at the base of the corolla, enabling the birds to get to the nectar. They used to belong to Coerebidae or Emberizidae, but are now part of Thraupidae.

RUSTY FLOWERPIERCER
Diglossa sittoides Pl. 270

Identification 11–13cm. Adult male bluish neutral grey above, darker on head, mask darker still but not black; underparts cinnamon, palest on throat, richest on flanks and undertail-coverts; thighs grey; eyes brown, bill black above, flesh below with brown tip, legs and feet brown. Female olive above, wings and tail slightly browner with off-white fringes, underparts sulphur-yellow, streaked and flammulated olive. Immature male like adult female but flushed cinnamon on flanks and thighs, undertail-coverts solid pale cinnamon. Juvenile browner above than female, streaks below browner, closer and more diffuse; juvenile male has undertail-coverts washed cinnamon. Adult male distinctly bicoloured and unlikely to be confused with any *Diglossa* (but see Fawn-breasted Tanager, montane conebills and female Tit-like Dacnis).

Ssp. *D. s. coelestis* (Perijá, Ve) top of head concolorous with back and uniform pale cinnamon below; female olive-brown above with buffy fringes to wings and tail, yellow below with soft brown streaks, belly clear yellow; juvenile more greenish above and streaks below weaker and more diffuse
D. s. decorata (Ec) forehead paler and brighter than back, tertials tipped buffy-white to cinnamon
D. s. dorbignyi (C Co, W Ve) as described
D. s. hyperythra (NE Co, N Ve) like *dorbignyi* below but head-sides plumbeous (vs. blackish slate)
D. s. mandeli (NE Ve) dark bluish-grey above, top and sides of head deep fuscous, uniform dense cinnamon below, grey thighs

Habits Very active and quick as it forages alone or in pairs, sometimes in small flocks, in flowering trees and shrubs at forest edge and on cut-over slopes, for nectar and invertebrates, and rarely joins mixed-species flocks.
Status Uncommon to locally fairly common.
Habitat Tropical Zone to Páramo, at 600–3,400m but usually 1,200–2,800m, in fairly arid to humid forest and woodland edge, second growth, overgrown clearings, bushy pastures, scrubby thickets and hedgerows, even gardens with many flowers, usually avoiding interior of closed-canopy forests.
Voice A loud sharp *cheek*. Songs alternate between short thin twitters and high-pitched trilling series of notes followed by a lower pitched burry note lasting *c*.2 s, e.g. *trrrtrrrtrr'trrrr* (F&K, I&I, R&G).
Note Formerly considered a race of Slaty Flowerpiercer *D. baritula* from Middle America (R&T).

VENEZUELAN FLOWERPIERCER

Diglossa venezuelensis Pl. 269

Identification 12.7–14cm. Adult male all black with white sides (pectoral tufts and underwing-linings) which are smaller than in very similar male White-sided Flowerpiercer (no overlap). Subadult male duller brown. Adult female dark olive-brown above with olive head and more yellowish face, and dark olive-brownish below with white sides, rather similar to female and especially juvenile White-sided Flowerpiercer, but usually darker and more olive (less buffy-brown) below. Overlapping, smaller female Rusty Flowerpiercer is streaked below and lacks white sides.

Ssp. Monotypic (NE Ve)

Habits Very active and quick as it forages, alone or in pairs at all levels. Does not usually join mixed-species flocks.

Status Endangered. Endemic to north-east Venezuela, where now only reliably found at 3 localities in Cordillera de Caripe (on borders of Anzoátegui, Monagas and Sucre), from Cerro Negro and Los Cumbres de San Bonifacio (not recently on Serranía de Turimiquire) and in westernmost Paria Peninsula (Sucre), specifically on Cerro Humo. Population of a few thousand individuals endangered by continuing habitat conversion for agriculture, especially coffee plantations, within its small and fragmented range.

Habitat Tropical to Temperate Zones, at 900–2,500m, in humid forest edges, young to mature second growth, and shrubby areas adjacent to forests.

Voice Song a complex but somewhat repetitive series of soft, low, rapid notes, lasting up to 25 s, rising and falling several times (Hilty).

WHITE-SIDED FLOWERPIERCER

Diglossa albilatera Pl. 269

Identification 12.2–13.2cm. Adult male blackish-slate with white sides (pectoral tufts and underwing-linings). Adult female dark olive-brown above and paler buffy-brown below, with buffy-olive flanks, white sides and central rear underparts. Immature male like female but much duller brown with blurry dusky streaks on breast. Juvenile dark grey-brown with feathers faintly dark-tipped. Only if white sides missed might be confused with Black Flowerpiercer. See also Rusty Flowerpiercer and Venezuelan Flowerpiercer (no overlap).

Ssp. *D. a. albilatera* (Ec, Co, W Ve) as described
D. a. federalis (N Ve) male greyer than nominate
D. a. schistacea (SW Ec) male has bluish gloss

Habits Very active and quick as it forages, mostly in pairs, also alone or in small flocks, mostly from under- to midstorey (sometimes on canopy flowers), for nectar and invertebrates, and sometimes joins mixed-species flocks.

Status Uncommon to locally common.

Habitat Subtropical to Temperate Zones, at 1,200–3,200m, but mostly 1,800–2,800m, at edges of humid forest, woodland and second growth (including stunted cloud forest), and in adjacent shrubby clearings, bushy hillsides, parks and gardens.

Voice Flat buzzy trills when disturbed and chirps during wing-spreading display. Song a distinctive even-pitched, fairly loud rattle-trill, usually preceded by 2 faint higher pitched, shrill notes, e.g. *SWEE-ti'ti'ti'ti't'ti'ti'ti'ti'ti'ti'ti*, lasting just over 1 s; in Northern Cordillera in Venezuela, preceding note descends slightly (R&T, F&K, Hilty).

BLACK-THROATED FLOWERPIERCER

Diglossa brunneiventris Pl. 270

Identification 15cm. Adult black above with bluish-grey shoulders and rump, and chestnut below with black central throat and bluish-grey flanks and sides. Subadult dusky-olive above and buffy-chestnut with faint dusky streaks below. Juvenile brownish above and buffy below with faint dusky streaks. Chestnut-bellied Flowerpiercer has all-black throat and upper breast (see also Blue-backed Conebill).

Ssp. *D. b. vuilleumieri* (W Co)

Habits Not well known, but presumably similar to congeners.

Status Race *vuilleumieri* endemic to Colombia and highly disjunct from nominate subspecies in Peru, Bolivia and Chile. It occurs at 2 localities: in high mountains around Medellín and in Paramillo Mts., at north end of West Andes.

Habitat Upper Subtropical Zone to Páramo, at 2,000–3,900m, in shrubby woodland.

Voice Song very similar to Black Flowerpiercer (H&B).

Note Also called Carbonated Flowerpiercer. Formerly considered a subspecies of Grey-bellied Flowerpiercer *D. carbonaria*.

CHESTNUT-BELLIED FLOWERPIERCER

Diglossa gloriosissima Pl. 270

Identification 14–15cm. Adult glossy-black except bluish-grey shoulders, dark slate rump and chestnut lower breast, belly and vent with dusky smudged streaks. See Black-throated Flowerpiercer (and Blue-backed Conebill).

Ssp. *D. g. gloriosissima* (Cauco, Co) as described
D. g. boylei (Antioquia, Co) clear cinnamon underparts

Habits Poorly known but presumably similar to congeners.

Status Endangered. Endemic to Colombia, very local and scarce in West Andes, recorded at 5 localities: Cerro Munchique (west Cauca), Páramo Frontino, Cerro Paramillo, Jardin and Farallones del Citará (Antioquia). No records between 1965 and 2003. Threatened by extensive deforestation within its tiny range, due to clearance for livestock grazing and associated fires.

Habitat Temperate Zone to Páramo, at 3,000–3,800m, near timberline at edge of semi-humid to humid montane scrub and elfin forests, apparently ranges only just below páramo edge.

Voice Unknown.

Note Formerly considered a race of Glossy Flowerpiercer (BirdLife International 2004).

GLOSSY FLOWERPIERCER

Diglossa lafresnayii Pl. 269

Identification 14–14.5cm. Adult glossy-black except bluish-grey shoulders. Juvenile duller dark greyish-brown with only a hint of shoulder patch. Very similar race *humeralis* Black Flowerpiercer is slightly smaller with proportionately smaller bill, duller black coloration (less gloss) and more greyish (less blue) shoulders, a faster song, and is generally found in drier and more open habitats (but identification often impossible).

Ssp. *D. l. lafresnayii* (Ec, C Co, W Ve)

Habits Very active and quick as it forages, for nectar and invertebrates, from under- to midstorey (sometimes higher in flowering trees). Usually alone or in pairs, sometimes joins mixed-species flocks.

Status Uncommon to locally common, most common just below treeline.

Habitat Upper Subtropical Zone to Páramo, at 2,000–3,750m but usually above 2,700m. Dense shrubs and trees at edges of humid, cloud, elfin and stunted mossy forests, also in hedges, gardens, overgrown pastures, shrubby clearings and hillsides, humid páramo shrubs, second growth and riparian thickets (not tied to forests, though usually more so than Black Flowerpiercer).

Voice A *chut*, *chip*, *chick-chick* and fine *zi-zi*. Song, often given from high exposed perch, a rapid twittering series of continuous single or doubled chirps, either thin and high or stronger and lower, and may continue for several minutes, e.g. *chiff chiff chee chiff chiff chee…* (F&K, I&I).

COAL-BLACK FLOWERPIERCER

Diglossa gloriosa Pl. 270

Identification 12.5–13.5cm. Adult black (no gloss) with bluish-grey eyebrow, shoulder and rump, chestnut lower breast, belly and vent, and grey flanks (see larger Blue-backed Conebill). Juvenile olive-brown above with faint dusky streaks, and dusky-brownish below with broad buffy streaks.

Ssp. Monotypic (Andes in Ve)

Habits Active and quick as it forages alone or in pairs, sometimes joins mixed-species flocks.

Status Endemic to Venezuela, uncommon to locally common.

Habitat Temperate Zone to Páramo, at 2,500–4,150m, in dry and rather open habitats, e.g. at forest edges and in patchy stunted woodland (dwarf and elfin forests), low shrubs and trees in highland valleys, also bushy open páramo and hedgerows, parks and gardens.

Voice A long, thin trill. Performs a song-flight (F&K).

Notes Also called Carbonated Flowerpiercer or Mérida Flowerpiercer. Formerly considered a subspecies of Grey-bellied Flowerpiercer *D. carbonaria*.

BLACK FLOWERPIERCER

Diglossa humeralis Pl. 269

Identification 13–14cm. Adult uniform, slightly glossy black with subtle blue gloss; eyes brown, bill black with grey base. Female duller black with no blue gloss; wings and tail fuscous-brown. Juvenile duller, dark greyish-brown above and paler with indistinct dusky streaks above and below. Bluish Flowerpiercer is dull dark blue but can appear black in bad light. See very similar Glossy Flowerpiercer (and less similar White-sided Flowerpiercer).

Ssp. *D. h. aterrima* (Ec, S Co) as described

D. h. humeralis (E Andes in N & C Co, SW Ve) male uniform dull black with small bluish shoulder and poorly defined grey rump (rarely has chestnut vent, near Bogotá: H&B); female very dark brown, grey rump less clear

D. h. nocticolor (Santa Marta in Co, Perijá in Ve) all black with only slight gloss and dark grey rump (hard to see in field), female slightly duller than male

Habits Forages for nectar and invertebrates, actively and quickly; usually rather low (sometimes higher in flowering trees). Alone or in pairs; rarely joins mixed-species flocks.

Status Fairly common to locally common.

Habitat Subtropical Zone to Páramo, at 2,175–4,000m but mostly 2,700–3,400m, in dense thickets at edges of wet to humid dwarf and elfin forests, and in scattered vegetation, e.g. *Polylepis* ravines, *Eucalyptus* plantations, shrubby clearings, hedgerows, parks and gardens (mostly a non-forest bird that has probably benefited from forest clearance).

Voice Song a rapid series of squeaky trills and twitters even faster than Glossy Flowerpiercer, but very similar to song of Cinereous Conebill (H&B).

Notes Also called Carbonated Flowerpiercer. Formerly considered a race of Grey-bellied Flowerpiercer *D. carbonaria*.

SCALED FLOWERPIERCER

Diglossa duidae Pl. 270

Identification 13–14cm. Adult uniform dull greyish-black above, darkest on head with slight bluish tone, wings and tail brownish; underparts dull bluish-grey with paler grey subterminal crescents on breast and belly, fringes of feathers darker and bluish, producing scaled pattern; dark grey undertail-coverts with vestigial white fringes. Reddish-brown eyes. Female virtually identical, slightly duller but not distinguishable in field. Juvenile like female, slightly smaller, dusky grey above with blackish crown and usually with whitish tips to median and greater wing-coverts (bolder on latter), giving 2 faint grey wingbars. No similarly uniform *Diglossa* species in range.

Ssp. *D. d. duidae* (C Amazonas in Ve) as described

D. d. georgebarrowcloughi (SW Ve) larger than others, darker and more blackish above with slight bluish gloss, particularly on head of male; more boldly and extensively spotted/scaled below

D. d. hitchcocki (N Amazonas in Ve: Cerros de Yavi and Paraque) more lustrous above than *duidae*; vestigial brownish spots/scales below, spots larger and browner on belly; undertail-coverts have broad white fringes; juvenile has solid white tips to median and greater wing-coverts producing 2 clear short wingbars, spots on belly large and without dark fringes, thus lacks scaling

Habits Not well known, but presumably similar to congeners.
Status Presumably fairly common to common.
Habitat Subtropical to Temperate Zones, at 1,400–2,600m (2,100–2,300m on Yavi, and 1,400–1,600m on Paraque). Low brushy forests on tepuis of southern Venezuela, and scattered low shrubs and trees in more open country.
Voice A short thin whistle (I&I).

GREATER FLOWERPIERCER

Diglossa major Pl. 270

Identification 16.5–17.3cm. Obviously large, dark bluish-grey flowerpiercer, with fringes of remiges and rectrices pale bluish-white, black mask, pale grey to white malar streak (variable) and chestnut undertail-coverts; reddish-brown eyes, strongly hooked bill, legs and feet black. Juvenile dusky-brown above and grey-brown with dirty white streaks below. No other *Diglossa* in range.

Ssp. *D. m. chimantae* (Chimantá, Ve) pale blue shaft-streaks on upperparts, well-defined black mask, forecrown pale blue, merging into rear crown, malar dotted white, mostly distally; fairly uniform dark neutral grey underparts, undertail-coverts dark chestnut

D. m. disjuncta (tepuis of C, S & W Bolívar in Ve) similar above to *chimantae* but slightly darker, distinctly more bluish below; malar has few white spots in single line

D. m. gilliardi (Auyán-tepui, Ve) slightly glossy above and below; bright blue shaft-streaks from rear crown to uppertail-coverts, malar line of a few white spots; richest blue below

D. m. major (tepuis in SE Ve) pale blue patches on top of head becoming narrower on nape and shaft-streaks on back to uppertail-coverts, white spotting on malar; vent to undertail-coverts rufous-chestnut; juvenile slightly paler below with patchy grey and some small chestnut tips on centre of breast and belly to vent

Habits Active and quick as it forages alone or in pairs, from understorey to canopy, but usually high, for nectar, sometimes joins mixed-species flocks.
Status Uncommon to abundant (e.g. Cerro Roraima) depending on locality, with seasonal altitudinal movements, at least in some localities.
Habitat Subtropical to Temperate Zones, 1,400–2,850m but mostly above 1,800m, in humid to wet low forests, including cloud forest, edges, shrubby clearings and dense mossy second growth on tepuis, and scattered low shrubs and trees in more open country.
Voice Song given alone or in duet consists of fast, chattering high, squeaky, tinkling or low-pitched, harsh, flat notes, more or less repeated again and again, lasting 0.5–5 minutes, sounding like radio static (Hilty).

INDIGO FLOWERPIERCER

Diglossa indigotica Pl. 269

Identification 11–11.5cm. Adult has bright red eyes and is indigo-blue with turquoise wing- and tail-feather fringes. Juvenile has dull bluish-green feathers with black fringes. Much larger but similarly coloured Masked Flowerpiercer is duller blue, with obvious black mask, not just lores and eye-ring, and usually occurs at higher elevations.

Ssp. Monotypic (NW Ec, W Co)

Habits Forages alone or in pairs from midstorey to canopy, sometimes lower, often joins mixed-species flocks.
Status Fairly common to common but local in Colombia, very rare to rare and local in Ecuador.
Habitat Tropical to Subtropical Zones, at 700–2,200m but mostly 1,000–1,500m in Colombia and 1,600–2,000m in Ecuador, in very wet mossy forests, including cloud forests, edges and mature second growth.
Voice A high, thin *chip* and an oft-repeated deliberate *squik* (H&B).
Note Also placed in genus *Diglossopis* (R&G).

DEEP-BLUE FLOWERPIERCER

Diglossa glauca Pl. 269

Identification 11.4–13cm. Adult male dark blue with distinctive golden eyes and black forehead, lores and chin. Adult female slightly duller. Juvenile sooty with yellow (not black) base to lower mandible.

Ssp. *D. g. tyrianthina* (E Ec)

Habits Active and quick as it forages alone, in pairs or small flocks mostly from midstorey to canopy (lower at edges) for invertebrates, fruits, seeds and nectar; almost always with mixed-species flocks.
Status Uncommon to common.
Habitat Upper Tropical to Upper Subtropical Zones, at 1,000–2,300 m, in humid to wet forests (especially mossy forests) and edges.
Voice A *ti-ti-dweeee* and high, pure, mechanical-sounding *keeeee*, often doubled. Song a fast series of high but descending chips and squeaks, accelerating and very jumbled at end, higher pitched than Bluish Flowerpiercer (H&B, R&G).
Notes Also called Golden-eyed Flowerpiercer. Has also been placed in genus *Diglossopis* (R&G). Race *tyrianthina* may not be valid, making this species monotypic (R&G).

BLUISH FLOWERPIERCER

Diglossa caerulescens Pl. 269

Identification 12.5–16cm. Essentially dull bluish-grey with some pretty blue tones in sunlight. Races all very similar with only tonal differences. Adult male dull greyish-blue (slightly paler below, especially on belly) with black forehead, lores and chin; undertail-coverts fringed narrowly white. Orange-red to dark-red eyes. Female duller above. Juvenile slightly greyer with faint streaks on upper belly and yellow (not black) base to lower mandible. Can appear all black in poor light (see

Black Flowerpiercer and other black flowerpiercers above). Larger Masked Flowerpiercer is usually brighter blue (not in juveniles) but always has larger black mask, and usually occurs at higher altitudes.

Ssp. *D. c. caerulescens* (N Ve) largest race; adult male almost uniform bluish-grey above, leading edge of primaries paler, underparts duller, slightly paler and greyer in centre of belly and on vent; general impression blue-grey – in sunlight seems brighter and bluer; eyes red, bill, legs and feet black

D. c. ginesi (NW Ve) slightly paler and duller above than either *caerulescens* or *saturata*, but indistinguishable from *saturata* in field, mask narrower and fades into lower cheeks and ear-coverts; pale sea blue below with grey belly and vent

D. c. media (S Ec) brighter, clearer blue than *saturata*, throat and breast deep blue, as in *saturata* and *caerulescens*, but less purplish-violet; breast and abdomen uniform pale greyish-blue and contrast with bluish-white of underparts, undertail-coverts fringed very broadly white

D. c. saturata (Co, SW Ve) darker and slightly more purplish above, darker slate blue below; undertail-coverts barely fringed white: from *caerulescens* by much darker, purplish-blue dorsal surface, face-sides and neck; underparts much darker slate blue with centre decidedly darker

Habits Active and quick as it forages alone or in pairs mostly from midstorey to canopy (lower at edges) for invertebrates, fruits, flowers and nectar; often joins mixed-species flocks.
Status Uncommon to locally common, seasonal movements at least in some localities.
Habitat Subtropical to Temperate Zones, at 1,400–3,200m (once at 250m in Colombia), in humid to very wet forests, including cloud and elfin forests, woodlands, edges, shrubby clearings, mature second growth and scrub, often on windswept ridges and areas with poor soils.
Voice Distinctive sharp high *tsin*, a hard, metallic *tiink* and distinctive flute-like note in flight. Song consists of a few slow high notes, followed by an accelerating and descending series of squeaky, twittering staccato notes, e.g. *eeeEET, esa-eet, eat'tsu-ti'tip-ta-leep'ta-lip'chlip, chee-ep, cheelip'liz'si…*, lasting *c.*2.5 s or longer, sometimes repeated regularly with pauses of *c.*5.5 s (F&K, I&I, R&G, Hilty).
Note Has also been placed in genus *Diglossopis* (R&G).

MASKED FLOWERPIERCER
Diglossa cyanea Pl. 269

Identification 13.5–15cm. Essentially marine/ultramarine-blue, slightly glossy – can look bright in good light, dull in poor); wings and tail fuscous with blue fringes to all feathers; clearly defined black mask (forehead, lores, chin, cheeks and ear-coverts); bright red eyes, hooked bill, legs and feet all black. Adult female paler blue on crown, slightly paler and less luminous blue above, with greyish tinge below. Juvenile even duller greyish-blue with dark brown eyes and yellow (not black) base to lower mandible, legs and feet brown. Adult male similar to Bluish Flowerpiercer (see also smaller Indigo Flowerpiercer in west Andes).

Ssp. *D. c. cyanea* (Ec, Co, W Ve) as described

D. c. dispar (SW Ec) like *cyanea*, but blue less violaceous and more greenish

D. c. obscura (NW Ve) like *cyanea* but generally deeper and darker blue

D. c. tovarensis (NC Ve) brighter and paler blue, particularly on forehead, darkening slightly on nape; mask more contrasting against blue; wings, tail and underparts like *cyanea*, perhaps slightly paler; female like *cyanea* but brighter and more extensive blue on head; juvenile duller above, almost entirely dull deep neutral grey below

Habits Forages alone, in pairs or small to large flocks, at all levels but usually high, for invertebrates, fruits, seeds and nectar, and often joins mixed-species flocks.
Status Fairly common to common, seasonal and altitudinal movements at least in some localities.
Habitat Subtropical Zone to Páramo, at 1,450–3,600m, in humid to wet forests, including cloud and elfin forests, edges, second growth, thickets and adjacent bushy clearings and slopes, isolated shrubs and gardens.
Voice A fine *zit* or *zik*. Song a series of 2–3 distinctive very high, thin *zeet* notes, followed by a accelerating, increasingly complex and descending series of twitters lasting *c.*3 s, often ending with 2 thin *zeet* notes, also transcribed as *tzi tzi tzi tzi tzideweedeleedeeleede* (starting with fine notes and ending in cascade), *trr te tziie tee tee tee* (third note accented, last part descending) or *tzirr tr tr tr tee tee tee* (first note accented) (H&B, F&K, Hilty).
Note Has also been placed in genus *Diglossopis* (R&G).

GLISTENING-GREEN TANAGER
Chlorochrysa phoenicotis Pl. 261

Identification 12.5–13.5cm. Adult male emerald-green, with grey tufts below eyes, grey, orange-tipped tufts behind eyes, and brilliant grey wing-coverts (often hidden). Adult female slightly duller. Subadult (possibly juvenile) dull green and lacks grey patches. All somewhat similar species are considerably duller (e.g. female Green Honeycreeper, Emerald Tanager, female and immature Multicoloured Tanager, immature Bay-headed and Rufous-winged Tanagers and various other immature *Tangara*).

Ssp. Monotypic (W Ec, W Co)

Habits Forages alone, in pairs or small flocks from higher understorey to canopy (where easily overlooked unless call known). Runs along limbs and gleans outer foliage for insects, fruits and berries, quite acrobatic. Almost always joins mixed-species flocks.
Status Uncommon in Ecuador, fairly common but very local in Colombia.
Habitat Tropical to Subtropical Zones, at 600–2,400m but

usually 1,000–1,500m, in very wet mossy and cloud forests, edges and mature second growth, sometimes in isolated large trees in adjacent clearings and pastures.
Voice Distinctive, high, weak, lisping *czee*, repeated 3–4 times, sometimes varied as *ee-see-seez-seez* or *tsi-tsi-tseeuw-tseeuw-tseeuw* in a short, descending series (H&B, I&I, R&G).

ORANGE-EARED TANAGER
Chlorochrysa calliparaea Pl. 261

Identification 12–13.5cm. Adult easily identified by emerald-green plumage with orange crown, orange rump and small orange patches bordering black (in male) or grey (in female) throat. Juvenile duller without orange or blue, yellowish eye-ring, buffy green-tipped throat-feathers and pale bill base (compare female Green Honeycreeper and various other immature *Tangara*).

Ssp. *C. c. bourcieri* (E Ec, C Co, W Ve)

Habits Forages alone, in pairs or small flocks from higher understorey to canopy (where easily overlooked unless call known). Runs along limbs and gleans outer foliage for insects, fruits and berries. Almost always joins mixed-species flocks.
Status Fairly common to locally common in Ecuador, fairly common in Colombia, with several sight records from San Isidro road, north-west Barinas, in western Venezuela (Hilty).
Habitat Tropical to Subtropical Zones, at 900–2,000m but usually 1,200–1,700m, in humid to wet mossy forests, cloud forests, edges and second growth, regularly in isolated large trees in adjacent clearings and pastures.
Voice A high, wheezy *seeep* or *tsip* (H&B, R&G).

MULTICOLOURED TANAGER
Chlorochrysa nitidissima Pl. 261

Identification 12–13cm. Adult male has yellow face and throat, gleaming green hindcrown and nape, black patches on neck-sides bordered by chestnut below, yellow mantle and greenish-blue rump, emerald-green wings and tail, bright blue underparts with black median breast and belly. Female similar but duller, lacking yellow mantle and black on underparts. If seen poorly, might be confused with Saffron-crowned Tanager, which has short black mask and black throat. Also compare immature Multicoloured Tanager, which is mostly dull green, to Glistening-green Tanager, female Green Honeycreeper and various other immature *Tangara*.

Ssp. Monotypic (W Co)

Habits Forages alone, in pairs or small flocks from higher understorey to canopy (where easily overlooked unless call known). Runs along limbs and gleans outer foliage for insects, fruits and berries. Almost always joins mixed-species flocks.
Status Vulnerable. Endemic to Colombia, in West and north Central Andes (Antioquia, Caldas, Risaralda, Quindío, Valle del Cauca and Cauca), with post-1951 records in Central Andes only from Ucumarí Regional Park, Risaralda, and near Anorí, Antioquia, and most modern records are from Valle del Cauca, West Andes. Formerly common, but now infrequently recorded because of continuing habitat loss in many parts of its range, notably, in the Cauca Valley, Cerro Tatamá, along the Buenaventura–Cali–Buga roads, and around Medellín, but remains fairly common locally, even in forest fragments.
Habitat Tropical to Subtropical Zones, at 900–2,200m but usually 1,400–2,000m, in humid to wet mossy and cloud forests, edges, mature second growth, and sometimes in isolated large trees in adjacent clearings and pastures.
Voice Calls include 1+ wheezing *ceeet* notes (H&B).

Tangara is the largest genus in the family, with many brightly-coloured small to medium-sized birds with complex and extremely varied plumage patterns. They are generally monomorphic, with several species travelling together in a feeding flock.

PLAIN-COLOURED TANAGER
Tangara inornata Pl. 261

Identification 12–12.2cm. Adult grey, paler below becoming white on belly, with dusky black lores, ocular region, wings and tail, and blue lesser wing-coverts (often hidden). Larger Blue-grey and Palm Tanagers lack white belly. Subadult has pale buff on belly and vent.

Ssp. *T. i. inornata* (N Co) as described
T. i. languens (NW Co) distinctly paler grey above (neutral grey vs. deep neutral grey), blue tinge on forehead and rump far less pronounced, throat and sides much paler grey with virtually no bluish tone

Habits Often flicks wings and tail. Forages rapidly and noisily in pairs or small flocks, usually in canopy. Looks for invertebrates and fruits, and sometimes joins mixed-species flocks.
Status Uncommon.
Habitat Tropical Zone, to 1,200m, rarely to 2,000m. Mostly in semi-open habitats, e.g. humid forest edges (especially beside water), lighter woodlands and second growth, gallery forest, shaded plantations, and isolated large trees in adjacent clearings and pastures.
Voice Series of high sibilant *tst* and *jeet* notes (often given rapidly and by many birds simultaneously), and sometimes a moderate-pitched kissing note and *tsrrr* when flying off. Song a series of *c.*15 notes delivered in *c.*2.5 s with pauses of equal duration, each series beginning with a few rapid sibilant *tsst* notes, but slows rather than accelerates (I&I).

TURQUOISE TANAGER
Tangara mexicana Pl. 261

Identification 12–14cm. Adult black on nape and back, wings and tail, also around bill, deep blue-violet on rump and uppertail-coverts, head-sides to breast and, in some races, on breast-sides and flanks; lesser wing-coverts turquoise-blue; underparts yellow with some black scalloping at sides; eyes brown, bill, legs and feet black. From distance looks black with yellow belly. Masked Tanager has paler blue hood, blue-green wing-coverts, darkish breast and white belly. Smaller White-bellied Dacnis mostly blue with white belly.

Ssp. *T. m. boliviana* (E Ec, E Co: western Amazonia) lesser wing-coverts more cerulean-blue, upper breast-sides rich yellow, forming small patch, broad swathe of violet-blue with black scallops runs from centre of breast to flanks and thighs

T. m. lateralis (extreme S Ve) forehead and head-sides and from central breast to flanks rich violet-blue, lesser wing-coverts and fringes of median coverts bright blue, breast-sides rich yellow with a few black spots distally and on rear flanks

T. m. media (E Co, S & E Ve) turquoise eyebrow, lesser wing-coverts bright turquoise, swathe of black scallops from breast to flanks with little violet-blue

T. m. mexicana (Guianas) faint turquoise eyebrow, very narrow yellow patch on breast-sides, belly to undertail-coverts pale to sulphur-yellow

T. m. vieilloti (Tr) blue of head and breast darker than *media*, more vivid and intense yellow below; turquoise in wing-coverts

Habits Forages noisily mostly in small flocks of up to 10, usually in canopy, but rarely joins mixed-species flocks.
Status Fairly common to common in Ecuador, fairly common in Colombia and Venezuela, common in Trinidad, Guyana, Suriname and French Guiana.
Habitat Tropical Zone, to 2,000m but usually below 600m, in humid *terra firme* and *várzea* (but rather rare in extensive forests), edges, open woodland, second growth, gallery forest, river islands, shaded plantations, parks, gardens and large trees and bushes in savannas.
Voice Calls include high, thin, chipping *tic* notes, often rapidly repeated or trilled, and often uttered by several individuals, especially as flock takes flight, thus a continuous twittering is heard (H&B, I&I, Hilty).
Notes Race *lateralis*, which occupies a significant range in northern Brazil, usually and confusingly recognised as being of hybrid origin (e.g. by I&I, either *media* × *mexicana* × *boliviana* or more simply *mexicana* × *boliviana*. We are not persuaded, as consistency of Venezuelan specimens clearly suggests that it is a valid race.

GREY-AND-GOLD TANAGER
Tangara palmeri Pl. 261

Identification 14.5–15cm. Quite unmistakable. Adult has complicated pattern of grey, with contrasting yellow and black: mantle moss-green, lower back to tail dark grey, scalloped lightly white, scapulars and wings black, with grey wash on lesser coverts, white fringes to median and greater coverts, tertials and remiges finely fringed white; top of head and neck grey, eyebrow, ear-coverts to chin and upper breast whitish, short black mask, pectoral band deep yellow, bordered above and below and scalloped at sides with black, rest of underparts mid grey; eyes brown, bill black, legs and feet vinaceous-grey. Juvenile similar but duller, and lacks black and yellow breast-band.

Ssp. Monotypic (W Ec, W Co)

Habits Forages noisily, mostly in pairs or small flocks of up to 8, from midstorey to canopy for fruits, berries and some invertebrates, and often joins mixed-species flocks.
Status Uncommon to locally fairly common in Ecuador, fairly common in Colombia.
Habitat Tropical Zone, to 1,100m (mostly above 300m), in humid to very wet forests and edges, often on steep hillsides, sometimes in second growth or large trees in adjacent clearings.
Voice Various musical and staccato notes, e.g. a frequently heard, loud, high and distinctive *chup, chup-sweeeeet* (last note rising), or any of these singly or repeated (H&B, I&I, R&G).

PARADISE TANAGER
Tangara chilensis Pl. 261

Identification 12–14cm. Adult unmistakable: black on nape, back, wings, uppertail-coverts and tail, central belly, vent and undertail-coverts, upper back bright crimson-red, rump bright rich yellow, full cowl (from forehead to crown surrounding eyes and ear-coverts to lower cheeks) grass green, eye-ring black, chin and throat deep ultramarine-blue, lesser wing-coverts, breast and flanks sea blue, median wing-coverts ultramarine-blue; eyes dark brown, bill, legs and feet black. Juvenile shows some key differences: lower back and rump ochre-yellow, lesser wing-coverts black as back, green head speckled slightly black, chin turquoise, blue of breast and flanks more turquoise with some black scalloping, legs and feet grey.

Ssp. *T. c. chilensis* (E Ec, SE Co) lower back and rump entirely bright crimson-red

T. c. coelicolor (E Co, S Ve) as described

T. c. paradisea (Guianas) lesser and median wing-coverts ultramarine as throat

Habits Noisily (constantly utters high *zeee* chirps) forages in small to large flocks of up to 20 (largest in non-breeding season, December–April) usually in canopy (lower at edges or in clearings) for fruits, berries and invertebrates, and sometimes joins mixed-species flocks.
Status Fairly common to common in Ecuador, common in Colombia, Venezuela and French Guiana, and uncommon (?) in Suriname.
Habitat Tropical Zone, to 1,700m but usually below 1,200m, in humid *terra firme* and *várzea*, edges, second growth, shaded plantations, or large trees in adjacent clearings.
Voice A sharp, moderate-pitched *chak* and high, thin, rising *zeee*, uttered singly, together or in an irregular series; also high, thin *sizit* given singly or in rapid series, or when taking flight. Dawn song a *chak-zeet* repeated every 2 s, but in Ecuador a high, upslurred *sweee?* repeated frequently, interspersed with lower pitched *tsut* notes (I&I, R&G, Hilty).

BLUE-WHISKERED TANAGER
Tangara johannae Pl. 261

Identification 13–13.5cm. Adult has forecrown to lower back black, feathers with greenish-yellow fringes producing a scaled appearance, rump greenish-yellow, uppertail-coverts black, subterminally blue with narrow greenish-yellow fringes, wings and tail similar but no blue in tertials; face to breast black with slight greenish-blue crescent from mid cheeks to mid ear-coverts (like a handlebar moustache), rest of underparts yellowish-green; eyes brown, bill black, legs and feet flesh-grey. Juvenile similar but lacks decorated black face, is paler scaled greenish above and pale greyish yellow-green from chin on down.

Ssp. Monotypic (NW Ec, W Co)

Habits Forages in pairs, usually in canopy, for fruits and invertebrates, and often joins mixed-species flocks.

Status Near Threatened. Rare to locally fairly common in Pacific lowlands from north Antioquia, Colombia, south through north-west Ecuador to Los Ríos. Although described as least numerous Pacific lowland *Tangara*, common in several parts of Nariño, Colombia, but its Chocó forests are threatened by rapid deforestation, with destruction most severe in its lowland habitats. As a result, probably now extinct south of north-west Pichincha and considered Vulnerable in Ecuador (R&G).

Habitat Tropical Zone, to 1,000m but usually below 800m, in humid to wet forest edges, adjacent clearings, and second growth around landslides, road edges and slashed clearings.

Voice A shrill, buzzy, very high *tzzeee* (H&B).

GREEN-AND-GOLD TANAGER

Tangara schrankii Pl. 261

Identification 12–14cm. Adult male mainly black above with bold yellow lower back and rump, feathers fringed bright green, rather bluish on wings and tail; top of head bright yellow, forehead black; ear-coverts and below black, neck-sides, lores, chin, basal malar, throat, breast-sides to flanks and thighs bright green, centre of breast, belly and undertail-coverts yellow; eyes brown, bill black, legs vinaceous. Female and subadult male similar but black-spotted nape extends to crown, becoming yellow only at point where black forehead starts, rump only slightly yellow-green. Juvenile has entire crown and nape concolorous with mantle, only hint of yellow on rump, and central underparts greenish-yellow instead of yellow.

Ssp. *T. s. schrankii* (E Ec, SE Co) yellow rump broader and pure (not washed slightly green), yellow patch more noticeable

T. s. venezuelana (S Venezuela) as described

Habits Forages in pairs or small flocks of up to 8 from midstorey to canopy (lower at edges or in fruiting trees, and sometimes with understorey flocks in forest). Often joins mixed-species flocks (especially with Paradise Tanager).

Status Fairly common to common in Ecuador, fairly common in Colombia, uncommon in Venezuela.

Habitat Tropical Zone, to 1,600m but usually below 1,100m, in humid *terra firme* and *várzea*, edges, second growth, sometimes in isolated large trees in adjacent coffee plantations, clearings and pastures.

Voice Calls include thin *chit* notes (Hilty).

EMERALD TANAGER

Tangara florida Pl. 261

Identification 12–13cm. Adult male has black back, with feathers fringed green, wings and tail black with yellowish fringes to median and greater coverts, forehead green, ear-coverts ochre, patch below ear-coverts black, chin dusky, throat to breast and flanks bright green, rest of underparts yellow; eyes brown, bill black, legs and feet grey. Female and subadult male duller, with green crown and paler yellow belly. Juvenile has yellowish-green head and underparts pale greenish-yellow, washed green.

Ssp. Monotypic (W Co, NW Ec)

Habits Often searches moss-covered limbs. Forages alone, in pairs or small flocks at all levels but usually in canopy. Searches for fruits, berries, invertebrates and a few flowers. Often joins mixed-species flocks.

Status Locally uncommon to fairly common but somewhat local (because of habitat preference), suffering locally from deforestation.

Habitat Tropical Zone, 100–1,200m, in very wet, mossy cloud forests and edges, sometimes in second growth, but rarely in isolated large trees in adjacent clearings and pastures.

Voice A sharp *tsit* and raspy, penetrating, moderate- to high-pitched *jree* or *dzreee*, even burrier than Golden or Silver-throated Tanagers, and repeated randomly or sometimes accelerated as a twitter. Probable song involves burry high *zeeeeeee* notes repeated regularly with 3-s pauses, lasting 2–3 minutes (H&B, I&I).

GOLDEN TANAGER

Tangara arthus Pl. 262

Identification 13–14cm. Considerable racial variation, but black ear-coverts on golden-yellow head good field mark, black-streaked back, black wings with feathers fringed yellow, and black tail constant in all races. Eyes brown, bill black, legs and feet grey.

Ssp. *T. a. aequatorialis* (E Ec) throat and foreneck washed dull orange-rufous grading into golden-yellow belly (some have more brownish throat), larger than *goodsoni*, with more extensive black lores and chin spot, green fringes to wing-feathers, tinged orange on head

T. a. arthus (N & E Ve) mostly black above with yellow fringes to back, wings and uppertail-coverts, golden lower back and rump, entire head golden with black ear-coverts, underparts chestnut, with yellow belly; juvenile has black-streaked nape to crown, back and rump washed dull brown, underparts largely washed brown, centre of belly yellowish

T. a. aurulenta (C Co, NW Ve) underparts same golden-yellow as head; juvenile has black-streaked crown to nape and lower back and rump, underparts from breast washed dull brown

T. a. goodsoni (W Ec) clean bright yellow head and body; some have brownish throat

T. a. occidentalis (W Co) top of head distinctly orange, underparts washed cinnamon

T. a. palmitae (C Co) like *goodsoni* but has much smaller bill, stripes on back green; less orange than *aurulenta*

T. a. sclateri (E Co) broad yellow streaks on back, entire underparts rich cinnamon

Habits Forages for fruits, invertebrates (often on mossy limbs) and flowers, alone, in pairs or small flocks of up to 6 (rarely 30). Usually from midstorey to canopy, and often joins mixed-species flocks.

Status Common.

Habitat Tropical to Subtropical Zones, 550–2,500m but usually 1,000–2,000m, in humid to wet mossy forests (especially cloud forests) and shrubby edges, sometimes in second growth or large trees in adjacent clearings and pastures.

Voice A slightly buzzy, penetrating high *seet* when foraging, less buzzy than Silver-throated or Emerald Tanagers; also a short *tsk*, smacking *chup* and various moderate-pitched, chipping, staccato phrases, e.g. *CHID-it, CHID-id-id-it* or *CHID-id-id-it chup*, usually pausing 2–6 s between phrases, and during longer pauses utters single sharp moderate- to high-pitched *tsick* notes (H&B, I&I, R&G, Hilty).

SILVER-THROATED TANAGER

Tangara icterocephala Pl. 262

Identification 13–13.5cm. Adult almost entirely yellow, with black wings and tail, black-streaked back, yellow fringes to black feathers, a black line like a moustache from lores under cheeks and ear-coverts, bordering silvery white throat; eyes brown, bill black, legs and feet grey. Female slightly duller; juvenile lacks white throat and is duller yellow and dull dark brown instead of black, washed greyish-brown over most of body. Adult should be unmistakable, from Golden Tanager by black-bordered white throat and absence of black ear-patch. Dingy immature may be confused, but usually shows some faint adult markings.

Ssp. *T. i. icterocephala* (W Ec, W Co)

Habits Forages noisily at all levels for fruits and invertebrates (often on mossy limbs). Sometimes alone or in pairs, but usually in flocks of up to 15; often joins mixed-species flocks.

Status Uncommon to locally fairly common in Ecuador, common in Colombia.

Habitat Tropical to Subtropical Zones, at 150–2,100m but usually 500–1,300m, in wet forests, edges and mature second growth, sometimes in large trees in adjacent clearings.

Voice A distinctive harsh buzzy moderate-pitched *schreet* or *jjeut*, or high, insect-like, slightly upward-inflected *bzeeet*, harsher than Emerald or Golden Tanagers, and often given in flight; also a high *tic*; all notes may be paired but not given in a series (H&B, I&I, R&G).

SAFFRON-CROWNED TANAGER

Tangara xanthocephala Pl. 262

Identification 12.5–13.5cm. Adult has almost entire body pale beryl-green, with yellow head and belly to undertail-coverts; black-streaked back and black wing- and tail-feathers all fringed beryl-green; short black mask from forehead and chin to just beyond eyes with black line from chin below cheeks to encircle head; eyes dark brown, bill black, legs and feet grey. Juvenile mostly dingy greyish-green, with faint beryl-green rump and yellowish head, centre of breast to undertail-coverts buffy.

Ssp. *T. x. venusta* (Ec, Co, W Ve)

Habits Forages for fruits and berries and some invertebrates, alone, in pairs or flocks of up to 25. Occurs at all levels but usually in canopy, and often joins mixed-species flocks.

Status Fairly common, but rare to uncommon on west slope of Andes in Ecuador.

Habitat Tropical to Subtropical Zones, at 1,100–2,400m (most numerous in upper elevational range, and once at 3,150m in Colombia). In humid to wet mossy and cloud forests, but usually at edges and in mature second growth, sometimes in shaded plantations and large trees in adjacent clearings and pastures.

Voice A high *chit* or *tsit* repeated at short intervals when foraging, extended into a rapid series when excited. Probable song a short series of high squeaky notes (I&I, Hilty).

GOLDEN-EARED TANAGER

Tangara chrysotis Pl. 262

Identification 14cm. Male has back, wings and tail black, finely fringed beryl-green, lower back to uppertail-coverts, breast and flanks beryl-green; crown to nape black, forehead to neck-sides and ear-coverts yellow-orange, lores to chin and short thick malar that runs below ear-coverts black; throat pale yellow, centre of lower breast to undertail-coverts rufescent cinnamon; eyes brown, bill black, legs and feet grey. Female is but a pallid version above, chin to flanks beryl-green, vent to undertail-coverts pale greenish-buffy. Juvenile lacks black markings on head, has dark wings and tail with beryl fringes as female, beryl-green from forehead to neck-sides, with dark streaks from crown to nape, head-sides yellowish, chin to undertail-coverts pastel beryl-green, suffused buffy from centre of breast to vent.

Ssp. Monotypic (E Ec, S Co)

Habits Forages usually alone or in pairs but sometimes in small flocks, from midstorey to canopy for fruits, berries and invertebrates (often on mossy limbs), and often joins mixed-species flocks.

Status Uncommon to locally fairly common in Ecuador, fairly common in Colombia (though somewhat less common in Upper Magdalena Valley, where only found above 1,700m).

Habitat Tropical to Subtropical Zones, at 850–2,400m but usually above 1,100 m, in humid to wet forests, edges and mature second growth, sometimes in large trees in adjacent clearings.

Voice A *tsuck* that is lower pitched than most other *Tangara*. Song in captivity a series of high hissing and rattling notes (I&I).

FLAME-FACED TANAGER

Tangara parzudakii Pl. 262

Identification 14–15cm. Adult has black back, wings and tail, lesser wing-coverts with pale green tips, median coverts have solid pale blue tips forming a wingbar, greater coverts have blue distal outer fringes, tail-coverts broadly fringed bright blue; lower back to rump pale sulphate green, top of head to nape, with line around neck-sides bright yellow, forecrown, cheeks and ear-coverts blood red, lores, eye-ring, small patch behind eyes and irregular line bordering ear-coverts to bib, black; breast to flanks pale sulphate green becoming yellowish on central belly, whole rather opalescent, then ochre on vent and undertail-coverts; eyes brown, bill black, legs and feet vinaceous-grey. Juvenile has black streaks from top of head to mantle, wings and tail weaker version of adult, head ochraceous-yellow where adult red, with vestigial black marks; whitish throat, rest of underparts buffy, streaked vaguely beryl-green.

Ssp. *T. p. lunigera* (W Ec, W Co) smaller and quite distinct; with yellow-orange forecrown and lower cheeks, less extensive yellow on hindneck, narrow yellow patch on neck-sides that joins yellow scapulars, duller and less opalescent underparts

T. p. parzudakii (E Ec, C & E Co, SW Ve) larger, with red forecrown and lower cheeks; subadult has orange-yellow ear-coverts, forehead admixed blackish and less iridescent green underparts

Habits Forages rather lethargically, despite being quite active, usually in pairs or small flocks at all levels but principally from midstorey to canopy. Searches for fruits, berries and invertebrates, often on mossy limbs, in lichen tufts and hanging mossy clumps, and almost always joins mixed-species flocks.

Status Fairly common in Ecuador and Colombia, but only a few records from south-west Venezuela.

Habitat Tropical to Subtropical Zones, 700–2,500m but usually above 1,500m, mostly in humid to wet mossy cloud forests, only sometimes at edges and in second growth and large trees in adjacent clearings and pastures.

Voice High, sharp *chit!* notes that sometimes run into a short twittering trill (a possible song), and a *seeet* call reminiscent of Golden Tanager (I&I, Hilty).

YELLOW-BELLIED TANAGER

Tangara xanthogastra Pl. 262

Identification 11–12.7cm. Adult emerald-green with black centres to feathers of upper body, wings and tail, except yellow belly and undertail-coverts; eyes brown, bill dark grey, legs and feet pale grey. Similar Spotted Tanager has greyer face and throat and white on breast; Speckled Tanager has yellow forehead and turquoise-tinged white underparts.

Ssp. *T. x. phelpsi* (S Ve) slightly larger, and noticeably yellow below

T. x. xanthogastra (E Ec, E Co, S Ve) as described

Habits Forages alone, in pairs or small flocks, usually from midstorey to canopy (lower at edges) for fruits and invertebrates, and often joins mixed-species flocks.

Status Uncommon to locally fairly common in Ecuador, uncommon in Colombia and Venezuela (*xanthogastra*), except on tepuis (*phelpsi*) where locally common.

Habitat Tropical Zone, to 1,350m but usually below 1,100m (*xanthogastra*) or at 1,000–1,800 m (*phelpsi*), mostly in humid *terra firme* and *várzea*, less often at shrubby edges and in mature second growth and large trees in adjacent clearings; *phelpsi* mostly in humid forests and especially in mossy, Melastome-dominated second growth on sandy soils.

Voice Calls include weak *chit* and *seet* notes (Hilty).

Note Races *phelpsi* and *xanthogastra* may be separate species (Hilty).

SPOTTED TANAGER

Tangara punctata Pl. 262

Identification 11–13cm. A green and white bird heavily spotted blackish. Mostly black above with grass-green fringes to all feathers, except rump and uppertail-coverts which are entirely grass-green, face greyish with black at base of bill, top of head flushed turquoise, breast and sides also black with broad white fringes, becoming all white on central belly and vent, flanks to undertail-coverts pale apple-green; eyes brown, bill black, legs and feet grey. Adult often confused with Speckled Tanager which has yellowish (not greyish-turquoise) head and turquoise (not green) wing fringes, lacks yellowish-green flanks and usually at higher elevations (where Spotted Tanager rather uncommon). Also see Yellow-bellied Tanager.

Ssp. *T. p. punctata* (S Ve, Guianas) as described

T. p. zamorae (E Ec) larger, primary-coverts and primaries fringed green instead of blue

Habits Active, with quick movements as it forages for fruits, berries and invertebrates. Alone, in pairs or small flocks, usually in canopy but lower at edges and in fruiting shrubs. Often joins mixed-species flocks.

Status Fairly common in Ecuador (and may occur in Colombia), uncommon in Venezuela, fairly common in Suriname, uncommon but widespread in French Guiana.

Habitat Tropical Zone, to 1,700m but usually below 1,500m in Ecuador and 1,100m in Venezuela, in humid forests (especially *terra firme* in Amazonia and mossy forests in Andes), edges and mature second growth, sometimes in large trees in adjacent clearings, in Suriname also in savanna forests.

Voice A high, dry *chip* delivered in rapid staccato manner, which becomes an even-pitched, chipping trill (I&I).

SPECKLED TANAGER

Tangara guttata Pl. 262

Identification 12–13.5cm. Adult bright green above, yellowish-green on head, more yellowish on forehead/eyebrow, lores black, black centres to all feathers from forecrown to rump with broad green fringes, wings and tail black with broad turquoise fringes to wing-feathers, green on tail; chin to belly white, small black lines on throat become semi-circular spots on malar and 'teardrops' on breast, fading to streaks on upper belly, flanks green, vent to undertail-coverts yellow. Female similar but yellow-green of forehead and eyebrow less extensive. Subadult female is duller. Adult often confused with

Spotted or Yellow-bellied Tanagers, which have green heads and yellow or green underparts.

Ssp. *T. g. bogotensis* (E Co, W Ve) as described
T. g. chrysophrys (Ve) adult bright yellow-green above, with yellow forehead and eyebrow/eye-ring more pronounced; juvenile dull yellowish-green above, washed dingy yellowish below, with streaks instead of spots
T. g. guttata (SE Ve) above like *bogotensis*, below like *chrysophrys* but throat unmarked, black spots below smaller
T. g. tolimae (C Co) like *bogotensis*, but throat and breast much more heavily spotted; undertail-coverts have broad black shaft-streaks
T. g. trinitatis (Tr) like *chrysophrys* but deeper golden-yellow on forehead and eyebrow, larger spots both above and below, including on throat

Habits Forages in canopy, coming lower at edges for fruits, berries and invertebrates. Pairs or small flocks of up to 8; often joins mixed-species flocks.
Status Fairly common in Colombia and Trinidad, common in Venezuela, collected once in Suriname (H&M) and also sighted there. Rare sight records in central French Guiana.
Habitat Tropical to Subtropical Zones, at 1,000–1,800m in Colombia and 400–2,000m in Venezuela (mainly above 500m in Trinidad), in humid forests, edges, shrubby second growth, light woodland, shaded plantations, and large trees in adjacent clearings.
Voice High, clear, weak twittering and chipping notes, e.g. somewhat metallic, bell-like *tit*, *chit* or *tit-a-chit*, often accelerated into a rapid trill on taking flight (H&B, I&I, Hilty).

DOTTED TANAGER *Tangara varia* Pl. 262

Identification 11–11.5cm. Adult male bright-green with black lores, turquoise wings and tail, and very faint spots on crown, throat and breast (hard to see in field). Adult female entirely green (albeit paler and more yellowish, especially on belly) with very faint spots or completely lacks them. Easily confused with adults of similar Yellow-bellied, Spotted and Speckled Tanagers, or female Blue Dacnis, but especially with immatures of these species (and other *Tangara*, e.g. Bay-headed and Green-and-gold Tanagers). Best to look for combination of small size, greenish underparts and blue wings (male only).

Ssp. Monotypic (E Co, S Ve, Guianas)

Habits Forages alone or in pairs, usually from midstorey to canopy, for fruits and invertebrates. Almost always joins mixed-species flocks.
Status Uncommon to fairly common in Venezuela, with an old and poorly documented record from Suriname (H&M), and also recorded in a few central and northern localities in French Guiana (Tostain *et al.*).
Habitat Tropical Zone, to 300m, in humid forest, edges, second growth, and clearings along rivers.
Voice Unknown.

RUFOUS-THROATED TANAGER
Tangara rufigula Pl. 262

Identification 12cm. Small and quite distinct tanager. Adult black above with golden-green scales on back, golden-green lower back and rump, black wings and tail with silvery-green fringes, chin, throat and malar reddish-rufous, rest of underparts greenish-yellow with conspicuous blackish spots, becoming white on belly and pale yellow-buff on undertail-coverts.

Ssp. Monotypic (NW Ec, W Co)

Habits Forages in pairs or small flocks, usually high, looking for fruits, berries, invertebrates, and some flowers and buds. Often joins mixed-species flocks.
Status Locally fairly common in Ecuador, fairly common to common in Colombia.
Habitat Tropical to Subtropical Zones, 400–2,100m, in wet mossy cloud forest, shrubby edges, second growth, favouring broken forest, with small openings, on steep slopes.
Voice Calls include excited bursts of ticking and twittering, e.g. *tic-ti-ti-ti-ti…*, especially in flight. Song a stuttered high chatter (H&B, R&G).

BAY-HEADED TANAGER
Tangara gyrola Pl. 263

Identification 12–14cm. Generally green above with yellow on nape and shoulder, head bay or chestnut, blue and green below. Juvenile lacks bay head and is pale green below. Eyes dark brown, bill brown, legs and feet horn to grey. Adult unmistakable, but compare Rufous-winged Tanager which even in juveniles usually has some rufous in wings (overlap on Pacific slope of Andes in western Colombia and north-west Ecuador, where usually at lower elevations), female Blue-naped Chlorophonia and Glistening-green Tanager. Subadult and juvenile are green with rufous-tinged face and have blue-tinged underparts in those subspecies with blue underparts; easily confused with female Green Honeycreeper which has thinner bill, and with immature Rufous-cheeked Tanager which usually has rufous-tinged cheeks and vent.

Ssp. *T. g. catharinae* (E Ec, E Co) conspicuous golden nuchal band and shoulders, deep bay-coloured head, blue from throat to vent, green undertail-coverts
T. g. deleticia (N Co) brighter on rear head, only small touch of yellow on neck-sides otherwise like *catharinae*
T. g. gyrola (S Ve, Guianas) narrow yellow nuchal band, yellow on shoulder, pale blue breast and belly
T. g. nupera (W Ec, SW Co) bright, paler head, narrow pale nuchal line, faint yellowish on shoulder, pale blue throat to flanks
T. g. parva (SE Co, S Ve) slightly smaller, conspicuous golden nuchal band and shoulders, crown to nape dark brown, medium blue throat to flanks
T. g. toddi (N Co, N Ve) narrow yellow nuchal band, weak yellow on shoulders, all green below; from

viridissima by paler rufous head, underparts brighter, less bluish-green, bill slightly longer
T. g. viridissima (NW Ve, Tr) narrow yellow nuchal band, green rump and underparts

Habits Forages deliberately, alone, in pairs or small flocks from midstorey to canopy (lower at edges and in fruiting trees). Hunts for fruits, berries, invertebrates (mostly on larger bare limbs), and some flowers and buds. Often joins mixed-species flocks.
Status Uncommon to fairly common in Ecuador and Colombia, common in Trinidad and Venezuela, with some minor seasonal or local parts of Suriname, but rare in lowlands, and uncommon but widespread in French Guiana.
Habitat Tropical to Subtropical Zones, to 2,100m and usually above 300m, in humid to wet *terra firme* and *várzea* (more common in former), edges, second growth and shaded plantations, sometimes in large trees in adjacent clearings, pastures and gardens.
Voice A thin, buzzy, nasal *seeaawee*, falling then rising in pitch, a short, scratchy, high *tssit*, also twitters and coarse *shree* often in flight. Song in Trinidad a slow *seee, seee, seee, tsou tsooy*, with last 2 notes lower (H&B, ffrench, I&I, Hilty).
Note Some races may prove to be specifically distinct (I&I).

RUFOUS-WINGED TANAGER
Tangara lavinia Pl. 263

Identification 12–13.2cm. Yellow nuchal band grades into pale green back, with tertials and tail slightly darker, wings largely rufous-chestnut from shoulder to secondaries, top and sides of head bright rufous-chestnut, chin to undertail-coverts green with blue flush on centre from chin to vent; eyes dark brown, bill brown above, yellowish-horn below, legs and feet vinaceous -grey. Juvenile has top of head to mantle dark, scaled green, wings weaker rufous, undertail-coverts yellow, otherwise similar to adult. Always shows some rufous in wings (compare Glistening-green and Bay-headed Tanagers, and female Green Honeycreeper).

Ssp. *T. l. lavinia* (NW Ec, W Co)

Habits Similar to Bay-headed Tanager, but somewhat more active and noisy.
Status Uncommon to locally common in Ecuador, fairly common in Colombia.
Habitat Tropical Zone, to 1,000m but usually below 500m, in humid to wet forests, edges and second growth, sometimes in large trees in adjacent clearings.
Voice A weak *tst*, sometimes given almost constantly, and a hummingbird-like, staccato, moderate- to high-pitched *deet-a-deet-a* and *deet deet deet* in flight. Possible song in Costa Rica is a weak, lisped, high *see'tsir, tzi'rtsir, tsi'rtsir* (H&B, I&I).

BURNISHED-BUFF TANAGER
Tangara cayana Pl. 263

Identification 13–14cm. Adult male has entire body, except black mask, wings and tail, creamy yellow, washed orange or tawny on head, blue, lavender or violet on throat and breast, and buffy undertail-coverts; feathers of wings and tail have pale blue fringes, but vary in tone. Plumage lustrous, with much individual variation in all races. Female and immature duller and more greyish-green, but still retain male's pertinent characters. Juvenile dull brown on nape, back, wings and tail, rest of body drab with some hues of adult plumage. Adult male easily distinguished by combination of straw-coloured plumage, black mask and habitat (but note that highly iridescent plumage may vary according to light). Somewhat similar Scrub Tanager has better-defined rufous crown and is even duller and more greenish; may soon overlap in north-east Colombia if continues to spread.

Ssp. *T. c. cayana* (E Co, S Ve, Guianas) as described
T. c. fulvescens (C Co) similar to *cayana* but larger and paler, more silvery and less buffy throughout

Habits Forages alone or in pairs, but sometimes in small flocks, at all levels in shrubs and trees, mostly for fruits, berries and seeds, and a few insects. Rarely joins mixed-species flocks but regularly attends feeding aggregations at fruiting trees.
Status Fairly common in Colombia, common in Venezuela, Suriname and French Guiana, with some seasonal or local migrations, probably in response to fruit availability.
Habitat Tropical to Subtropical Zones, to 2,500m but mostly below 1200m (locally higher in Venezuela), in drier semi-open habitats, e.g. savannas and ranchlands with scattered vegetation, second growth, gallery and open woodland edges, palm groves, and in gardens or around ranch buildings in *llanos*.
Voice A squeaky, moderate- to high-pitched *tsweek* and buzzy abrupt *tzzit*. Song consists of accelerating alternation of these 2 call notes, becoming a pulsating, buzzing, thin, high trill *sizza'sizza'sizza'…*, consisting of 10+ notes lasting 2–5 s (H&B, I&I, Hilty).
Note Also called Rufous-crowned Tanager.

SCRUB TANAGER
Tangara vitriolina Pl. 263

Identification 14cm. Adult violaceous-grey above, bright pale violet on rump, uppertail-coverts pale blue, wings and tail black with bluish to violet fringes, top of head rufous; black mask, throat violet, breast and flanks blue, belly cream, lower flanks to undertail-coverts warm pinkish-buffy; paler fringes to most body-feathers lend subtle mottling or scaling; eyes brown, bill, legs and feet grey. Juvenile has same pattern and markings but all softer and paler. Adult rather similar to Burnished-buff Tanager, but colours darker and more intense.

Ssp. Monotypic (NW Ec, W & C Co)

Habits Similar to Burnished-buff Tanager, but apparently feeds more on invertebrates.
Status Fairly common in Ecuador and common in Colombia. Spreading into deforested, previously humid forest areas, and will possibly reach Venezuela soon.
Habitat Tropical to Temperate Zones, at 300–3,000m but usually 1,000–2,200m, in drier semi-open habitats, e.g. overgrown pastures and other areas with scattered vegetation, open woodland, shaded plantations, and trees and shrubby vegetation around habitation.

Voice A shrill, buzzy *ziit* (H&B).
Note Sometimes considered to be possibly a subspecies of Burnished-buff Tanager (H&B).

RUFOUS-CHEEKED TANAGER
Tangara rufigenis Pl. 263

Identification 12–13cm. Adult dark bluish-grey from rear crown to back, feathers fringed paler, rump and uppertail-coverts pale blue, wings and tail blackish with bright fringes, pale blue fringes to lesser wing-coverts, duller greenish-blue to greater coverts, rufescent fringes to tertials and remiges, pale greyish-blue fringes to rectrices; mask clearly defined and bright rufous, bordered above by bright green, which surrounds ear-coverts and covers breast to flanks, central belly pale to whitish, becoming warm creamy buff from vent to undertail-coverts; eyes and bill dark brown, legs and feet vinaceous-grey. Female similar but with less blue on back of head.

Ssp. Monotypic (N Ve)

Habits Forages from midstorey to canopy, coming lower at edges for fruits, berries and invertebrates. Alone, in pairs or small flocks of up to 8. Often joins mixed-species flocks.
Status Endemic to Venezuela where uncommon (but regularly seen near pass on Rancho Grande road in Henri Pittier National Park, Aragua), perhaps moving downslope during wet season, May–September.
Habitat Tropical to Lower Subtropical Zones, 900–2,050m, in wet forests and edges, especially in disturbed or landslide areas with many Melastome trees and shrubs.
Voice Unknown.

GOLDEN-NAPED TANAGER
Tangara ruficervix Pl. 263

Identification 11.5–13cm. Adult male almost entirely rich blue, paler on lesser wing-coverts, wings and tail black with blue fringes, hindcrown bright yellow, bordered black, centre of belly to undertail-coverts bright yellow; eyes brown, bill black, legs and feet grey. Female similar but hindcrown patch smaller. Immature turquoise-blue above with dark crown, greyish-dusky mantle, and greyish below with buffy belly and vent. Juvenile has grey on crown and nape, and is pale grey below. May be confused with Metallic-green Tanager (different head and wing pattern), Blue-and-black Tanager (different head and wing pattern, and all-blue underparts), male Black-capped Tanager (different-coloured underparts) and male Swallow Tanager (for black throat and white belly).

Ssp. *T. r. leucotis* (W Ec) deeper and more intense blue, hindcrown patch rufescent, smaller and duller on female
T. r. ruficervix (Co) paler blue above and below, hindcrown patch deep orange on male with some blue on forecrown, paler, duller and smaller in female, and black mask quite apparent; white belly; juvenile warm grey to blackish above with dull violaceous-grey fringes, sides of face and rump violaceous-grey, greyish on breast gradually becoming dull creamy yellow distally
T. r. taylori (E Ec, SE Co) as described

Habits Forages alone, in pairs or small flocks from midstorey to canopy, for fruits, berries, seeds and invertebrates (often on larger bare limbs, but also in twigs and foliage). Often joins mixed-species flocks.
Status Uncommon to fairly common in Ecuador, fairly common in Colombia.
Habitat Tropical to Subtropical Zones, at 900–2,400m but usually above 1,500m, in humid to wet forests, edges, second growth, and large trees in adjacent clearings.
Voice Unknown.

METALLIC-GREEN TANAGER
Tangara labradorides Pl. 263

Identification 11.5–13cm. Adult mostly lustrous silvery blue-green (usually appears quite pale but note that iridescent plumage can vary in colour), with diagnostic broad black stripe from centre of crown to mid nape, and a small black mask and chin, forehead greenish-golden; central belly whitish, undertail-coverts creamy yellow, eyes brown, bill black and legs and feet grey. Juvenile duller, with central underparts yellowish-white tinged grey. Blue-browed Tanager has green-blue supercilium behind eyes, distinct black forehead and black back. Beryl-spangled Tanager has black back and lacks stripe on back of head. Male Black-capped Tanager has all-black crown, no supercilium, and bluish wings, whilst female has entirely dusky crown, no supercilium, and greenish wings.

Ssp. *T. l. chaupensis* (SE Ec) markedly more opal-green, especially on foreneck and lesser wing-coverts, with less golden sheen on forehead
T. l. labradorides (W Ec, W Co) more opal-blue

Habits Forages in pairs or small flocks at all levels for fruits and invertebrates. Often joins mixed-species flocks.
Status Rare to locally fairly common in Ecuador, locally common in Colombia.
Habitat Tropical to Subtropical Zones, at 500–2,400m but usually 1,300–2,000m, in humid forests, edges and second growth, and in large trees in adjacent clearings (less forest-based than most congeners).
Voice A moderate- to high-pitched, coarse *jitt*, squeaky high *eeek*, a wheeze and ticking twitter given in flight (H&B, F&K, I&I).

BLUE-BROWED TANAGER
Tangara cyanotis Pl. 263

Identification 11–12.2cm. Adult mostly silvery blue-green (brighter than Metallic-green Tanager) with black back, silvery blue-green lesser wing-coverts, greater wing-coverts broadly tipped pale blue, forming bold wingbar; diagnostic, conspicuous silvery blue-green supercilium behind eyes completely surrounded by black; central belly cream, undertail-coverts warm ochraceous. Female is duller with 2 narrow wingbars. Beryl-spangled Tanager lacks supercilium and has spotted underparts. Male Black-capped Tanager has all-black crown, no supercilium, and bluish wings, whilst female has entirely dusky crown, no supercilium, and greenish wings.

Male Black-faced Dacnis has yellow eyes, blue crown and much thinner bill. Compare also Metallic-green Tanager.

Ssp. *T. c. lutleyi* (E Ec, S Co)

Habits Forages in pairs, sometimes alone or in small flocks in canopy, for fruits and invertebrates, and sometimes joins mixed-species flocks.
Status Uncommon to locally fairly common in Ecuador, uncommon in Colombia (except in Cueva de los Guácharos National Park where fairly common).
Habitat Tropical to Subtropical Zones, 1,400–2,200m, in humid to wet mossy forests and edges, and wooded ravines.
Voice Calls similar to congeners

BLUE-NECKED TANAGER
Tangara cyanicollis Pl. 264

Identification 12–13cm. Four rather different races, but all have blue head with black lores and short line through eyes, golden wing-patch contrasts strongly with black back and breast (and some or all underparts). Female has paler blue head with black scallops reaching nape. Juvenile mostly brownish-grey above, with pale lemon rump, much paler below, with hint of adult colours on ear-coverts and wing-fringes. In subadult stages, yellow wing-patch appears and black on mantle, with some mottled black on body and a little blue on head. Adult should be unmistakable, but compare Golden-masked Tanager (golden hood and white belly), Masked Tanager (paler head and white belly), and male Scarlet-thighed Dacnis (red eye and much thinner bill).

Ssp. *T. c. caeruleocephala* (E Ec, Co) face indigo-blue, paler on crown and upper ear-coverts, back black, rump and uppertail-coverts creamy yellow, as are wing-coverts (greater coverts lemon-yellow), underparts black, becoming bluish on flanks and greyish on vent and undertail-coverts

T. c. cyanopygia (W Ec) black on back and breast, yellow lesser and median coverts only, lower back to uppertail-coverts, belly and flanks blue, vent to undertail-coverts green

T. c. granadensis (C Co) like *caeruleocephala* but pale green rump and tail-coverts, greater coverts black, broadly fringed yellow

T. c. hannahiae (E Co, NW Ve) lower back opalescent, rump pale yellow, uppertail-coverts greenish-yellow, chin and throat violaceous, rest of underparts black

Habits Forages noisily for fruits, berries and some flower buds and invertebrates at all levels. Usually in pairs but sometimes alone or in small flocks. Occasionally joins mixed-species flocks and feeding aggregations at fruiting trees.
Status Common in Ecuador and Colombia, uncommon to fairly common in Venezuela, spreading due to deforestation.
Habitat Tropical to Subtropical Zones, at 100–2,400m but usually 300–1,800m (above 1,000m in Andes), in semi-open habitats, e.g. humid forest edge, lighter woodland, second growth, shaded plantations, bushy pastures, and partially cultivated areas and gardens; essentially a non-forest tanager absent from very humid and arid regions.
Voice A weak *chip*, high *seet* and complaining moderate-pitched *che*, which may be rapidly repeated and followed by a louder *chep* or *seep* (I&I, Hilty).

GOLDEN-HOODED TANAGER
Tangara larvata Pl. 264

Identification 12–13cm. Adult has black back and pale blue lower back to rump, wings and tail, black tertials, remiges and uppertail-coverts fringed pale, scapulars, lesser and median wing-coverts fringed pale blue; head golden-orange with small black mask, edged turquoise that blends into gold; breast and sides black, flanks pale turquoise-blue, belly white, undertail-coverts yellowish; eyes brown, bill black, legs and feet vinaceous-grey. Juvenile greyish above, darker on wings and tail, with soft blue tones to lesser and median wing-coverts, emergent black mask; entire underparts whitish, sulphur-yellow wash on sides with hint of grey flammulations on sides and breast, and cinnamon-tinged rear underparts. Adult has diagnostic golden hood with small black and blue face mask, but overall pattern similar to Grey-and-gold and Blue-necked Tanagers.

Ssp. *T. l. fanny* (NW Ec, W Co)

Habits Forages noisily for fruits, berries and some flower buds and invertebrates at all levels. Usually in pairs but sometimes alone or in small flocks. Occasionally joins mixed-species flocks and feeding aggregations at fruiting trees.
Status Uncommon to fairly common in Ecuador, common in Colombia.
Habitat Tropical Zone, to 1,800m but usually below 500m in Ecuador and below 1,100m in Colombia, in semi-open habitats, e.g. humid forest edge, lighter woodland, second growth, shaded plantations, bushy pastures, and partially cultivated areas and gardens.
Voice A weak, sharp, moderate- to high-pitched, dry or buzzy *dzit* or *tsip*, often repeated rapidly, especially in flight, and sometimes accelerated into a trill of clearer metallic *tik* or *tsick* notes (probable song); also a dry chatter and wheezy *nyaaa* (H&B, I&I, R&G).
Notes Also called Golden-hooded Tanager. Considered conspecific with Masked Tanager by some authors (e.g. H&B).

MASKED TANAGER
Tangara nigrocincta Pl. 264

Identification 12–13cm. Adult has black mantle, blue lesser wing-coverts, lower back to uppertail-coverts, rest of wings black with broad greenish-blue fringes to median and greater coverts, and secondaries almost obscuring base colour); entire head rich turquoise becoming almost purplish-blue on nape, small black mask; breast and sides black becoming deep purplish-blue on upper flanks then turquoise, belly to vent white, undertail-coverts black with broad white fringes. Juvenile significantly duller above; grey breast and flanks to undertail-coverts. Overall pattern similar to Turquoise and Blue-necked Tanagers. Smaller White-bellied Dacnis is mostly blue with white belly and much thinner bill.

Ssp. Monotypic (E Ec, E Co, S Ve, Gu)

Habits Similar to Blue-necked Tanager.

Status Uncommon to locally fairly common in Ecuador, uncommon and local in Colombia and Venezuela.

Habitat Tropical Zone, to 1,400 m but usually at 300–900 m, mostly in semi-open habitats, e.g. humid forest edge, lighter woodland, second growth, shaded plantations, shrubby pastures and clearings, and partially cultivated areas and gardens, sometimes in canopy of *terra firme* and *várzea*.

Voice A dry chatter, and high *tsit* or *chit* notes, sometimes accelerated into short trills *tsit tsit-it-it-it-it*, or bursts of high, staccato ticking notes with gravelly quality, sometimes ending with 3 wheezy moderate-pitched *cheou* notes. Song a complex series of weak, jumbled notes followed by buzzy or sibilant, very high trill, or consists of 3 wheezy high *tseeee* whistles, with last note slurred to moderate pitch, lasting *c.*3 s and repeated after a pause interspersed with several *tsit* notes (I&I, R&G, Hilty).

Notes Also called Black-banded Tanager. Considered conspecific with Golden-masked Tanager by some authors (e.g. H&B).

GREEN-NAPED TANAGER

Tangara fucosa Pl. 264

Identification 12cm. Adult blackish above with pale green-spangled nape and neck-sides, turquoise rump, black wings with broad turquoise fringes to lesser and median coverts; black throat with blue spangles on breast, sides and flanks, latter with some dusky spotting, and cinnamon-buff distally.

Ssp. Monotypic (NW Co)

Habits Forages in small flocks for fruits, berries and invertebrates, sometimes joins mixed-species flocks, especially in heavily fruiting trees.

Status Near Threatened. Known in our region only from sight record by Pearman (1993) of a bird near ridge of Cerro Tacarcuna, northern Chocó, very close to Panama border, and otherwise only known from Cerro Pirre, Cerro Malí, Cerro Tacarcuna and Serranía de Jungurudó in east Darién, Panama, where fairly common. Very small range susceptible to any habitat loss or degradation, which may ensue from gold-mining operations currently operational below this species' altitudinal range, and from soon-to-be-completed Pan-American Highway through Darién.

Habitat Subtropical Zone, usually above 1,350m but once to 550m (in Panama), in montane evergreen and elfin forests.

Voice High *tsit* or more squealing *tsset*, given singly or rapidly in various combinations of 2–4 (sometimes even 5+) notes (I&I).

Note Considered a subspecies of Spangle-cheeked Tanager *T. dowii* by some authors (I&I).

BERYL-SPANGLED TANAGER

Tangara nigroviridis Pl. 264

Identification 12–13cm. Adult has black back, black wings and tail with broad turquoise fringes, lower back and rump turquoise, black mask and chin, rest of head and underparts very heavily spangled turquoise on black, paler on belly and vent, top of head paler to opalescent. Female slightly duller. Juvenile medium brown above with pale eyebrow that reaches nape and runs around ear-coverts, wing-coverts fringed pale buffy, below spangled brown and buffy with slight touch of pale blue. Adult has diagnostic spangles on underparts and head, combined with a black face mask. Male Black-capped Tanager has black crown and lacks spangles (though it has greenish-blue breast streaks). Also see Metallic-green Tanager.

Ssp. *T. n. cyanescens* (W Ec, N & W Co, N Ve) all blue distinctly more turquoise than *nigrocincta*, breast-sides and flanks narrowly uniform turquoise with white belly to vent more extensive, undertail-coverts more clearly black and white

T. n. lozanoana (W Ve) larger; generally more turquoise on crown; larger and brighter spots below, lesser wing-coverts fringed pale blue; bill black above, brown below; differs from *cyanescens* by black lesser wing-coverts and more opalescent, creamy crown

T. n. nigroviridis (E Ec, E Co) as described

Habits Searches mostly thin, bare, outer twigs in canopy, especially those hanging down. Quickly forages in pairs or small to large flocks of up to 25+ at all levels for fruits, berries and invertebrates, and often joins mixed-species flocks.

Status Fairly common to common in Ecuador, common in Colombia and commonest *Tangara* in Venezuela.

Habitat Tropical to Temperate Zones, at 900–3,000 m but usually 1,400–2,600 m, in humid to wet and mossy forests, edges, second growth, clearings with large trees and light woodland with many Melastomes.

Voice High *sit* and *chit* notes, given singly or in bursts. Song a high, thin, weak *see, sit sit, see see, tzle'tzle'tzeet* (Hilty).

Note Race *lozanoana* described by Aveledo & Pérez (1994).

BLUE-AND-BLACK TANAGER

Tangara vassorii Pl. 264

Identification 12.5–14cm. Adult male almost entirely deep warm blue with black wings and tail, and small black mask; eyes brown, bill black, legs and feet vinaceous-grey. Female similar, but slightly duller, noticeable when pair together. Juvenile is dull, blue-tinged, slightly brownish-grey above, with blackish lores, wings and tail, paler grey below, softly flammulated with darker and faint washes of blue. Adult mostly dark blue (which may easily look black in field), and may be confused with Golden-naped Tanager, male Capped Conebill or any blue/black-coloured flowerpiercer.

Ssp. *T. v. vassorii* (Andes in Ec, Ve & Co)

Habits Forages in a fast-moving manner; may occur in pairs or flocks of up to 25, often joins mixed-species flocks and feeding aggregations, especially at fruiting Melastomes. Forages at all levels.

Status Uncommon to fairly common in Ecuador, fairly common in Colombia and Venezuela.

Habitat Temperate Zone to Páramo, 1,800–3,600m but

usually 2,000 3,300m in Ecuador, 2,400–2,900m in Colombia and 2,200–2,600m in Venezuela, in broken humid to wet and elfin forests, edges, mature Melastome-dominated second growth and overgrown pastures with shrubs and trees, to near treeline.

Voice Very thin, rapid, high *tsit* and *chip* notes while foraging, sometimes given in rapid series, especially on taking flight, and a distinct *tzrr tzit* in flight; also a slightly lower *swit!*, sometimes repeated several times or varied to a harder *SWIT-it*. Song a high, thin *tsiit, tsiit tsiit tsiit* or *zieeu- zie-zie-zizizizeee*, starting slowly and then accelerating, lasting 2–3 s and repeated every 15 s (F&K, I&I, Hilty).

BLACK-CAPPED TANAGER

Tangara heinei Pl. 265

Identification 13–13.5cm. Adult male silvery grey-blue above with black crown and nape, pale greenish-blue face, throat and upper breast (latter two with dusky streaks), and rest of underparts dull grey-blue. Female mostly greenish with a dusky crown and nape. Subadult and juvenile even duller than female. Adult male may be confused with Golden-naped, Beryl-spangled and Metallic-green Tanagers. Adult female may be confused with Rufous-throated, Rufous-cheeked and Metallic-green Tanagers, as well as female Silvery Tanager, which has buffy face, or female Black-headed Tanager, which has bluish (not greenish) wing-fringes, mottled grey (not silvery green) throat and yellowish (not greenish) rear underparts, and is overall paler and greyer on head and breast.

Ssp. Monotypic (Ec, N & W Co, NW Ve)

Habits Forages alone, in pairs or small flocks, usually from midstorey to canopy; rarely joins mixed-species flocks or feeding aggregations.

Status Uncommon in Ecuador, uncommon to locally fairly common in Colombia and Venezuela, with downslope movements to 1,000 m during early rainy season in Venezuela; probably spreading due to deforestation, as not recorded in western Ecuador until 1980.

Habitat Tropical to Subtropical Zones, 700–2,800m but usually at 1,500–1,900m, in edges of humid to wet and cloud forests, open woodland, mature second growth, and shrubs and trees in clearings and pastures, usually not inside forests.

Voice Calls include 2 kinds of nasal, scratchy *zheet* notes, first high-pitched and other more nasal and moderate-pitched; also clear, high *tsit*. Song an alternation of 2 *zheet* notes, usually starting with a few even-pitched notes, then becoming louder and faster, ending in a scratchy wheedling, repeated 3–5 times, or, in Venezuela, a mechanical-sounding, ringing, very fast *t'kling-t'kling-t'kling*…, both types lasting to 12 s; pauses between songs irregular and contain call notes (I&I, Hilty).

SILVERY TANAGER

Tangara viridicollis Pl. 265

Identification 12.5–13cm. Adult male bright pale turquoise from mantle to uppertail-coverts, top of head, including lores and broad eye-ring, nape, neck-sides to breast, belly, rear flanks and undertail-coverts, wings and tail all black, breast-sides and flanks turquoise; lower cheeks, ear-coverts to chin and throat orange-buffy; eyes brown, bill black, legs and feet grey. Female has top of head including lores, nape and neck-sides grey-brown, and face a paler version of male, entire body soft green, wings and tail darker with bluish fringes to remiges. Orange-buffy face in both sexes should separate them from somewhat similar Straw-backed Tanager which has same plumage pattern, but has blue-green face and yellow back, and note male Silvery has bold, clear sides and flanks. Similar-patterned Black-capped Tanager does not overlap.

Ssp. *T. v. fulvigula* (S Ec)

Habits Forages at all levels but often quite low, looking for fruits, berries, and invertebrates. Occurs in pairs or small flocks (sometimes of up to 20), and often joins mixed-species flocks.

Status Uncommon to locally fairly common and rather local.

Habitat Tropical to Subtropical Zones, 1,300–2,750m but usually 1,500–2,000m, in humid forest, dwarf cloud forests, edges, wooded ravines, second growth and trees in adjacent clearings, often in areas with patchy forest and overall less dependent on extensive forest than most *Tangara*.

Voice A fine *tziu* and lower *pew*, distinctive and not as thin as other *Tangara* (F&K, I&I).

Note Also called Silver-backed or Silvery-backed Tanager.

STRAW-BACKED TANAGER

Tangara argyrofenges Pl. 265

Identification 13cm. Adult male bright straw colour from mantle to uppertail-coverts, top of head, including lores and broad eye-ring, nape, neck-sides to breast, belly, rear flanks and undertail-coverts, wings and tail all black, breast-sides and flanks straw, flecked black; lower cheeks, ear-coverts to chin and throat pale turquoise; eyes brown, bill black, legs and feet grey. Female has top of head including lores, nape and neck-sides grey-brown, and face paler than male, entire body soft yellowish-green, wings and tail darker with pale fringes to remiges. Subadult has greenish flight-feather fringes and dusky cream back. Same plumage pattern as Silvery Tanager, and could be confused in poor light, but note that male of latter has bold, clear sides and flanks.

Ssp. *T. a. caeruleigularis* (SE Ec)

Habits Similar to Silvery Tanager.

Status Rare, and considered Data Deficient in Ecuador (R&G). Thus far only found on east slope of Andes at Panguri, in southern Zamora-Chinchipe, in extreme south-east Ecuador.

Habitat Tropical to Subtropical Zones, 1,350–1,600m, in canopy and edges of humid montane forest.

Voice Unknown.

Note Formerly called Green-throated Tanager.

BLACK-HEADED TANAGER

Tangara cyanoptera Pl. 265

Identification 13–14cm. Adult male has black hood and entire body yellowish-opal, wings and tail black with rich bluish fringes; eyes brown, bill black, legs and feet dark grey. Female has head grey, merging into turquoise-tinged nape and flammulated upper breast, pale green above and yellowish wash below. Immature male duller and more flecked or mottled dusky; juvenile brownish-grey above with paler fringes to wing-coverts, whitish below but well flammulated with diffuse grey streaks. Adult male should be unmistakable, but compare adult female with female Rufous-cheeked and female Black-capped Tanagers (also young and rather drab Burnished-buff Tanager).

Ssp. *T. c. cyanoptera* (N Co, NW Ve) as described
T. c. whitelyi (S Ve, Gu) male noticeably duller with less opalescence, strong mottled effect below, lacks blue wing-fringes, female very dingy, with pronounced flammulations on underparts

Habits Forages for fruits, berries and invertebrates, mainly from midstorey to canopy. Singly, in pairs or small flocks; sometimes joins mixed-species flocks.

Status Common in Colombia, uncommon to locally fairly common in Venezuela.

Habitat Tropical to Subtropical Zones, 450–2,200m but usually above 800m (north Colombia, north-west Venezuela) or at 1,100–2,250 (south Venezuela, Guyana), in moist to moderately humid forests, lighter woodland and wooded ravines, but mainly at edges, in mature second growth and large trees in plantations, clearings and pastures (north Colombia, north-west Venezuela), or in humid to wet forests and stunted, mossy, Melastome-dominated second growth on tepuis (south Venezuela, Guyana).

Voice High buzzy or lisped notes when foraging, e.g. a slightly quivering, lisping, high *djeet*. Song of *cyanoptera* a high, thin *weeu weeu, weeu*; another song described as a quivering, piercing, moderate- to high-pitched squeal (like running fingernail across a blackboard) without inflection, lasting 1–2 s and regularly repeated with call notes uttered irregularly during pauses (I&I, Hilty).

Note May involve more than one species (Hilty).

OPAL-RUMPED TANAGER

Tangara velia Pl. 264

Identification 12–14.5cm. Top of head, neck-sides, back, wings and tail black, lesser and median wing-coverts blue, broad blue fringes to flight-feathers, lower back bright opalescent, becoming greenish-opal then blue, with uppertail-coverts deep purplish-blue; head-sides, upper cheeks and outer ear-coverts cerulean-blue, throat and malar mottled blue and black, lower throat violet, breast, sides and flanks purplish-blue, central belly to undertail-coverts reddish-chestnut; eyes bright brown, bill dark horn, legs and feet dusky. Female generally paler, with less intense shades of same colours, and juvenile similar but has much darker face. Rather similar to Opal-crowned Tanager with which it often occurs, but readily separated by broad opal forecrown and eyebrow and black (not chestnut) lower belly and undertail-coverts.

Ssp. *T. v. iridina* (E Ec, SE Co, S Ve) male has face deeper, purplish-blue, body and wings significantly more purplish-blue, lower rump and uppertail-coverts solid deep purplish-blue, undertail-coverts redder; female not quite so intensely coloured, particularly on face where blue is pale enough to contrast with black
T. v. velia (E Ve, Guianas) as described

Habits Forages in pairs or small flocks (of up to 15) mainly from subcanopy to canopy (sometimes lower at edges) and usually on outer, thinner branches and stems. Feeds on fruits, berries, and invertebrates. Often joins mixed-species flocks.

Status Uncommon, except in French Guiana where common (but probably often overlooked as fairly common in canopy around Surumoni Crane in southern Venezuela).

Habitat Tropical Zone, to 1,200m but usually below 500m, mostly in humid *terra firme* and *várzea* forests and edges, sometimes in mature second growth, shaded plantations and tall trees in clearings.

Voice High, thin, rapid burst of *sit* or *sis* notes when foraging (singly or repeated up to 6 times), and high twitter in flight. Song a series of high, thin, weak notes that quickly rise and then descend in pitch, e.g. *tiz-tiz-tiz-ti'ti-ti-E'E-ti-ti-ti-tz* (I&I, Hilty).

OPAL-CROWNED TANAGER

Tangara callophrys Pl. 264

Identification 14–14.7cm. Centre of nape and neck-sides, back and wings and tail black; tail-coverts, lesser wing-coverts, face-sides and underparts rich violaceous-blue; forehead to crown, broad line on nape-sides, lower back and rump creamy opal, thighs black, eyes brown, rather large bill black, legs and feet horn. Rather similar to Opal-rumped Tanager with which it often occurs, but readily separated by black head and lower belly (not reddish-chestnut).

Ssp. Monotypic (E Ec, SE Co)

Habits Forages in pairs or small groups, sometimes flocks of up to 15, mainly from subcanopy to canopy (sometimes lower at edges) and tends to be on inner, thicker branches and stems. Feeds on fruits, berries and invertebrates. Often joins mixed-species flocks.

Status Uncommon to fairly common in Ecuador (where usually commoner than Opal-rumped Tanager), rare to uncommon in Colombia (where usually less common than Opal-rumped).

Habitat Tropical Zone, to 750m but usually below 500m, mostly in humid *terra firme* and *várzea* forests and edges, sometimes in mature second growth, shaded plantations and tall trees in clearings.

Voice A high *zit*, usually quickly repeated 2–4 times (H&B).

GOLDEN-COLLARED HONEYCREEPER

Iridophanes pulcherrimus Pl. 267

Identification 11–12cm. Black hood separated from black upper mantle by band of golden-yellow, lower mantle streaked black and opal, becoming opal on lower back and rump, lesser coverts pale blue, rest of wings black with blue fringes, tail-coverts and tail black with blue fringes, underparts opalescent, becoming whitish undertail-coverts; dark-red eyes, slightly thin, pointed and slightly curved bill, legs and feet grey. Adult female olive above with yellowish rump, pale bluish-green fringes on wing-coverts and inner remiges, faint yellow-orange nuchal collar, and pale yellowish-buff below with greenish-tinged sides. Older immature male like female but has brown eyes and silvery (not yellow) base of mandible; in later stages is mottled with black. Adult male much like Black-capped Tanager (no overlap).

Ssp. *I. p. aureinucha* (W Ec) noticeably longer bill, male has dull, sooty hood and is generally paler, except blue shoulder which is deeper
I. p. pulcherrimus (E Ec, C Co) shorter bill

Habits Rapidly forages alone, in pairs or small flocks of up to *c.*9, often with mixed-species flocks, from midstorey to canopy, for fruits, invertebrates, flowers and possibly nectar.
Status Uncommon to locally fairly common in Ecuador, rare and local in Colombia (less common on Pacific slope of Andes).
Habitat Tropical to Subtropical Zones, at 650–2,150m, in very humid forests, edges, mature second growth and tall trees in adjacent clearings.
Voice Calls include a high, lisping, buzzy *czee*, sometimes doubled (H&B).
Note Formerly placed in genus *Tangara*.

Dacnis are small, colourful birds of humid forest canopy, rather warbler-like in shape and jizz, with short, pointed bills. Several are local and scarce. Turquoise Dacnis was at one time placed in a separate monotypic genus, *Pseudodacnis*.

TURQUOISE DACNIS
Dacnis hartlaubi Pl. 266

Identification 11–11.4cm. Adult male mostly blue with black mask (except blue eye-ring), throat, mantle, tail and wings (except blue scapulars and tertial fringes); yellow eyes, bill slightly stubbier and shorter than *Dacnis*. Adult female dull olive-brown above, greyer on head, with buff fringes to tertials and scapulars, and greyish-buff below, becoming yellowish-white on belly and undertail-coverts. Very similar male Black-faced Dacnis is brighter turquoise, with thinner bill and white belly. Male Blue Dacnis has red eyes and lacks black mask. Female Black-faced Dacnis more olive above, more yellowish below and lacks buffy wing-fringes.

Ssp. Monotypic (W Co)

Habits Forages rather sluggishly in subcanopy to canopy for fruits and invertebrates. Sometimes joins mixed-species flocks.
Status Vulnerable. Endemic to Colombia, rare, local and declining due to ongoing habitat loss, found only in Andes in Valle de Cauca, Huila, Quindío, Antioquia, Risaralda, Cundinamarca and Boyacá. A significant population may exist in Serranía de las Quinchas, Boyacá, but only other post-1980 records are from río Bogotá drainage (west-central Cundinamarca), 2 sites in Támesis, Antioquia, and one in Risaralda.
Habitat Tropical to Subtropical Zones, 300–2,200m but usually above 1,350m, in humid forest and edges, adjacent second growth and clearings with tall trees, and sometimes in shade plantations (especially where *Inga* and *Cordia alliodora* are commonest).
Voice Unknown.
Note Previously placed in monotypic genus *Pseudodacnis* and called Turquoise Dacnis-Tanager.

WHITE-BELLIED DACNIS
Dacnis albiventris Pl. 266

Identification 10–11.7cm. Adult male almost all cobalt-blue with small black mask and white belly and undertail-coverts; yellow eyes, dark, sharply pointed bill, grey legs and feet. Adult female has olive-green upperparts, brightest on rump, contrasting with pale olive underparts, whitish on throat and yellowish on belly; pale-brown to pale greyish-brown eyes. Immature male like female but flight-feathers contrastingly blackish, gradually acquiring adult plumage and eye colour. Compared to Turquoise and Masked Tanagers, male is much darker and richer, purplish-blue with more extensive white belly than Black-faced Dacnis. Female Black-faced Dacnis has yellow eyes, and female Yellow-bellied Dacnis has red eyes, and both have less contrasting plumage.

Ssp. Monotypic (E Ec, E Co, S Ve)

Habits Forages for fruits and invertebrates in outer foliage of subcanopy to canopy (lower at edges). Alone, in pairs or flocks of up to *c.*10, and sometimes follows mixed-species canopy flocks.
Status Very rare to rare.
Habitat Tropical Zone, to 400m, in humid *terra firme* and *várzea*, edges and second growth.
Voice In flight a soft, silky *seeeee* (Hilty).

BLACK-FACED DACNIS
Dacnis lineata Pl. 266

Identification 11–11.5cm. Adult male mostly rich turquoise-blue with black mask (except blue eye-ring) that joins mantle, scapulars blue, wings and tail black with narrow white fringes to tertials, central belly, thighs and undertail-coverts pure white; yellow eyes, bill dark with pale base, legs and feet grey. Adult female uniform olive-brown above and pale greyish-buff below becoming whiter on belly and undertail-coverts, eyes duller yellow. Juvenile like female. Male Blue Dacnis has red eyes, black throat, blue belly and lacks black mask. Adult female has either whitish or yellowish belly (compare female Turquoise Dacnis and female White-bellied Dacnis). Female Yellow-bellied Dacnis has red eyes, olive back and mottled underparts, female Scarlet-thighed Dacnis has red eyes, blue-tinged back and buffy underparts, and female Viridian Dacnis has pale olive (not yellowish) belly.

Ssp. *D. l. aequatorialis* (W Ec) like *lineata* but more greenish on shoulder, rump and underparts; underwing-coverts rich golden-yellow

D. l. egregia (C Co) quite different, male blue-green with pale yellow underwing-coverts and small yellow patch at breast-sides, belly and undertail-coverts yellow; female greenish-olive above, paler below with yellow belly and undertail-coverts, eyes slightly orange and duller

D. l. lineata (E Ec, E Co, S Ve, Guianas) as described; white underwing

Habits Rapidly forages alone, in pairs or flocks of up to 12, from subcanopy to canopy for fruits, berries, nectar and invertebrates, and often joins mixed-species flocks.

Status Fairly common in Ecuador and Suriname, and uncommon in Colombia, Venezuela and French Guiana.

Habitat Tropical Zone, to 1,700m but usually below 1,300m, in humid *terra firme* and *várzea*, edges, second growth and adjacent clearings with tall trees, sometimes in savanna and gallery forests.

Voice Calls include weak, high *tzit* notes and a *tsleyp* call (I&I, R&G, Hilty).

Note Race *egregia* (including *aequatorialis*) appears to be a separate species, called Yellow-tufted Dacnis by R&T, R&G, but proposal for recognition rejected by SACC on basis of insufficient published evidence.

YELLOW-BELLIED DACNIS

Dacnis flaviventer Pl. 266

Identification 11–13cm. Adult male unmistakable: black mask reaches nape and mantle, wings and tail also black, as is large teardrop-shaped bib; crown deep green; rest of body, including scapulars bright yellow; eyes bright red, slender and slightly curved bill black, legs and feet grey. Adult female olive-brown above, yellowish-white below with faint dusky brownish mottles on throat, breast and sides, becoming buffy on vent (red eyes distinguish from female White-bellied and Black-faced Dacnis).

Ssp. Monotypic (E Ec, SE Co, SC Ve)

Habits Rapidly forages alone or in pairs, sometimes in flocks of up to 15, from midstorey to canopy (lower at edges) for fruits, berries, nectar and invertebrates, and sometimes joins mixed-species flocks.

Status Uncommon to fairly common in Ecuador, uncommon to locally common in Colombia, uncommon in Venezuela.

Habitat Tropical Zone, to 1,050m but usually below 500m, in humid *terra firme* and *várzea* and edges (favouring forests near water, e.g. along rivers and on river islands), and adjacent shrubby or mature second growth, and other disturbed areas with isolated large trees.

Voice Short, high *zeet* and a coarse, buzzy, moderate- to high-pitched *zrreet*. Song a sharp and high *whuh-zeeé* (I&I, R&G).

SCARLET-THIGHED DACNIS

Dacnis venusta Pl. 266

Identification 12–12.2cm. Adult male has forehead to uppertail-coverts turquoise-blue, scapulars black with outer fringes turquoise; mask, throat and underparts black except scarlet thighs; eyes bright red, bill sharply pointed, legs and feet blackish. Adult female dusky blue-green above, brightest on ear-coverts, rump and scapulars, and buffy grey-brown below with cinnamon tinge on belly and undertail-coverts – combination of blue above and unstreaked buffy below a good field mark (compare subadult Blue Dacnis and White-eared Conebill). Red eyes. Subadult male like female but has black throat; juvenile like a pallid female, rather more greenish above than bluish. Adult male has diagnostic scarlet thighs which are often hidden, but even then is rather unmistakable (compare Blue-necked Tanager). Like female Black-faced Dacnis, female Viridian Dacnis has yellow eyes and olive underparts and lacks blue-tinged upperparts.

Ssp. *D. v. fuliginata* (NW Ec, W Co)

Habits Forages very rapidly at all levels, for fruits, berries, and invertebrates. Alone, in pairs or small groups, occasionally up to *c.*15, and sometimes joins mixed-species flocks.

Status Rare to locally uncommon in Ecuador, uncommon to fairly common in Colombia.

Habitat Tropical Zone, to 1,100m but usually 150–700m, in humid to very wet forests, edges, second growth, shaded plantations and large trees in adjacent clearings in lowlands, and broken forests and shrubby edges in foothills.

Voice A metallic *urp*, *zirp*, *rit* or *wurt*, and buzzy *wuzt* or *rezt*, and when excited utters a low, nasal, metallic *wheu wheu* (I&I).

BLUE DACNIS *Dacnis cayana* Pl. 266

Identification 11–12.7cm. Adult male bright lustrous turquoise-blue (or bluish-violet), more bluish on top of head and back; black mask, throat, mantle, tail and wings, all blue-fringed; dark red eyes, pointed bill is purplish-black, pink legs. Adult female bright leaf green, except greyish throat and diagnostic bluish (or bluish-violet) head. Immature male like female but with mask and bib, mantle slightly dusky. Older birds range from yellowish-green to brilliant green. Immature male like female but has black patches on mantle; head as male but colours less pure (slight greenish or greyish wash); breast mixed green and turquoise; underparts green. Juvenile like female but blue on head much more restricted and underparts more yellowish, juvenile male has darker mask than female. Rather unmistakable when combined with eye and leg colour (see male Turquoise Dacnis and male Black-faced Dacnis). Male Viridian Dacnis has yellow eyes and more greenish plumage, including throat. Compare female with female Capped Conebill, female Green Honeycreeper (green head and decurved, yellowish bill) and female Viridian Dacnis (yellow eyes and lacks bluish head).

Ssp. *D. c. baudoana* (W Ec, W Co) compared to *coerebicolor* blue with purple tinge; purplish-blue compared to *ultramarina*; female has bluish-violet head

D. c. cayana (E Co, Ve, Tr, Guianas) as described

D. c. coerebicolor (C Co) male most deeply coloured of all with bluish-violet to purplish tone, female has bluish-violet head

D. c. glaucogularis (S Co) male turquoise-blue, female

has much deeper blue on top and sides of head

D. c. napaea (N Co) male intermediate between *coerebicolor* and *ultramarina*, intense cobalt-blue; female with bluish-violet head is like female *coerebicolor*

D. c. ultramarina (NW Co) male blue, not turquoise; female has whiter throat and bluer sides of head

Habits Forages restlessly and nervously from midstorey to canopy but lower at edges. Takes invertebrates, fruits, berries and nectar. Alone, in pairs or small groups, rarely flocks of up to *c.*12, but often joins mixed-species flocks.

Status Fairly common to common, usually commonest *Dacnis* in range.

Habitat Tropical Zone, to 1,600m but usually below 1,000m, in humid *terra firme* and *várzea*, edges, mature second growth and shrubby clearings, shaded plantations, parks and gardens with large trees, sometimes in gallery and savanna forests.

Voice A high *tsit* and harsh, moderate- to high-pitched *chit* or *chid-it*. Probable song a lisped note often repeated (I&I, Hilty).

VIRIDIAN DACNIS *Dacnis viguieri* Pl. 266

Identification 10–11.5cm. Adult male almost entirely pale opalescent turquoise-green with black mantle, rather more greenish on head, bluer distally, scapulars and wings similar colour with black line caused by outer fringes of scapulars, and primaries also blackish, tail and lores black; eyes yellow, dark bill sharply pointed, legs and feet grey. Adult female blue-tinged olive above with black lores and primaries, and paler olive below with yellow tinge on belly and undertail-coverts. Subadult male resembles female. Adult male may resemble male Blue Dacnis at distance. Compare female with female Black-faced, Scarlet-thighed and Blue Dacnis. Larger female Green Honeycreeper has greener plumage, dark eyes and longer, decurved, yellowish (not dark) bill.

Ssp. Monotypic (NW Co)

Habits Similar to congeners, but not well known, tends to stay within high treetops.

Status Near Threatened. Rare within small range in north Chocó, north-west Antioquia and south-west Córdoba in north-west Colombia. Perhaps formerly locally common on both slopes of north Serranía de Baudó, north-west Chocó, but very few recent records. In Urabá lowlands and Sinú Valley, most habitat converted for agriculture. Extensive, largely intact forests remain in Panama and Chocó, but these threatened by Pan-American Highway link through Darién.

Habitat Tropical Zone, to 700m, mostly in dry to humid forests, sometimes edges and scrub.

Voice Unknown.

SCARLET-BREASTED DACNIS
Dacnis berlepschi Pl. 266

Identification 12cm. Yellow eyes. Adult male mostly ultramarine-blue, with silver-blue streaks on mantle and silver-blue rump, blackish wings and tail, and diagnostic scarlet lower breast fading to buff on belly and vent (compare Blue-backed Conebill). Adult female olive-brown above, paler and buffier below with diagnostic reddish-orange breast-band becoming straw yellow on belly and vent.

Ssp. Monotypic (NW Ec, SW Co)

Habits Forages, usually in pairs, in canopy, and often joins mixed-species flocks

Status Vulnerable. Rare to uncommon and local on Pacific slope and in lowlands of Esmeraldas, Imbabura, Pichincha (north-west Ecuador) and Nariño (south-west Colombia); in latter, few recent records despite numerous field studies. Habitat loss and fragmentation due to logging, mining and agricultural conversion has already been severe (with certain extinction in some former localities), and is predicted to increase further.

Habitat Tropical Zone, to 1,200m, in humid to very wet forests, cloud forests, edges and mature second growth.

Voice A very high-pitched, piercing *tz* or *tze*, often repeated as *tz-tz-tz-tz*, when foraging. Song a very fast, high and even-pitched series of thin notes, e.g. *tsit-sitsitsitsitsitsitsiti* (R&G).

Honeycreepers are generally small, usually bright blue or purplish (males) or greenish above and streaked below (females) with slender, slightly decurved bills and brightly coloured legs, often yellow or red. They are sociable, sometimes travelling in small groups.

GREEN HONEYCREEPER
Chlorophanes spiza Pl. 267

Identification 14cm. Adult male almost entirely turquoise-green, paler on hindneck, bluest on underparts, dusky on wings and tail with broad turquoise fringes and washed same colour, cowl black; eyes red, long slightly curved and pointed bill yellow with black culmen, legs and feet grey. Adult female soft powdery green, paler below, yellowish on undertail-coverts, basally dusky on wings and tail. Juvenile grey-green olive above, paler and more yellowish below; eyes brown, bill dull horn, legs and feet dull grey. Immature male like female but becomes mottled green and turquoise with age. Best mark is pointed, slightly decurved and bright yellow bill (duller in female) with black culmen. Adult male unmistakable. Adult female's best marks are bill and almost entirely grass-green coloration (compare Glistening-green Tanager, immature Orange-eared, Multicolored, Bay-headed and Rufous-winged Tanagers, and female Blue and Viridian Dacnis).

Ssp. *C. s. caerulescens* (E Ec, SE Co) male turquoise (bluer than *exsul*)

C. s. exsul (W Ec, SW Co) male shining-green (less blue than *caerulescens*)

C. s. spiza (E Co, Ve, Tr, Guianas) male intermediate between *caerulescens* and *exsul*; female has yellowish-green underparts with paler throat

C. s. subtropicalis (Co, W Ve) male resembles *caerulescens*, though black of crown extends slightly further back; female has yellowish throat and central underparts

Habits Flicks wings constantly. Forages restlessly with

quick movements, alone or in pairs, rarely in small flocks. From midstorey to canopy (lower at edges), searching for invertebrates, fruits, berries and nectar. Sometimes or often (perhaps depending on season or location) joins mixed-species flocks, where often very aggressive towards other species.
Status Fairly common throughout, but common in Trinidad, Suriname and French Guiana.
Habitat Tropical Zone, to 1,100m in Ecuador, 2,300m in Colombia and 1,400m in Venezuela, in humid *terra firme* and *várzea*, gallery and river island forests, edges, mature second growth and shaded plantations, but only sometimes in adjacent clearings, also in savanna forests in Suriname.
Voice High *psit* and *tseet* notes, a weak or strong *tsip* or *chip*, given singly or in a hummingbird-like chipping (I&I, Hilty).

SHORT-BILLED HONEYCREEPER
Cyanerpes nitidus Pl. 267

Identification 9–10.7cm. Adult male mostly glossy, rich cobalt-blue with black lores, throat, wings, tail, central belly and undertail-coverts; eyes brown, short and only slightly decurved bill is black, pinkish-red (male) or pale pink (female) legs. Adult female grass-green above including head-sides, with blackish lores and inconspicuous short blue malar, and greenish-flammulated white underparts, with buffy throat and pale buff belly. Juvenile like female above but dull, washed-out grass green below, with pale throat and vent. Shining Honeycreeper does not overlap. Male Purple Honeycreeper has smaller black throat patch, yellow legs and longer bill. Male Red-legged Honeycreeper has azure crown, blue throat, black back, red legs and longer bill. Female Purple Honeycreeper has longer bill, greenish-grey legs and cinnamon forehead, lores and head-sides. Female Red-legged Honeycreeper has longer bill, more reddish legs and yellow (not buffy-white) underwing-coverts.

Ssp. Monotypic (E Ec, Co, S Ve)

Habits Forages actively, from midstorey to canopy, seeking fruits, berries and invertebrates. Alone or in pairs, and often joins mixed-species flocks.
Status Rare and local in Ecuador, uncommon in Colombia, fairly common in Venezuela. Seems rare and local in Suriname and NW French Guiana.
Habitat Tropical Zone, to 400m, in humid *terra firme* and *várzea* (apparently less often in latter), edges, second growth and in adjacent clearings with tall trees.
Voice Unknown.

SHINING HONEYCREEPER
Cyanerpes lucidus Pl. 267

Identification 10–11.4cm. Adult male largely glossy, deep purple-blue with black wings and tail, shining sky blue touch on forehead and base of malar; eyes brown, bill slender, slightly curved and blackish, legs and feet bright yellow with dark nails. Female soft grass-green above, brownish on wings and tail, white throat, rest of underparts yellowish, streaked brownish from face-sides to flanks. Adult male not always safely separated from male Purple Honeycreeper (sometimes even considered the same species), but Purple Honeycreeper has slightly smaller black throat patch and slightly longer bill. Compare also Red-legged Honeycreeper, whilst Short-billed Honeycreeper does not overlap. Female Shining Honeycreeper much easier to separate from female Purple Honeycreeper, as female Shining has bluish-flammulated underparts, greyish forehead, lores and head-sides, and bluish-grey crown contrasting with green back.

Ssp. *C. l. isthmicus* (NW Co)

Habits Like Purple Honeycreeper.
Status Colombia, where only known from río Juradó drainage in north-west Chocó.
Habitat Tropical Zone, to 100m in Colombia (800m in Panama), in humid forest, edges and second growth, and in adjacent clearings with tall trees.
Voice Calls (outside Colombia) include a high, cricket-like and oft-repeated *zee*, slightly rasping *tsrrrp*, hard, metallic *click* or *tick*, and sharp, high *tsip*, *pssst* or *tsik*, sometimes trilled. Possible Song a monotonous single note, repeated every 1 s and lasting up to 15 minutes (H&B, I&I).
Note May or may not overlap with closely related Purple Honeycreeper on Panama/Colombia border (H&B).

PURPLE HONEYCREEPER
Cyanerpes caeruleus Pl. 267

Identification 10–11.4cm. Adult male largely glossy, deep purple-blue with black wings and tail; eyes brown, bill slender, decurved and blackish, legs and feet bright yellow with dark nails. Female soft grassy green above, brownish on wings and tail, supraloral spot and small eyebrow to middle of eyes, face-sides and underparts yellowish, streaked bluish from upper breast to flanks. Immature male like female but heavily streaked blue above and below. Adult male from Red-legged Honeycreeper by leg and crown colour, blue back and black throat (also compare male Short-billed and Shining Honeycreepers). Adult female from female Red-legged Honeycreeper by leg colour and absence of white eyebrow (also compare female Short-billed and Shining Honeycreepers).

Ssp. *C. c. caeruleus* (Co, Ve, Su, FG) as described
- *C. c. chocoanus* (W Ec, W Co) smaller; shorter bill, male has forecrown pale blue, female far less blue streaking below, thus more yellow
- *C. c. hellmayri* (Gu: Potaro Highlands) distinguished by larger size, bill in particular longer and heavier; adult male differs from nominate race by more violaceous-blue coloration; female larger, exposed culmen distinctly longer and more robust, fringes to breast and body-sides more greenish, less bluish-green, chin and throat darker cinnamon-buff, ear-coverts apparently rather more brownish, with darker, less whitish shaft-lines
- *C. c. longirostris* (Tr) like *caeruleus* but has noticeably longer bill
- *C. c. microrhynchus* (E Ec, Co, W & S Ve) like *caeruleus* but has noticeably shorter bill

Habits Forages alone, in pairs or small to sometimes large flocks from midstorey to canopy (lower at edges and sometimes even in forest interior or on ground to pick fallen fruits), looks for fruits, berries, invertebrates and nectar. Often joins mixed-species flocks and feeding aggregations at flowering or fruiting trees.

Status Fairly common to common in Ecuador, uncommon to locally common in Colombia, fairly common in Venezuela, common on Trinidad, possibly also on Tobago, fairly common in Suriname, common in French Guiana, with some seasonal migration in response to increased rainfall (when may move to drier regions which it otherwise shuns) in many parts of range, e.g. Colombia and Suriname, where sometimes invades coffee plantations in large numbers to feed on flowering *Erythrina*.

Habitat Tropical Zone, to 1,800m but usually below 1,200m, in humid to wet *terra firme* and *várzea*, edges, mature second growth, shaded plantations and sometimes in adjacent clearings and gardens with tall trees (usually in more humid and densely forested areas than Red-legged Honeycreeper, but considerable overlap), also savanna forests in Suriname (though less common there than Red-legged Honeycreeper).

Voice A high, lisping and sometimes repeated *zzree*, and less often a *tsik* (I&I, R&G, Hilty).

Notes May or may not overlap with closely related Shining Honeycreeper on Panama/Colombia border (H&B). Snyder (1966) wrote that race *hellmayri* was not generally accepted, however it is recognised in Dickinson (2003); we have not seen specimens.

RED-LEGGED HONEYCREEPER

Cyanerpes cyaneus Pl. 267

Identification 11.5–13cm. Adult male in breeding plumage almost entirely glossy, deep, rich purple-blue, crown bright blue, mantle, neck-sides, wings, tail and undertail-coverts black; eyes bright brown, bill long, thin and decurved (varies significantly according to race), legs and feet bright coral red. Adult male acquires post-breeding eclipse plumage which resembles female plumage but has black back, wings and tail. Immature male also like female but acquires mostly black wings and blue patches fairly rapidly. Adult female soft, slightly greyish-green (sage) above, with whitish eyebrow and throat, underparts grading from white to greenish-yellow, streaked densely with sage-green. Long and decurved bill, bright red (male) or dull red to pinkish (female) legs. Compare adults with other *Cyanerpes*, all of which are smaller and lack yellow underwing-coverts.

Ssp. *C. c. carneipes* (NW Co) very similar to *cyaneus*, but pale blue cap of breeding male smaller and separated from black mantle by much broader purplish-blue band; female much more yellowish below, especially on throat and mid breast to belly

C. c. cyaneus (SE Ve, Tr, Guianas) as described

C. c. dispar (Co, S Ve) much shorter and thicker bill, pale blue crown grades into nape

C. c. eximius (N Co, N Ve, Bo) longer, more decurved bill; paler blue crown more extensive, to nape

C. c. gemmeus (NE Co: Guajira Peninsula) largest race with heaviest bill; crown of male darker blue; female more greyish above, less vivid green

C. c. gigas (Gorgona I., Co) male like *pacificus* in pale underwing-coverts but darker and more purplish; female darker and more yellowish below

C. c. pacificus (W Ec, W Co) small deep sea blue crown patch

C. c. tobagensis (To) long, fairly straight and heavy bill, long deep sea blue crown patch

Habits Forages restlessly and rapidly for fruits, berries, invertebrates and nectar, alone, in pairs or flocks of up to 20, from midstorey to canopy (lower at edges). Often joins mixed-species flocks and feeding aggregations at flowering or fruiting trees (where up to 100 observed).

Status Rare to uncommon and local in Ecuador, but locally or seasonally common in Colombia and Venezuela, fairly common in Trinidad & Tobago, and common in Suriname and French Guiana, with some seasonal migration in at least some parts of range, in response to flowering and fruiting of favoured trees, e.g. Venezuela and Suriname, where sometimes invades coffee plantations in large numbers to feed on flowering *Erythrina*.

Habitat Tropical Zone, to 2,000m but only below 300m in Ecuador, usually in more semi-open habitats than Purple Honeycreeper, e.g. dry to humid forest edges, shrubby or mature second growth, lighter woodland, gallery forest, shaded plantations and adjacent clearings, also in mangrove edges and savanna forests in Suriname (where more common than Purple Honeycreeper), but sometimes also in canopy of *terra firme* and low-lying forests.

Voice A high, wheezy, ascending *shree* and constant, weak, high *tsip*, *tsst* or *zzee* notes either perched or in flight. Utters nasal, mewing, moderate-pitched *chaa* or *dzey* in intraspecific contests or given randomly. In alarm, a pebbly *chink*, more metallic than Bananaquit. At dawn, utters weak series of *tsip* or *chaa* calls, repeated for up to 20 minutes or more, with pauses of 1–4 s; a possible courtship song is a barely audible melodic warble consisting of a short note whistled twice, a longer ascending note and a rapid double note whistled 5 times (H&B, ffrench, I&I, Hilty).

TIT-LIKE DACNIS

Xenodacnis parina Pl. 265

Identification 12–14cm. Stubby bill is distinctive. Adult male entirely deep blue with soft pale blue streaks, especially above. Adult female greyish-brown above with blue forecrown and fringes to wing- and tail-feathers, and pale cinnamon-rufous below, becoming buffy-white on central belly. Subadult male bluish olive-brown above and pale cinnamon-rufous mixed with blue below. Juvenile like female but has crown and wings like back, wing-coverts with clay-coloured tips, and buffy underparts with very faint, broad clay-coloured streaks.

Ssp. *X. p. bella* (S Ec) see note below

Habits Very noisily forages alone, in pairs or small flocks, usually quite low, for invertebrates (especially small cicadas, aphids and their sugary secretions on undersides of *Gynoxys* shrubs and *Polylepis* trees), and sometimes joins mixed-species flocks.

Status Near Threatened. Fairly common but very local, and Near Threatened status in Ecuador confirmed by (R&G).

Habitat Páramo, 3,700–4,000m, in patchy, low shrubby woodlands dominated by *Gynoxys*, in *Polylepis* groves, and understorey to midstorey of cloud forest edges.

Voice Various loud calls, e.g. *tchiú tchiú tchiú* or *huit huit huit*, a fine *zit*, snarling *wheit*, and scratchy, moderate-pitched *jeeup*, sometimes extended as hissing notes. Song a fast and variable series of loud, penetrating whistles, e.g. *tiu tiu tiu ziet ziet zitzit* or *zwit-zwit-zwit-zwit-zhweet-zhweet-zhweet* (*zwit* notes liquid, low whistles, *zwheet* moderate- to high-pitched, and number, quality and accent variable), often interspersed with high or scratchy notes, e.g. loud calls and trilled *ziet*. In duet, male begins, female joins in, and female ends with several raspy notes (F&K, I&I, R&G).

Note Race in Ecuador is perhaps *petersi* and not *bella*, but they are extremely similar and perhaps should be synonymised (R&G).

SWALLOW TANAGER

Tersina viridis Pl. 265

Identification 14–15cm. Adult male almost entirely bright turquoise-blue with blackish remiges and centre of rectrices, full black mask dips onto throat, flanks barred black, central belly and undertail-coverts white; eyes reddish-brown, bill broad, flat and black, legs and feet dark grey. Adult female is slightly bluish bright green instead of blue, and yellow instead of white, with barring on face instead of mask. Immature male like female but has irregular patches of blue and emergent mask. Adult male should be unmistakable (but compare male Spangled, Blue and Plum-throated Cotingas, and Golden-naped Tanager). Adult female also rather unique, with its chunky body and barred flanks (compare greenish tanagers).

Ssp. *T. v. grisescens* (Santa Marta, Co) male similar to *occidentalis*; female differs by having green tracts duller, more greyish-green, especially noticeable posteriorly

T. v. occidentalis (Ec, Co, Ve, Tr, Guianas) as described

Habits Perches high on exposed branches from where commences sallying flights, strong, swift and swallow-like. Gregarious and noisy as it forages, usually in small to large monospecific flocks of up to 100+ (larger in non-breeding season), usually high (lower at edges or in more open habitats), for invertebrates, fruits and berries (especially of Lauraceae).

Status Locally fairly common to common and widespread, with apparently erratic, nomadic or migratory movements, with numbers fluctuating greatly between seasons and years, but usually not found in arid areas; rather rare and local on Trinidad.

Habitat Subtropical Zone, to 2,100m but mostly 600–900m, in moist to humid forest, edges, second growth, gallery forest and other riparian habitats, lighter woodland and clearings with tall trees, locally in dry semi-deciduous forests.

Voice Distinctive, loud, explosive, unmusical, slightly buzzy, moderate- to high-pitched *tchee* given perched and in flight, and repeated every 5–6 s; also disyllabic *sieee*, very sharp *tse-it tsu-it* in territory defence, and 3–6 rather long, nasal *tsee wee it* in aggression. Squeaky, twittering song of up to 7 syllables recalls Blue-grey Tanager; another song is *tchee* call followed by rapid, shrill, metallic, moderate- to high-pitched *WHEE-chy WHEE-chy WHEE-chy*; subadult males also give long musical song (H&B, R&T, ffrench, I&I, Hilty).

PLUSHCAP

Catamblyrhynchus diadema Pl. 265

Identification 13–14cm. Adult has upperparts uniform dark mouse grey, remiges and rectrices with dark brown tone, plush, bristly cap to rear crown bright rich orange, bordered narrowly mahogany; lores, narrow eyebrow and nape fuscous; face to undertail-coverts deep mahogany-red, deepest on face and brightest distally; eyes brown, small conical bill, legs and feet black. Immature uniform brownish-olive above, including crown, which might show a few small orange flecks, face to undertail-coverts tawny-cinnamon, washed dusky on face; older birds show emergent adult coloration, most notably on crown. Juvenile has greyish forehead and is plain olive-brown below lacking any tawny wash.

Ssp. *C. d. diadema* (Andes in Ec, Co & Ve) as described

C. d. federalis (Coastal Range in N Ve) slightly brighter and paler mahogany-red on vent to undertail-coverts, orange cap smaller and duller; bill, legs and feet grey; female appears slightly smaller and paler, with olive legs and feet; juvenile like *diadema* but paler olive brown below

Habits Apparently a bamboo specialist, but not wholly dependent on it. Forages restlessly, continually active on *Chusquea* bamboo stalks, clinging upright or upside-down, switching with agility, and pressing its short bill deep into dense leaf whorls at each node, sometimes tugging vigorously or alternatively running its bill along stem with series of rapid biting motions. Works along stem to outermost part. Bamboo foliage, ferns and other temperate vegetation also searched (Hilty 1979). Forages alone, in pairs or small groups 1–4m above ground, occasionally higher, and often with mixed-species flocks.

Status Uncommon to locally fairly common in Ecuador, uncommon and local in Colombia.

Habitat Subtropical Zone to Páramo, 2,000–3,500m, in undergrowth of humid to wet mossy forests, elfin woodland, second growth and dense edges, especially in *Chusquea* bamboo stands.

Voice Soft, high-pitched *chip* and twittering notes when foraging. Song in Peru a weaving, twittering series of unmusical, almost random, hummingbird-like chips and twitters, lasting 15–60 s (R&T, F&K, Hilty).

Note Also called Plush-capped Finch.

BLACK-BACKED BUSH TANAGER

Urothraupis stolzmanni Pl. 260

Identification 15–16cm. Tail slightly graduated. Adult black above including head-sides, and white becoming dark grey posteriorly below, with barred, speckled or mottled effect on throat and breast that separates it from similar *Atlapetes* brush finches (Slaty Brush Finch most similar, which has chestnut crown, black malar and white wing-spot; also compare Black-headed Hemispingus).

Ssp. Monotypic (C Ec, C & S Co)

Habits Forages in small flocks of up to 9 in dense undergrowth for invertebrates and berries, and often follows mixed-species flocks.

Status Uncommon to locally fairly common or common.

Habitat Páramo, 3,000–4,000m, in elfin woodland, dense edges, *Polylepis* groves and humid *páramo* shrubbery mixed with bamboo, especially near or just below timberline.

Voice High weak chipping and trilling notes when foraging, e.g. fine *zie*, *tsit* or *tzi* contact calls (H&B, F&K).

GENERA INCERTAE SEDIS

The following species are currently considered Incertae Sedis by the SACC, pending formal proposals or decisions as to their most appropriate placement. Some genera, like North American *Piranga* tanagers are pretty well accepted as belonging in Cardinalidae. To learn the latest, refer to www.museum.1su.edu/~Remsen/SACCBaseline.html.

Additional reference for these genera: Isler & Isler (1987, hereafter I&I).

The ant tanagers are a homogeneous genus of uncertain affinities, previously placed in Thraupidae, but DNA evidence suggests they are closer to the Cardinalidae and it is probable that they will be placed there eventually. They are solid, bulky birds with long conical bills, and strong legs and feet. Males are more or less reddish, with short to long crests, 2 of the females are mostly yellowish below and olive above, the others being umber. Forage in dense undergrowth, and have harsh shrill cries and sweet songs.

CROWNED ANT TANAGER

Habia rubica Pl. 253

Identification 17–19cm. Adult male all red, rather dusky above and brownish on rear underparts, with an inconspicuous, semi-concealed bright red coronal stripe narrowly bordered black Adult female olive-brown above with a tawny-orange central crown and pale buffy below with ochraceous undertail-coverts. Juvenile male like female, but darker. Rather similar male Red-throated Ant Tanager has brighter throat, lacks black in crown and is overall less rosy, female Red-throated has conspicuous ochre-yellow throat, lacks tawny crown patch and is overall browner. Also compare female Crimson-backed, White-lined, Fulvous-crested and Olive Tanagers.

Ssp. *H. r. coccinea* (NC Co, W Ve: Andes and east of Lake Maracaibo) redder brown above, with scarlet crest, throat scarlet, breast blood red, rest of underparts pale jasper-red; blackish bill

H. r. crissalis (NE Ve) brick red above with darker head, coral red chin and throat, breast and sides grey washed coral pink, grenadine-pink from belly to undertail-coverts

H. r. mesopotamia (SE Ve) known only from holotype, paler than *rubra*, salmon-pink below, bill pale horn

H. r. perijana (Perijá: Co & Ve) morocco red above with scarlet crest and carmine tail, coral chin and throat, dull scarlet breast, rose-pink belly to undertail-coverts, washed brick red on flanks

H. r. rhodinolaema (E Ec, SE Co) rosy-red throat, breast and belly washed grey

H. r. rubra (Tr) like *coccinea* but more pinkish below

Habits When alarmed, flits wings and flips from side to side, or lowers wings and cocks tail. Rather retiring and wary as it forages for invertebrates, fruits, and berries, moving rapidly, in pairs or small flocks. Mostly in dense undergrowth, sometimes to subcanopy. Usually in pairs or loose groups. Often joins mixed-species flocks; regularly follows army ants in Trinidad.

Status Rare to locally common in Ecuador, Colombia and Venezuela, but has suffered locally from deforestation (e.g. Maracaibo area, Venezuela), probably most common on Trinidad.

Habitat Tropical Zone, up to 1,400m. In humid forest and woodland, especially dense vegetation in ravines, near streams or in treefalls, but less common at edges. Also in riverine undergrowth, low-lying forests, tall scrub and second growth near forests.

Voice Distinctive rough, grating and scolding calls include oft-repeated, rapid staccato *chak*, *chat*, *chrrr*, *chit* or *chiup* notes (softer than those of Red-throated Ant Tanager), in Trinidad often followed by a musical *pee-pee-pee*. Sharp note like pebbles being knocked together which is repeated, sometimes becoming a long rolling call. Dawn song, mainly heard in breeding season, varies geographically, but consists typically of up to 6 slowly whistled, 2–4-syllable phrases, e.g. *tjee, dear-dear-dear*, the first note harsh and rest trailing off melancholically. Day song simpler, e.g. an indistinct *cree-chree* varying to *chee-cher, chur-chee, chereeher* (H&B, R&T, ffrench, I&I, R&G, Hilty).

Notes Sometimes called Red-crowned Ant Tanager. Willis (1972) suggested that the southern population, the *rhodinolaema* group, might be specifically distinct from northern *coccinea*.

RED-THROATED ANT TANAGER

Habia fuscicauda Pl. 253

Identification 18–20cm. Male has upperparts almost entirely deep reddish-umber, with a stubby, crimson crest; chin and throat deep reddish-pink, with rest of underparts deep dusky reddish-pink. Female greenish-olive, paler below, yellow on chin and throat. Juvenile and immature resemble female. Similar to, but much darker than Crowned Ant Tanager above (no overlap), and female further separated by lack of crest.

Ssp. *H. f. erythrolaema* (N Co)

Habits Forages in small flocks, mostly in dense undergrowth. Moves rapidly. Sometimes joins mixed-species flocks, but mostly follows army ants.

Status Poorly known in Colombia, formerly considered 'not rare'in Serranía de San Jacinto, in Bolívar and Sucre (Haffer 1975), but has apparently suffered from massive deforestation there since, and is probably at risk in Colombia (H&B).

Habitat Tropical Zone, to 200m. In drier Caribbean forest, woodland, edges and second growth.

Voice Vocalisations of Colombian race unpublished and because there is variation between races, we feel it inappropriate to describe the voice in Central America.

SOOTY ANT TANAGER

Habia gutturalis Pl. 253

Identification 19–20cm. Adult male all dark grey with conspicuous scarlet crest and rosy-red throat. Adult female duller with a pinkish-white throat.

Ssp. Monotypic (NW Co)

Habits Rather noisy as it forages, mostly for invertebrates and rarely fruits, in dense undergrowth from ground to midstorey. Usually in pairs or groups, often joins mixed-species flocks and regularly follows army ants.

Status Near Threatened. Endemic to and apparently rare (albeit locally fairly common) in north-west Colombia, where it occurs in Upper Sinú Valley at northern end of West Andes, and east along north base of the Andes to middle Magdalena Valley. The middle and lower Magdalena Valley has been extensively deforested since 19th century, and clearance in foothills near total since 1950s, with remaining suitable habitat unprotected and fragmented.

Habitat Tropical Zone, 100–1,100m. Humid forests, edges, gaps, mature second growth and patchy woodland, apparently preferring dense streamside and landslide habitats in extensive unbroken forest.

Voice Calls include a fast alarm chatter *chak-cha-cha-cha…* of 5–15 notes at *c.*5 notes per s, and single *chak* notes whilst foraging; also contact notes, e.g. *wik*, and short rattles. Very musical dawn and dusk song is usually 2–3 rich thrush-like whistles, *pong, peh, whee*, repeated frequently, or a more complex variation of 6–11 notes at *c.*2 notes per s, e.g. *wheh, hee, whereeheh, wher'erer*, the female often answering with a chatter and static (H&B, I&I).

CRESTED ANT TANAGER

Habia cristata Pl. 253

Identification 19cm. Adult male is dark crimson above and grey tinged crimson below, with distinctive scarlet crest and throat; black bill. Adult female is duller and lacks bright red tone to upperparts, with an obviously duller red face and bib, as well as a much shorter crest. Juvenile is all rufous-cinnamon, paler below.

Ssp. Monotypic (W Co)

Habits Rather noisy as it forages in pairs or small flocks, usually low in dense tangled vegetation, for invertebrates and fruits, often joins mixed-species flocks and regularly follows army ants.

Status Endemic to Colombia, where locally fairly common on Pacific slope (and even more locally on east slope), but has probably suffered from massive deforestation in its range, and is probably at risk (H&B).

Habitat Tropical to Subtropical Zones, at 700–1,800m. Humid forest, edges and mature second growth, apparently preferring low, dense vegetation in steep ravines or landslides along montane streams, only rarely crossing openings to reach isolated woodlots or trees in pastures.

Voice A very loud and sharp scolding *chiv-eek* or *guy-eek* directed at intruders, repeated 2–4 times at *c.*2 notes per s, also sharp loud *chip* contact calls and a series of *chee* notes. Dawn song a series of 1–12 unmusical, monotonous *che'ik* notes at *c.*2 notes per s, often from perches overhanging rivers (H&B, I&I).

Chlorospingus bush tanagers are rather noisy and gregarious but fairly cryptically coloured birds of forest and woodland. Predominantly yellowish-olive above, and grey below, with some yellowish and white. Most have pale to white eyes, somewhat variable (probably an age factor).

COMMON BUSH TANAGER

Chlorospingus ophthalmicus Pl. 249

Identification 13–14.5cm. Olive-green above with head black, dark brown or grey, and sometimes a white postocular spot (varies racially), throat varies from heavily speckled to almost white (see below), breast yellow, rest of underparts whitish with variable green wash to sides and flanks (see below). Juvenile has brown eyes, yellow-olive throat and crown concolorous with back. More crisp-coloured Ashy-throated Bush Tanager always has dark eyes, no postocular spot, and whiter, unmarked throat contrasting sharply with narrower but more sharply defined, brighter yellow breast-band. Pirre Bush Tanager easily confused but no overlap in range.

Ssp. *C. o. eminens* (E Andes in Co) white postocular spot, near-white throat

C. o. exitelus (W & C Andes in Co) no postocular spot

C. o. falconensis (NE Ve) white postocular spot

C. o. flavopectus (E Andes in Co) dark eyes, no postocular spot, near-white throat

C. o. jacqueti (Co: E Andes, N Ve: Coastal Cordillera) white postocular spot,

C. o. macarenae (Macarena Mts., Co) no postocular spot, near-white throat, white belly

C. o. nigriceps (C Andes & Upper Magdalena Valley, Co) no postocular spot, but white eyes contrast with very dark head, heavily speckled throat

C. o. phaeocephalus (Ec) dingiest race, no postocular spot, but has pale yellow-orange to pinkish eyes, slightly speckled pale buff throat
C. o. ponsi (Co, Perijá in Ve) white postocular spot
C. o. trudis (E Andes in Co) no postocular spot, near-white throat
C. o. venezuelanus (Andes in Ve) white postocular spot, well-speckled throat

Habits Constantly flicks tail sideways and flashes white underwings as it noisily forages for invertebrates, fruits, flowers, nectar and seeds. Travels in pairs or small to large flocks at all levels and often joins mixed-species flocks.
Status Generally common in forest and at edges, less so in clearings and second growth. Less common and more local in Ecuador.
Habitat Tropical to Subtropical Zones, at 700–3,000m, but usually 1,000–2,500m in humid to wet mossy forests with lots of epiphytes, also edges, dense second growth and patchy trees near forest.
Voice Hard, short contact calls include an easily overlooked *chep* or *chup* and a buzzy *tsit*, sometimes given in trilled series *t-z-z-z-z-z-z-z-zit*. Dawn song a long rhythmic series of *chit* or *chup* notes at *c*.1 note per s, sometimes ending in a descending trill or chatter (R&T, I&I, R&G, Hilty).

TACARCUNA BUSH TANAGER
Chlorospingus tacarcunae Pl. 249

Identification 13–14cm. Dark olive above, slightly browner on head but effectively concolorous, no postocular spot, yellow throat, olivaceous-green breast and most of underparts, paler and dull whitish centre of belly. Eyes white or yellow, bill dark, legs and feet vinaceous-grey. Juvenile similar, duller and has brown eyes. No overlap with any other bush tanager.

Ssp. Monotypic (NW Co: Cerro Tacarcuna, Darién range)

Habits Forages for invertebrates, in small flocks, mostly in understorey, but at all levels in stunted elfin forest. Travels in small flocks in understorey like Common Bush Tanager, often joins mixed-species flocks.
Status Locally fairly common on east slope of Cerro Tacarcuna in north-west Chocó, Colombia.
Habitat Tropical Zone, at 1,100–1,500m. In tall as well as stunted cloud forest and edges.
Voice Unknown.
Note Sometimes considered a subspecies of Common Bush Tanager.

PIRRE BUSH TANAGER
Chlorospingus inornatus Pl. 249

Identification 15cm. Dark olive-green above with dark grey head, yellow throat with dusky spots, olivaceous-green on breast, sides and flanks, cream or yellowish eyes, dark bill and grey legs and feet. Looks much like Common Bush Tanager, but no overlap with any other bush tanager, though cf. Tacarcuna Bush Tanager which has paler head and lacks throat spots.

Ssp. Monotypic (NW Co: Cerro Nique)

Habits Forages for invertebrates and fruits in small flocks, mostly in dense and vine entangled midstorey to canopy. Sometimes joins mixed-species flocks.
Status Found on Cerro Nique in Chocó, north-west Colombia.
Habitat Tropical Zone, at 800–1,700m. In forests and edges, also stands of bamboo in elfin forest.
Voice Calls include 3 buzzy thin high notes, *SPEETza*, *tsip* and *chuweet*, given singly or repeated up to 4 times (I&I).
Note Sometimes considered a subspecies of Common Bush Tanager.

DUSKY-BELLIED BUSH TANAGER
Chlorospingus semifuscus Pl. 249

Identification 14–15cm. Very plain, rather dark bush tanager with dark brownish-olive head, olive upperparts and brownish-grey underparts, buffier on throat, palest on belly and more olive on flanks and vent. Yellow-throated Bush Tanager has obvious yellow throat. Yellow-green Bush Tanager has brown eyes and uniform olive underparts. Larger Ochre-breasted Tanager has heavier bill and buffy underparts.

Ssp. *C. s. livingstoni* (W Co) pale yellowish eyes, dark grey head with small postocular spot, olive flanks and vent with rest of underparts purer grey than *semifuscus*; juvenile has faint grey streaks on belly and greyish throat
C. s. semifuscus (SW Co, NW Ec south to W Cotopaxi) pale reddish-brown eyes; juvenile has olive-tinged crown and head-sides

Habits Noisily forages in pairs or small to large flocks, mostly at lower levels, often joins mixed-species flocks.
Status Fairly common to common.
Habitat Tropical to Subtropical Zones, at 700–2,500m, in wet mossy cloud forest, clearings and second growth. More confined to forest interior than Common Bush Tanager, but visits edges to seek fruits
Voice Calls include a very high, oft-repeated *seet* and high buzzy trill. Crepuscular song is a series of high *tsit* notes becoming *tsit-it* notes before usually ending in a buzzy trill (I&I).
Note Also called Dusky Bush Tanager.

SHORT-BILLED BUSH TANAGER
Chlorospingus parvirostris Pl. 249

Identification 14–14.7cm. Olive upperparts, distinctive broad orange-yellow sweeping up from throat- to neck-sides, paler on central throat, brownish-grey underparts, yellowish undertail-coverts, pale greyish eyes, dark bill and grey legs. Yellow-throated Bush Tanager (race *flavigularis*) has pale grey (not olive) lores and more extensive yellow throat neatly separated from grey underparts, and usually occurs at lower elevations.

Ssp. *C. p. huallagae* (Ec, C & S Co)

Habits Forages for invertebrates, fruits and seeds in pairs

or small flocks, at all levels, lower at forest edges. Often joins mixed-species flocks.
Status Uncommon to fairly common but local.
Habitat Subtropical Zone, at 1,200–2,500m. Mossy forest and shrubby edges, sometimes along montane streams.
Voice Calls include an incessant *tsip*, and higher pitched vibrating *seep*, sometimes preceded by an abrupt thin *tsip* (F&K, I&I).
Note Also called Yellow-whiskered Bush Tanager.

YELLOW-THROATED BUSH TANAGER

Chlorospingus flavigularis Pl. 249

Identification 15cm. Adult has olive upperparts except yellow wing fringes, distinctive pure yellow throat neatly separated from rest of grey underparts, pale to white on belly, olive-tinged flanks and vent. Eye colour varies locally from hazel to brownish-orange. See Dusky-bellied Bush Tanager and Short-billed Bush Tanager. Yellow-green Bush Tanager has olive underparts.

Ssp. *C. f. flavigularis* (E Ec, C & NW Co) as described
C. f. marginatus (W Ec, W Co) pale eyes, yellow limited to throat-sides with central throat grey (but no overlap with similar Short-billed Bush Tanager above)

Habits Noisy and conspicuous as it forages alone, in pairs or small to large flocks at all levels (lower at edges) for invertebrates, fruits, flowers, nectar and seeds; often joins mixed-species flocks.
Status Fairly common to common.
Habitat Tropical Zone, at 300–2,100m, but usually below 1,800m, in humid to wet mossy forest and shrubby edges, especially along montane streams, also in second growth but rarely outside forest.
Voice Calls include an incessant spitting low- to moderately pitched *swit* or *chit*. Dawn song of *flavigularis* a steady series of alternating *tsuw-tseét* notes; that of *marginatus* a monotonous series of weak high *tsit* notes at *c*.2 notes per s (I&I, R&G).

YELLOW-GREEN BUSH TANAGER

Chlorospingus flavovirens Pl. 249

Identification 14–14.5cm. Very dull, almost unicoloured bush tanager with olive upperparts, black lores, dusky ear-coverts and yellow-olive underparts (most yellow on throat and vent). Brown eyes. See Dusky-bellied and Yellow-throated Bush Tanagers. Larger Olive Tanager (no overlap) has heavier bill. Larger Ochre-breasted Tanager has heavier bill and buffy underparts. Oleaginous Hemispingus is more ochraceous below with indistinct supercilium and smaller bill.

Ssp. Monotypic (NW Ec, SW Co)

Habits Noisily forages for invertebrates, fruits, and flowers in pairs or small flocks, mostly from midstorey to canopy. Often joins mixed-species flocks.
Status Vulnerable. Known only from a few locations, where fairly common to common, within small range on lower Pacific slope of Andes in north-west Ecuador (around El Placer, Esmeraldas, and at least historically in Pichincha, where now probably extinct) and south-west Colombia (4 sites in Nariño and 2 sites in Valle del Cauca). Habitat loss is occurring at a significant rate due to road building, logging, small-scale agriculture and gold mining.
Habitat Tropical Zone, around 500–1,100m in humid to wet mossy cloud forest and edges, also adjacent clearings with scattered tall trees.
Voice Calls include a loud, hoarse raspy and oft-repeated *chut* (I&I).

ASHY-THROATED BUSH TANAGER

Chlorospingus canigularis Pl. 249

Identification 13–14cm. Bright yellowish olive-green above with grey head, paler on chin and throat, distinctive yellowish breast-band and undertail-coverts, rest of underparts pale grey, slightly darker and more olivaceous on sides and flanks. Dark reddish-brown eyes, bill black above, slate below, legs and feet blue-grey. See Common Bush Tanager.

Ssp. *C. c. canigularis* (C Co, SW Ve) as described
C. c. conspicillatus (NW Ec, W Co) very close to *canigularis* but yellowish breast deeper in tone and broader, green body-sides more extensive
C. c. paulus (SW Ec) similar to both *canigularis* and *conspicillatus* but smaller, head clearer grey and back paler green, sometimes with narrow white postocular streak
C. c. signatus (E Ec) darker grey head, especially cheeks and ear-coverts which are nearly black, with conspicuous white postocular streak

Habits Forages for invertebrates and fruits in pairs or small flocks, from midstorey to canopy (lower at forest edges). Often joins mixed-species flocks.
Status Uncommon to locally fairly common.
Habitat Tropical to Temperate Zones, 300–2,600m. Humid to wet tall mossy forest and vine-strewn edges, often along montane streams, also in adjacent clearings and second growth.
Voice Calls include chips, thin twitters and rapid chittering notes, much like congeners (F&K, Hilty).
Note Also called Ash-throated Bush Tanager.

Piranga is a genus long considered to be typical tanagers, but recent DNA evidence suggests they should be placed within the typical cardinals in Cardinalidae, though they are currently regarded by the AOU as being incertae sedis. They are all medium-sized, with males being mostly bright red in breeding plumage, olivaceous-green and yellow when not breeding, when they resemble the females. They have stout bills, generally occur in pairs and are arboreal, keeping in the main to woodland of various types. Two species breed in North America, visiting our region in the boreal winter. The rest are resident.

HIGHLAND HEPATIC TANAGER

Piranga lutea Pl. 255

Identification 18cm. Adult male Brazil red above (like deep scarlet washed oxblood brown), with fine white streaks on ear-coverts, slightly paler below, rosiest on belly, and pale red eye-ring; eyes pale brown, bill, legs and feet grey. Adult female yellowish-olive (bright citron) above with yellow eye-ring and faint grey lores, yellow below with olive-tinged sides and flanks. Subadult male like female but has irregular red-tinged patches and is brighter yellow below. Juvenile like female but has dark brown streaks above and below. Similar male Summer Tanager has uniform bill, varying from pale to medium horn, lacks dusky lores, and is more rose-coloured below; female greener above and brighter yellow below, some are apparently slightly tinged orange below, unlike female Highland Hepatic Tanager (R&G).

Ssp. *P.l. desidiosa* (SW Co) male darker, deeper red than *lutea*, ear-coverts not streaked with white and no red eye-ring; female darker, with more olive back

P. l. faceta (N Co, N Ve, Tr) as described

P. l. haemalea (S Ve, W Gu, Su, FG) male darker than *faceta*, entirely oxblood red above with dusky grey lores, scarlet throat and belly has weak oxblood wash on breast; eyes pale brown, and more noticeably 2-tone bill, dark horn above, bone white below, legs and feet olive; female also darker than *faceta*, with more obviously olive-tinged upperparts; juvenile like female but has dusky streaks on sides and flanks

P. l. lutea (W Ec, SW Co) entirely bright red with fine white streaks on ear-coverts, red eye-ring; paler below, bill dusky above, pale greyish below, more so at base of mandible; female olive above, yellow below, washed olive on sides and flanks; immature male like female but has reddish lores and forehead

P. l. toddi (C Co) close to *faceta* but lores blackish, more bluish-red above, less scarlet, below washed grey on flanks, more like begonia rose on abdomen; female deeper yellow below, almost orange on throat with very dark flanks, like female *desidiosa*

Habits Usually in pairs and often in mixed flocks. Forages rather deliberately, at all levels but most frequently in canopy.
Status Uncommon to fairly common in Ecuador and Colombia, uncommon in Venezuela, and Trinidad, whilst scarce to locally common at higher altitudes in Suriname or French Guiana perhaps spreading due to deforestation in Ecuador.
Habitat Tropical to Subtropical Zones. To 1,900m on west slope in Ecuador and 1,000–1,350m on east slope, to 2,200m in Colombia, 450–2,050m north of Orinoco in Venezuela, 800–1,800m south of it, and in Suriname and French Guiana reported at 500–800m. Very much a forest bird.
Voice Calls include a frequent *chup* or *chup-chitup*, and *chup* or *tjik* in alarm; sometimes a *chuktik* or *chuktiti*, creaky *weez* and *yuhtitdit*, which sometimes ends with an added *yuh*, given perched or in flight. Race *haemalea* in Suriname gives short toneless chirps, *chip, chip, chipchipchip*… Song a leisurely, choppy series of typically 4–8 sweet, musical phrases which rise and fall, e.g. *wueep, purty, churdik, wudik, purty, wordik, chueet, breep, cheet* or *whip, chew'whip, worry, jury, keép-fit*; dawn song similar but longer (F&K, ffrench, I&I, R&G, Hilty, H&M).
Notes Previously considered part of an expanded species, Hepatic Tanager *Piranga flava*, which embraced both Highland Hepatic Tanager and Northern Hepatic Tanager as defined by I&I and substantiated by DNA analysis (Burns 1998). Subspecies *haemalea* has been treated as separate species, e.g. H&M, called Blood-red Tanager, and may be confirmed as such. IOC-recommended English name is Tooth-billed Tanager.

LOWLAND HEPATIC TANAGER

Piranga flava Pl. 255

Identification 18cm. Adult male bright brick red with dark bill. Adult female yellowish-olive above with yellow eye-ring, faint grey lores and yellow below with olive-tinged sides and flanks. Subadult male like female but has irregular red-tinged patches. Juvenile like female but has dark brown streaks above and below. Only all bright red tanager in range in our region, race *haemalea* of Highland Hepatic Tanager is much deeper and richer blood red, *macconnelli* is scarlet to grenadine below and is paler above.

Ssp. *P.f. macconnelli* (SW Gu: Roraima to SE) as described

P.f. saira (Su; Sipaliwini savanna, FG) the 2 races virtually identical, but *saira* is slightly deeper and richer red above and uniform bright scarlet-pink below; female deep olive-grey above

Status Moderately common in the Sipaliwini savanna, where considered to be race *saira* by Mees (H&M) but 'probably' *macconnelli* by I&I; fairly common in southern Guyana.
Habitat Tropical to Temperate Zones, 200–2400m, but usually at 700–1,500m; *macconnelli* is highland race and *saira* lowland, according to Mees (1974). Edges of deciduous to moist and even humid forests, lighter woodlands, more open tall second growth, and tall trees in clearings, riverine vegetation, plantations, orchards, parks and gardens, and even scattered scrub, tree groves and *Mauritia* palms in savannas.
Voice Calls include a soft *chef* and *chu chu*, a loud chip or *tcherit*, and song is a frequently repeated *tschip-tschurr* (I&I).
Notes Previously part of a broader species, Hepatic Tanager *Piranga flava*, which embraced both Highland Hepatic Tanager and Northern Hepatic Tanager as defined by I&I and substantiated by DNA analysis (Burns 1998). IOC-recommended English name is Red Tanager.

SUMMER TANAGER

Piranga rubra Pl. 255

Identification 16.5–18cm. Adult male pale carmine above with brown lores, rose-scarlet below; eyes sepia, bill horn, slightly darker above, legs and feet grey. First-year male like female, but often with red patches in plumage. Adult male and female easily confused with Hepatic Tanager.

Ssp. *P. r. rubra* (boreal migrant in Ec, N Co, N & SE Ve, T&T, Cu)

Habits Forages for invertebrates and fruits, rather deliberately, usually alone but sometimes in pairs. At all levels. Sometimes joins mixed-species flocks.
Status Uncommon to locally fairly common (mostly October–April, but also in September, January–February and May), primarily in foothill and montane habitats in northern South America, on also migration observed in Curaçao (early autumn and April). Uncommon in coastal French Guiana.
Habitat Tropical to Subtropical Zones, to 3,100m but usually below 2,000m. Humid forest, edges, forested swamps, second-growth woodland, plantations, shrubby clearings and gardens with scattered trees.
Voice Calls include a distinctive, staccato *TIC-a-tup*, *pit-ti-tuck*, *pit-tiuc-tiuc-tiuc* or *pi-tuk*. Not known to sing in northern South America (ffrench, I&I, R&G, Hilty).
Note Comprises 2 races, eastern race *rubra* and western *cooperi*, but only *rubra* has been observed in northern South America.

SCARLET TANAGER

Piranga olivacea — Pl. 255

Identification 16–18 cm. On arrival on wintering grounds (October), non-breeding adult male is olive above and olive-yellow below, with black wings and tail, but gradually becomes mottled red patches and assumes distinctive red-and-black breeding plumage (January–May). Adult female like non-breeding male, but has wings and tail dusky brownish-olive. First-year male like female or has orange tinge (young sometimes also have faint reddish or yellowish wingbars). Juvenile streaked brownish. Unmarked dark wings should distinguish this tanager from congeners (but compare Vermilion Tanager which has black bib).

Ssp. Monotypic (boreal migrant to Ec, W & C Co, W Ve, T&T)

Habits Forages for invertebrates, fruits and berries. Usually alone but sometimes in pairs or small flocks (mostly in spring). At all levels but usually high up.
Status Uncommon to occasionally fairly common in Ecuador (October–April) and Colombia (October–May), uncommon in Aruba (October, April), Bonaire and Curaçao (October–November, April–May), rare passage migrant in Venezuela, vagrant to Trinidad (April) and Tobago (April–May).
Habitat Tropical Zone, to 3,000m on migration but usually below 1,500m. Humid forests, edges, second growth, open woodland, clearings, parks and gardens with scattered trees.
Voice Calls include an abrupt throaty *chip-burrr*, first part moderate-pitched and second low, and sometimes shortened to *chip*. Not known to sing in our region (H&B, I&I, R&G, Hilty).

WHITE-WINGED TANAGER

Piranga leucoptera — Pl. 255

Identification 13–14.5cm. Smaller than other *Piranga*. Adult male carmine-red except black wings with 2 bold, pure white wingbars and all-black tail. Adult female typically olive-green above and yellow below but has black wings with white wingbars, and blackish tail. Diagnostic black wings with 2 white wingbars make species unmistakable.

Ssp. *P. l. ardens* (Ec, SW Co) as described
P. l. venezuelae (Co, Ve) virtually identical but for wider white wingbars

Habits Often forages lethargically, sometimes actively in pairs or sometimes alone or in small flocks in canopy (sometimes lower at edge) for invertebrates, fruits, berries and seeds, often joins mixed-species flocks.
Status Uncommon to locally fairly common in Ecuador and Colombia, fairly common in Venezuela.
Habitat Tropical to Subtropical Zones, 600–2,500m but mostly at 1,200–2,000m. Humid forest (especially epiphyte-laden cloud forest), edges, mature second growth, plantations and scattered adjacent trees, and especially in drier areas where forest is disturbed and broken.
Voice Calls include a frequently heard, distinctive *pit-sweet!* or *pit-sweet-sweet!* (alternatively *tsupeét* or *wheet, tsupeét*), the *sweet* notes rising and musical; also various sharp buzzy *weet* and *chip* notes, often rapidly repeated, and a trill of 6–10 notes. Song a thin, wiry *e-seé-se-whEET* (alternatively, *tsee-tsee-tsu-tsu*) (H&B, R&T, I&I, R&G, Hilty).
Note Sometimes placed in genus *Spermagra* (R&G).

RED-HOODED TANAGER

Piranga rubriceps — Pl. 255

Identification 17–19cm. Adult male bright olive-green above with black wings and yellow shoulders, and a striking, complete red hood. Adult female has hood restricted to chin but is otherwise similar. Subadult has orange instead of red, or partially red-and-orange hood, and yellow wingbars. Juvenile yellowish-olive above with broken yellow eye-ring, 2 narrow buffy wingbars and pale yellow below with faint dusky streaks on breast and sides, and ochraceous tone to vent. Should be unmistakable, although some congeners are somewhat similar, e.g. moulting immature male Scarlet Tanager or Summer Tanager.

Ssp. Monotypic (W Ec, W Co)

Habits Forages for invertebrates, fruits, seeds, seemingly rather sluggishly. May be alone, in pairs or small flocks. Mostly in canopy. Sometimes joins mixed-species flocks.
Status Rare to uncommon and local.
Habitat Subtropical to Temperate Zones, at 1,700–3,000m. Humid to wet open forest and edges.
Voice Calls include a rapid *ti-t-t-t-DEE* and sharp, piercing *tsee-ee-ee-ee*. Song a rapid, thin, high trill, *ti-ti-ti-ti-ti-ti*, alternated with a sweet, evenly paced, moderate-pitched *da-dee-dee*, *da-dee-da-dee-dee* or *tswe, weéteetseetsee*, with pauses of c.2–4 s between phrases, and sometimes additional moderate to high-pitched phrases such as *weet-check* or a hoarse *whirt* or *wirst* interspersed (I&I, R&G).

WESTERN TANAGER

Piranga ludoviciana Pl. 256

Identification 17cm. Adult male yellow with black mantle, wings and tail; wings have yellow patch near bend of wing formed by lesser and median wing-coverts, tips of greater wing-coverts white, forming a bar. In breeding plumage, head bright red, but at other times the yellow upperparts are washed olive-green, and the red largely replaced by olive-green, leaving only red as a heavy tinge to face. Bill is pale horn, legs and feet grey. Normal female olive-green above, paler and yellower on rump and uppertail-coverts, wings blackish, olive on lesser wing-coverts, median coverts yellow, forming wingbar, the greater coverts have white tips forming second bar; below yellow. Grey-morph female has back and lesser wing-coverts greyish, and breast to flanks and vent pale grey. Nearest similar species is Red-hooded Tanager, separable by uniform greenish back and rump, but restricted to Andes. Female Western Tanager separated from female Scarlet Tanager by dusky back contrasting with paler more greenish head (Scarlet is uniform from head to rump) and more orange-horn bill.

Ssp. Monotypic (Bo)

Habits Usually solitary but may form flocks during migration.

Status Accidental. A single July record from Bonaire (adult male), which was photographed.

Habitat Apparently prefers pine or pine–oak woodlands, low scrubby forest, forest edge and plantations, open areas with scattered trees. On migration may be found in more open habitats (I&I). On Bonaire, seen in shrubbery and scattered trees in a garden area, feeding in bushes and on ground, catching insects (Wells & Wells 2002).

Voice Quiet on migration. Call in flight a soft whistle, *howee* or *weet* (Sibley).

Tiaris grassquits are currently categorised by SACC as Incertae Sedis, with the added complication that the type species, *olivaceus*, appears not very closely related to its congeners. They are likely to settle in *Thraupidae* as a distinct group of tanager-finches. Round-bodied little birds with sharp bills, males have black on the face and greenish upperparts; females are duller. They usually keep in undergrowth, though may forage higher. Their natural history is not well known.

DULL-COLOURED GRASSQUIT

Tiaris obscurus Pl. 274

Identification 10.5cm. Entire upperparts are hair brown tending to dark drab on flight-feathers, with buffy eye-ring, and entirely olivaceous-drab below; sexes; alike; bill dark brown to blackish above, horn-coloured below, especially at base. Much like female Black-faced Grassquit, but usually found at higher elevations.

Ssp. Monotypic (E Ec, SW & NE Co, NW & NC Ve)

Habits Normally singly, in pairs or occasionally in small groups. Very retiring, shy and inconspicuous, keeping to cover of understorey. Usually one only sees a male as it rises on a stem to reach an inflorescence, or to sing.

Status Uncommon to scarce. Has retreated in face of human settlement of northern cordilleras of Venezuela (once bred in Caracas), and probably elsewhere as well.

Habitat Upper Tropical to Subtropical Zones, at 1,480m and 2,180m in Tambito National Park, south-west Colombia, below 1,600m in Perijá and north and east slopes of Santa Marta, and to 2,100m in central Colombia; in Venezuela at 900–1,300m. Cultivated areas, clearings, open vegetation and scrub, subtropical second-growth woodland, along trails with *Panicum maximum*, and generally at woodland edges.

Voice Song is composed, smooth and melodious (Canevari *et al.* 1991), and an explosive, buzzy *zeetig, zeezeezig!* (R&T), a trilling *zerisleree-zerisleree* (Koepcke 1970) and *szwee-yee-chittytitee* (J. V. Moore recording from Ecuador).

Notes We follow Bates (1997) in considering *S. obscurus* monotypic. Name *Tiaris* is masculine; therefore correct spelling is *obscurus*, not *obscura* (David & Gosselin 2002).

YELLOW-FACED GRASSQUIT

Tiaris olivaceus Pl. 274

Identification 10cm. Adult male bright olive-green above, blackish on face with bright orange-yellow supraloral spot that becomes a vestigial supercilium which terminates just behind eyes, crescent below eyes and bib same colour; buffy-olive below. Amount of black depends on age and varies from forehead, fore cheeks and upper breast in first-year to effectively entire head, breast and sides, trailing off on belly in older bird. Female duller and slightly browner version of male with yellow restricted to frontal band and supraloral, and a small bib. Juvenile like female but lacks any yellow. Female is not as dark nor as large as female Sooty Grassquit.

Ssp. *T. o. pusillus* (N Ec, W Co, Táchira in Ve)

Habits Forages alone, usually in pairs but also in groups within larger flocks of seed-eaters. Song is often first evidence of their presence. In wet season appears to feed almost exclusively on seeds of various grasses, both from ground and stem, clinging to one stem and grasping another with its bill, and feeds on several stems from single position. Occasionally takes seeds of other herbs as well as small white protein bodies, favoured by ants, from hairy brown cushions at bases of petioles of *Cecropia* trees. Also forages in crowns of low trees like wood warblers, taking small fruits, tender shoots and insects; observed sipping nectar from flowers.

Status Common in Colombia, rare in Venezuela.

Habitat In Venezuela in rain and cloud forest edges, semi-open grassy fields with scattered trees and bushes, cultivated and suburban areas, at 500–2,300m. In Colombia, open country, in pastures and clearings and other grassy areas and forest edges; also favours marshy localities with tall grass.

Voice A high thin *tsit*, sharp *tsik*, *sik*, or *tsi* or *tssip!* most often uttered from low perch. Song only heard during breeding season, a long-drawn, rapid trill, weak but sweet in tone. Alternatively, a series of high, thin rapid trills, varying in pitch, speed and notation, often prolonged, and sometimes delivered by several males perched together in a shrub (Skutch 1954).; typically, a weak, buzzy trill, *tttttt-tee* (H&B).

Note Name *Tiaris* is masculine, thus correct spelling is *olivaceus*, not *olivacea*, and race is *pusillus* (David & Gosselin 2002).

BLACK-FACED GRASSQUIT

Tiaris bicolor Pl. 274

Identification 10cm. Young adult male olive-green above, with black face extending to breast, greenish-buffy below. Amount of black age-related, birds older than 3 years have black extending right over head and covering entire underparts, with undertail-coverts fringed buffy. Bill black, legs and feet vinous-flesh. Female also olive-green above, buffy below, bill horn. Juvenile indistinguishable from female, but males start to show some black on face at *c*.3–5 months. Male could be confused with larger, deeper green Sooty Grassquit, but they rarely overlap, as latter is normally above 1,000m. Female could be mistaken for Dull-coloured Grassquit, but is generally more greenish above and sandy below, and Dull-coloured Grassquit has 2-tone bill.

Ssp. *T. b. huilae* (Magdalena Valley, C Co) palest race, dull sandy

T. b. johnstonei (Blanquilla & Hermanos Is., Ve) richer and greener above, black underparts more extensive, no pale fringes to undertail-coverts

T. b. omissa (NE Co, N Ve) as described

T. b. sharpei (ABC) variable, but usually paler with slate rather than black

T. b. tortugensis (Tortuga I., Ve) like *sharpei* but larger; heavier bill

Habits Readily forages on ground, where continually wing-flicks, alone, in pairs or small (sometimes large) groups and usually feeding on seeding *Panicum maximum* at roadsides and on wasteland, but also takes seeds of other herbs as well as small white protein bodies, favoured by ants, from hairy brown cushions at bases of petioles of *Cecropia* trees. Forages in crowns of low trees like wood warblers, for small fruits, tender shoots and insects; observed feeding on nectar of flowers of Scarlet Cordia tree *Cordia sebestena* in manner akin to Bananaquits. Crop content analysis showed traces of fruit of 2 species of cactus.

Status Uncommon and local in Colombia, fairly common in Venezuela.

Habitat Tropical Zone, to 1,300 in Colombia, to 1,000m in Venezuela, in open thorn scrub, dry *Acacia* and cactus scrub, open sandy places, particularly those with rich vegetation of herbs and dry grasses, and very dry xerophytic scrub. Also, possibly commonest species in Caracas, where occurs in dense scrub and lush second growth on hillsides, visiting feeders in gardens; also listed for rice fields (Meyer de Schauensee 1971).

Voice Contact a weak *tsit*. Early in breeding season, male performs variations of display-flight, flying very slowly with rapid shallow wingbeats, sometimes gliding momentarily, giving somewhat buzzy, *zit, di-diddle-dideee-dideee* and occasionally adding a couple of extra sweet notes, *zit, di-diddle-didee-didee-swee-swee* (Restall 1976). In Aruba song more like *chit-chitzy-chtzy*. In contrast, Voous (1983) notes a pleasant buzzing or rather twittering *tsee-tsee-tsee seeseesee*.

SOOTY GRASSQUIT

Tiaris fuliginosus Pl. 274

Identification 11.5cm. Adult male dark brown to fuscous, blacker on face and breast, with a rich olive-green wash on back, and in fresh breeding plumage has almost lustrous green glow, but leading edge of primaries paler. First-year male browner, and pale on chin; underwing-coverts sayal brown and undertail-coverts tend to cinnamon; bill black or dark neutral grey on upper mandible, lower perhaps slightly paler, and gape-sides pink, more noticeable in some, and bright rosy in adult breeding male; legs and feet from horn, dark vinous, brown to dark brown, to blackish, claws brown or horn. Immature to first-year male has upper mandible black and lower brown. Adult female is uniform drab, greyish-brown or dull olive-brown. Some totally lack any olive, whilst others possess a strong wash, especially on back. Others tend to cinnamon on underparts, and some are noticeably paler on abdomen. Underwing-coverts pale olive drab to light drab, in general paler than male. Juvenile is surprisingly bright olive-green and distinguished by noticeably 2-tone bill; upper mandible dark brown, lower mandible pale horn. Neither Black-faced nor Dull-coloured Grassquit has black on back, and unusual to find Black-faced above 1,000m and Sooty rarely below 1,000m. In side-by-side comparison, Dull-coloured has lower mandible paler than that of female Sooty, but some birds have all-black bills, and juvenile Sooty Grassquit has bicoloured bill.

Ssp. *T. f. fumosus* (N Ve, Tr) fully adult male decidedly darker above and below

T. f. zuliae (Perijá, Ve) more greyish-olive upperparts, below olive; elsewhere in NW Ve (Trujillo) both sexes distinctly duller with no green lustre above, bill, legs and feet dusky

Habits Encountered singly, in pairs or in small groups and not normally associated with other species. Forages in grass or low in shrubs and is easily overlooked.

Status Presumed uncommon and irregular, and invariably local, but also transient. Being nomadic and connected to seeding bamboo, true status unknown.

Habitat Tropical to Subtropical Zones, sight records to 2,300m but usually encountered above 800m and commonest around 2,000m. Grassy and weed-grown clearings within forest, second growth, open fields, scrub, and rice and corn fields. Usually found in seeding bamboo throughout range, and bamboo-forested areas are probably its preferred habitat.

Voice Generally quiet, but utters a simple *tchee*, sometimes repeated, also soft, penetrating *szit*. Song a short series of thin, high-pitched notes that run together and reminiscent of a scratchy, high-pitched violin, lasts 3 s. Sits somewhat puffed up, opens mouth, and tilts head so bright rose-coloured gape is very noticeable, starts with an outburst of finch-like *peep* notes, then *pizz-i-pizz-i-pizz-zii-zii-ziii-ziiii*, tailing off. In flight a continually repeated *tsizisizisizi* song similar to Black-faced Grassquit, but higher pitched and less structured (Restall pers. obs.).

Notes Considered probably monotypic (Bates 1997), but we found a distinct difference between live birds in Venezuela. Name *Tiaris* is masculine, so correct spelling of specific and subspecific names is *fuliginosus* and *fumosus* (David & Gosselin 2002).

Bananaquit has had and continues to enjoy a checkered taxonomic history, from being the sole representative of a family to being very closely related to *Tiaris*. Currently it is categorised by the AOU as Incertae Sedis, next to *Tiaris*. Small birds with long, curved bills, most races are similar with the exception of some extreme variants on islands, some are very common and others extremely rare.

BANANAQUIT *Coereba flaveola* Pl. 266

Identification 10cm. Adult has dark grey back, black wings with white speculum at base of primaries, yellowish rump, black tail with white tips to outer feathers, black top of head with bold white superciliary from base of bill to sides of nape, black lores and ear-coverts, extensive grey throat, underparts yellow except white undertail-coverts. Juvenile duller with a shorter bill and more olivaceous upperparts.

Ssp. *C. f. bolivari* (E & NE Ve) pale sulphur-yellow below, white speculum

C. f. bonairensis (Bo) pale wingbars, paler above, narrower, white throat

C. f. caucae (W Co) closest to *columbiana* but white supercilia much narrower, pale grey throat finely variegated, dusky on malar region

C. f. columbiana (SW Co, SC Ve) throat edged white, more greenish above

C. f. ferryi (Tortuga Is., Ve) full white forehead, extended white speculum

C. f. frailensis (Los Frailes & Los Hermanos Is., Ve) grey throat, large speculum, flanks and thighs olive grey

C. f. gorgonae (Gorgona Is., Co) nearest to *intermedia* but throat-sides and malar finely barred dusky, back sooty, speculum very small, white spots at tip of tail very small

C. f. guianensis (E Ve, Gu) vestigial speculum, no white on tail

C. f. intermedia (Ec, SW Co, SW Amazonas, Ve) paler olive above, white speculum

C. f. laurae (Los Testigos Is., Ve) all black

C. f. lowii (Los Roques, Ve) sage-washed back, head, wings and tail black, sides, flanks and lower belly to undertail-coverts sage, throat to upper belly black

C. f. luteola (N Co, N Ve, T&T) deep black above, white speculum, olive-grey thighs, greenish flanks

C. f. melanornis (Cayo Sal, Ve) black, with sage vent, thighs, rear flanks and undertail-coverts

C. f. minima (E Co, S Ve, Su, FG) smallest, pale grey chin and throat, no speculum

C. f. montana (SW Ve) extended white speculum, grades to pale

C. f. obscura (NE Co, W Ve) dark grey chin and throat, dusky above, white speculum, no white in tail

C. f. roraimae (S & SE Ve, S Gu) small, pale yellow breast, gradually becoming paler on undertail-coverts

C. f. uropygialis (Ar, Cu) broad supercilium, vent to undertail-coverts white

Habits A fearless little busybody that suspends its nest from tall bushes, small trees and seaside coconut palms, and many are dormitories, not being used for breeding. In some areas has learned to visit tables to steal sugar and jams. Usually seen alone, as pairs maintain only loose contact when foraging, mostly dipping for nectar, but almost as frequently piercing holes in bases of flowers to acquire nectar.

Status Common on north coast and most islands, less common inland.

Habitat Tropical and Lower Subtropical Zones Most common in lowlands below 100m, but frequent to 1,000m and records to 2,000m, in light second growth and open woodland, plantations, parks and gardens, coastal coconut groves and mangroves, but rare to absent from humid and heavy forests, and xerophytic areas. Otherwise, typical of the canopy of tall *terra firme* forest in French Guiana.

Voice Song a cheerful and endless repetition of buzzing, chipping and whistling notes, oddly suggestive of Black-faced Grassquit gone berserk, with much regional variation.

EMBERIZIDAE – New World Sparrows, Brush Finches and Allies

Emberizidae is a large and rather complex family of generally sparrow-sized birds. Recent DNA-based taxonomic research (e.g. Burns 1997, 1998, 2002) has resulted in a major revision to the Neotropical part of the family. Several subfamilies have been accorded family rank, including Thraupidae (tanagers) and Cardinalidae (cardinals and grosbeaks). Some subfamilies have been removed to other families, with euphonias and chlorophonias having been transferred to Fringillidae. Saltators have joined cardinals and grosbeaks in Cardinalidae, and other genera are undoubtedly en route to new niches, but currently placed in limbo of Incertae Sedis, including *Sporophila* seedeaters and *Tiaris* grassquits, which seem bound for Thraupidae where they will presumably be known collectively as tanager-finches. North American *Piranga* tanagers and dull red *Habia* ant tanagers are also in Incertae Sedis, pending presumed SACC ratification of their transfer to Cardinalidae. The result is a slimmed-down and more homogeneous family that roughly comprises 2 groups. The first is the cryptically plumaged buntings that are essentially North

American. American sparrows are small to medium-sized, often fairly slim, with streaked plumages of black, brown and white. In cases where sexes are distinct, the juvenile is like the adult female. They are birds of the ground, invariably foraging for seeds and insects in the leaf-litter, shuffling under bushes and through shrubby grasses. Some are birds of open grassland where they creep around bases of the grass like mice, seldom being seen in the open, and when disturbed fly a short distance, keeping low and dropping quickly back into cover. All are cheerful but seldom very accomplished songsters and a territorial male may often be the only sign of a species' presence. The second group is purely Neotropical and the birds usually more brightly coloured. In most cases sexes are alike and the rarely seen juveniles are duller above and heavily streaked below. They are far more arboreal, many seeming to spend their entire lives within bushes. In addition to seeds and insects, they take berries and small buds. Distribution is often irregular and fragmented, and recent field work suggests that many species with widespread but fragmented ranges might prove to constitute more than one species.

Sparrows of the genera *Zonotrichia* and *Melospiza* are perky songbirds, normally retiring as they forage amongst leaf-litter, under shrubs and bushes, but appear not to be consciously evasive of man, and once spotted are usually easily observed. They are also invariably cryptic, coloured predominantly in combinations of black and brown, streaked on grey. *Zonotrichia* is a large and widespread genus in North America, but only a single species is resident in South America, although this is extremely widespread and well adapted. Two other sparrows are rare visitors from the north.

LINCOLN'S SPARROW

Melospiza lincolnii Pl. 271

Identification 14cm. Adult brown above, streaked blackish from nape to long uppertail-coverts, with pale to whitish tips to tertials, median and greater coverts, top of head grey with chestnut stripe either side of crown, streaked finely black, head-sides and malar pale cinnamon-brown that continues on breast, sides and flanks to undertail-coverts streaked narrowly black; chin, throat, centre of belly to vent white with fine black streaks. Bill fairly fine, sharp and pointed with flat culmen, almost decurved, dark above and horn below, legs and feet pale horn. Could undoubtedly be mistaken for and dismissed as juvenile Rufous-collared Sparrow, but latter has white superciliary (streaked finely black) and is largely white below, with rufous flush on breast and sides, streaks shorter and thicker than Lincoln's Sparrow.

Ssp. *M. l. lincolnii* (boreal vagrant to N Ve)

Habits Skulker, creeps about silently among leaf-litter like a mouse.

Status Single confirmed record from Portachuelo Pass, Henri Pittier National Park, northern Venezuela.

Habitat Bird in Venezuela was mist-netted at 900m, within primary forest. In West Indies, where a rare migrant and possibly a non-breeding resident, inhabits moist highland forest thickets, especially around clearings and coastal thickets, and borders of dense forests (Raffaele *et al.* 1998). In Panama, where a casual winter visitor, favours dense lower growth in shrubby clearings and woodland borders, to 1,500m (Ridgely & Gwynne).

Voice Not known if it sings in winter; a flat *tschup* or *chip*, repeated rapidly when agitated, and a buzzy *zeee* (Byers *et al.* 1995).

RUFOUS-COLLARED SPARROW

Zonotrichia capensis Pl. 271

Identification 13.5–18cm. Adult brown above, streaked black from mantle to uppertail-coverts, wings and tail blackish, all feathers broadly fringed brown, rufescent on tertials, solid white tips to median coverts and slightly whitish tips to greater coverts. Bright rufous band across nape, reaching breast-sides. Top and sides of head grey with black line either side of crown, edge of cheeks and ear-coverts also black, chin, throat and malar white with terminal black patch, a few irregular black spots or arrowheads across upper breast, between black patches; rest of underparts pale buffy, washed olive on sides and flanks. Juvenile has brown head with whitish supercilium and whitish spots at ends of median and greater coverts, streaked finely but clearly black, underparts streaked cleanly black from throat to undertail-coverts. Considerable variation in size and coloration across different subspecies. Rufous collar separates adult from any similar bird, but juvenile can be perplexing if not seen with adults, and might be mistaken for a vagrant North American sparrow. Whitish eyebrow separates it from Lincoln's Sparrow.

Ssp. *Z. c. bonnetiana* (C Co) compared to *costaricensis*, black marks on neck-sides very small and white between them broad, back dark, dense and less red, with narrower and more black lines; darker than *roraimae* with black lines above broader, darker grey, below very contrasting white belly and brownish wash on sides and flanks

Z. c. capensis (FG) 13.5–14cm; small, rather pale grey head with contrasting narrow black lines, almost pure white below

Z. c. costaricensis (Ec, Co, W Ve) 14–14.5cm; as described; juvenile has top of head brown with short dark streaks, breast rusty, rufescent wash, and streaks do not extend beyond breast and sides

Z. c. inaccessibilis (Neblina, extreme S Ve) 15cm; dark above, dark head, throat and breast washed grey, finely streaked dusky, white belly and edges to undertail-coverts; juvenile has top of head brown, streaked faintly blackish, underparts washed yellowish-white with extensive streaking

Z. c. insularis (Ar, Cu) 14cm; paler, more sandy above, pale orange collar, grey of head pale, all white below

Z. c. macconnelli (Roraima, SE Ve) 16cm; larger, darker

above with duller, vestigial rufous collar, buffy wash to malar, breast, sides and flanks; small black streaks on throat and breast, undertail-coverts streaked brown

Z. c. perezchinchillae (Marahuaca, S Ve) 18cm; very large. darker brown above, head dark grey, underparts mostly dark, buffy-grey; juvenile has top of head almost all black with vestigial brown in centre, feathers of back fringed black and streaked chestnut, giving more reddish appearance than immature or adult, very yellow below and heavily streaked; immature darker above with white spots on tips of tertials and narrow rufous collar, dull, dark buffy-grey below with heavy black arrowhead streaks throughout

Z. c. roraimae (SE Co, S & E Ve, W Gu) 14–16cm; duller and darker above, small white tips to tertials, duller rufous collar, greyish drab underparts from chin to undertail-coverts, only whitish centre of belly; juvenile usually washed buffy-yellow below, but some whiter and have blacker streaks

Z. c. venezuelae (N Ve) 13.5cm; similar to but smaller than *costaricensis*, underparts white with grey wash on flanks, juvenile has crown dark with greyish stripe on centre, whole crown finely streaked black, beige to off-white below, streaks extend to beyond flanks and over belly

Habits Confiding and apparently unconcerned by man, though in fact as wily and cautious of him as House Sparrow, hops on ground surrounding houses and buildings, roads and gardens, foraging for tiny seeds and insects. Even races in distant tepuis seem as confiding and unafraid of man. Forages singly, often in close pairs, and sometimes groups with other species.

Status Common to very common in Ecuador and Colombia, very common in Venezuela in highlands north of Orinoco. Very local in central and southern French Guiana, on rocky outcrops.

Habitat Tropical Zone to Páramo, 900–3,500m in Ecuador 850–3,500m in Colombia, in Venezuela 800–4,000m north of Orinoco, 850–2,800m south of it, with a local population below 200m around Caicara, north-west Bolívar. Varied habitats from open grassy scrub and burned savanna, to urban gardens, light open woodland and regenerating second growth, forest edges, cultivation, farms and plantations, but never in dense or continuous woodland.

Voice Often sings at night. Variation throughout range, both local accents and by subspecies, but always includes drawn-out whistle, *zeeeeu* and/or a trill, e.g. *zeelit-zeeeeu trrrrt* (F&K). Typical song a sudden, short, cheerful outburst of whistles followed by a trill, *tre-tre-tre-tre-tréeeeeng* (R&G) or *tee-teeooo, e'e'e'e'e'e'* (Hilty) or *tee-teeoo, t-e-e-e-e* (R&T) or 3–5 clear whistles followed by a cheerful trill or accelerating stutter (Byers *et al.* 1995). Calls include *tsip*, *chink* and *chip*, etc.

WHITE-THROATED SPARROW

Zonotrichia albicollis Pl. 271

Identification 17cm. Adult rich brown on back, wings and tail, feathers with dusky to blackish centres giving streaked effect, rump and uppertail-coverts greyish-olive, also streaked dusky, top of head black with narrow white line on centre of crown and broad white supercilium, broad white malar separated from white chin and throat by narrow black line; vague white terminal spots on median and greater coverts, face-sides grey; underparts white with some greyish-buff streaks on breast-sides and forming necklace on lower throat. A morph has superciliary buffy-tan and underparts washed lightly greyish-buffy. First-year more distinctly and extensively streaked on sides and flanks. From Rufous-collared Sparrow by grey breast-sides instead of bright rufous and black.

Ssp. Monotypic (occasional boreal migrant to S Caribbean islands)

Status Uncertain in Aruba, Curaçao or Bonaire (Stotz *et al.* 1996), casual to Aruba (Voous).

Habitat Winters in scrub and gardens, with preference for woody and shrubby areas.

Voice A soft, lisping *tsssp* or *tseet* and a harder *chink* (Byers *et al.* 1995).

GRASSHOPPER SPARROW

Ammodramus savannarum Pl. 271

Identification 11.5cm. Nondescript with a short, apparently ragged, spiky tail. Adult dusky brown above, feathers have buffy fringes lending a streaked, cryptic appearance, bend of wing yellow, but not easily seen in field, dark cap with pale line through middle; supraloral spot with very short extension to above eyes and ear-coverts orange, chin and throat white, breast flushed orange, rest of underparts white, washed olive on sides and flanks. Cone-shaped bill horn. Juvenile slightly duller and more heavily washed and streaked brown below.

Ssp. *A. s. caribaeus* (Bo, Cu) as described

A. s. caucae (N Ec, Co) more sandy brown on supraloral, ear-coverts and breast; juvenile washed olive on breast and flushed buffy on underparts, except white belly.

Habits Extremely difficult to see unless flushed, keeps to ground and seems to creep like a mouse. In Ecuador or Colombia could be mistaken for a Grass Wren.

Status Very rare in Ecuador, no modern records and very probably extinct there. Very local in Colombia, and on Curaçao and Bonaire

Habitat Pichincha highlands of Ecuador, 2,800–2,900m. Around 1,000m in Colombia, in pastures and fields with tall grass. On Curaçao and Bonaire found in open scrub with scanty dry grass and low herbs, often in shade of scattered *Acacia*, peanut fields and areas with long grass.

Voice Song on islands a very thin and high-pitched, insect-like buzzing *pee-tsee-zee-zee-zee-zee-zee…*, preceded by a subdued and not always audible *chirpich*. Song delivered from top of grass stem or low *Acacia* branch, with head tilted and bill opened as in trance (Voous).

GRASSLAND SPARROW

Ammodramus humeralis Pl. 271

Identification 13cm. Adult warm olivaceous-grey from

forehead to tail, with centre of feathers chestnut and a black streak giving cryptic appearance, fringes of tertials and inner secondaries rather chestnut; pale, whitish eye-ring, supraloral spot and bend of wing yellow, latter not easily seen Chin and upper throat whitish, sides, breast and flanks buffy brownish-grey, much paler on belly and vent, undertail-coverts off-white, bill cone-shaped, dark horn above, paler below. Juvenile more buffy to yellow above and below, lacks yellow supraloral spot and wing bend, well streaked with brown below; immature loses yellow tone to underparts and is pale buffy with dark streaks. Separation from Yellow-browed Sparrow discussed below.

Ssp. *A. h. colombiana* (Co, Cauca & Valle, Ve, E of Andes) duller, with breast brownish-grey, rest of underparts washed greyish-white, bill all dark; from Portuguesa and northern Barinas head black and grey, whilst back striped dark brown and grey, from southern Barinas broader black streaks throughout
A. h. humeralis (C & E Ve, Gu, Su) as described
A. h. pallidulus (NE Co & Ve, Guajira Peninsula) paler and brighter pale buffy-grey above with distinctly less streaking, breast pale buffy, belly and vent to undertail-coverts white

Habits Occurs with and not easily separated from Yellow-browed Sparrow, in which yellow extends over eye. Both sing early morning and early evening, from an exposed perch, often a fence or tall stem, when their presence is most evident and when most easily identified. During day they forage on ground, running between clumps of grass, and only appearing when almost trodden on. Grassland takes-off in a rapid zigzag, quickly dropping back into grass and running off unpredictably.
Status Locally common in Colombia, common in Venezuela, Guyana and Suriname. Uncommon along N coastal French Guiana.
Habitat Tropical to Lower Subtropical Zones, to 500m in Colombia; in Venezuela to 1,300m north of Orinoco and to 1,750m south of river. Grassy savannas, open grassy plains, both with and without scattered trees, tall grassland and more regular grassy areas.
Voice Song a thin, high, but quite musical *eee teleee, teeeee* that lacks buzzy quality of Yellow-browed Sparrow (R&T), a high, wiry *tii he-he heeee* (H&B) and a high, thin *j-EE-ee geee*, with first note lowest, last trilled slightly, alternating with *j-EE kitjiiii* (P. Schwartz), and a thin, delicate, musical *tic-JEEE-tic'wazeee,* somewhat buzzy at end (Hilty).
Note Formerly placed in genus *Myospiza*.

YELLOW-BROWED SPARROW

Ammodramus aurifrons Pl. 271

Identification 13cm. Adult dusky above with greyish-brown fringes giving streaked appearance, yellow superciliary from supraloral to just beyond eye, with small yellow crescent below eyes and basal half of mesial yellow, bend of wing yellow, chin and throat pale to whitish, rest of underparts pale grey to whitish. Juvenile generally slightly browner well streaked dusky on breast, sides and flanks, no yellow on face or bend of wing. Immature has small yellowish supraloral, paler than Grassland Sparrow, is paler below, with less and finer streaking restricted to breast; bend of wing whitish. See Grassland Sparrow; yellow on face not restricted to supraloral and, unlike Grassland Sparrow, runs across open ground and is less likely to hide or flush.

Ssp. *A. a. apurensis* (CN & E Co, W Ve) mesial, chin and throat quite white, grading into pale buffy breast and flanks, rest of underparts very pale buffy
A. a. aurifrons (E Ec, SE Co) as described, has most yellow face
A. a. cherriei (E Co) less yellow on face than *aurifrons*
A. a. tenebrosus (SE Co, SW Ve) eyebrow and bend of wing orange-yellow, mesial greyish-brown as face-sides, chin and throat pale, rest of underparts greyish, more buffy on undertail-coverts

Habits See Grassland Sparrow.
Status Common and widespread
Habitat Tropical Zone, to 500m, locally to 1,000m. Wide variety of open grassy areas from landing strips to gardens, roadsides to open savanna.
Voice Song repeated endlessly, even during heat of day, a high, insect-like buzz, *tic, zzzzzz zzzzzz......* (H&M) or *tic, tzzz-tzzzzz...* (R&T, Hilty).
Note Formerly placed in genus *Myospiza.*

TUMBES SPARROW

Aimophila stolzmanni Pl. 271

Identification 14.5cm. Adult rufous-brown above, from mantle to tail-sides, streaked black on mantle and scapulars, wings black with chestnut fringes, quite broad on tertials and coverts, head grey except white chin and throat, and dark brown lines either side of crown and through eyes; underparts white, washed slightly ochraceous on flanks and thighs. Long, conical bill is dark above, horn below, legs and feet greyish-olive. Female much like male but darker on head-sides and throat. Amount of rufous on back might confusingly recall Rufous-collared Sparrow, but lack of rufous and black patches on breast-sides separates them, and latter usually at higher elevations than Tumbes Sparrow.

Ssp. Monotypic (SW Ec)

Habits Usually forages on ground, in pairs. Not particularly shy but tends to keep in cover. Male sings from exposed perch during rainy season only.
Status Uncommon to locally common.
Habitat Tropical Zone, to *c.*1,300m, in open, arid scrub, semi-desert with scattered trees and cacti and grassy areas of open woodland.
Voice Song a series of ringing, metallic notes, e.g. *chew-chew-chew-chew* or *tre-tre-tre-tre-trέeeeng* (R&G), metallic chipping notes interspersed with trills and usually ending with raspy or

buzzing note. A sharp, high-pitched *tsip* repeated regularly (Byers *et al.* 1995).

Coryphospingus and *Rhodospingus* finches are rounded, rather flycatcher- or warbler-like birds of light, scrubby woodland with rather warbler-like behaviour.

PILEATED FINCH

Coryphospingus pileatus Pl. 272

Identification 13.5cm. Mid-sized rotund finch with comparatively delicate bill. Adult male mid bluish-grey above with whitish band on rump, wings and tail blackish with broad grey fringes, crest black at sides, bright red in centre, and when raised, in excitement or agonistic context, red is bifurcated. White eye-ring and loral spot. Entire underparts white, flushed grey on breast, sides, flanks and thighs. Bill conical, black above, pale below, legs and feet grey. Female much warmer brownish-grey above, with shorter brown crest, paler eye-ring; below white, suffused warm brownish-grey on breast and thighs. Juvenile greyish-brown above with white chin and throat, breast, sides and flanks warm buffy-brown with darker striations, belly to undertail-coverts white. Unlikely to be confused, despite lack of obvious field marks, too large and small-billed to be mistaken for a seedeater, and more like a tyrannid in form and posture.

Ssp. *C. p. rostratus* (C Co) bill longer and slightly more curved, white loral spot variable, possibly paler on vent

C. p. brevicaudus (Santa Marta in Co, N Ve) as described

Habits Forages alone or in loose pairs, close to or on ground, in open woodland and second growth, at roadsides, in hedges and dry scrub. Surprisingly discreet and seldom seen. Reportedly occurs in loose groups, but we have not found it to do so.

Status Two discrete populations, *rostratus* in Upper Magdalena Valley, central Colombia, where apparently locally common, then (*brevicaudus*) from east side of Santa Marta across most of Venezuela north of Orinoco where fairly common. Sight records in French Guiana (Stotz *et al.* 1996) deserve investigation.

Habitat Tropical Zone, to 450m in Colombia and 750m in Venezuela,

Voice Song infrequently heard, a series of flat, rather vireo-like phrases, *tslip tslip tsweet, tslip tslip* (Hilty). A lisping, slightly querulous *tsiip*.

RED-CRESTED FINCH

Coryphospingus cucullatus Pl. 272

Identification 13cm. Mid-sized, rotund finch with comparatively delicate bill. Adult male essentially deep red, brownish on nape and mantle, more maroon on body, rather carmine on rump and uppertail-coverts, wings and tail deep maroon with brighter red fringes to feathers. Crest covers top of head, with black on sides, rest bright scarlet. When raised, as in excitement or agnostic context, crest is bifurcated. Pale, whitish eye-ring; eyes dark, bill conical and black above, silvery below, legs and feet grey. Female paler, though wings and tail are same, undertail-coverts pink. Juvenile rich brown, darker above, paler below. Unlikely to be confused with any other species, despite lack of clear field marks, too large and small-billed to be mistaken for a seedeater, too small for a *Ramphocelus* tanager, and more like a tyrannid in form and posture. Vermilion Flycatcher is much brighter red, and is brightly contrasting red and black, as is Red Siskin. Pale eye-ring is a clincher.

Ssp. *C. c. cucullatus* (Guianas) as described

C. c. fargoi (extreme SE Ec) richer colours, more reddish below.

Habits Forages alone or in loose pairs, close to or on ground, in open woodland and second growth, and usually in cover. Sometimes gathers in large loose flocks with other finches. Male sings from both within cover or on exposed perch.

Status Uncommon in Ecuador, rare in Suriname, no recent record for French Guiana.

Habitat Tropical to Subtropical Zones, at 1,100–1,400m in Ecuador, northern lowlands in Guyana and Suriname, in second growth, open woodland, scrub, agricultural land, parks and gardens.

Voice Song in Guyana *hweeawit-hweeawit-hweeawit* or *tuttyhweet-tuttyhweet-tuttyhweet*. A high thin *tsis*, perhaps in series, *tsis-tsis-tsis-tsis* (Snyder 1966). Sings mostly after dawn, a simple phrase repeated 3–6 times with short introductory and final notes, e.g. *chewit, weet-chewit, weet-chewit, weet-chewit, weet-chewit, chewit* (R&T).

CRIMSON FINCH

Rhodospingus cruentus Pl. 272

Identification 11cm. Adult male all black above except crimson crest, from forehead to top of crown; chin to undertail-coverts pure crimson; eyes dark, bill small, pointed but conical and black, legs and feet grey. Immature male deep brown above with shorter scarlet crest, and ochraceous below, flushed scarlet on breast and sides. Female warm mid brown above and cinnamon below, ochraceous on chin and upper throat, and vent to undertail-coverts. Juvenile as female above, with pale fringes to tertials and wing-coverts, powdery beige below, washed pale grey. Bill horn above and flesh below. Male unmistakable, but female and juvenile could be confused with female *Sporophila* seedeaters, particularly Variable Seedeater, which has heavier, more conical bill.

Ssp. Monotypic (W Ec, Gorgona I., Co)

Habits Frequently consorts with Variable Seedeater in dry season.

Status Common, widespread and conspicuous in south in wet season, but moves in flocks with other finches during dry season, north to more humid and wooded areas. One record for Gorgona I. and logically should be present in Nariño, Colombia, at this season, but no records appear to exist.

Habitat Lower Tropical Zone, to 500m, in agricultural areas, open grassy country, dry scrub, light woodland and forest borders.

Voice Song a *buzzy tsee-tzztzz*, with quality of Blue-black Grassquit, repeated frequently (R&G); a series of 7–8 sweet, harmonious whistles. Contact-call *chirrup* (Armani 1985).
Note Sometimes called Crimson-breasted Finch, e.g. by R&G.

Sierra finches are ground finches of the high Andes which forage on ground from treeline upwards. In 2 species, adult males are grey, and females and juveniles cryptically streaked dark brown and black, in the third both sexes are grey.

PLUMBEOUS SIERRA FINCH

Phrygilus unicolor Pl. 272

Identification 15cm. Fairly large rotund finch with a fine-pointed black bill. Adult male plumbeous grey with black wings and tail that have broad grey fringes; eyes dark, bill long and slightly conical, legs and feet vinous-grey. Female dusky above with buffy fringes to feathers, thus looks streaked, white on throat and undertail-coverts, rest buffy, streaked dusky. Bill dark above with pale lower mandible. Juvenile resembles female, but young males lack streaks on belly and are generally brownish-grey in that area, females all streaked below and have belly more beige. Ash-breasted Sierra Finch is smaller, streaked above and has whitish supercilium and bib, juvenile is far more lightly streaked below, and only on breast, sides and flanks.

Ssp. *P. u. nivarius* (Co, Andes in Ve) as described
P. u. geospizopsis (Ec, C & E Andes in S Co) female buffier on ear-coverts and throat

Habits Usually in pairs or small groups, and forages on ground; flies to top of an *Espeletia* to feed on seeds then drops back to ground. Fairly confiding and usually permits close approach. Will crouch low and still before flushing. Male will flit to top of rock to look out, flicking its wings sideways continually and then drop back to ground. Females do not flick their wings.
Status Fairly common in Ecuador
Habitat Temperate Zone to Páramo, 3,000–4300m with a record at 4,800m on Chimborazo volcano, Ecuador. Páramo and grassland, at treeline, and open land with shrubs and bushes.
Voice Generally quiet, song a brief *zhree* (R&G) or snarling *wheeze*, slightly vibrating and liquid, and slightly accented at end. Contact a faint *zee*, and flight-call a timid *chip* (F&K).
Note Birds from Venezuela attributed to race *montosus*, on basis of blacker and denser streaking on underparts of female, but not consistently recognised. In fact, many Venezuelan birds share such characters and an equal number match description of *nivarius*, thus it seems best to recognise this population as either variable or polymorphic.

ASH-BREASTED SIERRA FINCH

Phrygilus plebejus Pl. 272

Identification 11cm. Rotund finch with a fine-pointed black bill. Adult umber-grey on back, streaked black, with black wings and tail, broadly fringed grey on flight-feathers, particularly pale on tertials and greater wing-coverts, median and lesser coverts fringed umber-grey. Head, breast and belly, sides and flanks plumbeous grey, with slight whitish supercilium, white throat, and white vent to undertail-coverts. Eyes dark, bill long and slightly conical, legs and feet yellow. Juvenile dusky above with buffy fringes to feathers, thus appears streaked, and entire underparts yellow-buffy, washed lightly olive on breast and flanks, and softly streaked dusky. Bill horn-coloured. Similar but larger male Band-tailed Sierra Finch has yellow bill and clear white eye-ring. Female Band-tailed distinctly darker and more heavily streaked on breast and sides. In flight, white band on tail is a sure discriminator. Larger Plumbeous Sierra Finch is unicoloured without any streaking, and female is heavily streaked below.

Ssp. *P. p. ocularis* (Ec)

Habits Forages in pairs, small groups and sometimes quite large flocks, often associated with other ground-feeding birds and sierra finches.
Status Fairly common to common.
Habitat Tropical Zone to Páramo, usually at 1,500m to *c.*3500m, but recorded as low as sea level, and often in small numbers in desert scrub at 200–400m. Open arid country with grasses, shrubs or scrub, most common on grassy páramo.
Voice A short buzzy trill, *trzzt*, *tzrrrt* or *tzzzzzzzzi* (R&G). Song a fine trill, usually followed by 2–3 notes, *treedele tzie tzie* or *treeeetzie tzie tzi*, lasting *c.*1 s, or just a series of short trills, repeated every couple of seconds, sometimes doubled. Also a very fine *tsi* from ground and in flight (F&K).

BAND-TAILED SIERRA FINCH

Phrygilus alaudinus Pl. 272

Identification 14.5cm Male has entire head and nape, to breast and sides slate grey, with white eye-ring, blackish chin contrasting abruptly with underparts, back umber to black, as are wings and tail, feathers broadly fringed grey to whitish, all tail-feathers except central pair with broad white band across middle that is very obvious in flight. Eyes dark, bill orange-yellow when breeding, more yellow with a blackish culmen at other times, legs and feet horn. Female deep buffy-brown over entire head, back, breast, sides and flanks, streaked black, wings and tail as male, but grey fringes darker; chin white, belly to undertail-coverts white; bill, legs and feet horn. Similar but smaller male Band-tailed Seedeater has similar tail pattern in flight, but also has white speculum. It too has yellow bill, but shorter and stubbier, and chestnut undertail-coverts should be obvious.

Ssp. *P. a. bipartitus* (W Ec) as described
P. a. humboldti (S Ec) smaller and paler

Habits Usually seen singly or in pairs. Said by R&G not to occur in groups nor join mixed flocks, but reportedly sometimes with other finches (F&K). Forages on ground
Status Uncommon and local.
Habitat Tropical Zone to Páramo, 1,200–3,000m, in arid highlands and valleys, with sparse grasses, scattered bushes and

poor cover, sandy, stony, scattered rocks (*bipartitus*), and also in arid lowlands or semi-desert of western Guayas (*humboldti*).
Voice Song usually given in display-flight; male flies in circles 20–30m above ground, singing *chit-chitdedrrrrr-tju tju tju tju* during descent (F&K), further described as a fairly musical series of gurgling phrases ending in a long, buzzy *zzhhhhhh* as it glides to earth. Another song occasionally given from exposed perch or from ground, *dzi, dzi-dzi-dzíuw* (R&G).

CINEREOUS FINCH

Piezorhina cinerea Pl. 278

Identification 16.5cm. Adult a rather solid finch, essentially all grey, subtly darker on wings and tail, paler below, white on chin and belly to undertail-coverts. Bill hefty and yellow, with black feathering at base, eyes amber, legs and feet yellowish.

Ssp. Monotypic (extreme SW Ec)

Habits Usually singly or in pairs, sometimes in small groups that wander coastal desert scrub of northern Peru, Apparently does not flee man's presence instantly, often perching in open, especially noticeable at roadsides, e.g. on fences and telegraph poles.
Status A rare and casual wanderer to border with Peru, known only from sight records in Ecuador.
Habitat Lower Tropical Zone: coastal desert scrub and arid land with scattered trees, shrubs and some grasses.
Voice Dawn song a pleasant, rather slowly delivered series of loud notes and jumbled phrases, e.g. *chew, che-wét-chú, chee, che-wi-cher-chu-wit, che-weé…* (P. Coopmans).

SLATY FINCH *Haplospiza rustica* Pl. 272

Identification 12.5cm. Adult male uniform almost bluish slate grey, slightly paler below; wings and tail black with broad grey fringes and underwing-coverts grey; eyes brown, bill black, conical but long and pointed, legs and feet slate grey. Intermediate male dark grey above, wings slightly richer and darker than female, warm dark grey below with slate streaks on breast, paler on belly, vent and undertail-coverts. Female dull olive-brown above, wings and tail dusky with rust-brown fringes, underparts slightly paler brown, streaked dark from lower throat to breast and sides. Similar coloration to much larger Plumbeous Sierra Finch, which occurs at much higher elevations and female much paler below, contrasting with heavier streaking. Male Blue-black Grassquit is smaller and blacker (with a bright blue gloss), and female is paler; fractional overlap in some areas.

Ssp. *H. r. arcana* (S Ve) blacker, more sooty grey above and darker below
H. r. rustica (Ec, Co, N Ve) as described

Habits Usually forages in undergrowth, on or near ground, near woodland edges, open grassy land with shrubs and scattered trees near woodland. Particularly associated with *Chusquea* bamboo and breeding is associated with seeding bamboo when bird is numerous and males maintain small territories within seeding area. Territorial males sing both from exposed perch and in flight.
Status Like all bamboo-followers, very difficult to assess status as birds vary from locally numerous to absent, in a manner totally unrelated to season or weather, as they wander in search of flowering bamboo. Usually considered rare, scarce or uncommon, but within parameters of fairly specialist natural history probably maintaining level numbers and its future balanced with survival of *Chusquea* bamboo.
Habitat Upper Tropical to Subtropical Zones, at 1,500–3,300m in Ecuador and 1,900–2,800m in Venezuela.
Voice Song a complex fast series of chips, buzzes and trills, often ending in a descending raspy trill (R&G); varied, ranging from short complicated bursts of buzzy chips and trills that recall Bananaquit to long complex songs. Whether long or short, songs begin as thin rapid trills (almost an electrical hum) that increase in loudness and complexity at end, e.g. *iiiiiiiiittttttttTTTez'ezja'wEEz'let'ti* (*c*.3.5 s), repeated at short intervals. Songs in flight are much shorter than those given when perched (Hilty).

Poospiza warbling finches are mid-sized finches of light woodland and scrubby areas throughout the Andes. Generally they are found at higher altitudes, only one species reaches our region, and that is found in comparatively lower country.

COLLARED WARBLING FINCH

Poospiza hispaniolensis Pl. 272

Identification 13.5cm. Adult male olive on back, slightly streaked darker, grey on rump to blackish with grey fringes on tail-coverts and tail, inner webs of outer tail-feathers white, wings black with whitish fringes forming single wingbar, top of head grey, black at front and on fringes of crown-feathers, superciliary white, eyestripe black, white eye-ring, chin and throat, curving under ear-coverts; black bar on breast, grey at sides, washed olivaceous-grey on sides and flanks to thighs, which are finely barred black, sides of undertail-coverts cinnamon, rest of underparts white; eyes dark, bill dark blackish above, variable below from grey to pink, legs and feet flesh. Female follows same pattern, but is brown on back with dark streaks, ruddy-brown fringes to tertials, median and greater coverts, grey head with white supercilium, washed olive on breast, sides and flanks to undertail-coverts, central belly and vent white. Birds on Isla de la Plata have orange or partially orange bills. Contrasting black-and-white face and breast pattern ensure identification, also white outer tail-feathers show well in flight.

Ssp. Monotypic (SW Ec and Isla de la Plata)

Habits Usually seen in pairs or small groups, foraging both in trees and shrubs, and on ground. Birds on I. de la Plata apparently most numerous and tame, and commonly occur in flocks. Males sing in late wet season and well into dry season, usually from perch in foliage, but occasionally exposed (R&G).
Status Uncommon to locally common.
Habitat Upper Tropical Zone, 940–1,450m, in arid scrub of coastal lowlands.

Voice Vigorous and far-carrying song a ringing, well-enunciated series, e.g. *swik-swik-sweéu* (R&G).

Yellow finches of genus *Sicalis* are medium-sized, mostly yellowish birds, washed and streaked brown above, all with slightly forked tails, and occur over most of our region. They forage in small flocks and when not breeding may wander in large flocks. They feed on the ground but also perch in bushes and trees. All are surprisingly difficult to identify with certainty when glimpsed at a distance, foraging in scrubby grassland.

STRIPE-TAILED YELLOW FINCH

Sicalis citrina Pl. 273

Identification 12cm. Adult male olive-green above, yellowish on front of head and rump to uppertail-coverts, streaked dusky from nape to lower back, wings and tail dusky with greenish-yellow fringes, large elliptical white spots on inner webs of 2 outermost tail-feathers, narrow pale eye-ring; yellow below, washed olivaceous on breast. Eyes dark, bill sharp, blackish above with pale base to mandible, legs and feet grey. Female brown above, streaked dusky, yellowish-white on throat through yellowish breast and belly to yellowish-white undertail-coverts, streaked finely dusky from throat to flanks. Juvenile similar, perhaps warmer brown above, richer yellow below suffused cinnamon on breast and sides, and streaks more diffuse than on adult female. White spots in tail show in flight and are diagnostic.

Ssp. *S. c. browni* (C & NE Co, S Ve, Gu, Su)

Habits Seldom with other *Sicalis*, but forages with other grassland finches. Usually forages in seeding grass or on ground, when disturbed flies short distance and perches in shrub to observe cause of disturbance. Observed foraging on freshly burned land. Males have display-flight, fluttering upwards but also sings from perch.

Status Fairly common but local, and wanders extensively.

Habitat Tropical to Temperate Zones, 600–2,800m in Colombia, to 1,900m in Venezuela, Open grassland, agricultural land and pastures, scrub and along roadsides.

Voice Song in flight a musical *chu'u'u'u'u'u'u'u, zew-tew-tew-you*, chattering at end being low-pitched. Perched song a weak, semi-musical warble, mostly on same pitch, *chi-chew-chew, chewa-chew-chew-chew-chewee-chee* (H&B, Hilty).

ORANGE-FRONTED YELLOW FINCH

Sicalis columbiana Pl. 273

Identification 11–12cm. Adult male green above, diffusely streaked dark olive from nape to uppertail-coverts, wings and tail somewhat dusky with broad greenish fringes, front of crown to forehead orange; underparts yellow, washed and subtly streaked olive on breast and sides. Eyes dark, bill horn, legs and feet flesh. Female greyish-brown above, streaked dusky, fringes of tertials and rectrices yellow; chin, central belly and vent white, throat and undertail-coverts yellowish, breast, sides and flanks washed buffy with soft streaks. Juvenile like female though more warm buffy on face and chin to breast, streaking more diffuse; legs and feet dull, greyish. More robust and like Saffron Finch than other *Sicalis*, orange front may contrast boldly. Smaller than Grassland Yellow Finch, and smaller and more greenish than Saffron Finch and female much more olive – reasonably obvious when studied up close.

Ssp. *S. c. columbiana* (E Co, S & E Ve)

Habits Usually in pairs that stay within comparatively small breeding territory, but will wander afield to join flocks, including Saffron Finches. Forages on ground, but flies to tree or bush when flushed.

Status Common, though local in both Colombia and Venezuela. Listed as uncertain on Trinidad (Stotz *et al.* 1996) but actually long gone, due to combination of habitat loss and trapping for bird trade. Tends to occur in flocks out of breeding season.

Habitat Tropical Zone, to 400m. Open grassy land, pastures, open scrub near forest edges, always in vicinity of water, and often around ranches and farms, though not in towns like Saffron Finch.

Voice Song a short, chippy series of unmusical notes (Hilty), flight-call a soft, quick *chu-re-reet* (Hilty).

SAFFRON FINCH

Sicalis flaveola Pl. 273

Identification 14cm. Adult male olivaceous yellow-green above, tertials and flight-feathers dusky with greenish-yellow fringes, head and underparts yellow, suffused bright orange on crown. Conical bill black above, pale grey below, legs and feet grey. Female slightly more greenish above, with soft dusky-green streaks on back and crown weaker orange. Virtually impossible to sex lone adults, but in pairs appear different. Juvenile beige above, streaked dusky with soft flush of yellowish-olive, off-white below, with faint brown streaks on breast and sides. This plumage lasts only a few months and birds acquire slightly more yellow-olive plumage above and more yellow below; a yellowish collar wraps round to become a breast bar, and is twice as wide on males as females. From all other yellow finches, by size and amount of yellow in plumage.

Ssp. *S. f. flaveola* (N & E Co, N Ve, Tr, Gu) as described
S. f. valida (Ec) darker above, redder orange on forecrown, green on back extends to nape, bill heavier with more pronounced horn base, legs and feet flesh

Habits Pairs stay close and are only apart when female is brooding. Family stays together until juveniles acquire intermediate plumage when they drift away together, to join another flock or young depart whilst adults raise another brood. Forage on ground and often not seen until flushed when they fly to a nearby bush or tree to survey surroundings.

Status Fairly common to common in Ecuador, common to locally abundant in Colombia and Venezuela, though city populations appear to be declining.

Habitat Tropical Zone, locally to 2,000m in Ecuador, to 1,000m in Colombia and 1,850m in Venezuela, in semi-open areas and scrub with scattered trees and grass in foothills, pastures and ranches. Particularly fond of overgrown lawns in parks and gardens in cities. Generally found in drier areas than Orange-fronted Yellow Finch, and flocks leave areas during heavy or consistent rains.
Voice In Ecuador vigorous song a somewhat variable series of well-enunciated, cheery notes, e.g. *tsip, tsee-tit, tsee, tseeti, tsee, tsee, tseeti* (R&G). In Venezuela a dry chattering, rather monotone series of *weezip, weezip, tsit, tsit, weezip, tstsit, weezip, weezip, tsik, ta-sik, weezip, tsit*… and so on, often for a minute or more, rambling and lazy (Hilty). Call a dry *tsit!*, difficult to place.

GRASSLAND YELLOW FINCH
Sicalis luteola Pl. 273

Identification 12–13cm. Slightly small head and long tail. Adult olive-green above, streaked dusky, except rump, tertials fringed whitish, yellowish lores, white eye-ring, yellow chin to undertail-coverts, wrapping around below ear-coverts, with slight olive wash on breast. Bill pointed, black above, pale grey below, legs and feet olive-grey. Female distinctly browner above and buffier yellow-below, softly flammulated brown on breast and sides. Juvenile more distinctly and heavily streaked below.

Ssp. *S. l. bogotensis* (E Ec, E Andes in Co, W Ve) as described.
S. l. luteola (Co, N Ve, Gu) shorter and proportionately more stocky, more greenish above, paler, more yellowish head, and less suffused olive on breast, only streaked faintly on sides, bill more conical, base of mandible flesh; female darker on head and softly flammulated olive on breast, sides and flanks

Habits Usually forage on ground, but also take seeds from grass stems.
Status Uncommon to fairly common in Ecuador, locally common in Colombia and uncommon to locally fairly common in Venezuela.
Habitat Race *bogotensis* from Upper Tropical Zone to Páramo, from 1,300m but usually at 2,200–3,200m in Ecuador, 1,000–3,300m in Colombia and 2,800–3,000m in Venezuela; race *luteola* to 500m in Colombia and 1,200m in Venezuela. Highland birds occur in grassy areas and marshes, around lakes and rivers and nearby fields and pastures. Lowland birds occur in open grassland and wet areas, being particularly fond of rice-growing parts of *llanos* in Venezuela.
Voice Song of *bogotensis* a series of mixed, buzzy and more musical trilled notes, usually given in hovering display-flight, but sometimes from low perch, when rump is fluffed (R&G). Flight-call *tzi-tzit* (N. Krabbe in R&G). Song of *luteola* a fast series of high chips, buzzes and trills given perched or in display-flight high overhead. In display, typically flies high, then flutters earthwards slowly singing. Call in flight or perched, a short high, semi-musical *kreéz-zip* or *tease-zip*, with complex quality (Hilty).

SULPHUR-THROATED YELLOW FINCH
Sicalis taczanowskii Pl. 273

Identification 12cm. Large-headed, large-billed and short-tailed finch virtually devoid of yellow or green, quite unlike typical yellow finch. Adult greyish-brown above with dusky streaks, weaker on rump and uppertail-coverts, narrow whitish fringes to median and greater coverts; lores yellow merging into white superciliary, and white eye-ring, white mesial wraps below and behind ear-coverts, almost joining supercilium. Underparts white with flush of yellow on chin and soft flush of greyish-brown on breast, becoming flammulated on sides, perhaps flushed yellow on vent and undertail-coverts. Eyes dark, massive compressed bill greyish-horn, legs and feet flesh-grey. Quite nondescript, but combination of massive bill and yellow on lores and chin should separate it from female Parrot-billed Seedeater.

Ssp. Monotypic (SW Ec)

Habits Typically in open semi-desert and arid land, where it arrives in flocks and scatters to forage on ground. When disturbed rises en masse and swirls around to fly some distance away.
Status Rare and local in Ecuador, apparently an irregular and erratic non-breeding visitor from northern Peru (where its movements also appear to be erratic). Prolonged and heavy rains in Ecuador appear to have discouraged it in recent years, for records have become few and far between.
Habitat Lower Tropical Zone, to 50m. Open semi-desert and scrub to barren stony landscapes, e.g. western Santa Elena peninsula.
Voice Unknown.

Emberizoides is a small genus of grass finches, distinguished by the long heavy bill and long, heavy tail. They are found in tall grass in open country, with or without scattered shrubs and trees. They are usually hidden within grass as they forage on ground.

WEDGE-TAILED GRASS FINCH
Emberizoides herbicola Pl. 273

Identification 19cm. Adult streaked brown and black above, with yellow fringes to tertials and remiges, wing bend yellow, lores, short eyebrow and a few feathers below eyes whitish; below buffy, paler on throat, washed brown on sides, flanks, thighs and vent to undertail-coverts. Tail long, about half total length, with 2 central feathers finely pointed; eyes deep red, bill black above and yellow-horn below, legs and feet horn. Juvenile similar above, albeit richer, warmer brown, and lacks yellow fringes to remiges, and yellowish below, with brown to cinnamon flush on sides and flanks, streaked dusky; tail shorter and rounded; eyes brown, legs and feet dark horn. Proportions unique among grassland finches, only confusion being with Duida Grass Finch in very localised range. Duida Grass Finch slightly larger, with brown eyes, clear white supraloral and eye-ring, underparts more contrastingly defined, with extensive white throat and belly.

Ssp. *E. h. apurensis* (E Co, W Ve) darker greyish-brown above with blackish streaks, whiter below with fine streaks on flanks

E. h. sphenurus (N Co, Ve, Guianas) as described

Habits Usually seen when male sings from tall stem or fencepost. Otherwise stays on or near ground in tall grasses (usually knee-high) and is only seen when flushed, when flies short distance and drops back down Best to listen and watch for birds singing at dawn and in evening. Song may be given during short song-flight.

Status Few records but appears to be fairly common. Uncommon on the northern savannas of French Guiana.

Habitat Tropical to Lower Subtropical Zones, to 1,800m, in open grassland and sandy savannas, with or without scattered shrubs, bushes or trees.

Voice Song of *sphenurus* given as *ch,ch,ch,r,r,ree-chwee,ye* (H&M), *apurensis* as *tit-tit-zur-rreéeet* (H&M) and dawn song in Venezuela varies from *t'chíll'ip* to *t-t-chíll'ip* (Hilty).

DUIDA GRASS FINCH

Emberizoides duidae Pl. 273

Identification 22cm. Adult mostly cinnamon-brown, streaked dusky to blackish above, with white throat and belly extending to sides; tail very long and pointed. Juvenile less white below, streaked on sides and flanks.

Ssp. Monotypic (S Ve on Mt. Duida)

Habits As Wedge-tailed Grass Finch

Status Near Threatened Endemic to Venezuela where known only from savanna on slopes of Mt Duida, and long thought to be race of Wedge-tailed Grass Finch, which occurs at lower levels, until they were found in sympatry.

Habitat Tropical to Subtropical Zones, at 1,300–2,000m.

Voice Unknown.

The only member of its genus, and ranges from Mexican border with Texas to N Argentina. Adult male is unmistakable once known, but female and juveniles can be problematic unless seen well.

BLUE-BLACK GRASSQUIT

Volatinia jacarina Pl. 286

Identification 10cm. Small but surprisingly noticeable; rounded head when relaxed, flat when alert. Adult male glossy blue-black, with tuft of white feathers at base of wing, and axillaries and underwing-coverts variably and partially white; eyes dark chestnut, bill conical, but longish and pointed, black above and pale grey to flesh depending on condition, legs and feet vinous-grey. Female sepia-brown above, wings and tail dusky broadly fringed sepia, and underparts and underwing-coverts slightly creamy white, with brown-streaked breast, sides and flanks. Juvenile warmer buffy below with less well-defined markings, streaks below slightly diffuse. Males moult into basic plumage within 1 year, but have broad buffy fringes to most body-feathers which partially abrade and are replaced by fresh feathers also with buffy fringes. Old males of 3 years have fine buffy fringes to top of head, mantle and breast that abrade within 1–2 months, leaving bird wholly blue-black with bright blue and purple glosses. Though similar to several other dark blue finches, unmistakable in its habitat and even cryptic female easy to identify.

Ssp. *V. j. peruviensis* (W Ec) adult male retains brown leading edge in second year, and primaries have underwing-coverts and outer trailing edge of remiges white

V. j. splendens (Co, Ve, Tr, Guianas) as described

Habits Males have advertisement and territorial display involving flying straight up 0.5m, stalling with flash of white shoulder patch and burst of song, dropping back to (usually) same spot. Spends most time searching stems of seeding grasses and weeds for small insects, taking seeds from heads of grasses as well. Appears to be a stem-feeding seedeater but spends considerable time searching for insects within foliage and grasses near ground. Both sexes habitually pop up from amongst grass and look around, then drop back down, but males more noticeable.

Status Common to very common throughout, possibly commonest species in Neotropics.

Habitat Tropical and Subtropical Zones, to *c.*2,000m. Open areas, from overgrown clearings in cities where *Panicum maximum* has taken hold and weeds abound, to grassy savannas. Numerous in drier areas with well-grown grasses, but occurs in wet areas too.

Voice Song an explosive *dzuwee'ir!* given at top of display flight ('jump'), but slightly more relaxed, sometimes more intense, versions given from perch at edge of territory.

Sporophila seedeaters are widespread throughout our region, mainly in scrub and grassland. They mostly perform seasonal movements, several migrating and few are resident. Essentially they are stem feeders, and may be seen clinging to grasses and sedges, most frequently tall stands of *Panicum maximum* besides highways. However, all are to some extent insectivorous as well and search foliage of trees like a warbler, and hawk flying alates like many other birds when presented with opportunity. Males are generally easy to identify, but females and juveniles look alike and are best identified by accompanying males! With experience, shapes and subtleties that separate females become second nature, but juveniles are guaranteed to confuse even the experienced.

SLATE-COLOURED SEEDEATER

Sporophila schistacea Pl. 275

Identification 10.5–12cm. Two basic morphs occur in both sexes and at all ages. In addition, several stages of plumage development may occur, in an odd variation of delayed plumage maturation. Normal (grey) morph old adult male deep slate to blackish on face, grading through deep slate, to slate to cold grey on rump and long uppertail-coverts; wings black with fine, pale grey fringes in fresh plumage, innermost 3 (rarely 4) median coverts have white tips, greater coverts have white tips forming a wingbar, base of middle primaries white, but patch is partially covered by primary-coverts; white crescent below eye, chin may be white, throat, sides and flanks to breast slate grey, with a variable white crescent from lower throat below cheeks, central belly to undertail-coverts white. Bill waxy orange, deep and broad, with well-curved culmen and mandible twice as deep as maxilla; legs and feet greenish olive-grey with claws pale horn to yellowish. Younger males usually lack white tips to inner median coverts, but usually have complete fine eye-ring (white or yellow), and reduced white neck-side patches. Some males in their first grey plumage literally identical to Grey Seedeater, including in soft-part colours, and are only separated by very different-shaped bill. Fully adult female dark olive above, wings and tail dark olive to dusky with olive fringes, no primary patch; buffy below, washed darker on breast and undertail-coverts warm buffy, washed cinnamon; bill very dark brown, and legs and feet greenish-olive with pale claws. Juvenile like female, but bill less deep brown, and juvenile male always has underside of mandible horn and does not have white at base of primaries; legs and feet variable, from greyish through brown to greenish-olive, usually with pale (but not yellow) claws. Citron-olive morph adult male distinctly citron-olive above, with white of grey male yellow, except patch at base of primaries which is white but not always present! Intermediate male identical to adult citron-olive female, but initially has horn to orange base of bill, and eventually a bright orange bill, but with none of pale patches of male. Female like male but lacks pale markings. Compared to normal morph, juvenile more greenish-olive above (slightly duller than adult), olive on breast, sides and flanks, and bright yellow on central underparts to vent, undertail-coverts pale cinnamon. In some plumages impossible to separate from Grey Seedeater, but normally latter is uniform grey from head to tail. Ring-necked Seedeater has pale band on rump in male, and females of both are smaller, more rounded and more buffy-cinnamon. Undoubtedly Grey or Ring-necked Seedeater, especially if pale neck-side patches evident, are mistaken for Slate-coloured; greenish legs and pale claws a certain diagnostic if seen, but does not always have them.

Ssp. *S. s. incerta* (Ec, SW Co) large bill and longer wings
S. s. longipennis (W Co, Ve, Guianas) wings longer
S. s. schistacea (N Co) as described

Habits Very poorly known. Travels in flocks of several dozens or more when not breeding, searching for bamboo in flower. Visit rice fields in small flocks but not recorded to do so in Venezuela, probably due to lack of observers. Otherwise in pairs in mixed forest, mostly in foothills. Appears in numbers when *Guadua* bamboo is in seed and will breed in response, but also breeds in non-flowering bamboo and in light woodland.

Status Nomadic and associated with bamboo in mast. Status very difficult to assess as varies from being locally numerous to absent, as they wander in search of flowering bamboo. Thus usually rated as rare, scarce or uncommon, but is probably maintaining level numbers and its future depends on *Chusquea* bamboo. In Venezuela and Guyana, at least several hundreds are trapped annually to supply both local demand and export trade in cagebirds, but this is not likely to affect species seriously as it is widespread and apparently thinly distributed.

Habitat Tropical Zone, to 2,000m but mostly 500–1,000m, in transit through foothill woodland and feeding in *Panicum maximum*-dominated grasslands adjacent to forests, sometimes in numbers.

Voice Call a distinct, 2-note, *chit-chut*, second part slightly lower. Dawn song a declarative burst of 3–5 notes followed by short series of sibilant whistles, lasting 1–2 s, e.g. *chit-chew-chew-chit-chtsziszisziszi*. Short version possibly given in contact, and is uttered constantly, every *c.*20 s during first hour or so of day and frequently throughout day, *tsts'tiu-chew-chiu-tsii-tsii*. Fuller song a series of fine, high-pitched sibilant notes run together, followed by loud, rather plaintive triplet and an extended series of sibilant notes, *pseetseetseetseetseeTCHIIT-CHIEW-CHIIEEEWtseetseetseetseetseetseetsee*.

Note Several subspecies recognised, but characters are scattered throughout entire population and described discriminators for described races fall well within variation of nominate race. Species is almost certainly monotypic and definitely polymorphic. Plumages complex and only partially understood, but are being investigated (Restall in prep.).

PLUMBEOUS SEEDEATER

Sporophila plumbea Pl. 275

Identification 10.5cm. Adult male French grey above, with black wings and tail, feathers broadly fringed grey; white patch at base of central primaries, white lower lores, becoming a crescent below eyes, white chin and trailing from base of malar; central belly to undertail-coverts white. First-year male duller grey with less white on face. Bill black and stubby, legs and feet blackish. Female olive-brown above, buffy below, palest on vent and undertail-coverts; bill dark above and horn below, legs and feet dark brown. Juvenile very similar to adult female but has all-horn bill, sometimes darker above and paler below. Male easily separated from all other grey seedeaters by black bill; female less distinctive, as bill offers no guarantee of identify, unless bicoloured.

Ssp. *S. p. colombiana* (W & NC Co) paler grey with more white on face and entire throat white
S. p. whiteleyana (E Co, S & E Ve, Guianas) as described

Habits Unless breeding, travels in mixed-species flocks, but also in small groups of a few males and several female-type birds, foraging mainly in seeding grasses. Males sing from exposed perches, usually shrubs and small lone trees in savanna.

Status Fairly common but never numerous, both a breeding resident in south, and a non-breeding visitor from further south. Reports of breeding on Trinidad (e.g. Belcher & Smooker 1934) are in error, the species involved being Ring-necked Seedeater.

Habitat Tropical Zone, to 1,500m in Colombia and 1,400m in southern foothills of Coastal Cordillera in Venezuela; mostly in southern savannas, preferring well-watered areas.

Voice Before starting to sing, male utters series of querulous, thin, high-pitched whistles, *tseeep?* as if asking if anyone is listening. A gentle, sweet-whistled canary-like song, starting with 2 upward-slurred notes, *sweet sweet*, continuing with extended, complex and frequently varied notes, trills and warbles (Belton 1985), and may include fragments of songs of other species (Sick 1993), but not noticed by us. A captive male in a large planted aviary sang a soft, continuous series of complex constructions which answered well to Belton's description well. One of 2 females kept in an aviary in Caracas sang. It was at least 2 years old and had moulted fully several times. It began singing shortly after wet season had finished, in December, a short *pit-pchtychty-chtychty-t'cho* when relaxed and perched in sun. When more active, song was slightly longer and sweeter; *per chitty chitty pt-ti-ti-chitty pt'cho*.

Note Race *plumbea* in Brazil does not reach our region. Reports that some specimens have yellow bills only apply to that race, and not applicable in northern South America.

GREY SEEDEATER

Sporophila intermedia Pl. 275

Identification 10cm. Adult uniform grey above, slightly paler on rump and uppertail-coverts, with blackish wings and tail, with broad grey fringes, a white base to central primaries that appears as a white patch on closed wing but is partially concealed by primary-coverts, and grey below grading from ear-coverts to throat which becomes an inverted grey V on sides and flanks, with white central belly to undertail-coverts. Adult male in first grey plumage significantly duller, but at 3+ years is deeper bluish-grey, darkening on face and top of head. Bill conical, compressed, with a steep culmen, and straw yellow with paler cutting edges; legs and feet brownish-grey, and claws always dark. Female olive-brown above, dusky on wings and tail with olive fringes, buffy below, paler on belly and vent; bill slightly larger than male's and dark brown, legs, feet and claws brown. Juvenile resembles female, though underwing-coverts usually greyish (white to beige on females). Young male does not acquire white on primaries until first full moult. Easily confused with Ring-necked Seedeater and, although they differ in habitat preferences, they are often sympatric. Male Ring-necked has slightly fuzzy white bar on rump, but females are indistinguishable in field.

Ssp. *S. i. agustini* (Co) palest race; from *bogotensis* in being paler grey and uniform above, from *intermedia* by whitish bar on throat, albeit vague and not clearly defined

S. i. anchicayae (Valle, Co) darkest race, adult male darker than *bogotensis*, being blackish rather than grey above, pale neck patches are pure white, white and pale grey of throat developed as a stripe, extending over malar and encircling grey chin, belly and undertail-coverts more extensively white and more sharply contrasting with dark neutral grey breast, rump has a few white-tipped feathers rather than uniform grey; in both sexes bill partially yellow

S. i. bogotensis (Cauca in Co) differs from *intermedia* in pale whitish bar on throat, most noticeable as white patch on neck-sides.

S. i. intermedia (C & E Co, N Ve, Tr, Gu) as described

Habits Usually in tall grass, clinging to tops of stems to feed on heads, but also forages in forbs and shrubs, though less frequently in trees, unlike Ring-necked Seedeater. Travels in loose bands and joins other seedeaters in open grassland.

Status Locally common and widespread.

Habitat Tropical Zone, to 2,300m in Colombia, but only to 1,200m north of Orinoco in Venezuela and to 500m south of river. Often around farms and may be seen in *Panicum maximum* in overgrown lots in cities, but is primarily a bird of open grassland.

Voice A sharp and anxious-sounding *tseep?* when fleeing danger. Male an accomplished songster and sings loudly from lookout when proclaiming territory, repeated short bursts of same song when chasing another male and sometimes in pursuit of female. Males breed in subadult or female-type plumage, and sing in this plumage too. Males in full adult plumage vigorously chase singing males in subadult plumage. An accomplished mimic, there are reports of songs with phrases from many different passerines and other sounds, including squeaking gates and frog peeps!

Note Race *anchicayae* considered to be a misidentified Variable Seedeater (H&B). Stiles (1996b) considered *anchicayae* a hybrid *S. intermedia* × *S. corvina hicksii* and *agustini* a local variant of *bogotensis*.

RING-NECKED SEEDEATER

Sporophila insularis Pl. 275

Identification 10cm. Adult grey above, grading slightly from darker head to paler mantle and much paler on rump and uppertail-coverts, a slightly indistinct but definite whitish band on rump, with blackish wings and tail, both with broad grey fringes, a white base to central primaries that appears as a white patch on closed wing but is partially concealed by primary-coverts, inner 3–4 median coverts fringed white in old males; grey below, throat paler than ear-coverts, with a fairly clean division across breast, being white on central belly to undertail-coverts. Adult male in first grey plumage significantly duller, but at 3+ years is deeper bluish-grey, darkening on face and top of head. Bill conical, compressed and with a steep culmen, straw yellow, with paler cutting edges and mandibles of equal depth; legs and feet brownish-grey, claws always dark. Female olive-brown above, dusky on wings and tail with olive fringes, buffy below, paler on belly and vent; bill dark brown and slightly smaller than male's; legs, feet and claws brown. Juvenile resembles female. Young male does not acquire white on primaries until first full moult. Easily confused with Grey Seedeater, so look for male exposing rump, whilst presence of white fringes to inner median coverts also helpful, but females effectively identical, though when several of each to compare, Ring-necked is generally more cinnamon below.

Ssp. Monotypic (N Ve)

Habits Forages in grass like other seedeaters but also particularly inclined to search for insects under leaves of outer branches, much like a warbler. More likely to be encountered in scrub and grassy areas near woodland in foothills, less so in open savanna.
Status Uncertain, but seems fairly common across most of northern Venezuela.
Habitat Tropical to Lower Subtropical Zones, to 1,000m.
Voice Song a sweet continuum of trills and whistles, typical of *Sporophila* seedeaters, with varied structure and length, not unlike Grey Seedeater, but shorter and without invention and imitation. Considered a stronger and sweeter songster than Grey Seedeater on Trinidad, where trapped to extinction.
Note Formerly considered a race of Grey Seedeater (Restall 2002).

VARIABLE SEEDEATER
Sporophila corvina Pl. 276

Identification 10cm. Adult male entirely black above except large white rump and small patch at base of primaries, with a small white crescent below eye; chin, malar and throat, continuing onto neck-sides, white, narrow black bar on breast, rest of underparts except black thighs, white; eyes dark, bill black, conical and compressed, legs and feet black. Female olive above with darker wings and tail, chin white, merging into pale cinnamon throat to belly and flanks, paler buffy vent and undertail-coverts; bill dark horn. Juvenile resembles female.

Ssp. *S. c. ophthalmica* (W Ec, SW Co) all-white rump, white crescent below eyes, malar all white
S. c. hicksii (NW Co) white rump usually suffused or streaked blackish, malar black, bar across breast broader, sides and flanks smudged blackish

Habits Almost always in small flocks and usually with other seedeaters and Blue-black Grassquits. Females and juveniles appear to dominate in flocks. Usually found in tall grassland, clinging to grass stems to feed.
Status Common along Pacific slope and east of Andes at Leticia.
Habitat Tropical Zone, from sea level to 1,500m, in marshy grassland, second growth, tropical evergreen forest edge, tropical deciduous forest, roadsides, old fields, bushy pastures and grassy edges of streams.
Voice Call uttered by both sexes is a clear *cheeeu!*, sounds like a sharp *cht!* or *ts't!* Territorial song of male *ophthalmica* in north-west Ecuador (J. V. Moore recording) usually starts with a buzzing *tzzwirrrt*! then launches into full *tzetzetze-pt-chirt-ptchirt-chirp-chirp-ptt-tzzirrrt!*
Notes The validity of the race *hicksii* was examined by Olson (1981e), and the entire Variable Seedeater complex was reviewed by Stiles (1996b), who proposed several new species. We follow Stiles here. Alternative name, Black Seedeater, for *corvina* seems far preferable to Variable seedeater, which covers what is now recognised as a superspecies or species group.

CAQUETÁ SEEDEATER
Sporophila murallae Pl. 276

Identification 10cm. Adult male black above, with a white rump finely streaked black, median coverts tipped white and greater coverts have small white terminal spots, with a white patch at base of primaries; throat and tip of malar white, black band across upper breast, partial at sides, some irregular black smudging on flanks and rest of underparts white. Small bill is black, as are thighs, legs and feet. Female olive above with darker wings and tail, chin white, becoming soft cinnamon on throat to belly and flanks, paler buffy vent and undertail-coverts; bill dark horn. Juvenile resembles female.

Ssp. Monotypic (E Ec, SE Co)

Habits Feeds primarily on seeds of grasses and weeds, of which *Paspalum* and feral *Panicum maximum* are favoured. Also feeds on flowers and buds, and fruit high in trees. Borges & Macêdo (2001) mention birds feeding in *Cecropia*, consuming fruit and also taking Müllerian bodies from leaves, petioles and stems.
Status Fairly common.
Habitat Tropical Zone, from sea level to 1,500m, in scrub, tropical lowland evergreen forest edge, tropical deciduous forest and secondary forest. Howell (2002) watched a singing male, in July 2001, in Zamora-Chinchipe, notably further south than any other Ecuadorian records, suggesting the species is extending its range in response to forest clearance.
Voice Call uttered by both sexes is a clear *cheeeu!*
Note Formerly considered a race of the widespread and complex Wing-barred Seedeater. Stiles (1996b) revised this group and considered it to consist of several species: Caquetá Seedeater has since been recognised by R&G, and we also follow Stiles.

WING-BARRED SEEDEATER
Sporophila americana Pl. 276

Identification 11cm. Full-bodied, rather heavily built seedeater, with a bill at least as large as Grey Seedeater. Adult male black above with extensive grey rump sometimes flecked or barred white, lesser coverts have narrow white or grey fringes that may abrade completely, median coverts white, greater coverts finely tipped white, and a white patch at base of central primaries, small white crescent below eye; chin, throat, malar and patch on lower ear-coverts white, breast, sides and flanks grey, streaked and smudged black and white, lower breast to undertail-coverts white; bill, thighs, legs and feet black. Bill rather variable in size and shape, and may be quite large and heavy, occasionally like that of Parrot-billed Seedeater. In fresh plumage, usually has fine grey fringes to black feathers, but these wear off. Adult female buffy-olive above, olive on face and breast, then olive-ochre to chamois on thighs and central belly; overall impression is of a very olivaceous bird. Bill is dark brown. Juvenile similar to female, but more gingery below, especially undertail-coverts. Subadult male plumage has wings and tail darker than adult and white at base of primaries evident, but body as juvenile and below is even more gingery than female; wings definitely darker than female. Uncertain how long intermediate plumage is retained, almost certainly one year or more. Subsequently, moults to adult plumage; in transition, male acquires black patches, especially on head, and white patches on underparts. Both Lesson's and Lined Seedeaters have black on throat and are smaller, with smaller bills, and neither has wingbars.

Ssp. *S. a. americana* (NE Ve, To, Guianas)

Habits Usually encountered singly or in pairs, but sometimes in flocks (females and juveniles far outnumber adult males), including mixed-species flocks. Feeds primarily on seeds of grasses and weeds, of which *Paspalum* and feral *Panicum maximum* are favoured. Also feeds on flowers and buds, and fruit high in trees (Perrins 1990). Borges & Macêdo (2000) observed this species feeding on *Cecropia* fruit and taking Müllerian bodies from leaves, petioles and stems.

Status Extremely rare to casual in north-east Venezuela, formerly common but now scarce to locally uncommon in Guyana, where heavily trapped for bird trade, was common in Suriname, common in French Guiana.

Habitat Tropical Zone, to just 50m in Venezuela.

Voice Call a clear *cheeeu!* uttered by both sexes (Perrins 1990). An attractive (Junge & Mees 1961) but repetitive and rather sweet *titty-ootaw* (Snyder 1966).

Note Formerly treated as the nominate race of a widespread and complex superspecies, but which Stiles (1996b) considered to comprise several species, separating *americana* and *dispar* (Brazil) to form present species.

LESSON'S SEEDEATER

Sporophila bouvronides Pl. 275

Identification 10cm. Adult male black above with a white rump flushed grey and blackish streaks, a white patch at base of primaries, black over entire head except white malar, grading as flecks and smudges into white breast, with some smudging on sides and flanks, and rest of underparts white. Young adult male in first basic plumage often has short row of small white spots on forecrown, which has been assumed to be a result of hybridisation between Lesson's and Lined Seedeaters, but these disappear with moult into definitive basic plumage. Young adult also has far more grey and black smudging of on underparts. Small bill is black, thighs, legs and feet also black. Female greyish-olive above and yellowish-buffy or white below; bill dark horn above and pale flesh below. Juvenile resembles female, as does immature male but latter slightly darker and greyer above with an all-horn bill. Very similar to male Lined Seedeater, both of which have prominent white moustachial, but distinguished by having top of head all black; females and juveniles impossible to separate in field. They are also very similar indeed to females of several other seedeaters, but tend to be greyer olive above, and paler, more yellowish-buffy to white below.

Ssp. Monotypic (NE Co, N Ve, Tr, Guianas; tropical migrant – breeds in north and winters S to Amazonia)

Habits Most commonly seen in grassy areas at edges of woodland. (Lined Seedeater, in comparison, is not breeding and is usually feeding in open savanna.) Males establish territories on arrival and sing persistently from exposed perches on tall bushes or small trees in clearings and at edges of woodland. In Venezuela, in July–August, there are confirmed reports of singing Lesson's Seedeaters, with adult-plumaged Lined Seedeaters in same flocks. The Lined Seedeaters were neither singing nor breeding, though they were in full adult plumage.

Status Breeds in northern South America in May–November, some arriving earlier or leaving later. Rare in Ecuador, uncommon to local in Colombia, fairly common to common in Venezuela, fairly common in Guyana, rather local in Suriname, rare in French Guiana. Lined Seedeater, with which Lesson's Seedeater is often confused, has reverse pattern of movement, breeding in southern countries and migrating north when not breeding. Theoretically, they are thus always apart, but there are many records of them together.

Habitat Tropical Zone, to *c.*1,000m, and seems to prefer open spaces in forest and edges, rather than open savanna.

Voice A few harsh notes then melodious phrases, *chaaw, cheee, childedee-chea-chea-chea*, varying to *jaaaw, geee, chutchutchut-jeet* (P. Schwartz in Hilty).

LINED SEEDEATER

Sporophila lineola Pl. 275

Identification 10cm. Adult male black above with white rump only slightly flushed grey, white patch at base of primaries, black over entire head except clear white line on centre of crown and broad white malar, ending on throat; underparts white. Small bill is black, thighs, legs and feet black. Female greyish-olive above and yellowish-buffy to white below; bill dark horn above and pale flesh below. Juvenile resembles female, as does immature males but latter slightly darker and greyer above with all-horn bill. Very similar to male Lesson's Seedeater, both have prominent white moustachial, but distinguished by pure white breast (*S. bouvronides* has grey and blackish smudges on breast-sides) and white line on centre of head from forehead to rear crown. Females and juveniles are virtually impossible to separate, and are also very similar to females of several other seedeaters.

Ssp. Monotypic (austral migrant to E Ec, Ve, Guianas)

Status Fairly common throughout most of range, but irregular and uncommon in French Guiana. An austral migrant, seasonal throughout its range except central and western Amazonas where recorded almost year-round (Cardoso da Silva 1995). Whether these migrate at different times of year or whether some are resident is unknown.

Habitat Tropical Zone, to 500m, although observed, presumably on passage, to 1,500m. Essentially a bird of open grassy savanna.

Voice Calls a dull trill, *krrrr* (Howe in Snyder 1966). Two distinct populations, each with its own song (Cardoso da Silva 1995): eastern population, which winters in eastern Venezuela and breeds eastern Brazil, and other winters in central and western Venezuela and Colombia, and breeds central and western Brazil (latter not known to sing in our region). Song of eastern birds a short rubbery trill followed by abrupt *tu-weet* or sometimes a few *tic* notes and a trill, then either a pause or more *tic* notes. Sometimes just a short rattle, *drdrdrdrdrdr* (Hilty). Song in Brazil described as a rapid, somewhat metallic warbling that becomes a typical, quite resonant cadence, *chuh, chuh, chuh*, or even *ch, ch, ch, ch-HOOch* (Sick 1993), though it is not known which population this refers to.

Notes Originally described as a species then lumped with *S. bouvronides* (Paynter 1970), now again recognised specifically (e.g. R&T, Hilty, Dickinson 2003). It seems that the 2 populations (see Voice) are genetically distinct, but to what extent awaits comparative DNA analysis. Subspecies *restricta* (north-central Colombia) described from single specimen with characters that fall well within range of *lineola*; synonymised under *lineola* by Hellmayr, but inexplicably recognised by Paynter (1970) and Dickinson (2003) as a race of *bouvronides*, but is clearly invalid.

BLACK-AND-WHITE SEEDEATER

Sporophila luctuosa Pl. 276

Identification 11cm. Adult male glossy black above, including entire hood, usually with small white crescent below eye, and white patch at base of central primaries; gloss on black usually slightly bluish, but occasionally reflects green or purple. All white below, with black thighs; eyes dark, bill conical and pale greyish-blue, legs and feet pale bluish-grey. In fresh plumage, black feathers on back and rump, to lesser extent on head and wings, have fine brown fringes that gradually abrade. With each moult, amount of brown fringes is reduced. Intermediate male dark, greenish-olive above, with white patch at base of primaries, usually white crescent below eyes, pale, creamy yellow below, washed on sides and flanks with olive; bill may be pale horn or pale greyish-blue. Adult female olive-brown above, usually with white crescent below eyes, dull buffy below, paler on belly and vent, undertail-coverts buffy; bill pale greyish-horn. Juvenile warmer brown than female with variable tawny to orange fringes to wing-coverts, rump washed cinnamon and underparts pale cinnamon; bill dark olive, legs and feet dark grey. Clean black-and-white pattern without white collar rump or wingbars, separates male from all similar seedeaters, except Yellow-bellied, which is olive-green above and lacks white primary patch. Male of latter always separated from intermediate Black-and-white Seedeaters by hood effect.

Ssp. Monotypic (Ec, Co, extreme W Ve: Táchira)

Habits Usually singly or in pairs when breeding, and may forage in tall grasses with other grassland finches. At other times, gathers in flocks that vary considerably in size, and becomes far more noticeable in grasslands. Birds in female-type plumage significantly outnumber black-and-white males, but include many intermediate males, and flocks may also contain significant numbers of other grassland finches.

Status Uncommon to locally common in Ecuador and Colombia, and rare in Venezuela. Breeds at higher elevations and descends lower when not breeding.

Habitat Tropical to Temperate Zones, to 2,400m in Ecuador and at 100–3,200m in Colombia but more common at 1500–2,500m. Similarly, recorded at 250–3100m in Venezuela, but mostly at 900–3,100m. In Ecuador found in grassy areas, shrubby clearings and roadsides, on both sides of Andes and in inter-Andean valleys, on or near ground in *Chusquea* bamboo, and is perhaps partially dependent on flowering bamboo (F&K). Typical habitat second growth at edges of humid forest, in riparian shrubbery in semi-arid regions and bushy patches on grassy slopes; in Venezuela in cloud and dwarf forest.

Voice Males sing in all plumages, a distinctive, quite unmusical series of 6–8 rapidly delivered harsh notes, sometimes 2-parted, with almost icterid-like quality and unlike any other *Sporophila*, *tsu tsu tsu chew-see'see-sa-héet*, or similar variation, last note typically higher and accented (Hilty). Not known to sing in lowlands (R&G).

YELLOW-BELLIED SEEDEATER

Sporophila nigricollis Pl. 276

Identification 10.5cm. Adult male olive-green above, duskier on wings and tail; *no* white patch at base of primaries, head all black, extending to embrace breast and sides completely, rest underparts pale yellow, thighs black. Eyes dark, bill pale greyish-blue, legs and feet flesh. Variation includes those with more extensive or far less extensive black hoods, brown or grey backs, and white underparts. Immature male like female but has black emerging on face and throat. Female olive-brown above, with buffy to olive wash on breast and sides, paler on chin, belly and undertail-coverts, all sometimes with yellow tone. Juvenile lacks pale chin and is warmer, more cinnamon below. At end of wet season, birds in juvenile plumage wander in small groups and can be quite difficult to identify in absence of an adult.

Ssp. *S. n. nigricollis* (Co, Ve, To, Tr, Guianas) as described
S. n. vivida (W Ec, SW Co) slightly greener above and more intense yellow below

Habits Usually encountered in pairs or small groups. Normally resident, particularly in riparian and marshy areas that are wet year-round, but responds to periods of extended drought, when grasses drop their seeds and die, by wandering in search of food.

Status Locally common and widespread throughout its range, though never abundant. Very rare in coastal French Guiana.

Habitat Tropical to Subtropical Zones, to 2,400m across region, though more common at lower elevations. Widespread wherever grassy areas are found, from weedy edges in deciduous woodland and second growth, to once-cultivated areas overgrown with grasses, especially tall *Panicum maximus*. From rural parks and gardens to open savannas, and often in citrus groves and gardens.

Voice Song a short but sweet outburst of twittering rolling notes that ends rather abruptly. J. V. Moore recording of race *vivida* sounds like *tsee-ptitachee-chee-chee-ptitti-chitty-chitty-chuayeezzz*. A short musical *tsu tsu tsu chew-seesee-héet, tsu tsu tsu tswidle wés hére*, etc., with last note typically higher (F&K). In Guyana *cici cici cici bee* (Snyder 1966). In Caracas, variations on *pschweetdle-shleeweetle-chiwee-cchweewee-chwee-eet!* In Andes, *bd-dli-yer!* repeated every few seconds, sometimes prefaced by a single note, thus *bd!…bd!…bd-dly-yer!* (Restall).

DOUBLE-COLLARED SEEDEATER

Sporophila caerulescens Pl. 275

Identification 11.5cm. Adult male has back and wings dusky, with paler, brownish-grey fringes, rump and uppertail-coverts greyish-brown, wings and tail dusky, median and greater coverts with ashy fringes; forehead, lores and head-sides black grading into dark grey rear crown and nape. Line of tiny white feathers above and below eye, mesial white, chin and throat narrowly black, broadening at upper throat to join black head-sides, lower throat white with black bar across upper breast; lower breast to undertail-coverts white with some grey mottling on sides and flanks. Note this species does *not* have white patch at base of primaries typical of most *Sporophila*; bill yellowish to yellowish dark grey. Immature male as full adult but tinged brown above, black feathers of chin and throat fringed brownish-grey, belly washed slightly buffy and flanks washed greyish-brown. Female generally olive-brown above, wings and tail dusky with olive-brown fringes; head-sides and underparts ochraceous brown washed olive-yellow, throat paler, vent yellowish-white, thighs brown, undertail-coverts ochraceous white; bill flesh-coloured.

Ssp. *S. c. yungae* (austral migrant to SE Co, S Ve?)

Habits During migration and in winter, usually joins mixed flocks of small seedeaters that may be several hundred strong.
Status Austral migrant that is irregular and occasional in northern extremities of range, in Amazonian Colombia (Remsen & Hunn 1979). Unknown in Venezuela, but for a photograph of a bird claimed to have been trapped in the south and brought to Phelps Collection for identification (1997).
Habitat Tropical Zone. Brushy areas and open scrub, dry forest, and areas cleared by man, including fields, parks and gardens, overgrown fields and wasteland; often near water.
Voice A basic *pio*, male has loud, startled *chirp!* And song is a very fast, short, high-pitched mixture of sweet trills and warbles, sometimes beginning with 2–3 *sweet* notes, often ending with a burred trill (Belton 1985). A modulated outburst composed of short syllables in rapid sequence on descending scale, as *Wiyidilisiblidichrrchechidlbli!* (Canevari *et al.* 1991).

WHITE-BELLIED SEEDEATER

Sporophila leucoptera Pl. 275

Identification 12cm. Adult male grey above, with blackish wings and tail and grey fringes, white patch at base of central primaries is partially covered by primary-coverts, below all white, flushed grey on sides and flanks. Intermediate male dark brown above, wings and tail blackish with brown fringes, chin and throat white, breast buffy-grey and rest of underparts buffy; eyes dark, bill yellow-horn, paler at base and on cutting edges, legs and feet vinous-grey. Birds breed in and may retain intermediate plumage for years, some never attaining definitive grey-and-white plumage. Female umber-brown above, with wings dusky and feathers fringed brown, tending to rufous on rump; below pale tawny. Juvenile is similar to female. Female could be confused with female Chestnut-bellied Seed Finch, but latter has a near-black bill.

Ssp. *S. l. cinereola* (S Su) subspecies tentative and requires confirmation (H&M)

Habits Gregarious, usually seen in flocks of mixed seedeaters, including Plumbeous and Lined Seedeaters, feeding on grass seeds in drier parts of Sipaliwini savanna.
Status Known in region only from Sipaliwini, in southern Suriname.
Habitat Tropical Zone: a characteristic bird of riparian thickets and thick brush alongside rivers in the Cerrado of north-eastern Brazil, and also occurs in gallery forest (Sick 1955). Found in savanna and bushy scrub (Canevari *et al.* 1990).
Voice Calls (race *leucoptera*?) include a melancholic, ascending *Jüi, jüi, jüi*, repeated at short intervals (Canevari *et al.* 1990), characteristic part of song an ascending whistle, *ew-EE, ew-EE, ew-EE…* repeated unhurriedly (race *cinereola*?) (Sick 1993).

PARROT-BILLED SEEDEATER

Sporophila peruviana Pl. 276

Identification 11cm. Adult male in fresh plumage grey above, darker on wings and tail, uppertail-coverts and tertials have buffy fringes, median coverts white, forming a solid, white bar, greater coverts tipped white and fringed tawny, forming a diffuse bar; chin, centre and lower throat black, in an egg-timer shape, with white patches either side, rest of underparts white, washed greyish on sides and flanks, thighs grey. In worn plumage buffy fringes to wings and uppertail-coverts wear off and wingbars are reduced. Size of bib and extent of black on face is age-related, with older birds having more black. Also, bib appears partially obscured by pale buffy tips in post-breeding moult. Eyes dark brown; large, heavily decurved bill is yellowish-horn, paler below and darker on culmen and tip; legs and feet violaceous-horn in young males and dark greyish-horn in older males. Adult female slightly smaller and is warmer and paler than male, with bib pale greyish and underparts cream; bill and legs horn-coloured. Recently fledged juvenile resembles adult female though tail is noticeably shorter, may be slightly duller and wingbars not so clearly defined. Young male shows touches of black in bib at *c.*10 weeks. Female could be mistaken for a female Drab Seedeater, but larger bill is a sure discriminator.

Ssp. *S. p. devronis* (SE Ec)

Habits Forages on ground, usually with other ground-feeding finches, and is quite cryptic on dry bare soil. Habitually crouches across perch when alert or suspicious.
Status Fairly common, but irregular, and prone to wandering in flocks of mixed seedeaters when not breeding. Most common on Santa Elena peninsula, Ecuador.
Habitat Tropical Zone, to 800m but records to 1,400m in interior El Oro and Loja. A bird of the arid coastal strip,

in shrubby areas, agricultural smallholdings and farms, plantations, and riversides with bushy or park-like vegetation.
Voice Call (*peruviana*) a harsh *chay* or *chiep* (Koepcke 1964), not unlike chirrup of a House Sparrow. Song a short *jew-jee-jew* or *jee-jew* (R&T, R&G) or *tee-chey-tee-chey-tee-chey* (Koepcke 1964). Somewhat husky and lacks clear notes usually associated with *Sporophila* song (Restall pers. obs.). Double phrase repeated continually, thus becoming a crude, rolling, chattering song. Young males and females sing (Sabel 1990), but more softly and less frequently.

DRAB SEEDEATER

Sporophila simplex Pl. 276

Identification 11cm. Adult drab brownish-grey above and pale buffy below: male has 2 white wingbars, female 2 buffy less noticeable wingbars, and bill is conical and compressed, bicoloured in male (dark horn above, pale below), entirely horn in female; legs and feet buffy grey. Could be mistaken for female Parrot-billed Seedeater, which has much heavier, horn-coloured bill and dark line on centre of throat, whilst twin wingbars of male Drab Seedeater is another clear discriminator.

Ssp. Monotypic (SE Ec)

Habits Forages on ground in open, often with other ground-feeding finches, but also in foliage like a warbler, particularly looking below leaves, apparently searching for small insects. May also be seen nipping buds and taking small leaves.
Status Rare to uncommon and local.
Habitat Tropical to Lower Subtropical Zones, from *c*.650–1,900m but mostly below 1,000m, in arid lowlands on Pacific slopes to arid montane scrub, *Acacia*, riparian thickets, agricultural land and light open woodland edges with scrub.
Voice Song a fairly simple but sweet roll of notes, repeated frequently from favourite perch usually within cover but not shy; described as a series of short, harsh phrases, e.g. *tche-tzjetzjee-tche-tzjeee-tzjeee-tzjit* (R&G).

CAPPED SEEDEATER

Sporophila bouvreuil Pl. 277

Identification 9cm. Adult male in definitive basic plumage entirely pale pinkish-tawny, with black cap, black wings and tail, tawny fringes to feathers of wings and tail, grey on tertials and secondaries, and a clear white patch at base of central primaries. Intermediate male similar but paler tawny-pink and has nape to mantle and scapulars dusky, the feathers fringed tawny-pink, thus appearing scaly, and uppertail-coverts more brownish. Intensity of body coloration acquired with age, rarely deep and richly coloured, the majority, younger birds, paler and pinker. Female buffy-brown above, with dusky wings and tail as male, underparts pale tawny, paler and slightly greyish on belly to undertail-coverts. Juvenile resembles female. Very small, with black cap, brownish back and pale underparts, sets male apart from other small grassland seedeaters; female just like all other female grassland seedeaters of the capuchino group.

Ssp. *S. b. bouvreuil* (S Su)

Habits Usually found foraging among seeding tall grasses, in mixed flocks with *S. plumbea*
Status Common.
Habitat Tropical Zone. Weeds and tall grasses in open marshy areas of Sipaliwini Savanna.
Voice Song may be given from atop tall stem or in flight. One of the *Sporophila* that is particularly adept at picking notes, phrases and even complete songs from other species, it sings continually, running from its own phrases into those of another seedeater and back to its own without pause. One description (probably race *pileata*) is *it-iit-iilo-it* also *tzarrr-tzarr-tzarrretarre* (Canevari *et al.* 1991).

RUDDY-BREASTED SEEDEATER

Sporophila minuta Pl. 277

Identification 9.5cm. Adult male brownish-grey above, including head-sides, but not rump and short uppertail-coverts, which are pale orange-rufous, wings and tail dusky with buffy fringes to coverts and tertials. Small white patch at base of primaries and usually a small white spot at base of malar. Males vary in intensity of body coloration with age, taking up to 3 years to attain full reddish-rufous coloration. Back and head colour varies from brown to grey geographically, and may indicate different populations. Eyes dark, bill dark brown to grey, legs and feet grey. Female buffy-brown above (also varies geographically, but far less extreme than male) and pale cinnamon-buffy below; bill dark horn. Juvenile resembles female but uniformly slightly darker below; bill tends to be bicoloured, paler on lower mandible. Throughout most of range, male is only small seedeater with such plumage and instantly recognisable. Female and juvenile are like most other small *Sporophila*, though few are quite as small. In east, may be confused with young male Rufous-rumped Seedeater and, in extreme south-west Colombia, with Chestnut-throated and Tumaco Seedeaters, and it is impossible to identify lone females and juveniles with any certainty.

Ssp. *S. m. minuta* (NW Ec, Co, Ve, T&T, Guianas)

Habits A small finch that is invariably seen in groups or flocks where tall seeding grasses are found, though singles and pairs may also be seen, especially in breeding season. Flocks usually move slowly across grass in rolling waves, birds at rear of party flying forward over those feeding, but chaotic disorder at times. Sentinel birds cling to tall stems, usually males and when an intruder, e.g. a human is seen, fly away followed by the other birds. They soon drop back into grass, but after a couple of disturbances will fly from sight. In Delta Amacuro, Venezuela, small flocks forage along paths through lagoons and marshes, feeding on soft, unripe seeds of prostrate *Digitaria* grass.
Status Generally common and widespread, but rare to uncommon in Ecuador. Fairly sedentary and resident, moving only when seeding grasses dry out. Thus in an area with a short dry season resident year-round, but in a long dry season will disappear elsewhere. At end of breeding season, when grasses are still in full seed, forms large flocks, but as seeds start to fall,

flocks begin to break up and smaller groups wander off.

Habitat Tropical Zone, to 1,600m, generally in wet grassland but also in semi-arid areas with grasses, along trails and in clearings, open savanna, pastures, tall seeding grasses along roadsides, overgrown and fallow farmland, and fields left to grass. Generally, prefers wetter areas or grassland near water, including rice fields.

Voice All sexes and ages utter a fine, somewhat ventriloquial *tseep* in contact; alarm-call a distinct *chirp!*; female has harsh scolding call reminiscent of House Sparrow. Song may be *tsip-tsip-tsip-tsee* (Snyder 1966) or sound like buzzing grasshoppers, persistently uttering *pt-zwitty-ptzwitty-tzzwitty-pzit-tchiea* (Restall). First-year males, still in female-like plumage sing persistently in dry season before older males begin. A male in Ecuador (J. V. Moore recording) uttered a clear *chit! chit! chit!*, before singing a clear and melodious, full length *pt-sitty-sitty-tsititty-ptcheer*.

CHESTNUT-BELLIED SEEDEATER

Sporophila castaneiventris Pl. 277

Identification 10cm. Adult male slate grey from head, including sides, to uppertail-coverts, body-sides and flanks, wings and tail black with grey fringes; chin to undertail-coverts deep reddish-chestnut, small white spot at base of malar; eyes dark, bill black, legs and feet dark grey. Intermediate male has slightly less extensive red below and colour weakens on vent, being pale on undertail-coverts; lower mandible grey. First-year male has red even less extensive, like an large bib that extends to belly, where it becomes buffy to undertail-coverts; bill dusky above, grey below. Female buffy-brown above, pale buffy below; bill horn. Juvenile like female above, but richer and darker below, especially on breast. Female virtually identical to female Ruddy-breasted Seedeater.

Ssp. *S. c. castaneiventris* (E Ec, SE Co, S Ve, Guianas)

Habits During breeding season occurs singly and in pairs, males sit very upright on prominent exposed perches singing boldly, but females rarely seen. Apart from seeds of grasses, takes both fruits of *Cecropia* and Müllerian bodies, but always pecks at fruit that has previously been opened by larger species. Forages on ground for seeds of prostrate grasses and weeds.

Status Common throughout most of range. Essentially Amazonian, associated with riverine habitat, it is expanding and occasional at edges of range, especially in Venezuela where it has reached Puerto Ayacucho on the Orinoco.

Habitat Tropical Zone, to 1,300m in Ecuador, 500m in Colombia and 200m in Venezuela, being widespread and common in open savannas, second growth, even towns, but prefers habitats associated with rivers; floating vegetation, shrubs and small trees.

Voice Common call is given as *seeoo* (Snyder) or *cheeu* (R&G) and *chéeeoo* (Hilty). Song a pleasant warbling (R&G), a short series of sweet notes (J. V. Remsen in H&B) and sometimes long rambling series of melodic and varied notes with many repeated phrases (Hilty), given as *toto-seet…toto-seet…*(Snyder 1966).

[RUFOUS-RUMPED SEEDEATER

Sporophila hypochroma] Pl. 277

Identification 10cm. Adult male grey from forehead to back and lesser wing-coverts, and all uppertail-coverts, with paler grey fringes, and tail black with grey fringes to feathers; face-sides, chin to undertail-coverts, and rump deep reddish-chestnut; small white eye-ring, white patch at base of primaries. Intermediate male has grey replaced by deep brown. Female buffy-brown above, with dusky wings and pale grey fringes to wing-coverts and tertials; very pale buffy below.

Ssp. Monotypic (Gu?)

Status Mentioned by Snyder (1966) for Guyana, based on a report of a single bird, but not accepted by Braun *et al.* (2000). Rufous-rumped Seedeater is a poorly known species that breeds in northern Argentina and Uruguay, and migrates to southern Brazil and Paraguay.

Note A single bird described, in a Guyana newspaper, as a subspecies of Rufous-rumped Seedeater *S. hypochroma rothi* (Singh 1960) was considered to be a probable hybrid between Chestnut-bellied and Ruddy-breasted Seedeaters by Short (1969). However, it is perfectly possible that it was an aberrant, or particularly richly coloured old male Ruddy-breasted Seedeater, which was found in small numbers in Delta Amacuro, Venezuela, by Restall and Lentino. Included here to cover listing in Snyder.

CHESTNUT-THROATED SEEDEATER

Sporophila telasco Pl. 277

Identification 10.5–12cm. Adult male greyish-brown above with dusky streaking throughout, wings and tail dusky with greyish-brown fringes, white band on lower rump, and base of outer tail-feathers white, but invisible when perched as white is covered by uppertail-coverts; clear white base to all primaries except outer 2–3, and also at base of secondaries; underparts whitish, and underwing-coverts have unique black bar that runs across middle, from next to body to outer coverts; in breeding season has deep maroon-chestnut bib that is lost or largely obscured in post-nuptial moult. Non-breeding male without bib virtually identical to adult female. First-year male has bib, but no white rump, nor white at base of secondaries; they are washed pale buffy and lightly streaked on breast and flanks. Adult female like male above, though white primary patch (one of few *Sporophila* in which female has speculum) is smaller than in male and white on secondaries restricted to inner webs; below whitish, as male. Intermediate female more creamy white below and lightly streaked on breast and flanks. Juvenile similar to intermediate female, but slightly warmer, pale buffy below, and more intensely streaked.

Ssp. Monotypic (W Ec, SW Co)

Status Fairly common.

Habitat Tropical Zone, below 500m but locally to 1,400m, in grassy and shrubby areas. In Colombia reportedly favours marram grassland without bushes. Resident in bushy areas and in cultivated fields in valleys and hillsides on coast and lower foothills, but does not penetrate mountains. Usually common where cereal crops are grown.

Voice Call a fine *zeeteep* and *cheep* (H&B). Very characteristic song, a short, staccato musical warbling, sometimes with little sputter at end (R&G). A warbling *tsee-chey-wee-chey-wee-chey*... (Koepcke 1970).

TUMACO SEEDEATER

Sporophila insulata Pl. 277

Identification 10.5–12cm. Appears to have as complex a series of plumages as Chestnut-throated Seedeater, with which it share unique white at base of outer remiges and outer rectrices. Following is based on type series. Adult male in fresh plumage brownish-grey above with darker wings and tail, pale grey fringes to wing- and tail-coverts, white base to all primaries except outer 2–3 continues across base of secondaries; outermost, greater underwing-coverts black, forming crescent between white underwing-coverts and white base to remiges. From chin to undertail-coverts deep reddish-chestnut, relieved by a grey bar between throat and breast, and whitish vent. Clear white spot at base of malar, and band of reddish-chestnut on lower rump. Bill is dark horn. Intermediate plumage as described, but red fades at sides and undertail-coverts pale reddish-chestnut. What appears to be a first-year has red extending only to upper breast, rest of underparts being white. Sequence of plumages follows Chestnut-throated Seedeater. Female greyish-buffy above, darker on wings and tail, with white primary patch (one of few *Sporophila* species in which female has speculum), and very pale buffy below; horn-coloured bill.

Ssp. Monotypic (Tumaco Is., Co)

Habits Appears to associate with foraging Chestnut-throated Seedeaters and they both occur in grasslands with scrub, but does not occur in marram grassland without bushes. On mainland, all sightings of Tumaco Seedeater have been in company of Variable Seedeater and some of these flocks have included Chestnut-throated Seedeater, but not all.

Status Critically Endangered. Endemic to Colombia.

Habitat Tropical Zone. Type series thought to have been collected in open grassy and shrubby areas. Recent observations of Tumaco Seedeater on Is. Boca Grande suggest it is dependent on early successional vegetation on sandy soil, exclusively favouring marram grassland with scrub, where it feeds on seeding grasses, generally keeping near or on ground. Searches over large areas of such grassland without bushes (favoured habitat of *S. telasco*) were unsuccessful (P. G. W. Salaman, L. G. Olarte and R. Strewe pers. comm.).

Voice Vocalisation differences between *S. insulata* and *telasco* at Is. Boca Grande have confirmed their species ranking (L. G. Olarte pers. comm.). J. C. de las Casas (pers. comm.) recorded a male '*insularis*' in Sanquianga National Park with a 6-part song, commencing with a short sweet note uttered twice, a doubling of same note, a doubled guttural chatter and ending with two repeats of earlier double note, lasting a couple of seconds and with a cohesive structure, *ptsi-ptsi-ptsitsi-ptsiurghtsurgh-ptitsui-ptitsie*.

Note Taxonomy and specific status unresolved. Described in 1921 by Chapman, with comment '...evidently deserves full specific rank. It is known as yet only from island of Tumaco, but whether an island form or not, it appears to be insulated from its nearest relative, since our researches have thus far failed to discover any other representatives [either *S. telasco*, or *S. minuta*] on coasts of either Colombia or Ecuador.' Subsequently, *S. telasco* extended its range north beyond this area, but it was many decades before forest clearance in Colombia permitted *S. minuta* from north to colonise coastal south-west Colombia. Meanwhile, Tumaco Seedeater appeared to have disappeared from island, prompting several hypotheses as to its provenance, included erythristic Chestnut-throated Seedeaters, and hybridisation between Chestnut-throated and Ruddy-breasted Seedeaters (though neither occurs in region). Recent expeditions have revealed both hybrid *telasco* × *minuta*, which is assumed to be true *insulata* on basis of mtDNA analysis (J. C. de las Casas, pers. comm.), and an undescribed subspecies of *S. minuta*. Field investigations and laboratory analyses continue.

Large-billed *Oryzoborus* seed finches are pursued by trappers across their entire range and all are threatened as a result. The function of the extraordinary compressed bill is unknown, but appears to be related to hard seeds of sedges. With one exception, males are all black, and females and juveniles are all rich brown. There is considerable variation in the shape and size of bill within all species, and differences shown in the plate and described below are based on comparisons of the mean in each case. They are birds of open grassland, especially wetlands where sedges and other large grasses grow. Close to *Sporophila* taxonomically, but how close is a matter of ongoing debate; it appears that *Oryzoborus* may be embedded within *Sporophila*.

LARGE-BILLED SEED FINCH

Oryzoborus crassirostris Pl. 277

Identification 14.5cm. Adult male entirely black except white speculum, axillaries and underwing-coverts; massive bill is smooth, glossy white. Female rich dark brown above, paler below, with white underwing-coverts and blackish bill. Juvenile resembles female but slightly paler below, more so on throat and undertail-coverts; bill horn-coloured. In Ecuador, male from Black-billed Seed Finch by white bill; Black-billed has a more massive and heavier bill, but lone female not easily identified. In Venezuela and Guianas, from slightly larger and even more massive-billed Great-billed Seed Finch by smooth bill. Great-billed has a lined and aged-looking bill; female significantly darker above and below. Chestnut-bellied Seed Finch smaller with smaller bill, but females can be confused.

Ssp. *O. c. crassirostris* (E Co, Ve, Guianas) as described

O. c. occidentalis (NW Ec, W Co) black axillaries and sooty fringes to white underwing-coverts, and smaller speculum

Habits Generally found singly or in pairs, foraging for grain and seeds in low bushes and thickets. Lill (1974) watched 2 males defending adjoining territories, alternately chasing each other and each temporarily supplanting the rival. They sang from tops of *Mauritia* palms and saplings 2–3 ft above water. He saw 2 pairs jointly mob a large anaconda *Eunectes murinus*, which is known to prey on birds in wetlands.
Status Near Threatened. Locally scarce in Ecuador, locally fairly common in Colombia, scarce in Venezuela, locally scarce and increasingly rare in Guyana and Suriname where trapping is at its worst, very rare in coastal French Guiana.
Habitat Tropical Zone, to 700m in Ecuador, 1,000m in Colombia and 500m in Venezuela north of Orinoco, but only to 200m south of it. Grassland, especially with scattered trees and bushes near water, marshes and wet areas with tall sedges and grasses. In Venezuela rain forest, second growth, clearings, cultivated areas, savannas with scattered, tangled vegetation, In Guyana, Lill found it in *Mauritia flexuosa* palm swamps adjoining lowland forest much disturbed by Amerindian cultivation, along Nappi river in Rupununi savanna. Water was 70cm deep and emergent sedges were *Scleria pratensis* and *Fuerena umbellata*, with hydrophilic grass *Panicum zizanoides* also fairly common.
Voice Varied calls, including *chwit!*, *chweeoo! peep! tweet!* and a loud explosive *tchweet!* Females feeding alone give a *wit-wit-wit-oo* call, possibly to maintain contact with male. In song-flight display male flies high over above territory, uttering terminal trills and warbles not heard in perched song. (Lill 1974). Song a rich and melodic warbling that starts slowly than speeds up (R&G). A notably rich, mellow, whistled *twee teer, d'd'd'd twé-teer, twée-teer, twét-ear, du-weet, du-weet,* also *chut-eet, wheet-wheet-wheet*, and other variations (P. Schwartz recording).

BLACK-BILLED SEED FINCH

Oryzoborus atrirostris Pl. 277

Identification 16.5cm. Adult male entirely glossy black, with white speculum and underwing-coverts; truly massive bill is all black. Female rich dark brown above, paler below, with white underwing-coverts and blackish bill. Juvenile resembles female but is slightly paler below, more so on throat and undertail-coverts; bill horn-coloured. Male Large-billed Seed Finch has all-white bill, females virtually identical but bill somewhat smaller.

Ssp. Monotypic (S Ec)

Status Near Threatened. Rare and local.
Habitat Tropical Zone, to 600m. Grassy areas in clearings and open land with scattered trees in marshy country or near rivers and lakes with reeds, sedges and other grasses.
Voice Unknown, assumed to be similar to other seed finches.

GREAT-BILLED SEED FINCH

Oryzoborus maximiliani Pl. 277

Identification 16.5cm. Adult male entirely glossy black with a blue sheen, white speculum and underwing-coverts; truly massive bill is deeper than it is long and is dull, matt bone white, lined and aged-looking. Immature male acquires harlequin plumage that is retained *c*.5–6 months before moulting to all black. Female deep olive-brown above, slightly paler but still dark olive-brown below and underwing-coverts white; bill black. Juvenile like female. Large-billed Seed Finch has comparatively slightly smaller and smoother bill; white bill of male is glossy smooth.

Ssp. *O. m. magnirostris* (Ec, Co, E & SE Ve, Tr, Gu, Su)

Habits Usually seen singly, occasionally in pairs when breeding. Does not form groups, nor join those of other seedeaters. Male raises wings in courtship to reveal white and may be almost hidden by wing, which is turned towards female. In addition, vibrates wings and moves long tail upward and to sides, pausing with tail in whatever position (Sick 1993). A pair was seen performing an aerial display twice, wherein male perched on a dead tree in a marsh, and pursued female that flew, both birds gaining considerable altitude and then abruptly tumbling towards canopy at edge of marsh, whereupon they gained perches in foliage (Davis 1993).
Status Near Threatened. Very local and rare throughout its range.
Habitat Tropical Zone, to 100m. Open grassy or weedy areas and farmland, wet grassland and marshes, riverine grassland with sedges and reeds and other grasses.
Voice Both sexes are accomplished songsters, female equally good as male and may occasionally better him! Young male twitters as early as 3 weeks out of nest; at 5 months sings a little and by 7 months song is loud and complete. By one year old notes are pure and crystalline (Sick 1993). Loud complex songs composed mainly of sweet musical notes, trills and short rattles, usually beginning with 2–3 musical whistles, then a rattle-trill, then musical notes and so on. Many variations, but all more varied and creative than other *Oryzoborus* (Hilty).

CHESTNUT-BELLIED SEED FINCH

Oryzoborus angolensis Pl. 277

Identification 13cm. Adult male all black above with a small white speculum, head entirely black covering whole breast, white underwing-coverts, rest of underparts deep chestnut or bay; bill, legs and feet black. Considerable variation in size of bill, quite unrelated to age or location, in addition, top of culmen enlarges and recedes into feathers of forehead with age. Female olive-brown above, slightly paler and cinnamon below, with white underwing-coverts; bill dark brown. Juvenile like female.

Ssp. *O. a. angolensis* (E Ec, E Co, Ve, Tr, Guianas) as described
O. a. theobromae (Co) underparts slightly greyish chocolate-brown

Habits Often found singly or in pairs, usually in cover, but may also occur in loose wandering flocks with other seedeaters in open savanna. When perched, frequently flits its wings in a quick nervous manner, displaying the white undersurface. Attracted to recently burnt woodland and also feeds on *Cecropia* fruits and Müllerian bodies from leaves, petioles and stems.
Status Commonest far from areas frequented by man and bird

trappers. Uncommon to locally common in Ecuador, fairly common in Colombia, fairly uncommon to locally rare in Venezuela north of Orinoco, where it is trapped and illegally taken to Guyana for bird trade, but in eastern Bolívar, south of Orinoco, it is more frequent. A most sought-after finch and thus increasingly uncommon to rare in Guyana, uncommon to locally rare in Suriname and N French Guiana due to trapping, but locally common in the interior on rocky outcrops, and in coastal reserves.

Habitat Tropical Zone, to 1,700m in Ecuador, 1,600m in Colombia and 1,400m in Venezuela, but more common below 1,000m in all 3 countries. In Ecuador, R&G stress that it is found in shrubby clearings that are usually *not* grassy, and tends to avoid areas of intensive agriculture. Elsewhere, in a wide variety of locations, from within dense montane second-growth woodland at 1,200m, several km from open grassland, to wet, swampy grasslands with grasses up to 2m tall and scattered with *Mauritia* palms, and from recently burned open grassland on Gran Sabana, to a garden in Caracas.

Voice Both sexes utter a monosyllabic *chint!* (Lill 1974), *Chweel!* (Snyder 1966) or *chiut!* and a sharp alarm-call *tchirrrp!* (Restall). Males sing from high treetops and on bushes and saplings, frequently moving between perches and also sing while feeding. Male utters series of notes in phrases of *c.*6 syllables, falling in pitch, rising on fourth and falling again, thus: *hwee-hwee-hwee-HWEE-hwee-hwee*, often augmenting this with long terminal trills and warbles (Lill 1974). First part said to sound like an Indigo Bunting *techu techu chu chi techu chu chi*… and so on, often with trills at end (Hilty). J. V. Moore recording sounds like *swee-chiupchiup-tsee-chiupchiup-tse-tchiu-tse-tchiuchiuchiu-tciu-tseechiu-sweet* with some variation.

Notes Race *torridus* described on basis of measurements, but is well within range of *angolensis*. Has been considered conspecific with Thick-billed Seed Finch *O. funereus* but they are recognised specifically by AOU (1998). Has been called Lesser Seed Finch.

THICK-BILLED SEED FINCH

Oryzoborus funereus Pl. 277

Identification 12.5cm. Adult male entirely glossy black, with small white speculum and white underwing-coverts; bill dark fuscous, horn at base of mandible, legs and feet black, claws brown. Female and subadult male have underparts deep buffy, brown of breast and upperparts suffused with a greyish-olivaceous wash; bill dull dark brown, paler on lower mandible and cutting edges, legs, feet and claws dark grey.

Ssp. *O. f. aethiops* (W Ec, SW Co) as described
O. f. ochrogyne (W Co) female and subadult male darker, breast and upperparts suffused reddish-brown

Habits Feeds with other small seed-eaters in grassy areas, but not really gregarious bird and is usually found alone or in pairs. Occasionally found in company of other males at mid levels in trees.

Status Uncommon to locally common.

Habitat Tropical Zone, mostly below 900m, but records to 1,700m. Shrubby clearings, forest borders and grassy areas adjacent to open grassland.

Voice Call *ik!* or *ek!* or gentle *chihk!* or *jiit!* (Howell & Webb 1995). An abrupt, slurred *tchew* or staccato *dik* or *dit* (Stiles & Skutch 1989). Song described as a sweet warble, clear and musical but not loud: a deliberate, slow-paced, uninterrupted series (often 8–12 s) of similar, mellow whistles, ending in a rising querulous note. In some areas song is a medley of slurred whistles and short warbles; in others more complex, incorporating trills and twitters to produce a jumbled, rich-toned, varied performance commonly lasting 4–8 s, or up to 20 s. Resembles Variable Seedeater but is sweeter and longer (Stiles & Skutch 1989), and usually given from conspicuous perch. Immature male, looking much like a female, also sings, often as well as older, all-black males.

> *Amaurospiza* blue seedeaters are representatives of a small poorly known genus that appears to be a bamboo semi-obligate, although little is known of their natural history. It seems that they are resident in comparatively small areas and not particularly nomadic like other bamboo-related seedeaters. From limited experience with Carrizal Seedeater and observations of other blue seedeaters, we believe relationship with bamboo is less to do with seeds, but more connected to particular insects that live in bamboo.

BLUE SEEDEATER

Amaurospiza concolor Pl. 286

Identification 12.5cm. Adult male uniform dull indigo-blue, somewhat blackish on face, with white underwing-coverts, bill blackish, greyish base to mandible, legs and feet dark grey. Female tawny-brown above, ochre below. Juvenile like female but has horn-coloured bill.

Ssp. *A. c. aequatorialis* (Ec, SW Co)

Habits Generally in pairs or mixed groups, in uppermost tangles of *Chusquea* bamboo, where feeding method very similar to if not same as Plushcap (detailed by Hilty *et al.* 1979). Feeds on buds and small leaf fragments of *Chusquea* and other bamboos, and insects, and it seems likely that their feeding strategy is very much like Plushcap.

Status Rare and local.

Habitat Tropical to Subtropical Zones, to 2,300m. In Ecuador, generally very high in wispy mature *Guadua* bamboo and have also been reported in *Chusquea* bamboo (J. Lyons, pers. comm.).

Voice Males very vocal and territorial in breeding season, with beautiful warbling *Dendroica*-like song that becomes more intense/rapid in response to playback, when both sexes come low (J. Lyons, pers. comm.).

Note Lentino & Restall (2003) raised the possibility that race *aequatorialis* might be specifically distinct from the remainder of the *concolor* group (Slate-blue Seedeater) in Middle America, whilst Howell & Webb (1995) reported vocal differences between *concolor* and the west Mexican endemic *relicta*.

CARRIZAL SEEDEATER

Amaurospiza carrizalensis Pl. 286

Identification 12cm. Adult male entirely blue-black (actually sooty black, washed indigo-blue), with dusky tone to wings; rump and uppertail-coverts brighter blue and lesser coverts brighter still; underwing-coverts white. Eyes dark brown, bill, legs and feet black. Female rich olive-brown above, clay-coloured below. Bill horn, legs and feet grey. Superficially similar Blue-black Grassquit is smaller and bill more delicate and pointed. Female grassquit quite different, being paler brown above and streaked brown on whitish below.

Ssp. Monotypic (NC Ve)

Habits Stomach analysis revealed both vegetable matter and parts of a species of weevil. It is tempting to see similarities between it and Blue Seedeater in feeding behaviour.

Status Clearly data deficient but obviously seriously rare. Only 3 specimens found, and since unknown in life. Since its discovery on an island in río Caroni, in 2001, the area was converted to a dam lake, making the species' current status unclear. Attempts to raise a follow-up expedition repeatedly founder on bureaucracy.

Habitat Tropical Zone; only known from dense spiny *Guadua* bamboo forest on Is. Carrizal. Presumably persists in similar habitat in area, but spiny bamboo is dangerous without protective eyewear and is seldom, if ever, entered by birders.

Voice Unknown.

Note Originally named Carrizal Blue-black Seedeater to denote relationship with *Amaurospiza* group of blue seedeaters, but shortened to Carrizal Seedeater by SACC.

WHITE-NAPED SEEDEATER

Dolospingus fringilloides Pl. 278

Identification 13cm. Adult male has entire head black, with small white crescent below eye, narrow white collar separating head from black back, which in turn is separated from black uppertail-coverts and tail by broad white band on lower rump, wings black with white median coverts forming solid bar, white terminal teardrop spots on outer webs of greater coverts, and large white speculum, which covers basal third of inner 7 primaries, inner underwing-coverts off-white, fringed grey or blackish, with outer coverts black. Underparts white, washed irregularly with grey on flanks, thighs barred black and white. Eyes brown, bill whitish-horn, conical, long and pointed, legs and feet dark grey. Female rich olive-brown above, only slightly more cinnamon on lower rump and undertail-coverts, rest of underparts white. Immature male resembles female but has darker wings and tail and some emergent black on head and back. Juvenile very similar to adult female. Bill horn, legs and feet brownish-horn. Male is rather like a typical black-and-white *Sporophila* in plumage coloration, but is easily distinguished by its larger size and proportionately more slender build. It also has a longer bill than any seedeater, but white nape not clearly visible in field.

Ssp. Monotypic (E Co, S Ve, S Gu)

Habits Males sing from conspicuous perches and also perch silently for long periods. In contrast, females are furtive and retiring, tending to keep within dense shrubs and rarely perching in view.

Status Apparently very local, but common in suitable areas.

Habitat Tropical Zone, to 700m, generally in understorey of white-sand forests in northern Amazonia. Also found in tall grasses at edges of woodland and in seasonally-flooded scrub with scattered small trees alongside rivers.

Voice Call a sharp *tzink!* Song a loud, fast, musical *ne-ne-ne, te-te-te, ge-ge-ge, jiii-jiii-jiii, tuE tuE tuE*, and a common variation, *te'e'e'se, te'e'e'se, chuEE-chuEE-chuEE-chuEE, jreet-jreet-jreet* or similar. Some songs contain only triplets, others are more varied, e.g. *te'e'se-te'e'se, tuee-tuee, threy-threy-threy* (Hilty).

> *Catamenia* seedeaters are Andean birds of open, scrub and shrubby country, distinguished from other small finches in their habitat by the rufous undertail-coverts.

BAND-TAILED SEEDEATER

Catamenia analis Pl. 278

Identification 12–13.5cm. Adult male in fresh plumage clear slate grey above, paler below, blackish around bill, wings and tail black with grey fringes, whitish on inner secondaries and tertials, basal remiges except outermost primaries white, and a large white patch on inner webs of tail-feathers except central pair, undertail-coverts cinnamon. In worn plumage pale fringes to wing-feathers and uppertail-coverts wear off, and bird is noticeably darker as a result. Conical, compressed bill is yellow in breeding season, otherwise more yellowish-horn and dark-tipped; legs and feet flesh-horn. Adult female brownish above with dark streaks, wings dusky with buffy to whitish fringes to coverts and tertials; greyish below, palest on vent and undertail-coverts, streaked dusky from throat to breast, and sides and flanks; white on basal remiges covered by greater and primary-coverts and similarly white patches on inner webs of rectrices smaller and less noticeable. In worn plumage noticeably darker on wings. Juvenile like female but generally darker with much more extensive and denser streaking, reaching flanks, thighs and belly. May be mistaken for a *Sporophila* seedeater, but white in wings and tail usually obvious in flight. It is a fast and elegant flyer, with an undulating jizz, like that of a *Carduelis* finch; black and white markings of wings and tail prominent on taking flight.

Ssp. *C. a. alpica* (Santa Marta, Co) largest race; like *schistaceifrons* but less white in tail

C. a. schistaceifrons (C Co) smallest race

C. a. soderstromi (NC Ec) almost as small as *schistaceifrons*, undertail-coverts darker than other races, outer fringes and base of outer webs of primaries pure white

Habits Generally in pairs, small family groups or small flocks, and often seen with other species, occasionally in company of Páramo Seedeater in Venezuelan Andes. Agile and elegant, it grasps slender grass stems to extract seeds from inflorescences, but is shy and remains in cover of when disturbed. Keeps to low bushes and weeds most of time, but occasionally a male appears atop a tall bush or stem to sing

Status Uncommon, or locally fairly common to abundant. Widespread.

Habitat Subtropical to Temperate Zones, at 1,500–3,000m in Ecuador, 2,600–3,200m in Colombia, in open areas with grasses and weeds, scattered low bushes and trees, weedy patches near irrigation ditches or small streams, and on rock-strewn slopes above.

Voice A clear *ts!*, *twt!* and slightly querulous *twt?* uttered by both sexes. Both adults utter a soft but sharp *tsit!* of warning to nestlings and fledglings, this effectively silences them. Song a short *tzzz,* which might be preceded by soft *ts*, repeated every 7–9 s. A flat buzzy trill *tic bzzzzz*, lasting *c.*1 s and repeated at 7–8-s intervals, and also a weak soft twittering (F&K). Wetmore (1926) felt that their soft notes suggested those of a *Carduelis* rather than a seedeater. A male in captivity sang sweetly, a continuous gurgling, squeaky burble that went on and on (Restall 1984).

PLAIN-COLOURED SEEDEATER

Catamenia inornata Pl. 278

Identification 12–13cm. Nondescript, grey, medium-sized finch. Adult darkish grey above, with dusky streaks to centres of feathers of back, wings and tail dusky with dark grey fringes; underparts grey, becoming buffy on abdomen, vent and undertail-coverts chestnut. Bill bright salmon-pink in breeding season, otherwise flesh-horn. Female buffy-brown above, streaked dusky, slightly paler buffy-brown below with some streaking on sides of throat and breast, paler on belly, vent and undertail-coverts chestnut. Juvenile warm brown above, streaked fairly heavily dusky from forehead to uppertail-coverts, pale buffy below, streaked dusky from chin to undertail-coverts. Sympatric Band-tailed Seedeater distinguished by lack of noticeable white wing and tail bands.

Ssp. *C. i. minor* (Ec, E & C Co, W Ve) smallest race, with smaller and finer bill

C. i. mucuchiesi (Mérida, Ve) larger; heavier and more conical bill; uniform dark grey above with fine blackish streaks on back, breast grey, contrasting pale buff belly

Habits Found singly, in pairs or small flocks, and also join mixed flocks of foraging seed-eaters. In Mérida, found in open areas, foraging on ground in small flocks with Páramo Seedeater (M. R. Cuesta, pers. comm.).

Status Fairly common and widespread in Ecuador and Colombia, but less common and rather local in Venezuela

Habitat Temperate Zone to Páramo, 2,000–3,800m in Ecuador and Colombia, mostly above 2,600m, but higher in Venezuela, 3,250–4,200m. Open scrub and scrubby areas with scattered low trees and bushes, stony ground, high grasses, dry grassy slopes, among *Polylepis* shrubs and on *Espeletia* páramos, and dwarf forest.

Voice Contact a pleasant whistle, *tsee* (MdS&P). Song quite variable, a short series of piping whistles followed by buzzing trills, *chit-tita zree, bzzz, bree* and may last 3–6 s, repeated every 5–10 s (F&K), in north-east Colombia, *chit ta'ta zreeee, bzzzz, breeee* (Hilty).

PÁRAMO SEEDEATER

Catamenia homochroa Pl. 278

Identification 13cm. Adult uniform dark grey above and over most of body, slightly paler and browner on sides, flanks and belly, undertail-coverts deep chestnut; bill pale and slightly variable, from pinkish to yellowish, legs and feet grey. First-year male like darker female, more finely streaked below, with paler undertail-coverts; bill flesh with dark tip. Adult female olive-brown to greyish on head-sides, dark streaks that fade on rump, greyish-buffy below, very finely streaked on breast and flanks, vent cinnamon, undertail-coverts chestnut. Juvenile slightly paler and brighter brown than female, flushed cinnamon on belly to undertail-coverts; more heavily streaked blackish above and finely but noticeably streaked on head-sides and underparts to belly and flanks; 2-tone bill dark above, pale horn below, legs and feet horn.

Ssp. *C. h. duncani* (S Ve, Bolívar & Neblina) browner on belly and broad brown fringes to tertials contrast much more with black centres than *homochroa*; bill pale horn

C. h. homochroa (Ec, Co, W Ve) as described, darker on throat and breast and browner above than *duncani*

C. h. oreophila (Santa Marta, Co) less striped above than *homochroa*, washed brown on breast, flanks, rump and uppertail-coverts (rather than olive-brown), tail longer and broader, bill shorter

Birds from Sierra la Neblina, Ve–Brazil border (nominally *duncani*) are distinctly darker and rather richer coloured than those from tepuis, each plumage phase being roughly like that of tepui birds but a phase older

Habits In Colombia and Ecuador, *homochroa* is shy, moving restlessly, in pairs or small groups (possibly families?). Keeps to undergrowth and ground in cover, seldom on open ground. A bamboo specialist, thriving when bamboo is in flower, and subsisting between flowerings. F&K identified 2 genera of bamboo, *Chusquea* and *Swallenochloa* that Páramo Seedeater is linked with. In Venezuela, same race (?) does not occur on páramos but at lower elevations in elfin forest. Race *duncani* on tepuis in Bolívar usually seen singly, occasionally in pairs, possibly more often in loose pairs and is certainly not a bamboo specialist. Readily seen in open, popping onto exposed rocks to sing. On Neblina, also nominally *duncani*, but see above, is found primarily in *Brocchinia* scrub.

Status Rare to uncommon and local in Ecuador, fairly common in Colombia and local in Venezuela.

Habitat Temperate Zone to Páramo: in Santa Marta, Colombia (*oreophila*), at 2,200–3,300m; in Perijá (*homochroa*) to 3,400m, elsewhere at 2,800–3,800m. Throughout most of

Andean range, *homochroa* occurs in humid páramo shrubbery, and where there is bamboo, but in Venezuelan Andes usually at lower elevations in elfin forest and edges of cloud forest. In Bolívar, Venezuela (*duncani*), usually on open summits of tepuis, in open and sparse tepui scrub, at 1,600–2,450m (MdS&P). On Cerro Neblina, collected at 1,800–2,475m, where it was moderately common.

Voice Contact of Andean *homochroa* a double-noted *ts-ip!* Flight-call a high-pitched *tsit-tsit* (F&K). Song a series of repeated chattering notes and trills. Race *duncani* sings a long, low-pitched whistle (D. Ascanio). Voice of Neblina birds unknown.

Note Appears to merit serious comparative field study as implications for recognising hitherto ignored differences are clear.

> *Arremon* sparrows are solid finches with strong bills, black heads with white and/or grey, greenish bodies often with a prominent touch of yellow. They forage on or close to the ground where their bright colouring is surprisingly cryptic.

ORANGE-BILLED SPARROW

Arremon aurantiirostris Pl. 279

Identification 15–16cm Adult olive above, with yellow at wing bend, head pale grey with broad black stripe on crown-sides above supercilium, joining black on supraloral and extending to ear-coverts and malar; neck-sides pale grey, chin and throat white, black band on breast, rest of underparts white, flushed lightly grey and olive. Bill waxy orange, legs and feet flesh. Juvenile almost entirely brown, warmer than adult, with whitish supercilium, black-fringed rear ear-coverts, and white chin and throat; bill dusky.

Ssp. *A. a. erythrorhynchus* (N Co) as described

A. a. spectabilis (E Ec, SE Co) grey on head much darker, though still pale at lores and supraloral, wing bend wing reddish-orange

A. a. occidentalis (NW Ec, W Co) head dark grey, supercilium white, wing bend rich orange, tertials and remiges darker brown, contrasting with olive wing-coverts, black breast-band broad

A. a. santarosae (SW Ec) grey head almost concolorous with back, lores black, frontal supercilium buffy, breast broadly olive with black limited to centre, wing bend orange

A. a. strictocollaris (NW Co) black on face far more extensive, supercilium very narrow, throat grey, black on breast crescent-shaped

Habits Retiring and unobtrusive, generally foraging quietly in leaf-litter in undergrowth and lower levels; seldom deep in forest and seldom with other species.

Status Uncommon to fairly common in Ecuador and Colombia.

Habitat Tropical Zone, to 1,100m with a record at 1,800m in Colombia. Undergrowth and understorey of humid and advanced second-growth forest and woodland.

Voice In west Ecuador (*occidentalis*, *santarosae*) song a fast series of jumbled, very high-pitched notes, e.g. *tsu-t-t-ti-tu-ti-t-t* that lasts *c.*1 s. In east, *spectabilis* has very different series of buzzy notes, e.g. *tzeeeee-zee-zee-zeeeeeeet* (R&G). In Colombia, H&M report a very high, squeaky *t'sue-e-te-t'sue-ee-sweet-eet* or similar, repeated at 10–15 s intervals; but do not give a location or indication of race.

GOLDEN-WINGED SPARROW

Arremon schlegeli Pl. 279

Identification 15cm. Adult male has silvery grey mantle grading to dark yellowish-green lower back to uppertail- and wing-coverts, outer lesser coverts rich yellow, rest of wings and tail dark grey, head black, including chin and lobe of black to breast-sides, throat white, narrowing between black lobes, broadening on white underparts, washed narrowly on sides and flanks, thighs grey. Bill rich yellow, legs and feet flesh. Female similar but pale buffy below instead of white. Juvenile slightly browner than adult above, but yellowish-olive on head and below brownish, streaked dusky from throat-sides to flanks, belly and thighs. Unknown how soon black starts to appear, but first on chin, then in spots on head. From other sparrows by lack of stripes on head.

Ssp. *A. s. canidorsum* (E Andes in Co) entirely grey above, retaining yellow and olivaceous wing-coverts, black of head fragments on upper mantle

A. s. fratruelis (Guajira in Co) like *schlegeli* but generally larger, with a larger bill

A. s. schlegeli (NE Co, N Ve) as described

Habits Forages on ground and in undergrowth, but may also be found at higher levels.

Status Fairly common.

Habitat Tropical to Lower Subtropical Zones, to 1,300m, generally in arid areas, deciduous woodland and second growth.

Voice Song described as *soot-soot-soot-see* (R&T) and *zeut-zeut-zeut-zeee* (Hilty).

PECTORAL SPARROW

Arremon taciturnus Pl. 279

Identification 15cm. Olive above with yellowish tone, wing bend and carpal golden-yellow, head black with grey stripe on centre, white superciliary from eye, white throat that joins superciliary via a white line that wraps around black ear-coverts, underparts white except broad black band from neck-sides across breast, greyish thighs, grey wash on sides and flanks, undertail-coverts pale buffy; bill black, legs and feet vinaceous. Female, like male but wing bend less extensive, with buffy-grey breast-band and entire underparts warm buffy to pale cinnamon, buffy throat quite noticeable. Juvenile entirely dark olive-green above, with dull wing bend, black of head restricted to sides, below heavily washed and streaked dark olive-green on buffy-yellow ground that is only really visible on belly and vent. Bill all black. Immature dark brown above, with short white superciliary, underparts cinnamon-buffy, washed grey except undertail-coverts.

Ssp. *A. t. axillaris* (W Ve) more greenish-olive above, lesser and median wing-coverts golden-yellow with yellow fringes to greater coverts, only partial black breast-band, interrupted by white; female has orange coronal stripe, wing-coverts far more orange and lacks breast-band; bill black above and yellow below

A. t. taciturnus (E Co, SE Ve, Guianas) as described

Habits Retiring and unobtrusive, usually hops in leaf-litter or explores low undergrowth.

Status Fairly common throughout.

Habitat Tropical Zone, to 1,000m north of Orinoco and to 1,500m south of river, in open undergrowth of humid forest and mature second growth, light woodland and coffee plantations – especially in adjacent humid wooded ravines (Hilty).

Voice Song an extremely high, thin, buzzy *zitip-zeeee-zeeee-zeeee* (R&T) and *chit-tic-tzzzzzz, tzzzzzz, tzzzzzz*, or varied to *tzzz, tzzz, tzzz, zzz zzzzzzzzzzzit* (Hilty).

BLACK-CAPPED SPARROW

Arremon abeillei Pl. 279

Identification 15cm. Adult male moss-green above, including wing-coverts and tail, median and greater coverts fringed white (wingbars), tertials and secondaries grey with white fringes, nuchal collar and neck-sides grey, head black with white superciliary from base of bill, and chin and throat white; somewhat crescent-shaped black bar on chest, rest of underparts white; bill black, legs and feet salmon. Black-striped Sparrow is grey and black on head, whereas Orange-billed Sparrow is olive-green above and has orange bill.

Ssp. *A. a. abeillei* (SW Ec) all grey above with moss-green only on outer wing, long uppertail-coverts and tail, white superciliary from eye (supraloral black)

A. a. nigriceps (extreme SW Ec, Marañón drainage) as described

Habits Fairly retiring within undergrowth of forest or woodland, only occasionally venturing into adjacent scrub and second growth.

Status Fairly common.

Habitat Tropical Zone, to 800m, occasionally to 1,600m, in undergrowth of deciduous forest and mature second-growth woodland.

Voice Song of *abeillei* less high-pitched and sibilant than Orange-billed Sparrow, a fast *tseeét, tsi-tsi-tsi-tseeét* (R&G) or *tsee, tsew, tee-tee, ti-i-i-i-i* (R&T). Song of *nigrescens* similar, but slower, e.g. *sweée, sweée, si-si-si-si-si* (P. Coopmans in R&G).

Note Possibility that *nigriceps* is a separate species was raised by R&G.

Arremenops sparrows are comparatively small finches that spend most of their time on the ground foraging amongst leaf-litter in undergrowth. Generally dull olive with black and grey-striped heads, their plumage is overall highly cryptic.

TOCUYO SPARROW

Arremonops tocuyensis Pl. 279

Identification 13cm. Adult pale greenish-olive above, darker on wings (pale yellow at bend) and tail with paler fringes, greyish head with long black stripe on crown-sides above supercilium, narrow black eyestripe to nape-sides, whitish throat and belly, soft olive wash on breast, sides, flanks and thighs, vent and undertail-coverts warm buffy; eyes dark brown, bill dark above, horn below, legs and feet greyish-flesh. Juvenile warm olive above, streaked dusky from forecrown to back, faintly streaked rump to uppertail-coverts, clear pale superciliary, pale buffy throat, warm pale cinnamon below, streaked dusky on breast and sides, fading on flanks and belly; bill dark horn above, paler below; legs and feet flesh. Larger Black-striped Sparrow favours more humid areas, is more solid grey on head and darker, more greyish-olive above; juvenile lacks pale superciliary, is darker above and below, but has white belly, immature darker and only slightly striped on head.

Ssp. Monotypic (NE Co, NW Ve)

Habits Usually found singly or in pairs, foraging on or near ground. Male sings from concealed perch in undergrowth or within dense foliage.

Status Uncommon and fairly local.

Habitat Tropical Zone, mostly to 200m but occasional in Venezuela to 1,100m. Arid country, mostly at borders of dry, deciduous woodland and scrub, and thorn scrub.

Voice Dawn song a short sweet *tit,tit'ti'ti'ti'tsueetsuee* or *sweeu, sweeu, eeee, tu'tu'tu'tu* (*eeee* very high-pitched, followed by chatter) and *tsuee, tsuee, tzEE, tu'tu'tu'tu*. Song obviously variable, but usually in 3 parts (Hilty).

BLACK-STRIPED SPARROW

Arremonops conirostris Pl. 279

Identification 16.5cm. Adult dull olive above, wing bend yellow, yellowish fringes on wings less obvious than on tail, with grey head, a black stripe on crown-sides and black lores and eyestripe, grey cheeks and ear-coverts to neck-sides; chin and throat white, washed grey on sides, soft buffy centre to breast, becoming grey on flanks and thighs, and dull buffy on undertail-coverts; bill dusky to black above, grey below, legs and feet vinous-flesh. Juvenile dull olive-brown above, streaked dusky, wings and tail dusky with olive fringes, breast, sides and flanks olive streaked dusky, thighs olive, throat pale yellowish, centre of breast to vent powdery yellow, undertail-coverts olive-yellow; bill black above, base yellow. Immature retains pale yellowish throat with some olive and dusky streaking on upper breast, but have grey and whitish underparts of adult. Similar Tocuyo Sparrow is smaller, somewhat paler with less defined pattern, and occurs in drier habitats.

Ssp. *A. c. conirostris* (N & E Co, N & S Ve) largest race; as described

A. c. inexpectatus (CW Co) like *conirostris* but much smaller and duller with wings and tail bright yellowish-green

A. c. striaticeps (W Ec, W Co) bright olive-green above with pure grey head, flanks washed faintly brown, undertail-coverts yellow; juvenile brighter

A. c. umbrinus (NC Co, NW Ve) smallest race; uniform bright citrine above, inner flanks washed greenish, undertail-coverts bright yellowish-buff

Habits Occurs singly and in well-separated pairs, foraging on ground or in undergrowth up to a couple of metres.

Status Uncommon to locally fairly common in Ecuador, fairly common in Colombia and Venezuela.

Habitat Tropical to Lower Subtropical Zones, to 1,400m in Ecuador, 1,600m in Colombia, and to 1,300m north of Orinoco in Venezuela but to only 300m south of it. Shrubby clearings in light woodland, thickets and copses in agricultural areas, hedgerows, and plantations.

Voice Sings more readily and loudly than Tocuyo Sparrow. Song of *striaticeps* in Ecuador a series of inflected, whistled *ho-wheet* notes, less often a series of well-enunciated notes delivered deliberately at first then accelerating, e.g. *cho; cho; cho, chocho-cho-cho-chochochochochch* (R&T). Call, *kluk* (P. Coopmans). In Colombia, *conirostris* has similar structure, *wélop, wélop, te-tutututututu-te* (H&B), but in Melgar, near Tolima, *inexpectatus* (?) delivers *chort-tea, tu-a, wepepepe, chóiter, chóiter, chóiter*... up to 10+ times. Dusk song of *inexpectatus*, near Altamira, Huila, *tsu-leép, tsuk-tsuk-tsuk-tsuk* (H&B). Race *conirostris* in Falcón, *wü...wee, chivit, chivit, chivit, chivit, chivit* or *tsweet, tsweet, tsweet-tseeu, ti-ti-ti-ti*, ending in a slow trill. In Aragua (also *conirostris*), *tur, cheee, tu, chup-chup-chup-chup-chup*... with variable number of *chup* notes (Hilty).

Note Race *inexpectatus* with somewhat distinctive plumage and different song could be a distinct species (S. Olson in H&B, Byers *et al.* 1995).

Buarremon brush finches were formerly included within *Atlapetes*, both being essentially montane, but were separated on basis of plumage – considered to be closer to *Arremon* sparrows, genetically they are closer to *Lysurus* – voice (song structure is different) and habits (more secretive).

CHESTNUT-CAPPED BRUSH FINCH

Buarremon brunneinucha Pl. 283

Identification 19cm. Large brush finch, very distinctive. Adult deep olivaceous-green above, crown to nape bright chestnut, edged orange, broad black mask from frontal band and gape to beyond ear-coverts, with clear white supraloral spot; neck-sides grey, chin to undertail-coverts white, narrow black band on throat varies geographically; bill black, legs and feet olive-grey. Juvenile very deep greenish-olive with postocular superciliary (corresponding to orange edges to crown in adult), slightly paler throat with dark streaks, slightly paler streaks on breast and flanks; bill black above and pale yellow-horn below. Immature has dull chestnut crown, whitish streaks on throat and emergent white patches on belly. Intermediate has all-white throat, dark chestnut crown with bright buffy-orange postocular line and much white below; bill 2-toned. White-winged Brush Finch has white speculum on primaries, Bay-crowned Brush Finch is decidedly grey above, washed heavily with grey on sides, Moustached Brush Finch clearly yellow below, Slaty Brush Finch has no white below.

Ssp. *B. b. allinornatus* (NW Ve) all-white breast, no band, shorter, thicker bill

B. b. frontalis (Ec, Co, N & W Ve) as described, but note considerable variation of breast-band, from solid and even (Táchira) to fragmented and vestigial (Yaracuy), 3 white marks on frontal band, not 2 of other races; heavy bill

B. b. inornatus (CW Ec) irregular black marks on breast-sides

B. b. xanthogenys (NC Ve) 2 distinct forms, from Cerro El Candelo, Yaracuy, with vestigial breast-band, other from Carabobo to Miranda, with broad black band; long slender bill

Habits A skulker, and may be difficult to see, but is curious. Forages alone, quietly hopping through leaf-litter in undergrowth of humid montane forest and mature second growth. Does not join mixed flocks.

Status Fairly common throughout its range.

Habitat Tropical to Temperate Zones, mostly 700–2,500m in Ecuador, occasionally to 550m and 3,150m; 800–2,500m in Colombia, occasionally to 3,000m; and 1,000–3,100m in Andes and to 2,400m in Coastal Cordillera of Venezuela.

Voice Song 3–4 thin, squeaky and very high-pitched notes with second usually low, followed by thin trill, *tseee, tep, wee-teeeeeeeee* (H&B). In Venezuela a P. Schwartz recording, *peetee-zeeer-peetee-súueet* and from Mérida (*frontalis*), *pit't'zeet seee seee seee tzu-seet* or similar (Hilty).

Note Formerly placed in genus *Atlapetes* (Hackett 1992, Remsen & Graves 1995).

BLACK-HEADED BRUSH FINCH

Buarremon atricapillus Pl. 283

Identification 19cm. Adult olive-green above, top and sides of head black, chin and underparts white, washed grey on sides and olive on flanks, thighs and undertail-coverts; bill black, legs and feet vinaceous. Juvenile slightly more olive above than adult and entirely cinnamon below; bill dark horn. Adult quite distinct, juvenile could be mistaken for a *Lysurus*, but juvenile Olive Finch decidedly darker below. Juvenile Stripe-headed Brush Finch is striped below and has 2-tone bill.

Ssp. *B. a. atricapillus* (E & C Andes in N Co)

Habits Forages at lower levels and on ground, usually singly but perhaps in pairs, skulks and keeps to cover, but is curious.

Status Uncommon and local.

Habitat Tropical Zone, 700–1,000m, in undergrowth of humid montane and mossy cloud forests, particularly at borders and edges.

Voice High-pitched, penetrating *tsit*. Song thin and weak, also high-pitched trill of *tsit* notes (H&B).

Note Formerly placed in genus *Atlapetes* and also considered a race of Stripe-headed Brush Finch (Hackett 1992, Remsen & Graves 1995).

STRIPE-HEADED BRUSH FINCH

Buarremon torquatus Pl. 283

Identification 19cm. Adult olive-green above, with yellow wing bend, black on top and sides of head with grey coronal stripe and partial or complete supercilium that is grey, with maybe some vestigial white depending on race; white chin, throat and upper breast with black bar on breast, below white, with grey on neck- and breast-sides, becoming olive on flanks and undertail-coverts; bill black, legs and feet dark olivaceous. Orange-billed and Pectoral Sparrows are both brighter and more greenish above, have orange or yellow bills and pale legs and feet.

Ssp. *B. t. assimilis* (C & N Ec, Andes in Co, Mérida in Ve) medium olive above, clear grey coronal stripe and superciliary, with white supraloral, no breast bar, white from chin to vent, washed grey at sides, becoming cinnamon on flanks and undertail-coverts; juvenile even paler, including top and sides of head, white from chin to vent, washed cinnamon on sides, flanks and undertail-coverts, with some dusky streaks on sides, flanks and thighs

B. t. basilicus (N Co) like *assimilis* but more heavily washed on sides with grey, becoming buffy on flanks, undertail-coverts brownish

B. t. larensis (N Andes in Ve) broad grey superciliary with white spots from supraloral to above eyes, grey streaks and spots on nape; juvenile as *phygas* but lacks clear superciliary, in transition, black breast bar and white both above and below, apparently first adult feathers to show

B. t. nigrifrons (SW Ec) like *assimilis* but grey coronal stripe less extensive, not reaching forehead, grey postocular streak reduced and almost lacking

B. t. perijanus (E Andes in NC Co, NW Ve) grey supraloral and postocular line, cinnamon wash on sides and flanks

B. t. phaeopleurus (Coastal Cordillera, N Ve) complete greyish-white superciliary from supraloral to nape-sides, sides and flanks ochraceous-buffy

B. t. phygas (NE Ve) grey coronal line vestigial and fragmented, white on head only from rear ear-coverts to neck-sides; juvenile deep brown above and deep greyish-cinnamon below, heavily streaked dusky from chin to undertail-coverts, bill black above, grey below

Habits Forages in open undergrowth and on ground in heavy forest and is very easy to overlook, though white of underparts very obvious, if movement catches eye. Generally unafraid. Sometimes in mixed-species flocks.

Status Uncommon to fairly common, but is probably more common than records suggest.

Habitat Subtropical to Temperate Zones, 1,900–3,500m in north Ecuador, 900–3,000m in south, 1,700–3,600m in Colombia but most frequent at 2,500–3,000m; in Venezuela 900–1,800m, and more numerous at lower levels within this band. Undergrowth of humid montane forest, especially near borders and edges.

Voice Call a thin, penetrating *tsit* or *tsint*. Also a vibrating *chirr* (F&K). Song in Ecuador, *tseek-o-tseé* (R&T) and *tsué tsu-zeét tseiuw* (R&G). In Colombia a thin, weak, 5-note, *twee-eet? twee-o-phew* (H&B) and in Venezuela a very high-pitched *zu-zeet, aah-z-teee*. In north Monagas *EE-sit, ezzaweet...EE-sit...ezzaseet...ease-sit...tsEE-a-teet...* and so on in a rather irregular fashion, rambling without clear break (Hilty). Song a high-pitched *tziiie-tzie tz ieeee wee tzee tzee wee tzee tzee wee tzeee tziiu trrrrrr tzie wee tzi...*, song of female weaker than male F&K).

Note Formerly placed in genus *Atlapetes* (Hackett 1992, Remsen & Graves 1995).

Lysurus finches are very much like *Atlapetes*, and are poorly known birds of humid montane forest undergrowth.

SOOTY-FACED FINCH

Lysurus crassirostris Pl. 283

Identification 18cm. Adult dark olive-green above, slightly darker on wings and tail, entire top of head chestnut, head-sides slate grey with fine white eye-ring, fragmented, white malar and small irregular white bars on chin; underparts browner and centre of belly deep yellow; eyes brown, bill black, legs and feet flesh. Juvenile browner, richer colour above, suffused deep umber on head and back, slightly paler below, centre of belly yellow, with irregular bars and vestigial white malar. Juvenile Black-headed Brush Finch lacks yellow belly, juvenile Chestnut-capped Brush Finch also lacks yellow belly and has 2-tone bill, as does juvenile Stripe-headed Brush Finch.

Ssp. Monotypic (extreme NW Co: Cerro Tacarcuna)

Habits Forages singly and in pairs, sometimes in small groups, often near water (streams in ravines, for example). Responds to playback.

Status Rare, as its presence in region is marginal extension of range in Panama, where uncommon and local.

Habitat Subtropical Zone, mostly 800–1,300m in Panama, in tangled and deep undergrowth of humid montane forests.

Voice Most frequently heard call or song, *psu-psee* (R&T) or *pu-peee* (H&B).

Note Considered likely to be conspecific with *L. castaneiceps* by S&M.

OLIVE FINCH

Lysurus castaneiceps Pl. 283

Identification 15cm. Adult greyish olive-green, slightly darker on wings and tail, entire top of head rich chestnut, rest of head slate grey; bill dark above, paler below, legs and feet vinaceous-flesh. Juvenile all dark olive-green, somewhat suffused umber on head and grey on face. Possible confusion with juvenile Chestnut-capped Brush Finch, which has strongly 2-tone bill, and dark legs and feet. All other brush finches with chestnut on head have very distinctive, usually white, marks to separate them.

Ssp. Monotypic (W Ec, W Co)

Habits Forages on ground or in heavy undergrowth, singly and in pairs, sometimes in small groups, often near water (streams in ravines, for example).
Status Rare to uncommon in Ecuador, rare and local in Colombia, though undoubtedly under-reported.
Habitat Tropical to Subtropical Zones, 800–1,800 in Ecuador, 700–2,200m in Colombia, in humid and wet montane forest.
Voice Song a fast series of very high-pitched sibilant notes, e.g., *tsee-tsi-tsi-tititi-tsi-tsi-tsü-tsii*, hard to hear over sound of rushing water! Call a short flat, but high-pitched trill, *tsi-d-d-d-d-d-d-d* (P. Coopmans).

TANAGER FINCH
Oreothraupis arremonops Pl. 280

Identification 20cm. Adult large, finch-like, with black head and upper throat, broad silver-grey coronal stripe and eyestripe reaching to nape, ferruginous body, brighter on breast, grey belly and central lower breast, and blackish tail. Juvenile duller, with faint head pattern, brownish body and ferruginous back, black wings and tail.

Ssp. Monotypic (NW Ec, SW Co)

Status Vulnerable. Known from few locations in small range on Pacific slope of West Andes of Co (Antioquia, Valle del Cauca, Cauca, Nariño) and north-west Ecuador (Pichincha, Imbabura), with recent records from Tandayapa area, Pichincha, and Cotacachi-Cayapas National Park, Imbabura. Population in Munchique National Park, Cauca, probably global stronghold with *c.*1,000 individuals. Its apparent rarity may in part result from inaccessibility of its very wet, often steep-sloped environment; nevertheless, its habitat is threatened by accelerating loss, degradation and fragmentation due to logging and unplanned colonisation following completion of major roads.
Habitat Subtropical Zone, 1,200–2,700m, in dense undergrowth of humid forest (mostly dense, wet, mossy cloud forest).
Voice Sharp *tsip* during foraging, a thinner *sink* and soft frog-like whistle *wert*. Song a series of sharp, thin, high *tsip* notes (BirdLife 2004).

> *Atlapetes* brush finches form a large and apparently homogeneous genus of large, montane finches, found throughout the region. They forage in undergrowth and sometimes on ground, for insects, small fruits and seed. All have very high-pitched voices and often duet.

YELLOW-THROATED BRUSH FINCH
Atlapetes gutturalis Pl. 280

Identification 18cm. Adult unmistakable: dusky grey above, darkest on head, with white coronal stripe, chin and throat yellow, rest of underparts white, washed lightly olive on flanks and undertail-coverts; bill dusky, legs and feet grey. Juvenile brownish-grey above, with buffy fringes to wing-feathers, spots on greater coverts, producing a wingbar, coronal stripe paler grey, underparts yellowish-white, streaked finely dusky from breast to undertail-coverts. Juvenile Pale-naped Brush Finch has similar pattern but distinctly darker and no wingbar; juvenile White-winged Brush Finch does not reach Colombia.

Ssp. Monotypic (Co: W & C Andes)

Habits Usually seen foraging in pairs or small groups, often on ground, but less so than other brush finches. Usually in thick undergrowth.
Status Fairly common.
Habitat Upper Tropical to Subtropical Zones, 800–2,600m, most frequent at 1,500–2,200m. Shrubby clearings and forest borders, thickets at edges of woodland and in pastures, second growth and recently disturbed areas.
Voice Weak, thin song rarely heard, transliterated by Skutch (1967) as *O see me, o see, I'm weary, pity me.*
Note Formerly considered a race of White-naped Brush Finch called *A. albinucha* (S&M).

PALE-NAPED BRUSH FINCH
Atlapetes pallidinucha Pl. 280

Identification 18cm. Adult olivaceous-grey above with broad white stripe over crown to nape, tinged cinnamon at front; underparts yellow with olive suffusion depending on race. Juvenile slightly paler, more olive-brown above, coronal stripe and underparts streaked dusky. Rufous-naped Brush Finch has entire coronal stripe deep cinnamon-rufous and underparts entirely deep yellow; Tricoloured Brush Finch is not sympatric.

Ssp. *A. p. pallidinucha* (C Andes in Co, Táchira in Ve) coronal stripe has cinnamon extending to rear crown, yellow to belly and vent, washed greenish-olive on flanks and undertail-coverts; bill black, legs and feet dark grey; juvenile has pale base to crown and underparts, streaks noticeable.

A. p. papallactae (Ec, C Andes in Co) coronal stripe has weak cinnamon reaching centre of crown, olive-brown wash starts on breast, bill dark grey, legs and feet grey; juvenile dark on crown and below, almost obscuring streaks on both

Habits Pairs and small groups forage in undergrowth and understorey, often on ground, and also join mixed-species flocks.
Status Fairly common in Ecuador and Colombia.
Habitat Subtropical Zone to Páramo, at 2,400–3,900m, but more numerous at mid elevations in both countries.
Voice Song in Colombia a weak, very high-pitched series of trills and sibilant notes (J. Silliman in H&B). Dawn song, *tsie… tsie weu, tsi…tsie weu tsie seu, ti…ti wee tsits we weee* or *tsie…tsie tsieu*, first notes alike or descending, *tsiu* sharply rising. Advertisement-song *wheet-tew-tew-tew*, often given in duet (F&K).

RUFOUS-NAPED BRUSH FINCH

Atlapetes latinuchus Pl. 280

Identification 17cm. Adult slate grey above with top of head rich rufous, head-sides black, chin to undertail-coverts rich deep yellow. Varies considerably, though rather subtly, by subspecies: may have white speculum, white loral spot and pale supraloral spot. Also, be aware, birds in first year of adult plumage are not as richly coloured or as well marked as older birds; it has not been possible to access, or even know details of all these variants. Juvenile lacks rufous crown, being concolorous with dark greenish-olive back, but has black head-sides, and darker wings and tail; yellow below, washed olive-brown on breast, sides and flanks, vent and undertail-coverts. Tricoloured Brush Finch has orange top of head, olive wash on flanks and undertail-coverts, and occurs at lower elevations. Pale-naped has distinctly pale nape and at least as much olive below as Tricoloured.

Ssp. *A. l. caucae* (W & C Andes in Co) largest white speculum, crown deep, dark rufous, pale loral spot, malar yellow washed olive

A. l. comptus (SW Ec) yellow supraloral spot, malar black, thighs washed olive

A. l. elaeoprorus (C Andes in N Co) upperparts more greenish-olive than slate grey, small pale supraloral spot, large white speculum

A. l. latinuchus (SE Ec) large speculum, pale loral spot, malar yellow, possibly washed olive

A. l. phelpsi (E Co & NW Ve: Perijá range) malar black, no white or pale spots, flanks, thighs and undertail-coverts washed olive

A. l. simplex (E Andes in Co) back brownish, very small white speculum, malar pale olive-brown

A. l. spodionotus (N Ec, SW Co) vestigial supraloral spot yellow, malar pale olive

A. l. yariguierum (C Co: E Andes) all-black back, fine yellow supraloral

Habits Fairly arboreal, though does forage on ground at woodland edges. Pairs and small groups work understorey, but seldom join mixed-species flocks. Fairly tolerant of disturbed areas.

Status Locally common in all 3 countries.

Habitat Subtropical to Temperate Zones, 1,600–3,700m in Colombia, 1,100–2,200m in Venezuela.

Voice Fast, complicated, energetic song, of 2–3 s, *t't't't't'ut, weet-weet-weet-tu-tu-few-few-few*, with variations. Trill at start is characteristic (H&B).

Notes Separated from *A. rufinucha* of Bolivia by García-Moreno & Fjeldså (1999). Race *yariguierum* described by Donegan & Huertas (2006). In same paper authors propose synonymising *simplex* under *spodionotus*.

WHITE-RIMMED BRUSH FINCH

Atlapetes leucopis Pl. 280

Identification 18cm. Adult greenish-black above, paler on uppertail-coverts, entire top of head rufous-orange, head-sides black, significant white eye-ring extending behind eyes, entire underparts dark olive-green. Juvenile undescribed.

Ssp. Monotypic (SW Co, W Ec)

Habits An inconspicuous bird that is almost certainly under-reported. Secretive and retiring, but curious and often joins mixed-species flocks.

Status Near Threatened. Rare and local in Ecuador and at least local in Colombia.

Habitat Temperate Zone, at 2,200–3,100m in Ecuador and 2,300–3,000m in Colombia, in dense undergrowth within humid montane forest and at forest borders.

Voice Song a forceful series of pretty melodic notes and phrases, often including repetitions, rather different from other brush finches (N. Krabbe recording in R&G). In Colombia, a soft, chipping warble, begins *twoo-twoo*… and ends with 4–5 musical chips (J. Silliman in H&B).

SANTA MARTA BRUSH FINCH

Atlapetes melanocephalus Pl. 281

Identification 17cm. Adult slate grey above, almost entire head black, with silvery white lining on ear-coverts giving patch effect, chin black, throat to undertail-coverts deep yellow, washed olive on flanks and undertail-coverts; eyes red, bill black, legs and feet dark grey. Juvenile slightly paler and duller above, dull buffy-yellow below, streaked finely with dusky from chin to flanks. Rufous-naped Brush Finch has clear rufous crown; juvenile alike, but Rufous-naped has dark brown eyes, but they are unlikely to overlap.

Ssp. Monotypic (N Co: Santa Marta)

Habits A conspicuous and fairly easily seen Santa Marta endemic that forages in pairs or small groups in understorey and undergrowth, less on ground, and often joins mixed-species flocks.

Status Very common. Endemic to Colombia.

Habitat Subtropical to Temperate Zones, from 1,300m (recorded at 600m) to 3,200m. Humid shrubs and thickets at roadsides, forest edges, regenerating areas and second growth.

Voice Loud cascading song of chipping and twittering notes (H&B, F&K).

YELLOW-HEADED BRUSH FINCH

Atlapetes flaviceps Pl. 281

Identification 18cm. Adult yellowish-olive above, darker on wings and tail, head paler yellowish-olive with pale yellow eye-ring; colour of head somewhat variable, for reasons unknown, possibly increasingly yellow with age? Juvenile not known.

Ssp. Monotypic (C Andes in Co)

Habits Assumed to be rather like Dusky-headed Brush Finch, fairly arboreal, foraging in pairs or perhaps small groups in understorey and undergrowth. Appears to feed on small fruits, insects and some seeds.

Status Endangered. Endemic to Colombia.

Habitat Upper Tropical to Subtropical Zones, 1,300–2,150m, in second growth, borders and edges, plantations and

areas with fruit trees and shrubs, groves of trees and forest fragments.
Voice Unknown.
Note Sometimes called Olive-headed Brush Finch.

DUSKY-HEADED BRUSH FINCH
Atlapetes fuscoolivaceus Pl. 281

Identification 18cm. Adult dark olive above with vestigial white speculum, head darker to blackish; chin and throat to mesial deep yellow and blackish malar; rest of underparts deep yellow, washed narrowly olive on sides and flanks; bill dusky to blackish, legs and feet flesh. Juvenile just slightly paler above, blackish on head restricted to lores and base of cheeks and ear-coverts, malar dusky with mesial olivaceous, as neck-sides and wash over most of underparts, except throat which is clear yellow, and belly is fairly yellow, paler underparts streaked dark olive; bill horn-coloured.

Ssp. Monotypic (C Co: head of Magdalena Valley)

Habits Arboreal, forages in pairs and small groups, moving animatedly through thickets and tangles.
Status Near Threatened. Endemic to Colombia, where common in its very small range.
Habitat Subtropical Zone, 1,600–2,400m, at edges and borders of humid montane forest, second growth, shrubby clearings, bushy, overgrown pastures and copses in farmland.
Voice Distinctly 3-part song, very rapid, chippy, *ti-ti-ti-ti-ti-ti, tch-tch-tch-tch,chew-chew-chew*, slower and lower pitched at end (H&B).

TRICOLOURED BRUSH FINCH
Atlapetes tricolor Pl. 281

Identification 18cm. Adult dark olive above, black on head-sides, broad orange streak from bill to nape, underparts deep yellow washed narrowly on sides with olive, broadly on flanks to thighs and undertail-coverts; bill dusky, legs and feet horn. Juvenile slightly paler above, washed entirely olive below and finely streaked dusky; bill greyish-horn. Similar Rufous-naped Brush Finch greyer above and lacks olive wash on rear underparts, but note race *spodionotus* that overlaps has neither a white speculum nor a pale loral or supraloral spot, which otherwise would reinforce distinction; and Rufous-naped generally occurs at higher elevations.

Ssp. *A. t. crassus* (Ec, W Andes in Co)

Habits Arboreal, forages in pairs or small groups in dense understorey and shrubbery. Usually independent of mixed-species flocks.
Status Locally fairly common in Ecuador, fairly common in Colombia.
Habitat Tropical to lower Subtropical Zones, 600–2,400m in Ecuador, 300–2,000m in Colombia, with extremes varying locally in both countries. Lower growth of wet, mossy cloud forest borders and secondary woodland.
Voice Song high-pitched with wheezy quality (R&G). Dawn song in Colombia an excited *EEeu-tsit-tsit-tsueet* or *EEeu-tsit tsit-tsit-t't't't't't-eet* with first note downslurred (H&B). A long series of slowly accelerating notes terminated with a dry trill *tzit-tzit-tzit-tzit-tju-tju-tju-tju-tjrrrr*, sometimes initiated with falling note. Also a squeak, followed by 2 chirps and a sweet *churr*, or even *EEuu-tsit-tsit-tsueet* (F&K).
Note Race *crassus* probably a separate species (García-Moreno & Fjeldså 1999).

MOUSTACHED BRUSH FINCH
Atlapetes albofrenatus Pl. 281

Identification 17.5cm. Adult uniform olive-green above, with top of head broadly cinnamon-rufous, head-sides to nape-sides black, mesial broadly white, malar narrowly black, rest of underparts deep yellow with greenish wash on sides, broad on flanks and thighs; eyes red, bill black, legs and feet pink. Juvenile uniform olive-green above, darker on head-sides, malar black, deep yellow below, well washed with green from breast to undertail-coverts; eyes and bill dark, legs dull greyish-pink. Rufous-naped Brush Finch similar but lacks distinctive black and white moustachial on head-sides, and White-winged has same pattern but is dark grey-brown above with a white speculum.

Ssp. *A. a. albofrenatus* (E Andes in Co) white chin and throat, black malar heavier
A. a. meridae (W Ve) as described

Habits Arboreal, forages in trees and bushes in pairs or groups, active and fairly easy to see. Tolerant of disturbed habitat and occasionally travels with mixed-species flocks.
Status Fairly common throughout its range.
Habitat Upper Tropical to Subtropical Zones, in Colombia from 1,000m, though more frequently encountered above 1,600m, to 2,500m, in Venezuela at 2,100–2,500m. Borders of humid forest and moist oak woodland, to dry scrubby brush, and dry lower woodland, treefall clearings to regenerating second growth.
Voice In Colombia, a thin high-pitched *eeespe,* sometimes trebled (Hilty in H&B), in Venezuela, a variable dawn song is given a few times, typically a few notes then a longer, faster series, e.g. *czeet, czeet, czeet, czeet, tswit-tswit-tswit-tsu-tsu-tsu-tsu-tsu-tsu*, last notes rapid and clattery (F&K, Hilty).

SLATY BRUSH FINCH
Atlapetes schistaceus Pl. 280

Identification 18cm. Adult varies according to subspecies, but essentially is uniform dark grey above, blackish on head with a broad orange to deep rufous stripe on centre of head, white mesial line that extends below ear-coverts, and paler grey below. Juvenile similar but duller, streaked to some extent, and darker below. No similar species in range.

Ssp. *A. s. castaneifrons* (Andes in Ve) bright rufous crown extends to and broadens on nape, white supraloral spot, broad white mesial finely streaked black, greyish-cream throat finely streaked black, legs and feet horn; juvenile dark brown below, finely streaked on drab mesial and chin to flanks

A. s. fumidus (E Co, Perijá in Ve) slightly paler and drabber than *castaneifrons*, legs and feet dark vinaceous-grey; juvenile also slightly paler and more drab, but distinctly more heavily streaked below

A. s. tamae (CE Co, Táchira in Ve) dark rufous on head, underparts dark grey, streaked finely with white on chin and throat, legs and feet horn; juvenile very dark with obscure black streaking

A. s. schistaceus (E Ec, Andes in Co) brightest and cleanest-looking grey, slate above with large white speculum (the only race with this clear field mark); bold curving white mesial, white chin and throat, French grey below, legs and feet vinaceous-grey; juvenile palest and most clean grey, clearly streaked dusky on back and breast to flanks, large white spot on lores and supraloral, short white mesial, vestigial white speculum

Habits Restless and shy. Forages in pairs and small groups, and often joins mixed-species flocks. Usually in lower undergrowth, but moves higher and becomes more apparent with passing of a mixed-species flock, which it will follow for a while.
Status Uncommon in Ecuador, common in Colombia and Venezuela.
Habitat Subtropical to Temperate Zones, mostly at 2,500–3,400m in Ecuador and Colombia, and 2,000–3,800m in Venezuela. Bushes and thickets at borders of forest, from treefall clearings and gaps in humid mossy forest to treeline.
Voice Contact a fine *tzit-tzit-tzit*. Alarm a fine *krryt krryt* (F&K). Song phrases short, e.g. *weyé-chuw* (R&G). Often sings persistently for brief period at dawn, typically *tsuu, tweet-tweet*, slowly, with first note downslurred. Pairs sing poorly coordinated duets of high-pitched notes and trills that end with distinctive *chewy-chewy-chewy*, or *t'chew, t'chew, t'chew*. Utter fine thin *tseet* notes while foraging (Hilty).

BAY-CROWNED BRUSH FINCH
Atlapetes seebohmi Pl. 281

Identification 16–17cm. Adult grey above, with darker wings and tail, top of head rufous, head-sides black, from base of ear-coverts to throat white, with straggly black malar, breast and sides grey, mixed cinnamon on flanks and pure cinnamon on undertail-coverts, central belly and vent white. Eyes brown, bill grey, legs and feet dusky flesh.

Ssp. *A. s. simonsi* (extreme SSW Ec) larger, brownish-grey above, rich rufous on head from level with eyes but entire frontal band black to malar, breast pale grey, flanks olivaceous and undertail-coverts mid cinnamon

A. s. celicae (SW Ec) smaller, pure grey above, pale orange-rufous on head from supraloral (small amount by nostrils, black,) base of chin and reduced malar black, breast, sides and flanks darker grey, undertail-coverts pale cinnamon

Habits Usually in close pairs or small groups, foraging in undergrowth; relatively slow and deliberate in its movements. Rather arboreal and seldom forages on ground.
Status Rare to locally fairly common.
Habitat Tropical to Temperate Zones, mostly at 1,300–2,300m, in undergrowth of dry scrub and woodland and adjacent regenerating areas.
Voice Alarm, *dee dee tee tee*… Call a very high-pitched, repeated *zee*. Song *tschia-tschia-ziay-ziay-ziayziay*, sometimes terminated with a trill. (F&K, given for *A. nationi*, which then included *seebohmi*, *simonsi* and *celicae*).
Note F&K point out that *celicae* was described from a possibly aberrant *simonsi* specimen. Validity of both races contended by R&G due to occurrence of *simonsi* near type locality of *celicae*, which implies that they are mere variants of a single, variable population.

WHITE-WINGED BRUSH FINCH
Atlapetes leucopterus Pl. 281

Identification 16cm. Adult grey above with a large white speculum, top of head orange-rufous, head-sides black with white supraloral spot, mesial to neck-sides and throat, and entire underparts white, with a short narrow black malar and greyish wash on sides, flanks and thighs; eyes red, bill black, legs and feet grey. Juvenile soft olive-brown above with buffy head-stripe, white below, washed pale cinnamon, flanks and thighs pale olive. Somewhat similar Slaty Brush Finch is distinctly darker below and lacks speculum; it also occurs at higher elevations.

Ssp. *A. l. dresseri* (SW Ec) pale orange-rufous of head starts on rear crown, has a white eye-ring, and large supraloral is orange-buffy, underparts pale cinnamon from central belly to undertail-coverts; race is unusual in that it may exhibit extremely variable amounts of white on face (see plate) to point where head almost completely white (Fitzpatrick 1980)

A. l. leucopterus (W Ec) as described, larger bill

A. l. paynteri (N Peru to Ec border) broad frontal band black, with cream-coloured supraloral spot, broad band from above eyes to nape buffy, washed cinnamon only over eyes, vent to undertail-coverts pale cinnamon

Habits Occurs in pairs and small groups that forage actively and restlessly in undergrowth and at lower levels.
Status Locally fairly common in Ecuador,
Habitat Tropical to Temperate Zones, 1,000–2,600m in Ecuador, in light woodlands and shrubby areas in dry country; abandoned cultivation, plantations, farms and gardens on dry hillsides.
Voice Unknown.

WHITE-HEADED BRUSH FINCH
Atlapetes albiceps Pl. 281

Identification 16cm. Adult slate grey above, black wings and tail have grey fringes to feathers, top of head to nape and neck-sides black, rest of head white, including chin and throat and underparts to vent; sides and flanks narrowly washed grey, undertail-coverts pale cinnamon. Eyes dark, bill, legs and feet black. Juvenile undescribed. White-winged Brush Finch has rufous on rear of head, and white speculum. Pale-headed has entire head white, lightly tinged cinnamon on top, undertail-coverts white.

Ssp. Monotypic (SE Ec)

Habits Pairs and small groups forage in undergrowth and at lower levels.
Status Uncommon to locally fairly common.
Habitat Tropical Zone, in Dry, lowland deciduous forest and scrub, to *c*.1,100m.
Voice Unknown.

PALE-HEADED BRUSH FINCH

Atlapetes pallidiceps Pl. 281

Identification 16cm. Adult slate grey above, black wings and tail have grey fringes to feathers, white speculum, head entirely white, washed pale cinnamon above, greyish lores; underparts from chin to undertail-coverts white, washed narrowly with grey on flanks. Eyes dark, bill black, legs and feet dark grey. Juvenile apparently similar but has dark brown cheeks. Unique and cannot be confused with any other species.

Ssp. Monotypic (S Ec: río Jubones drainage)

Habits Singles and pairs forage up to 20m apart, maintaining contact with distinctive, high-pitched note. Every 5–20 minutes, pair comes together briefly before separating again. Forages in bushes and scrub within 2m of ground, also on ground, sometimes in open but never far from cover.
Status Critically Endangered. Very rare and local endemic to Ecuador. Rediscovered in 1989 and population in 1998 thought to number just *c*.10 breeding pairs. More recently, careful efforts to control brood parasitism by cowbirds have brought population to *c*.50 pairs (E. Restall-Orr, pers. comm.).
Habitat Upper Tropical to Lower Subtropical Zones, at 1,500–2,200m, in dense arid scrub on ungrazed land in intermontane valleys
Voice Reunited pairs utter a rapid burst of notes in a cascade, typical of all *Atlapetes*, but differs in being higher pitched and lacking any pure loud whistles, and trills are slower. Sometimes a pair will sing duet in perfect synchronisation. Another call, shorter and slightly lower pitched than contact, and relatively similar to Stripe-headed Brush Finch (which occurs in same area) was uttered frequently when joined mixed-species flocks Agreda *et al.* 1999).

OCHRE-BREASTED BRUSH FINCH

Atlapetes semirufus Pl. 282

Identification 18cm. Adult olive-green above, with entire head, breast and sides ochraceous-orange, rest of underparts yellow, flushed olive-green on flanks, thighs and undertail-coverts; eyes red, bill black above, pale bluish-grey below, legs and feet vinaceous-pink. Immature has distinct intermediate plumage following complete moult where after head still as juvenile, but throat yellow and rest of body as adult. Juvenile slightly softer olive-green above, including head and malar stripe, with pale mesial; chin and throat yellowish, rest of underparts yellow streaked olive; bill horn, legs and feet flesh. Bright orange-rufous head and green upperparts are distinctive and striking.

Ssp. *A. s. albigula* (NE Táchira, Ve) head paler orange, mesial white, throat- to breast-sides pale orange, throat whitish, breast to belly bright yellow, flanks washed green, undertail-coverts cinnamon, bill horn
A. s. benedettii (NW VE) like *semirufus*, but paler orange on breast, brighter green on flanks, undertail-coverts yellowish; juvenile has blackish flush to lower cheeks and blackish malar, bill black
A. s. denisei (Coastal Cordillera, N Ve) deeper orange to rufous head, darker green on sides and flanks and washed on undertail-coverts; juvenile has pale spots at tips of median and greater coverts (unlike other juveniles), well washed dark olive-green below and streaked dusky from breast to undertail-coverts; bill and legs dusky to dark grey
A. s. majusculus (C Andes, Co) paler orange head with whitish flush to lores, upper ear-coverts, face-sides and throat, bill horn above, pale horn to flesh below, undertail-coverts yellow, washed slightly green
A. s. semirufus (E Andes in C Co) as described
A. s. zimmeri (NC Co, Ve) like *majusculus*, but brown bill and pale orange undertail-coverts

Habits Forages quietly, alone and in close pairs, also in small groups. Usually seen as it emerges on outer branches of foliage *c*.2 m from ground, and frequently forages on ground, but seldom with mixed-species flocks.
Status Local in Colombia, fairly common in Venezuela. Tolerates some disturbance of habitat and may be a garden resident, but retreats in face of urbanisation.
Habitat Subtropical Zone to Páramo, at 1,600–3,500m in Colombia, mostly above 2,500m, and at 500–2,700m in Venezuela.
Voice Song a short, monotonous, whistled *wheet, peet, p'tsu-tsu-tsu* or *eeet, wheet, sweet-sweet-sweet*, or a shorter *swiit, chew-chew-chew* or similar variation, typically first notes rising (P. Schwartz recording).

TEPUI BRUSH FINCH

Atlapetes personatus Pl. 282

Identification 18cm. Adult very dark olive-green above, entire head except chin and throat rich deep rufous, chin and throat to breast and centre of belly yellow, rest of underparts deep olive-green; eyes brown, bill dusky above, horn below, legs and feet dusky. Juvenile like adult above, with head concolorous with back, but spots of rufous start to show early; below a duller version of adult. Only brush finch in range, and is much darker than Ochre-breasted Brush Finch.

Ssp. *A. p. collaris* (Gran Sabana, Ve) like *personatus* it has a yellow throat, but chin is rufous and underparts much more heavily washed green and streaked dusky from breast, bill dark above, horn below; juvenile densely washed rufous on underparts and streaked dusky, bill dark greenish-horn

A. p. duidae (Mt. Duida, Ve) entire head and nape, entire breast and sides deep rufous; immature similar but has deep olive-green streaks on yellow belly; juvenile washed heavily with deep reddish-brown, belly and flanks yellow, streaked deep reddish-brown

A. p. jugularis (SE Amazonas, Ve) head and upper breast bright rufous, lower breast to undertail-coverts yellow, with patchy green on sides and flanks, washed on undertail-coverts, which have yellow edges; juvenile paler olive-green above, with blackish streaks on back, underparts yellow streaked irregularly green from chin to belly, then a heavy wash, bill greenish-horn

A. p. paraquensis (NW Amazonas, Ve) head, chin and throat rufous, blackish wash on fore face, underparts yellow, washed heavily green on flanks to undertail-coverts, immature has rusty-brown head, with blackish wash on face, irregular black malar, chin and throat pale yellow, rest as adult; juvenile dark olive above with pale eye-ring, yellow from chin to belly washed irregularly olive and streaked finely dusky, undertail-coverts brown

A. p. parui (N Amazonas, Ve) very dark olive-green above with head to breast and sides very deep rufous, belly deep yellow, flanks to undertail-coverts deep olive-green, latter with clear yellow edges; bill, legs and feet black; juvenile unknown

A. p. personatus (Roraima and nearby tepuis in Ve & Gu) as described; has yellow throat

Habits Pairs and small groups forage together and often join mixed-species flocks. Mostly in undergrowth near ground, comes into view at ends of branches or if their curiosity prevails.

Status Common throughout its range.

Habitat Tropical to Subtropical Zones, 1,000–2,500m, at edges of forest, shrubbery and second growth.

Voice Dawn song on Sierra de Lema, by both sexes, an unmusical *speek! speek! speeu-TEE-tu'tu'tu*, with middle note loudest and highest. When excited, pairs duet, a crescendo of rapid, chattery forceful *tsit* and *ti* notes ending with 2–4 buzzy notes squeezed out, *ti'ti'ti'ti'ti'ti'ti'ti'tsit'tsit'tsit'tsit'chi'chi' chi'che'che'chewee-chewee*. Generally quiet, with only a few exuberant outbursts at dawn.

Paroaria cardinals are treated here as separate species on basis of DNA results presented in an unpublished PhD thesis, with paper in prep. (A. Porzecanski, pers. comm.). They are sympatric in extreme south-west Venezuela, with no evidence of hybridisation. Much of the literature is unfortunately not specific as to which bird is being referred to, and we have ignored all such equivocal data. They are birds of open areas, undoubtedly favouring sites near water and appear to have a propensity for nesting on branches overhanging water. They forage at roadsides, in open scrubby, nearly bare grassland and in trees, and quickly become used to man if not trapped, readily visiting feeding stations.

RED-CAPPED CARDINAL

Paroaria gularis Pl. 283

Identification 16cm Adult glossy black with some blue reflections above, white below; head bright glistening crimson-red with a short black streak from lores to just behind eyes, chin also crimson, but throat, extending as slightly lanceolate feathers onto white breast, is black, slight black shading on upper breast, and thighs barred black and white; eyes vermilion-red, bill black above and pink, through orange below, legs and feet black. Immature dark greyish-olive above, olive on top and sides of head, encircling eyes and as a short crescent over fore ear-coverts, with salmon-buffy lores, lower cheeks and rear ear-coverts; chin and throat pale greyish-buffy, entire underparts white; first adult feathers show as spots on throat; eyes orange, bill black above, pale greyish below, legs and feet grey. Juvenile like immature but concolorous olive from head to tail, eyes pale brown, bill dusky grey above, pale grey below.

Ssp. Monotypic (E Ec, E Co, extreme S Ve in SW Amazonas, SE Ve, Guianas)

Habits Seen alone, but usually in pairs or small groups on ground, taking fallen seeds, mostly confiding and fearless, and often perches boldly. Sometimes forages on floating vegetation, and perches on sticks protruding from water.

Status Fairly common to common. Reportedly very common in savannas of interior Guyana but rare and restricted in W Suriname, and rare vagrant in N French Guiana.

Habitat Tropical Zone, in Ecuador to 400m but mostly below 300m, usually in fairly open to open areas, *várzea* and grasslands near water.

Voice Song a variable series of short sweet phrases, often repeated for long periods, e.g. *chit-tweet-tu… chit-tweet-tu…* R&G). A medium–high *chwee* and a squeaky *wiss…wiss… wiss…* (Snyder 1966).

Note For taxonomy see introductory note to genus, above.

MASKED CARDINAL

Paroaria nigrogenis Pl. 283

Identification 16cm. Adult black above, white below; head glistening silky crimson-red with broad black streak from lores through eyes to neck, and crimson extends as slightly lanceolate feathers onto white breast, thighs barred black and white; eyes vermilion-red, bill black above and white to yellow below, legs and feet dark grey. Immature dark olive above, concolorous with top and sides of head, slightly salmon-buffy on lower cheeks, underparts white; red of head appears as bold irregular spots; bill black above, pale grey below, legs and feet grey. Juvenile olive above including head, with salmon-buffy lower cheeks, chin and throat, entire underparts creamy buffy; first adult feathers show as spots on throat; eyes pale brown, bill all grey, legs and feet grey.

Ssp. Monotypic (EC Co, Ve, Tr: río Apure to Orinoco, thence to Delta Amacuro and Tr, but not upstream from Puerto Ayacucho)

Habits Active to point of being restless, but walks steadily in

surprisingly open spaces, e.g. car parks. A popular cagebird, escapees occur in city centres and other unexpected places. Often forages on muddy ground at water's edge and on plants in water, inspecting emergent branches and stumps.
Status Common in Llanos of Venezuela and on Trinidad, where restricted to northern mangrove swamps.
Habitat Tropical Zone, to 300m, in open habitats, wet savannas and edges of gallery forest near water.
Voice Call a sharp *tchep* (ffrench) or soft *chuép* (Hilty). Song different from birds in Peru (*gularis*) (D. Ascanio, pers. comm.), in a P. Schwartz recording, *suwee-chú… suwee-chu… suwee* rising and *chu* falling, repeated at short intervals (Hilty). Recording at Hato El Cedral by D. Ascanio, *ptchiu wheet pt pt chiu chiieuw wheet chiu chiieer wheet pt pt chiu* (Restall transcription).
Note The English name is tentative in the absence of formal recognition of the species. For taxonomy see introductory note to genus, above.

CARDINALIDAE – Cardinals, Grosbeaks, Saltators and Allies

Cardinalidae is an interesting family, long considered part of Emberizidae and currently in a shake-down process with some genera being transferred into the family from Thraupidae and Emberizidae. Saltators, on the other hand, might be removed from this family since genetic support for their inclusion is weak (Klicka *et al.* 2000). The family contains many brightly coloured and often exquisitely beautiful birds, some of which have large, heavy bills and many of which are fine songsters. It is distributed throughout the Americas, from Argentina to Canada, and some members occur in most habitats, from desertic, xerophytic areas at sea level, through tropical forests to temperate zone woodland. Some inhabit dense and dark forests, and others light second growth, gallery forests, plantations, parks and gardens. Their diets range from insectivorous, or semi-ripened seeds during the breeding season and dry seeds when not breeding, to entirely vegetarian, including berries, fruits, leaves and flowers. The heavy, often massive bills might be taken for an adaptation to crack large hard seeds, and in some cases this is so, but in many cases these are adapted for nipping buds and the corollas of flowers. All build cup-shaped nests, which vary from small and neat to large and apparently messy. Young are usually precocial, fledging in some cases in as few as 9–15 days.

DICKCISSEL *Spiza americana* Pl. 284

Identification 15cm. Adult male brown above, streaked blackish on back and tertials, most wing-coverts chestnut, flight-feathers dark, broadly fringed pale brown, head grey with whitish superciliary and mesial, very narrow black line at edge of malar joins black throat which grades into breast, bib white; underparts yellow, becoming white on vent and undertail-coverts; eyes dark, bill horn, legs and feet grey. Black throat may have fresh, white-tipped feathers, thus can appear to have anything from black bib to none at all. Female slightly smaller and slimmer, brownish on head and has irregular black spots on malar that tend to curve around throat forming a necklace, but no breast patch, and is slightly streaked brownish below. Immature much like female, with paler head and bill, and slightly heavier streaking below.

Ssp. Monotypic (boreal migrant mainly to W Llanos in Ve, also N Ec, E Co, T&T, Gu, Su)

Habits Leaves roosts after dawn, in small groups of a few dozens to few hundreds, dispersing over entire rice-growing area, using rice, sorghum and any other cultivated cereal fields, where they are surprisingly difficult to see. Late afternoon they begin to desist from their foraging and gradually flocks merge, swirling and wheeling until they look like a horde of locusts. Eventually, after period of *c.*1 hour, they fly towards cane beds where they roost.
Status The wintering area appears to vary over time, for Dickcissels are far less numerous on Trinidad now than formerly, and the majority of the entire population descends on rice-growing areas of Venezuela, where they are poisoned, burned in their roosts and shot. Hundreds of thousands are still regular, but the flocks of several million of a few decades ago are now rare. Comparatively small numbers occur on Trinidad and in Colombia annually, and small numbers are also reaching northern Ecuador. First recorded on Tobago in 1998. It remains to be seen what effect the dramatically changing weather patterns in the Caribbean and Gulf of Mexico have on its movements.
Habitat Tropical Zone, recorded at altitude crossing Coastal Cordillera, but generally in Lower Tropical Zone of central and north-east Llanos where rice is grown year-round.
Voice Roosts at midday and great flocks engage in twittering, audible over some distance, similarly birds coming to roost at night twitter continually and only gradually become quiet after nightfall.

Pheucticus grosbeaks are arboreal birds with attractive voices and large heavy bills. The 2 resident species have particularly melodious voices, yellow and black garb and particularly massive bills. The 2 boreal migrants are slightly smaller and do not sing whilst in our region. They are even more arboreal, being mainly birds of the canopy.

GOLDEN-BELLIED GROSBEAK *Pheucticus chrysogaster* Pl. 284

Identification 20cm. Adult essentially all yellow with black wings and tail, the male streaked blackish on back, with large white terminal spots on median and greater wing-coverts, tertials and long uppertail-coverts, which wear over time, leaving bird looking blacker; leading edge of primaries whitish with a black band across middle. Eyes dark brown, bill massive and dark horn to dusky. Female has brown wings (not black), is streaked dusky from crown to lower rump and slightly streaked on head-sides, breast-sides and flanks. White spots tend slightly smaller. Young very much like female, but have lower mandible pale horn.

Ssp. *P. c. chrysogaster* (Ec, SW Co) all-yellow rump
P. c. laubmanni (N Co, N Ve) streaked rump

Habits Male defends territory, which is roughly size of a football pitch, by constantly flying between points and singing loudly for *c*.10 minutes at each stop, usually a treetop. Easier to hear than see and just as an observer approaches the singer, it flies off again to another corner! At other times perches quietly for long periods and may be easy to approach.
Status Uncommon to locally fairly common throughout. Recently recorded on Trinidad (perhaps an escape).
Habitat Tropical to Subtropical Zones, to 3,500m in Ecuador, 1700–2,800m in Colombia and 950–2,000m in Venezuela. Light woodland and arid scrub, partially cultivated areas with scattered trees, deciduous woodland and scrub, cultivated areas, parks and gardens.
Voice Song rich, mellow and melodious, liquid and full, rather thrush-like, and each bird has repertoire of variations. In Ecuador (*chrysogaster*) said to be a fast carolling (R&G), in Colombia and Venezuela (*laubmanni*) a series of liquid slow phrases (Hilty).
Note Formerly considered a subspecies of Yellow Grosbeak *P. chrysopeplus*. Called Southern Yellow-grosbeak in R&G and Hilty, but Golden-bellied Grosbeak by AOU and Dickinson (2003).

BLACK-BACKED GROSBEAK

Pheucticus aureoventris Pl. 284

Identification 22cm. Adult male has entire head and upperparts black except yellow rump, and underparts yellow. Bold white speculum on basal third of primaries except outermost and basal quarter of secondaries on inner webs, with large white spots on median and greater wing-coverts, and whitish tips to most outer tail-feathers. In worn plumage, white much reduced. Eyes dark brown; massive bill steel grey to blackish, legs and feet grey. Female lacks black head and has brown wings and tail, and is heavily streaked brown to dusky. Juvenile very much like female. Rose-breasted Grosbeak smaller and immature male invariably has some rose on breast, with white underparts; female whitish and streaked below. Black-headed Grosbeak not yet recorded on mainland, though immature male can be very buffy below, it has horn-coloured bill and noticeable broad white malar stripe.

Ssp. *P. a. crissalis* (Ec, SW Co) 2 white wingbars and white spot at tip of each tertial, yellow rump, and white spot at end of each long uppertail-covert
P. a. meridensis (Mérida, Ve) greater coverts largely white, appearing as block of white on wing, rather than 2 wingbars, large white spots on tertials and long uppertail-coverts much reduced when worn; some black flecking on yellow rump
P. a. uropygialis (W Co) 2 clear wingbars, rump and all tail-coverts black with yellow fringes, giving a roughly scaled effect

Habits Forages at all levels, including ground, but usually in treetops. Typically permits fairly close approach.
Status Uncommon and local in Ecuador, fairly common in Colombia and uncommon to rare in Venezuela.
Habitat Tropical to Temperate Zones, 1,500–3,200m in Ecuador, 1,700–3,000m in Colombia and 1,450–2,500m in Venezuela.
Voice Vocalisations like those of Golden-bellied Grosbeak (R&G, H&B, Hilty).

ROSE-BREASTED GROSBEAK

Pheucticus ludovicianus Pl. 284

Identification 18cm. Adult male has head, back, wings and tail black, with white rump, speculum and median wing-coverts, and white tips to greater coverts; centre of breast rose-red, sides and rest of underparts white, washed buffy on flanks, streaked finely dusky. Eyes dark brown, bill horn, legs and feet grey. Non-breeding male has vestigial white malar and superciliary, brown fringes to black feathers that wear during winter, and rose breast scaled white with a few blackish spots and streaks, or is more like female with rose flush on breast. Female dark brown above, streaked dusky on back and rump, pale spots on wing-coverts and tertials; white below, washed yellow-buff, streaked dusky from chin to breast, and on sides and flanks. Bill horn, legs and feet grey. Unlikely to be confused.

Ssp. *P. l. ludovicianus* (boreal migrant to E Ec, E & N Co, Ve, Tr, ABC)

Habits Invariably seen foraging high in canopy, though occasionally perches quietly, moving little and slowly.
Status Rare and uncommon in Ecuador, uncommon in Colombia, both as transient and winter resident, and very uncommon in Venezuela, uncommon passage migrant to Aruba, Curaçao and Bonaire. Very rare on Trinidad, but perhaps both a passage migrant and winter resident. Arrives in Colombia from mid October and all have left by late April.
Habitat Tropical to Subtropical Zones, to 2,000m in Ecuador and Venezuela, 3,800m in Colombia.
Voice Flight-call a soft wheezy *wheek*, calls include a sharp squeaky *iik* (Sibley), high-pitched metallic *eek* (H&B, Hilty) and metallic *pink* (R&G). Does not sing in our region.

BLACK-HEADED GROSBEAK

Pheucticus melanocephalus Pl. 284

Identification 18cm. Adult male has black head, wings and tail, with white rump, speculum, median wing-coverts and tips to greater coverts; back yellowish-cinnamon with rows of black streaks, rump, collar to throat and breast cinnamon, becoming white on vent and undertail-coverts. Immature and winter male have cinnamon paler, feathers fringed buffy, and black on head and mantle also fringed buffy, with vestigial coronal stripe. Female like immature male but more buffy below, finely streaked dusky on sides and flanks, pale stripe over crown, pale superciliary and pale throat more clearly defined. Immature and female from Rose-breasted by bicoloured bill, dark above, pale below.

Ssp. *P. m. maculatus* (boreal migrant, vagrant to Cu)

Habits No details of behaviour on Curaçao.
Status Rare visitor to Curaçao, possibly just stragglers; similar status in Panama.
Habitat Only recorded at sea level in our region.
Voice Flight-call a soft wheezy *wheek*, calls include a high, sharp *pik* (Sibley).

VERMILION CARDINAL
Cardinalis phoeniceus Pl. 284

Identification 20cm. Adult male appears entirely scarlet-red with small black surround at base of bill, wings and tail brown, the feathers broadly fringed scarlet. Crest long and slender, points vertically up, though when depressed projects beyond profile of head. Eyes dark brown, bicoloured bill is compressed, the black upper mandible shallow and curved, lower mandible grey, legs and feet grey. Female soft chamois above, with darker wings that have feather fringes chamois, a red flush to tail, grey top and sides of head with pinkish-red crest, and nape intermediate with back, lower head-sides and throat whitish, chin black, underparts warm cinnamon. Juvenile paler and duller than female with shorter tail and shorter crest, lacks any grey on head and is more yellowish below. Only superficially resembles well-known Red Cardinal of North America, being decidedly more slender and with longer crest. Unique and not to be confused with other red birds.

Ssp. Monotypic (NE Co, N Ve)

Habits Scattered and usually in loose pairs, occasionally a few together. Usually observed at distance, perched vertically on an exposed high branch of a thorn tree, and does not permit easy approach.
Status Fairly common, but hunted by trappers for the cagebird trade and thus usually wary and flighty.
Habitat Tropical Zone, to 150m. Xerophytic scrub, thorn thickets and *Acacia* woodland.
Voice Call a loud, clear chip. The song is a loud, eloquent *cheer, o-weet, toweet toweet toweet or cheer, cheer, heera toweer* (P. Schwartz recording, H&B), and *swit-sweet, swit-sweet chee-chEEo, swit-sweet, chee-chEEo cheeu, tsuu*, etc. (Hilty).

YELLOW-GREEN GROSBEAK
Caryothraustes canadensis Pl. 284

Identification 16.5cm. Adult bright yellow-olive above and yellow with olive tone below, black surround to base of bill, extending over lores to end in a point just behind eyes, bicoloured bill blackish above and pale blue-grey at base below, legs and feet grey. Juvenile appears identical in field but mask sooty rather than pure black, and bill all dark. Unique plumage coloration and pattern.

Ssp. *C. c. canadensis* (SE Co, S Ve, Guianas)

Habits Usually in pairs or small groups, occasionally up to 20, moving noisily through upper storey and canopy, their noise attracting other species that may join them.
Status Uncommon to locally fairly common, common in Suriname.
Habitat Tropical Zone, to 250m in Colombia, 1,000m in Venezuela, Usually in humid forest, only occasionally at edges or clearings.
Voice Call a buzzy *bzzit* and loud oft-repeated *teach-yerp* (H&B). Chirping song, given from treetops (H&M). A loud buzzy *dzzeet* or *dzreet*, sometimes followed by repeated *chew-chew-chew-chew*, or latter series given alone (R&T). Loud buzzy rattle when foraging, *b'z'zz'et!* and loud, oft-repeated *teach-yerp* with rising then falling inflection. Dawn song rather monotonous *chap, chap, cheeweep…* with scarcely a pause (Hilty).
Note Previously called Green Grosbeak (AOU 1983).

YELLOW-SHOULDERED GROSBEAK
Parkerthraustes humeralis Pl. 284

Identification 16.5cm Adult olive-green above with yellowish shoulder, top and sides of head slate grey with black frontal band and black mask to ear-coverts, mesial white with faint black barring, malar black, chin and throat barred black and white, underparts grey except yellow vent and undertail-coverts. Large heavy bill black above, grey below. Legs and feet grey. Juvenile and immature generally duller with facial markings less clearly defined and white mesial barred like throat. Unlikely to be confused with any other bird in its range.

Ssp. Monotypic (E Ec, S Co?)

Habits Usually singly or in pairs, and often with mixed-species flocks in canopy. Will perch on an exposed branch surveying its surroundings.
Status Rare to locally uncommon. Uncertain in Colombia (Stotz *et al.* 1996).
Habitat Tropical Zone, 200–1,000m but mostly below 600m. Humid lowland forest.
Voice Call, a sharp, high-pitched *cheét-swit* or *suweet*. Song a jumbled series of similar, twittered notes (R&G).
Note Species recognised as distinct from *Caryothraustes* and elevated to monotypic genus level (Remsen 1997).

RED-AND-BLACK GROSBEAK
Periporphyrus erythromelas Pl. 284

Identification 20cm. Adult male entirely crimson-red except all-black hood and paler red undertail-coverts. Eyes dark brown, massive bill black, legs and feet dark. Female olive-green above, darker on wings and tail, with reddish fringes to remiges and rectrices; below yellow with olive tone, the yellow reaching neck-sides, bordering black of hood until it barely meets at the nape; lower mandible pale grey at base. Juvenile undescribed.

Ssp. Monotypic (SE Ve, Guianas)

Habits Usually in pairs or small groups, with males singing almost continually (H&M), at middle and lower levels in Venezuela, mid levels in Suriname, mid levels and canopy in

French Guiana. Forages restlessly and is wary and not easy to follow, moving around over large area. Does not join mixed-species flocks. Both sexes sing.

Status Rare to very uncommon in Venezuela, fairly common in Suriname, uncommon in French Guiana.

Habitat Tropical Zone, to 1,000m. Primary lowland forest.

Voice Calls a high-pitched, sharp *spink!* and *psack!* (Hilty). Loud, sweet whistle, varied phrases ascending and descending (Beebe, in Snyder 1966). Striking song consists of long, slow whistles, ascending and descending, *feeyoo-feeyoo-feeyoo-weeyoo-weeyoo-wee* (H&M), or an exceptionally sweet and syrupy (*sic*) series of halting phrases that slide up and down, *UuureEE, ss'PEeeeeuu, reet-here…UuureEEcheer, preEEer, psek!… Pseet cheer REeechur, rEEar…* and so on, given slowly with pauses (Hilty).

Saltators are a fairly homogeneous genus of large arboreal grosbeaks that largely feed on buds and small leaves, berries and fruits. Generally quiet and reclusive, though not shy of man, they usually announce their presence by continually repeated songs. They all have large to heavy bills, mostly with pale eyebrows and dark malar stripes bordering pale throats.

SLATE-COLOURED GROSBEAK

Saltator grossus Pl. 285

Identification 20cm. Adult male slate grey with white chin and throat, white underwing-coverts; face black, embracing white bib. Eyes red, massive bill waxy red, legs and feet black. Female entirely grey, paler than male without any black on face nor round white bib. Juvenile distinctly warmer grey, white on throat much narrower and slightly shorter, underparts flammulated cinnamon and grey, the feather shafts paler, and the whole washed lightly with grey.

Ssp. *S. g. grossus* (E Ec, S Ve, Guianas) as described
S. g. saturatus (W Ec, N & W Co) darker slaty blue, underparts of female dark olive-grey with slight buffy-brownish tinge; juvenile has no white bib

Habits Pairs maintain large territory and are rather discreet and retiring. Forages in upper and mid levels, coming lower at edges and clearings. Sometimes joins mixed-species flocks. Fond of high vine tangles (Hilty).

Status Fairly common in Ecuador, Colombia and Venezuela.

Habitat Tropical Zone, mostly below 1,200m in Ecuador and Colombia, but to 1,300m in Venezuela. Lower and mid levels of humid and wet montane forest, tall second growth.

Voice Calls include *peek!* (Ridgely & Gwynne). Song sometimes very similar to Black-billed Peppershrike. Song of *grossus* a loud, full-bodied *whistlewHEchit, chee-chEEEr, tur-cHEit* or *prEEtuur, püü-TREEit*, or *three-more-BEErs*, or similar variation, with a soft quiet rendition as well (Hilty). Song of *saturatus*, *witcheeweeweeoo-cheéoo-cheer*, often with a querulous note at end.

Notes Also called Slaty Grosbeak. Formerly placed in genus *Pitylus* (Demastes & Remsen 1994).

BUFF-THROATED SALTATOR

Saltator maximus Pl. 285

Identification 20cm. Adult bright yellow-olive above, darker on primaries, head grey with short white supercilium, black malar, and white chin and throat; upper breast bright cinnamon-buff, as are vent and undertail-coverts, lower breast to flanks and thighs ochraceous-grey; eyes dark, conical bill black with bluish-grey base, long and heavy, legs and feet dark grey. Juvenile has head greyish with only vestigial white eyebrow, malar short and blackish, chin and upper throat buffy; lower throat to flanks and thighs dark buffy-grey, finely streaked dusky, undertail-coverts cinnamon; bill blackish with flesh-coloured base. Similar Greyish Saltator can appear very similar in canopy, but has a greyish back (not yellow-olive) and underparts are far less washed grey, only on breast and sides. Streaked Saltator also much paler below, the white belly reaching well onto centre of breast, and also has a white eye-ring.

Ssp. *S. m. iungens* (NW Co) more yellowish undertail-coverts, less fulvous; duller above, less yellowish-green
S. m. maximus (E Ec, E & NE Co, Ve, Guianas) as described

Habits A quiet and rather retiring bird. Individuals, pairs and sometimes small groups forage for fruits at all levels, but seems to most often be in canopy where it feeds on leaves and flowers.

Status Fairly common to common in Ecuador, common in Colombia, Venezuela and Guyana, fairly common in Suriname and French Guiana.

Habitat Tropical to Subtropical Zones, to 1,700m in Colombia. Light, semi-open forests, edges and second growth in humid or wet areas.

Voice Song of *iungens* a series of repeated, sweet musical phrases, *cheéaweet, cheyoo* or *cheeareet chweyoo*, sometimes suggesting a *Turdus* (Ridgely & Gwynne). Song of *maximus* recalls several *Turdus* thrushes, typically a rather soft *cheete-lewert, weete-wert, sweetle-e-er, e-te-were* etc. (Hilty). Song of *maximus* in Guyana variable and sweet, recalling Moriche Oriole and a peppershrike, e.g. *tih-teeoh-tiwee-tiwee* and *hee-seela-heesay-yoo* (Snyder 1966). In Suriname, a sweet warble, somewhat reminiscent of a European Robin *Erithacus rubecula* (H&M).

BLACK-WINGED SALTATOR

Saltator atripennis Pl. 285

Identification 20 cm. Adult olive-green above, blackish wings and tail with broad olive-green fringes to feathers, top and sides of head black, with broad white supercilium that curves behind ear-coverts, chin to flanks, thighs and vent white, undertail-coverts cinnamon-buffy. No overlap with Orinoco Saltator. Head pattern distinct.

Ssp. *S. a. atripennis* (NW Ec, W Co) pure white below, pale cinnamon-buffy undertail-coverts

S. a. caniceps (W Ec, Co) back more olive-green, grey nape less extensive; faint grey shading on sides and flanks, undertail-coverts slightly darker with pale fringes

Habits Sometimes alone, occasionally in noisy groups. Forages mid levels to canopy.
Status Uncommon to locally fairly common in Ecuador, fairly common in Colombia.
Habitat Tropical to Subtropical Zones, 200–1,700m, mostly at 500–1,500m, but 400–2,200m in Colombia, where usually above 800m. Dense forests and well-developed second growth in very humid or wet areas.
Voice Song, *twee twaa, toou, toweer, tweeeeear*, descending but enthusiastic. Calls vary in different areas, e.g. a loud *tsink*, a descending *cheeeer*, or a descending then rising *cheeeeeeer, tr-e-e-e-e* (H&B).
Note Differences in bill size used to define the 2 races unconvincing, as there is individual variation and much overlap. R&T suggested races invalid due to extent of variation.

GREYISH SALTATOR

Saltator coerulescens Pl. 285

Identification 20cm. Adult uniform dark grey above with short white supercilium, malar stripe black, chin and throat white; breast and sides grey, buffy on flanks and paler on belly, undertail-coverts buffy.

Ssp. *S. c. azarae* (E Ec, E Co) as described
S. c. brewsteri (NE Co, N Ve, Tr) warmer, more olivaceous-grey above, paler on breast, more uniform below, almost pastel cinnamon
S. c. olivascens (S Ve, Guianas) darkest race, colder grey above and darker breast
S. c. plumbeus (N coast of Co) paler, mouse grey above, paler below, and much more grayish; juvenile is much more heavily streaked

Habits Inconspicuous and forages alone or in pairs. Often seen in an open tree or on exposed branch. Draws attention by endlessly singing during breeding season; singing birds tend to stay in same spot without moving.
Status Fairly common to common in Ecuador, common in Colombia, Venezuela, Guyana, Suriname and French Guiana.
Habitat Tropical Zone, to 1,300m in Ecuador and Colombia, and 850m north of Orinoco in Venezuela but only 300m south of it. Dry scrub, open deciduous woodland, pastures, towns and gardens. Open, somewhat humid secondary forest. Borders of *várzea* forest and riparian habitats.
Voice Calls include a metallic *tchink!* in Ecuador and forced squeaky *tseet!* in Venezuela (R&G, Hilty). Song varies. In Ecuador, race *azarae* generally utters series of clear notes *chu-chu-chu-cheeú* (R&G), whilst those from Marañón drainage have more oriole-like song, often given at dawn, *tewe-chóo-weee-tcho-tchewée!* (P. Coopmans). In northern Colombia, *plumbeus* has a musical but broken *wheer, cheer, pe-chéer, po-chéer, whitwhit-sit-wheet*; also a greeting *d'wicker, d'wicker, d'wicker, d'weeter* (H&B), given by *azarae* as *wikewi-kewi-kewi-kewi-kewi-kewi* (R&G). In Falcón, Venezuela (*brewsteri*) sings *wee chopcheeEEeer* (middle note drops), but in western Apure (*olivascens*) a halting, jerky series of emphatic phrases, *yur-FEET!, yur SEAT! tduur*, or similar, with variations somewhat musical (Hilty). In Amazonas (race?), a sweet, slow, whistling *chúrk, churk-churk-churk chalk-weéeer* (H&B). In Guyana race *olivascens* has a scratchy phrase that affords it vernacular name of 'pitchoil', and sings *WHIT-tom-PIT-choil* or *WHITchitty-WHITchitty-WHIT-chitty*… (Snyder 1966).
Note Alternative English name, Southern Greyish Saltator (e.g. Hilty) not used by SACC.

ORINOCO SALTATOR

Saltator orenocensis Pl. 285

Identification 19cm. Adult grey above, black wings and tail with broad grey fringes to feathers, grey extends over top of head to culmen, white superciliary narrows on neck-sides, head- and neck-sides black, small white spot at base of lower mandible, chin and throat white, grading into rich cinnamon breast and sides to undertail-coverts. Eyes brown, heavy compressed bill black, legs and feet grey. Juvenile is generally smaller.

Ssp. *S. o. orenocensis* (CN & E Ve) white throat extends over breast to centre of belly, sides, flanks and thighs to undertail-coverts mid cinnamon.
S. o. rufescens (NE Co, NW Ve) as described

Habits Inconspicuous and quiet, forages alone, in pairs or small groups, from low levels to tops of small trees, usually in open. Quite territorial and responds well to playback.
Status Fairly common.
Habitat Tropical Zone, to 500–600m. From dry to fairly humid semi-open, gallery and deciduous forests, brush and open scrub with scattered trees.
Voice Song of *rufescens* in Colombia, repetitions of *cheert*, then a squeaky *pit-cher-each-er pitch-a pit-cher-each-er*... and more repetitions of *cheert* (H&B). In Falcón, Venezuela, *rufescens* has a loud exuberant song, heard mainly at dawn, often given by a pair in duet, a spirited, rollicking *chup'ep FEETSer'chup, chup'er FEETS er'chup*… (with *FEETS* note much higher pitched). Birds in western Apure sing different songs (Hilty). Tremendous variation in Venezuela, and species would make a perfect candidate for a study of dialects. Further notes on vocalisations come from D. Ascanio (pers. comm.). Remember that Orinocan Saltator occurs both in desert scrub (north-west Venezuela) and in gallery forest (elsewhere in Venezuela), and in most cases song is most probably a duet. Single birds singing are rarely reported. Three distinctive songs: first by birds in north-west Venezuela (desert scrub), whistles at intermediate frequency, *few-be! twiste-turetú* repeated more than 7 times; birds in low *llanos* have a slower and less musical, *pheé-few! pheé-few! pheé-feeu!*... repeated several times, with last phrase sometimes occurring first or in middle; and, finally, in Bolívar (south-east Venezuela) have a longer, fairly fast and cleaner voice, *fuew-beh-tuh! fuew-beh-tuh! fuew-beh-tuh!*... repeated insistently.

BLACK-COWLED SALTATOR

Saltator nigriceps Pl. 285

Identification 22cm. Adult rich grey above with white terminal band on tail, complete black hood, underparts paler grey with central belly and undertail-coverts cinnamon-buffy. Eyes brown, bill bright wax-red, legs and feet dark vinaceous.

Ssp. Monotypic (S Ec)

Habits Usually in pairs and can be noisy. Sometimes with mixed-species flocks. Generally discreet and tends to remain in cover.

Status Uncommon.

Habitat Tropical to Subtropical Zones, 1,000–2,000m. Humid montane forest, scrub, second growth.

Voice Song a simple, but ringing and explosive *kurt, sweee-it!* (R&G).

MASKED SALTATOR

Saltator cinctus Pl. 285

Identification 21.5cm. Adult grey above, wings and tail black with grey fringes to feathers, and white tip to graduated tail (from below large white spots obvious); head grey with full black mask that extends to breast and embraces white crescent on upper breast; centre of belly whitish, sides, flanks and thighs grey, undertail-coverts barred black and grey. Eyes pale orange to red, bill contrastingly black with variable amount of distal part lacquer red, legs and feet vinous. More red on bill of adult female and less on young birds. Slate-coloured Grosbeak is all dark below and white on throat is vertical, not lateral.

Ssp. Monotypic (E Ec)

Habits Wary, retiring and generally keeps to cover, and in a stand of dense *Chusquea* bamboo is very difficult to follow. Forages in pairs or small groups, but occasionally joins mixed-species flocks.

Status Near Threatened. Rare and local.

Habitat Subtropical to Temperate Zones, 2,000–2,700m. Undergrowth of humid montane forest, generally associated with *Chusquea* bamboo.

Voice Song a melodic *chu-chu-chu-chuwit* (P. Coopmans in R&G).

STREAKED SALTATOR

Saltator striatipectus Pl. 285

Identification 20cm. Adult olive-green above, head, rump and tail greyer, short white eyebrow and white eye-ring, white below, streaked olive on breast-sides and flanks; eyes dark brown, bill black with yellow tip, legs and feet grey. Juvenile more yellowish-olive above, flushed yellow below, streaked and faintly washed olive on breast and sides, pale olive thighs.

Ssp. *S. s. flavidicollis* (W Ec, SW Co) olive above with long broad, white superciliary, lores to cheeks and ear-coverts greyish-olive, including malar region, uniform yellowish below with virtually no streaking, flushed slightly yellow, bill tip yellow; juvenile has variable amount of streaking below

S. s. perstriatus (NE Co, N Ve, Tr) whitish supraloral spot reaches top of eye in very short eyebrow, whitish eye-ring, black malar streak, most adults have tinge of yellow on breast but a few (older birds?) are more contrastingly marked and lack all trace of yellow; bill all black; juvenile has small yellow supraloral spot and yellow eye-ring; bill black above, yellow below with black tip

S. s. peruvianus (extreme S Ec: Marañón drainage) more olive above and more streaked below than *striatipectus*, reduced eyebrow and mostly black bill

S. s. striatipectus (W Co) as described, olive malar streak

Habits Conspicuous, in pairs or small groups, foraging at all levels from fruiting trees to low garden shrubs.

Status Locally common in Ecuador, common in Colombia and Venezuela.

Habitat Tropical to Subtropical Zones, to 2,500m in Ecuador, 2,700m in Colombia and 2,000m in Venezuela; everywhere, more likely to be found around 1500m and lower. Dry to arid scrub, clearings, pastures, gardens, scattered trees (increasing with deforestation).

Voice Song in Ecuador a loud and melodic, oft-repeated *tchew-tchew-tchew, tcheeér*. In Colombia, a lazy whistled *o-chúck, chukweéear* or repeated *chuck-wéear* with variations (H&B). In Venezuela similar, *chuck WEET chuck wEEr* (Hilty).

Note All four subspecies were formerly included within *S. albicollis*, and it is possible that further revision may be warranted (Seutin *et al.* 1993).

The 2 *Cyanocompsa* grosbeaks are residents; the males are deep rich blue and the females rich deep brown. They are generally found at lower levels of humid forests. The 2 *Passerina* species are boreal migrants that only reach our region as vagrants, the males in winter plumage, with their blues concealed by browns, and the females with buffy fringes. *Cyanocompsa* placed in genus *Passerina* by some authorities (e.g. H&M, SFP&M), but this treatment is not widely accepted. They are sister genera (Klicka *et al.* 2000).

BLUE-BLACK GROSBEAK

Cyanocompsa cyanoides Pl. 286

Identification 16cm. Adult male deep blue-black, slightly brighter blue on forehead and at base of bill; eyes dark brown, bill massive, black, culmen almost straight, legs and feet black. Female deep brown; bill black above, dark horn below. Juvenile like female but immature male is completely mottled black and brown. Male only separated with difficulty from slightly smaller Ultramarine Grosbeak. Bill of latter shorter, more conical with a curved culmen, and bright blue shoulder more noticeable. Comparing live birds in Venezuela, Restall found that the pale blue areas of the face differ (see illustration): see also comparative profile of the culmens.

Ssp. *C. c. cyanoides* (CW Ec, E Andes in N Co, NW Ve) as described

C. c. rothschildii (E Ec, E Co, NE & S Ve, Tr, Guianas) larger; female significantly darker and uniformly coloured

Habits Usually forages in pairs that keep to dark, dense and tangled undergrowth, and are not at all easy to see, although often utters loud song. Often occurs in areas near water. Seldom if ever seen in the open.

Status Uncommon to fairly common in Ecuador, fairly common in Colombia and Venezuela, widespread but not common in Guyana and appears fairly common in Suriname.

Habitat Tropical Zone, to 1,700m in Ecuador, to 1,400m in Colombia and Venezuela north of the Orinoco, but to 1,000m south of it. Undergrowth of humid forest, mature second growth.

Voice Calls include a sharp metallic *chink!* or *chink-chink!* (Hilty). Songs differ between races but comparative material not easy to find. Song generally described as having some slow, introductory notes, then a jumble of descending notes and fades away, loud, melodious, but short (R&G, Hilty, H&M). Birds of Northern Cordillera of Venezuela and in Andes have faster and shorter songs than those in Guianan region, and birds recorded in Beni sound similar to Guianan birds (D. Ascanio). From Anchicayá Valley in Colombia (*cyanoides*), *weep-e-aa pee-e-u wegeeahere-see* (H&B), and Guyana (*rothschildii*), a melancholy series of 8–11 syllables, falling by a half-tone after a short pause, then rising to original pitch, *did-day-day-day-did-dididid-dee* (Snyder 1966).

Note *Cyanocompsa* inexplicably placed in genus *Passerina* by some authorities (e.g. H&M, SFP&M), but this is not widely accepted.

Comparison between heads of two live males of Blue-black Grosbeak Cyanocompsa cyanoides rothschildii *(left) and Ultramarine Grosbeak* C. brissonii minor, *in Venezuela; note how pale blue on malar area reaches bill on Blue-black, but is separated from the bill by black on Ultramarine*

ULTRAMARINE GROSBEAK

Cyanocompsa brissonii Pl. 286

Identification 15cm. Adult male is deep blue-black with brighter blue on forehead (extending slightly as an eyebrow), malar area and shoulder of wing. Eyes brown, bill black, pale at base of mandible, legs and feet black. Female all brown, but distinctly paler below. Juvenile like female but immature male stays in 'harlequin' plumage for 6 months before wholly blue-black plumage is attained. Male separated only with difficulty from slightly larger Blue-black Grosbeak, but bill of latter is longer and due to straighter culmen appears more pointed; the pale blue shoulder is barely noticeable. Comparing live birds in Venezuela, Restall found that the pale blue areas of the face differ (see illustration): see also comparative profile of the culmens.

Ssp. *C. b. caucae* (W Co) decidedly purer blue, more ultramarine

C. b. minor (N Ve) blue has distinct purplish tone

Habits Usually in pairs, though male far more likely to be seen. Far less retiring than Blue-black Grosbeak, and may be seen flying over clearings and early successional growth, and perching in full view on tops of bushes.

Status Fairly common to locally common.

Habitat Tropical Zone, to 1,600m but more usually below 1,000m. Undergrowth and edges of semi-arid country, including scrub, second growth, agricultural areas and even in towns and overgrown land in cities.

Voice Call a sharp, metallic *pik!* Song a fast series of high-pitched warbles that rise and fall, *wee-se-weep wee-so-weeep wee see wee-so-weep* (Hilty).

BLUE GROSBEAK

Passerina caerulea Pl. 286

Identification 16cm. Adult male mostly rich warm blue with black wings and tail, rufous median wing-coverts and rufous tips to greater coverts (2 wingbars), rufous fringes to tertials, blue fringes to secondaries and whitish fringes to primaries, but almost all body-feathers have broad terminal fringe of rufous-brown or pale buffy that largely obscures blue, lending an oddly motley appearance to bird. Heavy bill is bicoloured, black above and silvery grey below, legs and feet dark grey. Female olive-brown above, dusky wings and tail, with tawny or buffy fringes to feathers; below, including head-sides, tawny, richer on chin and throat, washed olive on breast and sides, tending to buffy on belly. Twin wingbars separate it from any other blue grosbeak.

Ssp. *P. c. caerulea* (boreal migrant to E Ec, E Co)

Habits Often twitches tail sideways and fans it open momentarily. Favours dense growth, usually near the ground, but may be seen high on a prominent perch.

Status Boreal migrant to Central America, and rare vagrant to Colombia and Ecuador (October–March).

Habitat In Panama found in shrubby and scrubby areas with scattered bushes and trees.

Voice Call a very metallic, hard *tink!* or *chink!* (Sibley).

Note Formerly placed in genus *Guiraca*, but now generally subsumed within *Passerina*.

INDIGO BUNTING

Passerina cyanea Pl. 286

Identification 13.5cm. Adult male olive-brown above, pale buffy below with irregular cerulean-blue feathers on head, over much of wings, rump and short uppertail-coverts, and even more irregularly on breast. Eyes brown, neat bill is conical, black above and pale whitish-horn below, legs and feet grey. Female also olive above, finely streaked dusky, with some blue on wings, pale buffy below with olive wash on sides and flanks. Smaller than any of the blue grosbeaks and unlikely to be confused with either *Amaurospiza* blue seedeaters or Blue-black Grassquit.

Ssp. Monotypic (occasional boreal migrant to Co, W Ve, ABC, Tr)

Habits Quiet and inconspicuous, likely to be seen feeding on ground in grass or among weeds with other finches. Rarely sings in winter but presumably more likely to do so just before departing.

Status Boreal migrant to Central America and Caribbean, and a rare but almost certainly regular visitor to our region. Several sightings on north coast unconfirmed, and apparently often mistaken for a grassquit (Voous).

Habitat Tropical Zone. Second growth and edges of light woodland, shrubby and scrubby areas with scattered bushes and trees, parks and gardens.

Voice Call a dry, sharp *spik!* Flight-call a relatively long, shrill buzz (Sibley). Song a high sharp warbling of paired phrases, somewhat musical and metallic, *ti ti, whee whee, zerre zerre* (Sibley). Call an emphatic *twit* (Raffaele *et al.* 1998).

PARULIDAE – New World Warblers

New World warblers are small, slender-billed birds, generally colourful and predominantly yellow. In resident species, females and immatures are usually like males, but North American migrants are usually duller and much alike. Migrant males acquire a winter plumage similar to that of females, and identification can be problematic. Warblers generally feed on invertebrates and may be quite specialised in this respect. *Myioborus*, *Basileuterus* and other residents build cup nests below bushes, close to or on the ground. The breeding season commences with the onset of rains. Very few juvenile plumages have been described (most illustrated here) because when fledglings leave nest they have usually already begun moulting into basic plumage, starting with small patches of yellow on the breast and belly. Fledglings are very difficult to see, for they tend to skulk under cover and their fluffy, dusty juvenile plumage is moulted within weeks. Northern migrants that winter in northern South America generally pass through a number of plumage phases, some subtle, but others quite distinct. Yearlings have normally begun to acquire first-winter plumage by the time they commence their migration to the Neotropics. Almost all respond well to pishing, squeaking and playback.

In addition to all guides and regular literature for region used throughout this book, we also referred to Curson, Quinn & Beadle (1994, hereafter CQB), Dunn & Garrett (1997, hereafter DG) and Sibley (2000).

Boreal migrants – With few exceptions all warblers on the first 5 plates are boreal migrants. Males in breeding plumages are wonderfully distinctive and easily identified but seldom occur here. In winter plumage, like females and juveniles, they can be difficult to separate, and as they moult while on the winter grounds, there are endless variations of plumage. The species accounts rely more heavily than usual on reference to the plates for a better understanding of the plumages of these birds. Most favour forest understorey, second growth and edge habitats, including shade coffee plantations, and are frequently observed with mixed-species flocks.

BLUE-WINGED WARBLER

Vermivora pinus Pl. 287

Identification 11–12cm. Adult male has yellow crown, olive upperparts, grey tail, obvious black eyestripe, yellow underparts and white vent, and greyish-blue wings with 2 broad white wingbars. Female duller with duller eyestripe, narrower wingbars and yellow only on forehead (juvenile even duller). Hybrids may be confusing (see below). Female and juvenile Prothonotary, Wilson's and Yellow Warblers lack black eyestripe and white wingbars (and Wilson's and Yellow Warblers lack white in tail and vent).

Ssp. Monotypic (N Co, NW Ve, ABC)

Habits Frequently flicks tail when foraging, showing its white sides. Gleans invertebrates from trees and shrubs, mainly at mid levels. Tends to be territorial but often joins mixed-species flocks in winter quarters.

Status Winters in Central America, rare even in West Indies and Panama as far east as Chepo, eastern Panama province, in March (Ridgely & Gwynne). Vagrant to Santa Marta, north Colombia, in March, and near Turiamo, Aragua, northern Venezuela, in October.

Habitat Tropical to Lower Subtropical Zones, to 1,500m, in successional habitats in North and Central America, but may be seen anywhere on migration. More partial to second growth and open areas than Golden-winged.

Voice Calls include a sharp, dry *chik*, and *zzip*, *zzee* or *tzzii* in flight (CQB, DG), song a harsh, buzzy *beeee-BZZZZZ*, first part high and thin, second part low and rough, also an alternative, more complex song (Sibley).

Notes Formerly placed in genus *Dendroica*. Cline of hybrids between Blue-winged and Golden-winged Warblers, some of which were once thought to be species. Most notable types are illustrated, but there are several intermediates. 'Brewster's Warbler' was named *V. leucobronchialis*, and is commonest, dominant type; 'Lawrence's Warbler' *V. lawrencii*, is recessive and rare hybrid.

GOLDEN-WINGED WARBLER

Vermivora chrysoptera Pl. 287

Identification 11–12cm. Adult male has bold facial pattern, with yellow crown and black ear-coverts and throat interrupted by white lines above and below eye, rest of plumage grey except white vent and large yellow patch on wing-coverts. Female duller with greenish crown, and grey face and throat but retains yellow wing patch (juvenile like female), and overall pattern unmistakable. In both sexes, extensive white on tail is conspicuous as birds regularly fan tail.

Ssp. Monotypic (boreal migrant to N & W Co, NW & N Ve and occasionally to N Ec, T&T, ABC)

Habits Forages for invertebrates in trees and shrubs at all levels but often in canopy, usually higher than Blue-winged, solitary and territorial in winter quarters but joins mixed-species flocks.

Status Near Threatened. Winters slightly further south than Blue-winged Warbler, being fairly common in West Andes of Colombia (September–March), becoming rarer to east, and uncommon in north-west and northern Venezuela, even rarer to east. Rare in West Indies, and only 2 sight records from Trinidad (December–January) and one on Tobago (June). At least 3 sight records in north Ecuador (January–March). Declining in southern part of breeding range.

Habitat Tropical to Temperate Zones, at 500–2,000m but occasionally to 3,000m, in early successional habitats in North America, e.g. brushy meadows and fields, second-growth woodland, and winters in similar habitats in Central and South America, but also found at various heights of more mature forest, plantations, cloud forests and high-elevation dwarf woodland. May be seen anywhere on migration.

Voice Calls include a sharp, dry *chik*, and *zzip* in flight, song a very fine, high buzzy *zeee-zaa-zaa-zaa* or *bzee-bzz-bzz-bzz* with first note higher, and following notes varying at 1–4, but usually 3, also an alternative, more complex song (DG, Sibley).

Note See Blue-winged Warbler for comments on hybrids.

TENNESSEE WARBLER

Vermivora peregrina Pl. 287

Identification 11–12cm. Adult male olive above with distinctive grey head, white superciliary and dusky eyestripe, white below including vent, and dusky wings (with faint wingbar in fresh plumage). Female similar, but yellowish tinge on head and upper breast (juvenile even more greenish-yellow overall, including yellow-tinged vent). Several vireos may appear similar to male Tennessee Warbler but all lack thin bill, white vent and obvious contrast between grey head and bright olive back, and movements slower. Greenlets, female conebills and juvenile Yellow Warbler all lack white superciliary (greenlets only have eye-ring).

Ssp. Monotypic (boreal migrant to N Co, NW Ve and occasionally to N Ec, ABC and T&T, FG)

Habits Forages high in trees for invertebrates, but also at lower levels (typically lower in autumn than spring), usually solitary but often joining mixed-species flocks in winter when many flowers in bloom. May defend territory around small flowering tree, e.g. *Erythrina*, and face may be stained reddish-orange with pollen. Migrates in groups.

Status Winters in Central America and north-west South America where common in north Colombia (September–April), becoming rarer to south and east, still common in north-west Venezuela but uncommon in Coastal Cordillera of north Venezuela and on Bonaire (November–April), and very rare in north Ecuador (October–March). Two sight records for French Guiana.

Habitat Tropical to Temperate Zones, to 2,300m, occasionally 3,000m, but commonest in Upper Tropical to Lower Subtropical Zones, in open second-growth forest and edges, clearings, plantations and gardens. Moves widely in search of flowering trees, and may be seen anywhere on migration.

Voice Calls include a soft, sharp *tsit*, sharp, high, smacking *stik*, and slightly husky *tseet* or thin, clear *see* in flight. Sings on spring migration, a trill of sharp high chips, usually in 3 parts, each with different tempo and pitch, e.g. *tip- tip- tip- tip, teepit- teepit- teepit- teepit, ti- ti- ti- ti- ti- ti- ti* or *ticka-ticka-ticka-ticka-swit-swit-swit-sit-sit-sit-sit-sit-sit*, last part faster (CQB, DG, Sibley).

NORTHERN PARULA

Parula americana Pl. 287

Identification 10–12cm. Compact body with short tail. Adult male grey-blue above with olive mantle, distinctive broken white eye-ring, 2 broad white wingbars, yellow throat and upper breast, with red-and-black breast-band, and rest of underparts white. Bill black above, lower mandible yellow. Female slightly duller, with breast-band fainter (almost or completely absent in juveniles, which also have broken extended eye-ring, giving impression of 2 lines instead of 2 arcs). White in outer tail-feathers visible in flight. Tropical Parula lacks broken eye-ring and black in male's breast-band. Juvenile Magnolia Warbler has different body shape, more extensive yellow below and different tail pattern.

Ssp. Monotypic (boreal vagrant to northern South America)

Habits Tends to forage amongst outermost branches in mid to upper levels, lower in autumn. Usually forages alone in winter quarters, but may join mixed-species flocks occasionally.

Status Winters in northern Central America and Caribbean where common and widespread in August–May, but only vagrant further south, e.g., a few records from Panama (January, March), San Andrés I., Bonaire and Curaçao (October–March), 4 from Tobago and one on Trinidad (November–February), 2 from Los Roques, Venezuela (October), and one near Adícora, Paraguaná peninsula, Falcón, Venezuela (November).

Habitat Tropical to Lower Subtropical Zones, in semi-arid scrub and dry deciduous forests, but also evergreen forest, mangroves, plantations and gardens, on Bonaire and Curaçao mostly in shrubs around pools.

Voice A strong, clear *chip* or *tsip*, high, sweet, musical *chip*, and a frequently repeated, weak high descending *tsif* in flight; song a rather unmusical, rising buzz with sharp final note *zeeeeeeeeeee-tsup* or *zid-zid-zid-zeeeeee-tsup* with final note often missing (CQB, DG, Sibley).

Note According to DG, perhaps comprises 2 subspecies, *ludoviciana* (wintering in Central America) and *americana* (wintering in West Indies).

TROPICAL PARULA

Parula pitiayumi Pl. 287

Identification 10.2–11.4cm. Adult male like male Northern Parula, except lack of black in breast-band and white eye-ring (with impression of black mask) and broader yellow throat.

Female slightly duller, with almost no breast-band (wholly absent in juvenile). Some have very faint broken eye-ring, but not as expressive as Northern Parula. White in outer tail-feathers visible in flight. Juvenile Magnolia Warbler has different body shape, more extensive yellow below and different tail pattern.

Ssp. *P. p. alarum* (E Ec) slightly duller than *pacifica*, with medium-sized olive mantle
P. p. elegans (Co, Margarita I., N Ve, T&T) duller than *roraimae*, especially on throat and breast, with smaller mantle patch
P. p. nana (NW Co) like *elegans* but smallest, with noticeably smaller olive mantle patch
P. p. pacifica (SW Co, W Ec) brighter than *alarum*, brighter blue above, more orange on throat
P. p. roraimae (S Ve, Gu, W Su) like *pacifica* but very bright with relatively small olive mantle

Habits Forages alone, in pairs or small groups for invertebrates and fruits, mostly in subcanopy and canopy (but closer to ground in scrub), gleaning undersides of leaves, often amongst outer branches, and often joins mixed-species flocks.
Status Fairly common to common and widespread, including on Trinidad, but no recent records from Tobago, local in Guianas.
Habitat Tropical to Subtropical Zones, to 2,600m (once to 3,000m in Venezuela), but commonest in foothills, in deciduous and gallery woodlands, plantations, edges, clearings, second growth, *chaco* scrub, usually avoiding humid regions except in montane areas. Often found along streams in dry forest.
Voice Calls include some similar to those of Northern Parula, e.g. a thin slurred *chip* (DG) and *chit*, often in series (F&K). Song also like Northern Parula but slightly more insect-like, with final note more buzzy (Sibley), a series of high-pitched notes speeding into a buzzy trill, e.g. *tsip-tsip-tsip-tsip-tsip-tsrrrrrrrrrip* (R&T) or *tsuey-twuey-twuey-tu-tu-tu-ti-ti'ti'ti'ti'ti'zip* (Hilty). Sings even at midday (R&G).

YELLOW WARBLER

Dendroica petechia Pl. 288

This incredible complex species possesses at least 43 currently recognised subspecies, with almost certainly more on Venezuelan offshore islands awaiting description. It is usual to separate them into three groups (Browning 1994), which are sometimes considered separate species (e.g. R&G, Hilty). MtDNA evidence suggests that *aestiva* might be separable, but there is no DNA support for splitting all 3 (Klein & Brown 1994, DeBenedictis 1997), and AOU (1998) retains them as a single species. It is virtually impossible to separate three groups in the field satisfactorily. Note that even whilst the plate shows 26 distinct plumages there are further intermediates when birds are moulting, combined with individual variation. Only males can be identified with any certainty, and familiarity with songs is helpful.

Northern Yellow Warbler, ***aestiva* group** – male has yellow head (migrant from North America and northern Central America)

Identification 11.4–12.5cm. From other groups by larger bill and longer primaries. Adult male is bright yellow to yellowish-olive above and bright yellow below, except dusky wings and distinctive rufous streaks on breast, upper belly and flanks. Female always yellowish-olive above, lacks breast streaks and has white fringes to tertials. Juvenile much duller, either mostly grey or pale yellowish-brown with yellowish vent, pale fringes to tertials and pale yellow eye-ring and lores (making dark eye very prominent, as in adult). First-year female Hooded Warbler has larger eyes, pale white (not yellow) in outer tail and dark lores, Tennessee Warbler always has superciliary, and Prothonotary Warbler has contrasting grey-blue wings, whilst female and juvenile conebills lack yellow undertail and prominent dark eye.

Ssp. *D. p. aestiva* (boreal migrant to Ec, Co, Ve) as described
D. p. amnicola (boreal migrant to Ec, Co, Ve, FG) duller and slightly darker above than *aestiva*, with male having slightly narrower and darker breast streaks; female greyer above
D. p. morcomi (boreal migrant to Ec, Co, Ve, FG) similar to *amnicola*, but male has slightly broader and paler breast streaks
D. p. sonorana (boreal migrant to Ec, Co) significantly paler than other races
Unidentified subspecies (boreal migrant to ABC, T&T, Guianas) see above; in addition, *rubiginosa* is similar to *amnicola* but even duller, darker and greyer above and paler below, male's crown is concolorous with upperparts; *dugesi* is similar to *sonorana*, but has stronger breast streaks and faint pale orange wash on crown

Habits Forages at all heights for invertebrates and fruits, but usually low. Fairly solitary and territorial (may sing to establish territory and generally vocal), only occasionally joining mixed-species flocks. Responds well to pishing and playback.
Status Winters in Central and northern South America, where fairly common to common migrant (August–April), but scarce in Ecuador. Sight records (unidentified to subspecies): Aruba, Curaçao, Bonaire, Trinidad & Tobago, Guyana, Suriname and French Guiana (SFP&M).
Habitat Tropical to Temperate Zones, to 1,000m but sometimes 3,000m on migration, in semi-open, brushy habitats, often near water, e.g. riverine thickets, scrub bordering marshes, humid second growth, overgrown clearings and plantations, shrubbery, hedges, and gardens, but may be seen anywhere on migration.
Voice A weak *sit*, loud clear *chip*, and high clear trill *tzip* in flight. Song a series of sweet and high notes with sharp upslurs followed by sharp downslurs and an emphatic staccato warble, e.g. *sweet-sweet-sweet-ti-ti-ti-to-soo*, also an alternative, more complex song (F&K, CQB, DG, Sibley).

Golden Warbler, ***petechia* group** – male has chestnut crown (resident in West Indies and N coast of Venezuela)
Identification 11.4–13cm. Adult male differs from male Northern Yellow Warbler by well-defined chestnut crown and

darker olive upperparts. Female and juvenile very similar to respective plumages of Northern Yellow Warbler. Cf. female conebills which have dark orange irides, no yellow in tail, and less contrast between upper- and underparts.

Ssp. *D. p. aurifrons* (NE Ve) as described
D. p. cienagae (N & NW Ve) male differs by having rufous streaks on throat, breast and flanks
D. p. obscura (C offshore islands off Ve)
D. p. rufopileata (E offshore islands off Ve, ABC) similar to *petechia*, but males have slightly paler crown, and females have paler underparts
Unidentified subspecies (Colombia) – another 13 subspecies have been described but not identified in N. S. Am. besides the 4 mentioned above (CQB)

Habits Forages for invertebrates and fruits at all heights, fairly solitary and territorial. Responds well to pishing and playback.
Status Common and sedentary in mangrove (more common on offshore islands than mainland where only locally common). Sight records of unidentified subspecies from Colombia (SFP&M).
Habitat Lower Tropical Zone, to 100m, almost exclusively in mangroves and nearby bushes and shrubs.
Voice A loud *chip* and *tsip* when foraging, slightly stronger and drier than Northern Yellow Warbler (CQB). Song like Northern Yellow Warbler, but shorter and more melodic, typically with a few bright notes, then 2 emphatic notes, e.g. *e'sa-e'sa-swEEa-swEEa* (Hilty).

Mangrove Warbler, *erithachorides* group – larger than *aestiva* group, shorter, more rounded wings, smaller bills and males have chestnut head (resident in coastal Central Am. and northern South America)
Identification 11.4–13cm. Adult male like Northern Yellow Warbler, but has chestnut head and throat. Juvenile distinguished from other groups by white belly. Female and juvenile similar to respective plumages of Northern Yellow and Golden Warblers, but usually much duller and greyer. Cf. female conebills which have dark orange irides, no yellow in tail, and less contrast between upper- and underparts.

Ssp. *D. p. chrysendeta* (NE Co, NW Ve) intermediate between *erithachorides* and *paraguanae* in pattern of underparts
D. p. erithachorides (Co) as described
D. p. jubaris (W Co) paler head, throat streaked with yellow, head-sides suffused with yellow giving a dark, capped appearance
D. p. paraguanae (NW Ve) male differs from *chrysendeta* in that only cap is solid rufous, head-sides mottled yellow and chestnut, and throat has chestnut streaks
D. p. peruviana (W Ec, SW Co) male differs in that only crown is chestnut

Habits Forages mainly for invertebrates, including amongst mangrove roots and on mud at low tide, apparently tolerating wintering Northern Yellow Warblers, but excluding Bicoloured Conebills. Responds well to pishing and playback.
Status Locally common and sedentary in mangrove.
Habitat Lower Tropical Zone, to 100m, almost exclusively in mangroves, especially Red Mangrove *Rhizophora mangle*.
Voice A loud constantly uttered *chip*, slightly stronger than Northern Yellow Warbler; song similar to latter, but more monotonous and less musical, emphasising higher pitched terminal note, lively and fast, typically a short series of *swee* notes followed by a warble or fast *chip* (CQB, R&G).

CHESTNUT-SIDED WARBLER
Dendroica pensylvanica Pl. 289

Identification 12–13cm. Adult breeding male has unmistakable combination of yellow crown, black eyestripe and moustachial enclosing white cheeks, and white underparts with chestnut sides. Adult non-breeding male has narrow white eye-ring, 2 yellowish-white wingbars on black wings, olive upperparts, grey face and whitish underparts, thus somewhat recalls adult non-breeding Bay-breasted Warbler, which has buffy-tinged underparts, faint dark eyestripe and buffy superciliary, and lacks narrow eye-ring. Adult breeding female like male, with more smudgy face and less chestnut on sides (in non-breeding plumage, almost or wholly absent). First-winter female like non-breeding male, but has grey not chestnut sides, thus an essentially olive-grey-white bird with yellowish white wingbars and white eye-ring (again, Bay-breasted has different underparts and face). Drab first-year Yellow Warbler lacks eye-ring and wingbars.

Ssp. Monotypic (boreal migrant to Ec, Co, Ve, Tr, ABC)

Habits Forages with tail cocked and wings drooped. Frequently flicks tail, showing flash of white. Looks for invertebrates, fruits and seeds at various heights, but usually low. Solitary and territorial, but often joins mixed-species flocks.
Status Winters in southern Central America and is rare straggler to northern South America. Rare from north-west Ecuador to north-west Venezuela with a handful of records in each country. Steady decline of breeding population probably due to maturation of secondary forests in North America.
Habitat Tropical to Upper Subtropical Zones, to 1,300m in moist submontane forests, but mostly in dry deciduous to humid forests, edges and second growth, clearings, brushy thickets, plantations, parks and gardens below 1,000m in Venezuela, but anywhere on migration.
Voice A husky, possibly slurred or flat *tchip*, and rough *breet* or *zeet* in flight (CQB, DG, Hilty).

MAGNOLIA WARBLER
Dendroica magnolia Pl. 289

Identification 12–13cm. Adult characterised by grey-and-black upperparts with yellow rump and some white around eyes, yellow underparts with heavy black streaks on breast and flanks, and black tail with white subterminal band. Blackburnian Warbler lacks yellow rump and has more prominent supercilium tinged yellow-orange (not white as in Magnolia). First-winter Prairie Warbler has different face, rump and tail patterns, and narrow yellowish (not white) wingbars. First-year Canada Warbler lacks yellow rump and white in wings and tail. Frequently spreads tail showing white patches (Prairie Warblers frequently wag or bob their tails).

Ssp. Monotypic (boreal vagrant to N Co, N Ve, T&T)

Habits Solitary, but joins mixed feeding flocks. Usually at lower levels but will venture to canopy.

Status Winters in Central America with a few records from northern Colombia and north Venezuela, and several sight records from Trinidad & Tobago.

Habitat Tropical to Lower Subtropical Zones, to 1,700m, but usually in lowlands, in forested and successional habitats, e.g. evergreen and deciduous forests and forest edge, clearings, second growth, semi-arid scrub, hedgerows, plantations, parks and gardens.

Voice A full, soft *tship*, a harsh, grating, vireo-like *tshekk*, nasal *nieff, schlep, tlep* or *tzek*, and a high buzzy *tzee* in flight, (CQB, DG).

CAPE MAY WARBLER

Dendroica tigrina Pl. 289

Identification 12–13cm. Adult male has distinctive head pattern, with black crown and eyestripe, chestnut ear-coverts and yellow supercilium and neck; also note yellow rump and white wing patch formed by greater coverts, underparts yellow becoming white on belly and vent, with heavy black streaks from throat to belly. Female similar but much duller, mostly grey above and yellowish-white below, but distinctive face pattern, greenish rump and streaked underparts characteristic. First-winter female even duller, with almost no yellow, but still retains overall pattern; look for pale grey neck, faint grey streaks on underparts and pale-tipped wing-coverts forming 2 faint whitish wingbars. Male Blackburnian Warbler lacks yellow rump and has different face pattern tinged yellow-orange (not yellow separated from chestnut as in Cape May). Female similar to especially Yellow-rumped, Pine and Palm Warblers, but separated by facial pattern, greenish rump and streaked underparts (also note yellow vent and constant tail-pumping in Palm, greener upper- and yellower underparts in Blackpoll, and greener upperparts and no streaking on underparts in Tennessee Warbler).

Ssp. Monotypic (boreal vagrant to N Co, N Ve, T&T, ABC)

Habits Feeds more on nectar and fruits than other warblers, and defends such resources, but also forages for invertebrates in canopy. Population apparently fluctuates with food availability, especially spruce budworms, which affect numbers reaching our region.

Status Winters in West Indies but only a rare visitor to northern South America with reports from northern Colombia to Tobago, where seen fairly frequently. Numbers appear to be increasing on Venezuelan coast (October–May).

Habitat Tropical to Lower Subtropical Zones, to 1,000m, mainly in open woodlands and second-growth forests, edges, clearings and mangroves, mostly near coast, but anywhere on migration. Attracted to flowering trees, especially *Erythrina*, but also to exotic trees in parks and gardens.

Voice A thin high-pitched *seet* or *tsip*, a soft buzzy *zeet* in flight, and very high, slightly descending *tsee-tsee*, usually in flight but occasionally when feeding (CQB, DG).

BLACK-THROATED BLUE WARBLER

Dendroica caerulescens Pl. 288

Identification 12–13cm. In most plumages, white wing patch at base of primaries (combined with lack of wingbars) is diagnostic. Adult male striking blue above and white below, with black face and flank stripes. Adult female much duller, brownish-olive above and pale greyish-yellow below, with pale yellowish supercilium, bluish tint on forehead, wings and tail, and wing patch is diagnostic (e.g. lacking in Tennessee Warbler, which is also greener and lacks dark ear-coverts of Black-throated Blue). First-year female has less or no bluish tint and sometimes lacks wing patch. Drab first-year Cerulean Warbler has diagnostic supercilium and wingbars.

Ssp. *D. c. caerulescens* (boreal vagrant to Ec, Co, Ve) as described

D. c. cairnsi (probably a vagrant to ABC, Tr, possibly To) noticeably darker above, much larger white wing patch

Habits Forages low for invertebrates, fruits, nectar and seeds, though males tend to forage higher than females, to the canopy, whilst females usually in dense understorey of second growth or scrub, often joining mixed-species flocks. Both defend territories. Frequently holds wings partially spread open.

Status Winters in Caribbean and West Indies, with a few records from northern South America and offshore islands (October–April, exceptionally to June in Ecuador).

Habitat Tropical to Lower Subtropical Zones, to 1,900m, in forested and successional habitats, e.g. primary and secondary, evergreen and deciduous forests and edges, scrub, mangroves, plantations and gardens, but anywhere on migration.

Voice A soft *tsip*, *thik*, *dit* or *twik*, and prolonged *tseet* in flight (CQB, DG).

YELLOW-RUMPED WARBLER

Dendroica coronata Pl. 288

Identification 13.5–14.5cm. Yellow patch on breast-sides and yellow rump distinctive in all plumages: adult male also has yellow crown, grey upperparts, large white wing patch, yellow throat, black breast-band, and rest of underparts white; female duller, with grey crown. First-year even duller and paler, with overall buffy to brownish-grey appearance, pale throat and greyish-black streaks on breast and upperparts. First-year Cape May Warbler more greenish, especially rump. First-year Palm Warbler has duller yellow rump, yellow vent and constantly pumps tail.

Ssp. *D. c. coronata* (boreal vagrant to N Co, Ve, ABC, To) white throat and pale superciliary

D. c. auduboni (boreal vagrant to Ve) pastel yellow throat, lacks eyebrow and is less streaked in all plumages

Habits Gregarious, in both single- and mixed-species flocks, at all levels seeking invertebrates and fruits, but often low and regularly on ground in fairly open areas, flying up to trees when disturbed.

Status Winters in North and Central America and the

Caribbean, rare in east Panama, with a few records from northern Colombia to Tobago (October–May).

Habitat Tropical to Temperate Zones, to 3,000m in Venezuela, in a wide variety of habitats, depending on food supply because of fondness for berries, and also flowers of *Agave braceara*, but anywhere on migration.

Voice A sharp *chek* that is quite distinctive and sure field mark. Very vocal, utters varied *chip, chup* or *chek* notes, often in series. Flight-call a high clear *see* (CQB, DG).

Note Races *auduboni* and *coronata* previously considered specifically as Myrtle and Audubon's Warbler, respectively.

TOWNSEND'S WARBLER

Dendroica townsendi Pl. 288

Identification 12–13cm. Adult male has distinctive yellow and black face pattern, olive upperparts, 2 white wingbars on grey wings, yellow breast, white belly and vent, and bold black streaks on flanks. Female duller, with white throat (first-year female has yellow throat) and black on head and flanks replaced by olive. Black-throated Green Warbler has paler, more yellowish-green crown, ear-coverts and upperparts, and yellow restricted to upper breast and narrow band on vent. First-winter Blackburnian has different back coloration and pattern, being more greyish-brown (less greenish than Townsend's) and more striped black and pale (latter missing in Townsend's).

Ssp. Monotypic (boreal vagrant to N Co)

Habits Forages at all levels for invertebrates (rarely seeds), joining mixed-species flocks. Males may defend territory.

Status Winters in North and Central America, rare even in west Panama, with a single vagrant record from Serranía. Macuira, Guajira peninsula, north Colombia, in January.

Habitat Tropical to Temperate Zones, to at least 2,000m, almost exclusively in montane pine–oak and cloud forests but has been found in, e.g. semi-deciduous or evergreen forests, especially on migration.

Voice A sharp *tip* or *tsik*, similar to Black-throated Green but slightly sharper and higher, though very difficult to separate. Flight-call a thin high *see*, lacking buzzy quality (DG).

BLACK-THROATED GREEN WARBLER

Dendroica virens Pl. 288

Identification 12–13cm. Rather like Townsend's Warbler in all plumages, but always has paler, more yellowish-green crown, ear-coverts and upperparts, and yellow restricted to upper breast and narrow band on vent. Immature and female Blackburnian Warblers have more greyish-brown (less greenish) and more striped-looking upperparts than Black-throated Green Warbler.

Ssp. Monotypic (boreal migrant to N Ec, N Co, N Ve, Tr, ABC)

Habits Usually forages lower than Townsend's Warbler for invertebrates and some fruits, solitary or in single- or mixed-species flocks.

Status Winters in Central America and Caribbean, but rare in eastern Panama and in northern South America only sporadic records from across north of region (October–May).

Habitat Tropical to Temperate Zones, to at least 3,400m, primarily in montane forest of all kinds, including cloud, pine–oak and coniferous, but also in, e.g. evergreen forests, and often in semi-open and edge habitats, e.g. clearings, parks and gardens, but anywhere on migration.

Voice A sharp *tip* or *tsip*, similar to Townsend's but slightly lower, and very difficult to separate. Flight-call a thin high *see*, lacking any buzzy quality (DG).

BLACKBURNIAN WARBLER

Dendroica fusca Pl. 287

Identification 12–13cm. Adult male unmistakable by bright orange and black face pattern (cf. Magnolia and Cape May Warblers). Adult female duller, but retains distinctive pattern and yellowish-orange head coloration. First-winter female may be confused with various warblers. Townsend's, Black-throated Green and Cerulean have more greenish upperparts (less greyish-brown than Blackburnian) without pale stripes (form 2 distinctive lines in all plumages of Blackburnian). First-winter female Cerulean also has paler, more yellowish-green ear-coverts and lemon wash on underparts. First-winter female Bay-breasted and Blackpoll Warblers frequently bob their tails and lack strong supercilium combined with dusky ear-coverts and pale back stripes of Blackburnian.

Ssp. Monotypic (boreal migrant throughout region)

Habits Forages at all levels but mostly in canopy, frequently cocking its tail and drooping its wings hunting for invertebrates and occasionally berries. Usually solitary, holding winter territory but joins single- and mixed-species flocks, in small flocks on migration.

Status Winters mostly in Andes (more common on eastern slopes), where fairly common to common, but could be found in any part of region between August and May.

Habitat Tropical to Temperate Zones, to 3,600m but usually at 1,000–2,500m. Montane evergreen forest and edge, mature second growth, clearings, plantations, gardens and dwarf forests, but anywhere on migration. Favours mature forests more than most warblers.

Voice A rich *chip* or *tsip* and buzzy *zzee* in flight (CQB, DG). No winter song recorded.

YELLOW-THROATED WARBLER

Dendroica dominica Pl. 288

Identification 12.5–14cm. Similar in all plumages. Adult male has striking yellow, white and black face pattern with distinctive white neck spot, yellow throat and upper breast, rest underparts white with greyish-black streaks on flanks, clean grey upperparts except white in tail and 2 wingbars. Female and first-year slightly duller with buffy tinge to flanks. First-year Blackburnian Warbler has different facial pattern with yellow (not white) supercilium and a greyish-brown pale-streaked (not uniform) back, lacking white neck spot.

Townsend's, Black-throated Green and Cerulean Warblers have yellow supercilium and greenish upperparts.

Ssp. *D. d. albilora* (boreal vagrant to N Co, T&T)

Habits Usually forages high for invertebrates, in canopy or subcanopy, with slow, rather deliberate movements, and often creeps along branches like Black-and-white Warbler and is rather attracted to epiphytes, joins mixed-species flocks.
Status Winters in North, Central America and Caribbean, with 3 sight records from northern Colombia.
Habitat Tropical Zone, to 1,350m, in wide variety of habitats but generally open areas with scattered trees, often in mangroves, plantations, gardens, farms, parks and orchards.
Voice A loud sharp high *chip* or *tsip* and clear high *see* in flight (CQB, DG).

PINE WARBLER

Dendroica pinus (not illustrated)

Identification 13-13.5cm. A fairly large and well-built bird with a rather heavy bill and a longish tail. The adult is unstreaked olive above, darker and rather brownish on the wings, with two large white wingbars, the edges of the greater-coverts and the remiges being similar olive to the back; the tail above is also darkish with olive edges to all rectrices; there is a yellowish loral line that joins a clear yellow eye-ring; throat to belly yellow, with an olive wash on the sides and flanks, belly and undertail-coverts are white, as is most of the undertail, being brownish at the very base of the rectrices. Females are slightly duller and paler below than males, and immatures browner still. Confusion species are Blackpoll and Bay-breasted Warblers, but Pine Warbler has tail extending significantly past the tip of the undertail-coverts; Blackpoll and Bay-breasted Warblers have their undertail-coverts reaching almost to the tip of the tail, while the tail of Pine Warbler extends well past the coverts. Also Blackpoll and Bay-breasted have only the distal half of the undertail white.

Ssp. *D. p. pinus* (boreal migrant to Co)

Pine Warbler shows a largely white undertail

Habits It seems to be rather sluggish in its foraging behaviour, creeping along branches and spending time probing into crevices and bunched leaves and litter, but also agile, when white undertail shows well. Feeds on fruits, seed and berries, as well as insects. Usually in groups or small flocks during winter, but stragglers this far away from base may well be singletons, and likely to be in mixed-species flocks.
Status Winters in southern North America, and rarely in Mexico; it is a very rare straggler to Central America, listed as hyypothetical for Panama by Ridgely & Gwynne; with a single record for northern South America, in N Colombia.
Habitat Wintering birds are not restricted to pines, and may occur in various forest and woodland, to fairly open areas on farms and plantations.
Voice Calls include a strong *tzip* (Raffaelle *et al.*), a loud smacking *tchip* (CQB), a high, flat *chip*, and a flight call a high, descending *seet* (Sibley) or a buzzy *zeet* (DG).

PRAIRIE WARBLER

Dendroica discolor Pl. 289

Identification 11.5–12cm. Similar to Northern Yellow Warbler, but adult male Prairie has distinctive face pattern including dark eyestripe, rufous streaks on mantle and black streaks on flanks, and frequently bobs and wags its tail. Adult female duller with rufous and black streaks fainter, yellow in face replaced by white. First-winter female even duller, with no rufous or black streaking and greyish head, but retains distinctive pattern of white face traversed by dark eyestripe and dark lower border to cheeks. First-winter Magnolia Warbler has white wingbars, different tail pattern and does not bob its tail.

Ssp. *D. d. discolor* (boreal migrant to West Indies, sometimes C America, rarely in N Co) brighter
D. d. paludicola (boreal migrant to West Indies, sometimes C America, rarely in Ar, Cu, Tr) duller, with less distinct streaking; above olive-grey, below paler yellow

Habits Forages at all levels for invertebrates and nectar (especially fond of flowering *Agave braceara*) and often joins mixed-species flocks.
Status Race *discolor* winters mostly in Caribbean, but also in Central America and race *paludicola* breeds in coastal mangroves of Florida, with records from Aruba (October–November) and single records from Córdoba, northern Colombia, in August 1977 (H&B), Curaçao, in April 1979 (Voous 1983) and Trinidad, in March 1978 (ffrench).
Habitat Tropical to Lower Subtropical Zones, to 2,000m, in variety of semi-open, scrubby and successional habitats, e.g. relatively open deciduous forest, edges and clearings, mangroves, scrub, plantations, overgrown fields, parks and gardens.
Voice A low sharp smacking *tchip* or *tuip* (similar to Palm Warbler), drier *chip* (similar to Canada Warbler), and high thin *seep* in flight. Departing birds start to sing, a distinctive, high-pitched series of thin buzzy notes that rise in pitch sharply (CQB, DG).

PALM WARBLER

Dendroica palmarum Pl. 291

Identification 12.5–14cm. Breeding adult (April–August) has rufous crown, olive rump, yellow throat and vent, whilst non-breeder is mostly dull grey-brown, with yellow vent, olive rump and a dark eyestripe bordering pale supercilium. Prairie Warbler (also pumps tail) has different facial pattern and lacks contrasting olive rump.

Ssp. *D. p. palmarum* (boreal vagrant to N Co, N Ve, Ar, Cu)

Habits Feeds mostly on open ground (often several close together) for invertebrates (but also takes fruits and seeds), and constantly pumps tail (more than any other warbler). Joins mixed-species flocks and defends *Agave braceara* plants against intruders.

Status Race *palmarum* winters in eastern North America and Caribbean, where common, but only a vagrant further south in Lesser Antilles, on Aruba and Curaçao (winter 1956–57), on I. Providencia and I. San Andrés, Colombia, with one record from continental South America at Laguna Mucubají, Mérida, western Venezuela.

Habitat Tropical to Temperate Zones, to 3,600m, but principally lowlands where prefers open habitats with short grass, e.g. pastures, fields, prairies, marshes, shrubby areas, dunes, beaches, pastures, parks and gardens. Often in towns and villages.

Voice A distinctive sharp, musical *tchik* or *tsup* (similar to Prairie Warbler), and high-pitched, slightly husky *tseet or tseet-tseet* in flight (CQB, DG).

Note Race *palmarum* is sometimes called Western Palm Warbler.

BAY-BREASTED WARBLER

Dendroica castanea Pl. 289

Identification 13–14cm. In winter essentially pale olive-green above with 2 white wingbars, and white patch on undersides of 2 outer tail-feathers, below buffy with some chestnut on flanks. Spring female has more extensive chestnut wash to throat, male develops black mask with chestnut crown and variable chestnut on throat, breast and flanks. Adult breeding male unmistakable, but non-breeding and first-winter plumages are like Blackpoll Warbler. Bay-breasted has buff unstreaked underparts (not yellowish and faintly streaked), often with some rufous on flanks, fainter eyestripe, and buffy or creamy (not pure white or pale lemon) vent. Overall tone of Bay-breasted is buffier and that of Blackpoll Warbler more olive, but despite these subtle differences, first-winters may be indistinguishable in field. Also, Bay-breasted Warbler winters mostly west of Andes whilst Blackpoll is mostly east of Andes (but both occur on both sides on migration). Female and first-winter Blackburnian and Cerulean Warblers have different face patterns with stronger supercilia. Cf. also Chestnut-sided Warbler.

Ssp. Monotypic (boreal migrant to N Ec, Co, N & W Ve, T&T, Cu, Bo)

Habits Moves fairly sluggishly and deliberately, even pumping its tail slowly and perch-gleans from upper surfaces of leaves. Usually forages solitary (but joins mixed-species flocks and forms flocks on migration) for invertebrates, fruits and nectar at all levels, but usually at middle to upper levels.

Status Winters in southern Central America and north-west South America. Common October–April, mostly west of Andes, in Colombia; fairly common on west slope of Andes in Venezuela but very small numbers east of Andes, with just a few records from northern Ecuador, Bonaire, Curaçao, Trinidad & Tobago.

Habitat Tropical Zone, usually to 1,500m but to 3,600m on migration. Evergreen, deciduous and cloud forests and edges, clearings and second growth, lighter open woodland with scrub, mangrove and riverine growth, but anywhere on migration.

Voice A loud, buzzy *sip*, see or *chip*, and sharp buzzy *seet* in flight or when feeding – indistinguishable from Blackpoll Warbler (CQB, DG).

BLACKPOLL WARBLER

Dendroica striata Pl. 289

Identification 13–14cm. In winter essentially greyish-olive above with 2 narrow white wingbars and white patch on undersides of 2 outer tail-feathers, pale yellowish below, with very little streaking on breast and belly but fairly heavy streaking on breast-sides and flanks. Adult breeding male unmistakable, but non-breeding and first-winter plumages rather like Bay-breasted Warbler though Blackpoll winters mostly east of Andes whilst Bay-breasted Warbler is mostly to west (both may occur either side on migration). Female and first-winter Blackburnian and Cerulean Warblers have different face patterns with stronger supercilia. Cf. Chestnut-sided Warbler.

Ssp. Monotypic (boreal migrant to E Ec, E Co, S Ve, Tr, ABC, Guianas)

Habits Moves fairly sluggishly and deliberately, even pumping its tail slowly. Usually forages solitarily (but joins mixed-species flocks and forms flocks on migration). Searches for invertebrates, fruits and seeds at all levels, but usually at middle to upper levels.

Status Winters in north-western South America and is fairly common in eastern Ecuador (October–April, few September–May) and eastern Colombia (September–April), but rare western Ecuador and western Colombia. Fairly common in Venezuela (August–May), in winter mostly south of Orinoco, common in Aruba, Bonaire and Curaçao (September–November, once in January, March–May), with a few records from Trinidad & Tobago (October–April), uncommon to rare in Guianas.

Habitat Tropical Zone, usually to 1,000m but sighted to 3,350m on migration. In forests and edges, clearings and second growth, also lighter open woodland with scrub, mangrove, gardens and riverine growth, but anywhere on migration.

Voice A loud, buzzy *sip, see* or *chip*, and sharp buzzy *seet* in flight or when feeding – indistinguishable from Bay-breasted Warbler (CQB, DG).

CERULEAN WARBLER

Dendroica cerulea Pl. 291

Identification 11–12cm. Male always blue-grey above, streaked black on back, 2 strong white wingbars and white patches on undersides of outer tail-feathers, white below with narrow black bar on breast, from which run rows of black streaks on sides and flanks. Spring plumage essentially as autumn but brighter and more contrasting. First-year and female pale bluish-grey or greyish-olive above, with 2 wingbars, pale yellow below with vestigial streaks on sides and flanks. Adult breeding male unmistakable, but non-breeding and first-winter plumages rather similar to several other warblers. Note short tail and short, heavy bill (cf. Blackburnian Warbler). First-year female has unstreaked bluish-green back (greyish-brown with pale stripes in Blackburnian), more lemon-coloured belly (more buffy-white in Blackburnian) with faint streaks, and different and fainter face pattern than Blackburnian. Yellow, Tennessee and Black-throated Blue Warblers lack bold supercilium and wingbars of Cerulean, and Bay-breasted and Blackpool Warblers have much fainter supercilia.

Ssp. Monotypic (boreal migrant to N Ec, Co, W & N Ve, Bo)

Habits Mainly midstorey to canopy, and easy to overlook as it gleans invertebrates from leaves, but comes lower at edges and on migration. Territorial, but sometimes joins mixed-species flocks, and forms pre-migratory flocks with Tennessee Warblers.

Status Vulnerable. Populations have declined precipitously in last few decades. Winters in southern Central America and north-west and central-west South America. Uncommon in northern Ecuador (October–April, once each August and September) and Colombia (October–March), uncommon to fairly common in west and north Venezuela (October–March), and a few autumn records from Bonaire and one from Tobago (November).

Habitat Upper Tropical to Lower Subtropical Zones, mainly 500–2,000m. Mostly in primary evergreen forest and edges in east Andean foothills, but sometimes in light woodland, second growth and plantations (including coffee), and occasionally in lowland evergreen forest east of Andes. May be seen anywhere on migration.

Voice An emphatic sharp (CQB), slurred DG), or hissing (F&K) *chip* or *tsip*, and loud buzzy *zzee* in flight (CQB, DG). Sometimes a short buzzy *zree-zree-zree-zree-zreeeeet* sung prior to spring migration (H&B).

BLACK-AND-WHITE WARBLER

Mniotilta varia Pl. 290

Identification 12–13cm. All plumages black above with white outer fringes to all feathers except remiges, creating bold streaking and 2 bold wingbars, fringes of tertials broadly edged white creating lateral line that joins larger wingbar to form distinctive T shape. Below variably streaked black and white, according to age, sex, and season, right to undertail-coverts. Unmistakable in all plumages, with black and white streaks all over and distinctively slightly curved bill.

Ssp. Monotypic (boreal migrant to Ec, Co, W & N Ve, T&T, ABC)

Habits Creeps rapidly up and down trunks and along and below branches in search of invertebrates at all levels (only other warbler with such nuthatch-like behaviour is Yellow-throated Warbler; unlike creepers, does not use tail as prop). Usually solitary, but joins mixed-species flocks, with some males singing and establishing territories.

Status Winters in North and Central America, the Caribbean and north-west South America. Rare to uncommon in Ecuador (September–April), uncommon to fairly common in Colombia (August–April), uncommon to fairly common in west and north Venezuela (September–April), fairly common in Trinidad (winter) and Tobago (January), and casual in Aruba, Bonaire and Curaçao (September–March, once in June).

Habitat Tropical to Subtropical Zones, usually at 400–2,200m and commonest at lower elevations, but migrants may occur to 3,000m, mostly in cloud, montane and submontane evergreen or deciduous forests, edges and second growth, but also in plantations, parks and gardens, and anywhere on migration.

Voice A sharp *tik* that may run into a chatter of alarm, soft sweet *tsip* or *tzeet* (sometimes doubled) when feeding and in flight (CQB, DG). Also, a rarely heard, weak *chip* (F&K). Song a chanting *see wee-see wee-see wee-see wee-see wee-see wee-see...* sometimes ending in a warble, may be given on arrival in wintering grounds, in flight and when defending territory (DG).

AMERICAN REDSTART

Setophaga ruticilla Pl. 290

Identification 12.5–13cm. Adult male black above to breast, with basal half of all but central tail-feathers orange, an orange patch on body-sides appears to join broad swath of orange across wing, with belly and undertail-coverts white. Female has dark brown instead of black, and yellow instead of orange. Juvenile uniform soft greenish-olive above, save basal half of tail-feathers (except central pair) yellow, underparts pale yellow. Virtually unmistakable due to distinctive tail pattern and constant wing- and tail-fanning (cf. *Myioborus* redstarts which have white in tail).

Ssp. Monotypic (boreal migrant to Ec, Co, Ve, T&T, ABC, Guianas)

Habits Solitary and often territorial, tame and easily seen at all levels, foraging mostly for invertebrates but also fruits and seeds. Adult males tend to establish territories in optimum forest habitat, excluding non-territorial females and immatures, which are thus more likely to occur in mangroves and second growth, and to join mixed-species flocks.

Status Winters in southern Central America, the Caribbean and north-west South America. Uncommon in western Ecuador and rare in east (October–March, once each August and April), fairly common in Colombia (August–May) and Venezuela (August–May), common in Trinidad & Tobago (September–April, once in August), uncommon to fairly common in Aruba, Bonaire and Curaçao (August–May), but rare in Suriname.

Habitat Tropical to Lower Subtropical Zones, usually below 1,500m but migrants to 3,600m. In wide variety of forest, woodland and scrub, edges, gaps, second growth and clearings, but also mangroves, thickets, plantations, parks and gardens, and anywhere on migration.

Voice A thin, sibilant but clear *tsip* or *chip*, and rising *tsweet* in flight (DG, Sibley).

Note Race *tricolor* described, from north-west of breeding range, as smaller with a longer tail, but now generally accepted as being within range of individual variation and species therefore considered monotypic.

PROTHONOTARY WARBLER

Protonotaria citrea Pl. 289

Identification 13–14cm. Adult always has largely or all-yellow head, greenish-olive above with unmarked bluish-grey wings, yellow below with white undertail-coverts and long white patches from base over two-thirds length of tail. Juvenile has top of head as back, but is almost as distinctive. Combination of yellow head, blue-grey wings and white vent diagnostic. Yellow Warbler and female Hooded and Wilson's Warblers lack blue-grey wings and solid spike-like bill, Yellow Warbler has yellow (not white) in tail and usually some faint breast streaks, and first-winter female Blue-winged has dark eyestripe and white wingbars.

Ssp. Monotypic (boreal migrant to N Ec, Co, N Ve, T&T, ABC, Gu, Su, FG)

Habits Solitary or in pairs, foraging deliberately around fallen wood, rotten trunks, pool edges, etc. for invertebrates, fruits, seeds and nectar, on or near ground to mid levels. Occasionally with mixed-species flocks.

Status Winters in southern Central America, the Caribbean and northern South America. Commonest near coast, casual in northern Ecuador (October–March), common in Colombia (August–April), fairly common to common in northern Venezuela (September–March), uncommon in Trinidad & Tobago (October–March), casual in Aruba, Bonaire and Curaçao (August–December, February–May), and rare in Suriname and French Guiana.

Habitat Lower Tropical Zone, usually below 1,000m, commonest below 500m but migrants to 3,300m. Common in wet, shady areas: mangroves, lowland swamps, riparian and wet woodlands, second growth, adjacent clearings and plantations, usually near water, occasionally in semi-open cattle country with patchy trees, drier woodland and even arid scrub (usually only during wet season), but anywhere on migration.

Voice A loud ringing *tsip* or *chink*, and softer, sibilant *psit* (CQB). Flight-call a loud *seeep* without any buzzy tones, also given when perched (DG).

WORM-EATING WARBLER

Helmitheros vermivorum Pl. 290

Identification 13–14cm. Two morphs: 'normal' is bright olive above, pale buffy-yellow on face and pale buffy on breast, fading to white on undertail-coverts and undertail uniform greyish, the 'cinnamon' is slightly warmer above, distinctly creamier buff on face and orange-buffy on breast and belly, paler on undertail-coverts. Adults have 4 diagnostic black stripes on head. Juvenile has fainter head-stripes and cinnamon tips to tertials, median and greater coverts. Swainson's Warbler has longer bill, white underparts (with lemon wash in fresh plumage, but not buffy like Worm-eating), and different and fainter head pattern (but cf. juvenile Worm-eating). Three-striped Warbler has more olive upperparts, more yellowish underparts and dark ear-coverts (not just dark eyestripe).

Ssp. Monotypic (boreal vagrant to Ec, Co, N Ve)

Habits Solitary and territorial, but sometimes joins mixed-species flocks. Forages on ground amongst dead leaves and searches dead leaf clusters in lower to middle levels, occasionally creeps along trunks and branches like Black-and-white Warbler.

Status Winters in Central America and Caribbean, vagrant to northern Ecuador (K. A. Boyla *in litt.*) and recorded in Colombia (SFP&M), with 2 records in northern Venezuela (October, March).

Habitat Tropical to Lower Subtropical Zones, mainly below 1,500m but occasionally to 2,000m, in lowland evergreen and deciduous forests with well-developed understorey and plentiful hanging clusters of dead leaves, but may be seen anywhere on migration.

Voice Calls include a *chip* similar to Swainson's Warbler but softer. Also, a double-noted *zeep-zeep, zeet-zeet* or *zit-zit*, sometimes in series (CQB, DG).

SWAINSON'S WARBLER

Limnothlypis swainsonii Pl. 290

Identification 13–14cm. Two morphs: 'normal' is bright olive above and on face-sides, with white throat, yellowish-buffy breast and belly, washed olive on sides and flanks, white undertail-coverts, undertail uniform greyish, and 'grey', being slightly greyer above and on face-sides, with distinctly paler, greyish-buffy breast, sides and flanks, and white undertail-coverts. Both sexes have 4 diagnostic black head-stripes, but juvenile has fainter head-stripes and faint cinnamon tips to tertials, median and greater coverts. Cf. Worm-eating Warbler and juvenile waterthrushes which have at least some faint streaks on breast.

Ssp. Monotypic (boreal migrant to NW Ve)

Habits Solitary and territorial, secretive terrestrial foraging behaviour makes it difficult to observe in dense undergrowth, amongst fallen leaves searching for invertebrates, but reacts well to playback, though it rarely sings in response. In Cuba, regularly observed following Ovenbirds, examining leaves it has tossed aside.

Status Winters in Central America and Caribbean, with single sight record on Ana Maria Campos peninsula, east of Maracaibo, Zulia, north-west Venezuela, February 1994 (Hilty).

Habitat Lower Tropical Zone, usually below 1,000m, in dense lowland or montane evergreen and semi-deciduous forests with dense understorey and plenty of leaf-litter, locally in mangroves and wooded gardens.

Voice An emphatic *sship*, similar to Worm-eating Warbler but longer and more forceful (CQB). Distinctive *chip* louder and sweeter than Prothonotary Warbler, which often is in same habitat. Also *tshup*, suggestive of Kentucky Warbler or soft Northern Waterthrush. Flight-call a very high, thin, slightly buzzy *swees*, sometimes doubled (DG).

Waterthrushes are easy to separate from other warblers, but are not so easy to tell apart until learned. They are uniformly coloured above, without wingbars or tail markings and are essentially terrestrial. In winter they can be quite difficult, and on migration even different habitat preferences are lost. Ovenbird appears smaller with a prominent eye-ring; it cocks its tail and then slowly lowers it, the others have distinct supercilia and constantly bob their tails. All are brown above and streaked on breast and flanks.

OVENBIRD *Seiurus aurocapilla* Pl. 290

Identification 13–15cm. Olive above with prominent white eye-ring, orange coronal stripe, bordered darker olive, below, white with black streaks on mesial, breast and flanks. Whilst orange crown-stripe is not easily seen in field, pink legs and feet are noticeable.

Ssp. Monotypic (boreal migrant to Ec, N Co, NW Ve, T&T, ABC)

Habits Forages on forest floor, walking deliberately (similar-looking *Catharus* thrushes hop), constantly bobbing head and cocking tail, then slowly lowering it (waterthrushes bob tails), turning leaves and gleaning invertebrates in leaf-litter (other waterthrushes prefer aquatic habitats); sometimes takes fruits and seeds.

Status Winters mainly in Central America and Caribbean. Two records for Ecuador (November, March). Rare in Santa Marta, north Colombia (October, January–February), in north-west Venezuela (September–November, February, April), on Trinidad & Tobago (November, January, March) and on Aruba, Bonaire and Curaçao (September–May).

Habitat Tropical to Lower Subtropical Zones, mostly below 1,500m, usually in extensive primary or well-developed secondary forest, with shady, dense undergrowth and plenty of leaf-litter, also locally in shrubby thickets, mangroves and shade coffee plantations, but anywhere on migration.

Voice A variety of sharp *chip*, *tsick*, *tsuck* notes and a high-pitched *seee* or *seek* in flight. May sing prior to spring migration, *TEE-cher TEE-cher TEE-cher*... and *cher-TEE cher-TEE cher-TEE*...or simply *teach-teach-*... (DG). Alternate transliterations *CHERTEE*... and *CHREET*... (Sibley).

NORTHERN WATERTHRUSH *Seiurus noveboracensis* Pl. 290

Identification 13–15cm. Two plumage types: 'yellow type' which to greater or lesser extent has yellow on superciliary and underparts, and 'white type' which have whitish supercilium and underparts. All are olive-brown above, with dusky streaks on upper breast, sides and flanks, and supercilia narrow and tapering; dull to dusky pink legs and feet. Northern and much scarcer Louisiana Waterthrush are very similar, but distinguished by morphology. Northern is slimmer, with shorter and smaller bill, spotted (not white) central throat, narrower supercilium tapering at rear, dusky pink (not bright pink) legs and heavier streaks below (but lacks buffy rear flanks of Louisiana). In behaviour, Louisiana bobs tail more slowly and exaggeratedly and in a semicircular fashion, involving more body motion; calls also differ. For habitat differences, see below. Birds with yellowish eyebrow and underparts are Northern Waterthrush, but those with white eyebrow and underparts can be either. Differences often slight, may overlap and should be combined for identification.

Ssp. Monotypic (boreal migrant to Ec, Co, Ve, T&T, ABC, Guianas)

Habits Territorial and usually singly, but territory small so several may be encountered in fairly small area, foraging on ground at edge of water or damp places, walking sedately with constant slow tail-bobbing and tossing leaves in search of invertebrates, e.g. water snails, worms and crustaceans.

Status Winters in Central America, Caribbean and northern South America. Rare in Ecuador (October–April), common in Colombia (September–April), Venezuela (September–May, rarely June), Trinidad & Tobago (September–May) and in Aruba, Bonaire and Curaçao (August–May). Uncommon in Suriname and French Guiana.

Habitat Tropical to Subtropical Zones, commonest below 1,500m but to 3,000m on migration, generally preferring wooded slow-moving streams, small springs and irrigation channels, still waters (permanent and temporary lakes, pools and puddles) and damp areas (unlike Louisiana Waterthrush), especially in mangroves, but also in wet thickets, swampy woodland and plantations, bogs, marshlands, and even wooded urban areas, but may be found well away from water on migration.

Voice A very loud sharp, metallic *chink* that may be given in series when excited, and in flight, as well as a high buzzy slightly rising *zeet* or *zzip* in flight (CQB, DG, Sibley). Occasionally sings weakly prior to migration (Hilty).

Note Irregular cline across breeding range of species, with birds in north-east and far north-west having yellowish or white superciliary and underparts, respectively. Within this cline, 3–4 subspecies sometimes recognised, but there is such individual variation within any population that attempting to identify birds to subspecies out of their breeding range is impossible and undermines validity of described races.

LOUISIANA WATERTHRUSH *Seiurus motacilla* Pl. 290

Identification 13.5–15.5cm. Brown above with white superciliary that broadens and flares at end. Below, white, washed pinkish or buff and streaked dusky on breast and sides. Legs and feet bright pink, bill long and strong, and may appear slightly upturned due to straight culmen and gonydeal angle.

More common Northern Waterthrush is very similar, but may be distinguished by careful comparison (see that species).

Louisiana Waterthrush (left) has a longer and slightly heavier bill with a straighter culmen than Northern Waterthrush (right), but difficult to see in field

Ssp. Monotypic (boreal migrant to Co, Ve, Tr, ABC)

Habits Retiring and wary, flushes readily and flies good distance before settling again. Establishes territory usually along a stream and is vocal in its defence, usually foraging close to or even in water, probing crannies in streamside rocks and roots, with prey items including larger invertebrates and even small vertebrates.

Status Winters in Central America, Caribbean and north-west South America. Rare in Colombia (November–February), Venezuela (September–October, February), Aruba (October), Bonaire (October–December) and Curaçao (February).

Habitat Tropical to Subtropical Zones, usually below 2,000m but higher on migration, generally beside fast-flowing clear-water streams in montane woodland, locally along lowland streams, rarely or never beside still water or in mangroves, unlike Northern Waterthrush. However, this difference is not applicable during migration, when both may be found even far from water.

Voice A sharp, resonant *spich* or *chik* similar to, but even louder than, Northern Waterthrush, and slightly lower pitched, less metallic and hard, that may be extended as a chatter when excited (Sibley). Loud buzzy *zeet* in flight. Song loud and musical, 3–4 shrill descending notes followed by a warbling twitter (CQB).

KENTUCKY WARBLER

Oporornis formosus Pl. 291

Identification 13–13.5cm. Uniform olive-green above, bright yellow below, broad bright yellow supraloral runs over and around eye, curling back below eye but not joining (hook-shaped). Variable black on head, from virtually none in juvenile to over forehead and crown, lores, ear-coverts and onto sides of neck in spring male, depending on sex and season. Distinctive face pattern with bold yellow spectacles and all-yellow belly distinguish Kentucky Warbler in all plumages from all yellowthroats as well as female and juvenile Hooded, Canada and Mourning Warblers.

Ssp. Monotypic (boreal migrant to N Co, NW Ve, Ar, Bo)

Habits Tail usually cocked and often flicked. Solitary, territorial and rather reclusive (best located by call), but sometimes follows army ants. Forages low by gleaning undersides of leaves and is quite terrestrial, running or hopping, turning leaf-litter on ground, searching for invertebrates.

Status Winters mainly in Central America, with some reaching northern South America each year. Rare in northern Colombia (October–January), north-west Venezuela (October–March), Aruba and Bonaire (September–October).

Habitat Tropical Zone, usually below 1,200m but occasional to 1,850m, usually in dense undergrowth in lowland forest, but also in well-developed second growth and light woodland, occasionally deciduous scrub that is in leaf, but anywhere on migration.

Voice A low, hollow, sharp *chup, chuck, chok* or *tship*, sharper and continual when agitated CQB, DG). Flight-call a loud buzzy *zeep* (CQB) or *drrt* (Sibley).

Note Formerly placed in genus *Geothlypis*.

CONNECTICUT WARBLER

Oporornis agilis Pl. 290

Identification 14–15cm. Rather thrush-like in posture; olive above with distinct white or pale yellow eye-ring, greyish to greyish-brown head, pale throat, olivaceous breast, rest of underparts yellow. Male always greyer on face and breast than female. Complete broad white eye-ring in all plumages, which usually distinguishes chunkier short-tailed Connecticut Warbler from smaller and much commoner Mourning Warbler. Some adult male Mourning Warblers show traces of a complete, albeit narrow eye-ring; also has bright yellow (not pale or drab yellow) underparts, tail projects well beyond undertail-coverts (nearly reach tail tip in Connecticut Warbler) and different voice.

Ssp. Monotypic (boreal migrant to Ec, Co, Ve, ABC)

Habits Long-legged and long-toed and is only *Oporornis* that does not hop but walks on ground. Yellowthroats also only hop, but much smaller, slimmer and longer tailed, with different coloration below. Distinctive walking gait is coupled with slight tail-bobbing, head-bobbing, and peers sideways and upwards, searching for invertebrates on ground, but often on undersides of leaves, stretching or jumping up. Usually solitary and retiring.

Connecticut Warbler is the only member of its genus that walks as it forages on ground

Status Winters in North and Central America, with a few reaching northern South America. Vagrant to Ecuador (November), rare in Colombia (October, December–January, April), uncommon in Venezuela (September–October, April–May) and Aruba, Bonaire and Curaçao (September–November). Rare in French Guiana.

Habitat Lower Tropical Zone, mostly below 1,800m but may reach 4,200m on migration. Occurs in evergreen forests, shrubby woodland, edges, clearings, plantations, parks and gardens, almost any habitat with trees and shrubs, particularly fond of moist dense thickets and tall grass, but anywhere on migration.
Voice A distinctive sharp, metallic *plink*, also a buzzy *zee* in flight (CQB). A rarely heard call is loud nasal *chimp* or *poitch*, lacking raspy quality of Mourning Warbler (DG).
Note Formerly placed in genus *Geothlypis*.

MOURNING WARBLER
Oporornis philadelphia Pl. 290

Identification 13–14cm. Generally olive-green above, grey head with variable amounts of black on breast according to season. First-year male has just a necklace of scallops on breast, but older male in spring plumage has black lores and a solid black 'cushion' on breast. Female lacks any black but greyish on head, juvenile lacks even grey. Compared with less common Connecticut Warbler, any bird with black is clearly distinct, but female may be confused, and is separated by having much paler throat and breast.

Ssp. Monotypic (boreal migrant to N Ec, Co, NW Ve, Ar, Cu)

Habits Solitary, forages close to or on ground in dense undergrowth, skulks in and below shrubbery and thickets, for invertebrates (although sometimes feeds in *Cecropia* trees), most often near water. Sings during spring migration.
Status Winters in southern Central America and north-west South America. Rare in north-west Ecuador (November–March), uncommon in Colombia (October–April), locally fairly common in Venezuela (October–April), rare in Aruba (October–November) and Curaçao (November). Rare in French Guiana (February).
Habitat Tropical Zone, to 1,400m but to 3000m on migration. Forest edges, in grassy clearings and overgrown plantations, also on river islands and damp floodplain thickets dominated by *Gynerium* cane, but anywhere on migration.
Voice A distinctive rough, sharp *chip* or *chak* that may run into a loose series when agitated, also clear high *svit* in flight (Sibley). Song a rolling series that may begin with some single notes and end with a lower pitched, weaker warble, e.g. *churree-churree-churree-turi-turi* (Sibley).
Note Formerly placed in genus *Geothlypis*.

Yellowthroats are small warblers with olive upperparts and yellow underparts, males distinguished by black masks. Very similar Kentucky Warbler distinguished by unique spectacles. They are often found skulking in underbrush, tall grasses and damp weedy areas.

COMMON YELLOWTHROAT
Geothlypis trichas Pl. 291

Identification 11.5–13cm. Olive-green above, broad black frontal band runs back through eyes and over ear-coverts, ending in small patch on neck-sides; unlike other yellowthroats, adult male has distinctive pale grey edge above mask. Below, all yellow. Female and immature similar but buffy or creamy yellow below, and first-year male has vestigial black on lores and cheeks. Kentucky Warbler has different face pattern with bold yellow spectacles and all-yellow belly.

Ssp. *G. t. trichas* (boreal migrant to Co, Ve, Ar, Tr) as described
G. t. campicola (unconfirmed but possible boreal migrant) male has slightly whiter forecrown band, female a distinctly creamy belly

Habits Hard to see as it forages for invertebrates, rather wren-like in its demeanor, close to or on ground in dense vegetation, often near water. Occasionally climbs a vertical stem.
Status Winters in Central America and Caribbean, rare in Colombia (October, January, March–April, once June) and Venezuela (old specimen of uncertain date and locality), vagrant on Aruba (January), and 2 unconfirmed reports from Trinidad (March) and Tobago (undated).
Habitat Tropical to Temperate Zones, to 2,500m though normally in lowlands, in dense, damp to wet stands of reeds and rushes in swamps, in tall-grass and weedy fields, shrubby areas surrounding them and in second growth and forest edge, often near water. May be seen anywhere on migration.
Voice A variety of notes ranging from short and dry to longer, softer and descending, e.g. *pik*, *djip*, *tchek*, *tschep* or *jierrk*, also a short low buzzy *zeet* in flight (CQB, R&T, Sibley, DG).

Comparative drawing of heads of male yellowthroats, showing, left to right, Common, Olive-crowned, Masked and Black-lored Yellowthroats

OLIVE-CROWNED YELLOWTHROAT
Geothlypis semiflava Pl. 291

Identification 13.5cm. Adults essentially olive above, yellow below, with male having deep black mask extending to mid crown. No overlap with Masked Yellowthroat, but does so with Black-lored Yellowthroat in west Ecuador, though latter favours drier habitats; male Black-lored Yellowthroat has significantly smaller black mask bordered grey above, and female Black-lored Yellowthroat has greyish tone to crown and cheeks and yellow supraloral and eye-ring (which may be difficult to see in field). Similar and rare Common Yellowthroat male has upper part of mask bordered pale grey and white.

Ssp. *G. s. semiflava* (W Ec, W Co)

Habits Hard to see as it forages in dense cover, except when male sings from high perch or in display-flight.
Status Uncommon to fairly common in Ecuador, common but local in Colombia, benefiting from deforestation and probably more common than observations suggest.
Habitat Tropical to Subtropical Zones, to 2,300m but usually

below 1,500m, in dense, tall grasses, shrubbery, thickets and undergrowth in clearings and pastures, at forest edges and roadsides, and favours damp areas and vicinity of water.

Voice A coarse *chuk* and harsh nasal *chee-uw, cheh-chee-uw* or *chreeuw*. Song a *Sporophila*-like musical series starting with several 2-syllable phrases, developing into a sweet jumble, longer and more complex than Black-lored Yellowthroat (CQB, R&G, R&T).

MASKED YELLOWTHROAT

Geothlypis aequinoctialis Pl. 291

Identification 14cm. Olive-green above, broad black frontal band through eyes and over ear-coverts; adult male has pale grey tone above mask but nothing like whitish-grey fringe of Common Yellowthroat. Below, all yellow. Female lacks all black and is washed olive on flanks. Immature similar, but has buffy cheeks, sides and flanks, males usually show some black on lores and below eyes. Formerly considered conspecific with Black-lored Yellowthroat, thus differences between Olive-crowned and Black-lored Yellowthroats described above also relevant to Olive-crowned and Masked Yellowthroats, although they are not known to overlap in Colombia. Compare also rare migrant Common Yellowthroat.

Ssp. Monotypic (NE Co, Ve, Tr, Guianas)

Habits Often circles tail, even cocking it almost upright. Hard to see as it restlessly forages for invertebrates, alone or in pairs in dense cover. Occasionally climbs a vertical stem or sings from high exposed perch.

Status Locally common in Colombia, fairly common but local in Venezuela, uncommon in *llanos*, locally common in Trinidad and locally common along coastal Suriname and French Guiana.

Habitat Tropical to Subtropical Zones, mostly below 900m but sometimes to 1,500m, in tall grass, dense shrubs and thickets in damp to wet marshes, fields (even cane in Trinidad), pastures (sometimes savannas) and at woodland edges, favouring damp areas and vicinity of water (but generally less humid habitats than Olive-crowned).

Voice A descending, fast chatter, fine sharp *chip* and plaintive *chiew* (CQB). Song a sweet, musical warbled *tee-chee-chee teeche weet teecheweet* (P. Schwartz recording) or *tjip tjip tjip rreh dideledie diei* (F&K), sometimes pairs duet a harsh *treep reh tri rreh trrep tri*, last note given by female (F&K).

BLACK-LORED YELLOWTHROAT

Geothlypis auricularis Pl. 291

Identification 13–14cm. Olive-green above, broad black frontal band that runs back through eyes and over ear-coverts; below, all yellow. Female similar but lacks black and is washed olive on flanks. Immature similar, but has buffy cheeks, sides and flanks, male usually shows some black on lores and below eyes. Only overlaps with Olive-crowned Yellowthroat, but has significantly smaller black mask.

Ssp. *G. a. auricularis* (W Ec) as described
G. a. peruviana (SE Ec) larger, otherwise similar

Habits Usually in pairs foraging in dense shrubbery, emerging occasionally at woodland edges, but males much more visible in wet season when they perch in open spots to sing.

Status Uncommon to fairly common in Ecuador.

Habitat Tropical Zone, to 1,650m but mostly below 1,100m. Usually in clearings and along woodland edges in lowlands and foothills.

Voice Song of race *auricularis* is a short vigorous series of clear notes ending in a warble, *swee-swee-swee-swee-chuchuchcu* whilst *peruviana* has a pleasant warble becoming a faster descending series of shorter notes *weche-chewi-chewi-we-titititittititi* (P. Coopmans in R&G), suggesting that *peruviana* might be a separate species?

Note Formerly considered conspecific with Masked Yellowthroat (Escalante-Pliego 1991, CQB, R&G).

Wilsonia warblers comprise three North American species that winter in Central America and the Caribbean, reaching northern South America as stragglers and accidentals. They are generally birds of lower growth in woodlands.

HOODED WARBLER

Wilsonia citrina Pl. 291

Identification 13–14cm. Adult male olive above and yellow below, with obvious black eyes offset by yellow face framed by black hood, dark lores (may be hard to see) and white outer tail-feathers (constantly flashed, more than once per second) are also important characteristics. Adult female similar, but less black in head, whilst juvenile has no black, making it an essentially olive-yellow bird, thus black eye framed by dark lores and yellow face and white in tail become important. First-year Wilson's and Yellow Warblers have smaller eyes, no dark lores or white in tail, and Wilson's is smaller whilst Yellow Warbler has pale yellow fringes to flight-feathers. Prothonotary Warbler also has white in tail but separated by blue-grey wings and white vent. Flavescent and Kentucky Warblers have different face patterns and no white in tail.

Ssp. Monotypic (boreal migrant to N Co, N Ve, Tr, Ar, Bo)

Habits Forages for invertebrates close to or on ground in dense vegetation. Territorial, but joins mixed-species flocks.

Status Rare in Colombia (November, January–February), Venezuela (October–November, March), Trinidad (once December) and Aruba and Bonaire (November–April).

Habitat Tropical Zone. Usually in well-developed undergrowth in extensive evergreen forests, edges and second growth, but susceptible to forest fragmentation. Segregated by sex: males in taller, more humid forests, whilst females prefer drier, more open woodlands and even shrubby fields, but may be seen anywhere on migration.

Voice A loud, sharp metallic *chip* or *tchink*, more complex *chippety-chup* in aggressive encounters, and soft buzzy *zrrt* in flight. On migration occasionally sings, a short, loud series of rising notes, e.g. *wee-tee, wee-teeWEE-to-WEE* (CQB, DG).

CANADA WARBLER

Wilsonia canadensis Pl. 291

Identification 11.5–13.5cm. All plumages uniform grey above without any white in wings or tail, have spectacles consisting of yellow supraloral and complete white eye-ring, underparts bright yellow adorned with streaked necklace (black in adult male, grey in adult female and faint grey or sometimes absent in first-year female), white vent and undertail-coverts. Magnolia Warbler has yellow rump and white in wings and tail. First-year Wilson's has different face pattern, olive upperparts and yellow vent. Cf. female and juvenile Kentucky Warbler.

Ssp. Monotypic (boreal migrant to Ec, Co, Ve)

Habits Forages alone or in small flocks at all levels in dense undergrowth for invertebrates, often with mixed-species flocks. Frequently holds wings slightly drooped and tail slightly cocked (and often fanned).

Status Common in Colombia (September–May), fairly common on east slope in Ecuador, scarcer on west slope (October–April). Scarce in north-west Venezuela, rarer in easterly submontane regions (October–March, June).

Habitat Upper Tropical to Temperate Zones, usually at 500–2,600m, in lowlands principally on migration. Dense undergrowth of humid and semi-humid forests and second growth in submontane and montane regions, and dense shrubbery in clearings and at forest edges, but anywhere on migration.

Voice A faint *chip* (Hilty), sharp *tchup* or *chik*, soft lisping *tsip*, high-pitched *zeee* in flight (CQB) and sharp, pebbly *sprit* (F&K). Sings regularly on northbound passage, and may give a snatch of its jumbled warbled song at other times (R&G).

WILSON'S WARBLER

Wilsonia pusilla Pl. 291

Identification 12cm. Olive-green above with narrow but clean yellow eye-ring, yellow below. Adult male has neat black cap, yellow crown-sides and forehead, female less of a cap, usually just forecrown, and immature has little to none and much less yellow on head-sides. Female, especially first-year, difficult to separate from female Hooded Warbler, which is larger with larger eyes within different facial pattern, dark lores and white in tail (visible when fanned, Wilson's does not fan tail). Canada Warbler has different face pattern, grey upperparts and white vent. Yellow Warbler has pale yellow fringes to flight-feathers and yellow in tail. Prothonotary has blue-grey wings and white vent. Blue-winged has black eyestripe and white in wingbars, vent and tail.

Ssp. Three subspecies recognised; it is not known which have reached the region (NW Co)

W. p. chryseola (Pacific coast, British Columbia, Canada, to southern California, USA) bright yellow-green above and rich cadmium-yellow below, forehead always bright yellow, even in fall female and juvenile, female has more black in cap than other races

W. p. pileolata (Alaska to north-east California) much brighter yellow on forehead and underparts than *pusilla*, lores clear yellow

W. p. pusilla (central Canada to Newfoundland) face-sides have more olive-green wash and very narrow yellow eye-ring, with touch of green on lores, especially in female and juvenile, and female has less black on crown than other races

Habits Extremely active and noisy, with frequent hovering and sally-gleaning, much tail- and wing-flicking, chipping continually. Forages for invertebrates and sometimes fruits at all levels, but usually in dense undergrowth to mid levels. In small flocks on migration, solitary and territorial during winter, but joins mixed-species flocks.

Status Winters in Central America where common, becoming rare in central and eastern Panama. One seen close to Panama border, below ridge of Tacarcuna at 1,250m, in October.

Habitat Tropical Zone to Páramo, to 3,500m, regularly in stunted growth above treeline in páramos of Costa Rica, in forest canopy and edge, mangroves, treeline scrub, second growth, plantations, hedgerows, gardens, brushy fields and clearings. In Panama, not confirmed for lowlands, thus likely in Darién highlands if seen in Colombia.

Voice A highly distinctive, somewhat nasal *timp* or *chimp*, a loud, flat, fairly low-pitched *chet*, also a hard *flik* and sharper downslurred *chip* or *tsip* in flight (CQB, DG).

Redstarts are a quite homogeneous genus of very attractive birds that draw attention by their habit of constantly drooping their wings and fanning their tails, showing bold white patches in latter. They are sometimes given the rather more appropriate name whitestart (e.g. R&G, Hilty).

SLATE-THROATED REDSTART

Myioborus miniatus Pl. 292

Identification 12–14cm. Deep slate above including head and breast, with outer tail-feathers white and crown chestnut; lower breast, belly and flanks yellow, vent and undertail-coverts white. Juvenile dusky brown instead of slate, and completely lacks chestnut on crown, lower breast, belly and flanks dark olivaceous, vent and undertail-coverts yellow with darker centres to feathers, undertail-coverts grey (not white) and white on undertail restricted to long elliptical patches. Slate-coloured throat distinguishes it from all other adult redstarts, which have yellow throats.

Ssp. *M. m. ballux* (Ec, Andes in Co & N Co, Andes in Ve, NW Ve) broad orange wash on upper breast between black and warm yellow underparts

M. m. pallidiventris (Coastal Range in N Ve) bright acid lemon yellow below, some with vestigial band of orange between black and yellow

M. m. sanctaemartae (Santa Marta, Co) like *pallidiventris*, but white patches on tail-feathers much smaller

M. m. subsimilis (SW Ec) dull grey above, forehead and crown-sides less black on centres of feathers than in other races, thus more grey, but chin and throat more deep black and breast-sides deeper grey, and deeper lemon-yellow below

M. m. verticalis (SE Ec, S & SE Ve, W Gu) as *ballux* but orange restricted to upper breast, rich warm yellow below

Habits Forages actively, alone, in pairs or small loose flocks from mid to higher levels, constantly drooping wings and flashing tail, and pirouetting to flush and catch invertebrates. Often joins mixed-species flocks.

Status Fairly common to common in Ecuador, very common in Colombia, common in Venezuela.

Habitat Tropical to Temperate Zones, 500–3,000m but usually at 700–2500m, in submontane and montane humid and wet forests, edges, second growth and adjacent clearings, tolerating considerable habitat disturbance.

Voice A sharp *tic* (CQB). Song a short accelerating series of 5–6 (sometimes 10) weak *see* notes on same pitch or rising slightly, accelerating at end, e.g. *sit-see-see-see-seet* (CQB, R&G, Hilty).

TEPUI REDSTART

Myioborus castaneocapillus Pl. 292

Identification 13–13.5cm. Adult has yellow throat, white lores and broken eye-ring (faint spectacles). Juvenile dusky brown above, darkest on wings, palest on head, especially throat, dark upper breast grades into rufous lower breast and flanks, with grey belly, vent and undertail-coverts. Overlaps on lower slopes with Slate-throated, which has grey head including throat, with no white, and smaller chestnut crown patch.

Ssp. *M. c. castaneocapillus* (Gran Sabana, S Ve, W Gu) mid yellow below

M. c. duidae (Amazonas tepuis, S Ve) orange-yellow below

M. c. maguirei (Neblina, S Ve) pale yellow below

Habits Forages in pairs or small groups from low to mid levels, frequently cocking and fanning tail, less often drooping wings, often joins mixed-species flocks.

Status Common and widespread in Tepui region. Restricted-range species, but not threatened.

Habitat Subtropical Zone, usually at 1,200–2,200m, does occur lower but apparently with little altitudinal movement, in premontane and montane forests, second growth, edges and adjacent shrubby clearings.

Voice A sharp *tsip* (CQB). Song a long thin, high-pitched, slowly accelerating and rising (Hilty) or falling (CQB, R&T) trill, *tszzzzzzzzeeeeeeeee*, also an occasional slow warbling trill (CQB, Hilty). Aggressively responds to playback March–June (D. Ascanio, pers. comm.).

Notes Formerly considered races of Brown-capped Redstart *M. brunniceps* (R&T). Possibly conspecific with Saffron-breasted and White-faced Redstarts.

PARIA REDSTART

Myioborus pariae Pl. 292

Identification 12.7–13cm. Dusky slate above with extensive bright rufous crown. White lores join bold white eye-ring. Entire underparts yellow, washed dusky on breast-sides. Immature lacks eye-ring and is much paler below, almost pale grey rather than pale yellow. Only redstart with yellow spectacles in its range. Only other redstart on Paria peninsula is Slate-fronted Redstart, which has completely grey head and throat.

Ssp. Monotypic (NE Ve: Paria)

Habits Forages alone or in pairs from low to mid levels, occasionally higher, for invertebrates, occasionally joins mixed-species flocks, particularly with Bananaquits and greenlets.

Status Endangered. Endemic to and uncommon in Parque Nacional Península de Paria, in north-east Sucre, Venezuela, which only covers 37,500 ha and suffers increasing disturbance.

Habitat Upper Tropical Zone, mostly at 800–1,150m but sometimes to 400m. Usually in humid montane and cloud forests, but largely absent from forest interior and rather more often at edges and in second growth, gaps, clearings and coffee plantations.

Voice A soft, liquid *tship* (CQB). Song bright and lively, louder and rising at end, e.g. *wheetsa- wheetsa- wheetsa-wesee, tezsa-sweet-see-ZEE-ZEET*, often variable (Hilty).

Note Also called Yellow-faced Redstart.

WHITE-FACED REDSTART

Myioborus albifacies Pl. 292

Identification 13cm. Dusky above, outer tail-feathers white, black on head with pure white line from lores over and below eyes, joining white cheeks and ear-coverts. From chin to belly orange, with vent and undertail-coverts white. Juvenile dark brown above, buffy on chin and throat, and belly to undertail-coverts, breast, sides and flanks deep rusty-brown. Only redstart with white face and orange underparts. Only other redstart in range is Slate-fronted which has completely grey head and throat.

Ssp. Monotypic (S Ve: tepuis of northern Amazonas)

Habits Virtually unknown in life but presumed similar to congeners.

Status Endemic to Venezuela. Unknown but possibly fairly common. A restricted-range species, but not threatened.

Habitat Upper Tropical to Subtropical Zones, at 900–2,250m, in rain and cloud forests.

Voice Unknown.

Note Perhaps conspecific with Saffron-breasted and Tepui Redstarts.

SAFFRON-BREASTED REDSTART

Myioborus cardonai Pl. 292

Identification 13–13.5cm. Dusky above with white patches on outer 3 tail-feathers, and white supraloral line back over eyes but does not join white crescent below eyes. Chin and ear-coverts dusky like top of head, throat to belly orange, vent and undertail-coverts white. Juvenile dark brown above, also on entire head, breast, sides and flanks; rest of underparts pale orange, darkest on belly, lightest on undertail-coverts. Slate-fronted Redstart has completely grey head and throat and yellow underparts.

Ssp. Monotypic (SE Ve: Cerro Guaiquinima)

Habits Forages from lower to mid levels.

Status Near Threatened. Restricted-range species endemic to Venezuela, on middle and upper slopes of Cerro Guaiquinima, in northern Amazonas, where common and no current threats known.

Habitat Upper Tropical to Lower Subtropical Zones, at 700–1,700m but mostly at 1,200–1,600m, in montane humid, cloud and gallery forests, and dense scrub. Usually within forest, but also occurs at edges and in adjacent scrub.

Voice Unknown.

Notes Also called Guaiquinima Redstart. Perhaps conspecific with Tepui and White-faced Redstarts.

SPECTACLED REDSTART

Myioborus melanocephalus Pl. 292

Identification 13–14.5cm. Dark brown above with outer 3 tail-feathers all white, head black with chestnut crown, yellow eye-ring and lores, giving spectacled effect. Chin to flanks yellow, white from vent to undertail-coverts. Juvenile greyish-olive above, paler and slightly more greyish on chin to breast and body-sides, rest of underparts pale yellow, very pale on undertail-coverts. Only redstart with yellow spectacles in its range, where only other *Myioborus* is Slate-fronted Redstart which has all-grey head and throat.

Ssp. *M. m. ruficoronatus* (Ec, SW Co)

Habits Hyperactively forages in pairs or small flocks at all levels, but usually high, constantly drooping wings and fanning tail, catching invertebrates with sallies and perch-gleans, joins mixed-species flocks.

Status Common in Ecuador and fairly common in Colombia.

Habitat Upper Subtropical Zone to Páramo, at 2,000–4,000m (or treeline), in montane, elfin and cloud forests, edges, second growth and adjoining clearings and scrub.

Voice A constantly uttered, high-pitched *tsip* or *tsit*. Song of male is *vee vee vee vee te-ttttt-t-t-t* (or similar) for up to 20 s, answered by female *tk-tk-tk-tk* (F&K, CQB).

GOLDEN-FRONTED REDSTART

Myioborus ornatus Pl. 292

Identification 13–14cm. Dark brown above with outer 2 tail-feathers all white, rear crown and neck-sides black with vertical white line parallel to ear-coverts, front of head and underparts to flanks yellow, vent to undertail-coverts white. Juvenile greyish-olive above, slightly paler and more greyish chin to breast and body-sides, rest of underparts yellow, almost to undertail-coverts. Only redstart with yellow or white-and-yellow head in range, in which only other *Myioborus* is Slate-fronted Redstart which has all-grey head and throat. Juvenile like juvenile Spectacled except throat and breast more brownish-olive.

Ssp. *M. c. chrysops* (W & C Andes in C & S Co) face entirely yellow

M. c. ornatus (C Co, SW Táchira in SW Ve) top of head and underparts yellow, lores, broad line above and below eye, cheeks and ear-coverts pure white

Habits Forages actively, in pairs or small flocks at all levels, but usually high, constantly drooping wings and flicking tail, catching invertebrates with sallies and perch-gleans, joins mixed-species flocks.

Status Common, sometimes apparently the commonest species at high elevations.

Habitat Subtropical to Páramo Zones, at 1,800–3,400m, commonest 2,400m to near treeline. Found in mid- to high-altitude montane, cloud, elfin and dwarf forests and edges, stunted woodland near treeline and adjacent scrub.

Voice A soft *tssip*, repeated regularly, also given in flight (CQB, R&T). Song a series of jumbled *tsit* and *tswwet* notes with no pattern, lasting 10–15 s, e.g. *pit-it, t'chittswit, tsweet, pits whewsits sweet iit...* (F&K).

WHITE-FRONTED REDSTART

Myioborus albifrons Pl. 292

Identification 13-14cm. Dark brown above with outer tail-feathers white, front of head black, crown rich chestnut, nape and head-sides black, white lores run back above and below eyes (spectacles). Chin to flanks yellow, vent to undertail-coverts white. Juvenile dark grey above (no spectacles), with pale grey throat and breast, yellow belly and white vent. Only redstart with bold white spectacles. Only other redstart in range is Slate-fronted Redstart which has all-grey head and throat.

Ssp. Monotypic (Andes in Ve)

Habits Forages actively, in pairs or small flocks at all levels, but usually high, constantly drooping wings and flicking tail, catching invertebrates with sallies and perch-gleans, often joins mixed-species flocks. Male perches on high exposed branch to sing and display in defence of territory.

Status Near Threatened, restricted-range species endemic to Venezuela. Fairly common to common, but although some large forest tracts remain, habitat degradation continues due to logging, cattle ranching, agriculture, mining and road building.

Habitat Temperate Zone to Páramo, at 2,000–4,000m but usually 2,200–3,200m. Mostly in montane, cloud, dwarf and elfin forests, edges, clearings and second growth, with lots of mosses and epiphytes, but not above dwarf forest or páramo scrub.

Voice A constant high-pitched *tsip*. Song a prolonged rambling series of jumbled twitters and warbles lasting up to 30 s, more varied, musical and lively than most redstarts, e.g. *swit-swit-wesee-wasee-tsee-tsee-ree-ree-ree-sit-pee-pee-swit-swit-...*, and sometimes in duet with female uttering high *tzee* notes (CQB, Hilty). Does not appear to respond to playback (D. Ascanio, pers. comm.).

YELLOW-CROWNED REDSTART

Myioborus flavivertex Pl. 292

Identification 12.5–14cm. Only redstart with yellow and black head pattern in range. Only other *Myioborus* in range is Slate-fronted Redstart which has all-grey head and throat. Female American Redstart differs most noticeably by yellow in wing and lack of yellow on crown. Juvenile olive-brown above and yellowish-buffy below.

Ssp. Monotypic (Santa Marta, Co)

Habits Conspicuous as it constantly calls and wags its tail. Forages rather hyperactively in pairs or small flocks at all levels, but usually high, catching invertebrates with sallies and perch-gleans, often joins mixed-species flocks.
Status Endemic to Colombia. Common. A restricted-range species, but not threatened.
Habitat Subtropical to Temperate Zones, at 1,500–3,050m but usually above 2,000m, in montane and cloud forests, lighter woodland and edges.
Voice A constantly uttered sharp *chip*. Song a series of high, weak, sibilant *chwee* notes on even pitch (CQB).
Note Also called Santa Marta Redstart.

Basileuterus warblers are stripe-headed, olivaceous-backed, yellow-bellied birds of understorey. The lack of white in the tail distinguishes them from *Myioborus* redstarts. All have pale legs and feet, orange, pink or yellow. There is little difficulty in identifying them, if one takes care with plumage details and distribution. Ground-dwellers are more difficult because they are reclusive and not easy to see, making vocalisations important. Very responsive to pishing and playback.

GREY-AND-GOLD WARBLER

Basileuterus fraseri Pl. 294

Identification 14cm. Bluish-grey above with greenish-olive mantle, top of head blackish with distinct yellow stripe, clearly bordered black, on centre of crown, and large white supraloral spot; underparts yellow. Juvenile olive above and rather duller yellow below, tinged greyish-white. Only *Basileuterus* in much of its range, and white supraloral, blue-grey upperparts with olive mantle and yellow underparts distinguish it from congeners (similar Golden-crowned Warbler does not overlap). Cf. immature Canada Warbler.

Ssp. *B. f. fraseri* (CW & SW Ec) yellow central crown-stripe
B. f. ochraceicrista (W Ec: except El Oro and Loja) orange central crown-stripe and smaller supraloral spot

Habits Not wary, but usually stays well in cover. Forages in pairs or small flocks from ground to mid levels for invertebrates, sometimes joins mixed-species flocks.
Status Fairly common to locally common. May move locally in dry season. A restricted-range species, but not threatened.
Habitat Tropical Zone, to 2,100m but usually below 400m, in undergrowth and edges of deciduous and humid forests, woodland and second growth, also scrub, favours wet gulleys in drier areas.
Voice Call unknown. Song a short varied series of *c.*7 *tew* notes, rising and accelerating at end (CQB), e.g. *tee-tididideedeecheechee* or *titu-titu-tituyuteechee* (R&T, R&G).

TWO-BANDED WARBLER

Basileuterus bivittatus Pl. 293

Identification 13.5–14cm. Adult bright olive above with distinctive head pattern of reddish-orange central line on crown, bordered black; underparts yellow. Bill black above, brown below. Very similar Golden-bellied Warbler does not overlap. Golden-crowned Warbler much paler grey above with white superciliary (and usually at lower elevations where overlaps), and some races of Golden-crowned have white or near-white undertail-coverts.

Ssp. *B. b. roraimae* (SE Ve)

Habits Not wary, but usually stays well in cover. Forages for invertebrates, in pairs or small flocks from ground to mid levels, often joins mixed-species flocks. Often flicks tail down. Climbs vertical stems.
Status Locally fairly common.
Habitat Tropical to Lower Subtropical Zones, at 700–1,800m, in dense, undisturbed understorey and edges of humid submontane, montane and cloud forests, and bamboo thickets.
Voice Regularly repeated harsh, scolding *fit* (CQB). Song a series of bouncy *tic* notes accelerating and ending in smooth buzz *tis, tis-tis-tic'tic'tic't't't'z'zzzzzzzZZZZE*, and more stuttering, slightly rising and accelerating *tis, tis tis my wish-wish-to'go'wee'wee* (Hilty).
Notes Sometimes considered conspecific with Golden-bellied Warbler. Race *roraimae* recognised as separate species, Roraiman Warbler *B. roraimae*, by Hilty without explanation.

GOLDEN-BELLIED WARBLER

Basileuterus chrysogaster Pl. 293

Identification 13cm. Adult dark olive above with distinctive head pattern of reddish-orange central line on crown, bordered by black; below all yellow. Very similar Two-banded Warbler does not overlap. Golden-crowned Warbler much paler grey above with white superciliary.

Ssp. *B. c. chlorophrys* (NW Ec, SW Co)

Habits Forages for invertebrates, in pairs or small flocks from understorey to subcanopy (higher than most *Basileuterus*), often joins mixed-species flocks.
Status Fairly common to locally common in Ecuador, poorly known in Colombia.
Habitat Tropical Zone, at 300–1,200m, in dense, undisturbed understorey and shrubby edges of humid lowland, submontane and montane forests, and adjacent second growth.

Voice Calls unknown. Song an accelerating series of thin, buzzy notes *t-t-t-t-t-t-t-zzzzzzz* (CQB).
Notes Sometimes considered conspecific with Two-banded Warbler. Race *chlorophrys* separated as Chocó Warbler from nominate race of Peruvian Andes by R&G on basis of 'utterly different song'.

[PALE-LEGGED WARBLER
Basileuterus signatus] Pl. 294

Identification 13–14cm. Bright olive-green above with dark line from lores through eyes, yellow lines above and below eyes and yellow underparts. Juvenile dark brown except slightly paler, buffy belly. Very similar to race *luteoviridis* of Citrine Warbler, but superciliary does not extend much beyond eye, and crescent below eye clearer and brighter yellow. Citrine is also fuller bodied, bigger billed and longer legged with an olivaceous-green wash to belly, flanks and undertail-coverts. Flavescent Warbler is brighter and cleaner-cut in plumage, with different voice, behaviour and altitudinal range.

Ssp. Unidentified (C Co)

Habits Moves tail in circular motion as moves through dense undergrowth, and only sometimes seen at edges. Forages alone, in pairs or small flocks near ground (somewhat lower than Citrine Warbler). Often joins mixed-species flocks.
Status Known from single June specimen, collected at 3,400m on edge of Páramo de Guasca, north-east of Bogotá, in Cundinamarca (its normal range is Peru to Argentina). Identification in doubt as specimen resembles Citrine Warbler (F. G. Stiles in CQB).
Habitat In southern South America occurs from Subtropical to Temperate Zones, at 1,500–3,050m, in undisturbed understorey and shrubby edges of montane forests, especially in dense undergrowth along streams.
Voice Regularly repeated scolding *fit*, soft *tsit*, slightly snarling *chiff* and harsh *tscheck* alarm that may be extended as a chatter. Song a fast, long series of jumbled high notes, first rising then falling in pitch, and increasing in volume (similar to Citrine Warbler but slightly shorter, slower and less trilling, with individual notes clearer and more separated; CQB), e.g. 2–3 notes in varying order *tjidewitcheedewitchechiffewitcheedee…* (F&K).
Note Sometimes considered part of 'citrine' superspecies including Citrine and Black-crested Warblers.

CITRINE WARBLER
Basileuterus luteoviridis Pl. 293

Identification 14-14.5cm. Dark olive-green above with dark line from lores through eye and narrow superciliary, vestigial yellow crescent below eyes; underparts yellow, washed olivaceous-green on flanks, vent and undertail-coverts. Bill black. Juvenile brown-olive above, darkest on head, throat and breast, with yellowish supraloral and dull yellow rear underparts. Race *luteoviridis* very similar to Pale-legged Warbler. Flavescent Warbler brighter and cleaner-cut, with different voice, behaviour and altitudinal range. Race *luteoviridis* easily confused with yellow-browed Venezuelan race of Superciliaried Hemispingus (*chrysophrys*), but Citrine Warbler is slightly smaller and less contrastingly coloured, with broader but shorter supercilium contrasting less with olive forehead, yellowish-brown (not slate horn) legs, rounded (not square) tail, olive wash on flanks extending to undertail-coverts, and lacks small blackish patch at base of primaries of Superciliaried Hemispingus. Oleaginous Hemispingus much duller and more uniform olive, with little yellow below and almost no supercilium, and usually at lower elevations. Grey-capped Hemispingus is even duller, with no supercilium. Brighter Black-crested Warbler has black crown- and eye-stripes bordering longer supercilium.

Ssp. *B. l. luteoviridis* (E Ec, E Co, SW Ve) as described
B. l. quindianus (C Andes in Co) intermediate between others, generally duller than *luteoviridis*, with yellowish-white supercilium
B. l. richardsoni (W Andes in Co) brighter olive-green above with shorter white supercilia, white chin and throat, grading into yellow on breast

Habits Forages for invertebrates in pairs or small flocks, from low to mid levels. Often joins mixed-species flocks.
Status Uncommon to fairly common in Ecuador, common in Colombia, fairly common at higher elevations in Venezuela.
Habitat Temperate Zone to Páramo, at 1,700–3,400 m but mostly above 2,300 m, in dense undergrowth and edges of humid montane and dwarf forests, especially near treeline.
Voice A sharp high *tsit* or *tick-tick-tick*. Song a fast, undulating trill, often with a few clear notes at start or end, e.g. *ch'ch'chu'u'chu-cheeet*, *te'e'e'e'ee-te-teet* or *trit-trit-chet-chet-seewit-seewit-seewit-tri'i'i'e'e'E'E'e'e'e'u'u* (faster, longer and more trilling than Pale-legged Warbler). Pairs may duet, first bird chattering, other uttering high, thin or squeaky notes (CQB, Hilty).
Notes Sometimes considered part of 'citrine' superspecies including Pale-legged and Black-crested Warblers. Race *richardsoni* sometimes considered specifically (CQB).

BLACK-CRESTED WARBLER
Basileuterus nigrocristatus Pl. 294

Identification 12.5–14.5cm. Pale olive-green above with top of head black, yellow supercilia and large, vaguely yellowish crescent below eyes, underparts yellow, washed slightly greenish on sides and flanks. Bill black. Immature duller (more greyish on head and mantle) with narrow and short yellow supercilium. Juvenile mid brown above with 2 dull wingbars, paler brown below. Bill black above, yellow-grey below. Separated from Pale-legged and Citrine Warblers by brighter, more clean-cut appearance and black crown- and eye-stripes bordering longer supercilia. Juvenile could be confused with only other juvenile *Basileuterus* to have wingbars, Rufous-capped Warbler, but latter has whitish eyebrow and is white from belly to undertail-coverts.

Ssp. Monotypic (E Ec, Co, SW Ve)

Habits Hard to see as usually keeps to dense cover but responds well to pishing. Forages for invertebrates low in understorey, bushes and bracken (lower than most *Basileuterus*), alone, in pairs or small flocks and often joins mixed-species flocks. Male sings from exposed perch at mid levels.
Status Fairly common to common in Ecuador, Colombia and Venezuela.
Habitat Subtropical Zone to Páramo, at 1,300–3,500m (lower in Ecuador, higher in Colombia and Venezuela), but usually above 2,500m. Dense undergrowth and shrubby edges of montane, cloud, elfin and dwarf forests and scrub to treeline, and adjacent second growth, clearings, riparian thickets, even hedgerows, also at edge of *Chusquea* bamboo stands, but avoids forest interior.
Voice A sharp, low *tzut*, *tchik* or *chit* that may run into a chatter (H&B, CQB). Song a series of rising and accelerating musical notes, e.g. *chit-chit-chit-chit-chit-chitty-chitty-chew* (R&T), *ti-ti-ti-ti-ti-tierrr* (F&K), *tuk, tuk-ti-ti-ti, ti ti ti ti rrr* (H&B, R&G), sometimes repeated several times (Hilty).
Note Sometimes considered part of 'citrine' superspecies including Pale-legged and Citrine Warblers.

GREY-HEADED WARBLER
Basileuterus griseiceps Pl. 293

Identification 14cm. Olive-green above, distinctive grey head with white supraloral, all yellow below. Bill black. Juvenile all brown, warmer and slightly brighter below, centre of breast and belly edged buffy. Bill dark brown above, orange below. Golden-crowned and Three-striped Warblers have different head patterns.

Ssp. Monotypic (E coastal range in NE Ve)

Habits Quite acrobatic as it forages low down early in day but gradually moves to higher levels and associates with mixed-species flocks (Boesman & Curson 1995). Also forages with Slate-throated Redstart. Responds well to pishing and playback.
Status Endangered, endemic to Venezuela. Clearance of understorey for coffee plantations, even in protected areas, but still present in small forest patches on high slopes of Cerro Negro (Monagas state) and a few surrounding localities.
Habitat Subtropical Zone, at 1,000–2,440m but mainly 1,400–2,100m, seems to require dense understory in undisturbed cloud forest, though occasionally ventures to forest edge and adjacent bamboo, *Heliconia* patches, natural clearings and second growth in coffee plantations.
Voice A harsh *thack*, *chack* or *tseck* (Brooks 2000) and pairs keep contact with thin soft *tik*, *tsip*, *teik* or *tsank*. Song a lively slurred, melodic and loud *(hu) wee-chee*, repeated several times, to which partner may respond with *chack* or *tseng* (Boesman & Curson 1995, Hilty).

SANTA MARTA WARBLER
Basileuterus basilicus Pl. 293

Identification 14–14.5cm. Distinctive head pattern: white stripe on centre of crown and long superciliary, white crescent below rear of eye and vertical white crescent at edge of ear-coverts, chin and throat white, rest of underparts rich golden-yellow. Juvenile has duller head with black and white replaced by dark greyish brown and buffy. Distinguished from very different White-lored Warbler (sympatric) and similar Three-striped Warbler (not sympatric) by head pattern.

Ssp. Monotypic (Santa Marta, NE Co)

Habits Difficult to observe as it forages low for invertebrates, in pairs or small flocks, and often joins mixed-species flocks.
Status Vulnerable. Restricted-range species endemic to Santa Marta region of Colombia where rare to locally common, but habitat increasingly degraded and fragmented due to cattle ranching, agriculture, logging and *Pinus* plantations, even in protected areas, though is tolerant of moderate habitat disturbance.
Habitat Upper Subtropical to Temperate Zones, at 2,100–3,000m but usually above 2,300m, in dense understorey, edges and second growth of stunted humid montane forest and second growth, also on brush-covered slopes and frequent along streams and in ravines, strongly associated with *Chusquea* bamboo.
Voice Call a short weak trill. Song unknown.

GREY-THROATED WARBLER
Basileuterus cinereicollis Pl. 294

Identification 14–14.5cm. Olive-green above with entire head grey, except black top, highlighted by bright yellow patch on crown; vestigial pale supraloral, chin and throat paler grey, centre of breast to undertail-coverts sulphur-yellow, flanks well washed olive-green. Bill black. Juvenile like adult but crest less well developed and more concealed. Races very much alike and cannot be identified in field, differences are very marginal. Russet-crowned Warbler has different head pattern, and Connecticut and Mourning Warblers longer bills, paler backs, no crown-stripes and forage deep in undergrowth.

Ssp. *B. c. cinereicollis* (E Andes in Co) slightly deeper, almost greenish-yellow
B. c. pallidulus (NE Co, NW Ve) as described
B. c. zuliensis (Perijá, Ve) slightly paler and brighter sulphur-yellow below

Habits Actively forages in understorey where difficult to observe.
Status Near Threatened. Rare to uncommon and local, formerly common in Sierra de Perijá on border of Colombia and Venezuela, but slopes severely degraded below 2,000 m, as have slopes in much of rest of range.
Habitat Upper Tropical to Subtropical Zones, at 800–2,100m, in dense understorey and edges of humid submontane forests and second growth, and on steep slopes with tangled vegetation, e.g. overgrown landslides and treefalls.
Voice Song a series of 3–6 high-pitched wispy notes that run together at end, eg. *swee-swee-se-SEET* or *we, we-E-E-a WEEK* (Hilty).

WHITE-LORED WARBLER

Basileuterus conspicillatus Pl. 293

Identification 13.5–14.2cm. Greenish-olive above with slightly paler fringes to wing-coverts, head grey with bold black stripe on crown-sides, lores black running through eye but barely beyond, supraloral white, fading as it reaches eyes. Chin and throat pale grey, rest of underparts yellow. Juvenile dark greenish-olive above, slightly paler and more greenish on throat and breast, even paler below, and more yellowish on belly and vent. Adult has white on head restricted to supraloral and eye-crescents, thus immediately distinguishing it from Santa Marta or Golden-crowned Warblers, and female Connecticut and Mourning Warblers are only vaguely similar.

Ssp. Monotypic (Santa Marta in N Co)

Habits Actively forages in low to mid levels.
Status Near Threatened. Endemic to Santa Marta, northern Colombia, where fairly common above 450 m. Apparently tolerates some habitat degradation, but only 15% of natural vegetation remains in its range, with rapid degradation and loss continuing.
Habitat Tropical to Subtropical Zones, at 450–2,200m, in humid forest, edges, mature second growth and shade coffee plantations.
Voice Unknown.

RUSSET-CROWNED WARBLER

Basileuterus coronatus Pl. 293

Identification 14–15cm. Olive-green above with grey head that has black stripes through lores and eye to rear ear-coverts, from base of bill over top of head, either side of orange-rufous coronal stripe. Underparts vary subspecifically. Bill black. Juvenile dull olive-brown with vague, narrow cinnamon wingbars and whitish to yellow flush on belly to undertail-coverts. Golden-crowned Warbler smaller and smaller billed, with narrower crown-stripes, paler superciliary and all-yellow underparts, and Grey-throated Warbler has different head pattern and grey extending further over breast.

Ssp. *B. c. castaneiceps* (SW Ec) greyish-olive above, underparts all white, with distinct flush of buffy-olive on breast-sides
B. c. elatus (W Ec, SW Co) olive-green above, underparts olive-yellow to yellow
B. c. orientalis (E Ec) greyish olive-green above, throat whitish-grey grading into pale yellow rest of underparts
B. c. regulus (CW Ve) bronzy olive-green above, pale olive-yellow on chin and throat, rest of underparts yellow, washed olive-green on flanks

Habits Wags tail in slow circular movement. Forages in pairs or small flocks in dense undergrowth and tangled vines from low to mid levels; often joins mixed-species flocks.
Status Fairly common to common throughout range.
Habitat Subtropical to Temperate Zones, at 1,300–3,100m, in dense understorey of humid montane and cloud forests, edges and mature second-growth.
Voice A short, high slightly trilled *trilip* or *tridlip*, buzzy, ascending *bzhreeep*, wheezy *wheeee*, and nasal *rrr-rrr-rrr* or *tack-tack* or pulsating, low-pitched *pl-b* or *pl-b-b* when disturbed. Sings at dawn, charming and melodic, stuttering series of 6–8 *tee* or *chee* notes at start, distinctly rising at end with a warble, e.g. *tee-tee-teehe-weede wéeh*. Pairs sing antiphonally, but song of female falls at end (CQB, F&K, R&G, R&T). Also *teet tut't't'u'u'treeeeeeEEE* or *tzinkle tzinkle tzinkle zuuurrreeeeEE* (Hilty).

GOLDEN-CROWNED WARBLER

Basileuterus culicivorus Pl. 293

Identification 12–13cm. Rather small and small-billed, races rather variable, but all have distinctive head pattern (though colours vary) and yellow underparts (white or yellow undertail-coverts according to subspecies-group), giving more clean-cut appearance than congeners. Juvenile dull olive-brown above including head, 2 narrow and faint buffy wingbars, with dull sulphur-yellow vent and undertail-coverts. This complex species has 13 races forming a steady cline from Mexico to Argentina, which are usually split into 3 groups that are sometimes regarded as species (CQB, Restall 2005). Two of them occur in our region. Three-banded Warbler is not sympatric, Two-banded and Golden-bellied Warblers (compared to *auricapillus* group) have brighter olive upperparts and olive-yellow supercilium, Russet-crowned Warbler is larger with grey throat, and Grey-headed and White-lored Warblers have distinctly different head patterns.

Ssp. **Cabanis's Warbler, *cabanisi* group,** upperparts grey, coronal stripe yellowish, undertail-coverts white:
B. c. austerus (C Co) brownish-grey above, some orange in stripe
B. c. cabanisi (NE Co, NW Ve) illustrated, bill black
B. c. indignus (Santa Marta in Co) illustrated, bill black above, brown below
B. c. occultus (W & NC Co) like *cabanisi* but stripe rather obscure and ear-coverts darker
Golden-crowned Warbler, *auricapillus* group, upperparts olive, coronal stripe orange, undertail-coverts yellow:
B. c. olivascens (E Co, NE Ve, Tr) illustrated, bill dark brown
B. c. segrex (SE Ve, W Gu) illustrated, pale crescent below eye edged dark, bill black above, orange below

Habits Often flicks wings and cocks tail. Forages at low to mid levels alone, in pairs or small flocks for invertebrates and berries, but responds well to pishing and playback. Often joins mixed-species flocks.
Status Fairly common to common throughout.
Habitat Tropical to Subtropical Zones, at 200–1,700m, occasionally to 2,100m, in dense understorey of dry and humid forests, edges, second growth, plantations and gallery forest.
Voice A chipping *pits* and buzzy *vreet* whilst foraging (Hilty), also a loud, sharp *chip*, soft *tchuck* and repeated sharp, high

tsip that may run into *tsip-l-it* or wren-like churring rattle. Song a variable series of whistled notes that rises in pitch and volume at end, eg. *e-whew-whew-we-see?* (CQB, DG). Also, high thin, chattery song, *pits-seet-seet-seet-seet* or *seet-seet-seet-seet-SEET-sit* (Hilty).

THREE-BANDED WARBLER

Basileuterus trifasciatus Pl. 293

Identification 12.5cm. Olive-green above with pale grey head that has black stripe either side of pale grey crown (tinged yellow in fresh plumage), lores grey, becoming black near eyes, running back through eyes to rear ear-coverts where forms solid black triangle on neck-sides; breast washed greyish-olive, rest of underparts yellow. Juvenile apparently undescribed. Similar to Golden-crowned Warbler but grey of head is paler and brighter, with central crown-stripe, incomplete eyestripe (lores pale grey) and black-framed cheeks. Race *tristriatus* of Three-striped Warbler (not known to be sympatric) has different head pattern with more extensive black on head-sides and dull yellow underparts.

Ssp. *B. t. nitidior* (SW Ec)

Habits Forages for invertebrates, alone, in pairs or small flocks mainly at low to mid levels, and sometimes joins mixed-species flocks.

Status Endemic to Tumbesian region where uncommon to locally fairly common. A restricted-range species, but not threatened.

Habitat Tropical to Temperate Zones, at 500–2,400m, locally to 3,000m, in dense understorey of humid forest, edges, mature second growth, shrubby clearings and riparian thickets in dry forests.

Voice A frequent, sharp *tsit*. Song a pulsating, warbling trill, rising slightly in pitch (CQB).

Rufous-capped Warbler has a distinctive jizz, usually holding its tail at right angles to body

RUFOUS-CAPPED WARBLER

Basileuterus rufifrons Pl. 294

Identification 12-13cm. Olive-green above, with distinctive rufous and white head: top of head and ear-coverts rufous, supraloral and superciliary white, lores black, reaching just beyond eyes, white crescent below eyes; underparts yellow with pale belly. Juvenile soft sandy brown above with 2 buffy wingbars, vestigial white eyebrow and crescent below eyes; mesial line white, chin and throat soft tawny-buffy, becoming white on breast and over rest of underparts. Quite distinct, both adult and juvenile.

Ssp. *B. r. mesochrysus* (N Co, W Ve)

Habits Tail held cocked at 45°, forages alone or in pairs in low scrub (sometimes higher), gleaning foliage for invertebrates and berries in a slow, deliberate manner with much scanning. Male sings from top of a bush. Pairs maintain territory year-round.

Status Fairly common, but less so in Santa Marta area of northern Colombia.

Habitat Tropical to Subtropical Zones, to 1,900m in Colombia but only to 1,000m in Venezuela, in thickets, brush and scrub at forest edges and in overgrown clearings, plantations and often along watercourses even in arid zones, e.g. in brushy ravines.

Voice A hard *tchek*, *chik* or *tik* that becomes a chatter when agitated (DG). Song a variable series of jumbled notes, starting with a few chirps and ending accented upwards, e.g. *chi-cha-chup-cha-chu-weépa* (R&T), *tis-tis weecha weecha beecher* (H&B) or *tis-tis-weecha weecher BEEcher* (Hilty).

PIRRE WARBLER

Basileuterus ignotus Pl. 293

Identification 13–13.5cm. Olive-green above, with top of head chestnut, yellow superciliary bordered below with black; underparts very pale yellow. Juvenile unknown. Only *Basileuterus* within its range with chestnut crown and broad pale yellow eyebrow.

Ssp. Monotypic (NW Co: Cerro Tacarcuna, NW Chocó)

Habits Forages in pairs or small flocks at low to mid levels, sometimes with Pirre Bush Tanagers and others.

Status Vulnerable. Tiny range in south-east Panama and north-west Colombia (<100 km^2), where uncommon to fairly common. Ongoing habitat degradation and loss place it at risk.

Habitat Subtropical Zone, above 1,200m, mainly 1,350–1,650m. Humid montane woodland and forest, especially fond of undergrowth of elfin forests.

Voice Calls include a distinctive and penetrating *tseeut* or *tseeit* (CQB).

THREE-STRIPED WARBLER

Basileuterus tristriatus Pl. 294

Identification 12–13cm. Pale stripes along head, not black ones. Juvenile entirely olive-brown, darker on wings and tail, 2 dull buffy wingbars and slight indication of head pattern, slightly paler and more greenish below with hint of buffy belly; bill all brown. All subspecies illustrated, somewhat variable but all have distinctive black and yellowish-buffy head and dull olive upperparts. Similarly patterned Worm-eating Warbler has less contrasting and striking head pattern and buffy-brown (not yellowish) underparts. Similar Santa Marta and Three-banded Warblers not sympatric.

Ssp. *B. t. auricularis* (E & SW Andes in Co, Táchira in Ve)
head clearly striped black and buffy-white, thick crescent below eye, straw yellow below; bill black above, flesh below

B. t. baezae (E Ec) rich amber-yellow below
B. t. bessereri (Coastal Cordillera, NE Ve) ear-coverts pale, generally palest race with no olive on sides or flanks; bill black above, horn below
B. t. daedalus (W Ec, W Co) olive-green above, lores and ear-coverts black, buffy-yellow below
B. t. meridanus (W Ve) duller and darker greenish-olive above, ear-coverts olive, stripes on head dull buffy, underparts dull yellow; bill black above, brown below
B. t. pariae (Paria, NE Ve) slightly darker above, coronal stripe almost concolorous with back, underparts dull olive-green with pale sulphur on centre to undertail-coverts; bill black above, yellow below
B. t. tacarcunae (NW Co) ear-coverts olive, coronal stripe dull orange

Habits Flicks tail frequently and twists body sideways. Not wary as it actively forages for invertebrates in dense undergrowth alone or in small to large chattering flocks (of up to 30), often joining mixed-species flocks, especially with Common Bush Tanagers. Responds well to pishing.
Status Fairly common to common throughout range.
Habitat Upper Tropical to Subtropical Zones, at 300–3,400m but mostly 1,000–2,300m, in dense understorey of humid and cloud forests, edges and mature second growth, often with bamboo.
Voice A sharp *tchp* or *tsik*, extended into chatter when agitated, and constantly repeated, husky and high *che-weep*. Song a single very long whistle followed by a fast and jumbled, twittering series of siskin-like notes that falls then rises in crescendo, eg. *tsit-tsit-tsit-ee-tse-te'ti'ti'ti'ti'ti'chi-chi-chi-e-e-ez-ez* (F&K, Hilty).

FLAVESCENT WARBLER
Basileuterus flaveolus Pl. 293

Identification 14–14.5cm. Olive-green above, yellow below with dark line from lores through eye, yellow supercilia and vestigial yellow crescent below eyes. Bill brown. Brighter and cleaner-cut than very similar Citrine and Pale-legged Warblers which have black bills and different voice, habits and altitudinal range. Similar Superciliaried Hemispingus occurs at higher elevations. Hooded Warbler has different face pattern and white in tail. First-year female Kentucky Warbler has slightly different face, including shorter supercilium, and different voice but similar habits. Female Masked Yellowthroat has narrower yellow supercilium, greyer head and different habits.

Ssp. Monotypic (NE Co, W & NC Ve)

Habits Continually pumps tail, slightly spreading it on downward pump. Forages alone or in pairs on or near ground, turning leaves in search of invertebrates, sometimes joins mixed-species flocks.
Status Locally fairly common to common.
Habitat Tropical Zone, to 1,350m in cloud forest but usually below 1,000m. Dense undergrowth of dry deciduous, semi-deciduous, moist and gallery forests, woodland, edges and second growth, shrubby or thorn thickets and overgrown clearings, but also ventures into open.
Voice A sharp *tschick* and short chatter of alarm (CQB). Song is sharp, fast, loud and variable, e.g. *ek, Ease-a Ease-a, E chew-chew-chew* or *seeka-seeka-SEETA, chew-chew-chew* (Hilty).
Note Sometimes placed in genus *Phaeothlypis*.

BUFF-RUMPED WARBLER
Basileuterus fulvicauda Pl. 294

Identification 13.5cm. Olive back and wings and distal third of tail, top of head and nape slightly paler olive, with dark lores and line through eye that reaches neck-sides; base of tail, rump and uppertail-coverts, superciliary and rear underparts cream colour. Juvenile darker olive-brown above, including rump and uppertail-coverts, leaving only basal half of tail creamy, head and breast also dark olive-brown, rest of underparts pale creamy. Similar to River Warbler but with very noticeable pale buff base to tail.

Ssp. *B. f. motacilla* (CW Co) tail almost entirely pale cream, with only tip olive, throat and centre of breast whitish
B. f. fulvicauda (E Ec) distal third of tail dark, cream colour warmer and more buffy, especially from rump to tail, throat to belly whitish
B. f. semicervina (E & W Ec, W Co) entirely buffy-cream below

Habits Continually swings tail side to side. Forages on or near ground, on fallen logs, muddy tracks, at edges of streams, around puddles, etc., for invertebrates. Pairs defend territory year-round.
Status Uncommon to fairly common in Ecuador (less common in eastern lowlands), common in Colombia.
Habitat Tropical Zone, mainly below 1,000m (once to *c*.1,600m in Ecuador). Always near water, e.g. near rivers, streams or swampy areas, in humid forest and edges.
Voice A sharp *tschick* like Northern Waterthrush but lacks metallic quality (CQB). Very loud song commences with short warble followed by vigorous and accelerating, somewhat variable series of *tew*-like notes always ending with an emphatic *chew*, e.g. *ee-ee-due-ee-ee-chew-chee* or *ee-ee-titichew chew* (R&G).
Note Sometimes placed in genus *Phaeothlypis*.

RIVER WARBLER
Basileuterus rivularis Pl. 294

Identification 13.5–14cm. Dark to umber-brown above, darkest on head, superciliary and head-sides cinnamon-buff, underparts white, variably flushed creamy to buffy, apparently independent of age or sex. Juvenile similar above, but lacks paler, cinnamon-buff superciliary or cheeks, chin and throat are mottled buffy grading rapidly into dark brown breast and sides, fading through flammulations to paler brown of lower underparts.

Ssp. *B. r. mesoleuca* (NE Ve, Guianas)

Habits Similar to but not sympatric with Buff-rumped Warbler which has essentially same habits, except that River Warbler generally prefers slower-moving waters and more swampy areas with standing water (although Buff-rumped Warbler's apparent preference for faster-moving waters may be due to availability), runs though heavy undergrowth, over logs, with body almost always horizontal, continually opening and closing its tail. Usually draws attention to itself by its loud song.

Status Fairly common throughout, though absent from coastal Suriname.

Habitat Tropical Zone, to 1,100m, always near water, e.g. near rivers, streams or swampy areas, in humid forest and edges.

Voice Loud alarm-call similar to Buff-rumped Warbler. Very loud but low-pitched song is a soft 2-noted warble followed by many loud, clear notes, nightingale-like in quality (H&M) e.g. *tseeu, tseeu, teeu, tee tee chu-chu-chu-chu-chu-CHU-CHEW-CHEW-CHEW…* c.20–25 notes (Hilty).

Notes Sometimes placed in genus *Phaeothlypis*. IOC-recommended English name is Riverbank Warbler.

GENUS INCERTAE SEDIS – Rose-breasted Chat

Rose-breasted Chat has distinctive jizz, horizontal posture, with wings slightly drooped and tail cocked and fanned, and frequently bobbed up and down

ROSE-BREASTED CHAT

Granatellus pelzelni Pl. 292

Identification 12–13cm. Adult male has upperparts slate grey, remiges and rectrices black, head black except pure white line that starts above eye and runs to rear ear-coverts; chin and throat white. Breast and centre of belly and undertail-coverts deep grenadine-red, sides of lower breast and upper flanks grey, lower flanks and vent white. Male has 4 distinct plumage phases: juvenile, which is greyish dusky throughout, flushed pale on throat and central belly (and in which sexes are alike), before acquiring a female-like plumage, distinguished by having distinct grenadine flush to breast, thereafter plumage much like definitive male, but lacks white postocular line, and has some buffy flecking on cheeks, breast-sides flecked black and grenadine breast fades into orange belly before white of vent. Female greyish-dusky above, warm buffy on supercilia and head-sides, chin to vent white, flushed buffy, most heavily on sides and flanks, undertail-coverts pale grenadine-red. Adult male distinctive, adult female separated from conebills by more clean-cut grey-buff pattern, especially on head, and contrasting reddish vent.

Ssp. *G. p. pelzelni* (SE Co, SE Ve, Gu, Su)

Habits Perches horizontally, usually carries wings slightly drooped and holds tail slightly fanned and cocked, bobbing it upwards. Forages, usually in pairs, at all levels, but most often in mid levels to subcanopy, where especially fond of vine tangles, and often joins mixed-species flocks.

Status Uncommon to fairly common in Venezuela, widespread but uncommon in Guyana and Suriname.

Habitat Tropical Zone, to 850m, in deciduous, moist semi-deciduous and humid evergreen forests, mature second growth and riparian woodland, occasionally at edges, e.g. along streams and rivers, but generally within forest, especially around overgrown treefalls.

Voice An oft-repeated short dry *jrrt* and nasal *tank*. Song a series of 4–8 clear sweet even-pitched notes, e.g. *weech weech wech…* (H&M), *sweet, t-weet, t-weet, t-weet…* (R&T), *sweet, tu-wee, tu-wee, tu-wee…* (CQB) or *wheet-wheet-wheet…* (Hilty).

Note This species' taxonomic position continues to be uncertain, (Lovette & Bermingham 2002), having traditionally been placed with warblers, next to conebills, but is currently considered Incertae Sedis by AOU (2006).

ICTERIDAE – Oropendolas, Orioles, Blackbirds and Allies

Despite a wide variety of sizes and colours, all icterids display an obvious family resemblance, a mixture of traits that permits the observer to immediately recognise them. Adult male plumages range from very contrasting combinations of red, orange or yellow with black, in orioles and caciques, to the most extreme of all black in grackles. Between these extremes are cryptic plumages (Bobolink) and luminous mixes (Russet-backed Oropendola). The largest of the oropendolas is 3 times the size of the smallest blackbird. There is their impudent, boastful personality, and there is the bill – sharp, dagger-like, strong and relatively long – like a pair of scissors. Orians & Angell (1985) concluded that it is the ability to gape, to open the bill against strong resistance, and thus access a much wider variety of foods hidden in tough places that ultimately gave icterids the necessary advantage for their amazing adaptive radiation. It also gave them the flexibility to explore all kinds of breeding systems, from the simple, energy-saving brood parasitism of the cowbirds, to the almost Homeric complexity of the oropendolas' societies and sex lives. Icterids are also flexible in the range of habitats and climates they adapt to. They can be found from Newfoundland to Tierra del Fuego and from sea sides to mountaintops. However, most species reside between Guatemala and the Amazon, making them important, permanent and numerous members of all bird communities in northern South America.

Additional references in preparing notes for this family: Orians (1985) and Jaramillo & Burke (1999, hereafter J&B).

Oropendolas (*Psarocolius* and *Ocyalus*) are amongst the most distinctive genera of Neotropical birds because they breed in colonies, suspending long tear-shaped nests from the undersides of tall trees where they are easily seen but virtually impossible to reach. They are large birds, invariably a shade or shades of brown with a highlight of yellow. The base of the bill is swollen and expanded, often into a plate, shield or casque on the forehead. Sexes are alike, albeit with subtle differences. Juveniles are like females, without the richly developed soft-parts colorations, and their eyes are invariably dark.

CASQUED OROPENDOLA

Psarocolius oseryi Pl. 295

Identification Male 36–38cm, female 28–30cm. Adult deep chestnut above, with rich yellow on tail-feathers 3–5, and yellow fringes to remiges, grey throat and yellowish-olive breast. Eyes white or pale blue, bill creamy, darker at tip, and casque larger in male, legs and feet dusky. Slightly duller juvenile has dark eyes and looser plumage. Larger Russet-backed Oropendola lacks casque and yellowish-olive breast. Larger Green and Olive Oropendolas lack casque and have different-coloured bill, face and body plumage.

Ssp. Monotypic (E Ec)

Habits Colonies often in large trees overhanging forest rivers. Forages in small flocks in canopy, sometimes with other oropendolas and caciques.
Status Rare to uncommon and local. Moves to foothills in search of food.
Habitat Lower Tropical Zone, to 300m. In *terra firme* and *várzea* primary and mid-successional secondary forests, rarely at clearings and edges.
Voice Calls include various loud, squawking calls, e.g. *zhrak* and a repeated *zhreeo*, also a low *whook*, buzzy *whEEoo*, muffled *fffttt-fffttt*, a *chhh-hhppp*, and loud piercing whistled alarm that descends evenly. Males have several vocalisations accompanying their showy courtship displays, including the loud, startlingly unique song *OOP-Koooheee* (the *heee* given simultaneously at much higher pitch than the *Kooo*) and a *squa-a-a-a-a-oook* lasting *c.*2 s (J&B, R&G)
Note Sometimes placed in monotypic genus *Clypicterus* (R&G).

CRESTED OROPENDOLA

Psarocolius decumanus Pl. 295

Identification Male 41–48cm, female 30–38cm. Adult all black except distinctive white bill, blue eyes, dark chestnut rump and vent and yellow edges to tail. Juvenile duller, with brownish eyes and bill. Smaller Chestnut-headed Oropendola has noticeable casque and chestnut head and neck. Smaller Band-tailed has grey upper mandible, chestnut head and neck, black rump and vent, and black band at tail tip. Also see similar but smaller caciques.

Ssp. *P. d. decumanus* (E Ec, E Co, Ve) as described
P. d. insularis (Paria Peninsula in Ve, T&T) smaller than nominate with more chestnut on wings and lower back
P. d. melanterus (NW Co) darker than nominate

Habits Conspicuous as it forages alone or in small flocks from midstorey to canopy (sometimes on ground) for large invertebrates, fruits and nectar, and sometimes joins mixed-species flocks, e.g. with other oropendolas, caciques and jays.
Status Uncommon to common, but exterminated in parts of Colombia.
Habitat Tropical to Temperate Zones, to 2,600m but usually below 1,200m. Primary and mature secondary, fairly dry to humid forests, clearings and edges, also gallery forest, plantations and other semi-open habitats with scattered forests, e.g. disturbed agricultural areas or urban parks. Benefits from forest clearance. Nests colonially in tall trees well away from forest.
Voice A melodious *kaueek* and loud *wak*, repeated in alarm. A rising or falling hoarse trill during territorial disputes. Females utter a whining scold when confronting other females or Giant Cowbirds. Males usually quiet except during breeding season when they sing during showy displays. Song a loud, liquid, descending or ascending *crreeeEEEoooooooooooo*, sometimes amended to *wooo-poooo* and accompanied by bill-snapping and wing-beating, sometimes a hoarse *tsreee-kleee* (J&B).

GREEN OROPENDOLA

Psarocolius viridis Pl. 295

Identification Male 43–51cm, female 35–38cm. Adult olive-green above, becoming chestnut on rump but olive-green on uppertail-coverts. Wings and tail dark with greenish fringes to wing-coverts, all but central pair of tail-feathers rich yellow, and outer web of outermost feather olive; brighter green on throat and breast, becoming dark chestnut on flanks, thighs and rest of underparts. Eyes blue, bill bright green with bright red tip. Female often has brown eyes, as does juvenile which is also duller. Adult has olive outer web to outermost tail-feathers, lacking on larger Olive Oropendola which has sharply divided olive and chestnut extending further up and including wings, bare pink cheeks, black (not pale to yellowish-green) base to bill, and brown (not pale blue) eyes in males. See also Casqued Oropendola.

Ssp. Monotypic (E Ec, E Co, S & E Ve, Guianas)

Habits Noisy and conspicuous as it forages in small flocks in canopy for large invertebrates, fruits and nectar. Sometimes joining mixed-species flocks, e.g. other oropendolas. Nests colonially, with up to 30 long, pendant nests high on terminal branches of large tree.
Status Rare to locally fairly common, more common in east.
Habitat Tropical Zone, to 1,100m but usually below 500m. Mostly in primary *terra firme* and *várzea* forests, mature second growth, clearings and edges, but also in gallery forest and semi-

open habitats, appears more tolerant of forest disturbance in Venezuela than in western Amazonia.

Voice Calls include *chak-chak*, *chut-ut* and scratchy *queea*. Males perform showy courtship displays, bowing deeply and uttering very loud, rapid and liquid *Qu-Q-Q-q-q-q-q D'D'D'CLOCK*, *agoogoo*, *zweeeEEE-whopwheerupwhopwheerup*, *zeeeeeEEE-papaparaparapUUUp*, or *zeeeeeeEEWHaruuuup*, with initial high screech distinctive (J&B, Hilty).

RUSSET-BACKED OROPENDOLA

Psarocolius angustifrons Pl. 295

Identification Male 44–49cm, female 34–38cm. Adult varies from dull olive to dark rufous, with considerable variation in bill colour; each subspecies distinct. Nevertheless should not be confused in most of range. Eyes dark, bill yellow. Juvenile has yellow or buffy wash on head and olivaceous-yellow on tail, and always has dark eyes. Chestnut-headed Oropendola smaller and lacks yellow forehead. See Casqued Oropendola.

Ssp. *P. a. alfredi* (SE Ec) head dark yellowish-olive, small yellow forehead patch, tail intense yellow including outermost feathers, eyes pale blue-grey or pale greyish-brown; female paler-faced than other races, pale yellow bill, pale blue-grey or greyish-brown eyes

P. a. angustifrons (E Ec, SE Co) variable green caste to face, throat and breast, eyes dark but occasionally pale blue, bill black

P. a. atrocastaneus (W Ec) bill orange-yellow, body very rufescent

P. a. neglectus (E slope of E Andes in Co, NW Ve) buffy to orange-yellow bill, yellow of forehead extends over superciliary, outer web of outer tail-feathers olive only on basal half, rump chestnut

P. a. oleagineus (N Ve) smallest race, very olivaceous, yellow only on forehead, all wing-feathers fringed yellow-olive, leading edge of primaries yellow, bill pale greenish, pale bluish at base of mandible; bill of juvenile pinkish-white

P. a. salmoni (W & C Andes in Co) head dark with yellow extending as noticeable eyebrow, rump and uppertail-coverts bright russet

P. a. sincipitalis (E Andes and W slope in Co) very similar to but somewhat paler than *salmoni*, yellow on face slightly more extensive

Habits Noisy and conspicuous as it forages in small to large flocks from midstorey to canopy looking for fruits, nectar and invertebrates. Often in epiphytes. Sometimes joins mixed-species flocks, e.g. with other oropendolas, caciques, jays and tanagers. Nests colonially, with up to 20 long, pendant nests in large, isolated tree, and often roosts in very large flocks on Amazonian river islands.

Status Common in Amazon and Orinoco basins, but rare to locally common elsewhere (e.g. Rancho Grande, north Venezuela). Appears to have spread due to forest clearance, e.g. in eastern Ecuador.

Habitat Tropical to Temperate Zones, 400–2,500m. Semi-open areas within primary and tall secondary, humid to wet forests, especially *várzea*, e.g. riparian areas, river islands, and edges of lakes, swamps and forests, also clearings, lighter woodlands and plantations.

Voice A low resonant *chugh-chugh-chugh* or *quip-quip-quip* (*angustifrons*), a softer muffled *whuup* and sharp hollow *chak-chak-chak*. Song a sequence of rattles, progressing into louder plopping notes like water drops, culminating in a long low whistle. Varies by subspecies: *atrocastaneus* in western Ecuador has a loud *g-kyoooyk*, *angustifrons* in eastern Ecuador and south-east Colombia *g-g-guh-guh-gágok*, *salmoni* in western Colombia *Whoop-KE-chot*, *neglectus* in eastern Colombia *wooEEL-tiii-oop*, but in north-west Venezuela *ou-ouu-ouu PLOP*, *oleaginous* in north-central Venezuela a melodious, chime-like series of 3–6 notes, but in north-east Venezuela *u-pu-pU-POIK* (J&B, R&G, Hilty).

Note Some authors separate all forms other than nominate as a separate species called Yellow-billed Oropendola *P. alfredi* (e.g. J&B).

CHESTNUT-HEADED OROPENDOLA

Psarocolius wagleri Pl. 296

Identification Male 34–36cm, female 27–28cm. Adult black all over, except deep chestnut head, including nape and upper breast, tail yellow except central pair and outer edges to outermost feathers. Eyes bright sky blue, bill creamy white with well-developed frontal shield in male, much less so on female, which is also smaller with shorter wings. Juvenile has brownish eyes, duller bill, and duller, more brownish plumage. Larger Crested Oropendola also has blue eyes but outer tail-feathers are all yellow. Band-tailed Oropendola (no overlap) has grey (not yellow) upper mandible and black band at tail tip.

Ssp. *P. w. ridgwayi* (W Ec, W Co)

Habits Noisy and conspicuous as it forages for large invertebrates, small vertebrates, fruits and nectar from midstorey to canopy. Often joins mixed-species flocks, e.g. other oropendolas and caciques.

Status Rare to uncommon and local in Ecuador, but fairly common in Colombia.

Habitat Tropical Zone, to 1,000m but usually below 700m. Primary and mature secondary, humid to wet forests, clearings and edges, often along rivers inside continuous forest, sometimes in plantations.

Voice A deep *chok*, an alarmed *cack-cack* and gurgling notes, e.g. *plup, plup, plup, plup-loo-upoo*. Females also utter a gurgled *wee-chuck-chuck-chuck*, and males a liquid *guaa* or *wauu*. Males do not bow in courtship displays but raise their heads and make rattling wing noises using the pronounced emarginations on their primaries; song *guu-guu-PHRRRRTTTT*. Each colony has its own variation (H&B, J&B, R&G).

Note Sometimes placed in monotypic genus *Zarynchus* (e.g. R&G).

OLIVE OROPENDOLA

Psarocolius yuracares Pl. 295

Identification Male 47–53cm, female 41–43cm. Olive-green head, mantle and breast, and central tail-feathers. Lower back to uppertail-coverts and entire underparts rich deep chestnut. Eyes brown, bill black with orange to reddish tip, and area of skin surrounding base of bill bright pinkish-flesh. Female smaller and has less swollen bill and shorter crest. Juvenile duller and bare skin at base of bill dull flesh. Rather similar to Green Oropendola but is clearly contrasting brown and green, with largely black bill.

Ssp. *G. y. yuracares* (E Ec, SE Co, Ve)

Habits Forages alone or in small flocks in canopy, sometimes joins mixed-species flocks, e.g. with other oropendolas. Nests colonially, with up to 17 (but usually many fewer) long, pendant nests in large, isolated tree.
Status Uncommon to locally fairly common.
Habitat Lower tropical Zone, to 600m. Humid *terra firme*, sometimes also *várzea*, mostly in forest interior but sometimes at edges, in small clearings and semi-open treefalls.
Voice A loud *chak*, a *drrOT*, nasal *raap* or *whrup*, mewing *nhye* and soft *dwot* in flight. Song in 2 parts, first a descending grating or crackling with metallic overtone, followed by an explosive whip-like liquid sound, e.g. *tek-tek-ek-ek-ek-ek-oo-guhloop*, *cc-rr-rr-rr-rr-whh-heeeeeooooppp* or *psooEE-OH,o,o,o,o,o,o,o*, performed while bowing and sometimes followed by audible wingbeats (J&B, Hilty).
Note Taxonomy unclear, sometimes considered conspecific with Pará Oropendola *P. bifasciatus* (R&T, Dickinson 2003, SACC), but also treated as specifically distinct (J&B, R&G).

BAUDÓ OROPENDOLA

Psarocolius cassini Pl. 296

Identification Male 44–46cm, female 38–41cm. Adult has mantle to uppertail-coverts, wings and lower half of body deep chestnut, head, including nape, entire breast and sides, and thighs black. Tail entirely yellow except 2 central feathers, which are shorter and black, looking slightly yellow-tipped. Large and distinctive patch of bright pink skin on face-sides and another wattle-like strip below which loops up to join it; eyes brown, bill black with orange tip. Female similar but smaller and duller. Juvenile like female, duller perhaps, with facial skin dull flesh and bill dull black. Slightly smaller and smaller billed Black Oropendola has blue (not pink) cheeks and black (not chestnut) upper mantle, flight-feathers and flanks, and tip of tail has much broader yellow band.

Ssp. Monotypic (Chocó in NW Co)

Habits Forages in flocks of 2–10 in canopy, and joins mixed-species flocks, e.g. with Chestnut-headed Oropendola.
Status Endangered. Endemic to Colombia, known historically only from foothills and lowlands around Serranías de los Saltos and Baudó, in Chocó, but recently also from north of Ensenada de Utría National Park and a nesting colony at headwaters of río Acandí. Ongoing habitat loss probably threatens its already small range and population.
Habitat Lower Tropical Zone, 100–365m. Wet sandy soil forests and edges along large rivers in areas of high, semi-open canopy and epiphyte abundance.
Voice Calls include a loud nasal whining *wak* in contact. Song has 2 parts, first a series of bubbly, tinkling notes overlaid by metallic sounds, followed by a long, loud, liquid gurgle *skol-l-l-l-l-woollii*, performed while bowing.
Notes Also called Chestnut-mantled Oropendola. Formerly placed in genus *Gymnostinops*.

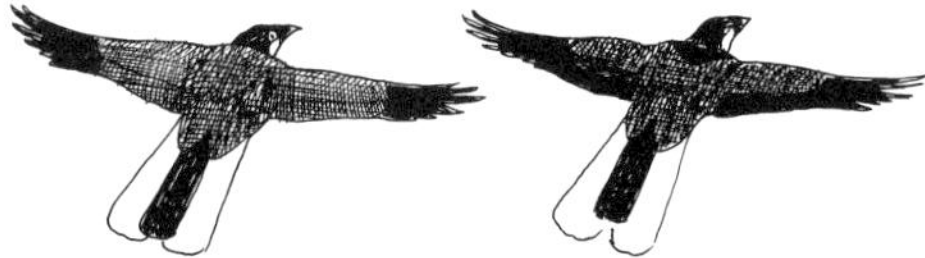

The different tail pattern produced by the shorter central tail-feathers is most apparent in flight, when the different amount of black in the wings is also noticeable; Baudó Oropendola (left) and Black Oropendola

BLACK OROPENDOLA

Psarocolius guatimozinus Pl. 296

Identification Male 44–48cm, female 38–41cm. Adult deep chestnut from lower back over wing-coverts to uppertail-coverts, and rest of body black, the tail all yellow except central pair which are black and significantly shorter, creating a yellow band at tip of tail. Orbital skin flesh, extending slightly behind eyes, bare skin on face-sides is bright powder blue, whilst strip below, which curves up to join other, is pink; bill black with a red tip. Female similar but smaller. Juvenile undescribed but almost certainly like female with facial skin dull flesh and bill all dark.

Ssp. Monotypic (NW Co)

Habits Forages in pairs or small to large flocks in canopy. Nests colonially, often along rivers.
Status Uncommon to locally common.
Habitat Lower Tropical Zone, to 800m. Humid to wet primary forest, edges and clearings with scattered trees, appears to shun forest interior and usually along edges and rivers, sometimes in drier forests.
Voice A low *cruk*. Song a loud resonant *skol-l-l-l-l-wool*, sometimes followed by a series of high *kwee* or *kee-a* notes (H&B, J&B).
Note Formerly placed in genus *Gymnostinops*.

BAND-TAILED OROPENDOLA

Ocyalus latirostris Pl. 296

Identification Male 32–34.5cm, female 23–26cm. Adult all black except deep chestnut top of head and nape, and outer 3 tail-feathers yellow with broad black tips and black outer web to outermost feathers. Eyes sky blue, bill 2-tone but not easy to see (upper grey, lower creamy white). Female similar but smaller. Look for grey upper mandible and distinctive black band at tail tip (sometimes hard to see) to separate from Chestnut-headed Oropendola, although they are not sympatric. Also, see Crested Oropendola and Chestnut-headed Oropendola (no overlap), and similar but smaller caciques.

Ssp. Monotypic (E Ec, SE Co)

Habits Forages alone or in small flocks from midstorey to canopy for invertebrates and fruits, and sometimes joins mixed-species flocks, e.g. other oropendolas and caciques.

Status Very rare.

Habitat Lower Tropical Zone, to 300m. Usually in *várzea* or swampy forests and edges, along rivers and on river islands, but sometimes in *terra firme*.

Voice Calls include liquid chortles, e.g. *chewop*, *ke-cho*, and *skeedelop-chop*, also *ch-zzp*, *zeeoo*, *chuue* and *chuk*. Males display by fluffing throat-feathers and bowing slightly while singing. Song a long, loud sequence of whistles, rattles and liquid notes, e.g. *chh-tooUUUUU*. Each colony has its own variation (J&B, R&G).

Note Formerly placed in genus *Psarocolius*.

Caciques (*Cacicus* and *Amblycercus*) are smaller than oropendolas, and regularly join them in mixed-species flocks. They are predominantly black, with highlights in yellow or red, and generally forage in noisy groups difficult to miss. Nest in colonies, suspending their pouch nests from the lower branches of tall, isolated trees, and sometimes set up a colony 'next door' to oropendolas, occasionally mixing with them.

YELLOW-RUMPED CACIQUE

Cacicus cela Pl. 297

Identification Male 27–29.5cm, female 23–25cm. Essentially black except bright yellow patch on wing-coverts and rear half of body – rump to basal third of tail, and vent and flanks to undertail-coverts. Eyes pale blue, bill yellow fading to pale bluish at base. Juvenile duller, with the black parts brownish-ashy and eyes brown. The typical, widespread and familiar black-and-yellow cacique, with yellow rump and wing patch. Mountain Cacique has a longer rounded (not square) tail and black (not yellow) basal tail and vent, and occurs at higher altitudes.

Ssp. *C. c. cela* (E of Andes, Tr) as described

C. c. flavicrissus (W Ec) duskier bill, less yellow on tail than nominate

C. c. vitellinus (N Co) larger with less yellow than nominate (and yellow is more orange), restricted to basal part of tail and innermost greater wing-coverts; song lacks mechanical sounds and imitations

In north-west Colombia, Yellow-rumped Cacique (race vitellinus*) has less yellow on wings and tail than the widespread nominate race, here on left, compared with Mountain Cacique (right) from the same region*

Habits Very noisy and conspicuous as it forages for invertebrates, fruits and nectar, alone, in pairs or small flocks at all levels (but not usually low) inside closed forest. Often joins mixed-species flocks. Nests colonially, with 5–75 pendant nests in large, isolated tree.

Status Fairly common to very common and widespread, least common in drier habitats. Has benefited from forest clearance.

Habitat Tropical Zone, to 1,000m. In humid forest, woodland, second growth and edges, especially in *várzea* and open swamp forests and often in semi-open habitats, e.g. along rivers and roads, and around habitation.

Voice Calls include a loud, harsh and often-repeated *tchak*, loud liquid *schweeooo* and loud downscale *sheek…we-er, wrup* (often just *we-er, wrup*). Females utter a rough *rrrrrr*. Males display showily while singing sequence of 4 notes (the first a species-distinctive screech) lasting *c.*2 s, a mix of screeches and whistles that changes between years or even seasons, and is sung by each male in colony. A second more complex and harsh song may last up to 20 minutes and includes loud whistles, *tchak* calls and imitations, e.g. sounds of birds, frogs, machinery, etc. (H&B, J&B, Hilty).

The three red-rumped caciques are all black with blue eyes, a pale greenish-yellow bill and a red rump and so similar that differences in body size and length of tail and bill are not much help when a single bird is seen in an uncertain location. They are, however, allopatric, although Subtropical Cacique is effectively parapatric with the other two. Note that Subtropical Cacique is the only one found in montane Andean forests while Scarlet-rumped Cacique is found west while Red-rumped Cacique east of the Andes. Beware that the red rump is easily concealed by the folded wings when perched, leaving the bird looking very similar to Yellow-billed Cacique or Solitary Black Cacique.

RED-RUMPED CACIQUE

Cacicus haemorrhous Pl. 296

Identification Male 25–29.5cm, female 20–24cm. Adult male all black with bluish gloss, with crimson lower back and rump. Eyes blue, bill yellow, paler at base. Female noticeably smaller and a little duller, less glossy. Juveniles and immatures have brown eyes and are duller, noticeably on rump which may be more orange than red and also has brownish barring. Parapatric and slightly larger Subtropical Cacique has smaller and duller red rump and lacks blue gloss to plumage. Red-rumped Cacique also has a straighter culmen, deeper bill and shorter slightly notched (not rounded) tail. Scarlet-rumped Cacique does not overlap.

Ssp. *C. h. haemorrhous* (E Ec, SE Co, S Ve, Guianas)

Habits Forages alone or in small flocks from midstorey to canopy, often with mixed-species flocks. Nests colonially, with up to 40 nests in large trees usually near rivers, clearings or other semi-open sites (in east Venezuela often over water), where noisy and conspicuous. One noisy colony in town of San Carlos de Río Negro, in Amazonas, Venezuela, had *c.*15 nests.

Status Common in east, but becoming rarer towards west.

Habitat Tropical Zone, to 1,000m. Various forested habitats (more forest-based than Yellow-rumped Cacique), both *terra firme* and *várzea*, although rare in latter, and sometimes at edges and in adjacent clearings and other semi-open areas.
Voice Calls include a drawn-out *zhweeeeeo*, loud *tjew* at colony, a *zhap-zhap-zhap* or *quack* when foraging, and a reedy *shoowip* and harsh often-repeated *gwash* or *chwak* in flight. Females give series of loud shrieks. Males have showy displays, accompanied by soft series of *ke* notes, followed by harsh grating bell-like *klang-klang* or *weuu-kleuu*. Another song, often given when female arrives at colony, is *dang-da-dang* (H&B, R&T, J&B, R&G, Hilty).

SUBTROPICAL CACIQUE

Cacicus uropygialis Pl. 296

Identification Male 28–30.5cm, female 25–25.5cm. All black with slight blue gloss, crimson rump, eyes blue, bill yellow. Female smaller and duller. Juvenile duller with rump patch more orange than red. Parapatric and smaller Scarlet-rumped Cacique has shorter and squared or notched, not rounded tail, with shorter red rump and more slender bill.

Ssp. Monotypic (E Ec, W & E Andes in Co, NW Ve)

Habits Noisy and conspicuous as it forages for invertebrates, fruits and nectar, alone or in small flocks at all levels, but mostly in canopy. Often joins mixed-species flocks. Nests colonially, one colony with 12 nests was in a semi-isolated tree above a steep ravine, in west Venezuela.
Status Uncommon to locally fairly common.
Habitat Tropical to Subtropical Zones, 1,000–2,300m, mostly in semi-open humid to wet forests, cloud forest, mature second growth and edges with lots of bromeliads and other epiphytes, but sometimes ventures into adjacent clearings with some large trees.
Voice Calls include a frequent, loud, jay-like, oft-repeated *greer*, loud ringing *qua-qua-qua-quee-quEE-QUEET*, fast *chi-chi-zi-zi-zi-zi-zi-jéw*, a *keeyoow-keeyoow-keeyoow*, repeated *weee-de-rit*, liquid oft-repeated *wurt* or *whuit*, loud *wheeeop*, nasal descending *q-ok*, liquid *cawik*, and raspy *ckrr-ckrr-ckrr* also given along with an odd whinny. Song a series of *wheeop* whistles followed by repeated *wheep*'s (J&B, R&G, Hilty).
Note Formerly considered conspecific with Scarlet-rumped Cacique.

SCARLET-RUMPED CACIQUE

Cacicus microrhynchus Pl. 296

Identification Male 23–27cm, female 20.5–23cm. Adult male all black with scarlet rump. Eyes blue, bill yellow. Juvenile duller with brown eyes.

Ssp. *C. m. pacificus* (W Ec, W Co)

Habits Noisy and conspicuous as it forages in pairs or small to large flocks at all levels, but mostly in canopy, for invertebrates, fruits and nectar, and often joins mixed-species flocks. Colonial.
Status Uncommon to common.
Habitat Tropical Zone, to 1,300m, but usually below 900m, in humid primary and very mature secondary forests, preferring forest interior, but sometimes venturing to edges as well as orchards and plantations.
Voice Soft calls and whistles when foraging, e.g. liquid sometimes-repeated *teeo* or *keeo*, a drawn-out and sometimes-repeated *shweeeeee*, *shweee-ooooo*, or *sheeeoooo*, a loud, ringing *treeo, trew-trew-trew-trew*, a guttural *kraaaaa*, and a peculiar gurgling sound. Song a melancholy descending *whip-wheeo-wheeo-wheeo* or series of bubbling whistles in ascending and descending sequences. Duets between sexes common. Vocalisations vary geographically (J&B, R&G).
Note Formerly considered conspecific with Subtropical Cacique. The race *pacificus* has different vocalisations and morphology from the nominate and is likely a separate species for which the name Pacific Cacique would be appropriate (R&T, J&B).

MOUNTAIN CACIQUE

Cacicus chrysonotus Pl. 297

Identification Male 27–30.5cm, female 23–25.5cm. Adult all black with yellow from lower back to rump, and patch of yellow on inner wing-coverts. Eyes pale blue, bill yellow, grading to bluish on base. Female slightly smaller. Juvenile duller, dark brownish-black with duller yellow only on rump, and a smaller, dull bill and brown eyes.

Ssp. *C. c. leucoramphus* (E Ec, Andes in Co, Táchira in Ve)

Habits Noisy and conspicuous as it forages for invertebrates, fruits and nectar, alone, in pairs or small flocks at all levels, but usually above mid level. Often joins mixed-species flocks.
Status Uncommon to locally fairly common.
Habitat Subtropical to Temperate Zones, 1,700–3,200m. Humid to wet, tall, primary forest, cloud forest and edges, especially tall stands of *Chusquea* bamboo and sometimes in adjacent clearings, but never far from contiguous forest.
Voice A nasal gull-like oft-repeated *kay*, *caa*, *kee-a* or *skeeuh* (typically doubled as *kay-kay*), a more jay-like, whining oft-repeated *krek*, *wheehnk* or *whaak*, a quavering *wree-wree-wree-wreeuh*, but sometimes just a single sharp descending *tsweeeeee*, *tjiue*, *wree* or *kreeuh* whistle, or *tweeaaaweee*, descending then rising, and long whistled sequences such as *arr tjie tjie tiuee arr arr tiue kik…kik tjiue*; sometimes a bird utters *arrhee-arrhee-*… and another answers with a long, descending, hawk-like *weeeeeeee* (H&B, R&T, F&K, J&B, R&G, Hilty).
Note The northern race is sometimes split as a separate species, Northern Mountain Cacique *C. leucoramphus*.

ECUADORIAN CACIQUE

Cacicus sclateri Pl. 297

Identification Male 23–23.5cm, female 19–20cm. Compared to other caciques, a smaller, more slender bird with a small slender bill. Entirely black, the eyes are sky blue, and bill pale blue. Female slightly smaller. Juvenile duller and dusky, with pale horn bill which is pale greyish at base. Larger Solitary Cacique has heavier and deeper pale (not whitish-blue) bill, dark brown (not pale blue) eyes (beware juveniles which may also have dark eyes), a longer tail, and is much more skulking, in dense low vegetation, usually near water.

Ssp. Monotypic (E Ec)

Habits Forages for invertebrates, fruits and nectar, alone, in pairs or small flocks, from midstorey to canopy, usually higher than Solitary Cacique. Joins mixed-species flocks.

Status Usually rare but fairly common at a few localities in Ecuador.

Habitat Lower Tropical Zone, to 750m but usually below 400m, in humid forest, mature second growth and edges, especially *várzea* and riparian vegetation, also nearby plantations.

Voice A repeated *chee-ker* sometimes followed by jay-like *k-cheeyow*, a doubled *kip-pheew* with second note lower, also just the *kip* note, often repeated, a series of mellow *tweeew* notes, sometimes doubled, and loud *tchak-tchak* (J&B, R&G). Song 2 low notes followed by a long, loud whistle lasting *c.*1 s, *wha-kuu-CHEEAAA*, but also a ringing *pee-churr, pee-churr, pee-churr, chur-chur-chur* (J&B), or a mournful clear *kleeéur* often preceded by several soft *wop* notes, a penetrating *kweeyh-kweeyh-kweeyh-kweeyh-wonhh* and *wo-wo-wo-wowo-waaahh* (R&G).

Note Also called Ecuadorian Black Cacique.

SOLITARY CACIQUE

Cacicus solitarius Pl. 297

Identification Male 27–28cm, female 23–24cm. Adult entirely black, eyes dark, bill whitish, tinged greenish-yellow except pale bluish-grey base. Juvenile more brownish-black, remiges distinctly dark brown, bill duller. Only all-black cacique that skulks in dense low vegetation up to midstorey (see Ecuadorian Cacique). Similar Yellow-billed Cacique does not overlap. Much smaller Velvet-fronted Grackle has smaller black bill. Much larger Giant Cowbird is much glossier with dark bill and yellow or red eyes, but juvenile has less gloss, pale bill and dark eyes. To avoid confusion, look for accompanying parents, small-headed look, decurved (not straight) culmen and square (not rounded) tail of Giant Cowbird. Carib Grackle has yellow eyes. Just occasionally overlaps with Pale-eyed Blackbird, which is significantly smaller.

Ssp. Monotypic (E Ec, E Co, NW Ve)

Habits Forages alone or in pairs for invertebrates, and often joins mixed-species flocks. Does not nest colonially, but solitarily, in penduline basket in free-standing tree, sometimes overhanging water. Sings from hidden perch without noticeable display.

Status Uncommon to fairly common.

Habitat Lower Tropical Zone, to 750m. In dense low vegetation, e.g. vine thickets near water in humid and gallery forests and mature second growth (e.g. on river islands or overgrown clearings), edges of *várzea* forests, swamps and *cochas*, or in *Heliconia* or bamboo stands and grassy patches along rivers.

Voice Very wide variety of reported vocalisations. A *quek-quek* contact call, single whistles, and fast, rising and falling sequences of whistles and tweets, e.g. *whup whup tew tew tew tew tew ti ti ti ti ti or whoo tewee kaaaaaa kuuuu* (J&B), also a penetrating *keeyoh keeyoh keeyoh* or *kyoong kyoong kyoong*, an oft-repeated *kway*, nasal *wheeeah* or *wheeeah-ah* similar to *Donacobius*, an extended descending *skeeeeeeunh* (R&G) and kitten-like *mee-er*, a liquid *E'yup*, a oft-repeated resounding *TSONK* and a strange series of electric sounds (Hilty).

Note Also called Solitary Black Cacique.

YELLOW-BILLED CACIQUE

Amblycercus holosericeus Pl. 297

Identification Male 21.5–25cm, female 21–23cm. Adult entirely black, eyes yellow and long slender bill is pale yellow with a greyish base. Juvenile distinctly duller, greyish-brown with darker fringes to feathers, and duller bill. The only all-black cacique in its range (no overlap with similar Ecuadorian or Solitary Caciques).

Ssp. *A. h. australis* (E Ec, Co, NW Ve) as described
A. h. flavirostris (W Ec, W Co) slightly smaller with chisel-shaped, all-yellow bill
A. h. holosericeus (N Co) chisel-shaped (flattened culmen) and slightly thicker bill

Habits Forages for invertebrates, alone, in pairs or small flocks, usually in dense undergrowth sometimes higher, mostly to visit flowers. Sometimes joins mixed-species flocks.

Status Generally uncommon, but fairly common at a few localities within its fragmented range. More common in north, and appears to be spreading due to forest clearance.

Habitat Tropical to Temperate Zones, to 3,300m. In dense low vegetation of deciduous woodland as well as humid to wet forests and edges, riparian thickets, overgrown clearings and treefalls, especially in *Chusquea* bamboo, also tall grasses in savannas and fallow fields.

Voice An oft-repeated *kuhkuhkuhkuhkuh*, a low gravelly grating *gr'ra'ra'ra'ra'ra*, and a harsh *waak* when foraging (F&K, R&G, Hilty). Pairs form permanent bond and sing duets during breeding season. Male's phrase described as pair of whistles, *chewee-chewo, chewee-chewo*, and female answers *churr* (J&B). In western lowland Ecuador, song a series of loud ringing whistles *pee-pee-peeo-peeo-peeo*… often paired with oft-repeated *whew-whew* and sometimes answered by female *wheee-chrrrr*, but in Andes of Ecuador song is a higher and shriller series of *teeeee* whistles sometimes answered by female *wheee-chrrrr* (R&G).

Notes Sometimes called Chapman's Cacique. Formerly placed in genus *Cacicus* but DNA evidence revealed it to be sufficiently distinct as to merit generic separation (S. M. Lanyon in J&B).

The genus *Icterus* comprises a number of brightly-coloured orioles and troupials, all clad in varying combinations of black and yellow, or orange, some with white. They have distinctive calls and attractive songs, as well as longish tails that are often flicked sideways, and they engage in many coquettish postures. Some are boreal migrants. Generally arboreal, they occur in light woodland in the lowlands. Troupials have the distinction of having juveniles in effectively the same plumage as adults, whereas the rest of the genus has more cryptic, greenish plumages that lack the display elements. This has led to speculation that they might constitute a separate genus.

TROUPIAL *Icterus icterus* Pl. 299

Identification 23–24cm (*icterus* and *metae*), 25–27cm (*ridgwayi*). Adult has broad black band across back, black wings with pure white on some wing-coverts forming an angled patch that runs diagonally across wing to join white outer tertials. Touch of orange at shoulder. Entire hood black, with black feathers of breast lanceolate, and rest of body rich, bright orange, becoming paler, slightly yellowish on thighs, vent and undertail-coverts. Orbital skin pale blue and eyes yellow, bill black with base of mandible bright bone-coloured. Juvenile duller with orange replaced by rather washed-out yellow, the black is brownish and dull, and orbital skin grey. Orange-backed Oriole has orange (not black) crown and back, and less white in wing. Smaller Baltimore Oriole has dark (not yellow-orange) eyes, orange on tail and lacks orange collar.

Ssp. *I. i. icterus* (E Co, N Ve) as described

I. i. metae (Meta river, Co & Ve) orange of mantle extends to nape, white on wing divided into 2 patches by all-black greater wing-coverts, orange patch on shoulder larger: juvenile has only vestigial white and yellow on lesser wing-coverts, with only white of tertials clear

I. i. ridgwayi (N Co, NW Ve, Margarita I., ABC) larger, longer billed and stronger legged than nominate, more uniformly orange below

Habits Forages alone, in pairs or small flocks at all levels, for invertebrates, fruits and nectar. Often visits flowering trees and bird feeders, and raids nests to take eggs or chicks. Rarely builds own nest, instead takes over other species' nests, especially thornbirds, but also kiskadees, caciques or even oropendolas.

Status Uncommon to common. Designated National Bird of Venezuela in 1950s and is a treasured cagebird there and overseas, severely depleting its numbers in some areas. Introduced to Bonaire.

Habitat Tropical Zone, to 1,300m. In dry to moist, open to semi-open habitats, e.g. dry deciduous forest and woodland, gallery forest, arid xerophytic scrub, savanna, pastures and other cultivated areas with scrub or scattered trees, plantations, orchards, parks, gardens and suburbs, rarely in mangroves.

Voice Calls include mellow whistles and nasal sounds. The name is onomatopoeic both in English and Spanish, originating from the loud and musical but repetitive whistled song *tru-pial…*, *tru*-note low *pi*-note high and *al*-note lower, delivered from high perch, sounds clearly across open country, farm and parkland, and is unmistakable.

Note Also called Venezuelan Troupial. See AOU (1998) for comments.

ORANGE-BACKED TROUPIAL
Icterus croconotus Pl. 299

Identification 22–23.5cm. Adult orange from crown to short uppertail-coverts, scapulars and most of wings black, lesser wing-coverts orange and outer halves of tertials white. Frontal band, mask, bib and central throat black, reaching point on breast; underparts orange, but paler, more yellowish on vent to undertail-coverts. Orbital skin blue, eyes yellow, and bill black with bright bone-coloured base to mandible. Juvenile same except lesser wing-coverts black and is duller with yellow replacing orange and black replaced by brownish-black.

Ssp. *I. c. croconotus* (E Ec, SE Co, Gu)

Habits Forages for invertebrates, alone, in pairs or small flocks, from subcanopy to canopy (lower in dense growth at edges and in clearings), often in dead leaves. Frequently visits fruiting and flowering trees. Takes over nests of other orioles, kiskadees or caciques.

Status Uncommon to locally fairly common in Ecuador, Colombia and Guyana, at the northern limit of its mainly Amazonian distribution. Trapped for cagebird trade.

Habitat Lower Tropical Zone, to 750m. In *várzea* and other very humid lowland forests (rarely in *terra firme*) and adjacent second growth, especially along rivers, lagoons, lakes and ponds, and at edges, including treefalls, clearings, tracks and roads.

Voice Several songs, all of monotonous and slowly repeated loud, rich, musical whistles, the most widespread variation being *Its Tues-DAY* with the first 2 notes descending and the third slightly higher (sometimes first note is missing). In Guyana, also a slow rich whistled *who-hu-chu-who-hu-chee-oo-oo*. Sexes frequently duet, often from high perch (J&B).

Note Formerly considered a subspecies of Troupial (H&B, Freeman & Zink 1995, AOU 1998, J&B, R&G, Dickinson 2003).

MORICHE ORIOLE
Icterus chrysocephalus Pl. 297

Identification 20.5–22cm. Adult all black except yellow rump, yellow patch on wing-coverts, yellow cap from forecrown to nape, and yellow thighs. Eyes dark, bill black. Juvenile duller, with black parts brown, and yellow both reduced and distinctly duller. Unmistakable black-and-yellow plumage. Epaulet Oriole has black (not yellow) head, rump and thighs (although some may have yellow thighs).

Ssp. Monotypic (E Ec, S & E Co, S & E Ve, Tr, Guianas)

Habits Often jerks tail nervously. Noisy and conspicuous as it forages alone, in pairs or small flocks at all levels, but usually in canopy, for invertebrates and nectar, and sometimes joins mixed-species flocks.

Status Uncommon to locally fairly common. Has decreased in some areas due to trapping for cagebird trade.

Habitat Tropical Zone, to 1,200m. Mainly in groves of Moriche Palm *Mauritia flexuosa* and in gallery forests in savannas, open marshy areas near lakes and swampy bogs in

semi-arid savannas provided scattered trees are present, also humid forest canopies, edges and semi-open second growth and clearings. Always breeds in crowns of the Moriche.
Voice A *meow*, grackle-like *chek*, a *twik-tweeeu-twik-tweeeu*, chattering *ch-ch-ch-ch*... and *chwut- chwut- chwut*... Songs are often duets or males sing near the nest, and consist mostly of varying slow sequences of 2–3 sweet rising and falling wren-like whistles, e.g. *weet, sa-weet, ... say-su-weet, ... he, your-he, sa-lee, ee, su-lee ... your sa-wee, ... jur, sa-lee-ee ...*, including some short trills (J&B, R&G, Hilty).
Note Formerly considered conspecific with Epaulet Oriole. Apparent hybrids with Epaulet Oriole are known, suggesting possible conspecificity (Hilty, Dickinson 2003) but they occur sympatrically in many localities without interbreeding, and are thus best regarded as species (R&T, J&B).

EPAULET ORIOLE

Icterus cayanensis Pl. 297

Identification 20cm. All black with distinctive yellow patch on uppermost wing-coverts. Eyes dark and slender, pointed bill is black. Juvenile is brownish-grey and pale yellow. All-black plumage with yellow epaulette is distinct and unmistakable.

Ssp. Monotypic (S Gu, S Su, FG)

Habits Often jerks tail nervously. Usually quiet as it forages from midstorey to canopy looking for invertebrates, fruits and nectar; alone or in pairs but sometimes in small flocks.
Status Uncommon to fairly common in some localities, especially those distant from settled areas, it being much sought after by the cagebird trade. Status in south-east Colombia uncertain. In French Guiana, uncommon in gardens on the coastal plain as in the primary *terra firme* forest of the interior.
Habitat Lower Tropical Zone, to 900m. In open and semi-open patchy woodland, savannas with scattered trees, gallery forest, thickets near swamps, light deciduous forest and edges, and even forest clearings and gardens with scattered trees. Also canopy in the tall primary forest of French Guiana, always in relation to palm trees.
Voice Calls include a sharp *kit*, *chik* or *spik*, a clear *oint* or *oint-oint*, nasal *whhaaa*, sweet high *twee-swee* whistle and low *wheee*. Songs are variable sequences of pleasant and melodious whistles, sometimes more squeaky and shrill, given in deliberate clear phrases of one to several notes with obvious pauses between phrases (J&B).
Note See note for previous species.

YELLOW-BACKED ORIOLE

Icterus chrysater Pl. 298

Identification 21.5–22cm. Entire body orange-yellow, with black wings, tail, frontal mask and throat. Virtually no difference between sexes, but some variation in intensity of yellow and orange suffusion, and on average males are more intensely orange. Eyes dark and bill 2-toned, black with pale bluish-grey base. Juvenile duller olive-yellow with dark olive-brown wings and tail, and no black on head; bill horn-coloured, dark above and pale below, especially at base. Only other yellow-backed oriole is slightly smaller Yellow Oriole which has smaller black bib and yellow (not black) forehead, and white-edged (not all-black) wings; it also lacks the ochre outline to the bib usually present in Yellow-backed Oriole, and occurs at lower altitudes.

Ssp. *I. c. giraudii* (NE Co, NW & N Ve) smaller than nominate with more extensive black face; female like male without olive wash
I. c. hondae (upper Magdalena Valley, Co) known only from two specimens; very deep orange and long slender bills

Habits Conspicuous as it forages alone, in pairs or small flocks of up to 12 (especially outside breeding season) from midstorey to canopy (especially in mosses, bromeliads and other epiphytes), mainly for invertebrates but sometimes fruits and nectar. Sometimes joins mixed-species flocks, e.g. other icterids and jays. Pairs often duet; appears to pair-bond for life.
Status Uncommon to fairly common and widespread in some regions, especially highlands. Has benefited from forest clearance. Possibly present in north-west Ecuador.
Habitat Tropical to Temperate Zones, to 2,900m. Deciduous woodlands in dry foothills to humid and cloud forest edges and mature second growth in highlands, also other semi-open habitats, e.g. lighter woodlands and plantations, tall shrubbery on montane slopes, clearings and pastures with scattered trees, and thorn scrub.
Voice Calls include a musical *chert*, an oft-repeated *whink* in alarm, a chattering *kzwee-kzwee-kzwee-kzwee* or *nyeh-nyeh-nyeh-nyeh*. Song a loud, clear leisurely series of sweet rising and falling whistles, e.g. *WEET, wa, WEET, waa, wee wee wa WEET ... wa, WEET* ... or *where-hee who-hee who-hee ha-heet, wita-wita-wita*, sometimes more varied and complex, e.g. a series of oft-repeated jerky *weet* or *jur-keet* notes (H&B, J&B, Hilty).

YELLOW ORIOLE

Icterus nigrogularis Pl. 298

Identification 20.5–21cm. Considerable variation in intensity of colour, but easily recognised. Adult male has entire body yellow with orange wash to parts adjoining black mask, with black tail, black wings with white fringes to greater coverts, tertials and remiges; rest of wing-coverts yellow, with some darkish centres to smaller feathers. Narrow black mask from lores through eyes with an extended, diamond-shaped black bib. Eyes dark and steel grey bill is long and pointed. Female lacks any orange wash and is comparatively greenish above. Female may be very greenish, just like juvenile, but has full black bib breeds in this plumage. Both sexes may have olive wash on nape to back, warmer in male, with pale brown shaft-streaks. Juvenile duller olive above with olive-brown wings and tail, and no black on head, but retains conspicuous wing edgings, and is olive-washed yellow below. Note broad white fringes to tertials and greater wing-coverts may wear-off completely. Orange is variable, occasionally quite intense and ranges to simply yellow. From Yellow-backed Oriole by white fringes to wing-feathers. Juvenile somewhat similar to juveniles of Orchard Oriole (which is smaller and more greenish and has 2 wingbars not one), Yellow-tailed Oriole (different wing pattern and yellow-olive outer tail) and Orange-crowned Oriole (which has different wing pattern and orange head). Subspecies mostly impossible to identify in the field, so go by geography. In all races, yellow varies from intense to orange; in the wings white tips and edges vary from heavy white in fresh plumage to very little or no white in worn plumage.

Ssp. *I. n. curasoensis* (ABC) distinct pure, cold yellow below, distinct greenish wash to upperparts; noticeably longer, thinner bill
I. n. helioeides (Margarita I.) larger, larger bill
I. n. nigrogularis (N Co, N & C Ve, Guianas) as described
I. n. trinitatis (Ve: Paria peninsula, Tr) primaries not fringed white in adult plumage (i.e. second-year or older)

Habits Usually conspicuous as it forages alone, in pairs or small flocks at all levels, for invertebrates, fruits and nectar. A frequent visitor to flowering trees and bird feeders.
Status Fairly common to common almost everywhere but scarce on some islands. Popular cagebird in some regions.
Habitat Tropical to Lower Subtropical Zones, to 1,800m but mostly below 500m. Semi-open mostly drier habitats (absent from humid areas with closed forest), e.g. forest, mangrove and swamp edges, gallery forest, open to semi-open deciduous or xerophytic woodland and scrub, plantations, towns, parks and gardens.
Voice Calls include a sharp oft-repeated *cack* or *ka-chek*, chattering *chuck-uch-ch-ch* and an unpleasant alarm-call *chet-chet-chet*, sometimes followed by a cat-like whine *cheeeh*. During breeding season, males often sing from treetops, a sweet soft sequence of flute-like whistles, usually in pairs of a lower and a higher note or trios, mixed with imitations and throaty notes such as *tik*, *brrrzz* and *cluk*, e.g. *chwit-chwoot-cht-cht-cht-chwit-chu*, *swet-weet-weet-weet-pit-tear*, or *tur-a-leet, tur-sweet, tuu…tweet, tweet…* (Voous, ffrench, J&B, Hilty).

YELLOW-TAILED ORIOLE
Icterus mesomelas Pl. 298

Identification 21.5–23cm. Adult male has back and wings black, with yellow on lesser wing-coverts and inner greater coverts as an elongated patch; rump and short uppertail-coverts yellow, long uppertail-coverts and tail black with 2 outermost pairs of feathers yellow; face black from supraloral to just behind eye, on fore cheeks and extended bib. Eyes dark, bill is steel grey to blackish. Female has back feathers fringed olive-yellow and rump to short uppertail-coverts olive-yellow, otherwise like male. Juvenile olive-yellow from crown to tail, tail and wings darker but feathers broadly fringed olive-yellow, rest of the head and underparts to undertail-coverts greenish-yellow, with some vestigial (and variable according to age) black on bib. Bill horn with paler base and dark tip. Distinctive black tail with yellow outer tail-feathers separates adults from all other orioles. Smaller Orange-crowned Oriole has longer all-black bill and tail and lacks white wing fringes (long bill and lack of yellow in long tail plus orange head should distinguish even juveniles). Slightly smaller White-edged Oriole has white-tipped tail with white outer tail-feathers and different wing pattern (which should distinguish even juveniles). See also juvenile Yellow Oriole.

Ssp. *I. m. carrikeri* (N & W Co, NW Ve) as described, no white on wing
I. m. taczanowskii (W Ec) white fringes to tertials

Habits Fans and flicks tail in flight. Forages for invertebrates and nectar, alone, in pairs or small flocks at all levels, but usually in dense undergrowth. Sometimes joins mixed-species flocks and often visits flowering trees.
Status Fairly common to common.
Habitat Tropical to Lower Subtropical Zone, to 1,750m. Humid to wet forest edges, preferring riparian or swampy habitats near water with dense undergrowth, but also in second growth, damp overgrown clearings, bamboo stands, marshes, plantations (especially *Musa* bananas), agricultural areas, orchards and gardens.
Voice Calls include a loud oft-repeated *pik-drup* or *pik, pik-drup* whistle, a mellow *chup-cheet* or *chup-chup-cheet*, and repeated *kip-chur*. In breeding season, males perch high near nest (even on wires) and sing for long periods, sometimes duetting with the female, even from nest. Males particularly gifted whistlers, with varied repertoire of very musical 5–6 note songs. Females sing shorter phrases (H&B, R&G).

ORANGE-CROWNED ORIOLE
Icterus auricapillus Pl. 298

Identification 19–20.5cm. Adult has back black, rump and short uppertail-coverts yellow, wings black except yellow lesser coverts, tail all black; top of head, nape and rear ear-coverts orange, most intense on face, palest on nape, mask and bib black, joining black breast, but breast-sides and rest of underparts yellow. Eyes dark, and sharp, pointed bill black. Juvenile yellow-olive above, palest on head and lower rump, darkest on wings and tail, with pale fringes to wing-feathers appearing as 2 weak wingbars. Adult Yellow-tailed Oriole has significantly smaller less black on face and breast, and less intense orange on head. Separating juvenile Yellow Oriole is less easy, look for more obvious clean white fringes to wing-feathers, and generally darker, greener upperparts.

Ssp. Monotypic (N Co, N & C Ve)

Habits Forages for invertebrates and nectar, alone or in pairs, mostly in canopy. Often visits flowering trees.
Status Mostly uncommon, but locally fairly common. Less common in arid regions.
Habitat Tropical to Lower Subtropical Zones, to 1,900m. Mostly in humid wooded habitats (always near water in arid regions), from dense to partially open habitats, e.g. dry to humid forests and edges, more open deciduous woodland, mature second growth, gallery forest, palm stands, and clearings and cultivated areas with scattered trees.
Voice Calls include a short chatter, a complaining buzzy *wheea*, a sharp *ze'e't*, and loud clear *krEEEa* given when

foraging. Song consists of 4 loud musical whistles *weer, cheet-your-kurr* repeated for up to 20 minutes delivered from high perch, sometimes also a slower, longer and more rambling series (J&B, Hilty).

WHITE-EDGED ORIOLE

Icterus graceannae Pl. 298

Identification 20.5cm. Adult has back black, rump and short uppertail-coverts yellow, tail black with outermost feathers white, wings black with lesser coverts yellow and outer half of tertials white; entirely yellow head except small black mask and bib to throat. Yellow of head and breast is suffused pale orange; eyes dark and bill steel-grey to blackish. Immature or subadult like adult but duller, browner wings and tail, and yellow is less bright with no orange tones. Juvenile has dark olive back and dark brownish wings and tail, less white on tertials; head and underparts are duller somewhat greenish-yellow, with a less extensive black bib. White wing patch and white (not yellow) in tail separates White-edged from similar Yellow-tailed Oriole.

Ssp. Monotypic (SW Ec: Tumbes)

Habits Forages alone, in pairs or small flocks at all levels.
Status Uncommon to locally fairly common, endemic to Tumbesian region.
Habitat Tropical Zone, to 1,700m but mostly below 400m. Lighter deciduous woodlands and adjacent xerophytic desert scrub, second-growth scrub and riparian thickets in dry coastal lowlands.
Voice A distinctive throaty *jori-jori* or *cheerwik-cheerwik*, and warbled *phreeee* or *phreet-phreet*. Song consists of rapid sequences of whistles such as *wheeet-wheeo-wit-wit* delivered from treetops, also rich musical phrases each repeated several times before going to next with a distinctive nasal *weeeenh-weh*, e.g. *chiro-chowee… weeeenh-weh… chiro-chowee… piro, chiro-chowee…weeeenh-weh…piro, chiro-chowee…* (R&T, J&B, R&G).

BALTIMORE ORIOLE

Icterus galbula Pl. 298

Identification 17.5–20cm. Adult male has back, head and throat black, wings black with orange line on uppermost wing-coverts, pale orange median coverts, white tips to greater coverts and white fringes to tertials and secondaries, lower back to short uppertail-coverts orange, tail black with outer feathers orange, breast deep orange, becoming slightly less intense on undertail-coverts. Eyes dark, bill steel grey, paler and bluer at base. Immature or first-year male blackish where adult is black, and feathers have brown fringes, the wings no orange, rather the median coverts are white (thus 2 white wingbars), and underparts paler and somewhat buffy-orange. Juvenile male lacks black on head and is completely dark above, with paler fringes to feathers, 2 whitish wingbars and is buffy-yellow below. Adult female not very different from first-year male, but lacks dark throat and has orange line on uppermost wing-coverts like adult male, thus has 3 wingbars, the uppermost being orange. Immature female like juvenile male but paler below with darker ear-coverts. Juvenile female is paler on head and even paler below. Possible confusion with larger Troupial, but Troupial's pale eyes and large white area on wings should quickly clarify identity. Similar but smaller female and juvenile Orchard Orioles are more greenish and lack orange wash on breast.

Ssp. *I. g. galbula* (boreal migrant to N Co, NW Ve, T&T, Ar, Bo)

Habits Forages for invertebrates and fruits, alone, but sometimes in small flocks, at all levels. Often forages in hanging bunches of dead leaves; several will gather in flowering trees (especially *Erythrina*) where they defend nectar-producing flowers. Often joins mixed-species flocks. Roosts in tall grass or cane stands with other orioles and blackbirds.
Status Boreal migrant that winters in Central and north-west South America, rare to locally fairly common in Colombia (October–May), especially common in Santa Marta Mts., but only rare to uncommon in north-west Venezuela (October, January–March), Tobago (February), Trinidad (December–January, March), Aruba (September, November) and Bonaire (October, May).
Habitat Tropical to Lower Subtropical Zones, to 1,600m. Varied habitats (but usually not inside closed-canopy forest), e.g. humid forest edges, second growth and overgrown clearings, light deciduous woodland, gallery forest, plantations, small forest patches, tree stands and shrubby thickets in Llanos, pastures, agricultural and suburban areas, e.g. parks and gardens, but may be seen anywhere on migration.
Voice Calls include slurred whistles and chatters of various lengths during aggressive encounters. Rarely sings parts of its song (a low double whistle) on South American wintering grounds (J&B).
Note Also called Northern Oriole.

ORCHARD ORIOLE

Icterus spurius Pl. 298

Identification 15–17cm. Adult male with its black-and-chestnut plumage is only superficially similar to female Silver-beaked Tanager, which has much thicker bill, or male Lesser Seed Finch, which is smaller and has a massive whitish bill. For females and juveniles (which may, due to their small size, even be confused with a warbler), see Yellow and Baltimore Orioles.

Ssp. *I. s. spurius* (boreal migrant to N Co, NW Ve)

Habits Often jerkily flicks its tail in flight. Forages, often in small flocks, from understorey to canopy, searching thickets and visiting flowering trees (especially *Erythrina* sp.). Roosts consisting of a few individuals (but up to hundreds in Central America) gather at dusk in dense bushes, trees, tall grasses or beds of cattails.
Status Winters in Central and north-western South America, where rare to locally uncommon in Colombia (August–May) and Venezuela (September–March), at the southernmost limit of its wintering range.
Habitat Lower Tropical Zone, to 500m (once at 1,000m). Semi-open habitats with scattered trees (avoids closed-canopy

forests), e.g. forest edges and clearings, second growth, light woodland, plantations (especially bananas) and even suburban areas, but may be seen anywhere on migration.
Voice Calls include a sharp *chuck* and alarmed chatter (J&B). May sing (a lively rich warble of varied notes) in March while still on South American wintering grounds.

ORIOLE BLACKBIRD
Gymnomystax mexicanus Pl. 299

Identification Male 28–30.5cm, female 26.5cm. Adult entirely black except patch of yellow on lesser wing-coverts, head yellow with heavy black mask and black malar streak. Eyes brown, blackish bill sharply angled, with straight culmen and base, tapering to sharp point, legs and feet blackish. Juvenile slightly paler yellow, lacking both yellow wing patch and black mask, but has a black cap. Unmistakable large oriole with heavy bill, black back and no bib, usually seen foraging on ground. Yellow epaulets show well in flight.

Ssp. Monotypic (E Ec, C & NW Co, Ve: N of Orinoco, NW Gu, Su?)

Habits Usually noisy and conspicuous as it forages for invertebrates, fruits and seeds (can be a pest in cornfields). Forages alone, in pairs or small and sometimes even large flocks at all levels, and frequently on ground, where walks sedately and deliberately. A frequent visitor to feeders, where it 'lords' over other species. When not breeding may roost in flocks of up to several hundred.
Status Fairly common to common in Colombia and Venezuela, but uncommon in Ecuador, local in Guyana.
Habitat Tropical Zone, to 1,400m but usually below 1,000m. Wide variety of open to semi-open, mostly moist, marshy and grassy habitats near water with scattered trees and bushes (avoids closed-canopy forests), e.g. deciduous and gallery forests, young second growth, marshes, *llanos*, savannas, moist grassy pastures, agricultural areas, parks and gardens (even centre of towns and cities), and also on riverbanks around lagoons, river islands and adjacent riparian vegetation.
Voice Common is long screech, like a rusty gate, a high metallic *cleek*, ringing sharp *kring* or *kyeeng*, *chrick-chaa* when flying off, and *wreg-kreg* in flight. Both sexes have same harsh unmusical song, comprising duos of nasal notes, e.g. *ting-ting-wreg-wreg-gri-gri* or a wheezy, buzzy *shssveek* repeated up to 4 times, sometimes preceded and/or followed by a few grating *grt* notes (R&G, Hilty). Song also described as *chaa-chaa-chrick-chaa*, the third note rising in pitch and the others quite nasal (J&B).

PALE-EYED BLACKBIRD
Chrysomus xanthophthalmus Pl. 299

Identification 20.5cm. Adult has distinctive pale eyes lacking in all other overlapping black icterids. Juvenile more brownish above and streaked buffy-yellow to ochre-brown below. J&B note that pale-eyed Solitary Caciques may occur, which would be difficult to distinguish; Solitary Cacique is larger with a greenish bill and slightly crested appearance, and also forages in trees. Velvet-fronted Grackle and Shiny Cowbird have dark eyes. Giant Cowbird has orange eyes and is much larger.

Ssp. Monotypic (NE Ec)

Habits Retiring and wary as it forages alone or in pairs for invertebrates, near water level in reeds and bushes surrounding waterbodies. It is more conspicuous in early morning when it may perch and sing atop vegetation.
Status Rare and very local in Napo (where main site is Limoncocha), north-east Ecuador, and considered Near Threatened in Ecuador because of its rarity and fragmented distribution due to specialised habitat requirements. Possibly makes local movements in response to changing water levels.
Habitat Lower Tropical Zone, 200–300m. Grassy and shrubby marshes and wetlands bordering oxbow lakes and *cochas*, where floating thickets of reeds, grasses, sedges and other emergent water plants are tall and abundant.
Voice Calls include a harsh *chrk* or *chek*, smacking *tsuck* and staccato trill. Song comprises loud piercing sequences of repeated *tew* or higher pitched *swit* whistles (H&B, J&B, R&G).
Notes Also called Pale-eyed Marsh Blackbird. Formerly placed in genus *Agelaius*.

YELLOW-HOODED BLACKBIRD
Chrysomus icterocephalus Pl. 299

Identification Male 17–18.5cm, female 16–16.5cm. Short-tailed. Adult male all black except distinctive yellow head (crown and nape have olive tips in fresh plumage). Female similar overall but duller, with black parts dull olive-brown with obscure streaks, and greyish-olive crown, nape and cheeks framing yellow supercilium. Immature male like female, but has brighter yellow throat and usually some black feathers below. Juvenile even duller than female, especially yellow throat which merges more gradually with buffy underparts.

Ssp. *C. i. bogotensis* (Bogotá plateau, E Co) larger than nominate, female darker with less yellow on head and more grey below, black (not dark olive) belly and vent
C. i. icterocephalus (N, E & SE Co, N & C Ve, Tr, Gu, N Su, FG) see above

Habits Forages, roosts and nests in small to large flocks. Very noticeable as birds fly along predictable routes to the roosts. Feeds mostly on invertebrates, but also seeds, causing damage when foraging in rice fields.
Status Fairly common to locally common and very abundant at some localities, especially in rice cultivations, e.g. central Llanos, Venezuela, in coastal Suriname and French Guiana. Migrates seasonally depending on water levels and rice cycles, and vagrants recorded on Bonaire and Curaçao.
Habitat Lower Tropical Zone, usually below 600m (although *bogotensis* occurs to 2,600m). In very wet open land and marshes with extensive reed, sedge or cattail beds and emergent shrubbery, also open grassy riverbanks and islands in Amazonia, and sometimes roosts in mangrove or sugarcane on Trinidad outside breeding season; away from marshes in tall wet grassland, pastures and farmland, rice paddies, and man-made ponds, borrowing pits and ditches.

Voice Calls include low *cluck*, a drier *chek* or *ship*, and descending *tieeewww* whistle. Song comprises varied long, loud wheezes, chucks, whistles and warbles, with primary song being a wheezy, drawn-out note, often preceded by *chuck* call and terminated with *cluck* or *tik* note, e.g. *cluck-tooWEEEZ-tik*, the first note weak, but the *tooWEEEZ* loud and raspy, and sometimes followed by a musical *te-diddle-de-de-do-dee* (J&B, Hilty).
Note Formerly placed in genus *Agelaius*.

CHESTNUT-CAPPED BLACKBIRD
Chrysomus ruficapillus Pl. 299

Identification 18.5cm. Short-tailed. Adult male all black except distinctive chestnut cap and throat (may be hard to see at distance or in bad light). Immature male similar, but has heavy buffy-grey tips producing scaly pattern. Female dull olive-brown with obscure streaks and faint supercilium, buffier below with yellowish-buffy throat. Juvenile more buffy-brown and more heavily streaked below. Very similar female and juvenile Shiny Cowbird have proportionately shorter bill but longer tail, and have pale greyish- (not yellowish-) buffy throat.

Ssp. *C. r. frontalis* (NE FG)

Habits Forages, roosts and nests in small to large flocks of up several thousand. Feeds mostly on invertebrates, but also seeds, causing damage when foraging in rice paddies.
Status Locally common to abundant in most of range, but rare in eastern French Guiana (Tostain *et al.* 1992), at northern limit of its range. Migrates seasonally depending on water levels and rice cycles.
Habitat Lower Tropical Zone, usually below 500m, breeding in marshes and reedbeds, but outside breeding season also uses various other wet habitats, e.g. tall wet grassland, pastures and farmland, rice fields, and man-made ponds, borrowing pits and ditches, and even found well away from water, e.g. in agricultural fields.
Voice A sharp *chee*, high *tip*, slow *che-che-che-*... chatter, and *pewt*, *tsiew* and *chat* calls. Song varied, with soft, musical whistles followed by harsh drawn-out descending screeches, e.g. *teep- teep...tcheeeeerrrrrrr* or *si-si-si-grahh*, also a shorter and higher *tic-tic-WHEEE*, and canary-like song of sweet whistles and trills (J&B).
Note Formerly placed in genus *Agelaius*.

RED-WINGED BLACKBIRD
Agelaius phoeniceus Pl. 299

Identification 22cm. Male all black with distinctive yellow-and-red shoulder patch. Female and juvenile dark brown with narrow buffy streaks above and broad buffy streaks below, and conspicuous buffy supercilium.

Ssp. Subspecies unknown (vagrant, Tr)

Habits Forages and roosts in small to large flocks in marshy vegetation.
Status Populations from northern North America winter in southern North and Central America, rarely in southern Caribbean, with a single vagrant record on Trinidad, from June 1980 to mid 1981 (ffrench).
Habitat Lower Tropical Zone, in shallow freshwater marshes and coastal wetlands with sedges or reedbeds.
Voice No data on vocalisations during winter, but calls include a *check*, and song consists of 3 notes *ko-low-ee*, the last a buzzy trill (ffrench).

RED-BREASTED BLACKBIRD
Sturnella militaris Pl. 301

Identification 19cm. Short-tailed. Adult male all black except distinctive red throat and breast (with buff tips in fresh plumage). Adult female dark brown with narrow buffy streaks above, distinctive buffy supercilium, buffy below with narrow dark brown streaks on breast, some pinkish feathers on belly (brighter red in fresh plumage), and broad dark brown streaks on flanks and vent (compare female Peruvian Meadowlark which does not overlap). Juvenile lacks pinkish feathers but has dark brown streaks on belly. Quite distinctive in its habitat.

Ssp. *S. m. militaris* (E Ec, Co, Ve, T&T, Guianas)

Habits Spends long periods singing from lookout on bush, rock, grass stem, fencepost, wire, etc. Forages alone, in pairs or small flocks on ground and low in tall grassy vegetation for invertebrates, seeds (especially rice) and sometimes berries. In non-breeding season, forages and roosts in small to large flocks of up to 100 individuals.
Status Uncommon to locally common, spreading due to extensive deforestation in most of its range, but local in Andes or in areas where deforestation is only recent. Wanders erratically in non-breeding season.
Habitat Tropical to Lower Subtropical Zones, to 1,750m in Colombia. Open moist to wet savannas, grassland, pastures, rice fields and other cultivated areas, and sometimes in moist to wet semi-open scrub, also open sandy savanna in Suriname where less common.

Red-breasted Blackbirds spend long periods in the open, and frequently sing from prominent exposed perches like meadowlarks

Voice Common *ee* call, a dry rattle, an alarmed *pist*, hard *pleek*, and *chit-chit*, *chirt*, *cha* and *kwak* notes. Song varies regionally, but usually consists of 3–6 weak, high metallic whistles followed by loud, drawn-out buzzy trill, e.g. *ti-ti-pee-pee-KWWAAAAHHH* or *chert-zeeeeee-e-e-e*, but in north-east Meta, Colombia, also a very different *keet...dear* song. Often delivered during showy flight displays, during which males ascend several metres then parachute down while singing (H&B, J&B, R&G, Hilty).
Note Formerly placed in genus *Leistes*.

PERUVIAN MEADOWLARK

Sturnella bellicosa Pl. 301

Identification 20.5–21cm. Short-tailed. Adult male has distinctive streaky upperparts, red breast and pale underwings (visible in flight). Female has black restricted to crown and cheeks, and red tone only on lower breast (compare female Red-breasted Blackbird which does not overlap). Juvenile has more streaking and lacks red below.

Ssp. *S. b. bellicosa* (W Ec)

Habits Forages alone, in pairs or small flocks on ground, but most conspicuous when perches on telephone poles and lines, posts, fences, wires, stumps, rocks, tall stems, bushes or low trees, which male also uses for singing and from which it may also commence short display flight. Flies in undulating sequences of flapping alternated with gliding.

Status Common.

Habitat Tropical to Temperate Zones, to 3,000m but usually below 2,500m. Open habitats, e.g. arid native grassland, open woodland, grassy pastures, irrigated fields and other cultivation, meadows along rivers, hedgerows, urban parks, desert scrub and other islands of greenery in deserts. Wintering flocks of up to 50+ move locally, sometimes into brushier habitats.

Voice A sharp raspy *chuck* and buzzing *tzp*. Song combines whistles, harsh phrases and buzzing notes and starts with several short notes followed by a long wheezy descending note, e.g. *tee-tee-zho-zhweeeeee*, whilst flight-song is longer and more varied (R&T, J&B, R&G).

Notes Also called Peruvian Red-breasted Meadowlark. Formerly considered conspecific with Red-breasted Blackbird.

EASTERN MEADOWLARK

Sturnella magna Pl. 301

Identification 21.5–24 cm. Short-tailed. Adult dark brown above with buffy fringes giving a streaked and scaled appearance, pale buffy supercilium from lores over eye to nape-sides, blackish line from eye to neck-sides, pale brown cheeks and pale mesial, unmistakable yellow underparts with black crescent on breast and black streaks on sides and flanks to undertail-coverts. White outer tail-feathers in flight. Eyes dark, bill sharply pointed, blackish above, blue-grey below, legs and feet grey. Juvenile has more buffy-yellow underparts with crescent composed of spots.

Ssp. *S. m. meridionalis* (C Co, NW Ve) longest-billed subspecies, darker with broader barring on rectrices and tertials, chestnut wing panel
S. m. paralios (N Co, C Ve) more buffy nape, paler cheeks contrasting with dark eyeline
S. m. praticola (E Co, SE Ve, Guianas) smaller than *meridionalis* or *paralios*, more chestnut above
S. m. quinta (Su) greyer fringes to coverts and secondaries than *paralios* or *praticola*

Habits Usually forages alone, in pairs or small flocks on ground for invertebrates, but most conspicuous when it perches on telephone poles and lines, posts, fences, wires, stumps, rocks, tall stems, bushes or low trees, which male also uses for singing. Flies in undulating sequence of rapid shallow flapping alternated with gliding on stiffly downcurved wings.

Status Fairly common to locally common, spreading due to deforestation.

Habitat Tropical Zone to Páramo, to 3,500m. Exclusively in moist open habitats with grass and leaf-litter, e.g. savannas, grassland, pastures, planted and fallow fields and other agricultural areas, grazed shore meadows, and man-made clearings.

Voice Year-round song is melodious series of 3–5 slurred whistles with some regional variation, e.g. *cheewa-seea, chewa-chorra* in western Venezuela (R&T, Hilty).

Note Race *monticola* is a synonym of *praticola*.

RED-BELLIED GRACKLE

Hypopyrrhus pyrohypogaster Pl. 300

Identification Male 30–31.5cm, female 27cm. Long-tailed. All-black adult has unmistakable red belly to undertail-coverts, pale yellow eyes and narrow, glossy lanceolate feathers over entire head, nape and throat. Juvenile blackish-brown with orange belly to undertail-coverts and greyish-yellow eyes.

Ssp. Monotypic (W Andes & southernmost E & C Andes in Co)

Habits Noisy and conspicuous as it forages alone or in pairs in breeding season and in small flocks of up to 16 or so, during non-breeding season. Searches foliage, vine tangles, and cracks and tufts of moss from subcanopy to canopy, for invertebrates and fruits. Sometimes joins mixed-species flocks with large tanagers, Masked Tityras, Green Jays, caciques and oropendolas.

Status Endangered. Endemic to Colombia where only found in a few, well-separated localities (e.g. Cordillera de los Picachos, Cueva de los Guácharos, Las Orquideas and Tatamá National Parks, Ucumarí Regional Park and several other reserves), where it may be fairly common. Fragmented distribution certainly due to widespread and continuing deforestation. Also persecuted as a maize crop-pest and trapped for cagebird trade.

Habitat Tropical to Temperate Zones, 800–2,700m. Humid primary forest and edges on montane slopes, often in more open habitats, e.g. scrubby growth, mature second growth and even plantations of non-native trees.

Voice Variety of typically liquid, gurgling or wheezy grackle sounds, e.g. *glok-glok*, *shleee-o*, *shleee* (R&T), with a loud shrieking *peep* in contact (J&B).

VELVET-FRONTED GRACKLE

Lampropsar tanagrinus Pl. 300

Identification Male 20.3–23.5cm, female 19–21cm. Adult male entirely black with very slight blue gloss, short thin conical bill and long fan-shaped tail. Shows rounded wings in flight. Adult female slightly duller below. Juvenile has more brownish plumage with no gloss and looser texture. See Pale-eyed Blackbird and Solitary Cacique. Carib Grackle has yellow eyes and short tail. Male Shiny Cowbird has thicker bill, shorter tail and bluer gloss.

Ssp. *L. t. guianensis* (Ve, NW Gu) smaller with more blue gloss below and browner underwings than nominate
L. t. tanagrinus (NE Ec, E Co) as described

Habits Noisy (constantly calling) but retiring as it forages for invertebrates in foliage, bromeliads and other epiphytes, cracks in bark, tangles and hanging bunches of dead leaves, and sometimes on ground or floating vegetation for invertebrates and fruits, Travels in pairs (possibly only in breeding season) or flocks of usually <10 (but sometimes <100) individuals, from understorey to canopy. Joins mixed-species flocks, e.g. with tanagers and caciques.

Status Uncommon and local in north-east Ecuador, uncommon to fairly common in east Colombia, very local but fairly common in Venezuela.

Habitat Lower Tropical Zone, to 400m. Almost invariably at humid forest edges near water, e.g. in *igapó* and *várzea* forests along rivers and around river islands, oxbow lakes, *cochas* and ponds, also in low-lying gallery forests and mangroves.

Voice Soft *pwit* whistles mixed with scolding *trrrrrr* rattles, a *chack* in flight and higher semi-whistled *cheziit* and fast chuckling *ch-ch-ch-ch-ch* when foraging. Song (most frequently crepuscular) begins with several soft *chuck*'s and ends in a liquid, fairly melodious 3-note phrase, e.g. *chuh-duh-duhree, chá-chá, gluk-gluk-glí-gluk*, or *puk, chur-cal-a-wík* varied to *chek, chuk, churcal-a- wík* or *chuk-your-Wheat* (H&B, J&B, R&G, Hilty).

GOLDEN-TUFTED GRACKLE

Macroagelaius imthurni Pl. 300

Identification Male 28cm, female 25–25.5cm. All-black adult male has slim body, long slim bill, very long tail, dark eyes and diagnostic golden axillary tufts (sometimes hidden, visible in flight). Adult female has slightly shorter tail. Juvenile duller blackish-brown with brown chin and no blue gloss. Habitat, habits and voice distinguish this grackle. Glossier and chunkier Carib Grackle and Shiny Cowbird only occur at lower elevations.

Ssp. Monotypic (Ve, Gu)

Habits Noisy and conspicuous as it forages in flocks (of up to 40) for invertebrates and fruits, in canopy. Apparently follows but does not join mixed-species flocks.

Status Uncommon to locally fairly common, but very poorly known.

Habitat Tropical to Lower Subtropical Zones, 500–2,000m. Humid to wet forests and edges with abundant epiphytes on higher slopes of tepuis, and more semi-open habitats, e.g. stunted and cloud forests, overgrown clearings, riparian corridors and even roadsides.

Voice A flat *chup* and ringing *whee* whistle in flight. Squeaky, jumbled, tinkling and variable calls and/or song given both in flight and when foraging. Song includes squeaks, *chup* calls, whistles and other shrill notes, and often includes some duetting: male sings high *ku-tlée*, female responds antiphonally *E-tlit* (or similar), whilst chorus of up to 25 individuals may sound like a cheerful tinkling *kut…ku-tlée, E-lit…kiew! tut… skreedle-E-churk…jerk-jerk-ET…* (J&B, Hilty).

Notes Also called Tepui Mountain Grackle and Golden-tufted Mountain Grackle, and sometimes considered conspecific with Mountain Grackle.

MOUNTAIN GRACKLE

Macroagelaius subalaris Pl. 300

Identification Male 28–30cm, female 26–28cm. All-black adult has slim body, long slim bill, very long tail, dark eyes, diagnostic chestnut epaulets, wing-linings and axillary tufts (all may be hard to see). Juvenile duller blackish-brown with less and only patchy blue gloss. Habitat and habits (similar to Golden-tufted Grackle but very poorly known) distinguish this grackle. Glossier and chunkier Carib Grackle, Shiny Cowbird and Giant Cowbird (also much larger with distinctive neck ruff) only occur at lower elevations.

Ssp. Monotypic (W slope of E Andes in Co)

Habits Usually observed in small groups.

Status Critically Endangered. Endemic to Colombia where recently only found at one small locality (Reserva Natural Guanentá-Alto Río Fonce, Santander, *c.*100km^2), where common but threatened by continuing deforestation. May occur at other forested localities elsewhere.

Habitat Subtropical to Temperate Zones, 1,750–3,150m. Humid forests and edges of montane slopes.

Voice Unknown.

Notes Also called Colombian Mountain Grackle. Sometimes considered conspecific with Golden-tufted Grackle.

SCRUB BLACKBIRD

Dives warszewiczi Pl. 300

Identification Male 24cm, female 23cm. Adult male all black with slight greenish-blue gloss, dark eyes and rather heavy bill. Rounded wings in flight. Female slightly duller. Juvenile even duller blackish-brown with less and only patchy blue gloss. Much larger Great-tailed Grackle has yellow eyes, longer wedge-shaped and creased tail, more gloss and occurs only near coast. Much smaller Shiny Cowbird is smaller billed and glossed purple. Much larger Giant Cowbird has yellow or red eyes and more gloss.

Ssp. *D. w. warszewiczi* (W Ec)

Habits Noisy and conspicuous as it forages alone, in pairs or small flocks on ground, sometimes around cattle, always near bushes or trees where it often perches and sings.

Status Fairly common to common, especially in moderately arid to semi-humid coastal lowlands and lower foothills in south, spreading north due to deforestation and irrigation, and will probably soon reach south-west Colombia.

Habitat Tropical to Subtropical Zones, to 2,800m but usually below 1,000m. Open and semi-open habitats with scattered large trees, e.g. forest edge, light woodland, shrubby areas, agricultural land, tree groves, hedgerows, orchards, urban parks and gardens. In desert habitats, found in irrigated lands, oases and riparian areas.

Voice Calls include a series of sharp *teeeew* given in flight. Song a loud ringing series of clear melodious whistles, interspersed with shrill notes, sharp buzzes and short chatters, e.g. *wr-tzzzeeét, worgleeo, wor-gleeo-glezeé*; sexes often bob and toss their heads while duetting complex songs (Shiny Cowbird does not bob) (J&B, R&G).

GREAT-TAILED GRACKLE

Quiscalus mexicanus Pl. 300

Identification Male 43–46cm, female 32–34cm. Adult male has yellow eyes, greenish-blue gloss, long, heavy bill, and very long, creased, keel- and wedge-shaped tail. Adult female has yellowish to pale brown eyes, shorter tail and is dusky brown above with buffy supercilium and paler buffy-brown below, becoming duskier towards vent. Juvenile has brown eyes and thin dark brown streaks below. Much smaller Carib Grackle has proportionately shorter tail. Somewhat smaller Giant Cowbird has shorter bill, shorter, rounded and flat tail and often has distinctive neck ruff.

Ssp. *Q. m. peruvianus* (coastal W Ec, Co, NW Ve)

Habits Conspicuous, noisy and bold as it forages, sometimes alone but mostly in flocks on ground, often on muddy shorelines, scavenging anything edible. Roosts and nests in sometimes very large flocks in mangroves or trees.

Status Locally fairly common to common, may be spreading inland along larger rivers.

Habitat Lower Tropical Zone, to 100m. Open and semi-open habitats with scattered large trees near coast, e.g. beaches, estuaries, coastal rivers, mangroves, savannas, pastures, marshes, agricultural fields, and especially coastal towns, waterfronts, parks and gardens. In Ecuador, tied to at least remnant patches of mangroves.

Voice A fast sharp oft-repeated *trit* and harsh guttural *chak* often given in flight. Male utters shrill, quavering, drawn-out *kuuueeeeeeee*. Song consists of some snapping notes followed by undulating *chewe-chewe* notes, faster snapping notes, and finally several loud *cha-wee* notes (R&G, Hilty).

Note Formerly placed in genus *Cassidix* (R&G).

CARIB GRACKLE

Quiscalus lugubris Pl. 300

Identification Male 24.5–27.5cm, female 20.5–23cm. Adult male is all glossy black with strong purple gloss, and distinctive somewhat creased, keel- and wedge-shaped tail with rounded end. Eyes pale yellow. Subspecies differ slightly in size, female coloration and voice. Adult female dark brown above without gloss, paler below, especially on throat, and flat tail. Juvenile like female but has dark eyes, and juvenile male has patchy blue gloss. See Solitary Cacique and Velvet-fronted Grackle, and non-overlapping Golden-tufted, Mountain and Great-tailed Grackles. Smaller Shiny Cowbird has dark eyes and shorter bill and tail. Larger Giant Cowbird has different body shape.

Ssp. *Q. l. insularis* (Margarita & Los Frailes Is., off Ve) larger than nominate, but smaller than *luminosus*
Q. l. lugubris (NE Co, N Ve, T&T, N Gu, N Su, N FG) as described
Q. l. luminosus (Los Testigos I., off Ve) thinner and longer bill than *insularis*, extensive violet gloss on head and body, female slightly paler than *insularis*, juvenile more densely streaked than other subspecies
Q. l. orquillensis (Los Hermanos Is., off Ve) like *insularis* but central tail-feathers without gloss

Habits Struts upright and displays frequently. Conspicuous, noisy and bold as it forages, sometimes alone but mostly in flocks on ground, scavenging anything edible. Roosts and nests in sometimes very large flocks in mangroves, trees or palms. Will defend nest area by dive-bombing passers-by and hitting them on the head, sometimes yanking hair. Males gather on exposed perch, such as a TV aerial, and sing, competitively in kind of chaotic lek – not visited by females!

Status Locally fairly common to abundant. Introduced to Tobago and Aruba, vagrant to Bonaire, March 1980 (ffrench). Possibly some local seasonal movements in Llanos. Spreading due to deforestation.

Habitat Lower Tropical Zone, to 850m. Open and semi-open habitats with scattered large trees, e.g. beaches, planted or open fields and other agricultural lands, around farms in *llanos*, urban areas, parks, golf courses and gardens, especially abundant in seaside areas, also at edge of gallery forests, but avoids closed-canopy forests. Young mangroves in French Guiana.

Voice Calls include alarm *chuck* and oft-repeated, loud ringing *queek*, both bell-like and metallic. Also *tick*, a rapid *chi-chi-chi-chi* and loud descending *keerr*. Song a series of harsh squeaks and clucks, often ending in ringing bell-like tone, e.g. *wee-tsi-ke-tsi-ke-tsi-ke*, *queek-queek-queek*, *etsywee* or *tickita-tick-tick-tickita-tickita-ting* on Trinidad (ffrench, J&B, Hilty).

SHINY COWBIRD

Molothrus bonariensis Pl. 301

Identification Male 18–22cm, female 17–19cm. Adult male all black with strong purple-blue gloss, dark eyes, short thick conical bill and square tail. Subspecies differ slightly in size and female coloration. Adult female greyish-brown above with faint pale supercilium, and paler below. Juvenile like female but has faint brown streaks below, with juvenile male darker than female appearing blackish-grey, whilst juvenile female is more yellowish-buffy than female. Overall small-headed, barrel-chested, short-billed and short-tailed, whilst dark eyes, habits and voice further help to distinguish this species (especially drabber females which are, however, mostly accompanied by males) from similar Chestnut-capped, Pale-eyed and Scrub Blackbirds, and Velvet-fronted, Golden-tufted Grackle, Mountain and Carib Grackles. Slightly smaller, more brownish and shorter-tailed Bronzed Cowbird has red eyes as adult.

Ssp. *M. b. aequatorialis* (W Ec, SW Co) female very dark with more prominent pale supercilium

M. b. cabanisii (NW, W & C Co) largest race, most purple gloss on male
M. b. minimus (T&T, Guianas) smallest race
M. b. occidentalis (SW Ec) palest female, greyish-white with more prominent pale supercilium and faint dusky streaks below
M. b. riparius (E Ec) female darker above and paler below, with throat distinctly paler
M. b. venezuelensis (E Co, Ve, recorded Curaçao: Debrot & Prins 1992) female pale below

Habits Walks with tail slightly cocked. Forages for invertebrates, sometimes around cattle and sometimes picking ticks off them, also a pest in maize fields and rice paddies. Sometimes alone, occasionally in small single-sex groups, but more often in small to large flocks, mostly on ground. Roosts in large flocks of up to several thousand, preferably in reedbeds, but also in mangroves and trees.
Status Fairly common to abundant. Widespread, and spreading to Caribbean islands and Florida, colonising deforested areas very quickly.
Habitat Tropical to Subtropical Zones, to 2,700m but usually below 2000m. Dry to humid open and semi-open, mostly disturbed, habitats with scattered trees and bushes (avoids closed-canopy forests), e.g. clearings, second growth, open woodland, plantations, tree groves, savannas, grassland, pastures, river and lake shores, floodplains, riparian thickets, hedgerows, agricultural land and urban areas.
Voice A *chuck* note and several clear high whistles in flight. Female does not sing and only utters harsh chatters and rattles. Male song usually given from prominent perch and is complex musical twittering, warbling and whistling with a few harsh notes, often preceded by several wheezing notes as male puffs himself up with feathers ruffled, e.g. several liquid purrs followed by high whistle, *purr-purr-purr-pe-tssss-teeeee*, sometimes followed by more twittering and flight whistles (ffrench, J&B, R&G, Hilty).
Note Also called Glossy Cowbird.

BRONZED COWBIRD
Molothrus aeneus Pl. 301

Identification 18.5–20cm. Short-tailed. Adult male all black with strong bronze gloss to upperparts and purple and turquoise gloss on wings, dark red eyes (sometimes hard to see), and small neck ruff (lacking in male Shiny Cowbird). Female only very slightly smaller and duller, and is much darker than female Shiny Cowbird, which is much paler greyish-brown, especially below. Juvenile dark brown with faint dark streaks, no gloss and dark eyes (also much darker than juvenile Shiny Cowbird).

Ssp. *M. a. armenti* (N coast of Co)

Habits Walks with tail slightly cocked. Forages on ground for invertebrates and seeds (sometimes rice), alone or in small flocks. Often joins other cowbirds, blackbirds, grackles and anis.
Status Very rare and local, with populations apparently diminishing (recent records only from western half of Isla de Salamanca National Park, north-west Magdalena, but previously also reported from provinces further west, possibly to Córdoba). Reports from Leticia, south-west Colombia, erroneous (H&B).
Habitat Lower Tropical Zone, near sea level, in open dry habitats with scattered vegetation, e.g. lightly wooded, xerophytic areas, dry brush and scrub, sandy grasslands and roadsides, and sometimes farmlands, e.g. rice fields.
Voice Song not melodious, e.g. *eez-eez-dzlee* or somewhat similar, usually given whilst puffing up head and neck feathers (H&B).
Note Race *armenti* endemic to Colombia and sometimes considered a separate species called Bronze-brown Cowbird (H&B, R&T, J&B).

GIANT COWBIRD
Scaphidura oryzivora Pl. 301

Identification Male 35–38cm, female 28–33cm. Adult male all black with purplish-blue gloss, large, black downcurved bill with small but diagnostic frontal shield, orange-red to pale yellow eyes, and distinctive long-tailed and small-headed body shape, appearing hunched because of distinctive neck ruff ('bull neck'). In flight has small head, deep chest, long wings and tail (less so in female). Adult female has less gloss and no neck ruff, thus appearing larger headed but retaining distinctive cowbird body shape. Juvenile male is blackish-brown with no gloss, pale bill, brown, greyish or even whitish-yellow eyes, and no neck ruff (thus looking most like Solitary Cacique). See also Pale-eyed Blackbird, Mountain Grackle, Scrub Blackbird and Great-tailed Grackle.

Ssp. *S. o. oryzivora* (Ec, Co, Ve, Tr, To, Guianas)

Habits Long pointed wings of male make obvious flight noise. Flies in distinctive undulating sequences of a few rapid flaps alternated with brief closed-wing glides. Obligate brood parasite of oropendolas or caciques, and even solicits preening from hosts and other species. Walks with tail slightly cocked. Males often sit quietly on high exposed perches, whilst warier females are seldom seen. Forages alone, in pairs or small flocks on ground for invertebrates, sometimes around cattle and may pick ticks off them, as well as in tree canopies, searching for invertebrates in cracks and holes by ripping bark from trees or by gleaning leaves, but also for fruits and nectar. Frequently visits *Erythrina* trees, and corn and rice.
Status Uncommon to locally common, partially dependent on abundance of host species, but disperses widely, with vagrants found far from host colonies, and possibly spreading due to deforestation. Recently colonised Tobago.
Habitat Tropical to Subtropical Zones, to 2,200m but mostly below 1,500m. Semi-humid to humid forests and mature second growth (unlike other cowbirds), also forest edges, semi-open and disturbed forest and woodland, plantations, river and lake shores, pastures and farmland – anywhere with colonies of oropendolas or caciques which it parasitises.
Voice Rather silent, thus differs from many other icterids,

especially grackles, but also fruitcrows and jays. Calls sharp and chattering, including a *chechk-chechk*, longer *chrrik rrik-rrik-rrik-rrik-rrik-rrik*, a high *mew* (*meew* in juveniles), low *dak*, grating *dzt-dzt-dzt*, and musical *pernt* in flight. Male song an unmusical sequence of a screechy whistle followed by 3+ short, metallic and often paired notes, e.g. *tchwweeeee twi-dlee tic-tic* or *shhweaa t-pic-pic*, *tew-tew-hee* on Trinidad. Male also utters nasal, metallic *neek* or *neck-neck* when foraging (ffrench, J&B, Hilty).
Note Formerly placed in genus *Cassidix* or *Scaphidura*, but probably best placed with *Molothrus* (J&B).

BOBOLINK *Dolichonyx oryzivorus* Pl. 301

Identification 17–18cm. Thick conical bill, short, graduated and spiky tail. Non-breeding adult male and female are sparrow-like: distinctive buffy head with dusky stripes, black and buffy streaks above and yellowish-buffy underparts with narrow dusky streaks on sides and flanks. Breeding male (only encountered on northbound migration in April–May) is unmistakable with its buffy nape and otherwise black-and-white plumage, but may still be moulting in spring. Immature has richer coloration, faint breast streaks and buffy (not whitish) throat. Juvenile has streaking confined to sides of breast.

When alarmed whilst foraging on ground, Bobolinks stand still in an upright position and watch alertly, ready to fly low over grass to alight further on

Ssp. Monotypic (boreal migrant; in transit through northern South America)
Habits Forages in fields of rice or wild grasses, and often roosts in reedbeds. Migrants often pause only briefly at stopovers and are wary and retiring. Whilst southbound flocks may number many thousands, northbound flocks tend to be much smaller.
Status Breeds in North America and winters mainly in temperate South America, passing through northern South America (including Aruba, Bonaire and Curaçao). Rarer in western Ecuador than in east, and passage throughout region is generally in September–November and February–May (but also noted in June and October on Trinidad, February and October on Tobago). Irregular and local, and rarer in spring.
Habitat Tropical Zone, usually below 500m but to 4,000m on migration. In rice fields, reedbeds, open marshes, wet pastures and riparian thickets, but may be seen anywhere on migration. Autumn migration route tends to be more westerly than spring.
Voice Calls include a soft low *chuk* and distinctive soft, musical and clear *peenk* or *bink*. Rarely heard song in spring is rapid series of cheerful bubbly notes on widely different pitches (J&B, Sibley, Hilty).

FRINGILLIDAE – Finches

Siskins and Goldfinches

The large family Fringillidae, formerly represented solely by the carduelids, now contains two subfamilies in the Neotropics, the present Carduelinae, and the Euphoniinae which follows. New World siskins are part of the same family that ranges across the Old World, some being called goldfinches. With a unique exception, they are yellow and black, each colour varying significantly, and there are infusions of green in the plumage, especially on juveniles. All have bright yellow wing panels and forked tails that act as clear social signals in flight, and they generally have a distinctive, undulating jizz when flying. Siskins and goldfinches sing sweetly, and the entire family is a favourite of the cagebird fraternity, whilst cross-breeding males with female canaries is a favourite pastime throughout the world. This has resulted in many species being hunted to the brink of extinction, and attempts to establish thriving strains of domesticated birds to meet this demand have faltered regularly.

They are usually birds of open woodland, parks and gardens, grassland and scrub, and as such are always evident. They build small, cup-shaped nests, usually placed a few metres above ground, and produce 2 broods a year. They tend to flock and wander over shrubby grassland when not breeding, and fly only a short distance when disturbed, although repeated disturbance may cause them to fly further afield out of sight.

Additional reference used to prepare this family: Clement, Harris & Davis (1993, hereafter CHD).

ANDEAN SISKIN
Carduelis spinescens Pl. 302

Identification 9.5–11cm. Adult male olive above with black cap, typical wing and distinctive tail pattern, and yellowish-olive below. Base of secondaries and primaries pure yellow, the tertials fringes white. In worn plumage, white on tertials significantly reduced and perhaps even almost absent. Basal third of outer tail-feathers yellow. Adult female lacks cap, is much duller overall and whiter below, but retains distinctive wing pattern (albeit with slightly less yellow). Immature male like female but has black cap and darker centres to feathers of mantle darker. Juvenile paler than female, with male greener above, female slightly buffier above, and paler, slightly buffy below. Both sexes of Yellow-faced Siskin (no overlap) are brighter yellow below and have different habitat preferences. Female Yellow-bellied Siskin is darker above and more 3-toned below with greyish-olive chin and throat, olive-yellow breast and belly, and paler yellowish-white lower belly and vent. In area of overlap (northern Ecuador / southern Colombia), female Hooded Siskin has whitish (not yellowish) underparts. Lesser Goldfinch has white wingbars.

Ssp. *C. s. spinescens* (Santa Marta & E Andes in Co, N & W Ve) black tail with yellow at base of outer feathers, female differs from male (see above)
C. s. nigricauda (N Ec, C & W Andes in Co) all-black tail, female almost like male but slightly duller, with black cap and yellowish-olive underparts, lacks yellow base to outer tail-feathers

Habits Forages alone, in pairs or small flocks at all levels, but often on ground (only occasionally high) mainly for seeds, and sometimes joins mixed flocks of other finches.
Status Rare to locally fairly common in Ecuador, in rest of range locally fairly common to common, but presence often seasonal, apparently due to propensity for nomadic wandering.
Habitat Subtropical Zone to Páramo, 1,500–4,100m. Moist to humid, semi-open habitats, e.g. open woodland, cloud or elfin forest and edges near treeline, thickets, open hillsides, pastures, agriculture, suburbs with scattered vegetation and páramos with scrub, low bushes and *Espeletia* species (a favourite food plant).
Voice Calls include a goldfinch-like *tsweee*, often given in flight. Song a lively, rambling, long-sustained series of high chips, twitters and trills (H&B, Hilty).
Note Nominate *spinescens* (together with *capitanea*, which we consider to be a synonym) may be a separate species from *nigricauda* (Robbins *et al.* 1994).

YELLOW-FACED SISKIN *Carduelis yarrellii* Pl. 302

Identification 10cm. Adult male greenish above, including median and lesser wing-coverts, black wings and tail with yellow markings. Tips of greater wing-coverts broadly yellow forming bold wingbar, lower rump and all tail-coverts bright yellow; black cap and clear pale yellow below. Female similar but lacks cap. Juvenile paler below than female, and significantly buffy above with no pale fringes to tertials. Lack of bib separates it from Andean Siskin, also pure yellow underparts and uppertail-coverts, and no overlap in habitat or range. Female Yellow-bellied Siskin is more 3-toned below with greyish-olive chin and throat, olive-yellow breast and belly, and paler yellowish-white lower belly and undertail-coverts. Lesser Goldfinch has white wingbars.

Ssp. Monotypic (Ve: see status)

Habits In its Brazilian range, forages for seeds and small fruits.
Status Vulnerable. In north-east Brazil threatened by habitat loss, pesticide application and heavy bird trade. Status in Venezuela and Guyana quite uncertain. Specimens exist from 2 sites in Carabobo, Venezuela, but these were probably escapes, although cagebird breeders maintain that a population persists in southern Carabobo, and there are rumours of another, larger population in western Monagas, but recent confirmed records are non-existent: perhaps all records refer to escaped cagebirds, which begs the issue of their origin. Recent reports claim of a roost site near the Brazilian border, at Santa Elena de Uairén, Bolívar state. Nothing published.
Habitat Lower Tropical Zone, to 500m. Humid lowland forest and mature second growth, mostly at edges, farmland with stands of trees, coffee and cocoa plantations.
Voice Song is a complex and varied series of high, sweet twitters and warbles typical of genus (BirdLife 2004).

RED SISKIN *Carduelis cucullata* Pl. 302

Identification 10–11cm. Brown back and wing-coverts washed red, lower back to uppertail-coverts red, wings black with red panel and wingbar, white fringes to tertials that abrade gradually; tail black with basal third of outer feathers red, dark centres to long uppertail-coverts; hood deep black, underparts crimson-red. Female essentially warm grey, with some brownish wash on top of head, back and wing-coverts, washed pale red on breast, red rump and short uppertail-coverts, wings and tail black with same red panels as male and white fringes to tertials. Immature male like female but somewhat browner and more uniform above. Young female greyer than male, and juveniles similar, but duller and darker above, and paler, almost yellowish below. Adult male unmistakable, but adult female, which has only red rump, wingbars, primary bases and reddish tone to flanks, may look like female Vermilion Flycatcher at a glance, at rest and if alone.

Ssp. Monotypic (NE Co, N & NW Ve, SW Gu)

Habits Forages alone, in pairs and small to (formerly) large flocks at all levels for seeds, nectar, flower buds, and small fruits, e.g. mistletoes, cacti and *Ficus* species.
Status Endangered. Probably only a few thousand remain in Colombia and Venezuela due to relentless illegal trapping for cagebird trade, and habitat loss due to expanding agriculture. Now very rare and local throughout its mostly Venezuelan range, and extremely rare and local in Norte de Santander, Colombia. Most recent records in Venezuela are from edges of coffee plantations on Andean slopes in Barinas and from scrub in valleys at western end of Coastal Cordillera. Seems to move semi-nomadically and altitudinally, both daily and seasonally, making accurate censuses difficult, although range within which it wanders unknown and may be fairly restricted. Formerly rare in Trinidad but trapped to extinction in early 1960s (ffrench). The few ornithologists who know of populations keep them secret for fear of trappers, and similarly trappers keep their locations secret to safeguard their resources. A recently discovered population in Guyana (Robbins *et al.* 2003) is already being reduced by trappers and it is hoped that urgently taken conservation action may not prove too late.
Habitat Tropical Zone, 100–1,300m (once at 1,700m). Drier to moist semi-open deciduous woodland and edges of humid forest, and more open areas with weeds, grasses and scattered shrubs and trees.
Voice Calls include a raspy, piercing *chut* or *jut*, often doubled as *chut-chut* or *chi-tit*, a clear, high, bell-like *ta-lee*, the second

note rising, and various high twitters and trills. Song a long, twittering series of semi-musical trills and chatters (H&B, CHD, Hilty).

HOODED SISKIN

Carduelis magellanica Pl. 303

Identification 10–11.5cm. Adult male olive-green above with black hood, yellow rump and uppertail-coverts, typical wing pattern of yellow panel and white fringes to tertials, black tail with basal quarter of outer feathers yellow, but not easy to see unless uppertail-coverts are worn, all-black hood and throat, and all yellow below. In worn plumage, tertials fringes abrade and may wear off completely. Bill blackish. Adult female lacks black on head, in fresh plumage is brighter and paler green above and whiter below, but retains distinctive wing and tail pattern, and blackish bill. In worn plumage pale fringes to upperparts abraded and dark centres to feathers much more apparent, whilst white fringes to tertials are lost. Juvenile has fine dark streaks on upperparts, but looks more uniform above than adult female, and is slightly duller buffier grey than female. Immature male may show some irregular black spotting or streaking on head. In worn plumage, female very difficult to separate from female Andean Siskin, except for darker bill, but juveniles have similar bill. Olivaceous Siskin very similar to race *capitalis*, but has slightly brighter, more olive-yellow coloration (especially below and especially in females), different habitat preferences (mostly forest-based, rarely feeds on ground) and little overlap, usually occurring at lower elevations (but hybridises with Hooded where they do). Very similar male Saffron Siskin generally brighter with more golden-olive back (lacks faint dark feather centres of Hooded) and more pure yellow underparts, and usually occurs at lower elevations. Female and juvenile Saffron Siskins are generally much brighter yellow than Hooded Siskin, especially below. Female Yellow-bellied Siskin is darker above and more 3-toned below with greyish-olive chin and throat, olive-yellow breast and belly, and paler yellowish-white lower belly and undertail-coverts. Lesser Goldfinch has white wingbars.

Ssp. *C. m. capitalis* (C & S Co, Ec) male has black on head extending only to chin and throat, very small yellow base to all tail-feathers; darker olive above, with yellow rump more concolorous with upperparts, and deeper golden-yellow below; female yellow above with pale-grey underparts and pale yellowish-olive tinge to throat and breast

C. m. longirostris (SE Ve, Gu) black hood extends over throat, whitish central belly and vent; pale green rump and uppertail-coverts in both sexes, yellow base to outer tail-feathers slightly more extensive, female distinctly pale grey on vent and undertail-coverts

C. m. paula (S Ec) male has less-streaked mantle and back, contrasting yellow rump and more extensive yellow in wings and tail, reaching fully halfway on outer tail-feathers; female greyer above, also with contrasting yellow rump, very similar to male but lacks black head

Habits Rapid undulating flight. Restless as it forages in pairs or small (sometimes large) flocks at all levels including ground, for seeds, buds, leaves and insects, often joins other finches.

Status Common and widespread in Ecuador, where the most common siskin, rare to locally fairly common in Colombia, uncommon and local in Venezuela, and uncertain in Guyana. Nomadic in some areas during non-breeding season.

Male Hooded Siskin in threat display

Habitat Tropical Zone to Páramo, 100–3,500m but usually above 1,000m (R&G), locally to *c*.4,000m (R&T) or even 5,000m (F&K). Dry to humid semi-open woodland, edge of humid, gallery and swamp forest, second growth, scrub and savannas or cultivated areas with scattered vegetation, e.g. edges of cocoa and palm plantations, hedgerows, parks and gardens.

Voice Calls include an oft-repeated, soft, sweet *djey* or *tseeu*, and long *trrrrrr* trill. Song a rapid, extended series of various short, twittering phrases, e.g. *tseet-tseet*, *tseet-weet*, or *tseet-weet-a-weeta*, given from perch or in flight, sometimes by several males simultaneously (H&B, F&K, CHD, R&G, Hilty).

SAFFRON SISKIN

Carduelis siemiradzkii Pl. 303

Identification 10–11cm. Uniform bright olive-green above, from rear crown to lower back, rump and uppertail-coverts yellow, long uppertail-coverts washed pale greenish; wings black with typical pattern of yellow panel and white fringes to tertials in fresh plumage, tail black with basal half of outer feathers bright yellow, clear bright yellow below. Female lacks black hood, but otherwise very similar. Juvenile slightly duller than female with less extensive yellow on wings. Male has a much smaller hood than other black-headed siskins, and uniform upperparts.

Ssp. Monotypic (SW Ec)

Habits Forages in pairs or flocks of up to 30. Restless as it forages in pairs or small (sometimes large) flocks, readily taking flight if disturbed. Forages at all levels including ground, for seeds, buds, leaves and insects, and often joins other finches.

Status Vulnerable. Probably only a few thousand individuals remain in Ecuador and extreme north-west Peru due to clearance of deciduous forests for agriculture and settlements, but appears highly tolerant of disturbed habitats. Found in only 3 protected areas: Machalilla National Park (Manabí), Cerro Blanco Protection Forest, and Manglares-Churute Ecological Reserve (both Guayas), otherwise uncommon to locally fairly common. Possibly nomadic, or undertakes seasonal and climate-driven movements, e.g. during El Niño events, but extent of movements unknown, though apparently limited.

Habitat Tropical Zone, to 1,300m but usually below 600m. Arid to dry semi-open habitats, e.g. deciduous forest, edges, second growth and scrub, along roadsides, streambeds and semi-dry ravines (especially weedy areas in quebradas and washes), and in scrubby farmland and pastures, suburbs and urban parks (even in central Guayaquil).
Voice Calls include a high twittering flight-call. Song similar to Hooded Siskin (R&G).

OLIVACEOUS SISKIN

Carduelis olivacea Pl. 303

Identification 10–11cm. Dark olive-green above, with darker centres to feathers, yellow rump and uppertail-coverts, latter with greenish tinge; strong yellow wingbar and typical yellow wing panel, but yellow (not white) fringes to tertials, hood completely black, reaching back further than hood of Saffron Siskin, yellow below tinged olive, reaching to border of black hood, where forms narrow collar between it and dark mantle. Bill blackish. Female similar, though less dark on mantle, lacks black hood and bill not quite as dark. In worn plumage both sexes lack fringes to tertials and become darker above. Juvenile duller, more buffy-brown than female, with brown streaks above and below, and a horn-coloured bill. Immature male resembles female but has spots or small patches of black on head.

Ssp. Monotypic (SE or E Ec?)

Habits Forages in pairs or small to large flocks in canopy and edges of montane forest, rarely visiting ground, and usually staying within or close to forest, but otherwise as Hooded Siskin.
Status Uncommon to locally fairly common in Ecuador, perhaps in southern Colombia.
Habitat Tropical to Lower Subtropical Zones, 750–1,700m but usually above 900m and mostly at 1,200–3,000m (R&T). In canopy, edges and clearings of dry forest, especially open spaces with scattered trees on upper slopes.
Voice Calls and song similar to Hooded Siskin, with flocks calling constantly (CHD).

YELLOW-BELLIED SISKIN

Carduelis xanthogastra Pl. 303

Identification 10–11.5cm. Adult male entirely black above, with typical yellow wing panel and basal half of tail-feathers, except central pair, but latter usually concealed by long black uppertail-coverts; black rump may be washed lightly or noticeably olivaceous-green, and black hood extends to breast. Sides of breast and rest of underparts pure deep yellow, sometimes faintly washed black, lending a slightly dirty or olivaceous tone, but which wears off. Immature male dark olivaceous on rump and uppertail-coverts, flight-feathers and tertials dark brown with vestigial pale fringes which abrade gradually, and yellow below is duller than older male. Adult female olive-green above, darker on back, brighter, yellowish on rump; chin whitish, throat and breast yellow well washed olive and very slightly flammulated, belly yellow, vent and undertail-coverts white. Juvenile buffy-grey above and paler and buffier than female below. Adult male unmistakable. Lesser Goldfinch has white wingbars, is more vocal and less tied to forest.

Ssp. *C. x. xanthogastra* (W Ec, Co, NW & N Ve)

Habits Forages for seeds, in pairs or small to large flocks of up to 30, at all levels but usually high.
Status Rare to uncommon and local in Ecuador, locally fairly common but erratic in Colombia and Venezuela (most common in southern Táchira). Probably nomadic in some areas. Males are prized by cagebird enthusiasts for cross-breeding with canaries, the resulting hybrids being valued songsters, and is this trapped in some areas.
Habitat Tropical to Temperate Zones, 500–3,000m, but usually at 1,400–2,000m. Canopy and edges of humid forest and coffee plantations, hedgerows, pastures, clearings, partially denuded slopes with stands of trees, and drier slopes with scattered bushes, rocks and farmland, but usually not in mainly open, deforested areas.
Voice Calls include a high *pee*. Song a fast, bubbling, complex series of melodious twitters, buzzy notes and musical sputtering, almost as if randomly generated, mixing high and thin with low nasal notes, the whole lasting 5–30 s (CHD, R&G, Hilty).

LESSER GOLDFINCH

Carduelis psaltria Pl. 302

Identification 10–10.5cm. Adult male in fresh plumage is black from forehead to tail, with white wing panel but no wingbar, and large white panel on underside of outer tail-feathers (but no markings on uppertail). Tertials broadly fringed white. From chin and mesial to undertail-coverts lemon-yellow. Bill shorter and more cone-shaped than siskins and is very pale. In worn plumage, white on tertials is completely abraded. Adult female in fresh plumage soft olive-green from forehead to uppertail-coverts, black wings and tail with broad white fringes to tertials, and no wing panel. Juvenile duller, buffy-grey above and paler buffy-brown below. Wings and tail dark brown, with pale fringes. Only siskin in northern South America with white (not yellow) wing panel in male, and complete lacks wingbar and panel in female and juvenile. Similar male euphonias have yellow foreheads and lack white in wing.

Ssp. *C. p. columbiana* (N & W Ec, N & C Co, N Ve)

Habits Forages alone or in pairs, but usually in small to large flocks of up to 50, at all levels for seeds.
Status Rare and local in Ecuador, common in Colombia, fairly common to common in Venezuela. Nomadic in non-breeding season when may be seen almost anywhere, and benefits from forest clearance.
Habitat Tropical to Temperate Zones, to 3,100m. Open to semi-open, dry to humid, weedy areas with scattered woody and bushy vegetation, e.g. deciduous woodland with thorn scrub, edges, shrubby clearings, grassy slopes, rushbeds, agriculture, hedgerows, roadsides, waste areas, suburban areas, parks and gardens.
Voice Calls include a sad, descending *pseee*, *peee-ee* or *kleeu*,

a grating, rattling *ch-ch-ch-ch*, and *chek-ek*, all frequently given in flight. Female has a plaintive and very distinct *chi-ru-lee* call and male a sad, descending *tsweee*. Rambling song is a disconnected, rising and falling series of musical twitters and scratchy notes (H&B, R&T, F&K, Hilty).

Note Also called Dark-backed Goldfinch.

Euphonias and Chlorophonias

Euphonias and chlorophonias were long considered part of the large subfamily Thraupinae, the tanagers, but recent DNA work, most notably by Burns (1997, 2002), Klicka *et al.* (2000), García-Moreno *et al.* (2001), Sato *et al.* (2001) and Yuri & Mindell (2002) has revealed that they are closest to siskins and goldfinches, a conclusion consistent with aspects of their voice, feeding and breeding behaviour. Euphonias are short-tailed, rather rotund-looking finches, brightly clad in dark blues and bright yellows, with various shades of green. Many species are confusingly similar, a situation compounded by racial variation, perhaps more amongst females than males, which are difficult enough, and it pays to keep careful notes of character, plumage (the white discs on the undertails are helpful) and behaviour, to construct a mental or actual portfolio of differences. They are generally arboreal and often seen in small groups in woodland treetops, where they frequently feed on their favourite mistletoe berries. Some species occur in more open areas and even in savannas with scattered trees. Generally indifferent to human presence, some are regularly found in city parks and gardens.

PLUMBEOUS EUPHONIA

Euphonia plumbea Pl. 304

Identification 9.5cm. Very small. Adult male has glossy steel grey (washed yellow) upperparts and hood, black wings and tail with olivaceous coverts; mid breast to undertail-coverts yellow-orange with grey-mottled sides, flanks, thighs and underwing-coverts white. Eyes dark brown, bill black, base pale grey, legs and feet plumbeous. Adult female paler, more yellow-washed grey above, especially yellowish on rump and uppertail-coverts, with grey head and nape, olive-yellow below with paler yellow-washed grey throat and breast, belly to undertail-coverts olive washed yellow. Eyes dark, bill, legs and feet dark grey. Larger male Rufous-bellied Euphonia is darker overall (more bluish above and orange below). Female White-lored Euphonia has white lores and pale grey underparts. Female White-vented Euphonia has distinct pale grey throat, central belly and vent.

Ssp. Monotypic (S Ve, Guianas)

Habits Forages for fruit and berries, from mid to upper levels of bushes and trees. Usually in pairs, sometimes in small flocks, and sometimes joins mixed-species flocks.

Status Uncommon to locally common in Venezuela, but only sight records from north-east Guainía in SE Colombia, and rare and local in the Guianas.

Habitat Tropical Zone, usually below 300m but to 1,000m in Venezuela. Scrubby open woodland, savanna woodland and edges, shrubby clearings, scattered vegetation in savanna, and scrub around large rocky outcrops in white sandy soil regions; sometimes also at edges of tall forest.

Voice Calls include a clear, high, slightly nasal, even- and moderately-pitched *dee* or *dee-dee*, or *dee, dee-dee*, given slowly or rapidly and often repeated; also a soft, short *wit* when foraging. Song, usually delivered atop tall vegetation, a long series of squeaky, jumbled and twittering notes at moderate to high pitch, e.g. *o'fiddle-de-wEET!*, *WEET sweet-a-swee-swee*, *weetu-chit*, or *witchay-chewit … witchay-chewit*, often mixed with *dee-dee* calls (Snyder, H&B, R&T, I&I, Hilty).

PURPLE-THROATED EUPHONIA

Euphonia chlorotica Pl. 304

Identification 9–10cm. Adult male glossy purplish (sometimes appears violet), white inner webs to basal half of all remiges except outer primary, and bold white spot on underside of outer tail-feathers, with bright yellow forecrown, breast, belly and undertail-coverts. Adult female olive above with faint grey tinge (lacking in Trinidad Euphonia) and orange-yellow forehead and throat (also lacking in Trinidad Euphonia), dusky lores, and mostly greyish below with yellowish sides and flanks, yellow undertail-coverts. Subadult male like female but has dull yellow underparts and tail more distinctly marked with white. Juvenile female all yellow below. Juvenile male like female but has full yellow forehead and throat, plus a few black feathers on throat and a few rich yellow feathers on breast. Virtually identical to Trinidad Euphonia, but only limited overlap, mostly just south of Orinoco (thus best separated by range). Male Trinidad Euphonia has yellow crown extending further behind eyes, and a more steely blue gloss. Slightly larger male Orange-bellied Euphonia has slightly more ochraceous forecrown and underparts. Slightly larger female Thick-billed and Violaceous Euphonias both have heavier build, thicker bill and yellow-olive underparts, and female White-vented has more extensively olive-yellow underparts.

Ssp. *E. c. chlorotica* (Guianas) as described, yellow on crown ends at rear crown

E. c. cynophora (NE Co, S Ve) strong violaceous gloss above and on throat, more extensive yellow cap and deeper yellow below

E. c. taczanowskii (río Marañón drainage, SE Ec) more purple above, paler yellow crown patch ends level with middle of eye, and paler yellow below; juvenile female is far less extensive grey below

Habits Forages actively and vociferously, in pairs but sometimes alone or in small flocks. Usually high (but lower at edges and in scrub) looking for fruit, berries (especially mistletoe), seeds and invertebrates. Sometimes joins mixed-species flocks.

Status Uncommon to fairly common in Ecuador, where only occurs around Zumba in río Marañón drainage of southern Zamora-Chinchipe, fairly common in Colombia and Venezuela, and fairly common in Guyana, rare in Suriname and French Guiana.

Habitat Tropical Zone, 650–1,100m in Ecuador, to 500m in Colombia, to 300m north of Orinoco in Venezuela but to 900m south of it. In seasonally relatively moist forest, humid forest (including *várzea* and *terra firme*), gallery forest, mangrove, and their edges, also adjacent clearings, savanna thickets and scrub; in Ecuador, in deciduous forest, second growth and scattered vegetation in partially cleared and cultivated areas.

Voice Vocalisations similar to Trinidad Euphonia. Calls include a plaintive, clear and high *pee-pee* or *pee-pee-pay* whistle (sometimes 1 or 4 whistles), even-pitched or second note slightly higher; also a rising *wheeet* when excited, repeated up to 4 times; 3–6 rapid *dee* notes, a clear, moderate-pitched *TI-a TI-a*, and a harsh, flat, very rapid *chid-d-d-d-d-d-d-d* (H&B, I&I, Hilty). Song a high-pitched, toneless *weet-teeeoo* or *peep-eeoo* (Snyder 1966).

TRINIDAD EUPHONIA

Euphonia trinitatis Pl. 304

Identification 9.5–10cm. Adult male deep glossy blue from rear crown, with bright yellow forehead and crown; lower breast, belly and undertail-coverts bright yellow. Bill black above, neat white base to lower mandible, legs and feet grey. Adult female olive above with yellowish supraloral spot, and mostly pale sulphur-yellow below, with pale grey centre of breast and belly to vent, flanks and undertail-coverts. Subadult male like female but has dull yellow underparts and usually small irregular patches of blue-black on face and throat; tail more distinctly marked with white. Juvenile like female, but young male often shows a few black spots on chin and upper throat. Male very similar to Purple-throated Euphonia but in areas of overlap latter has smaller yellow crown patch. Female and juvenile Purple-throated entirely greenish yellow below, lacking pale grey central band.

Ssp. Monotypic (Co, Ve, Tr)

Habits Forages actively and vociferously, in pairs but sometimes alone or in small flocks. Usually high (but lower at edges and in scrub) looking for fruit, berries (especially mistletoe), seeds and invertebrates. Sometimes joins mixed-species flocks.

Status Common in Colombia and Venezuela, most abundant in arid regions; uncommon in Trinidad.

Habitat Tropical Zone, to 1,100m. Mostly dry to moist forests, light deciduous woodland, gallery forest, second growth, and their edges, also adjacent clearings, arid scrub, scattered vegetation in savannas and partially cleared and cultivated agricultural and residential areas; in more humid regions mostly at forest edges.

Voice Very similar to Purple-throated Euphonia. Commonest calls a clear whistled *tee, dee* on same pitch and *duu-dee*, first note lower. Song a short jumble of musical and scratchy unmusical notes, mostly unaccented. Song and calls often alternated (Hilty). Song 3 similar notes, first 2 on even pitch, last higher, *féé-féé-féé* (Junge & Mees 1958).

VELVET-FRONTED EUPHONIA

Euphonia concinna Pl. 304

Identification 9–10cm. Adult male steely blue above, glossed purplish on back, forehead black, yellow on crown; underparts ochraceous-yellow, no white in tail. Eyes brown, bill black with whitish base, legs and feet grey. Female dull olive above, grey wash on nape (but not a clear grey band), yellow forehead, underparts dull yellow, washed slightly ochre on breast and sides. Adult male is only *Euphonia* in range with yellow confined to forecrown, as similar Orange-bellied Euphonia has more extensive yellow forecrown and white undertail spots. Adult female lacks grey nape of female Orange-bellied Euphonia and has buffy-grey underparts. See also slightly larger female Thick-billed Euphonia which has heavier build, thicker bill and lacks yellowish forecrown of female Velvet-fronted Euphonia.

Ssp. Monotypic (C Co)

Habits Similar to those of other non-forest euphonias; sometimes feeds on mistletoe in canopy alongside Orange-bellied Euphonias.

Status Endemic to Colombia, primarily found in arid semi-open parts of Upper Magdalena Valley where it is uncommon. Greatly outnumbered by Orange-bellied Euphonia, which occurs in same area (H&B).

Habitat Tropical Zone, to 1,800m in Cundinamarca but usually below 1,000m. Open dry woodland, hedgerows, trees bordering streams and agricultural areas with scattered trees.

Voice Song perhaps warbler-like (I&I).

ORANGE-CROWNED EUPHONIA

Euphonia saturata Pl. 304

Identification 10cm. Adult male dark, glossy purplish-black above and over head to breast, with orange patch from forehead over crown, lower breast to undertail-coverts orange, white spots on undertail. Eyes dark, bill black with pale base, legs and feet dark grey. Female uniform bright olive-green above, paler yellowish-green below and more greenish on breast and sides. Adult male is only *Euphonia* in range with entire crown orange-yellow, as similar Orange-bellied has smaller and yellower forecrown and yellower underparts (despite its name!). Adult female is olive above with dull yellowish forehead and olive-yellow below, brightest on belly. Slightly larger female Thick-billed Euphonia has slightly heavier build and thicker bill, and a pale loral spot (generally accompanying males helpful in diagnosis).

Ssp. Monotypic (W Ec, W Co)

Habits Forages alone or in pairs from midstorey to canopy, and often joins mixed-species flocks.

Status Uncommon to locally fairly common in Ecuador, locally uncommon in Colombia.

Habitat Tropical Zone, to 1,500m. Trees in semi-open areas, e.g. fairly dry to wet forest edges, broken forest on steep hillsides, deciduous woodland, mature second growth, clearings and agriculture with scattered trees, woodlots, parks, gardens, riparian woodland and tree-lined streams.

Voice Calls include a distinctive, high *pee-deet* or *beem-beem*, usually doubled, similar to Purple-throated and Trinidad Euphonias. Song a leisurely series of *tsit* notes, nasal *tcheeur* notes and fast *tididit* phrases (H&B, I&I, R&G).

FINSCH'S EUPHONIA

Euphonia finschi Pl. 305

Identification 9–10.2cm. One of the smallest euphonias. Adult male steel blue above, dusky on wings, rich yellow forehead to forecrown; belly yellow with sides, thighs and belly to undertail-coverts strongly washed orange-chestnut. Female yellow-green above, blackish wings and tail, slightly more yellowish on forehead and uppertail-coverts; face and underparts greenish-yellow. Adult male has same pattern as male Purple-throated, but yellow parts more orange-ochraceous. Adult female olive has slightly yellowish forecrown and faint dusky eyestripe, and is yellowest on belly; best identified by accompanying male, as easily confused with very similar but slightly larger and larger-billed female Violaceous Euphonia or with female Purple-throated which lacks yellowish forecrown.

Ssp. Monotypic (E Ve, Guianas)

Habits Forages in pairs or small flocks for fruit, e.g. mistletoe berries.

Status In Venezuela, known only from single specimen taken at Arabopó, near Cerro Roraima, and 2 sight and tape records from near Santa Elena de Uairén. Uncommon to fairly common in Guyana and Suriname, with rare scattered records for coastal French Guiana (Tostain *et al*. 1992).

Habitat Tropical Zone, to 1,200m. Shrubby forest borders and river-edge habitats, gallery forest, second growth, open woodland and bushy savanna, in Suriname primarily in coastal swamp forest and gallery forest in savanna.

Voice Calls include a clear *dee* whistle, repeated 2–4 times, delivered slightly slower than Purple-throated and Trinidad Euphonias; also a clear *beeee* (Hilty).

VIOLACEOUS EUPHONIA

Euphonia violacea Pl. 304

Identification 10–11.5cm. Adult male bicoloured, being deep glossy purplish-blue above, with white on wing appearing as a bar in flight, and large white panels on underside of outer tail-feathers; forehead, lores to throat and underparts rich orange-yellow, cleaner yellow from vent to undertail-coverts. Female olive-green above, pale olive-yellow below. In most of range, adult male is only euphonia with all-yellow underparts (no black throat). In Sucre and northern Monagas (north-east Venezuela), male Thick-billed has larger yellow forehead patch extending to behind eyes, heavier bill (hard to gauge in field) and less orange throat and breast. Adult female dark olive above (lack of any grey and yellow on forehead characteristic) and olive-yellow below, becoming deep yellow on rear underparts (lack of white or rufous characteristic); compare with female Purple-throated, Trinidad and Finsch's Euphonias. Female Thick-billed has grey lores and more yellow (less olive) underparts, but probably inseparable in field unless accompanied by male.

Ssp. *E. v. rodwayi* (E Ve, T&T) as described
E. v. violacea (Guianas) orange forehead ends almost midway above eyes; very rich purple gloss on back to tail, reddish-purple on nape, bluish on wings

Habits Forages alone, in pairs or small flocks at all levels, but usually fairly high for fruits, sometimes joins mixed-species flocks.

Status Common in Venezuela and Guyana, the commonest euphonia in Suriname, common in French Guiana and on Trinidad, but less common on Tobago.

Habitat Tropical Zone, to 1,100m. Humid forest, mangrove, gallery forest, edges, mature second growth and plantations, and in isolated trees and shrubs in clearings, cultivated areas, around habitation and even in savanna.

Voice Calls include a loud, harsh, moderate-pitched *che-ep* alarm and a loud chatter when disturbed or alarmed. A high-pitched *chi-chi-chi* and *pee-eep* rising in pitch. Song, lasting up to 2 minutes, is a sputtering, rambling series of relatively distinct phrases alternating abruptly between short buzzy trills, squeaks, chatters, musical (e.g. *di-sweet!* or *peeep!*) and harsh, raspy (e.g. *chi-chi* or *tzer*) notes, and many imitations of other birds, with buzzes, chatters and short trills being most characteristic (ffrench, I&I, Hilty). Described as canary-like and rapid, uttered at rate of one song per minute, *weewee-weeweewee-chrrr-eheur-heur-heur-cheur* (Snyder 1966).

Note Subspecies *rodwayi* probably a synonym of *violacea* (Hilty).

THICK-BILLED EUPHONIA

Euphonia laniirostris Pl. 304

Identification 10–11.5cm. One of the largest euphonias, an impression aided by larger bill. Adult male deep glossy blue-black above including head-sides and malar, with yellow cap, narrow yellow chin and throat and underparts. Considerable subspecific variation. Eyes brown, bill large and deep, blackish with pale base to lower mandible, legs and feet violaceous. Immature male has black mask and yellow forehead before any other adult coloration, in other respects like female, and appears to retain this plumage for one year. Female yellowish olive-green above, greenish-yellow below, palest on undertail-coverts. Thicker bill than other euphonias, but hard to see in field. Female Orange-bellied has yellowish forehead, grey nape and mostly buffy-grey underparts with contrasting yellowish-olive sides. A solitary immature male can be quite a puzzle.

Ssp. *E. l. crassirostris* (C Co, W Ve) yellow on head covers forehead and crown, pure yellow below, large white panels on underside of outer tail-feathers; immature has small grey panels on undertail.
E. l. hypoxantha (W Ec) lemon-yellow on head covers nape, underparts lemon-yellow
E. l. melanura (E Ec, SE Co, S Ve) yellow on head stops level with eyes, breast to flanks rich orange flushed yellow, no white on undertail

Habits Forages alone, in pairs or small flocks at all levels, but usually fairly high for fruits, and sometimes joins mixed-species flocks.
Status Uncommon to common in Ecuador where commonest in west, usually common in Colombia, and fairly common in Venezuela; may be spreading due to deforestation.
Habitat Tropical to Subtropical Zones, to 2,200m. Relatively dry to humid regions, in forest canopy and edges (mostly *várzea* in Amazonia), open deciduous woodland, gallery forest, mature second growth, plantations, woodlots and in isolated trees and shrubs in clearings, cultivated areas and around habitation.
Voice Calls include a sweet, musical, downward-inflected *chweet* or *wheep*, a loud, sharp, often-doubled *preet!* or *peem*, an upward-inflected *beeee*, a hoarse *wee*, a drawn-out *chweéyoo*, harsh, buzzy rattles, semi-musical phrases and imitations of other birds. Song similar to Violaceous Euphonia, but with fewer imitations (H&B, R&T, I&I, Hilty).

GOLDEN-RUMPED EUPHONIA
Euphonia cyanocephala Pl. 305

Identification 10.5–11cm. Adult male has black frontal band, forehead to nape warm lustrous sky blue; mantle and lower back black with a cobalt to purplish gloss; wing-coverts and tertials black with slight blue gloss; rectrices dark brown with dull yellowish olive-green outer webs and narrow dark fringes; rump and short uppertail-coverts rich orange-yellow; long uppertail-coverts blackish-blue, tail dusky; face, chin and throat black, breast to undertail-coverts yellowish-orange. Eyes brown, bill black, legs and feet grey. Immature male as adult but blue crown patch slightly smaller, duller and scaled with dark grey fringes; remiges entirely dark brown without greenish outer webs. Adult female has frontal bar broadly rufous-orange, with upper head lustrous sky blue; upperparts olivaceous-green, palest and brightest on lower rump and short uppertail-coverts; remiges and rectrices dark fuscous with olive-green fringes; face to undertail-coverts citron, darker on ear-coverts (effectively as back); bill black, legs and feet grey. Juvenile is duller version of adult female, but top of head differs by sex, bill black above, grey below: juvenile male has forehead and frontal bar pale orange, top of head deep olive-green washed pale blue with grey fringes; juvenile female has frontal bar yellowish, top of head dull dark olive-green. Blue-hooded male unmistakable. Adult female recalls larger female Chestnut-breasted Chlorophonia which is much brighter green (not olive) above, has chestnut line under blue crown and a green/yellow demarcation on underparts.

Ssp. *E. c. cyanocephala* (N & SE Ve, Tr, Guianas) as described
E. c. insignis (S Ec) forehead in male slightly ochraceous-orange, with a narrow blackish line behind; rump and underparts same orange; female has shining green back
E. c. pelzelni (W Ec, S Co) larger; rump and underparts decidedly paler than *intermedia* (a paler mix of ochraceous-yellow and pale orange)

Habits Forages in pairs or small flocks at all levels, but usually fairly high for fruits (especially mistletoe) and sometimes invertebrates. Rarely joins mixed-species flocks.
Status Uncommon to fairly common and rather local, rare on Trinidad. Scattered records in French Guiana.
Habitat Tropical to Subtropical Zones, to 3,000m and usually above 500m, in relatively dry to humid regions in forest edges, woodland, mature second growth, plantations and isolated trees and shrubs in clearings, cultivation and around habitation; not in continuous forest.
Voice Calls include a soft, plaintive, low- to moderate-pitched, slightly descending *tweer* or *teer* whistle, sometimes repeated up to 4 times, and *chit* or *chuk*. Song a fast, complex, squeaky, twittering series of high notes interspersed with low- to moderate-pitched *cheep* or *chup* notes and other chittering sounds, lasting 10–30 s with pauses of up to 22 s, the longer pauses sometimes interrupted by hard, sharp, moderate-pitched *tic*, *teek* or soft *chup* calls. Sometimes mixes calls and song (H&B, I&I, R&G, Hilty).
Note *E. cyanocephala* formerly treated as *aureata* subspecies group of expanded Blue-hooded Euphonia *E. musica* (I&I), and sometimes even called *E. aureata* (Tostain *et al.* 1992).

FULVOUS-VENTED EUPHONIA
Euphonia fulvicrissa Pl. 304

Identification 9–11cm. Adult male steel-blue above, including entire head to upper breast, with large yellow patch on forehead, underparts yellow, washed fulvous on undertail-coverts. Female pale yellowish olive-green above and below, with a fulvous patch on forehead, hint of grey on nape, paler below and somewhat more yellowish on throat, central belly and vent, fulvous on undertail-coverts. Adult male and female similar to many other euphonias, except for diagnostic contrasting fulvous undertail-coverts.

Ssp. *E. f. fulvicrissa* (NW Co) as described
E. f. omissa (C Co) like *fulvicrissa* but male has upperparts and sides of head and throat decidedly steel blue without any greenish tone; metallic gloss is intermediate between bluish bottle green of *fulvicrissa* and pale purplish-blue of *purpurascens*
E. f. purpurascens (NW Ec, SW Co) like *omissa* but upperparts and throat glossed purplish-blue, inclining to violet, outermost rectrix lacks, or has very little white on inner web

Habits Forages in pairs, sometimes alone or in small flocks, at all levels but quite often low, for fruits and invertebrates, and often joins mixed-species flocks.
Status Uncommon to locally fairly common.
Habitat Tropical Zone, to 1,000m but usually below 500m. Humid to wet forests, edges, and shrubby second growth and clearings.
Voice Calls include a distinctive, dull gravelly, chattering, low- to moderately-pitched *tr-r-r-r* rattle, repeated 1–3 times, and sometimes a moderate- to high-pitched upward-inflected *wheet*, repeated after pauses averaging 3.5 s. Song a fast,

jumbled series of high notes interspersed with lower pitched trills (H&B, I&I, R&G).

GOLDEN-BELLIED EUPHONIA

Euphonia chrysopasta Pl. 304

Identification 10–11.5cm. Adult male olive-green above, paler on uppertail-coverts, hint of bluish-grey on nape, supraloral, lores and base of malar white, underparts greenish-yellow, yellowest on undertail-coverts. Female similar but greyish from throat to belly. Distinctive white lores should distinguish both sexes from other euphonias (e.g. Bronze-green, which has bright yellow forehead patch). Female Golden-sided Euphonia has grey (not yellow) vent, whilst female Rufous-bellied Euphonia has rufous (not yellow) vent.

Ssp. *E. c. chrysopasta* (E Ec, SE Co) brighter, bluer on nape and more yellowish below.
E. c. nitida (E Co, S Ve, Guianas) as described; smaller than *chrysopasta*

Habits Forages noisily for fruit, berries and invertebrates. Alone, in pairs or small flocks and usually high (but lower at edges). Sometimes joins mixed-species flocks.
Status Uncommon to usually fairly common in Ecuador and Colombia, common in Venezuela and possibly quite common in the Guianas.
Habitat Tropical Zone, to 1,200m. Tall humid *terra firme* and *várzea*, especially where large clumps of mistletoe are found, and in large trees in adjacent second growth, plantations, clearings and pastures.
Voice Calls include a sharp smacking, explosive *spitz!* or *spitz weét!* with second note rising slightly, repeated at short intervals; also *weét!* repeated alone, or *pitzaweek*. Song a long jumbled series of sputtering notes and phrases, e.g. *chit*, *sit*, *spitz* or *week* put together in more or less random pattern, e.g. *P-pfits'et cheéu…sit, fits…pa'fits-a-whew!…* or *si-si-WILL-ow*, with male spreading and wagging tail and sometimes pumping body while singing (H&B, I&I, R&G, Hilty).
Note Also called White-lored Euphonia, which is a much more appropriate name.

BRONZE-GREEN EUPHONIA

Euphonia mesochrysa Pl. 304

Identification 9–10cm. Adult male bronzy-olive above with grey-tinged nape and distinctive yellow forehead, and yellowish-olive below with central breast, belly and vent deep orange-yellow. Adult female slightly paler and more yellowish, lacks yellow forehead, with a grey central lower breast and belly. Larger female Rufous-bellied Euphonia has grey underparts reaching further on throat and upper belly, and tawny (not deep yellow) vent. Female Orange-bellied is duller olive above with dull yellow or chestnut forehead, and duller buffy below, especially on vent (which is deep yellow in Bronze-green Euphonia). Immature male Thick-billed may look similar to male Bronze-green Euphonia when acquires yellowish forecrown, but retains mainly olive plumage.

Ssp. *E. m. mesochrysa* (E Ec, C Co)

Habits Forages from midstorey to canopy (lower at edges) for fruit and berries, often joins mixed-species flocks.
Status Uncommon to locally fairly common, perhaps often overlooked.
Habitat Tropical to Subtropical Zones, 500–2,300m but usually above 1,000m and thus at higher elevations than other euphonias except Orange-bellied. Humid forest and edges, sometimes in isolated large trees in adjacent clearings and pastures.
Voice Calls include a distinctive, soft gravelly, moderate-pitched *tr-r-r-r-r*, repeated 1–3 times or shortened, e.g. *tr-r-r-r tr-r-r*; also a sweeter, moderate- to high-pitched *chip*, sometimes doubled, tripled or extended as a chitter. Song consists of 2 clear notes followed by a musical trill, e.g. *tee-teeu-trrrrrt*, or a low whistle followed by a trill, e.g. *whurt tr-r-r tr-r-r tr-r-r tr-r-r*, lasting 2 s with 4–8 s pauses, and often overlaid with *chip* notes (R&T, I&I, R&G).

WHITE-VENTED EUPHONIA

Euphonia minuta Pl. 305

Identification 9–10.2cm. Adult male dark steel blue above, including entire head, except small yellow forehead. Breast and sides yellow, becoming white on belly to undertail-coverts, and white panels on underside of outer tail-feathers, and slight dusky scalloping on flanks. Subadult male yellowish-green above with yellow forehead, and yellow below becoming greenish-yellow on sides, with violet-blue throat. Female olive-green above, pale grey on throat, yellowish-green breast to flanks, then whitish to undertail. Small size, small bill and distinctive white (or mostly white) belly to undertail distinguishes both sexes from other euphonias (e.g. Bronze-green), and also note male's small yellow forehead and female's yellowish pectoral band (compare female Plumbeous, Purple-throated and Trinidad Euphonias).

Ssp. *E. m. humilis* (W Ec, W Co) larger yellow forehead
E. m. minuta (E Co, S Ve, Guianas) as described, very small forehead patch

Habits Often wags or twitches partly spread tail sideways, showing white tail spots. Forages for fruit (especially mistletoe) and invertebrates, usually in canopy (lower at edges). Alone, in pairs or small flocks of up to 6, rarely to 12. Often joins mixed-species flocks.
Status Rare to locally uncommon in Ecuador, fairly common in rest of range.
Habitat Tropical Zone, to 1,000m. Humid to wet *terra firme* and *várzea* forests, edges, and mature second-growth, and sometimes in isolated large trees in adjacent clearings and pastures but, in Suriname, even in plantations, savanna forests, parks and gardens.
Voice Calls include a single (rarely doubled), sharp *veet*, a *seeu* or sputtering moderate-pitched *wee-chu* and high, oft-repeated *pheet-pheet* (H&M). Song a loud, shrill series of sharp staccato, moderate- to high-pitched notes, e.g. *tu VEEVEET, ch VEET, cheewit, chewit,… VEET… ch-VEET, tsik, veEE, vic-squik, veEE, squik squik, veEE…*, with loud *VEET* and *veEE* notes characteristic (I&I, R&G, Hilty).

TAWNY-CAPPED EUPHONIA

Euphonia anneae Pl. 304

Identification 11–12cm. Adult male has distinctive tawny-rufous crown and white vent (the only similar male are those subspecies of Orange-bellied Euphonia which have a less extensive rufous cap and yellowish-rufous vent, but no known overlap). Adult female dark olive above with grey nape and distinctive rufous forehead (only present in female Fulvous-vented Euphonia and some subspecies of Orange-bellied), greyish below (yellow-olive with rufous tinge in female Fulvous-vented and Orange-bellied Euphonias), with yellowish-rufous belly and vent, and olive-yellow sides and flanks.

Ssp. *E. a. rufivertex* (NW Co)

Habits Similar to Orange-bellied Euphonia.
Status Not well known, only found west of Gulf of Urabá, Chocó, along border with Panama.
Habitat Tropical Zone, to 1,500m, in humid forest, edges and second growth.
Voice Calls include a harsh, unmusical and usually doubled *enk*, a cat-like *mya*, moderate-pitched burry *dee-dee-dee*, and trills and chatters. Song comprises 2–4 repetitions of single notes or phrases, with typical moderate- to high-pitched phrases being *whee whee whee* or *wheer wheer* whistles, a nasal *nah-a-a-ak*, a whining upward-inflected *eeeenk*, a squeezed-out *seeet*, and other sputtering phrases (H&B, I&I).

ORANGE-BELLIED EUPHONIA

Euphonia xanthogaster Pl. 305

Identification 9–11cm. Adult male has either rufous (compare Tawny-capped Euphonia) or yellow (compare Purple-throated, Trinidad and Orange-crowned Euphonias) forecrown (see below). Adult female distinguished by combination of distinctive grey nape, some rufous on forecrown and buffy-grey underparts with yellowish-olive sides (compare Velvet-fronted and Bronze-green Euphonias). Female Rufous-bellied has yellowish-olive forecrown, more greyish underparts and tawny (not buffy-yellowish) vent.

Ssp. *E. x. badissima* (NW Co, W Ve) male has rufous forecrown
E. x. brevirostris (E Ec, E Co, S Ve, Gu) male has yellow forecrown
E. x. chocoensis (NW Ec, W Co) male has yellow forecrown
E. x. dilutior (SE Co) male has yellow forecrown
E. x. exsul (NE Co, N Ve) male has rufous forecrown
E. x. quitensis (W Ec) male has yellow forecrown

Habits Forages alone, in pairs or small flocks at all levels but more often low for fruit, berries, flowers and invertebrates, and often joins mixed-species flocks in both understorey and canopy.
Status Common.
Habitat Tropical to Subtropical Zones, to 2,750m but usually at 650–2,000m, in humid to wet (especially cloud) forests, edges, mature second growth and plantations, sometimes in isolated large trees in adjacent clearings and pastures.
Voice Calls include a clear *ding-ding-ding*, an upslurred *kueé*, a nasal, gravelly *nay nay* or *chee chee*, a *zhurr-deet* or *zhurr dit-dit-dit*, and distinctive, buzzy, somewhat complaining, moderate-pitched *dee* (1–4 notes, mostly 3). Song a rambling, almost random series of semi-musical phrases given leisurely, e.g. *deeu deeu… deet deet deet… jew jew… chu chu chu… jew, ju-du-du-du…* (I&I, R&G, Hilty).
Notes Race *lecroyana*, described by Aveledo & Pérez (1994), is a synonym of *badissima* (Hilty, Lentino in prep.). Vocal differences between subspecies may indicate that several species are involved (Hilty).

RUFOUS-BELLIED EUPHONIA

Euphonia rufiventris Pl. 305

Identification 10–11.5cm. Adult male has diagnostic blue-black head and upperparts; lower breast and sides to undertail-coverts orange-rufous, with a touch of yellow-orange at sides of breast. Female dark olive above with yellowish-olive forecrown and greyish nape, and grey below with olive-yellow chin, incomplete breast-band and flanks, and diagnostic rufous belly and vent (compare female Golden-bellied, Bronze-green, Orange-bellied and Golden-sided Euphonias).

Ssp. *E. r. carnegiei* (S Ve) male has orange-yellow entire sides of body to past flanks
E. r. rufiventris (E Ec, E Co) as described

Habits Forages alone or in pairs from midstorey to canopy (where easily overlooked unless voice known), but sometimes lower at edges, for fruits (especially those of epiphytes and mistletoe), and often joins mixed-species flocks.
Status Uncommon to fairly common in Ecuador, uncommon in Colombia and common in Venezuela.
Habitat Tropical Zone, to 1,100m but mostly below 500m, in humid *terra firme* and *várzea*, and sometimes at edges, second growth, plantations or isolated large trees in adjacent clearings and pastures.
Voice Calls include a fast, raspy, moderate-pitched *bz-bz-bz-bz* or *drrt-drrt-drrt-drrt*, and a low, harsh *j'a'a'a'a* rattle, repeated 2–6 times, sounding insect-like (H&B, I&I, R&G, Hilty).

GOLDEN-SIDED EUPHONIA

Euphonia cayennensis Pl. 305

Identification 11–11.5cm. Adult male unmistakable. Adult female dark-olive above with brownish crown, and grey below with olive-yellow chin and throat-sides to flanks. Extensively grey underparts separate female from female Golden-bellied and Rufous-bellied Euphonias.

Ssp. Monotypic (S Ve, Guianas)

Habits Often twitches tail sideways. Forages alone, in pairs or small flocks in canopy (lower at edges and interior of forests) for fruit, berries and invertebrates, and sometimes joins mixed-species flocks.
Status Spottily distributed in eastern Venezuela, rare in Suriname, but fairly common to common in rest of range, e.g. interior forests of Suriname and French Guiana.

Habitat Tropical Zone, to 1,100m but mostly below 600m, in humid forest, edges, second growth, shaded plantations and savanna woodland.
Voice Calls very similar to Rufous-bellied Euphonia; a harsh, gravelly, insect-like, low- to moderate-pitched *j'a'a'a'a* or *bzzz-bzzz-bzzz*, given slow or fast and repeated 2–6 times, a longer, buzzy *bjjjjjjjjjjjjjjjjjjjjj* rattle, lasting *c*.2 s, and a higher, softer, nasal *ruee-e-et* (I&I, Hilty).

YELLOW-COLLARED CHLOROPHONIA
Chlorophonia flavirostris Pl. 305

Identification 10–10.2cm. Adult male unmistakable. Duller female and immature male best told by white eyes, yellow eye-ring and median rear underparts, and salmon-orange bill and legs.

Ssp. Monotypic (W Ec, SW Co)

Habits Forages in pairs or small to large flocks of up to 30 or even 80 (with adult males always rare). Usually in canopy (where easily overlooked unless call known) for fruit, berries and some invertebrates, and rarely joins mixed-species flocks.
Status Rare to locally fairly common in Ecuador (less common south), fairly common in Colombia; possibly some nomadic or seasonal migrations.
Habitat Tropical to Subtropical Zones, to 1,900m but usually below 1,500m, in wet and cloud forests, edges and second growth, and sometimes in isolated large trees in adjacent clearings and pastures.
Voice Calls include a soft, moderate-pitched *pek*, and more nasal, plaintive, drawn-out, high and thin *peeeeeeee*, often given in flight, sometimes interspersed with short, clear *winh* calls. Possible song is a brief, slow, high, rattling buzz followed by up to several soft, moderate-pitched whistles (H&B, I&I, R&G).

BLUE-NAPED CHLOROPHONIA
Chlorophonia cyanea Pl. 305

Identification 10.5–11.5cm. Adult male unmistakable and even adult female and immature male easily distinguished by yellowish forehead (in some races), narrow blue nape and distinctive blue rump. Juvenile green with yellow tinge below. Female Chestnut-breasted Chlorophonia has blue (not green) crown. Also compare larger and duller green immature Bay-headed Tanager and immature Rufous-cheeked Tanager.

Ssp. *C. c. frontalis* (N Ve) both sexes have green back, female has yellow forehead
C. c. intensa (W Co) male has blue back, female green back and forehead
C. c. longipennis (Andes in Ec, Co & Ve) male has blue back, female green back and forehead
C. c. minuscula (NE Ve) both sexes have green back, female has yellow forehead
C. c. psittacina (N Co) both sexes have green back, female has yellow forehead
C. c. roraimae (S Ve, Gu) male has blue-tinged back, female a green back and yellow forehead

Habits Forages in a seemingly sluggish manner, in pairs or small flocks of up to 12 (with adult males always rare) usually in canopy (where easily overlooked unless call known) for fruits (especially mistletoe) and invertebrates, and sometimes joins mixed-species flocks.
Status Rare and local in Ecuador, uncommon in Colombia and uncommon to fairly common in Venezuela; possibly some nomadic or seasonal migrations.
Habitat Tropical to Subtropical Zones, 210–2.500m but usually above 500m away from Andes and above 1,400m in Andes. Humid to wet forests, edges, mature second growth, shaded plantations and sometimes in isolated large trees in adjacent clearings and pastures.
Voice Calls include a low *chaak*, soft *pleee*, nasal, plaintive, soft, moderate-pitched *peent*, *ek* or *erk*, a short, gravelly *didle-itle-itle* rattle, and plaintive, downslurred, low- to moderate-pitched *teeeu* whistle (sometimes repeated regularly, a possible song). Another possible song consists of a rapid delivery of all these calls mixed with lower pitched *chew* notes (F&K, I&I, R&G, Hilty).

CHESTNUT-BREASTED CHLOROPHONIA
Chlorophonia pyrrhophrys Pl. 305

Identification 11.7–12cm. Adult male, adult female and immature male all have distinctive blue crown and (in adult male) chestnut underparts (compare female Blue-hooded and Golden-rumped Euphonias and female Blue-naped Chlorophonia).

Ssp. Monotypic (E Ec, Co, W Ve)

Habits Slowly forages alone, in pairs or small flocks, usually in epiphyte-laden canopy (lower at edge and in shrubs) for fruits (especially mistletoe) and invertebrates, and sometimes joins mixed-species flocks.
Status Rare to locally uncommon, perhaps most common in Venezuela.
Habitat Subtropical Zone to Páramo, 1,400–3,600m but mostly at 1,800–2,500m, in mature epiphyte-rich humid and cloud forests (even elfin forest in Venezuela), edges and mature second growth, and sometimes in isolated large trees in adjacent clearings and pastures.
Voice Calls include a soft, nasal *neck-nuur*, repeated frequently, a nasal, downslurred, sweet, clear *teeeur* contact, a higher pitched *peeeee* and a sharp, moderate-pitched, forceful but somewhat mournful *KEEE!* or *ta-KEE!* Song a long, rambling series with variable, nasal, low- to moderate-pitched notes and phrases (some with a mewing quality), e.g. *eeh, eeeah, uhh, tut-tut-tut too-dée too-dée*… or *na-deár na-deár*… *to-d'leép* (F&K, I&I, R&G, Hilty).

EXOTIC PASSERINES – Estrildidae, Ploceidae, Passeridae

It is interesting, if not significant, that the majority of feral, exotic passerines established in the Neotropics belong to the Ploceidae family of weavers and their allies, and the

Estrildidae waxbills, munias and grass finches. These families are those most commonly trapped in their native countries for the worldwide trade in live birds. They are generally easy to keep in captivity, living well on a simple diet of dry seed. They are colourful, but they are not great songbirds. Thus some individuals find themselves free, often having been released deliberately, occasionally by accident, by which means a significant number of birds escape. If suitable habitat is available, there is every chance that exotics will survive. Nest predation is probably the greatest cause of mortality amongst passerines in the Neotropics, and native species have evolved strategies to cope with it. Often, exotics have breeding strategies born of a different set of circumstances and if those circumstances are not approximated here and the situation favours the newcomers, then the results can be extraordinary. The case of Tricoloured Munia in Venezuela is a good example. Should the newcomers be persecuted and eradicated? There are arguments for and against. It seems that most have found their own virtually vacant niches and are not displacing local species. The threat of the House Sparrow in Venezuela is that it will displace local Saffron Finches by usurping nest sites, at a time when roofing is far less prone to broken tiles and holes under eaves than ever before, but so far all records are along the coast, where Saffron Finch is scarce or absent. The problem with exotics in general is that no one takes them seriously until it is too late, so all observations should be published quickly for the benefit of researchers.

The term 'exotic' in the bird sense at least, means non-indigenous and introduced by man, directly or indirectly. Thus, it is considered redundant to refer to each bird here as 'introduced'. The town of Maracay, in Carabobo, Venezuela, has a well-developed bird-keeping fraternity. That frequent escapes occur is evident by the individuals that have been collected or trapped in the vicinity of Lago de Valencia, most of them weavers or bishops of the family Ploceidae. This situation must be repeated around the region where there are local bird-keeping cultures but data is seldom published, and then only locally. It should also be noted that domesticated budgerigars, lovebirds, cockatiels, canaries and others frequently escape and are often seen apparently flying and living freely. There have been no cases, as far as we can tell, where any of these birds have become established, even temporarily. We have dealt here only with those that seem to be genuinely established.

There is no local literature to draw upon. The following accounts draw on the personal experience of the authors, reports received from around the region, plus Lever (1987), Clement, Harris & Davis (1993), Restall (1996), Raffaele *et al.* (1998), Mullarney *et al.* (1999) and Borrow & Demey (2001).

The Estrildidae is a large, Old World family of small birds, known as waxbills (named for their wax-red bills), mannikins and munias, and grass finches, most of which inhabit open grasslands and savannas. Most species occur in sub-Saharan Africa, but there are many species locally or widespread, right across India and the Asia–Pacific region to Australia. They thrive on dry seeds, are usually quite pretty, have quaint songs and are generally undemanding and easy to maintain in captivity. Their breeding biology is such that a pair may produce 2–3 broods of 4–5 a year, which gather and forage across the scrubby savannas in flocks. Thus they are easily caught in numbers. Common Waxbill was first brought to Brazil on slave ships from Africa, as other estrildids arrived in the West Indies by the same agency. They are generally sedentary and non-migratory, so local feral populations are easy to establish, and also to eliminate. The waxbill appears to be totally complementary and non-competitive, and is not a pest. The same cannot be said of the munias for they are avid feeders in rice fields and can breed more young in a year than any local species. But they do not appear to be competitors for natural resources and are not aggressive.

COMMON WAXBILL

Estrilda astrild Pl. 306

Identification 10cm. Adult pale brown above, very finely barred from forehead to tip of tail; bill wax-red, and there is a red stripe through eye, from lores and base of bill to rear ear-coverts. Underparts are paler, more buffy, almost white on chin and throat, warmest and darkest on sides and flanks, and also very finely barred, with a bright red patch on belly, vent to undertail-coverts black. Female has undertail-coverts dusky or fuscous. Juvenile distinguished by black bill, but otherwise is a slightly paler version of adult, with much fainter barring, and brown undertail-coverts instead of black. There is another estrildid that regularly escapes from captivity, Red-eared or Black-rumped Waxbill *E. troglodytes*, which is distinguished by its black rump. So far it has not established itself in our region, although it occurs on several islands of the West Indies, the closest being Guadeloupe and Martinique.

Ssp. 16 subspecies, unknown which occurs in our region; native to sub-Saharan Africa (Tr)

Habits Commonly seen clinging to stems of tall *Panicum maximum* grass, feeding on unripe seeding heads and flicking its tail from side to side. Also forages for seeds and small insects in weeds and open undergrowth, and commonly forages on ground for fallen dry seeds, in the same manner and locations favoured by ground-doves. Highly social and usually seen in flocks.

Status Locally common and expanding its range in north-central Trinidad.

Habitat Tropical Zone, lowland grasslands. Tall grasses and open areas with mixed scrub and grasses.

Voice Calls continually, soft *tchit*, *tsit*, *chit* and *pit*. In flight a *cherr-cherr* or *cher-peee*, with a flock chittering as they go. Song is a short, harsh series of buzzy notes.

TRICOLOURED MUNIA

Lonchura malacca Pl. 306

Identification 11cm. Adult chestnut-brown above, glossy

orange on uppertail-coverts and rich maroon on tail, entire head, centre of belly and undertail-coverts black, broad band on breast and down body-sides to flanks white. Eyes dark, bill pale bluish silvery grey, legs and large feet grey. Juvenile sandy-cinnamon above, darker on wings and tail, pale buffy below. Variations or morphs have not been studied, and their genetic make-up is not known; these are, black scalloping on flanks instead of a clean straight division between black and white, fine scallops of chestnut (like fringes) and cinnamon instead of white. Latter has been taken as evidence of hybridisation between Tricoloured and Chestnut Munias, but in error. Latter morph is highly variable from pale cinnamon to much brighter, and occurs regularly in Venezuela. Quite unique and unlikely to be mistaken, although locals catch them for the local pet shop trade, where they are often bought on the assumption that they are *Oryzoborus* seed-eaters, which are renowned for their song.

Ssp. Monotypic; native to southern India and Sri Lanka (Co: Tolima, Ve: NW Llanos)

Habits Usually seen in tall *Panicum maximum* lining ditches that separate roads from rice fields. Easily disturbed, they take-off and fly en masse, looking like clockwork-toy birds, calling as they go. They then sit up in an isolated tree, watching and resting, until they all take off together. When foraging in rice or tall grass, only a few individuals are ever seen, and some then fly up a few metres before dropping back down in front of the previous group to do so.

Status Sedentary. Very common in rice-growing parts of Portuguesa and Barinas states, Venezuela, and probably so in other areas where rice is grown year-round. Uncommon around Lago de Valencia where originally established in 1946, but development of irrigated, year-round rice gave Tricoloured Munia the perfect conditions for a population explosion. Sightings from Tolima, Colombia, confirmed by photographs (D. C. Ayala, pers. comm.).

Habitat Tropical Zone, to 100m. Natural habitat is marshy, seasonally flooded grassland. Nests in grass and rice, low over water. Year-round water essential for population growth, otherwise numbers decline in the dry season.

Voice Calls include a *pit* or *peet*, and similar, in contact a *peet!* loud and clear. Song a short series of almost inaudible squeaks and bill clicks, ending in a clear, descending *peeeeeee*.

Note Mistakenly considered conspecific with Chestnut Munia and often still treated as such under common name Black-headed Munia, but has different plumage variation characteristics, nesting behaviour, vocalizations and gape markings in nestlings, and whilst DNA reveals them to be closest relatives, it does not show them to be conspecific (Restall 1995, 1996).

CHESTNUT MUNIA

Lonchura atricapilla Pl. 306

Identification 11cm. Adult chestnut-brown with a full black hood; central belly and undertail-coverts vary from chestnut to black, depending on race. Juvenile is sandy-cinnamon above, darker on wings and tail, pale buffy below (and identical to juvenile Tricoloured Munia).

Ssp. 10 subspecies, unknown which occurs in our region; ranges from NW India across virtually all of SE Asia, except Sumatra and New Guinea (SE Ec: Guayas province)

Status Sightings near Puerto Inca and in Río Palenque reserve, Ecuador, but unknown whether species is established. Occurs on several islands in West Indies, the closest being Martinique. Natural expansion, island by island, established in Indonesia, and such leapfrogging has probably also occurred in Caribbean (Raffaele *et al.* 1998), but must have arrived in Ecuador by human agency.

Habitat Tropical Zone. Seen in reedbeds near a pond, *c.*35 km south-east of Guayaquil. Prefers marshy ground, but often found in colonies in parks and gardens across Asia and water not essential for successful breeding. Non-migratory but certainly more mobile than sedentary Tricoloured Munia.

Voice Calls include *pee*, *pew*, *peet* and a loud contact *pink! pink!* An in-flight triple *chirp* is recorded in the literature but we have only heard *fleep! fleep!* from one race, and *seep! seep!* from another. Pairs call antiphonally. Song begins with a series of virtually inaudible *clik* notes followed by a clear, descending *weeeeeee*.

Note See previous species.

JAVA SPARROW

Lonchura oryzivora Pl. 306

Identification 13–14cm. Quite unmistakable. Adult delicate French grey from nape to rump, including wings, but tail-coverts and tail all black, as are primaries. Head black with white cheeks, grey breast, flesh-pink belly and flanks tending to rosy on flanks, white vent and undertail-coverts. Eyes dark, the eyelids pink like bill, legs and feet. Male has eyelids and base of bill swollen and redder or rosier when breeding, thus permitting sexes to be separated. Juvenile warmer, slightly buffy-grey above including uppertail-coverts, tail and primaries blackish. Top of head dark grey to blackish, face-sides and chin to undertail-coverts pale buff with some grey flammulations on breast. Bill horn-coloured, becoming pink with time, eyes dark, eyelids grey, legs and feet flesh.

Ssp. Monotypic; native to Java and Bali, Indonesia (established in NW Llanos of Ve)

Habits Originally must have been a bamboo specialist that adapted and became totally dependent on rice. Tends to gather in same trees and rooftops every evening, and then before nightfall moves to preferred roost. Like other munias, when foraging in rice usually below top level of plants, as its weight causes stems to bend.

Status Vulnerable. Rare in native range due to unremitting trapping combined with persecution by the farmers. In Venezuela, appears well established but nowhere as common as Tricoloured Munia, in rice-growing areas of Portuguesa state, and possibly around Lake Valencia, in Carabobo state. Trapped in small numbers and sold to the pet trade where they are mixed with the much more expensive domesticated birds imported from Cuba and Holland.

Habitat Tropical Zone, to 100m. Rice-growing areas and adjacent bamboo and light forest.

Voice Basic contact call is a *tchuk* or slight variation, contact in flight variants of *tik, tek, tuk* and *tchuk*. In a group, occasional bird will utter a rolling *crrrrkrkrkrkrkrkrkrkrkr kr*. Song a series of *dik, tchuk* and *wee*, the whole jangling, unmusical racket ending with a *weeeeee*.

Note Formerly placed in the genus *Padda* (Restall 1996). This species has been domesticated and various mutants (white, fawn, harlequin etc.) are sold in pet shops – wild-caught grey birds are mixed with these and sold at the same high prices.

The large Ploceidae family is primarily African, with a few species in Asia. The characteristic weaver is yellow with dark rufous or black, and a large sharp bill. Generally highly social, breeding in colonies and taking their common name from the male's habit of weaving a nests that is suspended from a tall tree. Many are very attractive and their weaving antics most entertaining. They are favourites in the bird trade. Males have an eclipse plumage after breeding, when they lose their bright colours and long plumes. During this period they become rather dull as cage birds and are often released to make room for another species. They do not appear to be a pest, although they certainly take rice, neither do they seem to compete with local species for specialised food or other resources.

VILLAGE WEAVER

Ploceus cucullatus Pl. 306

Identification 15cm. A large yellow bird with very distinctive habits. Adult male golden-yellow above, with variable black centres to feathers of mantle and almost entirely black scapulars, appearing as an irregular V-shaped mark on back, wings black with broad golden-yellow fringes, tail olive washed yellow. Entire hood black, with deep rufous on nape, breast yellow, flushed warm orange and rest of underparts golden-yellow. Eyes red, massive black bill, legs and feet horn to flesh. Male enters eclipse plumage post-breeding, when resembles female, though more heavily striated on back and wings darker, and retains near-black bill. Female lacks black hood and is much more olivaceus above and on flanks, whitish on belly, bill horn-coloured, eyes red, legs and feet horn or flesh. Juvenile inseparable from female. Breeding male quite distinct, female/juvenile likely to be confused and best separated by heavy bill. Male from Masked Weaver by black hood and larger size.

Ssp. *P. c. cucullatus*, native to West Africa (N Ve: Lago de Valencia, Carabobo)

Habits Nests suspended from lower branches of high trees. Males are occupied in nest building for months, seeming never to take time out for foraging! Once built, male displays to attract a female and, if fails, builds another nest nearby. Many nests with several birds and pairs may be seen in a single tree. Unafraid of man and in natural range are a common sight in towns and villages.

Status Local and uncommon. Caught in small numbers and sold locally. Trapping is apparently keeping the population at sustainable levels, but is restricting expansion.

Habitat Tropical Zone, to 200m. Open areas with trees near Lago de Valencia, the region is partly marshy, partly agricultural.

Voice Calls include harsh chattering and twittering notes. Song a series of rasping chatters, ending in a drawn-out wheeze, *Chi-chit-ttt-t-t-t-t-t-shirrrzzzwrrerr* (Borrow & Demey).

Note Sometimes called Black-headed Weaver.

VITELLINE MASKED WEAVER

Ploceus vitellinus Pl. 306

Identification 14cm. Adult male olive above with a slightly yellowish rump and olive tail, wings black with yellow fringes to feathers, top of head golden-yellow with black mask running from lores to rear ear-coverts and to chin, with diffuse rufous border, rest of underparts golden-yellow, with rufous extending to centre of upper breast. Eyes red, bill heavy and sharp, legs and feet flesh. Non-breeding male and adult female alike; no mask, dull brownish-olive above, streaked dusky on mantle, greenish on rump, throat pale yellow, buffy breast, white belly, undertail-coverts pale, washed yellow; bill horn. Male from Village Weaver by black mask, not black hood. Females and juveniles more problematic and are best separated by their bill.

Ssp. *P. v. vitellinus*, native to sub-Saharan Africa, (NC Ve: Acarigua, Portuguesa state)

Habits Fairly solitary and forages alone or in pairs, but are based in small colonies.

Status Unconfirmed sight reports from Acarigua, Portuguesa, Venezuela (K. Castelain & D Lauten, pers. comm.). Has not been seen in the local bird trade.

Habitat Tropical Zone, to 100m. Pair seen in farmland, amidst rice country. Naturally favours dry woodland and thorn scrub,

Voice Calls include a sharp *tzik!* or *tchek!* Song a series of jumbled chattering and wheezy notes (Borrow & Demey).

Bishops and widowbirds of the genus *Euplectes* are amongst the most spectacular of African savanna birds. Most are either bright orange or scarlet and black, or bright yellow and black. When displaying, males erect the bright colours and fly in a kind of semi-hovering slow motion, hop up and down and sing ridiculous-sounding series of whirring clicks and squeaks. When not breeding, they assume plumage like that of their females and are difficult to identify. They are great favourites of the bird trade and are exported worldwide. Odd females regularly appear in pet shops in Venezuela, sometimes having been caught with Java

Sparrows and Tricoloured Munias, sometimes donated by disillusioned owners who find them 'just eating machines'. More often than not, they are released and a few make it to suitable habitat. Those released in the Valencia–Maracay area of northern Venezuela have established a small population in the reedbeds near the lake, where they are easy to trap. Their nests are usually placed in the reeds at about head height and are vulnerable to human predation at night.

NORTHERN RED BISHOP

Euplectes franciscanus Pl. 306

Identification 11cm. Adult male in breeding plumage has black forecrown and face-sides, black wings with buffy fringes to feathers, and black belly and vent; rest scarlet-red with some dark streaking on mantle; bill black. Non-breeding male, female and juvenile very similar, being sturdy and rotund, brown above with buffy fringes to feathers, a pale buffy superciliary, crescent below eyes and entire underparts; faint brownish flammulations on breast, whitish belly and undertail-coverts; bill horn. Note tail is particularly short for size of bird. Breeding male absolutely unmistakable. But, if only females or juveniles are seen, unless studied carefully is likely to remain a mystery, or be shoe-horned into the nearest illustration in Hilty, e.g., juvenile Grassland Yellow Finch or juvenile Saffron Finch (bill too small and lacks clear superciliary), possibly even a female Red-breasted Blackbird (too large, bill bicoloured).

Ssp. *E. f. franciscanus*, native to tropical savanna from Senegal to Somalia (N Ve)

Habits Highly social and lives in colonies in reedbeds. Forages singly or in pairs, but spends all non-foraging time in colony. Males sing and posture constantly, attempting to attract females to the round nests they have woven amongst the stems.
Status Rare.
Habitat Tropical Zone, to 100m. Savanna and marshy grasslands, but by preference, reedbeds near water, also cane and rice fields.
Note Two closely allied species could also be found, namely Southern Red Bishop *E. orix*, which differs in breeding male only by having black of forehead more restricted and short black tail protruding beyond red upper- and undertail-coverts, and Yellow-crowned Bishop *E. afer*, which is all black with a bright golden-yellow forehead to nape, yellow tuft on breast-sides, and lower back to upper- and undertail-coverts; rest is black. Females, non-breeding males and juveniles of both species cannot be safely distinguished from Northern Red Bishop.

The true sparrows, Passeridae, were placed as a subfamily within Ploceidae before gaining family recognition comparatively recently. A small assemblage of generally brown and grey birds, only one is worldwide in its distribution, with a little help from man. House Sparrow established a relationship with man in the days of horse and cart, and open farms where grain was used for animal feed, the sparrow found holes in roofs of houses within which it nested, and established a perfect symbiosis. Today, in many cities of the west, with modern farming methods, disappearance of horses and stables, and most of all, houses with sealed roofing, plus the widespread use of insecticides, House Sparrow is in serious decline. In northern South America it is a comparatively recent arrival and is still actively colonising. Whether it is a pest, as claimed or assumed by some writers, is very much in doubt and a totally detached analysis of the data suggests that on balance it is not. When breeding, it specialises in those insects harmful to crops and is undoubtedly beneficial. Post-breeding, the young flock to open country, feeding on fallen seeds and whatever else edible they find. In some areas this includes fruit crops, where the bird is destructive, and in rice-growing country it would undoubtedly be a pest. Old males stay at the nest site, defending it year-round. So, once established, their presence can always be verified.

HOUSE SPARROW

Passer domesticus Pl. 306

Identification 15cm. Adult male is a robust bird that is surprisingly handsome when examined closely. The use of the word 'sparrow' to denote something drab and nondescript can only refer to a female. Adult male in breeding plumage is rich chestnut above, with black streaks, white median wing-coverts (forming a solid wingbar), pale grey crown grey and cheeks; chin, throat and bib black, rest of underparts grey, flammulated slightly darker grey; bill black, legs and feet deep vinous-red. Post-breeding, in fresh plumage, feathers have buffy or greyish fringes, and entire plumage, especially black bib, appears much duller: bill horn-coloured. Female duller mid brown, lacking any rich chestnut, crown pale brown with a buffy superciliary, cheeks and underparts grey with a buffy tone and flammulated, especially on flanks. Juvenile like female, but young males soon show vestigial black on chin and throat. Similar colours to Rufous-collared Sparrow, but bright collar and black throat necklace of latter should suffice for identification. Both forage on ground, hopping onto and below bird feeders, and when glimpsed from above may be confused.

Ssp. Unidentified subspecies (introduced to Ec, Co, Ve, Ar, Cu, Bo, FG)

Status Sight records on Aruba and confirmed to occur along much of coastal Venezuela and offshore islands (RR, C. Sharpe, D. Ascanio, A. Azpiroz, pers. comm.). Now in French Guiana, where a well-established population at Kourou.
Habitat Tropical to Subtropical Zones, to 3,800m,
Voice Calls include much simple chirruping, *chirp, chirp, chirp* proclaims a nesting territory or an advertising male. Also, a scolding *cher'r'r'r'r'r'r* (Mullarney *et al.* 1999).
Note The entire House Sparrow population of the New World, from Alaska to Tierra del Fuego, is currently listed by Dickinson (2003) by default as *P. d. domesticus*.

A DISCOGRAPHY OF NORTHERN SOUTH AMERICAN BIRD VOICES

Compiled by Shaun Peters

Introduction

The aim of this discography is to list where recordings can be found for as many species as possible, but concentrating on titles that feature recordings made in the area covered by this guide, rather than trying to be entirely comprehensive. The list of titles is broken down into three sections. The first (nos. 1–22 & 51) are regional titles dealing with countries covered by this guide; the second (nos. 23–41) are family titles (mainly covering the New World) and the final group (nos. 42–50) are extralimital titles covering nearby countries. Included in this last section are the two most comprehensive North American productions, so that North American migrants that 'winter' in South America are included.

Each species is followed by a code indicating the title the recordings are on (a number) followed by letter codes indicating the country where the recordings were made (in upper case). For the countries covered by this guide and the neighbouring countries of Brazil and Peru the department/province/state locality is also given, where possible (in lower case); the reason for this is to reflect the geographic variation over the large area covered by this guide. Note that in Ecuador, Napo, Orellana and Sucumbíos are lumped together. This is because the old province of Napo has recently been split into three, with Napo itself being the western half, and the eastern half split into Orellana (north of the río Napo) and Sucumbíos (south of the río Napo). Several titles predate this spilt and it was felt better to use the 'old' region of Napo. In the list of localities given below, departments/provinces for Ecuador, Colombia and Venezuela are given alphabetically, whilst those for Brazil and Peru are ordered from north to south. Where there is more than one recording per title, departments/provinces/states for each country are separated by commas, and countries are separated by a semi-colon; countries are listed alphabetically, first those in the area covered by this guide and then extralimital countries. There are a few recordings from outside the New World and these countries are given in full, e.g. China, Norway and UK. Thus, an example from the discography:

Agami Heron *Agamia agami* 12Ena 19Ena

This means that recordings from Napo in Ecuador can be found on title no. 12 (*Ecuador – More Bird Vocalizations from the Lowland Rainforest*, vol. 3), and no. 19 (*Birds of Ecuador/Aves de Ecuador*).

The taxonomy used in this list largely follows that used in the book. As a number of English and scientific names have been modified to match the text entries, some species may not be named in precisely the same way on the recordings themselves.

Titles

1 *Cantos de Aves de la Cordillera Oriental de Colombia* (75 spp)
Mauricio Álvarez-Rebolledo (2000) Instituto de Investigación de Recursos Biológicas Alexander von Humboldt. One CD.

2 *Guia Sonora de las Aves del Departmento de Caldas – Colombia* (83 spp)
Mauricio Álvarez-Rebolledo & Sergio Córdoba-Córdoba (2002)
Instituto de Investigación de Recursos Biológicas Alexander von Humboldt. One CD.

3 *Guia Sonora de las Aves del Departmento de Norte de Santander – Colombia* (45 spp)
Sergio Córdoba-Córdoba & Mauricio Álvarez-Rebolledo (2003)
Instituto de Investigación de Recursos Biológicas Alexander von Humboldt. One CD.

4 *Guia Sonora de las Aves del Departmento del Valle del Cauca – Colombia* (65 spp)
Mauricio Álvarez-Rebolledo, Sergio Córdoba-Córdoba & J. A.López (2003)
Instituto de Investigacion de Recursos Biologicas Alexander von Humboldt. One CD.

5 *Birds of Venezuela/Aves de Venezuela* (666 spp)
Peter Boesman (1999) Bird Songs International BV. CD-ROM.

6 *Birdsongs of Ecuador* (86 spp)
Scott Connop (1996) Turaco Nature Inc. One cassette.

7 *Birdsongs of Ecuador* (Second edn.) (108 spp)
Scott Connop (2004) Turaco Nature Inc. One cassette.

8 *Birds of Eastern Ecuador* (99 spp)
Peter H. English & Theodore A. Parker (1992) Cornell Laboratory of Ornithology. One cassette.

9 *Sounds of La Selva* (120 spp)
John V. Moore (1993) John V. Moore Nature Recordings. One cassette.

10 *Ecuador – More Bird Vocalizations from the Lowland Rainforest*, vol. 1 (105 spp)
John V. Moore (1994) John V. Moore Nature Recordings. One cassette.

11 *Ecuador – More Bird Vocalizations from the Lowland Rainforest*, vol. 2 (117 spp)
John V. Moore (1996) John V. Moore Nature Recordings. One cassette.

12 *Ecuador – More Bird Vocalizations from the Lowland Rainforest*, vol. 3 (131 spp)
John V. Moore (1997) John V. Moore Nature Recordings. One cassette.
13 *Birds of Cabañas San Isidro, Ecuador* (154 spp)
John V. Moore & Mitch Lysinger (1997) John V. Moore Nature Recordings. Two cassettes.
14 *Birds of the Ecuadorian Highlands* (246 spp)
Niels Krabbe, John V. Moore, Paul Coopmans, Mitch Lysinger & Robert S. Ridgely (2001) John V. Moore Nature Recordings. Four CDs.
15 *The Birds of Northwest Ecuador, vol. 1: Upper Foothills & Subtropics* (189 spp)
John V. Moore, Paul Coopmans, Robert S. Ridgely & Mitch Lysinger (1999) John V. Moore Nature Recordings. Three CDs.
16 *The Birds of Northwest Ecuador, vol. 2: The Lowlands & Lower Foothills* (253 spp)
Olaf Jahn, John V. Moore, Patricio Mena Valenzuela, Niels Krabbe, Paul Coopmans, Mitch Lysinger & Robert S. Ridgely. (2002) John V. Moore Recordings. Two CDs.
17 *The Birds of Southwest Ecuador* (235 spp)
Paul Coopmans, John V. Moore, Niels Krabbe, Olaf Jahn, Karl S. Berg, Mitch Lysinger, Lelis Navarrete & Robert S. Ridgely. (2004) John V. Moore Nature Recordings. Five CDs.
18 *The Birds of Eastern Ecuador, vol. 1: The Foothills & Lower Subtropics* (217 spp)
Mitch Lysinger, John V. Moore, Niels Krabbe, Paul Coopmans, Daniel F. Lane, Lelis Navarrete, Jonas Nilsson & Robert S. Ridgely (2005) John V. Moore Nature Recordings. Five CDs.
19 *Birds of Ecuador/Aves de Ecuador* (1,184 spp)
Niels Krabbe & Jonas Nilsson (2003) Bird Songs International BV. DVD-ROM.
20 *Birds of Trinidad & Tobago* (179 spp)
John Hammick (2004) Mandarin Productions. Three CDs.
21 *Birds of Trinidad & Tobago* (38 spp)
William L. Murphy (1991) Peregrine Enterprises Inc. One cassette.
22 *Birds of Trinidad & Tobago* (32 spp)
Terry White (1977) Privately published. One cassette.
23 *Voices of the Tinamous* (38 spp)
John W. Hardy, Jacques Vielliard & Roberto Straneck (1995 edn.) ARA Records (ARA-18). One cassette.
24 *Voices of the New World Quails* (26 spp)
John W. Hardy & Ralph J. Raitt (1995) ARA Records (ARA-22). One cassette.
25 *Voices of the New World Rails* (40 spp)
John W. Hardy, George B. Reynard & Terry Taylor (1996) ARA Records (ARA-23). One cassette.
26 *Voices of the New World Pigeons & Doves* (59 spp)
John W. Hardy, George B. Reynard & Ben B. Coffey (1989) ARA Records (ARA-14). One cassette.
27 *Voices of New World Parrots* (140 spp)
Bret M. Whitney, Theodore A. Parker, Gregory F. Budney, Charles A. Munn & Jack W. Bradbury (2002) Cornell Laboratory of Ornithology. Three CDs.
28 *Voices of the New World Cuckoos and Trogons* (52 spp)
John W. Hardy, George B. Reynard & Ben B. Coffey (1987 edn.) ARA Records (ARA-11). One cassette.
29 *Voices of the New World Owls* (57 spp)
John W. Hardy, Ben B. Coffey & George B. Reynard (1999 edn.) ARA Records (ARA-16). One cassette.
30 *Voices of the New World Nightjars and their Allies* (46 spp)
John W. Hardy, George B. Reynard & Ben B. Coffey (1994 edn.) ARA Records (ARA-15). One cassette.
31 *A Sound Guide to Nightjars and Related Birds* (107 spp)
Richard Ranft & Nigel Cleere (1998) Pica Press/The British Library National Sound Archive. One CD.
32 *Voices of the Toucans* (34 spp)
John W. Hardy, Theodore A. Parker & Terry Taylor (1996) ARA Records (ARA-24). One cassette.
33 *Voices of the Woodcreepers* (51 spp)
John W. Hardy, Theodore A. Parker & Ben B. Coffey (1998 edn.) ARA Records (ARA-17). One cassette.
34 *Songs of the Antbirds (Thamnophilidae, Formicariidae and Conopophagidae)* (274 spp)
Phyllis R. Isler & Bret M. Whitney (2002) Cornell Laboratory of Ornithology. Three CDs.
35 *Voices of all the Mockingbirds, Thrashers and their Allies* (34 spp)
John W. Hardy, Jon C. Barlow & Ben B. Coffey (1987) ARA Records (ARA-12). One cassette.
36 *Voices of the New World Thrushes* (66 spp)
John W. Hardy & Theodore A. Parker (1992 edn.) ARA Records (ARA-10). One cassette.
37 *Voices of the Wrens* (74 spp)
John W. Hardy & Ben B. Coffey (1996 edn.) ARA Records (ARA-2). One cassette.

38 *Voices of the Neotropical Wood Warblers* (63 spp)
John W. Hardy, Ben B. Coffey & George B. Reynard (1994) ARA Records (ARA-21). One cassette.
39 *Voices of the Vireos and their Allies* (45 spp)
Jon C. Barlow (1995 edn.) ARA Records (ARA-7). One cassette.
40 *Voices of the Troupials, Blackbirds and their Allies* (96 spp)
John W. Hardy, George B. Reynard & Terry Taylor (1998) ARA Records (ARA-25). Two cassettes.
41 *Voices of the New World Jays, Crows and their Allies* (49 spp)
John W. Hardy (1990 edn.) ARA Records (ARA-9). One cassette.
42 *Voices of Amazonian Birds: Birds of the Rainforest of Southern Peru and Northern Bolivia* (297 spp)
Thomas S. Schulenberg, Curtis A. Marantz & Peter H. English (2000) Cornell Laboratory of Ornithology. Three CDs.
43 *Voices of Andean Birds, vol. 1: Birds of the Hill Forest of Southern Peru and Bolivia* (99 spp)
Thomas S. Schulenberg (2000) Cornell Laboratory of Ornithology. One CD.
44 *Voices of Andean Birds, vol. 2: Birds of the Cloud Forest of Southern Peru and Bolivia* (99 spp)
Thomas S. Schulenberg (2000) Cornell Laboratory of Ornithology. One CD.
45 *Birds of Bolivia 2.0/Aves de Bolivia* 2.0 (941 spp)
Sjoerd Mayer (2000) Bird Songs International BV. CD-ROM.
46 *Voices of Costa Rican Birds – Caribbean Slope* (220 spp)
David L. Ross & Bret M. Whitney (1995) Cornell Laboratory of Ornithology. Two CDs.
47 *Songs of the Birds of Argentina* (487 spp)
Roberto Straneck (1990) LOLA. Four cassettes.
48 *Stokes Field Guide to Bird Songs: Eastern Region* (372 spp)
Lang Elliott with Donald & Lillian Stokes (1997) Time Warner AudioBooks. Three CDs.
49 *Stokes Field Guide to Bird Songs: Western Region* (551 spp)
Kevin J. Colver with Donald & Lillian Stokes (1999) Time Warner AudioBooks. Four CDs.
50 *Birds of Brazil – MP3 Sound Collection* (1,031 spp)
Peter Boesman (2006) Peter Boesman/Birdsounds.nl. One mp3 CD.
51 *Birds of Venezuela – MP3 Sound Collection* (952 spp)
Peter Boesman (2006) Peter Boesman/Birdsounds.nl. One mp3 CD.

Localities

E ECUADOR
Eaz Azuay
Ebo Bolívar
Ecn Cañar
Eca Carchi
Ech Chimborazo
Eco Cotopaxi
Eeo El Oro
Ees Esmeraldas
Egu Guayas
Eim Imbabura
Elo Loja
Elr Los Ríos
Ema Manabí
Ems Morona-Santiago
Ena Napo + Orellana + Sucumbíos
Epa Pastaza
Epi Pichincha
Etu Tungurahua
Ezc Zamora-Chinchipe

C COLOMBIA
Cam Amazonas
Can Antioquia
Car Arauca
Cat Atlántico
Cbo Bolívar

V VENEZUELA
Vam Amazonas
Van Anzoátegui
Vap Apure
Var Aragua
Vba Barinas
Vbo Bolívar
Vca Carabobo
Vco Cojedes
Vda Delta Amacuro
Vdf Distrito Federal
Vfa Falcón
Vgu Guárico
Vla Lara
Vma Margarita
Vme Mérida
Vmi Miranda
Vmo Monagas
Vpo Portuguesa
Vsu Sucre
Vta Táchira
Vya Yaracuy
Vzu Zulia

G GUYANA

S SURINAME

P PERU
Ptu Tumbes
Ppi Piura
Pla Lambayeque
Pca Cajamarca
Plo Loreto
Pam Amazonas
Pll La Libertad
Psm San Martín
Pan Ancash
Phu Huánuco
Puc Ucayali
Ppa Pasco
Pli Lima
Pju Junín
Pcu Cuzco
Pmd Madre de Dios
Pap Apurímac
Pay Ayacucho
Ppu Puno
Par Arequipa

ES EL SALVADOR

PA PANAMA

HO HONDURAS

C COLOMBIA (cont.)
Cby Boyacá
Cca Caldas
Ccq Caquetá
Ccc Cauca
Ccs Casanare
Cce Cesar
Cch Chocó
Cco Córdoba
Ccu Cundinamarca
Cgu Guajira
Cgn Guainía
Chu Huila
Cma Magdalena
Cme Meta
Cna Nariño
Cns Norte de Santander
Cpu Putumayo
Cqu Quindío
Cri Risaralda
Csa Santander
Csu Sucre
Cto Tolima
Cvc Valle del Cauca
Cva Vaupés
Cvi Vichada

M MEXICO

BE BELIZE

CR COSTA RICA

GT GUATEMALA

BO BOLIVIA

F FRENCH GUIANA

T TRINIDAD & TOBAGO

N NETHERLANDS ANTILLES
Nar Aruba
Nbo Bonaire
Ncu Curaçao

B BRAZIL
Bro Roraima
Bap Amapá
Bam Amazonas
Bpa Pará
Bma Maranhão
Bpi Piauí
Bce Ceará
Bpb Paraíba
Bpe Pernambuco
Bal Alagoas
Bse Sergipe
Brd Rondônia
Bac Acre
Bba Bahia
Bmg Mato Grosso
Bgo Goiás
Bbr Distrito Federal
Bmi Minas Gerais
Bes Espírito Santo
Brj Rio de Janeiro
Bsp São Paulo
Bpn Paraná
Bsc Santa Catarina
Brg Rio Grande do Sul

NC NICARAGUA

A ARGENTINA

PY PARAGUAY

CH CHILE

CN CANADA

USA USA

GL GREENLAND

AN ANTARCTICA

H HISPANIOLA

MO MONSERRAT

J JAMAICA

DR DOMINICAN REPUBLIC

BA BAHAMAS

MA MARTINIQUE

GC GRAND CAYMAN

CB CUBA

PR PUERTO RICO

Systematic list

TINAMIDAE

Grey Tinamou *Tinamus tao* 5Vca,fa 18Ems 19Ems 23Var; Bmg 45BO 50Vca 51Vca

Black Tinamou *Tinamus osgoodi* 18Ena 19Ena 23Pcu 43Pcu

Great Tinamou *Tinamus major* 5Vbo; PA 8Plo 16Ees 19Ees,na 23CR 42Ena 45BO 46CR 50Bpa; PA 51PA

White-throated Tinamou *Tinamus guttatus* 11Ena 19Ena 23Plo 42Pmd 51V

Highland Tinamou *Nothocercus bonapartei* 5Var 18Ena,zc 19Ena 23CR 51Var

Tawny-breasted Tinamou *Nothocercus julius* 14Eca 19Eca,lo 23Elo

Cinereous Tinamou *Crypturellus cinereus* 5Vam; Pmd 6Ena 7Ena 8Plo 19Ena 23Bpa; Puc 42Pmd 45BO 50Bpa 51Vam

Berlepsch's Tinamou *Crypturellus berlepschi* 16Ees 19Ees 23Ees

Little Tinamou *Crypturellus soui* 1Csa 2Cca 3Csa 4Cvc 5Vbo,fa,mo 6Epi 8Pmd 12Ena 16Ees,pi 19Ees,gu,lr,na,pa,pi 20T 23Bes; CR 42BO; Pmd 45BO 46CR 50Bse 51Vbo

Brown Tinamou *Crypturellus obsoletus* 5Vfa,me 18Epa 19Ems,pa 23Bmg,rg,sp; Phu 43BO; Ppa 45BO 47A 50Bsp 51Vme

Undulated Tinamou *Crypturellus undulatus* 5BO 8Pmd 19Ena 23Plo,md 42Pmd 45BO 50Bmg 51Bmg

Pale-browed Tinamou *Crypturellus transfasciatus* 17Elo 19 Eeo,lo 23Eeo

Slaty-breasted Tinamou *Crypturellus boucardi* 23CR 46CR

Red-legged Tinamou *Crypturellus erythropus* 5Vfa,mo 23V 50Vbo 51Vbo,fa

Chocó Tinamou *Crypturellus kerriae* 23PA

Variegated Tinamou *Crypturellus variegatus* 5Vbo 8Bam 19Ena 23Vbo; Bap 42Vbo; Bam 50Vbo 51Vbo

Bartlett's Tinamou *Crypturellus bartletti* 8Pmd 19Ena 23Pmd 42Pmd

Barred Tinamou *Crypturellus casiquiare* 23Vam 51V

Tataupa Tinamou *Crypturellus tataupa* 18Ezc; Psm 19Pca 23Bsp 45BO 47A 50Bmg

Andean Tinamou *Nothoprocta pentlandii* 17Elo 19Eaz,lo 23A 45BO 47A

Curve-billed Tinamou *Nothoprocta curvirostris* 19Epi

ANHIMIDAE

Horned Screamer *Anhima cornuta* 5Vca 9Ena 17Egu 19Egu,na 45BO 50Vca 51Vca

ANATIDAE

Fulvous Whistling Duck *Dendrocygna bicolor* 17Ema 19Ema 45BO 47A 48USA 50Brg 51USA

White-faced Whistling Duck *Dendrocygna viduata* 20T 45Bba 47A 50Brg 51V

Black-bellied Whistling Duck *Dendrocygna autumnalis* 5Vca,fa 17Eeo,gu,lo 19Egu 20T 45BO 48USA 49USA 50Vfa 51Vfa

Orinoco Goose *Neochen jubata* 12Epa 19Epa

Comb Duck *Sarkidiornis melanotos* 17Elo

Brazilian Teal *Amazonetta brasiliensis* 47A 50Bpn 51Bpn

American Wigeon *Anas americana* 48CN; USA 49USA 51USA

Green-winged Teal *Anas carolinensis* 48USA 49USA 51USA

Mérida Speckled Teal *Anas altipetens* 5Vme 51Vme

Andean Teal *Anas andinum* 14Eaz,co 19Eco

Northern Pintail *Anas acuta* 48USA 49USA

Yellow-billed Pintail *Anas georgica* 14Eaz,na 19Eaz 47A

White-cheeked Pintail *Anas bahamensis* 17Eeo,gu

Blue-winged Teal *Anas discors* 17Egu 48CN; USA 49CN; USA 50USA 51USA

Cinnamon Teal *Anas cyanoptera* 48USA 49USA

Northern Shoveler *Anas clypeata* 48USA 49CN; USA 51USA

Southern Pochard *Netta erythrophthalma* 45Bba

Ring-necked Duck *Aythya collaris* 48USA 49USA

Lesser Scaup *Aythya affinis* 48USA 49USA

Andean Duck *Oxyura ferruginea* 14Ech 19Eaz

CRACIDAE

Rufous-vented Chachalaca *Ortalis ruficauda* 5Vfa,mo 20T 22T 51Vfa

Rufous-headed Chachalaca *Ortalis erythroptera* 17Egu,lo,lr 19Egu,lo,lr

Speckled Chachalaca *Ortalis guttata* 8Pmd 9Ena 11Ena 19Ena,pa 42Pmd 45BO

Colombian Chachalaca *Ortalis columbianus* 2Cca 4Cvc

Little Chachalaca *Ortalis motmot* 5Vbo 50Vbo 51Vbo

Band-tailed Guan *Penelope argyrotis* 5Var,la,me 51Vya

Bearded Guan *Penelope barbata* 14Elo 19Elo,zc

Baudó Guan *Penelope ortoni* 16Ees

Andean Guan *Penelope montagnii* 5Vtr 13Ena 14Ena,pi,tu 19Eaz,im,na,tu 44BO; Pll,pa 45BO 51Vtr

Marail Guan *Penelope marail* 5Vbo 50Vbo 51Vbo

Spix's Guan *Penelope jacquacu* 5Vam,bo 8Pmd 9Ena 11Ena 19Ena 42Pmd 45BO 50Vbo 51Vbo

Crested Guan *Penelope purpurascens* 5CR 16Ees 19Egu 46Var; CR 51CR

Cauca Guan *Penelope perspicax* 4Cvc

Trinidad Piping Guan *Pipile pipile* 20T

Blue-throated Piping Guan *Pipile cumanensis* 5Vam 9Ena 11Ena 19Ena,pa 42Pmd 45BO 51Vam

Wattled Guan *Aburria aburri* 1Ccq 3Cns 13Ena 18Ena 19Ena 43Psm

Sickle-winged Guan *Chamaepetes goudotii* 13Ena 15Epi 19Eca,na,pi 45BO

Nocturnal Curassow *Nothocrax urumutum* 8Ena 19Ena

Salvin's Curassow *Mitu salvini* 8Plo 19Ems,na

Razor-billed Curassow *Mitu tuberosum* 42Pmd 45BO

Helmeted Curassow *Pauxi pauxi* 5Var 51Var

Great Curassow *Crax rubra* 16Ees 46CR

Yellow-knobbed Curassow *Crax daubentoni* 51V

Black Curassow *Crax alector* 5Vam 50Vam 51Vam

ODONTOPHORIDAE

Crested Bobwhite *Colinus cristatus* 5Vam,mo 24CR 50Vsu 51Vmo

Marbled Wood Quail *Odontophorus gujanensis* 5Vam,bo 8Plo 12Ena 19Ems,na 24Ena 42Plo 45BO 50Vam 51Vam,bo

Black-fronted Wood Quail *Odontophorus atrifrons* 5Cma 24Cma 51Cma

Rufous-fronted Wood Quail *Odontophorus erythrops* 16Ees 17Eeo 19Eeo,es,lo,pi 24Epi

Chestnut Wood Quail *Odontophorus hyperythrus* 4Cvc 24Cri

Dark-backed Wood Quail *Odontophorus melanonotus* 15Cna; Epi 19Eca,pi 24Cna

Rufous-breasted Wood Quail *Odontophorus speciosus* 18Ena,zc 19Ena,zc 24Pll 43BO 45BO

Gorgeted Wood Quail *Odontophorus strophium* 1Csa

Venezuelan Wood Quail *Odontophorus columbianus* 5Var,ta 51Var

Starred Wood Quail *Odontophorus stellatus* 24Pmd 42Pmd

Tawny-faced Quail *Rhynchortyx cinctus* 16Ees 19Ees

PODICIPEDIDAE

Least Grebe *Tachybaptus dominicus* 5Vca,la 20T 45Bba 49USA 50Vla 51Vla

Pied-billed Grebe *Podilymbus podiceps* 14Ech 19Egu 45Bba 47A 48USA 49USA

Silvery Grebe *Podiceps occipitalis* 14Ena

PHAETHONTIDAE

Red-billed Tropicbird *Phaethon aethereus* 20T

PHALACROCORACIDAE

Neotropic Cormorant *Phalacrocorax brasilianus* 5Vca 17Eeo,ma 47A 49T 50Bmg 51Van

ANHINGIDAE

Anhinga *Anhinga anhinga* 17Ema 48USA

ARDEIDAE

Whistling Heron *Syrigma sibilatrix* 45BO 47A

Tricoloured Heron *Egretta tricolor* 17Ema 48USA 50Vfa 51Vfa

Snowy Egret *Egretta thula* 17Ema 47A 48USA 49USA 50Bmg 51USA

Little Blue Heron *Egretta caerulea* 17Ema 48USA

Capped Heron *Pilherodius pileatus* 45BO 50Bmg 51Bmg

Great Blue Heron *Ardea herodias* 20T 48USA 49USA

Cocoi Heron *Ardea cocoi* 5Vap 9Ena 17Eeo,ma 45BO 47A 50Bmg 51Vap

Great Egret *Ardea alba* 5Vap 17Egu,ma 45BO 47A 48USA 49USA 50Bmg 51M

Cattle Egret *Bubulcus ibis* 5Vap 17Eeo 47A 48USA 49USA 50M 51M

Striated Heron *Butorides striata* 5Vap 11Ena 17Eeo,gu,ma 19Eeo,gu 20T 45BO 47A 50Vbo 51Vap,bo

Green Heron *Butorides virescens* 5Vfa 20T 48USA 49USA 51USA

Agami Heron *Agamia agami* 12Ena 19Ena
Yellow-crowned Night Heron *Nyctanassa violacea* 17Eeo,ma 19Eeo 20T 48USA
Black-crowned Night Heron *Nycticorax nycticorax* 17Ema 19Ema 20T 45BO 47A 48USA 49USA 50Bmg 51Vfa
Boat-billed Heron *Cochlearius cochlearius* 9Ena 19Ena 50Bmg 51Bmg
Rufescent Tiger Heron *Tigrisoma lineatum* 9Ena 19Ees,na 45BO 47A 50Bmg 51Bpa
Zigzag Heron *Zebrilus undulatus* 5Ena; Vam 8Ena 9Ena 19Ena 50Bmg 51Ena
Least Bittern *Ixobrychus exilis* 5Vmo; BO 12Ena 17Ema 19Ema,na 45BO 47A 48USA 49CN 50BO 51Vmo
Stripe-backed Bittern *Ixobrychus involucris* 5Vca 47A 50Vca 51Vca
Pinnated Bittern *Botaurus pinnatus* 17Ema 19Ema

THRESKIORNITHIDAE

White Ibis *Eudocimus albus* 17Ema 48USA
Scarlet Ibis *Eudocimus ruber* 5Vfa 51Vfa
White-faced Ibis *Plegadis chihi* 47A 49USA
Sharp-tailed Ibis *Cercibis oxycerca* 50Vba 51Vba
Green Ibis *Mesembrinibis cayennensis* 5Vam 10Ena 19Ena 42Vam 45BO 46Vco 47A 50Vsu 51Vsu
Bare-faced Ibis *Phimosus infuscatus* 5Vap 50Vap 51Vap
Buff-necked Ibis *Theristicus caudatus* 5Vap 45BO 50Brg 51Vap
Andean Ibis *Theristicus branickii* 14Eco,na 45BO
Roseate Spoonbill *Platalea ajaja* 47A

CICONIIDAE

Jabiru *Jabiru mycteria* 45A
Wood Stork *Mycteria americana* 48USA

CATHARTIDAE

Black Vulture *Coragyps atratus* 50Vca 51Vca

PHOENICOPTERIDAE

Greater Flamingo *Phoenicopterus ruber* 5Vfa 50Vfa 51Vfa
Chilean Flamingo *Phoenicopterus chilensis* 17Egu 45CH 47A

PANDIONIDAE

Osprey *Pandion haliaetus* 13Ena 17Ena 20T 48USA 49USA 51CR

ACCIPITRIDAE

Grey-headed Kite *Leptodon cayanensis* 12Ena 16Epi 19Ees,na 20T 46CR 50Vmo 51Vmo
Hook-billed Kite *Chondrohierax uncinatus* 11Ena 17Egu 19Egu 49V
Swallow-tailed Kite *Elanoides forficatus* 5BO 15Epi 19Eca,gu 45BO 47A 48USA 50Vca 51Vca
Pearl Kite *Gampsonyx swainsonii* 17Egu 19Egu
White-tailed Kite *Elanus leucurus* 47A 49USA
Snail Kite *Rostrhamus sociabilis* 5Vca 17Ema 45BO 48USA 50Bmg 51Vca
Slender-billed Kite *Heliocolestes hamatus* 5Vmo 7Ena 12Ena 50Vmo 51Vmo
Double-toothed Kite *Harpagus bidentatus* 11Ena 16Ees 19Ees,ms,pi 46PA
Mississippi Kite *Ictinia mississippiensis* 48USA 49USA
Plumbeous Kite *Ictinia plumbea* 16Egu 45BO 47A
Northern Harrier *Circus cyaneus* 48USA 49CN
Cinereous Harrier *Circus cinereus* 14A 45CH
Long-winged Harrier *Circus buffoni* 47A
Tiny Hawk *Accipiter superciliosus* 5Vbo 16Ees 19Ena 45BO 50Vbo 51Vbo
Semicollared Hawk *Accipiter collaris* 19Epi
Plain-breasted Hawk *Accipiter ventralis* 14Elo,na 15Epi 19Eim,na
Cooper's Hawk *Accipiter cooperii* 48USA 49USA
Bicoloured Hawk *Accipiter bicolor* 5Vca 15Ees 46CR 50Vca 51Vca
Crane Hawk *Geranospiza caerulescens* 5Vmo 10Ena 19Ena 45A; Bba; BO 50M 51M
Plumbeous Hawk *Leucopternis plumbeus* 16Ees 19Ees,pi
Slate-coloured Hawk *Leucopternis schistaceus* 5Ena 6Ena 7Ena 10Ena 11Ena 19Ena 45BO 50Ena 51Ena
Barred Hawk *Leucopternis princeps* 15Eeo,pi 19Eeo,es,pi 46CR
Black-faced Hawk *Leucopternis melanops* 12Ena 19Ena 50Vbo 51Vbo
Semiplumbeous Hawk *Leucopternis semiplumbeus* 16Ees 19Ees 46CR
White Hawk *Leucopternis albicollis* 45BO 46CR
Grey-backed Hawk *Leucopternis occidentalis* 17Egu 19Eeo,gu
Grey-lined Hawk *Asturina nitida* 5Cma; Vca 17Egu,im,lr 19Egu,lr 20T 45BO 49USA 50Bpa 51Vta
Common Black Hawk *Buteogallus anthracinus* 20T 49USA 51Van
Mangrove Black Hawk *Buteogallus subtilis* 17Egu
Great Black Hawk *Buteogallus urubitinga* 5Vam 12Epa 17Eeo,lo 19Elo 45BO 46CR 51Eeo 51Vam
Savanna Hawk *Buteogallus meridionalis* 5Vap 17Ema 19Ema 20T 45BO 47A 50Vap 51Vap
Solitary Eagle *Harpyhaliaetus solitarius* 5Eeo 18Ena 19Eeo 44Pcu 45BO
Black-collared Hawk *Busarellus nigricollis* 5Vca 12Plo 45BO 47A 50Bmg 51Vca
Black-chested Buzzard-Eagle *Geranoaetus melanoleucus* 14Eaz,lo 19Eaz,lo 45Bba 47A
Harris's Hawk *Parabuteo unicinctus* 17Eaz,gu,lo 19Eaz,gu 45CH 49USA
Roadside Hawk *Buteo magnirostris* 1Ccu 4Cvc 5Vca,la 6Ena 7Ena 12Ena,pa 13Ena 16Ees,pi 19Ems,na,pi,zc 45BO 47A 50Bsp 51Vca,la
Broad-winged Hawk *Buteo platypterus* 5Vla 13Ena 19Eca,na 48USA 50Vla 51Vla
White-rumped Hawk *Buteo leucorrhous* 13Ena 15Epi 19Elo,na,pi 44Ppa 45BO
Short-tailed Hawk *Buteo brachyurus* 17Ena
White-throated Hawk *Buteo albigula* 14Pcu
Swainson's Hawk *Buteo swainsoni* 48CN 49USA
White-tailed Hawk *Buteo albicaudatus* 45Bmg; BO 49USA
Red-backed Hawk *Buteo polyosoma* 14Eca,na,pi 17Egu 19Eca,gu 45BO 47A
Zone-tailed Hawk *Buteo albonotatus* 17Elo 19Elo 49USA
Red-tailed Hawk *Buteo jamaicensis* 48CN; USA 49USA
Crested Eagle *Morphnus guianensis* 9Ena 19Ena
Harpy Eagle *Harpia harpyja* 5Vbo 50Vbo 51Vbo
Black Hawk-Eagle *Spizaetus tyrannus* 5Vbo,mo 12Epa 16Epi 19Ees,ms 42Var 45BO 46CR 50Bsp 51Vbo
Ornate Hawk-Eagle *Spizaetus ornatus* 5Var 11Ena 16Ees 20T 42Bam 45BO 46CR 50Bmg 51Bmg
Black-and-chestnut Eagle *Oroaetus isidori* 13Ena 15Epi 19Elo

FALCONIDAE

Black Caracara *Daptrius ater* 5Vda 8Pmd 19Ena 42Pmd 45BO 50Vda 51Vam

Red-throated Caracara *Ibycter americanus* 5Vam,bo 8Phu,md 16Egu 19Ena,pa 42Pmd 45BO 50Bpa 51Vbo

Carunculated Caracara *Phalcoboenus carunculatus* 14Epi,tu 19Etu

Mountain Caracara *Phalcoboenus megalopterus* 14Pam,cu 45BO

Northern Caracara *Caracara cheriway* 17Egu 47A 48USA 49USA 50Van 51Van,bo

Yellow-headed Caracara *Milvago chimachima* 20T 45BO 47A 50Brj 51Vla

Laughing Falcon *Herpetotheres cachinnans* 5Vap 8Epi; Vbo 16Ees,lr 19Ees,na,pi 42Vba 45Bba; BO 46CR 50Brj 51Vda

Barred Forest Falcon *Micrastur ruficollis* 1Cns 3Cns 4Cvc 5Vbo,ca,ta 11Ena 16Ees,pi 19Eeo,es,im,na,pi,zc 42Pmd 45A; BO 46CR 47A 50Bmg 51Vbo

Plumbeous Forest Falcon *Micrastur plumbeus* 16Epi 19Ees,ma,pi

Lined Forest Falcon *Micrastur gilvicollis* 5Vbo 7Ena 10Ena 12Ena; Plo 19Ems,na 42Pmd 45BO 50Vbo 51Vbo

Slaty-backed Forest Falcon *Micrastur mirandollei* 5Vbo 7Ena 12Ena 19Ena 42Plo 45BO 46CR 50Vbo 51Vbo

Collared Forest Falcon *Micrastur semitorquatus* 5Vam,bo 12Ena 13Ena 16Eco 19Eco,gu,na 42Pmd 45BO 46CR 47A 50Vta 51Vta

Buckley's Forest Falcon *Micrastur buckleyi* 11Ena 12Ena,pa 19Ena 42Pmd

American Kestrel *Falco sparverius* 14Eim,lo 17Elo 19Eim 45BO; CH 48USA 49USA

Merlin *Falco columbarius* 48CN 49USA

Bat Falcon *Falco rufigularis* 12Epa 16Ees 19Ees,lr 45Bba; BO 50Bpa 51M

Orange-breasted Falcon *Falco deiroleucus* 12Ena 18Ena 19Ena

Aplomado Falcon *Falco femoralis* 45BO 50M 51M

Peregrine Falcon *Falco peregrinus* 14A 17Egu 47A 48GL; USA 49CN; USA

ARAMIDAE

Limpkin *Aramus guarauna* 5Vca,da 10Ena 17Egu,ma 19Ena 45BO 47A 48USA 50Bmg 51Vsu

PSOPHIIDAE

Grey-winged Trumpeter *Psophia crepitans* 5Vbo 8Plo 9Ena 19Ena 50Vbo 51Vbo

RALLIDAE

Ocellated Crake *Micropygia schomburgkii* 25Bbr 45BO; PY 50Vbo 51Vbo,ca

Clapper Rail *Rallus longirostris* 17Ema 19Ems 20T 25USA 48USA 49USA

Plain-flanked Rail *Rallus wetmorei* 51Vfa

Virginia Rail *Rallus limicola* 14Eco 19Eaz 25USA 48USA 49USA

Bogotá Rail *Rallus semiplumbeus* 25Ccu

Brown Wood Rail *Aramides wolfi* 16Epi 19Ees 25Epi

Grey-necked Wood Rail *Aramides cajanea* 5Vbo 8Pmd 9Ena 19Ena 25Pmd 42Pmd 45BO 46CR 47A 50Bmi 51Vbo

Rufous-necked Wood Rail *Aramides axillaris* 17Egu; Ptu 19Ptu 25Egu 51V

Red-winged Wood Rail *Aramides calopterus* 18Ena

Uniform Crake *Amaurolimnas concolor* 16Ees 19Ees 25CR 45BO 46CR 50M 51M

Chestnut-headed Crake *Anurolimnas castaneiceps* 9Ena 10Ena 19Ems,na,pa 25Plo 42Plo

Russet-crowned Crake *Anurolimnas viridis* 18Ezc; Psm 19Ezc 25Bsp 45BO 50Bpa 51Vbo

Black-banded Crake *Anurolimnas fasciatus* 12Ena 19Ena,pa 25Plo

Rusty-flanked Crake *Laterallus levraudi* 5Vca,fa,la 25Vca 51Vca

Rufous-sided Crake *Laterallus melanophaius* 5Pmd 12Ena,pa 19Ezc 25Pmd 45BO 47A 50Pmd 51Pmd

White-throated Crake *Laterallus albigularis* 16Ees 17Eeo,ma 19Egu 25PA 46CR

Grey-breasted Crake *Laterallus exilis* 10Ena 16Ees 17Ees 19Ees,na 25Puc 45BO 46CR 50Bmg 51Bpa

Black Rail *Laterallus jamaicensis* 48USA 49USA

Yellow-breasted Crake *Porzana flaviventer* 25DR; J; PR

Ash-throated Crake *Porzana albicollis* 25Bsp 45BO; PY 47A 50Bsc 51Vbo

Sora *Porzana carolina* 25USA 48USA 49USA 51USA

Paint-billed Crake *Neocrex erythrops* 25Vbo 50Vda 51Vda

Spotted Rail *Pardirallus maculatus* 25CB; PY

Blackish Rail *Pardirallus nigricans* 18Ena,pa 19Epa 25Bes 45Bba 47A 50Bba 51Pmd

Plumbeous Rail *Pardirallus sanguinolentus* 17Elo 19Elo 25Pcu 45A 47A 50Brg

Common Moorhen *Gallinula chloropus* 5Vca 17Egu,ma 19Ema 20T 25CB; CR; USA 47A 48USA 49USA 50Brg 51Vca

Purple Gallinule *Porphyrula martinica* 5Vca 17Egu,ma 19Egu,ma 20T 25CB; J 47A 48USA 50Vbo 51Vbo

Azure Gallinule *Porphyrula flavirostris* 20T 25Bpi

Caribbean Coot *Fulica caribaea* 5Vla 25J 51Vla

Slate-coloured Coot *Fulica ardesiaca* 14Eaz,ch 25Ech 45BO

HELIORNITHIDAE

Sungrebe *Heliornis fulica* 11Ena 19Ena 45BO 46CR 47A

EURYPYGIDAE

Sunbittern *Eurypyga helias* 5Vam 9Ena 19Ena 42Pmd 45Cam; BO 46Pmd 50Vba 51Vba

CHARADRIIDAE

Pied Lapwing *Vanellus cayanus* 45BO 50Bmg 51Vap

Southern Lapwing *Vanellus chilensis* 5Vfa 19Eim 20T 21T 45BO 47A 50Bsc 51Vbo

Andean Lapwing *Vanellus resplendens* 14Ech,co,na 19Eaz,co 45BO 47A

American Golden Plover *Pluvialis dominica* 14Eco 17Eco 19Eco 48USA 49USA 50USA 51USA

Pacific Golden Plover *Pluvialis fulva* 49USA

Black-bellied Plover *Pluvialis squatarola* 5Vfa 17Egu 48USA 49USA 50M 51Vfa

Semipalmated Plover *Charadrius semipalmatus* 17Egu 20T 48USA 49USA 50USA 51USA

Piping Plover *Charadrius melodus* 48USA

Wilson's Plover *Charadrius wilsonia* 17Ema 19Eeo 48USA 50Vsu 51Vsu

Killdeer *Charadrius vociferus* 17Egu 48USA 49USA 51USA

Snowy Plover *Charadrius alexandrinus* 17Egu 4USA 49USA

Collared Plover *Charadrius collaris* 5Vfa 10Ena 17Ena 19Ena 47A 50Brg 51Vfa

Tawny-throated Dotterel *Oreopholus ruficollis* 47A

HAEMATOPODIDAE

American Oystercatcher *Haematopus palliatus* 17Egu 47A 48USA

RECURVIROSTRIDAE

Black-necked Stilt *Himantopus mexicanus* 5Vfa 17Egu,ma 19Eeo 48USA 49USA 50Bpe 51Van

American Avocet *Recurvirostra americana* 48USA 49USA

BURHINIDAE

Double-striped Thick-knee *Burhinus bistriatus* 5Vca 50Vca 51Vca

Peruvian Thick-knee *Burhinus superciliaris* 17Elo; Ppi 19Egu,lo

SCOLOPACIDAE

Wilson's Snipe *Gallinago delicata* 48USA 49USA

South American Snipe *Gallinago paraguaiae* 45BO 47A 50Brg 51Vbo

Puna Snipe *Gallinago andina* 14Pju,pu 19Pam,ju,pu 45Pju,pu

Noble Snipe *Gallinago nobilis* 14Eca,co 19Eca,co,lu,tu

Giant Snipe *Gallinago undulata* 45BO; PY 50Brg 51Vbo

Andean Snipe *Gallinago jamesoni* 5Pcu 14Ems,pi 19Eco,im,ms,pi,tu 45BO 51Pcu

Imperial Snipe *Gallinago imperialis* 14Epi 19Epi,zc

Short-billed Dowitcher *Limnodromus griseus* 17Egu 48USA 49USA

Long-billed Dowitcher *Limnodromus scolopaceus* 48USA 49USA

Hudsonian Godwit *Limosa haemastica* 48USA 49USA

Bar-tailed Godwit *Limosa lapponica* 49USA

Marbled Godwit *Limosa fedoa* 48CN; USA 49USA

Whimbrel *Numenius phaeopus* 17Ema 19Eeo 20T 45CH 48CN 49USA 50M 51M

Long-billed Curlew *Numenius americanus* 48USA 49USA

Upland Sandpiper *Bartramia longicauda* 14Ena 47A 48USA 49CN

Greater Yellowlegs *Tringa melanoleuca* 14Eco,na 17Egu,ma 45Pli 48CN; USA 49USA 50Brg 51Brg

Lesser Yellowlegs *Tringa flavipes* 14Eco,na 17Eim,ma 19Eco 20T 45Pli 47A 48USA 49USA 50Vfa 51Vfa

Solitary Sandpiper *Tringa solitaria* 5Vam,da 20T 45Bba 48USA 49CN; USA 50Bpe 51Vam

Willet *Catoptrophorus semipalmatus* 17Ema 48USA 49USA 50M 51USA

Wandering Tattler *Heteroscelus incanus* 49USA

Spotted Sandpiper *Actitis macularius* 17Egu,lo 48CN; USA 49USA 50Bba 51Bba

Ruddy Turnstone *Arenaria interpres* 17Eeo,gu 48USA 49USA

Black Turnstone *Arenaria melanocephala* 49USA

Surfbird *Aphriza virgata* 49CN

Red Knot *Calidris canutus* 49CN

Sanderling *Calidris alba* 17Egu 48USA 49CN; USA

Semipalmated Sandpiper *Calidris pusilla* 5Vfa 17Egu,ma 19Egu 48USA 49USA 50Vfa 51Vfa

Western Sandpiper *Calidris mauri* 48USA 49USA

Least Sandpiper *Calidris minutilla* 17Egu,ma 19Egu 48USA 49USA 50M 51Vsu

White-rumped Sandpiper *Calidris fuscicollis* 14Eco 19Eco; A 45A 47A 48USA 49CN 50USA 51USA

Baird's Sandpiper *Calidris bairdii* 14Eco 19Eco,pa 45BO 47A 49CN

Pectoral Sandpiper *Calidris melanotos* 14Pmd 17Pmd 19A 45A 48USA 49USA 50USA 51USA

Dunlin *Calidris alpina* 48USA 49USA

Stilt Sandpiper *Calidris himantopus* 17Egu 19Egu 48USA 49CN

Buff-breasted Sandpiper *Tryngites subruficollis* 49USA

Wilson's Phalarope *Phalaropus tricolor* 48USA 49USA

Red-necked Phalarope *Phalaropus lobatus* 49USA

Red Phalarope *Phalaropus fulicarius* 49USA

THINOCORIDAE

Rufous-bellied Seedsnipe *Attagis gayi* 7Epi 14Ech,na 19Ech 45A; CH

Least Seedsnipe *Thinocorus rumicivorus* 47A

JACANIDAE

Wattled Jacana *Jacana jacana* 5Vca 9Ena 17Ema 20T 45BO 47A 50Bmg 51Vbo

STERCORARIIDAE

South Polar Skua *Stercorarius maccormicki* 49AN

Pomarine Jaeger *Stercorarius pomarinus* 49CN

Parasitic Jaeger *Stercorarius parasiticus* 49USA

Long-tailed Jaeger *Stercorarius longicaudus* 49USA

LARIDAE

Ring-billed Gull *Larus delawarensis* 48CN 49USA

California Gull *Larus californicus* 49USA

Great Black-backed Gull *Larus marinus* 48USA

Kelp Gull *Larus dominicanus* 17Egu 47A

American Herring Gull *Larus smithsonianus* 48CN; USA 49USA

Lesser Black-backed Gull *Larus fuscus* 51Belgium

Grey-hooded Gull *Larus cirrocephalus* 17Egu 47A

Brown-hooded Gull *Larus maculipennis* 47A 50Brg

Bonaparte's Gull *Larus philadelphia* 48USA 49USA

Andean Gull *Larus serranus* 14Eco,na 19Eim 45BO 47A

Laughing Gull *Larus atricilla* 17Ema 20T 48USA 49USA 50USA 51USA

Franklin's Gull *Larus pipixcan* 17Egu 45CH 48USA 49USA

Brown Noddy *Anous stolidus* 48USA

Sooty Tern *Onychoprion fuscatus* 48USA

Least Tern *Sternula antillarum* 48USA 49USA 50USA 51USA

Yellow-billed Tern *Sternula superciliaris* 9Ena 19Ena 45BO 50Brg 51Van

Large-billed Tern *Phaetusa simplex* 5Vam,fa 12Ena 19Ena 20T 45BO 47A 50Bmg 51Vam

Gull-billed Tern *Gelochelidon nilotica* 17Eeo,gu 48USA 49USA 50M 51M

Caspian Tern *Hydroprogne caspia* 48USA 49USA 51M

Black Tern *Chlidonias niger* 49USA

Common Tern *Sterna hirundo* 48USA 49CN 50Belgium 51Belgium

Roseate Tern *Sterna dougallii* 48USA

Arctic Tern *Sterna paradisaea* 48USA 49USA

South American Tern *Sterna hirundinacea* 47A

Sandwich Tern *Thalasseus sandvicensis* 17Egu 20T 48USA 50USA 51USA

Royal Tern *Thalasseus maximus* 17Egu,ma 20T 47A 48USA 49USA 50USA 51USA

Elegant Tern *Thalasseus elegans* 49USA

RYNCHOPIDAE

Black Skimmer *Rynchops niger* 45BO 48USA 49USA 50USA 51USA

OPISTHOCOMIDAE

Hoatzin *Opisthocomus hoazin* 5Pmd 9Ena 19Ena 45BO 50Pmd 51Vsu

COLUMBIDAE

White-crowned Pigeon *Patagioenas leucocephala* 26DR; USA

Scaled Pigeon *Patagioenas speciosa* 5Vam,bo 16Ees 18Ees, ms,na 19Ees,ms,pa 20T 26Puc 42Pmd 45BO 50Vmo 51Vmo

Scaly-naped Pigeon *Patagioenas squamosa* 26DR

Bare-eyed Pigeon *Patagioenas corensis* 5Vfa 26Ncu 51Vfa

Band-tailed Pigeon *Patagioenas fasciata* 2Cca 14Eca,lo,zc 15Elo,pi,zc 19Eca,lo 26Ppa; USA 45BO 49USA 50M 51Vbo

Pale-vented Pigeon *Patagioenas cayennensis* 4Cvc 5Vfa 8Pmd 16Egu 17Egu 19Egu,na 20T 21T 26Pmd 42Pmd 45BO 47A 50Bmi 51Vfa

Marañón Pigeon *Patagioenas oenops* 18Pam 19Ezc

Plumbeous Pigeon *Patagioenas plumbea* 8Pmd 9Ena 12Ena 15Eeo,pi 19Eca,ms,na,pi 26Bac,ma,rj 42Pmd 45BO 50Bmg,sp 51Vbo,me

Ruddy Pigeon *Patagioenas subvinacea* 5Vmo 8Bmg 9Ena 16Ees,pi 19Eca,es,ms,na,pa 26Epi; Bpa 42Pmd 45BO 46CR 50Vda 51Vda

Short-billed Pigeon *Patagioenas nigrirostris* 26CR; M 46CR

Dusky Pigeon *Patagioenas goodsoni* 16Ees 19Ees,lr,pi 26Epi

White-winged Dove *Zenaida asiatica* 48USA 49USA

Pacific Dove *Zenaida meloda* 17Egu,ma; Ppi 19Egu 26Pli

Eared Dove *Zenaida auriculata* 14Epi 17Eaz,lo,pi 19Eaz,pi 20T 26Ppi 45BO 47A 50Bmg 51Vsu

Mourning Dove *Zenaida macroura* 26J; USA 48USA 49USA

Common Ground Dove *Columbina passerina* 5Vfa 14Epi 19Epi 26USA 48USA 49USA 50Vsu 51Vsu

Plain-breasted Ground Dove *Columbina minuta* 17Egu 19Egu 26Brj 50Bpe 51Vbo

Ruddy Ground Dove *Columbina talpacoti* 5Vmo 20T 26Puc 45BO 47A 49M 50Vbo 51Vbo

Ecuadorian Ground Dove *Columbina buckleyi* 17Egu,ma 19Eeo,gu 26Eeo

Scaled Dove *Columbina squammata* 5Vca,fa 26Cma 45PY 50Vsu 51Vsu

Picui Ground Dove *Columbina picui* 26Brg 45BO 47A 50Bba

Croaking Ground Dove *Columbina cruziana* 17Egu,ma 19Egu 26Pli

Blue Ground Dove *Claravis pretiosa* 5Vbo 11Ena 16Egu 17Elr,ma 19Ema,na 26M 45BO 47A 50Bce 51Vbo

Maroon-chested Ground Dove *Claravis mondetoura* 14Pcu 26Pcu 44Pcu

Black-winged Ground Dove *Metriopelia melanoptera* 14Ena; Par 19Par 45BO

White-tipped Dove *Leptotila verreauxi* 5Vfa 11Ena 14Elo,pi 17Egu,lo,pi 19Eca,gu,lo,na 20T 22T 26A; BE; M 42Phu 45BO 47A 48CR 49USA 50Bmg 51Vla

Pallid Dove *Leptotila pallida* 16Ees 19Elr,ma 26Epi

Grey-headed Dove *Leptotila plumbeiceps* 4Cvc 26M 46CR

Grey-fronted Dove *Leptotila rufaxilla* 5Vbo,mo 8Pmd 9Ena 19Ems 20T 26Ena; Pmd; Bpe 42Pmd 45BO 47A 50Bpa 51Vda

Caribbean Dove *Leptotila jamaicensis* 26J; M

Grey-chested Dove *Leptotila cassini* 26CR

Ochre-bellied Dove *Leptotila ochraceiventris* 17Ema 19Egu,lo,ma 26Eeo

Russet-crowned Quail-Dove *Geotrygon goldmani* 26PA

Sapphire Quail-Dove *Geotrygon saphirina* 11Ena 16Epi 19Ees,ms,na 26Puc

Olive-backed Quail-Dove *Geotrygon veraguensis* 16Ees

Lined Quail-Dove *Geotrygon linearis* 1Ccu 5Var,ca,me 51Vca

White-throated Quail-Dove *Geotrygon frenata* 7Epi 12Ena 14Eco,lo,na 15Epi 19Eaz,ca,co,im,lo,na 26Phu 43Phu 45A; BO 47A

Violaceous Quail-Dove *Geotrygon violacea* 26Bsp

Ruddy Quail-Dove *Geotrygon montana* 4Cvc 11Ena 16Ees 19Ems,na 26Bpa:J 42Pmd 45BO 50Bba 51Vbo

PSITTACIDAE

Blue-and-yellow Macaw *Ara ararauna* 5Vmo 9Ena 19Ena 27Ena; Bmg; Pmd; PA 42BO; Pmd 45BO 50Vmo 51Vmo

Military Macaw *Ara militaris* 1Ccq 18Ena; Pca 19Ems,na 27Var,gu; M; Psm 44Psm 45BO 51Vme

Great Green Macaw *Ara ambiguus* 16Ees 17Egu 19Ees,gu 27PA 46CR

Scarlet Macaw *Ara macao* 5Vap 9Ena 19Ena 27G; Vgu; Bmg; Pmd 42Pmd 45BO 50Vap 51Vap

Red-and-green Macaw *Ara chloropterus* 5Vfa,bo 27Vbo,zu; Bpa 42BO; Pmd 45BO 50Bpa 51Vbo

Chestnut-fronted Macaw *Ara severus* 5Vap,ca 9Ena 16Epi 19Ena,pa 27Vba; Bpa; Pmd 42Pmd 45BO 50Bpa 51Vca

Red-bellied Macaw *Orthopsittaca manilata* 5Ena 9Ena 19Ena 20T 27G; Vbo; BO; Plo 42Plo 45BO 50Bmg 51Vmo

Red-shouldered Macaw *Diopsittaca nobilis* 27Vbo; Bgo 45BO 50Vbo 51Vbo

Yellow-eared Parrot *Ognorhynchus icterotis* 14Eco 15Eco 19Eco 27Eco

Blue-crowned Parakeet *Aratinga acuticaudata* 27Van,ap,la; A; Bmg; BO 45BO 47A 50Bba 51Vbo

Scarlet-fronted Parakeet *Aratinga wagleri* 1Cns 4Cvc 5Vca 27Vmo; Pam 51Vme

Red-masked Parakeet *Aratinga erythrogenys* 17Eeo,lo 19Eeo,gu,lo 27Elo

White-eyed Parakeet *Aratinga leucophthalma* 5Vmo 11Ena 19Ems,pa,zc 27Vbo; Bmi; BO; Plo 42Plo 45BO 47A 50Bmg 51Vmo

Sun Parakeet *Aratinga solstitialis* 27Bpa

Dusky-headed Parakeet *Aratinga weddellii* 9Ena 19Ena 27Pcu,lo,md 42Pmd 45BO

Peach-fronted Parakeet *Aratinga aurea* 27Bbr,pa; Pmd 45BO 50Bmg

Brown-throated Parakeet *Aratinga pertinax* 5Var 27Vbo,gu 50Var 51Var

Golden-plumed Parakeet *Leptosittaca branickii* 14Ezc 19Elo,ms,zc 27Pcu

Maroon-faced Parakeet *Pyrrhura leucotis* 5Vca,su 27Vmi; Bce,es,go 51Vmo

Painted Parakeet *Pyrrhura picta* 5Vbo 27G; Vbo; Bac,am,mg,pa; BO 42Pmd 45BO 50Bmg 51Vbo

Santa Marta Parakeet *Pyrrhura viridicata* 27Cma

Fiery-shouldered Parakeet *Pyrrhura egregia* 27Vbo 50Vbo 51Vbo

Maroon-tailed Parakeet *Pyrrhura melanura* 5Ena 12Ena 16Ees,pi 18Ems,na 19Ees,ms,na 27Chu; Eca,es,na; Plo,sm 50Ena 51Ena

El Oro Parakeet *Pyrrhura orcesi* 17Eaz,eo 19Eaz,eo 27Eeo
White-breasted Parakeet *Pyrrhura albipectus* 18Ezc 19Ems,zc 27Ezc
Flame-winged Parakeet *Pyrrhura calliptera* 27Ccu
Red-eared Parakeet *Pyrrhura hoematotis* 5Vla 27Var 51Vla
Rose-headed Parakeet *Pyrrhura rhodocephala* 5Vme 27Var,ta 51Vme
Barred Parakeet *Bolborhynchus lineola* 13Ena 14Ena,pi 15Epi 19Eaz,ms,na,pi 27M; Pcu 45BO 51Vta
Green-rumped Parrotlet *Forpus passerinus* 5Vca,fa 20T 27Vbo,gu 50Vda 51Vca
Blue-winged Parrotlet *Forpus xanthopterygius* 11Ena 19Ena 27Bpa; Plo 45BO 47A 50Bmg
Spectacled Parrotlet *Forpus conspicillatus* 2Cca 27PA
Dusky-billed Parrotlet *Forpus modestus* 12Epa 19Epa 27Vbo; Bam,mg,pa 42Vbo; Pmd 50Bmg 51Bmg
Pacific Parrotlet *Forpus coelestis* 17Elo 19Ees,gu,lr 27Egu,lo; Pla,pi
Canary-winged Parakeet *Brotogeris versicolurus* 27Plo 50Bmg
Grey-cheeked Parakeet *Brotogeris pyrrhoptera* 17Egu,lo 19Egu,lo,ma 27Elo; Ptu
Orange-chinned Parakeet *Brotogeris jugularis* 5Vap 27CR; ES 46CR 51Vap
Cobalt-winged Parakeet *Brotogeris cyanoptera* 8Plo 9Ena 19Ena,pa 27Ena; Bac,am; BO; Plo,md 42Plo,md 45BO 51Pmd
Golden-winged Parakeet *Brotogeris chrysoptera* 5Vbo,mo 27Vbo; Bam,mg,pa 50Bmg 51Vbo
Tui Parakeet *Brotogeris sanctithomae* 12Plo 19Plo 27Bam; Plo
Tepui Parrotlet *Nannopsittaca panychlora* 5Vbo 27Vbo 50Vbo 51Vbo
Lilac-tailed Parrotlet *Touit batavicus* 5Var 20T 27S
Scarlet-shouldered Parrotlet *Touit huetii* 5Vmo 19Plo 27G; BO 42BO 50Vmo 51Vmo
Blue-fronted Parrotlet *Touit dilectissimus* 15Eco 19Epi 27PA 46PA
Sapphire-rumped Parrotlet *Touit purpuratus* 11Ena 19Ena 27Ena; Bam
Spot-winged Parrotlet *Touit stictopterus* 18Ena,zc; Plo 19Ena 27Ems
Black-headed Parrot *Pionites melanocephalus* 5Vam,bo 8Vbo; Plo 9Ena 19Ena 27Ena; S; Plo 50Vam 51Vbo
Brown-hooded Parrot *Pionopsitta haematotis* 27M; PA 46CR
Rose-faced Parrot *Pionopsitta pulchra* 16Ees 19Ees,pi
Orange-cheeked Parrot *Pionopsitta barrabandi* 9Ena 19Ena 27Bmg,pa; Pmd 42Pmd
Saffron-headed Parrot *Pionopsitta pyrilia* 27Vba 51Vba,me
Caica Parrot *Pionopsitta caica* 27Vbo; Bam 50Vbo 51Vbo
Rusty-faced Parrot *Hapalopsittaca amazonina* 27Vta
Red-faced Parrot *Hapalopsittaca pyrrhops* 14Elo,ms 19Eaz,lo,ms 27Elo
Short-tailed Parrot *Graydidascalus brachyurus* 12Plo 19Plo 27Bam,pa; Plo
Blue-headed Parrot *Pionus menstruus* 2Cca 5Vam 9Ena 16Ees 19Ees,gu,lr,ms,na,pa 20T 27Epi; Bam,es,mg,pa; CR; Pcu,lo,md; PA 42Bam; Plo,md 45BO 50Bmg 51Vbo
Red-billed Parrot *Pionus sordidus* 5Var 13Ena 15Eco,pi 19Eaz,eo,na 27Chu; Var; BO 42Epi 45BO 51Var
White-capped Parrot *Pionus seniloides* 5Vme 13Ena 14Eim,na,pi 15Eim,pi 19Eim,lo,pi 27Vta 51Vme
Bronze-winged Parrot *Pionus chalcopterus* 5Eeo 6Epi 7Epi 16Ees,pi 19Eeo,gu,pi 27Epi; Ptu 51Vme
Dusky Parrot *Pionus fuscus* 5Vbo 27Vbo; Bam,pa 50Vbo 51Vbo
Red-lored Parrot *Amazona autumnalis* 16Ees 17Egu 19Egu 27Bam; BE; GT; M; PA 46CR 50M 51M
Blue-cheeked Parrot *Amazona dufresniana* 27G; Vbo 51Vbo
Festive Parrot *Amazona festiva* 10Ena 19Ena 27Ena; Vbo
Yellow-shouldered Parrot *Amazona barbadensis* 5Vfa 27Nbo; Vfa 51Vfa
Yellow-crowned Parrot *Amazona ochrocephala* 5Vfa 9Ena 19Ena,pa 27Vgu; Bpa; BE; CR; GT; M; Pmd 42Pmd 45BO 50Vbo 51Vfa
Orange-winged Parrot *Amazona amazonica* 5Vbo 9Ena 19Ena 20T 21T 22T 27Vbo; Bes,pa 45BO 50Vbo 51Vbo
Scaly-naped Parrot *Amazona mercenaria* 1Ccq 5Cma; Vtr 13Ena 14Ems,na,pi,zc 19Eaz,ca,co,ms,na,pi,zc 27Vta; BO; Phu,pa,sm 43Ppa 45BO 51Vtr
Mealy Parrot *Amazona farinosa* 5Vbo 9Ena 16Ees 19Ees,lr,na 27Ena; Bam,es; BO; CR; Pmd 42BO; Pmd 45BO 46CR 50Vbo 51Vbo
Red-fan Parrot *Deroptyus accipitrinus* 12Epa 19Epa 27S; Vbo; Bam,mg,pa 50Bpa 51Bpa

CUCULIDAE

Dwarf Cuckoo *Coccyzus pumilus* 28Vgu
Ash-coloured Cuckoo *Coccyzus cinereus* 47A
Black-billed Cuckoo *Coccyzus erythropthalmus* 28USA 48USA
Yellow-billed Cuckoo *Coccyzus americanus* 28CB; USA 48USA 49USA 50USA 51USA
Pearly-breasted Cuckoo *Coccyzus euleri* 19Ema 28B
Mangrove Cuckoo *Coccyzus minor* 28DR; J 48USA
Dark-billed Cuckoo *Coccyzus melacoryphus* 28Vbo 45BO 47A 51Vbo,su
Grey-capped Cuckoo *Coccyzus lansbergi* 5Vca 17Eeo,gu 19Egu,ma 28Vzu 51Vzu
Squirrel Cuckoo *Piaya cayana* 4Cvc 5Vbo,ca,fa 9Ena 12Ena 13Ena 16Epi 19Ees,lo,ms,zc 20T 28Ena; M; Puc 42Eaz,na; Plo,md,pu 45BO 46CR 47A 50Brj,mg 51Vbo,ca,su
Black-bellied Cuckoo *Piaya melanogaster* 12Ena 19Ena 42Bam,rd; BO 50Bmg 51Bmg
Little Cuckoo *Piaya minuta* 5Vca,mo 10Ena 16Epi 19Elr,ms 20T 28Puc 45BO 50Vca 51Vca
Greater Ani *Crotophaga major* 5Ena; Vmo 8Ena 9Ena 19Ena 28Puc 45BO 47A 50Vsu 51Vsu
Smooth-billed Ani *Crotophaga ani* 4Cvc 5Vap,bo 9Ena 13Ena 16Ees,pi 17Eeo,es,ma,pi 19Epi 20T 21T 22T 28Phu,uc 45BO 47A 48USA 50Bba 51Van
Groove-billed Ani *Crotophaga sulcirostris* 5Vmo 17Elo,ma 19Eaz,eo,gu 28M 48USA 49USA 51Vmo
Guira Cuckoo *Guira guira* 28Brg 45BO 47A 50Bpe
Striped Cuckoo *Tapera naevia* 5Vfa,mo 6Epi 7Epi 16Ees 17Eaz,es,gu,lo,ma 19Eaz,es,gu 20T 28M; PA 45BO 46CR 47A 50Bba 51Vda,mo
Pheasant Cuckoo *Dromococcyx phasianellus* 12Plo 19Epa 28M 42Plo 45BO 50Bmg 51Bmg
Pavonine Cuckoo *Dromococcyx pavoninus* 5Vme 28BO 42Pmd 45BO 47A 50Vme 51Vme
Rufous-vented Ground Cuckoo *Neomorphus geoffroyi* 28Bsp

Banded Ground Cuckoo *Neomorphus radiolosus* 16Ees 19Ees

Rufous-winged Ground Cuckoo *Neomorphus rufipennis* 5Vbo 50Vbo 51Vbo

TYTONIDAE

Barn Owl *Tyto alba* 29J; Puc 45BO 47A 48USA 49USA

STRIGIDAE

Tropical Screech Owl *Megascops choliba* 5Vca 7Ena 12Plo 19Ena 20T 29Plo 42Plo 45BO 47A 50Bpa 51Vca

Peruvian Screech Owl *Megascops roboratus* 17Elo 18Ezc 19Eeo,gu,lo,zc 29Pam,ca,tu

Bare-shanked Screech Owl *Megascops clarkii* 29CR

Colombian Screech Owl *Megascops colombianus* 4Cvc 15Cna; Eca 19Eca,pi 29Eca

Rufescent Screech Owl *Megascops ingens* 3Csa 5Pcu 18Ems; Psm 19Ems,na 29Vme 43BO; Pju 45BO 51Pcu

Cinnamon Screech Owl *Megascops petersoni* 18Ezc 19Ems,zc 29Pca

Northern Tawny-bellied Screech Owl *Megascops watsonii* 5Vbo 8Ena 9Ena 19Ena 29Ena 50Vbo 51Vbo

Southern Tawny-bellied Screech Owl *Megascops usta* 29Pmd 42Pmd 45BO 50Bpa; Pmd

Vermiculated Screech Owl *Megascops vermiculatus* 5Var 16Ees 19Eeo,es,pi 29Cri; Var; CR; PA 46CR 51Var

Roraima Screech Owl *Megascops roraimae* 50Vbo 51Vbo

Río Napo Screech Owl *Megascops napensis* 18Ems,zc 19Ems,na,pa 29Phu 43Psm 45Epa

White-throated Screech Owl *Megascops albogularis* 1Ccu 5Vta 14Eca,na 19Eaz,ca,lo,na 29Pay 45BO 51Vta

Crested Owl *Lophostrix cristata* 5Vbo 7Ena 8Pmd 9Ena 16Ees 19Ees,na,pi 29Vzu 42Pmd 45BO 46CR 50Bpa 51Vbo

Spectacled Owl *Pulsatrix perspicillata* 8Ena 16Ees 19Eeo,es,ma,na,pa 20T 29Puc 42Ena 45BO 46CR 50Vmo 51Vmo; Bpa

Band-bellied Owl *Pulsatrix melanota* 1Cna 18Ena 19Ems,na,zc 29Phu 43BO 45BO

Great Horned Owl *Bubo virginianus* 14Eaz,na 19Eaz,pi 29USA 45BO 47A 48USA 49USA 51V

Mottled Owl *Ciccaba virgata* 5Var,ca,la 8Eca 16Ees 19Eaz,eo,es,gu,im,na,pi 20T 29M 42Ppu 45BO 46Bar; CR 47A 51Vca

Black-and-white Owl *Ciccaba nigrolineata* 5Vca 16Epi 19Eeo,gu 29Var 46Vme; CR 51Vca

Black-banded Owl *Ciccaba huhula* 5Ena; Vbo 8Ena 9Ena 19Ena 29Ena; Plo 42Pmd 45A; BO 47A 50Ena 51Ena

Rufous-banded Owl *Ciccaba albitarsis* 5Vla 6Ena 7Ena 13Ena 14Eca,na,pi 19Eca,im,lo,na,pi 29Phu 44Pju 45BO 51Vla

Cloud-forest Pygmy Owl *Glaucidium nubicola* 15Epi 19Eca,pi 29Eca

Andean Pygmy Owl *Glaucidium jardinii* 14Eaz,im,pi 19Eaz,co,im,ms,pi 29Ccu; Vta

Subtropical Pygmy Owl *Glaucidium parkeri* 18Ena 19Ems 29Ezc 43Ems 45BO

Central American Pygmy Owl *Glaucidium griseiceps* 16Ees 19Ees 29CR 46CR 50PA

Amazonian Pygmy Owl *Glaucidium hardyi* 29Brd; Pmd 42Pmd 45BO 50Bpa 51Bpa

Ferruginous Pygmy Owl *Glaucidium brasilianum* 5Vca 8Epi 9Ena 19Ena,pa 20T 21T 22T 29Cam,ma; A 42Phu 45BO 47A 50Bmg 51Vmo

Ridgway's Pygmy Owl *Glaucidium ridgwayi* 29M 49USA

Peruvian Pygmy Owl *Glaucidium peruanum* 17Elo,ma 19Eaz,eo,gu,lr,lo,ma 29Elo; Pan

Burrowing Owl *Athene cunicularia* 14Eim 17Egu,lo 19Egu,lo 29Bmi; CB; DR 45BO; CH; PY 47A 48CN 49USA 50Bba 51Bmi

Buff-fronted Owl *Aegolius harrisii* 14Eaz 19Eaz 29Bce 44A 45BO

Striped Owl *Asio clamator* 17Egu 19Egu 29Vmi; Phu 47A

Stygian Owl *Asio stygius* 14Ccc; Ppi 29A; Bsp; BE 51Vbo

Short-eared Owl *Asio flammeus* 29Vdf; CN; DR 48CN; USA 49CN; USA

STEATORNITHIDAE

Oilbird *Steatornis caripensis* 5Vmo 16Ees 18Ems; Vmo 19Ees,ms 20T 30Phu 31T; Vba 45BO 50Vmo 51Vmo

NYCTIBIIDAE

Great Potoo *Nyctibius grandis* 5Vap,bo 8Plo 19Ena 30Ena; Pmd 31Ena; Pmd 42Plo 45BO 46CR 50Vap 51Vap

Long-tailed Potoo *Nyctibius aethereus* 5Ena 8Plo 9Ena 19Ena 30Puc 31Plo 42Plo 45BO 47A 50Ena 51Ena

Common Potoo *Nyctibius griseus* 1Cby 4Cvc 5Vmo; Pmd 8Bam 9Ena 16Ena 17Elo 19Eca,es,na 20T 30Ena; Pmd 31Cam; Ena 42Plo 45BO 46CR 47A 50Bce 51V

Andean Potoo *Nyctibius maculosus* 13Ena 19Ena 30Ppa 31Ena 44Ppa

White-winged Potoo *Nyctibius leucopterus* 30Bam 31Bam

Rufous Potoo *Nyctibius bracteatus* 12Ena 19Ena 30Bam 31Ena

CAPRIMULGIDAE

Short-tailed Nighthawk *Lurocalis semitorquatus* 19Egu,pa 30Var; Bba 31Egu; A 45BO; PY 47A 50Bmg 51Vca

Rufous-bellied Nighthawk *Lurocalis rufiventris* 13Ena 14Eim,na 19Eim,ms,na 31Eim 44Vme

Least Nighthawk *Chordeiles pusillus* 30Bma 31Bma 45BO 50Bpe 51Vam

Sand-coloured Nighthawk *Chordeiles rupestris* 11Ena 19Ena 30Pmd 31Pmd

Lessser Nighthawk *Chordeiles acutipennis* 5Vam 17Egu,lo 19Egu; Pca 30V; USA 48no data 49USA 50Vam 51Vam

Common Nighthawk *Chordeiles minor* 30USA 31USA 48USA 49USA 50M 51USA

Antillean Nighthawk *Chordeiles gundlachii* 30DR 31GC; J 48USA

Band-tailed Nighthawk *Nyctiprogne leucopyga* 5Vap 30Bmg 31Bmg 45BO 50Bmg 51Bmg

Nacunda Nighthawk *Podager nacunda* 30Vgu; Bmg,rg 31Vgu; Bmg 47A 50Bmg 51Bmg

Pauraque *Nyctidromus albicollis* 4Cvc 5Vbo,fa 8Ems 9Ena 16Ees,pi 19Eaz,gu,im,lo,ma,pi 20T 30Phu,uc 31Ena; GT; Pmd 42Pmd 45BO 46CR 47A 48USA 49USA 50M 51Vfa

Ocellated Poorwill *Nyctiphrynus ocellatus* 12Epa 19Ena 30Pmd 31Bes; BO 42Pmd 45BO 47A 50Bmg

Chocó Poorwill *Nyctiphrynus rosenbergi* 16Ees 19Ees,im,pi 30Ees 31Ees

Chuck-will's-widow *Caprimulgus carolinensis* 30USA 31USA 48USA 51USA

Rufous Nightjar *Caprimulgus rufus* 5Vam,ca 18Psm 20T 30Bpe 31Vbo; A 45BO 47A 50Bce 51Vca

Silky-tailed Nightjar *Caprimulgus sericocaudatus* 30A; Puc 31A; Puc 45BO 47A 50Bpa

Band-winged Nightjar *Caprimulgus longirostris* 2Cca 13Ena 14Ebo,ma,pi 19Eaz,bo,im,lo,ms,na,pi 30Cna 31A; Pli 45BO 50Vla 51Vla

White-tailed Nightjar *Caprimulgus cayennensis* 5Vca 14Eim 20T 30Var 31Vma 50Vsu 51Vsu

Spot-tailed Nightjar *Caprimulgus maculicaudus* 30M 31M 45BO 50M 51M

Little Nightjar *Caprimulgus parvulus* 30Vfa; Puc 31Vfa; Bpe 45BO 47A 50Bba 51V

Scrub Nightjar *Caprimulgus anthonyi* 17Egu; Ppi 19Egu,ma 30Eeo 31Egu

Blackish Nightjar *Caprimulgus nigrescens* 12Ena 18Ena; Psm 19Ena 30V 31V 50Bmg,pa 51Vbo; Bpa

Ladder-tailed Nightjar *Hydropsalis climacocerca* 30S 31Plo 45BO

Scissor-tailed Nightjar *Hydropsalis torquata* 30A 31A 45BO 47A

Swallow-tailed Nightjar *Uropsalis segmentata* 14Epi 15Epi 19Ena,pi 30Puc 31Puc 45BO

Lyre-tailed Nightjar *Uropsalis lyra* 15Ena 18Ena 19Ena 30BO 31BO 44BO 45BO

APODIDAE

Spot-fronted Swift *Cypseloides cherriei* 15Epi

White-chinned Swift *Cypseloides cryptus* 18Ena

Black Swift *Cypseloides niger* 49USA

White-chested Swift *Cypseloides lemosi* 18Ena

Chestnut-collared Swift *Streptoprocne rutila* 5BO 13Ena 15Eaz 19Eaz,lo 45BO 51BO

Tepui Swift *Cypseloides phelpsi* 51Vbo

White-collared Swift *Streptoprocne zonaris* 5Vme 13Ena 14Ems 15Epi 19Ems,na,zc 45BO 50M 51Vme

Band-rumped Swift *Chaetura spinicaudus* 5Vbo 50Vbo 51Vbo

Grey-rumped Swift *Chaetura cinereiventris* 5Vca 19Ems,na,pi 20T 45BO 50Bsp 51Vme

Pale-rumped Swift *Chaetura egregia* 18Psm

Vaux's Swift *Chaetura vauxi* 49USA 51M

Chimney Swift *Chaetura pelagica* 48USA 51USA

Sick's Swift *Chaetura meridionalis* 45BO 47A 51Brj

Short-tailed Swift *Chaetura brachyura* 9Ena 17Elo; Ppi 19Eeo,na 45BO 51Vmo

White-tipped Swift *Aeronautes montivagus* 14Eaz 45BO 50Vla 51Vla

Fork-tailed Palm Swift *Tachornis squamata* 5Vam 10Ena 19Ena 20T 50Bmg 51Vam

TROCHILIDAE

White-tipped Sicklebill *Eutoxeres aquila* 1Ccu 15Eeo,pi 18Ena 19Eeo,na

Buff-tailed Sicklebill *Eutoxeres condamini* 18Ena

Bronzy Hermit *Glaucis aeneus* 16Ees

Rufous-breasted Hermit *Glaucis hirsutus* 5Vca,fa 12Plo 19Plo 20T 50Vfa 51Vfa

Band-tailed Barbthroat *Threnetes ruckeri* 5PA 16Ees 46CR 51PA

Pale-tailed Barbthroat *Threnetes leucurus* 19Ems 50Vbo 51Vbo

Streak-throated Hermit *Phaethornis rupurumii* 5Vbo 50Vbo 51Vbo

Little Hermit *Phaethornis longuemareus* 5Vmo 20T 22T 50Vmo 51Vmo

Black-throated Hermit *Phaethornis atrimentalis* 19Epa

Stripe-throated Hermit *Phaethornis striigularis* 5Vfa 16Ees 19Elr 51Vfa

Grey-chinned Hermit *Phaethornis griseogularis* 5Vla 18Ena,zc 19Ezc 50Vla 51Vla

Reddish Hermit *Phaethornis ruber* 5Vam,bo 45BO 50Bmg 51Vam

White-bearded Hermit *Phaethornis hispidus* 12Plo 19Plo

White-whiskered Hermit *Phaethornis yaruqui* 16Ees 19Eeo,es,lr,pi

Green Hermit *Phaethornis guy* 3Cns 18Ena,zc 19Ems,na,zc 20T 21T 46CR

Tawny-bellied Hermit *Phaethornis syrmatophorus* 6Ena 13Ena 15Cna; Epi 19Eca,na

Straight-billed Hermit *Phaethornis bourcieri* 11Ena 19Ems,na

Western Long-tailed Hermit *Phaethornis longirostris* 17Elo,ma 19Ema 46CR 51CR

Eastern Long-tailed Hermit *Phaethornis superciliosus* 5Vam 50Vam 51Vam

Great-billed Hermit *Phaethornis malaris* 9Ena 19Ena 45BO

Tooth-billed Hummingbird *Androdon aequatorialis* 16Ees 19Ees

Green-fronted Lancebill *Doryfera ludovicae* 15Epi 18Epi; Psm

Blue-fronted Lancebill *Doryfera johannae* 18Plo

Grey-breasted Sabrewing *Campylopterus largipennis* 11Ena 19Ena 45BO 50Bpa 51Bpa

White-tailed Sabrewing *Campylopterus ensipennis* 5Vmo 20T 51Vmo

Lazuline Sabrewing *Campylopterus falcatus* 1Ccq 5Vmi 51Vmi

Napo Sabrewing *Campylopterus villaviscensio* 18Ems 19Ems

Buff-breasted Sabrewing *Campylopterus duidae* 51Vbo

Swallow-tailed Hummingbird *Eupetomena macroura* 45BO 50Bmg

Brown Violetear *Colibri delphinae* 4Cvc 5Vbo,la 15Epi 19Eca,pi 45BO 46CR 50Vbo 51Vla

Green Violetear *Colibri thalassinus* 1Ccq 2Cca 5Var,mi 13Ena 15Epi 19Eaz,co,lo,na,pi 44Pju 45BO; Pcu 51Vya

Sparkling Violetear *Colibri coruscans* 2Cca 13Ena 14Eaz,ch,lo,pi 19Elo,pi 45BO 50Vme 51Vme

Black-throated Mango *Anthracothorax nigricollis* 19Ees,na 45BO

Fiery-tailed Awlbill *Avocettula recurvirostris* 50Bpa 51Bpa

Crimson Topaz *Topaza pella* 51Vbo

Ruby-topaz Hummingbird *Chrysolampis mosquitus* 20T 45Bba 50Vbo 51Vbo

Violet-headed Hummingbird *Klais guimeti* 1Cns 3Cns 5Vca 18Ems,na,zc 19Ems,zc 45BO 46CR 51Vca

Blue-chinned Sapphire *Chlorostilbon notata* 20T

Blue-tailed Emerald *Chlorostilbon mellisugus* 45BO

Western Emerald *Chlorostilbon melanorhynchus* 14Epi 19Epi

Green-crowned Wood-nymph *Thalurania fannyi* 16Ees 17Eeo

Fork-tailed Wood-nymph *Thalurania furcata* 5Vmo 18Ena 19Ems,na 45BO 50Vmo 51Vmo

Violet-bellied Hummingbird *Damophila julie* 16Ees

Rufous-throated Sapphire *Hylocharis sapphirina* 5Vam 45Bba 50Vam 51Vam

White-chinned Sapphire *Hylocharis cyanus* 45BO 50Vbo 51Vbo,ta
Blue-headed Sapphire *Hylocharis grayi* 14Eim 19Eim
Golden-tailed Sapphire *Chrysuronia oenone* 1Cns 3Cns 5Vsu,ta 18Ena 19Ena 45BO 50Vta 51Vla
White-tailed Goldenthroat *Polytmus guainumbi* 45BO 50Vbo 51Vbo
Buffy Hummingbird *Leucippus fallax* 5Vfa,la 51Vsu
Tumbes Hummingbird *Leucippus baeri* 17Elo 19Elo; Pla
Olive-spotted Hummingbird *Leucippus chlorocercus* 10Ena 19Ena
Many-spotted Hummingbird *Taphrospilus hypostictus* 18Ems
Rufous-tailed Hummingbird *Amazilia tzacatl* 5Vta 16Ees 19Eim 51M
Amazilia Hummingbird *Amazilia amazilia* 17Eaz,eo,gu,lo,ma 19Eaz,eo,gu,lo,ma
Versicoloured Emerald *Amazilia versicolor* 45PY 50Brj
White-chested Emerald *Amazilia brevirostris* 5Vmo 20T 50Vmo 51Vmo
Andean Emerald *Amazilia franciae* 15Eim,pi 18Ezc 19Eca,pi
Glittering-throated Emerald *Amazilia fimbriata* 10Ena 19Ena,zc 50Vca 51Vca
Blue-chested Hummingbird *Amazilia amabilis* 16Ees,lr 19Ees
Purple-chested Hummingbird *Amazilia rosenbergi* 16Ees 19Ees,pi
Green-bellied Hummingbird *Amazilia viridigaster* 5Vbo 50Vbo 51Vbo
Copper-rumped Hummingbird *Amazilia tobaci* 5Vca,la 20T 51Vla
White-vented Plumeleteer *Chalybura buffonii* 17Elo 19Ptu
Bronze-tailed Plumeleteer *Chalybura urochrysia* 16Ees
Speckled Hummingbird *Adelomyia melanogenys* 1Ccq 5Vla,ta 13Ena 14Ena,pi 15Epi 19Egu,na,pi,zc 44BO; Pju 45BO 51Vla
Ecuadorian Piedtail *Phlogophilus hemileucurus* 18Ena,zc 19Ems,na,zc
Velvet-browed Brilliant *Heliodoxa xanthogonys* 50Vbo 51Vbo
Black-throated Brilliant *Heliodoxa schreibersii* 11Ena 19Ems,na
Gould's Jewelfront *Heliodoxa aurescens* 45BO
Fawn-breasted Brilliant *Heliodoxa rubinoides* 13Ena 15Epi 19Ems,na,zc 44Pju
Green-crowned Brilliant *Heliodoxa jacula* 16Epi
Empress Brilliant *Heliodoxa imperatrix* 19Eca
Violet-fronted Brilliant *Heliodoxa leadbeateri* 5Vla 18Ena,zc 19Ems,zc 44BO 45BO 51Vca
Scissor-tailed Hummingbird *Hylonympha macrocerca* 5Vsu 51Vsu
White-tailed Hillstar *Urochroa bougueri* 15Epi 18Ena 19Ena
Buff-tailed Coronet *Boissonneaua flavescens* 1Ccu 2Cca 15Epi 19Eca,pi
Chestnut-breasted Coronet *Boissonneaua matthewsii* 13Ena 18Elo,na,zc 19Ezc
Velvet-purple Coronet *Boissonneaua jardini* 15Epi
Shining Sunbeam *Aglaeactis cupripennis* 14Eaz 19Eaz,pi
Ecuadorian Hillstar *Oreotrochilus chimborazo* 14Eco
Andean Hillstar *Oreotrochilus estella* 45BO
Mountain Velvetbreast *Lafresnaya lafresnayi* 14Eaz,na 19Eaz,im,na
Bronzy Inca *Coeligena coeligena* 1Ccq 2Cca 5Vta 13Ena 44Phu 51Vta
Brown Inca *Coeligena wilsoni* 15Cna; Epi 19Eca,pi
Collared Inca *Coeligena torquata* 13Ena 15Epi 19Eco,zc
Buff-winged Starfrontlet *Coeligena lutetiae* 2Cca 14Ems,pi 19Ems,na,pi
Rainbow Starfrontlet *Coeligena iris* 14Eaz; Ppi 19Eaz,lo
Sword-billed Hummingbird *Ensifera ensifera* 14Elo
Great Sapphirewing *Pterophanes cyanopterus* 14Eim,pi 19Ech,im,ms
Giant Hummingbird *Patagona gigas* 14Epi 19Epi
Orange-throated Sunangel *Heliangelus mavors* 5Vtr 51Vtr
Amethyst-throated Sunangel *Heliangelus amethysticollis* 5Elo; Vta 14Ems 19Ezc 45BO 51Vta
Mérida Sunangel *Heliangelus spencei* 5Vme 51Vme
Gorgeted Sunangel *Heliangelus strophianus* 15Epi 19Eca,pi
Tourmaline Sunangel *Heliangelus exortis* 2Cca
Flame-throated Sunangel *Heliangelus micraster* 14Elo; Pca 19Ezc
Purple-throated Sunangel *Heliangelus viola* 14Eaz,lo 19Eaz,lo
Glowing Puffleg *Eriocnemis vestita* 14Ems,na 19Ems,na
Black-thighed Puffleg *Eriocnemis derbyi* 14Cri
Sapphire-vented Puffleg *Eriocnemis luciani* 14Epi 19Epi
Emerald-bellied Puffleg *Eriocnemis alinae* 18Ena
Greenish Puffleg *Haplophaedia aureliae* 18Ena
Hoary Puffleg *Haplophaedia lugens* 15Cna 19Eca
Purple-bibbed Whitetip *Urosticte benjamini* 15Epi
Booted Racket-tail *Ocreatus underwoodii* 5Vla,ta 15Cna; Epi 18Ena,zc; Plo 19Eim,na 44Ems 51Vta
Black-tailed Trainbearer *Lesbia victoriae* 14Eaz,pi 19Eaz,pi
Green-tailed Trainbearer *Lesbia nuna* 14Elo,pi 19Elo 45BO
Purple-backed Thornbill *Ramphomicron microrhynchum* 2Cca 14Ena,pi 19Eaz,pi
Tyrian Metaltail *Metallura tyrianthina* 2Cca 5Vtr 14Eim,lo,pi,zc 19Eaz,ca,im,lo,ms,na,pi 45BO 51Vtr
Viridian Metaltail *Metallura williami* 14Eaz,ms,na 19Ems,na,tu
Violet-throated Metaltail *Metallura baroni* 14Eaz 19Eaz
Neblina Metaltail *Metallura odomae* 14Ezc; Pca 19Elo,zc
Rufous-capped Thornbill *Chalcostigma ruficeps* 19Ezc
Blue-mantled Thornbill *Chalcostigma stanleyi* 14Eaz,co 19Eaz
Rainbow-bearded Thornbill *Chalcostigma herrani* 14Eaz 19Eca
Mountain Avocetbill *Opisthoprora euryptera* 14Ena 19Ena
Long-tailed Sylph *Aglaiocercus kingi* 13Ena 19Ems,zc 45BO 51Vme
Violet-tailed Sylph *Aglaiocercus coelestis* 15Epi 17Eeo 19Epi
Venezuelan Sylph *Aglaiocercus berlepschi* 51Vmo
Wedge-billed Hummingbird *Schistes geoffroyi* 15Epi 18Ena 19Eca,na,pi 44Ppa
Purple-crowned Fairy *Heliothryx barroti* 16Ees 19Ees
Black-eared Fairy *Heliothryx auritus* 50Vbo 51Vbo
Long-billed Starthroat *Heliomaster longirostris* 17Ema 19Ema
Blue-tufted Starthroat *Heliomaster furcifer* 50Bmg
Amethyst Woodstar *Calliphlox amethystina* 51Vbo
Purple-throated Woodstar *Calliphlox mitchellii* 15Epi
Purple-collared Woodstar *Myrtis fanny* 14Eaz 19Eaz
Short-tailed Woodstar *Myrmia micrura* 17Egu,lo 19Egu

White-bellied Woodstar *Chaetocercus mulsant* 14Epi
Little Woodstar *Chaetocercus bombus* 17Ezc
Gorgeted Woodstar *Chaetocercus heliodor* 18Ena

TROGONIDAE

Western White-tailed Trogon *Trogon chionurus* 16Ees 19Ees,pi
Amazonian White-tailed Trogon *Trogon viridis* 5Vam,bo 6Ena 8Pmd 9Ena 19Ems,na 20T 21T 22T 28Pmd 42Pmd 45BO 50Bsp 51Vbo
Blue-crowned Trogon *Trogon curucui* 8Pmd 19Ems,na 28Bpi 42Pmd 45BO 47A 50Bce
Northern Violaceous Trogon *Trogon caligatus* 16Ees 17Eeo,gu 19Egu,pi 28GT 46CR 51M
Amazonian Violaceous Trogon *Trogon violaceus* 5Vam,mo 9Ena 19Ems,na 20T 22T 42Pmd 45BO 50Vmo 51Vmo
Collared Trogon *Trogon collaris* 4Cvc 5Var,ca,la,mo 11Ena 16Ees,pi 19Eeo,gu,lr,ms,na,pa 20T 21T 22T 28Cvc; M 42Pmd 45BO 50Bmg 51Vca,gu
Masked Trogon *Trogon personatus* 1Ccq 5Vla,me 13Ena 14Eaz,lo,na,pi 15Epi 19Eca,im,ms,na,pi,tu,zc 28Phu 43BO 45BO 50Vbo 51Vbo,me
Black-throated Trogon *Trogon rufus* 5Vbo 10Ena 16Ees 19Ees,na,pa 28CR 46CR 47A 50Brj 51Vbo
Slaty-tailed Trogon *Trogon massena* 16Ees 19Ees 28M 46CR
Blue-tailed Trogon *Trogon comptus* 16Ees,pi 19Ees 28Epi
Black-tailed Trogon *Trogon melanurus* 11Ena 17Elo 19Ees,lr,lo,na,pa 28Puc 42Pmd 45BO 50Bmg 51Vbo
Pavonine Quetzal *Pharomachrus pavoninus* 11Ena 19Ena,pa 28Pmd 42Pmd 51Pmd
Golden-headed Quetzal *Pharomachrus auriceps* 6Ena 7Ena 13Ena 15Epi 19Eca,na,pi 28Phu 43Phu 45BO 51Vme
White-tipped Quetzal *Pharomachrus fulgidus* 5Var 28Cma 51Var
Crested Quetzal *Pharomachrus antisianus* 1Cpu 6Ena 7Ena 13Ena 15Epi 19Eco,pi 28Psm 43Phu 45BO 51Vme

ALCEDINIDAE

Ringed Kingfisher *Megaceryle torquata* 5Vca 9Ena 16Ees,na 17Ema 19Eeo,gu,ma,na,pi 45BO 47A 49USA 50Bsp 51Vda
Belted Kingfisher *Megaceryle alcyon* 48USA 49USA
Amazon Kingfisher *Chloroceryle amazona* 11Ena 19Ena,pa 45BO 47A 50Bsp 51Bsp
Green Kingfisher *Chloroceryle americana* 16Ees 17Ees,ma 19Eeo 49USA
Green-and-rufous Kingfisher *Chloroceryle inda* 5Vmo 9Ena 16Ees 19Ena 50Vmo 51Vmo
American Pygmy Kingfisher *Chloroceryle aenea* 19Ees 20T 45BO 50Vsu 51Vsu

MOMOTIDAE

Broad-billed Motmot *Electron platyrhynchum* 8Pmd 16Ees,pi 19Eeo,lr,na,pi 42Pmd 45BO 46CR 50Bmg
Rufous Motmot *Baryphthengus martii* 16Ees 19Ees,lr,ms,na,pa,pi 42Plo,md 45BO 46CR 50Ees
Blue-crowned Motmot *Momotus momota* 4Cvc 5Vbo,ca,ta 9Ena 12Ena 17Eeo,lo,ma 19Eeo,lo,ma,na,pa,pi 20T 21T 22T 42Pmd 45BO 50Bmg 51Vbo
Highland Motmot *Momotus aequatorialis* 2Cca 13Ena 19Ena

GALBULIDAE

White-eared Jacamar *Galbalcyrhynchus leucotis* 10Ena 19Ena
Brown Jacamar *Brachygalba lugubris* 12Epa 19Epa 50Bpa 51Bpa
Yellow-billed Jacamar *Galbula albirostris* 5Vbo 12Ena 19Ena 50Vbo 51Vbo
Rufous-tailed Jacamar *Galbula ruficauda* 5Vca,fa,mo 16Ees 19Ees,lr,pi 20T 22T 45BO 46CR 50Bmg 51Vmo
Green-tailed Jacamar *Galbula galbula* 5Vbo 50Vbo 51Vbo
White-chinned Jacamar *Galbula tombacea* 7Ena 10Ena 19Ena
Bluish-fronted Jacamar *Galbula cyanescens* 42Pmd
Coppery-chested Jacamar *Galbula pastazae* 7Ena 18Ena,zc 19Ena,zc
Purplish Jacamar *Galbula chalcothorax* 7Ena 9Ena 19Ena
Paradise Jacamar *Galbula dea* 42Pmd 45BO 50Bpa 51Vbo
Great Jacamar *Jacamerops aurea* 5Vbo 7Ena 9Ena 12Ena,pa 16Ees 19Ees,ms,na,pa 42Pmd 46PA 50Bpa 51Vbo

BUCCONIDAE

White-necked Puffbird *Notharchus macrorhynchos* 5Vbo 10Ena 16Ees 19Ees,ma,na,pi 42Brd; Pmd 45BO 50Bmg 51Vbo
Black-breasted Puffbird *Notharchus pectoralis* 16Ees 19Ees
Pied Puffbird *Notharchus tectus* 11Ena 19Ees,na 46PA
Chestnut-capped Puffbird *Bucco macrodactylus* 42Puc
Spotted Puffbird *Bucco tamatia* 12Epa 19Bap 45Bap
Collared Puffbird *Bucco capensis* 11Ena 19Ena
Barred Puffbird *Nystalus radiatus* 16Epi 19Ees,pi
Striolated Puffbird *Nystalus striolatus* 18Ena,zc 19Ems,na,zc 42Pmd 45BO 50Bpa
Russet-throated Puffbird *Hypnelus ruficollis* 5Vam,fa,mo 51Vam
White-chested Puffbird *Malacoptila fusca* 10Ena 11Ena
White-whiskered Puffbird *Malacoptila panamensis* 16Ees,pi 19Ees 46CR
Black-streaked Puffbird *Malacoptila fulvogularis* 18Ems,na,zc 19Ems,na 43Ezc
Moustached Puffbird *Malacoptila mystacalis* 2Cca
Lanceolated Monklet *Micromonacha lanceolata* 12Ena 16Ees 19Ees,na 43Ezc
Brown Nunlet *Nonnula brunnea* 11Ena 19Ena
White-faced Nunbird *Hapaloptila castanea* 13Ena 15Epi 19Eca; Psm
Black Nunbird *Monasa atra* 5Vam 50Vam 51Vam
Black-fronted Nunbird *Monasa nigrifrons* 8Plo 19Ena 42Pmd 45BO 50Bmg
White-fronted Nunbird *Monasa morphoeus* 8Pmd 19Ena 42Pmd 45BO 46CR 50Bpa 51Bpa
Yellow-billed Nunbird *Monasa flavirostris* 9Ena 19Ena 42Ena; Plo
Swallow-winged Puffbird *Chelidoptera tenebrosa* 10Ena 12Ena,pa 19Epa

CAPITONIDAE

Scarlet-crowned Barbet *Capito aurovirens* 8Plo 19Ena
Orange-fronted Barbet *Capito squamatus* 16Ees,pi 19Ees
Five-coloured Barbet *Capito quinticolor* 16Cna; Ees 19Ees
Gilded Barbet *Capito auratus* 5Vam,bo 8Pmd 9Ena 12Ena 19Ems,na 42Pmd 45BO 50Vam 51Vbo
Lemon-throated Barbet *Eubucco richardsoni* 10Ena 19Ena,pa 42Pmd 45BO
Red-headed Barbet *Eubucco bourcierii* 1Cna 2Cqu 16Ees 18Ena; Pca 19Ems,zc 46CR 51Vta
Toucan Barbet *Semnornis ramphastinus* 6Epi 7Epi 15Epi 19Eca,pi

RAMPHASTIDAE

Emerald Toucanet *Aulacorhynchus prasinus* 1Cby 2Cca 3Cns 5Vla,me,tr 7Ena 13Ena 14Elo,na 19Elo,ms,na 32Cma; Vme; CR; M43BO 45BO 46CR 51Vla

Groove-billed Toucanet *Aulacorhynchus sulcatus* 5Var 32Var,mo 51Var

Yellow-billed Toucanet *Aulacorhynchus calorhynchus* 5Vme 51Vme

Chestnut-tipped Toucanet *Aulacorhynchus derbianus* 18Ems,na 19Ems,na 32BO 43BO 45BO 51Vbo

Crimson-rumped Toucanet *Aulacorhynchus haematopygus* 4Cvc 5Epi 6Epi 7Epi 15Eeo,pi 19Eeo,gu,im,lo,pi 32Epi 51Epi

Yellow-eared Toucanet *Selenidera spectabilis* 32CR 46CR

Golden-collared Toucanet *Selenidera reinwardtii* 9Ena 19Ems,na,pa 32Ena 42Pmd 45BO

Tawny-tufted Toucanet *Selenidera nattereri* 32Bam

Guianan Toucanet *Selenidera piperivora* 32Vbo 50Vbo 51Vbo

Green Araçari *Pteroglossus viridis* 32Bam

Lettered Araçari *Pteroglossus inscriptus* 32Pmd 42Pmd 50Bmg

Ivory-billed Araçari *Pteroglossus azara* 10Ena 19Ems 32Plo 42BO; Pmd

Black-necked Araçari *Pteroglossus aracari* 5Vbo,mo 32Vmo; Bes 50Bal 51Vbo

Chestnut-eared Araçari *Pteroglossus castanotis* 12Ena 32Cme 42Phu 45BO 47A 50Bmg

Many-banded Araçari *Pteroglossus pluricinctus* 5Vta 9Ena 19Ena 32Plo 50Vta 51Vta

Collared Araçari *Pteroglossus torquatus* 32M 46CR 51M

Stripe-billed Araçari *Pteroglossus sanguineus* 16Ees 19Ees

Pale-mandibled Araçari *Pteroglossus erythropygius* 16Epi 19Ees,gu,lr,pi 32Epi

Grey-breasted Mountain Toucan *Andigena hypoglauca* 2Cca 14Elo 19Eaz,lo 32Elo

Plate-billed Mountain Toucan *Andigena laminirostris* 6Epi 7Epi 15Epi 19Eca,co,pi 32Cna

Black-billed Mountain Toucan *Andigena nigrirostris* 3Cns 5Vtr 6Ena 7Ena 13Ena 19Ena 32Ccu; Ems 51Vla

Toco Toucan *Ramphastos toco* 32A 45BO 47A 50Bmg

Black-mandibled Toucan *Ramphastos ambiguus* 1Cna 5Vba,ta 16Ees 18Ena 19Ees,na,pi 32Vba,me; CR 46CR 51Vba

Red-billed Toucan *Ramphastos tucanus* 5Vmo 32S; Vmo 51Vbo

Cuvier's Toucan *Ramphastos cuvieri* 5Vam 8Bam 9Ena 19Ena 32Ena; Vam 42Pmd 45BO 50Bpa 51Vam

Keel-billed Toucan *Ramphastos sulfuratus* 5PA 32GT 46CR 51PA

Chocó Toucan *Ramphastos brevis* 6Epi 16Ees 19Ees,pi 32Epi

Channel-billed Toucan *Ramphastos vitellinus* 5Vbo,mo 20T 21T 22T 32Vmo 51Vbo

Citron-throated Toucan *Ramphastos citreolaemus* 51Vme

Yellow-ridged Toucan *Ramphastos culminatus* 8Pmd 9Ena 18Ems,na 32Ena; Pmd 42Pmd 45BO 50Bsc 51Vam

PICIDAE

Bar-breasted Piculet *Picumnus aurifrons* 45BO

Lafresnaye's Piculet *Picumnus lafresnayi* 12Ena 19Ems

Golden-spangled Piculet *Picumnus exilis* 50Bse 51Vbo

Black-dotted Piculet *Picumnus nigropunctatus* 51Vsu

Ecuadorian Piculet *Picumnus sclateri* 17Egu,lo 19Eeo,gu

Scaled Piculet *Picumnus squamulatus* 5Vca,fa,la 51Vca

White-bellied Piculet *Picumnus spilogaster* 50Vda 51Vda

White-barred Piculet *Picumnus cirratus* 45BO 47A 50Brj

Rufous-breasted Piculet *Picumnus rufiventris* 18Ena 19Ems 42Ena

Olivaceous Piculet *Picumnus olivaceus* 16Ees 19Epi 51PA

White Woodpecker *Melanerpes candidus* 45BO 50Bsp

Acorn Woodpecker *Melanerpes formicivorus* 4Cvc 49USA

Yellow-tufted Woodpecker *Melanerpes cruentatus* 5Vbo,ta 8Pmd 9Ena 12Ena 19Ems,na,pa 42Pmd 45BO 50Bpa 51Vta

Black-cheeked Woodpecker *Melanerpes pucherani* 16Ees 19Epi 46CR

Red-crowned Woodpecker *Melanerpes rubricapillus* 20T 22T 51Vla

Yellow-bellied Sapsucker *Sphyrapicus varius* 48USA

Scarlet-backed Woodpecker *Veniliornis callonotus* 16Ees 17Egu,lo 19Eeo,gu

Yellow-vented Woodpecker *Veniliornis dignus* 13Ena 15Epi 19Eca,co,na

Bar-bellied Woodpecker *Veniliornis nigriceps* 14Eca,ms,pi 19Eaz,ca,pi 45BO

Smoky-brown Woodpecker *Veniliornis fumigatus* 5Vla,ta 15Epi 17Eeo,lo 18Ems,na 19Eaz,lo,ms,pi 44Psm 45BO 51Vya

Little Woodpecker *Veniliornis passerinus* 10Ena 19Ena 42Bmg 45BO 50Bmg 51Bmg

Red-rumped Woodpecker *Veniliornis kirkii* 5Vmo 16Ees 19Epi 20T 50Vmo 51Vmo

Red-stained Woodpecker *Veniliornis affinis* 12Ena 19Ena 42Plo 45BO 50Bmg 51Bmg

White-throated Woodpecker *Piculus leucolaemus* 18Ems,na 19Ems 45BO

Lita Woodpecker *Piculus litae* 16Ees 19Ees

Yellow-throated Woodpecker *Piculus flavigula* 45BO 50Bsp 51Bsp

Golden-green Woodpecker *Piculus chrysochloros* 42BO; Pcu 45BO 47A

Golden-olive Woodpecker *Piculus rubiginosus* 2Cca 5Vmo 16Elo,pi 18Ena 19Eaz,ca,eo,es,ms,pi,zc 20T 43BO; Pll 45BO 46CR; Pmd 50Vmo 51Vmo

Crimson-mantled Woodpecker *Piculus rivolii* 3Cns 7Epi 13Ena 14Eca,lo,pi; Phu 15Epi 19Eaz,ca,co,lo,na,pi 45BO

Spot-breasted Woodpecker *Colaptes punctigula* 5Vca 11Ena 19Ena 50Vsu 51Vsu

Andean Flicker *Colaptes rupicola* 14Pan,ll 45BO

Campo Flicker *Colaptes campestris* 47A 50Brj

Cinnamon Woodpecker *Celeus loricatus* 16Ees 19Ees 46PA

Waved Woodpecker *Celeus undatus* 5Vbo,mo 50Vmo 51Vmo

Scale-breasted Woodpecker *Celeus grammicus* 5Ena;Vbo 10Ena 19Ena,pa 42BO 45BO 50Ena 51Vbo

Chestnut Woodpecker *Celeus elegans* 5Vmo 10Ena 19Ena 20T 42Pmd 50Vmo 51Vmo

Cream-coloured Woodpecker *Celeus flavus* 5Vmo 8Plo,md 9Ena 19Ena 42Plo,md 45BO 50Bpa 51Vmo

Rufous-headed Woodpecker *Celeus spectabilis* 12Ena 19Ena 42Pmd

Ringed Woodpecker *Celeus torquatus* 5Vmo 10Ena 19Ena 42Pmd 45BO 50Vmo 51Vmo

Lineated Woodpecker *Dryocopus lineatus* 5Vbo,me 9Ena 12Ena 16Ees 19Eeo,es,na,pi 20T 42BO; Plo 45BO 46CR 47A 50Vme 51Vbo,me

Powerful Woodpecker *Campephilus pollens* 3Cns 7Ena,pi 13Ena 14Epi 15Epi 19Eca,na,pi

Crimson-bellied Woodpecker *Campephilus haematogaster* 16Ees 18Ems,na;Pca 19Ees,ma 44Ems; Ppa

Red-necked Woodpecker *Campephilus rubricollis* 12Ena,pa 19Ems,pa 42Pmd 45BO 50Bpa 51Vbo

Crimson-crested Woodpecker *Campephilus melanoleucos* 4Cvc 5Vam 9Ena 19Ena 42BO; Plo 45BO 50Bmg 51Vam

Guayaquil Woodpecker *Campephilus guayaquilensis* 16Eeo,pi 19Eeo,es,gu

FURNARIIDAE

Slender-billed Miner *Geositta tenuirostris* 14Eco 19Eco 45BO

Stout-billed Cinclodes *Cinclodes excelsior* 14Eca,co,na,pi,tu 19Eaz,ca,pi,tu

Bar-winged Cinclodes *Cinclodes fuscus* 14Eaz,ca,co,na 19Eca,ms,tu 45BO

Pale-legged Hornero *Furnarius leucopus* 5Vfa 17Elo,ma 19Eeo,gu,lo,ma,ms,pi 45BO 50Bmg 51Vca

Lesser Hornero *Furnarius minor* 10Ena 19Ena

Andean Tit-Spinetail *Leptasthenura andicola* 5Vme 14Eco,na,tu 19Eca,pi,tu 51Vme

Ochre-browed Thistletail *Schizoeaca coryi* 5Vme 51Vme

White-chinned Thistletail *Schizoeaca fuliginosa* 5Ena 14Ena,pi,tu 19Eca,im,ms,na,pi,tu 51Ena

Mouse-coloured Thistletail *Schizoeaca griseomurina* 14Eaz,ms,zc 19Eaz,ms,zc

Azara's Spinetail *Synallaxis azarae* 2Cca 3Cns 5Vba 6Epi 7Epi 13Ena 14Eco,lo,na,pi 15Epi 19Eaz,co,eo,im,lo,pi 44BO; Pju 45BO 51Vba

Pale-breasted Spinetail *Synallaxis albescens* 5Vbo,da 20T 21T 45BO 47A 50Bmi 51Vca

Dark-breasted Spinetail *Synallaxis albigularis* 7Ena 10Ena 19Ems,na,zc 50Pmd

Ruddy Spinetail *Synallaxis rutilans* 5Vam 11Ena 19Ena 42Plo 45BO 50Vam 51Vam

Chestnut-throated Spinetail *Synallaxis cherriei* 12Ena 18Ena 19Ena 50Bpa

Rufous Spinetail *Synallaxis unirufa* 5Vtr 6Ena 7Ena 13Ena 14Eca,na,pi 15Epi 19Eca,co,na,zc 44Ppa 51Vtr

Black-throated Spinetail *Synallaxis castanea* 5Var 51Var

Slaty Spinetail *Synallaxis brachyura* 4Cvc 6Epi 7Epi 16Ees 17Eeo,gu 19Eeo,es,gu,pi 46CR

Blackish-headed Spinetail *Synallaxis tithys* 17Egu,lo,ma 19Eeo,gu,lo

White-bellied Spinetail *Synallaxis propinqua* 10Ena 19Ena,pa

McConnell's Spinetail *Synallaxis macconnelli* 50Vbo 51Vbo

Dusky Spinetail *Synallaxis moesta* 11Ena 18Ena 19Ems,na

Marañón Spinetail *Synallaxis maranonica* 18Ezc 19Ezc

Plain-crowned Spinetail *Synallaxis gujanensis* 5Vbo 11Ena 19Ena 42Pcu 45BO 50Vda 51Vda

White-whiskered Spinetail *Synallaxis candei* 5Vfa 51Vla

Stripe-breasted Spinetail *Synallaxis cinnamomea* 3Cns 5Var,ca,fa 20T 21T 22T 51Vca

Necklaced Spinetail *Synallaxis stictothorax* 17Egu 19Eeo,gu

White-browed Spinetail *Hellmayrea gularis* 5Vta,tr 14Eaz,ch,pi 19Eaz,bo,ch,na,pi,zc 51Vtr

Rusty-backed Spinetail *Cranioleuca vulpina* 5Vam 45BO 50Bmg 51Vda

Parker's Spinetail *Cranioleuca vulpecula* 5Ena 10Ena 19Ena

Crested Spinetail *Cranioleuca subcristata* 5Vfa,la,mo 51Vla

Red-faced Spinetail *Cranioleuca erythrops* 4Cvc 6Epi 15Epi 19Egu,pi

Tepui Spinetail *Cranioleuca demissa* 5Vbo 50Vbo 51Vbo

Streak-capped Spinetail *Cranioleuca hellmayri* 5Cma 51Cma

Line-cheeked Spinetail *Cranioleuca antisiensis* 17Eaz,lo 19Eaz,lo

Ash-browed Spinetail *Cranioleuca curtata* 6Ena 7Ena 18Ena,zc 19Ems,na 43Ezc; Ppa 45BO

Speckled Spinetail *Cranioleuca gutturata* 12Plo 19Plo 42Pmd

Yellow-chinned Spinetail *Certhiaxis cinnamomeus* 5Vap,ca 20T 45BO 47A 50Bpe 51Van

Plain Softtail *Thripophaga fusciceps* 42Pmd 45BO

Streak-backed Canastero *Asthenes wyatti* 5Vme 14Eaz,pi 19Eaz,ch,lo 45BO 51Vme

Many-striped Canastero *Asthenes flammulata* 14Eaz,co,zc 19Eaz,ca,tu,zc

Rufous-fronted Thornbird *Phacellodomus rufifrons* 5Vca,mo 18Ezc; Pca 19Ezc 45BO 47A 50Bmg 51Vgu

Orange-fronted Plushcrown *Metopothrix aurantiaca* 10Ena 19Ena

Double-banded Greytail *Xenerpestes minlosi* 16Epi

Equatorial Greytail *Xenerpestes singularis* 18Ezc; Psm 19Ems

Rusty-winged Barbtail *Premnornis guttuligera* 13Ena 15Epi 19Ena

Spotted Barbtail *Premnoplex brunnescens* 1Cna 2Cca 13Ena 15Epi 19Ems,na,pi 43Pju 45BO 46CR

White-throated Barbtail *Premnoplex tatei* 5Vsu 51Vsu

Pearled Treerunner *Margarornis squamiger* 5Eaz 13Ena 14Ena,pi 19Eaz,bo,ms,na,tu 45BO 51Vla

Buffy Tuftedcheek *Pseudocolaptes lawrencii* 15Eeo 19Eeo

Streaked Tuftedcheek *Pseudocolaptes boissonneautii* 13Ena 14Elo 15Epi 19Elo,zc 44Phu,ju 45BO 51Vya

Point-tailed Palmcreeper *Berlepschia rikeri* 5Vam 8Pmd 9Ena 19Vam 42Pmd 50Bmg 51Vam

Scaly-throated Foliage-gleaner *Anabacerthia variegaticeps* 15Cna; Epi 19Eca,pi

Montane Foliage-gleaner *Anabacerthia striaticollis* 5Vca 6Ena 7Ena 18Ena 19Elo,ms,na 43BO 45BO 51Vya

Guttulated Foliage-gleaner *Syndactyla guttulata* 5Vca 51Vca

Lineated Foliage-gleaner *Syndactyla subalaris* 1Ccq 5Vla 6Epi 7Epi 13Ena 15Epi 19Eca,es,im,ms,na,pi,zc 44Ems; Pam 46CR 51Vla

Buff-browed Foliage-gleaner *Syndactyla rufosuperciliata* 18Ezc 19Ezc 44BO 45BO 47A 50Bsp

Rufous-necked Foliage-gleaner *Syndactyla ruficollis* 17Elo 19Elo

Chestnut-winged Hookbill *Ancistrops strigilatus* 9Ena 12Ena,pa; Plo 19Ena 42Brd; Pmd 45BO

Striped Woodhaunter *Hyloctistes subulatus* 9Ena 16Ees 19Ees,ms,na,pi 42Pcu,md 45BO 46CR

Rufous-tailed Foliage-gleaner *Philydor ruficaudatum* 18Ena 19Ems 42Pmd 50Bpa 51Bpa

Slaty-winged Foliage-gleaner *Philydor fuscipenne* 16Epi 19Eeo

Rufous-rumped Foliage-gleaner *Philydor erythrocercum* 11Ena 18Ena,pa 19Ems,na 42Pmd 43BO 45BO 50Bmg

Chestnut-winged Foliage-gleaner *Philydor erythropterum* 11Ena 12Ena 19Ena 42Plo,md

Buff-fronted Foliage-gleaner *Philydor rufum* 15Epi 18Ems 19Ems,pi 45BO 50Bsp 51Vca

Cinnamon-rumped Foliage-gleaner *Philydor pyrrhodes* 11Ena 19Ena,pa 42Pmd 45BO 50Vam; Bmg 51Vam

Dusky-cheeked Foliage-gleaner *Anabazenops dorsalis* 10Ena 18Ena 19Ena 42Pcu 50Bmg

Uniform Treehunter *Thripadectes ignobilis* 15Cna; Epi 19Eeo

Streak-capped Treehunter *Thripadectes virgaticeps* 7Epi 13Ena 15Epi 19Eca,eo,im,na,pi 51Vla

Black-billed Treehunter *Thripadectes melanorhynchus* 1Ccq 7Ena 18Ena 19Ems,na 43Ezc

Striped Treehunter *Thripadectes holostictus* 5Elo; Pmd 7Epi 13Ena 15Epi 19Eca,pi 44Ppa 45BO 51Elo

Flammulated Treehunter *Thripadectes flammulatus* 7Ena 14Ena,zc 15Epi 19Ena,pi,tu

Buff-throated Foliage-gleaner *Automolus ochrolaemus* 5Vam; PA 9Ena 16Ees,gu 19Ees,gu,lr,ma,na,pa 42Plo 45BO 46CR 50Bmg 51Vbo

Olive-backed Foliage-gleaner *Automolus infuscatus* 5Ena 9Ena 19Ena,pa 42Plo,md 45Pmd 50Ena 51Ena

Brown-rumped Foliage-gleaner *Automolus melanopezus* 9Ena 19Ena,pa 42Pmd

White-throated Foliage-gleaner *Automolus roraimae* 5Vbo 50Vbo 51Vbo

Ruddy Foliage-gleaner *Automolus rubiginosus* 5Cma; Epi 6Epi 7Epi 12Ena 16Ees 18Ena 19Ees,na,zc 42BO 50M 51M

Chestnut-crowned Foliage-gleaner *Automolus rufipileatus* 5Vbo,ta 6Ena 7Ena 11Ena 19Ena,pa 42Pcu,md 50Bmg 51Vbo

Henna-hooded Foliage-gleaner *Hylocryptus erythrocephalus* 17Egu,lo 19Elo

Tawny-throated Leaftosser *Sclerurus mexicanus* 5Vba 12Epa 16Ees 19Ees,ms 43BO 45BO 46CR 50Bpa 51Vba

Short-billed Leaftosser *Sclerurus rufigularis* 11Ena 19Ena

Black-tailed Leaftosser *Sclerurus caudacutus* 5Ena; Vbo 7Ena 11Ena 19Ems,na 42BO; Pmd 50Ena 51Ena

Scaly-throated Leaftosser *Sclerurus guatemalensis* 16Ees 19Ees,gu 46CR

Grey-throated Leaftosser *Sclerurus albigularis* 5Var 18Ems,na,zc 19Ems,na 20T 21T 43Pcu 45BO 46CR 50Bba 51Var

Sharp-tailed Streamcreeper *Lochmias nematura* 18na,zc 43Ena 45BO 47A 50Bpn 51Bpn

Rufous-tailed Xenops *Xenops milleri* 42Pmd

Slender-billed Xenops *Xenops tenuirostris* 12Ena 19Ena

Plain Xenops *Xenops minutus* 5Vfa,la 10Ena 16Ees,pi 19Eeo,ma,na 42BO 50Bpa 51CR

Streaked Xenops *Xenops rutilans* 15Eeo,lo 17Eeo,lo,ma,pi 18Ena,zc 19Eeo,ma,ms 43Ppa 45BO 47A 51Vla

Tyrannine Woodcreeper *Dendrocincla tyrannina* 1Ccu 13Ena 15Epi 19Eca,na,pi 33Epi 44Ezc

Plain-brown Woodcreeper *Dendrocincla fuliginosa* 5Vbo,ca 10Ena 16Ees 19Eeo,es,gu,lr,ma,ms,na,pa,pi 20T 33Epi; CR; Pmd 42Pmd 45BO 50Vbo 51Vbo,ca

White-chinned Woodcreeper *Dendrocincla merula* 33Bam; Plo 42Pmd

Ruddy Woodcreeper *Dendrocincla homochroa* 33M

Long-tailed Woodcreeper *Deconychura longicauda* 18Ems,na 19Ems 33CR; Pmd 42Pmd 45BO 50Bmg 51Bmg

Spot-throated Woodcreeper *Deconychura stictolaema* 19Ena 33Ena; Bpa 50Bpa 51Bpa

Olivaceous Woodcreeper *Sittasomus griseicapillus* 5Vam,ar,ca 10Ena 17Egu,ma,lr 19Egu,na,zc 20T 33Brg; GT 42Pmd 45BO 47A 50Brj 51Vam,ca

Wedge-billed Woodcreeper *Glyphorynchus spirurus* 1Ccu 5Vam,bo 11Ena 16Ees 19Eeo,es,ms,na 33CR; Pmd 42Plo 45BO 46CR 50Vbo 51Vbo

Long-billed Woodcreeper *Nasica longirostris* 5Ena; Vam 8Pmd 9Ena 19Ena 33Pmd 45BO 50Bmg 51Ena

Cinnamon-throated Woodcreeper *Dendrexetastes rufigula* 5Ena 8Pmd 9Ena 19Ena 33Pmd 42Pmd 45BO 50Bmg 51Vbo

Red-billed Woodcreeper *Hylexetastes perrotii* 33Bam

Strong-billed Woodcreeper *Xiphocolaptes promeropirhynchus* 1Ccq 5Vmo,ta 10Ena 14Eco,im,pi 15Epi 19Eco,im,lo,ms,na,pa,pi 33Vta; BO; M 42Plo,md 44BO 45BO 46CR 50Bmg 51Vya

Northern Barred Woodcreeper *Dendrocolaptes sanctithomae* 5CR; PA 16Ees 19Epi 33Epi; M; PA 46CR 51PA

Amazonian Barred Woodcreeper *Dendrocolaptes certhia* 10Ena 19Ems,na 33Ena; Brd; Plo 42Plo 45BO 50Bmg 51Vbo

Black-banded Woodcreeper *Dendrocolaptes picumnus* 5Vam,ca,fa,mo 11Ena 19Ena 33Ena 42Bam 45BO 46Var 47A 50Vam 51Vam,ca

Straight-billed Woodcreeper *Xiphorhynchus picus* 5Vap,fa 9Ena 19Ena 20T 33S 42Pmd 45BO 50Bpa 51Vda

Striped Woodcreeper *Xiphorhynchus obsoletus* 5Vmo 8Plo 19Ena 33Plo 42Plo 45BO 50Bmg 51Vmo

Ocellated Woodcreeper *Xiphorhynchus ocellatus* 8Pmd 19Ems 33Pmd 45BO

Elegant Woodcreeper *Xiphorhynchus elegans* 33Brd; Plo 45BO 50Bmg

Spix's Woodcreeper *Xiphorhynchus spixii* 12Ena 19Ena,pa 33Bpa; Pmd 42Pmd 45BO 50Bpa

Chestnut-rumped Woodcreeper *Xiphorhynchus pardalotus* 5Vbo 33S; Vbo 50Vbo 51Vbo

Cocoa Woodcreeper *Xiphorhynchus susurrans* 2Cca 4Cvc 5Var,ca,fa 20T 22T 33T; CR 46CR 51Vca,su

Buff-throated Woodcreeper *Xiphorhynchus guttatus* 5Vbo 8Pmd 9Ena 11Ena 19Ems,na,pa 33Ena; Bam,mg,pa 42Pmd 45BO 50Bmg 51Vbo

Black-striped Woodcreeper *Xiphorhynchus lachrymosus* 16Ees 19Ees 33CR 46CR

Spotted Woodcreeper *Xiphorhynchus erythropygius* 15Epi 19Eeo,es,pi 33CR 46CR

Olive-backed Woodcreeper *Xiphorhynchus triangularis* 13Ena 18Ems,na,zc 19Ems,na,zc 33Psm 44Pcu,sm 45BO 51Var

Streak-headed Woodcreeper *Lepidocolaptes souleyetii* 5Vla,me,mo 16Ees,pi 17Elo 19Eeo,gu,lo 20T 33M 50Vca 51Vca

Narrow-billed Woodcreeper *Lepidocolaptes angustirostris* 33BO 45BO 47A 50BO

Montane Woodcreeper *Lepidocolaptes lacrymiger* 13Ena 14Eca,lo,na,pi 15Epi 19Eca,co,im,lo,na,pi 33M; Phu 44P 45BO 51Vme

Lineated Woodcreeper *Lepidocolaptes albolineatus* 5Vbo 11Ena 19Ena 33Vam; Pmd 42BO; Pmd 45BO 50Bmg 51Vbo

Greater Scythebill *Campylorhamphus pucherani* 14Elo

Red-billed Scythebill *Campylorhamphus trochilirostris* 5Vca,fa,su 9Ena 16Ees 17Egu,lo 19Eeo,gu,lr,ma,na,pi,zc 33Var; Bmg 42BO 45BO 50Bmg 51Vme,ta

Curve-billed Scythebill *Campylorhamphus procurvoides* 33Vbo 50Vbo; Bmg 51Vbo

Brown-billed Scythebill *Campylorhamphus pusillus* 2Cca 5PA 13Ena 15Eeo 18Ems,na 19Ees,ms,na 33Cme; CR 46CR 51PA

THAMNOPHILIDAE

Fasciated Antshrike *Cymbilaimus lineatus* 5Vbo 6Ena 10Ena 16Ees 19Ees,ms,na,pa 34Plo 42Plo 45BO 46CR 50Bpa 51Vbo

Black-throated Antshrike *Frederickena viridis* 34Vbo 50Vbo 51Vbo

Undulated Antshrike *Frederickena unduligera* 6Ena 7Ena 8Ems 11Ena 19Ena 34Plo 42Pmd 50Ena

Great Antshrike *Taraba major* 5Vam,bo,ca 8Pam 16Ees 19Eeo,lr,na 20T 34Vbo 42Pam 45BO 47A 50Bba 51Vca

Black-crested Antshrike *Sakesphorus canadensis* 5Vam,ca,da,fa 20T 21T 34Vbo,zu 50Vam 51Vam,la

Collared Antshrike *Sakesphorus bernardi* 17Eeo,gu,lo; Ppi 19Eeo,gu,lo 34Pca,la

Black-backed Antshrike *Sakesphorus melanonotus* 5Vfa 34Vla 51Vfa

Band-tailed Antshrike *Sakesphorus melanothorax* 34S

Barred Antshrike *Thamnophilus doliatus* 5Vca 11Ena 19Ena 20T 21T 22T 34Vdf 42Pmd 45BO 50Bpe 51Vca

Chapman's Antshrike *Thamnophilus zarumae* 17Elo 19Elo 34Pla

Bar-crested Antshrike *Thamnophilus multistriatus* 2Cca 4Cvc 34Cca

Lined Antshrike *Thamnophilus tenuepunctatus* 1Ccq 7Ena 18Ena,zc 19Ena,zc 34Ena

Black Antshrike *Thamnophilus nigriceps* 34PA

Cocha Antshrike *Thamnophilus praecox* 8Ena 9Ena 19Ena 34Ena

Blackish-grey Antshrike *Thamnophilus nigrocinereus* 5Vam 34Bam 50Vam 51Vam

Castelnau's Antshrike *Thamnophilus cryptoleucus* 6Ena 7Ena 10Ena 19Ena 34Bam 50Ena

White-shouldered Antshrike *Thamnophilus aethiops* 5Vam,bo 10Ena 19Ems,na 34Pmd 42Pmd 45BO 50Bpa 51Vbo

Uniform Antshrike *Thamnophilus unicolor* 1Ccq 2Cca 15Epi 19Eaz,ca,eo,ms,pi,zc 34Cvc

Black-capped Antshrike *Thamnophilus schistaceus* 8Pmd 12Ena 19Ems,na,pa 34Pmd 42Pmd 45BO 50Bmg

Mouse-coloured Antshrike *Thamnophilus murinus* 5Vbo 6Ena 8Ena 12Ena,pa 19Ena 34Ena 45BO 50Vbo 51Vbo

Western Slaty Antshrike *Thamnophilus atrinucha* 2Cca 5Epi; PA 16Ees 19Ees,gu,lr 34PA 46CR 51PA

Eastern Slaty Antshrike *Thamnophilus punctatus* 5Vbo 18Ezc; Pca 19Ezc 34Vbo 50Vbo 51Vbo

Amazonian Antshrike *Thamnophilus amazonicus* 5Vam 12Ena 19Ena 34S 45BO 50Bmg 51Vam

Streak-backed Antshrike *Thamnophilus insignis* 34Vbo 50Vbo 51Vbo

Pearly Antshrike *Megastictus margaritatus* 10Ena 19Ena 34Plo

Black Bushbird *Neoctantes niger* 10Ena 19Ena,pa 34Plo

Russet Antshrike *Thamnistes anabatinus* 15Eeo,pi 18Ena,zc 19Ees,na,pa,pi 34BE; BO 43Psm

Plain Antvireo *Dysithamnus mentalis* 2Cca 4Cvc 5Var,la,mo 17Egu,lo,pi 18Ena; Pam,ca 19Egu,ms,na,pi 20T 34Var 43BO 45BO 46CR 47A 50Brj 51Var,la

Spot-crowned Antvireo *Dysithamnus puncticeps* 16Ees 19Eca,es,pi 34PA

Bicoloured Antvireo *Dysithamnus occidentalis* 13Ena 19Eca,na 34Ena

White-streaked Antbireo *Dysithamnus leucostictus* 1Cna 5Vca 18Ena 19Ems,na 34Ena; Var 51Vca

Dusky-throated Antshrike *Thamnomanes ardesiacus* 5Vbo 6Ena 7Ena 8Plo 11Ena 19Ems,na,pa 34Plo 42Plo,md 50Vbo 51Vbo

Cinereous Antshrike *Thamnomanes caesius* 5Vbo 8Plo 11Ena 19Ena,pa 34Plo 45Bba 50Bpa 51Vbo

Speckled Antshrike *Xenornis setifrons* 34PA

Spot-winged Antshrike *Pygiptila stellaris* 9Ena 19Ena 34Pmd 42Pmd 45BO 50Bpa 51Bpa

Checker-throated Antwren *Myrmotherula fulviventris* 16Ees 19Ees,pi 34Ees 46PA

Brown-bellied Antwren *Myrmotherula gutturalis* 34S

Stipple-throated Antwren *Myrmotherula haematonota* 5Vbo 11Ena 12Ena 34Plo 50Vbo 51Vbo

Brown-backed Antwren *Myrmotherula fjeldsaai* 19Ena 34Epa

Foothill Antwren *Myrmotherula spodionota* 18Ena,zc 19Ems,na 34Ena 43Pcu

Ornate Antwren *Myrmotherula ornata* 11Ena 19Ems,na 34Pmd 42Pmd 50Bpa

Rufous-tailed Antwren *Myrmotherula erythrura* 7Ena 10Ena 19Ems,na 34Ena 43Ppu

Pygmy Antwren *Myrmotherula brachyura* 5Vbo 8Phu 12Ena 19Ems,na 34Bpa 42Phu 45BO 50Vbo 51Vbo

Moustached Antwren *Myrmotherula ignota* 6Ena 7Ena 8Plo 12Ena 16Ees 19Ees,na,pa,pi 34Plo 50Ena

Yellow-throated Antwren *Myrmotherula ambigua* 34Bam

Guianan Streaked Antwren *Myrmotherula surinamensis* 5Vbo 34Vbo 50Vbo 51Vbo

Amazonian Streaked Antwren *Myrmotherula multostriata* 10Ena 19Ena 34BO 42BO 45BO 50Bpa 51Bpa

Pacific Antwren *Myrmotherula pacifica* 16Ees 19Ees,lr,pi 34Epi

Cherrie's Antwren *Myrmotherula cherriei* 5Vam 34Vam 50Vam 51Vam

Stripe-chested Antwren *Myrmotherula longicauda* 18Ems,na; Psm 19Ems,na 34Pmd 43Pcu 45BO

Plain-throated Antwren *Myrmotherula hauxwelli* 6Ena 7Ena 10Ena 19Ena 34Plo 42Plo 50Bmg

Rufous-bellied Antwren *Myrmotherula guttata* 5Vbo 34Bam 50Vbo 51Vbo

White-flanked Antwren *Myrmotherula axillaris* 5Ena; Vam,bo,mo 6Ena 7Ena 10Ena 16Ees 19Ees,ms,na,pi 20T 34Bes; Plo,md 42Pmd 45BO 46CR 50Bse 51Ena; Vmo

Slaty Antwren *Myrmotherula schisticolor* 5Var,ca 15Epi 18Ems,na 19Eca,ms,na 34Ena 44Ena; Pcu 51Vca

Río Suno Antwren *Myrmotherula sunensis* 19Epa 34Ena

Long-winged Antwren *Myrmotherula longipennis* 5Vbo 11Ena 19Ena,pa 34G; Bmg; Pmd 42Pmd 50Vbo 51Vbo

Plain-winged Antwren *Myrmotherula behni* 18Ena 19Ena 34Ena

Grey Antwren *Myrmotherula menetriesii* 6Ena 7Ena 9Ena 12Ena; Plo 19Ena,pa 34Vbo; Pmd 42Pmd 45BO 50Bpa 51Vbo

Leaden Antwren *Myrmotherula assimilis* 34Plo 45BO

Banded Antbird *Dichrozona cincta* 9Ena 11Ena 19Ena 34Pmd 42Pmd 50Bmg 51Bmg

Spot-tailed Antwren *Herpsilochmus sticturus* 5Vbo 34Vbo 50Vbo 51Vbo

Dugand's Antwren *Herpsilochmus dugandi* 10Ena 12Ena 19Ena 34Ena

Todd's Antwren *Herpsilochmus stictocephalus* 5Vbo 34Vbo 50Vbo 51Vbo

Ancient Antwren *Herpsilochmus gentryi* 19Epa 34Plo

Spot-backed Antwren *Herpsilochmus dorsimaculatus* 34Bam

Roraiman Antwren *Herpsilochmus roraimae* 5Vbo 34Vbo 50Vbo 51Vbo

Yellow-breasted Antwren *Herpsilochmus axillaris* 18Ems,na 19Ems,na 34Phu 43Ems

Rufous-winged Antwren *Herpsilochmus rufimarginatus* 5Vca,fa 16Elr,pi 18Ems,na; Psm 19Ees,ms,na 34Vbo; Bba; PA 43BO 45BO 47A 50Bpa,sc 51Vfa

Dot-winged Antwren *Microrhopias quixensis* 12Epa 16Ees,pi 19Eca,es,ma,lr,pa 34Pmd; PA 42Pmd 46CR 50Bmg

White-fringed Antwren *Formicivora grisea* 5Vca,fa,mo 20T 21T 34Vam 50Bpa 51Vca,fa; Bpa

Rusty-backed Antwren *Formicivora rufa* 34Bba; BO 45BO 50Bmg

Striated Antbird *Drymophila devillei* 18Ena 19Ena 34Pmd 42Pmd 45BO 50Bmg

Long-tailed Antbird *Drymophila caudata* 1Ccq 5Cma; Var 6Ena 7Ena 13Ena 14Ena,pi,zc 15Epi 19Eca,na,pi,zc 34Epi; Var 44Phu,ju 45BO 51Vfa

Rufous-rumped Antwren *Terenura callinota* 15Cna; Epi 18Cna; Epi 19Epi 34Chu

Chestnut-shouldered Antwren *Terenura humeralis* 11Ena 19Ena,pa 34Pmd 42Pmd

Ash-winged Antwren *Terenura spodioptila* 12Ena 19Ena 34Vbo 50Vbo 51Vbo

Grey Antbird *Cercomacra cinerascens* 5Vam,bo 8Ems 11Ena 19Ems,na 34Plo 42Pmd 45BO 50Bpa 51Vbo

Dusky Antbird *Cercomacra tyrannina* 1Cns 3Cns 5Vbo 16Ees 19Eca,es,lr,pi 34Ees 46CR 50Vbo 51Vbo

Parker's Antbird *Cercomacra parkeri* 34Cri

Blackish Antbird *Cercomacra nigrescens* 6Ena 7Ena 10Ena 18Ena,zc 19Ems,na,zc 34Bac,mg 42Pmd 45BO 50Bpa

Black Antbird *Cercomacra serva* 6Ena 11Ena 19Ems,na,pa,zc 34Plo 43BO 45BO 50Ena

Jet Antbird *Cercomacra nigricans* 2Cca 5Vda,mo 17Ees,lr 19Ees 34PA 51Vda

Rio Branco Antbird *Cercomacra carbonaria* 34Bro

White-backed Fire-eye *Pyriglena leuconota* 17Egu,lr 18Ena,zc 19Egu,ms,na,pi,zc 34Ena 43BO 45BO 50Bpa

White-browed Antbird *Myrmoborus leucophrys* 5Vbo,ta 12Epa 19Ena 34Vbo 42Pmd 45BO 50Bmg 51Vbo,ta

Ash-breasted Antbird *Myrmoborus lugubris* 12Ena; Plo 19Ena; Plo 34Bam

Black-faced Antbird *Myrmoborus myotherinus* 5Ena 6Ena 7Ena 8Ems 9Ena 11Ena 19Ems,na,pa 34Plo,md 42Pmd 45BO 50Bpa 51Ena; Bpa

Warbling Antbird *Hypocnemis cantator* 5Vam,bo 8Plo 10Ena 19Ena,pa 34G; Vbo; Bac,am,mg,pa 42Pmd 45BO 50Vam,bo; Bpa 51Vbo

Yellow-browed Antbird *Hypocnemis hypoxantha* 8Plo 12Ena; Plo 19Ena,pa 34Plo 50Ena

Black-chinned Antbird *Hypocnemoides melanopogon* 5Vam,mo 10Ena 19Ena 34Vam 50Vam 51Vmo

Black-and-white Antbird *Myrmochanes hemileucus* 10Ena 19Ena 34Plo 45Ena

Bare-crowned Antbird *Gymnocichla nudiceps* 34PA 46CR

Silvered Antbird *Sclateria naevia* 5Vmo 8Pmd 11Ena 19Ena 20T 21T 34Pmd 42Pmd 45BO 50Vsu 51Vsu

Black-headed Antbird *Percnostola rufifrons* 34Vam; Plo

Slate-coloured Antbird *Schistocichla schistacea* 12Plo 34Plo

Spot-winged Antbird *Schistocichla leucostigma* 5Ena 6Ena 10Ena 19Ems,na,pa 34G; Bpa; Plo 43Ppu 50Ena 51Vbo

Caura Antbird *Schistocichla caurensis* 34Vbo

White-bellied Antbird *Myrmeciza longipes* 5Vbo,fa,mo 20T 34Vmi 50Vmo 51Vfa

Chestnut-backed Antbird *Myrmeciza exsul* 6Epi 7Epi 16Ees 19Ees,pi 34CR 46CR

Ferruginous-backed Antbird *Myrmeciza ferruginea* 5Vbo 34G 50Vbo 51Vbo

Dull-mantled Antbird *Myrmeciza laemosticta* 34PA 46CR

Esmeralda's Antbird *Myrmeciza nigricauda* 6Epi 7Epi 15Eim,pi 19Eeo,es,im,pi 34Cvc

Stub-tailed Antbird *Myrmeciza berlepschi* 16Ees 19Ees 34Cvc

Grey-bellied Antbird *Myrmeciza pelzelni* 34Bam

Northern Chestnut-tailed Antbird *Myrmeciza castanea* 19Epa 34Bmg; Plo 42Pmd 45BO 50Pmd

Black-throated Antbird *Myrmeciza atrothorax* 5Vam,bo 7Ena 11Ena 19Ena 34Pmd 42BO 45BO 50Vbo 51Vbo

White-shouldered Antbird *Myrmeciza melanoceps* 6Ena 7Ena 8Plo 9Ena 11Ena 19Ena,pa 34Plo 50Ena

Plumbeous Antbird *Myrmeciza hyperythra* 6Ena 7Ena 8Pmd 9Ena 10Ena 19Ena 34Pmd 42Pmd 45BO 50Ena

Sooty Antbird *Myrmeciza fortis* 6Ena 7Ena 8Ems 11Ena 19Ems,na,pa 34Ena 42Pmd 50Ena

Immaculate Antbird *Myrmeciza immaculata* 3Cns 5Ees; PA 7Epi 15Eeo,pi 19Eeo,es,gu,im,pi 34Ecn 46CR 51Vta

Yapacana Antbird *Myrmeciza disjuncta* 34Vam

Grey-headed Antbird *Myrmeciza griseiceps* 17Elo 19Elo 34Ptu

Wing-banded Antbird *Myrmornis torquata* 12Ena 19Ena 34Vbo; Bmg 50Vbo 51Vbo

White-plumed Antbird *Pithys albifrons* 5Vbo 11Ena 19Ems,na 34Plo 50Vbo 51Vbo

Bicoloured Antbird *Gymnopithys leucaspis* 6Ena 7Ena 9Ena 16Ees 19Ees,na 34PA; Plo 46PA 50Ena

Rufous-throated Antbird *Gymnopithys rufigula* 5Vbo 34Vbo 50Vbo 51Vbo

Lunulated Antbird *Gymnopithys lunulatus* 7Ena 12Ena,pa 19Ena 34Plo

Chestnut-crested Antbird *Rhegmatorhina cristata* 34Bam

Hairy-crested Antbird *Rhegmatorhina melanosticta* 9Ena 19Ena 34Pmd 42Pmd 45BO

Spotted Antbird *Hylophylax naevioides* 16Ees 19Ees 34PA

Spot-backed Antbird *Hylophylax naevius* 5Vbo 6Ena 10Ena 19Ems,na,pa 34Pcu,lo 42Ppu 45BO 50Bmg 51Vbo

Dot-backed Antbird *Hylophylax punctulatus* 5Ena 8Brd 11Ena 19Ena 34Plo 50Bpa 51Ena

Scale-backed Antbird *Hylophylax poecilinotus* 6Ena 7Ena 9Ena 11Ena 19Ems,na 34Bam,pa 42Pmd 45BO 50Bpa 51Vbo

Black-spotted Bare-eye *Phlegopsis nigromaculata* 6Ena 9Ena 11Ena 19Ena 34Bpa 42Pmd 45BO 50Bmg

Reddish-winged Bare-eye *Phlegopsis erythroptera* 11Ena 19Ena,pa 34Plo 45Ena

Ocellated Antbird *Phaenostictus mcleannani* 16Ees 19Ees 34PA 46CR

FORMICARIIDAE

Rufous-capped Antthrush *Formicarius colma* 5Vbo 8Pmd 11Ena 19Ena 34Pmd 42Pmd 45BO 50Bpa 51Vbo

Black-faced Antthrush *Formicarius analis* 3Cns 5Vca,la 6Ena 7Ena 8Ena 9Ena 11Ena 19Ems,na 20T 21T 22T 34M; PA; Pmd 42Pmd 45BO 46CR 50Bpa 51Vsu

Black-headed Antthrush *Formicarius nigricapillus* 6Epi 7Epi 16Ees 19Ees,lr,pi 34PA 46CR

Rufous-breasted Antthrush *Formicarius rufipectus* 5Epi; Vta 6Epi 7Epi 15Cna; Epi 18Ena 19Eca,eo,im,ms,na 34PA 44Pcu 46CR 51Vta

Short-tailed Antthrush *Chamaeza campanisona* 1Ccq 5Vca 18Ena 19Ems,na 34Var; Bce 43BO 45BO 47A 50Bpa 51Vca

Striated Antthrush *Chamaeza nobilis* 6Ena 7Ena 8Pmd 11Ena 19Ena 34Bmg; Pmd 42Pmd 45Ena 50Bmg

Schwartz's Antthrush *Chamaeza turdina* 1Ccu 5Var 34Var 51Var

Barred Antthrush *Chamaeza mollissima* 6Ena 7Ena 13Ena 19Ena 34Pam 45BO

Black-crowned Antpitta *Pittasoma michleri* 34CR 46CR

Rufous-crowned Antpitta *Pittasoma rufopileatum* 16Ees 19Ees 34Ees

Undulated Antpitta *Grallaria squamigera* 1Cby 2Cca 5Elo 6Epi 7Epi 14Ebo 19Eaz,bo,im,lo,pi 34Ccu 45BO 51Elo; Vme

Giant Antpitta *Grallaria gigantea* 15Eco 19Eco,na,pi 34Ena

Great Antpitta *Grallaria excelsa* 5Vla 34Vla 51Vla

Variegated Antpitta *Grallaria varia* 34Plo 47A 50Bpa 51Bpa

Scaled Antpitta *Grallaria guatimalensis* 1Ccu 5Vmo 7Epi 10Ena 15Elo 19Eca,im,lo,ms,na,pi,zc 20T 34Vbo 43Phu 45BO 46Vbo 50Vta 51Vta

Moustached Antpitta *Grallaria alleni* 15Epi 19Ena,pi 34Ena

Plain-backed Antpitta *Grallaria haplonota* 5Var 15Eeo 18Ena 19Eeo,ms,na,zc 34Var 51Var

Ochre-striped Antpitta *Grallaria dignissima* 9Ena 11Ena 19Ena 34Plo

Chestnut-crowned Antpitta *Grallaria ruficapilla* 1Ccu 2Cca 3Cns 5Var,me 13Ena 14Elo,na,pi 15Epi 19Eaz,ca,co,lo,na,pi 34Vta 51Vla

Watkins's Antpitta *Grallaria watkinsi* 17Egu,lo 19Egu,lo 34Elo

Santa Marta Antpitta *Grallaria bangsi* 34Cma

Cundinamarca Antpitta *Grallaria kaestneri* 1Ccu 34Cme

Grey-naped Antpitta *Grallaria griseonucha* 5Vta 34Vta 51Vta

Bicoloured Antpitta *Grallaria rufocinerea* 14Ena 19Eca 34Cna

Jocotoco Antpitta *Grallaria ridgelyi* 14Ezc 19Ezc 34Ezc

Chestnut-naped Antpitta *Grallaria nuchalis* 2Cca 13Ena 14Elo,na,pi 19Eaz,na,pi,zc 34Pca

Yellow-breasted Antpitta *Grallaria flavotincta* 15Epi 19Eca,pi 34Ccc

White-bellied Antpitta *Grallaria hypoleuca* 1Ccq 6Ena 7Ena 13Ena 19Ena,ms,zc 34Ppi

Rufous Antpitta *Grallaria rufula* 3Cns 5Cma; Elo; BO 6Epi 7Epi 14Ena,pi,tu 19Eaz,bo,ca,im,lo,na,pi,tu 34Ccu; Ezc; BO; Pca,cu,hu,pa 45BO

Tawny Antpitta *Grallaria quitensis* 6Epi 7Epi 14Eco,lo,na,pi,tu 19Eaz,ca,co,im,lo,ms,na,pi,tu 34Ppi

Brown-banded Antpitta *Grallaria milleri* 34Cto

Streak-chested Antpitta *Hylopezus perspicillatus* 16Ees 19Ees 34CR 46CR

Spotted Antpitta *Hylopezus macularius* 5Vbo 34Vbo; Bmg 50Vbo 51Vbo

Thicket Antpitta *Hylopezus dives* 34CR 46CR

White-lored Antpitta *Hylopezus fulviventris* 7Ena 10Ena 19Ena,pa 34Plo

Thrush-like Antpitta *Myrmothera campanisona* 5Vbo 6Ena 7Ena 8Pmd 9Ena 11Ena 19Ems,na,pa 34Plo 42Plo 45BO 50Bmg 51Vbo

Tepui Antpitta *Myrmothera simplex* 5Vbo 34Vbo 50Vbo 51Vbo

Ochre-breasted Antpitta *Grallaricula flavirostris* 15Cna 18Ena 19Eca,eo 34Ena 43Ppa 45BO

Rusty-breasted Antpitta *Grallaricula ferrugineipectus* 2Cca 5Var,fa 17Ppi 19Elo; Ppi 34Var 44Ppa 45BO; Pcu,sm 51Vfa

Slate-crowned Antpitta *Grallaricula nana* 1Cby 2Cca 3Cns 5Var,su 6Ena 7Ena 13Ena 14Ena,zc 19Eaz,na 34Ppi 51Vsu

Crescent-faced Antpitta *Grallaricula lineifrons* 14Eca 19Eca,lo,ms,na 34Eca

CONOPOPHAGIDAE

Chestnut-belted Gnateater *Conopophaga aurita* 8Plo 9Ena 34Bmg; Plo 50Bpa

Ash-throated Gnateater *Conopophaga peruviana* 11Ena 19Ena,pa 34Plo 42Plo

Chestnut-crowned Gnateater *Conopophaga castaneiceps* 1Ccq 4Cvc 18Ems,na 19Ems 34Ena 43Elo; Ppa,sm

RHINOCRYPTIDAE

Rusty-belted Tapaculo *Liosceles thoracicus* 1Cna 6Ena 7Ena 8Ena 11Ena 19Ems,na 42Pmd 45Epa 50Pmd

Ash-coloured Tapaculo *Myornis senilis* 6Ena 13Ena 14Eim,lo,ms 19Eim,lo,ms,na,pi,zc

Blackish Tapaculo *Scytalopus latrans* 5Elo; Vta 6Ena,pi 7Ena 13Ena 14Eaz,im,lo,ms,na,pi 19Eaz,bo,ca,cn,co,im,lo,ms,na,pi,tu,zc 51Vta

Long-tailed Tapaculo *Scytalopus micropterus* 1Ccu 7Ena 13Ena 19Ems,na,zc

White-crowned Tapaculo *Scytalopus atratus* 3Cns 6Ena 7Ena 18Ems,na 19Ems,na,zc 51Vta

Chocó Tapaculo *Scytalopus chocoensis* 15Cna; Ees,im 19Ees

Ecuadorian Tapaculo *Scytalopus robbinsi* 17Eeo 19Eaz,eo

Nariño Tapaculo *Scytalopus vicinior* 7Epi 15Cna; Epi 19Eca,im,pi

Mérida Tapaculo *Scytalopus meridanus* 5Vla,me,ta,tr 51Vla,me,ta,tr

Caracas Tapaculo *Scytalopus caracae* 5Var 51Var

Spillmann's Tapaculo *Scytalopus spillmanni* 2Cca 7Ena 13Ena 14Eco,im,na,pi 15Epi 19Ech,co,ms,na,pi,tu

Chusquea Tapaculo *Scytalopus parkeri* 14Elo,ms,zc 19Elo,ms,zc

Páramo Tapaculo *Scytalopus canus* 14Eaz,ca,na,tu,zc 19Eaz,ca,ms,na,pi,tu,zc

Ocellated Tapaculo *Acropternis orthonyx* 5Vta 7Ena 13Ena 14Epi 19Ena,pi 51Vta

Elegant Crescentchest *Melanopareia elegans* 17Egu,lo,ma 19Egu,lo,ma

Marañón Crescentchest *Melanopareia maranonica* 18Ezc; Pca 19Ezc

TYRANNIDAE

Rough-legged Tyrannulet *Phyllomyias burmeisteri* 18Ena; Pcu,lo 19Ena 43BO 45BO 46CR

Sooty-capped Tyrannulet *Phyllomyias griseiceps* 4Cvc 5Vla 7Epi 12Ena 16Ees 17Ees,gu,pi 18Ems,na; Psm 19Ees,gu,ms,pi 50Vbo 51Vla

Black-capped Tyrannulet *Phyllomyias nigrocapillus* 2Cca 7Epi 14Eaz,zc 19Eaz,ca,lo,pi,zc

Ashy-headed Tyrannulet *Phyllomyias cinereiceps* 13Ena 15Epi 19Eeo,im,pi 44Ena

Tawny-rumped Tyrannulet *Phyllomyias uropygialis* 5Epi; BO 14Elo 19Eaz,im,lo,pi,zc 45BO 51Epi

Plumbeous-crowned Tyrannulet *Phyllomyias plumbeiceps* 18Ena 19Ems,zc 44Ppa

Yellow-crowned Tyrannulet *Tyrannulus elatus* 5Vam 6Ena 7Ena 8Epi 16Ees 19Ena 42Pmd 45BO 50Bpa 51Vam

Forest Elaenia *Myiopagis gaimardii* 5Vca,mo 6Ena 7Ena 12Ena 19Ems 20T 42Pmd 45BO 50Bpa 51Vmo

Grey Elaenia *Myiopagis caniceps* 11Ena 12Ena 16Ees 19Ees,na,pi 42Plo 45A; BO; PY 50Bmg 51Bmg

Foothill Elaenia *Myiopagis olallai* 18Ena,zc 19Ems,na,zc

Pacific Elaenia *Myiopagis subplacens* 17Egu,lo 19Eaz,eo,gu,lo

Yellow-crowned Elaenia *Myiopagis flavivertex* 5Vmo 10Ena 19Ena 50Vmo 51Vmo

Greenish Elaenia *Myiopagis viridicata* 17Egu,ma 19Egu,ma 45BO; Bmi 50Vbo 51Vbo

Yellow-bellied Elaenia *Elaenia flavogaster* 5Vca,ta 16Elr,zc 17Elr,ma 19Elr,zc 20T 45BO; PY 46CR 47A 50Bmg 51Vbo

Large Elaenia *Elaenia spectabilis* 45BO 47A

White-crested Elaenia *Elaenia albiceps* 14Elo,pi,tu 19Eaz,co,lo,tu 45BO 47A

Small-billed Elaenia *Elaenia parvirostris* 45BO 47A

Slaty Elaenia *Elaenia strepera* 45BO 47A

Mottle-backed Elaenia *Elaenia gigas* 10Ena 11Ena 19Ems,na,pa 45BO

Plain-crested Elaenia *Elaenia cristata* 50Vbo 51Vbo

Lesser Elaenia *Elaenia chiriquensis* 5Vca 18Ezc 19Ees 45BO; Bmi 51Vbo

Mountain Elaenia *Elaenia frantzii* 2Cca 3Cns 5Var 51Var

Highland Elaenia *Elaenia obscura* 14Elo 19Elo 45BO 47A 50Bsc

Sierran Elaenia *Elaenia pallatangae* 5Vbo; BO 14Eim; Psm 19Eaz,ca,eo,im,lo,ms,zc 45BO 50Vbo 51Vbo

Brown-capped Tyrannulet *Ornithion brunneicapillus* 16Ees 19Ees,gu,lr 51Vme

White-lored Tyrannulet *Ornithion inerme* 5Vbo 7Ena 12Ena 19Ena 42Plo 45BO 50Bmg 51Vbo

Southern Beardless Tyrannulet *Camptostoma obsoletum* 5Vca 6Epi 10Ena 14Elo,pi 17Ees,gu,lo 18Ezc; Pam,sm 19Egu,lo,na,pi 20T 45BO 47A 50Bsp 51Vbo,ca

Suiriri Flycatcher *Suiriri suiriri* 45A; BO; Bba 47A 50BO

White-tailed Tyrannulet *Mecocerculus poecilocercus* 7Ena 13Ena 15Eco,pi 19Eaz,co,pi 44Phu

White-banded Tyrannulet *Mecocerculus stictopterus* 2Cca 5Vta 7Epi 14Eaz,im,lo 19Eim,lo,ms,na,pi 45BO 51Vta

White-throated Tyrannulet *Mecocerculus leucophrys* 1Cby 5Var,me,ta,tr 14Ems,na,pi 19Eaz,ca,im,ms,na,pi,tu 45BO 47A 50Vtr 51Vtr

Rufous-winged Tyrannulet *Mecocerculus calopterus* 15Eeo,lo 17Eeo,lo 19Eeo,lo

Sulphur-bellied Tyrannulet *Mecocerculus minor* 13Ena 19Eca,na

Black-crested Tit-Tyrant *Anairetes nigrocristatus* 14Elo 19Elo

Tufted Tit-Tyrant *Anairetes parulus* 14Eca,pi 19Eaz,ca,im,pi 45BO 47A

Agile Tit-Tyrant *Anairetes agilis* 5Vta 14Ebo,co,pi 19Ebo,co,lo,ms,pi 51Vta

Torrent Tyrannulet *Serpophaga cinerea* 13Ena 15Cna; Epi 19Ems

River Tyrannulet *Serpophaga hypoleuca* 5Vam 12Ena,pa 19Ena 50Vam 51Vam

Mouse-coloured Tyrannulet *Phaeomyias murina* 5Vca,fa 17Egu,lo 19Egu,na 45BO 50Bpe 51Vbo,fa

Yellow Tyrannulet *Capsiempis flaveola* 5Vmo 16Epi 17Egu,pi 18Ena 19Egu,ms,na,pa 45BO 46CR 47A 50Brj 51Vmo

Bearded Tachuri *Polystictus pectoralis* 47A

Crested Doradito *Pseudocolopteryx sclateri* 45BO

Subtropical Doradito *Pseudocolopteryx acutipennis* 14A 45BO

Bronze-olive Pygmy Tyrant *Pseudotriccus pelzelni* 13Ena 15Cna; Epi 18Ena,zc 19Eeo,zc 44Ems; Ppa

Rufous-headed Pygmy Tyrant *Pseudotriccus ruficeps* 1Ccu 7Ena 13Ena 14Ena,pi 15Eim,pi 19Ena,pi 45BO

Ringed Antpipit *Corythopis torquatus* 5Pmd 11Ena 19Ems,na 42Pmd 45BO 50Bmg 51Pmd

Tawny-crowned Pygmy Tyrant *Euscarthmus meloryphus* 5Vca 17Egu,lo,ma 19Eeo,gu 45BO 47A 50Bpe 51Vla

Rufous-sided Pygmy Tyrant *Euscarthmus rufomarginatus* 45BO

Grey-and-white Tyrannulet *Pseudelaenia leucospodia* 17Egu,ma 19Egu

Lesser Wagtail-Tyrant *Stigmatura napensis* 5Vam 10Ena 19Ena 50Bba 51Vam

Paltry Tyrannulet *Zimmerius vilissimus* 46CR

Venezuelan Tyrannulet *Zimmerius improbus* 5Vla,me 51Vdf

Red-billed Tyrannulet *Zimmerius cinereicapilla* 18Ena 43BO; Pmd 45BO

Slender-footed Tyrannulet *Zimmerius gracilipes* 5Vbo 10Ena 19Ena 42Plo,md 45BO 50Bce 51Bce

Golden-faced Tyrannulet *Zimmerius chrysops* 1Ccu 2Cca 4Cvc 5Vla,ta 11Ena 15Epi 17Elo; Ppi 18Ems,na,zc 19Eca,es,lo,ms,na,pi,zc 51Vla,su

Variegated Bristle Tyrant *Phylloscartes poecilotis* 13Ena 19Eca,na 44Vme 51Vla

Chapman's Tyrannulet *Phylloscartes chapmani* 5Vbo 50Vbo 51Vbo

Marble-faced Bristle Tyrant *Phylloscartes ophthalmicus* 6Epi 7Epi 13Ena 15Ena; Epi 19Ems,na 43BO 45BO 51Vya

Venezuelan Bristle Tyrant *Phylloscartes venezuelanus* 5Var 51Vca

Spectacled Bristle Tyrant *Phylloscartes orbitalis* 18Ena 19Ems,na 43Ems

Ecuadorian Tyrannulet *Phylloscartes gualaquizae* 6Ena 18Ena 19Ems,pa,zc

Black-fronted Tyrannulet *Phylloscartes nigrifrons* 5Vbo 50Vbo 51Vbo

Rufous-browed Tyrannulet *Phylloscartes superciliaris* 18Ems,zc 19Ems

Streak-necked Flycatcher *Mionectes striaticollis* 2Cca 4Cvc 15Cna; Epi 19Eca,ms 44Ppa 45BO

Olive-striped Flycatcher *Mionectes olivaceus* 4Cvc 5Vme,mo 15Ees,pi 18Ena 19Eeo 43Ena 51Vme

Ochre-bellied Flycatcher *Mionectes oleagineus* 4Cvc 10Ena 16Ees 19Ees,lr,na 20T 42Plo 45BO 46CR 50Bpa 51Bpa

McConnell's Flycatcher *Mionectes macconnelli* 42BO 45BO
Sepia-capped Flycatcher *Leptopogon amaurocephalus* 5Vbo,ta 12Epa 19Epa 42Pmd 45BO 47A 50Bmg 51Vbo
Slaty-capped Flycatcher *Leptopogon superciliaris* 5Vca 15Epi 18Ena 19Eeo,ms,na,pi 20T 43BO 45BO 46CR 51Vgu
Rufous-breasted Flycatcher *Leptopogon rufipectus* 2Cca 3Cns 13Ena 19Ena
Northern Scrub Flycatcher *Sublegatus arenarum* 5Vfa 51Vfa
Amazonian Scrub Flycatcher *Sublegatus obscurior* 51Vbo
Slender-billed Inezia *Inezia tenuirostris* 5Vfa 51Vfa
Pale-tipped Inezia *Inezia caudata* 5Vfa 50Vfa 51Vfa
Ornate Flyactcher *Myiotriccus ornatus* 6Ena 15Eeo,im,pi 18Ena,zc 19Ees,ms,na,pi 43Pcu
Black-capped Pygmy Tyrant *Myiornis atricapillus* 16Ees 19Ees,pi
Short-tailed Pygmy Tyrant *Myiornis ecaudatus* 5Vbo,fa,mo 12Plo 19Plo 42Pmd 45BO 50Bpa 51Vbo
Scale-crested Pygmy Tyrant *Lophotriccus pileatus* 3Cns 4Cvc 5Vca 6Epi 7Epi 16Epi 18Ena,zc 19Eca,eo,es,lo,ma,pi,zc 43Phu,pa 46CR 51Vca
Double-banded Pygmy Tyrant *Lophotriccus vitiosus* 6Ena 7Ena 8Ems,na 19Ena,pa
Helmeted Pygmy Tyrant *Lophotriccus galeatus* 5Vbo 50Bpa 51Vbo
Pale-eyed Pygmy Tyrant *Atalotriccus pilaris* 5Vca 51Vca
Snethlage's Tody-Tyrant *Hemitriccus minor* 45BO 50Bpa 51Bpa
White-eyed Tody-Tyrant *Hemitriccus zosterops* 11Ena 19Ems,na,pa 42Pmd 45BO 50Bal,mg 51Bpa
Johannes's Tody-Tyrant *Hemitriccus iohannis* 12Epa 19Pmd 42Pmd 45BO 50Pmd
Stripe-necked Tody-Tyrant *Hemitriccus striaticollis* 45BO 50Bse
Pearly-vented Tody-Tyrant *Hemitriccus margaritaceiventer* 5Vbo,fa 45BO 47A 50Bpe 51Vbo,fa
Black-throated Tody-Tyrant *Hemitriccus granadensis* 1Ccq 5Pcu 14Can; Ena,zc 19Ems,na,zc 44Pcu 45BO 51Pcu
Cinnamon-breasted Tody-Tyrant *Hemitriccus cinnamomeipectus* 18Ezc; Psm 19Ezc
Buff-throated Tody-Tyrant *Hemitriccus rufigularis* 18Ena 19Ems,na 43Pmd 45BO
Rufous-crowned Tody-Tyrant *Poecilotriccus ruficeps* 6Ena 7Ena 13Ena 15Epi 19Eaz,ca,na
Black-and-white Tody-Tyrant *Poecilotriccus capitalis* 12Epa 18Ena 19Ems,na 50Bpa
Ruddy Tody-Flycatcher *Poecilotriccus russatus* 5Vbo 50Vbo 51Vbo
Rusty-fronted Tody-Flycatcher *Poecilotriccus latirostris* 12Epa 19Ems,pa 42Pam 45BO 50Bmg
Slate-headed Tody-Flycatcher *Poecilotriccus sylvia* 2Cca 4Cvc 5Vmo 50Vmo 51Vmo
Golden-winged Tody-Flycatcher *Poecilotriccus calopterus* 12Epa 18Ena,pa 19Ems,na,pa
Black-chested Tyrant *Taeniotriccus andrei* 50Bpa 51Bpa
Spotted Tody-Flycatcher *Todirostrum maculatum* 12Epa; Plo 19Ena 42Plo,md 45BO 50Bmg 51Bmg
Common Tody-Flycatcher *Todirostrum cinereum* 4Cvc 5Vap,da 16Ees 17Egu,ma 18Ezc 19Eeo,es,ma,ms,pa,zc 50Brj 51Vda
Maracaibo Tody-Flycatcher *Todirostrum viridanum* 5Vfa 51Vfa
Black-headed Tody-Flycatcher *Todirostrum nigriceps* 5Vta 16Ees 19Epi 51Vme
Painted Tody-Flycatcher *Todirostrum pictum* 5Vbo,da 50Vbo 51Vbo
Yellow-browed Tody-Flycatcher *Todirostrum chrysocrotaphum* 8Phu 19Ems 42Phu 45BO 50Bpa
Brownish Twistwing *Cnipodectes subbrunneus* 10Ena 19Ema,na,pa 45BO 50PA
Olivaceous Flatbill *Rhynchocyclus olivaceus* 5Vfa 12Epa 19Ems 42Pmd 45BO 50Vfa 51Vfa,su
Pacific Flatbill *Rhynchocyclus pacificus* 16Ees 19Ees
Fulvous-breasted Flatbill *Rhynchocyclus fulvipectus* 15Epi 18Ezc 44Eca,na
Yellow-olive Flycatcher *Tolmomyias sulphurescens* 5Vca 17Egu,lo 18Ena,zc 19Eeo,lo,ma,na,zc 20T 45BO 46CR 47A 50Bsp 51Vbo
Orange-eyed Flycatcher *Tolmomyias traylori* 12Epa; Plo 19Plo
Yellow-margined Flycatcher *Tolmomyias assimilis* 7Ena 11Ena 16Ees 19Ees,na 42BO 45BO 46PA 50Vbo 51Vbo
Grey-crowned Flycatcher *Tolmomyias poliocephalus* 5Vbo 7Ena 11Ena 19Ems,na,pa 42Plo 45BO 50Bpa 51Vda
Yellow-breasted Flycatcher *Tolmomyias flaviventris* 5Vbo,ca 11Ena 12Ena 18Ena,pa 19Ems,na,pa 20T 42BO; Plo 45BO 50Bba 51Vca
Cinnamon-crested Spadebill *Platyrinchus saturatus* 50Vam 51Vam
White-throated Spadebill *Platyrinchus mystaceus* 4Cvc 5Vca 6Epi 16Eeo,pi 18Ena 19Eca,eo,ms,na,pi 20T 44BO 45BO 46CR 47A 50Bce 51Vca
Golden-crowned Spadebill *Platyrinchus coronatus* 8Pmd 16Ees 19Ees,na,pa,pi 42Pmd 45BO 46CR 50Bmg 51Bmg
Yellow-throated Spadebill *Platyrinchus flavigularis* 18Ems; Pca 19Ems 44Ems
White-crested Spadebill *Platyrinchus platyrhynchos* 19Epa 42Pmd 50Bmg 51Bmg
Amazonian Royal Flycatcher *Onychorhynchus coronatus* 10Ena 19Ena; BO 42Pmd 45BO 50Bpa
Pacific Royal Flycatcher *Onychorhynchus occidentalis* 17Egu 19Egu,ma
Flavescent Flycatcher *Myiophobus flavicans* 2Cca 5Vla 6Ena 7Epi 13Ena 15Eim,pi 19Eca,im,pi 44Ppa 51Vla
Orange-crested Flycatcher *Myiophobus phoenicomitra* 15Ees 18Ezc 19Ees,ms,na,zc
Unadorned Flycatcher *Myiophobus inornatus* 45BO
Roraiman Flycatcher *Myiophobus roraimae* 44Ems
Handsome Flycatcher *Myiophobus pulcher* 13Ena 15Epi 19Ena
Orange-banded Flycatcher *Myiophobus lintoni* 14Ezc 19Elo,zc
Olive-crested Flycatcher *Myiophobus cryptoxanthus* 18Ena,zc 19Ems,na,pa
Bran-coloured Flycatcher *Myiophobus fasciatus* 5Vca; Pmd 16Elr 17Eeo,lo,lr,pi 19Eaz,lo 45A; BO 47A 50Brj 51Vca
Tawny-breasted Flycatcher *Myiobius villosus* 18Psm 44Ena 45BO
Whiskered Flycatcher *Myiobius barbatus* 5Ena 11Ena 19Ena 50Bsc 51Ena
Sulphur-rumped Flycatcher *Myiobius sulphureipygius* 16Ees 19Epi

Ruddy-tailed Flycatcher *Terenotriccus erythrurus* 5Vbo 11Ena 16Ees 19Elr,ms,na 42Pmd 45BO 50Bpa 51Vbo

Cinnamon Tyrant *Neopipo cinnamomeus* 18Epa; Plo 19Ena

Cinnamon Flycatcher *Pyrrhomyias cinnamomea* 1Ccq 2Cca 5Vta 6Ena 13Ena 15Epi 19Eco,lo,na,pi 43Phu 45BO 51Vya

Cliff Flycatcher *Hirundinea ferruginea* 18Ena,zc 19Ena 45BO 50Bsp 51Vbo

Euler's Flycatcher *Lathrotriccus euleri* 5Vca 12Ena 19Ena,pa 20T 42Pmd,pu 45BO 47A 50Brj 51Vca

Grey-breasted Flycatcher *Lathrotriccus griseipectus* 17Egu,lo,lr,ma 19Eeo,gu,lo,ma,pi

Fuscous Flycatcher *Cnemotriccus fuscatus* 5Vfa 11Ena 12Ena,pa 19Ena,pa 20T 21T 45BO 47A 50Bce 51Vap

Acadian Flycatcher *Empidonax virescens* 19Ees,lr 48USA 51Vta; USA

Willow Flycatcher *Empidonax traillii* 5Vta 19Ena 48USA 49USA

Alder Flycatcher *Empidonax alnorum* 45BO 48USA 49USA 51USA

Olive-sided Flycatcher *Contopus cooperi* 3Cns 18Ems,na; Pcu 19Eca,ms,na 48USA 49USA

Smoke-coloured Pewee *Contopus fumigatus* 3Cns 5Vba,ca 13Ena 15Cna; Epi 19Eca,eo,na,pi 44Var; Psm 45BO 50Vbo 51Vca,me

Western Wood Pewee *Contopus sordidulus* 15Ena,pi 18Ena,zc 19Eim,ms,na,pi,zc 46CR 49USA

Eastern Wood Pewee *Contopus virens* 5Vme 11Ena 19Ena 45BO 48USA 50M 51Vme

Tropical Pewee *Contopus cinereus* 5Vca 17Egu; Pam 19Eaz,eo,gu 20T 21T 45A 46CR 47A 50Bsp 51Vsu

Blackish Pewee *Contopus nigrescens* 12Ems 18Ems; Plo 19Epa 50Bpa

Tufted Flycatcher *Mitrephanes phaeocercus* 16Ees 19Ees 46CR

Olive Tufted Flycatcher *Mitrephanes olivaceus* 44Pju,pa 45BO

Black Phoebe *Sayornis nigricans* 5Vta 13Ena 15Epi 45BO 47A 49USA 51Vta

Vermilion Flycatcher *Pyrocephalus rubinus* 14Elo,pi 17Egu,lo 19Egu,pi 47A 49USA 50M 51Vap

Rufous-tailed Tyrant *Knipolegus poecilurus* 18Ena; Psm 19Psm

Riverside Tyrant *Knipolegus orenocensis* 12Ena 19Ena

Drab Water Tyrant *Ochthornis littoralis* 10Ena 19Ena 45BO

Spot-billed Ground Tyrant *Muscisaxicola maculirostris* 14Epi 45CH

Plain-capped Ground Tyrant *Muscisaxicola alpinus* 14Eaz,co,na

Black-billed Shrike-Tyrant *Agriornis montanus* 14Eco,pi 19Etu 45BO

White-tailed Shrike-Tyrant *Agriornis andicola* 14Elo,pi 19Elo,pi

Grey Monjita *Xolmis cinereus* 45PY 47A

Streak-throated Bush Tyrant *Myiotheretes striaticollis* 14Eca,lo,pi 19Eaz,ca,im,pi 45BO 51Vme

Smoky Bush Tyrant *Myiotheretes fumigatus* 2Cca 13Ena 14Ems,na 19Eaz,ca,co,im,ms,na,zc 51Vme

Red-rumped Bush Tyrant *Cnemarchus erythropygius* 14Ena 19Epi

Pied Water Tyrant *Fluvicola pica* 5Vap,ca 20T 45Bba 47A 50Vca 51Vca

Masked Water Tyrant *Fluvicola nengeta* 17Ema 19Egu,pi 50Bal

White-headed Marsh Tyrant *Arundinicola leucocephala* 20T 50Van 51Van

Crowned Chat-Tyrant *Ochthoeca frontalis* 14Ebo,na,zc 19Ebo,na,zc

Jelski's Chat-Tyrant *Ochthoeca jelskii* 14Elo 19Elo

Yellow-bellied Chat-Tyrant *Ochthoeca diadema* 5Vtr 13Ena 14Eim,na,pi 15Eim,pi 19Eaz,ca,co,im,na,pi 51Vtr

Slaty-backed Chat-Tyrant *Ochthoeca cinnamomeiventris* 3Cns 5Pcu 13Ena 14Ems,na,pi 15Epi 19Ems,na,zc 44BO 45BO

Rufous-breasted Chat-Tyrant *Ochthoeca rufipectoralis* 5BO 14Eaz,ca 19Eaz,ca,im,na,pi,zc 45BO

Brown-backed Chat-Tyrant *Ochthoeca fumicolor* 5Ena 13Eaz,ch,na,pi 19Eaz,ca,ch,na,pi,tu 45BO 51Ena

White-browed Chat-Tyrant *Ochthoeca leucophrys* 14Elo 19Elo 45BO

Long-tailed Tyrant *Colonia colonus* 5Vbo 16Ees 18Ena,zc 19Ees,pi 46CR 47A 50Bmg 51Vbo

Short-tailed Field Tyrant *Muscigralla brevicauda* 17Egu,lo 19Egu

Cattle Tyrant *Machetornis rixosa* 5Vap 45BO 47A 50Vap 51Vap

Piratic Flycatcher *Legatus leucophaius* 5Vbo 10Ena 16Ees 19Ema,na,pa 20T 42BO 45BO 47A 50Vbo 51Vca

Rusty-margined Flycatcher *Myiozetetes cayanensis* 4Cvc 5Vca,ta 16Epi 19Ees 45BO 50Bmg 51Vca

Social Flycatcher *Myiozetetes similis* 5Ena 10Ena 16Ees 17Ema 19Eeo,es,gu,na,pa,zc 45BO 46CR 47A 50Bsp 51Bsp

Grey-capped Flycatcher *Myiozetetes granadensis* 5Vbo 10Ena 16Ees 19Eca,es,na,pa 46CR 50Vbo 51Vbo

Dusky-chested Flycatcher *Myiozetetes luteiventris* 5Vam,bo 7Ena 12Ena 19Ems,na 42Pmd 50Bpa 51Vbo

White-bearded Flycatcher *Phelpsia inornata* 51V

Great Kiskadee *Pitangus sulphuratus* 4Cvc 5Vca,mo 9Ena 19Ena 20T 21T 22T 45BO 46CR 47A 48USA 49USA 50Vsu 51Vsu

Lesser Kiskadee *Philohydor lictor* 5Vbo,fa 9Ena 19Ena 45BO 50Bmg 51Vfa

White-ringed Flycatcher *Conopias albovittatus* 5Ees 19Ees 46CR

Yellow-throated Flycatcher *Conopias parvus* 19Plo 50Vbo 51Vbo

Three-striped Flycatcher *Conopias trivirgatus* 19BO 47A 50Bsp 51Bsp

Lemon-browed Flycatcher *Conopias cinchoneti* 5Pcu 13Ena 18Ems,na,zc 19Ems,na,zc 43Psm 51Pcu

Golden-crowned Flycatcher *Myiodynastes chrysocephalus* 2Cca 5Cma; Vta 13Ena 15Epi 18Ena,zc 19Eca,eo,na,pi 43BO 45BO 51Vme

Baird's Flycatcher *Myiodynastes bairdii* 17Elo,ma 19Egu; Pla

Sulphur-bellied Flycatcher *Myiodynastes luteiventris* 7Ena 12Ena 45BO 46CR 49USA 50M

Streaked Flycatcher *Myiodynastes maculatus* 5Var,ca,mo 12Plo 17Ees,gu,lo 19Egu,lo 20T 45BO 47A 50Vbo 51Vbo

Boat-billed Flycatcher *Megarhynchus pitangua* 5Vda,mo 9Ena 16Ees,pi 17Eeo,gu,lo 19Eca,gu,ma,pa 20T 21T 45BO 46CR 47A 50Bpa 51Vmo

Sulphury Flycatcher *Tyrannopsis sulphurea* 10Ena 19Ena 20T 42Pmd 51Vmo

Variegated Flycatcher *Empidonomus varius* 5BO 12Ena 19Ena 45Bba 47A 50BO 51BO

Snowy-throated Kingbird *Tyrannus niveigularis* 17Ees,gu; Ptu 19Egu

Tropical Kingbird *Tyrannus melancholicus* 5Vam,ca,fa,mo 9Ena 12Ena 13Ena 16Ees,pi 19Ezc 20T 45BO 47A 49USA 50Vmo 51Vam

Scissor-tailed Flycatcher *Tyrannus forficatus* 48USA 49USA

Fork-tailed Flycatcher *Tyrannus savana* 5Vam 47A 50Vam 51Vam

Eastern Kingbird *Tyrannus tyrannus* 48USA 49USA 50USA 51USA

Grey Kingbird *Tyrannus dominicensis* 20T 21T 48USA

Rufous Mourner *Rhytipterna holerythra* 16Ees 19Ees,ma,pi 46CR

Greyish Mourner *Rhytipterna simplex* 5Vbo,mo 8Bes; Pmd 19Ena 42Pmd 45BO 50Bsp 51Vbo,mo

Pale-bellied Mourner *Rhytipterna immunda* 5Vam 50Vam 51Vam

Sirystes *Sirystes sibilator* 5PA 6Ena 8Pmd 11Ena 16Ees 19Ena 42Pmd 45BO 47A 50Bba 51Bba

Dusky-capped Flycatcher *Myiarchus tuberculifer* 5Vba,ta 15Elo,pi 17Eeo,lo 19Eaz,ca,eo,gu,lo,na 20T 43A; Ppi 45BO 49USA 50Vbo 51Vta

Swainson's Flycatcher *Myiarchus swainsoni* 19Ena 45BO 47A 50Bba 51Vbo

Venezuelan Flycatcher *Myiarchus venezuelensis* 5Vca 20T 51Var

Short-crested Flycatcher *Myiarchus ferox* 5Vbo 10Ena 19Ems,pa 42Pmd 45BO 50Bmi 51Vbo

Apical Flycatcher *Myiarchus apicalis* 4Cvc

Sooty-crowned Flycatcher *Myiarchus phaeocephalus* 17Eeo,gu,lo,ma 18Pca 19Eeo,gu,lo

Pale-edged Flycatcher *Myiarchus cephalotes* 2Cca 5Vla 13Ena 19Es,na,zc 43Ccc; Ppa 45BO 51Vla

Great Crested Flycatcher *Myiarchus crinitus* 48USA 51USA

Brown-crested Flycatcher *Myiarchus tyrannulus* 5Vca,fa 18Pam,ca 20T 45BO 47A 49USA 50Bpe 51Vca,fa

Large-headed Flatbill *Ramphotrigon megacephalum* 5Pmd 6Ena 18Ena 19Ena 42Pmd 45BO 50Bmg 51Pmd

Rufous-tailed Flatbill *Ramphotrigon ruficauda* 5Vam 12Ena 19Ena 42Pmd 45BO 50Vam 51Vam

Dusky-tailed Flatbill *Ramphotrigon fuscicauda* 18Ena; Pmd 19BO 42BO; Pmd 45BO 50Bmg

Cinnamon Attila *Attila cinnamomeus* 5Vbo,mo 6Ena 8Ena; Vbo 9Ena 19Ena 45BO 50Bpa 51Vsu

Ochraceous Attila *Attila torridus* 17Ees,lr,ma 19Eeo,gu,lo

Citron-bellied Attila *Attila citriniventris* 5Vam 10Ena 19Ena

Dull-capped Attila *Attila bolivianus* 42Pmd 45BO 50Bmg

Bright-rumped Attila *Attila spadiceus* 5Var,mo,ta 8Pmd 11Ena 16Ees 19Ees,lr,ms,na,pi 20T 22T 42Pmd 45BO 46CR 50Bmg 51Var

OXYRUNCIDAE

Sharpbill *Oxyruncus cristatus* 5PA 18Ems 19Ems 43Psm 45BO 46CR 50Bba 51PA

COTINGIDAE

Red-crested Cotinga *Ampelion rubrocristatus* 5Vta 14Ebo,pi 19Ebo,pi 45BO 51Vta

Chestnut-crested Cotinga *Ampelion rufaxilla* 14Ezc 19Pam 44Ppa 45BO

Green-and-black Fruiteater *Pipreola riefferii* 3Cns 5Vla,me 7Ena 13Ena 15Epi 19Ena,pi 51Vme

Barred Fruiteater *Pipreola arcuata* 2Cca 5Vta 14Epi 19Eim,ms,zc 45BO 51Vta

Golden-breasted Fruiteater *Pipreola aureopectus* 5Var,mi 51Vla

Orange-breasted Fruiteater *Pipreola jucunda* 7Epi 15Epi

Black-chested Fruiteater *Pipreola lubomirskii* 13Ena 19Ezc

Fiery-throated Fruiteater *Pipreola chlorolepidota* 19Ena,zc

Scarlet-breasted Fruiteater *Pipreola frontalis* 18Ena 19Ems

Red-banded Fruiteater *Pipreola whitelyi* 51Vbo

Scaled Fruiteater *Ampelioides tschudii* 7Epi 15Epi 19Eca,es,lo,na,pi 43Phu 45BO

Guianan Cock-of-the-Rock *Rupicola rupicola* 50Vbo 51Vam

Andean Cock-of-the-Rock *Rupicola peruvianus* 1Ccu 5Vba 6Ena 7Ena 13Ena 15Epi 19Eim,ms,na,pi 43Phu 45BO 51Vba

Black-necked Red Cotinga *Phoenicircus nigricollis* 11Ena 19Ena

Plum-throated Cotinga *Cotinga maynana* 10Ena 19Ena

Spangled Cotinga *Cotinga cayana* 19Pmd

White Bellbird *Procnias albus* 5Vbo 50Bpa 51Vbo

Bearded Bellbird *Procnias averano* 5Vbo,fa 20T 21T 22T 50Bce 51Vbo

Dusky Piha *Lipaugus fuscocinereus* 13Ena 19Ems,na

Rufous Piha *Lipaugus unirufus* 16Ees 19Ees 46CR

Screaming Piha *Lipaugus vociferans* 5Vbo 8Pmd 9Ena 11Ena 19Ena,pa 42Pmd 45BO 50Bpa 51Vbo

Grey-tailed Piha *Snowornis subalaris* 18Ems,na 19Ems 43Psm

Olivaceous Piha *Snowornis cryptolophus* 19Epi

Purple-throated Cotinga *Porphyrolaema porphyrolaema* 11Ena 19Ena

Pompadour Cotinga *Xipholena punicea* 19Plo

Black-tipped Cotinga *Carpodectes hopkei* 19Ees

Purple-throated Fruitcrow *Querula purpurata* 5Vbo 8Ena 16Epi 19Ena 42Pmd 45BO 46CR 50Bpa 51Vbo

Red-ruffed Fruitcrow *Pyroderus scutatus* 15Cri 47A

Capuchinbird *Perissocephalus tricolor* 5Vbo 50Vbo 51Vbo

Amazonian Umbrellabird *Cephalopterus ornatus* 10Ena 18Ena 19Ena 45BO

Long-wattled Umbrellabird *Cephalopterus penduliger* 16Ees 19Ees

PIPRIDAE

Dwarf Tyrant-Manakin *Tyranneutes stolzmanni* 5Vam 8Pmd 10Ena 19Ems,na 42Bmg; Ppu 45BO 50Bpa 51Bpa

Golden-winged Manakin *Masius chrysopterus* 15Cna; Eeo,pi 18Pca,sm 19Epi 51Vba

White-ruffed Manakin *Corapipo altera* 5PA 46CR

Club-winged Manakin *Machaeropterus deliciosus* 15Epi 19Epi

Striped Manakin *Machaeropterus regulus* 4Cvc 8Plo 9Ena 19Ems,na

Fiery-capped Manakin *Machaeropterus pyrocephalus* 42Pmd 45BO 50Bmg 51Bmg

Blue-crowned Manakin *Lepidothrix coronata* 5CR 8Plo 9Ena 10Ena 16Ees 19Ees,na,pa 42Pmd 45BO 50CR 51CR

Orange-bellied Manakin *Lepidothrix suavissima* 50Vbo 51Vbo

Blue-rumped Manakin *Lepidothrix isidorei* 1Ccq 18Ena 19Ems,na,zc

White-bearded Manakin *Manacus manacus* 5Epi; Vta 10Ena 12Ena,pa; Plo 16Ees,pi 19Ees,lr,na,pi 20T 21T 22T 45BO 50Bsp 51Vbo

Golden-collared Manakin *Manacus vitellinus* 2Cca

Lance-tailed Manakin *Chiroxiphia lanceolata* 5Var,ca,fa 51Var

Blue-backed Manakin *Chiroxiphia pareola* 6Ena 10Ena 19Ems,na,pa 20T 21T 22T 42Bmg 50Bpa 51Vbo

Green Manakin *Xenopipo holochlora* 16Ees 18Ems 19Ees,ms

Olive Manakin *Xenopipo uniformis* 50Vbo 51Vbo

Jet Manakin *Xenopipo unicolor* 18Ems; Pcu 19Ems

Orange-crowned Manakin *Heterocercus aurantiivertex* 11Ena 19Ena

Yellow-crowned Manakin *Heterocercus flavivertex* 50Vam 51Vam

White-crowned Manakin *Dixiphia pipra* 5Vla 10Ena 18Ena 19Ems,na 46CR 51Vla

Crimson-hooded Manakin *Pipra aureola* 5Vmo 50Vmo 51Vmo

Wire-tailed Manakin *Pipra filicauda* 5Ena 9Ena 19Ena 50Ena 51Ena

Scarlet-horned Manakin *Pipra cornuta* 50Vbo 51Vbo

Red-capped Manakin *Pipra mentalis* 16Ees 19Ees 46CR

Golden-headed Manakin *Pipra erythrocephala* 5Vam,bo 8Plo 12Ena 19Ems,na,pa 20T 50Vbo 51Vbo

TITYRIDAE

Black-crowned Tityra *Tityra inquisitor* 47A

Black-tailed Tityra *Tityra cayana* 5Vam,mo 10Ena 19Ena 20T 42Plo 45BO 47A 50Vme 51Vme

Masked Tityra *Tityra semifasciata* 4Cvc 6Epi 12Ena 16Ees,pi 19Epi 42BO 45BO 46CR 50M 51M

Várzea Schiffornis *Schiffornis major* 5Ena 9Ena 12Ena 19Ena 42Pmd 45BO 50Ena 51Ena

Thrush-like Schiffornis *Schiffornis turdina* 5Vam,bo,fa,ta 10Ena 16Ees 18Ems,na 19Eeo,es,ms,na 42Pmd 45BO 46CR 50Bmg 51Vam,fa

Speckled Mourner *Laniocera rufescens* 16Ees

Cinereous Mourner *Laniocera hypopyrra* 5Vam,bo,mo 9Ena 19Ena 42Pmd,pu 45BO 50Bmg 51Vbo

White-browed Purpletuft *Iodopleura isabellae* 5Vam 10Ena 19Ena 51Vam

Elegant Mourner *Laniisoma elegans* 18Ems 19Ems 43Psm 50Bes

White-naped Xenopsaris *Xenopsaris albinucha* 45Bba 50Bpe 51Vbo

Green-backed Becard *Pachyramphus viridis* 45Bba 47A 50Bpa 51Brj

Yellow-cheeked Becard *Pachyramphus xanthogenys* 18Ezc 19Ena

Barred Becard *Pachyramphus versicolor* 5Pcu 13Ena 14Ena 15Epi 19Ena,pi 44Ppi 45BO 51Vme

Slaty Becard *Pachyramphus spodiurus* 17Egu,lo

Cinereous Becard *Pachyramphus rufus* 5Vap 50Vap 51Vap

Cinnamon Becard *Pachyramphus cinnamomeus* 5Vta 16Ees 19Ees,pi 46CR 51Vta

Chestnut-crowned Becard *Pachyramphus castaneus* 5Vca 12Ena 19Ena 45BO 47A 50Bsp 51Vca

White-winged Becard *Pachyramphus polychopterus* 10Ena 15Epi 19Eca,im,ms,na,pa 20T 42Plo,md 45BO 46CR 47A 50Bal 51Vca

Black-and-white Becard *Pachyramphus albogriseus* 15Eeo 17Eeo,gu 18Ems,na 19Ems,na,pi 46CR 51Vme

Black-capped Becard *Pachyramphus marginatus* 5Vmo 12Ena 19Ena 42Plo,md 45BO 50Bmg 51Vbo

One-coloured Becard *Pachyramphus homochrous* 17Eeo,lo,lr 19Elo

Pink-throated Becard *Pachyramphus minor* 12Ena 19Ena,pa 42Plo 45BO 50Bpa 51Bpa

INCERTAE SEDIS

Wing-barred Piprites *Piprites chloris* 5Vbo,ca 8Pmd 19Ems,na 42Pmd 45BO 47A 50Bmg 51Vbo

SAPAYOIDAE

Broad-billed Sapayoa *Sapayoa aenigma* 16Ees 19Ees

VIREONIDAE

Rufous-browed Peppershrike *Cyclarhis gujanensis* 2Cca 5Vam,ca,da 17Egu,lo,ma 18Ezc; Pca 19Eaz,gu,lo,ms,zc 20T 21T 22T 39F; Vdf; BE; M 45BO 46CR 47A 50Bpe 51Vsu

Black-billed Peppershrike *Cyclarhis nigrirostris* 4Cvc 7Ena 13Ena 15Epi 18Ena 19Eca,es,na 39Chu

Yellow-browed Shrike-Vireo *Vireolanius eximius* 5PA 51PA

Slaty-capped Shrike-Vireo *Vireolanius leucotis* 5Vbo 6Epi 10Ena 16Ees 19Ees,ms,na,pa 39Vbo 43Pmd 45BO 50Bmg 51Vbo

Yellow-throated Vireo *Vireo flavifrons* 39USA 48USA 51USA

Chocó Vireo *Vireo masteri* 15Cna

Brown-capped Vireo *Vireo leucophrys* 5Vca 13Ena 15Epi 19Eaz,ca,eo,na,pi 39Vdf 43BO 45BO 51Vca,me

Philadelphia Vireo *Vireo philadelphicus* 39CN 48USA

Red-eyed Vireo *Vireo olivaceus* 5Vca 12Plo 17Egu,lo,ma 18Ezc 19Egu,lo,zc 20T 39Var; Bsp; CN; USA 45BO 47A 48USA 49CN 50Bse; USA 51Vca

Yellow-green Vireo *Vireo flavoviridis* 39M 49USA 50M 51M

Black-whiskered Vireo *Vireo altiloquus* 39BA; J; MO 49USA

Lemon-chested Greenlet *Hylophilus thoracicus* 5Vbo 12Epa 19Ena,pa 39Pmd 42Pmd 45BO 51Vbo

Grey-chested Greenlet *Hylophilus semicinereus* 39Bpa 45BO 51Bpa

Ashy-headed Greenlet *Hylophilus pectoralis* 39S 45BO 51Bmg

Tepui Greenlet *Hylophilus sclateri* 5Vbo 39Vbo 50Vbo 51Vbo

Rufous-naped Greenlet *Hylophilus semibrunneus* 4Cvc 18Ena 19Ena 39Cvc

Golden-fronted Greenlet *Hylophilus aurantiifrons* 5Vca,fa,mo 20T 39T 51Vsu

Dusky-capped Greenlet *Hylophilus hypoxanthus* 11Ena 19Ems,na 39Pmd 42Pmd 45BO 50Bpa 51Bpa

Buff-cheeked Greenlet *Hylophilus muscicapinus* 5Vbo 39Vbo 45BO 50Vbo 51Vbo

Scrub Greenlet *Hylophilus flavipes* 5Vda,fa 20T 21T 22T 39Ccc; Vma 51Vda

Olivaceous Greenlet *Hylophilus olivaceus* 6Ena 18Ena,zc 19Ems,na,zc 39Phu

Tawny-crowned Greenlet *Hylophilus ochraceiceps* 5Vam,bo 10Ena 16Ees 19Ems,na,pi 39Vbo 43Pmd 45BO 46CR 50Bpa 51Vbo

Lesser Greenlet *Hylophilus decurtatus* 16Ees 19Eeo,es,gu,pi 39BE 46CR

CORVIDAE

Black-collared Jay *Cyanolyca armillata* 5Vta,tr 14Ena 19Ena 41Vta 51Vla

Turquoise Jay *Cyanolyca turcosa* 7Epi 13Ena 14Eaz,co,lo,na, ms,pi 15Epi 19Eaz,co,lo,ms,na,pi,zc 41Ppi

Beautiful Jay *Cyanolyca pulchra* 15Epi 19Eca,pi 41Ccc; Epi

Violaceous Jay *Cyanocorax violaceus* 5Vbo 9Ena 12Ena 19Ena 41Vba 42Pmd 50Pmd 51Vbo

Black-chested Jay *Cyanocorax affinis* 5Cma; Vme; PA 41PA 46PA 51Vme

White-tailed Jay *Cyanocorax mystacalis* 17Egu,lo 19Egu,lo 41Ppi,tu

Cayenne Jay *Cyanocorax cayanus* 5Vbo 41Vbo 50Vbo 51Vbo

Azure-naped Jay *Cyanocorax heilprini* 41Vbo

Green Jay *Cyanocorax yncas* 1Ccu 3Cns 5Vmo,ta 13Ena 18Ezc 19Ena 41GT; Phu; USA 44BO; Pam,sm 45BO 48USA 49USA 51Vta

ALAUDIDAE

Horned Lark *Eremophila alpestris* 48CN 49USA

HIRUNDINIDAE

Bank Swallow/Sand Martin *Riparia riparia* 48USA 49USA

Tree Swallow *Tachycineta bicolor* 48USA 49USA 51USA

Tumbes Swallow *Tachycineta stolzmanni* 17Ppi 19Pla

White-winged Swallow *Tachycineta albiventer* 5Vam 10Ena 19Ena,pa 45Bba 50Vam 51Vam

Chilean Swallow *Tachycineta meyeni* 47A

Violet-green Swallow *Tachycineta thalassina* 49USA

Brown-chested Martin *Progne tapera* 11Ena 19Ena 45BO 47A

Purple Martin *Progne subis* 48USA 49USA 50USA 51USA

Caribbean Martin *Progne dominicensis* 20T

Grey-breasted Martin *Progne chalybea* 5Vmo 11Ena 17Ema 19Egu 20T 45BO 50Vmo 51Vco

Southern Martin *Progne elegans* 47A

Blue-and-white Swallow *Notiochelidon cyanoleuca* 5Vba 13Ena 14Elo,pi 19Eca,pi 45BO 50Bsp 51Vba

Brown-bellied Swallow *Notiochelidon murina* 5Vme 14Eaz,co 19Etu 45BO 51Vme

Pale-footed Swallow *Notiochelidon flavipes* 5Vla,tr 13Ena 14Elo,zc 19Ezc 45BO 51Vla,me

White-banded Swallow *Atticora fasciata* 9Ena 19Epa 45BO; Pmd

Black-collared Swallow *Atticora melanoleuca* 5Vam 50Vam 51Vam

White-thighed Swallow *Neochelidon tibialis* 16Ees 18Ena 19Epa 50Bsp 51Bpa

Tawny-headed Swallow *Alopochelidon fucata* 47A 50Bmi 51Bmi

Northern Rough-winged Swallow *Stelgidopteryx serripennis* 48USA 49USA

Southern Rough-winged Swallow *Stelgidopteryx ruficollis* 5Vfa 16Ees 18Ena,zc 45A; BO 47A 50Vfa 51Vfa

Barn Swallow *Hirundo rustica* 14Par 48USA 49USA 50USA 51USA

Cliff Swallow *Petrochelidon pyrrhonota* 48USA 49USA 50USA 51USA

Cave Swallow *Petrochelidon fulva* 49USA

Chestnut-collared Swallow *Petrochelidon rufocollaris* 17Elo,zc

TROGLODYTIDAE

Southern Nightingale Wren *Microcerculus marginatus* 4Cvc 5Var,fa 8Pmd 16Ees 19Elr,ms,na,pi 37Phu,md 42Pmd 45BO 50Bpa 51Var,fa

Flutist Wren *Microcerculus ustulatus* 5Vbo 37Vbo 50Vbo 51Vbo

Wing-banded Wren *Microcerculus bambla* 5Vbo 12Ena 18Ena 19Ems,na 37Bam 50Vbo 51Vbo

Grey-mantled Wren *Odontorchilus branickii* 16Ees 18Ena,zc 19Ees 37BO 43BO

Southern House Wren *Troglodytes musculus* 4Cvc 5Vca 11Ena 14Ena,pi 16Ees,pi 17Ees,lo 19Eca,es,gu,lo,pi 20T 22T 37Cam;A 45BO 47A 50Brj 51Vca

Mountain Wren *Troglodytes solstitialis* 5BO 13Ena 14Ena,zc 15Epi 19Eaz,lo,ms,na,pi 37Vta 44BO 45BO 47A 51Vla

Tepui Wren *Troglodytes rufulus* 37Vbo

Sedge Wren *Cistothorus platensis* 2Cca 3Cns 5Vmi,ta 14Eco,na,tu 19Eca,co,im,pi,zc 37Cna; USA 45A; BO 47A 48USA 50Vta 51Vmi,ta

Mérida Wren *Cistothorus meridae* 37Vme

Apolinar's Wren *Cistothorus apolinari* 37Ccu

White-headed Wren *Campylorhynchus albobrunneus* 37PA

Band-backed Wren *Campylorhynchus zonatus* 16Ees 19Ees,pi 37Cma 46CR

Stripe-backed Wren *Campylorhynchus nuchalis* 5Vca,mo 37Vgu 51Vsu

Fasciated Wren *Campylorhynchus fasciatus* 17Elo 19Eeo,gu,lo 37Ppi

Bicoloured Wren *Campylorhynchus griseus* 5Vmo 37Cma 50Vla 51Vla,su

Thrush-like Wren *Campylorhynchus turdinus* 8Plo 9Ena 11Ena 19Ems,na,pa,zc 37Cam 42Pmd 45BO 50Bpa

Sooty-headed Wren *Thryothorus spadix* 37PA

Black-bellied Wren *Thryothorus fasciatoventris* 37Cto

Plain-tailed Wren *Thryothorus euophrys* 6Epi 13Ena 14Epi,zc 15Epi 19Eaz,co,lo,ms,na,pi,zc 37Epi

Whiskered Wren *Thryothorus mystacalis* 1Cns 2Cca 3Cns 5Var,ba,ca 16Eeo,lr 19Eeo,lr,pi 37Ccc; Ema 51Vba,ca

Coraya Wren *Thryothorus coraya* 5Vbo 7Ena 9Ena 19Ems,na,pa 37Plo 50Bpa 51Vbo

Rufous-breasted Wren *Thryothorus rutilus* 1Ccq 5Vca,fa,la,ta 20T 22T 37Cme 51Vmo

Speckle-breasted Wren *Thryothorus sclateri* 2Cca 4Cvc 17Egu,lo,lr 18Ezc 19Eeo,gu,lo,zc

Bay Wren *Thryothorus nigricapillus* 6Epi 16Ees,pi 19Eeo,es,pi 37PA 46CR

Stripe-throated Wren *Thryothorus leucopogon* 16Ees 19Ees 37PA

Rufous-and-white Wren *Thryothorus rufalbus* 5Vca,mo 37Cma 51Vca

Buff-breasted Wren *Thryothorus leucotis* 5Vam,fa,bo,mo 8Ena 11Ena 19Ena 37Puc 42Pmd 45BO 50Bmg 51Vda

Superciliated Wren *Thryothorus superciliaris* 17Eeo,gu,lo,ma 19Eeo,gu 37Ppi

Rufous Wren *Cinnycerthia unirufa* 2Cca 3Cns 5Elo 13Ena 14Elo,na,pi,tu 19Elo,ms,na,pi,tu,zc 37Pca 51Elo

Sharpe's Wren *Cinnycerthia olivascens* 6Ena 7Epi 13Ena 15Epi 19Eaz,na

White-breasted Wood Wren *Henicorhina leucosticta* 2Cca 4Cvc 5Vbo 6Ena 8Ees 9Ena 16Ees 19Ees,ms,na,pa 37HO; M 46CR 50Vbo 51Vbo

Grey-breasted Wood Wren *Henicorhina leucophrys* 1Ccq 2Cca 3Cns 5Vla,ta,tr 6Ena 13Ena 14Ena,pi 15Epi 17Eeo,lo 19Eaz,bo,ca,co,eo,na,pi,zc 37M 43Phu,sm 45BO 46CR 51Vca

Bar-winged Wood Wren *Henicorhina leucoptera* 18Ezc 19Ezc 37Pca

Chestnut Wren *Cyphorhinus thoracicus* 18Ena 37Cvc 43Phu 45BO

Song Wren *Cyphorhinus phaeocephalus* 16Ees 19Eeo 37Epi; CR 46CR

Musician Wren *Cyphorhinus arada* 5Vbo 8Pmd 19Ems,na 37Ena; Vda 42Pmd 45BO 50Bmg 51Vbo

POLIOPTILIDAE

Collared Gnatwren *Microbates collaris* 12Plo 19Plo

Tawny-faced Gnatwren *Microbates cinereiventris* 10Ena 16Ees 19Ems,na,pi 43Ems; Plo 46CR

Long-billed Gnatwren *Ramphocaenus melanurus* 5Vbo,fa 11Ena 16Egu 17Egu 19Egu,lr,ma,na,pa 20T 21T 42Ppu 45BO 46CR 50Bpa 51Vfa

Tropical Gnatcatcher *Polioptila plumbea* 5Vca,fa 12Epa 16Ees 17Ees,gu,lo,ma 19Egu,lo,na 46CR 50Bba 51Vca,su

Slate-throated Gnatcatcher *Polioptila schistaceigula* 16Ees 19Ees

INCERTAE SEDIS

Black-capped Donacobius *Donacobius atricapilla* 5Vca,mo 9Ena 11Ena 19Ena,pa 37Puc 45BO 47A 50Bmg 51Vca,mo

CINCLIDAE

White-capped Dipper *Cinclus leucocephalus* 14Ena 19Epi

BOMBYCILLIDAE

Cedar Waxwing *Bombycilla cedrorum* 48USA 49USA 51M

TURDIDAE

Varied Solitaire *Myadestes coloratus* 36PA

Andean Solitaire *Myadestes ralloides* 1Ccq 2Cca 3Cns 4Cvc 5Vla,tr 13Ena 15Epi 19Eca,eo,es,im,ms,na,pi,zc 36Pll 44Pju 45BO 51Vla

Orange-billed Nightingale-Thrush *Catharus aurantiirostris* 5Vla 36Ccc; M 51Vla

Slaty-backed Nightingale-Thrush *Catharus fuscater* 5Cma; Vla,ta,tr 15Elo,pi 19Eaz,lo 36CR 44BO; Pju 45BO; Psm 46CR 51Vla

Spotted Nightingale-Thrush *Catharus dryas* 1Ccq 3Cns 15Egu,pi 18Ems,na; Pca 19Egu,ms,na 36BO; Phu 43Phu 45BO 51Vme

Veery *Catharus fuscescens* 36USA 48USA 49USA

Grey-cheeked Thrush *Catharus minimus* 36CN; USA 48USA 49USA

Swainson's Thrush *Catharus ustulatus* 15Ena,pi 18Eaz,na 19Eca 36USA 45BO 48CN; USA 49USA 50M 51M

Wood Thrush *Hylocichla mustelina* 36USA 48USA

Black Solitaire *Entomodestes coracinus* 15Cna 19Eca

Rufous-brown Solitaire *Cichlopsis leucogenys* 15Cna; Ees 19Ees 36Bes

Yellow-legged Thrush *Turdus flavipes* 5Vfa,la 20T 36Cma 50Bsp 51Vfa

Pale-eyed Thrush *Turdus leucops* 13Ena 15Epi 19Eca,im,lo,zc 36Eeo; Psm 43Psm

Chiguanco Thrush *Turdus chiguanco* 14Ech,lo 19Eaz,lo 36BO; Pcu,pi 45BO 47A

Great Thrush *Turdus fuscater* 2Cca 5Vme 13Ena 14Eaz,ca,co,ms,na,pi,zc 19Eaz,ca,co,im,lo,na,pi,tu,zc 36Cna 45BO 51Vme

Glossy-black Thrush *Turdus serranus* 5Vla 13Ena 14Ena,pi 15Epi 19Eaz,ca,lo,na,pi 36Var; Phu 44Pju 45BO 51Vla

Andean Slaty Thrush *Turdus nigriceps* 17Elo 36A 45BO 47A

Plumbeous-backed Thrush *Turdus reevei* 17Elo 19Eeo,lo 36Egu

Black-hooded Thrush *Turdus olivater* 5Vfa,la 36Var,bo 50Vfa 51Vla

Marañón Thrush *Turdus maranonicus* 18Ezc 19Ezc 36Pca

Chestnut-bellied Thrush *Turdus fulviventris* 13Ena 19Ems,na,zc 36Vta

Pale-breasted Thrush *Turdus leucomelas* 5Vca 36Cma; Var 45BO 47A 50Bpa 51Vca

Black-billed Thrush *Turdus ignobilis* 5Vta 9Ena 11Ena 19Ena 36V; Puc 42Plo 45BO 51Vme

Lawrence's Thrush *Turdus lawrencii* 5Ena 8Plo 9Ena 12Ena,pa; Plo 19Ena,pa 36Ena; Bac 42Pmd 45BO 50Bmg 51Ena

Pale-vented Thrush *Turdus obsoletus* 16Ees 46CR

Cocoa Thrush *Turdus fumigatus* 5Vmo 20T 21T 22T 36T; Vbo 50Vsu 51Vsu

Hauxwell's Thrush *Turdus hauxwelli* 12Ena; Plo 19Plo 35Plo,md 42Plo 45BO

Clay-coloured Thrush *Turdus grayi* 36CR; M 46CR 48M

Bare-eyed Thrush *Turdus nudigenis* 5Vca 20T 22T 36Vdf 50Vca 51Vca

Ecuadorian Thrush *Turdus maculirostris* 17Egu,lo 19Eaz,eo,gu,lo,ma

Dagua Thrush *Turdus daguae* 16Ees 19Ees

White-necked Thrush *Turdus albicollis* 5Vca 11Ena 19Ems,na 20T 21T 22T 36Bsp 42Pmd 45BO 47A 50Bpa 51Vca

Northern Wheatear *Oenanthe oenanthe* 36Norway; UK 49USA

MIMIDAE

Grey Catbird *Dumetella carolinensis* 35USA 48USA 49USA

Tropical Mockingbird *Mimus gilvus* 1Cby 5Vfa 19Eim 20T 21T 35M 50Vme 51Vme

Long-tailed Mockingbird *Mimus longicaudatus* 17Egu,lo 19Egu,lo 35Egu

Chalk-browed Mockingbird *Mimus saturninus* 35A 45BO; Bba 47A 50Bba

Brown Thrasher *Toxostoma rufum* 35USA 48USA

Pearly-eyed Thrasher *Margarops fuscatus* 35MO

STURNIDAE

European Starling *Sturnus vulgaris* 48USA 49USA

MOTACILLIDAE

Yellowish Pipit *Anthus lutescens* 45BO 47A 50Bmg 51Bmg

White Wagtail *Motacilla alba* 49China

Páramo Pipit *Anthus bogotensis* 14Eca,co,pi 19Eca,pi 45BO

THRAUPIDAE

Black-faced Tanager *Schistochlamys melanopis* 18Ezc 19Ezc 45BO 50Bmg 51Vbo

Magpie Tanager *Cissopis leverianus* 1Ccu 10Ena 12Ena,pa 19Ems 45BO 47A 50Bpa 51Bpa

Black-and-white Tanager *Conothraupis speculigera* 17Elo 19Eaz,gu,lo

Red-billed Pied Tanager *Lamprospiza melanoleuca* 50Bpa

White-capped Tanager *Sericossypha albocristata* 3Cns 5Eaz 13Ena 14Ena 19Ena 51Eaz

Hooded Tanager *Nemosia pileata* 5Vca 45Bba 50Bmg 51Vca
Rufous-crested Tanager *Creurgops verticalis* 18Eca,na,zc 19Eca
Black-capped Hemispingus *Hemispingus atropileus* 13Ena 14Eco,lo,ma,na 19Eaz,co,lo,na,zc
Superciliaried Hemispingus *Hemispingus superciliaris* 5Vta 14Eaz,lo,pi 19Eaz,im,lo,pi 51Vla
Grey-capped Hemispingus *Hemispingus reyi* 5Vta,tr 51Vla
Oleaginous Hemispingus *Hemispingus frontalis* 5Var,tr 13Ena 42Phu 51Var
Black-eared Hemispingus *Hemispingus melanotis* 13Ena 15Epi 19Eco,lo,na 44BO 45BO
Black-headed Hemispingus *Hemispingus verticalis* 14Elo,ms 19Elo,na,zc
Grey-hooded Bush Tanager *Cnemoscopus rubrirostris* 5Eaz 13Ena 14Ems,na 19Elo,na 51Eaz
Fulvous-headed Tanager *Thlypopsis fulviceps* 5Vla 51Vla
Rufous-chested Tanager *Thlypopsis ornata* 14Eaz,ms 19Eaz,lo
Orange-headed Tanager *Thlypopsis sordida* 47A 50Brj
Buff-bellied Tanager *Thlypopsis inornata* 18Ezc 19Pam
White-rumped Tanager *Cypsnagra hirundinacea* 45BO 50Bmg
Grey-headed Tanager *Eucometis penicillata* 5Var 9Ena 45BO 50Vca 51Vca
Flame-crested Tanager *Tachyphonus cristatus* 50Bsp 51Vam
Fulvous-crested Tanager *Tachyphonus surinamus* 19Ena 50Vbo 51Vbo
White-shouldered Tanager *Tachyphonus luctuosus* 5Vbo,mo 16Epi 20T 45BO 50Vbo 51Vbo
Tawny-crested Tanager *Tachyphonus delatrii* 16Ees 19Ees,pi 46CR
White-lined Tanager *Tachyphonus rufus* 5Vfa 16Ees,zc 18Ems,zc 19Ems,pa 20T 50Vfa 51Vam
Red-shouldered Tanager *Tachyphonus phoenicius* 50Vbo 51Vbo
Fulvous Shrike-Tanager *Lanio fulvus* 5Vbo 10Ena 19Ems,na 50Vbo 51Vbo
Masked Crimson Tanager *Ramphocelus nigrogularis* 9Ena 11Ena 19Ems,na
Crimson-backed Tanager *Ramphocelus dimidiatus* 4Cvc 5Vta 51Vme
Silver-beaked Tanager *Ramphocelus carbo* 5Vca,mo 9Ena 10Ena 19Ems,na,pa 20T 21T 45BO 50Vbo 51Vbo
Flame-rumped Tanager *Ramphocelus flammigerus* 16Ees 19Eca,eo,es
Blue-grey Tanager *Thraupis episcopus* 5Vam 10Ena 13Ena 16Ees 17Egu,lo 19Egu,pi,zc 20T 50Vam 51Vam
Glaucous Tanager *Thraupis glaucocolpa* 5Vfa 51Vfa
Palm Tanager *Thraupis palmarum* 4Cvc 5Vca 10Ena 16Ees,pi 19Eeo,es 20T 45BO 50Vsu 51Vsu
Blue-capped Tanager *Thraupis cyanocephala* 5Var,ta 15Epi 19Eaz,lo,pi 44Ppa 45BO 51Var
Blue-and-yellow Tanager *Thraupis bonariensis* 14Ech,im,pi 19Elo,pi 45BO 47A
Vermilion Tanager *Calochaetes coccineus* 18Ena; Psm 19Ena
Golden-chested Tanager *Bangsia rothschildi* 16Ees
Moss-backed Tanager *Bangsia edwardsi* 15Ees 19Ees
Orange-throated Tanager *Wetmorethraupis sterrhopteron* 18Pam 19Pam
Hooded Mountain Tanager *Buthraupis montana* 2Cca 13Ena 14Ebo,ca,lo,na,pi,zc 19Ebo,ca,im,na,pi 45BO
Black-chested Mountain Tanager *Buthraupis eximia* 14Ems,pi 19Eim,lo,ms,pi
Masked Mountain Tanager *Buthraupis wetmorei* 14Eaz,ms,na 19Eaz,ms
Lacrimose Mountain Tanager *Anisognathus lacrymosus* 2Cca 5Vtr 13Ena 14Elo,ms,na,zc 19Ena,zc 51Vtr
Scarlet-bellied Mountain Tanager *Anisognathus igniventris* 2Cca 14Ena,pi 19Eaz,co,im,lo,ms,na,pi,z c 45BO
Blue-winged Mountain Tanager *Anisognathus somptuosus* 2Cca 13Ena 15Cna; Eco,pi 19Eca,co,pi,zc 44BO 45BO 51Vya
Black-chinned Mountain Tanager *Anisognathus notabilis* 15Epi
Grass-green Tanager *Chlorornis riefferii* 13Ena 14Elo,pi 15Epi 19Eca,na,pi 45BO
Buff-breasted Mountain Tanager *Dubusia taeniata* 2Cca 5Vla 14Elo,na,pi,zc 19Eaz,bo,na,pi,zc 51Vla
Purplish-mantled Tanager *Iridosornis porphyrocephalus* 15Cna; Epi
Yellow-throated Tanager *Iridosornis analis* 18Ems,zc 19Ems,na,zc 44Pju
Golden-crowned Tanager *Iridosornis rufivertex* 14Eaz,ms,zc
Fawn-breasted Tanager *Pipraeidea melanonota* 3Cns 4Cvc 5Eeo 13Ena 14Eaz,na,pi 15Eeo,pi 19Eaz,ca,eo,na,pi 45BO 47A 50Vme 51Vme
Glistening-green Tanager *Chlorochrysa phoenicotis* 15Epi 19Epi
Orange-eared Tanager *Chlorochrysa calliparaea* 18Ena,zc 19Ena,zc
Grey-and-gold Tanager *Tangara palmeri* 16Epi 19Ees,pi
Turquoise Tanager *Tangara mexicana* 45BO 50Vbo 51Vbo
Paradise Tanager *Tangara chilensis* 10Ena 19Ems,pa 45BO 50Vbo 51Vbo
Blue-whiskered Tanager *Tangara johannae* 16Ees
Green-and-gold Tanager *Tangara schrankii* 11Ena 19Ena 45BO
Emerald Tanager *Tangara florida* 19Ees,pi
Golden Tanager *Tangara arthus* 2Cca 4Cvc 5Vla 15Epi 18Ena,zc 19Elo,na,pi 51Vla
Silver-throated Tanager *Tangara icterocephala* 16Eeo 19Eeo,gu 46CR
Saffron-crowned Tanager *Tangara xanthocephala* 13Ena 19Eca 51Vla
Golden-eared Tanager *Tangara chrysotis* 18Ena
Flame-faced Tanager *Tangara parzudakii* 13Ena 15Epi
Yellow-bellied Tanager *Tangara xanthogastra* 12Ena 19Ena,pa 45BO 50Vbo 51Vbo
Spotted Tanager *Tangara punctata* 18Ena
Speckled Tanager *Tangara guttata* 5Var 50Vbo 51Vbo
Rufous-throated Tanager *Tangara rufigula* 15Eeo,pi
Bay-headed Tanager *Tangara gyrola* 4Cvc 5Vfa 16Egu 19Egu,ms,zc 20T 45BO 50Vfa 51Vfa
Rufous-winged Tanager *Tangara lavinia* 16Ees 19Ees
Burnished-buff Tanager *Tangara cayana* 5Vam 45BO; PY 50Vam 51Vam
Scrub Tanager *Tangara vitriolina* 4Cvc 14Epi 19Eim,pi
Golden-naped Tanager *Tangara ruficervix* 15Epi 18Pca 19Eca,pi
Metallic-green Tanager *Tangara labradorides* 15Epi 18Ezc 19Eca,zc
Blue-browed Tanager *Tangara cyanotis* 18Ena; Pca 19Ezc
Blue-necked Tanager *Tangara cyanicollis* 16Ees 18Ena 19Egu,ms,zc 50Vla 51Vla

Golden-hooded Tanager *Tangara larvata* 16Epi
Masked Tanager *Tangara nigrocincta* 11Ena 19Ena 45BO
Beryl-spangled Tanager *Tangara nigroviridis* 2Cca 13Ena 15Epi 19Eca,pi 51Vla
Blue-and-black Tanager *Tangara vassorii* 5Vta 14Eco,pi 19Eca,co,pi 51Vta
Black-capped Tanager *Tangara heinei* 5Vla 13Ena 15Epi 51Vme
Silvery Tanager *Tangara viridicollis* 17Elo 19Elo
Black-headed Tanager *Tangara cyanoptera* 50Vbo 51Vbo
Opal-rumped Tanager *Tangara velia* 10Ena 19Ena 50Vbo 51Vbo
Opal-crowned Tanager *Tangara callophrys* 9Ena
Swallow Tanager *Tersina viridis* 4Cvc 5Var 12Plo 16Epi 20T 45BO 47A 50Var 51Var
Yellow-bellied Dacnis *Dacnis flaviventer* 10Ena 19Ena
Blue Dacnis *Dacnis cayana* 50Vbo 51Vbo
Scarlet-breasted Dacnis *Dacnis berlepschi* 16Ees 19Ees
Purple Honeycreeper *Cyanerpes caeruleus* 5Vta 16Ees 50Vta 51Vta
Red-legged Honeycreeper *Cyanerpes cyaneus* 16Ees 20T 45BO 50Bse 51M
Green Honeycreeper *Chlorophanes spiza* 16Ees 19Ees,na 45BO
Golden-collared Honeycreeper *Iridophanes pulcherrimus* 18Ena
Scarlet-browed Tanager *Heterospingus xanthopygius* 16Ees 19Ees
Guira Tanager *Hemithraupis guira* 5Vta 16Epi 18Pca 19Eeo,gu 45BO 47A 50Vbo 51Vbo
Yellow-backed Tanager *Hemithraupis flavicollis* 11Ena 19Ems 45BO
Scarlet-and-white Tanager *Chrysothlypis salmoni* 16Ees 19Ees,pi
Chestnut-vented Conebill *Conirostrum speciosum* 18Ena; Pcu 19Ena 45BO 47A 50Bmg 51Bmg
White-eared Conebill *Conirostrum leucogenys* 5Vca 51Vca
Bicoloured Conebill *Conirostrum bicolor* 20T 50Van 51Van
Cinereous Conebill *Conirostrum cinereum* 14Eaz,pi 19Eaz,pi,tu 45BO
Blue-backed Conebill *Conirostrum sitticolor* 2Cca 5Vta; BO 14Elo,ms,pi 19Eca,lo,na 45BO 51V
Capped Conebill *Conirostrum albifrons* 5Var 13Ena 14Eco,na,pi 15Epi 19Eca,co,na,pi 44Ppa 51Var
Giant Conebill *Oreomanes fraseri* 14Eaz,na 19Eaz 45BO
Tit-like Dacnis *Xenodacnis parina* 14Eaz 19Eaz
Rusty Flowerpiercer *Diglossa sittoides* 14Eaz,lo,pi 19Eaz,pi
Glossy Flowerpiercer *Diglossa lafresnayii* 2Cca 5Vtr 14Epi,zc 19Eca,ch,ms,zc 51Vtr
Black-throated Flowerpiercer *Diglossa brunneiventris* 45BO
Venezuelan Flowerpiercer *Diglossa venezuelensis* 5Vmo 51Vmo
White-sided Flowerpiercer *Diglossa albilatera* 2Cca 5Var,tr 13Ena 14Elo,pi 15Epi 19Eim,lo,ms,na,pi 44Pju 51Vmi
Greater Flowerpiercer *Diglossa major* 51Vbo
Black Flowerpiercer *Diglossa humeralis* 14Eco,pi 19Eaz,ch,im,lo,pi
Indigo Flowerpiercer *Diglossa indigotica* 15Cna
Deep-blue Flowerpiercer *Diglossa glauca* 18Ena 19Ems,na,zc 43BO 45BO
Bluish Flowerpiercer *Diglossa caerulescens* 5Vtr 13Ena 19Ems,na 43Psm 51Vtr
Masked Flowerpiercer *Diglossa cyanea* 5Var,la 13Ena 14Elo,na,pi 15Epi 19Eaz,bo,ca,ch,im,na 44BO 45BO 51Var
Plushcap *Catamblyrhynchus diadema* 14Elo,pi 15Elo 19Eca,pi 45Epi; BO
Black-backed Bush Tanager *Urothraupis stolzmanni* 14Eaz,na

INCERTAE SEDIS

Common Bush Tanager *Chlorospingus ophthalmicus* 2Cca 3Cns 5Vta,tr 13Ena 19Eeo,na 44BO; Pju 45BO 46CR 47A 51Vca,tr
Dusky-bellied Bush Tanager *Chlorospingus semifuscus* 15Epi 19Eca,pi
Short-billed Bush Tanager *Chlorospingus parvirostris* 13Ena 19Ena
Yellow-throated Bush Tanager *Chlorospingus flavigularis* 15Eeo,pi 18Ems,na,zc 19Eeo,ms,na,zc
Yellow-green Bush Tanager *Chlorospingus flavovirens* 19Ees
Ashy-throated Bush Tanager *Chlorospingus canigularis* 15Epi 17Eeo 18Ena,zc 19Ems,na,zc 44Psm
Highland Hepatic Tanager *Piranga lutea* 17Egu,lo 19Elo 20T 45BO 49USA
Summer Tanager *Piranga rubra* 1Ccu 2Cca 4Cvc 5Vla,ta 13Ena 14Elo,na,pi 19Eaz,ms,pi 48USA 49USA 50Vta 51Vta; USA
Scarlet Tanager *Piranga olivacea* 48USA
Western Tanager *Piranga ludoviciana* 49USA
Red-hooded Tanager *Piranga rubriceps* 13Ena 14Ena,zc 19Elo,na
White-winged Tanager *Piranga leucoptera* 15Epi 18Ems,pi,zc 19Ems,pi 43BO 45BO 50Vbo 51Vbo
Crowned Ant Tanager *Habia rubica* 1Cns 3Cns 10Ena 12Ena,pa 19Ena 20T 42Pmd 45BO 47A 50M 51M
Red-throated Ant Tanager *Habia fuscicauda* 46CR
Carmiol's Tanager *Chlorothraupis carmioli* 18Ena 43Pmd 45BO 46CR
Lemon-spectacled Tanager *Chlorothraupis olivacea* 16Ees 19Ees
Ochre-breasted Tanager *Chlorothraupis stolzmanni* 16Ees,pi 19Eeo,es,im,pi
Dusky-faced Tanager *Mitrospingus cassinii* 16Ees 19Ees,pi
Olive-backed Tanager *Mitrospingus oleagineus* 50Vbo 51Vbo
Rosy Thrush-Tanager *Rhodinocichla rosea* 5Vfa 51Vfa
Bananaquit *Coereba flaveola* 1Ccu 5Vam,fa,mo,ta 16Ees 18Ezc 19Ema,na 20T 21T 22T 45BO 46CR 47A 50Bba 51Vsu
Yellow-faced Grassquit *Tiaris olivaceus* 15Eim 19Eim,pi 46CR 51M
Dull-coloured Grassquit *Tiaris obscurus* 16Ezc 17Eaz,zc 19Eaz 45BO
Sooty Grassquit *Tiaris fuliginosus* 20T 50Bba 51Bba
Black-faced Grassquit *Tiaris bicolor* 5Vfa 20T 51Vla

EMBERIZIDAE

Lincoln's Sparrow *Melospiza lincolnii* 48USA 49USA
Rufous-collared Sparrow *Zonotrichia capensis* 2Cca 3Cns 5BO 13Ena 14Ech,na,pi 10Eim,lo,ms,na,pi,zc 45BO 47A 50Bpa 51Vmo
White-throated Sparrow *Zonotrichia albicollis* 48USA
Grasshopper Sparrow *Ammodramus savannarum* 48USA 49USA
Grassland Sparrow *Ammodramus humeralis* 45BO; PY 47A 50Bpe 51Vbo

Yellow-browed Sparrow *Ammodramus aurifrons* 5Vda; Pcu 10Ena 12Ena 19Ems,pa,zc 45BO 50Vba 51Vba

Tumbes Sparrow *Aimophila stolzmanni* 17Elo 19Elo

Plumbeous Sierra Finch *Phrygilus unicolor* 14Eco 19Elo 45A; BO

Ash-breasted Sierra Finch *Phrygilus plebejus* 14Ech,lo,pi 19Eeo,pi 45A; BO 47A

Band-tailed Sierra Finch *Phrygilus alaudinus* 14Ech 17Egu 19Eaz,ch,gu 45BO 47A

Slaty Finch *Haplospiza rustica* 14Epi 15Epi 19Eca,lo,pi

Cinereous Finch *Piezorhina cinerea* 17Pla,pi

Collared Warbling Finch *Poospiza hispaniolensis* 17Egu,lo,ma 19Egu

Stripe-tailed Yellow Finch *Sicalis citrina* 45BO; Bmi 50Vbo 51Vbo

Saffron Finch *Sicalis flaveola* 5Vap,fa 17Elo; Ptu 20T 45BO 47A 50Vap 51Vfa

Grassland Yellow Finch *Sicalis luteola* 5Vda 14Eaz,pi 19Eaz,im,pi 20T 45CH 47A 50Brg 51Vda

Sulphur-throated Yellow Finch *Sicalis taczanowskii* 17Egu

Wedge-tailed Grass Finch *Emberizoides herbicola* 5Vbo 18Psm 45BO; PY 47A 50Vbo 51Vbo

Blue-black Grassquit *Volatinia jacarina* 4Cvc 5Vmo 16Epi 17Elo,ma 19Egu,lo,pi,zc 20T 45BO 46CR 50Bpe 51Vbo

Slate-coloured Seedeater *Sporophila schistacea* 16Ees 19Eca,es 45BO

Grey Seedeater *Sporophila intermedia* 5Vap,mo 51Vap

Plumbeous Seedeater *Sporophila plumbea* 45BO; PY 50Vbo 51Vbo

Variable Seedeater *Sporophila corvina* 16Ees 46CR

Wing-barred Seedeater *Sporophila americana* 9Ena 19Ena

Lesson's Seedeater *Sporophila bouvronides* 5Vca 50Vca 51Vca

Lined Seedeater *Sporophila lineola* 45BO; Bmi 50Bpe 51Bpe

Black-and-white Seedeater *Sporophila luctuosa* 5Vme 12Ena,pa 14Ena,pa,pi 15Elo 19Eaz,na,pi 50Vme 51Vme

Yellow-bellied Seedeater *Sporophila nigricollis* 4Cvc 5Vca 14Eeo,pi 16Ees,pi 18Ezc 19Eca,es,im,pi 50Bba 51Vta

Double-collared Seedeater *Sporophila caerulescens* 45BO; PY 47A 50BO

White-bellied Seedeater *Sporophila leucoptera* 45BO

Parrot-billed Seedeater *Sporophila peruviana* 17Egu 19Egu

Drab Seedeater *Sporophila simplex* 17Elo; Pca 19Elo; Pca

Capped Seedeater *Sporophila bouvreuil* 50Bba

Ruddy-breasted Seedeater *Sporophila minuta* 5Vca,fa 16Eim 50Vbo 51Vbo

Chestnut-bellied Seedeater *Sporophila castaneiventris* 10Ena 19Ems,na 51V

Rufous-rumped Seedeater *Sporophila hypochroma* 45BO

Chestnut-throated Seedeater *Sporophila telasco* 17Elo,ma 19Egu

Thick-billed Seed Finch *Oryzoborus funereus* 19Ema 46CR

Chestnut-bellied Seed Finch *Oryzoborus angolensis* 5Vbo,ca 12Plo 16Ees 19Ema,na,pa 45BO 47A 50Bba 51Vbo

Large-billed Seed Finch *Oryzoborus crassirostris* 5Vmo 17Ees 19Egu,im,na 50Vmo 51Vgu

Great-billed Seed Finch *Oryzoborus maximiliani* 11Ena 45BO

Black-billed Seed Finch *Oryzoborus atrirostris* 18Epa,zc 19Epa,zc 45BO

Blue Seedeater *Amaurospiza concolor* 15Epi 19Eaz,gu

Band-tailed Seedeater *Catamenia analis* 14Ech,pi 45BO 47A

Plain-coloured Seedeater *Catamenia inornata* 5Vme 14Eco,na,pi,tu 19Epi,tu 45BO 51Vme

Páramo Seedeater *Catamenia homochroa* 5Cma 14Ena,pi 19Ems,pi,zc 45BO 50Cma 51Cma

Tocuyo Sparrow *Arremonops tocuyensis* 51Vla

Black-striped Sparrow *Arremonops conirostris* 2Cca 5Vbo,ca 16Ees 19Eeo,es,pa 51Vbo

Pectoral Sparrow *Arremon taciturnus* 5Vbo 45BO 50Bce 51Vbo

Orange-billed Sparrow *Arremon aurantiirostris* 12Epa 16Ees 17Eeo 18Ena,pa,zc 19Eeo,es,gu,lr,ma,ms,na,pa,pi 46CR

Golden-winged Sparrow *Arremon schlegeli* 5Vca 51Vca

Black-capped Sparrow *Arremon abeillei* 17Egu,lo,ma 18Ezc 19Egu,lo,zc

Chestnut-capped Brush Finch *Buarremon brunneinucha* 1Ccq 2Cca 3Cns 4Cvc 5Var,la 13Ena 14Ees,gu,na 15Epi 19Eaz,ca,gu,ms,na,pi 44Psm 46CR 51Vya

Stripe-headed Brush Finch *Buarremon torquatus* 2Cca 5Vmo 13Ena 14Eaz,ch,ms,pi 19Eaz,ch,co,im,lo,na,pi 45A; BO 47A 51Var

Tanager Finch *Oreothraupis arremonops* 15Ccc; Epi 19Epi

Sooty-faced Finch *Lysurus crassirostris* 46CR

Olive Finch *Lysurus castaneiceps* 15Cna 18Ena,zc 43Ena

Moustached Brush Finch *Atlapetes albofrenatus* 51Vme

Ochre-breasted Brush Finch *Atlapetes semirufus* 5Var,fa,mo,ta 51Var

Tepui Brush Finch *Atlapetes personatus* 50Vbo 51Vbo

Yellow-throated Brush Finch *Atlapetes gutturalis* 2Cca

Pale-naped Brush Finch *Atlapetes pallidinucha* 14Eaz,na,tu,zc 19Ech,lo,na,tu,zc

Tricoloured Brush Finch *Atlapetes tricolor* 7Epi 15Epi 19Epi 44Pju

White-rimmed Brush Finch *Atlapetes leucopis* 13Ena 14Eim,na 19Eim,na

Rufous-naped Brush Finch *Atlapetes latinuchus* 14Epi,zc 19Eaz,ca,co,eo,im,lo,ms,zc

Slaty Brush Finch *Atlapetes schistaceus* 1Cns 2Cca 3Cns 5Vta 14Ena 19Eca,ms,na 51Vta

White-winged Brush Finch *Atlapetes leucopterus* 14Eim,pi 17Elo 19Elo

White-headed Brush Finch *Atlapetes albiceps* 17Elo

Pale-headed Brush Finch *Atlapetes pallidiceps* 17Eaz 19Eaz

Bay-crowned Brush Finch *Atlapetes seebohmi* 17Elo 19Elo

Pileated Finch *Coryphospingus pileatus* 50Bpe

Red-crested Finch *Coryphospingus cucullatus* 18Ezc; Pam 19Ezc 45BO 47A 50Bmg 51Vco

Crimson-breasted Finch *Rhodospingus cruentus* 17Egu,ma 19Egu

Red-capped Cardinal *Paroaria gularis* 5Vam 9Ena 11Ena 19Ena 20T 51V

CARDINALIDAE

Dickcissel *Spiza americana* 20T 48USA 50USA 51USA

Golden-bellied Grosbeak *Pheucticus chrysogaster* 5Cma 14Egu,lo,pi 17Elo,ma 19Eaz,gu,lo,pi 51Cma

Black-backed Grosbeak *Pheucticus aureoventris* 14Ech,co 19Ech 45BO 47A

Rose-breasted Grosbeak *Pheucticus ludovicianus* 48USA

Black-headed Grosbeak *Pheucticus melanocephalus* 48USA 49USA

Vermilion Cardinal *Cardinalis phoeniceus* 5Vfa 51Vfa,su

Yellow-green Grosbeak *Caryothraustes canadensis* 5Vbo 50Bba 51Vbo

Yellow-shouldered Grosbeak *Parkerthraustes humeralis* 19Ena 45BO

Red-and-black Grosbeak *Periporphyrus erythromelas* 50Vbo 51Vbo

Slate-coloured Grosbeak *Saltator grossus* 5Vbo 8Pam 9Ena 12Ena,pa 16Ees 19Eeo,es,gu,lr,ms,na,pi 45BO 46CR 50Bpa 51Vbo

Buff-throated Saltator *Saltator maximus* 5Vca 10Ena 16Ees 19Eeo,es,gu,lo,na,zc 42Pmd 45BO 46CR 50Vbo 51Vta

Black-winged Saltator *Saltator atripennis* 15Epi 19Eaz,eo,es,im

Greyish Saltator *Saltator coerulescens* 5Vca 9Ena 11Ena 18Ezc 19Ems,na,pa,zc 20T 22T 45BO 46CR 47A 50Bmg 51Vsu

Orinoco Saltator *Saltator orenocensis* 5Vla 51Vla

Black-cowled Saltator *Saltator nigriceps* 17Elo 19Elo

Streaked Saltator *Saltator striatipectus* 5Vca,fa 14Eim 17Elo,ma 18Ezc; Pca 19Egu,im,lo,zc 51Vfa

Masked Saltator *Saltator cinctus* 14Ena 19Egu

Blue-black Grosbeak *Cyanocompsa cyanoides* 5Vbo,ca 11Ena 16Ees 19Egu,ma,ms,na,pa,zc 42Pmd 45BO 46CR 50Bpa 51Vca

Ultramarine Grosbeak *Cyanocompsa brissonii* 5Vca 45BO 47A 50Bpe 51Vla

Blue Grosbeak *Passerina caerulea* 48USA 49USA

Indigo Bunting *Passerina cyanea* 48USA 49USA 51USA

PARULIDAE

Golden-winged Warbler *Vermivora chrysoptera* 48USA

Blue-winged Warbler *Vermivora pinus* 48USA

Tennessee Warbler *Vermivora peregrina* 48CN; USA 51USA

Northern Parula *Parula americana* 48USA 51USA

Tropical Parula *Parula pitiayumi* 5Vfa,mo 13Ena 15Epi 17Egu,lo 19Eeo,lo,ma,na,pi 20T 21T 38A; M; NC 43BO 45BO 46CR 47A 49M 50Brj 51Vbo

Chestnut-sided Warbler *Dendroica pensylvanica* 48CN; USA 51USA

Yellow Warbler *Dendroica petechia* 5Vfa 17Ema 19Eeo 20T 38Eeo; CB; USA 48USA 49USA 50Vfa 51Vfa; M; USA

Blackpoll Warbler *Dendroica striata* 5Vta 48CN; USA 49USA 50Vta 51Vta; USA

Bay-breasted Warbler *Dendroica castanea* 48USA

Blackburnian Warbler *Dendroica fusca* 5Vla 13Ena 19Ena 48CN; USA 50Vla 51Vla

Magnolia Warbler *Dendroica magnolia* 48USA 51M

Cerulean Warbler *Dendroica cerulea* 48USA 51USA

Cape May Warbler *Dendroica tigrina* 48USA

Black-throated Blue Warbler *Dendroica caerulescens* 48USA

Yellow-rumped Warbler *Dendroica coronata* 48CN; USA 49USA 51M

Black-throated Green Warbler *Dendroica virens* 48USA 51M

Townsend's Warbler *Dendroica townsendi* 49USA

Yellow-throated Warbler *Dendroica dominica* 48USA

Prairie Warbler *Dendroica discolor* 48USA

Palm Warbler *Dendroica palmarum* 48USA

American Redstart *Setophaga ruticilla* 48CN; USA 49USA 50M 51Vco; USA

Black-and-white Warbler *Mniotilta varia* 5Vla 48CN; USA 51Vla; USA

Prothonotary Warbler *Protonotaria citrea* 48USA 51USA

Worm-eating Warbler *Helmitheros vermivorum* 48USA

Swainson's Warbler *Limnothlypis swainsonii* 48USA

Ovenbird *Seiurus aurocapilla* 48USA 51M; USA

Northern Waterthrush *Seiurus noveboracensis* 5Vam,fa 20T 48CN; USA 49USA 50Vfa 51Vfa

Louisiana Waterthrush *Seiurus motacilla* 48USA 51BE

Kentucky Warbler *Oporornis formosus* 48USA 51USA

Connecticut Warbler *Oporornis agilis* 48CN

Mourning Warbler *Oporornis philadelphia* 48CN; USA 51Vta

Common Yellowthroat *Geothlypis trichas* 38USA 48USA 49USA 51USA

Olive-crowned Yellowthroat *Geothlypis semiflava* 15Eeo,pi 17Eeo,gu 19Eeo,gu,pi 38CR 46CR

Masked Yellowthroat *Geothlypis aequinoctialis* 17Eaz,gu,lo 18Ezc 19Eaz,lo,zc 20T 38Ema; A; PA 45PY 47A 50Bsp 51Van

Hooded Warbler *Wilsonia citrina* 48USA 51USA

Wilson's Warbler *Wilsonia pusilla* 48CN; USA 49USA

Canada Warbler *Wilsonia canadensis* 13Ena 19Ena,zc 48USA

Slate-throated Redstart *Myioborus miniatus* 1Cby 4Cvc 5Vla 13Ena 15Epi 19Eaz,ca,pi,zc 38M 43Ems; Ppa 45BO 46CR 50Vgu 51Vgu

Tepui Redstart *Myioborus castaneocapillus* 38Vbo 50Vbo 51Vbo

Saffron-breasted Redstart *Myioborus cardonai* 51Vbo

Golden-fronted Redstart *Myioborus ornatus* 2Cca

Spectacled Redstart *Myioborus melanocephalus* 13Ena 14Ena,pi 15Epi 19Ebo,ca,im,lo,na,pi 38Pll 45BO

White-fronted Redstart *Myioborus albifrons* 5Vla,ta 51Vme

Grey-and-gold Warbler *Basileuterus fraseri* 17Eeo,gu,lo,lr,ma 19Eeo,gu,lo,ma 38Ema

Two-banded Warbler *Basileuterus bivittatus* 5Vbo 38BO 43BO 45BO 47A 50Vbo 51Vbo

Golden-bellied Warbler *Basileuterus chrysogaster* 16Ees,pi 19Ees,pi 38Epi 43Pcu

Citrine Warbler *Basileuterus luteoviridis* 2Cca 5BO 13Ena 14Elo,na,zc 19Elo,ms,na 38Pcu 45BO

Pale-legged Warbler *Basileuterus signatus* 38Pcu 45BO 47A

Black-crested Warbler *Basileuterus nigrocristatus* 1Cby 2Cca 3Cns 5Vta 13Ena 14Elo,pi,zc 15Epi 19Ech,lo,na 38Vme 51Vla

Grey-headed Warbler *Basileuterus griseiceps* 5Vmo 51Vmo

Grey-throated Warbler *Basileuterus cinereicollis* 5Vme 51Vme

White-lored Warbler *Basileuterus conspicillatus* 38Cma

Russet-crowned Warbler *Basileuterus coronatus* 1Cby 2Cca 5Vme 13Ena 14Eaz,lo,na,pi 15Epi 19Eca,co,im 38Cvc; Eaz; Phu 43Pju 45BO 51Vla

Three-banded Warbler *Basileuterus trifasciatus* 17Elo 19Eeo,lo 38Elo

Golden-crowned Warbler *Basileuterus culicivorus* 4Cvc 5Vca,mo 20T 38M 45BO 46CR 47A 49M 50Brj 51Vbo,fa

Rufous-capped Warbler *Basileuterus rufifrons* 38CR; M

Three-striped Warbler *Basileuterus tristriatus* 1Ccu 5Var,la 13Ena 15Epi 19Eca,im,ms,na,pi 38CR 43Ppa 45BO 46CR 51Vla

Flavescent Warbler *Basileuterus flaveolus* 5Vca 38Bsp 45BO 50Bpa 51Vca

Buff-rumped Warbler *Basileuterus fulvicauda* 2Cca 10Ena 12Ena 16Ees 19Ees,gu,na,pi,zc 38CR 42Pmd 45BO 46CR

River Warbler *Basileuterus rivularis* 5Vbo,mo 38Vbo 45BO 47A 50Bsp 51Vbo

INCERTAE SEDIS

Rose-breasted Chat *Granatellus pelzelni* 5Vbo 38Vbo 45BO 50Vbo 51Vbo

ICTERIDAE

Russet-backed Oropendola *Psarocolius angustifrons* 1Ccq 5Vca,la 9Ena 12Ena 13Ena 15Epi 19Eca,ms,na,pi 40Var; Pcu 42Pmd 45BO 50Vca 51Vca

Green Oropendola *Psarocolius viridis* 5Vbo,mo 11Ena 19Ena 40S; Vbo:Plo 50Vbo 51Vbo

Chestnut-headed Oropendola *Psarocolius wagleri* 16Ees 40Cch; M 46CR

Crested Oropendola *Psarocolius decumanus* 5Vca 9Ena 12Ena 19Ems,na 20T 21T 22T 40Cch; A 42Pmd 45A; BO 50Bmg 51Vca

Black Oropendola *Psarocolius guatimozinos* 40PA

Olive Oropendola *Psarocolius yuracares* 5Vam,bo 9Ena 19Epa 40Ena; Vam; Pmd 42Pmd 45BO 50Vbo 51Vbo

Casqued Oropendola *Psarocolius oseryi* 9Ena 10Ena 19Ems,na 40Pmd 42Pmd

Band-tailed Oropendola *Ocyalus latirostris* 40Plo

Mountain Cacique *Cacicus chrysonotus* 2Cca 3Cns 5BO 13Ena 14Ems,na 19Ena 40Ccu; Ena; Pcu 45BO

Ecuadorian Cacique *Cacicus sclateri* 11Ena 12Ena,pa 19Ena 40Ena; Pam

Solitary Cacique *Cacicus solitarius* 11Ena 19Ena 40Bap; Puc 42Plo,md 45BO 47A 50Bmg 51Bmg

Yellow-rumped Cacique *Cacicus cela* 5Vap 8Pmd 9Ena 17Egu 19Egu,ms,na 20T 40Cch; Ena 42Pmd 45BO 50Bpa 51Vap

Red-rumped Cacique *Cacicus haemorrhous* 5Vbo 19Ena 40A; Bsp; PY 45BO 47A 50Brj 51Vbo

Subtropical Cacique *Cacicus uropygialis* 5Vba 7Ena 13Ena 19Ems,na,zc 40Ena,zc 51Vba

Scarlet-rumped Cacique *Cacicus microrhynchus* 16Ees,pi 19Eeo,es,pi 40Elr; CR 46CR

Yellow-billed Cacique *Amblycercus holosericeus* 5Elo; Var 13Ena 14Eaz,na 16Ema 19Eaz,gu,ms 40CR 44Ena 45BO 46CR 51Var; M

Troupial *Icterus icterus* 5Vfa 40Vco; PR 51Vfa

Orange-backed Troupial *Icterus croconotus* 11Ena 12Ena; Plo 19Ena 40Puc 45BO 50Bmg

White-edged Oriole *Icterus graceannae* 17Egu,lo 19Eeo 40Pla

Yellow-tailed Oriole *Icterus mesomelas* 5Elo 16Epi 17Egu,lo 19Egu,lo 40M 51Elo

Epaulet Oriole *Icterus cayanensis* 40BO; PY 42Pmd 45BO 47A 50Bpa

Moriche Oriole *Icterus chrysocephalus* 5Ena; Vbo 10Ena 11Ena 19Ems 40Bam 50Ena 51Ena

Orchard Oriole *Icterus spurius* 40M; USA 48USA

Orange-crowned Oriole *Icterus auricapillus* 5Vca 40Vfa 51Vca

Yellow-backed Oriole *Icterus chrysater* 4Cvc 5Vme,po 40Cma; Var; M; NC 51Vta

Baltimore Oriole *Icterus galbula* 40USA 48USA 51M; USA

Yellow Oriole *Icterus nigrogularis* 5Vfa 20T 40Cma; Vca 50Vfa 51V

Scrub Blackbird *Dives warszewiczi* 17Egu,lo,pi 19Egu,lo,ma 40Epi; Pli

Mountain Grackle *Macroagelaius subalaris* 1Csa 3Cns

Golden-tufted Grackle *Macroagelaius imthurni* 5Vbo 40Vbo 50Vbo 51Vbo

Oriole Blackbird *Gymnomystax mexicanus* 5Vap,fa 11Ena 19Ena 40Vam; Plo 50Vca 51Vap

Red-bellied Grackle *Hypopyrrhus pyrohypogaster* 1Ccq 40Chu

Velvet-fronted Grackle *Lampropsar tanagrinus* 5Vmo 10Ena 19Ena 40G; Plo 45BO 50Vmo 51Vmo

Red-winged Blackbird *Agelaius phoeniceus* 40M; USA 48USA 49USA

Pale-eyed Blackbird *Chrysomus xanthophthalmus* 40Pmd

Chestnut-capped Blackbird *Chrysomus ruficapillus* 40A 45Bba 47A

Yellow-hooded Blackbird *Chrysomus icterocephalus* 5Vca 20T 21T 40Vco; Plo 50Vbo 51Vbo

Giant Cowbird *Scaphidura oryzivora* 11Ena 16Ees 19Epi 20T 40Plo 45BO

Bronzed Cowbird *Molothrus aeneus* 40CR 49USA

Shiny Cowbird *Molothrus bonariensis* 10Ena 11Ena 16Ees 17Ees,ma 19Eaz,gu 20T 40A; DR 45BO 47A 50Bmg 51Vap

Carib Grackle *Quiscalus lugubris* 20T 21T 40MA 50Vsu 51Vsu

Great-tailed Grackle *Quiscalus mexicanus* 17Eeo,ma 19Eeo,es 40Cma; M 48USA 49USA 51M

Red-breasted Blackbird *Sturnella militaris* 20T 40Vco; PA

Peruvian Meadowlark *Sturnella bellicosa* 14Eaz,gu,lo 17Egu,lo,ma 19Eaz,gu,lo 40Pca

Eastern Meadowlark *Sturnella magna* 5Vap,ta 40Vbo; CB; CR; USA 48USA 49USA 50Vbo 51Vap

Bobolink *Dolichonyx oryzivorus* 40USA 48USA 49USA

FRINGILLIDAE

Andean Siskin *Carduelis spinescens* 5Cma 14Eca 19Eca 51Cma

Hooded Siskin *Carduelis magellanica* 5Elo 14Eaz,ca,pi,zc 19Eca,pi,zc 45BO 47A 50Brg 51Elo

Saffron Siskin *Carduelis siemiradzkii* 17Egu,lo 10Egu,lo

Olivaceous Siskin *Carduelis olivacea* 13Ena 18Ena 44Ppa 45BO

Yellow-bellied Siskin *Carduelis xanthogastra* 2Cca 5Vta 15Epi 19Ees,pi 45BO 51Vta

Lesser Goldfinch *Carduelis psaltria* 5Vca 18Elo; Pla 49USA 51Vla

Plumbeous Euphonia *Euphonia plumbea* 5Vam 50Vam 51Vam

Purple-throated Euphonia *Euphonia chlorotica* 5Vam; BO 18Ezc; Pam,ca 45A; BO 47A 50Vam 51Vam

Trinidad Euphonia *Euphonia trinitatis* 5Vca 20T 51Vla

Orange-crowned Euphonia *Euphonia saturata* 16Ees,lo,pi

Finsch's Euphonia *Euphonia finschi* 50Vbo 51Vbo

Violaceous Euphonia *Euphonia violacea* 5Vbo 20T 47A 50Bpa 51Vbo

Thick-billed Euphonia *Euphonia laniirostris* 5Vca,ta 10Ena 16Ees,gu 17Eeo,gu,lo,ma 19Eeo,gu,lo,ma,na 42Phu,lo 45BO 50Vca 51Vca,ta

Golden-rumped Euphonia *Euphonia cyanocephala* 4Cvc 5Vla 13Ena 14Eaz,na,pi 15Epi 19Eaz,im,pi 44Ppi 45A; BO 47A 50Vla 51Vla

Fulvous-vented Euphonia *Euphonia fulvicrissa* 16Ees,pi 19Ees

Golden-bellied Euphonia *Euphonia chrysopasta* 5Vam 10Ena 19Ems,na,pa 42Pmd 45BO 50Bmg 51Vam

Bronze-green Euphonia *Euphonia mesochrysa* 1Cna 18Ena 19Ems,na,zc 43Ems; BO 45BO

White-vented Euphonia *Euphonia minuta* 5PA 12Ena; Plo 16Ees 19Ees,ms,na 42Pmd

Tawny-capped Euphonia *Euphonia anneae* 46CR

Orange-bellied Euphonia *Euphonia xanthogaster* 3Cns 5Var,bo,ta 12Ena; Plo 13Ena 15Epi 18Ena 19Eca,eo,es,ms,na,pa,pi,zc 43Pmd 45BO 50Vbo 51Vbo

Rufous-bellied Euphonia *Euphonia rufiventris* 5Vbo 10Ena 19Ena 42Pmd 45BO 50Bpa 51Vbo

Golden-sided Euphonia *Euphonia cayennensis* 50Vbo 51Vbo

Blue-naped Chlorophonia *Chlorophonia cyanea* 4Cvc 5Vtr 18Ena 19Ezc 43Pmd 45BO 50Brj 51Vtr

Chestnut-breasted Chlorophonia *Chlorophonia pyrrhophrys* 13Ena 14Elo,na 19Eca,lo 51Vme

Yellow-collared Chlorophonia *Chlorophonia flavirostris* 15Epi 19Ees,pi

ESTRILDIDAE

Common Waxbill *Estrilda astrild* 50Brj

PASSERIDAE

House Sparrow *Passer domesticus* 17Elo,ma 45CH 48USA 49USA 50M 51M

Acknowledgements

I would like to thank Mauricio Álvarez-Rebolledo and Richard Ranft for supplying details of the Norte de Santander and Valle del Cauca CDs, Scott Connop for supplying recording localities for his Ecuador tapes, John V. Moore for supplying details of his eastern Ecuador CDs, and Peter Boesman for supplying details of some errors on his 1999 Venezuela CD-ROM.

GLOSSARY

Albino: an organism lacking pigment. Such birds are entirely white and have red or pink eyes and pink or flesh-coloured soft parts. White morphs, on the other hand, have the soft parts normally coloured, whilst leucistic birds have the colours simply paler, typically fawn of pale buffy. Partially white birds are frequent, and are usually but incorrectly referred to as partial albinos.
Allopatric: two or more taxa that occur in separate geographical areas, sometimes very widely separated. (See also sympatric and parapatric.)
Bare parts (or soft parts): the non-feathered parts of a bird, i.e. the eyes, eye-ring or orbital ring, cere, bill, legs and feet.
Binomial: the specific scientific name given to a bird, i.e. the name of the species, e.g., *pertinax* in *Aratinga pertinax*.
Cline: change involving one or more characters, across a bird's range. Birds that are recognised as having subspecific populations but in which the variation follows a gradual cline are often subject to taxonomic debate, and in some cases the races are rejected by some authors.
Coffee shade: tall trees that provide shade for coffee plants.
Congeneric: of the same genus but implicitly referring to a different species.
Conspecific: belonging to the same species.
Contour feathers: those body feathers that are generally large and form the shape of the bird.
Dimorphic: having two morphs, usually applied to species where males and females are different (i.e. sexually dimorphic).
Emergent trees: those trees which grow taller than surrounding trees in a forest; regularly covered with flowers.
Endemic: restricted to a defined area (e.g. a country or island), but does not occur elsewhere.
Genus: a group of taxa considered closely related and (normally) of single origin, with certain characteristics in common. Always the first word in a binomial or trinomial name, e.g., *Aratinga* in the case of *Aratinga pertinax*.
GIS: acronym for General Impression and Shape, used originally by Royal Air Force aircrew when learning identification of flying aircraft. Pronounced and usually written as 'jizz'. In Britain, the term came to be used for the specific characteristics of a bird unrelated to plumage (e.g. posture and behavioural movements as well as flight characteristics).
Hoary: a white fringe to feathers that gives a hoary appearance to the plumage. The word derives from the covering of frost on plants in early morning on winter days at temperate latitudes.
Hybrid: the result of crossbreeding between two different species. Some birds with unusual plumage are referred to as being hybrids, despite there being an absence of field observations or credible DNA evidence. Some families seem far more prone to hybridisation then others, e.g. Laridae, Anatidae and Trochilidae. The Biological Species Concept generally considers that evidence of crossbreeding indicates conspecificity, but this is too simplistic.
Immature: bird with plumage intermediate between juvenile and adult, but does not mean the bird is necessarily sexually immature, as males of many species sing and defend territories while in immature plumage, and some breed successfully.
Intergrade: an individual that occurs in the area between those occupied by different and allopatric taxa, and which shows intermediate characteristics or traits.
Jizz: see GIS above.
Juvenile: a bird in its first full plumage upon leaving the nest.
Leucistic: a pigmentation deficiency, refers to birds that are unusually pale in coloration. The term is sometimes used for birds which have partial pale areas.
Monomorphic: single morph or colour type.
Monospecific: genus with a single species.
Monotypic: a species without any subspecies, or a genus with only a single species.
Morph: one of possibly several different types of coloration.
Morphology: the study of body characteristics, usually including all measurements of a bird.
Nomen dubium: a name for which the available evidence is insufficient to permit recognition of the zoological species to which it was applied.
Nominate (subspecies): that form of a species to be first described. When another subspecies is described, the first takes the species name as its trinomial, e.g., *Aratinga pertinax pertinax,* normally written as *Aratinga p. pertinax*.
Parapatric: two taxa whose ranges meet (see also sympatric).
Perch-gleaning: to glean insects from leaves while remaining perched, either by simply reaching at a nearby leaf, or more agile stretching and acrobatic movements.
Polymorphic: a species with more than one morph within a sex or age phase, particularly common among raptors.
Polytypic: a species divided into two or more subspecies.
Race: a subspecies.
Raptor: all birds of prey, including owls. In the broadest sense it means all birds that feed primarily on animal food, and thus includes scavengers, like vultures. Raptors are often divided into nocturnal (i.e. owls) and diurnal raptors, which may be confusing, as some owls are diurnal.
Rectrices: tail-feathers.
Remiges: the main flight-feathers of the wing, i.e. primaries and secondaries.
Sally, Sallying: to fly out to snatch an insect from the air and return to a perch.
Sexual dimorphism: where males and females of a species exhibit different plumages.

Stitching: term used to describe the manner in which some shorebirds patrol the water's edge or soft muddy soil, pumping their bill up and down into the ground or water, in a rhythmic manner reminiscent of a sewing-machine needle.
Subspecies: name(s) given to distinct allopatric divisions within a species, usually on the basis of a combination of plumage characteristics and measurements.
Superspecies: two or more similar species which are (usually) allopatric, closely related and presumably recent in origin as distinct species.
Sympatric: two or more species that occur in the same area usually when breeding, and where applied to species in their non-breeding ranges this is usually specifically stated.
Synonym: (as a nomenclatural term), an alternative name for the same taxon, usually as a result of a taxon being named independently by different authors.
Systematics: the study of classification; virtually synonymous with taxonomy, but used in a wider sense to embrace species origins and strictly is the science dealing with the diversity of organisms.
Taxon (plural **taxa**): a taxonomic unit of any rank, most frequently applied to species or subspecies.
Taxonomy: the theory and practice of classifying organisms, covering the disciplines of classification, nomenclature and systematics.
Trap-lining: a behaviour of some hummingbirds that follow a regular route between locations, foraging at different flowering trees and shrubs on the way.
Trinomial: the subspecific scientific name of a species.
Type (more correctly holotype): the individual specimen first (or primarily) used to describe a species or taxon.

ORGANISATIONS

International

BirdLife International (Americas Division)
Casilla 17-17-717, Vicente Cardenas E5-75 y Japon, Quito, Ecuador.
Publication: e-mail newsletter
Web: www.birdlife.org

BirdLife International
Wellbrook Court, Girton Road, Cambridge CB3 0NA, UK.
Publication: *World Birdwatch* (four issues per annum) and, by separate subscription, *Bird Conservation International* (four issues per annum)
Web: www.birdlife.org

Neotropical Bird Club
Publication: *Cotinga* (bi-annual) and *Neotropical Birding* (annual)
Web: www.neotropicalbirdclub.org

Neotropical Ornithological Society
Publication: *Ornitología Neotropical* (four issues per annum)
Web: www.neotropicalornithology.org

National

Colombia:

Fundación ProAves
Carrera 20 No. 36-61, Bogotá DC, Colombia.
Web: www.proaves.org

Asociación Colombiana de Ornitología (ACO)
Publication: *Ornitología Colombiana* (annual)
Web: http://www.ornitologiacolombiana.org

Sociedad Antioqueña de Ornitología (SAO)
Publication: *Boletín SAO* (bi-annual)
Web: http://www.sao.org.co/index.html

Ecuador:

Aves & Conservación (Corporación Ornitológica del Ecuador, formerly CECIA) (BirdLife Partner)
Pasaje Joaquín Tinajero E3-05 y Jorge Drom, Casilla 17-17-906, Quito, Ecuador.
E-mail: aves_comunicacion@yahoo.com
Web: www.avesyconservacion.org

French Guiana:

Comité d'Homologation Ornithologique de Guyane (French Guiana rarities committee)
E-mail: alex.renaudier@wanadoo.fr

Guyana:

Guyana Amazon Tropical Birds Society
E-mail: guyanabirdsociety@yahoo.com

South Rupununi Conservation Society
E-mail: rupununi_jaguar@yahoo.com

Suriname:

Foundation for Nature Conservation in Suriname
(STINASU) (BirdLife Affiliate)
Cornelis Jongbauwstraat 14, PO Box 12252, Paramaribo, Suriname.
E-mail: research@stinasu.sr
Web: www.stinasu.sr

Venezuela:

Colección Ornitológica Phelps (COP)
Avenida Abraham Lincoln, Edificio Gran Sabana, piso 3, Sabana Grande, Caracas 1050, Venezuela
E-mail: restall@cantv.net

Sociedad Conservacionista Audubon de Venezuela (SCAV)
(BirdLife Affiliate)
Apartado 80.450, Caracas 1080-A, Venezuela.
E-mail: audubon@cantv.net
Web: www.audubonvenezuela.org

Estación Ornitológica La Mucuy - Parque Nacional Sierra Nevada
Coleccion de Aves de la Universidad de los Andes, Facultad de Ciencias, Mérida, 5101, Venezuela.
E-mail: crengifo@ula.ve

BIBLIOGRAPHY

Adams, J., & E.R. Slavid. 1984. Cheek plumage pattern in Colombian Ruddy Duck *Oxyura jamaicensis*. *Ibis* 126: 405–407.

Ágreda, A., N. Krabbe & O. Rodriguez. 1999. Pale-headed Brush-finch *Atlapetes pallidiceps* is not extinct. *Cotinga* 11: 50–54.

Ágreda, A., J. Nilsson, L. Tonato, & H. Román. 2005. A new population of Cinnamon-breasted Tody-tyrant *Hemitriccus cinnamomeipetus* in Ecuador. *Cotinga* 24: 16–18.

Agro, D.J., & R.S. Ridgely. 1998. First record of Striped Manakin *Machaeropterus regulus* in Guyana. *Bull. Brit. Orn. Club* 118: 122–123.

Aguilera, E. 1982. La comunidad de ibises en los Llanos de Venezuela. *Mem. Soc. Cienc. Nat. La Salle* 48: 59–75.

Aleixo, A. 2002. Molecular systematics and the role of the "várzea"– "terra firme" ecotone in the diversification of *Xiphorhynchus* woodcreepers (Aves: Dendrocolaptidae). *Auk* 119: 621–640.

Aleixo, A. 2004. Historical diversification of a terra-firme forest bird superspecies: a phylogeographic perspective on the role of different hypotheses of Amazonian diversification. *Evolution* 58: 1303–1317.

Aleixo, A., & B.M. Whitney. 2002. *Dendroplex* (=*Xiphorhynchus*) *necopinus* Zimmer 1934 (Dendrocolaptidae) is a junior synonym of *Dendrornis kienerii* (=*Xiphorhynchus picus kienerii*) Des Murs 1855. *Auk* 119: 520–523.

Alström, P., & K. Mild. 2003. *Pipits & Wagtails of Europe, Asia and North America*. Christopher Helm, London.

Altman, A., & B. Swift. 1993. *Checklist of the Birds of South America*. Third edn. Privately published, Ashland, Ohio.

Altman, A., & C. Parrish. 1978. Sight records of Wilson's Phalarope, Ruff, and other shorebirds from Venezuela. *Amer. Birds* 32: 309–310.

Álvarez-Alonso, J.A., & B.M. Whitney. 2003. Eight new bird species for Peru and other distributional records from white-sand forests of the northern Peruvian Amazon, with implications for biogeography of northern South America. *Condor* 105: 552–566.

Amadon, D. 1982. A revision of the sub-buteonine hawks (Accipitridae: Aves). *Amer. Mus. Novit.* 2741: 1–20.

Amadon, D., & J. Bull. 1988. Hawks and owls of the world: a distributional and taxonomic list. *Proc. Western Found. Vert. Zool.* 3: 294–357.

American Ornithologists' Union (AOU). 1983. *Check-list of North American Birds*. Sixth edn. AOU, Washington, D.C.

American Ornithologists' Union (AOU). 1998. *Check-list of North American Birds*. Seventh edn. AOU, Washington, D.C.

American Ornithologists' Union. 2000. Forty-second supplement to the American Ornithologists' Union *Check-list of North American Birds*. *Auk* 117: 847–858.

Ames, P.L. 1971. *The Morphology of the Syrinx in Passerine Birds*. Peabody Mus. Nat. Hist., Yale Univ. Bull. 37. New Haven, Conn. Pp. 194.

Ames, P.L., M.A. Heimerdinger, & S.L. Warter. 1968. The anatomy and systematic position of the ant pipits *Conopophaga* and *Corythopis*. *Postilla* 114: 1–32.

Andersson, M. 1999. Phylogeny, behaviour, plumage evolution and neoteny in skuas Stercorariidae. *J. Avian Biol.* 30: 205–215.

Armani, G. 1985. *Guide des Passereaux Granivores*. Soc. Nouvelle des Editions Boubée, Brussels.

Armenta, J.K., J.D. Weckstein, & D.F. Lane. 2005. Geographic variation in mitochondrial DNA sequences of an Amazonian non-passerine: the Black-spotted Barbet complex. *Condor* 107: 527–536.

Arndt, T. 1992–96. *Lexicon of Parrots*. Verlag Arndt & Müller, Bretten.

Atwood, J.L. 1988. Speciation and geographic variation in Black-tailed Gnatcatchers. *Orn. Monogr.* 42: 1–74.

Aveledo-H., R. & Gines Rdo. Hno. 1950. Descripción de cuatro aves nuevas de Venezuela. *Mem. Soc. Cien. Nat. La Salle*, X (26): 59-71.

Aveledo, R. 1998. Nueva subespecie de la familia Picidae del estado Lara. *Bol. Soc. Venez. Cienc. Nat.* 46(150): 3–7.

Aveledo, R., & L. Pérez. 1989. Tres nuevas subespecies de aves (Picidae, Parulidae, Thraupidae) de la Sierra de Perijá, Venezuela, y lista hipotetica para la avifauna colombiana de Perijá. *Bol. Soc. Venez. Cienc. Nat.* 63(146): 7–24.

Aveledo, R., & L. Pérez. 1991. Dos nuevas subespecies de aves (Trochilidae y Formicaridae) de la region oriental y occidental de Venezuela. *Bol. Soc. Venez. Cienc. Nat.* 43(147): 7–25.

Aveledo, R., & L. Pérez. 1994. Descripción de nueve subespecies nuevas y comentarios sobre dos especies de aves de Venezuela. *Bol. Soc. Venez. Cienc. Nat.* 44(148): 229–257.

Avise, J., W. Nelson, & C.G. Sibley. 1994. DNA sequence support for a close phylogenetic relationship between some storks and New World vultures. *Proc. Nat. Acad. Sci. Phil.* 91: 5173–5177.

Bahr, N. 1995. Additions to the list of new species of birds described from 1981 to 1990. *Bull. Brit. Orn. Club* 115: 114–116.

Bangs, O. & G.K. Noble. 1918. List of birds collected on the Harvard Peruvian expedition of 1916. *Auk* 35: 442-463.

Bangs, O. & T.E. Penard. 1918. Notes on a collection of Suriname birds. *Bull. Mus. Comp. Zool.* 62: 25-93.

Banks, R.C. 1997. The name of Lawrence's Flycatcher. Pp. 21–24 *in* Dickerman, R.W. (compiler) *The Era of Allan R. Phillips: A Festschrift*. Horizon Communications, Albuquerque, New Mexico.

Banks, R.C., & M.R. Browning. 1995. Comments on the status of revived old names for some North American birds. *Auk* 112: 633–648.

Banks, R.C., C. Cicero, J.L. Dunn, A.W. Kratter, P.C. Rasmussen, J.V. Remsen, J.D. Rising, & D.F. Stotz. 2002. Forty-third supplement to the American Ornithologists' Union *Check-list of North American Birds*. *Auk* 118: 897–906.

Banks, R.C., C. Cicero, J.L. Dunn, A.W. Kratter, P.C. Rasmussen, J.V. Remsen, J.D. Rising, & D.F. Stotz. 2004. Forty-fourth supplement to the American Ornithologists' Union *Check-list of North American Birds*. *Auk* 120: 923–931.

Banks, R.C., & C. Dove. 1992. The generic name for Crested Caracaras (Aves: Falconidae). *Proc. Biol. Soc. Wash.* 105: 420–425.

Baptista, L.F., P.W. Trail, & H.M. Horblit. 1997. Family Columbidae (pigeons and doves). Pp. 60–243 *in* del Hoyo, J., A. Elliott, & J. Sargatal (eds.) *Handbook of the Birds of the World*, vol. 4. Lynx Edicions, Barcelona.

Barker, F.K. 2004. Monophyly and relationships of wrens (Aves: Troglodytidae): a congruence analysis of heterogeneous mitochondrial and nuclear DNA sequence data. *Mol. Phylogen. Evol.* 31: 486-504.

Barker, F.K., A. Cibois, P. Schikler, J. Feinstein and J. Cracraft. 2004. Phylogeny and diversification of the largest avian radiation. *Proc. Nat. Acad. Sci.* 101: 11040-11045.

Barnett, A., R. Shapley, P. Benjamin, E. Henry, & M. McGarrell. 2002. Birds of the Potaro Plateau, with eight new species for Guyana. *Cotinga* 18: 19–36.

Barrowclough, G.F., & P. Escalante-Pliego. 1990. Notes on the birds of the Sierra de Unturán, southern Venezuela. *Bull. Brit. Orn. Club* 110: 167–169.

Barrowclough, G.F., P. Escalante-Pliego, R. Aveledo-Hostos, & L.A. Pérez-Chinchilla. 1995. An annotated list of the birds of the Cerro Tamacuarí region, Serranía de Tapirapecó, Federal Territory of Amazonas, Venezuela. *Bull. Brit. Orn. Club* 115: 211–219.

Barrowclough, G.F., R.M. Lentino, & P.R. Sweet. 1997. New records of birds from Auyán-tepui, Estado Bolívar, Venezuela. *Bull. Brit. Orn. Club* 117: 194–198.

Bates, J.M. 1997. Distribution and geographic variation in three South American grassquits (Emberizinae, *Tiaris*). Pp. 91–110 *in* Remsen, J.V. (ed.) Studies in Neotropical ornithology honoring Ted Parker. *Orn. Monogr.* 48.

Bates, J.M., S.J. Hackett, & J.M. Goerck. 1999. High levels of mitochondrial DNA differentiation in two lineages of antbirds (*Drymophila* and *Hypocnemis*). *Auk* 116: 1093–1106.

Bates, J.M., & R.M. Zink. 1994. Evolution into the Andes: molecular evidence for species relationships in the genus *Leptopogon*. *Auk* 111: 507–515.

Belton, W. 1985. Birds of Rio Grande do Sul, Brazil, Pt. 2. *Bull. Amer. Mus. Nat. Hist.* 180: article 1.

Berg, K. 1994. New and interesting records of birds from a dry forest reserve in south-west Ecuador. *Cotinga* 2: 14–19.

Berlioz, M.J. 1936. Étude critique del Capitonidés de la Région neotropicale. *Oiseau & RFO* 6: 28–56.

Bertram, B.C.R. 1996. Family Heliornithidae (finfoots). Pp. 210–217 *in* del Hoyo, J., A. Elliott, & J. Sargatal (eds.) *Handbook of the Birds of the World*, vol. 3. Lynx Edicions, Barcelona.

Best, B.J. 1994. Focus on: Ochre-bellied Dove *Leptotila ochraceiventris*. *Cotinga* 1: 30–33.

Bierregaard, R.O. 1994a. Family Accipitridae (hawks and eagles): Neotropical species accounts. Pp. 108–205 *in* del Hoyo, J., A. Elliott, & J. Sargatal (eds.) *Handbook of the Birds of the World*, vol. 2. Lynx Edicions, Barcelona.

Bierregaard, R.O. 1994b. Family Falconidae (falcons and caracaras): Neotropical species accounts. Pp. 249–268 *in* del Hoyo, J., A. Elliott, & J. Sargatal (eds.) *Handbook of the Birds of the World*, vol. 2. Lynx Edicions, Barcelona.

Bierregaard, R.O., M. Cohn-Haft, & D.F. Stotz. 1997. Cryptic biodiversity: an overlooked species and new subspecies of antbird (Aves: Formicariidae) with revision of *Cercomacra tyrannina* in northeastern South America. Pp. 111–128 *in* Remsen, J.V. (ed.) Studies in Neotropical ornithology honoring Ted Parker. *Orn. Monogr.* 48.

BirdLife International. 2000. *Threatened Birds of the World.* BirdLife International, Cambridge, UK& Lynx Edicions, Barcelona.

BirdLife International. 2004. *Threatened Birds of the World 2004*. CD-ROM. BirdLife International, Cambridge, UK.

Birdsley, J.S. 2002. Phylogeny of the tyrant flycatchers (Tyrannidae) based on morphology and behavior. Auk 119: 715–734.

Blake, E.R. 1958. Birds of Volcán Chiriquí, Panama. *Fieldiana Zool.*, 36(5): 499-577.

Blake, E.R. 1977. *Manual of Neotropical Birds*, vol. 1. University of Chicago Press, Chicago.

Blake, E.R., & P. Hocking. 1974. Two new species of tanager from Peru. *Wilson Bull.* 86: 321–324.

Bliss, N.B. & L.M. Olsen. 1996. Development of a 30-arc-second digital elevation model of South America, in: *Pecora Thirteen, Human interactions with the environment-perspectives from space, held at Souix Falls, South Dakota, August 20-22, 1996.*

Bock, W.J. 1985. Is *Diglossa* (Thraupinae) monophyletic? Pp. 319–332 *in* Buckley, P.A., M.S. Foster, E.S. Morton, R.S Ridgely & F.G. Buckley (eds.) Neotropical ornithology. *Orn. Monogr.* 36.

Boesman, P. 1998. Some new information on the distribution of Venezuelan birds. *Cotinga* 9: 27–39.

Boesman, P., & J. Curson. 1995. Grey-headed Warbler *Basileuterus griseiceps* in danger of extinction? *Cotinga* 3: 35–39.

Bonaccorsi, G. 1998. Observation du Canard souchet *Anas clypeata* au Venezuela. *Alauda* 66: 69.

Bond, J. 1956. Additional notes on Peruvian birds II. *Proc. Acad. Nat. Sci. Phil.* 108: 227–247.

Bond, J. & R. Meyer de Schauensee. 1940. The Birds of Bolivia, pt. ll. *Proc. Acad. Nat. Sci. Philadelphia* 95: 167-221.

Borges, S. H., & I. Torres de Macêdo. 2001. *Cecropia* fruits and Müllerian bodies in the diet of Chestnut-bellied Seedeater *Sporophila castaneiventris*. *Cotinga* 15: 17–18.

Borrero, J.I., & J. Hernández-Camacho. 1958. Apuntes sobre aves colombianas. *Caldasia* 8: 253–294.

Borrow, N. & R. Demey. 2001. *Birds of Western Africa.* Christopher Helm, London.

Bosque, C. 1987. The passage of North American migratory land birds through xerophytic habitats on the western coast of Venezuela. *Biotropica* 19: 267–273.

Botero, J.E., & J.C. Verhelst. 2001. Turquoise Dacnis *Dacnis hartlaubi*, a Colombian endemic in shade coffee plantations. *Cotinga* 15: 34–36.

Braun, M.J., & R.T. Brumfield. 1998. Enigmatic phylogeny of skuas: an alternative hypothesis. *Proc. Roy. Soc. Lond., Ser. B.* 265: 995–999.

Braun, M.J., D.W. Finch, M.R. Robbins & B.K. Schmidt. 2000. *A Field Checklist of the Birds of Guyana.* Smithsonian Institution, Washington, D.C.

Braun, M.J., M.L. Isler, P.R. Isler, J.M. Bates, & M.R. Robbins. 2005. Avian speciation in the Pantepui: the case of the Roraiman Antbird (*Percnostola* [*Schistocichla*] "*leucostigma*" *saturata*). *Condor*: 107: 327–341.

Braun, M.J., & T.A. Parker. 1985. Molecular, morphological, and behavioural evidence concerning the taxonomic relationships of "*Synallaxis*" *gularis* and other synallaxines. Pp. 333–346 *in* Buckley, P.A., M.S. Foster, E.S. Morton, R.S Ridgely & F.G. Buckley (eds.) Neotropical ornithology. *Orn. Monogr.* 36.

Braun, M.J., M.R. Robbins, C.M. Milensky, B.J. O'Shea, B.R. Barber, W. Hinds & W.S. Prince. 2003. New birds for Guyana from Mts. Roraima and Ayanganna. *Bull. Brit. Orn. Club* 123: 24–33.

Brewer, D., & MacKay, B.K. 2001. *Wrens, Dippers, and Thrashers*. Christopher Helm, London.

Brooke, R.K. 1974. Nomenclatural notes on and the type-localities of some taxa in the Apodidae and Hirundinidae (Aves). *Durban Mus. Novit.* 10 (9): 127-137.

Brooks, T. 2000. Finding Grey-headed Warbler *Basileuterus griseiceps* on Cerro Negro, Monagas, Venezuela. *Cotinga* 14: 30–32.

Brown, L., & D. Amadon. 1968. *Eagles, Hawks and Falcons of the World*. Country Life Books, Feltham.

Browning, M.R. 1989. The correct name for the Olivaceous Cormorant, "Maiague" of Piso (1685). *Wilson Bull.* 101: 101–106.

Bruce, M.R. 1999. Family Tytonidae (barn-owls). Pp. 34–75 *in* del Hoyo, J., A. Elliott, & J. Sargatal (eds.) *Handbook of the Birds of the World*, vol. 5. Lynx Edicions, Barcelona.

Brumfield, R.T., & M.J. Braun. 2001. Phylogenetic relationships in bearded manakins (Pipridae: *Manacus*) indicate that male plumage color is a misleading taxonomic marker. *Condor* 103: 248–258.

Brumfield, R.T., & J.V. Remsen 1996. Geographic variation and species limits in *Cinnycerthia* wrens of the Andes. *Wilson Bull.* 108: 205–227.

Brumfield, R.T., D.L. Swofford & M.J. Braun. 1997. Evolutionary relationships among the potoos (Nyctibiidae) based on isozymes. Pp. 129–145 *in* Remsen, J.V. (ed.) Studies in Neotropical ornithology honoring Ted Parker. *Orn. Monogr.* 48.

Bryan, D.C. 1996. Family Aramidae (Limpkin). Pp. 90–95 *in* del Hoyo, J., A. Elliott, & J. Sargatal (eds.) *Handbook of the Birds of the World*, vol. 3. Lynx Edicions, Barcelona.

Buckley, P.A., & F.G. Buckley. 1984. Cayenne Tern new to North America, with comments on its relationship to Sandwich Tern. *Auk* 101: 396–398.

Buckley, P.A., M.S. Foster, E.S. Morton, R.S. Ridgely & F.G. Buckley (eds.) 1985. Neotropical ornithology. *Orn. Monogr.* 36.

Bühler, P. 1996. Die neotropischen Tukane (Ramphastidae) als Model einer ökomorphologischen Evolutionsanalyse. *Ökol. Vögel* 18: 127–162.

Burger, J., & M. Gochfeld. 1996. Family Laridae (gulls). Pp. 572–623 *in* del Hoyo, J., A. Elliott, & J. Sargatal (eds.) *Handbook of the Birds of the World*, vol. 3. Lynx Edicions, Barcelona.

Bündgen, R. 1999. Species accounts of Trochilidae (p.573) in: del Hoyo, J., A. Elliott & J. Sargatal (eds) 1999. *Handbook of the Birds of the World*, vol. 5. Lynx Edicions, Barcelona.

Burns, K.J. 1997. Molecular systematics of tanagers (Thraupinae): evolution and biogeography of a diverse radiation of Neotropical birds. *Mol. Phyl. & Evol.* 8: 334–348.

Burns, K.J. 1998. A phylogenetic perspective on the evolution of sexual dichromatism in tanagers (Thraupinae): the role of female versus male plumage. *Evolution* 52: 1219–1224.

Byers, C., U. Olsson & J. Curson. 1995. *Buntings and Sparrows: A Guide to the Buntings and North American Sparrows*. Pica Press, Robertsbridge.

Caballero, L., A. Wilinski & A.E. Seijas. 1984. Una nueva especie de *Rallus* (Gruiformes: Rallidae) para Venezuela. *Bol. Soc. Venez. Cienc. Nat.* 39(142): 107–110.

Cabot, J. 1992. Family Tinamidae (tinamous). Pp. 112–138 *in* del Hoyo, J., A. Elliott, & J. Sargatal, eds. *Handbook of Birds of the World*, vol. 1. Lynx Edicions, Barcelona.

Cabot, J., & T. de Vries. 2003. *Buteo polyosoma* and *Buteo poecilochrous* are two distinct species. *Bull. Brit. Orn. Club* 123: 190–207.

Cabot, J., & T. de Vries. 2004. Age- and sex-differentiated plumages in the two colour morphs of the Variable Buzzard *Buteo polyosoma*: a case of delayed maturation with subadult males disguised in definitive adult female plumage. *Bull. Brit. Orn. Club* 124: 272–285.

Cabot, J., T. de Vries, & F.G. Stiles. 2006. Aberrant distributional records of Cordilleran Buzzard (Hawk) *Buteo poecilochrous* in Colombia reflect confusion with White-tailed Buzzard (Hawk). *Bull. Brit. Orn. Club* 126: 65–68.

Cade, T.J. 1982. *The Falcons of the World*. Cornell University Press, Ithaca, New York.

Cade, T.J., J.M. Enderson, C.G. Thelander, & C.M. White. 1988. *Peregrine Falcon Populations: Their Management and Recovery*. The Peregrine Fund, Boise, Idaho.

Calchi, R. 1995. Primer registro de *Cinclodes fuscus* (Aves: Furnariidae) para el Páramo de Tamá, frontera colombo-venezolana. *Orn. Neotrop.* 6: 121–123.

Canevari, M. 1991. *Nueva Guia de las Aves Argentinas*. Vols I & II. Fundacion Acindar, Buenos Aires.

Canevari, P., G. Castro, M. Sallabery, & L.G. Naranjo. 2001. *Guía de los Chorlos y Playeros de la Región Neotropical*. American Bird Conservancy, WWF-US, Manomet Center for Conservation Science & Asociación Calidris, Santiago de Cali, Colombia.

Capparella, A.P., G.H. Rosenberg, & S.W. Cardiff. 1997. A new subspecies of *Percnostola rufifrons* (Formicariidae) from northeastern Amazonian Peru, with a revision of the *rufifrons* complex. Pp. 165–170 *in* Remsen, J.V. (ed.) Studies in Neotropical ornithology honoring Ted Parker. *Orn. Monogr.* 48.

Carboneras, C. 1992a. Family Sulidae (gannets and boobies). Pp. 312–325 *in* del Hoyo, J., A. Elliott, & J. Sargatal (eds.) *Handbook of Birds of the World*, vol. 1. Lynx Edicions, Barcelona.

Carboneras, C. 1992b. Families Anhimidae (screamers) and Anatidae (ducks, geese and swans). Pp. 527–628 *in* del Hoyo, J., A. Elliott, & J. Sargatal (eds.) *Handbook of Birds of the World*, vol. 1. Lynx Edicions, Barcelona.

Carboneras, C. 1992c. Families Diomedeidae (albatrosses), Procellariidae (petrels and shearwaters) and Hydrobatidae (storm-petrels). Pp. 197–278 *in* del Hoyo, J., A. Elliott & J. Sargatal (eds.) *Handbook of Birds of the World*, vol. 1. Lynx Edicions, Barcelona.

Carriker, M.R. 1935. Descriptions of new birds from Peru and Ecuador, with critical notes on other little-known species. *Proc. Acad. Nat. Sci. Philadelphia* 87: 343-359.

Carroll, J.P. 1994. Family Odontophoridae (New World quails). Pp. 412–433 *in* del Hoyo, J., A. Elliott, & J. Sargatal (eds.) *Handbook of the Birds of the World*, vol. 2. Lynx Edicions, Barcelona.

Casler, C. 1996. First record of the Great Black-backed Gull (*Larus marinus*) in Venezuela. *Bol. Ctr. Invest. Biol. LUZ* 30: 1–8.

Casler, C., & E. Esté. 1997. Record of Swainson's Warbler (*Limnothlypis swainsonii*) in northern South America. *Bol. Ctr. Invest. Biol. LUZ* 31: 95–98.

Casler, C., & D. Pirella. 2005. Seasonal abundance of Parasitic Jaegers (Aves: Stercorariidae) on the southwestern coast of the Gulf of Venezuela. *Bol. Ctr. Invest. Biol. LUZ* 39: 145–158.

Castaño R., A.M., & G.J. Colorado Z.. 2002. First records of Red-tailed Hawk *Buteo jamaicensis* in Colombia. *Cotinga* 18: 102.

Chantler, P. 1999. Family Apodidae (swifts). Pp. 388–457 *in* del Hoyo, J., A. Elliott, & J. Sargatal (eds.) *Handbook of the Birds of the World*, vol. 5. Lynx Edicions, Barcelona.

Chantler, P., & G. Driessens. 2000. Swifts: *A Guide to the Swifts and Treeswifts of the World*. Second edn. Pica Press, Robertsbridge.

Chapman, F.M. 1917. The distribution of bird-life in Colombia. A contribution to a biological survey of South America. *Bull. Amer. Mus. Nat Hist*. 36: 1–729.

Chapman, F.M. 1921. Descriptions of proposed new birds from Colombia, Ecuador, Peru and Brazil. *Amer. Mus. Novit*., No. 18.

Chapman, F.M. 1926. The distribution of bird-life in Ecuador. A contribution to a study of the origin of Andean bird-life. *Bull. Amer. Mus. Nat. Hist*. 55: 1–784.

Chapman, F.M. 1929. Descriptions of new birds from Mt. Roraima. *Amer. Mus. Novit*. 341: 1-7.

Chapman, F.M. 1931 The upper zonal bird-life of Mts. Roraima and Duida. *Bull. Amer. Mus. Nat. Hist*. 63: 1–135.

Chesser, T. 1994. Migration in South America: an overview of the austral system. *Bird Conserv. Intern*. 4: 91–107.

Chesser, R.T. 1999. Molecular systematics of the Rhinocryptid genus *Pteroptochos*. *Condor* 101: 439–446.

Chesser, R.T. 2000. The phylogenetics of *Muscisaxicola* ground-tyrants. *Mol. Phyl. & Evol*. 15: 369–380.

Chesser, R.T. 2004a. Systematics, evolution, and biogeography of the South American ovenbird genus *Cinclodes*. *Auk* 121: 752–766.

Chesser, R.T. 2004b. Molecular systematics of New World suboscine birds. *Mol. Phyl. & Evol*. 32: 11–24.

Clark, G.A. 1974. Foot-scute differences among certain North American oscines. *Wilson Bull*. 86: 104–109.

Clark, W.S., & R.C. Banks 1992. The taxonomic status of the White-tailed Kite. *Wilson Bull*. 104: 571–579.

Clark, W.S., & B.K. Wheeler. 2001. *Hawks of North America*. Second edn. Houghton Mifflin, Boston.

Cleere, N. 1999. Family Caprimulgidae (nightjars). Pp. 302–386 *in* del Hoyo, J., A. Elliott, & J. Sargatal (eds.) *Handbook of the Birds of the World*, vol. 5. Lynx Edicions, Barcelona.

Cleere, N., & J. Ingels. 2002. First record of the Rufous Potoo *Nyctibius bracteatus* and in-flight drinking by the Semi-collared Nighthawk *Lurocalis semitorquatus* in French Guiana. *Bull. Brit. Orn. Club* 122: 154–155.

Cleere, N., & D. Nurney 1998. *Nightjars: A Guide to the Nightjars and Related Nightbirds*. Pica Press, Robertsbridge.

Clement, P., A. Harris, & J. Davis 1993. *Finches & Sparrows: An Identification Guide*. Christopher Helm, London.

Clement, P., & R. Hathaway. 2000. *Thrushes*. Christopher Helm, London.

Clements, J.F. 1991. *Birds of the World: A Checklist*. Fourth edn. Two Continents, New York.

Clements, J.F., & N. Shany. 2001. *A Field Guide to the Birds of Peru*. Ibis Publishing, Temecula, California.

Cody, M.L. 2005. Family Mimidae (mockingbirds and thrashers). Pp. 448–495 *in* del Hoyo, J., A. Elliott, & D.A. Christie (eds.) *Handbook of the Birds of the World*, vol. 10. Lynx Edicions, Barcelona.

Cohen, B.L., A.J. Baker, K. Blechschmidt, D.L. Dittmann, R.W. Furness, J.A. Gerwin, A.J. Helbig, J. de Korte, H.D. Marshall, R.L. Palma, H.U. Peter, R. Ramli, I. Siebold, M.S. Willcox, R.H. Wilson, & R.M. Zink. 1997. Enigmatic phylogeny of the skuas (Aves: Stercorariidae). *Proc. Roy. Soc. Lond. Ser. B* 264: 181–190.

Cohn-Haft, M. 1993. Rediscovery of the White-winged Potoo (*Nyctibius leucopterus*). *Auk* 110: 391–394.

Cohn-Haft, M. 1999. Family Nyctibiidae (potoos). Pp. 288–301 *in* del Hoyo, J., A. Elliott, & J. Sargatal (eds.) *Handbook of the Birds of the World*, vol. 5. Lynx Edicions, Barcelona.

Collar, N.J. 1997. Family Psittacidae (parrots). Pp. 280–477 *in* del Hoyo, J., A. Elliott, & J. Sargatal (eds.) *Handbook of the Birds of the World*, vol. 4. Lynx Edicions, Barcelona.

Collar, N.J. 2001. Family Trogonidae (trogons). Pp. 80–127 *in* del Hoyo, J., A. Elliott, & J. Sargatal (eds.) *Handbook of the Birds of the World*, vol. 6. Lynx Edicions, Barcelona.

Collar, N.J. 2005. Family Turdidae (thrushes). Pp. 514–807 *in* del Hoyo, J., A. Elliott, & D.A. Christie (eds.) *Handbook of the Birds of the World*, vol. 10. Lynx Edicions, Barcelona.

Collar, N.J. & P. Andrew. 1988. *Birds to Watch: the ICBP world check-list of threatened birds*. International Council for Bird Preservation, Cambridge, UK.

Collar, N.J., M.J. Crosby, & A.J. Stattersfield. 1994. *Birds to Watch 2: The World List of Threatened Birds*. BirdLife International, Cambridge, UK.

Collar, N.J., L.P. Gonzaga, N. Krabbe, A. Madroño Nieto, L.G. Naranjo, T.A. Parker, & D.C. Wege. 1992. *Threatened Birds of the Americas: The ICBP/IUCN Red Data Book*. International Council for Bird Preservation, Cambridge, UK.

Collins, C.T. 1969. A review of the shearwater records for Trinidad and Tobago. *Ibis* 111: 251–253.

Collins, C.T. 1972. A new species of swift of the genus *Cypseloides* from northeastern South America. *Contrib. Sci., Nat. Hist. Mus. Los Angeles County* 229.

Colorado Z., G.J., & P.C. Pulgarín R. 2003. Snowy-bellied Hummingbird *Saucerottia edward*, new to Colombia and South America. *Cotinga* 20: 99, 100.

Colston, P.R. 1985. Trogons and mousebirds. Pp. 264–265 *in* Perrins, C.M., & A.L.A. Middleton (eds.) *The Encyclopaedia of Birds*. Allen & Unwin, London

Colvee N.J. 1999. First report on the Rose-ringed Parakeet (*Psittacula krameri*) in Venezuela and preliminary observations on its behaviour. *Orn. Neotrop*. 10: 115–117.

Coopmans, P., & N. Krabbe. 2000. A new species of flycatcher (Tyrannidae: *Myiopagis*) from eastern Ecuador and eastern Peru. *Wilson Bull*. 112: 305–312.

Coopmans, P., N. Krabbe, & T.S. Schulenberg. 2001. Vocal evidence of species rank for nominate Unicoloured Tapaculo *Scytalopus unicolor*. *Bull. Brit. Orn. Club* 121: 208–213.

Córdoba-Córdoba, S. & M.A. Echeverry-Galvis. 2006. Two new hummingbirds for Colombia, Many-spotted Hummingbird *Taphrospilus hypostictus* and Violet-chested Hummingbird *Sternoclyta cyanopectus*. *Bull. Brit. Orn. Club* 126: 194-195.

Cory, C.B. 1918. Catalogue of birds of the Americas and the adjacent islands in Field Museum of Natural History, part II(1). *Field Mus. Nat. Hist. Zool. Ser*. 13(200): 1–315.

Cory, C.B. 1919. Catalogue of birds of the Americas and the adjacent islands in Field Museum of Natural History, part II(2). *Field Mus. Nat. Hist. Zool. Ser.* 13(203): 317–607.

Cory, C.B., & Hellmayr, C.E. 1924. Catalogue of birds of the Americas and the adjacent islands in Field Museum of Natural History, part III. *Field Mus. Nat. Hist. Zool. Ser.* 13(223): 1–369.

Cory, C.B., & Hellmayr, C.E. 1925. Catalogue of birds of the Americas and the adjacent islands in Field Museum of Natural History, part IV. *Field Mus. Nat. Hist. Zool. Ser.* 13(224): 1–390.

Cracraft, J. 1981. Towards a phylogenetic classification of the recent birds of the world (Class Aves). *Auk* 98: 681–714.

Crochet, P.A., J.D. Lebreton, & F. Bonhomme. 2002. Systematics of large white-headed gulls: patterns of mitochondrial DNA variation in Western European taxa. *Auk* 119: 603–620.

Cuadros, T., & W. Weber. 2000. En busca de la "i" perdida. *Bol. SAO* 11 (20–21): 78–84.

Cuervo, A.M., C.D. Cadena, N. Krabbe & L.M. Renjifo. 2005. *Scytalopus stilesi*, a new species of tapaculo (Rhinocryptidae) from the Cordillera Central of Colombia. *Auk* 122: 445–463.

Cuervo, A.M., P.G.W. Salaman, T.M. Donegan & J.M. Ochoa. 2001. A new species of piha (Cotingidae: *Lipaugus*) from the Cordillera Central of Colombia. *Ibis* 143: 353–368.

Curson, J., D. Quinn & D. Beadle. 1994. *Warblers of the Americas: An Identification Guide*. Christopher Helm, London.

Dallmeier, F.G., & A. Cringan. 1989. *Biology, Conservation and Management of Waterfowl in Venezuela*. Ed. Ex Libris, Caracas.

Daszkiewicz, P., & J.-C. de Massary. 2006. Overlooked historical testimony as to the presence of Red-billed Tropicbird *Phaethon aethereus* in French Guiana. *Bull. Brit. Orn. Club* 126: 71–73.

David, N., & M. Gosselin. 2000. The supposed significance of originally capitalized species-group names. *Bull. Brit. Orn. Club* 120: 261–266.

David, N., & M. Gosselin. 2002a. Gender agreement of avian species names. *Bull. Brit. Orn. Club* 122: 14–49.

David, N., & M. Gosselin. 2002b. The grammatical gender of avian genera. *Bull. Brit. Orn. Club* 122: 257–282.

Davies, N.B. 2000. *Cuckoos, Cowbirds and other Cheats*. T. & A. D. Poyser, London.

Davies, S.J.J.F. 2002. *Ratites and Tinamous*. Oxford University Press, Oxford.

Davis, T.J., & J.P. O'Neill. 1986. A new species of antwren (Formicariidae: *Herpsilochmus*) from Peru, with comments on the systematics of other members of the genus. *Wilson Bull.* 98: 337–352.

Debrot, A., & T. Prins. 1992. First record and establishment of the Shiny Cowbird in Curaçao. *Carib. J. Sci.* 28: 104–105.

del Hoyo, J., & A. Motis. 2004. In: Delacour, J. and Amadon, D. *Curassows and Related Birds*. Lynx Edicions, Barcelona.

Delacour, J. 1956. *The Waterfowl of the World*, vol. 2. Country Life, London

Delacour, J. 1959. *The Waterfowl of the World*, vol. 3. Country Life, London

Delacour, J., & D. Amadon. 1973. *Curassows and Related Birds*. Amer. Mus. Nat. Hist., New York.

Delgado, F., & S. Francisco. 1985. A new subspecies of the Painted Parakeet (*Pyrrhura picta*) from Panama. Pp. 17–22 *in* Buckley, P.A., M.S. Foster, E.S. Morton, R.S Ridgely & F.G. Buckley (eds.) Neotropical ornithology. *Orn. Monogr.* 36.

Dick, J.A., W. McGillivray & D.M. Brooks. 1984. A list of birds and their weights from Saül, French Guiana. *Wilson Bull.* 96: 347–365.

Dickerman, R.W. 1987. Notes on the plumages of *Diglossa duidae* with the description of a new subspecies. *Bull. Brit. Orn. Club* 107: 42–44.

Dickerman, R.W. 1988. An unnamed subspecies of *Euphonia rufiventris* from Venezuela and northern Brazil. *Bull. Brit. Orn. Club* 108: 20–22.

Dickerman, R.W., G.F. Barrowclough, P.F. Cannell, W.H. Phelps, & D.E. Willard. 1986. *Philydor hylobius* Wetmore & Phelps, is a synonym of *Automolus roraimae* Hellmayr. *Auk* 103: 431–432.

Dickerman, R.W., & K.C. Parkes. 1968. Notes on the plumages and generic status of the Little Blue Heron. *Auk* 85: 437–440.

Dickerman, R.W., & W.H. Phelps Jr. 1982. An Annotated List of the Birds of Cerro Urutaní on the Border of Estado Bolívar, Venezuela, and Territorio Roraima, Brazil. *Amer. Mus. Novit.* 2732. Pp 1-20.

Dickinson, E.C. (ed.) 2003. *The Howard & Moore Complete Checklist of the Birds of the World*. Third edn. Christopher Helm.

Dilger, W.C. 1956. Adaptive modifications and ecological isolating mechanisms in the thrush genera *Catharus* and *Hylocichla*. *Wilson Bull.* 68: 171–199.

Donahue, P.K. 1985. Notes on some little known or previously unrecorded birds of Suriname. *Amer. Birds* 39: 229–230

Donald, P.F. 2004. Horned Lark *Eremophila alpestris*. Pp. 589–590 *in* del Hoyo, J., A. Elliott, & J. Sargatal (eds.) *Handbook of the Birds of the World*, vol. 9. Lynx Edicions, Barcelona.

Donegan, T.M., & B.C. Huertas. 2002. First mainland record of Worm-eating Warbler *Helmitheros vermivorus* for Colombia. *Cotinga* 17: 77–78.

Donegan, T.M., & B. Huertas. in press. A new brush-finch in the *Atlapetes latinuchus* complex from the Yariguíes Mountains and adjacent Eastern Andes of Colombia. *Bull. Brit. Orn. Club* 126.

Donegan, T.M., B.C. Huertas H., & E.R. Briceño L. 2005. Discovery of a population stronghold of Gorgeted Wood-quail *Odontophorus strophium*, a critically endangered Colombian endemic, with notes on ecology and vocalisations. *Cotinga* 23: 74–77.

Dove, C.J., & R.C. Banks. 1999. A taxonomic study of Crested Caracaras (Falconidae). *Wilson Bull.* 111: 330–339.

Downing, C. 2005. New distributional information for some Colombian birds, with a new species for South America. *Cotinga* 24: 13–15.

Downing, C., & Hickman, J. 2004. New record of Hooded Antpitta *Grallaricula cucullata* in the Western Cordillera of Colombia. *Cotinga* 21: 76.

Dunn, J., & K. Garrett 1997. *Warblers*. Houghton Mifflin, Boston.

Dunne, P., D. Sibley, & C. Sutton. 1988. *Hawks in Flight*. Houghton Mifflin, Boston.

Eberhard, J.R. & E. Bermingham. 2005. Phylogeny and comparative biology of *Pionospitta* parrots and *Pteroglossus* toucans. *Mol. Phylog. Evol.* 36: 288-304.

Eisenmann, E. 1958. The spelling of *Notharchus macrorhynchos hyperrynchus*. *Auk* 75: 101.

Eley, J.W. 1982. Systematic relationships and zoogeography of the White-winged Guan (*Penelope albipennis*) and related forms. *Wilson Bull.* 94: 241–432.

Eley, J.W., G.R. Graves, T.A. Parker, & D.R. Hunter. 1979. Notes on *Siptornis striaticollis* (Furnariidae) in Peru. *Condor* 81: 319.

Elliott, A. 1992a. Family Ciconiidae (storks). Pp. 466–471 *in* del Hoyo, J., A. Elliott, & J. Sargatal (eds.) *Handbook of the Birds of the World*, vol. 1. Lynx Edicions, Barcelona.

Elliott, A. 1992b. Family Pelecanidae (pelicans). Pp. 290–311 *in* del Hoyo, J., A. Elliott, & J. Sargatal (eds.) *Handbook of the Birds of the World*, vol. 1. Lynx Edicions, Barcelona.

Elphick, C.J., & D. Sibley. 2001. *The Sibley Guide to Bird Life and Behaviour*. Christopher Helm, London.

English, P.H., & T. A. Parker. 1992. *Birds of Eastern Ecuador*. Cornell Lab. of Ornithology. Ithaca, New York.

Ericson, P.G.P., Zuccon, D., Ohlson, J.I., Johansson, U.S., Alvarenga, H. & Prum, R.O. 2006. Higher level phylogeny and morphological evolution of tyrant flycatchers, cotingas, manakins and their allies (Aves: Tyrannida). *Molecular Phylogenetics and Evolution* 40: 471-483.

Erwin, R.M. 1990. Feeding activities of Black Skimmers in Guyana. *Colonial Waterbirds* 13 (1): 70-71.

Escalante, P., & A.T. Peterson 1992. Geographic variation and species limits in Middle American woodnymphs (*Thalurania*). *Wilson Bull.* 104: 205–338.

Estela, F.A., Garcia, C., Johnston-Gonzales, R., Soler, G. & Bessudo, S. Parkinson's Petrel *Procellaria parkinsoni* in the Colombian Pacific: a new record for Colombia or a continuous misinformation about seabirds. Submitted to *Cotinga.*

Eva, H.D., A.S. Belward, E.E. de Miranda, C.M. Di Bella, V.Gond, O.Huber, S.Jones, M. Sgrenzaroli & S. Fritz. 2004. A land cover map of South America. *Global Change Biology*, 10 (5): 732-745.

Fairbank, R.J. 2002. Ring-billed Gull *Larus delawarensis* and Lesser Black-backed Gull *L. fuscus* in Venezuela. *Cotinga* 17: 78.

Farquhar, C.C. 1998. *Buteo polyosoma* and *B. poecilochrous*, the "Red-backed Buzzards" of South America are conspecific. *Condor* 100: 27–43.

Feduccia, J.A. 1970. The systematic position of the avian species *Metopothrix aurantiacus*. *J. Grad. Res. Center Southern Methodist Univ*. 38: 61–66.

Ferguson-Lees, J., & D.A. Christie. 2001. *Raptors of the World*. Christopher Helm, London.

ffrench, R. 1976. *A Guide to the Birds of Trinidad and Tobago*. Revised edn. Harrowood Books, Valley Forge, Pennsylvania.

ffrench, R. 1996a. *Checklist of the Birds of Tobago*. Asa Wright Nature Centre, Trinidad.

ffrench, R. 1996b. *Checklist of the Birds of Trinidad*. Asa Wright Nature Centre, Trinidad.

ffrench, R., & M. Kenefick. 2003. Verification of rare bird records from Trinidad and Tobago. *Cotinga* 19: 75–79.

Fisher, D.J. 1998. The first record of Spotted Redshank *Tringa erythropus* for South America. *Cotinga* 9: 21.

Fitzpatrick, J.W. 1980. A new race of *Atlapetes leucopterus* with comments on widespread albinism in *A. l. dresseri*. *Auk* 97: 883–887.

Fitzpatrick, J.W. 2004. Family Tyrannidae (tyrant-flycatchers). Pp. 170–462 *in* del Hoyo, J., A. Elliott, & D.A. Christie (eds.) *Handbook of the Birds of the World*, vol. 9. Lynx Edicions, Barcelona.

Fitzpatrick, J.W., & J.P. O'Neill. 1979. A new tody-tyrant from northern Peru. *Auk* 96: 443–447.

Fitzpatrick, J.W. & J.P. O'Neill. 1986. *Otus petersoni*, a new species of screech-owl from the eastern Andes, with systematic notes on *O. colombianus* and *O. ingens*. *Wilson Bull.* 98(1): 1-14.

Fitzpatrick, J.W. & D.F. Stotz. 1997. A new species of tyrannulet (*Phylloscartes*) from the Andean foothills of Peru and Bolivia. Pp 37-44 in Remsen 1997.

Fitzpatrick, J.W., J.W. Terborgh & D.E. Willard. 1977. A new species of wood-wren from Peru. *Auk* 94: 195–201.

Fitzpatrick, J.W., & D.E. Willard. 1982. Twenty one bird species new or little known from the Republic of Colombia. *Bull. Brit. Orn. Club* 102: 153–158.

Fjeldså, J. 1983. Geographic variation in the Andean Coot *Fulica ardesiaca*. *Bull. Brit. Orn. Club* 103: 18–22.

Fjeldså, J. 1985. Origin, evolution and status of the avifauna of Andean wetlands. Pp. 85–112 *in* Buckley, P.A., M.S. Foster, E.S. Morton, R.S. Ridgely & F.G. Buckley (eds.) 1985. Neotropical ornithology. *Orn. Monogr*. 36.

Fjeldså, J. 1996. Family Thinocoridae (Seedsnipes). Pp. 538–545 in del Hoyo, J., A. Elliott, & J. Sargatal (eds.) *Handbook of the Birds of the World*, vol. 3. Lynx Edicions, Barcelona.

Fjeldså, J., & N. Krabbe. 1990. *Birds of the High Andes*. Zool. Mus., Univ. of Copenhagen, & Apollo Books, Svendborg.

Fjeldså, J., D. Zuccon, M. Irestedt, U.S. Johansson & P.G.P. Ericson. 2003. *Sapayoa aenigma*: a New World representative of "Old World suboscines". *Proc. Royal Soc. Lond. Ser. B* 270 (Suppl.): S238–S241.

Forrester, B.C. 1995. Brazil's northern frontier sites: in search of two Rio Branco endemics. *Cotinga* 3: 51–53.

Forshaw, J.M. 2006 *Parrots of the World: An Identification Guide*. Princeton University Press, Princeton.

Forshaw, J.M., & W.T. Cooper. 1989. *Parrots of the World*. Third edn. Lansdowne Editions, Brisbane.

Franke, R., & L.G. Naranjo. 1994. Primer registro del Pingüino de Magallanes en costas colombianas. *Trinea* 5: 401–406.

Freeman, S. & R.M. Zink. 1995. A phylogenetic study of the blackbirds based on variation in mitochondrial DNA restriction sites. *Syst. Biol*. 44: 409-420.

Freile, J.F., & J.A. Chaves. 1999. Photospot: Colombian Screech-Owl *Otus ingens colombianus*. *Cotinga* 12: 95–96.

Friesen, V., D.A. Anderson, T. Steeves, H. Jones & E.A. Schreiber. 2002. Molecular support for species status of the Nazca Booby (*Sula granti*). *Auk* 119: 820–826.

Fry, C.H. 1980. The evolutionary biology of kingfishers (Alcedinidae). *Living Bird* 18: 113–160.

Fry, C.H., K. Fry & A. Harris. 1992. *Kingfishers, Bee-eaters and Rollers of the World*. Christopher Helm, London.

Furness, R.W. 1985. *The Skuas*. T. & A.D. Poyser, Calton, UK.

Furness, R.W. 1996. Family Stercorariidae (skuas). Pp. 556–571 in del Hoyo, J., A. Elliott, & J. Sargatal (eds.) *Handbook of the Birds of the World*, vol. 3. Lynx Edicions, Barcelona.

Gandy, D. 1995. Lanceolated Monklet (*Micromonacha lanceolata*). *Cotinga* 3: 80.

García-Moreno, J., P. Arctander & J. Fjeldså. 1999. A case of rapid diversification in the Neotropics. Phylogenetic relationships among *Cranioleuca* spinetails (Aves, Furnariidae). *Mol. Phyl. & Evol*. 12: 273–281.

García-Moreno, J., & J. Fjeldså. 1999. Re-evaluation of species limits in the genus *Atlapetes* based on mtDNA sequence data. *Ibis* 141: 199–207.

Garcia-Moreno, J., J. Ohlson & J. Fjeldså. 2001. MtDNA sequences support monophyly of *Hemispingus* tanagers. *Molec. Phylog. Evol.* 21: 424-435.

Garrido, O.H., & J.V. Remsen. 1996. A new subspecies of the Pearly-eyed Thrasher *Margarops fuscatus* (Mimidae) from the island of St. Lucia, Lesser Antilles. *Bull. Brit. Orn. Club* 116: 75–80.

Garrido, O.H., A.T. Peterson & O. Komar. 1999. Geographic variation and taxonomy of the Cave Swallow (*Petrochelidon fulva*) complex, with the description of a new subspecies from Puerto Rico. *Bull. Brit. Orn. Club* 119: 80–90.

Gerwin, J.A., & R.M. Zink. 1989. Phylogenetic patterns in the genus *Heliodoxa* (Aves: Trochilidae): an allozymic perspective. *Wilson Bull.* 101: 525–544.

Gibbs, D., E. Barnes & J. Cox. 2001. *Pigeons and Doves. A Guide to the Pigeons and Doves of the World.* Christopher Helm, London.

Gilliard, E.T. 1958. *The Living Birds of the World.* Doubleday & Co., Garden City, New York._

Gochfeld, M., & J. Burger. 1996. Family Sternidae (terns). Pp. 624–667 *in* del Hoyo, J., A. Elliott, & J. Sargatal (eds.) *Handbook of the Birds of the World*, vol. 3. Lynx Edicions, Barcelona.

Goodall, J.W. 1964. Seedsnipe. Pp. 721–722 *in* Thomson, A.L. (ed.) *A New Dictionary of Birds.* Nelson, London.

Goodwin, D. 1976. *Crows of the World.* Cornell Univ. Press, Ithaca, New York.

Goodwin, D. 1982. *Estrildid Finches of the World.* Brit. Mus. (Nat. Hist.), London & Cornell Univ. Press, Ithaca, New York.

Goodwin, D. 1983. *Pigeons and Doves of the World.* 3rd edition. Cornell Univ. Press. Ithaca.

Gould, J. 1834. *A Monograph of the Ramphastidae or Family of Toucans.* Smith, Elder & Co., London.

Gould, J. 1851. *Introduction to the Trochilidae.* London.

Gould, J. 1854. *Monograph of the Trochilidae*, vol. 4. London.

Grant, P.J. 1986. *Gulls: A Guide to Identification.* Second edn. T. & A. D. Poyser, Calton.

Graves, G.R. 1980. A new species of metaltail hummingbird from northern Peru. *Wilson Bull.* 92: 1–7.

Graves, G.R. 1980. A new subspecies of *Diglossa* (*carbonaria*) *brunneiventris*. *Bull. Brit. Orn. Club* 100: 230–232.

Graves, G.R. 1982. Speciation in the Carbonated Flower-piercer (*Diglossa carbonaria*) complex of the Andes. *Condor* 84: 1–14.

Graves, G.R. 1986. The systematic status of *Cranioleuca furcata* Taczanowski (Furnariidae). *Condor* 88: 120–122.

Graves, G.R. 1986. Systematics of the gorgeted woodstars (Aves: Trochilidae: *Acestrura*). *Proc. Biol. Soc. Wash.* 99: 218–224.

Graves, G.R. 1988. *Phylloscartes lanyoni,* a new species of bristle-tyrant (Tyrannidae) from the lower Cauca Valley of Colombia. *Wilson Bull.* 100: 529–534.

Graves, G.R. 1990a. Systematics of the "green-throated sunangels" (Aves: Trochilidae): valid taxa or hybrids? *Proc. Biol. Soc. Wash.* 103: 6–25.

Graves, G.R. 1990b. A new subspecies of *Diglossa gloriosissima* (Aves: Thraupinae) from the western Andes of Colombia. *Proc. Biol. Soc. Wash.* 103: 962–965.

Graves, G.R. 1991. Taxonomic status of the Sword-billed Hummingbird *Ensifera ensifera caerulescens*. *Bull. Brit. Orn. Club* 111: 139–140.

Graves, G.R. 1992. Diagnosis of a hybrid antbird (*Phlegopsis nigromaculata* × *Phlegopsis erythroptera*) and the rarity of hybridization among suboscines. *Proc. Biol. Soc. Wash.* 105: 834–840.

Graves, G.R. 1993. Relic of a lost world: a new species of sunangel (Trochilidae: *Heliangelus*) from "Bogotá". *Auk* 110: 1–8.

Graves, G.R. 1997. Colorimetric and morphometric gradients in Colombian populations of Dusky Antbirds (*Cercomacra tyrannina*), with a description of a new species *Cercomacra parkeri*. Pp. 21–36 *in* Remsen, J.V. (ed.) Studies in Neotropical ornithology honoring Ted Parker. *Orn. Monogr.* 48.

Graves, G.R. 1998. Diagnoses of hybrid hummingbirds (Aves: Trochilidae). 5. Probable hybrid origin of *Amazilia distans* Wetmore & Phelps. *Proc. Biol. Soc. Wash.* 111: 28–34.

Graves, G.R. 1999. Taxonomic notes on hummingbirds (Aves: Trochilidae). 2. *Popelairia letitiae* (Bourcier & Mulsant, 1852) is a valid species. *Proc. Biol. Soc. Wash.* 112: 804–812.

Graves, G.R., & M.B. Robbins. 1987. A new subspecies of *Siptornis striaticollis* (Aves: Furnariidae) from the eastern slope of the Andes. *Proc. Biol. Soc. Wash.* 100: 121–124.

Graves, G.R., & D. Uribe-Restrepo. 1989. A new allopatric taxon in the *Hapalopsittaca amazonina* (Psittacidae) superspecies from Colombia. *Wilson Bull.* 101: 369–376.

Griffiths, C.S. 1994. Monophyly of the Falconiformes based on syringeal morphology. *Auk* 111: 787-805.

Guzman, H.M., & R.W. Schreiber. 1987. Distribution and status of Brown Pelicans in Venezuela in 1983. *Wilson Bull.* 99: 275–279.

Hackett, S.J. 1993. Phylogenetic and biogeographic relationships in the Neotropical genus *Gymnopithys* (Formicariidae). *Wilson Bull.* 105: 301–315

Hackett, S.J., & K.V. Rosenberg. 1990. Comparison of phenotypic and genetic differentiation in South American antwrens. *Auk* 107: 473–489.

Hackett, S.J., & C.A. Lehn. 1997. Lack of genetic divergence in a genus (*Pteroglossus*) of Neotropical birds: the connection between life-history characteristics and levels of genetic divergence. Pp. 267–279 *in* Remsen, J.V. (ed.) Studies in Neotropical ornithology honoring Ted Parker. *Orn. Monogr.* 48.

Haffer, J. 1967. Speciation in Colombian forest birds west of the Andes. *Amer. Mus. Novit.* 2294: 1–57.

Haffer, J. 1970. Art-Entstehung bei einigen Waldvögeln Amazoniens. *J. Orn.* 111: 285–331.

Haffer, J. 1974. *Avian Speciation in Tropical South America, With a Systematic Survey of the Toucans (Ramphastidae) and Jacamars (Galbulidae)*. Publ. Nuttall Orn. Club. 14: 1–390.

Haffer, J. 1975. Avifauna of northwestern Colombia, South America. *Bonn Zool. Monogr.* 7: 5–182.

Haffer, J. 1997. Contact zones between birds of southern Amazonia. Pp. 281–305 *in* Remsen, J.V. (ed.) Studies in Neotropical ornithology honoring Ted Parker. *Orn. Monogr.* 48.

Haffer, J. & J.W. Fitzpatrick. 1985. *Geographic variation in some Amazonian forest birds.* Pp 147-168, in Buckley *et al.* 1985.

Hancock, J., & J. Kushlan. 1984. *The Herons Handbook*. Croom Helm, London.

Hancock, J., & H. Elliott. 1978. *The Herons of the World*. Harper & Row, London.

Hancock, J., J. Kushlan, & M. Kahl. 1992. *Storks, Ibises and Spoonbills of the World*. Academic Press, London.

Hardy, J.W., T.A. Parker, & B.B. Coffey. 1998. *Voices of the Woodcreepers*. Third edn. Cassette tape. ARA Records, Gainesville.

Harris, M.P. 1968. Black-browed Albatross (*Diomedea melanophris*), and other seabirds near Guayaquil, Ecuador. *Ardea* 56: 284–285.

Harrison, P. 1983. *Seabirds: An Identification Guide*. Croom Helm, Beckenham.

Harrison, P. 1987. *Seabirds of the World: A Photographic Guide*. Christopher Helm, London.

Hartert, E. 1899. Further notes on humming-birds. *Novit. Zool.* 6: 72–75.

Hartert, E. 1900. *Das Tierreich. Eine Zusammenstellung und Kennzeichnung der rezenten Tierformen. Herausgegeben von der Deutschen Zoologischen Gesellschaft*. 9. Lieferung. Aves: Trochilidae. R. Friedlander und Sohn, Berlin.

Hartert, E. 1901. [Descriptions of some new South American birds]. *Bull. Brit. Orn. Club* 11: 37–40.

Haverschmidt, F., & G.F. Mees. 1994. *Birds of Suriname*. VACO Press, Paramaribo.

Hayes, F.E. 2001. Geographic variation, hybridization, and the leapfrog pattern of evolution in the Suiriri Flycatcher (*Suiriri suiriri*) complex. *Auk* 118: 457–471.

Hayes, F.E. 2004. Variability and interbreeding of Sandwich Terns and Cayenne Terns in the Virgin Islands, with comments on their systematic relationship. *North Amer. Birds* 57: 566–572.

Hayes, F.E., & M. Kenefick. 2002. First record of Black-tailed Godwit *Limosa limosa* for South America. *Cotinga* 17: 20–22.

Hayes, F.E., & G.L. White. 2001. Status of the Little Egret (*Egretta garzetta*) in Trinidad and Tobago. *Pitirre* 14: 54–58.

Hayes, F.E., G.L. White, M.D. Frost, B. Sanasie, H. Kilpatrick, & E.B. Massiah. 2002. First records of Kelp Gull *Larus dominicanus* for Trinidad and Barbados. *Cotinga* 18: 85–88

Hayes, F.E., G.L. White, M. Kenefick, & H. Kilpatrick. 2002. Status of the Lesser Black-backed Gull *Larus* [*fuscus*] *graellsii* in Trinidad and Tobago. *Atlantic Seabirds* 4: 91–100.

Hayman, P., J. Marchant & T. Prater. 1986. *Shorebirds: An Identification Guide.* Croom Helm, Beckenham.

Heidrich, P., C. König & M. Wink. 1995. Bioakustik, Taxonomie ind molkulare Systematik americanischer Sperlingskäuze (Strigidae: *Glaucidium* spp.). *Stuttgarter Beiträge Naturkunde*, ser. A. 534: 1-47.

Hekstra, G.P. 1982. "I don't give a hoot…": a revision of the American Screech Owls (*Otus*, Strigidae). Dissertation. Univ. of Amsterdam, Amsterdam.

Hekstra, G.P. 1982. Description of 24 new subspecies of American *Otus* (Aves, Strigidae). *Bull. Zoöl. Mus. Univ. Amsterdam* 9: 49–63.

Hellmayr, C.E. 1925. Catalogue of birds of the Americas and the adjacent islands in Field Museum of Natural History, part IV. *Field Mus. Nat. Hist. Zool. Ser. XIII*, 234: 1–390.

Hellmayr, C.E. 1927. Catalogue of birds of the Americas and the adjacent islands in Field Museum of Natural History, part V. *Field Mus. Nat. Hist. Zool. Ser. XIII*, 242: 1–517.

Hellmayr, C.E. 1929. Catalogue of birds of the Americas and the adjacent islands in Field Museum of Natural History, part VI. *Field Mus. Nat. Hist. Zool. Ser. XIII*, 266: 1–258.

Hellmayr, C.E. 1934. Catalogue of birds of the Americas and the adjacent islands in Field Museum of Natural History, part VII. *Field Mus. Nat. Hist. Zool. Ser. XIII*, 330: 1–531.

Hellmayr, C.E. 1935. Catalogue of birds of the Americas and the adjacent islands in Field Museum of Natural History, part VIII. *Field Mus. Nat. Hist. Zool. Ser. XIII*, 347: 1–541.

Hellmayr, C.E. 1936. Catalogue of birds of the Americas and the adjacent islands in Field Museum of Natural History, part IX. *Field Mus. Nat. Hist. Zool. Ser. XIII*, 365: 1–458.

Hellmayr, C.E. 1937. Catalogue of birds of the Americas and the adjacent islands in Field Museum of Natural History, part X. *Field Mus. Nat. Hist. Zool. Ser. XIII*, 381: 1–228.

Hellmayr, C.E. 1938. Catalogue of birds of the Americas and the adjacent islands in Field Museum of Natural History, part XI. *Field Mus. Nat. Hist. Zool. Ser. XIII*, 430: 1–662.

Hellmayr, C.E., & B. Conover. 1942. Catalogue of birds of the Americas and adjacent islands in Field Museum of Natural History, part I(1). *Field Mus. Nat. Hist. Zool. Ser. XIII*, 514: 1–636.

Hellmayr, C.E., & B. Conover. 1948. Catalogue of birds of the Americas and adjacent islands in Field Museum of Natural History, part I(2). *Field Mus. Nat. Hist. Zool. Ser. XIII*, 615: 1–434.

Hellmayr, C.E., & B. Conover. 1948. Catalogue of birds of the Americas and adjacent islands in Field Museum of Natural History, part I(3). *Field Mus. Nat. Hist. Zool. Ser. XIII*, 616: 1–383.

Hellmayr, C.E., & B. Conover. 1949. Catalogue of birds of the Americas and adjacent islands in Field Museum of Natural History, part I(4). *Field Mus. Nat. Hist. Zool. Ser. XIII*, 634: 1–358.

Henry, P.-Y. 2005. New distributional records of birds from Andean and western Ecuador. *Cotinga* 25: 27–32.

Herklotz, G.A.C. 1961. *The Birds of Trinidad & Tobago*. Collins, London.

Hernández-Camacho J.I., & H. Romero. 1978. Descripción de una nueva subespecie de *Momotus momota* para Colombia. *Caldasia* 12: 353–358.

Hernández-Camacho, J.I., & J.V. Rodríguez. 1979. Dos nuevos taxa del género *Grallaria* (Aves: Formicariidae) del alto valle del Magdalena (Colombia). *Caldasia* 12: 573–580.

Heynen, I. 1999. Genus *Heliangelus*, family Trochilidae (hummingbirds). Pp. 595–605 *in* del Hoyo, J., A. Elliott, & J. Sargatal (eds.) *Handbook of the Birds of the World*, vol. 5. Lynx Edicions, Barcelona.

Hilty, S. 1994. *Birds of Tropical America*. Chapters Publishing Ltd., Shelburne.

Hilty, S. 1999. Three bird species new to Venezuela, and notes on the behaviour and distribution of other poorly known species. *Bull. Brit. Orn. Club* 119: 220–235.

Hilty, S. 2003. *Birds of Venezuela*. Second edn. Princeton University Press, Princeton.

Hilty, S.L., & W.L. Brown 1986. *A Guide to the Birds of Colombia*. Princeton University Press, Princeton.

Hilty, S., T.A. Parker & J. Silliman. 1979. Observations on Plush-capped Finches in the Andes with a description of the juvenile and immature plumages. *Wilson Bull.* 91: 145–148.

Hinkelmann, C. 1988a. Comments on recently described new

species of hermit hummingbirds. *Bull. Brit. Orn. Club* 108: 159–169.

Hinkelmann, C. 1996. Systematics and geographic variation in long-tailed hermit hummingbirds, the *Phaetornis superciliosus–malaris–longirostris* species group (Trochilidae), with notes on their biogeography. *Orn. Neotrop.* 7: 119–148.

Hinkelmann, C. 1999. Genera *Ramphodon, Eutoxeres, Glaucis, Threnetes, Anopetia* and *Phaethornis*, family Trochilidae (Hummingbirds). Pp. 537–547 *in* del Hoyo, J., A. Elliott, & J. Sargatal (eds.) *Handbook of the Birds of the World*, vol. 5. Lynx Edicions, Barcelona.

Hinkelmann, C., & K.-L. Schuchmann. 1997. Phylogeny of the hermit hummingbirds (Trochilidae: Phaethornithinae). *Stud. Neotrop. Fauna & Environ.* 32: 142–163.

Hockey, P. 1996. Family Haematopodidae (oystercatchers). Pp. 308–325 *in* del Hoyo, J., A. Elliott, & J. Sargatal (eds.) *Handbook of the Birds of the World*, vol. 3. Lynx Edicions, Barcelona.

Houston, D.C. 1994. Family Cathartidae (New World vultures). Pp. 24–41 *in* del Hoyo, J., A. Elliott, & J. Sargatal (eds.) *Handbook of the Birds of the World*, vol. 2. Lynx Edicions, Barcelona.

Houston, D.C. 2001. *Condors and Vultures.* Voyager Press, Stillwater.

Howell, S.N.G. 1994. The specific status of Black-faced Antthrushes in Middle America. *Cotinga* 1: 20–25.

Howell, S.N.G. 2002. Additional information on the birds of Ecuador. *Cotinga* 18: 62–65.

Howell, S.N.G., & A. Whittaker. 1995. Field identification of Orange-breasted and Bat Falcons. *Cotinga* 4: 36–43.

Howell, S.N.G., & M.B. Robbins. 1995. Species limits of the Least Pygmy-Owl (*Glaucidium minutissimum*) complex. *Wilson Bull.* 107: 7–25.

Howell, S.N.G., & S. Webb. 1995. *A Guide to the Birds of Mexico and Northern Central America.* Oxford University Press, Oxford.

del Hoyo. 1992. Family Phoenicopteridae (flamingos). Pp. 508–526 *in* del Hoyo, J., A. Elliott, & J. Sargatal (eds.) *Handbook of Birds of the World*, vol. 1. Lynx Edicions, Barcelona.

del Hoyo, J. 1994. Family Cracidae (chachalacas, guans and curassows). Pp. 310–363 *in* del Hoyo, J., A. Elliott, & J. Sargatal (eds.) *Handbook of the Birds of the World*, vol. 2. Lynx Edicions, Barcelona.

Hu, D., L. Joseph & D.J. Agro. 2000. Distribution, variation, and taxonomy of *Topaza* hummingbirds (Aves: Trochilidae). *Orn. Neotrop.* 11: 123–142.

Hudson, R. 1985. Button quails and other relatives. Pp. 156–157 *in* Perrins, C.M., & A.L.A. Middleton (eds.) *The Encyclopaedia of Birds.* Allen & Unwin, London.

Hughes, J.M., & A.J. Baker. 1999. Phylogenetic relationships of the enigmatic Hoatzin (*Opisthocomus hoazin*) resolved using mitochondrial and nuclear gene sequences. *Mol. Biol. Evol.* 16: 1300–1307.

Hume, R.A. 1996. Family Burhinidae (thick-knees). Pp. 348–363 *in* del Hoyo, J., A. Elliott, & J. Sargatal (eds.) *Handbook of the Birds of the World*, vol. 3. Lynx Edicions, Barcelona.

Irestedt, M., J. Fjeldså, & P.G.P. Ericson. 2004. Phylogenetic relationships of woodcreepers (Aves: Dendrocolaptinae) – incongruence between molecular and morphological data. *J. Avian Biol.* 35: 280–288.

Irestedt, M., J. Fjeldså, U.S. Johansson & P.G.P. Ericson. 2002. Systematic relationships and biogeography of the tracheophone suboscines (Aves: Passeriformes). *Mol. Phyl. & Evol.* 23: 499–512.

Irestedt, M., U.S. Johansson, T. Parsons & P.G.P. Ericson. 2001. Phylogeny of major lineages of suboscines (Passeriformes) analysed by nuclear DNA sequence data. *J. Avian Biol.* 32: 15–25.

Irestedt, M., J.I. Ohlson, D. Zuccon, M. Källersjö & P.G.P. Ericson. 2006. Nuclear DNA from old collections of avian study skins reveals evolutionary history of the Old World suboscines (Aves, Passeriformes). *Zoologica Scripta.*

Isler, M.L. 1997. A sector-based ornithological geographic information system for the Neotropics. Pp. 345–354 *in* Remsen, J.V. (ed.) Studies in Neotropical ornithology honoring Ted Parker. *Orn. Monogr.* 48.

Isler, M.L., J. Álvarez-Alonso, P.R. Isler, T. Valqui, A. Begazo, & B.M. Whitney. 2002. Rediscovery of a cryptic species and description of a new species in the *Myrmeciza hemimelaena* complex (Thamnophilidae) of the Neotropics. *Auk* 119: 362–378.

Isler, M.L., J. Álvarez-Alonso, P.R. Isler, & B.M. Whitney. 2001. A new species of *Percnostola* antbird (Passeriformes: Thamnophilidae) from Amazonian Peru, and an analysis of species limits within *Percnostola rufifrons. Wilson Bull.* 113: 164–176.

Isler, M.L., & P.R. Isler. 1987. *The Tanagers: Natural History, Distribution and Identification.* Smithsonian Institution Press, Washington, D.C.

Isler, M.L., P.R. Isler, & R.T. Brumfield. 2005. Clinal variation in vocalizations of an antbird (Thamnophilidae) and implications for defining species limits. *Auk* 122: 433–444.

Isler, M.L., & P.R. Isler. 2003. Species limits in the Pygmy Antwren (*Myrmotherula brachyura*) complex (Aves: Passeriformes: Thamnophilidae). Part 1. The taxonomic status of *Myrmotherula brachyura ignota. Proc. Biol. Soc. Wash.* 116: 23–28.

Isler, M.L., P.R. Isler, & B.M. Whitney. 1997. Biogeography and systematics of the *Thamnophilus punctatus* (Thamnophilidae) complex. Pp: 355–381 *in* Remsen, J.V. (ed.) Studies in Neotropical ornithology honoring Ted Parker. *Orn. Monogr.* 48.

Isler, M.L., P.R. Isler, & B.M. Whitney. 1998. Use of vocalizations to establish species limits in antbirds (Passeriformes: Thamnophilidae). *Auk* 115: 577–590.

Isler, M.L., P.R. Isler, & B.M. Whitney. 1999. Species limits in antbirds: the *Myrmotherula surinamensis* complex. *Auk* 116: 83–96.

Isler, M.L., P.R. Isler, B.M. Whitney, & B. Walker. 2001. Species limits in antbirds: the *Thamnophilus punctatus* complex continued. *Condor* 103: 278–286.

Jahn, O., M.B. Robbins, P. Valenzuela, P. Coopmans, R.S. Ridgely & K.-L. Schuchmann. 2000. Status, ecology, and vocalizations of Five-coloured Barbet *Capito quinticolor*, in Ecuador, with notes on the Orange-fronted Barbet *C. squamulatus. Bull. Brit. Orn. Club* 120: 16–22.

Jahn, O., B. Palacios & P.M. Valenzuela. Ecology, population and conservation status of the Chocó Vireo *Vireo masteri*, a species new to Ecuador. (In press) *Bull. Brit. Orn. Club.* 127.

James, C., & C. Hislop. 1988. Status and conservation of two cracid species – the Trinidad Piping Guan (*Pipile pipile*) and the Cocrico (*Ortalis ruficauda*) in Trinidad & Tobago. *Proc. II Intern. Cracid Symp., Caracas, March 1988.*

Jaramillo, A. 2003. *Birds of Chile.* Christopher Helm, London.

Jaramillo, A., & P. Burke. 1999. *New World Blackbirds: The Icterids*. Christopher Helm, London.

Jenni, D.A. 1996. Family Jacanidae (jacanas). Pp. 276–291 *in* del Hoyo, J., A. Elliott, & J. Sargatal (eds.) *Handbook of the Birds of the World*, vol. 3. Lynx Edicions, Barcelona.

Johnsgard, P.A. 1981. *The Plovers, Sandpipers, and Snipes of the World*. University of Nebraska Press, Lincoln.

Johnsgard, P.A. 1988. *The Quails, Partridges and Francolins of the World*. Oxford University Press, Oxford.

Johnsgard, P.A. 1993. *Cormorants, Darters and Pelicans of the World*. Smithsonian Inst. Press, Washington, D.C.

Johnsgard, P.A., & M. Carbonell. 1996. *Ruddy Ducks and Other Stifftails: Their Behavior and Biology*. University of Oklahoma Press, Norman.

Johnson, N.K., & R.M. Zink 1985. Genetic evidence for relationships in the avian family Vireonidae. *Condor* 90: 428–445.

Johnson, N.K., R.M. Zink & J.A. Maarten 1988. Genetic evidence for relationships among the Red-eyed, Yellow-green, and Chivi Vireos. *Wilson Bull.* 97: 421–435.

Johnson, K.P., & M.D. Sorensen. 1999. Phylogeny and biogeography of dabbling ducks (genus *Anas*): a comparison of molecular and morphological evidence. *Auk* 116: 792–805.

Jones, H.L. 2003. *Birds of Belize.* Univ. of Texas Press, Austin.

Joseph, L. 1992. Notes on the distribution and natural history of the Sun Parakeet *Aratinga solstitialis*. *Orn. Neotrop.* 3: 17–26.

Joseph, L. 1996. Preliminary climatic overview of migration patterns in South American austral migrant passerines. *Ecotropica* 2: 185–193.

Joseph, L. 2000. Beginning an end to 63 years of uncertainty: the Neotropical parakeets known as *Pyrrhura picta* and *P. leucotis* comprise more than two species. *Proc. Acad. Nat. Sci. Phil.* 150: 279–292.

Joseph, L. 2002. Geographical variation, taxonomy and distribution of some Amazonian *Pyrrhura* parakeets. *Orn. Neotrop.* 13: 337–363.

Joseph, L. & D.R.B. Stockwell. 2002. Climatic modeling of the distribution of some *Pyrrhura* parakeets of northwestern South America with notes on their systematics and special reference to *Pyrrhura caniceps* Todd, 1947. *Orn. Neotrop.* 13: 1-8.

de Juana, E., F. Suarez, & P.G. Ryan. 2004. Family Alaudidae (larks). Pp. 496–601 *in* del Hoyo, J., A. Elliott, & D.A. Christie (eds.) *Handbook of the Birds of the World*, vol. 9. Lynx Edicions, Barcelona.

Junge, G.C.A. & G.F. Mees. 1958. The Avifauna of Trinidad & Tobago. *Zool. Verh.* 37: 1-172.

Juniper, T., & M. Parr 1998. *Parrots: A Guide to the Parrots of the World*. Pica Press, Robertsbridge.

Kear, J. (ed). 2005. *The Ducks, Geese and Swans.* Oxford Univ. Press, Oxford.

Kenefick, M. 2004. Verification of rare bird records from Trinidad & Tobago. *Cotinga* 22: 101–103.

Kennedy, M. & R.D.M. Page, 2002. Seabird Supertrees combining partial estimates of procellariiform phylogeny. *Auk* 119: 88-108.

Kirwan, G.M., & T. Marlow. 1996. A review of avifaunal records from Mindo, Pichincha province, north-western Ecuador. *Cotinga* 6: 47–57.

Kirwan, G.M., & C.J. Sharpe. 1999. Range extensions and notes on the status of little-known species from Venezuela. *Bull. Brit. Orn. Club* 119: 38–47.

Klein, N., K. Burns, S.J. Hackett, & C. Griffith. 2004. Molecular phylogenetic relationships among the wood warblers (Parulidae) and historical biogeography in the Caribbean basin. *J. Carib. Orn.* 17: 3–17.

Klein, N.K., & W.M. Brown. 1994. Intraspecific molecular phylogeny in the Yellow Warbler (*Dendroica petechia*) and implications for avian biogeography in the West Indies. *Evolution* 48: 1914–1932.

Kleinschmidt, O. 1943. *Katalog meiner ornithologischen Sammlung.* Germany.

Klicka, J., K.P. Johnson, & S.M. Lanyon. 2000. New World nine-primaried oscine relationships: constructing a mitochondrial DNA framework. *Auk* 117: 321–336.

Koepcke, M. 1964. *Las Aves del Departamento de Lima*. Ed. Gráfica Morsom, Lima.

Koepcke, M. 1970. *The Birds of the Department of Lima*. Livingston Publishing, Wynnewood.

König, C. 1991. Zur Taxonomie und Ökologie der Sperlingskäuze (*Glaucidium* spp.) des Andenraumes. *Ökol. Vögel* 13: 15–76.

König, C. 1994. Lautäuberungen als interspezifische Isolationmechanismen bei Eulen der Gattung *Otus* aus dem südlichen Südamerika. *Stuttgarter Beitr. Naturk. Ser. A* 511: 1–35.

König, C., & R. Straneck. 1989. Eine neue Eule (Aves: Strigidae) aus Nordargentinien. *Stuttgarter Beitr. Naturk. Ser. A* 428: 1–20.

König, C., F. Weick & J.H. Becking. 1999. *Owls*. Pica Press, Sussex.

Krabbe, N. 1992a. A new subspecies of the Slender-billed Miner *Geositta tenuirostris* (Furnariidae) from Ecuador. *Bull. Brit. Orn. Club* 112: 166–169.

Krabbe, N. 1992b. Notes on distribution and natural history of some poorly-known Ecuadorean birds. *Bull. Brit. Orn. Club* 112: 169–174.

Krabbe, N. 2000. Rediscovery of *Asthenes wyatti azuay* (Chapman 1923) with notes on its plumage variation and taxonomy of the *Asthenes anthoides* superspecies. *Bull. Brit. Orn. Club* 120: 149–153.

Krabbe, N. 2004. A record of Pale-legged Hornero *Furnarius leucopus* from Ecuador. *Bull. Brit. Orn. Club* 124: 226–227.

Krabbe, N., D.J. Agro, N.H. Rice, M. Jácome, L. Navarrete & F. Sornoza. 1999. A new species of antpitta (Formicariidae: *Grallaria*) from the southern Ecuadorian Andes. *Auk* 116: 882–890.

Krabbe, N., & P. Coopmans. 2000. Rediscovery of *Grallaria alleni* (Formicariidae) with notes on its range, song and identification. *Ibis* 142: 183–187.

Krabbe, N., G. DeSmet, P. Greenfield, M. Jácome, J.C. Matheus, & F. Sornoza. 1994. Giant Antpitta *Grallaria gigantea*. *Cotinga* 2: 32–34.

Krabbe, N., P. Flórez, G. Suárez, J. Castaño, J. Arango, P.C. Pulgarín, W. Muñera, F.G. Stiles, & P.G.W. Salaman. 2005. Rediscovery of the Dusky Starfrontlet *Coeligena orina*, with a description of the adult plumages and re-assessment of its taxonomic status. *Orn. Colombiana* 3: 28–35.

Krabbe, N., M.L. Isler, P.R. Isler, B.M. Whitney, J. Álvarez-Alonso, & P.J. Greenfield 1999. A new species in the *Myrmotherula haematonota* superspecies (Aves: Thamnophilidae) from the western Amazonian lowlands of Ecuador and Peru. *Wilson Bull.* 111: 157–165.

Krabbe, N., & J. Palacios. 1999. Range extensions of Bicolored Antvireo *Dysithamnus occidentalis* in Ecuador. *Cotinga* 11: 48.

Krabbe, N., & T.S. Schulenberg. 1997. Species limits and natural history of *Scytalopus* tapaculos (Rhinocryptidae), with descriptions of the Ecuadorian taxa, including three new species. Pp: 47–88 *in* Remsen, J.V. (ed.) Studies in Neotropical ornithology honoring Ted Parker. *Orn. Monogr*. 48.

Krabbe, N., & T.S. Schulenberg. 2003a. Family Formicariidae (ground antbirds). Pp. 682–731 *in* del Hoyo, J., A. Elliott, & D.A. Christie (eds.) *Handbook of the Birds of the World*, vol. 8. Lynx Edicions, Barcelona.

Krabbe, N., & T.S. Schulenberg. 2003b. Family Rhinocryptidae (tapaculos). Pp. 748–787 *in* del Hoyo, J., A. Elliott, & D.A. Christie (eds.) *Handbook of the Birds of the World*, vol. 8. Lynx Edicions, Barcelona.

Krabbe, N., & T.S. Schulenberg. 2005. A mystery solved: the identity and distribution of Kalinowski's Tinamou *Nothoprocta kalinowskii*. *Bull. Brit. Orn. Club* 125: 253–260.

Krabbe, N., P.G.W. Salaman, A. Cortés, A. Quevedo, L. Ortega, & C.D. Cadena. 2005. A new species of *Scytalopus* tapaculo from the Upper Magdalena Valley, Colombia. *Bull. Brit. Orn. Club* 125: 3–18.

Krabbe, N., & F. Sornoza. 1994. Avifaunistic results of a subtropical camp in the Cordillera del Condor, southeastern Ecuador. *Bull. Brit. Orn. Club* 114: 55–61.

Kratter, A.W. 1993. Geographic variation in the Yellow-billed Cacique (*Amblycercus holosericeus*), a partial bamboo specialist. *Condor* 95: 641–651.

Kratter, A.W. 1997. Bamboo specialization by Amazonian birds. *Biotropica* 29: 100–110.

Kratter, A.W., & T.A. Parker. 1997. Relationship of two bamboo-specialized foliage-gleaners: *Automolus dorsalis* and *Anabazenops fuscus* (Furnariidae). Pp. 383–397 *in* Remsen, J.V. (ed.) Studies in Neotropical ornithology honoring Ted Parker. *Orn. Monogr*. 48.

Kroodsma, D.E., & D. Brewer. 2005. Family Troglodytidae (wrens). Pp. 356–447 *in* del Hoyo, J., A. Elliott, & D.A. Christie (eds.), *Handbook of the Birds of the World*, vol. 10. Lynx Edicions, Barcelona.

Kushlan, J.A., & J.A. Hancock. 2005. *The Herons*. Oxford University Press, Oxford.

Lack, D. 1956. A review of the genera and nesting habits of the swifts. *Auk* 73: 1–32.

Lane, D.F. 1999. A phylogenetic analysis of the American barbets using plumage and vocal characters (Aves: Family Ramphastidae; Subfamily Capitonidae). MSc thesis. Louisiana State University, Baton Rouge.

Lanyon, S.M. 1985. Molecular perspective on higher-level relationships in the Tyrannoidea (Aves). *Syst. Zool*. 34: 404–418.

Lanyon, S.M., & R.M. Zink. 1987. Genetic variation in Piciform birds: monophyly and genetic and familial relationships. *Auk* 104: 724–732.

Lanyon S.M., & W.E. Lanyon. 1989. The systematic position of the plantcutters, *Phytotoma*. *Auk* 106: 422–432.

Lanyon, W.E. 1978. Revision of the *Myiarchus* flycatchers of South America. *Bull. Amer. Mus. Nat. Hist*. 161: 427–627.

Lanyon, W.E. 1984. A phylogeny of the kingbirds and their allies. *Amer. Mus. Novit*. 2797: 1–28.

Lanyon, W.E. 1985. A phylogeny of the Myiarchine flycatchers. Pp. 361–380 *in* Buckley, P.A., M.S. Foster, E.S. Morton, R.S. Ridgely & F.G. Buckley (eds.) 1985. Neotropical ornithology. *Orn. Monogr*. 36.

Lanyon, W.E. 1986. A phylogeny of the thirty-three genera in the *Empidonax* assemblage of tyrant flycatchers. *Amer. Mus. Novit*. 2846: 1–64.

Lanyon, W.E. 1988a. A phylogeny of the thirty-two genera in the *Elaenia* assemblage of tyrant flycatchers. *Amer. Mus. Novit*. 2914: 1–64.

Lanyon, W.E. 1988b. The phylogenetic affinities of the flycatcher genera *Myiobius* Darwin and *Terenotriccus* Ridgway. *Amer. Mus. Novit*. 2915: 1–11.

Lanyon, W.E. 1988c. A phylogeny of the flatbill and tody-tyrant assemblage of tyrant flycatchers. *Amer. Mus. Novit*. 2923: 1–41.

Lanyon, W.E., & J.W. Fitzpatrick. 1983. Behavior, morphology, and systematics of *Sirystes sibilator* (Tyrannidae). *Auk* 100: 98–104.

Lanyon, W.E., & C.H. Fry. 1973. Range and affinity of the Pale-bellied Mourner (*Rhytipterna immunda*). *Auk* 90: 672–674.

Lanyon, W.E., & S.M. Lanyon. 1986. Generic status of Euler's Flycatcher: a morphological and biochemical study. *Auk* 103: 341–350.

Leeuwen van, M., & C. Hoogeland. The first Pale-winged Trumpeter *Psophia leucoptera* in Colombia. *Cotinga* 21: 76–77, 85.

Leger, D., & D. Mountjoy. 2003. Geographic variation in song of the Bright-rumped Attila (Tyrannidae: *Attila spadiceus*): implications for species status. *Auk* 120: 69–74.

Lentino, M. 1988. *Notiochelidon flavipes*, a swallow new to Venezuela. *Bull. Brit. Orn. Club* 108: 70–71.

Lentino, M. 1994. Suplemento. Pp. 487–497 *in* Phelps Jr., W.H., & R. Meyer de Schauensee. *Una Guia de las Aves de Venezuela*. Ed. Ex Libris, Caracas.

Lentino, M. 1997. Lista actualizada de las aves de Venezuela. Pp: 145–202 *in* La Marca, E. (ed.) *Vertebrados actuales y fósiles de Venezuela*. Mus. de Cienc. y Tec. de Mérida, Mérida.

Lentino, M., F. Bisbal, B. Ospino & R. Rivero. 1984. Nuevos registros y extensiones de distribución para especies de aves en Venezuela. *Bol. Soc. Venez. Cienc. Nat*. 39: 111–119.

Lentino, M., & R. Restall. 2003. A new species of *Amaurospiza* blue seedeater from Venezuela. *Auk* 120: 600–606.

Lentino, M., & C. Rodner. 2002. Los Roques: una muestra de la riqueza de nuestra avifauna insular. Pp. 143–165 *in* Zamarro, J. (ed.) *Guía del Parque Nacional Archipiélago Los Roques*. Agencia de Cooperación Española y Embajada de España en Venezuela, Caracas.

Lesson. 1829. Hist. Nat. Colibris, Suppl. Hist. Nat. Ois.-Mouches.

Lesterhuis, A.J., & R.P. Clay. 2003. The first record of Dunlin (*Calidris alpina*) in Paraguay and a summary of South American records of the species. *Hornero* 18: 65–67.

Leveque, R. 1964. Notes on Ecuadorian birds. *Ibis* 106: 52–62.

Lever, C. 1987. *Naturalized Birds of the World*. Longman, Harlow.

Ligon, J. 1967. Relationships of the Cathartid vultures. *Occ. Pap. Mus. Zool. Univ. Mich*. 651: 1–26.

Livezey, B.C. 1986. A phylogenetic analysis of recent Anseriform genera using morphological characters. *Auk* 103: 737–754.

Livezey, B.C. 1991. A phylogenetic analysis and classification of recent dabbling ducks (Tribe Anatini) based on comparative morphology. *Auk* 108: 471–517.

Livezey, B.C. 1995. Phylogeny and comparative ecology of stiff-tailed ducks (Anatidae, Oxyurini). *Wilson Bull.* 107: 214–234.

Livezey, B.C. 1997. A phylogenetic classification of waterfowl (Aves: Anseriformes), including selected fossil species. *Ann. Carnegie Mus.* 66: 457–496.

Llimona, F., & J. del Hoyo. 1992. Family Podicipedidae (grebes). Pp: 174–196 *in* del Hoyo, J., A. Elliott, & J. Sargatal (eds.) *Handbook of the Birds of the World*, vol. 1. Lynx Edicions, Barcelona.

Loaiza, J.M., F.A. Sornoza, A.E. Agreda, J. Aguirre, R. Ramos, & C. Canaday. 2005. The presence of Wavy-breasted Parakeet *Pyrrhura peruviana* confirmed for Ecuador. *Cotinga* 23: 37–38.

Lock, L., R.S.R. Williams, I. Olmedo, & I. Munoz. 2003. An unusual altitudinal record of White-cheeked Pintail *Anas bahamensis* in Ecuador. *Cotinga* 19: 79.

Londoño, G.A. & C.D. Cadena. 2003. The nest and eggs of the Cinereous Mourner (*Laniocera hypopyrra*). *Wilson Bull.* 115: 115-118.

Low, R. 2005. *Amazon Parrots: Aviculture, Trade, and Conservation.* Dona Publishing, Czech Republic.

Lowery G.H., & D.A. Tallman. 1976. A new genus and subspecies of nine-primaried oscine of uncertain affinities from Peru. *Auk* 93: 415–428.

Lowery, G.H. & J.P. O'Neill. 1969. A new species of antpitta from Peru and a revision of the subfamily Grallariinae. *Auk* 86: 1–12.

Mader, W.J. 1979. First nest description for the genus *Micrastur* (forest falcons). *Condor* 81: 320.

Madge, S., & H. Burn. 1988. *Waterfowl: An Identification Guide to the Ducks, Geese and Swans of the World.* Houghton Mifflin Co., Boston.

Madge, S., & H. Burn. 1993. *Crows and Jays: A Guide to the Crows, Jays and Magpies of the World.* Helm Information, Robertsbridge.

Madge, S., & P. McGowan. 2002. *Pheasants, Partridges, and Grouse: A Guide to the Pheasants, Partridges, Quails, Grouse, Guineafowl, Buttonquails and Sandgrouse of the World.* Christopher Helm, London.

Mann, N.I. 2006. Molecular data delineate four genera of *Thryothorus* wrens. *Mol. Phylogen. Evol.*

Mansell, W. & G. Low. 1980. *North American Birds of Prey.* Morrow, New York.

Marantz, C.A. 1997. Geographic variation of plumage patterns in the woodcreeper genus *Dendrocolaptes* (Dendrocolaptidae) in South America. Pp. 399–429 *in* Remsen, J.V. (ed.) Studies in Neotropical ornithology honoring Ted Parker. *Orn. Monogr.* 48.

Marantz, C.A., A. Aleixo, R.L. Bevier & M.A. Patten. 2003. Family Dendrocolaptidae (woodcreepers). Pp. 358–447 *in* del Hoyo, J., A. Elliott, & D.A. Christie (eds.) *Handbook of the Birds of the World*, vol. 8. Lynx Edicions, Barcelona.

Marantz, C.A., & J.V. Remsen. 1991. Seasonal distribution of the Slaty Elaenia, a little-known austral migrant of South America. *J. Field Orn.* 62: 162–172.

Marchant, S. 1960. The breeding of some southwestern Ecuadorian birds. *Ibis* 102: 349–382, 584–599.

Marín, M. 1993. Patterns of distribution of swifts in the Andes of Ecuador. *Avocetta* 17: 117–123.

Marín, M. 1997. Species limits and distribution of some New World spine-tailed swifts (Chaetura spp.). Pp. 431–443 *in* Remsen, J.V. (ed.) Studies in Neotropical ornithology honoring Ted Parker. *Orn. Monogr.* 48.

Marín, M. 2000. Species limits, distribution, and biogeography of some New World grey-rumped, spine-tailed swifts (*Chaetura*, Apodidae). *Orn. Neotrop.* 11: 93–107.

Marín, M., & B.J. Carrión. 1994. Additional notes on nests and eggs of some Ecuadorian birds. *Orn. Neotrop.* 5: 121–124.

Marín, M., B.J. Carrión, & F.C. Sibley. 1992. New distributional records for Ecuadorian birds. *Orn. Neotrop.* 3: 27–34.

Marín, M., & F.G. Stiles. 1993. Notes on the biology of the Spot-fronted Swift (Cypseloides cherriei). *Condor* 95: 479–483.

Marinkelle, C.J. 1970. Birds of the Serranía de Macuira, Guajira Peninsula, Colombia. *Mitt. Inst. Colombo-Alemán Investig. Cient.* 4: 15–34.

Marks, J.S., R.J. Cannings, & H. Mikkola. 1999. Family Strigidae (typical owls). Pp. 76–242 *in* del Hoyo, J., A. Elliott, & J. Sargatal (eds.) *Handbook of the Birds of the World*, vol. 5. Lynx Edicions, Barcelona.

Marshall, J.T., & B.F. King. 1988. Subfamily Striginae typical owls, genus *Otus*. *Proc. Western Found. Vert. Zool.* 3: 331–347.

Martin, P.R., R.C. Dobbs, H.F. Greeney, M. Doveston, & H. Creber. 2004. First record of Black-throated Blue Warbler *Dendroica caerulescens* for Ecuador. *Cotinga* 21: 60–62.

Martínez, I. 1992. Family Spheniscidae (penguins). Pp: 140–160 *in* del Hoyo, J., A. Elliott, & J. Sargatal (eds.) *Handbook of Birds of the World*, vol. 1. Lynx Edicions, Barcelona.

Martínez-Vilalta, A., & A. Motis. 1992. Family Ardeidae (herons). Pp: 376-429 *in* del Hoyo, J., A. Elliott, & J. Sargatal (eds.) *Handbook of Birds of the World*, vol. 1. Lynx Edicions, Barcelona.

Marturet de Monaldi, A., C. Rivero de Rodner, & E. Cordero de Nutt. 1994. *Los Tucusitos de Paria.* Fundación Thomas Merle & Fundación Proyecto Paria, Caracas.

Matheu, E. & J. del Hoyo. 1992. Family Threskionithidae (Ibises and Spoonbills). In del Hoyo, J. *et al.* 1992. *Handbook of the Birds of the World,* Vol. 1. Lynx Edicions, Barcelona.

Mayr, E. & D. Amadon. 1951. A classification of recent birds. *Amer. Mus. Novit.* 1496: 1-42.

Mayr, E., & G.W. Cottrell (eds.) 1986. *Check-list of Birds of the World*, vol. 11. Mus. Comp. Zool., Cambridge, Mass.

Mayr, E., & J.C. Greenway (eds.) 1960. *Check-list of Birds of the World*, vol. 9. Mus. Comp. Zool., Cambridge, Mass.

Mayr, E., & J.C. Greenway (eds.) 1962. *Check-list of Birds of the World*, vol. 15. Mus. Comp. Zool., Cambridge, Mass.

Mayr, E., & R.A. Paynter (eds.) 1964. *Check-list of Birds of the World*, vol. 10. Mus. Comp. Zool., Cambridge, Mass.

Mayr, E., & F. Vuilleumier. 1983. New species of birds described from 1966 to 1975. *J. Orn.* 124: 217–232.

Mazar Barnett, J., & G.M. Kirwan. 2004. Notes on the nest of the Striated Softtail (*Thripophaga macroura*) with comments on a nest of Plain Softtail (*T. fusciceps*) and relationships of the genus based on nest architecture. *Orn. Neotrop.* 15: 257–263.

McNeil, R., J.R. Rodriguez, & F. Mercier. 1985. Winter range expansion of the Long-billed Curlew (*Numenius americanus*) to South America. *Auk* 102: 174–175.

McNutt, W.J., D. Ellis, C. Peres G., T. Roundy, W. Vasina & C. White. 1980. Distribution and Status of the Peregrine Falcon in South America. Pp. 237–249 *in* Cade, T.J., J.H.

Enderson, C.G. Thelander, & C.M. White. *Peregrine Falcon Populations: Their Management and Recovery*. The Peregrine Fund, Boise.

Mees, G.F. 1974. Additions to the Avifauna of Suriname. *Zool. Meded., Leiden,* 48: 55-67.

Mena, P.V., & O. Jahn. 2003. First record of the Whistling Heron *Syrigma sibilatrix* for Ecuador. *Bull. Brit. Orn. Club* 123: 285–287.

Mercier, F., R. McNeil, & J. Rodríguez. 1987. First occurrence of Bar-tailed Godwit in South America, and status of the Marbled Godwit in northeastern Venezuela. *J. Field Orn.* 58: 78–80.

Meyer de Schauensee, R. 1948. The birds of the Republic of Colombia (part 1). *Caldasia* 5: 251–379.

Meyer de Schauensee, R. 1949. The birds of the Republic of Colombia (part 2). *Caldasia* 5: 381–644.

Meyer de Schauensee, R. 1950. The birds of the Republic of Colombia (part 3). *Caldasia* 5: 645–871.

Meyer de Schauensee, R. 1951. The birds of the Republic of Colombia (part 4). *Caldasia* 5: 873–1112.

Meyer de Schauensee, R. 1952. The birds of the Republic of Colombia (part 5). *Caldasia* 5: 1115–1214.

Meyer de Schauensee, R. 1966. *The Species of Birds of South America and Their Distribution.* Livingston Publishing, Narberth.

Meyer de Schauensee, R. 1967. *Eriocnemis mirabilis*, a new species of hummingbird from Colombia. *Notulae Naturae* 402: 1–2.

Meyer de Schauensee, R. 1970. A review of the South American finch *Oryzoborus crassirostris*. *Notulae Naturae* 428: 1–6.

Meyer de Schauensee, R. 1970. *A Guide to the Birds of South America.* Livingston Publishing, Wynnewood.

Meyer de Schauensee, R. 1982. *A Guide to the Birds of South America.* Second edn. Acad. Nat. Sci., Philadelphia.

Meyer de Schauensee, R., & W.H. Phelps, Jr. 1978. *A Guide to the Birds of Venezuela.* Princeton University Press, Princeton.

Mlodinow, S.G. 2004. First records of Little Egret, Green-winged Teal, Swallow-tailed Kite, Tennessee Warbler, and Red-breasted Blackbird from Aruba. *North Amer. Birds* 57: 559–661.

Mobley, J.A., & R.O. Prum 1995. Phylogenetic relationships of the Cinnamon Tyrant, *Neopipo cinnamomea*, to the tyrant flycatchers (Tyrannidae). *Condor* 97: 650–662.

Monroe, B.L., & M.R. Browning. 1992. A re-analysis of *Butorides*. *Bull. Brit. Orn. Club* 112: 81–85.

Monroe, B.L., & C.G. Sibley. 1993. *Checklist of Birds of the World.* Yale University Press, New Haven.

Morales, J.E. 1988. Confirmación de la presencia de *Spheniscus humboldtii* Meyen (Aves: Spheniscidae) para Colombia. *Caldasia* 16: 209–214.

Moreno, J., R. de Ayala, & L.G. Naranjo. 1999. Expansión del rango de la paloma coroniblanca *Columba leucocephala* al territorio continental de Colombia. *Caldasia* 21: 112–113.

Morony, J.J. 1985. Systematic relations of *Sericossypha albocristata* (Thraupinae). Pp. 382–389 *in* Buckley, P.A., M.S. Foster, E.S. Morton, R.S. Ridgely & F.G. Buckley (eds.) 1985. Neotropical ornithology. *Orn. Monogr.* 36.

Mountjoy, D.J. 2005. Family Bombycillidae (waxwings). Pp. 304–319 *in* del Hoyo, J., A. Elliott, & D.A. Christie (eds.) *Handbook of the Birds of the World*, vol. 10. Lynx Edicions, Barcelona.

Moynihan, M. 1966. Display patterns of Tropical American "Nine-primaried" songbirds. IV. The Yellow-rumped Tanager. *Smithsonian Misc. Coll.* 149, No. 5. Pp. 1-34.

Mullarney, K., L. Svensson, D. Zetterström, & P.J. Grant. 1999. *Birds of Europe*. Princeton, New Jersey.

Murphy, R.C. 1936. *Oceanic Birds of South America*. Amer. Mus. Nat. Hist., New York.

Murphy, W.L. 2002. Observations of pelagic seabirds wintering at sea in the southeastern Caribbean. Pp. 104–110 *in* Hayes, F.E., & S.A. Temple (eds.) *Studies in Trinidad & Tobago Ornithology Honouring Richard ffrench*. Occ. Paper 11. Dept. Life Sciences, University of the West Indies, St. Augustine.

Murphy, W.L., & W. Nanan. 1987. First confirmed record of Western Reef-Heron (*Egretta gularis*) for South America. *Amer. Birds* 41: 392–394.

Naranjo, L.G. 1991. Confirmación de la presencia de *Limnodromus scolopaceus* (Aves: Scolopacidae) en Colombia. *Trianea* 4: 559–561.

Navarrete, L. 2003. White-breasted Parakeet *Pyrrhura albipectus*: a new record for Peru. *Cotinga* 19: 79.

Navarrete, L., J.V. Moore, & R.A. Moore. 2002. Rediscovery of the Striated Antbird *Drymophila d. devillei* in Ecuador and several new elevational records. *Cotinga* 17: 53.

Navarrete, L., A. Swash, & G. Swash. 2003. The first confirmed record of Marañón Crescentchest *Melanopareia maranonica* for Ecuador. *Cotinga* 20: 100, 103.

Navarro, A.A., T. Peterson, E. Lopez-Medrano & H. Benítez-Díaz. 2001. Species limits in Mesoamerican *Aulacorhynchus* toucanets. *Wilson Bull.* 113: 363-494.

Navas, J.R., & N.A. Bo. 1982. La posicion taxonomica de Thripophaga sclateri y T. Punensis (Aves: Furnariidae). *Com. Mus. Argentino Cienc. Nat." Bernardino Rivadavia", Zool.* 4: 85–93.

Nelson, J.B. 1978. *The Sulidae – Gannets and Boobies*. Oxford Univ. Press, Oxford.

Nilsson, J., R. Jonsson, & N. Krabbe. 2001. First record of Bicoloured Antpitta *Grallaria rufocinerea* from Ecuador, with notes on the species' vocalisations. *Cotinga* 16: 105–106.

Norberg, R. Å. 1977. Occurrence and independent evolution of bilateral ear asymmetry in owls and implications on owl taxonomy. *Phil. Trans. Roy. Soc. London (ser.B)*. 280: 375-408.

Nørgaard-Olesen, E. 1974. *Tanagers*, vol. 2. Skibby Books, Skibby.

Norton, R.L. 1984. Cayenne × Sandwich terns nesting in Virgin Islands, Greater Antilles. *J. Field Orn.* 55: 243–246.

Nunn, G.B., J. Cooper, P. Jouventin, C.J.R. Robertson, & G.G. Robertson. 1996. Evolutionary relationships among extant albatrosses (Procellariiformes: Diomedeidae) established from complete cytochrome-*b* gene sequences. *Auk* 113: 784–801.

Ocampo, S. 2005. La Reinita Gorrinegra *Wilsonia pusilla* (Parulidae), nuevo registro para las Andes de Colombia. *Orn. Colombiana* 3: 74–75.

Olrog, C.C. 1968. *Las Aves Sudamericanas: Una Guia de Campo*. Fundación Instituto Miguel Lillo, Tucuman.

Olsen, K.M., & H. Larsson. 1995. *Terns of Europe and North America*. Christopher Helm, London.

Olsen, K.M., & H. Larsson. 1997. *Skuas and Jaegers: A*

Guide to the Skuas and Jaegers of the World. Pica Press, Robertsbridge.

Olsen, K.M., & H. Larsson. 2003. *Gulls of Europe, Asia, and North America*. Christopher Helm, London.

Olson, S.L. 1980a. Geographic variation in the Yellow Warblers (*Dendroica petechia*, Parulidae) of the Pacific coast of Middle America and South America. *Proc. Biol. Soc. Wash.* 93: 473–480.

Olson, S.L. 1980b. Revision of the Tawny-faced Antwren, *Microbates cinereiventris* (Aves: Passeriformes). *Proc. Biol. Soc. Wash.* 93: 68–74.

Olson, S.L. 1981a. A revision of the subspecies of *Sporophila* ("*Oryzoborus*") *angolensis* (Aves: Emberizinae). *Proc. Biol. Soc. Wash.* 94: 43–51.

Olson, S.L. 1981b. Systematic notes on certain oscines from Panama and adjacent areas (Aves: Passeriformes). *Proc. Biol. Soc. Wash.* 94: 363–373.

Olson, S.L. 1981c. Interaction between the two subspecies groups of the seed-finch *Sporophila angolensis* in the Magdalena Valley, Colombia. *Auk* 98: 379–383.

Olson, S.L. 1981d. A revision of the northern forms of *Euphonia xanthogaster*. *Proc. Biol. Soc. Wash.* 94: 101–106.

Olson, S.L. 1981e. The nature and variability in the Variable Seedeater of Panamá (*Sporophila americana*, Emberizinae). *Proc. Biol. Soc. Wash.* 94: 380–390.

Olson, S.L. 1983. Geographic variation in *Chlorospingus ophthalmicus* in Colombia and Venezuela (Aves: *Thraupidae)*. *Proc. Biol. Soc. Wash.* 96: 103–109.

Olson, S.L. 1995. The genera of owls in the Asioninae. *Bull. Brit. Orn. Club* 115: 35–39.

Olson, S.L. 2006. Reflections on the systematics of *Accipiter* and the genus for *Falco superciliosus* Linnaeus. *Bull. Brit. Orn. Club* 126: 69–70.

O'Neill, J.P. 1966. Notes on the distribution of *Conothraupis speculigera* (Gould). *Condor* 68: 598–600.

O'Neill, J.P., D.F. Lane, A.W. Kratter, A.P. Capparella, & C.F. Joo. 2000. A striking new species of Barbet (Capitonidae: *Capito*) from the Eastern Andes of Peru. *Auk* 117: 569–577.

O'Neill, J.P., & T.A. Parker. 1977. Taxonomy and range of *Pionus seniloides* in Peru. *Condor* 79: 274.

O'Neill, J.P., & T.A. Parker. 1981. New subspecies of *Pipreola riefferii* and *Chlorospingus ophthalmicus* from Peru. *Bull. Brit. Orn. Club* 101: 294–299.

O'Neill, J.P., & T.A. Parker. 1997. New subspecies of *Myrmoborus leucophrys* (Formicariidae) and *Phrygilus alaudinus* (Emberizidae) from the upper Huallaga Valley, Peru. Pp. 485–492 *in* Remsen, J.V. (ed.) Studies in Neotropical ornithology honoring Ted Parker. *Orn. Monogr.* 48.

Oren, D.C. 1985. Two new subspecies of birds from the canga vegetation, Serra dos Carajás, Pará, Brazil, and one from Venezuela. *Publ. Avul. Mus. Paraensis Emilio Goeldi* 40: 94–100.

Orians, G.H. 1985. *Blackbirds of the Americas*. University of Washington Press, Seattle.

Ormerod, S.J., & S.J. Tyler. 2005. Family Cinclidae (dippers). Pp. 332–355 *in* del Hoyo, J., A. Elliott & D. Christie, eds., *Handbook of the Birds of the World*, vol. 10. Lynx Edicions, Barcelona.

Orta, J. 1992a. Family Anhingidae (darters). Pp. 354–361 *in* del Hoyo, J., A. Elliott, & J. Sargatal (eds.) *Handbook of Birds of the World*, vol. 1. Lynx Edicions, Barcelona.

Orta, J. 1992b. Family Fregatidae (frigatebirds). Pp. 362–374 *in* del Hoyo, J., A. Elliott, & J. Sargatal (eds.) *Handbook of Birds of the World*, vol. 1. Lynx Edicions, Barcelona.

Orta, J. 1992c. Family Phaethontidae (tropicbirds). Pp. 280–289 *in* del Hoyo, J., A. Elliott, & J. Sargatal (eds.) *Handbook of Birds of the World*, vol. 1. Lynx Edicions, Barcelona.

Orta, J. 1992d. Family Phalacrocoracidae (cormorants). Pp. 326–353 *in* del Hoyo, J., A. Elliott, & J. Sargatal (eds.) *Handbook of Birds of the World*, vol. 1. Lynx Edicions, Barcelona.

Ortiz-Crespo, F., & J.M. Carrión. 1991. *Introducción a las Aves de Ecuador.* FECODES, Quito.

Ortiz-von Halle, B. 1990. Additions to the avifauna of Colombia: new species for Gorgona Island (Pacific Ocean). *Caldasia* 16: 209–214.

Ottema, O. 2002a. The occurrence of the Short-billed Honeycreeper *Cyanerpes nitidus* in Surinam. *Cotinga* 17: 78–79.

Ottema, O. 2002b. A possible population of Fasciated Tiger-heron *Tigrisoma fasciatum* on the upper Coppename, Surinam. *Cotinga* 18: 103.

Ottema, O. 2002c. Crimson Fruitcrow *Haematoderus militaris* feeding on *Cecropia sciadophylla*. *Cotinga* 18: 103–104.

Ottema, O. 2004a. First sight record of Alpine Swift *Tachymarptis melba* for South America, in French Guiana. *Cotinga* 21: 70–71.

Ottema, O. 2004b. Sight records of birds new to Suriname. *Cotinga* 22: 103–104.

Ottema, O., & F.C. Joe. in press. Records of three bird species new to Suriname. *Cotinga* 26.

Ouellet, H. 1992. Speciation, zoogeography and taxonomic problems in the Neotropical genus *Sporophila* (Aves: Emberizidae). *Bull. Brit. Orn Club* 112: 225–235.

Ouellet, H. 1993. Bicknell's Thrush: taxonomic status and distribution. *Wilson Bull.* 105: 545–572.

Pacheco, J.F., & B.M. Whitney. 2006. Mandatory changes to the scientific names of three Neotropical birds. *Bull. Brit. Orn. Club* 126: 242-244.

Paredes, R., C.B. Zavalaga, G. Battistini, P. Majluf, & P. McGill. 2003. Status of the Humboldt Penguin in Peru, 1999–2000. *Waterbirds* 26: 129–137.

Parker, T.A., A. Castillo U., M. Gell-Mann, & O. Rocha. 1991. Records of new and unusual birds from northern Bolivia. *Bull. Brit. Orn. Club* 111: 120–138.

Parker, T.A., & J. O'Neill. 1985. A new species and a new subspecies of *Thryothorus* wren from Peru. Pp: 9–15 *in* Buckley, P.A., M.S. Foster, E.S. Morton, R.S. Ridgely & F.G. Buckley (eds.) 1985. Neotropical ornithology. *Orn. Monogr.* 36.

Parker, T.A., & S.A. Parker. 1980. Rediscovery of *Xenerpestes singularis* (Furnariidae). *Auk* 97: 203–205

Parker, T.A., S.A. Parker & M.A. Plenge. 1982. *An Annotated Checklist of Peruvian Birds*. Buteo Books, Vermillion.

Parker, T.A., & J.V. Remsen. 1987. Fifty-two Amazonian bird species new to Bolivia. *Bull. Brit. Orn. Club* 107: 94–107.

Parker III, T.A., T.S. Schulenberg, G.R. Graves & M.J. Braun. 1985. The avifauna of the Huancabamba region, northern Peru. Pp. 169-197 in: Buckley *et al.* (1985).

Parker, T.A., D.F. Stotz, & J.W. Fitzpatrick. 1996. Ecological and distributional databases for Neotropical birds. Pp. 131–436 in Stotz, D.F., J.W. Fitzpatrick, T.A. Parker, & D. Moskovits (eds.) *Neotropical Birds: Ecology and Conservation*. University of Chicago Press, Chicago.

Parkes, K.C. 1970. The races of the Rusty-breasted Nunlet (*Nonnula rubecula*). *Bull. Brit. Orn. Club* 90: 154–157.

Parkes, K.C. 1993. Taxonomic notes on the White-collared Swift (*Streptoprocne zonaris*). *Avocetta* 17: 95–100.

Paulson, D. 1993. *Shorebirds of the Pacific Northwest*. University of Washington Press. Seattle.

Paulson, D. 2005. *Shorebirds of North America*. Christopher Helm, London.

Payne, R.B. 1997. Family Cuculidae (cuckoos). Pp. 508–607 *in* del Hoyo, J., A. Elliott, & J. Sargatal (eds.) *Handbook of the Birds of the World*, vol. 4. Lynx Edicions, Barcelona.

Payne, R.B. 2005. *The Cuckoos*. Oxford University Press, Oxford.

Paynter, R.A. (ed.) 1967. *Check-list of Birds of the World*, vol. 12. Mus. Comp. Zool., Cambridge, Mass.

Paynter, R.A. (ed.) 1970. *Check-list of Birds of the World*, vol. 13. Mus. Comp. Zool., Cambridge, Mass.

Paynter, R.A. 1972. Notes on the furnariid *Automolus* (*Hylocryptus*) *erythrocephalus*. *Bull. Brit. Orn. Club* 92: 154–155.

Paynter, R.A. 1978. Biology and evolution of the avian genus *Atlapetes* (Emberizinae). *Bull. Amer. Mus. Comp. Zool.* 148: 323–369.

Paynter, R.A. Jr., 1982. *Ornithological Gazeteer of Venezuela*. Mus. Comp. Zool., Cambridge, Mass.

Paynter, R.A., Jr., 1992. *Ornithological Gazeteer of Bolivia*, second edition. Mus. Comp. Zool., Cambridge, Mass.

Paynter, R.A., Jr., 1993. *Ornithological Gazeteer of Ecuador*, second edition. Mus. Comp. Zool., Cambridge, Mass.

Paynter, R.A., Jr., 1997. *Ornithological Gazeteer of Colombia*, second edition. Mus. Comp. Zool., Cambridge, Mass.

Paynter, R.A., Jr., & M. A. Traylor, Jr., 1991. *Ornithological Gazeteer of Brazil*, second edition. Mus. Comp. Zool., Cambridge, Mass.

Pearman, M. 1993. Some range extensions and five species new to Colombia, with notes on some scarce or little known species. *Bull. Brit. Orn. Club* 113: 66–75.

Peña, M.R. de la, & M. Rumboll. 1998. *Birds of Southern South America and Antarctica*. HarperCollins, London.

Penhallurick, J. & M. Wink. 2004. Analysis of the taxonomy and nomenclature of the Procellariiformes based on complete nucleotide sequences of the mitochondrial cytochrome *b* gene. *Emu* 104 (2): 125-147.

Peréz-Emán, J.L. 2005. Molecular phylogenetics and biogeography of the Neotropical redstarts (*Myioborus*; Aves, Parulinae). *Mol. Phyl. & Evol.* 32: 511–528.

Perrins, C.M. (ed). 1990. *Illustrated Encyclopaedia of the Birds of the World*. Prentice Hall.

Peters, J.L. 1931. *Check-list of Birds of the World*, vol. 1. Mus. Comp. Zool., Cambridge, Massa.

Peters, J.L. 1934. *Check-list of Birds of the World*, vol. 2. Mus. Comp. Zool., Cambridge, Mass.

Peters, J.L. 1937. *Check-list of Birds of the World*, vol. 3. Mus. Comp. Zool., Cambridge, Mass.

Peters, J.L. 1940. *Check-list of Birds of the World*, vol. 4. Mus. Comp. Zool., Cambridge, Mass.

Peters, J.L. 1945. *Check-list of Birds of the World*, vol. 5. Mus. Comp. Zool., Cambridge, Mass.

Peters, J.L. 1948. *Check-list of Birds of the World*, vol. 6. Mus. Comp. Zool., Cambridge, Mass.

Peters, J.L. 1951. *Check-list of Birds of the World*, vol. 7. Mus. Comp. Zool., Cambridge, Mass.

Peters, J., & G.L. Brewer. 1999. Observations of Andean Teal [*Anas flavirostris* (= *andium*) *andium*] in southern Ecuador. *Proc. VI Neotrop. Orn. Congr.*: 190–191. Monterrey, Mexico.

Petersen, W.R., & D. McRae. 2002. Noteworthy bird records for Trinidad and Tobago, including first reports of Wood Sandpiper (*Tringa glareola*) and White-eyed Vireo (*Vireo griseus*). Pp. 204–206 *in* Hayes, F.E., & S.A. Temple (eds.) *Studies in Trinidad and Tobago Ornithology Honoring Richard ffrench*. Occ. Paper 11. Dept. Life Sciences, University of the West Indies, St. Augustine.

Peterson, A.T., N.H. Rice, & A.G. Navarro-Sigüenza. 2004. Geographic variation in the Rosy Thrush-tanager (*Rhodocincla rosea*) complex of Mesoamerica. *Biota Neotropica* 4(2).

Phelps Jr., W.H. 1972. Adiciones a la *Lista de Aves de Sur America, Brasil, y Venezuela* y notas sobre aves venezolanas. *Bol. Soc. Venez. Cienc. Nat.* 30 (124/125): 23–40.

Phelps, W.H., Jr. 1976. Descripción de una raza geográfica de *Crypturellus obsoletus* (Aves: Tinamidae) de los Andes de Venezuela. *Bol. Soc. Venez. Cienc. Nat.* 32: 15–22.

Phelps, W.H., Jr. 1977. Aves colectadas en las mesetas de Sarisariñama y Jaua durante tres expediciones al Macizo de Jaua, estado Bolívar. Descripciones de dos nuevas subespecies. *Bol. Soc. Venez. Cienc. Nat.* 33: 15–42.

Phelps, W.H., Jr. 1977. Una nueva especie y dos nuevas subespecies de aves (Psittacidae, Furnariidae) de la Sierra de Perijá cerca de la divisoria colombo–venezolana. *Bol. Soc. Venez. Cienc. Nat.* 33: 43–53.

Phelps W.H., Jr. & R. Aveledo H. 1984. Dos nuevas subespecies de aves (Troglodytidae, Fringillidae) del Cerro Marahuaca, Territorio Amazonas, Venezuela. *Bol. Soc. Venez. Cienc. Nat.* 39: 5–10.

Phelps W.H., Jr. & R. Aveledo H. 1987. Cinco nuevas subespecies de aves (Rallidae, Trochilidae, Picidae, Furnariidae) y tres extensiones de distribucion para Venezuela. *Bol. Soc. Venez. Cienc. Nat.* 41: 7–26.

Phelps, W.H. Jr., & R.W. Dickerman. 1980. Cuatro subespecias nuevas de aves (Furnariidae, Formicariidae,) de la región de Pantepui, Estado Bolívar y Territorio Amazonas, Venezuela. *Bol. Soc. Venez. Cienc. Nat.* 35: 139-147

Phelps, W.H., Jr. & R. Meyer de Schauensee. 1978. *Una Guía de las Aves de Venezuela*. Graf. Armitano, Caracas.

Phelps W.H., Jr., & R. Meyer de Schauensee. 1994. *Una Guia de las Aves de Venezuela*. Second edn. Ex Libris, Caracas.

Phelps, W.H. & W.H. Phelps, Jr. 1946. Descripción de cuatro aves nuevas de los Cerros Paraque y Ptari-tepui y notas sobre *Bubuculus ibis, Myioborus cardonai* and *Platycichla leucops*. *Bol. Soc. Ven. Cien. Nat.*, 10 (67): 229-240.

Phelps, W.H. & W.H. Phelps, Jr. 1950. Lista de las aves de Venezuela con su distribución, parte 2, Passeriformes. *Bol. Soc. Venez. Cienc. Nat.* 12: 1–427.

Phelps, W.H. & W.H. Phelps Jr. 1953. Eight new subspecies of birds from the Perijá Mountains, Venezuela. *Proc. Biol. Soc. Wash.* 66: 1-12.

Phelps, W.H. & W.H. Phelps, Jr. 1958. *Lista de las Aves de Venezuela con su Distribución. Parte I: No Passeriformes*. Ed. Sucre, Caracas.

Phelps, W.H. & W.H. Phelps, Jr. 1958. Lista de las aves de Venezuela con su distribución. Tomo 2, Parte 1, No-Passeriformes. *Bol. Soc. Venez. Cienc. Nat.* 19: 1–317.

Phelps, W.H. & W.H. Phelps, Jr. 1962. Two new subspecies of birds from Venezuela. *Proc. Biol. Soc. Wash.* 75: 199–203.

Phelps, W.H., & W.H. Phelps, Jr. 1963. Lista de las aves de Venezuela con su distribución. Tomo 1, Parte 2. Passeriformes. Second edn. *Bol. Soc. Venez. Cienc. Nat.* 24: 1–479.

Phillips, A.R. 1994. A review of the northern *Pheucticus* grosbeaks. *Bull. Brit. Orn. Club* 114: 162–170.

Pierce, R.J. 1996. Family Recurvirostridae (stilts and avocets). Pp. 332–347 *in* del Hoyo, J., A. Elliott, & J. Sargatal (eds.) *Handbook of the Birds of the World*, vol. 3. Lynx Edicions, Barcelona.

Piersma, T., J. van Gils, & P. Wiersma. 1996. Family Scolopacidae (sandpipers, snipes and phalaropes). Pp. 444–533 *in* del Hoyo, J., A. Elliott, & J. Sargatal (eds.) *Handbook of the Birds of the World*, vol. 3. Lynx Edicions, Barcelona.

Piersma, T., & P. Wiersma. 1996. Family Charadriidae (plovers). Pp. 384–442 *in* del Hoyo, J., A. Elliott, & J. Sargatal (eds.) *Handbook of the Birds of the World*, vol. 3. Lynx Edicions, Barcelona.

Pinto, O.M. de O., & E.A. de Camargo. 1957. *Papeis Avulsos Sao Paolo* 13.

Pinto, O.M. de O., & E.A. de Camargo. 1961. *Archivos de Zoologica do Estado de San Paolo* 11: 193-284.

Pitman, R.C. 1964. Thick-knee. Pp. 815–816 *in* Thomson, A.L. (ed.) *New Dictionary of Birds*. Nelson, London.

Pitman, R.L., & J.R. Jehl. 1998. Geographic variation and reassessment of species limits in the "Masked Boobies" of the eastern Pacific Ocean. *Wilson Bull.* 110: 155–170.

Poole, A.F. 1994. Family Pandionidae (Osprey). Pp. 42–51 *in* del Hoyo, J., A. Elliott, & J. Sargatal (eds.) *Handbook of the Birds of the World*, vol. 2. Lynx Edicions, Barcelona.

Poulsen, B.O. 1985. Observations of the White-fronted Manakin (*Pipra serena*) in Suriname. *Auk* 102: 384–387.

Poulsen, B.O. 1992. Range extensions of Orange-cheeked Parrot and White-browed Purpletuft in Amazonian Venezuela. *Bull. Brit. Orn. Club* 112: 276–277.

Poulsen, B.O. 1993. A contact zone between Mountain and Caruncŭlated Caracaras in Ecuador. *Wilson Bull.* 105: 688–691.

Poulsen, M.K., & D.C. Wege. 1994. Coppery-chested Jacamar *Galbula pastazae*. *Cotinga* 2: 60–62.

Prum, R.O. 1986. The displays of the White-throated Manakin *Corapipo gutturalis* in Suriname. *Ibis* 128: 91–102.

Prum, R.O. 1990a. A test of monophyly of the manakins (Pipridae) and of the cotingas (Cotingidae) based on morphology. *Occ. Papers Mus. Zool., Univ. Mich.* 723: 1–44.

Prum, R.O. 1990b. Phylogenetic analysis of the evolution of display behavior in the Neotropical manakins (Aves: Pipridae). *Ethology* 84: 202–231.

Prum, R.O. 1992. Syringeal morphology, phylogeny, and evolution of the Neotropical manakins (Aves: Pipridae). *Amer. Mus. Novit.* 3043: 1–65.

Prum, R.O. 1994. Species status of the White-fronted Manakin, *Lepidothrix serena* (Pipridae), with comments on conservation biology. *Condor* 96: 692–702.

Prum, R.O. 2001. A new genus for the Andean green pihas (Cotingidae). *Ibis* 143: 307–309.

Prum R.O., & A.E. Johnson. 1987. Display behavior, foraging ecology, and systematics of the Golden-winged Manakin (*Masius chrysopterus*). *Wilson Bull.* 99: 521–539.

Prum R.O., J.D. Kaplan, & J.E. Pierson. 1996. Display behavior and natural history of the Yellow-crowned Manakin (*Heterocercus flavivertex:* Pipridae). *Condor* 98: 722–735.

Prum R.O., & W.E. Lanyon. 1989. Monophyly and phylogeny of the *Schiffornis* group (Tyrannoidea). *Condor* 91: 444–461.

Prum R.O., N.H. Rice, J. Mobley, & W. Dimmick. 2000. A preliminary phylogenetic hypothesis for the cotingas (Cotingidae) based on mitochondrial DNA. *Auk* 117: 236–241.

Pyle, P., S.N.G. Howell, R.P. Yunick, & D.F. DeSante. 1987. *Identification Guide to North American Passerines*. Slate Creek Press, Bolinas.

Raffaele, H., J. Wiley, O. Garrido, A. Keith & J. Raffaele. 1998. *A Guide to the Birds of the West Indies*. Princeton, New Jersey.

Raikow, R.J. 1994. A phylogeny of the woodcreepers (Dendrocolaptinae). *Auk* 111: 104–114.

Raikow, R.J., & J. Cracraft. 1983. Monophyly of the Piciformes: a reply to Olson. *Auk* 100: 134–138.

Ralph, C.J. 1975. Life style of *Coccyzus pumilus*, a tropical cuckoo. *Condor* 77(1): 60-72.

Raposo, M.A., & E. Höfling. 2003. Alpha taxonomy of the *Xiphorhynchus spixii* species group with validation of *X. juruanus* Ihering 1904. *Cotinga* 20: 72–80.

Rasmussen, P.C., & N.J. Collar. 2002. Family Bucconidae (puffbirds). Pp. 102–138 *in* del Hoyo, J., A. Elliott, & J. Sargatal (eds.) *Handbook of the Birds of the World*, vol. 7. Lynx Edicions, Barcelona.

Remsen, J.V. 1981. A new subspecies of *Schizoeaca harterti* (Aves: Furnariidae) with notes on taxonomy and natural history of *Schizoeaca*. *Proc. Biol. Soc. Wash.* 94: 1068–1075.

Remsen, J.V. 1984. Geographic variation, zoogeography, and possible rapid evolution in some *Cranioleuca* spinetails (Furnariidae) of the Andes. *Wilson Bull.* 96: 515–523.

Remsen, J.V. 1993. Zoogeography and geographic variation in *Atlapetes rufinucha* (Aves: Emberizinae), including a distinctive new subspecies, in southern Peru and Bolivia. *Proc. Biol. Soc. Wash.* 106: 429–435.

Remsen, J.V. 1997. A new genus for the Yellow-shouldered Grosbeak. Pp. 89–90 *in* Remsen, J.V. (ed.) Studies in Neotropical ornithology honoring Ted Parker. *Orn. Monogr.* 48.

Remsen J.V. 2001. True winter range of the Veery (*Catharus fuscescens*): lessons for determining winter ranges of species that winter in the tropics. *Auk* 118: 838–848.

Remsen, J.V. 2003. Family Furnariidae (ovenbirds). Pp. 162–357 *in* del Hoyo, J., A. Elliott, & D.A. Christie (eds.) *Handbook of the Birds of the World*, vol. 8. Lynx Edicions, Barcelona.

Remsen, J.V., & W.S. Graves. 1995. Distribution patterns and zoogeography of *Atlapetes* brush-finches *(Emberizinae)* of the Andes. *Auk* 112: 210–224.

Remsen, J.V., & W.S. Graves. 1995. Distribution patterns of *Buarremon* brush-finches (Emberizinae) and interspecific competition in Andean birds. *Auk* 112: 225–236.

Remsen, J.V., A. Jaramillo, M. Nores, J.F. Pacheco, M.B. Robbins, T.S. Schulenberg, F.G. Stiles, J.M. Cardoso da Silva, D.F. Stotz, & K.J. Zimmer. A classification of the bird species of South America. Version January 2006. American Ornithologist's Union. http://www.museum.lsu.edu/~Remsen/SACCBaseline.html

Remsen, J.V., & T.A. Parker. 1990. Seasonal distribution of the Azure Gallinule (*Porphyrula flavirostris*), with comments on vagrancy in rails and gallinules. *Wilson Bull.* 102: 380–399.

Remsen, J.V., C.G. Schmitt & D.C. Schmitt. 1988. Natural

history notes on some poorly known Bolivian birds, part 3. *Gerfaut* 78: 363-381.

Renjifo, L.M. 1991. Discovery of the Masked Saltator in Colombia, with notes on its ecology and behaviour. *Wilson Bull.* 103: 685–690.

Renjifo, L.M. 1994. First record of the Bay-vented Cotinga *Doliornis sclateri* in Colombia. *Bull. Brit. Orn Club* 114: 101–103.

Renjifo, L.M., A.M. Franco, J.D. Amaya, G.H. Kattan, & B. López (eds.) 2002. *Libro Rojo de las Aves de Colombia.* Serie Libros Rojos de Colombia. Instituto Alexander von Humboldt & Ministry of Environment, Bogotá.

Restall, R.L. 1976. The Black-faced Grassquit, *Tiaris bicolor. Avic. Mag.* 82: 15–159.

Restall, R.L. 1984. More finches and other seedeating birds. *Avic. Mag.* 90: 145–173, 198–208.

Restall, R.L. 1995. Proposed additions to the genus *Lonchura* (Estrildidae). *Bull. Brit. Orn. Club* 115: 140–157.

Restall, R.L. 1996. *Munias & Mannikins.* Pica Press, Robertsbridge.

Restall, R.L. 2002. Is the Ring-necked Seedeater (*Sporophila insularis*) from Trinidad extinct, or is it a cryptic species widespread in Venezuela? Pp. 37–44 *in* Hayes, F.E., & S.A. Temple (eds.) *Studies in Trinidad and Tobago Ornithology Honoring Richard ffrench.* Occ. Paper 11. Dept. Life Sciences, Univ. West Indies, St. Augustine.

Rheindt, F.E. & J.J. Austin. 2005. Major analytical and conceptual shortcomings in a recent revision of the Procellariiformes – a reply to Penhallurick and Wink (2004). *Emu* 105: 181-186.

Ribas, C.C., R. Gaban-Lima, C.Y. Miyaki, & J. Cracraft. 2005. Historical biogeography and diversification within the Neotropical parrot genus *Pionopsitta* (Aves: Psittacidae). *Jour. Biogeog.* 32: 1409-1427.

Ribot J.H. Distribution of birds in Suriname. http://webserv.nhl.nl/~ribot/php4/verspreiding.html

Rice, N.H. 2000. *Phylogenetic Relationships of the Ground Antbirds (Aves: Formicariidae) and their relatives.* PhD dissertation. Univ. Kansas, Lawrence, Kansas.

Rice, N.H. 2005a. Phylogenetic relationships of antpitta genera (Passeriformes: Formicariidae). *Auk* 122: 673–683.

Rice, N.H. 2005b. Further evidence for paraphyly of the Formicariidae (Passeriformes). *Condor* 107: 910–915.

Richford, A.S. 1985. Jacanas and other waders. Pp. 178–187 *in* Perrins, C.M., & H. Middleton (eds.) *The Encyclopaedia of Birds.* Allen & Unwin, London.

Ridgely, R.S., & J. Gwynne. 1989. *A Guide to the Birds of Panama.* Revised edn. Princeton University Press, Princeton.

Ridgely, R.S., & P.J. Greenfield. 2001. *The Birds of Ecuador.* Cornell University Press, Ithaca.

Ridgely, R.S., P.J. Greenfield, & M. Guerrero 1998. *Una Lista Anotada de las Aves de Ecuador Continental / An Annotated List of the Birds of Mainland Ecuador.* Fundación Ornitológica del Ecuador, CECIA, Quito.

Ridgely, R.S., & M.B. Robbins 1988. *Pyrrhura orcesi,* a new parakeet from southwestern Ecuador, with systematic notes on the *Pyrrhura melanura* complex. *Wilson Bull.* 100: 173–182.

Ridgely, R.S., & G. Tudor 1989. *The Birds of South America*, vol. 1. University of Texas Press, Austin.

Ridgely, R.S., & G. Tudor 1994. *The Birds of South America*, vol. 2. University of Texas Press.

Ridgway, R. 1907. The Birds of North and Middle America. Part IV. *Bull. U.S. Nat. Mus.* Washington, D.C.

Riesing, M.J., L. Kruckenhauser, A. Gamauf & E. Haring. 2003. Molecular phylogeny of the genus *Buteo* (Aves: Accipitridae) based on mitochondrial marker sequences. *Mol. Phyl. & Evol.* 27: 328–342.

Ripley, S.D. 1964. Family Muscicapidae, Subfamily Turdidae. Pages 13-227. In: *Checklist of Birds of the World.* Vol. 10 (E. Mayr & R.A. Paynter, Jr., eds). Mus. Comp. Zool. Harvard, Cambridge, Mass.

Ripley, S.D. 1977. *Rails of the World: A Monograph of the Family Rallidae.* David R. Godine, Boston.

Rising, J. 1996. *A Guide to the Identification and Natural History of the Sparrows of the United States and Canada.* Academic Press, San Diego.

Robbins, M.B., M.J. Braun & D.W. Finch. 2003. Discovery of a population of the endangered Red Siskin (*Carduelis cucullata*) in Guyana. *Auk* 120 (2): 291-310.

Robbins, M.B., & S.N.G. Howell. 1995. A new species of pygmy-owl (Strigidae: *Glaucidium*) from the Eastern Andes. *Wilson Bull.* 107: 1–6.

Robbins, M.B., N. Krabbe, G.H. Rosenberg & F. Sornoza. 1994. Geographic variation in the Andean Siskin *Carduelis spinescens* with comments on its status in Ecuador. *Orn. Neotrop.* 5: 61–63.

Robbins, M.B., & T.A. Parker. 1997. Voices & taxonomy of *Caprimulgus* (*rufus*) *otiosus* (Caprimulgidae), with a re-evaluation of the *Caprimulgus rufus* subspecies. Pp: 601–608 *in* Remsen, J.V. (ed.) Studies in Neotropical ornithology honoring Ted Parker. *Orn. Monogr.* 48.

Robbins, M.B., & R.S. Ridgely 1986. A new race of *Grallaria haplonota* (Formicariidae) from Ecuador. *Bull. Brit. Orn. Club* 106: 101–104.

Robbins, M.B., & R.S. Ridgely 1990. The avifauna of an upper tropical cloud forest in southwestern Ecuador. *Proc. Acad. Nat. Sci. Phil.* 142: 59–71.

Robbins, M.B., & R.S. Ridgely 1991. *Sipia rosenbergi* (Formicariidae) is a synonym of *Myrmeciza* (*laemosticta*) *nigricauda,* with comments on the validity of the genus *Sipia. Bull. Brit. Orn. Club* 111: 11–18.

Robbins, M.B., & R.S. Ridgely 1992. Taxonomy and natural history of *Nyctiphrynus rosenbergi* (Caprimulgidae). *Condor* 94: 984–987.

Robbins, M.B., & R.S. Ridgely 1993. A new name for *Myrmeciza immaculata berlepschi* (Formicariidae). *Bull. Brit. Orn. Club* 113: 190.

Robbins, M.B., R.S. Ridgely & S.W. Cardiff. 1994. Voice, plumage and natural history of Anthony's Nightjar (*Caprimulgus anthonyi*). *Condor* 96: 224–228.

Robbins, M.B., G.H. Rosenberg & F. Sornoza. 1994. A new species of cotinga (Cotingidae: *Doliornis*) from the Ecuadorian Andes, with comments on plumage sequence in *Doliornis* and *Ampelion. Auk* 111: 1–7.

Robbins, M.B., G.H. Rosenberg, F. Sornoza & M. Jácome. 1997. Taxonomy and nest description of the Tumbes Swallow (*Tachycineta* [*albilinea*] *stolzmanni*). Pp. 609–612 *in* Remsen, J.V. (ed.) Studies in Neotropical ornithology honoring Ted Parker. *Orn. Monogr.* 48.

Robbins, M.B., & F.G. Stiles. 1999. A new species of pygmy-owl (Strigidae: *Glaucidium*) from the Pacific slope of the northern Andes. *Auk* 116: 305–315.

Robbins, M.B., & K.J. Zimmer. 2005. Taxonomy, vocalisations and natural history of *Philydor dimidiatum* (Furnariidae), with comments on the systematics of *Syndactyla* and *Simoxenops*. *Bull. Brit. Orn. Club* 125: 212–228.

Robertson, C.J.R. & R. Gales. 1998. Towards a new taxonomy for Albatrosses. Pp.13-19 in: *The Albatross: Biology and Conservation* (G. Robertson and R. Gales, eds). Beatty & Sons, Chipping Norton.

Rodner, C., M. Lentino, & R. Restall. 2000. *Checklist of the Birds of Northern South America*. Pica Press, Robertsbridge.

Rodríguez, G., & M. Lentino. 1997. Range expansion and summering of Palm Warbler *Dendroica palmarum* in Venezuela. *Bull. Brit. Orn. Club* 117: 76–77.

Rodríguez, J.V. 1980. Notas sobre *Dumetella carolinensis* (Linnaeus) y primer registro de *Hylocichla mustelina* (Gmelin) (Aves: Mimidae y Turdidae) en Colombia. *Lozania* 30: 7–8.

Rodríguez, J.V. 1982. *Aves del Parque Nacional Los Katios*. INDERENA, Bogotá.

Rodríguez, J.V., & J.I. Hernández-Camacho. 2002. *Loros de Colombia*. Conservation International, Bogotá.

Rojas, R., W. Piragua, F.G. Stiles, & T. McNish. 1997. Primeros registros para Colombia de cuatro taxones de la familia Tyrannidae (Aves: Passeriformes). *Caldasia* 19: 523–525.

Romero-Zambrano, H. 1977. Status taxonómico de *Catamenia oreophila* Todd. *Lozania* 23: 1–7.

Romero-Zambrano, H. 1980. Una nueva subespecie colombiana de *Campylorhamphus pusillus*. *Lozania* 31: 1–4.

Romero-Zambrano, H., & J. Hernández-Camacho. 1979. Una nueva subespecie Colombiana de *Haplophaedia aureliae*. *Lozania* 30: 1–6.

Romero-Zambrano, H., & J. Morales-Sanchez. 1981. Descripción de una nueva subespecie de *Leptotila verreauxi* Bonaparte 1855 (Aves: Colombidae) del sureste de Colombia. *Caldasia* 13: 291–299.

Romero-Zambrano, H., & J.V. Rodriguez. 1980. Hallazgo de *Oncostoma cinereigulare* (Sclater) (Aves: Tyrannidae) en Colombia. *Lozania* 31: 5–6.

Rosenberg, G.H. 1990. Habitat specialization and foraging behaviour by birds of Amazonian river islands of northeastern Peru. *Condor* 92: 427–443.

Roy, M.S., J.C. Torres-Mura, & F. Hertel. 1999. Molecular Phylogeny and evolutionary history of the tit-tyrants (Aves: Tyrannidae). *Molec. Phylog. Evol.* 11 (1): 67-76.

Rudge, D.W., & R.J. Raikow. 1992. The phylogenetic relationships of the *Margarornis* assemblage (Furnariidae). *Condor* 94: 760–766.

Ryan, R. 1997. First record of Little Egret *Egretta garzetta* from Guyana. *Cotinga* 8: 92.

Salaman, P, P. Coopmans, T.M. Donegan, M. Mulligan, A. Cortés, S.L. Hilty & L.A. Ortega. 2003. A new species of wood-wren (Troglodytidae: *Henicorhina*) from the Western Andes of Colombia. *Orn. Colombiana* 1: 4–21.

Salaman, P., T. Cuadros, J.G. Jaramillo, & W.H. Weber. 2001. *Lista de Chequeo de las Aves de Colombia*. Soc. Antioqueña de Ornitología, Medellín.

Salaman, P., T.M. Donegan & A.M. Cuervo. 1999. Ornithological Surveys in Serranía de los Churumbelos, southern Colombia. *Cotinga* 12: 29-39.

Salaman, P.G.W., & F.G. Stiles. 1996. A distinctive new species of vireo (Passeriformes: Vireonidae) from the western Andes of Colombia. *Ibis* 138: 610–619.

Salaman, P.G.W., F.G. Stiles, C.I. Bohórquez, M. Álvarez-R., A.N. Umaña, T. Donegan, & A. Cuervo. 2002. New and noteworthy bird records from the east slope of the Andes in Colombia. *Caldasia* 24: 157–189.

Salcedo, M., D. Ascanio, & C. Molina. 2006. Smoky-fronted Tody-tyrant *Todirostrum frumifrons*, a new species for Venezuela. *Cotinga* 25: 41–42.

Salvin, O. 1892. *Catalogue of the Birds of the British Museum*, vol. 16. Trustees of the Brit. Mus., London.

Salvin, O., & F.D. Godman. 1896. *Biologica Central Americana*. London.

Sato, A., H. Tichy, C. O'Huigin. P.R. Grant, B.R. Grant, & J. Klein. 2001. On the origin of Darwin's finches. *Mol. Biol. Evol.* 18: 299-311.

Schreiber, E.A., & R.W. Schreiber, 1985. Pelicans and gannets. Pp. 52–56 *in* Perrins, C.M., & A.L. Middleton (eds.) *The Encyclopaedia of Birds*. Allen & Unwin. London.

Schuchmann, K.L. 1999. Family Trochilidae (hummingbirds). Pp. 468–680 in del Hoyo, J., A. Elliott, & J. Sargatal (eds.) *Handbook of the Birds of the World*, vol. 5. Lynx Edicions, Barcelona.

Schuchmann, K.L., & K. Duffner 1993. Geographical variation and speciation patterns in the Andean hummingbird genus *Aglaiocercus* Zimmer 1930. *Mitt. Zool. Mus. Berlin 69 Suppl.: Ann. Orn.* 17: 75–92.

Schuchmann, K.L., A. Weller., & I. Heynen. 2001. Systematics and biogeography of the Andean genus *Eriocnemis* (Aves: Trochilidae). *J. Orn.* 142: 433–481.

Schulenberg, T.S. 1983. Foraging behavior, eco-morphology and systematics of some antshrikes (Formicariidae: *Thamnomanes*). *Wilson Bull.* 95: 505–521.

Schulenberg, T.S., & T.A. Parker. 1997. A new species of tyrant flycatcher (Tyrannidae: *Tolmomyias)* from the western Amazon basin. Pp: 723–731 *in* Remsen, J.V. (ed.) Studies in Neotropical ornithology honoring Ted Parker. *Orn. Monogr.* 48.

Schulenberg, T.S., & M.D. Williams. 1982. A new species of antpitta (*Grallaria*) from northern Peru. *Wilson Bull.* 94: 105–240.

Schwartz, P. 1968. Notes on two Neotropical nightjars, *Caprimulgus anthonyi* and *C. parvulus*. Condor 70: 223–227.

Schwartz, P. 1972a. *Micrastur gilvicollis*, a valid species sympatric with *M. ruficollis* in Amazonia. *Condor* 74: 399–415.

Schwartz, P. 1972b. On the taxonomic rank of the Yellow-billed Toucanet (*Aulacorhynchus calorhynchus)*. *Bol. Soc. Venez. Cienc. Nat.* 29: 459–476.

Schwartz, P. 1975. Solved and unsolved problems in the *Sporophila lineola / S. bouvronides* complex (Aves: Emberizidae). *Ann. Carnegie Mus.* 45: 277–285.

Schwartz, P. 1977. Some clarifications about *Ramphastos "aurantiirostris"*. *Auk* 94: 775–777.

Schwartz, P., & M. Lentino. 1984a. Relaciones de los Tinamidos venezolanos del grupo *Crypturellus noctivagus,* indicadas por su voz (Aves: Tinamidae). MARNR. *Serie Informes Científicos de la DGSIIA* 23: 1–42.

Schwartz, P., & M. Lentino. 1984b. Estudio sobre la posición sistemática de *Myrmornis torquata* (Aves: Formicariidae). MARNR. *Serie Informes Científicos de la DGSIIA* 24: 1–19.

Schwartz, P., & M. Lentino. 1985. Notas sobre la reproducción de *Odontophorus columbianus* (Aves: Phasianidae). MARNR. *Serie Informes Científicos de la DGSIIA* 25: 1–xx.

Schwartz, P., & D. Snow. 1979. Display and related behavior of the Wire-tailed Manakin. *Living Bird* 17: 51–78.

Sclater, P.L. 1882. *Monograph of Jacamars and Puff-Birds*. London

Sclater, P.L., & O. Salvin. 1877. Descriptions of two new antbirds of the genus *Grallaria*, with a list of the known species of the genus. *Ibis* (4) 1: 437–451.

Serna, M.A., & J.V. Rodríguez. 1979. Una nueva parulida registrada por primera vez en Colombia: *Dendroica discolor discolor* (Aves: Parulidae). *Lozania* 29: 1–2.

Seutin, G., J. Brawn, R.E. Ricklefs & E. Bermingham 1993. Genetic divergence among populations of a tropical passerine, the Streaked Saltator (*Saltator albicollis*). *Auk* 104: 97–108.

Sharpe, C.J., D. Ascanio & R. Restall. 1997. Three species of exotic passerine in Venezuela. *Cotinga* 7: 43–44.

Sheldon, F.H. & F.B. Gill. 1996. A reconsideration of birdsong phylogeny, with emphasis on the evolution of titmice and their sylvioid relatives. *Syst. Biol.* 45: 473-495.

Sherman, P.T. 1996. Family Psophiidae (trumpeters). Pp. 96–107 *in* del Hoyo, J., A. Elliott, & J. Sargatal (eds.) *Handbook of the Birds of the World*, vol. 3. Lynx Edicions, Barcelona.

Short, L.L. 1982. *Woodpeckers of the World*. Monogr. 4. Delaware Mus. Nat. Hist., Greenville.

Short, L.L., & J.F.M. Horne. 2001. *Toucans, Barbets and Honeyguides*. Oxford University Press, Oxford.

Short, L.L., & J.F.M. Horne. 2002a. Family Capitonidae (barbets). Pp. 140–219 *in* del Hoyo, J., A. Elliott, & J. Sargatal (eds.) *Handbook of the Birds of the World*, vol. 7. Lynx Edicions, Barcelona.

Short, L., & J.F.M. Horne. 2002b. Family Ramphastidae (toucans). Pp. 220–272 *in* del Hoyo, J., A. Elliott, & J. Sargatal (eds.) *Handbook of the Birds of the World*, vol. 7. Lynx Edicions, Barcelona.

Sibley, C.G. & J.E. Ahlquist. 1985. Phylogeny and classification of New World suboscine passerine birds (Passeriformes: Oligomyodi: Tyrannides). Pp 396-428 in: Buckley *et al.* 1985.

Sibley, C.G., & J.E. Ahlquist. 1990. *Phylogeny and Classification of Birds: A Study in Molecular Evolution*. Yale University Press, New Haven.

Sibley, C.G., S.M. Lanyon & J.E. Ahlquist. 1984. The relationships of the Sharpbill (*Oxyruncus cristatus*). *Condor* 86: 48-52.

Sibley, C.G., & B.L. Monroe, Jr. 1990. *Distribution and Taxonomy of Birds of the World*. Yale University Press, New Haven.

Sibley, C.G., & B.L. Monroe, Jr. 1993. *A Supplement to Distribution and Taxonomy of Birds of the World*. Yale University Press, New Haven.

Sibley, D.A. 2000. *The Sibley Guide to Birds*. Knopf, New York.

Sick, H. 1993. *Birds in Brazil: A Natural History*. Princeton University Press, Princeton.

Siegel-Causey, D. 1998. Phylogeny of the Phalacrocoracidae. *Condor* 90: 885-905.

Silva, J.L. 1999. Notes on the distribution of *Pauxi pauxi* and *Aburria aburri* in Venezuela. *Wilson Bull.* 111: 564–569.

Skutch, A.F. 1954. *Life Histories of Central American Birds*. Cooper Orn. Soc., Berkeley.

Skutch, A.F. 1983. *Birds of Tropical America*. University of Texas Press, Austin.

Skutch, A.F. 1996. *Orioles, Blackbirds and Their Kin: A Natural History*. University of Arizona Press, Tucson.

Slud, P. 1964. The birds of Costa Rica. Distribution and ecology. *Bull. Amer. Mus. Nat. Hist.* 128: 1–430.

Smith, W.J. & F. Vuilleumier. 1971. Evolutionary relationships of some South American ground tyrants. *Bull. Mus. Comp. Zool.*, 141: 259-286.

Snow, B.K. 1961. Notes on the behaviour of three Cotingidae. *Auk* 78: 150–161.

Snow, B.K. 1970. A field study of the Bearded Bellbird in Trinidad. *Ibis* 112: 299–329.

Snow, D.W. 1971. Observations on the Purple-throated Fruit-crow in Guyana. *Living Bird* 10: 5–17.

Snow, D.W. 1973. The classification of the Cotingidae (Aves). *Breviora* 409: 1–27.

Snow, D.W. 1975a. *Laniisoma elegans* in Peru. *Auk* 92: 583–584.

Snow, D.W. 1975b. The classification of the manakins. *Bull. Brit. Orn. Club* 95: 20–27.

Snow, D.W. 1976. *The Web of Adaptation*. Quadrangle, New York.

Snow, D.W. 1982. *The Cotingas*. Brit. Mus. (Nat. Hist.), London & Cornell University Press, Ithaca.

Snow, D.W. 1985. Systematics of the *Turdus fumigatus/hauxwelli* group of thrushes. *Bull. Brit. Orn. Club* 105: 30–37.

Snow, D.W. 2001. Family Momotidae (motmots). Pp. 264–284 *in* del Hoyo, J., A. Elliott, & J. Sargatal (eds.) *Handbook of the Birds of the World*, vol. 6. Lynx Edicions, Barcelona.

Snow, D.W. 2004a. Family Cotingidae (cotingas). Pp. 32–108 *in* del Hoyo, J., A. Elliott, & D.A. Christie (eds.) *Handbook of the Birds of the World*, vol. 9. Lynx Edicions, Barcelona.

Snow, D.W. 2004b. Family Pipridae (manakins). Pp. 110–169 *in* del Hoyo, J., A. Elliott, & D.A. Christie (eds.) *Handbook of the Birds of the World*, vol. 9. Lynx Edicions, Barcelona.

Snyder, D. 1966. *The Birds of Guyana*. Peabody Museum, Salem, Mass.

Souza, D. 2006 *All the Birds of Brazil: An Identification Guide*. 2nd edition. Subbuteo Natural History Books, Shrewsbury. UK.

Stattersfield, A.J., M.J. Crosby, A.J. Long & D.C. Wege. 1998. *Threatened Birds of the World: Priorities for Biodiversity Conservation*. BirdLife International, Cambridge, UK.

Stephens, L. & M.A. Traylor, Jr., 1983. *Ornithological Gazeteer of Peru*, second edition. Mus. Comp. Zool., Cambridge, Mass.

Stephens, L. & M.A. Traylor, Jr., 1985. *Ornithological Gazeteer of the Guianas*, second edition. Mus. Comp. Zool., Cambridge, Mass.

Stiles, F.G. 1981. The taxonomy of Rough-winged Swallows (*Stelgidopteryx*; Hirundinidae) in southern Central America. *Auk* 98: 282–293.

Stiles, F.G. 1983. The taxonomy of *Microcerculus* wrens (Troglodytidae) in Central America. *Wilson Bull.* 95: 169–183.

Stiles, F.G. 1992. A new species of antpitta (Formicariidae: *Grallaria*) from the Eastern Andes of Colombia. *Wilson Bull.* 104: 389–399.

Stiles, F.G. 1995a. Distribución y variación en el Hermitaño Carinegro (*Phaethornis anthophilus*) en Colombia. *Caldasia* 18: 119–129.

Stiles, F.G. 1995b. Dos nuevas subespecies de aves de la Serrania del Chiribiquete, Departamento del Caqueta, Colombia. *Lozania* 66: 1–16.

Stiles, F.G. 1995c. La situación del Tororoi Pechicanela (*Grallaria haplonota*, Formicariidae) en Colombia. *Caldasia* 17: 607–610.

Stiles, F.G. 1996a. A new species of emerald hummingbird (Trochilidae, *Chlorostilbon*) from the Sierra de Chiribiquete, southeastern Colombia, with a review of the *C. mellisugus* complex. *Wilson Bull.* 108: 1–27.

Stiles, F.G. 1996b. When black plus white equals grey: the nature of variation in the Variable Seedeater complex (Emberizinae: *Sporophila*). *Orn. Neotrop.* 7: 75–107.

Stiles, F.G. 1999. Species accounts of Trochilidae *in* del Hoyo, J., A. Elliott, & J. Sargatal (eds). 1999. *Handbook of Birds of the World*. Vol. 5. Lynx Editions, Barcelona.

Stiles, F.G. 2004. The Tumaco Seedeater (*Sporophila insulata*; Emberizidae): a species that never was? *Orn. Neotrop.* 15: 17–30.

Stiles, F.G. 2004. Austral migration in Colombia: the state of knowledge, and suggestions for action. *Orn. Neotrop.* 15: 349–355.

Stiles, F.G., & H. Alvarez-López. 1995. La situación del Tororoi Pechicanela (*Grallaria haplonota*) Formicariidae. *Caldasia* 17: 607-610.

Stiles, F.G., L. Rossellini & C.I. Bohórquez. 1999, New and noteworthy records of birds from the middle Magdalena Valley of Colombia. *Bull. Brit. Orn. Club* 119 (2): 113-129.

Stiles, F.G., & A.F. Skutch. 1989. *A Guide to the Birds of Costa Rica*. Cornell University Press, Ithaca.

Storer, R.W. 1969. What is a tanager? *Living Bird* 8: 127–136.

Storer, R.W. 1976. The behavior and relationships of the Least Grebe. *Trans. San Diego Soc. Nat. Hist.* 18: 113–125.

Storer, R.W., & T. Getty. 1985. Geographic variation in the Least Grebe (*Tachybaptus dominicus*). Pp. 31–39 *in* Buckley, P.A., M.S. Foster, E.S. Morton, R.S. Ridgely & F.G. Buckley (eds.) 1985. Neotropical ornithology. *Orn. Monogr.* 36.

Stotz, D.F. 1990. The taxonomic status of *Phyllomyias reiseri*. *Bull. Brit. Orn. Club* 110: 184–187.

Stotz, D.F., J.W. Fitzpatrick, T.A. Parker & D. Moskovits. 1996. *Neotropical Birds: Ecology and Conservation*. University of Chicago Press, Chicago.

Strewe, R. 2001a. First record of Rufous-headed Chachalaca *Ortalis erythroptera* for Colombia. *Cotinga* 15: 63.

Strewe, R. 2001b. Segundo registro de *Buteo jamaicensis* para Colombia. *Boletin SAO* 12: 80–81.

Strewe, R., & C. Navarro. 2004. New and noteworthy records of birds from the Sierra Nevada de Santa Marta region, north-eastern Colombia. *Bull. Brit. Orn. Club* 124: 38–51.

Summers-Smith, J.D. 1963. *The House Sparrow*. Collins, London.

Tarroux, A., R. McNeil, & P. Legendre. 2003. Influence of rainfall on the composition of a tropical avian assemblage in north-eastern Venezuela. *Ecotropica* 9: 15–31.

Taylor, B., & B. van Perlo 1998. *Rails: A Guide to the Rails, Crakes, Gallinules, and Coots of the World*. Pica Press, Robertsbridge.

Taylor, P.B. 1996. Family Rallidae (rails, gallinules and coots). Pp. 108–209 *in* del Hoyo, J., A. Elliott, & J. Sargatal (eds.) *Handbook of the Birds of the World*, vol. 3. Lynx Edicions, Barcelona.

Taylor, M. 2002. The first Terek Sandpiper *Xenus cinereus* in Trinidad and Tobago. *Cotinga* 16: 66.

Terborgh, J.W. & J.S. Weske. 1972. Rediscovery of the Imperial Snipe in Peru. *Auk* 89: 497-505.

Texeira, D.M., J. Nacinovic & M. Tavares. 1986. Notes on some birds of northeastern Brazil. (Part 1). *Bull. Brit. Orn. Club* 106: 70–74.

Texeira, D.M., J. Nacinovic & F. Pontual. 1987. Notes on some birds of northeastern Brazil. Part 2. *Bull. Brit. Orn. Club* 107: 151–157.

Texeira, D.M., J. Nacinovic & F. Pontual. 1988. Notes on some birds of northeastern Brazil. Part 3. *Bull. Brit. Orn. Club* 108: 75–79.

Texeira, D.M., J. Nacinovic & G. Luigi. 1989. Notes on some birds of northeastern Brazil. Part 4. *Bull. Brit. Orn. Club* 109: 152–157.

Thiollay, J.M. 1994. Family Accipitridae (hawks and eagles). Pp. 52–105 *in* del Hoyo, J., A. Elliott, & J. Sargatal (eds.) *Handbook of the Birds of the World*, vol. 2. Lynx Edicions, Barcelona.

Thomas, B.T. 1996. Family Eurypygidae (Sunbittern). Pp. 226–233 *in* del Hoyo, J., A. Elliott, & J. Sargatal (eds.) *Handbook of the Birds of the World*, vol. 3. Lynx Edicions, Barcelona.

Thomas, B.T. 1996. Family Opisthocomidae (Hoatzin). Pp. 24–32 *in* del Hoyo, J., A. Elliott, & J. Sargatal (eds.) *Handbook of the Birds of the World*, vol. 3. Lynx Edicions, Barcelona.

Thomas, B.T. 1999. Family Steatornithidae (Oilbird). Pp. 244–251 *in* del Hoyo, J., A. Elliott, & J. Sargatal (eds.) *Handbook of the Birds of the World*, vol. 5. Lynx Edicions, Barcelona.

Tobias, J.A. 2002. Family Galbulidae (jacamars). Pp. 74–101 *in* del Hoyo, J., A. Elliott, & J. Sargatal (eds.) *Handbook of the Birds of the World*, vol. 7. Lynx Edicions, Barcelona.

Todd, W.E.C. 1947. The Venezuelan races of *Piaya cayana*. *Proc. Biol. Soc. Wash*. 60: 59–60.

Todd, W.E.C. 1948. Critical remarks on the ovenbirds. *Ann. Carnegie Mus*. 31: 33-43.

Todd, W.E.C., & M.A. Carriker. 1922. The birds of the Santa Marta region of Colombia: a study in altitudinal distribution. *Ann. Carnegie Mus*. 14: 3–661.

Tomkins, R.J. & B.J. Milne. 1991. Differences among Dark-rumped Petrel (*Pterodroma phaeopygia*) populations within the Galapagos Archipelago. *Notornis* 38: 1-35.

Tostain, O., J.L. Dujardin, C. Érard & J.M. Thiollay 1992. *Oiseaux de Guyane*. Société d'Études Ornithologiques, Cayenne.

Trail, P.W. & P. Donahue. 1991. Notes on the behavior and ecology of Red-Cotingas (Cotingidae: Phoenicircus). *Wilson Bull.* 103: 539-551.

Traylor, M.A. 1958. Variation in South American Great Horned Owl. *Auk* 75: 143–148.

Traylor, M.A. 1977. A classification of the tyrant flycatchers (Tyrannidae). *Bull. Mus. Comp. Zool.* 148: 129–184.

Traylor, M.A. 1982. Notes on tyrant flycatchers (Aves: Tyrannidae). *Fieldiana, Zool. N. Ser.* 13: 1–22.

Traylor, M.A. 1985. Species limits in the *Ochthoeca diadema* species-group (Tyrannidae). Pp. 430–442 *in* Buckley, P.A., M.S. Foster, E.S. Morton, R.S. Ridgely & F.G. Buckley (eds.) 1985. Neotropical ornithology. *Orn. Monogr.* 36.

Traylor, M.A. (ed.) 1979. *Check-list of the Birds of the World*, vol. 8. Mus. Comp. Zool., Cambridge, Mass.

Traylor, M.A., & J.W. Fitzpatrick. 1982. A survey of the tyrant-flycatchers. *Living Bird* 19: 7–50.

Trevis, B. 1994. Photospot: Andean Potoo (*Nyctibius maculosus*). *Cotinga* 1: 35.

Turner, A., & C. Rose. 1989. *Swallows and Martins of the World*. Christopher Helm, London.

Turner, A.K. 2004. Family Hirundinidae (swallows and martins). Pp. 602–685 *in* del Hoyo, J., A. Elliott, & D.A. Christie (eds.) *Handbook of the Birds of the World*, vol. 9. Lynx Edicions, Barcelona.

Tyler, S.J. 2004. Family Motacillidae (pipits and wagtails). Pp. 686–786 *in* del Hoyo, J., A. Elliott, & D.A. Christie (eds.) *Handbook of the Birds of the World*, vol. 9. Lynx Edicions, Barcelona.

USGS. 1997. GTOPO30 Documentation, available online at the USGS website: http://edcwww.cr.usgs.gov/landdaac/gtopo30.

Van Gils, J., & T. Wiersma. 1996. Family Scolopacidae (sandpipers, snipes and phalaropes). Pp. 444–533 *in* del Hoyo, J., A. Elliott, & J. Sargatal (eds.) *Handbook of the Birds of the World*, vol. 3. Lynx Edicions, Barcelona.

Vaurie, C. 1962. A systematic study of the Red-backed Hawks of South America. *Condor* 64: 277–290.

Vaurie, C. 1964. Systematic notes on the bird family Cracidae. No. 1. Geographic variation of *Ortalis canicollis* and *Penelope marail*. *Amer. Mus. Novit*. 2197: 1–8.

Vaurie, C. 1965a. Systematic notes on the bird family Cracidae. No. 3. *Ortalis guttata*, *Ortalis superciliaris*, and *Ortalis motmot*. *Amer. Mus. Novit*. 2232: 1–21.

Vaurie, C. 1965b. Systematic notes on the bird family Cracidae. No. 4. *Ortalis garrula* and *Ortalis ruficauda*. *Amer. Mus. Novit*. 2237: 1–16.

Vaurie, C. 1966a. Systematic notes on the bird family Cracidae. No. 5. *Penelope purpurascens*, *Penelope jacquacu*, and *Penelope obscura*. *Amer. Mus. Novit*. 2250: 1–23.

Vaurie, C. 1966b. Systematic notes on the bird family Cracidae. No. 6. Reviews of the nine species of *Penelope*. *Amer. Mus. Novit*. 2251: 1-30.

Vaurie, C. 1967a. Systematic notes on the bird family Cracidae. No. 7. The genus *Pipile*. *Amer. Mus. Novit*. 2296: 1–16.

Vaurie, C. 1967b. Systematic notes on the bird family Cracidae. No. 8. The genera *Aburria*, *Chamaepetes*, and *Penelopina*. *Amer. Mus. Novit*. 2299: 1–12.

Vaurie, C. 1967c. Systematic notes on the bird family Cracidae. No. 9. The genus *Crax*. *Amer. Mus. Novit*. 2305: 1–20.

Vaurie, C. 1967d. Systematic notes on the Bird Family Cracidae. No. 10. The genera *Mitu* and *Pauxi,* and the generic relationships of the Cracini. *Amer. Mus. Novit*. 2307: 1–20.

Vaurie, C. 1968. Taxonomy of the Cracidae (Aves). *Bull. Amer. Mus. Nat. Hist*. 138: 131–260.

Vaurie, C. 1971. *Classification of the ovenbirds (Furnariidae)*. H.F. & G. Witherby, London.

Vaurie, C. 1971a. *Cranioleuca furcata* Taczanowski (Furnariidae) is a valid species. *Ibis* 113: 517–519.

Vaurie, C. 1971b. Notes systématiques sur des Furnariidés rare des genres *Philydor* et *Xenerpestes*, et parallélisme de la forme du bec au type *Xenops*. *L'Oiseau & RFO* 41: 117–126.

Vaurie, C. 1971c. Systematic status of *Synallaxis demissa* and *Synallaxis poliophrys*. *Ibis* 113: 520–521.

Vaurie, C. 1980. Taxonomy and geographical distribution of the Furnariidae (Aves: Passeriformes). *Bull. Amer. Mus. Nat. Hist*. 166: 1–357.

Vaurie, C., & P. Schwartz 1972. Morphology and vocalizations of *Synallaxis unirufa* and *Synallaxis castanea* (Furnariidae, Aves), with comments on other *Synallaxis*. *Amer. Mus. Novit*. 2483: 1–13

Verea, C., & A. Solórzano. 2001. La comunidad de aves del sotobosque de un bosque deciduo tropical en Venezuela. *Orn. Neotrop*. 12: 235–253

Vielliard, J. 1989. Una nova especie de *Glaucidium* (Aves: Strigidae) da Amazonia. *Rev. Bras. Zool*. 6: 685–693.

Voelker, G. & G.M. Spellman. 2004. Nuclear and mitochondrial DNA evidence of polyphyly in the avian superfamily Muscicapidae. *Mol. Phylogen. Evol*. 30: 386-394.

Voous, K.H. 1957. The birds of Aruba, Curaçao and Bonaire. *Stud. Fauna Curaçao and other Caribbean Islands* 7(29): 1–260.

Voous, K.H. 1964. Wood Owls of the genera *Strix* and *Ciccaba*. *Zool. Med*. 39: 471-478.

Voous, K.H. 1982. Straggling to islands. South American birds in the islands of Aruba, Curaçao and Bonaire, south Caribbean. *J. Yamashina Inst. Orn*. 14: 171–178.

Voous, K.H. 1983. *Birds of the Netherlands Antilles*. Foundation for Science Research in Suriname and the Netherlands Antilles, Utrecht.

Voous, K.H. 1985. Additions to the avifauna of Aruba, Curaçao and Bonaire, south Caribbean. Pp: 247–254 *in* Buckley, P.A., M.S. Foster, E.S. Morton, R.S. Ridgely & F.G. Buckley (eds.) 1985. Neotropical ornithology. *Orn. Monogr*. 36.

Voous, K.H. 1986. Striated or Green herons in the South Caribbean islands? *Aus. Naturhist. Mus. Wien* 88/89: 101–106.

Vuilleumier, F. 1984. Zoogeography of Andean birds: two major barriers, and speciation and taxonomy of the *Diglossa carbonaria* superspecies. *Natl. Geogr. Soc. Res. Rep*. 16: 713–731.

Vuilleumier, F., & E. Mayr 1987. New species of birds described from 1976 to 1980. *J. Orn*. 128: 137–150.

Wattel, J. 1973. Geographical differentiation in the genus *Accipiter*. Publ. Nuttall Orn. Club 13: 1–231.

Welford, M.R., & T. Nunnery. 2001. Behaviour and use of human trail by a Giant Antpitta *Grallaria gigantea*. *Cotinga* 16: 67–68.

Weller, A.-A. 1999. Species accounts of Trochilidae (p.598) in: del Hoyo, J. *et al*. 1999. *Handbook of the Birds of the World*, Vol. 5. Lynx Edicions, Barcelona.

Weller, A.-A. 2000a. Biogeography, geographic variation and habitat preference in the Amazilia Hummingbird *Amazilia amazilia* Lesson (Aves, Trochilidae) with notes on the status of *Amazilia alticola* Gould. *J. Orn*. 141: 93–101.

Weller, A.-A. 2000b. A new hummingbird subspecies from southern Bolívar, Venezuela, with notes on biogeography and taxonomy of the *Saucerottia viridigaster–cupreicauda* species group. *Orn. Neotrop*. 11: 143–154.

Weller, A.-A., & C. Rengifo G. 2003. Notes on the avifauna of the Cordillera de Mérida, Venezuela. *Bull. Brit. Orn. Club* 123: 261–270.

Weller, A.-A., & S.C. Renner. 2001. A new subspecies of *Heliodoxa xanthogonys* (Aves: Trochilidae) from southern Pantepui highlands, with biogeographical and taxonomic notes. *Ararajuba* 9: 1–5.

Weller, A.-A. & K-L Schuchmann. 1997. The hybrid origin of a Venezuelan trochilid, *Amazilia distans* Wetmore & Phelps 1956. *Orn. Neotropical* 8(1): 107-112.

Wells, J.V., & A. Childs Wells. 2001. First sight record of

Philadelphia Vireo (*Vireo philadelphicus*) for Curaçao, Netherlands Antilles, with notes on other migrant songbirds. *El Pitirre* 14: 49–60.

Wells, J.V., & A. Childs Wells. 2002. Extreme extralimital summer record of Western Tanager *Piranga ludoviciana* from Bonaire, Netherlands Antilles. *Cotinga* 18: 96–97.

Weske, J.S. 1985. A new subspecies of Collared Inca hummingbird (*Coeligena torquata*) from Peru. Pp: 41–46 *in* Buckley, P.A., M.S. Foster, E.S. Morton, R.S. Ridgely & F.G. Buckley (eds.) 1985. Neotropical ornithology. *Orn. Monogr.* 36.

Weske, J.S., & J.W. Terborgh. 1981. *Otus marshalli*, a new species of screech owl from Peru. *Auk* 98: 1–7.

Wetmore, A. 1926. Observations on the birds of Argentine, Paraguay, Uruguay and Chile. *U.S. Nat. Mus. Bull. 133*. Smithsonian Inst., Washington D.C. 449pp.

Wetmore, A. 1946. New birds from Colombia. *Smithsonian Misc. Coll.* 106: 1–14.

Wetmore, A. 1953. Further additions to the birds of Panama & Colombia. *Smithsonian Misc. Coll.* 122: 1–12.

Wetmore, A. 1958. Additional subspecies of birds from Colombia. *Proc. Biol. Soc. Wash.* 71: 1–4.

Wetmore, A. 1960. *A classification for the birds of the world.* Smithsonian. Misc. Coll. 139 (11): 1-36.

Wetmore, A. 1965a. Additions to the list of birds of the Republic of Colombia. *L'Oiseau* 35: 156–162.

Wetmore, A. 1965b. *The Birds of the Republic of Panamá*, part 1. Smithsonian Institution Press, Washington, DC.

Wetmore, A. 1968. *The Birds of the Republic of Panamá*, part 2. Smithsonian Institution Press, Washington, DC.

Wetmore, A. 1970. Descriptions of additional forms of birds from Panamá and Colombia. *Proc. Biol. Soc. Wash.* 82: 767–776.

Wetmore, A. 1972. *The Birds of the Republic of Panamá*, part 3. Smithsonian Institution Press, Washington, DC.

Wetmore, A., R.F. Pasquier & S.L. Olson. 1984. *The Birds of the Republic of Panamá*, part 4. Smithsonian Institution Press, Washington, DC.

Wheeler, B.K., & W.S. Clark. 2003. *A Photographic Guide to North American Raptors*. Princeton University Press, Princeton.

White, C.M. 1994a. Family Accipitridae (hawks and eagles): Nearctic species accounts. Pp. 117–184 *in* del Hoyo, J., A. Elliott & J. Sargatal (eds.) *Handbook of the Birds of the World*, vol. 2. Lynx Edicions, Barcelona.

White, C.M. 1994b. Family Falconidae (falcons and caracaras): Nearctic species accounts. Pp. 261–275 *in* del Hoyo, J., A. Elliott & J. Sargatal, eds. *Handbook of the Birds of the World*, vol. 2. Lynx Edicions, Barcelona.

White, C.M., P.D. Olsen & L.F. Kiff. 1994. Family Falconidae (falcons and caracaras). Pp. 216–247 *in* del Hoyo, J., A. Elliott, & J. Sargatal (eds.) *Handbook of the Birds of the World*, vol. 2. Lynx Edicions, Barcelona.

Whitney, B.M. 1992. Observations on the systematics, behaviour and vocalizations of *"Thamnomanes" occidentalis* (Formicariidae). *Auk* 109: 302–308.

Whitney, B.M. 2003. Family Conopophagidae (gnateaters). Pp. 732–747 *in* del Hoyo, J., A. Elliott, & D.A. Christie (eds.) *Handbook of the Birds of the World*, vol. 8. Lynx Edicions, Barcelona.

Whitney, B.M., & J. Álvarez-Alonso. 1998. A new *Herpsilochmus* antwren (Aves: Thamnophilidae) from northern Amazonian Peru and adjacent Ecuador: the role of edaphic heterogeneity of terra firme forests. *Auk* 115: 559–576.

Whitney, B.M., & J. Álvarez-Alonso. 2005. A new species of gnatcatcher from white-sand forests of northern Amazonian Peru, with revision of the *Polioptila guianensis* complex. *Wilson Bull.* 117: 113–210.

Whitney, B.M., & J.F. Pacheco. 1997. Behavior, vocalizations, and relationships of some *Myrmotherula* antwrens (Thamnophilidae) in eastern Brazil, with comments on the "plain-winged" group. Pp. 809–819 *in* Remsen, J.V. (ed.) Studies in Neotropical ornithology honoring Ted Parker. *Orn. Monogr.* 48.

Whitney, B.M., J.F. Pacheco & R. Parrini. 1995. Two species of *Neopelma* in southeastern Brazil and diversification within the *Neopelma/Tyranneutes* complex: implications of the subspecies concept for conservation (Passeriformes: Tyrannidae). *Ararajuba* 3: 43–53.

Whitney, B.M., & G.H. Rosenberg. 1993. Behavior, vocalizations and possible relationships of *Xenornis setifrons* (Formicariidae), a little-known Chocó endemic. *Condor* 95: 227–231.

Whittingham, M.J., & R.S.R. Williams. 2000. Notes on morphological differences exhibited by Royal Flycatcher *Onychorhynchus coronatus* taxa. *Cotinga* 13: 14–16.

Wiedenfeld, D.A., T.S. Schulenberg & M.B. Robbins. 1985. Birds of a tropical deciduous forest in extreme northwestern Peru. Pp. 305–315 *in* Buckley, P.A., M.S. Foster, E.S. Morton, R.S. Ridgely & F.G. Buckley (eds.) 1985. Neotropical ornithology. *Orn. Monogr.* 36.

Willard, D.E., M.S. Foster, G.F. Barrowclough, R.W. Dickerman, P.F. Cannell, S.L. Coates, J.L. Cracraft, & J.P. O'Neill. 1991. The birds of the Cerro de la Neblina, Territoro Federal Amazonas, Venezuela. *Fieldiana Zool.* 65: 1–80.

Williams, R.S.R., & D. Beadle. 2003. Eurasian Wigeon *Anas penelope* in Venezuela: a new bird for South America. *Cotinga* 19: 71.

Willis, E.O. 1969. On the behaviour of five species of *Rhegmatorhina*, ant-following antbirds of the Amazon basin. *Wilson Bull.* 81: 363–395.

Willis, E.O. 1972. Taxonomy, Ecology and Behaviour of the Sooty Ant-Tanager (*Habia gutturalis*) and other ant-tanagers (Aves). *Amer. Mus. Novit.* 2480: 1-38.

Willis, E.O. 1983. Toucans (Rasmphastidae) and hornbills (Bucerotidae) as ant followers. *Gerfaut* 73: 239–242.

Willis, E.O. 1983. Trans-Andean *Xiphorhynchus* (Aves, Dendrocolaptidae) as army ant followers. *Rev. Brasil. Biol.* 43: 125–131.

Willis, E.O. 1984. Antshrikes (Formicariidae) as army ant followers. *Pap. Avulsas Zool.* 35: 177–182.

Willis, E.O. 1992. Three *Chamaeza* antthrushes in eastern Brazil (Formicariidae). *Condor* 94: 110–116.

Willis, E.O. & E. Eisenmann. 1979. A Revised List of Birds of Barro Colorado Island, Panama. *Smiths. Contrib. Zool.* No. 291: 1-31.

Wilmore, S.B. 1977. *Crows, Jays and Ravens*. David & Charles, Newton Abbott.

Winkler, H. & D.A. Christie. 2002. Family Picidae (woodpeckers). Pp. 296–555 *in* del Hoyo, J., A. Elliott & J. Sargatal, eds. *Handbook of the Birds of the World*, vol. 7. Lynx Edicions, Barcelona.

Winkler, H., D.A. Christie & D. Nurney 1995. *Woodpeckers: An Identification Guide to the Woodpeckers of the World.* Pica Press, Robertsbridge.

Woodall, P.F. 2001. Family Alcedinidae (kingfishers). Pp. 130–

249 *in* del Hoyo, J., A. Elliott, & J. Sargatal (eds.) *Handbook of the Birds of the World*, vol. 6. Lynx Edicions, Barcelona.

Worth, B. 1969. Hooded Warbler in Trinidad, West Indies. *Wilson Bull.* 81: 215.

Yuri, T. & D.P. Mindell. 2002. Molecular phylogenetic analysis of Fringillidae, "New World nine-primaried oscines" (Aves: Passeriformes). *Mol. Phylog. Evol.* 23: 229-243.

Zimmer, J.T. 1930. Birds of the Marshall Field Peruvian Expedition 1922-1923. *Publications of the Field Museum of Natural History (Zool. Ser.)* 282, pt. 17(7). Pp 480.

Zimmer, J.T. 1931a. Studies of Peruvian birds. I New and other birds from Peru, Ecuador, and Brazil. *Amer. Mus. Novit.* 500: 1–23.

Zimmer, J.T. 1931b. Studies of Peruvian birds. II Peruvian forms of the genera *Microbates*, *Ramphocaenus*, *Sclateria*, *Pyriglena*, *Pithys*, *Drymophila*, and *Liosceles*. *Amer. Mus. Novit.* 509: 1–20.

Zimmer, J.T. 1932a. Studies of Peruvian birds. III The genus *Myrmotherula* in Peru, with notes on extralimital forms. Part 1. *Amer. Mus. Novit.* 523: 1–19.

Zimmer, J.T. 1932b. Studies of Peruvian birds. IV The genus *Myrmotherula* in Peru, with notes on extralimital forms. Part 2. *Amer. Mus. Novit.* 524: 1–16.

Zimmer, J.T. 1932c. Studies of Peruvian birds. V The genera *Herpsilochmus*, *Microrhopias*, *Formicivora*, *Hypocnemis*, *Hypocnemoides*, and *Myrmochanes*. *Amer. Mus. Novit.* 538: 1–27.

Zimmer, J.T. 1932d. Studies of Peruvian birds. VI The Formicarian genera *Myrmoborus* and *Myrmeciza* in Perú. *Amer. Mus. Novit.* 545: 1–24.

Zimmer, J.T. 1932e. Studies of Peruvian birds. VII The genera *Pygiptila*, *Megastictus*, *Dysithamnus*, *Thamnomanes*, *Cercomacra*, and *Phlegopsis*. *Amer. Mus. Novit.* 558: 1–25.

Zimmer, J.T. 1932f. Studies of Peruvian birds. VIII The Formicarian genera *Cymbilaimus*, *Thamnistes*, *Terenura*, *Percnostola*, *Formicarius*, *Chamaeza*, and *Rhegmatorhina*. *Amer. Mus. Novit.* 584: 1–20.

Zimmer, J.T. 1933a. Studies of Peruvian birds. IX The Formicarian genus *Thamnophilus*. Part I. *Amer. Mus. Novit.* 646: 1–22.

Zimmer, J.T. 1933b. Studies of Peruvian birds. X The Formicarian genus *Thamnophilus*. Part II. *Amer. Mus. Novit.* 647: 1–27.

Zimmer, J.T. 1933c. Studies of Peruvian birds. XI The genera *Taraba* and *Sakesphorus*. *Amer. Mus. Novit.* 668: 1–17.

Zimmer, J.T. 1934a. Studies of Peruvian birds. XII Notes on *Hylophylax*, *Myrmothera*, and *Grallaria*. *Amer. Mus. Novit.* 703: 1–21.

Zimmer, J.T. 1934b. Studies of Peruvian birds. XIII The genera *Dendrexetastes*, *Campylorhamphus*, and *Dendrocincla*. *Amer. Mus. Novit.* 728: 1–20.

Zimmer, J.T. 1934c. Studies of Peruvian birds. XIV Notes on the genera *Dendrocolaptes*, *Hylexetastes*, *Xiphocolaptes*, *Dendroplex*, and *Lepidocolaptes*. *Amer. Mus. Novit.* 753: 1–26.

Zimmer, J.T. 1934d. Studies of Peruvian birds. XV Notes on the genus *Xiphorhynchus*. *Amer. Mus. Novit.* 756: 1–20.

Zimmer, J.T. 1934e. Studies of Peruvian birds. XVI Notes on the genera *Glyphorhynchus*, *Sittasomus*, *Deconychura*, *Margarornis*, *Premnornis*, *Premnoplex*, and *Sclerurus*. *Amer. Mus. Novit.* 757: 1-22.

Zimmer, J.T. 1935a. Studies of Peruvian birds. XVII Notes on the genera *Syndactyla*, *Anabacerthia*, *Philydor*, and *Automolus*. *Amer. Mus. Novit.* 785: 1–24.

Zimmer, J.T. 1935b. Studies of Peruvian birds. XVIII Diagnoses of new species and subspecies of Furnariidae from Perú and other parts of South America. *Amer. Mus. Novit.* 819: 1–8.

Zimmer, J.T. 1936a. Studies of Peruvian birds. XIX Notes on the genera *Geositta*, *Furnarius*, *Phleocryptes*, *Certhiaxis*, *Cranioleuca* and *Asthenes*. *Amer. Mus. Novit.* 860: 1–17.

Zimmer, J.T. 1936b. Studies of Peruvian birds. XX Notes on the genus *Synallaxis*. *Amer. Mus. Novit.* 861: 1–26.

Zimmer, J.T. 1936c. Studies of Peruvian birds. XXI Notes on the genera *Pseudocolaptes*, *Hyloctistes*, *Hylocryptus*, *Thripadectes*, and *Xenops*. *Amer. Mus. Novit.* 862: 1–25.

Zimmer, J.T. 1936d. Studies of Peruvian birds. XXII Notes on the Pipridae. *Amer. Mus. Novit.* 889: 1–29.

Zimmer, J.T. 1936e. Studies of Peruvian birds. XXIII: Notes on *Doliornis*, *Pipreola*, *Attila*, *Laniocera*, *Rhytipterna*, and *Lipaugus*. *Amer. Mus. Novit.* 893: 1–15.

Zimmer, J.T. 1936f. Studies of Peruvian birds. XXIV Notes on *Pachyramphus*, *Platypsaris*, *Tityra*, and *Pyroderus*. *Amer. Mus. Novit.* 894: 1–26.

Zimmer, J.T. 1937a. Studies of Peruvian birds. XXV Notes on the genera *Thamnophilus*, *Thamnocharis*, *Gymnopithys*, and *Ramphocaenus*. *Amer. Mus. Novit.* 917: 1–16.

Zimmer, J.T. 1937b. Studies of Peruvian birds. XXVI Notes on the genera *Agriornis*, *Muscisaxicola*, *Myiotheretes*, *Ochthoeca*, *Colona*, *Knipolegus*, *Phaeotriccus*, *Fluvicola* and *Ramphotrigon*. *Amer. Mus. Novit.* 930: 1–27.

Zimmer, J.T. 1937c. Studies of Peruvian birds. XXVII Notes on the genera *Muscivora*, *Tyrannus*, *Empidonomus*, and *Sirystes*, with further notes on *Knipolegus*. *Amer. Mus. Novit.* 962: 1–28.

Zimmer, J.T. 1937d. Studies of Peruvian birds. XXVIII Notes on the genera *Myiodynastes*, *Conopias*, *Myiozetetes*, and *Pitangus*. *Amer. Mus. Novit.* 963: 1–28.

Zimmer, J.T. 1938. Studies of Peruvian birds. XXIX The genera *Myiarchus*, *Mitrephanes*, and *Cnemotriccus*. *Amer. Mus. Novit.* 994: 1–32.

Zimmer, J.T. 1939a. Studies of Peruvian birds. XXX Notes on the genera *Contopus*, *Empidonax*, *Terenotriccus*, and *Myiobius*. *Amer. Mus. Novit.* 1042: 1–13.

Zimmer, J.T. 1939b. Studies of Peruvian birds. XXXI Notes on the genera *Myiotriccus*, *Pyrrhomyias*, *Myiophobus*, *Onychorhynchus*, *Platyrinchus*, *Cnipodectes*, *Sayornis*, and *Nuttallornis*. *Amer. Mus. Novit.* 1043: 1–15.

Zimmer, J.T. 1939c. Studies of Peruvian birds. XXXII The genus *Scytalopus*. *Amer. Mus. Novit.* 1044: 1–18.

Zimmer, J.T. 1939d. Studies of Peruvian birds. XXXIII The genera *Tolmomyias* and *Rhynchocyclus*, with further notes on *Ramphotrigon*. *Amer. Mus. Novit.* 1045: 1–23.

Zimmer, J.T. 1940a. Studies of Peruvian birds. XXXIV The genera *Todirostrum*, *Euscarthmornis*, *Snethlegea*, *Poecilotriccus*, *Lophotriccus*, *Myiornis*, *Pseudotriccus*, and *Hemitriccus*. *Amer. Mus. Novit.* 1066: 1–23.

Zimmer, J.T. 1940b. Studies of Peruvian birds. XXXV Notes on the genera *Phylloscartes*, *Euscarthmus*, *Pseudocolopteryx*, *Tachuris*, *Spizitornis*, *Yanacea*, *Uromyias*, *Stigmatura*, *Serpophaga*, and *Mecocerculus*. *Amer. Mus. Novit.* 1095: 1–19.

Zimmer, J.T. 1941a. Studies of Peruvian birds. XXXVI The genera *Elaenia*, and *Myiopagis*. *Amer. Mus. Novit.* 1108: 1–23.

Zimmer, J.T. 1941b. Studies of Peruvian birds. XXXVII The genera *Sublegatus*, *Phaeomyias*, *Camptostoma*, *Xanthomyias*, *Phyllomyias*, and *Tyranniscus*. *Amer. Mus. Novit.* 1109: 1–25.

Zimmer, J.T. 1941c. Studies of Peruvian birds. XXXVIII The genera *Oreotriccus*, *Tyrannulus*, *Acrochordopus*, *Ornithion*, *Leptopogon*, *Mionectes*, *Pipromorpha*, and *Pyrocephalus*. *Amer. Mus. Novit.* 1126: 1–25.

Zimmer, J.T. 1941d. Studies of Peruvian birds. XXXIX The genus *Vireo*. *Amer. Mus. Novit.* 1127: 1–20.

Zimmer, J.T. 1942a. Studies of Peruvian birds. XL Notes on the genus *Veniliornis*. *Amer. Mus. Novit.* 1159: 1–12.

Zimmer, J.T. 1942b. Studies of Peruvian birds. XLI The genera *Hylophilus*, *Smaragdolanius*, and *Cyclarhis*. *Amer. Mus. Novit.* 1160: 1-16.

Zimmer, J.T. 1942c. Studies of Peruvian birds. XLII The genus *Polioptila*. *Amer. Mus. Novit.* 1168: 1-7.

Zimmer, J.T. 1942d. Studies of Peruvian birds. XLIII Notes on the genera *Dacnis*, *Xenodacnis*, *Coereba*, *Conirostrum*, and *Oreomanes*. *Amer. Mus. Novit.* 1193: 1–16.

Zimmer, J.T. 1942e. Studies of Peruvian birds. XLIV. Notes on the genera *Diglossa* and *Cyanerpes*, with Addenda to *Ochthoeca*. *Amer. Mus. Novit.* 1203: 1–15.

Zimmer, J.T. 1943a. Studies of Peruvian birds. XLV The genera *Tersina*, *Chlorophonia*, *Tanagra*, *Tanagrella*, *Chlorochrysa*, and *Pipraeidea*. *Amer. Mus. Novit.* 1225: 1–24.

Zimmer, J.T. 1943b. Studies of Peruvian birds. XLVI The genus *Tangara*. Part 1. *Amer. Mus. Novit.* 1245: 1–14.

Zimmer, J.T. 1943c. Studies of Peruvian birds. XLVII The genus *Tangara*. Part 2. *Amer. Mus. Novit.* 1246: 1–14.

Zimmer, J.T. 1944a. Studies of Peruvian birds. XLVIII The genera *Iridosornis*, *Delothraupis*, *Anisognathus*, *Buthraupis*, *Compsocoma*, *Dubusia*, and *Thraupis*. *Amer. Mus. Novit.* 1262: 1–21.

Zimmer, J.T. 1944b. Studies of Peruvian birds. XLIX. Notes on *Frederickena* and *Ochthoeca*. *Amer. Mus. Novit.* 1263: 1–5.

Zimmer, J.T. 1944c. Two new subspecies of *Catharus aurantiirostris*. Auk 61: 404–408.

Zimmer, J.T. 1945. Studies of Peruvian birds. L The genera *Ramphocelus*, *Piranga*, *Habia*, *Lanio*, and *Tachyphonus*. *Amer. Mus. Novit.* 1304: 1–26.

Zimmer, J.T. 1947a. Studies of Peruvian birds. LI The genera *Chlorothraupis*, *Creurgops*, *Eucometis*, *Trichothraupis*, *Nemosia*, *Hemithraupis*, and *Thlypopsis*, with additional notes on *Piranga*. *Amer. Mus. Novit.* 1345: 1–23.

Zimmer, J.T. 1947b. Studies of Peruvian birds. LII The genera *Sericossypha*, *Chlorospingus*, *Cnemoscopus*, *Hemispingus*, *Conothraupis*, *Chlorornis*, *Lamprospiza*, *Cissopis*, and *Schistochlamys*. *Amer. Mus. Novit.* 1367: 1–26.

Zimmer, J.T. 1948. Studies of Peruvian birds. LIII The family Trogonidae. *Amer. Mus. Novit.* 1380: 1–56.

Zimmer, J.T. 1949. Studies of Peruvian birds. LIV The families Catamblyrhynchidae and Parulidae. *Amer. Mus. Novit.* 1428: 1–59.

Zimmer, J.T. 1950a. Studies of Peruvian birds. LV The hummingbird genera *Doryfera*, *Glaucis*, *Threnetes*, and *Phaethornis*. *Amer. Mus. Novit.* 1449: 1–51.

Zimmer, J.T. 1950b. Studies of Peruvian birds. LVI The genera *Eutoxeres*, *Campylopterus*, *Eupetomena*, and *Florisuga*. *Amer. Mus. Novit.* 1450: 1–14.

Zimmer, J.T. 1950c. Studies of Peruvian birds. LVII The genera *Colibri*, *Anthracothorax*, *Klais*, *Lophornis*, and *Chlorestes*. *Amer. Mus. Novit.* 1463: 1–28.

Zimmer, J.T. 1950d. Studies of Peruvian birds. LVIII The genera *Chlorostilbon*, *Thalurania*, *Hylocharis*, and *Chrysuronia*. *Amer. Mus. Novit.* 1474: 1–31.

Zimmer, J.T. 1950e. Studies of Peruvian birds. LIX The genera *Polytmus*, *Leucippus*, and *Amazilia*. *Amer. Mus. Novit.* 1475: 1–27.

Zimmer, J.T. 1951a. Studies of Peruvian birds. LX The genera *Heliodoxa*, *Phlogophilus*, *Urosticte*, *Polyplancta*, *Adelomyia*, *Coeligena*, *Ensifera*, *Oreotrochilus*, and *Topaza*. *Amer. Mus. Novit.* 1513: 1–45.

Zimmer, J.T. 1951b. Studies of Peruvian birds. LXI The genera *Aglaeactis*, *Lafresnaya*, *Pterophanes*, *Boissonneaua*, *Heliangelus*, *Eriocnemis*, *Haplophaedia*, *Ocreatus*, and *Lesbia*. *Amer. Mus. Novit.* 1540: 1–55.

Zimmer, J.T. 1952. Studies of Peruvian birds. LXII The hummingbird genera *Patagona*, *Sappho*, *Polyonymus*, *Ramphomicron*, *Metallura*, *Chalcostigma*, *Taphrolesbia*, and *Aglaiocercus*. *Amer. Mus. Novit.* 1595: 1–29.

Zimmer, J.T. 1953a. Studies of Peruvian birds. LXIII The hummingbird genera *Oreonympha*, *Schistes*, *Heliothryx*, *Loddigesia*, *Heliomaster*, *Rhodopis*, *Thaumastura*, *Calliphlox*, *Myrtis*, *Myrmia*, and *Acestura*. *Amer. Mus. Novit.* 1604: 1–26.

Zimmer, J.T. 1953b. Studies of Peruvian birds. LXIV The swifts: Family Apodidae. *Amer. Mus. Novit.* 1609: 1–20.

Zimmer, J.T. 1953c. Studies of Peruvian birds. LXV The jays (Corvidae) and pipits (Motacillidae). *Amer. Mus. Novit.* 1649: 1–27.

Zimmer, J.T. 1955. Studies of Peruvian birds. LXVI The swallows (Hirundinidae). *Amer. Mus. Novit.* 1723: 1–35.

Zimmer, J.T. 1959. Further notes on tyrant flycatchers. *Amer. Mus. Novit.* 1749: 3–7.

Zimmer, K.J. 1997. Species limits in *Cranioleuca vulpina*. Pp: 849–864 *in* Remsen, J.V. (ed.) Studies in Neotropical ornithology honoring Ted Parker. *Orn. Monogr.* 48.

Zimmer, K.J. 2002. Species limits in Olive-backed Foliage-gleaners (*Automolus:* Furnariidae). *Wilson Bull.* 114: 20–37.

Zimmer, K.J., & M.L. Isler. 2003. Family Thamnophilidae (typical antbirds). Pp. 448–681 *in* del Hoyo, J., A. Elliott, & D.A. Christie (eds.) *Handbook of the Birds of the World*, vol. 8. Lynx Edicions, Barcelona.

Zimmer, K.J., & A. Whittaker. 2000. Species limits in Pale-tipped Tyrannulets (*Inezia:* Tyrannidae). *Wilson Bull.* 112: 51–66.

Zimmer, K.J., & A. Whittaker. 2004. Observations on the vocalizations and behaviour of Black-chested Tyrant *Taeniotriccus andrei* from the Serra dos Carajás, Pará, Brazil. *Cotinga* 22: 24–29.

Zink, R.M. & N.K. Johnson. 1984. Evolutionary genetics of flycatchers. L. Sibling species in the genera *Empidonax* and *Contopus*. *Syst. Zool.*, 33: 205-216.

Züchner, T. 1999. Genus *Coeligena*, family Trochilidae (hummingbirds). Pp. 626–629 *in* del Hoyo, J., A. Elliott, & J. Sargatal (eds.) *Handbook of the Birds of the World*, vol. 5. Lynx Edicions, Barcelona.

Zusi, R.L. 1996. Family Rynchopidae (skimmers). Pp. 668–677 *in* del Hoyo, J., A. Elliott, & J. Sargatal (eds.) *Handbook of the Birds of the World*, vol. 3. Lynx Edicions, Barcelona.

Zyskowski, K., & R.O. Prum. 1999. Phylogenetic analysis of the nest architecture of Neotropical ovenbirds (Furnariidae). *Auk* 116: 891–911.

INDEX

abbreviatus, Ramphastos ambiguus 312
abditivus, Manacus manacus 550
abdominalis, Mionectes oleagineus 447
abdominalis, Veniliornis dignus 320
abeillei, Arremon 707
aburri, Aburria 47
Aburria 47
Accipiter 88
ACCIPITRIDAE 83
accipitrinus, Deroptyus 193
accola, Myiopagis viridicata 467
acer, Zimmerius gracilipes 460
Acestrura 276
acrolophites, Schiffornis turdina 557
Acropternis 445
Actitis 134
acuflavidus, Thalasseus sandvicensis 153
acuta, Anas 39
acuticauda, Hylophilus flavipes 574
acuticaudata, Aratinga 173
acutipennis, Chordeiles 212
acutipennis, Pseudocolopteryx 477
acutirostris, Xenops tenuirostris 362
Adelomyia 252
adjacens, Myiobius atricaudus 496
adusta, Roraimia 347
Aegolius 209
aemulus, Hylophilus thoracicus 571
aenea, Chloroceryle 285
aenea, Schiffornis turdina 557
aeneicauda, Chalybura buffonii 252
aeneosticta, Adelomyia melanogenys 252
aeneus, Glaucis 225
aeneus, Molothrus 762
aenigma, Sapayoa 566
aenigmaticus, Campylorhynchus turdinus 588
aequalis, Stelgidopteryx ruficollis 585
aequatorialis, Amaurospiza concolor 703
aequatorialis, Anairetes parulus 476
aequatorialis, Androdon 230
aequatorialis, Asthenes wyatti 344
aequatorialis, Campylopterus largipennis 231
aequatorialis, Cercomacra nigrescens 407
aequatorialis, Chordeiles acutipennis 213
aequatorialis, Cistothorus platensis 591
aequatorialis, Dacnis lineata 669
aequatorialis, Dysithamnus mentalis 390
aequatorialis, Eubucco bourcierii 303
aequatorialis, Falco sparverius 107
aequatorialis, Gymnopithys leucaspis 419
aequatorialis, Heliodoxa rubinoides 253
aequatorialis, Herpsilochmus axillaris 402
aequatorialis, Lepidocolaptes lacrymiger 377
aequatorialis, Lesbia victoriae 277
aequatorialis, Megascops albogularis 204
aequatorialis, Molothrus bonariensis 761
aequatorialis, Momotus 289
aequatorialis, Neomorphus geoffroyi 198
aequatorialis, Penelope purpurascens 45
aequatorialis, Petrochelidon rufocollaris 587
aequatorialis, Rallus limicola 114
aequatorialis, Rupicola peruvianus 536
aequatorialis, Sittasomus griseicapillus 366
aequatorialis, Tangara arthus 659
aequatorialis, Thamnistes anabatinus 389
aequatorialis, Tolmomyias sulphurescens 486
aequinoctialis, Buteogallus 93
aequinoctialis, Geothlypis 736
aequinoctialis, Procellaria 59
aequinoctialis, Rhynchocyclus olivaceus 485
Aeronautes 223
aeruginosa, Aratinga pertinax 175
aestiva, Dendroica petechia 725
aethereus, Aglaiocercus coelestis 277
aethereus, Nyctibius 211
aethereus, Phaethon 64
aetherodroma, Chaetura spinicauda 221
aethiops, Oryzoborus funereus 703
aethiops, Thamnophilus 385
affinis, Aythya 42
affinis, Cyanocorax 577
affinis, Eucometis penicillata 635
affinis, Glaucis hirsutus 225
affinis, Lophotriccus vitiosus 482
affinis, Suiriri suiriri 464
affinis, Veniliornis 320
agami, Agamia 70
Agamia 70
Agelaius 758
agilis, Anairetes 476
agilis, Oporornis 734
agilis, Veniliornis passerinus 320
Aglaeactis 258
Aglaiocercus 276
Agriornis 508
agustini, Sporophila intermedia 694
ajaja, Platalea 79
alamoris, Anisognathus somptuosus 647
alarum, Parula pitiayumi 725
alarum, Xiphorhynchus lachrymosus 375
ALAUDIDAE 578
alaudinus, Phrygilus 688
alba, Ardea 74
alba, Calidris 136
alba, Gygis 148
alba, Motacilla 624
alba, Tyto 200
Albatross, Black-browed 56
  Black-footed 56
  Waved 56
  Yellow-nosed 56
albertaensis, Larus californicus 144
alberti, Crax 49
albescens, Synallaxis 333
albicans, Thamnophilus doliatus 383
albicans, Troglodytes musculus 598
albicauda, Caprimulgus cayennensis 216
albicauda, Penelope argyrotis 44
albicaudatus, Buteo 97
albiceps, Atlapetes 713
albiceps, Elaenia 468
albicilius, Campylorhynchus griseus 587
albicincta, Streptoprocne zonaris 220
albicollis, Leucopternis 92
albicollis, Nyctidromus 215
albicollis, Porzana 116
albicollis, Turdus 621
albicollis, Zonotrichia 685
albicrissa, Heliomaster longirostris 272
albidiadema, Ochthoeca frontalis 504
albidiventris, Cinclodes fuscus 329
albifacies, Myioborus 738
albifrons, Anser 36
albifrons, Conirostrum 651
albifrons, Myioborus 739
albifrons, Pithys 418
albigula, Atlapetes semirufus 714
albigula, Buteo 98
albigula, Myrmotherula axillaris 398
albigularis, Hemithraupis flavicollis 632
albigularis, Laterallus 112
albigularis, Microcerculus bambla 603
albigularis, Sclerurus 360
albigularis, Synallaxis 334
albigularis, Thryothorus fasciatoventris 592
albigularis, Zimmerius chrysops 461
albilatera, Diglossa 653
albilateralis, Henicorhina leucosticta 600
albilinea, Patagioenas fasciata 157
albilinea, Tachycineta 579
albilora, Dendroica dominica 729
albilora, Muscisaxicola 509
albiloris, Grallaria ruficapilla 430
albimarginatus, Myiarchus swainsoni 517
albinucha, Xenopsaris 559
albipectus, Pyrrhura 178
albipectus, Thryothorus leucotis 597
albirostris, Galbula 290
albitarsis, Ciccaba 205
albitorques, Tityra inquisitor 556
albiventer, Geotrygon violacea 169
albiventer, Tachycineta 579
albiventer, Turdus leucomelas 617
albiventris, Dacnis 669
albiventris, Ramphocaenus melanurus 605
albivertex, Elaenia chiriquensis 471
albivitta, Aulacorhynchus prasinus 305
albivitta, Columbina passerina 162

albobrunneus, Campylorhynchus 588
albocaudatus, Mecocerculus stictopterus 474
albocinereus, Sirystes sibilator 516
albocristata, Sericossypha 627
albofrenatus, Atlapetes 712
albogriseus, Mimus longicaudatus 622
albogriseus, Pachyramphus 562
albogriseus, Sirystes sibilator 516
albogularis, Contopus 502
albogularis, Megascops 203
albogularis, Platyrinchus mystaceus 489
albogularis, Schistes geoffroyi 271
albogularis, Tyrannus 520
albolineatus, Lepidocolaptes 377
albonotatus, Buteo 100
albovittatus, Conopias 524
albus, Eudocimus 77
albus, Procnias 538
ALCEDINIDAE 285
alcyon, Megaceryle 286
alector, Crax 49
alexandri, Falco tinnunculus 107
alexandrinus, Charadrius 124
alfredi, Psarocolius angustifrons 748
alice, Chlorostilbon 240
aliciae, Amazilia tobaci 250
aliciae, Catharus minimus 612
alinae, Eriocnemis 266
alixii, Clytoctantes 389
alleni, Grallaria 428
alleni, Piculus rubiginosus 322
allinornatus, Buarremon brunneinucha 708
alnorum, Empidonax 502
alopecias, Cranioleuca vulpina 342
Alopochelidon 585
alpestris, Eremophila 578
alpica, Catamenia analis 704
alpina, Calidris 138
alpinus, Muscisaxicola 509
altera, Corapipo 547
alticola, Amazilia 251
alticola, Cistothorus platensis 591
alticola, Elaenia cristata 470
alticola, Grallaria quitensis 433
altiloquus, Vireo 570
altipetens, Anas 38
altirostris, Xiphorhynchus picus 371
altissima, Streptoprocne zonaris 220
amabilis, Amazilia 248
amacurense, Todirostrum maculatum 455
amacurensis, Glyphorynchus spirurus 367
amarcurensis, Celeus undatus 325
amaruni, Topaza pyra 255
amaurocephalus, Leptopogon 448
amaurogaster, Thryothorus mystacalis 593
Amaurolimnas 115
Amaurospiza 703
Amazilia 247
amazilia, Amazilia 251
amazilia, Columbina minuta 161
Amazon, Blue-cheeked 191
Festive 190
Mealy 192
Orange-winged 192
Red-lored 190
Scaly-naped 192
Yellow-crowned 191
Yellow-shouldered 191
Amazona 190
amazona, Capsiempis flaveola 463
amazona, Chloroceryle 286
amazona, Schiffornis turdina 557
Amazonetta 37
amazonica, Amazona 192
amazonicus, Thamnophilus 387
amazonicus, Trogon rufus 282
amazonina, Hapalopsittaca 185
amazonum, Conirostrum speciosum 650
amazonus, Myiarchus swainsoni 517
amazonus, Sittasomus griseicapillus 366
ambigua, Myrmotherula 393
ambigua, Nothoprocta pentlandi 33
ambiguus, Ara 171
ambiguus, Ocreatus underwoodii 278
ambiguus, Ramphastos 312
Amblycercus 752
americana, Anas 38
americana, Chloroceryle 285
americana, Fulica 119
americana, Mycteria 80
americana, Parula 724
americana, Recurvirostra 126
americana, Spiza 716
americana, Sporophila 695
americanus, Anous minutus 148
americanus, Ibycter 103
americanus, Numenius 132
amethysticollis, Heliangelus 263
amethystina, Calliphlox 273
Ammodramus 685
amnicola, Dendroica petechia 725
Ampelioides 535
Ampelion 531
Anabacerthia 353
anabatinus, Thamnistes 389
Anabazenops 355
anachoreta, Henicorhina leucophrys 601
anaethetus, Onychoprion 148
Anairetes 476
analis, Catamenia 704
analis, Formicarius 424
analis, Iridosornis 648
Anas 38
ANATIDAE 34
anatum, Falco peregrinus 109
anchicayae, Sporophila intermedia 694
Ancistrops 350
andaquiensis, Grallaria alleni 428
andersoni, Patagioenas cayennensis 157
andicola, Agriornis 508
andicola, Leptasthenura 331
andicola, Ramphomicron microrhynchum 268
Andigena 309
andina, Gallinago 129
andina, Oxyura ferruginea 36
andinus, Chaetocercus jourdanii 275
andinus, Hemitriccus granadensis 453
andinus, Podiceps 54
andinus, Polytmus guainumbi 245
andinus, Sclerurus mexicanus 360
andium, Anas 39
andrei, Chaetura 222
andrei, Crypturellus soui 29
andrei, Dysithamnus mentalis 390
andrei, Taeniotriccus 451
Androdon 230
angolensis, Oryzoborus 702
angustifrons, Psarocolius 748
angustirostris, Lepidocolaptes 376
angustirostris, Myrmoborus leucophrys 409
angustirostris, Sayornis nigricans 503
Anhima 34
ANHIMIDAE 34
Anhinga 68
anhinga, Anhinga 68
ANHINGIDAE 68
ani, Crotophaga 198
Ani, Greater 197
Groove-billed 198
Smooth-billed 198
Anisognathus 646
anneae, Euphonia 772
annectens, Pseudotriccus pelzelni 449
annectens, Thraupis cyanocephala 643
Anous 148
Anser 36
antarcticus, Podilymbus podiceps 54
Antbird, Amazonas 412
Ash-breasted 409
Banded 400
Bare-crowned 411
Bicoloured 419
Black 407
Black-and-white 411
Black-chinned 410
Black-faced 409
Black-headed 412
Black-throated 417
Blackish 407
Caura 413
Chestnut-backed 414
Chestnut-crested 420
Dot-backed 421
Dull-mantled 415
Dusky 406
Esmeraldas 414
Ferruginous-backed 415
Grey 406
Grey-bellied 416
Grey-headed 417
Hairy-crested 420

Immaculate 417
Jet 408
Long-tailed 404
Lunulated 419
Northern Chestnut-tailed 416
Ocellated 423
Parker's 406
Plumbeous 416
Rio Branco 408
Roraiman 413
Rufous-throated 418
Scale-backed 421
Silvered 411
Slate-coloured 412
Sooty 417
Spot-backed 421
Spot-winged 413
Spotted 420
Striated 404
Stub-tailed 413
Warbling 410
White-bellied 414
White-browed 409
White-masked 418
White-plumed 418
White-shouldered 416
Willis's 407
Wing-banded 419
Yapacana 415
Yellow-browed 410
antelius, Pionus sordidus 189
anteocularis, Polioptila plumbea 606
Anthocephala 252
anthoides, Corythopis torquata 457
anthonyi, Caprimulgus 217
anthophilus, Phaethornis 228
anthracinus, Buteogallus 94
Anthracothorax 234
Anthus 624
antillarum, Buteo platypterus 98
antillarum, Sternula 149
antioquensis, Picumnus granadensis 317
antioquiae, Ampelion rufaxilla 531
antioquiae, Anisognathus somptuosus 647
antioquiae, Machaeropterus regulus 547
antioquiae, Piprites chloris 566
antioquiae, Zenaida auriculata 160
antisianus, Pharomachrus 283
antisiensis, Cranioleuca 341
Antpipit, Ringed 457
Antpitta, Bicoloured 431
Black-crowned 426
Brown-banded 433
Chestnut-crowned 430
Chestnut-naped 432
Crescent-faced 437
Cundinamarca 431
Giant 427
Great 427
Grey-naped 431
Hooded 437
Jocotoco 431
Moustached 428
Ochre-breasted 436
Ochre-striped 430
Peruvian 437
Plain-backed 429
Rufous 433
Rufous-crowned 426
Rusty-breasted 436
Santa Marta 431
Scaled 428
Scallop-breasted 437
Slate-crowned 436
Spotted 434
Streak-chested 434
Táchira 429
Tawny 433
Tepui 435
Thicket 434
Thrush-like 435
Undulated 427
Variegated 428
Watkins's 430
White-bellied 432
White-lored 434
Yellow-breasted 432
Antshrike, Amazonian 387
Band-tailed 382
Bar-crested 383
Barred 382
Black 384
Black-backed 382
Black-capped 386
Black-crested 381
Black-throated 380
Blackish-grey 384
Castelnau's 385
Chapman's 383
Cinereous 392
Cocha 384
Collared 382
Dusky-throated 392
Eastern Slaty 386
Fasciated 379
Great 380
Guianan Slaty 386
Lined 384
Mouse-coloured 386
Pearly 388
Plain-winged 386
Russet 389
Speckled 389
Spot-winged 388
Streak-backed 387
Undulated 380
Uniform 385
Western Slaty 387
White-shouldered 385
Antthrush, Barred 426
Black-faced 424
Black-headed 424
Rufous-breasted 425
Rufous-capped 424
Schwartz's 426
Short-tailed 425
Striated 425
Antvireo, Bicoloured 391
Plain 390
Spot-crowned 391
White-streaked 391
Antwren, Amazonian Streaked 394
Ancient 402
Ash-winged 405
Brown-backed 396
Brown-bellied 395
Checker-throated 396
Cherrie's 394
Chestnut-shouldered 405
Dot-winged 403
Dugand's 400
Foothill 397
Grey 399
Guianan Streaked 393
Leaden 399
Long-winged 399
Moustached 393
Ornate 397
Pacific 394
Plain-throated 395
Plain-winged 398
Pygmy 393
Río Suno 398
Roraiman 401
Rufous-bellied 395
Rufous-rumped 405
Rufous-tailed 397
Rusty-backed 404
Slaty 398
Spot-backed 401
Stipple-throated 396
Stripe-chested 395
Todd's 401
White-eyed 396
White-flanked 397
White-fringed 403
Yellow-breasted 402
Yellow-throated 393
Anurolimnas 111
anxia, Anabacerthia striaticollis 353
apertus, Caprimulgus cayennensis 216
aphanes, Chaetura vauxi 223
Aphanotriccus 499
Aphriza 135
apicalis, Amazilia fimbriata 247
apicalis, Myiarchus 519
apicalis, Phaethornis guy 226
APODIDAE 219
apolinari, Cistothorus 591
apurensis, Ammodramus aurifrons 686
apurensis, Athene cunicularia 209
apurensis, Cranioleuca vulpina 342
apurensis, Emberizoides herbicola 692
apurensis, Picumnus squamulatus 316
aquila, Eutoxeres 224
aquilonalis, Turdus fumigatus 619

Ara 170
aracari, Pteroglossus 308
Araçari, Black-necked 308
Chestnut-eared 308
Collared 308
Green 307
Ivory-billed 308
Lettered 307
Many-banded 309
Pale-mandibled 309
Stripe-billed 309
arada, Cyphorhinus 604
ARAMIDAE 109
Aramides 114
Aramus 109
aranea, Gelochelidon nilotica 150
ararauna, Ara 170
Aratinga 173
arboricola, Progne subis 581
arcana, Haplospiza rustica 689
arcuata, Pipreola 532
Ardea 73
ARDEIDAE 69
ardens, Piranga leucoptera 680
ardesiaca, Fulica 119
ardesiacus, Thamnomanes 392
ardosiacus, Contopus fumigatus 500
Arenaria 135
arenarum, Sublegatus 463
argentata, Sclateria naevia 411
argenticinctus, Momotus momota 288
argentinus, Lathrotriccus euleri 498
argyrofenges, Tangara 667
argyrotis, Penelope 44
aripoensis, Grallaria guatimalensis 429
aristeguietana, Drymophila caudata 404
armata, Merganetta 41
armenti, Molothrus aeneus 762
armillata, Cyanolyca 575
Arremon 706
Arremonops 707
arremonops, Oreothraupis 710
arthuri, Turdus ignobilis 618
arthus, Tangara 659
arubensis, Aratinga pertinax 175
arubensis, Athene cunicularia 209
Arundinicola 512
asemus, Tolmomyias sulphurescens 486
aserriensis, Chordeiles minor 213
asiatica, Zenaida 161
Asio 209
assimilis, Buarremon torquatus 709
assimilis, Hyloctistes virgatus 351
assimilis, Myrmotherula 399
assimilis, Puffinus 61
assimilis, Pyrrhomyias cinnamomeus 497
assimilis, Tolmomyias 487
assimilis, Trogon personatus 283
Asthenes 344
astreans, Chaetocercus 274
astrild, Estrilda 776
Atalotriccus 483
ater, Daptrius 103
aterrima, Diglossa humeralis 654
aterrima, Schistochlamys melanopis 625
athalassos, Sternula antillarum 149
Athene 208
atlantica, Chiroxiphia pareola 550
atlanticus, Anser caerulescens 36
Atlapetes 710
atopus, Troglodytes musculus 598
atra, Monasa 299
atratus, Coragyps 80
atratus, Scytalopus 440
atricapilla, Donacobius 606
atricapilla, Lonchura 775
atricapillus, Buarremon 708
atricapillus, Myiornis 481
atricaudus, Myiobius 496
atriceps, Myiarchus tuberculifer 517
atriceps, Thryothorus euophrys 593
atricilla, Larus 146
atrifrons, Odontophorus 51
atrigularis, Metallura williami 269
atrigularis, Synallaxis candei 339
atrimentalis, Phaethornis 230
atrinucha, Thamnophilus 387
atripennis, Fluvicola nengeta 511
atripennis, Saltator 719
atripennis, Thraupis palmarum 643
atrirostris, Cyclarhis nigrirostris 567
atrirostris, Oryzoborus 702
atrirostris, Sublegatus arenarum 463
atrocastaneus, Psarocolius angustifrons 748
atrocyaneum, Conirostrum albifrons 652
atrogularis, Penelope montagnii 45
atronitens, Xenopipo 552
atropileus, Hemispingus 627
atrosericeus, Turdus serranus 615
atrothorax, Myrmeciza 417
atrura, Fulica ardesiaca 120
Attagis 140
Atticora 584
Attila 513
Attila, Bright-rumped 514
Cinnamon 513
Citron-bellied 514
Dull-capped 514
Ochraceous 513
Rufous-tailed 513
audax, Aphanotriccus 499
audax, Pachyramphus validus 565
auduboni, Dendroica coronata 727
augusti, Phaethornis 229
Aulacorhynchus 304
aura, Cathartes 81
aurantiaca, Metopothrix 346
aurantiicinctus, Capito auratus 302
aurantiifrons, Hylophilus 573
aurantiigena, Pionopsitta barrabandi 188
aurantiirostris, Arremon 706
aurantiirostris, Catharus 610
aurantiivertex, Heterocercus 552
aurantioatrocristatus, Griseotyrannus 523
auratus, Capito 302
aurea, Aratinga 174
aureatus, Myiobius sulphureipygius 495
aureinucha, Iridophanes pulcherrimus 669
aureliae, Haplophaedia 267
aureocincta, Bangsia 645
aureola, Pipra 553
aureopectus, Machaeropterus regulus 547
aureopectus, Pipreola 533
aureoventris, Pheucticus 717
aurescens, Heliodoxa 253
aureus, Jacamerops 292
aureus, Phyllomyias nigrocapillus 459
auricapillus, Icterus 755
auriceps, Pharomachrus 284
auricrissa, Thraupis cyanocephala 643
auricularis, Basileuterus tristriatus 744
auricularis, Geothlypis 736
auricularis, Pyrrhura emma 177
auriculata, Zenaida 159
aurifrons, Ammodramus 686
aurifrons, Dendroica petechia 726
aurifrons, Picumnus 313
aurigularis, Hemithraupis flavicollis 632
aurita, Conopophaga 438
auritus, Heliothryx 271
auritus, Phalacrocorax 68
aurocapilla, Seiurus 733
aurora, Coeligena iris 261
aurosus, Piculus chrysochloros 323
aurovirens, Capito 301
aurulenta, Tangara arthus 659
aurulentus, Tolmomyias flaviventris 488
austerus, Basileuterus culicivorus 743
australis, Amblycercus holosericeus 752
australis, Geranoaetus melanoleucus 96
australis, Rhynchortyx cinctus 53
australis, Schistocichla caurensis 413
australis, Trogon massena 283
australis, Zenaida asiatica 161
Automolus 357
autumnalis, Amazona 190
autumnalis, Dendrocygna 35
auyantepui, Elaenia dayi 471
auyantepui, Hemitriccus margaritaceiventer 452
aveledoi, Synallaxis cinnamomea 338
averano, Procnias 539
avilae, Grallaria ruficapilla 430
Avocet, American 126
Avocetbill, Mountain 271
Avocettula 235
Awlbill, Fiery-tailed 235
axillaris, Aramides 114
axillaris, Arremon taciturnus 707
axillaris, Herpsilochmus 402
axillaris, Myrmotherula 397
axillaris, Sittasomus griseicapillus 366
Aythya 41
azara, Pteroglossus 308
azarae, Saltator coerulescens 720

azarae, Synallaxis 333
azuay, Asthenes wyatti 344
badissima, Euphonia xanthogaster 772
badius, Automolus infuscatus 357
badius, Colinus cristatus 50
badius, Pachyramphus cinnamomeus 561
baeri, Leucippus 246
baezae, Anisognathus somptuosus 648
baezae, Basileuterus tristriatus 745
baezae, Veniliornis dignus 321
bahamensis, Anas 40
bahamensis, Momotus momota 288
bairdii, Calidris 137
bairdii, Myiodynastes 525
baliola, Ortalis ruficauda 43
ballux, Myioborus miniatus 737
balzarensis, Geranospiza caerulescens 90
bambla, Microcerculus 603
Bananaquit 683
bangsi, Grallaria 431
bangsi, Henicorhina leucophrys 601
bangsi, Manacus manacus 550
bangsi, Porzana flaviventer 116
Bangsia 644
barbacoae, Hylopezus dives 434
barbadensis, Amazona 191
barbadensis, Vireo altiloquus 570
barbaritoi, Catharus aurantiirostris 610
barbata, Penelope 44
barbatulus, Vireo altiloquus 570
barbatus, Myiobius 495
Barbet, Black-spotted 302
Five-coloured 302
Gilded 302
Lemon-throated 303
Orange-fronted 301
Red-headed 303
Scarlet-crowned 301
Spot-crowned 301
Toucan 304
White-mantled 301
Barbtail, Roraiman 347
Rusty-winged 348
Spotted 348
White-throated 348
Barbthroat, Band-tailed 226
Sooty 225
White-tailed 226
bardus, Rhynchocyclus olivaceus 485
Bare-eye, Argus 422
Black-spotted 422
Reddish-winged 422
bargei, Tyto alba 200
barinensis, Dendrocincla fuliginosa 364
barinensis, Piaya minuta 196
barnesi, Colinus cristatus 50
baroli, Puffinus assimilis 61
baroni, Metallura 268
baroni, Phaethornis longirostris 227
baroni, Thryothorus superciliaris 598
barrabandi, Pionopsitta 187
barringeri, Phlegopsis 422
barroti, Heliothryx 271
barrowcloughianus, Thryothorus coraya 594
bartletti, Amazilia lactea 248
bartletti, Crypturellus 32
bartletti, Dendrocincla merula 364
Bartramia 132
Baryphthengus 288
Basileuterus 740
basilicus, Basileuterus 742
basilicus, Buarremon torquatus 709
batavicus, Touit 183
baudoana, Dacnis cayana 670
Becard, Barred 560
Black-and-white 562
Black-capped 563
Chestnut-crowned 561
Cinereous 564
Cinnamon 561
Crested 565
Glossy-backed 563
Green-backed 560
One-coloured 564
Pink-throated 565
Slaty 564
White-winged 561
Yellow-cheeked 560
beebei, Rhodinocichla rosea 633
behni, Myrmotherula 398
belcheri, Larus 143
beldingi, Charadrius wilsonia 124
bella, Goethalsia 244
bella, Xenodacnis parina 673
Bellbird, Bearded 539
White 538
bellicosa, Sturnella 759
bellus, Masius chrysopterus 546
bellus, Myiophobus pulcher 493
benedettii, Atlapetes semirufus 714
benjamini, Urosticte 267
Bentbill, Northern 483
Southern 483
beringiae, Limosa fedoa 131
berlepschi, Aglaiocercus 276
berlepschi, Anthocephala floriceps 252
berlepschi, Chaetocercus 275
berlepschi, Conopias trivirgatus 524
berlepschi, Crypturellus 29
berlepschi, Dacnis 671
berlepschi, Mitrephanes phaeocercus 499
berlepschi, Myrmeciza 413
berlepschi, Myrmoborus lugubris 409
berlepschi, Patagioenas subvinacea 158
berlepschi, Phaeochroa cuvierii 231
berlepschi, Phimosus infuscatus 78
berlepschi, Pipra erythrocephala 554
berlepschi, Pseudotriccus pelzelni 449
berlepschi, Pyrrhura melanura 178
berlepschi, Thamnophilus tenuepunctatus 384
berlepschi, Thraupis episcopus 642
berlepschi, Tolmomyias sulphurescens 486
Berlepschia 350
berliozi, Heterospingus xanthopygius 636
bernardi, Sakesphorus 382
bessereri, Basileuterus tristriatus 745
bicinctus, Hypnelus 296
bicolor, Accipiter 90
bicolor, Campylorhynchus griseus 588
bicolor, Conirostrum 650
bicolor, Dendrocygna 34
bicolor, Gymnopithys leucaspis 419
bicolor, Tachycineta 579
bicolor, Tiaris 682
bidentatus, Harpagus 86
bilineata, Polioptila plumbea 606
bipartitus, Phrygilus alaudinus 688
birchalli, Catharus aurantiirostris 610
Bishop, Northern Red 777
bistriatus, Burhinus 126
Bittern, Least 71
Pinnated 71
Stripe-backed 72
bivittatus, Basileuterus 740
Blackbird, Chestnut-capped 758
Oriole 757
Pale-eyed 757
Red-breasted 758
Red-winged 758
Scrub 760
Yellow-hooded 757
Blossomcrown 252
Bobolink 763
Bobwhite, Crested 50
bodini, Amazona festiva 190
bogotensis, Anthus 624
bogotensis, Asio flammeus 210
bogotensis, Camptostoma obsoletum 462
bogotensis, Chrysomus icterocephalus 757
bogotensis, Cinnycerthia olivascens 591
bogotensis, Colinus cristatus 50
bogotensis, Contopus cinereus 501
bogotensis, Gallinula melanops 118
bogotensis, Ixobrychus exilis 72
bogotensis, Myiopagis gaimardii 465
bogotensis, Patagioenas plumbea 159
bogotensis, Polystictus pectoralis 477
bogotensis, Sicalis luteola 691
bogotensis, Sporophila intermedia 694
bogotensis, Tangara guttata 662
bogotensis, Thryothorus leucotis 597
Boissoneaua 261
boissonneautii, Pseudocolaptes 350
Bolborhynchus 179
bolivari, Coereba flaveola 683
bolivari, Dixiphia pipra 552
bolivari, Synallaxis cinnamomea 338
boliviana, Tangara mexicana 657
bolivianus, Attila 514
bolivianus, Lathrotriccus euleri 498
bombus, Acestrura 276
Bombycilla 608
BOMBYCILLIDAE 607

bonairensis, Coereba flaveola 683
bonairensis, Margarops fuscatus 623
bonairensis, Vireo altiloquus 570
bonapartei, Coeligena 260
bonapartei, Nothocercus 28
bonariensis, Molothrus 761
bonariensis, Thraupis 643
bonnetiana, Zonotrichia capensis 684
Booby, Blue-footed 66
Brown 67
Masked 66
Nazca 66
Peruvian 66
Red-footed 67
borealis, Calonectris diomedea 59
borealis, Cypseloides niger 219
borealis, Numenius 131
borreroi, Anas cyanoptera 40
Botaurus 71
bottomeana, Chloroceryle americana 285
boucardi, Crypturellus 31
boucardi, Myrmeciza longipes 414
bougainvillii, Phalacrocorax 68
bougueri, Urochroa 257
bourcieri, Chlorochrysa calliparaea 657
bourcieri, Geotrygon frenata 169
bourcieri, Phaethornis 228
bourcierii, Eubucco 303
bouvreuil, Sporophila 699
bouvronides, Sporophila 696
boydi, Puffinus assimilis 61
boylei, Diglossa gloriosissima 653
braccata, Amazilia saucerrottei 249
Brachygalba 289
brachyptera, Athene cunicularia 209
brachyptera, Elaenia chiriquensi 471
brachypterus, Donacobius atricapilla 607
brachyrhynchus, Tachybaptus dominicus 54
brachyura, Chaetura 221
brachyura, Myrmotherula 393
brachyura, Synallaxis 334
brachyurus, Buteo 98
brachyurus, Graydidascalus 186
brachyurus, Thamnophilus multistriatus 383
bracteatus, Nyctibius 211
brangeri, Cymbilaimus lineatus 379
branickii, Leptosittaca 175
branickii, Odontorchilus 590
branickii, Theristicus melanopis 79
brasilianum, Glaucidium 207
brasilianus, Phalacrocorax 67
brasiliensis, Amazonetta 37
brasiliensis, Coragyps atratus 80
brasiliensis, Leptotila verreauxi 165
brevicarinatus, Ramphastos sulfuratus 311
brevicauda, Muscigralla 510
brevicaudus, Coryphospingus pileatus 687
brevipennis, Campylorhamphus trochilirostris 378
brevipennis, Campylorhynchus nuchalis 589
brevipennis, Falco sparverius 107
brevipennis, Polystictus pectoralis 477
brevipes, Tachyphonus surinamus 637
brevirostris, Campylorhynchus zonatus 589
brevirostris, Crypturellus 32
brevirostris, Euphonia xanthogaster 772
brevirostris, Galbula ruficauda 290
brevirostris, Piculus rivolii 322
brevirostris, Rhynchocyclus 485
brevirostris, Sublegatus modestus 464
brevis, Ramphastos 311
breweri, Hemitriccus margaritaceiventer 452
brewsteri, Empidonax traillii 502
brewsteri, Saltator coerulescens 720
bricenoi, Thripadectes flammulatus 357
Brilliant, Black-throated 254
Empress 254
Fawn-breasted 253
Green-crowned 254
Pink-throated 255
Velvet-browed 254
Violet-fronted 253
brissonii, Cyanocompsa 722
brooki, Penelope montagnii 45
Brotogeris 181
browni, Elaenia frantzii 471
browni, Sicalis citrina 690
brunnea, Myrmeciza immaculata 417
brunnea, Nonnula 298
brunneicapillus, Ornithion 461
brunneicaudalis, Synallaxis moesta 335
brunneiceps, Galbula dea 292
brunneiceps, Henicorhina leucophrys 601
brunneiceps, Hylophilus 572
brunneiceps, Myiarchus tuberculifer 517
brunneidorsalis, Hellmayrea gularis 340
brunneifrons, Ochthoeca fumicolor 505
brunneinucha, Buarremon 708
brunneiventris, Diglossa 653
brunnescens, Anurolimnas viridis 111
brunnescens, Automolus rubiginosus 359
brunnescens, Myiarchus ferox 518
brunnescens, Penelope purpurascens 45
brunnescens, Premnoplex 348
brunnescens, Sclerurus rufigularis 360
brunneus, Sclerurus caudacutus 361
brunnitorques, Streptoprocne rutilus 220
Buarremon 708
Bubo 204
Bubulcus 73
Bucco 294
BUCCONIDAE 292
buckleyi, Columbina 163
buckleyi, Laniisoma elegans 559
buckleyi, Micrastur 106
buckleyi, Odontophorus gujanensis 51
buckleyi, Tityra inquisitor 556
buenavistae, Piculus rubiginosus 322
buenavistae, Xiphorhynchus elegans 373
buesingi, Thraupis cyanocephala 643
buffoni, Circus 87
buffoni, Picumnus exilis 314
buffonii, Chalybura 252
bulleri, Puffinus 60
bulunensis, Hylophilus ochraceiceps 574
Bulweria 59
bulwerii, Bulweria 59
bunites, Phyllomyias burmeisteri 457
Bunting, Indigo 722
BURHINIDAE 126
Burhinus 126
burmeisteri, Phyllomyias 457
burrovianus, Cathartes 81
Busarellus 95
Bushbird, Black 388
Recurve-billed 389
Buteo 97
Buteogallus 93
Buthraupis 645
Butorides 73
Buzzard-Eagle, Black-chested 96
cabanisi, Basileuterus culicivorus 743
cabanisi, Cnemotriccus fuscatus 498
cabanisi, Syndactyla rufosuperciliata 352
cabanisi, Cnemotriccus fuscatus 498
cabanisii, Chloroceryle americana 285
cabanisii, Molothrus bonariensis 762
cachinnans, Herpetotheres 105
Cacicus 750
Cacique, Ecuadorian 751
Mountain 751
Red-rumped 750
Scarlet-rumped 751
Solitary 752
Subtropical 751
Yellow-billed 752
Yellow-rumped 750
cacozelus, Turdus fuscater 615
caerulea, Egretta 76
caerulea, Passerina 722
caerulea, Thraupis episcopus 642
caeruleiceps, Pyrrhura 176
caeruleigularis, Tangara argyrofenges 667
caeruleocephala, Tangara cyanicollis 665
caeruleogaster, Chalybura buffonii 252
caeruleoventris, Iridosornis rufivertex 649
caerulescens, Anisognathus lacrymosus 647
caerulescens, Anser 36
caerulescens, Chlorophanes spiza 671
caerulescens, Dendroica 727
caerulescens, Diglossa 655
caerulescens, Geranospiza 90
caerulescens, Sporophila 698
caeruleus, Cyanerpes 672
caeruleus, Pterophanes cyanopterus 257
caesius, Thamnomanes 392
caica, Pionopsitta 188
caicarae, Xiphorhynchus obsoletus 372
Cairina 37
cairnsi, Dendroica caerulescens 727
cajamarcae, Myiotheretes fumigatus 507

cajanea, Aramides 114
Calidris 135
californicus, Larus 144
caligatus, Trogon 279
caligris, Nyctanassa violacea 72
callinota, Terenura 405
calliparaea, Chlorochrysa 657
Calliphlox 273
calliptera, Pyrrhura 179
callogenys, Aratinga leucophthalma 174
callonotus, Veniliornis 319
callophrys, Tangara 668
Calonectris 59
calopterus, Aramides 115
calopterus, Mecocerculus 473
calopterus, Poecilotriccus 456
calorhynchus, Aulacorhynchus 305
calurus, Buteo jamaicensis 99
camanii, Myrmotherula behni 399
campanisona, Chamaeza 425
campanisona, Myrmothera 435
Campephilus 327, 328
campestris, Colaptes 324
campicola, Geothlypis trichas 735
Camptostoma 462
Campylopterus 231
Campylorhamphus 377
Campylorhynchus 587
cana, Thraupis episcopus 642
canadensis, Caryothraustes 718
canadensis, Sakesphorus 381
canadensis, Wilsonia 737
canariensis, Falco tinnunculus 107
Canastero, Many-striped 344
Streak-backed 344
candei, Synallaxis 339
candelae, Myadestes ralloides 609
candidus, Melanerpes 318
canescens, Contopus nigrescens 501
canescens, Pachyramphus homochrous 565
canicauda, Grallaria squamigera 427
caniceps, Attila spadiceus 514
caniceps, Myiopagis 465
caniceps, Poecilotriccus latirostris 454
caniceps, Saltator atripennis 720
canidorsum, Arremon schlegeli 706
canigularis, Chlorospingus 678
canipalliata, Amazona mercenaria 192
canipennis, Thamnophilus murinus 386
cantator, Hypocnemis 410
cantica, Cyclarhis gujanensis 567
canus, Scytalopus 444
canutus, Calidris 135
capense, Daption 58
capensis, Bucco 295
capensis, Zonotrichia 684
capistratus, Piculus chrysochloros 323
capitalis, Carduelis magellanica 765
capitalis, Poecilotriccus 450
capitalis, Ramphocelus carbo 640
capitalis, Thamnophilus schistaceus 386
Capito 301
CAPITONIDAE 300
CAPRIMULGIDAE 212
Caprimulgus 215
Capsiempis 463
Capuchinbird 544
caquetae, Automolus rubiginosus 359
caquetae, Brachygalba lugubris 290
caquetae, Crypturellus soui 29
caquetae, Hylopezus fulviventris 435
caquetae, Lepidothrix coronata 548
caquetensis, Synallaxis rutilans 337
caracae, Scytalopus 443
Caracara 104
Caracara, Black 103
Carunculated 103
Mountain 104
Northern 104
Red-throated 103
Yellow-headed 104
carbo, Ramphocelus 639
carbonaria, Cercomacra 408
carbonata, Lepidothrix coronata 548
Cardinal, Masked 715
Red-capped 715
Vermilion 718
CARDINALIDAE 716
Cardinalis 718
cardonai, Cranioleuca demissa 341
cardonai, Myioborus 738
Carduelis 763
caribaea, Fulica 119
caribaeus, Ammodramus savannarum 685
caribaeus, Chlorostilbon mellisugus 239
caribbaeus, Myiarchus cephalotes 518
caripensis, Myiophobus flavicans 492
caripensis, Steatornis 210
carmelitae, Grallaria guatimalensis 429
carmioli, Chlorothraupis 634
carnegiei, Euphonia rufiventris 772
carneipes, Cyanerpes cyaneus 673
carnifex, Phoenicircus 537
carnobarba, Procnias averano 539
carolina, Porzana 115
carolinensis, Anas 38
carolinensis, Caprimulgus 215
carolinensis, Dumetella 621
carolinensis, Pandion haliaetus 83
carolinensis, Pelecanus occidentalis 65
Carpodectes 542
carri, Synallaxis cinnamomea 338
carrikeri, Athene cunicularia 209
carrikeri, Capito hypoleucus 301
carrikeri, Dubusia taeniata 649
carrikeri, Formicarius rufipectus 425
carrikeri, Icterus mesomelas 755
carrizalensis, Amaurospiza 704
carunculatus, Phalcoboenus 103
Caryothraustes 718
casiquiare, Crypturellus 32
casius, Turdus grayi 620
caspia, Hydroprogne 150
cassini, Falco peregrinus 109
cassini, Leptotila 166
cassini, Myrmeciza exsul 414
cassini, Psarocolius 749
cassini, Veniliornis 319
cassinii, Mitrospingus 633
castanea, Dendroica 730
castanea, Grallaria hypoleuca 432
castanea, Hapaloptila 299
castanea, Myrmeciza 416
castanea, Synallaxis 338
castaneiceps, Anurolimnas 111
castaneiceps, Basileuterus coronatus 743
castaneiceps, Conopophaga 438
castaneiceps, Lysurus 709
castaneifrons, Ara severus 171
castaneifrons, Atlapetes schistaceus 712
castaneiventris, Amazilia 251
castaneiventris, Sporophila 700
castaneocapillus, Myioborus 738
castaneotinctus, Lipaugus unirufus 540
castaneus, Amaurolimnas concolor 115
castaneus, Crypturellus obsoletus 30
castaneus, Gymnopithys leucaspis 419
castaneus, Pachyramphus 561
castaneus, Pithys 418
castaneus, Trogon collaris 282
castanonotus, Lochmias nematura 361
castanoptera, Pyriglena leuconota 408
castanotis, Pteroglossus 308
castelnau, Picumnus 316
castelnaudii, Glyphorynchus spirurus 367
castelnaui, Onychorhynchus coronatus 491
castilloi, Phacellodomus rufifrons 345
castro, Oceanodroma 63
Catamblyrhynchus 674
Catbird, Grey 621
catesbyi, Phaethon lepturus 65
catharinae, Tangara gyrola 662
Cathartes 81
CATHARTIDAE 80
Catharus 610
Catoptrophorus 134
caucae, Ammodramus savannarum 685
caucae, Atlapetes latinuchus 711
caucae, Camptostoma obsoletum 462
caucae, Coereba flaveola 683
caucae, Columbina talpacoti 163
caucae, Crypturellus soui 29
caucae, Cyanocompsa brissonii 722
caucae, Falco sparverius 107
caucae, Forpus conspicillatus 181
caucae, Pardirallus nigricans 117
caucae, Phyllomyias griseiceps 458
caucae, Semnornis ramphastinus 304
caucae, Synallaxis brachyura 334
caucae, Turdus olivater 616
caucae, Vireo olivaceus 569
caucae, Zenaida auriculata 160
caucensis, Haplophaedia aureliae 267
caucensis, Pitangus sulphuratu 529
caudacutus, Sclerurus 361
caudata, Aglaiocercus kingi 276

caudata, Amazilia tobaci 250
caudata, Drymophila 404
caudata, Inezia 475
caudatus, Theristicus 78
caurensis, Amazilia tobaci 250
caurensis, Bucco macrodactylus 294
caurensis, Microcerculus bambla 603
caurensis, Schistocichla 413
caurensis, Thryothorus coraya 594
caurensis, Xiphorhynchus pardalotus 373
caurinus, Limnodromus griseus 130
cautor, Turdus leucomelas 617
cavicola, Petrochelidon fulva 587
cayana, Cotinga 538
cayana, Dacnis 670
cayana, Tangara 663
cayana, Tityra 555
cayanensis, Icterus 754
cayanensis, Leptodon 83
cayanensis, Myiozetetes 526
cayanus, Cyanocorax 577
cayanus, Vanellus 121
cayennensis, Caprimulgus 216
cayennensis, Euphonia 772
cayennensis, Mesembrinibis 78
cayennensis, Nyctanassa violacea 72
cayennensis, Panyptila 223
cayennensis, Patagioenas 157
cayennensis, Thamnophilus murinus 386
cayennensis, Vanellus chilensis 121
cecilii, Veniliornis kirkii 321
cedrorum, Bombycilla 608
cela, Cacicus 750
Celeus 325
celicae, Atlapetes seebohmi 713
centralandium, Conirostrum albifrons 652
centralis, Megascops 202
centunculorum, Myrmeciza castanea 416
Cephalopterus 544
cephalotes, Myiarchus 518
cephalus, Phaethornis longirostris 227
Cercibis 78
Cercomacra 406
cerdaleus, Laterallus albigularis 113
certhia, Dendrocolaptes 370
certhia, Leptasthenura andicola 331
Certhiaxis 343
cerula, Capsiempis flaveola 463
cerulea, Dendroica 730
cervicalis, Automolus infuscatus 357
cervina, Adelomyia melanogenys 252
cervina, Leucippus fallax 246
cervinicauda, Threnetes leucurus 226
cervinigularis, Heliodoxa rubinoides 253
cerviniventris, Crypturellus obsoletus 30
Chachalaca, Chestnut-winged 42
  Colombian 43
  Grey-headed 42
  Little 44
  Rufous-headed 43
  Rufous-vented 43
  Speckled 43
Chaetocercus 274
Chaetura 220
chakei, Cinnycerthia unirufa 590
chalcocephala, Galbula albirostris 290
chalcopterus, Pionus 189
Chalcostigma 269
chalcothorax, Galbula 291
chalybea, Progne 582
chalybeus, Lophornis 237
Chalybura 252
Chamaepetes 47
Chamaeza 425
chaplinae, Grallaria haplonota 429
chapmani, Amazona farinosa 192
chapmani, Chaetura 221
chapmani, Conopophaga castaneiceps 438
chapmani, Formicivora rufa 404
chapmani, Mecocerculus leucophrys 472
chapmani, Myiodynastes maculatus 525
chapmani, Oceanodroma leucorhoa 63
chapmani, Patagioenas plumbea 159
chapmani, Phylloscartes 479
chapmani, Pulsatrix perspicillata 206
chapmani, Pyrrhura melanura 178
CHARADRIIDAE 121
Charadrius 123
Chat, Rose-breasted 746
Chat-Tyrant, Brown-backed 505
  Crowned 504
  Jelski's 504
  Rufous-breasted 505
  Slaty-backed 505
  White-browed 506
  Yellow-bellied 504
Chauna 34
chaupensis, Tangara labradorides 664
chavaria, Chauna 34
Chelidoptera 300
cheriway, Caracara 104
cherriei, Ammodramus aurifrons 686
cherriei, Cypseloides 219
cherriei, Myrmotherula 394
cherriei, Synallaxis 337
cherriei, Thripophaga 345
cherriei, Tolmomyias sulphurescens 486
chiguanco, Turdus 614
chihi, Plegadis 78
chilensis, Elaenia albiceps 468
chilensis, Phoenicopterus 82
chilensis, Stercorarius 141
chilensis, Tangara 658
chilensis, Vanellus 121
chimachima, Milvago 104
chimantae, Diglossa major 655
chimantae, Lochmias nematura 361
chimborazo, Oreotrochilus 256
chionogaster, Chamaeza turdina 426
chionopectus, Amazilia 247
chionurus, Trogon 282
chiribiquetensis, Hemitriccus margarita-ceiventer 452
chiriquensis, Elaenia 470
Chiroxiphia 550
chivi, Vireo olivaceus 569
Chlidonias 151
Chlorestes 238
chlorion, Piprites chloris 566
chloris, Piprites 566
chlorocercus, Leucippus 246
Chloroceryle 285
Chlorochrysa 656
chlorolepidota, Pipreola 534
chloronota, Buthraupis eximia 646
chloronotus, Mionectes oleagineus 447
Chlorophanes 671
Chlorophonia 773
Chlorophonia, Blue-naped 773
  Chestnut-breasted 773
  Yellow-collared 773
chlorophrys, Basileuterus chrysogaster 740
chloropogon, Metallura tyrianthina 270
chloropterus, Ara 171
chloropus, Gallinula 118
chlororhynchos, Thalassarche 56
Chlorornis 626
Chlorospingus 676
Chlorostilbon 239
Chlorothraupis 634
chlorotica, Euphonia 767
chocoana, Malacoptila panamensis 297
chocoanus, Cyanerpes caeruleus 672
chocoanus, Cyphorhinus phaeocephalus 603
chocoanus, Phaenostictus mcleannani 423
chocoensis, Conopophaga castaneiceps 438
chocoensis, Euphonia xanthogaster 772
chocoensis, Grallaria guatimalensis 429
chocoensis, Nyctibius aethereus 211
chocoensis, Scytalopus 441
chocoensis, Veniliornis 320
choicus, Xiphorhynchus picus 371
choliba, Megascops 201
Chondrohierax 84
Chordeiles 212
chrysater, Icterus 754
chrysauchen, Melanerpes 319
chrysendeta, Dendroica petechia 726
chryseola, Wilsonia pusilla 737
chrysocephalum, Neopelma 545
chrysocephalus, Icterus 753
chrysocephalus, Myiodynastes 525
chrysochloros, Piculus 323
chrysocrotaphum, Todirostrum 456
chrysogaster, Basileuterus 740
chrysogaster, Chlorostilbon gibsoni 239
chrysogaster, Megarhynchus pitangua 523
chrysogaster, Pheucticus 716
Chrysolampis 235
chrysomelas, Chrysothlypis 632
Chrysomus 757
chrysonotus, Cacicus 751
chrysopasta, Euphonia 771
chrysophrys, Aratinga pertinax 175

chrysophrys, Hemispingus superciliaris 628
chrysophrys, Tangara guttata 662
chrysopis, Thlypopsis sordida 631
chrysops, Myioborus ornatus 739
chrysops, Zimmerius 461
chrysoptera, Brotogeris 182
chrysoptera, Vermivora 723
chrysopterus, Masius 546
Chrysoptilus 323
Chrysothlypis 632
chrysotis, Tangara 660
Chrysuronia 244
chthonia, Grallaria 429
chubbi, Cichlopsis leucogenys 609
Chuck-will's-widow 215
chunchotambo, Xiphorhynchus 372
Ciccaba 204
Cichlopsis 609
Ciconia 80
CICONIIDAE 79
cienagae, Dendroica petechia 726
cinchoneti, Conopias 524
CINCLIDAE 607
Cinclodes 329
Cinclodes, Bar-winged 329
Stout-billed 330
Cinclus 607
cincta, Dichrozona 400
cinctus, Rhynchortyx 53
cinctus, Saltator 721
cineracea, Nonnula rubecula 298
cineraceus, Contopus fumigatus 500
cinerascens, Cercomacra 406
cinerascens, Myiodynastes chrysocephalus 525
cinerascens, Rynchops niger 154
cinerea, Ardea 73
cinerea, Myiopagis canicep 465
cinerea, Piezorhina 689
cinerea, Serpophaga 474
cinereicapilla, Zimmerius 460
cinereicapillus, Colaptes rupicola 324
cinereiceps, Grallaria varia 428
cinereiceps, Ortalis 42
cinereiceps, Phyllomyias 459
cinereiceps, Thamnophilus amazonicus 388
cinereicollis, Basileuterus 742
cinereifrons, Pseudelaenia leucospodia 467
cinereigulare, Oncostoma 483
cinereiventris, Chaetura 220
cinereiventris, Hellmayrea gularis 340
cinereiventris, Microbates 605
cinereiventris, Myrmotherula menetriesii 399
cinereiventris, Pachyramphus polychopterus 562
cinereola, Sporophila leucoptera 698
cinereoniger, Thamnophilus nigrocinereus 385
cinereum, Conirostrum 651
cinereum, Todirostrum 455
cinereus, Circus 88
cinereus, Contopus 501
cinereus, Crypturellus 29
cinereus, Xenus 134
cinereus, Xolmis 507
cinnamomea, Neopipo 496
cinnamomea, Synallaxis 338
cinnamomea, Tringa solitaria 133
cinnamomeigula, Automolus rubiginosus 359
cinnamomeipectus, Hemitriccus 453
cinnamomeiventris, Ochthoeca 505
cinnamomeus, Attila 513
cinnamomeus, Certhiaxis 343
cinnamomeus, Furnarius leucopus 330
cinnamomeus, Pachyramphus 561
cinnamomeus, Picumnus 315
cinnamomeus, Pyrrhomyias 496
cinnamominus, Charadrius wilsonia 124
Cinnycerthia 590
Circus 87
cirratus, Picumnus 315
cirrocephalus, Larus 145
cisandina, Cranioleuca curtata 341
Cissopis 626
Cistothorus 591
citrea, Protonotaria 732
citreolaemus, Ramphastos 311
citreopygius, Celeus elegans 326
citrina, Sicalis 690
citrina, Wilsonia 736
citriniventris, Attila 514
clamator, Asio 209
Claravis 164
clarior, Deconychura stictolaema 365
clarisse, Heliangelus 263
clarkii, Megascops 200
clarus, Myiobius villosus 495
clarus, Picumnus exilis 314
clarus, Turdus fuscater 615
cleavesi, Chaetocercus heliodor 274
climacocerca, Hydropsalis 218
clypeata, Anas 40
Clytoctantes 389
Cnemarchus 506
Cnemoscopus 627
Cnemotriccus 497
Cnipodectes 484
coccinea, Habia rubica 675
coccineipes, Anurolimnas castaneiceps 111
coccineus, Calochaetes 638
coccinicollaris, Pionopsitta haematotis 187
Coccyzus 193
Cochlearius 71
cochlearius, Cochlearius 71
Cock-of-the-Rock, Andean 536
Guianan 535
cocoi, Ardea 74
coelestis, Aglaiocercus 277
coelestis, Diglossa sittoides 652
coelestis, Forpus 181
coelestis, Thraupis episcopus 642
coelicolor, Tangara chilensis 658
Coeligena 258
coeligena, Coeligena 259
coelina, Lepidopyga coeruleogularis 241
Coereba 683
coerebicolor, Dacnis cayana 670
coeruleogularis, Lepidopyga 241
coerulescens, Saltator 720
cognatus, Aulacorhynchus prasinus 305
Colaptes 324
Colibri 233
Colinus 50
collaris, Accipiter 89
collaris, Atlapetes personatus 714
collaris, Aythya 41
collaris, Charadrius 125
collaris, Microbates 604
collaris, Trogon 282
collingwoodi, Tolmomyias flaviventris 488
collinus, Thryothorus leucotis 597
colma, Formicarius 424
colombiana, Ammodramus humeralis 686
colombiana, Merganetta armata 41
colombiana, Neocrex 116
colombiana, Penelope argyrotis 44
colombiana, Sporophila plumbea 693
colombianum, Electron platyrhynchum 287
colombianum, Philydor rufum 355
colombianus, Bubo virginianus 204
colombianus, Megascops 203
colombianus, Turdus obsoletus 619
colombica, Thalurania 241
Colonia 512
colonus, Buteo albicaudatus 97
colonus, Colonia 512
coloratus, Hypnelus ruficollis 295
coloratus, Myadestes 609
coloratus, Piculus rubiginosus 322
coloratus, Premnoplex brunnescens 348
Columba 155
columbae, Troglodytes musculus 598
columbarius, Falco 107
columbiana, Carduelis psaltria 766
columbiana, Chamaeza campanisona 425
columbiana, Coeligena coeligena 259
columbiana, Coereba flaveola 683
columbiana, Fulica americana 119
columbiana, Sicalis 690
columbiana, Synallaxis gujanensis 336
columbiana, Tityra semifasciata 556
columbianus, Cinclodes excelsior 330
columbianus, Crypturellus erythropus 31
columbianus, Microbates collaris 604
columbianus, Mionectes striaticollis 446
columbianus, Muscisaxicola alpinus 509
columbianus, Myiozetetes similis 527
columbianus, Odontophorus 52
columbianus, Ortalis 43
columbianus, Phaethornis syrmatophorus 227
columbianus, Thryothorus sclateri 596

COLUMBIDAE 155
Columbina 161
comptus, Atlapetes latinuchus 711
comptus, Trogon 281
conboschas, Anas platyrhynchos 39
concentricus, Micrastur ruficollis 105
concinna, Euphonia 768
concinnus, Trogon violaceus 280
concolor, Amaurolimnas 115
concolor, Amaurospiza 703
condamini, Eutoxeres 225
Condor, Andean 82
Conebill, Bicoloured 650
Blue-backed 651
Capped 651
Chestnut-vented 650
Cinereous 651
Giant 652
Rufous-browed 651
White-eared 650
conexus, Momotus momota 288
confinis, Lepidopyga coeruleogularis 241
confusa, Pipreola riefferii 532
confusus, Picumnus cirratus 315
confusus, Scytalopus atratus 441
confusus, Tolmomyias sulphurescens 486
conirostris, Arremonops 707
Conirostrum 650
connectens, Adelomyia melanogenys 252
connectens, Deconychura longicauda 365
connectens, Formicarius analis 424
connectens, Grallaria ruficapilla 430
connectens, Thryothorus nigricapillus 596
connectens, Xiphorhynchus guttatus 374
Conopias 524
Conopophaga 438
CONOPOPHAGIDAE 438
Conothraupis 626
conoveri, Leptotila 167
conradi, Turdus chiguanco 614
conradii, Coeligena torquata 258
consita, Coeligena bonapartei 260
consobrinus, Automolus rufipileatus 359
consobrinus, Microrhopias quixensis 403
consobrinus, Thryothorus mystacalis 593
conspicillatus, Basileuterus 743
conspicillatus, Chlorospingus canigularis 678
conspicillatus, Forpus 181
contempta, Tyto alba 200
continentalis, Veniliornis kirkii 321
continentis, Colinus cristatus 50
Contopus 500
contrerasi, Cyclarhis gujanensis 567
conversii, Popelairia 238
cooperi, Contopus 500
cooperii, Accipiter 89
Coot, American 119
Caribbean 119
Slate-coloured 119
Coquette, Festive 237
Peacock 237
Racket-tailed 238
Rufous-crested 236
Spangled 237
Tufted 236
cora, Thaumastura 278
coracina, Dixiphia pipra 552
coracinus, Entomodestes 610
Coragyps 80
corallinus, Pionus sordidus 189
Corapipo 546
coraya, Thryothorus 594
cordobae, Hyloctistes virgatus 351
corensis, Patagioenas 156
Cormorant, Double-crested 68
Guanay 68
Neotropic 67
cornuta, Anhima 34
cornuta, Pipra 554
cornutus, Heliactin 272
coronata, Dendroica 727
coronata, Lepidothrix 548
coronatus, Basileuterus 743
coronatus, Onychorhynchus 491
coronatus, Pachyramphus albogriseus 563
coronatus, Platyrinchus 490
Coronet, Buff-tailed 262
Chestnut-breasted 262
Velvet-purple 262
coronobscurus, Glyphorynchus spirurus 367
coronulatus, Masius chrysopterus 546
corrasus, Microcerculus marginatus 602
coruscans, Colibri 234
coruscus, Phaethornis guy 226
CORVIDAE 575
corvina, Sporophila 695
coryi, Schizoeaca 332
Corythopis 457
costaricensis, Asturina nitida 93
costaricensis, Cypseloides niger 219
costaricensis, Leucopternis albicollis 92
costaricensis, Zonotrichia capensis 684
Cotinga 537
cotinga, Cotinga 538
Cotinga, Black-necked Red 536
Black-tipped 542
Blue 537
Chestnut-bellied 531
Chestnut-crested 531
Guianan Red 537
Plum-throated 537
Pompadour 541
Purple-breasted 538
Purple-throated 541
Red-crested 531
Spangled 538
COTINGIDAE 530
Coturnicops 111
Cowbird, Bronzed 762
Giant 762
Shiny 761
CRACIDAE 42
Crake, Ash-throated 116
Black-banded 112
Chestnut-headed 111
Colombian 116
Grey-breasted 113
Ocellated 111
Paint-billed 116
Rufous-sided 112
Russet-crowned 111
Rusty-flanked 112
Speckled 111
Uniform 115
White-throated 112
Yellow-breasted 116
Cranioleuca 340
crassirostris, Euphonia laniirostris 769
crassirostris, Forpus xanthopterygius 180
crassirostris, Lysurus 709
crassirostris, Oryzoborus 701
crassirostris, Xiphocolaptes promeropirhynchus 368
crassus, Atlapetes tricolor 712
Crax 48
Creagrus 147
creatopus, Puffinus 60
crepitans, Psophia 110
Crescentchest, Elegant 445
Marañón 445
Creurgops 636
crinitus, Myiarchus 519
crissalis, Chordeiles acutipennis 213
crissalis, Formicarius analis 424
crissalis, Habia rubica 675
crissalis, Onychoprion fuscatus 149
crissalis, Pheucticus aureoventri 717
crissalis, Trogon violaceus 280
cristata, Elaenia 470
cristata, Eucometis penicillata 635
cristata, Habia 676
cristata, Lophostrix 205
cristata, Rhegmatorhina 420
cristatellus, Tachyphonus cristatus 636
cristatus, Colinus 50
cristatus, Oxyruncus 530
cristatus, Phyllomyias griseiceps 458
cristatus, Tachyphonus 636
croconotus, Icterus 753
Crotophaga 197
crucigerus, Megascops choliba 201
cruentatus, Melanerpes 318
cruentus, Rhodospingus 687
cruziana, Columbina 163
crypterythrus, Myiophobus fasciatus 494
cryptoleuca, Progne 582
cryptoleucus, Thamnophilus 385
cryptolophus, Snowornis 541
cryptoxanthus, Myiophobus 494
Crypturellus 29
cryptus, Cypseloides 220
cuchiverum, Philydor rufum 355
Cuckoo, Banded Ground 199
Black-bellied 196

Dwarf 193
Guira 198
Little 196
Pavonine 197
Pheasant 196
Red-billed Ground 199
Rufous-vented Ground 198
Rufous-winged Ground 199
Striped 196
CUCULIDAE 193
cucullata, Buthraupis montana 645
cucullata, Carduelis 764
cucullata, Grallaricula 437
cucullatus, Coryphospingus 687
cucullatus, Ploceus 776
culicivorus, Basileuterus 743
culminatus, Ramphastos 311
cumanensis, Grallaricula nana 436
cumanensis, Pipile 46
cumanensis, Thryothorus rufalbus 597
cumanensis, Turdus serranus 615
cumanensis, Zimmerius chrysops 461
cumbreanus, Dysithamnus mentalis 390
cuneicauda, Thinocorus rumicivorus 140
cunicularia, Athene 208
cupreicauda, Amazilia 250
cupreicauda, Trogon rufus 282
cupreoventris, Eriocnemis 266
cupripennis, Aglaeactis 258
curasoensis, Icterus nigrogularis 755
Curassow, Black 49
Blue-billed 49
Great 48
Helmeted 48
Lesser Razor-billed 47
Nocturnal 47
Razor-billed 48
Salvin's 48
Wattled 49
Yellow-knobbed 49
curiosus, Phaethornis augusti 229
Curlew, Eskimo 131
Long-billed 132
cursitans, Crypturellus erythropus 31
curtata, Cranioleuca 341
curucui, Trogon 281
curvirostris, Campylorhynchus zonatus 589
curvirostris, Nothoprocta 33
cuvieri, Ramphastos 312
cuvierii, Phaeochroa 231
cyanea, Chlorophonia 773
cyanea, Diglossa 656
cyanea, Passerina 722
Cyanerpes 672
cyanescens, Galbula 290
cyanescens, Pionus chalcopterus 190
cyanescens, Tangara nigroviridis 666
cyaneus, Circus 88
cyaneus, Cyanerpes 673
cyanicollis, Tangara 665
Cyanicterus 644
cyanicterus, Cyanicterus 644
cyanifrons, Amazilia 249
cyanocalyptra, Buthraupis eximia 646
cyanocephala, Euphonia 770
cyanocephala, Thraupis 643
cyanochroum, Conirostrum leucogenys 650
Cyanocompsa 721
Cyanocorax 576
cyanodorsalis, Cyanocorax yncas 577
cyanoides, Cyanocompsa 721
cyanolaemus, Aulacorhynchus prasinus 305
cyanolaemus, Oxypogon guerinii 268
cyanoleuca, Notiochelidon 583
Cyanolyca 575
cyanonotum, Conirostrum albifrons 652
cyanopectus, Sternoclyta 255
cyanophanes, Forpus passerinus 180
cyanoptera, Anas 40
cyanoptera, Brotogeris 182
cyanoptera, Tangara 667
cyanopterus, Anisognathus somptuosus 648
cyanopterus, Pterophanes 257
cyanopygia, Tangara cyanicollis 665
cyanotis, Tangara 664
cyanotus, Colibri thalassinus 234
cyanus, Hylocharis 243
Cyclarhis 567
Cymbilaimus 379
cynophora, Euphonia chlorotica 767
cypereti, Rallus longirostris 113
Cyphorhinus 603
Cypseloides 219
Cypsnagra 625
Dacnis 669
Dacnis, Black-faced 669
Blue 670
Scarlet-breasted 671
Scarlet-thighed 670
Tit-like 673
Turquoise 669
Viridian 671
White-bellied 669
Yellow-bellied 670
Yellow-tufted 670
dacotiae, Falco tinnunculus 107
dactylatra, Sula 66
daedalus, Basileuterus tristriatus 745
daguae, Gymnopithys leucaspis 419
daguae, Polioptila plumbea 606
daguae, Turdus 621
Damophila 242
Daption 58
Daptrius 103
darienensis, Deconychura longicauda 365
darienensis, Henicorhina leucosticta 600
darienensis, Hylophilus decurtatus 575
darienensis, Threnetes ruckeri 226
darwinii, Thraupis bonariensis 643
daubentoni, Crax 49
davidwillardi, Elaenia pallatangae 472
dayi, Elaenia 471
debellardiana, Adelomyia melanogenys 252
debilis, Turdus ignobilis 618
decaocto, Streptopelia 159
decolor, Hypnelus ruficollis 296
decolor, Leptotila verreauxi 165
Deconychura 365
decora, Pipreola aureopectus 533
decorata, Diglossa sittoides 652
decoratus, Colinus cristatus 50
decurtatus, Hylophilus 574
deiroleucus, Falco 108
delatrii, Tachyphonus 637
delattrei, Lophornis 236
delawarensis, Larus 143
deleticia, Tangara gyrola 662
delicata, Gallinago 128
delicata, Patagioenas plumbea 159
deliciosus, Machaeropterus 547
delphinae, Colibri 233
deltana, Dendrocincla fuliginosa 364
deltanus, Celeus elegans 326
deltanus, Piculus rubiginosus 322
deltanus, Xiphorhynchus picus 371
demissa, Cranioleuca 341
Dendrexetastes 368
Dendrocincla 363
Dendrocolaptes 369
Dendrocygna 34
Dendroica 725
denisei, Atlapetes semirufus 714
derbianus, Aulacorhynchus 305
derbyi, Eriocnemis 266
Deroptyus 193
desidiosa, Piranga lutea 679
destructus, Formicarius nigricapillus 424
devillei, Dendrexetastes rufigula 368
devillei, Drymophila 404
devronis, Sporophila peruviana 698
diadema, Catamblyrhynchus 674
diadema, Ochthoeca 504
dialeucos, Odontophorus 52
diaphora, Sclateria naevia 411
dichroura, Coeligena violifer 261
dichrous, Cyphorhinus thoracicus 603
Dichrozona 400
Dickcissel 716
difficilis, Myiodynastes maculatus 525
Diglossa 652
dignissima, Grallaria 430
dignus, Veniliornis 320
dilectissimus, Touit 184
dillonripleyi, Rallus longirostris 113
dilutior, Euphonia xanthogaster 772
dilutum, Ornithion brunneicapillus 461
dimidiatus, Ramphocelus 639
dimorpha, Thripophaga fusciceps 345
diodon, Harpagus 86
diomedea, Calonectris 59
DIOMEDEIDAE 55
Diopsittaca 172
Dipper, White-capped 607
discifer, Ocreatus underwoodii 278

discolor, Dendrocygna autumnalis 35
discolor, Dendroica 729
discors, Anas 40
Discosura 238
discrepans, Nothocercus bonapartei 28
disjuncta, Diglossa major 655
disjuncta, Myrmeciza 415
disjunctus, Vireo leucophrys 571
dispar, Cyanerpes cyaneus 673
dispar, Diglossa cyanea 656
dissita, Myrmotherula leucophthalma 396
dissors, Myrmothera campanisona 435
dissors, Ochthoeca leucophrys 506
dissors, Synallaxis rutilans 337
dissors, Tolmomyias flaviventris 488
distans, Amazilia 248
districta, Metallura tyrianthina 270
divaricatus, Thamnophilus amazonicus 388
diversus, Hylopezus macularius 434
diversus, Leptopogon amaurocephalus 449
diversus, Vireo olivaceus 569
Dives 760
dives, Hylopezus 434
Dixiphia 552
doliatus, Thamnophilus 382
Dolichonyx 763
Doliornis 531
Dolospingus 704
domesticus, Passer 777
dominica, Dendroica 728
dominica, Pluvialis 122
dominicanus, Larus 144
dominicensis, Progne 581
dominicensis, Tyrannus 522
dominicus, Nomonyx 35
dominicus, Tachybaptus 53
Donacobius 606
Donacobius, Black-capped 606
Doradito, Crested 477
Subtropical 477
dorbignyi, Diglossa sittoides 652
dorsale, Ramphomicron 269
dorsalis, Anabazenops 355
dorsalis, Mionectes oleagineus 447
dorsalis, Pachyramphus polychopterus 562
dorsimaculatus, Herpsilochmus 401
Doryfera 231
Dotterel, Tawny-throated 125
dougallii, Sterna 151
Dove, Black-winged Ground 164
Blue Ground 164
Caribbean 166
Common Ground 161
Croaking Ground 163
Eared 159
Ecuadorian Ground 163
Eurasian Collared 159
Grey-chested 166
Grey-fronted 166
Grey-headed 165
Maroon-chested Ground 164
Mourning 160
Ochre-bellied 167
Pacific 160
Pallid 165
Picui Ground 163
Plain-breasted Ground 161
Ruddy Ground 162
Scaled 162
Tolima 167
White-tipped 165
White-winged 161
Dowitcher, Long-billed 130
Short-billed 129
dresseri, Atlapetes leucopterus 713
Dromococcyx 196
dryas, Catharus 611
Drymophila 404
Dryocopus 326
dubius, Thamnophilus schistaceus 386
dubusi, Leptotila rufaxilla 166
Dubusia 649
Duck, Andean 36
Black-bellied Whistling 35
Comb 37
Fulvous Whistling 34
Masked 35
Muscovy 37
Ring-necked 41
Torrent 41
White-faced Whistling 35
dufresniana, Amazona 191
dugandi, Bucco capensis 295
dugandi, Chlorothraupis stolzmanni 635
dugandi, Herpsilochmus 400
dugandi, Liosceles thoracicus 439
dugandi, Xiphorhynchus picus 371
duidae, Amazilia cupreicauda 250
duidae, Atlapetes personatus 715
duidae, Aulacorhynchus derbianus 305
duidae, Automolus roraimae 358
duidae, Campylopterus 231
duidae, Chlorostilbon mellisugus 239
duidae, Contopus fumigatus 500
duidae, Crypturellus 32
duidae, Diglossa 654
duidae, Emberizoides 692
duidae, Glaucidium brasilianum 208
duidae, Hemitriccus margaritaceiventer 452
duidae, Hylophylax poecilinotus 422
duidae, Lepidocolaptes albolineatus 377
duidae, Lophornis pavoninus 237
duidae, Megascops choliba 201
duidae, Microcerculus ustulatus 602
duidae, Myioborus castaneocapillus 738
duidae, Myrmothera simplex 435
duidae, Nonnula rubecula 298
duidae, Phylloscartes chapmani 480
duidae, Platyrinchus mystaceus 489
duidae, Ramphocaenus melanurus 605
duidae, Roraimia adusta 347
duidae, Schiffornis major 556
duidae, Taraba major 380
duidae, Tolmomyias sulphurescens 486
duidae, Troglodytes rufulus 599
duidae, Trogon personatus 283
duidae, Turdus olivater 617
duidae, Xenopipo uniformis 551
duidae, Xiphorhynchus picus 371
duidaeCnemotriccus fuscatus 498
Dumetella 621
duncani, Catamenia homochroa 705
Dunlin 138
Dysithamnus 390
Eagle, Bald 91
Black-and-chestnut 102
Crested 100
Harpy 101
Solitary 95
earina, Hylocharis eliciae 243
ecaudatus, Myiornis 481
ecuadoriensis, Buteo magnirostris 97
edward, Amazilia 251
edwardsi, Bangsia 645
effutitus, Troglodytes musculus 598
egregia, Chaetura 222
egregia, Dacnis lineata 670
egregia, Pyrrhura 177
Egret, Cattle 73
Great 74
Little 76
Reddish 75
Snowy 76
Egretta 75
egretta, Ardea alba 74
eisenmanni, Picumnus olivaceus 316
eisenmanni, Tachybaptus dominicus 54
Elaenia 467
Elaenia, Brownish 470
Caribbean 467
Foothill 466
Forest 465
Great 471
Greenish 466
Grey 465
Highland 471
Large 468
Lesser 470
Mottle-backed 469
Mountain 471
Pacific 466
Plain-crested 470
Rufous-crowned 470
Sierran 471
Slaty 469
Small-billed 469
White-crested 468
Yellow-bellied 468
Yellow-crowned 466
elaeodes, Columbina minuta 161
elaeoprorus, Atlapetes latinuchus 711
Elanoides 85
Elanus 86
elatus, Basileuterus coronatus 743
elatus, Tyrannulus 464
Electron 287

elegans, Celeus 326
elegans, Melanopareia 445
elegans, Myrmoborus myotherinus 409
elegans, Parula pitiayumi 725
elegans, Progne 582
elegans, Thalasseus 153
elegans, Xiphorhynchus 373
elegantior, Synallaxis azarae 333
elegantissima, Amazilia fimbriata 247
elgasi, Anser albifrons 36
eliciae, Hylocharis 243
EMBERIZIDAE 683
Emberizoides 691
Emerald, Andean 249
Blue-tailed 239
Chiribiquete 239
Coppery 240
Glittering-throated 247
Green-tailed 240
Narrow-tailed 240
Plain-bellied 249
Red-billed 239
Sapphire-spangled 248
Short-tailed 240
Táchira 248
Versicoloured 247
West Andean 239
White-chested 247
emiliae, Phaethornis guy 226
eminens, Chlorospingus ophthalmicus 676
eminulus, Mitrephanes phaeocercus 499
emma, Pyrrhura 177
emmae, Aglaiocercus kingi 276
Empidonax 502
Empidonomus 522
endoecus, Furnarius leucopus 331
ennosiphyllus, Sclerurus guatemalensis 361
enochrus, Sittasomus griseicapillus 366
Ensifera 257
ensifera, Ensifera 257
ensipennis, Campylopterus 232
Entomodestes 610
eos, Coeligena 260
episcopus, Phaethornis ruber 229
episcopus, Thraupis 642
equifasciatus, Veniliornis nigriceps 321
Eremophila 578
Eriocnemis 265
erithachorides, Dendroica petechia 726
erithacus, Liosceles thoracicus 439
erythogenys, Tityra inquisitor 556
erythrocephala, Pipra 554
erythrocephalus, Hylocryptus 359
erythrocercum, Philydor 354
erythrogaster, Hirundo rustica 586
erythrogenys, Aratinga 173
erythrognatha, Crax alector 49
erythrognathus, Aulacorhynchus sulcatus 305
erythrolaema, Habia fuscicauda 676
erythromelas, Ixobrychus exilis 72
erythromelas, Periporphyrus 718
erythronotum, Philydor fuscipenne 354
erythronotus, Amazilia tobaci 250
erythropareia, Geotrygon frenata 169
erythrophrys, Myrmoborus leucophrys 409
erythrophthalma, Netta 41
erythrops, Cranioleuca 340
erythrops, Neocrex 116
erythrops, Odontophorus 51
erythroptera, Ortalis 43
erythroptera, Phlegopsis 422
erythropterum, Philydor 355
erythropus, Crypturellus 31
erythropus, Tringa 133
erythropygius, Cnemarchus 506
erythropygius, Pteroglossus 309
erythropygius, Xiphorhynchus 375
erythrorhynchus, Arremon aurantiirostris 706
erythrotus, Anisognathus igniventris 647
erythrura, Myrmotherula 397
erythrurus, Terenotriccus 494
esmeraldae, Chordeiles pusillus 213
esmeraldae, Lepidocolaptes souleyetii 376
estella, Oreotrochilus 257
Estrilda 774
ESTRILDIDAE 774
etesiaca, Sula leucogaster 67
Eubucco 303
eucharis, Henicorhina leucosticta 600
euchloris, Chlorostilbon poortmani 240
Eucometis 635
Eudocimus 77
euleri, Lathrotriccus 498
eumorphus, Trogon melanurus 280
euophrys, Thryothorus 593
Eupetomena 233
Eupetomena macroura 233
Euphonia 767
Euphonia, Bronze-green 771
Finsch's 769
Fulvous-vented 770
Golden-bellied 771
Golden-rumped 770
Golden-sided 772
Orange-bellied 772
Orange-crowned 768
Plumbeous 767
Purple-throated 767
Rufous-bellied 772
Tawny-capped 772
Thick-billed 769
Trinidad 768
Velvet-fronted 768
Violaceous 769
White-vented 771
Euplectes 777
eurygnathus, Thalasseus 153
euryptera, Opisthoprora 271
Eurypyga 120
EURYPYGIDAE 120
Euscarthmus 477, 478
Eutoxeres 224
examinatus, Tolmomyias assimilis 487
exasperatus, Oceanites oceanicus 62
excelsa, Grallaria 427
excelsior, Cinclodes 330
exigua, Nyctiprogne leucopyga 214
exiguus, Herpsilochmus rufimarginatus 402
exilis, Ixobrychus 71
exilis, Laterallus 113
exilis, Picumnus 314
eximia, Buthraupis 645
eximius, Cyanerpes cyaneus 673
eximius, Vireolanius 568
exitelus, Chlorospingus ophthalmicus 676
exoptatus, Trogon collaris 282
exortis, Heliangelus 264
exortivus, Tolmomyias sulphurescens 486
exsul, Brotogeris jugularis 182
exsul, Chlorophanes spiza 671
exsul, Euphonia xanthogaster 772
exsul, Myrmeciza 414
exterior, Leptasthenura andicola 331
extima, Leptasthenura andicola 331
extimus, Xiphorhynchus picus 371
extinctus, Capito hypoleucus 301
extremus, Dysithamnus mentalis 390
faceta, Piranga lutea 679
facilis, Polioptila guianensis 606
fagani, Chamaepetes goudotii 47
Fairy, Black-eared 271
Purple-crowned 271
falcatus, Campylopterus 232
falcinellus, Plegadis 77
Falco 107
Falcon, Aplomado 108
Barred Forest 105
Bat 108
Buckley's Forest 106
Collared Forest 106
Laughing 105
Lined Forest 106
Orange-breasted 108
Peregrine 109
Plumbeous Forest 105
Slaty-backed Forest 106
falconensis, Chlorospingus ophthalmicus 676
FALCONIDAE 103
falklandicus, Cathartes aura 81
fallax, Leucippus 246
fallax, Tachyphonus cristatus 636
fanny, Myrtis 273
fanny, Tangara larvata 665
fannyi, Thalurania 242
fargoi, Coryphospingus cucullatus 687
farinosa, Amazona 192
fasciata, Atticora 584
fasciata, Patagioenas 157
fasciatoventris, Thryothorus 592
fasciatum, Tigrisoma 70
fasciatus, , Cymbilaimus lineatus 379

fasciatus, Anurolimnas 112
fasciatus, Campylorhynchus 589
fasciatus, Harpagus bidentatus 86
fasciatus, Myiophobus 494
federalis, Catamblyrhynchus diadema 674
federalis, Diglossa albilatera 653
federalis, Hemitriccus granadensis 453
fedoa, Limosa 131
feliciae, Amazilia tobaci 250
feliciana, Damophila julie 242
femoralis, Falco 108
ferocior, Myiarchus swainsoni 517
ferox, Myiarchus 518
ferruginea, Calidris 138
ferruginea, Coeligena coeligena 259
ferruginea, Hirundinea 497
ferruginea, Myrmeciza 415
ferruginea, Ochthoeca fumicolor 505
ferruginea, Oxyura 36
ferrugineifrons, Bolborhynchus 180
ferrugineifrons, Hylophilus ochraceiceps 574
ferrugineipectus, Grallaricula 436
ferryi, Coereba flaveola 683
festatus, Pharomachrus fulgidus 284
festiva, Amazona 190
festiva, Pipreola aureopectus 533
fidelis, Monasa morphoeus 299
fidelis, Veniliornis passerinus 320
filicauda, Pipra 553
fimbriata, Amazilia 247
Finch, Ash-breasted Sierra 688
Band-tailed Sierra 688
Bay-crowned Brush 713
Black-billed Seed 702
Black-headed Brush 708
Chestnut-bellied Seed 702
Chestnut-capped Brush 708
Cinereous 689
Collared Warbling 689
Crimson 687
Duida Grass 692
Dusky-headed Brush 712
Grassland Yellow 691
Great-billed Seed 702
Large-billed Seed 701
Moustached Brush 712
Ochre-breasted Brush 714
Olive 709
Orange-fronted Yellow 690
Pale-headed Brush 714
Pale-naped Brush 710
Pileated 687
Plumbeous Sierra 688
Red-crested 687
Rufous-naped Brush 711
Saffron 690
Santa Marta Brush 711
Slaty 689
Slaty Brush 712
Sooty-faced 709
Stripe-headed Brush 709
Stripe-tailed Yellow 690
Sulphur-throated Yellow 691
Tanager 710
Tepui Brush 714
Thick-billed Seed 703
Tricoloured Brush 712
Wedge-tailed Grass 691
White-headed Brush 713
White-rimmed Brush 711
White-winged Brush 713
Yellow-headed Brush 711
Yellow-throated Brush 710
finschi, Euphonia 769
Fire-eye, White-backed 408
fissilis, Thalurania furcata 242
fjeldsaai, Myrmotherula 396
flabellifera, Florisuga mellivora 233
Flamingo, Chilean 82
Greater 82
flammeus, Asio 210
flammiceps, Pipra erythrocephala 554
flammigerus, Ramphocelus 640
flammulata, Asthenes 344
flammulatus, Thripadectes 357
Flatbill, Dusky-tailed 484
Eye-ringed 485
Fulvous-breasted 486
Large-headed 484
Olivaceous 485
Pacific 485
Rufous-tailed 485
flava, Piranga 679
flaveola, Capsiempis 463
flaveola, Coereba 683
flaveola, Sicalis 690
flaveolus, Basileuterus 745
flaveolus, Manacus manacus 550
flavescens, Boissonneaua 262
flavescens, Hypocnemis cantator 410
flavicans, Myiophobus 492
flavicapilla, Xenopipo 551
flaviceps, Atlapetes 711
flavicollis, Hemithraupis 632
flavicrissus, Cacicus cela 750
flavidicollis, Saltator striatipectus 721
flavidifrons, Zimmerius chrysops 461
flavidorsalis, Hemispingus frontalis 628
flavifrons, Vireo 568
flavigula, Melanerpes formicivorus 318
flavigula, Piculus 323
flavigularis, Chlorospingus 678
flavigularis, Machetornis rixosa 513
flavigularis, Platyrinchus 490
flavimentum, Phyllomyias nigrocapillus 459
flavipectus, Cyclarhis gujanensis 567
flavipectus, Philydor ruficaudatum 354
flavipes, Hylophilus 573
flavipes, Notiochelidon 583
flavipes, Tringa 133
flavipes, Turdus 613
flavirostris, Amblycercus holosericeus 752
flavirostris, Anser albifrons 36
flavirostris, Chlorophonia 773
flavirostris, Grallaricula 436
flavirostris, Monasa 300
flavirostris, Porphyrula 118
flavirostris, Pteroglossus azara 308
flaviventer, Dacnis 670
flaviventer, Porzana 116
flaviventris, Phylloscartes 480
flaviventris, Tachyphonus luctuosus 637
flaviventris, Tolmomyias 488
flavivertex, Myioborus 740
flavivertex, Myiopagis 466
flavogaster, Elaenia 468
flavoolivaceus, Tolmomyias sulphurescens 486
flavopectus, Chlorospingus ophthalmicus 676
flavotectus, Tolmomyias assimilis 487
flavotincta, Grallaria 432
flavotinctus, Picumnus olivaceus 316
flavovirens, Chlorospingus 678
flavoviridis, Vireo 569
flavus, Celeus 325
flavus, Rhynchocyclus olivaceus 485
Flicker, Andean 324
Campo 324
floriceps, Anthocephala 252
florida, Tangara 659
floridanus, Phalacrocorax auritus 68
Florisuga 233
Flowerpiercer, Black 654
Black-throated 653
Bluish 655
Chestnut-bellied 653
Coal-black 654
Deep-blue 655
Glossy 654
Greater 655
Indigo 655
Masked 656
Rusty 652
Scaled 654
Venezuelan 653
White-sided 653
fluviatilis, Amazilia fimbriata 248
fluviatilis, Muscisaxicola 509
Fluvicola 511
Flycatcher, Acadian 502
Alder 502
Amazonian Royal 491
Amazonian Scrub 464
Apical 519
Baird's 525
Black-billed 499
Black-tailed 496
Boat-billed 523
Bran-coloured 494
Brown-crested 519
Cinnamon 496
Cliff 497
Crowned Slaty 523

Dusky-capped 516
Dusky-chested 528
Euler's 498
Flavescent 492
Fork-tailed 521
Fuscous 497
Golden-crowned 525
Great Crested 519
Grey-breasted 499
Grey-capped 527
Grey-crowned 487
Handsome 493
Lemon-browed 524
McConnell's 448
Northern Royal 492
Northern Scrub 463
Ochre-bellied 447
Olive-chested 494
Olive-sided 500
Olive-striped 447
Olive Tufted 499
Orange-banded 493
Orange-crested 493
Orange-eyed 488
Ornate 492
Pacific Royal 491
Pale-edged 518
Panama 518
Piratic 528
Roraiman 493
Ruddy-tailed 494
Rufous 516
Rufous-breasted 448
Rusty-margined 526
Scissor-tailed 521
Sepia-capped 448
Short-crested 518
Slaty-capped 449
Social 527
Sooty-crowned 519
Southern Scrub 464
Streak-necked 446
Streaked 525
Suiriri 464
Sulphur-bellied 526
Sulphur-rumped 495
Sulphury 523
Swainson's 517
Tawny-breasted 495
Three-striped 524
Tufted 499
Unadorned 493
Variegated 522
Venezuelan 517
Vermilion 503
Whiskered 495
White-bearded 529
White-ringed 524
Willow 502
Yellow-breasted 488
Yellow-margined 487
Yellow-olive 486
Yellow-throated 524
foetens, Coragyps atratus 81
foetidu, Gymnoderus 542
Foliage-gleaner, Brown-rumped 358
Buff-browed 352
Buff-fronted 355
Buff-throated 357
Chestnut-crowned 359
Chestnut-winged 355
Cinnamon-rumped 354
Dusky-cheeked 355
Guttulated 351
Henna-hooded 359
Lineated 352
Montane 353
Olive-backed 357
Ruddy 358
Rufous-necked 352
Rufous-rumped 354
Rufous-tailed 354
Scaly-throated 353
Slaty-winged 354
White-throated 358
fontanieri, Accipiter superciliosus 89
forficatus, Elanoides 85
forficatus, Tyrannus 521
FORMICARIIDAE 423
Formicarius 424
Formicivora 403, 404
formicivorus, Melanerpes 318
formosa, Pipreola 534
formosus, Oporornis 734
Forpus 180
forreri, Vireo flavoviridis 570
fortis, Myrmeciza 417
fortis, Tityra semifasciata 556
fortis, Xiphocolaptes promeropirhynchus 368
fostersmithi, Syrigma sibilatrix 75
frailensis, Coereba flaveola 683
franciae, Amazilia 249
franciscanus, Euplectes 777
frantzii, Elaenia 471
fraseri, Basileuterus 740
fraseri, Conirostrum cinereum 651
fraseri, Oreomanes 652
frater, Herpsilochmus rufimarginatus 402
fraterculus, Onychorhynchus mexicanus 492
fraterculus, Thamnophilus doliatus 383
fratruelis, Arremon schlegeli 706
frederici, Rhytipterna simplex 515
Frederickena 380
Fregata 69
FREGATIDAE 69
frenata, Chlorothraupis 634
frenata, Geotrygon 169
Frigatebird, Great 69
Magnificent 69
frigidus, Lepidocolaptes lacrymiger 377
FRINGILLIDAE 763
fringilloides, Dolospingus 704
frontalis, Buarremon brunneinucha 708
frontalis, Chlorophonia cyanea 773
frontalis, Chrysomus ruficapillus 758
frontalis, Hemispingus 628
frontalis, Nonnula 298
frontalis, Ochthoeca 504
frontalis, Pipreola 534
frontata, Aratinga wagleri 173
Fruitcrow, Bare-necked 542
Crimson 543
Purple-throated 543
Red-ruffed 543
Fruiteater, Barred 532
Black-chested 533
Fiery-throated 534
Golden-breasted 533
Green-and-black 532
Handsome 534
Orange-breasted 533
Red-banded 535
Scaled 535
Scarlet-breasted 534
fucata, Alopochelidon 585
fucosa, Tangara 666
fuertesi, Hapalopsittaca 185
fulgidus, Pharomachrus 284
Fulica 119
fulica, Heliornis 120
fulicarius, Phalaropus 139
fuligidigula, Coeligena torquata 258
fuliginata, Dacnis venusta 670
fuliginosa, Catharus fuscescens 611
fuliginosa, Dendrocincla 364
fuliginosa, Schizoeaca 332
fuliginosus, Phaethornis anthophilus 228
fuliginosus, Tiaris 682
Fulmar, Southern 57
Fulmarus 57
fulva, Petrochelidon 587
fulva, Pluvialis 122
fulvescens, Chamaeza campanisona 425
fulvescens, Tangara cayana 663
fulvicauda, Basileuterus 745
fulviceps, Euscarthmus meloryphus 477
fulviceps, Thlypopsis 630
fulvicrissa, Euphonia 770
fulvidus, Nystalus radiatus 295
fulvigula, Tangara viridicollis 667
fulvigularis, Sclerurus rufigularis 360
fulvigularis, Terenotriccus erythrurus 494
fulvigularis, Troglodytes rufulus 599
fulvipectus, Rhynchocyclus 486
fulvipennis, Stelgidopteryx serripennis 585
fulviventris, Brachygalba lugubris 290
fulviventris, Hylopezus 434
fulviventris, Myrmotherula 396
fulviventris, Turdus 617
fulvogularis, Malacoptila 297
fulvus, Lanio 635
fumicolor, Ochthoeca 505
fumidus, Atlapetes schistaceus 713
fumifrons, Poecilotriccus 454

fumigata, Schizoeaca fuliginosa 332
fumigatus, Contopus 500
fumigatus, Myiotheretes 507
fumigatus, Turdus 619
fumigatus, Veniliornis 321
fumosa, Formicivora grisea 403
fumosus, Myiarchus swainsoni 517
fumosus, Sakesphorus canadensis 381
fumosus, Tiaris fuliginosus 682
fumosus, Cnemotriccus fuscatus 498
funereus, Oryzoborus 703
furcata, Tachornis 223
furcata, Thalurania 242
furcatus, Creagrus 147
furcifer, Heliomaster 272
FURNARIIDAE 328
Furnarius 330
fusca, Dendroica 728
fusca, Iodopleura 559
fusca, Malacoptila 296
fusca, Progne tapera 580
fuscater, Catharus 611
fuscater, Turdus 614
fuscatior, Cnemotriccus fuscatus 498
fuscatus, Cnemotriccus 497
fuscatus, Margarops 623
fuscatus, Onychoprion 148
fuscescens, Catharus 611
fuscicapillus, Colonia colonus 512
fuscicapillus, Hylophilus hypoxanthus 573
fuscicapillus, Lepidocolaptes albolineatus 377
fuscicapillus, Phaethornis anthophilus 228
fuscicauda, Cercomacra nigrescens 407
fuscicauda, Habia 675
fuscicauda, Ramphotrigon 484
fuscicauda, Scytalopus 444
fusciceps, Thripophaga 345
fuscicollis, Calidris 137
fuscifrons, Certhiaxis cinnamomeus 343
fuscipenne, Philydor 354
fuscipennis, Dryocopus lineatus 327
fuscivertex, Cranioleuca subcristata 342
fuscobrunneus, Turdus serranus 615
fuscocinereus, Lipaugus 539
fuscoolivaceus, Atlapetes 712
fuscorufa, Synallaxis 338
fuscus, Cinclodes 329
fuscus, Larus 145
fuscus, Pionus 190
gaimardii, Myiopagis 465
galapagensis, Anous stolidus 148
galapagoensis, Oceanites gracilis 62
Galbalcyrhynchus 289
galbanus, Hylophilus flavipes 574
galbinus, Mionectes olivaceus 447
galbraithii, Thryothorus leucotis 597
Galbula 290
galbula, Galbula 291
galbula, Icterus 756
GALBULIDAE 289
galeata, Gallinula chloropus 119
galeatus, Cyanocorax yncas 577
galeatus, Lophotriccus 483
Gallinago 128
Gallinula 118
Gallinule, Azure 118
Purple 118
Spot-flanked 118
gambeli, Anser albifrons 36
Gampsonyx 84
garrula, Ortalis 42
garzetta, Egretta 76
gayi, Attagis 140
Gelochelidon 150
gemmeus, Cyanerpes cyaneus 673
gentryi, Herpsilochmus 402
geoffroyi, Neomorphus 198
geoffroyi, Schistes 271
georgebarrowcloughi, Diglossa duidae 654
georgica, Anas 39
Geositta 329
geospizopsis, Phrygilus unicolor 688
Geothlypis 735
Geotrygon 167
Geranospiza 90
germanus, Colibri coruscans 234
gibsoni, Chlorostilbon 239
gigantea, Grallaria 427
giganteus, Macronectes 57
gigantodes, Turdus fuscater 615
gigas, Buthraupis montana 645
gigas, Cyanerpes cyaneus 673
gigas, Elaenia 469
gigas, Patagona 257
gigas, Turdus fuscater 615
gilliardi, Diglossa major 655
gilliardi, Pauxi pauxi 48
gilvicollis, Micrastur 106
gilvus, Mimus 622
gilvus, Nyctidromus albicollis 215
ginesi, Diglossa caerulescens 656
giraudii, Icterus chrysater 754
glaber, Sublegatus arenarum 463
glacialoides, Fulmarus 57
glareola, Tringa 133
glauca, Diglossa 655
Glaucidium 206
Glaucis 225
glaucocolpa, Thraupis 642
glaucogularis, Dacnis cayana 671
glaucus, Thamnomanes caesius 392
globulosa, Crax 49
gloriosa, Diglossa 654
gloriosissima, Diglossa 653
Glyphorynchus 366
Gnatcatcher, Guianan 606
Slate-throated 606
Tropical 605
Gnateater, Ash-throated 438
Chestnut-belted 438
Chestnut-crowned 438
Gnatwren, Collared 604
Long-billed 605
Tawny-faced 605
godini, Eriocnemis 265
Godwit, Bar-tailed 131
Black-tailed 130
Hudsonian 130
Marbled 131
goeringi, Brachygalba 289
goeringi, Hemispingus 629
Goethalsia 244
Goldenthroat, Green-tailed 245
Tepui 244
White-tailed 245
Goldfinch, Lesser 766
goldmani, Geotrygon 168
Goldmania 244
goodfellowi, Turdus ignobilis 618
goodsoni, Patagioenas 158
goodsoni, Tangara arthus 659
Goose, Greater White-fronted 36
Orinoco 36
Snow 36
gorgonae, Coereba flaveola 683
gorgonae, Thamnophilus atrinucha 387
goudoti, Lepidopyga 241
goudotii, Chamaepetes 47
gouldii, Lesbia nuna 277
graceannae, Icterus 756
gracilipes, Zimmerius 460
gracilis, Lesbia nuna 277
gracilis, Oceanites 62
gracilis, Piaya minuta 196
Grackle, Carib 761
Golden-tufted 760
Great-tailed 761
Mountain 760
Red-bellied 759
Velvet-fronted 759
graellsii, Larus fuscus 145
Grallaria 427
Grallaricula 436
grammicus, Celeus 325
granadensis, Hemitriccus 453
granadensis, Myiozetetes 527
granadensis, Picumnus 317
granadensis, Pyroderus scutatus 543
granadensis, Tangara cyanicollis 665
granadensis, Taraba major 380
Granatellus 746
grandior, Thamnophilus unicolor 385
grandis, Myiozetetes similis 527
grandis, Nyctibius 210
granti, Penelope jacquacu 46
granti, Sula 66
Grassquit, Black-faced 682
Blue-black 692
Dull-coloured 681
Sooty 682
Yellow-faced 681
gratiosa, Ochthoeca diadema 504
gravis, Puffinus 60
Graydidascalus 186
grayi, Hylocharis 243

grayi, Turdus 620
Grebe, Colombian 54
Great 54
Least 53
Pied-billed 54
Silvery 55
greenewalti, Lafresnaya lafresnayi 258
Greenlet, Ashy-headed 572
Brown-headed 572
Buff-cheeked 572
Dusky-capped 573
Golden-fronted 573
Grey-chested 571
Lemon-chested 571
Lesser 574
Olivaceous 574
Rufous-naped 573
Scrub 573
Tawny-crowned 574
Tepui 572
Greenshank, Common 132
Greytail, Double-banded 347
Equatorial 347
grisea, Formicivora 403
griseicapillus, Sittasomus 366
griseiceps, Atalotriccus pilaris 483
griseiceps, Basileuterus 742
griseiceps, Glaucidium 206
griseiceps, Lepidocolaptes angustirostris 376
griseiceps, Myrmeciza 417
griseiceps, Phyllomyias 458
griseicollis, Scytalopus 444
griseigula, Laniocera rufescens 557
griseigularis, Aulacorhynchus prasinus 305
griseigularis, Cranioleuca erythrops 340
griseigularis, Elaenia albiceps 468
griseigularis, Pachyramphus viridis 560
griseipecta, Aratinga pertinax 175
griseipectus, Lathrotriccus 499
griseipectus, Myrmeciza longipes 414
griseipectus, Thryothorus coraya 594
griseiventris, Hylophilus thoracicus 571
griseiventris, Neochelidon tibialis 584
griseobarbatus, Vireo olivaceus 569
griseocapillus, Phylloscartes superciliaris 481
griseodorsalis, Ramphocaenus melanurus 605
griseogularis, Phaethornis 229
griseola, Columbina passerina 162
griseolus, Poecilotriccus sylvia 455
griseomurina, Schizoeaca 333
griseonucha, Grallaria 431
griseonucha, Synallaxis brachyura 334
Griseotyrannus 523
griseoventris, Formicarius analis 424
grisescens, Tersina viridis 674
grisescens, Thryothorus leucopogon 596
griseus, Campylorhynchus 587
griseus, Limnodromus 129
griseus, Nyctibius 211
griseus, Puffinus 60
griseus, Sittasomus griseicapillus 366
groenvoldi, Gelochelidon nilotica 150
Grosbeak, Black-backed 717
Black-headed 717
Blue 722
Blue-black 721
Golden-bellied 716
Red-and-black 718
Rose-breasted 717
Slate-coloured 719
Ultramarine 722
Yellow-green 718
Yellow-shouldered 718
grossus, Saltator 719
gryphus, Vultur 82
guainumbi, Polytmus 245
guaiquinimae, Campylopterus duidae 231
guaiquinimae, Myrmothera simplex 435
gualaquizae, Phylloscartes 480
Guan, Andean 45
Band-tailed 44
Baudó 45
Bearded 44
Blue-throated Piping 46
Cauca 46
Crested 45
Marail 45
Orton's 45
Sickle-winged 47
Spix's 46
Trinidad Piping 46
Wattled 47
guapiensis, Campylorhamphus pusillus 378
guarauna, Aramus 109
guaricola, Conirostrum speciosum 650
guatemalensis, Amaurolimnas concolor 115
guatemalensis, Cyanocorax yncas 577
guatemalensis, Sclerurus 361
guatimalensis, Grallaria 428
guatimozinus, Psarocolius 749
guayae, Xenops rutilans 363
guayaquilensis, Ara ambiguus 171
guayaquilensis, Campephilus 328
guayaquilensis, Pachyramphus albogriseus 563
guerinii, Oxypogon 268
guianae, Piculus rubiginosus 322
guianensis, Chaetura cinereiventris 220
guianensis, Coereba flaveola 683
guianensis, Doryfera johannae 231
guianensis, Lampropsar tanagrinus 760
guianensis, Lophotriccus vitiosus 482
guianensis, Morphnus 100
guianensis, Myiopagis gaimardii 465
guianensis, Piculus chrysochloros 323
guianensis, Polioptila 606
guianensis, Rhynchocyclus olivaceus 485
guianensis, Terenura callinota 405
guimeti, Klais 236
Guira 198
guira, Guira 198
guira, Hemithraupis 631
guirina, Hemithraupis guira 631
gujanensis, Cyclarhis 567
gujanensis, Odontophorus 51
gujanensis, Synallaxis 336
gularis, Cichlopsis leucogenys 609
gularis, Egretta 75
gularis, Heliodoxa 255
gularis, Hellmayrea 339
gularis, Mecocerculus leucophrys 472
gularis, Paroaria 715
gularis, Piculus rubiginosus 322
gularis, Thamnistes anabatinus 389
Gull, American Herring 144
Andean 146
Belcher's 143
Black-headed 145
Bonaparte's 146
Brown-hooded 145
California 144
Great Black-backed 144
Grey 143
Grey-hooded 145
Kelp 144
Laughing 146
Lesser Black-backed 145
Little 147
Ring-billed 143
Swallow-tailed 147
gumia, Platyrinchus coronatus 490
gundlachii, Chordeiles 214
guttata, Myrmotherula 395
guttata, Ortalis 43
guttata, Tangara 661
guttatoides, Xiphorhynchus guttatus 374
guttatum, Todirostrum chrysocrotaphum 456
guttatus, Chrysoptilus punctigula 324
guttatus, Tinamus 28
guttatus, Xiphorhynchus 374
guttulata, Syndactyla 351
guttuligera, Premnornis 348
gutturalis, Atlapetes 710
gutturalis, Corapipo 546
gutturalis, Habia 676
gutturalis, Myrmotherula 395
gutturata, Cranioleuca 343
guy, Phaethornis 226
Gymnocichla 411
Gymnoderus 542
Gymnomystax 757
Gymnopithys 418
gyrola, Tangara 662
gyrola, Tangara gyrola 662
Habia 675
haemalea, Piranga lutea 679
haemastica, Limosa 130
Haematoderus 543
haematogaster, Campephilus 327
haematonota, Myrmotherula 396

HAEMATOPODIDAE 125
Haematopus 125
haematopygus, Aulacorhynchus 306
haematotis, Pionopsitta 187
haemorrhous, Cacicus 750
Haliaeetus 91
haliaetus, Pandion 83
hamatus, Helicolestes 85
hanieli, Hemispingus frontalis 628
hannahiae, Tangara cyanicollis 665
Hapalopsittaca 185
Hapaloptila 299
haplonota, Grallaria 429
Haplophaedia 267
Haplospiza 689
hardyi, Glaucidium 207
hargitti, Pharomachrus auriceps 284
Harpagus 86
Harpia 101
harpyja, Harpia 101
Harrier, Cinereous 88
Long-winged 87
Northern 88
harrisi, Parabuteo unicinctus 96
harrisii, Aegolius 209
harterti, Campylorhynchus albobrunneus 588
harterti, Crypturellus soui 29
harterti, Picumnus olivaceus 316
harterti, Pittasoma rufopileatum 426
harterti, Rhodinocichla rosea 633
hartlaubi, Dacnis 669
hasitata, Pterodroma 58
hauxwelli, Henicorhina leucosticta 600
hauxwelli, Mionectes oleagineus 447
hauxwelli, Myrmotherula 395
hauxwelli, Turdus 619
Hawk, Barred 91
Bicoloured 90
Black-collared 95
Black-faced 91
Broad-winged 98
Common Black 94
Cooper's 89
Crane 90
Great Black 94
Grey-backed 91
Grey-bellied 88
Grey-lined 93
Harris's 96
Mangrove Black 94
Plain-breasted 89
Plumbeous 92
Puna 100
Red-backed 99
Red-tailed 99
Roadside 97
Rufous Crab 93
Savanna 95
Semicollared 89
Semiplumbeous 93
Short-tailed 98
Slate-coloured 92
Swainson's 99
Tiny 89
White 92
White-rumped 98
White-tailed 97
White-throated 98
Zone-tailed 100
Hawk-Eagle, Black 102
Black-and-white 101
Ornate 101
hederaceus, Mionectes olivaceus 447
heilprini, Cyanocorax 576
heinei, Tangara 667
helenae, Neopipo cinnamomea 496
Heliactin 272
Heliangelus 262
helianthea, Coeligena 261
helias, Eurypyga 120
Helicolestes 85
heliodor, Chaetocercus 274
Heliodoxa 253
helioeides, Icterus nigrogularis 755
Heliomaster 272
Heliornis 120
HELIORNITHIDAE 120
Heliothryx 271
Hellmayrea 339
hellmayri, Celeus elegans 326
hellmayri, Cranioleuca 341
hellmayri, Cyanerpes caeruleus 672
hellmayri, Dendrocincla tyrannina 364
hellmayri, Drymophila caudata 404
hellmayri, Hemithraupis flavicollis 632
hellmayri, Leptotila rufaxilla 166
hellmayri, Myiozetetes cayanensis 526
hellmayri, Rhynchocyclus brevirostris 485
hellmayri, Tyto alba 200
hellmayri, Xenops tenuirostris 362
Helmetcrest, Bearded 268
Helmitheros 732
helvinus, Hylophilus aurantiifrons 573
hemileucurus, Phlogophilus 253
hemileucus, Myrmochanes 411
Hemispingus 627
Hemispingus, Black-capped 627
Black-eared 629
Black-headed 630
Grey-capped 628
Oleaginous 628
Piura 629
Slaty-backed 629
Superciliaried 628
Western 629
Hemithraupis 631
Hemitriccus 451
hendersoni, Limnodromus griseus 130
Henicorhina 600
henryi, Chordeiles minor 213
herbicola, Emberizoides 691
Hermit, Black-throated 230
Bronzy 225
Eastern Long-tailed 227
Great-billed 227
Green 226
Grey-chinned 229
Little 229
Pale-bellied 228
Reddish 229
Rufous-breasted 225
Sooty-capped 229
Straight-billed 228
Streak-throated 229
Stripe-throated 230
Tawny-bellied 227
Western Long-tailed 226
White-bearded 228
White-whiskered 227
hernandezi, Cistothorus apolinari 591
hernandezi, Leptotila verreauxi 165
herodias, Ardea 74
Heron, Agami 70
Bare-throated Tiger 70
Black-crowned Night 72
Boat-billed 71
Capped 75
Cocoi 74
Fasciated Tiger 70
Great Blue 74
Green 72
Grey 73
Little Blue 76
Purple 74
Rufescent Tiger 70
Striated 73
Tricoloured 75, 76
Western Reef 75
Whistling 75
Yellow-crowned Night 72
Zigzag 71
Herpetotheres 105
Herpsilochmus 400
herrani, Chalcostigma 270
hershkovitzi, Tinamus osgoodi 27
hesperia, Progne subis 581
hesperis, Chordeiles minor 213
hesperus, Coeligena iris 261
Heterocercus 552
heterogynus, Thamnophilus schistaceus 386
heteropogon, Chalcostigma 270
Heteroscelus 134
Heterospingus 636
heterurus, Caprimulgus parvulus 217
heterurus, Cinclodes fuscus 329
heterurus, Eutoxeres aquila 224
heterurus, Xenops rutilans 363
hiaticula, Charadrius 123
hicksii, Sporophila corvina 695
hilaris, Henicorhina leucophrys 601
hilaris, Veniliornis affinis 320
Hillstar, Andean 257
Ecuadorian 256
White-tailed 257

Himantopus 126
himantopus, Calidris 138
hirsutus, Glaucis 225
hirundinacea, Cypsnagra 625
hirundinacea, Sterna 151
Hirundinea 497
HIRUNDINIDAE 578
Hirundo 586
hirundo, Sterna 152
hispaniolensis, Poospiza 689
hispidus, Phaethornis 228
hitchcocki, Diglossa duidae 654
hoactli, Nycticorax nycticorax 72
Hoatzin 154
hoatzin, Opisthocomus 154
hoematotis, Pyrrhura 179
hoffmanni, Trogon massena 283
holerythra, Rhytipterna 515
hollandi, Amazilia versicolor 247
holochlora, Xenopipo 551
holosericeus, Amblycercus 752
holostictus, Thripadectes 356
homochroa, Catamenia 705
homochroa, Dendrocincla 365
homochroa, Oceanodroma 64
homochrous, Pachyramphus 564
hondae, Formicivora grisea 403
hondae, Icterus chrysater 754
Honeycreeper, Golden-collared 668
  Green 671
  Purple 672
  Red-legged 673
  Shining 672
  Short-billed 672
Hookbill, Chestnut-winged 350
hopkei, Carpodectes 542
hormotus, Microbates cinereiventris 605
hornbyi, Oceanodroma 64
Hornero, Lesser 330
  Pacific 330
  Pale-billed 330
  Pale-legged 330
horvathi, Colinus cristatus 50
howelli, Chordeiles minor 213
huachamacarii, Chamaeza campanisona 425
huallagae, Chlorospingus parvirostris 677
huallagae, Synallaxis gujanensis 336
huambina, Hemithraupis guira 632
hudsonia, Calidris alpina 138
hudsonicus, Numenius phaeopus 131
hudsonius, Circus cyaneus 88
huetii, Touit 183
huhula, Ciccaba 204
huilae, Malacoptila fulvogularis 297
huilae, Tiaris bicolor 682
humboldti, Phrygilus alaudinus 688
humboldti, Pteroglossus inscriptus 307
humboldti, Spheniscus 55
humboldtii, Hylocharis 244
humeralis, Ammodramus 685
humeralis, Diglossa 654
humeralis, Parkerthraustes 718
humeralis, Terenura 405
humilis, Euphonia minuta 771
Hummingbird, Amazilia 251
  Blue-chested 248
  Buffy 246
  Chestnut-bellied 251
  Copper-rumped 249
  Copper-tailed 250
  Giant 257
  Green-bellied 250
  Indigo-capped 249
  Loja 251
  Many-spotted 246
  Olive-spotted 246
  Purple-chested 248
  Ruby 235
  Rufous-cheeked 244
  Rufous-tailed 250
  Sapphire-bellied 241
  Sapphire-throated 241
  Scaly-breasted 231
  Scissor-tailed 255
  Shining-green 241
  Snowy-breasted 251
  Speckled 252
  Steely-vented 249
  Swallow-tailed 233
  Sword-billed 257
  Tooth-billed 230
  Tumbes 246
  Violet-bellied 242
  Violet-capped 244
  Violet-chested 255
  Violet-headed 236
  Wedge-billed 271
HYDROBATIDAE 61
Hydroprogne 150
Hydropsalis 218
Hylexetastes 368
Hylocharis 243
Hylocichla 613
Hylocryptus 359
Hyloctistes 351
hylodroma, Grallaria gigantea 427
hylodromus, Xiphorhynchus triangularis 375
Hylomanes 287
Hylonympha 255
Hylopezus 434
Hylophilus 571
Hylophylax 420
hyperrynchus, Notharchus macrorhynchos 293
hyperythra, Diglossa sittoides 652
hyperythra, Myrmeciza 416
hyperythrus, Campylopterus 232
hyperythrus, Odontophorus 51
Hypnelus 295
hypochlora, Thalurania fannyi 242
hypochroma, Sporophila 700
Hypocnemis 410
Hypocnemoides 410
hypoglauca, Andigena 310
hypoglaucus, Oxyruncus cristatus 530
hypoleuca, Grallaria 432
hypoleuca, Nemosia pileata 633
hypoleuca, Serpophaga 474
hypoleuca, Zenaida auriculata 160
hypoleucus, Capito 301
hypoleucus, Thryothorus leucotis 597
hypomelaena, Jacana jacana 141
hypophaea, Thraupis cyanocephala 643
hypopolia, Petrochelidon pyrrhonota 586
hypopyrra, Laniocera 558
Hypopyrrhus 759
hypospodius, Buteo albicaudatus 97
hypospodius, Thryothorus rutilus 595
hyposticta, Cranioleuca gutturata 343
hypostictus, Campylorhynchus turdinus 588
hypostictus, Taphrospilus 246
hypoxantha, Euphonia laniirostris 769
hypoxantha, Hypocnemis 410
hypoxanthus, Hylophilus 573
ibis, Bubulcus 73
Ibis, Bare-faced 78
  Black-faced 79
  Buff-necked 78
  Glossy 77
  Green 78
  Scarlet 77
  Sharp-tailed 78
  Whispering 78
  White 77
  White-faced 78
Ibycter 103
ICTERIDAE 746
icterocephala, Tangara 660
icterocephalus, Chrysomus 757
icteronotus, Ramphocelus 641
icterophrys, Conopias cinchoneti 525
icterophrys, Satrapa 512
icterotis, Ognorhynchus 176
Icterus 753
icterus, Icterus 753
Ictinia 87
idoneus, Crypturellus erythropus 31
ignicapillus, Iridosornis rufivertex 649
igniventris, Anisognathus 647
ignobilis, Hemispingus frontalis 628
ignobilis, Phaethornis striigularis 230
ignobilis, Thripadectes 356
ignobilis, Turdus 618
ignota, Myrmotherula 393
ignotus, Basileuterus 744
ignotus, Xiphocolaptes promeropirhynchus 368
imatacae, Platyrinchus mystaceus 489
immaculata, Cercomacra cinerascens 406
immaculata, Myrmeciza 417
immarginata, Pyrrhura hoematotis 179
immunda, Rhytipterna 515
imperatrix, Heliodoxa 254

imperialis, Gallinago 129
impiger, Hemitriccus margaritaceiventer 452
implacens, Myiopagis viridicata 467
improbus, Zimmerius 460
imthurni, Macroagelaius 760
inaccessibilis, Zonotrichia capensis 684
inaequalis, Synallaxis albescens 333
Inca, Black 259
Bronzy 259
Brown 259
Collared 258
Purple 259
inca, Larosterna 151
incanescens, Phaethornis augusti 229
incanus, Heteroscelus 134
incerta, Sporophila schistacea 693
incomptus, Turdus grayi 620
incomta, Phaeomyias murina 462
inda, Chloroceryle 286
indigotica, Diglossa 655
inerme, Ornithion 461
inexpectata, Conopophaga aurita 438
inexpectatus, Arremonops conirostris 707
Inezia 475
Inezia, Amazonian 475
Pale-tipped 475
Slender-billed 475
infasciatus, Scytalopus griseicollis 444
infusca, Geotrygon linearis 168
infuscata, Schistocichla leucostigma 413
infuscatus, Acropternis orthonyx 445
infuscatus, Automolus 357
infuscatus, Phimosus 78
ingens, Megascops 202
innotata, Polioptila plumbea 606
innotatus, Celeus loricatus 325
inops, Crypturellus tataupa 33
inornata, Amazona farinosa 192
inornata, Catamenia 705
inornata, Henicorhina leucosticta 600
inornata, Myrmotherula behni 399
inornata, Phelpsia 529
inornata, Tangara 657
inornata, Thlypopsis 630
inornatus, Buarremon brunneinucha 708
inornatus, Catharus aurantiirostris 610
inornatus, Catoptrophorus semipalmatus 134
inornatus, Chlorospingus 677
inornatus, Myiophobus 493
inornatus, Phacellodomus rufifrons 345
inquisitor, Tityra 556
inscriptus, Pteroglossus 307
insidiatrix, Buteo magnirostris 97
insignis, Catharus aurantiirostris 610
insignis, Euphonia cyanocephala 770
insignis, Sclerurus caudacutus 361
insignis, Synallaxis albescens 333
insignis, Thamnophilus 387
insolens, Myiodynastes maculatus 526
insolitus, Phaethornis malaris 228
insolitus, Xiphorhynchus erythropygius 375
insulanus, Vireo flavoviridis 570
insularis, Caprimulgus cayennensis 216
insularis, Hylophilus flavipes 574
insularis, Platyrinchus mystaceus 489
insularis, Psarocolius decumanus 747
insularis, Quiscalus lugubris 761
insularis, Sporophila 694
insularis, Zonotrichia capensis 684
insularum, Glaucis hirsutus 225
insulata, Sporophila 701
integratus, Glyphorynchus spirurus 367
intensa, Chlorophonia cyanea 773
intensa, Thlypopsis fulviceps 630
intensus, Anisognathus lacrymosus 647
intensus, Hemitriccus granadensis 453
intensus, Mionectes oleagineus 447
intensus, Thryothorus rutilus 595
intercedens, Nothocercus bonapartei 28
intercedens, Tachyphonus cristatus 636
interfluvialis, Nonnula rubecula 298
interior, Manacus manacus 550
interior, Myrmotherula schisticolor 398
interior, Thryothorus rutilus 595
intermedia, Chalybura urochrysia 252
intermedia, Coereba flaveola 683
intermedia, Formicivora grisea 403
intermedia, Inezia caudata 475
intermedia, Jacana jacana 141
intermedia, Sporophila 694
intermedium, Conirostrum sitticolor 651
intermedius, Cymbilaimus lineatus 379
intermedius, Larus fuscu 145
intermedius, Pachyramphus castaneus 561
intermedius, Sakesphorus canadensis 381
intermedius, Thamnistes anabatinus 389
interpositus, Thamnophilus punctatus 386
interpres, Arenaria 135
interstes, Micrastur ruficollis 105
involucris, Ixobrychus 72
Iodopleura 558
iodura, Amazilia viridigaster 250
iohannis, Hemitriccus 452
iracunda, Metallura 270
iridescens, Anthracothorax nigricollis 235
iridina, Tangara velia 668
Iridophanes 668
Iridosornis 648
iris, Coeligena 260
irrorata, Phoebastria 56
isabellae, Iodopleura 558
isabellinus, Falco sparverius 107
isaurae, Chalybura urochrysia 252
isidorei, Lepidothrix 549
isidori, Jacamerops aureus 292
isidori, Oroaetus 102
iteratus, Hemispingus frontalis 628
iungens, Saltator maximus 719
Ixobrychus 72
Jabiru 80
Jacamar, Bluish-fronted 290
Bronzy 292
Brown 290
Coppery-chested 291
Dusky-backed 289
Great 292
Green-tailed 291
Pale-headed 289
Paradise 292
Purplish 291
Rufous-tailed 290
White-chinned 291
White-eared 289
Yellow-billed 290
Jacamerops 292
Jacana 140
jacana, Jacana 140
Jacana, Wattled 140
JACANIDAE 140
jacarina, Volatinia 692
Jacobin, White-necked 233
jacquacu, Penelope 46
jacqueti, Chlorospingus ophthalmicus 676
jacula, Heliodoxa 254
jacupeba, Penelope marail 45
Jaeger, Long-tailed 142
Parasitic 142
Pomarine 142
jamaicensis, Buteo 99
jamaicensis, Laterallus 112
jamaicensis, Leptotila 166
jamesoni, Gallinago 129
jamesoni, Heliodoxa jacula 254
jamesonii, Oreotrochilus chimborazo 256
jardinei, Xiphorhynchus susurrans 374
jardini, Boissonneaua 262
jardinii, Glaucidium 207
Jay, Azure-naped 576
Beautiful 576
Black-chested 577
Black-collared 575
Cayenne 577
Green 577
Turquoise 575
Violaceous 576
White-tailed 577
jelambianus, Rhynchocyclus olivaceus 485
jelskii, Ochthoeca 504
jesupi, Ochthoeca diadema 504
Jewelfront, Gould's 253
johannae, Doryfera 231
johannae, Tangara 658
johnsoni, Pseudocolaptes lawrencii 349
johnstonei, Tiaris bicolor 682
josephae, Vireo leucophrys 571
josephinae, Hemitriccus 451
josephinae, Synallaxis albescens 333
jota, Cathartes aura 81
jourdanii, Chaetocercus 275
jubaris, Dendroica petechia 726
jubata, Neochen 36
jucunda, Amazilia tzacatl 250
jucunda, Pipreola 533

jugularis, Atlapetes personatus 715
jugularis, Brotogeris 182
juliae, Lesbia victoriae 277
julie, Damophila 242
julius, Nothocercus 28
jumanus, Celeus elegans 326
juninensis, Podiceps occipitalis 55
juruanus, Pachyramphus rufus 564
kaestneri, Grallaria 431
kalimayae, Geositta tenuirostris 329
kathleenae, Herpsilochmus roraimae 401
kathleenae, Pipreola whitelyi 535
kelsalli, Oceanodroma tethys 63
kemptoni, Turdus olivater 617
kerdeli, Colibri thalassinus 234
kerriae, Crypturellus 31
Kestrel, American 107
  Common 107
  Eurasian 107
kienerii, Xiphorhynchus 371
Killdeer 124
Kingbird, Eastern 522
  Grey 522
  Snowy-throated 520
  Tropical 520
  White-throated 520
Kingfisher, Amazon 286
  American Pygmy 285
  Belted 286
  Green 285
  Green-and-rufous 286
  Ringed 286
kingi, Aglaiocercus 276
kirkii, Veniliornis 321
Kiskadee, Great 529
  Lesser 528
Kite, Double-toothed 86
  Grey-headed 83
  Hook-billed 84
  Mississippi 87
  Pearl 84
  Plumbeous 87
  Rufous-thighed 86
  Slender-billed 85
  Snail 85
  Swallow-tailed 85
  White-tailed 86
klagesi, Drymophila caudata 404
klagesi, Lophornis chalybeus 237
klagesi, Thripadectes virgaticeps 356
klagesi, Tolmomyias poliocephalus 488
Klais 236
kleei, Tinamus tao 27
Knipolegus 510
Knot, Red 135
knoxi, Crypturellus obsoletus 30
koenigi, Aratinga acuticaudata 173
kollari, Synallaxis 339
krameri, Psittacula 172
kukenamensis, Grallaricula nana 436
kulczynskii, Thamnophilus nigrocinereus 385
kunanensis, Sclerurus albigularis 360
labradorides, Tangara 664
lachrymosus, Xiphorhynchus 375
lacrymiger, Lepidocolaptes 376
lacrymosus, Anisognathus 647
lactea, Amazilia 248
laemosticta, Myrmeciza 415
laeta, Cercomacra 407
laetus, Thryothorus rutilus 595
Lafresnaya 258
lafresnayei, Dendrocincla fuliginosa 364
lafresnayi, Lafresnaya 258
lafresnayi, Lepidocolaptes lacrymiger 376
lafresnayi, Picumnus 314
lafresnayii, Diglossa 654
laireti, Amazilia cupreicauda 250
laminirostris, Andigena 309
Lampropsar 759
Lamprospiza 626
Lancebill, Blue-fronted 231
  Green-fronted 231
lanceolata, Chiroxiphia 550
lanceolata, Micromonacha 298
langsdorffi, Popelairia 238
languens, Tangara inornata 657
laniirostris, Euphonia 769
Laniisoma 559
Lanio 635
Laniocera 557
lanyoni, Phylloscartes 479
lapponica, Limosa 131
Lapwing, Andean 122
  Pied 121
  Southern 121
larensis, Buarremon torquatus 709
larensis, Picumnus cinnamomeus 315
larensis, Tinamus tao 27
largipennis, Campylopterus 231
LARIDAE 143
Lark, Horned 578
Larosterna 151
Larus 143
larvata, Tangara 665
lasallei, Formicarius rufipectus 425
latebricola, Scytalopus 442
lateralis, Andigena hypoglauca 310
lateralis, Tangara mexicana 658
Laterallus 112
Lathrotriccus 498
laticlavius, Heliangelus amethysticollis 263
latifascia, Nyctiprogne leucopyga 214
latifrons, Tinamus major 27
latinuchus, Atlapetes 711
latirostris, Chaetura spinicauda 221
latirostris, Ocyalus 749
latirostris, Poecilotriccus 454
latitabunda, Synallaxis albescens 334
latrans, Scytalopus 440
latreillii, Attagis gayi 140
laubmanni, Pheucticus chrysogaster 717
laurae, Coereba flaveola 683
lautus, Aulacorhynchus prasinus 305
lavinia, Tangara 663
lawrencei, Lathrotriccus euleri 498
lawrencei, Chaetura cinereiventris 221
lawrencii, Cyphorhinus phaeocephalus 604
lawrencii, Pseudocolaptes 349
lawrencii, Turdus 618
leadbeateri, Heliodoxa 253
Leaftosser, Black-tailed 361
  Grey-throated 360
  Scaly-throated 361
  Short-billed 360
  Tawny-throated 360
Legatus 528
lehmanni, Aratinga pertinax 175
lehmanni, Grallaria gigantea 427
lehmanni, Hemitriccus granadensis 453
lemae, Hyloctistes subulatus 351
lemos, Cypseloides 219
leonae, Gampsonyx swainsonii 84
leopetes, Caprimulgus cayennensis 216
leotaudi, Celeus elegans 326
Lepidocolaptes 376
lepidonotus, Hylophylax poecilinotus 422
Lepidopyga 241
Lepidothrix 548
Leptasthenura 331
Leptodon 83
Leptopogon 448
Leptosittaca 175
Leptotila 165
lepturus, Phaethon 65
Lesbia 277
lessoni, Lophornis delattrei 236
leucaspis, Gymnopithys 419
Leucippus 246
leucocephala, Arundinicola 512
leucocephala, Patagioenas 155
leucocephalus, Cinclus 607
leucocephalus, Haliaeetus 91
leucochlamys, Manacus manacus 550
leucogaster, Amazilia 249
leucogaster, Sula 67
leucogaster, Thamnophilus punctatus 386
leucogastra, Galbula 292
leucogenis, Merganetta armata 41
leucogenys, Cichlopsis 609
leucogenys, Conirostrum 650
leucogonys, Phyllomyias burmeisteri 457
leucolaemus, Piculus 323
leucomelas, Turdus 617
leuconota, Colonia colonus 512
leuconota, Pyriglena 408
leucophaius, Legatus 528
leucophrys, Capsiempis flaveola 463
leucophrys, Henicorhina 600
leucophrys, Mecocerculus 472
leucophrys, Myrmoborus 409
leucophrys, Ochthoeca 506
leucophrys, Vireo 571
leucophthalma, Aratinga 174
leucophthalma, Myrmotherula 396

leucopis, Atlapetes 711
leucopogon, Thryothorus 596
leucops, Turdus 614
leucoptera, Henicorhina 601
leucoptera, Piranga 680
leucoptera, Psophia 110
leucoptera, Sporophila 698
leucoptera, Thraupis episcopus 642
Leucopternis 91
leucopterus, Atlapetes 713
leucopterus, Nyctibius 211
leucopus, Furnarius 330
leucopyga, Nyctiprogne 214
leucoramphus, Cacicus chrysonotus 751
leucorhoa, Oceanodroma 63
leucorodia, Platalea 79
leucorrhoa, Corapipo 547
leucorrhous, Buteo 98
leucorrhous, Polytmus theresiae 245
leucospodia, Pseudelaenia 467
leucosticta, Henicorhina 600
leucostictus, Dysithamnus 391
leucostigma, Schistocichla 413
leucotis, Colinus cristatus 50
leucotis, Galbalcyrhynchus 289
leucotis, Tangara ruficervix 664
leucotis, Thryothorus 597
leucotis, Vireolanius 568
leucura, Urochroa bougueri 258
leucurus, Elanus 86
leucurus, Threnetes 226
leverianus, Cissopis 626
levis, Sittasomus griseicapillus 366
levraudi, Laterallus 112
lherminieri, Puffinus 61
lictor, Philohydor 528
lilacina, Amazona autumnalis 190
lilliae, Lepidopyga 241
limicola, Rallus 114
Limkpin 109
Limnodromus 129, 130
Limnothlypis 732
Limosa 130
limosa, Limosa 130
lincolnii, Melospiza 684
lindenii, Oxypogon guerinii 268
linearis, Geotrygon 168
lineata, Dacnis 669
lineata, Dacnis lineata 670
lineaticeps, Lepidocolaptes souleyetii 376
lineatocapilla, Xiphorhynchus ocellatus 372
lineatum, Tigrisoma 70
lineatus, Cymbilaimus 379
lineatus, Dryocopus 326
lineifrons, Grallaricula 437
lineola, Bolborhynchus 179
lineola, Sporophila 696
lintoni, Myiophobus 493
Liosceles 439
Lipaugus 539
liriope, Lafresnaya lafresnayi 258
litae, Myiophobus phoenicomitra 493
litae, Piculus 323
litae, Xenopipo holochlora 551
littoralis, Colinus cristatus 50
littoralis, Lepidocolaptes souleyetii 376
littoralis, Ochthornis 506
littoralis, Synallaxis albescens 334
littoralis, Xenops minutus 363
livia, Columba 155
livingstoni, Chlorospingus semifuscus 677
lobatus, Phalaropus 139
Lochmias 361
Loddigesia 278
Lonchura 774
longicauda, Bartramia 132
longicauda, Deconychura 365
longicauda, Myrmotherula 395
longicaudatus, Mimus 622
longicaudatus, Nyctibius aethereus 211
longicaudus, Discosura 238
longicaudus, Stercorarius 142
longipennis, Chlorophonia cyanea 773
longipennis, Myrmotherula 399
longipennis, Sporophila schistacea 693
longipes, Myrmeciza 414
longipes, Thryothorus euophrys 593
longirostris, Caprimulgus 216
longirostris, Carduelis magellanica 765
longirostris, Chrysuronia oenone 244
longirostris, Cyanerpes caeruleus 672
longirostris, Furnarius leucopus 331
longirostris, Heliomaster 272
longirostris, Nasica 367
longirostris, Phaethornis 226
longirostris, Rallus 113
longirostris, Xiphorhynchus picus 371
longuemareus, Phaethornis 229
Lophornis 236
Lophostrix 205
Lophotriccus 482
lorata, Sternula 150
loretoyacuensis, Sakesphorus canadensis 381
loricata, Grallaricula 437
loricatus, Celeus 325
lovejoyi, Picumnus squamulatus 316
lowii, Coereba flaveola 683
lozanoana, Tangara nigroviridis 666
lubomirskii, Pipreola 533
luciani, Eriocnemis 265
lucianii, Pyrrhura picta 176
lucidus, Cyanerpes 672
luctisomus, Megascops choliba 201
luctuosa, Sporophila 697
luctuosus, Tachyphonus 637
ludovicae, Doryfera 231
ludoviciana, Piranga 681
ludovicianus, Pheucticus 717
lugens, Haplophaedia 267
lugubris, Brachygalba 290
lugubris, Myiotheretes fumigatus 507
lugubris, Myrmoborus 409
lugubris, Quiscalus 761
luminosa, Lepidopyga goudoti 241
luminosus, Quiscalus lugubris 761
lunatipectus, Microcerculus ustulatus 602
lunigera, Tangara parzudakii 661
lunulatus, Anisognathus igniventris 647
lunulatus, Gymnopithys 419
Lurocalis 212
lutea, Piranga 679
luteifrons, Hylophilus ochraceiceps 574
luteiventris, Myiodynastes 526
luteiventris, Myiozetetes 528
luteola, Coereba flaveola 683
luteola, Sicalis 691
luteoviridis, Basileuterus 741
lutescens, Anthus 624
lutescens, Chlorothraupis carmioli 634
lutetiae, Coeligena 261
lutleyi, Tangara cyanotis 665
lyra, Uropsalis 218
Lysurus 709
macabrum, Megascops albogularis 204
macao, Ara 171
macarenae, Chlorospingus ophthalmicus 676
macarenae, Xiphocolaptes promeropirhynchus 368
Macaw, Blue-and-yellow 170
Chestnut-fronted 171
Great Green 171
Military 170
Red-and-green 171
Red-bellied 172
Red-shouldered 172
Scarlet 171
macconnelli, Ciccaba virgata 205
macconnelli, Mionectes 448
macconnelli, Piranga flava 679
macconnelli, Sclerurus mexicanus 360
macconnelli, Synallaxis 335
macconnelli, Zonotrichia capensis 684
maccormicki, Stercorarius 141
Machaeropterus 547
Machetornis 512
macilvainii, Myiopagis gaimardii 465
maclovianus, Muscisaxicola 509
Macroagelaius 760
macrocerca, Hylonympha 255
macrodactylus, Bucco 294
Macronectes 57
macrorhamphus, Progne chalybea 582
macrorhyncha, Dendrocincla tyrannina 364
macrorhyncha, Myrmeciza immaculata 417
macrorhynchos, Notharchus 293
macroura, Eupetomena 233
macroura, Trogon melanurus 280
macroura, Zenaida 160
macrurus, Thryothorus mystacalis 593
macularius, Actitis 134
macularius, Hylopezus 434
maculata, Adelomyia melanogenys 252

maculata, Butorides virescens 73
maculata, Synallaxis stictothorax 339
maculatum, Todirostrum 455
maculatus, Catharus dryas 611
maculatus, Myiodynastes 525
maculatus, Pardirallus 117
maculatus, Pheucticus melanocephalus 718
maculicauda, Amazilia fimbriata 248
maculicaudus, Caprimulgus 216
maculicoronatus, Capito 301
maculifer, Myrmeciza exsul 415
maculifrons, Hemispingus superciliaris 628
maculipennis, Larus 145
maculipennis, Pygiptila stellaris 388
maculirostris, Muscisaxicola 508
maculirostris, Turdus 620
maculosus, Caprimulgus 217
maculosus, Nyctibius 211
magdalenae, Malacoptila panamensis 297
magdalenae, Microbates cinereiventris 605
magdalenae, Pachyramphus cinnamomeus 561
magdalenae, Thripadectes virgaticeps 356
magellanica, Carduelis 765
magellanicus, Spheniscus 55
magna, Sturnella 759
magnificen, Fregata 69
magnirostris, Buteo 97
magnirostris, Capsiempis flaveola 463
magnirostris, Ramphocelus carbo 640
magnolia, Dendroica 726
magnus, Gampsonyx swainsonii 84
magnus, Piculus flavigula 323
maguari, Ciconia 80
maguirei, Myioborus castaneocapillus 738
major, Crotophaga 197
major, Diglossa 655
major, Eurypyga helias 120
major, Podiceps 54
major, Schiffornis 556
major, Taraba 380
major, Tinamus 27
major, Veniliornis callonotus 319
majusculus, Atlapetes semirufus 714
malacca, Lonchura 774
malaris, Phaethornis 227
malherbii, Campephilus melanoleucos 328
Mallard 39
Manacus 549
manacus, Manacus 550
Manakin, Black 552
Blue-backed 550
Blue-crowned 548
Blue-rumped 549
Club-winged 547
Crimson-hooded 553
Fiery-capped 548
Golden-collared 549
Golden-headed 554
Golden-winged 546
Green 551
Jet 551
Lance-tailed 550
Olive 551
Orange-bellied 549
Orange-collared 549
Orange-crowned 552
Red-capped 553
Scarlet-horned 554
Striped 547
White-bearded 550
White-bibbed 547
White-crowned 552
White-fronted 548
White-ruffed 547
White-throated 546
Wire-tailed 553
Yellow-crowned 552
Yellow-headed 551
manapiare, Crypturellus undulatus 30
manastarae, Henicorhina leucophrys 601
mandeli, Diglossa sittoides 652
Mango, Black-throated 235
Green-breasted 234
Green-throated 234
manilata, Ara 172
manillensis, Psittacula krameri 172
maoriana, Pelagodroma marina 63
marabinus, Certhiaxis cinnamomeus 343
marahuacae, Troglodytes rufulus 600
marail, Penelope 45
maranonica, Melanopareia 445
maranonica, Synallaxis 336
maranonicus, Turdus 617
margarethae, Aglaiocercus kingi 276
margaritaceiventer, Hemitriccus 452
margaritae, Crypturellus erythropus 31
margaritae, Glaucidium brasilianum 208
margaritae, Megascops choliba 201
margaritae, Rallus longirostris 113
margaritae, Thraupis cyanocephala 643
margaritae, Xiphorhynchus susurrans 374
margaritatus, Megastictus 388
margaritensis, Aratinga pertinax 175
Margarops 623
Margarornis 349
marginatus, Chlorospingus flavigularis 678
marginatus, Microcerculus 602
marginatus, Pachyramphus 563
marginella, Zenaida macroura 160
marina, Pelagodroma 63
marinus, Larus 144
markhami, Oceanodroma 64
marmoratus, Odontophorus gujanensis 51
martii, Baryphthengus 288
Martin, Brown-chested 580
Caribbean 581
Cuban 582
Grey-breasted 582
Purple 581
Sand 578
Sinaloa 581
Southern 582
martinica, Elaenia 467
martinica, Porphyrula 118
Masius 546
massena, Trogon 283
masteri, Vireo 570
matthewsii, Boissonneaua 262
mauri, Calidris 136
mavors, Heliangelus 262
maximiliani, Oryzoborus 702
maximus, Manacus manacus 550
maximus, Saltator 719
maximus, Thalasseus 152
maynana, Cotinga 537
mayri, Roraimia adusta 347
mcleannani, Phaenostictus 423
Meadowlark, Eastern 759
Peruvian 759
Mecocerculus 472
media, Diglossa caerulescens 656
media, Synallaxis azarae 333
media, Tangara mexicana 658
media, Thlypopsis ornata 631
mediana, Thraupis episcopus 642
medianum, Glaucidium brasilianum 208
medius, Odontophorus gujanensis 51
megacephalum, Ramphotrigon 484
Megaceryle 286
megalopterus, Larus atricilla 146
megalopterus, Phalcoboenus 104
Megarhynchus 523
Megascops 200
Megastictus 388
melaena, Myrmotherula axillaris 398
melambrotus, Cathartes 81
melanantherus, Ocreatus underwoodii 278
melancholicus, Tyrannus 520
Melanerpes 317
melania, Oceanodroma 64
melanocephala, Arenaria 135
melanocephalus, Atlapetes 711
melanocephalus, Myioborus 739
melanocephalus, Pheucticus 717
melanocephalus, Pionites 186
melanoceps, Myrmeciza 416
melanochlamys, Bangsia 644
melanogaster, Petrochelidon pyrrhonota 586
melanogaster, Piaya 196
melanogenia, Galbula ruficauda 290
melanogenys, Adelomyia 252
melanogenys, Anisognathus 646
melanolaema, Pipreola riefferii 532
melanoleuca, Atticora 584
melanoleuca, Lamprospiza 626
melanoleuca, Tringa 132
melanoleucos, Campephilus 328
melanoleucus, Geranoaetus 96
melanoleucus, Spizastur 101
melanomystax, Poecilotriccus ruficeps 450
melanonota, Pipraeidea 649

melanonotus, Odontophorus 52
melanonotus, Sakesphorus 382
Melanopareia 445
melanopezus, Automolus 358
melanophaius, Laterallus 112
melanophrys, Thalassarche 56
melanopis, Schistochlamys 625
melanopis, Theristicus 79
melanopleura, Turdus flavipes 613
melanopogon, Hypocnemoides 410
melanops, Anisognathus lacrymosus 647
melanops, Gallinula 118
melanops, Leucopternis 91
melanoptera, Metriopelia 164
melanoptera, Thraupis palmarum 643
melanopterus, Mimus gilvus 622
melanopygia, Jacana jacana 141
melanorhynchus, Chlorostilbon 239
melanorhynchus, Thripadectes 356
melanornis, Coereba flaveola 683
melanosternon, Popelairia langsdorffi 238
melanosticta, Rhegmatorhina 420
melanota, Pulsatrix 206
melanothorax, Sakesphorus 382
melanotis, Hemispingus 629
melanotos, Calidris 137
melanotos, Sarkidiornis 37
melanterus, Psarocolius decumanus 747
melanura, Euphonia laniirostris 769
melanura, Pyrrhura 178
melanurus, Himantopus mexicanus 126
melanurus, Ramphocaenus 605
melanurus, Taraba major 380
melanurus, Trogon 280
melba, Tachymarptis 224
melleus, Hylophilus flavipes 574
mellisugus, Chlorostilbon 239
mellivora, Florisuga 233
meloda, Zenaida 160
melodus, Charadrius 124
meloryphus, Euscarthmus 477
Melospiza 684
mendiculus, Spheniscus 55
menetriesii, Myrmotherula 399
mengeli, Caprimulgus sericocaudatus 216
menstruus, Pionus 188
mentalis, Celeus loricatus 325
mentalis, Dysithamnus 390
mentalis, Muscisaxicola maclovianus 509
mentalis, Pipra 553
mentalis, Syndactyla subalaris 352
mercedesfosterae, Mionectes macconnelli 448
mercenaria, Amazona 192
Merganetta 41
meridae, Anthus bogotensis 624
meridae, Atlapetes albofrenatu 712
meridae, Cistothorus 592
meridae, Mionectes olivaceus 447
meridae, Piculus rivolii 322
meridae, Pseudocolaptes boissonneautii 350
meridana, Cyanolyca armillata 575
meridana, Henicorhina leucophrys 601
meridana, Ochthoeca diadema 504
meridana, Synallaxis unirufa 337
meridanus, Basileuterus tristriatus 745
meridanus, Scytalopus 443
meridensis, Megascops albogularis 204
meridensis, Notiochelidon murina 583
meridensis, Pheucticus aureoventris 717
meridensis, Piculus rubiginosus 322
meridensis, Thlypopsis fulviceps 630
meridionalis, Buteogallus 95
meridionalis, Cathartes aura 81
meridionalis, Chaetura 222
meridionalis, Dendrocincla homochroa 365
meridionalis, Pachyramphus versicolor 561
meridionalis, Sturnella magna 759
Merlin 107
merula, Dendrocincla 364
meruloides, Dendrocincla fuliginosa 364
mesaeus, Penelope argyrotis 44
Mesembrinibis 78
mesochrysa, Euphonia 771
mesochrysus, Basileuterus rufifrons 744
mesoleuca, Basileuterus rivularis 746
mesomelas, Icterus 755
mesonauta, Phaethon aethereus 65
mesopotamia, Habia rubica 675
mesurus, Trogon 280
metae, Forpus conspicillatus 181
metae, Icterus icterus 753
metae, Myrmeciza atrothorax 418
Metallura 268
Metaltail, Neblina 269
  Perijá 270
  Tyrian 269
  Violet-throated 268
  Viridian 269
Metopothrix 346
mexicana, Tangara 657
mexicanum, Tigrisoma 70
mexicanus, Gymnomystax 757
mexicanus, Himantopus 126
mexicanus, Megarhynchus pitangua 523
mexicanus, Onychorhynchus 492
mexicanus, Quiscalus 761
mexicanus, Sclerurus 360
meyeni, Tachycineta 580
micans, Chalybura buffonii 252
michleri, Pittasoma 426
micraster, Heliangelus 264
Micrastur 105
Microbates 604
Microcerculus 602
micromeris, Chordeiles acutipennis 213
Micromonacha 298
micropterus, Scytalopus 440
Micropygia 111
Microrhopias 403
microrhynchum, Ramphomicron 268
microrhynchus, Cacicus 751
microrhynchus, Cyanerpes caeruleus 672
microsoma, Oceanodroma 63
microstephanus, Momotus momota 288
microstictus, Microrhopias quixensis 403
micrura, Myrmia 275
mikettae, Vireolanius leucotis 568
militaris, Ara 170
militaris, Haematoderus 543
militaris, Sturnella 758
milleri, Grallaria 433
milleri, Manacus vitellinus 549
milleri, Polytmus 244
milleri, Xenops 362
millerii, Amazilia versicolor 247
Milvago 104
MIMIDAE 621
Mimus 622
mindoensis, Grallaricula flavirostris 436
mindoensis, Pionus sordidus 189
mindoensis, Snowornis cryptolophus 541
Miner, Slender-billed 329
miniatus, Myioborus 737
minima, Coereba flaveola 683
minima, Dixiphia pipra 552
minima, Neochelidon tibialis 584
minimus, Caprimulgus rufus 216
minimus, Catharus 612
minimus, Electron platyrhynchum 287
minimus, Molothrus bonariensis 762
minimus, Zimmerius chrysops 461
minlosi, Thryothorus rufalbus 597
minlosi, Xenerpestes 347
minor, Campylorhynchus griseus 588
minor, Catamenia inornata 705
minor, Chordeiles 213
minor, Cnipodectes subbrunneus 484
minor, Cyanocompsa brissonii 722
minor, Deconychura longicauda 365
minor, Fregata 69
minor, Furnarius 330
minor, Hemitriccus 451
minor, Hylophilus decurtatus 575
minor, Mecocerculus 474
minor, Myiodynastes chrysocephalus 525
minor, Odontorchilus branickii 590
minor, Pachyramphus 565
minor, Percnostola rufifrons 412
minor, Pipra mentalis 554
minor, Podager nacunda 214
minor, Xenopsaris albinucha 559
minus, Conirostrum bicolor 651
minuscula, Chlorophonia cyanea 773
minuscula, Lepidothrix coronata 548
minuta, Columbina 161
minuta, Euphonia 771
minuta, Piaya 196
minuta, Sporophila 699
minutilla, Calidris 137
minutissimus, Picumnus 315
minutus, Anous 148
minutus, Larus 147
minutus, Xenops 363
Mionectes 446

mirabilis, Eriocnemis 266
mirabilis, Loddigesia 278
mirandae, Vireo leucophrys 571
mirandollei, Micrastur 106
mirus, Rhynchocyclus olivaceus 486
miserabilis, Myiornis ecaudatus 481
mississippiensis, Ictinia 87
mitchellii, Calliphlox 273
Mitrephanes 499
Mitrospingus 633
Mitu 47
Mniotilta 731
Mockingbird, Chalk-browed 622
Long-tailed 622
Tropical 622
mocoa, Aglaiocercus kingi 277
mocquerysi, Colinus cristatus 50
modesta, Myrmothera campanisona 435
modestus, Forpus 181
modestus, Larus 143
modestus, Myiobius atricaudus 496
modestus, Sublegatus 464
modestus, Veniliornis passerinus 320
moesta, Synallaxis 335
mollissima, Chamaeza 426
molochinus, Ramphocelus dimidiatus 639
Molothrus 761
momota, Momotus 288
MOMOTIDAE 287
momotula, Hylomanes 287
Momotus 288
monachus, Tyrannus savana 521
Monasa 299
mondetoura, Claravis 164
Monjita, Grey 507
Monklet, Lanceolated 298
montagnii, Penelope 45
montana, Anabacerthia striaticollis 353
montana, Buthraupis 645
montana, Coereba flaveola 683
montana, Geotrygon 169
montanus, Agriornis 508
montensis, Mecocerculus leucophrys 472
monticola, Amazilia tobaci 250
monticola, Troglodytes 599
monticola, Veniliornis kirkii 321
montivagus, Aeronautes 223
moorei, Phaethornis malaris 228
Moorhen, Common 118
morcomi, Dendroica petechia 725
morinella, Arenaria interpres 135
Morphnus 100
morphoeus, Monasa 299
moschata, Cairina 37
mosquera, Eriocnemis 266
mosquitus, Chrysolampis 235
Motacilla 624
motacilla, Basileuterus fulvicauda 745
motacilla, Seiurus 733
MOTACILLIDAE 624
Motmot, Blue-crowned 288
Broad-billed 287
Highland 289
Rufous 288
Tody 287
motmot, Ortalis 44
Mourner, Cinereous 558
Greyish 515
Pale-bellied 515
Rufous 515
Speckled 557
mucuchiesi, Asthenes wyatti 344
mucuchiesi, Catamenia inornata 705
mulsant, Chaetocercus 274
multistriatus, Thamnophilus 383
multistrigatus, Dendrocolaptes picumnus 370
multostriata, Asthenes flammulata 344
multostriata, Myrmotherula 394
munda, Eutoxeres aquila 224
Munia, Chestnut 775
Tricoloured 774
munoztebari, Synallaxis unirufa 337
murallae, Sporophila 695
murina, Notiochelidon 583
murina, Phaeomyias 462
murinus, Thamnophilus 386
murinus, Turdus ignobilis 618
murphyi, Pelecanus occidentalis 65
MUSCICAPIDAE 608
muscicapinus, Hylophilus 572
Muscigralla 510
Muscisaxicola 508
musculus, Troglodytes 598
mustelina, Hylocichla 613
mustelinus, Certhiaxis 343
mustelinus, Crypturellus soui 29
mutabilis, Vireolanius eximius 568
Myadestes 609
Mycteria 80
mycteria, Jabiru 80
Myiarchus 516
Myiobius 495
Myioborus 737
Myiodynastes 525
Myiopagis 465
Myiornis 481
Myiotheretes 507
Myiotriccus 492
Myiozetetes 526
Myornis 439
myotherinus, Myrmoborus 409
Myrmeciza 413
Myrmia 275
Myrmoborus 409
Myrmochanes 411
Myrmornis 419
Myrmothera 435
Myrmotherula 393
Myrtis 273
mystacalis, Cyanocorax 577
mystacalis, Malacoptila 297
mystacalis, Thryothorus 593
mystaceus, Platyrinchus 489
nacunda, Podager 214
nacurutu, Bubo virginianus 204
naevia, Sclateria 411
naevia, Tapera 196
naevioides, Hylophylax 420
naevius, Hylophylax 421
nana, Columbina passerina 162
nana, Grallaricula 436
nana, Parula pitiayumi 725
Nannopsittaca 183
nanus, Pachyramphus marginatus 563
nanus, Xiphorhynchus susurrans 374
napaea, Dacnis cayana 671
napaeum, Camptostoma obsoletum 462
napensis, Campylorhamphus trochilirostris 378
napensis, Chiroxiphia pareola 550
napensis, Dysithamnus mentalis 390
napensis, Megascops 201
napensis, Psophia crepitans 110
napensis, Stigmatura 475
napensis, Xiphorhynchus chunchotambo 373
napoensis, Synallaxis cherriei 337
Nasica 367
naso, Micrastur semitorquatus 106
nattereri, Amazona ochrocephala 191
nattereri, Attila bolivianus 514
nattereri, Lurocalis semitorquatus 212
nattereri, Selenidera 307
nattererii, Cotinga 537
navai, Odontophorus atrifrons 51
neblinae, Xiphocolaptes promeropirhynchus 368
nebouxii, Sula 66
nebularia, Tringa 132
neglecta, Dendrocincla fuliginosa 364
neglectus, Falco tinnunculus 107
neglectus, Platyrinchus mystaceus 489
neglectus, Psarocolius angustifrons 748
neglectus, Tolmomyias assimilis 487
neglectus, Xenops minutus 363
negreti, Henicorhina 601
nelsoni, Onychoprion anaethetus 148
nematura, Lochmias 361
Nemosia 633
nengeta, Fluvicola 511
Neochelidon 584
Neochen 36
Neocrex 116
Neoctantes 388
Neomorphus 198
Neopelma 545
Neopipo 496
neotropicalis, Chordeiles minor 213
neoxena, Aratinga acuticaudata 173
nesiotis, Synallaxis albescens 334
nesophilus, Thraupis episcopus 642
Netta 41
nicefori, Aratinga leucophthalma 174
nicefori, Thryothorus 597
niceforoi, Anas georgica 39

niceforoi, Muscisaxicola maculirostris 509
niger, Capito 302
niger, Chlidonias 151
niger, Cypseloides 219
niger, Neoctantes 388
niger, Threnetes 225
Nighthawk, Antillean 214
Band-tailed 214
Common 213
Least 213
Lesser 212
Nacunda 214
Rufous-bellied 212
Sand-coloured 213
Short-tailed 212
Nightingale-Thrush, Orange-billed 610
Slaty-backed 611
Spotted 611
Nightingale-Wren, Southern 602
Nightjar, Band-winged 216
Blackish 217
Cayenne 217
Ladder-tailed 218
Little 217
Lyre-tailed 218
Roraiman 217
Rufous 215
Scissor-tailed 218
Scrub 217
Silky-tailed 216
Spot-tailed 216
Swallow-tailed 218
White-tailed 216
niglarus, Myrmeciza exsul 415
nigrescens, Bubo virginianus 204
nigrescens, Caprimulgus 217
nigrescens, Cercomacra 407
nigrescens, Contopus 501
nigrescens, Thamnophilus doliatus 383
nigricans, Cercomacra 408
nigricans, Pardirallus 117
nigricans, Sayornis 503
nigricans, Scytalopus atratus 441
nigricapillus, Formicarius 424
nigricapillus, Thryothorus 596
nigricauda, Automolus rubiginosus 359
nigricauda, Carduelis spinescens 764
nigricauda, Myrmeciza 414
nigriceps, Arremon abeillei 707
nigriceps, Chlorospingus ophthalmicus 676
nigriceps, Crypturellus soui 29
nigriceps, Mecocerculus leucophrys 472
nigriceps, Myiarchus tuberculifer 517
nigriceps, Piculus rubiginosus 322
nigriceps, Saltator 721
nigriceps, Thamnophilus 384
nigriceps, Tityra semifasciata 556
nigriceps, Todirostrum 456
nigriceps, Turdus 616
nigriceps, Veniliornis 321
nigricinctus, Phaethornis ruber 229
nigricollis, Anthracothorax 235
nigricollis, Busarellus 95
nigricollis, Phoenicircus 536
nigricollis, Sporophila 697
nigricristatus, Thamnophilus doliatus 383
nigrifrons, Buarremon torquatus 709
nigrifrons, Formicarius colma 424
nigrifrons, Hemispingus superciliaris 628
nigrifrons, Monasa 299
nigrifrons, Phylloscartes 480
nigrigula, Hemithraupis guira 632
nigripes, Phoebastria 56
nigrirostris, Andigena 310
nigrirostris, Cyclarhis 567
nigrirostris, Patagioenas 158
nigrita, Ochthoeca cinnamomeiventris 505
nigriventris, Pachyramphus polychopterus 562
nigrivestis, Eriocnemis 265
nigrocapillus, Phyllomyias 458
nigrocincta, Tangara 665
nigrocinereus, Thamnophilus 384
nigrocristatus, Anairetes 476
nigrocristatus, Basileuterus 741
nigrodorsalis, Donacobius atricapilla 607
nigrodorsalis, Tachornis furcata 223
nigrofasciata, Thalurania furcata 242
nigrofrontalis, Thamnophilus insignis 387
nigrofumosa, Synallaxis brachyura 334
nigrogenis, Paroaria 715
nigrogularis, Icterus 754
nigrogularis, Ramphocelus 639
nigrolineata, Ciccaba 204
nigrolineata, Grallaria ruficapilla 430
nigromaculata, Phlegopsis 422
nigropunctatus, Picumnus 314
nigroviridis, Tangara 666
nilotica, Gelochelidon 150
nitens, Chlorostilbon gibsoni 239
nitida, Asturina 93
nitida, Euphonia chrysopasta 771
nitidior, Basileuterus trifasciatus 744
nitidior, Capito auratus 302
nitidissima, Chlorochrysa 657
nitidus, Buteo 93
nitidus, Cyanerpes 672
nivarius, Phrygilus unicolor 688
niveiceps, Colonia colonus 512
niveigularis, Tyrannus 520
nivosus, Charadrius alexandrinus 124
noanamae, Bucco 294
nobilis, Chamaeza 425
nobilis, Diopsittaca 172
nobilis, Gallinago 128
nobilis, Myiodynastes maculatus 526
nocticolor, Diglossa humeralis 654
noctivagus, Lurocalis semitorquatus 212
Noddy, Black 148
Brown 148
Nomonyx 35
Nonnula 298
nortoni, Siptornis striaticollis 346
notabilis, Anisognathus 648
notata, Chlorestes 238
notatus, Coturnicops 111
notatus, Mecocerculus leucophrys 472
notatus, Xiphorhynchus obsoletus 372
Nothocercus 28
Nothocrax 47
Nothoprocta 33
Notiochelidon 583
noveboracensis, Seiurus 733
nubicola, Glaucidium 208
nuchalis, Campylorhynchus 589
nuchalis, Grallaria 432
nuchalis, Pteroglossus torquatus 308
nudiceps, Gymnocichla 411
nudigenis, Turdus 620
Numenius 131
nuna, Lesbia 277
Nunbird, Black 299
Black-fronted 299
White-faced 299
White-fronted 299
Yellow-billed 300
Nunlet, Brown 298
Grey-cheeked 298
Rusty-breasted 298
nupera, Tangara gyrola 662
Nyctanassa 72
NYCTIBIIDAE 210
Nyctibius 210
Nycticorax 72
nycticorax, Nycticorax 72
Nyctidromus 215
Nyctiprogne 214
Nystalus 295
oberholseri, Pseudocolaptes boissonneautii 350
oberi, Asio clamator 209
oberi, Dysithamnus mentalis 390
obfuscata, Ochthoeca rufipectoralis 505
obidensis, Thamnomanes ardesiacus 392
obscura, Chamaeza campanisona 425
obscura, Coeligena coeligena 259
obscura, Coereba flaveola 683
obscura, Dendroica petechia 726
obscura, Diglossa cyanea 656
obscura, Elaenia 471
obscura, Inezia subflava 475
obscura, Myrmotherula ignota 393
obscura, Pyrrhura egregia 178
obscura, Schistocichla saturata 413
obscura, Synallaxis moesta 335
obscuratus, Veniliornis fumigatus 321
obscuricauda, Amazilia fimbriata 247
obscuriceps, Brachygalba lugubris 290
obscuriceps, Thlypopsis fulviceps 630
obscuriceps, Tolmomyias assimilis 487
obscurior, Myiozetetes granadensis 527
obscurior, Sclerurus mexicanus 360
obscurior, Sublegatus 464
obscurior, Synallaxis macconnelli 335
obscuripectus, Mitrospingus oleagineus 634

obscuritergum, Leptopogon amaurocephalus 449
obscurodorsalis, Roraimia adusta 347
obscurostriatus, Machaeropterus regulus 547
obscurus, Automolus rubiginosus 359
obscurus, Hylomanes momotula 287
obscurus, Megascops albogularis 204
obscurus, Microcerculus ustulatus 602
obscurus, Taraba major 380
obscurus, Thryothorus coraya 594
obscurus, Tiaris 681
obsoleta, Grallaria nuchalis 432
obsoletum, Camptostoma 462
obsoletus, Crypturellus 30
obsoletus, Picumnus squamulatus 316
obsoletus, Turdus 619
obsoletus, Xenops minutus 363
obsoletus, Xiphorhynchus 372
occidentalis, Andigena nigrirostris 310
occidentalis, Ardea herodias 74
occidentalis, Arremon aurantiirostris 706
occidentalis, Celeus torquatus 326
occidentalis, Chaetura spinicauda 221
occidentalis, Charadrius alexandrinus 124
occidentalis, Conopophaga aurita 438
occidentalis, Dysithamnus 391
occidentalis, Eubucco bourcierii 303
occidentalis, Hypocnemoides melanopogon 410
occidentalis, Leucopternis 91
occidentalis, Microcerculus marginatus 602
occidentalis, Molothrus bonariensis 762
occidentalis, Myiozetetes granadensis 527
occidentalis, Onychorhynchus 491
occidentalis, Oryzoborus crassirostris 701
occidentalis, Patagioenas cayennensis 157
occidentalis, Pelecanus 65
occidentalis, Pipreola riefferii 532
occidentalis, Pyroderus scutatus 543
occidentalis, Tangara arthus 660
occidentalis, Tersina viridis 674
occidentalis, Chaetura cinereiventris 221
occipitalis, Podiceps 55
occipitalis, Pygiptila stellaris 388
occipitalis, Synallaxis albescens 334
occultus, Basileuterus culicivorus 743
oceanicus, Oceanites 62
Oceanites 62
Oceanodroma 63
ocellatus, Nyctiphrynus 215
ocellatus, Xiphorhynchus 372
ochracea, Synallaxis azarae 333
ochraceiceps, Hylophilus 574
ochraceicrista, Basileuterus fraseri 740
ochraceiventris, Grallaricula flavirostris 436
ochraceiventris, Leptotila 167
ochraceiventris, Phaethornis malaris 228
ochraceus, Falco sparverius 107
ochraceus, Hemispingus 629
ochrocephala, Amazona 191
ochrogyne, Oryzoborus funereus 703
ochrolaemus, Automolus 357
ochroptera, Psophia leucoptera 110
Ochthoeca 504
Ochthornis 506
Ocreatus 277
ocularis, Chrysothlypis chrysomelas 632
ocularis, Phrygilus plebejus 688
Ocyalus 749
ocypetes, Chaetura 221
odomae, Metallura 269
ODONTOPHORIDAE 50
Odontophorus 51
Odontorchilus 590
oecotonophilus, Thamnophilus multistriatus 383
Oenanthe 608
oenanthe, Oenanthe 608
oenone, Chrysuronia 244
oenops, Laterallus melanophaius 112
oenops, Patagioenas 158
ogilviegranti, Patagioenas subvinacea 158
Ognorhynchus 176
Oilbird 210
olallai, Myiopagis 466
oleagineus, Mionectes 447
oleagineus, Mitrospingus 634
oleagineus, Psarocolius angustifrons 748
olivacea, Carduelis 766
olivacea, Chlorothraupis 634
olivacea, Piranga 680
olivacea, Porzana albicollis 116
olivacea, Schiffornis turdina 557
olivacea, Syndactyla subalaris 352
olivaceiceps, Anisognathus lacrymosus 647
olivaceiceps, Penelope argyrotis 44
olivaceum, Camptostoma obsoletum 462
olivaceum, Glaucidium brasilianum 208
olivaceum, Oncostoma 483
olivaceus, Hylophilus 574
olivaceus, Mionectes 447
olivaceus, Mitrephanes 499
olivaceus, Myiotheretes fumigatus 507
olivaceus, Picumnus 315
olivaceus, Rhynchocyclus 485
olivaceus, Tiaris 681
olivaceus, Vireo 569
olivaceus, Xenops minutus 363
olivaresi, Chlorostilbon 239
olivaresi, Momotus momota 288
olivascens, Basileuterus culicivorus 743
olivascens, Cinnycerthia 590
olivascens, Grallaricula nana 436
olivascens, Neocrex erythrops 116
olivascens, Saltator coerulescens 720
olivater, Turdus 616
olivicyanea, Thraupis cyanocephala 643
olivina, Elaenia pallatangae 472
omissa, Euphonia fulvicrissa 770
omissa, Tiaris bicolor 682
Oncostoma 483
Onychoprion 148
Onychorhynchus 491
opacus, Scytalopus canus 445
opertaneus, Catharus fuscater 611
ophthalmica, Sporophila corvina 695
ophthalmicus, Chlorospingus 676
ophthalmicus, Phylloscartes 478
OPISTHOCOMIDAE 154
Opisthocomus 154
Oporornis 734
orbitalis, Phylloscartes 479
orcesi, Pyrrhura 178
ordii, Notharchus 293
orenocensis, Certhiaxis cinnamomeus 343
orenocensis, Formicivora grisea 403
orenocensis, Knipolegus 511
orenocensis, Pyroderus scutatus 543
orenocensis, Saltator 720
orenocensis, Thalurania furcata 242
orenocensis, Veniliornis affinis 320
orenocensis, Xiphocolaptes promeropirhynchus 368
oreobates, Cinclodes fuscus 329
Oreomanes 652
oreophila, Catamenia homochroa 705
Oreopholus 125
oreopola, Metallura tyrianthina 270
Oreothraupis 710
Oreotrochilus 256
orientalis, Basileuterus coronatus 743
orientalis, Eubucco bourcierii 303
orienticola, Amazilia chionopectus 247
orienticola, Penelope jacquacu 46
orina, Coeligena 260
orinocensis, Leptopogon amaurocephalus 449
orinocensis, Picumnus spilogaster 317
orinocensis, Sublegatus arenarum 463
orinocensis, Tachyphonus cristatus 636
orinocensis, Thlypopsis sordida 631
orinocensis, Turdus fumigatus 619
orinomus, Cnemarchus erythropygius 506
Oriole, Baltimore 756
  Epaulet 754
  Moriche 753
  Orange-crowned 755
  Orchard 756
  White-edged 756
  Yellow 754
  Yellow-backed 754
  Yellow-tailed 755
ornata, Hemithraupis flavicollis 632
ornata, Myrmotherula 397
ornata, Thlypopsis 631
ornatus, Cephalopterus 544
ornatus, Lophornis 236
ornatus, Myioborus 739
ornatus, Myiotriccus 492
ornatus, Spizaetus 101
ornatus, Xiphorhynchus elegans 373
Ornithion 461

Oropendola, Band-tailed 749
Baudó 749
Black 749
Casqued 747
Chestnut-headed 748
Crested 747
Green 747
Olive 748
Russet-backed 748
orquillensis, Quiscalus lugubris 761
Ortalis 42
orthonyx, Acropternis 445
ortoni, Penelope 45
oryzivora, Lonchura 775
oryzivora, Scaphidura 762
oryzivorus, Dolichonyx 763
Oryzoborus 701
oseryi, Psarocolius 747
osgoodi, Aulacorhynchus derbianus 305
osgoodi, Momotus momota 288
osgoodi, Tinamus 27
Osprey 83
Ovenbird 733
Owl, Amazonian Pygmy 207
Andean Pygmy 207
Band-bellied 206
Bare-shanked Screech 200
Barn 200
Black-and-white 204
Black-banded 204
Buff-fronted 209
Burrowing 208
Central American Pygmy 206
Chocó Screech 202
Cinnamon Screech 202
Cloud Forest Pygmy 208
Colombian Screech 203
Crested 205
Ferruginous Pygmy 207
Great Horned 204
Mottled 205
Northern Tawny-bellied Screech 202
Peruvian Pygmy 207
Peruvian Screech 203
Ridgway's Pygmy 208
Rio Napo Screech 201
Roraima Screech 201
Rufescent Screech 202
Rufous-banded 205
Short-eared 210
Southern Tawny-bellied Screech 203
Spectacled 206
Striped 209
Stygian 209
Subtropical Pygmy 206
Tropical Screech 201
Tumbes Screech 203
Vermiculated Screech 201
White-throated Screech 203
oxycerca, Cercibis 78
Oxypogon 268
OXYRUNCIDAE 529
Oxyruncus 530
Oxyura 36
Oystercatcher, American 125
pacaraimae, Myrmothera simplex 435
Pachyramphus 560
pacifica, Calidris alpina 138
pacifica, Malacoptila mystacalis 297
pacifica, Myrmotherula 394
pacifica, Parula pitiayumi 725
pacifica, Pyrrhura melanura 178
pacificus, Cacicus microrhynchus 751
pacificus, Cyanerpes cyaneus 673
pacificus, Megascops 203
pacificus, Mionectes oleagineus 447
pacificus, Phaenostictus mcleannani 423
pacificus, Puffinus 60
pacificus, Rhynchocyclus 485
palaearctica, Xema sabini 147
pallatangae, Elaenia 471
pallens, Galbula ruficauda 290
pallens, Hemitriccus minor 451
pallens, Myiopagis viridicata 467
pallens, Sublegatus arenarum 463
pallescens, Campylorhynchus fasciatus 590
pallescens, Monasa morphoeus 299
pallescens, Neopelma 545
pallescens, Nonnula frontalis 298
pallescens, Patagioenas plumbea 159
pallescens, Stercorarius longicaudus 143
palliata, Myrmeciza laemosticta 415
palliatus, Haematopus 125
palliatus, Xiphorhynchus obsoletus 372
pallida, Chelidoptera tenebrosa 300
pallida, Deconychura longicauda 365
pallida, Leptotila 165
pallida, Myrmotherula menetriesii 399
pallida, Nyctiprogne leucopyga 214
pallida, Petrochelidon fulva 587
pallida, Pionites melanocephalus 186
pallida, Syndactyla guttulata 352
pallidicaudus, Asio flammeus 210
pallidiceps, Atlapetes 714
pallidiceps, Machaeropterus pyrocephalus 548
pallidiceps, Phyllomyias griseiceps 458
pallidicrissa, Patagioenas cayennensis 157
pallididorsalis, Anisognathus lacrymosus 647
pallidigula, Cypsnagra hirundinacea 625
pallidigula, Gymnopithys rufigula 418
pallidigularis, Automolus ochrolaemus 357
pallidinucha, Atlapetes 710
pallidior, Hylopezus perspicillatus 434
pallidipectus, Leptotila rufaxilla 166
palliditergum, Mecocerculus leucophrys 472
pallidiventris, Griseotyrannus aurantio-atrocristatus 523
pallidiventris, Mionectes oleagineus 447
pallidiventris, Myioborus miniatus 737
pallidulus, Ammodramus humeralis 686
pallidulus, Basileuterus cinereicollis 742
pallidulus, Glyphorynchus spirurus 367
pallidus, Campylorhynchus griseus 588
pallidus, Conirostrum sitticolor 651
pallidus, Cyanocorax violaceus 576
pallidus, Gymnopithys rufigula 418
pallidus, Mionectes olivaceus 447
pallidus, Myiarchus tuberculifer 517
pallidus, Oreopholus ruficollis 125
pallidus, Ramphocaenus melanurus 605
palmarum, Dendroica 729
palmarum, Thraupis 642
Palmcreeper, Point-tailed 350
palmeri, Tangara 658
palmitae, Tangara arthus 660
palpebrosus, Anisognathus lacrymosus 647
paludicola, Dendroica discolor 729
panamense, Conirostrum leucogenys 650
panamensis, Amazona ochrocephala 191
panamensis, Chordeiles minor 213
panamensis, Cnipodectes subbrunneus 484
panamensis, Cochlearius cochlearius 71
panamensis, Formicarius analis 424
panamensis, Malacoptila 297
panamensis, Myiarchus 518
panamensis, Myrmeciza longipes 414
panamensis, Nyctibius griseus 211
panamensis, Philohydor lictor 528
panamensis, Piaya minuta 196
panamensis, Schiffornis turdina 557
panamensis, Scytalopus 441
panamensis, Tachyphonus luctuosus 637
panamensis, Tyrannulus elatus 464
Pandion 83
PANDIONIDAE 83
panerythrum, Philydor rufum 355
pantchenkoi, Pyrrhura caeruleiceps 176
panychlora, Nannopsittaca 183
Panyptila 223
papa, Sarcoramphus 81
papallactae, Atlapetes pallidinucha 710
paradisaea, Sterna 152
paradisea, Tangara chilensis 658
paraguaiae, Gallinago 128
paraguanae, Dendroica petechia 726
paraguanae, Melanerpes rubricapillus 317
paraguanae, Sakesphorus canadensis 381
paraguanae, Xiphorhynchus picus 371
paraguensis, Microbates collaris 604
Parakeet, Barred 179
Blue-crowned 173
Brown-breasted 179
Brown-throated 175
Cobalt-winged 182
Dusky-headed 174
El Oro 178
Fiery-shouldered 177
Golden-plumed 175
Golden-winged 182
Grey-cheeked 182
Maroon-tailed 178

Orange-chinned 182
Painted 176
Peach-fronted 174
Red-eared 179
Red-masked 173
Rose-headed 179
Rose-ringed 172
Rufous-fronted 180
Santa Marta 177
Scarlet-fronted 173
Sinú 177
Sun 174
Todd's 176
Tui 183
Venezuelan 177
White-breasted 178
White-eyed 174
White-winged 181
paralios, Sturnella magna 759
parambae, Attila spadiceus 514
parambae, Grallaria haplonota 429
parambae, Myiopagis canicep 465
parambae, Odontophorus erythrops 51
parambanus, Turdus obsoletus 619
paramillo, Eriocnemis vestitus 265
paramo, Cinclodes fuscus 329
paraquensis, Atlapetes personatus 715
paraquensis, Automolus roraimae 358
paraquensis, Knipolegus poecilurus 510
paraquensis, Piculus rubiginosus 322
paraquensis, Turdus olivater 617
parasiticus, Stercorarius 142
parcus, Mionectes oleagineus 447
pardalotus, Xiphorhynchus 373
Pardirallus 117
pardus, Campylorhynchus nuchalis 589
pareola, Chiroxiphia 550
pariae, Basileuterus tristriatus 745
pariae, Grallaria haplonota 429
pariae, Grallaricula nana 436
pariae, Leptopogon superciliaris 449
pariae, Myioborus 738
pariae, Pipreola formosa 534
pariae, Premnoplex tatei 348
pariae, Pyrrhomyias cinnamomeus 497
pariae, Synallaxis cinnamomea 338
parina, Xenodacnis 673
parkeri, Cercomacra 406
parkeri, Glaucidium 206
parkeri, Scytalopus 444
Parkerthraustes 718
parkinsoni, Procellaria 59
Paroaria 715
Parrot, Black-headed 186
Blue-headed 188
Bronze-winged 189
Brown-hooded 187
Caica 188
Dusky 190
Indigo-winged 185
Orange-cheeked 187
Red-billed 189
Red-faced 186
Red-fan 193
Rose-faced 187
Rusty-faced 185
Saffron-headed 187
Short-tailed 186
White-capped 189
Yellow-eared 176
Parrotlet, Blue-winged 180
Dusky-billed 181
Green-rumped 180
Lilac-tailed 183
Pacific 181
Red-winged 184
Sapphire-rumped 184
Scarlet-shouldered 183
Spectacled 181
Spot-winged 184
Tepui 183
parui, Atlapetes personatus 715
parui, Mecocerculus leucophrys 472
parui, Pachyramphus castaneus 561
Parula 724
Parula, Northern 724
Tropical 724
PARULIDAE 723
parulus, Anairetes 476
parva, Tangara gyrola 662
parvicristatus, Colinus cristatus 50
parvirostris, Attila spadiceus 514
parvirostris, Chlorospingus 677
parvirostris, Elaenia 469
parvistriatus, Picumnus sclateri 314
parvula, Columbina passerina 162
parvula, Heliodoxa leadbeateri 253
parvulus, Aglaeactis cupripennis 258
parvulus, Caprimulgus 217
parvus, Conopias 524
parvus, Cyclarhis gujanensis 567
parvus, Numenius americanus 132
parvus, Zimmerius vilissimus 459
parzudakii, Tangara 660
Passer 777
PASSERIDAE 777
Passerina 722
passerina, Columbina 161
passerinus, Forpus 180
passerinus, Veniliornis 320
pastazae, Galbula 291
Patagioenas 155, 156
Patagona 257
patagonica, Notiochelidon cyanoleuca 583
paucimaculatus, Thryothorus sclateri 596
paula, Carduelis magellanica 765
paulus, Chlorospingus canigularis 678
paulus, Euscarthmus meloryphus 477
Pauraque 215
Pauxi 48
pauxi, Pauxi 48
pauxilla, Gallinula chloropus 119
pavoninus, Dromococcyx 197
pavoninus, Lophornis 237
pavoninus, Pharomachrus 284
pax, Masius chrysopterus 546
paynteri, Atlapetes leucopterus 713
pealei, Falco peregrinus 109
pectorale, Ramphotrigon megacephalum 484
pectoralis, Hylophilus 572
pectoralis, Notharchus 293
pectoralis, Polystictus 476
pectoralis, Veniliornis nigriceps 321
pectoralis, Vireo olivaceus 569
pediacus, Burhinus bistriatus 127
pelagica, Chaetura 222
Pelagodroma 63
PELECANIDAE 65
Pelecanus 65
Pelican, Brown 65
Peruvian 65
pella, Topaza 256
pelodramus, Rallus longirostris 113
pelzelni, Elaenia 470
pelzelni, Euphonia cyanocephala 770
pelzelni, Granatellus 746
pelzelni, Myiarchus swainsoni 517
pelzelni, Myrmeciza 416
pelzelni, Pseudotriccus 449
penardi, Jacamerops aureus 292
penardi, Poecilotriccus fumifrons 454
penduliger, Cephalopterus 544
Penelope 44
penelope, Anas 38
Penguin, Galápagos 55
Humboldt 55
Magellanic 55
penicillata, Eucometis 635
peninsulae, Contopus sordidulus 500
peninsularis, Patagioenas subvinacea 158
pensylvanica, Dendroica 726
pentheria, Zenaida auriculata 160
pentlandi, Nothoprocta 33
Peppershrike, Black-billed 567
Rufous-browed 567
Percnostola 412
peregrina, Eremophila alpestris 578
peregrina, Vermivora 724
peregrinus, Falco 109
perezchinchillae, Zonotrichia capensis 685
perijana, Anabacerthia striaticollis 353
perijana, Grallaria ruficapilla 430
perijana, Habia rubica 675
perijana, Piprites chloris 566
perijana, Schizoeaca 332
perijanus, Asthenes wyatti 344
perijanus, Buarremon torquatus 709
perijanus, Dromococcyx pavoninus 197
perijanus, Myiophobus flavicans 492
perijanus, Picumnus cinnamomeus 315
perijanus, Platyrinchus mystaceus 489
perijanus, Sittasomus griseicapillus 366
perijanus, Xenops rutilans 363
periophthalmicus, Hylopezus perspicillatus 434

Periporphyrus 718
Perissocephalus 544
perlatus, Margarornis squamiger 349
pernix, Myiotheretes 507
perpallida, Synallaxis albescens 334
persaturatus, Picumnus cinnamomeus 315
personatus, Atlapetes 714
personatus, Trogon 283
perspicax, Penelope 46
perspicillata, Pulsatrix 206
perspicillatus, Hylopezus 434
perstriatus, Saltator striatipectus 721
pertinax, Aratinga 175
peruana, Hemithraupis flavicollis 632
peruana, Monasa morphoeus 299
peruanum, Glaucidium 207
peruanum, Todirostrum cinereum 455
peruanus, Knipolegus poecilurus 510
peruanus, Ocreatus underwoodii 278
peruanus, Thryothorus leucotis 598
peruviana, Conopophaga 438
peruviana, Dendroica petechia 726
peruviana, Geothlypis auricularis 736
peruviana, Grallaricula 437
peruviana, Patagonia gigas 257
peruviana, Sporophila 698
peruvianus, Celeus flavus 325
peruvianus, Charadrius vociferus 124
peruvianus, Falco sparverius 107
peruvianus, Lanio fulvus 635
peruvianus, Leptopogon amaurocephalus 449
peruvianus, Masius chrysopterus 546
peruvianus, Microbates cinereiventris 605
peruvianus, Phacellodomus rufifrons 345
peruvianus, Pithys albifrons 418
peruvianus, Poecilotriccus ruficeps 450
peruvianus, Pterophanes cyanopterus 257
peruvianus, Quiscalus mexicanus 761
peruvianus, Rupicola 536
peruvianus, Saltator striatipectus 721
peruvianus, Sclerurus mexicanus 360
peruvianus, Tinamus major 27
peruvianus, Tolmomyias sulphurescens 486
peruvianus, Trogon curucui 281
peruvianus, Xenops rutilans 363
peruvianus, Xiphorhynchus picus 371
peruviensis, Volatinia jacarina 692
petechia, Dendroica 725
petersi, Zimmerius improbus 460
petersoni, Megascops 202
petoensis, Falco rufigularis 108
Petrel, Black 59
Black-capped 58
Bulwer's 59
Cape 58
Galápagos 58
Parkinson's 59
Southern Giant 57
White-chinned 59
Petrochelidon 586
Pewee, Blackish 501
Eastern Wood 501
Smoke-coloured 500
Tropical 501
Tumbes 501
Western Wood 500
White-throated 502
Phacellodomus 345
Phaenostictus 423
phaeocephalus, Chlorospingus ophthalmicus 677
phaeocephalus, Cyphorhinus 603
phaeocephalus, Myiarchus 519
phaeocercus, Mitrephanes 499
phaeochroa, Dendrocincla fuliginosa 364
phaeochroa, Lepidopyga goudoti 241
phaeolaemus, Aulacorhynchus prasinus 305
Phaeomyias 462
phaeonotus, Myiarchus swainsoni 517
phaeopleurus, Buarremon torquatus 709
phaeoplurus, Catharus aurantiirostris 610
phaeopus, Numenius 131
phaeopygia, Pterodroma 58
phaeopygoides, Turdus albicollis 621
phaeopygus, Turdus albicollis 621
Phaethon 64
PHAETHONTIDAE 64
Phaethornis 226
Phaetusa 150
phainoleucus, Sakesphorus canadensis 381
phainopeplus, Campylopterus 232
PHALACROCORACIDAE 67
Phalacrocorax 67
phalaenoides, Glaucidium brasilianum 208
phalara, Xiphorhynchus picus 371
Phalarope, Red 139
Red-necked 139
Wilson's 139
Phalaropus 139
Phalcoboenus 103
phalerata, Coeligena 260
Pharomachrus 283
phasianellus, Dromococcyx 196
phelpsi, Atlapetes latinuchus 711
phelpsi, Cypseloides 219
phelpsi, Grallaria excelsa 428
phelpsi, Oxyruncus cristatus 530
phelpsi, Rallus longirostris 113
phelpsi, Tangara xanthogastra 661
phelpsi, Xenops rutilans 363
Phelpsia 529
Pheucticus 716
philadelphia, Larus 146
philadelphia, Oporornis 735
philadelphicus, Vireo 569
Philohydor 528
Philomachus 138
Philydor 354
Phimosus 78
Phlegopsis 422
Phlogophilus 253
Phoebastria 56
Phoebe, Black 503
phoeniceus, Agelaius 758
phoeniceus, Cardinalis 718
Phoenicircus 536
phoenicius, Tachyphonus 638
phoenicomitra, Myiophobus 493
PHOENICOPTERIDAE 82
Phoenicopterus 82
phoenicotis, Chlorochrysa 656
phoenicurus, Attila 513
phoenicurus, Myiotriccus ornatus 492
phoeopygus, Chlorostilbon mellisugus 239
Phrygilus 688
phygas, Buarremon torquatus 709
Phyllomyias 457
Phylloscartes 478
Piaya 196
pica, Fluvicola 511
picatus, Notharchus tectus 294
pichinchae, Athene cunicularia 209
pichinchae, Falco femoralis 108
PICIDAE 313
picirostris, Xiphorhynchus picus 371
picta, Pyrrhura 176
pictum, Todirostrum 456
picui, Columbina 163
Piculet, Bar-breasted 313
Black-dotted 314
Chestnut 315
Ecuadorian 314
Golden-spangled 314
Greyish 317
Guianan 315
Lafresnaye's 314
Olivaceous 315
Orinoco 313
Plain-breasted 316
Rufous-breasted 316
Scaled 316
White-barred 315
White-bellied 317
Piculus 321
Picumnus 313
picumnus, Dendrocolaptes 370
picus, Xiphorhynchus 371
Piedtail, Ecuadorian 253
Piezorhina 689
pifanoi, Phylloscartes poecilotis 479
Pigeon, Band-tailed 157
Bare-eyed 156
Dusky 158
Feral Rock 155
Marañón 158
Pale-vented 157
Plumbeous 159
Ruddy 158
Scaled 156
Scaly-naped 156
Short-billed 158
White-crowned 155
Piha, Chestnut-capped 539

Dusky 539
Grey-tailed 541
Olivaceous 541
Rose-collared 540
Rufous 540
Screaming 540
pilaris, Atalotriccus 483
pileata, Nemosia 633
pileatus, Coryphospingus 687
pileatus, Leptopogon amaurocephalus 449
pileatus, Lophotriccus 482
pileatus, Pilherodius 75
pileolata, Wilsonia pusilla 737
Pilherodius 75
pinnatus, Botaurus 71
Pintail, Northern 39
White-cheeked 40
Yellow-billed 39
pinus, Dendroica 729
pinus, Vermivora 723
Pionites 186
Pionopsitta 187
Pionus 188
piperivora, Selenidera 307
Pipile 46
pipile, Pipile 46
Pipit, Páramo 624
Yellowish 624
pipixcan, Larus 147
Pipra 553
pipra, Iodopleura 558
Pipraeidea 649
Pipreola 532
PIPRIDAE 545
Piprites 566
Piprites, Wing-barred 566
Piranga 679
pitangua, Megarhynchus 523
Pitangus 529
Pithys 418
pitiayumi, Parula 724
Pittasoma 426
piurae, Hemispingus 629
piurae, Pyrocephalus rubinus 503
piurae, Sakesphorus bernardi 382
Platalea 79
platensis, Cistothorus 591
platensis, Mimus longicaudatus 622
platypterus, Buteo 98
platyrhynchos, Anas 39
platyrhynchos, Platyrinchus 490
platyrhynchum, Electron 287
Platyrinchus 489
plebejus, Phrygilus 688
Plegadis 77
PLOCEIDAE 776
Ploceus 776
Plover, American Golden 122
Black-bellied 122
Collared 125
Common Ringed 123
Grey 122
Pacific Golden 122
Piping 124
Semipalmated 123
Snowy 124
Wilson's 123
plumbea, Euphonia 767
plumbea, Ictinia 87
plumbea, Patagioenas 159
plumbea, Polioptila 605
plumbea, Sporophila 693
plumbeiceps, Leptotila 165
plumbeiceps, Myadestes ralloides 609
plumbeiceps, Nothocercus bonapartei 28
plumbeiceps, Phyllomyias 458
plumbeiceps, Polioptila plumbea 606
plumbeus, Leucopternis 92
plumbeus, Micrastur 105
plumbeus, Saltator coerulescens 720
Plumeleteer, Bronze-tailed 252
White-vented 252
pluricinctus, Pteroglossus 309
Plushcap 674
Plushcrown, Orange-fronted 346
Pluvialis 122
Pochard, Southern 41
Podager 214
Podiceps 54
podiceps, Podilymbus 54
PODICIPEDIDAE 53
Podilymbus 54
poecilinotus, Hylophylax 421
poecilocercus, Knipolegus 510
poecilocercus, Mecocerculus 473
poecilochrous, Buteo 100
poecilonota, Colonia colonus 512
poecilotis, Phylloscartes 479
Poecilotriccus 450
poecilurus, Knipolegus 510
poliocephalus, Tolmomyias 487
poliogaster, Accipiter 88
poliogastra, Ochthoeca rufipectoralis 505
polionota, Turdus flavipes 613
polionotus, Thamnophilus aethiops 385
poliopis, Malacoptila panamensis 297
Polioptila 605
POLIOPTILIDAE 604
pollens, Campephilus 327
polychopterus, Pachyramphus 561
polyosoma, Buteo 99
Polystictus 476
polystictus, Ocreatus underwoodii 278
polystictus, Xiphorhynchus guttatus 374
Polytmus 244
pomarinus, Stercorarius 142
ponsi, Chlorospingus ophthalmicus 677
ponsi, Pionus sordidus 189
poortmani, Chlorostilbon 240
Poorwill, Chocó 215
Ocellated 215
Poospiza 689
Popelairia 237
popelairii, Popelairia 237
porcullae, Phaethornis griseogularis 229
porphyrocephalus, Iridosornis 648
Porphyrolaema 541
porphyrolaema, Porphyrolaema 541
Porphyrula 118
portovelae, Myiobius atricaudus 496
Porzana 115
Potoo, Andean 211
Common 211
Great 210
Long-tailed 211
Rufous 211
White-winged 211
praecox, Thamnophilus 384
praevelox, Chaetura brachyura 221
prasinus, Aulacorhynchus 304
praticola, Sturnella magna 759
prattii, Haematopus palliatus 125
Premnoplex 348
Premnornis 348
pretiosa, Claravis 164
prevostii, Anthracothorax 234
Prickletail, Spectacled 346
primolina, Metallura williami 269
princeps, Leucopternis 91
Procellaria 59
PROCELLARIIDAE 57
procerus, Xiphocolaptes promeropirhynchus 369
Procnias 538
procurvoides, Campylorhamphus 378
Progne 580
promeropirhynchus, Xiphocolaptes 368
propinqua, Synallaxis 336
propinquus, Cyphorhinus phaeocephalus 604
propinquus, Sclerurus albigularis 360
Protonotaria 732
prunellei, Coeligena 259
psaltria, Carduelis 766
psammochrous, Stelgidopteryx serripennis 585
Psarocolius 747
Pseudelaenia 467
pseudoaustralis, Myrmotherula longicauda 395
Pseudocolaptes 349
Pseudocolopteryx 477
Pseudotriccus 449
PSITTACIDAE 170
psittacina, Chlorophonia cyanea 773
Psittacula 172
Psophia 110
PSOPHIIDAE 110
ptaritepui, Crypturellus 30
ptaritepui, Dysithamnus mentalis 390
ptaritepui, Platyrinchus mystaceus 489
ptaritepui, Trogon personatus 283
Pterodroma 58
Pteroglossus 307, 308
Pterophanes 257
pucherani, Campylorhamphus 377

pucherani, Melanerpes 318
pucheranii, Neomorphus 199
pudica, Elaenia frantzii 471
Puffbird, Barred 295
Black-breasted 293
Black-streaked 297
Brown-banded 293
Chestnut-capped 294
Collared 295
Moustached 297
Pied 293
Russet-throated 295
Sooty-capped 294
Spotted 294
Striolated 295
Swallow-winged 300
Two-banded 296
White-chested 296
White-necked 293
White-whiskered 297
Puffinus 60
puffinus, Puffinus 61
Puffleg, Black-breasted 265
Black-thighed 266
Colourful 266
Coppery-bellied 266
Emerald-bellied 266
Glowing 265
Golden-breasted 266
Greenish 267
Hoary 267
Racket-tailed 277
Sapphire-vented 265
Turquoise-throated 265
pugnax, Philomachus 138
pulchellus, Sakesphorus canadensis 381
pulcher, Melanerpes chrysauchen 319
pulcher, Myiophobus 493
pulcherrimus, Iridophanes 668
pulchra, Cyanolyca 576
pulchra, Pionopsitta 187
pulmentum, Bucco tamatia 294
Pulsatrix 206
pumilus, Chlorostilbon melanorhynchus 239
pumilus, Coccyzus 193
pumilus, Picumnus 313
punctata, Tangara 661
punctatus, Capito auratus 302
punctatus, Thamnophilus 386
puncticeps, Dysithamnus 391
punctigula, Chamaeza campanisona 425
punctigula, Chrysoptilus 323
punctigula, Lophornis pavoninus 237
punctipectus, Chrysoptilus punctigula 324
punctipectus, Dendrocolaptes sanctithomae 369
punctitectus, Dysithamnus occidentalis 392
punctulatus, Hylophylax 421
punensis, Athene cunicularia 209
punensis, Contopus cinereus 501
punicea, Xipholena 541
Purpletuft, Buff-throated 558
Dusky 559
White-browed 558
purpurascens, Euphonia fulvicrissa 770
purpurascens, Penelope 45
purpurata, Geotrygon 167
purpurata, Querula 543
purpuratus, Touit 184
purpurea, Ardea 74
purpurea, Coeligena 259
purpureotincta, Patagioenas subvinacea 158
purus, Phylloscartes ophthalmicus 478
purusianus, Xenops rutilans 363
pusilla, Calidris 136
pusilla, Wilsonia 737
pusillum, Camptostoma obsoletum 462
pusillus, Campylorhamphus 378
pusillus, Chordeiles 213
pusillus, Tiaris olivaceus 681
Pygiptila 388
pyra, Topaza 255
Pyriglena 408
pyrilia, Pionopsitta 187
Pyrocephalus 503
pyrocephalus, Machaeropterus 548
Pyroderus 543
pyrohypogaster, Hypopyrrhus 759
pyrrhodes, Philydor 354
pyrrholaemum, Electron platyrhynchum 287
Pyrrhomyias 496
pyrrhonota, Myrmotherula haematonota 397
pyrrhonota, Petrochelidon 586
pyrrhophrys, Chlorophonia 773
pyrrhops, Hapalopsittaca 186
pyrrhops, Hemitriccus granadensis 453
pyrrhops, Hemitriccus margaritaceiventer 452
pyrrhoptera, Brotogeris 182
pyrrhopterus, Pyrrhomyias cinnamomeus 497
Pyrrhura 176
quaesita, Thraupis episcopus 642
Quail, Black-fronted Wood 51
Chestnut Wood 51
Gorgeted Wood 52
Marbled Wood 51
Rufous-breasted Wood 52
Rufous-fronted Wood 51
Starred Wood 53
Tacarcuna Wood 52
Tawny-faced 53
Venezuelan Wood 52
Quail-Dove, Indigo-crowned 167
Lined 168
Olive-backed 168
Ruddy 169
Russet-crowned 168
Sapphire 167
Violaceous 169
White-throated 169
Querula 543
quesadae, Muscisaxicola alpinus 509
Quetzal, Crested 283
Golden-headed 284
Pavonine 284
White-tipped 284
quimarinus, Pachyramphus homochrous 565
quindiana, Asthenes flammulata 344
quindianus, Basileuterus luteoviridis 741
quindio, Turdus fuscater 615
quindiuna, Cyanolyca armillata 575
quindiuna, Piculus rivolii 322
quinta, Sturnella magna 759
quinticolor, Capito 302
Quiscalus 761
quitensis, Columbina passerina 162
quitensis, Euphonia xanthogaster 772
quitensis, Grallaria 433
quitensis, Metallura tyrianthina 270
quixensis, Microrhopias 403
radiatus, Nystalus 295
radiolatus, Dendrocolaptes certhia 370
radiolosus, Neomorphus 199
Rail, Black 112
Blackish 117
Bogotá 114
Brown Wood 115
Clapper 113
Grey-necked Wood 114
Plain-flanked 114
Plumbeous 117
Red-winged Wood 115
Rufous-necked Wood 114
Spotted 117
Virginia 114
RALLIDAE 110
ralloides, Myadestes 609
Rallus 113
RAMPHASTIDAE 304
ramphastinus, Semnornis 304
Ramphastos 310
Ramphocaenus 605
Ramphocelus 639
Ramphomicron 268
Ramphotrigon 484
rara, Grallaricula ferrugineipectus 436
rarum, Glaucidium griseiceps 206
recisa, Metallura williami 269
recognita, Onychoprion anaethetus 148
Recurvirostra 126
RECURVIROSTRIDAE 126
recurvirostris, Avocettula 235
Redshank, Spotted 133
Redstart, American 731
Golden-fronted 739
Paria 738
Saffron-breasted 738
Slate-throated 737
Spectacled 739
Tepui 738

White-faced 738
White-fronted 739
Yellow-crowned 740
reevei, Turdus 616
refulgens, Thalurania furcata 242
regalis, Heliangelus 263
regulus, Basileuterus coronatus 743
regulus, Grallaria guatimalensis 429
regulus, Machaeropterus 547
reinwardtii, Selenidera 306
remoratus, Xenops minutus 363
remseni, Doliornis 531
resplendens, Vanellus 122
restricta, Myiopagis viridicata 467
reyi, Hemispingus 628
Rhegmatorhina 420
RHINOCRYPTIDAE 439
Rhodinocichla 633
rhodinolaema, Habia rubica 675
rhodocephala, Pyrrhura 179
Rhynchocyclus 485
Rhynchortyx 53
Rhytipterna 515
richardsoni, Basileuterus luteoviridis 741
richardsoni, Eubucco 303
richardsoni, Falco columbarius 107
richmondi, Leucippus fallax 246
ridgelyi, Grallaria 431
ridgwayi, Anous stolidus 148
ridgwayi, Buteogallus urubitinga 94
ridgwayi, Columbina squammata 162
ridgwayi, Dendrocincla fuliginosa 364
ridgwayi, Fregata minor 69
ridgwayi, Glaucidium 208
ridgwayi, Icterus icterus 753
ridgwayi, Jacamerops aureus 292
ridgwayi, Psarocolius wagleri 748
ridgwayi, Stelgidopteryx serripennis 585
ridgwayi, Thryothorus coraya 594
ridibundus, Larus 145
riefferii, Chlorornis 626
riefferii, Pipreola 532
riisii, Elaenia martinica 467
rikeri, Berlepschia 350
Riparia 578
riparia, Riparia 578
riparius, Molothrus bonariensis 762
ripleyi, Neocrex colombiana 116
riveti, Philydor rufum 355
rivolii, Piculus 321
rivularis, Basileuterus 745
rivularis, Cinclus leucocephalus 607
rixosa, Machetornis 512
robbinsi, Scytalopus 441
robinsoni, Butorides striata 73
roboratus, Megascops 203
robustus, Asio stygius 209
rodolphei, Synallaxis albigularis 335
rodriguezi, Scytalopus 442
rodwayi, Euphonia violacea 769
roehli, Picumnus squamulatus 316
romeroana, Grallaria rufocinerea 431
roraimae, Automolus 358
roraimae, Basileuterus bivittatus 740
roraimae, Caprimulgus longirostris 216
roraimae, Chlorophonia cyanea 773
roraimae, Coereba flaveola 683
roraimae, Grallaria guatimalensis 429
roraimae, Hemithraupis guira 632
roraimae, Herpsilochmus 401
roraimae, Mecocerculus leucophrys 473
roraimae, Megascops 201
roraimae, Mionectes macconnelli 448
roraimae, Myiophobus 493
roraimae, Parula pitiayumi 725
roraimae, Patagioenas fasciata 157
roraimae, Pteroglossus aracari 308
roraimae, Trogon personatus 283
roraimae, Turdus olivater 617
roraimae, Zonotrichia capensis 685
Roraimia 347
rosae, Chaetocercus jourdanii 275
rosea, Rhodinocichla 633
rosenbergi, Amazilia 248
rosenbergi, Nyctiphrynus 215
rosenbergi, Rhytipterna holerythra 515
rosenbergi, Schiffornis turdina 557
rosenbergi, Xiphorhynchus susurrans 374
rostrata, Hylocharis cyanus 243
rostratus, Colibri coruscans 234
rostratus, Coryphospingus pileatus 687
rostratus, Mimus gilvus 622
rostratus, Premnoplex brunnescens 348
rostratus, Xiphocolaptes promeropirhynchus 369
Rostrhamus 85
rostrifera, Thalurania colombica 241
rothschildi, Bangsia 644
rothschildii, Cyanocompsa cyanoides 722
rubecula, Nonnula 298
rubellula, Ochthoeca diadema 504
ruber, Eudocimus 77
ruber, Phaethornis 229
ruber, Phoenicopterus 82
ruberrima, Patagioenas subvinacea 158
rubica, Habia 675
rubicundulus, Ochthoeca rufipectoralis 505
rubida, Calidris alba 136
rubida, Chamaeza nobilis 425
rubidior, Pipreola formosa 534
rubiginosus, Automolus 358
rubiginosus, Piculus 322
rubinoides, Heliodoxa 253
rubinus, Pyrocephalus 503
rubra, Crax 48
rubra, Piranga 679
rubricapillus, Melanerpes 317
rubriceps, Piranga 680
rubricollis, Campephilus 327
rubrigularis, Pionus menstruus 188
rubrilateralis, Capito maculicoronatus 301
rubripes, Zenaida auriculata 160
rubripileus, Piculus rubiginosus 322
rubrirostris, Cnemoscopus 627
rubrocristatus, Ampelion 531
ruckeri, Threnetes 226
rufa, Calidris canutus 136
rufa, Formicivora 404
rufalbus, Thryothorus 597
rufaxilla, Ampelion 531
rufaxilla, Leptotila 166
rufescens, Egretta 75
rufescens, Laniocera 557
rufescens, Muscisaxicola maculirostris 509
rufescens, Saltator orenocensis 720
Ruff 138
ruficapilla, Grallaria 430
ruficapillus, Chrysomus 758
ruficauda, Galbula 290
ruficauda, Ortalis 43
ruficauda, Ramphotrigon 485
ruficauda, Zenaida auriculata 160
ruficaudatum, Philydor 354
ruficaudatus, Thryothorus mystacalis 593
ruficaudus, Xenops minutus 363
ruficeps, Chalcostigma 269
ruficeps, Dendrocincla homochroa 365
ruficeps, Elaenia 470
ruficeps, Grallaria nuchalis 432
ruficeps, Gymnopithys leucaspis 419
ruficeps, Poecilotriccus 450
ruficeps, Pseudotriccus 450
ruficervix, Caprimulgus longirostris 216
ruficervix, Tangara 664
ruficollis, Cathartes aura 81
ruficollis, Egretta tricolor 75
ruficollis, Hypnelus 295
ruficollis, Micrastur 105
ruficollis, Oreopholus 125
ruficollis, Stelgidopteryx 585
ruficollis, Syndactyla 352
ruficoronatus, Myioborus melanocephalus 739
ruficrissa, Ortalis ruficauda 43
ruficrissa, Urosticte 267
rufifrons, Basileuterus 744
rufifrons, Percnostola 412
rufifrons, Phacellodomus 345
rufigenis, Poecilotriccus ruficeps 450
rufigenis, Tangara 664
rufigula, Dendrexetastes 368
rufigula, Gymnopithys 418
rufigula, Tangara 662
rufigularis, Falco 108
rufigularis, Glyphorynchus spirurus 367
rufigularis, Hemitriccus 453
rufigularis, Sclerurus 360
rufimarginatus, Herpsilochmus 402
rufinus, Empidonomus varius 522
rufipectoralis, Ochthoeca 505
rufipectus, Automolus rubiginosus 359
rufipectus, Formicarius 425
rufipectus, Leptopogon 448
rufipennis, Columbina talpacoti 163
rufipennis, Myiophobus roraimae 493

rufipennis, Myiozetetes cayanensis 526
rufipennis, Neomorphus 199
rufipennis, Pitangus sulphuratu 529
rufipileatus, Automolus 359
rufiventer, Tachyphonus 638
rufiventris, Euphonia 772
rufiventris, Formicivora grisea 403
rufiventris, Lurocalis 212
rufiventris, Picumnus 316
rufiventris, Ramphocaenus melanurus 605
rufivertex, Euphonia anneae 772
rufivertex, Iridosornis 649
rufocinerea, Grallaria 431
rufocollaris, Petrochelidon 586
rufomarginatus, Euscarthmus 478
rufomarginatus, Mecocerculus leucophrys 473
rufopectus, Ochthoeca rufipectoralis 505
rufopileata, Dendroica petechia 726
rufopileatum, Pittasoma 426
rufosuperciliata, Syndactyla 352
rufula, Grallaria 433
rufulus, Troglodytes 599
rufum, Conirostrum 651
rufum, Philydor 355
rufum, Toxostoma 623
rufus, Caprimulgus 215
rufus, Pachyramphus 564
rufus, Tachyphonus 638
rufus, Trogon 282
rumicivorus, Thinocorus 140
rupestris, Chordeiles 213
Rupicola 535
rupicola, Colaptes 324
rupicola, Rupicola 535
rupurumii, Phaethornis 229
russata, Haplophaedia aureliae 267
russatus, Chlorostilbon 240
russatus, Poecilotriccus 454
rustica, Haplospiza 689
rustica, Hirundo 586
ruticilla, Setophaga 731
rutila, Streptoprocne 220
rutilans, Synallaxis 337
rutilans, Xenops 363
rutilus, Thryothorus 595
RYNCHOPIDAE 153
Rynchops 154
sabini, Xema 147
Sabrewing, Buff-breasted 231
Grey-breasted 231
Lazuline 232
Napo 232
Rufous-breasted 232
Santa Marta 232
White-tailed 232
sadiecoatsae, Myiophobus roraimae 493
sagitta, Heliodoxa leadbeateri 253
saira, Piranga flava 679
Sakesphorus 381
salicicola, Catharus fuscescens 611
salmoni, Brachygalba 289
salmoni, Chrysothlypis 632
salmoni, Myrmotherula fulviventris 396
salmoni, Psarocolius angustifrons 748
salmoni, Tigrisoma fasciatum 70
Saltator 719
Saltator, Black-cowled 721
Black-winged 719
Buff-throated 719
Greyish 720
Masked 721
Orinoco 720
Streaked 721
saltuarius, Crypturellus erythropus 31
saltuensis, Grallaria rufula 433
saltuensis, Thryothorus mystacalis 594
salvini, Amazona autumnalis 190
salvini, Cyphorhinus arada 604
salvini, Eutoxeres aquila 224
salvini, Knipolegus poecilurus 510
salvini, Mitu 48
salvini, Neomorphus geoffroyi 198
salvini, Pachyramphus albogriseus 563
salvini, Sclerurus guatemalensis 361
sanctaeluciae, Lophotriccus pileatus 482
sanctaemartae, Asthenes wyatti 344
sanctaemartae, Catharus fuscater 611
sanctaemartae, Lepidocolaptes lacrymiger 376
sanctaemartae, Myioborus miniatus 737
sanctaemartae, Myrmotherula schisticolor 398
sanctaemartae, Ramphocaenus melanurus 605
sanctaemartae, Scytalopus 440
sanctaemartae, Trogon personatus 283
sanctaemartae, Turdus olivater 617
sanctaemartae, Tyrannus savana 521
sanctaemartae, Xiphocolaptes promeropirhynchus 369
sanctamartae, Gymnocichla nudiceps 411
sanctamarthae, Chamaepetes goudotii 47
sanctithomae, Brotogeris 183
sanctithomae, Dendrocolaptes 369
Sanderling 136
Sandpiper, Baird's 137
Buff-breasted 138
Curlew 138
Least 137
Pectoral 137
Semipalmated 136
Solitary 133
Spotted 134
Stilt 138
Terek 134
Upland 132
Western 136
White-rumped 137
Wood 133
sandvicensis, Thalasseus 152
sanguineus, Pteroglossus 309
sanguineus, Veniliornis 319
sanguinolentus, Pardirallus 117
sanguinolentus, Rupicola peruvianus 536
sanluisensis, Henicorhina leucophrys 601
santarosae, Arremon aurantiirostris 706
sanus, Campylorhamphus procurvoides 378
Sapayoa 566
Sapayoa, Broad-billed 566
SAPAYOIDAE 566
saphirina, Geotrygon 167
Sapphire, Blue-chinned 238
Blue-headed 243
Blue-throated 243
Golden-tailed 244
Humboldt's 244
Rufous-throated 243
White-chinned 243
Sapphirewing, Great 257
sapphirina, Hylocharis 243
Sapsucker, Yellow-bellied 319
sarayacuensis, Corythopis torquata 457
Sarcoramphus 81
Sarkidiornis 37
sasaimae, Automolus rubiginosus 359
Satrapa 512
satrapa, Tyrannus melancholicus 521
saturata, Diglossa caerulescens 656
saturata, Euphonia 768
saturata, Hypocnemis cantator 410
saturata, Myrmotherula ornata 397
saturata, Schistocichla 413
saturatior, Cercomacra tyrannina 406
saturatior, Xiphorhynchus picus 371
saturatus, Automolus rubiginosus 359
saturatus, Contopus sordidulus 500
saturatus, Formicarius analis 424
saturatus, Hylophilus aurantiifrons 573
saturatus, Pachyramphus castaneus 561
saturatus, Phaethornis striigularis 230
saturatus, Pionus sordidus 189
saturatus, Platyrinchus 489
saturatus, Pyrocephalus rubinus 503
saturatus, Saltator grossus 719
saturatus, Tinamus major 27
saturninus, Mimus 622
saucerrottei, Amazilia 249
saul, Lafresnaya lafresnayi 258
savana, Tyrannus 521
savannarum, Ammodramus 685
savannophilus, Euscarthmus rufomarginatus 478
Sayornis 503
Scaphidura 762
scapularis, Jacana jacana 141
Scaup, Lesser 42
schaeferi, Lurocalis semitorquatus 212
schaeferi, Myiobius villosus 495
Schiffornis 556
Schiffornis, Thrush-like 557
Várzea 556
schistacea, Diglossa albilatera 653
schistacea, Schistocichla 412
schistacea, Sporophila 692

schistacea, Chaetura cinereiventris 221
schistaceifrons, Catamenia analis 704
schistaceigula, Polioptila 606
schistaceus, Atlapetes 712
schistaceus, Leucopternis 92
schistaceus, Thamnophilus 386
schisticolor, Myrmotherula 398
Schistochlamys 625
Schistocichla 412
Schizoeaca 332
schlegeli, Arremon 706
schomburgki, Hydropsalis climacocerca 218
schomburgkii, Micropygia 111
schottii, Thryothorus nigricapillus 596
schrankii, Tangara 659
schreibersii, Heliodoxa 254
sclateri, Attila spadiceus 514
sclateri, Cacicus 751
sclateri, Camptostoma obsoletum 462
sclateri, Chaetura cinereiventris 221
sclateri, Forpus modestus 181
sclateri, Hirundinea ferruginea 497
sclateri, Hylophilus 572
sclateri, Knipolegus orenocensis 511
sclateri, Monasa morphoeus 299
sclateri, Picumnus 314
sclateri, Pseudocolopteryx 477
sclateri, Tangara arthus 660
sclateri, Thripadectes virgaticeps 356
sclateri, Thryothorus 595
sclateri, Todirostrum cinereum 455
sclateri, Tolmomyias poliocephalus 488
Sclateria 411
Sclerurus 360
scolopaceus, Limnodromus 130
SCOLOPACIDAE 127
Screamer, Horned 34
Northern 34
scutatus, Pyroderus 543
Scytalopus 440
Scythebill, Brown-billed 378
Curve-billed 378
Greater 377
Red-billed 378
secunda, Deconychura stictolaema 365
seebohmi, Atlapetes 713
Seedeater, Band-tailed 704
Black-and-white 697
Blue 703
Capped 699
Caquetá 695
Carrizal 704
Chestnut-bellied 700
Chestnut-throated 700
Double-collared 698
Drab 699
Grey 694
Lesson's 696
Lined 696
Páramo 705
Parrot-billed 698
Plain-coloured 705
Plumbeous 693
Ring-necked 694
Ruddy-breasted 699
Rufous-rumped 700
Slate-coloured 692
Tumaco 701
Variable 695
White-bellied 698
White-naped 704
Wing-barred 695
Yellow-bellied 697
Seedsnipe, Least 140
Rufous-bellied 140
segmentata, Uropsalis 218
segrex, Basileuterus culicivorus 743
seilerni, Dendrocolaptes picumnus 370
Seiurus 733
Selenidera 306
selvae, Thamnophilus multistriatus 383
semibrunneus, Hylophilus 573
semicervina, Basileuterus fulvicauda 745
semicinereus, Dysithamnus mentalis 390
semicinereus, Hylophilus 571
semicinnamomeus, Celeus flavus 325
semifasciata, Tityra 555
semifasciatus, Taraba major 380
semiflava, Geothlypis 735
semiflavus, Myiobius sulphureipygius 495
semifuscus, Chlorospingus 677
semipagana, Elaenia flavogaster 468
semipalmatus, Catoptrophorus 134
semipalmatus, Charadrius 123
semiplumbeus, Leucopternis 93
semiplumbeus, Rallus 114
semirufus, Atlapetes 714
semirufus, Baryphthengus martii 288
semirufus, Myiarchus 516
semitorquatus, Lurocalis 212
semitorquatus, Micrastur 106
Semnornis 304
semota, Tachornis squamata 224
senex, Herpsilochmus axillaris 402
senex, Platyrinchus platyrhyncho 490
senilis, Myornis 439
seniloides, Pionus 189
sennetti, Chordeiles minor 213
septentrionalis, Cathartes aura 81
septentrionalis, Chloroceryle americana 285
septentrionalis, Chordeiles pusillus 213
septentrionalis, Hemitriccus margaritaceiventer 453
septentrionalis, Myiozetetes luteiventris 528
septentrionalis, Tinamus tao 27
septentrionalium, Anas cyanoptera 40
serena, Lepidothrix 548
sericocaudatus, Caprimulgus 216
Sericossypha 627
Serpophaga 474
serranus, Larus 146
serranus, Turdus 615
serripennis, Stelgidopteryx 585
serus, Spizaetus tyrannus 102
serva, Cercomacra 407
setifrons, Xenornis 389
Setophaga 731
setophagoides, Mecocerculus leucophrys 473
severus, Ara 171
sexnotatus, Aulacorhynchus haematopygus 306
Sharpbill 530
sharpei, Tiaris bicolor 682
Sheartail, Peruvian 278
Shearwater, Audubon's 61
Buller's 60
Cory's 59
Galápagos 61
Great 60
Little 61
Manx 61
Pink-footed 60
Sooty 60
Wedge-tailed 60
Shoveler, Northern 40
Shrike-Tanager, Fulvous 635
Shrike-Tyrant, Black-billed 508
White-tailed 508
Shrike-Vireo, Slaty-capped 568
Yellow-browed 568
sibilator, Sirystes 516
sibilatrix, Syrigma 75
Sicalis 690
Sicklebill, Buff-tailed 225
White-tipped 224
siemiradzkii, Carduelis 765
signata, Myrmothera campanisona 435
signata, Terenura spodioptila 405
signatum, Todirostrum maculatum 455
signatus, Basileuterus 741
signatus, Chlorospingus canigularis 678
signatus, Knipolegus 510
signatus, Terenotriccus erythrurus 494
similis, Myiozetetes 527
similis, Pachyramphus polychopterus 562
simonsi, Atlapetes seebohmi 713
simonsi, Pardirallus sanguinolentus 117
simplex, Atlapetes latinuchus 711
simplex, Crypturellus undulatus 30
simplex, Myrmothera 435
simplex, Phaetusa 150
simplex, Rhytipterna 515
simplex, Sporophila 699
simulatrix, Nonnula rubecula 298
sinaloae, Progne 581
sincipitalis, Psarocolius angustifrons 748
singularis, Xenerpestes 347
Siptornis 346
Sirystes 516
Siskin, Andean 763
Hooded 765
Olivaceous 766

Red 764
Saffron 765
Yellow-bellied 766
Yellow-faced 764
Sittasomus 366
sitticolor, Conirostrum 651
sittoides, Diglossa 652
Skimmer, Black 154
Skua, Chilean 141
Great 141
South Polar 141
skua, Stercorarius 141
smaragdinipectus, Eriocnemis vestitus 265
smaragdula, Topaza pella 256
smithsonianus, Larus 144
sneiderni, Lepidocolaptes lacrymiger 376
Snipe, Andean 129
Giant 128
Imperial 129
Noble 128
Puna 129
South American 128
Wilson's 128
Snowornis 541
sociabilis, Rostrhamus 85
soderstromi, Catamenia analis 704
soderstromi, Myrmotherula longicauda 395
soederstroemi, Oreotrochilus chimborazo 256
soederstroemii, Odontophorus speciosus 52
Softtail, Orinoco 345
Plain 345
solimoensis, Vireo olivaceus 569
Solitaire, Andean 609
Black 610
Rufous-brown 609
Varied 609
solitaria, Tringa 133
solitarius, Agriornis montanus 508
solitarius, Cacicus 752
solitarius, Harpyhaliaetus 95
solitarius, Myiodynastes maculatus 526
solitarius, Troglodytes solstitialis 599
solstitialis, Aratinga 174
solstitialis, Troglodytes 599
somptuosus, Anisognathus 647
sonnini, Colinus cristatus 50
sonorana, Dendroica petechia 725
Sora 115
sordida, Thlypopsis 631
sordidulus, Contopus 500
sordidus, Pionus 189
sororius, Lochmias nematura 361
souancei, Pyrrhura melanura 178
soui, Crypturellus 29
souleyetii, Lepidocolaptes 376
Spadebill, Cinnamon-crested 489
Golden-crowned 490
White-crested 490
White-throated 489
Yellow-throated 490
spadiceus, Attila 514
spadix, Pyrrhomyias cinnamomeus 497
spadix, Thryothorus 592
Sparrow, Black-capped 707
Black-striped 707
Golden-winged 706
Grasshopper 685
Grassland 685
House 777
Java 775
Lincoln's 684
Orange-billed 706
Pectoral 706
Rufous-collared 684
Tocuyo 707
Tumbes 686
White-throated 685
Yellow-browed 686
sparverius, Falco 107
spatha, Momotus momota 288
spatiator, Grallaria rufula 433
Spatuletail, Marvellous 278
speciosa, Patagioenas 156
speciosum, Conirostrum 650
speciosus, Chrysoptilus punctigula 324
speciosus, Odontophorus 52
spectabilis, Arremon aurantiirostris 706
spectabilis, Celeus 326
spectabilis, Elaenia 468
spectabilis, Selenidera 306
speculigera, Conothraupis 626
spencei, Crypturellus erythropus 31
spencei, Heliangelus 262
spengeli, Forpus xanthopterygius 180
SPHENISCIDAE 55
Spheniscus 55
sphenurus, Emberizoides herbicola 692
Sphyrapicus 319
spillmanni, Scytalopus 443
spilogaster, Picumnus 317
spilorhynchus, Andigena nigrirostris 310
spinescens, Carduelis 763
Spinetail, Ash-browed 341
Azara's 333
Black-throated 338
Blackish-headed 336
Chestnut-throated 337
Crested 342
Dark-breasted 334
Dusky 335
Hoary-throated 339
Line-cheeked 341
Marañón 336
McConnell's 335
Necklaced 338
Pale-breasted 333
Parker's 342
Plain-crowned 336
Red-and-white 343
Red-faced 340
Ruddy 337
Rufous 337
Rusty-backed 342
Rusty-headed 338
Silvery-throated 336
Slaty 334
Speckled 343
Streak-capped 341
Stripe-breasted 338
Tepui 341
White-bellied 336
White-browed 339
White-whiskered 339
Yellow-chinned 343
spinicauda, Anas georgica 39
spinicaudus, Chaetura 221
spirurus, Glyphorynchus 366
spixii, Xiphorhynchus 373
Spiza 716
spiza, Chlorophanes 671
Spizaetus 101
Spizastur 101
splendens, Campephilus haematogaster 327
splendens, Volatinia jacarina 692
spodiolaemus, Turdus albicollis 621
spodionota, Myrmotherula 397
spodionotus, Atlapetes latinuchus 711
spodionotus, Dysithamnus mentalis 390
spodioptila, Terenura 405
spodiurus, Pachyramphus 564
Spoonbill, Eurasian 79
Roseate 79
Sporophila 692
spurius, Icterus 756
squamaecrista, Lophotriccus pileatus 482
squamata, Tachornis 224
squamatus, Capito 301
squamiger, Margarornis 349
squamigera, Grallaria 427
squamipectus, Pipreola frontalis 534
squammata, Columbina 162
squamosa, Patagioenas 156
squamulatus, Microcerculus marginatus 602
squamulatus, Picumnus 316
squatarola, Pluvialis 122
stanleyi, Chalcostigma 270
Starfrontlet, Blue-throated 261
Buff-winged 261
Dusky 260
Golden 260
Golden-bellied 260
Rainbow 260
Violet-throated 261
White-tailed 260
Starling, European 623
Starthroat, Blue-tufted 272
Long-billed 272
Steatornis 210
STEATORNITHIDAE 210
Stelgidopteryx 585
stellaris, Pygiptila 388
stellata, Dichrozona cincta 400
stellatus, Margarornis 349

stellatus, Myiotriccus ornatus 492
stellatus, Odontophorus 53
stenorhyncha, Schiffornis turdina 557
stenura, Zenaida auriculata 160
stenurus, Chlorostilbon 240
STERCORARIIDAE 141
Stercorarius 141
Sterna 151
Sternoclyta 255
Sternula 149
sterrhopteron, Wetmorethraupis 646
stictocephalus, Herpsilochmus 401
stictolaema, Deconychura 365
stictolophus, Lophornis 237
stictoptera, Myrmornis torquata 420
stictopterus, Mecocerculus 474
stictopterus, Touit 184
stictothorax, Synallaxis 338
sticturus, Herpsilochmus 400
Stigmatura 475
stilesi, Scytalopus 442
Stilt, Black-necked 126
stoicus, Hypnelus bicinctus 296
stolzmanni, Aimophila 686
stolzmanni, Chlorothraupis 635
stolzmanni, Oreotrochilus estella 257
stolzmanni, Tachycineta 579
stolzmanni, Tyranneutes 545
stolzmanni, Urothraupis 675
Stork, Maguari 80
  Wood 80
Storm-petrel, Ashy 64
  Band-rumped 63
  Black 64
  Hornby's 64
  Leach's 63
  Least 63
  Markham's 64
  Ringed 64
  Sooty 64
  Wedge-rumped 63
  White-faced 63
  White-vented 62
  Wilson's 62
Streamcreeper, Sharp-tailed 361
strepera, Elaenia 469
Streptopelia 159
streptophorus, Lipaugus 540
Streptoprocne 220
striata, Butorides 73
striata, Dendroica 730
striaticeps, Arremonops conirostris 708
striaticeps, Pseudocolaptes boissonneautii 350
striaticeps, Thripadectes melanorhynchus 356
striaticollis, Anabacerthia 353
striaticollis, Hemitriccus 452
striaticollis, Hypnelus ruficollis 296
striaticollis, Mionectes 446
striaticollis, Myiotheretes 507
striaticollis, Siptornis 346
striatidorsus, Thripadectes holostictus 356
striatigularis, Chrysoptilus punctigula 324
striatipectus, Saltator 721
striatipectus, Synallaxis cinnamomea 338
striatulus, Troglodytes musculus 598
striatus, Accipiter 89
stricklandi, Lophostrix cristata 205
strictocollaris, Arremon aurantiirostris 706
STRIGIDAE 200
strigilatus, Ancistrops 350
striigularis, Phaethornis 230
striolata, Syndactyla subalaris 352
striolatus, Machaeropterus regulus 548
striolatus, Nystalus 295
strophianus, Heliangelus 264
strophium, Odontophorus 52
stuartae, Heliomaster longirostris 272
stuarti, Stelgidopteryx serripennis 585
stuebelii, Oxypogon guerinii 268
stulta, Nonnula frontalis 298
Sturnella 759
Sturnidae 623
Sturnus 623
stygius, Asio 209
suavissima, Lepidothrix 549
subalaris, Macroagelaius 760
subalaris, Puffinus lherminieri 61
subalaris, Snowornis 541
subalaris, Syndactyla 352
subandeana, Tyto alba 200
subandina, Pyrrhura 177
subbrunneus, Cnipodectes 484
subcinerea, Thraupis cyanocephala 643
subcinereus, Scytalopus latrans 440
subcinereus, Thamnophilus atrinucha 387
subcristata, Cranioleuca 342
subflava, Inezia 475
subfulvum, Philydor erythrocercum 354
subfurcatus, Chlorostilbon mellisugus 239
subgrisea, Geotrygon frenata 169
subis, Progne 581
Sublegatus 463
sublestus, Glyphorynchus spirurus 367
subochraceus, Hylophylax punctulatus 421
subpallida, Pipra filicauda 553
subplacens, Myiopagis 466
subplumbea, Schistocichla leucostigma 413
subpudica, Synallaxis 336
subrufescens, Glyphorynchus spirurus 367
subrufescens, Momotus momota 288
subrufescens, Phaethornis striigularis 230
subruficollis, Tryngites 138
subsimilis, , Iridosornis rufivertex 649
subsimilis, Myioborus miniatus 738
substriata, Malacoptila fulvogularis 297
subtectus, Notharchus tectus 294
subtilis, Buteogallus 94
subtropicalis, Chlorophanes spiza 671
subtropicalis, Streptoprocne zonaris 220
subtropicalis, Thalurania fannyi 242
subtropicalis, Trogon collaris 282
subulatus, Hyloctistes 351
subvinacea, Patagioenas 158
suffusa, Myrmotherula hauxwelli 395
suffusa, Xenopipo holochlora 551
suffusus, Dysithamnus mentalis 391
Suiriri 464
suiriri, Suiriri 464
Sula 66
sula, Sula 67
sulcatus, Aulacorhynchus 305
sulcirostris, Crotophaga 198
sulfuratus, Ramphastos 310
SULIDAE 66
sulphuratu, Pitangus 529
sulphurea, Tyrannopsis 523
sulphureipygius, Myiobius 495
sulphurescens, Tolmomyias 486
sulphureus, Trogon rufus 282
sumaco, Thripadectes virgaticeps 356
Sunangel, Amethyst-throated 263
  Bogotá 264
  Flame-throated 264
  Gorgeted 264
  Longuemare's 263
  Mérida 262
  Orange-throated 262
  Purple-throated 264
  Royal 263
  Tourmaline 264
Sunbeam, Shining 258
Sunbittern 120
sunensis, Myrmotherula 398
Sungem, Horned 272
Sungrebe 120
superciliaris, Burhinus 127
superciliaris, Hemispingus 628
superciliaris, Leptopogon 449
superciliaris, Phylloscartes 481
superciliaris, Platyrinchus coronatus 490
superciliaris, Poecilotriccus sylvia 455
superciliaris, Sternula 149
superciliaris, Thryothorus 598
superciliosa, Ochthoeca fumicolor 505
superciliosus, Accipiter 89
superciliosus, Phaethornis 227
Surfbird 135
surinama, Aratinga pertinax 175
surinamensis, Chlidonias niger 151
surinamensis, Contopus cinereus 501
surinamensis, Myrmotherula 393
surinamensis, Nemosia pileata 633
surinamus, Pachyramphus 563
surinamus, Tachyphonus 637
sussurus, Phaethornis longirostris 227
susurrans, Xiphorhynchus 374
swainsoni, Buteo 99
swainsoni, Catharus ustulatus 612
swainsoni, Myiarchus 517
swainsonii, Gampsonyx 84
swainsonii, Limnothlypis 732
swainsonii, Ramphastos 312
Swallow, Bank 578

Barn 586
Black-collared 584
Blue-and-white 583
Brown-bellied 583
Cave 587
Chestnut-collared 586
Chilean 580
Cliff 586
Mangrove 579
Northern Rough-winged 585
Pale-footed 583
Southern Rough-winged 585
Tawny-headed 585
Tree 579
Tumbes 579
Violet-green 580
White-banded 584
White-thighed 584
White-winged 579
Swallow-wing 300
Swift, Alpine 224
Amazonian 222
Ashy-tailed 222
Band-rumped 221
Black 219
Chapman's 221
Chestnut-collared 220
Chimney 222
Fork-tailed Palm 224
Grey-rumped 220
Lesser Swallow-tailed 223
Pale-rumped 222
Pygmy 223
Short-tailed 221
Sick's 222
Spot-fronted 219
Tepui 219
Tumbes 221
Vaux's 222
White-chested 219
White-chinned 220
White-collared 220
White-tipped 223
Sylph, Long-tailed 276
Venezuelan 276
Violet-tailed 277
sylvia, Poecilotriccus 454
sylvicola, Sarkidiornis melanotos 37
Synallaxis 333
Syndactyla 351
Syrigma 75
syrmatophorus, Phaethornis 227
tacarcunae, Basileuterus tristriatus 745
tacarcunae, Chlorospingus 677
tacarcunae, Oxyruncus cristatus 530
tacarcunae, Syndactyla subalaris 352
tachina, Petrochelidon pyrrhonota 586
tachirae, Grallaria griseonucha 431
tachirensis, Campylorhamphus pusillus 378
tachirensis, Picumnus olivaceus 316
tachirensis, Sittasomus griseicapillus 366
tachirensis, Thripadectes virgaticeps 356
tachirensis, Thryothorus mystacalis 594
Tachornis 223
Tachuri, Bearded 476
Tachybaptus 53
Tachycineta 579
Tachymarptis 224
Tachyphonus 636
taciturnus, Arremon 706
taczanowskii, Euphonia chlorotica 767
taczanowskii, Icterus mesomelas 755
taczanowskii, Sicalis 691
taeniata, Dubusia 649
taeniatus, Microcerculus marginatus 602
Taeniotriccus 451
talpacoti, Columbina 162
tamae, Anisognathus lacrymosus 647
tamae, Atlapetes schistaceus 713
tamae, Cistothorus platensis 591
tamae, Henicorhina leucophrys 601
tamae, Lafresnaya lafresnayi 258
tamae, Zimmerius improbus 460
tamai, Coeligena helianthea 261
tamatia, Bucco 294
tamborensis, Rhynchocyclus olivaceus 486
Tanager, Ashy-throated Bush 678
Bay-headed 662
Beryl-spangled 666
Black-and-gold 644
Black-and-white 626
Black-and-yellow 632
Black-backed Bush 675
Black-capped 667
Black-chested Mountain 645
Black-chinned Mountain 648
Black-faced 625
Black-headed 667
Blue-and-black 666
Blue-and-yellow 643
Blue-backed 644
Blue-browed 664
Blue-capped 643
Blue-grey 642
Blue-necked 665
Blue-whiskered 658
Blue-winged Mountain 647
Buff-bellied 630
Buff-breasted Mountain 649
Burnished-buff 663
Carmiol's 634
Common Bush 676
Crested Ant 676
Crimson-backed 639
Crowned Ant 675
Dotted 662
Dusky-bellied Bush 677
Dusky-faced 633
Emerald 659
Fawn-breasted 649
Flame-crested 636
Flame-faced 660
Flame-rumped 640
Fulvous-crested 637
Fulvous-headed 630
Glaucous 642
Glistening-green 656
Gold-ringed 645
Golden 659
Golden-chested 644
Golden-crowned 649
Golden-eared 660
Golden-hooded 665
Golden-naped 664
Grass-green 626
Green-and-gold 659
Green-naped 666
Grey-and-gold 658
Grey-headed 635
Grey-hooded Bush 627
Guira 631
Highland Hepatic 679
Hooded 633
Hooded Mountain 645
Lacrimose Mountain 647
Lemon-rumped 641
Lemon-spectacled 634
Lowland Hepatic 679
Magpie 626
Masked 665
Masked Crimson 639
Masked Mountain 646
Metallic-green 664
Moss-backed 645
Multicoloured 657
Ochre-breasted 635
Olive 634
Olive-backed 634
Opal-crowned 668
Opal-rumped 668
Orange-eared 657
Orange-headed 631
Orange-throated 646
Palm 642
Paradise 658
Pirre Bush 677
Plain-coloured 657
Purplish-mantled 648
Red 679
Red-billed Pied 626
Red-hooded 680
Red-shouldered 638
Red-throated Ant 675
Rufous-cheeked 664
Rufous-chested 631
Rufous-crested 636
Rufous-throated 662
Rufous-winged 663
Saffron-crowned 660
Santa Marta Mountain 646
Scarlet 680
Scarlet-and-white 632
Scarlet-bellied Mountain 647
Scarlet-browed 636
Scrub 663

Short-billed Bush 677
Silver-beaked 639
Silver-throated 660
Silvery 667
Sooty Ant 676
Speckled 661
Spotted 661
Straw-backed 667
Summer 679
Swallow 674
Tacarcuna Bush 677
Tawny-crested 637
Tooth-billed 679
Turquoise 657
Vermilion 638
Western 681
White-capped 627
White-lined 638
White-rumped 625
White-shouldered 637
White-winged 680
Yellow-backed 632
Yellow-bellied 661
Yellow-crested 638
Yellow-green Bush 678
Yellow-throated 648
Yellow-throated Bush 678
tanagrinus, Lampropsar 759
Tangara 657
tao, Tinamus 27
Tapaculo, Ash-coloured 439
Blackish 440
Brown-rumped 442
Caracas 443
Chocó 441
Chusquea 444
Ecuadorian 441
Lara 444
Long-tailed 440
Mattoral 444
Mérida 443
Nariño 442
Ocellated 445
Pale-throated 441
Páramo 444
Rusty-belted 439
Santa Marta 440
Spillmann's 443
Stiles's 442
Upper Magdalena 442
White-crowned 440
tapanahoniensis, Nonnula rubecula 298
Tapera 196
tapera, Progne 580
Taphrospilus 246
Taraba 380
tataupa, Crypturellus 33
tatei, Premnoplex 348
Tattler, Wandering 134
taylori, Tangara ruficervix 664
Teal, Andean 39
Blue-winged 40
Brazilian 37
Cinnamon 40
Green-winged 38
Mérida Speckled 38
tectus, Notharchus 293
telasco, Sporophila 700
temperatus, Trogon personatus 283
temporalis, Anabacerthia variegaticeps 353
tenebrosa, Chelidoptera 300
tenebrosa, Myrmeciza atrothorax 418
tenebrosus, Ammodramus aurifrons 686
tenebrosus, Pachyramphus polychopterus 562
tenebrosus, Xiphocolaptes promeropirhynchus 369
tenellus, Trogon rufus 282
tenuepunctatus, Thamnophilus 384
tenuifasciatus, Thamnophilus tenuepunctatus 384
tenuirostris, Geositta 329
tenuirostris, Inezia 475
tenuirostris, Xenops 362
Terenotriccus 494
Terenura 405
Tern, Arctic 152
Black 151
Bridled 148
Caspian 150
Cayenne 153
Common 152
Elegant 153
Gull-billed 150
Inca 151
Large-billed 150
Least 149
Peruvian 150
Roseate 151
Royal 152
Sandwich 152
Sooty 148
South American 151
White 148
Yellow-billed 149
ternominatus, Charadrius vociferus 124
terrestris, Synallaxis cinnamomea 338
Tersina 674
tertia, Laniocera rufescens 558
tethys, Oceanodroma 63
texensis, Chordeiles acutipennis 213
thagus, Pelecanus 65
Thalassarche 56
Thalasseus 152
thalassina, Tachycineta 580
thalassinus, Colibri 233
Thalurania 241
Thamnistes 389
Thamnomanes 392
THAMNOPHILIDAE 379
Thamnophilus 382
Thaumastura 278
theobromae, Oryzoborus angolensis 702
theresae, Hapalopsittaca amazonina 185
theresae, Hylophylax naevius 421
theresiae, Polytmus 245
Theristicus 78
Thick-knee, Double-striped 126
Peruvian 127
THINOCORIDAE 140
Thinocorus 140
Thistletail, Mouse-coloured 333
Ochre-browed 332
Perijá 332
White-chinned 332
Thlypopsis 630
thoracicus, Campylorhamphus trochilirostris 378
thoracicus, Cyphorhinus 603
thoracicus, Formicarius rufipectus 425
thoracicus, Hylophilus 571
thoracicus, Liosceles 439
Thornbill, Black-backed 269
Blue-mantled 270
Bronze-tailed 270
Purple-backed 268
Rainbow-bearded 270
Rufous-capped 269
Thornbird, Rufous-fronted 345
Thorntail, Black-bellied 238
Green 238
Wire-crested 237
Thrasher, Brown 623
Pearly-eyed 623
THRAUPIDAE 625
Thraupis 642
Threnetes 225
THRESKIORNITHIDAE 77
Thripadectes 356
Thripophaga 345
Thrush, Andean Slaty 616
Bare-eyed 620
Black-billed 618
Black-hooded 616
Chestnut-bellied 617
Chiguanco 614
Clay-coloured 620
Cocoa 619
Dagua 621
Ecuadorian 620
Glossy-black 615
Great 614
Grey-cheeked 612
Hauxwell's 619
Lawrence's 618
Marañón 617
Pale-breasted 617
Pale-eyed 614
Pale-vented 619
Plumbeous-backed 616
Swainson's 612
White-necked 621
Wood 613
Yellow-legged 613
Thrush-Tanager, Rosy 633
Thryothorus 592

thula, Egretta 76
Tiaris 681
tibialis, Neochelidon 584
tigrina, Dendroica 727
tigrinus, Bolborhynchus lineola 180
Tigrisoma 70
TINAMIDAE 27
Tinamou, Andean 33
Barred 32
Bartlett's 32
Berlepsch's 29
Black 27
Brown 30
Chocó 31
Cinereous 29
Curve-billed 33
Great 27
Grey 27
Grey-legged 32
Highland 28
Little 29
Pale-browed 30
Red-legged 31
Rusty 32
Slaty-breasted 31
Tataupa 33
Tawny-breasted 28
Tepui 30
Undulated 30
Variegated 32
White-throated 28
Tinamus 27
tinnunculus, Falco 107
tinochlora, Boissonneaua flavescens 262
Tit-Spinetail, Andean 331
Tit-Tyrant, Agile 476
Black-crested 476
Tufted 476
tithys, Synallaxis 336
Tityra 555
Tityra, Black-crowned 556
Black-tailed 555
Masked 555
TITYRIDAE 554
tobaci, Amazilia 249
tobagensis, Cyanerpes cyaneus 673
tobagensis, Formicivora grisea 403
tobagensis, Leptotila verreauxi 165
tobagensis, Mimus gilvus 622
tobagensis, Myiodynastes maculatus 526
tobagensis, Patagioenas cayennensis 157
tobagensis, Piculus rubiginosus 322
tobagensis, Thamnophilus doliatus 383
tobagensis, Thryothorus rutilus 595
tobagensis, Troglodytes musculus 599
tobagensis, Vireo olivaceus 569
tocantinsi, Oxyruncus cristatus 530
toco, Ramphastos 313
tocuyensis, Arremonops 707
tocuyensis, Dysithamnus leucostictus 391
toddi, Piranga lutea 679
toddi, Tangara gyrola 662
Todirostrum 455
Tody-Flycatcher, Black-headed 456
Common 455
Golden-winged 456
Maracaibo 455
Painted 456
Ruddy 454
Rusty-fronted 454
Slate-headed 454
Smoky-fronted 454
Spotted 455
Yellow-browed 456
Tody-Tyrant, Black-and-white 450
Black-throated 453
Boat-billed 451
Buff-throated 453
Cinnamon-breasted 453
Johannes's 452
Pearly-vented 452
Rufous-crowned 450
Snethlage's 451
Stripe-necked 452
White-eyed 452
tolimae, Athene cunicularia 209
tolimae, Chalcostigma herrani 271
tolimae, Cistothorus platensis 591
tolimae, Tangara guttata 662
tolimensis, Mimus gilvus 622
Tolmomyias 486
tombacea, Galbula 291
tomentosum, Mitu 47
Topaz, Crimson 256
Fiery 255
Ruby 235
Topaza 255
torquata, Coeligena 258
torquata, Hydropsalis 218
torquata, Megaceryle 286
torquata, Myrmornis 419
torquatus, Buarremon 709
torquatus, Celeus 326
torquatus, Corythopis 457
torquatus, Microbates collaris 605
torquatus, Pteroglossus 308
torridus, Attila 513
torridus, Furnarius 330
tortugensis, Aratinga pertinax 175
tortugensis, Columbina passerina 162
tortugensis, Tiaris bicolor 682
tortuguensis, Sublegatus arenarum 463
Toucan, Black-billed Mountain 310
Black-mandibled 312
Channel-billed 311
Chestnut-mandibled 312
Chocó 311
Citron-throated 311
Cuvier's 312
Grey-breasted Mountain 310
Keel-billed 310
Plate-billed Mountain 309
Red-billed 312
Toco 313
Yellow-ridged 311
Toucanet, Chestnut-tipped 305
Crimson-rumped 306
Emerald 304
Golden-collared 306
Groove-billed 305
Guianan 307
Tawny-tufted 307
Yellow-billed 305
Yellow-eared 306
Touit 183
tovarensis, Diglossa cyanea 656
tovarensis, Ochthoeca diadema 504
townsendi, Dendroica 728
Toxostoma 623
trachelopyrus, Campephilus rubricollis 327
traillii, Empidonax 502
Trainbearer, Black-tailed 277
Green-tailed 277
transandeanus, Taraba major 380
transfasciatus, Crypturellus 30
transfluvialis, Cyphorhinus arada 604
transilis, Aratinga wagleri 173
traylori, Tolmomyias 488
Treehunter, Black-billed 356
Flammulated 357
Streak-capped 356
Striped 356
Uniform 356
Treerunner, Fulvous-dotted 349
Pearled 349
triangularis, Xiphorhynchus 375
trichas, Geothlypis 735
tricolor, Atlapetes 712
tricolor, Egretta 75
tricolor, Furnarius leucopus 331
tricolor, Phalaropus 139
trifasciatus, Basileuterus 744
Tringa 132
trinitatis, Euphonia 768
trinitatis, Geotrygon linearis 168
trinitatis, Icterus nigrogularis 755
trinitatis, Manacus manacus 550
trinitatis, Myiopagis gaimardii 465
trinitatis, Piculus rubiginosus 322
trinitatis, Pitangus sulphuratu 529
trinitatis, Pulsatrix perspicillata 206
trinitatis, Ramphocaenus melanurus 605
trinitatis, Sakesphorus canadensis 381
trinitatis, Synallaxis albescens 334
trinitatis, Tangara guttata 662
tristis, Pachyramphus polychopterus 562
tristriatus, Basileuterus 744
trivirgatus, Conopias 524
TROCHILIDAE 224
trochilirostris, Campylorhamphus 378
Troglodytes 598
TROGLODYTIDAE 587
Trogon 279
Trogon, Amazonian Violaceous 280
Amazonian White-tailed 281

Black-tailed 280
Black-throated 282
Blue-crowned 281
Chocó 281
Collared 282
Ecuadorian 280
Masked 283
Northern Violaceous 279
Slaty-tailed 283
Western White-tailed 282
TROGONIDAE 279
Tropicbird, Red-billed 64
White-tailed 65
tropicus, Anas cyanoptera 40
Troupial 753
Orange-backed 753
trudis, Chlorospingus ophthalmicus 677
Trumpeter, Grey-winged 110
Pale-winged 110
Tryngites 138
tschudii, Ampelioides 535
tschudii, Chamaepetes goudotii 47
tschudii, Piprites chloris 566
tschuktschorum, Xema sabini 147
tuberculifer, Myiarchus 516
tuberosum, Mitu 48
tucanus, Ramphastos 312
Tuftedcheek, Buffy 349
Streaked 350
tumbezana, Phaeomyias murina 462
tundrae, Charadrius hiaticula 123
tundrius, Falco peregrinus 109
turcosa, Cyanolyca 575
TURDIDAE 608
turdina, Chamaeza 426
turdina, Schiffornis 557
turdinus, Automolus ochrolaemus 357
turdinus, Campylorhynchus 588
Turdus 613
Turnstone, Black 135
Ruddy 135
turturilla, Zenaida macroura 160
Twistwing, Brownish 484
tyleri, Elaenia dayi 471
typica, Deconychura longicauda 365
Tyranneutes 545
TYRANNIDAE 446
tyrannina, Cercomacra 406
tyrannina, Dendrocincla 364
Tyrannopsis 523
Tyrannulet, Ashy-headed 459
Black-capped 458
Black-fronted 480
Brown-capped 461
Ecuadorean 480
Golden-faced 461
Grey-and-white 467
Mouse-coloured 462
Olive-green 481
Paltry 459
Plumbeous-crowned 458
Red-billed 460
River 474
Rough-legged 457
Rufous-browed 481
Rufous-lored 480
Rufous-winged 473
Slender-footed 460
Sooty-headed 458
Southern Beardless 462
Sulphur-bellied 474
Tawny-rumped 459
Torrent 474
Tumbes 463
Urich's 457
Venezuelan 460
White-banded 474
White-lored 461
White-tailed 473
White-throated 472
Yellow 463
Yellow-crowned 464
Tyrannulus 464
tyrannulus, Myiarchus 519
Tyrannus 520
tyrannus, Spizaetus 102
tyrannus, Tyrannus 522
Tyrant, Amazonian Black 510
Andean 510
Antioquia Bristle 479
Black-capped Pygmy 481
Black-chested 451
Bronze-olive Pygmy 449
Cattle 512
Chapman's Bristle 479
Cinnamon 496
Dark-faced Ground 509
Double-banded Pygmy 482
Drab Water 506
Helmeted Pygmy 483
Little Ground 509
Long-tailed 512
Marble-faced Bristle 478
Masked Water 511
Pale-eyed Pygmy 483
Pied Water 511
Plain-capped Ground 509
Red-rumped Bush 506
Riverside 511
Rufous-headed Pygmy 450
Rufous-sided Pygmy 478
Rufous-tailed 510
Santa Marta Bush 507
Scale-crested Pygmy 482
Short-tailed Field 510
Short-tailed Pygmy 481
Smoky Bush 507
Spectacled Bristle 479
Spot-billed Ground 508
Streak-throated Bush 507
Tawny-crowned Pygmy 477
Variegated Bristle 479
Venezuelan Bristle 479
White-browed Ground 509
White-headed Marsh 512
Yellow-browed 512
Tyrant-Manakin, Dwarf 545
Pale-bellied 545
Saffron-crested 545
Tiny 546
tyrianthina, Diglossa glauca 655
tyrianthina, Metallura 269
Tyto 200
TYTONIDAE 199
tzacatl, Amazilia 250
uaireni, Lepidocolaptes souleyetii 376
ucayalae, Glaucidium brasilianum 208
ujhelyii, Chrysoptilus punctigula 324
ultramarina, Dacnis cayana 671
umbraticus, Xenerpestes minlosi 347
Umbrellabird, Amazonian 544
Long-wattled 544
umbrinus, Arremonops conirostris 708
umbrosus, Manacus manacus 550
uncinatus, Chondrohierax 84
undatus, Celeus 325
underwoodii, Ocreatus 277
undulata, Gallinago 128
undulatus, Crypturellus 30
undulatus, Picumnus exilis 314
undulatus, Zebrilus 71
unduligera, Frederickena 380
unibrunnea, Cinnycerthia unirufa 590
unica, Dixiphia pipra 553
unicinctus, Parabuteo 96
unicolor, Phrygilus 688
unicolor, Ramphocelus carbo 640
unicolor, Thamnophilus 385
unicolor, Xenopipo 551
uniformis, Xenopipo 551
unirufa, Cinnycerthia 590
unirufa, Synallaxis 337
unirufus, Lipaugus 540
urbanoi, Cyphorhinus arada 604
urichi, Phyllomyias 457
Urochroa 257
urochrysia, Chalybura 252
Uropsalis 218
uropygialis, Cacicus 751
uropygialis, Coereba flaveola 683
uropygialis, Pheucticus aureoventris 717
uropygialis, Phyllomyias 459
uropygialis, Stelgidopteryx ruficollis 585
Urosticte 267
Urothraupis 675
urubitinga, Buteogallus 94
urubitinga, Cathartes burrovianus 81
urumutum, Nothocrax 47
urutani, Automolus roraimae 358
usta, Megascops 203
ustulatus, Catharus 612
ustulatus, Microcerculus 602
valencianus, Certhiaxis cinnamomeus 343
valida, Sicalis flaveola 690
validus, Dendrocolaptes picumnus 370
validus, Pachyramphus 565

Vanellus 121
vanrossemi, Gelochelidon nilotica 150
varia, Grallaria 428
varia, Mniotilta 731
varia, Tangara 662
variegata, Sula 66
variegaticeps, Anabacerthia 353
variegatus, Crypturellus 32
variegatus, Odontophorus atrifrons 51
varius, Empidonomus 522
varius, Sphyrapicus 319
vassorii, Tangara 666
vauxi, Chaetura 222
Veery 611
velezi, Hapalopsittaca amazonina 185
velia, Tangara 668
veliei, Contopus sordidulus 500
Velvetbreast, Mountain 258
venezuelae, Aratinga pertinax 175
venezuelae, Buthraupis montana 645
venezuelae, Camptostoma obsoletum 462
venezuelae, Malacoptila fusca 296
venezuelae, Myrmeciza laemosticta 415
venezuelae, Piranga leucoptera 680
venezuelae, Zonotrichia capensis 685
venezuelana, Anabacerthia striaticollis 353
venezuelana, Chamaeza campanisona 425
venezuelana, Grallaricula cucullata 437
venezuelana, Premnornis guttuligera 348
venezuelana, Serpophaga hypoleuca 474
venezuelana, Tangara schrankii 659
venezuelana, Terenura callinota 405
venezuelanus, Anisognathus somptuosus 648
venezuelanus, Automolus rubiginosus 359
venezuelanus, Chlorospingus ophthalmicus 677
venezuelanus, Knipolegus poecilurus 510
venezuelanus, Leptopogon rufipectus 448
venezuelanus, Megascops ingens 202
venezuelanus, Myiophobus flavicans 492
venezuelanus, Phylloscartes 479
venezuelanus, Thryothorus leucotis 598
venezuelense, Laniisoma elegans 559
venezuelense, Ramphotrigon megacephalum 484
venezuelensis, Atalotriccus pilaris 483
venezuelensis, Campylorhamphus trochilirostris 378
venezuelensis, Diglossa 653
venezuelensis, Henicorhina leucophrys 601
venezuelensis, Leptopogon superciliaris 449
venezuelensis, Mionectes olivaceus 447
venezuelensis, Molothrus bonariensis 762
venezuelensis, Myadestes ralloides 609
venezuelensis, Myiarchus 517
venezuelensis, Picumnus cinnamomeus 315
venezuelensis, Pipraeidea melanonota 649
venezuelensis, Ramphocelus carbo 640
venezuelensis, Synallaxis candei 339
venezuelensis, Terenotriccus erythrurus 494
venezuelensis, Threnetes ruckeri 226
venezuelensis, Turdus flavipes 613
Veniliornis 319
ventralis, Accipiter 89
ventralis, Platyrinchus mystaceus 490
venusta, Dacnis 670
venusta, Tangara xanthocephala 660
veraguensis, Geotrygon 168
verdiscutatus, Heliangelus clarisse 263
vermiculatus, Megascops 201
Vermivora 723
vermivorum, Helmitheros 732
verreauxi, Leptotila 165
verreauxii, Celeus grammicus 325
verreauxii, Lophornis chalybeus 237
versicolor, Amazilia 247
versicolor, Pachyramphus 560
versicolurus, Brotogeris 181
verticalis, Creurgops 636
verticalis, Hemispingus 630
verticalis, Myioborus miniatus 738
verticeps, Thalurania fannyi 242
vestita, Eriocnemis 265
vicarius, Spizaetus ornatus 102
vicina, Cercomacra tyrannina 406
vicinior, Scytalopus 442
vicinus, Chordeiles gundlachii 214
victoriae, Lesbia 277
victorini, Anisognathus somptuosus 648
viduata, Dendrocygna 35
vieilloti, Tangara mexicana 658
vieillotioides, Pyrrhomyias cinnamomeus 497
viguieri, Dacnis 671
vilissimus, Zimmerius 459
villaviscensio, Campylopterus 232
villosus, Myiobius 495
vinaceorufa, Zenaida auriculata 160
viola, Heliangelus 264
violacea, Euphonia 769
violacea, Geotrygon 169
violacea, Nyctanassa 72
violaceus, Cyanocorax 576
violaceus, Trogon 280
Violetear, Brown 233
  Green 233
  Sparkling 234
violiceps, Goldmania 244
violiceps, Heliangelus clarisse 263
violifer, Coeligena 261
violilavata, Thraupis palmarum 643
virens, Contopus 501
virens, Dendroica 728
virenticeps, Cyclarhis gujanensis 567
Vireo 568
Vireo, Black-whiskered 570
  Brown-capped 571
  Chocó 570
  Philadelphia 569
  Red-eyed 569
  Yellow-green 569
  Yellow-throated 568
Vireolanius 568
VIREONIDAE 566
virescens, Butorides 72
virescens, Empidonax 502
virescens, Formicarius analis 424
virescens, Phylloscartes 481
virescens, Tyranneutes 546
virgata, Aphriza 135
virgata, Ciccaba 205
virgaticeps, Thripadectes 356
virgatus, Hyloctistes 351
virgatus, Xiphocolaptes promeropirhynchus 369
virginalis, Trogon collaris 282
virginianus, Bubo 204
viridanum, Todirostrum 455
viridicata, Myiopagis 466
viridicata, Pyrrhura 177
viridiceps, Amazilia franciae 249
viridiceps, Hylophilus semicinereus 571
viridiceps, Mionectes striaticollis 446
viridiceps, Phyllomyias burmeisteri 457
viridiceps, Tolmomyias flaviventris 488
viridiceps, Touit purpuratus 184
viridicollis, Tangara 667
viridicordatus, Anthracothorax prevostii 234
viridi dorsalis, Anisognathus somptuosus 648
viridigaster, Amazilia 250
viridigula, Anthracothorax 234
viridipectus, Thalurania furcata 242
viridipennis, Chaetura 222
viridis, Anurolimnas 111
viridis, Dysithamnus mentalis 391
viridis, Frederickena 380
viridis, Pachyramphus 560
viridis, Psarocolius 747
viridis, Pteroglossus 307
viridis, Tersina 674
viridis, Trogon 281
viridissima, Tangara gyrola 663
viridissimus, Forpus passerinus 180
viridissimus, Piculus rubiginosus 322
viridiventris, Hylocharis cyanus 243
viridiventris, Manacus vitellinus 549
vitellinus, Cacicus cela 750
vitellinus, Manacus 549
vitellinus, Ploceus 776
vitellinus, Ramphastos 311
vitiosus, Lophotriccus 482
vitriolina, Tangara 663
vivida, Sporophila nigricollis 697
vividior, Vireo olivaceus 569
vividus, Platyrinchus flavigularis 490
vocifer, Burhinus bistriatus 127
vociferans, Lipaugus 540
vociferus, Charadrius 124
Volatinia 692
vorax, Tyrannus dominicensis 522
vuilleumieri, Diglossa brunneiventris 653
vulgaris, Sturnus 623

vulpecula, Cranioleuca 342
vulpina, Cranioleuca 342
Vultur 82
Vulture, Black 80
Greater Yellow-headed 81
King 81
Lesser Yellow-headed 81
Turkey 81
wagae, Phaeomyias murina 462
wagleri, Aratinga 173
wagleri, Psarocolius 748
Wagtail, White 624
Wagtail-Tyrant, Lesser 475
waimiri, Cercomacra laeta 407
wallacei, Mionectes oleagineus 447
wallacei, Patagioenas plumbea 159
wallacii, Schiffornis turdina 557
Warbler, Bay-breasted 730
Black-and-white 731
Black-crested 741
Black-throated Blue 727
Black-throated Green 728
Blackburnian 728
Blackpoll 730
Blue-winged 723
Buff-rumped 745
Cabanis's 743
Canada 737
Cape May 727
Cerulean 730
Chestnut-sided 726
Citrine 741
Connecticut 734
Flavescent 745
Golden-bellied 740
Golden-crowned 743
Golden-winged 723
Grey-and-gold 740
Grey-headed 742
Grey-throated 742
Hooded 736
Kentucky 734
Magnolia 726
Mourning 735
Pale-legged 741
Palm 729
Pine 729
Pirre 744
Prairie 729
Prothonotary 732
River 745
Rufous-capped 744
Russet-crowned 743
Santa Marta 742
Swainson's 732
Tennessee 724
Three-banded 744
Three-striped 744
Townsend's 728
Two-banded 740
White-lored 743
Wilson's 737
Worm-eating 732
Yellow 725
Yellow-rumped 727
Yellow-throated 728
warscewiczi, Amazilia saucerrottei 249
warscewiczi, Lepidocolaptes lacrymiger 377
warszewiczi, Dives 760
Waterthrush, Louisiana 733
Northern 733
watkinsi, Grallaria 430
watsonii, Megascops 202
Waxbill, Common 774
Waxwing, Cedar 608
Weaver, Village 776
Vitelline Masked 776
weberi, Lipaugus 539
websteri, Sula sula 67
weddellii, Aratinga 174
weddellii, Xiphorhynchus ocellatus 372
wedeli, Lophostrix cristata 205
wetmorei, Buthraupis 646
wetmorei, Phyllomyias burmeisteri 457
wetmorei, Rallus 114
wetmorei, Thamnophilus aethiops 385
wetmorei, Troglodytes rufulus 600
Wetmorethraupis 646
Wheatear, Northern 608
Whimbrel 131
whiteleyana, Sporophila plumbea 693
whitelianus, Aulacorhynchus derbianus 305
whitelyi, Amazilia chionopectus 247
whitelyi, Caprimulgus 217
whitelyi, Phaethornis bourcieri 228
whitelyi, Pipreola 535
whitelyi, Tangara cyanoptera 668
Whitetip, Purple-bibbed 267
Rufous-vented 267
Wigeon, American 38
Eurasian 38
Willet 134
williami, Metallura 269
williaminae, Leucopternis albicollis 92
wilsoni, Coeligena 259
Wilsonia 736
wilsonia, Charadrius 123
wolfi, Aramides 115
Woodcreeper, Amazonian Barred 370
Black-banded 370
Black-striped 375
Buff-throated 374
Chestnut-rumped 373
Cinnamon-throated 368
Cocoa 374
Elegant 373
Lineated 377
Long-billed 367
Long-tailed 365
Montane 376
Narrow-billed 376
Northern Barred 369
Ocellated 372
Olivaceous 366
Olive-backed 375
Plain-brown 364
Red-billed 368
Ruddy 365
Spix's 373
Spot-throated 365
Spotted 375
Straight-billed 371
Streak-headed 376
Striped 372
Strong-billed 368
Tschudi's 372
Tyrannine 364
Wedge-billed 366
White-chinned 364
Zimmer's 371
Woodhaunter, Eastern 351
Western 351
Woodnymph, Fork-tailed 242
Green-crowned 242
Violet-crowned 241
Woodpecker, Acorn 318
Bar-bellied 321
Black-cheeked 318
Blood-coloured 319
Chestnut 326
Chocó 320
Cinnamon 325
Cream-coloured 325
Crimson-bellied 327
Crimson-crested 328
Crimson-mantled 321
Golden-collared 319
Golden-green 323
Golden-naped 319
Golden-olive 322
Guayaquil 328
Lineated 326
Lita 323
Little 320
Powerful 327
Red-crowned 317
Red-necked 327
Red-rumped 321
Red-stained 320
Ringed 326
Rufous-headed 326
Scaly-breasted 325
Scarlet-backed 319
Smoky-brown 321
Spot-breasted 323
Waved 325
White 318
White-throated 323
Yellow-throated 323
Yellow-tufted 318
Yellow-vented 320
Woodstar, Amethyst 273
Esmeraldas 275
Gorgeted 274
Little 276

Purple-collared 273
Purple-throated 273
Rufous-shafted 275
Santa Marta 274
Short-tailed 275
White-bellied 274
woznesenskii, Xema sabini 147
Wren, Apolinar's Marsh 591
Band-backed 589
Bar-winged Wood 601
Bay 596
Bicoloured 587
Black-bellied 592
Buff-breasted 597
Chestnut-breasted 603
Coraya 594
Fasciated 589
Flutist 602
Grey-breasted Wood 600
Grey-mantled 590
Mountain 599
Munchique Wood 601
Musician 604
Niceforo's 597
Páramo 592
Plain-tailed 593
Rufous 590
Rufous-and-white 597
Rufous-breasted 595
Santa Marta 599
Sedge 591
Sharpe's 590
Song 603
Sooty-headed 592
Southern House 598
Speckle-breasted 595
Stripe-backed 589
Stripe-throated 596
Superciliated 598
Tepui 599
Thrush-like 588
Whiskered 593
White-breasted Wood 600
White-headed 588
Wing-banded 603
wyatti, Asthenes 344
xanthocephala, Tangara 660
xanthochlorus, Piculus chrysochloros 323
xanthogaster, Euphonia 772
xanthogastra, Carduelis 766
xanthogastra, Tangara 661
xanthogenia, Aratinga pertinax 175
xanthogenys, Buarremon brunneinucha 708
xanthogenys, Pachyramphus 560
xanthogonys, Heliodoxa 254
xanthophthalmus, Chrysomus 757
xanthopterygius, Forpus 180
xanthopygius, Heterospingus 636
xanthoscela, Turdus flavipes 613
Xema 147
Xenerpestes 347
Xenodacnis 673
Xenopipo 551
Xenops 362
Xenops, Plain 363
Rufous-tailed 362
Slender-billed 362
Streaked 363
Xenopsaris 559
Xenopsaris, White-naped 559
Xenornis 389
Xenus 134
Xiphocolaptes 368
Xipholena 541
Xiphorhynchus 371
Xolmis 507
xyostictus, Chordeiles rupestris 213
yananchae, Thryothorus mystacalis 594
yapura, Crypturellus undulatus 30
yariguierum, Atlapetes latinuchus 711
yarrellii, Carduelis 764
yaruqui, Phaethornis 227
yavii, Chamaeza campanisona 425
yavii, Myrmotherula behni 399
yavii, Synallaxis macconnelli 335
yavii, Troglodytes rufulus 600
Yellowlegs, Greater 132
Lesser 133
Yellowthroat, Black-lored 736
Common 735
Masked 736
Olive-crowned 735
yetapa, Elanoides forficatus 85
yncas, Cyanocorax 577
yungae, Sporophila caerulescens 698
yuracares, Psarocolius 748
zamorae, Formicarius analis 424
zamorae, Platyrinchus mystaceus 489
zamorae, Sclerurus albigularis 360
zamorae, Tangara punctata 661
zapluta, Leptotila verreauxi 165
zarumae, Contopus fumigatus 500
zarumae, Grallaricula flavirostris 436
zarumae, Thamnophilus 383
Zebrilus 71
Zenaida 159
zimmeri, Amazilia lactea 248
zimmeri, Atlapetes semirufus 714
zimmeri, Buthraupis eximia 646
zimmeri, Campylorhynchus griseus 588
zimmeri, Myrmotherula longipennis 399
Zimmerius 459
zonaris, Streptoprocne 220
zonatus, Campylorhynchus 589
zonothorax, Micrastur ruficollis 105
Zonotrichia 684
zosterops, Hemitriccus 452
zuliae, Chrysoptilus punctigula 324
zuliae, Lepidopyga goudoti 241
zuliae, Myiopagis viridicata 467
zuliae, Patagioenas subvinacea 159
zuliae, Tiaris fuliginosus 682
zuliana, Coeligena coeligena 259
zulianus, Machaeropterus regulus 548
zuliensis, Basileuterus cinereicollis 742
zuliensis, Piculus rivolii 322
zuliensis, Thryothorus leucotis 598
zuliensis, Tinamus major 28
zuloagae, Coeligena coeligena 259
zusii, Heliangelus 264